south america
on a shoestring

Danny Palmerlee, Sandra Bao, Charlotte Beech, Krzysztof Dydyński, Molly Green, Carolyn Hubbard, Morgan Konn, Andrew Dean Nystrom, Ginger Adams Otis, Regis St. Louis, Lucas Vidgen, Emily K Wolman

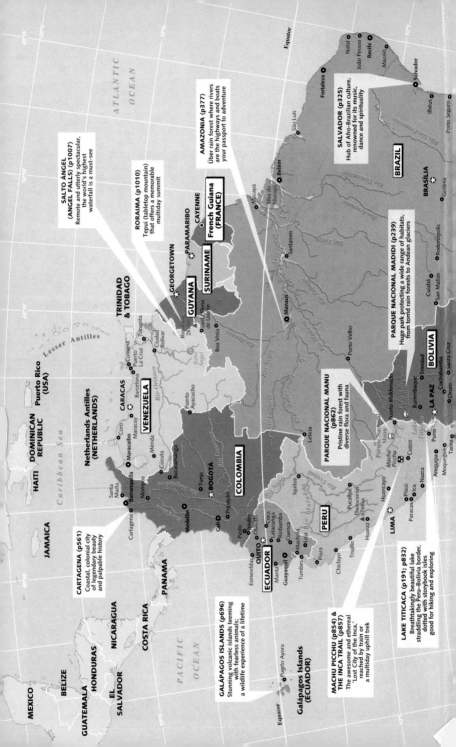

SALTO ÁNGEL
(ANGEL FALLS) (p1007)
Remote and utterly spectacular,
the world's highest
waterfall is a must-see

RORAIMA (p1010)
Tepui (tabletop mountain)
that offers a memorable
multiday summit

AMAZONIA (p377)
Über rain forest where rivers
are the highways and boats
your passport to adventure

SALVADOR (p325)
Hub of Afro-Brazilian culture,
renowned for its music,
dance and spirituality

PARQUE NACIONAL MADIDI (p239)
Huge park protecting a wide range of habitats,
from torrid rain forests to Andean glaciers

PARQUE NACIONAL MANU
(p862)
Pristine rain forest with
diverse flora and fauna

CARTAGENA (p561)
Coastal, colonial city
of legendary beauty
and palpable history

LAKE TITICACA (p191; p832)
Breathtakingly beautiful lake
straddling the Peru-Bolivia border,
dotted with storybook isles
good for hiking and exploring

MACHU PICCHU (p854) &
THE INCA TRAIL (p857)
The awesome and ethereal
'Lost City of the Inca,'
reached by train or
a multiday uphill trek

GALÁPAGOS ISLANDS (p696)
Stunning volcanic islands teeming
with fearless animals;
a wildlife experience of a lifetime

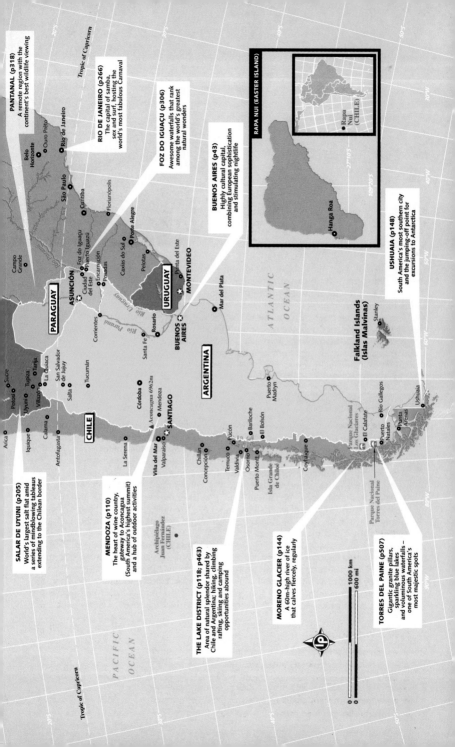

PANTANAL (p318)
A remote region with the continent's best wildlife viewing

RIO DE JANEIRO (p266)
The capital of samba, sex and surf, hosting the world's most fabulous Carnaval

FOZ DO IGUAÇU (p306)
Awesome waterfalls that rank among the world's greatest natural wonders

BUENOS AIRES (p43)
Highly cultural capital, combining European sophistication and stimulating nightlife

RAPA NUI (EASTER ISLAND)

USHUAIA (p148)
South America's most southern city and the jumping-off point for excursions to Antarctica

SALAR DE UYUNI (p205)
World's largest salt flat amid a series of mindblowing tableaus extending to the Chilean border

MENDOZA (p110)
The heart of wine country, gateway to Aconcagua (South America's highest summit) and a hub of outdoor activities

THE LAKE DISTRICT (p118; p463)
Area of natural splendor shared by Chile and Argentina; hiking, climbing, rafting, skiing and camping opportunities abound

MORENO GLACIER (p144)
A 60m-high river of ice that calves fiercely, regularly

TORRES DEL PAINE (p507)
Gigantic granite pillars, sparkling blue lakes, and voluminous waterfalls – one of South America's most majestic spots

Tropic of Capricorn

PACIFIC OCEAN

ATLANTIC OCEAN

PARAGUAY

URUGUAY

CHILE

ARGENTINA

Falkland Islands (Islas Malvinas)

Belo Horizonte
Ouro Prêto
Rio de Janeiro
São Paulo
Curitiba
Florianópolis
Porto Alegre
Caxias do Sul
Pelotas
Campo Grande
ASUNCIÓN
Foz do Iguaçu
Puerto Iguazú
Ciudad del Este
Encarnación
Posadas
MONTEVIDEO
Punta del Este
Corrientes
Rio Paraná
Rio Uruguay
Rosario
Santa Fe
BUENOS AIRES
Mar del Plata
Córdoba
Aconcagua 6962m
SANTIAGO
Mendoza
Viña del Mar
Valparaíso
La Serena
Arica
Iquique
Calama
Antofagasta
Potosí
Sucre
Uyuni
Tupiza
Villazón
Tarija
La Quiaca
San Salvador de Jujuy
Salta
Tucumán
Archipiélago Juan Fernández (CHILE)
Chillán
Concepción
Temuco
Valdivia
Osorno
Pucón
Bariloche
El Bolsón
Puerto Montt
Isla Grande de Chiloé
Coyhaique
Parque Nacional Los Glaciares
El Calafate
Puerto Natales
Parque Nacional Torres del Paine
Punta Arenas
Río Gallegos
Ushuaia
Puerto Madryn
Stanley
Rapa Nui (CHILE)
Hanga Roa

Tropic of Capricorn

0   1000 km
0   600 mi

Responsible Travel

One of the joys of travel is leaving responsibilities behind, so who really wants to think about responsible travel? But responsibility clings to us like a good backpack, and no matter how, we still have an impact on the communities and natural habitats we visit. The question is how to make that impact a positive one.

Throughout this book we recommend ecotourism operations (businesses that help preserve natural environments and their communities through tourism) and community tourist projects (projects created and controlled – at least significantly – by the communities people visit, rather than outside entrepreneurs). Community-managed tourism is especially important when visiting indigenous communities (such as those throughout the Amazon region) which are often exploited by businesses which channel little money back into the community.

TIPS TO KEEP IN MIND

- **Learn the lingo** Take a Spanish or Portugese class before or during your travels. Knowing the language shows respect.
- **Spend at the source** Try to buy crafts directly from the artisans themselves.
- **Ask before taking someone's photo** This is especially true of indigenous people, who may not like to be photographed.
- **Don't litter** Sure, many locals do it, but many also frown upon it.
- **Pay your porter, tip your guide** Porters, guides and cooks are often despicably underpaid. Tip as much as you can.
- **Support community** Try to seek out community-based services that keep dollars local. Ask where your operator is based and where the money ends up.
- **Hire responsible guides** When you hire a guide, make sure they have a good reputation and will respect the environment and communities you'll visit.
- **Have shower willpower** Don't take hot showers if the water is heated by wood fire, especially in rural areas where gathering wood damages local ecosystems.
- **Don't shell out cash for the coral** Avoid buying souvenirs or products made from endangered species.
- **Respect local traditions** Dress appropriately if visiting churches and shrines and consider the effect of your presence.

INTERNET RESOURCES

- **www.planeta.com** Ron Mader's outstanding ecotourism website.
- **www.peruweb.org/porters/index.html** info on hiring porters.
- **www.ecotourism.org** the International Ecotourism Society offers loads of links to businesses devoted to ecotourism (according to their respective definitions of the term).
- **www.tourismconcern.org.uk** UK-based organization dedicated to promoting ethical tourism.
- **www.transitionsabroad.com** eponymous website focusing on immersion and responsible travel.

Contents

6

The Authors

DANNY PALMERLEE   Coordinating Author, Ecuador
Danny has spent nearly every waking moment of the past three years traveling in and writing about Latin America – a region he's been infatuated with since he first backpacked through Mexico and Central America in 1991. He began traveling at age 12 when he and a friend floated too far from home down a California creek in an abandoned bathtub. Since then, he's traveled extensively through Latin America, Europe and Morocco, trekked through Montana and Wyoming, managed a hostel in Scotland, owned a lucrative body jewelry business in San Francisco and filled the many gaps with freelance writing. For some reason – probably the bus rides – he keeps returning to South America.

Danny contributed to the last editions of LP's *South America on a Shoestring*, *Argentina, Uruguay & Paraguay* and *Ecuador & the Galápagos Islands*, and he coordinated *Mexico's Pacific Coast*.

SANDRA BAO   Argentina
'I don't need to learn English; I'm an Argentine!' enthused little nine-year-old Sandra, after emigrating to the United States. Soon she started missing her native *bife de chorizo* (sirloin steak) and *alfajores* (cookie sandwiches), while being shocked to learn 'Midnight Special' wasn't written by a fellow Argentine. Much later Sandra met her future husband, Ben Greensfelder, whom she originally thought a total geek (as he did her). Now they adore each other.

Sandra's hobbies include rockclimbing, notecard-making and alligator wrestling. Her future hopes include being a homeowner, silverworker and kick-ass gardener. Any tomato-growing tips are appreciated and can be sent to her care of Lonely Planet, as can any tips relating to travel in the world's best country – Argentina.

CHARLOTTE BEECH   Peru
Charlotte spent most of 2002 all but sleeping in her hiking boots as she traveled through Latin America from Venezuela to Bolivia. Finding herself totally smitten by empanadas and Carlos Vives, she gave up a job editing travel books to return to the continent at every opportunity to write for Lonely Planet. While covering Peru for *South America on a Shoestring*, she was overjoyed to find that her studies in archaeology at Cambridge were useful after all, and at long last it was an important skill to tell an Inca from a Moche. When not traveling, Charlotte hangs up her boots in London, where she lives with her Colombian partner. She has also worked on Lonely Planet's *Peru* and *Venezuela*.

KRZYSZTOF DYDYŃSKI   Colombia, Venezuela
A native Pole from Warsaw, Krzysztof caught the travel bug in his teens and traveled extensively across Europe and Asia. It was, however, Latin America that knocked him out, and what was intended to be a one-year postgraduate study on geography kept him in Colombia for four years. Based at Bogotá, he traveled pretty much everywhere from Mexico to Argentina. He now lives in Australia, yet as a migratory bird, he regularly returns to Latin America to explore new paths. Krzysztof is the author of LP's *Colombia, Venezuela, Poland* and *Kraków*.

MOLLY GREEN   Brazil
In the same year, both Ilê Ayê and Olodum rocked Molly's home town of Santa Cruz, California with Afro-Brazilian rhythms, and the victorious Brazilian World Cup team spurred spontaneous street parties, inspiring her to learn to samba and embark on a nine-week tour of Brazil. An obsession was born, which led to an intensive study of Brazilian dance, an impressive collection of *axé* music, university-level studies in Brazilian Portuguese and literature, and further hours on Brazil's freezing buses and sweaty beaches. While researching this edition, Molly broadened her repertoire of *lambada* moves and learned what to do when the drive shaft drops out the bottom of a 4WD in remote Piauí. Molly has lived with local families and studied in Argentina and Venezuela, surfed in Mexico, eaten chicken-foot soup in Guatemala, fainted from altitude in Peru, lived out of a van in Australia and been robbed by monkeys in Indonesia.

CAROLYN HUBBARD
Chile

Four years ago, Carolyn embarked on her first trip to Chile, traveling from tip to bottom and relishing every discovery. A trip every year since has convinced her that Chile is a treasure trove of adventure. She is both proud and embarrassed to say she knows Chile better than California where she lives, and the majority of parks she's trekked in are closer to Antarctica than to her front door.

MORGAN KONN
Paraguay

After travels through French Polynesia, Southeast Asia, Europe and finally South America, Morgan could not resist getting off the beaten path and heading to Paraguay. Originally introduced to Paraguay through the evocative photos of a Peace Corp volunteer, she knew the people would win her heart. Upon her arrival, the trickling sweat behind her knees, dusty horse-drawn carts and the languid movement of it all assured her she was far from her native Berkeley, California. Morgan started her Lonely Planet affair in the US marketing department before trying her hand at writing. She has contributed to Lonely Planet's *Mexico* guidebook.

ANDREW DEAN NYSTROM
Bolivia

Andrew's fascination with Bolivia began while playing Santa Cruz' famous *fútbol* (soccer) club Tahuichi to a tie in a Texas tournament. A summer of scientific investigation of geothermal features in Yellowstone National Park's wild backcountry inspired a quest for the world's highest soakable hot springs. Seven months of tramping from the Antarctic Peninsula to the Central Andes revealed several surreal candidates...but the search must go on. When not out rambling, Andrew hangs his sombreros in a garden cottage that straddles an earthquake fault in Alta California.

GINGER ADAMS OTIS
Brazil

Ginger Adams Otis is a freelance writer based in New York City. She graduated from Boston University in 1993 with a degree in comparative literature, but after six depressing months of trying to find work in an unfriendly job market, she chucked it all in and began traveling. Ginger's been supplementing her globe-trotting addiction with freelancing writing for more than ten years, and she files regularly for the *Village Voice*, *In These Times*, *MS. Magazine*, the *Ex-Berliner* and many other publications.

REGIS ST. LOUIS
Brazil

Raised on a diet of *futebol* (soccer) and old Gal Costa records, Regis became infatuated with Brazil at an early age. His dream of traveling widely around the Americas was first realized in the late 1990s when he sold all his possessions and took off for the tropics. Regis speaks Portuguese, Spanish and Russian and has traveled widely throughout Latin America, Eastern Europe and the Middle East. When not bumping along rugged terrain for Lonely Planet, he makes his living as a freelance writer and editor in New York City.

LUCAS VIDGEN   Argentina, Uruguay

Lucas started wandering away from his mother in shopping malls when he was about five and has never really stopped. Since then he has lived, traveled and worked in more than 20 countries, many of which don't supply free milk and crayons when you get lost.

Lucas first went to South America in the early '90s and has been pining for it ever since, getting cheap fixes from Marquez novels and late-night soccer games on TV. When LP asked him to go back it took him about two seconds to say '¡Olé!' He has previously contributed to *India* and *Central America on a Shoestring*.

EMILY K WOLMAN   The Guianas

Since the day when young Emily's grandfather bestowed upon her a pilfered piece of one of the Pyramids of Giza wrapped in an old paper towel (yes, he's since learned about responsible travel), she has been striving to match his record of 168 countries visited. Her genetic propensity for being unable to sit still has led her across five continents, with long-term stops in Australia, New Zealand, Thailand, Fiji, and Colombia. Raised in New York, educated there and in Paris, and still growing in Oakland, California, Emily edited for several companies, including Lonely Planet, before trying her hand at travel writing. Her trip to the Guianas taught her that the solo travel she'd done in the past and thought was challenging was actually cake, comparatively, and that there is only one way to prepare for off-the-beaten-track travel: off-the-beaten-track travel.

CONTRIBUTING AUTHOR

Dr David Goldberg MD wrote the Health chapter (p1053). David completed his training in internal medicine and infectious diseases at Columbia-Presbyterian Medical Center in New York City, where he has also served as voluntary faculty. At present, he is an infectious diseases specialist in Scarsdale, New York State, and the editor-in-chief of the website MDTravelHealth.com.

Destination South America

Aymara people celebrating Año Nuevo (New Year's Day) in Juli

Beware – you're toying with obsession, and once the magic of South America grips you, it owns you. From the crashing glaciers of Patagonia to the steaming Amazon jungles, the continent is so fantastically diverse and packed with adventure, you'll forever wonder what's coming next. Strap on your crampons and climb, climb, climb the snowcapped volcanoes of the Andes. Trek the Inca Trail to the awe-inspiring remains of Machu Picchu, marvel at the colonial architecture of Cartagena, let loose to the hedonism of Brazil's Carnaval, doze to frog songs in the Amazon and wake up to the thundering magnificence of Iguazú Falls. You can stay in jungle lodges, cloud-forest campgrounds, backpacker party pads or indigenous shelters. You can down an aperitif before dinner on a deluxe bus in Argentina, race the tide in the back of a rusty truck or ride the roof of a boxcar down the Andes. What's more, South America is an incredible cultural kaleidoscope, where Lake District towns seem plucked from the Bavarian Alps, cities rival their European counterparts, and delicacies range from football-sized steaks to pint-size piranhas and spit-roasted guinea pigs. And the music? With every adventure there's a soundtrack, from modern break-beat bossa nova to traditional tango to the haunting panpipes of the Andean *páramo* (grasslands). Add to the mix the gregarious, open nature of South Americans, and you have a traveler's paradise. Whatever travel fantasy you can dream up, South America's got it, so start obsessing–and make your trip there as long as you can!

The stunning glacial backdrop of Parque Nacional Torres del Paine (p507)

HIGHLIGHTS

BEST ADRENALINE RUSHES

Paragliding, Iquique ■ fly over the sand dunes backing this Chilean beach resort and close the afternoon with a beer on the beach (p445)

Downhill mountain biking, Volcán Cotopaxi ■ dare the downhill descent on the slopes of this spectacular, snowcapped volcano, the second highest in Ecuador (p650)

Skiing & snowboarding, Valle Nevado & Cerro Catedral ■ carve up the powdery slopes of these kick-ass ski resorts…in July! (p418; p127)

Surfing, Peru ■ rip up the epic lefts that grace Peru's northern coast, a paradise of reef and point breaks, and wild coastal desert scenery (p871)

Rafting & kayaking ■ Río Futaleufú (p496), Río Misahuallí (p553) and Río Apurímac (p845) are all so fun and so beautiful we had to name them all

BEST PARKS & NATURAL ATTRACTIONS

Iguazú Falls ■ boggle your mind beneath the thundering roar of one of the world's most magnificent waterfalls (Argentina p79; Brazil p306)

Parque Nacional Madidi ■ marvel at the abundant wildlife of the continent's most biodiverse ecosystems, a protected area in Bolivia spanning terrain from steaming rain forest to frigid Andean peaks (p239)

Parque Nacional Torres del Paine ■ hike among shimmering lakes, azure icebergs and the spectacular granite pillars of Chile's Torres del Paine (p507)

Roraima ■ trek the strenuous trail to the top of this surreal, cliff-edge table mountain, the highest of the *tepuis* (sandstone-capped mesas) jutting from Venezuela's Gran Sabana (p1010)

The Pantanal ■ experience the continent's best wildlife viewing in this vast Brazilian wetland. It's half the size of France and boasts the greatest concentration of fauna in the New World (p318)

Giant tortoises at the Charles Darwin Research Station in the Galápagos Islands (p705)

BEST BEACHES & ISLANDS

Galápagos Islands ▪ stare down iguanas, snorkel with penguins, share a moment with a tortoise and witness the dance of the blue-footed booby on this unique archipelago famous for its fearless wildlife (p696)

Tierra del Fuego ▪ island-hop at the world's edge, hike the Dientes de Navarino, watch Antarctic cruisers come to shore, trek historic missionary trails and gorge yourself on butter-smothered king crab (Argentina p146; Chile p510)

Ilha Grande ▪ kiss reality goodbye and venture to this remote Brazilian island of tropical beaches, Atlantic rain forest and long, quiet walks (p289)

Parque Nacional Tayrona ▪ hit the jungle-covered coast and explore some of Colombia's finest beaches within this coastal national park (p560)

Archipiélago Los Roques ▪ fly out to this stunning archipelago of coral islands in Venezuela and snorkel, scuba dive, fish, camp, windsurf and island-hop by fishing boat (p962)

BEST FESTIVALS & EVENTS

Carnaval ▪ get hot, heavy and hedonistic to the rhythm of samba, parading dancers and the Bacchanalian frenzy of one of the world's wildest, sexiest parties (Rio p277; Salvador p328)

Diablos Danzantes ▪ watch dancing devils shimmy and whirl down the streets of San Francisco de Yare in Venezuela at this colorful fiesta blending Spanish and African traditions (p962)

Círio de Nazaré ▪ witness Brazil's biggest religious festival, when some one million people pay homage to the image of NS de Nazaré. Then drink, dance and be merry for the following two-week bash (p365)

Copa Libertadores ▪ scream, cry, jump, laugh, sing and boo with the fans at a match during South America's most prestigious soccer tournament. Check www.soccerage.com for upcoming cup matches (p26)

La Diablada ▪ get down with the devils at Bolivia's biggest bash, the Dance of the Devils, Oruro's version of Carnaval (p197)

Ethereal Machu Picchu, the lost city of the Inca, Peru (p854)

BEST PLACES TO SEE THE HISTORY OF SOUTH AMERICA

Machu Picchu mystify your mind at South America's most famous and spectacular archaeological site (p854)

Ciudad Perdida trek through the jungle to the 'Lost City' of the Tayronas, one of the largest pre-Columbian cities discovered in the Americas (p561)

Rapa Nui (Easter Island) fly to one of the world's most remote inhabited islands and marvel at the colossal stone *moai* (large anthropomorphic statues carved from volcanic tuff), whose history is still shrouded in mystery (p513)

Jesuit missions explore the beautifully preserved and sometimes hauntingly decrepit ruins of the 17th-century Jesuit missions in northeast Argentina (p77) and southern Paraguay (p780)

Potosí visit this historic Bolivian silver-mining city, which was once the largest and wealthiest in Latin America, and tour its stunningly hellish co-operative mines. At 4090m, it's also the highest city in the world (p223).

BEST CITIES

Buenos Aires (Argentina) explore San Telmo, birthplace of tango, colorful La Boca and ritzy Recoleta; eat massive steaks, catch a football match between La Boca and River Plate and dance the night away (p43)

Rio de Janeiro (Brazil) fall in love with the world's most beautifully set city and the *cariocas* (people from Rio) themselves, dance to samba, and see what Copacabana and Ipanema are all about (p266)

Cartagena (Colombia) steep yourself in history as you meander within the walled old-town districts of South America's most beautiful colonial city (p561)

Salvador (Brazil) succumb to the city of spontaneous festivals, rich African culture, beautiful beaches and music, music, music (p325)

Ushuaia (Argentina) c'mon, it's the southernmost city in the world – and it feels like it! (p148)

ITINERARIES

ANDEAN ROUTE

How long?
Partial route:
3 weeks;
full route:
6 weeks

When to go?
May–Sep:
best trekking;
Jun–Aug:
best weather

Budget?
US$10–25/day
(Galápagos trip extra)

For rugged adventure, unparalleled alpine vistas, rich indigenous cultures, fabulous crafts and some of the best, most colorful markets on the continent, the Ecuador–Peru–Bolivia circuit is the way to go. What's more, you can shoot downhill to lush Amazon Basin rain forest in any of these countries.

Ecuador is one of the best places to study Spanish in South America and a great place to start. Take a crash course in **Quito** (p627), **Baños** (p653) or **Cuenca** (p661) and travel south with your new Spanish tongue through the volcano-studded Andes, detouring if you need (go on, you have time) to the tropical **beaches** (p677) of Ecuador's coast, the best along this stretch. Cross into Peru and take pause at **Huaraz** (p883) for Peru's best trekking and climbing. Peru's big must, of course, is **Machu Picchu** (p854) and the four-day hike along the **Inca Trail** (p857) to get there. From there beat it south to shimmering **Lake Titicaca** (p832) and cross into Bolivia for more hiking, trekking and mountaineering in the **Yungas** (p189) and **Cordillera Real** (p189). Then head south to the hallucinogenic landscapes around **Salar de Uyuni** (p205). You can mix this up by starting in Lima, Peru, but starting in La Paz, Bolivia, is trickier – flying there is expensive, and the altitude (it's the world's highest capital) can literally be sickening.

The Andean route winds through the rugged Andean highlands for over 3000km (side trips not included), passing snow-capped volcanoes, indigenous villages and exciting cities. Three weeks makes a great trip, but six weeks allows for fabulous side trips.

The most obvious (and most expensive) side trip is a flight from Ecuador to the **Galápagos Islands** (p696). For something more rugged, hunker down with livestock, foodstuffs and the locals in a cargo boat and chug down the Río Napo from **Coca** (p669), in Ecuador, to **Iquitos** (p896), in Peru, on the Río Amazonas. Some of the world's most remote natural areas, including **Parque Nacional Manu** (p862) in Peru, or **Parques Nacionales Madidi** (p239) and **Noel Kempff Mercado** (p168) in Bolivia, await those who want to skip the trodden trail. Colombia makes an easy detour from Ecuador, and you'll surely lose the travelin' crowds and be amazed by its wonders, especially the popular (and safe) Caribbean coast and its spectacular colonial city of **Cartagena** (p561). The dangers of travel in parts of the country are serious, however, and you should fully assess them before going.

BRAZILIAN ROUTE

A veritable paradise buzzing with surf, sun, samba and the spices of life, Brazil is one of the world's greatest outdoor-travel spots. You could spend weeks tripping up and down the 7400km coastline charring your buns on idyllic beaches near **Natal** (p351), **Ilha de Santa Catarina** (p308), **Ilha do Mel** (p305) and **Rio** (p266). Time it right and you'll catch the hedonistic Carnaval celebrations in **Rio** (p277) or **Salvador** (p328), although the latter is alive with parties all year long.

From **Belém** (p362) in the north, head inland by boat along the Río Amazonas to **Manaus** (p374), from where you can explore the river's mighty headwaters and the surrounding jungle. In southern Brazil, you can venture inland from Rio or São Paulo to the wondrous **Pantanal**

How long?
Partial route:
3 weeks;
full route:
2 months

When to go?
Feb–Aug: best
beach weather;
Jun–Aug:
best surfing;
Feb/Mar: Carnaval

Budget?
US$25–40/day

Traveling the Brazilian route will take you to tropical Caribbean beaches, along the mighty Amazon River and across the wildlife-rich wetlands of the Pantanal. Segments of the route can be done in two or three weeks, but to really cover some territory allow at least two months.

(p318), a vast wetland half the size of France with the best wildlife viewing on the continent. Further south, beat it due west of **Curitiba** (p302) to behold one of the world's most spectacular waterfalls, **Foz do Iguaçu** (p306), on the Argentine border.

In the north, Manaus is an important hub for side trips into Venezuela and Guyana. You can bus it north to **Bonfim** (p380), Brazil, and cross into Guyana and head into the **Kanuku Mountains** (p759). Before Bonfim, you could alternately veer northwest to **Santa Elena de Uairén** (p1011), cross into southern Venezuela and set out for the fascinating **Roraima trek** (p1012), another of the continent's highlights. If you're aching for more boat travel, take one of the Amazon tributaries from Manaus to the Triple Frontier region of Brazil–Peru–Colombia; or the boat-and-bus combination from Manaus to **Porto Velho** (p380) through to Bolivia.

From **Campo Grande** (p322) in the Pantanal (we're back in southern Brazil now), you could travel down to **Ponta Porã** (p324), cross into central Paraguay, work down to **Concepción** (p784) and hop a cargo boat for a taste of authentic, untouristed river life along the **Río Paraguay** (p784). From Campo Grande, you can also turn your toes west to the Brazilian border town of **Corumbá** (p323), jump into Bolivia at Quijarro and take the train to **Santa Cruz** (p228).

SOUTHERN CONE ROUTE

Outdoor enthusiasts and nature junkies will score their ultimate fix in Chilean and Argentine **Patagonia** (p132). Camping in the south is so popular that campsites (often free or dirt cheap) can be found just about anywhere. The **Lake District** (p118), on both sides, provides incomparable

How long?
Partial route:
2 weeks;
full route:
6–8 weeks
When to go?
Dec–Mar:
long days & dry
weather in Patagonia;
Mar–May:
stable temperatures
& less wind;
Jun–Sep: ski season
Budget?
US$30–35/day
(more if you ski)

hikes among azure mountain lakes and lush forest. Heading further south, Chile abounds with some awesome rafting opportunities and hidden inlets, and the country also boasts the serene archipelago of **Chiloé** (p489). Over the Andes in Argentina, the dry landscape widens and becomes impressively desolate, with access to the wildlife reserve at **Península Valdés** (p136), where the whale-watching is supreme. Further south, where enormous glaciers creep, you'll find the impressive national parks of **Los Glaciares** (p144) and **Torres del Paine** (in Chile; p507), both necessary stops for anyone with hiking shoes in the pack. **Tierra del Fuego** (p510) is the tip of the cone, with mystic forests, trekking, and an end-of-the-world feel you can't get elsewhere.

Before the magic of Patagonia sucks you in, hit some of the must-sees to the north: **Cerro Aconcagua** (p114), South America's highest peak; bustling **Buenos Aires** (p43); thundering **Iguazú Falls** (p79); and in Chile, the colorful port city **Valparaíso** (p419) or laidback **Valle del Elqui** (p435).

When it comes to nightlife, Argentina rules the roost, but in large cities on both sides of the Andes, partying till the crack of dawn is as natural as drinking *maté*.

Ideas for splitting from the route include heading up through **San Pedro de Atacama** (p442) in Chile and across the stunning *salares* (salt plains) to Bolivia or chugging on the slow train from **Calama** (p439) to **Uyuni** (p202), with other trains into Bolivia. If you have the cash, fly off to enigmatic **Easter Island** (p513) or to the **Falkland Islands** (Islas Malvinas; p36) for unparalleled wildlife-viewing.

The Southern Cone route covers over 8000km, from the salt flats of southern Bolivia down the spine of the Andes to Tierra del Fuego and back up through Buenos Aires to Iguazú Falls. Sections can be done in two to three weeks, but at least two months is needed to cover it all.

Getting Started

Psyching yourself up for the trip (some call it planning) is half the fun. This section is intended to help you decide when to go and predict what kind of cash you'll drop, and offer a glimpse at what to expect while bouncing around South America. Also check out the South America Directory at the back of this book (p1025), which has sections ranging from Health and Dangers & Annoyances to Activities and Festivals & Events.

WHEN TO GO

South America spans from the tropics – where the sweltering lowlands are sometimes only hours from the chilly Andean highlands – nearly to Antarctica, so when to go depends on where you go.

Climbing and trekking in the Andes of Ecuador, Peru and Bolivia is best in the drier months from May to September. Travel in the Amazon is possible year-round: even during rainy season, storms are usually short and broken with sunshine (see regional chapters for the varying rainy seasons throughout the Amazon). River levels, however, fluctuate greatly between dry and rainy seasons, which affects boat travel. Ski season in Argentina and Chile is June to September (rub *that* in the faces of northern-hemi friends). Patagonia is best visited during the region's summer months of December to April.

See under Climate in the Directory section of each country chapter for country-specific information.

The continent's wild array of colorful festivals (see Festivals & Events, p1033) is also a consideration; Carnaval, the most famous celebration of all, is in late February/early March.

South Americans love to travel during the two- to three-week period around Semana Santa (Holy Week) and Easter and during the Christmas/New Year holidays. Throughout most of South America, both foreign and national tourists are out in droves from late June to early September (especially in July and August). During these tourist high seasons, prices peak, hotels fill up quickly and public transportation gets slammed. The flip side is the celebratory, holiday atmosphere that can be wonderfully contagious. High season in the Southern Cone, when campgrounds and trails are slammed, is December through March. June through September (ski season) can also get busy in and around the ski areas of Chile and Argentina.

COSTS & MONEY

Brazil, Chile, Venezuela, Uruguay and the Guianas are the most expensive countries, while Bolivia, Ecuador, Colombia and – surprise, surprise – Argentina are the cheapest.

Generally, it will cost less (per person) if you travel in twos or threes, shun big cities where possible and travel slowly. Costs rack up as you tag on comforts like air-conditioning and a private bathroom, expensive tours to places such as the Galápagos Islands, or activities like skiing or clubbing.

UH-OH! *by Sandra Bao*

I was in search of a hostel. Spotting my destination, I walked right in the unlocked door. 'Buenas tardes,' I chirped to the man at a computer. A woman and child sat at a nearby table, and everyone just stared at me without saying a word. 'How rude!' I thought, but just remarked, 'I'd like to stay here – isn't this the hostel?' The man was kind enough to inform me that the hostel was two doors down, and polite enough not to mention I'd walked into his family's living room.

WHAT TO TAKE?

Packing (and unpacking and packing again) can be nerve wracking, so remember this: you can buy just about anything you'll need in most towns of significant size throughout South America. Certain items, however, can be hard to find or painfully expensive. Remember, the lighter you pack the more mobile you are (important for long huffs across towns or if you want to carry your pack on the bus).

- **Alarm clock** Ding! Don't miss that bus.
- **Books** Bring a couple. New and used books in English are available in larger cities and at the occasional hotel book exchange, but they tend to be expensive.
- **Camping gear** If you plan to camp, you're best off bringing all the gear you'll need (except for the fuel in your stove). Good equipment is available in the bigger cities and in popular trekking areas, but it's usually expensive.
- **Contraceptives** Condoms and birth-control pills are available in the larger towns of most countries, but it's convenient to bring your own, especially pills.
- **Duct tape** The handiest material on earth; make your own mini roll around a pencil and use the tape to patch holes in your rain gear, attach a mosquito net to the wall, repair busted sandals, seal leaks in your tent, reinforce your journal or to tape your travel mate's mouth shut.
- **Film** 35mm print film can be found in cities, but it's easier to bring your own. Slide film is harder to come by. High-speed film (faster than ASA 400) is useful in the jungle, but hard to find.
- **Flashlight** Yes. Mini pack-lights are hard to find outside larger cities.
- **Medicine** Bring a small first-aid kit. General medication and first-aid gear are available in larger towns.
- **Photocopies of important documents** Absolutely. Copy your passport, your airline ticket, visas, traveler's check serial numbers and pack them separately.
- **Photos** Snaps of folks from back home satisfy the inherent curiosity South Americans seem to have about family.
- **Pocket knife** You're guaranteed to use it; make sure it has a can-opener.
- **Rain gear** Bring a thin waterproof jacket. A rainproof sack for your pack is a godsend; on bus roofs, in boats and while hiking, your pack is just begging to get stormed upon.
- **Repellent** Indispensable in the tropical lowlands, but unnecessary in the Andes.
- **Safety pins** The ultimate fixer.
- **Sleeping bag** If you're camping or planning to stay in mountain refuges or basic, out-of-the-way shelters, bring one. Although even the cheapest hotels provide bedding, the Andes get cold, and a warm bag-liner (which takes up little space in a pack) is often handy.
- **Tampons** Difficult to find outside the biggest cities.
- **Toilet paper** With a wipe, wipe here and a wipe, wipe there…
- **Travel mug** Great for hot drinks to go and avoiding bacteria-swaps from common glasses at drink stalls.
- **Universal sink plug** Definitely; makes washing clothes in hotel sinks a breeze.
- **Water purifiers** If you plan any remote travel, lengthy river trips, or low-budget tours, always have iodine tablets on hand. Filter pumps are great for trekking, but take up space in your backpack.
- **Zip-close plastic bags** Great for keeping things dry.

THE PRICE YOU'LL PAY (ROUGHLY)

To give a very rough idea of relative costs, let's assume you're traveling with another person, mostly by bus, staying in cheap but clean hotels, eating in local restaurants and food stalls, with the occasional splurge on sightseeing or a night out dancing. In all countries, especially the Guianas, you'll spend much more with juicy side trips and/or tours into interior regions. You could expect the following as a minimum per person/per day budget:

Argentina – US$20
Bolivia – US$20 or less
Brazil – US$25 to US$35
Chile – US$30
Colombia – US$15 to US$25
Ecuador – US$15 to US$20
  (substantially more with a Galápagos trip)

French Guiana – US$50 minimum
Guyana – US$20 to US$30
Paraguay – US$15 to US$25
Peru – US$25 to US$30
Suriname – US$25
Uruguay – US$15 to US$25
Venezuela – US$20 to US$30

Traveler's checks (best if in US dollars) are the safest way to carry money. While it is worth ensuring you have some on hand, they usually entail waiting in lines during standard bank hours, which makes an ATM card much more appealing. ATMs are available in most cities and large towns. Many ATMs accept personal identification numbers (PINs) of only four digits; find out whether this applies to your destinations before heading off.

For more information on money, see Money in the individual country chapter directories and in the South America Directory at the back of this book (p1025).

LIFE ON THE ROAD

There's nothing worse than the working-stiffs back home giving you hell for traipsing around a foreign continent living a 'carefree' life on the road. What they don't know is that it's not all mangos and sunshine. The road means getting up at the crack of dawn to catch a bus after being kept awake all night by the blaring soccer game and squeaking bedsprings in the hotel room next door. It means sucking dust on a long bus ride while manically trying to guess which of the towns you keep passing through is the one you intended to visit. It means blissful relief when you finally arrive and find your pack still on the roof. It's the sight of begging children, the arduous haul to the hotel, a screaming bladder and the excitement of a new town all catapulting your mind from one emotional extreme to another.

The hotel manager says the showers are hot, but the water hitting the skin is as cold as the bottom of Lake Titicaca. There's no seat on the toilet. (At least the bowels are behaving.) You call that a fan? Sounds like a helicopter! OK – food. Leave the pack in the corner, get out the map, locate the market, grab the passport (or leave behind?) and go. The sun feels great. Then you get lost, your mood turns sour as your blood-sugar crashes, you find the market, smell the mangos and try to haggle but have no clue what the fruit seller is saying. You finally hand over the cash – did I just get ripped off? – and walk out to find a good place to eat. Is this easy? Travel in South America certainly has its trials, but that's why we do it. And it sure beats working!

CONDUCT
Dress

Casual dress has become more acceptable recently, but most South Americans still take considerable pride in their personal appearance. Foreign visitors should, at the very least, be clean and neatly dressed if

WHOOPS!

You know you're in South America when you sit on a plaza bench and a monkey jumps on your lap, steals your smoke, puts it in its mouth, looks up at you and then pisses all over your lap when you laugh at it.

DANNY PALMERLEE

10 TIPS TO STAY ON A BUDGET

- Make a group when taking tours; your bargaining power increases the more people you have.
- Camp when you can, especially in southern Argentina and southern Chile.
- Wash your clothes in hotel sinks.
- Skip the taxi and walk or take local buses.
- Buy food at open-air markets instead of eating all meals at restaurants.
- Eat where the locals do rather than at pricier tourist-oriented restaurants.
- Take overnight buses in countries such as Argentina and Brazil to save a night's hotel costs.
- Take 2nd-class buses.
- Travel in a group of two or more to save on food and hotel costs.
- Visit museums on free days.

they wish to conform to local standards and be treated with respect by officials, businesspeople and professionals.

To people of modest means, even shoestring travelers possess considerable wealth. Flaunting items such as expensive cameras, watches and jewelry is likely to attract thieves. Police and military officials are often poorly paid and may resent affluent visitors who do not behave appropriately. (Read: bribery attempts could be coming your way.)

Indigenous People
Using the term 'indio/a' to refer to indigenous people is considered derogatory; rather, the word indígena for indigenous men and women is used.

Access to many remote Amazon Basin areas where people retain the most traditional ways of living is restricted, and it is essential to respect these restrictions. Such regulations help to deflect unwanted interference and protect the communities from diseases to which they have little immunity.

Introductions
In general, South Americans are gregarious, not easily offended, and will want to exchange pleasantries before starting a conversation; skipping this part of any social interaction is considered unrefined and tactless. Public behavior can be very formal, especially among government officials, who expect respect and deference.

Sex
Sexual contact between locals and visitors, male and female, straight and gay, is quite common, and some areas could be described as sex-tourism destinations. Prostitution exists, but is most common in Brazil, where the distinction between prostitution and promiscuity can be hazy. Child prostitution is not common but, sadly, exists. There are harsh penalties for those convicted of soliciting children and real risks of entrapment. AIDS is widespread among gay and straight people alike, so always protect yourself.

Taking Photographs
Don't photograph individuals without obtaining their permission first, especially indigenous people. If someone is giving a public performance, such as a street musician or a dancer at Carnaval, or is incidental to a photograph, in a broad cityscape for example, it's usually not necessary to request permission – but if in doubt, ask or refrain.

Snapshots

CURRENT EVENTS

Argentina headlined South America's entrance into the 21st century by stumbling into it in complete economic turmoil. Protesting Argentines, infuriated by the government's handling of the crisis, forced the resignation of President Fernando de la Rúa in December 2001, and three interim presidents resigned by the time Eduardo Duhalde took office in January 2002. He was the fifth president in two weeks. Argentina defaulted on its US$140 billion loan later that year, and the ragged economy was bequeathed in May 2003 to President Néstor Kirchner.

Brazil's 2002 presidential election swung the country's political agenda to the left when Workers Party (PT) candidate Luíz Inácio 'Lula' da Silva won 61% of the vote. Lula (as he's fondly called) secured the vote by promising to curb hunger and create jobs. Brazil's other big boy of the year was Ronaldo, the oddly coiffed football striker whose two goals against Germany in the World Cup final captured the cup – the country's fifth title – for Brazil.

One of the most fiery issues in South America these days is the proposed Western Hemisphere free-trade agreement known as the Free Trade Area of the Americas (FTAA; ALCA in Spanish), slated for implementation in 2005. To learn why so many are criticizing it, visit www.globalexchange .org/ftaa or www.stopftaa.org.

In Chile, former dictator Augusto Pinochet was to be tried in July 2002 for numerous human rights violations he allegedly committed during his rule from 1973 to 1990, but the Chilean Supreme Court dropped all charges against him, deeming him mentally unfit to stand trial. In mid-2003 headlines turned to booze, as Chile heatedly battled with Peru over ownership rights to *pisco*, a brandy-like liquor which both countries claim is their national drink. (Take the side of the country you're in.)

Peruvian ex-president Alberto Fujimori faced being extradited from Japan, where he fled in 2000 after Peruvian TV aired a video of his spy chief and right-hand man, Vladimir Montesinos, bribing an opposition politician to switch parties. At the time of writing, Montesinos, who filmed himself bribing politicians and Peruvian elite, was on trial in Peru in a bullet-proof courtroom facing corruption charges. President Alejandro Toledo (elected in 2001) continued to pressure Japan for Fujimori's extradition.

In October 2003, Bolivian president Gonzalo Sánchez de Lozada was forced to resign after weeks of protests paralyzed the nation and left more than 65 people dead. Widespread protests by indigenous poor, labor unions and students against Sánchez de Lozada's free-market policies (specifically, in the end, his plan to sell natural gas to the US and Mexico) had rocked Bolivia during the months leading up to the president's October 17 resignation. Sánchez de Lozada was replaced by vice president Carlos Mesa, who was supposed to serve out the ex-president's term until 2007, though he called for early elections. At the time of writing, Mesa has been given a 90-day mandate to roll back the policies that sparked the uprisings that led to Sánchez de Lozada's resignation.

TIMELINE

1524–26: Spanish navigator Francisco Pizarro begins preliminary explorations down South America's Pacific coast

1816–30: Spanish colonies, beginning with Argentina and Chile, win independence from Spain

1935: First official samba parade performed at Rio's Carnaval

1400   1500   1600   1700   1800   1850   1900   1910   1920   1930

1430–40: Inca victory over the Chankas marks beginning of rapid expansion of the Inca empire

1535: Lima founded as the capital of the new viceroyalty of Peru

1930: First World Cup held in Montevideo, Uruguay

In Colombia, Álvaro Uribe came to power in 2002 promising to crack down on armed rebels, which have paralyzed the country for decades. He ditched peace talks and, with continued aid from the US, increased coca eradication and military funding. Political kidnappings and murders by the Fuerzas Armadas Revolucionarias de Colombia (FARC) increased dramatically.

In neighboring Venezuela a failed coup in April 2002 nearly unseated President Hugo Chávez, and nationwide strikes (mostly by middle-class Venezuelans) between December 2002 and February 2003 paralyzed the country. At the close of this edition, Chávez still held power.

HISTORY

Back in the salad days (sometime between 12,500 and 70,000 years ago), humans migrated from Asia to Alaska over a land bridge across the Bering Strait and slowly hunted and gathered their way south. Settled agriculture developed in South America between 5000 BC and 2500 BC in and around present-day Peru, and the emerging societies ultimately developed into major civilizations, of which the Inca empire was the most sophisticated.

> At its peak, the Inca empire governed at least 12 million people from 100 separate cultures and 20 language groups. Its highways traversed more than 8000km of the Andes.

At the time of the Spanish invasion in the early 16th century, the Inca empire was at its peak, governing at least 12 million people from northern Ecuador to central Chile and northern Argentina, where native peoples of the Araucanian language groups fiercely resisted incursions from the north.

The Spanish first arrived in Latin America in 1492, when Christopher Columbus, who was bankrolled by Queen Isabella of Spain to find a new route to Asia's spice islands, accidentally bumped into the Caribbean islands. Meanwhile, the Portuguese navigator Vasco da Gama founded the new sea route to Asia. These spectacular discoveries raised the stakes in the brewing rivalry between Spain and Portugal, and to sort out claims of their newly discovered lands, they decided it was treaty time.

Spanish and Portuguese representatives met in 1494 to draw a nice little line at about 48° west of Greenwich, giving Africa and Asia to Portugal and all of the New World to Spain. Significantly, however, the treaty placed the coast of Brazil (not discovered until six years later) on the Portuguese side of the line, giving Portugal access to the new continent.

Between 1496 and 1526, Spanish exploration from Panama intensified. Rumors surfaced of a golden kingdom south of Panama, prompting Francisco Pizarro to convince Spanish authorities to finance an expedition of 200 men.

When Pizarro encountered the Inca, the empire was wracked by dissension and civil war and proved vulnerable to this invasion by a very small force of Spaniards. Pizarro's well-armed soldiers terrorized the population, but his deadliest weapon was infectious disease, to which

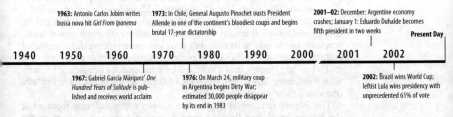

1963: Antonio Carlos Jobim writes bossa nova hit *Girl From Ipanema*	1973: In Chile, General Augusto Pinochet ousts President Allende in one of the continent's bloodiest coups and begins brutal 17-year dictatorship	2001–02: December: Argentine economy crashes; January 1: Eduardo Duhalde becomes fifth president in two weeks

Present Day

1940	1950	1960	1970	1980	1990	2000	2001	2002

1967: Gabriel García Márquez' *One Hundred Years of Solitude* is published and receives world acclaim	1976: On March 24, military coup in Argentina begins Dirty War; estimated 30,000 people disappear by its end in 1983	2002: Brazil wins World Cup; leftist Lula wins presidency with unprecedented 61% of vote

indigenous people lacked any immunity. The Inca ruler Huayna Capac died, probably of smallpox, in about 1525.

Lima, founded in 1535 as the capital of the new viceroyalty of Peru, was the base for most of the ensuing exploration and conquest, and became the seat of all power in Spanish South America. By 1572 the Spanish had defeated and killed two successive Inca rulers – Manco Inca and Tupac Amaru – and solidified Spain's dominance over much of the continent.

Following the conquest, the Spaniards, who above all else wanted gold and silver, worked the indigenous populations mercilessly in the mines and the fields. Native American populations declined rapidly, however, due to introduced diseases. In several parts of the continent, African slaves were introduced to make up for the lack of indigenous labor, notably in the plantations of Brazil and the mines of Bolivia.

The movement for independence by the Spanish colonies began around the end of the 18th century, when Spain, devoting its energy and troops to the war against France, began to lose control of the colonies. By the end of the war in 1814, Venezuela and Argentina had effectively declared independence from Spain, and over the next seven years, the other Spanish colonies followed suit. Brazil became autonomous in 1807 and declared independence in 1822.

After independence, conservative rural landowners, known as caudillos, filled the power vacuum left by the departed colonial regime. Strong dictatorships, periods of instability and the gross inequality between powerful elites and the disfranchised masses have since characterized most South American countries.

After WWII, which marked the beginning of industrialization throughout South America, most countries turned to foreign loans and investment to make up for their lack of capital. This set the stage for the massive debt crises of the 1970s and 1980s, as South American governments accelerated their borrowing, and profits from industry and agriculture made their way into Western banks and the pockets of corrupt South American officials. Dictatorships provided a semblance of stability, but oppression, poverty and corruption bred violent guerrilla movements in many countries, most notably (and most recently) in Peru and Colombia (see those chapters for details). Many of the problems facing South America today are a direct result of foreign debt and the systems of corruption and inequality that date back to colonial and post-independence years.

THE CULTURE
Indigenous Culture

When foreigners imagine indigenous South Americans, odds are they imagine either the colorfully dressed *indígenas* (indigenous people) of the Andean highlands or the people of the Amazon rain forests. The Quechua and other linguistic groups of the Bolivian, Ecuadorian and Peruvian highlands have coexisted with the *mestizo* (people of mixed indigenous and European decent) majority – although not without conflict – for centuries. Their cultures are strong, autonomous and reticent to change and have influenced their country's culture (through music, food, language and so on) to its core. For travelers, experiencing these highland cultures firsthand can be as simple as getting on a bus, shopping in a market or hanging around a village. Many indigenous people are friendly with foreigners; but many are wary of them, as outsiders have brutally oppressed their people for centuries.

The lives of rain-forest peoples are usually vastly different from what the tourist brochures floating the world would suggest. Except under

You know you're in South America when the bus driver says, 'get on, get on, we're leaving!' and then waits 45 minutes before starting the bus.
DANNY PALMERLEE

You know you're in South America when you start to like Nescafé instant coffee.
CAROLYN HUBBARD

unique circumstances, travelers generally will not encounter indigenous people of the rain forest traditionally dressed, unless they're doing so specifically for the sake of tourism – not an inherently negative situation, but one to approach with awareness. Most rain-forest communities have only recently been hit with the Western world. Many are facing the complete upheaval – if not annihilation – of their cultures and lives, and the culture one encounters as a visitor is one in the throes of dramatic change.

Bolivia, Peru and Ecuador have the highest percentages of indigenous people, most of whom live in the highlands. Other important groups include the Tikuna, Yanomami and Guaraní of Brazil, the Mapuche of northern Patagonia, the Aymara of Bolivia, and the Atacameños and Aymara of Chile's altiplano.

Music

How do you spell 'life' in South America? M-u-s-i-c. Turn it off, and the continent would simply grind to a halt. South America's musical landscape is incredibly varied, and its more popular styles – samba, lambada and bossa nova from Brazil, the Argentine tango, Colombian salsa and Andean *musica folklorica* – are known internationally. But there are countless regional styles that will likely be new to foreign ears, including *vallenato* in Colombia, Afro-Peruvian music, *joropó* in Venezuela, *chamamé* in Argentina and *forró* and *carimbo* in Brazil. For those who happen to have more Western pop sensibilities, there's a rich history of *rock en español* (Spanish-language rock) and Nueva Canción (political folk music) in Argentina and Chile. The musical influences on South American music are equally diverse, with Eastern European polkas, African rhythms and North American jazz and rock all factoring into the equation.

You know you're in South America when you realize that not only do all the men dance, but they all dance darn well! Now that's culture shock.

CHARLOTTE BEECH

Population & People

Over three-quarters of all South Americans live in cities, while large areas such as the Amazon Basin and Atacama Desert are almost uninhabited. Population growth and internal migration have led to the emergence of supercities, such as São Paulo (population 17 million), Buenos Aires (13 million), Rio de Janeiro (seven million), Lima (7.7 million) and Bogotá (seven million). These megalopolises concentrate some of the most severe social and environmental problems on the continent.

Infant mortality rates are shockingly high in some countries, most notably Bolivia, Brazil and Peru. South America has a high proportion of people younger than 15 years old (30%), but some of the countries (in particular Bolivia, Brazil, Columbia, Ecuador, Peru, and Venezuela) have even more youthful populations, with nearly 40% of the people younger than 15. It's likely that populations will continue to burgeon as these individuals reach childbearing ages, and it's doubtful that local economies will be able to provide employment for so many in such a short period of time.

You know you're in South America when you're playing a card game whose sole premise is cheating.

DANNY PALMERLEE

Although the majority of South Americans are *mestizos*, a large percentage of the Peruvian, Ecuadorian and Bolivian populations are self-identified indigenous. Many Brazilians claim African heritage, and the Guianas are a mosaic of East Indians, Indonesians, Africans, Creoles, Chinese and their descendants. Even in the most racially homogeneous countries (eg Argentina, Chile and Paraguay), Syrian, Chinese, Japanese and other immigrants and their descendants are represented in the population.

Religion

About 90% of South Americans are at least nominally Roman Catholic. Virtually every city, town and village has a central church or cathedral and a calendar loaded with Catholic holidays and celebrations. Spreading the faith was a major objective of colonization.

Among indigenous peoples, allegiance to Catholicism was often a clever veneer adopted to disguise traditional beliefs ostensibly forbidden by the church. Similarly, black slaves in Brazil gave Christian names and forms to their African gods, whose worship was discouraged or forbidden. Syncretic beliefs and practices such as Candomblé in Brazil have proliferated to this day, but they do not exclude Christianity. There is no conflict between attending mass one day and seeking guidance from a *brujo* (witch) the next.

In recent decades, various Protestant sects have made inroads among the traditionally Catholic population. This is partly because of evangelical efforts, partly as a response to the uncertainty created by rapid social and economic change, and perhaps partly due to complacency in the established Catholic Church. There is also a small number of Jews and Muslims sprinkled throughout the continent.

Sports

Baseball, bullfighting, cockfighting and the rodeo are important in some South American countries, but nothing unites most South Americans like football (in the soccer sense, that is). It's the national passion in every South American country. Brazil won its fifth World Cup final in 2002, snatching the world record for most titles taken. Argentina's Boca Juniors are one of the world's most famous teams. If you want to get anyone blabbing, just bring up former Boca Junior star Diego Maradona's infamous 'Hand of God' goal that knocked England out of the 1986 World Cup. He scored with his hand. The passion can reach extremes: in 1994, after Colombian defender Andreas Escobar scored an own goal in a World Cup game against the US, he was shot ten times outside a Medellín nightclub. According to police, the gunman shouted *'Gol!'* after each shot. To say the least, football is serious. The annual South American championship is the Copa Libertadores. The Copa América is a continent-wide championship played in odd-number years, and non–South American teams are invited.

Volleyball has become extremely popular throughout South America, especially in Brazil. There, people also play a variation called *futvolei*, in which players use their feet instead of their hands.

Rallies (dirt- and off-road auto races) are big in Chile, Argentina, Bolivia and Brazil. Argentina is famous for polo, Buenos Aires being the best place to see a match.

ENVIRONMENT
Land

'Glaciers on the equator – whoa, this place is weird.'

TRAVELER REFLECTING ON HER WHEREABOUTS

The Cordillera de los Andes, the longest continuous mountain system on earth, forms the western margin of the continent, snaking nearly 8000km from Venezuela to southern Patagonia. Riddled with volcanoes, the Andes are part of the volcanic 'ring of fire' running from Asia to Alaska to Tierra del Fuego. East of the Andes, the Amazon Basin – the largest river basin in the world – covers parts of Bolivia, Venezuela, Colombia, Peru, Ecuador, the Guianas and Brazil. In the center of the continent (in parts of Brazil, Bolivia and Paraguay), the vast Pantanal is the largest inland wetland on earth. Yep, this place is *big*.

On the geographical sidestage, other physical features include the Orinoco River Basin, which drains the *llanos* (plains) of Venezuela; the barren Chaco of southern Bolivia, northwestern Paraguay and the northern tip of Argentina; the extensive Paraná–Paraguay river system; the fertile pampas of Argentina and Uruguay; and arid, mystical Patagonia, in the far south.

Wildlife

AMAZON BASIN RAIN FORESTS

Tropical rain forest is the earth's most complex ecosystem. Check out the Amazon: it contains an estimated 50,000 species of higher plants, one-fifth of the world's total. In some of its two-hectare plots, it's possible to find more than 500 tree species; a comparable plot in a midlatitude forest might have three or four. One study found 3000 species of beetle in five small plots and estimated that each tree species supported more than 400 unique animal species. The rain-forest canopy is so dense, however, that little to no sunlight penetrates to the forest floor, and nearly all life is found in the trees.

TROPICAL CLOUD FORESTS

In remote valleys at higher elevations, tropical cloud forests retain clouds that engulf the forest in a fine mist, allowing wonderfully delicate forms of plant life to survive. Cloud-forest trees have low, gnarled growth, dense, small-leafed canopy, and moss-covered branches supporting orchids, ferns and a host of other epiphytes (plants that gather moisture and nutrients without ground roots). Such forests are the homes of rare species such as the woolly tapir, the Andean spectacled bear and the puma.

HIGH-ALTITUDE GRASSLANDS

Even higher than the cloud forest, the *páramo* is the natural sponge of the Andes and is characterized by a harsh climate, high levels of ultraviolet light and wet, peaty soils. It is an enormously specialized habitat unique to tropical America and is found only from the highlands of Costa Rica to the highlands of northern Peru. Flora of the *páramo* is dominated by hard grasses, cushion plants and small herbaceous plants, and features dense thickets of the *queñoa* tree, which, along with Himalayan pines, share the world altitude record for trees.

CENTRAL ANDEAN REGION

Another unique ecosystem exists between the coast and the cordillera, from northern Chile to northern Peru. The coastal Atacama Desert, the world's driest, is almost utterly barren in the rain shadow of the Andes. The cold Peru current (also called the Humboldt current) moderates the temperature at this tropical latitude and produces convective fogs (*garúa* or *camanchaca*) that support hillside vegetation (*lomas*) in the coastal ranges.

TROPICAL DRY FORESTS

Hot areas with well-defined wet and dry seasons support the growth of dry forests. In South America these climatic conditions are mostly found near the coast in the northern part of the continent. Because many of these coastal regions have a dense and growing population, tropical dry forest is a fast-disappearing habitat – only about 1% remains undisturbed.

The Amazon River, from its inconspicuous source in the Peruvian highlands, to its mouth near Belém, Brazil, measures more than 6200km. Its flow is 12 times that of the Mississippi, it carries one-fifth of the world's freshwater and its discharge into the Atlantic every 24 hours equals that of the Thames in a full year.

GOING TO THE SOURCE *by Regis St. Louis*

Jaguars, piranhas and scorpions were all part of the scenery in Catherine Clark's 4000-mile journey along the length of the Amazon.

As a born and bred urbanite with a healthy horror of insects and no specialist knowledge of the rain forest, Catherine Clark seemed among the least-suitable candidates for a six-month journey along the Amazon. But her lack of experience was precisely what inspired her. 'I wanted to test myself,' she explained, 'to see if I could rise to the challenge of surviving in a culture and habitat so alien to everything I had known before.'

Indeed, in her 4000-mile trek from the mouth of the Amazon on the Atlantic coast to the river's source in the Andes, Catherine experienced things she never would have imagined, from fleeing pirates along the Río Ucayali to sampling the saliva-fermented yucca drink *masato*. She visited remote tribes, dined on piranhas, and traveled for weeks along vast waterways without seeing another foreigner. Her journey turned out to be one of the greatest trips she'd undertaken, and her lack of experience in the region didn't seem to inhibit her. 'The Amazon is without doubt a mystery and a challenge,' she noted, 'but it is a region that anyone can enter with the right amount of respect and awe.'

Although this was Catherine's first trip to the Amazon, she's no stranger to long trips abroad. From an early age, she traveled with her parents all over Western Europe and the United States during school breaks. At eighteen, she spent the better part of a year in Mexico, working as a volunteer in a children's home, before returning to England to study French and Spanish at Oxford University. Since then she has traveled further in Europe and India while also working in communications. At present, Catherine lives in Peru where she is writing a book about her recent trip. It is entitled *Eye of the Amazon: Travels from the Mouth to the Source of the Great River.*

When Lonely Planet heard of Catherine's adventures, we contacted her to get the lowdown on her epic journey.

Lonely Planet: When did you first decide to undertake a trip along the Amazon?

Catherine Clark: The Amazon region has always intrigued me with its tales of legendary tribes of female warriors, its attraction to adventurers throughout the ages, and its turbulent past and present. Amazonia is a watery land of superlatives and mystery: the world's biggest rain forest, its most powerful river, and one of its wildest frontiers, with roughly 50 uncontacted tribes living in the Brazilian Amazon alone. It was the river itself that attracted me most.

What's your fondest memory of traveling in the Amazon?

The hospitality I received in Sachapapa, a community of the Aguaruna tribe in the province of Alto Amazonas. Arriving at the community after nine hours stumbling over the muddy hills of the jungle, I found I couldn't walk more than a hundred yards without being invited into a house for a bowl of the traditional indigenous drink, *masato*. The drink is made from the yucca plant, which is boiled, then chewed so that saliva kick-starts the fermentation process. Afterwards, it is spat into large vats, where it ferments within a day or two in the heat and humidity of the jungle. A visitor risks grave offense in refusing an offer of food or drink, so I floated around the community with a happy smile for the next few days, accepting bowls of *masato* for breakfast, lunch and dinner. They gave me an Aguaruna name, as is the custom for a first-time visitor, and from now on I was to be Yampan, named after the industrious wife of the sun Etsa in Aguaruna legend.

What was your favorite place?

Of the many favorites, I would include the Pacaya-Samiria reserve in the Peruvian Amazon. It's a giant wonderland – uninhabited and virtually untouched. I spent seven days paddling with a local guide up the river Samiria, with the mighty trees of the forest towering up to 200ft above us. It felt like stepping into a David Attenborough documentary with all the birds and animals around: gold and blue macaws, toucans, river turtles, crocodiles, electric eels and dolphins, with monkeys munching in branches less than 10ft away. My encounters with the local insect population were somewhat less enjoyable, as I was stung by a scorpion falling from a tree into our canoe. An Amazonian saying is that newcomers need to be bitten 'for the jungle to get to know you,' but it was an intimacy I could have done without.

Any particularly difficult experiences?

One of the most difficult moments was when my guide and I were being stalked by a jaguar in the forest near the river Urubu in Brazil. It was the longest three-hour walk of my life as we hurried back to our canoe. I swallowed my rising panic as my guide warned me to watch our backs – jaguars follow their prey from behind until they're sure of their target. In those three hours, every twitch of a leaf or crackle of the undergrowth transformed itself in my imagination into the spring of a hungry jaguar.

How was it traveling solo as a woman in the region?

I can't say that it was always easy, but in many ways it worked in my favor. I was struck time and time again by the kindness and hospitality of local villagers. On almost every boat ride I encountered a middle-aged woman who took it upon herself to adopt me for the duration of the journey, and who would ask after me if she hadn't see me in a while. On one boat, the passengers thought I'd been left behind when we stopped to unload cargo and were on the point of sending out a speedboat to try and find me. Luckily they searched the ship first and found me lounging on the top deck.

Did you eat any grubs? Other exotic foods?

No grubs. There are large worms – served fried – that are popular around Iquitos, but I couldn't bring myself to eat them. I tried crocodile, which is delicious and tastes like a cross between chicken and fish. I also grew fond of piranha fishing, and found satisfaction in hauling the vicious creatures, with their bad-tempered expressions, out of the water. The only other thing I really couldn't eat was monkey. I'd been prepared to try anything while with the Aguaruna community in Sachapapa, but when they brought out a whole monkey's arm with a tiny hand attached I had to make my excuses.

Where did your trip end?

At the source of the river Amazon, the 'Eye of the Amazon', set high on the 18,000ft Mount Mismi near Colca Canyon in southern Peru. After a torturous ascent, crossing high plains and climbing snow-clad ridges, I arrived at the spot where a mere trickle of water came gushing out of a dark wall of rock, starting the 4000-mile journey I'd just traveled in reverse. It was one of the happiest moments of my life, and that day I had one of the best drinks I've ever tasted – the ice-cold water from the Eye of the Amazon.

Any advice for someone thinking of undertaking an Amazonian expedition?

Above all, don't be afraid of the unknown. Try to get out of the major cities to the smaller Amazonian towns and villages, where life is lived at a different pace. Yes, there are many dangers in the region, but follow the example of the locals – don't bathe where they don't, don't walk where they don't and, if in doubt, ask someone for help or advice. They're more than willing to give it to you.

MANGROVES

Found in coastal areas of Brazil, Colombia, Ecuador, the Guianas and Venezuela, mangroves are trees with a remarkable ability to grow in saltwater. They have a broadly spreading system of intertwining stilt roots to support the tree in unstable sandy or silty soils. Mangrove forests trap sediments and build up a rich organic soil, which in turn supports other plants. Mangrove roots provide a protected habitat for many types of fish, mollusc and crustacean, while the branches provide nesting areas for sea birds.

National Parks

There are over 200 national parks in South America and a staggering number of provincial parks and private reserves. They are undeniably one of the continent's highlights, covering every terrain imaginable, from tropical rain forest and cloud forest to Andean *páramo* to tropical and temperate coastal regions. The most popular parks have well-developed tourist infrastructures and high-season crowds and are fairly easy to reach. Some parks have only faint trails, basic camping facilities or refuges and, if you're lucky, a park ranger to answer questions. Others are impossible to reach without 4WD transport or a private boat. Maps are generally tough to come by, so if you plan to do any trekking, research the park first and check larger cities for topographical map sources. See Maps in both the South America Directory, p1035, and in individual country directories for information on where to obtain maps.

Environmental Issues

Deforestation – of the Amazon rain forest, the temperate forests of Chile and Argentina, the coastal mangroves and cloud forests of Ecuador, and the Chocó bioregion of pacific Panama, Colombia and Ecuador – is perhaps the single greatest environmental problem facing South America. Oil exploration has opened pristine tracts of Amazon rain forest to colonization and has lead to large-scale toxic spills and the poisoning of rivers and streams. Conservation of Brazil's Pantanal, the largest wetland in the world, may soon take back seat to more profitable industrial projects such as a natural gas pipeline, a thermal electric plant and steel mills. The list goes on, and the best way to help is to study up and get involved. The following websites are great starting points:

Amazon Watch (www.amazonwatch.org)
Ancient Forests International (www.ancientforests.org)
Conservation International (CI; www.conservation.org)
Rainforest Action Network (RAN; www.ran.org)

Argentina

HIGHLIGHTS

- **Buenos Aires** – beautiful European buildings, tasty restaurants, colorful neighborhoods, great shopping, thick tango culture and a raging nightlife that throbs till dawn (p43)
- **Southern Patagonia** – from the crashing icebergs of dynamic Moreno Glacier to the world-class hikes and climbs streaming from the hamlet of El Chaltén (p132)
- **Lake District** – a recreational paradise: enjoy hiking, white-water rafting, horse riding, mountain biking, fishing and skiing. And try the chocolate, will you? (p118)
- **Iguazú Falls** –thundering cascades stretching more than 2km and enclosed by thick, toucan-filled jungles. Probably the most amazing waterfalls on earth (p79)
- **Off the beaten track** – running north of Jujuy towards the Bolivian border, the Quebrada de Humahuaca is dotted with cobbled Quechuan hamlets and historic churches (p98)
- **Best journey** – gravelly Ruta 40, running the length of Argentina along the Andean spine and reaching an almost mythical stature among adventurous Argentines, is a bleak, expansive terrain of flat isolation occasionally dotted with quirky towns (p144)

FAST FACTS

- **Area:** 2.8 million sq km (roughly the size of India)
- **Budget:** US$20 a day
- **Capital:** Buenos Aires
- **Costs:** hostel US$6, steak dinner US$5, four-hour bus ride US$6
- **Country code:** ☎ 54
- **Electricity:** 220V, 50Hz; adapters – two rounded prongs or three angled flat prongs
- **Famous for:** *gauchos* (cowboys), tango, steak and Maradona
- **Languages:** Spanish; Quechua in the Andean northwest
- **Money:** US$1 = 2.90 pesos
- **Phrases:** *genial, barbaro* (cool), *asqueroso* (disgusting), *fiesta, partusa, pachanga* (party)
- **Population:** 37 million
- **Time:** GMT minus 3 hours

- **Tipping:** 10% in restaurants; leftover change in taxis
- **Traveler's checks:** very hard to cash outside Buenos Aires; ATMs are the way to go
- **Visas:** not needed by North American and most European citizens

---

TRAVEL HINTS

Pack light; if you forget anything, you can probably find it in Argentina. Bring nice clothes if hanging out in Buenos Aires. In Patagonia, pack layers and foul weather gear – even in summer. A few photos from home, especially of the family, will always be a hit when getting to know the locals.

There are absolutely no ifs, ands or buts about it: for budget backpackers doing the South America circuit, Argentina is now the place to be. Thinking of learning the seductive tango? Always wanted to traverse the Patagonian steppe? Hungry for thick and juicy steaks? Need to take some Spanish classes? What about catching a really passionate game of soccer? Don't forget the incredible nightlife in cosmopolitan Buenos Aires, raging on till 6am! And finally, wait till you see how much it'll all cost – you won't believe your eyes at what bargains this country has to offer. But you need more convincing, right?

You can see South America's highest peaks, rising to almost 7000m and perpetually blanketed in virgin snow; the painted northern Andean deserts, dotted with colonial cities and lanky cactus; the Lake District, with blue-green shimmering lakes and lush mountain forests; astounding southern glaciers calving huge slivers of ice that smash into lakes below; the legendary Iguazú Falls, a massive stream of 70m-high cataracts extending as far as your eye can see; and wildlife ranging from strange guanacos (llama-like animals), rheas (large flightless birds) and capybaras (large amphibious rodents) to the more familiar flamingos, whales and penguins. And then there's Patagonia, instilling a romantic tingle and wanderlust to those who dream of someday visiting this vast and bleak outback land, ringed to the west by some of the world's most impressive mountain formations and extending all the way south toward Ushuaia and the edge of the world.

Argentina is safe, amazing, accessible and downright hot and affordable these days, so whatever you do, don't miss seeing this country. It's what everyone's talking about, and a great place to visit.

HISTORY
Pre-Columbian Times
Before the Spanish arrived, nomadic hunter-gatherers roamed the wilds of ancient Argentina. The Yámana (or Yahgan) developed canoes and gathered shellfish in Patagonia, while on the pampas the Querandí used *boleadoras* (weights on cords) to hunt rhea (ostrich-like birds) and guanaco (animals similar to the llama). Up in the subtropical northeast, the Guaraní settled down long enough to cultivate maize, while in the arid northwest the Diaguita developed an irrigation system for crops.

In 1536 the Querandí were unfortunate enough to meet exploring Spaniards in search of gold and silver. After refusing to be subjugated, they attacked their tormentors and a few years later managed to drive them away to Asunción, Paraguay. (Left behind were cattle and horses, which multiplied giving rise to the legendary *gaucho*, or cowboy). In 1580 when the Spaniards returned to the area they established Buenos Aires – but trade restrictions from Spain limited the development of the new settlement. The northern colonies of Tucumán, Córdoba and Salta, however, thrived by providing mules, cloth and foodstuffs for the silver mines of Bolivia. Meanwhile, Spaniards from Chile moved into the Andean Cuyo region, which produced wine and grain.

Growth & Independence
In 1776 Buenos Aires was a designated capital of the new viceroyalty of the Río de la Plata. A rogue British force, hoping to snag a piece of the trade pie, invaded in 1806 but was expelled soon after by the settlers. With newfound power, confident colonists revolted against Spain, which they still resented for trade restrictions. Complete independence was finally declared six years later in 1816.

Despite the unity hatched by independence, provincial strongmen resisted Buenos Aires' authority. Argentina split allegiances between the inhabitants of Buenos Aires (Unitarists) and the country folk (Federalists). A civil war ensued, and the two parties' bloody, vindictive conflicts nearly exhausted the country.

In 1829 Juan Manuel de Rosas came into power as a Federalist, but applied his own brand of Unitarist principles to centralize control in Buenos Aires. He built a large army, created the *mazorca* (a ruthless secret police) and forced overseas trade through the port city. Intellectual Domingo F Sarmiento, who later became president, wrote in his book *The Human Background of Dictatorship, the Gaucho* (1868) that Rosas 'applied the knife of the *gaucho* to the culture of Buenos Ayres, and destroyed the work of centuries – of civilization, law

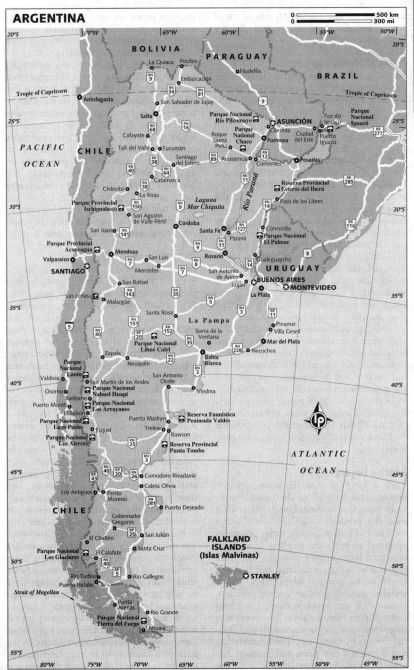

and liberty'. The Unitarists, and some of Rosas' former allies, forced the dictator from power in 1852.

Roots of Modern Argentina

Settled in power, the Unitarists issued a liberal constitution that opened the country to foreign investment, trade and immigration. In the following decades, sheep, cattle and cereal products were freely exported while Spanish, Italian, French and other European immigrants filled key roles in crafts and commerce. British capital built the extensive rail network that fanned out from Buenos Aires. Prosperity arrived at last, and Argentina became one of the richest countries in the world – although much of that wealth belonged to relatively few landowners and urban elite.

This was a tenuous opulence, as global economic fluctuations brought about new foreign trade restrictions that mostly benefited rich producers of wheat, wine and sugar. After the 1880s poor immigrants continued to flood in and nearly doubled Buenos Aires' population, increasing it to one million residents. Old colonial buildings were torn down, major streets were widened and urban services improved. The industrial sector could not absorb all the immigrants and their needs, however, and the gap between rich and poor widened. In 1929 the military took power from an ineffectual civilian government, but an obscure colonel – Juan Domingo Perón – was the first leader to really confront the developing social crisis.

Perón's Legacy

From a minor post in the labor ministry, and with the help of his charismatic soon-to-be wife, Eva Duarte (Evita), Juan Perón won the presidency in 1946. His social welfare and new economic order programs appealed to both the working class, who benefited from improved wages, job security and working conditions, and to more conservative groups. Remarkably, Perón avoided alienating either sector, despite a virtual civil war between them. His heavy control over the country, however, was tinged with fascism: he abused his presidential powers by using excessive intimidation and squelched free press and political dissent. Dynamic Evita, meanwhile, used her

growing influence for her own sometimes vindictive political ends, though she was mostly championed for her charitable work and women's rights campaigns.

Rising inflation and economic difficulties (due especially to a shortage of capital from war-torn Europe) undermined Perón's second presidency in 1952; Evita's death the same year was another blow. After a coup against him in 1955, Perón retreated to Spain to plot his return. The opportunity came almost two decades later when Héctor Cámpora resigned the presidency in 1973. Perón won the elections easily, but his death in mid-1974 sucked the country back into the governmental coups and chaos that had plagued it since his exile. In 1976 military rule prevailed once again, and Argentina entered its darkest hour.

Dirty War (1976–83)

In the late 1960s, a left-wing, highly organized Perónist guerrilla group called the Montoneros formed to resuscitate Evita's anti-elitist doctrine, sometimes by violent means. The mostly educated, middle-class youths bombed foreign businesses, kidnapped executives for ransom and robbed banks to finance their armed struggle and to spread their social messages. After Perón's death, General Jorge Videla's regime instituted an unparalleled reign of terror, the so-called Process of National Reorganization. In theory, the Proceso (as it came to be called) was to create a basis for enduring democracy by stabilizing the economy and eliminating corruption. In practice, it was an orgy of corruption in the name of development, accompanied by state-sponsored violence and anarchy – and their primary target was the Montoneros.

True numbers may never be known, but some estimate that up to 30,000 people died in the infamous Guerra Sucia (Dirty War). The dictatorship did not distinguish between the revolutionary guerrillas or those who assisted them, those who sympathized with them, or those who simply expressed reservations about the dictatorship's indiscriminate brutality. To 'disappear' meant to be detained, tortured and probably killed, without legal process. Any person could become a target, whisked off suddenly in the back of a black Ford Falcon; intellectuals, writers, doctors, factory workers, liberals –

anyone at all who might have been in the wrong place at the wrong time.

The government rarely acknowledged detentions, though it sometimes reported deaths of individuals in 'battles with security forces.' A few courageous individuals and groups, including Nobel Peace Prize winner Adolfo Pérez Esquivel and the Madres de la Plaza de Mayo (women who to this day keep a vigil for their disappeared children in Buenos Aires' Plaza de Mayo) kept the story in public view, but the Dirty War ended only when the government forces attempted a real military objective – the repossession of the Islas Malvinas (Falkland Islands).

Falklands War

In early 1981 General Roberto Viola replaced Videla as de facto president, but General Leopoldo Galtieri soon replaced the ineffectual Viola. When continuing economic deterioration and general discontent brought mass demonstrations, a desperate Galtieri, trying to draw attention away from his flailing government, invaded the British-ruled Islas Malvinas in April 1982.

The brief occupation of the Malvinas, claimed by Argentina for 150 years, unleashed a wave of nationalist euphoria that lasted about a week. Then the Argentines realized that iron-clad British prime minister Margaret Thatcher was not a woman to be crossed, especially when she had political troubles of her own. Britain fought back, sending a naval contingent to set things straight, and Argentina's mostly teenaged, ill-trained, and poorly motivated forces surrendered after 74 days.

The war cost the two countries almost 2000 men (mostly Argentines) and US$2 billion. The military, stripped of its reputation and emasculated before the eyes of the country and world, finally withdrew from government. In 1983, Argentina elected Raúl Alfonsín, of the Radical Civic Union, to the presidency.

Argentina Today

Alfonsín brought democracy back to Argentina, and at least the first part of his tenure proved successful, solving some territorial disputes with Chile and managing to curb inflation somewhat. And Alfonsín's pledge to try military officers for human rights violations brought convictions of kidnapping, torture and murder for Videla, Viola and others – but he couldn't pull the long-struggling country back onto its feet again.

Carlos Menem, president from 1989 to 1999, brought brief prosperity to Argentina by selling off many private industries and borrowing heavily. He also practically stopped inflation in its tracks by pegging the peso with the US dollar, but this was only a quick fix. Argentina's economy just couldn't keep up with the United States', and after a few years the peso became so overvalued that Argentine goods weren't competitive enough on the global market. Toward the end of Menem's rule major scandals and even house arrest plagued his presidency, while unemployment spiraled steadily upwards.

In December 1999 Fernando de la Rúa was sworn into office. He inherited an almost bankrupt government which witnessed yet another economic downturn, even higher unemployment and a widespread lack of public confidence. Seeing him as an inept, powerless figure, the public lost faith in their banks and in late 2001 – after Argentina failed to acquire IMF loan guarantees – began withdrawing massive amounts of savings. To avoid complete insolvency the government imposed a weekly cash-withdrawal limit of US$250, but subsequent rioting (in which 27 people were killed) proved this a bad idea. After de la Rúa resigned in December 2001, the country went through three more presidents within two weeks before finally putting transitory *jefe* (leader) Eduardo Duhalde in the hot seat.

Duhalde's tolerable 17th-month presidency dealt with the aftermath of the peso crash, Argentina's $140 billion debt default and the use of provincial bonds as currency, not to mention a further shrinking of the country's economy, sustained high unemployment and continued lack of funds from an exasperated IMF. At least inflation had been kept mostly in check, and toward the end of his reign the Argentine economy was actually starting to stir a little.

In May 2003 the left-leaning Néstor Kirchner was handed the presidential reins after he won by default against comeback kid

WHEN THE EDGE OF THE WORLD JUST ISN'T FAR ENOUGH – FALKLAND ISLANDS/ISLAS MALVINAS

Fast Facts

- **Area:** 12,173 sq km (slightly smaller than Northern Ireland or the US state of Connecticut)
- **Budget:** US$70–90 a day
- **Capital:** Stanley
- **Costs:** B&B in Stanley £20 per person per night, main course at nice restaurant £15, short taxi ride £2
- **Country code:** ☎ 500
- **Electricity:** 240V, 50 Hz; UK-type plugs

- **Famous for:** sheep, penguins and a war
- **Languages:** English
- **Money:** US$1 = £0.58 Falkland Islands pound
- **Phrases:** baaaaaa
- **Population:** 3500 humans, 700,000 sheep
- **Time:** GMT minus 4 hours
- **Tipping:** generally not practiced
- **Traveler's checks:** readily accepted
- **Visas:** North American and most European citizens need only a valid passport

The sheep boom in Tierra del Fuego and Patagonia owes its origins to a cluster of islands 300 miles (500km) to the east in the South Atlantic Ocean. These islands, the Islas Malvinas (to the Argentines) or Falkland Islands (to the British) were explored, but never fully captured either country's interest. Very little transpired on the islands until the mid-19th century wool boom in Europe, when the Falkland Islands Company (FIC) became the islands' largest landholder. The population, mostly stranded mariners and *gauchos*, grew rapidly with the arrival of English and Scottish immigrants. In an unusual exchange, the South American Missionary Society in 1853 began transporting Yahgan Indians from Tierra del Fuego to Keppel Island to catechize them.

Argentina has laid claim to the islands since 1833, but it wasn't until 1982 that Argentine president Leopoldo Galtieri decided that reclaiming the islands would unite his country behind him. However, English Prime Minister Margaret Thatcher (who was also suffering in the polls) didn't hesitate for a moment in striking back, thoroughly humiliating Argentina in what became known as the Falkland Islands War. A severe blow to Argentina's nationalist pride, the ill-fated war succeeded in severing all diplomatic ties between the two nations.

On July 14 1999 a joint statement issued by the British, Falkland Islands and Argentine governments promised closer cooperation on areas of economic mutual interest. In August 2001 British Prime Minister Tony Blair visited Argentina in an effort to further improve ties between the countries. Nevertheless, relations with Argentina are still distinctly cool, many islanders remain deeply suspicious of Argentine motives, and most trade with the South American continent goes via Chile.

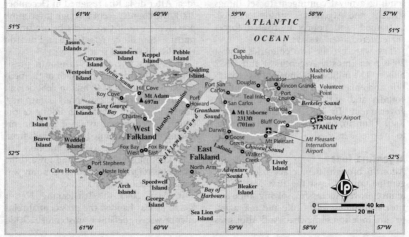

Besides being an unusually polemic piece of property, what is there about the Falklands that might intrigue the intrepid traveler? Bays, inlets, estuaries and beaches create a tortuous, attractive coastline that is home to abundant wildlife. Striated and crested caracaras, cormorants, oystercatchers, snowy sheathbills, sheldgeese and a plethora of penguins – Magellanic, rockhopper, macaroni, gentoo and king – share top billing with elephant seals, sea lions, fur seals, killer whales and some five species of dolphins.

Stanley is an assemblage of brightly painted metal-clad houses and is a good place to throw down a few pints and listen to island lore. 'Camp' – as the rest of the islands is known as – is home to settlements that began as company towns (hamlets where coastal shipping could collect wool) and now provide lodging and a chance to experience pristine nature and wildlife.

Planning

The best time to visit is from October to March, when migratory birds and mammals return to beaches and headlands. Fun events around which to plan a trip are the sports meetings featuring horse racing, bull riding and sheepdog trials, which take place in Stanley between Christmas and New Year's, and on East and West Falkland in late February. Summer never gets truly hot (maximum high is 24°C or 75°F), but high winds can chill the air.

Information

Everyone entering the Falkland Islands is required to have an onward ticket, proof of sufficient funds (credit cards are fine) and prearranged accommodations for the first few nights.

The **Falkland Islands Tourist Board** (☎ 22281; www.tourism.org.fk; Ross Rd; ⏰ 9am-5pm Mon-Sat, 10am-4pm Sun summer & when cruise ships are in port, 11am-2pm Wed & Fri-Sun winter), at the public jetty in Stanley, distributes excellent brochures on things to do in and around Stanley. The *Visitor Accommodation Guide* lists lodgings and places that allow camping around the islands. In the UK there's the **Falkland House** (☎ 020-7222-2542; fax 020-7222-2375; manager@figo.u-net.com; 14 Broadway, Westminster, London SW1H 0BH).

Pound sterling and US dollars in cash or traveler's checks are readily accepted, but the exchange rate for US currency is low. There's no need to change money to FK£, which are not accepted off the islands. The only bank is **Standard Chartered Bank** (☎ 21352; fax 22219), in Stanley; ATMs do not exist. In peak season, expect to spend US$70 to US$90 per day, not including airfare, within the islands (less if camping or staying in self-catering cottages).

Getting There & Around

From South America, LANChile flies to Mt Pleasant International Airport (near Stanley) every Saturday from Santiago, Chile, via Puerto Montt, Punta Arenas and – one Saturday each month – Río Gallegos, Argentina. Round-trip fares are US$680 from Santiago, US$490 from Punta Arenas. Book a week in advance to save $30 to $70.

From RAF Brize Norton, in Oxfordshire, England, there are regular flights to Mt Pleasant (16 hours, plus an hour layover on Ascension Island). The round-trip fare is UK£2490, but reduced Apex fares cost UK£1530 with 30-day advance purchase. Travelers continuing on to Chile can purchase one-way tickets for half the fare. Contact the travel coordinator at **Falkland House** (☎ 020-7222-2542).

From Stanley, **Figas** (☎ 27219; figas.fig@horizon.co.fk) serves outlying destinations in nine-passenger aircraft. Travel within the Falklands costs approximately FK£1 per minute.

Byron Marine Ltd (☎ 22245; fax 22246; byron@horizon.co.fk; Byron House, H Jones Rd, Stanley) carries a few passengers on its freighter MV Tamar while delivering wool and other goods to outlying settlements. Berths are limited; day trips cost FK£20, overnights cost FK£25. Meals are included.

Several Stanley operators run day trips to East Falkland settlements, including **Discovery Tours** (☎ 21027; fax 22304; www.discoveryfalklands.com), **Ten Acre Tours** (☎ 21155; fax 21950; www.tourism.org.fk/pages/tenacres-tours.htm) and **South Atlantic Marine Services** (☎ 21145; fax 22674; www.falklands-underwater.com). **Hebe Tours** (☎ 21561; www.tourism.org.fk/pages/hebe-tours.htm) conducts fishing and wildlife tours. **Seaview** (☎ 22669; fax 22670) can arrange visits to Kidney Island, which has colonies of rockhopper penguins and sea lions.

Carlos Menem, who had pulled out of the race just a few days before the final vote (which he probably would've lost by a landslide). Perónist Kirchner now has the pleasure of negotiating talks with Argentina's unfortunate creditors and getting the economy back on track. Best of luck, Néstor.

THE CULTURE
The National Psyche
Ask any other South American what they think of their Argentine neighbors and you're likely to get an unfavorable response. Argentines have a world-wide reputation for being spoiled, stuck-up and egotistical. They seem to think they're better than anyone else, and that they belong in Europe rather than at the tail end of a third-world continent like South America. It's no wonder people make fun of them – just ask any Argentine to tell you an Argentine joke. Most of these jokes aren't flattering, but they are funny.

Well, it wouldn't be a stereotype if it weren't a little bit true, but most Argentines simply don't fit this profile. Maybe it's because when folks think of Argentines, they think of *porteños*, or residents of Buenos Aires. While a huge number of people do live in the capital and its suburbs, a full two-thirds live in the rest of Argentina – where attitudes and egos are more modest. In fact, many folks outside the capital don't even *like porteños*. And, not all *porteños* are sniffy aristocratic wannabes who go around disparaging everyone else and their mother. Quite a few, as you'll find out, are very friendly, helpful and hospitable, and curious about where you come from and what you think. They're mostly great folks – just give them a chance.

It's not hard to see how Argentines got their reputation. They live in a fabulous country rich in scenery, culture and natural resources. Their capital, Buenos Aires, is a gorgeous city full of history and life. They have sultry tango, high fashion, great soccer and the best steaks in the world. Why wouldn't they be proud of what they've created? Perhaps what some may see as a superior attitude is partly a veiled frustration for seeing their country – a country that once was one of the richest in the world – collapse over the decades into a corrupt entity now forced to ask for financial handouts.

It's downright embarrassing, and if Argentines can maintain their proud spirit and polished self-importance in the face of this adversity, then let them – they deserve it.

Lifestyle
A shocking 50% of the total population is now considered to be living in poverty, with most of the poor in rural areas. To save resources and maintain family ties, two or three generations often live under one roof. Argentines don't really look poor, however; they're very image conscious and many will dress 'richer' than they really are, especially in Buenos Aires.

Families are pretty close, and Sundays (when many businesses close) are often reserved for the family *asado* (barbecue). Guests are often invited, so if you get a chance to go to one, don't miss it – you'll get a good insight into Argentine relationships. Friends are also highly valued, and being the social butterflies they are, Argentines love to go out in large groups. Something that surprises many travelers are all those little cheek kisses family and friends give each other every time they meet. Even introduced strangers, men and women alike, will get a kiss.

It'll also soon become apparent to you that this culture likes to stay out *late;* dinner is often at 9pm or later, and finishing dessert around midnight on a weekend is the norm. Bars and discos often stay open until 6am or so – even in smaller cities.

One last thing to keep an eye out for is the highly important culture of maté. You'll probably see Argentines sipping this bitter herb drink at home, work and play. They carry, without fail, their gourds and hot-water thermoses while traveling and on picnics. Consider yourself honored if you're invited to partake in a maté-drinking ritual.

People
About 90% of the country's population lives in urban areas. Argentina's literacy rate is over 95%.

Nineteenth-century immigration created a large population with feisty Italian or Spanish blood, though many other European nationalities are represented. Fresh mixes include Japanese, Koreans and Chinese (rarer outside the capital), and other South American nationalities such as Peruvians, Bolivians, Paraguayans and Uruguayans.

The major indigenous groups (thought to make up less than 2% of Argentina's population) are the Quechua of the northwest and the Mapuche of Patagonia, and smaller groups of Guaraní, Matacos, Tobas and Wichi inhabit other northern pockets. Around 15% of the country's population is *mestizo*, or of mixed indigenous and European ancestry; most *mestizo* reside up north.

ARTS
Cinema
Argentine cinema has achieved international stature through such directors as Luis Puenzo (*The Official Story*), Eliseo Subiela (*Man Facing Southeast*), Héctor Babenco (*Kiss of the Spider Woman*), Adolfo Aristarain (*A Place in the World*) and the late María Luisa Bemberg (*Camila*, *Miss Mary*).

Literature
Jorge Luis Borges, known for his short stories and poetry, is a world literary figure who created bizarre labyrinthine worlds and elaborate time circles with vivid and imaginative style. Ernesto Sábato's psychological novel *On Heroes and Tombs*, a favorite among Argentine youth in the 1960s, explores people and places in Buenos Aires.

Julio Cortázar fudged the lines between real and magical worlds with strange metaphors and whimsical descriptions of man's unseen realities. Manuel Puig's novel *Kiss of the Spider Woman* details a relationship between political prisoners. Adolfo Bioy Casares' *The Invention of Morel* deals with the inability or unwillingness to distinguish between fantasy and reality. His wife, Silvina Ocampo, wrote poetry and children's stories. In Osvaldo Soriano's novel *Shadows*, the protagonist is lost in an Argentina where the names are the same, but all the familiar landmarks and points of reference have lost their meaning.

Music
Argentina has produced a legion of great musicians, both past and present.

Legendary figures like Carlos Gardel, Julio Sosa and Astor Piazzolla popularized the tango as music and dance, while contemporaries like Susana Rinaldi, Eladia Blásquez, Adriana Varela and Osvaldo Pugliese carry on the tradition. Folk musicians Mercedes Sosa, Tarragó Ross, Leon Gieco and the Conjunto Pro Música de Rosario are popular performers. Gato Barbieri is an internationally known jazz musician.

Rock star Charly García is Argentina's best-known musician, but other popular groups include Los Divididos, Memphis La Blusera, Fito Páez, Pappo's Blues, Los Babasónicos, Las Blacanblus, Soda Stereo and Patricio Rey y Sus Redonditos de Ricota. Los Fabulosos Cadillacs won a 1998 Grammy for best alternative Latin rock group. Les Luthiers, who build many unusual instruments from scratch, satirize nationalist sectors in the middle class and the military.

Performing Arts
The monumental Teatro Colón, home of the Buenos Aires Opera, is one of the world's finest acoustic facilities. Classical music and ballet, as well as modern dance performances, are held here and at similar venues. Buenos Aires has a vibrant theater community, and even in the provinces live theater is an important medium of expression.

Visual Arts
Well-known painters include Xul Solar, who painted busy, Klee-inspired dreamscapes that combined dark yet bright disjointed images; Guillermo Kuitca, who meshed cartographic illustrations with historical German themes; and Víctor Hugo Quiroga, who concentrated on provincial topics and the impact of modern society on *criollo* (South American of European descent) life.

Famous sculptors are Graciela Sacco, dabbling in audio, video and life's common objects; Rogelio Yrurtia, whose art centers on the struggles of the working people; and Alberto Heredia, who enjoyed ridiculing solemn official public art.

Buenos Aires' Galerías Pacifico, on Av Florida, has restored ceiling murals by Antonio Berni and Lino Spilimbergo, two European-influenced artists who also dealt with political themes.

RELIGION

Almost 90% of Argentina's population is Roman Catholic, but there are other popular beliefs. Spiritualism and veneration of the dead, for instance, are widespread – visitors to Recoleta and Chacarita cemeteries will see endless processions of pilgrims communing with icons like Juan and Evita Perón, Carlos Gardel and psychic Madre María. Cult beliefs like the Difunta Correa of San Juan province attract hundreds of thousands of fans, evangelical Protestantism is growing and what is probably South America's largest Islamic mosque was built in Palermo. Buenos Aires is also home to one of the largest Jewish populations outside Israel.

SPORT

Rugby, field hockey, tennis, polo, golf, motor racing, skiing and cycling are popular sports, but soccer is an obsession. The national team has twice won the World Cup, once in 1978 and again in 1986, when Diego Maradona (Argentina's bad-boy, rags-to-riches soccer star) surreptitiously punched in a goal to beat England in the quarterfinals. If you get a chance to see a *fútbol* game, take it. The game between River Plate and Boca Juniors is a classic match not to be missed, as the rivalry between the two teams is intense (see p57).

ENVIRONMENT
Land

The glorious Andes line the edge of northwest Argentina, where only hardy cactus and scrubby vegetation survive the extreme temperatures. Here, soaring peaks and salt lakes give way to the more subtropical lowland provinces of Salta and Santiago del Estero. To the south, the hot and scenic Tucumán, Catamarca and La Rioja provinces harbor agriculture and viticulture.

Toward Paraguay, drier thornlands of the western Andean foothills give way to the forked river valleys and hot lowlands of Formosa and Chaco provinces. Rainfall is heaviest to the northeast, near Brazil, where swampy forests and subtropical savannas thrive. Misiones province, densely forested and surrounded on three sides by Brazil and Paraguay, contains the awe-inspiring Iguazú Falls. Rivers streaming off these immense cataracts wind their way around the alluvial grasslands of Corrientes and Entre Ríos provinces. Summers in this region are very hot and humid.

The west-central Cuyo region (Mendoza, San Juan and San Luis provinces) pumps out most of San Juan's world-class wine vintages. Central Argentina has the mountainous Córdoba and richly agricultural Santa Fe provinces. The Pampas is a flat, rich plain full of agriculture and livestock. Along the Atlantic Coast are many popular and attractive beaches.

Patagonia spans the lower third of Argentina. Most of this region is flat and arid, but toward the Andes rainfall is abundant and supports the lush Lake District. The southern Andes boasts huge glaciers, while down on the flats cool steppes pasture large flocks of sheep.

The Tierra del Fuego archipelago mostly belongs to Chile. Its northern half resembles the Patagonian steppe, while dense forests and glaciers cover the mountainous southern half. The climate can be relatively mild, even in winter (though temperatures can also drop below freezing). The weather in this region is very changeable year round.

Wildlife

The famous Pampas is mostly sprawling grasslands and home to many birds of prey and introduced plant species; most of the region's remaining native vegetation survives up north along the Río Paraná. Also in the northern swamplands live the odd-looking capybara (the world's largest rodent), swamp deer, the alligator-like caiman and many large migratory birds.

The main forested areas of Argentina are in subtropical Misiones province, near Brazil, and on the eastward-sloping Andes from Neuquén province south, where southern beech species and coniferous woodlands predominate; look for the strange monkey-puzzle tree (*Araucaria araucana* or *pehuén*) around the Lake District. In the higher altitudes of the Andes and in much of Patagonia, pasture grasses are sparse. Northern Andean saline lakes harbor pink flamingos, and on the Patagonian steppe you're likely to see guanacos, rheas, Patagonian hares, armadillos, crested caracaras and gray foxes. Pumas and condors live in southern Andean foothills, but sightings are rare.

Coastal Patagonia, especially around Península Valdés, supports dense and viewable concentrations of marine fauna, including southern right whales, sea lions, southern elephant seals, orcas and Magellanic penguins.

National Parks

Argentina's national and provincial park systems protect the country's incredibly varied environments. The most notable parks are Parque Nacional Iguazú, famous for its waterfalls (p79); Reserva Provincial Esteros del Iberá, home to swamp-dwelling wildlife (p70); Parque Provincial Aconcagua, home to the continent's highest peak (p114); Reserva Faunística Península Valdés, famous for coastal fauna (p136); Parque Nacional Nahuel Huapi, boasting vivid alpine scenery (p127); Parque Nacional Los Alerces, site of ancient alerce (false larch) forests (p131); Parque Nacional Los Glaciares, world-renowned for its continental glaciers (p144) and alpine towers; and Parque Nacional Tierra del Fuego, known for its beautiful beech forests and coastal fauna (p151).

Environmental Issues

Argentina doesn't have a huge rain forest to destroy, but does claim some environmental problems.

Since 90% of Argentina's population is urban, many large cities have serious air and noise pollution. Some rural areas suffer soil erosion from improper land use or flood control, as well as river pollution from pesticide or fertilizer runoff.

Argentina has lost about two-thirds of its forests in the last century. Practically all the pampas is now cattle grazing land, and the Patagonian steppe region suffers from overgrazing and desertification. Some celebrities, such as Kristine McDivitt Tompkins (ex-CEO of clothing company Patagonia) and Ted Turner, have bought huge tracts in Patagonia with the idea of protecting much of the land. For more information check www.vidasilvestre.org.ar and www.patagonialandtrust.com.

TRANSPORT

GETTING THERE & AWAY
Air

Cosmopolitan Buenos Aires is linked to most of the capitals in South America.

Argentina's main international airport is Buenos Aires' Aeropuerto Internacional Ministro Pistarini (known as Ezeiza). Aeroparque Jorge Newbery (known simply as Aeroparque) is the capital's domestic airport. For information on getting into town from the airports, see p43. A few other Argentine cities have 'international' airports, but they mostly serve domestic destinations.

International passengers leaving from Ezeiza are required to pay a US$18 departure tax in either pesos or US dollars.

Boat

Ferries link Buenos Aires to several points in Uruguay. For more information, see p59.

Bus

It's possible to cross into Argentina from Bolivia (La Quiaca, Aguas Blancas, Pocitos), Paraguay (Clorinda, Posadas, Puerto Iguazú), Brazil (Puerto Iguazú, Paso de los Libres, Santo Tomé), Uruguay (Gualeguaychú, Colón, Concordia) and Chile (numerous). See each city section for details on transport.

GETTING AROUND
Air

The airline situation in Argentina is constantly in flux, with minor airlines regularly going in and out of business. Ticket prices are also unpredictable, though they are always highest during holiday times (including late December, January, February, July, and on long weekends). Certain flights in extensive Patagonia are comparable to bus fares when you consider time saved.

Some airlines have adopted a two-tier system where foreigners pay a much higher fare than Argentine residents. Unless you're legally living in Argentina and can prove it, you'd better get used to being quoted (and paying) the higher price.

The major airlines are Aerolíneas Argentinas (AR), Austral (AR's domestic partner), LAPA, Southern Winds and LADE (the air force's passenger service, which serves mostly Patagonian destinations with cheap but infrequent flights). There's a list of principal airline offices, both international and domestic, in the Buenos Aires section (see p58), and addresses of regional offices appear in each city entry.

There may be special air-pass deals available when you plan to travel. It's best to check with a travel agency specializing in Latin America, since deals come and go regularly. One theme with these passes is that they need to be purchased outside Argentina (sometimes in conjunction with an international ticket), you need to be a foreign resident to use them, and they're often limited to travel within a certain time period.

For more information, see p1046.

Bicycle

Cycling around the country has become popular among travelers. Beautiful routes in the north include the highway from Tucumán to Tafí del Valle, the direct road from Salta to Jujuy, and the Quebrada de Cafayate. The Lake District also has scenic roads. Drawbacks include the wind (which can slow progress to a crawl in Patagonia) and reckless motorists. Less-traveled secondary roads carrying little traffic are good alternatives. Rental bikes are common in tourist areas and a great way to get around.

Bus

Long-distance buses are modern, fast, comfortable and usually the best budget way to get around Argentina. Journeys over six hours or so will either have pit stops for refreshments or serve drinks, sweet snacks and sometimes simple meals. All have bathrooms, though they're sometimes grungy. The most luxurious companies offer more expensive *coche cama* recliners (overnight trips save hotel costs), but regular buses are usually fine even on long trips.

Bus terminals usually have kiosks, restrooms, cheap eats and luggage storage. Fares quoted in this book tend toward the low range, but paying a little more will get you better services. Calculate around US$1.50 per hour of travel; Patagonia often costs more. In small towns you'll want to be aware of the timetable of your next bus out (and possibly buy a ticket), since some routes run infrequently. During holiday periods like January, February or July, buy advance tickets.

Car

Unless you really want to get off the beaten path, renting a car in Argentina is unnecessary – and expensive. Figure around US$50

per day for the cheapest model with some free mileage. The minimum driving age in Argentina is 17 or 18 years depending on the province, but car rental offices may require drivers to be at least 21.

Forget driving in Buenos Aires; traffic is unforgivable and parking is a headache, while public transport is great.

If the police stop you they may conduct meticulous document and equipment checks; minor violations and tickets carry large fines. Offer a *coma* (bribe) only if certain that it is 'appropriate' and unavoidable. Ask, *¿Como poems irregular ester as unto?* (How can we solve this problem?). If uncertain of your rights, calmly state your intention to contact your consulate.

The Automobile Club Argentina (ACE) has offices, service stations and garages in major cities. If you're a member of an overseas affiliate (like AAA in the United States) you may be able to obtain vehicular services like towing, or discounts on maps and certain accommodations. ACA's main headquarters is in **Buenos Aires** (☎ 011-4802-6061; www.aca.org.ar; Av del Libertador 1850, Palermo).

Hitching

Good places for a pickup are at gas stations on the outskirts of large cities, where truckers refuel their vehicles. In Patagonia, distances are great and vehicles few, so expect long waits and carry snack foods and warm, windproof clothing. Carry extra water as well, especially in the desert north.

Hitching is fairly safe for women in Argentina; however, don't do it alone, don't get in a car with two men and don't do it at night. There is also nothing especially unsafe about hitching in rural Argentina.

Local Transport

Even small towns have good bus systems. A few cities use magnetic fare cards, which are usually bought at kiosks. Pay attention to placards indicating an ultimate destination, since identically numbered buses may cover slightly different routes.

Taxis have digital-readout meters that start at about US$0.40. Tipping isn't expected, but you can leave extra change. *Remises* are taxis that you book over the phone, or regular cars without meters; any hotel or restaurant should be able to call one for you. They're considered more secure than taxis since an established company sends them out. Ask the fare in advance.

Buenos Aires is the only city with a subway system, known as Subte.

Train

The British-built train system in Argentina is not as widespread as it once was, and currently bus travel is faster, more flexible and more reliable. There are long-distance services from Buenos Aires to Mar del Plata (and other Atlantic beach resorts), Rosario and Santa Rosa, and from Viedma to Bariloche. Buenos Aires and Rosario have commuter routes to their suburbs.

The very scenic, famous and expensive Tren a las Nubes chugs from Salta, in the north, towards Chile. In Patagonia there are a couple of short touristy train rides (both narrow-gauge) like *La Trochita*, which originates in Esquel or El Maitén, and *El Tren del Fin del Mundo*, in Ushuaia.

BUENOS AIRES

Here's the honest-to-goodness truth: from a budget traveling standpoint, Buenos Aires is a bargain. Where else in the world can you chow down on a US$5 steak, watch a tango show for US$4, grab a couple of US$1 beers at a midnight happy hour and spend the night in a clean, US$6 hostel bed? Where can you party till the sun comes up, shop for bargain leather jackets till you drop and lie back in elegant leafy parks in a sophisticated city filled with grand European architecture? Jump on the bandwagon and follow the savvy crowds, because more and more travelers are discovering this amazing city and leaving with unforgettable experiences.

Counting its extensive suburbs, Buenos Aires is home to 13 million proud *porteños* (port city dwellers). The busy *microcenter* (city center) is adorned with elegant buildings while well-dressed inhabitants strut about stylishly, chat into their cell phones and sip coffee in atmospheric cafés. To the north lies upper-crust Recoleta, where an amazing cemetery provides eternal sleep to the top-drawer class. Even farther north, Palermo is the middle-classes' romping grounds, featuring ethnic cuisine, extensive grassy parks and stately monuments. Down south is where the blue-collar class hangs:

tango-mecca San Telmo has charming cobbled streets and colonial mansions, while rough-housing La Boca offers up colorful buildings and its world-famous *fútbol* team. There's enough bustle in this city to keep you busy all day and all night.

ORIENTATION

Buenos Aires is a very large city, but sights are within the compact downtown area and you can easily access surrounding *barrios* (neighborhoods) via public transport. The major thoroughfare is broad Av 9 de Julio, which runs from gritty Plaza Constitución to the exclusive northern suburbs. Except for Av 9 de Julio, all north-south street names change at Av de Mayo.

Most *porteños* live in *barrios* that tourists rarely see, but a few main ones contain most of the capital's attractions. The *microcentro* (north of Av de Mayo and east of Av 9 de Julio) includes the popular pedestrian streets

---

GETTING INTO TOWN

If you fly into Buenos Aires from outside Argentina, you'll probably land in **Ezeiza** (Aeropuerto Internacional Ministro Pistarini; ☎ 011-5480-6111; www.aa2000.com.ar), some 35km south of the city center. The best way into town is to take a frequent shuttle service; competitors Manuel Tienda León and Transfer Express both greet you as you leave customs, and charge US$5 for the 40-minute ride. The cheapest way into town is Bus 86 (US$0.50, two hours), which leaves from the Aerolíneas Argentinas terminal. Taxis charge US$13. Shuttle transfers from Ezeiza to Aeroparque cost US$5.80.

Most domestic flights land in **Aeroparque** (Aeroparque Jorge Newbery; ☎ 011-5480-6111; www.aa2000.com.ar), only a few kilometers north of the city center. Manuel Tienda León and Transfer Express shuttles to the city center cost US$2.25 (15 minutes). Buses include Nos 33 and 45; take them going south (to the right as you leave the airport; US$0.30). Taxis cost about US$8.

Retiro bus station is about 1km north of the city center. Hundreds of BA's local bus lines converge here; outside, it's a seething mass and not to be figured out after a 14-hour bus ride. Take a taxi to your hotel – they're cheap.

of Florida and Lavalle, and the commercial and entertainment areas of Avs Corrientes, Córdoba and Santa Fe. To the north are chic Recoleta, Barrio Norte and Palermo, while to the south lie the working-class San Telmo and La Boca.

The waterside *barrio* Puerto Madero, with its modernized brick warehouses and promenades, lines the eastern side of the town center. Trendy restaurants and bars have planted stakes here, along with some fancy apartments and offices.

INFORMATION
Bookshops
ABC (Córdoba 685) Stocks English and German books, and many Lonely Planet guides.
El Ateneo Microcentro (Florida 340); Barrio Norte (Santa Fe 1860) Carries large selection of books in English.

Cultural Centers
Biblioteca Lincoln (Maipú 672; ☉ 10am-6pm Mon-Fri) English-language newspapers and magazines.
Centro Cultural Recoleta (☎ 011-4803-1040; www.centroculturalrecoleta.org in Spanish; Junín 1930) Inexpensive exhibitions and theater.
Centro Cultural San Martín (☎ 011-4374-1251; Sarmiento 1551) Cheap galleries, theater, lectures and films.

Emergency
Tourist Police (☎ 011-4346-5748, 4346-7000; turista@ policiafederal.gov.ar; Corrientes 436; ☎ 24 hr) Can provide help (to a certain extent) if you've been robbed or ripped off. Officers speak English, French, Italian and Portuguese.

Immigration Offices
Immigration (☎ 011-4317-0200; www.migraciones.gov .ar; Av Antártida Argentina 1335; ☉ 8am-1pm Mon-Fri) Extensions are available here for US$36, but lines and bureaucracy may make you wish you'd just taken the short boat trip to Uruguay instead (and thus got a new re-entry stamp; check if your nationality needs an Uruguayan visa.

Internet Access
Internet access is available everywhere. Charges run about US$0.50 per hour.

Medical Services
British Hospital (☎ 011-4304-1081; Perdriel 74)
Hospital Municipal Juan Fernández (☎ 011-4808-2600; Cerviño 3356)

Money
The 2001 peso crash stimulated a grey market for US dollars. You may hear people on pedestrian Florida call out '*cambio, cambio*', but it's wiser to change money at a bank or *cambio* (exchange house) – scams and counterfeit bills do exist.

Some banks won't change less than US$300, and may require ID. *Cambios* have slightly poorer exchange rates, but are usually much quicker and have fewer limitations. US dollars are accepted at many retail establishments at a pretty fair rate.

Travelers' checks are hard to cash (try exchange houses rather than banks) and incur bad exchange rates – one exception is **American Express** (Arenales 707). Visa and MasterCard holders can get advances at many banks, and ATMs are everywhere.

Post
Correo Postal Internacional (☎ 011-4316-1770; www.correoargentino.com.ar in Spanish; Av Antártida Argentina; ☉ 10am-5pm Mon-Fri) Near Retiro bus station. Accepts parcels 2-20kg; check website for prices.
DHL (☎ 011-4630-1000; www.dhl-usa.com; Moreno 927)
FedEx (☎ 011-0810-333-3339; www.fedex.com; Maipú 753)
Main post office (☎ 011-4316-3000; Sarmiento 151; ☉ 9am-8pm Mon-Fri) Several branches in Buenos Aires; parcels under 2kg also accepted.

Telephone & Fax
The easiest way to make a call is from a *locutorio* (telephone office), where you enter a booth and make calls in a safe, quiet environment. Costs are comparable to street telephones, and you don't need change. Most *locutorios* offer reasonably priced fax and Internet services as well.

Public phones are numerous; use coins, or buy a magnetic phone card from any kiosk.

Tourist Offices
Florida tourist kiosk (cnr Florida & Av Roque Sáenz Peña; ☉ 10am-1pm & 2-6pm Mon-Fri, 10am-4pm Sat)
Puerto Madero tourist kiosk (Av Alicia Moreau de Justo, dique 4; ☉ noon-3pm & 4-8pm)
Recoleta tourist kiosk (cnr Av Quintana & RM Ortiz; ☉ noon-3pm & 4-8pm)
Secretaría de Turismo de la Nación (☎ 011-4312-2232; ☎ 0800-555-0016; www.turismo.gov.ar; Santa Fe 883; ☉ 9am-5pm Mon-Fri) Good information on Buenos Aires and Argentina.

Travel Agencies

Asatej (☎ 011-4114-7515; www.almundo.com in Spanish; Florida 835, 3rd fl) This busy and crowded student travel agency seeks out cheap airfares and tours, but often has long waits. ISIC cards sold here.

Say Hueque (☎ 011-5199-2517; sayhueque@arnet .com.ar; Viamonte 749, 6th fl) Friendly place that offers budget travelers cheap trips in Argentina and South America.

Tije (☎ 011-4326-5665; www.tije.com in Spanish; San Martín 674, 3rd fl) Another discount travel agency serving mostly students and people aged 35 and under.

DANGERS & ANNOYANCES

Many folks who have never been to Buenos Aires seem to think it's an overly dangerous place. Don't believe that what you see in newspapers or on TV happens all the time. The majority of tourists who visit this great city have fabulous experiences – and without a scrape. As long as you don't forget that you are indeed in a big city, and take the usual precautions (watch those valuables in crowded places!) you should be fine. In many neighborhoods old folks walk their dogs after midnight, and women often walk alone without fear at 4am.

The worst neighborhoods you, as a tourist, will encounter are La Boca (stick to those few tourist streets like glue, even in daylight), Av Florida (dodgy only very, very late at night), Constitución (plaza and train station area – again, be careful at night) and possibly some borderline areas

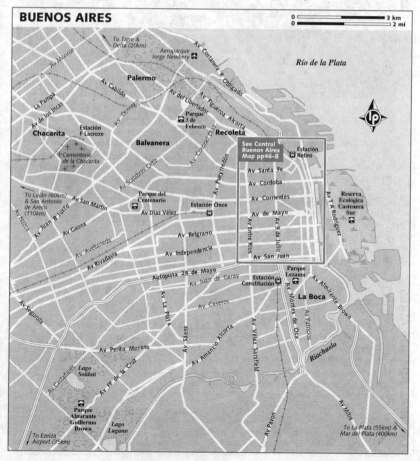

BUENOS AIRES

ARGENTINA

CENTRAL BUENOS AIRES

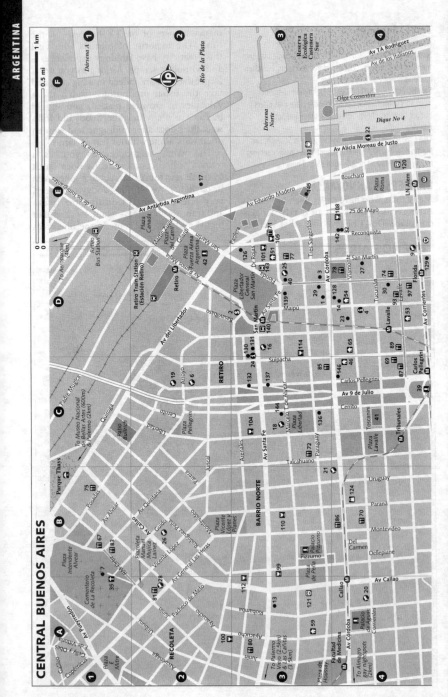

Río de la Plata

Dársena A

Dársena Norte

Reserva Ecológica Costanera Sur

Av TA Rodríguez

Av de los Italianos

Olga Cossentini

Dique No 4

Av Alicia Moreau de Justo

Bouchard

Plaza Roma

LN Alem

Av Antártida Argentina

Av Eduardo Madero

25 de Mayo

Reconquista

San Martín

Florida

Av Corrientes

Retiro Bus Station

Plaza Canadá

Retiro Train Station (Estación Retiro)

Plaza Libertador General San Martín

Maipú

Av del Libertador

RETIRO

Suipacha

Carlos Pellegrini

Av 9 de Julio

Cerrito

Plaza Lavalle

Tribunales

Av Santa Fe

Marcelo T de Alvear

Plaza Libertad

Paraguay

Talcahuano

Uruguay

Parque Thays

Parque Bullrich

Av Alvear

Av Quintana

Posadas

Av Callao

Plaza Intendente Alvear

Plaza Manuel Mujica Láinez

Plazoleta Carlos Pellegrini

Guido

Vicente López

Plaza Vicente López y Planes

BARRIO NORTE

Av General Las Heras

Montevideo

Del Carmen

Dellepiane

Parana

Del

Av Callao

Av Cordoba

Pizzurno

Palacio Pizzurno

Plaza de Pena

Facultad de Medicina

Plaza del Houssay

To Almagro gay nightspots (2km)

Cementerio de La Recoleta

RECOLETA

Ayacucho

Junin

Uriburu

Azcuénaga

Larrea

Riobamba

Palacio de Aguas Corrientes

Av de Mayo

Callao

Vittoria

Kelly y Díaz

Plaza Mitre

To Museo Nacional de Bellas Artes (600m) & Palermo (2km)

To Aeroparque (4km)

To Palermo Viejo (2.5km) & Las Cañitas (3.5km)

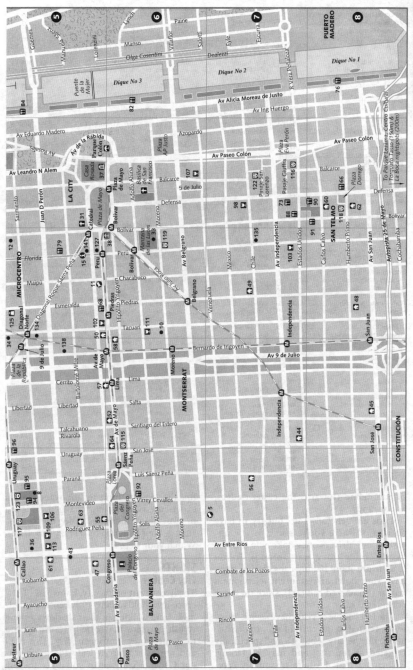

of San Telmo (towards the eastern edges; ask around).

Taxis are generally safe, but try to have an idea of where you're going. A few unscrupulous drivers may take you on the 'scenic' route (long way around). If you feel unsure about hailing cabs on the street, have your hotel or restaurant telephone a *remise* (unmarked call taxi), since these are considered safer.

The last couple of years have seen a crime wave, related to the current economic situation, hit the city – but it's not specifically targeted at tourists, and may be fading. Remember that if you're reasonably care-ful, the closest thing to annoyance you'll experience is being shortchanged, stepping in those ubiquitous piles of dog dirt or possibly getting flattened by a crazy bus driver. Watch your step.

SIGHTS
City Center
The lively heart of the city, known as El Microcentro, holds many 19th-century buildings – and walking in their shadows among stylish *porteños* may briefly transport you to some fancy European city. Downhill and northwards from leafy Plaza Libertador General San Martín you'll see the Big

Ben lookalike, **Torre de los Ingleses** (English Tower); there's a good, free view from the top. Stroll south on the Florida and Lavalle *peatonales* (pedestrian streets) to avoid street traffic and do some shopping, but prepare to dodge masses of hurried businesspeople, angling leather salespeople and ubiquitous fellow tourists. The theater district is centered on lively Corrientes – where there are also many bookstores – and here, super broad Av 9 de Julio is decisively punctuated by the famous white **Obelisco**.

The remodeled 18th-century **Museo del Cabildo** (admission US$0.35; 12:30-6pm Wed-Fri, 1-6pm Sat & Sun) is all that's left of the colonial arches that once surrounded Plaza de Mayo. Nearby, the neoclassical **Catedral Metropolitana** (finished in 1827) contains the tomb of liberator José de San Martín, Argentina's most venerated historical figure. A block east you'll see the pink presidential palace, **Casa Rosada**, and the famous balcony where vibrant Evita energized adoring crowds during her heyday in the 1940s. Around the southern side of the building is **Museo de la Casa Rosada** (admission US$0.35; 10am-6pm Mon-Fri, 2-6pm Sun), whose most interesting feature is the catacombs of the Fuerte Viejo, an 18th-century colonial ruin. Free tours of the Casa Rosada are given at 5pm Monday to Friday (English tours only on Friday); reserve in person beforehand, and take identification.

A block south of Plaza de Mayo is **Manzana de las Luces** (Block of Enlightenment), a solid square of 18th-century buildings that includes **Iglesia San Ignacio**, Buenos Aires' oldest church, and **Colegio Nacional**, an elite secondary school. Underground are old defensive military tunnels; tours of these and the buildings above are available at Perú 272.

Over to the west, at the other end of Av de Mayo, is the green-domed **Palacio del Congreso** (modeled on Washington, DC's Capitol Building). It was completed in 1906 and faces pigeon-filled Plaza del Congreso and its **Monumento a los Dos Congresos**, whose granite steps symbolize the Andes.

Since its opening in 1908, visitors have marveled at magnificent **Teatro Colón** (011-4378-7133), a bit farther north at Cerrito and Tucumán. The luxurious seven-story building seats 2500 spectators on plush red-velvet chairs and surrounds them with tiers of gilded balconies – it's a world-class facility for opera, ballet and classical music. Several daily tours in English and Spanish are given (US$3.75).

San Telmo

Six blocks south of Plaza de Mayo, San Telmo has attracted artists with low rents and aging mansions. Here you'll also find Buenos Aires' richest concentration of tango culture. The neighborhood was a fashionable place until 1870, when a series of epidemics over 20 years drove the rich elite to higher ground; many houses were then subdivided and turned into cramped immigrant shelters.

On Sundays, **Plaza Dorrego** buzzes with its famous **antiques fair** – hordes of tourists clash elbows for rusty pocketwatches, vintage dresses, ancient crystal and metalware, delicate china, old coins and creative knick-knacks. Good tango exhibitions add excitement and photo ops, but don't forget to drop some change into the hat. Surrounding the plaza are pleasant cafés where you can sip anything from cognacs to *cortados* (coffee with a little milk) while lazily people-watching. Afterwards, stroll the cobbled streets to take in the local atmosphere while window-shopping for that perfect *victrola* (gramophone) – you just may find it. At night check out the clubs that put on those famous tango shows.

Four blocks south at Defensa and Brasil is leafy **Parque Lezama**, the presumptive site of Buenos Aires' foundations; mix with the locals playing chess, or visit nicely presented **Museo Histórico Nacional** (admission US$0.35; 12:30-7:30pm Tue-Fri, 9:30am-7:30pm Sat & Sun). Showcased are plenty of portraits of historical figures and their sideburns.

La Boca

Vivid, working-class La Boca, situated along the old port and at the mouth *(boca)* of the Río Riachuelo, was built by Italian immigrants from Genoa. Its main attraction is colorful **Caminito** (named for a popular tango song), a short pedestrian walk lined with corrugated-metal buildings. Local artists display their brightly colored paintings, adding to the vibrant ambience. The neighborhood is also home to the Boca Juniors soccer team, and on a rowdy home-game day you'll see blue and gold banners, flags and T-shirts joyously paraded everywhere.

Boca's standing as an artists' enclave is the legacy of painter Benito Quinquela Martín; his old home and studio is **Museo de Bellas Artes de La Boca** (Pedro de Mendoza 1835; admission free).

Find yourself a good *cantina* (snack bar) and enjoy some local pizza, but be aware that this is one of the poorer *barrios* of Buenos Aires and, whether day or night, you shouldn't wander from the beaten path of tourist hangouts. Bus Nos 130 and 152 run to La Boca.

Recoleta

One of Buenos Aires' prime tourist attractions, **Cementerio de la Recoleta** sits in the plushest of neighborhoods, ritzy Recoleta. High walls surround this necropolis where, in death as in life, generations of Argentina's elite rest in ornate splendor. It's fascinating to wander around and explore this extensive mini-city of lofty statues, detailed marble façades and earthy-smelling sarcophagi, all the while reading family names of those with enough social points to make it in here. Follow the crowds and you'll find Evita's grave.

Next to the cemetery is colonial **Iglesia de Nuestra Señora de Pilar** (1732), an historical monument, and **Centro Cultural Recoleta**, which hosts cultural events. A weekend hippie fair takes place on the surrounding paths, attracting lively performers and crowds of tourists. Sit at a café and take in the nearby attractive greenery of **Plaza Alvear** – don't miss the amazing giant ombú trees. If you're lucky you'll spot a *paseaperros* (professional dog-walker) strolling along, surrounded by 15 or so leashed canines of all shapes and tails.

The **Museo Nacional de Bellas Artes** (Libertador 1473; admission free; 12:30-7:30pm Tue-Fri, 9:30am-7:30pm Sat & Sun) houses works by famous French impressionists and Argentine artists. Farther north is the excellent **Museo de Arte Latinoamericano de Buenos Aires** (MALBA; Av Figueroa Alcorta 3415; www.malba.org.ar; admission US$1.50, Wed free; noon-8pm Mon, Thu-Fri, noon-9pm Wed, 10am-8pm Sat & Sun).

Palermo

Full of green parks, imposing statues, elegant embassies and large sporting complexes, Palermo on a sunny Sunday afternoon is a *porteño* yuppie's wet dream. **Jardín Botánico Carlos Thays** (the botanical gardens) is good for a stroll, while the **Jardín Zoológico** (the zoo) has mostly humane animal enclosures and some attractive classic structures to boot. The **Rosedal** (rose garden) is great for smooching with your honey, but stretch out on the grass and the keeper may blow his whistle. On weekends, rent bikes and cruise the lakes of **Parque 3 de Febrero**, where the nearby *boliches* (dancing clubs) come to life at 2am.

Not too far from these green spots is **Museo Evita** (Lafinur 2988; admission US$0.75; 2-7:30pm Tue-Sun), chronicling this legendary and effervescent woman's life and work. Palermo also contains the **Campo de Polo** (polo grounds), **Hipódromo** (racetrack) and **Planetario** (observatory). Some of these places were obviously not for the masses, but it's a more democratic place these days.

COURSES
Language

It's official: Buenos Aires is a hot destination for Spanish-learners. There are plenty of schools and even more private teachers, so ask around for recommendations. Some good standbys include:

Centro de Estudio del Español (CEDIC; /fax 011-4315-1156; www.cedic.com.ar; Reconquista 715, 11th fl)

Instituto de Lengua Española para Extranjeros (ILEE; /fax 011-4372-0223; www.argentinailee.com, Av Callao 339, 3rd fl)

International Bureau of Language (IBL; /fax 011-4331-4250; www.ibl.com.ar; Florida 165, 8th fl)

Tradfax (011-4372-8584; www.tradfax.com; Callao 194, 1st fl)

Tango

Check tango magazines like *La Tanguata* or *BA Tango*, available at tourist offices, for many more options for tango classes and *milongas* (dances).

Academia Nacional del Tango (011-4345-6967; www.turismo.gov.ar/cultura/ant/ant.htm; Av de Mayo 833) Perched right above Café Tortoni, the academy has classes (US$1.75) on weekday nights.

Centro Cultural Torquato Tasso (011-4307-6506; www.tangotasso.com in Spanish; Defensa 1575) Old San Telmo venue that offers classes (US$1.75-3.75) and *milongas* with a live tango band – unusual in Buenos Aires.

Confitería Ideal (15-5006-4102; Suipacha 384) A bulletin board with extensive schedules of classes and *milongas* greets you at the door of this old café. The dancing happens upstairs.

TOURS

Big cruising buses stuffed with languid sightseers certainly exist in BA, but a better choice is the more creative tours on offer.

Eternautas (☎ 011-4781-8868; www.eternautas.com) Guided by historians, Eternautas runs educational and affordable two-hour walks (US$1.75-3.75; some in English) with a political, social and historical bent. Longer tours also available.

Gobierno de la Ciudad Autonoma de Buenos Aires (☎ 011-4114-5775; www.buenosaires.gov.ar in Spanish) Free tours, some with historical-figure themes (Evita, Gardel, Borges) are given on weekends by the city – but they're all in Spanish.

Bike Tours (☎ 011-4311-5199; www.biketours.com.ar; Florida 868, 13th fl) Spin your wheels and see Buenos Aires at the same time – daily 3½- to 4-hour tours (US$20) include bike rental and cover the city's major *barrios*. Longer trips and English-speaking guides are available.

Urban Biking (☎ 011-4371-1338; www.urbanbiking .com) Offers similar trips to Bike Tours.

Tangol (☎ 011-4312-7276; www.tangol.com; Florida 971, Suite 59, 1st fl) Works with other agencies to organize adventurous activities such as sky-diving, *estancia* (ranch) visits, helicopter flights and night tours of BA. They also go to *fútbol* games.

SLEEPING
Hostels

The number of hostels in Buenos Aires has mushroomed from under ten in 2001 to over fifty in 2003. Note that private rooms (and even dorm beds) in some hostels can cost more than rooms in a cheap hotel. All hostels listed here include kitchen access and a light breakfast; the first three are HI-affiliated.

Milhouse (☎ 011-4345-9604; www.milhousehostel .com; Hipólito Yrigoyen 959; dm US$8.50, dm with HI card US$7.30, s with card $18-20, without card $20-22, d with/ without card $20/26; ☐) This huge, central and modern hostel offers over 100 beds, a large cafeteria area, free Internet, artsy decor and many services, including tours. Clean and comfortable spaces.

Tango Back-Packers (☎ 011-4776-6871; www.tango bp.com; Thames 2212; dm US$7-9, d with/without HI card US$18/22; ☐) Good if you want to eat and party in trendy Palermo Viejo, a 10-minute bus ride from downtown. Free Internet, a pleasant rooftop patio and small-hostel feel are all part of this converted mansion.

St Nicholas Hostel (☎ 011-4373-8841; www.snhostel .com; Bartolomé Mitre 1691; dm with/without HI card US$20/24, d with/without HI card US$19/22) Colorful atmosphere and an awesome rooftop terrace add personality to these digs, located in the Congreso area. Spacious rooms ring an open central lightwell on two floors, and baths are clean. Credit cards accepted.

Nomade (☎ 011-4300-7641; www.hostelnomade .com; Carlos Calvo 430; dm US$6.50, d US$19) For San Telmo, you can't beat Nomade's location as it's a mere block from Plaza Dorrego. A sunny terrace, pleasant patios and nice four-bed dorms in an old mansion make for a great stay.

Urbano (☎ 011-4372-5494; www.urbanohostel .ar; Av de Mayo 1385, 6th fl; dm US$6.30) Beautiful terraces, bright rooms and marble floors add charm to this lofty hostel, located in a nicely converted old building. It's fairly intimate, with 35 beds sharing just four baths.

Lime House (☎ 011-4383-4561; www.limehouse argentina.com; Lima 11; dm US$5.80, s/d US$11/18; ☐) Funkier than most, this friendly place offers a central but busy location and large rooftop terrace with views of Av 9 de Julio. Most dorms have four to eight beds (one has 11 beds) and almost all rooms, including the doubles, share baths.

Milonga (☎ 011-4815-1827; www.milongahostel .ar; Ayacucho 921; dm US$6-7, d US$20; ☐) West of downtown in fancy Recoleta, this good tango-themed hostel has 38 beds. The old mansion sports a sunny second-floor patio, nice rooms and a good kitchen. Internet is free, and there's a pool table.

V&S Hostel Club (☎ 011-4322-0994; www.argentina hostels.com; Viamonte 887; dm US$7.80-12, s US$23-25, d US$26-28; ☐) The snazziest (and most expensive) of BA's hostels, V&S offers a very central location, great common room, good dorms and decent services. There's a small outdoor patio and cooking area. Prices vary depending on the length of your stay.

Garden House (☎ 0114304-1824; www.garden houseba.com.ar; San Juan 1271; dm US$6, d US$18; ☐) There's no real garden and the location is off-center, but this friendly place has an intimate feel. It sports a good kitchen, pleasant (though noisy) terrace and free Internet access. Two of the doubles share baths and a shady patio. Free pickup from Ezeiza airport.

Palermo House (☎ 011-4832-1815; www.palermo house.com.ar; Thames 1754; dm US$7.30, s/d US$16/20; ☐) Located in Palermo Viejo, this isn't your typical hostel – there's just one four-bed dorm and six private rooms, all of which share baths. A large common space sits on the second floor (kitchen access available); the whole layout is odd but cool enough.

Hostel-Inn Tango City (☎ 011-4300-5764; www .hostel-inn.com; Piedras 680; dm US$3-7, d US$20; 🖳 🐱) Cut-throat prices and a large range of free services make this large, 100-bed hostel a fierce competitor in BA's hostel market. Spaces are nicely decorated, there's an elevator to access the six floors, and a bar-like area downstairs is good for partying and chatting up fellow travelers. Credit cards accepted; free pickup from Ezieza airport.

Hostel-Inn Buenos Aires (☎ 011-4300-7992; www.hostel-inn.com; Humberto Primo 820; dm US$3-5, d US$16; 🖳 🐱) A bit cozier than its big brother four blocks north is this colorful 66-bed hostel, offering similar free services like Spanish classes, massages and Internet access. The San Telmo neighborhood brings tango closer to home. Credit cards accepted; free pickup from Ezieza airport.

Hotels

Paying with credit card may incur a fee of up to 10%. All but the very cheapest hotels have cable TV, though air-con is rare in this price range.

Hotel Central Cordoba (☎ 011-4311-1175; fax 011-4315-6860; San Martín 1021; s/d US$14/19) Good-value rooms are on tap at this downtown hotel, located within swilling distance of BA's two most popular bars. Pass out on the satin bedsheets and you won't notice the lobby's spiffier than the older but decent rooms. Breakfast included.

Hotel Alcazar (☎ 011-4345-0926; Av de Mayo 935; s/d US$5.50/7.30, with bath US$10/13) Breakfast isn't included, the mattresses can be mushy and street-facing rooms are noisy, but this charming old standby comes with good showers and efficient management. Get an inside room for more tranquility.

Gran Hotel Hispano (☎ 011-4345-2020; www .hhispano.com.ar; Av de Mayo 861; s/d US$16/18; 🖳 🐱) Excellent modern rooms surround a bright, glass-topped indoor patio, and there's a nice area for breakfast (dish out a few extra pesos). The whole place is well-run and clean and there's free Internet access, though the marble lobby's a tight squeeze.

Goya Hotel (☎ 011-4322-9269; www.goyahotel .com.ar; Suipacha 748; s US$16-25, d US$22-29) Two main types of comfortable rooms are on

offer here, with the 'superior' offering slightly more modern amenities and bathtubs rather than open showers. A 'presidential' suite is also available (US$43) and has jets in the tub. Breakfast included.

Residencial Carly (☎ 011-4361-7710; Humberto Primo 464; s/d US$4.25/5.80, with bath US$5/6.50) You can't get any closer to Plaza Dorrego than these cheap digs. Basic, high-ceilinged old rooms line open hallways and tiled patios. There's even a funky kitchen for cooking up homemade treats.

Hotel Brisas del Mar (☎ 011-4300-0040; Humberto Primo 826; s/d US$4.25/5.50, with bath US$5.50/7.30) This friendly San Telmo hotel offers good, no-nonsense rooms and a family atmosphere; there's also kitchen access. Find it right next door to Hostel-Inn Buenos Aires.

Maípu (☎ 011-4322-5142; Maípu 735; s/d US$7.30/9, with bath US$9/11) Well-kept, spacious rooms, along with a great old feel and friendly service, make this place a good and central choice. Don't expect things to be too modern though – this building has been around a long time.

Gran Hotel Oriental (☎ 011-4951-6427; Mitre 1840; s/d US$9.80/12) Call ahead if you want to stay here – this place is popular for its very nice, well-priced and modern rooms, which face a long outdoor hallway. The decor is pretty tasteful, considering the small spaces; breakfast is included.

Hotel Plaza (☎ 011-4371-9747; Av Rivadavia 1691; s/d US$4.25/7.30, d with bath & TV US$9) Grand it ain't, but if you're looking for dirt cheap in the Congreso area you'll find it here. Dark, bleak rooms and homely industrial halls are a bit depressing, though.

Hotel El Cabildo (☎ 011-4322-6745; Lavalle 748; s/d US$13/16) Rooms are simple and clean (but good), and the location is right on pedestrian Lavalle. You'll have to speak loudly to the manager, though, as he's a bit hard of hearing.

Hotel Chile (☎ 011-4383-7877; hotelchile@argentina.com; Av de Mayo 1297; s/d US$11/16; ✖) Comfortable rooms, friendly service and a free breakfast keep this popular place hopping with tourists. Street-facing rooms are noisy but some come with balcony and views of the Congreso building.

Nuevo Hotel Callao (☎ 011-4374-4222; www.hotelcallao.com.ar; Av Callao 292; s/d US$18/22; ☐ ✖) Offering a great deal in the Congreso area, this modern and more upscale hotel occupies a charming older building. Some rooms have balconies overlooking busy Callao, with the best nestled under the corner cupola. Breakfast is included.

Long-Term Stays
Any hostel or hotel listed earlier should offer a significant discount for a long-term stay.

La Casa de Etty (☎ 011-4384-6378; www.angelfire.com/pq/coret; Luis Sáenz Peña 617; r per person per month US$90-107) Señora Esther Corcias offers four basic double-occupancy rooms in her house, all with shared bath and kitchen access. She can also help students and travelers find long-term apartment rentals.

EATING
You'll dine very well in Buenos Aires, whether you eat meat or not. Most restaurants serve a standard fare of *parrillada* (mixed grill), pastas, pizzas or *minutas* (short orders), but in the last few years Buenos Aires has seen a trend toward ethnic foods such as Vietnamese, Japanese and Mexican. These restaurants tend to be upscale and most are located in the hip neighborhoods of Palermo Viejo and Las Cañitas (both in Palermo). Other relatively expensive areas to dine are Recoleta and Puerto Madero, though you'll find more steaks than stir-fries there.

Cafés
You can't beat the elegance of Buenos Aires' famous cafés, where *porteños* spend hours solving their own, the country's and the world's problems over a chessboard and a *cortado* (coffee with milk).

Café Tortoni (Av de Mayo 829) The Cadillac of BA's cafés, Tortoni takes you back in time with its charming old-time atmosphere.

Service can be sniffy as well as spotty, though the nightly tango shows (US$4.25) are good.

Richmond (Florida 468) Another elegant and traditional java stop, with crystal chandeliers swinging upstairs and chess-playing locals sitting downstairs. Blue-haired ladies abound.

La Biela (Av Quintana 596) The upper-crust elite dawdle for hours at this classy joint in Recoleta. Outside seating costs 20% more but is irresistible on a warm sunny day. Prices are relatively expensive; Irish coffee (with whiskey and cream) goes for US$4.75.

Café de la Paix (Quintana 600) Across from La Biela, this is another place to rub elbows with the rich. Sit on the sunny patio and take in the glorious views, but note that the caffeine (and snacks) aren't cheap here, either.

Bar Plaza Dorrego (cnr Defensa & Humberto Primo) Sit among dark wood surroundings smack on Plaza Dorrego at this old-fashioned café and watch the world stroll by. On Sunday afternoons this place buzzes to the hilt, with sidewalk tables at a premium.

Librería de las Madres (Hipólito Yrigoyen 1440; ✖ 10am-11pm Mon-Sat) Whether or not you believe in their cause, you could still drop in for a cup of good coffee. It's a very modest café, though, so don't expect fancy doilies or snappy service. Proceeds help the Madres de Plaza de Mayo (whose children 'disappeared' during the Dirty War).

Italian
Pizzería Güerrín (Av Corrientes 1368) Go for quick, cheap, standup slices, or sit down if you must. Tempting pastries out front lead you in.

El Cuartito (Talcahuano 937) Another excellent, inexpensive standup pizzeria, full of gray-haired businessmen wolfing down US$0.75 slices on weekdays. Great sports posters.

Filo (San Martín 975) Creative artsy decor and trendy music liven up this hip spot, as does the full bar. Pizzas, pastas and tons of other things are available.

Las Marías (Bolívar 949) Unpretentious, tasty and well-priced pasta served under old-time photos on the wall brings in the diners at this traditional San Telmo joint.

Il Gatto (Alicia Moreau de Justo 1190) An affordable choice in pricey Puerto Madero, this casual spot offers Italian dishes and cheerful decor.

Parrillas

Don't leave without indulging yourself on Argentina's succulent grilled meat; it doesn't come any better or cheaper than at *parrillas* (steak houses) here.

La Estancia (Lavalle 941) Exceptional, moderately priced fare on popular, pedestrian Lavalle – check out the *gaucho* wannabes by the huge front grills.

Dora (Alem 1016) Popular with tourists and businesspeople alike for its comfortable local atmosphere and large selection of good food. There are even rabbit dishes.

Pippo (Paraná 356; Montevideo 341; until 4am) Economical, casual, no-nonsense and some waiters with over 40 years of experience.

Parrilla al Carbón (Lavalle 645; daily specials US$1.60-3) A great deal if you're looking for cheap, good steak cuts. Generous daily specials come with sides. Central and quick.

La Vieja Rotisseria (Defensa btwn Carlos Calvo & Estados Unido) Hopelessly stuffed on Sunday afternoons, this cheap San Telmo *parrilla* offers good atmosphere, tango tunes and excellent meats. Weekdays are calmer.

El Desnivel (Defensa 855) The occasional singing waiter and some of the most tender *vacío* (ribs) in town jam this San Telmo favorite with loyal patrons. Did we mention it's cheap?

Quick Eats

Coto supermarket cafetería (Viamonte 1581; 8am-10pm Mon-Sat, 9am-4pm Sun) Has cheap grub upstairs.

El Patio (Florida btwn Lavalle & Tucumán; lunch to 4pm) Sit down and relax in some style, but only after you've cued up for quick salads, beef and pasta. Havanna has a trendy café here.

Galerías Pacífico (cnr Florida & Córdoba) Step on downstairs for the glitziest food court in town. There's free tango at 8pm on Friday and Saturday.

SPLURGE – PARRILLAS

Estilo Campo (Alicia Moreau de Justo 1840) Located on the strip known as Puerto Madero, this dock-side *parrilla* offers set menus of US$8.50 (US$10 with wine) along with à la carte selections. The atmosphere's excellent, with rabbit or wild boar dishes also available.

Vegetarian

Unlike in the rest of the country, you'll find a good range of vegetarian restaurants in the capital.

La Esquina de las Flores (Córdoba 1587; 8:30am-7:30pm Mon-Fri, 8:30am-3pm Sat) Buenos Aire's most enduring veggie haven; entreé selections change daily, and there's takeout. Includes a small store selling wheat breads.

Lotos (Av Córdoba 1577; 11:30am-6pm Mon-Fri) Next door to La Esquina, this vegetarian spot also serves fresh and healthy meals. The **store** (8:30am-8pm Mon-Fri, 8:30am-4pm Sat) downstairs has longer hours and sells goodies like *seitan* (chewy wheat gluten), brown rice and lentils.

La Huerta (Lavalle 895; meals US$2.25) Central and very casual is this all-you-can-eat *cafetería* – meals include drink and dessert. The whole-wheat bread is delicious, and even the salt is healthy. Closed Sunday dinner.

Granix (Florida 165; meals US$4.75; lunch Mon-Fri) Popular with businessfolk, Granix offers plenty of good, tasty choices for an all-inclusive price. Enter Galería Güemes and take the first flight of stairs to your right.

Other

La Farmacia (Bolívar 898) Fantastic wall art accompanies creative cuisine at this great San Telmo eatery. Sit on the rooftop terrace if it's warm, or inside the old house for a more cozy atmosphere.

El Sanjuanino (Posadas 1515) A cheap choice in pricey Recoleta, this small, casual place serves up regional dishes like *locro* (meat, corn and potatoes, US$1.75), tamales (US$1.75) and plenty of empanadas (US$0.40 each).

China Doll (Suipacha 544; meals US$2) One of BA's many *tenedor libres* (all-you-can-stuff restaurants), this one comes cheap.

Grant's (Junín 1155; Las Heras 1925) The grandest of all *tenedor libres* is this chain of large buffets. The US$2.50 lunch is a great deal, but prices rise a few pesos for dinner and weekend meals.

The following few selections are all in Palermo Viejo or Las Cañitas, which have dozens more specialty restaurants.

Krishna (Malabia 1833; Tue-Sun) A tiny, tight joint full of Indian drapes, mosaic tables and prayer flags. Wash down your thalis, tofu and seitan with lassi and chai. Limited menu.

Cielito Lindo (El Salvador 4999) Colorful festive decor complements good Mexican grub; the margaritas are *muy buenas* (very good – so says one waiter). Reserve weekends before 10pm; afterwards there's a waiting list.

María Fulo (Honduras 4795) Brazilian goodies are on tap at this snappy corner restaurant: order *feijoada* (meat stew with rice and beans; US$5.80) and follow it with a *caipirinha* (Brazilian drink, US$1.50). The menu's limited but adequate when you're missing Bahia.

Sudestada (cnr Fitzroy & Guatemala; dishes US$3.75-7.30) Nibble specialties from Thailand, Vietnam and Malaysia at this simple, elegant and popular restaurant.

Mark's Deli and Coffeehouse (cnr Armenia & El Salvador) Enjoy the casual yet elegant unmatched furniture and nice patio. Sandwiches come recommended by a homesick expat.

Soul Café (Báez 246) This slick, self-proclaimed 'boogie restaurant' located in trendy Las Cañitas has some interesting choices on the menu, but come for the moody red lighting and groovy tunes. A bar takes over here in the wee hours.

Narguile (Báez 317) Middle-Eastern specialties rule at this exotic Las Cañitas joint. Sample the schwarma, shish-kebab and baklava. Hot falafels are available at 4am Saturday nights.

DRINKING
Bars

This great city has heaps of excellent bars in which to quench that travelin' thirst of yours. For cheap thrills, buy some bottles of brew and hang out with the masses in Plaza Serrano (Palermo Viejo) on a weekend night; it's the most happenin' place in town.

Full Bar (Av Rivadavia 878) Expat-run and decked out in black and white, this hip joint offers microbrews, cocktails and hard-to-find liquor like Kahlúa and Southern Comfort. The cool tunes and staff wearing 'Fuck Bush' T-shirts add interest.

Gibraltar (Perú 895) 'You don't need to shower to come here' says the owner. This translates into an unpretentious atmosphere attracting a heady mix of backpackers and locals. Sofas, curried foods and happy hour 'til 1am keep everyone comfortably numb.

Milión (Paraná 1048; cocktails US$3.75) Slick as all get-out is this richly elegant bar/restaurant.

Head on upstairs, sit under the kaleidoscopic wall projection and watch hipsters softly illuminated by candlelight. The terrace overlooks a leafy garden.

Gran Bar Danzón (Libertad 1161) This trendy wine bar is popular with the youthful, long-haired crowd. The dining section offers exotic treats like *nigiri* salmon rolls with mango and cream cheese; otherwise it's tall barstools or black sofas for you.

Kilkenny (Marcelo T de Alvear 399) Too popular for its own good is this so-called Irish bar. Weekend nights find patrons squashed together in the dark smoky spaces, so come early for some breathing room.

Druid In (Reconquista 1040) Half a block from Kilkenny is this more intimate drinking venue, offering classic Irish pub fare and live Celtic music on Fridays and Saturdays.

Le Cigale (25 de Mayo 722) This hip and moody place is especially popular on Tuesday nights. Cycles of electronic tunes frequently crank out of live instruments; otherwise you'll be listening to music like Beck – not too shabby.

Shamrock (Rodríguez Peña 1220) This popular Barrio Norte saloon sports a downstairs disco from Thursday to Saturday nights. It's more artsy than Irish, despite the dangling dartboard – your dart's as likely to end up in the bullseye as in some hip chick's ass.

Deep Blue (Ayacucho 1240) Enter this futuristic corrugated tube for the 11 pool tables – upstairs the felt is orange. The DJ music is pretty genial, the cocktails are positively luscious-looking, and the waitresses wear skimpy tops.

Acabar (Honduras 5733) It's a restaurant before midnight, so come late to take in the colorful, creative environment and play board games – that's what folks do here. It's a hip and casual joint in Palermo Viejo, with plenty of cocktails to sip in between moves.

Mundo Bizarro (Guatemala 4802) You'll be seeing red at this cool Palermo Viejo watering hole – lights give the whole lounge a vermilion glow. Monday has Japanese snacks and jazz, Wednesday sees beer specials, and Thursday is ladies night.

Van Koning (Báez 325) Find yourself thirsty in the trendy Las Cañitas neighborhood? Check into this medieval, Dutch-themed pub. Three bars lurk among the dark, cozy spaces and multi-levels.

Live Music

Many bars often have live music. For tango shows, see Entertainment, p57.

Notorious (☎ 011-4815-8473; Callao 966; admission US$1.75-5.50) Live jazz is often played here, but anything from tango to acid funk goes. Up front, headphoned patrons listen to CDs; out back there's a café/restaurant.

Club de Vino (☎ 011-4833-8330; Cabrera 4737) Visit this upscale Palermo Viejo venue for good jazz (call for a current schedule). There's a fancy restaurant in front.

Café Tortoni (☎ 011-4342-4328; www.cafetortoni .com.ar; Av de Mayo 829) Yet another place for jazz is the classic Tortoni, where bands play nightly from Thursday to Sunday (US$2.25 to US$3).

La Trastienda (☎ 011-4342-7650; Balcarce 460) Salsa, merengue, rock, blues, Latin pop and tango – it's all here in San Telmo and coming at you live. Call for current schedules.

Bar Seddon (☎ 011-4342-3700; Defensa 695) Brazilian beats play live on Tuesday and Wednesday, while jazz and rock liven things up Friday and Saturday. Shows start around 10:30pm.

El Samovar de Rasputín (☎ 4302-3190; Del Valle Iberlucea 1251) and **Blues Special Club** (☎ 4854-2338; Almirante Brown 102) are both in La Boca, but unless you're a die-hard fan or in a large group you'll want to avoid this rough neighborhood at night.

Clubbing

Buenos Aires loves its nightclubs. To join in the fun, dress well, take a nap before heading out at 2am or 3am – when the clubs really start to hop – and plan on staying up 'til the early morning light. Cover charges will vary according to the night or in some cases the DJs, but are usually between US$3.75 and US$7.30. Drinks can be pricey.

Club Niceto (☎ 011-4779-9396; Niceto Vega 5510; admission women/men US$2.50/3.75) Thursday is *the* night, when a raucous, '*muy* hot' transvestite show has everyone riled; gates open at 1:30am. Also open Friday and Saturday nights. It's on the western edge of Palermo Viejo.

Pachá (☎ 011-4788-1500; Av Costanera Norte near Av La Pampa) DJs from all over keep cover prices high, but the masses still line up faithfully – probably the coolest disco in town. As one taxi driver explained, it's the '*templo de la música electrónica*'.

BA News (☎ 011-4778-1500; cnr Av de la Infanta Isabel & Freyre; admission women/men US$3.75/5.50; ☽ Thu-Sat) Still popular after all these years, this classic has multi-level dance floors, strobe lights and dry ice effects, which make for a wild night out.

Mint (☎ 011-4806-8002; cnr Costanera norte & Sarmiento; admission US$3.75/7.30; ☽ 9pm-3am Wed-Sat) The place to party on Wednesday nights, this club also rocks loudly from Thursday to Saturday nights. Draped tent-like areas add an exotic feel to otherwise simple spaces. Admission varies depending on the night.

La France (☎ 011-4382-4418; Sarmiento 1662; admission US$3.75; ☽ Sat night) After 2am this place is for the 25 and up crowd; youngsters shake it earlier on. Bars line a large space punctuated by sofas and spotlights while videos play above. It's packed.

Sudaca (☎ 011-4371-0802; Sarmiento 1752; admission women/men US$2.50/4.75, free Sun) On Friday live bands play, while Saturday is *caña libre* (all-you-can-drink). Two floors of music bring in the denim-clad crowds, who start lining up at 2am.

Maluco Beleza (☎ 011-4372-1737; Sarmiento 1728; ☽ Wed, Fri-Sun) Brazilian music and stage dancers keep the hordes entertained below, while upstairs more intimate spaces provide smoochy privacy. The decor keeps changing but is always catchy. Cover charges vary.

Gay & Lesbian Venues

The gay scene in Buenos Aires is not completely out, but it's the best in Argentina and you'll find enough choices for some good fun.

Amerika (☎ 011-4865-4416; Gascon 1040; ☽ Fri-Sun) Saturday is all-you-can-drink, sticky-floors night. It's a mix of hets and homos (especially on Saturday), but everyone appreciates the beefy men in tanktops. Occasional live shows; located in the Almagro neighborhood.

Sitges (☎ 011-4861-3763; Córdoba 4119; ☽ Fri-Sun) Mainly a bar, this place is sardine city on a Saturday night – to the point of being a serious fire hazard. If you want to take the risk, check out the dance floor in back. Close to Amerika in Almagro.

Bach Bar (Cabrera 4390; ☽ Tue-Sun) A rowdy place for both gays and lesbians, this intimate joint has something different going on every night. You may end up seeing drag shows, singing karaoke, playing the telegram game or taking advantage of two-for-one drink specials. Friday and Saturday nights are for dancing.

Palacio Alsina (☎ 011-4331-1277; Adolfo Alsina 934) It is indeed palatial, with flowing drapes and fancy columns. The half-naked show dancers can be pretty hot, and keep the packed floor happy. Friday and Sunday are mostly gay, while Thursday and Saturday are mixed.

Contramano (Rodríguez Peña 1082; ☽ Wed-Sun) One of the city's oldest gay venues, this Recoleta joint isn't huge or fancy but does sport a mirrored dance floor. Stripper shows raise the flagpoles on Sunday nights when the sluices open at 8pm.

UNNA (Suipacha 927; admission US$3; ☽ from 1am Sat) Buenos Aires' only lesbians-only spot. Glide through the metal (or penis) detector and descend into a dark, steamy room where people smooch in the shadows; beyond the swinging doors is a dance floor crowded with bare bodies and thumping heartbeats.

ENTERTAINMENT

The *carteleras* (ticket offices) along Av Corrientes sell discounted tickets for a limited selection of movies, theater and tango shows; buy tickets in advance. **Cartelera Vea Más** (☎ 011-6320-5319; Suite 2, Corrientes 1660) is in the Paseo La Plaza complex, while **Cartelera Baires** (☎ 011-4372-5058, Corrientes 1382) is in the Galería Apolo.

Cinemas

The main cinema zones run along Lavalle (west of Florida) and on Avs Corrientes and Santa Fe, though there are good theaters all over the city. Foreign films from around the world can be seen in their original languages with Spanish subtitles. Many sell half-price tickets on Wednesday and for the first show of the day. Check the *Buenos Aires Herald* for screening times.

Classical Music & Performing Arts

Av Corrientes, between 9 de Julio and Callao, is Buenos Aires' answer to Broadway.

Teatro Colón (☎ 011-4378-7133; www.teatrocolon .org.ar; cnr Tucumán & Cerrito) The capital's most prestigious performing arts venue is richly opulent and an excellent place to see opera, ballet, theatre and classical music. Some events are surprisingly affordable.

Teatro General San Martín (☎ 011-4371-0111/ 0119; www.teatrosanmartin.com.ar; Av Corrientes 1530) Inexpensive shows and events (cheapest on Wednesday) are on offer here, but practically all are in Spanish.

Luna Park (☎ 011-4312-2135; cnr Corrientes & Bouchard) This prominent building serves as a venue for operas, dances, rock concerts, sporting gigs or any other large event. For current listings check with the ticket office or local newspapers.

Sport

If you're lucky enough to witness a *fútbol* match, you'll encounter a passion unrivaled in any other sport. The most popular teams are **Boca Juniors** (☎ 011-4362-2260; www.bocajuniors.com.ar; Brandsen 805) in La Boca and **River Plate** (☎ 011-4788-1200; www.carp.org.ar in Spanish; Alcorta 7597) in Belgrano.

Entradas populares (US$3.75) are the cheapest seats and attract the more emotional fans of the game; don't show any signs of wealth in this section, including watches, necklaces or fancy cameras. *Plateas* (fixed seats) cost US$5.50 to US$11. Ticket prices can ultimately depend on the rivalry of the teams playing, however. If you don't want to go by yourself, you can join a tour with **Tangol** (☎ 011-4312-7276; www.tangol.com; Florida 971, Suite 59, 1st fl), which charges US$35 for a ticket, transfers and tour guide. For more information on *fútbol* in Argentina see www.afa.org.ar.

Polo is most popular from October through December at Campo de Polo in Palermo. Rugby, horseracing and *pato* (a traditional Argentine game played on horseback) are also spectating possibilities.

Tango

Your best chance for 'free' (donation) tango shows is on Sunday at San Telmo's Plaza Dorrego, on weekends at other touristy places like La Boca or Recoleta, or by chance on pedestrian Av Florida (check in front of Galerías Pacifico). Galerías Pacifico has free performances at 8pm Friday and Saturday in the food court downstairs. Many restaurants combine dinner with shows (especially in San Telmo), though these can be costly.

Café Tortoni (☎ 011-4342-4328; www.cafetortoni .com.ar in Spanish; Av de Mayo 829; shows US$4.25) For good, inexpensive tango in the back of an atmospheric old café, the Tortoni can't be beat. Shows run at 9:30pm and 11:30pm nightly.

Bar Sur (☎ 011-4362-6086; www.bar-sur.com.ar; Estados Unidos 299; shows US$16) This very intimate, long-running San Telmo venue offers nightly tango shows; admission includes all the pizza you can eat. Reservations are a good idea.

El Balcón (☎ 011-4362-2354; Humberto Primo 461) Grab a balcony seat early on Sunday, and watch tango both here and in the plaza below – it's free as long as you buy something to nibble. Nearby is the similar **Mitos Argentinos** (☎ 011-4362-7810; Humberto Primo 489).

Café Homero (☎ 011-4701-7357; Cabrera 4946) In Palermo Viejo, this nice-sized venue, features tango singers and musicians more than dancers. The admission fee varies depending on who's on, but usually runs under US$7.30. Call for reservations.

Club de Vino (☎ 011-4833-8330; Cabrera 4737) Near Café Homero, this upscale joint comes complete with fancy restaurant up front. Call for reservations.

For sensational dinner/tango shows – oriented at wealthy tourists – try **El Querandí** (☎ 011-4345-1770; www.querandi.com.ar; Perú 302; shows US$45), **Señor Tango** (☎ 011-4303-0231; Vieytes 1653; shows US$39) or **Taconeando** (☎ 011-4307-6696; www.taconeando.com; Balcarce 725; shows US$22). Shows only (without dinner) cost about 25% less. Reserve in advance.

If you tire of the tango, try **Avila Bar** (☎ 011-4383-6974; Av de Mayo 1384; shows US$14; ☼ Thu-Sat). You can dine on tapas, seafood or paella, then watch an intimate flamenco show; reserve in advance.

SHOPPING

For modern shopping needs, walk along Avs Florida, Lavalle and Santa Fe. The San Telmo antiques fair, on Plaza Dorrego, takes place on Sunday. Heaps of homemade crafts, both creative and kitschy, are on display weekends at the hippy *feria artesana* (craft market), in front of Recoleta's cemetery.

Feria de Mataderos (☎ 011-4374-9664 Mon-Fri, ☎ 011-4687-5602 Sun; cnr Av de los Corrales & Lisandro de la Torre) Way out west in the Mataderos *barrio* is this great market, offering up good craft buys along with *gaucho* traditions. It's open Saturday nights in summer, and Sunday days the rest of the year – check the tourist office for exact schedules. Bus No

180 (which is also No 155) gets you there in about an hour.

Ski Center (☎ 011-4326-1207; Esmeralda 346) Despite the name, this store also sells a decent selection of camping supplies.

Eurocamping (☎ 011-4374-5007; Paraná 761) A good place to find quality outdoor clothing, along with tents and sleeping bags.

GETTING THERE & AWAY
Air

Most international flights leave from Ezeiza. **Manuel Tienda León** (☎ 011-4314-3636; www.tiendaleon.com; Santa Fe 790) and **Transfer Express** (☎ 011-4480-9538; Florida 1045) run frequent buses to Ezeiza (US$5.80, 40 minutes). The cheapest way to get there, however, is by local bus No 86 (US$0.50, about two hours); be sure it says 'Ezeiza,' since not all No 86s go there. Taxis cost US$11, including tolls.

Manuel Tienda León and Transfer Express charge US$2.25 for the 20-minute ride to Aeroparque. Or take city bus No 45 from Plaza San Martín (US$0.30). Taxis cost US$3.

Argentina's departure tax is US$18, payable in US dollars or pesos. The following is a list of airline offices:

Aerolíneas Argentinas/Austral (☎ 0810-222-86527; Alem 1134; Perú 2)
Air Canada (☎ 011-4393-9090; Córdoba 656)
Air France (☎ 011-4317-4700; San Martín 344, 23rd fl)
Alitalia (☎ 011-4310-9999; Santa Fe 887)
American Airlines (☎ 011-4318-1111; Santa Fe 881)
British Airways (☎ 011-4320-6600; Pellegrini 1163)
Delta (☎ 011-4312-1200; Reconquista 737, 3rd fl)
Dinar Líneas Aéreas (☎ 011-4327-8000; Roque Sáenz Peña 933)
KLM (☎ 011-4326-8422; Suipacha 268, 9th fl)
LADE (☎ 0810-810-5233; Perú 714)
LanChile (☎ 011-4378-2200; Cerrito 866)
LAPA (☎ 011-4114-5336; Carlos Pellegrini 1075)
Lloyd Aéreo Boliviano (LAB; ☎ 011-4323-1900; Carlos Pellegrini 141)
Lufthansa (☎ 011-4319-0600; Marcelo T de Alvear 590, 6th fl)
Pluna (☎ 011-4342-4420; Florida 1)
Southern Winds (☎ 0810-777-7979; Santa Fe 784)
Swissair (☎ 011-4319-0000; Santa Fe 846, 1st fl)
TransBrasil (☎ 011-4312-0856; Reconquista 737, 4th fl)
Transportes Aéreos de Mercosur (TAM; ☎ 011-4819-4800; Cerrito 1026)
United Airlines (☎ 0-810-777-864833; Eduardo Madero 9000)
Varig (☎ 011-4329-9211; Córdoba 972, 3rd fl)

Boat

There are several daily trips to Colonia (US$17 to US$30, one to 2¾ hours) and Montevideo (US$56, 2½ hours) from the **Buquebus port** (☎ 011-4316-6500; www.buquebus.com in Spanish; cnr Av Antártida Argentina & Córdoba), and also combination boat-bus services to Punta del Este, Uruguay's top beach resort. Buquebus also has an office in Recoleta's Patio Bullrich mall. More services and higher prices exist in the summer season, when it's a good idea to buy your ticket an hour in advance. Some nationalities may need visas to enter Uruguay.

Bus

Retiro (☎ 011-4310-0700; cnr Av Antártida Argentina & Ramos Mejía) is a huge bus station with slots for 75 buses. It has restaurants, bathrooms, stores, luggage storage, 24-hour information and telephone offices with Internet.

The entries in the table are only a sample of very extensive schedules. Prices listed are at the low end of the range and vary depending on the season, the company and the economy. During holidays, buy your tickets to popular destinations in advance; you may have to go to the station to do so.

Domestic destinations include:

Destination	Duration in Hours	Cost
Bahía Blanca	9	US$13
Bariloche	24	US$32
Comodoro Rivadavia	24	US$25
Córdoba	10	US$11
Mar del Plata	5½	US$11
Mendoza	14	US$18
Neuquén	16	US$22
Puerto Iguazú	18	US$24
Puerto Madryn	20	US$22
Resistencia	13	US$14
Rosario	4	US$7.30
Salta	21	US$23
Santa Fe	6½	US$10
Santa Rosa	9	US$11
Tucumán	16	US$20

International destinations include:

Destination	Duration in Hours	Cost
Asunción	18	US$18
Foz de Iguazú	19	US$22
Montevideo	8	US$23
Punta del Este	10½	US$30
Rio de Janeiro	44	US$88
Santiago	20	US$29
São Paulo	38	US$71

Train

Rail travel in Argentina is generally cheaper but not nearly as fast, frequent or comfortable as bus travel. Each train station has its own *subte* stop.

Estación Constitución (☎ 011-4304-0028) Service to La Plata, Bahía Blanca, Atlantic beach towns.

Estación Once (☎ 011-4861-0043) Service to Luján, Santa Rosa.

Estación Retiro (☎ 011-4317-4000) Service to Tigre, Rosario.

GETTING AROUND
Bicycle

Bike Tours (☎ 011-4311-5199; www.biketours.com.ar; Florida 868, 13th fl) You can rent bicycles and have them delivered to your door. They cost US$3.75 per 24 hours, including helmet and lock.

Bus

Sold at many kiosks and bookstores, *Lumi* (US$3.75) and *Guia T* (pocket version US$0.75) are bus guides that detail some 200 bus routes. Fares depend on distance, but most rides are US$0.30 (about Arg$0.80) – say 'ochenta' to the driver, then place coins in the machine behind him (change given). Offer front seats to elderly folk.

Subway

Buenos Aires' Subte (www.metrovias.com.ar) is fast, efficient and costs only US$0.25 per ride. Four of the five lines (Líneas A, B, D and E) run from the *microcentro* to the capital's western and northern outskirts, while Línea C links Retiro and Constitución. Trains operate from approximately 5am to 10:30pm except Sunday and holidays (when hours are 8am to 10pm); they run frequently on weekdays, less so on weekends.

Taxi & Remise

Metered black-and-yellow cabs are common and reasonably priced. Make sure the driver uses the meter; if he just quotes you a price, especially to a tourist destination, it may be jacked up. Rides start at US$1.12; tips are unnecessary, but you can leave some change.

Remises are unmarked taxis with set fares comparable to taxis. They are considered a bit safer than street taxis, since you phone an established company to send out a car. Any business should be able to call a *remise* for you.

AROUND BUENOS AIRES

TIGRE

Just off the Río de la Plata, this favorite *porteño* weekend destination is an hour away from the capital and is a great starting point for exploring the Delta del Paraná. You can shop at **Mercado de Frutos** (a daily crafts market; best on weekends), see a couple of museums, check out the popular riverfront, or take a relaxing boat ride.

Tigre's **tourist office** (☎ 011-4512-4497; www .tigre.gov.ar; Mitre 305; ☺ 9am-5pm) is next door to McDonald's. Nearby are ticket counters for commuter boats that cruise the waterways; the tourist office has recommendations for destinations you can go to for walks or camping. Tigre is also the push-off point for Isla Martín García.

To get to Tigre, you have several options. The fastest is taking the Tigre train line from Estación Retiro (US$0.35, 50 minutes, frequent); the final station is almost at the tourist office and docks. For a touristy journey take the Mitre line from Estación Retiro to Estación Bartolome Mitre (US$0.85), where you board the **Tren de la Costa** (US$0.75 to US$0.90), an upgraded train line that has stops at cafés and a fancy shopping center. The final station (Estación Delta) is near a tacky amusement park popular with families; the tourist office is a 10-minute walk away, but the Mercado de Frutos is a few blocks southeast. You can also take bus Nos 59, 152, and 60 to the Bartolome Mitre station. Bus No 60 also goes all the way to Tigre itself and takes up to two hours (US$1.35).

ISLA MARTÍN GARCÍA

As you navigate the densely forested channels of the delta en route to historic Martín García, it's easy to imagine colonial smugglers hiding out among the rushes. Just off the Uruguayan littoral, the island was infamous as a prison camp; four Argentine presidents have put in time here, and it's still used as a halfway house for prisoners near the end of their terms. At present, though, it's mostly a combination of historical monument, nature reserve and recreational retreat for the bustling capital.

The most affordable way to the island is by guided tour with **Cacciola** (☎ 011-4749-0329;

www.cacciolaviajes.com), across from Estación Fluvial in Tigre; tickets are also available at the company's **Buenos Aires office** (☎ 011-4393-6100; Florida 520, 1st fl). The boat leaves Tigre at 9am Tuesday, Thursday and weekends, returning around 5:30pm (US$16 round trip). It's possible to spend a night or two on the island; contact Cacciola for more information.

LUJÁN

Legend says that in 1630 a wagon would not budge on a rutted cart road until *gauchos* removed from it an image of the Virgin brought from Brazil. The image's devoted owner built a chapel on the spot, 65km west of Buenos Aires. Argentina's patron saint now occupies the neo-Gothic **Basílica Nuestra Señora de Luján** and this spot is the country's most important devotional site. Her day is May 8. Luján's other attractions are a colonial museum complex and a commercial yet pleasant riverfront area. Weekends are liveliest, with folks bringing their babies from all over the country to be baptized at the basilica.

To get here take Transportes Atlántida's bus No 57 (US$1.75, 1½ hours), which leaves from Plaza Italia in Palermo, or Metrolíneas' bus No 52 (US$1.75, one hour), which leaves from Plaza Miserere in Once.

SAN ANTONIO DE ARECO

Dating from the early 18th-century construction of a chapel in honor of San Antonio de Padua, this serene village is the symbolic center of Argentina's vestigial *gaucho* culture. It's also host to the country's biggest *gaucho* celebration, Día de la Tradición, in November. Narrow tree-lined streets make this low-rise, stoplight-free town pleasant to stroll, so walk to **Parque Criollo y Museo Gauchesco Ricardo Güiraldes**, which honors the author of the classic gauchesque novel *Don Segundo Sombra*.

Plaza Ruiz de Arellano is beautifully landscaped and sports a parroquial church, while local artisans are known for producing maté paraphernalia, *rastras* (silver-studded belts) and *facones* (long-bladed knives). The tourist office is at the northern end of Arellano.

Frequent buses from Buenos Aires to San Antonio take 1½ hours (US$3.75). Chevallier has the most departures.

LA PLATA

On Plaza Moreno is La Plata's beautiful neo-Gothic **cathedral**; it took 115 years to finish and was finally completed in 2000. North of town, the extensive 60-hectare **Paseo del Bosque** is home to the ancient but excellent **Museo de La Plata** (☎ 0221-425-7744; www.fcnym.unlp.edu.ar/museo; admission US$1; ☽ 10am-6pm Tue-Sun). On display are heaps of interesting exhibits such as taxidermy specimens, dried insects, musty mummies and dinosaur skeletons. Nearby are the **Observatorio Astronómico** and a small **Jardín Zoológico** (☎ 0221-427-3925; admission US$0.75; ☽ 9am-6pm Tue-Sun).

La Plata is easily seen on a daytrip from Buenos Aires, but there are plenty of hotels if you want to hang around. Near the bus terminal is plain and homely **Hotel Roca** (☎ 0221-421-4916; Calle 42 No 309; s/d US$9/13); TV and private bath cost an extra US$1.75. Much ritzier is **Benevento Hotel** (☎ 0221-423-7721; www.hotelbenevento.com.ar; Calle 2 No 645; s/d US$14/26), with elegant and clean rooms; breakfast is included. Hang with a friendly beer at venerable **Cervecería Modelo** (Calles 54 & 5).

To get to La Plata, take frequent Costera Metropolitana buses (one way/round trip US$4.50/8, one hour). They run all night and depart from Retiro train station. La Plata's bus terminal is at Calles 4 and 42, while its train station (cnr Av 1 and Calle 44) has half-hourly services to Constitución (US$0.50, 1¼ hours).

URUGUAY

Day trips to small, charming, cobbled **Colonia** are popular with tourists. It's also possible to travel to nearby **Montevideo**, Uruguay's capital, for a couple of days to enjoy its beaches and experience a different big city feel than Buenos Aires. Farther east, **Punta del Este** (where droves of rich *porteños* flock in summer) is Uruguay's most popular beach resort and only a few hours away from Argentina's capital. There are many buses and ferries that link the two countries; see p59. For more information on visiting any of these destinations, see the Uruguay chapter, p910.

NORTHEAST ARGENTINA

The area between the Paraná and Uruguay Rivers, traditionally known as Mesopotamia, offers varied recreational opportunities on the rivers and in the parks of Entre Ríos and Corrientes provinces. Subtropical Misiones province, nearly surrounded by Paraguay and Brazil, features ruined Jesuit missions and the spectacular Iguazú Falls. Across the Río Paraná, the Gran Chaco is Argentina's 'empty quarter' (a sparsely populated area of the country).

HISTORY

This was Guaraní country first. They were semi-sedentary agriculturalists, raising sweet potatoes, maize, manioc and beans and eating river fish until the Spanish arrived in 1570, pushing their way south from Paraguay. Santa Fe was founded in 1573, Corrientes a few years later. The Jesuits came soon after, herding the Guaraní into 30 *reducciones* (settlements) in the upper Paraná in the hope of converting them by way of prayer (and hard work). The *reducciones* were doing a roaring trade in *yerba maté* (herb maté) production until Carlos III, busy with nation-building back in Spain, decided that the Jesuit's growing power base was too much of a distraction, and booted them all off the Americas in 1767.

Some Guaraní were still out there, though, in the steamy thorn forests of Chaco and Formosa, resisting the newcomers. They lasted until 1850 when the woodcutters from Corrientes came through, looking for the *quebracho* (axe-breaker) tree to satisfy their tannin lust. After the land had been cleared (in more ways than one), the Guaraní who were left were kept busy picking the newly planted cotton and raising cattle.

The War of the Triple Alliance (1865–70) put an end to Brazil and Paraguay's claims on the territory and for a few years Entre Ríos was an independent republic, before joining the Buenos Aires-based Unitarist coalition under Rosas. Local *caudillo* (chief) Justo José Urquiza brought about Rosas' defeat and the eventual adoption of Argentina's modern constitution.

ROSARIO

Che Guevara was born in Rosario. Situated on the banks of the Paraná, 320km from Buenos Aires, the town has cheap camping, beautiful buildings and a rockin' nightlife (but only on weekends). There are also plenty of artists and musos around, the

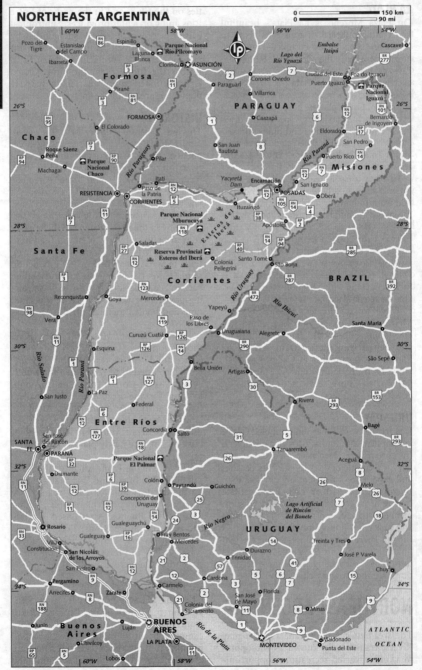

NORTHEAST ARGENTINA

galleries are good, the beaches close, and the riverside happening – we should all be there right now, basically.

After independence, the railway brought agricultural exports from Córdoba, Mendoza and Tucumán, and the city quickly superseded the provincial capital of Santa Fe as the area's economic powerhouse.

Orientation

The long-distance **bus terminal** (☎ 0341-437-2384; Cafferata 702), is 4km west of center. Many local buses (marked 'Centro' or 'Plaza Sarmiento') go to the center; buy US$0.50 magnetic cards at kiosks before you board. Bus No 138 is the one to catch from the train station.

Information

The informative **tourist office** (☎ 0341-480-2230; Av del Huerto; ⏱ 7am-7pm) is on the waterfront.

Cambios along San Martín and Córdoba change traveler's checks; there are many banks and ATMs on Santa Fe between Mitre and Entre Ríos. **Hacker Cibercafé** (3 de Febrero 1280) charges US$3 per hour for Internet access.

Sights

Prices, dates and hours change throughout the year. Check with the tourist office to be sure.

The colossal **Monumento Nacional a la Bandera** (Monument to the Flag; ⏱ 9am-7pm), located behind Plaza 25 de Mayo, contains the crypt of flag designer General Manuel Belgrano. You can take the elevator (US$0.30) to the top for a dizzying view of the river and surrounds.

Parque Independencia's **Museo Histórico Provincial Dr Julio Marc** (⏱ 9am-5pm) has excellent displays on indigenous cultures from all over Latin America, as well as colonial and religious artifacts and the most ornate collection of maté paraphernalia you ever did see. The **Museo Municipal de Bellas Artes Juan B Castagnino** (cnr Pellegrini & Oroño; ⏱ 2-8pm) focuses on European and Argentine fine art. The **Museo Provincial de Ciencias Naturales Dr Ángel Gallardo** (Moreno 750; ⏱ 3-6pm) is a huge collection of stuffed animals and other grisly items. The crumbling mansion that it's housed in nearly steals the show and the spider and insect exhibits will make

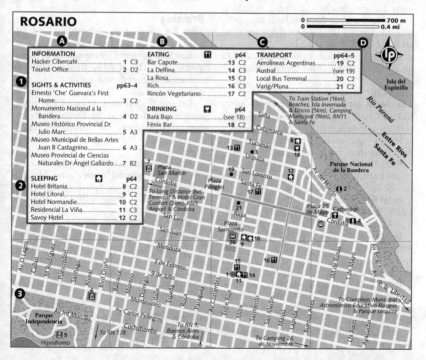

ROSARIO

0 — 700 m
0 — 0.4 mi

Isla del Espinillo

Río Paraná

Entre Ríos

Santa Fe

To Train Station (1km),
Beaches, Isla Invernada
& Discos (5km), Camping
Municipal (9km), RN11
& Santa Fe

Salta

Catamarca

Tucumán

Urquiza

Parque Nacional
de la Bandera

Plaza
San Martín

San Lorenzo

Córdoba

Plaza
Pringles

Santa Fe

To Long Distance Bus
Terminal & Hotel Gran
Comfort (2km), RN9,
Airport & Córdoba

Rioja

Plaza 25
de Mayo

Cathedral

Córdoba

San Juan

Plaza
Sarmiento

Mendoza

3 de Febrero

9 de Julio

San Luis

M de Rosas

M de Rosas

M de Mayo

Av de la Libertad

Av Lagos

Callao

M Rodríguez

Pueyrredón

Santiago

Alvear

Bvd Oroño

Balcarce

Moreno

Dorrego

Italia

España

Roca

Paraguay

Av Corrientes

Entre Ríos

Mitre

Sarmiento

San Martín

Maipú

Laprida

Buenos Aires

Ln Alem

Ayacucho

Montevideo

Av Carlos Pellegrini

Cochabamba

To RN 178

To RN 9,
Buenos Aires
& Córdoba

To Camping 26
de Noviembre

To Complejo Municipal
Astronómico Educativo Rosario
& Parque Urquiza

Parque
Independencia

Hipodromo

Av Int Morcillo

you want to rush out and buy a mosquito net immediately.

The **planetarium** (Complejo Astronómico Municipal, Parque Urquiza; admission US$1) has weekend shows at 5pm and 6pm.

Renowned architect Alejandro Bustillo designed the apartment building at **Entre Ríos 480** where, in 1928, Ernesto Guevara Lynch and Celia de la Serna resided after the birth of their son Ernesto Guevara de la Serna, popularly known as Che. There's heated historical debate over whether he was born in May or June, but this was certainly his first home.

Wanna go to the beach? Take bus No 153 from the center of town north 6km to Av Puccio (here the bus turns inland). Stroll up the **rambla** (boardwalk) along Catalunya beach and look for a spot to lay your towel. There are plenty of restaurants around. If you keep walking along the boardwalk, in 20 minutes you'll hit private beach Florida, which charges US$1 for access to a wider stretch of sand. Beyond it is Estación Costa Alta (the boat dock), where you can take a 15-minute ride across the Paraná (round trip US$1) to **Isla Invernada** – land of woodsier, more natural beaches (camping possible). To get to the boat dock without the stroll, take bus No 103 from the local bus terminal on San Luis; it stops close by.

Back in town, there's a weekend **crafts fair** on Belgrano south of the tourist office.

Sleeping

The **Savoy Hotel** (☎ 0341-448-0071; San Lorenzo 1022; s/d US$6/10) A grand old place with high ceilings and ornate fittings that's obviously fallen on hard times. All rooms have private baths and most have balconies.

Hotel Litoral (☎ 0341-421-1426; Entre Ríos 1045; s/d with breakfast US$7/11) Clean and new. Most rooms have TV and balcony.

Hotel Normandie (☎ 0341-421-2694; Mitre 1030; s/d US$5/8, with bath US$7/10) Friendly and central. Rooms are adequate if a bit sterile.

Residencial La Viña (☎ 0341-421-4549; 3 de Febrero 1244; s/d with bath US$7/10) Has a range of rooms that must be good value – some of the locals use them by the hour.

Hotel Britania (☎ 0341-440-6036; San Martín 364; s/d US$3/5, with bath US$5/7) Proves without doubt that you get what you pay for. Popular, friendly but none too clean.

Hotel Gran Confort (☎ 0341-438-0486; Pasaje Quintanilla 657; s/d US$7/10) Near the long-distance bus terminal (but nothing else). A bit pokey, but good for late-night arrivals.

The best, most natural camping sites are on **Isla Invernada** (campsites per person US$1); see Sights previous for details on how to get there. On the mainland, **Camping Municipal** (☎ 0341-471-4381; campsites per person US$1) is about 9km north of the city – take bus No 35 from the center to Barra 9.

Eating

There are many café hangouts on the pedestrian streets, and up north the coast has beach-oriented eateries.

Bar Capote (cnr Urquiza & Av Corrientes) Tastefully decorated with atmospheric lighting in a beautifully restored older building; they'll serve your basic café fare at decent prices.

Rich (San Juan 1031) Fine Italian food with a budget *rotisería* (takeaway section) next door.

La Rosa (Entre Ríos 1271; 🕑 Mon-Sat) Serves vegetarian Chinese, pizza, empanadas and other basic vegetarian dishes.

Rincón Vegetariano (Mitre 720) Another meat-free alternative.

Drinking

Fénix Bar (cnr San Martín & Tucumán) Good for cheap drinks and a young crowd.

Bara Bajo (San Martín 370; admission US$3; 🕑 2am-dawn Fri & Sat) This bar-like dance club plays house, techno and *rock nacional* and usually gets packed.

During the summer, most of the nightclub action moves to the Costanera Norte mega-discos along Av Colombres and E Carrasco. The following are only a few of them.

Timotea (Colombres 1340, south of Av Puccio; admission US$3-4; 🕑 year round, Sat only in winter) *Marcha*, techno and the usual house rhythms keep a young crowd going wild into the wee hours.

Blue Velvet (Colombres 1698, south of Av Puccio), **Pancho Villa** (Av Puccio 122, at Colombres) and **El Faro** (north of Costa Alta), are similar mainstream discos that stay packed through the summer and busy on off-season weekends. They all charge around US$4 a head, which includes a free drink.

Getting There & Away

Aerolíneas Argentinas (☎ 0341-424-9517; Santa Fe 1412) and **Austral** (☎ 0341-424-9517; Santa Fe

1412), have several daily flights to Buenos Aires (US$45). International services are with Varig and **Pluna** (☎ 0341-425-6262; Córdoba 1015, 2nd fl); they go to Brazil (US$410) and Uruguay (US$88).

Sample bus fares from Rosario include Buenos Aires (US$6, four hours), Córdoba (US$8, six hours), Santa Fe (US$4, 2¼ hours) and Mendoza (US$12, 12 hours), as well as Montevideo, Uruguay (US$23, 10 hours). Prices for tickets go up in high season.

The **train station** (☎ 0341-430-7272 Av del Valle 2700), 3km northwest of the center of town, has service to Buenos Aires (US$4, five hours), leaving at 6am Monday through Saturday.

SANTA FE

Santa Fe is a sassy little town, perfect for the late riser; the locals eat late, go out late and – you guessed it – go home late. The university ensures a young population, out and about on the lively riverfront or in the happening bar district, La Recoleta.

Relocated during the mid-17th century because of hostile indigenous groups, floods and isolation, the city duplicates the original plan of Santa Fe La Vieja (Old Santa Fe), but a 19th-century neo-Parisian building boom and more recent construction have left only isolated colonial buildings, mostly near Plaza 25 de Mayo.

Av San Martín, north of the plaza, is the main commercial artery. The airport

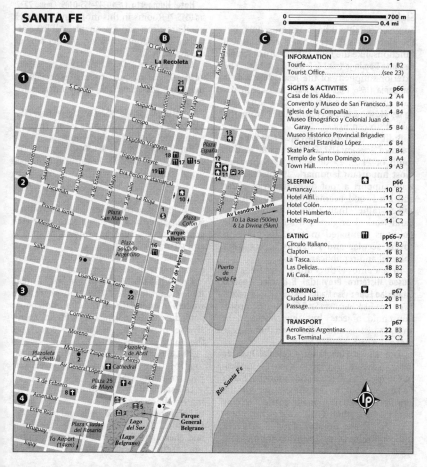

SANTA FE

0	700 m
0	0.4 mi

is 15km south of town. The bus marked 'L (aeropuerto)' goes past San Luis and Hipólito Yrigoyen (US$0.50, 45 minutes). From the bus terminal, ask at Tata Rapido or Rio Coronda for their express airport service (US$0.50). A taxi should set you back about US$4.

Information
The **municipal tourist office** (☎ 0342-457-4123; ◷ 7am-1pm & 3-8pm) is in the bus terminal at Belgrano 2910.

Tourfe (San Martín 2500) collects 3% commission on traveler's checks; there are several ATMs along the San Martín *peatonal*. There's a **post office** (Av 27 de Febrero 2331) and a *locutorio* at the bus terminal.

Sights
Some colonial buildings are museums, but the churches still serve their ecclesiastical functions, like the mid-17th-century **Templo de Santo Domingo** (cnr 3 de Febrero & 9 de Julio). The exterior simplicity of the Jesuit **Iglesia de la Compañía** (1696; Plaza 25 de Mayo) masks an ornate interior. The restored, two-story **Casa de los Aldao** (Buenos Aires 2861) dates from the early 18th century.

Built in 1680, the **Convento y Museo de San Francisco** (Amenábar 2257; ◷ 10am-noon & 4-6:30pm), south of Plaza 25 de Mayo, is Santa Fe's most important landmark. Its meter-thick walls support a roof of Paraguayan cedar and hardwood beams fitted with wooden spikes rather than nails. The doors are hand-worked originals, while the baroque pulpit is laminated in gold. Its museum covers secular and religious topics from colonial and republican eras.

In a damp 17th-century building, the **Museo Histórico Provincial Brigadier General Estanislao López** (San Martín 1490; ◷ 8:30am-noon & 4-7pm Mon-Fri, 5:30-8:30pm Sat & Sun) shows mostly household objects, but the collection of antique pistols and solid silver horse gear make it worth a quick visit.

The **Museo Etnográfico y Colonial Juan de Garay** (25 de Mayo 1470; ◷ 8:30am-noon & 4-7pm Mon-Fri, 4:30-7pm Sat & Sun) has a scale model of Santa Fe La Vieja, but the real show-stopper is the *gaucho* 'campchair' – made entirely of cow bones and leather. Gruesome – but comfortable! There are also colonial artifacts, indigenous basketry, Spanish ceramics and a *gaucho*'s stuffed horse.

The little **skate park** on the shores of Lago de Sur has a half-pipe, ramps and rails. If you've got the moves, you can probably borrow a deck and impress the locals. If not, you can probably still borrow one and give them something to laugh at. Your call.

Sleeping
The surprisingly seedy area around the bus terminal is the budget hotel zone. It's not dangerous – just the town center for various unsavory transactions.

Hotel Colón (☎ 0342-452-1586; San Luis 2862; s/d US$7/10) A block from the bus terminal, this hotel has large carpeted rooms with TV and private bath.

Hotel Humberto (☎ 0342-455-0409; Crespo 2222; s/d US$5/7) Rooms in this mom-and-pop-run hotel are clean and reasonable. All have attached bath. Some cheaper, smaller singles are available.

Amancay (☎ 0342-456-5052; 25 de Mayo 2692; s/d US$5/7) Clean, quiet rooms (especially at the rear). May have too many mirrors for some.

Hotel Royal (☎ 0342-452-7359; Irigoyen Freire 2256; d US$5, s/d with bath US$5/7) Small and friendly with basic, slightly shabby rooms.

Hotel Alfil (☎ 0342-453-5044; Belgrano 2859; s/d US$3/7, with bath US$5/8) Features functional, wood paneled rooms.

Eating
On Belgrano, across from the bus terminal, several good, inexpensive places serve Argentine staples such as empanadas, pizza, and *parrillada*.

Clapton (San Martín 2300) A chic café/bar/ restaurant with cheap set-meal deals.

Círculo Italiano (Hipólito Yrigoyen 2457) A real find. Come for the ritzy atmosphere, the waiters in linen jackets, the complimentary paté, the extensive wine list or the inexpensive set meals. Stay for the classic rock on the sound system.

Mi Casa (San Martín 2777) Mostly Chinese food, warmly recommended by locals (all you can eat for US$6).

La Tasca (San Martín 2846) Nothing mindblowing on the menu here, but it's got a great old-time feel with tiled walls and hardwood furniture. Breakfast and snacks are good and cheap and there are occasional exhibitions featuring local artisans.

Las Delicias (cnr San Martín & Hipólito Yrigoyen) Good for coffee, sandwiches and outstanding pastries in a swanky ambience with decent prices.

Drinking

Santa Fe's rock-steady nightlife centers on the intersection of San Martín and Santiago del Estero, an area known as La Recoleta. Things hot up from Thursday to Saturday. Bars come and go in this area – it's worth going for a wander and seeing where the crowds are. The following are a couple of old faithfuls.

Ciudad Juarez (25 de Mayo 3424) It's been around for years, but the combination of loud music and Tex-Mex decor keeps 'em coming back for more.

Passage (San Martín 3243; admission US$1) Although *slightly* bigger than a passage, this is the place to get your groove on before hitting the *boliches* (disco).

La Divina (Costanera Este s/n) This huge tent-like structure is the city's definitive summertime disco. Come and you'll hear everything from *cumbia* (big on horns and percussion) and *marcha español* (aggressive drum beats, bleepy noises and chanted lyrics) through to mainstream house and techno.

La Base (cnr Leandro Alem & Necochea; admission US$2-3) The biggest of Santa Fe's *boliches*, this multiplex dance club attracts the crowds when La Divina shuts down for the winter.

Getting There & Around

Aerolíneas Argentinas (☎ 0342-459-6313; Lisandro de la Torre 2633) has 45 weekly non-stop flights to Buenos Aires (US$41).

The **bus information office** (☎ 0342-457-4124; ☼ 7am-9pm) at the bus terminal posts fares for all destinations.

Buses leave hourly for Paraná (US$1, one hour). Sample long-distance fares include Rosario (US$4, two hours), Buenos Aires (US$10, six hours), Corrientes (US$12, 10 hours) and Posadas (US$13, 12 hours). Other carriers go to Córdoba and its sierras, Mendoza and Patagonian destinations.

International services go to Porto Alegre (US$36, 18 hours) and Rio de Janeiro, Brazil (US$66, 40 hours); Asunción, Paraguay (US$18, 13 hours); and Montevideo, Uruguay (US$20, 11 hours).

PARANÁ

On the hilly banks of its namesake river, Paraná rolls out with a relaxed and stately assurance, a fitting counterpart to hectic Santa Fe across the river. If you arrive in Paraná on a Sunday, you could be forgiven for thinking that the town had been evacuated – in a way it has. This is the day when everybody heads down to the *costanera* (seaside promenade), and the grassy riverside strip transforms into a sea of folding lawn chairs and a flurry of maté sipping activity. It's a good place for strolling at any time, especially around sundown when the promenaders come out.

The city's irregular plan has several diagonals, curving boulevards and complex intersections. From Plaza Primero de Mayo, the town center, Calle San Martín is a *peatonal* for six blocks. Bus No 1 goes from the bus terminal past the center to the riverside.

Information

Paraná's municipal tourist office has branches at the bus terminal and at the **Oficina Parque** (☎ 0343-420-1837; cnr Bajada San Martín & Av Laurencena; ☼ 8am-8pm) on the riverfront. The **provincial tourist office** (☎ 0343-422-3384; ☼ 8am-9pm) is located at Laprida 5. The freecall number for the **municipal tourist office** (☎ 0800-555-9575) is very handy if you suddenly find yourself in need of on-the-spot, low-cost tourist information.

There are several ATMs along the San Martín *peatonal*. The post office is at Av 25 de Mayo and Monte Caseros, and there's a *locutorio* on San Martín between Uruguay and Pazos. **Ciber** (Urquiza 521) has Internet access.

Sights

Plaza Primero de Mayo has had an **Iglesia Catedral** since 1730, but the current building dates from 1885. When Paraná was capital of the confederation, the Senate deliberated at the **Colegio del Huerto**, at 9 de Julio and 25 de Mayo.

A block west, at Corrientes and Urquiza, are the **Palacio Municipal** (1889) and the **Escuela Normal Paraná**, a school founded by noted educator (later President) DF Sarmiento. Across San Martín is the **Teatro Municipal Tres de Febrero** (Av 25 de Mayo 60), dating from 1908. At the west end of the

San Martín *peatonal*, on Plaza Alvear, the **Museo Histórico de Entre Ríos Martín Leguizamón** (7:30am-12:30pm & 3-7:30pm Tue-Fri, 9am-noon & 4-7pm Sat, 9am-noon Sun) flaunts provincial pride, as knowledgeable guides go to rhetorical extremes extolling the role of local *caudillos* in Argentine history. The adjacent subterranean **Museo de Bellas Artes Pedro E Martínez** (9am-noon & 4-9pm Mon-Fri, 10:30am-12:30pm & 5:30-8pm Sat, 10:30am-12:30pm Sun) displays works by provincial artists. Both museums welcome the US$0.30 voluntary contribution.

The modern **Museo de la Ciudad** (Parque Urquiza; admission free; 8am-noon Tue-Fri, 4-8pm Tue-Sun, 9am-noon Sat) focuses on Paraná's urban past and surroundings. Winter hours are slightly shorter.

From the Puerto Nuevo at Av Laurencia and Vélez Sársfield, the **Paraná Rowing Club** (0343-431-6518) conducts hour-long **river excursions** (tickets US$3; Fri-Sun) at 3:30pm and 5pm.

Sleeping

Hotel Latino (0343-431-1036; San Juan 154; s/d US$5/8) Simple and clean rooms opening onto an enclosed patio. Nice tilework, too.

Residencial Las Brisas (0343-422-0517; Bavio 125; s/d with bath US$5/8) Central, basic and a bit shabby, but good value for the price.

Hotel City (0343-431-0086; Racedo 231; s/d with TV & bath US$7/11) Opposite the railway station, this is a good budget choice. It's tranquil and leafy with cool rooms and high ceilings.

Hotel Bristol (0343-431-3961; Alsina 221; s/d US$3/7, d with bath US$12) Well-kept and quiet, right across the road from the bus terminal.

Camping Balneario Thompson (0343-420-1583; campsites per person US$2) is the most convenient campground. Bus Nos 1 and 6 ('Thompson') link it to downtown.

Eating

A good place to stock up on food is the **Mercado Central** (cnr Pellegrini & Bavio).

La Brava (Costanera s/n; opposite the rowing club) This is a great place for a sunset beer on the balcony overlooking the river. Fish and *parrillada* are on the menu.

Club Atlético Estudiantes (cnr Los Vascos & Bertozzi) Inside the athletic club on the western end of Parque Urquiza is one of the best seafood restaurants in town. The upscale

atmosphere is at odds with the very reasonable prices.

Petra (25 de Mayo 32; lunch/dinner US$2/3) A very popular *tenedor libre* offering a huge selection.

Giovani (Urquiza 1045) A highly regarded *parrilla*, which also serves great pasta.

Drinking

Coyote (Linieres 334; midnight-dawn Thu-Sat) This Tex-Mex-flavored dance club on the river plays the usual mix of mainstream *marcha* house and salsa.

Las Piedras (cnr Rivadavia & Córdoba; 9am-1pm & 6pm-late) This bar-cum-sandwich shop has live music on Friday and Saturday nights, usually followed by dancing. It's a small, fun place.

Getting There & Around

Aerolíneas Argentinas (0343-423-2425; Corrientes 563) has offices in town; flights leave from Santa Fe's airport (see p67).

The **bus terminal** (0343-422-1282) is on Av Ramírez between Posadas and Moreno. Roughly hourly throughout the day and night, Etacer and Fluvial buses leave for Santa Fe (US$3, one hour). Other services and fares closely resemble those to and from Santa Fe.

GUALEGUAYCHÚ

On a tributary of the Río Uruguay, Gualeguaychú is the first sizable city north of Buenos Aires and a popular gateway for Uruguay. It retains a relaxed, provincial feel with low 19th-century buildings lining wide tree-lined avenues. In February, the city springs into action with Argentina's foremost Carnaval celebrations.

Plaza San Martín marks the city center. The **tourist office** (03446-422900; 8am-8pm) is on the Plazoleta de los Artesanos. Several banks have ATMs.

The colonial **Casa de Andrade** (cnr Andrade & Borques) once belonged to 19th-century poet, journalist, diplomat and politician Olegario Andrade.

At the former Estación Ferrocarril Urquiza, at the south end of Maipú, the **Museo Ferroviario** has a free open-air exhibit of locomotives, dining cars and a steam engine. Alongside the station the **Corsódromo** (Blvd Irazusta) is the main site for Gualeguaychú's lively Carnaval.

Boats circumnavigate Isla Libertad in the Río Gualeguaychú on Friday, Saturday and Sunday afternoons (US$3, one hour); inquire at the port, on Costanera Norte JFM Bernard, 800m east of the Corsódromo.

Sleeping & Eating

Hotel Amalfi (☎ 03446-426818; 25 de Mayo 571; s/d US$5/8) Rooms have high ceilings, polished floors and balconies. Prices rise in January and February.

Pensión Gualeguaychú (☎ 03446-424132; Av 25 de Mayo 456; campsites per person US$3) Practically derelict from the outside, but has serviceable singles.

Hotel Brutti (☎ 03446-426048; Bolívar 591; s/d with bath & TV US$5/8) Good value but often full.

Camping Costa Azul (☎ 03446-423984; campsites per person US$3) Good facilities overlooking the Río Gualeguaychú, 200m north of Puente Méndez Casariego.

Ducal (cnr San Lorenzo & Andrade) Overlooks the river – the fish and pasta are recommended.

París (Pellegrini 62) This spacious restaurant serves *parrillada*, fish etc. Check out the carpeted columns and the good wine list.

Getting There & Away

The sparkling **bus terminal** (☎ 03446-440688; cnr Blvd Jurado & General Artigas) is 1km southwest of downtown. Several companies go to Buenos Aires (US$8, 3½ hours), Paraná (US$6, five hours), and north toward Corrientes. At noon and 7pm Monday through Friday, Ciudad de Gualeguay goes to Fray Bentos, Uruguay (US$2.50, one hour), continuing to Mercedes.

PARQUE NACIONAL EL PALMAR

The yatay palm (*Syagrus yatay*) covered much of the littoral until 19th-century agriculture, ranching and forestry destroyed palm savannas and inhibited their reproduction. On the west bank of the Río Uruguay, 360km north of Buenos Aires, surviving yatays of 8500-hectare El Palmar have again begun to thrive, under protection from fire and grazing. Reaching 18m in height, the larger specimens punctuate a soothing subtropical landscape.

To see wildlife, walk along the watercourses or through the palm savannas early in the morning or just before sunset. The most conspicuous bird is the rhea (*Rhea americana*, ñandú in Spanish), but look for parakeets, cormorants, egrets, herons, storks, caracaras, woodpeckers and kingfishers too. The *carpincho* (capybara), a semiaquatic rodent weighing up to 60kg, and the vizcacha, a relative of the chinchilla, are among the most conspicuous mammals.

At night, squeaking vizcachas infest the campground at Arroyo Los Loros and gigantic toads invade the showers and toilets, but both are harmless. The *yarará* is a highly poisonous pit viper. Bites are unusual, but watch your step and wear high boots and long trousers when hiking.

Sights

The park's **Centro de Interpretación** (☎ 03447-493031), across from the campground, offers evening slide shows and contains a small **reptile house**. At the Arroyo Los Loros campground, rental canoes are available for exploring the placid river. A short hike from the campground, **Arroyo Los Loros** is a good place to observe **wildlife**.

Five kilometers from the campground, **Arroyo El Palmar** is a pleasant stream with a beautiful **swimming hole**, and a good site for **bird-watching**. Crossing the ruined bridge, you can walk several kilometers along a palm-lined road being reclaimed by savanna grasses.

Sleeping & Eating

Camping Arroyo Los Loros (☎ 03447-493031; campsites per person US$1.50) Good sites, hot showers, a shop and a *confitería*. There's an additional US$1.50 charge per tent for the first day only.

Getting There & Away

Any northbound bus from Buenos Aires to Concordia can drop you at the entrance to **Parque Nacional El Palmar** (admission US$4). No public transport serves the Centro de Interpretación and campground, but hitching is feasible.

PASO DE LOS LIBRES

Paso de los Libres, 700km north of Buenos Aires, lies directly across the Río Uruguay from Uruguaiana (Brazil), connected by a bridge about 10 blocks southwest of central Plaza Independencia. Apart from a lively **Carnaval**, there's little else to see or do here.

The bus terminal is a very depressing half-hour walk from the center – the US$0.60 bus fare is a good investment.

Libres Cambio (Av Colón 901) will change cash and **Cahuil** (Av Colón 585) is an Internet café.

Sleeping & Eating

Residencial 26 de Febrero (☎ 03772-425867; Uruguay 1297; s/d US$3/7) The cheapest joint in town; rooms with balconies are less drab.

Hotel Las Vegas (☎ 03772-423490; Sarmiento 554; s/d US$5/9; 🔀) may be worth the extra expense. It's clean and friendly, and the rooms have private bath and air-con.

La Giralda (Av Colón 887) A popular breakfast spot. They also serve pizza, *lomitos* (steak sandwiches), pastas, burgers and beer.

La Farola (cnr Madariaga & Mitre) Good for snacks.

Getting There & Away

From the **bus terminal** (☎ 03772-425600; cnr Av San Martín & Santiago del Estero), there are services to Corrientes (US$5, five hours) and Santo Tomé via Yapeyú (US$3, 1½ hours). There are also daily buses to Paraná (US$10, 5½ hours) and Santa Fe (US$10, seven hours).

Expreso Singer and Crucero del Norte buses pass near Paso de los Libres regularly en route between Buenos Aires and Posadas and can drop you off at the Esso station on RN 14, where a taxi can take you the 16km into town. Expect to pay around US$6.

YAPEYÚ

Yapeyú is a mellow little place 72km north of Paso de los Libres. You're more likely to smell bread baking than the car fumes you may have become accustomed to. Founded in 1626, it once had a population of 8000 Guaraní, who tended up to 80,000 cattle; after the Jesuits' expulsion, the indigenous people dispersed and the mission fell into ruins, but villagers built many houses of salvaged red sandstone blocks. National hero General José de San Martín was born here.

The **Museo de Cultura Jesuítica** (admission free), consisting of several modern kiosks on the foundations of mission buildings, has a sundial, a few other mission relics and interesting photographs.

Plaques cover the walls of the pretentious temple sheltering the **Casa de San Martín**, but San Martín's birthplace is little more than a crumbling ruin.

Hotel San Martín (☎ 03772-493120; Sargento Cabral 712; s/d US$5/7) has cheerful rooms that face an inner courtyard. Near the river **Camping Paraíso** (Maipo s/n; campsites per person US$2) has good hot showers. Insects can be abundant, and low-lying sites can flood in heavy rain.

Comedor El Paraíso (next to the Casa de San Martín) serves passable meals and has good river views.

Crucero del Norte stops three times daily at the small **bus terminal** (cnr Av del Libertador & Chacabuco), en route between Paso de los Libres and Posadas.

RESERVA PROVINCIAL ESTEROS DEL IBERÁ

Esteros del Iberá is a wildlife cornucopia comparable to Brazil's Pantanal do Mato Grosso. Aquatic plants and grasses, including 'floating islands,' dominate this wetlands wilderness that covers 13,000 sq km in north-central Corrientes. Trees are relatively few. The most notable wildlife species are reptiles like the caiman and anaconda; mammals like the maned wolf, howler monkey, neotropical otter, capybara, and pampas and swamp deer; and more than 350 bird species.

For independent travelers, the settlement of **Colonia Pellegrini**, 120km northeast of Mercedes on Laguna Iberá, within the park's boundaries, is the easiest place to organize trips into the marshes. One hour **launch tours** (US$3) are outstanding values.

Posada Ypa Sapukai (☎ 03773-420155; s/d with breakfast US$17/20, with full board US$27/36) is the best deal in Colonia Pellegrini. Run by the same owners, **Hysteria Ñandé Retá** (☎ 03773-420155) is a bit more rustic, but still comfortable and right next door. Prices are similar. They can also organize photo safaris and horse riding excursions into the park for an extra charge.

Camping is possible at Colonia Pellegrini and costs about US$1 per person.

Plenty of buses run from Corrientes and Paso de los Libres to Mercedes, where Itatí buses to Colonia Pellegrini (US$4, 2½ hours) leave at noon. The buses return to Mercedes at 5am Monday to Friday, and also at 11am Saturday.

CORRIENTES

Just below the confluence of the Paraná and Paraguay Rivers, Corrientes is one of

Argentina's oldest cities. The city's colorful streets and early-20th-century balconied buildings rising up from the muddy waters of the Río Paraná were the setting for Graham Greene's novel *The Honorary Consul*. The once-moribund **Carnaval Correntino** has experienced a revival and is now attracting crowds of up to 80,000.

Plaza 25 de Mayo is the center of Corrientes' extremely regular grid plan, but public buildings are more dispersed than in most Argentine cities. The commercial center is the Junín *peatonal*, between Salta and Catamarca, but the most attractive areas are Parque Mitre and the shady riverside along Av Costanera General San Martín. If you're wondering where everybody is

in the late afternoon, check the riverbank, a favorite spot for maté drinking and fishing. Sunset across the Río Paraná is particularly spectacular. Bus No 106 runs between San Lorenzo downtown and the bus terminal.

Information

The helpful **provincial tourist office** (☎ 03783-427200; 7am-1pm & 3-9pm Mon-Fri, 8am-noon & 4-8pm Sat & Sun) is at 25 de Mayo 1330 and the **municipal tourist office** (☎ 03783-428845; 7am-1pm & 3-8pm) is in Plaza Cabral.

Cambio El Dorado (9 de Julio 1341) changes cash and traveler's checks; there are several banks with ATMs around 9 de Julio. There's a **post office** (cnr San Juan & San Martín) and there are *locutorios* throughout town. **Cibercafé** (Mendoza 787)

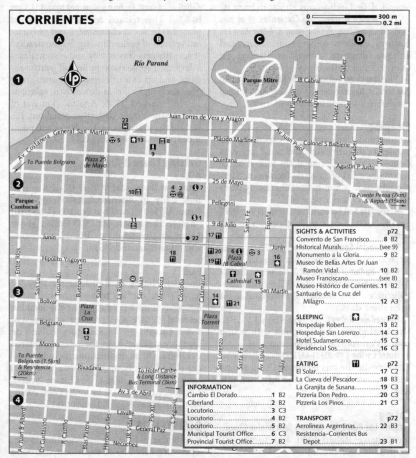

CORRIENTES

0 — 300 m
0 — 0.2 mi

SIGHTS & ACTIVITIES	p72
Convento de San Francisco	8 B2
Historical Murals	(see 9)
Monumento a la Gloria	9 B2
Museo de Bellas Artes Dr Juan Ramón Vidal	10 B2
Museo Franciscano	(see 8)
Museo Histórico de Corrientes	11 B2
Santuario de la Cruz del Milagro	12 A3

SLEEPING	p72
Hospedaje Robert	13 B2
Hospedaje San Lorenzo	14 C3
Hotel Sudamericano	15 C3
Residencial Sos	16 C3

EATING	p72
El Solar	17 C2
La Cueva del Pescador	18 B3
La Granjita de Susana	19 C3
Pizzería Don Pedro	20 C3
Pizzería Los Pinos	21 C3

TRANSPORT	p72
Aerolineas Argentinas	22 B3
Resistencia–Corrientes Bus Depot	23 B1

INFORMATION	
Cambio El Dorado	1 B2
Ciberland	2 B2
Locutorio	3 C3
Locutorio	4 B2
Locutorio	5 B2
Municipal Tourist Office	6 C3
Provincial Tourist Office	7 B2

ARGENTINA

and **Ciberland** (Pellegrini 1239) both charge just US$1 an hour for Internet access.

Sights

The colonial **Convento de San Francisco** has been converted into a **museum** (Mendoza 450; admission free; ☼ 8am-noon & 5-9pm Mon-Fri). The east side of San Juan, between Plácido Martínez and Quintana, is a shady, attractive area whose **Monumento a la Gloria** honors the Italian community; a series of striking historical **murals**, extending over 100m around the corner, chronicles local history since colonial times.

On Belgrano between Buenos Aires and Salta, visit the **Santuario de la Cruz del Milagro**, whose 16th-century cross, according to local legend, defied indigenous efforts to burn it.

The **Museo Histórico de Corrientes** (9 de Julio 1044; admission free; ☼ 8am-noon & 4-8pm Mon-Fri) features exhibits of weapons, coins and antique furniture, as well as displays on religious and civil history.

The **Museo de Bellas Artes Dr Juan Ramón Vidal** (San Juan 634; admission free; ☼ 9am-12:30pm & 5-8:30pm) emphasizes sculpture and modern art.

Sleeping

Accommodations tend to be expensive and single rooms are often the same price as doubles. During Carnaval, the tourist office maintains a list of *casas de familia* (accommodations in a family home) ranging from US$4 to US$12 per person.

Hospedaje San Lorenzo (San Lorenzo 1136; d US$7) Small, but the best budget option in the center.

Residencial Sos (Hipólito Yrigoyen 1771; r with bath per person US$5) Super basic but friendly.

Hotel Sudamericano (☎ 03783-469058; Hipólito Yrigoyen 1676; d with bath & air-con US$10; ❄) Probably nice once, though it's looking a bit tired these days.

Hospedaje Robert (La Rioja 415; s/d US$5/10) Shabby, but somehow popular with young couples on romantic trysts.

Hotel Caribe (☎ 03783-442197; Maipú 2590; US$8/12) Opposite the bus terminal. Good rooms with private bath and student discounts of 15%.

Eating

Pizzería Los Pinos (cnr Bolívar & San Lorenzo) Good, inexpensive Italian food and some very toothsome beer snacks.

El Solar (San Lorenzo 830) An extensive vegetarian selection, as well as meat dishes; food is priced by weight. The atmosphere's better than the food.

La Granjita de Susana (cnr San Lorenzo & Hipólito Yrigoyen) A good budget option, serving empanadas, burgers and steaks at sidewalk tables across from Plaza Cabral.

Pizzería Don Pedro (Junín 1410; ☼ 24 hr) Serving pizza, burgers, sandwiches etc.

La Cueva del Pescador (Hipólito Yrigoyen 1255) A very fine fish restaurant with good atmosphere. Prices are considerable but not outrageous.

Entertainment

Puente Pexoa (☎ 451687; RN 12 at La Retonda Virgen de Itatí roundabout; ☼ from 8:30pm, first band at 11:30pm Fri & Sat) This relaxed restaurant is a great place to check out *chamamé*, a sort of Guaraní version of polka dancing. Sound deadly? It actually gets very rowdy and is sometimes hilarious. People show up in full *gaucho* regalia, and up to four *conjuntos* (bands) may play each night. From downtown, take bus No 102 marked '17 de Agosto' 7km out of town to the Virgen de Itatí roundabout. It's just off the roundabout; the driver will point it out. A taxi back costs US$4 to US$6.

Getting There & Around

AIR

Aerolíneas Argentinas (☎ 03783-427442; Junín 1301) flies daily to Buenos Aires' Aeroparque (from US$80). Local bus No 105 (US$0.40) goes to the **airport** (☎ 03783-458358), about 15km east of town on RN 12. A *remise* should cost around US$3.

BUS

Frequent buses to Resistencia (US$0.50) leave from the **bus terminal** (cnr Av Costanera General San Martín & La Rioja). From the **local bus terminal** (☎ 03783-458322; Av Maipú), southeast of town, Ciudad de Posadas goes to Paso de los Libres via Mercedes for access to Esteros del Iberá. Other destinations include Posadas (US$7, four hours), Formosa (US$5, 3½ hours), Puerto Iguazú (US$12, nine hours), Buenos Aires (US$12, 11 hours) and Asunción, Paraguay (US$9, five hours).

RESISTENCIA

Resistencia is Fat City for sculpture lovers. There are over 300 of them dotted around the streets for anyone to see and ponder. A good range of styles are represented, too (not just the who's-that-guy-on-horseback school) – figurative, abstract, religious, even a few funky '70s numbers. While the woman in the tourist office may save her most lavish praise for nearby Corrientes, Resistencia is still worth a brief stopover. It's also capital of Chaco province and a major crossroads for Paraguay, Santa Fe and trans-Chaco routes to the northwest. Delightful Plaza 25 de Mayo, a riot of tall palms and comical *palo borracho* trees, marks the city center.

Resistencia's airport is 6km south of town on RN 11; Bus No 3 (marked 'aeropuerto/ centro') goes to Plaza 25 de Mayo. A taxi will cost around US$2.

Bus Nos 3 and 10 go from the bus terminal to Plaza 25 de Mayo.

The **tourist office** (☎ 03722-423547; Santa Fe 178; ☽ 7am-8pm Mon-Fri, 8am-noon Sat) is well stocked and there's a **tourist kiosk** (☎ 03722-458289; Plaza 25 de Mayo; ☽ 7am-8pm) about 500 yards away. Handy.

Cambio El Dorado (Jose María Paz 36) changes traveler's checks at reasonable rates. There are several ATMs near Plaza 25 de Mayo. The **post office** (Sarmiento & Yrigoyen) faces the plaza. There's a *locutorio* at JB Justo 136. **Edunet** (Alberdi 449) offers cheap Internet access at just US$1 an hour.

Sights

There's insufficient space to detail the number of **sculptures** in city parks and on the sidewalks, but the tourist office distributes a map with their locations that makes a good introduction to the city. The best starting point is the open-air **Parque de las Esculturas Aldo y Efraín Boglietti** (cnr Avs Laprida & Sarmiento), a 2500-square-meter area alongside the old French railroad station (1907). The station is now the **Museo de Ciencias Naturales** (admission free; ☽ 8:30am-12:30pm Mon-Fri, 5-8:30pm Sat). On Sunday evenings there's also a good **artisan market** in the park.

El Fogón de los Arrieros (Brown 350; admission US$1; ☽ 8am-noon & 4-8pm & 9-11pm Mon-Sat) is the driving force behind the city's progressive displays of public art and is famous for its eclectic assemblage of art objects from around the Chaco, Argentina and the world.

The **Museo del Hombre Chaqueño** (Museum of Chaco Man; Arturo Illia 655; admission free; ☽ 8:30am-

12:30pm Mon-Sat) focuses on the colonization of the Chaco.

The **Museo Policial** (Roca 223; free guided tours) is better than one might expect, partially redeeming its trite drug-war rhetoric with absorbing accounts of *cuatrerismo* (cattle-rustling – still widespread in the province) and social banditry.

Sleeping

El Hotelito (Alberdi 311; s/d US$5/8) Airy, white-washed rooms. Prices include breakfast and the owners speak some English.

Residencial Bariloche (☎ 03722-421412; Obligado 239; s/d US$7/10) Clean rooms with TV face a central patio.

Residencial San José (☎ 03722-426062; Frondizi 304; s/d with bath US$3/8) A bit grimy, but spacious.

Camping Parque 2 de Febrero (Av Avalos 1100; campsites US$2) Excellent facilities.

Eating & Drinking

Several attractive *confiterías* and ice-creameries have rejuvenated the area north and northwest of Plaza 25 de Mayo – you should try, for instance, the bohemian **Café de la Ciudad** (Pellegrini 109), formerly a sleazy bar, for slightly pricey sandwiches, burgers and beer.

La Bianca (Colón 102; dishes US$2-4) Has character and charm along with fish, pasta and steaks.

Barrilito (Lavalle 269) A beer-garden restaurant offering the inevitable *parrillada* etc.

Los Campeones (cnr Perón & Necochea) A popular pizza joint with sidewalk seating.

Bahia (cnr Colón & JB Justo) Cheap meal deals and icy cold beer.

Máyeli Maxi Kiosk (273 JB Justo) Has all of your fast-food faves and a young crowd at its sidewalk tables.

Kebon (cnr Güemes & Don Bosco) Probably Resistencia's best restaurant (budget-watchers will find its next-door *rotisería* a bargain for take-out food).

The Har Bar (Donovan & Perón; ☽ 24 hrs) A good place for a game of pool and a few beers. There's a young crowd.

Monarca (Perón 393; admission US$2). The kids come on Friday, the older crowd on Saturday. The street out front gets nearly as lively as the dance floor and the music requires plenty of drinks. One drink is included in the admission price.

Getting There & Away

AIR
Aerolíneas Argentinas (☎ 03722-445550; JB Justo 184) has twice-daily flights to Buenos Aires' Aeroparque (from US$80) except Sunday (one flight).

BUS
The **bus terminal** (☎ 03722-461098) is at Av MacLean and Islas Malvinas. An urban service (marked 'Chaco-Corrientes') provides a shuttle service between Resistencia and Corrientes for US$0.30 that you can catch in front of the post office on Plaza 25 de Mayo.

La Estrella goes to the village of Capitán Solari, near Parque Nacional Chaco, four times daily (US$2). Godoy goes to Laguna Naick-Neck and Laguna Blanca, near the Parque Nacional Río Pilcomayo (US$6).

Several companies go south to Santa Fe (US$12), Rosario (US$39) and Buenos Aires (US$17), north to Formosa and Asunción, Paraguay, and east to Posadas (US$7) and Puerto Iguazú (US$13, 10½ hours). There is daily service to Córdoba (US$17) and across the Chaco to Salta (US$21, 14 hours).

PARQUE NACIONAL CHACO
This little-visited park, 115km northwest of Resistencia, preserves 15,000 hectares of marshes, grasslands, palm savannas, scrub and dense forests in the humid eastern Chaco. Mammals are few, but birds include rheas, jabiru storks, roseate spoonbills, cormorants and caracaras. The most abundant species is the mosquito, so visit in the relatively dry, cool winter (June to August) and bring insect repellent.

Hiking and bird-watching are best in the early morning or around sunset. Some swampy areas are accessible only on horseback – inquire in Capitán Solari (5km east of park entrance) for horses and guides.

The **Administración** (☎ 03725-496166) is located at the park entrance. Rangers are extremely hospitable and will accompany visitors if their duties permit.

The shaded **camping** (free) area has clean toilets and showers, but a tent is essential. There is no food available so make sure you bring supplies from Resistencia, although you should be able to purchase basics in Capitán Solari.

La Estrella runs four buses daily from Resistencia to Capitán Solari (US$2, 2½ hours); from there you must walk or catch a lift to the park entrance (5km). You could also try enquiring at **Remis Satur** (☎ 421-004; Alberdi 770) about a share *remise* (US$3 per person).

FORMOSA
Things get pretty Paraguayan this far north – the cheap *liquados* (fruit juice made in a vitamizer), the street markets, the scooter races. Formosa is also a transport hub – most people are heading for Paraguay, but others are going to Jujuy, Salta and Bolivia. In November, the week-long **Fiesta del Río** features an impressive nocturnal religious procession in which 150 boats from Corrientes sail up the Río Paraguay.

Residencial Seti (☎ 03717-435901; Brandsen 37; s/d US$5/7) is one of Formosa's few budget accommodations.

Mercobus (☎ 03717-431469; Av Lelong 899) has regular buses to Clorinda, Laguna Naick-Neck and Laguna Blanca (Parque Nacional Río Pilcomayo), departing daily at 6:30am, 9:30am, 12:30pm and 4pm.

PARQUE NACIONAL RÍO PILCOMAYO
West of Clorinda, the wildlife-rich wetlands of 60,000-hectare Parque Nacional Río Pilcomayo hug the Paraguayan border. The park's outstanding feature is shimmering **Laguna Blanca** where, at sunset, *yacarés* (alligators) lurk on the lake surface. Other wildlife, except for birds, is more likely to be heard than seen among the dense aquatic vegetation.

Parque Nacional Río Pilcomayo's free camping facilities are basic but little used except on weekends; just outside the park entrance, a small shop sells basic food and cold drinks, including beer. There is a bus service (run by Mercobus) from Formosa and Clorinda along RN 86 to Laguna Naick-Neck and the park entrance at Laguna Blanca ranger station (US$5, 2½ hours).

POSADAS
On the south bank of the upper Paraná, Posadas (population 250,000) became the capital of the new territory of Misiones in the 1880s. Travelers stopping here en route to Iguazú should not miss the Jesuit ruins

at San Ignacio Miní, about 50km east, or at Trinidad (Paraguay), across the river. Posadas itself appeals to many – it's an attractive and friendly city of leafy parks, plazas and a lively riverfront.

Plaza 9 de Julio is the center of Posadas' standard grid. Streets were renumbered several years ago, but local preference for the old system occasionally creates confusion.

Bus Nos 8, 15, 21 and 24 go downtown from the bus terminal.

Information

The provincial **tourist office** (☎ 03752-5550297; turismo@misiones.gov.ar; Colón 1985; ⏰ 7am-8pm Mon-Fri, 8am-noon, 4-8pm Sat & Sun) is well informed and has a wealth of printed material.

You can change traveler's checks at **Cambios Mazza** (Bolívar btwn San Lorenzo & Colón). There are several downtown ATMs. The post office is at Bolívar and Ayacucho. There's a **locutorio** (cnr Bolívar & Colón); **WEBe.ar** (Junín 2168) and **3CL Cyber Café** (Av Azara 2067) both charge US$1 per hour for Internet access.

Sights

The **Museo Provincial Andres Guacurarí** (General Paz 1865; admission free; ⏰ 8am-noon) is basic but has interesting photographs of the Jesuit mission at San Ignacio Miní before restoration, as well as some archaeological objects.

The **Museo de Arte Juan Yapari** (Sarmiento 319; admission free; ⏰ 8am-noon) has a small range of odd exhibits.

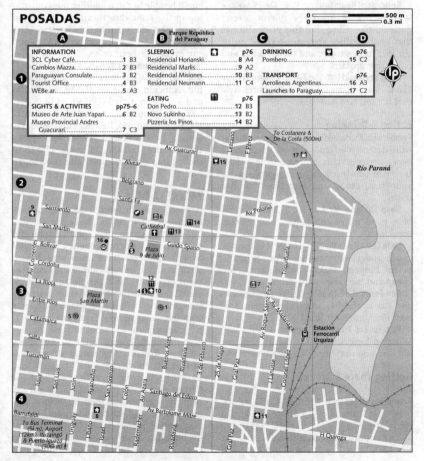

POSADAS

0	500 m
0	0.3 mi

INFORMATION
3CL Cyber Café...........................1 B3
Cambios Mazza...........................2 B3
Paraguayan Consulate.................3 B2
Tourist Office.............................4 B3
WEBe.ar.....................................5 A3

SIGHTS & ACTIVITIES pp75–6
Museo de Arte Juan Yapari.........6 B2
Museo Provincial Andres
  Guacurarí..................................7 C3

SLEEPING 🛏 p76
Residencial Horianski....................8 A4
Residencial Marlis.........................9 A2
Residencial Misiones....................10 B3
Residencial Neumann...................11 C4

EATING 🍴 p76
Don Pedro.................................12 B3
Novo Sukinho............................13 B2
Pizzería los Pinos.......................14 B2

DRINKING 🍷 p76
Pombero....................................15 C2

TRANSPORT p76
Aerolíneas Argentinas.................16 A3
Launches to Paraguay.................17 C2

ARGENTINA

In the cool of the afternoon the **costanera** (riverside promenade) comes alive. It's a favorite spot for joggers, cyclists, dog walkers, maté sippers, hotdog vendors and young couples staring wistfully at the lights of Paraguay across the water.

Sleeping

Residencial Misiones (☎ 03752-430133; Av Azara btwn La Rioja & Córdoba; s/d US$6/9) This place is friendly and very central with a well-equipped kitchen.

Residencial Marlis (☎ 03752-4257664; Av Corrientes 1670; s/d US$6/9) Spacious, clean and surprisingly quiet rooms for the busy location. The Brady Bunch decor may not be for everyone.

Residencial Neumann (☎ 03752-424675; Av Roque Sáenz Peña 665; s/d US$5/7) The mirrors aren't quite on the ceiling, but this place still has that kind of vibe. They don't come much cheaper in this town, and there's a bar and pool table upstairs.

Hotel Horianski (☎ 03752-422673; Líbano 2655; s/d US$5/8) Poky rooms set around a motel-style parking lot. Not *bad* value.

Eating & Drinking

Pombero (cnr Rivadavia & Guacurari) A bar/restaurant with decent food and a good selection of beers and cocktails at reasonable prices. It's open late (even on weeknights), gets a young(ish) crowd and sometimes has live music.

Novo Sukinho (Av Azara 1629) Sidewalk tables, good juices and better than average breakfasts.

De la Costa (Costanera 1536) The best of the riverside budget eateries. No surprises here – pizzas, burgers, steaks – but the drinks are cheap and the views unbeatable.

Don Pedro (Córdoba 1827) Offers good pizzas and pastas and has an excellent value *tenedor libre* lunch for just US$2.

Pizzería Los Pinos (cnr Sarmiento & Buenos Aires) Worth a look, if only for the magnificent old building that began life as a pharmacy.

Getting There & Around
AIR
Aerolíneas Argentinas (☎ 03752-422036; cnr Ayacucho & San Martín) flies 13 times weekly to Aeroparque in Buenos Aires (US$85).

The airport, 12km southwest of town via RN 12, is served by the No 8 bus from San Lorenzo between La Rioja and Entre Ríos. A *remise* costs about US$4.

BOAT
Launches across the Paraná to Encarnación (US$1) continue to operate despite the bridge. They leave from the dock at the east end of Av Guacurarí but bear in mind that there are no immigration procedures on this route.

BUS
Buses to Encarnación, Paraguay (US$1) leave every 20 minutes from Mitre and Junín, passing through downtown before crossing the bridge (get off for immigration procedures and hang on to your ticket – you'll be able to catch another bus continuing in the same direction). Horianski and Aguila Dorada buses to San Ignacio Miní (US$1.50, one hour) start at 5:15am and run every half-hour or so.

The **bus terminal** (☎ 03752-4526106; cnr Ruta 12 & Av Santa Catalina) has international departures for Asunción, Paraguay (US$8, six hours) and São Paulo, Brazil (US$50, 24 hours).

Typical domestic fares include Corrientes (US$7, four hours), Resistencia (US$8, five hours), Puerto Iguazú (US$8, 5½ hours), Buenos Aires (US$13, 13 hours; US$18 in *coche cama* sleepers) and Salta (US$26, 15 hours).

YACYRETÁ DAM
A vivid lesson in foreign debt, this gigantic hydroelectric project has been plagued by delays, corruption and disgraceful cost overruns since the outset. The dam, which submerges the Paraná over 200km upstream, has already caused the displacement of some 12,000 people and it's estimated that a further 50,000 people, mostly Paraguayans, will be displaced. Despite vigorous campaigning from environmental groups, plans are afoot to raise the reservoir from its current level of 76m above sea level to 83m. This would submerge a further 80,000 hectares in Paraguay and 29,000 hectares in Argentina. Parts of the Paraguayan city of Encarnación are already being flooded out and there has been a serious loss of wild lands and endemic species, not to mention people's homes and livelihoods. As a presidential candidate, Carlos Menem called it 'a monument to

corruption,' but his and successive governments continued its construction.

At Ituzaingó, 1½ hours from Posadas by bus, the Argentine–Paraguayan Entidad Binacional Yacyretá is still trying to put this boondoggle in the best possible light, the task falling to their public relations **office** (☎ 03786-420050), which runs free guided tours (leaving at 10am, 11am, 3pm, 4pm and 5pm).

Camping Mattes (☎ 03786-421272; 4-6 person cabanas US$12-18) is 2km south of Ituzaingó. They don't offer camping anymore, but the cabanas aren't bad value for groups.

Hotel Géminis (☎ 03786-420324; Corrientes 9430; s/d US$7/15) is the place to stay if you really want to stay in town.

Empresa Ciudad de Posadas and Singer link Ituzaingó with Posadas (US$3).

SAN IGNACIO MINÍ

At its peak, in 1733, the **mission of San Ignacio Miní** (admission US$1; ☺ 7am-7pm) had an indigenous population of nearly 4500. Italian Jesuit Juan Brasanelli designed the enormous redsandstone church, embellished with bas-relief sculptures in 'Guaraní baroque' style. Adjacent to the tile-roofed church were the cemetery and cloisters; the same complex held classrooms, a kitchen, a prison and workshops. On all sides of the Plaza de Armas were the living quarters. There is a sound and light show at 7pm nightly.

San Ignacio Miní is 56km east of Posadas via RN 12 at the village of San Ignacio. It is an easy day trip from Posadas, but staying overnight allows more time to explore the mission ruins.

Sleeping & Eating

Hospedaje Aleman Los Salpeterer (☎ 03752-470362; campsites/r per person US$1/3) Near the bus terminal, and offers kitchen facilities.

Hospedaje Italia (San Martín 1291; r per person US$4) Inside a local artist's house, it only has two beds, but there's plenty of character to compensate.

Hospedaje El Descanso (☎ 03752-470207; Pellegrini 270; r/cabanas per person US$3/4) Further from the ruins, but has spotless rooms and friendly German-speaking management. Breakfast is US$2 extra. Plus it's kind of fun to sleep in a Bavarian-style cabana.

Coco (Medina 501; dinners from US$2) Opposite the exit to the ruins. First-rate, home-style dinners.

Don Valentín (Alberdi 444; set meals US$2-5) Mains can be a bit pricey, but the set meals are good value.

La Carpa Azul (Rivadavia 1295) Pretty much an assembly-line *comedor* (basic cafeteria), but the swimming pool can provide relief from the heat.

Getting There & Away

The bus terminal is at the west end of Av Sarmiento, the main road into town. Services are frequent between Posadas (US$3, one hour) and Puerto Iguazú (US$7, 4½ hours) with several companies, but buses along RN 12 also stop readily en route in either direction.

PUERTO IGUAZÚ

Puerto Iguazú hosts most visitors to the Argentine side of Iguazú Falls but the town has thankfully managed to avoid tacky trappings and retains a pleasant resort feel (for details of the Brazilian side, see p306). The falls are definitely a superstar among tourist attractions – you'll meet plenty of people who have come straight from Buenos Aires, and are heading straight back afterwards. There's a steady backpacker population and a correspondingly jumpin' hostel and restaurant scene. Puerto Iguazú's very irregular street plan is compact enough for relatively easy orientation. The main drag is the diagonal Av Victoria Aguirre.

Information

The main **tourist office** (☎ 03757-420800; Av Victoria Aguirre 311; ☺ 8am-noon Mon-Fri, 4-8pm daily) is in town. There's also a tourist kiosk at the bus terminal which keeps irregular hours.

Banco de Misiones has an ATM at Av Victoria Aguirre 330. Before buying Brazilian currency, ask other travelers about trends in Foz do Iguaçu.

The post office is at Av San Martín 780.

Telecentro Internet (cnr Av Victoria Aguirre Eppens) is a *locutorio* that also has Internet access.

No visa is required for entry into Paraguay, but US citizens entering Brazil will need one. They must submit one passport photo, have six months validity on their passport, pay US$100 (a reciprocal fee equal to that which Brazilians pay when entering the States) and have a return/onward ticket.

Sleeping

Corre Camino (☎ 03757-420967; P Amarante 48; dm with/without HI card US$3/3.50) A well-appointed hostel with a lively atmosphere – a great place to go to meet up with other travelers.

Residencial Uno (☎ 03757-420529; Fray Luis Beltrán 116; dm US$3, d US$10) The local HI affiliate. Rooms are spotless and there are some good common areas.

Residencial Noelia (☎ 03757-420729; Fray Luis Beltrán 119; d US$7) Good-value rooms with fan, private bath and breakfast.

Hostería San Fernando (☎ 0357-4212429; cnr Avs Córdoba & Guaraní; s/d US$18/25) Leafy and quiet. The reasonable rooms have attached bath. Prices include breakfast.

Hospedaje Lola (☎ 0357-423954; Av Córdoba 255; r per person US$3) Basic rooms with private bath. Kitchen facilities are available.

Camping El Pindo (☎ 03757-421795; per tent US$2.50 plus per person US$2.20) At km 3.5 of RN 12 on the edge of town.

Eating

Jardín del Iguazú (Av Misiones) Tables arranged in a leafy outdoor setting. Offers *parrillada* and

---

SPLURGE!

Sheraton Iguazú (lunch buffet US$10) Now this is a room with a view. On your left there's Brazil. On the right, Argentina. Smack in the middle, the star of the show – the Garganta del Diablo (p79). If you can take your eyes off it, you'll notice another breathtaking sight – the Sheraton's lunch buffet spread. Local and international cuisine, a plethora of tropical fruits and more desserts than you could possibly sample (although it *is* fun trying). You don't even have to dress up – all the guests are in their finest 'backpacker' gear: hiking boots, photojournalist vests, collapsible hats – you'll blend right in.

---

an impressive salad bar. Live music (no guarantees on quality) is sometimes on offer.

Charo (Av Córdoba 118) The usual range of *parrillada* offerings, with outdoor seating and some good value set meals.

JB (Eppens 294) A huge menu of cheap, filling food. Don't come for the atmosphere.

PUERTO IGUAZÚ

BRAZIL

Porto Meira

Río Paraná

Puerto Iguazú

Río Iguazú

Av Costanera

ARGENTINA

Av Tres Fronteras

Av Córdoba

Félix de Azara

Paraguay

Uruguay

San Lorenzo

Av San Martín

El Urú

Moisés Bertoni

Av Misiones

Bompland

El Mensú

Plaza

Av Brasil

Av Moreno

Eppens

Bompland

Alvar Núñez

Av Guaraní

P Amarante

Av Victoria Aguirre

Belgrano

Av Córdoba

Fray Luis Beltrán

Equil

Quiroga

Ushuaia

Apepú

Los Cedros

Aguay

Curupy

El Pombero

Los Yerbales

Chenes

Tareferos

To Camping El Pindo (1km),
Parque Nacional Iguazú (15km)
& Airport (18km)

0 ────── 500 m
0 ────── 0.4 mi

The outdoor **food court** (cnr Av Victoria Aguirre & Shuardz) has fast food, *parrillada*, pizza, beer and ice cream in a (family-oriented) rockin' nighttime environment.

Getting There & Around

AIR

Aerolíneas Argentinas (☎ 03757-420168; Av Victoria Aguirre 295) flies four times daily to Buenos Aires (US$100).

Caracol (☎ 03757-420064; Aguirre 563) charges US$2 to the airport and makes hotel pick-ups; phone for reservations. *Remises* run about US$9.

BUS

The **bus terminal** (☎ 03757-423006; cnr Avs Córdoba & Misiones) has departures for Posadas (US$8, 5½ hours), Buenos Aires (US$23, 20 hours) and intermediate points. Frequent buses leave to Parque Nacional Iguazú (US$1), and there are also international buses to Foz do Iguaçu (US$1) and Ciudad del Este, Paraguay (US$1).

TAXI

For groups of three or more hoping to see both sides of the falls as well as Ciudad del Este and the Itaipú hydroelectric project, a shared cab or *remise* can be a good idea; figure about US$45 for a full day's sightseeing. Contact the **Asociación de Trabajadores de Taxis** (☎ 03757-420282), or simply approach a driver.

PARQUE NACIONAL IGUAZÚ

Even the most hardened of waterfall yawners will be taken aback by the Iguazú Falls. This is more than your average gee-isn't-gravity-neat type of experience. The power, size and sheer noise of the falls are truly spectacular. You could try coming early, but you're unlikely ever to have the place to yourself. The **park** (admission US$10) quickly fills with Argentines, backpackers, families and, on the day of research, several men wearing only red speedos and the Brazilian flag.

Guaraní legend says that Iguazú Falls originated when a jealous forest god, enraged by a warrior escaping downriver by canoe with a young girl, caused the riverbed to collapse in front of the lovers, producing a precipitous falls over which the girl fell and, at their base, turned into a rock. The

warrior survived as a tree overlooking his fallen lover.

The falls' geological origins are more prosaic. In southern Brazil, the Río Iguazú passes over a basalt plateau that ends just above its confluence with the Paraná. Before reaching the edge, the river divides into many channels to form several distinctive *cataratas* (cataracts).

The most awesome is the semicircular **Garganta del Diablo** (Devil's Throat), a deafening and dampening part of the experience, approached by launch and via a system of *pasarelas* (catwalks). There's no doubt that it's spectacular – there's only one question: where's the bungy jump?

Despite development pressures, the 55,000-hectare park is a natural wonderland of subtropical rain forest, with over 2000 identified plant species, countless insects, 400 bird species and many mammals and reptiles.

Information

Buses from Puerto Iguazú will drop passengers off at the **Centro de Informes** (☎ 03757-420180), near the Hotel Internacional, where there's a small natural history museum. There's also a photo-developing lab, gift shop, bar and many other services, including restaurants and snack bars.

Dangers & Annoyances

The Río Iguazú's currents are strong and swift; more than one tourist has been swept downriver and drowned near Isla San Martín.

The wildlife is potentially dangerous – in 1997, a jaguar killed a park ranger's infant son. Visitors should respect the big cats and, if you should encounter one, do not panic. Speak calmly but loudly, do not run or turn your back, and try to appear bigger than you are, by waving your arms or clothing, for example.

Human predators may abscond with your personal belongings, so watch your things while hiking. This is not exactly epidemic, but it's not unheard of either.

Iguazú Falls

Before seeing the falls themselves, grab a map, look around the museum, and (if it has reopened) climb the nearby tower for a good overall view. Plan hikes before the

ARGENTINA

mid-morning tour-bus invasion. Descending from the visitor center, you can cross by free launch to **Isla Grande San Martín**, which offers unique views and a refuge from the masses on the mainland.

Several *pasarelas* (catwalks) give good views of smaller falls, and, in the distance, the **Garganta del Diablo**. A train from the visitor center operates regularly to shuttle visitors from site to site. At the last stop, follow the trail to the lookout perched right on the edge of the mighty falls. Of all sights on earth, this must come closest to the experience of sailing off the edge of the earth imagined by early European sailors, as the deafening cascade plunges to a murky destination, blurred by the rising vapor soaking the viewer.

Activities

Best in the early morning, the Sendero Macuco nature trail leads through dense forest, where a steep sidetrack goes to the base of a hidden waterfall. Another trail goes to the *bañado*, a marsh abounding in bird life. Allow about 2½ hours round trip (6km) for the entire Sendero Macuco trail.

To get elsewhere in the forest, hitch or hire a car to take you out along RN 101 toward the village of Bernardo de Irigoyen. Few visitors explore this part of the park, and it is still nearly pristine forest. **Iguazú Jungle Explorer** (☎ 03757-421696), at the visitor center, can arrange 4WD excursions on the Yacaratía trail to Puerto Macuco as well as thrilling speedboat trips below the falls (US$23).

Moonlight walks (☎ 03757-491-469; guided walks US$5) to the falls are offered at 8:30pm and 10:45pm on full moon nights. Call to reserve a place and arrange for free transport to the park.

Getting There & Away

For information on getting here by bus, see p9. Park admission includes the launch to Isla Grande San Martín. For Brazilian visa information, see p77.

NORTHWEST ARGENTINA

The northwest comprises the provinces of Jujuy, Salta, Tucumán, La Rioja, Catamarca, Santiago del Estero and Córdoba. Its pre-Columbian and colonial past makes the trip to the Argentine heartland a journey through time as well as space.

HISTORY

The Central Andean population spread never got much further than what is now northwest Argentina. Before the Spanish arrived, the place was crawling with indigenous tribes – the Lule south and west of modern Salta, the Tonocote of Santiago del Estero, and the Diaguita, doing the roaming nomad thing. Even today, the northern provinces resemble the Andean countries, and Quechuan communities reach as far south as Santiago del Estero.

Diego de Almagro's expedition came through Jujuy and Salta on the way from Cuzco to Chile in 1535, but it wasn't until 1553 that the first city of the region – Santiago del Estero – was established. Spirited local resistance meant slow going for the conquistadors in these parts, but eventually San Miguel de Tucumán (1565), Córdoba (1573), Salta (1582), La Rioja (1591) and San Salvador de Jujuy (1593) were founded. It took Catamarca another hundred years to find its feet. Unimpressive in their infancy, these settlements still established the basic elements of colonial rule: the *cabildo* (town council), the church, and the rectangular plaza with its clustered public buildings.

As the double horns of disease and exploitation decimated indigenous populations and the *encomiendas* (grant of land and native inhabitants given to settlers) lost their economic value, the region's focus shifted. Tucumán provided mules, cotton and textiles for the mines of Potosí, and Córdoba became a center for education and arts. The opening of the Atlantic to legal shipping in late colonial times diminished Jujuy's and Salta's importance as trade posts, but Tucumán grew in stature as the local sugar industry boomed.

CÓRDOBA

The streets of Argentina's historic university city swarm with undergraduates, giving Córdoba a young and lively buzz. Famed for its medical faculty, the city is often referred to simply as 'La Docta' (The Scholar). Córdoba is also one of Argentina's more Catholic cities; there are 21 churches in the downtown area alone, and Holy

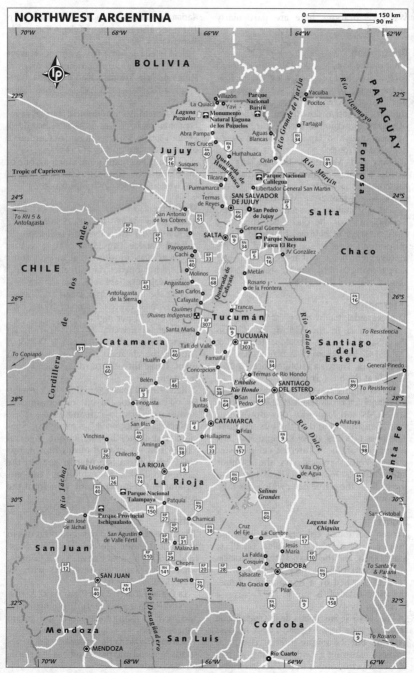

NORTHWEST ARGENTINA

0 —————————— 150 km
0 —————————— 90 mi

BOLIVIA

Villazón
La Quiaca Yavi
Yacuiba
Pocitos
Parque Nacional Baritú
Laguna Pozuelos
Monumento Natural Laguna de los Pozuelos
Tartagal
Río Grande de Tarija
PARAGUAY
Abra Pampa
Aguas Blancas
Río Pilcomayo
Tres Cruces
Jujuy
RN 9
RN 40
RN 34
Humahuaca
Orán
Río Martín
RN 81
Formosa
RP 16
Susques
Tropic of Capricorn
Quebrada de Humahuaca
Tilcara
Purmamarca
Parque Nacional Calilegua
Libertador General San Martín
Termas de Reyes
SAN SALVADOR DE JUJUY
RP 5
Salta
San Antonio de los Cobres
RP 51
RN 66
San Pedro de Jujuy
To RN 5 & Antofagasta
La Poma
RP 27
General Güemes
SALTA
RN 9
RN 34
Parque Nacional Finca El Rey
Chaco
los Andes
Payogasta
Cachi
RP 17
RP 33
RP 5
RN 16
JV González
de
Molinos
RP 40
RN 68
Metán
Angastaco
RP 43
San Carlos
Rosario de la Frontera
Cordillera
Antofagasta de la Sierra
Cafayate
Quebrada de Cafayate
RN 16
Quilmes (Ruines Indígenas)
Tucumán
Trancas
To Resistencia
Santa María
RP 307
TUCUMÁN
Río Salado
Catamarca
Tafí del Valle
RN 40
RN 9
RP 303
Santiago del Estero
To Copiapó
31
Hualfín
Famaillá
General Pinedo
RN 60
Concepción
Termas de Río Hondo
Belén
RP 46
Embalse Río Hondo
SANTIAGO DEL ESTERO
RN 89
To Resistencia
RP 3
RN 38
RN 64
San Pedro
RN 64
Suncho Corral
Tinogasta
Las Juntas
CATAMARCA
RP 4
Frías
Añatuya
San Blas
Vinchina
RN 40
RN 38
Huillapima
RP 33
RN 157
RN 9
Río Dulce
RN 98
Santa Fe
Aminga
RP 26
Chilecito
LA RIOJA
RP 5
RN 60
Villa Ojo de Agua
RN 34
Villa Unión
RP 26
RP 74
La Rioja
Salinas Grandes
San Cristóbal
RN 40
Parque Nacional Talampaya
Patquía
RN 60
Laguna Mar Chiquita
Parque Provincial Ischigualasto
RP 150
RP 27
Chamical
Cruz del Eje
La Cumbre
RP 17
RP 10
San José de Jáchal
San Agustín de Valle Fértil
RN 79
RN 38
Jesús María
Río Jáchal
RP 29
RP 28
RP 31
Malanzán
La Falda
Cosquín
RP 510
RP 29
Chepes
RP 20
RP 28
CÓRDOBA
To Santa Fe & Paraná
San Juan
RP 12
RP 141
Ulapes
RN 79
Salsacate
RN 19
SAN JUAN
RN 40
RN 141
Alta Gracia
Pilar
Río Desaguadero
RN 158
To Santa Fe & Paraná
Mendoza
San Luis
RN 36
RN 9
Córdoba
RN 9
To Rosario
◎ MENDOZA
Río Cuarto

CHILE

Week celebrations here are particularly animated.

Orientation

Sited on the south bank of the Río Primero (or Suquía), 400m above sea level at the foot of the Sierra Chica, the city has sprawled north of the river and into the countryside. Its attractive downtown, a labyrinth of plazas and colonial architecture shaded by jacaranda and lapacho trees, is easily explored on foot.

Plaza San Martín is the nucleus for Córdoba's one million inhabitants, but the commercial center is northwest of the plaza, where the 25 de Mayo and Indarte pedestrian malls intersect. Calle Obispo Trejos, south of the plaza, has the finest concentration of colonial buildings. Local buses don't serve the bus terminal, but it's an easy eight-block walk to the center – just keep moving towards the big steeple. A taxi should cost less than US$1.

Information

The **provincial tourist office** (☎ 0351-428-5856; 🕑 8am-8pm) is in the historic *cabildo* on Plaza San Martín. The **municipal tourist office** (☎ 0351-428-5600; Rosario de Santa Fe 39) has the same hours. There's a satellite **office** (☎ 0351-433-1980) at the bus terminal.

For changing traveler's checks, try **Cambio Barujel** (cnr Buenos Aires & 25 de Mayo). There are ATMs and *locutorios* downtown near Plaza San Martín and at the bus terminal. The post office is at Av General Paz 201. A number of cheap Internet cafés cluster on Av Vélez Sársfield; try the 24-hour **Internet Club** (Av Vélez Sársfield 214; US$1 per hr), at the back of the Lihue café, which has ISIC discounts.

Sights

To see Córdoba's colonial buildings and monuments, start at the **cabildo**, on Plaza San Martín, and the **Casa del Obispo Mercadillo** (Rosario de Santa Fe 39). At the plaza's southwest corner, crowned by a Romanesque dome, the **Iglesia Catedral** (begun in 1577) mixes a variety of styles.

The 1645 Jesuit **Iglesia de la Compañía de Jesús** (cnr Obispo Trejos & Caseros) has a modest exterior, but its unique interior is a masterpiece featuring a timber ceiling shaped like an inverted ship's hull. The **Universidad**

Nacional de Córdoba (Obispo Trejos 242), dates from 1613; see also the nearby **Colegio Nacional de Monserrat** (1782).

The **Iglesia de Santa Teresa** and its **convent** also have a museum of religious art, the **Museo de Arte Religioso Juan de Tejeda** (Independencia 122; admission US$0.50; 🕑 9:30am-12:30pm Wed-Sat).

The **Museo Histórico Provincial Marqués de Sobremonte** (Rosario de Santa Fe 218; admission US$0.50; 🕑 10am-4pm Tue-Sat) is set in one of Córdoba's oldest surviving houses (1752).

Córdoba has many good cinemas; one of the oldest is the **Cine Teatro Córdoba** (27 de Abril 275) which features art-house films.

Sleeping

Hotel Garden (☎ 0351-421-4729; 25 de Mayo 35; s/d with bath US$8/13) Attractive and well kept.

Hotel Claridge (☎ 0351-421-5741; 25 de Mayo 218; s/d US$3/7) Run-down balconied rooms overlooking a pedestrian street.

Hospedaje Susy (Entre Ríos 528; s/d with bath US$5/8) Near the bus terminal; clean and attractive. There is secure off-street parking next door for US$1 per night.

Residencial Helvetia (☎ 0351-421-7297; San Jerónimo 479; s/d US$4/5, with bath & TV US$6/7) Among the cheapest accommodations in town. Large threadbare rooms face a central patio.

Hotel Termini Roma (☎ 0351-421-8721; Entre Ríos 687; s/d US$7/9) Modern but rather soulless. Rooms have private bath and TV.

Municipal campground (per person US$1) Spacious but basic, in the Parque General San Martín, 13km west of downtown. Bus No 1 from Plaza San Martín goes to the Complejo Ferial, an exhibition and entertainment complex about 1km from the park.

Eating

There are many cheap bars and pizzerias in the student haunts around Plaza Vélez Sársfield and in the area known as La Cañada, where Blvd San Juan intersects with Av Marcelo T de Alvear.

La Candela (Corrientes near Obispo Trejos) A rustic student hangout featuring empanadas and *locro* (a filling meat, corn and potato concoction).

Macondo (Av Alcorta 376; 🕑 evenings only) Serves salads, seafood and pasta and has live music on weekends.

ARGENTINA

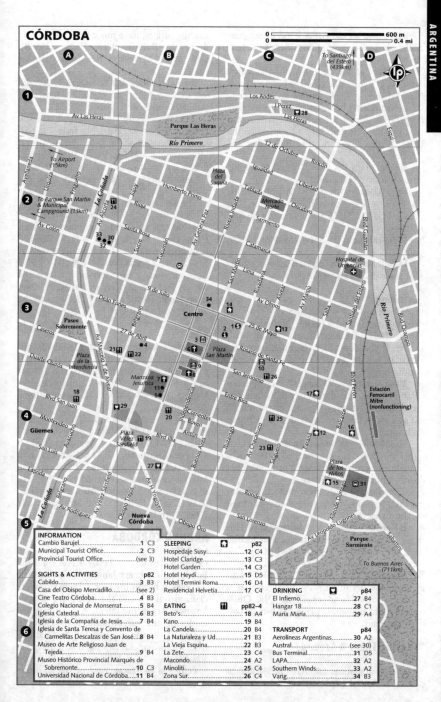

CÓRDOBA

0 — 600 m
0 — 0.4 mi

Beto's (Blvd San Juan 450) A good cheap *parrilla* whose *lomitos* are considered the best in town.

Zona Sur (San Jerónimo 263) A popular lunch choice, offering a large salad bar as well as meat dishes in a self-service-style canteen.

La Naturaleza y Ud (Belgrano 180) A busy, tiny vegetarian lunch joint. Vegetarians hanging out for a protein hit will appreciate the tofu, brown rice and other Asian-inspired dishes.

Minoliti (Entre Ríos 358) A good, bargain-priced Italian restaurant.

Kano (Av Hipólito Yrigoyen near Obispo Trejos) This is a more expensive Italian choice, but has a US$4 to US$5 fixed-price lunch and dinner.

La Zete (Corrientes 455) Serves Middle Eastern food.

La Vieja Esquina (cnr Belgrano & Caseros) Popular for their divine empanadas.

Drinking

Córdoba's drink of choice is Fernet (a strong, medicinal tasting, herbed liquor from Italy), almost always mixed with Coke. If you don't mind a rough morning, start in on the Fernet con Coke – it gets addictive.

María María (Blvd San Juan 230) Across from Patio Olmos, this dark, cozy bar often gets excellent bands playing a variety of music. It's a comfortable place good for dancing or sitting around.

El Infierno (cnr Independencia & Montevideo; 🕙 11pm-late Wed-Sat) A variety of music and a boisterous crowd make for a fun, noisy bar with dim parlor ambience.

The closest nightclub zone to the center is the Mercado Abasto (the *zona roja* or red light district).

El Mariscal (Bajada Alvear 69, Mercado Abasto) This is a smaller club where house and techno are the standards. As usual, when the DJs are good, it's good.

Hangar 18 (Blvd Las Heras 118, Mercado Abasto) Córdoba's definitive gay disco attracts a diverse crowd and excellent DJs. On a good night the whole place can lose its collective head.

Getting There & Around
AIR
Aerolíneas Argentinas (🕾 0351-410-7690; Av Colón 520) and **Austral** (🕾 0351-410-7690; Av Colón 520),

sharing offices, have more than 100 weekly flights to Buenos Aires (from US$80). **LAPA** (🕾 0351-425-8000; Av Colón 534) has similar prices.

Southern Winds (🕾 0351-426-6626; Av Colón 544) flies to Mendoza (US$32), Bariloche (US$70) and Buenos Aires (US$55).

Córdoba's only international service is three times weekly with **Varig** (🕾 0351-425-6262; 9 de Julio 40, 7th fl) to Porto Alegre, Florianópolis and São Paulo, Brazil, but all flights go via Buenos Aires, so you're better off going there first and getting a cheaper flight.

The **airport** (🕾 0351-465-0392) is 15km north of town via Av Monseñor Pablo Cabrera. Bus No A5 (marked Aeropuerto) leaves from Plaza San Martín. Buy a US$0.30 *cospel* (token) from a kiosk before traveling. For US$1, **Agencia Ecuador** (🕾 0351-475-9199) runs an hourly bus service between the airport and the city center; transport leaves from Hotel Heydi at Illia 615. Taxis to the airport cost about US$4.

BUS
Córdoba's **bus terminal** (🕾 0351-433-1988; Blvd Perón 380) is for all practical purposes a shopping mall, with supermarkets and restaurants. More than 50 bus companies serve local, provincial, national and international destinations.

Sample destinations and fares include to Tucumán (US$10, eight hours), Buenos Aires (US$12, 10 hours), Mendoza (US$12, 10 hours), Posadas (US$23, 18 hours) and Salta (US$17, 13 hours). There are also international bus services to Florianópolis, Brazil (US$45, 32 hours); Montevideo, Uruguay (US$27, 15 hours) and Santiago, Chile (US$23, 16 hours).

AROUND CÓRDOBA
Cosquín
Cosquín's nine day Festival Nacional del Folklore, held every January for more than 30 years, is becoming increasingly commercialized but it's still the best place to spot hot new Argentine talent. A good base for exploring the surrounding area, Cosquín is one of the more appealing destinations near the provincial capital, 63km away via RN 38.

Cerro Pan de Azúcar, east of town, offers good views of the sierras and the city of

Córdoba. Hitch or walk (buses are few) 7km to a saddle, where an *aerosilla* (chairlift; US$3) climbs to the top, or take a steep 25-minute walk to the 1260m summit. Also at the saddle is a *confitería* whose owner, a devotee of Carlos Gardel, has decorated the grounds with Gardel memorabilia, including a mammoth statue.

Hospedaje Siempreverde (☎ 03541-450093; Santa Fe 525; s/d US$7/11) is housed in an attractive building with a leafy garden. **Hospedaje Remanso** (☎ 03541-452681; General Paz 38; s/d with breakfast US$7/11) is quiet and well run.

Pizzería Raffaeli (Av San Martín) and **Pizzería Riviera** (Av San Martín) are both warmly recommended. The **Club de Ajedrez** (Plaza del Folklore) serves enormous tasty *lomitos* for only US$3.50.

La Calera and Ciudad de Córdoba have buses from Córdoba to Cosquín (US$2, 1½ hours).

La Falda

Surrounded by extensive woodland at the western base of the Sierra Chica, 78km from Córdoba, La Falda is a fairly large and noisy resort with the ubiquitous video arcades lining the main street, but it's a good jumping-off point for visiting the neighboring villages of La Cumbre, Huerta Grande and Valle Hermosa. The **tourist office** (☎ 03548-423007; España 50) opens erratically, but they're very helpful.

The **Museo de Trenes en Miniatura** (Miniature Train Museum; admission US$2; ☽ 9:30am-8pm) warrants a quick visit.

Hostería Marína (☎ 03548-422640; Güemes 134; r per person with breakfast US$4) is La Falda's best value lodging and **Hospedaje San Remo** (☎ 03548-424875; Av Argentina 108; r per person with breakfast US$5) is another good bet.

There are many *parrillas* and pizzerias along Av Edén. **La Parrilla de Raúl** (Av Edén 1000) is one of the best *parrillas* in town and at **Pizza & Pasta Libre** (Av Edén 500) you can eat all the pizza and pasta you want for US$2 – sweet!

La Calera run buses to and from Córdoba (US$2, two hours).

Jesús María

After losing their operating funds to pirates off the coast of Brazil, the Jesuits produced and sold wine from Jesús María to support their university in colonial Córdoba. These days the town, 51km north of Córdoba via RN 9, hosts the annual **Fiesta Nacional de Doma y Folklore**, a celebration of *gaucho* horsemanship and customs, during early January.

Museo Jesuítico Nacional de Jesús María (admission US$0.70; ☽ 8am-7pm Mon-Fri, 9am-noon, 3-7pm Sat & Sun) is housed in the old church and convent in very attractive grounds.

The colonial posthouse of **Sinsacate** (admission US$0.30; ☽ 2-7pm Mon-Fri), five kilometers away was the site of a wake for murdered La Rioja *caudillo* Facundo Quiroga in 1835.

Ciudad de Córdoba operates buses between Córdoba and Jesús María (US$1, one hour).

Alta Gracia

Only 35km southwest of Córdoba, the colonial mountain town of Alta Gracia is steeped in history. Its illustrious residents range from Jesuit pioneers to Viceroy Santiago Liniers, Spanish composer Manuel de Falla and revolutionary Ernesto 'Che' Guevara. In the first half of the 20th century, the town (whose architecture closely resembles parts of Mar del Plata) was a summer retreat for the Argentine oligarchy, but it's not the social center it once was.

From 1643 to 1762, Jesuit fathers built the **Iglesia Parroquial Nuestra Señora de la Merced**, on the west side of the central Plaza Manuel Solares; the nearby Jesuit workshops of **El Obraje** (1643) are now a public school. Liniers, one of the last officials to occupy the post of Viceroy of the Río de la Plata, resided in what is now the **Museo Histórico Nacional del Virrey Liniers** (admission US$0.70; ☽ 9am-7pm, Tue-Sun), alongside the church.

Some blocks west, on Av Vélez Sársfield, squatters inhabit the crumbling **Sierras Hotel**, which, during Alta Gracia's social heyday, was the meeting place for the elite (including Che's black sheep family). From 1939 until his death in 1946, Falla lived in **Villa Los Espinillos** (cnr Carlos Pellegrini & Calle Manuel de Falla), which is now a museum. Though the Guevaras lived in several houses in the 1930s, their primary residence was **Villa Beatriz** (Avellaneda 501) in Villa Carlos Pellegrini.

Hostal Hispania (☎ 03547-426555; Vélez Sársfield 57; s/d with breakfast US$10/17) is airy and many of the rooms have balconies. **Hostería Asturias** (☎ 03547-423668; Vélez Sársfield 127; s/d US$3/8) is charming but often full.

Trattoria Oro (España 18) has a varied menu and excellent service, and **Hispania** (Urquiza 90) is another good choice that specializes in large portions.

From the **bus terminal** (cnr Av Perón & Butori), Satag runs every 15 minutes to and from Córdoba (US$1, one hour).

LA RIOJA

La Rioja is often dubbed the 'City of Orange Trees,' fabulous examples of which can be seen in the city's attractive plazas. Summer temperatures are often searing – folks here take their siesta very seriously.

In 1591, Juan Ramírez de Velasco founded Todos los Santos de la Nueva Rioja, at the base of the Sierra del Velasco, 154km south of Catamarca. An earthquake in 1894 destroyed many buildings, but the restored commercial center, near Plaza 25 de Mayo, replicates colonial style.

The province produced some memorable historical figures, including *caudillos* (provincial strongmen) like Facundo Quiroga, and also nurtured intellectuals like Joaquín V González, founder of La Plata University. Facundo's modern counterparts, including former president Carlos Menem's *riojano* (La Rioja dwellers) family, are politically influential. Corruption and nepotism are widespread.

Information

La Rioja's **tourist office** (☎ 03882-453982; Pelagio Luna 345; ☼ 8am-10pm) has a blurry city map and brochures of other provincial destinations. The **provincial tourist office** (☎ 03822-428839; Perón & Urquiza; ☼ 8am-12:30pm & 4-9pm Mon-Fri) is also helpful with a better city map.

La Rioja has no *cambios*, but several banks have ATMs. The **post office** is at Perón 764 and there's a *locutorio* at Perón 1066. Internet access is available at **Cyber Hall** (Rivadavia 763; US$2 per hr; ☼ until 1am) is expensive.

Sights

Museums welcome the US$1 voluntary contribution.

The **Museo Folklórico** (Pelagio Luna 811; ☼ 9am-noon Tue-Sat), described by one contented visitor as having a 'good smell', is in a wonderful 19th-century house. It displays ceramic reproductions of mythological figures from local folklore as well as *gaucho* paraphernalia and colorful weavings.

The **Museo Inca Huasi** (Alberdi 650; ☼ 9am-noon Tue-Sat) exhibits over 12,000 pieces, from tools and artifacts to Diaguita ceramics and weavings.

Built by the Diaguita under Dominican overseers, the **Convento de Santo Domingo** (1623; cnr Pelagio Luna & Lamadrid), is the country's oldest. The **Convento de San Francisco** (cnr Av 25 de Mayo & Bazán y Bustos) houses the Niño Alcalde, a Christ-child icon symbolically recognized as the city's mayor. The **Iglesia Catedral** (cnr San Nicolás & Av 25 de Mayo) contains the image of patron saint Nicolás de Bari, another devotional object.

Festivals & Events

The December 31 ceremony El Tinkunako re-enacts San Francisco Solano's mediation between the Diaguitas and the Spaniards in 1593. When accepting peace, the Diaguitas imposed two conditions: resignation of the Spanish mayor and his replacement by the Niño Alcalde.

Sleeping

Residencial Florida (☎ 03822-426563; 8 de Diciembre 524; r per person US$5) Cozy rooms with private bath; disturb the senora during her siesta at your own peril.

Residencial Don José (☎ 03822-426365; Perón 419; s/d US$5/8) Dark but clean rooms with private bath.

Pensión 9 de Julio (☎ 03822-426955; cnr Copiapó & Vélez Sársfield; s/d with breakfast US$7/10) Large rooms with private bath and a lovely shaded courtyard overlooking Plaza 9 de Julio.

Residencial Petit (☎ 03822-427577; Lagos 427; r per person US$6) A maze of rooms, all with private bath.

Residencial Anita (☎ 03822-424835; Lagos 476; s/d US$8/12) Family-oriented but friendly (as long as you don't mind the large pet dogs).

Country Las Vegas (campsites per person US$1.50) The campground is at km 8 on RN 75 west of town; to get there, catch city bus No 1 southbound on Perón.

Eating

Places serving both regional specialties and standard Argentine dishes like *parrillada* include **La Vieja Casona** (Rivadavia 427) and **La Querencia** (Perón 1200).

La Stanzza (Dorrego 160) Offers fine dining, seafood and a healthy wine list.

Alike (cnr Yrigoyen & Vélez Sársfield) Has a variety of dishes, including *parrillada*.

Café del Paseo (cnr Pelagio Luna & 25 de Mayo) An appealing *confitería*, with tables around a shaded courtyard.

La Aldea de la Virgen de Lujan (Rivadavia 756) Serves excellent homemade pasta and regional specialties.

Complejo Roginá (cnr 25 de Mayo & Rivadavia) Informal stalls selling cheap pizzas and hot dogs.

Getting There & Away

Aerolíneas Argentinas (☎ 03822-426307; Belgrano 63) flies Monday to Saturday to Buenos Aires (US$90).

La Rioja's small **bus terminal** (☎ 03822-425453) is at Artigas and España.

Facondo travels daily to provincial destinations. La Riojana goes to Chilecito (US$3, three hours). Sample long-distance fares include Catamarca (US$3.50, two hours), Tucumán (US$7, five hours), Córdoba (US$7, 5½ hours), San Luis (US$9, eight hours), San Juan (US$6, six hours), Mendoza (US$10, eight hours), Salta (US$12, 10 hours) and Buenos Aires (US$25, 16 hours).

CATAMARCA

Quiet, conservative and extremely Catholic, San Fernando del Valle de Catamarca wasn't settled until 1683. Known commonly as Catamarca, the city has remained an economic backwater, but major holidays attract many visitors. Flanked by the Sierra del Colorado to the west and the Sierra Graciana in the east, 156km northeast of La Rioja, Catamarca enjoys a spectacular setting. Shady Plaza 25 de Mayo offers refuge from summer heat in an otherwise fairly treeless city but beware of La Zonda, a fierce mountain wind that can cause dramatic temperature increases. The bus terminal is five blocks south of the center – as you walk out of the terminal turn right, walk along Güemes until you get to Plaza 25 de Agosto, then hang a right up Yrigoyen until you bump into Plaza 25 de Mayo.

Information

The municipal **tourist office** (☎ 03833-437413; Sarmiento 450; ⊗ 7am-1pm & 2:30-8pm Mon-Fri) is inside the Instituto Cultural.

Several downtown banks have ATMs. Banco Catamarca, on Plaza 25 de Mayo,

can change traveler's checks in 24 hours (open mornings only). The post office is at San Martín 753. There's a *locutorio* at Rivadavia 758. Access the Internet at **Cool Net** (Maipú 665; US$1.50 per hr), which appears to be run by teenagers.

Sights

The neocolonial **Iglesia y Convento de San Francisco** (cnr Esquiú & Rivadavia) contains the cell of Fray Mamerto Esquiú, famous for his vocal defense of the 1853 constitution. After being stolen and left on the roof years ago, a crystal box containing his heart (perched rather grotesquely on a velvet cushion) is on display in the church. Squeamish visitors should give it a miss.

In the **Museo Arqueológico Adán Quiroga** (Sarmiento btwn Esquiú & Prado), tedious presentation undermines outstanding materials, including two 500-year-old mummified bodies discovered in the province. Opposite Plaza 25 de Mayo, a temple behind the **cathedral** contains the Virgen del Valle, one of northern Argentina's most venerated images.

Festivals & Events

On the Sunday after Easter, thousands of pilgrims from across Argentina honor the Virgen del Valle in the Fiesta de Nuestra Señora del Valle. On December 8, a colorful procession carries the Virgin through the town. A more provincial event is the Fiesta del Poncho, held during two weeks in July.

Sleeping

The tourist office keeps a list of *casas de familia* charging from US$6.

Hospedaje del Peregrino (☎ 03833-431203; Sarmiento 653; dm US$3) The cheapest option in town is this pilgrims dormitory. Nothing fancy and cheaper if you supply your own bedding.

Hotel Comodoro (☎ 03833-423490; República 855; d US$3, with bath US$7) It looks better from outside – the rooms with shared bath are small and dark; the ones with attached baths are slightly better.

Residencial Delgado (☎ 03833-426109; San Martín 788; s/d US$5/9) Better than it looks from outside and very central.

Autocamping Municipal (campsites per tent/person US$2/1) This place gets heavy use on weekends and holidays, and also has some ferocious mosquitoes. It's about 4km from downtown. To get there take bus No 10 (marked 'camping') from Convento de San Francisco, on Esquiú.

Eating
The least expensive eateries cater to pilgrims.

Comedor El Peregrino (2 courses with/without meat US$3.50/2) In the gallery behind the cathedral, this place offers *empanadas* and pasta.

Open Plaza (República 580) Electric neon red-and-blue lighting gives this funky place a nightclub feel, which is probably where most of its patrons are coming from in the wee hours. The food is simple and filling and they also have a good range of cocktails.

La Tinaja (Sarmiento 533) La Tinaja has low prices and sometimes live music. It's handy if you're staying in the center.

Trattoria Montecarlo (República 548) Specializes in pasta and other simple, wholesome dishes.

Sociedad Española (Av Virgen del Valle 725) Traditional Spanish dishes, including seafood.

Shopping
For hand-tied rugs, a Catamarcan specialty, visit the **Mercado Artesanal Permanente y Fábrica de Alfombras** (Av Virgen del Valle 945), which also sells ponchos, blankets, jewelry, red onyx sculptures, musical instruments, hand-spun wool and baskets.

Getting There & Away
AIR
Aerolíneas Argentinas (☎ 03833-424460; Sarmiento 589) flies to Buenos Aires' Aeroparque (US$82) from Monday to Saturday. **LAPA** (☎ 03833-434772; Sarmiento 506), flies to Buenos Aires via La Rioja on Monday, Wednesday, Friday and Sunday (US$85).

BUS
Catamarca's **bus terminal** (☎ 03833-423415; Av Güemes 850) has many departures including to La Rioja (US$3, two hours), Tucumán (US$5, three hours), Santiago del Estero (US$5, five hours), Córdoba (US$6, 5½ hours), Salta (US$8, eight hours), San Juan (US$8, seven hours) Mendoza (US$9, 10 hours) and Buenos Aires (US$18, 16 hours).

SANTIAGO DEL ESTERO
Founded in 1553, hot and dusty Santiago del Estero (population 224,000) is Argentina's oldest city; unfortunately it also has the reputation of being one of the most boring. The pace of life is ploddingly slow, grinding to a standstill during the siesta, but things tend to liven up a bit in the evening when *santiagueños* (people from Santiago) gather in cafés around Plaza Libertad. In 1993, the city's famously laid-back attitude was temporarily put aside when provincial employees, who had gone without pay for four months, set fire to the Casa de Gobierno and Palacio Legislativo. The buildings have since been restored but little colonial architecture remains. Santiago del Estero was once a stopover between the Pampas and the Bolivian mines, but irrigated cotton now supports the economy. Accommodation options listed below are all near Santiago's aging **bus terminal** (☎ 0385-421-3746; cnr Pedro León Gallo & Saavedra), eight blocks south of Plaza Libertad. A *remise* from the airport costs around US$2.

Information
The provincial **tourist office** (☎ 0385-421-3253; Av Libertad 417; ☽ 7:30am-1:30pm & 3-9pm Mon-Sat) keeps slightly longer hours in the summer.

Several banks in the downtown area have ATMs but it is difficult to change traveler's checks. The post office is at Buenos Aires and Urquiza and there are a number of *locutorios* downtown.

Sights
The **Museo de Ciencias Antropológicas y Naturales** (Avellaneda 355; ☽ 7:30am-1:30pm & 2-8pm Mon-Fri, 10am-noon Sat & Sun) offers free guided tours of its well-presented collection of fossils, funerary urns and Chaco ethnography.

Exhibits at the **Museo Histórico Provincial** (Urquiza 354; admission free; ☽ 8am-noon & 2-8pm Mon-Fri, 9am-noon Sat) emphasize postcolonial history. Opposite the museum, a copy of the Turin Shroud can be seen in the **Convento de Santo Domingo.**

Sleeping & Eating
Residencial Emaus (☎ 0385-421-5893; Moreno Sur 673; s/d US$5/8) It only has five rooms, but they're all spotless, with TV, bath and breakfast.

Residencial Iovino (☎ 0385-421-3311; Moreno Sur 602; s/d US$5/9) A large, dark and ragged place, the Iovino offers reasonable value.

Residencial Santa Rita (☎ 0385-422-0625; Santa Fe 273; s/d US$5/7) A good budget choice near the bus terminal.

Campamento Las Casuarinas (Parque Aguirre; campsites per person US$1) Offers shady campsites less than a kilometer from Plaza Libertad.

Mercado Armonía (Tucumán btwn Pellegrini & Salta) It's cheap, but less appealing than some Argentine markets.

El Quebracho (cnr Pellegrini & Roca) Recommended for mouth watering food and an extensive wine list.

Mía Mamma (24 de Septiembre 15) Moderately priced with an extensive Italian menu, plus a good, inexpensive salad bar.

Tequila (Independencia 46) On Plaza Libertad, this popular café/bar has Internet access upstairs.

Getting There & Around

Aerolíneas Argentinas (☎ 0385-422-4335; Urquiza 235) flies daily to Buenos Aires (US$100).

There are hourly buses to Tucumán (US$3, two hours) and other destinations such as Catamarca (US$5, five hours) and Buenos Aires (US$16, 13 hours).

TUCUMÁN

You're still likely to see horse-drawn carts from the countryside rattling down the streets of San Miguel de Tucumán (Tucumán for short). It's a vibrant, colorful and energetic city, and notable colonial remnants are preserved near Plaza Independencia. Fruits and sugar cultivated in the area have earned Tucumán the title as the 'Garden of Argentina,' but visitors in the summer months may find the city very hot and oppressive. Independence Day (July 9) celebrations are especially vigorous in Tucumán, which hosted the congress that declared Argentine independence in 1816. The bus terminal is a few blocks from the center – an easy walk if you don't want to fork out the US$0.80 fare. Tucumán's **airport** (☎ 0381-426-5072) is 8km east of downtown. Catch bus No 120, which passes the center on the way to the bus terminal (US$1). A taxi there will cost US$4.

Information

The **tourist office** (☎ 0381-430-3644; 24 de Septiembre 484; ☽ 8am-10pm) is on Plaza Inde-pendencia. There is also a booth at the bus terminal.

Maguitur (San Martín 765) cashes traveler's checks (2% commission), and ATMs are numerous. The post office is at 25 de Mayo and Córdoba. There's a *locutorio* at Maipú 480. For Internet access, try **Tucumán Cyber-center** (San Juan 612; US$1 per hr). Some downtown *locutorios* also have Internet access for the same price.

Sights

Spectacularly lit up at night, Tucumán's most imposing landmark is the **Casa de Gobierno**, which replaced the colonial *cabildo* on Plaza Independencia in 1912.

Museo Folklórico Manuel Belgrano (24 de Septiembre 565; admission free; ☽ 8am-noon & 4-8pm Mon-Fri, 9am-1pm & 4-9pm Sat & Sun) displays horse gear, indigenous musical instruments, weavings, woodcarvings, Quilmes pottery and samples of *randa* (a Puerto Rican lace technique that doesn't require a bobbin to sew it, only a needle and thread). The museum shop sells some items.

Museo Iramain (Entre Ríos 27; ☽ 8am-noon & 4-8pm Mon-Fri) focuses on Argentine art and sculpture.

Museo de Bellas Artes Timoteo Navarro (9 de Julio 44; ☽ 8am-noon & 4-8pm) showcases fine arts from around the country. A US$0.30 donation is welcome at both of these museums.

Casa Histórica de la Independencia (Congreso 151; admission US$1; ☽ 8am-noon & 4-8pm Mon-Fri) is a dazzlingly white colonial house where Unitarist lawyers and clerics declared independence on July 9, 1816 (Federalists boycotted the meeting).

Casa del Obispo Colombres (Parque 9 de Julio; admission free; ☽ 8am-noon & 4-8pm) is an 18th-century house which preserves the first ox-powered *trapiche* (sugar mill) of Tucumán's post-independence industry. Guided tours in Spanish explain the mill's operations.

Sleeping

Hotel Petit (☎ 0381-421-3902; Crisóstomo Álvarez 765; s/d with bath US$4/7) A maze of leafy patios. Definitely the best budget choice in town. Rooms with shared bath are cheaper.

Hotel La Vasca (☎ 0381-421-1288; Mendoza 289; s/d with bath US$6/8) Another good budget choice; rooms have classy hardwood furniture and face a pretty courtyard.

ARGENTINA

TUCUMÁN

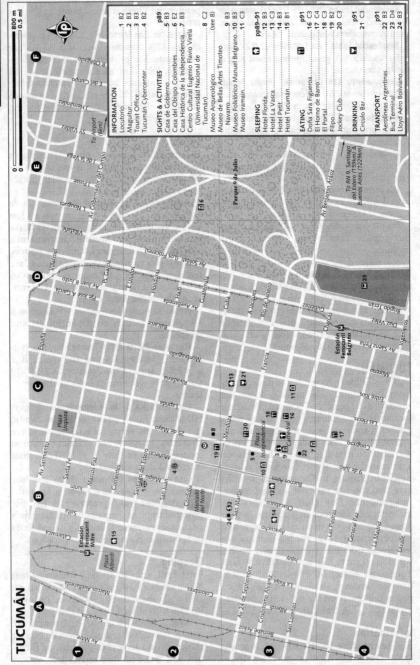

INFORMATION	p89
Locutorio............................1	B2
Maguitur...........................2	B3
Tourist Office....................3	B3
Tucumán Cybercenter..........4	B2

SIGHTS & ACTIVITIES	p89
Casa de Gobierno...............5	B3
Casa del Obispo Colombres...6	E2
Casa Histórica de la Independencia...7	B3
Centro Cultural Eugenio Flavio Virela (Universidad Nacional de Tucumán)..........8	C2
Museo Arqueológico..........(see 8)	
Museo de Bellas Artes Timoteo Navarro...........................9	B3
Museo Folklórico Manuel Belgrano...10	B3
Museo Iramain....................11	C3

SLEEPING	pp89–91
Hotel Florida....................12	B3
Hotel La Vasca..................13	C3
Hotel Petit........................14	B3
Hotel Tucumán..................15	B1

EATING	p91
Doña Sara Figueroa..........16	C3
El Horno de Barro..............17	C4
El Portal...........................18	C3
Filipo...............................19	B2
Jockey Club......................20	C3

DRINKING	p91
Círculo Bar.......................21	C3

TRANSPORT	p91
Aerolíneas Argentinas........22	B3
Bus Terminal....................23	D4
Lloyd Aéro Boliviano.........24	B3

ARGENTINA

Hotel Tucumán (☎ 0381-422-1809; Catamarca 573; s/d US$3/5) Offers basic, tidy rooms. Student discounts are sometimes available.

Hotel Florida (☎ 0381-422-6674; Av 24 de Septiembre 610; s/d with bath US$5/8) Just off Plaza Independencia, it's friendly, quiet and central but very small; upstairs rooms have better light.

Eating & Drinking

Stalls at the Mercado del Norte, with an entrance at Mendoza and Maipú, serve good cheap food and great pizza.

Filipo (Mendoza 202) Does good breakfast, including excellent coffee and croissants.

El Portal (Av 24 de Septiembre s/n) Half a block east of Plaza Independencia. Does chicken empanadas, *humitas* (a concoction of corn, onions, cheese and flour wrapped and served in a corn leaf) and other regional specialties.

Doña Sara Figueroa (Av 24 de Septiembre 358) Serves Middle Eastern food as well as the standard empanadas.

Jockey Club (San Martín 451) Don't let the old-time elegance fool you – the US$4 set lunches are a real bargain.

El Horno de Barro (cnr Congreso & San Lorenzo) Cheap set meals for under US$1 and *parrillada*.

Círculo Bar (Mendoza 240; ☾ 11:30am-3pm & 6pm-late) Easily the funkiest bar in town, this place is small and has cool music and a student atmosphere. It gets going late and there is live music on Tuesday and Sunday, a free movie on Wednesday and DJs on other nights.

Getting There & Around

AIR

Aerolíneas Argentinas (☎ 0381-431-1030; 9 de Julio 112) flies daily to Buenos Aires' Aeroparque (US$110). **Lloyd Aéreo Boliviano** (LAB; ☎ 0381-422-3030; San Martin 667, 4th fl) flies Wednesday, Friday and Saturday to Santa Cruz, Bolivia (US$185) from Salta.

BUS

Tucumán's **bus terminal** (☎ 0381-422-2221; Brígido Terán 350) has a post office, *locutorios*, a supermarket, bars and restaurants, all blissfully air-conditioned. There's also a left-luggage service opposite stand 10 (US$1 per day).

Aconquija goes to Tafí del Valle (US$3, 2½ hours) six times daily, to Amaichá del Valle (US$5) four times daily, and to Cafa-

yate (US$8, seven hours) three times a day, once via Santa María.

Some long-distance destinations from Tucumán include Santiago del Estero (US$3, two hours), Córdoba (US$12, eight hours), Salta (US$6, 4½ hours), Corrientes (US$16, 12 hours), La Rioja (US$7, five hours) and Buenos Aires (US$23, 16 hours).

TAFÍ DEL VALLE

Southwest of Tucumán, RP 307 snakes up a narrow gorge, opening onto a misty valley where *tucumanos* (people from Tucumán) seek relief in the cool heights around Tafí del Valle. Beyond Tafí, the road zigzags over the 3050m Abra del Infiernillo, an alternate route to Cafayate and Salta.

At 2000m, a temperate island in a subtropical sea, Tafí grows seed potatoes, sends fruits (apples, pears and peaches) to Tucumán, and pastures cattle, sheep and, at higher altitudes, llamas. It also produces some exceedingly good handmade cheese and the **cheese festival** held during the second week in February will be worth a look (and, possibly, a nibble). Out of season, Tafí has a quiet, slightly deserted feel and many houses stand empty, but come the summer the town's population triples and you may be hard-pressed to find accommodation.

The helpful **Casa del Turista** (☎ 03867-421084; ☾ 8am-8pm) is in Tafí's central plaza. **Banco Tucumán** (Av Miguel Critto) has an ATM. Long-distance telephones are in the plaza.

Sights

At **Parque Los Menhires**, at the south end of La Angostura reservoir, stand more than 80 indigenous granite monuments collected from nearby archaeological sites. Some say they resemble the standing stones of the Scottish Hebrides.

Tafí's 18th-century Jesuit chapel **Capilla La Banda** (1718) contains a worthwhile museum (cross the bridge at the end of Av Perón and follow the road round for about 1km).

Sleeping & Eating

Hospedaje El Valle (☎ 03867-421641; Av Perón 56) Above the artisan shops; undoubtedly the best budget option in town.

Hospedaje Celia Correa (☎ 03867-421170; Av Belgrano 423; r per person US$3) Friendly and good value. Prices go up over the cheese festival.

Autocamping del Sauce (☎ 03867-421084; campsites/cabanas per person US$2/3) The tiny cabanas with bunks would be very cramped at their maximum capacity of four people.

Pub El Ciervo (Av Perón, next to the YPF station) Popular with locals and serves good short orders and excellent trout. The open fireplace and English menu are other bonuses.

Bar El Paraíso (Juan de Perón 176) This is where the locals congregate to dine cheaply on sandwiches and set meals while watching Segal or Stallone videos. A pleasant patio overlooks Juan de Perón.

Getting There & Around

Mountain bikes can be rented from the elegant **Hotel Rosada** (Av Belgrano 322) for US$1 an hour.

CAFAYATE

At the mouth of the Valles Calchaquíes, 1600m above sea level, Cafayate's dry, sunny climate is responsible for producing some of Argentina's best wine. Surrounded by vineyards that practically engulf the town itself, Cafayate is a popular destination for Argentine tourists and a hangout for young artisans. February's **La Serenata** music festival draws big crowds. RN 40 (Av Güemes) goes northwest to the colonial villages of Molinos and Cachi, while RN 68 goes to Salta.

The **tourist information kiosk** (☑ 9am-9pm Mon-Fri, 10am-8pm Sat & Sun) is at the northeast corner of Plaza San Martín. Both banks have ATMs. Telecentros Cafayate is at Güemes and Belgrano.

Sights

The **Museo Arqueológico** (Calle Colón; admission US$1; ☑ daylight hrs) in the late Rodolfo Bravo's house displays his personal collection of Calchaquí (Diaguita) ceramics. Colonial and other artifacts include elaborate horse gear and wine casks.

The **Museo de Vitivinicultura** (Güemes near Colón; admission US$0.50; ☑ 10am-1pm & 5-8pm Mon-Fri) details the history of local wines. Three nearby **bodegas** (wine cellars) offer tours and tasting; try the fruity white *torrontés*. From Av 25 de Mayo, a five kilometer walk southwest leads you to the Río Colorado. Follow the river upstream for about two hours to get to a 10m **waterfall**, where you can swim. Look out for hidden rock paintings on the way (for a small tip, local children will guide you).

Sleeping

El Hospedaje (☎ 03868-421680; cnr Salta & Quintana de Niño; s/d US$3/7) One of the best budget choices in town. It offers comfortable rooms and a good breakfast for an extra US$1.

Hospedaje Colonial (☎ 03868-421655; Diego de Almagro 134; s/d US$3/6) In an attractive colonial building with quiet patios.

Hostal Del Valle (☎ 03868-421039; San Martín 243; s/d US$4/8) Comfortable, clean and friendly.

Camping Lorahuasi (☎ 03868-421051; per car, person & tent US$1) Has hot showers, a swimming pool and a grocery.

Eating

Cheap eats can be found at the various *comedores* inside the **Mercado Central** (cnr San Martín & 11 de Noviembre).

El Cafayateño (cnr Quintana de Niño & Nuestra Señora del Rosario) A good spot for breakfast in the sun or a light meal, this café is a popular little place.

El Rancho (cnr Av Güemes & Belgrano) Serving regional specialties, El Rancho has a large fireplace surrounded by tables, perfect for warming the tush on chilly winter nights.

Heladería Miranda (cnr Av Güemes & Quintana de Niño) Sells imaginative wine-flavored ice cream with a considerable alcoholic kick.

Getting There & Around

El Indio (Belgrano btwn Av Güemes & Salta) has four buses daily to Salta (US$4, 3½ hours) except Sunday (three only). There are three daily to San Carlos, up the Valle Calchaquí, and one to Angastaco (US$2.50).

Take one of the daily buses to Santa María to visit the ruins at Quilmes (see p93), in Tucumán province. **El Aconquija** (Mitre 77) has three daily buses to Tucumán (US$8, seven hours) all passing through Tafí del Valle; one also goes via Santa María.

Bike rental from **Rudi** (Av Güemes Norte 175) costs US$3 a day.

AROUND CAFAYATE
Quebrada de Cafayate

From Cafayate, RN 68 slices through the Martian-like landscape of the Quebrada de Cafayate on its way to Salta. About 50km north of Cafayate, the eastern Sierra de Carahuasi is the backdrop for distinctive sandstone landforms like the Garganta del Diablo (Devil's Throat), El Anfiteatro (The Amphitheater), El Sapo (The Toad),

El Fraile (The Friar), El Obelisco (The Obelisk) and Los Castillos (The Castles). Nearer Cafayate is an extensive dunefield at Los Médanos.

Other than car rental or brief, regimented tours, the best way to see the Quebrada is by bike or on foot, but bring plenty of water and go in the morning, as unpleasant, strong winds kick up in the afternoon. At Cafayate, cyclists can load their bikes onto any El Indio bus heading to Salta and disembark at the impressive box canyon of Garganta del Diablo. From here, the 50-odd kilometers back to Cafayate can be biked in about four hours, but it's too far on foot. When they've had enough, walkers should simply hail down another El Indio bus on its way back to Cafayate.

Valles Calchaquíes

In this valley north and south of Cafayate, once a principal route across the Andes, the Calchaquí people resisted Spanish attempts to impose forced labor obligations. Tired of having to protect their pack trains, the Spaniards relocated many Calchaquí to Buenos Aires, and the land fell to Spaniards, who formed large rural estates.

CACHI

Northwest of Cafayate is Cachi. Its scenic surroundings, 18th-century church and archaeological museum make it the most worthwhile stopover in the Valles Calchaquíes. For accommodations, check out the municipal campground and hostel, or **Hotel Nevado de Cachi** (☎ 03868-491004; r per person US$3), a modest, good value hotel. Cheap restaurants surround the plaza.

You can only reach Cachi from Cafayate if you have your own transport or are prepared to hitchhike a stretch of RN 40 between Angastaco and Molinos. It's easier to take a Marcos Rueda bus from Salta (US$5), which uses the scenic Cuesta del Obispo route past Parque Nacional Los Cardones.

QUILMES

This pre-Hispanic *pucará* (indigenous Andean fortress), in Tucumán province only 50km south of Cafayate, is probably Argentina's most extensive preserved ruin. Dating from about AD 1000, this complex urban settlement covered about 30 hectares, housing perhaps 5000 people. The

Quilmes people abided contact with the Incas but could not outlast the Spaniards, who, in 1667, deported the last 2000 to Buenos Aires.

Quilmes' thick walls underscore its defensive functions, but evidence of dense occupation sprawls north and south of the nucleus. Camping is possible near the small museum, where US$1 admits you to the ruins. **Parador Ruinas de Quilmes** (☎ 03892-421075; s/d US$30/60) also has a restaurant. Buses from Cafayate to Santa María pass the junction, but from there, it's five kilometers to the ruins by foot or thumb.

SALTA

Surrounded by verdant peaks, 1200m above sea level, Salta's wonderful climate and attractive colonial architecture have long captivated visitors to the city. With good trekking, horse riding and rafting nearby, this is a great base to explore the surrounding area, but you will also have fun soaking up the Andean atmosphere and wandering through the city's colonial streets.

Salta's commercial center is southwest of the central Plaza 9 de Julio. Alberdi and Florida are pedestrian malls between Caseros and Av San Martín. Bus No 5 connects the train station, downtown and bus terminal.

Information

The **provincial tourist office** (☎ 0387-431-0950; Buenos Aires 93; 9am-9pm) is very central. The **municipal tourist office** (☎ 0387-437-3341; cnr Av San Martín & Buenos Aires; 9am-8pm) runs an information kiosk in the bus terminal in high season. The **Administración de Parques Nacionales** (APN; ☎ 0387-431-0255; Santa Fe 23; 10am-noon & 3-5pm Mon-Fri), has information on the province's national parks.

Cambio Dinar (B Mitre 101) changes cash and traveler's checks, although banks may give you a better rate. There are ATMs downtown and a **post office** (Deán Funes 140). Many downtown *locutorios* offer Internet access. **Chat Café** (Vicente López 117; US$1 per hr) is open late.

Sights
CERRO SAN BERNARDO
For spectacular views of Salta and the Lerma valley, take the **teleférico** (gondola; round trip US$3; 10am-7:45pm) from Parque San

ARGENTINA

Martín up to the top and back, or climb the winding staircase trail that starts behind the Güemes monument.

MUSEUMS

The **Museo Histórico del Norte** (Caseros 549; admission US$0.50; 🕑 9:30am-1:30pm & 3:30-8:30pm) is in the 18th-century **cabildo**. It houses religious and modern art, period furniture, historic coins, paper money and horse-drawn vehicles.

The **Museo de Bellas Artes** (Florida 18; 🕑 9am-1pm & 4-8pm) in the colonial Casa Arias Rengel displays modern painting and sculpture.

CHURCHES

The 19th-century **Iglesia Catedral** (España 596) guards the ashes of General Martín Miguel de Güemes, a hero of the wars of independence. So ornate it's almost gaudy, the **Iglesia San Francisco**, at Caseros and Córdoba, is a Salta landmark. Only Carmelite nuns can enter the 16th-century adobe **Convento de San Bernardo**, at Caseros and Santa Fe, but anyone can admire its carved *algarrobo* (carob tree wood) door or peek inside the chapel during Mass, held at 8am daily.

EL TREN A LAS NUBES

From Salta, the Tren a las Nubes (Train to the Clouds) makes countless switchbacks and spirals to ascend the Quebrada del Toro and reach the high puna (Andean plateau). Its La Polvorilla viaduct, crossing a broad desert canyon, is a magnificent

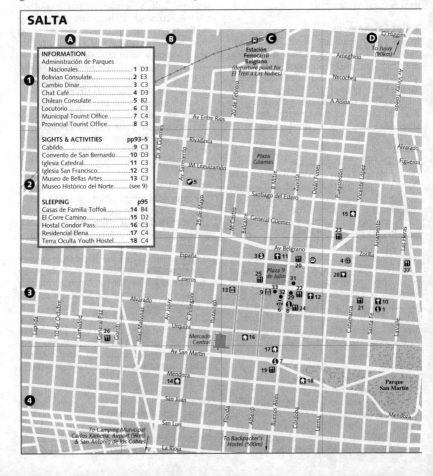

SALTA

INFORMATION
Administración de Parques
Nacionales.............................1 D3
Bolivian Consulate.....................2 E3
Cambio Dinar...........................3 C3
Chat Café..............................4 D3
Chilean Consulate......................5 B2
Locutorio..............................6 C3
Municipal Tourist Office...............7 C4
Provincial Tourist Office..............8 C3

SIGHTS & ACTIVITIES   pp93–5
Cabildo................................9 C3
Convento de San Bernardo..............10 D3
Iglesia Catedral......................11 C3
Iglesia San Francisco.................12 C3
Museo de Bellas Artes.................13 C3
Museo Histórico del Norte.........(see 9)

SLEEPING   p95
Casas de Familia Toffoli..............14 B4
El Corre Camino.......................15 D2
Hostal Condor Pass....................16 C3
Residencial Elena.....................17 C4
Terra Oculta Youth Hostel.............18 C4

engineering achievement at 4220m above sea level.

Turismo Tren a las Nubes (☎ 0387-401-2000; Buenos Aires 44) operates full-day excursions as far as La Polvorilla; most trips take place on Saturday only from April to November, but can be more frequent during July holidays. The US$70 fare does not include meals, which cost around US$7.

Sleeping

Hostal Condor Pass (☎ 0387-4221050; Urquiza 675; dm US$3, d US$6) About as accommodating as accommodation gets, with rooms for two to five people, laundry, kitchen, good bathrooms, even a babysitter! All smack in the middle of town.

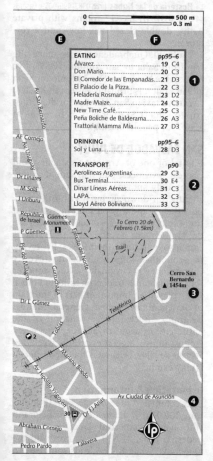

EATING   pp95–6
Álvarez.............................19 C4
Don Mario.......................20 C3
El Corredor de las Empanadas...21 D3
El Palacio de la Pizza........22 C3
Heladería Rosmari.............23 D2
Madre Maize....................24 C3
New Time Café.................25 C3
Peña Boliche de Balderama....26 A3
Trattoria Mamma Mia..........27 D3

DRINKING   pp95–6
Sol y Luna.......................28 D3

TRANSPORT   p90
Aerolíneas Argentinas.........29 C3
Bus Terminal....................30 E4
Dinar Líneas Aéreas...........31 C3
LAPA...............................32 C3
Lloyd Aéreo Boliviano........33 C3

Terra Oculta Youth Hostel (☎ 0387-421-8769; Córdoba 361; dm US$3, d US$7) A real 'backpacker's' vibe. Dorms are spacious; there's a ping pong table, cheap Internet access and two kitchens. A sunny roof terrace with bar and BBQ are further bonuses.

El Corre Camino (☎ 0387-431-4579; Vicente López 353; dm US$3, d US$7) In an attractive building with good kitchen facilities.

Casas de Familia Toffoli (☎ 0387-432-0813, Mendoza 915; ☎ 0387-421-2233, Mendoza 917; ☎ 0387-431-8948, Mendoza 919; r per person US$4) The three Toffoli sisters provide private lodging. All houses have pleasant patios, kitchen facilities and spotless bathrooms.

Residencial Elena (☎ 0387-421-1529; Buenos Aires 256; s/d US$7/9) In an attractive neocolonial building with an interior patio; has good rooms but a very odd atmosphere.

Camping Municipal Carlos Xamena (☎ 0387-423-1341; Av Libano; campsites per person/tent US$1/1) Features a gigantic swimming pool. Take bus No 3B from the corner of Mendoza and Lerma near the bus terminal.

Eating & Drinking

Mercado Central (cnr Florida & Av San Martín) At this large, lively market you can supplement inexpensive pizza, empanadas and *humitas* with fresh fruit and vegetables.

El Corredor de las Empanadas (Caseros 117) Serves excellent regional dishes as well as empanadas.

Peña Boliche Balderama (Av San Martín 1126) Has cheap set lunches and puts on 'folklore and music' shows with dinner.

Madre Maize (Alvarado 508) Does better than average vegetarian food – brown rice, tofu, seaweed etc in an earthy environment.

El Palacio de la Pizza (Caseros 437) A tried and trusted choice for pizza.

New Time Café (cnr Mitre & Caseros; breakfast US$1-2; snacks US$2-4) The ultimate in plaza-side cafés... shady tables, great views of the *cabildo*, Cerro San Bernado and cathedral, a leafy plaza across the way... they also serve coffee and food.

Trattoria Mamma Mia (Pasaje Zorrilla 1) Does superb pasta at reasonable prices.

Don Mario (España 492; set lunch US$3) With friendly service and much cheaper meals than other restaurants on nearby Plaza 9 de Julio.

Heladería Rosmari (Pueyrredón 202) One of Salta's many fine ice-creameries.

Sol y Luna (España 211) A small groovy bar which is good for a drink and has live music, usually starting at about 11pm on weekends (free entry). If there's no live music, the background vibe will be mellow homegrown grooves.

Getting There & Around

AIR

Aerolíneas Argentinas (☎ 0387-431-1331; Caseros 475) flies two or three times daily to Buenos Aires' Aeroparque (US$120).

Dinar Líneas Aéreas (☎ 0387-431-0500; Caseros 492) flies nonstop every weekday to Buenos Aires (US$120) and daily via Tucumán. **LAPA** (☎ 0387-431-7081; Buenos Aires 24) flies at least once daily to Buenos Aires (US$120).

Lloyd Aéreo Boliviano (LAB; ☎ 0387-431-0320; Caseros 529) flies Tuesday, Thursday and Sunday to Santa Cruz (Bolivia). **LanChile** (☎ 0387-421-7330; Buenos Aires 88) has seasonal flights over the Andes.

Transport to Salta's **airport** (☎ 0387-423-1648), 9km southwest of town on RP 51, leaves from airline offices about 1½ hours before the flight (US$2).

BUS

Salta's **bus terminal** (☎ 0387-401-1143; Av Hipólito Yrigoyen), southeast of downtown, has frequent services to all parts of the country.

Géminis flies to the Chilean destinations of San Pedro de Atacama (US$21, 12½ hours) and Calama, Chile (US$21, 14 hours) on Tuesday and Friday mornings, connecting to Antofagasta, Iquique and Arica.

El Indio has four buses daily to Cafayate (US$5, 3½ hours) except Sunday (three only); El Cafayateño goes twice daily Monday to Saturday and once on Sunday. El Quebradeño leaves for San Antonio de los Cobres at 3pm daily.

Empresa Marcos Rueda serves the Altiplano village of Cachi (US$6, four hours) twice daily except Monday and Wednesday (once only); it also goes to Molinos daily except Tuesday and Thursday (US$8, seven hours).

Long-distance services are frequent in all directions. Some sample fares include Tucumán (US$7, 4½ hours), La Quiaca (US$8, seven hours), Resistencia (US$18, 14 hours), Rosario (US$25, 16 hours), Mendoza (US$25, 18 hours) and Buenos Aires (US$30, 21 hours).

SAN ANTONIO DE LOS COBRES

Colonial pack trains to Peru usually took the Quebrada de Humahuaca, but an alternative crossed the Puna de Atacama to the Pacific. For travelers on this route, bleak San Antonio (3700m) must have seemed an oasis. Well into the 20th century, it was a stopover for drovers moving stock to Chile's nitrate mines, but railways and roads have now supplanted mules.

San Antonio is a largely indigenous town with posters and political graffiti that tell you it's still part of Argentina.

Hospedaje Belgrano (☎ 0387-490-9025; r per person US$3) and **Hospedaje Los Andes** (r per person US$4) both offer basic lodging; the latter has a restaurant.

Hostería de las Nubes (☎ 0387-490-9059; Caseros 441; s/d US$12/17) has 12 rooms with private baths, double-glazed windows and a restaurant.

Daily El Quebradeño buses make the trip from Salta to San Antonio (US$5, five hours); the bus leaves San Antonio for Salta at 9am. But it is probably easier (and faster) to catch a taxi in San Antonio for the return trip to Salta (US$7 per person, based on at least four people sharing).

SAN SALVADOR DE JUJUY

Capital of one of Argentina's smallest and poorest provinces, San Salvador de Jujuy (commonly known as Jujuy) has a shabby, slightly run-down air, but it's a bustling city nonetheless and a good jumping-off point for exploring the spectacular Quebrada de Humahuaca to the north. Travelers can also entertain themselves by trying to pronounce the town's name correctly (huoy-*huoyy*!). Originally a key stopover for colonial mule-traders en route to Potosí, Jujuy played an important part in the wars of independence when General Manuel Belgrano directed the evacuation of the entire city to avoid royalist capture; every August Jujuy's biggest event, the weeklong **Semana de Jujuy**, celebrates the *éxodo jujeño* (Jujuy exodus).

Orientation & Information

The colonial center of the city (population 200,000) is Plaza Belgrano. Belgrano (the main commercial street) is partly a pedestrian mall. RN 9 leads north up the Quebrada, while RN 66 leads southeast to

RN 34, the main route to Salta. To get to the center from the bus terminal, walk north along Dorrego and across the river, keeping the hill at your back.

Staff at the **provincial tourist office** (☎ 0388-422-1326; Av Urquiza 354; ☷ 7am-10pm) in the old railway station are helpful, speak English and have abundant maps and brochures on hand.

ATMs are common on Belgrano and banks should be able to change traveler's checks. The post office is at Lamadrid and Independencia; there's a **locutorio** (Belgrano 952) that also has Internet facilities for US$1 per hour.

Sights

Opposite Plaza Belgrano, Jujuy's **Iglesia Catedral** (1763) features a gold-laminated Spanish baroque pulpit, built by local artisans under a European master. In a small square next to the church is the **Paseo de los Artesanos**, a colorful arts market. On the south side of Plaza Belgrano, the imposing **Casa de Gobierno** is built in the style of a French palace and houses Argentina's first

national flag. On the north side of the plaza, the colonial **cabildo** deserves more attention than the **Museo Policial** within.

Museo Histórico Provincial (Lavalle 256; admission US$0.50; ☷ 8am-8pm Mon-Fri, 8am-noon & 4-8pm Sat) has rooms dedicated to distinct themes in provincial history.

Iglesia Santa Barbara (cnr Lamadrid & San Martín) contains several paintings from the colonial Cuzco school; you can slip in during mass on Saturday morning at 7am.

Museo Arqueológico Provincial (Lavalle 434; admission US$0.50; ☷ 8am-1pm & 3-9pm) has a small but interesting collection of ceramics from Yavi culture, as well as a number of human skulls.

Mercado del Sur opposite the bus terminal, is a bustling Indian market where Quechuan men and women swig *mazamorra* (a cold maize soup) and surreptitiously peddle coca leaves (unofficially tolerated for indigenous people).

Don't leave Jujuy without wallowing in the **thermal baths** (US$1) at **Hostería Termas de Reyes** (☎ 0388-492-2522), 20km northwest of downtown, overlooking the scenic canyon

SAN SALVADOR DE JUJUY

INFORMATION	
Bolivian Consulate	1 B2
Locutorio	2 C2
Provincial Tourist Office	3 D1

SIGHTS & ACTIVITIES	p97
Cabildo	4 D2
Casa de Gobierno	5 D2
Iglesia Catedral	6 D2
Iglesia Santa Barbara	7 B2
Mercado del Sur	8 C3
Museo Arqueológico Provincial	9 C1
Museo Histórico Provincial	10 C2
Museo Policial	(see 4)
Paseo de los Artesanos	11 D2

SLEEPING	⌂	p98
Residencial Chung King	12 C1
Residencial los Andes	13 D3
Residencial Norte	14 D1
Residencial Río de Janeiro	15 C3
Residencial San Antonio	16 C3

EATING	▯	p98
Carena	17 C2
Chung King	(see 12)
Confitería La Royal	18 C2
Madre Tierra	19 C2
Manos Jujeñas	20 B2
Ruta 9	21 C2
Sociedad Española	22 B2
Tía Violeta	23 D1

TRANSPORT	p98
Aerolíneas Argentinas	24 B2

of the Río Reyes, easily reached from Jujuy's Plaza Belgrano on Bus No 14. Bring food, since the *hostería's* restaurant is expensive.

Sleeping

Residencial Chung King (☎ 0388-422-8142; Alvear 627; s/d US$3/5, with bath US$5/7) Good rooms, but make sure you're at the back away from the noisy restaurant downstairs.

Residencial Norte (☎ 0388-423-8475; Alvear 444; dm/d US$2/4) Rock-bottom accommodations with shared bathroom; the central courtyard is pleasant but very run-down.

Residencial San Antonio (☎ 0388-422-5998; L de la Torre 933; s/d US$4/6) Directly opposite the bus terminal – it's convenient, clean and basic.

Residencial Los Andes (☎ 0388-422-4315; República de Siria 456; s/d with bath & TV US$5/8) A few blocks east of the terminal; a good hotel in an unexciting area.

Residencial Río de Janeiro (☎ 0388-422-3700; José de la Iglesia 1356; dm US$2, r per person US$3) West of the bus terminal with rather cramped rooms. Expect to pay more for a private bath.

Camping El Refugio (☎ 0388-490-9344; per tent US$1 & per person US$1) About 3km west of downtown. Bus No 9 goes there from downtown or the bus terminal.

Eating

Upstairs at the **Mercado Municipal** (cnr Alvear & Balcarce), several eateries serve inexpensive regional specialties that are generally spicier than elsewhere in Argentina – try *chicharrón con mote* (stir-fried pork with boiled maize).

Chung King (Alvear 627) An extensive Argentine menu and fine service. Its *rotisería* and pizzeria next door are good budget options.

Tia Violeta (cnr Alvear & Gorriti) Does sandwiches, *minutas* (short-order snacks), chopp beer (draft beer) and has live music some evenings.

Ruta 9 (Lavalle 2870) Serves up huge portions, making it a classic local choice.

Sociedad Española (Belgrano 1102) A traditional Spanish restaurant serving good seafood.

Madre Tierra (Belgrano 619) Excellent vegetarian fare, but only open for lunch.

Carena (cnr Belgrano & Balcarce) A traditional ambience and excellent coffee.

Manos Jujeñas (cnr Senador Pérez & San Martin) Famed for its regional food, including empanadas and *humitas*.

Confitería La Royal (Belgrano 766) One of the best cafés in town.

Getting There & Around

AIR

Aerolíneas Argentinas (☎ 0388-422-2575; Belgrano 1056), flies to Buenos Aires' Aeroparque (US$120) Tuesday to Friday at 8:20pm.

Jujuy's **airport** (☎ 0388-491-1103) is 32km southeast of town. The airline provides transport to the airport.

BUS

Jujuy's scruffy **bus terminal** (☎ 0388-422-1375; cnr Av Dorrego & Iguazú), blends in with the Mercado del Sur. It has provincial and long-distance services, but Salta has more alternatives.

Chile-bound buses from Salta to Calama (US$23 to US$40; prices depend on whether it's a day or night bus) pick up passengers in Jujuy on Tuesday and at 8:45am Friday; make reservations in advance if possible at the Géminis office at the terminal.

El Quiaqueño goes to La Quiaca (US$6, five hours), Humahuaca (US$3, two hours) and Tilcara (US$2, 1¼ hours). Cota Norte goes three times a day to Libertador General San Martín (US$2, two hours), from where you can access Parque Nacional Calilegua. It also goes to Tilcara and Humahuaca several times a day.

Many carriers serve Buenos Aires and intermediate points. Sample fares include Salta (US$2, 2½ hours), Tucumán (US$6, five hours), Córdoba (US$16, 13½ hours), Mendoza (US$15, 14 hours), Resistencia (US$20, 14 hours) and Buenos Aires (US$30, 20 hours).

QUEBRADA DE HUMAHUACA

North of Jujuy, RN 9 snakes its way through the Quebrada de Humahuaca, a painter's palette of color on barren hillsides, dwarfing hamlets where Quechua peasants scratch a living from growing maize and raising scrawny livestock. On this colonial post-route to Potosí, the architecture and other cultural features recall Peru and Bolivia.

Earthquakes leveled many of the adobe churches, but they were often rebuilt in the

17th and 18th centuries with solid walls, simple bell towers, and striking doors and wood paneling from the *cardón* cactus. Andean villages such as Tilcara and Humahuaca offer excellent examples of rural Andean life.

Tilcara

Tilcara's hilltop *pucará*, a pre-Hispanic fortress with unobstructed views, is its most conspicuous attraction, but the village's museums and its reputation as an artists colony help make it an appealing stopover. At 2461m above sea level, Tilcara (population 2919) has an irregular street plan beyond the central Plaza Prado. The **tourist office** (Plaza Prado; ☽ 8am-noon & 3-8pm) in the municipal offices distributes a useful map. There are *locutorios* on Lavalle, on the north side of Plaza Prado; Banco Macro, also on the plaza, has an ATM.

SIGHTS

Several worthwhile museums are on Plaza Prado. The well-organized **Museo Arqueológico Dr Eduardo Casanova** (admission US$1; ☽ 9am-6pm) displays regional artifacts in a beautiful colonial house. The admission fee includes entry to El Pucará (see following). The **Museo Ernesto Soto Avendaño** (admission US$0.50; ☽ 9am-1pm & 3-6pm Wed-Sun), displays the work of a sculptor who spent most of his life here; he created the Monumento a la Independencia in Humahuaca. The **Museo José Antonio Terry** (admission US$0.50, free Thu; ☽ 7am-7pm Tue-Sun) honors a Buenos Aires-born painter whose themes were largely rural and indigenous.

The **Museo Irureta de Bellas Artes** (cnr Bolívar & Belgrano; admission free; ☽ 10am-1pm & 3-6pm), half a block west of Plaza Prado, displays an appealing collection of contemporary Argentine art.

Rising above the sediments of the Río Grande valley, an isolated hill is the site of **El Pucará** (admission US$1; ☽ 9am-noon & 3-6pm), 1km south of central Tilcara. There are fantastic views of the valley from the top of the fort, which has been brilliantly reconstructed in parts. The admission fee includes entry to the Museo Arqueológico Dr Eduardo Casanova (see earlier).

Only a few kilometers south of Tilcara, the hillside cemetery of **Maimará** is a can't-miss photo opportunity.

SLEEPING & EATING

Albergue Malka (☎ 0388-495-5197; tilcara@hostels .org.ar; dm US$4) Excellent hilltop accommodations four blocks from Plaza Prado at the east end of San Martín (free pickup from the bus terminal). Discounts are available for HI cardholders. The owners can arrange trekking and vehicle tours of the Quebrada.

Posada Wiphala (☎ 0388-495-5015; Jujuy 549; r per person US$5) Friendly accommodations with good communal areas and shared bath.

Posada con Los Angeles (☎ 0388-4955153; Gorriti s/n; r per person US$4, with bath US$6) Near the bus terminal with lovely rooms, a large garden, and a kitchen.

Autocamping El Jardín (☎ 0388-495-5128; campsites per person US$1.50) At the west end of Belgrano near the river, this congenial place has hot showers and attractive vegetable and flower gardens. There's an adequate free site, with picnic tables but no toilets or potable water, near the YPF gas station along the highway.

El Cafecito (cnr Belgrano & Rivadavia) Opposite the post office, this café seems appropriate to a more urbane setting, but it's an agreeable spot for coffee and snacks.

Pacha Mama (Belgrano 590) A large eatery with a good bar, this place has a decent menu, although it's a bit expensive. Get here early if you like your *medialunas* (croissants) and forget the toasties – they're *tiny*.

La Peñalta A folkloric *peña* (folk club) with live music on the north side of Plaza Prado.

GETTING THERE & AROUND

Both northbound and southbound buses leave from the bus terminal on Exodo, three blocks west of Plaza Prado. Sample destinations include Jujuy (US$2, 1½ hours), Humahuaca (US$1, 40 minutes) and La Quiaca (US$3, 3¾ hours).

Bike rental can be arranged opposite Autocamping El Jardín for US$3 per day.

Humahuaca

Straddling the Río Grande, nearly 3000m above sea level, Humahuaca (population 6200) is a mostly Quechuan village of narrow cobbled streets lined with adobe houses. Carnaval celebrations are particularly boisterous here, and on February 2, the village holds a festival in honor of the town's patron saint – the Virgen de la Candelaria. The **tourist office** (cnr Tucumán & Jujuy) in the *cabildo* is rarely open, but Federico Briones, who runs Bar El Portillo (see Sleeping & Eating), is a good source of local information, can organize trekking in the Quebrada and also speaks English. The post office is across from the plaza. There's a **locutorio** (Jujuy 399), behind the Municipalidad.

SIGHTS

From the clock tower in the **cabildo**, a life-size figure of San Francisco Solano emerges daily at noon. Arrive early, since the clock is erratic and the figure appears only very briefly.

Humahuaca's patron saint resides in the colonial **Iglesia de la Candelaria**, which contains 18th-century oil paintings by Cuzco painter Marcos Sapaca. Overlooking the town, Tilcara sculptor Ernesto Soto Avendaño's **Monumento a la Independencia** is a textbook example of *indigenismo*, a distorted, romantic nationalist tendency in Latin American art and literature.

Museo Folklórico Regional (Buenos Aires 435/447; admission US$2.50; ☹ 8am-8pm) is run by local writer Sixto Vázquez Zuleta (who prefers his Quechua name 'Toqo'). It's open for formal tours only.

Ten kilometers north of Humahuaca by a dirt road on the east side of the bridge over the Río Grande, northwestern Argentina's most extensive pre-Columbian **ruins** cover 40 hectares at **Coctaca**. Many appear to be broad agricultural terraces on an alluvial fan, but there are also obvious outlines of clusters of buildings.

SLEEPING & EATING

Albergue Juvenil (Buenos Aires 435; dm US$4, r per person US$4) No longer an HI affiliate, although it likes to claim otherwise. The building is a bit shoddy, but it has a good feel.

Posada El Portillo (☎ 03887-421288; r per person US$4) Formerly El Sol, it's out of town across the bridge but well worth the 10-minute walk uphill. Eclectic, hand-built rooms give the effect of sleeping in a tree house and there's a big kitchen.

Residencial Humahuaca (☎ 03887-421141; Córdoba 401; s/d US$3/7, with bath US$7/10) Half a block from the bus terminal, it's clean, modern and friendly.

The municipal campsite across the bridge remains closed, but it's possible to park or pitch a tent there for free.

La Tejerina (Av Belgrano) This local favorite is next to the market. The food is much better than the bleak decor.

Mercado Municipal (Av Belgrano) Has a great selection of seasonal fruits.

Half a block east of the plaza Bar El Portillo serves pizza as well as regional dishes like *humitas* and tamales and vegetarian food.

GETTING THERE & AWAY

From the bus terminal at Belgrano and Entre Ríos, several carriers run southbound buses to Salta and Jujuy, and northbound buses to La Quiaca (US$3, three hours).

LA QUIACA

North of Humahuaca, graveled RN 9 climbs steeply to the Altiplano, where agriculture is precarious and peasants subsist on llamas, sheep, goats and the few cattle that can graze on the sparse ichu grass. At the end of the road are La Quiaca and its Bolivian twin, Villazón, across an ugly concrete bridge with immigration and customs. The border is open between 6am and 8pm daily. For more details on the crossing and a map, see Villazón & La Quiaca in the Bolivia chapter, p212.

La Quiaca has no tourist office, but the ACA station on RN 9 has maps. If Banco de la Nación will not cash traveler's checks, try Universo Tours in Villazón.

There's not much to do or see in La Quiaca, although the **Manca Fiesta** held in mid-October may be worth a look; *campesinos* (rural dwellers) pour in from the surrounding countryside to barter goods and dance.

Sleeping & Eating

Hotel Cristal (☎ 03885-422255; Sarmiento 543; s/d US$7/11) A bit run down, but probably the best budget choice in town.

Hotel Frontera (☎ 03885-422269; cnr Belgrano & Árabe Siria; r per person US$3) Unimpressive, but it will do in a pinch.

Ragu (cnr 9 de Julio & Árabe Siria) This bar serves simple meals (such as chicken, *milanesa* – a thin, breaded steak – and *lomito*) and is endowed with a terrific potbellied stove for those frosty nights. Check out the stylish cash register.

Parrillada La Cabaña (Av España 550) Serves regional specialties and is very popular with locals. The set lunch (US$1.50) is an absolute bargain.

Getting There & Away

From the **bus terminal** (cnr Belgrano & Av España), several carriers provide frequent connections to Jujuy (US$6, five hours), Salta and intermediate points, plus long-distance services.

AROUND LA QUIACA

At the village of **Yavi**, 16km east of La Quiaca, the 17th-century **Iglesia de San Francisco** is renowned for its altar, paintings, carved statues and gold leaf-covered pulpit. The nearby **Casa del Marqués Campero** belonged to a nobleman whose marriage to the holder of the original *encomienda* created a family that dominated the region's economy in the 18th century.

Friendly **Hostal de Yavi** (☎ 03887-490508; Güemes 222; d US$16 with breakfast) has clean facilities in a cozy building.

Shared taxis leave from La Quiaca's **Mercado Municipal** (Av Hipólito Yrigoyen) and charge US$1 per person.

ATLANTIC COAST

In summer, millions of *porteños* take a break from friends, families and co-workers, only to run into them on the beaches of Buenos Aires province. Mar del Plata is the chief tourist draw, with sunbathing, swimming and surfing among the popular activities for fun-seeking Argentines. Mixing with them here requires stamina for partying and patience to deal with lively vacationing crowds.

North of Mar del Plata, gentle dunes rise behind narrow beaches, while southwest toward Miramar, steep bluffs highlight a changing coastline. Beyond here, broad sandy shores delight bathers, fishing enthusiasts and windsurfers. To truly relax, get off the beaten track and find your own small, laid-back Atlantic resort; there are many to choose from.

Prices all along the coast are highest around mid-December to March, while in the off-season many hotels and restaurants close down, and most resorts look like ghost towns.

MAR DEL PLATA

It's worth going to Mar del Plata on a summer weekend if only so you'll never again be tempted to say 'gee this beach is crowded'. There's a couple of places where you could get a few strokes in without taking somebody's eye out, but mostly it's shoulder to shoulder sun-frazzled *porteños*. During the week, and especially in the nonsummer months, the crowds disperse, hotel prices drop and the place takes on a much more relaxed feel.

Founded in 1874, this most popular of Argentine beach destinations is 400km south of Buenos Aires. First a commercial and industrial center, then a resort for upper-class *porteño* families, Mardel (as it's often called) now caters mostly to middle-class vacationers.

Filled with skyscrapers built without much planning, this city nevertheless has charming older buildings and neighborhoods left over from its more elite days. The wide and attractive beach bustles with activity during summer, there are some interesting museums in town, and nightlife can be just as kick-ass as Buenos Aires when warm nights come around.

South of town, the salty port offers closeup viewing of a sea lion colony (you'll smell 'em before you see 'em) and of colorful fishing boats with their catches. Mardel's airport is 9km away (take bus No 542); taxis there cost US$4, more in summer. To get from the bus terminal to the center, take the No 511 bus, a taxi (US$2) or walk 20 minutes. You can rent bikes at **Bicicletería Madrid** (Yrigoyen 2249) on Plaza Mitre, for US$2/6 per hour/day.

Information

The **tourist office** (☎ 0223-495-1777; Blvd Marítimo 2240) is near Plaza Colón and the beach.

Most *cambios*, banks and ATMs are near the intersections of San Martín/Córdoba and Independencia/Luro. For Internet access there's **Calíz Computación** (Santa Fe 1914; US$0.80 per hr) and **Milenium** (Santa Fe 1779; US$0.80 per hr).

Sights

Now the Italian consulate, **Villa Normandy** (Viamonte 2216), dating from 1919, is one of few surviving examples of the French style that underwent a renovation craze in the

ARGENTINA

MAR DEL PLATA

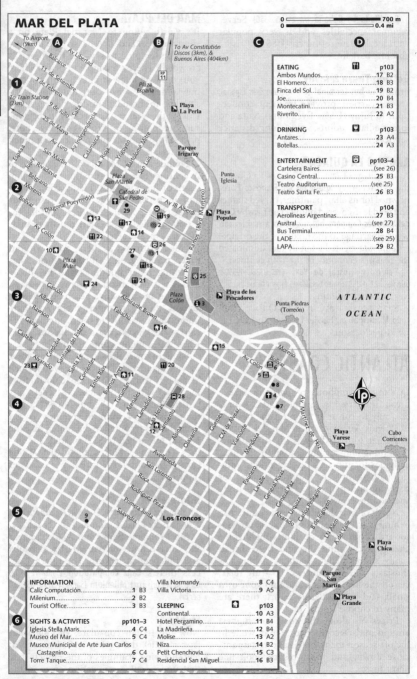

0 ————— 700 m
0 ————— 0.4 mi

EATING		p103
Ambos Mundos	17	B2
El Hornero	18	B3
Finca del Sol	19	B2
Joe	20	B4
Montecatini	21	B3
Riverito	22	A2

DRINKING		p103
Antares	23	A4
Botellas	24	A3

ENTERTAINMENT		pp103–4
Cartelera Baires	(see 26)	
Casino Central	25	B3
Teatro Auditorium	(see 25)	
Teatro Santa Fe	26	B3

TRANSPORT		p104
Aerolíneas Argentinas	27	B3
Austral	(see 27)	
Bus Terminal	28	B4
LADE	(see 25)	
LAPA	29	B2

INFORMATION		
Calíz Computación	1	B3
Milenium	2	B2
Tourist Office	3	B3

SIGHTS & ACTIVITIES		pp101–3
Iglesia Stella Maris	4	C4
Museo del Mar	5	C4
Museo Municipal de Arte Juan Carlos		
Castagnino	6	C4
Torre Tanque	7	C4

Villa Normandy	8	C4
Villa Victoria	9	A5

SLEEPING		p103
Continental	10	A3
Hotel Pergamino	11	B4
La Madrileña	12	B4
Molise	13	A2
Niza	14	B2
Petit Chenchovia	15	C3
Residencial San Miguel	16	B3

1950s. A block away near the top of the hill, **Iglesia Stella Maris** has an impressive marble altar; its virgin is the patron saint of local fishermen. On the summit, **Torre Tanque** (8am-3pm Mon-Fri) offers outstanding views.

Museo del Mar (adult/student US$1/0.50), opposite Villa Normandy, is probably the most extensive seashell museum you'll ever see. Based around central cafés on two floors are a small tide pool and an aquarium. Nicely presented shells are everywhere. It's a good place to rest and have tea; opening hours vary but are extensive. Just downhill a block is **Museo Municipal de Arte Juan Carlos Castagnino** (adult/student US$1/0.50; free Tue; Fri-Wed), an art museum in an interesting mansion. Hours vary widely throughout the year, but it's open mostly in the afternoons.

Away from center is **Villa Victoria** (Matheu 1851; admission US$1; 6-9pm summer, 1-7pm Mon-Fri, 1-8pm Sat & Sun other times), a beautiful prefab Norwegian house that's now a cultural center with classes and changing exhibits. Famous Argentine writer Victoria Ocampo, who founded the journal *Sur* in the 1920s, lived here and hosted literary salons.

Sleeping

Remember that prices are about 30% higher in January and February, when it's worth making reservations. Prices for the following hotels are per person, and all include private bath.

Residencial San Miguel (0223-495-7226; Tucumán 2383; s/d US$5/10 with breakfast) Situated above a good, cheap *salteña* (from Salta) restaurant, this quirky place has spacious rooms with dilapidated baths.

Continental (0223-495-2392; Yrigoyen 2281; s/d with breakfast US$4/8) Well-run and homey on Plaza Mitre.

La Madrileña (0223-451-2072; Sarmiento 2957; s/d US$4/8) Close to the bus terminal, modest and friendly.

Molise (0223-495-2762; Bartolomé Mitre 1989; s/d with breakfast US$5/10) Comfy and clean.

Petit Chenchovia (Sarmiento 2258; s/d with breakfast US$5/10) Good value but the rooms at the front can get noisy.

Niza (0223-495-1695; Santiago del Estero 1843; s/d with breakfast US$5/10) Central with a happy-family atmosphere.

Hotel Pergamino (0223-495-7927; Tucumán 2728; dm US$5) The hostel here isn't a great deal – cramped dorm rooms with shared bath in a rundown hotel.

Rates at Mardel's crowded campgrounds, mostly south of town, are around US$2 per person; the tourist office prints out information about their facilities.

Eating

Around the bus terminal you can find cheap *minutas* or sandwiches, and there are many *tenedor libres* in the center of town, especially on the pedestrian streets, for US$3 to US$4, not including mandatory drink purchase. It's very tempting to look at these buffets from outside the window, and they're a great deal if you're a big eater.

Riverito (cnr Bartolomé Mitre & Bolívar; pastas US$3, meats US$4) A homey atmosphere and decent prices for their pastas and meats.

Joe (cnr Lamadrid & Alberti; meals around US$4) A bit sparse on atmosphere, but serves great pizza and calzones.

Finca del Sol (San Martín 2463) A US$3 vegetarian *tenedor libre*.

Montecatini (cnr Av Colón & Corrientes) Popular and serves standard Argentine food.

Ambos Mundos (Rivadavia 2644) Good for *lomitos* (US$2), snacks and big steaks.

El Hornero (Moreno 2376) A home-style feel and US$0.60 empanadas.

Near the port is a cluster of seafood restaurants, but they aren't cheap.

Drinking

The area southwest of Plaza Mitre is particularly conducive to bar-hopping.

Botellas (Córdoba 2355; 9pm-late daily & Sat afternoons) Due to friendly staff and an excellent atmosphere, it can be difficult to leave this eclectically decorated pub.

Antares (Córdoba 3025; 8pm-late) The six homebrews on tap at Mar del Plata's only microbrewery include imperial stout, pale ale and barley wine – excellent cures for the Quilmes blues. Food is available.

The discos on Av Constitución heat up late on the weekends. Check out Sobremonte, Chocolate or Azúcar, all of which charge US$6 to US$8 admission. Bus No 551 runs from the center all night.

Entertainment

When Buenos Aires shuts down in January, many shows come here, and there are also several cinemas and a casino. **Cartelera Baires**

(Santa Fe 1844) sells discount tickets in summer; another *boletería* (ticket office) in the casino building is open all year. Check the monthly activity guide *Guía de Actividades* (available from the tourist office) for happenings.

Plaza Colón's 'dancing waters' fountain puts on strangely entertaining nightly summer shows. During off-season you'll see the jets spurting only on weekends.

Getting There & Away
AIR
Aerolíneas Argentinas (☎ 0223-496-0101; Moreno 2442) and **Austral** (☎ 0223-496-0101; Moreno 2442) scoot to Buenos Aires (US$65) often, as does **LAPA** (☎ 0223-495-9694; San Martín 2648). **LADE** (☎ 0223-493-8211), in the casino building, is cheapest to Buenos Aires (US$45) and also serves Patagonia.

BUS
From Mardel's busy **bus terminal** (☎ 0223-475-6076; Alberti 1602), many buses go to Buenos Aires (US$7 to US$9, 5½ hours). There are also services to Pinamar (US$3, 2¼ hours), Villa Gesell and Necochea (US$3, two hours), La Plata (US$9, five hours), and Bahía Blanca (US$7, seven hours).

TRAIN
The **train station** (☎ 0223-475-6076; cnr Luro & Italia) is about 20 blocks from the beach, but there's an **office** (☎ 0223-451-2501) at the bus terminal. In summer there are tourist trains seven times daily to Buenos Aires for US$12 in *turista* and US$16 in *primera* (those under 25 get a discount in the off-season). The trip takes about 5½ hours.

VILLA GESELL
Smaller than Pinamar and more relaxed than Mar del Plata, this laid-back dune community harbors charming summer cottages (and grander retreats) along its windy, sandy back roads. The lively main street, Avenida 3, is three blocks from the beach and sees most of the action; a section of it becomes a pedestrian mall in summer, when young vacationing *porteños* stream in to party the warm nights away.

Information
There's a central **tourist office** (☼ Av 3 near Paseo 108; ☼ summer only); another **tourist office** (☎ 02255-458596; Av Buenos Aires), about a 20-

minute walk northwest of town, is open all year. Banks and their ATMs run along Av 3. Get your Internet fix at **Gesell.net** (Paseo 105 No 289). The main **bus terminal** (cnr Av 3 & Paseo 140) is on the south side of town; bus No 504 will get you to the center. Short- and medium-distance buses stop at the mini terminal, which is at Blvd Gesell (known as 'Boulevard') and Paseo 100 (at Av Buenos Aires). It's about a 20-minute walk from the center.

Sights
Gesell's long **beach** and boardwalk draw swimmers, sunbathers and horse riders. There's year-round **fishing** from the pier, and surfers can rent gear from **Windy** (Paseo 104) on the beachfront. Likewise, cyclists can rent their cruisers at **Casa Macca** (cnr Av Buenos Aires & Paseo 204). In January and February, a national **choir competition** takes place at the local amphitheater. Also, check out the nightly summer **crafts fair** on Av 3 at Paseo 112.

Sleeping
The most affordable *hospedajes* are north of Av 3. It's important to book ahead in summer, especially in the second half of January, when prices rise even more. Summer rates are listed here.

Parada 6 (☎ 02255-466256; Av 6, near Paseo 105; r per person US$5) Small, friendly and among the cheapest. Prices include breakfast. It's family-run, basic and clean.

Viya (☎ 02255-462757; Av 5 btwn Paseos 105 & 106; r per person US$6) Another friendly place with a pretty garden.

Las Lajas (☎ 02255-460401; r per person US$6) Across from, Viya, this place has a leafy area in back. Price includes breakfast.

Gesell's dozen campgrounds charge US$5 to US$8 per person. Most close at the end of March, but three clustered at the south end of town on Av 3 are open all year. These are **Casablanca** (☎ 02255-470771), **Mar Dorado** (☎ 02255-470963) and **Monte Bubi** (☎ 02255-470732).

Eating
Cantina Arturito (Av 3 No 2580 btwn Paseos 126 & 127; dishes US$2-5). This owner-operated cantina serves large portions of exquisite risotto and homemade pasta, as well as shellfish and home-cured ham.

Nearby Torino Bar has attractive outdoor seating to complement its sandwiches, salads, coffees and beers.

El Estribo (cnr Av 3 & Paseo 109) The hot favorite for the *parrillada* in town. A *bife de chorizo* will set you back US$3 and the *parrillada* for two (with enough meat for three) costs US$7.

La Jirafa Azul (Av 3 near Paseo 102; meals US$3-4) Serves a good, cheap standard menu.

Jalisco (cnr Av 4 & Paseo 104) Offers pizza and tacos in *trés* hip surrounds. More hipness is available at the beachside restaurants, but you'll need a thicker wallet.

Entertainment

Anfiteatro del Pinar (☎ 02255-467123; cnr Av 10 & Paseo 102) Performances in January, February and Semana Santa. Gesell's Encuentros Corales take place annually in this lovely amphitheater.

Cine Teatro Atlas (☎ 02255-462969; Paseo 108 btwn Avs 3 & 4) Such rock-and-roll greats as Charly García and Los Pericos have played this small theater which doubles as a cinema during off-season months. Call here or the tourist office for information.

Shopping

Feria Artesanal (Regional y Artística; Av 3 btwn Paseos 112 & 113) This excellent arts and crafts fair takes place every evening from mid-December through mid-March. The rest of the year it's a weekend-only event.

Getting There & Away

Aerolíneas Argentinas (☎ 02255-458331; cnr Av Buenos Aires & Av 10) has daily summer flights to Buenos Aires (US$72).

Sample bus destinations include Buenos Aires (US$11, six hours), Mar del Plata (US$8, two hours) and Pinamar (US$2, 40 minutes).

PINAMAR

Bathed by a tropical current from Brazil, Pinamar's waters are pleasantly warm, and its clean beaches slope gradually into a sea abundant with fish. Its extensive forests, sandy streets, luxury homes and hotels, chic shops and posh restaurants have made Pinamar the 'in' place for wealthy Argentine families.

Many places are only open on weekends and in summer, but at other times you can stroll peacefully in bordering pine forests and along the wide, attractive **beach** without being trampled by holidaymakers.

Pinamar acquired notoriety in early 1997 with the murder of photojournalist José Luis Cabezas, which was linked to bodyguards of shady businessman Alberto Yabrán, who committed suicide barely a year later.

Av Libertador, roughly paralleling the beach, and perpendicular Av Bunge are the main drags; streets on each side of Bunge form large fans, making orientation tricky. The **tourist office** (☎ 02254-491680; Bunge 654) has a good map with useful descriptions of Pinamar and surrounding resorts. The **bus terminal** (Shaw & Del Pejerrey) is 12 blocks from the beach and seven from the center (inland budget accommodation is not far from the bus terminal). The train station is a couple of kilometers north of town, near Av Bunge.

Sleeping & Eating

The following rates listed are for summer.

Albergue Bruno Valente (☎ 02254-482908; cnr Mitre & Nuestras Malvinas, Ostende; HI members with/ without breakfast $5/4, nonmembers with breakfast US$6) About eight blocks south of Pinamar's center, this large youth hostel gets packed in summer and then left cold and empty in winter. The kitchen is huge and the bathrooms are institutional. The building itself is a decaying historic hotel that was built in 1926.

Other affordable accommodations, all acceptable, are mostly inland.

Hospedaje Las Acacias (☎ 02254-485175; Del Cangrejo 1358; d around US$13) Cheerful, airy rooms opening onto a small grassy area.

Hospedaje Valle Fértil (☎ 02254-484799; Del Cangrejo 1110; d around US$13) A small, slightly disheveled place on a woodsy street.

Modern **Hotel La Gaviota** (☎ 02254-482079; Del Cangrejo 1332; d around US$13) and friendly **Hotel Rose Marie** (☎ 02254-482522; Las Medusas 1381; d around US$13) are other reasonable choices.

Several campgrounds, charging about US$5 for two, line the coast between Ostende and Pinamar.

Most restaurants are on Bunge and along the beach. Your best bet is to stroll and choose.

Con Estilo Criollo (cnr Bunge & Marco Polo) Serves up some good grilled meats.

Paxapoga (cnr Bunge & Libertador) *Parrillada*, pizza and…wait for it…pasta!

Cantina Tulumei (☎ 02254-488696; Bunge 64) Reasonably priced, quality seafood, though garlic shrimp and octopus plates get pricey.

El Vivero (Bunge near Marco Polo) Serves high-quality vegetarian food.

Getting There & Away

Aerolíneas Argentinas (☎ 02254-483663) is across from the tourist office.

Bus schedules resemble those from Villa Gesell. Trains run in summer to Buenos Aires. Purchase tickets at the bus terminal.

NECOCHEA

The most attractive feature of this popular, family-oriented beach resort is **Parque Miguel Lillo**, a huge green space along the beach whose dense pine woods are good for cycling. Rent bikes at **Stop Bicicletas** (Av 79 & Calle 10). The Río Quequén, rich in trout and mackerel, allows for adventurous **canoeing**. At the village of **Quequén** at the river's mouth, several stranded shipwrecks offer good opportunities for exploration and **photography** below sculpted cliffs. Necochea is dead in winter, however.

The **tourist office** (☎ 02262-430158; cnr Av 2 & Calle 79) is on the beach. The **bus terminal** (☎ 02262-422470; cnr Av 58 & Ruta 86) is 4km from the beach. Bus No 502 winds its way to the coast via the town center (itself 2km from the beach).

Sleeping & Eating

The following hotels are near the coast. Many places close in the off-season.

Hotel Marino (☎ 02262-422140; Av 79 at Calle 4; s/d US$3.50/7) The star of the budget digs. Its got old-world charm, original fixtures and furniture *and* is the cheapest joint in town.

Hospedaje Bayo (☎ 02262-423334; Calle 87 No 338; s/d US$4/8) Basic but good value.

Hostal del Rey (☎ 02262-425170; Calle 81 No 335; s/d with breakfast US$4.50/9) A good deal.

Camping Americano (☎ 02262-435832; cnr Av 2 & Calle 101; campsites per person US$3) In Parque Lillo.

Pizzería Tempo (Calle 83 No 310) Has a menu that goes far beyond pizzas and stays cheap. *Milanesas* and the like average US$2, and a US$4 pizza serves three.

La Rueda (Calle 4 No 4144; 4 courses US$3) Serves excellent, well-priced *parrillada*, seafood and Italian dishes.

Getting There & Away

Bus destinations include Mar del Plata (US$3, two hours), Bahía Blanca (US$10, 5½ hours) and Buenos Aires (US$15, seven hours).

Ferrocarril Roca (☎ 02262-450028), in nearby Quequén, has three trains weekly to Buenos Aires.

BAHÍA BLANCA

While some may knock Bahía Blanca for seeming uninteresting, this coastal gateway to Patagonia (home sweet home to 300,000) has many nicely detailed older buildings spaced between modern ones; it's a good place for budding architects to wander around on the clean, tree-lined streets. South America's largest naval base is nearby, and the city is also a key port for grain and produce (you'll see fruit vendors on the outskirts of town).

The **tourist office** (☎ 0291-459-4007; Alsina 45; ☖ 8am-1pm Mon-Fri, 10am-1pm Sat) is almost overwhelmingly helpful. **Pullman Cambio** (San Martín 171) changes traveler's checks. The post office is at Moreno 34.

The most worthwhile sight is **Museo del Puerto** (Guillermo Torres 4180; Puerto Ingeniero White; ☖ 8am-11am Mon-Fri), a 'community museum' that's a whimsical tribute to the immigrant population of Bahía Blanca. From downtown, bus Nos 500 and 501 drop passengers almost at the front door. On weekends there's a **feria artesanal** (crafts fair) on Plaza Rivadavia.

Sleeping & Eating

Hotel Victoria (☎ 0291-452-0522; General Paz 84; r per person US$6, with bath & TV US$8) Leads the budget pack with its beautiful rooms in a nicely maintained older mansion with courtyard.

Hospedaje Chiclana (☎ 0291-450-1088; Chiclana 277; r per person US$7, s/d with bath US$10/15) Central, cheap, and worn – it's hard to beat with its tall-ceilinged older rooms lining a spacious courtyard, and there's kitchen access.

On Cerri, across from the train station, are no-frills **Residencial Roma** (☎ 0291-453-8500; r per person US$7, with bath US$3), and **Hotel Molinari** (☎ 0291-451-0413; s/d with bath US$6/8) which is run by an old guy who needs a big hug (go on, give him one). Rooms are dingy but passable.

The campground at **Balneario Maldonado** (☎ 0291-452-9511; campsites per person US$2) is 4km southwest of downtown. Bus No 514 gets you there.

Gambrinus (Arribeños 164) A lively atmosphere, tasteful decor and friendly service come with the sometimes imaginative food and beer.

El Molino (Chiclana 83) An excellent US$3 *tenedor libre* which includes a *parrillada* platter.

Pelicáno (Alsina 226) Good prices and sidewalk tables.

Other *parrillas* include **Víctor** (Chiclana 83), which also serves seafood, and **La Mark** (Chiclana 429).

Tía supermarket is on Brown between Colón and O'Higgins.

Getting There & Around
The airport is 15km east of town. **Austral** (☎ 0291-456-0561; San Martín 298) hops to Buenos Aires (US$75). **LADE** (☎ 0291-452-1063; Darregueira 21) flies cheaply but slowly to Patagonian destinations.

The bus terminal is about 2km east of Plaza Rivadavia; there are many local buses into town (fare is US$0.30; buy magnetic cards from kiosks). Destinations include Sierra de la Ventana (US$2, two hours), Buenos Aires (US$12, 10 hours), Santa Rosa (US$8, 4½ hours), Mar del Plata (US$8, seven hours), Neuquén (US$10, seven hours) and Río Gallegos (US$34, 30 hours).

The **train station** (☎ 0291-452-9196; Av Cerri 750) has nightly service to Buenos Aires. Cheapest fares are US$4.50/5.50 in *turista/ primera* class.

SIERRA DE LA VENTANA
Sierra de la Ventana, the mountain range in Parque Provincial Ernesto Tornquist, attracts hikers and climbers to its jagged peaks, which rise over 1300m. The nearby charming and leafy little namesake village, 125km north of Bahía Blanca, is a great place to come and relax, explore and swim in the river or in nearby recreational pools.

For a nice walk, go to the end of Calle Tornquist and cross the small dam (which makes a local **swimming hole**). On the other side you'll see **Cerro del Amor** – hike to the top for good views of town and pampas.

Near the train station is the **tourist office** (☎ 0291-491-5303; Roca 15).

Sleeping & Eating
Hospedaje La Perlita (☎ 0291-491-5020; Morón near Islas Malvinas; r with/without bath per person US$7/4) Has

a peaceful, relaxing garden in back. There's no sign; look for the awning behind overgrown trees.

Residencial Sosba (☎ 0291-491-5071; Punta Alta 276; r per person US$4) Across the river in Villa Arcadia, the Sosba offers good accommodations with bath.

Ymcapolis (☎ 0291-491-5004; r per person with breakfast US$3, full board US$10) At the east end of Coronel Suárez in a stylish older building.

There are several free campsites along the river, with bathroom facilities nearby at the pleasant and grassy municipal swimming pool (US$1). For organized campgrounds, try **Camping El Paraíso** (☎ 0291-491-5299; Diego Meyer), which has good facilities; opposite is **Camping Yapay** (☎ 156-44-9326). Both charge US$2 per person.

Sher, on Güemes, and El Establo, on San Martín between Islas Malvinas and Roca, both have shady sidewalk tables and good pizza, pasta and *parrillada* (the three Ps of Argentine food).

Getting There & Away
From in front of the *locutorio* on San Martín near Islas Malvinas, La Estrella has nightly buses to Buenos Aires (US$12, eight hours), plus an 8am service to La Plata (US$12). Expreso Cabildo goes to Bahía Blanca twice daily (US$2, two hours).

The **train station** (Av Roca) is near the tourist office. There's nightly train service to Buenos Aires on Tuesday, Thursday and Sunday for US$5/6 in *turista/primera* class.

AROUND SIERRA DE LA VENTANA
Popular for ranger-guided walks and independent hiking, 6700-hectare **Parque Provincial Ernesto Tornquist** (entry US$1) west of the village, is the starting point for the 1136m summit of **Cerro de la Ventana**. It's about two hours' routine hiking for anyone except the wheezing *porteño* tobacco addicts who struggle to the crest of what is probably the country's most climbed peak. Leave early: You can't climb after 11am in winter, noon in summer.

Friendly Campamento Base has shady campsites, clean baths and excellent hot showers for US$2 per person.

Buses traveling between Bahía Blanca and Sierra de la Ventana can drop you at the entrance, and there are also buses directly to the park from the village.

CENTRAL ARGENTINA

Argentina's agricultural heartland lies between the colorful deserts of historic northwest Argentina, the steamy forests and savannas of the northeast, and the windy expanses of Patagonia. This central area consists of arid and mountainous Mendoza, San Juan and San Luis provinces (which comprise the wine-producing Cuyo region) and rich, level La Pampa province (which is part of the verdant Pampas region).

Cuyo retains a strong characteristic individuality and has a substantial *mestizo* population that distinguishes it from the Pampas. It's also a key region for grape growing and is responsible for producing the vast majority of Argentina's very drinkable wines. Despite the rain-shadow effect of Aconcagua (6960m) and other formidable peaks, enough snow accumulates to sustain the rivers that irrigate these extensive vineyards. And with its varied terrain and climate, Cuyo offers outdoor activities all year round; you can go climbing, trekking, riding, white-water rafting, fishing and skiing. Many travelers visit Mendoza, but the other provinces, especially San Juan, provide off-the-beaten-track adventures.

These are the stomping grounds for ancient as well as present-day *gauchos*. There's plenty of pampas action in Central Argentina – huge flat grassy expanses of it. No sign of the cows, though – perhaps they're all off being eaten.

HISTORY

In the 16th century, Spaniards crossed from the Pacific over Uspallata Pass toward Mendoza to manage *encomiendas* among the indigenous Huarpe. Though politically and economically tied to the northern viceregal capital in Lima, Cuyo's isolation behind the barrier of the Andes fostered a strong independence and political initiative (this fortitude later provided the basis for present-day Cuyo's defined regional identity).

Irrigated vineyards became important during later colonial periods, but Cuyo's continued isolation limited the region's prosperity. It wasn't until the arrival of the railway in 1884 that prosperity arrived; improved irrigation systems also allowed for expansion of grape and olive cultivation, plus alfalfa for livestock. Vineyard cultivation grew from 6400 hectares in 1890 to 240,000 in the 1970s, and many vineyards remain relatively small, owner-operated enterprises to this day.

SAN LUIS

Capital of its province, San Luis (population 135,000) is 260km east of Mendoza. Its narrow, shady streets and leafy plazas make it a good place to walk around – which is lucky, 'cause there ain't much else to do. The commercial center is along the parallel streets of San Martín and Rivadavia, between Plaza Pringles on the north and Plaza Independencia to the south. You won't see many tourist buses here – most Argentine travelers come to visit outlying areas such as Merlo and Sierra de las Quijadas.

The **tourist office** (☎ 02652-423957) is across from the post office on Av Illia just off Plaza Pringles. It has an almost overwhelming amount of information on San Luis' surrounding areas. Several banks, mostly around Plaza Pringles, have ATMs. Cyber Colón, in the mall at Colón and Lavalle, has Internet access.

Sights

The 1930s **Iglesia de Santo Domingo**, on Plaza Independencia, replaced a 17th-century predecessor but kept its Moorish style; note the *algarrobo* doors on remaining parts of the old church next door. Alongside, on Av 25 de Mayo, the **Mercado Artesanal** (🕙 8am-1pm Mon-Fri, 9am-noon Sat) sells fine handmade wool rugs, as well as ceramics, onyx carvings and weavings. Check out the New York City-block-themed **casino** on Pederna and Rivadavia, if only for its incongruity here in San Luis.

Sleeping & Eating

Hotel Buenos Aires (☎ 02652-424062; Buenos Aires 834; s/d with bath US$5/10) The most central budget option. Good value, clean and friendly. There's a newer annex across the street.

Hotel Los Andes (☎ 02652-422033; Ejército de los Andes 1180; d US$7) A few blocks from the terminal, this is a good if somewhat uninspiring choice.

La Gran Avenida (Illia 168) Offers many pizza choices with good service and atmosphere.

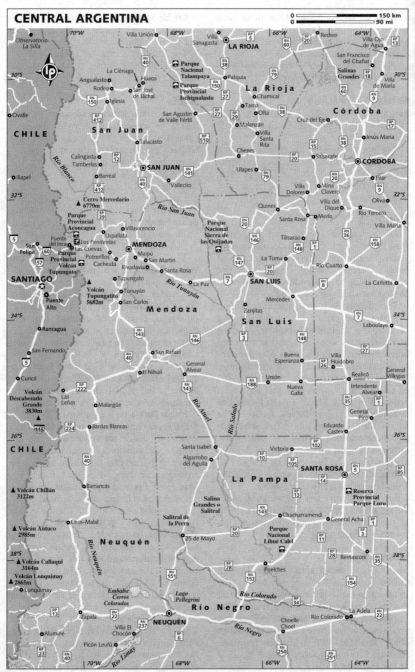

CENTRAL ARGENTINA

Sofía (cnr Colón & Bolívar) This place was closed at the time of research, but is worth a look in for Spanish cuisine seafood and evening entertainment.

There's a trendy café with many drink selections in the mall at Colón and Lavalle.

Getting There & Away

Austral (☎ 02652-423407; Colón 733) and **LAPA** (☎ 02652-431753; Pederna 863) fly daily to Buenos Aires.

The bus terminal is on España between San Martín and Rivadavia. Buses go to Mendoza (US$7, 3½ hours), San Juan (US$10, four hours), Rosario (US$18, 10 hours) and Buenos Aires (US$20, 12 hours).

MENDOZA

Those *mendocinos* (people from Mendoza) sure know how to live – wide, shady sidewalks, beautiful plazas, good restaurants and bars, a thriving cultural scene – if you've been traveling hard, Mendoza's a great place to stop and chill out for a while.

Founded in 1561, at an altitude of 760m, the provincial capital is a university city of almost a million inhabitants. Modern quake-resistant construction has replaced fallen historic buildings, but Mendoza retains a very pleasant and cool atmosphere.

The Mendoza region produces 70% of the country's wine, and this bounty is reflected in early March's **Fiesta Nacional de la Vendimia**, or wine harvest festival. The surrounding countryside offers **wine tasting**, **mountaineering**, **cycling** and **white-water rafting**, and many different tours of the area are available. The bus terminal is about 15 minutes walk from the center – catch the Villa Nueva trolley (which looks more like a bus) if you don't feel like walking. Mendoza's **airport** (☎ 0261-448-7128) is 6km north of the city. Bus No 60 (Aeropuerto) goes from Calle Salta straight there.

Information

The helpful **tourist kiosk** (☎ 0261-420-1333; Garibaldi near Av San Martín; ☼ 9am-9pm) is the most convenient information source and the staff speaks English. The **tourist office** (☎ 0261-420-2800; Av San Martín 1143; ☼ 8am-9pm Mon-Fri) is nearby. There's also an **information office** (☎ 0261-431-3001) in the bus terminal. Another kiosk with more limited hours is at Las Heras and Mitre.

Cambio Santiago (Av San Martín 1199) charges 2% for traveler's checks. Banks and ATMs are commonplace.

For Internet access, try **La red** (cnr LN Alem & San Juan; US$1 per hr). More central is **Internet Mendoza** (Sarmiento 25; US$1.50 per hr).

Sights

The spacious **Museo Fundacional** (admission US$1.50; ☼ 8am-8pm Tue-Sat, 2-8pm Sun, afternoon siesta break in summer), in the park at Alberdi and Videla Castillo, protects the foundations of the original *cabildo*, destroyed by an earthquake in 1861. There are also exhibits of items found at the site and scale models of old and new Mendoza, all nicely presented. Across the street, the scanty rubble of **Ruinas de San Francisco** (1638) were part of a Jesuit-built church/school later taken over by Franciscans.

The Virgen de Cuyo in the **Iglesia, Convento y Basílica de San Francisco** (Necochea 201) was the patron of San Martín's Army of the Andes. Unique **Museo Popular Callejero**, along the sidewalk at Las Heras and 25 de Mayo, consists of encased dioramas depicting the history of one of Mendoza's major avenues. The sun determines viewing hours, and it's free.

Funky, sparsely labeled **Museo Sanmartiniano** (Av San Martín 1843; admission US$1; ☼ 9:30am-1pm Mon-Fri) is full of historical costumes, guns, paintings and furniture; ring the bell.

Parque San Martín is a forested 420-hectare green space containing **Cerro de la Gloria** (nice views), a hillside **zoo** (pleasant, leafy, serpentine paths for people; many small cages for animals), several museums and a lake, among other things. Bus No 110 gets you here from Plaza Independencia, or better yet rent a bicycle and cruise around.

For a good orientation to Mendoza, take the municipality's **guided bus tour** (tickets US$2; ☼ 10am-8pm Jan 1-early Apr). At the corner of Garibaldi and San Martín, the Bus Turístico will pick you up and wind its way through the city to the summit of Cerro de la Gloria. Good for 24 hours, the ticket allows you to board and reboard at any of several fixed stops throughout the city.

Plaza Independencia has a **crafts fair** Thursday through Sunday night, while Plaza Pellegrini holds its own weekend **antique market** with music and dancing. Also check out the beautiful tile work in Plaza España.

WINERIES

Argentina's wines are getting better and better (especially in the higher-quality range) and consequently attracting international attention. Wine tasting is a popular activity at the many wineries in the area. Call first to confirm opening hours.

About 17km southeast of downtown in Maipú, is traditional **La Colina de Oro** (☎ 0261-497-6777; Ozamis 1040; ☽ 9am-6:30pm Mon-Sat, 11am-2pm Sun). Visit the museum next door. Bus Nos 160 and 170 go there from downtown Mendoza.

Also in Maipú is **La Rural** (☎ 0261-497-2013; Montecaseros; ☽ 9am-1pm & 2-5pm Mon-Sat, 10am-1pm Sun). Its museum displays wine-making tools used by 19th-century pioneers, as well as colonial religious sculptures from the Cuyo region. Bus Nos 170 and 173 leave from Rioja between Garibaldi and Catamarca.

Cyclists can consider biking a 40km circuit that would cover these wineries and more. Visit tourist information in Mendoza for an area map.

Sleeping

Note that prices, especially at the more expensive hotels, can rise from January to March and most notably during the wine festival in early March. At this time accommodations are difficult to find.

CAMPING

Bus 110 leaves from LN Alem just east of Av San Martín and from Av Sarmiento to El Challao, a neighborhood 6km northwest of town with several camping areas, including woodsy **Parque Suizo** (☎ 0261-444-1991; campsites for 2 US$4). It has hot showers, laundry facilities and a grocery.

HOSPEDAJES & HOTELS

Imperial Hotel (☎ 0261-423-4671; Av Las Heras 88; r per person with breakfast US$6) A no-frills, good-value place with clean, carpeted rooms for one to eight people.

Hotel Galicia (☎ 0261-420-2619; San Juan 881; s US$3.50, s/d with bath US$10/12) Pretty gloomy but friendly. Some of the singles are tiny – check out a few.

Hospedaje Garibaldi (☎ 0261-426-5618; Garibaldi 368; s/d with bath US$15/24) Stylish if cramped.

Hotel Petit (☎ 0261-423-2099; Perú 1459; s/d with bath US$9/13) Modern, clean and friendly. Most rooms have balconies, TV and phone.

Hotel Rincón Vasco (☎ 0261-423-3033; Av Las Heras 590; s/d US$9/15) A comfortable option, offering TV, private bath and temperature control. Rooms with balconies have street noise.

HOSTELS

Hostel Campo Base (☎ 0261-429-0707; Av Mitre 946; r per person with/without HI card US$3/4) Centrally located with good common spaces, it attracts many climbers, as they organize climbing tours. It has your basic services, but can get noisy.

Mendoza International Hostel (☎ 0261-424-0018; España 343; r per person with/without HI card US$3/4) A bit further out, but it's nice and clean and offers meals, email and organized tours.

Savigliano Hostel (☎ 0261-423-7746; Pedro Palacios 944; r per person US$3.50) Across from the bus terminal (take the store-lined pedestrian underpass). It's very pleasant and popular. There are good homey common areas with kitchen access. Call ahead for the popular private rooms.

Eating

Sidewalk restaurants on pedestrian Av Sarmiento are fine places to people-watch. The restaurants along Las Heras and Av San Martín offer good value set meals – see signboards for details.

Mercado Central (cnr Av Las Heras & Patricias Mendocinas) The best budget choice; its various stalls offer pizza, empanadas and sandwiches.

Rincón de La Boca (Av Las Heras 485) This is the place for more pizza.

Autentico Patio de Comidas (Av Las Heras 420; meal US$2-3) Set back from the road in a leafy patio. Prices are good and they have live tango and folk music Thursday to Saturday nights.

El Mesón Español (Montevideo 244) Typical Spanish food, moderately priced.

Onda Libre (Av Las Heras 446; lunch US$2) A huge *tenedor libre* lunch including *parrillada*.

Línea Verde (San Lorenzo 550; ☽ lunch only) A good vegetarian option, as is **Naturata** (☽ lunch only), in Plaza Pellegrini, where nicely shaded sidewalk tables tempt you to try the healthy US$3 *tenedor libre*.

The Green Apple (Av Colón 458) Gets raves from lots of travelers (and rightly so) for its US$3 home-cookin' style vegetarian *tenedor libre*. Don't miss the lemon meringue pie.

MENDOZA

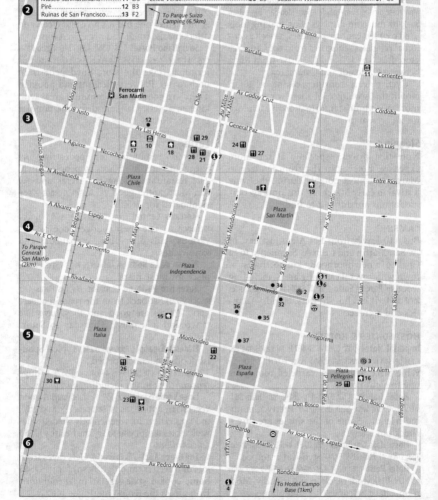

INFORMATION
Cambio Santiago...................1 D4
City Hall............................(see 4)
Internet Mendoza.................2 C5
La Red..............................3 D5
Municipal Tourist Office........4 C6
Municipal Tourist Office........5 C5
Provincial Tourist Office........6 C5
Tourist Kiosk......................7 B3

SIGHTS & ACTIVITIES   pp110–11
Iglesia, Convento y Basílica de San
Francisco.........................8 C4
Museo Fundacional...............9 F2
Museo Popular Callejero.......10 B3
Museo Sanmartiniano..........11 D3
Piré..................................12 B3
Ruinas de San Francisco......13 F2

SLEEPING   p111
Hospedaje Garibaldi............14 E5
Hostel Campo Base..............15 B5
Hotel Galicia......................16 D5
Hotel Petit.........................17 B3
Hotel Rincón Vasco..............18 B3
Imperial Hotel....................19 C4
Savigliano Hostel................20 E5

EATING   pp111–13
Autentico Patio de Comidas...21 B3
El Mesón Español................22 B5
Green Apple.......................23 B6
La Marchigiana...................24 C3
La Naturata.......................25 D5
Línea Verde.......................26 B5

Mercado Central...................27 C3
Onda Libre.........................28 B3
Rincón de La Boca...............29 B3

DRINKING   p113
Pop Bar.............................30 A5
Tenorio.............................31 B6

TRANSPORT   pp113–14
Aerolineas Argentinas...........32 C5
Austral.............................(see 32)
Bus Terminal.......................33 E6
Dinar Lineas Aéreas.............34 C5
Lan Chile...........................35 C5
LAPA.................................36 C5
Southern Winds..................37 C5

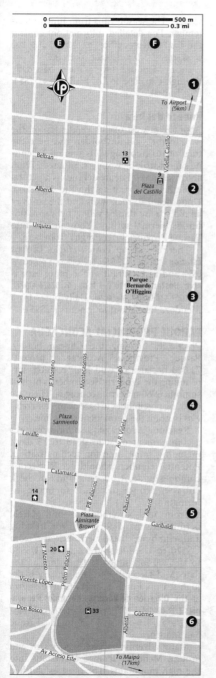

La Marchigiana (Patricias Mendocinas 1550; entrées US$4-11) Mendoza's finest Italian restaurant. It's relatively expensive, but worth the splurge.

Drinking

Av Colón is the place to go wandering in search of a watering hole. Here are a couple of suggestions to get you started.

Pop Bar (Av Colón 740) Of several popular bars along Av Colón, this spot, with its neo-minimalist pop-art bent, is the most hopping of the bunch.

Tenorio (Av Colón 462 ☽ 8am-late Mon-Sat, 6pm-late Sun). This is a relaxed place that's good for chatting or just hanging out; it's also a good choice to enjoy reading a book in the afternoon.

Getting There & Away

AIR

Aerolíneas Argentinas (☎ 0261-420-4185; Sarmiento 82), **Austral** (☎ 0261-420-4185; Sarmiento 82), **LAPA** (☎ 0261-423-1000; España 1012) and **Dinar Líneas Aéreas** (☎ 0261-420-4520; Sarmiento 119) all have daily flights to Buenos Aires for US$131.

Southern Winds (☎ 0261-429-3200; España 943) touches down in Córdoba (US$70), as well as other destinations in the northwest and Patagonia.

LanChile (☎ 0261-425-7900; Rivadavia 135) hops twice daily to Santiago.

BUS

The **bus terminal** (☎ 0261-431-1299) is about 10 blocks east of the town center. There are long-distance services to almost every province. The frequency to some of the following destinations, such as Las Leñas, Malargüe and Aconcagua, depends on the season.

Destination	Duration in Hours	Cost
Aconcagua	3½	US$4
Buenos Aires	14	US$22
Córdoba	10	US$12
Las Leñas	7	US$9
Los Penitentes	4	US$4
Malargüe	6	US$8
Neuquén	12	US$13
San Juan	2	US$3
San Luis	3¼	US$7
San Rafael	3¼	US$12
Tucumán	14	US$26
Uspallata	2	US$3
Valparaíso	8	US$8

Getting Around

Mendoza buses take magnetic fare cards, sold at kiosks in multiple values of the US$0.60 fare. Trolleys cost US$0.60 in coins.

For bike rentals, try **Piré** (Av Las Heras 615; per day US$5), or the **Hotel Petit** (☎ 0261-423-2099; Perú 1459; per day US$4). **Hostel Campo Base** (☎ 0261-429-0707; Av Mitre 946) also rents bikes.

USPALLATA

In an exceptionally beautiful valley surrounded by polychrome mountains, 105km west of Mendoza at an altitude of 1751m, this crossroads village along RN 7 is a good base for exploring the surrounding area, which served as a location for the Brad Pitt epic Seven Years in Tibet.

One kilometer north of the highway junction toward Villavicencio, a signed side road leads to ruins and a museum at the **Bóvedas Históricas Uspallata**, a metallurgical site since pre-Columbian times. About four kilometers north of Uspallata, in a volcanic outcrop near a small monument to San Ceferino Namuncurá, is a faded but still visible set of **petroglyphs**.

Sleeping & Eating

Residencial Viena (☎ 02624-420046; Las Heras 240; r per person with breakfast US$7) East of the highway junction, it's a bargain for its tidy rooms with private bath and cable TV.

Camping Municipal (campsites US$2; P ⊠ ✕) Uspallata's poplar-shaded campground is 500m north of the Villavicencio junction.

For food, try **Parrilla San Cayetano** and the Brad Pitt-themed **Café Tibet**.

Getting There & Away

Expreso Uspallata runs a few buses daily between Mendoza (US$3, two hours) and Uspallata. Santiago-bound buses will carry passengers to and across the border, but are often full; in winter, the pass can close to all traffic for weeks at a time.

AROUND USPALLATA
Los Penitentes

Both the terrain and snow cover can be excellent for downhill and Nordic skiing at Los Penitentes, two hours southwest of Uspallata at an altitude of 2580m. Lifts and accommodations are very modern; the maximum vertical drop on its 21 runs exceeds 700m. A day ski pass costs around US$23. The season runs from June to September. For detailed information, contact the **Los Penitentes office** (☎ 0262-442-0110; Paso de los Andes 1615, Departamento C, Godoy Cruz).

From Mendoza, several buses pass daily through Uspallata to Los Penitentes (US$4, four hours).

Puente del Inca

About 8km west of Los Penitentes, on the way to the Chilean border and near the turn-off to Aconcagua, is one of Argentina's most striking wonders. Situated 2720m above sea level, Puente del Inca is a natural stone bridge spanning the Río Mendoza. Underneath it, rock walls and the ruins of an old spa are stained yellow by warm, sulfurous thermal springs. You can hike into Parque Provincial Aconcagua from here.

There's a cheap hostel/refugio, **La Vieja Estacion** (☎ 0261-429-0707 in Mendoza; r per person US$4) and a restaurant at the more expensive **Hostería Puente del Inca** (☎ 02624-420222; ☎ 0261-438-0480 in Mendoza). Daily buses from Mendoza take about four hours (US$5).

PARQUE PROVINCIAL ACONCAGUA

Practically hugging the Chilean border, Parque Provincial Aconcagua protects 71,000 hectares of wild high country surrounding the Western Hemisphere's highest summit, 6960m Cerro Aconcagua. There are trekking possibilities to base camps and refugios beneath the permanent snow line.

Reaching Aconcagua's summit requires a commitment of at least 13 to 15 days, including some time for acclimatization. Potential climbers should get RJ Secor's climbing guide, Aconcagua, and can check out www.aconcagua.com.ar for more information.

From mid-November to mid-March, permits are mandatory both for trekking and climbing; these permits vary from US$20 to US$40 for trekkers and US$80 to US$200 for climbers, depending on the date. Mid-December to late January is the high season. Purchase permits in Mendoza at the **Dirección de Recursos Naturales Renovables** (☎ 0261-425-2090; Av Boulogne Sur Mer; ☼ 8am-8pm Mon-Fri, 8am-noon Sat & Sun) in the Parque San Martín.

Many adventure-travel agencies in and around Mendoza arrange excursions into the high mountains. The most established operators are **Fernando Grajales** (☎ 0261-428-3157; Necochea 2271) and **Aconcagua Trek** (☎ 0261-431-7003; Güiraldes 246); both are in Mendoza.

SAN JUAN

Clouds over the Pacific lose their moisture in the Andean *cordillera* (mountain range), where the hot, dry *zonda* (hot northerly wind) sweeps down into the sunny provincial capital of San Juan. Located 170km north of Mendoza and retaining the rhythm of a small town, San Juan is characterized by modern construction and wide, tidy tree-lined streets. It was here that Juan Perón's relief efforts, following the area's massive 1944 earthquake, first made him a public figure. Most local buses from the bus terminal pass through the center of town.

The **tourist office** (☎ 0264-421-0004; Sarmiento 24 Sur) has good information on the region. Cambio Santiago is at General Acha 52 Sur, and there are several ATMs. The post office is on Roza near Tucumán, and there's an Internet café at Roza and Sarmiento if you want to check your email.

Sights

The only surviving part of the earthquake-ravaged 17th-century **Convento de Santo Domingo** is the room occupied by San Martín in 1815; enter the complex at Laprida 96. Consecrated in 1979, the **Iglesia Catedral** (cnr Mendoza & Rivadavia) has a tower with an elevator – for US$0.30 you get a great view of the city in the evenings.

The following charge US$1 or less for admission. The **Museo de Ciencias Naturales** (☺ 9am-1:30pm Tue-Sun), now in the old train station at España and Maipú, has exhibits of Triassic dinosaur skeletons found in the area, and you can see the preparation labs. Nearby **Museo El Hombre y la Naturaleza** (☺ 9:30am-12:30pm & 5-9:30pm), at the edge of tackiness, is unsurpassed for ferocious taxidermy examples, including sea life and insects. There's also a full-grown stuffed Saint Bernard, obviously someone's beloved ex-pet.

Provincial governor Domingo Faustino Sarmiento, also president of Argentina from 1868 to 1874, was born in the colonial **Casa de Sarmiento** (Sarmiento 21 Sur; ☺ 9am-noon & 4-7pm). Nostalgic memorabilia recounts his childhood in this house.

Sleeping & Eating

Hotel Hispano Argentino (☎ 0264-421-0818; Estados Unidos 381 Sur; r per person US$3, with bath US$5) Basic rooms and friendly staff near the terminal.

Hotel Pehuen (☎ 0264-422-4391; Entre Ríos 180 Sur; r per person US$4, with bath US$7) Basic, comfortable rooms in the centre of town.

Petit Hotel Dibú (☎ 0264-420-1034; cnr San Martín & Patricias Sanjuaninas; s/d US$8/12; ☒) Spotless, modern rooms with TV. Air-con is available for US$2 extra.

Buses go to **Camping El Pinar** (campsites per person US$0.30, per tent US$1), the woodsy municipal site on Benavídez Oeste, 6km west of downtown.

Club Sirio Libanés (Entre Ríos 33 Sur) Moderately priced Middle Eastern food served among beautiful tiles and woodwork.

Soychú (Roza 223 Oeste) The US$3 vegetarian *tenedor libre* is worth going to Argentina for.

Un Rincón de Napoli (Rivadavia 175 Oeste) Good pizza + good beer = good restaurant.

Getting There & Away

Aerolíneas Argentinas (☎ 0264-422-0205; San Martín 215 Oeste) and **Austral** (☎ 0264-422-0205; San Martín 215 Oeste) fly daily to Buenos Aires for US$100.

The **bus terminal** (☎ 0264-422-1604; Estados Unidos 492 Sur) has buses to destinations including Mendoza (US$3, two hours), Córdoba (US$7, eight hours), San Agustín de Valle Fértil (US$4, four hours), La Rioja (US$6, six hours), Tucumán (US$35, 11 hours) and Buenos Aires (US$18, 15 hours).

AROUND SAN JUAN
Museo Arqueológico La Laja

With an emphasis on regional prehistory, **Museo Arqueológico La Laja** (☺ 9am-1pm Mon-Sat), housed in a Moorish-style building 25km north of San Juan in a village called La Laja, displays mummies, artifacts including baskets and tools, and plant remains. Outside are reproductions of the natural environment, farming systems, petroglyphs and ancient abodes. There are **thermal baths** next door, good for a long hot soak.

Bus No 20 will get you here from Av Córdoba in San Juan; there are a few daily.

Vallecito

According to legend, Deolinda Correa trailed her conscript husband on foot through the desert during the civil wars of the 1840s before dying of thirst, hunger and exhaustion, but passing muleteers found her infant son alive at her breast. Vallecito, 60km southeast of San Juan, is believed to be the site of her death.

Since the 1940s, the once simple and now offbeat **Difunta Correa Shrine** has become a small town, and continues to grow. Her cult may be the strongest popular belief system in Argentina, and truck drivers are especially devoted believers – all around the country, roadside shrines display her image surrounded by candles, small banknotes, and bottles of water left to quench her thirst.

Vallecito has an inexpensive *hostería* and a decent restaurant, but unless you're a true believer, it's a better day trip than an overnighter. Like the pilgrims, you can camp almost anywhere. Empresa Vallecito buses arrive regularly from San Juan, but any other eastbound bus will drop you at the site.

San Agustín de Valle Fértil

This relaxed, green little village is 250km northeast of San Juan and set amid colorful hills and rivers. It relies on farming, animal husbandry, mining and tourism. Visitors to Parques Ischigualasto and Talampaya use San Agustín as a base, and there are nearby **petroglyphs** and the Río Seco to explore.

The tourist office, on the plaza, can help set you up with tours of the area. There's camping and several cheap accommodations, and a couple of good *parrillas*. Change money before you get here.

Buses roll daily to and from San Juan (US$4, four hours).

Parque Provincial Ischigualasto

At every meander in the canyon of Parque Provincial Ischigualasto, a desert valley between sedimentary mountain ranges, the intermittent waters of the Río Ischigualasto have exposed a wealth of Triassic fossils and dinosaur bones – up to 180 million years old – and carved distinctive shapes in the monochrome clays, red sandstone and volcanic ash. The desert flora of *algarrobo* trees, shrubs and cacti complement the eerie moonscape, and common fauna include guanacos, condors, Patagonian hares and foxes.

Camping is (unofficially) permitted at the visitors center near the entrance, which also has a *confitería* with simple meals (breakfast and lunch) and cold drinks. There are toilets and showers, but water shortages are frequent and there's no shade.

Ischigualasto is about 80km north of San Agustín. Given its size and isolation, the only practical way to visit the park is by vehicle. After you pay the US$5 entrance fee, a ranger will accompany your vehicle on a two- or three-hour circuit over the park's unpaved roads, which may be impassable after rain.

If you have no transport, ask the tourist office in San Agustín about tours or hiring a car and driver, or contact the park (☎ 02646-491100). **Ischigualasto Tour** (☎ 0264-427-5060; Entre Ríos 203 Sur, San Juan), has tours for about US$30 per person (English-speaking guides may cost more). Some tours can be combined with **Parque Nacional Talampaya**, almost 100km northeast of Ischigualasto.

The infrequent Empresa Vallecito bus from San Juan to San Agustín and La Rioja stops at the Los Baldecitos checkpoint, about 5km from the park's entrance.

MALARGÜE

From pre-colonial times, the Pehuenche people hunted and gathered in the valley of Malargüe, but the advance of European agricultural colonists dispossessed the original inhabitants. Today petroleum is a principal industry, but Malargüe is also a year-round outdoor activity center: Las Leñas offers Argentina's best **skiing**, and there are archeological sites and fauna reserves nearby, as well as organized **caving** possibilities. Hotel prices go up in ski season.

The **tourist office** (☎ 02627-471659) is at the north end of town, directly on the highway.

Hotel Turismo (☎ 02627-471042; San Martín 224; r per person US$8) has plain but comfortable rooms (the upstairs ones are best) with TV and phone. **Hotel Bambi** (☎ 02627-471237; San Martín 410; r per person US$10) is clean and reasonable.

Open all year, **Camping Municipal Malargüe** (☎ 02627-470691; Alfonso Capdevila; campsites US$2) is at the north end of town.

La Posta (Roca 374) serves local specialties such as *chivito* (goat) and trout as well as good-value lunch specials.

The **bus terminal** (cnr Roca & Aldao) has regular services to Mendoza (US$8, six hours) and Las Leñas. There is a weekly summer service across the 2500m Paso Pehuenche and down the awesome canyon of the Río Maule to Talca, Chile.

AROUND MALARGÜE & LAS LEÑAS

Wealthy Argentines and foreigners alike come to Las Leñas, the country's most prestigious ski resort, to look dazzling zooming down the slopes and then spend nights partying until the sun peeks over the snowy mountains. Summer activities include hiking, horse riding and mountain biking. Despite the fancy glitter, it's not completely out of reach for budget travelers.

Open approximately July to October, Las Leñas is only 70km from Malargüe. Its 33 runs stand at a base altitude of 2200m, but the slopes reach 3430m for a maximum drop of 1230m. Lift tickets run about US$30 to US$41 (depending on the season) for a full day of skiing. The **ticket office** (☎ 02627-471100) can provide more information.

Budget travelers will find regular transport from Malargüe, where accommodations are cheaper. Buses from Mendoza (US$9) take seven hours.

SANTA ROSA

Around 600km from Buenos Aires is Santa Rosa, a tidy city of 82,000 that is the capital of La Pampa province. It's not a tourist destination and won't knock your socks off as such, but at least it's not ugly and there's a nearby recreational lake west of center. Santa Rosa is also the base for exploring Parque Nacional Lihué Calel, an isolated but pretty park that's home to a surprising assortment of vegetation and wildlife.

The **tourist office** (☎ 02954-425060; cnr Luro & San Martín; 🕑 7am-8pm Mon-Fri, 9am-1pm & 4-8pm Sat & Sun) is near the bus terminal. There's a **tourist information center** (🕑 24 hrs) at the bus terminal.

You'll find several ATMs near Plaza San Martín and there's a **post office** (Hilario Lagos 258).

Sights

The **Museo Provincial de Historia Natural** (Pellegrini 180) contains natural science, archaeological, and historical exhibits, among others.

The **Museo de Artes** (admission free; cnr 9 de Julio & Villegas) shows off works by local artists.

Laguna Don Tomás is the place for locals to boat, swim, play sports or just stroll.

Sleeping & Eating

Hostería Santa Rosa (☎ 02954-423868; Hipólito Yrigoyen 696; s/d US$7/10) Fine rooms with bath and a homey atmosphere.

Río Atuel (☎ 02954-422597; Luro 356; s/d US$8/10) Across from the bus terminal, has worn but functional rooms with TV, phone and bath.

Centro Recreativo Municipal Don Tomás (☎ 02954-455358; campsites per person US$1) Provides decent campsites at the west end of Av Uruguay. From the bus terminal, take the local Transporte El Indio bus.

Restaurant San Martín (Pellegrini 115) A routine but popular spot for *parrillada* and pasta.

La Tablita (Urquiza 336) A well-priced *parrilla* with a gut-busting buffet – come hungry.

Club Español (Hilario Lagos 237) Excellent Argentine and Spanish food at reasonable prices.

Getting There & Away

Austral (☎ 02954-433076) is on Rivadavia 256.

The **bus terminal** (☎ 02954-422952; Luro 365) services destinations including Bahía Blanca (US$6, five hours), Puerto Madryn (US$16, 10 hours), Buenos Aires (US$15, nine hours), Mendoza (US$17, 12 hours), Neuquén (US$11, 15 hours) and Bariloche (US$18, 21 hours).

The **train station** (☎ 02954-433451; cnr Alsina & Pellegrini) has sluggish service to Buenos Aires (*turista/primera* US$5/7) on Tuesday, Thursday and Sunday.

PARQUE NACIONAL LIHUÉ CALEL

This park's small, remote mountain ranges, 226km southwest of Santa Rosa, were a stronghold of Araucanian resistance during General Roca's Conquista del Desierto (Conquest of the Desert, or Patagonia). Its salmon-colored exfoliating granites, reaching 600m, offer a variety of subtle environments that change with the season and even with the day.

Sudden storms can bring flash floods to this 10,000-hectare desert and create spectacular, temporary waterfalls. Even when there's no rain, subterranean streams nourish the *monte*, a scrub forest of surprising botanical variety.

The most common mammals are gray foxes, guanacos, *maras* (Patagonian hares) and vizcachas (cute relatives of the chinchilla). Feathered species include *ñandú* (rhea) and birds of prey like the carancho (crested caracara).

Sights

From the park campground, a signed trail leads through a dense thorn forest of *caldén* (*Prosopis caldenia*) and similar trees, to a site with **petroglyphs**, unfortunately vandalized. From here, another trail reaches the 589m summit of **Cerro de la Sociedad Científica Argentina**, with outstanding views of the entire sierra, surrounding marshes and *salares* (salt lakes). The boulders are slippery when wet; look for flowering cacti between them.

Sleeping & Eating

ACA Hostería (02952-436101; r per person US$5) On the highway with rooms and a restaurant. There's not much else good that can be said about it.

The free campground near the visitor center has shade, picnic tables, firepits, cold showers and many birds. Bring food – the nearest supplies are at the town of Puelches, 35km south.

Getting There & Away

Tus leaves daily at 7am for US$5; Tersa takes you there Monday and Friday at 9:30pm. Note that these schedules are very changeable. The trip takes about four hours.

THE LAKE DISTRICT

Crystal-blue reflecting lakes, tree-blanketed glacial mountains, fresh, clean Andean air and the many opportunities to experience it attract travelers to this region all year round. Extending from Neuquén down through Esquel, most of the Argentine Lake District offers beautiful scenery at every turn, and despite some similarities to the Sierra Nevada of California, the European Alps, and practically any mountain range in Canada, there are distinct destinations here that are worth deeper exploration.

The original inhabitants of the area were the Puelches and Pehuenches, so named for their dependence on pine nuts from the *pehuén*, or monkey-puzzle tree (which you'll no doubt investigate curiously when you visit). Spaniards explored from the west in the late 16th century, but it was the Mapuche who eventually dominated the region until the Conquista del Desierto brought in a flood of European settlers in the 19th century. There are still Mapuche living in the area, especially on national park lands.

NEUQUÉN

At the confluence of the Limay and Neuquén Rivers, this provincial capital of almost 370,000 is the commercial and agricultural center for Río Negro valley, as well as the gateway to Patagonia and the Andean Lake District. It won't win any popularity contests with tourists, but Neuquén is nevertheless a pleasant, busy city with some eucalyptus-lined streets.

The **provincial tourist office** (☎ 0299-442-4089; Félix San Martín 182; ❤ 7am-8pm Mon-Fri, 8am-8pm Sat & Sun) is two blocks south of the bus terminal, which itself has an **information counter** (❤ 8am-8pm). **Cambio Pullman** (Ministro Alcorta 144; 8am-3pm Mon-Fri) and plenty of banks with ATMs keep your wallet happy. Other helpers include the **post office** (cnr Rivadavia & Santa Fe) and the **immigration office** (☎ 0299-422-2061; Santiago del Estero 466; ❤ 8am-1pm Mon-Friday).

Museo Nacional de Bellas Artes (cnr San Martín & Brown) offers changing exhibits by modern Argentine artists. Five blocks away, small **Museo de la Cuidad** (cnr Independencia & Córdoba; admission free; ❤ 8am-9pm Mon-Fri, 6-10pm Sat & Sun) has some good Mapuche jewelry, stone pipes and creative hair 'tweezers'. Hours vary slightly in winter.

Sleeping

Residencial Continental (☎ 0299-448-3812; Perito Moreno 90; s US$5.50-9, d US$7.30-11) A block from the bus terminal and OK in a pinch, with small rooms and stuffy baths.

Residencial Alcorta (☎ 0299-442-2652; Ministro Alcorta 84; s/d US$7.50/10) Also near the bus terminal and a nicer choice, with good if worn rooms.

Residencial Inglés (☎ 0299-442-2252; Félix San Martín 534; s/d US$5.50/9) Six blocks east, with tidy, homey old rooms run by an elderly Polish lady who takes a break in the afternoon.

Residencial Belgrano (☎ 0299-442-4311; Rivadavia 283; s/d US$7.30/12) More toward the center, with dark but good-value rooms with breakfast.

Eating & Drinking

El Norte supermarket (cnr Olascoaga & Moreno) For takeout.

Fatto dalla Mamma (cnr 9 de Julio & Belgrano) A womb of brick walls and cheerful tablecloths; serves cannelloni, trout or *milanesas*.

La Rayuela (Alberdi 59) Modern, large and offering a *tenedor libre parrillada* (US$5.50); also has à la carte selections.

Restaurant Alberdi (Alberdi 176) Offers cheap home-style cooking.

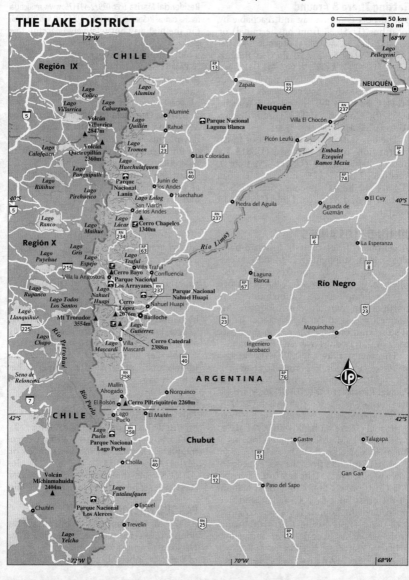

THE LAKE DISTRICT

Baco Wine Bar (Roca 293) More class can be found at this clean-cut place serving US$2.50 cocktails, exotic salads, fancy sandwiches and cheese plates.

Bar El Sol (Rivadavia 71) Has comfy sofas, artsy decor, neon lighting and rockin' music to help getting plastered along.

Getting There & Around

The airport is 6km away and reachable by local bus (US$0.35 from bus terminal) or taxi (US$3.75). **Aerolíneas Argentinas/Austral** (☎ 0299-442-2409; Santa Fe 52) flies to Buenos Aires (US$71). **LADE** (☎ 0299-443-1153; Brown 163; ☼ 9am-1pm Mon-Fri) favors Patagonian destinations, while **Southern Winds** (☎ 0299-442-0124; San Martín 107) travels to Bariloche (US$29), Córdoba (US$57) and Buenos Aires (US$94).

The bus station is in the center of town. Destinations include Bariloche (US$13, six hours), Bahía Blanca (US$11, 7½ hours), Viedma (US$11, 11½ hours), Mendoza (US$14, 12 hours), Buenos Aires (US$23, 16 hours) and Temuco, Chile (US$18, 14 hours).

JUNÍN DE LOS ANDES

Argentina's 'trout capital,' this laid-back, slow-paced, stoplight-free, friendly, pleasant, tranquil, tidy, monkey-puzzle-tree-filled, leafy little town of 12,000 is located on the beautiful Río Chimehuín, 42km north of San Martín de los Andes, and has the best access to Parque Nacional Lanín. It's the kind of place where you might see the same stray dogs over and over again.

The **tourist office** (☎ 02972-491160; turismo@jdeandes.com.ar; ☼ 8am-9pm) is on Plaza San Martín and issues fishing permits. Next door is **Parques Nacionales** (☎ 02972-491160; ☼ 8am-4pm Mon-Wed, 8am-7pm Tue-Fri). **Club Andino** (☎ 02972-492207; Alejandro Gonzalez) sits nearby in the Paseo Artesanal. There's a bank with ATM at San Martín and LaMadrid and there's Internet at Nogueira 635 (closed Sun).

Hike 15 minutes from the western edge of town to pine-dotted **Cerro de la Cruz**, where the Via Cristi project hopes to have 21 stations of the cross built by 2005 (admission free; open daylight hours). It's a very creative, well-done effort fusing Christian themes with Mapuche struggles. For indigenous artifacts, visit **Museo Mapuche** (Ponte 540; entry by donation; ☼ 9am-noon & 2-7pm Mon-Fri, 9am-noon Sat).

Fish fans head 7km north of town to **Centro Ecología Applicado Neuquén** (CEAN; ☎ 02972-491305; admission US$0.35; ☼ 8am-1pm Mon-Fri), a trout and salmon hatchery enhanced with guanaco and *ñandú*. Taxis cost US$2.50; buses run in summer.

Sleeping & Eating

Residencial Marisa (☎ 02972-491175; www.residencialmarisa.com.ar in Spanish; Rosas 360; s US$7.30-9, d US$9-13) On the highway but relatively peaceful, this place has good value rooms with TV and is a block from the bus terminal.

Posada Pehuén (☎ 02972-492246; posadapehuen@jandes.com.ar; Suárez 560; s/d US$9/14) On the other side of town (six blocks away), you'll find pleasant rooms in a nice home.

Hostería Chimehuín (☎ 02972-491132; cnr Suárez & 25 de Mayo; s US$7.30-14, d US$18-25) Two blocks down, this riverside spot offers flowery grounds and comfy rooms, the best with balconies. Apartments available.

Camping La Isla (☎ 02972-492029; campsites per person US$1.50) Three blocks east of the plaza and across from the river, has shady sites.

Laura Vicuña (☎ 02972-491149; campinglv@jandes.com.ar; campsites per person US$1.50, cabanas from US$16) More pleasant and open all year, with sunny, grassy riverside sites. Cabanas also available.

La Cumbre (cnr LaMadrid & Rosas Posada) The supermarket is good for when you don't want to eat out.

Pehuén (meals US$7.30) Serves delicious homemade meals in a living-room setting.

Ruca Hueney (on the plaza) Long-running place which cooks decent trout dinners.

Roble Bar (Ginés Ponte 331) Friendly, and Junín's main pizzeria; after dinner it becomes a bar.

Getting There & Away

The airport is 19km south towards San Martín de los Andes; for flights, see p122.

The bus station is three blocks west of the plaza. Destinations include San Martín de los Andes (US$1.75, 45 min), Bariloche (US$6.50, three hours) and Neuquén (US$9.80, six hours). Buses also go to Chile.

PARQUE NACIONAL LANÍN

At 3776m, snowcapped Volcán Lanín is the dominating centerpiece of tranquil Parque Nacional Lanín, where extensive stands of *lenga* (southern beech) and the curious monkey-puzzle tree flourish. Pleistocene glaciers left behind blue finger-shaped lakes, excellent for fishing and camping. For detailed information, contact the Parques Nacionales office in Junín or San Martín.

In summer **Lago Huechulafquen** is easily accessible from Junín; there are outstanding views of Volcán Lanín and several excellent hikes. Mapuche-run campgrounds include **Raquithue** (campsites per person US$1.50), **Piedra Mala** (campsites per person US$1.10) and **Bahía Cañicul** (campsites per person US$5). Purchase supplies in Junín de los Andes.

The forested **Lago Tromen** area, on the northern approach to Volcán Lanín, opens earlier in the season than the route from Huechulafquen.

From San Martín you can boat west on **Lago Lácar** to Paso Hua Hum and cross by road to Puerto Pirehueico (Chile), but there is also a bus service. Hua Hum has camping and hiking trails. Fifteen kilometers north of San Martín, serene **Lago Lolog** has good camping and fishing.

Summer vans from Junín's bus station go all along Lago Huechulafquen to Puerto Canoas (US$3.75). Buses to Chile over the Hua Hum and Tromen passes can also stop at intermediate points, but are often crowded.

SAN MARTÍN DE LOS ANDES

San Martín, with a population of 30,000 and nestled between two verdant mountains on the shores of Lago Lácar, is a fashionable vacation town with many wood and stone chalet-style buildings harboring chocolate stands, ice-cream stores and souvenir boutiques. Behind the touristy streets lie pleasant residential neighborhoods with pretty rose-filled gardens. There are nice forested trails in the area perfect for hiking and biking, and some upscale restaurants to savor. Note the separate but similarly-named streets, Perito Moreno and Mariano Moreno.

The **tourist office** (☎ 02972-427347; www.smandes.gov.ar; ◷ 8am-10pm) is on San Martín, near the plaza. Also here is **Parques Nacionales** (☎ 02972-427233; ◷ 8am-1pm Mon-Fri), where you can get fishing licenses. **Andina Internacional** (Capitán Drury 876) changes traveler's checks; there are several ATMs. The post office is at Pérez and Roca. Check email fast at PST *locutorio*, across from the tourist office.

Sights

The 2.5km hike to **Mirador Bandurrias** ends with awesome views of Lago Lácar. Start at Albergue Rukalhue (see Sleeping below) and follow Bandurrias to its end; bear right up a steep dusty trail and hike about 45 minutes. Tough cyclists can rent bikes at **Rodados** (San Martín 1061), and reach the *mirador* (viewing point) in about an hour via dirt roads. Follow Moreno east out of town, turn left at the top of the hill onto Los Pañiles and ride hard until you hit the T-intersection. Turn left and follow the signs. During the summer the Mapuche people charge US$0.75 for access to the tip of a promontory, where the unsurpassed view goes well with a small snack or lunch.

Walk, bike or hitch to **Playa Catrite**, 5km away down RN 234 (there's public transport in summer). Popular with families and young folk, this protected rocky beach has a laid-back restaurant with nice deck; there's camping nearby. Cerro Chapelco, a ski center 20km away, has a downtown **information office** (☎ 02972-427845; cnr San Martín & Elordi). You can book biking, rafting, fishing and horse riding excursions through them; there's bus transport in winter and summer seasons only.

From the pier, you can take daily boat trips to Paso Hua Hum (one way/round trip US$11/18) and Quila Quina (round trip US$5.50).

Numerous area tours include trips to nearby *miradores* and beaches, Volcán Lanín, Lagos Huechulafquen and Traful, Siete Lagos and Cerro Chapelco.

Sleeping

Prices listed here are for January and February – vacation months for Argentines, including those boisterous teenage school groups.

Puma Youth Hostel (☎ 02972-422443; www.hostels.org.ar; Fosbery 535; dm with/without HI card US$5.50/6.50, d US$16/14) Spacious, good dorms, one beautiful double and a pleasant common area. Bike rental available.

La Grieta Hostel (☎ 02972-429669; lagrieta@smandes.com.ar; Ramayón 767; dm US$5.50-6.50, d US$13) Intimate hostel in a cozy house on the east side of town. One double.

Albergue Rukalhue (☎ 02972-427431; www.rukalhue.com.ar; Juez del Valle 682; dm US$5.50, s/d US$14/18) Bleak halls and impersonal eating area, but

SPLURGE!

It's unpretentious and very comfortable, with gorgeous rooms sporting fluffy comforters and cable TV. The service is gracious and plenty of sitting areas are accented by plants or bookcases. There's even a small pool, and the neighborhood is woodsy. Where? **Plaza Mayor Hostería** (☎ 02972-427302; www.hosteriaplazamayor.com.ar; Pérez 1199; d with breakfast US$54)

OK rooms. Two and a half blocks north of the bus terminal.

Las Lucarnas Hostería (☎ 02972-427085; hosterialaslucarnas@hotmail.com; Pérez 631; s/d US$14/18) Beautiful, comfortable rooms with beamed ceilings. Good value; breakfast included.

Casa Alta (☎ 02972-427456; Obeid 659; d/tr US$22/29) Pleasant, with only three rooms and a beautiful garden. Breakfast included; English, German, Italian and French spoken.

Los Pinos (☎ 02972-427207; Almirante Brown 420; d US$18) Homey older house with wild garden. A bit run-down but fairly comfortable.

On the eastern outskirts is spacious **Camping ACA** (☎ 02972-429430; campsites per person US$2.75). There's also good camping at **Playa Catrite** (campsites per person US$6), 5km southwest. Bring supplies.

Eating

Abolengo (San Martín 806) Great for coffee, chocolate and croissants, but the low tables are for little people.

Pura Vida (Villegas 745) Small and good mostly vegetarian menu offering things like stuffed squash and soy *milanesas*.

El Tenedor (Villegas 776) *Parrillada libre* for US$5; trout and venison cost US$1.50 extra. There's a good salad bar; drink and dessert extra.

Ku (San Martín 1053) Very pricey *parrilla*, but the best. Also regional cuisine. Elegant in dark wood, so wear your finest threads.

Avataras (☎ 02972-427104; Ramayón 765; from 8:30pm Mon-Sat) Simple and sophisticated. Ethnic dishes from Afghanistan, India, Malaysia, Hungary, Greece, Mexico and Japan.

Drinking

Downtown Matias (cnr Coronel DíArizona & Calderon; closed Mon) Yuppie magnet on a hill (take a taxi there for US$0.90). Spacious and lofty, with pool tables, rock music and pricey drinks (Guinness US$4.25).

Avataras Pub (Ramayón 765) Small fancy pub with booths, bar stools or sofa. Plenty of drinks and upscale grub.

Zoo Café (Elordi 950) Futuristic bar with sparse furniture downstairs and a disco upstairs.

Getting There & Away

The **airport** (☎ 02972-428388) is 23km north of town (a taxi there costs about US$11). Airlines that serve San Martín include **Austral** (☎ 02972-427003; Capitán Drury 876) and **LADE** (☎ 02972-427672), at the bus station.

The bus station is five blocks west of Plaza San Martín. Destinations include Junín de los Andes (US$1.75, 45 minutes), Villa La Angostura (US$6.30, 3½ hours), Bariloche (US$7.80, 4½ hours), Buenos Aires (US$90, 22 hours), Temuco, Chile (US$25, eight hours) and Puerto Pirehueico, the Chilean border (US$9, two hours). The trip to Puerto Pirehueico takes you over Paso Hua Hum to Lago Pirehueico in Chile, from where you continue by ferry to Puerto Fuy – a beautiful trip. See Lago Pirehueico (p476) for ferry details.

VILLA LA ANGOSTURA

This easy-going, placid hamlet of 10,000 inhabitants takes its name from the narrow *(angosta)* 91m neck of land that connects it to the striking Península Quetrihué. Villa's a bit touristy, but pleasantly so; cute wood-and-stone alpine buildings line the main street. Autumn is a wonderfully colorful season to visit, when the hills light up in reds, yellows and oranges. In springtime, violet lupine blooms profusely, accenting the snow-dusted mountain landscape along with the vibrantly yellow scotch broom (both plants non-natives, unfortunately). There's skiing at nearby Cerro Bayo in winter.

El Cruce is the main part of town and contains the bus terminal and most hotels and businesses; the main street, Av Arrayanes, is just three blocks long. Woodsy La Villa, with a few restaurants, hotels and a nice beach, is 3km southwest and on the shores of Lago Nahuel Huapi.

The **tourist office** (☎ 02944-494124; 8am-9pm) is across from the bus station. There's a **national park office** (☎ 02944-494152; 8am-

2pm Mon-Fri) in La Villa. **Andina** (Arrayanes 256) changes traveler's checks. The **post office** (Suite 4, Paseo Inacayal) is at the east end of Arrayanes.

Parque Nacional Los Arrayanes

The cinnamon-barked *arrayán*, a myrtle relative, is protected in this small but beautiful national park on the Península Quetrihué (the peninsula itself is located within another much larger national park, Nahuel Huapi). The main *bosque*, or forest, of *arrayanes* is situated at the southern tip of the peninsula; it's reachable by a 35-minute boat ride (one way US$5.80 to US$7.80, round trip US$7.80 to US$11) or a relatively easy 12km trail from La Villa. There's a US$4.25 entry fee.

An adventurous way to reach the *arrayán* forest is to bike. The first section climbs so steeply you'll have to push your bike; after an equally steep cruise down, the trail evens out. Much of the route is gorgeous, rock-free, shady single-track mountain biking, with accessible lakes to add beauty and tree roots for plenty of (bouncing over) excitement.

It's possible to boat either there or back, hiking or biking half the way. Just make sure you know the boat schedule before you head out, and take water. Be out of the park by the closing time of 4pm in winter, 6pm in summer (approximately December 15th to March 15th).

At the start of the Arrayanes trail, near the beach, a steep 20-minute hike climbs to panoramic viewpoints over Lago Nahuel Huapi.

From the El Cruce part of town, a 3km walk north takes you to **Mirador Belvedere**; 1km farther on is **Cascada Inayacal**, a 50m waterfall (on a side trail). Three kilometers farther earns you the summit of Cerro Inayacal.

Sleeping

The following are all in El Cruce. Prices are for the January–February high season.

Hostel La Angostura (☎ 02944-494834; www .hostellaangostura.com.ar in Spanish; Barbagelata 157; dm US$6.50-7.30, d US$18) Excellent clean and central hostel with great spaces; kitchen access only outside peak times. Breakfast included; cheap dinners available.

Hostal Bajo Cero (☎ 02944-495454; www.bajocero hostel.com in Spanish; dm with/without HI card US$5.50/

6.50, d with/without HI card US$17/18) On Av 7 Lagos (1200m from the bus terminal) is this beautiful HI-affiliated hostel with bright, airy rooms and a full range of services.

Residencial Río Bonito (☎ 02944-494110; rio bonito@ciudad.com.ar; Topa Topa 260; d US$29, apartment US$29) Friendly, with five simple, homey rooms. Breakfast is included; there's also a large apartment.

Don Pedro (☎ 02944-494269; cnr Belvedere & Los Marquis; s/d US$13/18) Comfortable and pleasant rooms, welcoming living room area and all nicely decorated and surrounded by hedges. Breakfast included.

Camping Unquehué (☎ 02944-494688; campsites per person US$2.50) On the highway across from the YPF station and 600m west of the terminal. Grassy, shady sites.

Eating & Drinking

Nativa Café (cnr Arrayanes & Inacayal) Airy and bright; popular for pizza, hamburgers, coffee and beer. Nice terrace upstairs.

La Buena Vida (Arrayanes 167) Choose foods like risotto, soufflé or Hungarian goulash. Also regional items; well-priced.

La Macarena (☎ 495120; Cerro Bayo 65; ☼ Thu-Tue) Fine menu with entrées such as 'Sublime Bambi' (venison, US$9), 'Conejo Sauvignon' (rabbit, US$7.80) and 'Camélido fusión' (guanaco, US$9.30). Reservations recommended.

Tinto Bistro (☎ 02944-494924; Nahuel Huapi 34; ☼ dinner Mon-Sat) This place is owned by the Dutch princess' Argentine brother, and is therefore popular. Fine and exotic changing menu with extensive wine list. Reservations recommended.

Cervecería Epalufquen (Belvedere 69; ☼ from 6pm) Small bar serving the local microbrews, both draft and bottled. Snack food available.

Getting There & Around

From the **bus station** (cnr Avs Siete Lagos & Arrayanes), buses depart for Bariloche (US$3, 1¼ hours) and San Martín de los Andes (US$17, 3½ to four hours, depending on route). If heading into Chile, reserve ahead for the buses passing through.

Frequent local buses from the terminal connect to La Villa, where the boat docks and park entrance are located.

Good mountain bikes are available at **Ian** (Topa Topa 102) next to the bus terminal or **Free Bikes** (Las Retamas 121).

BARILOCHE

San Carlos de Bariloche, home to 120,000 people, is surrounded by snow-dusted mountains and beautifully situated on the shores of Lago Nahuel Huapi. It's a major tourist mecca with chocolate and jam shops elbowing souvenir and sportswear stores along the busy main streets. Travelers come here mostly to explore Parque Nacional Nahuel Huapi – in which Bariloche is located – where camping, trekking, rafting and fishing are popular activities. Skiing is the main attraction in winter, while summer brings vacationing gaggles of boisterous teenage school groups. Despite the heavy touristy feel, Bariloche offers good services and is a fun place to eat, party and just hang out to rest for a few days.

Information

There's an **immigration office** (☎ 02944-434694; Libertad 191; 🕑 9am-1pm Mon-Fri) if you need to extend your visa.

Internet access is available all over Bariloche. For cheap rates try **Cyber Firenze** (Suite 19, Quaglia 262). For medical services, visit **Hospital Privado Regional** (☎ 02944-525000; cnr 24 de Septiembre & 20 de Febrero).

Banco Columbia (Perito Moreno 105) and **Cambio Sudamérica** (Av Bartolomé Mitre 63) change traveler's checks, and banks with ATMs are common. The **post office** (Perito Moreno 175) is close to Banco Columbia.

If you are looking to polish up on your Spanish-language skills, take a look at **La Montaña** (☎ 02944-524212; www.lamontana.com; Elflein 251). Group classes cost US$6.50/hour; private classes cost US$9.80/hour. Family stays can be arranged.

The **municipal tourist office** (☎ 02944-429850; www.bariloche.org; 🕑 8am-9pm) is in Centro Cívico. There's also an **information kiosk** (☎ 02944-422623; cnr Perito Moreno & Villegas; 🕑 9am-9:30pm), a **provincial tourist office** (☎ 02944-423188; cnr 12 de Octubre & Emilio Frey) and an **Intendencia del Parques Nacionales** (☎ 02944-423188; San Martín 24), which has information on Parque Nacional Nahuel Huapi. **Club Andino** (☎ 02944-527966; info@activepatagonia.com.ar; 20 de Febrero 30) has trekking, *refugio* and guide information.

Many agencies in town will arrange area tours to surrounding sights. Try **Huilliches Turismo** (☎ 02944-425374; Suite 27, Galería del Sol, Av Bartolomé Mitre 340) or **Turisur** (☎ 02944-426109; www.bariloche.com/turisur; Av Bartolomé Mitre 209).

Sights & Activities

The heart of town is the Centro Cívico, a group of well-kept public buildings built of log and stone (architect Ezequiel Bustillo originally adapted Middle European styles into this form of architecture, now associated with the Lake District area). Here you'll find the diverse **Museo de la Patagonia** (admission US$0.90; 🕑 10am-12:30pm & 2-7pm Tue-Fri, 10am-1pm Mon & Sat), offering good displays of taxidermied critters and archaeological artifacts along with an explanation (in Spanish) of Mapuche resistance toward the European conquest.

Rafting and kayaking trips on the Río Limay (easy class II) or Río Manso (class III to IV) have become popular. They're generally 20km day trips and include all gear and transfers.

Sleeping

All rates are for January, February and holidays; prices may drop in off-seasons.

IN BARILOCHE

Periko's (☎ 02944-522326; www.perikos.com; Morales 555; dm with/without HI card US$4.75/5, d with shared bath US$12) A well-run, modern hostel with clean, pleasant atmosphere, grassy yard and big kitchen. Each dorm bed has a private shelf and light.

Patagonia Andina (☎ 02944-421861; www.elpatagoniaandina.com.ar; Morales 564; dm US$5, s US$6.30 d US$12-13) In an old house across from Periko's but with a much different atmosphere, like a college dorm. Good trekking information.

La Bolsa del Deporte (☎/fax 02944-423529; Palacios 405; dm US$4.75-5, d US$12) Popular for cozy common areas, attractive wood accents and hangout garden with a boulder wall. One double; free Internet access, bike and ski rental.

SPLURGE!

Attractive **Hostería El Ciervo Rojo** (☎ 02944-435241; ciervorojo@ciudad.com.ar; Elflein 115; d US$29), right in the center of town, offers a comfortable living area and plain but spacious rooms with cable TV – some have partial views. Two larger rooms with four beds are also available. English, Portuguese and Hebrew are spoken; breakfast is included.

ARGENTINA

Albergue Ruca Hueney (☎ 02944-433986; www .rucahueney.com; Elflein 396; dm US$4.25-5.50, d US$14) Casual place with large kitchen and dining room. OK dorms, some with partial lake views. One double.

Hostel 1004 (☎ 02944-432228; www.lamorada hostel.com; Edificio Bariloche Center, 10th fl; dm US$4.25-4.75, floor space US$2.50-3, d US$11-14) Ugly tall building, but sports a balcony with incredible views. Heavy hippy atmosphere, with folks (many Israelis) sacked out on the living room floor. Grungy dorms.

Hostería Portofino (☎ 02944-422795; Morales 439; s/d US$11/14) Central, intimate and comfortable place offers great value. Eight small but warm rooms come with good breakfast. Reserve ahead.

Residencial Güemes (☎ 02944-424785; Güemes 715; d US$13) A hike up the hill for plain and outdated rooms, but the fine living room has a fireplace and great views. Breakfast included; English spoken.

Arko (☎ 02944-423109; Güemes 691; r per person US$5.50) Homey and intimate rooms beside a pretty garden. There is a kitchen available and lawn space for a couple of tents (US$2.50 per person, call first to arrange). English spoken.

Hostería El Viejo Aljibe (☎ 02944-423316; nsegat@infovia.com.ar; Frey 571; d US$18) A pretty garden greets you out front, with simple but tidy rooms inside. It's friendly and breakfast is included. One apartment for five is available (US$36).

BARILOCHE

INFORMATION		SLEEPING	pp124-6	La Alpina	32 B3
Banco Colombia	1 B3	Albergue Ruca Hueney	16 C4	La Bohemia	33 B3
Cambio Sudamérica	2 B3	Arko	17 A4	La Esquina de las Flores	34 B3
Chilean Consulate	3 B4	Hostel 1004	18 B3	La Vizcacha	35 B3
Club Andino	4 B4	Hostería El Ciervo Rojo	19 B4	Simoca	36 C3
Cyber Firenze	5 B3	Hostería El Viejo Aljibe	20 C4		
Huilliches Turismo	6 C3	Hostería Portofino	21 B4	DRINKING	p126
Immigration	7 B3	La Bolsa del Deporte	22 C4	Cerebro	37 A3
Information Kiosk	8 B3	Patagonia Andina	23 B4	Pacha	(see 37)
La Montaña	9 B4	Periko's	24 B4	Pilgrim Pub	38 C3
Municipal Tourist Office	10 B3	Residencial Güemes	25 A4	Roket	(see 37)
Provincial Tourist Office	11 C3			South Bar	(see 34)
Turisur	12 B3	EATING	p126	Wilkenny	39 A3
		Cerros Nevados	26 C3		
SIGHTS & ACTIVITIES	p124	Días de Zapata	27 B3	TRANSPORT	p127
Catedral Turismo	13 C3	El Boliche de Alberto	28 B4	Aerolíneas Argentinas	40 B3
Dirty Bikes	14 C3	El Boliche de Alberto	29 B4	LADE	41 C3
Museo de la Patagonia	15 B3	El Vegetariano	30 B4	LAPA	42 B3
		Familia Weiss	31 C3	Southern Winds	(see 5)

OUT OF BARILOCHE

Albergue Alaska (☎ /fax 02944-461564; www.visit bariloche.com/alaska; Lilinquen 328; dm with/without HI card US$4.75/5, d US$9.30/10, 6-person apartments US$14-36) Tree-shaded, small spaces and a decent feel in a long A-frame building; one double available. Good services and bike rentals also. Located in a residential neighborhood 7.5km west of town; take bus Nos 10, 20 or 21.

La Morada (☎ 02944-442349; www.lamoradahostel .com; dm US$5, d per person US$6.30-7.30) Far up Cerro Otto's flanks and reachable only with a 4x4 (free ride from Hostel 1004) is this lofty haven. Hang out, read a book and enjoy the awesome view.

Hostel-Inn Bariloche (☎ 02944-467570; www .hostel-inn.com; Ruta 82 km 16; dm US$3-5, s/d US$7/8) About 20km southwest of Bariloche, on Lago Gutierrez, is this excellent hostel with beautiful spaces and great services. Credit cards accepted.

La Selva Negra (☎ 02944-441013; campingselva negra@infovia.com.ar; campsites per person US$3) Pleasant, terraced camping sites under trees, some with shelters, though all side-by-side. It's 3km west of town; take bus Nos 10, 20 or 21.

Eating

Regional specialties include *jabalí* (wild boar), *ciervo* (venison), and *trucha* (trout).

Familia Weiss (Palacios 167) Family restaurant specializing in smoked game and fish. Good atmosphere.

La Bohemia (Perito Moreno 48) Quirky surroundings with equally quirky dishes like trout and venison goulash.

SPLURGE!

Feel like treating yourself to a lazy afternoon of tea and pastry-stuffing? Twenty-five km outside town is Argentina's famous **Llao Llao Hotel** (afternoon tea US$6.50, served 4pm to 7:30pm daily), gracing a serene hilltop surrounded by fingers of blue lakes. includes unlimited visits to the pastry buffet, great service, posh wicker chairs and wonderful views of Lago Nahuel Huapi. Warm sunny days mean lounging on the stone terrace. Wear nice duds; bus No 20 (US$0.75) runs frequently and ends up right at the hotel.

La Vizcacha (Rolando 279) Try *bife de chorizo* (a thick sirloin steak) stuffed with ham and cheese or covered with two eggs and fried potatoes. Or don't.

El Boliche de Alberto (Villegas 347) Great *parrilla*. Its pasta restaurant (Elflein 163) is excellent. Large portions all around.

La Alpina (Perito Moreno 98) Nibble pan-fried lemon trout or smoked salmon ravioli in this cute alpine house. There are raspberry and apple shakes for dessert.

Días de Zapata (Morales 362) Munch Mexican food like burritos, tacos and enchiladas in a festive atmosphere. Throw back margaritas, too.

Cerros Nevados (Perito Moreno 388) Save up your appetite and come for the good US$4.75 *tenedor libre* (not including drink).

Simoca (Palacios 264) Non-touristy eatery serving Northern Argentine cuisine: spicy empanadas, *locro*, *humitas* and tamales.

El Vegetariano (20 de Febrero 730; meals US$5) Has good vegetarian meals. Homey atmosphere but the music (or Muzak) sucks.

La Esquina de las Flores (20 de Febrero 313) Health-food store selling whole-wheat bread and homemade vegetable tarts (order the day before). Cooking classes available.

Drinking

The most popular discos – **Roket**, **Cerebro** and **Pacha** – are clustered together by the lake on Av Juan Manuel de Rosas, west of center. At some discos admission is US$13 for foreigners, but some travelers keep their mouths shut and pay the US$5.50 residents rate.

Wilkenny (San Martín 435) The mother of all Bariloche's bars and ridiculously popular. Many kinds of music (sometimes live) are played in this traditional wood pub with wrap-around bar. Food served too.

Pilgrim Bar (Palacios 167) Softy lit and decorated with old photos. Yuppie-like, with decent music and Pilgrim beer.

South Bar (cnr Juramento & 20 de Febrero) Intimate, laid-back bar with Celtic theme. The music's trendy and cocktails like mojito, grasshopper or white lady are stirred up. Play chess, cards or darts.

Cervecería Blest (☎ 02944-461026; Bustillo km 11,600; ☯ noon-midnight) Touristy brewery/restaurant, but with a nice atmosphere. Try pilsner, lager, bock and even raspberry beers. Far outside town; take a taxi (US$4.25) or bus No 20.

Getting There & Around

AIR

The **airport** (☎ 02944-426162) is 15km east of town. Taxis to the airport charge US$5.50, but the Codao bus No 72 costs US$0.55.

Aerolíneas Argentinas (☎ 02944-422425; Av Bartolomé Mitre 185) hops to Buenos Aires (US$147) and El Calafate (US$156). **LAPA** (☎ 02944-425032; Villegas 316, 1st fl) skips to BA (US$147), El Calafate (US$232) and Ushuaia (US$225). **Southern Winds** (☎ 02944-423704; Quaglia 262) jumps to BA (US$90). **LADE** (☎ 02944-423562; Av Bartolomé Mitre 531) touches down weekly in Buenos Aires (US$80), Trelew (US$38) and Comodoro Rivadavia (US$42).

BUS

The bus terminal is 3km east of Bariloche; buses into town cost US$0.35, while taxis are US$1.25. Some companies have downtown offices.

Catedral Turismo (☎ 02944-425444; Palacios 263) arranges a beautiful 1½-day bus-boat combination tour over the Andes to Puerto Montt (US$140 for foreigners).

Destination	Duration in Hours	Cost
Buenos Aires	19	US$40
Comodoro Rivadavia	15	US$19
El Bolsón	2	US$3.75
Esquel	5	US$5.50
Junín de los Andes	3½	US$6.50
Mendoza	19	US$27
Neuquén	6	US$11
San Martín de los Andes	3½	US$7.80
Trelew	14	US$18
Villa La Angostura	1½	US$3
Osorno (Chile)	5	US$13
Puerto Montt (Chile)	7	US$13

TRAIN

The **train station** (☎ 02944-423172) is east of the town center about 2km. There's train service to Viedma (17 hours) twice weekly; *turista*/Pullman class US$20/16.

PARTY TIME IN BARILOCHE

'In San Martín they go to sleep at 11pm; in Villa la Angostura it's 10pm; but we're here in Bariloche now, so let's go!' – young Argentine woman, at an undisclosed Bariloche hostel around midnight, trying to rile up fellow travelers to party.

PARQUE NACIONAL NAHUEL HUAPI

Lago Nahuel Huapi, a glacial relic over 100km long, is the centerpiece of this gorgeous national park. To the west, 3554m Monte Tronador marks the Andean crest and Chilean border. Humid Valdivian forest covers its lower slopes, while summer wildflowers blanket alpine meadows.

The 60km **Circuito Chico** is probably Parque Nacional Nahuel Huapi's most popular excursion. Every 20 minutes, bus No 20 (from San Martín and Morales, US$0.85) does half the circuit along Lago Nahuel Huapi to end at Puerto Pañuelos, where boat trips leave a few times daily for beautiful **Puerto Blest**, pretty **Península Quetrihué**, and touristy **Isla Victoria**. Bus No 10 goes the other way, inland via **Colonia Suiza** (a small woodsy Swiss community), and ends at Bahía López, where you can hike a short way to the tip of the peninsula Brazo de la Tristeza. In summer, bus No 11 does the whole Circuito, connecting Puerto Pañuelos with Bahía López, but in winter you can walk the 6km stretch along the non-busy highway, with much of that being on a wonderfully woodsy nature trail. It's best to walk from Bahía López to Puerto Pañuelos rather than the other way around, since many more buses head back to Bariloche from Pañuelos.

Skiing is a trendy winter activity around **Cerro Catedral** (☎ 02944-423776), some 20km west of town. Catedral is one of the biggest ski centers in South America, with almost 70km of all-level runs, 32 lifts, a cable car and plenty of services. The best part, however, is the views: peaks surrounding the lakes are gloriously visible. The center is open year-round (there's hiking in summer), and ski lessons and equipment rentals available in winter.

Hard-core cyclists can bike the whole paved circuit. For rentals, try **Bikeway** (☎ 02944-424202; Eduardo O'Connor 867), or **Dirty Bikes** (☎ 02944-425616; Eduardo O'Connor 681), both in Bariloche.

Hikers can climb Cerros Otto (two hours), Catedral (four hours), López (three hours) and Campanario (30 minutes), as well as Monte Tronador (10 hours). If trekking, check with Club Andino for trail conditions; snow can block trails even in summer. If camping, get an area map (detailing campsites) at Bariloche's tourist office.

ARGENTINA

EL BOLSÓN

As close to Berkeley, California, as you can get in Argentina, artsy and liberal El Bolsón (population 20,000) draws alternate-lifestyle folks from all over the country. Calm, though not particularly attractive, this 'non-nuclear municipality' is located about 120km south of Bariloche and boasts some beautiful sur-rounding mountains with plenty of activities for nature-lovers. A warm microclimate and fertile valley support a cadre of organic farms devoted to hops, cheese, soft fruits such as raspberries, and orchards. And for hippie fun with friendly atmosphere, you shouldn't miss El Bolsón's famous **feria artesanal** (craft market); shoppers bus all the way from

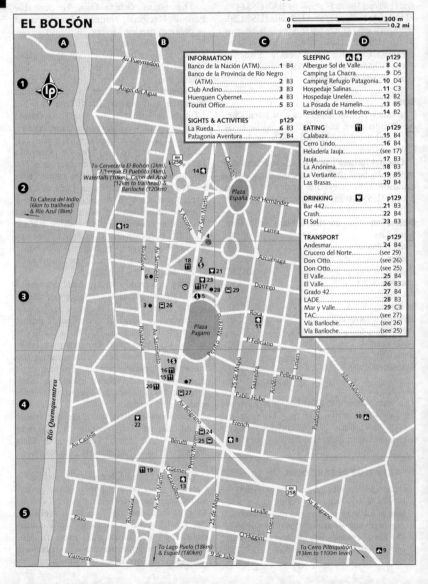

EL BOLSÓN

0 _____ 300 m
0 _____ 0.2 mi

INFORMATION	
Banco de la Nación (ATM)..........1	B4
Banco de la Provincia de Río Negro (ATM)................................2	B3
Club Andino..............................3	B3
Huerquen Cybernet...................4	B3
Tourist Office...........................5	B3

SIGHTS & ACTIVITIES	p129
La Rueda.................................6	B3
Patagonia Aventura.................7	B4

SLEEPING 🛏️	p129
Albergue Sol de Valle..............8	C4
Camping La Chacra..................9	D5
Camping Refugio Patagonia..10	D4
Hospedaje Salinas..................11	C3
Hospedaje Unelén..................12	B2
La Posada de Hamelin.............13	B5
Residencial Los Helechos........14	B2

EATING 🍴	p129
Calabaza..............................15	B4
Cerro Lindo...........................16	B4
Heladería Jauja...................(see 17)
Jauja...................................17	B3
La Anónima..........................18	B3
La Vertiente.........................19	B5
Las Brasas...........................20	B4

DRINKING 🍷	p129
Bar 442...............................21	B3
Crash...................................22	B4
El Sol...................................23	B3

TRANSPORT	p129
Andesmar............................24	B4
Crucero del Norte................(see 29)
Don Otto.............................(see 26)
Don Otto.............................(see 25)
El Valle................................25	B4
El Valle................................26	B3
Grado 42..............................27	B4
LADE....................................28	B3
Mar y Valle...........................29	C3
TAC....................................(see 27)
Vía Bariloche.......................(see 26)
Vía Bariloche.......................(see 25)

Bariloche for quality crafts and tasty health food. Experience it on Tuesdays, Thursdays and weekends (best on Saturdays).

The **tourist office** (☎ 02944-492604; ☺ 9am-11pm in summer, 9am-9pm Mon-Sat, 10am-9pm Sun other times) is next to Plaza Pagano. **Club Andino** (☎ 02944-492600; ☺ Jan-Apr) is on Sarmiento near Roca. Mountaineers get information on trail conditions and guide recommendations here. There are two ATMs in town. The post office is opposite the tourist office, and there's Internet access available at **Huerquen Cybernet** (Azcuénaga 465).

For area tours, contact **Grado 42** (☎ 02944-493124; Av Belgrano 406) or **Patagonia Aventura** (☎ 02944-492513; www.argentinachileflyfishing.com; Pablo Hube 418).

Sleeping

All rates listed are for summer.

Albergue El Pueblito (☎ 02944-493560; www .hostels.org.ar; dm with/without HI card US$3/3.25; d with/ without HI card US$9.80/11, cabana US$22) Cozy countryside hostel with large but comfortable wood dorms. Great hangout area and wonderfully tranquil atmosphere. One double and one cute two-room cabana are available; bike rentals can be arranged. Take a bus (it's 4km north of town) or taxi (US$1.25).

Camping Refugio Patagonia (☎ 15-63-5463; Islas Malvinas s/n; dm US$3.75) Beautiful dorms, kitchen access, large dining room and wonderful farm-like surroundings.

Residencial Los Helechos (☎ 02944-492262; Av San Martín 3248; s/d US$5.50/11) Modern, comfortable and spotless, with just four pretty rooms. Grassy garden and spiffy kitchen; look for the 'Kioscón' sign.

Hospedaje Salinas (☎ 02944-492396; Roca 641; r per person US$4.25) No-frills older rooms (all with shared bath), a nice veranda, tiny cooking facilities and a peaceful garden.

Hospedaje Unelén (☎ 02944-492729; Azcuenaga 134; dm US$5.50, d with/without bath US$22/14) Basic, plain and unpretentious. The doubles are pricey but include breakfast.

Albergue Sol de Valle (☎ 02944-492087; 25 de Mayo 2329; dm US$3.25, d US$6.50) Impersonal and lacking interesting décor, this large *albergue* (youth hostel) has tiled halls, small rooms and kitchen access.

Camping La Chacra (☎ 02944-492111; Av Belgrano; campsites per person US$2.50) On the eastern edge of town, this well-tended camping ground is pleasantly grassy and shady.

Camping Refugio Patagonia (☎ 15-41-1061; Calle Islas Malvinas; campsites per person US$1.75) Great sites in a tree-dotted field. There's kitchen access available.

Surrounding mountains offer plenty of camping opportunities, including at *refugios* (US$1.10 to US$1.50; also bunks for US$2.50 to US$4.25).

Eating

Food at the *feria artesanal* is not only great value; it's also tasty and healthy. Supermarket **La Anónima** (cnr Av San Martín & Dorrego) provides groceries.

Calabaza (Av San Martín 2518) Offers pastas, burgers and trout dishes, plus some vegetarian food.

Cerro Lindo (Av San Martín 2524) Next door to Calabaza and serving pizzas, veggies and local specialties.

La Vertiente (cnr Güemes & Rivadavia) A friendly spot, with well-priced homemade pastas.

Las Brasas (cnr Av Sarmiento & Pablo Hube) Eat a huge *bife de chorizo* (US$3.75) here.

Jauja (Av San Martín 2867) Modern and popular place offering a varied menu and country-time atmosphere. Next door, Heladería Jauja is not to be missed – how about some maté ice-cream?

Drinking

Crash (Av Castelli 120) Has comic book heroes gracing the walls while patrons down the goods; dancing occasionally breaks out.

El Sol (Dorrego 423) At night this place turns from a *pizzería* into a decent bar with good music, two pool tables and *fútbol* on TV.

Bar 442 (Dorrego 442; ☺ Wed & Fri-Sun in high season, Wed in low season) Across the street from El Sol, this disco hops at midnight.

Cervecería El Bolsón (☎ 02944-492595; Ruta 258; ☺ 8:30am-2am in summer, 10am-8pm Mon-Sat other times) Located 2km north of town, this place serves food and 11 kinds of brew (including fruit beers).

Getting There & Around

There's no central bus terminal. Bus companies are spread over town (see Map p128 for locations). Buses go to Bariloche (US$2.50 to US$3.75, two hours), Esquel (US$3, two hours), Puerto Madryn (US$17, 12 hours) and Buenos Aires (US$28, 19 hours).

Rent bikes at **La Rueda** (Av Sarmiento 2972; ☺ Mon-Sat) for US$3/4.25 a half/full day.

AROUND EL BOLSÓN

The spectacular granite ridge of 2260m **Cerro Piltriquitrón** looms to the east like the back of some prehistoric beast. From the 1100m level, reached by taxi (US$9) or an unpleasant dusty 13km hike, a further 30 minutes' hike leads to **Bosque Tallado** (admission US$0.90 Dec-Mar, free rest of year), a shady grove of about 25 figures carved from logs. Another 15 minutes' walk uphill is Refugio Piltriquitrón, where you can have a drink or even sack down (US$2.50, bring sleeping bag). From here it's two hours to the summit. The weather is very changeable, so bring layers.

On a ridge 6km west of town is **Cabeza del Indio** (admission US$0.35 Dec-Mar, free rest of year), a rock outcrop resembling a man's profile; the trail has great views of the Río Azul and Lago Puelo. A taxi to the trailhead is US$2.50.

Other attractions outside town include a couple of **waterfalls**, about 10km north of town, and the amazing narrow canyon of **Cajón del Azul** a few kilometers farther north; hike three hours along it until you reach Refugio de Atilio, where you can stay for the night (US$3.75). Town buses drop you 15 minutes' walk from the Cajón del Azul trailhead (US$1.25), or take a taxi (US$4).

About 18km south of El Bolsón is windy **Parque Nacional Lago Puelo** (☎ 02944-499064; admission US$4.25). You can camp, stay at a *refugio*, take a boat tour or a ferry to the Chilean border (US$11 return). Regular buses run from El Bolsón (US$0.75).

ESQUEL

Not exactly your pot-of-gold travel destination, homely Esquel (population 25,000), set in the dramatic hikeable foothills of western Chubut province, is the gateway to Parque Nacional Los Alerces (among other recreation areas). The pleasant Welsh stronghold, Trevelin, is a good daytrip away.

Esquel's **tourist office** (☎ 02945-451927; cnr Alvear & Fontana; ⏰ 7am-midnight in summer; 8am-8pm other times) and **post office** (Alvear 1192) are next to each other. Banks with ATMs are located on Alvear. There's Internet access available at 25 de Mayo and 9 de Julio.

La Trochita (The Old Patagonian Express) is Argentina's famous narrow-gauge steam train. It does short tourist runs from the station at Brown and Roggero (now also a museum) to Nahuel Pan, 20km east (one hour, US$5.50). At the other end of the tracks, 402km away, is El Maitén – the railroad's workshops are here. Check the tourist office for current schedules.

Tiny **Museo de Culturas Originarias Patagónicas** (Belgrano 330; admission free; ⏰ 8am-noon & 2-8pm Mon-Fri, 8am-noon & 5-9pm Sat, 5-8pm Sun) has good Mapuche artifacts.

For area excursions, try **Tierra** (☎ 02945-454366; cnr Rivadavia & Roca), which also rents bikes, or **Patagonia Verde** (☎ 02945-454396; patagoniaverde@ciudad.com.ar; 9 de Julio 926).

Sleeping

Hotel Argentino (☎ 02945-452237; 25 de Mayo 862; s/d US$3.75/7.30, with bath US$5.50/9) Atmospheric old digs with personality. Floor space to crash on is available for US$5.

Residencial El Cisne (☎ 02945-452256; Chacabuco 778; s/d US$5.50/9) A great deal; nine modern, comfortable and quiet rooms in two buildings (ring at No 777 if no answer at No 778). Limited dining facilities.

Casa de Familia Rowlands (☎ 02945-452578; Rivadavia 330; r per person US$3.75) Friendly with three homey, basic rooms (two share baths). About seven blocks from the town center.

Parador Lago Verde (☎ 02945-452251; Volta 1081; s/d US$6.50/10) Six small, tidy rooms. Supposedly a hostel, but has no kitchen or dorms; it's about six blocks from the town center.

Residencial Ski (☎ 02945-451646; elcalafate@ciudad.com.ar; San Martín 961; s/d US$11/14) Decent, no-nonsense, carpeted rooms with cable TV. Breakfast costs US$1.25.

El Hogar del Mochilero (☎ 02945-452166; Roca 1028; campsites per person US$1.75, dm US$3) A shady little camping paradise; kitchen available. Also has a huge 31 bed dorm; bring your own sleeping bag. If Carlos isn't around, check the house across the street.

Eating & Drinking

La Anónima supermarket (cnr Fontana & 9 de Julio) When you just don't want to get dressed up to eat out.

Parrilla La Barra (Sarmiento 638) *Tripa* (intestines), *riñon* (kidneys), *morcilla* (blood sausage) or other more palatable meat choices.

Mirasoles (Alvear 1069) Elegant, upscale spot cooking up creative, healthy dishes like tabouleh salad, stuffed squash and soy *milanesas*.

Pizzería Fitzroya (Rivadavia 1050) Small but popular, with creative pizzas, including low-calorie choices.

María Castaña (cnr 25 de Mayo & Rivadavia) Good for breakfast and drinks; bring your cigars and loaf in the overstuffed chairs.

Hotel Argentino (cnr 25 de Mayo 862) Old-time Wild West saloon bar and pool tables. There's a disco in back. Funky.

Wilkinson Irish Pub (San Martín & Roca) More like a yuppie watering hole, though the brick atmosphere is alright. Food available.

Getting There & Around

The airport is 20km east of town; taxis there cost US$4.75. **Aerolíneas Argentinas** and **Austral** (☎ 02945-453614; Fontana 408) fly to Buenos Aires (US$100) and Bariloche (US$32). **LADE** (☎ 02945-452124; Alvear 1085) ventures to Patagonian destinations.

The bus terminal is six blocks north of center, at Alvear and Brun. Destinations include Parque Nacional Los Alerces (US$2.25 to US$4), El Bolsón (US$3.75, two hours), Bariloche (US$16, four hours), Puerto Madryn (US$41, nine hours) and Comodoro Rivadavia (US$39, nine hours). Buses also go to Trevelin (US$0.75, 30 minutes) from the terminal, but stop at Alvear and 25 de Mayo on their way out.

TREVELIN

Only 24km south of Esquel, historic Trevelin is a calm, sunny and laid-back community of 6,000. There are a few teahouses, such as **Nain Maggie** (Perito Moreno 179) and **Las Mutisias** (San Martín 170), where you can conquer a platter of pastries for US$3.75 while keeping your ears pricked for locals speaking Welsh. Frequent buses run from Esquel to Trevelin (US$0.75).

The **tourist office** (☎ 02945-480120; ☻ 8am-10pm Mon-Fri, 9am-10pm Sat & Sun summer, 9am-8pm other times) is on Plaza Fontana.

Landmarks include **Museo Regional** (admission US$0.75; 10am-9pm summer), in a restored brick mill, and **Capilla Bethel**, a Welsh chapel from 1910. **Tumba de Malacara** (admission US$0.75; 3-8pm in summer), two blocks northeast of the plaza, is a monument to the horse that saved John Evans, Trevelin's founder. His granddaughter gives an animated talk in Spanish.

The best budget accommodation in town is friendly and serene **Hostel Casaverde** (☎ 02945-480091; www.hostels.org.ar; dm with/without HI card US$4.25/5, d US$14), on Alerces at the top of a small hill. The rooms, kitchen, atmos-

phere and views are wonderful – you'll be tempted to extend your stay. For camping, check out **Gold Country** (☎ 15-50-4963; campsites per person US$1.50; ☻ closed winter), with fine grassy sites. It's not signed. From San Martín, walk two blocks west on Coronel Holdich and turn left down the gravel road (the Esquel bus stops at Coronel Holdich).

PARQUE NACIONAL LOS ALERCES

West of Esquel, the spacious Andean **Parque Nacional Los Alerces** (admission US$4.25) protects extensive stands of alerce (*Fitzroya cupressoides*), a large and long-lived conifer of humid Valdivian forests. Other common trees include cypress, incense cedar, southern beeches and *arrayán*. The bamboo undergrowth is almost impenetrable.

The receding glaciers of Los Alerces' peaks, which barely reach 2300m, have left nearly pristine lakes and streams with charming vistas and excellent fishing. Westerly storms drop nearly 3m of rain annually, but summers are mild and the park's eastern zone is much drier. An **interpretative center** (☎ 02945-471015; ☻ 9am-6pm Mon-Fri) provides information.

The most popular excursion sails from Puerto Limonao (on Lago Futalaufquen) up the Río Arrayanes to Lago Verde (US$24). Launches from Puerto Chucao (on Lago Menéndez) cover the second segment of the trip to **El Alerzal**, an accessible stand of rare *alerces* (US$16). A one-hour stopover permits a hike around a loop trail that passes Lago Cisne and an attractive waterfall to end up at **El Abuelo** (The Grandfather), the finest single alerce specimen. You can buy boat tickets in Esquel.

Organized **campgrounds** (campsites per person US$1.75-2.50) at Los Maitenes, Lago Futalaufquen, Bahía Rosales, Lago Verde and Lago Rivadavia. There are also free sites near some of these locations. Lago Krüger, reached by foot (12 hours) from Villa Futalaufquen, has a campground and *refugio*, but these were closed in the 2003 season. **Cabañas Los Tepues** (☎ 02945-452129, cabins US$29), on Lago Futalaufquen, rents five-person cabins. **Motel Pucón Pai** (☎ 02945-471010; d US$22) has doubles with private bath and breakfast.

For getting there and away information, see Getting There & Around under Esquel above.

PATAGONIA

Few places in the world inspire the traveler's imagination like Patagonia. Those adventurous souls lucky enough to journey down here will find a mostly windy, barren expanse of flat bleakness that – at its Andean edge – has some of the most fantastic mountain scenery in the world, including awe-inspiring glaciers and resplendent waterways. The sky is wide, the clouds are airbrushed and the late sunsets can be spectacular. Perhaps because of these characteristics, Patagonia attracted tough outlaws Butch Cassidy and the Sundance Kid, provided the basis of some notable books by authors such as Darwin and Bruce Chatwin, and has drawn propertyseekers like Ted Turner and Sylvester Stallone. Previously relying on sprawling sheep *estancias* for its economy, it now depends more heavily on large oilfields in Chubut and Neuquén provinces and on the tourism from its Andean national parks.

Patagonia was thought to be named after the Tehuelche people's moccasins, which made their feet appear huge – in Spanish, *pata* means foot. The region has one of the lowest population densities in the world.

VIEDMA

This unexciting provincial capital (population 80,000) has some small museums, a river for afternoon kayaking and a willowy shoreline walk – not completely unappealing, though its sister city Carmen de Patagones has most of the family charm. In mid-January the world's longest kayak race, **La Regata del Río Negro**, ends in Viedma – about 500km away from the start in Neuquén.

The **tourist office** (☎ 02920-427171; viprotur@ impsat1.com.ar; cnr Costanera & Colón; ☒ 9am-8pm) is by the river, while the **provincial office** (☎ 02920-422150; Caseros 1425) is 15 blocks south of the town center. **Tritón Turismo** (☎ 02920-431131; Namuncurá 78) changes traveler's checks; there are ATMs in the town center. There's a **post office** (Rivadavia 151) and plenty of Internet access.

Sights & Activities

Check out deformed skulls and Tehuelche skeletons at **Museo Gobernador Eugenio Tello** (San Martín 263; admission free; ☒ 9am-noon & 4:30-7:30pm in summer). **Museo Cardenal Cagliero** (Rivadavia 34; admission free; ☒ 7:30am-1:30pm Mon-Fri) has some amaz-

ing ceiling paintings and a neat fish vertebrae cane (check out the cardinal's office). **Museo del Agua del Suelo y del Riego** (admission free; ☒ 9am-11am Mon-Fri in summer) has everything you need to know about Río Negro's waterscape.

Want to **kayak**? Head down 25 de Mayo to the river and look for afternoon rentals about a block north (left) of the small pier, or ask at Escuela Nautica, a block south of the pier.

The Atlantic shoreline, Patagonia's oldest lighthouse and the town of **Balneario El Condor** lie 30km southeast of Viedma; daily buses go from Plaza Alsina (Yrigoyen and Barros; US$0.75). A further 30km south is **Punta Bermeja**, a sea-lion colony. Buses from Viedma drop you 3km from the colony (US$1.50).

Triton Turismo (☎ 02920-431131; tritontur@speedy .com.ar; Namuncurá 78) does tours of the area.

Sleeping & Eating

Residencial Tosca (☎ 02920-428508; residencialtosca@ hotmail.com; Alsina 349; s/d US$9/14) Pleasant, simple rooms with TV and breakfast.

Residencial Luis Eduardo (☎ 02920-420669; Sarmiento 366; s/d US$9/13) Nearby Residencial Tosca and offers a similar deal.

Hotel Spa (☎ 02920-430459; piturburu@impsat1 .com.ar; 25 de Mayo 174; d US$11) Has good new rooms; a sauna, small indoor pool and gym can be used for US$1.75 each.

Camping Municipal (campsites per person US$1.50; ☒ mid-Nov–Mar) Riverside with bleak gravel sites; a taxi here will cost US$1.10.

Sahara Pizza & Pasta (Saavedra 336) Offers flashy decor and fine pizza.

Camila's Café (cnr Saavedra & Buenos Aires) Good for breakfast and sandwiches.

Dragon (366 Buenos Aires; lunch/dinner US$6/7) Good *Tenedor libre*.

La Anónima supermarket (cnr Alberdi & Rivadavia) has cheap takeout.

Getting There & Around

The airport is 15km southwest of town; taxis there cost US$3.75. At the time of research only **LADE** (☎ 02920-424420; Buenos Aires 320) provided air services.

Viedma's bus terminal is 13 blocks south of the center, at Guido and Perón. Buses (US$0.25) and taxis (US$1.10) go to the center. Destinations include Bahía Blanca (US$15, 3½ hours), Puerto Madryn (US$27, six hours), Comodoro Rivadavia (US$56, 12 hours), Bariloche (US$76, 14 hours) and Buenos Aires (US$60, 12 hours).

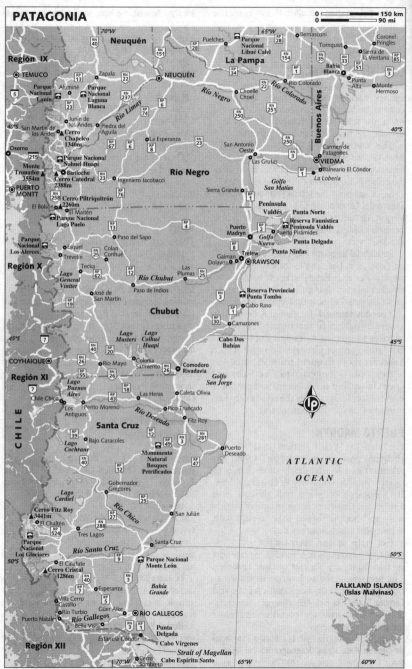

The **train station** (☎ 02920-422130) is on the southeast outskirts of town; there's service to Bariloche (15 hours, US$7.30/18 *turista/* Pullman class).

CARMEN DE PATAGONES

Across the Río Negro, picturesque 'Patagones' harbors cobbled streets and many colonial buildings. It's a relaxing walk around town, and there's a much more laid-back and historic feel here than in busy Viedma.

The **tourist office** (☎ 02920-461777 ext 253; Bynon 186; 7am-9pm Mon-Fri, 10am-1pm & 6-8pm Sat & Sun in summer) distributes maps and brochures describing the town's other historic sites.

Salesians built the **Iglesia Parroquial Nuestra Señora del Carmen** (1883); its image of the Virgin, dating from 1780, is southern Argentina's oldest. Also note flags captured in the 1827 victory over the Brazilians.

Residencial Reggiani (☎ 15-62-0091; Bynon 422; s/d US$6.50/9.30) has small, sometimes musty rooms. Better is **Hotel Percaz** (☎ 02920-464104; Comodoro Rivadavia 384; s/d US$8.30/13), offering good carpeted digs with TV and breakfast.

The **bus terminal** (cnr Barbieri & Méjico) has a surprisingly nice restaurant. There are services to Buenos Aires and Puerto Madryn (among other places) but long-distance buses are more frequent from Viedma.

Patagones is connected to Viedma by frequent buses, but the *balsa* (passenger boat) is more scenic. It crosses the river every few minutes (US$0.50, two minutes).

PUERTO MADRYN

Founded by Welsh settlers in 1886, this sheltered port city (population 74,000) has taken off as a tourist destination thanks to nearby wildlife sanctuary Península Valdés. It's a fine enough place itself, though, with a lively tourist street scene, popular boardwalk and hoppin' beach that throngs with activity on a hot summer day.

Get help at the **tourist office** (☎ 02965-453504; www.madryn.gov.ar; Av Roca 223; ☿ 7am-10pm Dec-Feb); hours are shorter outside summer. The bus terminal also has tourist information. There are many banks with ATMs, and **Cambio Thaler** (Av Roca 493) changes travelers' checks. *Locutorios* are plentiful and most have Internet access.

Highlights at the pretty **Museo Provincial de Ciencias Naturales y Oceanográfico** (cnr Domencq García & Menéndez; admission US$0.75; ☿ 9am-1pm &

4-8:30pm Mon-Fri, 4-8:30pm Sat Dec-Feb; 9am-1pm & 2:30-7pm Mon-Fri, 4-8:30pm Sat other times) include a giant preserved squid, a giant stuffed elephant seal and a giant dried mola (an enormous fish). The brilliant **EcoCentro** (☎ 02965-457470; Julio Verne 3784; admission US$3) offers cutting-edge exhibits of unique marine ecosystems and local sea life. There's a small touch-pool and a lofty, bright, glass tower with beach views. To get here, take the Linea 2 bus to the last stop (La Universidad) then walk 1km. Call for current hours.

Other area activities include scuba diving and windsurfing, or you can ride a bike 17km southwest to **Punta Loma** (admission US$3.50), a sea-lion rookery. See p136 for bike and windsurfing rentals.

Tours

There are many agencies selling tours to Península Valdés (US$22 plus US$9 entry) and Punta Tombo (US$22 plus US$5.35 entry). It's a long drive to both reserves, so take water; there's a lunch stop at a decent mid-range restaurant (for more information on the reserves, see p136 and p138). Whale-watching is popular from June to mid-December (US$14). Tour operators include:

Aike Tour (☎ 02965-450720; aiketour@hotmail.com; Av Roca 353)

Argentina Visión (☎ 0265-455888; www.argentina vision.com; Av Roca 536)

Cuyun-Co (☎ 02965-451845; www.cuyunco.com.ar; Av Roca 165)

Turismo Puma (☎ 02965-471482; 28 de Julio 46)

Sleeping

Prices listed are for the high season, approximately October to March, July and holidays. In the low season prices dip about 25%. All hostels have kitchen access.

El Gualicho (☎ 02965-454163; www.elgualichohostel .com.ar; Marcos A Zar 480; dm US$4.75-6.30, d US$14-16) Great place with clean dorms, comfortable living room, spacious kitchen and grassy yard. Some doubles share baths. Bike rentals and free pickup.

La Tosca (☎ 02965-456133; marianore@infovia.com .ar; Sarmiento 437; dm US$4.75) Recently built, this simple hostel has rooms lining an outdoor hall and garden. It also has free pickup.

Hostel Viajeros (☎ 02965-456457; info@hostelvia jeros.com; Gobernador Maíz 545; r per person US$5.50) All private (single, double and triple) rooms in this motel-like strip have TVs; dorms are

PUERTO MADRYN

coming. Has a grassy yard with large cabana and indoor grill. Good value; breakfast included.

Hostel Huefur (☎ 02965-453926; huefur53@hotmail .com; Estivariz 245; dm US$4.75; d US$18) Cramped, haphazard hostel with labyrinthine halls and large dorms sharing just two bathrooms. One double room with kitchen is available. Free breakfast and pickup.

Vaskonia (☎ 02965-472581; buce23@infovia.com.ar; 25 de Mayo 43; s/d US$9/13) Centrally located and a decent budget option, with tight, tidy rooms around a small, grassy area.

Hotel del Centro (☎ 02965-473742; 28 de Julio 149; s/d US$5.50/9, with bath US$7.30/11) Old standby with plant-filled halls and nice patio. Rooms are plain, dark and have saggy beds.

Some campgrounds are clustered 4km south of the town. Taxis there cost US$2, or take the Línea 2 bus to the last stop (La

> **SPLURGE!**
>
> Tired of roughing it down Patagonia's back roads? Head to **Hostería Torremolinos** (☎ 02965-453215; www.patagoniatorremolinos .com; Marcos A Zar 64; r US$32-36), where six beautiful and immaculate rooms greet your tired bones. Living areas are very tastefully decorated and the friendly proprietors make you feel right at home. Breakfast is included; reservations are essential in the high season.

Universidad) and walk about 800m. Tents and other camping gear can be rented at **Na Praia Bar & Restaurant** (Brown near Perlotti).

El Golfito (☎ 02965-454544; campsites per person US$1.60, dm US$2.75; ❨ all year) Best of the lot because of its location near the beach. OK gravel sites with trees.

ACA Camping (☎ 02965-452952; campsites for 2/4 US$5.50/6.50; ❨ Sep-Apr) Gravel sites with trees; some food service available.

Eating & Drinking

Supermarkets include **El Norte** (28 de Julio near Mitre) and **La Anónima** (cnr H Yrigoyen & 25 de Mayo).

Estela (Roque Saenz Peña 27; ❨ Tue-Sun) Popular, intimate and highly esteemed *parrillada*.

Mar y Meseta (Av Roca 485) Clever dishes like fish in honey, prawns in champagne and rabbit with chocolate. Artsy orange interior and small wood deck out front.

La Barra (Blvd Brown 779; ❨ until 2am) Specializes in pizzas like '*esótica*' (ham and *palmitos*, 'hearts of palm,' a common ingredient in Argentine pizza toppings) and *mágica* (egg soufflé – don't ask). Casual, colorful atmosphere.

Shanghai (cnr San Martín & 28 de Julio) Chinese *tenedor libre* for US$3.25 (not including drinks).

Asociación Pescadores Artesanales (APA; Blvd Brown) Fishing cooperative 3km from the town center, serving cheap and generous plates of seafood. Take Linea 2 bus to the last stop (La Universidad); the cooperative is opposite the stop. Taxis cost US$1.60.

Na Praia Bar & Restaurant (Blvd Brown near Perlotti) Cool dude waiters bring sandwiches, pizza, salads and maté. A small wood deck overlooks the beach.

Margarita Bar (cnr Av Roca & Roque Saenz Peña) Very trendy, hip place with brick walls, gentle lighting and suave Latin music.

La Oveja Negra (H Yrigoyen 144) Live music and plenty of drinks to make it sound even better.

Getting There & Away

Madryn has an airport, but most flights arrive at Trelew, 65km south (minibuses US$5.50).

LAPA (☎ 02965-451048; 25 de Mayo 141) takes off to Buenos Aires (US$99), Ushuaia (US$186), El Calafate (US$198). Much cheaper but less frequent is **LADE** (☎ 02965-451256; Roca 119), with mostly short-range flights.

The bus station is on H Yrigoyen and San Martín. Destinations include Puerto Pirámide (US$7, 1½ hours), Trelew (US$5, one hour), Comodoro Rivadavia (US$9, six hours), Viedma (US$8.50, seven hours), Esquel (US$45, nine hours), Bariloche (US$60, 15 hours) and Buenos Aires (US$20, 19 hours).

Getting Around

There are shuttles from Puerto Madryn's airport (US$1.75) as well as Trelew's airport (US$4.75). From Trelew you can also catch intercity buses on RN 3 (US$1.75).

Rent-A-Car (☎ 02965-450295; Av Roca 293) and **Localiza** (15-66-5230; Av Roca 536) charge about US$55 per day with 300km. For bike rentals, check **XT Mountain Bike** (Av Roca 742) or the beach stand next to Na Praia Bar & Restaurant (which also rents windsurf, kayak and bodyboarding equipment).

RESERVA FAUNÍSTICA PENÍNSULA VALDÉS

Shaped by two large bays and the Atlantic Ocean, this bleak-looking peninsula is really a wildlife wonderland. Sea lions, elephant seals, guanacos, rheas, maras (Patagonian hares), gray foxes, armadillos, Magellanic penguins and – if you're very, very lucky – orcas (who have been filmed here snatching pinnipeds straight off the beach) can be seen. June through mid-December is whale-watching season, penguins waddle around from October to March, and elephant seals and sea lions lounge around all year. The orca phenomenon happens during high tide from February to April.

As you enter the **Reserva Faunística Península Valdés** (admission US$9) you'll pass the thin 5km neck of the peninsula. If you're on a tour bus, it will stop at an interpretation center and lookout. Squint far off to your left, in Golfo San José, for a glimpse of **Isla de los Pájaros**. This small island inspired Antoine de Saint-Exupéry's description of a hat, or 'boa swallowing an elephant', in his book *The Little Prince* (from 1929 to 1931 Saint-Exupéry flew as a postal manager in the area). Also, keep an eye out for Argentina's lowest spots, salt flats **Salina Grande** and **Salina Chico** (42m below sea level).

At **Punta Delgada**, a large elephant seal colony is visible from the cliffs. **Caleta Valdés** is a bay sheltered by a long gravel spit; elephant seals haul ashore and guanacos stroll the beach here. Between Caleta Valdés and Punta Norte lives a substantial colony of burrowing Magellanic penguins. At **Punta Norte** a mixed group of sea lions and elephant seals snoozes.

Puerto Pirámide – a sunny, sandy, shrubby, one-street kinda town – is home to 300 souls. You can stay here, the peninsula's only sizable settlement, to enjoy a calmer spot and be closer to wildlife attractions. Services, however, are very limited compared to Puerto Madryn, though scuba diving and area tours are available. Boat rides (US$14) outside whale-watching season aren't really worth it unless you adore shorebirds and sea lions.

Sleeping & Eating
In summer, call ahead to reserve any of these places.

Camping Puerto Pirámides (☎ 02965-495084; campsites per person US$1.50) Gravel sites sheltered by shrubs and dunes.

Hospedaje El Español (☎ 02965-495025; r per person US$3.75) Basic and run-down with shared-bath rooms.

Better choices are **Casa de la Tia Alicia** (☎ 02965-495046; per person US$4.25) and **Hospedaje El Medano** (☎ 02965-495032; d US$11).

Estancia del Sol (☎ 02965-495007; s/d with breakfast US$14/17) Head here for comfort.

Among food options, La Estación, across from the YPF gas station, has a nice deck and atmosphere. There are many restaurants by the water, down the first street to the right as you enter town.

Getting There & Away
Buses from Puerto Madryn leave daily to Puerto Pirámide (US$7, 1½ hours) at 8:55am and 5pm from December to February. The rest of the year buses run only at 8:55am on Tuesday, Thursday and weekends.

TRELEW
This plain, modern city of 108,000 offers a pleasant bustling center with leafy plaza and some historical buildings. It's a convenient base for exploring the nearby Welsh villages of Gaiman and Dolavon, along with the noisy Punta Tombo penguin reserve. Trelew's major cultural event is late October's **Eisteddfod de Chubut**, celebrating Welsh traditions.

There's a **tourist office** (☎ 02965-420139; cnr San Martín & Mitre; ☷ 8am-9pm Mon-Fri, 9am-1pm &

3-8pm Sat & Sun) on the plaza, an **information desk** (☷ 4-8pm Mon-Fri, Jan-Mar) at the bus terminal and another **office** (☎ 02965-433433) at the airport. Many banks with ATMs can be found in the blocks around the plaza. There's a **post office** (cnr Av 25 de Mayo & Mitre); for Internet access, head to either **Telefonica** (cnr 9 de Julio & Rivadavia) or **Telecom** (cnr 25 de Mayo & Mitre).

In the former railway station, the nicely presented **Museo Regional** (cnr Fontana & 9 de Julio; admission US$0.75; ☷ 8am-8pm Mon-Fri, 5pm-8pm Sun) has good Welsh artifacts – check out the glass 'breast' bottle and the hat iron. Just behind the museum lies the excellent **Museo Paleontológico Egidio Feruglio** (admission US$3; ☷ 10am-8pm Sept 15-Mar 15, 10am-6pm Mon-Sat, 10am-8pm Sun other times) with realistic dinosaur exhibits. Don't miss the 1.7m ammonite or petrified spider body (*not* scary).

Tours
Travel agencies organizing tours to Península Valdés (US$22 plus US$9 entry) and Punta Tombo (US$22 plus US$5.35 entry) include **Patagonia Grandes Espacios** (☎ 02965-426098; surrel@infovia.com.ar; Belgrano 338), **Alcamar Travel** (☎ 02965-421213; alcamarsrl@infovia.com.ar; San Martín 146) and **Nievemar** (☎ 02965-434114; nievemar@internet.siscotel.com; Italia 20). Tours are similarly priced in Puerto Madryn. There are also tours to see black-and-white Commerson's dolphins (US$14, June to March). Request English-speaking guides beforehand.

For more information about the reserves, see p136 and p138.

Sleeping
Hotel Avenida (☎ 02965-434172; Lewis Jones 49; s/d US$4.25/3.75) Worn around the edges and everywhere else, but has cheap and serviceable rooms (all with shared bath).

Residencial Argentino (☎ 02965-436134; Moreno 93; s/d US$7.30/11) Full of funky murals, kitschy decor and plain rooms, some overlooking the plaza. Near the bus terminal; TV costs US$1.75 extra.

Residencial Rivadavia (☎ 02965-434472; www .cpatagonia.com/rivadavia in Spanish; Rivadavia 55; s/d US$4.75/9.30, with bath & TV US$7.80/14) The best and priciest rooms are upstairs, where it's brighter. All rooms are good and fairly modern.

Hotel Touring Club (☎ 02965-425790; htouring@ ar.inter.net; Fontana 240; s/d US$11/14) Worth it just for BBC on the TV. Classic old feel with marble touches and decent small rooms; breakfast is included.

Camping Patagonia (☎ 154-06907; campsites per person US$1.50) Seven kilometers outside town, off Ruta 7 on the way to Rawson (follow the signs). Green and clean.

Eating & Drinking

El Norte supermarket (cnr 9 de Julio & Rivadavia) Stocks sandwiches to socks, salads to sheets.

Comedor Universitario (9 de Julio & Fontana; 🕒 12:30-2pm & 9-10pm Mon-Fri, 12:30-2pm Sat) A funky space with cheap fixed-menu grub mostly for students. Travelers welcome.

Confitería Touring Club (Fontana 240) Wonderful old-time atmosphere and smoky male hangout, but comfortable for lone women too. Breakfast, sandwiches and alcoholic drinks.

Lo de Juan (Moreno 360; 🕒 8pm-2am) Best pizza in town (39 varieties). Toppings include asparagus, corn chowder, shrimp and anchovies.

Los Tres Chinos (San Martín 188) Signed as 'Girasol Restaurant'; Chinese-run *tenedor libre* costs US$3 (US$3.25 on weekends).

El Viejo Molino (Gales 250) Beautifully renovated old mill, with lofty and artsy interior. Specializes in *parrillada*, especially *cordero* (mutton; US$6.50). Upscale; uses only the best meats.

Vittorio (Belgrano 351) Trendy café with lots of drinks and live shows on weekends.

Genesis (Belgrano 361) Neon-lit and smothered in Latin beats; offers lots of drinks and pool tables in back.

Getting There & Away

Aerolíneas Argentinas (☎ 02965-420210; 25 de Mayo 33) goes to Buenos Aires (US$89), among other places. **LADE** (☎ 02965-435740), at the bus station, has infrequent flights to Bariloche (US$38) and Buenos Aires (US$63).

Trelew's bus station is six blocks northeast of downtown. There are frequent buses Puerto Madryn (US$1.75, one hour), Gaiman (US$0.60, 30 to 40 minutes), Rawson (US$0.50, 15 minutes), and services to Comodoro Rivadavia (US$6.80, five hours), Viedma (US$11, seven hours), Esquel (US$14, seven hours), Bariloche (US$19, 15 hours) and Buenos Aires (US$25, 20 hours).

Getting Around

The airport is 5km north of town; a taxi ride there costs US$3. Car rental stands are at the airport and in town; for mini-RV rentals contact **Motor Home Time** (☎ 02965-154-07412; infovaldes@gaibu.com; Salvador Allende 1064).

AROUND TRELEW
Gaiman

One of few demonstrably Welsh towns remaining in Patagonia, Gaiman is 17km west of Trelew and sports calm, wide streets and low-rise, mostly nondescript buildings. The typical tourist, however, comes here to down pastries at one of several good **Welsh teahouses**. Most open around 3pm and offer unlimited tea and homemade sweets for US$4.25 to US$5.50; only Plas y Coed opens in the morning. Tip: eat a very light lunch.

To place everything, grab a map at the **tourist office** (☎ 02965-491014; cnr Rivadavia & Belgrano; 🕒 9am-9pm Mon-Sat, 3-8pm Sun Oct-Feb, 9am-6pm Mon-Sat, 3-6pm Sun Mar-Sep).

The small **Museo Histórico Regional Gales** (admission US$0.35; 🕒 3-7pm Tue-Sun) details Welsh colonization with old pioneer photographs and household items. Support Joaquín Alonso's eccentricity at **Parque El Desafío** (admission US$1.75; 🕒 dawn-dusk), a garden-forest area methodically strewn with bottles, cans, and even old TV sets.

Gaiman is an easy day trip from Trelew, but if you want to stay try clean and comfortable **Hostería Gwesty Tywi B&B** (☎ 02965-491292; www.advance.com.ar/usuarios/gwestywi; MD Jones 342; s/d US$10/20), which offers gracious service and kitchen access. Another great choice is homey **Dyffryn Wirdd** (☎ 02965-491777; dyffrynwirdd@hotmail.com; Tello 103; s/d per person US$7.30), which has good new rooms and a pleasant, friendly atmosphere. There's also **camping** outside the town center (ask at the tourist office).

Frequent buses arrive from Trelew (US$0.60, 30 to 40 minutes).

Reserva Provincial Punta Tombo

From September to April, about a half-million Magellanic penguins breed at Punta Tombo, 115km south of Trelew (1½ hours by road). It's the largest penguin colony outside Antarctica. Other area birds include rheas, cormorants, giant petrels, kelp gulls and oystercatchers. You may also spy some land critters such as armadillos, foxes and guanacos on the way there.

You can get very, very close to the birds for photos, but don't try to touch them – they'll nip. To get there, arrange a tour in Trelew or Puerto Madryn (about US$22 per person) or hire a taxi (US$110). Car rentals are also a possibility. There's currently a US$5.35 entry fee. For more information, see Puerto Madryn (p134) and Trelew (p137).

COMODORO RIVADAVIA

Comodoro is a homely stopover for travelers and contains the ugliest cathedral you'll ever see. It's not a place you'd want to stay in for too long, although there is a flat, windy and shell-strewn beach 14km south at Rada Tilly (frequent buses make the 25-minute run).

Founded in 1901, Comodoro Rivadavia (population 160,000) boomed a few years later when well-diggers made the country's first major petroleum strike. The state soon dominated the sector through now-privatized YPF. Argentina is self-sufficient in petroleum, about one-third of it coming from this area; you'll see fuel storage tanks and pipelines along the coast.

Fanatical petroleum fans make the pilgrimage to **Museo del Petróleo** (☎ 0297-455-9558; admission US$1.60; ⊙ 8am-8pm Tue-Fri, 3-8pm Sat & Sun Dec-Feb; 9am-6pm Tue-Fri & 2-6pm at other times), which vividly exhibits early and modern oil technology while covering social and historical aspects of petroleum development. From downtown, take the No 7 Laprida or No 8 Palazzo bus (10 minutes); get off at La Anónima supermarket.

Information

There's an **information counter** (⊙ 8am-9pm) at the bus station and a nearby **tourist office** (☎ 0297-446-2376; www.comodoro.gov.ar in Spanish; Rivadavia 430; ⊙ 8am-3pm Mon-Fri).

Comodoro's other services include banks with ATMs (along San Martín), **Cambio Thaler** (San Martín 272; ⊙ 8am-1pm & 6-8pm Mon-Fri, 10am-1pm Sat) and the **post office** (cnr San Martín & Moreno).

For Internet access check **Cyber Patagonia** (Rivadavia 331; US$0.75 per hr) or **Jugados** (Pellegrini 930; ⊙ 24 hr).

Sleeping

The first three *hospedajes* listed are pretty basic.

25 de Mayo (☎ 0297-447-2350; 25 de Mayo 989; s/d US$4.25/9) Central and colorful, with an outdoor hall and kitchen access. One nicer double with private bath US$13; all others share bath.

Belgrano (☎ 0297-447-8439; Belgrano 546; s/d US$5/7.80, with bath US$7.30/11) Nice halls and homey rooms with pet dog and cat included.

Cari-Hue (☎ 0297-447-2946; Belgrano 563; s/d US$7.30/13) OK rooms with shared bath across from the Belgrano. The indoor patio is infested with plants and garden gnomes.

Hostería Rua Marina (☎ 0297-446-8777; Belgrano 738; s US$8.50-16, d US$13-21) The rooms are fine, if small, but are dark and face the indoor hallway. Best are rooms 18 to 20, with outside windows. Breakfast is included.

Eating & Drinking

El Norte supermarket (cnr Rivadavia & Pellegrini) Cheap takeout.

Patio de Comidas (cnr Güemes & San Martín) Flat broke? Come here and pounce on others' leftover plates.

La Rastra (Rivadavia 348) One of the better *parrillas* in town; popular and central.

Molly Malone (San Martín 292) Small and funky bar/restaurant with tea, snacks, meals and alcoholic drinks.

WALKING THE LONG WALK

Not many adventurers can say they're walking – *walking* – from the southern tip of South America to the northern edge of Alaska. Ian Reeves, however, is presently doing just this. Originally a high school teacher from Portland, Oregon, Ian started out in Bahía Windhond (south of Ushuaia) and plans to walk all the way to Barrow, Alaska. He was 33 as of March 2003 and figures he'll be 38 by the time it's all over. 'I wouldn't mind a shoe sponsor,' Ian said to me, looking down at his tattered sneakers.

What could possibly have inspired him to do this? Well, it all started out with a lovely llama. (For more information, check out his story at www.ianwalk.com.) And, if you're traveling through Columbia or Mexico over the next few years and are lucky enough to run into Ian, buy him a warm meal or drink – he could certainly use it by then.

Los Tres Chinos (Rivadavia 341) Chinese *tenedor libre* for US$3.25; good selection (including vegetarian choices).

Café del Sol (San Martín 502) Hip and softly lit café which doubles as a late-night bar. Cool food (including breakfast).

BaroBar (San Martín 626) Bar with creative art and live shows (tango, theatre, salsa). Colorful, trendy and yuppie.

Getting There & Around

From Av San Martín, the No 8 bus (Directo Standard or Palazzo; US$0.50) goes 8km east to the **airport** (☎ 0297-454-8190).

Aerolíneas Argentinas (☎ 0297-444-0050; 9 de Julio 870) hops frequently to Buenos Aires. **LAPA** (☎ 0297-447-2400; Rivadavia 396) skips to El Calafate (US$150), Puerto Madryn (US$32) and Ushuaia (US$85). **LADE** (☎ 0297-447-0585; Rivadavia 360) jumps to El Calafate (US$36), Bariloche (US$45), Rio Gallegos (US$39) and Ushuaia (US$60).

The bus terminal is in the center of town. There's an international service to Coyhaique, Chile (US$25, eight hours) at 8am on Tuesday and Saturday and to Puerto Montt (US$32, 30 hours) at 8am on Tuesday.

Destinations include Trelew (US$6.80, five hours), Los Antiguos (US$11, six hours), Esquel (US$14, 8½ hours), Bariloche (US$55, 14 hours), Río Gallegos (US$40, 12 hours) and Buenos Aires (US$110, 26 hours). Buses to El Calafate all go through Río Gallegos.

LOS ANTIGUOS

Aged Tehuelche people came to Los Antiguos to spend their last days. Travelers now come to cross the border into Chile. Getting here via RN 40 can be an adventure in itself. Situated on the shores of Lago Buenos Aires, this tidy, modern hamlet has rows of poplar trees sheltering *chacras* (farms) of cherries, strawberries, apples, apricots and peaches. Los Antiguos' **Fiesta de la Cereza** (cherry festival) occurs the first or second weekend in January, and the nearby countryside has good **hiking**, **horse riding** and **fishing**.

The **tourist office** (☎ 156-253231; www.losan tiguos-sc.com.ar in Spanish; 11 de Julio 446; 🕑 8am-8pm Dec-Feb, 8am-2pm Mon-Fri, 8am-8pm Sat & Sun other times) has transport information. There's one bank nearby (no ATM). For Internet access, try **CTC** (cnr Moreno & Patagonia Argentina).

Hospedaje Padillo (☎ 02963-491140; San Martín 44 Sur; dm US$4.25-5.50) is a friendly, family-run place right where Chaltén Travel stops; it has good dorms and a nice cooking area. For more comfort try **Hotel Argentino** (☎ 02963-491132; s/d US$9/16), which has decent modern rooms; it also runs the 'best' restaurant in town. Two kilometers east of the town center lies cypress-sheltered **Camping Municipal** (campsites per person US$0.75; one-time tent charge US$0.90). Windowless, 6-bunk log cabins are also available (US$7.30).

Buses cross the border to Chile Chico three times daily. From November through March, **Chaltén Travel** goes to El Chaltén on even-numbered days (US$50, 13 hours) – due to lop-sided demand, it's cheaper to travel from Los Antiguos to El Calafate than vice versa. There are also daily buses to Perito Moreno (US$2.50, one hour), Caleta Olivia (US$9.80, six hours) and Comodoro Rivadavia (US$12, seven hours). There's no public bus north to Esquel; you have to detour through Comodoro Rivadavia.

EL CHALTÉN

If you're looking for a place to camp, hike, climb or just hang out among some of the most gorgeous mountain scenery in the world, then El Chaltén is your mecca. This small, plain and growing village, set in a pretty river valley, is edged on one side by the extraordinary snow-capped towers of the Fitz Roy range. World-class mountaineers from around the globe come here for their chance to make it to the summit of 3441m Cerro Fitz Roy, as well as other peaks, and their success is largely based on the extremely changeable weather conditions. It can be very windy, rainy and cold even in summer, and views of the peaks are often obscured.

One popular hike goes to Laguna Torre and the base camp for skilled technical climbers attempting the spire of Cerro Torre (3128m). Another climbs from Camping Madsen to a signed junction, where a side trail leads to backcountry campsites at Laguna Capri. The main trail continues gently to Río Blanco, base camp for the Cerro Fitz Roy climb, and then very steeply to Laguna de los Tres. All water sources in the area are potable, so help keep them clean.

El Chaltén shuts down from April to October.

Information

Park headquarters (☎ 02962-493004; ♥ 9am-8pm Jan-Feb, 9am-6pm other times) On the left just before the bridge into town, the park headquarters has maps and hiking information; your bus may automatically stop here. You need to register if camping in the backcountry or at Laguna Torre. The **tourist office** (☎ 02962-493011; ♥ 9am-7pm Mon-Fri, 1-8pm Sat & Sun Jan-Feb; 9am-7pm Mon-Fri at other times) is across from the gas pumps after crossing the bridge.

Rancho Grande Hostel changes traveler's checks at poor rates. There's one *locutorio*, but no bank yet (the big supermarket will change US dollars). You can send and receive email (but not access the Internet) at Zafarrancho; the Internet will probably arrive here soon, however.

A decent selection of camping food and supplies is readily available in town. Gear like stoves, fuel, sleeping bags, tents and warm clothes can be bought or rented from Viento Oeste, a small store near Rancho Grande Hostel.

Sleeping

Prices below are for January and February, when you should book ahead. Hostels fill up quickly when buses arrive. Most places have their own restaurant and all hostels offer kitchen access.

Albergue Patagonia (☎ 0292-493019; alpatagonia@ infovia.com.ar; dm with/without HI card US$6.50/7.80) Cozy areas, an intimate homey feel and small dorms make for a friendly stay. Great restaurant; bike rentals available.

Rancho Grande Hostel (☎ 02962-493005; www .hostelspatagonia.com; dm with/without HI card US$6.50/ 7.80; d US$29) Spacious, modern and pleasant, with a large common room. Best for large groups.

Condor de los Andes (☎ 02962-493101; www.condor delosandes.com; dm US$7.80) Another good choice with more of a 'party' feel – it's run by young guys into rock music.

Nothofagus B&B (☎ 02962-493087; www.elchalten .com/nothofagus; s/d US$18/23) Just three simple rooms with shared bath, but friendly, small and family-run.

Albergue Los Nires (☎ 02962-493009; dm US$8.50, d with breakfast US$36) Good modern rooms for those needing more creature comforts, especially after those long hikes.

There are two free campsites. Confluencia is smaller and right at the entrance to

town. Camping Madsen, at the other end of town, is larger and a bit more private; it's also near the start of the Fitz Roy hike. Both have an outhouse and potable river water nearby. Carrilay Aike offers US$1.10 showers.

Eating & Drinking

Ruca Mahuida (☎ 02962-493018), behind Albergue Patagonia, is good for its creative cuisine.

Pangea (☎ 02962-493084) Next to the big supermarket, with a comfortable atmosphere and OK food.

Patagonicus (☎ 02962-493025) In the 'center.' Bakes kick-ass pizza.

Zafarranchos (☎ 02962-493005) A beautiful wood building on the street behind Rancho Grande and a great place to hang and eat pizza, pasta and meats. At night they show climbing films.

Bodegón El Chaltén (☎ 02962-493109) Has creative driftwood decor, good homemade brews and a feisty female beer-master.

Getting There & Away

The following schedules are for January and February. During other months services are less frequent or nonexistent.

There are several daily buses to El Calafate (US$14). Direct service to Río Gallegos is available depending on demand (ask at the tourist office). To Los Antiguos there's a daily shuttle for US$70 (13 hours).

EL CALAFATE

Few glaciers on earth can match the activity and excitement of the blue-hued Moreno Glacier. Its 60m jagged ice-peaks sheer off and crash-land with huge splashes and thunderous rifle-cracks, birthing small tidal waves and large bobbing icebergs – while your neck hairs rise a-tingling. To see it you'll have to base yourself in nearby El Calafate (80km away), which despite being touristy is a decent enough small town. You should definitely make reservations in the January–February peak season, when Argentines on vacation flood in faster than those ice-chunks can fall off the glacier.

In town, bird-watchers can flock to beautifully situated **Laguna Nimez** (admission US$0.75; ♥ 9am-9pm Oct-Mar), a wetlands sanctuary only 15 minutes' walk from center. Walk north on Alem, go over the small white bridge and at the *cervecería* (brewery restaurant) jog right, then left. There's also good horse riding in the area.

Information

The **tourist office** (☎ 02902-491090; 🕑 8am-11pm Mon-Fri, 9am-11pm Sat & Sun Oct-Apr; 8am-10pm rest of year) is at the bus terminal. **Parques Nacionales** (cnr Bustillo & Av del Libertador General San Martín; 🕑 8am-9pm) issues trekking permits, fishing licenses and hiking information. **La Cueva** (Moyano 839; 🕑 Sep-May) is a basic mountaineers *refugio* that organizes area treks.

There are three banks with ATMs in town. **Cambio Thaler** (Av del Libertador General San Martín 1242) changes traveler's checks. Send love letters from the **post office** (Av del Libertador General San Martín 1133) and check for emailed responses at **Telefónica** (Av del Libertador General San Martín 996; US$2.25 per hr; 🕑 8:15am-11:30pm).

Sleeping

Prices listed here are for January and February, when beds are hard to find (reserve ahead!). Prices and occupancy drop with the temperatures. Unless noted, the following all have kitchen access.

Albergue del Glaciar (☎ 02902-491243; www .glaciar.com; Los Pioneros 255; dm with/without HI card US$6.50/7.80, d from US$30) A 10-minute walk from the center, this pleasant and modern HI-affiliated hostel comes with small, clean dorms and spacious common areas. Pricey

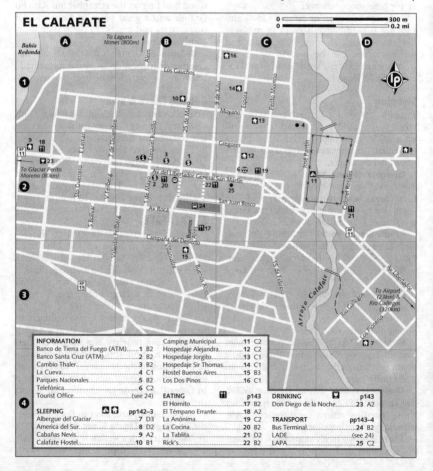

EL CALAFATE

0 ————— 300 m
0 ————— 0.2 mi

INFORMATION	
Banco de Tierra del Fuego (ATM)	1 B2
Banco Santa Cruz (ATM)	2 B2
Cambio Thaler	3 B2
La Cueva	4 C1
Parques Nacionales	5 B2
Telefónica	6 C2
Tourist Office	(see 24)

SLEEPING 🏠🏠	pp142–3
Albergue del Glaciar	7 D3
America del Sur	8 D2
Cabañas Nevis	9 A2
Calafate Hostel	10 B1

Camping Municipal	11 C2
Hospedaje Alejandra	12 C2
Hospedaje Jorgito	13 C1
Hospedaje Sir Thomas	14 C1
Hostel Buenos Aires	15 B3
Los Dos Pinos	16 C1

EATING 🍴	p143
El Hornito	17 B2
El Témpano Errante	18 A2
La Anónima	19 C2
La Cocina	20 B2
La Tablita	21 D2
Rick's	22 B2

DRINKING 🍸	p143
Don Diego de la Noche	23 A2

TRANSPORT	pp143–4
Bus Terminal	24 B2
LADE	(see 24)
LAPA	25 C2

Map labels: To Laguna Nimes (800m); Bahía Redonda; Alem; Los Gauchos; 9 de Julio; 25 de Mayo; Moyano; Espora; Perito Moreno; Eberhard; 7 de Diciembre; Ezequiel Bustillo; Gregores; José Pantín; Gobernador Moyano; Av del Libertador General San Martín; San Juan Bosco; Av Roca; Coronel Rosales; Campaña del Desierto; Buenos Aires; Villanueva; 15 de Febrero; Arroyo Calafate; Río Gallegos; Los Pioneros; Av Libertador; To Glaciar Perito Moreno (80km); To Glaciar Perito Moreno (80km); To Airport (23km) & Río Gallegos (320km); Elemein; Sito Guerrero; V Feilberg; 9 de Mayo; S Bolívar; Valentín Feilberg

> **SPLURGE!**
>
> **Cabañas Nevis** (☎ 02902-493180; www.caba nasnevis.com.ar; Av del Libertador General San Martín 1696; cabins US$45-60) Just outside the center are these 13 cute, two-story A-frame cabins best for families or groups (five to eight people). They're on a nice, grassy lot and all have kitchen and cable TV. English is spoken.

but good double rooms available. Free pickup from bus terminal.

America del Sur (☎ 02902-493525; www.america hostel.com.ar; Puerto Deseado near La Bamba; dm US$6.50, d US$29) Overlooking the town, this friendly hostel has airy spaces, a great common room and expansive views. It's 15 minutes' walk from the center and there's free pickup from the bus terminal. Breakfast included.

Calafate Hostel (☎ 02902-492450; www.hostels patagonia.com; Moyano 1226; dm US$7.30, d US$25) This huge, wood-beamed monster hostel is surrounded by balconies inside and out. It's beautiful but rather impersonal, and boasts all the services.

Hostel Buenos Aires (☎ 02902-491147; Buenos Aires 296; dm US$7.30, d US$18) A bit dark and maze-like homey choice with a cramped kitchen. It's near the bus terminal. Doubles share bath.

Los Dos Pinos (☎ 02902-491271; losdospinos@ cotecal.com.ar; 9 de Julio 358; dm with sheets US$5.50, with own sleeping bag US$4.25, d with/without bath US$32/18, apartment US$36) A mishmashed empire of halls and rooms, with something for everyone. Vie for a double, grab an 'apartment' or just camp. It's decent.

Hospedaje Alejandra (☎ 02902-491328; Espora 60; s/d US$11/14) One apartment and seven small, homey rooms with shared bath. Walk through the owner's living room to reach them.

Hospedaje Jorgito (☎ 02902-491323; Moyano 943; r with/without bath US$8.30/6.50) Twelve bright, warm and old-fashioned rooms, all in a large house.

Hospedaje Sir Thomas (☎ 02902-492220; www .cotecal.com.ar/hospedajesirthomas in Spanish; Espora 257; s/d US$25/29) Ten beautiful, modern rooms with bath. Friendly and intimate; breakfast available for US$2.50.

Camping Municipal (☎ 02902-492622; campsites per person US$1.75; ☼ Sep-Apr) Woodsy but well-used creekside sites with firepits. Nice common hang-out area (no kitchen) and hot showers available 24 hours. Also with decent campsites (same contact details) are **Los Dos Pinos** (US$2.50), which has small sites separated by hedges, and **Hospedaje Jorgito** (US$2.25), which sports pleasant orchard sites.

Eating

Rick's (Av del Libertador General San Martín 1105) *Parrillada libre* for US$5.50, but try the huge à la carte *bife de chorizo*.

La Cocina (Av del Libertador General San Martín 1245; ☼ dinner) This popular and upscale place has rustic decor and a good innovative Italian menu.

El Témpano Errante (Av del Libertador General San Martín 1630) Delicious healthy and creative cuisine. Good vegetarian dishes, pasta, meat and fish. Does not serve breakfast; only serves lunch January–February. Located three blocks west of the town center.

El Hornito (Buenos Aires 155; ☼ Thu-Tue) Boasts natural, healthy foods like homemade pastas, pizzas and crepes.

La Tablita (Colonel Rosales 28; ☼ closed Wed lunch) Very popular for its great *parrillada*. Bright and modern, and just outside center.

La Anónima (cnr Av del Libertador General San Martín & Perito Moreno) For stocking up.

Drinking

Don Diego de la Noche (Av del Libertador General San Martín 1603) Dinner runs until midnight, but at 9:45pm there's a folk or tango show. Drink until 6am in this cozy venue.

Shackleton Lounge (Av del Libertador General San Martín 3287) Three kilometers from center, but worth it for the good music, daiquiris and Shackleton theme. The mayor has thrown back shots here.

Right next to the post office, El Toldería is an easy stumble home if you're staying in the center.

Getting There & Around

The **airport** (☎ 02902-491230) is 23km east of town. **Aerobus** (☎ 02902-492492) has shuttle services for US$3; taxis cost US$7.80.

Rumbo Sur (☎ 02902-492155) and **Sunny Tour** (☎ 02902-492561) are agents for Aerolíneas Argentina, which flies to Bariloche (US$154), Trelew (US$105), Ushuaia (US$96) and Buenos Aires (US$105). Other airlines in town include **LADE** (☎ 02902-491262), in the bus terminal, and **LAPA** (☎ 02902-491171; Av del Libertador General San Martín 1015).

Bus destinations include Río Gallegos (US$11, five hours) and Puerto Natales, Chile (US$16, five to six hours; in winter must go via Río Gallegos). Several companies head to El Chaltén twice daily (US$14, 4½ hours; in winter once a week or less).

Overland Patagonia (☎ 02944-461564), based at Albergue del Glaciar, does a four-day tour from El Calafate to Bariloche on adventurous Ruta 40 for US$180 (from December to March only).

For information about the Moreno Glacier, see Parque Nacional Los Glaciares.

PARQUE NACIONAL LOS GLACIARES

Over millennia, Andean snowfields have compacted into ice and flowed eastward toward Lago Argentino and Lago Viedma, which in turn feed the Río Santa Cruz, southern Patagonia's largest river. The centerpiece of this conjunction of ice, rock and water is the dynamic **Moreno Glacier**, one of the earth's most active icefields. Due to its proximity to a nearby peninsula, you can see and hear the glacier safely from a series of catwalks and platforms in the **Parque Nacional Los Glaciares** (admission US$7.30).

Albergue del Glaciar (see Sleeping p142) offers a good US$23 Moreno Glacier tour that includes a hike and a boat ride. Most tour operators, however, charge US$18 just for transport and a few hours at the glacier (it's always best to get recommendations from other travelers). You can also hire a *remise* for about US$50 (negotiate rates, times and what is included) – this gives you more flexibility and the option to visit nearby *estancias*.

Launches from Puerto Bandera, 45km west of El Calafate, sail to the **Upsala Glacier**; from here you can hike to iceberg-choked Lago Onelli. It's possible to camp at the *refugio* there and return to Puerto Bandera another day. Tour operators in El Calafate run Upsala boat tours, which include four glaciers and a one-hour hike (US$60).

RÍO GALLEGOS

Most travelers stop in this coal-shipping, oil-refining and wool-raising port city of 95,000 just long enough to catch the next bus to El Calafate, Punta Arenas or Ushuaia. While rather bleak in appearance and not a destination on its own, Río Gallegos does have an active, tree-lined downtown, free museums and some of the best fly-fishing on the continent. Many modern buildings are going up, and the boardwalk is being improved – take a walk along the muddy shoreline and check out the amazingly low tides, which can dip down 14m.

The **Museo Padre Molina** (Ramón y Cajal; admission free; ☉ 8am-8pm Mon-Fri, 11am-7pm Sat & Sun) is an odd combination of dinosaur bones and strange modern art, an interactive area and geology exhibits; check out the giant armadillo reconstruction. In an 1890s house typical of southern Patagonia nestles the small and scanty **Museo de los Pioneros** (cnr Elcano & Alberdi; admission free; ☉ 10am-8pm). Note Saint-Exupéry's photo in the stairway.

Information

The **provincial tourist office** (☎ 02966-422702; tur ismosantacruz@speedy.com.ar; Av Roca 863; ☉ 9am-8pm Mon-Fri, 10am-8pm Sat, 10am-3pm & 5-8pm Sun summer, shorter hours winter) is good, but the **municipal tourist office** (cnr Av Roca & Córdoba; ☉ 8am-3pm Mon-Fri) needs to get its act together, even superficially. At the bus terminal is another **tourist office** (☎ 02966-442159; ☉ 7am-9pm Mon-Fri, 10am-1pm & 4-8pm Sat & Sun), helpful for finding transport and lodging.

Most banks with ATMs are on or near Av Roca. **Thaler Cambio** (cnr San Martín & Alcorta; ☉ 10am-3pm Mon-Fri, 10am-1pm Sat) changes travelers' checks. The post office is on the corner of Roca and San Martín. **J@va Cybercafé** (Av Roca 923; ☉ 8am-4am; US$0.75 per hr) has Internet access.

Río Gallegos has an **immigration office** (☎ 02966-420205; Urquiza 144; ☉ 9am-3pm Mon-Fri).

Sleeping

Casa de Familia Elcira Contreras (☎ 02966-429856; Zuccarrino 431; dm US$5.50) Clean and homey shared rooms have kitchen access. It's far from the town center, a 15-minute walk from the bus station (cross RN3; no sign; taxi US$0.75).

Residencial Laguna Azul (☎ 02966-422165; Estrada 298; s/d US$6.80/9.30) Good, warm rooms, some with bunks and tiled floors. Breakfast is US$0.75.

Hotel Nevada (☎ 02966-435790; Zapiola 480; s/d US$9/14) Nice, small and comfortable modern rooms with TV. Popular, so book ahead.

Hotel Sehuen (☎ 02966-425683; www.hotelse huen.unlugar.com in Spanish; Rawson 160; s US$13-17, d US$17-21) Serene new hotel with a bright lobby and beautiful rooms (all have TV).

Polideportivo Atsa (☎ 02966-420301; cnr Asturias & Yugoslavia; campsites per person US$1.75) The spot to camp lies 500m southwest of the bus terminal.

Eating

Panadería Zapiola (cnr Zapiola & Estrada; ☺ 24 hr) Great for baked goods.

La Vieja Esquina (cnr Vélez Sársfield & Zapiola) Clean and comfy; serves fine pasta and pizza.

El Dragón (9 de Julio 39) If you're hungry, head to this all-you-can-eat *tenedor libre*.

Restaurant Díaz (Av Roca 1143; ☺ 24 hrs) When the need for meat hits, this is definitely the place to go.

Monaco (cnr Avs Roca & San Martín) A (respectable) local male hangout in the mornings.

Club Británico (Av Roca 935) Classic atmosphere outshines passable food.

Getting There & Away

Río Gallegos' airport is 7km from center; taxis cost about US$3.25. **Aerolíneas Argentinas/ Austral** (☎ 02966-422020; Av San Martín 545) zoom to Buenos Aires (US$104). **LADE** (☎ 02966-422316; Fagnano 53) chugs infrequently but cheaply to Río Grande, El Calafate and Ushuaia. **LAPA** (☎ 02966-428382; Estrada 71) has an office but no flights from Río Gallegos at the time of research.

The bus station is about 3km from the center, on RN 3. Taxis to the center cost

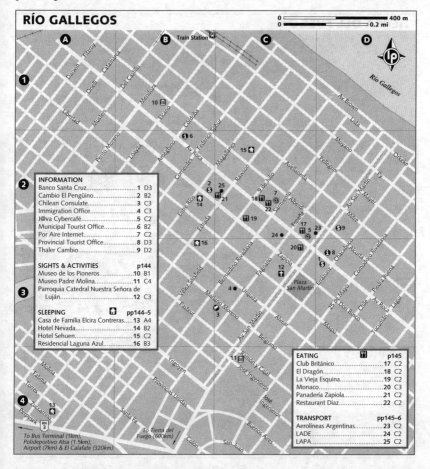

RÍO GALLEGOS

0 ——————— 400 m
0 ——————— 0.2 mi

To Bus Terminal (1km);
Polideportivo Atsa (1.5km);
Airport (7km) & El Calafate (320km)

To Tierra del
Fuego (600km)

about US$1.50; bus No 1 or 12 are US$0.45. Fewer bus services run in winter.

Chilean destinations from Río Gallegos include Punta Arenas (US$7.30, five hours) and Puerto Natales (US$11, six hours). Argentine destinations include El Calafate (US$11, 4½ hours), Ushuaia (US$27, 12 hours), Comodoro Rivadavia (US$14, 11 hours), Puerto Madryn (US$26, 20 hours) and Buenos Aires (US$49, 36 hours).

TIERRA DEL FUEGO

Surrounded by the stormy South Atlantic and the Strait of Magellan, Tierra del Fuego is full of scenic glaciers, lush forests, clear lakes and rivers, and a dramatic sea coast. It really is the end of the world, and while Ushuaia claims to be the 'southernmost city in the world' (a major draw for travelers), Puerto Williams – a Chilean naval settlement of 2500 – is just a bit farther south.

This group of islands got its name from distant shoreline campfires, seen by passing ships, that the Yámana (or Yahgan) people tended. In 1520, when Magellan came through, neither he nor any other European explorers were interested in the land – they wanted to find passage to the Asian spice islands. So the ships sailed by while the indigenous Ona (or Selknam) and Haush continued hunting land animals, and the Yámana and Alacalufe ('Canoe Indians') lived on seafood

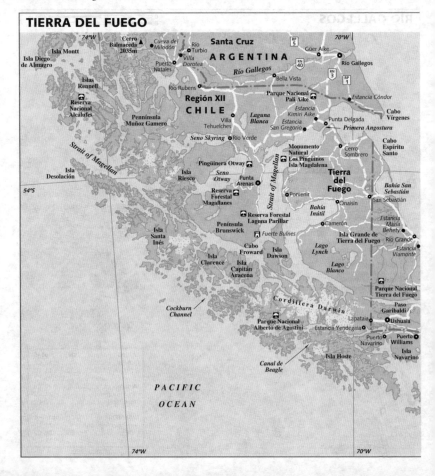

TIERRA DEL FUEGO

and marine mammals. Spain's withdrawal from the continent in the early 1800s, however, brought on European settlement.

In the mid-1800s, Chile and Argentina began scuffling here and have only recently (in 1984) resolved their border disputes. The archipelago is now owned mostly by Chile, though the largest cities of Río Grande and Ushuaia belong to Argentina.

RÍO GRANDE

Cold, bleak and windswept Río Grande, with an economy based on sheep and oil, is making an effort to improve and beautify itself – but it's got a long, long way to go. Most travelers pass through quickly, but pause and you'll find a couple of good museums, one of

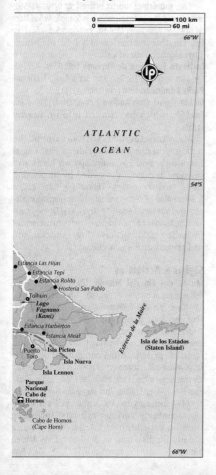

the world's lowest tides (5km out!), and surrounding countryside that harbors working *estancias* and some truly fine trout fishing.

Information

The tourist office (☎ 02964-431324; rg-turismo@netcom bbs.com.ar; ☼ 9am-9pm Dec-Apr, 9am-8pm Mon-Fri, 10am-5pm Sat May-Nov) is in the main plaza. There's also a **government tourist office** (☎ 02964-422887; ☼ 9am-5pm Mon-Fri) in the Hotel Yaganes, Belgrano 319.

There are banks with ATMs at San Martín and 9 de Julio. **Thaler Cambio** (☼ 10am-3pm Mon-Fri) is half a block from the park on Rosales. The post office is at Rivadavia 968.

There's Internet access at **Telefónica** (☼ 8am-midnight) and **Don Pepe** (☼ 24 hr) near the plaza. Don Pepe also sells maps of the town and fishing licenses.

Sights

The **Museo de la Ciudad** (cnr Alberdi & Belgrano; admission free; ☼ 9am-7pm Mon-Sat in summer) explains early navigation and colonization of the area and has displays on flora, fauna and military artifacts. The **Museo Salesiano** (☎ 02964-421642; admission US$0.75; ☼ 10am-12:30pm & 3-7pm Mon-Sat, 3-7pm Sun), 11km north of town, has exhibits on geology, natural history and ethnography. Take Línea B from San Martín.

Sleeping

Hotel Argentino (☎ 02964-422546; hotelargentino@yahoo.com; San Martín 64; dm US$5.50) *The* place for shoestringers, this old house has simple but homey dorms. Common areas are chummy; breakfast is included.

Hospedaje Noal (☎ 02964-427516; Rafael Obligado 557; s/d US$7.30/13) One block from Tecni-Austral is this tidy but cramped place with old wood-paneled rooms.

Hotel Rawson (☎ 02964-430352; Estrada 750; s/d US$7.80/12) Rough around the edges but friendly; offers small OK rooms with TV.

Hotel Isla del Mar (☎ 02964-422883; Güemes 963; s/d US$20/23) Need more comfort? This upscale hotel has good, modern rooms that include breakfast. Get one facing the sea.

Eating

La Nueva Piamontesa (Belgrano 464; ☼ 24 hrs) Has decent sandwiches, pasta and pizza.

Café Sonora (Perito Moreno 705) Pleasant, modern and bright; offers jolts of coffee and pizza.

La Nueva Colonial (Fagnano 669) This popular place is an old restaurant best for its pastas; it also bakes pizza.

Epa!!! Bar-café (Rosales 445) The hippest spot in town, with colorful booths, futuristic tables, long hours and standard dishes.

El Norte supermarket (cnr Piedra Buena & San Martín) Great when you just don't want to sit down to eat.

Getting There & Away

Aerolíneas Argentinas (☎ 02964-424467; San Martín 607) and **LADE** (☎ 02964-422968; Lasserre 425) have limited flights.

The bus terminal is on Belgrano near the coast. Lider, Transportes Montiel and Tolkeyen between them have many daily departures to Ushuaia (US$7.80). Buses Pacheco goes to Punta Arenas (US$18) at 9:30am Monday and 10:30am Tuesday, Thursday and Saturday.

Tecni-Austral (☎ 02964-430448; Moyano 516), eight blocks west of the bus terminal, leaves Ushuaia at 6pm Monday to Saturday (US$7.80), Río Gallegos on Monday, Wednesday, Thursday and Friday at 9:30am (US$18) and to Punta Arenas Monday, Wednesday and Friday at 10am (US$18).

USHUAIA

Many travelers come here just to say they've seen the southernmost city in the world. Fortunately for them, Ushuaia is a pleasant (if touristy) destination with a relatively moderate climate and a world-class backdrop. It nestles beside the frigid Beagle Channel while the spectacular 1500m glacial peaks of the Fuegan Andes tower behind; if you arrive by air, you'll be treated to some breathtaking views. The beautiful landscape surrounding Ushuaia offers hiking, trekking, skiing and boat trips, and the chance to go as far south as highways go: RN 3 ends at Bahía Lapataia, 3242km from Buenos Aires.

Over the past few decades, this fast-growing destination has evolved from a small village into a city of 55,000. Originally established as a notorious penal colony, Ushuaia became a key naval base in 1950. Gold, lumber, wool and fishing have all brought in revenue over the years, but tourism now drives the city's economy. Flights and hotels are full in January and Febru-

ary, when cruise ships arrive almost daily. Even the shoulder months of December and March see crowds and good (though changeable) weather.

There are no buses to/from the airport; fortunately, taxi rides are cheap (US$1.60).

Information

There's an **immigration office** (☎ 02901-422334; Beauvoir 1536; ⏰ 9am-noon Mon-Fri) in town. Visa extensions cost from US$36 and are good for up to 90 days.

Plenty of places on San Martín offer Internet access; they fill up when cruise boats dock. Several banks in town have ATMs. **Thaler Cambio** (Av San Martín 788) changes traveler's checks.

The **municipal tourist office** (☎ 02901-424550; www.tierradelfuego.org.ar/ushuaia in Spanish; Av San Martín 674; ⏰ 8am-10pm Mon-Fri, 9am-8pm Sat & Sun) is informative and has lots of helpful literature. Three other tourist offices to check out are **Instituto Fueguino de Turismo** (☎ 02901-423340; ⏰ 8am-9pm Mon-Fri, 9am-8pm Sat & Sun), **National Parks Administration** (☎ 02901-421315; Av San Martín 1395) and **Club Andino** (☎ 02901-422335; Juana Fadul 50), which has limited info on nearby trails.

Many travel agencies sell tours around the region; you can go horse riding, visit Lagos Escondido and Fagnano, spy on birds and beavers, and even get pulled by husky-dog sleds (winter only). **Tolkar** (⏰ 9am-12:30pm & 3-8pm Mon-Fri, 9am-1pm Sat) is a popular all-around agency. **Canal** (☎ 02901-435777; www.canalfun.com; Rivadavia 82) organizes adventure tours including trekking, kayaking, canoeing and 4x4 trips, but it's not cheap.

Sights & Activities

Museo del Fin del Mundo (Av Maipú 179; tierradelfuego.org.ar/museo in Spanish; admission US$1.75; ⏰ 10am-1pm & 3-7:30pm Oct-Apr, 3-7:30pm Mon-Sat May-Sept) has good exhibits on Ushuaia's indigenous and natural histories, including bone harpoons, elephant-seal skulls and some surprised stuffed penguins. The excellent **Museo Marítimo** (cnr Yaganes & Gobernador Paz; www.museomaritimo.com; admission US$4.75; ⏰ 10am-8pm Nov 15-May 1, 10am-7pm May 2-Nov 14) held up to 600 inmates in 380 small jail cells and now contains various exhibits, including ones on expeditions to Antarctica. There's a daily English tour at 3:30pm. Tiny **Museo Yámana** (Rivadavia 56; admission US$1.75; ⏰ 10am-8pm

Sept-Mar, 10am-6pm Tue-Sun Apr-Oct) has some history on the area's original folk.

After seeing the Moreno Glacier in El Calafate, the **Martial Glacier** here will seem like an overgrown ice-cube – but at least it's located in a beautiful valley with great views of Ushuaia and the Beagle Channel. Walk or bus (US$1.75) to a short chairlift 7km northwest of town; from here it's about two hours up to the glacier (a bit shorter if you take the chairlift, US$2.25).

Hop on a **boat tour** to the lighthouse and sea lion or penguin colonies (penguins waddle October through March). Tours range from US$18 to US$41 and depart twice daily in summer; buy tickets at the pier or from your hotel.

Hiking and trekking opportunities aren't limited to the national park – the entire mountain range behind Ushuaia, with its lakes and rivers, is an outdoorperson's wonderland. However, many trails are poorly marked, so check in beforehand with Club Andino (which occasionally organizes hikes). A multi-day trek worth asking about is the Sendero de Lucas Bridges, first created by Bridges to connect the *estancias* Harberton and Via Monte.

Plenty of ski resorts dot the nearby mountains – all accessed from RN 3 – with both downhill and cross-country options. Ski season runs June to mid-September.

The largest resort is Cerro Castor (27km from Ushuaia), with 15 slopes spanning 400

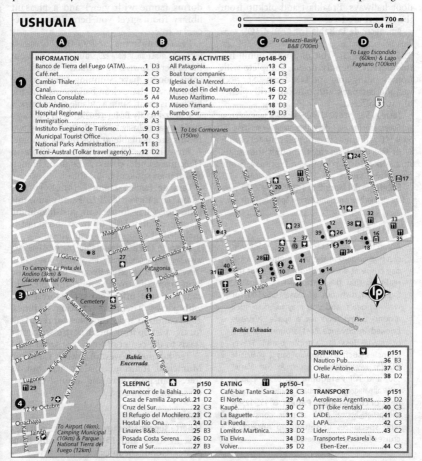

USHUAIA

0 — 700 m
0 — 0.4 mi

INFORMATION
Banco de Tierra del Fuego (ATM)	**1** D3
Café.net	**2** C3
Cambio Thaler	**3** C3
Canal	**4** D2
Chilean Consulate	**5** A4
Club Andino	**6** C3
Hospital Regional	**7** A4
Immigration	**8** A3
Instituto Fueguino de Turismo	**9** D3
Municipal Tourist Office	**10** C3
National Parks Administration	**11** B3
Tecni-Austral (Tolkar travel agency)	**12** D2

SIGHTS & ACTIVITIES pp148–50
All Patagonia	**13** C3
Boat tour companies	**14** D3
Iglesia de la Merced	**15** C3
Museo del Fin del Mundo	**16** D2
Museo Marítimo	**17** D2
Museo Yamaná	**18** D3
Rumbo Sur	**19** D3

To Galeazzi-Basily
B&B (700m)

To Lago Escondido
(60km) & Lago
Fagnano (100km)

To Los Cormoranes
(150m)

RN 3

To Camping La Pista del
Andino (3km) &
Glacier Martial (7km)

Bahía Ushuaia

*Bahía
Encerrada*

Pier

To Airport (4km),
Camping Municipal
(10km) & Parque
Nacional Tierra del
Fuego (12km)

SLEEPING p150
Amanecer de la Bahía	**20** C2
Casa de Familia Zaprucki	**21** D2
Cruz del Sur	**22** C3
El Refugio del Mochilero	**23** C2
Hostal Río Ona	**24** D2
Linares B&B	**25** B3
Posada Costa Serena	**26** D2
Torre al Sur	**27** B3

EATING pp150–1
Café-bar Tante Sara	**28** C3
El Norte	**29** A4
Kaupé	**30** C2
La Baguette	**31** C3
La Rueda	**32** D2
Lomitos Martinica	**33** D2
Tía Elvira	**34** D3
Volver	**35** D2

DRINKING p151
Nautico Pub	**36** B3
Orelie Antoine	**37** C3
U-Bar	**38** D2

TRANSPORT p151
Aerolíneas Argentinas	**39** D2
DTT (bike rentals)	**40** C3
LADE	**41** C3
LAPA	**42** C3
Lider	**43** C2
Transportes Pasarela & Eben-Ezer	**44** C3

ARGENTINA

hectares. Another large area (19km from town) is Altos del Valle, known for breeding Siberian Huskies – you can even get pulled in dog sleds here. Ski rental equipment is available at each resort, and shuttles run several times daily from town.

Sleeping

Hostels in Ushuaia are breeding like horny mosquitoes. All have kitchens and most offer Internet access. Accommodation prices usually drop 25% in the low season (April to October).

Los Cormoranes (☎ 02901-423459; www.loscor moranes.com; Kamshen 788; dm US$6.50) Ten minutes' walk north of center, this excellent hostel has good six-bed dorms facing outdoor hallways. Breakfast and pickup from the airport are free.

Amanecer de la Bahía (☎ 02901-424405; www .ushuaiahostel.com.ar in Spanish; Magallanes 594; dm US$5.50, d US$21-25) A bit of a walk uphill lies this decent, friendly hostel, complete with homey eating area and OK dorms. Services include car park and outdoor grill; plenty of tours offered.

Torre al Sur (☎ 02901-430745; www.torrealsur.com .ar; Gobernador Paz 1437; dm with/without HI card US$4.75/ 5.80) HI-affiliated, this popular hostel comes with the usual services, though the small, maze-like dorm rooms can be noisy. Some have great views.

El Refugio del Mochilero (☎ 02901-436129; www .refugiodelmochilero.netfirms.com in Spanish; 25 de Mayo

231; dm US$7.30, d US$20) Six- to eight-person dorms are central but a bit cramped and dark – try for the newer ones upstairs. Bike rentals available.

Cruz del Sur (☎ 02901-423110; www.xdelsur.com.ar; Deloquí 636; dm US$6.50) Cozy four- to six-bed dorms (some with view) and a pleasant library room greet you here. Internet access is free.

Posada Costa Serena (☎ 02901-437212; posadacosta serena@hotmail.com.ar; Roca 129; s/d US$23/29) Smack in the center of town is this attractive new place – some rooms have stunning views of the channel. All share clean bathrooms, and the kitchen is great. Suite available downstairs.

Galeazzi-Basily B&B (☎ 02901-423213; www.geo cities.com/galeazzibasily; Valdéz 323; r US$20) Only two rooms are available at this pleasant home. A large house (sleeps six) is available in December and February. English, French and Italian spoken; book ahead.

Casa de Familia Zaprucki (☎ 02901-421316; Deloquí 271; apartments US$25-72) Family-run, this little Eden has four clean, just-like-home apartments that hold up to six; breakfast is included. It's popular, so call ahead.

Camping La Pista del Andino (☎ 02901-435890; www.lapistadelandino.com.ar in Spanish; Alem 2873; camping/RV sites per person US$3; ☯ Oct-Apr) Some 3km from the town center, this pleasant camping spot offers grassy or forest sites with views. There are cooking facilities, good common areas and bikes for rent. Call for free pickup from the airport/town center (taxis to the center of town cost US$1.25).

Ten kilometers west of town is Camping Municipal. It has minimal services, but it's free. Transport there and around may eat up savings, however.

Eating

El Norte supermarket (cnr Lugones & Karukinká) Biggest in town and 15-minutes' walk from center. Good, cheap *cafetería*.

> **SPLURGE!**
>
> Yup, there is indeed high cuisine in Ushuaia. Just hike up the hill to **Kaupé** (☎ 02901-422704; Roca 470; entrées US$8.50-12), where you'll be served fine international food, wine and views. If you're looking for a romantic spot with soft music in the background you'll do fine here. Call for reservations.

Lomitos Martinica (Av San Martín 68) Cheap *parrillada* choices and set meals, no-non-sense service and stools for seats.

La Baguette (cnr Av San Martín & Don Bosco) Modern, small place with tempting breads and pastries. Pasta and sandwiches for takeout.

Café-bar Tante Sara (Av San Martín 701) Modern art on the walls and chatter in the air. Breakfasts, sandwiches and snacks.

La Rueda (Av San Martín 193) One of five *parrillas* on this stretch, with a good *tenedor libre* (US$5.80). Ushuaia's stray mutts gather outside.

Volver (Av Maipú 37) Basic meat, pasta and seafood in a busy, almost romantic setting. One plus (or minus) is the background accordion music.

Tía Elvira (Av Maipú 349) Another pricey seafood joint, but with plenty of meat and wine choices, if your hot date eschews mollusks.

Drinking

U-Bar (Av San Martín 245) Orange sofas, neon trim and futuristic tables knock Ushuaia so much into its hip future that it hurts. Come Saturdays for house and electronic music spun by DJs.

Orelie Antoine (Lasserre 108) Live music breaks out on weekends and the occasional Wednesday, and after midnight the dark, simple spaces become a disco. For big shows cover charges run US$1.75 to US$3.75.

Nautico Pub (cnr Maipú & Belgrano) A restaurant by day, this shoreline spot transforms into a popular disco on weekends. Cover charges depend on the day, your gender and what's going on, though they're not overly expensive and may include a drink.

Getting There & Away

In January and February it's a good idea to book your passage out of Ushuaia as early as possible or you might end up waiting days for an open seat to Punta Arenas.

Aerolíneas Argentinas (☎ 02901-421091; Roca 116) zooms to Buenos Aires (US$115), Río Gallegos (US$33), El Calafate (US$100) and Trelew (US$105). **LAPA** (☎ 02901-432112; 25 de Mayo 64) does Buenos Aires (US$115), Bariloche (US$215) and El Calafate (US$135). **LADE** (☎ 02901-421123; Av San Martín 542) can't be beat to Río Grande (US$13), Comodoro Rivadavia (US$60) or El Calafate (US$33), although service is infrequent.

Tecni-Austral (☎ 02901-431412; Roca 157) has buses to Río Grande at 6am Monday to Saturday (US$7.80, 3½ hours) and to Río Gallegos and Punta Arenas at 6am on Monday, Wednesday and Friday (both US$27, 12 hours). **Lider** (☎ 02901-420003; Gobernador Paz 921) has the most services to Rio Grande, with eight daily departures (US$7.80).

Getting Around

Taxis around town are cheap. Rent bikes at **DTT** (Av San Martín 903) for US$9 per day. Many bus companies provide transport to Lagos Escondido/Fagnano for US$13 return. For transport to Parque Nacional Tierra del Fuego, see p152.

PARQUE NACIONAL TIERRA DEL FUEGO

West of Ushuaia by 12km lies the beautiful **Parque Nacional Tierra del Fuego** (admission US$4.25), which extends from the Beagle Channel in the south to beyond Lago Fagnano in the north; only a small part of the park is accessible to the public, however. Despite a tiny system of short, easy trails more suited to day-trippers than backpacking trekkers, the views along the bays, rivers and forests are wonderfully scenic. Southern beeches like the evergreen coihue and deciduous lenga thrive on heavy coastal rainfall, and in autumn the hillsides of deciduous *ñire* burst out in red.

Plenty of bird life graces the coasts here. Keep your eyes peeled for upland geese *(cauquén)*, cormorants, oystercatchers, grebes, steamer ducks and even rare condors or albatross. The most common land critters are the European rabbit and North American beaver, introduced species that have wreaked havoc on the ecosystem. Foxes and the occasional guanaco may also be seen, but marine mammals are most common on offshore islands.

One good, moderate hike runs for 2½ hours along the north shores of Bahía Ensenada and Bahía Lapataia; it starts at the boat pier (rides to Isla Redonda US$14). For a longer hike, you can continue along the road, past the Lago Roca camping and *confitería* area, to the start of the Lago Roca trail – which goes for 5km to the Chilean border (best not to cross it). About 1.5km into this trail a side shoot to the right leads to steep Cerro Guanaco, with decent views (four hours). Taking the bus all the way to the end of RN 3 gives you access to some short scenic walks. For the complete picture, get a map of the area from the tourist office or Parques Nacionales in Ushuaia.

Park admission is collected between 8am and 8pm daily November through April. Weather can be very changeable, even in summer, so come prepared.

Sleeping
The only organized campground is **Lago Roca** (Oct-Apr). Pitch a tent for US$1.75/3 per person without/with hot shower; a *confitería* and tiny grocery are nearby. Tent rentals are available for US$5.50. Free campsites in the park include Las Bandurrias, Laguna Verde and Los Cauquenes, Ensenada and Río Pipo.

Getting There & Away
The many bus companies in Ushuaia providing service to the park charge US$5.50 to US$7.30 round trip (depending on destination). Transporte Pasarela and Eben-Ezer have the most departures and honor each other's tickets; they leave half-hourly 8am to 8pm daily from Maipú and 25 de Mayo. For a complete list of bus companies, see the tourist office.

If you've got money to burn, take **El Tren del Fin del Mundo** (2901-431600; www.trendelfin delmundo.com.ar) to the park. The one-hour, scenic narrow-gauge train ride comes with historical explanations in English and Spanish (US$17 return, not including park admission). The station is 8km from Ushuaia (taxi US$3 one way; bus US$3 return) and there are four departures daily in summer and one in winter. Reserve in January and February, when cruise ship tours take over.

ARGENTINA DIRECTORY

ACCOMMODATIONS
There's a good range of affordable hostels throughout Argentina, and whether they are Hostelling International-affiliated or not, most are friendly and offer quality services. Sheets are often included, towels are often available for hire and the majority of hostels have a few private rooms (book ahead). For information on two popular and excellent hostel organizations check out www.hostels.org.ar (Hostelling International) or www.argentina hostels.com (Argentina Hostel Club).

Residenciales are small hotels, while *hospedajes* are usually family homes with extra bedrooms and shared baths. Hotels can range from one to five stars, and usually come with private bath.

Camping is popular in Argentina, though sites aren't always near the center of town. National parks usually have organized sites, and some offer distant *refugios* (basic shelters for trekkers).

ACTIVITIES
Argentina's chock-full of awesome ways to get outdoors. Like to climb? Go scale Aconcagua (6960m), the highest peak outside Asia (p114). What about hiking or trekking? Heaps of trails await around Bariloche (p124), not to mention the fantastic Fitz Roy range (p140). White-water rafting can be enjoyed near Mendoza (as well as Bariloche p124) and horse riding is popular in many tourist areas.

Skiing is world-class, with major resorts at Cerro Catedral (Bariloche), Las Leñas (Malargüe, p116) and Chapelco (San Martín de los Andes, p121). In summer, these mountains turn into activity centers for mountain biking, among other things.

BOOKS
Lonely Planet's *Argentina, Uruguay & Paraguay* travel guide and *Buenos Aires* city guide are *número uno* for exploring Argentina in greater depth.

Travelogues on the country include *The Voyage of the Beagle* (Darwin on *gaucho* life), *The Uttermost Part of the Earth* (Lucas Bridges on Tierra del Fuego's indigenous folk), *In Patagonia* (Bruce Chatwin's classic) and *The Motorcycle Diaries: A Journey Around South America* (Che Guevara on adventurous travel with a dilapidated motorcycle).

For history, check out James Scobie's standard *A City and a Nation*, or David Rock's comprehensive *Argentina 1516–1987: from Spanish Colonization to Alfonsín*. DF Sarmiento's 19th-century classic *Life in the Argentine Republic in the Days of the Tyrants* eloquently criticizes Federalist *caudillos* (powerful landowners).

Pampas reading includes Richard W Slatta's *Gauchos and the Vanishing Frontier*, while Nicholas Shumway's *The Invention of Argentina* is an intellectual history of the country. Peron fans can peruse Joseph Page's *Perón: a Biography* and Robert Crassweller's *Perón & the Enigma of Argentina*. The Dirty War is chronicled in Jacobo Timerman's *Prisoner Without a Name, Cell Without a Number* and Horacio Verbitsky's *The Flight*. On the democratic transition, see Mónica Peralta-Ramos and Carlos Waisman's *From Military Rule to Liberal Democracy in Argentina*.

BUSINESS HOURS

Traditionally, businesses open by 9am, break at 1pm for lunch and then reopen at 4pm until 8pm or 9pm. This pattern is still common in the provinces, but government offices and many businesses in Buenos Aires have adopted the 9am to 5pm schedule.

CLIMATE

January and February are oppressively hot and humid in the subtropical north (including Iguazú Falls) and Buenos Aires. These are the best months, however, to visit the high Andes and southern Patagonia – and you'll still need warm clothes. Buenos Aires is best in spring or fall. Skiers enjoy the Andes during the winter months, June to September. For more information and climate charts see the South America Directory (p1028).

DANGERS & ANNOYANCES

Don't let anyone tell you otherwise: despite the public's constant dissatisfaction with its government and a lumbering economy that gives rise to occasional crime waves, Argentina remains one of the safest countries in Latin America. Most tourists who visit Buenos Aires leave happy and unscathed. Outside the big cities, serious crime is rare.

In general, the biggest dangers in Argentina are speeding cars and buses – be careful crossing streets, and *never* assume you have the right of way as a pedestrian. If you're sensitive to cigarette smoke, be aware that Argentines are truly addicted to nicotine – they'll light up in banks, post offices, restaurants, cafés and everywhere else. Other small concerns include loose sidewalk tiles, ubiquitous dog piles and the occasional hole in the ground.

For big-city advice, see Buenos Aires (p45). For general advice on traveling safely in South America, see the Directory (p1030).

EMBASSIES & CONSULATES
Embassies & Consulates in Argentina

The following is not a complete list. For locations of these and other consulates see individual city maps.

Australia Buenos Aires (☎ 011-4777-6580; Villanueva 1400, Belgrano)

Bolivia Buenos Aires (Map pp46-8; ☎ 011-4381-0539; Belgrano 1670, 1st fl, Montserrat); La Quiaca (☎ 03885-42-2283; cnr San Juan & Árabe Siria) Charges up to US$30 for visas, so it's best to get one elsewhere; Salta (Map p94; ☎ 0387-421-1040; Mariano Boedo 34); San Salvador de Jujuy (Map p97; ☎ 0388-424-0501; Independencia 1098)

Brazil Buenos Aires (Map pp46-8; ☎ 011-4515-6500; Carlos Pellegrini 1363, 5th fl, Retiro); Paso de Los Libres (☎ 03772-425444; Mitre 842) Requires 24 hours processing time for visas; Puerto Iguazú (Map p78; ☎ 03757-421348; Av Guaraní 70) Can turn around visa applications in as little as half an hour.

Canada Buenos Aires (☎ 011-4805-3032; Tagle 2828, Palermo)

Chile Bariloche (Map p125; ☎ 02944-422842; Av Juan Manuel de Rosas 180); Buenos Aires (Map pp46-8; ☎ 011-4394-6582; San Martín 439, 9th fl, San Nicolás); Comodoro Rivadavia (☎ 0297-446-2414; Brown 456, 1st fl); Mendoza (☎ 0261-425-4844; Paso de los Andes 1147); Neuquén (☎ 0299-442-2727; La Rioja 241); Río Gallegos (Map p145; ☎ 02966-422364; Mariano Moreno 136); Salta (Map p94; ☎ 0387-431-1857; Santiago del Estero 965); Ushuaia (Map p149; ☎ 02901-430909; Jainén 50)

France Buenos Aires (Map pp46-8; ☎ 011-4312-2409; Santa Fe 846, 4th fl, Retiro)

Germany Buenos Aires (☎ 011-4778-2500; Villanueva 1055, Palermo)

Israel Buenos Aires (Map pp46-8; ☎ 011-4338-2500; Av de Mayo 701, 10th fl, Montserrat)

Italy Buenos Aires (Map pp46-8; ☎ 011-4816-6132; Marcelo T de Alvear 1149, Retiro)

Netherlands Buenos Aires (Map pp46-8; ☎ 011-4334-4000; Av de Mayo 701, 19th fl, Montserrat)

New Zealand Buenos Aires (Map pp46-8; ☎ 011-4328-0634; Carlos Pellegrini 1427, 5th fl)

Paraguay Buenos Aires (Map pp46-8; ☎ 011-4802-3432; Viamonte 1851, Balvanera); Posadas (Map p75; ☎ 03752-423858; San Lorenzo 179) Has brochures and basic maps.

Peru Buenos Aires (Map pp46-8; ☎ 011-4811-4619; Córdoba 1345, 11th fl, Retiro)

South Africa Buenos Aires (Map pp46-8; ☎ 011-4317-2900; Marcelo T de Alvear 590, 7th fl)

Spain Buenos Aires (Map pp46-8; ☎ 011-4811-0070; Guido 1760, Recoleta)

Switzerland Buenos Aires (Map pp46-8; ☎ 011-4311-6491; Santa Fe 846, 10th fl, Retiro)

UK Buenos Aires (☎ 011-4803-7070; Dr Luis Agote 2412, Recoleta)

Uruguay Buenos Aires (Map pp46-8; ☎ 011-4807-3040; General Las Heras 1915, Recoleta); Gualeguaychú (☎ 03446-426168; Rivadavia 510)

USA Buenos Aires (☎ 011-5777-4533; Colombia 4300, Palermo)

Argentine Embassies & Consulates Abroad

Argentina probably has an embassy or consulate in your country; this is only a partial list.

Australia Canberra (☎ 02-6273 9111; 7 National Cct, Level 2, Barton, ACT 2600)

Canada Ottawa (☎ 613-236-2351; 90 Sparks St, Suite 910, Ottawa, Ontario K1P 5B4)

France Paris (☎ 01 45 53 33 00; 6 rue Cimarosa, Paris 75116)

Germany Bonn (☎ 0228-228010; Adenauerallee 50-52, 53113 Bonn)

New Zealand Wellington (☎ 04-472 8330; 142 Lambton Quay, Level 14, Wellington)

UK London (☎ 020-7318 1300; 65 Brook St, London W1K 4AH)

USA Los Angeles (☎ 213-954-9155; 5055 Wilshire Blvd, Suite 210, Los Angeles, CA 90036); New York (☎ 212-603-0400 ;12 W 56th St, New York, NY 10019); Washington (☎ 202-238-6400; 1600 New Hampshire Ave NW, Washington, DC 20009)

FESTIVALS & EVENTS

These are just a smattering of available festivals in Buenos Aires and Argentina; check your local tourist office for more information.

Wine Harvest Festival (dates vary) Folkloric events and parades in Mendoza.

Carnaval (usually in February) Especially rowdy in Gualeguaychú and Corrientes.

Buenos Aires Tango Festival (www.festivaldetango .com.ar; early March)

Feria del Libro (Buenos Aires' Book Fair; first three weeks in April)

Festival Internacional de Cine Independiente (Buenos Aires Independent Film Festival; www.bafilmfest.com in Spanish; mid to late April)

Día de la Virgen de Luján (May 8) Virgin Mary is honored in Luján.

Campeonato Mundial de Baile de Tango (Tango competitions; www.mundialdetango.com.ar; mid to late August)

Guitarras del Mundo (Buenos Aires Guitar Festival; www.festivaldeguitarras.com.ar in Spanish; mid to late October)

FILMS & VIDEOS

For a brief introduction to the country, check out Lonely Planet's *Argentina* video.

Madonna's *Evita* caused controversy as many Argentines resented her being cast in the title role. A creepy English-language film with a Dirty War theme, Martin Donovan's *Apartment Zero* depicts many amusing aspects of *porteño* life. Sally Potter's autobiographical *The Tango Lesson* is a tale of the sensual tango. And screen idol Brad Pitt can't be forgotten in *Seven Years in Tibet*, filmed in the high Andes west of Mendoza.

For films by Argentine directors, see Cinema, p39.

FOOD & DRINK
Argentine Cuisine

Most of Argentina won't astound you with a wide range of cuisine – folks here seem to survive mainly on meat, pasta and pizza – but the country's famous beef does live up to expectations. At a *parrilla* (steakhouse) or *asado* (private barbecue) try *bife de chorizo* (thick sirloin), *bife de lomo* (tenderloin) or a *parrillada* – a mixed grill of cheaper beef cuts and organ meats. Ask for *chimichurri*, a spicy sauce of garlic, parsley and olive oil. If you want your steak rare say *jugoso*; medium is *a punto*, but you're on your own with well-done.

The Italian influence is apparent in dishes like pizza, spaghetti, ravioli and chewy *ñoquis* (gnocchi). Vegetarian fare is available in Buenos Aires and other larger cities. *Tenedor libres* (all-you-can-eat buffets) are popular everywhere and are often great value. Middle Eastern food is common in the north, while the northwest has spicy dishes like those of Bolivia or Peru. In Patagonia lamb is king, while specialties like trout, boar and venison are served around the Lake District.

Confiterías usually grill sandwiches like *lomito* (steak), *milanesa* (a thin breaded steak) and hamburgers. *Restaurantes* have larger menus, professional waiters and more elaborate decor. Cafés are important social places for everything from marriage proposals to business deals to revolutions, and many also serve alcohol and simple meals.

Fast food places cluster around busy bus terminals. Large supermarkets often have a counter with good, cheap takeout. Western fast-food joints, such as McDonald's, exist in larger cities.

Breakfast is a simple affair of coffee, tea or maté with *tostadas* (toast), *manteca* (butter) and *mermelada* (jam). *Medialunas* (croissants) come either sweet or plain. Lunch is around 1pm, teatime around 5pm and dinner usually after 8pm (few restaurants open before this hour).

Empanadas are baked or fried turnovers with vegetables, beef, cheese or other fillings. *Sandwichitos de miga* (thin, crust-free sandwiches layered with ham and cheese) are great at teatime. Commonly sold at kiosks, *alfajores* are cookie sandwiches filled with *dulce de leche* (a thin milky caramel) or *mermelada* and covered in chocolate or meringue.

Postres (desserts) include *ensalada de fruta* (fruit salad), pies and cakes, *facturas* (pastries) and flan, which can be topped with *crema* (whipped cream) or *dulce de leche*. Argentina's Italian-derived *helados* (ice cream) are South America's best.

Drinks

ALCOHOLIC DRINKS

Argentines like to drink, and you'll find long lists of beer, wine, cognac, whiskey and gin at many (not necessarily upscale) restaurants. *Ginebra bols* (which differs from gin) and *caña* (cane alcohol) are specialties worth a 'shot'. Both Quilmes and Isenbeck are popular beers; in bars or cafés, ask for *chopp* (draft or lager).

Microbrews are widely available in the Lake District.

Some Argentine wines are world-class; both reds *(tintos)* and whites *(blancos)* are excellent, but Malbecs are especially well known. Good wineries include Norton, Lopez, Bianchi, Chandon, Navarro Correas, Rutini and Luigi Bosca. The major wine-producing areas are near Mendoza, San Juan, La Rioja and Salta.

NONALCOHOLIC DRINKS

Soft drinks are everywhere. For water, there's *con gas* (carbonated) or *sin gas* (non-carbonated) mineral water and the much cheaper *agua de siphon* (soda water), which comes in plastic siphon bottles and is available at most local eateries. Or ask for Argentina's usually drinkable *agua de canilla* (tap water).

For fresh-squeezed orange juice, ask for *jugo de naranja exprimido* to avoid canned juice. *Manzana* (apple), *pomelo* (grapefruit) and *ananá* (pineapple) are other common juices.

Licuados are milk-blended fruit drinks. Common flavors include banana, *durazno* (peach) and *pera* (pear).

Even in the smallest town, coffee will be espresso. *Café chico* is thick, dark coffee in a very small cup. *Café cortado* is a small coffee with a touch of milk; *cortado doble* is a larger portion. *Café con leche* (a latte) is served for breakfast only; after lunch or dinner, request a *cortado*.

Tea usually comes with two giant packs of sugar. If you don't want milk, avoid *té con leche*, a tea bag immersed in tepid milk; rather, ask for *un poquito de leche*, which will get you a little milk on the side. You shouldn't decline an invitation to maté, although until you acquire the taste it may seem like you're ingesting 'steeped horse shit' (anonymous).

GAY & LESBIAN TRAVELERS

Argentina is a strongly Catholic country, but enclaves of tolerance toward gays and lesbians do exist (especially in Buenos Aires). Argentine men are more physically demonstrative than you may be used to, so behaviors such as cheek kisses or a vigorous embrace are innocuous even to the local homophobe. Lesbians walking hand-in-hand should attract little attention, as heterosexual

ARGENTINA

Argentine women often do, but this would be suspicious behavior for males. In general, do your thing – but be discreet.

In Buenos Aires there are plenty of gay entertainment venues (see p56); check current happenings in *NX* magazine or in the free booklet *La Otra Guía*.

HEALTH

Argentina requires no vaccinations. Cholera and malaria are minor concerns in the more rural, lowland border sections of Salta, Jujuy, Corrientes and Misiones provinces. In the high Andes, watch for signs of altitude sickness and use more sunscreen.

Urban water supplies are usually potable, making salads and ice safe to consume. Many prescription drugs are available over the counter. Seek out an embassy recommendation if you need Western-type medical services. For more information, see the Health chapter (p1053).

HOLIDAYS

Government offices and businesses close on most national holidays, which are often moved to the nearest Monday or Friday to extend weekends. Provincial holidays are not listed here.

Año Nuevo (New Year's Day; January 1)
Jueves & Viernes Santo/Pascua (Good Thursday & Friday/Easter; March/April – dates vary)
Día del Trabajador (Labor Day; May 1)
Revolución de Mayo (May Revolution of 1810; May 25)
Día de las Malvinas (Malvinas Day; June 10)
Día de la Bandera (Flag Day; June 20)
Día de la Independencia (Independence Day; July 9)
Día de San Martín (Anniversary of San Martín's death; August 17)
Día de la Raza (Columbus Day; October 12)
Día de la Tradición (Gaucho Day; November 10)
Día de la Concepción Inmaculada (Immaculate Conception Day; December 8)
Navidad (Christmas Day; December 25)

INTERNET ACCESS

Argentina is online: Internet cafés exist even in small towns and prices are quite reasonable (usually US$0.75/hour). To type the @ *(arroba)* symbol, hold down the Alt-key while typing 64 on the keypad.

INTERNET RESOURCES

CDC Travelers' Health (www.cdc.gov/travel/temsam.htm) Health information for Argentina and surrounding regions.

Expat Village (www.expatvillage.com/home) Best for expats, but heaps of good information for travelers too.
Lanic (www.lanic.utexas.edu/la/argentina) A massive list of Argentine websites.
US Department of State Consular Information Sheet (www.travel.state.gov/argentina.html) How the American government views travel to Argentina.

LANGUAGE

Besides flamboyance, the unique pronunciation of *castellano* – Argentina's version of the Spanish language – readily identifies an Argentine elsewhere in Latin America or abroad. If you're in Buenos Aires you'll also hear *lunfardo*, the capital's colorful slang.

Some immigrants (like the Welsh in Patagonia) retain their language as a badge of identity. Quechua speakers, numerous in the Northwest, tend to be bilingual in Spanish. Many Mapuche speakers live in the southern Andes, while most Guaraní speakers live in northeastern Argentina.

See the Language chapter (p1064) for more information.

MAPS

If you plan to hang around the capital, grab a copy of Lonely Planet's laminated *Buenos Aires* map.

The **Automóvil Club Argentino** (ACA; www.aca .org.ar in Spanish), whose main branch is in **Palermo** (☎ 011-4802-6061; Av del Libertador 1850), publishes some excellent city and provincial maps – members of ACA's overseas affiliates get discounts with their card. True map nerds can visit the **Instituto Geográfico Militar** (☎ 011-4576-5576; Cabildo 381) in Palermo. Many newspaper kiosks and bookstores stock good maps.

MEDIA

The English-language daily, *Buenos Aires Herald* (www.buenosairesherald.com), covers the world from an Anglo-Argentine perspective.

Buenos Aires' most important Spanish dailies are *La Prensa, La Nación* and the middle-of-the-road tabloid *Clarín*, which has an excellent Sunday cultural section. *Página 12* provides a refreshing leftist perspective and often breaks important stories that mainstream newspapers are slow to cover. *Ámbito Financiero* is the voice of the business sector, but it also provides good cultural coverage.

MONEY

ATMs

ATMs are common, handy and the way to go in Argentina, whether you're in a big city or small town. Exchange rates are reasonable. Don't forget your four-digit code.

Cash

Bills come in denominations of two, five, 10, 20, 50 and 100 pesos. The peso is subdivided into 100 centavos. Coins come in one (rare), five, 10, 25 and 50 centavos and one peso. Some businesses will accept clean US bills at a decent exchange rate. Always carry change.

Although all prices in this book are quoted in US dollars, and many businesses in Argentina will indeed accept US dollars as currency, not all places will take them. Carry local currency for small purchases and patriotic merchants, or for government offices.

Credit Cards

The larger a hotel is, the greater the chance it will accept credit cards. Ditto for stores and other services. Many businesses add a *recargo* (surcharge) of up to 10% to credit card purchases; always ask before charging. MasterCard and Visa are the main honchos, but American Express is also commonly accepted.

Exchange Rates

Exchange rates at press time included the following:

Country	Unit		Arg$ (peso)
Australia	A$1	=	2.06
Canada	C$1	=	2.20
euro zone	€1	=	3.37
Japan	¥100	=	2.64
New Zealand	NZ$1	=	1.78
United Kingdom	UK£1	=	4.93
United States	US$1	=	2.90

Exchanging Money

US dollars and certain other currencies can be converted to Argentine pesos at most banks or *cambios* (exchange houses). Some banks will only exchange a minimum amount (say, US$300) so check before lining up. *Cambios* offer slightly poorer rates, but usually have fewer restrictions.

Since the major currency devaluation in January 2002, Buenos Aires' Av Florida

has seen a proliferation of shady figures offering 'cambio, cambio, cambio' to passing pedestrians. Using these unofficial street changers is not recommended; there are quite a few fake bills floating about.

Traveler's checks are very difficult to cash (even at banks) and suffer poor exchange rates. They're not recommended as your main source of traveling money.

Tipping & Bargaining

The usual *propina* (tip) at restaurants is 10% – provided a service charge hasn't already been included in the bill. There's no need to tip taxis, but you can leave them extra change.

Bargaining is possible in the northwest and in craft fairs countrywide. If you stay several days at a hotel, you can often negotiate a better rate. Many higher-range hotels will give discounts for cash payments.

POST

Letters and postcards (up to 20g) to the US cost US$1.60; they're US$1.90 to Europe and Australia. You can send packages under 2kg from any post office, but anything heavier needs to go through *aduana* (a customs office).

Correo Argentino (www.correoargentino.com.ar in Spanish) – the privatized postal service – has become more dependable over the years, but send essential mail *certificado* (registered). Private couriers, such as OCA, DHL and FedEx are available in some larger cities, but are much more expensive.

> ### WHAT'S THIS FUNNY-LOOKING MONEY?!?
>
> While you're traveling around Buenos Aires you may be given some money that doesn't look quite...right. You've likely stumbled upon *Patacones*, or bills that were issued by the province when the federal government stopped printing pesos for fear of runaway inflation. Starved for funds, many provinces were forced to print their own currency to pay employees. This official-looking 'money' (in reality, a type of bond) is accepted by many businesses and banks, but is worthless outside its original province of issue. Get rid of the bills before you move on, or don't take them in the first place.

ARGENTINA

STUDYING
Since devaluation of the peso, Argentina has become a hot (and cheap) destination in which to learn Spanish. For a partial list of Spanish schools in Buenos Aires, see p50. Other large cities, such as Bariloche, Mendoza and Córdoba, also have Spanish schools.

TELEPHONE
Telecom and Telefónica are the major Argentine phone companies. *Locutorios* (small telephone offices) are very common in any city; you enter private booths, make calls, then pay at the front counter. These may cost more than street phones but are better for privacy and quiet, and you won't run out of coins.

Calling the US, Europe and Australia from *locutorios* is expensive, but rates are discounted after 10pm and on weekends. Tell the operator beforehand if you want to make an international call. Some public phones use *tarjetas* (magnetic cards), available from kiosks.

To call someone in Argentina, you'll need to dial Argentina's country code (☎ 54), then the city's area code (noted in this guidebook before every telephone number in every city), then the number itself.

TWO-TIER COSTS IN ARGENTINA

Don't be surprised if, as a traveling foreigner, you're charged more than Argentine residents on occasion. Since the collapse of the peso in 2002, major airlines, most national parks, some hotels and even a few museums have adopted a two-tier price system. Rates for foreigners can be close to double the locals' price. While it's somewhat useless to complain to service personnel at government-run entities about this discrepancy, you can at least choose to stay at hotels that don't discriminate. Ask them point blank if they charge more for foreigners than locals, and if you don't like it go elsewhere – there are plenty of hotels that feel OK charging everyone the same.

By the way, no accommodation listed in this Argentina chapter has adopted this two-tier system; if you find that they have, please write in and tell us.

To call a cell phone you must first dial ☎ 15, unless you are calling from another cell phone.

TOURIST INFORMATION
All tourist-oriented cities in Argentina have a conveniently located tourist office, and many of them have English-speaking staff. In Buenos Aires, each Argentine province has a tourist office. Also in Buenos Aires is the excellent **Secretaría de Turismo de la Nación** (☎ 011-4312-2232; 0800-555-0016; www.turismo.gov.ar; Santa Fe 883; ☼ 9am-5pm Mon-Fri), which dispenses information on all of Argentina.

VISAS
Residents of Canada, the US, Australia, and many western European countries do not need visas to enter Argentina – they receive an automatic 90-day stamp on arrival. It's smart to double-check this information with your embassy before you leave, as changes often occur.

For visa extensions, visit *migraciones* (immigration offices) in the provincial capitals.

WOMEN TRAVELERS
Being a woman in Argentina is a challenge, especially if you are young, traveling alone and/or come with an inflexible liberal attitude. In some ways Argentina is a safer place for a woman than Europe, the USA and most other Latin American countries, but dealing with this *machismo* culture can be a real pain in the ass.

Some males brimming with testosterone feel the need to comment on a woman's attractiveness. This most often happens when a woman is alone and walking by on the street. Verbal comments include hisses, whistles and *piropos*, which are sometimes vulgar comments (though some can be poetically eloquent). Much as you may want to kick them where it counts, the best thing to do is completely ignore them. Most men don't necessarily mean to be insulting; they're just doing what males in their culture were taught to do.

On the plus side of *machismo*, expect men to hold a door open for you and let you enter first, including getting on buses; this gives you a better chance at grabbing an empty seat, so get in there quick.

WORKING

There are some English-teaching jobs in Buenos Aires and other major cities, but don't expect to get rich – most teachers make just enough to get by, maybe US$5 per hour. Having a TESOL or TESL certificate will be an advantage in acquiring work.

Many teachers work 'illegally' on tourist visas, which they must renew every three months (in Buenos Aires this usually means hopping to Uruguay a few times per year). Work schedules drop off during the holiday months of January and February, when those who can afford to take English classes can afford to travel around the country.

For job postings, check out the classifieds in the **Buenos Aires Herald** (www.buenosairesherald.com).

Bolivia

HIGHLIGHTS

- **Salar de Uyuni** – the southwest's hallucinogenic salt deserts, spurting geysers and eerie lagoons – some of the bleakest terrain on Earth – are more surreal than a Dali (p205)
- **Lake Titicaca island hopping** – ponder snow-tipped Andean peaks reflected in the sapphire blue waters of the world's highest major lake. Watching the sunset over ancient ruins on serene Isla del Sol is positively Mediterranean (p195)
- **Choro trek & the 'World's Most Dangerous Road'** – plunge from tundra to misty valleys then ascend to breathtaking vistas during a vertigo-inspiring ramble. Or, tackle the adrenaline-rushing descent from La Cumbre to Coroico on a mountain bike (p189)
- **Amazon Basin jungle & pampas trips** – penetrate deep into the lush pampas and rain forest of the Amazon lowlands. Riverboat trips await the gung-ho outside of Rurrenabaque (p236)
- **Off the beaten track** – head for far-flung, awe-inspiring protected areas like Parques Nacionales Madidi, Noel Kempff Mercado, Torotoro or Amboró (p167)
- **Best journey** – lazy river routes from Trinidad into the Brazilian Amazon are ripe for adventure. The road and rail routes to Brazil and Paraguay are not for the faint of heart

FAST FACTS

- **Area:** 1,098,580 sq km (France and Spain combined)
- **Budget:** US$15–25 a day
- **Capitals:** Sucre (constitutional), La Paz (de facto)
- **Costs:** La Paz bed US$2–4, 1L bottle of domestic beer US$1, four-hour bus ride US$2
- **Country code:** ☎ 591
- **Electricity:** 220V, 50Hz; US-type plugs
- **Famous for:** world's highest everything, being landlocked, *peñas*, coca
- **Languages:** Spanish, Quechua, Aymara, Guaraní
- **Money:** US$1 = 7.99 bolivianos
- **Phrases:** *genial* (cool), *la bomba* (party), *mugre* (disgusting)
- **Population:** 8.8 million (2003 UN estimate)
- **Time:** GMT minus 4 hours
- **Tipping:** 10% in better restaurants, small change elsewhere; don't tip taxis
- **Traveler's checks:** cashed at banks and *casas de cambio* (2–5% fee); ATMs are easier
- **Visas:** most North and South American and Western European citizens get a free 30-day tourist card (extendable for free for up to 90 days) upon arrival

TRAVEL HINTS

Take it easy in the first few days at altitude. Visit a toilet before boarding buses. Pack some cushioning for the long hauls. Wear sandals to ward off shoeshine boys. Request the *llapa* ('extra bit').

Unparalleled natural beauty. Vibrant indigenous cultures. Muy tranquilo (tranquil) cities. Whispers of ancient civilizations. Except for beaches, Bolivia has it all. Landlocked and lying astride the widest stretch of the Andes, its geography runs the gamut, from jagged soaring peaks and hallucinogenic salt flats to steamy jungles and wildlife-rich pampas (grasslands). Surprisingly, it still falls below many travelers' radar, so opportunities for unique adventures and off-the-beaten-path exploration abound.

Bolivia isn't called the Tibet of the Americas for nothing: it's the hemisphere's highest, most isolated and most rugged nation. It's also South America's most indigenous country, with over half of the population claiming pure Amerindian blood. Socially and politically, trouble simmers steadily thanks to an impotent economy, the US Drug War and a populace worn ragged by poverty, unemployment and disfranchisement. As a result, protests, marches and demonstrations (mostly peaceful) are a perpetual part of the country's mind-boggling landscape. Put on your high-altitude goggles and get ready to ramble.

HISTORY
Pre-Gringo Times
Sometime around 1500 BC, Aymara people, possibly from the mountains of modern central Peru, swept across the Bolivian Andes to occupy the altiplano. The years between AD 500 and AD 900 were distinguished by imperial expansion and increasing power and influence of the Tiahuanaco (or Tiwanaku) culture. The society's ceremonial center near Lake Titicaca rapidly became the highland's religious and political center. In the 9th century AD, however, Tiahuanaco's power waned. Ongoing submarine excavations in Lake Titicaca are attempting to identify the cause of Tiahuanaco's downfall.

Before the Spanish Conquest, the Bolivian altiplano had been incorporated into the Inca empire as the southern province of Kollasuyo. Modern Quechua speakers around Lake Titicaca are descended from those who immigrated under an Inca policy of populating newly conquered colonies with Quechua-speaking tribes.

There's considerable speculation that ruins on the scale of Machu Picchu, possibly the lost Inca city of Paititi, may be buried in the Bolivian rain forest.

Conquistadores
By the late 1520s, internecine rivalries began cleaving the Inca empire. However, it took the arrival of the Spaniards – initially thought to be emissaries of the Inca sun god – to seal the deal. The Inca emperor Atahualpa was captured in 1532, and by 1537 the Spanish had consolidated their forces in Peru and securely held Cuzco.

After the demise of the Inca empire, Alto Perú, as the Spaniards called Bolivia, fell briefly into the hands of the conquistador Diego de Almagro. Before long, Francisco Pizarro, dispatched his brother Gonzalo to subdue the rogue, silver-rich southern province. In 1538 Pedro de Anzures founded the township of La Plata (later renamed Chuquisaca and then Sucre), which became the political center of Spain's eastern territories.

In 1545 tremendous deposits of high-quality silver were discovered in Potosí. The settlement grew into one of the world's richest (and highest) cities on the backs of forced labor: appalling conditions in the mines led to the deaths of perhaps eight million African and Indian slaves. In 1548 Alonso de Mendoza founded La Paz as a staging post on the main silver route to the Pacific coast.

In 1574 the Spaniards founded the future granaries of Cochabamba and Tarija, which served to contain the uncooperative Chiriguano people. Hereafter, colonialism and Jesuit missionary efforts established settlement patterns that defined the course of Bolivian society.

Coups de Grâce
In 1781 a futile attempt was made to oust the Spaniards and reestablish the Inca empire. Three decades later a local government was established in the independence movement stronghold of Chuquisaca (Sucre). Chuquisaca's liberal political doctrines soon radiated throughout Spanish America.

In 1824, after 15 years of bloodshed, Peru was finally liberated from Spanish domination. However, in Alto Perú, the royalist general Pedro Antonio de Olañeta held out against the liberating forces. In 1825, when offers of negotiation failed, Simón Bolívar

BOLIVIA

dispatched an expeditionary force to Alto Perú under General Antonio José de Sucre. On August 6, 1825, independence was proclaimed, Alto Perú became the Republic of Bolivia, and Bolívar and Sucre became the new republic's first and second presidents.

In 1828 mestizo Andrés de Santa Cruz took power and formed a confederacy with Peru. This triggered protests by Chile, whose army defeated Santa Cruz in 1839, breaking the confederation and throwing Bolivia into political chaos. The confusion peaked in 1841, when three different governments claimed power simultaneously.

Such spontaneous and unsanctioned changes of government became commonplace and continued through the 1980s in a series of coups and military interventions. As of 2003, Bolivia had endured 192 changes of government in its 178 years as a republic.

Chronic Territorial Losses

By the mid-19th century, the discovery of rich guano and nitrate deposits in the Atacama Desert transformed the desolate region into an economically strategic area. Since Bolivia lacked the resources to exploit the Atacama, it contracted Chilean companies. In 1879, when the Bolivian government proposed taxing the minerals, Chile occupied Bolivia's Litoral department, prompting Bolivia and Peru to declare war on Chile.

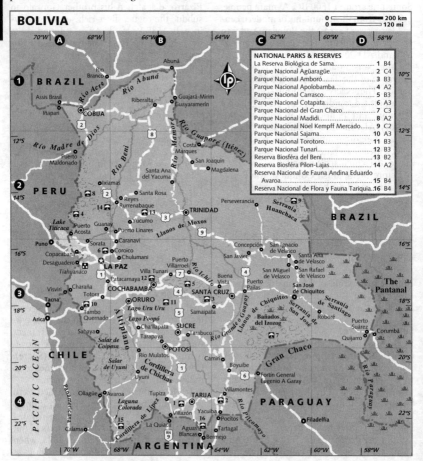

BOLIVIA

NATIONAL PARKS & RESERVES	
La Reserva Biológica de Sama	1 B4
Parque Nacional Agüaragüe	2 C4
Parque Nacional Amboró	3 B3
Parque Nacional Apolobamba	4 A2
Parque Nacional Carrasco	5 B3
Parque Nacional Cotapata	6 A3
Parque Nacional del Gran Chaco	7 C3
Parque Nacional Madidi	8 A2
Parque Nacional Noel Kempff Mercado	9 C2
Parque Nacional Sajama	10 A3
Parque Nacional Torotoro	11 B3
Parque Nacional Tunari	12 B3
Reserva Biosféra del Beni	13 B2
Reserva Biosféra Pilon-Lajas	14 A2
Reserva Nacional de Fauna Andina Eduardo Avaroa	15 B4
Reserva Nacional de Flora y Fauna Tariquia	16 B4

During the War of the Pacific (1879–83), Chile annexed 350km of coastline, leaving Bolivia landlocked. Though Chile offered to compensate Bolivia with a railway from Antofagasta to Oruro and duty-free export facilities, Bolivians refused to accept their *enclaustramiento* (landlocked status). The Bolivian government still lodges coastal claims but diplomatic relations with Santiago appear to be improving – at least now Chile and Bolivia are exchanging diplomatic representatives.

Bolivia's next loss came in 1903, when Brazil annexed a huge chunk of the rubber-rich Acre region, which stretched from Bolivia's present Amazonian border to halfway up Peru's eastern border.

Between 1932 and 1935, Bolivia lost a third – and particularly brutal – war to Paraguay for control of the Chaco region. Trouble started brewing when foreign oil companies began speculating about potential Chaco petrol deposits. A quarrel was sparked, with Standard Oil backing Bolivia and Shell siding with Paraguay. Although Bolivia had more firepower, the Chaco's hellacious fighting conditions favored the Paraguayans. A 1938 peace settlement granted 225,000 sq km of the Chaco to Paraguay. Ironically, oil reserves have still not been discovered – a waste of 80,000 lives.

Revolution & Counterrevolution

Following the Chaco War, friction between disenfranchised miners and their absentee bosses escalated. Radicals, especially in Oruro, gathered beneath the banner of the Movimiento Nacional Revolucionario (MNR). The turbulent 1951 presidential elections brought victory to the MNR's Victor Paz Estenssoro, but a military coup prevented him from taking power. The bloody revolution of 1952 forced the military to capitulate and Paz Estenssoro finally took the helm.

The new government spearheaded reforms aimed at ensuring the participation of all social sectors. Mining properties were nationalized and the sole right to export mineral products was vested in the state. Universal suffrage and an unprecedented policy of agrarian and educational reform were introduced, including a redistribution of estates among campesinos (farmers) and the introduction of universal elementary education. For the first time since the Spanish Conquest, indigenous people felt that they had a voice in the government.

The MNR government lasted an unprecedented 12 years under various presidents but had trouble raising the standard of living. Paz Estenssoro became increasingly autocratic as dissension in his own ranks percolated. Shortly after his second reelection in 1964, he was overthrown by his vice president, General René Barrientos, reviving Bolivia's political instability.

A series of repressive military governments ensued, starting with that of the right-wing general Hugo Banzer Suárez (1971–78). In 1982 a civilian government returned under Hernán Siles Zuazo and his left-wing Movimiento de la Izquierda Revolucionaria (MIR), but the country suffered from labor disputes, monetary devaluation and staggering inflation.

Under the Bolivian constitution, a candidate must earn 50% of the popular vote to become president in a direct election. When no candidate emerges with a clear majority, congress makes the decision, usually via a backroom deal between the major candidates. In 1989 the right-wing Acción Democrática Nacionalista (ADN) made a deal with the MIR, and the MIR's leader Jaime Paz Zamora was appointed president. In 1993 MNR leader Gonzalo Sánchez de Lozada ('Goni'; the Gringo) garnered the most votes, but had to ally with a campesino party to secure the presidency. He embarked on an ambitious privatization program, notable because much of the proceeds were invested in a public pension program. The new economic policies were met with protests and strikes, while anti-drug programs sparked more unrest.

In the 1997 elections, comeback king Hugo Banzer Suárez and his rightist ADN party won just 23% of the vote. Due to pressure from the International Monetary Fund (IMF), neoliberal economic reforms were instituted, the currency was stabilized and many major industries were privatized. In August 2001, Banzer resigned due to cancer and handed over the reins to his vice president Jorge Quiroga Ramirez. With strong US backing, Sánchez de Lozada returned to power in the 2002 elections, only to face a popular uprising in February 2003 that left the presidential palace bullet-riddled and capitalist symbols like the El Alto Coca-Cola factory ransacked.

As this book went to press, widespread demonstrations had forced Sánchez de Lozada to resign and a temporary government was established.

Although the GDP grew steadily in the 1990s, Bolivia remains the continent's poorest nation. Thanks to relentless IMF aid, the foreign debt is said to be under control. Making matters worse is the US-sponsored War on Drugs, which threatens the livelihood of impoverished *cocaleros* (coca farmers). Infrastructure shortcomings and high unemployment rates continue to plague the country.

Hypocrisy: the War On Drugs

Coca has been part of Bolivian culture from time immemorial: the Inca love goddess was represented holding coca leaves. Manco Capac, the son of the sun god, is believed to be responsible for bringing the divine leaf down to earth. When coca leaves are chewed with a catalyst (typically the ashes of other plants), the extracted juices result in insensitivity to hunger, cold, fatigue and pain, and indifference toward anxiety and hardship.

The alkaloid drug extracted from coca leaves has been widely used as a stimulant and topical anesthetic. Numerous 19th-century patent medicines, as well as Coca-Cola, were based on coca, and synthetic versions are still used in many medicines. When coca derivatives like cocaine became the recreational drug of choice (particularly in the USA), demand for Bolivian coca leaves exploded. Today, between 25,000 and 50,000 hectares are cultivated (statistics vary greatly depending on political spin), with most of the leaves refined into coca paste and smuggled to nearby countries for processing. The trade has resulted in widespread corruption and constant foreign intervention in Bolivian affairs.

As early as 1987, the USA sent its Drug Enforcement Agency (DEA) squadrons into the Chapare and Beni regions to 'assist' in coca eradication. Due to lax enforcement, corruption and skyrocketing profits, this program backfired and ultimately resulted in an increase in cocaine production. Moreover, powerful growers' unions formed in response to the programs.

Perturbed at their policy failures, the White House set eradication deadlines and demanded Bolivia's signature on an extradition treaty that would send drug traffickers to trial in the USA. If Bolivia failed to meet targets, US loans, aid and funding would be withheld. Protests erupted and the Coca Leaf Growers Association reiterated that the problem lay not with Bolivian growers, but with the growing US demand for 'blow.'

Bolivia tried to meet the targets by paying farmers US$2500 for each hectare destroyed, but this stretched already strained government resources. Naturally, this also created an incentive to plant more coca, and as the eradication campaign intensified in one area, cultivation shifted to other areas.

The Drug War arouses great cynicism in Bolivia, where it is widely seen as a pretext for US interference and a cover for its interests in the international drug trade. The real problem, most agree, is cocaine's profitability, which in large part is due to the insatiable drug market in the industrialized West. All the while, fighting between campesinos, guerrillas, paramilitary groups and armed forces rages on in the Chapare, Bolivia's main coca-growing region. US President George W Bush's March 2001 announcement of a US$100 million aid package for Bolivian eradication efforts (as part of the much larger Andean Regional Initiative) was seen as ominous. Many international observers fear that substantial portions of the Beni and Chapare regions could fall into the hands of drug-trafficking guerrilla groups, as has happened previously in Colombia and Peru.

THE CULTURE
The National Psyche

Bolivian attitude varies widely depending on climate and altitude. *Kollas* (highlanders) and *cambas* (lowlanders) enjoy expounding on what makes themselves different (ie better) than the other. Lowlanders are said to be warmer, more casual and more generous to strangers; highlanders are supposedly harder working but less open-minded. The reality is that seemingly every *camba* has a kind *kolla* relative living in La Paz and the jesting is good-natured.

Bolivians are all very keen on greetings and pleasantries. Every exchange is kicked off with the usual *buen(os) día(s)* (hello/ good day), but also with a *¿Cómo está?* or *¿Qué tal?* (How are you?). Bolivian Spanish is also liberally sprinkled with endearing diminutives such as *sopita* (a little soup) and *pesitos* (little pesos, as in 'it only costs 10 little pesos').

It's often said that Bolivia is like a beggar sleeping in a golden bed. The nation is among the top five recipients of foreign aid worldwide and always seems to have its hand out for more. Stubborn pride and an overriding desire to protect the country's natural wealth make it politically contentious to export abundant resources like oil or natural gas, even when the potential financial rewards are huge. A landlocked longing for the ocean is manifest in the military airline's logo, a lost pelican in a thunderstorm over Illimani.

Lifestyle

From ritual offerings to Pachamama (Mother Earth) to the habitual chewing of coca, Bolivia is long and strong in traditional culture. An entire canon of gods and spirits are responsible for bountiful harvests, safe travels and matchmaking. One especially unique tradition is the *tinku*, a ritual fistfight that establishes a pecking order, practiced during festivals in the northern Potosí department. The bloody, drunken battles (some fatal) go on for days, may feature rocks or other weapons and don't exempt women. Religious syncretism is most evident in the practice of Alasitas and reverence of Ekeko (Aymara god of abundance; see p245) and the *cha'lla* (ritual blessing) of vehicles at the cathedral in Copacabana.

People

Thanks to its amazing geographic diversity, Bolivia is anything but homogenous. More than half of the population claims pure indigenous heritage. Many campesinos continue to speak Quechua or Aymara as a first language and some still live by a traditional lunar calendar. Miraculously, the frigid altiplano region, where social and political strife are always simmering just above the surface, supports nearly 70% of the populace.

Most Bolivians' standard of living is alarmingly low, marked by substandard housing, nutrition, education, sanitation and hygiene. Bolivia suffers from a Third World trifecta: a high infant mortality rate (57 deaths per 1000 births); a high birth rate (3.3 per woman); and a low female literacy rate (77%).

Bolivia's economic landscape is bleak, but not completely dire, thanks to a thriving informal economy. The largest slice of the economic pie comes from coca exports, which exceed all legal agricultural exports combined.

ARTS
Architecture

Tiahuanaco's ruined structures and a handful of Inca remains are about all that's left of pre-Columbian architecture in Bolivia. The classic Inca polygonal-cut stones that distinguish many Peruvian sites are rare in Bolivia, found only on Isla del Sol and Isla de la Luna, in Lake Titicaca.

Some colonial-era houses and street facades survive, notably in Potosí, Sucre and La Paz. Most colonial buildings, however, are religious and their styles are divided into several major overlapping periods.

Renaissance (1550–1650) churches were constructed primarily of adobe, with courtyards and massive buttresses. One of the best surviving examples is in the village of Tiahuanaco. Renaissance churches indicating Moorish Mudejar influences include San Miguel, in Sucre, and Copacabana, on the shores of Lake Titicaca.

Baroque (1630–1770) churches were constructed in the form of a cross, with an elaborate dome. The best examples are the Compañía in Oruro, San Agustín in Potosí and Santa Bárbara in Sucre.

Mestizo style (1690–1790) is defined by whimsical decorative carvings including tropical flora and fauna, Inca deities and designs, and bizarre masks, sirens and gargoyles. See the wild results at San Francisco (in La Paz); San Lorenzo, Santa Teresa and the Compañía (in Potosí).

In the mid-18th century, the Jesuits in the Beni and Santa Cruz lowlands went off on neoclassical tangents, designing churches with Bavarian rococo and Gothic elements. Their most unusual effort was the mission church at San José de Chiquitos.

Since the 1950s many modern high-rises have appeared in the major cities. Though

BOLIVIA

most are pretty generic, there are some gems – look for triangular pediments on the rooflines, new versions of the Spanish balcony and hardwoods of differing hues. In La Paz, chalet-type, wooden houses are all the rage and the new cathedral in Riberalta sings the contemporary gospel of brick and cedar like nobody's business.

Dance

Traditional altiplano dances celebrate war, fertility, hunting prowess, marriage and work. After the Spanish arrived, European dances and those of the African slaves were introduced and evolved into the hybrid dances that now characterize most Bolivian celebrations.

Bolivia's de facto national dance is the *cueca*, derived from the Chilean original and danced by handkerchief-waving couples to three-quarter time, primarily during fiestas. The most unusual and colorful dances are performed at altiplano festivals, particularly during Carnaval. Oruro's La Diablada (Dance of the Devils) fiesta draws huge international crowds. The most famous and recognizable Diablada dance is *la morenada*, which reenacts the dance of African slaves brought to the courts of Viceroy Felipe III. The costumes consist of hooped skirts, shoulder mantles and devilish dark-faced masks adorned with plumes.

Music

Despite motley, myriad influences, each of Bolivia's regions has developed its own musical styles and instruments. Andean music, from the cold, bleak altiplano, is suitably haunting and mournful, while music from the warmer lowland areas like Tarija has more vibrant, colorful tones.

Although original Andean music was exclusively instrumental, popularization of the melodies has inspired the addition of bittersweet lyrics. Entertaining *peñas* (folk-music shows) operate in most larger cities. Under the military regimes, *peñas* became a venue for protest but this role has now diminished.

Major artists to look for include *charango* masters Celestino Campos, Ernesto Cavour and Mauro Núñez – look for the recording *Charangos Famosos*. Other groups worth looking for are Altiplano, Savia Andina,

Chullpa Ñan, K'Ala Marka, Rumillajta, Los Quipus, Wara, Los Masis and Yana-pakuna.

The ukulele-like *charango* was originally based on early forms of the guitar and mandolin. By the early 17th century, Andean Indians had adapted the Spanish designs into the *charango,* with five pairs of llama-gut strings and a *quirquincho* (armadillo carapace) soundbox that produced the pentatonic scale. Modern *charangos* are similar to the earliest models, though the soundbox is now usually made of wood. Another stringed instrument, the *violín chapaco,* originated in Tarija and is a variation on the European violin.

Prior to the advent of the *charango,* melody lines were carried exclusively by woodwind instruments. Best recognized are the *quena* (reed flute) and the *zampoña* (pan flute), which star in the majority of traditional musical ensembles. Both *quenas* and *zampoñas* come in a variety of sizes and tonal ranges. The *bajón,* an enormous pan flute with separate mouthpieces in each reed, accompanies festivities in the Moxos communities of the Beni lowlands.

Percussion also figures in most folkloric performances as a background for the typically lilting strains of the woodwind melodies. In highland areas, the most popular drum is the *huankara.* The *caja,* a tambourine-like drum played with one hand, is used exclusively in Tarija.

Bolivia has its share of pop groups, some of distinguishable talent. Currently in the mix are Azul Azul, Octavia and Los Kjarkas. The last are best know for their recording 'Llorando se Fue' which was lifted without permission and reshaped into the blockbuster hit 'Lambada.'

Weaving

Weaving methods have changed little in Bolivia for centuries. In rural areas, girls learn to weave before they reach puberty and women spend nearly all their spare time with a drop spindle or weaving on heddle looms. Prior to colonization, llama and alpaca wool were the materials of choice, but sheep's wool has now emerged as the least expensive material, along with synthetic fibers.

Bolivian textiles come in diverse patterns. The majority display a degree of skill that results from millennia of artistry and tradition. The most common piece is a *manta* or *aguayo*, a square shawl made of two handwoven strips joined edge to edge. Also common are the *chuspa* (coca pouch), the *falda* (skirt) with patterned weaving on one edge, woven belts and touristy items such as camera bags made from remnants.

Regional differences are manifest in weaving style, motif and use. Weavings from Tarabuco often feature intricate zoomorphic patterns, while distinctive red-and-black designs come from Potolo, northwest of Sucre. Zoomorphic patterns are also prominent in the wild Charazani country north of Lake Titicaca and in several altiplano areas outside La Paz, including Lique and Calamarka.

Some extremely fine weavings originate in Sica Sica, one of the many dusty and nondescript villages between La Paz and Oruro, while in Calcha, southeast of Potosí, expert spinning and an extremely tight weave – more than 150 threads per inch – produce Bolivia's finest textiles.

SPORT
Like in most of Latin America, the national sport is *futból* (soccer) and the national side typically fares quite well in *futsal* or *futból de salon* (five-versus-five minisoccer) world championships. Professional matches happen every weekend in big cities and its easy to pick up impromptu street games. On the altiplano, liberated women have been playing more and more in recent years – in full skirts. Bolívar and Canada Strongest (both from La Paz) usually represent (albeit weakly) in the Copa Libertadores. Racquetball, billiards, chess and *cacho* (dice) are also huge. The unofficial national sport, however, has to be festing and feting – competition between dancers and drinkers knows no bounds.

ENVIRONMENT
Land
Despite the loss of huge chunks of territory in wars and concessions, landlocked Bolivia is South America's fifth-largest country. Two Andean mountain chains define the west, with many peaks above 6000m. The western Cordillera Occidental stands between Bolivia and the Pacific coast. The eastern Cordillera Real runs southeast past

Lake Titicaca, then turns south across central Bolivia, joining with the other chain to form the southern Cordillera Central.

The haunting altiplano (high plain), which ranges from 3500m to 4000m, is boxed in by these two great cordilleras. It is an immense, nearly treeless plain punctuated by mountains and solitary volcanic peaks. At the north end of the altiplano, straddling the Peruvian border, Lake Titicaca is one of the world's highest navigable lakes. In the bottom left corner, the land is drier and less populated. Here are the remnants of two ancient lakes, the Salar de Uyuni and the Salar de Coipasa, which form an ethereal expanse of blindingly white desert plains when dry and hallucinogenic mirror images when under water.

East of the Cordillera Central are the Central Highlands, a region of scrubby hills, valleys and fertile basins. Olives, nuts, wheat, maize and grapes are cultivated in this Mediterranean-like climate.

North of the Cordillera Real, where the Andes abut the Amazon Basin, the Yungas form a transition zone between arid highlands and humid lowlands. More than half of Bolivia's total area is in the Amazon Basin. The northern and eastern lowlands are sparsely populated and flat, with swamps, savannas, scrub and rain forest.

In the country's southeastern corner lies the flat, nearly impenetrable scrubland of the Gran Chaco, which extends into northern Paraguay.

Wildlife
National parks and reserves comprise 35% of Bolivia's territory and harbor myriad animal and bird species. Several national parks and protected areas (Parque Nacional Amboró, for example) boast greater densities of species concentration than almost anywhere in the world. The new Vilcabamba-Amboró Conservation Corridor, being promoted by Conservation International, seeks to link Andean and Amazonian protected areas stretching from Apurímac in Peru to Amboró in Bolivia.

National Parks
Bolivia has declared 60 protected areas. Many of these, however, are just lines drawn on maps, with few on-the-ground facilities or conservation measures in place.

Areas that are accessible to visitors – albeit often with some difficulty – include:

Amboró Near Santa Cruz, home to the rare spectacled bear, jaguars and an astonishing variety of bird life (p234).

Apolobamba Excellent hiking in this remote park abutting the Peruvian border beneath the Cordillera Apolobamba.

Carrasco Remote extension to Amboró protects remaining stands of cloud forest in the volatile Chapare region.

Cotapata Most of the Choro trek passes through here, midway between La Paz and Coroico in the Yungas.

Madidi Protects a wide range of wildlife habitats; home to more than 1100 bird species (p239).

Noel Kempff Mercado Remote park on the Brazilian border contains a variety of wildlife and some of Bolivia's most inspiring scenery.

Reserva Nacional de Fauna Andina Eduardo Avaroa A highlight of the Southwest Circuit tour, including wildlife-rich lagoons and loads of pink flamingos (p206).

Sajama Adjoining Chile's magnificent Parque Nacional Lauca, contains Volcán Sajama (6542m), Bolivia's highest peak.

Torotoro Enormous rock formations with dinosaur tracks from the Cretaceous period, plus caves and ancient ruins.

Tunari Within hiking distance of Cochabamba, features the Lagunas de Huarahuara and lovely mountain scenery.

Environmental Issues

The 1990s saw a surge in international and domestic interest in Amazonian ecological issues. Though environmental organizations have crafted innovative ways to preserve selected spots (including debt-for-nature swaps), in other areas intensive development continues, often with governmental encouragement. Contact the following nonprofit groups for information on countrywide environmental conservation efforts:

Armonía (☎ /fax 03-356-8808; armonia@scbbs-bo.com; www.birdbolivia.com; Lomas de Arena 400, Santa Cruz) Everything you need to know about Bolivian birding and bird conservation.

Conservación Internacional (CI; ☎ 02-243-5225; www.conservation.org.bo in Spanish; Pinilla 291, San Jorge, La Paz) Promotes community-based biodiversity conservation and ecotourism.

Fundación Amigos de la Naturaleza (FAN; ☎ 03-355-6800; www.fan-bo.org; Santa Cruz & Samaipata) Working in Parques Nacionales Amboró and Noel Kempff Mercado.

Protección del Medioambiente del Tarija (Prometa; ☎ 04-664-5865; www.prometabolivia.org; Carpio E-659, Tarija) Working in Gran Chaco, Sama and Tariquía reserves, Parque Nacional Aguaragüe and El Corbalán Private Reserve.

Servicio Nacional de Areas Protegidas (Sernap; ☎ 02-243-4420/72; www.sernap.gov.bo in Spanish; 20 de Octubre 2659, La Paz) Bolivia's national park service manages all reserves and protected areas. Its website has a decent overview of each national park.

TRANSPORT

GETTING THERE & AWAY

Air

Only a few airlines are brave enough to offer direct services to La Paz' Aeropuerto El Alto (LPB), thus fares are as high as the altitude; flights to and from Chile and Peru are the cheapest. Many travelers land in Lima (Peru) or Santiago (Chile) and travel overland to enter Bolivia. Santa Cruz' Viru Viru International (VVI) is an increasingly popular entry point from Western European hubs and for regional destinations not linked to La Paz.

Direct flights serve Arica (Chile), Asunción (Paraguay), Bogotá (Colombia), Buenos Aires (Argentina), Caracas (Venezuela), Cordoba (Argentina), Cuzco (Peru), Iquique (Chile), Lima (Peru), Manaus (Brazil), Río de Janeiro (Brazil), Salta (Argentina), Santiago (Chile) and São Paulo (Brazil).

The international departure tax (US$25) is payable in cash only at the airport, no matter how long you have been in Bolivia. There's also a 15% tax on all international airfares purchased in Bolivia.

Boat

The Brazilian and Peruvian Amazon frontiers are accessible via irregular riverboats. A more popular crossing is across the Río Mamoré by frequent ferry from Guajará-Mirim (Brazil) to Guayaramerín (see p242). From there, you can travel overland to Riberalta and on to Cobija or Rurrenabaque and La Paz.

Bus & Camión

Daily *flotas* (long-distance buses) link La Paz with Buenos Aires (Argentina) via Bermejo or Yacuiba; Salta (Argentina) via Tupiza/Villazón; Corumbá (Brazil) via Puerto Suarez-Quijarro; and Arica and Iquique (Chile) via Tambo Quemado. Increasingly popular is the crossing to San Pedro de Atacama (Chile) as a detour from Salar de Uyuni tours (see p203). The most popular overland route to and from Puno and Cuzco (Peru) is via Copacabana (p192), but traveling via Desaguadero is quicker. Hotter-than-Hades Villamontes is the gateway for hearty souls attempting the Trans Chaco Rd, which now hits Paraguay at Fortín Infante Rivola and rambles all the way to Asunción. Cheaper *camiones* carry more contraband than passengers across borders, but they are useful for reaching obscure border crossings where there is little regularly-scheduled public transport.

Car, Bicycle & Motorcycle

While most travelers enter Bolivia from adjoining lands by bus, train and/or boat, a few thrill seekers pilot their own vehicles. Motoring and bicycling in Bolivia are certain to try your patience (and mechanic skills!) and fry your nerves, but might result in the trip of a lifetime. See Car & Motorcycle in the Transport chapter (p1049). Most rental agencies accept national driver's licenses, but if you plan on doing a lot of motoring bring an international license. For motorcycle and moped rentals, a passport is all that is normally required.

Train

Bolivia's only remaining international railway route detours west from the Villazón-Oruro line at Uyuni. It passes through the Andes to the Chilean frontier at Avaroa/Ollagüe then descends precipitously to Calama (see p441). Other adventurous routes deadend at the Argentine frontier at Villazón/La Quiaca (see p212) and Yacuiba/Pocitos and in the Brazilian Pantanal at Quijarro/Corumbá.

GETTING AROUND

You can get anywhere cheaply via bus, hitching or *camión*. Buses come in all shapes and sizes – and in all states of disrepair. Inevitably, the worst buses are relegated to running the worst roads, so think twice before booking that 24-hour trip into the jungle during the rainy season. Boats, planes and trains are a much better choice when river crossings are high and unpaved roads have turned to muck. Trains are always the best option in the far south and eastern lowlands and moto-taxis will zip you around cheaply in every Beni town. No matter how you are rolling, always have

a stash of snacks, warm clothes, water and toilet paper close at hand.

Air

Most domestic air services are operated by national carrier **Lloyd Aéreo Boliviano** (LAB; reservations ☎ 800-10-3001, info ☎ 800-10-4321; www .labairlines.com in Spanish) and the private **AeroSur** (www.aerosur.com). Both charge the same fares and have a wide network with frequent flights and services to virtually everywhere you might wish to go (and many places you don't!). LAB's service is relatively reliable, but delays and cancellations are common in the Amazon. AeroSur offers better in-flight service but isn't immune to inexplicable delays either.

The rough-and-ready military airline **Transportes Aéreos Militares** (TAM; in La Paz ☎ 02-212-1582/1585; tam@entelnet.bo) is a good alternative for Rurrenabaque and hard-to-reach places (there's even talk of a new La Paz–Sucre–Uyuni flight). Fares are cheap but the trade-offs are that seats are unreserved and flights are often late or canceled. The upstart carrier **Amaszonas** (www.amaszonas.com in Spanish) crash-landed at El Alto in 2001 but is back in business with two slick new 12-seat Cessnas and wings it from La Paz to Rurrenabaque twice daily.

AeroSur and LAB both offer four-flight, 45-day air passes (US$225) between any of the main cities. The only catch is that you can't pass through the same city twice, except to make connections. LAB also offers a similarly structured BeniPass that covers northern cities.

The domestic departure tax ranges from US$1 to US$2 and must be paid, plus any municipal taxes, after check-in.

Boat

Half of Bolivia's territory lies in the Amazon Basin, where rivers are the main (and during the rainy season often the only) transport arteries. The region's main waterways are the Beni, Guaporé (Iténez), Madre de Dios and Mamoré Rivers – all Amazon tributaries. Most cargo boats offer simple accommodations (cheap hammocks and mosquito nets are available in all ports) and carry everything from livestock to vehicles. Patience and plenty of spare time are key to enjoying these off-the-beaten-path journeys.

Bus, Camión & Hitching

Thankfully, the Bolivian road network is improving as more kilometers are paved. Unpaved roads range from good-grade dirt to mud, sand, gravel and 'only at own risk.' Modern coaches use the best roads, while older vehicles ply minor secondary routes.

Long-distance bus lines are called *flotas*. Large buses are called *buses* and small ones are called *micros*. A bus terminal is a *terminal terrestre*.

To be safe, reserve bus tickets at least several hours in advance; for the lowest fare, purchase immediately after the driver starts up the engine. Many buses depart in the afternoon or evening, to arrive at their destination in the wee hours of the morning. Often you can sleep on these buses until sunrise. On most major routes there are also daytime departures.

An alternative on many routes is a *camión* (truck), which normally costs around 50% of the bus fare. This is how campesinos travel, and it can be excruciatingly slow and rough, depending on the cargo and number of passengers. *Camiones* offer the best views of the countryside. Each town has places where *camiones* gather to wait for passengers; some even have scheduled departures. Otherwise, the best places to hitch a lift will be the *tranca*, the police checkpoint at every town exit.

On any bus or *camión* trip in the highlands, day or night, take plenty of warm clothing. Nights on the altiplano often mean temperatures below freezing. Even in the lowlands, nights can be surprisingly chilly. Expect much longer travel times (or canceled services) in the rainy season.

Taxi & Moto-taxi

Taxis are cheap but none are metered. Confirm the fare before departure or you're likely to be overcharged. Cross-town rides in large cities rarely exceed a couple of dollars (except to and from the airport) and short hops in smaller towns are less than US$1. Fares are sometimes higher late at night, with excessive luggage (bargain hard!) and are always more for uphill runs. Full-day taxi hire is often cheaper than renting a car.

Hourly moto-taxi rentals are common in balmy Beni towns and are a cheap and breezy way to cruise around.

Train

Since privatization, passenger rail services have been cut way back. The western network runs from Oruro to Uyuni and Villazón (on the Argentine border); a branch line runs southwest from Uyuni to Avaroa, on the Chilean border. Between Oruro, Tupiza and Uyuni, the comfortable *Expreso del Sur* trains run twice weekly. The cheaper *Wara Wara del Sur* also runs twice weekly between Oruro and Villazón.

In the east, there's a line from Santa Cruz to the frontier at Quijarro, where you cross to the Pantanal in Corumbá, Brazil. An infrequently used service goes south from Santa Cruz to Yacuiba on the Argentine border a couple of times a week.

Rail travel in Bolivia requires patience and determination. Most stations now have printed timetables, but they still can't be entirely trusted. In older stations, departure times may be scrawled on a blackboard and ticket lines are always long and sometimes hostile. When buying tickets, take your passport. For most trains, tickets are available only on the day of departure, but you can usually reserve seats on better trains through a local travel agent for a small commission.

LA PAZ

Setting eyes on the world's highest capital city (population 1.5 million), plopped in a chasm at a dizzying 3660m above sea level, is unforgettable. Bleak approaches give way to the poverty-plagued sprawl of El Alto (once a suburb, but now Latin America's fasting growing city), clinging precariously to the canyon's lip. Crest the edge and 400m below is Bolivia's largest city, filling the bowl and climbing the walls of a gaping canyon nearly 5km from rim to rim. On a clear day, the showy, snowy triple peak of Illimani (6402m) commands the background.

The city retains a mystery that reveals itself little by little. You can spend hours wandering the alleys and markets, visiting museums or kicking back in the plazas watching the crucible of life on high unfold. There are several worthwhile day trips from La Paz and the music scene is popping on weekends.

La Paz was founded by Alonso de Mendoza in 1548, following the discovery of gold in the Río Choqueyapu. Although gold fever soon fizzled, the town's location on the main silver route from Potosí to the Pacific assured stable progress. By the mid-20th century, La Paz was growing by leaps and bounds as campesinos migrated from the countryside in search of a better life. Although Sucre remains the judiciary capital, La Paz has usurped most political and financial power and is now the de facto capital.

Since La Paz is nearly 4km above sea level, warm clothing is essential. In the summer, the climate can be harsh and melancholy; it rains most afternoons and the city's steep streets become stream chutes. Daytime temperatures hover around 18°C (64°F), though dampness makes it seem colder and most establishments lack heat. In the winter, days are slightly cooler but the crisp, clear air is invigorating. While the sun shines, temperatures may reach the mid- to high teens, but at night it often dips below freezing; see p1059 for advice on dealing with altitude sickness.

ORIENTATION

It's nearly impossible to get lost in La Paz (winded, yes; lost, no). There's only one major thoroughfare, which follows the canyon of the Río Choqueyapu. It changes names several times from top to bottom: Autopista El Alto, Av Ismael Montes, Av Mariscal Santa Cruz, Av 16 de Julio (the Prado) and Av Villazón. At the lower end, it splits into Av 6 de Agosto and Av Aniceto Arce. If you become disoriented and want to return to this main street, just head downhill. Away from this thoroughfare, streets climb steeply uphill, and many are cobbled or unpaved.

The city has a number of districts, including the Zona Central (the blocks around and down from Plaza Pedro D Murillo), Sopocachi (the upmarket commercial and residential zone around Av 6 de Agosto), Miraflores (climbing the slope east of Zona Central) and Zona Sur (the most expensive residential area, farther down the valley). A handful of Zona Sur suburbs, including Obrajes, Calacoto and Cotacota have clinics, government offices and other services of interest to travelers.

The best tourist map of the city is the *Mapa Referencial de la Ciudad de La Paz* (US$1.50), available from the municipal tourist office. It also sells a map of a couple of La Paz–area treks (US$1) and assorted booklets on Bolivia's most touristed cities.

Ambulatory vendors prowl the Prado hawking a good selection of country and trekking maps; you'll often find them lurking around the entrance to the Gravity Assisted and America Tours office (Map pp174–5).

Instituto Geográfico Militar (IGM; Map pp174–5; ☎ 02-254-5090; off Rodríguez btwn México/Murillo & Linares) publishes Bolivia's best topographical maps. The most popular maps are often only available as photocopies (US$4.50 to US$7 per map). Head office is inconveniently located in Miraflores.

INFORMATION
Bookshops

Bookshops include:

Gisbert & Co (Map pp174–5; Comercio 1270) Good stock of maps and Spanish-language literature.

GETTING INTO TOWN

The main bus terminal is 1km uphill from the center. *Micros* (US$0.20) marked 'Prado' and 'Av Arce' pass the main tourist areas but are usually too crowded to accommodate swollen backpacks. If walking, snake your way down to the main drag, Av Ismael Montes, and keep descending for 15 minutes past several plazas and street markets until you see San Francisco Church on your right, where Calle Sagárnaga, the main tourist street, heads uphill.

Heading into town from El Alto Airport (10km outside the center) between 7:30am and 7pm, catch *micro* 212 (US$0.50) outside the terminal, which will drop you anywhere along the Prado. A proper taxi from the rank to the center should cost no more than US$6 for up to four people. Freelance cabs that frequent the main road 1km outside the airport should cost a few dollars less. If arriving by bus in Villa Fatima or the Cemetery District, take special care of your belongings. At night, it's best to take a cab (US$1), but not one shared with other passengers. By day, frequent *micros* run to the center from both locations.

BOLIVIA

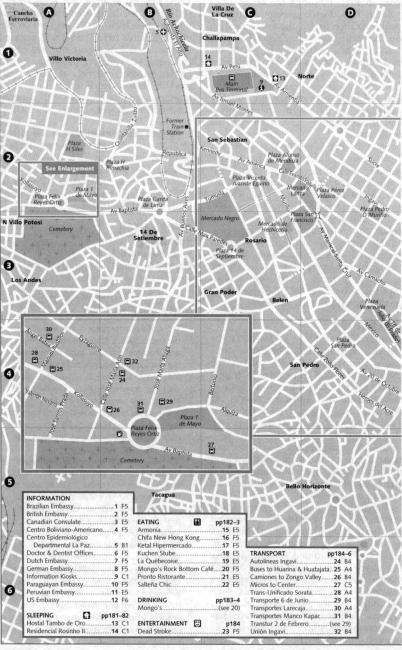

LA PAZ

INFORMATION
Brazilian Embassy...............................1 F5
British Embassy..................................2 F5
Canadian Consulate...........................3 E5
Centro Boliviano-Americano............4 F5
Centro Epidemiológico
  Departmental La Paz......................5 B1
Doctor & Dentist Offices...................6 F5
Dutch Embassy..................................7 F5
German Embassy.................................8 F5
Information Kiosks..............................9 C1
Paraguayan Embassy.......................10 E5
Peruvian Embassy............................11 E5
US Embassy......................................12 F6

SLEEPING pp181–82
Hostal Tambo de Oro.......................13 C1
Residencial Rosinho II......................14 C1

EATING pp182–3
Armonia...15 E5
Chifa New Hong Kong.....................16 F5
Ketal Hipermercado.........................17 E5
Kuchen Stube...................................18 E5
La Québécoise.................................19 E5
Mongo's Rock Bottom Café.............20 F5
Pronto Ristorante.............................21 F5
Salteña Chic....................................22 F5

DRINKING pp183–4
Mongo's.....................................(see 20)

ENTERTAINMENT p184
Dead Stroke.....................................23 F5

TRANSPORT pp184–6
Autolineas Ingavi............................24 B4
Buses to Huarina & Huatajata.........25 A4
Camiones to Zongo Valley...............26 B4
Micros to Center..............................27 C5
Trans-Unificado Sorata....................28 A4
Transporte 6 de Junio......................29 B4
Transportes Larecaja.......................30 A4
Transportes Manco Kapac...............31 B4
Transtur 2 de Febrero.................(see 29)
Unión Ingavi....................................32 B4

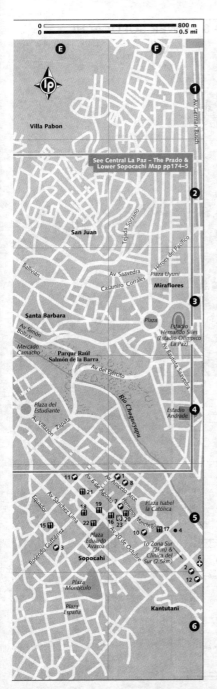

Los Amigos del Libro (Map pp174-5; Mercado 1315) Widest selection of foreign-language novels and periodicals, plus a good selection of travel guides.

Where there are gringos, there are book exchanges. Try any of the cheap hotels near Sagárnaga and the following, or check the stalls in Paseo María Nunez del Prado.

Ángelo Colonial (Map pp174-5; Linares 922; 🕙 9am-7pm)

America Tours (Map pp174-5; 16 de Julio 1490, Edificio Av, No 9)

Gravity Assisted Mountain Biking (Map pp174-5; 16 de Julio 1490, Edificio Av, No 10)

Café Sol y Luna (Map pp174-5; cnr Murillo & Cochabamba)

Cultural Centers

Centro Boliviano-Americano (Map pp172-3; ☎ 02-234-2582; www.cba.com.bo in Spanish; Parque Zenón Iturralde 121) Language classes and current US periodical library.

Goethe Institut (Map pp174-5; ☎ 02-244-2453; www.goethe.de; Av 6 de Agosto 2118) Films, language classes and good German-language library.

Emergency

To report a crime or file a *denuncia* (police report), contact the English-speaking **tourist police** (Policía Turistica; Map pp174-5; ☎ 02-222-5016, 800-10-8687; cnr Sagárnaga & Murillo).

Numbers for emergency services are the same in cities throughout the country:

Ambulance (☎ 118)
Fire department (☎ 119)
Police (Radio Patrol; ☎ 110)

Internet Access

La Paz has nearly as many cybercafés as shoeshine boys. Charges are from US$0.35 to US$0.50 an hour; connections are generally fastest in the morning or late evening.

Internet Alley (Map pp174-5; Pasaje Irrturalde) Just off Prado near Plaza del Estudiante. Fastest, cheapest connections in town.

Tolomeo's (Map pp174-5; cnr Loayza & Comercio) Warm and nonsmoking. Fast new machines and video conferencing – which can slow service down a bit.

Internet Resources

Happening (www.happening.tk in Spanish) Current culture and nightlife listings focusing on Sopocachi and San Miguel; pick up free weekly flyer at clubs and cafés.

La Paz municipal (www.ci-lapaz.gov.bo in Spanish) Flash site with good culture and tourism sections.

CENTRAL LA PAZ – THE PRADO & LOWER SOPOCACHI

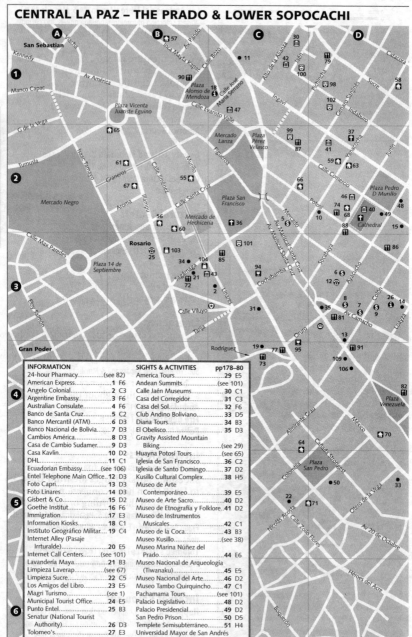

INFORMATION
24-hour Pharmacy..............(see 82)
American Express....................**1** F6
Angelo Colonial.......................**2** C3
Argentine Embassy..................**3** F6
Australian Consulate................**4** F6
Banco de Santa Cruz................**5** C2
Banco Mercantil (ATM)............**6** D3
Banco Nacional de Bolivia........**7** D3
Cambios América......................**8** D3
Casa de Cambio Sudamer.........**9** D3
Casa Kavlin............................**10** D2
DHL.......................................**11** C1
Ecuadorian Embassy...........(see 106)
Entel Telephone Main Office..**12** D3
Foto Capri.............................**13** D3
Foto Linares...........................**14** D3
Gisbert & Co..........................**15** D2
Goethe Institut......................**16** F6
Immigration..........................**17** E3
Information Kiosks..................**18** C1
Instituto Geográfico Militar....**19** C4
Internet Alley (Pasaje
  Irrituralde)..........................**20** E5
Internet Call Centers.........(see 101)
Lavandería Maya....................**21** B3
Limpieza Laverap................(see 67)
Limpieza Sucre.......................**22** C5
Los Amigos del Libro..............**23** D3
Magri Turismo...................(see 1)
Municipal Tourist Office.........**24** B3
Punto Entel............................**25** B3
Senatur (National Tourist
  Authority)...........................**26** D3
Tolomeo's...............................**27** E3
Tourist Police...................(see 101)
Travel Center (ATM)...............**28** E5
Western Union..................(see 11)

SIGHTS & ACTIVITIES   pp178–80
America Tours.........................**29** E5
Andean Summits................(see 101)
Calle Jaén Museums................**30** C1
Casa del Corregidor................**31** C3
Casa del Sol...........................**32** F6
Club Andino Boliviano............**33** D5
Diana Tours............................**34** B3
El Obelisco.............................**35** D3
Gravity Assisted Mountain
  Biking..............................(see 29)
Huayna Potosí Tours...........(see 65)
Iglesia de San Francisco..........**36** C2
Iglesia de Santo Domingo........**37** D2
Kusillo Cultural Complex..........**38** H5
Museo de Arte
  Contemporáneo..................**39** E5
Museo de Arte Sacro...............**40** D2
Museo de Etnografía y Folklore..**41** D2
Museo de Instrumentos
  Musicales............................**42** C1
Museo de la Coca...................**43** B3
Museo Kusillo...................(see 38)
Museo Marina Núñez del
  Prado................................**44** E6
Museo Nacional de Arqueología
  (Tiwanaku).........................**45** E5
Museo Nacional del Arte.........**46** C1
Museo Tambo Quirquincho......**47** C1
Pachamama Tours..............(see 101)
Palacio Legislativo..................**48** D2
Palacio Presidencial................**49** D2
San Pedro Prison....................**50** D5
Templete Semisubterráneo......**51** H4
Universidad Mayor de San Andrés
  (UMSA)..............................**52** E5
Valmar Tours..........................**53** E3
Vicuña Tours.....................(see 62)

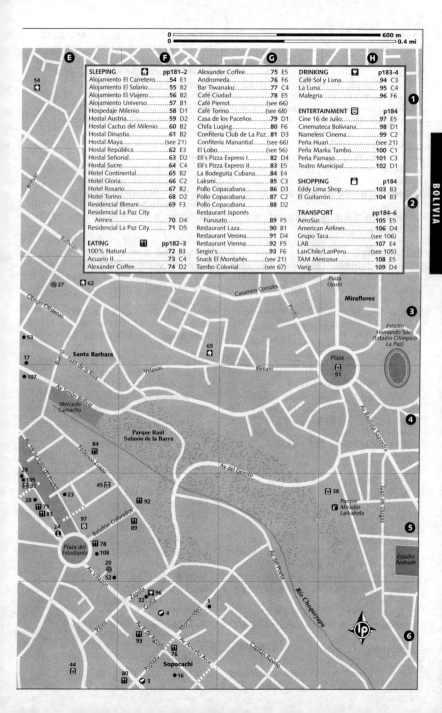

BOLIVIA

SLEEPING	pp181–2
Alojamiento El Carretero	54 E1
Alojamiento El Solario	55 B2
Alojamiento El Viajero	56 B2
Alojamiento Universo	57 B1
Hospedaje Milenio	58 D1
Hostal Austria	59 D2
Hostal Cactus del Milenio	60 B2
Hostal Dinastía	61 B2
Hostal Maya	(see 21)
Hostal República	62 E3
Hostal Señorial	63 D2
Hostal Sucre	64 C4
Hotel Continental	65 B2
Hotel Gloria	66 C2
Hotel Rosario	67 B2
Hotel Torino	68 D2
Residencial Illimani	69 F3
Residencial La Paz City Annex	70 D4
Residencial La Paz City	71 D5

EATING	pp182–3
100% Natural	72 B3
Acuario II	73 C4
Alexander Coffee	74 D2
Alexander Coffee	75 E5
Andromeda	76 F6
Bar Tiwanaku	77 C4
Café Ciudad	78 E5
Café Pierrot	(see 66)
Café Torino	(see 68)
Casa de los Paceños	79 D1
Chifa Luqing	80 F6
Confitería Club de La Paz	81 D3
Confitería Manantial	(see 66)
El Lobo	(see 56)
Eli's Pizza Express I	82 D4
Eli's Pizza Express II	83 E5
La Bodeguita Cubana	84 E4
Laksmi	85 C3
Pollo Copacabana	86 D3
Pollo Copacabana	87 C2
Pollo Copacabana	88 D2
Restaurant Japonés Furusato	89 F5
Restaurant Laza	90 B1
Restaurant Verona	91 D4
Restaurant Vienna	92 F5
Sergio's	93 F6
Snack El Montañés	(see 21)
Tambo Colonial	(see 67)

DRINKING	p183–4
Café Sol y Luna	94 C3
La Luna	95 C4
Malegria	96 F6

ENTERTAINMENT	p184
Cine 16 de Julio	97 E5
Cinemateca Boliviana	98 D1
Nameless Cinema	99 C2
Peña Huari	(see 21)
Peña Marka Tambo	100 C1
Peña Parnaso	101 C3
Teatro Municipal	102 D1

SHOPPING	p184
Eddy Lima Shop	103 B3
El Guitarrón	104 B3

TRANSPORT	pp184–6
AeroSur	105 E5
American Airlines	106 D4
Grupo Taca	(see 106)
LAB	107 E4
LanChile/LanPeru	(see 105)
TAM Mercosur	108 E5
Varig	109 D4

Laundry

La Paz' climate makes hand washing untenable – nothing ever dries, so *lavanderías* are the rule.

Calle Illampu, at the top of Sagárnaga, is lined with laundries. Most *residenciales* (budget accommodations) offer cheap hand-washing service. For quick, reliable same-day machine wash-and-dry service (US$1 per kilo), try the following:

Limpieza Laverap (Map pp174-5; Illampu 704; ☺ 9am-9pm Mon-Sat) Delivery to hotels with prepaid service.

Lavandería Maya (Map pp174-5; Sagárnaga 339) At Hostal Maya.

Limpieza Sucre (Map pp174-5; Nicolás Acosta) Near Plaza San Pedro.

Left Luggage

Most recommended places to stay offer inexpensive or free left-luggage storage, especially if you make a return reservation. Think twice about leaving anything valuable in deposit as there have been numerous reports of items going missing.

Media

La Razon (www.la-razon.com in Spanish), *El Diario* (www.eldiario.net in Spanish) and *La Prensa* (www.laprensa.com.bo in Spanish) are the major daily newspapers in La Paz. National media chains ATB (www.bolivia.com in Spanish) and Groupo Fides (www.fidesbolivia.com in Spanish) host websites with the most up-to-date news.

Medical Services

After-hours *farmacias de turno* (pharmacies) are listed in daily newspapers.

24-hour pharmacy (Map pp174-5; Av 16 de Julio at Bueno) A good pharmacy on the Prado.

Centro Epidemiológico Departamental La Paz (Centro Pilote; Map pp172-3; ☎ 02-245-0166; Vásquez 122 at Peru; ☺ 8:30-11:30am Mon-Fri) Off upper Av Ismael Montes near the brewery. Anyone heading for the lowlands can pick up cheap antimalarials, and rabies and yellow fever vaccinations.

Clínica del Sur (☎ 02-278-4001; Siles 3539, Obrajes) Frequently recommended by readers and embassies as friendly, knowledgeable and kind.

Dr Elbert Orellana Jordan (Unidad Medica Preventiva; ☎ 02-242-2342, 725-20964; asistmedbolivia@hotmail.com; cnr Freyre & Mujia) Gregarious English-speaking doctor makes emergency house calls around the clock for US$20.

Dr Fernando Patiño (Map pp172-3; ☎ 02-243-1664/0697, 772-25625; fpatino@ceibo.entelnet.bo; Av Aniceto Arce 2677, Edificio Illimani, 2nd fl) Opposite the US embassy. American-educated, English-speaking high-altitude medicine expert. He is opening a specialized travel clinic soon.

Dr Jorge Jaime Aguirre (Map pp172-3; ☎ 02-243-2682; Av Aniceto Arce 2677, Edificio Illimani, 1st fl) Frequently recommended dentist, from routine cleaning to root canals.

Money

Watch out for counterfeit US dollars, especially with *cambistas* (street moneychangers), who loiter around the intersections of Colón, Camacho and Santa Cruz. Outside La Paz you'll get 3% to 10% less for checks than for cash.

Casas de cambio in the city center are quicker and more convenient than banks. Most places open from 8:30am to noon and 2pm to 6pm weekdays and on Saturday mornings. Outside these times, try the following:

El Lobo (Map pp174-5; cnr Illampu & Santa Cruz)
Hotel Gloria (Map pp174-5; Potosí 909)
Hotel Rosario (Map pp174-5; Illampu 704)

The following places change traveler's checks for minimal commission:

Cambios América (Map pp174-5; Av Camacho 1223)
Casa de Cambio Sudamer (Map pp174-5; cnr Colón 206 & Camacho) Sells currency from neighboring countries.

Cash withdrawals of US dollars and Bolivianos are also possible at Enlace ATMs at major intersections around the city. For Visa and MasterCard cash advances (Bolivianos only) with no commission and little hassle, try the following:

American Express (Map pp174-5) This helpful representative does everything (including holding client mail) but doesn't change traveler's checks.

DHL/Western Union (Map pp174-5; Montes 693) For urgent international money transfers. Outlets are scattered all around town.

Banco de Santa Cruz (Map pp174-5; Mercado 1078)
Banco Mercantil (Map pp174-5; Mercado & Ayacucho)
Banco Nacional de Bolivia (Map pp174-5; Colón & Camacho)
Magri Turismo (Map pp174-5; ☎ 02-244-2727; www.magri-amexpress.com.bo; Capitán Ravelo 2101)

Photography

Casa Kavlin (Map pp174-5; ☎ 02-240-6046; Potosí 1130) Good for one-hour slide or print processing.

Foto Capri (Map pp174-5; ☎ 02-237-0134; Santa Cruz at Colón; ⏱ 10:30am-noon Mon-Fri) For camera problems, track down master repairman Rolando Calla. Otherwise, try him at home (☎ 02-222-3701; rccrcc@entelnet.bo; Victor Eduardo 2173, Parque Triangular; ⏱ 2:30-7:30pm).
Foto Linares (Map pp174-5; Loayza & Juan de la Riva, Edificio Alborda) Best choice for specialist processing.

Post

Ángelo Colonial (Map pp174-5; Linares 922; ⏱ 9am-7pm) Convenient, gringo-friendly branch with Internet access, tourist information and outgoing-only service.
Central post office (Ecobol; Map pp174-5; Santa Cruz & Oruro; ⏱ 8am-8pm Mon-Fri, 8am-6pm Sat, 9am-noon Sun) A tranquil oasis off the bustling Prado, and a quiet place to make card-phone calls while admiring the architecture. Holds *lista de correos* (poste restante) mail for three months.

Telephone

Convenient Punto Entels are scattered throughout the city. Street kiosks on nearly every corner offer brief local calls for B$1 and sell phone cards. Hawkers with mobiles on a leash offer cellular calls for B$1 per minute.
Internet Call Centers (Map pp174-5; Sagárnaga & Murillo, Galería Doryan; ⏱ 8am-8pm) Cheap worldwide Internet-based phone calls.
Main Entel office (Map pp174-5; Ayacucho 267; ⏱ 7am-10pm) Best place to receive incoming calls and faxes.

Tourist Offices

Ángelo Colonial (Map pp174-5; Linares 922) Privately run tourist information office with a book exchange, notice board and guidebook reference library.
Information kiosks Outside the main bus terminal (Map pp172-3) and on the southeast side of Plaza Alonso de Mendoza (Map pp174-5).
Municipal tourist office (Map pp174-5; ☎ 02-237-1044; north side of Plaza del Estudiante; ⏱ 8:30am-noon & 2:30-7pm Mon-Fri) Sells maps and has free brochures (mostly in Spanish, but some in English, French and German).

Travel Agencies

America Tours (Map pp174-5; ☎ 02-237-4204; www .america-ecotours.com; Av 16 de Julio 1490, ground fl, No 9) Warmly recommended English-speaking agency for help organizing trips to anywhere in the country, especially new routes and community-based ecotourism projects.
Travel Center (Map pp174-5; ☎ 02-231-1416, 715-76883; travelcenter2001@hotmail.com; 16 de Julio 1764) Best place to book flights. The owner is multilingual.
Valmar Tours (Map pp174-5; ☎ 02-220-1499/1519; www.valmartour.com in Spanish; Riva 1406, Edificio Alborada, 1st fl) Specializes in student travel and sells ISIC cards (US$15).

Visas

For information on embassies and consulates in La Paz, see p244.
Immigration (Migración; Map pp174-5; ☎ 02-237-0475; Camacho 1433; ⏱ 8:30am-4pm Mon-Fri) Extensions to length of stay granted with little ado.

DANGERS & ANNOYANCES

La Paz is a great city to explore on foot, but take local advice '*camina lentito, come poquito...y duerme solito*' ('walk slowly, eat only a little bit...and sleep by your poor little self') to avoid feeling the effects of

---

LIFE INSIDE THE WORLD'S MOST UNIQUE GAOL: SAN PEDRO PRISON

The 1000 prisoners living inside South America's unique penitentiary must engage in various activities to get the money they need to survive; the most successful (or ruthless) have 'cells' with all the conveniences of a five-star hotel. Those without money live in retched conditions. In the past, English-speaking inmates made money by giving tourists prison tours – like a zoo, but with people.

Official visiting days are Thursday and Sunday between 9am and 5pm, but since the Black February uprisings of 2003, San Pedro has officially been declared off-limits to tourists. You may be granted entrance if you approach the *capitan* (captain) on duty and request an *entrevista* (interview) with an incarcerated friend or 'relative'. Your embassy may be able to provide a list of names of jailed citizens. Bring picture ID and gifts of food, but no valuables or cameras. There's a crafts shop around the corner from the main gate selling *artesanias* (handicrafts) produced by inmates, a popular stop in January for locals shopping for Alasitas (the festival of abundance).

For a riveting account of life inside San Pedro, read *Marching Powder* (2003; www .marchingpowder.com), penned by Australian law graduate Rusty Young. Young, whose curiosity was aroused by Lonely Planet's description of San Pedro as 'the world's most bizarre tourist attraction,' spent four months inside the gaol interviewing a British prisoner. If you get in – and make it out – let us know how it goes....

soroche (altitude sickness). More annoying than dangerous, *lustrabotes* (shoeshine boys) hound everyone with footwear. Many affect a menacing and anonymous appearance, wearing black ski masks and baseball caps pulled so low you can just make out two eye sockets. It's said they do so often to avoid social stigma, as many are working hard to support families or pay their way through school – you can support their cause for B$1.

Scams
La Paz is incredibly *tranquilo* by South American standards, but there are still a number of ruses aimed at separating gringos from their goods. Authentic police officers will always be uniformed (undercover police are under strict orders not to hassle foreigners) and will never insist that you get in a taxi with them or that they search your person in public. If confronted by an imposter, refuse to show them your valuables (wallet, passport, money etc), try to get the attention of a uniformed police officer or insist on going to the nearest police station on foot. See p244 for a complete rundown of *en vogue* cons, swindles and rip-offs.

SIGHTS
When the sun shines, La Paz invites leisurely exploration. The steep city is short on breathtaking attractions but long on lively markets and colorful street life, which swirls to the beat of indigenous cultures. Keep your eyes peeled for fantastic glimpses of Illimani towering between the world's highest high-rises.

Plaza Pedro D Murillo Area
This plaza marks the formal city center, with various monuments, the imposing **Congreso Nacional**, the bullet-riddled **Palacio Presidencial** (Map pp174–5) and the 1835 **cathedral**. Inside the cathedral, the **Museo de Arte Sacro** (Map pp174-5; enter at Socabaya 432; admission US$0.75; ◐ 9:30am-12:30pm & 3-5:30pm Tue-Fri, 10am-1pm Sat) houses a collection of religious art and artifacts.

Just off the west side of the plaza, the **Museo Nacional del Arte** (Map pp174-5; Calle Comercio at Socabaya; admission US$1.35; ◐ 9am-12:30pm & 3-7pm Tue-Sat, 9am-12:30pm Sun) is in the superbly restored pink granite Palacio de los Condes de Arana (1775). The collection

of indigenous, colonial and contemporary arts is small but rewarding.

Walk a block west on Ingavi to see the impressive facade of the **Iglesia de Santo Domingo** (Map pp174-5; Yanacocha & Ingavi).

Calle Jaén Museums
Five blocks northwest of Plaza Murillo, colonial Calle Jaén has four small **museums** (Map pp174-5; combined admission US$0.50; ◐ 9:30am-12:30pm & 3-7pm Mon-Fri, 9am-1pm Sat & Sun) that can easily be appreciated in a few hours. The **Museo de Metales Preciosos Precolombinos** (Jaén 777) has amazing gold and silver artifacts; **Museo Casa Murillo** (Jaén 790) displays items from the colonial period; **Museo del Litoral Boliviano** (Jaén 789) laments the 1884 war in which Bolivia lost its Pacific coast; and **Museo Costumbrista Juan de Vargas** (Jaén & Sucre) has good displays on the colonial period.

At the foot of Calle Jaén is the impressive **Museo de Instrumentos Musicales** (Map pp174-5; ☎ 02-233-1075; Jaén 711; admission US$0.65; ◐ 10am-1pm & 2-6pm), with an exhaustive hands-on collection of unique instruments from Bolivia and beyond. It's a must for musicians. If you don't happen on an impromptu jam session, check out museum founder and *charango* master Ernesto Cavour's **Peña Marka Tambo** (see p184) across the street. You can also arrange *charango* and wind instrument lessons here for around US$5 per hour.

Other Central Museums
The terrific **Museo de la Coca** (Map pp174-5; ☎ 02-231-1998; Linares 906; admission US$1; ◐ 10am-7pm) looks at the sacred leaf's role in traditional societies, its use by the soft-drink and pharmaceutical industries, and the growth of cocaine as an illicit drug. The multilingual displays (ask for a translation) are educational, provocative and evenhanded.

Between the plaza and Calle Jaén, the free **Museo de Etnografía y Folklore** (Map pp174-5; ☎ 02-235-8559; Ingavi at Genaro Sanjinés; ◐ 9:30am-12:30pm & 3-7pm Tue-Sat, 9:30am-12:30pm Sun) explores the fascinating Chipaya culture and has an astounding exhibit of the country's finest textiles, all housed in a palatial 18th-century home.

Adjacent is the **Museo Tambo Quirquincho** (Map pp174-5; off Evaristo Valle at Plaza Alonzo de Mendoza; admission US$0.15; ◐ 9:30am-12:30pm & 3-7pm Tue-Fri, 9:30am-12:30pm Sat & Sun) is a former *tambo* (wayside market and inn) that displays old-

BOLIVIA

fashioned dresses, silverware, photos, art-work and a collection of Carnaval masks.

Near Plaza del Estudiante, the **Museo Nacional de Arqueología** (Map pp174-5; Tiwanaku 93; ☎ 02-231-1621; admission with guide US$1.35; ☯ 9am-12:30pm & 3-7pm Mon-Fri, 10am-12:30pm & 3-6pm Sat, 10am-1pm Sun) holds an interesting collection of Tiahuanaco (Tiwanaku) pottery, sculptures, textiles and other artifacts.

Over in Miraflores, the **Templete Semisubterráneo** (Map pp174-5; Museo al Aire Libre; Ilimani & Bautista Saavedra) is a free, open-air reproduction of part of the Tiahuanaco archaeological site that merits a look only if you can't make it out to the site itself.

In Sopocachi, the **Museo Marina Núñez del Prado** (Map pp174-5; ☎ 02-232-4906; Ecuador 2034; admission US$0.65; ☯ 9:30am-1pm & 3-7pm Tue-Fri, 9:30am-1pm Sat & Sun) is dedicated to Bolivia's most renowned sculptor. It's housed in her stunning mansion.

Back on the Prado, the private **Museo de Arte Contemporáneo** (Map pp174-5; ☎ 02-233-5905; Av 16 de Julio 1698; admission US$1.35; ☯ 9am-9pm) is as notable for its colonial building, a 19th-century mansion with glass roof and stained-glass panels designed by Gustave Eiffel, as it is for its pedestrian modern Bolivian art collection.

Parque Laikakota Mirador & Kusillo Cultural Complex

This complex overlooking La Paz has an awesome **mirador** (lookout; Map pp174-5; admission US$0.15; ☯ 9am-5:30pm) in a tranquil park setting. Across the street is the **Museo Kusillo** (Map pp174-5; Av del Ejército; ☎ 02-222-6187; admission Mon-Fri US$0.65, adult/child Sat & Sun US$1.35/1; ☯ 10:30am-6:30pm Tue-Sun), a hands-on museum of science and play that's a big hit with children.

For big kids, there's great sunset views from the café atop the **world's highest funicular**. The complex is a 20-minute walk east of the Prado along Av Zapata, which turns into Av del Ejército.

ACTIVITIES
Mountain Biking

For a memorable outing, try a trip with highly-regarded **Gravity Assisted Mountain Biking** (Map pp174-5; 16 de Julio 1490, Edificio Av, No 10) – see p250. Two of the most popular full-day options (US$49) are to zoom down from Chacaltaya to La Paz or from La Cumbre

down the 'World's Most Dangerous Road' to Coroico. Many other outfits on Sagárnaga offer the La Cumbre to Coroico trip for a few bucks less but consider what corners are being cut before you go plummeting downhill. Also, think twice before going with any of the agencies who offer these trips during the rainy season (January/February).

Skiing, Hiking & Climbing

The world's highest downhill skiing (5320m down to 4900m), strictly for enthusiasts, is on the slopes of **Chacaltaya**, a rough 35km drive north of La Paz. The ski season (February to late April) is increasingly uncertain because the piste is on a retreating glacier. There is just one primitive rope tow (constantly undergoing repair), and the high altitude means most people can manage only a couple of runs before they're gasping for oxygen.

Club Andino Boliviano (Map pp174-5; ☎ 02-232-4682; www.geocities.com/yosemite/trails/7553/cab1.html in Spanish; México 1638) operates the lift and the basic **lodge** (dm US$5), where you can buy hot drinks, rent ski gear and stay the night. It arranges weekend ski trips when conditions are suitable (US$10 to US$20, plus transportation); make sure you're well acclimatized and bring good UV protection.

Out of season, many La Paz tour agencies offer daily hiking tours to Chacaltaya (US$15), a fun and easy way to bag a high peak. For rock climbing and other extreme adventure possibilities, contact the Oruro-based **Club de Montañismo Halcones** (www.geocities.com/yosemite/gorge/1177), who have pioneered many routes around La Paz.

WALKING TOUR

A good starting point is **Iglesia de San Francisco (1)**, on the plaza of the same name. This imposing church was started in 1549 but went unfinished until the mid-18th century. Its architecture reflects the mestizo style, emphasizing natural forms. Watch for colorful wedding processions on weekend mornings.

From **Plaza San Francisco (2)**, huff up Sagárnaga, which is lined with shops and stalls selling beautiful weavings (ponchos, *mantas* and coca pouches), musical instruments, antiques, 'original' Tiahuanaco artifacts and handmade leather bags. Turn right at Linares and poke around the uncanny **Mercado**

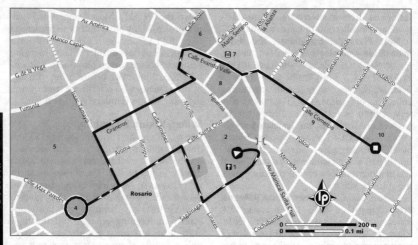

de Hechicería (3; Mercado de los Brujos or Witches Market), which is asses-to-elbows with herbs, magical potions and shriveled llama fetuses intended to cure ills and protect supplicants from malevolent spirits. If you're lucky, you might convince a *yatiri* (Aymara healer) to toss the coca leaves and tell your fortune, but they usually refuse gringo customers. Taking photographs here may be met with unpleasantness – unless you are a customer and first ask politely.

Heading up Santa Cruz to **Plaza 14 de Septiembre (4)** and Calle Max Paredes, you'll find the **Mercado Negro (5)**, a clogged maze of makeshift stalls that sprawls over several blocks. The name means 'black market,' but it's mostly above board and is a good place to bargain for clothing and household goods. It is, however, notorious for pickpockets.

From here, wander downhill, (along Graneros and left onto Figueroa, if that takes your fancy), north and east of the markets, through streets choked with people and *micros* to **Plaza Alonso de Mendoza (6)**. Visit the adjacent **Museo Tambo Quirquincho (7**; p178).

Continue past the bustling **Mercado Lanza (8)** along pedestrian-only **Calle Comercio (9)** to end at **Plaza Pedro D Murillo (10)**.

COURSES

Spanish classes are offered by the **Centro Boliviano-Americano** (CBA; see Cultural Centers, p173) and private teachers who charge around US$5 per hour. **Isabel Daza Vivado**

(☎ 02-231-1471; maria_daza@hotmail.com; Murillo 1046, 3rd fl) is frequently recommended for her professionalism.

For Bolivian-style guitar or *charango* lessons, stop by the **Museo de Instrumentos Musicales** (see p178).

Casa del Sol (☎ 02-244-0928; Goitia 127) offers yoga, tai chi and meditation classes. A single class costs US$2 and monthly memberships are US$25; ask about student discounts and massage services.

TOURS

Innumerable agencies operate tours in and around La Paz. In addition to those listed in the Directory section (see p250), try the English-speaking **Pachamama Tours** (Map pp174-5; ☎ 02-231-9740; Sagárnaga 189, Galería Doryan, 2nd fl) or **Vicuña Tours** (Map pp174-5; ☎ 02-239-0915; Comercio 1455, at Hostal República). With four to six people, a half-day city tour costs around US$10 per person and a day trip to Chacaltaya and Valle de la Luna or Tiahuanaco costs US$15.

FESTIVALS & EVENTS

Of the major festivals and holidays during the year, Alasitas (January 24), the festival of abundance, and El Gran Poder (late May to early June) are the most interesting to visitors. The Fiestas Universitarias take place during the first week in December, accompanied by riotous merrymaking and enough water-balloon bombs to sink the Chilean navy.

SLEEPING
Most backpackers beeline for Central La Paz to find a crash pad. The area between Plazas Mendoza and Murillo is chock full of cheap, popular places and many of the services travelers need. If you want to stay closer to movie theaters, a wider array of restaurants and a bar or two, consider staying around Plaza San Pedro in the Lower Prado area where there are a few choice cheapies.

The area around the Witches Market (between Santa Cruz and Sagárnaga) is about as close as Bolivia gets to a traveler's ghetto. Here you'll find scores of dives, hostels and some plusher digs all cheek by jowl with adventure tour operators, Krishna cafés and touristy *peñas*. In the cheapest accommodation, expect communal bathrooms, cold showers, no heat and lots of partying. Spend a bit more if you feel like sleeping soundly; always bargain during the low season. Some budget places impose a midnight curfew.

Alojamientos, Hospedajes & Residenciales
Hospedaje Milenio (Map pp174-5; ☎ 02-228-1263; Yanacocha 860; s/d US$3/5.35) Clean and simple with hot showers all day. This place has friendly staff, includes kitchen use, and is close to the bus terminal. The best rooms, including the single room in the tower, are upstairs. They organize cheap bus trips and extra blankets are available on request.

Alojamiento El Solario (Map pp174-5; ☎ 02-236-7963; elsolariohotel@yahoo.com; Murillo 776; dm/s/d US$2.65/3.35/6.25;) This mellow hangout has clean, spare rooms, hot showers, laundry service, a shared kitchen and luggage storage. Check out the sunny roof terrace.

Residencial La Paz City (Map pp174-5; ☎ 02-249-4565; Acosta 487; r per person US$3.50-4) A friendly, safe, helpful former Peace Corps favorite near Plaza San Pedro. The affiliated **Residencial La Paz City Annex** (Map pp174-5; ☎ 02-368-380; México 1539; r per person US$3.35) has some rooms with balconies and a good restaurant and cooking school in the courtyard below.

Alojamiento El Carretero (Map pp174-5; ☎ 02-228-5271; Catacora 1056; r per person US$2) A classic cheapie, with a kitchen, laundry and lots of traveler traffic – mind your gear.

Alojamiento Universo (Map pp174-5; ☎ 02-246-0731; Kapac 575; dm US$1.85, r per person US$2) A cheap, cleanish, friendly place with hot showers until noon. Go for a ground-floor unit and, as in all dormitory scenarios, keep your gear locked up.

Alojamiento El Viajero (El Lobo; Map pp174-5; ☎ 02-245-3465; cnr Illampu & Santa Cruz; dm US$2, r per person US$2.65;) Just like your college dorm, only colder and with everything in Hebrew. The few shared baths are grubby.

Residencial Illimani (Map pp174-5; ☎ 02-220-2346; Illimani 1817; s/d US$4.75/7.75) In a quiet (some would say dead) area near the stadium, this friendly family place has a laundry sink and leafy patio where you can cook.

Hostals & Hotels
Hostal Cactus del Milenio (Map pp174-5; ☎ 02-245-1421; Jiménez 818; r per person US$3) Smack in the middle of the Witches Market, this basic home has a communal kitchen, hot showers all day, a nice rooftop terrace and clean rooms with saggy beds.

Hostal Maya (Map pp174-5; ☎ 02-231-1970; maya hostal@hotmail.com; Sagárnaga 339; r per person US$6;) A new central budget favorite a stumble away from Peña Huari. All of the rooms are tidy and have good beds. Some have balconies but the ones in back are quieter. Breakfast included.

Hotel Torino (Map pp174-5; ☎ 02-240-6003; Socabaya 457; s/d/tr US$4/6.65/10, with bath US$6.50/10.50/16;) Central backpacker hangout in a modernized (in the '50s) colonial building that's seen better days. It's more popular for its services – restaurant, book exchange, luggage storage – than its comforts.

Hostal Señorial (Map pp174-5; ☎ 02-240-6042; Yanacocha 540; r with bath per person US$7.50) A family-run place with gas showers and kitchen facilities where you'll meet more Bolivians than foreigners. Rooms have TVs.

Hostal Austria (Map pp174-5; ☎ 02-240-8540; Yanacocha 531; r per person US$3.35-4) An old travelers' haunt known for overbooking (give a clear arrival time and don't be late) and treating its clientele like chattel (in English and French!), but you'll meet tons of people. It's a bit pricey for what you get (short beds, dicey shared bath), but worth it if the goal is to meet people. Hot showers and cooking facilities available. Note: some of the rooms are windowless cells.

Hotel Continental (Map pp174-5; ☎ 02-245-1176; Illampu 626; r per person US$4.50, s/d with bath & cable TV US$10/12) This older, two-star HI-affiliate is used by climbers, thrifty tour groups and Bolivian business types. It's clean, well-located and has terrific showers, but rooms without bath are cramped.

Hostal Dinastía (Map pp174-5; ☎ 02-245-1076; hosteldinastia@yahoo.com; Illampu 684; r per person US$4, with bath & cable TV US$6; 🖳) Basic, clean carpeted rooms in the middle of the action. The friendly owner speaks English and breakfast is available.

Hostal Sucre (Map pp174-5; ☎ 02-249-2038; Colombia 340; r per person US$6.50, s/d with bath & cable TV US$10/15) The management is helpful and the freshly painted rooms at this *hostal* facing Plaza San Pedro are set around a pleasant courtyard.

Near the Main Bus Terminal
There are a couple of decent places to crash opposite the main bus terminal.

Residencial Rosinho II (Map pp172-3; ☎ 02-228-1578; Perú 125; r per person US$3) This place has basic rooms with shared bath.

Hostal Tambo de Oro (Map pp172-3; ☎ 02-228-1565; Armentia 367; s/d US$5.25/8, with bath & cable TV US$9.50/12) A nice, quiet spot with good-value carpeted rooms with stylin' gas showers. Breakfast is available before early departures.

EATING
La Paz overfloweth with inexpensive eateries. Most budget places have set meals – typically *almuerzos* (lunch, the word normally refers to a set meal served at midday) but sometimes *cenas* (dinner) too – and a selection of common dishes such as *lomo, churrasco, milanesa* (breaded and fried beef or chicken cutlets) and *silpancho* (beef schnitzel), but go easy on the grease if attempting to acclimatize.

Breakfast & Cafés
Café Torino (Map pp174-5; Socabaya 457, at Hotel Torino; under US$2; 🕑 from 7:30am) Serves a good breakfast and big *almuerzos*.

Tambo Colonial (Map pp174-5; Illampu 704, at Hotel Rosario; breakfast US$2.50; 🕑 7-10:30am & 7-10:30pm) Offers an excellent fruity breakfast buffet.

Alexander Coffee (Av 16 de Julio Map pp174-5; Av 16 de Julio 1832; Potosí Map pp174-5; Potosí 1091) Trendy cafés serving all manner of java drinks, pastries and sandwiches.

Café Ciudad (Map pp174-5; Plaza del Estudiante; 🕑 24 hr) Slow service and ordinary food, but the full menu is available around the clock and they don't mind travelers lingering over coffee.

Café Pierrot (Map pp174-5; Potosí 909) At Hotel Gloria, another friendly coffee shop with good joe and fresh *salteñas*.

Kuchen Stube (Map pp172-3; Gutiérrez 461; 🕑 noon-8pm Mon, 10am-12:30pm & 2:30-7pm Tue-Fri) European coffee, quiche loraine, German pastries and other decadent homemade goodies.

100% Natural (Map pp174-5; Sagárnaga 345) A deservedly popular snack place with big breakfasts and tremendous, sanitary salads.

Confitería Club de La Paz (Map pp174-5; cnr Av Camacho & Santa Cruz) A haunt of politicians and other charismatic habitués is good for a strong espresso and a *salteña*. Avoid the stale pie.

Markets & Street Food
For cheap, filling eats hit the markets. Cheap DIY meals can easily be cobbled together from the abundance of fruit, produce and bread sold there.

Mercado Camacho (Map pp174-5; cnr Av Simon Bolivar & Bueno) There are stands selling *empanadas* (pillows of dough lined with cheese and deep fried), and chicken sandwiches and *comedores* (basic eateries) with sitting areas. A set feast of soup, a meat dish, rice and oca or potato comes in under US$1.

At Mercado Lanza (Map pp174-5), don't miss the rank of fruit drink stalls outside the Figueroa entrance. Hygiene in the *comedor* is questionable.

For excellent *empanadas,* go to the first landing on the steps between the Prado and Calle México. For US$0.20, you'll get an enormous beef or chicken *empanada* served with your choice of sauces – hot, hotter and hottest. In Sopocachi, the northwest border of Plaza Avaroa is lined with *salteña* stands; try **Salteña Chic** (Map pp172-3; Belsario Salinas s/n).

Quick Meals
Eli's Pizza Express I & II (Map pp174-5; Av 16 de Julio 1491 & 1800) A local favorite where you can choose between pizza, pasta, pastries and ice cream.

Pollo Copacabana (Map pp174-5; locations on Potosí, Calle Comercio & Socabaya; meals under US$2) Bolivia's undisputed king of quick chicken, where you'll get a greasy roast bird, chips and fried plantains smothered in condiments and *ají* (chili sauce).

Sergio's (Map pp174-5; Villazón near Aspiazu steps; evenings only) The best by-the-slice pizza in town. The hot dogs and chili are also winners.

Snack El Montañés (Map pp174-5; Sagárnaga 323) Convenient for good light meals, juices and desserts.

Restaurants
BOLIVIAN
Cheap set meals offered at countless hole-in-the-wall restaurants can be excellent, varied and cheap – look for the chalkboard menus out front.

Restaurant Laza (Map pp174-5; Calle Bozo 244, Plaza Alonso de Mendoza; lunch US$0.75) This place is a winner.

Bar Tiwanaku (Map pp174-5; Oruro & México; lunch US$0.75) Has a good set lunch and hosts live music some weekends.

Restaurant Verona (Map pp174-5; Colón near Calle Santa Cruz; mains US$1-2) Open daily for sandwiches, pizzas and *almuerzos*.

Casa de los Paceños (Map pp174-5; Sucre 856; mains US$3-6; lunch Tue-Sun, dinner Tue-Fri) For upscale versions of classic *paceño* (La Paz) dishes like *saice*, *sajta*, *fricasé* and *chairo*, try this friendly, family-run place.

INTERNATIONAL
Andromeda (Map pp174-5; Av Aniceto Arce; lunch US$1.75) Located at the bottom of Aspiazu steps, this is recommended for *almuerzos*. It has vegetarian options and fish on Friday.

El Lobo (Map pp174-5; cnr Calle Illampu & Santa Cruz; mains US$2-3) El Lobo is a favorite for inexpensive, filling meals. The curry, pasta and chicken dishes are better than the surly service; it's cluttered with whacky photos of naked Israelis and often open when everything else on Sagárnaga is shut.

Mongo's Rock Bottom Café (Map pp172-3; Manchego 2444; lunch US$3) Expats hang out at this hopping American-style bar. It has good set lunches and specialties include nachos, enormous burgers, Miller beer and NFL football on the big-screen.

Chifa New Hong Kong (Map pp172-3; cnr Salinas & 20 de Octubre) Inexpensive, MSG-laden heaps of Chinese grub. '*Sin agí-no-moto*' is the key phrase to avoid the glutamate.

Chifa Luqing (Map pp174-5; 20 de Octubre 2090; lunch US$1.75; 11am-11pm) Try this place for better, slightly pricier Chinese. It serves big *almuerzos* in a bright atmosphere.

Calle Rodríguez boasts several excellent *ceviche* restaurants, where a heap of Peruvian-style seafood fetches under US$2. The best is **Acuario II** (Map pp174-5; no sign), opposite Acuario I.

Other recommended international eateries (all of which are in the Lower Prado or Sopocachi area) include the following:

La Bodeguita Cubana (Map pp174-5; Federico Zuazo 1653; mains US$2.50-5) Go for the filling Cuban specialties.

Restaurant Japonés Furusato (Map pp174-5; Batallon Colorados & Federico Zuazo; mains US$3-6) Good, unpretentious Japanese fare.

Restaurant Vienna (Map pp174-5; 02-239-1660; Zuazo 1905; mains US$4-7) Classy and arguably La Paz' best continental restaurant.

La Québecoise (Map pp172-3; 02-212-1682; Av 20 de Octubre 2387; mains US$5-10; Mon-Sat) Lauded for its romantic atmosphere and excellent French-Canadian cuisine.

Pronto Ristorante (Map pp172-3; Jáuregui 2248 btwn Av 6 de Agosto & Av 20 de Octubre; mains US$4-7) An excellent choice for homemade pasta and other good-value Italian meals.

VEGETARIAN
Armonía (Map pp172-3; Ecuador 2286; buffet US$2.75; noon-2:30pm Mon-Fri) La Paz' best all-you-can-eat vegetarian lunch is found above Libería Armonia in Sopocachi.

Laksmi (Map pp174-5; Sagárnaga 213) Try this place for cheap and wholesome vegetarian lunches with cultish East Indian leanings.

Confitería Manantial (Map pp174-5; Potosí 909; buffet US$2.25) This place in Hotel Gloria has a popular veggie lunch and dinner buffet.

Self-Catering
Ketal Hipermercado (Map pp172-3; Av Aniceto Arce near Pinilla, Sopocachi) If you're headed off to picnic, load up on everything from olives to cheese, crackers and beer at Ketal, just beyond Plaza Isabel la Católica.

DRINKING
There are scores of cheap local drinking dens around the city, especially near the Prado. Women on their own should steer clear and only devoted sots will enjoy the drunken marathon that typifies Bolivian partying.

There are a few bars with a mixed traveler/Bolivian scene.

La Luna (Map pp174-5; Oruro 197) This central and friendly bohemian bar has live music and no cover charge.

Mongo's (Map pp172-3; Manchego 2444; 🕑 until 2am) The expat local gets crazy after the café shuts down around 11pm.

Malegria (Map pp174-5; Goitia 155) A good place to mingle with students. It features Afrobolivian drumming and dancing on Thursdays and live bands on weekends.

Café Sol y Luna (Map pp174-5; cnr Murillo & Cochabamba) This low-key Dutch-run hangout has big booths, a book exchange and extensive guidebook reference library, a dart alley and couches downstairs for watching TV. It serves cocktails and good coffee.

The local gilded youth mingle with upmarket expats at trendy bars and clubs along 20 de Octubre in Sopocachi and lower down in Zona Sur, where US-style bars and discos spread along Av Ballivián and Calle 21. You'll need more than a backpacker's clothes (and budget) to fit in here.

ENTERTAINMENT

The municipal tourist office distributes a free monthly cultural and fine arts schedule.

Teatro Municipal (Map pp174-5; Genaro Sanjinés & Indaburo) The theater has an ambitious program of folk-music concerts and foreign theatrical presentations.

Dead Stroke (Map pp172-3; Av 6 de Agosto 2460; 🕑 nightly) Billiards is incredibly popular – if you fancy a rack or two, check out this place.

Peñas

Typical of La Paz are folk music venues called *peñas*. Most present traditional Andean music, but they often include lavish guitar and song recitals. The cover charge for the places listed here is US$4 to US$5. The most touristy are **Peña Huari** (Map pp174-5; Sagárnaga 339) and **Peña Parnaso** (Map pp174-5; Sagárnaga at Murillo), which both serve dinner and advertise nightly shows but often only go off when tour groups are in town. **Casa del Corregidor** (Map pp174-5; Murillo 1040) and **Peña Marka Tambo** (Map pp174-5; Jaén 710) attract local music fans as well.

Cinemas

Cinemateca Boliviana (Map pp174-5; cnr Pichincha & Indaburo; tickets US$1.35) For classics and arty flicks, check out this cinema.

Modern cinemas on the Prado, including **Cine 16 de Julio** (Map pp174-5; near Plaza del Estudiante; admission US$2), show recent international releases, usually in the original language with Spanish subtitles; the **nameless cinema** (Map pp174-5; Calle Comercio near Sanjinés) does an afternoon double feature for US$1.35.

SHOPPING

Street stalls are the cheapest place to buy everything from batteries and film to bootleg CDs.

If you're low on clean skivvies or need a new fleece, head to the Mercado Negro (Map pp174-5) for garment bargains galore. Calle Sagárnaga (Map pp174-5) is the street for 'typical' souvenirs and the nearby Witches Market (Map pp174-5) is the place for oddities.

There are several good places for music and musical instruments. There are plenty of CD shops along Sagárnaga.

Eddy Lima Shop (Map pp174-5; Illampu 827) Try this shop for Bolivian CDs and a decent selection of instruments.

El Guitarrón (Map pp174-5; Sagárnaga 303) Specializes in stringed instruments.

GETTING THERE & AWAY
Air

Call **Aeropuerto El Alto** (☎ 02-281-0240) for flight information. Airline offices in La Paz include:

AeroSur (Map pp174-5; ☎ 02-243-0430, 02-231-3233; Av 16 de Julio 1616)

Amaszonas (☎ 02-222-0840/0848; Saavedra 1649, Miraflores)

American Airlines (Map pp174-5; ☎ 02-235-5384; www.aa.com; Plaza Venezuela 1440, Edificio Herrmann Busch)

Grupo Taca (Map pp174-5; ☎ 02-231-3132; www.taca .com; Av 16 de Julio 1479, Edificio San Pablo, 4th fl)

LAB (Map pp174-5; ☎ 02-237-1020/1024, 800-10-4321, 800-10-3001; Camacho 1460)

LanChile/LanPeru (Map pp174-5; ☎ 02-235-8377; www.lanchile.com, www.lanperu.com; Av 16 de Julio 1566, Edificio Ayacucho, Suite 104)

Transportes Aéreos Militares (TAM; ☎ 02-212-1582/1589, TAM airport ☎ 02-284-1884; Montes 738)

TAM Mercosur (Map pp174-5; ☎ 02-244-3442; www.tam.com.py in Spanish; Plaza del Estudiante 1931)

Varig (Map pp174-5; ☎ 02-231-4040; www.varig.com; Calle Santa Cruz 1392, Edificio Cámara de Comercio)

Domestic flight prices vary little between airlines, except for TAM, which is always the cheapest. Most travel agents sell tickets for internal flights for the same price as the airlines. The following schedule and price information is subject to change. Prices quoted are one way. Many domestic flights are not direct and often involve a change of plane, with legs usually lasting less than an hour.

Cobija US$85, 2 to 3 flights weekly with AeroSur or TAM.

Cochabamba US$43/27, 3 flights daily with AeroSur and LAB/TAM.

Guayaramerín US$130/88, 1 to 2 flights weekly with Amazonas/TAM.

Puerto Suarez US$110/95, 2 flights weekly via Santa Cruz with AeroSur/TAM.

Riberalta US$130/88, 2 to 3 flights weekly with Amazonas/TAM.

Rurrenabaque US$50, daily flights with Amazonas and TAM.

San Borja US$53, 2 to 3 flights weekly with Amazonas.

Santa Cruz US$96/67, 2 to 3 flights daily with AeroSur and LAB/TAM.

Sucre US$62/42, daily flights with AeroSur (direct) and LAB (via Cochabamba or Santa Cruz), 1 to 2 flights weekly with TAM.

Tarija US$97/75, daily flights with AeroSur (direct or via Santa Cruz), LAB (via Cochabamba or Santa Cruz) and TAM.

Trinidad US$63/60, daily flights with Amazonas (via San Borja) and LAB (via Cochabamba or Santa Cruz).

Yacuiba US$88, weekly flight (via Sucre & Tarija) with TAM.

Bus

There are three *flota* (bus) departure points in La Paz: the main terminal, the cemetery district and Villa Fátima. Fares are relatively uniform between companies, but competition keeps prices low. Allow for longer travel times (often double) in the rainy season.

MAIN TERMINAL

A few companies have ticket offices in the **terminal** (Map pp172-3; ☎ 02-228-0551), but their buses actually leave from the cemetery; you'll pay twice the price if you buy your passage here. There's a secure **left-luggage facility** (☼ 5am-10pm) and a B$2 terminal fee.

Approximate one-way fares and journey times from the main terminal are shown in the following table. Buses provide connections between major cities several times daily, and more expensive *bus cama* (sleeper) services are available on long overnight runs.

Destination	Duration in Hours	Cost
Arica, Chile	8	US$10-13
Cochabamba	7	US$2-3
Cuzco, Peru	12-17	US$15-20
Iquique, Chile	11-13	US$12-17
Oruro	3	US$2
Potosí	11	US$5-7
Puno, Peru	8	US$6-8
Santa Cruz	18	US$8-15
Sucre	14	US$8-10
Tarija	24	US$10-15
Trinidad	40	US$20
Uyuni	13	US$6-10
Villazón	23	US$7-12

CEMETERY AREA

Micros and minibuses run to the *cementerio* (cemetery) constantly from the center: catch them on Av Mariscal Santa Cruz and grab *micro* No 2 along Av Yanacocha. Heading into the city from the cemetery by day you can catch *micros* along Av Baptista. At night it's best to take a taxi.

Transportes Manco Kapac (Map pp172-3; Plaza Felix Reyes Ortiz) and Transtur 2 de Febrero run to Copacabana (US$2, three hours) all day from Calle José María Aliaga. Transporte 6 de Junio also goes to Copacabana between 5am and 8pm. Otherwise, for US$4 to US$5, try the more comfortable tourist minibuses (see p177) that do hotel pick-ups. From Copacabana, lots of *micros* and minibuses sprint to Puno (US$3 to US$4, three to four hours).

Between 5am and 6pm, **Autolíneas Ingavi** (Map pp172-3; Calle José María Asín) has departures every 30 minutes to Desaguadero (US$1, two hours) via Tiahuanaco. **Unión Ingavi** (Map pp172-3; Calle José Maria Asin) services the same route. Nearby is **Trans-Unificado Sorata** (Map pp172-3; Ángel Babia & Manuel Bustillos), which operates ten daily buses to Sorata (US$1.50, 4½ hours). Seats are in short supply, so book your ticket early; sit on the left for views. Buses to Huarina and Huatajata also leave from this area.

VILLA FÁTIMA

You can reach Villa Fátima by *micro* or minibus from the Prado or Av Camacho. Turbus Totai and Flota Yungueña minibuses to Coroico (US$2, four hours) leave from near the gas station. Flota Yungueña also has daily departures to Rurrenabaque (US$7, 18 to 20 hours) at 11am.

Turbus Totai has hourly departures to Chulumani (US$2, four hours) – a heinous

BOLIVIA

trip in the rainy season; a bus to Guanay (US$8, eight hours) at 9:30am daily; and another to Rurrenabaque (US$11, 16 hours) at 11:30am daily.

GETTING AROUND

La Paz is well serviced by public transport. There are full-size buses and *micros* (medium-size buses), which charge US$0.20 (B$1.50) for trips around the city center. *Kombi* minibuses charge B$1.80 around town and B$2 to the Zona Sur. Buses, *micros* and minibuses announce their route with signs on the windshield; barkers shout out destinations on minibuses ad nauseam. *Trufis* are shared taxis that follow a fixed route and charge B$2 per person around the center. Any of these vehicles can be waved down anywhere, except in areas cordoned off by the police.

Radio taxis, which you can phone or flag down, charge B$6 around the center and B$8 to the cemetery district, slightly more at night, slightly less coming downhill. Charges are for up to four passengers and include pickup, if necessary.

AROUND LA PAZ

VALLE DE LA LUNA

The **Valley of the Moon** (admission US$0.65) makes a pleasant half-day break from La Paz' bustle. It's not a valley but a bizarrely eroded maze of canyons and pinnacles technically known as badlands, 10km down the canyon of the Río Choqueyapu from the city center.

To get there, catch any *micro* marked 'Mallasa' or 'Zoológico' from Plaza del Estudiante. Get off after the **Cactario** at the junction for Malasilla Golf Course and walk for a few minutes uphill toward Mallasa village. When you see a green house on your right, you're at the top of the *valle*. Be careful walking here in the rainy season – the route is eroded and can be slippery.

Afterwards, you can visit La Paz' sprawling but underfunded **zoo** (☎ 02-274-5992; admission US$0.40; ☼ 10am-5pm), where you'll find a terrific array of animals amid a gorgeous backdrop. There are photo opportunities aplenty and feeding time (10am daily) is raucous. From the top of Valle de la Luna, catch another *micro* headed down the valley or continue a couple of kilometers on foot.

TIAHUANACO (TIWANAKU)

Tiahuanaco is Bolivia's most significant archaeological site, 72km west of La Paz on the road toward the Peruvian frontier at Desaguadero.

Little is known of the people who constructed this great ceremonial center on Lake Titicaca's southern shore. Archaeologists generally agree that the civilization that spawned Tiahuanaco rose in about 600 BC. The site was under construction around AD 700, but after AD 1200 the group faded into obscurity. However, evidence of its influence has been found throughout the area of the later Inca empire.

There are a number of megaliths (up to 175 tons in weight) strewn around the site, including a ruined pyramid and the remains of a ritual platform. Much has been restored, not always with total authenticity, and travelers fresh from Peru may be disappointed. Across the railway line from Tiahuanaco is a new **site museum** (admission US$2.35; ☼ 9am-5pm) and the ongoing excavation of **Puma Punku** (Gateway of the Puma). For a greater appreciation of Tiahuanaco's history, hire a guide. They hang around the fence and charge US$2 to US$3 after bargaining.

You can stop at Tiahuanaco en route between La Paz and Puno, Peru (via Desaguadero), but most travelers prefer to travel from La Paz to Puno via Lake Titicaca (p191) and visit Tiahuanaco as a day trip from La Paz. Autolíneas Ingavi *micros* depart every half-hour for Tiahuanaco (US$1, 1½ hours) from Calle José María Asín near the cemetery – some continue to Desaguadero. To return to La Paz, flag down a bus (expect to stand), or walk 1km west into Tiahuanaco village and catch one from the plaza.

Several La Paz tour agencies (see p180) offer guided tours to Tiahuanaco for US$10 to US$15.

CORDILLERA REAL & THE YUNGAS

Northeast of La Paz, the dramatic Cordillera Real rises before giving way to the Yungas, a beautiful region characterized by steep forested mountainsides that fall away into humid, cloud-filled gorges. The Yungas, which contain several Afrobolivian settlements, form a natural barrier between the altiplano and the Amazonian rain forests. Heading northeast from La Paz, the road winds up to La Cumbre (4600m), then descends a dramatic 4340m to the Beni lowlands. Tropical fruits, coffee and coca all grow here with minimal tending. The climate is moderate with misty rain possible at any time of year.

COROICO

Perched on the shoulder of Cerro Uchumachi (2548m), Coroico, with a population of 3500 and at an elevation of 1500m to 1750m, is a little Bolivian Eden. It's a weekend getaway for middle-class *paceños* (citizens of La Paz), an enclave for a few European immigrants and a popular base for short treks into the countryside. As many expats can attest, it's so laid-back that it's hard to break away.

Orientation & Information

Coroico is 7km uphill from the transport junction of Yolosa. There's no information office, but the friendly Ćamara Hotelera on the plaza has free town maps. The Parque Nacional Cotapata office is on the plaza; check here for permission to camp at the park's biological research station off the Choro trail (see p189).

Entel is on the western side of the plaza. MCM, near the bus offices, and Internet La Casa, one block east of the plaza, offer slothlike internet access for US$2 an hour.

Banco Unión offers cash advances and may change cash. **Hotel Esmeralda** (☎ 02-213-6017; www.hotelesmeralda.com) changes traveler's checks without commission (see below).

Sights & Activities

For pretty views, trek an easy 20 minutes up to **El Calvario** where the stations of the cross lead to a grassy knoll and **chapel**. To get there, head uphill toward Hotel Esmeralda. There are two good trailheads from El Calvario. The one to the left leads to the **cascadas**, a trio of waterfalls 6km (two hours) beyond the chapel. The trail to the right leads up to **Cerro Uchumachi** (a five-hour round trip), which affords terrific views of the valley. Don't set off on these routes on your own.

You can rent horses from **El Relincho** (☎ 719-23814), 100m past Hotel Esmeralda, for US$5 an hour or US$30 per day, which

includes a guide. Hotel Bella Vista (see below) rents bicycles.

Siria Leon (☎ 719-55431; siria_leon@yahoo.com; JZ Cuenca 062) is recommended for Spanish lessons (US$4 an hour).

Sleeping

Rates rise as much as 20% on weekends and holidays; bargain midweek and for longer stays. There are many more places to sleep than those listed here and most have restaurants as well.

Residencial Coroico (r per person US$1.75) One block north of the plaza, these are the cheapest digs in town. Try to score a rooftop room.

Hostal Sol y Luna (☎ 715-61626, in La Paz ☎ 02-236-2099; www.solyluna-bolivia.com; camping per person US$2, s/d per person from US$4/3.50, s/d cabañas with bath per person from US$10/7) This splendid German-run retreat is well worth the 20-minute walk east of town. It has scenic campsites, lovely self-contained cabins sleeping up to seven (nicer ones have views and a patio) and comfortable rooms, with shared bath, near the pool. Bonuses include a gringo-friendly restaurant with veggie options (recruit a group for the Indonesian buffet), a multilingual lending library and book exchange, Shiatsu massage (US$12 an hour) and a sublime slate hot tub (US$6.50 for up to three). Free taxi pickup is available for guests with reservations.

Hostal Cafetal (Rancho Beni; Miranda s/n; r per person weekdays/weekends US$3.35/4.50) A superlative option with stunning views, hammocks, great eats and pool in a lush garden setting. Follow the signs from the plaza.

Hostal Kory (in La Paz ☎ 02-243-1311; s/d US$4/7, r with bath per person US$6) Southwest of the plaza, with a pool, great views and small, clean rooms.

Hotel Bella Vista (☎ 715-69237, 02-213-6059; r per person US$5, with bath US$10) Two blocks north of the plaza with new, spotless rooms, racquetball courts and a small rooftop patio with expansive views.

Hotel Don Quixote (☎ 02-213-6007; d US$16) An exceptionally friendly *paceño* weekend favorite, with an indoor-outdoor restaurant and a big splash-about pool. A 10-minute flat walk northeast of the plaza. Breakfast included.

Hotel Esmeralda (☎ 02-213-6017; www.hotelesmeralda.com; r per person US$7-9, with bath US$12-15) Everyone (including most tour groups) seems to end up at Hotel Esmeralda, 400m uphill east of the plaza. The pool, sunny patio and restaurant have killer views. Avoid the dank, overpriced downstairs rooms without views or bath; the best rooms with both are upstairs. Big buffet meals run US$2 to US$3. Phone from the plaza for free pickup.

Eating & Drinking
Coroico has a good choice of eateries and most aren't budget busting.

La Taberna (on the plaza) Try this place for terrific pancakes, coffee and omelets.

Back-Stube Konditorei (opposite Hostal Kory) Good for breakfast, Yungas coffee and homemade German desserts.

Hostal La Casa (Radael Miranda s/n; ☺ Tue-Sun) Has fine European cuisine – book ahead for fondue or raclette.

Restaurante Los Osos (just north of the plaza) Large pizzas at budget prices.

Comedor popular (northwest of the plaza) Typical Bolivian meals all day for under US$1.

Coroico's culinary gold medal goes to Restaurante Cafetal, a French-run restaurant. It's worth every step of the 15-minute walk east of town for its phenomenal salads, crêpes, lasagnas and breezy atmosphere.

Bamboo's (Julio Zuazo Cuenca) For nightlife, try Bamboo's, half a block northeast of the plaza, which has live music, cocktails and Mexican food, or Taurus, a block further east and with a similar vibe.

Getting There & Away
Flanked by epic scenery and punctuated with waterfalls during the rainy season, the La Paz–Coroico road plunges over 3000m in 80km. It's called the 'World's Most Dangerous Road' because it sees the most fatalities annually (over 100 on average), but the road itself is not that treacherous. True, it's extremely narrow and can be muddy, slippery and deeply rutted, but Andean veterans will recall much worse routes in Peru and Ecuador. What makes the road so dangerous is the drivers – a combination of weekend warriors, macho bus drivers on sleep-deprived benders and tenderfooted tourists. To minimize the danger, travel on a weekday in a minivan rather than a big bus, or bicycle or trek in (see p189). Traveling at night is a death wish.

Buses and minibuses leave from near the gas station in La Paz' Villa Fátima neighborhood (see p185). A Flota Yungueña or Trans

Totai minibus (US$2, 3½ hours) is the best way to go. In Coroico, all transport leaves from the plaza. There are dozens of daily departures from Coroico/Yolosa to La Paz and daily buses to Rurrenabaque (US$7.25, 15 hours) at 1pm and 1:30pm. Minibuses stop first in Yolosa, from where many buses and trucks continue down to Guanay (US$5, six hours), Rurre and further into Bolivian Amazonia. Brave souls can risk the rough Coroico–Chulumani road (via Coripata) by hopping onto a *camión* in Coroico's plaza.

CHULUMANI
This placid town is the terminus of the **Yunga Cruz trek** (see p189) and a great detour off the gringo circuit. It's also the capital of Sur Yungas province and is in a main coca-growing region.

Banco Unión, on the plaza, changes cash and traveler's checks (5% commission).

There's an Entel office on the plaza and intermittent Internet access (US$2.65 per hour) a few doors down.

There are beautiful views from the **mirador** two blocks south of the plaza. The gregarious owner of the Country Guesthouse (see below) is full of ideas for hiking, biking, river tubing and camping outside the town. **Ramiro Portugal** (in La Paz ☎ 02-213-6016, 02-279-0381) takes groups on day trips (US$25 for up to five people) to **Bosque Apa Apa**, a cloud forest rich in birds and flora. Camping, including tents, is US$10 plus US$1 per person per night.

Sleeping & Eating
Alojamiento Daniel (r per person US$2, with bath US$3.25) Half a block uphill from the plaza, this place has clean rooms, hot shared showers and decent *almuerzos*. Next door is the similarly priced Alojamiento Chulumani.

Hotel Panorama (☎ 02-213-6109; Murillo at Andrade; r per person US$6) Moving up a notch in comfort, this hotel has good rooms with private bath, a pool and expansive views.

Country Guesthouse (camping per person US$2.65, with bath & breakfast US$6.65) The nicest place to stay is Xavier Sarabia's rustic guesthouse, an easy 10-minute walk southwest of the plaza. There's a pool, homey bar and good meals on request; hot showers are included.

Food choices are limited. Try the restaurant at the Country Guesthouse or one of the basic *comedores* at the tranca. The spic-n-span market also has good cheap meals.

El Mesón (on the plaza) dishes up filling set lunches. Across the plaza, **Restaurant Chulumani** has an upstairs dining terrace. The **café** (✪ from 7:30am) next to Entel on the plaza does good coffee, cakes and *empanadas*.

Getting There & Away

From Villa Fátima in La Paz (see p185), Turbus Totai buses go to and from Chulumani (US$2, four hours) when full from 8am to 4pm. From Chulumani, Trans San Bartolomé has daily departures for La Paz at 5:30am, noon and 2pm. Trans Chulumani and 24 de Agosto minibuses leave hourly from the *tranca* (police post). The Chulumani–Unduavi road (where the paved bit begins) is hazardous in the rainy season. Bring lots of snacks and water and expect delays.

It's possible to go to Coroico via Coripata: take a La Paz–bound bus and get off at the crossroads just after Puente Villa at Km 93. Here, wait for a bus or *camión* to Coripata and then change again for a lift to Coroico. It's a lo-o-o-ng, dusty trip, but worth it.

TREKKING IN THE CORDILLERA REAL

Several worthwhile treks run between the altiplano and the Yungas, all of which cross the Cordillera Real on relatively low passes. Most popular are the **Choro** (La Cumbre to Coroico, 70km), **Taquesi** (Takesi; 40km) and **Yunga Cruz** (114km). These two- to four-day treks all begin with a brief ascent, then head down from spectacular high-mountain landscapes into the riotous vegetation of the Yungas.

Trekking the Choro independently is only tricky at the trailhead: take any bus from La Paz to Coroico and alight at **La Cumbre**, the highest point on the road. The path begins on the left and is distinct for the first kilometer, but then gets harder to discern. Stay to your right and pass between two ponds (one often dry) before heading uphill. From here it's clear sailing to Coroico. Security is a concern as nasty incidents have been reported. Most La Paz tour agencies offer this as a three-day trip for around US$100, all-inclusive.

Serious trekkers should consult Lonely Planet's *Trekking in the Central Andes,* which includes maps and detailed descriptions of these treks, as well as other routes.

GUANAY

Isolated Guanay, 70km northwest of Caranavi, makes a good base for visits to the gold-mining operations along the Ríos Mapiri and Tipuani. If you can overlook the devastation of the landscape wrought by gold fever, a visit with the miners is interesting. Guanay is a detour from the Coroico–Rurrenabaque road, and it's at the end of the **Camino del Oro** trek from Sorata. Access to the mining areas is by jeep along the Llipi road, or by motorized dugout canoes up the Río Mapiri.

Guanay's gold dealers love to get their hands on dollars and Caranavi's Banco Unión does cash advances and changes traveler's checks.

Sleeping & Eating

Hotel Pahuichi (r per person US$2.50) A block downhill from the plaza, this is the best value in town.

Hospedaje Los Pinos (d US$4.50) This friendly spot near the dock has clean doubles with private bath and fan.

Several other basic but friendly places within a block of the plaza all charge around US$2 per person.

There are many restaurants on the main strip and around the plaza.

Getting There & Away

Four companies offer daily runs to and from La Paz via Caranavi and Yolosa (US$8, eight to 10 hours). For Coroico, get off at Yolosa and catch a lift up the hill. If you're heading to Rurrenabaque (US$7.50, 14 hours), get off in Caranavi and connect with a northbound bus.

Ask around at the dock if you're gung ho for a thrilling motorized canoe ride down the Río Beni to Rurre (US$10 to US$20), which departs only on demand. It's also sometimes possible to find rides through mining country to Mapiri in the early morning.

SORATA

Sorata, with a population of 2450 and at an elevation of 2670m, is a gem. It sits below the awesome snowcapped peaks of Illampu (6362m) and Ancohuma (6427m) at the confluence of the Ríos San Cristobal and Challa Suya. It's popular with mountaineers, trekkers and travelers needing a cool place to relax. Sunday is market day.

Although it's nothing to shout about, many visitors do the 12km trek to the **Gruta** de San Pedro (San Pedro Cave; admission US$1; ☺ 8am-5pm), a six-hour round trip from Sorata (a one-way taxi costs US$2). An attendant will crank up the lights inside the cave, where there is a tepid lagoon. Bring a flashlight, water and snacks – or, better yet, stop by Café Illampu en route.

Trekking

Peak hiking season is April to September. Ambitious adventurers can do the seven-day **Camino del Oro trek**, an ancient trading route between the altiplano and the Río Tipuani gold fields. Alternatively, there's the steep climb up to **Laguna Challata**, a long day trek; **Comunidad Lakathiya**, another long day trek; **Laguna Glacial**, a three-day trek; the challenging five-day **Mapiri Trail**; or the seven-day **Illampu circuit**. Go with guides and inquire locally about security before attempting any treks as many serious incidents continue to be reported.

The Spanish-speaking **Sorata Guides & Porters Association** (☎/fax 02-213-6698; guiasorata@hotmail.com; Sucre 302) rents equipment of varying quality and arranges many different treks. Budget on US$12 to US$20 per day for a group plus food, depending on the group size.

Sleeping

Hostal Las Piedras (r with shared bath per person US$2.65) This new, *simpático* (pleasant) German-run (English spoken) place has six artistically-decorated rooms with shared bath. The optional breakfast includes homemade wholemeal bread and yoghurt courtesy of Café Illampu. It's near the soccer field, a 10-minute walk from the plaza, down Calle Ascarrunz (a rough track) off the shortcut to the cave.

Camping Altai Oasis (☎ 715-19856; resaltai@hotmail.com; camping per person US$1.35, s/d US$2.65/6, r with bath US$10.65, cabins US$20-40) Campers love this beautiful riverside retreat, 20 minutes walk from town off the road to caves, and run by Bolivian hosts Johny and Roxana. There's a good bar/café, a book exchange, laundry service, hot showers and a communal kitchen. It's a 20-minute walk from the plaza, 1km down a winding detour of the road to San Pedro.

Hostal Mirador (☎ 02-289-5002/5008; Muñecas 400; r per person US$2.65) This HI-affiliate has a sunny terrace restaurant and great views down the valley. Breakfast included.

Residencial Sorata (☎ 02-279-3459; NE cnr of plaza; r per person US$2-5.50; 💻) The main attractions at this sprawling Canadian-run colonial mansion is the unkempt antique atmosphere. The cheapest rooms are basic and the beds are poor, but there's a restaurant, book exchange, nightly videos and good trekking information.

Hotel El Paraiso (☎ 02-213-6671; Villavicencio s/n; r per person US$3, with bath US$4.25) This family-run hotel has carpeted rooms, a restaurant and a sunny terrace.

Villa Sorata (☎ 02-213-6688; Guachalla 238; s/d US$8/11.50) There are four new rooms with bath and TV at this American-run B&B. There are great Illampu views from the sunny terrace. Breakfast included.

Hotel Landhaus Copacabana (☎/fax 02-213-6670; www.boliviatrek.com; r per person low/high season US$2/4, d with bath US$15/20; 💻) This German-run place has a sunny garden with hammocks, good restaurant and large video collection, but a sketchy local reputation. It's ten minutes from the plaza toward San Pedro.

Hostal Panchita (☎ 02-813-5038; south side of plaza; s/d with shared bath US$2.50/4) This popular hostel has ample rooms and a nice courtyard.

Alojamiento Sorata Central (north side of plaza; r per person US$1.35) This basic but friendly place is also the cheapest in town. It has plaza views and shared cold showers.

An obligatory stop on the way to San Pedro is the atmospheric Swiss-run Café Illampu (see p191), which has rental tents and grassy camping with hot showers and terrific views.

Eating & Drinking

Small, inexpensive restaurants around the market and the plaza sell cheap and filling *almuerzos*; Restaurant Sorata has veggie options.

For a quick B$1 burger piled high with weenies and fries, hit the hamburger stands on the northwest corner of the plaza, where snack stands do fry-ups until the wee hours.

Pete's Place (☎ 02-289-5005; on the plaza; ☺ 8:30am-10pm) For the latest trekking news and great food, this is the place. Healthy breakfasts and a yummy selection of veggie and international dishes will cure what ails you.

Camping Altai-Oasis (☎ 715-19856) The café here offers coffee, drinks and its trademark steaks, veggie treats and Eastern European specialties (see Sleeping, p190).

There are no less than four pizzerias on the plaza, all jokingly said to share the same kitchen – Bella Italia is the best.

Café Illampu (☼ Thu-Mon) On the road to San Pedro, this café, run by the jovial Stephan the Swiss pastry chef, is where you'll find killer coffee and cakes, plus *licuados* (fruit shakes) blended from garden-fresh berries.

Cocktails and occasional live music can be found at the cozy pub formerly known as the Spider Bar, which is 250m west of the plaza and due to re-open under new management, or across the way at the smokin' Casa Reggae, which also has cheap rooms to rent.

Getting There & Away

Sorata is far removed from the other Yungas towns and there are no direct connections to Coroico.

From La Paz, Trans Unificado Sorata departs the cemetery district 10 times daily (US$1.50, 4½ hours). From Sorata, La Paz–

bound buses depart from the plaza hourly from 4am to 5pm.

For Copacabana you must get off at the junction town of Huarina and wait for another, probably packed, bus.

LAKE TITICACA

Fabled Lake Titicaca is a brilliant splash of blue amid the sere no-man's-land of the altiplano. According to ancient legend, the sun was born here, and the Inca believe their first emperor rose from the rock called Titicaca ('Rock of the Puma') on the northern tip of Isla del Sol. The lake is still revered by the Aymara who populate its shores and the whole area pulsates with energy.

More than 230km long, 97km wide and at an elevation of 3820m, it's among the world's highest navigable lakes and covers over 9000 sq km. Straddling the Peru–Bolivia border, it's a remnant of the ancient inland sea known as Lago Ballivián, which covered much of the altiplano before the water level fell due to geological faults and evaporation.

BOLIVIA

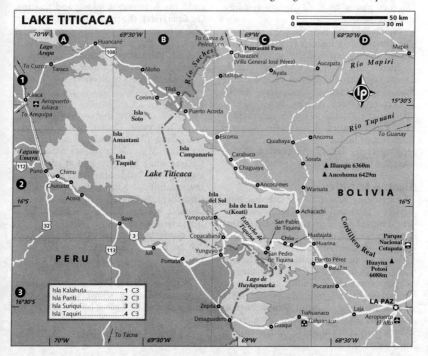

LAKE TITICACA

Isla Kalahuta	1 C3
Isla Pariti	2 C3
Isla Suriqui	3 C3
Isla Taquiri	4 C3

BOLIVIA

COPACABANA

Copacabana (Copa), with a population of 54,300 and at an elevation of 3800m, is a small, enchanting town on Lake Titicaca's southern shore. In the 16th century, Copacabana was presented with an image of the Virgin of Candelaria (now Bolivia's patron saint), sparking a slew of miracles. The town became a pilgrimage site and today is known for its cathedral, besotted fiestas and memorable views.

Neither literally nor figuratively the 'hottest spot north of Havana,' tourist-ready Copa does make a convenient base for visiting Isla del Sol and a handy stopover between La Paz and Puno or Cuzco (Peru). It rains in December and January but it's pleasant and sunny with chilly nights throughout the rest of the year.

Information

The best book exchanges are at La Cúpula (see p194) and Café Sol y Luna (see p194).

Alf@Net (cnr 6 de Agosto & 16 de Julio) is a popular hangout with speedy Internet access for US$2 an hour. There are a couple more Internet places on 6 de Agosto heading towards the lake.

Try **Mankha Uta** (6 de Agosto s/n) or **Coyote** (Plaza 2 de Febrero) for laundry (US$1.50 a kilo), but figure on a few days drying time.

There's no ATM in town but **Casa de Cambio Copacabana** (6 de Agosto s/n, at Hotel Playa Azul) changes cash and traveler's checks (5% commission). Nearby, Banco Unión changes checks and does cash advances, as does Prodem, a few doors down, which is open longer hours.

If open, the helpful **tourist office** (NE cnr of plaza) has lots of informative brochures.

Sights & Activities

The sparkling Moorish-style **cathedral**, built between 1605 and 1820, dominates town. The famous wooden **Virgen de Copacabana statue** is housed upstairs in the **Camarín de la Virgen** (admission by donation; ☉ 9am-noon & 2:30-6pm). Don't miss the **Capilla de Velas** (Candle Chapel), around the side of the cathedral, where thousands of candles illuminate an arched sepulchre and wax graffiti cakes the walls. The colorful **Benediciones de Movilidades** (*cha'lla*; blessing of automobiles) occurs daily at 10am and 2:30pm in front of the cathedral.

The hill north of town is **Cerro Calvario** (3966m), which can be reached in 30 minutes and is well worth the climb, particularly at sunset. Many pilgrims make this climb, placing stones at the stations of the cross as they ascend. Less impressive are the minor Inca sites around town: **Horca del Inca** (admission US$1.35), on the hill Niño Calvario; the **Tribunal del Inca** (☉ 9am-noon & 1-5pm), near the cemetery; and **Baño del Inca** (admission US$0.50), 2km north of town.

Head to the lakeshore to rent **bicycles**, **motorcycles**, **canoes** or **sailboats**.

Festivals & Events

One local tradition is the blessing of miniature objects, like cars or houses, at the **Alasitas festival** (January 24), as a prayer that the real thing will be obtained in the coming year. These miniatures are sold in stalls around the plaza and at the top of Cerro Calvario.

Following Alasitas, the **Fiesta de la Virgen de Candelari**a is celebrated on the first two days of February. Dervishes from Peru and Bolivia perform traditional Aymara dances amid much music, drinking and feasting. On **Good Friday**, the town fills with pilgrims, who join a solemn candlelit procession at dusk. The biggest fiesta lasts for a week around **Independence Day** (first week in August), featuring parades, brass bands, fireworks and lots of alcohol.

Sleeping

There is an incredible variety of cheap places to snooze. During fiestas, however, everything fills up and prices can jump threefold. Most places will store backpacks for free while you overnight at Isla del Sol and beyond. Wild camping is possible on the summits of Niño Calvario and Cerro Sancollani. Following are the cheapest acceptable options, asking US$1.25 to US$2 per person for rooms without bath.

Alojamiento Emperador (☎ 02-862-2083; Murillo 235) An upbeat place which has hot showers, a small kitchen, firm beds and a sunny mezzanine.

Alojamiento Aroma (☎ 02-862-2004; cnr Jáuregui & Destacamento) Hot showers, sunny patio and a superb lake view; best rooms on top floor.

Alojamiento Kotha Kahuaña (Av Busch 15) Family-run, with cooking facilities, good

BOLIVIA

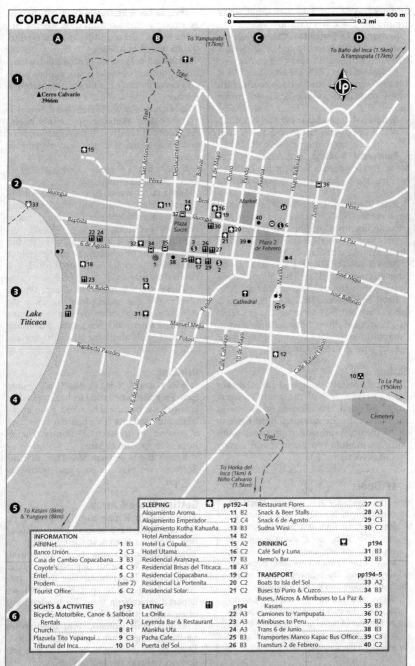

COPACABANA

0   400 m
0   0.2 mi

upstairs rooms with lake views, hot water around the clock and a mellow vibe.

Residencial La Porteñita (☎ 02-862-2006; cnr Jáuregui s/n & Pando) Friendly and clean, with a well-traveled, English-speaking owner.

Residencial Solar (☎ 02-862-2009; Jáuregui 140 at 3 de Mayo) Cramped roof-terrace rooms with sunny patio and panoramic views; go for room No 1.

Residencial Copacabana (☎ 02-862-2220, 02-2784130 in La Paz; Oruro 555) Wood floors and some nicer rooms with private bath.

Residencial Aransaya (☎ 02-862-2229; 6 de Agosto 121) New rooms with private bath, an inviting, sunny patio and a good restaurant below.

Hotel Utama (☎ 02-862-2013; Michel Peréz; r per person with breakfast US$5) In the mid-range, this friendly hotel has comfortable rooms with private bath (it often gets the overflow from the nearby La Cúpula).

Hotel Brisas del Titicaca (☎ 02-862-2178; r per person US$4, with bath US$5.35) This HI-affiliate is popular with groups and overlooks the lake.

Hotel Ambassador (☎ 02-862-2216; Jáuregui at Bolívar; r with bath & TV per person US$5.35-6) This ex-HI affiliate offers optional breakfast in the rooftop restaurant and piped-in shower music! Upstairs rooms are best.

Eating

The local specialty is farmed Lake Titicaca *trucha criolla*, one of the world's largest trout. As usual, the cheapest meals are in the market. In the morning, head there to smell the fish and sate your sweet tooth with *api morado* (purple api) and syrupy *buñuelos* (doughnuts).

SPLURGE!

For a treat, try the well-run **Hotel La Cúpula** (☎ 02-862-2029; www.hotelcupula.com; Michel Peréz 1-3; s/d/tr from US$6/8/20, with bath from US$14/20/28), on a shady, hammock-equipped hillside overlooking the lake. None of the 17 rooms are alike, but all are very inviting. The upstairs Mirador restaurant is superb and there's a TV/video room, library and shared kitchen, and laundry facilities. The staff speak a raft of languages and are full of travel tips. For lovers, there's a sweet honeymoon suite (US$32). Book ahead via the website.

Leyenda Bar & Restaurant You can hardly go wrong at this lakefront spot, where delicious juices, pizzas and trout are served to the strains of Bob Marley.

La Orilla (6 de Agosto s/n) With a full bar and huge portions of pasta pesto, stuffed trout and coconut curry, La Orilla is definitely a winner.

La Cúpula (☎ 02-862-2029; Michel Peréz 1-3; ☽ from 7:30am) Walking up to this hotel/ restaurant is worth it for the atmosphere and view as much as the tasty vegetarian dishes.

Mankha Uta (6 de Agosto s/n; set meals US$1.50) Features veggie options.

Sudna Wasi (Jáuregui 127; mains US$3-5) An interesting choice with delightful courtyard tables and a varied menu including many Bolivian specialties.

Pacha Cafe (cnr 6 de Agosto & Bolívar) Try the superlative hot chocolate and excellent pizza here, and listen to occasional live entertainment.

There are a number of cheap, typical places. On the main drag, Snack 6 de Agosto is a good value, or give Restaurant Flores or Puerta del Sol a shot. The snack and beer stalls along the lakeshore are another option.

Drinking

Café Sol y Luna (Av 16 de Julio, at Hotel Gloria; ☽ from 6pm) This atmospheric, kickback spot has java drinks, bar munchies and good cocktails, plus satellite TV, board games and a groovin' by-request CD library. Happy hour is from 7pm to 9pm.

Nemo's Bar (6 de Agosto 684) This British/ Bolivian-run place is cozy and warm for a tipple.

Getting There & Away

Trans Manco Kapac and Transturs 2 de Febrero both have several daily connections from La Paz (near the cemetery) via Tiquina to Copacabana (US$2, 3½ hours), with extra weekend departures. Faster Trans 6 de Junio minibuses depart frequently from 3am to 7pm. Note that buses depart Copacabana from Plaza Sucre, but often arrive at Plaza 2 de Febrero.

Comfortable nonstop tour buses from La Paz to Copacabana cost US$2 to US$4. Many go all the way to Puno, but you can arrange to break the journey in Copacabana and then continue with the same agency. You can do just the Copacobana-Puno leg (US$3 to US$4, three to four hours) or go all the way to Cuzco (US$9.50, 15 hours) – book ahead. These buses arrive and depart from Av 6 de Agosto.

The cheapest way to reach Puno (Peru) is via a minibus from Plaza Sucre to the border at Kasani/Yunguyo (US$0.50, 30 minutes), where you'll find frequent onward transport to Puno (US$1.50, 2½ to three hours), but it's worth the few extra ducats for a private transfer (US$2.50 to US$3) with agencies who help facilitate border crossing formalities.

Note that Peruvian time is one hour behind Bolivian time.

COPACABANA TO YAMPUPATA TREK

The 17km walk from Copacabana to Yampupata (just across the strait from Isla del Sol) takes three to four hours. The scenery along the trek rocks, and you can take a boat across to Isla del Sol for a few more days of hiking, and then hop on a boat back to Copacabana – it makes a phenomenal trip.

From Copacabana, head northeast along the road across the flat plain. After an hour or so, you'll reach the **Hinchaca reforestation project** on your left. Just beyond the project, cross the stream on your left and follow the obvious **Inca road** up the steep hill. This paved stretch makes a shortcut, rejoining the track at the hilltop. At the fork in the road, take the road to the left, which leads down to the village of **Titicachi**.

At **Sicuani**, the next village, **Hostal Yampu** (basic accommodations per person around US$1) has meals and reed boat rides. It's another hour to the piers at **Yampupata**, where you can hire a two-person rowboat to **Pilko Kaina** on **Isla del Sol** for around US$3 or a faster motorboat for US$1.35 per person with a larger group. Returning to Copacabana, some sort of *movilidad* (anything that moves) usually leaves Yampupata early in the morning or after lunch on most days (around US$0.50).

ISLA DEL SOL & ISLA DE LA LUNA

The Island of the Sun is the legendary Inca creation site and is the birthplace of the sun in Inca mythology. It was here that the bearded white god Viracocha and the first Incas, Manco Capac and his sister-wife

Mama Huaca (or Mama Ocllo), made their mystical appearances. **Isla de la Luna** (Koati; Island of the Moon), the site of a deteriorating convent housing the virgins of the sun, is smaller and less touristed; a small admission fee may be charged.

Isla del Sol is dotted with several villages, of which **Yumani** and **Cha'llapampa** are the largest. The island's Inca ruins include **Pilko Kaina** (admission US$0.65) at the southern end and the **Chincana** complex in the north, which is the site of the sacred rock where the Inca creation legend began. At Cha'llapampa, there's a **museum** with gold artifacts from the underwater excavations near Isla Koa, north of Isla del Sol. Due to community in-fighting, separate admission tickets are required for each site. The **Museo Templo de Sol** (admission US$0.65) near Cha'lla features a collection of all things Aymara, but opening hours are erratic.

Networks of **walking tracks** make exploration easy, but the sunshine and altitude can take their toll. You can see the island's main archaeological sites in one long day, but it's best to stay overnight. Bring food, water and sunscreen. On a day tour, the boat arrives at Cha'llapampa near the northern end of the island at about 10am. A Spanish-speaking guide shows groups around the museum and accompanies them to Chincana. From there it's a moderately strenuous three-hour walk along the ridgeline to Yumani, where food and accommodations are available. The **Escalera del Inca** (Inca Stairway) goes down to the jetty at **Fuente del Inca**, from where tour boats leave at 4pm for the return journey. Most tour boats stop to visit the Pilko Kaina ruins on the way back, finishing at Copacabana at around 6pm.

Most tour tickets theoretically let you return on a later day, so you can stay on the island to explore. But hooking up with your original company for the return isn't always easy. Half-day tours (US$2) only give a glimpse of either end of the island and are hardly worthwhile. The easiest solution is to purchase two separate one-way tickets, which allows flexibility and works out at around US$3.25.

Sleeping & Eating

Isla del Sol's infrastructure is basic but improving and there will no doubt be more options by the time you read this. Food is

BOLIVIA

more expensive than on the mainland and shops for self-catering are scarce. You can wild camp just about anywhere away from the village and cultivated land; the best spots are on beaches and on the west side of the island.

There are at least half-dozen *alojamientos* on the hilltop in Yumani. There's little to distinguish them: they all charge US$2 to US$3 per person with shared cold showers (but several are working on installing private electric showers), offer meals for under US$2 and enjoy spectacular views.

Hostal Inti Wayra (☎ 719-42015, in La Paz ☎ 02-2461765) This large, two-story and ever-expanding white house has new rooms with private baths.

Other options include the following:

Hostal Puerta del Sol (☎ 719-55181) A cheery white house.

Hostal Imperio del Sol Clean and friendly.

Hostal Templo del Sol Run-down.

Posada Inca del Mallku (r per person US$2.50) About 20 minutes north of Yumani on the coastal trail, this place has rooms perched over the lake.

Restaurant Imperio Aymará, on the hilltop, and Restaurant La Kantuta, at the top of the Escalera del Inca, are the best bets for simple meals.

At the north end of the island, you'll find lodging and meals in houses around Cha'llapampa's plaza.

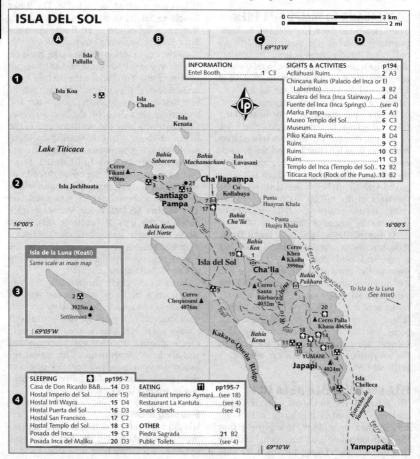

ISLA DEL SOL

INFORMATION	
Entel Booth	1 C3

SIGHTS & ACTIVITIES	p194
Acllahuasi Ruins	2 A3
Chincana Ruins (Palacio del Inca or El Laberinto)	3 B2
Escalera del Inca (Inca Stairway)	4 D4
Fuente del Inca (Inca Springs)	(see 4)
Marka Pampa	5 A1
Museo Templo del Sol	6 C3
Museum	7 C2
Pilko Kaina Ruins	8 D4
Ruins	9 C3
Ruins	10 C3
Ruins	11 C3
Templo del Inca (Templo del Sol)	12 B2
Titicaca Rock (Rock of the Puma)	13 B2

Isla de la Luna (Koati)
Same scale as main map

SLEEPING	pp195-7
Casa de Don Ricardo B&B	14 D3
Hostal Imperio del Sol	(see 15)
Hostal Inti Wayra	15 D4
Hostal Puerta del Sol	16 D3
Hostal San Francisco	17 C2
Hostal Templo del Sol	18 C3
Posada del Inca	19 C3
Posada Inca del Mallku	20 D3

EATING	pp195-7
Restaurant Imperio Aymará	(see 18)
Restaurant La Kantuta	(see 4)
Snack Stands	(see 4)

OTHER	
Piedra Sagrada	21 B2
Public Toilets	(see 4)

SPLURGE!

The peaceful four-room refuge known as **Casa de Don Ricardo B&B** (☎ 719-34427; birdyzehnder@hotmail.com; s/d US$12/20) is perched halfway up the hill from the Fuente del Inca. All the eager local kids who meet arrivals will know the way. Argentine community activist Ricardo runs this place with his friendly Aymara neighbors, cooks great meals on request and knows everything about the island. It's the perfect base camp and worth a stay for the spectacular sunrise and sunset views alone. Ask about guided boat trips on the lake. Rooms have private hot showers and rates include breakfast.

Hostal San Francisco is the most often recommended option.

Posada del Inca (r per person US$1.50; dinner US$2) Further down the east coast, on the utopian sandy beach at Bahía Kea, this friendly place has transcendent views. Cold drinks are available and the day's catch can be had for dinner. Ask the owners about the new place they are building on the ridge along the trail to the Chincana ruins.

Getting There & Away

Day tours by boat from Copacabana to Isla del Sol and back cost from US$2 to US$4 per person, plus admission charges; buy tickets at the kiosks on the beach or at agencies in town. Tours cost the same if you walk from Cha'llapampa to Yumani. You'll pay similar for a round-trip passage to the Pilko Kaina ruins but will end up spending more time on the water than on land. Boats leave Copacabana for Isla del Sol at 8:15am and 1:30pm, returning around 11am and 5pm. You can hop on a Copacabana-bound boat at the foot of the Escalera del Inca and have it drop you at Cha'llapampa in the north for US$1.50.

If you have the time and energy, it's more interesting to walk from Copacabana to Yampupata and across to Isla del Sol by boat (see p195).

THE SOUTHWEST

Geographically, Bolivia's untamed bottom-left corner consists of the southern altiplano and highlands. Aesthetically, it is ethereal, inspiring and unparalleled. The southern altiplano is an inhospitable wilderness of windswept basins, lonely volcanic peaks and glaring salt deserts – a dreamscape of mirages and indeterminable distances. Farther east, the altiplano drops into spectacular red-rock country and then, lower still, into dry, eroded badlands, before magically erupting with orchards and vineyards.

ORURO

The southern altiplano's main city (elevation 3700m) is immediately north of the seasonal **Uru Uru** and **Poopó lakes**, crowded against a motley range of mineral-rich hills. Oruro's 200,000 inhabitants, 90% of whom are pure Amerindian, call themselves *quirquinchos* (armadillos). The city is three hours south of La Paz by a decent (by Bolivian standards) paved road and is the northern limit of Bolivia's shrinking rail network.

It's fiercely cold and windy year-round, so come prepared. It's worth rearranging your itinerary to attend **La Diablada**, a wild annual fiesta on the Saturday before Ash Wednesday, during **Carnaval**. The main event is a spectacular parade of devils, performed by dancers in intricately garish masks and costumes. Accommodations and transportation are in high demand, so advance booking is essential and inflated prices are the norm.

Information

The **Tourist Police** (☒ 02-5251923; Plaza 10 de Febrero) only seem to be out in force during Carnaval. Extend your stay at **immigration** (☎ 02-5270239; Ayacucho 322, 2nd fl).

The best of several cheap Internet places (US$0.50 an hour) along 6 de Octubre is **Compumundo** (6 de Octubre) opposite the university. **Mundial Internet** (Bolívar 573; ☒ 9am-midnight) charges US$0.65 an hour for the best hookup in town.

Hotel Sucre (Sucre & 6 de Octubre) charges US$1.25 per dozen items for hand wash-and-dry laundry service.

Banco Boliviano Americano (Calle Bolívar & Soria Galvarro) and **Banco de Santa Cruz** (Calle Bolívar 460) change cash and traveler's checks (5% commission). There are a couple of Enlace ATMs on the plaza. Watch your cash stash – local pickpockets and bag-slashers are

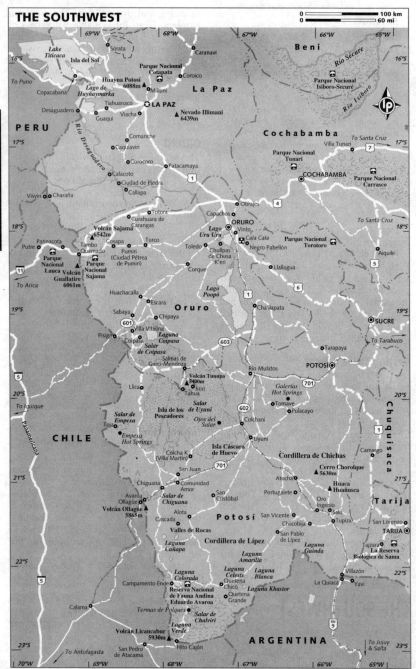

quite competent, especially during drunken festivals.

The helpful **tourist information office** (☎ 02-525-7881) is in a glass kiosk in front of Entel. The less helpful **municipal tourist office** (Plaza 10 de Febrero) is on the west side of the plaza.

Sights & Activities

In the **Casa de la Cultura**, the **Museo Patiño** (☎ 02-525-4015; Soria Galvarro 5755; admission US$0.80; 9am-noon & 2:30-6pm Mon-Fri) is a former residence of tin baron Simón Patiño. Exhibits include period furnishings, paintings, photographs and some fine toys.

Adjacent to the **Santuario de la Virgen del Socavón**, the intriguing subterranean **Museo Etnográfico Minero** (☎ 02-525-6954; admission for 1/2 museums US$0.40/0.60, camera use US$0.40; 9am-noon & 3-6pm) is in a defunct mine, with displays on mines, miners and the all-important, devilish miners' god, El Tío. Also here is the new **Museo Sacro Folklorico Arquelogico**.

At the south end of town, the **Museo Antropológico Eduardo López Rivas** (admission US$0.65; 8am-noon & 2-6pm) has artifacts from the early Chipaya and Uru tribes. Take *micro* C marked 'Sud' from the plaza's northwest corner or opposite the railway station and get off just beyond the tin foundry.

More gems: the **Museo Mineralógico** (☎ 02-526-1250; admission US$1; 8am-noon & 2-7pm Mon-Fri, 8am-noon Sat), on the university campus south of the center, has exhibits of minerals, precious stones, fossils and crystals. From the center, take *micro* A, also marked 'Sud.'

The **Obrajes hot springs** (admission US$0.35), 25km northeast of town, are the best of several nearby hot soak options. From the corner of Caro and Av 6 de Agosto, catch an 'Obrajes' *micro* (US$0.35, 30 minutes) which departs from 7:30am to 5pm daily; it also passes by the less appealing **Capachos hot springs**, 10km east of town. On weekends, local rock climbers flock to the area called **Rumi Campana**, 2km northwest of town – contact the **Club de Montañismo Halcones** (www.geocities.com/yosemite/gorge/1177) or ring Juan Pablo (☎ 02-524-4082).

Sleeping

Near the train station on Velasco Galvarro there are several handy, if not classy, *alojamientos*.

Alojamiento Copacabana (☎ 02-525-4184; Velasco Galvarro No 6352; r per person US$2, with bath US$4.65)

Bright, clean and friendly – the best on this strip.

Residencial San Salvador (☎ 02-527-6771; Velasco Galvarro No 6325; r per person US$2, with bath US$4.65) Recently improved, with firm beds and morning showers.

Alojamiento San Juan de Dios (☎ 02-527-7083; Velasco Galvarro No 6346; r per person US$2) A short step up from the bottom of the barrel.

Alojamiento Ferrocarril (☎ 02-527-4079; Velasco Galvarro No 6278; r per person US$2) Like a prison, but without the showers; new cells were being added at last look which may be a bit nicer.

Pub the Alpaca (☎ 02-525-5715; wcamargo_gallegos@hotmail.com; Av La Paz 690; r per person US$3.25) Near Plaza Ranchería, this place has a shared kitchen and the best beds in town. Book ahead for Carnaval, when the minimum stay is three nights (US$45 per person) and the maximum occupancy is 10 bodies. The pub is also a good place for a drink (see p201).

Hotel Bernal (☎ 02-527-9468; Av Brasil 701; r per person US$2.75, with bath US$5.35) Opposite the bus terminal, it's clean and well-run and popular with Brazilian business types. The helpful manager speaks English and Portuguese.

Hotel Samay Wasi (☎ 02-527-6737; samaywasioruro@hotmail.com; Av Brasil 392; s/d US$13/20;) This modern, high-rise HI-affiliate near the bus terminal has gas showers around the clock, cable TV and phones; rates include breakfast.

Other solid options include the following:
Residencial Ideal (☎ 02-527-7863; Calle Bolívar 386; r per person US$3.50, with bath US$4.50) Far from perfect.
Residencial San Miguel (☎ 02-527-2132; Calle Sucre 331; r per person US$3, with bath US$4.50)
Hostal Hidalgo (☎ 02-525-7516; 6 de Octubre 1616; r per person US$4.75, with bath US$8) A good newish option with big, clean rooms.

Eating

It's usually too cold for most places to open before 11am, so Mercado Campero is your best bet for an early breakfast. Stalls serve mostly *api* and pastries in the morning, but look out for *falso conejo* ('false rabbit,' a rubbery meat-based concoction), mutton soup, and beef and potatoes smothered with hot *llajhua* (spicy tomato-based sauce). For bargain lunch specials, check out the small eateries around the train station.

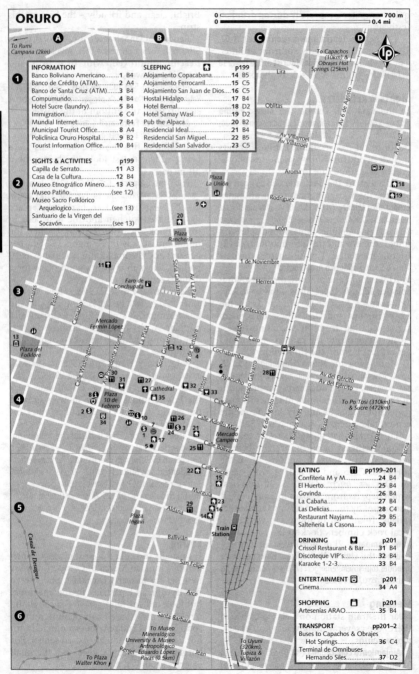

ORURO

0 ———— 700 m
0 ———— 0.4 mi

To Rumi
Campana (2km)

To Capachos
(10km) &
Obrajes Hot
Springs (25km)

INFORMATION
Banco Boliviano Americano.......1 B4
Banco de Crédito (ATM)...........2 A4
Banco de Santa Cruz (ATM).......3 B4
Compumundo............................4 B4
Hotel Sucre (laundry)...............5 B4
Immigration..............................6 C4
Mundial Internet.......................7 B4
Municipal Tourist Office............8 A4
Policlínica Oruro Hospital..........9 B2
Tourist Information Office.........10 B4

SIGHTS & ACTIVITIES   p199
Capilla de Serrato....................11 A3
Casa de la Cultura...................12 B4
Museo Etnográfico Minero......13 A3
Museo Patiño......................(see 12)
Museo Sacro Folklorico
  Arqueologico....................(see 13)
Santuario de la Virgen del
  Socavón...........................(see 13)

SLEEPING   p199
Alojamiento Copacabana...........14 B5
Alojamiento Ferrocarril.............15 C5
Alojamiento San Juan de Dios...16 C5
Hostal Hidalgo........................17 B4
Hotel Bernal...........................18 D2
Hotel Samay Wasi...................19 D2
Pub the Alpaca.......................20 B2
Residencial Ideal......................21 B4
Residencial San Miguel.............22 B5
Residencial San Salvador..........23 C5

EATING   pp199–201
Confitería M y M......................24 B4
El Huerto................................25 B4
Govinda..................................26 B4
La Cabaña...............................27 B4
Las Delicias.............................28 C4
Restaurant Nayjama.................29 B5
Saltería La Casona...................30 B4

DRINKING   p201
Crissol Restaurant & Bar...........31 B4
Discoteque VIP's......................32 B4
Karaoke 1-2-3.........................33 B4

ENTERTAINMENT   p201
Cinema...................................34 A4

SHOPPING   p201
Artesenías ARAO.....................35 B4

TRANSPORT   pp201–2
Buses to Capachos & Obrajes
  Hot Springs..........................36 C4
Terminal de Omnibuses
  Hernando Siles......................37 D2

Lira
Oblitas
Av Villarroel
Av Villarroel
Aroma
Rodríguez
León
Av 6 de Agosto
Av Brasil

Plaza
La Unión

Plaza
Ranchería

1 de Noviembre
Herrera

Faro de
Conchupata

Montecinos

Soria Galvarro
Av La Paz

Mercado
Fermín López

Plaza del
Folklore

Cochabamba
Ayacucho
Calle Junín
Calle Adolfo Mier
Calle Bolívar
Calle Sucre
Murguía
Aldana
Plaza
Ingaví

Av del Ejército
Av del Ejército

To Po Tosi (310km)
& Sucre (472km)

Buenos Aires
Brasil
Tejerina
Tarapacá
Tacna

Plaza
10 de
Febrero

Cathedral
Mercado
Campero

Train
Station

Canal de Desague

Ballivián
San Felipe
Arce
Santa Bárbara

To Museo
Mineralógico
University & Museo
Antropológico
Eduardo López
Rivas (0.5km)

To Plaza
Walter Khon

To Uyuni
(320km),
Tupiza &
Villazón

BOLIVIA

Salteñeria La Casona (Av Presidente Montes 5969) The best *salteñas* are found here, just off Plaza 10 de Febrero; it also has sandwiches for lunch and pizza in the evening.

Govinda (6 de Octubre 6089; mains US$1-2) For Hare-Hare veggie fare, try this godlike place.

El Huerto (Calle Bolívar near Pagador) Lunch for around US$1.35.

Las Delicias (Av 6 de Agosto 1278; set meals US$1-2, mains US$2-4) This lively spot is locally recommended for its attentive service and huge *parrilladas* (selection of grilled meats).

Confitería M y M (6 de Octubre s/n) A cheap fast food option...with slow service.

La Cabaña (Junín 609; mains US$1-4) Visit La Cabaña for juicy steaks and typical Bolivian dishes in a pleasant setting.

Drinking & Entertainment

Crissol Restaurant & Bar (02-525-3449; Calle Adolfo Mier at La Plata) The altiplano's classiest place for a game of pool or dice and live music and dancing on weekends is the auto-racing themed Crissol, which also has a full bar, full menu and sports TV lounge.

Pub the Alpaca (Av La Paz 690) This gringo-friendly pub is an interesting spot for a quiet quaff after 8:30pm. Styled after an English pub, the owner, professor Don Wily, speaks English and a range of European languages. There's also a library and book exchange.

If don't fancy another night of **Karaoke 1-2-3** (Potosí at Calle Junín) or drunken gyrating at **Discoteque VIP's** (Calle Junín at 6 de Octubre), there's always the **cinema** (Calle Bolivar; admission US$1), on the west side of the plaza, which screens relatively recent releases nightly.

Shopping

The design and production of artful Diablada masks and costumes is a booming cottage industry. There are many workshops selling these devilish things on Av La Paz, between León and Villarroel.

Artesanías ARAO (02-525-0331; Sorias Galvarro & Calle Adolfo Mier) Opposite the cathedral, this place stocks a diverse selection of fine fair-trade handicrafts from all over Bolivia.

Getting There & Around

BUS

All buses arrive and depart from **Terminal de Omnibuses Hernando Siles** (02-527-9535), a flat 15-minute walk northeast of the center. When the roads aren't blocked, buses to La

Paz (US$1.35 to US$2, three hours) run every 30 minutes. There are several daily services to Cochabamba (US$1.75, 4½ hours), Potosí (normal/*cama* US$4/9, eight hours) with connections to Tupiza and Villazón, and one nighttime service to Uyuni (US$3 to US$4, eight hours), but the train is the ticket on this rough route.

Basic services to Sucre (US$4.50, 10 hours) go via either Cochabamba or Potosí. Alternatively, there's a direct Trans Copacabana *bus cama* at 10:30pm nightly (US$13.50, 10 hours). For Santa Cruz (US$10, 18 to 20 hours), you must make a connection in Cochabamba.

There are daily departures for Arica, Chile (US$10.50, nine hours) via Tambo Quemado (passing through Parque Nacional Sajama) with connections to Iquique. Most travelers, however, prefer to enter Chile farther south at San Pedro Atacama via Uyuni and a *salares* (salt plains) tour.

TRAIN

Oruro became a railroading center thanks to its mines, but the only surviving passenger connection is with Uyuni and points south. You must take your passport to the **ticket window** (02-527-5676/4605; 8-11am & 3-6:30pm Sun-Fri); arrive early and purchase your ticket a day ahead to avoid long lines.

A taxi to the train station or center costs US$0.30 per person.

The privatized service is run by the Chilean **Empresa Ferroviaria Andina** (FCA; www.fca.com.bo in Spanish) and offers two services. The top-notch *Expreso del Sur* has two classes: the quite serviceable salon and top-of-the-line executive premier, which includes meals. Videos are shown and there's a dining car. It departs Oruro at 3:30pm on Monday and

---

SPLURGE!

Cordon Bleu cuisine on the altiplano? *Si señor.* The elegant, non-smoking **Restaurant Nayjama** (02-527-7699; Aldana 1880 at Pagador; mains US$3-6) is run by celeb chef Don Roberto. He has catered to jet-setters the world over – invite him for a glass of wine to find out who. The house specialties are novel, international interpretations of classic Bolivian dishes and vegetarian options are available on request

---

Friday for Uyuni (salon/executive US$4.75/10.25, 6½ hours); Tupiza (US$9.65/19.35, 11¾ hours); and Villazón (US$10.65/21.50, 15 hours). It's a thoroughly enjoyable trip with beautiful scenery as far as Uyuni, but unfortunately the stretch to Tupiza is after dark.

The *Wara Wara del Sur* is the 2nd-class train, departing Oruro at 7pm Wednesday and Sunday, stopping at numerous stations en route to Uyuni (salon/executive US$4/8, seven hours), Tupiza (US$6.75/13.75, 13 hours) and Villazón (US$8.25/16.75, 16¾ hours). The slightly cheaper third class is called *popular*: prime your wrestling persona before joining the fray. There's no dining car, but snacks are peddled at every stop.

UYUNI

This frigid, otherworldly middle-of-nowhere community (population 14,000; elevation 3675m) thrives on tourists flocking in to visit the astounding *salares* (salt plains). The town itself has but two notable sights: the archaeology museum and the rubbish-strewn **Cementerio de Trenes**

(a graveyard of rusting locomotives 3km south of town).

Servinet@Uyuni, the glass box in the middle of Bolívar, offers satellite Internet access for US$1 an hour. There are a couple of other less hectic Internet places opposite the plaza on Potosí and near the bus terminal.

You can break big boliviano notes and change cash at decent rates at **Banco de Crédito** (Av Potosí near Av Arce). Otherwise, try the streetchangers near the bank, bigger tour companies or popular restaurants; several places on Potosí buy Chilean and Argentine pesos.

Popular hotels are your best bet for laundry service.

The **tourist information office** (9am-12:30pm & 2-7:30pm) is near the plaza in the base of the wannabe Big Ben clock tower. The **Unidad Regional de Turismo** (Av Potosí at Av Arce) has useful area maps and is the place to file formal complaints against tour agencies. Sernap's friendly **Reserva National de Fauna Andina Eduardo Avaroa office** (REA; ☎ 02-293-2225; Avaroa at Ferroviaria) is more user-friendly than the park's name.

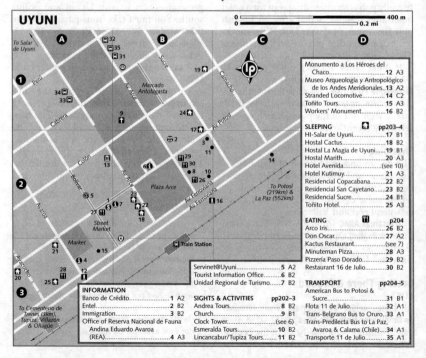

UYUNI

| | 0 ——————— 400 m |
| | 0 ——————— 0.2 mi |

INFORMATION	
Banco de Crédito	1 A2
Entel	2 B2
Immigration	3 B2
Office of Reserva Nacional de Fauna Andina Eduardo Avaroa (REA)	4 A3
Servinet@Uyuni	5 A2
Tourist Information Office	6 B2
Unidad Regional de Turismo	7 B2

SIGHTS & ACTIVITIES	pp202–3
Andrea Tours	8 B2
Church	9 B1
Clock Tower	(see 6)
Esmeralda Tours	10 B2
Lincancabur/Tupiza Tours	11 B2
Monumento a Los Héroes del Chaco	12 A3
Museo Arqueología y Antropológico de los Andes Meridionales	13 A2
Stranded Locomotive	14 C2
Toñito Tours	15 A3
Workers' Monument	16 B2

SLEEPING	pp203–4
HI-Salar de Uyuni	17 B1
Hostal Cactus	18 B1
Hostal La Magia de Uyuni	19 B1
Hostal Marith	20 A3
Hotel Avenida	(see 10)
Hotel Kutimuy	21 A3
Residencial Copacabana	22 B2
Residencial San Cayetano	23 B2
Residencial Sucre	24 B1
Toñito Hotel	25 A3

EATING	p204
Arco Iris	26 B2
Don Oscar	27 A2
Kactus Restaurant	(see 7)
Minuteman Pizza	28 A3
Pizzería Paso Dorado	29 B2
Restaurant 16 de Julio	30 B2

TRANSPORT	pp204–5
American Bus to Potosí & Sucre	31 B1
Flota 11 de Julio	32 A1
Trans-Belgrano Bus to Oruro	33 A1
Trans-Predilecta Bus to La Paz, Avaroa & Calama (Chile)	34 A1
Transporte 11 de Julio	35 A1

If you're traveling to Chile, you're best off picking up a Bolivian exit stamp (officially US$2) at the Las Vegasesque **immigration office** (Sucre & Potosí) since the hours of the Bolivian border post at Hito Cajón (just beyond Laguna Verde) are about as reliable as altiplano transport.

The trippy **Museo Arqueología y Antropológico de los Andes Meridionales** (cnr Av Arce & Colón; adults/students US$0.65/$0.35; ☉ 8:30am-noon & 2-6pm) features mummies, loads of skulls and Spanish-language descriptions of the practices of mummification and deformation.

Salar & Southwest Tours

At last count, more than 40 agencies were attempting to arrange *salar* tours from Uyuni. The explosion of competition has been a double-edged sword. On the positive side, it's meant more choice and cheaper tours. On the flip side, it's lowered quality and in many cases generated much corner-cutting and touting for business. Typically, tours are in 4WD vehicles of variable health, holding six (or, inadvisably, seven), passengers, a cook and a driver-guide. Bigger agencies may pack tour buses with up to 30 people in the high season. Whomever you go with, bring lots of film.

THREE OR FOUR DAYS IN A JEEP

The most popular trip is a four-day circuit visiting the Salar de Uyuni (p205), Laguna Colorada, Sol de Mañana and Laguna Verde. The last day of the standard circuit is a laborious drive back to Uyuni, but if you want to head into Chile, you can do three days of the tour, hop off at Laguna Verde and connect there with transport to San Pedro de Atacama (around US$10 per person). Before leaving Uyuni, get a Bolivian exit stamp – better tour agencies can often arrange stamps outside office hours. A trip continuing to San Pedro is one day and night shorter than the full circuit back but costs about the same.

CUSTOM TRIPS

Shorter trips traverse the northern crescent of the Salar de Uyuni, stopping overnight at the friendly village of Jiriri, with a climb on Volcán Tunupa. You can arrange longer custom trips visiting Llica, the Salar de Coipasa or Laguna Celeste via the world's highest motorable road near the Argentine border.

HOW TO CHOOSE AN AGENCY

The main costs are the vehicle and driver, so trips are a lot cheaper if you're in a group (easy to arrange in Uyuni). Six people is ideal. For transport, driver and food, budget US$75 to US$125 per person all in – plan on the higher figure during peak season (July to September) and a more professional operator, or if booking outside Uyuni. Cheaper operators inevitably cut corners on basics like food, water or vehicle maintenance. The US$4 entrance fee (probably rising in 2004) to the Reserva Eduardo Avaroa and bathroom stops en route are not included in the price.

The best operators have written itineraries outlining meals, accommodations and other trip details – bring snacks and ask what's available for vegetarians (eggs, eggs and more eggs, most likely). Accommodations are typically in super-basic *pensiones* and scientific or military camps.

If the trip is not as described notify the Uyuni tourist office. Small companies come and go, and they often share passengers to complete a group – it's common to book with one company but end up on a trip with another. It's very difficult to recommend one agency over another since so much depends on the driver. The best bet is to chat to returning travelers to get the latest scoop. The following agencies have been around for a few years and consistently receive good reports from readers:

AS Tours (☎ 02-693-2772; Av Ferroviaria s/n) Opposite the train station.

Andrea Tours (☎ 02-693-2638; Av Arce 26) Receives high marks for food and accommodation.

Colque Tours (☎ /fax 02-693-2199; Potosí 56) One of the most well-known companies and often recommended for travel to and from Chile. However, go in with your eyes open.

Esmeralda Tours (☎ 02-693-2130; Av Ferroviaria 11, at Hotel Avenida) Receives some of the best reports at the cheaper end of the scale.

Lincancabur/Tupiza Tours (☎ 02-693-2996/2988; licancatours@entelnet.bo; Sucre 86) Best choice for reverse circuit trips ending up in Tupiza.

Toñito Tours (☎ /fax 02-693-2094; www.bolivianexpeditions.com; Av Ferroviaria 152) Guarantees prices, even without a full group.

Sleeping

Uyuni's tourism boom means the best hotels fill up fast; advance booking is advisable in high season. In a pinch, crash out for free in the railway station's waiting room; it's toasty with all the bodies in there and quite safe.

Cheap places near the station come in handy since most trains arrive and depart at ungodly hours. If you're not shipping out, however, all the comings and goings can be sleep-depriving.

Hotel Avenida (☎ 02-693-2078; Av Ferroviaria 11; r per person US$2-3, with bath US$5-6) This popular, clean hotel has renovated rooms and laundry sinks. Hot showers are available from 7am to 1pm.

Hostal Cactus (SW side of Plaza Arce; r per person US$2.50) Refurbished Hostal Cactus provides a clean, cheap shelter with plenty of blankets. It's expanding in 2004.

Hostal Marith (☎ 02-693-2174; Av Potosí 61; r per person US$2, with bath US$4) Rooms at this quiet cheapie off the main drag can be dank but the showers are good. Extras include laundry sinks and a social patio.

Hotel Kutimuy (☎ /fax 02-693-2391/2199; kutimuy@ yahoo.com; cnr Av Potosí & Avaroa; r per person US$2.75, with bath & breakfast US$6.75) For something nicer, try this revamped hotel which, for better or worse, is affiliated with Colque Tours. The rooms are usually tidy and have good beds.

HI-Salar de Uyuni (☎ /fax 02-693-2228; pucara _tours@yahoo.com; www.hostellingbolivia.org; cnr Av Potosí & Sucre; dm US$2.65, d per person US$3.35; 🖳) This place has good beds and all the typical hostel amenities plus free pickup from the bus station, which is 300m away.

Hostal La Magia de Uyuni (☎ 02-693-2541; magia_uyuni@yahoo.es; Colón 432; s/d US$15/20) Spotless, homey rooms are arranged around a nice indoor courtyard. It's one of the nicest places in town, thus often overrun by squawking tour groups. Breakfast included.

SPLURGE!

The cheaper rooms at the brand-new **Toñito Hotel** (☎ 02-693-3186; www.boliviane xpeditions.com; Av Ferroviaria 60; r per person US$5, s/d/tr with bath & breakfast US$20/30/40) are deservedly popular with tour groups, so book ahead in the high season. If you have the dough, though, kick back in style in a suite. Just try to resist the aromatic waft of pizza from the all-you-can-eat buffet downstairs at Minuteman Pizza (see Eating, following). Go on, indulge yourself.

Other options include the following:
Residencial Sucre (☎ 02-693-2047; Sucre 132; r per person US$2) Marginal, with basic but sanitary rooms.
Residencial San Cayetano (N side of Plaza Arce; r per person US$2, shower US$0.50) Serviceable. Rise early to use the one decent shower.
Residencial Copacabana (N side of Plaza Arce; r per person US$2, shower US$0.50) Standoffish.

Eating

Minuteman Pizza (☎ 02-693-2094; Av Ferroviaria 60, at Hotel Toñito; breakfast US$3, dinner buffet US$4.65; 🕑 from 8am) Uyuni's best all-around eating choice, hands down, Minuteman Pizza is owned by a true blue Yankee from Amherst, Massachusetts. It's got homemade bagels, biscotti, Budweiser and a gas BBQ grill. The brick-oven pizza is as out-of-this-world as the *salar*. The all-you-can-eat dinner buffet hits the spot after four days of bland *'si, el chofer es* the cook *tambien'* ('yes, the driver is the cook, too') rations.

Comedor (Av Potosí & Avaroa) If you've got a strong stomach, cheap meals are on offer at the market *comedor* and nearby street food stalls. For a piquant dose of altiplano culture, look for *charque kan* (mashed hominy peppered with bits of dried llama meat), often found inside tamales. Good snack stands serving burgers, potato cakes, juice and ice cream are lined up like ducks in a row on Av Arce.

Arco Iris (north side Plaza Arce) The best spot to cobble together a tour group – you'll have plenty of time, as service is at armadillo pace. It's a warm place with good pizzas, cold beer and occasional live music.

Elsewhere, there are many choices – of flavors of pizza!

Pizzeria Paso Dorado (Arce 49; mains US$3, pizzas US$4-10) Serves non-round choices on the plaza.

The more upmarket **Restaurant 16 de Julio** (Arce 35; mains US$2-4; 🕑 from 7am) and **Kactus** (Av Potosí) dish out tasty pasta, international dishes and Bolivian fare in a pleasant atmosphere.

Don Oscar (cnr Av Potosí & Bolívar) This friendly spot opens early for breakfast and does decent dinners.

Getting There & Away

Arrive from Tupiza via the badlands to avoid the crowds. Getting out of isolated Uyuni can be problematic. Buy your bus ticket the day before or ask a tour agency how much they charge to purchase train tickets; lines are long and *quien es mas macho* (literally 'who is the most macho') shoving matches can break out for the limited seats. Proposed transport upgrades include an on-demand Ferrobus rail service to Potosí and TAM flights from La Paz via Sucre, though the latter is sketchy due to treacherous altiplano wind conditions.

BUS & JEEP

There's supposedly a new bus terminal in the works (funded by the US$0.15 'terminal fee'), but for now all buses leave from the west end of Av Arce.

American and Transporte 11 de Julio buses blast off at 10am daily for Potosí (US$2 to US$3, seven hours) and Sucre (US$4 to US$5, nine to 11 hours). Diana Tours runs the same service at 7pm daily. Flota 11 de Julio goes to Tupiza (US$4 to US$5, 10 to 12 hours) at 9am on Wednesday and Sunday, and Calama in Chile, via Avoroa (US$10, 12 to 15 hours), at 4am Monday and Thursday. Oruro (US$2 to US$3, eight to 10 hours) depart at 7pm daily. Roads and weather permitting, there are departures for Tarija (US$8, up to 24 hours) at 10am on Wednesday, and services to La Paz (US$6, 11 to 14 hours) on Wednesday and Sunday.

4WD Jeep services shuttle between Uyuni and Tupiza (US$6.50, seven to eight hours) when there's enough demand. Several companies depart around 7:30am after they've stuffed in as many as 10 passengers.

TRAIN

Uyuni has a modern, well-organized **train station** (☎ 02-693-2153); confirm hours on the blackboard inside as they often vary, then queue at least two hours before departure. Comfortable but crowded *Expreso del Sur* trains ramble to Oruro (salon/executive US$5/9; 6½ hours) at midnight on Tuesday and Friday. Departures south to Tupiza (US$4/9, five hours) and Villazón (US$6/13.75, 9½ hours) are at 10:20pm on Monday and Friday. If tickets sell out, you can try to sneak on the train (Bolivian-style) or take a bus 111km south to Atocha, where the train stops at 12:40am.

Chronically late *Wara Wara del Sur* trains are supposed to chug out of the station for Oruro (3rd/2nd/1st-class US$3.50/4/7.75, seven hours) at 1:40am on Monday and Thursday and at 2:40am on Wednesday and Sunday for Tupiza (US$2.75/3.25/5.75, 5½ hours) and Villazón (US$4/4.50/9, nine hours). These trains always seem to be chanting 'I think I can...think I can...'

At 3:30am on Monday, a recently improved train trundles west for the town of Avaroa (US$4.25), on the Chilean border, where you cross to Ollagüe and have to wait several hours to clear Chilean customs. Another train continues the journey to Calama (US$12). The whole trip takes 20 to 40 hours and is strictly for masochistic rail junkies.

SOUTHWEST CIRCUIT

Different times of year offer different experiences: from April to September, the *salares* are dry and blindingly white. In the rainy season, they're under water, projecting a perfect mirror image of clouds, sky and land to the horizon. At this time, roads may be quagmires, making passage difficult, and hail and snow are always a possibility.

Salar de Uyuni

The world's largest salt flat sits at a lofty 3653m and blankets an amazing 12,000 sq km. It was part of a prehistoric salt lake, Lago Minchín, which covered most of southwest Bolivia. When it dried up, it left a couple of seasonal puddles and several salt pans, including the **Salar de Uyuni** and **Salar de Coipasa**.

Towns of note include **Colchani** on the eastern shore and **Llica** on the west, where there are basic accommodations. A maze of tracks crisscrosses the *salar* and connects nearby settlements and several islands that pepper this blindingly-white desert. **Isla de los Pescadores** bears amazing stands of giant cactus and a marooned colony of vizcachas (long-tailed rodents related to chinchillas). **Isla Cáscara de Huevo** is known for its roselike salt formations.

At the time of research, the *salar's* famous salt hotels, Hotel Playa Blanca and the Palacio de Sal, were being deconstructed and moved block by block to the edge of salar near Colchani due to environmental concerns. Inquire at agencies in La Paz or Uyuni or at **Hidalgo Tours** (☎ 02-622-5186; www.salardeuyuni.net) in Potosí to find out when they might be up and running again.

BOLIVIA

Far Southwest

Several startlingly beautiful sights are hidden away in this remote corner. The surreal landscape is nearly treeless, punctuated by gentle hills and volcanoes near the Chilean border. Wildlife in the area includes three types of flamingos (most notably the rare James species), plus plenty of llamas, vicuñas, emus and owls.

The following sites comprise the major stops on most tours. **Laguna Colorada** is a bright adobe-red lake fringed with cakey white minerals, 25km east of the Chilean border. On its western shore is Campamento Ende and beside it the meteorological station, where those with marginal tour companies find shelter and visitors without tents can crash overnight. When open, the **Reserva Nacional de Fauna Andina Eduardo Avaroa** runs a better lodge with basic bunks and decent beds; there's a shared bath with running water.

The thin, clear air is bitterly cold and at night the temperature drops below -20°C (-4°F). The air is perfumed by *llareta* – a rock-hard, mosslike shrub that is broken apart to be burned for fuel.

Most independent transport to Laguna Colorada will be supplying or servicing mining and military camps or the on-hold geothermal project 50km south at **Sol de Mañana**. The main interest here is the 4950m-high **geyser basin**, with its boiling mud pots and sulfurous fumaroles. Tread carefully when approaching the site; any damp or cracked earth is potentially dangerous. The nearby **Termas de Polques** hot springs spout comfortable 30°C (86°F) sulfurous water and provide a relaxing morning dip at 4200m.

Laguna Verde, a splendid aquamarine lake, is tucked into Bolivia's southwestern corner at 5000m. Behind the lake rises the dramatic 5930m cone of **Volcán Licancabur**.

Getting There & Around

The easiest way to visit the far southwest is with a group from Uyuni (see p203). Some agencies in La Paz can arrange tours but Potosí agents tend to overcharge. Alternatively, you can set out from Tupiza (see p208) and end up in Uyuni, a very worthwhile option.

The sparsely populated far southwest region is even more remote than the *salares*, but there are several mining and military camps and weather stations that may provide a place to crash in an emergency. The determined can do it independently, but you'll need a compass, maps, camping gear, warm clothing, food, water, patience, fortitude, a loose screw and people skills (for when you get stuck).

TUPIZA

This tranquil but growing settlement (population 25,000; 2950m) is set in the friendly valley of the Río Tupiza, ringed by the rugged Cordillera de Chichas – an amazing landscape of rainbow-colored rocks, hills, mountains and canyons. Hiking, biking and horse riding opportunities (all possible in the same day!) abound and the variety of bizarre geologic formations, deep gorges and cactus forests are thrilling backdrops. It's the sort of place many people visit for a day and end up staying in for a week.

Reminiscent of the American Wild West, Tupiza served as an apt setting for the demise of Butch Cassidy and the Sundance Kid: after robbing an Aramayo payroll at Huaca Huañusca, some 40km north of Tupiza, the pair reputedly met their makers in the mining village of San Vicente in 1908. For more about Cassidy and the Kid, watch the documentary videos shown at most Tupiza hotels or check out the website ourworld.compuserve.com/homepages /danne.

Information

Several raucous Internet places on the plaza have decent connections for US$0.65 an hour. Around the corner from Hotel Mitru (and possibly moving into the hotel), the quiet, nonsmoking **Rocanet** (Florida & Chichas) has the best connections.

Most hotels offer same-day laundry service for around US$1 per kilo.

For maps, try the Instituto Geográfico Militar, upstairs inside the Municipalidad on the plaza.

Tupiza Tours (☎ /fax 02-694-3513; www.tupiza tours.com; Av Regimento Chichas 187, at Hotel Mitru) is a wealth of information, has a book exchange and gives cash advances for around 3% commission. To change cash, try the *casa de cambio* inside the *libería* (stationery store) on Avaroa or Banco de Crédito on the plaza's north side.

There's no tourist office.

Sights & Activities

A short trek up **Cerro Corazón de Jesús**, west of town, reveals lovely views over the town. Lively **street markets** convene on Thursday and Saturday morning near the train station. You can steam in a sauna (US$0.65) at **Los Alamos Club** (Chuquisaca) or play a set of tennis (US$1.35) on the clay courts at **Club Deportivo Ferroviaría** (set back from Av Serrano), about a block from the train station. Nonguests can enjoy Hotel Mitru's sparkling, solar-heated **swimming pool** all day for US$1. If desperate to kill time, there's a dusty **municipal museum** (admission free; ☯ noon-6pm Mon-Fri) off the plaza.

Tupiza's main attraction is the surrounding countryside, best seen on foot or horseback. Recommended destinations include **Quebrada de Palala** (10km round trip), **Quebrada de Palmira** (10km), **El Cañon** (10km), **Quebrada Seca** (10km to 20km) and **El Sillar** (32km).

Tours

Tupiza Tours (☎ /fax 02-694-3513; www.tupizatours .com; Av Regimiento Chichas, at Hotel Mitru) offers good-value day trips exploring Tupiza's rugged *quebradas* (ravines) for around US$20 per person. It also runs two-day tours along the Butch and Sundance trail to Huaca Huañusca and the lonely mining village of San Vicente where the outlaws' careers abruptly ended. They also arrange horseback trips for US$2.50/20 per hour/day

BOLIVIA

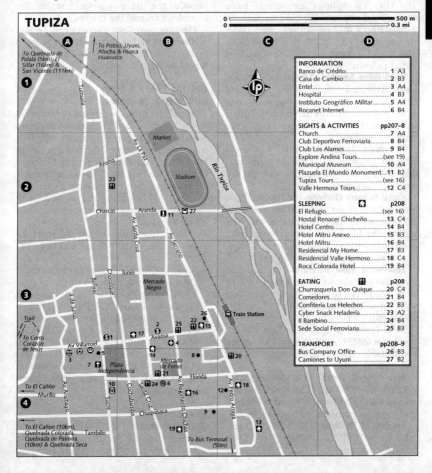

TUPIZA

0 — 500 m
0 — 0.3 mi

To Potosí, Uyuni,
Atocha & Huaca
Huañusca

To Quebrada de
Palala (5km), El
Sillar (16km) &
San Vicente (111km)

Market

Stadium

Río Tupiza

Charcas

Aranda

Junín

Mercado
Negro

Trail

To Cerro
Corazón
de Jesús

Av Villarroel

Plaza
Independencia

Mercado
de Ferias

Florida

To El Cañon
Murillo

Train Station

To El Cañon (10km),
Quebrada Colorada,
Quebrada de Palmira
(10km) & Quebrada Seca

Tambillo

To Bus Terminal
(50m)

INFORMATION	
Banco de Crédito	1 A3
Casa de Cambio	2 B3
Entel	3 A4
Hospital	4 B3
Instituto Geográfico Militar	5 A4
Rocanet Internet	6 B4

SIGHTS & ACTIVITIES	pp207–8
Church	7 A4
Club Deportivo Ferroviaría	8 B4
Club Los Alamos	9 B4
Explore Andina Tours	(see 19)
Municipal Museum	10 A4
Plazuela El Mundo Monument	11 B2
Tupiza Tours	(see 16)
Valle Hermosa Tours	12 C4

SLEEPING	p208
El Refugio	(see 16)
Hostal Renacer Chicheño	13 C4
Hotel Centro	14 B4
Hotel Mitru Anexo	15 B3
Hotel Mitru	16 B4
Residencial My Home	17 B3
Residencial Valle Hermoso	18 C4
Roca Colorada Hotel	19 B4

EATING	p208
Churrasquería Don Quique	20 C4
Comedores	21 B4
Confitería Los Helechos	22 B3
Cyber Snack Heladería	23 A2
Il Bambino	24 B4
Sede Social Ferroviaria	25 B3

TRANSPORT	pp208–9
Bus Company Office	26 B3
Camiones a Uyuni	27 B2

or you can embark on a recommended four-day, three-night tour from Tupiza to the Salar de Uyuni (see p205) for around US$100 per person (with six people). The innovative Triathlon tour visits Tupiza's best places in a full-day circuit by bicycle, horse and in a jeep (US$18.50 per person for group of six, with a minimum of two people for US$30).

Other agencies offering similar tours include **Explore Andina Tours** (☎ 02-694-3016; Av Regimento Chichasat Roca Colorada Hotel) and **Valle Hermoso Tours** (☎ 02-694-2370; Av Pedro Arraya). Most agencies also rent mountain bikes (around US$8 a day).

Sleeping

The cheapest options are several basic *residenciales* opposite the train station.

Hotel Mitru (☎ 02-694-3001; Av Regimento Chichas 187; r per person US$3, with bath US$5.50, suites US$20) This bright and airy hotel is one of the best values in town.

Hotel Mitru Anexo (☎ 02-694-3002; Avaroa at Serrano) Affiliated with the Mitru and located near the train station, this hotel is also one of the best values in town. A rooftop Jacuzzi with great views should be working by the time you read this.

El Refugio (Av Regimento Chichas; r per person US$2.85) This simple place amid a sunny garden setting extends laundry and kitchen privileges to guests.

Hostal Renacer Chicheño (☎ 719-53801; Barrio Ferro Caja No 18; renacer_ch@hotmail.com; r per person US$2) Closest to the bus terminal, this new kid on the block has bright rooms with good beds. Extras include kitchen use, laundry service and a sunny TV lounge.

Residencial Valle Hermoso (☎ 02-694-2370; www.bolivia.freehosting.net; Av Pedro Arraya 478; r per person US$2.50) A crowded, family-run place with a book exchange, optional breakfast and laundry service.

Hotel Centro (☎ 6942705; Av Santa Cruz 287; r per person US$2.35, with bath US$4) This clean, comfortable choice has perennially hot showers.

Roca Colorada Hotel (☎ 02-694-2633; Chicacas 220; d US$5.50, with bath US$7) This hotel has clean rooms with good beds, TV and telephone, and some nicer rooms with private bath.

Residencial My Home (☎ 02-694-2947; Avaroa 288; r per person US$2.50, with bath US$3.50) Also recommended.

Eating

Confitería Los Helechos (Avaroa) This place in Hotel Mitru Anexo is the only restaurant that reliably serves three meals a day. Breakfasts with real coffee (also served at Hotel Mitru) are especially nice. Later in the day, there's a salad bar, good chicken, burgers, *licuados* and cocktails.

Il Bambino (Florida & Santa Cruz) Try the southern altiplano's best *salteñas* at this friendly place which also has good *almuerzos* for US$1.25.

Residencial My Home (Avaroa 288) Serves a good *almuerzo*.

Cyber Snack Heladería (Chorolque 131; ☻ 8am-11pm) Serves snacks and ice cream.

Affordable street meals are also served outside the train station and at the *comedores* around the market.

Heartier *parrillada* dinners can be had at **Churrasquería Don Quique** (Av Pedro Arraya 21) or the more staid **Sede Social Ferroviaria** (cnr Avaroa & Ave Regimento Chichas).

Getting There & Away

BUS, JEEP & CAMIÓN

Buses depart from the **terminal** (Av Pedro Arraya) at the southern end of the *avenida*. Fares for Oruro-bound routes north double a month before Carnaval. Several companies have 10am and 8pm departures to Potosí (US$3.35, at least eight hours), with Sucre connections. Several services depart for Tarija (US$4, eight hours) at 8pm, with connections to Yacuiba. Many companies serve Villazón (US$1.35, three hours) at 4am and 2pm daily; sit on the right for views. There are daily departures to La Paz (US$12, 16 hours) via Potosí at 10am and 3:30pm. O'Globo leaves for Cochabamba at 10:30am and 8:30pm daily.

Flota Boquerón leaves on Monday and Thursday for Uyuni (US$5, 10 to 12 hours) but the train is much less nerve wracking. 4WD Jeep services to Uyuni (US$6.75, seven to eight hours) depart around 7:30am when there is enough demand. *Camiones* to Uyuni leave after 7am from just east off Plazuela El Mundo, a traffic circle around an enormous globe.

TRAIN

The **ticket window** (☎ 02-694-2529) has no set opening hours, so inquire about when to queue up or have Tupiza Tours buy your ticket for a small surcharge. The scenery is brilliant, so travel by day if possible. The *Expreso del Sur* trundles north to Uyuni (salon/executive US$4/9; five hours) and Oruro (US$9.65/19.35, 11¾ hours) at 6:20pm on Tuesday and Saturday. At 3:25am on Monday and Friday the *Expreso* speeds south to Villazón (US$1.25/2.50, three hours).

The cheaper *Wara Wara del Sur,* which are always late and crowded, leave at 7pm on Monday and Thursday for Uyuni (salon/executive US$2.75/5.75, six hours) and Oruro (US$8.25/16.75, 13¾ hours), and at 8:35am on Wednesday and Sunday for Villazón (US$1/2, three hours).

TARIJA

The architecture, attitude and vegetation of Tarija (population 130,000; elevation 1860m) lend it a distinct Mediterranean flavor. The main plaza is planted with stately date palms and the surrounding landscape combines wild badlands with lush grapegrowing valleys to form Bolivia's premier viticultural region. The valley's climate is idyllic, though winter nights can be cool; the dry season lasts from April to November.

Chapacos (as *tarijeños* refer to themselves) take their Argentine satellite status seriously and consider themselves more Spanish or Argentine than Bolivian. The region is known for its fiestas and the unique musical instruments used to celebrate them. A significant student population adds to the liveliness. Combined with a visit to a few wineries or surrounding nature reserves, Tarija is a relaxing stopover on the way to or from Argentina.

Orientation

Street numbers are preceded by an O *(oeste)* for those addresses west of Calle Colón and an E *(este)* for those east of Colón; addresses north of Av Las Américas (Av Victor Paz Estenssoro) take an N.

Information

Several Internet places around Plaza Sucre charge less than US$0.50 an hour and are open until midnight. The nonsmoking **Internet Bunker** (Saracho 456) is fast and open until 1am weekends.

Esmeralda Lavandería (☎ 04-664-2043; La Madrid 0-157) offers quick machine wash-and-dry service for US$0.80 per kilo.

Casas de cambio (Bolívar btwn Sucre & Daniel Campos) change US dollars and Argentine pesos. On the main plaza, Banco Bisa changes traveler's checks (up to US$1000 for US$6 fee). ATMs are numerous around the plazas.

Entel and the **post office** (cnr Sucre & Virginio Lema) are a block southeast of the plaza on Lema.

On the main plaza, the helpful **departmental tourist office** (☎ 04-663-1000; Sucre) sells an OK map of town (US$1). The **municipal tourist office** (☎ 04-663-8081; Bolívar & Sucre) is more friendly than helpful and rarely open.

Immigration (☎ 04-664-3450; Bolívar & Ballivían) is the place to get an entry/exit stamp if using the Bermejo border crossing on weekends.

Sights & Activities

It's worth a stroll around the center to see what remains of the colonial atmosphere. The free university-run **Museo de Arqueología y Paleontología** (Virginio Lema near General Bernando Trigo; ♥ 8am-noon & 3-6pm Mon-Fri, 9am-noon & 3-6pm Sat & Sun) provides an overview of the region's geology, history, early inhabitants and prehistoric creatures.

A GOOD DROP

To arrange visits to nearby wineries (including free tours and tastings), inquire at the winery offices, which sell bottles at factory prices: **Aranjuez** (☎ 04-664-2552; Calle 15 de Abril E-241); **Casa Real/Campos de Solana** (☎ 04-664-5498; Calle 15 de Abril E-259); and **Kohlberg** (☎ 04-663-6366; Calle 15 de Abril E-275). You may be able to arrange a lift with the friendly staff. The award-winning **La Concepción/Rujero** (☎ 04-664-3763; O'Conner N-642), which has vineyards in unique microclimates (up to 2800m) and promotes its vintages as the 'world's highest,' is regarded as Bolivia's best vintner.

Only the Aranjuez bodega is close to town, a short jaunt west across the river; Casa Real and Kohlberg are in Santa Ana, 17km east of Tarija via an indirect road which passes Campos de Solana. Concepción is 25km south of town, but worth the extra effort for enophiles. Rujero and Casa Real also produce *singani,* a distilled grape spirit best drunk with a mixer on ice in a *chuflay* cocktail.

BOLIVIA

TARIJA

Wealthy 19th-century merchant Moisés Navajas left behind a couple of curious buildings. One is the private, garish **Castillo de Moisés Navajas** (Castillo de Beatriz; Bolívar E-644), which is sometimes open for informal tours. The other is the recently-restored **Casa Dorada** (cnr Ingavi & Trigo), now the **Casa de la Cultura** and open for guided tours for a small fee. It's an imposing extravaganza of large, lurid and overdone rooms – kitsch for the rich.

One popular weekend retreat is **San Lorenzo**, 15km northwest, where there's a museum in the home of the Chapaco hero, Moto Méndez. San Lorenzo *micros* leave from Ingavi, near Daniel Campos; alternatively, San Lorenzo buses depart from in front of Iglesia de San Juan. Another nearby getaway is **Tomatitas**, 5km northwest, which has a natural swimming hole and a trek to 50m-high **Coimata Falls**. Tomatitas *micros* leave frequently from the west end of Av Domingo Paz. For Coimata Falls, walk or hitch 5km to Coimata, where there's a small cascade. The falls are a 40-minute walk upstream.

For reasonably-priced organized winery tours, and tours to the stunning Sama Biological Reserve and the varied Gran Chaco hinterlands, contact **Viva Tours** (www.viva-tours.cjb.net; La Paz ☎ 04-666-1169; La Paz 252; Sucre ☎ 04-633-8325; Sucre N-615).

Sleeping

Alojamiento Ocho Hermanos (☎ 04-664-2111; Sucre N-782; r per person US$4, with bath US$7) The best central budget choice. It has tidy, pleasant rooms near the market, with laundry service and sunny terrace. Closed for repairs but supposed to reopen in 2004.

Residencial Zeballos (☎ 04-664-2068; Sucre N-966; r per person US$3.35, with bath & cable TV US$6.35) Leafy with bright, comfortable rooms, laundry service and a sunny courtyard. Rates include breakfast.

Residencial El Rosario (☎ 04-664-2942; Ingavi 0-777; r per person US$3.35, with bath US$5.35) A favorite haunt of NGO workers. It has good gas showers, laundry sinks and cable TV room, and a good breakfast for US$1 extra.

Hostal Libertador (☎ 04-664-4231; Bolívar 0-649; s/d with bath US$8/12) Welcoming, family-run place with phone, cable TV and good optional breakfast.

Hostería España (☎ 04-664-1790; Corrado 0-546; r per person US$3.35, with bath US$5.35) A welcoming

and helpful place offering all-around value with hot showers and a flowery patio. It has many long-term university student residents.

Hostal Bolívar (☎ 04-664-2741; Bolívar E-256; s US$5.50-9.50, d US$10-16) Hostal Bolívar has hot showers, cable TV room and a sunny courtyard. Cheapest rooms lack TV.

Gran Buenos Aires Hostal (☎ 04-663-6802; Daniel Campos N-448; s/d with bath US$12/20) A comfortable, central option with breakfast.

Hostal Miraflores (☎ 04-664-3355; Sucre N-920; r per person US$3.75, d with bath US$10) Near the market, Hostal Miraflores' best rooms are upstairs. The cheapest rooms without bath are basic and windowless.

Alojamiento El Hogar (☎ 04-664-3964; Paz Estenssoro & La Paz; r per person US$2) The best of several dodgy options near the bus terminal is basic but friendly and family-run.

Eating

At the northeast corner of the Mercado Central, at Sucre and Domingo Paz, vendors sell local pastries and snacks unavailable in other parts of Bolivia, including delicious crêpelike *panqueques*. Breakfast is served at the back of the market, other cheap meals are available upstairs and fresh juices can be found in the produce section. Don't miss the huge bakery and sweets section off Bolívar.

Taverna Gattopardo (☎ 04-663-0656; N side of Plaza La Madrid; mains US$2-5, wine tasting US$6-10) Deservedly popular for its pizza, pasta, burgers and antique atmosphere. It has a wine-tasting bar where you can sample the region's best vintages between bites of local Serrano ham.

Heladería Napoli (Campero N-630) The ice-cream cones are simply divine.

Snack Vicky (La Madrid at Trigo) A local favorite for a quick bite.

Café/Pastelería Sarita (Av 15 de Abril 0-561) Serves cookies and rich coffee.

Changuito II (Lema 0-197) Delivers yummy US$1 *almuerzos*.

Snack Lulu (Campero N-525) The people's choice for *salteñas*.

Club Social Tarija (Plaza Luis de Fuentes y Vargas) Try this place, off the east side of the main plaza, for more old-fashioned US$1 set lunches.

Chifa New Hong Kong (Sucre N-235) Cheap cocktails and big US$2.25 Asian *almuerzos*.

Plaza Sucre is hopping with cafés, families, popcorn vendors and neohippie *artesanías*. Try the following.

Chingo's (Plaza Sucre) A local hangout serving pizza, chicken and other fried things.

Bagdad Café (Plaza Sucre) Has a full bar and light dinner menu.

Cafe Mokka (Plaza Sucre) A newcomer on the north side of the plaza; open all day for espresso, breakfast, cocktails and good light grub.

Mr Pizza (☎ 04-665-0505; Plaza Sucre; pies US$2-3.50) No-nonsense place delivering until midnight.

Drinking

Earplug alert: karaoke runs rampant around Plaza Sucre. For more tone-deafness try **Karaoke Tom-Thonn** (cnr 15 de Abril & Méndez) or the hip **Karaoke Discoteca Amor** (Sucre at La Madrid).

Entertainment

Cine Gran Rex (La Madrid at Colón) Screens double-feature first-run flicks for a couple of bucks.

Auto Mania (Sucre & Carpio) To watch big games, head to Tarija's only full-fledged sports bar.

Coliseo Deportivo (Campero) Entertaining basketball, *futsal* and volleyball games are played here.

Asociación Tarijeña de Ajedrez (Campero) After 6pm, chess heads can find a game next door to Coliseo Deportivo where you can play for free if you respect club rules: no smoking and quiet, please.

Getting There & Around

AIR

The **airport** (off Av Victor Paz Esstenssoro) is 3km east of town. **LAB** (☎ 04-664-2195; General Bernando Trigo N-329) has regular service to Cochabamba and a couple flights a week to Santa Cruz. **TAM** (☎ 04-664-2734; La Madrid 0-470) has Saturday flights to Santa Cruz (US$55) and Sunday flights to La Paz (US$75) via Sucre (US$40). **AeroSur** (☎ 04-663-0893; Ingavi at Sucre) flees three times a week to La Paz and Santa Cruz.

Taxis into town (US$1) cost twice as much from the terminal as from the road 100m outside. *Micro* A (US$0.20) will drop you two blocks from the airport and returns to the Mercado Central.

BUS

The **bus terminal** (☎ 04-663-6508) is at the eastern end of town, a 20-minute walk from the center. Cross the street from the bus stop to catch *micro* A to the center.

Several buses travel daily to Potosí (US$6.50, 12 to 15 hours), with connections to Oruro, Cochabamba and Sucre. For Tupiza (US$4 to US$5, nine to 10 hours), there are daily evening departures. Daily buses to Villazón (US$4 to US$5, 10 hours) follow a spectacular unpaved route. Daily buses for La Paz (US$15, 24 hours) leave at 7:30am. There's one daily departure for the rough ride to Uyuni (US$8, 20 hours) at 3:30pm.

Connections to Argentina, via Bermejo or Yacuiba, involve long hauls through beautiful scenery. There are also international services to Asunción (Paraguay), Iquique (Chile) and Montevideo (Uruguay).

VILLAZÓN & LA QUIACA (ARGENTINA)

Villazón (population 28,000; elevation 3440m) is the main Argentine–Bolivian border crossing. It's a dusty, haphazard burg that contrasts with sleepy La Quiaca (p100). Most travelers breeze through, as there aren't really any worthwhile sights or attractions here. Despite rampant smuggling, the frontier manages to avoid having a sinister feel. That said, you should still be on your guard: petty theft, scams and counterfeit US banknotes are not unheard of. From October to April, Bolivian time lags one hour behind Argentine time. The rest of the year, Argentina operates on Bolivian time (only a bit more efficiently).

Information

There's decent Internet places (US$1 per hour) opposite the bus station and several others north of the plaza along Av Independencia. Public phones are plentiful near the frontier.

Numerous *casas de cambio* along Av República Argentina offer reasonable rates for dollars and Argentine pesos, less for Bolivianos. **Casa de Cambio Beto** (Av República Argentina s/n) changes traveler's checks at similar rates, minus 5% commission. **Banco de Crédito** (Oruro 111) changes cash but lacks an ATM.

There's a **Bolivian consulate** (Sarmiento & Belgrano) in La Quiaca, three blocks east of the bus station.

VILLAZÓN & LA QUIACA (ARGENTINA)

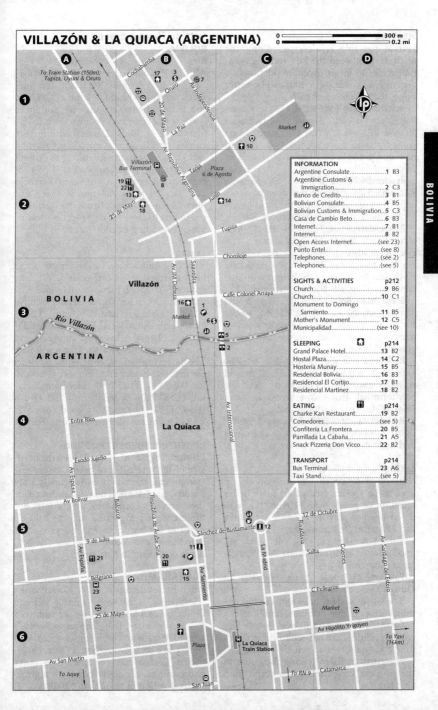

0 ————— 300 m
0 ————— 0.2 mi

BOLIVIA

INFORMATION
Argentine Consulate	1 B3
Argentine Customs & Immigration	2 C3
Banco de Credito	3 B1
Bolivian Consulate	4 B5
Bolivian Customs & Immigration	5 C3
Casa de Cambio Beto	6 B3
Internet	7 B1
Internet	8 B2
Open Access Internet	(see 23)
Punto Entel	(see 8)
Telephones	(see 2)
Telephones	(see 5)

SIGHTS & ACTIVITIES   p212
Church	9 B6
Church	10 C1
Monument to Domingo Sarmiento	11 B5
Mother's Monument	12 C5
Municipalidad	(see 10)

SLEEPING   p214
Grand Palace Hotel	13 B2
Hostal Plaza	14 C2
Hostería Munay	15 B5
Resdencial Bolivia	16 B3
Residencial El Cortijo	17 B1
Residencial Martínez	18 B2

EATING   p214
Charke Kan Restaurant	19 B2
Comedores	(see 5)
Confitería La Frontera	20 B5
Parrillada La Cabaña	21 A5
Snack Pizzeria Don Vicco	22 B2

TRANSPORT   p214
Bus Terminal	23 A6
Taxi Stand	(see 5)

Sleeping

Several passable *residenciales* along the main drag between the bus and train stations cater to locals. Accommodations on the Argentine side (see p100) can be better value, if a tad more expensive.

Hostería Munay (☎ 03885-423-924; www.munay hotel.jujuy.com in Spanish; Belgrano 51-61, La Quiaca; r per person US$3, with bath US$5) La Quiaca's best value for money accommodation is brand new and amiable and has sister hotels in Jujuy and Salta.

Residencial Bolivia (Belgrano 51-63; r per person US$2, with bath US$3.35) Fairly run-down beds occupy most of the room and padlocks barely secure doors, but it's a clean, cheap sleep.

Residencial Martínez (☎ 04-596-3353; 25 de Mayo 13; r per person US$2.75) The gas showers (no electric death-trap heater!) make this the best deal this side of Río Villazón, especially if you can score one of the rooms with private bath. Opposite the bus terminal.

Grand Palace Hotel (☎ 04-596-5333; 25 de Mayo 52; r per person US$2.65, with bath US$4.50-5) Really the bland palace, but the rooms (some windowless) are clean and the café does a good breakfast.

Residencial El Cortijo (☎ 04-596-2093; 20 de Mayo 338; d US$6.65, with bath & cable TV US$10.50) An old travelers' favorite two blocks north of the bus terminal. Hot showers cost an extra US$0.65 for rooms without bath.

Hostal Plaza (☎ 04-596-3535; Plaza 6 de Agosto 138; s/d US$4.65/6.65, with bath US$6.65/10.50) The nicest and most modern place in town.

Eating

Villazón's culinary choices are limited; hop over to La Quiaca (see p100) for a better selection of good cheap eateries. If you're determined to stay in Villazón, try **Charke Kan Restaurant** (Av República Argentina s/n), opposite the bus terminal, which is grimy but good. Better is **Snack Pizzeria Don Vicco** (Av República Argentina s/n) next door.

Parrillada La Cabaña (España at Belgrano) La Quiaca's best choice.

The fast-food stand at La Quiaca's bus terminal serves decent pizza and hamburgers.

Confitería La Frontera (Belgrano & Arabe Siria; everything under US$2) An old-school diner where four-course set meals fetch US$1.25.

Marginal *comedores* along the route to the *frontera* keep the human cargo train well fed.

Getting There & Around

BOLIVIA

Bus

All northbound buses depart from Villazón's central terminal (US$0.25 terminal fee). Daily buses head for Tupiza (US$1.35, two to three hours) at 7am, 3pm and 5pm. Some continue or make connections to Potosí (US$4.75, 10 to 12 hours) with further connections to Sucre, Oruro, Cochabamba and La Paz. Daily services along the rough but amazing route to Tarija (US$4.75, eight to 10 hours) continue to Bermejo and Yacuiba from Villazón at 11am and 8pm. Agencies across from the terminal sell tickets to most major Argentine destinations, including Buenos Aires.

Train

Villazón's train station is 600m north of the border crossing – a taxi costs US$2. The *Expreso del Sur* departs Tuesday and Saturday at 3:30pm for Tupiza (salon/executive US$2.15/4.50, 2¾ hours), Uyuni (US$7/13.60, eight hours) and Oruro (US$11.25/22.50, 15 hours). This is an enjoyable trip with superb scenery for the first few hours. The more crowded and basic *Wara Wara del Sur* departs Monday and Thursday at 3:30pm for Tupiza (US$1.25/2.50, three hours), Uyuni (US$4.25/8.75, 9½ hours) and Oruro (US$7/17, 17 hours). It's a good option as far as Tupiza, but after dark it turns tedious.

ARGENTINE BORDER CROSSING

Bolivian immigration (☼ 5am-8pm), on the north side of the international bridge, issues exit stamps and tourist cards (normally only for 30 days) – there is no official charge for these services. Formalities are minimal, but those entering Argentina may be held up south of the border by exhaustive custom searches at several control points. The border is open 6am to 8pm daily.

COCHABAMBA

After its founding in 1574, Cochabamba (elevation 2550m), with its fertile soil and mild climate, blossomed into the country's foremost granary. Long known as Bolivia's second city, it's now been knocked into third place by booming Santa Cruz. Nonetheless, Cochabamba remains a progressive and economically active city, with a growing population of more than 550,000.

The city is warm, dry and sunny – a welcome relief after the chilly altiplano. There's a congenial nightlife, thanks to the university population and good museums and shopping. Don't leave without sampling some *chicha cochabambina,* a traditional fermented corn brew quaffed throughout the region.

Orientation

Addresses north of Av de las Heroínas take an N, those below take an S. Addresses east of Av Ayacucho take an E and those west an O. The number immediately following the letter tells you how many blocks away from these division streets the address falls. Good maps are available at kiosks on the west side of the plaza or at the well-stocked Amigos del Libro (see below) which also carries guidebooks.

Information

Los Amigos del Libro (☎ 04-425-4114; Heroínas 3712) is the best-stocked bookshop.

Internet places are popping up so fast that nobody has time to come up with unique names. Try **CyberNet Café** (cnr Colombia & Baptista), **Black Cat** (cnr Bolívar & Aguirre) and **Internet Bolivia** (España at Ecuador).

For laundry, head to **Lavaya** (cnr Salamanca & Antezana).

Banks and *casas de cambio* will change traveler's checks and there are ATMs located all around town. Exprint-Bol, on the west side of the plaza, gives OK rates (2% to 3% commission). You'll find street moneychangers on Av Heroínas and around the **Entel** (Achá) office, which has cheap but slow Internet.

Bolivian immigration (☎ 04-222-5553; Arce & Jordán) can extend your length of stay. See p244 for details on consular representation in Cochabamba.

Sights & Activities

Museo Arqueológico (cnr Jordán & Baptista Aguirre; admission US$1.35; ☼ 8am-6pm Mon-Fri, 9am-noon Sat) has a fine collection of Bolivian mummies and artifacts. Exhibits date from as early as 12,000 BC and as late as the colonial period.

Tin baron Simón Patiño never actually lived in this pretentious **Palacio de Portales** (☎ 04-224-3137; admission with guide US$1.35; gardens ☼ 2:30-6:30pm Mon-Fri, 10:30am-12:30pm Sat & Sun),

a French-style mansion in the *barrio* of Queru Queru, north of the center. It was built between 1915 and 1925 and everything, except perhaps the bricks, was imported from Europe. Now the Simón I Patiño Cultural Center, it's used for music recitals and art exhibitions. The sumptuous house and its lovely garden can be visited only with a guide. Tours in Spanish/English start at 5pm/5:30pm from Monday to Friday, and 11am/11:30am on Saturday – call ahead to verify tour times. Don't miss the nice new **Natural History Museum** next door. Take *micro* 'E' north from Av San Martín.

The **Cristo de la Concordia** statue, which towers over the city's east side, can be reached by taxi (US$4.50 round trip from the center). There's a **teleférico** (cable car; round trip US$0.80; ☼ 10am-8pm) that climbs the 2900m to the top.

Courses

Cochabamba is a good spot for studying Spanish, Quechua or Aymara. Private teachers charge around US$5 per hour, but not all are experienced. Reader recommendations include the following:

Claudia Villagra (☎ 04-224-8685)
Gloria Ramírez (☎ 04-424-8697)
Maricruz Almanza Bedoya (☎ 04-422-7923; maricruz_almanza@hotmail.com)
Reginaldo Rojo (☎ 04-224-2322; frojo@supernet .com.bo)

Alternatively, ask for recommendations at the **Centro Boliviano-Americano** (CBA; ☎ 04-222-1288/2518; www.cbacoch.org in Spanish; 25 de Mayo N-365), the **Instituto Cultural Boliviano-Alemán** (ICBA; ☎ 04-222-8431; Sucre 693) or **Volunteer Bolivia** (see p251).

Tours

To visit nearby national parks and reserves, contact **Fremen Tours** (☎ 04-225-9392; www.andes -amazonia.com; Calle Tumusla N-245).

Festivals & Events

The Fiesta de la Virgen de Urcupiña (around August 15 to 18) is huge, with pilgrims converging on the village of Quillacollo, 13km west of Cochabamba.

Sleeping

For decent, thrifty accommodations, try **Alojamiento Cochabamba** (☎ 04-222-5067; Aguirre

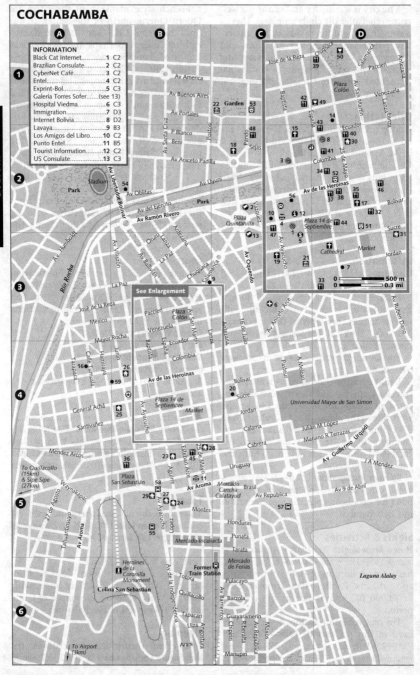

COCHABAMBA

INFORMATION

Black Cat Internet	1 C2
Brazilian Consulate	2 C2
CyberNet Café	3 C2
Entel	4 C2
Exprint-Bol	5 C3
Galeria Torres Sofer	(see 13)
Hospital Viedma	6 C3
Immigration	7 D3
Internet Bolivia	8 D2
Lavaya	9 B3
Los Amigos del Libro	10 C2
Punto Entel	11 B5
Tourist Information	12 C2
US Consulate	13 C3

S-591; r per person US$2), your basic flophouse. More attractive at this price is the clean but surly **Alojamiento San Juan de Dios** (López S-871; r per person US$2).

Hostal Elisa (☎ /fax 04-223-5102; helisa@super net.com.bo; López S-834; r per person US$6, with bath US$10) One of Bolivia's nicest inexpensive places, it's convenient to the bus station but in an unattractive location. Inside the door it's another world, with friendly management, gas-heated showers and a sunny courtyard.

Hostal Oruro (☎ 04-424-1047; López S-864; r per person US$3.25) If the Elisa is full, head next door to this secure, family-run place where the rooms are a bit bigger and shared bathrooms have solar-heated showers.

Hostal Florida (☎ /fax 04-225-7911; floridah@ elsitio.com; 25 de Mayo S-583; r per person US$3.25, with bath, phone & cable TV US$6; 🖥) Another excellent choice, where the chummy owner offers laundry service and organizes trips.

Hostal Colonial (☎ 04-222-1791; Junín N-134; r per person US$3, with bath US$4-5) Very clean and mellow, with pleasant rooms, especially the ones upstairs overlooking the courtyard garden.

Hostal Central (☎ 04-222-3622; General Achá 0-235; r with bath per person US$6) An excellent, quiet choice, including TV and continental breakfast.

Hostal Versalles (☎ 04-422-1096; Av Ayacucho S-714; r per person US$3.25, with bath US$4.50) The best choice nearest the bus terminal is a clean, friendly HI-affiliate where breakfast is included. More expensive rooms have cable TV.

Residencial Familiar (☎ 04-222-7988; Sucre E-554; r per person US$3.25, d with bath US$10) and the nicer **Residencial Familiar Anexo** (☎ 04-222-7986; 25 de Mayo N-234; r per person US$3.25, d with bath US$10) have poor beds but are popular with Bolivian and foreign travelers.

Eating

Markets are cheap for simple but varied and tasty meals – don't miss the huge, mouthwatering fruit salads. The most central market, on 25 de Mayo, is between Sucre and Jordán. Other markets include the Mercado de Ferias, just east of the old train station, and the giant, entertaining Mercado Cancha Calatayud, on Aroma between San Martín and Lanza. Street vendors on the corner of General Achá and Ayacucho sell

BOLIVIA

delicious *papas rellenas* (potatoes stuffed with meat or cheese).

Cristal (Heroínas E-352) Try this place for a big breakfast, great juice, eggs, coffee, pancakes and *salteñas*.

Café Express (Aguirre S-443) Pours Cochabamba's best espresso drinks. Other good coffee spots include **Café Francés** (España N-140) and **Café Express Bolívar** (Bolívar E-485).

Economical *almuerzos* are everywhere.

Restaurant Marvi (Cabrera at 25 de Mayo; lunch US$1.35) A nice, family-run place. At dinner you'll pay a bit more for hearty helpings of *comida típica*.

Restaurant Jose A convenient spot for lunch or dinner on the plaza, with inexpensive Bolivian and pseudo-Chinese meals.

Av Heroínas is fast-food row and is good for pizza, chicken, burgers and *salteñas*.

California Burgers & Donuts (25 de Mayo) Delivers on its premise and grinds decent coffee too.

Dumbo (Colombia & 25 de Mayo) May mouse around with Mickey's copyright but serves good light meals and ice cream.

El Prado Farther north on Ballivián, this upmarket ice-creamery has sidewalk seating.

Snack Uno's (Av de las Heroínas & Av San Martín; set lunch US$1.25) Cochabamba's best vegetarian food. Pizza and pasta dishes are also available and there's a good *salteñería* next door.

Gopal (España N-250) Vegetarian lunch or dinner with an Indian take.

Tea Room Zürich (Pando 1182; ☺ Wed-Mon) For something classier, take tea and éclairs at the tea room.

Much less refined are the smoky *churrasquerías* at the south end of Hamiraya.

Eli's (25 de Mayo N-254) Pizzas are the ticket here.

Metrópolis (España & Ecuador; mains US$2-4), a popular eating, drinking and socializing spot. It offers somewhat pricey soup, salad and pasta, among other more imaginative fare.

La Cantonata (España & Mayor Rocha; mains US$5-10) One of the city's best restaurants, one of the country's best Italian splurges.

Drinking

The liveliest nightlife is found up España and 25 de Mayo, which feature restaurants, bars, discos and revelers. On the Prado (Av Ballivián), there's more drinking and less eating at **Top Chopp** (Av Ballivián), a Bolivian beer barn, and the **Viking Pub** (Av Ballivián), which showcases loud music. Or, sing and boogie at any of the strip's discos and karaoke bars.

Pancho's (España N-460; cover US$2) The hard-rocking scene jams on Saturday nights here, when live bands cover Kiss, Metallica and Deep Purple.

Entertainment

Big, bright **Cine Heroínas** (Heroínas) and **Cine Astor** (Sucre & 25 de Mayo) both screen first-run movies.

Strike X Bowling (Pando at Portales) Local teens hangout at the fully-automated, 10-lane center and the go-kart track and arcade next door.

Getting There & Around

AIR

To reach Aeropuerto Jorge Wilsterman (CBB) take *micro* B from the main plaza or a taxi (US$1 per person). The airport is served regularly by **AeroSur** (☎ 04-440-0911; Villarroel 105) and **LAB** (☎ 04-425-0750; office at airport). LAB flies daily to La Paz, Santa Cruz and Sucre, and several times a week to Tarija and Trinidad. **TAM** (☎ 04-458-1552; Hamiraya N-122) lifts off from the military airport to Santa Cruz (US$40) on Tuesday morning and La Paz (US$27) on Tuesday afternoon.

BUS & CAMIÓN

Cochabamba's **central bus terminal** (☎ 155) is on Av Ayacucho, just south of Aroma. There's a US$0.35 terminal fee and comfortable *bus cama* service is available on the main routes for roughly double the regular price. There's frequent service to La Paz (US$2 to US$3, seven hours) and Oruro (US$2, four hours). Most buses to Santa Cruz (US$3 to US$6, 10 to 13 hours) leave before 9am or after 5pm. Several daily buses depart for Sucre (US$4, 10 hours); some then continue to Potosí (around US$7, 15 hours).

Micros and buses to Villa Tunari (US$1.75, three to four hours) and Puerto Villarroel (US$2, seven hours) in the Chapare region leave every hour or so from the corner of 9 de Abril and Oquendo.

AROUND COCHABAMBA

Two to three hours' walk from the village of **Sipe Sipe**, 27km southwest of Cochabamba, are the ruins of **Inca-Rakay**. It makes a good side trip for the scenery, rather than any archaeological grandeur, but there have been several serious reports of campers being assaulted here. Sunday is market day. Sipe Sipe is accessible by *micro* from **Quillacollo**, which is reached by *micro* from Cochabamba.

About 160km northeast of Cochabamba is the steamy, relaxed Chapare town of **Villa Tunari** and **Inti Wara Yassi** (Parque Machía; www.intiwarayassi.org), a wildlife refuge and mellow place to chill out and warm up after the altiplano. Volunteers are welcome (15-day minimum) and you can camp for US$2. In town, there are numerous places to stay and eat, though there is no bank.

SUCRE

Set in a valley surrounded by low mountains, Sucre (population 175,000; elevation 2790m) is a small, convivial city with a rich colonial heritage evident in its streetscapes, churches and 1991 Unesco Cultural Heritage designation. Although La Paz usurped most of the governmental power and is the de facto capital, the supreme court still convenes in Sucre and *sureños* (residents of Sucre) maintain that the real heart of Bolivian governance beats here.

Sucre was founded in 1538 (under the name La Plata) as the Spanish capital of the Charcas, a vast region stretching from southern Peru to Río de la Plata in present-day Argentina. In 1776, when new territorial divisions were created by the Spaniards, the city's name was changed to Chuquisaca. During the colonial period, it was the most important center in the eastern Spanish territories and heavily influenced Bolivia's history. Independence was declared here on August 6, 1825, and the new republic was created here and named after its liberator, Simón Bolívar. Several years later, the name of the city was changed again to Sucre in honor of the general who promoted the independence movement.

Information

For emergencies, ring the **tourist police** (☎ 04-648-0467).

In addition to the **post** (Junín & Estudiantes) and **Entel** (España & Urcullo) offices, Sucre has many Internet places including speedy, smoky **Internet 2000** (Ravelo s/n; ☽ until 11pm) and **Cyber-café Samael** (Estudiantes 33 & 79; ☽ until 11pm).

Laverap (Bolívar 617) is a reliable laundry and **Lavandería LG** (Loa 407) offers 90-minute service. Both charge about US$1/kilo.

Casas de cambio are around the main market. **Casa de Cambio Ambar** (San Alberto) changes traveler's checks at good rates. **Banco Nacional de Bolivia** (cnr Espana & Ravelo) changes traveler's checks (3% commission); there is an ATM here and at **Banco de Santa Cruz** (España & San Alberto), which also does cash advances. Street moneychangers operate along Hernando Siles, behind the main market.

The university runs a **tourist information desk** (in Museo Gutiérrez Valenzuela), on the plaza, which is sometimes staffed by enthusiastic English speakers – ask here about guided city tours. You may be able to extract some tourist information from the friendly English-speaking staff at the **Casa de la Cultura** (Argentina s/n).

Beg **immigration** (Pastor Sainz 117) for length of stay extensions. The **Peruvian consulate** (☎ 04-645-5592; Avaroa 462; ☽ 9:30am-2:30pm Mon-Fri) issues visas.

Sights & Activities

Ride the Dino Truck to Fancesa's cement quarry, **Cal Orcko** (☎ 04-645-1863; admission US$3.35), a sort of Grumman's Chinese theater for large and scaly types with hundreds of dinosaur tracks measuring up to 80cm in diameter. It departs from the plaza at 9:30am, noon and 2:30pm daily.

For a dose of Bolivian history, visit the **Casa de la Libertad** (☎ 04-645-4200; Plaza 25 de Mayo 11; admission US$1.35, free Sun; ☽ 9am-noon & 2:30-6:30pm Mon-Sat, 9am-noon Sun), an ornate house where the Bolivian declaration of independence was signed in 1825. It's now a museum displaying artifacts of the era.

The excellent **Museo de Arte Indígena** (ASUR; ☎ 04-645-3841; San Alberto 413; admission US$1.60; ☽ 8:30am-noon & 2:30-6pm Mon-Fri, 9:30am-noon Sat), in the Caserón de la Capellanía, displays fine Candelaria, Potolo and Tarabuco weavings – ask for English translations of the labels. It's part of a successful project to revitalize handwoven crafts. You can see weavers in action and browse the superb works for sale.

The **Museos Universitarios** (☎ 04-645-3285; Bolívar 698; admission US$1.35; ☽ 8:30am-noon & 2-6pm Mon-Fri, 9am-noon & 3-6pm Sat) are three separate museums housing colonial relics, anthropological artifacts and modern art. The university also operates the **Museo Gutiérrez Valenzuela** and **Museo de Historia Natural** (☎ 04-645-3828; SE cnr of Plaza 25 de Mayo; admission US$1.35; ⏰ 8:30am-noon & 2-6pm Mon-Fri; 9am-noon & 3-6pm Sat); the former is an old aristocrat's house with schmaltzy 19th-century decor. The **Museo de los Niños Tanga-Tanga** (☎ 04-644-0299; NW cnr of Plaza La Recoleta; adult/child US$1/0.65; ⏰ 9am-noon & 2:30-6pm Tues-Sun) hosts cultural and environmental programs for kids, including theater performances and ceramic classes. The café here is open from 9am to 7pm.

It's worth checking out the **Casa de la Cultura** (Argentina 65), which has art exhibitions, music recitals, a café and a library.

CHURCHES & RELIGIOUS ART
Sucre boasts several lovely colonial churches but opening hours are unpredictable. The **cathedral** (entrance at Nicolas Ortiz 61; ⏰ mornings only) dates from the 16th century, though major additions were made in the early 17th century. Just down the block is the **Museo Catedralico** (admission US$1.25; ⏰ 10am-noon & 3-5pm Mon-Fri, 10am-noon Sat) which holds an interesting collection of religious relics.

Iglesia La Merced (Pérez 512; admission US$0.80; ⏰ 10am-noon & 3-5pm Mon-Fri) has the finest interior of any Sucre church, but it's rarely open. Both **Iglesia de San Miguel** (Arenales 10; ⏰ 11:30am-noon Mon-Fri, mass on weekends) and **Iglesia de San Francisco** (Ravelo 1; ⏰ 7-9am & 4-7pm) reflect Mudejar influences, particularly in their ceiling designs. The beautiful **Convento de San Felipe Neri** (Nicolas Ortiz 165; admission US$1.35; ⏰ 4-6pm Mon-Fri, Sat during high season) has good rooftop views. If you're interested in sacred art or antique musical instruments, the 1639 **Museo y Convento de Santa Clara** (Calvo 212; admission US$0.65; ⏰ 9am-noon & 3-6pm Mon-Fri, 9am-noon Sat) has a renowned collection.

For spectacular city views, trek up to the **Iglesia de la Recoleta** and **Museo de la Recoleta** (Plaza Anzures; admission US$1.35; ⏰ 9:30-11:30am & 2:30-4:30pm Mon-Fri) which houses many religious paintings and sculptures.

Courses
Sucre has a great vibe and is becoming a favorite place to study Spanish.

The **Instituto Cultural Boliviano-Alemán** (ICBA; ☎ /fax 04-645-2091; www.icba-sucre.edu.bo in Spanish; Avaroa 326) offers recommended Spanish and

salsa lessons. **Academía Latinoamericana de Español** (☎ 04-646-0537; www.latinoschools.com/bolivia; Dalence 109) has a comprehensive program that features language, dance and cooking lessons, homestay options and volunteer opportunities.

The **Centro Boliviano-Americano** (CBA; ☎ 04-645-1982; www.cba.com.bo in Spanish; Calvo 437) gives referrals to private teachers. Recommended Spanish teachers include **Sofía Sauma** (☎ 04-645-1687; fsauma@hotmail.com; Loa 779) and **Stella Peredo** (contact through the CBA). Both offer one-on-one classes for US$5 an hour.

Sleeping
Sucre has plenty of budget accommodations around the market and along Ravelo and San Alberto, but it's also a good place to splurge on something a bit more stylish.

HI Sucre Hostel (☎ 04-644-0471; www.hostellingbolivia.org; Loayza 119; dm US$3-8, d US$16-20; 🖳) Bolivia's flagship, full-service hostel – the country's swankest – is 100m from the bus station (follow the signs). Some private rooms have Jacuzzis and cable TV. Reserve online.

Alojamiento El Turista (☎ 04-645-3172; Ravelo 118; r per person US$2) The best rooms at the dumpy but clean and friendly Turista are on the top floor.

Alojamiento San José (☎ 04-645-1475; Ravelo s/n; s/d US$3.25/5) A basic choice in an interesting old building.

Hostal Veracruz (☎ 04-645-1560; Ravelo 158; s/d US$5.35/9) A well-run tour group choice with a variety of rooms, some with bath. Breakfast available.

Hostal Charcas (☎ 04-645-3972; hostalcharcas@yahoo.com; Ravelo 62; s/d US$5.35/8.50, with bath US$8.50/13.50) One of Sucre's best values, with good showers and sparkling clean rooms.

Residencial Bolivia (☎ 04-645-4346; San Alberto 42; s/d US$4/6.65) Worn but clean and spacious rooms. There's a sunny patio, but alcohol isn't allowed. Breakfast included.

Hostal San Francisco (☎ 04-645-2117; hostalsf@cotes.net.bo; Aniceto Arce 191; r with bath per person US$6) A tranquil option with an inviting patio. Rates include breakfast.

Sucre's newest accommodation option is *casas de huéspedes* (guesthouses), which offer a distinctive, homey feel.

Casa de Huéspedes San Marcos (☎ 04-646-2087; Aniceto Arce 233; r per person US$4, with bath US$5) This place has clean, quiet rooms with kitchen and laundry access for guests.

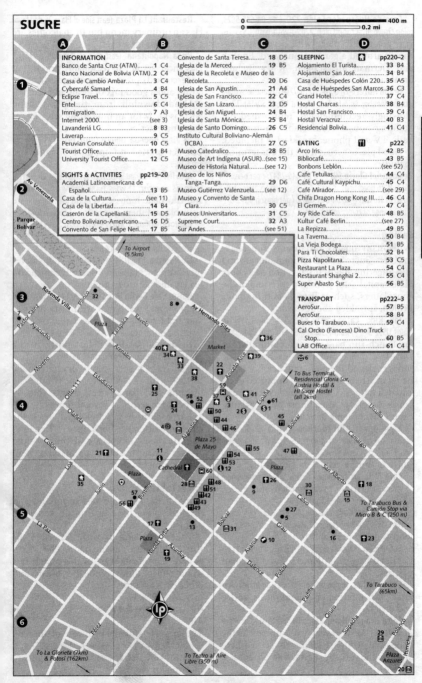

SUCRE

0 — 400 m
0 — 0.2 mi

INFORMATION

Banco de Santa Cruz (ATM)............1 C4
Banco Nacional de Bolivia (ATM)...2 C4
Casa de Cambio Ambar.................3 C4
Cybercafé Samael.........................4 B4
Eclipse Travel..............................5 C5
Entel..6 C4
Immigration................................7 A3
Internet 2000.........................(see 3)
Lavanderiá LG.............................8 B3
Laverap......................................9 C5
Peruvian Consulate.....................10 C5
Tourist Office.............................11 B4
University Tourist Office...............12 C5

SIGHTS & ACTIVITIES   pp219–20

Academiá Latinoamericana de
    Español.................................13 B5
Casa de la Cultura....................(see 11)
Casa de la Libertad....................14 B4
Caserón de la Capellaniá.............15 D5
Centro Boliviano-Americano........16 D5
Convento de San Felipe Neri........17 B5

Convento de Santa Teresa...........18 D5
Iglesia de la Merced...................19 B5
Iglesia de la Recoleta e Museo de la
    Recoleta...............................20 D6
Iglesia de San Agustín...............21 A4
Iglesia de San Francisco.............22 C4
Iglesia de San Lázaro.................23 D5
Iglesia de San Miguel................24 B4
Iglesia de Santa Mónica.............25 B5
Iglesia de Santo Domingo...........26 C5
Instituto Cultural Boliviano-Alemán
    (ICBA).................................27 C5
Museo Catedralico....................28 B5
Museo de Art Indígena (ASUR)..(see 15)
Museo de Historia Natural........(see 12)
Museo de los Niños
    Tanga-Tanga..........................29 D6
Museo Gutiérrez Valenzuela.....(see 12)
Museo y Convento de Santa
    Clara....................................30 C5
Museos Universitarios................31 C5
Supreme Court..........................32 A3
Sur Andes.............................(see 51)

SLEEPING   pp220–2

Alojamiento El Turista.................33 B4
Alojamiento San José.................34 B4
Casa de Huéspedes Colón 220....35 A5
Casa de Huéspedes San Marcos...36 C3
Grand Hotel..............................37 C4
Hostal Charcas..........................38 B4
Hostal San Francisco..................39 C4
Hostal Veracruz.........................40 B3
Residencial Bolivia.....................41 C4

EATING   p222

Arco Iris...................................42 B5
Bibliocafé.................................43 B5
Bonbons Leblón.....................(see 52)
Cafe Tetulias............................44 C4
Café Cultural Kaypichu...............45 C4
Café Mirador.........................(see 29)
Chifa Dragon Hong Kong III........46 C4
El Germén.................................47 B5
Joy Ride Cafe............................48 B5
Kultur Café Berlin...................(see 27)
La Repizza................................49 B5
La Taverna................................50 B4
La Vieja Bodega.........................51 B5
Para Ti Chocolates.....................52 B4
Pizza Napolitana........................53 C5
Restaurant La Plaza....................54 C4
Restaurant Shanghai 2...............55 C4
Super Abasto Sur.......................56 B5

TRANSPORT   pp222–3

AeroSur...................................57 B5
AeroSur...................................58 B4
Buses to Tarabuco......................59 C4
Cal Orcko (Fancesa) Dino Truck
    Stop....................................60 B5
LAB Office................................61 C4

Parque
Bolívar

To Airport
(5.5km)

Rosenda Villa

Pilinco

32

8

Av Hernando Siles

36

Pastor Saini

Tarapacá

Ravelo

Market

22

39

Ayacucho

Arenales

40
34
33

38

Moreno

Estudiantes

25

59

41

España

61

Otto-III

58 52

24

50

3

1

Olañeta

Arenales

14

44

46

45

Bolívar

Camargo

Urcullo

Colón

21

11

Plaza 25
de Mayo

54

55

47

San Alberto

Loa

Junín

Cathedral

28

60

12

53

48

51

42
43

49

26

30
9

15

18

To Tarabuco Bus &
Camión Stop via
Micro B & C (250 m)

Bustillos

35

57

56

Plaza

17

13

27

31

10

16

23

La Paz

Nicolás Ortíz

Aguirre

19

Bolívar

Aviaca

Grau

Calvo

Plaza
Loa

Dalence

Potosí

Padilla

To Tarabuco
(65km)

Oruro

Suipacha

Pelez

To La Glorieta (7km)
& Potosí (162km)

To Teatro al Aire
Libre (350 m)

29

Plaza
Anzures

Itimincha

Potolo

20

To Bus Terminal,
Residencial Gloria Sur,
Austria Hostal &
HI Sucre Hostel
(all 2km)

BOLIVIA

Casa de Huéspedes Colón 220 (☎ 04-645-5823; colon220@bolivia.com; Colón 220; d with bath US$5-16) is a great little place with seven spotless rooms around a garden courtyard. English and German are spoken. Rates include breakfast.

Grand Hotel (☎ 04-645-2104/2461; grandhot@mara .scr.entelnet.bo; Aniceto Arce 61; s/d US$13.50/16) This glowingly recommended, refurbished old building houses comfortable rooms with bath, TV and phone; breakfast is included.

Good places across from the bus terminal include:

Residencial Gloria Sur (☎ 04-645-2847; r per person US$3) With good beds.

Austria Hostal (☎ 04-645-4202; r per person US$3-6) With a range of comfy rooms.

Eating

With many quality restaurants and relaxing cafés, Sucre is ideal for lounging around and lingering about. It's also Bolivia's chocolate capital – for a fix pop into one of the chocolatiers, such as Para Ti and Bonbons Leblon, sprinkled about town.

Joy Ride Café (☎ 04-642-5544; Nicolas Ortiz; mains US$2-5; ☽ from 7:30am Mon-Fri, from 9am Sat & Sun) Dutch-run bar, café and cultural space with live music and book exchange. The tunes rock and the patio outback is a super hangout. There are plenty of imported beers and deli fixings you won't find elsewhere in South America. After hours on weekends, expect lots of table dancing.

Upstairs in the market, you'll find delicious breakfasts of *pasteles* (pastries) plus fruit salads and juices – try *jugo de tumbo* (juice of unripe yellow passion fruit).

Café Mirador (in Museo de los Niños Tanga-Tanga; ☽ from 9am) has a great garden and views, and opens for breakfast.

Café Cultural Kaypichu (San Alberto 168; ☽ 7:30am-2pm & 5-9pm Tue-Sun) Serves awesome vegetarian food and is super popular.

El Germén (San Alberto 231) Serves vegetarian food and has great *almuerzos* and German pastries.

Cafe Tetulias (north side of Plaza 25 de Mayo) An artsy place offering tasty light meals, coffee and snacks.

Chifa Dragon Hong Kong III (north side of Plaza 25 de Mayo) MSG lovers will appreciate the good-value Chinese *almuerzos* served here and at the nearby **Restaurant Shanghai 2** (Calvo).

Restaurant La Plaza (east side of Plaza 25 de Mayo) Has an ordinary menu but the balconies are a good place for a beer.

Pizza Napolitana (east side of Plaza 25 de Mayo) Has cheap set lunch, reasonably priced (but undercooked) pizza and pasta, excellent ice cream and a good mix of locals and visitors.

Head downhill from the plaza along Nicolas Ortiz for an interesting selection of bars and eateries.

La Vieja Bodega (Nicolas Ortiz) For US$5 you can get stuffed on fondue, lasagna and salads.

Arco Iris (Restaurant Suizo; Nicolas Ortiz) For delights such as *roeschti* (Swiss hash browns), fondue and chocolate mousse. Vegetarian meals are available and there's occasional live music.

Bibliocafé (Nicolas Ortiz; ☽ evenings) Serves light meals to '80s music. The pasta is recommended, as are the crêpes.

La Repizza (cnr Dalence & Nicolas Ortiz) Serves pizza and cocktails and hosts live music on Friday and Saturday nights.

Kultur Café Berlin (Avaroa 326) A German coffee shop and restaurant with tasty pastries and light meals – try the *papas rellenas* (stuffed potatoes).

La Taverna (Aniceto Arce) Just north of the plaza, Alliance Française runs this restaurant, which serves a savory ratatouille for US$1.75, as well as *coq au vin*, quiche lorraine and llama steak. Films (mostly French) are screened several times a week.

For back-to-basics Bolivian, check the chicken-and-chips shops on Av Hernando Siles, between Tarapaca and Junín. Super Abasto Sur on Bustillos is a massive, well-stocked grocery store.

Entertainment

Some of the bars and restaurants on and near the plaza have live music and *peña* nights.

For discos and karaoke, check Calle España just up from the plaza. The Teatro al Aire Libro, southeast of the center, is a wonderful outdoor venue for music and other performances.

Getting There & Away
AIR

The airport is 6km northwest of the city center. **AeroSur** (☎ 04-645-4895; Arenales 31) and **LAB** (☎ 04-691-3181; Bustillos 121) have flights to most major cities.

BUS & SHARED TAXI

The bus terminal, located 2km northeast of the city center, is accessed by *micro* A or 3 from the center (you can flag it down anywhere along Calle España), but the *micros* are too tiny to accommodate lots of luggage. There are numerous daily buses to Cochabamba (US$7 to US$10, 10 to 12 hours), leaving around 6pm or 7pm. Direct buses to Santa Cruz (ie, not via Cochabamba) run most days (US$7 to US$10, 15 to 20 hours). Several companies leave daily for Potosí (US$2 to US$2.50, three hours) around 7am and at 5pm; some continue to Tarija (US$9.50, 15 hours), Oruro and Villazón. Alternatively, most hotels can arrange shared taxis to Potosí (US$4 per person with four people). There is frequent *bus cama* service to La Paz (US$7 to US$10, 14 to 16 hours).

Getting Around

Local *micros* (US$0.15) take circuitous routes around Sucre's one-way streets. Most eventually converge on the stop on Hernando Siles, north of the market, but they can be waved down virtually anywhere. You can reach the airport on *micro* F or 1 (allow an hour) or by taxi (US$2 to US$3.50).

AROUND SUCRE
Tarabuco

This small, predominantly indigenous village, 65km southeast of Sucre, is known for its beautiful weavings and colorful, sprawling **Sunday market**. Plenty touristy, the market is overflowing with amazing woven ponchos, bags and belts as well as *charangos* (buy only wooden ones – have mercy on endangered armadillos). However, much of the work for sale is not local but acquired by traders, so don't expect many bargains.

You can visit Tarabuco with a tour (US$3.50) or take a *micro* from Sucre (on Ravelo in front of the market) at 7am on Sunday (US$1, 2½ hours). Buses and *camiones* returning to Sucre leave from the main plaza in Tarabuco between 1am and 3pm.

Cordillera de los Frailes

This range runs through much of western Chuquisaca and northern Potosí departments and offers scenic trekking opportunities. Sites in the Sucre area worth visiting include **Capilla de Chataquila**, the 6km **Camino del Inca**, the rock paintings of **Pumamachay**, the weaving village of **Potolo**, pastoral **Chaunaca**, dramatic **Maragua Crater** and the **Talula hot springs**.

There are plenty of **trekking routes**, but they traverse little-visited areas; to minimize cultural impact and avoid getting hopelessly lost, hire a local guide like **Lucho Loredo** (☎ 04-642-0752; Comarapa 127, Barrio Petrolero, Sucre). His family speaks some English and offers a variety of itineraries for around US$25 per person per day. Several Sucre travel agencies also arrange excursions – try **Sur Andes** (☎ /fax 04-645-2632; Nicolas Ortíz 6) or **Eclipse Travel** (☎ /fax 04-644-3960; eclipse@mara.scr .entelnet.bo; Avaroa 310).

POTOSÍ

Potosí has at turns been blessed, cursed, rich and depressed by its renowned silver deposits. The city was founded in 1545, following the discovery of ore in silver-rich Cerro Rico, the hill overlooking town. The veins proved so loaded that the mines quickly became the world's most prolific and Potosí, at a staggering altitude of 4070m, grew into Latin America's largest and wealthiest city. Millions of laborers were conscripted to work in the mines – both indigenous people and imported African slaves. Conditions were (and remain) appalling, with as many as eight million workers dying from diseases, accidents or contact with toxic chemicals during the three centuries of colonial rule.

In the early 19th century, good times turned bad when silver production began to wane. Nowadays, a renewed demand for lead and zinc keeps this Unesco World Heritage city alive, though small-scale silver extraction continues. Echoes of the once-grand colonial city reverberate through the

---

JOY RIDING

Joy Ride Bolivia (☎ 04-642-5544; www.joyride bol.com; Nicolas Ortiz 14) at Joy Ride Café runs guided, multilingual motorcycle, ATV and mountain bike tours and rents mountain bikes (US$2.50 per hour) for those who prefer to go it alone. Bicycle trips cost US$15 to US$40 per person and motorcycle/ATV excursions are US$68/$84.

narrow streets, bouncing from the formal balconied mansions and ornate churches.

Superlative buffs will appreciate Potosí's ranking as the **world's highest city**, an in-your-face fact when you're laboring up the streets while freezing at night…in the middle of 'summer.' Take it easy if you're arriving from the flatlands.

Information

Internet access is available for US$0.40 per hour at several places along the pedestrian mall and at **Tuko's Café** (Junín & Bolívar, upstairs).

Lots of businesses along Bolívar, Sucre and in the market change US dollars at reasonable rates. Cash advances are available at **Banco de La Paz** (Plaza 10 de Noviembre) on the plaza and ATMs are common in the center.

There is a pretty unhelpful **regional tourism office** (☎ 02-622-5288; Ayacucho & Bustillos). Better, but biased, is the **information kiosk** (Plaza 6 de Agosto), infrequently staffed by local tour agencies.

Sights

Potosí's central area contains a wealth of colonial architecture. The **cathedral** (Ayacucho; admission US$0.75; tours 9:30-10am & 3-5:30pm Mon-Fri, 9:30-10am Sat) has a particularly fine interior, while the **Iglesia de San Lorenzo** (Heroes del Chaco) is famous for its classic mestizo facade.

The **Casa Real de la Moneda** (Royal Mint; Ayacucho; admission for mandatory 2-3hr guided tour US$2.65; ☯ 9am-12:30pm & 3-7pm Tue-Sat, 9am-12:30pm Sun) is Potosí's star attraction and one of Bolivia's finest museums. The building, which occupies a full block, was constructed between 1753 and 1773 to control the minting of colonial coins. It now houses religious art, Tiahuanaco artifacts, ancient coins, wooden minting machines and the country's first locomotive. The knockout building itself has been painstakingly restored.

The highlight of the **Museo & Convento de San Francisco** (Nogales; admission US$1.35; ☯ 9-11:30am & 2:30-5:30pm Mon-Fri, 9am-12:30pm Sat) is the view from the roof. The **Museo & Convento de Santa Teresa** (Villavicenzio; admission US$2; ☯ 9am-noon & 3-5pm) is a must for flagellation fans.

Activities
COOPERATIVE MINE TOURS

A visit to the cooperative mines is demanding, shocking and memorable. Tours typically involve scrambling and crawling in low, narrow, dirty shafts and climbing rickety ladders – wear your gnarliest clothes. Working practices are medieval, safety provisions nearly nonexistent and most shafts are unventilated; chewing coca helps, but tours aren't recommended for claustrophobes and asthmatics. Work is done by hand with basic tools, and underground temperatures vary from below freezing to a stifling 45°C (113°F). Miners, exposed to myriad noxious chemicals, normally die of silicosis pneumonia within 10 years of entering the mines. They work the mine as a cooperative venture, with each miner milking his own claim and selling his ore to a smelter through the cooperative.

Most tours start at the **miners' street market** where you buy gifts for the miners – coca leaves, alcohol and cigarettes to start; dynamite and fuses if you're after an explosive experience. Then you're driven up to **Cerro Rico** where guides often give a **demonstration blast**. After donning a jacket and helmet, the scramble begins. You can converse with the miners (language permitting), take photos (with flash) and share gifts as a tip.

All guides work through tour agencies, and all must be licensed. Most guides speak Spanish – ask around the agencies if you need an English speaker. Expect to pay around US$5 per person for a three- to five-hour group tour. A group of 10 people or fewer is best. There are many agencies; some of the best include the following:

Altiplano Tours (☎ 02-622-5353; Ayacucho 19)

Koala Tours (☎ 02-622-4708; Ayacucho 7) Repeatedly recommended for its professional, personable service. Worth every bit of the US$10 per person price.

South American Tours (☎ 02-622-28919; Ayacucho 11) Visits San Miguel la Poderosa mine in addition to standard tours.

Sumaj Tours (☎ 02-622-4633; Oruro 143)

TransAmazonas (☎ 02-622-7175; Quijarro 12)

Victoria Tours (☎ 02-622-2132; Chuquisaca 148) Also runs Lagunas de Kari Kari and hot springs trips.

LAGUNAS & HOT SPRINGS

A good day trek is to **Lagunas de Kari Kari**, 8km southeast of town. These artificial lakes were constructed in the late 16th and early 17th centuries by indigenous slaves to provide water for the city and hydropower to run its 132 *ingenios* (smelters). Travel agencies offer full- and half-day tours to the *lagunas*. Alternatively, you can head off independently. There are several routes – you could walk there and back in a long day or get a lift at least part of the way, along the road to Tupiza. Pick up the 1: 50,000 topo map *6435-II, Potosí (Este)*, at an IGM office.

Outside Potosí are several **hot spring resorts**; the most popular is **Tarapaya**, in picturesque countryside 25km north of the city, where the pools hover around 30°C (86°F). There are a dozen similar pools in the surrounding area. *Camiones* leave every half hour or so from Plaza Chuquimia near the bus terminal. *Micros* (US$0.50, 20 minutes) also run until mid-afternoon.

Festivals & Events

The most popular annual party is the Fiesta de Chu'tillos around the end of August. It features traditional dancing from all over South America as well as special performances from other continents. Booking accommodations for this period is essential. Alternatively, show up a week early; the week preceding the festival is given over to practicing for the big event and can be nearly as exciting as the real thing.

Sleeping

Only top-end hotels have heating, and there may be blanket shortages in the cheapies, so you'll want a sleeping bag. Hardcore budget places may charge extra for hot showers.

Koala Den (☎ 02-622-6467; ktours_potosi@hot mail.com; Junín 56; dm US$2.65) Heating, round-the-clock gas showers, a shared kitchen, good book exchange and bar make Koala the current traveler's favorite.

Residencial Sumaj (☎ 02-622-3336; F Gumiel 12; r per person US$3.35) Near Plaza del Estudiante, this is a hopping budget place despite its fringe location. Small, dark rooms with shared bath downstairs aren't as good value as the upstairs rooms.

Hostal María Victoria (☎ 02-622-2144; Chuquisaca 148; dm US$2, d US$5.50) Cleanish and at the hub of the traveler's scene.

Hostal Compañía de Jesús (☎ 02-622-3173; Chuquisaca 445; r per person US$5, with bath & breakfast US$6) Friendly and better value than María Victoria, with quiet, clean, (and some carpeted) rooms.

Hostal Carlos V (☎ 02-622-5121; Linares 42; r per person US$3.25) In an old colonial building with a covered patio.

Hotel Central (☎ 02-622-2207; cnr Bustillos & Cobija; r per person US$3, with bath US$4.65) In a quiet part of town, with a traditional *potosino* overhanging balcony and loads of character.

Hotel Jerusalén (☎ 02-622-4633; hoteljer@cedro .pts.entelnet.bo; Oruro 143; s/d with bath & breakfast US$10-25) One of Potosí's best values is this friendly, mellow HI-affiliate with nice balconies; prices vary seasonally and all rooms include phone and TV. Breakfast included.

Hotel El Turista (☎ 02-622-2492; Lanza 19; s/d with bath US$8/12) Most Latin American towns have a hotel straight out of *The Shining*: Potosí's entrant is this sprawling place.

There are several passable places strung along Av Serrudo near Plaza Campero:

Residencial Felcar (☎ 02-622-4966; Av Serrudo 345; r per person US$2.65) A top pick for its sunny, flowery patio and clean rooms. Hot water runs from 8am to 4pm. Private baths coming soon.

Residencial Copacabana (☎ 02-622-2712; Serrudo 319; r per person US$2.65) Pales in comparison to Felcar but works for a night. Hot water runs from 6am to 6pm.

Hostal Santa María (☎ 02-622-3255; Av Serrudo 244; s/d US$7.50/12) Comfortable carpeted rooms with bath, TV and phone.

Eating & Drinking

The market *comedor* offers inexpensive breakfasts, and a couple of small bakeries along the pedestrian stretch of Padilla do continental breakfasts. Luckily, most *hostals* offer breakfast options (however meager), as nearly everything else is locked up until the frost melts midmorning.

Food stalls line the pedestrian street near the bus terminal; tasty, filling *almuerzos* with a fruit shake on the side are US$1.

Café Imma Sumac (Bustillos 987) For great *salteñas*, hit this spot.

Manzana Mágica (Bustillos & Ayacucho; lunch US$1.75) A good vegetarian restaurant serving muesli and yogurt for breakfast, a hearty *almuerzo* and dinners and snacks until 9pm.

Café Cultural Kaypichu (Millares 24; mains US$2; ☺ Tue-Sun) In the same veggie vein as Manzana Mágica.

Café-Restaurant Potocchi A pleasant and inexpensive place which hosts a *peña* (US$1.50 cover) several nights a week.

Confitería Capricornio (Padilla at Hoyos) Notable for its affordable meals, snacks and coffee.

Cherry's Salon de Té (Padilla) The spot for apple strudel, chocolate cake and lemon meringue pie – the coffee is mediocre.

BOLIVIA

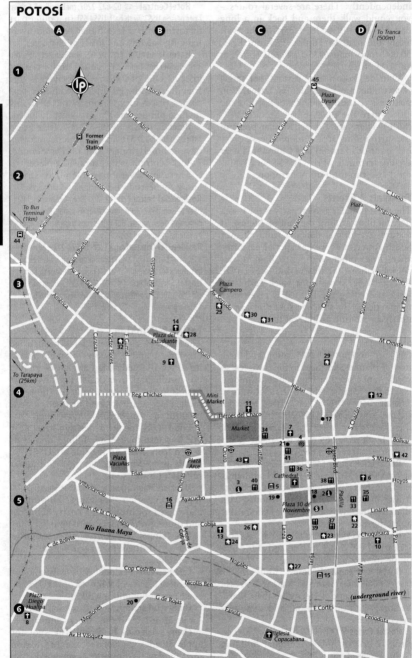

POTOSÍ

Sumac Orcko (Quijarro 46; lunch US$1.35; mains US$3) Offers filling, four-course *almuerzos*. In the evening it's a bit fancier, with à la carte options such as *trucha al limón* (lemon trout).

Chaplin's (S Matos near Quijarro) A friendly spot popular for lunch and international and Mexican dinner fare.

El Mesón (cnr Linares & Junín; mains US$3-5) For something a bit more formal, try locally recommended El Mesón, where US$5 gets you a fish or chicken meal with a glass of wine in a white-tablecloth atmosphere.

The best places for cocktails are **La Casona Pub** (Frias at Bustillos) or **La Bohemia Pub** (S Matos & La Paz).

Getting There & Around

The bus terminal is 1km northwest of town (30 minutes walk downhill from the center), reached by frequent *micros* (US$0.15) from the west side of the cathedral or by taxi (US$0.40 per person). Several companies serve La Paz (US$5 to US$10, 11 hours) daily. There are morning and evening buses to Oruro (US$4, eight hours), with connections to Cochabamba.

Buses to Sucre (US$2, three hours) leave daily at 5pm. There are also shared taxis to Sucre (US$4 per person, two hours) if you're rushed, and slow *camiones* and *micros* that leave from Plaza Uyuni if you're not.

Heading south, buses leave for Tupiza (US$3.35, eight hours) daily around 8am and 7pm with some continuing to Villazón (US$5.50, 10 to 12 hours). There are several daily buses to Tarija (US$7, 14 hours) and daily departures for Camargo, Yacuiba and Bermejo. Its better to go to Sucre or Cochabamba for buses to Santa Cruz, but there is one direct departure at 7am.

Buses to Uyuni (US$2 to US$3.50, six to seven hours) depart between 11am and 6pm – a scenic and popular route. Some go from the terminal, others from Av Universitario.

THE SOUTHEAST

This less-frequented area of Bolivia is rich and varied, with cultural highlights including beautifully restored Jesuit missions and natural wonders like Parque

Nacional Amboró. The Chaco is a wild frontier beckoning stalwart travelers into Paraguay, and the border crossing into Brazil at Quijarro (reached via the Death Train) is only a hop and a skip from the southern Pantanal.

SANTA CRUZ

Santa Cruz de la Sierra (elevation 415m) was founded in 1561 by Spaniard Ñuflo de Chaves, 220km east of its current location. Around the end of the 16th century, however, it proved vulnerable to indigenous attack and was moved to its present position, 50km east of the Cordillera Oriental foothills. Over the past four decades, Santa Cruz has mushroomed from a backwater cow town of 30,000 to its present position as Bolivia's second-largest city, with the population of the department now pushing 2 million. The concurrent explosion of the cocaine trade may not be coincidental.

Growth has slowed in recent years and the cosmopolitan city on the edge of a retreating wilderness manages to retain traces of its dusty past. It has direct flights to Miami and Europe, but, as a sign of the times, the sloths that used to laze in the main plaza have been relocated to the zoo. Visitors enjoy the frontier feel and tropical ambience, and it's a good base for exploring still-pristine rain forests and 18th-century Jesuit missions.

Orientation

When asked why he was planting onions and garlic in the city's new median strips, mayor Johnny Fernández responded: 'They are said to be good for circulation...' Santa C

Information

BOOKSHOPS

Lewy Libros (Junín 229) Stocks travel guides and has a selection of maps and used English- and German-language paperbacks.
Los Amigos del Libro (Ingavi 114) Slim pickings.

DANGERS & ANNOYANCES

You should beware of bogus immigration officials at the bimodal bus/train station. Carry your passport or, better yet, a legible photocopy at all times: if you're caught without ID, you may have to pay a 'fine' of about US$50 and waste several hours at the police station while someone shuffles paperwork.

IMMIGRATION

The main immigration office is north of the center, opposite the zoo's entrance. If you're arriving overland from Paraguay, pick up a length-of-stay stamp here. There's a more convenient office at the **train station** (10am-noon & 1:30-7pm) but the station is plagued by phony officials; use as a last-ditch resort. The most reliable office is at the airport. For those braving the Death Train, exit stamps are reportedly only available at the Brazilian frontier – ask around before departing.

For information on consulates in Santa Cruz, see p244.

INTERNET ACCESS

The arcade at España and Junín has a couple of swell Internet places.
Meganet (cnr España & Florida; US$0.50 per hr; until midnight) The best – hyper-fast and air-conditioned.

LAUNDRY

España Lavandería (España 160) Same-day service (drop off before noon) costs around US$1 per kilo.
Lavandería La Paz (La Paz 42) Central, efficient wash 'n' dry.
Nameless lavandería (Bolívar 490) Central, efficient wash 'n' dry – ring the bell.

MONEY

Casas de cambio Aleman (Plaza de Septiembre) Changes cash or traveler's checks (2% to 3% commission).
Banco de Santa Cruz (Junín) Cash advances and ATM. Less efficient but may have slightly better rates for changing traveler's checks.
Magri Turismo (03-334-5663; Warnes & Potosí) American Express agent but doesn't cash traveler's checks.

TELEPHONE

Punto Entel (Junín 284) Near the plaza; has land lines.
Telecom Stores (along Bolívar) Cheap international Internet calls.

TOURIST OFFICES

Departamental de Turismo (03-336-8901) Inside the Palacio Prefectural on the plaza's north side, along with the **tourist police** (03-322-5016).
Fundación Amigos de la Naturaleza (FAN; 03-355-6800; www.fan-bo.org; Km7-1/2, Carretera a Samaipata) Dispenses information on Amboró and Noel Kempff Mercado national parks. West of town (micro 44) off the old Cochabamba road.
Main tourist office (03-336-9595; 8:30am-noon & 2:30-6:30pm Mon-Fri) On the ground floor of the Casa de la Cultura, on the plaza's west side.

Sights
There are few attractions in Santa Cruz proper, but the shady **Plaza 24 de Septiembre** with its **cathedral** is an attractive place to relax by day or night. On the plaza's west side, the **Casa de la Cultura Raúl Otero Reiche** (☺ 8am-noon & 3-5:30pm Mon-Fri) hosts free music and contemporary art exhibitions in addition to theater performances.

Locals relax around the lagoon at **Parque El Arenal**, north of the center, where there's a handicrafts market and paddle boats for rent. Overlooking the lagoon is the **Museo Etno-Folklórico** (admission US$0.75), with a small collection of regional anthropological finds. Don't dawdle here at night.

The underfunded **Jardín Zoológico** (☎ 03-342-9939; adult/child US$0.65/$0.40; ☺ 9am-7pm) is worth a visit. The collection includes South American birds, mammals and reptiles – don't miss the sloths. Take any 'Zoologico' *micro* from the center.

Discover the wonder of sequins, big hats and gold rope trim at the cathedral's air-conditioned **Museo de Arte Sagrado** (Plaza 24 de Septiembre; admission US$0.65), with a dazzling collection of gowns, jewels and spooky paintings upstairs.

Sleeping
In a bind, there are several cheap, indistinguishable places to crash across from the new bimodal terminal. Otherwise, there are few stellar options.

Alojamiento Santa Bárbara (☎ 03-332-1817; Santa Bárbara 151; r per person US$2.65) Clean and friendly, with sunny courtyard. Despite poor beds it's popular with young Bolivians and travelers – be wary of using the safe-deposit boxes.

Residencial Bolívar (☎ 03-334-2500; Sucre 131; s/d US$6/11) A perennial travelers' favorite. Clean and bright with inviting courtyard hammocks and excellent communal showers. Call ahead or arrive early.

GETTING INTO TOWN

The bimodal bus/train station is beyond easy walking distance, but you can get to the center in about 10 minutes on *micro* 12 or 20. The airport minibus service (US$0.60, 30 minutes), stops along the 1st *anillo* every 20 minutes from 5:30am; a taxi costs US$6.

Residencial Ballivián (☎ 03-332-1960; residencial ballivian@yahoo.es; Ingavi; r per person US$4) A reasonable but run-down alternative, with a nice courtyard and decent rooms with shared bath.

Hotel Bibosi (☎ 03-334-8548; Junín 218; bibosi@ scbbs-bo.com; s/d US$13/20) Hotel Bibosi has helpful staff, a great rooftop view and clean, spacious rooms with fan, phone and bath. Breakfast included.

Hotel Amazonas (☎ 03-333-4583; Junín 214; leanch@ bibosi.scz.entelnet.bo; s/d US$10/14) Next door to Amazonas, with bath, TV and phone. Breakfast is included.

Hotel Copacabana (☎ 03-332-9924; Junín 217; s/d US$20/24) The new HI affiliate has small, well appointed disco '70s doubles with ceiling fans (US$4 extra for quiet remote-controlled air-con), firm beds and breakfast. Avoid the noisy ground-floor rooms and bargain during slow periods.

Eating
For simple, cheap eats, try Mercado La Ramada or the mall-like Mercado Los Pozos with food stalls on the top floor. The latter is especially good for unusual tropical fruits. Mercado Florida is wall-to-wall blender stalls serving exquisite juices and fruit salads for US$0.50.

Café Sofia (Velasco 40) Great coffee, juices and pastries are made fresh here.

La Romana (cnr Velasco & Mercado) Bakes stunning breads, croissants and addictive sweet buns.

Mama Rosa (Velasco near Av Irala) Serves feisty pizzas, chicken and big *almuerzos*.

El Galeón Peruano (Ingavi at Colón; lunch US$2, mains US$3) A local favorite lunch spot.

Pizzería Marguerita (☎ 03-337-0285; cnr Libertad & Junín) On the north side of the plaza, this pizzería does good pasta, pizzas and salads.

Bar Hawaii (Calle Ayacucho & Beni) A block east of the plaza, this expansive place is popular for ice cream, sundaes, cakes, light meals and good coffee. Similar in menu and style are **Dumbo's** (Calle Ayacucho 247) and **Kivón** (Calle Ayacucho 267), both a block west of the plaza.

Bar El Tapekuá (Ballivián & La Paz) The cozy Swiss/Bolivian-owned place serves pub grub from Wednesday to Saturday evenings, with live music (US$1 cover) most nights.

La Bella Napoli (Independencia 635; pizza & mains US$5-7) Serves fine pasta dishes in a rustic

BOLIVIA

BOLIVIA

SANTA CRUZ

INFORMATION
Argentine Consulate.....................1 D3
Banco de Bolivia (ATM)...............2 D4
Banco de Santa Cruz (ATM)........3 D3
Brazilian Consulate.......................4 C1
Cabinas Telefonicas & Internet
 Phone Calls..............................5 D3
Casa de Cambio Aleman...............6 D3
Departamental de Turismo......(see 17)
Entel Office..................................7 D4
España Lavandería........................8 C3
Honorary German Consul..............9 E4
Internet Arcade........................(see 16)
Lavanderiá La Paz.......................10 D3
Lavandería..................................11 E3
Lewy Libros................................12 C3
Los Amigos del Libro..................13 D4
Magri Turismo............................14 E4
Main Tourist Office....................15 D3
Meganet.....................................16 C3
Prefectura...................................17 D3
Punto Entel................................18 C3
Tourist Police.........................(see 17)

SIGHTS & ACTIVITIES   p229
Casa de la Cultura Raúl Otero
 Reiche..................................(see 15)
Museo de Arte Sagrado...............19 D3
Museo Etno-Folklórico...............20 D2

SLEEPING   p229
Alojamiento Santa Bárbara.........21 C3
Hotel Amazonas.........................22 C3
Hotel Bibosi...............................23 C3
Hotel Copacabana......................24 C3
Residencial Ballivián..................25 D3
Residencial Bolívar....................26 D3

EATING   pp229–31
Bar El Tapekuá...........................27 D1
Bar Hawaii.................................28 D3
Café Sofia..................................29 C3
Cozzolisi Pizza...........................30 D5
Crêperie El Boliche.....................31 D3
Dumbo's................................(see 33)
El Galeón Peruano.....................32 C4
Kívón..33 C3
La Bella Napoli..........................34 D5
La Casona..................................35 D3
La Romana.................................36 C4
Mama Rosa................................37 D5
Naturalia Natural Foods
 Grocery..................................38 D4
Pizzería Marguerita....................39 D3
Yorimichi...................................40 C1

DRINKING   p231
Bar Irlandés...............................41 D3
BED Disco..................................42 D3
Clapton's Blues Bar....................43 D3
La Cueva del Ratón....................44 D5
Victory Bar................................45 C3

ENTERTAINMENT   p231
Cine Arenal................................46 D2
Cine Palace................................47 D3

TRANSPORT   p232
AeroSur Office...........................48 C5
Expreso Samaipata Taxis.............49 C6
LAB Office.................................50 D4
Minibus to Airport.....................51 B3
Old Bus Terminal.......................52 C5
Taxis to Montero & Buena
 Vista.......................................53 C5

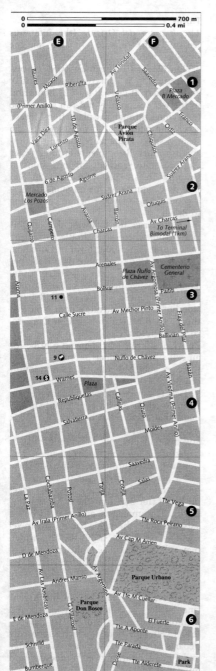

barn and at outside tables. It's good but pricey and requires a dark walk back to the center at night.

Cozzolisi Pizza (Independencia & La Riva) A reliable, cheap outpost of the national chain.

Yorimichi (☎ 03-334-7717; Av Busch 548; around US$10) Near the Campus Universitario, you should give this place a try if you're craving sashimi or udon. It's not cheap, but it's sushi.

Crêperie El Boliche (☎ 03-333-9053; Arenales 135) A splash-out option serving dinner only.

La Casona (☎ 03-337-8495; Arenales 222; mains US$5-7; ✆ Mon-Sat) German-run, 'am I really in Bolivia?' restaurant where the salad has arugula and the chicken balsamic vinaigrette.

Naturalia (Independencia 452) Organic grocery store with a wide selection of healthy goodies.

Drinking

Check Friday's *El Deber* for bar, club and music listings. Most places only jump after 11pm on weekends.

Victory Bar (cnr Junín & 21 de Mayo) Upstairs and a block from the plaza, this is one of several central sociable watering holes.

Bar Irlandés (cnr Junín & 24 de Septiembre) There's a hopping scene most nights and good plaza views from the balcony bar.

La Cueva del Ratón (La Riva 173) Barnlike bar with big-screen music videos.

Clapton's Blues Bar (Murillo at Arenales; ✆ Sat & Sun) Has fun live acts.

There's a full quota of discos and karaoke bars, but most are outside the central area, so you'll need a taxi (US$1 to US$2). Cover charges start at US$2 and drinks are expensive. In the center, try **BED** (Beni & Arenales). On Av San Martín in Barrio Equipetrol ask around for Mad, Varadero or Number One.

Entertainment

Cine Palace (Plaza 24 de Septiembre; admission US$2.25) First-run flicks are shown nightly at this cinema on the plaza's west side.

Cine Arenal (Beni 555; admission US$2) Older releases play at this cinema facing Parque Arenal.

Aqualand (☎ 03-385-2500; www.aqualand.com.bo in Spanish; half-day US$5-8, full-day US$7.50-10; ✆ 10am-5:30pm Fri-Sun) For a real splash, dive into this water park near the airport.

BOLIVIA

Getting There & Around

AIR

The modern **Viru Viru International Airport** (VVI; ☎ 181), 15km north of the center, handles domestic and international flights. Many flights from neighboring countries and Europe come direct to Santa Cruz and are worth considering if you're arriving from sea level and don't want to spend days acclimatizing in La Paz.

AeroSur (☎ 03-336-4446; Irala at Colón) and **LAB** (☎ 03-334-4896; Chuquisaca 126) both have flights most days to Cochabamba, La Paz, and Sucre, with connections to most other Bolivian cities. **TAM** (☎ 03-353-2639) flies direct to La Paz (US$67) on Monday morning and a couple more times a week from El Trompillo, the military airport south of the center. It also flies direct to Puerto Suárez (US$65) a couple of times a week.

BUS

The new, full-service **Terminal Bimodal** (☎ 03-348-8382; terminal fee US$0.40), a combo long-distance bus and train station, is 1.5km east of the center, just before the 3rd *anillo* at the end of Av Brasil. *Micro* No 4 heads straight to the center.

There are several daily morning and evening *bus cama* services to Cochabamba (US$4 to US$6, 10 to 12 hours), with connections to La Paz, Oruro, Sucre, Potosí and Tarija. Direct overnight buses to Sucre (ie, not via Cochabamba) depart between 5pm and 8pm (US$6 to US$12, 16 to 25 hours) and to La Paz (US$8 for *bus cama*) at 7pm.

There are also afternoon and night buses south to Yacuiba and Bermejo, with connections to Salta. Buses leave daily (during the dry season) at 6:30am for the grueling trip through the Chaco to Asunción (around US$50, 30 hours minimum). There are morning and evening buses to Vallegrande. At least four companies have nightly buses at 7pm and 7:30pm for Concepción (US$4, six hours) and San Ignacio de Velasco on the Mission Circuit; 31 del Este has additional daytime departures.

To Trinidad and beyond, several buses leave between 5:30pm and 8pm nightly (US$4 to US$10, at least 12 hours). Although the road is theoretically open year-round, the trip gets rough and buses are often rescheduled in the rainy season.

TRAIN

The *Expreso del Oriente* (the infamous Death Train) runs to Quijarro, on the Brazilian border, daily (except Sunday) at 3:30pm (2nd/1st/Pullman-class US$7/15.50/20), returning at 7pm Wednesday, Friday and Monday. It takes at least 21 hours and in the wet season may not run at all. The train chugs through soy plantations, forest, scrub and oddly shaped mountains to the steamy, sticky Pantanal region on the Brazilian frontier. Bring plenty of food, water and mosquito repellent for long stops in swampy areas. This train stops in San José de Chiquitos on the mission circuit – a good place to layover before continuing to Brazil.

Trains arrive the following day in Quijarro, from where taxis shuttle passengers to the Brazilian border town of Corumbá, 2km away. Don't pay more than US$2 per person for the taxi – rip-offs are common. You can change dollars or bolivianos into *reais* (pronounced *hay*-ice) on the Bolivian side, but the boliviano rate is poor. Note that there's no Brazilian consulate in Quijarro, so if you need a visa, get it in Santa Cruz. Bolivian officials may demand a bribe for an exit stamp at Quijarro. From Corumbá there are good bus connections into southern Brazil, but no passenger trains.

Tickets can be scarce and carriages are often so jammed with people and contraband that there's nowhere to sit. Ticket windows (supposedly) open at 8am, and you can only buy your ticket on the day of departure, when lines reach Cuban proportions. An adventurous alternative is to stake out a place in the *bodegas* (boxcars) of a mixed train and purchase a 2nd-class ticket on board (for 20% over the ticket-window price). The upmarket option is to buy a 1st-class ticket through a Santa Cruz travel agent – try **Bracha** (☎ 03-346-7795), which may still have an office in the train station. You must pay a national/international departure tax (US$1.35/4) after purchasing your ticket.

Rail service to Yacuiba (on the Argentine border) is a reasonably quick and comfortable *ferrobus* (3rd/2nd/1st-class $5/6.50/13.50, nine hours), which supposedly departs at 5pm on Monday, Wednesday and Friday, returning on Wednesday and Sunday at 8pm.

AROUND SANTA CRUZ
Samaipata
Amid the gorgeous foothills of the Cordillera Oriental, Samaipata (1660m) is a popular weekend destination and the perfect place to chill for a few days. You can also visit **Parque Nacional Amboró** from here. Highlights include the **Pajcha waterfalls**, giant ferns and the **Cueva Mataral cave paintings**. Forays to the site of **Che's last stand** near Vallegrande are also possible.

The area's main attraction is **El Fuerte** (adult/child US$2.65/$1.35 plus local tax US$0.25; 9am-5pm), a pre-Inca ceremonial site on a hilltop 10km southeast of town, from where there are memorable views. Hitching from the village is easiest on weekends, but it also makes a fine day-long walk. Taxis for the round trip, including a 1½-hour stop at the ruins, cost US$7.50 for up to four people. The ticket for the ruins is also valid for admission to the small **archaeological museum** (admission US$0.65; 8:30am-12:30pm & 2:30-6:30pm) in town.

Several agencies organize trips to nearby attractions (US$10 to US$50 per person per day), including the recommended **Bolviajes** (at La Víspera; www.samaipata.info); biologist **Michael Blendinger** (/fax 03-944-6186; mblendinger@cotas.com.bo; Bolívar s/n, in front of museum) for orchid, birding and full-moon tours in English and German; **Amboro Tours** (03-944-6293; erickamboro@yahoo.com) for park trips and bike rentals; and Olaf and Frank at **Roadrunners** (03-944-6153/93; dustyroad99@hotmail.com) for self-guided treks with GPS and guided tours in German- and English-speaking to Amboró and El Fuerte. Spanish-speaking Samaipata native **Don Gilberto** (03-944-6050) lived inside what is now the national park for many years.

Sernap has a new office 1km outside of town on the road to Santa Cruz. The **FAN office** (www.fan-bo.org; Sucre & Murillo) can arrange trips to the community of La Yunga at the edge of the park.

SLEEPING
Paola Hotel (03-944-6903; SW cnr of plaza; r per person US$2, with bath & breakfast US$3.35) This family-run place has clean rooms and good beds plus a shared kitchen, laundry sinks, cheap meals and a terrace overlooking the plaza.

Palacio del Ajedrez (Chess Club; 03-944-6196; paulin-chess@cotas.com.bo; Bolívar s/n; r per person US$5,

s/d with bath US$8/13) Next to the archaeology museum, has new rooms with good beds and a café. It's a great place to pick up a game of chess with Bolivian junior champions.

Residencial Chelo (03-944-6014; Sucre s/n; r per person US$2-4) A basic place just off the plaza with rooms with shared bath.

Residencial Kim (03-944-6161; r per person US$2.65, with bath US$3.35) A quiet, sunny place a half block north of the plaza.

Mi Casa Hostería (r per person US$3.35, with bath US$4.65) This recently restored place behind the church has a lush garden and rustic, clean rooms with a view.

Hostal Saldías (03-944-6023; Bolívar s/n; r per person US$1.35, with bath US$1.65) The funkiest acceptable option.

Mama Pasquala's (campsites per person US$3.50, cabins US$5) The basic camping at this secluded spot, 500m upstream from the river ford en route to El Fuerte, is a deal.

Achira Resort (in Santa Cruz /fax 03-352-2288; Km 113; camping per person US$3.50, cabañas per person US$5) This family-oriented complex, eight kilometers east of Samaipata, has cabins, campsites, baths, showers, a restaurant, pool and game room.

At Km 100, Las Cuevas is another recommended camping spot with good swimming.

EATING
La Pascana (southeast corner of plaza) This spot has cheap, filling *almuerzos*.

Bishus (south side of plaza) Bichus has a full bar, all manner of coffee drinks and Bolivian set lunch for US$1.35.

SPLURGE!

The lovely Dutch-run **Finca La Víspera** (/fax 03-944-6082; www.lavispera.org; camping per person with tent US$4, without tent US$5, guesthouse per person US$7, with bath US$12) is a 15-minute walk southwest of the plaza. The organic farm's accommodation options range from grassy camping and firm beds in the 'backpacker's house' to charming self-contained guesthouses. The food, views and hospitality are superb and the owners rent horses and organize Amboró treks. Bring a flashlight as there are no streetlights between the village and the farm.

La Chakana (Southern Cross; west side of plaza) This European-owned place is the main gringo hangout. It has vegetarian options, omelets and pancakes.

Landhaus (☯ Thu-Sun evening) For excellent gourmet fare, try this place below the airplane near the northern end of town.

Latina Café A cozy place for a meal or a drink.

GETTING THERE & AWAY

Four-passenger Expreso Samaipata Taxis (US$3.35 per person, 2½ hours) leave Santa Cruz for Samaipata when full from the corner of Chávez Ortíz and Solis de Olguin. Alternatively, a small bus departs from Av Grigotá at the third *anillo* at 4pm daily (US$2, three hours). From Samaipata, **shared taxis** (☎ 03-944-6133/6016) depart for Santa Cruz from the gas station on the highway. *Micros* leave from the plaza daily around 4:30am and between noon and 5pm on Sunday.

Parque Nacional Amboró

The village of Buena Vista, two hours (100km) northwest of Santa Cruz, is a staging point for trips into the spectacular forested northern lowland section of Parque Nacional Amboró. For a park entry permit and cabin reservations visit Buena Vista's **Sernap office** (☎ 03-932-2054), two blocks south of the plaza. Just off the plaza, **Amboró Tours** (☎ 03-932-2093) organizes tours starting at US$45 per person, per day.

There are several places to sleep and eat and camping is also possible in the park. Try the basic **Residencial Nadia** (☎ 03-932-2049), where the owner is a good source of park information. For food, Los Franceses has a savory menu and a jovial trés-French owner who loves to chat.

Jesuit Mission Circuit

From the late 17th century, Jesuits established settlements called *reducciones* in Bolivia's eastern lowlands, building churches, establishing farms and instructing the Indians in religion, agriculture, music and crafts in return for conversion and manual labor. A circuit north and east of Santa Cruz takes in some old mission sites, with buildings in various stages of reconstruction or decay. Santa Cruz agencies organize tours, or you can do it on your own with more time to spare. Food and lodging (sometimes basic) are available in most of the towns. Heading clockwise from Santa Cruz are the following:

San Ramón Noteworthy only as a transport junction.

San Javier The oldest mission (1692), recently and sympathetically restored.

Concepción An attractive town with a gaudy restored 1756 church.

San Ignacio de Velasco Much less attractive but still worth a stop, with an elaborate mission and church (1748) demolished in 1948.

San Miguel A sleepy town with a beautiful church (1721) that has been painstakingly restored.

Santa Ana A tiny village with a rustic 1755 church.

San Rafael's The 1740s church is noted for its fine interior.

San José de Chiquitos Has an impressive 1748 stone church situated in a complex of mission buildings.

If you opt to take the train, it's best to catch it to San José first and then proceed counterclockwise. You can also take buses to San Ignacio, visit the villages south of there as an excursion, skip San José and return by bus from San Ignacio or continue to Brazil. Renting a car in Santa Cruz is another option, affordable between a few people.

AMAZON BASIN

Bolivia's slice of the Amazon Basin encompasses half of the country's entire territory and is a prime place to experience pristine rain forest. Though the Brazilian Amazon is known worldwide and is more easily accessible, much of it is heavily populated and degraded. By contrast, northern Bolivia remains relatively undeveloped, though population pressures are increasing. Also, Bolivia's waterways are narrower, so riverboat travelers usually see more wildlife.

Cargo vessels that ply the northern rivers lack passenger comforts or scheduled services. Most passages include meals, but the menu is monotonous and the water comes straight from the river. Cabins are rarely available; bring a hammock or a sleeping bag. Other necessities are snacks, a water container, water purification tablets, antimalarials and mosquito protection. The most popular river routes are Puerto Villarroel to Trinidad on the **Río Ichilo** and Trinidad to Guayaramerín on the **Río Mamoré**. Tour agencies offer comfortable river trips focused on wildlife watching.

THE AMAZON BASIN

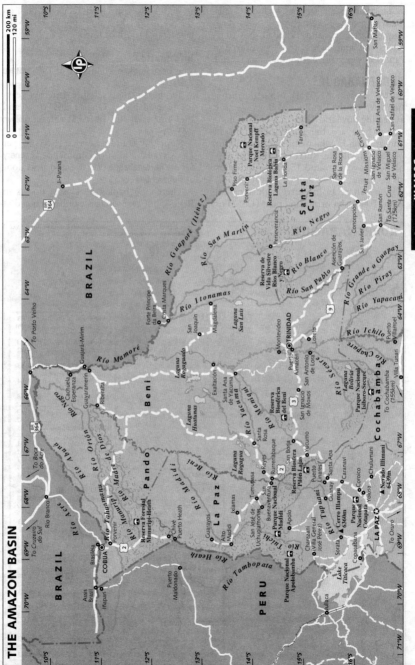

0   200 km
0   120 mi

BOLIVIA

BRAZIL

PERU

Santa Matías

San Ramón
To Santa Cruz
(125km)

Parque Nacional
Noel Kempff
Mercado

Reserva Biológica
Laguna Bahía

Porvenir
Piso Firme
La Florida

Santa Rosa
de la Roca

Jesuit Missions Circuit

Santa Ana de Velasco
San Rafael de Velasco
San Ignacio
de Velasco
San Miguel
de Velasco

Concepción

Ji-Paraná

BR
364

Reserva de
Vida Silvestre
Ríos Blanco
y Negro

Asención de
Guarayos

San Javier

**Santa
Cruz**

Rio San Martín

Rio Negro

Forte Principe
da Beira

Costa Marques

Rio Guaporé (Iténez)

Perseverancia

Rio Blanco

Rio San Pablo

Rio Grande o Guapay

Rio Piray

Rio Yapacani

To Porto Velho

Guajará-Mirim

Rio Itonamas

San
Joaquín

Magdalena

Laguna
San Luis

Montevideo

Loreto

TRINIDAD

Rio Ichilo

Puerto
Villarroel

Cachuela
Esperanza

Rio Mamoré

Guayaramerin

Riberalta

Laguna
Rogaguado

Exaltación

Puerto
Almacén

San Antonio
de Lora

Rio Sécure

Villa Tunari

Rio Chapare

To Cochabamba
(155km)

Cochabamba

Río Negro

Rio Orton

Rio Abuná

Rio Madre de Dios

Beni

Santa Ana
de Yacuma

Laguna
Huatunas

Rio Yacuma

Rio Maniqui

Santa
Rosa

Reserva
Biosférica
del Beni

San Ignacio
de Moxos

Parque Nacional
Isiboro-Sécure

Laguna
Bolivia

Pando

La Paz

Rio Branco

To Boca
do Acre

Rio Acre

Puerto
Maldonado

Rio Tahuamanu

Rio Manuripi

Rio Madidi

Rio Beni

Laguna
Rogagua

Reserva Biósfera
Pilón Lajas

San
Borja

Yucumo

San
Ignacio

Rio Heath

Rio Tambopata

Rio Tuichi

Parque Nacional
Apolobamba

Ullaca

Lake
Titicaca

Copacabana

Sorata

Charazani
Villa General
José Pérez

Apolo

San José de
Uchupiamonas

Buenaventura

Guarayos

Alto
Madidi

Chivé
Puerto Heath

Reserva Forestal
Manuripi-Heath

Porvenir

COBIJA

Brasiléia

Assis
Brasil

Iñapari

Rio Branco

To Cruzeiro
do Sul

BR
364

Ixiamas

Tumupasa

San
Buenaventura

Reyes

Rurrenabaque

Puerto
Linares

Guanay

Caranavi

Coroico

Yolosa

Chulumani

Santa Ana

Rio Tipuani

Cerro Illampu
6360m

Nevado Illimani
6439m

Parque
Nacional
Cotapata

LA PAZ

To Oruro

Rio Grande o Guapay

9

3

2

2

Towns with air services include Cobija, Guayaramerín, Reyes, Riberalta, Rurrenabaque, San Borja and Trinidad, but timetables vary and flights are often delayed or canceled, especially during the rainy season.

RURRENABAQUE

'Rurre' (elevation 105m), a bustling frontier town on the Río Beni, is Bolivia's most appealing lowland settlement. The main draws here are the surrounding forests and grasslands, which still support vibrant pockets of wildlife. Rurre's permanent population hovers around 15,000, with almost an equal number of annual visitors.

You can relax in Rurre's glorious **Balenario El Ambaibo** swimming pool (US$2) or,

in high season, at Hotel Tacuara's pool on the plaza. Or take a short uphill trek to the **mirador** just south of town.

Information

The best book exchange is at **Café Motacú** (Santa Cruz).

Temperamental satellite Internet service is available at **Camila's** (US$2 per hr) and the American-run **Libería Sembrador** (Bolivar; US$1.60 per hr).

Same-day laundry service (US$1.35 per kg) is available at the recommended **Laundry Service Rurrenabaque** (Vaca Diez) and next door at **Number One** (Vaca Diez).

There's no bank (the closest one is in Reyes), but cash dollars can be changed at

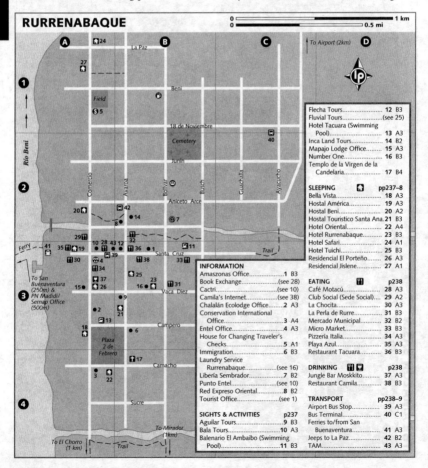

RURRENABAQUE

Flecha Tours	12 B3
Fluvial Tours	(see 25)
Hotel Tacuara (Swimming Pool)	13 A3
Inca Land Tours	14 B2
Mapajo Lodge Office	15 A3
Number One	16 B3
Templo de la Virgen de la Candelaria	17 B4

SLEEPING	pp237–8
Bella Vista	18 A3
Hostal América	19 A3
Hostal Beni	20 A3
Hostal Touristico Santa Ana	21 B3
Hotel Oriental	22 A4
Hotel Rurrenabaque	23 B3
Hotel Safari	24 A1
Hotel Tuichi	25 B3
Residencial El Porteño	26 A3
Residencial Jislene	27 A1

EATING	p238
Café Motacú	28 A3
Club Social (Sede Social)	29 A2
La Chocita	30 A3
La Perla de Rurre	31 B3
Mercado Municipal	32 B2
Micro Market	33 B3
Pizzería Italia	34 A3
Playa Azul	35 A3
Restaurant Tacuara	36 B3

INFORMATION	
Amazonas Office	1 B3
Book Exchange	(see 28)
Cactri	(see 10)
Camila's Internet	(see 38)
Chalalán Ecolodge Office	2 A3
Conservation International Office	3 A4
Entel Office	4 A3
House for Changing Traveler's Checks	5 A1
Immigration	6 B3
Laundry Service Rurrenabaque	(see 16)
Libería Sembrador	7 B2
Punto Entel	(see 10)
Red Expreso Oriental	8 B2
Tourist Office	(see 1)

SIGHTS & ACTIVITIES	p237
Aguilar Tours	9 B3
Bala Tours	10 A3
Balenario El Ambaibo (Swimming Pool)	11 B3

DRINKING	p238
Jungle Bar Moskkito	37 A3
Restaurant Camila	38 B3

TRANSPORT	pp238–9
Airport Bus Stop	39 A3
Bus Terminal	40 C1
Ferries to/from San Buenaventura	41 A3
Jeeps to La Paz	42 B2
TAM	43 A3

Cactri (Santa Cruz), next to Bala Tours. Some tour agencies change traveler's checks (4% to 5% commission), as will **Red Expreso Oriental** (Aniceto Arce), which can also handle overseas money orders. Tours can usually be paid for with credit cards and *simpático* bars, agencies and hotels may be willing to facilitate cash advances.

In addition to the **Punto Entel** (Santa Cruz & Comercio) there are several Entel card phones around town.

Keep an eye out for the new municipal tourist office a couple of doors down from the Amaszonas office, which plans to maintain a complaint registry and publish a qualitative ranking of Rurre's tour agencies, compiled from visitor evaluations. Sernap's **Parque Nacional Madidi's office** (☎ 03-892-2540), where independent visitors must pay a US$5.35 entrance fee, is across the river in San Buenaventura.

Extend your stay at **immigration** (☎ 03-892-2241) on the plaza's northeast corner.

Tours

Jungle and pampas tours are Rurre's bread and butter, but there's a number of emerging community-based ethno-ecotourism projects that also merit mention.

Jungle tours typically include a motorized canoe trip up the Beni and Tuichi rivers, with camping and rain-forest treks along the way. You'll most likely sleep on the river sand beneath a tarp surrounded by a mosquito net.

If you're more interested in watching wildlife, opt for a **pampas tour**, which visits the wetland savannas northeast of town. They include rewarding guided walks and daytime and evening animal-viewing boat trips. For a few bucks more, fly-in variations include horse riding and stays at ranches.

Rain, mud and insects make the wet season (especially January to March) unpleasant for jungle tours particularly, but some agencies have jungle camps set up for good wildlife watching at this time.

Another outstanding alternative is the community-run **Mapajo Lodge** (☎ 03-892-2317; www.mapajo.com; around US$35 per person per day) which offers all-inclusive (comfy individual cabañas, *simpático* guides, great food) overnight visits to the Mosetén-Chimán community of Asuncíon, three hours upriver

from Rurre just below the confluence of the Riós Beni and Tuichi on the Rió Quiquibey, inside the Pilon-Lajas Biosphere Reserve. Activities include bow-and-arrow fishing, rain-forest trekking and unchoreographed visits to the community.

Inquire at the tourist office about day-long **Day for the Community tours** (www.rurren abaquebolivia.com; tours US$25), which visit four altiplano immigrant colonies and highlight alternative sustainable development efforts, including agroforestry, organic foods and *artesanía* projects.

The community-based **San Miguel project** is Conservation International's latest foray into ethno-ecotourism, with plans for seven self-contained cabañas, community visits and interpretive trails tracing traditional Tacana hunting routes. It's scheduled to be up and running by mid-2004 – inquire at CI's office on the plaza in Rurre.

Jungle and pampas tours officially cost US$30 per person per day, including transport, guides and food. These trips are excellent values and most people are very happy with them, but the guide's treatment of the wildlife depends on your group's demands. A lack of drinking water and abundance of biting insects are the main complaints. All guides should be licensed – ask to see *la autorización*. Keep in mind that most guides speak Spanish and no agency has a sterling record. It's worth seeking out a local guide who can provide insight on the fauna, flora, indigenous people and forest lore. Most agencies have offices on Avaroa. Frequently-recommended agencies include the following:

Águilar Tours (☎ 03-892-2476/2478; Avaroa & Vaca Diez)

Bala Tours (☎ 03-892-2527; www.mirurrenabaque .com; Comercio s/n) Has its own jungle camp and pampas lodge away from other agencies.

Flecha Tours (☎ 03-892-2476/2478; Avaroa & Santa Cruz)

Fluvial Tours/Amazonia Adventures (☎ 03-892-2372; at Hotel Tuichi) The longest-running agency, with a good reputation.

Inca Land Tours (in La Paz ☎ 02-220-0829, ☎ 772-35261; Aniceto Arce & Avaroa) Best-known for touting at El Alto airport with snakes wrapped around them.

Sleeping

Hostal Touristico Santa Ana (☎ 03-892-2399; Avaroa btwn Diez & Campero; r per person US$3.35, with bath

BOLIVIA

US$5.35) Clean rooms, plus a couple of peaceful, leafy courtyards with hammocks under a shady *palapa* (thatched, palm-leaf-roofed shelter with open sides).

Hotel Oriental (☎ 03-892-2401; S side of Plaza 2 de Febrero; r per person US$3.35, s/d with bath US$9.25/13.35) A sedate, good-value place with garden hammocks and a book exchange.

Bella Vista (☎ 03-892-2328; NW cnr of Plaza 2 de Febrero; r per person US$2, with bath US$3.35) Korean-run, clean and simple place without matrimonial beds.

Hotel Rurrenabaque (☎ 03-892-2481, in La Paz ☎ 02-279-5917; Vaca Diez; s/d US$4.65/9, with bath & breakfast US$8/13.35) Friendly and far from the maddening late-night disco crowd. It has basic but clean rooms with fan and hammocks on a breezy balcony.

Residencial Jislene (☎ 03-892-2552; Comercio near Beni; r per person from US$2, with bath US$3) The Caldera family's riverside retreat makes up what it lacks in creature comforts with hospitality. The rooms with private bath are new, and the simple rooms with shared facilities have good fans and mosquito nets. Good meals are available on request.

Residencial El Porteño (☎ 03-892-2558; cnr Comercio & Vaca Diez; r per person US$3.35, with bath US$4.65) Good value, with clean albeit old-fashioned rooms and free all-you-can-drink starfruit juice.

Hotel Tuichi (☎ 03-892-2372; Avaroa s/n; dm US$2, r per person US$4-5.50) Classic, party-hearty backpackers' haunt with plain, decent rooms.

Hostal América (☎ 03-892-2413; r per person US$2.65) This basic *hostal* is worthwhile only for its top-floor rooms, which afford a superb view of the river and the hills.

Mid-range places include the **Hostal Beni** (☎ 03-892-2408; Comercio at Arce; s/d US$4/6.65, d with bath & TV US$9.35), near the river; and **Hotel Safari** (☎ /fax 03-892-2210; s/d US$20/30), which includes breakfast in its rates.

Eating

The market is full of good *comedores* and juice bars.

Café Motacú (Santa Cruz s/n; ☼ 8:30am-noon & 6:30-9:30pm Mon-Sat) Great cakes, pastries and coffee are homemade here.

Restaurant Camila (Santa Cruz s/n) A travelers hotspot with a full menu.

Restaurant Tacuara (Santa Cruz & Avaroa s/n) Opposite Camila, this friendly place is popular, especially for its lasagna.

Pizzería Italia (Commercio s/n) Has good you-know-what and delivers to Jungle Bar Moskkito next door.

Club Social (Commercio s/n; lunch US$1.25, mains US$2-4) A pleasant place to enjoy à la carte lunch or dinner, and cocktails from outdoor tables overlooking the river.

Several fish restaurants occupy shelters along the riverfront – they're all pretty good; try Playa Azul or La Chocita.

La Perla de Rurre (Bolivar s/n) The best bet for superlative service and fresh, tasty US$3 fish dinners.

Drinking

Jungle Bar Moskkito (Commercio) Rurre doesn't see a lot of action, but there are a couple of bars and discos, of which Jungle Bar Moskkito is the undisputed travelers' favorite. Happy hour runs 7pm to 9pm, you can request tunes from an extensive CD library and there are pool tables and darts. The English-speaking staff are super-friendly and it's the spot to form tour groups.

Otherwise, you can choose from a host of drunken, locals-only pool halls, thumping discos and karaoke bars.

Getting There & Around
AIR

The number of flights to Rurre is increasing all the time, but it's still easy to get sold out. Have your tour agency purchase your return ticket in advance. If you're stuck, try using the Reyes airport, an hour northeast by bus or shared taxi.

In theory, **TAM** (☎ 03-892-2398) has flights between La Paz and Rurre (US$50) on Monday, Wednesday, Thursday, Saturday and Sunday. In reality, they're often canceled in the rainy season. **Amaszonas** (☎ 03-892-2472) attempts to fly to and from La Paz (US$50) twice daily, but isn't any more reliable. SAVE offers charter flights (US$65) a couple of times a week; book through Inca Land Tours in La Paz. The humble airport is a grassy landing strip a few kilometers north of town. Airport transport costs US$0.65, whether by bus (which drops you in the center), packed taxi or, if you're traveling light, on the back of a breezy motorcycle.

BOAT

Thanks to the new Guayaramerín road, there's little cargo transport down the Río

Beni to Riberalta. Taxi ferries across the Río Beni to San Buenaventura (US$0.15) sail frequently all day long.

BUS

When the roads are dry, buses run daily between Rurrenabaque and La Paz (US$6.65, 16 hours), but it's best to break the journey at Coroico, which is 'only' 14 hours from Rurre – actually, you get off at Yolosa, 7km west of Coroico, where there's an *alojamiento* if you get stranded. Caranavi, with a couple of basic places to sleep and eat, is a less desirable stopover option and the transfer point for minibuses to Guanay (US$2, 2½ hours).

Twice-weekly buses to Trinidad (US$17, *bus cama* US$22, 16 to 17 hours) go via Yucumo, San Borja and San Ignacio de Moxos when the road is clear. There are also daily buses to Riberalta and on to Guayara-merín (US$22, 18 hours to three days!).

AROUND RURRENABAQUE
Parque Nacional Madidi

The Río Madidi watershed contains one of South America's most intact ecosystems. The most ecologically sound section is protected by Parque Nacional Madidi, which encompasses a huge range of wildlife habitats, from torrid rain forests to Andean glaciers at 5500m. Researchers have observed 1110 bird species – over 10% of the world's known avian species.

The park's populated bits along the Río Tuichi have been designated as a Unesco biosphere reserve, which allows indigenous people to continue with their traditional practices – hunting, fishing and utilizing other forest resources. So far, the Quechua, Araona and Tacana communities are coexisting successfully with the park.

Logging activity along the Tuichi and at the northern end of the park, however, is a major threat, with rogue timbermen still felling mahogany, cedar and other valuable trees. A proposed dam project has been slated for the Bala Gorge area for years, just upstream from Rurre, which would flood vast tracts of rain forest, destroy settlements and obliterate native flora and fauna. The kibosh appears to have been put on the dam, but a more pressing threat is the proposed road from Apolo to Ixiamas, which would bisect the park.

GETTING THERE & AWAY

Those erring on the side of adventure can visit the park's fringes independently, but must first register with the Sernap office in San Buenaventura and must be accompanied by an authorized guide. Penetrating deeper into Madidi will depend on luck, patience and the generosity of your hosts. Ixiamas-bound trucks, *micros* and buses depart daily from San Buenaventura for Tumupasa, 50km north of Rurre. From Tumupasa, it's a 30km trek through the forest to San José de Uchupiamonas. Travelers making this trip should be entirely self-sufficient. For a taste of just how wrong things can go, read *Return from Tuichi* (also published as *Heart of the Amazon*) by Yossi Ghinsberg.

TRINIDAD

The city of La Santísima Trinidad (the Most Holy Trinity) was founded on June 13, 1686, by Padre Cipriano Barace as the southern Beni's second Jesuit mission. 'Trini' (population 78,000; elevation 235m) may be the Beni's capital but it's still a backwater and the open sewers are a serious turnoff. Its main attraction is as a stopover between Santa Cruz and Rurrenabaque or as a place to organize a Mamoré river trip.

Sightseeing is limited to the locals maniacally zipping around the plaza on motorcycles – for US$1.35 per hour you can rent a bike and join the action. Or, there's a movie theater if you're up for something less

---

SPLURGE!

The Bolivian Amazonia's most notable community-based ecotourism project is **Chalalán Ecolodge**, fronting a wildlife-rich lagoon five hours up the Río Tuichi from Rurre. It has successfully provided employment for the Tacana villagers of San José de Uchupiamonas since 1995 and is often cited as a model for sustainable tourism. It's an incredible place. An all-inclusive three-day, two-night stay costs around US$280 per person (minimum four people). For details, visit the office in **Rurrenabaque** (☎ 03-892-2419; www.chalalan.com in Spanish; Avaroa btwn Diez & Campero) or contact América Tours (p177) in La Paz.

hazardous. Imbibers, keep an eyelid peeled for the forthcoming Drunken Boat Bar.

The lovely Ignaciano Indian village of **San Ignacio de Moxos** is 89km west of Trinidad. The annual **Fiesta del Santo Patrono de Moxos** (July 31) attracts revelers from around the country. Arrange boat passage at Puerto Barador.

Information

The **tourist office** (☎ 03-462-1722) seems to move all the time but isn't really worth tracking down. Full Internet, in a shopping center on the west side of the plaza, offers lickety-split access for US$0.50 an hour.

Tours

Tour agencies are along Av 6 de Agosto: **Fremen Tours** (☎ 03-462-1834/2276; www.andes -amazonia.com; Barace 332) and **Moxos Turismo** (☎ 03-462-1141; turmoxos@sauce.entelnet.bo; 6 de Agosto 114) both offer live-aboard boat trips.

Sleeping

Hotel Copacabana (☎ 03-462-2811; Villavicencio 627; r per person US$4, with bath US$9) A friendly, good-value hotel with basic rooms with fans.

Hostal Palmas (☎ 03-462-6979; La Paz 365; s/d US$3.25/5.35, with bath US$10/15.50) Nice rooms with TV and air-con upgrades for a bit extra.

Residencial Brasilia (☎ 03-462-1685; 6 de Agosto 46; r per person US$2) It's a dump, but hey, some of the beds are decent.

Hotel Paulista (☎ 03-462-0018; 6 de Agosto & Suárez; r per person US$2.65, s/d with bath US$8/13.50) This central hotel is welcoming but tat-tered. For this much money, you're better off at **Hotel Monte Verde** (☎ 03-462-2750; 6 de Agosto 76; s/d with bath US$10/13.50), where rooms have phones. Cable TV and air-con are extra.

Eating

Trinidad is cattle country, so beef is boun-tiful. If budget is the priority, hit the Mer-cado Municipal, where for a pittance you can try the local specialty, *arroz con queso* (rice with cheese), plus shish kebabs, *yuca*, plantain and salad. The plaza is home to plenty of popcorn, ice cream and *refresco* vendors.

La Casona (east side of plaza) This welcoming place has sidewalk tables, good pizza and inexpensive *almuerzos*.

Habib's (east side of plaza) A tiny place next to La Casona which grills great kebabs.

Carlitos Across the plaza inside the Social Club, aloof Carlitos dishes up popular *almuerzos* atop white tablecloths.

Heladería Kivón (east side of plaza) Serves snacks, light meals and full breakfasts – head upstairs for good views of the cruis-ing scene.

Feeling fishy? Drop anchor at **El Moro** (Bolívar & Velasco).

Getting There & Around

AIR

The airport is northwest of town, a feasi-ble half-hour walk from the center. Taxis charge around US$1 per person, but if you don't have much luggage, a motorcycle taxi is only US$0.65. **AeroSur** (☎ 03-462-3402/5443; 6 de Agosto s/n), **LAB** (☎ 03-462-1277; La Paz 322) and **TAM** (☎ 03-462-2363; Bolívar at Santa Cruz) fly (seasonally) several times a week to Cochabamba, La Paz, Santa Cruz, Riberalta and Guayaramerín.

BOAT

The closest ports are Puerto Almacén, on the Ibare, 8km southwest of town, and Puerto Barador, on the Río Mamoré, 13km in the same direction. Trucks charge around US$1 to Puerto Almacén and US$2 to Puerto Barador.

If you're looking for river transportation north to Guayaramerín or south to Puerto Villarroel, inquire at the Transportes Fluvi-ales office at Puerto Almacén. The Guayara-merín run takes up to a week (larger boats do it in three to four days) and costs around US$20, including food. To Puerto Villarroel, smaller boats take eight to 10 days.

BUS

The rambling bus terminal is on Rómulo Mendoza. Road conditions permitting, *flotas* depart nightly for Santa Cruz (normal/*cama* US$2.50/5.50, eight to 10 hours). Several companies head daily to Rurrenabaque (US$7, 12 hours) via San Borja. Flota Copa-cabana beelines direct to La Paz (US$24 *bus cama*, 30 hours) at 5:30am. Frequent *micros* and *camionetas* run to San Ignacio de Moxos (US$2.50, three hours) from the small terminal on Av La Paz. There are also daily dry-season departures to Riberalta and Guayaramerín.

RIBERALTA

Riverside Riberalta (population 76,000; elevation 115m), located on the Brazilian border, is Bolivia's major northern frontier settlement. Once a rubber-production center, its (legal) economy now revolves around – yawn – processing Brazil nuts. Since the opening of the La Paz road, Riberalta's importance as a Río Beni port has faded.

Riberalta is cursed with open sewers, but otherwise it's a laid-back kind of place. In the paralyzing heat of the day, strenuous activity is suspended in favor of lounging in the nearest hammock. Chilling in the Club Náutico's sparkling **riverside pool** (two blocks north of the plaza) is highly touted. On fine evenings backlit by technicolor sunsets, the plaza buzzes with cruising motorcycles, while the anomalous **cathedral** stands watch.

There are a couple banks and Internet is supposedly coming soon.

Sleeping

Residencial Los Reyes (☎ 03-852-8018; r per person US$3, with bath US$4) Near the airport, this spotless place is quite nice.

Residencial El Pauro (Salvatierra s/n; r per person US$2) A classic cheapie, where threadbare rooms offer good views of the neighbors.

Palace Hotel (☎ 03-852-2680; Molina 79; s/d with bath & fan US$4.50/7.50) Most rooms are cinderblock basic, but the hammocks, cafeteria and enthusiastic *señorita* add atmosphere.

Hotel Amazonas (☎ 03-852-2339; r with bath per person US$7) A good lower mid-range choice.

Hotel Campos (☎ 03-852-3691; Moreno s/n; r per person US$12) A few blocks from the plaza, modern Hotel Campos has it all – big doubles with air-con, TV, bath and breakfast.

Eating

The market is the best place to cobble together a classic breakfast of *api*, juice and *empanadas*. The most interesting eateries are around the plaza.

La Cabaña de Tío Tom Located on the plaza, it has good coffee, ice cream, juices and sandwiches as well as red meat and fish dishes.

Club Social Serves inexpensive set lunches, superb filtered coffee, drinks and fine desserts nearby La Cabaña de Tío Tom.

Pizzería Al Paso Has nice outdoor tables and good pizza, around the plaza.

Club Social Japonés Near the market, this place serves up Bolivian and Amazonian dishes – sorry, no sushi.

Churrasquería El Pahuichi Also near the market, there's al fresco seating and an endless supply of Beni beef here.

Getting There & Away

AIR

The airport is 15 minutes from the main plaza. **AeroSur** (☎ 03-852-2798) and **LAB** (☎ 03-852-2239; Martinez 77) have several flights a week to Trinidad, connecting to La Paz, Santa Cruz and Cochabamba, plus a few per week to Cobija. **TAM** (☎ 03-852-2646) flies from La Paz to Riberalta (US$88) Tuesday and Thursday, returning to La Paz on Wednesday and Saturday. TAM's 20-minute, five-times-a-week Riberalta to Guayara flight (US$20) is surely one of Bolivia's cheapest thrills.

BOAT

Boats up the Río Beni to Rurrenabaque are rare, but run when the road becomes impassable in the wet season. If you do find something, budget on US$20 to US$30 for the five- to eight-day trip. For details, visit the port captain's office.

BUS & CAMIÓN

Several *flotas* run daily between Riberalta and Guayaramerín (US$2.75, three hours), or wait for a car or *camión* along Av Héroes del Chaco. Daily *flotas* from Guayaramerín to Cobija, Rurrenabaque and La Paz stop at Riberalta en route. Sindicato de Guayaramerín has a 10am Thursday departure for Trinidad (US$25 – don't ask how long).

GUAYARAMERÍN

Bolivia's back door to Brazil (population 40,000; elevation 130m) lies on the banks of the Río Mamoré in the country's top right corner. The frontier settlement thrives on legal and illegal trade with the Brazilian town of Guajará-Mirim, just across the river. A new road links Guayaramerín to Riberalta, connecting south to Rurrenabaque and La Paz, and west to Cobija.

Information

Exchange US dollars at the Banco Mercantil, Hotel San Carlos or the *casas de cambio* on the plaza. For traveler's checks, try Bank Bidesa.

Sleeping & Eating

Hotel Santa Ana (☎ 03-855-3900, 25 de Mayo 611; r per person US$2.65, with bath US$3.50) The quiet, shady hotel is an attractive choice. Opposite is mellow Hotel Litoral, which charges the same.

Hotel Plaza Anexo (on the plaza; r per person US$3.25) This place has clean rooms with bath and a pleasant ambience.

Hotel Central (☎ 03-855-3911; s/d US$2.50/3.50) Down the block from Hotel Plazo Anexo, this is a friendly, well-kept place.

Hotel San Carlos (☎ 03-855-3555; s/d US$15/25) If you can't cope with the heat, seek refuge in the swimming pool and air-con here.

On the plaza, both Snack Paulita and Restaurant Los Bibosis serve yummy juices, burgers, beer and snacks. Rincón is a popular Brazilian place. Prices (quoted in *reais*) are generally higher than in Bolivian establishments.

Getting There & Away

BOLIVIA

Air

LAB (☎ 03-855-3540; 25 de Mayo 652) lands several times a week in Riberalta and Trinidad, with La Paz connections. **AeroSur** (☎ 03-855-3731) serves Cobija a couple times a week. **TAM** (☎ 03-855-3924) flies twice a week from La Paz to Riberalta and Guayaramerín, twice a week to Trinidad and once a week to Cochabamba and Santa Cruz.

Boat

Boats up the Río Mamoré to Trinidad leave almost daily (around US$25 with food). The notice board at the port captain's office lists departures.

Bus & Taxi

The bus terminal is at the western end of town, beyond the market. Buses go to Riberalta (US$2.75, three hours) several times daily. Shared taxis to Riberalta (US$4.25, two hours) leave from the terminal when they have four passengers. In the dry season, several foolhardy *flotas* head out daily for Rurrenabaque (US$18, 14 to 36 hours) and La Paz (US$21.50, 30 to 60 hours). There are four buses weekly to Cobija (US$14, 16 hours) and Trinidad (US$25, 22 hours).

BRAZILIAN BORDER CROSSING

Frequent motorboats (around US$1) link the two ports. There are no restrictions on shuttling between Guayaramerín and Guajará-Mirim, but if you intend to travel farther into Brazil or are entering Bolivia here, you must pick up entry-exit stamps.

Bolivian immigration (☆ 8am-8pm) is by the dock. In Brazil, have your passport stamped at the Polícia Federal. A yellow-fever vaccination certificate is officially required to enter Brazil.

BOLIVIA DIRECTORY

ACCOMMODATIONS

Bolivian accommodations are among South America's cheapest, though price and value are hardly uniform. Prices in this chapter reflect standard, mid-season rates – the high season (late June to early September) can be 10% to 20% more and rates can double during fiestas. Negotiate during slow times; a three-night stay may net you a deal. Room availability is only a problem during fiestas (especially Carnaval in Oruro) and at popular weekend getaway destinations (eg Coroico).

The Bolivian hotel-rating system divides accommodations into *posadas, alojamientos, residenciales, casas de huéspedes, hostales* and *hoteles*. This rating system reflects the price scale and, to some extent, the quality.

Posadas are the cheapest roof and bed available. They're frequented mainly by campesinos visiting the city, cost between US$1 and US$2 per person and provide minimal cleanliness and comfort. Shared bathrooms are stanky, some have no showers and hot water is unknown.

A step up are *alojamientos*, which are marginally better and cost slightly more, but are still pretty basic. Bathing facilities are almost always communal, but you may find a hot shower. Some are clean and tidy, while others are disgustingly seedy. Prices range from US$1.25 to US$5 per person.

Quality varies at *residenciales, casas de huéspedes* and *hostales*. Most are acceptable, and you'll often have a choice between shared or private bath. Plan on US$5 to US$20 for a double with a private bath, about 30% less without. Bolivia also has plenty of mid-range places and five-star luxury resorts when you're ready for a splurge.

Hostelling International (HI; www.hostellingbolivia .org) has recently affiliated with a network of 14 existing accommodations. Atypical of 'hostelling' networks in other countries, members range from two-star hotels to camping grounds, but few offer traditional dorm beds or amenities like shared kitchens. HI membership cards may be for sale at HI Sucre Hostel, the flagship hostel in Sucre (p220), or at Valmar Tours in La Paz (p177).

Bolivia offers excellent camping, especially along trekking routes and in remote mountain areas. Gear is easily rented in La Paz and popular trekking towns like Sorata. There are few organized campsites, but you can pitch a tent almost anywhere outside populated centers. Remember, however, that highland nights are often freezing. Theft from campers is reported in some areas – inquire locally about security.

ACTIVITIES

Hiking, trekking and mountaineering (see p250) in and around the Andes top the to-do list – opt for camping or fishing if you're feeling lazy. The most popular treks (see p189) begin near La Paz, traverse the Cordillera Real along ancient Inca routes and end in the Yungas. Jungle treks (see p237) are all the rage around Rurrenabaque.

An increasing number of La Paz agencies organize technical climbs and expeditions into the Cordillera Real and to Volcán Sajama (6542m), Bolivia's highest peak. Skiing (p179) is also possible – but not for long as the glacier is retreating, so hurry.

Mountain biking (p179) options around La Paz are endless. Kayaking and whitewater rafting are gaining popularity near Coroico and in the Chapare.

Countrywide, Bolivians are loco for karaoke, racquetball, billiards, chess, cacho and fútbol.

BOOKS

For in-depth coverage, pick up a copy of Lonely Planet's *Bolivia*.

If walking is on your itinerary, add LP's *Trekking in the Central Andes*, or *Trekking in Bolivia*, by Yossi Brain, to your kit. *Bolivian Andes*, by Alain Mesili, is a must for madcap mountaineers.

For a good synopsis of Bolivian history, politics and culture, check out *Bolivia in Focus*, by Paul van Lindert. If you'll be in-country for the long haul, pick up *Culture Shock! Bolivia*, by Mark Cramer.

The Fat Man from La Paz: Contemporary Fiction from Bolivia, a collection of 20 short stories edited by Rosario Santos, makes great roadside reading.

English-, German- and French-language publications are available from Los Amigos del Libro, in La Paz, Cochabamba and Santa Cruz. The books are pricey, but there's ample selection of popular novels, Latin American literature, dictionaries and coffeetable books.

Bibliophiles rejoice: used-book outlets and dog-eared book exchanges are now commonplace along the Bolivian part of the gringo trail.

BUSINESS HOURS

Few businesses open before 9am, though markets stir awake as early as 6am. Cities virtually shut down between noon and 2pm, except markets and restaurants serving lunch-hour crowds. Most businesses remain open until 8pm or 9pm. If you have urgent business to attend to, don't wait until the weekend as most offices will be closed.

CLIMATE

Bolivia has a wide range of altitude-affected climatic patterns. Within its frontiers, every climatic zone can be found, from stifling rain-forest heat to arctic cold.

Adventurers will likely encounter just about every climatic zone, no matter when they visit. Summer (November to April) is the rainy season. The most popular, and arguably most comfortable, time to visit is during the dry winter season (May to October).

The high season is from June to September, and the low season runs from October to May.

The rainy season lasts from November to March or April (summer). Of the major cities, only Potosí receives regular snowfall (between February and April), though flakes are possible in Oruro and La Paz toward the end of the rainy season. On the altiplano and in the highlands, subzero nighttime temperatures are frequent.

Winter in Cochabamba, Sucre and Tarija is a time of clear skies and optimum temperatures. The Amazon Basin is always hot

BOLIVIA

and wet, with the drier period falling between May and October. The Yungas region is cooler but fairly damp year-round.

For more information and climate charts, see the South America Directory chapter (p1028).

DANGERS & ANNOYANCES

Bolivia is a comparatively mellow travel destination, but certain dangerous and/or annoying instances may arise. First, there's a strong tradition of social protest – demonstrations are a weekly occurrence. These are usually peaceful, but police occasionally use force and tear gas to disperse crowds. The Bolivian workforce is heavily unionized and work stoppages by bus drivers, teachers and others can affect travelers. *Bloqueos* (roadblocks) and strikes by transportation workers often lead to long delays.

The rainy season means flooding, landslides and road washouts, which means more delays. Getting stuck overnight behind a slide is common: you'll be a happier camper with ample food, drink and warm clothes on hand.

Emergencies

Emergency service numbers in major cities are:

Ambulance (☎ 118)
Fire department (☎ 119)
Police (RadioPatrol; ☎ 110)

Scams

Psst, hey, my friend: one popular scam involves a shill spilling something on you and while you or they are wiping it off, another lifts your wallet or slashes your pack. The ruse often starts with a fat luggi or phlegm ball being spat on your shoulder; the perpetrator may be an innocent granny or young girl.

After dark outside dodgy bus stations, beware of hopping into shared cabs with strangers – several violent assaults have been reported in the past few years, usually targeting female travelers.

In general, travel in Bolivia is as safe or safer than in neighboring countries.

DISABLED TRAVELERS

The sad fact is that Bolivia's infrastructure is ill-equipped for disabled travelers. You will, however, see locals overcoming all manner of challenges and obstacles while making their daily rounds. If you encounter difficulties yourself, you're likely to find locals willing to go out of their way to lend a hand.

EMBASSIES & CONSULATES

See relevant city and town maps for the position of embassies and consulates.

Embassies & Consulates in Bolivia

Argentina Cochabamba (☎ 04-422-9347; Blanco 0-929); La Paz (Map pp174-5; ☎ 02-241-7737; embarbol@caoba.entelnet.co; Aspiazu 497); Santa Cruz (Map pp230-1; ☎ 03-334-7133; Junín 22) Above Banco de la Nación Argentina facing Plaza 24 de Septiembre; Tarija (Map p210; Ballivián N-699; ☑ 8:30am-12:30pm Mon-Fri) Issues visas and entry stamps; Villazón (Map p213; Saavedra 311; ☑ 9am-1pm Mon-Fri)

Australia La Paz (Map pp174-5; ☎ 02-244-0459; Av Ancieto Arce 2081, Edificio Montevideo)

Brazil Cochabamba (Map pp216-17; ☎ 04-425-5860; Edificio Los Tiempos II, 9th fl); Guayaramerín (☎ /fax 03-855-3766; Beni & 24 de Septiembre; ☑ 9am-1pm & 3-5pm Mon-Fri); La Paz (Map pp172-3; ☎ 02-244-0202; embajadabrasil@acelerate.com; cnr Av Ancieto Arce & Gutierrez, Edificio Multicentro); Santa Cruz (Map pp230-1; ☎ 03-334-4400; Av Busch 330)

Canada La Paz (Map pp172-3; ☎ 02-241-5021; lapaz@dfait-maeci.gc.ca; Sanjinés 2678, Edificio Barcelona, 2nd fl)

Chile La Paz (☎ 02-278-3018; Siles 5843, Obrajes); Santa Cruz (☎ 03-343-4272; Calle 5 Oeste 224, Barrio Equipetrol)

Colombia La Paz (☎ 02-278-6841; emcol@acelerate.com; Calle 9 No 7835, Calacoto)

Ecuador La Paz (Map pp174-5; ☎ 02-233-1588; mecuabol@entelnet.bo; Av 16 de Julio s/n, Edificio Herrmann, 14th fl)

France La Paz (☎ 02-278-6114; amfrabo@ceibo.entelnet.bo; cnr Siles 5390 & Calle 8, Obrajes); Santa Cruz (☎ 03-343-3434; 3rd Anillo btwn Alemana & Mutualista)

Germany Cochabamba (☎ 04-425-4024; Edificio La Promontora, 6th fl); La Paz (Map pp172-3; ☎ 02-244-0066, 244-1133/66; www.embajada-alemana-bolivia.org; Av Ancieto Arce 2395); Santa Cruz (Map pp230-1; ☎ 03-336-7585; dconsscz@cotas.com.bo; Nuflo de Chavez 437); Tarija (Map p210; ☎ 04-664-2062; Campero 321)

Italy Santa Cruz (☎ 03-353-1796; El Trompillo, Edificio Honnen, 1st fl)

Netherlands La Paz (Map pp172-3; ☎ 02-244-4040; nllapos@caoba.entelnet.bo; Av 6 de Agosto 2455, Edificio Hilda, 7th fl); Santa Cruz (☎ 03-358-1866; Aguilera 300, 3rd Anillo)

Paraguay Cochabamba (☎ /fax 04-425-0183; Edificio El Solar, 16 de Julio 211); La Paz (Map p172-3;

☎ 02-243-3176; embapar@acelerate.com; Av 6 de Agosto at Pinilla, Edificio Illimani)
Peru Cochabamba (☎ 04-424-6210; Pando 1143, Recoleta); La Paz (Map pp172-3; ☎ 02-244-1250; embbol@caoba.entelnet.bo; Guachalla 300, Sopocachi); Santa Cruz (☎ 03-336-8979; Edificio Oriente, 2nd fl)
Spain Santa Cruz (☎ 03-332-8921; Santiesteban 237)
UK La Paz (Map pp172-3; ☎ 02-243-3424; www.embassy ofbolivia.co.uk; Av Ancieto Arce 2732)
USA Cochabamba (Map p216-17; ☎ 04-425-6714; Torres Sofer, Oquendo E-654, Rm 601); La Paz (Map pp172-3; ☎ 02-243-3812; lapaz.usembassy.gov; Av Ancieto Arce 2780); Santa Cruz (☎ 03-333-0725; Guemes Este 6B, Barrio Equipetrol)

Bolivian Embassies & Consulates Abroad

Bolivia has diplomatic representation in most South American countries and also in the following countries:
Australia Honorary Consul (☎ 02-9247 4235; 305/4 Bridge St, Sydney NSW 2000)
Canada Embassy (☎ 613-236-5730; www.bolivia embassy.ca; 130 Albert St, Suite 416, Ottawa, Ontario K1P 5G4)
France Embassy (☎ 01-42 24 93 44; embolivia.paris@ wanadoo.fr; 12 Ave du President Kennedy, F-75016 Paris)
Germany Embassy (☎ 030 2639 150; www.bolivia.de; Wichmannstr. 6, PLZ-10787 Berlin)
UK Embassy (☎ 020-7235 4248/2257; www.embassyof bolivia.co.uk; 106 Eaton Square, London SW1W 9AD)
USA Consulate General (☎ 202-232-4828, 202-232-4827; bolivianconsulatewdc@starpower.net; 2120 L St NW, Suite 335, Washington, DC 20037)
Embassy (☎ 202-483-4410, 202-328-3712; www.bolivia -usa.org; 3014 Massachusetts Ave NW, Washington, DC 20008)

FESTIVALS & EVENTS

Bolivian fiestas are invariably of religious or political origin and typically include lots of music, drinking, eating, dancing, processions, rituals and general unrestrained behavior. Water balloons (gringos are sought-after targets!) and fireworks (all too often at eye-level) figure prominently.
Alasitas (Festival of Abundance; January 24) Best in La Paz and Copacabana.
Fiesta de la Virgen de Candelaria (Feast of the Virgin of Candelaria; first week in February) Best in Copacabana.
Carnaval (February/March – dates vary) All hell breaks loose in Oruro during La Diablada (see p197).
Semana Santa (Easter Week; March/April – dates vary)
Fiesta de la Cruz (Festival of the Cross; May 3) May or may not have anything to do with the cross Jesus hung on.

Corpus Christi (May – dates vary)
El Gran Poder (Great Power of Our Lord Jesús; late May or early June) In La Paz.
Fiesta del Santo Patrono de Moxos (Festival of the Patron Saint of Moxos; July 31) In San Ignacio de Moxos.
Fiesta de la Virgen de Urcupiña (Festival of the Virgen de Urcupiña; August 15–18) Best in Quillacollo.
Chu'tillos (late August) In Potosí.

FOOD & DRINK
Bolivian Cuisine

Generally, Bolivian food is palatable, filling and ho-hum. Figuring prominently, potatoes come in dozens of varieties, most of them small and colorful. *Chuño* or *tunta* (freeze-dried potatoes) often accompany meals and are gnarled looking and tasting, though some people love them. In the lowlands, the potato is replaced by *yuca* (cassava).

Beef, chicken and fish are the most common proteins. Campesinos eat *cordero* (mutton), *cabrito* (goat), llama and, on special occasions, *carne de chancho* (pork). The most common altiplano fish is *trucha* (trout), which is farmed in Lake Titicaca. The lowlands have a great variety of fresh-water fish, including *sábalo*, *dorado* and the delicious *surubí* (catfish). Pizza, fried chicken, hamburgers and *chifas* (Chinese restaurants) provide some variety.

The tastiest Bolivian snack is the *salteña*. These delicious meat and vegetable pasties originated in Salta, Argentina, but achieved perfection in Bolivia. They come stuffed with beef or chicken, olives, egg, potato, onion, peas, carrots and other surprises – watch the squirting juice. *Empanadas*, pillows of dough lined with cheese and deep fried, are toothsome early morning market treats.

Standard meals are *desayuno* (breakfast), *almuerzo* (lunch, the word normally refers to a set meal served at midday) and *cena* (dinner). For *almuerzo*, restaurants – from backstreet cubbyholes to classy establishments – offer bargain set meals consisting of soup, a main course and coffee or tea. In some places, a salad and simple dessert are included. *Almuerzos* cost roughly half the price of à la carte dishes – less than US$1 to US$5, depending on the class of restaurant. Reliable market *comedores* (basic eateries) and street stalls are always the cheapest option.

BOLIVIA

Some popular Bolivian set-meal standbys include the following:

Chairo Lamb or mutton stew with potatoes, *chuño* and other vegetables.

Fricasé Stew of various meats with ground corn.

Milanesa Breaded and fried beef or chicken cutlets.

Pacumutu Grilled beef (or sometimes fried chicken) chunks.

Pique a lo macho Heap of chopped beef, hot dogs and French fries topped with onions, tomatoes and whatever else.

Saice Spicy meat broth.

Sajta Chicken served in hot pepper sauce.

Silpancho Thinly pounded beef schnitzel.

Drinks
ALCOHOLIC DRINKS

Bolivia's wine region is centered around Tarija. The best – and most expensive – label is La Concepción's Cepas de Altura (from the world's highest vineyards), which sells for under US$10 a bottle. The same wineries also produce *singani,* a powerful spirit obtained by distilling grape skins and other by-products. The most popular cocktail is *chuflay,* a refreshing blend of *singani,* 7-Up (or ginger ale), ice and lemon.

Bolivian beers aren't bad either; popular brands include Huari, Paceña, Sureña and Potosina. Beer is ridiculously fizzy at the higher altitudes, where it can be difficult to get the brew from under the foam.

The favorite alcoholic drink of the masses is *chicha cochabambina,* obtained by fermenting corn. It is made all over Bolivia, especially in the Cochabamba region. Other versions of *chicha,* often nonalcoholic, are made from sweet potato, peanuts, cassava and other fruits and vegetables.

NONALCOHOLIC DRINKS

Beyond the usual coffee, tea and hot chocolate, *mate de coca* (coca leaf tea) is the most common boiled drink. *Api,* a sweet, hot drink made of maize, lemon and cinnamon and tasting like manna on bitter mornings, is served in markets; look for *mezclado,* mixed yellow and purple *api.* Major cola brands are available, as well as locally produced soft drinks of varying tastiness; grapefruit-flavored Wink is a winner. Don't miss *licuados,* addictive fruit shakes blended with milk or water. Be sure to request the *llapa* or *aumento* – the second serving remaining in the blender.

Zumos are pure fruit and vegetable juices. *Mocachinchi* is a ubiquitous market drink made from dried fruit and more sugar than water.

GAY & LESBIAN TRAVELERS

Naturally, homosexuality exists in Bolivia and is fairly widespread among rural indigenous communities. It's also perfectly legal (though the constitution does prohibit same-sex marriages), but the overwhelmingly Catholic society tends to both deny and suppress it. To be openly gay limits vocational and social opportunities and may cause family ostracism. The Bolivian government merely defines homosexuality as 'a problem.' Gay bars and venues are limited to the larger cities, but due to bashings and police raids, they come and go with some regularity. As for hotels, sharing a room is no problem as long as you don't request a double bed. The bottom line is that discretion is still in order.

Gay rights lobby groups are active in La Paz (MGLP Libertad), Cochabamba (Dignidad) and most visibly in progressive Santa Cruz. In June 2003, Santa Cruz organization La Comunidad Gay, Lésbica, Bisexual y Travestí (GLBT) replaced their fourth annual Marcha de Colores on Día del Orgullo Gay (Gay Pride Day, June 26) with a health fair called Ciudadanía Sexual in an effort to gain wider public acceptance. In La Paz, watch for flyers advertising drag performances by La Familia Galan, the capital's most fabulous group of cross-dressing queens.

HEALTH

Sanitation and hygiene are not Bolivia's strong suits, so pay attention to what you eat. Most tap water isn't safe to drink; stick to bottled water if your budget allows (your bowels will thank you). Carry iodine if trekking and avoid the nasty Viscachani brand, which is orifice-puckering.

The altiplano lies between 3000m and 4000m, and many visitors to La Paz, Copacabana and Potosí will have problems with altitude sickness. Complications like cerebral edema have been the cause of death in otherwise fit, healthy travelers. Diabetics should note that only the Touch II blood glucose meter gives accurate readings at altitudes over 2000m.

Bolivia is officially in a yellow fever zone, so a vaccination is recommended – it may be obligatory for return or onward travel. If you'll be in the lowlands, take precautions against malaria. Anyone coming from a yellow-fever infected area needs a vaccination certificate to enter Bolivia. Many neighboring countries, including Brazil, also require anyone entering from Bolivia to have proof of a yellow-fever vaccination. If necessary, a jab can often be administered at the border.

While medical facilities might not be exactly what you're used to back home, there are decent hospitals in the biggest cities and passable clinics in most towns. Still, in remote parts of the country you'll be hard pressed to find decent medical care. For more information on altitude sickness and other critical matters, see the Health chapter (p1053)

HOLIDAYS

On major holidays, banks, offices and other services are closed and public transport is often bursting at the seams; book ahead if possible.

Año Nuevo (New Year's Day; January 1)
Día del Trabajador (Labor Day; May 1) Watch out for dynamite in plazas.
Días de la Independencia (Independence Days; August 5-7)
Día de la Raza (Columbus Day; October 12)
Día de Todos los Santos (All Souls' Day; November 2)
Navidad (Christmas Day; December 25)

Not about to be outdone by their neighbors, each department has its own holiday: February 22 in Oruro, April 1 in Potosí, April 15 in Tarija, May 25 in Chuquisaca, July 16 in La Paz, September 14 in Cochabamba, September 24 in Santa Cruz and Pando, and November 18 in Beni.

INTERNET ACCESS

Nearly every corner of Bolivia has a cybercafé. Rates run from US$0.25 to US$3 per hour. In smaller towns, check the local Entel office for access.

INTERNET RESOURCES

A thorough, searchable index of Bolivian sites, in Spanish, can be found at www.bolivia.com.
Bolivia.com (www.bolivia.com in Spanish) Current news and cultural information.

Bolivia Web (www.boliviaweb.com) Makes a good starting point, with good cultural and artistic links.
Enlaces Bolivia (www.enlacesbolivia.net) Good collection of up-to-date links.
Lanic-Bolivia (www.lanic.utexas.edu/la/sa/bolivia) Outstanding collection of links from the University of Texas.

MAPS

Government topographical and specialty maps are available from the Instituto Geográfico Militar (IGM), with two offices in La Paz (see p171 for details). For Cordillera Real and Sajama trekking maps, the contour maps produced by Walter Guzmán are good. Good climbing maps are published by the Deutscher Alpenverein and distributed internationally. The excellent *New Map of the Cordillera Real*, published by O'Brien Cartographics, is available at various travelers' hangouts. O'Brien also publishes the *Travel Map of Bolivia*, which is about the best country map. South American Explorers (see p1034) distribute the O'Brien maps, plus maps of major cities.

MEDIA
Newspapers & Magazines

Bolivian towns with daily newspapers include Cochabamba (www.lostiempos.com in Spanish), La Paz, Potosí (www.elpotosi.net in Spanish) and Sucre (www.correodelsur.com in Spanish). The *Bolivian Times* (www.boliviantimes.com) is an accomplished (but on-again, off-again) English-language weekly. In La Paz and other gringo hangouts, look for the free *Llama Express* tourist newspaper. The *Miami Herald*, *International Herald Tribune* and major English-language news magazines are sold at Amigos del Libro outlets.

Radio

Bolivia has 125 radio stations broadcasting in Spanish, Quechua and Aymara. Recommended listening in La Paz includes noncommercial FM 96.5 for folk tunes and FM 100.5 if you're after a good English/Spanish-language pop mix. In Cochabamba, Radio Latina at FM 97.3 spins a lively mix of Andean folk, salsa and rock. For a good selection of recorded typical music, try Bolivia Web Radio (www.boliviaweb.com/radio).

TV

There are two government-run and several private TV stations. Cable (with CNN, ESPN and BBC) is available in most midrange and upmarket hotels.

MONEY

All prices listed in this chapter are in US dollars unless otherwise noted.

ATMs

Just about every sizable town has a *cajero automatico* (ATM) – look for the 'Enlace' sign. They dispense bolivianos in 50 and 100 notes (sometimes US$ as well) on Visa, Plus and Cirrus cards.

Cash

Finding change for bills larger than US$10 is a national pastime as change for larger notes seems to be scarce countrywide. When you're exchanging money or making big purchases, make sure you request small denominations. If you can stand waiting in the lines, most banks will break large bills.

Credit Cards

Brand-name credit cards, such as Visa, MasterCard and (less often) American Express, may be used in larger cities at better hotels, restaurants and tour agencies. Cash advances of up to US$1000 per day are available on Visa (and less often MasterCard) with no commission from Banco de Santa Cruz, Banco Mercantil and Banco Nacional de Bolivia. Travel agencies in towns without ATMs will often provide cash advances for clients for 3% to 5% commission.

Currency

Bolivia's unit of currency is the boliviano (B$), which is divided into 100 centavos. Bolivianos come in 10, 20, 50, 100 and 200 denomination notes; the coins are worth 10, 20 and 50 centavos. Often called pesos (the currency was changed from pesos to bolivianos in 1987), bolivianos are extremely difficult to unload once you're outside the country.

Exchange Rates

Exchange rates at press time included the following:

Country	Unit		Bol$ (boliviano)
Australia	A$1	=	5.61
Canada	C$1	=	6.01
euro zone	€1	=	9.18
Japan	¥100	=	7.29
New Zealand	NZ$1	=	4.90
United Kingdom	UK£1	=	13.43
United States	U$1	=	7.99

Exchanging Money

As a rule, visitors fare best with US dollars. Currency may be exchanged at *casas de cambio* and at some banks in larger cities. You can often change money in travel agencies and jewelry stores. *Cambistas* (street moneychangers) operate in most cities but only change cash dollars, paying roughly the same as *casas de cambio*. They're convenient after hours, but guard against rip-offs. The rate for cash doesn't vary much from place to place and there is no black-market rate. Currencies of neighboring countries may be exchanged in border areas and at *casas de cambio* in La Paz. Beware of mangled notes; unless both halves of a repaired banknote bear identical serial numbers, the note is worthless.

International Transfers

The fastest way to have money transferred from abroad is with Western Union. It has offices in all major cities but charges hefty fees. Your bank can also wire money to a cooperating Bolivian bank for a smaller fee, but it may take a couple of business days.

Traveler's Checks

The rate for traveler's checks (1% to 3% commission) is best in La Paz, where it nearly equals the rate for cash; in other large cities it's 3% to 5% lower, and in smaller towns it's sometimes impossible to change checks at all. American Express is the most widely accepted, though with persistence you should be able to change other major brands.

POST

Even small towns have post offices – some are signposted Ecobol (Empresa Correos de Bolivia). The post is generally reliable from major towns, but when posting anything important, pay the additional US$0.20 to have it certified.

Reliable free *lista de correos* (poste restante) is available in larger cities. Mail should be addressed to you c/o Poste Restante, Correo Central, La Paz (or whatever the city), Bolivia. Using only a first initial and capitalizing your entire last name will help to avoid any confusion. Mail is often sorted into foreign and Bolivian stacks, so those with Latin surnames should check the local stack.

A postcard costs US$0.65 to the USA, US$1.10 to Europe and US$1.25 to the rest of the world. A 2kg parcel will cost about US$50 to the USA or US$80 by air; to airmail it to Australia costs US$150. Posting by sea is s-l-o-w but considerably cheaper.

RESPONSIBLE TRAVEL

Traveling responsibly in Bolivia is a constant struggle. Trash cans (and recycling bins) are few and far between and ecological sensitivity is a relatively new – but growing – concept. Nearly every tour operator in the country claims to practice 'ecotourism,' but don't take their word for it. The best thing to do is grill agencies about their practices and talk to returning travelers to see if their experiences match the propaganda.

On the level of personal behavior, there are several things you can do to leave minimal impact (or maximize your positive impact) on the country. If you're taking a jungle or pampas tour around Rurrenabaque, request that your guide does not catch wildlife for the benefit of photo opportunities. Before visiting an indigenous community, ask if the guide is from the community or make sure that the agency has permission to visit. On the Salar de Uyuni, encourage drivers to haul out garbage that they pack in and to follow existing tire tracks to minimize damage to the fragile salt flats. In the Beni, don't eat fish out of season and resist the urge to purchase handicrafts made from endangered rain-forest species.

When it comes to dealing with begging, think twice about indiscriminately handing out sweets, cigarettes or money. Instead, teach a game, share a photograph of family or friends, or make a donation to an organization working to improve health, sanitation or education. Gifts of basic medical supplies or pens and notebooks are always appreciated in rural communities. If invited to someone's home for a meal, take something that won't undermine the local culture, like a handful of coca leaves or a few pieces of fruit.

SHOPPING

Compact discs and cassettes of *peñas*, folk and pop music make good souvenirs. Cassettes, however, may be low-quality bootlegs; higher-quality CDs cost around US$10. Selection is best in La Paz, but tapes are also available in the USA through the South American Explorers (see p1034).

Traditional instruments (eg *charangos, zampoñas*) are sold widely throughout the country but avoid buying ones made from endangered armadillos.

Bolivian woven ware is also a good buy. Touristy places such as the Witches Market (La Paz) and Tarabuco (near Sucre) have the greatest selection, but buying them here may be more expensive than buying direct from a craftsperson. Prices vary widely with the age, quality, color and extent of the weaving – a new and simple *manta* might cost US$20, while the finest antique examples will cost several hundred. Another good buy is alpaca goods, either finished or raw wool.

STUDYING

Sucre, Cochabamba and La Paz are all loaded with Spanish schools. Private lessons are starting to catch on in smaller retreats like Sorata and Samaipata. In bigger cities, it's also possible to find one-on-one music, weaving and other arts lessons. Instruction averages around US$5 an hour.

TELEPHONE

Entel, the Empresa Nacional de Telecomunicaciones, has telephone offices in nearly every town, usually open 7am to 11:30pm daily. Local calls cost just a few bolivianos from these offices. Punto Entels are small, privately-run outposts offering similar services. Alternatively, street kiosks are often equipped with telephones that charge B$1 for brief local calls. In some tiny villages, you'll find pay telephone boxes, but card phones are much more common. Cards come in both magnetic and computer-chip varieties, but phones only take one or the other. Both card types come in denominations of 10, 20, 50 and 100 bolivianos.

Two-digit area codes change by province – ☎ 02 for La Paz, Oruro and Potosí; ☎ 03 for Santa Cruz, Beni and Pando; and ☎ 04 for Cochabamba, Sucre and Tarija. In this book, telephone numbers are given with the area code. Drop the initial code if you're calling within a province. If calling from abroad, drop the 0 from the code. If ringing a local mobile phone, dial the 8-digit number; if the mobile is from another city, you must first dial '0' plus a two-digit carrier code.

Bolivia's country code is ☎ 591. The international direct-dialing access code is 00. Some Entel offices accept reverse-charge (collect) calls; others will give you the office's number and let you be called back. For reverse-charge calls from a private line, ring an international operator (beware that these calls are bank-breakers):

Canada (Teleglobe ☎ 800-10-0101)
UK (BT ☎ 800-10-0044)
USA (AT&T toll-free ☎ 800-10-1111; MCI ☎ 800-10-2222)

Calls from Entel offices are getting cheaper all the time to the USA (US$0.60 per minute), more expensive to Europe (US$1 per minute), Asia, Australia and Oceania (US$1.50 per minute). Reduced rates take effect at night and on weekends. Much cheaper Net2Phone Internet call centers, charging US$0.15 a minute to the USA and less than US$1 a minute to anywhere else in the world, are springing up in major cities.

See www.sittel.gov.bo/mennpn.htm for a thorough explanation (in Spanish) of the new numeration plan which took effect in late 2001.

TOILETS

Learn to live with the fact that toilet facilities don't exist in buses. Stanky *baños publicos* (public toilets) abound. Carry toilet paper with you wherever you go at all times! Don't put anything in the toilet that didn't come out of you unless you want to see it again.

TOURIST INFORMATION

The national tourist authority, Senatur, the Vice-Ministerio de Turismo, has an office in La Paz (see Map pp174-5). When functioning, its website is more helpful than the tourist office itself.

Municipal and departmental tourist offices are usually functional and, when open, distribute what little printed information is available.

TOURS

Tours are a convenient way to visit a site when you're short on time or motivation, and are frequently the easiest way to visit remote areas. They're also relatively cheap but the cost will depend on the number of people in your group. Popular organized tours include Tiahuanaco, the Chacaltaya ski slopes and excursions to remote attractions such as the Cordillera Apolobamba. Arrange organized tours in La Paz or the town closest to the attraction you wish to visit.

There are scores of outfits offering trekking, mountain climbing and rain-forest adventure packages. For climbing in the Cordilleras, operators offer customized expeditions. They can arrange anything from a guide and transport right up to equipment, porters and even a cook. Some also rent trekking equipment. Recommended La Paz–based agencies include the following:

América Tours (Map pp174-5; ☎ 02-237-4204; www.america-ecotours.com; 16 de Julio 1490, Edificio Av, No 9) English-speaking agency specializing in community-based ecotourism: PN Madidi, PN Sajama, Rurrenabaque and the Salar de Uyuni.

Andean Summits (Map pp174-5; ☎ 02-242-2106; www.andeansummits.com; Aranzaes 2974, Sopocachi) Mountaineering and trekking all over Bolivia, plus adventure tours and archaeology trips.

Colibri (☎ 02-237-8098; www.colibri-adventures.com; Sagárnaga 309) Offers comprehensive trekking, mountaineering, mountain biking, jungle trips and 4WD tours, and also rents gear. French and English spoken.

Diana Tours (Map pp174-5; ☎ 02-2375374; hotsadt@ceibo.entelnet.bo; Sagárnaga 328, Hotel Sagárnaga) Good-value city tours plus day trips to Tiahuanaco, Valle de la Luna, Chacaltaya and the Yungas; cheap tours to Copacabana and Puno.

Fremen Tours (☎ 02-240-7995; www.andes-amazonia .com; Santa Cruz & Socabaya, Galeria Handal, No 13) Upmarket agency specializing in the Amazon and Chapare; there is also an office in Cochabamba (Map pp216-17; ☎ 04-425-9392; Tumusla 0245).

Gravity Assisted Mountain Biking (Map pp174-5; ☎ 02-231-3849; www.gravitybolivia.com; 16 de Julio 1490, Edificio Av, No 10) Downhill mania on two wheels, from the 'World's Most Dangerous Road' to stylin' single-track. Ask about Customized Hell Missions and exploratory adventures.

Huayna Potosí Tours (Map pp174-5; ☎ /fax 02-274-0045; berrios@mail.megalink.com; Sagárnaga 398) Runs Refugio Huayna Potosí, which serves as an expedition base camp. Organizes good-value treks and climbs in the

Cordillera Real, Cordillera Apolobamba and elsewhere; English and French spoken.

Inca Land Tours (☎ 02-231-3589; incalandbolivia@ hotmail.com; Sagárnaga 213, No 10) Established Peruvian operation running tours out of Rurrenabaque and Coroico; it arranges its own charter flights to Rurre with SAVE and will book tickets in advance with TAM – at a premium.

Tawa Tours (☎ 02-232-5796; tawa@ceibo.entelnet.bo; Sagárnaga 161) French-speaking company with a wide selection of adventure options including mountaineering, jungle trips, trekking, horse riding and mountain biking.

VISAS

Passports must be valid for one year beyond the date of entry. Entry or exit stamps are free and attempts at charging should be met with polite refusal; ask for a receipt if the issue is pressed. Personal documents – passports, visas or photocopies of these items – must be carried at all times, especially in lowland regions.

Bolivian visa requirements can be arbitrarily changed and interpreted. Each Bolivian consulate and border crossing may have its own entry requirements, procedures and idiosyncrasies.

Citizens of most South American and Western European countries can get a tourist card on entry for stays up to 90 days. Citizens of the USA, Canada, Australia, New Zealand, Japan, South Africa, Israel and many other countries are usually granted 30 days – if you want to stay longer, ask at the point of entry for 90 days and officials will likely oblige. Otherwise, you have to extend your tourist card (easily accomplished at the immigration office in any major city – some nationalities pay for extensions) or apply for a visa. Visas are issued by Bolivian consular representatives, including those in neighboring South American countries. Costs vary according to the consulate and the nationality of the applicant – up to US$50 for a one-year multiple-entry visa.

Overstayers can be fined US$2 per day and may face ribbons of red tape at the border or airport when leaving the country. See the website of the **Ministerio de Relaciones Exteriores y Culto** (www.rree.gov.bo) for a complete list (in Spanish) of overseas representatives and current regulations.

VOLUNTEERING

Volunteer organizations in Bolivia include the following:

Comunidad Inti Wara Yassi (see p219; www.intiwara yassi.org; Parque Machía, Villa Tunari, Chapare) Volunteer-run wild animal refuge. The minimum commitment is 15 days and no previous experience working with animals is required.

Volunteer Bolivia (☎ 04-452-6028; www.volunteer bolivia.org; 342 Ecuador btwn 25 de Mayo & España, Cochabamba) Runs Cafe La Republika cultural center and arranges short- and long-term volunteer work, study and homestay programs throughout Bolivia.

WOMEN TRAVELERS

Women's rights in Bolivia are nearing modern standards. That said, avoid testing the system alone in a bar in a miniskirt. Conservative dress and confidence without arrogance are a must for foreign women. Men are generally more forward and flirtatious in the lowlands than in the altiplano.

WORKING

There are many voluntary and nongovernmental organizations working in Bolivia, but travelers looking for paid work shouldn't hold their breath. Qualified English teachers can try the professionally run Centro Boliviano-Americano (see p173) in La Paz; there are also offices in other cities. New, and as yet unqualified, teachers must forfeit two months' salary in return for their training. Better paying are private-school positions teaching math, science or social studies. Accredited teachers can expect to earn up to US$500 per month for a full-time position.

Brazil

HIGHLIGHTS

- **Rio de Janeiro** – drink caipirinhas on the world's most beautiful beaches, watch the mad spectacle of football at Maracanã, and dance till dawn at sexy samba clubs in Lapa (p266)
- **Salvador** – dance through the cobblestone streets at one of the many Bahian festivals, see *capoeira* on the beach, and spend a mystical evening at a ceremony of Afro-Brazilian Candomblé (p325)
- **Pantanal** – observe scores of animals in these vast southern wetlands, a region with the greatest concentration of fauna in the new world (p318)
- **Foz do Iguaçu** – visit the awe-inspiring spectacle of the massive falls, the world's largest, plunging over the mountains of Paraná (p306)
- **Off the beaten track** – a blend of tropical beach and Atlantic rainforest, the remote Ilha Grande offers the perfect island getaway (p289)
- **Best journey** – on the epic 4WD-journey from Tutoía to Parque Nacional dos Lençóis Maranhenses you'll roll past sand dunes and splash through creeks, ducking palms as the untouched landscape unfolds around you (p361)

FAST FACTS

- **Area:** 8,456,510 sq km (slightly smaller than the continental United States)
- **Budget:** US$25–35 a day
- **Capital:** Brasília
- **Country code:** ☎ 55
- **Electricity:** 110V and 220V (varies), 60Hz
- **Famous for:** Carnaval, the Amazon, soccer, beaches, bossa nova
- **Languages:** Portuguese and 180 indigenous languages
- **Money:** US$1 = 2.9 reais
- **Phrases:** *legal*, *bacana* (cool), *repugnante* (disgusting), *festa* (party)
- **Population:** 170 million
- **Time:** GMT minus 3 to minus 5 hours, depending on the region
- **Tipping:** 10% in restaurants, often included
- **Traveler's checks:** cashed at major banks and exchange offices
- **Visas:** some nationalities require visas (US$40–100), which must be arranged in advance (see Visas, p394)

TRAVEL HINTS

To save time and money, try local travel agents for booking rooms and buying bus tickets. Pack fewer clothes; buy them there for less.

One of the world's most seductive places, Brazil is South America's giant, a dazzling country of pristine beaches, tropical cities and lush jungles. From the Pantanal to the Amazon, Brazil has the widest variety of plant and animal life on the planet.

Birds and monkeys are only a small part of the wildlife in Brazil. Carnaval offers a rather different version and is just one manifestation of Brazil's celebratory spirit. Dancing and music are as integral here as eating and sleeping, and the country has as many musical styles as there are shades of people, from the sensual rhythms of *carimbó* (a folkloric dance with African and indigenous roots) in the Amazon to the samba-charged beats in Bahia.

For explorers, the only limits are your imagination: colorful colonial towns, remote tropical islands, *caboclo* (of mixed indigenous and Spanish ancestry) villages deep in the jungle and wide-open skies in the *gaúcho*-infused south all comprise the varied landscape.

With so much going for them, it's no wonder Brazilians say, *'Deus é brasileiro'* (God is Brazilian). The country seems to have received the lion's share of cultural riches, not least of all the people themselves: open and friendly, spontaneous and passionate, Brazilians are perhaps the biggest reason why visitors leave with hearts full of *saudade* (longing).

HISTORY
The Tribal Peoples

Little is known of Brazil's first inhabitants, but from the few fragments left behind (mostly pottery, trash mounds and skeletons), archeologists estimate that the first humans may have arrived 50,000 years ago, predating any other estimates in the whole American continent.

The population at the time of the Portuguese landing in 1500 is also a mystery, and estimates range from two to six million. There were likely over 1000 tribes living as nomadic hunter-gatherers or in more settled, agricultural societies. Life was punctuated by frequent tribal warfare, and at times, captured enemies were ceremonially killed and eaten after battle.

When the Portuguese first arrived, they had little interest in the natives, who were viewed as a Stone-Age people; and the heavily forested land offered nothing for the European market. All that changed when Portuguese merchants expressed interest in the red dye from Brazilwood (which later gave the colony its name), and slowly colonists arrived to harvest the land.

The natural (Portuguese) choice for the work, of course, was the Indians. Initially, the natives welcomed the strange, smelly foreigners and offered them their labor, their food and their women in exchange for the awe-inspiring metal tools and the fascinating Portuguese liquor. But soon, the newcomers abused the Indians' customs, took their best land, and ultimately enslaved them.

The Indians fought back and won many battles, but the tides were against them.

When colonists discovered that sugarcane grew quite well in the colony, the Indians' labor was more valuable than ever, and soon the sale of Indian slaves became Brazil's second-largest commercial enterprise. It was an industry dominated by *bandeirantes*, brutal men who hunted the Indians in the interior and captured or killed them. Their exploits, more than any treaty, secured the huge interior of South America for Portuguese Brazil.

Jesuit priests went to great lengths to protect the Indians, a few even arming them and fighting alongside them against *bandeirante* incursions. But they were too weak to stymie the attacks (and the Jesuits were later expelled from Brazil in 1759). Indians who didn't die at the hands of the colonists often died from introduced European diseases.

The Africans

During the 17th century, African slaves replaced Indian prisoners on the plantations. From 1550 until 1888, about 3.5 million slaves were shipped to Brazil – almost 40% of the total that came to the New World. The Africans were considered better workers and were less vulnerable to European diseases, but they resisted slavery strongly. *Quilombos*, communities of runaway slaves, formed throughout the colonial period. They ranged from *mocambos*, small groups hidden in the forests, to the great republic of Palmares, which survived much of the 17th century. Led by the African king Zumbí, Palmares had 20,000 residents at its height.

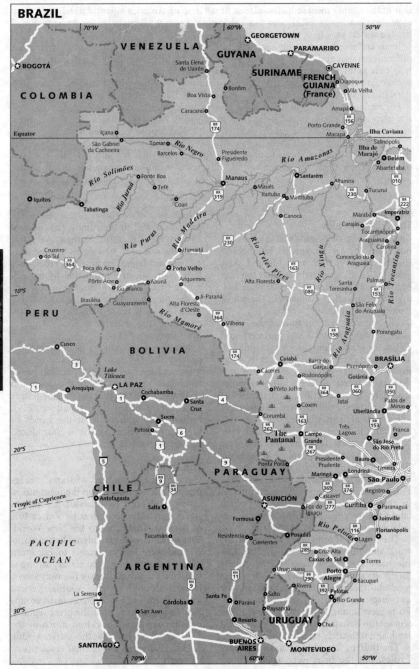

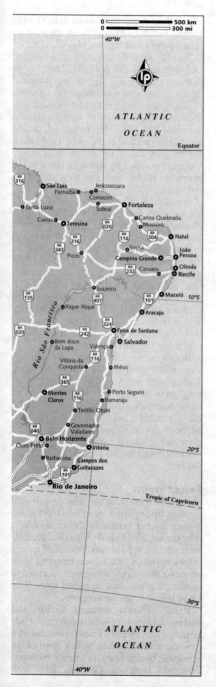

More than 700 villages that formed as Quilombos remain in Brazil today, their growth only stopped by abolition itself, in 1888.

Those who survived life on the plantation sought solace in their African religion and culture through song and dance. The slaves were given perfunctory instruction in Catholicism and a syncretic religion rapidly emerged (see Religion p258). Spiritual elements from many African tribes, such as the Yoruba, were preserved and made palatable to slave masters by adopting a facade of Catholic saints. Such were the roots of modern Candomblé and Macumba, prohibited by law until recently.

Life on the plantations was miserable, but an even worse fate awaited many slaves. In the 1690s gold was discovered in present day Minas Gerais, and soon the rush was on. Wild boomtowns like Vila Rica de Ouro Prêto (Rich Town of Black Gold) sprang up in the mountain valleys. Immigrants flooded the territory, and countless slaves were brought from Africa to dig and die in Minas.

The Portuguese

For years, the ruling powers of Portugal viewed the colony of Brazil as little more than a moneymaking enterprise. That attitude changed, however, when Napoleon marched on Lisbon in 1807. The prince regent (later known as Dom João VI) immediately transferred his court to Brazil. He stayed on even after Napoleon's Waterloo in 1815, and when he became king in 1816 he declared Rio de Janeiro the capital of a united kingdom of Brazil and Portugal, making Brazil the only New World colony to serve as the seat of a European monarch. In 1821, Dom João finally returned to Portugal, leaving his son, Pedro, in Brazil as regent.

The following year, the Portuguese parliament attempted to return Brazil to colonial status. According to legend, Pedro responded by pulling out his sword and shouting out 'Independência ou morte!' (Independence or death), crowning himself Emperor Dom Pedro I. Portugal was too weak to fight its favorite colony, so Brazil attained independence without bloodshed.

Dom Pedro I, by all accounts a bumbling incompetent, ruled for nine years. He scandalized the country by siring a string of illegitimate children, and was finally forced to abdicate in favor of his five-year-old son, Dom Pedro II. Until the future emperor reached adolescence, Brazil suffered a period of civil war. In 1840, Dom Pedro II ascended the throne with overwhelming public support. During his 50-year reign he nurtured an increasingly powerful parliamentary system, went to war with Paraguay, meddled in Argentine and Uruguayan affairs, encouraged mass immigration, abolished slavery and ultimately forged a state that would do away with the monarchy forever.

The Brazilians

During the 19th century, coffee replaced sugar as Brazil's primary export, at one time supplying three-quarters of world demand. With mechanization and the building of Brazil's first railroads, profits soared, and the coffee barons gained enormous influence over the country.

In 1889, a coffee-backed military coup toppled the antiquated Empire, sending the emperor into exile. The new Brazilian Republic adopted a constitution modeled on that of the USA, and for nearly 40 years Brazil was governed by a series of military and civilian presidents through which the armed forces effectively ruled the country.

One of the first challenges to the new republic came from a small religious community in the northeast. An itinerant holy man named Antônio Conselheiro had wandered for years through poverty-stricken backlands, prophesying the appearance of the Antichrist and the end of the world. He railed against the new government and in 1893 gathered his followers in the settlement of Canudos. Suspecting a plot to return Brazil to the Portuguese monarchy, the government set out to subdue the rebels. Only on the fourth attempt were they successful, but in the end, the soldiers killed every man, woman and child, and burned the town to the ground to erase it from the nation's memory.

Coffee remained king until the market collapsed during the global economic crisis of 1929. This weakened the planters of São Paulo, who controlled the government, and an opposition alliance formed with the support of nationalist military officers.

When their presidential candidate, Getúlio Vargas, lost the 1930 elections, the military seized power and handed him the reins.

Vargas proved a gifted maneuverer, and dominated the political scene for 20 years. At times his regime was inspired by the Italian and Portuguese fascist states of Mussolini and Salazar: he banned political parties, imprisoned opponents and censored the press. He remained in and out of the political scene until 1954, when the military called for him to step down. Vargas responded by writing a letter to the people of Brazil, then shooting himself in the heart.

Juscelino Kubitschek, the first of Brazil's big spenders, was elected president in 1956. His motto was '50 years' progress in five.' His critics responded with '40 years of inflation in four.' The critics were closer to the mark, owing in part to the huge debt Kubitschek incurred during the construction of Brasília. By the early 1960s, inflation gripped the Brazilian economy, and Castro's victory in Cuba had spread fears of communism. Brazil's fragile democracy was crushed in 1964 when the military overthrew the government.

Brazil remained under the repressive military regime for almost 20 years. Throughout much of this time, the economy grew substantially, owing in part to heavy borrowing from international banks. But it exacted a heavy toll on the country. At the neglect of all social reform, problems grew dire. Millions came to the cities, and *favelas* (shantytowns) grew at an exponential rate.

Recent Events

November 1989 saw the first presidential election by popular vote in nearly 30 years. Voters elected Fernando Collor de Mello over the socialist Luíz da Silva ('Lula'). Collor promised to fight corruption and reduce inflation, but in 1992 he was removed from office on charges of corruption – accused of heading a group that siphoned more than US$1 billion from the economy.

Itamar Franco replaced Collor and surprised his critics with a competent administration. In 1994 Franco introduced a new currency, the *real*, which sparked an economic boom. Franco's finance minister, Fernando Henrique Cardoso, later won a landslide presidential victory riding the *real's* success.

Cardoso presided through the mid-1990s over a growing economy and record foreign investment, and small efforts were made toward education, land reform and anti-poverty measures. But by the end of Cardoso's office, the social problems facing the country were dire.

Corruption and violent crime was rife. In the late 1990s murders were running at 700 a month in greater São Paulo, making it (along with Rio de Janeiro) among the most violent cities on earth. Fifty million Brazilians lived in serious poverty, many unable to earn enough just to feed themselves.

Given the numbers, it's not surprising that sooner or later a presidential candidate would campaign solely on a platform of social reform. What is surprising is that such a candidate could win, especially one who had run three times previously and lost.

In 2002 Lula ran for the fourth time and at last won. From a humble working class background, Lula rose to become a trade unionist and a strike leader in the early 1980s. He later founded the Workers Party (PT), a magnet for his many followers seeking social reform.

At his inauguration, Lula reaffirmed that his priorities were eliminating hunger and creating jobs. But he was also cautious not to alienate investors. This was a shift from the anti-capitalist rhetoric PT espoused years ago.

Still, this didn't stop conservative zealots in the US from labeling him a communist. (In a letter to Bush, Congressman Henry Hyde wrote, 'There is a real prospect that Castro, Chávez, and Lula da Silva could constitute an axis of evil in the Americas which might soon have nuclear weapons and ballistic missiles.')

Following Lula's first days in office, his harshest critics said that he had not moved fast enough; some even said that he was incapable of accomplishing his idealistic goals. Certainly, Lula's term won't be easy. Brazil entered the 21st century with a sickly healthcare system, urban overcrowding, rural landlessness and ongoing environmental abuse. Brazilians, and many around the globe, are watching to see if the Lula experiment can at last bring social justice to Brazil.

THE CULTURE
The National Psyche
Despite the country's social and economic woes, Brazilians take much pride in their country. The gorgeous landscape is a favorite topic, and although every Brazilian has a different notion of where to find paradise on earth, it will almost certainly be located within the country's borders. Soccer is another source of pride – less the national pastime than a countrywide narcotic to which every Brazilian seems to be addicted.

Famed for their Carnaval, Brazilians love to celebrate, and parties happen year round. But it isn't all samba and beaches in the land of the tropics. At times, Brazilians suffer from *saudade*, a nostalgic, often deeply melancholic longing for something. The idea appears in many works by Jobim, Moraes and other great songwriters, and it manifests itself in many forms – from the dull ache of homesickness to the deep regret over past mistakes.

When Brazilians aren't dancing the samba or drowning in sorrow, they're often helping each other out. Kindness is both commonplace and expected, and even a casual introduction can lead to deeper friendships. This altruism comes in handy in a country noted for its bureaucracy and long lines. There's the official way of doing things, then there's the *jeitinho*, or the little way around it, and a little kindness – and a few friends – can go a long way. One need only have patience, something Brazilians seem to have no shortage of.

Lifestyle
Although Brazil has the world's eighth largest economy, with abundant resources and developed infrastructure, the standard of living varies wildly. More than for its GDP, Brazil is known for having one of the world's widest income gaps between rich and poor.

Since the mass urban migration in the mid-19th century, the poorest have lived in *favelas* (urban slums) that surround every city. Many dwellings consist of little more than a few boards pounded together, and access to clean water, sewage, schools and healthcare are luxuries few *favelas* enjoy. Drug lords rule the streets, and crime is rampant.

BRAZIL

The rich often live just a stone's throw away, sometimes separated by nothing more than a highway. Many live in modern fortresses, with security walls and armed guards, enjoying a lifestyle not unlike the upper classes in Europe and America.

Carnaval brings the two together – albeit in different ways. The *favelas* take center stage, parading through the streets, while the rich enjoy the spectacle; and everyone wracks up a few sins before Lent brings it all to a close.

People

In Brazil the diversity of the landscape matches that of the people inhabiting it. Officially, 55% of the population is white, 6% black, 38% mixed and 1% other, but the numbers little represent the many shades and types of Brazil's rich melting pot. Indians, Portuguese, Africans (brought to Brazil as slaves), and their mixed-blood offspring made up the population until the late 19th century. Since then there have been waves of immigration by Italians, Spaniards, Germans, Japanese, Russians, Lebanese and others.

Immigration is only part of the picture when considering Brazil's diversity. Brazilians are more prone to mention regional types when speaking of the racial collage. Caboclos, who are descendents of the Indians, live along the rivers in the Amazon region and keep alive the traditions and stories of their ancestors. *Gaúchos* (herdsmen) populate Rio Grande do Sul, speak a Spanish-inflected Portuguese and can't quite shake the reputation for being rough-edged cowboys. By contrast, Baianos, descendents of the first Africans in Brazil, are stereotyped for being the most extroverted and celebratory of Brazilians. And let's not forget Cariocas (residents of Rio), Paulistanos (who inhabit Rio's rival city, São Paolo), Mineiros (who come from the colonial towns of Minas Gerais), and Sertanejos (denizens of the drought-stricken *sertão*). These groups represent but a handful of the many types that make up the kindhearted (but complicated, mind you) Brazilian soul.

RELIGION

Brazil is officially a Catholic country, but it's also noted for the diversity and flexibility of its many sects and religions. Without much difficulty you can find churchgoing Catholics who attend spiritualist gatherings or appeal for help at a *terreiro* (the house of an Afro-Brazilian religious group).

Brazil's principal religious roots comprise the animism of the indigenous people, Catholicism and African religions introduced by slaves. The latest arrival is evangelical Christianity, which is spreading all over Brazil, especially in poorer areas.

The Afro-Brazilian religions emerged when the colonists prohibited slaves from practicing their native religions. Not so easily deterred, the slaves simply gave Catholic names to their African gods and continued to worship them behind representations of Catholic saints. The most orthodox of the religions is Candomblé. Rituals take place in the Yoruba language in a *casa de santo or terreiro*, directed by a *pai de santo* or *mãe de santo* (literally, a saint's father or mother – the Candomblé priests). If you attend a Candomblé ceremony, it's best to go as the invited guest of a knowledgeable friend or commercial guide.

Candomblé gods are known as *orixás* and each person is believed to be protected for life by one of them. The *Jogo dos Búzios* (Casting of Shells) is a serious, respected ritual used to tell the future. In Bahia and Rio, followers of Afro-Brazilian cults turn out in huge numbers to attend festivals at the year's end – especially those held during the night of December 31 and on New Year's Day. Millions of Brazilians go to the beach at this time to pay homage to *Iemanjá*, the sea goddess, whose alter ego is the Virgin Mary.

ARTS

Brazilian culture has been shaped by the Portuguese, who gave the country its language and religion, and also by the Indigenous population, immigrants and Africans.

The influence of the latter is particularly strong, especially in the northeast, where African religion, music and cuisine have all profoundly influenced Brazilian identity. *Capoeira*, a martial art developed by slaves to fight their oppressors, enjoys wide popularity.

Architecture, Sculpture & Painting

Brazil has fine colonial architecture in cities like Salvador, Olinda, São Luís, Ouro Prêto, Diamantina and São João del Rei. Over the centuries, the names of two architects stand out: Aleijadinho, the genius of 18th-century baroque in Minas Gerais mining towns (he was a miraculous sculptor too) and Oscar Niemeyer, the 20th-century modernist/functionalist who was chief architect for the new capital, Brasília, in the 1950s and designed many other striking buildings around the country.

The best-known Brazilian painter is Cândido Portinari (1903–62) who early in his career made a decision to paint only Brazil and its people. He was strongly influenced by Mexican muralists like Diego Rivera.

Cinema

Cinema opened the world's ears to bossa nova, by way of Marcel Camus' romantic *Black Orpheus* (1958), set amid Rio's Carnaval. In the 1960s, the Cinema Novo movement, led by Glauber Rocha with films like *Black God, White Devil* (1963), forged a polemical national style using Afro-Brazilian traditions in conscious resistance to the influences of Hollywood.

The military dictatorship didn't exactly encourage creative cinematography. Hector Babenco's *Pixote* (1981), the tale of a street kid in Rio, did win the best film award at Cannes, however.

Since the end of the dictatorship, Brazil has enjoyed a film renaissance, even though much of the money and talent these days go into *telenovelas* (TV soap operas). *Carlota Joaquina – Princesa do Brasil* (1994) blends fable with historical drama in the satirical story of a Spanish princess married to the Portuguese prince regent (later Dom João VI) at the time of his arrival in Brazil.

Bruno Barreto's Oscar-nominated *O Que É Isso, Companheiro? (Four Days in September;* 1998) is based on the 1969 kidnapping of the US ambassador to Brazil by leftist guerrillas. Other directors who took on difficult subjects include Walter Salles, one of Brazil's greatest directors, who made many films dealing with the painful underbelly of society. *Central do Brasil (Central Station;* 1998), one of his more recent works, won much acclaim. The film tells the story of a lonely woman accompanying a young homeless boy on a search for his father into the real, unglamorized Brazil.

Eu, Tu, Eles (Me, You, Them; 2000), Andrucha Waddington's social comedy about a northeasterner with three husbands was also well received when it came out in 2000. It has beautiful cinematography and a score by Gilberto Gil that contributed to the recent wave of popularity for that funky northeastern music, *forró.*

Cidade de Deus (City of God), based on a true story by Paolo Lins, gives an honest and disturbing portrayal of life in a Rio *favela* (slum). After its release in 2002, it brought much attention to the plight of the urban poor.

Literature

Joaquim Maria Machado de Assis (1839–1908), the son of a freed slave, is widely regarded as Brazil's greatest writer. Assis had a great sense of humor and an insightful – though cynical – take on human affairs. His major novels were *Quincas Borba, The Posthumous Memoirs of Bras Cubas* and *Dom Casmurro.*

Brazil's most celebrated writer today is Jorge Amado (1912–2001), with his brilliantly clever portraits of the people and places of Bahia – notably *Gabriela, Clove and Cinnamon* and *Dona Flor and her Two Husbands.*

Paulo Coelho is Latin America's second most read novelist (after Gabriel García Márquez). Recent works like *Veronika Decides to Die* and *The Fifth Mountain* are more sophisticated than the new-age fables (*The Alchemist* and *The Pilgrimage*), which launched his career in the mid-1990s.

Music & Dance

Music is an integral part of Brazilian culture. No matter where you go in the country, you'll find dancing, singing and live music.

Samba, a Brazilian institution, has strong African influences and is intimately linked to Carnaval. Its most famous star, from the 1930s, was Carmen Miranda. The most popular form of samba today is *pagode,* a relaxed, informal genre whose leading exponents include singers Beth Carvalho, Jorge Aragão and Zeca Pagodinho.

Bossa nova, another Brazilian trademark, arose in the 1950s, and gained the world's attention in the classic *The Girl from Ipanema* composed by Antônio Carlos Jobim and Vinícius de Moraes. Bossa nova's founding father, guitarist João Gilberto, still performs, as does his daughter Bebel Gilberto, who has sparked renewed interest in the genre, combining smooth bossa sounds with electronic grooves.

Tropicalismo, which burst onto the scene in the late 1960s, mixed varied Brazilian musical styles with North American rock and pop. Leading figures such as Gilberto Gil and Caetano Veloso are still very much around. Gil, in fact, was chosen by Lula to be Brazil's new Minister of Culture. Another brilliant songwriter not to overlook is Chico Buarque, recently nominated Brazil's musician of the century by the weekly journal *Isto É*.

The nebulous term *Música Popular Brasileira* (MPB) covers a range of styles from original bossa nova-influenced works to some sickly pop. Jazz-influenced Milton Nascimento is one MPB artist who has kept his innovative touch.

Brazilian rock (pronounced 'hock') is highly popular. Groups and artists such as Zeca Baleiro, Os Tribalistas, Kid Abelha, Ed Motta, the punk-driven Legião Urbana and the reggae-based Skank are all well worth a listen. Racionais MCs, from São Paulo, lead Brazilian rap.

Wherever you go in Brazil you'll also hear regional musical styles. The most widely known is *forró* ('foh-*hoh*'), a lively, syncopated northeastern music, which mixes the beats of the *zabumba* (an African drum) with accordion sounds. Stars of this style include Luiz Gonzaga, Jackson do Pandeiro and São Paulo *forró* group Falamansa. *Axé* is a label for the samba/pop/rock/reggae/funk/Caribbean fusion music that emerged from Salvador in the 1990s, popularized especially by the flamboyant Daniela Mercury. In the Amazon, you'll encounter the seductive rhythms of Carimbó, along with the sensual dance that accompanies it.

SPORT

Futebol (soccer) is a national passion. Most people acknowledge that Brazilians play the world's most creative, artistic and thrilling style of football, and Brazil is the only country to have won five World Cups (1958, 1962, 1970, 1994 and 2002). Games are an intense spectacle – one of the most colorful pageants you're likely to see. Just don't take any valuables with you to the stadium. Tickets typically cost between US$3 and US$10. The season goes on nearly all year, with the national championship running from late July to mid-December. Local newspapers as well as the daily *Jornal dos Sports* and the website www.netgol.com list upcoming games. Major clubs include Botafogo, Flamengo, Fluminense and Vasco da Gama (all of Rio de Janeiro); Corinthians, Palmeiras and São Paulo (all of São Paulo); and Bahia (of Salvador), Sport (of Recife) and Cruzeiro (of Belo Horizonte).

ENVIRONMENT
Land

The world's fifth-largest country, after Russia, Canada, China and the USA, Brazil borders every other South American country except Chile and Ecuador. Its 8.5 million-sq-km area covers almost half the continent.

Brazil has four primary geographic regions: the coastal band, the Planalto Brasileiro, the Amazon Basin and the Paraná–Paraguai Basin.

The narrow, 7400km-long coastal band lies between the Atlantic Ocean and the coastal mountain ranges. From the border with Uruguay to Bahia state, steep mountains often come right down to the coast. North of Bahia, the coastal lands are flatter.

The Planalto Brasileiro (Brazilian Plateau) extends over most of Brazil's interior south of the Amazon Basin. It's sliced by several large rivers and punctuated by mountain ranges reaching no more than 3000m.

The thinly populated Amazon Basin, composing 42% of Brazil, is fed by waters from the Planalto Brasileiro to its south, the Andes to the west and the Guyana shield to the north. In the west the basin is 1300km wide; in the east, between the Guyana shield and the planalto, it narrows to 100km. More than half the 6275km of the Rio Amazonas lies in Peru, where its source is found. The Amazon and its 1100 tributaries contain an estimated 20% of the world's fresh water. Pico da Neblina (3014m) on the Venezuelan border is the highest peak in Brazil.

The Paraná–Paraguai Basin, in the south of Brazil, extends into neighboring Paraguay and Argentina and includes the large wetland area known as the Pantanal.

Wildlife

Brazil has more known species of plants (55,000), freshwater fish (3000) and mammals (520-plus) than any other country in the world. It ranks third for birds (1622) and fifth for reptiles (468). An abundance of these species live in the Amazon rain forest, which occupies 3.6 million sq km in Brazil and 2.4 million sq km in neighboring countries. It's the world's largest tropical forest and most biologically diverse ecosystem, with 20% of the world's bird and plant species, 10% of its mammals and 10 to 15 times as many fish species as Europe.

Many Brazilian species are widely distributed around the country. For example, the biggest Brazilian cat, the jaguar, is found in Amazon and Atlantic rainforests, the cerrado and the Pantanal.

Many other Brazilian mammals are found over a broad range of habitats, including five other big cats (puma, ocelot, margay, oncilla and jaguarundi); the giant anteater; several varieties of sloths (best seen in Amazonia) and armadillos; 75 primate species, including several types of howler and capuchin monkey, the little squirrel monkey (Amazonia's most common primate) and around 20 small species of marmosets and tamarin; the cute, furry, long-nosed coati (a type of raccoon); the giant river otter; the maned wolf; the tapir; peccaries (like wild boar); marsh and pampas deer; the capybara (the world's largest rodent at 1m in length); the pink dolphin, often glimpsed in the Amazon and its tributaries; and the Amazon manatee, an even larger river dweller.

Birds form a major proportion of the wildlife you'll see. The biggest is the flightless, 1.4m-high rhea, found in the cerrado and Pantanal. The gloriously colorful parrots, macaws, toucans and trogons come in dozens of species. In Amazonia or the Pantanal you may well see scarlet macaws and, if you're lucky, blue-and-yellow ones. Unfortunately, the macaws' beautiful plumage makes them a major target for poachers.

In Amazonia or the Pantanal you can't miss the alligators. One of Brazil's five species, the black caiman, grows up to 6m long. Other aquatic life in the Amazon includes the beautiful pirarucu, which grows 3m long. Its red and silvery-brown scale patterns are reminiscent of Chinese paintings. The infamous piranha comes in about 50 species, found in the basins of Amazon, Orinoco, Paraguai or São Francisco rivers or rivers of the Guianas. Only a handful of species pose a risk, and confirmed accounts of human fatalities caused by piranhas are *extremely* rare.

National Parks

Over 350 areas are protected as national parks, state parks or extractive reserves. Good parks for observing fauna, flora and/or dramatic landscapes include:

Parque Nacional da Chapada Diamantina Rivers, waterfalls, caves and swimming holes make for excellent trekking in this mountainous region in the northeast.

Parque Nacional da Chapada dos Guimarães On a rocky plateau northeast of Cuiabá, this canyon park features breathtaking views and impressive rock formations.

Parque Nacional da Chapada dos Veadeiros 200km north of Brasília, among waterfalls and natural swimming holes, this hilly national park features an array of rare flora and fauna.

Parque Nacional da Serra dos Órgãos Set in the mountainous terrain in the southeast, this park is a mecca for rock climbers and mountaineers.

Parque Nacional de Aparados da Serra Famous for its narrow canyon with 700m escarpments, this park in the southeast features hiking trails with excellent overlooks.

Parque Nacional dos Lençóis Maranhenses Spectacular beaches, mangroves, dunes and lagoons comprise the landscape of this park in the northeast.

Reserva de Desenvolvimento Sustentável Mamirauá Deep in Amazonia, the wildlife viewing is spectacular at this tropical rainforest reserve north of Manaus.

Environmental Issues

Sadly, Brazil is as renowned for its forests, as it is for the destruction of them. By the year 2000, about 14% of the Brazilian Amazon rain forest had been completely destroyed. All its major ecosystems are threatened and more than 70 mammals are endangered.

Environmental threats have come in many forms. In the 1970s the government cleared roads through the jungle in hope of giving drought-stricken northeasterners a chance to better their lives on the cleared land of Amazonia. Along with the new arrivals came loggers and cattle ranchers, both of whom

BRAZIL

further cleared the forests. The few settlers that remained (most gave up and moved to the *favelas* of Amazonia's growing cities) widely employed slash-and-burn agriculture with devastating consequences.

Further damage to the environment is delivered by the hands of *garimpeiros*, renegade miners, usually seeking gold. Mercury separation is used to extract gold from ore, which has led to large quantities of highly poisonous mercury washing into the rivers, creating a major health hazard.

One of the greatest immediate threats to the Amazon is the ironically named Avança Brasil (Advance Brazil), a program unveiled in 1999 by Cardoso. The plan includes paving 8000km of roads, opening gas pipelines, building power stations, and adding thousands of kilometers of new electric power lines all over Amazonia. Many environmentalists predict dire consequences if the project goes through (one ecologist feared that as much as 40% of the Amazon would be deforested or damaged in the next 20 years). At time of research, the government still hadn't implemented Avança Brasil.

TRANSPORT

GETTING THERE & AWAY

Brazil has several gateway airports and shares a border with every country in South America except Chile and Ecuador.

Air

The busiest international airports are Aeroporto Galeão (formally known as Aeroporto Internacional António Carlos Jobim) in Rio de Janeiro (p284) and São Paulo's Aeroporto Guarulhos (p295). Connecting flights to cities around the country leave regularly from both these airports. The other principal gateways are Manaus (p377), Macapá (p371) and Belém (p368), all located in the North. Varig, Brazil's largest airline, flies into Brazil from 11 South American cities.

For student fares, try the **Student Travel Bureau** (STB; ☎ 0xx21-2512-8577; www.stb.com.br; Rua Visconde de Pirajá 550, Ipanema, Rio), which has some 30 branches around the country. **Andes Sol** (☎ 0xx21-2275-4370; Av NS de Copacabana 209, Rio) is a good agency for arranging economi-

cal itineraries. Discount agencies in São Paulo include **US Tour** (☎ 0xx11-3813-1308, www.ustour.com.br).

Another website to search for cheap flights is www.viajo.com.br.

ARGENTINA

Round-trip flights from Buenos Aires to Rio or São Paulo are available on Varig, Aerolíneas Argentinas or Swissair. Other flights from Buenos Aires go to Foz do Iguaçu, Porto Alegre, Curitiba, Florianópolis, Salvador and Recife, and to Puerto Iguazú in Argentina, a short cross-border hop from Foz do Iguaçu.

BOLIVIA

Varig flies from La Paz to Rio or São Paulo. Lloyd Aéreo Boliviano (LAB) flies to Manaus from Santa Cruz.

The Bolivian towns Cobija, Guayaramerín and Puerto Suárez, across the border from the Brazilian towns Brasiléia, Guajará-Mirim and Corumbá, respectively, can all be reached by domestic flights from several cities inside Bolivia.

CHILE

Varig, TAM, LanChile and Swissair fly from Santiago to Rio and São Paulo.

COLOMBIA

From Bogotá you can fly to Leticia, and walk, taxi or take a combi across the border into Brazil. A Rio–Bogotá round-trip flight on Varig or Avianca is costly.

ECUADOR

Ecuatoriana flies to Manaus from Guayaquil and Quito.

THE GUIANAS

Surinam Airways flies between Georgetown (Guyana), Paramaribo (Suriname),

Cayenne (French Guiana), and Belém. Penta, a Brazilian regional airline, flies into Macapá and Belém from Cayenne. If you get the connections right, it's cheaper to fly with Air Guyane between Cayenne and St Georges, on the French Guiana–Brazil border and then between Oiapoque, on the Brazilian side of the same border, and Macapá with Penta.

PARAGUAY
Varig flies between Asunción and Rio or São Paulo. You can also fly from Asunción to Ciudad del Este, a short cross-border hop from Foz do Iguaçu, Brazil.

PERU
Varig flies round trips from Lima to Rio or São Paulo. From Iquitos, Peru, there's a seaplane to Santa Rosa on the Rio Amazonas on the Brazil–Peru–Colombia triple frontier. The carrier is **Tans** (☎ 0xx92-412-2045 in Tabatinga, Brazil), most easily contacted at the riverside Restaurante Blue Moon in Tabatinga.

URUGUAY
Varig and Pluna fly from Montevideo to Rio and São Paulo.

VENEZUELA
The flight to Boa Vista and Manaus is no longer available. A Varig round-trip flight from Caracas to Rio de Janeiro or São Paulo is US$785.

Boat
BOLIVIA
From Trinidad in Bolivia boats take about five days to sail down the Río Mamoré to Guayaramerín (Bolivia), opposite Guajará-Mirim (Brazil).

PERU
Fast passenger boats make the 400km trip along the Rio Amazonas between Iquitos (Peru) and Tabatinga (Brazil) in eight to 10 hours for US$40 to US$50. From Tabatinga you can continue to Manaus and Belém.

Bus
ARGENTINA
The main crossing used by travelers is Puerto Iguazú–Foz do Iguaçu, a 20-hour bus ride from Buenos Aires. Further south, you can cross from Paso de los Libres (Ar-

gentina) to Uruguaiana (Brazil), also served by buses from Buenos Aires, and at San Javier–Porto Xavier or Santo Tomé–São Borja on the Rio Uruguai.

Direct buses run between Buenos Aires and Porto Alegre (US$64, 20 hours) and Rio de Janeiro (US$141, 42 hours). Other destinations include Florianópolis, Curitiba and São Paulo.

BOLIVIA
Brazil's longest border runs through remote wetlands and forests, and is much used by smugglers.

The busiest crossing is between Quijarro (Bolivia) and Corumbá (Brazil), which is a good access point for the Pantanal. Quijarro has a daily train link with Santa Cruz, Bolivia. Corumbá has bus connections with Bonito, Campo Grande, São Paulo, Rio de Janeiro and southern Brazil.

Cáceres, in Mato Grosso (Brazil) has a daily bus link with Santa Cruz (Bolivia) via the Bolivian border town of San Matías.

Guajará-Mirim (Brazil) is a short river crossing from Guayaramerín (Bolivia). Both towns have bus links into their respective countries, but from late December to late February rains can make the northern Bolivian roads very difficult.

Brasiléia (Brazil), a 4½-hour bus ride from Rio Branco, stands opposite Cobija (Bolivia), which has bus connections into Bolivia. This route is less direct than the Guayaramerín–Guajará-Mirim option, and Bolivian buses confront the same wet season difficulties.

CHILE
Although there is no border with Chile, direct buses run between Santiago and Brazilian cities such as Porto Alegre (US$116, 36 hours), Curitiba, São Paulo and Rio de Janeiro (US$130, 62 hours).

COLOMBIA
Leticia, on the Rio Amazonas in far southeast Colombia, is contiguous with Tabatinga (Brazil). You can cross the border on foot, combi or taxi, but river and air are the only ways out of either town.

FRENCH GUIANA
The Brazilian town of Oiapoque, a rugged 560km bus ride (or a quick flight) from

BRAZIL

Macapá, stands across the Rio Oiapoque from St Georges (French Guiana). An unpaved road from St Georges to Régina, about halfway to the French Guiana capital, Cayenne, was expected to open officially in 2004. At the time of writing it was possible to get a truck along the road for around US$35. Taxi-buses between Régina and Cayenne cost US$10. St Georges–Cayenne flights cost US$40 (see Air, p262).

GUYANA

Lethem (southwest Guyana) and Bonfim (Roraima, Brazil) are a short boat ride apart. You can travel between Lethem and the Guyanese capital, Georgetown, by plane or truck. The latter takes between two days and two weeks, depending on weather conditions. Bonfim is a two-hour bus ride from Boa Vista, Roraima.

PARAGUAY

The two major border crossings are Ciudad del Este–Foz do Iguaçu and Pedro Juan Caballero–Ponta Porã. The latter gives access to the Pantanal. Direct buses run between Asunción and such Brazilian cities as Curitiba (US$40, 18 hours), São Paulo and Rio de Janeiro (US$69, 28 hours).

PERU

The only available land route across the long Peru–Brazil border is via Iñapari, a 10-hour minibus or truck ride north of Puerto Maldonado (Peru). You wade across the Rio Acre between Iñapari and the small Brazilian town of Assis Brasil, a three- to four-hour bus or 4WD trip from Brasiléia.

SURINAME

Overland travel between Suriname and Brazil involves first passing through either French Guiana or Guyana.

URUGUAY

The crossing most used by travelers is at Chuy (Uruguay)–Chuí (Brazil). Other crossings are Río Branco–Jaguarão, Isidoro Noblia–Aceguá, Rivera–Santana do Livramento, Artigas–Quaraí and Bella Unión–Barra do Quaraí. Buses run between Montevideo and Brazilian cities such as Porto Alegre (US$58, 12 hours), Florianópolis, Curitiba, São Paulo and Rio de Janeiro (US$130, 39 hours).

VENEZUELA

Paved roads run all the way from northern Venezuela to Boa Vista and Manaus, crossing the border at Santa Elena de Uairén–Pacaraíma. Buses run to Manaus from as far away as Puerto La Cruz on Venezuela's coast (US$80, 33 hours).

GETTING AROUND
Air
DOMESTIC AIR SERVICES

Brazil has three major national carriers: Varig, TAM and VASP. At least one of these serves every major city. Varig also has two affiliates, Nordeste and Rio Sul, which fly to smaller cities.

Other airlines serving Rio de Janeiro and various cities in the southeast, south and northeast include Fly, Trip and Gol. Amazonia has a host of regional carriers including Penta, TAVAJ, Rico and Meta.

In general, VASP is the cheapest of the big airlines, though smaller airlines often undercut the larger ones, and the resulting price wars make going to a travel agent all the more worthwhile.

Overall, Brazilian airlines operate efficiently, but schedules can change and it's always important to reconfirm your flights. Most airlines have national telephone numbers for reservations and confirmations.

Fly (☎ 0300-313-13 23; www.voefly.com.br)
Gol (☎ 0300-789-21 21; www.voegol.com.br)
TAM (☎ 0300-123-10 00; www.tam.com.br)
Trip (☎ 0800-701-87 47; www.airtrip.com.br)
Varig (☎ 0300-788-70 00; www.varig.com.br)
VASP (☎ 0300-789-10 10; www.vasp.com.br)

In order to secure a seat, book as far ahead as possible during busy seasons — from Christmas to Carnaval, Holy Week and Easter, July and August. At other times, you can buy tickets for same-day flights, with no added cost.

Embarkation tax on domestic flights ranges from US$1.50 at minor airports to US$5 at major ones. If it isn't already included in the price of your ticket, you have to pay it in cash (reais only) at check-in. The check-in clerks never have any change.

AIR PASSES

If you're combining travels in Brazil with other countries in southern South America, it's worth looking into the Mercosur Airpass (see Air Passes in the Transport chapter p1046).

For flights solely within Brazil, Varig, TAM and VASP all offer a Brazil Airpass, giving you five domestic flights within 21 days for around US$500. Up to four further flights can usually be added for US$100 each.

The Brazil Airpass must be purchased outside Brazil and to do so you need an international round-trip ticket to Brazil. You have to book your airpass itinerary at the time you buy it, and there are usually penalties for changing reservations. On most airpasses you're not allowed to visit the same city twice. Airpasses often include the domestic departure tax.

The VASP Brazil Airpass costs US$452 and travel must be completed within 21 days. You can buy it in conjunction with an international ticket on any airline.

TAM's Brazil Airpass can also be bought in conjunction with an international ticket on any airline. It's valid for 21 days and costs US$511.

The Varig Brazil Airpass provides the most destinations, but it is also the most expensive. It costs US$542 and must be bought in conjunction with an international ticket on Varig or other specified airlines (American, British Airways, United and many others). It can be used on Varig, Nordeste and Rio Sul flights.

Boat

The Amazon region is one of the last great bastions of river travel in the world. The Rio Negro, the Rio Solomões and the Rio Madeira are the highways of Amazonia, and you can travel thousands of kilometers along these waterways (which combine to form the mighty Rio Amazonas), exploring the vast Amazon basin traveling to or from Peru or Bolivia. Travel may be slow and dull along the river (with distances measured in days rather than kilometers), but it is cheap. And in the Amazon, apart from flying, *barcos* (large floating tubs which sputter along the river) are the only option.

Most passengers travel *rede* (hammock) class, which entails staking out a spot (get their early) on one of the decks and stringing up your own hammock. The other option is booking a *camarote* (cabin), which

costs about double the hammock price. Cabins typically sleep two to four and allow more privacy than the overcrowded decks, but they are hot, stuffy and extremely basic.

Boats provide three basic meals a day (usually a variation of the same meal), and access to a toilet facility (make sure you're bunking far from it), as well as fresh water, but you are advised to bring your own snacks and bottled water.

For more information, see River Travel in the North section (p362).

Bus

Buses are the backbone of long-distance transportation in Brazil, and if you do any amount of traveling in the country, you'll become intimately acquainted with them. Bus services are generally reliable and cheap, and all major cities have frequent departures.

Road quality varies from well-paved roads in the south, to decent highways along the coast, to ravaged stretches of pockmarked terrain in the northeast interior. In Amazonia the handful of long-distance roads in the region are among the worst, with very few exceptions such as the good paved road from Manaus to Venezuela.

There are three main classes of long-distance buses. The cheapest, *comum*, is fairly comfortable with reclining seats and usually a toilet. The *executivo* provides roomier seats, costs about 25% more and makes fewer stops. *Leitos*, the leer jets of the bussing world, can cost twice as much as *comum* and have spacious, fully reclining seats with pillows, air-conditioning, and often an attendant serving sandwiches and drinks. Overnight buses, regardless of the class, often make fewer stops.

All big cities, and most small ones, have one central bus terminal (*rodoviária*, pronounced 'hoe-doe-vee-*ah*-rhee-ya'), often located on the outskirts of town. Usually you can simply show up at the station and buy a ticket for the next bus out, but on weekends and holidays (particularly from December to February) it's a good idea to book ahead. Some travel agents in major cities sell tickets for long-distance buses, which can save you a time-consuming trip out to the bus station.

BRAZIL

Bus fares average US$2.50 per hour in comum: the six-hour Rio–São Paulo trip costs US$15/32 in *comum/leito*, and the 20-hour trip from Rio to Florianópolis is US$45/80 *comum/leito*.

Car & Motorcycle

Brazilian roads can be dangerous, especially busy highways such as the Rio to São Paulo corridor. The number of fatalities caused by motor vehicles in Brazil is estimated at 80,000 per year. Driving at night is particularly hazardous because other drivers are more likely to be drunk and road hazards are less visible. Another peril is the police, who rarely lack reasons to impose fines.

All that said, driving can be a convenient way to get around Brazil. A small four-seat rental car costs around US$35 a day with unlimited kilometers (US$45 with air-con). Maximum insurance runs another US$20 a day. Ordinary gasoline costs around US$1.20 a liter. Familiar multinationals dominate the car-rental business and getting a car is safe and easy if you have a driver's license, credit card and passport and are over the minimum age (25 with most firms, 21 with others). You should also carry an international driver's license.

Renting a motorcycle is as expensive as renting a car, and riding one poses a serious risk to your health. If you do rent one, be sure to get an off-road bike.

Hitching

Hitchhiking in Brazil, with the possible exception of the Pantanal and a few other areas where it's commonplace among locals, is difficult. The best way to hitch is to ask drivers when they're not in their vehicles – for example, by waiting at a gas station or a truck stop. But even this can be difficult. The Portuguese for 'lift' is *carona*.

Local Transport

BUS

Local bus services are frequent and cheap, and their routes are usually extensive. Many buses list their destinations in bold letters on the front, making it easier to identify the one you need. This comes in handy when you see your bus, since drivers don't stop unless someone flags them. To hail one, hold out your arm and wave them down.

Typically, you enter the bus at the back and exit from the front. The price is displayed near the money collector, who sits at a turnstile just inside the entrance and provides change for the fare (usually about US$0.50). You'll have difficulty getting a bulky backpack through the narrow turnstile, but try to avoid lingering in the back – where pickpockets and thieves are more likely to be. Avoid riding the bus after 11pm and at peak (read packed) times: noon–2pm and 4–6pm in most areas.

TAXI

City taxis are reasonably priced, and are quite useful for avoiding potentially dangerous walks and late-night bus rides, or if your baggage is too bulky for public transport. Most meters start around US$1 and rise by US$1 or so per kilometer (prices increase at night and on Sunday). Make sure the driver turns on the meter when you get in. Sometimes the fare is fixed – typically on trips between the airport and the city center.

If possible, orient yourself before taking a taxi, and keep a map handy in case you find yourself being taken on a wild detour.

The worst place to get a cab is where the tourists are. Don't get one near one of the expensive hotels.

TRAIN

Passenger train service has been scaled down to almost nothing in recent years. One of the few remaining lines runs from Curitiba to Paranaguá, descending the coastal mountain range. With unforgettable views, it's worth the trip.

RIO DE JANEIRO

With its lush peaks, breathtaking beaches and urban ambience, the *cidade maravilhosa* (marvelous city) occupies one of the most spectacular settings on the planet. *Cariocas* (inhabitants of Rio) are no less striking. Sensual and free-spirited, with a love for samba and celebration, they welcome visitors to their tropical city, sharing beaches, caipirinhas (*cachaça*-fueled cocktails) and their wild Carnaval with all who are willing to fall under the Carioca *encanto* (spell).

In spite of its many charms, Rio de Janeiro, with over 7 million inhabitants, has its share of problems: poverty, violence, drug abuse and police corruption are widespread.

Don't miss people-watching on the beaches of Ipanema and Copacabana, samba dancing in Lapa, the ride up Pão de Açúcar, a stroll through Santa Theresa, the view from Cristo Redentor and football madness at Maracanã.

HISTORY

The city earned its name from the ignorance of an explorer named Gaspar de Lemos. The Portuguese sailor entered the huge bay (Baía de Guanabara) in January 1502, and mistaking it for a river, named it Rio de Janeiro (January River). The French were actually the first settlers along the bay, establishing the colony of Antarctic France in 1555. The Portuguese, fearing that the French would take over, gave them the boot in 1567 and remained from then on. Thanks to sugar plantations and the slave trade, their new colony developed into an important settlement, and grew substantially during the Minas Gerais gold rush of the 18th century.

In 1763, with a population of 50,000, Rio replaced Salvador as the colonial capital. By 1900, after a coffee boom, heavy immigration from Europe and internal migration by ex-slaves, Rio had 800,000 inhabitants.

The 1920s to 1950s were Rio's golden age. It became a romantic, exotic destination for international high society. Brasília took over as Brazil's political capital in 1960, but Rio remains the cultural capital of the country.

ORIENTATION

Rio is a city of unusual urban diversity, with beaches, mountains, skyscrapers and the omnipresent *favelas* all woven into the fabric of the landscape. The city can be divided into two zones: the *zona norte* (north zone), consisting of industrial, working-class neighborhoods, and the *zona sul* (south zone), full of middle- and upper-class neighborhoods and well-known beaches. Centro, Rio's business district and the site of its first settlement, marks the boundary between the two, and a number of the important museums and colonial buildings are there.

BRAZIL

GETTING INTO TOWN

Rio's Galeão international airport (GIG) is 15km north of the city center on Ilha do Governador. Santos Dumont airport, used by some domestic flights, is by the bay in the city center, 1km east of Cinelândia metro station.

Real Auto Bus (☎ 0800-240-850) operates safe air-con buses from the international airport (outside the arrivals floor of terminal 1 or the ground floor of terminal 2) to Novo Rio bus station, Avenida Rio Branco (Centro), Santos Dumont airport, southward through Glória, Flamengo and Botafogo and along the beaches of Copacabana, Ipanema and Leblon to Barra da Tijuca (and vice-versa). The buses (US$2, every 20 to 30 minutes) run from 5:20am to 12:10am, and will stop wherever you ask. You can transfer to the metro at Carioca station.

Heading to the airports, you can catch the Real bus from in front of the major hotels along the main beaches, but you have to look alive and flag them down.

Taxis from the international airport may try to rip you off. The safest course, a radio taxi for which you pay a set fare at the airport, is also the most expensive. A yellow and blue common (*comum*) taxi should cost around US$25 to Copacabana if the meter is working. A radio taxi costs about US$35.

If you arrive in Rio by bus, it's a good idea to take a taxi to your hotel, or at least to the general area you want to stay. Don't try walking into town with all your gear – **Rodoviária Novo Rio** (Map p268; ☎ 0xx21-2291-5151; Av Francisco Bicalho), the bus station, is in a seedy area – and traveling on local buses with all your belongings is a little risky. A small booth near the Riotur desk on the first floor of the bus station organizes the yellow cabs in the rank out front. Say where you want to go and the clerk will write a price on a ticket, which you then give to the driver of the first cab in line, paying the stated fare. Sample fares are US$12 to the international airport and US$10 to Copacabana or Ipanema.

Local buses, should you decide to take them, leave from stops outside the station. For Copacabana, the best are Nos 127, 128 and 136; for Ipanema, Nos 128 and 172. For the budget hotels in Catete and Glória, take No 136 or 172.

BRAZIL

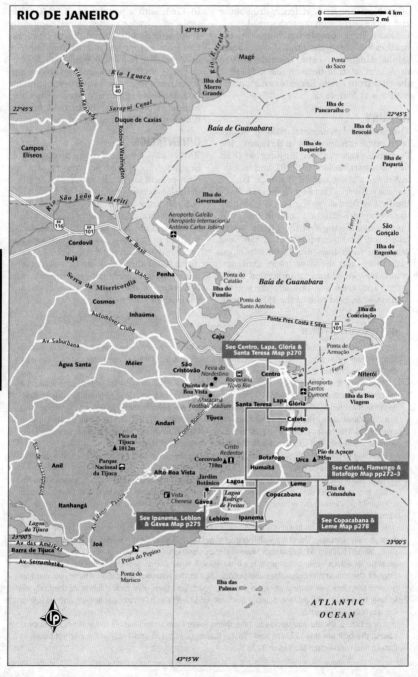

RIO DE JANEIRO

0 — 4 km
0 — 2 mi

43°15'W

Magé

Ponta do Saco

Rio Iguaçu

BR 40

Ilha do Morro Grande

Ilha de Pancaraíba

22°45'S

Sarapuí Canal

22°45'S

Duque de Caxias

Baía de Guanabara

Ilha de Brocoió

Ilha do Boqueirão

Ilha de Paquetá

Campos Elíseos

Rodovia Washington

Rio São João de Meriti

BR 116

BR 101

Av Brasil

Ilha do Governador

Aeroporto Galeão (Aeroporto Internacional Antônio Carlos Jobim)

São Gonçalo

Ilha do Engenho

Cordovil

Av Uranos

Irajá

Penha

Ponta do Catalão

Baía de Guanabara

Serra da Misericórdia

Ilha do Fundão

Ponta de Santo Antônio

Ilha da Conceição

Cosmos

Bonsucesso

Automóvel Clube

Inhaúma

Ponte Pres Costa E Silva

BR 101

Av Suburbana

Caju

Ponta de Armação

Água Santa

Méier

São Cristóvão

Feira do Nordestino

See Centro, Lapa, Glória & Santa Teresa Map p270

Centro

Aeroporto Santos Dumont

Niterói

Quinta da Boa Vista

Rodoviária Novo Rio

Santa Teresa

Lapa

Glória

Ilha da Boa Viagem

Maracanã Football Stadium

Catete

Andari

Av Conde Bonfim

Tijuca

Flamengo

Pico da Tijuca ▲1012m

Cristo Redentor

Botafogo

Pão de Açúcar ▲395m

Anil

Parque Nacional da Tijuca

Corcovado▲ 710m

Urca

Humaitá

Alto Boa Vista

Jardim Botânico

Lagoa

Leme

Ilha da Cotunduba

Av Edson Passos

Vista Chenesa

Gávea

Lagoa Rodrigo de Freitas

Copacabana

Itanhangá

See Ipanema, Leblon & Gávea Map p275

Leblon

Ipanema

See Copacabana & Leme Map p278

Lagoa da Tijuca

23°00'S

Av das Américas

Joá

23°00'S

Barra de Tijuca

Av Sernambetiba

Praia do Pepino

Ponta do Marisco

Ilha das Palmas

ATLANTIC OCEAN

43°15'W

The parts of Rio you are most likely to explore stretch along the shore of the Baía de Guanabara and the Atlantic Ocean. South from Centro are the neighborhoods of Lapa, Glória, Catete, Flamengo, Botafogo and Urca – where the striking peak of Pão de Açúcar (Sugar Loaf) dominates the landscape. Further south lie the neighborhoods of Copacabana, Ipanema and Leblon, the first and only stop for many travelers to the city.

Other areas of interest include the quaint, colonial neighborhood of Santa Theresa on a hill overlooking Centro and just south of there the looming statue of Cristo Redentor (Christ the Redeemer), situated atop Corcovado and offering fabulous views of both zones of the city.

Aside from the bus station, Maracanã football stadium and the international airport, most travelers have few reasons to visit the *zona norte*.

Lonely Planet produces an excellent city map for Rio de Janeiro, and Riotur, the city's tourist information center, provides free street maps at their offices. For tourist maps of Brazil and the region, check kiosks in the center of town. For physical and topographical maps, head to **Editora Geográfica Paulini** (Map 270; ☎ 0xx21-220-0181; Rua Senador Dantas 75, Loja J).

INFORMATION
Bookshops
Livraria Letras & Expressões (Map p275; Rua Visconde de Pirajá 276, Ipanema) An Ipanema favorite with English-language newspapers and magazines, and a good café on the 2nd floor.
Nova Livraria Leonardo da Vinci (Map p270; Edifício Marquês de Herval; Avenida Rio Branco 185, Centro) Rio's largest bookstore, with a good collection of books in English, including travel guides.

Cultural Centers
Centro Cultural do Banco do Brasil (Map p270; Rua Primheiro do Março 66; www.ccbb.com.br; admission free; ⏲ Tue-Sun) Beautiful building housing exhibition halls, a cinema and ample performance space, the Centro Cultural has ongoing music and dance programs throughout the year.

Emergency
If you have the misfortune to be robbed, you should report it to the **Tourist Police** (Map p275; ☎ 0xx21-3399-7170; Rua Afrânio de Melo Franco 119, Leblon; ⏲ 24hr), who can provide you with a police form to give to your insurance company.

Internet Access
Youth hostels and larger hotels provide Internet access, as do the following:
Central Fone (Map p270: Largo da Carioca plaza, Centro) In the kiosk.
Eurogames (Map pp272-3; Rua Correia Dutra 39B, Catete)
Post Office (Map p275; Praça General Osório, Ipanema) Offers 15 minutes free access.
Tele Rede (Map p278; Avenida NS de Copacabana 209A, Copacabana)

Internet Resources
RioGayGuide.com One of the best online guides for gay and lesbian visitors to the city.
www.ipanema.com Dubbed 'the insider's guide to Rio de Janeiro,' this colorful website provides an excellent introduction to the city.
www.rio.rj.gov.br/riotur Riotur has a more comprehensive website, though you'll need some Portuguese to navigate its pages.

Laundry
Sadly, laundry isn't cheap in Brazil. To save cash inquire at your hotel: often housekeepers wash clothes at home to make a few extra *reais*. If things are desperate, the following locations provide drop off wash-and-fold service for around US$0.80/kg:
Laundromat (Map pp272-3; Rua Arturo Bernardes 14, Catete)
Laundromat (Map p278; Rua Barata Ribeiro 181B, Copacabana) Across from the metro station.
Laundromat (Map p278; Av Nossa Senhora de Copacabana 1226, Copacabana)
Laundromat (Map p275; Rua Farme de Amoedo, Ipanema) Near Rua Visconde de Pirajá.

Medical Services
Galdino Campos Cárdio Copa (Map p278; ☎ 0xx21-2548-9966; Av Nossa Senhora de Copacabana 492) Twenty-four-hour clinic with English- and French-speaking staff.
Cardio Trauma Ipanema (Map p275; ☎ 0xx21-287-2322; Rua Farme de Amoedo 88) Has a 24-hour emergency room.

Money
ATMs for most card networks can be found throughout the city; Banco do Brasil, Bradesco, Citibank and HSBC are the best ones to try when using a debit or credit card.

In addition to ATMs, Banco do Brasil and Citibank also have currency exchange facilities at the following locations:
Banco do Brasil Centro (Map p270; Rua Senador Dantas 105); Copacabana (**Map p278; Av Nossa Senhora de**

BRAZIL

BRAZIL

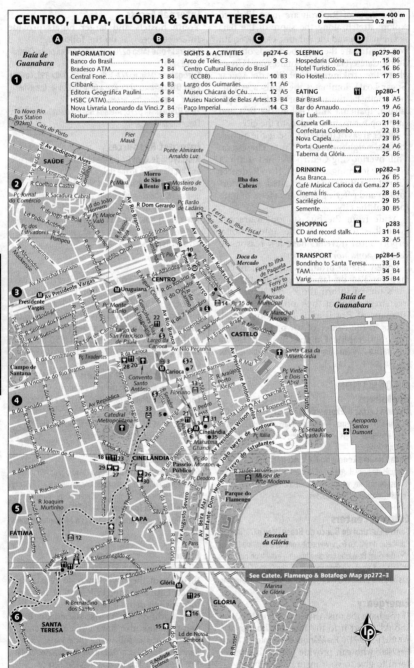

CENTRO, LAPA, GLÓRIA & SANTA TERESA

| 0 | 400 m |
| 0 | 0.2 mi |

INFORMATION
Banco do Brasil.............................1 B4
Bradesco ATM...............................2 B4
Central Fone.................................3 B4
Citibank.......................................4 B3
Editora Geográfica Paulini..............5 B4
HSBC (ATM).................................6 B4
Nova Livraria Leonardo da Vinci.....7 B4
Riotur..8 B3

SIGHTS & ACTIVITIES   pp274–6
Arco de Teles................................9 C3
Centro Cultural Banco do Brasil
  (CCBB)....................................10 B3
Largo dos Guimarães....................11 A6
Museu Chácara do Céu................12 A5
Museu Nacional de Belas Artes....13 B4
Paço Imperial.............................14 C3

SLEEPING   pp279–80
Hospedaria Glória.......................15 B6
Hotel Turístico...........................16 B6
Rio Hostel.................................17 B5

EATING   pp280–1
Bar Brasil..................................18 A5
Bar do Arnaudo..........................19 A6
Bar Luís....................................20 B4
Cazuela Grill.............................21 B4
Confeitaria Colombo....................22 B3
Nova Capela.............................23 B5
Porta Quente............................24 A5
Taberna da Glória.......................25 B6

DRINKING   pp282–3
Asa Branca................................26 B5
Café Musical Carioca da Gema.27 B5
Cinema Íris...............................28 B4
Sacrilégio................................29 B5
Semente..................................30 B5

SHOPPING   p283
CD and record stalls...................31 B4
La Vereda................................32 A5

TRANSPORT   pp284–5
Bondinho to Santa Teresa............33 B4
TAM..34 B4
Varig......................................35 B4

Baía de Guanabara

To Novo Rio
Bus Station
(92km)

SAÚDE

CENTRO

Presidente
Vargas

Campo de
Santana

CINELÂNDIA

FÁTIMA

LAPA

SANTA
TERESA

GLÓRIA

CASTELO

Baía de
Guanabara

Aeroporto
Santos
Dumont

Ilha das
Cabras

Ilha Fiscal

Enseada
da Glória

Marina
de Glória

See Catete, Flamengo & Botafogo Map pp272–3

Copacabana 594); International Airport (Map p268; Terminal 1, 3rd fl)
Citibank Centro (Map p270; Rua da Assembléia 100); Ipanema (Map p275; Rua Visconde de Pirajá 459A)
HSBC (Map p270; Av Rio Branco 108, Centro) Has ATMs.

The international airport has Banco do Brasil machines on the third floor and currency exchange booths on the **arrivals floor** (☺ 6:30am-11pm).

In Copacabana, *casas de cambio* (exchange places) cluster behind the Copacabana Palace Hotel on Avenida NS de Copacabana. Ipanema has several places scattered along Rua Visconde da Pirajá near Praça General Osório.

In Centro, some travel agencies double as exchange offices on Avenida Presidente Rio Branco, just north of Avenida Presidente Vargas. Be cautious when carrying money in the city center and don't take much to the beach.

Post

Correios (post offices) are prevalent throughout Rio, and easily identified by their yellow and blue signage. Any mail addressed to Posta Restante, Rio de Janeiro, Brazil, ends up at the **central post office** (Map p270; Rua Primeiro de Março 64, Centro).

Other branches include:
Botafogo (Praia de Botafogo 324)
Copacabana (Av Nossa Senhora de Copacabana 540)
Ipanema (Rua Prudente de Morais 147)

Telephone

To make an international call, try:
Central Fone (Map p270; Largo da Carioca plaza) In the center of town.
Rodoviária Novo Rio (Map p268; Bus Station)
Tele Rede (Map p278; Av Nossa Senhora de Copacabana 209).
Telemar (Map p278; Av Nossa Senhora de Copacabana 540)

Tourist Offices

Riotur (☎ 0xx21-2542-8080; ☺ 8am-8pm) The very useful city tourism bureau operates a tourist information hotline. The receptionists speak English. Staff at Riotur will phone around to make you a hotel reservation.

Riotur operates the following offices and booths:
Bus station (Map p268; Rodoviária Novo Rio; ☺ 6am-midnight) Booth.

Centro (Map p270; Rua da Assembléia 10, 9th fl; Carioca)
Copacabana (Map p278; Avenida Princesa Isabel 183; ☺ 8am-8pm)
International airport (Map p268; ☺ 5am-11pm) Booth.
Pão de Açúcar (☺ 8am-7pm) Booth.

Travel Agencies

Andes Sol (Map p278; 0xx21-2275-4370; andessol@uol .com.br; Av Nossa Senhora de Copacabana 209) A friendly, multilingual agency that can help arrange discounted flights and help you save on accommodations within Rio.

DANGERS & ANNOYANCES

Rio, like other metropolitan destinations, has its share of crime and violence. But if you travel sensibly when visiting the city, you will likely suffer nothing worse than a few bad hangovers. All the same, theft is not uncommon, but you can take precautions to minimize the risks.

Buses are well-known targets for thieves. Avoid taking them after dark, and keep an eye out while aboard. Take taxis at night to avoid walking along empty streets and beaches. That holds especially true for Centro, which becomes deserted in the evening and on weekends, and is better explored during the week.

Copacabana and Ipanema beaches are safer than others, owing to a police presence there, but don't get complacent. Avoid taking anything of value to the beach, and always stay alert – especially during holidays (such as Carnaval) when the sands get fearfully crowded.

Get in the habit of carrying small bills separate from your wallet so you don't have to flash a wad when you pay for things. Maracanã football stadium is worth a visit, but take only spending money for the day and avoid the crowded sections. Don't wander into the *favelas* at any time.

If you have the misfortune of being robbed, hand over the goods. Thieves in the city are only too willing to use their weapons if given provocation.

See the Brazil Directory (p387) for other tips on how to avoid becoming a victim.

Scams

A common beach scam is for one thief to approach you from one side and ask you for a light or the time. While you're distracted, the thief's partner grabs your gear from the other side.

CATETE, FLAMENGO & BOTAFOGO

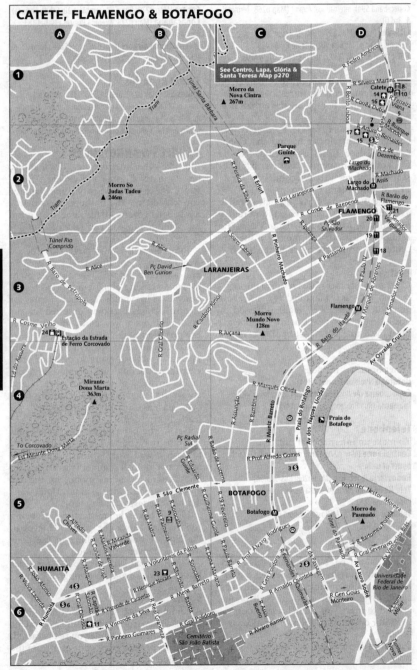

BRAZIL

See Centro, Lapa, Glória &
Santa Teresa Map p270

R Pedro Américo

Túnel Santa Bárbara

Tram

Morro da
Nova Cintra
▲ 267m

R Silveira Martins
Catete
R Bento Lisboa
R Corrêa Dutra
R Ferreira
Viana
8
14
10
16
5
@
7
R Buarque
de Macedo
R Arturo
Bernardes
17
15
R 2 de
Dezembro

Parque
Guinle

Largo do
Machado

R Machado
Assis

Largo do
Machado

R Barão do
Flamengo

Morro So
Judas Tadeu
▲ 246m

Tram

R Pereira da Silva

R Erfurt

R das Laranjeiras

R Conde de Baependi

FLAMENGO
21
20
19
18

Pç São
Salvador

R Iplanga

Túnel Rio
Comprido

R Baro de Petrópolis

R Alice

R Alice

R Soures Cabral

Pç David
Ben Gurion

LARANJEIRAS

R Pinheiro Machado

R Passandu

R Paulo IV

R Marquês de Abrantes

R Cosme Velho

24

Estação da Estrada
de Ferro Corcovado

R Gral Glicério

R Cardoso Júnior

Morro
Mundo Novo
128m
▲

R Juçana

Flamengo
M

R Baro do Itambi

R Senador Vergueiro

Ld do Ascurra

Mirante
Dona Marta
363m
▲

To Corcovado
Est Mirante Dona Marta

R Assunção

R Bambina

R Marqués Olinda

Pç Radial
Sul

R Barão de Lucerna

R Eduardo
Guinle

R Prof Alfredo Gomes

R Muniz Barreto

Praia do Botafogo

Av das Nações Unidas

Praia do
Botafogo

3

Av Reporter Nestor Moreira

R Alfredo
Chaves

R Martins Ferreira

R Conde de Irajá

R da Matriz

R das Palmeiras

R São Clemente

R Guilherme Guinle

R 19 Fevereiro

R Sorocaba

9

BOTAFOGO

Botafogo
M

R Prof Álvaro Rodrigues

Morro do
Pasmado
▲

Túnel do Pasmado

R Bartolomeu Portela

HUMAITÁ

R Vilela Lacerda

R João Afonso

R Humaitá

R Gral Dionísio

R Visconde de Caravelas

R Capitão
Salomão

R Visconde de Silva

R Real Grandeza

R Miranda Valverde

R Voluntários da Pátria

R São João Batista

R Henrique Novais

R Dona Mariana

R Paulo Barreto

R Mena Barreto

R Gral Polidoro

23

R Assis
Bueno

R São Polidoro

R Gen Polidoro

R Fernandes

R Arnaldo Quintela

2

R da Passagem

R Gral Severiano

Av Laura Sodré

Av Venceslau Brás

Universidade
Federal de
Rio de Janeiro

4

11

R Pinheiro Guimares

R Álvaro Ramos

Cemitério
São João Batista

R Gen Goiás
Monteiro

R Gen Severiano

Túnel
Novo

R Radm
Müller

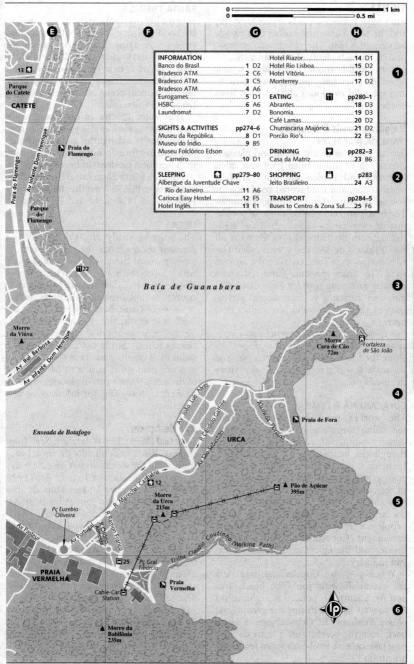

0 ————— 1 km
0 ————— 0.5 mi

INFORMATION
Banco do Brasil...................1 D2
Bradesco ATM......................2 C6
Bradesco ATM......................3 C5
Bradesco ATM......................4 A6
Eurogames...........................5 D1
HSBC....................................6 A6
Laundromat.........................7 D2

SIGHTS & ACTIVITIES   pp274–6
Museu da República............8 D1
Museu do Índio....................9 B5
Museu Folclórico Edson
    Carneiro..........................10 D1

SLEEPING   pp279–80
Albergue da Juventude Chave
    Rio de Janeiro.................11 A6
Carioca Easy Hostel..............12 F5
Hotel Inglês.........................13 E1

Hotel Riazor........................14 D1
Hotel Rio Lisboa..................15 D2
Hotel Vitória.......................16 D1
Monterrey...........................17 D2

EATING   pp280–1
Abrantes.............................18 D3
Bonomia.............................19 D3
Café Lamas..........................20 D2
Churrascaria Majórica..........21 D2
Porcão Rio's........................22 E3

DRINKING   pp282–3
Casa da Matriz.....................23 B6

SHOPPING   p283
Jeito Brasileiro.....................24 A3

TRANSPORT   pp284–5
Buses to Centro & Zona Sul....25 F6

Parque
do Catete
CATETE

Praia do
Flamengo

Praia do Flamengo

Av Infante Dom Henrique

Parque
do
Flamengo

Baía de Guanabara

Morro
da Viúva

Av Rui Barbosa

Av Infante Dom Henrique

Enseada de Botafogo

Morro
Cara de Cão
72m

Fortaleza
de São João

Praia de Fora

Av João Luís Alves

R Cândido Gaffrée

Al São Sebastião

Alameda Portolano

URCA

Pão de Açúcar
395m

Pç Euzebio
Oliveira

R Marechal Cantuária

Morro
da Urca
215m

R Ramon Franco

Av Portugal

Av Pasteur

Trilha Claudio Coutinho (Walking Path)

**PRAIA
VERMELHA**

Pç Gral
Tibúrcio

Praia
Vermelha

Cable-Car
Station

Morro da
Babilônia
235m

BRAZIL

SIGHTS

Rio's most famous attractions are sand, sky and the sea of beautiful bodies that parade between the two. The *cidade maravilhosa*, however, boasts plenty of other attractions – historic neighborhoods, colorful museums, colonial churches, picturesque gardens and splendid overlooks all lie within Rio's borders.

Neighborhoods & Beaches

IPANEMA & LEBLON

Boasting a magnificent beach and pleasant streets full of music-filled bars and cafés, Ipanema and Leblon are Rio's loveliest destinations, and the favored residence for young, beautiful (and wealthy) Cariocas. The beach attracts a broad range of people, mixing over games of volleyball and football beneath the tropical rays. Posto 9, off Rua Vinícius de Moraes, is also called Garota de Ipanema (named after the famous song 'Girl from Ipanema') and remains a popular gathering spot for old leftists, hippies and artists; a younger crowd arrives later in the day to watch the sunset over beers or joints.

Arpoador, between Ipanema and Copacabana, is Rio's most popular surf spot. All along the beach the waves can get big, and the undertow is strong – swim only where the locals do.

COPACABANA & LEME

The world's most famous beach runs for 4.5km along one of the world's most densely populated residential areas. Although the beaches aren't as pristine as Ipanema's, Copacabana pulses with an energy unknown elsewhere. Praia do Leme in the east end contains dozens of restaurants and bars lining the walk overlooking the sea, and at all times of day, offers people-watching at its finest. For pure city excitement, Copacabana is Rio's liveliest theater and the epicenter of Brazil's tourism industry.

When you visit Copacabana, take only the essentials with you. The beach area and Av Atlântica is policed at night, so it's OK to walk around during the evening. Av Nossa Senhora de Copacabana, a block back from the beachfront, is more dangerous; take care on weekends when few locals are around.

SANTA THERESA

Set on a hill overlooking the city, the neighborhood of Santa Theresa, with its cobbled streets and aging mansions, retains the charm of days long past. Currently the residence of a new generation of artists and bohemians, Santa Theresa has a small but lively music scene on weekends around Largo dos Guimarães.

The **Museu Chácara do Céu** (Map p270; Rua Murtinho Nobre 93; admission US$2, free Sunday; 🕐 noon-5pm Wed-Mon) is a delightful art and antiques museum in a former industrialist's mansion with beautiful gardens and great views.

To reach Santa Theresa, take the **bondinho** (streetcar; tickets US$0.50) from the station on Rua Profesor Lélio Gama, behind Petrobras.

URCA

The peaceful, shady streets of Urca offer a pleasant escape from the urban bustle of other parts of the city. Along the seawall, which forms the northwestern perimeter of Pão de Açucar, fishermen cast for dinner as couples lounge beneath palm trees, taking in views of Guanabara Bay and Christ the Redeemer off in the distance. Tiny Praia Vermelha in the south is one of Rio's prettiest beaches – but is not clean enough to swim in. At night musicians play here, and you can hear great samba or MPB in one of the city's finest open-air locales. See Pão de Açucar, following, for information getting there.

Pão de Açucar

Sugar Loaf (Map p273) is dazzling. Seen from its peak, Rio is undoubtedly the most beautiful city in the world. Sunset on a clear day is the most spectacular time to go. Try to avoid going between 10 and 11am or 2pm and 3pm, when most tourist buses arrive. To reach the summit, 396m above Rio and the Baía de Guanabara, you have to take two cable cars (US$8), changing from one to the other at Morro da Urca (215m). The first cable car departs from Praça General Tibúrcio at Praia Vermelha in Urca about every 30 minutes from 8am to 10pm daily. The second car continues the journey to Pão de Açucar's summit, departing every 30 minutes from 8:15am to 10pm. To get there take an 'Urca' bus – (No 107 from Centro or Flamengo, No 500, 511 or 512 from the zona sul).

IPANEMA, LEBLON & GÁVEA

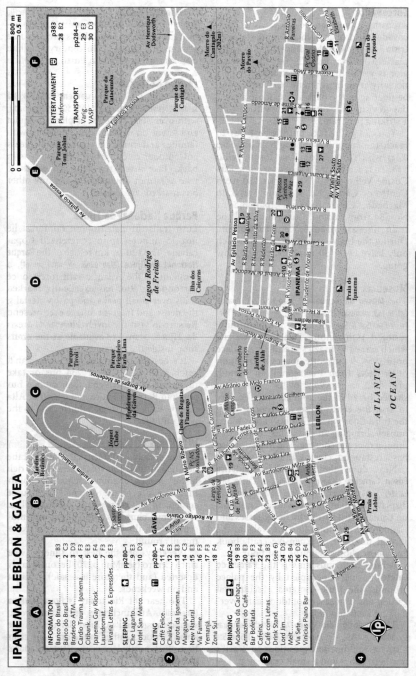

INFORMATION
Banco do Brasil...................1	B3
Banco do Brasil...................2	C3
Bradesco ATM.....................3	D3
Cardio Trauma Ipanema........4	F3
Citibank.............................5	F3
Ipanema Gay Kiosk..............6	F4
Laundromat........................7	F3
Livraria Letras & Expressões...8	E3

SLEEPING pp280-1
Che Lagarto.......................9	E3
Hotel San Marco................10	D3

EATING pp280-1
Caffè Felice.......................11	F4
Chaika's............................12	E3
Garota da Ipanema............13	E3
Manguaça..........................14	C3
New Natural.......................15	F3
Via Farme..........................16	F3
Yemanjá.............................17	F3
Zona Sul............................18	F4

DRINKING pp282-3
Academia da Cachaça..........19	B3
Armazém do Café...............20	E3
Bar Bofetada.....................21	F3
Cafeína..............................22	F4
Café com Letras.................23	B3
Drink Stand...................(see 6)
Lord Jim............................24	D3
Melt..................................25	B4
Via Sete............................26	D3
Vinicius Piano Bar...............27	E4

ENTERTAINMENT
Plataforma.........................28	B2

TRANSPORT pp284-5
Varig.................................29	E3
VASP.................................30	D3

BRAZIL

Parque Tom Jobim

Parque Tivoli

Parque Brigadeiro Faria Lima

Parque da Catacumba

Parque do Cantagalo

Jardim Botânico

Joquei Clube

Hipódromo da Gávea

Clube de Regatas Flamengo

Lagoa Rodrigo de Freitas

Ilha dos Caiçaras

Jardim de Alah

Morro do Cantagalo (202m)

Morro do Pavão

ATLANTIC OCEAN

Praia do Arpoador

Praia do Ipanema

Praia de Leblon

GÁVEA

LEBLON

IPANEMA

0   800 m
0   0.5 mi

Corcovado

Atop the 710m-high peak known as Corcovado (Hunchback), the looming statue of **Cristo Redentor** (Christ the Redeemer; Map p268) gazes placidly out over Rio. The outstretched savior is visible from all over the city, particularly at night, when he often appears to be floating in the dark sky. Choose a clear day to visit, and you will be rewarded with a striking panorama.

You can go by taxi, but the best way to reach the summit is by **cog train** (round trip US$8), which leaves from Rua Cosme Velho 513. To reach the train take a taxi or a 'Rua Cosme Velho' bus – No 184 or 180 from Centro or Glória, No 583 from Largo do Machado, Copacabana or Ipanema or No 584 from Leblon. Corcovado and the train line are open 8:30am to 6:30pm. During the high season, the trains, which only leave every 30 minutes, can be slow going.

Museums

The **Museu da República** (Map pp272-3; Rua do Catete 153; admission US$2, free Wed; ☾ noon–5pm Tue-Fri, 2-6pm Sat & Sun) occupies the beautifully restored 19th-century Palácio do Catete, which served as Brazil's presidential palace until 1954. It currently houses a collection of artifacts from the republican period, providing an overview of the events that shaped Brazil in the 20th century. Be sure to visit the eerily preserved rooms along the third floor where Getúlio Vargas killed himself, bringing an end to his 20-year dominion over the country. The museum also has a restaurant, cinema and bookstore.

Next door, the small **Museu Folclórico Edson Carneiro** (Map pp272-3; Rua do Catete 181, Catete; ☾ 11am-6pm Tue-Fri, 3-6pm Sat, Sun & holidays) displays Brazilian folk art with an emphasis on Bahian artists. Colorful headdresses and Candomblé costumes line the walls of the second floor. An inexpensive craft, book and music shop sits on the first floor.

Behind both museums is the **Parque do Catete**. Formerly occupied by the palace grounds, the park contains a sculptural garden and a pleasant outdoor café overlooking a small pond.

The **Museu do Índio** (Map pp272-3; Rua das Palmeiras 55; admission US$2; ☾ 9am-5:30pm Tue-Fri, 1-5pm Sat & Sun) has multimedia expositions on Brazil's northern tribes and a small craft shop.

Museu Nacional de Belas Artes (Map p270; Av Rio Branco 199; admission US$3, free Sun; ☾ 10am-6pm Tue-Fri, 2-6pm Sat, Sun & holidays), Rio's premier fine art museum, houses 20th-century Brazilian classics such as Cândido Portinari's *Café*.

Jardim Botânico

This exotic 1.41-sq-km **garden** (Map p268; Jardim Botânico 920; admission US$1.50; ☾ 8am-5pm), with over 5000 varieties of plants, is quiet and serene on weekdays and blossoms with families and music on weekends. A pleasant outdoor café overlooks the gardens in back. Take insect repellent. To get there take a 'Jardim Botânico' bus, or any other bus marked 'via Jóquei.'

Parque Nacional da Tijuca

Lush trails through tropical rainforest lie just 15 minutes from concretized Copacabana. The 120-sq-km refuge of the **Parque Nacional da Tijuca** (Map p268; ☾ until sunset), a remnant of the Atlantic rain forest once surrounding Rio, has excellently marked trails over small peaks and past waterfalls, the dense and fragrant foliage ever present. Be sure to visit the lovely Floresta (Forest) da Tijuca. Maps are available at the crafts shop inside the entrance.

It's best to go by car, but if you can't, catch a No 221, 233 or 234 bus or take the metro to Saens Peña, then catch a bus going to Barra da Tijuca and get off at Alta da Boa Vista, the small suburb close to the park entrance.

WALKING TOUR

Although lacking the sensual charms of the beaches in the *zona sul*, central Rio's rich history makes for some fascinating exploring. The site of the original Portuguese settlement 500 years ago is today a collage of colonial churches, wide plazas and museums, with the bustle of commerce teeming all around.

Weekdays are the best to time to visit since Centro (see Map p270) becomes fairly deserted (and therefore less safe) at night and on weekends.

The heart of Rio today is **Praça Floriano** (Cinelândia). At lunchtime and after work, samba music and political debate fills the air as Cariocas gather in the open-air cafés here. Just north looms the **Museu Nacional de Belas Artes (1)**.

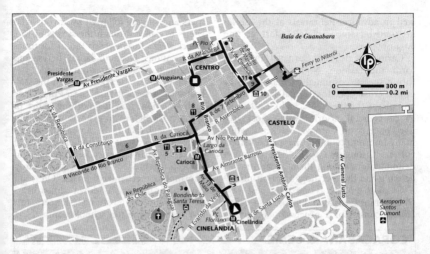

From Praça Floriano leave its northwest corner and walk along pedestrian-only **Avenida 13 de Maio**, home to some of Rio's best *suco* (juice) bars. Cross Av Almirante Borroso and you're in the Largo da Carioca. Up on the hill is the recently restored **Convento de Santo Antônio (2)**, whose eponymous statue is an object of great devotion to many Cariocas in search of a husband.

From the convent, you'll notice the **Petrobras (3)** building (rather like the old Rubik's cube) and the ultramodern **Catedral Metropolitana (4)**. If you have time for a side trip, take the **bondinho** (streetcar, US$0.75) up to Santa Theresa. (See Neighborhoods & Beaches, p274).

Not far from the cathedral, you'll find old shops lining 19th-century **Rua da Carioca**. Stop at **Bar Luís (5)**, a Rio institution with good food and beer (see Eating p280). At the end of the block you'll emerge into the bustle of **Praça Tiradentes (6)**, once a fabulous part of the city. It's worth exploring as far as **Campo de Santana (7)** – a pleasant park where Emperor Dom Pedro I declared Brazil's independence from Portugal in 1822.

Back near Avenida Rio Branco, hit the elegant coffee house **Confeitaria Colombo** (8; Rua Gonçalves Dias 30) for good espresso and decadent desserts beneath the stained-glass skylight. From here, cross Av Rio Branco and continue along Rua 7 de Setembro into **Praça 15 de Novembro (9)**. Beside this square stands the **Paço Imperial (10**; admission free; noon-6:30pm Tue-Sun), formerly the royal palace and seat of government. Today it houses temporary exhibits and a couple of popular cafés. Across the square is the **Arco de Teles (11)**, an arch formed by part of an old aqueduct. Walking through into **Travessa de Comércio**, you'll find a number of outdoor bars, restaurants and simple colonial churches. It's a colorful area.

From Praça 15 de Novembro, you can stroll over to the **waterfront**, where frequent ferries leave to **Niterói**, on the east side of the Baía de Guanabara. If you want to extend your walking tour, go back through Arco de Teles and follow the street around toward Rua Primeiro de Março. Walk north to the **Centro Cultural do Banco do Brasil (12**; see p269). From here, head back to Av Rio Branco and try to imagine how it was in 1910: a tree-lined boulevard with sidewalk cafés – the Champs Elysées of the tropics.

FESTIVALS & EVENTS

Colorful, outrageous, hedonistic – words do little justice to capture the bacchanalian spectacle of Carnaval that lends the country much notoriety. Foreigners arrive in droves to join Brazilians as they drink, dance, celebrate and chalk up a few sins before Ash Wednesday brings it all (somewhat) to a close. Wild and unforgettable it may be, but cheap it isn't: room rates and taxi fares triple and quadruple; and some thieves keep in the spirit of things by robbing in costume.

Carnaval officially lasts from Friday to Tuesday preceding Lent, but revelry begins well in advance. Rehearsals at the *escolas de samba* (samba schools) start around August.

Cariocas celebrate Carnaval in every form and fashion. Nightclubs and bars throw special costumed events, while the upper crust opts for formal balls. Parks and plazas (Largo do Machado, Cathedral, Praça General Osório) often host free live concerts on Carnaval weekend, while many impromptu parties happen on street corners throughout town. The common denominators among them all are music, dancing and the ever-flowing caipirinha.

Going to a *banda* is one of the best ways to celebrate Carnaval. *Bandas,* also called *blocos*, consist of a procession of drum-mers and singing followed by anyone who wants to dance through the streets of Rio. Check *Veja*'s Rio insert or Riotur for times and locations. *Blocos* in Santa Theresa and Ipanema come highly recommended.

The main parade takes place in the **sambódromo** (Rua Marques do Sapuçaí) near Praça Onze metro station, and it's nothing short of spectacular. Before an exuberant crowd of some 30,000, each of 14 samba schools has their hour to dazzle the audience. Painted dancers wearing feather headdresses and rhinestone-studded G-strings gyrate atop enormous, mechanized floats. On foot, rows of drummers lay down samba beats as thousands of costumed dancers fol-low behind. The top schools compete on

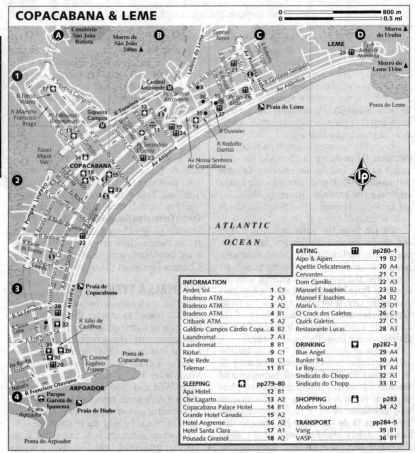

COPACABANA & LEME

INFORMATION	
Andes Sol	1 C1
Bradesco ATM	2 A3
Bradesco ATM	3 A2
Bradesco ATM	4 B1
Citibank ATM	5 A2
Galdino Campos Cárdio Copa	6 B2
Laundromat	7 A3
Laundromat	8 B1
Riotur	9 C1
Tele Rede	10 C1
Telemar	11 B1

SLEEPING	pp279–80
Apa Hotel	12 B1
Che Lagarto	13 A2
Copacabana Palace Hotel	14 B1
Grande Hotel Canada	15 A2
Hotel Angrense	16 A3
Hotel Santa Clara	17 A1
Pousada Girassol	18 A2

EATING	pp280–1
Aipo & Aipim	19 B2
Apetite Delicatessen	20 A4
Cervantes	21 C1
Dom Camillo	22 A3
Manoel E Joachim	23 B2
Manoel E Joachim	24 B2
Mariu's	25 D1
O Crack dos Galetos	26 C1
Quick Galetos	27 C1
Restaurante Lucas	28 A3

DRINKING	pp282–3
Blue Angel	29 A4
Bunker 94	30 A4
Le Boy	31 A4
Sindicato do Chopp	32 A3
Sindicato do Chopp	33 B2

SHOPPING	p283
Modern Sound	34 A2

TRANSPORT	pp284–5
Varig	35 B1
VASP	36 B1

BRAZIL

Carnaval Sunday and Monday (February 6 and 7 in 2005; February 26 and 27 in 2006; February 18 and 19 in 2007).

The metro runs round the clock during Carnaval and is by far the safest way to reach the *sambódromo*.

For information on buying sambódromo tickets at official prices (around US$40), stop by **Riotur** (www.rio.rj.gov.br/riotur) or visit its website. By Carnaval weekend most tickets are sold out, leaving you to the mercy of the scalpers (they'll find you), or to simply show up at the sambódromo around midnight, three or four hours into the show, when you can get tickets at the grandstand for about US$10.

For on-the-spot Carnaval information, get Riotur's special Carnaval guide and *Veja* magazine with the Rio insert, which has details of all the balls and *bandas*.

If you fancy really getting into the swing of Carnaval, it's not hard to join an *escola de samba* and take part in the parades yourself.

SLEEPING

The neighborhood of Catete (kah-teh-chee) remains popular with backpackers, though there isn't much nightlife around. If you plan on going out a lot, remember to factor in the extra dough you'll pay on the cab fare. Copacabana and Ipanema offer both the lure of the beach and the distractions of the evening, but accommodations cost noticeably more.

Reservations are a good idea, especially for expensive places. Booking in advance, or on the spot through a Rio travel agency, will often gain you a discount of around 30% — except with some online bookings. Try Andes Sol (p271). Around New Year's Eve and Carnaval, prices rise and rooms disappear, but you should be able to find one somewhere.

Hostels

Che Lagarto Copacabana (Map p278; ☎ 0xx21-2256-2776; Rua Anita Garibaldi 87; www.chelagarto.com; dm/d US$12/30); Ipanema (Map p275; ☎ 0xx21-2247-4582; Rua Barão de Jaguaripe 208; dm/d US$14/34) With locations in Copacabana and Ipanema, Che Lagarto is popular with backpackers. The hostel in Copacabana attracts a young crowd that gathers around the pool table in the evening for cocktails and pickup games.

The friendly staff is particularly keen on arranging nights out for guests. In Ipanema the hostel lies on a quiet, shady street one block from Lagoa and runs an outdoor bar (until 11pm) with a view of Corcovado.

Rio Hostel (Map p270; ☎ 0xx21-3852-0827; www.riohostel.com; Rua Joaquim Murtinho; dm/d US$11/34; ▣) Situated in lovely Santa Teresa, the hostel boasts sweeping views over downtown and is ideal for travelers interested in being near Rio's most bohemian neighborhoods. Brazilian run, the sunny hostel has ample space for lounging and a lovely patio with a swimming pool.

Carioca Easy Hostel (Map pp272-3; ☎ 0xx21-2295-7805; www.cariocahostel.com.br; Rua Marechal Cantuária 168; dm US$13) Another locally run hostel, Carioca Easy lies below Pão de Açucar in the tranquil neighborhood of Urca. The friendly owner has a wealth of information about Rio.

Albergue da Juventude Chave Rio de Janeiro (Map pp272-3; ☎ 0xx21-2286-0303; www.riohostel.com.br; Rua General Dionísio 63; dm US$10) The HI hostel in Botafogo is a model youth hostel that attracts a lively international crowd, as well as Brazilians. It gets busy, so you need to make reservations. From Novo Rio bus station, catch bus No 170, 172 or 173 and ask to get off at the Largo dos Leões. Go up Rua Voluntários da Pátria to Rua General Dionísio, then turn left. Non-members pay 50% more and can only stay 24 hours, but you can buy an HI card there for US$10.

Hotels
GLÓRIA, CATETE & FLAMENGO

Hotel Turístico (Map p270; ☎ 0xx21-2557-7698; Ladeira da Glória 30; s/d US$13/23) On a quiet street up from Glória metro station, lies one of Rio's most popular budget hotels, with a helpful staff and clean, safe rooms. A laid-back vibe permeates the open lobby.

Hotel Riazor (Map pp272-3; ☎ 0xx21-2225-0121; Rua do Catete 160; s/d $15/20) A few steps from the Catete metro, Hotel Riazor has clean aircon apartments and standard rooms.

Hotel Vitória (Map pp272-3; ☎ 0xx21-2205-5397; Rua do Catete 172; s/d US$13/18) The rugged quarters here have seen better days, but Hotel Vitória remains popular with budget travelers – particularly groups of Israelis.

The **Monterrey** (Map pp272-3; ☎ 0xx21-2265-9899, Rua Artur Bernardes 39; s/d quartos US$8/13, s/d apartamentos US$10/16) and **Hotel Rio Lisboa** (Map pp272-3;

☎ 0xx21-2265-9599; Rua Artur Bernardes 29; s quartos US$7, s/d apartamentos US$12/16), on the same quiet street, are two of the cheapest hotels in Catete. Rooms are spare, clean and a bit short on natural light. Breakfast in the Rio Lisboa is brought to your room.

Hotel Inglês (Map pp272-3; ☎ 0xx21-2558-3052; www.hotelingles.com.br; Rua Silveira Martins 20; s/d US$25/32) This two-star hotel in a good location has friendly staff and excellent rooms. Good value if you can swing it.

Hospedaria Glória (Map p270; ☎ 0xx21-2558-8064; Rua do Catete 34; r per person US$5) The dreary, men-only quarters are perhaps the cheapest digs in Rio, if also the least inspiring.

COPACABANA & IPANEMA

Pousada Girassol (Map p270; ☎ 0xx21-2256-6951; pousadagirassol@infolink.com.br; Travessa Angrense 25A; s/d US$26/33) The budget price (for Copacabana) and the big cheerful *apartamentos* (with ceiling fans) make this a travelers' favorite in the zona sul. Friendly staff.

Hotel Angrense (Map p278; ☎ 0xx21-2548-0509; angrense@antares.com.br; Travessa Angrense 25; s/d quartos US$22/29, s/d apartamentos US$27/35) Just next door to Girassol, you'll find clean but dreary *quartos* and slightly more spacious *apartamentos*. English is spoken.

Hotel Santa Clara (Map p278; ☎ 0xx21-2256-2650: reserva@hotelsantaclara.com.br; Rua Décio Vilares 316; s/d US$31/34) A delightful Copacabana option on a shady street off the main drag. Sunny rooms, some with balconies.

Apa Hotel (Map p278; ☎ 0xx21-2548-8112; apa@apahotel.com.br; Rua República do Peru 305; s/d US$35/40) Three blocks from the beach, the Apa has decent rooms and friendly, English-speaking staff.

Grande Hotel Canada (Map p278; ☎ 0xx21-2257-1864; hotel.canada@uol.com.br; Av Nossa Senhora de Copacabana 687; s/d US$40/55) The sleek and somewhat imposing edifice has modern *apartamentos*, some with ocean views.

Hotel San Marco (Map p275; ☎ 0xx21-2540-5032; email@sanmarcohotel.net; Rua Visconde de Pirajá 524; s/d US$34/37) In one of the best locations in the city, near Ipanema beach, the San Marco has small air-con *apartamentos* with TVs and refrigerators. Laundry service on site.

EATING

Rio has a wealth of dining options, and it's not hard to find good, inexpensive food. For lunch, self-serve buffets offering Brazilian

dishes, salads, fruits and roasted meats cost around US$7 per kg (full plates cost about $3.50). Lunch counters serve *pratos feitos* for about US$4. For cafés, head to Ipanema with its abundance of coffee shops – good for lingering over pastries and espresso.

CENTRO

Bar Luís (Map p270; ☎ 0xx21-2262-6900; Rua da Carioca 39; ☒ lunch & dinner to midnight Mon-Sat) A Rio institution since 1887. You'll find filling portions of German food and Rio's best dark beer at moderate prices.

Confeitaria Colombo (Map p270; Rua Gonçalves Dias 34) Stained-glass windows and polished brocade provide the setting for java and mouth-watering desserts (try anything with chocolate in it).

Cazuela Grill (Map p270; Alcindo Guanabara 20A; per kg US$7) A recent favorite with Rio's working stiffs who pack this tasty lunchtime buffet, getting their fill of meats, pastas and fresh-squeezed juices.

LAPA & SANTA THERESA

Nova Capela (Map p270; Av Mem de Sá 96) Respected for traditional Portuguese cuisine since the early 1900s. Nova Capela attracts a garrulous late-night crowd, with its staples of good, cheap, entrees and legendarily bad-tempered waiters. The *cordeiro* (lamb) is tops.

Bar Brasil (Map p270; Av Mem de Sá 90) Next door, chefs at Bar Brasil prepare German dishes with Brazilian invention, and one entree easily feeds two.

In Santa Theresa on weekends, the restaurants around Largo dos Guimarães are lively, with music spilling onto the street.

Bar do Arnaudo (Map p270; Rua Almirante Alexandrino 316B) The view overlooking the city below Bar do Arnaudo is excellent, as are the northeastern Brazilian dishes. Try the excellent *carne do sol* (grilled salt meat).

Porta Quente (Map p270; cnr Largo dos Guimarães & Rua Almirante Alexandrino) A hip café that serves lighter fare like salads and delicious sandwiches. On weekends, it stays open late.

Taberna da Glória (Map p270; Rua do Russel 32B) Pleasant open-air spot with friendly service and good, inexpensive food such as pepper steak (US$6) and *moqueca* (US$5).

GLÓRIA, CATETE & FLAMENGO

Churrascaria Majórica (Map pp272-3; Rua Senador Vergueiro 11) A carnivore's delight in a kitschy, gaúcho-themed dining room. Good steaks cost US$7.

Just east, a number of restaurants line Rua Marquês de Abrantes, and the street is quite lively in the evening.

Café Lamas (Map pp272-3; Rua Marquês de Abrantes 18A) One of Rio's most renowned eateries, operating since 1874 – and the waiters here aren't much younger. Meats reign supreme. Try the *grilled linguiça* (sausage, US$7) or filet mignon with garlic (US$8).

Bonomia (Map pp272-3; Rua Marquês de Abrantes 38) Flamengo's best juice bar, serving over 30 different juices. Try Amazonian flavors like the smooth *cupuaçu* or the dark, rich *açai*.

Abrantes (Map pp272-3; Rua Marquês de Abrantes 38) This restaurant and café with outdoor seating prepares a tasty dinner and dessert crepes (US$2).

Porção Rio's (Map pp272-3; Av Infante Dom Henrique-Aterro) Top-notch *churrascaria* churning out plates and plates of the grilled stuff in Parque do Flamengo. Great views of Pão de Açúcar. All taxi drivers know it.

COPACABANA & LEME

Apetite Delicatessen (Map p278; Av Rainha Elizabeth 122, Copacabana). Cappuccinos go well with the fresh baked goods.

Aipo & Aipim (Map p278; Av Nossa Senhora de Copacabana 391B; 1kg US$7) The wide spread of tasty dishes at Aipo & Aipim makes for self-serve dining at its finest. Get there early to beat the crowds.

Cervantes (Map p278; Av Prado Junior 335B; sandwiches US$5) Rio's best sandwich joint and a colorful late-night hangout. Meat sandwiches come with pineapple. The beer, steak and fries are excellent too.

For finger-licking good chicken that doesn't come from a bucket, head to **O Crack dos Galetos** (Map p278; Av Prado Junior 63) or **Quick Galetos** (Map p278; Rua Duvivier 28A).

Restaurant Lucas (Map p278; Av Atlântica 3744; dishes from US$10) A popular beachfront spot serving reasonably priced seafood and German dishes.

Dom Camillo (Map p278; Av Atlântica 3056) Another ocean-facing spot, this one serving good Italian dishes just like Mom – or Dom, rather – used to make. The seafood pasta and tiramisu always gets rave reviews.

Manoel e Joaquim (Map p278; cnr Rua Siqueira Campos 12 & Avenida Atlântica 1936) Large portions of good, inexpensive Brazilian cuisine.

IPANEMA & LEBLON

The **Zona Sul supermarket** (Map p275; Rua Gomes Carneiro 29) is a good place to assemble cheap meals, which are great for picnics on the beach.

Cafeína (Map p275; Rua Farme de Amoedo 43, Ipanema) Waffles, desserts, dark coffees and espressos in the heart of Ipanema.

Armazém do Café (Map p275; Rua Maria Quitéria 77G, Ipanema) Snacks, coffee and desserts, with locations throughout the zona sul.

Café com Letras (Map p275; Av Bartolemeu Mitre 297, Leblon) Besides coffee and fresh juices, this stylish bistro serves up live music on weekend nights.

New Natural (Map p275; Rua Barão da Torre 167) A backpackers' favorite, offering a delicious organic buffet at lunchtime and a menu stocked with vegetarian items.

Manguaçu (Map p275; Av Ataulfo de Paiva 427) Enjoy hearty *pratos feitos* for US$2, or catch football on the tube at this popular Brazilian joint.

Chaika's (Map p275; Rua Visconde de Pirajá 321) This neon wonder has a stand-up fast-food bar and a restaurant in the back serving delicious hamburgers and the sweetest pastries.

Yemanjá (Map p275; Rua Visconde de Pirajá 128A) You'll find Bahian food at reasonable prices, something hard to find in Rio. The excellent seafood *moquecas* for US$20 are enough for two. Adorable wait staff.

Garota de Ipanema (Map p275; Rua Vinícius de Moraes 49) Lively open-air dining and delicious appetizers. There are always a few foreigners checking out the spot where Tom Jobim and Vinícius de Moraes composed 'The Girl from Ipanema.'

Via Farme (Map p275; Rua Farme de Amoedo 47; dishes US$15) A wide-ranging menu, filling pastas and good ambience make this an excellent choice. Plates serve two.

SPLURGE!

Mariu's (Map p278; Av Atlântica 290; buffet US$16). In addition to the heart-stopping array of delicious meats brought to your table, this Leme *churrascaria* has a lavish buffet table to end all buffet tables. Oysters on the half-shell, sushi, roasted vegetables with fresh herbs – just a sample of what you'll experience. At peak hours, be prepared to drain a few caipirinhas while you wait for a table.

BRAZIL

DRINKING

Ipanema and Leblon upstage other parts of the city when it comes to nightlife – though in recent years Lapa has surged as the top destination to hear live music. Copacabana's beachfront bars are good for a few drinks early in the evening, but things get seedy as the night wears on. Wherever you go, you're likely to meet a few Cariocas, who are not among the most noted introverts. For the latest on what's going on, check the entertainment section of *Jornal do Brasil* or the *Veja Rio* insert in *Veja* magazine, which comes out on Sunday.

Bars

Bar Brasil (Map p270; Avenida Mem de Sá 90) This bohemian hangout in Lapa always packs a crowd, and it's in a neighborhood brimming with music in the evenings.

Lord Jim (Map p275; Rua Paul Redfern 63) Foreigners knock each other down (really) to get at the Guinness flowing from the taps at this Ipanema pub.

Sindicato do Chopp (Map p278; Av Atlântica 3806 & Rua Santa Clara 18) Both Copacabana locations of this bar/restaurant attract a pre-partying crowd enticed by ice-cold glasses of *chopp* (pale blond pilsener draft beer).

Garota de Ipanema (Map p275; Rua Vinicius de Moraes 49) Fine place to be merry and watch the lively street scene unfolding.

Bar Bofetada (Map p275; Rua Farme do Amoedo 87A) This festive Ipanema favorite claims to be the most Carioca place in all of Rio, namely for its mixed and free-spirited crowd. Weekends they host live bossa nova and *choró*.

Academia de Cachaça (Map p275; Rua Conde de Bernadotte 26A) Fire water is the name of the game, and this Leblon institution has every variety under the tropical sun. For a treat (and/or a bad hangover), try the passion fruit caipirinha.

Via Sete (Map p275; Garcia d'Avila 125) Attracts a hip, downtown crowd sipping frozen cocktails and checking each other out on the front patio.

Nightclubs

Nothing happens before midnight. Cover charges range from US$3 to US$7, and in general women pay less than men, if at all.

Casa da Matriz (Map pp272-3; casadamatriz.com.br; Rua Henrique Novaes 107, Botafogo) Artwork lines the walls of this avant-garde space in Botafogo. With numerous little rooms to explore – lounge, screening room, dance floors – this old two-story mansion embodies the most creative side of the Carioca spirit. Check website for party listings – click 'festas.'

Bunker 94 (Map p278; www.bunker94.com.br; Rua Raul Pompéia 94, Copacabana) Hipsters and non-hipsters alike mix it up to drum 'n' bass, electropop and house music in one of three rooms in this Copacabana club.

Cinema Íris (Map p270; ☎ 0xx21-2262-1729, Rua da Carioca 51) Progressive house and techno are the fare at this Centro-based club that doubles as a porn theater by day. The Íris often hosts extravagant dance parties and raves.

Melt (Map p275; ☎ 0xx21-2249-9309; Rua Rita Ludolf 47, Leblon) This upscale Leblon restaurant and lounge transforms into a sexy dance space late in the evenings. Rotating parties attract eclectic DJs spinning world beats, trip-hop and samba, often accompanied by live percussionists.

Gay & Lesbian Venues

Rio's gay community, largely localized in Ipanema, is neither out nor flamboyant most of the year, except at Carnaval. Still, there is a large gay and lesbian scene in Rio, and gay couples are welcome almost everywhere.

On the beaches, you'll find gay-friendly drink stands across from the Copacabana Palace Hotel in Copacabana and opposite Rua Farme de Amoedo in Ipanema.

Blue Angel (Map p278; Rua Júlio de Castilhos 15) Good DJs lay down mellow grooves in this cozy, Copacabana club. A mixed crowd gathers during the week, while weekends belong to the boys.

Le Boy (Map p278; Rua Raul Pompéia 94) Speaking of boys, this is one of Copa's best (and largest) gay clubs. DJs spin house and drum 'n' bass on weekends. Drag shows are the fare during the week.

Caffe Felice (Map p275; Rua Gomes Carneiro 30) This quaint Ipanema café-cum-restaurant gathers a young gay crowd after 10pm.

Bar Bofetada (Map p275; Rua Farme do Amoedo 87A) Though not exclusively a gay bar, gay couples are part of the mix at this lively spot.

Live Music

Shows can happen any night of the week, but it's best to call or check the paper for listings. Cover charges vary from US$2 to US$5 (which sometimes includes a drink). Most venues don't get going until after 11pm.

Semente (Map p270; 0xx21- 2242-5165; Rua Joaquim Silva 138) A diverse crowd packs this bar in the rugged hood of Lapa for some of the best chorinho and samba in the city.

Asa Branco (Map p270; 0xx21-2224-2342; Avenida Mem de Sá 79) Housed in an old mansion, the pounding rhythms of samba here are not for wallflowers – nor is the spacious dance floor.

Other entertaining music places nearby include **Sacrilégio** (Map p270; 0xx21-3970-1461; Avenida Mem de Sá 81) and **Café Musical Carioca da Gema** (Map p270; 0xx21-2221-0043; Avenida Mem de Sá 79).

Vinícius Piano Bar (Map p275; 0xx21-2523-4757; Rua Prudente de Morais 34) Top bossa nova acts perform at this charming Ipanema spot.

ENTERTAINMENT
Samba

In addition to venues that host samba nights in Lapa (see Live Music, above), you can get your fill of the Brazilian beat at samba schools. Carnaval rehearsals in the top schools start around August and are wild, festive affairs generally open to the public. If you go, it's best to go with a Carioca or with a group as many of the schools lie in sketchy neighborhoods. Check with Riotur for schedules and locations. The best ones for tourists include:

Salgueiro (☎ 0xx21-2238-5564; Rua Silva Teles 104, Andaraí; admission US$3) Rehearsals at 10pm on Saturday.

Mangueira (☎ 0xx21-2567-4637; Rua Visconde de Niterói 1072, Mangueira; entry US$8) Rehearsals at 7pm on Saturday.

Plataforma (Map p275; ☎ 0xx21-2274-4022; Rua Adalberto Ferreira 32) If you don't mind rubbing elbows with groups of tourists, Plataforma hosts beautifully staged shows, though lacking the vibe you'd find at a samba school.

Sports

Nearly every boy in Brazil dreams of playing in Maracanã, Rio's enormous shrine to football (Map p268). Matches here rate among the most exciting in the world, and the behavior of the fans is no less colorful. The devoted pound huge samba drums as their team takes the field, and if things are going badly – or very well – fans are sometimes driven to sheer madness. Some detonate smoke bombs in team colors,

while others launch beer bottles, cups full of urine or dead chickens into the seats below.

Games take place year round and can happen any day of the week. Rio's big four clubs are Flamengo, Fluminense, Vasco da Gama and Botafogo.

To get to the **stadium** (Rua Professor Eurico Rabelo e Av Maracanã), take the metro to Maracanã station then walk along Avenida Osvaldo Aranha. Alternatively, catch any bus marked 'Maracanã' (from the *zona sul*, No 434, 464 or 455; from Praça 15 in Centro, No 238 or 239) and leave a couple of hours before kickoff.

The safest seats are on the lower level *cadeira*, where the overhead covering protects you from descending objects. The ticket price is US$5 for most games.

After the game, avoid the crowded buses, and go by metro or taxi.

SHOPPING
Markets

Feira do Nordestino (Map p268; Pavilhão de São Cristóvão near the Quinta da Boa Vista; ☺ until 3pm Sun). Northeastern in character with lots of food, drink and samba – well worth a visit.

Hippie Fair (Praça General Osório; ☺ 9am-6pm Sun) An Ipanema favorite with good souvenirs and even better people-watching.

Other places where you can purchase Brazilian handicrafts include Jeito Brasileiro, next to the Corcovado train terminal in Cosme Velho (Map p273), and **La Vereda** (Map p270; Rua Almirante Alexandrino 428) in Santa Teresa.

Music

On weekdays along Rua Pedro Lessa (Map p270) record and CD venders hawk their wares, ranging from American indie rock to vintage Brazilian funk. You'll pay less for music here than at stores, and most sellers will let you listen to anything – new or used – on portable CD players at their stands.

Modern sound (Map p278; www.modernsound.com.br; Rua Barata Ribeiro 502D) Rio's answer to Western megastores boasts the largest CD selection in the country. Knowledgeable staff can direct you to some of the better samba, bossa nova and MPB artists, and live bands perform daily in the adjoining café.

BRAZIL

GETTING THERE & AWAY

Air

Most flights depart from Aeroporto Galeão (also called Aeroporto António Carlos Jobim), 15km north of the center. Shuttle flights to/from São Paulo, and some flights for other nearby cities, use Aeroporto Santos Dumont in the city center. Also see Getting Into Town (p267).

In addition to ticket counters at the airport, Brazil's principal airlines have the following offices in the city:

TAM Centro (Map p270; ☎ 0xx21-2524-1717; Avenida Rio Branco 245, Centro)

Varig Centro (Map p270; ☎ 0xx21-2534-0333; Avenida Rio Branco 277); Copacabana (☎ 0xx21-2541-6343; Rua Rodolfo Dantas 16); Ipanema (Map p275; ☎ 0xx21-2523-0040; Rua Visconde de Pirajá 351)

VASP Centro (☎ 0xx21-3814-8000; Rua Santa Luzia 735); Copacabana (☎ 0xx21-3814-8094; Av Nossa Senhora de Copacabana 262); Ipanema (Map p275; ☎ 0xx21-3814-8098; Rua Visconde de Pirajá 444)

Many international airlines have offices on or near Avenida Rio Branco, Centro.

The following price information and schedule is subject to change. Prices quoted are one way and leave from Galeão.

Belém VASP, US$173, daily; Varig, US$264, 3 daily; Gol, US$292, Sun-Fri; TAM, US$354, daily.

Fortaleza Gol, US$190, 2 daily; VASP, US$210, 3 daily; TAM, US$242, 4 daily; Varig, US$267, 4 daily.

Foz do Iguaçu Varig, US$181, 2 daily; VASP, US$189, daily; TAM, US$195, daily.

Manaus VASP, US$204, 2 daily; Gol, US$205, Sun-Fri; Varig, US$286, 2 daily with extra services on Tue, Thu & Sun.

Recife VASP, US$146, 3 daily; Rio Sul US$165, 2 daily; Gol, US$194, daily; TAM, US$207, 4 daily; Varig, US$225, 4 daily.

Salvador VASP, US$99, 2 daily; Gol, US$100, 4 daily Sun-Fri, 3 daily Sat; Rio Sul, US$125, 2 daily; TAM, US$142, 4 daily; Varig, US$175, 3 daily, extra service Tue.

São Paolo VASP, US$80, 2 daily; TAM, US$81, 8 daily; Varig, US$88, 3 daily, extra service Tues, Thu & Sun; Gol, US$145, 4 daily.

Bus

Buses leave from the **Rodoviária Novo Rio** (Map p268; ☎ 0xx21-2291-5151; Av Francisco Bicalho) about 2km northwest of Centro. Several buses depart daily to most major destinations, but it's a good idea to buy tickets in advance. Excellent buses leave Novo Rio every 15 minutes or so for São Paulo (US$15, six hours). Approximate traveling times and fares to sample destinations are:

Destination	Duration in Hours	Cost
Asunción (Paraguay)	30	US$42
Belém	52	US$85
Buenos Aires (Argentina)	46	US$91
Belo Horizonte	7	US$12
Florianópolis	18	US$34
Foz do Iguaçu	22	US$29
Ouro Prêto	7	US$12
Parati	4	US$9
Petrópolis	1½	US$4
Porto Alegre	26	US$58
Porto Velho	54	US$88
Recife	42	US$60
Salvador	26	US$50
Santiago (Chile)	60	US$106

GETTING AROUND

Bus & Van

Rio buses are fast, frequent and cheap, and because Rio is long and narrow it's easy to get the right bus and usually no big deal if you're on the wrong one. Nine out of 10 buses going south from the center will go to Copacabana, and vice versa. The buses are, however, often crowded, stuck in traffic, and driven by raving maniacs. They're also the sites of many of the city's robberies, and it's not wise to ride late at night.

Board buses at the back and exit from the front. Money collectors sit at a turnstile in the rear, with the fare displayed nearby. To avoid pickpockets and muggers, pay and go through the turnstile, rather than lingering at the back of the bus. Avoid packed buses.

Minibuses (Cariocas call them vans) provide a faster alternative between Avenida Rio Branco in Centro and the *zona sul* as far as Barra da Tijuca. The destination is written in the front window. The flat fare runs US$1.50.

Metro

Rio's two-line subway system is an excellent and speedy way to get around some parts of the city. It's open from 6am to 11pm Monday to Saturday. The main line from Copacabana to Saens Peña has 17 stops. The first 14, from Copacabana to Estácio, are shared with the second line which diverges northward at Estácio to São Cristóvão, Maracanã and beyond.

Each ride costs US$0.70 and you can buy singles, returns or 10-ride tickets. Free subway maps are available at most stations.

Taxi

Rio's taxis are reasonably priced and particularly useful late at night and when you are carrying valuables. The flat rate is US$1, plus around US$0.50 per km – slightly more on nights and Sundays. **Radio-taxis** (☎ 0xx21-2260-2022) are 30% more expensive than others, but safer.

THE SOUTHEAST

The southeast is Brazil's economic powerhouse, but there's a lot more going on here than just mundane money-making. The region covers 11% of Brazil's total land mass and is comprised of four individual states:

Rio de Janeiro, São Paulo and Espírito Santo on the coast, and Minas Gerais (easily the biggest) inland. And with more than 44% of Brazil's population living here, it's definitely diverse: Japanese, German and French and a few indigenous languages are nearly as common as Portuguese.

Each year thousands of migrant workers flock to the Industrial Triangle of Rio de Janeiro, São Paulo and Belo Horizonte – Brazil's three richest and largest cities. But there's also a continuous influx of surfers and nature-lovers heading for pristine beach towns like Saquarema, Arraial do Cabo and fashionable Búzios (all in Rio state). History buffs marvel at the colonial splendors of Ouro Prêto, São João del Rei, Tiradentes

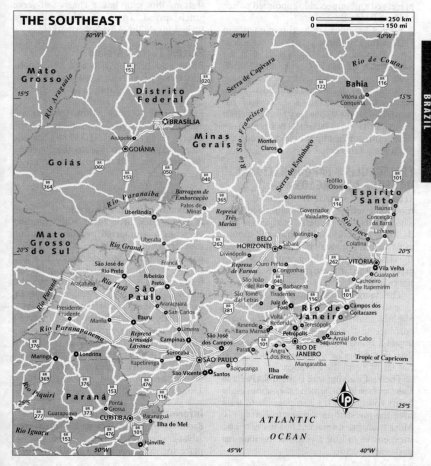

and Diamantina in Minas Gerais, and national parks dot the landscape all the way to the mega-metropolis of São Paulo.

PETRÓPOLIS

Petrópolis (population 270,000) was once the summer home of the Portuguese Imperial Family and is now back in vogue as a weekend retreat for stressed-out urbanites.

The main attractions are the **Catedral São Pedro de Alcântara**, housing the tombs of Brazil's last emperor, Dom Pedro II, and his wife and daughter; the **Casa de Santos Dumont**, summer home of Brazil's diminutive father of aviation and inventor of the wristwatch; and above all the **Museu Imperial** (admission US$2; ☻ noon-5:30pm Tue-Sun), in the perfectly preserved and impeccably appointed palace of Dom Pedro II.

Budget lodgings are hard to come by in Petrópolis – definitely bargain on weekdays. **Pousada 14 Bis** (☎ 0xx24-2231-0946; Rua Santos Dumont 162; dm US$13, s or d with bath US$20) is an attractive renovated colonial house with four-bed dorms near the bus station. Nearby **Comércio** (☎ 0xx24-2242-3500; Rua Dr Porciuncula 55; s/d US$10/16) has very basic but clean rooms. **Kafta** (Rua 16 de Março 52) is a great Arab restaurant, and just up the block Frango Bip has a great self-serve buffet.

TERESÓPOLIS & PARQUE NACIONAL DA SERRA DOS ÓRGÃOS

Teresópolis (population 115,000) is a mountain retreat, 95km northeast of Rio. The city itself is modern, prosperous and dull: the attraction is the dramatic mountains around it, which make Teresópolis the climbing and trekking center of Brazil – especially the fantastic rock pinnacles of the national park.

The **tourist office** (☎ 0xx21-2742-3352; Praça Olímpica; ☻ 8am-6pm) is in central Teresópolis. Slightly south of Teresópolis is the main entrance to the **Parque Nacional da Serra dos Órgãos** (☎ 0xx21-2642-1070; Hwy BR-116; admission US$3; ☻ 8am-5pm Sun-Tue). The **visitor center** is not far up from the entrance.

The best walking trail is the **Trilha Pedra do Sino** (admission US$10), which takes about eight hours round trip. It's also possible to walk over the forested mountains to Petrópolis. Most trails are unmarked but it's easy and inexpensive to hire a guide at the national park visitor center.

Sleeping & Eating

Hotel Comary (☎ 0xx21-2742-3463; Avenida Almirante Lúcio Meira 467; s/d US$7/10, with bath US$12/16) A big hit with Brazilians on weekends and holidays.

Várzea Palace Hotel (☎ 0xx21-2742-0878; Rua Prefeito Sebastião Teixeira 41/55; s/d US$10/15, with bath US$20/26) A grand old white building with red trim and classy rooms.

Pousada Refúgio do Parque (☎ 0xx21-9221-9147; r per person US$11) This place, a few kilometers past the national park's main entrance, services hungry hikers with hearty breakfasts and soup for dinner.

Cheiro de Mato (Rua Delfim Moreira 140) A decent vegetarian restaurant.

Sand's (Av Almirante Lúcio Meira) Near the bus station, this spot has a cheap self-serve lunch spread. There's another self-serve tucked inside the ABC Supermarket.

Getting There & Around

Buses run between Rio and Teresópolis about every half hour from 5am to 10pm (US$6, 1½ hours). From Teresópolis, a few daily buses run to Petrópolis and Nova Friburgo. To get to the national park's main entrance from central Teresópolis, take the hourly 'Soberbo' bus (US$0.60), or the more frequent 'Alto' bus to the Praçinha do Alto, then walk a short way south to the entrance.

SAQUAREMA

Saquarema, 100km east of Rio de Janeiro, is a laid-back little town with stunning stretches of unmarred beaches. Polluting industries are forbidden in the municipality; the waters are clean and fish and shrimp are abundant. The shoreline attracts surfers, sport fishing enthusiasts and sun worshippers. To the west are **Boqueirão**, **Barra Nova** (8km) and **Jaconé** (15km), which is reachable by local buses. East of town is **Praia Itaúna** (3km), probably Saquarema's most beautiful beach and one of the best surf spots in Brazil (US$3 by taxi from the center). Saquarema's NS de Nazaré masses on September 7 and 8 attract around 150,000 pilgrims.

Information

Banco do Brasil (Av Saquarema 539) offers cash advances on credit cards. The nearest place for exchange is in Cabo Frio. Lakes

Shopping, a tiny mall built to look like a log cabin on the road to Praia Itaúna, has an ATM, lots of eateries, and Internet access at the computer repair shop on the first floor.

The **Secretaria de Turismo** (☎ 0xx24-2651-2178; City Hall; ☻ 9am-8pm Mon-Fri) is friendly and useful.

Sleeping & Eating

In high season you'll pay about 30% more than the prices given here.

Youth Hostel Ilhas Gregas (☎ 0xx24-2651-1008; Rua do Prado 671; r per person US$10) Check out this hostel, which has kitchen and laundry facilities.

Pousada Itaúna Inn (☎ 0xx24-2651-5147; Av Oceânica; s/d with bath US$15/22) Surfers will like this place right on the beachfront: it has an ugly access, but a lovely view to the surf break.

Espuma da Praia (☎ 0xx22-2651-2848; s/d with bath US$16/25) A good off-season bargain with beautiful cabins two steps from the water.

Itaúna's (☎ 0xx24-2651-1711; Rua dos Tatuis 999) This place off Av Oceânica has camping facilities.

Restaurante Marisco, just opposite the bus stop in Saquarema, has good and inexpensive self-serve food.

Crepe e Cia (Avenida Nazareth 160) Come here for delicious crêpes.

Pizza na Pedra (Avenida Nazareth 487) Good for pizzas and pasta.

Getting There & Around

The bus stop in Saquarema is on the main central *praça*. From Rio to Saquarema, buses leave about hourly from 6:30am to 8pm (US$6, two hours). For Cabo Frio, take a local bus from Saquarema to Bacaxá, where buses depart for Cabo Frio every half-hour.

ARRAIAL DO CABO

Arraial do Cabo, 45km east of Saquarema, is surrounded by gleaming white sand dunes and offers all the beauty of Búzios with half the fuss. Lately it's become a favorite for fishing enthusiasts, which has somewhat lessened the area's charm (not to mention fish supply), but overall it still maintains a welcoming working-class demeanor.

For information, visit the **tourist office** (☎ 0xx24-2620-5039; Praça da Bandeira).

Sights & Activities

Today Praia dos Anjos has beautiful turquoise water but too much boat traffic for comfortable swimming. Favorite beaches within short walking distance of town are Prainha to the north, Praia do Forno to the northeast (reached by a 1km walking trail from Praia dos Anjos) and Praia Grande to the west. Praia Grande and its continuation, Praia Maçambaba, stretch 40km to Itaúna near Saquarema.

Ilha do Cabo Frio is reachable by boat from Praia dos Anjos. Praia do Farol, on the protected side of the island, is a gorgeous beach with fine white sand. The Gruta Azul (Blue Cavern) on the southwest side of the island is another beautiful spot. Be alert, though: the entrance to the cavern is submerged at high tide. **Barracuda Tour** (☎ 0xx24-2622-1340) and **Gruta Azul** (☎ 0xx24-2622-1033) run boat trips for around US$12 per person.

Arraial do Cabo has some good diving sites. Operators such as **Arrail Sub** (☎ 0xx24-2622-1145) run diving trips. The tourist office has information on these and other options.

Sleeping & Eating

This town isn't easy on the pocket, and you can expect room prices to rise by 30% in high season.

Camping Club do Brasil (☎ 0xx24-2622-1023; Avenida da Liberdade 171; campsites per person US$8) This campground is near Praia dos Anjos.

Hotel Praia Grande (☎ 0xx24-2622 1369; Rua Dom Pedro 41; s/d US$8/14) A good cheapie in the center of town.

Porto dos Anjos (☎ 0xx24-2622-1629; Avenida Luis Correa 8; d with bath US$20) This spot at Praia dos Anjos has great sea views at bargain prices.

Garrafa de Nansen Restaurante (Rua Santa Cruz 4; dishes US$8-10) A classy seafood spot where you can eat very well without draining the exchequer.

Cheaper eats are available at the self-serve **Água na Boca** (Av Litorânea; dishes US$3) on Praia Grande. Also try **Todos Os Prazeres** (Rua José Pinto Macedo) for self-serve seafood.

Getting There & Away

Direct buses run from Rio to Arraial, the first at 5am and the last at midnight (US$11, three hours). An alternative is to catch one of the more frequent buses to Cabo Frio, then take the municipal bus, which runs every 20 minutes to Arraial (US$1) from the bus stop just up to the left as you leave the Cabo Frio bus station.

BÚZIOS

Búzios, a lovely beach resort, lies 30km northeast of Arraial do Cabo on a peninsula scalloped by 17 beaches. A simple fishing village until the early 1960s, when it was 'discovered' by Brigitte Bardot, Búzios is now littered with boutiques, fine restaurants, fancy villas and posh *pousadas*. During the holiday season (when the population explodes from 8000 to 100,000!) prices here are twice those in the rest of Brazil.

Orientation & Information

Búzios is actually a grouping of four settlements. Ossos, which is set on the tip of the peninsula, is the oldest and most attractive. Manguinhos, on the isthmus, is the most commercial, while Armação, in between, boasts the best restaurants, along with necessities such as international telephones and a bank. Rasa is northwest along the coast.

Malízia Tour (☎ 0xx24-2623-1226; Rua das Pedras; Praia dos Ossos; Shopping Praia do Canto, loja 16) will change money in its offices. The town's website is www.buzioturismo.com.

The **Secretaria de Turismo** (☎ 0800-249999; ☒ 24hr) sits right at the entrance to Búzios. Another **information booth** (☎ 0xx24-2623-2099; Praça Santos Dumont, Armação) is open during weekday business hours.

Beaches

In general, the southern beaches are trickier to get to, but are prettier and have better surf. Geribá and Ferradurinha (Little Horseshoe), south of Manguinhos, are beautiful beaches with good waves, but the Búzios Beach Club has built condos here. Next on the coast is Ferradura, large enough for windsurfing. Praia Olho de Boi (Bull's Eye Beach), at the eastern tip of the peninsula, is a pocket-size beach reached by a little trail from the long, clean Praia Brava. Near the northern tip of the promontory, João Fernandinho, João Fernandes and the topless Azedinha and Azeda are all good for snorkeling. Praia da Tartaruga is quiet and pretty.

Sleeping

Lodging is expensive from December to March, and in July, but similarly priced to Arraial do Cabo at other times. Prices here are for the low season.

Albergue de Juventude Praia dos Amores (☎ 0xx24-2623-2422; Avenida Bento Riberio 92; r per person US$13) The youth hostel is about 20 minutes walk from Praia da Tartaruga. It fronts a busy road but is otherwise very pleasing.

Zen-Do (☎ 0xx24-2623-1542; d US$23) A private home with rooms to let. Yesha Vanicore speaks English and runs a friendly and progressive household.

Brigitta's Guest House (☎ 0xx24-2623-6157; brigittas@mar.com.br; Rua das Pedras 131; s/d US$12/18) A four-room *pousada* overlooking the water.

Pousada Axé (☎ 0xx24-2623-2008; Rua do Sossego 200; s/d US$14/18) A good deal, with a pool and light breakfast included in the rates.

Casa da Ruth (☎ 0xx24-2623-2242; Rua dos Gravatás, Geribá; s/d US$13/15, with bath US$18/23) Spartan but clean rooms.

Eating & Drinking

For good, cheap food, eat grilled fish right on the beaches. Brava, Ferradura and João Fernandes beaches have little thatched-roof fish and beer restaurants.

Botequim do Baiano (Rua Luis Joaquim Pereira 265; near Praça Santos Dumont; dishes US$3) The best *prato feito* in town – fish or meat with rice, beans and salad for a few dollars.

Restaurante Boom (Rua Turíbio de Farias 110; buffet per kg US$10) An excellent and varied buffet.

Chez Michou Crêperie (Rua das Pedras 90) A popular hangout because of its incredible crepes – any kind you want. The outdoor bar has delicious piña coladas.

Most of the nightlife is located on Rua das Pedras after midnight.

Getting There & Away

Seven buses run daily from Rio to Búzios, the first at 6:30am and the last at 7:15pm (US$9, three hours). Municipal buses run between Cabo Frio and Búzios (Ossos), a 50 minute, 20km trip.

Getting Around

The schooner **Queen Lory** (☎ 0xx24-2623-1179) makes daily trips out to Ilha Feia, and to Tartaruga and João Fernandinho beaches

(US$15 to US$20 for two to five hours). These are good value, especially since caipirinhas, soft drinks, fruit salad and snorkeling gear are included. **Bike Tour** (☎ 0xx24-2623-6365; Rua das Pedras 2660) has the best rentals in town for US$10 per day.

ILHA GRANDE

If you really want to get away from it all, Ilha Grande may well be the place to go. This island, off the coast about 150km west of Rio de Janeiro, is almost all tropical beach and Atlantic rain forest, with only three settlements. You can take a boat trip from Vila do Abraão, the main settlement, or follow trails through the steamy forest to beaches around the island. It's a 2½-hour hike from Abraão to Praia Lopes Mendes, which some claim to be the most beautiful beach in Brazil. Praia de Parnaioca also ranks up there.

Vila do Abraão

Busy on weekends and tranquil during the week, Abraão has a gorgeous, palm-studded beachfront of pale, faded homes.

In Angra dos Reis on the mainland, the helpful **Centro de Informações Turísticas** (☎ 0xx24-3365-1175; Ave Júlio Maria 10; ☻ 9am-5pm) has information about Ilha Grande, including accommodation options. Change money before leaving the mainland.

Sleeping & Eating

Some locals rent rooms cheaply; just ask around. From December to February, most pousadas double the prices given here.

Camping das Palmeiras (Rua Getúlio Vargas; campsites per person US$3) Reasonable facilities.

Pousada Beira Mar (☎ 0xx24-3361-5051; beiramar2000@uol.com.br; s/d US$20/40) This is a good option right on the beach, 300m from the dock.

Tropicana (☎ 0xx24-3361-5047; pousadatropicana@uol.com.br; Rua da Praia 28; s/d US$27/40) A very laid-back place.

Beto's Pousada (☎ 0xx24-3361-5312; Travessa do Beto 63; s/d US$30/30) Beto's offers spotless rooms.

Youth Hostel (☎ 0xx21-2264-6147; Rua Pres Vargas; r per person US$6) The local hostel is probably the cheapest place in town.

For finger-lickin' eats, try **Restaurant Minha Deusa** (Rua Getúlio Vargas) and **Café com Banana Internet Café** (Rua Getúlio Vargas), next to the creek.

Getting There & Away

You reach the island by catching a Conerj ferry to Abraão from Mangaratiba or Angra dos Reis on the mainland. Ferries leave Mangaratiba at 8am Monday to Friday, and 9am Saturday and Sunday, returning from Abraão at 5pm daily. The ferry from Angra dos Reis departs at 3:30pm daily, returning from Abraão at 10am the next day. The 1½ hour ride costs US$2 from Monday to Friday, and US$6 on Saturday and Sunday. Angra dos Reis is linked to Rio de Janeiro (US$9, three hours) by hourly buses and to Parati (US$2, two hours) by several buses daily.

PARATI

Set on a shoreline of jutting peninsulas and secluded beaches, Parati is backed by steep, jungled mountains that seem to leap down towards the hundreds of islands dotting the clear, warm waters. The town grew up and grew wealthy as a stopover between Rio and the Minas Gerais goldfields in the early 18th century, but started to decline when a new Rio–Minas road via the Serra dos Órgãos was opened in the 1720s. Parati is crowded and lively from Christmas to Carnaval and most weekends, but at other times is delightfully quiet.

Information

Banco do Brasil (Av Roberto Silveira; ☻ 9am-3pm) changes cash and traveler's checks. **Internet access** is available at nearly every corner. The **Centro de Informações Turísticas** (☎ 0xx24-3371-1897/1222; Av Roberto Silveira; ☻ 9am-9pm) is staffed by friendly locals.

Sights & Activities

Parati's 18th-century prosperity is reflected in its beautiful old homes and churches. Three main churches served separate races. The 1725 **Igreja NS do Rosário e São Benedito dos Homens Pretos** (Rua Dr Samuel Costa) was built by and for slaves. The 1722 **Igreja de Santa Rita dos Pardos Libertos** (Praça Santa Rita) was the church for freed mulattos. The 1800 **Capela de NS das Dores** (Rua Dr Pereira) was the church of the colonial white elite.

Forte Defensor Perpétuo is on Morro da Vila Velha, a hill 20-minutes walk north of town. It was built in 1703 to defend gold in transit from pirate attacks and now houses the **Casa de Artista e Centro de Artes e Tradições**

BRAZIL

Populares de Parati. If hiking is your thing, ask at the tourist office for information on **The Gold Trail**, a partially cobbled mountain road once used by miners.

BEACHES

Parati has some 65 islands and 300 beaches in its vicinity. **Praia do Forte**, a quick walk north from the center, is clean, relatively secluded and frequented by a youngish crowd. **Praia do Jabaquara**, 2km past the town beach **Praia do Pontal**, is a big, spacious beach with great views, shallow waters, a small restaurant and a better campground than those in town. About an hour from Parati by boat are the **Vermelha** and **Lulas** beaches, both to the northeast, and Saco, to the east. These beaches are small and idyllic; most have barracas (stalls) serving beer and fish and, at most, a handful of beachgoers. **Praia de Parati-Mirim**, 27km east of Parati, is hard to beat for accessibility, cost and beauty, and it has barracas and houses to rent. You can get there by municipal bus (US$1, 40 minutes) from Parati bus station at 5:30, 6:30 or 9am, or 12:40, 3:40 or 5:10pm. Return buses start at 6am.

To visit the less accessible beaches, many tourists take one of the schooners from the docks. Tickets cost US$15 per person; lunch is an additional US$10. The boats make three beach stops of about 45 minutes each. An alternative is to rent one of the many small motorboats at the port. For US$10 per hour (more in summer), the skipper will take you where you want to go.

Sleeping

From December to February hotels get booked up and room prices double those quoted here. Reservations are a good idea but, inconveniently, many places require the full amount to be paid in advance – usually into their bank account in Rio or São Paulo. The rest of the year, finding inexpensive accommodations is easy, especially outside the historic district.

Pousada do Careca (☎ 0xx24-3371-1291; www.pousadadocareca.cjb.net; Praça do Chafariz s/n; s/d with bath US$10/14) At the edge of the old town, this is a great place to stay. Rooms are clean and bright, and guests can use the kitchen.

Villaggio (☎ 0xx24-3371-1870; www.paraty.com.br/villaggio.htm; Rua José Viera Ramos 280; s/d with bath US$12/17) For lodgings just a few minutes from the old town, try Villagio, which has a pool and big airy rooms.

Pouso Familiar (☎ 0xx24-3371-1475; Rua José Vieira Ramos 262; s/d with bath US$15/25) A recommended place.

Pousada Marendaz (☎ 0xx24-3371-1369; pousada-marendaz@uol.com.br; Rua Dr Derly Ellena 9; r per person US$13) Run by five sisters, this place is more family home than hotel.

Pousada Konquista (☎ 0xx24-3371-1308; Rua Jango Pádua 20; s/d with bath US$13/20) Konquista has clean and rustic air-con rooms.

Pousada Coco Verde (☎ 0xx24-3371-1039; abilio carlos@uol.com.br; Rua João Luiz do Rosário 3; s/d with bath US$10/16) Quaint rooms in a faux log cabin setting.

There are a few campgrounds on the edge of town, just over the bridge.

Eating & Drinking

Sabor da Terra (Rua Roberto Silveira 80) To beat the inflated prices in the old part of town, try this self-serve.

Beija Flor (corner of Rua Dr Pereira & Rua Beira Rio) In the old town, this place has sandwiches, soups and juices.

More substantial food is served at **Galeria do Engenho** (Rua da Lapa; dishes US$10), with particular emphasis on large, juicy steaks, and **Margarida Café** (Praça do Chariz).

Paraty 33 (☎ 0xx24-3371-7311; Paraty 33, Rua Maria Jacomé de Mello) A popular restaurant/bar with live music in the same area.

Expect cover charges of US$3 to US$5 at live music venues. Young locals avoid the tourist crush by gathering on the far side of the historic district, on Rua da Cadeia near the beach.

Getting There & Away

The bus station is on Rua Jango Pádua, 500m west of the old town. Eight daily buses run to/from Rio (US$13, four hours) and four to/from São Paulo (US$11, six hours).

SÃO PAULO

Talk about a city within a city! An estimated 17 million people live in 'Greater São Paulo' (the city proper and its environs), making it the third largest metropolis on earth. It's home to more ethnic groups than any other part of the country, and contains Brazil's biggest and best-educated middle class. Sampa – as the city's known to locals – is

GETTING INTO TOWN

A taxi from Aeroporto Congonhas to the center costs about US$17. For buses (one hour), walk out of the terminal and then to your right, where you'll see a busy street with a pedestrian overpass. Head to the overpass but don't cross; you should see a crowd of people waiting for the buses along the street, or ask for the bus to Terminal Bandeiras. The last bus departs at around 1am.

From a stop just in front of the arrivals terminal at Aeroporto Guarulhos, buses run to Praça da República, Terminal Tietê bus station and Congonhas airport every 30 to 40 minutes (US$8). The same buses will also take you out to the airport from these places. A taxi from Aeroporto Guarulhos to the center costs about US$30.

an intoxicating place, with art and entertainment on par with any world capital. *Paulistanos* (inhabitants of the city; inhabitants of São Paulo state are called *paulistas*) believe in working hard and playing harder, and despite constantly complaining about street violence, clogged highways and pollution, most wouldn't dream of living anywhere else.

Orientation

You can reach many places on the *metrô*, São Paulo's subway system, which is one of the best in the world.

The key downtown squares are Praça da Sé, with the Sé metrô interchange station, and Praça da República, with República metrô station. In ethnic terms, the Liberdade area, just south of Praça da Sé, is the Asian neighborhood. Bela Vista (also called Bixiga), to the southwest, is Italian. A large Arab community is based around Rua 25 de Março, northeast of Praça da Sé.

Avenida Paulista, running southeast to northwest a kilometer or two southwest of downtown and accessible by metro, is an avenue of skyscrapers.

Information

EMERGENCY

Deatur (☎ 0xx11-214-0209; Avenida São Luís 95; ⏰ 9am-5pm Mon-Fri) A special police force just for tourists.

INTERNET ACCESS

Monkey Lan House (☎ 0xx11-3253-8627; main office Alameda Santos 1217) Its Internet cafés all over the city are open 24 hours per day.

MEDICAL SERVICES

Einstein Hospital (☎ 0xx11-3747-1233; Av Albert Einstein 627) One of the best hospitals in Latin America. It's in the southwestern corner of the city (catch bus No 7241 to Jardim Colombo from Rua Xavier de Toledo).

MONEY

Except on weekends, changing money is easy. Many travel agencies and exchange offices around the city offer good rates, but avoid the smaller ones downtown – some are illegal and will rip you off.

Action Cambio (Shopping Light, Loja 130A; ⏰ 10am-7pm Mon-Fri, 10am-4pm Sat)

Citibank (Avenida Paulista 1111) These machines accept Visa cards.

Itaú Bank (Rua Coriselheiro Crispiniano) Has ATMs and accepts MasterCard and Cirrus cards.

POST

Post office (Rua Líbero Badaró) The safest place to drop letters is at this main branch.

TELEPHONE

Cabinas (Rua 7 de Abril) Long-distance phone calls can be made from about 200m from Praça da República.

TOURIST OFFICES

Located at strategic points around the city, the Centrais de Informação Turistica (CIT) booths are very helpful. One of the most helpful for non-Portuguese speakers is at **Avenida Ipiranga** (☎ 0xx11-231-2922; Praça da República; ⏰ 9am-6pm). Other booths are on the ground floor of Shopping Light and near MASP (Museu de Arte de São Paulo) on Avenida Paulista, as well as in Ibirapuera Park, Terminals 1 and 2 at the airport, and in the Tietê bus station.

Dangers & Annoyances

Reports of crime in the city have increased, and São Paulo is said to be less safe than Rio. Be especially careful in the center at night, as well as in the cheap hotel area around Rua Santa Efigênia. Watch out for pickpockets on buses and at Praça da Sé. If you're driving, be aware that car-jackings and red-light robberies are common after dark. The situation has become so bad that

BRAZIL

CENTRAL SÃO PAULO

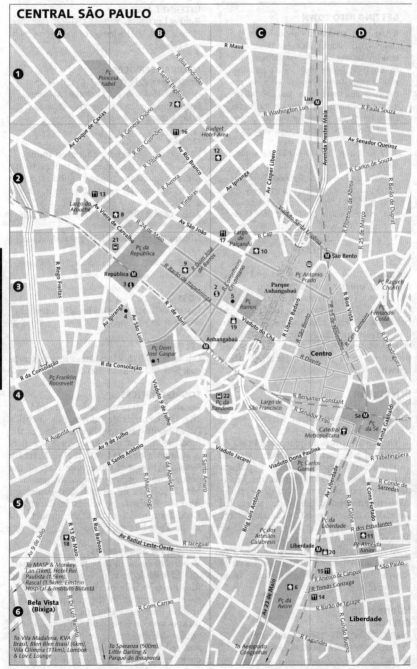

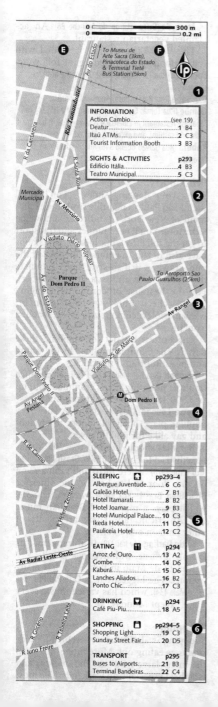

INFORMATION
Action Cambio.............................(see 19)
Deatur...1 B4
Itaú ATMs.......................................2 C3
Tourist Information Booth..........3 B3

SIGHTS & ACTIVITIES   p293
Edifício Itália.................................4 B3
Teatro Municipal..........................5 C3

SLEEPING   pp293–4
Albergue Juventude..................6 C6
Galeão Hotel.................................7 B1
Hotel Itamarati............................8 B2
Hotel Joamar.................................9 B3
Hotel Municipal Palace............10 C3
Ikeda Hotel..................................11 D5
Pauliceía Hotel............................12 C2

EATING   p294
Arroz de Ouro..............................13 A2
Gombe...14 D6
Kaburá...15 D6
Lanches Aliados.........................16 B2
Ponto Chic...................................17 C3

DRINKING   p294
Café Piu-Piu................................18 A5

SHOPPING   pp294–5
Shopping Light............................19 C3
Sunday Street Fair.....................20 D5

TRANSPORT   p295
Buses to Airports.......................21 B3
Terminal Bandeiras....................22 C4

São Paulo recently changed a traffic law – it's now legal (and recommended) to just slow down at red lights at night. If there's no traffic, continue without stopping.

Sights & Activities

The old center of São Paulo lies between Praça da Sé, Luz metrô station and Praça da República. The city's pride is the baroque-cum-art nouveau **Teatro Municipal** just west of Viaduto do Chá. Another beloved landmark is the 41-story **Edifício Itália** (cnr Av São Luís & Av Ipiranga) which has a restaurant/piano bar/viewing terrace at the top (no cover charge).

Museu de Arte de São Paulo (MASP; Av Paulista 1578; M Trianon-Masp; adult/student US$4/2; 11am-5pm Tue-Sun), has Latin America's best collection of western art. Highlights include the works by the great Brazilian artist Cândido Portinari and many French Impressionist paintings.

The large **Parque do Ibirapuera**, 4km from the city, contains several museums, monuments and attractions, notably the **Museu de Arte Moderna** (admission US$3; noon-6pm Tue, Wed & Fri, noon-10pm Thu, Sat & Sun) with a huge collection of art from 1930 to 1970. Take bus No 5121 'Santo Amaro' from Praça da República.

The **Museu de Arte Sacra** (Av Tiradentes 676, M Tiradentes; admission US$2; 11am-6pm Tue-Fri, 10am-7pm Sat & Sun) is the best of Brazil's many museums of religious art.

The **Instituto Butantã** (0xx11-3726-7222; admission free; 9am-3pm Tue-Sun), one of São Paulo's most popular attractions, is a snake farm with over 1000 serpents, from which it milks venom for the production of vaccines and anti-venins. Take bus No 702-U 'Butantã-USP' from Praça da República.

Sleeping

The areas surrounding the Estação da Luz train station and central downtown are rife with crime, prostitution, and extremely cheap hotels. If you decide to stay in one of them, use extreme caution with your belongings and your person at all times. Reports of muggings (and worse) are common and the neighborhood is often the site of gang-related violence. Safer accommodations can be had in other parts of the city for just a bit more money.

BRAZIL

Albergue da Juventude Praça da Árvore (☎ 0xx11-5071-5148; Rua Pageú 266; r with bath for members/non-members US$12/16) A cheap, secure option just a few minutes' walk from Praça da Árvore metrô station.

Hotel Municipal Palace (☎ 0xx11-228-7833; Av São João 354; r per person US$9) Basic but clean rooms.

Hotel Joamar (☎ 0xx11-221-3611; Rua Dom Jose de Barros 187; s/d with bath US$10/14) A quaint place on a quiet pedestrian street.

Hotel Itamarati (☎ 0xx11-222-4133; Av Vieira de Carvalho 150; s with bath US$14) A well-kept old establishment with helpful staff.

Hotel Rei Paulista (☎ 0xx11-3885-1362; Alameda Lorena 21; s/d with bath US$15/22) This place has gone a bit upscale, but is still a good deal considering its location (near Av Paulista).

The Pauliceía Hotel (☎ 0xx11-220-9733; Rua Timbiras 216; s/d US$10/16, s/d with bath US$20) Clean and safe.

Galeão Hotel (☎ 0xx11-220-8211; Rua dos Gusmões 394; s/d US$20/26, d with bath US$35) This friendly place offers good value, and discounts are possible if you sweet talk the management.

Ikeda Hotel (☎ 0xx11-278-3844; Rua dos Estudantes 134; s/d US$14/25, with bath US$30/40) In the quieter, safer and nocturnally more interesting Liberdade area, this hospitable hotel has immaculate rooms and impeccable service.

Eating

Eating is a much-loved activity in Sampa – and it goes on well into the wee hours every day. Almost every type of cuisine imaginable can be found.

Ponto Chic (Largo Paiçandu 27; dishes US$4) A few blocks from Praça da República this informal spot serves a famous sandwich, the *bauru*, which is made with beef, tomato, pickle and melted cheeses on French bread.

Lanches Aliados (cnr Av Rio Branco & Rua Vitória) A cheap and cheerful lunch spot with excellent food.

Praça de Alimentação (Shopping Light, 5th fl, Viaduto do Chá) This food court has inexpensive and popular per-kilo restaurants.

Rascal (Rua Eugenio de Lima) A popular franchise off Av Paulista, and also found in shopping malls, that serves fresh-cooked salmon and other fish, as well as pizzas, salads, a huge self-serve buffet and delectable desserts at bargain prices.

Arroz de Ouro (Largo do Arouche 88) An acclaimed vegetarian restaurant.

The Bela Vista district is loaded with Italian-food spots, including the following:
Speranza (Rua 13 de Maio 1004) One of the best pizzerias.
C.Q. Sabe (Rua Rui Barbosa) Another favorite.
Gombe (Rua Tomás Gonzaga 22; meals for 2 US$24) This Japanese restaurant in Liberdade is always full. It has great sushi and sashimi, and excellent sukiyaki.
Kaburá (Rua Galvão Bueno 346) Another Japanese favorite.

Drinking

Bring your dancing shoes – you'll need them! São Paulo's nightlife rivals the excitement of New York's (and costs almost the same too). You'll need money and transport to get the full effect, but luckily Paulistanos have also begun to embrace the joys of the pub crawl – British-style pubs populate the Jardins area and Rua Franz Schubert. For the best list of constantly-changing events, check out www.baladas.com.br, www.mariolevi.com.br, and www.obaodba .com.br.

The hottest district for clubbing these days is Vila Olímpia, mobbed by the young and beautiful round the clock.

Lombok (Rua Olimpiadas 272) Plays electronica on three pulsating floors crammed with up to 3,500 18- to 25-year-olds per night.

Lov.e Lounge (Rua Pequetita 189) This very popular place opens its doors to straight and gay alike for nightly raves.

Bar flies should head to the Vila Madalena district to check out **KVA Brasil** (Rua Cardeal Arco Verde 2978), where forró and samba reign on one floor and techno on the other, or **Blen Blen Brasil** (Rua Inacio Pereira da Rocha 520) which plays a mixture of Brazilian music and American rap. There are plenty of other bars on every corner.

Little Darling (Av Irai 229) In Ibirapuera, this is a big favorite, with live rock-n-roll.

Rua 13 de Maio in Bela Vista has many options. The biggest bar is **Café Piu-Piu** (Rua 13 de Maio 134), which has varied music every night except Monday.

Shopping

Shopping is almost as important to *Paulistanos* as eating out. More interesting than the many large malls are the markets and fairs held especially on weekends. The most popular is on Praça da República from 8am to 2pm Sunday – offerings include Brazilian precious stones, leather gear, woodcarvings and some excellent paintings.

Liberdade, the Asian district, has a big street fair with great food all day Sunday, surrounding Liberdade metrô station.

One of the most popular malls is **Shopping Light** (☎ 0xx11-6445-2380; Rua Coronel Xavier de Toledo 23, Centro), an upscale shopping mall with boutiques and restaurants across from the Teatro Municipal.

Getting There & Away
AIR
São Paulo is the Brazilian hub for many international airlines and thus the first stop for many travelers. Most major airlines have offices on Avenida São Luís, near Praça da República. Before buying a domestic ticket, check which of the city's airports the flight departs from.

Aeroporto Guarulhos (☎ 0xx11-6445-2945), the international airport, is 30km east of the center. Flights to Rio (Santos Dumont airport) depart every half hour (or less) from **Aeroporto Congonhas** (☎ 0xx11-5090-9000), 14km south of the center. You can usually go to the airport, buy a ticket and be on a plane within the hour.

BUS
The enormous **Terminal Tietê bus station** (☎ 0xx11-235-0322), with buses to destinations throughout Brazil, is adjacent to Tietê metrô station. International buses from here go to Buenos Aires (US$125, 36 hours), Santiago do Chile (US$120, 56 hours) and Asunción (US$50, 20 hours). Frequent buses go to Rio de Janeiro (US$15, six hours). Other destinations within Brazil include Brasília (US$37, 14 hours), Belo Horizonte (US$21, eight hours), Foz do Iguaçu (US$40, 15 hours), Cuiabá (US$40, 13 hours), Salvador (US$68, 32 hours), Curitiba (US$15, six hours) and Florianópolis (US$30, 12 hours). A tip for people coming into the city: try to pick buses that won't arrive during early morning or late afternoon – traffic jams are enormous at those times.

Getting Around
METRO
A combination of *metrô* and walking is the best way to see the city. The metrô is cheap,

safe, fast and runs from 5am to midnight. A single ride costs US$0.80; a *multiplo 10* ticket gives 10 rides for US$7.

BUS
Buses are slow, crowded during rush hours and not too safe. The main transfer points are Praça da República and the bustling Terminal Bandeiras. The tourist booths are excellent sources of bus information.

BELO HORIZONTE
Belo Horizonte, the third largest city in Brazil, is a rapidly-growing industrial giant with soaring skyscrapers that blot out the surrounding mountains. It's equally rapidly-growing pollution problem will bring tears to your eyes, but the sooty streets have an undeniably edgy appeal. Most travelers only come to the sprawling capital of Minas Gerais en route to the colonial towns of Ouro Prêto or Diamantina.

If you have time to spare here, head for the **Parque Municipal**, a sea of green 10 minutes' walk southeast of the bus station along Avenida Afonso Pena, and visit the park's **Palácio das Artes**, an art gallery and performing arts center.

Belo Horizonte has had a rise in petty crimes of late. Pay close attention to your surroundings in the crowded area around the bus station and don't wander late at night unless you are with a large group of people.

Information
Centro de Cultura Belo Horizonte (Rua da Bahia 1149; US$3 per hr) offers Internet access.

Nascente Turismo (Rua Rio de Janeiro 1314) is a convenient currency exchange place.

Belotur (☎ 0xx31-3277-7666; Av Afonso Pena 1055; ⊗ 8am-8pm Mon-Fri, 8am-4pm Sat & Sun), the municipal tourist organization, puts out an excellent monthly guide in Portuguese, English and Spanish. There are booths at the bus station, **Bahia Shopping** (Rua da Bahia, 1022), and the city's two airports.

Sleeping
Albergue de Juventude Chalé Mineiro (☎ 0xx31-3467-1576; Rua Santa Luzia 288; r per person US$10) Good dorm rooms, with discounts for HI members. It's about 2km east of the Parque Municipal. You can get there by bus No 9801 'Saudade/Santa Cruz' from

BRAZIL

Rua dos Caetés near the bus station, or the metrô to Santa Theresa station, from which you cross a pedestrian bridge to Rua Santa Luzia.

Pousadinha Mineira (☎ 0xx31-3446-2911; Rua Araxá 514; r per person US$7) Very bare bones accommodations. From the bus station, follow Avenida Santos Dumont to Rua Rio de Janeiro, turn left and go up a couple of blocks to Avenida do Contorno. Cross it and follow Rua Varginha a few blocks to Rua Araxá.

There's a cluster of budget hotels in the sleazy red-light district just south of the bus station.

Hotel Gontijo (☎ 0xx31-3272-1177; Rua Dos Tupinambás 731; s/d US$12/15, with bath US$18/23) Rooms vary here; ask for a clean one and don't pay until you've seen it.

Eating & Drinking

Lanchonetes and fast-food places cluster around Praça Sete, on Avenida Afonso Pena, 400m southeast of the bus station.

Padaria Zona Sul (Avenida Paraná 163; dishes US$2) Just southwest of the bus station, this place has super roast chickens.

Shopping Cidade (Rua Rio de Janeiro) and **Bahia Shopping** (Rua da Bahia 1022) both have food courts.

A lot of great restaurants are in Savassi.

Naturalis (Rua Tome de Souza 689; dishes US$5) Terrific vegetarian lunch specials are served here.

Cafe com Letras (Rua Antônio Albuquerque 785) The coolest place to hang out, snack and sip wine by the glass. It also has a bookstore with English-language books.

Rococo (Afonso Pena 941) Before and after shows local musicians and music-lovers alike gather at Rococo.

Getting There & Away

Belo's two airports have flights to just about anywhere in Brazil. Flights to/from Rio, Brasília, Vitória and São Paulo by VASP, Varig and Transbrasil are frequent. Most airlines use Aeroporto Confins, 40km north of the city, but some use Aeroporto da Pampulha, 7km north of the center.

The **bus station** (Praça da Rodoviária) is in the north of the city center, near the north end of Avenida Afonso Pena. Buses will take you to Rio (US$13, seven hours), São Paulo (US$16, 9½ hours), Brasília (US$30,

12 hours) and Salvador (US$56, about 22 hours). There are 17 daily departures for Ouro Prêto (US$5, 2¾ hours), 21 to Mariana (US$6, two hours), six to Diamantina (US$17, 5½ hours) and seven to São João del Rei (US$9, 3½ hours). For Vitória, it's cheaper and more enjoyable to take the beautiful train trip (regular/executivo class US$12/16; 14 hours) from the train station just north of the Parque Municipal.

OURO PRÊTO

For much of the wild, violent and debauched 18th century, slaves in Minas Gerais were digging up half the gold being produced in the world. The baroque churches and sacred art that some of this loot paid for – especially the sculptures by Aleijadinho (see Congonhas p299) – account for over half of Brazil's national monuments. Of all the exquisite colonial towns scattered around Minas Gerais, Ouro Prêto (population 56,000), 87km southeast of Belo Horizonte, might be the jewel in the crown.

Vila Rica de Ouro Prêto (Rich Town of Black Gold), as it was originally known, was founded in 1711 amid the western hemisphere's richest gold deposits. At the height of the gold boom in the mid-18th century, there were 110,000 people (mainly slaves) in Ouro Prêto. As the boom tapered off toward the end of the 18th century, the miners found it increasingly difficult to pay the taxes demanded by Portugal, and in 1789 the poet-dentist Joaquim José da Silva Xavier (nicknamed Tiradentes, 'Tooth-Puller') and others hatched a famous revolutionary plot called the Inconfidência Mineira. The rebellion was crushed in its early stages and Tiradentes ended up being drawn and quartered.

Orientation

Ouro Prêto is divided into two parishes. If you stand in Praça Tiradentes, the central square, facing the Museu da Inconfidência, the parish of Pilar is to the right (west), the parish of Antônio Dias to the left (east).

Information

The **Cyberhouse** (Rua Bobadela 109) does tea and offers Internet access.

It's impossible to change traveler's checks in Ouro Prêto, but most of the jewelry stores will change cash dollars. **Banco**

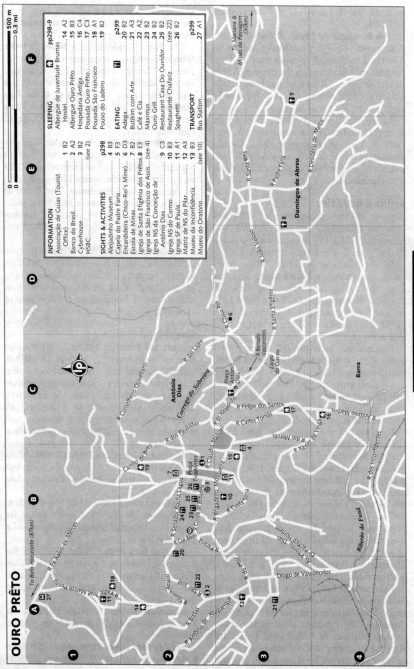

OURO PRÊTO

To Belo Horizonte (87km)

To Mariana & Minas da Passagem (50km)

BRAZIL

do Brasil (Rua São José 195) is right next door to HSBC.

The **Associação de Guias** (☎ 0xx31-3559-3269; Praça Tiradentes 41; ⏰ 8am-6pm Mon-Fri, 8am-5pm Sat & Sun) is a useful and friendly source of information. A leaflet gives the opening hours of all the sights. Official guides here charge US$30 for four hours, or US$60 for four to eight hours, for up to 10 people.

Lately the town's become a bit seedy at night, particularly around the bus station. Anyone lodging near there should absolutely not walk around after dark, especially if you've been in the center having a few drinks.

Sights & Activities

Almost all the museums and churches close on Monday. Most charge admission of around US$2, but in some cases a ticket to one gives free entrance to another.

Ideally, start out at about 7:30am from Praça Tiradentes and walk along Rua das Lajes for a panoramic morning view. In the east of town, the **Capela do Padre Faria** is one of Ouro Prêto's oldest chapels (1701–1704) and one of the richest in gold and artwork.

Descending back toward town, you'll come to the **Igreja de Santa Efigênia dos Prêtos**, built between 1742 and 1749 by and for the black slave community. This is Ouro Prêto's poorest church in terms of gold, and its richest in artwork. The exterior image of **NS do Rosário** is by Aleijadinho.

Back toward the center, the **Igreja NS da Conceição de Antônio Dias** was designed by Aleijadinho's father, Manuel Francisco Lisboa, and built between 1727 and 1770. Aleijadinho is buried near the altar of Boa Morte. Nearby is the **Encardideira mine** (Rua Dom Silvério 108; ⏰ daily). This mine was owned by Chico-Rei, an African tribal king enslaved at Ouro Prêto who bought his own freedom and then that of his entire tribe. Gold from here financed the building of the Igreja de Santa Efigênia dos Prêtos. The mine is fantastic, but it is full of crumbling passageways.

The **Igreja de São Francisco de Assis** (Rua do Ouvidor aka Rua Cláudio Manoel) two blocks east of Praça Tiradentes and not far west of NS da Conceição de Antônio Dias, is the most important piece of Brazilian colonial art after the Prophets in Congonhas. Its entire exterior was carved by Aleijadinho and the

inside was painted by his long-term partner, Manuel da Costa Ataíde. An **Aleijadinho museum** adjoins the church.

On Praça Tiradentes, the **Museu da Inconfidência** contains documents of the Inconfidência Mineira, Tiradentes' tomb, torture instruments and important works by Ataíde and Aleijadinho. The **Escola de Minas** (Praça Tiradentes) in the old governor's palace has a very fine museum of with displays on metals and mineralogy.

The **Igreja NS do Carmo** (Rua Brigadeiro Mosqueira), southwest of Praça Tiradentes, was built as a group effort by the most important artists of the area. Built between 1766 and 1772, its facade is by Aleijadinho. The **Museu do Oratório**, next door, has a fabulous, well-displayed collection of oratories (niches containing saints' images to ward off evil spirits).

The **Matriz de NS do Pilar** (Rua Brigador Mosqueira Castilho Barbosa s/n, in Praça Monsenhor João Castilho Barbosa), further southwest, boasts 434kg of gold and silver in its ornamentation and is one of Brazil's finest showcases of artwork.

Sleeping

Pousada São Francisco (☎ 0xx31-3551-3456; Rua Padre José Marcos Penna 202; dm US$10, s/d with bath US$20/27) A short walk from the bus station, this friendly place is close to the Igreja de São Francisco de Paula (not São Francisco de Assis). If you come in on a late bus, call to announce your arrival and someone will pop over to walk you back (it gets very dark at night!).

Albergue de Juventude Brumas Hostel (☎ 0xx 31-3551-2944; r per person US$8) A very basic but inexpensive option nearby Pousada São Francisco.

Pouso do Ladeira (☎ 0xx31-3551-3654; Camilo de Brito 50; s/d with bath US$15/23) A great choice. Its English and Spanish speaking owners make everyone feel at home.

Albergue Ouro Prêto (☎ 0xx31-3551-6705; Rua Costa Sena 30, Largo de Coimbra; r per person US$10) This place has a large dorm facing the Igreja de São Francisco de Assis and discounts apply for HI cardholders.

Hospedaria Antiga (☎ 0xx31- 3551-2203; Rua Xavier da Veiga 01; s/d US$13/27) A classy budget option.

Pousada Ouro Prêto (☎ 0xx31-3551-3081; Largo Musicista José dos Anjos Costa 72; s/d with bath US$16/28)

Prices at this very lovely *pousada* are a bit steep, plus an extra US$6 per person during the high season, but worth the splurge.

Eating

Most restaurants cluster along lively Rua Conde de Bobadela (known as Rua Direita) and Rua São José. The typical Minas dish is *tutu a mineira*, a black-bean *feijoada*, and **Restaurante Casa Do Ouvidor** (Rua Direita 42), though a bit on the expensive side, is the best place to try it.

Spaghetti (Rua Direita 138A) serves pancakes and pizza and features live music nightly.

Maximus (Rua Direita 151) This is where locals go to self-serve.

Ouro Grill (Rua Senador Rocha Lagoa 61) All the meat you can eat.

Adega (Rua Teixeira Amaral 24) Vegetarians will delight in the plethora of fresh dishes here.

Butikim.com Arte (Rua Gabriel Santos) Way off the beaten track, this place has a new 'cultural night bar' that also does lunch. It's run by Pousada São Francisco.

Café e Cia (Rua São José 187; meals per kg US$6) An old favorite for lunch and dinner.

Restaurante Chafariz (Rua São José 167; buffets US$9) An incredibly sumptuous all-you-can-eat buffet of *cozinha mineira*, with a free shot of *cachaça* to aid digestion.

Getting There & Away

The **bus station** (Rua Rolimex-Merces) is northwest of town. Seventeen daily buses run between Belo Horizonte and Ouro Prêto (US$5, 2¾ hours). During peak periods, buy your tickets a day in advance. From Ouro Prêto a bus goes to Rio at 11pm (US$16, seven hours), and there are two daily buses to São Paulo.

CONGONHAS

Congonhas, 72km south of Belo Horizonte, would be a very ordinary industrial town if it weren't for the brooding and beautiful presence of Aleijadinho's Prophets, his and possibly Brazil's most famed works of art. If you're in the region and don't see them, you're really missing out.

Congonhas' Jubileu do Senhor Bom Jesus do Matosinhos, held from September 7 to 14, is one of Brazil's biggest religious festivals, attracting 600,000 pilgrims each year.

The **tourism office** (☎ 0xx31-3731-1300, ext 114; Alameda das Palmeiras), located in the Romaria, a new structure that houses several small

---

ALEIJADINHO

Aleijadinho (Antônio Francisco Lisboa, 1730–1814), son of a Portuguese architect and an African slave, lost the use of his hands and legs at the age of 30 but, with a hammer and chisel strapped to his arms, he advanced art in Brazil from the excesses of baroque to a finer, more graceful rococo. This Brazilian Michelangelo sculpted the **12 Old Testament Prophets**, his masterworks, at the **Basílica do Bom Jesus de Matosinhos**, between 1800 and 1805. Aleijadinho was also responsible for the six chapels here, and their wooden statues representing the Passion of Christ, which together are just as impressive as the prophets.

---

museums, is very helpful. It can give directions to a new camping ground about 7 km from the city center.

Colonial Hotel (☎ 0xx31-3731-1834; Praça da Basílica 76; s/d US$6/12, with bath US$10/18) Now somewhat faded, remnants of the former glory of this hotel are apparent in the huge hallways and immensely high ceilings. Best of all, it's right across the street from the Prophets. Breakfast is included and dinner is available in the restaurant downstairs.

Six daily buses run from Belo Horizonte to Congonhas (US$3, 1¾ hours). Local buses run between Congonhas bus station and the Basílica (US$0.50, 15 minutes).

Buses leave Congonhas every 45 minutes for Conselheiro Lafaiete (US$1, 30 minutes), where buses leave for Ouro Prêto (US$4, 2½ hours) at 7:05am, 9am, noon, 3pm and 6pm from Monday to Saturday, and 6am, 3pm and 6pm on Sunday.

Seven daily buses run from Congonhas to São João del Rei (US$4, two hours).

SÃO JOÃO DEL REI

São João del Rei (population 74,000), 182km south of Belo Horizonte, has a fascinating old center and is the gateway to the picture-perfect village of Tiradentes. Tiradentes is busy on weekends and quiet during the week, São João is pretty empty on Sundays.

City10 (Av Andrade Reis 120; US$3 per hr) offers Internet access. The useful **tourist office** (☎ 0xx32-3372-7338; Praça Frei Orlando 90; ☯ 8am-5pm) sits opposite São Francisco de Assis church.

Sights & Activities

The following churches and museums are all open from 9am to 5pm, Tuesday to Sunday, but close each day for lunch.

The baroque **Igreja de São Francisco de Assis** (Rua Padre José Maria Xavier), built in 1774 and overlooking a palm-lined plaza, was Aleijadinho's first complete project. Though much of his plan was not realized, the exterior, with an Aleijadinho sculpture of the Virgin and several angels, is one of the finest in Minas. The **Igreja de NS do Carmo** (Rua Getúlio Vargas), which was begun in 1732, was also designed by Aleijadinho. In the second sacristy is a famous unfinished sculpture of Christ.

Construction of the **Catedral de NS do Pilar** (Largo do Rosário) began in 1721. It has exuberant gold altars and fine Portuguese tiles.

The **Museu Regional do Sphan** (Rua Marechal Deodoro, 12; admission US$1) has a small but impressive art collection from the city's churches.

The **Maria Fumaça** (steam train; São João station; ☉ Fri-Sun & holidays; one way/round trip US$5/8) is pulled by 19th-century locomotives, and chugs along a picturesque 13km track from São João to Tiradentes. It's a great half-hour ride. It departs São João at 10am and 3pm and returns at 1pm and 5pm. Train tickets include admission to the very interesting Railway Museum, or **Museu Ferroviário** (São João station; admission to museum alone US$1.50).

Sleeping & Eating

There are several inexpensive hotels in the old section of the city. Book ahead in December, when the town is filled with students taking exams.

Hotel Provincia de Orense (☎ 0xx32-3371-7960; Rua Marechal Deodoro 131; s/d US$9/18, with bath US$11/20) This hotel has clean, elegant rooms and a sumptuous breakfast buffet.

Pousada Casarão (☎ 0xx32-3371-7447; Rua Ribeiro Bastos 94; s/d US$12/24) Up on the hill behind the Igreja de São Francisco is this lovely converted mansion.

Restaurante Vileiros (Rua da Prata 132) Near the tourist office, Vileiros has a varied menu and pleasant courtyard.

Pizzeria Primus (Rua Arthur Bernardes 97) Good, inexpensive pizza.

Pelourinho (Hermilio Alvea) In the center, offering an excellent per-kilo lunch.

Restaurante & Pousada Portal del-Rey (Praça Severiano Resende; dishes US$4) A good self-serve buffet and clean, welcoming rooms.

Getting There & Around

Four direct daily buses run to São João from Rio de Janeiro (US$13, 5½ hours). Seven daily buses run from São João to Belo Horizonte (US$9, 3½ hours) via Congonhas (US$6, two hours). For Ouro Prêto, catch the São Paulo–Mariana bus departing São João at 3:30am and 5:30pm daily (US$13, four hours). For the 3:30am you need to buy tickets the day before.

Yellow buses run to the town center from São João's bus station on Rua Cristóvão Colombo (US$0.30, 10 minutes). From the center to the bus station, buses go from the small bus stop in front of the train station.

TIRADENTES

They don't make towns any prettier than little Tiradentes, São João del Rei's golden-era rival, 14km east down the valley with the blue Serra de São José as a backdrop. It's undeniably gorgeous, although the recent influx of antique shops and boutiques might be a bit too cloying for some visitors. It's named for the martyred hero of the Inconfidência Mineira (see Ouro Prêto section p296), who was born at a nearby farm.

The useful **Secretária de Turismo** (☎ 0xx32-3355-1212; Rua Resende Costa 71; ☉ 9am-4pm Mon-Fri) is the only three-story building in town. Drop in for a map – for a small town, Tiradente can be very confusing.

Sights & Activities

The town's colonial buildings run up a hillside, where they culminate in the beautiful **Igreja Matriz de Santo Antônio** (☉ 9am-5pm), which was begun in 1710 and has a facade by Aleijadinho.

The **Igreja Nossa Senhora Rosário dos Pretos** (☉ noon-4pm Thu-Tue), another beautiful church, dates from 1708. The **Museu do Padre Toledo** (☉ 9am-4:30pm Thu-Tue) is dedicated to another hero of the Inconfidência, and was his home.

At the foot of the Serra de São José is a 1km-wide band of protected Atlantic rain forest, with several hiking trails. The most popular and direct leads to the Mãe d'Agua spring, reached by a 25-minute walk from the Chafariz de São José fountain in town. Other walks include the two-hour Caminho do Mangue, which heads up the Serra from the west side of town, and A Calçada, a stretch of the old road between Ouro Prêto and Rio de Janeiro. Locals advise against trekking alone. For guides (US$9 to US$30 per walk) ask at the tourist office or Hotel Solar da Ponte. Tiradente native **Adriano** (☎ 0xx32-9966-5864; US$10 per hour) rents horses with guides.

Sleeping & Eating
At weekends, Tiradentes gets crowded and prices can double.

Pousada do Laurito (Rua Direita 187; s/d with bath US$12/17) The best cheapie in town.

Pousada Tiradentes (☎ 0xx32-3355-1232; s/d with bath US$12/23) Next to the bus station, this place has a small measure of charm.

Pousada da Bia (☎ 0xx32-3355-1173; Rua Frederico Ozanan 330; s/d US$20/37) Down the hill from Santo Antônio church, it's like a home. Prices go up a few dollars on weekends.

Pousada Quatro Encantos (☎ 0xx32-3355-1609; Rua da Camara; s/d with bath US$23/46) Around the corner from Pousada da Bia, these cozy rooms have tiny courtyard gardens.

Pasta & Cia (Rua Frederico Ozanan 327) Has good Italian-style cooking.

Estalagem (Rua Ministro Gabriel Passos 280) Does a mean *feijão com lombo* (beans with pork).

Sabor de Minas (Rua Ministro Gabriel Passos 62) and **Bar do Celso Restaurante** (Largo das Forras) on the main square, have good regional food at reasonable prices.

Getting There & Around
The best approach to Tiradentes is the wonderful train trip from São João del Rei (see the São João del Rei section), but buses (US$1, 20 minutes) also come and go between the two towns approximately every 90 minutes.

DIAMANTINA
One of Brazil's prettiest and least visited colonial gems, Diamantina boomed when diamonds were discovered in the 1720s. Because of its isolation, it's a well-preserved colonial town and the center has changed little in 200 years. None of the gentrification so evident in Tiradentes is visible here.

Diamantina is about 300km north of Belo Horizonte. The stark landscape of northern Minas, with its rocky outcrops and barren highlands, poses a sharp contrast to the lush southern hills.

Information
Banco do Brasil (main square) has a Visa/Plus ATM but neither it nor **Itaú bank** offers currency exchange. The **municipal tourist office** (☎ 0xx38-3531-1857; Praça Monsenhor Neves 44) hands out a guide and map in Portuguese. Also try the office on the third floor of the **Casa de Cultura** (☎ 0xx38-3531-1636; Praça Antônio Eulálio).

Sights & Activities
Most Diamantina sights open in the early afternoon from Tuesday to Saturday and on Sunday mornings.

The **Igreja de NS do Carmo** (admission US$1), built in 1760–65, is Diamantina's most opulent church. It's worth a look inside. The tower was built at the rear lest the bells awaken Chica da Silva, the famous mistress and ex-slave of diamond contractor João Fernandes de Oliveira. Oliveira's mansion on Praça Lobo de Mesquita, known as the Casa de Chica da Silva, gives an idea of their extravagant lifestyle.

The **Museu do Diamante** (west of Praça JK; admission US$0.50) is actually inside the house of Padre Rolim, one of the Inconfidêntes. It houses furniture, instruments of torture and other relics of the good old diamond days.

The Saturday **food and craft market** (Centro Cultural David Ribeiro, Praça Barão Guaicuí), with live music, is an interesting occasion. The Centro has a small museum with fascinating old photos.

Juscelino Kubitschek, the 1960s Brazilian president who founded Brasília, was born in Diamantina. The small **Casa de Juscelino Kubitschek** (Rua São Francisco 241), reflects his simple upbringing.

While you're here, walk a couple of kilometers down the **Caminho dos Escravos** (built by slaves) to the **Serra da Jacuba.**

Sleeping & Eating
Camping is allowed at the waterfall just outside of town.

Chalé Pousada (☎ 0xx38-3531-1246; Rua Macau de Baixo 52; r per person US$10, with bath US$16) A cute old house in a great position with friendly staff.

Pousada Gameleira (☎ 0xx38-3531-1900; Rua do Rosário 209; r per person US$13) This little place is also excellent value.

Dália Hotel (☎ 0xx38-3531-1477; Praça JK 25; s/d US$14/24, with bath US$26/36) The quaint Dália

BRAZIL

Hotel is a pleasantly aged building with a big buffet breakfast.

Reliquias do Tempo (☎ 0xx38-3531-1627; Rua Macau de Baixo 104; s/d with bath US$16/30) A gorgeous historical house with immaculate rooms.

Pensão Comercial (Praça Monsenhor Neves; s/d US$8/12) Very basic.

Restaurante Grupiaria (Rua Campos Carvalho 12; dishes US$7-10) A popular place serving *mineiro* dishes.

Apocalipse (Praça Barão Guaicuí) Has excellent per-kilo food.

Cantinha do Marinho (Rua Direita 113; dishes US$3) On the main square, this is another favorite.

Capistrana, near Cathedral Square, is good, as is Santo Antônio in the center of town.

Getting There & Away
Six daily buses run from Belo Horizonte (US$17, 5½ hours).

THE SOUTH

Brazil's south is a kaleidoscope of cultures and traditions, a place where *gaucho's* still cling to the cowboy lifestyle on the wide plains bordering Argentina and Uruguay, and the influence from millions of German, Italian, Swiss and Eastern European settlers is evident in the Old World feel of inland and coastal villages. Echoing throughout the region is the thunderous call of Foz do Iguaçu's mighty waterfall.

The region comprises of three relatively prosperous states: Paraná, Santa Catarina and Rio Grande do Sul. The climate is generally subtropical, but snow is not uncommon in the interior highlands in winter. The must-see attraction is the Iguaçu waterfalls in southwest Paraná – it's Brazil's most spectacular natural wonder. Santa Catarina and Paraná have some of the country's best beaches, a few with excellent surfing, others mimicking the Caribbean's clear turquoise water.

CURITIBA
Curitiba, the capital of Paraná (population 1.6 million), is one of Brazil's urban success stories, with parks, well-preserved historic buildings, little traffic congestion and a large university population. It's a good place for a pit stop, but there's not much to hold your attention beyond a few days.

You can find free Internet access 24 hours a day at **Digitando o Futuro** (Rua 24 Horas). If there's a big queue (and there often is) a number of places in the same area have cheap access. **Paraná Turismo** (Loja 18, Rua 24 Horas) is a helpful information booth in the city's big pedestrian mall.

Sights & Activities
Wander around the **Largo da Ordem**, the cobbled historic quarter, with beautifully restored buildings, art galleries, bars and restaurants, and music after dark. Stroll in the **Passeio Público** (Avenida Presidente Carlos Cavalcanti; ☽ Tue-Sun), a park complex where Curitibanos have relaxed since 1886. **Rua 24 Horas** is a pedestrian mall and arcade – always open, and very crowded around 3am – with gift shops, restaurants, bars and Internet kiosks.

Sleeping
There are plenty of cheap hotels across from the bus station.

Hotel Maia (☎ 0xx41-264-1684; Avenida Presidente Afonso Camargo 355; s/d US$10/20) The well-run Maia is a few blocks from the bus station.

Hotel Cristo Rei (☎ 0xx41-264-9093; Avenida Presidente Afonso Camargo 381; s/d US$7/14) This hotel has basic *quartos*, but no breakfast.

Golden Hotel (☎ 0xx41-323-3603; Rua Tobias de Macado 26; s/d with bath US$10/16) In the center of town, this might not be much to look at but it offers excellent value, with a huge breakfast and very helpful staff.

Estacão Palace (☎ 0xx41-322-9840; Rua des Westphalen 126; s/d with bath US$10/16) This minimalist but immaculate place has slightly stark surroundings.

AJ de Curitiba Youth Hostel (☎ 0xx41-233-2746; ajcwb@uol.com.br; Av Padre Agostinho 645; r per person US$7) A short walk from Rua 24 Horas, with clean dorm rooms, shared bathrooms and basic amenities.

Eating
Alfândego (Rua das Flores 424; buffet US$3) On the 2nd floor of the Galeria Schaffer, this is a pretty spot for a cheap buffet lunch.

Restaurante Déa (Mercado Municipal; dishes US$3) Good lunches with meat and salad near the bus station.

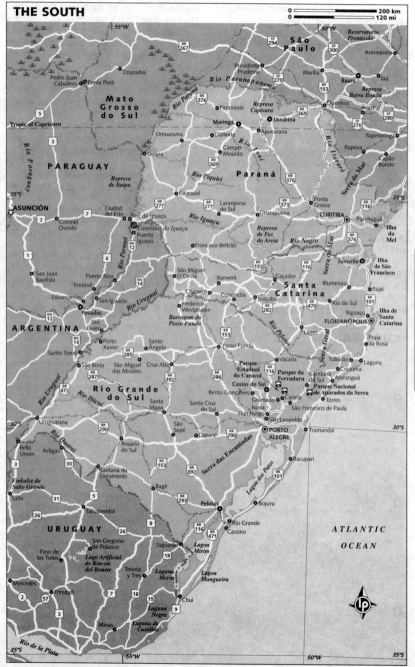

THE SOUTH

0 — 200 km
0 — 120 mi

Reservatorio Promissão

São Paulo

SP 294

SP 300

Araraquara

Pedro Juan Caballero
Ponta Porã
Dourados

Presidente Prudente

Marília

Bauru

Jaú

Represa Barra Bonita

Mato Grosso do Sul

BR 267

Rio Paranapanema

SP 270

BR 153

Quinhos

Avaré

SP 280

BR 376

Paranavaí

Represa Capivara

Londrina

BR 369

SP 270

Tropic of Capricorn

5

3

Umuarama

Maringá

Cianorte

Apucarana

Itapetininga

Rio Paraná

Guaíra

Campo Mourão

Rio Ivaí

Itapeva

Capão Bonito

PARAGUAY

Represa de Itaipu

BR 369

Rio Piquiri

Paraná

BR 376

Serra do Mar

25°S

ASUNCIÓN

2

Coronel Oviedo

7

Ciudad del Este

BR 277

Foz do Iguaçu

Cascavel

BR 277

Laranjeiras do Sul

Guarapuava

BR 373

Ponta Grossa

CURITIBA

BR 116

Paranaguá

25°S

Cataratas do Iguaçu

RN 12

Puerto Iguazú

Rio Iguaçu

Represa de Foz do Areia

Rio Negro

BR 376

Ilha do Mel

1

6

Francisco Beltrão

BR 153

Caçador

BR 116

Joinville

Ilha de São Francisco

San Juan Bautista

Puerto Rico

São Miguel D'Oeste

Xanxerê

Santa Catarina

Blumenau

Itajaí

Rio do Sul

BR 101

Ilha de Santa Catarina

Trinidad

RN 14

Chapecó

Concordia

Joaçaba

BR 470

Biguaçu

FLORIANÓPOLIS

Encarnación

San Ignacio

Frederico Westphalen

BR 282

Lages

ARGENTINA

Posadas

San Javier

Barragem do Passo Fundo

BR 153

Praia da Rosa

RN 14

Porto Xavier

Santo Ângelo

Passo Fundo

Vacaria

Serra Geral

Tubarão

Laguna

Santo Tomé

BR 285

Cruz Alta

BR 386

Parque Estadual do Caracol

BR 116

Parque da Ferradura

Cambará do Sul

Criciúma

Araranguá

São Borja

São Miguel das Missões

BR 392

Caxias do Sul

Parque Nacional de Aparados da Serra

BR 287

BR 472

Rio Grande do Sul

Santa Maria

Santa Cruz do Sul

Bento Gonçalves

Gramado

Canela

Torres

Rio Ibicuí

Nova Hamburgo

São Francisco de Paula

Uruguaiana

BR 290

Rio Uruguai

São Sepé

Capané

BR 290

São Leopoldo

PORTO ALEGRE

Tramandaí

30°S

Bella Unión

Rio Quaraí

Artigas

Rosário do Sul

BR 153

BR 392

Serra das Encantadas

Bacupari

30°S

3

30

Santana do Livramento

BR 101

Lagoa dos Patos

Salto

Embalse de Salto Grande

31

5

Bagé

BR 293

Pelotas

Bojuru

ATLANTIC OCEAN

26

Tacuarembó

8

BR 116

Rio Grande

San Gregorio de Polanco

Jaguarão

BR 471

Cassino

Paso de los Toros

Lago Artificial de Rincón del Bonete

18

Lagoa Mirim

URUGUAY

26

Treinta y Tres

Laguna Merín

Lagoa Mangueira

Mercedes

2

7

18

15

Chuí

57

Trinidad

3

Minas

Laguna Negra

9

Laguna de Castillos

Río de la Plata

55°W

50°W

35°S

BRAZIL

Largo da Ordem has several reasonably priced restaurants including:

Saccy Restaurante (Rua São Francisco 350; dishes US$8) Serves large steak, chicken or fish dishes for two and has a pleasant view of the plaza.

Getting There & Away

You can fly from Curitiba to any major city in Brazil.

BUS

Frequent buses run to São Paulo (US$20, 6½ hours), Rio de Janeiro (US$32, 12 hours), Foz do Iguaçu (US$30, 10 hours) and all major cities to the south. If you should miss the train to Paranaguá (see following), there are plenty of buses.

Direct buses run to Asunción (US$40, 18 hours), Buenos Aires (US$66, 28 hours) and Santiago (US$120, 52 hours).

TRAIN

The railway from Curitiba (altitude 900m) to the port of Paranaguá is the most exciting in Brazil, with sublime panoramas.

The *trem* (regular train) and the *litorina* (tourist train) both take 3½ to four hours each way. The *trem* leaves Curitiba at 8am daily except Monday, starting back from Paranaguá at 4pm. There are three classes: *executivo*, *turístico* and *convencional*. One-way/round-trip *convencional* tickets from Curitiba cost US$15/20 for a left-side seat going down (giving the best views) and US$13/18 on the right side.

The air-con *litorina* leaves Curitiba at 9am on weekends, starting back at 3pm. From June to August and December to February it also runs on Tuesday and Wednesday. One-way/round-trip tickets cost US$46/66 (left side) and US$36/60 (right side).

Schedules change frequently so check in advance by calling ☎ 0xx41-323-4007 or logging on to www.serraverdeexpress.com.br.

Getting Around

Alfonso Pena airport is 18km from the city (US$22 by taxi). An Aeroporto–Centro bus (US$0.70, 35 minutes) leaves every 20

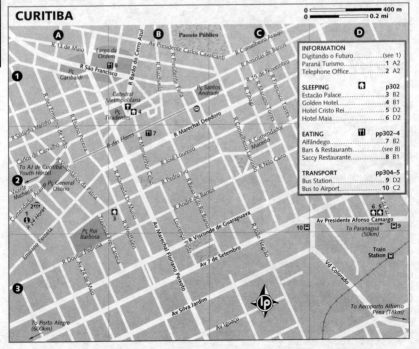

minutes from Avenida Presidente Afonso Camargo. There is a shuttle bus that goes direct but it only makes selected stops – ask at your hotel if there's a pick-up nearby.

PARANAGUÁ

The scenic train ride from Curitiba isn't the only reason to go to Paranaguá (population 122,000), one of Brazil's major ports. It's a colorful city, with a historic section near the waterfront that's in the midst of restoration but still has a feeling of tropical decadence. A great swath of Atlantic rainforest is visible across the bay. Paranaguá also provides access to Ilha do Mel.

The main **tourist office** (☎ 0xx41-422-6882; Rua General Carneiro), along the waterfront, is very helpful.

Sights

Don't miss the **Museu de Arqueologia e Etnologia** (Rua 15 de Novembro 567; admission US$1.50; ⊙ noon-5pm Tue-Sun), near the waterfront. Housed in a beautifully restored 18th-century Jesuit school, it has many indigenous artifacts and folk art, and some fascinating old machines.

Sleeping & Eating

There are some cheap places near the waterfront, but the area can be a bit seedy at night.

Hotel Ponderosa (☎ 0xx41-423-2464; Rua Prescilinio Corrêa 68; s/d with bath US$12/18) In a restored colonial building, this is a bargain – with light, clean, tasteful rooms.

Hotel Litoral (☎ 0xx41-423-1734; Rua Correia de Freitas 65; r per person US$7, with bath US$13) Closer to the train station, Hotel Litoral is run by a group of lovely old ladies.

Karibe (☎ 0xx41-422-1177; Simas 86; r per person US$9) A popular spot for backpackers.

Mercado Municipal do Café, a restored café and good spot for lunch, has five small cafés serving cheap seafood and snacks.

Gato Nerô (Rua Benjamin Constant) A good mid-range place that stays open later in evenings and has cheap pizza and chopp, when many shut down in Bela Vista, on the waterfront.

Getting There & Away

Out-of-town buses leave from the bus station on the waterfront. There are frequent buses to Curitiba (US$5.50, 1½ hours).

Southward, hourly buses go to Guaratuba, where you can catch another bus to Joinville.

For details on the train ride to/from Curitiba, see p304.

ILHA DO MEL

This oddly shaped island at the mouth of the Baía de Paranaguá has excellent beaches, good waves for surfing, and scenic walks. A young party crowd descends on the island from January to Carnaval, and over Easter. Otherwise, it's a tranquil, relatively isolated place.

Ilha do Mel consists of two parts joined by the beach at Nova Brasília. The larger, northern part is mostly an ecological station, little visited except for Praia da Fortaleza, where the remains of an 18th-century fort are worth a look, and Praia Ponta do Bicho. The best beaches are on the ocean side (east) – Praia da Fora, Praia do Miguel and Praia Ponta do Bicho. The best walks are also along the ocean side, from the southern tip of the island up to Praia da Fortaleza. There are bichos de pé (parasites that burrow under the skin), so keep your shoes on. When the surf is big, the walk from Praia da Fora to Praia Grande should only be done at low tide.

Sleeping & Eating

If you arrive on the island on a summer weekend or other peak time, rooms will be hard to find, but you can rent space to sling a hammock. There are plenty of **camping areas** (campsites per person US$3) at Encantadas and Nova Brasília and two at Praia do Farol.

The biggest concentration of pousadas is at laid-back Praia do Farol, along the track to the right from Nova Brasília. Praia do Farol is popular with surfers because it's near the Praia Grande waves. Prices here increase 20% to 50% in the high season.

Pousada das Meninas (☎ 0xx41-426-8023; r per person US$14, with bath US$20) A relaxed little place, with rustic rooms.

Pousada das Palmas (☎ 0xx41-335-6028; r per person US$10) A good cheapie closer to the pier. Ask for a discount for longer stays.

Pousada Colméia (☎ 0xx41-426-8029; r per person US$16) Further out towards the lighthouse, Pousada Colméia has a lovely shady balcony that invites loafing.

BRAZIL

The quieter Praia Ponta do Bicho has three pousadas: the last you reach, **Pousada dos Prazeres** (☎ 0xx41-978-3221; r per person US$16) is a friendly place with a seafood café.

Encantadas, in the southwest of the island, is small, and crowded on summer weekends.

Pousada da Tia Maria (☎ 0xx41-9978-3352; s/d with bath US$14/28) A good-value place with clean, comfortable *apartamentos*.

There are *barracas* (stalls) with food and drinks at Nova Brasília, Encantadas and Praia da For. On Friday and Saturday nights you'll find some live music and probably a beach party. Toca do Abutre, in Nova Brasília, is a surf bar/seafood restaurant/music venue rolled into one.

Getting There & Away

Boats for Nova Brasília and Encantadas leave the jetty opposite the tourist office in Paranaguá at 3pm Monday to Friday, 9:30am and 1pm Saturday and 9:30am Sunday (US$3.50, 1½ to two hours). Returning, they leave Nova Brasília at 8am Monday to Friday and 3:30pm on Sunday.

Alternatively, get an hourly bus from Paranaguá to Pontal do Sul (US$0.80, 1½ hours), on the mainland opposite Encantadas, and from there take a boat for the 4km crossing to Encantadas (US$3, 30 to 40 minutes). In high season, the boats leave at least hourly from 8am to 7pm (call ☎ 0xx41-455-1144 for schedules).

FOZ DO IGUAÇU

The stupendous roar of 275 different waterfalls crashing 80m into the Rio Iguaçu seems to create a low-level buzz of excitement all over the small town of Foz, even though the famed Cataratas are a good 20km southeast of city center. Even on the sleepiest, hottest afternoon, nature's relentless churning power is present. There's little to see in Foz beyond the Cataratas and Itaipu dam, the largest hydro-electric power plant in the world and one of the 'seven modern wonders,' but those two experiences alone are enough to leave you sated.

Information

The Secretaria Municipal de Turismo (colloquially known as FozTur) is one of the best-run tourism offices in Brazil. The staff speak a variety of languages and are ex-tremely well-informed about the area. The **Foztur Information Booth** (☎ 0800-451516; Av Jorge Schimmelpfeng) is downtown just past the yellow building that houses the local police. Other booths can be found at the local and international bus stations (☯ 6am-6pm) and at the airport (☯ 8am-last plane).

Dozens of exchange houses broker better deals than the banks, but traveler's checks aren't widely accepted and often get a lower exchange rate than cash. It's not safe to walk near the riverfront at anytime; be on guard for pickpockets at the bridge to Ciudad del Este in Paraguay.

Sights

To see the falls properly, which takes at least two full days, you must visit both sides – Brazil gives the grand overview and Argentina the closer look. The best time to come is August to November. A great local tour guide who can fix up just about any trip is **Neri Enio Krug** (☎ 0xx45-529-7110; discoveryneri@yahoo.com.br; Rua Marechal Floriano 1851). He speaks English, Spanish, Portuguese, Italian and German with equal ease. **Iguazu Jungle Explorer** (www.iguazujunglexplorer.com), on the Argentine side, has a variety of hikes and stellar boat rides. **Macuco Safari** (www.macucosafari.com.br) offers under-the-falls trips from the Brazilian side. To include **Itaipu dam** (☎ 0xx45-520-6985; www.itaipu.gov.br) schedule at least three days in town; remember the Brazilian side of the falls is closed on Monday mornings, and Itaupi is closed on Sunday.

Sleeping

Albergue Paudimar Campestre (☎ 0xx45-529-6061; www.paudimar.com.br; Av das Cataratas; r per person US$9) Foz's youth hostel, 12km from town on the way to the falls, has an information desk at the bus station, open 5am to 6pm, and will pay half your taxi fare to the hostel if there's two or more people headed out there and you stay at least two nights. It's more like a mini resort, with a swimming pool, bar, cheap meals and Internet access.

Hotel Rouver (☎ 0xx45-574-2916; rouver@fnn.net; Av Jorge Schimmelpfeng 872; s/d with bath US$8/14, ste US$18) Possibly the best deal in town, this family-run hotel is clean airy and bright, and offers free Internet access.

Pousada Evelina (☎ 0xx45-574-3817; pousada .evalina@foznet.com.br; Rua Irlan Kalichewski 171; r per person with bath US$11) This good budget place,

3.5km from Foz toward the falls, has spotless rooms.

Hotel Del Rey (☎ 0xx45-523-2027; www.hoteldelreyfoz.com.br; Rua Tarobá 1020; s/d with bath US$16/24) Spacious rooms in town.

Eating & Drinking

There's lots of both going on in Foz, especially along Av Schimmelpfeng at night.

Tropicana (Avenida Juscelino Kubitschek 198; meals per kg US$3) A popular student hang-out with something for everyone – food per kilo, meat or pizza *rodízio* or salad-and-meat buffet.

Búfalo Branco (Rua Rebouças 530; dishes US$10) Foz's longest-established churrascaria is always crowded.

Nissei (Juscelino Kubitscheck 94; dishes US$3.50) Brazilian lunches and Japanese dinners daily.

Barbarela's (Av Brasil 1119; menu items US$4). Delicious all-natural food and great fruit smoothies.

Jardim Da Cerveja (Schimmelpfeng 700) Check out this place or the neighboring Bier Garten. Both have cheap *chopp*, inexpensive food (with huge portions) and stay open to the wee hours.

Getting There & Away

BRAZIL

There are frequent flights from Foz to Asunción, Rio, São Paulo and Curitiba. Buses go to Curitiba (US$20, 9½ hours, 14 daily), São Paulo (US$40, 16 hours, six daily), Rio

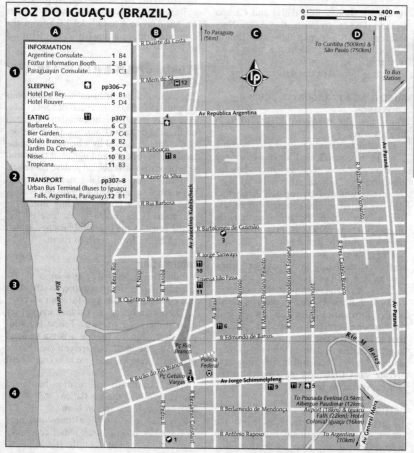

FOZ DO IGUAÇU (BRAZIL)

INFORMATION	
Argentine Consulate	1 B4
Foztur Information Booth	2 B4
Paraguayan Consulate	3 C3

SLEEPING	pp306–7
Hotel Del Rey	4 B1
Hotel Rouver	5 D4

EATING	p307
Barbarela's	6 C4
Bier Garden	7 C4
Búfalo Branco	8 B2
Jardim Da Cerveja	9 C4
Nissei	10 B3
Tropicana	11 B3

TRANSPORT	pp307–8
Urban Bus Terminal (Buses to Iguaçu Falls, Argentina, Paraguay)	12 B1

BRAZIL

(US$50, 22 hours, four daily) and Campo Grande (US$24, 16 hours, two daily). Note that some bus lines depart at the same time as competitors; although there are many buses to Curitiba, for example, most leave at the same time instead of throughout the day.

ARGENTINE & PARAGUAYAN BORDER CROSSINGS

There are also frequent flights to/from Buenos Aires.

Crossing borders in this area has become a lot more complicated since September 11. Paraguay now requires entry visas for Americans and several other nationalities – the list is updated frequently. Argentina also has added several countries to its visa list, mostly Asian. Brazilian authorities might not worry about exit and entry stamps if you are just leaving for the day, but neighboring countries are becoming real sticklers. Bring your passport when visiting Argentina's falls.

Local bus drivers stop at the border if you ask, but rarely wait while you finish border formalities. You can always grab the next one; service is stopped at 7pm. It's wise to consult a FozTur agent upon arrival to get the latest update on who needs what stamps. Many hotels and hostels now have private vans that ferry passengers to the falls in Argentina to avoid hassle.

Getting Around

To get to the airport, 16km from the center, catch a 'P Nacional' bus (US$2, 30 minutes) from any stop on Av Juscelino

Kubitschek after Rua Barbosa. A taxi is around US$14.

Going from the bus station (6km out) into town, catch any 'Centro' bus (US$0.60). A taxi costs US$5.50.

The Parque Nacional No 400 bus (US$1) runs to the Brazilian side of the waterfalls from the urban bus terminal on Av Juscelino Kubitschek, every half hour until midnight, daily except Monday morning.

For the Argentine side of the falls, catch a Puerto Iguazú bus (US$1.50) in front of the urban bus terminal or any stop along Av Juscelino Kubitschek. They pass about every 10 minutes (every 50 minutes on Sunday) until 7pm. At Puerto Iguazú bus station, transfer to a bus to the falls (see Puerto Iguazú in the Argentina chapter p77).

Buses run every 10 minutes (30 minutes on Sunday) to Ciudad del Este from the army base opposite the urban bus terminal in Foz.

FLORIANÓPOLIS & ILHA DE SANTA CATARINA

The beautiful beach town of Florianópolis (population 322,000), capital of Santa Catarina state, is half on the mainland and half on the Ilha de Santa Catarina. The two sides of the city are joined by a bridge; the mainland side is modern and ugly, but the island side beckons with cobbled pedestrian streets and sun-faded colonial buildings around the central square, Praça 15 de Novembro. This place is a favorite among Brazilians and tourists, as much for the relaxed feel of the town as the beautiful beaches, which stretch 52km from north to south.

Information

Moncho (Rua Tiradentes 181), run by a super-friendly Argentinian couple, is the best place for phone calls and Internet access.

There's an active street black market for cash dollars on the Rua Felipe Schmidt pedestrian block. There's a **Banco do Brasil** (Praça 15 de Novembro, 20) where you can change traveler's checks and make credit card withdrawals.

There are handy information booths in Florianópolis at the **bus station** (☎ 0xx48-224-2777; Rua Paulo Fontes) and in **town** (☎ 0xx48-222-4906; Rua Paulo Fontes, near Parque Metropolitano), next to the old customs house. Staff can make reservations for hotels on the island.

Ilha de Santa Catarina

The island's **east-coast beaches**, facing the ocean, are the cleanest and most beautiful, with the biggest waves and greatest expanses of empty sand. They're the most popular for day trips and have few hotels. The **north-coast beaches** have become heavily developed and crowded. For more on individual beaches, see Sleeping & Eating, following. To help you decide which beach to stay at, or whether you'd prefer to stay in town and make day trips to take an island tour. **Veleiro Tur** (☎ 0xx48-225-9939; Rua Silva Jardim 1050) in the suburb of Prainha, runs several different tours to the main beaches and places of interest; half-day tours cost US$14.

Lagoa da Conceição, in the interior, is very beautiful, though it can also get very busy. The views of the lagoon, surrounding peaks and sand dunes make for great walks or boat rides. Boats for up to 10 people can be hired at the bridge (around US$15 for two hours). Boat tours to beautiful, undeveloped **Ilha do Campeche**, off the island's east coast (US$15), are fun: you can check out ancient inscriptions and snorkel in pretty lagoons. Call **Scuna Sul** (☎ 0xx48-224-1806) or **Scuna Central** (☎ 0xx48-225-9939).

Sleeping & Eating

Most of the budget places are in the center of town. At the beaches, it's possible to economize by renting an apartment with a group of people. There are also many places to camp.

TOWN

Albergue da Juventude Ilha de Catarina (☎ 0xx48-225-3781; Rua Duarte Schutel 227; r per person US$6) In town, the welcoming HI hostel is a 10-minute walk from the bus station.

Felippe Hotel (☎ 0xx48-222-4122; Rua João Pinto; r per person US$9) A cheap place to lay your head, but it doesn't rank high on atmosphere (or cleanliness).

Sumare (☎ 0xx48-222-5359; Rua Felipe Schmidt 423; s/d US$12/16) The rooms that are a bit dark and stuffy, but in general the place is clean and the staff friendly.

Restaurante Villa (Rua Trajano 91; lunch US$5) This central restaurant is a great, breezy, per-kilo lunch spot with good salads.

BRAZIL

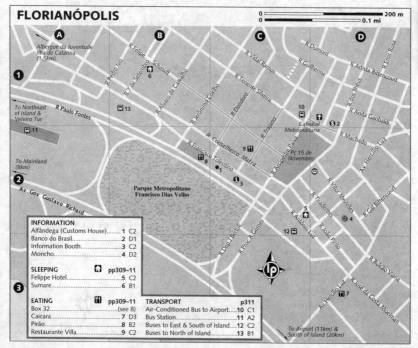

FLORIANÓPOLIS

INFORMATION	
Alfândega (Customs House)	1 C2
Banco do Brasil	2 D1
Information Booth	3 C2
Moncho	4 D2

SLEEPING	pp309–11
Felippe Hotel	5 C2
Sumare	6 B1

EATING	pp309–11
Box 32	(see 8)
Caicara	7 D3
Pirão	8 B2
Restaurante Villa	9 C2

TRANSPORT	p311
Air-Conditioned Bus to Airport	10 C1
Bus Station	11 A2
Buses to East & South of Island	12 C2
Buses to North of Island	13 B1

Parque Metropolitano
Francisco Dias Velho

To Northeast of Island & Veleiro Tur

To Mainland (8km)

To Airport (11km) & South of Island (20km)

0   200 m
0   0.1 mi

BRAZIL

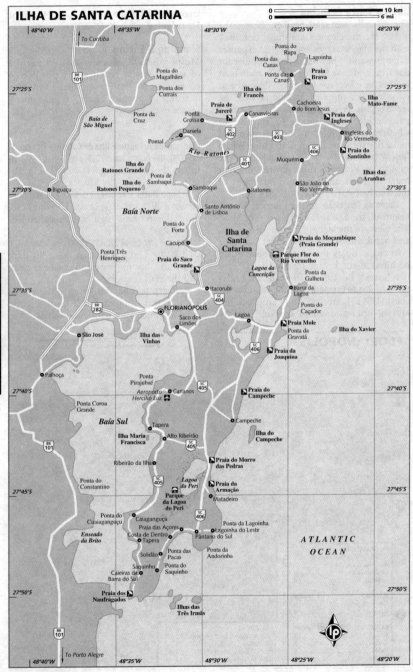

ILHA DE SANTA CATARINA

0 — 10 km
0 — 6 mi

Caicara (Av Hercílio Luz; lunch US$5, dinner US$9) Caicara serves cheap lunch and dinner. The old market is full of character, a good place to drink *chopp*, snack and watch people in the late afternoon. Interesting seafood restaurants include: **Pirão** (dishes US$5), with great seafood dishes, and **Box 32** (Rua Francisco Tolentino; dishes US$2-6), which is known for delicious late-afternoon snacks. Both are popular places at night and get crowded with locals looking for fun.

BEACHES
East coast prices can double between December and February. At the north end of the east coast, Praia dos Ingleses is a nice beach but quite developed.

Pousada Sol & Mar (☎ 0xx48-269-1271; Rua Dom João Backer; s/d with bath US$16/28) Has the best-value accommodations right on the beach.

Praia do Santinho, a little further south, is one of the most beautiful beaches and is relatively uncrowded. It also has a surf school.

Pousada do Santinho (☎ 0xx48-269-2836; pous adasantinho@ig.com.br; s/d with bath US$24/30) This place has large, comfortable *apartamentos*, and chalets that work out cheaper for bigger groups. The food is good here, and the Ingleses bus from Florianópolis stops right at the door. To rent houses at Santinho, ask at the little yellow hut on the roadside.

The next beach south, Praia do Moçambique, is 14km long and undeveloped. A pine forest hides it from the road (SC-406) that runs a couple of kilometers inland. At the south end is Barra da Lagoa, a big, curved stretch of beach that's still home to fishermen and has quite a few hotels and restaurants, and plenty of houses to rent.

Hotel Cabanas (☎ 0xx48-232-7032; Rua Altomire Barcellos 1504; r per person US$10) A rustic place with a bar and grill in the front and small *cabanas* out the back. There's a communal kitchen and English and German are spoken.

Continuing south, Praia da Joaquina hosts the Brazilian surfing championship in January. About 1km back along the approach road, **Pousada Felicidade da Ilha** (d with bath US$20) has basic *apartamentos* with cooking facilities.

The beaches to the south are more remote and quite spectacular, but beware of strong currents.

Pousada Vila Tamarindo (☎ 0xx48-237-3464; tamarindo@fastlane.com.br; d with bath US$40) A friendly and great place to stay about 3km from Campeche on the road heading north to Lagoa da Conceição. It has large gardens with a pool, and is just a short walk over dunes to the long, uncrowded Praia do Campeche.

Praia da Armação is similarly undeveloped. Accommodation is hard to find and involves asking around, or inquiring at the tourist office when you arrive. The area is unrivalled for observing birds and other wildlife, and there are some great walks along the hilly trails.

Getting There & Away
There are daily flights to São Paulo and Porto Alegre, and connections to most other cities. Long-distance buses link Florianópolis with Porto Alegre (US$20, 6½ hours), Curitiba (US$17, 4½ hours), São Paulo (US$28, 12 hours), Rio de Janeiro (US$42, 18 hours), Foz do Iguaçu (US$32, 15 hours), Buenos Aires (US$88, 24 hours) and Montevideo (US$62, 20 hours).

Getting Around
The airport is 12km south of the city. To get there, you can take a taxi (US$16), Correador Sudoeste local buses from the bus station (US$0.60), or by air-con Correador Sudoeste bus (US$1.50) from the stop next to the cathedral on Praça 15 de Novembro.

Local buses and yellow microbuses (which take surfboards) serve all the beaches. Buses for the east and south of the island (including Lagoa da Conceição) leave from the local bus terminal in town on Rua Antônio Luz. Buses for the north leave from the local bus terminal on Rua Francisco Tolentino, close to the main bus station.

TORRES
This small town, 205km northeast of Porto Alegre, is a great spot to take a rest while traversing the Rio Grande do Sul coast. It has fine beaches, beautiful rock formations and good surrounding country for walks. There are numerous surfing competitions held here throughout the year and the nearby **Ilha dos Lobos**, a rocky island about 2km out to sea, is home to sea lions in the winter months.

BRAZIL

The **HI Albergue da Juventude São Domingos** (☎ 0xx51-664-1865; Rua Júlio de Castilhos 875) is open in summer; reservations are required. The friendly, family-run **Hotel Costa Azul** (☎ 0xx51-664-3291; Avenida José Bonifácio 382; s/d with bath US$14/20), near the bus station, has comfy rooms with breakfast. **Central** (☎ 0xx51-664-2580; Rua Borges de Medeiros 296) is another good cheapie. Camping is allowed at **Praia de Itapeva** (☎ 0xx51-605-5112), about 5km from town.

Bem Gosto (Rua Rio Branco 242) is a delicious *churrascaria* and **Sol Macrobiótico** (Júlio de Castilhos 875) has heart-healthy fare.

Hourly buses run to/from Porto Alegre (US$10, three hours).

PARQUE NACIONAL DE APARADOS DA SERRA

This magnificent **national park** (admission US$4; ✹ 9am-4pm Wed-Sun) is 70km northeast of São Francisco de Paula and 18km from Cambará do Sul. The big attraction is the **Cânion do Itaimbezinho**, a fantastic narrow canyon with sheer escarpments of 600m to 720m. Two waterfalls drop into this deep incision. There are three hiking trails in the park: **Trilha do Vértice** (2km each way) and **Trilha Cotovelo** (2½ hours return) go to waterfalls and offer canyon vistas; **Trilha do Rio do Boi**, best approached from Praia Grande, east of the national park, follows the base of the canyon for 7km. It's for experienced hikers and is closed during the rainy season. A guide is highly recommended.

The Parque Nacional de Aparados da Serra **visitors center** (☎ 0xx54-251-1262; guides per person US$2) has maps, a café and guides for Trilha Cotovelo. Guides can also be hired through **Acontur** (☎ 0xx54-251-1320; Cambará do Sul), the local guide association, and **Praia Grande** (☎ 0xx48-532-1414), a tour operator.

Sleeping

Cambará do Sul has small pousadas and many families rent rooms in their houses.

Pousada Itaimbeleza (☎ 0xx54-251-1367; Rua Dona Ursula; r per person US$10) Close to the bus station, this is the best set up for travelers.

Hotel e Churrascaria Sabrina (☎ 0xx54-251-1147; Av Getúlio Vargas; r per person US$10) You can also try this hotel.

Getting There & Around

A bus leaves Porto Alegre at 6:15am daily for São Francisco de Paula and Cambará

do Sul (US$8, five hours). Buy tickets the night before. From Torres on the coast, a bus runs to Praia Grande and Cambará do Sul at 4pm daily.

No buses go to the park itself. Sr Rezende at Pousada Itaimbeleza can organize a van (US$30 for up to six people), or grab a taxi at the bus station (round trip US$22, including waiting time) for up to four people.

CANELA

North of Porto Alegre is the Serra Gaúcha, a popular area for walking. The bus ride from the city is beautiful, as are the mountain resorts of Canela and (more expensive) Gramado. In winter there are occasional snowfalls and in spring the hills are blanketed with flowers.

Canela's tourist office (☎ 0xx54-282-1287; Lago da Fama 227) is right in the center of town.

Adventure tourism – rock climbing, rappelling, rafting, mountain biking, bungee jumping – is the latest thing here. Ask at the tourist office, or the agencies **At!tude** (☎ 0xx54-282-6305; Av Osvaldo Avanha 391) or **JM Rafting** (☎ 0xx54-282-1542; Av Osvaldo Avanha 1038). Prices are reasonable – for example, a 2½ hour rafting trip costs US$35.

Parque Estadual do Caracol & Parque da Ferradura

Nine kilometers north from Canela, the major attraction of this park (admission US$2.50; ✹ 8:30am-5:30pm) is the spectacular Cascata do Caracol, a 130m waterfall which is incredibly beautiful in the morning sun. If you're feeling fit, you can walk down 927 stairs to the base (and then back up) of the waterfall down. The Linha Turística bus runs there from the tourist office every two hours from 9:30am to 5:30pm Tuesday to Sunday.

Parque da Ferradura (admission US$3; ✹ 9am-5:30pm), is a 6km hike from the Parque do Caracol entrance. It's a stunning 420m horseshoe-shaped canyon with three lookouts along well-marked trails.

Sleeping & Eating

Camping Sesi (☎ 0xx54-282-1311; Rua Francisco Bertolucci 504) This campsite is 2.5km from town.

Pousada do Viajante (☎ 0xx54-282-2017; Rua Ernesto Urban 132; r per person US$10) The HI youth hostel is next to the bus station.

Hotel Turis (☎ 0xx54-282-2774, Av Osvaldo Aranha 223; r per person US$14) This central hotel offers basic but pleasant lodgings.

All the restaurants are on or just off the main street, Av Osvaldo Aranha.

Churrascaria Espelho Gaúcho (☎ 0xx54-282-4348; Rua Baden Powel, 50; dishes US$14) Big meat eaters will enjoy this barn-sized place where the juicy steaks are large enough for two.

Restaurante e Pizzeria Scur (☎ 0xx-54-282-3688; Avenida Osvaldo Aranha, 151) Offers a per-kilo lunch and 32 different pizzas for dinner.

Getting There & Around

Frequent buses run to/from Porto Alegre (US$8.50, 2¼ hours) via Gramado. There are also buses to São Francisco de Paula (US$1.50, one hour), from where you can connect to Cambará do Sul to get to the Parque Nacional de Aparados da Serra.

The Linha Turística buses make it easy (and cheap) to get to most attractions. Pick up a schedule from the tourist office.

PORTO ALEGRE

The capital city of Rio Grande do Sul is a flourishing port town on the banks of the Rio Guaíba, which in turn empties its waters into the huge Lagoa dos Patos. This lively, modern city is filled with green parks, interesting museums, good restaurants and nightlife, not to mention friendly gaúcho hospitality.

Information

Phone Express (Rua Uruguai 279) has long-distance phone cabinas as well as Internet access, for US$3 per hour. There are handy and helpful tourist offices at the **long-distance bus station** (☎ 0xx51-3225-0677; Largo Vespasiano Julio Veppo; ☒ 8am-9pm), the **Mercado Público** (Praça 15 de Novembro; ☒ 9am-6pm) and the airport.

Activities

The 1869 **Mercado Público** (Public Market), and the adjacent Praça 15 de Novembro, constitute the city's heart. Shops in the market sell the *gaúchos*' unique tea-drinking equipment, the *cuia* (gourd) and *bomba* (silver straw). The interesting **Museu Histórico Júlio de Castilhos** (Rua Duque de Caxias 1231; admission US$2; ☒ 10am-5pm Tue-Sun) contains diverse objects related to Rio Grande do Sul's history, such as special moustache cups. The **Museu de Arte do Rio Grande do Sul** (Praça da Alfândega;

☒ 10am-5pm Tue-Sun) has a good collection of gaúcho art. Near Lake Guáiba is the Usina do Gasômetro, an abandoned thermoelectric station that's been turned into a showcase for art, dance and film.

Sleeping

Hotel Ritz (☎ 0xx51-3225-3423; Avenida André da Rocha 225; r per person US$7) Porto Alegre's non-HI youth hostel sits in the funky Cidade Baixa quarter.

Hotel Uruguai (☎ 0xx51-3228-7864; Rua Dr Flores 371; s/d US$9/14, with bath US$15/20) Secure and cheap.

Hotel Palácio (☎ 0xx51-3225-3467; Rua Vigário José Ignácio 644; s/d US$7/12, with bath US$14/20) A friendly place, very popular with South Americans.

Hotel Praça Matriz (☎ 0xx51-3225-5772; Largo João Amorim de Albuquerque 72; s/d US$7/13) An ornate old building, with very good value rooms.

América Hotel (☎ 0xx51-3226-0062; Av Farrapos 119; s/d US$7/14) Not exactly in the city center, but it's still a good find for the price.

Eating & Drinking

Wherever you go, a tender steak will be nearby.

La Churrasquita (Rua Riachuelo 1331; dishes US$12) The enormous steaks easily feed two.

Bar Lider (Av Independência 408; dishes US$10) A carnivore fave.

Ilha Natural Restaurante Vegetariano (Rua General Camara 60) Packs in locals for a vegetarian buffet lunch.

Nova Vida (Av Borges de Medeiros 100; ☒ 11am-3pm Tue-Sun) A veg-oriented place.

The Mercado Público has a central food hall with inexpensive food and a bunch of cafés on its perimeter for lunch.

A great Alegre tradition is to have a late-afternoon *chopp* beer at Chalé da Praça XV, built in 1885, on Praça 15 de Novembro – a great place to people-watch.

Dr Jekyll (Travessa do Carmo 76; ☒ 11pm-dawn Mon-Sat) Cidade Baixa's favorite late-night watering hole.

Wanda Bar (Rua Comendador Coruja 169) A popular gay club, although anyone's welcome.

Getting There & Away

The busy bus station at Largo Vespasiano Julio Veppo has separate terminals for destinations in and outside Rio Grande do

BRAZIL

BRAZIL

PORTO ALEGRE

0 — 400 m
0 — 0.2 mi

INFORMATION
Tourist Office...1 B2
Tourist Office...2 D1

SIGHTS & ACTIVITIES   p313
Mercado Público..................................(see 1)
Museu de Arte do Rio Grande do Sul....3 A2
Museu Histórico Júlio de Castilhos.........4 B3

SLEEPING   p313
Hotel Palácio..5 C3
Hotel Pç Matriz..6 B3
Hotel Ritz..7 C3
Hotel Uruguai...8 C2

EATING   pp313–14
Bar Lider...9 D2
Chaleé da Pç XV..10 B2
Ilha Natural Restaurante Vegetariano....11 B2
La Churrasquita..12 B3
Nova Vida...13 B3

TRANSPORT   p314
Bus Station..14 D1

Sul. International buses run to Montevideo (US$58, 12 hours), Buenos Aires (US$64, 20 hours) and Santiago (US$116, 36 hours). Other buses go to Foz do Iguaçu (US$41, 15 hours), Florianópolis (US$17, seven hours), Curitiba (US$30, 11 hours) and Rio de Janeiro (US$70, 24 hours).

Getting Around

Porto Alegre has an efficient one-line metrô. The most useful stations are Estação Mercado Modelo (by the port), Estação Rodoviária (the next stop) and the airport (three stops beyond). A ride costs US$0.70.

JESUIT MISSIONS

In the early 17th century Jesuit missionaries established a series of Indian missions in a region straddling northeast Argentina, southeast Paraguay and neighboring bits of Brazil. Between 1631 and 1638, after devastating attacks by slaving expeditions from São Paulo and hostile Indians, activity was concentrated in 30 more easily defensible missions. These became centers of culture

as well as religion – in effect a nation within the colonies, considered by some scholars an island of utopian progress and socialism, which at its height in the 1720s had over 150,000 Guarani Indian inhabitants.

Seven of the now-ruined missions lie in the northwest of Brazil's Rio Grande do Sul state, eight are in Paraguay and 15 in Argentina.

The town of Santo Ângelo is the main jumping-off point for the various Brazilian missions, and has a **tourist office** (☎ 0xx55-3381-1294; www.missoesturismo.com.br). São Miguel das Missões (53km southwest, reachable by four daily buses) is the most interesting and intact of the missions. Admission is US$4; the evening sound-and-light show is US$2.50. See the sections on San Ignacio Miní in the Argentina chapter (p77) and Trinidad & Jesús in the Paraguay chapter (p780) for information on missions in those countries.

Sleeping & Eating

Pousada das Missões (☎ 0xx55-3381-1202; www.alber gues.com.br/saomiguel; dm US$9, s/d with bath US$16/25)

A new HI youth hostel right next to São Miguel mission.

Hotel Barichello (☎ 0xx55-3381-1327, Av Borges do Canto 1559; s/d US$12/18) Also in São Miguel, this hotel has a good *churrascaria* on site.

Santo Ângelo's cheapies are on or near Praça Rio Branco.

Hotel Comércio (☎ 0xx55-3312-2542; Av Brasil 1178; s & d US$18) Has nice amenities for a decent price.

Getting There & Away
There are six daily buses from Porto Alegre to Sânto Angelo (US$28, 6½ hours).

It's possible to enter Argentina by crossing the Rio Uruguai from Porto Xavier to San Javier, or from São Borja to Santo

Tomé, or at Uruguaiana, 180km south of São Borja (with buses to Buenos Aires). But if you're heading for the Argentine missions, more frequent buses (seven daily) depart from Puerto Iguazú (across the border from Foz do Iguaçu) for San Ignacio Miní (US$20, five hours). For the Paraguayan missions, daily buses go to Encarnación from Ciudad del Este, Paraguay, also opposite Foz do Iguaçu.

THE CENTRAL WEST

The Central West is a region of amazing contrasts. The lush Amazon jungle comes to rest against the dry bushes of Brazil's

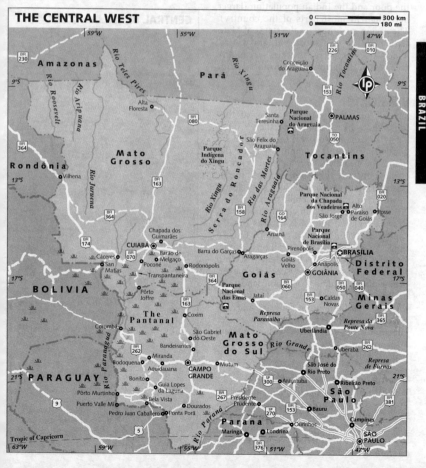

central high plains, and dramatic *chapadas* (tablelands) rise like brilliant red giants from the dark green cerrado backdrop to the east. In the southwest, The Pantanal spreads its watery tentacles over an area half the size of France, reaching into Paraguay and Bolivia and housing some 600 species of birds, not to mention fish, deer and about a million other creatures.

Also here is the modern national capital, Brasília, lying in a special Distrito Federal (Federal District) carved out of Goiás state. The Central West is in some ways Brazil's Wild West – though still relatively thinly populated, it's the scene of some intense, sometimes violent, competition for land between agribusiness road builders, miners, the poor and the Indian population (larger here than in most parts of the country). The region encompasses the states of Mato Grosso, Mato Grosso do Sul, and Goiás, which – if you believe the tales – regularly receives tourists from even the most distant galaxies.

BRASÍLIA

There's no other city in the world that looks quite like Brasília, and there's quite a few Brazilians who will tell you that's a good thing. Shooting up out of a sparse flat plain, the heavily skyscrapered city looks (from a distance) like some kind of futuristic experiment gone right. Get a little closer, however, and it's a different story.

Built from nothing in about three years, Brasília replaced Rio de Janeiro as Brazil's capital in 1960. Today it's one of Brazil's biggest cities, with two-million people. Its chief creators were President Juscelino Kubitschek, architect Oscar Niemeyer, urban planner Lucio Costa and landscape architect Burle Marx. Unfortunately, the city was built more for cars and air-conditioners than people. Distances are enormous, the sun blazes without mercy, and no one walks. Accommodations are expensive too.

Orientation & Information

The central area is shaped like an airplane and it's divided into an Asa Norte (North Wing) and an Asa Sul (South Wing). The government buildings and monuments are located in the fuselage, along the Eixo Monumental.

The **airport tourist office** (☎ 0xx61-364-9135; ☽ 7am-11pm) is the best place for tourist information. Staff can organize hotel discounts for you, but generally only have information on the more expensive places. The airport also has a variety of ATMs, most with Cirrus/MasterCard/Visa networking, a post office and a VIP center with Internet connection all conveniently lined up next to each other – something you won't find again until you leave the city. Take advantage while you can.

Banks with exchange facilities are in the areas of the city known as the Setor Bancário Sul (SBS, Banking Sector South) and Setor Bancário Norte (SBN, Banking Sector North), both close to the local bus station.

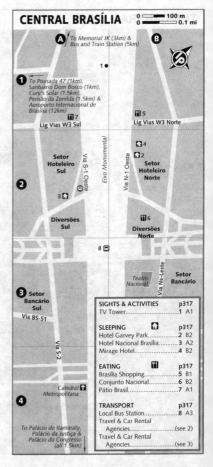

CENTRAL BRASÍLIA

SIGHTS & ACTIVITIES	p317
TV Tower................................1 A1	

SLEEPING	☐	p317
Hotel Garvey Park..................2 B2		
Hotel Nacional Brasília............3 A2		
Mirage Hotel..........................4 B2		

EATING	🍴	p317
Brasília Shopping....................5 B1		
Conjunto Nacional..................6 B2		
Pátio Brasil...........................7 A1		

TRANSPORT	p317
Local Bus Station....................8 A3	
Travel & Car Rental Agencies..................(see 2)	
Travel & Car Rental Agencies..................(see 3)	

Sights & Activities

Brasília's major edifices are mostly spread along a 5km stretch of the Eixo Monumental and are listed in northwest-to-southeast order here. To visit them you can take a **bus tour** (half-day US$20), rent a car or combine buses from the local bus station (No 104 and 108 are the most useful) with some long walks.

Start at the **Memorial JK** (admission US$2; 9am-5pm Tue-Sun), which houses the tomb of President Kubitschek and has exhibits on Brasília's construction. Then head to the observation deck of the **TV Tower** (8am-8pm Tue-Sun, 2-8pm Mon). About 1km southwest along Via W3 Sul, off the Eixo Monumental, is the **Santuário Dom Bosco** (8am-6pm), a church with very beautiful blue stained-glass windows.

The **Catedral Metropolitana**, with its curved columns, stained glass and haunting statues of the four evangelists, is worth seeing too. The most interesting government buildings, the **Palácio do Itamaraty**, **Palácio da Justiça** and **Palácio do Congresso**, are in the 'cockpit' of the airplane ground-plan.

Sleeping & Eating

Good budget accommodations are hard to come by. If you plan to stay over a weekend, a lot of mid-range and high-end hotels often slash prices by almost half. The most inexpensive places to stay are on or near Via W3 Sul, 1 or 2km southwest of the Eixo Monumental, but hygiene is not a top priority in many and your safety (and that of your belongings) is far from guaranteed.

Cury's Solar (0xx61-244-1899; Quadra 707, Bloco I, Casa 15; s/d US$9/16) If you don't mind a little crowding, this is a good option. It's clean, family-run, very safe, and guests are welcome to use the kitchen and washer/dryer. Add US$2 for breakfast.

Pensão da Zenilda (0xx61-224-7532; Quadra 704, Bloco Q, Casa 29; r per person US$9) An apartment with rooms to let. It sleeps five and has kitchen and laundry facilities for guest use.

Mirage (0xx61-225-7150; Quadra 2, Bloco N; s/d US$14/25) Small rooms with fans.

Taxi drivers often tell tourists to stay in hotels outside the city center – usually the suburbs of Taguatinga or Núcleo Bandeirante. There are some decent options there, but be careful in Núcleo, which has a lot of *favelas*.

Eating is also expensive. Locals flock to three central, air-conditioned shopping malls – **Brasília Shopping** (Asa Norte, SCN QD 5, lote 2), **Pátio Brasil** (Asa Sul, W3, SCS) and **Conjunto Nacional** (Asa Norte, SCN) – to chow down. All have small cafés and food courts with enough variety to satisfy most tastes.

Getting There & Away

With so many domestic flights making a stopover in Brasília, it's easy to catch a plane to almost anywhere in Brazil.

From the giant long-distance bus and train station *(Rodoferroviária)*, 5km northwest of the center along the Eixo Monumental, daily buses go almost everywhere, including Goiânia (US$10, three hours), Rio (US$78, 17 hours), Salvador (US$85, 24 hours), Pirenópolis (US$7, three hours), Cuiabá (US$35, 20 hours) and Belém (US$113, 34 hours).

Getting Around

The airport is 12km south of the center. From the local bus station, take bus No 102 (US$2, 40 minutes) or minibus No 30 (US$2, 25 minutes). A taxi from the airport to the center costs US$15 through the tourist office.

From the local bus station to the long-distance bus and train station, take bus No 131.

There are car rental agencies at the airport, the Hotel Nacional Brasília and the Hotel Garvey Park.

PARQUE NACIONAL DA CHAPADA DOS VEADEIROS

Just over 220km north of Brasília, this spectacular park showcases the unique landscape and flora of high-altitude cerrado. Big skies, hills rising like waves from the plains, scenic waterfalls and natural swimming pools make for a sublime landscape. Wildlife you're likely to see includes maned wolves, giant anteaters and 7-foot-tall rheas.

There's an excellent **tourist office** (0xx61-646-1159; Ave Ari Valadão; 8am-5pm Mon-Sat, 9am-noon Sun), 200m from the bus station in the town of Alto Paraíso de Goiás, southeast of the park. But the former crystal mining hamlet of São Jorge, 40km west and 2km from the national park entrance, is the best place to stay.

BRAZIL

Sights & Activities

The lunar landscape and otherworldly atmosphere of the **Vale da Lua** (Moon Valley; admission US$2), make it the most unusual sight in the area. It's around 5km from São Jorge on a well-marked walking trail, and it's outside the national park, so you're not obliged to go with a guide.

Visitors to the national park itself must go with an accredited guide (US$20 for up to 10 people). You can organize this at the park entrance or at most hotels in São Jorge. Main attractions include the canyons (**Cânion I** and **Cânion II**) along the Rio Preto, the waterfalls (**Salto do Rio Preto I & II**; 80m and 120m high, respectively), and **Morro da Baleia**, a humpback hill with a 2.5km trail to the top.

Sleeping & Eating

There are plenty of **campgrounds** (campsites per person US$5), mostly backyards, in São Jorge.

Two good *pousadas* lie close together two blocks from São Jorge's main street.

Pousada Trilha Violeta (☎ 0xx61-9985-6544; s/d with bath US$14/23) This friendly place features large rooms and a good breakfast.

Pousada Aguas de Marco (☎ 0xx61-347-2082; s/d with bath US$12/24) An atmospheric little place. All prices rise by up to 30% on weekends.

Villa São Jorge (dishes US$7) A laid-back, outdoor restaurant and bar with great a atmosphere and great pizzas.

Getting There & Away

Buses to Alto Paraíso de Goiásleave Brasília depart at 10am, 3pm and 10:30pm (US$9, 3½ hours), for Goiânia at 9pm (US$18, six hours), and for Palmas (Tocantins) at 9:30pm (US$16, seven hours). The Palmas bus goes via Natividade. One daily bus goes from Alto Paraíso de Goiásto São Jorge (US$2, one hour) at 4pm, returning at 8am.

GOIÂNIA

The capital of the state of Goiás, 205km southwest of Brasília, Goiânia (population 1.1 million) is of little interest except as a staging post for the state's historic towns or national parks.

Ask for discounts at all hotels on weekends. Centrally located **Goiânia Palace** (☎ 0xx62-224-4874; Av Anhanguera; s/d US$15/22, with bath US$ 29/36) is one of the best budget options in town. The homey **Principe Hotel** (☎ 0xx62-224-0085; Av Anhanguera 2936; s/d US$23/40) is another good deal.

The best per-kilo lunch in the center is at **Argu's** (Rua 4 No 811).

Varig, TAM and VASP all fly to Goiânia. Buses leave regularly for Brasília (US$8, three hours), Cuiabá (US$28, 13 hours) and Goiás Velho (US$8, three hours).

GOIÁS VELHO

As dusk falls in this little town 145km northwest of Goiânia and the churches light their bell towers, a palpable quiet settles over the village and – except for the black jungle mountains silhouetted against the darkening sky – one might almost be in 18th century Portugal. Goiás Velho is among the most picturesque of the Central West's colonial towns.

The most impressive of several baroque churches is the oldest, **Igreja da Paula** (Praça Zaqueu Alves de Castro), built in 1761.

The **Museu das Bandeiras** (Praça Brasil Caiado; ☺ 8am-5pm Tue-Sat & 8am-noon Sun), with varied antiques from around the world, is well worth a visit. Also have a look at the Palácio Conde dos Arcos (the old governor's residence).

It's a good idea to book ahead if you're arriving on a weekend or during Holy Week.

Pousada do Ipê (☎ 0xx62-371-2065; Rua do Forum 22; s/d with bath US$15/25) The best place, with rooms around a shady courtyard and a pool.

Pousada do Sol (☎ 0xx62-371-1717; Rua Dr Americano do Brasil 17; s/d with bath US$17/24) An atmospheric choice.

Hotel Araguaiá (☎ 0xx62-371-1462; Av Dr Deusdeth Ferreira de Moura 8; s/d with bath US$9/17) A 15-minute hike from the bus station.

Restaurant Flor do Ipê (Praça da Boa Vista; dishes US$10) Across from the Pousada do Ipê, this place serves good regional food in shady garden settings.

Dona Maninha (Rua Dom Cândido) Serves regional food at bargain prices.

THE PANTANAL

This vast natural paradise is Brazil's major ecological attraction and – being *somewhat* more effectively preserved than the Amazon – offers a density of exotic wildlife not found anywhere else in South

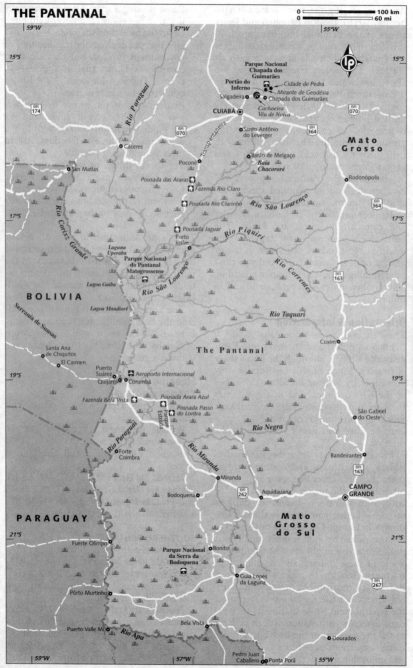

THE PANTANAL

0 _____ 100 km
0 _____ 60 mi

59°W   57°W   55°W

15°S   15°S

Rio Paraguai

BR 174

Parque Nacional
Chapada dos
Guimarães

Portão do
Inferno   Cidade de Pedra
Salgadeira   Mirante de Geodésia
    Chapada dos Guimarães

CUIABÁ   Cachoeira
Véu de Noiva

BR 070

Cáceres

BR 070

Transpantaneira

Santo Antônio
do Leverger

BR 364

Mato
Grosso

San Matias

Poconé

Barão de Melgaço
Baía
Chacororé

Rodonópolis

Pousada das Araras

Fazenda Rio Claro

Rio São Lourenço

17°S   17°S

Pousada Rio Clarinho

BR 364

Rio Cortiz Grande

Pousada Jaguar
Porto
Jofre

Rio Piquiri

Rio Correntes

Laguna
Uperaba

Parque Nacional
do Pantanal
Matogrossense

Rio São Lourenço

BR 163

Lagoa Gaiba

BOLIVIA

Lagoa Mandioré

Rio Taquari

Serrania de Suusas

Santa Ana
de Chiquitos
El Carmen

The Pantanal

Coxim

19°S   19°S

Puerto
Suárez   Aeroporto Internacional
Quijarro   Corumbá

Fazenda Bela Vista

Pousada Arara Azul

Pousada Passo
do Lontra

São Gabriel
do Oeste

Parque
Estada

Rio Negra

Rio Paraguai

Forte
Coimbra

Bandeirantes

BR 163

Rio Miranda

Miranda

CAMPO
GRANDE

PARAGUAY

Bodoquena

BR 262

Aquidauana

Mato
Grosso
do Sul

21°S   21°S

Fuerte Olimpo

Parque Nacional
da Serra da
Bodoquena

Bonito

Guia Lopes
da Laguna

BR 267

Pôrto Murtinho

Bela Vista

Puerto Valle Mi   Rio Apa

Dourados

Pedro Juan
Caballero   Ponta Porã

59°W   57°W   55°W

BRAZIL

America. During the rainy season (October to March), the Rio Paraguai and lesser rivers of the Pantanal inundate much of this low-lying region, creating cordilheiras (patches of dry land where animals cluster). The waters rise as much as 3m above low-water levels around March in the northern Pantanal and in June in the south. This seasonal flooding has severely limited human occupation of the area but it provides an enormously rich feeding ground for wildlife. The waters teem with fish; birds fly in flocks of thousands and gather in enormous rookeries.

Altogether the Pantanal supports 650 bird species and 80 mammal species, including jaguars, ocelots, pumas, maned wolf, deer, anteaters, armadillos, howler and capuchin monkeys and tapirs. The most visible mammal is the capybara, the world's largest rodent, often seen in family groups or even large herds. And you can't miss the alligators, which, despite poaching, still number somewhere between 10 and 35 million.

Orientation & Information

The Pantanal covers some 230,000 sq km (89,000 sq miles) and stretches into Paraguay and Bolivia, although the lion's share is Brazil's. Much of this territory is only accessible by boat or on foot. It's muggy at the best of times, and in the summer the heat and mosquitoes are truly vicious. Stock up on sunscreen and bug repellent, because you won't find any in the interior.

Bringing tourists into the Pantanal is now a big business, and seemingly overnight the three cities that serve as jumping off points to the region have been flooded with tour operators – some of dubious repute. Whether you arrive in Cuiabá, Corumbá, or Campo Grande you can expect to be approached by a guide fairly rapidly – at peak times you might even be stampeded! Some of these individuals are simply opportunists looking to make a buck out of Brazil's eco-tourism, but there are still a few old-timers out there who work to protect the environment while sharing its tremendous diversity with visitors. It can be hard to tell the good from the bad, but here are some suggestions to ensure you have a safe and enjoyable trip:

- Resist making a snap decision, especially if you've just come off an overnight bus.
- Go to the local tourism office. Most can't give independent advice because they're government funded, but they do keep complaints books that you're free to peruse. There's a lot to be gleaned from other traveler's experiences.
- Remember that the owner or salesperson is not always your guide, and it's the guide you're going to be with in the wilderness for three to five days. Ask to meet your guide if possible.
- Try to get things in writing and don't hand over your cash to any go-betweens.
- Compare your options. Most operators work out of the local bus station or airport, so it's easy to shop around.

There's no obligation to go with a tour operator. You can drive or hitchhike across the Transpantaneira road that starts in the northwest (Mato Grosso state), or the Estrada Parque that loops around the south (Mato Grosso do Sul).

The Transpantaneira is generally considered the best road for hitching or driving. It heads 145km south from Poconé, south of Cuiabá. You'll see a lot of wildlife even without a guide.

Sleeping & Eating

TRANSPANTANEIRA

There are quite a lot of accommodations on and off the road.

Pousada das Araras (☎ 0xx65-682-2800; Km 30; www.araraslodge.com.br; s/d with bath US$54/108) This good spot includes full board in its prices.

Fazenda Rio Claro (☎ 0xx65-9982-0796; Km 42), **Pousada Rio Clarinho** (☎ 0xx65-9977-8966; Km 42) and **Pousada Jaguar** (☎ 0xx65-345-1545; Km 105), all offer full board for US$45/70.

SOUTHERN PANTANAL

Prices quoted are for high season.

Pousada Passo do Lontra (☎ 0xx67-231-6136; www.passodolontra.com.br; r per person US$60) A classic Pantanal wood-on-stilts structure with lots of wildlife around.

Pousada Arara Azul (☎ 0xx67-384-6114; www.pousadaararaazul.com.br; r per person around US$60) Located deep in the heart of the Pantanal.

Fazenda Bela Vista (☎ 0xx67-9987-3660; r per person US$55) Easily reached from Corumbá.

BRAZIL

CUIABÁ

The capital of Mato Grosso state, Cuiabá (population 476,000) is a lively frontier boom town and a good starting point for visiting the Pantanal or the Chapada dos Guimarães, the geological center of South America.

Sedtur (☎ 0xx65-624-9060; Praça da República; ✆ 8:30am-6pm Mon-Fr) is the Mato Grosso tourist authority.

With exhibits on the Xavante, Bororo and Karajá tribes, the **Museo do Índio** (Av Fernando Correia da Costa; ✆ 8-11am daily, & 2-5pm Mon-Fri) is worth a visit. Catch bus No 406 on Avenida Tenente Coronel Duarte heading for the university.

Sleeping

Pousada Ecoverde (☎ 0xx65-624-1386; Rua Pedro Celestino 391; r per person US$6) Very good value, if a little rustic. There's a delightful courtyard and garden, and laundry facilities are available.

Hotel Samara (☎ 0xx65-322-6001; Rua Joaquim Murtinho 270; r per person US$9; s/d with bath US$11/17) Offers basic, boxy rooms.

Portal do Pantanal Youth Hostel (☎ 0xx65-624-8999; www.portaldopantanal.com.br; Av Isaac Póvoas 655; r per person US$6) Laundry and kitchen facilities are available to guests for a small fee.

Eating & Drinking

Cuiabá offers some great fish dishes.

Miranda's (Rua Commandante Costa; dishes US$4) This place in the center does wholesome self-serve dishes.

Restaurante Hong Kong (Av Getúlio Vargas 647; buffet US$5) Offers a tasty Chinese lunch and dinner buffet.

Choppão (Rua Getúlio Vargas; US$11) At Praça 8 de Abril, Choppão serves obscenely large meat, fish and salad meals for two.

The two main nightlife clusters in town are along Av Getulio Vargas and Av Mato Grosso.

Getting There & Away

Varig, TAM, Gol and VASP fly to/from many Brazilian cities, with the notable omission of Corumbá.

The bus station is 3km north of the center on the Chapada dos Guimarães highway. Destinations include Cáceres (US$12, 3½ hours, six buses daily), Porto Velho (US$50, 24 hours, several daily), Goiânia (US$27, 13 hours, frequently),

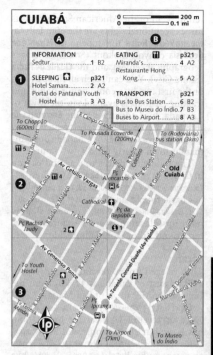

Brasília (US$35, 20 hours, one bus in the morning and one at night) and Campo Grande (US$26, 10 hours, eight daily).

Car rental agencies just outside the airport grounds tend to be cheaper than those inside. The best vehicles for the Transpantaneira are a VW Golf or Fiat Uno.

Getting Around

The airport is in Varzea Grande, 7km south of the center. The 'Rodoviaria/Marajoara,' '24 de Dezembro' and 'Pireneus' buses, from opposite the Las Velas Hotel near the airport, go to the center. Buses from the center to the airport depart from the east side of Praça Ipiranga.

'Centro' buses from inside the bus station go to Praça Alencastro. More frequent 'Centro' buses from outside the bus station will drop you along Av Isaac Póvoas.

AROUND CUIABÁ
Parque Nacional da Chapada dos Guimarães

This rocky plateau beginning about 60km northeast of Cuiabá is a beautiful region reminiscent of the American Southwest. Its three exceptional sights are the 60m falls **Cachoeira Véu de Noiva**, the stupendous **Mirante de Geodésia** canyon lookout (South America's geographical center), and the **Cidade de Pedra** (Stone City). You can reach all three by car, or the first two by a combination of bus and walking. A map is available in the town of Chapada dos Guimarães at the **Secretária de Turismo** (☎ 0xx65-301-2045; Av Perimentral S/N).

Buses leave Cuiabá for Chapada dos Guimarães town hourly (US$9, two hours).

The following places to stay and eat are in Chapada town. **Hotel São José** (☎ 0xx65-301-1563; Rua Vereador José de Souza 50; r per person US$5) has basic rooms, and **Rios Hotel** (☎ 0xx65-301-1126; Rua Tiradentes; s/d US$10/16) offers a slightly more upscale atmosphere. Restaurants cluster around Praça Dom Wunibaldo.

Cáceres

This relaxed town on the Rio Paraguai 215km west of Cuiabá is 115km from the Bolivian border town of San Matías.

Capri Hotel (☎ 0xx65-223-1711; Rua Getúlio Vargas 99; s/d with bath US$6/12), near the bus station, has basic but clean rooms and a few spacious *apartamentos*. Closer to the river and center, **Rio Hotel** (☎ 0xx65-223-3084; Praça Major João Carlos; s/d US$9/13, with bath US$14/20) is a good option.

A bus leaves Cáceres at 6am daily for San Matías and Santa Cruz, Bolivia (US$24, 24 hours). You can get a Brazilian exit stamp from Cáceres' Polícia Federal, 4km from the center on Av Getúlio Vargas (US$8 round trip by taxi).

Poconé

The Transpantaneira 'highway' starts just outside this town 100km southwest of Cuiabá.

The best places to stay, especially if you're trying to organize a lift down the Transpantaneira, are a couple of kilometers out of town near the beginning of the road. **Pousada Pantaneira** (☎ 0xx65-345-1630; r per person US$8), has grim rooms, but its restaurant's *rodízio* is pretty good.

Six daily buses run from Cuiabá to Poconé (US$5, 2½ hours).

CAMPO GRANDE

The lively capital of Mato Grosso do Sul state is a major gateway to the Pantanal.

The **tourist office** (☎ 0xx67-324-5830; Av Afonso Pena & Av Noroeste; ☯ 8am-7pm Tue-Sat, 9am-noon Sun), three blocks from the bus station, has friendly staff and an extensive database on Mato Grosso do Sul. It does its best to give independent advice.

The **Museu Dom Bosco** (Rua Barão do Rio Branco 1843; ☯ 8-11am & 1-5pm) has an excellent collection of wildlife, interesting exhibits on the Indians of the region, and inexpensive handicrafts for sale.

Sleeping & Eating

The following inexpensive hotels are clustered around the bus station. It's a good area during the day, but don't walk it around alone late at night.

Hotel Iguaçu (☎ 0xx67-784-4621; Rua Dom Aquino 761; s/d with bath US$10/18) A clean friendly place just opposite the bus station.

Novo Hotel (☎ 0xx67-721-0505; Rua Joaquim Nabuco 185; s/d with bath US$10/15) Novo has basic rooms.

Nacional (☎ 0xx67-383-2461; Rua Dom Aquino 610; s/d US$7/12, with bath US$10/16) This hotel is always busy but if you can get in, it's a great deal.

Campo Grande Youth Hostel (☎ 0xx 67-382-3504/67-321-0505; Rua Joaquim Nabuco 185; r per person US$6) Directly opposite the bus station, the youth hostel is open 24 hours a day.

Vitórios (Av Afonso Pena; dishes US$5) Serves hearty meat, fish and chicken dishes.

Viva a Vida (Rua Dom Aquino 1324; buffet US$3.50) A delectable vegetarian/vegan buffet, with takeout available too.

Getting There & Away

Varig, TAM and VASP provide daily flights to/from São Paulo, Cuiabá, Rio and Brasília.

Six daily buses run to Corumbá (US$20): the four direct services take around six hours, but if you want to get off at Estrada Parque take a non-direct one. Other services include Cuiabá (US$24, 10 hours), Ponta Porã (US$14, seven hours), São Paulo (US$46, 14 hours) and Foz do Iguaçu (US$22, 16 hours).

Getting Around

Buses to the center (7km) go from the stop on the main road outside the airport. To get from the center to the airport, take the Indubrasil bus.

CORUMBÁ

This port of 86,000 people on the Rio Paraguai is a gateway both to the Pantanal and to Bolivia, which is only 15 minutes away. At night the river sunsets are beautiful, and although the city has a reputation for poaching and drug trafficking, travelers are generally left alone.

To change cash or traveler's checks, try **Casa de Câmbio** (Rua Frei Mariano 361).

Sematur (☎ 0xx67-231-7336; Rua Manoel Cavassa 275) can provide a list of Pantanal guides, tour companies, hotels and boat trips.

Sleeping

Hotel Selette (☎ 0xx67- 231-3768; Rua Delamare 893; s/d US$6/10, with bath US$12/16) This great choice in the center has clean spacious rooms and a good breakfast.

Pousada Green Track (☎ 0xx67-231-2258; Rua Antônio João 216; r per person US$6) A converted old house with big airy rooms and a friendly, dorm-like setting.

Hotel Santa Rita (☎ 0xx67-231-5453; Rua Dom Aquino 860; s/d with bath US$14/20) This place has big *apartamentos*.

Premier Hotel (☎ 0xx67-231-4937; Rua Antônio Maria Coelho; r per person US$10) Good-value rooms with breakfast.

Eating

Churrascaria e Restaurante Rodeio (Rua 13 de Junho 760) This is the snazziest per-kilo lunch spot, with 43 salad dishes and plenty of tasty meat as well.

Restaurante Paladar (Rua Antônio Maria Coelho; dishes US$6) A travelers' favorite for pizza and pasta.

For as much fish, meat and pizza as you can eat, try **Laco do Ouro** (Rua Frei Mariano; dishes US$6), or **Restaurante Galpão** (Rua Antônio Maria Coelho).

Getting There & Away

BRAZIL

GENSA (☎ 0xx67-232-3851) has three weekly flights into Corumba on varying days.

Nine daily buses go to Campo Grande (US$24, six hours if direct). A bus to Bonito (US$22, seven hours) leaves at 2pm.

BOLIVIAN BORDER CROSSING

The Fronteira–Corumbá bus (US$0.75, every 30 minutes) from Praça Independência on Rua Dom Aquino goes to the Bolivian border. Coming from the border the bus runs to Rua Frei Mariano and the local bus terminal on Rua 13 do Junho. A motorcycle taxi is US$2, and a taxi costs US$6.

All Brazilian border formalities must be completed in Corumbá at the *rodovíaria*. If you're just crossing into Bolivia for a few hours to buy train tickets, you don't need a Brazilian exit stamp. You won't be allowed to enter Brazil without a yellow fever vaccination certificate: there's a medical van at the border, or get one at **Sucum** (Rua Ladário 788, Corumbá).

Moneychangers at the frontier accept US, Brazilian and Bolivian cash.

The Bolivian border town of Quijarro is little more than a collection of shacks. Taxis run the 4km between the border and Quijarro train station for US$2.50. See Santa Cruz (p232) in the Bolivia chapter for details of the train trip between Quijarro and Santa Cruz.

Getting Around

From the bus stop outside Corumbá bus station, the Cristo Redentur bus (US$0.60) runs to the local bus terminal on Rua 13 de Junho. You can take a motorcycle taxi (US$1) from the local bus station if your luggage is light. A taxi costs US$3.50.

BONITO

This small town in southwest Mato Grosso do Sul is undergoing an ecotourism boom due to the surrounding area's caves, waterfalls and incredibly clear, forest-lined rivers where divers can swim eyeball to eyeball with hundreds of fish.

Only local travel agencies are authorized to hire guides to the area's attractions, so you're obliged to book tours through them. The main street is lined with agencies, all with the same prices. The better ones include **Muito Bonito Tourismo** (☎ 0xx67-255-1645; Rua Coronel Pilad Rebua 1448) and **Ygarapé Tour** (☎ 0xx67-255-1733; Rua Coronel Pilad Rebua 1853). Trip prices don't include transportation, so you might want to try tacking onto a group that has already organized transport.

At **Aquário Natural Baía Bonita** 7km from Bonito, you can swim among 30 varieties of fish and float gently downstream; it costs US$28 for three hours, including wetsuits and snorkel. **Gruta do Lago Azul** (20km, US$7) is a large cave, with a luminous

BRAZIL

underground lake and stalactites. The **Balneário Municipal** (7km, US$6) is a natural swimming pool with lots of fish (and no guide needed). The **Abismo de Anhumas** (22km, US$100, including rappelling and snorkeling) is a 72m abyss with an underground lake and incredible stalactites.

In December–February, July and other holiday periods, prices rise about 25% and some tours are filled months ahead.

Sleeping

Accommodation is tight, and more expensive on weekends and during high season.

HI hostel Albergue da Juventude do Ecoturismo (☎ 0xx67-255-1462; Rua Lúcio Borralho 716; r per person US$11) The hostel is 1.5km from the center.

Pousada Muito Bonito (☎ 0xx67-255-1645; muito bonito@uol.com.br; Rua Coronel Pilad Rebua 1448; r per person US$8, s/d with bath US$10/14) In town, this very beautiful *pousada* has a gorgeous courtyard and comfortable cabins.

Pousada Caramachão (☎ 0xx67-255-1674; www .caramanchao@caramanchao.com.br; Rua das Flores 1203; s/d with bath US$14/19) A friendly, upmarket place off the main drag.

Pousada do Mineiro (r per person US$3/4) The cheapest place in town, directly across from the bus station. Run by a little old Brazilian lady, the rooms are clean with shared baths (no hot water).

Eating

Restaurante da Vovó (Rua Felinto Muller) Serves excellent per-kilo regional food.

O Casarão (Rua Coronel Pilad Rebua 1843) A popular per-kilo restaurant, specializing in fish.

Lanchonete Tutti Frutti (Rua Coronel Pilad Rebua; dishes US$2) Fill up on fresh pastries, pies and juices here.

Getting There & Away

Three daily buses go from Campo Grande to Bonito (US$13, 5½ hours) and vice-versa. Buses leave for Ponta Porã (US$14, six hours) at 12:10pm (except Sunday) and for Corumbá (US$19, seven hours) at 6am (except Sunday).

PONTA PORÃ

Ponta Porã is a border town divided from the Paraguayan town of Pedro Juan Caballero by Av Internacional. For information on Pedro Juan Caballero, see the Paraguay chapter.

For Brazilian entry/exit stamps, go to the **Polícia Federal** (☎ 0xx67-431-1428; Av Presidente Vargas; ☼ 8am-5pm), near the Paraguayan consulate. Paraguay now requires entry visas from US citizens, which can be obtained at the same consulate.

Sleeping & Eating

This area is now heavily patrolled by Brazilian and Paraguayan authorities. Drug trafficking is on the rise and it's a good idea to limit your night time activities.

Hotel Internacional (☎ 0xx67-431-1243, Av Internacional 2604; s/d US$6/12, with bath US$14/24) A safe, inexpensive option.

Choppão (Rua Marechal Floriano 1877; dishes US$5) A popular spot with an extensive menu of meat, fish and pasta.

Getting There & Around

From the bus station in Ponta Porã (about 4km from the center), 9 daily buses go to Campo Grande (US$10, 5½ hours). There's one bus to Corumba via Bonito; it's usually at 6am but it changes frequently. If you're coming into town from the Brazilian side, the bus can drop you at the local bus terminal on Avenida Internacional, near the hotels.

THE NORTHEAST

It's a sin to visit Brazil and not travel the northeast, a tropical paradise of year-round warmth and sensual culture. These are the lands the Portuguese first set foot on; later they constructed the cities of Salvador, Olinda and São Luís, restored colonial gems that are highlights of any trip. These cities and their hinterlands absorbed more African slaves than anywhere else in the world, visible today in the faces of their people as well as in the trademark culture of the region.

The northeast has endless white beaches, which cradle most of the region's population. Along these palm-studded shores are the happening villages of Trancoso, Arraial d'Ajuda, Morro de São Paulo, Praia da Pipa and Jericoacoara, not one of which should be missed. Chapada Diamantina and Lençóis Maranhenses national parks also cannot be skipped.

The northeast faces massive social problems, including underemployment, housing shortages, inadequate education and an absence of basic services such as sanitation. The interior of this region is made up of the *sertão*, a drought-prone backlands whose inhabitants often live in extreme poverty, especially in the more northerly states. Despite these setbacks, northeasterners are extremely proud of their land's human and geographical beauty.

SALVADOR

Salvador da Bahia, often abbreviated to Bahia, is the northeast's brightest cultural gem. Salvador is Brazil's third-largest city, the largest in the northeast, and its most African influenced. In Salvador, blacks preserved the roots of their African culture more than anywhere else in the New

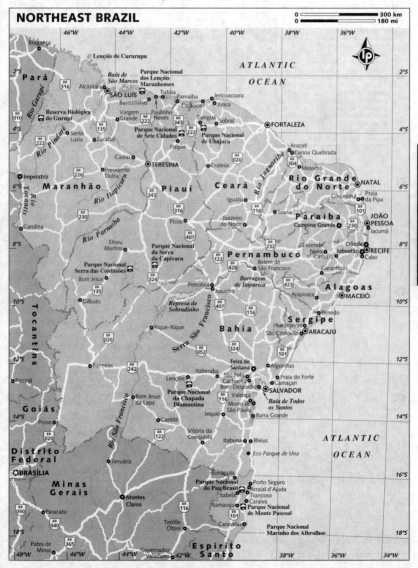

NORTHEAST BRAZIL

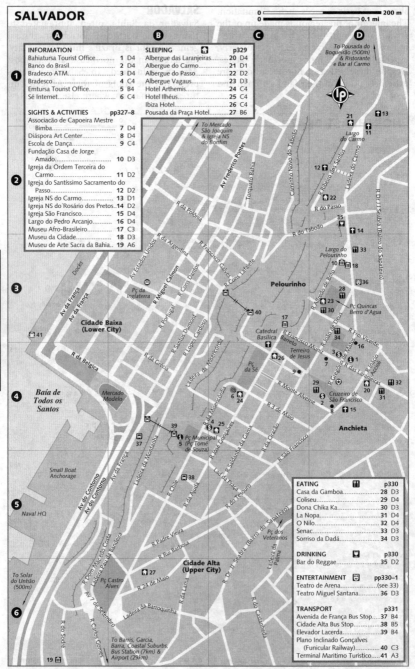

SALVADOR

0 — 200 m
0 — 0.1 mi

INFORMATION	
Bahiatursa Tourist Office..........	**1** D4
Banco do Brasil.........................	**2** D4
Bradesco ATM...........................	**3** D4
Bradesco..................................	**4** C4
Emtursa Tourist Office...............	**5** B4
Sé Internet...............................	**6** C4

SIGHTS & ACTIVITIES	pp327–8
Associação de Capoeira Mestre	
Bimba....................................	**7** D4
Diáspora Art Center..................	**8** D4
Escola de Dança.......................	**9** C4
Fundação Casa de Jorge	
Amado...................................	**10** D3
Igreja da Ordem Terceira do	
Carmo..................................	**11** D2
Igreja do Santíssimo Sacramento do	
Passo....................................	**12** D2
Igreja NS do Carmo..................	**13** D1
Igreja NS do Rosário dos Pretos..	**14** D2
Igreja São Francisco.................	**15** D4
Largo do Pedro Arcanjo............	**16** D4
Museu Afro-Brasileiro...............	**17** C3
Museu da Cidade.....................	**18** D3
Museu de Arte Sacra da Bahia..	**19** A6

SLEEPING	p329
Albergue das Laranjeiras..........	**20** D4
Albergue do Carmo..................	**21** D1
Albergue do Passo...................	**22** D2
Albergue Vagaus......................	**23** D3
Hotel Arthemis.......................	**24** C4
Hotel Ilhéus...........................	**25** C4
Ibiza Hotel.............................	**26** C4
Pousada da Praça Hotel...........	**27** B6

EATING	p330
Casa da Gamboa......................	**28** D3
Coliseu..................................	**29** D4
Dona Chika Ka........................	**30** D3
La Nopa..................................	**31** D4
O Nilo....................................	**32** D4
Senac.....................................	**33** D3
Sorriso da Dadá......................	**34** D3

DRINKING	p330
Bar do Reggae.........................	**35** D2

ENTERTAINMENT	pp330–1
Teatro de Arena......................	(see 33)
Teatro Miguel Santana............	**36** D3

TRANSPORT	p331
Avenida de França Bus Stop.....	**37** B4
Cidade Alta Bus Stop...............	**38** B5
Elevador Lacerda.....................	**39** B4
Plano Inclinado Gonçalves	
(Funicular Railway)..............	**40** C3
Terminal Marítimo Turístico.....	**41** A3

To Pousada do Boqueirão (500m) & Ristorante e Bar al Carmo

Largo do Carmo

To Mercado São Joaquim & Igreja NS do Bonfim

Av Frederico Pontes

Torquato Bahia

Caminho Novo do Taboão

Ladeira do Carmo

R do Passo

R do Taboão

R da Polônia

Ladeira do Carmo

R J J Seabra (Bairro do Sapateiro)

Ribeiro dos Santos

Largo do Pelourinho

Pelourinho

R Cons Lafaiete

R Francisco Gomes

R Cons Dantos

R Santos

Alfredo de Brito

R de Jesus

Pç Quincas Berro d'Agua

R João de Deus

R Saldanha da Gama

R Frei Vicente

R Gregório de Mattos

R do Taboão

Docks

Av da França

Av da França

Cidade Baixa (Lower City)

R da Argentina

R Miguel Calmon

R Portugal

R Santos Dumont

R Lopes Cardoso

R da Grécia

Pç da Inglaterra

R Estados Unidos

R da Bélgica

Ladeira da Montanha

Ladeira da Misericórdia

R da Misericórdia

Catedral Basílica

R Francisco Muniz Barreto

Terreiro de Jesus

Pç da Sé

R Monte Alverne

Cruzeiro de São Francisco

Anchieta

R das Laranjeiras

R Alfredo de Almeida

R Crisógono

R 3 de Maio

R Orozio

R São Francisco

Baía de Todos os Santos

Mercado Modelo

Small Boat Anchorage

Naval HQ

To Solar do Unhão (500m)

R Dom Marcelo Costa

Ladeira da Água Brusca

R Carlos Gomes

R do Sodré

Av 7 de Setembro

Pç Castro Alves

R 24 de Maio

Ladeira da Barroquinha

R da Laima

R Ruy Barbosa

R Padre Vieira

Cidade Alta (Upper City)

R da Ajuda

R Chile

R do Tesouro

R da Piaça

Pç Municipal (Pç Tomé de Souza)

R José Gonçalves

R Saldanha da Gama

Ladeira da Praia

Pç dos Veteranos

Ladeira de Palma

R J J Seabra (Bairro do Sapateiro)

R do Castanheda

Av do Contorno

Av do Contorno

Av da França

To Barris, Garcia, Barra, Coastal Suburbs, Bus Station (7km) & Airport (29km)

BRAZIL

World, successfully transforming them into thriving culinary, religious, martial art, dance and musical traditions. You may want to dedicate the better part of a week to checking out the Pelourinho, the vibrant restored historical city, and experiencing the nightlife of this incredibly musical city.

History
Founded in 1549 as Brazil's first capital, Salvador remained influential for two centuries, growing rich on exports of sugarcane, tobacco, gold and diamonds, imports of African slaves, and the profits of cattle ranching in the interior. With the decline of the sugarcane industry the capital was shifted to Rio, leaving this city, renowned for its sensuality and decadence, to slip into economic decline. Only recently has it begun to move forward with new industries such as petroleum, chemicals and tourism.

Orientation
For Cidade Alta, cross the footbridge from the bus station (8km from the center) to Shopping Iguatemí and catch the Praça da Sé minibus. Catch the same bus from the airport (over 30km from the center). For Barra, catch the Barra 1 bus in front of the bus station.

Salvador sits on a peninsula at the mouth of the Baía de Todos os Santos. The city center is on the bay side of the peninsula and is divided by a steep bluff into two parts: the historic Cidade Alta (Upper City) and the Cidade Baixa (Lower City), containing the commercial center and port. The heart of the historic center, which attracts most of the tourists and nightlife, is called the Pelourinho. This roughly refers to the area from Largo do Pelourinho to Terreiro de Jesus. South, at the tip of the peninsula, is the well-to-do Barra neighborhood. Other interesting beachside suburbs, such as Rio Vermelho, stretch northeast along the coast.

Information
EMERGENCY
Deltur (☎ 0xx71-322-7155; Cruzeiro de São Francisco 14, Pelourinho) Twenty-four-hour tourist police.

INTERNET ACCESS
Sé Internet (Praça da Sé, Pelourinho; US$1 per hr) The city's cheapest Internet access, with one-hour intervals only.

MONEY
Travel agents along Cruzeiro de São Francisco change traveler's checks and cash. Or try:
Banco do Brasil (Cruzeiro de São Francisco 11, Pelourinho) Has ATMs.
Bradesco (Rua da Miserecordia, Cidade Alta) Also with ATMs in Pelourinho.

POST
Central post office (Praça da Inglaterra, Cidade Baixa)
Branch offices (Cruzeiro de São Francisco & Rua 3 de Maio, Pelourinho)

TOURIST OFFICES
Bahiatursa (☎ 0xx71-321-2463; Rua Francisco Muniz Barreto 12, Pelourinho; ☻ 8:30am-9pm Mon-Thu, 8:30am-10pm Fri-Sun) The State tourism authority is multilingual. Other offices are located at the bus station, airport, Mercado Modelo, Shopping Iguatemí and Shopping Barra.
Emtursa (☎ 0xx71-371-1580; Elevador Lacerda, Cidade Alta; ☻ 9am-8pm Mon-Fri, 9am-6pm Sat, 9am-1pm Sun) The city's tourism office is often the most helpful. English and French are spoken.

Dangers & Annoyances
Salvador has a reputation for theft and muggings, though the Pelourinho area has become increasingly safer. Safe neighborhoods shift quickly into sketchy ones. Avoid wandering into areas in which you have no business being. Don't hesitate to use taxis after dusk.

Women will attract annoying attention from men, especially in the Pelourinho. The best tactic is to simply ignore the comments and hissing.

Sights
PELOURINHO
While wandering around and checking out the huge number of churches and museums in the Pelô, open your eyes to the schools, galleries and cultural houses that pack the historical center.

Museu Afro-Brasileiro (Terreiro de Jesus; admission US$0.65; ☻ 9am-5pm Mon-Fri) is probably the most interesting museum in the city. It has a room of amazing representations of the *orixás* (Afro-Brazilian gods) carved in wood, and exhibits tying Brazilian and African traditions.

Salvador has a church for every day of the year, but the one you should pop your head into is the baroque **Igreja São Francisco**

(Cruzeiro de São Francisco; admission US$1; ❤ 8:30am-5:30pm), crammed with displays of wealth and splendor. The African slave artisans who were forced to build this church while prohibited from practicing their own religion responded through their work: some angels have huge sex organs and others appear pregnant.

The steep **Largo do Pelourinho** is where slaves were auctioned and publicly beaten on a *pelourinho* (whipping post).

The **Fundação Casa de Jorge Amado** (Largo do Pelourinho; ❤ 9am-6pm Mon-Sat) will only be interesting to this famous novelist's readers. Next door, the **Museu da Cidade** (Largo do Pelourinho; admission US$0.35; ❤ 9am-6pm Mon-Fri, 1-5pm Sat, 9am-1pm Sun) exhibits Candomblé *orixá* costumes and the personal effects of the Romantic poet Castro Alves, one of the first public figures to protest against slavery.

Museu de Arte Sacra da Bahia (Rua do Sodré 276; admission US$2; ❤ 11:30am-5:30pm Mon-Fri) displays sacred art in a beautifully restored 17th-century convent.

CIDADE BAIXA & BARRA
Solar do Unhão, an old sugar estate mansion and shipping area on the bay housing the **Museu de Arte Moderna** (❤ for special exhibits), is a cool spot to check out when the museum is open. Take a taxi there from the base of the Elevador Lacerda, as the desolate walk is known for tourist muggings.

Barra's waterfront is a good area for a walk. Contemplate the sunset at Bahia's oldest fort, **Forte de Santo Antônio da Barra** (1598).

ITAPAGIPE PENINSULA
To discover the meaning behind the colored ribbons wrapped around believer's wrists, take the Bonfim or Ribeira bus from the base of the Elevador Lacerda to the **Igreja NS do Bonfim** (❤ closed noon-2pm & Mon). Built in 1745, the church is famous for its power to effect miraculous cures and is Salvador's most important church for *candomblistas*. In a side room are replicas of body parts devotees claim were cured. If you walk up the hill in front of the church and stick to the left, there is a great view back to the center.

Activities
BEACHES
Praia do Porto in Barra is a great place to people-watch and listen to singing vendors. Head out to Piatã, Itapoã or beyond for less crowded beaches and to swim in an unpolluted Atlantic.

CANDOMBLÉ
Much of Bahian life revolves around the Afro-Brazilian religion Candomblé. A night in a *terreiro* promises hours of ritual and possession, so wear clean, light-colored clothes out of respect for the house and go well fed. Bahiatursa can provide addresses and monthly schedules.

Courses
CAPOEIRA, DANCE & PERCUSSION
Associacão de Capoeira Mestre Bimba (Rua das Laranjeiras 1; show US$1.50; show 7-9pm Mon-Fri) offers classes in *capoeira*, *maculêlê* (stick fighting), percussion and *berimbau*. The 'show' is probably just an advanced class offering quite an eye full.

Escola de Dança (Rua da Oracão 1) and **Diáspora Art Center** (Largo de São Francisco 21, 3rd fl) both offer classes in traditional and contemporary Afro-Brazilian dance, *capoeira* and percussio.

LANGUAGE
Casa do Brasil (☎ 0xx71-245-5866; Rua Milton de Oliveira 231, Barra) runs language and culture classes.

At **Diálogo** (☎ 0xx71-264-0007; info@dialogo-brazil study.com; Rua Dr João Pondé 240, Barra) homestays are possible.

Festivals & Events
CARNAVAL
Salvador's Carnaval is the second largest in Brazil and, according to young people, the best. It is characterized by slow-moving parades of bands playing *axé* and *pagode* atop long trucks loaded with huge *trios-electricos* (speakers). The band and it's fans grouped in a roped-off area around the truck form a *bloco*. People pay up to US$150 for the *abadá* (shirt required for entry to the *bloco*) for their favorite band, mostly for prestige and the safety of those ropes. Choosing to *fazer pipoca* (be popcorn) in the street is still a fine way to spend Carnaval, and you'll be spared the hassle involved with picking up the *abadá*.

There are three main Carnaval areas: the beachside Barra to Rio Vermelho circuit (where most tourists hang out), the narrow Campo Grande to Praça Castro Alves circuit, and the Pelourinho (no *trios* here, mostly concerts and parading drum corps). Get a schedule of events from Bahiatursa, or pick up the fantastic *Guia do Ócio* entertainment guide, available in many bookstores.

Crowds clearing to escape a fight pose the greatest threat during Carnaval, so be aware of your surroundings. Hands will be all over you, searching your pockets and groping the ladies. To ensure a trouble-free Carnaval, take note of the following:

- carry only a small amount of money and stash it in your shoe
- leave *any* jewelry, watches, or nice-looking sunglasses in your hotel
- don't challenge pickpockets – they usually fight back
- women should not walk alone or wear skirts (hands will be up them in no time)

OTHER FESTIVALS

Carnaval receives the greatest emphasis, but Salvador stages many other festivals – particularly in January and February – which are often a more colorful cultural experience. Check with Bahiatursa for festival dates.

Sleeping

Travelers prefer the Pelourinho in order to be close to the action, but make sure the party isn't next door. Hotels from Praça da Se toward the Cidade Alta are more run-down and within walking distance to the Pelô. Beachside Barra is mellower and only a short bus ride away from the Pelô. Reservations are absolutely necessary everywhere during Carnaval.

PELOURINHO

Albergue do Carmo (☎ 0xx71-326-3750; albergue carmo@veloxmail.com.br; Largo do Carmo 6; dm US$8; 🖳) This all-star hostel is divided into bright and modern suites, each with a loft, two bathrooms and a kitchen. As if that isn't enough, the location is great and guests get free Internet use.

Albergue das Laranjeiras (☎ 0xx71-321-1366; albergue@alarans.com.br; Rua Inácio Acciolli 13; dm US$8, s/d US$12/20) This stylish and well-organized hostel has staggered beds like hanging trays.

Hotel Arthemis (☎ 0xx71-322-0724; artemis@ artemishotel.com.br; Praça da Sé 398, Edifício Themis; s/d

US$13/17) The view over the bay and Pelourinho makes a stunning accompaniment to your breakfast at this hotel occupying the entire seventh floor of an apartment building. The rooms are large and modern.

Ibiza Hotel (☎ 0xx322-6929; Rua do Bispo 6/8; d US$13) Don't let the 80's paint job scare you away, the rooms are small, well-finished and the location is choice.

Also recommended are:

Albergue do Passo (☎ 0xx71-326-1951; passoyouth hostel@yahoo.com; Rua Ribeiro dos Santos 3; dm/d US$7/17) A clean and tidy spot.

Albergue Vagaus (☎ 0xx71-322-1179; vagaus@ hotmail.com; Rua Alfredo Brito 25; dm US$4) You can't find cheaper than this hostel.

CIDADE ALTA

Pousada da Praça Hotel (☎ 0xx71-321-0642; pousadadapraca@terra.com.br; Rua Rui Barbosa 5; dm US$5, s/d US$10/12, with bath US$13/15) This place has slightly more charm than others in this area, and an open breakfast porch.

Hotel Ilhéus (☎ 0xx71-322-7240; www.hotelilheus .com.br; Ladeira da Praça 4; s/d US$7/8, with bath US$8/10) A pretty run-down hotel with a couple of decent bright rooms for the undemanding guest.

BARRA

Âmbar Pousada (☎ 0xx71-264-6956; ambarpousada@ ambarpousada.com.br; Rua Afonso Celso 485; dm US$9, s/d with bath US$20/25) Âmbar is brightly colored with a grassy inner courtyard.

Casa da Barra (☎ 0xx71-264-1289; casabarra@uol .com.br; Rua Alfonso Celso 447; dm US$5) A hallway with rooms off it, this place will do the trick if you want something cheap. No breakfast.

> ### SPLURGE!
> **Pousada do Boqueirão** (☎ 0xx71-241-2262; boqueirao@terra.com.br; Rua Direita do Santo Antônio 48; s/d US$20/25, s/d with bath US$40/50) Along Rua do Carmo and its extension Rua Direita do Santo Antônio are several colonial homes that have been renovated into classy *pousadas*. Boqueirão is one of the more elegant and, surprisingly, reasonably priced. Spacious common rooms with high ceilings back onto a porch with a fantastic view over the bay, and the breakfast buffet is superb.

BRAZIL

Eating

The Pelourinho is packed with restaurants, some of them quite good but reluctant to make dishes for one. Restaurants in the coastal suburbs such as Barra are often clustered near the water. Be aware of cover charges for live music.

PELOURINHO

Coliseu (Cruzeiro de São Francisco; per kg US$5.30) Look for a costumed woman handing out receipts in the doorway to find this upstairs buffet restaurant. Vegetarians will love the huge salad bar, and many of the dishes are regional.

Senac (Largo do Pelourinho 13; buffet US$6) A cooking school offering an all-you-can-eat buffet of 40 regional dishes.

O Nilo (Rua Laranjeiras 44; dishes US$2.50-5) Excellent falafel and other Middle Eastern specialties – great for the vegetarian.

La Nopa (Rua Santa Isabel 13) Try the fresh ricotta ravioli (US$3) in orange-mint sauce at this fine Italian restaurant.

Ristorante e Bar Al Carmo (Rua do Carmo 66) Fantastic Italian cuisine is served on a roof-top terrace at this classy restaurant.

Recommended for traditional Bahian food are:

Sorriso da Dadá (Rua Frei Vicente 5) Tasty seafood.

Dona Chika Ka (Rua Frei Vicente) Its *bobó de camarão* (shrimp in flavored manioc paste) gets rave reviews (US$15 for two).

Casa da Gamboa (Rua João de Deus 32) Great ambiance and delicious *moqueca de camarão* (coconut milk shrimp stew; US$20 for two).

BARRA & COASTAL SUBURBS

Yemanjá (Av Otávio Mangabeira, Jardin Armação) Even the stars come here for the best Bahian food in the city.

Touché (Rua Belo Horizonte 114, Jardim Brasil, Barra) The world's flavors wrapped in crepes are served in a courtyard setting.

Drinking

Salvador easily has the most happening music and nightlife scene in the northeast, with action almost every night of the week. Pick up a free copy of *BahiaCultural* from Bahiatursa for listings.

PELOURINHO

Pelourinho is Salvador's nightlife capital and is filled with bars offering outside tables

or inside ambience. Its cobbled streets and restored buildings create the perfect setting for a mellow drink with friends or sambaing 'til you drop. The city sponsors free live music in the inner courtyards of the Pelô – Largo de Tereza Batista, Largo de Pedro Arcanjo and Praça Quincas Berro d'Água – and on the Terreiro de Jesus. Tuesdays have traditionally been a happening night in the Pelô.

Bar do Reggae (Largo do Pelourinho) may not have the best sound system, but always attracts a crowd for frequent concerts.

COASTAL SUBURBS

There is often live music on weekends on Alameda Marques de Leão in Barra. The Rio Vermelho neighborhood has a somewhat Bohemian reputation, with many restaurant/bars along its waterfront, and live music along the Largo da Mariquita. It is in this suburb that people line up to get *acaraje* (fried bean dumplings filled with dried shrimp, spiced manioc paste and sauces) from the most famous stand in the city – Acaraje da Dinga.

The young, hip and wealthy head out to **Aeroclube Plaza Show** (Av Otávio Mangabeira, Boca do Rio), an outdoor mall that includes a couple of bars and dance clubs such as Rock in Rio and Café Cancún, for those over 21.

GAY & LESBIAN VENUES

Gloss (Rua Afonso Celso 60, Barra) This dance club attracts a mostly male crowd.

Queens Club (Rua Teadoro Sampaio 160, Barris) There are gay-specific and mixed nights at this dance spot.

Off (Rua Dias D'Ávila 33, Barra) Nights of grooving for mostly lesbian crowd over 18.

Café Odeon (Pelourinho) A gay-friendly hangout.

Beco dos Artistas (Av Cerqueira Lima, Garcia) Enter the alley next to Pizzaria Giovanni off Rua Leovigildo Filgueira, and you'll find a few bars that attract a young, gay-friendly crowd.

Entertainment

FOLKLORIC SHOWS

Seeing a folkloric show in the Pelourinho shouldn't be missed. The shows include displays of *afro* (Afro-Brazilian dance), *samba de roda* (flirtatious samba performed in a circle), dances of the *orixás* (which imitate Candomblé followers possessed by their gods), maculêlê, capoeira, live percussion and vocals that will blow your mind.

Balé Folclórico da Bahia (Teatro Miguel Santana, Rua Gregório de Mattos 49; admission US$3; ☽ 8pm Wed-Mon) This is the highest quality show.

Grupo Folclórico SESC (Teatro de Arena, Largo do Pelourinho; admission US$2; ☽ 8pm Thu-Sat) Second-best but still extremely professional.

LIVE MUSIC
Many popular music groups in Salvador hold ensaios (public rehearsals), which seem suspiciously like concerts and carry a similar price tag – from US$7 to US$13. Ensaios are often held weekly, mostly in the six months leading up to Carnaval, but ask Bahiatursa about who's on now.

Some of the more traditional groups (characterized by strong afro drum corps) that rehearse for the public are Ilê Aiyê, the first exclusively black Carnaval group; Muzenza; and Dida, which is all women. More pop and with strong percussion sections are Olodum, a Pelourinho institution, Araketu and Timbalada, brainchild of master composer and musician Carlinhos Brown. The queens of Salvador pop music – Margareth Menezes, Ivete Sangalo and Daniela Mercury – also often 'rehearse' publicly.

Shopping
MALLS
Shopping Iguatemí is Salvador's largest mall and a convenient place to see a movie while you wait for your bus, since the bus station is right across the road. The twin malls of **Shopping Lapa** and **Shopping Piedade** (off Av 7 de Setembro behind Praça da Piedade) are much smaller than Shopping Barra, but walking distance from the Pelourinho.

MARKETS
The perfect place to pick up local handicrafts from musical instruments to T-shirts is the **Mercado Modelo** (☽ 9am-7pm Mon-Sat, 9am-2pm Sun), a lively enclosed tourist market at the base of the Elevador Lacérda. Capoeira demonstrations and live music are often performed out back. The die-hard market fan will like the Mercado São Joaquim, a small city of sketchy waterfront stalls about 3km north of the Mercado Modelo.

Getting There & Away
AIR
Salvador's airport is serviced by Varig, VASP, TAM and Gol. There are daily flights to any Brazilian destination. It's worth checking up on airline specials as flying can sometimes be nominally more expensive than the bus.

BUS
Most Salvador buses coming from the south go around the Baía de Todos os Santos, but alternately you can go to Bom Despacho on the Ilha Itaparica, and catch a ferry into Salvador (45min).

Destination	Duration in Hours	Cost	Frequency
Aracaju	4½	US$8–13	11 daily
Belo Horizonte	24	US$58–61	daily
Fortaleza	20	US$38	daily
Ilhéus	8	US$19	6 daily
João Pessoa	14	US$33	daily
Lençois	6	US$10	2 daily
Natal	21	US$36	2 daily
Porto Seguro	11	US$27	2 daily
Recife	11	US$26–30	2 daily
Rio	24–28	US$48–56	4 daily
São Paulo	33	US$53–58	2 daily
Vitória	18	US$37	daily

Getting Around
Linking the lower and upper cities in the center are the newly renovated **Elevador Lacerda** (5 centavos; ☽ 24 hr), and the more thrilling **Plano Inclinado Gonçalves** (Funicular; 5 centavos; ☽ 7am-7pm Mon-Fri, 7am-1pm Sat). When catching the bus, watch out for pricey air-con minibuses.

PRAIA DO FORTE
Praia do Forte is a tiny tourist village currently being developed as an upmarket ecological beach resort. It has beaches with white fluffy sand and a beautiful ruined fortress, the **Castelo do Garcia d'Ávila** (admission US$1.50; ☽ 8am-6pm), 3km from town. Visit during the week to avoid crowds and higher accommodation prices. There are no banks.

The **Projeto Tamar** (admission US$1; ☽ 9am-5:30pm) station, on the beach next to the church at Praia do Forte, is part of a national project working with local communities to preserve sea turtle breeding

BRAZIL

grounds and educate the public about the endangered turtles. It has tanks of sea turtles from 10cm to a meter long, as well as urchins, eels and other sea life. The center has a multimedia display (some in English) and is definitely worth a visit.

Albergue Praia do Forte (☎ 0xx71-676-1094; praiadoforte@albergue.com.br; Rua da Aurora 3; dm/d US$8/20) offers discounts for HI members in its nice six-bed dorm rooms surrounding a grassy central courtyard.

Pousada dos Artistas (☎ 0xx71-676-1147; pousada dosartistas@terra.com.br; Praça dos Artistas; s/d US$20/28) seems ready to negotiate on its beautiful rooms, which open onto a lush garden.

There's a **campground** about 10 minutes from the beach. **Sabor da Vila** (Alameda do Sol) offers tasty typical Bahian dishes.

Two buses run from Salvador to Praia do Forte daily (US$2.50, one hour, 40 minutes). Buses for the return trip depart every 40 minutes from 7am to 6:40pm, or catch a *kombi* (US$1.50).

CACHOEIRA & SÃO FELIX

The beautiful colonial town of Cachoeira, unblemished by modern buildings or tourism, is home to a wood sculpting tradition with a heavy African flavor. This is the best place to get a glimpse of the Recôncavo, the green, fertile region surrounding Baía de Todos os Santos, whose sugar and tobacco plantations made it the economic heartland of colonial Brazil. Checking out Cachoeira and its twin town São Felix, just on the other side of the Rio Paraguaçu, is a perfect day trip.

There is a tiny **tourist office** (Praça da Aclamaçã, Cachoeira; ☺ Sat & Sun) and banks in both towns.

Sights & Activities

Cachoeira is an important center for Candomblé. Long, mysterious ceremonies are held in small shacks in the hills, usually on weekend nights. The tourist office is sometimes reluctant to give out information, but show an interest in Candomblé and respect for its traditions and they may divulge.

Partially dressed prostitutes and Christ are running themes in the block prints and paintings at the **Museu Hansen Bahia** (Rua 13 de Maio; ☺ 9am-5pm Tue-Fri, 9am-2pm Sat & Sun), which displays the work of this German-Brazilian artist. For a small donation, members of the exclusively female Boa Morte (Good Death) Candomblé cult will lead you around their barren one-room **Museu da Boa Morte** (Rua 13 de Maio; ☺ 10am-6pm). There are some good photos and usually members sitting around smoking their pipes and gossiping.

Igreja da Ordem Terceira do Carmo (Rua Inocência Bonaventura; admission US$0.65; ☺ 1-5pm Tue-Thu & Sat, 2-6:30pm Fri) is an ornately gilded church featuring a gallery of suffering Christs with genuine ruby blood. Across the bridge in São Felix, visit the riverfront **Centro Cultural Dannemann** (Av Salvador Pinto 39; gallery ☺ 8am-noon, 1-5pm Tue-Sat, 1-5pm Sun) which, in addition to contemporary art displays, has a room of women at work rolling cigars.

Festivals & Events

The fascinating Festa da NS de Boa Morte, organized by the Boa Morte sisterhood, falls on the Friday closest to August 15 and lasts for three days: descendants of slaves pay tribute to their liberation with dance and prayer in a mix of Candomblé and Catholicism. The Festa de São João (June 22–24) is the largest popular festival of Bahia's interior.

Sleeping & Eating

Pousada do Paraguassú (☎ 0xx75-438-3386; p-para guassu@uol.com.br; Av Salvador Pinto 1; s/d US$10/15) Located on the river in São Felix, this modern *pousada* is easily the nicest economical option on either side of the bridge.

Pousada do Pai Thomaz (☎ 0xx75-425-1288; Rua 25 de Junho 12; r per person US$7) Though the rooms are much more simple than the downstairs restaurant jam packed with local wood carvings, they are comfortable and bright.

Gruta Azul (Praça Manoel Vitorino 2; dishes US$5) Cachoeira's best restaurant. Try *maniçoba*, a spicy local meat-and-manioc dish.

Nair (Rua 13 de Maio; dishes US$1) This simple restaurant concocts excellent *moquecas* and *prato feito*.

Getting There & Away

Buses depart from Salvador to Cachoeira/São Felix (US$3, two hours, hourly) every day from 5:30am to 9:30pm. Hourly return buses can be caught in either town from 4:20am to 6:30pm. You can also continue on to Feira de Santana (US$1, 1½ hours, 12 daily) to make further connections.

LENÇÓIS

Lençóis is the prettiest of the old diamond mining towns in the Chapada Diamantina, a mountainous wooded oasis in the dusty *sertão*. While the town itself is a draw – cobbled streets, brightly painted 19th-century buildings, nestled between lush green hills – it is the surrounding area bursting with caves, waterfalls and plateaus promising panoramic views that are the real attraction.

There is a **Banco do Brasil** (Praça Horácio de Mattos). A recommended local tour agency is **Lentur** (☎ 0xx75-334-1271; Rua da Baderna).

Sights

If the tour company photo albums left you unconvinced, the photo gallery of **Calil Neto** (Praça Horácio de Mattos 82; ⏰ 8am-1pm & 6-11pm Wed-Mon, 6-11pm Tue) will leave no question about this area's beauty. Small prints of the artists shots are sold. The **Prefeitura Municipal** (Praça do Coreto 8) is a pretty building with interesting old photos of Lençóis. Also worth a visit is **Zacão**, a small museum of mining relics and artifacts run by local historian Mestre Oswaldo.

Activities

WALKS & SWIMMING

There are a couple of walks just outside town that you can easily take without a guide. One is a 3km walk past the bus station and out of town, following the Rio Lençóis upstream. You will see the **Salão de Areias Coloridas** (Hall of Colored Sands), where artisans gather material for bottled sand paintings, **Poço Halley** (the swimming hole), **Cachorinha** (little waterfall) and finally **Cachoeira da Primavera** (waterfall of the spring), with good views back to Lençóis along the way. Another relaxing 4km hike is to follow Rua São Benedito out of town to **Ribeirão do Meio**, a series of swimming holes with a natural waterslide. For more swimming, catch the morning bus to Seabra and hop off at Mucugêzinho Bar. About 2km downstream is **Poço do Diabo** (Devil's Well), a swimming hole with a 25m waterfall.

TREKS

Just to the southwest of Lençóis is **Parque Nacional da Chapada Diamantina**, comprising 1520 sq km of breathtaking scenery, waterfalls, rivers, monkeys and a lot to interest geologists. The park has very little infrastructure for visitors and bus services are scarce, making it difficult to penetrate. The best way to see it is to hire a guide certified by the ACVL guide association. Two knowledgeable native English speaking guides are **Roy Funch** (☎ 0xx75-334-1305; Rua Pé de Ladeira 212) and **Olivia Taylor** (☎ 0xx75-334-1229; oliviadosduendes@zaz.com.br; Rua do Pires), owner of Pousada dos Duendes.

Recommended Brazilian guides (some of whom speak English) are **Virgínia Vieira** (☎ 0xx75-334-1530), **Rao** (☎ 0xx75-334-1544), **João** (☎ 0xx75-334-1221), **Trajano** (☎ 0xx75-334-1143), Zoi (ask around), **Luiz Krug** (☎ 0xx75-334-1102; Pousada Lençóis), **Henrique Gironha** (☎ 0xx75-334-1326) and **Rosa** (☎ 0xx75-334-1916; Pousalegre).

Treks can last anywhere from two to eight days, and usually involve a combination of camping, staying in local homes and *pousadas*. Prices run around US$9 per day, including food and lodging. Gear can be rented in town.

Tours

This is not the time to pinch pennies – take a tour. Local tour agencies organize day long car trips and hikes for around US$10 per person, not including admission fees if there are any. Car tours almost always include some swimming and walking. Some stand-out sights are **Poço Encantado**, the Lençóis poster child: a cave filled with stunningly beautiful blue water; **Poço Azul**, another rainwater filled cave you can swim in; **Gruta da Lapa Doce**, a cave with impressive formations; **Morro do Pai Inácio**, the most prominent peak in the area affording an awesome view over a plateau-filled valley; and **Cachoeira da Fumaça**, at 420m, Brazil's longest waterfall.

Sleeping

Reservations are required for all major holidays. If you arrive by night bus, most *pousadas* allow you to stay the rest of the night, only charging for breakfast.

Pousada Casa de Hélia (☎ 0xx75-334-1143; casa dehelia@ig.com.br; Rua da Muritiba; dm/d US$7/20) Quiet and beauty prevail in this multilevel *pousada* built into a hillside. This backpacker's favorite is up a dirt road from the bus station.

Pousada dos Duendes (☎ 0xx75-334-1229; olivia dosduendes@zaz.com.br; Rua do Pires; dm US$5, s/d US$7/13, with bath US$10/13) Nicely finished with a

BRAZIL

very social atmosphere, this pretty *pousada* perched above town puts on open group dinners. It's a good place to pick up new reading material.

Pousada Lavramor (☎ 0xx75-334-1280; Praça João Colosso; dm US$5-7, s/d US$8/13, d with bath US$20) On the hill across from town, Lavramor offers newish rooms with a breeze and an amazing view.

Pousada da Fonte (☎ 0xx75-334-1953; pousada dafonte@hotmail.com; Rua da Muritiba; dm/d US$7/15) With stone walls and a breakfast porch surrounded by forest, this quaint *pousada* has the feel of a weekend home. Just past Casa de Hélia.

Pousada & Camping Lumiar (☎ 0xx75-334-1241; lumiar@sendnet.com.br; Praça do Rosário 70; campsites per person US$2, s/d US$12/23) A converted colonial family home, this *pousada* offers shady campsites within its groomed gardens. Guests have use of the kitchen.

Eating
Gaia Comida Natural (Praça Horácio de Mattos 114; sandwiches US$1) The sandwiches come on thick slices of homemade whole wheat bread at this veggie café.

Pizza na Pedra (Rua Gal Viveiros) Renowned as the best in town, this pizzeria is tucked away on the road leaving town.

Ristorante Italiano os Artistas da Massa (Rua da Baderna 49) Homemade pastas are served to the tunes of jazz, which you can also order off the menu.

Picanha na Praça (Praça Otáviano Alves 62; dishes US$5) The half-portion of fish – sizzling on its own grill with heaping side dishes – feeds two.

Neco's Bar (Rua da Baderna; meals US$3) Place your order a day ahead and experience excellent Bahian food.

Getting There & Away
Buses to Salvador (US$10, six hours) leave at 11:30pm daily, at 1:15pm every day but Saturday, and at 7:30am on Monday, Wednesday and Friday. All Salvador buses stop in Feira de Santana (US$7, 4½ hours), where connections can be made to just about anywhere, but are not always well timed.

MORRO DE SÃO PAULO
Remotely perched at the tip of Ilha de Tinharé is the picturesque holiday village of Morro de São Paulo, where wheelbarrows are the primary mode of transport on sand streets lined with shops and restaurants. The beaches, with their shallow, warm water, disappear with the tides, liberating you for a hike to the waterfall, a trip to nearby **Boipeba**, or to catch the sunset from the lighthouse or fort. There are no banks.

Sleeping
Reservations for Morro's 100 or so *pousadas* are required for all major holidays, especially Carnaval and *resaca* (five days of post-Carnaval hangover). Second Beach is where the nightly party is, so staying there means sleeping to pounding beats.

Pousada Gaucho (☎ 0xx75-483-1243; pousada gaucho@ligbr.com.br; Caminho da Praia; s/d US$7/12; ▨) Gaucho has a great location on the main drag, with nice, bright rooms.

Pousada Ninho da Águia (☎ 0xx75-483-1537; mlso@zipmail.com.br; s/d US$7/10; ▨) The view is spectacular from these well-finished rooms on the hill by the lighthouse.

Pousada Cairu (☎ 0xx75-483-1074; Rua da Fonte; r per person US$3; ▨) The rooms are dark and a little small, but upstairs hammocks are prime for people-watching. Pay more for air-con.

Pousada Aradhia (☎ 0xx75-483-1099; pousada aradhia@ieg.com.br; Terça Praia; s/d US$12/13; ▨) One of the cheaper options on Third Beach, Aradhia boasts a pool and rooms with TV and mini-fridge.

Eating
There are many restaurants along Camino da Praia.

Ponte de Encontro (Camino da Praia) Veggie sandwiches and pasta dishes are served up on mosaic tiled tables at this chic restaurant.

Oh La La! Crepes (Camino da Praia) Your genuine French-made crepe meal can turn into your nights' party at this hip creperia/bar.

Espaguetaria Strega (Camino da Praia) The pasta is so well-priced that you can afford to choose a chaser from the bar, which has over 40 different *cachaça* (sugarcane rum) infusions.

Restaurante Tinharé (Camino da Praia) Hidden down some stairs, huge portions of excellent Bahian cuisine are served to those in the know. Don't order any extra for your third person.

Getting There & Away

The catamaran *Gamboa do Morro* (US$13, 1¾ hours, two to three daily) and the boat *Ilha Bela* (US$15, two hours, daily) sail between Morro and Salvador's Terminal Maritimo Turistico (behind the Mercado Modelo). The catamaran can be a bit of a vomit-fest, so come fairly empty-stomached and focus on a fixed point on land if seas get rough. If you come by land, Valença is the gateway city where you get a boat upriver to Morro (US$1, 1½ hours, hourly) from 7:30am to 5:30pm, stopping first in Gamboa.

ILHÉUS

Bright turn-of-the-century architecture and oddly angled streets lend Ilhéus a vibrant

and rather playful air. The town's fame comes from its history as a prosperous cocoa port, as well as being the hometown of Jorge Amado (Brazil's best-known novelist) and the setting of one of his greatest novels (*Gabriela, Cravo e Canela*). All this combined with the chance to visit the Atlantic rain forest make Ihéus worth a quick stop.

A **tourist information office** (Traverse Leite Mendes) is in a kiosk between the cathedral and the water. An **Internet café** (Rua General Câmara) is next door to Albergue da Ilha. Change money at **Banco do Brasil** (Rua Marquês de Paranagua).

Sights & Activities

The best thing to do in Ilhéus is just wander. The hill of the Convento NS da Piedade

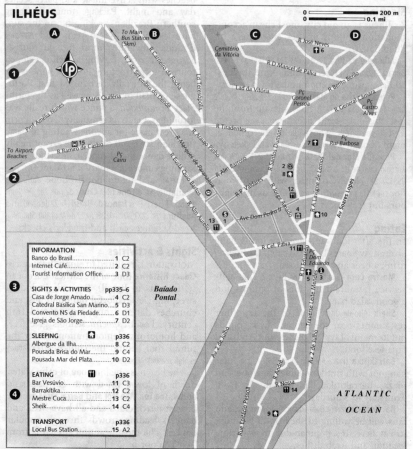

ILHÉUS

INFORMATION
Banco do Brasil.................... 1 C2
Internet Café....................... 2 C2
Tourist Information Office....3 D3

SIGHTS & ACTIVITIES pp335–6
Casa de Jorge Amado..............4 C2
Catedral Basílica San Marino...5 D3
Convento NS da Piedade........6 D1
Igreja de São Jorge.................7 D2

SLEEPING   p336
Albergue da Ilha....................8 C2
Pousada Brisa do Mar.............9 C4
Pousada Mar del Plata..........10 D2

EATING   p336
Bar Vesúvio.........................11 C3
Barrakitika.........................12 C2
Mestre Cuca........................13 C2
Sheik.................................14 C4

TRANSPORT   p336
Local Bus Station.................15 A2

BRAZIL

is a great place to catch the sunset and get a view of the city. **Casa de Jorge Amado** (Rua Jorge Amado 21; admission US$0.35; ☺ 9am-noon & 2-6pm) is where the author was raised and wrote his first novel. The displays will be most interesting to his readers.

Igreja de São Jorge (Praça Rui Barbosa; ☺ Tue-Sun), built in 1534, is the city's oldest church and houses a small sacred-art museum.

Eco Parque de Una (☎ 0xx73-633-1121) gives two-hour tours of its Atlantic rain forest reserve, which includes a suspended tree canopy walkway and swimming ponds. It lies 70km south of Ilhéus. Make a direct appointment or go through a tour agency.

The best beaches, such as **Praia dos Milionários**, are to the south.

Sleeping

As Ilhéus is an old city, most cheap accommodation options in the center are a bit dilapidated.

Albergue da Ilha (☎ 0xx73-231-8938; Rua General Câmara 31; dm US$5) Friendly and secure, this hostel has a prime location in the town center.

Pousada Brisa do Mar (☎ 0xx73-231-2644; Av 2 de Julho 136; s/d US$10/17) A huge step up from the rest, this place really does have a sea breeze *and* a sea view. The walk to the center at night, though short, is desolate and sketchy.

Pousada Mar del Plata (☎ 0xx73-231-8009; Rua Antonio Lavigne de Lemos 3; s/d US$8/12, s/d with bath US$12/18) Newly painted with hardwood floors, this *pousada* is as simple as its neighbors but feels nicer.

Eating

In the afternoon and evening locals hang around Av Soares Lopez to catch the breeze, drink a beer and eat seafood.

Mestre Cuca (Rua Eustá Quio Bastos) This self-service restaurant has lots of options and a good salad bar.

Sheik (Alto de Oitero) One of the few finer restaurants near the center, Sheik rounds out its menu of typical dishes with Arab and Japanese food.

Barrakítika (Praça Antonio Muniz 39) A popular hangout with outdoor tables, seafood and pizza, Barrakítika has live music from Thursday to Saturday.

Bar Vesúvio (Praça Dom Eduardo) Jorge Amado fans will be willing to shell out a bit more to eat here. It's popular due to its prime location and Arab dishes.

Getting There & Away

Frequent buses go to Valença (US$6, five hours, four daily), Salvador (US$11 to US$29, seven hours, five daily), Porto Seguro (US$8, six hours, three daily), Vitoria (US$19 to US$28, 13 hours, two daily) and Rio (US$35 to US$44, 22 hours, two to three daily). More frequent connections can be made in Itabuna, 30km inland. Local buses to Itabuna leave from the local bus station on Praça Cairu and from outside the main (long-distance) bus station (US$0.65, 40 minutes) every 15 minutes.

PORTO SEGURO

For decades Porto Seguro has epitomized the Bahian tourism attraction of gorgeous beaches with active music and party scenes day and night. Package tours (bringing southern Brazilians seeking fun in the sun) have lessened in recent years, and Arraial d'Ajuda now lures most foreign tourists across the river, leaving a well-developed tourism infrastructure. Porto is famous for being the officially recognized first Portuguese landfall in Brazil, as well as the birthplace of *lambada*, a dance which really was forbidden due to its sensuality. Today Porto is a great place for anyone wanting to party Brazilian-style and catch some exceptionally skilled dancers and *capoeiristas* (those performing *capoeira*, a martial art/dance).

Email and international phone calls are available at **@Fone** (Rua Cidade da Fafe 78; ☺ 9am-11pm). There is a **Banco do Brasil** (Av 22 de Abril) and **Adeltur** (☎ 0XX73-288-1888; Av 22 de Abril 100, Shopping Avenida) changes cash and traveler's checks.

Sights & Activities

Motivation is required to climb the stairs to **Cidade Histórica** (one of the earliest European settlements in Brazil). Rewards include a sweeping view, colorful old buildings, and churches dating from early to mid-16th century. Local *capoeira* schools give free, and humorous, demonstrations under the round roof behind the churches (☺ hourly in high season).

The beach is one long bay of calm water, north of town, lined with *barracas* and clubs. **Toa Toa**, **Axé Moi** and **Barramares** are the biggest beach clubs and all have MCs and dancers leading crowds through popular dances. The most beautiful stretch is from Toa Toa north.

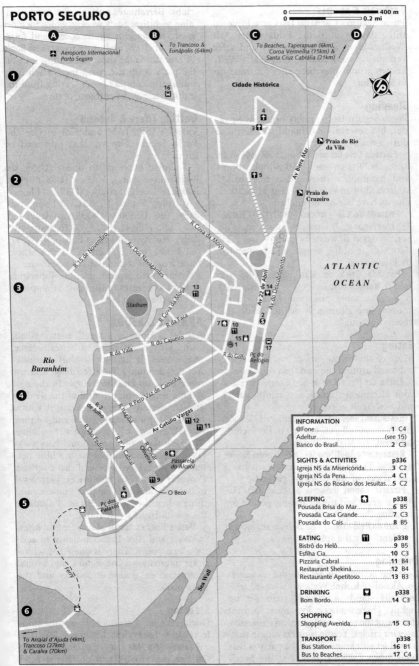

PORTO SEGURO

0 ──────── 400 m
0 ──────── 0.2 mi

To Trancoso & Eunápolis (64km)

To Beaches, Taperapuan (6km), Coroa Vermelha (15km) & Santa Cruz Cabrália (21km)

Aeroporto Internacional Porto Seguro

Cidade Histórica

Praia do Rio da Vila

Praia do Cruzeiro

ATLANTIC OCEAN

R Cova da Moça

Av Beira Mar

Av do Descobrimento

Av 22 de Abril

R 15 de Novembro

Av Dos Navegantes

R Cova da Moça

R da Faca

Stadium

Rio Buranhém

R do Cajueiro

R da Vala

R Pero Vaz de Caminha

R 2 de Julho

R Itagibá

R São Pedro

R PA Cabral

R Oscar Oliveira

Av Getúlio Vargas

Passarela do Álcool

O Beco

Pç dos Pataxós

R do Golfo

Pç do Relógio

Ferry

Sea Wall

To Arraial d'Ajuda (4km), Trancoso (27km) & Caraíva (70km)

BRAZIL

INFORMATION
@Fone...1 C4
Adeltur...(see 15)
Banco do Brasil...................................2 C3

SIGHTS & ACTIVITIES   p336
Igreja NS da Misericórida.....................3 C2
Igreja NS da Pena.................................4 C1
Igreja NS do Rosário dos Jesuítas...5 C2

SLEEPING   p338
Pousada Brisa do Mar..........................6 B5
Pousada Casa Grande..........................7 C3
Pousada do Cais...................................8 B5

EATING   p338
Bistrô do Helô......................................9 B5
Esfiha Cia...10 C3
Pizzaria Cabral....................................11 B4
Restaurant Shekiná.............................12 B4
Restaurante Apetitoso........................13 B3

DRINKING   p338
Bom Bordo...14 C3

SHOPPING
Shopping Avenida...............................15 C3

TRANSPORT   p338
Bus Station..16 B1
Bus to Beaches...................................17 C4

Festivals & Events

Porto Seguro's Carnaval lasts an additional three days – until the Friday after Ash Wednesday – and is a smaller and safer version of Salvador's Carnaval. Well-known groups play here after finishing up in Salvador.

Sleeping

Porto Seguro has as many hotels as Salvador, but reservations should still be made during major holidays.

Pousada Casa Grande (☎ 0xx73-268-3564; Av dos Navegantes 107; r per person US$3) Simple rooms and hammocks surround a tree-shaded courtyard in an extremely central location. Guests have use of the kitchen.

Pousada do Cais (☎ 0xx73-288-2112; Av Portugal 382; r per person US$7) Upstairs rooms roast on sunny days, downstairs rooms are a bit dark. It's friendly, simple and frequented by Europeans.

Pousada Brisa do Mar (☎ 0xx73-288-2943; Praça Dr Manoel Ribeiro Coelho 188; r per person US$5) A quiet, somber place run by an elderly couple, but gleamingly white inside the rooms and out.

Eating

Most of the nicest dinner restaurants are clustered around the Passarela do Álcool.

Esfíha Cia (Rua Cidade de Fafe) Come here for your afternoon spinach and ricotta pastry and fresh fruit juice.

Restaurant Shekiná (Rua Augusto Borges 102; buffet US$1) A simple all-you-can-eat buffet including meats roasted on the spot.

Restaurante Apetitoso (Av dos Navegantes 404; per kg US$4.50) This self-service restaurant has a good selection and is always packed.

Pizzaria Cabral (Passarela do Álcool 272) The pizza is great and the location is perfect for watching the night action.

Bistrô do Helô (O Beco) The Bahian seafood is excellent – try the spicy *moqueca*.

Drinking

Evening action centers on the Passarela do Álcool (Alcohol Walkway), where fruit cocktails stands and craft stalls set up nightly. There is always live music in front of some of the restaurants and, on weekends, *capoeira* circles. Young hipsters selling tickets will let you know where the party is that night, often called a *luau* if at the beach

clubs. Barramares puts on the most stunning nighttime party weekly, which includes *lambada*, *capoeira*, an *axé* cover band, *forró*, *samba* or *MPB*, and other treats. **Bom Bordo** (Av 22 de Abril) is the most fun club in town. If the party is up the coast, there are usually round-trip courtesy buses leaving from the traffic circle at the entrance of town.

Getting There & Around

Varig, VASP, TAM and Gol service the Porto Seguro airport, 2km northeast of town.

Frequent buses go to Ilhéus (US$8, six hours, three daily), Valença (US$28, eight hours, two daily), Salvador (US$28, 11 hours, two daily), Vitoria (US$21, 10 hours, two daily), Rio (US$30 to US$38, two daily) and São Paulo (US$41 to US$53, 26 hours, two daily). Hourly buses go to Eunápolis (US$2, one hour) from 5:30am to 9:30pm, where more frequent connections can be made.

From Porto Seguro, take the Taperapuã or Rio Doce buses to the beach, Campinho or Cabralia to get back.

ARRAIAL D'AJUDA

Arraial d'Ajuda is a small, pretty village with stone roads winding beneath large, shady trees. It sits atop a bluff overlooking the dreamlike **Praia de Pitinga** and the more built up **Praia de Mucugê**. In the past Arraial was the playground of the wealthy and connected, a legacy leaving it with a trickle of up-market tourism and keeping the slicker side of its infrastructure alive. The new wave of international backpackers and nouveau hippies mesh a little better with the relaxed vibe and rustic setting. Probably due to its low prices, high level of comfort, and because they know a good thing when they find it, 'Israel d'Ajuda' is thick with Israelis year round.

Mestre Bimba's school (Rua da Capoeira) offers *lambada* and Afro-Brazilian dance in addition to *capoeira*. There is one ATM with a fickle international connection, and several Internet cafés around Broadway and the main plaza.

Sleeping

During the off-season, check out the mid-level hotels for backpacker range deals.

Pousada Alto Mar (☎ 0xx73-575-1935; Rua Bela Vista; r per person US$8) Turn down the road on the right side of the church to find this quiet cheapie with comfortable, basic *apartamentos*.

Pousada Republica das Bananas (☎ 0xx73-575-3336; Rua Santo Antonio; r per person US$3; 🌂 🍴) Two lines of simple rooms, some with porches and hammocks, stand close together at this backpacker favorite without a sign.

Condomínio Abner Xavier (☎ 0xx73-575-1766; abnerxavier@uol.com.br; Alameda das Eugênias 26; r per person US$7-10; 🌂 🍴) These fully furnished, two-bed, two-bath condominiums with a full kitchen are a fantastic deal. There's a two person minimum in the low season, four person minimum in the high season.

Pousada Mir a Mar (Rua Jatobar; campsites US$1.50, r per person US$3) At the end of the street parallel to Broadway, one block closer to the beach, Mir a Mar has a row of simple rooms facing an undeveloped yard where they allow camping.

Eating
A Portinha (Rua Manoel C. Santiago) This is possibly the best per kilo food in Brazil, including mashed pumpkin, veggie quiches and fresh fish. It's on the road parallel to the main plaza away from the beach.

Mão na Massa (Rua Bela Vista 125) Serves tasty pasta and fish dishes on the edge of the bluff with a fantastic view.

Manguti (Rua Caminho da Praia; dishes US$3) A recommended Italian restaurant known for its gnocchi. Try the *filé manguti*.

Beco dos Cores (Caminho da Praia) This attractive galleria has great sushi, crepes, pizza and fancier food with Asian flavors.

Drinking
Lambart (Broadway) This is the happening spot for *lambada* and *forró*.

Girasol (Caminho da Praia) The pool tables are often cleared away for bands or dancing, and pillowed window seats offer a comfortable vantage point.

Beco dos Cores (Caminho da Praia) Fantastic atmosphere and live music from Thursday through Saturday.

Getting There & Away
Two ferries travel between Porto Seguro and Arraial d'Ajuda (US$0.60, five minutes). The passenger ferry runs half-hourly from 7:30am to 10pm. The car ferry runs half-hourly from 7am to midnight, hourly

from midnight to 7am. From the dock, jump on a bus or *kombi* to Arraial. It's also possible to walk the lovely 4km along the beach.

TRANCOSO
Very hip with the international hippy crowd, Trancoso is a tiny rustic village atop a grassy bluff overlooking fantastic beaches. The town is characterized by its *quadrado* (central square), which is lined with big trees and small, colorful colonial buildings, and lit by paper lanterns at night. 'Transecoso' is famous for its full moon beach raves, but when those aren't on, there is still some nightlife on weekends – just follow the music. There are no banks.

Sleeping
Reservations are a must during January and major holidays.

Café Esmeralda (☎ 0xx73-668-1527; Quadrado; s/d US$7/10) A Canadian/Brazilian couple have a row of simple rooms behind their café.

Pousada Quarto Crescente (☎ 0xx73-668-1014; quartocrescente@trancoso.tv; Rua Itabela; s/d US$8/13; 🍴) Lovely gardens surround comfortable rooms and a well-stocked library; the breakfast is superb. It's on the road into town.

Eating
A Portinha (Quadrado) This is some of possibly the best per kilo food in Brazil, including mashed pumpkin, veggie quiches, and fresh gnocchi.

Cantinho Doce (Quadrado) The portions are gigantic at this tree-shaded restaurant serving Bahian cuisine and creative meat and fruit dishes.

Jonas and **Amendoeira** have good, cheap seafood on the asphalt road to the right of the Quadrado. **Raios do Sol** is a beach bar that prepares delicious *peixe amendoeira* – fish wrapped in the leaves of an almond tree.

Getting There & Away
It is possible to walk the beautiful 13km along the beach from Arraial d'Ajuda. If that doesn't appeal, hourly buses depart from Arraial d'Ajuda from 7:20am to 8:30pm (US$1, 50 minutes) and return hourly from 7am to 8pm. Three daily buses travel between Trancoso and Porto Seguro (US$3, 1½ hours).

BRAZIL

CARAIVA

Without electricity, cars or throngs of tourists, the hamlet of Caraiva, 42km south of Trancoso by dirt road, is primitive and beautiful. Its beaches are long and deserted, with churning surf. Boat journeys up the Rio Caraiva, trips to the Parque Nacional de Monte Pascoal and horse riding to a Pataxó Indian village are easy to organize here. Several rustic *pousadas* will put you up for around US$10 per person.

Buses for Caraiva leave from Arraial d'Ajuda (US$2, 2½ hours, two daily) and Trancoso (US$2, two hours, three daily). A daily 7am bus leaves Caraiva for Itabela, for connections north and south.

ARACAJU

You're in Aracaju, the capital of Sergipe, because for some reason you absolutely have to be. The plazas are leafy, but the beaches are mediocre and the sights barely interesting.

The helpful **Bureau de Informações Turísticas** (☎ 0xx79-3179-1947; Praça Olímpio Campos) is reachable by walking through the **Rua 24 Horas** (Rua Laranjeiras) shopping arcade, where there is an Internet café. The Rodoviária Nova (New Bus Terminal) is 4km east of the center.

Weekend and nighttime action is mostly limited to the sandy barrier island of Santa Luzia at the mouth of the Rio Sergipe. **Nova Orla** is the most popular weekend beach, and is lined with *barracas* and restaurants. While you're out there, look down the mouth of an eel and watch rays swim in a 50,000L tank at Projeto Tamar's **Oceanário** (aquarium; Av Santos Dumont, Praia de Atalaia; admission $6; ☼ 2-8pm Tue-Fri, noon-9pm Sat & Sun).

Sleeping

There are many hotels at Praia de Atalaia, but the ones in the center are more convenient and better value.

Hotel Amado (☎ 0xx79-211-9937; hotelamado@ infonet.com.br; Rua Laranjeiras 532; s/d US$25/38; 🐱) Almost pretty, with potted plants lining the porch and an old house feel, Amado is the best budget option.

Hotel Brasília (☎ 0xx79-214-2964; Rua Laranjeiras 580; s/d US$36/55; 🐱) A no-frills, presentable option with a 10% discount for cash payment.

Eating

Cacique Chá (Praça Olímpio Campos) This garden restaurant is a popular meeting place.

Sal e Pimenta (Praça da Imprensa) A good self-serve lunch place in the center.

Gonzaga (Rua Santa Amaro) and **O Miguel** (Av Antônio Alves 340) are recommended for northeastern specialties like carne do sol.

Praia de Atalaia has a lot of bars and restaurants and is a good spot to wander if you're looking for cheap eats at night.

Getting There & Around

BRA, TAM, Varig and VASP service Aracaju's airport.

Frequent buses go to Maceió (US$7, four hours, four daily), Penedo (US$3, three hours, daily), Recife (US$18, 23 hours, daily) and Salvador (US$8, 4½ hours, eight daily). Internal city buses leave from the **Rodoviária Velha** (Old Bus Terminal; Av Divina Pastora).

LARANJEIRAS

Nestled between three green, church-topped hills, Laranjeiras is the colonial gem of Sergipe. This may not be saying much, but it is still a pretty little town. Simple, bat-filled churches, a good museum and walks in the picturesque surrounding hills make it worth visiting. Laranjeiras is a mellow day trip from Aracaju but also has a decent *pousada*.

A knowledgeable docent will lead you around informative displays on sugar production, slave torture, Afro-Brazilian religions and Laranjeiras' cultural traditions at the **Museo Afro-Brasileiro** (Rua José do Prado Franco; admission US$0.35; ☼ 10am-5pm Tue-Fri, 1-5pm Sat & Sun).

Buses run between Laranjeiras and Aracaju's Rodoviária Velha (US$1, 35 minutes) half hourly from 5:30am to 9:30pm.

PENEDO

Penedo is a riverfront colonial city almost untouched by tourism. Attractions include many baroque churches and colonial buildings and the opportunity to travel the jade-colored waters of the Rio São Francisco. People come from surrounding villages to buy or sell everything from papayas to faux jewels in the markets that cram Penedo's streets.

The helpful **tourist office** (☎ 0xx82-551-2727; Praça Barão de Penedo; ☼ 7:30am-5:30pm) in the Casa da Aposentadoria can hook you up with Portuguese-speaking guides for a one-hour walking tour. Catch the view from the second floor while you are in there.

Saturday is the major market day and the easiest day to find a boat up or down the São Francisco. Boats (US$0.35) leave every half-hour for Neópolis, a few kilometers downriver, or Carrapicho (Santana do São Francisco), a nearby village noted for its ceramics. The tourist office can inform you about longer trips.

Sleeping

Pousada Colonial (☎ 0xx82-551-2355; Praça 12 de Abril 21; d US$17) This beautifully restored colonial house on the waterfront has hardwood floors and antique furniture. Try to get a room with a view of the river.

Hotel Turista (☎ 0xx82-551-2237; Rua Siqueira Campos 143; s/d US$5/8) A little rundown but the most comfortable budget option.

Eating

There are plenty of cheap *luncheonettes* and self-service restaurants in the center.

Forte da Rocheira (Rua da Rocheira 2; dishes US$8-20) For some thing nicer, this old replica fort overlooking the river serves abundant portions of seafood and meat.

Getting There & Away

The bus station sits on a traffic island on the riverfront. For Maceió, take the normal (US$5, 2½ hours, three daily) or the *pinga litoral* (coastal drip; US$5, four hours, four daily) bus. The latter gives you a thorough tour of every nook and cranny on the stretch, which can be great. Only one bus a day goes to Aracaju (US$3, three hours) or Salvador (US$11, nine hours), so it may be more convenient to take a ferry to Neópolis (US$2, hourly), which has more frequent buses.

MACEIÓ

Maceió's greatest gifts are the beachfronts of Ponta Verde and Pajuçara, where jade-colored water laps beaches lined with palms and brightly painted *jangadas* (traditional sailboats), and locals weave their evening walks between thatched-roof restaurants and *futbol* courts. The nightlife is pretty happening too. Maceió Fest, a Salvador-style, out-of-season Carnaval in the second week of December, is the city's largest festival.

Internet Cybercafé (Av Dr Antônio Gouveia 1113; US$1 per hr) is buried in the Ana Maria building right across the street from Alseturs. There's a branch of **Banco do Brasil** (Rua do

Sol). The **Alsetures** (☎ 0xx82-315-1503; Av Dr Antônio Gouveia 1143, Pajuçara; ◷ 8am-6pm Mon-Fri) tourist information booth is staffed by teenagers, so you may actually find the city's **tourism office** (☎ 0xx82-336-4409; Rua Sá e Albuquerque 310; ◷ 8am-2pm Mon-Fri) to be more helpful.

Sights & Activities

High quality examples of Alagoas' popular culture are displayed at **Museu Théo Brandão** (Av da Paz 1490; ◷ 9am-noon & 2-5pm Tue-Fri, 3-6pm Sat & Sun), including festival headpieces modeled after churches, which are loaded with mirrors, beads and multicolored ribbons, and weigh up to 35kg.

Organize your own tour to nearby islands and beaches by heading out to Pontal da Barra, west of town, where small boats depart daily around 9:30am for a five-hour cruise (without/with lunch US$3/5). From Praia de Pajuçara, *jangadas* sail 2km out to natural pools formed by the reef (US$3).

City beaches are polluted, but gorgeous beaches are not far away. Two spots renowned for their beauty are Praia do Francês (24km) and Barra de São Miguel (34km).

Sleeping

There is no reason to torture yourself by staying in the center – beachside Pajuçara is much more tranquil.

PAJUÇARA

Pousada Rex (☎ 0xx82-231-4358; Rua Dr Antônio Pedro de Mendonça 311; s/d US$6/9) Tiled from floor to ceiling, Rex is pretty sterile but friendly and family-run.

Mar Amar (☎ 0xx82-231-1551; Rua Dr Antônio Pedro de Mendonça 343; s/d US$7/10; ✖) It wouldn't pass a white glove test, but it has that cluttered, homey feeling.

Hotel Praia Bonita (☎ 0xx82-231-2565; Av Dr Antônio Gouveia 943; s/d US$13/17; ✖) Right on the waterfront, this is a proper hotel with a shiny, modern lobby and marble floors.

CENTRO

Hotel Maceió (☎ 0xx82-336-0954; Rua Dr Pontes de Miranda 146; r per person US$3) *Apartamentos* are clean and cell-like with no natural light or breakfast.

Hotel dos Palmares (Praça dos Palmares 253; r per person US$3) This place feels more like a tenement than a hotel. Breakfast is not available.

BRAZIL

Eating

The beachfronts of Pajuçara and Ponta Verde are packed with **stands** and **restaurants** serving every type of food imaginable. **Massagueira**, a fishing village 12km northwest of town, has stands on the Lagoa Mundaú selling seafood at very reasonable prices.

The northeastern specialty *beiju de tapioca* must be tried. *Tapioca* **stands** clustered on the beachfronts make these taco-like folds with sweet or savory fillings (US$1) by heating manioc flour until it solidifies.

Viver (Av Professor Vital Barbosa 554, Ponta Verde) A vegetarian restaurant with a good selection.

Gouveia (Av Dr Antônio Gouveia 293, Pajuçara) The menu at this popular hangout is much the same as elsewhere, but the prices are good.

Zumbi (Av Senador Robert Kennedy, Ponta da Terra) Seafood and typical Brazilian dishes are served right on the beachfront.

Alecrim (Rua da Alegria 213, Centro) A good self-service restaurant with lots of salads.

Getting There & Away

BRA, Gol, TAM, VASP and Varig service Maceió's airport, 20km north of the center.

There are daily flights to every Brazilian destination.

The bus station is 4km north of town. There are frequent buses to Recife (US$7, 3½ hours, 13 daily), Penedo (2½ hours, three daily; *pinga litoral,* 4½ hours, four daily; US$5), Aracaju (US$7, four hours, four daily) and Salvador (US$12, nine hours, four daily).

RECIFE

Recife is the capital of one of the more culturally rich states in the northeast, Pernambuco, where it's argued the musical traditions of *forró* and *frevo* (fast-paced, popular music) were born. Unfortunately, it can be difficult to perceive this outside of Carnaval time among the gritty high rises of this big city, the third largest in the region and a major industrial center. Culture is not packaged for the tourist here, so keep your eyes peeled as you enjoy the museums and take advantage of Recife's happening nightlife and you'll probably find something. Recife's sights can easily be seen through day trips from its sister city Olinda,

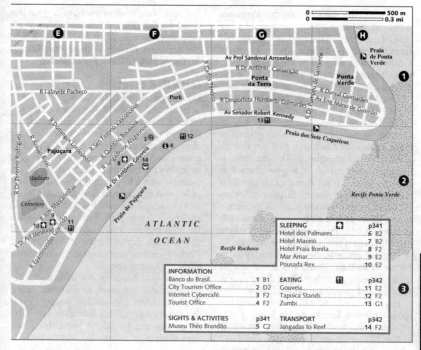

SLEEPING p341
Hotel dos Palmares..................6 B2
Hotel Maceió...........................7 B2
Hotel Praia Bonita....................8 F2
Mar Amar................................9 E2
Pousada Rex..........................10 E2

INFORMATION
Banco do Brasil........................1 B1
City Tourism Office.................. 2 D2
Internet Cybercafé...................3 F2
Tourist Office...........................4 F2

EATING p342
Gouveia.................................11 E2
Tapioca Stands.......................12 F2
Zumbi....................................13 G1

SIGHTS & ACTIVITIES p341
Museu Théo Brandão................5 C2

TRANSPORT p342
Jangadas to Reef....................14 F2

which travelers consistently agree is a more pleasant place to stay.

Orientation

The heart of Recife ranges along the river-front in the Boa Vista district, across the Rio Capibaribe to the Santo Antônio district and then across to Ilha do Recife which holds the historical Recife Antigo district. All are connected by bridges. Boa Viagem is a wealthy beachside neighborhood 6km south of the center which is divided into three zones called *jardins*.

Information
INTERNET ACCESS
Instituto Porto Digital (Av Barbosa Lima 149, Recife Antigo) Offers one hour free Internet access from 4pm to 6pm on weekdays.

Multilink (Av Conselheiro Aguiar 2966, Loja 4, Boa Viagem; 24 hrs Thu-Sun) Near Albergue Maracatus.

Telefe (Av Conde da Boa Vista 56; US$1.50 per hr; until 10:30pm)

MONEY
Bradesco (Av Guararapes, Boa Vista)

TOURIST OFFICES
Tourist Information booths are in the following locations:
Airport (0xx81-3462-4960; 24 hr)
Boa Viagem (0xx81-3463-3621; Praça de Boa Viagem; 8am-8pm)
Recife Antigo (0xx81-3224-2361; 9am-9pm)
TIP (7am-7pm)

TRAVEL AGENCIES
Andratur (0xx81-3465-8588; Av Conselheiro Aguiar 3150, Loja 5, Boa Viagem) Provides tickets at discounted prices.

Sights & Activities

Serpents gape, buttocks bulge, reptiles emerge from their shells and jaws gape skyward at the **Oficina Cerâmica Francisco Brennand** (Várzea; admission US$1; 8am-5pm Mon-Thu, 8am-4pm Fri). The artist revitalized his family's abandoned roof and floor tile factory to create his own line of decorative ceramic tiles. The rest of the huge space is dedicated to a seemingly exhaustive exhibition of his bizarre sculptures, including extensive gardens with Moorish arches and gliding swans.

BRAZIL

A trip out to this forested suburb is a regional highlight, so bring a picnic and spend some time. To get there, take the UR7-Várzea bus from the main post office downtown on Av Guararapes to the end of the line (35 minutes). From there catch a taxi (US$2) as the several kilometers walk is not safe.

The **Museu do Homem do Nordeste** (Av 17 de Agosto 2187, Casa Forte; admission US$2; ☺ 11am-5pm Tue-Fri, 1-5pm Sat & Sun) has anthropological exhibits on northeastern life ranging from slave chains to Carnaval costumes, with good photos throughout. The museum is extensive and well-done, so give yourself at least an hour. To get there, catch the Dois Irmãos bus from the main post office on Av Guararapes downtown. Also worthwhile is the **Museu de Arte Moderna** (Rua da Aurora 265; admission US$0.35; ☺ noon-6pm Tue-Sun), where exhibits depart the realm of the serious. A great place to be on a Sunday is in **Parque 13 de Maio**. Brazilians don't just sit around their parks, they break dance, argue politics, and practice their back flips.

Highlights of the old city include the **Igreja da Ordem Terceira de São Francisco** (Rua Imperador Pedro II; ☺ 8-11am, 2-5pm Mon-Fri, 8-11:30am Sat), a church dating from 1697 whose Capela Dourada (Golden Chapel) is one of the finest examples of Brazilian baroque. The **Forte das Cinco Pontas** (Tr do Fortes; ☺ 9am-5pm Tue-Fri, 1-5pm Sat & Sun) is down to four points after having one removed by the Portuguese to make it less Dutch, but is only worthwhile for those with a deep affection for forts.

GETTING INTO TOWN

The Terminal Integrado de Passageiros (TIP) – a combined long-distance bus station and metro terminal – is 14km southwest of the center. From the TIP to all Recife and Olinda destinations, catch a metro train to the Estacão Recife stop (US$0.30, 25 minutes) and catch a bus or *kombi* from there. For Boa Viagem, catch the Setubal (Príncipe) bus. For Olinda, catch the Rio Doce/Princesa Isabel bus.

From the airport (10km south of the center), the Aeroporto bus goes to Boa Viagem and then Av Dantas Barreto in the center. For Olinda, take this bus to Recife's Av NS do Carmo and pick up a Casa Caiada bus there.

Locals don't seem to have a problem going to the beach in Boa Viagem to escape Recife's muggy heat, but you'll find cleaner water further south at **Praia Enseada dos Corais**, **Praia Gaibu** or **Praia Calhetas**.

Festivals & Events

Recife and Olinda hold one of Brazil's most colorful and folkloric Carnavals. The few months leading up to Carnaval, which are filled with parties and public rehearsals, are almost as fun as the actual event. Carnaval groups and spectators deck themselves out in elaborate costumes such as *maracatu* (warrior with a huge headpiece and a flower in his mouth), *caboclo* (indigenous/African mix), colonial era royalty, harlequin, bull, and *frevo* (crop tops with ruffled sleeves for both genders and a tiny umbrella), and shimmy for days to frenetic *frevo* music. Recife's action concentrates downtown along Av Guararapes.

Recife also hosts an out-of-season Carnaval in the last week in October called Recifolia. Over two million people crowd the streets during this Salvador-style Carnaval, dancing to Bahian bands for seven days straight.

Sleeping

The *centro* is close to nightlife, but Boa Viagem is more pleasant.

BOA VIAGEM

Albergue Maracatus do Recife (☎ 0xx81-3326-1221; alberguemaracatus@yahoo.com; Rua Maria Carolina 185; dm/d US$7/13; ☁) Dorm rooms have only four beds and kitchen privileges are offered at this hostel, though sheet and towel rental is US$2. It offers HI member discount.

Albergue Boa Viagem (☎ 0xx81-3326-9572; albergueboaviagem@ieg.com.br; Rua Aviador Severiano Lins 455; dm US$7, s/d US$12/13; ☁) This hostel sprung up recently. Sheet and towel rental is US$2.

CENTRO

Hotél Central (☎ 0xx81-3423-6411; info@hotelcentral.com.br; Rua Manoel Borba 209; s/d US$8/11, s/d with bath US$11/13) Bright rooms with high ceilings and a location on a tree-shaded street make this semi-shabby 1930s hotel the best budget option in the center.

Hotel Park 13 de Maio (☎ 0xx81-3231-7627; hotelpark@ieg.com.br; Rua do Hospício 671; s/d US$7/8, with bath US$9/11; ❌) It has a little of that fading tropical grandeur look going for it, but is basically just a passable hotel on a busy street.

Eating

Vinagreto (Rua do Hospício 203) or the nearby **Salada Mista** (Rua do Hospício 50) are classy self-service lunch restaurants in the center.

At night it should be easy to find something to your liking around the lively Pátio de São Pedro, a colonial inner patio lined with restaurants and bars. The partially-restored Recife Antigo offers a wide variety of flavors.

Brotfabrik (Rua da Moeda 87) This place serves high-quality pastries and snacks.

Sabor de Beijo (Av Conselheiro Aguiar 2994) It's a very popular self-service lunch place.

Venetia (Rua Júlio Pires, Segunda Jardim) Serves up pizza, pasta and meat dishes.

Boa Viagem has many restaurants, but apart from those in the Polo Pina area (see p346, Drinking), which has a concentrated assortment of bars and restaurants, they're scattered.

Drinking

Recife Antigo (aka Polo Bom Jesus) comes alive at night, with small, arty bars and lots of outdoor tables, concentrated along Rua Bom Jesus. Popular dancing spots include **O Depois** (Av Rio Branco 66), **Downtown** (Rua Vigário Tenório 105) and **Calypso** (Rua Bom Jesus 147), which

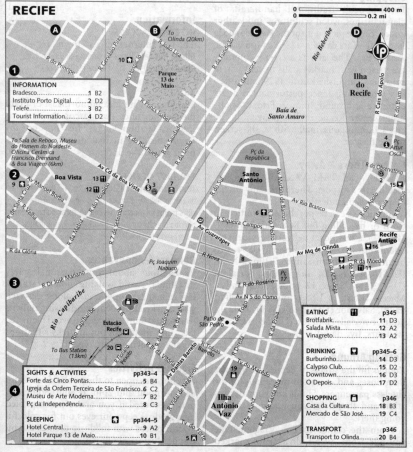

have live music and DJ nights. Rua da Moeda and **Burburinho** (Rua Tomzinha 106) are known to be frequented by the 'alternative' crowd. Another favourite hangout is the Patio de São Pedro in the *centro*, with a night of Afro-Brazilian rhythms such as *afoxé* and *maracatu* called Terça Negra (Black Tuesday).

As for Boa Viagem, bars are concentrated in the less interesting Polo Pina, and there is one dance club.

Theatro (Av Boa Viagem 760, Segunda Jardim) This place plays everything from *pagode* to electronica.

Sala de Reboco (Rua Gregorio 264, Cordeiro) The best *forró* in the city can be found here.

Shopping

Pernambuco's traditional handicrafts of clay figurines, wood sculptures and leather goods, can be picked up at the **Mercado do São José** or the **Casa da Cultura** (🕑 9am-7pm Mon-Sat, 9am-2pm Sun). The later is a creepy colonial-era prison with market stalls in cells where prisoners languished until 1979, and often has music and dance performances at its entrance at around 3pm on Friday. Shopping Center Recife in Boa Viagem is the city's humongous mall with a six-screen movie theater.

Getting There & Away

BRA, Fly, Gol, TAM, VASP and Varig service Recife's airport. There are daily flights to any Brazilian destination.

Bus tickets can be purchased at outlets in town or by calling **Disk Rodoviária** (🕿 0xx81-3452-3990), a bus ticket delivery service. Frequent buses go to João Pessoa (US$4, two hours, hourly) from 5am to 7:30pm, Natal (US$10, 4½ hours, nine daily), Fortaleza (US$23 to US$33, 12 hours, four daily), Maceio (US$6 to US$9, four hours, eight daily), Salvador (US$26 to US$30, 11 to 12 hours, two daily) and Rio (US$58 to US$70, 42 hours, five daily).

Getting Around

Kombis fill the streets of Recife, are quicker than buses and are often more helpful for clueless passengers. Shout out your destination and they'll let you know if they're going there.

From the center to Boa Viagem, take any bus from Av NS do Carmo marked

Aeroporto, Shopping Center, Candeias or Piedade. To return to the center, take any bus marked Dantas Barreto along Av Engenheiro Domingos Ferreira, three blocks from the beach.

OLINDA

The part of Olinda that will interest you is the historical center: sleepy streets lined with pastel-colored houses and packed with churches wind their way around a few hills with an ocean backdrop. Since most buildings are private homes, it may take a few days to penetrate to the artists, students and bohemians that fill this neighborhood. This is one of Brazil's best-preserved colonial cities and, together with Recife, is one of the major cultural centers of the northeast.

Information

INTERNET ACCESS

The two Internet cafés in town are:
Olinda Net Café (Praça do Carmo 5-B; US$2 per hr)
Olind@.com (Praça João Pessoa 15; US$2 per hr)

MONEY

Many banks are located northeast of Praça do Carmo, once Av Marcos Freire turns into Av Getulio Vargas. Just hop on any *kombi* heading in that direction and it'll drop you at the door.

TOURIST OFFICES

Tourist Information Post (🕿 0xx81-3305-1048; Praça do Carmo 100; 🕑 8am-noon, 2-5:30pm Mon-Fri) The city's tourist information has English-speaking pre-teens offering church tour maps, basic information and their services as a free guide.

Dangers & Annoyances

Be cautious about your personal safety in Olinda. Avoid walking alone or carrying valuables at night, and along deserted streets. The city recommends using only its free yellow-shirted guides to avoid being fed false information or put in sticky situations involving payment discrepancies.

Sights & Activities

All churches open to the public do so from 8am to noon and 2pm to 5pm. Some can only be toured if you arrive accompanied by a guide. Keep your eyes out for colorful graffiti pieces with folkloric themes as you wander historical Olinda.

Climb Rua de São Francisco to the **Alto da Sé** (Cathedral Heights), where there are craft stalls and an awesome view. The 1537 **Igreja da Sé** (Rua Bispo Coutinho) has had its facade redone at least four times to change with architectural fashions. There is often a *capoeira* or dance show around 3pm on Sunday afternoons in front of **Gres Preto Velho**. The 1696 **Museu de Arte Sacra de Pernambuco** (Rua Bispo Coutinho; admission US$0.35; ☉ 9am-1pm Mon-Fri) has displays on the city and sacred-art, including a modern representation of Christ bearing the cross dressed as a communist. Just down the street is **Loja Ecológica** (Rua Bispo Coutinho), a row of shops facing a courtyard where dancers will put on a *frevo* demonstration and mini-lesson for a small donation.

If you'd like to check out a *capoeira* school, **Angola Mãe** (Rua Ilma Cunha 243) makes for an almost spiritual experience. To get there, turn up the dirt alley and rap the metal gate painted in zebra stripes. The school welcomes visitors to take classes or watch an open *roda* (circle) at 6pm on Sunday. Come with a respectful attitude and unaccompanied by a guide.

Museu do Mamulengo (Rua do Amparo 59; admission US$0.35; ☉ 8am-5pm Tue-Fri, 10am-5pm Sat & Sun) displays wooden hand puppets typical of the northeast, including an animated display of bandits attacking white plantation owners, complete with puppet blood. A couple of doors down, the **Casa dos Bonecos Gigantes** (Rua do Amparo 45; admission

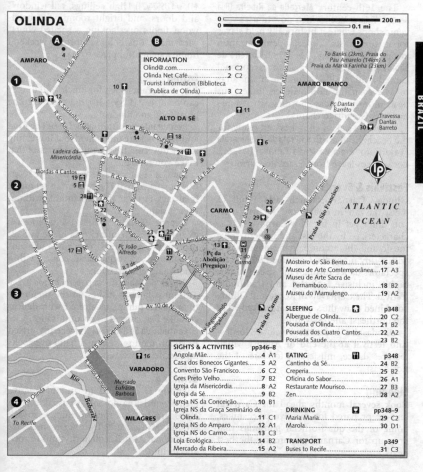

US$0.65; 🕑 8am-1pm, 2-6pm Mon-Sat) houses giant papier-mâché Carnaval puppets that can weigh up to 13kg. The dolls are mostly of known local figures, but politicians and major companies also have them created in their likeness as propaganda.

Though capable of putting on some interesting exhibits, the most fascinating thing about the **Museu de Arte Contemporânea** (Rua 13 de Maio; admission US$0.35; 🕑 9am-noon, 2-5pm Tue-Fri, 2-5pm Sat & Sun) is its past as an 18th-century Inquisition jail. Men and women were kept separated, probably not a lasting arrangement as there is a deep toilet hole in the wall over which they could pass. Guards kept an eye on the whole thing through the holes in the heavy wooden doors.

The 16th-century **Mercado da Ribeira** (Rua Bernardo Vieira de Melo), which now houses souvenir shops where it historically held slaves for auction, hosts a *capoeira* demonstration at 6pm on Saturday. The 1582 **Mosteiro de São Bento** (Rua São Bento) has an exceptional carved and guilded wooden main altar to awe even the non-believer. Poke your head in on a Sunday morning when mass includes Gregorian chants.

If you are sick of churches and ready for the beach, head north to **Praia do Pau Amarelo** (14km) or **Praia da Maria Farinha** (23km). Local buses leave from Praça do Carmo.

Festivals & Events

Olinda's Carnaval, which lasts a full 11 days, has an intimacy and security that you don't get in big city Carnavals. It is characterized by the fast and frenetic *frevo* music and the accompanying dance done with a tiny umbrella. Costumed *blocos* and spectators dance through the streets in this highly inclusive, colorful and traditional festival. The Carnavals of Recife and Olinda combined draw the second largest crowd in the northeast after Salvador.

Olinda also hosts the Folclore Nordestino festival at the end of August which features dance, music and folklore of the northeast.

Sleeping

Book several months ahead for Carnaval and be prepared for massive price hikes. Some of the quasi-official *pousadas* that crop up for Carnaval are among the best deals.

Pousada d'Olinda (☎ 0xx81-3494-2559; sbai@pousadadolinda.com.br; Praça João Alfredo 178; dm US$6, s/d US$12/17; 🅿️ 🖫) A central table area and lawn make this pretty *pousada* very social, and rooms are well-finished. Isa loves to dance and is always gathering groups to go out.

Albergue de Olinda (☎ 0xx81-3429-1592; alberguedeolinda@alberguedeolinda.com.br; Rua do Sol 233; dm/d US$7/16; 🖫) Modern rooms have a pretty garden, but the traffic noise is constant. It offers HI member discount.

Pousada Saude (☎ 0xx81-3494-6123; Rua 7 de Setembro 8; s/d US$5/10) Staying here feels like renting a room in a not very plush home. Guests have use of the kitchen.

Pousada dos Quatro Cantos (☎ 0xx81-3429-0220; hotel@pousada4cantos.com.br; Rua Prudente dos Morais 441; s/d US$20/24) High ceilings, tall windows and doors, and bright rooms with hardwood floors overlooking a shaded courtyard make this colonial former weekend home a delightful place to stay.

Eating

Few restaurants open for lunch, and dinner can be pricey (US$5–10), but there is some great food in Olinda.

Restaurante Mourisco (Praça do Carmo) The food and salad bar are quite good, but it is eating under towering trees wrapped in vines that make you return.

Zen (Rua Bernardo Veira de Melo 157; 🕑 1-8:30pm Mon-Sat; set menu US$3) The vegetarian set menu is always tasty at this restaurant, without even a sign.

Creperia (Praça João Alfredo 168; salad for two US$2) The spinach and ricotta crepe (US$2) makes for a nice break from rice and beans and the mixed veggie salad comes with a true vinaigrette dressing.

Oficina do Sabor (baked pumpkin for two US$10) The most famous dishes on the menu are their baked pumpkins stuffed with delicacies like fish cooked in coconut sauce.

Cantinho da Sé (Ladeira da Sé) Decently priced Brazilian food served on a patio overlooking Recife.

Drinking

Nightlife is clustered in an unattractive area around Rua do Sol. As usual, certain clubs are hot on specific nights, so ask around. Music varies from *forró* and *afoxé* (traditional Afro-Brazilian rhythm) to rock and techno.

Maria Maria (Rua do Sol 225) A good dance floor with a gay-friendly reputation.

Marola (Travessa Dantas Barreto) A small waterfront bar with a twinkling light ambience and live *MPB*.

Getting There & Around
From outside Recife's central metro station, catch a Rio Doce/Princesa Isabel bus and get off at Praça do Carmo. Any Rio Doce, Casa Caiada or Jardim Atlantico bus will take you from central Recife to Olinda. *Kombis* are often a quicker and cheaper way to get around, plus everyone inside will help you get to your destination.

CARUARU
Modern and without architectural appeal, this inland market city contains unexpected cultural riches. Known as the Capital of Forró, Caruaru hosts the largest *forró* festival in the country – 30 straight days of couples swaying to the accordion and triangle. It is also South America's center for ceramic-figurine art, famous for brightly painted little people captured enacting daily activities such as chasing chickens or getting teeth pulled.

Off Rua José de Vasconcelos, on the broad Patio do Forró is a tall brick smokestack. Below it is the **Museu do Forró** (8am-5pm Tue-Sat, 9am-1pm Sun) displaying every bit of memorabilia on Luis Gonzaga, the father of *forró* music, they could get their hands on. There is a side bonus room on the singer Elba Ramalho, which includes her Playboy shots. Upstairs is the **Museu do Barro**, displaying the ceramics of accomplished local potters, including the most famous of all, Mestre Vitalino. He began creating figurines as a child for his own amusement, accidentally discovering his pastime could be lucrative while hanging out at the market one day. It's worth going out to **Alto de Moura**, 6km out of town, where Vitalino lived and worked and where his descendents carry on the tradition. Prices are usually better here and you can see the artists at work. Figurines and other crafts are also available at the **Feira do Artesenato** (Mon-Sat), an open-air market in the city center. Wednesday and Saturday are the big days for the adjoining **Feira Livre**, a huge market selling everything from undies to cashews.

Moto-taxis are a thrilling and cheap way to get around in Caruaru. Buses run between Recife and Caruaru every half hour (*opcional* US$4, one hour and 40 minutes; *comun* US$3, two hours and 10 minutes). The bus station is 3km from the center – ask to be let off close to the market.

JACUMÃ
Jacumã has a long, thin beach featuring colored sandbars, natural pools and mineral springs by day, and *forró* bars by night. There are beautiful beaches nearby, such as **Praia do Amor** to the north, and **Praia dos Coqueirinhos** and **Praia de Tambaba** (the only official and regulated nudist beach in the northeast) to the south. If you are looking for a simple, unpolished fishing village with a relatively mellow tourism scene, this is it. There are no banks.

The Swedish-owned **Hotel Viking** (0xx83-290-1015; info@hotelviking.com.br; s/d US$10/13;), perched on a hill overlooking town, is easily identified by the Viking ship on its water tower. It has comfortable, decorated rooms and a pool area with theme park touches. The adjoining restaurant has live music in summer. It's a quick walk from the final bus stop.

For a more natural environment, try **Pousada das Flores** (0xx83-9309-0414; r per person US$10), south of Jacumã on Praia de Carapibus. Round bungalows are scattered through a gorgeous garden, and guests have kitchen use. It's a long, hot walk out from town, so catch the Jacumã PB008 bus from João Pessoa and ask to be let off at Carapibus.

Peixada de Jacumã, on the waterfront in the center of town, serves up the town's fresh seafood. **Zekas**, near the main road leading to Praia de Carapibus, has great views and tasty traditional meat and bean soups.

Traveling north from Pernambuco on Hwy BR-101, ask to be dropped off at the Conde/Jacumã turn-off and catch a local bus from there. In João Pessoa, 'Jacumã' buses (US$1, 1¼ hours, hourly until 9:10pm) leave from the third platform in front of the long-distance bus station. The last bus to João Pessoa leaves at 10:20pm from the main road in Jacumã's center.

JOÃO PESSOA
João Pessoa is an unremarkable seaside capital without a whole lot going on. The

beachfront area of Tambaú is 7km east of the center and much more pleasant.

David, the American owner of **Gameleira Internet** (Av João Maurício 157, Manaira; US$1 per hr), just north of Tambaú, is a good information source. The **Tourist Information** (☎ 0xx800-281-9229; Av Almirante Tamandaré 100, Tambaú; ☻ 8am-8pm) has English-speakers and a post in the airport.

Sights & Activities

Allow at least an hour for a docent-led tour of the **Centro Cultural de São Francisco** (admission US$0.65; ☻ 9am-noon, 2-5pm). The center is a beautiful, architecturally confused religious complex built over three centuries due to interrupting battles with the Dutch and French. None of its chapels are still in use. It is worth touring to see floor tiles inlaid with myrrh resin, bats hanging from the ornate Baroque chapel carvings and the extremely good popular-art collection that fills the upper floor.

The city beaches of **Praia Cabo Branco** and **Praia Tambaú** are rather built up but tranquil. It is a gorgeous 15km walk south from Praia Cabo Branco to **Ponta de Seixas**, the easternmost tip of South America. The northern beaches are nice as well.

Sleeping

It's worth spending a bit extra to stay near Praia Tambaú.

Pousada do Caju (☎ 0xx83-247-8231; reservas@pousadadocaju.com.br; Rua Helena Meira Lima 269, Tambaú; s/d US$15/22; ☒ ☒) A colorful, sprawling maze of pools and plants.

Hotel Pousada Mar Azul (☎ 0xx83-226-2660; Av João Maurício 315, Tambaú; d US$8) A no-frills place on the waterfront with large, well-priced rooms with kitchenettes.

Hotel Aurora (☎ 0xx83-241-3238; Praça João Pessoa 41, Centro; s/d US$6/12; ☒) A dark but adequate hotel with cheap *quartos* too.

Hotel Rio Verde (☎ 0xx83-241-6141; Rua Duque de Caxias 111, Centro; s/d US$4/6; ☒) The quality of the breakfast surpasses that of the simple windowless, cement block *apartamentos*.

Eating

At Tambaú, tons of restaurants and bars sit two blocks deep along the waterfront.

Peixada do Duda (Av General Édson Ramalho 147, Tambaú) The inexpensive seafood and *ensopado de caranguejo* (crab stew) are superb.

Mangai (Av General Édson Ramalho 696, Tambaú) The regional buffet is excellent at this alcohol-free restaurant.

Cassino da Lagoa (Centro) The seafood and chicken dishes are recommended at this restaurant overlooking the Lagoa.

Natural (Rua Rodrigues de Aquino 177, Centro) Serves a good vegetarian lunch.

Getting There & Around

TAM, VASP and Varig service João Pessoa's airport (11km west of the center).

Frequent buses go to Recife (US$4, two hours, hourly), from 5am to 7pm, Natal (US$5, three hours, eight daily), Fortaleza (US$16, 10 hours, two daily) and Salvador (US$31, 14 hours, daily). Bus Nos 510 and 511 go to Tambaú from the first platform in front of the bus station. Most local buses also pass the Lagoa in the center.

PRAIA DA PIPA

A living tourism brochure, Pipa is one of the northeast's hippest beach towns with dolphin-filled waters and pristine beaches backed by tall cliffs. Don't let the few boutiques along the main drag fool you; a youthful, laidback vibe dominates Pipa and natural beauty abounds. The nightly tradition is to see and be seen in the center and then head up the main road to the dance clubs pumping *forró*, reggae and techno. On Saturday nights the *capoeira* school takes over the street in front of the hotspot **Blue Bar**. There are no banks and Internet access is pricey.

Southernmost of the beaches is **Praia do Amor**. North of town, **Praia dos Golfinhos** is accessible only via the beach and is closed off by high tide. You can get to **Praia do Madeiro** from Golfinhos or by catching a *kombi* leaving town, then descend the stairs at Village Natureza. Surf lessons and boards are available in town.

On the road leading into town is **Santuário Ecológico** (admission US$1; ☻ 8am-5pm Mon-Sat, 8am-1pm Sun), a small flora and fauna reserve worth visiting just for the spectacular views.

Sleeping

Reservations are required for all major holidays.

Pousada da Pipa (☎ 0xx84-246-2271; pousadadapipa@uol.com.br; Rua do Cruzeiro; s/d US$8/13) A green front patio and an entire porch of hammocks with a sea view make this a very social *pousada*. Located on a cul-de-sac down from the pharmacy.

Pousada Manolo (☎ 0xx84-246-2328; pousada manolo@pipa.com.br; Rua do Bem-te-Vis; s/d US$8/17) The rooms are well-ventilated and the location is good.

Pousada Aconchego (☎ 0xx84-246-2439; aconch ego@bluemail.ch; Rua do Céu 100; s/d US$13/17) Spacious bungalows with hammocks with a few green, flowery bushes. Up the street from the bookshop.

Camping Refugio Capitão (☎ 0xx84-246-2206; refugcap@bol.com.br; Rua do Bem-te-Vis; camping/cabins per person US$3/7) This spacious, shady campground has a well-equipped outdoor kitchen. It also has a couple of decent cabins.

Eating
Casa da Farinha (main street) An excellent bakery with a sandwich grill.

Chez Liz (main street; soup US$1) Tasty meat or veggie soups are the only thing on the menu at this French-owned café.

Altas Horas (main street) A decent *prato feito (pf)* at a decent price.

Tá Massa (Rua da Gameleira; pastas US$2) A cozy nook with well-seasoned pastas.

Companhia da Sopa (Rua da Gameleira; cakes US$1) Searching for the best chocolate cake in Brazil? It's here.

Getting There & Away
Seven buses leave Natal daily for Pipa (US$3, one hour and 40 minutes), with three on Sunday. If you're coming from the south, get off at Goaininha, 1½ hours from João Pessoa. *Kombis* (US$0.85, 40 minutes) for Pipa leave from behind the church. Taxis cost US$8.

Pipa Tour Ecotourismo, behind Blue Bar, posts bus schedules.

NATAL
Brazil's 'sun city,' Natal, is a clean, well laid-out capital. Even the center seems under control in this rather bland city. Most travelers stop here long enough to race down the faces of the sand dunes in a beach-buggy or on a sandboard (even though this risks damaging the dunes). Another draw is Carnatal, Natal's Salvador-style, out-of-season Carnaval in the first week of December.

Information
There is a bar offering **Internet access** (US$2 per hr; ☉ 8:30pm-5am) on Praia das Artistas. There is a **Banco do Brasil** (Av Rio Branco) and a **Bradesco** (Av Rio Branco) in the center. There are **tourist information** booths with very limited information at the airport, Rodoviária Nova, Praia dos Artistas, Casa da Cultura and Praia Shopping.

Sights & Activities
Enjoy a *tapioca* ice cream where the Portuguese struggled to repel French invasion in the late 16th century at the **Forte dos Reis Magos** (US$0.65; ☉ 8am-4:30pm). The views of the city and the dunes across the Rio Potengi are fantastic from this prime location at the tip of a peninsula north of town.

Natal's city beaches stretch over 9km south from the fort to Farol de Mãe Luiza lighthouse. To the north are the dunes of **Genipabu**, which can be toured on beach-buggy excursions offered by a host of would-be Ayrton Sennas. You'll be asked if you want the trip *com emoção* (with emotion) and if you agree, you'll be treated to thrills such as Wall of Death and Vertical Descent. An eight-hour trip costs around US$13 per person and can be lined up through tour agencies. It is possible to go all the way to Fortaleza by beach buggy – 760km of beautiful coastline.

Sleeping
Most backpackers stay with Tia Helena. If you don't, Praia das Artistas is far preferable to the center, where budget hotels are dilapidated.

Albergue Pousada Meu Canto (☎ 0xx84-212-2811; Rua Ana Neri, Petrópolis; dm US$5) Within minutes Tia Helena will add you to her international family at this simple *pousada* with pretty greenery. Take bus No 21 and get off at the first stop on Rua Manoel Dantas.

Hotel Beira Mar (☎ 0xx84-202-1470; Av Presidente Café Filho 886, Praia das Artistas; s/d US$8/10; ⊠) Basic rooms are rounded out by the TV, mini-fridge and hammock at this breezy, oceanfront hotel.

Hotel Miami Beach (☎ 0xx84-202-3377; Av Governador Sílvio Pedrosa 24, Praia das Artistas; s/d US$10/15; ⊠) The entire hotel has recently been renovated and hung with shiny, stylish fixtures.

BRAZIL

Hotel Sol (☎ 0xx84-221-1157; Rua Dr Heitor Carrilho 107, Centro; s/d US$10/13; ❄) Bright, decent rooms equipped with mini-fridge, TV and a view.

Hotel Natal (☎ 0xx84-222-2792; hotelnatal@terra .com.br; Av Rio Branco 740, Centro; s/d US$4/6; ❄) The rooms need a paint, but Natal is one of the better downtown budget hotels.

Eating

A Macrobiótica (Rua Princesa Isabel 528, Centro; per kg US$4) The food may be a bit flavorless, but the veggies and soy abound.

Center Pão (Av Rio Branco 553, Centro) This place is packed with locals picking up tasty savory and sweet snacks. Great for a light lunch.

O Crustáceo (Rua Apodi 414, Centro) This place has a good atmosphere and tasty seafood. It serves lunch only.

Mamma Itália (Rua Silvio Pedrosa 43, Praia das Artistas, Centro; dishes US$5) The spinach and ricotta ravioli is divine at this fine Italian restaurant.

Drinking

Piató Café (Rua Apodi 222, Centro) A walled refuge with tables set out on a lawn and live music on Friday.

Chaplin (Av Presidente Café Filho 27, Praia dos Artistas; cover US$5) Thursday and Saturday are the happening nights at this huge club with six dance floors playing different music. Look for a flier at your hotel for 50% off the cover. On Thursday, women get in free.

NATAL

0 — 200 m
0 — 0.1 mi

To Forte dos Reis Magos
(1km) & Genipabu (20km)

Praia do Meio

ROCAS

R Décio Fonseca
R São João de Deus
R São Sebastião
São Jorge
Pinto
R Simões
R do Areial

Av Presidente Café Filho
R da Esperança

Port Area
Av Duque de Caxias
Rio Potengi
R Branco
R Silva Jardim
R Gen Elyceno

Praia dos Artistas

ATLANTIC OCEAN

Av Tavares de Lira
Rua Gen Gustavo C de Farias
Av Getúlio Vargas

Praia da Areia Preta

AREIA PRETA

RIBERIA
Pç Augusto Severo
R Sachet
Train Station
R Henrique Castriciano
R Manoel Dantas
Av Deodoro da Fonseca
Av Floriano Peixoto
R Ana Neri
Av Nilo Peçanha

PETRÓPOLIS

R Juvino Barreto
R Train
Av Hermes da Fonseca

To Farol de Mãe Luiza (8km)
& Ponta Negra (13km)

R Auta de Souza
R Mipibu
To Airport (15km)
R Caldas
R Mossoró
Av Campos Sales
Av Rodrigues Alves
Av Prudente de Morais
Av Afonso Pena

CENTRO
R João Pessoa
R Açu
R Barcelonel
R Princesa Isabel
Rua Dr Heitor Carrilho
R Jundiaí

Rua Profesor Zuza
To Rodoviária
Nova (6km)
R Apodi

Forró com Turista (Centro do Tourismo, Rua Aderbal Figueiredo 980; ☽ Thu night) The name of this local staple may be cheesy, but dancing to live *forró* in an open courtyard is actually a blast.

The rest of the city's nightlife concentrates in Ponta Negra, 14km south.

Getting There & Around

Natal's airport is served by BRA, Fly, Trip, TAM, Varig, and VASP. Flights out of Natal are more expensive than those out of Recife or Fortaleza.

Long-distance buses leave the Rodoviária Nova (new bus station), 6km south of the center, for Fortaleza (US$13, eight hours, eight daily), Recife (US$11, 4½ hours, nine daily), João Pessoa (US$5, three hours, eight daily) and Salvador (US$35, 20 hours, two daily). The Rodoviária Velha (old bus station) is the hub for destinations in the city, such as Praia dos Artistas (Nos 21 and 38) and beaches as far north as Genipabu.

Bus A-Aeroporto runs between the Rodoviária Velha and the airport (15km south). Bus Nos 38 and 20 connect the two bus stations.

CANOA QUEBRADA

A quiet fishing village of aging hippies, Canoa Quebrada is perched between white dunes and sienna ocean cliffs. A healthy variety of restaurants and a few shops line one main sand street, and mellow nightlife is limited to the weekends. The narrow beaches are not Brazil's best, but a buggy tour of the surrounding dunes and beaches like **Morro Branco** will reveal the area's beauty. There are no banking facilities.

Many *pousadas* and restaurants are foreign-owned and high quality. Two clean, basic options are the friendly **Pousada do Holandês** (☎ 0xx88-421-7129; Rua Nascer do Sol 128; r per person US$7) and **Pousada Alternativa** (Rua Francisco Craço; r per person US$5). **Pousada Oásis do Rei** (☎ 0xx88-421-7081; Rua Nascer do Sol 112; s/d US$12/17; ⚒) has well-finished but poorly ventilated rooms in a garden setting and a great breakfast view. On the cliffs at the end of the main road, **Pousada Lua Morena** (☎ 0xx88-421-7030; luamorena@secrel.com.br; s/d US$13/20; ⚒) is a breezy seafront village of cottages.

At **Cabana** (main road; dishes US$3) a single portion of sumptuous chicken Roquefort can feed two if you aren't starving.

From Natal, catch a bus to Aracati (US$8, six hours, four daily) and then a bus (last one at 6:30pm Sunday to Wednesday) or taxi (US$4) the remaining 13km to Canoa. There are four daily buses from Fortaleza to Canoa (US$4, 3½ hours).

FORTALEZA

Fortaleza is the northeast's second-largest city and a major fishing port and commercial center. There are a few historical buildings with pretty facades scattered around the center, but Fortaleza is mostly a gritty, modern city. There are no extremely unique sights but the nightlife is pretty happening, so for most travelers this is just a necessary stop. In the last week of July, Bahian tunes shake up Fortaleza during Fortal, a Salvador-style, out-of-season Carnaval.

Orientation

To get to Praia Iracema from the bus station, cross busy Av Borges de Melo and catch the Mucuripe bus in front of the Telemar building. The air-con Guanabara Top Bus loops from the airport and bus station (both about 6km south of the center) through the center and on to Praias Iracema and Meireles.

Information

INTERNET ACCESS

Limatur (Av Almirante Barroso 977; US$1 per hr) Offers the cheapest Internet access in Iracema and sells bus tickets.

MONEY

Banco do Brasil (Centro Cultural Dragão do Mar) The ATM here takes Visa.

TOURIST OFFICES

There are tourist information booths at the bus station, airport, **Praça da Ferreira** (☽ 9am-1pm & 2-5pm Mon-Fri), **Centro de Turismo** (Ensetur; ☽ 8am-6pm Mon-Sat, 8am-noon Sun), Mercado Central, **Praia do Iracema** (☽ 9am-1pm & 2-10pm) and **Praia do Nautico in Meireles** (☽ 9am-1pm, 2-10pm). The state also operates a toll-free tourism hotline (☎ 0800-99-1516).

Dangers & Annoyances

Travelers have reported pickpocketing in the city center, petty theft on the beaches, and solicitous females who cuddle up to male travelers on the beaches, drug their drinks and take their valuables.

BRAZIL

BRAZIL

Sights & Activities

The **Centro Cultural Dragão do Mar** includes a planetarium, cinemas, theaters, galleries and the **Museu de Arte Contemporanea** (admission US$0.65; 9am-5:30pm Tue-Thu, 2-9:30pm Fri-Sun). There are good exhibits on the state's history and anthropology at the **Museu do Ceará** (Rua São Paulo 51; admission US$0.65; 8:30am-5pm Tue-Sat, noon-5pm Sun), including one on four fishermen who sailed from Praia de Iracema to Rio in 1941 to bring their life of 'misery and suffering' to the attention of the federal government. Above the tourist office in the Centro de Turismo is the one-room **Museu de Arte e Cultura Populares** (admission US$0.35), displaying folk art from woodblock prints to incredibly intricate colored sand bottles.

Praia de Iracema has a bit of a bohemian atmosphere, but **Praia do Meireles** has a much more attractive waterfront with leafy trees and active daytime beach bars. Locals pack **Praia do Futuro** on weekends, the cleaner and more popular of the three city beaches. **Praia Icaraí** (16km west) is a good out-of-town beach.

Sleeping

Praia de Iracema tends to be the cheaper of the two beach areas, which are much nicer places to stay than the center.

Albergue da Juventude Atalaia (0xx85-219-0658; pousada@pousadaatalaia.com.br; Av Beira Mar 814, Praia de Iracema; dm US$7, s/d US$13/17;) The rooms are bright and modern at this hostel, which is the nicest in Iracema.

Aquarius Pousada (0xx85-248-0778; aquarius@aquariuspousada.com.br; Rua Carlos Vasconcelos 308, Praia de Iracema; s/d US$12/15;) Away from the waterfront, Aquarius' comfortable rooms surround a green, inner courtyard.

Turismo Praia Hotel (0xx85-219-6133; turismo praia@aol.com.br; Av Beira Mar 894, Praia de Iracema; s/d US$12/17;) Rooms are bright, well-finished and equipped with a mini-fridge and TV.

Pousada Abril em Portugal (0xx85-219-9509; Av Almirante Barroso 1006, Praia de Iracema; r per person US$5) This dark, run-down *pousada* has Iracema's cheapest private rooms and for unknown reasons persists as a backpacker haven.

Backpackers, CE (0xx85-3091-8997; backpackers@hotmail.com; Rua Monsenhor Bruno 742, Praia de Meireles;

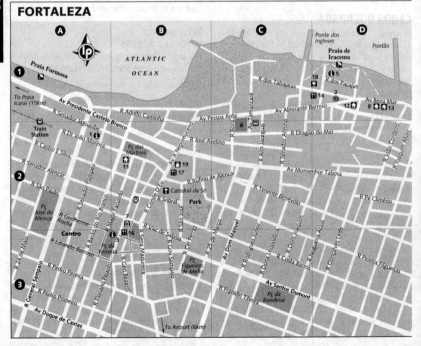

FORTALEZA

r per person US$5) The vibe is super informal at this hostel in the home of two young women. Guests have use of the kitchen and washing machine.

Hotel Passeio (☎ 0xx85-226-9640; Rua Dr João Moreira 221, Centro; s/d US$10/13; 🛇) The rooms here are nicer than the average city center accommodations.

Eating

Praia do Meireles is packed with restaurants, many of which are up-market. Praia de Iracema is also loaded with restaurants and is a total scene with waiters and street venders vying for your attention. For more options, head to the Centro Cultural Dragão do Mar, which is surrounded by renovated buildings that house bars and restaurants with outdoor tables.

Self L'Escale (Rua Guilherme Rocha, Centro; per kg US$5) A self-service restaurant with fancy foods and salads and an airy upstairs dining room.

Um, Dois, Feijão com Arroz (Av Alberto Nepomuceno 339, Centro; per kg US$2.50; 🛇) Down a flight of stairs, this restaurant is a project aimed

at giving street kids marketable restaurant skills. But that isn't why the place is packed at lunchtime – the food is actually quite good!

Picanha do Raul (Rua Joaquim Alves, Iracema) On a quiet, shady street Raul serves up your usual Brazilian meat and fish lunches and dinners at prices far below restaurants near the waterfront.

El Gaucho (Rua dos Tabajaras 368, Iracema) At the end of a row of pricey eateries, El Gaucho serves decently priced barbeque meats, side soups and salads.

Al Mare (Av Beira Mar 3821, Meireles) Good seafood is served in a breezy location right on the beach.

Drinking

The restaurant areas are also the nightlife zones.

Pirata Bar (Rua dos Tabajaras 325, Praia de Iracema; cover US$4) This spot puts on a really fun night of *forró*, deemed 'the craziest Monday on the planet'. There is often live music around the Centro Cultural Dragão do Mar from Thursday to Sunday.

BRAZIL

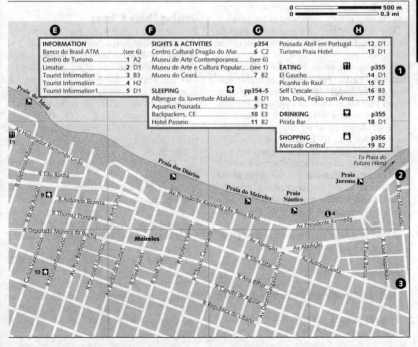

INFORMATION	**SIGHTS & ACTIVITIES** p354	Pousada Abril em Portugal........12 D1
Banco do Brasil ATM.............(see 6)	Centro Cultural Dragão do Mar.......6 C2	Turismo Praia Hotel..................13 D1
Centro de Turismo.................1 A2	Museu de Arte Contemporanea.......(see 6)	
Limatur...........................2 D1	Museu de Arte e Cultura Popular....(see 1)	**EATING** 🍴 p355
Tourist Information 3 B3	Museu do Ceará........................7 B2	El Gaucho...........................14 D1
Tourist Information 4 H2		Picanha do Raul....................15 E2
Tourist Information1.............5 D1	**SLEEPING** 🛏 pp354–5	Self L'escale.......................16 B3
	Albergue da Juventude Atalaia..........8 D1	Um, Dois, Feijão com Arroz.......17 B2
	Aquarius Pousada.....................9 E2	
	Backpackers, CE......................10 E3	**DRINKING** 🍷 p355
	Hotel Passeio.......................11 B2	Pirata Bar...........................18 D1
		SHOPPING 🛍 p356
		Mercado Central......................19 B2

Shopping

Fortaleza is one of the northeast's most important craft centers. Lacework, embroidery, leather goods, ceramics, straw articles and hammocks can be picked up cheaply at the Mercado Central and the Centro de Turismo.

Getting There & Around

BRA, Gol, Fly, TAM, Trip, VASP and Varig serve Fortaleza's airport. There are daily flights to any Brazilian destination.

Buses run daily to Natal (US$18, eight hours), Teresina (US$22, 10 hours), São Luís (US$36, 16 hours), Recife (US$30, 12 hours), Belém (US$55, 22 hours), Salvador (US$55, 22 hours) and Rio (US$112, 48 hours).

To get to the bus station from Praia Iracema, catch the Aguanabi 1 or Siqueira/Mucuripe bus across Av Tamancaré from Centro Cultural Dragão do Mar.

JERICOACOARA

Jericoacoara is a tiny, remote fishing village facing a broad grey beach, shouldered by a huge yellow sand dune and rolling green hills. Hip Brazilians, backpackers and windsurfers love the extremely relaxed vibe, usually finding their stay extended by days.

The cheapest Internet access is at **Pousada Tirol** (Rua São Francisco 202; US$3 per hr). There are no banks here.

Daytime activities include a beautiful 3km walk east to **Pedra Furada**, or highly recommended **buggy trips** (US$8) to surrounding dunes and lakes, such as Lagoa do Paraíso. Around sunset everyone gathers atop the dune or down on the beach to watch the local *capoeiristas* fly in circles around each other. Later, have a drink at **Planeta Jeri** and then move on to the night's hotspot, either **Forró Encanto do Momento** (Rua do Forró) or **Mama Africa** (Rua das Dunas). Before crashing, drop by **Padaria Santo Antonio** and use some of their fresh-from-the-oven breads to absorb all those caipirinhas.

Avoid *bichos de pé* (burrowing foot parasites) by not walking barefoot.

Sleeping

There is no shortage of places to stay or eat in Jeri, and many are foreign owned and high quality.

Pousada Senzala (☎ 0xx88-669-2328; pousadase nzala@hotmail.com; Beco da Padaria; r per person US$7)

New, simple rooms surround a small chill area with hammocks and chairs. Guests have use of the kitchen.

Pousada do Véio (☎ 0xx88-669-2015; Rua Principal; s/d US$7/10) Nice rooms with hammocks and lots of woodwork line up in the lush garden behind a family home.

Casa Suíça Brasileira (☎ 0xx88-669-2037; adriano@ jericoacoara.tur.br; Rua da Matriz 201; r per person US$8) Fine rooms surround a huge central garden on the edge of town.

Posada do Serrote (campsites per person US$1.50) This *pousada*, just up from the church, allows camping in their yard and has bathroom facilities.

Eating

Carcara (Rua do Forró) At the top of the street, Carcara serves amazing pastas and meat dishes flavored with herbs from its garden and prepared with the utmost care.

For fantastic seafood go to Isabel on the beach. Though there are competitors, **Pizzaria Dellacasa** has the best pizza, and the crepes at beachfront **Naturalmente** are divine.

Cafe Brasil (in a side alley off Rua Principal) For excellent snacks, sandwiches and juices.

Getting There & Away

Buying your ticket from Fortaleza to Jericoacoara (US$9, six hours, three daily) at **Velastur** (Av Monsenhor Tabosa 1273, Meireles) allows you to board the bus at its office, saving you the trip to the bus station. The 10:30am bus goes along the beach for the last stretch, the others go to Jijoca, where you are transferred to an open, 4WD truck (included in the ticket price) for a one-hour rodeo ride over the dunes to Jeri.

For those coming from the west, catch the 11:15am bus to Jijoca from Sobral (US$7, three hours) and connect with the Fortaleza bus there. Alternately, catch the 6:45am bus from Parnaíba to Camocim (US$4, two hours). From Camocim's central market a jeep leaves at about 10:30am for Jijoca, and will carry on to Jericoacoara if there's sufficient demand.

For those heading west from Jeri, catch the 10:30pm truck to Jijoca (US$0.85). Once there, locate the minibus to Sobral (US$5, three hours), from Monday to Saturday, that should be parked nearby, and they will let you snooze inside until it leaves at 2am.

PARQUE NACIONAL DE UBAJARA

The main attraction in Brazil's smallest **national park** (admission US$0.35; ☺ Tue-Sun) is an eight-chamber cave system with impressive limestone formations extending over half a kilometer into the side of a mountain. The landscape is green and lush in this area 850m above sea level, and the expansive views out over the plains of the *sertão* have a depth rare in the relatively flat northeast. The park has free guides for a 6km hike past the park's waterfalls and down into the valley containing the cave; groups depart from 8am to 11am for the 4½ hour trip, or you can take a freakily steep **cable car** (one way US$0.65; ☺ 9am-2:30pm). Many of the area's gems such as **Cachoeira do Fraude** lie outside the park, but there's no public transport. Trips can be arranged through *pousada* Sitio do Alemão.

There is a **Banco do Brasil** on the main street.

Staying near the park entrance is recommended. **Pousada Neblina** (☎ 0xx88-634-1270; s/d US$8/13; ☒) has groomed grounds and a variety of well-finished *apartamentos*. Right across the street, **Pousada Gruta de Ubajaras** (☎ 0xx88-634-1375; s/d US$5/8) has a strip of simple, tiled *apartamentos*. Both have restaurants. **Sitio do Alemão** (☎ 0xx88-9961-4645; cabins per person US$5), 1km up a dirt road, is a grouping of simple cement cabins with steep peaked roofs surrounded by lush forest and coffee plants (not for arachnophobes). Perks include private view points, homemade jams, and loads of information about local attractions. If you'd rather stay in town, rooms at **Pousada da Neuza** (☎ 0xx88-634-1261; Rua Juvêncio Luís Pereira 370; r per person US$3) are dark but fine, and **Avoar** is a decent restaurant.

Taxis and moto-taxis are available for the 3km stretch between town and the park entrance. There are buses to Ubajara from Fortaleza (US$11, six hours) and Teresina (US$11, six hours). From other cities, get a bus or *kombi* to Tianguá and then a *kombi* to Ubajara.

PARQUE NACIONAL DE SETE CIDADES

Ancient rock paintings, arches and caves grace **Parque Nacional Sete Cidades** (admission US$1; ☺ 8am-5pm), but the highly unusual rock formations rising up from the surrounding flat, dry land cannot be forgotten. Some people, educated scientists among them, claim the rocks are everything from seven ruined, 190-million-year-old cities to alien creations. At the park center, 6km from the entrance, pick up your obligatory guide (US$7 per group). The 13km walk to all seven cities takes two to three hours, leaving two more hours for a swim in a pond or stunning waterfall (February to July only). Start your hike early and bring snacks, plenty of water and protection from the unrelenting sun.

In Piripiri, **California Hotel** (☎ 0xx86-276-1645; Rua Dr Antenor Freitas 546; s/d US$7/10; ☒) has several, newly-renovated rooms with TVs. Just outside the park entrance is **Hotel Fazenda Sete Cidades** (☎ 0xx86-276-2222; s/d US$12/16; ☒ ☒), with expansive grounds, farm animals, a restaurant and rooms that don't live up to the quality of the rest of the hotel. Ibama runs the **Parque Hotel Sete Cidades** (☎ 0xx86-223-3366; www.hotelsetecidades .com.br; s/d US$13/17, campsites per person US$3; ☒), located on park grounds 2km from the park center, with a restaurant and natural swimming pool. The nice rooms all have mini-fridges and verandas.

Transport between the park and Piripiri (26km) is via moto-taxi, taxi, or the free park employee bus, which leaves at 7am from the Telemar building on Praça da Bandeira and 5pm from the park. Several daily buses run to Piripiri from Fortaleza (US$11, seven hours), Tianguá (US$3, 3½ hours) and Teresina (US$4, three hours).

PARNAÍBA

Parnaíba is a peaceful port on the mouth of the Rio Parnaíba, with many good beaches to its northeast. Porto das Barcas, the town's restored riverfront warehouse area, has a few art galleries, bars and restaurants, but is nothing grand. The reason to come here is to check out the **delta**, a 2700-sq-km expanse of islands, beaches, lagoons, dunes and mangroves, with abundant wildlife. The 8½ hour trip costs US$10 per person (including two meals) and only occurs when there is sufficient interest, so call ahead. Contact the agencies **Igaratur** (☎ 0xx86-322-2141) or **Morais Brito** (☎ 0xx86-321-1969) in Porto das Barcas.

Sleeping & Eating

Casa Nova Hotel (☎ 0xx86-322-3344; Praça Lima Rebelo 1094; s/d US$5/10, with bath US$8/13; ☒) A sterile, very white hotel a short walk from Porto das Barcas.

BRAZIL

Hotel Cívico (☎ 0xx86-322-2470; Av Governor Chagas Rodrigues 474; s/d US$8/12; 🖭 🖭) A proper hotel some 10 blocks from Porto das Barcas with backpacker range deals in the off-season.

In Porto das Barcas are **Pousada Porto das Barcas** (☎ 0xx86-322-2307; Av Getúlio Vargas 53; r per person US$5; 🖭), a friendly, musty converted warehouse with a duck pen, and **Rio's Restaurante & American Bar**, which serves seafood and pasta dishes, often to live music.

Getting There & Away

Parnaíba can be a jumping off point for Jericoacoara (p356) or Parque Nacional dos Lençóis Maranhenses (p361).

The bus to Teresina (US$8, six hours, eight daily) stops in Piripiri (US$5, three hours), and the bus to Fortaleza (US$13, three daily) stops in Camocim and Sobral. Frequent buses go to Tutoía (US$3, three hours, three daily), and São Luís (US$13, nine hours, two daily). Boats to Tutoía leave most days of the week from Porto das Barcas (US$4, seven hours).

TERESINA

Teresina, famed as the hottest city in Brazil, is a pleasant but un-noteworthy capital where tourists are rare. Micarina, the city's Salvador-style, out-of-season Carnaval, is held in mid-July. From the bus station to the center, catch the Rodoviaria Circular bus from the stop across the road or a Potivelho or Dirceuit *kombi*.

Check your email at **Jeff Networks** (Rua Álvaro Mendes 2121; US$0.35 per hr; 🕒 8am-10pm Mon-Sat, 1-10pm Sun). The state operates a **tourist information booth** (Praça Dom Pedro II; 🕒 8am-noon Mon-Fri) inside the Central de Artesanato.

The **Central de Artesanato** (🕒 8am-6pm Mon-Fri, 8am-4pm Sat) is a row of craft shops surrounding a courtyard full of parked cars, but is not a bad place to drink an *agua de coco*. The **Casa da Cultura** (Rua Rui Barbosa 348; admission US$0.15; 🕒 8am-5:30pm Mon-Fri, 8am-noon Sat) is a cultural center offering art and music classes with good displays.

Sleeping & Eating

Hotel São Raimundo (☎ 0xx86-222-0181; Rua Senador Teodoro Pacheco 1199; s/d US$3/5) This simple and central hotel has surprisingly decent *quartos* and *apartamentos*.

Piauí Palace Hotel (☎ 0xx86-221-5548; Rua Barroso 124; s/d US$12/20; 🖭) A proper, business-person

hotel which you can infiltrate by taking a perfectly fine basement room.

Bom Bocado (Rua Paissandu 120) Across the street from the Casa da Cultura, this fancy self-service restaurant has freshly grilled meats and an indoor waterfall.

Camarão do Elias (Av Pedro Almeida 457) Try this place for seafood.

Forno e Fogão (Praça da Bandeira 310; buffet US$5) Inside the Luxor Piauí hotel, this place has an all-you-can-eat, fine dining buffet every day but Sunday, which includes many regional dishes.

Getting There & Away

Teresina's airport (6km north of center) is served by BRA, TAM, VASP, and Varig.

Frequent buses go to Parnaíba (US$10, five hours, eight daily), Belém (US$23, 14 hours, seven daily) and over a terrible road to São Luís (US$12, seven hours, six daily). The bus to Fortaleza (US$15, 10 hours, four daily) stops in Piripiri (US$4, three hours), Tianguá (US$11, six hours) and Sobral (US$13, seven hours).

SÃO LUÍS

São Luís do Maranhão's unpretentious colonial charm and one of the richest folkloric traditions in Brazil, make it a highlight for travelers in the northeast. Its restored colonial center is one of Brazil's architectural gems, unique due to the many facades covered with *azulejos* (Portuguese painted tiles) to combat the predominant damp heat. São Luís was developed slowly by the French and then the Portuguese as a port for exporting sugar and later, cotton.

Orientation

São Luís is divided into two peninsulas by the Rio Anil. On the southernmost, the city center sits on a hill above the historic core of Praia Grande, called Projeto Revivir by locals. On the northern peninsula lie the more modern and wealthy suburbs, such as São Francisco, as well as the city's beaches. Many city streets in the center have multiple names, but this shouldn't prevent you from navigating easily by foot.

Information

For Internet access, head to **Poeme-se** (Rua Humberto de Campos; US$1 per hr). Moneychangers on Praça Benedito Leite change cash and traveler's checks, or head to **Banco do Brasil** (Travessa Boa Ventura). There are tourist offices at the **bus station** (⊗ 8am-10pm), **airport** (⊗ 8-2:30am) and **Praça Benedito Leite** (⊗ 8am-7pm Mon-Fri, 9am-5pm Sat & Sun).

Sights & Activities

You will be unable to resist wandering the entire historical district, from the waterfront east to Praça João Lisboa, and from Praça Dom Pedro II south to Rua Jacinto Maia. Restoration of these colorful colonial mansions lining cobbled streets started in the late 1980s, resulting in the revitalization of this neighborhood now dotted with restaurants, bars, shops and no shortage of museums.

The Centro de Cultura Popular has a trio of excellent museums that should not be missed. Admission is free and the museums are open 9am to 7pm Tuesday through Sunday. The **Casa da Festa** (Rua do Giz 221) has four floors of colorful costumes and props from local festivals and religious practices. The **Casa do Maranhão** (Rua do Trapiche), housed in a gigantic converted warehouse, has what amounts to a multimedia state tourism brochure downstairs, and a second floor dedicated entirely to the different regional flavors of Bumba Meu Boi (see below) costumes. Items from Maranhão quotidian life, from delicate wooden fish traps to children's toys made from trash, are displayed at the **Casa do Nhozinho** (Rua Portugal 185).

The **Museu Histórico do Estado de Maranhão** (Rua do Sol 302; admission US$0.65; ⊗ 9am-6pm Tue-Fri, 2-6pm Sat & Sun) is a restored 1836 mansion with attractive, historical displays of wealthy families' belongings. The city's main cathedral is the neo-classical **Catedral da Sé**, constructed by Jesuits in 1629.

Local beaches are broad and flat. Locals and their cars pack the beautiful **Praia do Calhau** on weekends. To get there, take the 'Calhau' bus from the Praia Grande bus terminal.

Festivals & Events

São Luís' folklore is best seen in the streets during major festivals and the months of rehearsal that preceed them. Carnaval and the combined festivals of São João and Bumba Meu Boi, from late June to the second week of August, are the biggies. The latter is a famous festival celebrated all over the northeast in which celebrants engage in music, dance, theater and ritual based around a legend of the death and resurrection of a bull. Marafolia, the out-of-season Carnaval in mid-October, mimics Salvador's with *trios electricos* of famous Bahian musicians.

Sleeping

Staying close to the action in Projeto Revivir is an intelligent choice for convenience and safety.

Solar das Pedras (☎ 0xx98-232-6694; Rua da Palma 127; dm US$5, s/d US$7/8) Backpackers gravitate toward this attractive hostel in a restored colonial home for good reason. All rooms have shared bath, and discounts are offered for HI members.

Pousada Victória do Lopez (☎ 0xx98-222-9937; Rua do Giz 129; s/d US$7/10, with bath US$13/17; ⊠) A plain but sweet colonial building in good condition with simple rooms.

Hotel Lord (☎ 0xx98-221-4655; Rua de Nazaré 258; s/d US$7/10, with bath US$10/13) No one has touched the 1960s decor in this place since the day it was laid down, leaving it slightly shabby but decent.

Walking to the following places at night is a bit desolate and only recommended for groups.

Pousada Solar dos Nobres (☎ 0xx98-232-5705; Rua de São João 82a; s/d US$8/12; ⊠) An attractive hotel with modern rooms surrounding a palm-shaded stone courtyard. Fantastic breakfast.

Hotel Casa Grande (☎ 0xx98-231-5265; Becos dos Barracos 94; s/d US$6/8) You won't be tripping over your backpack in these very simple, gigantic *apartamentos* with hardwood floors.

SPLURGE!

Pousada Colonial (☎ 0xx98-232-2834; Rua Afonso Pena 112; s/d US$17/22; ⊠) Looking for colonial charm with a touch of elegance and snappy service? Pousada Colonial offers comfortable *apartamentos* and luxurious suites in a restored colonial mansion with fantastic views over the old city. The building is covered inside and out with unique raised *azulejos*, which the tourism authority has adopted as their mascot for brochure covers. A 20% discount is offered for cash payment.

BRAZIL

BRAZIL

SÃO LUÍS

INFORMATION
Banco do Brasil.................1 A3
Poeme-se.........................2 B3
Tourist Information............3 B2

SIGHTS & ACTIVITIES   p359
Casa da Festa....................4 B3
Casa do Maranhão.............5 A2
Casa do Nhozinho.............6 A2
Museu Histórico do Estado de
    Maranhão.....................7 C2

SLEEPING   p359
Hotel Casa Grande.............8 C2
Hotel Lord........................9 B2
Pousada Colonial...............10 B3
Pousada Solar dos Nobres...11 D1
Pousada Victória do Lopez...12 B3
Solar das Pedras...............13 B3

Eating

Most restaurants surrounding Projeto Revivir are closed at night. Dinner spots are mostly on the other side of the bridge.

Gula Gula (Rua da Paz 414; per kg US$4.25) Retreat from the heat in the air-con dining room upstairs at this big time self-service lunch restaurant.

Senac (Rua de Nazaré 242; buffet US$5) This cooking school offers a high-class, all-you-can-eat buffet lunch that features regional dishes.

Crioula (Beco da Pacotilha 42; dishes US$3.25) You can get a good salad at this local spot, which serves tasty regional dishes loaded with seafood.

Naturista Alimentos (Rua do Sol 517; per kg US$4.25) Offering a vegetarian buffet lunch daily.

Le Papagaio Amarelo (Rua da Estrela 210; dishes US$2) Slightly less of a tourist trap than its neighbor Antigamente, the four-cheese pasta is one of the better dishes here.

Valéry (Rua do Gis) This French-owned bakery has tasty pastries, croissants, quiches and, of course, fantastic breads.

Drinking

São Luís is known for its reggae bars, such as **Bar do Nelson** (Av Litorânea, Calhau). Some can be a bit sketchy, so ask the tourist office for a list of safe venues.

Action in the old city usually centers around **Restaurante Antigamente** (Rua Alfândega 210), but **Bar do Porto** (Rua do Trapiche 49) and **Café Bagdá** (Rua Portugal) also have live music often. Leaving Revivir, the Japanese restaurant/bar **Kitaro Lagoa** (Lagoa da Jansen, São Francisco) and **Crepe's Bier House** (Av dos Holandeses, Ponta do Farol) are both happening spots that often have live music.

Getting There & Around

TAM, VASP and Varig will take or connect you to anywhere you want to go from São Luís' airport.

Frequent buses go to Belém (US$25, 12 hours, twice daily), Barreirinhas (US$7, five hours, four daily), Teresina (US$11, seven hours, nine daily) and Fortaleza (US$27, 18 hours, four daily).

Rather than risking it, take moto-taxis and taxis – the best way to get around at night.

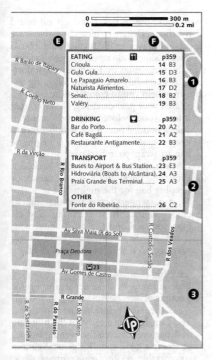

EATING	🍴	p359
Crioula	14	B3
Gula Gula	15	D3
Le Papagaio Amarelo	16	B3
Naturista Alimentos	17	D2
Senac	18	B2
Valéry	19	B3

DRINKING	🍷	p359
Bar do Porto	20	A2
Café Bagdã	21	A2
Restaurante Antigamente	22	B3

TRANSPORT		p359
Buses to Airport & Bus Station	23	E3
Hidroviária (Boats to Alcântara)	24	A3
Praia Grande Bus Terminal	25	A3

OTHER		
Fonte do Ribeirão	26	C2

ALCÂNTARA

Across the Baía de São Marcos from São Luís is a colonial architectural treasure slipping regally into decay. Built in the early 17th century with extensive slave labor, Alcântara was the hub of the region's sugar and cotton economy and home to Maranhão's rich landowners.

As you walk around this picturesquely decrepit town, have a look at Brazil's best preserved **pelourinho** (whipping post; Praça da Matriz) and the **Museu Histórico** (Praça da Matriz; admission US$0.35; 🕑9am-2pm Mon-Sat, 9am-1pm Sun), displaying the personal effects of 18th and 19th century residents. The Festa do Divino (first Sunday after Ascension Day, usually in May) consists of children dressed up like royalty, drum corps of black women dressed in red, and lots of sweets and pink frilly tissue paper; it shouldn't be missed. There are no banks.

Alcântara makes a fine day trip, but if you want to stay, **Pousada do Mordomo Régio** (☎ 0xx98-337-1197; Rua Grande 134; s/d without bath US$12/20, with bath US$30) has rooms in a restored colonial home. Down on the beach, a bit of a

walk from town, **Pousada dos Guarás** (☎ 0xx98-337-1339; pousadadosguaras@aol.com; s/d US$7/14) has simple thatched-roof bungalows in a tropical garden. Silvia at **Planeta Alcântara** (Rua das Mercês 400) rents rooms in her home, but you should also stop by to try her *doce de especie*, the local cookie/sweet made from coconut and the juice of orange tree leaves.

Boats to Alcântara depart from São Luís' *hidroviária* (boat terminal), or, when the tide is out, from Praia Ponta d'Áreia. Buy your ticket in advance as boats fill up, and try to leave from the *hidroviária* as delays involved with being bused to the beach (included in ticket price) can be frustrating. The *Diamantina* (US$3, one hour) leaves at 7am and 9:30am daily. For the more adventurous, the crowded sailing boats *Newton Belle* and the *Mensageiro da Fé* leave weekdays according to the tides (US$1.50, 1½ to two hours, twice daily).

PARQUE NACIONAL DOS LENÇÓIS MARANHENSES

The best time to visit this remote park is between March and September, when crystal-clear rainwater pools form between the immense white sand dunes that dominate the landscape. Highly recommended day trips over the dunes to **Lagoa Azul** or **Lagoa Peixe**, and upriver to the oceanfront village **Caburé**, run from US$8 to US$12 per person with local tour agencies. Two-day hikes through the park can also be arranged. Tranquility seekers will want to take the regular boat (US$1.50, three to four hours) upriver and stay in Caburé or Atins. In Atins, Lucia is famous for putting up anyone who is willing to walk the hour and a half out to her home, and for her wonderful cooking. The setting is gorgeous – just ask locals for directions once you arrive.

Access to the park is through the pretty town of Barreirinhas, which has a **Banco do Brasil** on the main street.

Most budget accommodation options are dark and musty, but **Pousada do Porto** (☎ 0xx98-349-1690; Rua Acleto de Carvalho; s/d US$7/13) is riverfront, modern and airy. **Restaurante do Carlão** (Rua Coronel Godinho), in the Pousada Victória do Lopez, is duly famous for its fish in mango sauce (US$6 for two).

Transport between Parnaíba and Barreirinhas is a recommended adventure.

BRAZIL

The journey involves a bus or boat from Parnaíba to Tutóia, a 4WD truck to Rio Novo/Paulinho Neves (US$1.50, two hours), and another extremely rough truck ride to Barreirinhas (US$3, two hours). Transport for both truck segments only leaves in the morning and afternoon, so a night in Rio Novo is required. Luckily it is a nice town within walking distance of the rest of the park.

Transport to São Luís is via van (US$8, four hours), which departs in the morning and evening and will drop you at your requested destination, or by bus (US$7, five hours, four daily).

THE NORTH

Vast jungle covers the north of Brazil, with the many tributaries of the Amazon coursing through the region like the earth's dark veins. Along the riverbanks lie tropical cities, *caboclo* (Indian descendent) villages and great stretches of uninhabited rain forest, inspiring the imagination with its unknown mysteries.

The Amazon basin has 80,000km of navigable rivers, and ocean-going vessels can sail 3800km inland to Iquitos, Peru. Upstream from its confluence with the Rio Negro to the end of Brazilian territory at Tabatinga, the Amazon is known locally as the Rio Solimões. Below and above that stretch it's called the Amazonas.

Most of the rivers are so wide you won't see much flora and fauna from boats. To see Amazonian wildlife – alligators, monkeys, sloths, pink and gray dolphins, anacondas, toucans, macaws – you must explore the *igarapés* (narrower channels cutting through the jungle). Trips are best when the water level is high – March to July in most areas. At high water, canoes slide through the flooded forests almost at jungle canopy level, bringing you closer to the wildlife.

River Travel

When looking for travel routes on a map of Amazonia, look for water; rivers are the highways here. Except for a couple of routes, bus travel is not an option. If time is on your side, boats are a great way to experience the north. To join the locals, just invest in a

hammock, buy a ticket and get on board a riverboat. Distances along the rivers are great, and travel on the regular public boats is always slow and crowded, often wet and smelly, sometimes dull and never comfortable. It's certainly cheap. The following few tips may help you to enjoy it more.

- Watch your gear carefully. Never entrust it to anyone, before or after departure.
- Take a hooded poncho or windbreaker to keep yourself dry, a cloth or large plastic bag to wrap your backpack in, a hammock, rope to suspend your backpack above the deck, and a sheet, blanket or sleeping bag for the nights.
- Most passengers travel *rede* (hammock) class: you just sling your hammock wherever you can find the most convenient space. Before embarking, the boats get very crowded with people and baggage, and it's not hard to get to know your traveling companions!
- Boats often moor at the departure port for a couple of days before sailing, so you can check them out before buying your ticket. You can also board early on the morning of departure (or even the evening before) to secure a good spot. It's generally more comfortable on the cooler upper deck, preferably towards the bow.
- Fares from A to B vary little between boats. Three basic meals a day – mainly rice, beans and meat – and drinks are included in fares, but it's advisable to bring bottled water and snacks.
- Most boats have a few *camarotes* (cabins) for up to four people, costing about double the hammock fare per person. Cabins are bare and basic and can be hot and stuffy, but they provide a little privacy.
- Downstream travel is considerably faster than upstream, but boats heading upriver go closer to the shore, which makes for a more scenic trip.

BELÉM

A city of mango tree-lined boulevards, historic neighborhoods, looming churches and a vibrant arts and music scene, Belém is the gateway to the Amazon. It's also one of the most Brazilian of cities, a fascinating hybrid of cultures in one of the world's rainiest zones. Founded in 1616, Belém was the base for the Portuguese conquest of Amazonia. Today it's the economic center of the north.

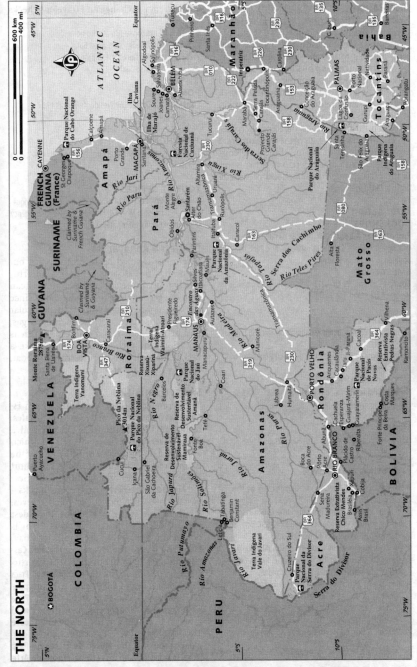

Orientation

Belém lies 120km from the Atlantic where the Rio Guamá (a tributary of the mighty Amazonas) empties into the Baía de Guajará. Belém's most prominent feature is its busy port, which has a bustling market (Mercado Ver-o-Peso), a shopping esplanade and the shipping and transportation hub north of there. Av Presidente Vargas, Belém's main street, heads east from the waterfront to the leafy central park, Praça da República. Between the park and the port is the Comercio area, where most of Belém's hotels are concentrated. South of Comercio near the water is the picturesque neighborhood of Cidade Velha (Old Town).

Information

BOOKSHOPS

Emporio das Artes (2nd fl, Estação das Docas) Photography and coffee-table books on Belém and Pará, in addition to traditional music.

EMERGENCY

Tourist Police (☎ 0xx91-212-0948; Praça Waldemar Henrique s/n) Available 24 hours.

INTERNET ACCESS

Cybercafé (top fl, Iguatemi shopping center; US$1.50 per hr; ☯ daily)

Telemar (cnr Av Presidente Vargas & Rua Riachuelo; US$2 per hr; ☯ daily)

MEDICAL SERVICES

Hospital Adventista (☎ 0xx91-246-8686; Av Almirante Barroso 1758)

MONEY

HSBC (Av Presidente Vargas 670) Has ATMs.

GETTING INTO TOWN

Aeroporto Val de Cães is 8km north of the center. Bus 'Pratinha-P Vargas' runs between the traffic circle outside the airport and Avenida Presidente Vargas (US$0.60, 40 minutes). Taxis cost about US$8.

The bus station is on Avenida Almirante Barroso, 3km east of the center. For a city bus to Avenida Presidente Vargas, catch any 'Aero Club' or 'P Vargas' bus from the far side of Av Almirante Barroso. Going out to the bus station, take an 'Aeroclube' or 'Pratinha-P Vargas' bus from Av Presidente Vargas. Taxis to points along Av Presidente Vargas cost around US$5

For currency exchange and traveler's checks visit:

Banco da Amazônia (Rua Carlos Gomes; ☯ 9am-7pm Mon-Fri, 9am-noon Sat)

Fitta (Estação das Docas, mezzanine level; ☯ noon-7pm Mon-Sat)

POST

Central Post Office (Av Presidente Vargas 498; ☯ 9am-5pm Mon-Fri)

TELEPHONE

Telemar (cnr Av Presidente Vargas & Rua Riachuelo; ☯ daily)

TOURIST OFFICES

Paratur (☎ 0xx91-212-0669; Praça Waldemar Henrique s/n; ☯ 8am-6pm Mon-Fri) Friendly state tourism agency with lots of helpful information.

Dangers & Annoyances

Belém has cleaned up in recent years, but crime has not disappeared, and unfortunately tourists are still a target. Sunday can be a dangerous time to wander alone since the streets are fairly empty. In particular watch yourself on Av Presidente Vargas, and at the Mercado Ver-o-Peso, which is notorious for pickpockets. Always take a taxi at night. If you plan to travel by boat, watch your gear carefully.

Sights & Activities

Three renovated port warehouses form **Estação das Docas**, an attractive area with cafés, restaurants, exhibitions, a cinema and a 500m riverside promenade (all of which are closed on Monday), near the foot of the main street, Av Presidente Vargas. A short distance southwest, the teeming, centuries-old **Mercado Ver-o-Peso** spans several blocks – be very alert for pickpockets and thieves. South of here is the **Cidade Velha**, the oldest part of Belém; walking around at night is not recommended, but don't miss it by day. Here you'll find the riverbank **Forte do Castelo**, on the site of the original 1616 Portuguese fortification; **Palácio Antonio Lemos** (Praça Felipe Patron), a grand 1880s rubber-boom palace housing the **Museu de Arte de Belém** (Praça Felipe Patron), with opulent furnishings and modern Brazilian art; the **Palácio Lauro Sodré** (Praça Felipe Patron), the 18th-century governors' palace housing the **Museu do Estado do Pará** (Praça Fr Brandão); the excellent **Museu de Arte**

Sacra (Praça Fr Brandão), comprising a fascinating old baroque church and adjoining bishop's palace, with its brilliant carved works by Indian artisans; and the 1750s **Catedral da Sé**. The three museums close Monday and each costs around US$1.50.

The lavish **Teatro da Paz** (Praça da República; admission US$1.50; ☺ normally Tue-Fri) is one of Belém's finest rubber-boom buildings. About 1.25km east along Av Nazaré is the 1909 **Basílica de NS de Nazaré**, with a fine marble interior housing the tiny image of the Virgin of Nazaré (see Festivals below). Take an Aero Club or Cid Nova 6 bus from Av Presidente Vargas to get there. Another couple of blocks east is the not-to-be-missed **Museu Emílio Goeldi** (Av Governador Magalhães Barata 376; admission to each section US$0.70; ☺ 9-11:30am, 2-5 pm Tue-Thu, 9-11:30am Fri, 9am-5pm Sat, Sun & holidays), comprising a zoobotanic garden with many exotic and rare species of Amazonian wildlife, an aquarium and an indoor museum with Amazonia's best archaeological displays.

Festivals & Events
On the second Sunday in October, Belém explodes with fireworks as the churches ring out the feast of Círio de Nazaré, one of Brazil's biggest religious festivals. A million people accompany the image of the Virgin of Nazaré, a supposedly miraculous statue believed to have been sculpted in Nazareth, from the Catedral da Sé to the Basílica de NS de Nazaré. Two weeks of serious partying follow the procession.

Sleeping
Hotel Fortaleza (☎ 0xx91-212-1055; Travessa Frutuoso Guimarães 276; dm US$3, s/d US$4/6) This longstanding backpackers' favorite has a lively atmosphere and is a good place to meet other travelers. The rooms themselves are a bit shabby: thin walls and mattresses match the slender prices.

Hotel Central (☎ 0xx91-242-4800; Av Presidente Vargas 290; s/d quartos with fan US$6/10, with breakfast US$8/11, s/d apartamentos US$13/17) An Art Deco gem who's beauty still shines despite the years. The somewhat haunting rooms are large and decent – though a little bare. To get a night's sleep above noisy Av Presidente Vargas, ask for a room in the back

Hotel Ver-o-Peso (☎ 0xx91-241-2022; Boulevard Castilhos França 208; s/d apartamentos US$10/13; ☒)

Drab air-con rooms are the norm in this waterfront location.

Hotel Vitória Régia (☎ 0xx91-212-2077; Travessa Frutuoso Guimarães 260; s/d US$8/11) Friendly Belém standard with clean and featureless *apartamentos*.

Hotel Novo Avenida (☎ 0xx91-242-9953; avenida@hotelavenida.com.br; Av Presidente Vargas 404; s/d quartos US$11/12, apartamentos US$15/18) Not much atmosphere, but centrally located, with comfortable rooms and hot showers.

Eating
Belém's cuisine features a wide variety of fresh seafood. Food stands throughout the city serve dishes such as *dourada* (a tasty catfish), *pato no tucupi* (lean duck cooked in a sauce made from manioc juice) or the delicious *tacacá* (a rich, shrimp-filled soup).

Estação das Docas (Av Castilho Franca s/n) has about a dozen places to eat. They're not cheap but the riverside location is great.

Spazzio Verdi (upstairs, Estação das Docas, Av Castilho Franca s/n; meals per kilo US$7; ☺ lunch & dinner Tue-Sun) Quality self-serve.

Other self-serve lunch places include the vegetarian **Restaurante Belo Centro** (Rua Santo Antônio 264; meals per kilo US$4); **Inter Restaurant** (Rua 28 de Setembro 304; meals per kilo US$5), also serving *prato feito* for US$2.50; **Restaurante Zimbro** (Rua 15 de Novembro 314; meals per kg US$5), east of the center; and the main branch of **Spazzio Verdi** (Avenida Braz de Aguiar 824; meals per kilo US$7), with quality fare.

Bistrô da Rita (Rua Ferreira Cantão 279; prato feitos US$2.50) Hearty *pratos feitos* by day and a full menu by night, this café showcases the work of local artists. In the evenings it's a lively spot.

Kanshari (Rua Gama Abreu 83; juices US$1, buffets per kilo US$7) Friendly all-vegetarian lunch buffet with a variety of fresh squeezed fruit and vegetable juices. Try the orange and beet juice.

Xícara da Silva (Av Visconde de Souza 978A; sandwiches US$3, large pizzas US$7) Stylish café and pizzeria with tasty sandwiches and pizzas in a chalet-style house with a vine-covered patio out front.

Deli Cidade (Av Braz de Aguiar 168) Fresh-baked breads, juices, cappuccinos and sandwiches at low prices on a quiet, shady street. Excellent choice for java and pastries in the morning.

BRAZIL

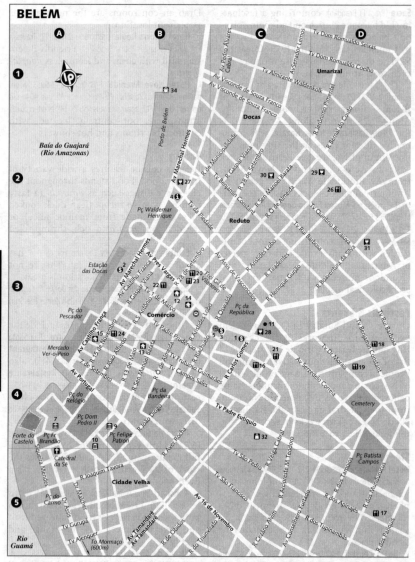

BELÉM

Baía do Guajará
(Rio Amazonas)

Porto de Belém

Pç Waldemar
Henrique

Estação
das Docas

Pç do
Pescador

Mercado
Ver-o-Peso

Comércio

Pç da
República

Umarizal

Docas

Reduto

Pç da
Bandeira

Pç do
Relógio

Pç Dom
Pedro II

Pç Felipe
Patron

Forte do
Castelo

Pç Fr
Brandão

Catedral
da Sé

Pç do
Carmo

Cidade Velha

Cemetery

Pç Batista
Campos

Rio
Guamá

To Mormaço
(600m)

BRAZIL

Café Imaginario (Rua Apinagés, btwn Mundurucus & Pariquis) A colorful late-night eatery and drinking spot that serves delicious pizzas and attracts a Bohemian crowd. The artwork of some of the regulars decorates the walls.

Restaurante Casa Portuguesa (Rua Senador Manoel Barata 897; dishes US$5) Serving basics

such as fish and shrimp dishes, this pleasant dining room offers decent service at affordable prices. The savory *bacalhau* costs a mere US$16, and it's big enough for two.

Cantina Italiana (Travessa Benjamin Constant 1401; pastas US$5) Get your fill of big plates of pasta at this quaint eatery.

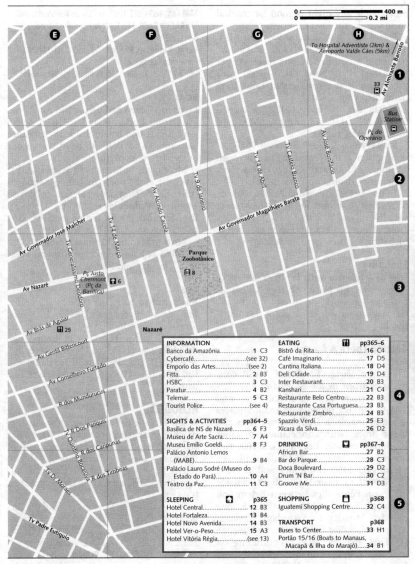

INFORMATION	
Banco da Amazônia	1 C3
Cybercafé	(see 32)
Emporio das Artes	(see 2)
Fitta	2 B3
HSBC	3 C3
Paratur	4 B2
Telemar	5 C3
Tourist Police	(see 4)

SIGHTS & ACTIVITIES	pp364–5
Basílica de NS de Nazaré	6 F3
Museu de Arte Sacra	7 A4
Museu Emilio Goeldi	8 F3
Palácio Antonio Lemos (MABE)	9 B4
Palácio Lauro Sodré (Museu do Estado do Pará)	10 A4
Teatro da Paz	11 C3

SLEEPING	p365
Hotel Central	12 B3
Hotel Fortaleza	13 B4
Hotel Novo Avenida	14 B3
Hotel Ver-o-Peso	15 A3
Hotel Vitória Régia	(see 13)

EATING	pp365–6
Bistrô da Rita	16 C4
Café Imaginario	17 D5
Cantina Italiana	18 D4
Deli Cidade	19 D4
Inter Restaurant	20 B3
Kanshari	21 C4
Restaurante Belo Centro	22 B3
Restaurante Casa Portuguesa	23 B3
Restaurante Zimbro	24 B3
Spazzio Verdi	25 E3
Xicara da Silva	26 D2

DRINKING	pp367–8
African Bar	27 B2
Bar do Parque	28 C3
Doca Boulevard	29 D2
Drum 'N Bar	30 C2
Groove Me	31 D3

SHOPPING	p368
Iguatemi Shopping Centre	32 C4

TRANSPORT	p368
Buses to Center	33 H1
Portão 15/16 (Boats to Manaus, Macapá & Ilha do Marajó)	34 B1

Drinking

Estação das Docas (Av Castilho Franca s/n) The cafés facing the river make a scenic spot for a drink in the evening. Try the **Cervejaria Amazonas** brewery.

Mormaço (☎ 0xx91-9983-4320; Praço do Arsenal; ⏳ Sat & Sun) At the end of the pier, this open-air space overlooking the water is difficult to find, but worth the effort: it's one of the best places to see live music in the city. Sunday afternoons are often dedicated to the swirling rhythms of *carimbó*.

Drum 'N Bar (Travessa Quintina Bocaiuva 582) DJs spin more than just drum 'n' bass in this stylish café in a former industrial hood. Wednesday nights are devoted to Cuban beats, while any night is good for tropical cocktails like the kiwi caipiroscas.

Groove Me (Rua Boaventura da Silva; cover US$2-4) This small club holds techno and house parties in a non-pretentious space. As per the name, it's a good place to get your groove on if the Amazonian rains have dampened your spirits.

African Bar (☎ 0xx91-241-1085; Av Marechal Hermes) Colorful space hosting samba groups most Saturday nights.

Bar do Parque (Praça da República s/n) This outdoor spot near the Teatro da Paz stays open 24 hours and attracts a range of travelers, bohemians, drunks and prostitutes.

In the 'Docas' area along Av Visconde de Souza Franco, numerous bright bars, some with live music, fill with a lively 20s and 30s crowd. Doca Boulevard building has several, including the rock-frenzied **Bulldog** bar.

Shopping

Feira de Artesanato crafts fair (Praça da República; ☼ weekends) This place sells regional handicrafts and artwork. Be sure to stop by the CD stalls for a wide selection of traditional music.

Getting There & Away

AIR

There are Varig, TAM and VASP connections from major Brazilian cities. Regional carriers such as Meta, Penta and TAVAJ connect Belém with smaller places around Amazonia. Daily average fares and flight times (with connections) to cities in Brazil include: Brasília (US$100, two hours), Fortaleza (US$110, four hours), Manaus (US$150, two hours) and Salvador (US$200, four hours). For flights outside of Brazil, Penta flies between Belém and Cayenne, French Guiana (US$215; one per day Monday to Saturday). Surinam Airways also flies from Belém to Cayenne (US$208, two per week), continuing on to Paramaribo (Suriname; US$270), and Georgetown (Guyana; US$323). Surinam also flies to destinations in the Caribbean. Varig flies daily to/from Miami (USA).

The following airlines have offices in Belém:

Meta (☎ 0xx91-223-1082; Av Assis de Vasconcelos 448)
Penta (☎ 0xx91-222-6000; Av Assis de Vasconcelos 396)
Surinam Airways (☎ 0xx91-212-7144; Rua Gaspar Viana 488)

TAM (☎ 0xx91-223-1082; Av Assis de Vasconcelos 265)
TAVAJ (☎ 0xx91-212-1201; Rua Senador Manoel Barata 925)
Varig, Nordeste, Rio Sul (☎ 0xx91-211-3344; Av Presidente Vargas 768)
VASP (☎ 0xx91-224-5588; Av Presidente Vargas 345)

BOAT

Boats to Macapá and up the Rio Amazonas leave from Portão (Gate) 15/16 of Belém port. Ticket booths are inside the entrance here and it's advisable to buy tickets a day or two before departure.

Most boats to Manaus (five days) call at seven or eight ports including Santarém (three days). They depart at 6pm or 7pm on Monday, Wednesday and Friday. On most, the hammock fare including food is US$61 to Manaus and US$42 to Santarém.

Boats to Macapá (hammock/cabin US$26/ 32, 20 to 24 hours) depart at 10am on Tuesday, Thursday and Friday.

BUS

Buses run to São Luís (US$24, 12 hours, four daily), Fortaleza (US$55, 25 hours, four daily), Recife (US$62, 34 hours, one daily), Salvador (US$70, 36 hours, one daily), Palmas (US$32, 19 hours, two daily), Brasília (US$65, 34 hours, three daily) and Rio de Janeiro (US$85, 50 to 55 hours, one daily).

ALGODOAL

A small, rustic fishing village of windswept beaches, mangrove forests and freshwater lagoons, Algodoal is an idyllic remnant of the past – a place where cars are absent, electricity is scarce and the charm of village life rejuvenates even the weariest of travelers.

Algodoal lies on the west coast of the Ilha de Maiandeua, 180km northeast of Belém, and in addition to weekending Brazilians, attracts a handful of foreign travelers.

Beautiful **Praia da Princesa**, backed by dunes and palms, stretches the length of the east coast, while inland the lush Lagoa da Princesa (Princess lake) lies just behind it.

Sleeping

From the boat pier, it's a 10-minute walk to the main road, Rua Principal, where you'll find a number of rustic accommodations, as well as the following places.

Pousada Kakuri (☎ 0xx91-3854-1138 in Belém; pousadakakuri@hotmail.com; Rua Principal; cabanas without/with bath US$9/13) A backpackers' favorite, it has a lively atmosphere with decent rooms and a friendly English-speaking owner.

Cabanas do Cesar (no tel; Rua Principal; cabanas s/d US$3/8) Just up the road, this place lacks the travelers' vibe, but has good, clean cabanas with mosquito nets and shared baths for a bit less.

Pousada da Sereia (no tel; Rua Principal; r US$3) On the other side of Kakuri, this is the cheapest place to stay, with small, very basic rooms.

Eden (☎ 0xx91-9967-9010 in Belém; jardimdoeden@hotmail.com; campsite/room/chalet per person US$5/15/22) Positioned on an idyllic seaside spot near the northern tip of the island, it's a 20- to 30-minute walk from the boat pier (or you can hire a horse and cart). Run by a friendly, English-speaking, Brazilian-and-French couple, guests are hosted in the main house or in two beautiful bungalows in the forest. Breakfast is included. They also lead tours around the island.

Eating & Drinking

Most places serve portions big enough for two. Unfortunately, not a lot of these places have addresses and roads are unsigned (it's a town of just two sandy paths with some simple dwellings scattered along the road).

Eden (dishes US$7) Just north of town, Eden prepares delicious lunches and dinners, with vegetarian options.

Restaurant Prato Cheio (dishes US$2) West of Rua Principal on the town beach, this place has plates of chicken or fish.

Kakuri (Rua Principal; dishes US$4-5) Serves shrimp, fish and chicken dishes. A few doors down at Mata Broca, you'll find similar offerings for a bit less.

Hotel Bela Mar (Rua Principal; dishes US$6) At the base of the street, this hotel makes a decent *caldeirada* (seafood stew).

During the busy season, beach bars near the tip of the island fill with visitors downing batches of fried fish and *carangueijo toc-toc* (whole crab).

For a lively music scene on the weekends, head to Bar do Carimbó, around the corner from Kakuri.

Getting There & Away

Access is via the mainland village of Marudá. Rápido Excelsior buses (US$3.50) and microbuses (US$4.50) leave Belém bus station for Marudá (3½ hours, four or five daily). To be sure of getting onto the island the same day, leave Belém by 12:30pm. In Marudá, take a boat from the Maré Mansa port to Algodoal (US$1.75, 40 minutes).

ILHA DE MARAJÓ

On the enchanting Ilha de Marajó bicycles and buffalo rule the grassy lanes, and its 250,000 inhabitants are among the friendliest people you'll meet. In addition to the abundance of wildlife that covers the island, Marajó is known for its sensuous *carimbó* – the colorful dance of Pará – and its mouthwatering platefuls of fresh seafood.

Slightly larger than Switzerland, this verdant, 50,000-sq-km island lies in the middle of the mouth of the Amazon. For half the year most of it lies under water, but there's little rain between August and November.

Joanes

Arriving from the Camará port, Joanes is 5km off the main road and the first coastal village of any size that you can reach. It's a quiet place, with livestock wandering among the fragments of an old Jesuit church and a fine sandy beach nearby. The popular **Pousada Ventania do Rio-Mar** (☎ 0xx91-3646-2067; ventaniapousada@hotmail.com; s/d US$13/19) sits atop a breezy headland overlooking the beach and has good rooms. The amiable Belgian owner can arrange all kinds of excursions to see the plentiful wildlife in the area, but she's sometimes booked, so call ahead. Breakfast is included in rates. Two **peixarias** lie on the beach, and they serve hearty plates of fish for around US$2.

Salvaterra

Larger, livelier Salvaterra (population 5800) lies 18km north of Joanes. It has a good beach, Praia Grande.

The helpful state **tourist office** (Av Victor Engelhard 56) provides information about nearby attractions. The friendly **Pousada Bosque dos Aruãs** (☎ 0xx91-3765-1115; Segunda Rua; s/d with fan US$10/12, with air-con US$12/14; 🖳), immediately above the ocean at the end of Segunda Rua, has comfortable, clean wooden cabins with bathrooms and a good breakfast. Its **restaurant** also serves delicious fish and shrimp dishes (US$4). Bosque dos Aruãs rents bicycles for US$3 a day.

BRAZIL

Soure & Around

Soure (population 17,000), Marajó's principal town, sits on the north bank of the mouth of the Rio Paracauari, almost opposite Salvaterra. **Banco do Brasil** (Rua 3; ☺ 10am-3pm Mon-Fri) offers Visa cash advances. The beaches near Soure are excellent: you can easily cycle or walk the 3km north to **Praia Barra Velho** by following the street Travessa 14 out of town (passing the gate into the *fazenda*; ranch) till you see the path to the beach diverging to the right. A bit farther (if there's a boat on hand to take you across the intervening river) is **Praia de Araruna**, the most beautiful beach, several kilometers long and practically deserted. **Praia do Pesqueiro**, 9km from town (head inland along Rua 4), is Soure's popular weekend beach, with stalls serving great crab.

The **Soure Hotel** (☎ 0xx91-741-1202, Rua 3 No 1347; s/d apartamentos with fan US$10/13, with air-con US$16/24; ✂) in the center of town has drab *apartamentos*. **Hotel Araruna** (☎ 0xx91-741-1347; Travessa 14; s/d with air-con US$20/30; ✂) is better, with clean rooms.

Bar Batú Anu (Rua 2; dishes US$2), just off the ferry landing, serves hearty shrimp, beef and chicken *pratos feitos*.

Getting There & Around

From Belém port (Portão 15/16), boats depart for the small port of Foz do Rio Camará (often called simply Camará) on the Ilha do Marajó at 6:30am and 2pm, Monday, Wednesday and Friday. Boats also leave at 10:30am on Tuesday, Thursday and Saturday, and at 10am on Sunday. Boats return to Belém at 3pm Tuesday, Thursday, Saturday and Sunday; and 10:30am on Monday, Wednesday and Friday. The three-hour crossing costs US$4.

Buses and minivans (US$0.75) meet the boats at Camará to carry passengers the 27km to Salvaterra, or a few kilometers further to the bank of the Rio Paracauari facing Soure. Some of them may go into Joanes. If not, get off at the Joanes junction (trevo) and walk or hitchhike the remaining 5km. Small motorboats carry passengers across the Paracauari for US$0.30, or you can travel free on the hourly vehicle ferry.

MACAPÁ

Lying on the north side of the Rio Amazonas estuary, Macapá (population 270,000) is an orderly, safe place, with a pleasant waterfront and delectable sea breezes (though it's rather humid). The city is the capital of the small state of Amapá, which stretches north to the border of French Guiana.

The Amapá tourism department, **Detur** (☎ 0xx96-212-5335; Rua Independência 29; ☺ 9:30am-noon & 2:30-6pm Mon-Fri), has a helpful information desk.

Sights & Activities

The large, impressive fortress, **Fortaleza de São José de Macapá** (admission free; ☺ 9am-6pm Tue-Fri, 10am-7pm Sat, Sun & holidays) was built by the Portuguese between 1764 and 1782 to defend the north side of the Amazon against French incursions from the Guianas. The **Museu Sacaca de Desenvolvimento Sustentável** (Av Feliciano Coelho 1509; admission free; ☺ 8:30am-noon & 3-6pm Mon-Fri, 3-6pm Sat) focuses on projects related to Amapá state's admirable sustainable development program. Exhibits include medicinal uses of plants and traditional shamanic healing practices.

Sleeping

Hotel Santo Antonio (☎ 0xx96-222-0226; Av Coriolano Jucá 485; dm per person US$6, s/d with air-con US$14/18; ✂) This hotel has the best budget accommodations in town with a range of clean, decent rooms.

América Hotel (☎ 0xx96-223-2819; Av Coaracy Nunes 333; s/d quartos US$8.50/13.50, s/d apartamentos US$16.50/25.50) A step up, this place has friendly service and good rooms – get the breezy ones in front.

Hotel Glória (☎ 0xx96-222-0984; Rua Leopoldo Machado 2085; s/d US$17/29; ✂) Neat rooms and hot showers.

Eating

Two of Macapá's best restaurants have beautifully breezy settings on the waterfront Av Beira Rio, a few hundred meters south of the fort.

Peixaria Amazonas (Rio Macacoari; dishes for 2 around US$10) Serves good fish dishes.

Cantinho Baiano (Av Beira Rio 328) Has tasty Bahian food at similar prices to Amazonas.

Bom Paladar Kilos (Av Presidente Getúlio Vargas 456; meals per kg US$8) Try this place for good per kilo food.

Chalé Restaurant (Avenida Presidente Vargas 499; dishes for 2 US$10-20) A classy spot serving two-person seafood, chicken and pasta dishes.

Getting There & Away

AIR

Varig, VASP and TAM all fly to other main Brazilian cities. Most flights from Macapá leave early in the morning and you'll at least touch down in Belém if not change planes there. Regional airline Penta has flights to Cayenne (French Guiana) and Oiapoque. Average flights from Belém cost US$34 on Gol, US$55 on Varig and take one hour.

BOAT

Boats to Belém, Santarém and Manaus go from Santana, 25km southwest of Macapá. You can buy tickets in Macapá at **Agencia Sonave** (Rua São José 2145). Buses to Santana (US$0.70) depart from any northbound stop on Rua São José in central Macapá.

Slower boats (hammock/air-con US$40/46, 20 to 24 hours) leave every morning at 7am except Wednesday and Sunday.

Boats to Santarém (hammock US$40, about 2½ days) and Manaus (US$80, five days) leave at 6pm Monday and Friday.

BUS

Hwy BR-156 runs 532km north to the border town Oiapoque. Only the first 140km are paved. Most days there are supposed to be at least two daily buses in each direction but during the rainiest months (roughly January to June) buses may not go every day. The trip (US$20) should take between 12 and 24 hours depending on the season. In the wet season, the going can be rough.

Getting Around

The airport is 3.5km northwest of the center; a taxi is around US$6.

Buses Jardim I/Bairro and Brasil Novo/Universidade (US$0.70) run to the bus station, in Bairro São Lázaro on the northern edge of the city, from Praça Veiga Cabral in the center.

OIAPOQUE

This is the remote town on the Brazilian side of the French Guiana border. Across the Rio Oiapoque (a US$5, 15-minute motorboat ride) lies St. Georges, French Guiana.

The Brazilian Polícia Federal post is open daily except Sunday for immigration procedures. Oiapoque has no exchange facilities except for cash. There are a few cheap places to stay: the **Hotel do Governo** (☎ 0xx96-521-1809) and **Hotel Kayama** (☎ 0xx96-521-1448) are probably the best options.

Oiapoque is linked to Macapá by bus and plane (see p371).

PALMAS

Palmas (population 131,000) is a clean, modern city that makes a good base for exploring the rich, wildlife areas around Tocantins state. Tocantins' attractions are mostly ecotouristic and not cheap, but if you have the money and time to get well off the beaten track, the Ilha do Bananal (the world's largest river island, on Tocantins' western borders) and the unique, hardly inhabited Jalapão region in eastern Tocantins are excellent choices. The best people to organize visits are **Bananal Ecotour** (☎ 0xx63-215-4333; travel@bananalecotour.com.br; Quadra 103-S, Conjunto 03, Rua SO 11, Lote 28, Palmas).

Sleeping & Eating

Alvorada Hotel (☎ 0xx63-215-3401; Quadra 103-N, Conjunto 2, Rua NO 1, Lotes 20 & 21; s/d with fan US$6/7, with air-con US$7/8; 🔀) A block north of the central Praça dos Girassó, this is the best budget place in town. The upstairs rooms are better.

Hotel Brasília (☎ 0xx63-215-2707; Avenida JK, Quadra 103-N, Conjunto 1, Lote 20; s/d with fan US$8/12, with air-con US$16/24; 🔀) Just west of the central Praça dos Girassó, a plain but adequate choice.

Palmas Shopping mall, immediately south of Praça dos Girassóis, has a **food court** with a dozen fairly economical eateries.

Getting There & Away

TAM and Nordeste fly daily to/from Brasília. TAM also serves Belém. The airport lies 30km outside of town. Bus 71, Expresso Miracema, runs to the center (US$0.50).

The **bus station** (APMSE 125 Avenida LO27), in the center of town, is a 10-minute walk to the Palácio Araguaia. Bus connections include Alto Paraíso de Goiás (US$10, seven hours, daily), Belém (US$32, 19 hours, one or more daily), Brasília (US$22, 14 hours, daily) and Natividade (US$5, three to four hours, three daily).

NATIVIDADE

With a charming historic center of cobbled streets and one-story, 18th- and 19th-century houses, Natividade is Tocantins'

BRAZIL

oldest town. It was founded in 1734 after a minor gold rush in the green, wooded Serra Geral, which lies nearby, and it sits 230km southeast of Palmas.

The most evocative building is the shell of the tall stone **Igreja NS do Rosário dos Pretos**, built in 1828 by and for slaves (who were not allowed to use the whites' church). Half a kilometer from town are the **Poções**, a series of small waterfalls and natural bathing pools, from which a trail leads up the Serra Geral to the remains of **São Luiz**, the original settlement of the 1720s gold prospectors. Children from the town will lead you up there for a few *reais* – allow several hours for the outing.

Small central *pousadas* such as **Hotel Brazão** (no tel; Rua Deocleciano Nunes; s/d quartos US$3/6, apartamentos US$9/11) and **Hotel July** (no tel; Rua 7 de Setembro; s/d quartos US$3/6, apartamentos US$9/11) are good values, offering plain simple rooms. **Hotel Serra Geral** (☎ 0xx63-372-1160; s/d US$13/17; ✷), 1.7km north of the center, has bigger, decent air-con *apartamentos*.

Natividade lies between Palmas in Alto Paraíso de Goiás (where you can access

Parque Nacional da Chapada dos Veadeiros) and Brasília. Three daily buses run to Natividade from Palmas (US$5, four hours). There are also daily buses to/from Lençóis, Salvador, Alto Paraíso de Goiás and Brasília.

SANTARÉM

A pleasant town on the Rio Amazonas, Santarém (population 177,000) is a sleepy backwater compared with Manaus and Belém, which lies about halfway between. Nearby is the lovely river-beach resort, Alter do Chão.

Cyber Café (Av Tapajós 418) offers Internet access. Banks are on Avenida Rui Barbosa, notably **HSBC** (Av Rui Barbosa 553). Santarém has no tourist office, but you can get information and book excursions and flights at English-speaking **Santarém Tur** (☎ 0xx93-522-4847; Rua Adriano Pimentel 44).

Sights

The **walkway** overlooking the river is the centerpiece of the town. At night it's a pleasant place to stroll among the fishermen,

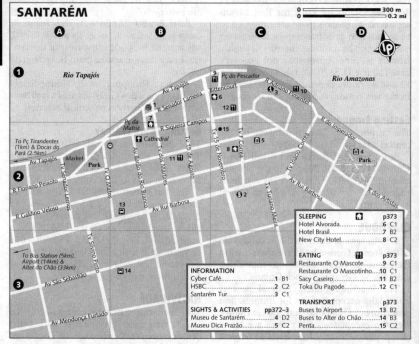

SANTARÉM

0   300 m
0   0.2 mi

Rio Tapajós

Rio Amazonas

To Pç Tirandentes (1km) & Docas do Pará (2.5km)

To Bus Station (5km), Airport (14km) & Alter do Chão (33km)

INFORMATION	
Cyber Café	1 B1
HSBC	2 C2
Santarém Tur	3 C1

SIGHTS & ACTIVITIES	pp372–3
Museu de Santarém	4 D2
Museu Dica Frazão	5 C2

SLEEPING	p373
Hotel Alvorada	6 C1
Hotel Brasil	7 B2
New City Hotel	8 C2

EATING	p373
Restaurante O Mascote	9 C1
Restaurante O Mascotinho	10 C1
Sacy Caseiro	11 B2
Toka Du Pagode	12 C1

TRANSPORT	p373
Buses to Airport	13 B2
Buses to Alter do Chão	14 B3
Penta	15 C2

food vendors and handholding couples. The **Museu de Santarém** (admission US$0.50; 8am-5pm Mon-Fri) facing the waterfront just east of the center, has a small collection of stone and pottery works (including figurines and burial urns) from the Tapajoara culture, which flourished more than 6000 years ago. The **Museu Dica Frazão** (Rua Floriano Peixoto 281; daily), run by the eccentric 80-something Dona Dica Frazão herself, displays the beautiful clothing and tapestries she makes from natural fibers found in the Amazon. Some of her handicrafts are for sale.

Sleeping

Hotel Brasil (0xx93-523-5177; Travessa dos Mártires 30; s/d US$7/10) A charming old family-run place with clean rooms, some with large, shuttered windows overlooking the street. Breakfast included.

Hotel Alvorada (0xx93-522-5340; Rua Senador Lameira Bittencourt 179; s/d quartos US$5/8, s/d apartamentos US$9/12) Hotel Alvorada offers a range of basic rooms. The airy front rooms with river views are nice.

New City Hotel (0xx93-522-0355; Travessa Francisco Correa 200; s/d US$15/20;) Decent air-con *apartamentos* run by friendly staff. Free pick-up from the airport.

Eating

In the evening look for snack carts along Avenida Tapajós and around Praça do Pescador – especially the woman selling delicious Brazilian-style crepes.

Sacy Caseiro (Rua Floriano Peixoto 521; buffet per kilo US$5) It's hard to beat the selection of good food at this lunch buffet.

Toka Du Pagode (Siqueira Campos 164; buffet per kilo US$3) Covered courtyard lunch buffet with a good selection of freshly roasted meats.

Restaurante O Mascote (Praça do Pescador 10; dishes from US$4) Tasty plates of fish and decent steaks serve two, and the open-air locale is pleasant.

Restaurante O Mascotinho (Rua Adrian O Pimentel) Further east, on a large terrace overlooking the river, you'll find snacks and standards – beer, burgers and pizza.

Getting There & Around

AIR

Penta (0xx93-523-2220; 15 de Novembre 187) flies to/from Belém and Manaus daily for around US$50. Varig has flights for quite a bit more. Regional airlines also serve many smaller Amazonian cities.

The airport is 14km west of the center; buses (US$0.50) run to the airport nine times between 5:30am and 5:30pm, and to the city nine times between 6:15am and 6:15pm. Taxis cost US$8. The New City hotel offers free transportation from the airport for guests.

BOAT

Boats to and from Manaus, Belém and Macapá (each two days from Santarém) dock at the Docas do Pará, 2.5km west of the center. Tickets are sold at booths outside the dock's entrance. Boats usually leave for Manaus (hammock US$33) around 3pm daily except Sunday. Simon Soare has express boats to Manaus at 5pm on Saturday (US$40; 24 hours). Boats for Belém (US$33) depart around noon from Tuesday to Sunday; and for Macapá (US$30) at 6pm daily. Cabins are normally already taken by passengers embarking in Manaus or Belém.

Boats to Monte Alegre (US$6, 3½ hours) depart from in front of Praça Tiradentes at 2pm from Monday to Friday and noon on Saturday.

The Orla Fluvial bus shuttles between the center and Docas do Pará until about 7pm (US$0.50).

BUS

The BR-163 to Cuiabá is paved for only 84km south from Santarém. The remaining unpaved 700km can take a week in the wet season. The bus station is 5km southwest of the center. From about June to November only, a daily bus runs to Cuiabá (US$50, about three days).

ALTER DO CHÃO

With its white-sand beaches and tropical ambience, the village of Alter do Chão is one of Amazonia's most beautiful places to unwind. The town, 33km west of Santarém, overlooks the Rio Tapajós at the entrance to a picturesque lagoon, Lago Verde.

Large crowds descend on Alter do Chão in the second week of September for the Festa do Çairé, a lively folkloric festival with dancing and processions.

The beaches are usually submerged in June and July.

Sleeping & Eating

Except for weekend nights, little happens in the sleepy town after dark. For excursions onto the lake ask at your *pousada*.

Pousada Alter-do-Chão (☎ 0xx93-522-3411; Rua Lauro Sodré 74; s/d with fan US$7/10, s&d with air-con US$13; 🔀) A beachside location with comfortable rooms. A decent breakfast is included in the price.

Pousada Vila da Praia (☎ 0xx93-527-1130; Rua Copacabana 145; s&d US$10, chalets US$13; 🔀) A block inland, this friendly place has good air-con suites for one or two people and 'chalets' for up to five. Rates include breakfast.

Pousada Tia Marilda (☎ 0xx93-527-1144; Travessa Agostinho A. Lobato 559; s/d quartos US$6/7, s/d apartamentos US$8/12; 🔀) Cramped rooms with air-con lie on the ground floor. Upstairs the breezier, bigger *quartos* are a better value. Breakfast included.

The several **restaurants** in town offer pretty much the same range of beef, chicken and fish dishes for around US$4 to US$8 for two.

Getting There & Away

Buses to Alter do Chão (US$0.60, one hour) leave Santarém about 10 times daily. From Monday to Saturday they depart from a stop on Av São Sebastião, east of Travessa Silvino Pinto; on Sunday and holidays buses depart from Praça Tiradentes, 1km west of Santarém center.

GETTING INTO TOWN

Aeroporto Internacional Eduardo Gomes is 13km north of the city center. Smaller regional airlines use the separate Terminal 2, 'Eduardinho,' about 600m east of the main one. Bus No 306 'Aeroporto Centro' runs about every half hour between the airport and the city center bus terminus on Praça da Matriz (US$0.50, 30 minutes). It's not a good idea to take it before 6am or after 11pm. The official airport-to-center taxi fare is US$15, but if you walk out to the airport bus stop you'll often get one for US$8 or so.

The bus station is 6km north of the center at Rua Recife 2784 (US$8 by taxi). Bus No 306 'Aeroporto Centro' (see the preceding section) stops on Avenida Constantino Nery, a one-minute walk away.

MANAUS

Once billed as the Paris of the tropics for its opera house, its wrought-iron market (modeled on Paris's Les Halles) and its refined aristocracy, Manaus exuded extravagance in the late 19th century. Today one might be more prone to call it the Cleveland of the Tropics, owing to its blighted coastline and the ruined landscape surrounding the city. Still, Manaus is not without its charm, and beneath the worn facade you'll find a fascinating place. Today many travelers visit Manaus only to arrange jungle trips, and agencies – good and bad – abound.

Manaus lies on the Rio Negro, 10km upstream from its confluence with the Rio Solimões, beyond which the mighty combined river is called the Rio Amazonas. The city is an international port some 1500km from the mouth of the Amazonas.

Though the Portuguese built a fort here in 1669, Manaus remained a minor outpost till the rubber boom of the late 19th century. Impoverished northeasterners came to work as rubber tappers in the jungles, under a rich elite of plantation owners, rubber traders and bankers. Ocean-going steamships brought luxuries up the Amazon and left laden with latex. When the rubber boom ended, around 1914, Manaus fell into decline.

Orientation

Downtown Manaus stretches from the Rio Negro to the Teatro Amazonas (opera house) area, about 1km. The streets nearest the main passenger dock, the Porto Flutuante (Floating Dock), are crowded and noisy. A little inland is an area of shopping streets known as the Zona Franca. This ends at Praça da Polícia, a focal point.

Budget lodgings mostly cluster a few streets southeast of the Zona Franca.

Information

EMERGENCY

Centro de Atendimento ao Turista (Tourist Assistance Center; ☎ 0xx92-231-1998; Av Eduardo Ribeiro; ⊙ daily) There's a police post here.

INTERNET ACCESS

The following places charge about US$1 an hour:

Amazon Cyber Café (cnr Rua Getúlio Vargas &10 de Julho)

Cybercity Café (Av Getúlio Vargas 188)

Discover Internet (Rua Marcílio Dias 304)

MEDICAL SERVICES
Unimed (☎ 0xx92-633-4431; Av Japurá 241) The best private hospital in the city.

MONEY
Amazônia Turismo (Rua Dr Moreira 88) Changes cash and traveler's checks.
Banco do Brasil (Rua Guilherme Moreira 315 & at the airport) Has ATMs.
HSBC (Rua Dr Moreira 226) Has ATMs.

POST
Main post office (Rua Marcílio Dias 160; ☼ 9am-5pm Mon-Fri, 8am-noon Sat).

TOURIST OFFICES
The Amazonas state tourism secretariat runs information offices.
Airport (☎ 0xx92-652-1120)
Centro de Atendimento ao Turista (Tourist Assistance Center; ☎ 0xx92-231-1998; Av Eduardo Ribeiro)

Dangers & Annoyances
At the airport, avoid the vultures touting jungle trips or city accommodations. Some have reportedly hustled people off

to be robbed. After 11pm steer clear of the port area and take care around Praça da Matriz.

Sights & Activities
Mercado Municipal is one of several bustling markets near the waterfront. This sprawling, cast-iron, Art-Nouveau wonder opened in 1882. In addition to herbal and traditional medicines of the Amazon, you'll find crafts and souvenirs.

A little farther east lies the newer, smellier **Feira do Produtor**, a lively food market.

The British-designed **Porto Flutuante** (Floating Dock) dates from 1902 and rises and falls up to 10m with seasonal water levels.

The famous **Teatro Amazonas** (admission US$1.50; ☼ 9am-4pm Mon-Sat) was built in 1896 in eclectic neoclassical style at the height of the rubber boom. You can take an interesting guided tour in English.

Museu do Homem do Norte (Av Sete de Setembro 1385; admission free; ☼ 9am-noon & 1-5pm Mon-Fri) displays both household and ceremonial instruments used by Amazonian tribes, and gives an overview of some of their legends.

BRAZIL

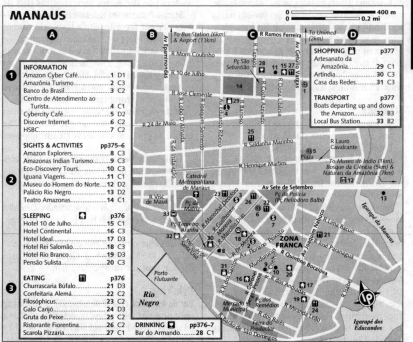

MANAUS

0 — 400 m
0 — 0.2 mi

INFORMATION
Amazon Cyber Café.....................1 D1
Amazônia Turismo.......................2 C3
Banco do Brasil...........................3 C2
Centro de Atendimento ao
   Turista....................................4 C1
Cybercity Café.............................5 D2
Discover Internet.........................6 C3
HSBC..7 C2

SIGHTS & ACTIVITIES pp375-6
Amazon Explorers........................8 C3
Amazonas Indian Turismo...........9 C3
Eco-Discovery Tours...................10 C3
Iguana Viagens...........................11 C1
Museu do Homem do Norte.......12 D2
Palácio Rio Negro.......................13 D2
Teatro Amazonas........................14 C1

SLEEPING p376
Hotel 10 de Julho.......................15 C1
Hotel Continental........................16 C3
Hotel Ideal.................................17 D3
Hotel Rei Salomão......................18 D3
Hotel Rio Branco........................19 D3
Pensão Sulista............................20 C3

EATING p376
Churrascaria Búfalo....................21 D3
Confeitaria Alemã.......................22 C2
Filosóphicus...............................23 C2
Galo Carijó.................................24 D3
Gruta do Peixe...........................25 C2
Ristorante Fiorentina..................26 C3
Scarola Pizzaria..........................27 C1

SHOPPING p377
Artesanato da
   Amazônia.............................29 C1
Artíndia.....................................30 C3
Casa das Redes...........................31 C3

TRANSPORT p377
Boats departing up and down
   the Amazon............................32 B3
Local Bus Station........................33 B2

DRINKING pp376-7
Bar do Armando.........................28 C1

To Bus Station (6km)
& Airport (13km)

To Unimed
(2km)

R Ramos Ferreira

Av Epaminondas

R Mons Coutinho

Pç São
Sebastião

R 10 de Julho

R José Clemente

R 24 de Maio

R Lobo D'Almada

R Joaquim Sarmento

R Eduardo Ribeiro

R Costa Azevedo

R Dona Libânia

Av Getúlio Vargas

R Saldanha Marinho

R Henrique Martins

Catedral
Metropolitana
de Manaus

Av Sete de Setembro

R da Instalação

R Visc
de Mauá

Pç da
Matriz

Pç da Polícia
(Pç Heliodoro Balbi)

R Marechal Deodoro

R Guilherme
Moreira

R Marcílio Dias

R Dr Moreira

R Lauro
Cavalcante

To Museu do Índio (1km),
Bosque da Ciência (5km) &
Naturais da Amazônia (7km)

Plaza

Pç Tenreiro
Aranha

R Rocha dos Santos

R Quintino Bocaiúva

ZONA
FRANCA

R José Paranaguá

R Joaquim Nabuco

R Lima Bacuri

Munduruca

R Pororoca

R dos Andradas

R Isabel

Porto
Flutuante

Rio
Negro

R dos Barés

R Miranda Leão

Mercado
Municipal

R dos
Remédios

Feira do
Produtor

Av Lourenço de São Domingos

Igarapé de Manaus

Igarapé dos
Educandos

The ornate **Palácio Rio Negro** (Av Sete de Setembro 1546; admission free; 🕑 10am-5pm Tue-Fri, 4-8pm Sat) is a rubber baron's mansion turned cultural center. It houses changing expositions, a coffee shop and the uninspiring state art gallery.

Museu do Índio (Rua Duque de Caxias 356, off Av Sete de Setembro; admission US$1.75; 🕑 8am-noon, 2-5pm Mon-Fri, 8am-noon Sat) features good exhibits on the Yanomami and other peoples of the northwest. The shop downstairs sells Indian crafts. Bus No 606 from Avenida Floriano Peixoto opposite Praça Heliodoro Balbi (also known as Praça da Polícia) stops almost outside the door.

Bosque da Ciência (Rua Otávio Cabral; admission US$1.75; 🕑 9-11am & 2-5pm Tue-Sun) The tranquil 'Forest of Science,' 5km northeast of the center, belongs to the National Amazonian Research Institute and has a collection of giant otters, manatees, alligators and other creatures on 130,000 sq m of rain forest. Bus No 519 from Praça da Matriz stops at the entrance.

Along with an array of stuffed fish and colorful butterflies, **Museu de Ciências Naturais da Amazônia** (Estrada Belém s/n, Colônia Cachoeira Grande; students/adults US$1.75/3; 🕑 9am-5pm Mon-Sat) has a small aquarium with beautiful, 2m-long pirarucu fish. Take bus No 519 from Praça da Matriz or onward from the Bosque da Ciência: tell the conductor you want the Museu de Ciências Naturais, then from the stop walk 15 minutes, following 'Museu' signs.

Sleeping

The main cluster of respectable budget hotels is around Rua dos Andradas.

Hotel Ideal (☎ 0xx92-622-0038; Rua dos Andradas 491; s/d with fan US$5/8, with air-con US$8/11; 🔀) A popular choice for backpackers, given the clean rooms, friendly staff and decent breakfast. Rooms lack natural light.

Hotel 10 de Julho (☎ 0xx92-232-6280; htdj@ internext.com.br; Rua 10 de Julho 679; s/d US$11/13; 🔀) Young travelers flock to the modern digs near the Teatro Amazonas. It has good, comfy rooms and a nice breakfast.

Hotel Rio Branco (☎ 0xx92-233-4019; Rua dos Andradas 484; s/d with fan US$5/8, with air-con US$6/12; 🔀) Lacking the travelers' vibe but not the budget prices, *quartos* here are dark and mournful. Bigger rooms with air-con are a little brighter. Simple breakfasts are included in the rates.

Pensão Sulista (☎ 0xx92-234-5814; Av Joaquim Nabuco 347; s/d with fan US$5/8, with air-con US$12; 🔀) A Manaus standard with basic, clean rooms.

Hotel Continental (☎ 0xx92-233-3342; Rua Coronel Sergio Pessoa 189; s/d US$11/13; 🔀) A good value for Manaus, with amiable staff, air-con *apartamentos*, hot showers and a fine breakfast.

Hotel Rei Salomão (☎ 0xx92-234-7374; Rua Dr Moreira 119; s/d US$13/18; 🔀) Offers decent air-con *apartamentos* in a modern building near the plaza. Rates are higher if you don't pay in cash.

Eating

At street stalls bold palates can sample *tacacá*, a gummy soup made from manioc root, dried shrimp and lip-numbing jambu leaves. Praça da Saudade has several **barracas de tacacá** (*tacacá* stalls), open from about 4pm.

Churrascaria Búfalo (Av Joaquim Nabuco 628; lunch buffet per kg US$7.50) A meat-lovers' paradise with gigantic steaks and an extensive lunch buffet. By night, skewers of meat flash like swords as sausage- and brisket-bearing waiters pile the plates high (*rodízio* US$8).

Scarola Pizzaria (Rua 10 de Julho 739; pizzas from US$6) An open-air favorite with a tasty selection of pizzas, good service and ice-cold chopp.

Ristorante Fiorentina (Rua José Paranaguá 44; lunch buffet per kg US$7.50) This handsome spot on Praça Heliodoro Balbí offers a good lunch spread and equally good Italian à la carte fare in the evening (pastas around US$5).

Gruta do Peixe (Rua Saldanha Marinho 609; dishes around US$7) Inside the grotto-like dining room, *moços* (waiters) serve steaming plates of fresh fish.

Confeitaria Alemã (Rua José Paranagua 126; lunch buffet per kg US$6) Small but good lunch buffet plus fast-food options in the no-nonsense dining room.

Filosóphicus (top fl, Av Sete de Setembro 752; buffet per kg US$4) Weekday lunch buffet with vegetarian dishes.

Galo Carijó (cnr Rua dos Andradas & Rua Pedro Botelho; dishes US$1.50-5; 🕑 Mon-Sat) Good lunch and dinner spot for inexpensive fish.

Drinking

Bar do Armando (Rua 10 de Julho 593) A drinking spot popular with a few travelers as well as a Manaus crowd bent on solving the world's social problems.

On Friday and Saturday nights, Praça Heliodoro Balbí and Praça da Saudade are lively places to grab a drink under the open sky.

Shopping

Good places to buy Indian crafts include:
Artíndia (Praça Tenreiro Aranha)
Artesanato da Amazônia (Rua José Clemente 500)
Museu do Índio (Rua Duque de Caxias 356)

For hammocks try **Casa das Redes** (Rua Rocha dos Santos) or the street vendors around Praça Tenreiro Aranha.

Getting There & Away

AIR

Manaus has several international flights on Varig and LAB, as well as numerous domestic connections on Varig, TAM, VASP and Rico. Sample destinations and one-way fares include the following:

Belém US$140, 6 per day.
Brasília US$115, 7 per day.
Miami, US US$800, 1 per day Mon & Fri on LAB, 1 per day Sun on Varig.
Santa Cruz, Bolivia US$260, 1 per day Tue & Thu on LAB.
Santarém US$165, 4 per day Mon, 3 per day Tue-Sat, 1 per day Sun.
Tabatinga US$175, 3 per day Tue, Thu, Sat, 1 per day Sun.

BOAT

Nearly all passenger boats arrive and depart from the Porto Flutuante. Tickets are sold at the booths just inside the entrance. The following table shows information for the main riverboat destinations. Departures are usually between 3pm and 6pm.

Destination	Duration	Cost	Frequency
Belém	4 days	upper/lower deck US$76/70	Mon & Wed
Porto Velho	4 days	upper/lower deck US$65/63	Tue & Fri
Santarém	30-36 hrs	upper/lower deck US$37/31	Mon-Sat
Tabatinga	6 days	upper deck US$86	departs irregularly
Tefé	2½ days	upper/lower deck US$37/32	Wed, Thu & Sat

BUS

The only long-distance road link is the highway north to Boa Vista, which contin-ues to Santa Elena de Uairén, Venezuela, and the Caribbean. Five daily air-con buses go to Boa Vista (US$22, 12 hours). One continues to Santa Elena and to Puerto de la Cruz (US$52, 33 hours) on the Vene-zuelan coast.

Buses south to Porto Velho have been suspended since 1991.

Getting Around

Try to avoid moving around the city be-tween 1pm and 2pm, and 5pm and 7pm, when city buses and downtown streets get fearfully crowded.

AROUND MANAUS
Encontro das Águas & Parque Ecológico Janauary

The Encontro das Águas (Meeting of the Waters) is where the dark, violet Rio Negro meets the café au lait Rio Solimões, a few kilometers downstream from Manaus. The two flow side by side without mingling, and make a fascinating sight. Agencies such as **Amazon Explorers** (Praça Tenreiro Aranha) run daily excursions (US$30) to the Encontro das Águas followed by a visit to the nearby Parque Ecológico Janauary. However, the 'park' is anything but ecological, and there's a seriously packaged feel to these tours.

You can visit the same sites by motor-ized canoe for around US$50 for four people. Find an Associação dos Canoeiros member at the Porto Flutuante to organize this (see p378).

Another way of seeing the Meeting of the Waters is from the free hourly *balsa* (ferry) between Ponta do Catalão, 12km east of downtown Manaus, and Careiro on the far shore of the Amazonas. From the same dock, motorboats regularly depart for Careiro (US$1.75, 40 minutes). You can reach the ferry by taxi or by bus No 713 from Praça da Matriz (last stop).

Careiro is a quaint village and worth a look around. Just up the main road from the dock you'll find **Silva and Silva**, an inexpensive restaurant that serves big portions of fried fish or grilled chicken for US$2.50.

Jungle Trips

Taking a jungle trip is the top priority for most visitors to Manaus, and the city offers Brazilian Amazonia's greatest concentration

BRAZIL

of agencies and guides for arranging either a short jaunt or a longer, more adventurous excursion.

Standard activities on trips lasting at least one night include piranha fishing, a jungle walk, a visit to a rustic *caboclo* home (where you'll meet riverbank dwellers of indigenous descent), and nighttime alligator spotting. You'll probably see *botos* (river dolphins) along the way and observe abundant bird life.

On a trip of just a few days from Manaus, don't expect to meet remote tribal peoples or encounter many free-ranging beasts. If you have five or six days you can start to think about reaching areas of primary forest with chances of spotting more wildlife.

Once you've decided what kind of trip you want, take the time to compare the options closely and consider the following:

- Whether you and your guide have languages in common.
- How much time is spent getting to and from your destination.
- Whether the tour includes travel in small boats (without use of motor) along *igarapés*.
- What the cost breakdown (food, drinks, lodging, fuel, guides) is. You may want to buy some of your own food, or pay some expenses en route, thereby avoiding fanciful mark-ups. Unless the agency is very well established, you should insist on paying only part of the price at the beginning of the trip, settling the rest at the end.

Allow at least a day to agree a deal, change money and buy provisions. If you're solo, you can try to join a group to make the trip more economical. Several of the agencies mentioned here can bring travelers together to reduce per-person costs.

Try to meet the actual guide prior to committing yourself to a trip. Don't scrimp on water – you need at least 4L of bottled water per person per day. Last but not least, insist on life jackets.

AGENCIES & GUIDES

Of the dozens of agencies operating in Manaus, some offer packaged jungle tours, which feel about as authentic as a visit to Disneyland. It's best to go with established guides. Talk to other travelers returning from the jungle to get an idea of what to expect.

For a basic trip most agencies will ask about US$50 per person per day, but you should be able to negotiate a price between US$30 and US$40. This should include all meals, drinking water and transportation. Most agencies can set up almost anything, but some have particular experience and expertise. An attractive trip that several agencies can organize is to Lago Mamori, a lake with plentiful bird life some 60km south of Manaus (about a six-hour trip by road, ferry and motorized canoe). Accommodation is in cabanas or simple local homes.

Jungle Experience (☎ 0xx92-233-2000; Hotel Ideal, Rua do Andrades, Manaus) Run by experienced guide Chris Gomes. Travelers recommend the trips to Lago Juma. The quoted daily price is US$50 per person.

Iguana Viagens (☎ 0xx92-9111-0554; iguanatour@ hotmail.com; Rua 10 de Julho 667, Manaus) With a variety of excursions from one to ten days, guides Gerry Hardy and Wilson Castro are favored for leading educational and ecological excursions. The quoted price is US$50 per person, with a four-person minimum, but they'll bring travelers together to make up the numbers.

Gero Mesquita (☎ 0xx92-9983-6273; geromesquita@ hotmail.com; Hotel 10 de Julho, Rua 10 de Julho 679, Manaus) Gero, a friendly English-speaking guide, arranges trips to Lago Mamori and up the Negro and Solimões rivers, which travelers report on favorably. For Mamori, Gero quoted daily prices of around US$200 for a group of up to four people.

Amazonas Indian Turismo (☎ 0xx92-633-5578; Rua dos Andradas 311) A prominent budget agency that gets generally satisfactory reports, Amazonas uses English-speaking Indian guides and a camp with rustic cabanas on the Rio Urubú, northeast of Manaus (200km by bus and motorized canoe). Trips can last from two to 10 days and there's a virgin rain forest area to the northeast.

Eco-Discovery Tours (☎ 0xx92-232-6898; www.eco discovery.hpg.com.br; Rua Leovigildo Coelho 360) A budget outfit running trips to the Rio Urubú. Typical trips of three days and two nights run at US$40 per day.

Associação dos Canoeiros (no tel; Porto Flutuante) This association of independent, licensed boatmen is the best place to go if you're thinking of setting up your own trip. They take travelers up the Rio Negro and Solimões to stay with *caboclo* families, who then lead treks into the jungle. The association, run by English-speaking Antonio Franco, has many members of indigenous descent. Look for them at the Porto Flutuante, wearing green jackets. Independent guides like Marcelo (marcelotours@hotmail.com) work closely with the Canoeiros, and can arrange anything from a simple two-day excursion to a 15-day overland journey to Guyana and Venezuela. While a canoe trip may be less predictable than an organized tour, it may be more authentic. A four-day jungle trip should cost US$40 to US$60 a day, plus provisions and anything you pay for accommodation.

JUNGLE LODGES

At least a dozen jungle lodges lie within 250km of Manaus. These rustic but comfortable wooden hotels boast waterside settings, and visits are normally made on a (somewhat costly) package deal, which includes transportation from/to Manaus, all meals and a program of outings and activities.

Terra Verde Lodge (bookings ☎ 0xx92-622-7305; terraverde@internext.com.br; Room 304, Hotel Mônaco, Rua Silva Ramos 20, Manaus) A small, friendly place about 50km west of Manaus, located off Lago Acajatuba. Two-/three-day packages cost US$220/270 per person.

Acajatuba Jungle Lodge (☎ 0xx92-233-7642; www.acajatuba.com.br; upstairs, Rua Lima Bacuri 345, Manaus) Two-/three-day packages on Lago Acajatuba itself start at US$310/340 per person. Reserve through Anaconda Turismo.

Amazon Lodge (☎ 0xx92-656-6033; www.nature safaris.com; Rua Flavio Espirito Santo 1, Kissia II, Manaus) A small floating lodge on Lago Juma, 60km southeast of Manaus, this lovely lodge caters to 28 guests. Three-day packages cost US$495 per person, with a minimum of two people.

MAMIRAUÁ RESERVE

If you're going to splash out on one ecotourism program in Brazilian Amazonia, the Reserva de Desenvolvimento Sustentável Mamirauá (Mamirauá Sustainable Development Reserve) is the place to do it. This floodplain forest between the Rio Solimões and Rio Japurá, a little over halfway be-

tween Manaus and the Peruvian frontier, is a beautiful, pristine environment of jungle, rivers and lakes. Its excellent ecotourism program provides some of the best wildlife viewing in Amazonia. On a three-day visit one traveler reported seeing four species of monkey (including howlers and the bizarre white uacari with its crimson face and shaggy white coat), dozens of pink dolphins and alligators, numerous gray dolphins, sloths, squirrels and piranhas, and many of the reserve's 400-odd recorded bird species.

Accommodation is in comfortable floating bungalows. Prices include all meals, river trips, guided walks and boat transfers from/to the town of Tefé. A three-day/ two-night package in a double suite costs US$315 per person.

To arrange a visit or to get more information, contact the **Mamirauá office** (☎ 0xx97-343-4160; ecoturismo@mamiraua.org.br; www.mamiraua .org.br; Av Brasil 173 & 197, Tefé).

Varig flies to Tefé from Manaus (US$111, one way) three days a week and from Tabatinga (US$117) twice weekly. Rico flies from both places daily (US$80 from Manaus; US$120 from Tabatinga). Plenty of riverboats ply the Rio Solimões to Tefé from Manaus and Tabatinga. The hammock fare to/from Manaus is around US$37, taking about two days, with departures in both directions most days.

TRIPLE FRONTIER

The Brazilian town of Tabatinga and the Colombian town of Leticia, on the northeast bank of the Amazon about 1100km west of Manaus, are separated by nothing except an international border. The opposite bank of the river here, and the islands in the middle of it, are Peru. This 'triple frontier' provides travel routes between all three countries and is a good area from which to take jungle trips. For information, see Leticia (p597) in the Colombia chapter.

BOA VISTA

A planned city on the banks of the Rio Branco, Boa Vista (population 197,000) feels quite isolated and has few attractions to draw travelers. For many it's just somewhere to pass through between Venezuela and Manaus (645km south). Roraima, of which Boa Vista is the capital, includes most of the Brazilian territories of the Yanomami, one of Amazonia's largest surviving indigenous peoples.

Useful moneychangers in the center exchange US, Venezuelan and Guyanese currencies including **Edson Ouro Safira Joyas** (Av Benjamin Constant 64 W) and **Pedro José** (Rua Araújo Filho 287), who also exchanges US dollar traveler's checks.

Codetur (☎ 0xx95-623-1230; Rua Coronel Pinto 241; ☉ 7:30am-1:30pm Mon-Fri), the state tourism office, provides information. It also has a desk at the airport, open when flights arrive, and another at the bus station, which rarely opens.

Parque Anauá

This vast park on Avenida Brigadeiro Eduardo Gomes, about 2.5km northwest of the center, contains gardens, a lake and the **Museu Integrado de Roraima** (admission free; ☉ 8am-6pm daily). The museum is small but wide-ranging, and free guided tours – available in English most mornings – make this an interesting visit.

Sleeping & Eating

Hotel Ideal (☎ 0xx95-224-6342; Rua Araújo Filho 533; s/d with fan US$11/15, with air-con US$15/20; ✖) The best budget place in town, with clean but bare *apartamentos*, all with breakfast.

Hotel Monte Libano (☎ 0xx95-224-7232; Av Benjamin Constant 319 W; s/d quartos with fan US$10/13, with air-con US$13/16; ✖) The second-best option, with drab, tired rooms and no breakfast provided.

Restaurant Ver O Rio (Praça Barreto Leite; 1/2-person fish plates US$6/12) This fine spot just above the river (there's even a breeze sometimes) serves good fish plates.

Macuchik Restaurante (lunch buffet US$5) Just behind Restaurant Ver O Rio, overlooking the river, this place serves a good-value lunch buffet and à la carte fare from pizzas to fish.

Getting There & Away

AIR

Varig and Meta fly direct daily to/from:
Brasília US$175; 2 per day Mon, Wed, Fri; 1 per day Tue, Thu, Sat & Sun.
Manaus US$125; 2 per day Mon, Wed, Fri; 1 per day Tue, Thu, Sat, Sun.
Rio de Janeiro US$242; 2 per day Mon, Wed, Fri; 1 per day Tue, Thu, Sat & Sun.

Meta also flies to:
Georgetown, Guyana US$235, 1 per day Tue, Thu, Sat.
Paramaribo, Suriname US$275, 1 per day Tue, Thu.

BUS

Eucatur buses leave for Manaus (US$33, 12 hours) six times daily (five have air-con). It also has three departures to Santa Elena de Uairén, Venezuela (US$6, 3½ hours), one of which continues all the way to Puerto La Cruz on Venezuela's Caribbean coast (US$46, 20 hours).

Getting Around

Taxis marked 'Lotação' go along roughly fixed routes for US$1 per passenger. Just ask if they're going where you want – they'll sometimes deviate a bit for you. The airport is 3.5km northwest of the city center (around US$8 by taxi). The **bus station** (Avenida das Guianas) is 2.5km southwest of the center (US$4 by taxi, but Joquei Clube buses go there from the municipal bus terminal on Av Dr Silvio Botelho).

BONFIM

The small town of Bonfim, 125km northeast of Boa Vista, is a possible stepping stone to Guyana (p759). The Guyanese town of Lethem is about 5km away across the Rio Tacutu. Whichever direction you're traveling in, start early to get to your destination before nightfall.

The Polícia Federal (for Brazilian immigration) are between Bonfim bus station and the river, so you have to walk or get taxis (about US$1.25 each time) to the police and onward from them. You can either wade the river or get a canoe across for US$3.

Accommodations in and around Lethem are much better, but if you're stuck in Bonfim try **Pousada Fronteira** (☎ 0xx95-552-1294; Rua Aluísio de Menezes 26; d around US$9).

Amatur buses travel three or four times daily each way between Boa Vista bus station and Bonfim (US$6, two hours).

PORTO VELHO

Breathtaking cloud formations, the red soil of the Amazon, and the inescapable heat are the first things you'll notice upon arrival in Porto Velho (population 262,000). Stretched along the muddy banks of the Rio Madeira, the city has the rugged feel of a frontier town. Slums of straw-roofed shacks lay scattered on the outskirts and newspapers give grisly accounts of shoot-outs between the polícia and smugglers. Rubber, once the commerce of choice for those on the make, has long since been usurped by cocaine, and the states of Acre and Rondônia are the conduits for most of the stuff entering Brazil from Bolivia and Peru. Travelers are generally left alone if they mind their own business.

Orientation & Information

The Rio Madeira forms the western boundary of the city, with the main street, Av Sete de Setembro, running east from there. Boats depart just south of the Madeira-Mamoré Railroad museum. The **bus station** (Av Jorge Teixeira) is 3km from the river, with the airport a further 3km beyond.

Casa de Câmbio Marco Aurélio (Rua José de Alencar 3353; ⊙ 8:30am-3pm Mon-Fri) changes US dollars and traveler's checks. For ATMs, try **Banco do Brasil** (Rua Dom Pedro II 607). You can purchase international phone cards at **Telemania** (Carlos Gomes 728). The state tourism office, **Embratur**

(Av Presidente Dutra 3004; ⊙ Mon-Fri), can provide limited information in Portuguese, as can travel agents.

Shops and offices generally close between noon and 2pm.

Sights & Activities

Porto Velho's only real tourist attraction, **Museu da Estrada de Ferro Madeira-Mamoré** (end of Avenida Sete de Setembro; admission free; ⊙ 8am-6pm), the museum of the Madeira-Mamoré Railroad, houses fascinating displays of old railway relics, dating from the line's early days until its demise in 1972. The museum and the old ruins rusting near the waterfront serve as a plaintive reminder of a dark era in Amazonia's history.

Instrumental in bringing inland rubber to the navigable port, the 364km railroad was built between 1907 and 1912. When completed, it was known as the Railway of Death, owing to the thousands of workers who died during its construction. At least 5000 – 25,000 by some accounts – perished from tropical diseases, Indian and animal attacks, gunfights, accidents and disappearances.

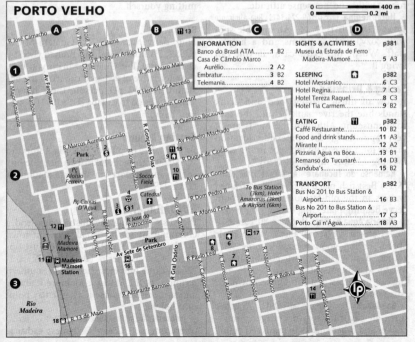

PORTO VELHO

0 — 400 m
0 — 0.2 mi

INFORMATION		SIGHTS & ACTIVITIES	p381
Banco do Brasil ATM	1 B2	Museu da Estrada de Ferro	
Casa de Câmbio Marco		Madeira-Mamoré	5 A3
Aurélio	2 A2		
Embratur	3 B2	SLEEPING	p382
Telemania	4 B2	Hotel Messianico	6 C3
		Hotel Regina	7 C3
		Hotel Tereza Raquel	8 C3
		Hotel Tia Carmem	9 B2

EATING		p382
Caffé Restaurante	10 B2	
Food and drink stands	11 A3	
Mirante II	12 A2	
Pizzaria Agua na Boca	13 B1	
Remanso do Tucunaré	14 D3	
Sanduba's	15 B2	

TRANSPORT		p382
Bus No 201 to Bus Station &		
Airport	16 B3	
Bus No 201 to Bus Station &		
Airport	17 C3	
Porto Cai n'Água	18 A3	

Recently the Maria Fumaça (Smoking Mary) steam locomotive was restored, allowing visitors to ride the historic line to and from Santo Antônio, 7km southwest of Porto Velho (US$2 return) on Sunday. At press time, the engine was no longer running, but there was talk of restoration. Ask at the museum for more information.

Sleeping

Hotel Tereza Raquel (☎ 0xx69-223-9234; Rua Tenreiro Aranha; s/d US$7/10; ✷) The friendly staff, bright rooms and decent breakfast make this a good value hotel for Porto Velho.

Hotel Tia Carmem (☎ 0xx69-221-7910; Av Campos Sales 2895; s/d quartos US$5/8, apartamentos US$9/12; ✷) Rooms here range from monastic cells to airier quarters with TV and air-con. Good location on a quiet street.

Hotel Messianico (☎ 0xx69-221-9348; Av Sete de Setembro 1180; s/d quartos US$3/5, apartamentos US$7/8) Clean, basic, rather cramped rooms at rock-bottom prices. The street stays noisy day and night.

Hotel Amazonas (☎ 0xx69-221-7735; Av Carlos Gomes 2838; s quartos US$3, s/d apartamentos US$4/7) Near the bus station. Fairly clean, secure rooms with a no-nonsense attitude.

Hotel Regina (☎ 0xx69-224-3411; Rua Almirante Barroso 1127; s/d US$13/22; ✷) An amiable spot with cozy, spotless rooms and a helpful staff. Worth the extra cash, if you can swing it.

Eating & Drinking

A row of music-blaring food and drink stands line the riverbank behind the railroad museum. Although the meals aren't very appetizing, the waterside location makes for a nice drinking spot in the early evening – before things get seedy.

Remanso do Tucunaré (Av Brasília 1506; dishes US$5-7) Best fish place in town. Poker-faced waiters in the old-fashioned dining room serve heaping plates, big enough for two.

Pizzaria Agua na Boca (Av Calama 201; pizza US$4-10; ✹ 6pm-midnight Tue-Sun) Pleasant, open-air space serving good pizzas – some with rather daring ingredient combinations. Wednesday nights offer *rodízio*-style dining: all the pizza you can choke down for three bucks.

Sanduba's (Av Campos Sales 2913) Another open-air favorite, serving burgers, milkshakes and other snacks to famished young

diners. Big multi-ingredient burgers with trimmings cost US$2.

Caffé Restaurante (Av Carlos Gomes 1097; buffet per kilo US$5) Don't let the generic name keep you from the good daily lunch buffet.

Mirante II (Rua Dom Pedro II; dishes around US$4.50) Along with a nice view overlooking the river, you'll find straightforward plates of fried fish. Live, often very loud, music serenades diners most nights.

Getting There & Away

AIR

Varig and VASP both fly daily to/from Manaus, Rio Branco, Brasília, Rio de Janeiro and São Paulo. TAM operates further long-distance flights, while Rico and Tavaj provide regional flights.

BOAT

Boats to Manaus via the Rio Madeira and Rio Amazonas usually leave around 6pm on Tuesday and Friday from Porto Cai n'Água, at the end of Rua 13 de Maio. The trip should take three to 3½ days (hammock US$23 to US$33). Check out the boat for unsavory characters before committing yourself.

BUS

Four daily buses run to Guajará-Mirim (US$9, 5½ hours) and Rio Branco (US$14, eight hours). For Guajará-Mirim you have the alternative of a shared cab from the bus station (US$12 per person, three hours). Other buses go to Cuiabá (US$30, 21 hours, four daily).

Getting Around

Bus No 201, Hospital de Base via Aeroporto (US$0.50), runs the 6km between the city center and airport via the bus station. A taxi is US$8.

GUAJARÁ-MIRIM

Bicyclists pedaling the dusty roads lend a charming air to this small, pleasant town on the edge of the Rio Mamoré. Just opposite Guayaramerín (Bolivia), Guajará-Mirim came into existence as the southern terminus of the Madeira-Mamoré Railway, and some travelers use it as an entry point into Bolivia.

Informática (Av Presidente Dutra 331; US$2 per hr) offers Internet access. A signless **exchange**

BRAZIL

considered one of the founders of modern Spanish-language poetry. The importance of metaphor continues with contemporary poet Nicanor Parra.

One of Chile's best-known contemporary writers is Isabel Allende, many of whose novels are based in or reference Chile. She, as well as playwright-novelist-essayist Ariel Dorfman, lives in the USA but maintains close links to her homeland. Other important literary figures include José Donoso, whose novel *Curfew* offers a view of life under dictatorship through the eyes of a returned exile, and Antonio Skármeta, who wrote the novel *Burning Patience*, upon which the award-winning Italian film *Il Postino* (The Postman) is based. Luis Sepúlveda (1949–) is one of Chile's most prolific writers, with such books as *The Name of the Bullfighter* and the novella *The Old Man Who Read Love Stories*, a fictional account of life and society on Ecuador's Amazonian frontier.

Marcela Serrano (1951–) is considered to be one of the best Latina authors in the last decade. Pedro Lemebel (1950–) writes of homosexuality, transgender issues and other controversial subjects with top-notch shock value. Alberto Fuguet's (1964–) novella *Sobredosis* has been considered the spark that set off the 'new Chilean narrative'.

Music & Dance

Chile's contemporary music spans from the revolutionary tunes of the 1960s and 70s to Andean folklore to today's one-hit-wonder sexy crooners and hip-hoppers.

La Nueva Canción Chilena (New Chilean Song Movement) grew as the country's folk singers lyricized about the social hopes and political issues of the day. Its most legendary figure is Violeta Parra, best known for her enduring theme 'Gracias a la Vida' (Thanks to Life). Her children Isabel and Angel, also performers, established the first of many *peñas* (musical and cultural centers) in Santiago in the mid-1960s. The movement also gave strength to performers such as Victor Jara and groups Quilapayún and Inti-Illimani.

Immediately following the coup, many musicians were imprisoned. Victor Jara was brutally murdered in the National Stadium. Music groups went into exile and found success in Europe, such as Paris-based Los Jaivas, Los Prisioneros and La Ley (based in Mexico). Los Prisioneros broke up for a long time, but have since reunited and attracted a whole new fan base. La Ley has won a Grammy for best alternative rock group. The only 'traditional' Chilean dance is La Cueca. Dancers, each with a bandana that they twirl above their heads or hide behind their backs, prance around each other, in a sort of fight or flirt provocation.

SPORT

Soccer is by far the most popular spectator sport; the main teams are Colo Colo, Universidad de Chile and Universidad Católica. But tennis matches are equally popular, thanks to Marcelo 'El Chino' Rios, who rose quickly in the ranks of tennis stars, and Fernando González, a new rising star on the courts. Horse racing is also a national past-time. Okay, betting on the horses is more the sport. Jockey José Santos took third place on Funny Cide in the Triple Crown in 2003.

RELIGION

About 90% of Chileans are Catholic, with Evangelical Protestantism covering most of the rest of the population.

ENVIRONMENT
Land

Continental Chile stretches 4300km from Peru to the Strait of Magellan. Less than 200km wide on average, the land rises from sea level to above 6000m in some areas, with a narrow depression running through the middle.

Mainland Chile, dry topped and glacial heavy, can be easily broken into particular temperate and geographic zones, with the length of the Andes running alongside. From the Peruvian border to Chañaral is the Norte Grande, dominated by the Atacama Desert, the most arid desert in the world, and the *altiplano* (Andean high plain) leading toward Bolivia.

From Chañaral to, more or less, the Río Aconcagua, is the Norte Chico, where scrubland and forest grow denser with more southern rainfall. Here mining gives way to agriculture in the major river valleys.

From Río Aconcagua, you'll find wide river valleys down to Concepción and the Río Biobío. This section, called Middle

house (Av Mendonça Lima 145; ✆ 8am-noon Mon-Fri) exchanges cash, US and Bolivian currencies. The door is immediately east of Drogaria Fialho.

The **Polícia Federal**, for Brazilian immigration formalities, is near the end of Avenida Presidente Dutra (when walking toward the river turn right onto Dutra).

The **Museu Histórico Municipal** (admission free; ✆ daily), in the old Madeira-Mamoré train station, has two old steam locomotives and some aging natural history exhibits inside.

Sleeping & Eating

Two hotels facing each other on Avenida 15 de Novembro are better than their drab exteriors suggest.

Fênix Palace Hotel (☎ 0xx69-541-2326; Av 15 de Novembro 459; s/d quartos US$5/8, apartamentos US$7/10; ✆) There's a variety of rooms – the airy street-facing ones with air-con aren't bad.

Hotel Mini-Estrela Palace (☎ 0xx69-541-1140; Av 15 de Novembro 460; s/d apartamentos US$6/8; ✆) Across the road, this hotel offers much the same, with basic air-con apartamentos. Those upstairs are better.

Hotel Pousada Tropical (☎ 0xx69-541-3308; Av Benjamin Constant 376; s/d apartamentos with fan US$5/9, with air-con US$7/10; ✆) A few blocks north, this friendly place offers small but clean rooms.

There are several decent restaurants on Avenida 15 de Novembro.

Restaurante Oásis (Av 15 de Novembro No 460; buffet per kilo US$5) This is Guajará-Mirim's best restaurant, with a good lunch buffet.

Pizzaria Disk Stop (Av 15 de Novembro No 620) Decent pizzas.

Panificadora Central (Av 15 de Novembro No 632) For breakfast or snacks try the tasty food at this place.

Getting There & Around

The bus station is 2km east of the center (US$2.75 by taxi). Four daily buses run to/from Porto Velho (US$9, 5½ hours), and one to/from Rio Branco (US$12, eight hours).

Passenger launches across the Rio Mamoré to/from Guayaramerín depart about every 15 minutes in both directions from 7am to 6pm. From 6pm to 7am they leave when they have 10 passengers. Fare for the five-to-10-minute trip is US$1. The port is in front of the Museu Histórico Municipal.

RIO BRANCO

A chaotic city on the banks of the Rio Acre, Rio Branco was founded in 1882 by rubber tappers. Aside from a few museums documenting its rubbery past, the capital of Acre has few attractions.

Razec Informática (Rua Benjamin Constant 331) offers Internet access. **Banco do Brasil** (Rua Benjamin Constant 830) exchanges US dollars and has ATMs.

Sights

The **Casa do Seringueiro** (Av Getúlio Vargas 309; admission free; ✆ Mon-Fri) has exhibits portraying the life of a *seringueiro* (rubber tapper). The **Museu da Borracha** (Rubber Museum; Av Ceará 1441; admission free; ✆ Mon-Fri) has displays on archaeology, Indian artifacts, and the local cult of Santo Daime, centered around the hallucinogenic drink ayahuasca.

Sleeping

Chalé Hotel (☎ 0xx68-221-5633; Rua Palmeiral 334; s/d US$8/12) Just outside the bus station. Friendly staff and decent rooms. Breakfast included.

Albemar Hotel (☎ 0xx68-224-1938; Rua Franco Ribeiro 99; s/d US$7/9; ✆) Small, clean air-con *apartamentos* in a good location.

Hotel Triângulo (☎ 0xx68-224-9206; Rua Floriano Peixoto 727; s/d US$8/12; ✆) An excellent value, with spacious air-con *apartamentos* and a good breakfast.

Eating

Anexo Espaço Gastronômico (Rua Franco Ribeiro 99; buffet per kilo US$5.75) Excellent per-kilo lunches.

Churrascaria Triângulo (Rua Floriano Peixoto 727; dishes from US$3) The Hotel Triângulo's evening *rodízio* is a crowd pleaser with carnivores.

Pizzaria Tutti Frutti (Avenida Ceará 1132; pizza from US$3) Open-air dining. Good pizzas and ice-cold chopp.

Getting There & Away

Varig and VASP fly daily to Porto Velho, Manaus and Brasília. Tavaj and Rico operate regional flights. The airport is 20km west of town: a taxi costs US$13 or **Inácio's Tur** (Rua Rui Barbosa 450) runs a bus to, but not from, the airport (US$7).

Buses run from Rio Branco to Porto Velho (US$14, eight hours, four daily),

BRAZIL

Guajará-Mirim (US$12, eight hours, one daily), and Brasiléia (US$9, 4½ hours, four daily), 235km southwest. West of Rio Branco is paved as far as Sena Madureira (170km). The road from Rio Branco to Brasiléia is also paved, but Acre has few other paved roads. Bus Norte-Sul (US$0.50) from outside the bus station runs the 1.25km to the city bus terminal on Rua Benjamin Constant.

XAPURI

A tidy town of neat wooden houses, Xapuri was home to rubber tapper and environmental martyr Chico Mendes, who was murdered in 1988 after years of successful campaigning against the destruction of forests by loggers and ranchers.

The **Fundação Chico Mendes** (Rua Dr Batista de Moraes; admission free; ☑ 7-11am & 1-5pm Mon-Fri), a block from the bus station, displays Mendes memorabilia. The visit includes Mendes' rustic house across the street where he was fatally shot.

Pousada das Chapurys (☎ 0xx68-542-2253; Rua Sadala Koury 1385; s/d US$10/20; ☒), half a block from the central square, has decent rooms and a nice breakfast.

Buses to Xapuri leave Rio Branco at 7am and 1:45pm (US$7, 3½ hours), returning at 6am and 1pm. Buses leave Brasiléia for Xapuri at 10am and 4:30pm (US$3.50, two hours).

BRASILÉIA

This small border town is separated from Cobija, Bolivia, by the meandering Rio Acre and Igarapé Bahia. The Polícia Federal, where you need to obtain an exit/entry stamp if you're leaving or entering Brazil, is in the neighboring town of Epitáciolândia: you can ask buses coming from the Rio Branco direction to drop you there.

Accommodations in Cobija are cheaper, but Brasiléia's **Pousada Las Palmeras** (☎ 0xx68-546-3284; Avenida Geny Assis 425; s/d US$13.50/27; ☒) is a pleasant place, near the church in the center. Clean *apartamentos* come with an excellent breakfast. **La Felicitá** (Avenida Prefeito Rolando Moreira 361; buffet per kilo US$5.75), nearby, serves a reasonably good buffet.

Four buses run daily to Rio Branco (US$9, 4½ hours). In the dry season (roughly June to October) two daily buses take the unpaved road west to Assis Brasil

(US$6.75, about three hours). The rest of the year, 4WD vehicles make the trip (US$13.50, about four hours), departing from the bus station. Assis Brasil stands across the Rio Acre from Iñapari, Peru, which has minibus and truck transportation to Puerto Maldonado, Peru, about 10 hours south.

You can enter Cobija from Brasiléia by the international bridge, 1km off Epitáciolândia's main street, Avenida Santos Dumont, or by a rowboat ferry across the Rio Acre from behind the Ministério de Fazenda building on Avenida Prefeito Rolando Moreira in central Brasiléia. A taxi from the Polícia Federal to Bolivian immigration on the international bridge, then on to one of Cobija's bus terminals costs US$5 or so.

BRAZIL DIRECTORY

ACCOMMODATIONS

Brazilian accommodations are simple yet usually clean and reasonably safe, and nearly all come with *café da manhã* (breakfast) – though it may consist of nothing more than instant coffee and a dry roll. Private rooms with communal bathrooms are called *quartos*. Rooms with private bathrooms are *apartamentos*.

Where there are no hotels or *pousadas* (guesthouses) – as in parts of Amazonia and the northeast – a hammock and mosquito net are essential. With these basics (inexpensively bought in almost any town) and friendly locals, you can get a good night's rest anywhere.

Camping

Camping is a viable alternative in many parts of the country for travelers on limited budgets or for those wanting to explore some of the national parks, as long as you're prepared to carry a tent and the other necessary gear. The **Camping Clube do Brasil** (www.campingclube.com.br in Portuguese) has 48 camping grounds as far apart as Fortaleza and Porto Alegre.

Hostels

Youth hostels are called *albergues da juventude*. The **Federação Brasileira dos Albergues da Juventude** (FBAJ; www.hostel.org.br) has over 50 hostels, including many in state capitals and popular travel destinations. Many hostels are excellent, and they're great places to meet young Brazilians. A dormitory bed costs between US$7.50 and US$16 per person. Non-HI members usually pay 50% extra, but you can buy an HI guest card for US$15 at many hostels and at youth hostel association offices in Brazil.

The FBAJ's website lists all FBAJ hostels, often with links to the hostels' own sites. Booklets listing the hostels are available free at hostels, hostel offices and some travel agents.

There are also a few dozen non-FBAJ hostels around the country, many of which are fine.

Hotels

Brazil has good, modern, luxury hotels; old, shabby, moldy hotels; and everything in between. A clean, comfortable, air-con room including private bathroom with no frills can cost as little as US$15 to US$25 a double.

A very cheap hotel can cost as little as US$5/7 for single/double *quartos*. For that kind of price, expect a bare, shabby room with nothing but a bed and maybe a fan.

Prices are often flexible. Many mid-range and top-end hotels will give you a discount of up to 40% from their posted prices just for asking '*Tem desconto?*' ('Is there a discount?'). The discount is sometimes available only if you pay cash, or if you stay a few days; sometimes it's available to anyone who asks for it. Prices usually rise during high seasons. Hotels in business-oriented cities such as Curitiba and Brasília readily give discounts on weekends.

Pousadas

Budget travelers often stay at *pousadas* where a room with shared bath can go for as little as US$7 per person. Their small scale can make them some of the most pleasant places to stay in Brazil. Not that they're all cheap; the most luxurious cost US$100 for a double room with breakfast.

ACTIVITIES

Brazilians are seeking evermore radical ways to spend their time, so opportunities for fresh-air adventure are on the rise. The websites www.360graus.com.br

and www.guiaverde.com.br (both in Portuguese) are valuable resources on a host of activities, from canyoning, paragliding, kitesurfing or wakeboarding to plain old rafting, surfing, trekking, diving or mountain climbing.

Hiking & Climbing

These popular activities are best during the cooler months, April to October. Outstanding hiking areas include the national parks of Chapada Diamantina in Bahia (p333), Serra dos Órgãos in Rio de Janeiro state (p286), Chapada dos Veadeiros in Goiás (p317) and the Serra de São José near Tiradentes in Minas Gerais (p300).

Within 40 minutes of central Rio de Janeiro, the hub of Brazilian climbing, are some 350 documented climbs. Serra dos Órgãos and Itatiaia (Rio de Janeiro) and Caparaó (Minas Gerais) national parks also have some particularly good climbs.

Brazilian hiking and climbing clubs are an unbeatable source of information, as well as the best meeting place for likeminded people. They generally welcome visitors. Try Rio's **Centro Excursionista Brasileiro** (☎ 0xx21-2252-9844; www.ceb.org.br in Portuguese; Av

---

RESERVATIONS

In tourist centers, especially Rio, during vacations (July and from Christmas to Carnaval), reservations are a good idea for mid-range hotels or the most popular budget ones. The same goes for any vacation mecca (eg Búzios) on weekends. Most mid-range places, at least, should have someone who'll understand some English or Spanish on the phone. For ultrapeak times (eg Carnaval in Rio, Salvador or Olinda) make contact weeks or months ahead; during Carnaval hotels only accept reservations for four nights or more.

At any time, a phone call from the airport or bus station can establish whether your preferred lodgings have a free room.

Another good reason for making reservations in mid-range or top-end hotels is that the price may be up to 30% cheaper than if you just walk in off the street. However, there have been reports of travelers being forced to upgrade on the spot after reserving a room over the Internet.

Almirante Barroso 2, 8th fl, Centro). It lists upcoming excursions on its website, and often has meetings during the week to discuss the weekend's program, usually geared toward trekking and day hikes.

Surfing

Surfing is very popular, and there's surf virtually all along the coast; it's particularly good in the south and southeast. The best surfing beaches are in Santa Catarina state, at places like Ilha de Santa Catarina (p309) and São Francisco do Sul. Ilha do Mel (p305), Búzios (p288) and Rio de Janeiro (p274) also have great breaks. The waves are best in the Brazilian winter (June to August).

Rentals of boogie boards and surfboards are easy to arrange on the beach wherever you go.

Windsurfing

Búzios in Rio state has good conditions, and access to rental equipment. But Brazil's hardcore windsurfing mecca is the Ceará coast northwest of Fortaleza, from July to December. Here, Jericoacoara (p356) and the small fishing village of Icaraizinho are the most popular spots.

BOOKS

Lonely Planet's *Brazil*, *Rio de Janeiro* and (in French) *Brésil* guides have all the information needed for travelers making a more in-depth exploration of the country. Lonely Planet also publishes an excellent Brazilian phrasebook.

Quatro Rodas: Guia Brasil, available for US$15 at most Brazilian newsstands and bookstores, has detailed listings of accommodations and restaurants (except the cheapest) in over 900 cities and towns, plus some information on sights. It also comes with an excellent foldout map of the country.

Travelers' Tales Brazil, edited by Scott Doggett and Annette Haddad, is a fine anthology of travel adventures with good portraits of life in Brazil. One of the great classics of travel writing is Peter Fleming's *Brazilian Adventure*, a hilarious account of an expedition into Mato Grosso in the 1930s. Claude Levi-Strauss' *Tristes Tropiques* (1955) was an anthropological milestone for its study of Indian peoples in

the Brazilian interior. It's also a beautifully written travelog.

Two recent books on Brazil's fascinating history are *A Concise History of Brazil* by Boris Fausto and *Brazil: Five Centuries of Change* by Thomas Skidmore. The story behind Euclides da Cunha's masterly *Rebellion in the Backlands* (which describes the 19th-century Canudos mystics' rebellion) is told by Mário Vargas Llosa in his darkly entertaining novel *The War of the End of the World*.

A brief introduction to the plight of Indians in Brazil today is provided in *Disinherited: Indians in Brazil* by Fiona Watson, Caroline Pearce and Stephen Corry. *The Brazilians*, by Joseph A Page, is a readable and penetrating portrait of the country and its people. For a well-illustrated, accessible introduction to Brazilian popular music, get *The Brazilian Sound* by Chris McGowan and Ricardo Pessanha. For insight into the country's favorite addiction, read *Futebol: The Brazilian Way*, a rich and entertaining account of the culture behind the sport.

Amazon Watershed by George Monbiot delves into the root causes of the destruction of the Amazon forests. Sy Montgomery's captivating *Journey of the Pink Dolphins* recounts her magical experiences while studying these elusive Amazonian river creatures. Similarly, Mark Plotkin's *Tales of a Shaman's Apprentice* tells of his mystical encounters in the Amazon with some of the world's greatest healers.

BUSINESS HOURS

Most shops and government services (including post offices) are open 9am to 6pm Monday to Friday and 9am to 1pm Saturday. Banks are generally open 9am or 10am to 2pm or 3pm.

CLIMATE

Most of Brazil experiences only moderate temperature changes throughout the year, though southern states like Río Grande do Sul have more extreme seasonal changes like those in Europe and the US. In general as you go from north to south, the seasonal changes are more defined.

During the summer, which runs from December to February (school holidays coinciding), Rio and the northeast have temperatures in the high 30s. The rest of the year temperatures are generally in the mid-20s to low 30s. The south has much wider temperature variations, ranging from 15°C in the winter (June through August) to 35°C in the summer.

The Amazon region rarely gets hotter than 27°C, but it is humid there. As one might expect, considerable rain falls over tropical Amazonia throughout the year. In some parts of the North, December to March is considered winter, since that's when most of the rain falls.

Owing to generally temperate weather year-round, there is no bad time to visit Brazil. But unless you have your heart set on attending Carnaval, you may want to avoid the summer crowds (and heat), and visit from April to November. Treks into the Amazon are best then – especially during July and August, when the downpours don't last for days and the river is still not at its lowest.

For more information and climate charts see the South America Directory (p1028).

DANGERS & ANNOYANCES

Brazil receives a lot of bad press about its violence and high crime rate. By using common sense, there is much you can do to reduce the risks, including taking the general precautions applicable throughout South America (see Dangers & Annoyances in the South America Directory, p1030). At the time of research there were reports of heightened security issues all along Brazil's southeastern border from Foz do Iguaçu to Cuiaba. Please take extra precaution in these areas, and make sure your papers are in order before crossing the border.

In Brazil there are many basic precautions you should take to minimize the risks of getting mugged. Don't start your trip by wandering around touristy areas in a jetlagged state soon after arrival: you'll be an obvious target. Accept the fact that you might be mugged, pickpocketed or have your bag snatched while you're in the country. If you carry only the minimum needed for the day, and don't try to resist thieves, you're unlikely to come to any real harm. Other tips:

- Dress down, with casual clothes that blend in. Clothes bought in Brazil are a good choice.
- Keep small change handy so you don't have to flash a wallet to pay a bus fare.

- Don't wander around with a camera in view – keep it out of sight. Consider carrying it in a plastic bag from a local store.
- Before arriving in a new place take a map or at least have a rough idea of the area's orientation. Use taxis to avoid walking through risky areas.
- Be alert and walk purposefully. Criminals will home in on dopey, hesitant, disoriented-looking individuals.
- Use ATMs inside buildings. When using any ATM or exchanging money, be aware of those around you. Robbers sometimes watch these places looking for targets.
- Check windows and doors of your room for security, and don't leave anything valuable lying around.
- If you're suspicious or uneasy about a situation, don't hesitate to make excuses and leave, change your route, or do whatever else is needed to extricate yourself.
- Don't take anything to city beaches except your bathing suit, a towel and just enough money for lunch and drinks. No camera, no bag, no jewelry.
- After dark, don't walk along empty or nearly-empty streets or into deserted parks.
- Don't wander into *favelas* (slums) at any time.

If something is stolen from you, report it to the police. No major investigation is going to occur, but you will get a police report to give to your insurance company.

DISABLED TRAVELERS

Unfortunately, disabled travelers don't have an easy time in Brazil. Rio de Janeiro is probably the most accessible city for disabled travelers. The streets and sidewalks along the main beaches have curb cuts and are wheelchair accessible, but most other areas do not have cuts and many restaurants have entrance steps.

There is one Brazilian travel agency in São Paulo specializing in travel for persons with disabilities: **Fack Tour** (☎ 0xx11-4335-7662; facktour@originet.com.br).

EMBASSIES & CONSULATES
Embassies & Consulates in Brazil
Argentina Rio de Janeiro (☎ 0xx21-2553-1646; Praia de Botafogo 228, No 201, Botafogo)

Australia Rio de Janeiro (☎ 0xx21-3824-4624; Av Presidente Wilson 231, 23rd fl, Centro)

Bolivia Manaus (☎ 0xx92-236-9988; Av Efigênio Salles, Condomínio Greenwood, Quadra B, Casa 20); Rio de Janeiro (☎ 0xx21-2552-5490; Av Rui Barbosa 664, No 101, Flamengo)

Canada Rio de Janeiro (☎ 0xx21-2543-3004; Av Atlântica 1130, 5th fl, Copacabana)

Chile Rio de Janeiro (☎ 0xx21-2552-5349; Praia do Flamengo 344, 7th fl, Flamengo)

Colombia Belém (☎ 0xx91-246-5662; Av Almirante 71, Apto 601, Bloco B); Manaus (☎ 0xx92-234-6777; Rua Dona Libânia 62); Rio de Janeiro (☎ 0xx21-2552-5048; Praia do Flamengo 284, No 101, Flamengo)

Ecuador Rio de Janeiro (☎ 0xx21-2491-4113; Av das Americas 500, Bldg 21, No 305, Barra da Tijuca)

Germany Rio de Janeiro (☎ 0xx21-2553-6777; Rua Presidente Carlos de Campos 417, Laranjeiras)

Ireland Rio de Janeiro (☎ 0xx21-2501-8455; Rua 24 de Maio 347, Riachuelo)

Israel Rio de Janeiro (☎ 0xx21-2235-5588; Av NS de Copacabana 680, Copacabana)

Netherlands Rio de Janeiro (☎ 0xx21-2552-9028; Praia de Botafogo 242, 10th fl, Botafogo)

Paraguay Rio de Janeiro (☎ 0xx21-2553-2294; Praia de Botafogo 242, 2nd fl, Botafogo)

Peru Manaus (☎ 0xx92-236-5012; Rua HI 12, Morada do Sol, Alexio); Rio de Janeiro (☎ 0xx21-2551-9596; Av Rui Barbosa 314, 2nd fl, Flamengo)

UK Belém (☎ 0xx91-222-5074; Av Governador J. Malcher 815 Ed Palladium Center); Manaus (☎ 0xx92-613-1819; Rua Poraquê 240, Distrito Industrial); Rio de Janeiro (☎ 0xx21-2555-9603; Praia do Flamengo 284, 2nd fl, Flamengo)

Uruguay Rio de Janeiro (☎ 0xx21-2553-6030; Praia de Botafogo 242, 6th fl, Botafogo)

US Belém (☎ 0xx91-223-0800; Rua Oswaldo Cruz 165); Manaus (☎ 0xx92-633-4907; Rua Recife 1010, Adrianopolis); Rio de Janeiro (☎ 0xx21-2292-7117; Av Presidente Wilson 147, Centro)

Venezuela Belém (☎ 0xx91-222-6396; Rua Presidente Pernambuco 270); Manaus (☎ 0xx92-233-6004; Ferreira Pena 179); Rio de Janeiro (☎ 0xx21-2551-5248; Praia de Botafogo 242, 5th fl, Botafogo)

Brazilian Embassies & Consulates Abroad

Countries with Brazilian embassies and/or consulates include the following:

Australia Embassy (☎ 02-6273-2372; brazil.org.au; 19 Forster Cres, Yarralumla, Canberra ACT 2600); consulate (☎ 02-9267-4414; www.brazilsydney.org; Level 17, 31 Market St, Sydney NSW 2000)

Canada Embassy (☎ 613-237-1090; 450 Wilbrod St, Ottawa, Ontario K1N 6M8); Montreal consulate (☎ 514-499-0968); Toronto consulate (☎ 416-922-2503; www.consbrastoronto.org; 77 Bloor Street West, Suite 1109 & 1105, Toronto, Ontario M5S 1M2)

France Embassy (☎ 01 45 61 63 00; www.bresil.org; 34 Cours Albert, 1er, 75008 Paris)

Germany Embassy (☎ 030-726280; www.brasilianische-botschaft.de; Wallstrasse 57, 10179 Berlin-Mitte)

New Zealand Embassy (☎ 04-473-3516; 10 Brandon St, Level 9, Wellington 1)

UK Embassy (☎ 020-7399-9000; www.brazil.org.uk; 32 Green St, London W1Y 4AT); consulate (☎ 020-7930-9055; 6 St Alban's St, London SW1Y 4SQ)

USA Embassy (☎ 202-238-2828; www.brasilemb.org; 3006 Massachusetts Ave NW, Washington, DC 20008); Boston consulate (☎ 617-542-4000; www.consulatebrazil.org; 20 Park Plaza, Suite 810, Boston, MA 02116); Chicago consulate (☎ 312-464-0244; 401 North Michigan Ave, Suite 3050, Chicago, IL 60611); Houston consulate (☎ 713-961-3063; www.brazilhouston.org; 1233 West Loop South, Park Tower North, Suite 1150, Houston, TX 77027); Los Angeles consulate (☎ 323-651-2664; 8484 Wilshire Blvd, Suites 711-730, Beverly Hills, CA 90211); Miami consulate (☎ 305-285-6200; www.brazilmiami.org; 2601 South Bayshore Drive, Suite 800, Miami, FL 33133); New York consulate (☎ 917-777-7777; www.brazilny.org; 1185 6th Ave, 21st Fl, New York, NY 10036); San Francisco consulate (☎ 415-981-8170; www.brazilsf.org; 300 Montgomery St, Suite 900, San Francisco, CA 94104)

FESTIVALS & EVENTS

Festa de Iemanjá (Festival of Iemanjá; January 1) Festival in Rio de Janeiro on New Year's Day.

Procissão do Senhor Bom Jesus dos Navegantes (Procession of the Lord Jesus of Boatmen; January 1) In Salvador, Bahia on New Year's Day.

Lavagem do Bonfim (Washing of Bonfim church; 2nd Thursday in January) A Candomblé festival culminating in the ritual cleansing of Bonfim church in Salvador, Bahia.

Carnaval (Friday to Tuesday preceding Ash Wednesday) Carnaval celebrations usually start well before the official holiday.

Semana Santa (Holy Week; the week before Easter) Festival in Congonhas, Ouro Prêto, Goiás Velho.

Dia do Índio (Indian Day; April 19)

Festas Juninas (June Festivals; throughout June) Celebrated throughout in Rio state and much of the rest of the country.

Boi-Bumbá (June 28–30) Celebrated in Parintins, Amazonas.

Bumba Meu Boi (late June to second week of August) Festival in São Luís.

Fortal (out-of-season Carnaval; last week of July) Celebrated in Fortaleza.

Jubileu do Senhor Bom Jesus do Matosinhos (Jubilee of the Savior of Matosinhos; September 7–14) Celebrated in Congonhas.

Círio de Nazaré (Festival of the Virgin of Nazaré; starting second Sunday in October) Festival in Belém.

Carnatal (Carnaval in Natal; first week of December) Natal's answer to Brazil's big celebration comes in December (Natalese simply can't wait for the *other* Carnaval).

FOOD & DRINK
Brazilian Cuisine

Brazilian eateries serve some of the biggest portions on the planet, and many plates are designed for two. It's hard to go hungry, even on a modest budget. The basic Brazilian diet revolves around *arroz* (white rice), *feijão* (black beans) and *farinha* (flour from the root of manioc or cassava). The typical Brazilian meal, called *prato feito* (set meal, often abbreviated 'pf' in restaurants) or *refeição*, consists of these ingredients plus either meat, chicken or fish and costs US$2 to US$4 in most eateries.

Another good option for travelers is the *por quilo* (per-kilogram) lunch buffet. You pay by the weight of what you serve yourself: typically around US$7 per kilogram, with a big plateful weighing around half a kilo. Per-kilo places are good for vegetarians too, but go early for lunch: many places start serving around 11:30am, and by 2pm there may not be much left. The fixed-price *rodízio* is another deal, and most *churrascarias* (meat barbecue restaurants) offer *rodízio* dining, where they bring skewers and skewers of meat to you, till you can eat no more.

In many restaurants frequented by tourists, overcharging and shortchanging are almost standard procedure. It's all part of the game. They good-naturedly overcharge and you can good-naturedly hassle them until the check is fixed. They're used to it.

Despite many similarities there are regional differences in Brazilian cuisine. The *comida baiana* of the northeastern coast has a distinct African flavor, using peppers, spices and the delicious but strong oil of the *dendê* palm tree. The Amazon region offers some unique and tasty varieties of fish (including piranha!). Rio Grande do Sul's *comida gaúcha* features much meat. Common Brazilian dishes include the following:

Açaí An Amazonian fruit with a berrylike taste and deep purple color. Ground up with crushed ice, it makes a great, sorbetlike dish to which you can add granola, ginseng, honey etc.

Acarajé *Baianas* (Bahian women) traditionally sell this on street corners throughout Bahia. It's made from peeled brown beans, mashed in salt and onions, and then fried in wonderful-smelling *dendê* (palm) oil. Inside is *vatapá*, dried shrimp, pepper and tomato sauce.

Barreado A mixture of meats and spices cooked in a clay pot for 24 hours, it's served with banana and *farofa*. It's the state dish of Paraná.

Bobó de camarão Manioc paste cooked and flavored with dried shrimp, coconut milk and cashews.

Caldeirada Stew with big chunks of fish, onions and tomato.

Carne do sol Tasty salted beef, grilled and served with beans, rice and vegetables.

Caruru One of the most popular Afro-Brazilian dishes, this is prepared from okra or other vegetables cooked in water, plus onions, salt, shrimp, *malagueta* peppers, *dendê* oil and fish.

Casquinha de carangueijo or siri Stuffed crab, prepared with manioc flour.

Cozido A stew usually made with many vegetables (eg potatoes, sweet potatoes, carrots and manioc).

Dourada Scrumptious catfish found throughout Brazil.

Farofa Manioc flour gently toasted and mixed with bits of onion or bacon; it's a common condiment.

Feijoada Brazil's national dish, this pork stew is served with rice and a bowl of beans, and is traditionally eaten for Saturday lunch. It goes well with *caipirinhas*.

Frango a passarinho Small chunks of crisp fried chicken make a delicious *tira-gosto* (appetizer or snack).

Moqueca A stew flavored with *dendê* oil and coconut milk, often with peppers and onions. The word also refers to a style of covered clay-pot cooking from Bahia: fish, shrimp, oyster, crab or a combination can all be done *moqueca*-style.

Pato no tucupi Very popular in Pará, this roast duck dish is flavored with garlic and cooked in the *tucupi* sauce made from the manioc juice and *jambu*, a local vegetable.

Peixada Fish cooked in broth with vegetables and eggs.

Peixe a delícia Broiled or grilled fish, usually prepared with bananas and coconut milk.

Prato de verão Literally 'summer plate,' basically a fruit salad – served at many juice bars in Rio.

Sanduich Covers a multitude of inexpensive bites from the *X-tudo* (hamburger with everything) to the dependable *misto quente* (toasted ham-and-cheese sandwich). *Sanduiches* are a mainstay of *lanchonetes* (snack bars).

Tacacá Indian dish made of dried shrimp cooked with pepper, *jambu*, manioc and much more.

Tucunaré Tender, tasty Amazonian fish.

Tutu á mineira Black-bean *feijoada*, often served with *couve* (a type of kale). Typical of Minas Gerais.

Vatapá Perhaps the most famous Brazilian dish of African origin, a seafood dish with a thick sauce made from manioc paste, coconut and *dendê* oil.

Drinks

The incredible variety of Brazilian fruits makes for some divine *sucos* (juices). Every town has plenty of juice bars, often offering 30 or 40 different varieties at around US$1 for a good-sized glass.

Cafezinho (coffee), as typically drunk in Brazil, is strong, hot and sweet. It's served as an espresso-sized shot with plenty of sugar but no milk. *Cafezinho* is taken often and at all times. It's sold in stand-up bars and dispensed free from large thermoses in restaurants and at hotel receptions.

Refrigerantes (soft drinks) are found everywhere and are cheaper than bottled water. *Guaraná* 'champagne,' made from the fruit of an Amazonian plant, is about as popular as Coke. It's cold, carbonated and sweet, and the fruit has all sorts of supposedly marvelous properties, so you can tell yourself it's healthy too!

The two key alcoholic drinks in Brazil are *cachaça* (more politely called *pinga*), a high-proof sugarcane rum, and *cerveja* (beer). *Cachaça* ranges from excrementally raw to tolerably smooth, and is the basis of that celebrated Brazilian cocktail the *caipirinha*. Of the common beer brands, Antarctica and Brahma are generally the best. Chopp (*shoh*-pee) is pale blond pilsener draft beer, and stands pretty much at the pinnacle of Brazilian civilization. Key phrase: '*Moço, mais um chopp!*' ('Waiter, another chopp!').

GAY & LESBIAN TRAVELERS
Brazilians are pretty laid back about sexual issues. Especially in Rio, Salvador and São Paulo, the gay bars are all-welcome affairs attended by fun-loving GLS (*Gays, Lesbians e Simpatizantes*) crowds of heterosexuals, homosexuals and who-gives-a-sexuals. But the degree to which you can be out varies from region to region, and in some smaller towns flamboyance is not appreciated.

There is no law against homosexuaity in Brazil. The age of consent is 18 years, the same as for heterosexuals. Useful websites for gay and lesbian travelers are www.riogayguide.com and www.pridelinks.com/Regional/Brazil.

HEALTH
A yellow fever vaccination certificate is required for travelers who, within three months of arriving in Brazil (or applying for a Brazilian visa), have been in Bolivia, Colombia, Ecuador, French Guiana, Peru, Venezuela or any of about a dozen African countries. The list of countries can vary, so check with a Brazilian consulate. At some Brazilian borders there are vaccination posts where you can have the jab and get the certificate immediately, but it's sensible to do this in advance.

Travelers to the Amazon should take an appropriate malaria preventitive, such as mefloquine or doxycycline (chloroquine is inadequate here), and cover up as much as possible to prevent mosquito bites (dengue, for which there is no medication is also prevalent in the Amazon).

Tap water is safe to drink in urban areas like Rio and São Paulo. In other areas, filter your own or stick to bottled water.

Throughout Brazil, and especially along the coast, the sun is powerful, and travelers should be mindful of heatstroke, dehydration and plain old sunburn. Drink plenty of water, wear a strong sunscreen and allow your body time to acclimatize to high temperatures before attempting strenuous activities.

See the Health chapter (p1053) for more information.

HOLIDAYS
Official national holidays in Brazil are:
Ano Novo (New Year's Day; January 1)
Carnaval (Friday to Tuesday preceding Ash Wednesday, February/March) Carnaval celebrations usually start well before the official holiday.
Paixão & Páscoa (Good Friday & Easter Sunday; dates vary, March/April)
Tiradentes (Tiradentes Day; April 21)
Dia do Trabalho (May Day/Labor Day; May 1)
Corpus Christi (60 days after Easter, Sunday May/June)
Dia da Independência (Independence Day; September 7)
Dia da Nossa Senhora de Aparecida (Day of Our Lady of Aparecida; October 12)
Finados (All Souls' Day; November 2)
Proclamação da República (Proclamation of the Republic Day; November 15)
Natal (Christmas Day; December 25)

INTERNET ACCESS
You can find Internet cafés and other public Internet services in just about any town of medium-size and above. Charges are generally about US$1.50 an hour, but in smaller towns prices are much higher.

INTERNET RESOURCES

lanic.utexas.edu/la/brazil The University of Texas' extensive collection of Brazil links.

www.brazil.org.uk Site of the Brazilian embassy in London, with much practical info for tourists and links to local tourism sites in Brazil.

www.brazilmax.com Self-proclaimed hip gringo's guide to Brazilian culture and society; decent selection of articles and links.

www.brazzil.com Web version of the monthly magazine published in the US; features in-depth articles on the country's politics, economy, literature, arts and culture.

www.terra.com.br/turismo Portuguese-language travel site with up-to-date info on entertainment, nightlife and dining options in dozens of cities around Brazil.

LEGAL MATTERS

Be wary of (but of course respectful to) Brazilian police. Some allegedly plant drugs and sting gringos for bribes.

Stiff penalties are in force for use and possession of drugs; the police don't share most Brazilians' tolerant attitude toward marijuana. Police checkpoints along the highways stop cars and buses at random. Police along the coastal drive from Rio to São Paulo are notorious for hassling young people and foreigners. Border areas are also dangerous.

A large amount of cocaine is smuggled out of Bolivia and Peru through Brazil. If you're entering Brazil from one of the Andean countries and have been chewing coca leaves, be careful to clean out your pack first.

MAPS

Brazil is vast, and decent maps that give a clear idea of scale are extremely useful. Good maps for general planning include Bartholomew's *Brazil & Bolivia World Travel Map*, GeoCenter's *Brazil, Bolivia, Paraguay, Uruguay* and the *South America* sectional maps published by International Travel Map Productions (ITM).

A good source of Brazil maps is **Omni Resources** (www.omnimap.com), which ships worldwide.

In Brazil the useful Quatro Rodas series is widely available at newsstands and some bookstores. These include the *Atlas Rodoviário* road atlas (it fits into a backpack – just), and excellent street atlases for the main cities. Each costs between US$10 and US$16.

Good topographical maps are published by the IBGE, the government geographical service, and the DSG, the army geographical service. They cost around US$6 and US$15, respectively, per map. Availability is erratic, but IBGE offices in most state capitals sell IBGE maps. Office locations can be found on the IBGE website (www.ibge.gov.br).

Searchable street maps of 128 Brazilian cities are online at the Portuguese-language website www.terra.com.br/turismo. Telephone directories in many states include city maps.

MEDIA
Newspapers & Magazines

The weekly Portuguese-language *Veja* is an irreverent current-affairs magazine of range, depth and insightful analysis. In seven or eight major cities it comes with *Vejinha*, a good pullout guide to the local music, arts and nightclub scene. The *Folha de São Paulo* and Rio's *Jornal do Brasil* newspapers have good national and international coverage and a socially liberal stance. *O Estado de São Paulo* and Rio's *O Globo* are a little more comprehensive in their coverage and more right wing. All these papers are available nationwide.

English-language publications *Newsweek* and the daily *International Herald Tribune* are widely available. European and US newspapers are sold at some newsstands in tourist and business areas of Rio and São Paulo, but they are expensive.

TV

Brazilian TV consists mostly of game shows, football matches, bad American films dubbed into Portuguese and the universally watched *telenovelas* (soap operas). Major hotels and some bars and restaurants have pay-TV with CNN and occasionally other English-language programs.

MONEY
ATMs

ATMs are the easiest way of getting cash in big cities and are widely available. In many smaller towns, ATMs exist but rarely work for non-Brazilian cards. Make sure you have a four-digit PIN. In general HSBC, Banco de Brasil and Bradesco are the best ATMs to try. Look for the stickers on the machines that say Cirrus, Visa, or whatever system your card uses – though this may not mean the machine will necessarily work.

Bargaining

A little bargaining for hotel rooms is standard – see Accommodations, p384. On unmetered cab rides, arrange the fare before departing.

Credit Cards

You can use credit cards to pay for many purchases and to make cash withdrawals from ATMs and at banks. Visa is the most commonly accepted card, followed by MasterCard. American Express and Diners Club cards are also useful. Visa cash advances are widely available, even in small towns that have no other currency exchange facilities – but the process can be time consuming. Credit-card fraud is widespread. Keep your card in sight at all times, especially in restaurants.

Exchange Rates

Exchange rates at press time included the following:

Country	Unit		R$ (reais)
Australia	A$1	=	2.0
Canada	C$1	=	2.2
euro zone	€1	=	3.3
Japan	¥100	=	2.6
New Zealand	NZ$1	=	1.8
United Kingdom	UK£1	=	4.8
United States	US$1	=	2.9

Exchanging Money

Cash and traveler's checks, in US dollars, can be exchanged in banks or in *casas de cambio* (exchange offices). Banks are slower but on the whole give better exchange rates (however, Banco do Brasil charges US$20 commission for every traveler's check transaction). You'll usually get a 1% or 2% better exchange rate for cash than for traveler's checks.

American Express is the most recognized traveler's check.

POST

A postcard or letter weighing up to 20g costs US$0.75 to the USA, US$0.85 to Europe and US$1 to Australia. There are mailboxes on the streets, but it's safer to go to a *correios* (post office). Airmail letters to the USA and Europe arrive in a week or so. The *posta restante* system functions reasonably well. Post offices hold mail for 30 days.

RESPONSIBLE TRAVEL

Most places you'll go in Brazil welcome tourism, but be sensitive to local ways of doing things – especially with indigenous peoples who have some delicate traditions and unique beliefs. Many are wary about having their photo taken – only snap them if you're sure (probably having asked first) that they won't mind.

As for Brazil's environment, we all have an obligation to protect it. You can do your bit by using environmentally friendly tourism services wherever possible. Using the services of local community groups and enterprises – as guides, hosts, artisans or whatever – ensures that your money goes directly to those helping you, as does buying crafts and other products directly from the artisans or from their trusted representatives.

SHOPPING

Recorded music, musical instruments, local crafts (indigenous and otherwise) and artwork all make good souvenirs.

Glitzy, air-con shopping malls – imaginatively called *'shoppings'* – are a feature of every self-respecting city and often contain decent music stores. Browsing the many markets and small streetside stalls yields, for better or worse, less predictable results. Street stalls sell bootleg CDs for around US$3, against about US$12 for the official releases in stores.

Brazil's many varieties of percussion, wind and string instruments make good souvenirs and presents. You can often find inexpensive ones at craft markets as well as in music stores.

For genuine Indian arts and crafts, look in the Artíndia stores of Funai (the government Indian agency) and museum gift shops.

Artisans in the northeast produce a rich assortment of artistic items. Salvador and nearby Cachoeira are notable for their rough-hewn wood sculptures. Ceará specializes in fine lace. The interior of Pernambuco, in particular Caruaru, is famous for wildly imaginative ceramic figurines.

Candomblé stores are a good source of curios, ranging from magical incense guaranteed to increase sexual allure, wisdom and health, to amulets and ceramic figurines of Afro-Brazilian gods.

STUDYING

It's easy to arrange Portuguese classes through branches of the IBEU (Instituto Brasil Estados Unidos), where Brazilians go to learn English. There will be one in every large city. For more on language schools, try the **National Registration Center for Study Abroad** (www.nrcsa.com) or the website www.onestoplanguage.net.

TELEPHONE
Domestic Calls

You can make domestic calls from normal card pay telephones on the street and in telephone offices. The cards cost US$1.40 per 30 units at telephone offices and around US$2 from vendors, newsstands and anywhere else advertising *cartões telefônicos*. Cards for 20, 60 or 90 units are also sometimes available.

Local calls (within the city you're in) cost only one or two units. Just dial the number without any area code. To make a local collect call dial ☎ 9090, then the number.

For calls to other cities, dial ☎ 0, then the code of your selected long-distance carrier, then the two or three digits representing the city, followed by the local number. You need to choose a long-distance carrier that covers both the place you are calling from and the place you're calling to. Carriers advertise their codes in areas where they're prominent, but you can always use Embratel (code 21) or Intelig (code 23) because they cover the whole country.

City codes are thus usually given in the format '0xx digit digit', with the two x's representing the carrier code. As an example, to call from Rio de Janeiro to the number ☎ 219-3345 in Fortaleza (city code ☎ 0xx85) in the state of Ceará, you dial ☎ 0 followed by 21 or 23 or 31 or 85 (the codes of the four carriers that cover both Rio and Ceará), followed by 85 for Fortaleza, followed by the number 219-3345.

A long-distance call usually eats up five to 10 phonecard units per minute.

To make an intercity collect call, dial ☎ 9 before the 0xx. A recorded message in Portuguese will ask you to say your name and where you're calling from, after the tone.

International Calls

Brazil's country code is ☎ 55. When calling internationally to Brazil, omit the initial 0xx of the area code.

International calls from Brazil typically cost about US$1 a minute to the USA or Canada and US$1.75 a minute to Europe or Australia (20% less between 8pm and 6am daily and all day Sunday).

The regular card pay telephones found on the streets are of little use for international calls unless you have an international calling card or are calling collect. Most pay telephones are restricted to domestic calls, and even if they aren't, a 30-unit Brazilian phonecard may last less than a minute internationally.

Without an international calling card, your best option is to find a *posto telefônico* (telephone office – nearly every town has one), where you pay in cash after you finish talking. You can also call from your hotel, but do establish costs beforehand.

For international *a cobrar* (collect) calls, dial ☎ 000107 from any phone. This only works to some countries. Alternatively, you can get a Brazilian international operator by dialing ☎ 000111 or ☎ 0800-703-2121. Failing that, you need to locate a phone that handles international calls. Home Country Direct services get you through to an operator in the country you're calling, and will connect the collect call for you. For most Home Country Direct services, dial ☎ 00080 followed by the country code (for North ☎ 16 for Sprint; for Australia, dial ☎ 0008006112).

Mobile Phones

Celular (mobile) phones have eight-digit numbers starting with a 9, and calls to them run through your phonecard units much faster than calls to regular numbers. Mobiles have city codes like normal phone numbers, and if you're calling from another city you have to use them.

TOILETS

Public toilets are available at every bus station and airport; there's usually a small entrance fee of US$0.50 or so. Elsewhere,

BRAZIL

public toilets are not common, though Brazilians are generally quite nice about letting you use facilities in restaurants and bars. As in other Latin American countries, toilet paper isn't flushed but placed in the smelly basket next to the toilet. Sadly, few of the country's bathrooms are handicapped accessible.

TOURIST INFORMATION

Tourist offices in Brazil are nearly all run by individual states or municipalities. With the exception of Rio de Janeiro – which has abundantly helpful staff at its tourism offices – most of the country's information centers are woefully inadequate. You're likely to encounter staff members who view visitors less as people to assist and more of an object to get rid of as quickly as possible. Keep your sense of humor, don't expect too much, and you may be pleasantly enlightened following a visit to an *embratur* office.

Brazilian consulates and embassies can provide limited tourist information (several do so on their websites); the embassy in the UK actually has a tourist office (see p388 for contact details). Riotur, the Rio de Janeiro city tourist board, maintains US offices in **New York** (☎ 212-375-0801; natalia@myriad.cc) and **Manhattan Beach, California** (☎ 310-643-2638; rio@myriad.cc).

VISAS & DOCUMENTS

When you arrive in Brazil you should be able to show your ticket out of Brazil or evidence of adequate funds (such as an international credit card).

Entry/Exit Card

On entering Brazil, all tourists must fill out a *cartão de entrada/saída* (entry/exit card); immigration officials keep half, you keep the other. They will also stamp your passport. If for any reason they are granting you less than the usual 90-day stay, the number of days will be written in the stamp in your passport. When you leave Brazil, the second half of the entry/exit card will be taken by immigration officials. Don't lose it in the interim. If by some misfortune you do, immigration officials are likely to be understanding if you leave Brazil within the time limit indicated by your passport stamp. You can go to the Polícia Federal

(see Visa Extensions, below) for a replacement card, but their procedures may be time consuming.

Visas

Citizens of the UK, France and Germany do not require visas for entry into Brazil, though citizens of the US, Australia, Canada and New Zealand do.

Tourist visas are valid for arrival in Brazil within 90 days of issue and then for a 90-day stay. The fee depends on your nationality and where you are applying; it's usually between US$40 and US$60; though for US citizens visas cost a whopping US$100. In many Brazilian embassies and consulates it takes only a couple of hours (or less) to issue a visa if you go in person. You'll generally need to present one passport photograph and a round-trip or onward ticket (or a photocopy of it or a statement from a travel agent that you have it) and, of course, a valid passport.

People under 18 years of age who wish to travel to Brazil without a parent or legal guardian must have a notarized letter of authorization from the nontraveling parent(s)/guardian(s), or from a court. Such a letter must also be presented when applying for a visa, if one is required. Check with a Brazilian consulate well in advance about this.

If you decide to return to Brazil, your visa is valid for five years.

VISA EXTENSIONS

These are handled by Brazil's Polícia Federal, who have offices in the state capitals and border towns. You must apply before your entry/exit card or visa lapses, and don't leave it until the last minute. When you go, dress nicely! Some Fed stations don't take kindly to people in shorts. Granting an extension seems to be pretty automatic, but they may ask to see a ticket out of the country and proof of sufficient funds; and sometimes they may not give you the full 90 days. If you get the maximum 90-day extension and then leave the country before the end of that period, you cannot return until the full 90 days have elapsed.

VOLUNTEERING

Action Without Borders (www.idealist.org) lists volunteer openings on its website. Also look at the site of the **International Study and Travel Center** (www.istc.umn.edu). **Earthwatch** (www.earthwatch.org) runs environmental and archaeological projects in Brazil, but you have to pay to take part in them (around US$2000 for 15 days). International NGOs (nongovernmental organizations) working in Brazil are worth contacting, too, if you have some particular interest or a skill to offer.

A little door-knocking can help you find volunteer work with welfare organizations in Brazil – and they could certainly use the help. One traveler reportedly walked to the front door of a Catholic home for abandoned children in Recife and asked if there was anything he could do. The priests gave him a bed and he spent two months helping out with the cooking, keeping the children out of trouble and telling them stories. He said it was the highlight of his trip.

WOMEN TRAVELERS
In the cities of the southeast and South, foreign women without traveling companions will scarcely be given a sideways glance. In the more traditional rural areas of the northeast, blonde-haired and light-skinned women, especially those without male escorts, will certainly arouse curiosity.

Machismo is less overt in Brazil than in Spanish-speaking Latin America. Flirtation – often exaggerated – is a common form of communication, but it's generally regarded as innocent banter; no sense of insult, exploitation or serious intent should be assumed.

It's advisable to adapt what you wear to local norms. The brevity of Rio beach-suburb attire generally is not suitable for the streets of interior cities, for instance.

In the event of unwanted pregnancy or the risk thereof, most pharmacies in Brazil stock the morning-after pill, which costs about US$7.

WORKING
Brazil has high unemployment, and tourists are not supposed to take jobs. However, it's not unusual for foreigners to find language-teaching work in the bigger cities, either in language schools or through private tutoring. The pay is not great (around US$10 an hour), but if you can work for three or four days a week you can live on it.

Chile

HIGHLIGHTS

- **Torres del Paine** – trek around awe-inspiring Los Cuernos and Torres peaks and to glacier lookouts, then relax with a box of *vino* and share your stories of blisters and blusters (p507)
- **Lake District** – get immersed in the green, eat cakes laden with cream, soak in hot springs until your skin raisins, climb, hike, raft, ski, kayak…need we say more? (p463)
- **Atacama Desert** – see for miles across the driest desert, a spectacle of pastel salt flats and fuming geysers, adobe villages and welcoming oases (p428)
- **Off the beaten track** – explore Cochamó, on the Seno de Reloncaví, with an adorable village and old cattle trails leading into incredible valleys (p485)
- **Best journey** – Carretera Austral is the ultimate in road trips: minivans go up and down, but grab friends and pickup and do it your way – quirky towns, impenetrable forests and mountainous beauty at every curve (p493)

FAST FACTS

- **Area:** 748,800sq km land, 8150 sq km water, 6435km of coastline
- **Budget:** US$25 a day
- **Capital:** Santiago
- **Costs:** *hospedaje* with breakfast US$8–10, bottle of red US$2, national park entrance US$2–11
- **Country code:** ☎ 56
- **Electricity:** 220 volts, 50 cycles; two and three rounded prongs
- **Famous for:** politics, *pisco* (brandy-like liquor; the national drink) and Patagonian peaks
- **Languages:** Spanish, Mapudungun, Rapanui
- **Money:** US$1 = 644 pesos
- **Phrases:** *choro*, *bacán* (cool), *chancho*, *asco*, *punga* (disgusting), *carrete* (party)
- **Population:** 15.5 million
- **Time:** GMT minus 4 hours (minus 3 hours in summer)
- **Tipping:** 10% in better restaurants; tip all guides
- **Traveler's checks:** cashed at Banco del Estado and most exchange houses; ATMs are easier
- **Visas:** North American, Australian and most European citizens need only a valid passport

TRAVEL HINTS

When exchanging money, ask for some of it in small bills; lots of places can't make change. Waiters will immediately hand you a menu, but ask for the *menú del día* instead – a cheaper and more filling alternative.

Think extremes: Chile's 4300km stretch from Peru to the Strait of Magellan, all ocean on one side and almost all Andes on the other. The driest desert in the world is here, as is the second highest peak in South America and the second-largest lake. More than 50 volcanoes string along this needle of land like a bellowing charm bracelet. Going from extreme desert to wineries to ice fields all within one country is a traveling highlight. A well-trodden 'gringo trail' extends from top to bottom, and for those with limited time, hitting the most obvious sites provides enough of a sense of Chile's variety. What lies just off the beaten track, however, represents the country's true nature: head to beaches outside of cities for endless stretches of isolation, spend time in less-visited parks, rest a bus-weary body at small Patagonian hamlets. Santiago is the booming capital with fabulous restaurants and skyscrapers dwarfed by the Andes. It's chaotic and smoggy, but fun for a few days. Chile is a very easy country to travel. Thanks to its more or less stable economy, begging is rare and things work: buses and trains leave and arrive almost to the minute. Added pleasures are the country's bounty of fresh seafood and world-class wines. From dry desert top to ice-capped south, Chile's got something for everyone. And if you are willing to go the distance, Rapa Nui (Easter Island) mystifies, while Isla Robinson Crusoe lets the most urban of us play castaway.

HISTORY
Early History
Inca rule touched Chile, but northern Aymara and Atacameño farmers and herders predated the lords of Cuzco, while Changos fished coastal areas and Diaguitas farmed the interior of Coquimbo. Beyond the central valley, Araucanian (Mapuche) Indians resisted Inca aggression. Cunco Indians fished and farmed on the island of Chiloé. Groups in the south, such as Selk'nam and Yahgan, long avoided European contact, but are now nearly extinct.

Colonial Times
A year after leaving Peru in 1540, conquistador Pedro de Valdivia reached the Mapocho valley to found the city of Santiago. Mapuche assaults threatened the fledgling capital, but Valdivia gradually worked southward, founding Concepción, Valdivia and Villarrica. Spanish invaders set up *encomiendas* (forced labor systems) to exploit the north's relatively large, sedentary population, but south of the Río Biobío, the Mapuche fought European colonization for over three centuries. When the *encomiendas* lost value, Valdivia rewarded loyalists with land grants. Landless and 'vagrant' Spaniards became tenants on agricultural *haciendas* or *fundos*. These estates (*latifundios*), many remaining intact into the 1960s, became the dominant force in Chilean society. Other groups, like immigrant Basques, purchased large properties as their families flourished in commerce.

Revolutionary Wars & the Early Republic
As part of the Viceroyalty of Peru, Chile stretched roughly from modern Chañaral to Puerto Aisén. By 1818, José de San Martín's Ejército de los Andes (Army of the Andes), marched from Argentina into Chile, took Santiago and sailed north to Lima. San Martín appointed the Chilean Bernardo O'Higgins, the son of an Irishman, to be his second-in-command, and O'Higgins became 'supreme director' of the Chilean republic.

O'Higgins dominated politics for five years after independence, decreeing political, social, religious and educational reforms, but landowners' objections to his egalitarian measures forced his resignation.

The landowners' spokesman was businessman Diego Portales, who, as interior minister, was de facto dictator until his execution in 1837. His custom-drawn constitution centralized power in Santiago and established Catholicism as the state religion.

Expansion & Development
At independence, Chile was small and compact, but triumphs over Peru and Bolivia in the War of the Pacific (1879–83) and treaties with the Mapuche placed the nitrate-rich Atacama Desert and the southern lake district under Chilean rule. Chile also annexed remote Rapa Nui (Easter Island) in 1888.

British, North American and German capital turned the Atacama into a bonanza, as nitrates brought prosperity to certain sectors of society and funded the government. The nitrate ports of Antofagasta and Iquique grew rapidly until the Panama Canal (1914) reduced traffic around Cape Horn and the development of petroleum-based fertilizers made mineral nitrates obsolete.

Mining also created a new working class and a class of nouveau riche, both of which challenged the landowners. Elected in 1886, President José Manuel Balmaceda promoted government services and public works to tackle the dilemma of unequally distributed wealth and power. However, in 1890 a congressional attempt to depose him triggered a civil war that resulted in 10,000 deaths, including his own suicide.

20th-Century Developments

As late as the 1920s, up to 75% of Chile's rural population still lived on *latifundio* holding 80% of prime agricultural land. As industry expanded and public works advanced, urban workers' welfare improved, but that of rural workers declined, forcing day laborers to the cities.

Elected by a narrow vote in 1920, President Arturo Alessandri Palma instituted land and income taxes – despite hard times due to declining nitrate income – to fund health, education and welfare reforms. However, military right-wing opposition forced his resignation in 1924. For several years the dictatorial General Carlos Ibáñez del Campo held the presidency, but opposition to his policies, and economic woes caused by the Great Depression, forced him to resign in 1931.

Stalinists, Trotskyites and other radicals and reformists created a bewildering mix of new political entities in the 1930s and 1940s, but the democratic left dominated politics. Corfo, the state development corporation, played a major economic role, and North American companies gained control of copper mines, now the cornerstone of Chile's economy.

In 1952, Ibáñez del Campo again won the presidency, but his attempts to curtail landowners' power faltered. In the 1958 presidential elections, Arturo Alessandri's son, popular Jorge Alessandri Rodríguez, won a close race, defeating leftist Salvador Allende Gossens and Christian Democrat Eduardo Frei Montalva.

In the 1964 presidential election, Frei decisively defeated Allende. Frei's genuinely reformist policies threatened both the elite's privileges and the left's working-class base. Opportunistically attacking the US-dominated export sector, Frei advocated 'Chileanization' of the copper industry, in which the government took just over 50% ownership of the mines that were controlled

CHILE (NORTH)

0 — 150 km
0 — 90 mi

PERU

Arica
Putre
Oruro

BOLIVIA

Región I

20°S

IQUIQUE

Panamericana

PACIFIC
OCEAN

Calama
Chuquicamata

Región II
San Pedro
de Atacama

Tropic of Capricorn

ANTOFAGASTA

Atacama
Desert

25°S

Región III

Bahía Inglesa
Caldera
COPIAPÓ

RN 40

Vallenar

La Rioja

30°S
LA SERENA

Ovalle
RN 40
RN 38

Región IV
5

San Juan
RN 141

Región V
RN 20

Viña del Mar
San Felipe
VALPARAÍSO
Mendoza
To Isla
Robinson
Crusoe
(670km)
Isla Negra
SANTIAGO
RN 7
San Luis

Pichilemu
RANCAGUA
RN 143

Región VI
Curicó

35°S

TALCA

Región VII
ARGENTINA

Chillán
CONCEPCIÓN

70°W

by US companies, thus prompting higher returns for Chile from the industry.

Considered too reformist by the right and too conservative by the left, Frei's Christian Democratic administration faced many challenges, including from violent groups like MIR (the Leftist Revolutionary Movement), which found support among coal miners, textile workers and other urban laborers, and also agitated for land reform. As the 1970 election grew near, the Christian Democratic party, unable to satisfy society's expectations for reform, grew weaker.

Allende Comes to Power
In 1970 Allende's Unidad Popular (Popular Unity or UP) coalition offered a radical program advocating nationalization of industry and expropriation of *latifundio*. After winning a small plurality and agreeing to constitutional guarantees, Allende took office with congressional approval, but the coalition quarreled over the administration's objectives.

Allende's program included state control of many private enterprises and massive income redistribution. Politics grew more confrontational as peasants, frustrated with agrarian reforms, seized land. Harvests declined, and expropriation of copper mines and other enterprises, plus conspicuously friendly relations with Cuba, provoked US hostility.

Pinochet's Dictatorship
However, in October 1988, voters rejected Pinochet's bid to extend his presidency until 1997. In 1989, 17 parties formed the coalition Concertación para la Democracia (Consensus for Democracy), whose candidate Patricio Aylwin easily defeated both Pinochet's protégé, Hernán Büchi, and right-wing independent Francisco Errázuriz. Pinochet's custom-made constitution limited Aylwin's presidency, which, however, did see the publication of the Rettig report, documenting deaths and disappearances during the dictatorship.

Recent Politics
In September 1998, Pinochet was arrested in London at the request of Spanish judge Báltazar Garzón, who was investigating human rights abuses of Spanish citizens

in the aftermath of the coup. Pinochet returned to Chile in March 2000 to much speculation. Documents about Pinochet's role in the 'caravan of death' came to light, and in January 2001, Judge Juan Guzmán put Pinochet under house arrest and ordered the 1978 self-imposed amnesty be lifted.

Both the Court of Appeals (in 2000) and the Supreme Court (2002) ruled him unfit to stand trial, thereby ending any judicial effort to hold him accountable. As a consequence of the court's decision – that he suffers from dementia – Pinochet stepped down from his post as lifetime senator, finally ending his political career. President Ricardo Lagos was elected in March 2000; he is Chile's first Socialist leader since Salvador Allende. The next election is due in December 2005.

THE CULTURE
The National Psyche
Chile is going through some radical social changes. The Catholic Church is losing ground and after years hunkering down during a dictatorship and slowly overcoming it, Chileans are starting to show some cultural rebellion. One of the more 'expressive' gestures happened on a bitterly cold morning in 2002, when US artist Spencer Tunick advertised his need for 400 souls to pose naked for a photo shoot and over 3000 showed up. Chileans love to psychoanalyze things, trying to figure out what makes their society tick; no wonder that reality TV shows have become quite the hit. While most Chileans are quite proud of their heritage, there's a palpable lack of patriotism and an increasing level of individualism.

Lifestyle
Travelers crossing over from Peru or Bolivia may wonder where the stereotypical 'South America' went. Chilean lifestyle has many similarities to European counterparts, albeit at a lessened economic level. Long lunches and afternoon teas are de rigueur. Dress for adults is usually conservative, leaning toward business formal. Exceptions being the scantily clad coffee-bar waitresses, and teenage fashion slaves. The average Chilean focuses energy on family, home and work. They are very kid-oriented and make little effort to shush screaming tykes. That said,

they don't have huge families. The Chilean government has yet to create a law making divorce legal. This lack doesn't keep families together as much as it has increased the acceptance of couples living together and having children out of wedlock. Chileans work a lot, often six days a week, but are always eager for a good *carrete* (party).

People
About 75% of Chile's population occupies just 20% of the country's total area – in the main agricultural region of Middle Chile. This region includes Gran Santiago (the capital and its suburbs), where over a third of the country's estimated 15.1 million people reside. More than 85% of Chileans live in cities.

Chile's people are mainly of Spanish ancestry, but the Irish and English also made a mark. Germans began immigrating in 1848 and left quite a stamp on the Lake District. Other immigrants came from France, Italy, Croatia (especially to Magallanes and Tierra del Fuego) and Palestine. The northern Andean foothills are home to around 20,000 Aymara and Atacameño peoples. Over 900,000 are, or consider themselves, Mapuche (population statistics vary widely as a consequence), many of whom consider the south (La Araucanía) their home. Their name stems from the words *mapu* for land, and *che* for people. About 2000 Rapa Nui, of Polynesian ancestry, live on Easter Island.

ARTS
Cinema
Before the 1973 coup, Chilean cinema was among the most experimental in Latin America and is now returning to reclaim some of this status. Recent films that have received praise and awards at international film festivals include *Taxi Para Tres* (2001) by Orlando Lubbert, *La Fiebre del Loco* (2001) by Andrés Wood, *El Chacotero Sentimental* (The Sentimental Teaser; 1999) and Diego Izquierdo's *Sexo con Amor* (2002).

Literature
If there's one art form Chile is famous for, it's poetry, mainly due to the Nobel Prize poets Gabriela Mistral and Pablo Neruda, as well as Vicente Huidobro, who is

Chile, is the main agricultural and wine-growing region. South of the Biobío to Puerto Montt is Chile's Lake District, with extensive native forests, snowcapped volcanoes and foothill lakes. South of Puerto Montt, Chiloé is the country's largest island, with dense forests and a patchwork of pasturelands. On the mainland, famed Patagonia begins with the Aisén region's rugged, mountainous area, takes in the Campo de Hielo Sur (the southern continental ice field), and ends in Magallanes, which includes Tierra del Fuego.

Mostly for political reasons, the country is divided into 13 regions, using roman numerals. Travel brochures do refer to them, and some people express their regional destinations using these names. One of the only obvious signs that you're going from one region to the next is pulling over on the bus. Between Region I and II, you'll be checked for produce and duty-free items. The regions are I Tarapacá, II Antofagasta, III Atacama, IV Coquimbo, V Valparaíso (includes Rapa Nui and Archipiélago Juan Fernández), Región Metropolitana (not numbered), VI Libertador General Bernardo O'Higgins, VII Maule, VIII Biobío, IX La Araucanía, X Los Lagos, XI Aisén del General Carlos Ibáñez del Campo and XII Magallanes y Antártica Chilena.

Wildlife

Bounded by ocean, desert and mountain, Chile is home to a unique environment that developed much on its own, creating a number of endemic species.

Within the desert reaches of the north, candelabria cacti grow, spaced well apart for maximum *camanchaca* (fog) absorption. You can spot guanaco, vicuña, llama and alpaca (as well as the ostrich-like rhea – called *ñandú* in Spanish) and the vizcacha (a wild relative of the chinchilla). Parque Nacional Lauca contains a variety of bird life, from Andean gulls and giant coots to three species of flamingo.

To the south are protected forests of monkey-puzzle tree (*Araucaria araucana*; *pehuén* in Spanish) as well as cypress and southern beech, while further south is the alerce, cousin to the Northern Hemisphere's sequoia. Throughout, the Valdivian temperate rain forest provides a substantial variety of plants. In the Andes,

the wide-ranging puma has been seen, although rarely, as have wild boars. The rare and diminutive deer (*pudú*) hides out in thick forests throughout the south. The awkward looking ibis, which makes a loud knocking call, is seen in pastures, while the *chucao* (a small red bird), may approach you out of curiosity. The *queltehue*, with black, white and gray markings, has a loud call used to protect its ground nests.

On Chiloé and in Aisén, the *nalca* is the world's largest herbaceous plant, with enormous leaves that grow from a single stalk. Off the northwestern coast of Chiloé is a colony of Humboldt and Magellanic penguins.

In the far south of Aisén and Magallanes, verdant upland forests consist of several species of the widespread genus *Nothofagus*, while on the eastern plains of Magallanes and Tierra del Fuego, decreased rainfall creates extensive grasslands. Reserva Nacional Tamango, near Cochrane, has the largest concentration of the elusive *huemul* (Andean deer). Guanaco, now protected, have made a successful comeback within Torres del Paine, where rheas, *caiquenes* (upland geese) and several species of foxes can also be spotted. Colonies of Magellanic penguins and cormorants are found near Punta Arenas. Chile's long coastline features many marine mammals, including sea lions, otters and fur seals.

National Parks

With the exception of Torres del Paine, Chile's protected areas are underutilized. Hikers have their pick of trails and solitude is easily found – if you avoid the summer high season. As part of its Sistema Nacional de Areas Silvestres Protegidas del Estado (Snaspe, or National System of State-Protected Wild Areas), the government has created a variety of parks and reserves that are administered by Conaf (Corporación Nacional Forestal). Unfortunately, Conaf is under-funded and struggles to maintain the vast amount of parks. Before leaving Santiago, travelers should visit **Conaf** (☎ 02-3900282; www.conaf.cl in Spanish; Av Bulnes 291) for inexpensive maps and brochures, which may be in short supply in the parks themselves.

Chilean law permits the creation of private nature reserves, and conservationists have taken advantage of this to protect lands from massive deforestation. They may be 'privately held' but are open to the public. The most notable is Parque Pumalín in the Aisén region. Other important private reserves are Alto Huemul, in Region VII; El Cañi, near Pucón; Monte Verde, on Isla Riesco north of Punta Arenas; and Bahía Yendegaia, on Tierra del Fuego. In all, there are about 104 privately protected areas throughout Chile.

The following lists the most popular and accessible national parks from north to south. A couple of them are actually national reserves.

Lauca East of Arica, with active and dormant volcanoes, clear blue lakes, abundant bird life, *altiplano* villages and extensive steppes.

Los Flamencos In and around San Pedro de Atacama, a reserve protecting salt lakes and high-altitude lagoons, flamingos, eerie desert landforms and hot springs.

Nevado Tres Cruces East of Copiapó, includes a 6330m-high namesake peak and 6900m-high Ojos del Salado.

Llanos de Challe On the coastal plain of the Norte Chico, best site to view 'flowering of the desert' after rare heavy rains.

La Campana Close to Santiago, protects forests of native oaks and Chilean palms.

Altos del Lircay A reserve with views of the Andean divide and a loop trek to Radal Siete Tazas.

Nahuelbuta In the high coastal range, preserves the area's largest remaining araucaria forests.

Conguillío Mixed forests of araucaria, cypress and southern beech surrounding the active, snowcapped Volcán Llaima.

Huerquehue Near Pucón, hiking trails through araucaria forests, with outstanding views of Volcán Villarrica.

Villarrica The smoking symmetrical cone of Volcán Villarrica is playground for trekkers and climbers, snowboarders and skiers.

Puyehue Near Osorno, with fancy hot-springs and ski resort, and a popular hike through volcanic desert, up the crater, to thermals and geyser fields.

Vicente Peréz Rosales Chile's oldest national park includes spectacular Lago Todos los Santos and Volcán Osorno.

Alerce Andino Near Puerto Montt, this park preserves stands of alerce trees.

Chiloé Features broad sandy beaches, blue lagoons and the forbidding forests that fostered the island's colorful folklore.

Hornopirén Largely undeveloped, with verdant rain forest and secluded lakes.

Queulat Wild evergreen forest, mountains and glaciers stretch across 70km of the Carretera Austral.

Torres del Paine Chile's showpiece near Puerto Natales, with a very popular trail network circuiting some of the country's most awesome mountain peaks.

Environmental Issues

Dubious hydropower and forestry projects threaten Chile's revered whitewater rivers and native forest. From Region VIII south, native forest continues to lose ground to plantations of fast-growing exotics, such as eucalyptus and Monterey pine. Native forests of araucaria and alerce have declined precipitously over the past decades. Salmon farming in the south threatens to pollute both the freshwater and saltwater as well as endanger marine life. Another issue is the intensive use of agricultural chemicals and pesticides to promote Chile's fruit exports. In the north, mining and agricultural pesticides threaten the limited water supply. The growing hole in the ozone layer over Antarctica has become such an issue that medical authorities recommend wearing protective clothing and heavy sunblock to avoid cancer-causing ultraviolet radiation, especially in Patagonia.

That said, environmental awareness is growing, thanks to the increasing number of conservation organizations that have managed to influence legislation and bully forestry companies to pack up their saws.

TRANSPORT

GETTING THERE & AWAY
Air

Santiago's Aeropuerto Internacional Arturo Merino Benítez is the main port of entry. Some other cities have international service to neighboring countries. Only LanChile flies to Rapa Nui (Easter Island). Lacsa (Grupo Taca), LanChile and LanPeru all have nonstop flights to/from Lima, Peru. Most travelers access Chile by taking a cheaper Peruvian flight to Tacna. There are no direct flights between Cuzco and Santiago. LAB and LanChile fly to/from La Paz, Bolivia. Other flights from Santiago include Santa Cruz and Cochabamba.

Aerolíneas Argentinas and LanChile often have Internet specials from Santiago to Buenos Aires. European airlines, such as Lufthansa and British Airways, picking up passengers in Buenos Aires before going long-haul, offer competitive fares. Dap Air-

CHILE

DEPARTURE TAX & ENTRY FEES

Chilean departure tax for international flights is US$26 or its equivalent in local currency. Reciprocity fees are applied to US (US$100), Australian (US$34) and Canadian (US$55) citizens upon arrival at Santiago's international airport. The stamp given is valid for the life of the passport. Fees must be paid in exact amounts in cash, and preferably in US dollars.

lines flies between major destinations in Patagonia.

Land

For details on road conditions at the border crossings, the **carabineros** (☎ 133) in the nearest towns to the borders are good resources. For Peru, Tacna to Arica is the only land crossing. Connections between Chile and Bolivia are much improved, but many of these routes are long, arduous trips. The most accessible crossings are:

Arica to La Paz Hwy completely paved, goes through Parque Nacional Lauca, many buses; hitching is feasible.

Calama to Ollagüe Clunky long train ride with connections to Oruro and La Paz.

Iquique to Oruro Goes via Colchane/Pisiga; hwy almost all paved, regular buses, passes by Parque Nacional Volcán Isluga; keep an eye out for wildlife.

San Pedro de Atacama to Uyuni Popular 4WD tour; with more choices leaving from Bolivia.

Except in far southern Patagonia and Tierra del Fuego, travel to Argentina involves crossing the Andes; some passes close in winter. Crossings in the Lake District and Patagonia are very popular, especially in summer months, so booking early is advised.

Chile Chico to Los Antiguos Frequent bus service.

Coyhaique to Comodoro Rivadavia Several weekly bus services, usually heavily booked, go through Río Mayo.

Futaleufú to Esquel Regular *colectivo* service goes to the border, from where other transport is readily available.

Iquique, Calama & San Pedro de Atacama to Jujuy & Salta Paso de Jama (4200m) is most often used; Paso de Lago (4079m) is an excellent trip through little-visited *salar* (salt pans) country; book early.

Osorno to Bariloche Quickest land route in the Lake District; frequent buses use Paso Cardenal Samoré, often called Pajaritos, year-round.

Puerto Montt & Puerto Varas to Bariloche Year-round, touristy bus–ferry combination tours.

Puerto Natales to El Calafate Many buses in summer; limited off-season.

Punta Arenas to Río Gallegos Many buses ply this six-hour route daily.

Punta Arenas to Tierra del Fuego Three-hour ferry ride to Porvenir, with two buses weekly to Río Grande, connecting to Ushuaia; direct buses via Primera Angostura.

Santiago to Mendoza Tons of options crossing Libertadores; *colectivos* cost more, but are faster.

Temuco to San Martín de los Andes Very popular route with regular summer buses using the Mamuil Malal pass (Paso Tromen to Argentines).

Temuco to Zapala & Neuquén Regular but thin bus service via Pino Hachado (1884m); Icaima (1298m) is an alternative.

Valdivia to San Martín de los Andes Bus–ferry combination crosses Lago Pirehueico to Paso Hua Hum, from where buses continue to San Martín de los Andes.

GETTING AROUND

Air

LanChile (☎ 600-526-2000; www.lanchile.com) and **Sky Airline** (☎ 600-600-2828; www.skyairline.cl in Spanish) provide domestic flights. In the south, small airlines link the more inaccessible regions. The *taza de embarque* (departure tax) is US$7. LanChile's 30-day Visit Chile Pass is available to nonresidents only and must be purchased outside Chile. If your international flight is with LanChile, the pass costs US$250 for three flight coupons, plus US$60 for any additional coupons. Changes in routing, which must be determined upon purchase, cost US$30. Discount fares to Rapa Nui may also be available to pass-holders. If you enter Chile with another carrier, the pass is US$350, plus US$80 for additional coupons. This pass is worthwhile if traveling long distances – from Arica to Santiago to Punta Arenas, for example. Otherwise, special deals on flights are cheaper. Weight limit for carry-on items is 10kg.

Boat

Passenger and car ferries and catamarans connect Puerto Montt with points along the Carretera Austral, including Caleta Gonzalo (Chaitén) and Coyhaique, and also connect Quellón and Castro, Chiloé to Chaitén. Ferries from La Arena to Puelche, Hornopirén to Caleta Gonzalo only run in summer.

A highlight for many travelers is the trip from Puerto Montt to Puerto Natales on board Navimag's *Magallanes*. Book with **Navimag** (☎ 02-442-3120; www.navimag.com; Av El Bosque Norte 0440, Santiago) far in advance and remember that this is really a cargo vessel that has been outfitted for tourism; it's not a cruise ship. Cabins and beds are quite comfortable, but the cheapest beds are the farthest down and closest to farm animal smells and most vulnerable to the tossing waves. Meals are passable; vegetarians need give notice when booking and also bring along some extra food. Pack motion sickness remedies, snacks and drinks, which are expensive at the bar.

Another route goes between Puerto Montt and Puerto Chacabuco; it's not very comfortable, but accesses some out of the way corners. It is imperative to check the latest schedules and reconfirm a week before departure. Navimag has other offices in Puerto Montt.

Bus

The Chilean bus system is fabulous. Tons of companies vie for customers with *ofertas* promotions, discounts and added luxuries like movies and meal service. Long-distance buses are comfortable, fast and punctual. They usually have toilets and either serve meals or make regular food stops. Make advance bookings on popular long-distance routes (mainly those heading to Argentina) in the summer and on or close to major holidays. Luggage holds are safe, but a lockable sack is always a good idea and keeps the pack grime-free. Two of the largest, most convenient and reliable companies, Pullman Bus and Tur Bus have membership clubs you can join for US$5 and get 10% discounts on long-distance trips and access to an Internet or phone reservation system.

Hitching

Especially among Chileans packing around in summer, hitching is a favored form of getting around the country. Vehicles are often packed with families but truckers can be helpful – try asking for rides at *servicentros* on the Panamericana. In Patagonia, where distances are great and vehicles few, expect long waits and keep accessible some warm, windproof, waterproof clothing. Also carry snacks and water, especially in the desert. Women who opt to hitch should do so with someone else.

Local Transport

All main towns and cities have taxis, most of which are metered. Some have set fees for tourist-oriented destinations. Confirm the price before going. *Colectivos* are taxis with fixed routes, shown on the placards on the roof. Rates are about US$0.35 per ride. *Micros* are city buses, clearly numbered and with a sign indicating their destination. Pay your fare and the driver will give you a ticket, which may be checked by an inspector. Santiago has a clean, quick and easy-to-use metro system, which connects the most visited and popular neighborhoods.

Train

The **Empresa de Ferrocarriles del Estado** (EFE; ☎ 02-376-8500; www.efe.cl in Spanish) runs a southbound passenger service from Santiago to Chillán, Concepción, Temuco and intermediates. Classes of service are *turista* and *salón*, both with reclining seats, *cama pasillo* (sleeper), and *clase departamento*, the most luxurious with two-bed private chambers and washbasin. The costlier *cama* class has upper and lower bunks. The charming between-the-wars sleepers that were a trip highlight for some travelers have been replaced with modern models.

SANTIAGO

Santiago has a strong European and US feel to it: classic sidewalk cafés and fast-food outlets line the streets under glassy skyscrapers that dwarf colonial buildings. Its stately, dignified boulevards and neoclassical architecture, swanky suburbs, efficient metro system and, above all, general state of orderliness are reflections of a culture that is hard-working and business-minded. After miles of desert or pasture, entering into this smoggy city may be quite daunting, but it's an essential stopover and there's more than enough to make your time here enjoyable. In Bellavista, innovative restaurants and nightclubs line the streets, while Barrio Brasil offers a bohemian buzz. Providencia and Las Condes, Santiago's wealthier neighborhoods, are worth a jaunt to explore the cafés, bookstores and, mostly, to see how this slice of Chile lives. One of the best things about Santiago is its proximity

CHILE

406 SANTIAGO •• Orientation

to the mighty Andes. There's something kind of great about being smack in the middle of a metropolis and then looking up and seeing, to your surprise, the second-highest mountain range in the world just a few kilometers away.

Mapuche warriors nearly obliterated Santiago six months after Pedro de Valdivia founded it in 1541. But the Spanish prevailed. Building dams to control the Río Mapocho, plus railway tracks to the main port of Valparaíso, helped the city grow. Due to earthquakes, few colonial buildings remain, Iglesia San Francisco being the exception.

ORIENTATION

'El Centro' is a compact, triangular area bounded by the Río Mapocho and Parque Forestal in the north, the Vía Norte Sur in the west, and Av General O'Higgins (the Alameda) in the south. Key public buildings line Plaza de Armas, from which there is a busy graph of shopping arcades and pedestrian streets. North and east of the center is Barrio Bellavista, with Cerro San Cristóbal (Parque Metropolitano). To the west is Barrio Brasíl, the bohemian enclave of the city. At the tip of this triangle and extending east are the wealthy *comunas* (communes) of Providencia and Las Condes, accessed via the Alameda.

INFORMATION
Bookshops
Books (Map pp412-13; Manuel Montt, Av Providencia 1652, Local 6) Sells used English-language paperbacks.
Chile Ilustrado (Map pp412-13; ☎ 02-2358145) In the same complex as Books.
Feria Chilena del Libro (Paseo Huérfanos 623) Best stocked, even has an assorted collection of Lonely Planet books.
Librería Inglesa (Paseo Huérfanos 669, Local 11; Av Pedro de Valdivia 47, Providencia)

Cultural Centers
Instituto Chileno-Británico (Map pp412-13; ☎ 02-6382156; Santa Lucía 124)
Instituto Chileno-Norteamericano (Map pp412-13; ☎ 02-6963215; Moneda 1467)

Emergency
Ambulance (☎ 131)
Fire Department (☎ 132)
Police (☎ 133)

Internet Access
Most budget lodgings have Internet access or can direct you to the closest Internet café. The average price is about US$0.75 per hour.
Axcesso Internet (Map pp412-13; Agustinas 869, Galería Imperio, 2nd fl) Sixty computers and fast connections.
Cyber.sur (Map pp408-9; Maturana 302; ☾ till 11pm) On the corner of the Barrio Brasil plaza.
Dity Office (Fidel Oteíza 1930, Providencia)

Laundry
Self-service laundries are hard to find in Santiago, but most budget lodgings offer laundry services. Laundries listed below charge about US$2.50–3 per kg to wash, dry and fold.
Lavandería Autoservicio (Map pp412-13; Monjitas 507) South of Parque Forestal.
Lavandería San Miguel (Map pp408-9; Moneda 2296) In Barrio Brasil.

Left Luggage
All the main bus terminals have a *custodia*, where you can stash your bags for about US$1 per day, but we suggest storing luggage at a reputable lodging, many of which don't charge.

Medical Services
Clínica Alemana de Santiago (☎ 02-2101111; Av Vitacura 5951) In Vitacura, well recommended.
Farmacia Ahumada (☎ 02-2319861; Av Providencia 2128; ☾ 24 hr) Near Av Ricardo Lyon.
Posta Central (Map pp412-13; ☎ 02-6341650; Portugal 125, metro Universidad Católica) English-speaking staff.

GETTING INTO TOWN

Aeropuerto Internacional Arturo Merino Benítez (☎ 02-6019001) is in Pudahuel, 20km northwest of downtown Santiago. **Tur Bus** (Map pp412-13; ☎ 02-6717380; Moneda 1529), runs every 15 minutes between 6:30am and 9pm (US$2, 30 minutes). Centropuerto provides a similar, slightly cheaper service from Los Héroes metro station. A door-to-door shuttle service (US$5.50) is provided by **New Transfer** (☎ 02-6773000) and **Transfer** (Map pp412-13; ☎ 02-7777707). A cab ride to the center costs about US$20. All of the main bus stations are right off the Alameda, at which you can find metro stations to access your final destination.

Money

Many *casas de cambio* are downtown along Agustinas between Bandera and Ahumada. They change cash and traveler's checks and are open regular business hours. Some are open Saturday morning. ATMs (Redbanc) are found throughout the city. **Blanco Viajes** (☎ 02-6369100; General Holley 148, Providencia) is the American Express representative.

Post

Main post office (north side Plaza de Armas; ☑ 8am-10pm Mon-Fri, 8am-6pm Sat) Handles poste restante. There's a minor pick-up fee & mail is held for 30 days. Other locations: in the Centro at Moneda 1155 & in Providencia at Av Providencia 1466.

Tourist Offices

Conaf (Map pp412-13; ☎ 02-3900282; Paseo Bulnes 291; ☑ 9:30am-5:30pm Mon-Thu, 9:30am-4:30pm Fri) Distributes brochures (in Spanish) with maps to all of the parks and reserves, and has topographic maps to photocopy.
Municipal tourist office (Map pp412-13; ☎ 02-6327785; www.ciudad.cl/turismo; Merced 860; ☑ 10am-6pm Mon-Fri) In Casa Colorada, near the Plaza de Armas.
Sernatur (☎ 02-2361420; Av Providencia 1550; ☑ 9am-5pm Mon-Fri, 9am-1pm Sat) Abundant leaflets on the entire country and English-speaking staff. There are other offices at the airport and at the San Borja bus terminal.

Travel Agencies

Student Flight Center (☎ 02-3350395, 800-340034; www.sertur.cl in Spanish; Hernando de Aguirre 201, Oficina 401, Providencia) STA representative, bargains on air tickets.

DANGERS & ANNOYANCES

Santiago is relatively safe, but has a growing reputation for pickpockets, especially in the Centro (the first two blocks of San Antonio going north from Alameda are notorious), around Mercado Central (near the river) and on Cerro Santa Lucía. Be alert but not obsessed with personal security, and take special care with your belongings when seated at sidewalk cafés in heavily traveled areas. Women should avoid walking alone at night, and it's probably safest to avoid walking through parks at night, even in groups. Also of note is Santiago's smog, which can make your eyes burn and throat hurt.

SIGHTS
Museums

Most museums are free on Sunday and closed on Monday. Regular hours are usually from 10am to 6pm or 7pm Tuesday to Saturday and 10am to 2pm Sunday. Admission to most is US$1.

If you have time to visit only one museum, **Museo Chileno de Arte Precolombino** (Map pp412-13; Bandera 361; admission US$3) should be it. In the 1805 Real Casa de Aduana (royal customs house), this museum chronicles 4500 years of pre-Columbian civilization in four different geographic regions: Mesoamerica, and central, northern and southern Andes.

The **Museo Histórico Nacional** (Plaza de Armas 951), inside the Palacio de la Real Audencia, documents colonial and republican history. There's a small room with indigenous artifacts, early colonial furniture and house fittings, and an interesting exhibit on 20th-century politics.

Modeled on the Petit Palais in Paris, Santiago's early-20th-century fine arts museum, **Palacio de Bellas Artes** (Map pp412-13; José M de La Barra near Av José María Caro), fronts an entire block in the Parque Forestal. It has permanent collections of French, Italian, Dutch and Chilean paintings.

Museo de la Solidaridad Salvador Allende (Map pp408-9; Herrera 360, Barrio Brasil), housed in an old mansion with a pretty central courtyard, is a '70s art time-capsule. Having begun in 1971 with donations from artists around the world in sympathy with Chile's socialist experiment, the museum went underground after the coup of 1973 – the entire collection spent 17 years in the warehouses of the Museo de Arte Contemporáneo, awaiting the return of civilian rule.

Isidora Goyenechea (widow of Luis Cousiño of the prominent wine family, with successes also in coal, silver and shipping) helped mastermind what is probably Santiago's most glorious mansion, **Palacio Cousiño** (Map pp408-9; Dieciocho 438; admission US$2). Dating from 1871, the house is embellished with French-style artwork and features one of the country's first elevators. The palace is south of the Alameda. Admission includes an informative guided tour in Spanish, or sometimes in English.

La Chascona (Map pp412-13; Museo Neruda; Márquez de La Plata 0192; admission US$5), Pablo Neruda's ship-like house, shows off the poet's eclectic collection of furniture and knick-knacks. Tours, conducted on a first-come, first-served basis, last an hour and are very thorough.

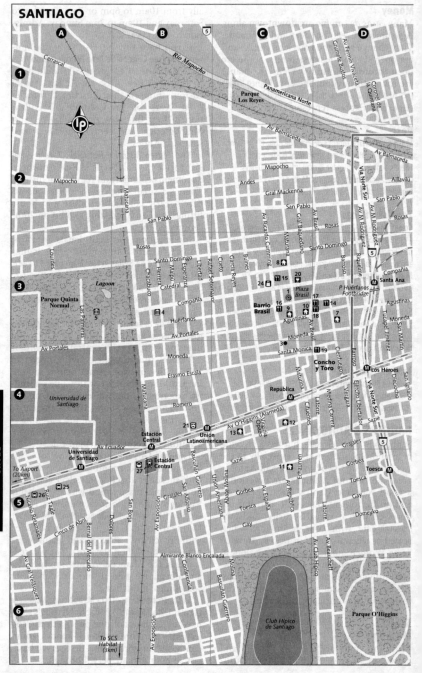

SANTIAGO

CHILE

To Airport (20km)

To SCS Habitat (3km)

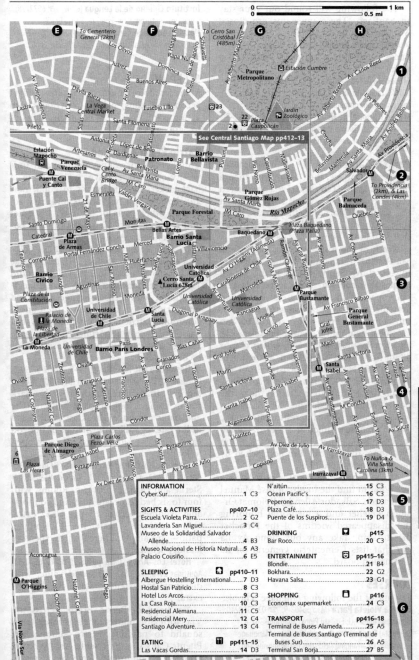

CHILE

INFORMATION	
Cyber.Sur..1	C3

SIGHTS & ACTIVITIES	pp407–10
Escuela Violeta Parra.......................2	G2
Lavandería San Miguel.....................3	C4
Museo de la Solidaridad Salvador	
Allende..4	B3
Museo Nacional de Historia Natural...5	A3
Palacio Cousiño...............................6	E5

SLEEPING	pp410–11
Albergue Hostelling International......7	D3
Hostal San Patricio..........................8	C3
Hotel Los Arcos..............................9	C3
La Casa Roja.................................10	C3
Residencial Alemana.......................11	C5
Residencial Mery............................12	C4
Santiago Adventure........................13	C4

EATING	pp411–15
Las Vacas Gordas............................14	D3

N'aitún...15	C3
Ocean Pacific's..............................16	C3
Peperone......................................17	D3
Plaza Café.....................................18	D3
Puente de los Suspiros....................19	D4

DRINKING	p415
Bar Roco.......................................20	C3

ENTERTAINMENT	pp415–16
Blondie...21	B4
Bokhara..22	G2
Havana Salsa.................................23	G1

SHOPPING	p416
Economax supermarket...................24	C3

TRANSPORT	pp416–18
Terminal de Buses Alameda.............25	A5
Terminal de Buses Santiago (Terminal de	
Buses Sur)..................................26	A5
Terminal San Borja.........................27	B5

The following will round out your stay in Santiago. These museums are closed Monday; admission is US$1–2:

Museo Colonial de San Francisco (Map pp412-13; Londres 4) Inside Iglesia de San Francisco, Santiago's oldest church.

Museo de Artes Visuales (Map pp412-13; Lastarria 307, Plaza Mulato Gil de Castro, Centro) Clean, modern space showing contemporary Chilean sculptures.

Museo Nacional de Historia Natural (Map pp408-9; Quinta Normal) Fun old-style dioramas, butterfly collection and a sampling of dinosaur bones.

Parks & Gardens   Map pp408–9

Once a hermitage, then a convent, then a military bastion, **Cerro Santa Lucía** has offered respite from the city chaos since 1875. At the southwest corner is the Terraza Neptuno, with fountains and curving staircases that lead to the summit.

North of the Río Mapocho, 870m **Cerro San Cristóbal** ('Tapahue' to the Mapuche) towers above Santiago and is the site of **Parque Metropolitano**, the capital's largest open space, with an unimpressive zoo, two very nice pools, a botanical garden and art museum. The most direct route to San Cristóbal's summit is via the **funicular** (US$2; 1-8pm Mon, 10am-8pm Tue-Sun), which climbs 485m from Plaza Caupolicán, at the north end of Pío Nono in Bellavista. From the Terraza, the 2000m-long *teleférico* (US$2 round trip) runs to a station near the north end of Av Pedro de Valdivia Norte, accessing most of the interesting sites in the park. Purchase a funicular/*teleférico* combo for US$3 from either end of the park. From Pío Nono, the top can also be reached by bus, or a rocky uphill hike.

At the **Cementerio General** (north end of Av La Paz), you can find the tombs of José Manuel Balmaceda, Salvador Allende, diplomat Orlando Letelier and a memorial honoring the 'disappeared' victims of the Pinochet dictatorship. Take any bus along Av La Paz that lists Cementerio General on its destination board.

COURSES

Try one of the following language schools:

Escuela Violeta Parra (Map pp408-9; 02-7358240; vioparra@chilesat.cl; Ernesto Pinto Lagarrigue 362-A; Bellavista) Emphasizing the social context of language instruction by arranging field trips to community and environmental organizations, vineyards and the like.

Instituto Chileno de la Lengua (ICHIL; 6972728; www.cmet.net/ichil; Riquelme 226, Barrio Brasil)

Natalis Language Center (Map pp412-13; 02-2228721; www.natalislang.com; Vicuña Mackenna 6, 7th fl)

SLEEPING

Many family-oriented *residenciales* (budget accommodations) lock the front doors from 2am to 7am, so ask first before heading out to Santiago's nightlife.

Barrio Brasil & Beyond

This bohemian, young, family- and university-oriented enclave is becoming a backpackers center, thanks to good, new and hostels, fun restaurants and easy access to other parts of the city. It's quiet and relatively safe. Metro stations are Los Héroes or Santa Ana.

La Casa Roja (Map pp408-9; 02-6964241; info@lacasaroja.tie.cl; Av Agustinas 2113; dm US$6, s&d with bath US$17, breakfast US$2.50) This splendid 19th-century mansion makes a good meeting point, with elegant lounge areas and interior patios, a large back garden and a communal kitchen. Can get a bit noisy, but has a fun, friendly atmosphere. Free luggage storage and bulletin board. Reservations recommended.

Hostal San Patricio (Map pp408-9; 02-6719045; Catedral 2235; s without/with bath US$9/10) Local family atmosphere, with slightly dark rooms along a long crooked hallway. The and baths are huge. Breakfast is included in the rate regardless of whether or not you eat it. There's a kitchen and TV room open to lodgers.

Albergue Hostelling International (Map pp408-9; 02-6718532; Cienfuegos 151; dm/s/d US$9/18/20) Sterile and lacking in charm. Rooms, with four to six beds each, are quiet and comfortable. Nonmembers of HI pay US$2 extra. Common areas – cafeteria, TV lounge, patio – are ample. There's an inexpensive laundry service.

Hotel Los Arcos (Map pp408-9; 02-6990998; Agustinas 2173; s/d US$22/30) Good value, with discounts for extended stays. Breakfast is extra.

Northeast of Barrio Brasil, across the Via Norte Sur, budget lodgings range from squalid to passable. Metro stations are Puente Cal y Canto or Santa Ana. Women may feel uncomfortable here late at night,

CHILE

especially on General Mackenna, where many prostitutes hang out.

Hotel Indiana (Map pp412-13; ☎ 02-6714251; Rosas 1339; r per person without/with bath US$5/6.50). Popular with Israelis and has all the backpacker services, from kitchens and barbecues to Internet access, but also pithy petty rules. Can get too rowdy and is generally uninviting.

Hotel Caribe (Map pp412-13; ☎ 02-6966681; San Martín 851; US$6.50) Well known and cheap, but little to recommend it. The rooms in back are quieter. The beds probably keep local chiropractors in business.

Nuevo Hotel (Map pp412-13; ☎ 02-6715698; Morandé 791; US$4) A bit better and a bit cheaper, this one has kitchen privileges and a TV lounge. All rooms share baths with hot water.

El Centro & Barrio París Londres

Places around the center are more expensive, but are right in the heart of things. Barrio París Londres (metro Universidad de Chile) is an attractive, quiet cobblestone enclave south of the Alameda. Barrio Santa Lucía (metro Santa Lucía), on the other side, is equally quaint and more upscale.

Residencial Londres (Map pp412-13; ☎ 02-6382215; Londres 54; r per person US$11, d/tr with bath US$25/37) Great for couples – romantic, old-fashioned rooms with double beds the best but there aren't many singles and most are small. Very attractive and well maintained old mansion with enough baths, good breakfast (US$1) and polished staff. It's popular – make reservations. Doors locked at 2am.

Hotel París (Map pp412-13; ☎ 02-6640921; París 813; s/d US$23/27) Not as charming, but secure and ample rooms with courteous staff.

Hotel Foresta (Map pp412-13; ☎ 02-6396262, fax 632-2996; Subercaseaux 353; s/d US$30/36) Close to bars and restaurants in the Barrio Santa Lucía, this hotel is cute and cozy and a first-rate choice. All rooms have private bath, hot water and breakfast is included.

República   Map pp408–9

South of the Alameda and east of Estación Central, the area around Av República has a predominantly university atmosphere. A few quality budget options have sprung up here. Metro is República.

Santiago Adventure (☎ 02-6715529; santiago _adventure@terra.cl; Cabo Arestey 2468; dm US$9, d with bath US$21) Praised by travelers for its quiet location, communal kitchen, laundry, Internet and traveler info. Prices include breakfast. Other meals can be ordered. It's in an alley off Av España – one street west of República.

Residencial Alemana (☎ 02-6712388; República 220; r per person US$11) A charming old world place and a great option, all rooms have shared bath and breakfast included.

Residencial Mery (☎ 02-6968883; Pasaje República 36; r without/with bath US$13/18) In a quiet alley, Mery isn't as charming, but is still quiet. Doors are locked at 2am.

SCS Habitat (☎ 02-6833732; scshabitat@yahoo.com; San Vicente 1798; dm US$6) In a tranquil, middle-class neighborhood about 10 minutes south of Estación Central by *micro* or taxi, Scott, the owner, has cramped but airy rooms. It's not known for being spit-spot clean, but is a good place to gather and exchange travel tips around the communal table. There are some private rooms or you can pitch a tent on the patio. From Estación Central, take *micro* 335, 358 or 360 down Exposición to San Vicente and walk east one block.

EATING

The best bets for lunch are in the center; for dinner try Barrio Bellavista, Brasil or Providencia. Lots of cafés focus more on drinking than eating after 9pm, so it's best not to order something on the menu that takes time to prepare – you might have to wait a long time and end up buying more drinks.

Center   Map pp412–13

Have lunch or *onces* (a snack) in the center, but don't expect to find much open for dinner. Along the southern arcade of the **Plaza de Armas**, vendors serve *completos* (hot dogs) and *empanadas* (fried snacks) of varying quality.

Mercado Central (🕙 6am-4pm Sun-Thu, 6am-8pm Fri, 6am-6pm Sat) These days it's more a stage for touristy restaurants than a market. Restaurants along the periphery cost a fraction of what Donde Augusto does – none are outstanding, but the ambiance is fun. Across 21 de Mayo is a large produce market – a lot more fun than a grocery store.

Bar Central (San Pablo 1063) Near Mercado Central, serves generous portions of seafood and Santiago atmosphere at lunchtime. Popular with locals and tourists alike.

CHILE

CENTRAL SANTIAGO

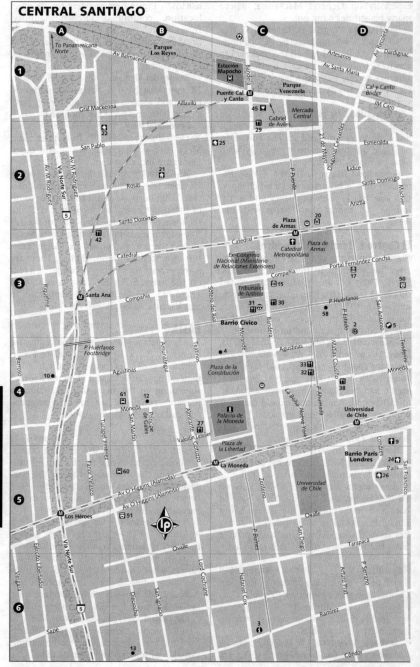

To Panamericana Norte

Av Balmaceda

Parque Los Reyes

Estación Mapocho

Puente Cal y Canto

Parque Venezuela

Artesanos

Av Santa María

Cal y Canto Bridge

JM Caro

Gral Mackenna

Aillavilú

45

Gabriel de Aviles

29

Mercado Central

21 de Mayo

21 de Mayo

Esmeralda

San Pablo

25

Lidice

Santo Domingo

Rosas

21

Ariztía

Santo Domingo

P Puente

Plaza de Armas

20

42

Catedral

Catedral Metropolitana

Plaza de Armas

Catedral

Ex-Congreso Nacional (Ministerio de Relaciones Exteriores)

Compañía

Portal Fernández Concha

17

50

Santa Ana

Compañía

Tribunales de Justicia

15

P Huérfanos

58

5

P Huérfanos Footbridge

Barroso

10

Agustinas

Barrio Cívico

31

30

Agustinas

2

Matías Cousiño

33

32

38

Moneda

Plaza de la Constitución

4

Universidad de Chile

61

12

Príncipe de Gales

27

Palacio de la Moneda

Plaza de la Libertad

Universidad de Chile

Barrio París Londres

9

24

26

Valentín Letelier

La Moneda

Paris

60

Av O'Higgins (Alameda)

Los Héroes

51

Av O'Higgins (Alameda)

Universidad de Chile

Ovalle

Tarapacá

Ovalle

3

13

Cóndor

CHILE

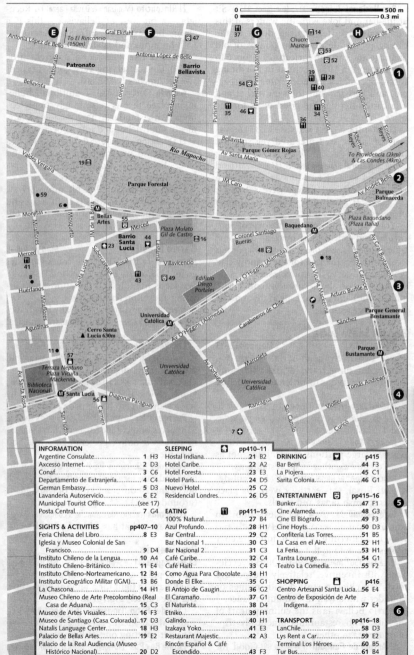

CHILE

Bar Nacional (Bandera 317; Huérfanos 1151) Sit at the bar and joke with the waiters at this lunchtime favorite, or head down to the dining rooms, decorated in photos of old Santiago and cartoon caricatures. From 6 to 10pm there's a 10% discount in the dining room. Specialties include: *crudos* (carpaccio) and *borgoña*, but the sandwiches and a la carte offerings are good deals for the price.

El Naturista (Moneda 846; mains US$3.50-6) Variety of salads, well-prepared veg specials, fresh juices.

100% Natural (Valentín Letelier 1319) Clean and green and west of La Moneda, order up a veg *menu del día* (inexpensive set meal) for US$3.50, sandwiches (US$2.50), juices or *onces*, weekdays only.

You can drink up the history of *machismo* and get a good buzz at the same time at one of these original *café con piernas* ('cafe with legs' named for the scantily clad women who serve the coffee), serving good strong espresso shots, *cortados* (coffee with a little milk) and cocoa: Café Haití and **Café Caribe** (Paseo Ahumada).

Barrios Santa Lucía & Bellavista   Map pp412–13

These two lively neighborhoods are top choices for dinner and drinks. But don't even bother trying to order dinner before 9pm.

Middle Eastern cafés (Merced) In Santa Lucía; serve excellent sweets, spinach *empanadas* and Turkish coffee.

Izakaya Yoko (Merced 456; mains US$5-6) Inexpensive, large portions of sushi, but not as good quality as other sushi restaurants.

Rincón Español (Rosal Interior 346) In a cul-de-sac off Rosal, this earthy cavernous place serves Spanish tapas and meals.

Café Escondida (Rosal 346) Next door to Rincón Español; serves omelets, salads and wine in a labyrinth of small, intimate cozy rooms overlooking the alley.

R (Lastarria 307; mains US$7.50-11) Quirky yet elegant with inventive, relatively inexpensive food. Try chicken stuffed with prunes or flounder with a walnut and butter sauce.

Barrio Bellavista is the culinary heart of the city, with restaurants practically tripping over each other.

El Antojo de Gauguin (Pío Nono 69) Good for cheap, tasty Middle Eastern fare.

El Rinconcito (Manizano & Dávila Baeza) In Recoleta – a bit west of Bellavista – this is a cheap but excellent informal restaurant with hummus and falafel sandwiches.

Donde La Elke (Dardignac 68) A bright little café-like place serving very good inexpensive set lunches (US$2.80).

Galindo (Dardignac 098) Traditional, bohemian place that is refreshingly unpretentious, with standard, hearty Chilean fare, meaty sandwiches and lots of beer.

El Caramaño (Purísima 257) There's no sign out front, so just ring the door bell and enter this graffiti decorated favorite, serving well-prepared Chilean specialties.

Etniko (Constitución 172) A bit more pricey, but cool and stylish, this is both a bar and place to order large wok stir fries (US$6.60) and sushi (US$5–7).

Barrio Brasil   Map pp408–9

Plaza Café (Av Brasil 221) Three-course lunches go for US$2 or try a pizza (around US$3.50). Service is friendly and the atmosphere inviting and unpretentious.

N'aitun (Ricardo Cumming 453) Daily lunch specials for US$2 in a cool, pleasant, musical spot.

Las Vacas Gordas (Cienfuegos 280) Fabulous *parrillada* (grilled meat), decent pastas and great service; call ahead.

Ocean Pacific's (Ricardo Cumming 221) Reasonable, family-style seafood restaurant with friendly service and superb homemade bread.

Puente de los Suspiros (Brasil 75) Hands down, Santiago's best choice for Peruvian dishes – in case you didn't get enough while you were there.

Peperone (Huérfanos 1954) Candlelit neighborhood café serving tea, coffee, beer, fresh juices and 20 different kinds of *empanadas* (around US$1).

Economax (cnr Ricardo Cumming & Compañía) Large supermarket that has a bit of everything.

Providencia

La Mia Pappa (11 de Septiembre 1351; pasta US$2, menú US$2) Popular all-you-can-eat pasta joint – you'll have to fight for a table at lunchtime. Definite cafeteria flavor to it.

Café del Patio (Providencia 1670, Local 8-A) Veg and seafood menu; servings are huge, so consider splitting one dish between two.

Phone Box Pub (Providencia 1670; US$7-8) Homesick Brits can find pub lunches here.

El Huerto (Orrego Luco 054) Best veg restaurant in the city – stylish and imaginative. The adjacent café, La Huerta, has a limited menu, but is kinder on the wallet.

La Pizza Nostra (Providencia 1975; mains US$8) Open when most other places are closed (eg on Sunday), it offers a good range of pastas (sauces overly creamy), pizzas and salads.

DRINKING

Santiago's main nightlife districts are Barrio Bellavista (metro: Baquedano), Providencia's Av Suecia (metro: Los Leones), Plaza Ñuñoa (most easily reached by bus or taxi) and Barrio Brasil (metro: República or Unión Latinoamericana). The metro closes at 10:30pm – around the time most of these places get interesting.

La Piojera (Map pp412-13; Aillavilú 1030) Rowdy, cavernous drinking hall near the Mercado Central, packed with atmosphere and *chicha* (popular drink, often alcoholic) drinkers, even during the day.

Bar Berri (Map pp412-13; Rosal 321) In Barrio Santa Lucía, this low-ceilinged, dark, old-

style bar is one of Santiago's liveliest, with a fashionable crowd. Also good is nearby **Café Escondida** (see Eating p414).

Bar Roco (Map pp408-9; Compañía 2085, 2nd fl) Low lit, with ambient music and creatively mixed drinks, this is a relaxed space right on Plaza Brasil.

In Barrio Bellavista, many of the restaurants listed above are good for drinks, especially Etniko. Also check out:

Sarita Colonia (Map pp412-13; Dardignac 50) Velvet curtains, gorgeous upstairs lounge, great drinks and superb food.

HBH Brewery (Irarrázaval 3176, Ñuñoa) Beer buffs crowd for the two styles of homebrew.

Flannery's Irish Geo Pub (Encomenderos 83, Las Condes) Guinness and Boddington's on tap and an assortment of imported beers.

CLUBBING

Many dance clubs close their doors in February and move to Valparaíso and Viña del Mar. Also, don't bother showing up to any of these places earlier than 1am.

Confitería Las Torres (Map pp412-13; Alameda 1570) Near the center, an old world place dating from 1879; has live tango music on weekends.

Fausto (Av Santa María 0832, Providencia; metro: Salvador) Another fun venue; stylish, multilevel club with techno-pop music and a gay crowd.

Blondie (Map pp408-9; Alameda 2879, Barrio Brasil) In a spectacular old theater, with a massive video screen looming over the dance floor.

The following are all in Bellavista:

Bokhara (Map pp408-9; Pío Nono 430) Primarily a gay venue – small but with lots of mirrors.

Bunker (Map pp412-13; Bombero Núñez 159) One of the venues that makes Bellavista the focus of Santiago's gay life.

Havana Salsa (Map pp408-9; Dominica 142) Cleverly recreates the ambience of Old Havana.

La Feria (Map pp412-13; Constitución 275) The place to go for electronic music.

Tantra Lounge (Map pp412-13; Ernesto Pinto Lagarrigue 154) Very cool; music is strictly techno and house.

ENTERTAINMENT
Cinemas

Many cinemas offer Wednesday discounts.

Cine Hoyts (Map pp412-13; Paseo Huérfanos 735) Paseo Huérfanos, in the center, has a few multiplexes, including this one.

Art-house cinemas include:

Cine Alameda (Map pp412-13; Alameda 139)

CHILE

Cine El Biógrafo (Map pp412-13; Lastarria 181, Barrio
Santa Lucía; US$3.50)
Cine Tobalaba (Providencia 2563, Providencia)

Live Music & Theater
N'Aitún (Map pp408-9; Ricardo Cumming 453) This is
Santiago's *peña*, a comfortable, intellectual
bookstore pub with live folk music.

La Casa en el Aire (Map pp412-13; Antonia López
de Bello 0125) Great place to hear and see live
music, poetry readings and theater.

Estación Mapocho (Map pp412-13; ☎ 02-3611761;
cnr Bandera & Balmaceda) Passenger trains to
Viña del Mar and Valparaíso once arrived
and departed here, now it's Santiago's main
cultural center, offering live theater, concerts, exhibits and a café.

Performing arts venues include the prestigious **Teatro Municipal** (☎ 02-3690282; Agustinas
794) and the well-established **Teatro La Come-
dia** (Map pp412-13; ☎ 02-6391523; Merced 349), near
Cerro Santa Lucía, offering contemporary
drama Thursday through Sunday.

Sport
Estadio Nacional (Av Grecia & Marathon, Ñuñoa) Catch
a soccer match here. Any match involving
Colo Colo is likely to be fairly exciting, as
they have the biggest fan base. Tickets can
be bought at the stadium.

Horseracing takes place every Saturday
from 2:30pm and on alternate Thursdays
at **Hipódromo Chile** (Av Independencia 1715) in the
comuna of Independencia; and every Monday from 2:30pm and on alternate Wednesday at **Club Hípico de Santiago** (Almirante Blanco
Encalada 2540; metro Unión Latinoamericana), south of
the Alameda near Parque O'Higgins.

SHOPPING
For artisan crafts try the following:
Centro de Exposición de Arte Indígena (Map pp412-
13; Alameda 499) At the southwestern corner of Cerro
Santa Lucía; indigenous crafts from Mapuche and Aymara
people as well as from Rapa Nui.
Centro Artesanal Santa Lucía (Map pp412-13; Carmen
& Diagonal Paraguay) On other side of Cerro Santa Lucía;
lapis lazuli jewelry, sweaters, copperware and pottery.
Cooperativa Almacén Campesina (Purísima 303)
In Bellavista; shawls and scarves, as well as pottery and
jewelry.
Centro Artesanal de Los Dominicos (Av Apoquindo
9085; ⏰ 11am-7:30pm year-round) At the Dominican
monastery in Las Condes is Santiago's largest crafts selection, with goods imported from throughout the country

and also made on site. Take the metro to Escuela Militar
and then catch a taxi (US$4) or bus (look for one marked
'Los Dominicos') out along Av Apoquindo. It's also possible
to catch bus No 327 from Av Providencia, No 344 from
the Alameda or Av Providencia, No 229 from Catedral or
Compañía, or No 326 from Alameda and Miraflores.

GETTING THERE & AWAY
Air
Aeropuerto Internacional Arturo Merino Benítez
(☎ 02-6019001) is in Pudahuel, 20km northwest of downtown Santiago. It takes about
half an hour to 45 minutes to get there,
and airlines require you to be there one
hour before a flight, so plan accordingly.
Domestic carrier offices are **LanChile** (Map
pp412-413; ☎ 600-5262000; Huérfanos 926 & Providencia 2006) and **Sky Airline** (☎ 02-3533100; Andres de
Fuenzalida 55, Providencia). Following are some
approximate fares.

Destination	Cost
Antofagasta	US$60–90
Arica	US$225
Concepción	US$117
Iquique	US$130
La Serena	US$30
Osorno	US$157
Pucón	US$180
Puerto Montt	US$180
Punta Arenas	US$300
Temuco	US$157
Valdivia	US$157

Bus
Santiago has four main bus terminals, from
which buses leave to northern, central and
southern destinations. Bus transportation
within Chile is reliable, prompt, safe and
comfortable. It's one of the best things
about traveling here. The largest and most
reputable bus company is Tur Bus. Frequent travelers can pay US$5 to become
card-carrying members of the Tur Bus club,
which provides a 10% discount on one-way
fares (if paying in cash), a phone or Internet
reservation system, and a tad more attention at the counter. You can join at any Tur
Bus office. Pullman Bus is also very good. In
the south, Cruz del Sur is the best.

Terminal San Borja (Map pp408-9; ☎ 02-7760645;
Alameda 3250) is at the end of the shopping
mall alongside the main train station. The
ticket booths are divided by region, with
destinations prominently displayed. Desti-

nations are from Arica down to the *cordillera* (mountain range) around Santiago.

Terminal de Buses Alameda (Map pp408-9; ☎ 02-7762424; cnr Alameda & Jotabeche; metro: Universidad de Santiago) is home to **Tur Bus** (☎ 02-7780808) and **Pullman Bus** (☎ 02-7781185). For northern and central coastal destinations, contact Pullman Bus; for middle Chile, **Pullman del Sur** (☎ 02-7762426); and for every destination along the Panamericana, Tur Bus.

Terminal de Buses Sur (Terminal de Buses Santiago; Map pp408-9; ☎ 02-7791385; btwn Ruiz Tagle & Nicasio Retamales, Alameda 3850) has the most service to the central coast, international and southern destinations (the Lake District and Chiloé).

Terminal Los Héroes (Map pp412-13; Tucapel Jiménez), near the Alameda in the Centro, is a convenient and less chaotic terminal. It provides service to nearby northern destinations, south and a few Argentine destinations. Some long-distance buses from Terminal de Buses Santiago make a stop here for passengers. There's Internet service upstairs.

Fares can vary dramatically among companies, so explore several possibilities. Promotions can reduce normal fares by half; student reductions by 25%. Discounts are common outside the peak summer season, and bargaining may even be possible. Try it if the bus is leaving soon and appears to have empty seats. Book in advance to travel during holiday periods. Fares between important destinations are listed throughout this chapter. Approximate one-way fares and journey times are shown in the following table.

Destination	Duration in Hours	Cost: Pullman	Cost: Salón Cama
Antofagasta	18	US$31	US$42
Arica	28	US$38	US$56
Castro	19	US$27	US$45
Chillán	6	US$9	n/a
Concepción	8	US$14	n/a
Copiapó	11	US$20	US$30
Iquique	26	US$37	US$46
La Serena	7	US$15	US$22
Osorno	14	US$19	US$32
Puerto Montt	16	US$20	US$35
Punta Arenas	60	US$100	n/a
Temuco	11	US$14	US$29
Valdivia	13	US$17	US$32
Valparaíso	2	US$4	n/a
Villarrica	13	US$15	US$29
Viña del Mar	2	US$4	n/a

Train

All trains depart Santiago from the Estación Central. Tickets are sold at that **ticket office** (Map pp412-13; ☎ 02-3768500; Alameda 3170; ☯ 7am-9:45pm) and at **Metro Universidad de Chile** (Map pp412-13; ☎ 02-6883284; ☯ 9am-8pm Mon-Fri, 9am-2pm Sat).

GETTING AROUND
Bus
Santiago's yellow exhaust-spewing buses (known as *micros*) go everywhere cheaply. Check the destination signs in their windows or ask other passengers waiting at the stop. Many buses now have signed, fixed stops, but may stop at other points. Fares vary slightly depending on the bus, but most are US$0.50 per trip; hang on to your ticket, since inspectors may ask for it.

Car
Renting a car to drive around Santiago is a sure-fire way to have a bad day. But if you must, here are some agencies. Most also have offices at the airport.

Automóvil Club de Chile (Acchi; ☎ 02-2125702; Vitacura 8620, Vitacura)

Budget (☎ 02-3623232; Bilbao 1439, Providencia)

First (☎ 02-2256328; Rancagua 0514, Providencia)

Hertz (☎ 02-2359666; Av Andrés Bello 1469, Providencia)

Lys (Map pp412-13; ☎ 02-6337600; Miraflores 541) Lys also rents mountain bikes for US$12 a day.

Colectivo
Quicker and more comfortable than buses, taxi *colectivos* carry up to five passengers on fixed routes. The fare is about US$0.75 within the city limits, more to outlying suburbs. They look like regular taxis, but have an illuminated roof sign indicating their route.

Metro
The clean, quick and efficient metro operates from 6am to 10:30pm Monday to Saturday and 8am to 10:30pm Sunday and holidays. The three lines interlink to form a network to most places of interest for the traveler. Fares vary slightly depending on time of day, but range from US$0.30 to US$0.45. Tickets are single use, so purchase a few at a time to avoid waiting in line. Within some of the subterranean stations you can also find ticket offices for bus companies, call centers and places for quick eats.

CHILE

Taxi

Santiago's abundant metered taxis – black with yellow roofs – are moderately priced. Most drivers are honest, courteous and helpful, but a few take roundabout routes and a handful have 'funny' meters. Flag fall *(bajar la bandera)* costs about US$0.25 and about US$0.12 per 200m. There is also a system of radio taxis, which can be slightly cheaper. Hotels and restaurants are usually happy to make calls for clients.

AROUND SANTIAGO

SKI RESORTS

Chilean ski resorts are open from June to October, with lower rates in early and late season. Most ski areas are above 3300m and treeless; the runs are long, the season is long, and the snow is deep and dry. Snowboarders are welcome at all the resorts. Three major resorts are barely an hour from the capital, while the fourth is about two hours away on the Argentine border. **El Colorado & Farellones** (full-day lift ticket US$33), 45km east of the capital, close enough together to be considered one resort, has 19 lifts and 22 runs from 2430m to 3330m. **Centro de Ski El Colorado** (☎ 02-2463344; Av Apoquindo 4900, Local 48, Las Condes) has the latest information on snow and slope conditions. The tourist desk at **El Colorado** (☎ 02-3211006) can arrange discount lodging at nearby hotels, but expect to pay around US$60 per person.

Only 4km from the Farellones ski resort, **La Parva** (full-day lift ticket US$22.50-28, interconnected with Valle Nevado US$33-38) has 30 runs from 2662m to 3630m. For the latest information, contact **Centro de Ski La Parva** (☎ 02-2641466; La Concepción 266, Providencia).

Another 14km beyond Farellones well-planned **Valle Nevado** (☎ 02-2060027; Gertrudis Echeñique 441, Las Condes; full-day lift ticket US$24-30) has 27 runs from 2805m to 3670m, some up to 3km in length.

In a class of its own, **Portillo** (full-day lift ticket US$34), 145km northeast of the capital on the Argentine border, has a dozen lifts and 23 runs from 2590m to 3330m, with a maximum vertical drop of 340m. Contact **Centro de Ski Portillo** (☎ 02-2630606; Renato Sánchez 4270, Las Condes) for the latest details.

SkiTotal (☎ 02-2466881; Av Apoquindo 4900, Local 42-46, Las Condes) arranges transportation (about US$10) to all of the preceding resorts, leaving at 8:45am and returning at 5:30pm. It also rents equipment (US$20–22 for the full package) for slightly cheaper than on the slopes. **KL Adventure Ski** (☎ 02-2179101; Av Las Condes 12207, Las Condes) heads to the slopes daily at 8:30am, returning at 5:30pm; it also rents ski and snowboarding equipment (US$15–20 per day) and carries out repairs. It can also arrange transport to Portillo.

WINERIES

The cheapest way to enjoy the bounty of Santiago's nearby wineries is to go to the closest store and buy a few bottles. Winery tours are still considered an elite affair and include a thorough tour of the grounds, explanations on wine production, then a couple of tastings, all at steep prices (US$20). Tours arranged directly with the winery are usually free and include a tour of the grounds and one glass of wine (not really a tasting), but you have to get yourself there. Make reservations a couple of days before. Here's a list of some accessible wineries:
Viña Concha y Toro (☎ 02-8217069; Pirque) South-east of Santiago; one of the country's largest and oldest wineries. Tours cost US$4 and include three tastings. English-language tours are at 11:30am and 3pm Mon-Fri, 10am and noon on Saturday; Spanish-language tours are at 10:30am and 3:30pm weekdays, and 11am Saturday. Reservations must be made at least four days before the date you want to go. Take metro Línea 5 to Bellavista de la Florida, then catch connecting metrobus No 74 or 80, or a taxi *colectivo* at Paradero 14.
Viña Cousiño Macul (☎ 02-3514100; Av Quilín 7100) Tours daily at 11am. Take bus No 39 or 391 from Santo Domingo out Américo Vespucio Sur to Av Quilín.
Viña Santa Carolina (☎ 02-5115778; Rodrigo de Araya 1341) In Ñuñoa, tours take place at 11am daily.
Viña Undurraga (☎ 02-3722865; ☺ 10am-1pm & 2:30-4:20pm Mon-Fri) Southwest of Santiago by 34km on the old Melipilla road; take Buses Peñaflor's 'Talagante' *micro* from Terminal San Borja, Alameda 3250.

CAJÓN DEL MAIPO

Southeast of the capital, the Cajón del Maipo (Río Maipo canyon) is a major weekend destination for *santiaguinos*, who come to camp, hike, climb, bike, raft and ski. Rafting descents run from September to April, lasting a little over an hour on mostly Class III rapids. Full-day trips cost about US$70, less if you provide your own transport and food. The Maipó is murky

CHILE

in comparison to rivers to the south. **Cascadas Expediciones** (☎ 02-8611777; www.cascada-expediciones.com; Cam Al Volcán 17710, Casilla 211, San José de Maipó) and **Altué Active Travel** (☎ 02-232-1103; www.chileoutdoors.com; Encomenderos 83, Las Condes) arrange the fun.

Near the village of San Alfonso, **Cascada de las Animas** (☎ 02-8611303; www.cascadadelasanimas .cl; campsites/cabins US$8/67) is a 3500-hectare private nature reserve and working horse ranch. Riverside campsites are flat and woodsy; the four-person cabins have kitchens and log fires. A lively restaurant serves adventurous food on a terrace with views over the valley, *and* there's a large attractive pool of natural spring water, a sauna and massage facility. You can arrange any number of hiking, riding and rafting options here, too. This is a top out-of-the-city destination. (Note that lodging and activities are discounted from May to September.)

Only 93km from Santiago, 3000-hectare **Monumento Natural El Morado** (admission US$2; ☉ closed May-Sep) rewards hikers with views of 4490m Cerro El Morado at Laguna El Morado, a two-hour hike from the humble hot springs of **Baños Morales** (US$1.75). There are free **campsites** around the lake.

Refugio Alemán Lo Valdés (☎ 02-2342430; s US$33) Run by the German Alpine Club, this is a hidden away mountain chalet. Rates include breakfast, other meals also available. Eleven kilometers from here is **Baños Colina** (☎ 02-2099114; per person incl campsite US$15), where there are terraced hot springs overlooking the valley.

Buses San José de Maipo (☎ 02-6972520) leave every 30 minutes, from 6am till 9pm, from Terminal San Borja (but stopping at Parque O'Higgins metro station) for San José de Maipo. The 7:15am bus continues to Baños Morales daily in January and February; from March to October it runs to Baños Morales on weekends only.

Turismo Arpue (☎ 02-2117165; US$5) runs buses on Saturday and Sunday beginning at 7:30am from Santiago's Plaza Italia (the Baquedano metro station) directly to Baños Morales; call to confirm departure times. From October to mid-May, **Buses Manzur** (☎ 02-7774284) runs to the baths from Plaza Italia on Wednesday, Saturday and Sunday at 7:15am. Try also **Buses Cordillera** (☎ 02-777-3881) from Terminal San Borja.

VALPARAÍSO

Valparaíso (population 270,000), 120km northwest of Santiago, has two styles of charm: the macho rough-and-tumble port that has turned gray and dirty in its forgotten state, and the more feminine rolling hills, grandiose mansions, and poetic alleys. Most major streets in the congested center, known as El Plan, are on the lower level parallel to the shoreline, which curves toward Viña del Mar. The rest is a maze of cobblestone streets and irregular intersections. The hills above and behind downtown, for the most part residential, are connected to the lower level by steep footpaths and Valparaíso's famous marvels of engineering, the hillside *ascensores* (elevators), which were built between 1883 and 1916.

The port, a strategic stopover along the Cape Horn route, attracted foreign merchants and capital and became Chile's financial powerhouse. Valparaíso's population at independence (1818) was barely 5000, but demand for Chilean wheat (brought on by the California gold rush) prompted such a boom that shortly after the mid-18th century the city's population was about 55,000. After a railway to Santiago was completed in 1880, the population exceeded 100,000. the heydays soon ended, first with the devastation of the 1906 earthquake, then with the opening of the Panama Canal in 1914, followed by a reduced demand for minerals after the Great Depression in the 1930s. Today, 'Valpo' is capital of the V Region, site of the National Congress, a university, lots of historical lore, a fabulous antique market, one of Neruda's homes and some neat museums.

Information
INTERNET ACCESS
Expect to pay about US$1.40 per hour. Many *hospedajes* (budget accommodations with shared bath) also have Internet.
World Next Door Ciber Cafe (Blanco 692) Near Plaza Sotomayor, has superfast connections and Internet-based phone calls; run by Canadians.
Valparaíso Mi Amor (☎ 032-749992; Papudo 612) Up on Cerro Concepción; open late.

LAUNDRY
Most *hospedajes* offer laundry service.
Lavanda Café (Almirante Montt 454) On Cerro Alegre.

CHILE

VALPARAÍSO

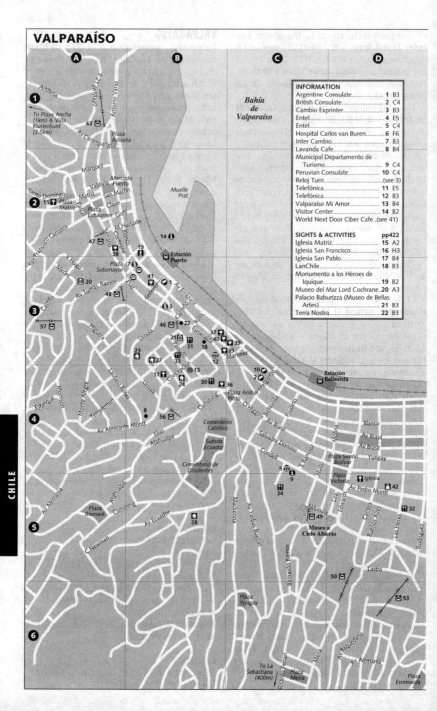

Bahía de Valparaíso

INFORMATION		
Argentine Consulate	1	B3
British Consulate	2	C4
Cambio Exprinter	3	B3
Entel	4	E5
Entel	5	C4
Hospital Carlos van Buren	6	F6
Inter Cambio	7	B3
Lavanda Cafe	8	B4
Municipal Departamento de Turismo	9	C4
Peruvian Consulate	10	C4
Reloj Turri	(see 3)	
Telefónica	11	E5
Telefónica	12	B3
Valparaíso Mi Amor	13	B4
Visitor Center	14	B2
World Next Door Ciber Cafe	(see 41)	

SIGHTS & ACTIVITIES	pp422	
Iglesia Matriz	15	A2
Iglesia San Francisco	16	H3
Iglesia San Pablo	17	B4
LanChile	18	B3
Monumento a los Héroes de Iquique	19	B2
Museo del Mar Lord Cochrane	20	A3
Palacio Baburizza (Museo de Bellas Artes)	21	B3
Terra Nostra	22	B3

Muelle Prat

Estación Puerto

Estación Bellavista

Museo a Cielo Abierto

To La Sebastiana (400m)

CHILE

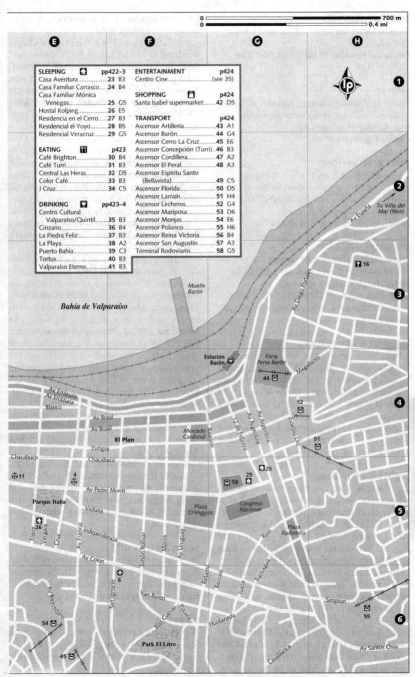

0   700 m
0   0.4 mi

SLEEPING 🏠   pp422–3
Casa Aventura.................**23** B3
Casa Familiar Carrasco.....**24** B4
Casa Familiar Mónica
  Venegas..................**25** G5
Hostal Kolping...............**26** E5
Residencia en el Cerro....**27** B3
Residencial el Yoyo.........**28** B5
Residencial Veracruz.......**29** G5

EATING 🍴   p423
Café Brighton.................**30** B4
Café Turri......................**31** B3
Central Las Heras............**32** D5
Color Café......................**33** B3
J Cruz............................**34** C5

DRINKING 🍷   pp423–4
Centro Cultural
  Valparaíso/Quintil......**35** B3
Cinzano.........................**36** B4
La Piedra Feliz................**37** B3
La Playa.........................**38** A2
Puerto Bahía..................**39** C3
Tortus...........................**40** B3
Valparaíso Eterno...........**41** B3

ENTERTAINMENT   p424
Centro Cine.................(see 35)

SHOPPING 🛍   p424
Santa Isabel supermarket.......**42** D5

TRANSPORT   p424
Ascensor Artillería.............**43** A1
Ascensor Barón................**44** G4
Ascensor Cerro La Cruz......**45** E6
Ascensor Concepción (Turri)..**46** B3
Ascensor Cordillera............**47** A2
Ascensor El Peral..............**48** A3
Ascensor Espíritu Santo
  (Bellavista).................**49** C5
Ascensor Florida...............**50** D5
Ascensor Larraín...............**51** H4
Ascensor Lecheros.............**52** G4
Ascensor Mariposa............**53** D6
Ascensor Monjas..............**54** E6
Ascensor Polanco..............**55** H6
Ascensor Reina Victoria.......**56** B4
Ascensor San Augustín........**57** A3
Terminal Rodoviario..........**58** G5

E   F   G   H

1

2

To Viña del
Mar (9km)

Av España

🏠 16

3

Av Diego Portales

Bahía de Valparaíso

Muelle
Barón

Estación
Barón 🚉

Feria
Persa Barón

Magallanes

44 🚠

52 🚠

4

Av Errázuriz
Av Errázuriz
Blanco

Av Brasil

Av Brasil

Yungay

El Plan

Mercado
Cardonal

Rawson

12 de Febrero

Av Argentina

Av Argentina

Eusebio Lillo

51 🚠

Chacabuco

Chacabuco

🛜 11

4
🛜

Av Pedro Montt

🚠 58

29 🏠

25 🏠

Plaza
O'Higgins

Congreso
Nacional

Plaza
Radomiro

5

Parque Italia

Freire
Vergara

🏠 26

Cruz

Av Francia

Independencia

Victoria

Simón Bolívar

Morris

Av Uruguay

Retamo

Barroso

Juana

Rancagua

Ross

Av Colon

San Ignacio

✚ 6

Van Buren

Blas Cuevas

Pocuro

Hontaneda

Casablanca

Simpson

55 🚠

6

Av Baquedano

54 🚠

45 🚠

Park El Litre

Av Santos Ossa

CHILE

MEDICAL SERVICES

Hospital Carlos van Buren (☎ 032-204000; Av San Ignacio 725)

Farmacia Ahumada (☎ 032-215524; Pedro Montt 1881; ☼ 24 hr)

MONEY

Both of these exchange traveler's checks and cash and are open weekdays only.

Inter Cambio (Plaza Sotomayor)

Cambio Exprinter (Prat 895)

POST & TELEPHONE

The post office is on Plaza Sotomayor.

Call centers are abundant in the center.

Telefónica (Esmeralda 1054; Pedro Montt 2023 & bus terminal)

Entel (Condell 1495; cnr Av Pedro Montt & Cruz)

TOURIST OFFICES

Municipal Departamento de Turismo (☎ 32-939108; Condell 1490; ☼ 8:30am-2pm & 3:30-5:30pm Mon-Fri) Has walking tour maps.

Bus station office (☼ 10am-2pm & 3-6pm Tue-Sun) Has lists of lodgings and can be more helpful; limited hours off-season.

Dangers & Annoyances

Valpo has a reputation for petty thievery, so take precautions. Watch for suspicious characters in the area west of Plaza Sotomayor and downtown. Avoid poorly lit areas at night, and if possible, walk with a companion. Women should not go out at night alone. Large gangs of dogs roam the streets. While you may want to show them some affection, refrain.

Sights & Activities

The **Muelle Prat**, at the foot of Plaza Sotomayor, is lively on weekends, but is rather tackily touristy. Harbor tours are offered (US$1.50). Note that photographing naval vessels while on tours or anywhere around here could land you a special tour to military custody. From here, head up through Plaza Sotomayor, where there's a subterranean mausoleum, **Monumento a los Héroes de Iquique**, paying tribute to Chile's naval martyrs of the War of the Pacific.

To the west of the plaza, on Calle Merlet (take Ascensor Cordillera), the **Museo del Mar Lord Cochrane** (1842) housed Chile's first observatory and now displays a good collection of model ships. Back on the lower level,

take Serrano to Plaza Echaurren. A block north is the **Iglesia Matriz**, a national monument dating from 1842; the original chapel was built in 1559. Back by Plaza Sotomayor, near the Tribunales (law courts), **Ascensor El Peral** goes to Cerro Alegre, where on Paseo Yugoslavo the Art Noveau **Palacio Baburizza** (1916) houses the **Museo de Bellas Artes** (☼ 9:30am-6pm Tue-Sun), worth a visit if only for the architecture and grounds. From here, continue on Paseo Yugoslavo to Urriola to access Cerro Alegre and Cerro Concepción, the most well-known and typical of the hill areas. Pasaje Galvez or Templeman lead to Paseo Gervasoni. **Iglesia San Pablo**, on Pilcomayo and Templeman, has organ concerts Sunday at 12:30pm. Take **Ascensor Concepción (Turri)** down to reach **Reloj Turri** (Esmeralda & Gómez Carreño), a landmark clock tower.

Further east, near Plaza Victoria off Aldunate, **Ascensor Espíritu Santo** accesses Cerro Bellavista, which has become an open-air museum of murals, called **Museo a Cielo Abierto**. From here, take Av Ramos and then Ferrari to get to Neruda's least-known house, **La Sebastiana** (☎ 032-256606; Ferrari 692; adult/student US$3.75/2; ☼ 10:30am-2:30pm & 3:30-6pm Tue-Sun, till 7pm Jan & Feb). In this wind-whipped locale, the poet's eclectic taste, humor and his passion for ships come to life. Another way to get here is to take the Verde Mar bus 'O' or 'D' on Serrano north of Plaza Sotomayor and disembark in the 6900 block of Av Alemania, a short walk from the house.

Chile's imposing but uninspiring **Congreso Nacional** (National Congress) is at the junction of Av Pedro Montt and Av Argentina, opposite the bus terminal. Of engineering interest is **Ascensor Polanco**, on the east side of Av Argentina, near Simpson, but the area around it is rather depressing and possibly dangerous.

Festivals & Events

Año Nuevo (New Year's) is one of Valparaíso's biggest events thanks to the massive fireworks display that brings hundreds of thousands of spectators to the city.

Sleeping

If you don't have to race out of town, look for a place up on the hills – you might pay a smidgen more, but it's a lot more charming.

Villa Kunterbunt (☎ 32-288873; villakunterbunt valpo@yahoo.de; Quebrada Verde 92, Cerro Playa Ancha; r per person US$10-15; 🖳) The very welcoming and fun German–Chilean family make you feel right at home in their colonial house, with nice rooms, good pillows, clawfoot tub (take a bath), a romantic room in the tower and backyard patio. Hearty breakfast included. It's in a safe neighborhood, accessed by *colectivo* No 150, 151 or buses Nos 1, 2, 3, 5, 17 and 111 from the bus terminal.

Casa Aventura (☎ 032-755963; casatur@ctcinternet .cl; Pasaje Galvez 11, Cerro Alegre; US$10) Comfortable, friendly and airy hostal, with great breakfast (included), kitchen use, organized hiking trips and Spanish courses. Walk up Urriola until it's intersected by Alvaro Besa to the right and tiny Pasaje Galvez is to the left.

Residencia en el Cerro (☎ 032-495298; pierreloti51 .hotmail.com; Pierre Loti 51 btwn Abtao & Pilcomayo, Cerro Concepción; r per person US$9-10; 🖳) In a gorgeous old house on a small alleyway bedecked in bougainvillea. Some rooms are airy, light; others dark. An abundant breakfast costs US$1.50. There's no kitchen access, but good common areas and an outside garden for barbecues.

Residencial el YoYo (☎ 032-591087; elyoyo355@ latinmail.com; Subida Ecuador 355; r per person US$6; 🖳) Basic backpacker place with washing machine, large shared rooms, miniscule kitchen and large-screen TV in a small common area. Easy access to bars and pubs. Rooms that aren't shared cost US$1.50 extra. Breakfast is included.

Casa Familiar Carrasco (☎ 032-210737; Abtao 668, Cerro Concepción; r per person US$12) Rooms in this kaleidoscopic mansion are clean, decent; some have views and antique furnishings. The annex, however, is unimpressive. Offers a good breakfast, cordial owners and rooftop deck.

Residencial Veracruz (☎ 032-253583; Pedro Montt 2881; s/d US$8/12) Near the bus terminal, Veracruz has nice common areas and kitchen access, but rooms get a lot of street noise. Run by a friendly family, it has laundry but no breakfast.

Casa Familiar Mónica Venegas (☎ 032-215673; Av Argentina 322-B; r per person US$8) Also near the terminal, large rooms, some with saggy beds and loud street noise, are shared in this very friendly family environment. Breakfast is US$2; some kitchen access.

Hostal Kolping (☎ 032-216306; Vergara 622; s/d US$13/20) Across from Parque Italia, Kolping is safe, secure and has kind staff; ask to use the kitchen. All rooms have private baths.

Eating
Mercado Cardonal (cnr Yungay & Rawson; ☯ daily) Valparaíso's attractive and busy produce market takes up the entire block. This is the best place to pick up fresh veg, goat cheese and olives. Upstairs **cocinerías** serve *paila marina* (fish and shellfish chowder) for US$3.50 or daily specials (US$1.75).

Mercado Puerto (Blanco & San Martín) Smaller, fishier, scruffier, but also has some good meal deals.

Santa Isabel (Av Pedro Montt btwn Las Heras & Carrera; ☯ 9am-9pm) This supermarket has a cafeteria upstairs with US$2 lunch specials and a variety of hot plates.

Central Las Heras (cnr Las Heras & Independencia; ☯ till 10pm Mon-Sat, 4pm Sun) Fast and popular with students, this is another cafeteria-style place, with more choices, including lentils, *empanadas*, pastas and salads – all dirt cheap.

J. Cruz (Jota Cruz; Condell 1466; ☯ 2:30pm-3am) Across from Hotel Prat, nautical and quirky Jota Cruz is the place to go late at night for bow-tied service and *chorrillana* (a plate of spicy pork, onions and fried eggs, buried under fries) – one serving easily feeds two.

Terra Nostra (Esmeralda 978; ☯ Mon-Fri lunch & dinner) Enjoy plush pastas (US$3.50) and espresso drinks at this attractive café (the upstairs restaurant is more posh). It's right across from Reloj Turri.

Color Café (Papudo 526; Cerro Concepción) Cute café with an artistic flare, a variety of veg specialties and sandwiches (US$2–4). Live music on weekends.

Café Turri, at the upper exit of Ascensor Concepción, and **Café Brighton** (Pasaje Atkinson 151) are out-of-budget restaurants, but fun for sipping a *pisco sour* and soaking up the spectacular sea views.

Drinking
Cinzano (Anibal Pinto 1182) Not to be missed, Cinzano dates back to 1896. Old crooners sing tango songs to crowds of people enjoying *vino con chirimoya* (white wine with apple-custard fruit) and *chorrillana*.

Valparaíso Eterno (Señoret 150, 2nd fl) Offering bohemian atmosphere in abundance, and

CHILE

usually with live music. Admire the graffiti mural created by Chilean artists covering a much older mural.

La Subida Ecuador (Av Ecuador) Pubs line both sides of this street. Check out long-standing favorites Mr Egg at No 50, or Leo Bar at No 24. Best not to go alone.

Centro Cultural Valparaíso (Esmeralda 1083) With a comfortable café on one side and a lively bar on the other.

Tortus (Blanco 1049) Come here for quieter nights and acoustic one-act shows.

La Playa (Cochrane 568) Popular with students; order cheap pitchers of beer here.

Clubbing

Dance clubs change from year to year, so ask around for the latest hot spots. They usually charge from US$5 to US$12 to get in, with one drink free.

Puerto Bahía (Errázuriz 1090) With two floors for dancing, one for hard-core *salsoteca*.

La Piedra Feliz (Errázuriz 1054) For tango with live music.

Shopping

Feria de Antiguedades y Libros La Merced (Plaza O'Higgins; ☼ Sat, Sun & holidays) This antiques and books fair is great fun. Goods aren't cheap, but the selection is outstanding.

Getting There & Away

LanChile (☎ 032-251441; Esmeralda 1048) can help with bus tickets, but most service is from Viña. The **Terminal Rodoviario** (Av Pedro Montt 2800) is across from the Congreso Nacional. Bus service from Valparaíso is almost identical to that from Viña del Mar. Many buses go to points north and south, with fares and times similar to Santiago. On weekends, get your ticket to Santiago in advance; Tur Bus has the most departures (US$4, two hours). Most buses to the north leave at night, while many to the south leave in the morning.

Fénix Pullman Norte (☎ 032-257993) runs to Mendoza (US$10–15, eight hours) as does **Tas Choapa** (☎ 032-252921 in Valparaíso, 882258 in Viña del Mar), which continues to San Juan and Córdoba. Buses stop in Viña del Mar, but bypass Santiago. Pullman Bus will store luggage from 7:30am to 10:30pm for US$0.60.

Getting Around

Micros (local buses, US$0.50) run to and from Viña and all over the city, as

do *colectivos* (US$0.60). During the day, avoid the traffic to Viña by hopping on *Merval*, a commuter train that leaves from the Estación Puerto, Plaza Sotomayor 711 (corner Errázuriz). Other stations are at Bellavista, Pudeto and Muelle Barón. Trains run till 10pm. Valpo's **ascensores** (☼ 7am-8pm or 8:30pm) cost, on average, 100 pesos each way. Ascensor Cordillera runs from 6am to 11:30pm.

ISLA NEGRA

Even more outlandish than La Chascona in Santiago, Pablo Neruda's favorite **house** (☎ 035-461284; admission with English-speaking guide US$4; ☼ 10am-8pm Tue-Sun in summer, 10am-2pm & 3-6pm Tue-Fri, 10am-8pm Sat & Sun in winter) sits atop a rocky headland that's roughly 80km south of Valparaíso. The **Museo Neruda** houses the poet's collections of ships in bottles, bowsprits, nautical instruments, as well as other memorabilia. His tomb is also located here. Isla Negra, is *not*, by the way, an island.

Reservations are imperative for the half-hour tours. From Valparaíso's Terminal Rodoviario, take Pullman Bus Lago Peñuelas (US$2, 1¼ hours). From Santiago, take a bus from Terminal Sur. Unfortunately, Neruda's house is poorly signposted from the bus stop; ask for directions.

VIÑA DEL MAR

Viña del Mar (population 299,000), or just Viña for short, is as much a bustling city as a beach resort. Its main attraction is the many gardens and parks that have earned the city the nomenclature 'Ciudad Jardín', or Garden City. After the railway linked Santiago and Valparaíso, people soon flocked to Viña and built grand houses and mansions away from the congested port. Today, you can see the contrast between the area's working class neighborhoods and the ostentatious wealth. Areas north of Viña have much better beaches (see Around Viña del Mar p427). Visitors hoping for balmy summer weather are often disappointed; Viña and the entire central coast are subject to cool fogs that don't burn off until early afternoon, and ocean temperatures are downright chilly. Summer is the pickpocket season, so keep a close eye on your belongings, especially on the beach.

VIÑA DEL MAR

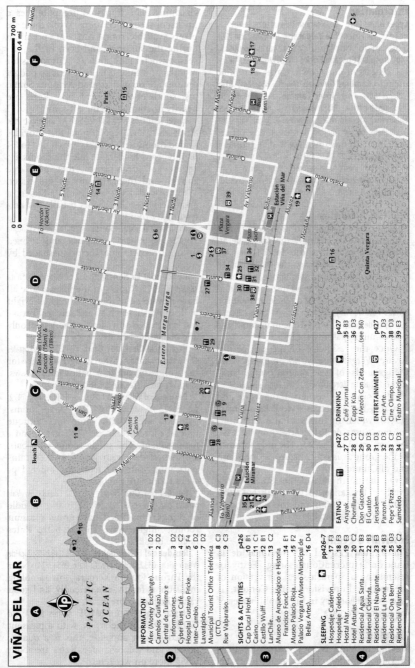

PACIFIC OCEAN

To Beaches (100m), & Concón (15km) & Quintero (38km)

To Horcón (40km)

Estero Marga Marga

To Valparaíso (8km)

Estación Miramar

Estación Viña del Mar

Plaza Vergara

Plaza Sucre

Quinta Vergara

Plaza México

Puente Casino

Park

Terminal

INFORMATION		p426
Afex (Money Exchange)...	1	D2
Cambios Guiñazú...	2	D2
Central de Turismo e		
Informaciones...	3	D2
Cyber Blues Café...	4	C2
Hospital Gustavo Fricke...	5	F4
Inter-Cambio...	6	D2
Lavarápido...	7	D2
Municipal Tourist Office Telefónica		
(CTC)...	8	C3
Rue Valparaíso...	9	C3

SIGHTS & ACTIVITIES		p426
Cap Ducal Hotel...	10	B1
Casino...	11	C1
Castillo Wulff...	12	B1
LanChile...	13	C2
Museo de Arqueológico e Historia		
Francisco Fonck...	14	E1
Museo Palacio Rioja...	15	F2
Palacio Vergara (Museo Municipal de		
Bellas Artes)...	16	D4

SLEEPING		pp426–7
Hospedaje Calderón...	17	F3
Hospedaje Toledo...	18	E3
Hostal Mar...	19	E3
Hotel Asturias...	20	C2
Residencial Agua Santa...	21	B3
Residencial Clorinda...	22	B3
Residencial El Navegante...	23	E3
Residencial La Nona...	24	B3
Residencial Ona Berri...	25	D3
Residencial Villarrica...	26	C2

EATING		p427
Anayak...	27	D2
Chorrillana...	28	C2
Don Giacomo...	29	C2
El Guatón...	30	D3
Jerusalem...	31	D3
Panzoni...	32	D3
Pepe's Pizza...	33	C3
Samoledo...	34	D3

DRINKING		p427
Café Journal...	35	B3
Cappi Kúa...	36	D3
El Mezón Con Zeta...	(see 36)	

ENTERTAINMENT		p427
Cine Arte...	37	D3
Cine Olimpo...	38	D3
Teatro Municipal...	39	E3

CHILE

Information

Cyber Blues Café (Av Valparaíso 196) offers Internet access, as does **Rue Valparaíso** (Av Valparaíso 286). You can do your laundry at **Lavarápido** (Arlegui 440). **Hospital Gustavo Fricke** (☎ 032-680041; Álvarez 1532) is east of downtown. *Casas de cambio* include **Cambios Guiñazú** (Arlegui 684/686), **Afex** (Arlegui 641) and **Inter-Cambio** (1 Norte 655-B). The **post office** (Plaza Vergara) is near Puente Libertad. **Telefónica** (Valparaíso 628; cnr Valparaíso & Villanelo; cnr Av Libertad & 1 Norte) has offices scattered around town. **Central de Turismo e Informaciones** (☎ 032-269330; north of Plaza Vergara; ☯ 9am-7pm Mon-Sat in summer, 9am-2pm & 3-7pm Mon-Fri, 10am-2pm & 4-7pm Sat in winter) provides an adequate map.

Sights & Activities

Specializing in Rapa Nui archaeology and Chilean natural history, the **Museo de Arqueológico e Historia Francisco Fonck** (4 Norte 784; admission US$1.70; ☯ 9:30am-6pm Tue-Fri, till 2pm Sat & Sun) has a *moai* statue, Mapuche silverwork, Peruvian ceramics, a good insect room and lots of stuffed birds. Two blocks east, at the **Museo Palacio Rioja** (Quillota 214; ☯ 10am-1:30pm & 3-5:30pm Tue-Sun), is a one-time mansion that's now a municipal museum.

Once the residence of the prosperous Alvarez-Vergara family, now a public park, the grounds of the magnificently landscaped **Quinta Vergara** (☯ 7am-7pm) showcases plants from many corners of the world and contains the Venetian-style **Palacio Vergara** (1908), which in turn contains the uninspiring **Museo de Bellas Artes** (admission US$1; ☯ 10am-2pm & 3-6pm Tue-Sun). The only entrance to the grounds is on Errázuriz at the south end of Quinta.

On the north side of the estuary is the overly glitzy **casino**; to the south is **Castillo Wulff**, built in 1880; and the fancy boat-shaped **Cap Ducal hotel**.

Festivals & Events

The annual Festival Internacional de la Canción (International Song Festival), resembling a Spanish-speaking version of the insipid Eurovision Song Contest, is held every February in the amphitheater of the Quinta Vergara.

Sleeping

Staying in Viña is more expensive than in Valpo, and the choices aren't nearly as charming. The tourist office publishes a full list of accommodations. While there are plenty available, rooms can be at a premium during the summer, and even in the off-season when many students rent rooms for months at a time. The best quality budget options are on and around Av Agua Santa, just south of the railway line. Rates are heavily discounted in the off-season.

Hotel Asturias (☎ 032-691565; Av Valparaíso 299; HI members US$10) A regular hotel that provides shared rooms with breakfast included to HI or ISIC card holders. While the rooms are square and drab-brown, they are large enough and there's plenty of hot water. Well located and professional, this is a great deal. Regular clients usually get better-quality rooms.

Residencial Agua Santa (☎ 032-901531; Agua Santa 36; s/d US$10/20) Peaceful and relaxed in an attractive blue Victorian shaded by trees.

Residencial La Nona (☎ 032-663825; Agua Santa 48; s/d US$12/20) Rooms in the main house all have private bath; those in the glow-bright pink annex share a bath and kitchen. Breakfast is included and there is a very matronly and charming laundry service.

Residencial Clorinda (☎ 032-623835; Diego Portales 47; s without/with bath US$10/15) A great choice for the wonderful outdoor patios, great views, laundry facilities and kitchen use.

Residencial Villarrica (☎ 032-881484; Arlegui 172; s/d US$12/20, with bath US$17/25) Clean rooms, common areas with some nice antique touches, Internet access, TV and friendly management. The single rooms with bath are awkward – with just flimsy curtains separating your bed from the toilet. Upstairs rooms are the best.

Residencial Ona Berri (☎ 032-688187; Av Valparaíso 618; s/d US$9/22) Right in the middle of things, Ona Berri has sunny, pleasant rooms; singles have shared bath. Rates include breakfast.

Residencial El Navigante (☎ 032-482648; Alcalde Prieto Nieto 0332; without/with bath US$12/14) Near the Parque Quinta Vergara, this rambling mansion, is family-run, friendly, and good value, including breakfast.

Hostal Mar (☎ 032-884775; Alvares 868-A; s/d US$17/27; Ⓟ) Off the street, with a pleasant shaded garden and dog, this is a quaint, private, and secure choice. Rates are about US$3 more on weekends.

Hospedaje Calderón (☎ 032-970456; Batuco 147; US$10) and **Hospedaje Toledo** (☎ 032-881496, Batuco 160; US$10) are both near the bus terminal and without signs. Friendly, comfortable, basic places; no breakfast, no kitchen.

Eating

The pedestrian area around Av Valparaíso is the best bet for a variety of cheap eats.

El Guatón (Av Quinta 232) For US$3 you get an immense sandwich with all the extras, and US$1 buys a platter of French fries.

Jerusalem (Quinta 259) A stand-up place with sumptuous falafel sandwiches (US$1–2) and other Middle Eastern delicacies.

Pepe's Pizza (Av Valparaíso near Ecuador) The best thin-crust pizza, order by the pie or slice (US$10 buys a large with free sodas).

Panzoni (Paseo Cousiño 12-B) Friendly service and fine Italian specialties make this a favorite, especially for lunch.

Chorrillana (Valparaíso 176) Dig into an artery-plugging platter of *chorrillana* (US$4–6.50). Choose from the usual, or pile on some more stuff to really stop the system. Platters are easily shared.

Don Giacomo (Villanelo 135, 2nd fl) Lasagna and pasta dishes for around US$2 at lunch are the order of the day.

For sandwiches, coffee and yummy desserts served in elegance you can try either **Anayak** (Quinta 134) or **Samoiedo** (Valparaíso 637). Come for *onces* or breakfast.

Drinking

Café Journal (cnr Santa Agua & Alvarez; ⏾ till 4am Fri & Sat) Buzzes with students enjoying the loud music, beers on tap and walls covered in old newspapers, magazines and posters.

Pubs along Pasaje Cousiño are worth checking out, including **Cappi Kúa** (Pasaje Cousiño 11, Local 4) and **El Mezón con Zeta** (Pasaje Cousiño 9), which has live music. For more dancing and bar-hopping, head to Valparaíso.

Entertainment

Teatro Municipal (Plaza Vergara) Stages plays and concerts.

For movies, try **Cine Arte** (Plaza Vergara 142) and **Cine Olimpo** (Quinta 294).

Getting There & Away

LanChile (☎ 600-526-2000; Ecuador 80) runs a shuttle (US$7) to Santiago's Padahuel airport from the corner of three Norte and

Libertad. Or take a bus toward Santiago and ask to be dropped off at 'Cruce al Aeropuerto' to shave about an hour from the trip. Taxis from this point charge US$4 to the airport.

The **bus terminal** (cnr Valparaíso & Quilpué), four blocks east of Plaza Vergara, is less chaotic than Valpo's and most buses from Valparaíso pick up passengers here, though a few lines start in Viña. Sol de Pacífico has the cheapest seats to destinations as far south as Concepción. Direct buses to Mendoza, Argentina, leave daily (US$10–15, eight hours).

Getting Around

Buses marked 'Puerto' or 'Aduana' go to Valparaíso from Av Arlegui and from Von Shroeders. A faster way to get to Valparaíso is on the commuter train, *Merval*, which stops at two stations: Miramar (at Alvarez and Agua Santa) and Viña del Mar (at the southeast corner of Plaza Sucre). Sol del Pacífico *micros* run along Av Libertad en route to northern beach resorts.

AROUND VIÑA DEL MAR

Beach towns immediately north of Viña have better beaches, but lack character now that they are overbuilt suburbs with apartment buildings crowding the beaches. **Concón**, 15km from Viña, is worth a trip for its informal seafood restaurants. **La Picá Horizonte** (San Pedro 120, Caleta Higuerillas) is one of the best. Also look out for Las Deliciosas, considered to make the best *empanadas* in the area.

Another 23km beyond Concón is **Quintero**, a sleepy town with beaches nestled between rocks. Lodging includes **Residencial María Alejandra** (☎ 032-930266; Cochrane 157; s US$10) and **Hotel Monaco** (☎ 032-930939; 21 de Mayo 1530; s US$6, d with bath US$30).

Further north, **Horcón** is a quaint fishing port and relaxed artists' colony with a picturesque cove and narrow footpaths snaking through the neighborhoods. Before reaching the cove, a road on the right follows a rocky, crescent moon bay. Wild camping is possible, although it gets dirty. At the far end is a nudist beach, 'Playa La Luna'. '**La Negra**' (☎ 032-796213; Calle Principal; camping US$3) has a small shaded yard for camping, plus a couple of rooms to share in her artsy, airy house for US$7. There are good camp facilities and use of kitchen. Ask the bus driver to stop at 'Agua Potable'; La Negra is next door. **Juan Esteban** (☎ 032-796056; Pasaje Miramar 2) has shared dorm rooms in his nautical motif house overlooking the tiny church and cove. Call for price. **Santa Clara** (Pasaje La Iglesia; fish dishes US$3-5) cooks up enormous and delicious fish platters with side dishes. The 2nd floor has good views.

Keep going north 35km to reach Zapallar, a more exclusive resort but with good public access to the beaches, and a gem of a place, **El Chiringuito** (Caleta de Pescadores; fish mains US$8), with superb seafood, a spectacular location by the water, a wall of windows and a floor carpeted with crushed shells.

Sol del Pacífico buses from Viña's Av Libertad or the station run frequently through all of the above towns, including Horcón (US$1.25, two hours). On weekdays there's less traffic. If heading to more northerly places, hop on buses at Zapallar or Papudo (10km north of Zapallar) to La Ligua. Buses going north pick up passengers at Dulces Teresa, just before the intersection. Pay your fare to the driver.

NORTHERN CHILE

From beach resorts to ghost towns, observatories to desert oases, Chile's 2000km northern stretch offers travelers a diversity of geography and a glimpse into its mineral-rich past. Politically, the north takes in the first four regions: I Tarapacá, II Antofagasta, III Atacama, and IV Coquimbo. The IV and III are often referred to as Norte Chico, or 'region of 10,000 mines,' a semiarid transition zone from the Valle Central to the Atacama Desert (roughly from Ovalle to Parque Nacionale Pan de Azúcar). The main attractions in this area are the beaches, La Serena, Valle Elqui and the observatories.

Continuing north, the desolate Atacama Desert, one of the world's driest, takes up the first two regions, dubbed Norte Grande. After the War of the Pacific, Chile took this mineral-rich region from Peru and Bolivia. *Nitrate oficinas* (mining towns) like Humberstone, which flourished in the early 20th century, are now ghost towns, while copper is still extracted at a number of mines, including at Chuquicamata, the world's largest open-pit copper mine. Relaxing beach

time can be had at Arica before heading into the *altiplano*. Iquique sports restored buildings and is the place to surf waves or jump off a cliff and fly. Inland, stretches of *salares* (salt pans), *altiplano* geysers and lakes, and moon-like landscapes are all accessible from San Pedro de Atacama. Indigenous roots are evident in the huge, stylized geoglyphs of humans and animals on barren hillsides throughout the region. Aymara peoples still farm the *precordillera* and pasture llamas and alpacas in the highlands.

Many buses make trips from city to city at night – a recommended time to travel as it is cooler and the view out the window doesn't change much at all. Take precautions against altitude sickness and avoid drinking tap water in the desert reaches. Coastal *camanchaca* keeps the climate cool along the beach, while *altiplano* temperatures change drastically from day to night.

OVALLE

If planning trips to Parque Nacional Fray Jorge or Valle del Encanto, Ovalle (population 97,000) is the best base. Otherwise, it's a quiet town with a decent museum and that's about it. There's a **tourist kiosk** (Alameda) at the corner of Benavente and Ariztia Oriente. Also try **Limtur** (☎ 053-630057; Vicuña Mackenna 370). **Tres Valles Turismo**

SPLURGE!

Feel like seeing the land from a saddle instead of a bus seat? Want to skinny down to your birthday suit and sit riverside with a good book? How about rambling leisurely on goat paths through cactus-dotted hills? Overlooking the lush banks of Río Hurtado, intimate **Hacienda Los Andes** (☎ 053-691822; www.haciendalosandes.com; camping/s/d US$4/32/40) provides all that. Horse riding tours start at US$60 for a five- to six-hour ride. Along the river are places to relax, including one secluded nudist nook. Campsites are nestled away next to the river. Campers can use the hacienda showers and buy meals (US$7–12) at the big house.

Take the daily bus from Ovalle to Hurtado; the hacienda is 3km before Hurtado, just before the bridge. German and English are spoken.

NORTHERN CHILE (NORTE CHICO)

0 — 100 km
0 — 60 mi

Región II

To Antofagasta

Taltal

Cifuncho

5

Cerro Galán
6600m

Parque Nacional
Pan de Azúcar

El Salvador

Salar de
Pedernales

Antofagasta
de la Sierra

Chañaral

Diego de
Almagro

Porterillos

Catamarca

Río Salado

Región III

Parque
Nacional
Nevado
Tres Cruces

Laguna
Verde

Santuario Naturaleza
Granito Orbicular

31

Camping

Paso de San
Francisco
4727m

PACIFIC

Caldera

Cerros
Tres
Cruces
6330m

Ojos
del
Salado
6893m

Palo Blanco

OCEAN

Bahía Inglesa

Río Copiapó

Laguna
Santa Rosa

COPIAPÓ

Tierra Amarilla

Laguna
del Negro
Francisco

Cerro Pissis
6779m

Belén

Mina El Tránsito

Nantoco

RN
60

Pabellón

Los Loros

Cerro Bonito
Chico 6850m

Chañarcillo

Tinogasta

RP
3

RN
40

Carrizal Bajo

Parque Nacional
Llanos de Challe

La Rioja

San Blas

Huasco

Vallenar

Vinchina

RN
40

Freirina

Alto del Carmen

ARGENTINA

Reserva Nacional
Pingüino de Humboldt

Domeyko

5

San Félix

Observatorio
Las Campanas

Chilecito

Caleta de Choros

Observatorio
La Silla

Villa Unión

LA RIOJA

Choros

Caleta Hornos

Observatorio
Cerro
Mamalluca

Chapilca

LA SERENA

Río Blanco

RN
40

RP
26

RN
74

Coquimbo

41

Paihuano

Monte Grande

Paso del
Agua Negra
4765m

San José
de Jáchal

RN
150

Observatorio
Cerro Tololo

Vicuña

Tongoy

Pisco Elqui

Cochiguaz

Pismanta

RP
28

Región IV

Ovalle

San Juan

Parque Nacional
Fray Jorge

Valle del
Encanto

RP
436

San Agustín
de Valle Fértil

Termas
de Socos

Tulahuén

RP
510

Combarbalá

RP
12

Panamericana

Illapel

Salamanca

Los Vilos

SAN JUAN

RN
141

Pichidangui

Cerro Mercedario
6770m

RN
20

Papudo

La Ligua

Zapallar

RP
39

Horcón

San Felipe

Cerro Aconcagua
6960m

Mendoza

Río Desaguadero

Quintero

VALPARAÍSO

Viña del Mar

60

Las Cuevas

RN
7

MENDOZA

San Luis

RN
20

Colina

Isla Negra

Cordillera de los Andes

SANTIAGO

RN
40

Cajón de Maipo

CHILE

72°W   70°W   68°W
26°S   28°S   30°S   32°S

(☎ 053-629650; Libertad 496) organizes tours and exchanges money. ATMs can be found along Victoria, at the plaza.

The **Museo del Limarí** (cnr Covarrubias & Antofagasta; admission US$1, Wed free; ☎ 9am-1pm & 3-7pm Tue-Fri, 10am-1pm Sat & Sun) in the restored train station, stresses the trans-Andean links between the Diaguita peoples of coastal Chile and northwestern Argentina. **Feria Modelo** (🕑 Mon, Wed & Fri) is a lively fruit and vegetable market with several restaurants. It occupies the former railway workshops: look for the large yellow building a block from the bus station.

Sleeping & Eating

Hotel Roxy (☎ 053-620080; Libertad 155; s/d US$9/14, with bath US$12/19) Serene interior patio and conscientious staff. Rooms get lots of light, are clean and attractive, but some of the beds are too soft. Breakfast is US$1 extra.

Hotel Quisco (☎ 053-620351; Maestranza 161; r US$9, s/d with bath & breakfast US$17/22) Quirky mix of furniture and helpful owners. Most rooms have windows to narrow hallways and lack light. Close to bus terminal.

Portal del Gourmet (Coquimbo 282; fixed-price lunch US$3, mains US$1.50-3) Best place to eat in town, with tasty Arabic-inspired dishes – stuffed grape leaves, summer squash or red peppers, baklava – and Chilean specialties. Also does take out.

Also try:

Casino Olmedo (Libertad 199) With homemade sherbets so refreshingly delicious (try the cinnamon) they make the trip into town worth it.

D'Oscar (Miguel Aguirre 292) For sandwiches, fresh fruit juice and cakes.

El Quijote (Arauco 295) For beers.

Getting There & Away

From the **bus terminal** (Terrapuerto; cnr Maestranza & Balmaceda) plenty of buses go to Santiago (US$9, six hours), La Serena (US$1.50, one hour) and more northerly points. A faster way to La Serena is by **Colectivos Tacso** (Ariztía Pontiente 159; US$2.50). To get to Hurtado, look for buses at the Feria Modelo.

AROUND OVALLE

The **Monumento Arqueológico Valle del Encanto**, 19km west of Ovalle, is a rocky tributary canyon of the Río Limarí, with petroglyphs, pictographs and mortars from the El Molle culture (AD 200–700); best seen at mid-

day. Camping is possible. Any westbound bus will drop you at the highway marker, where it's an easy 5km walk on a clearly marked road.

Parque Nacional Fray Jorge (admission US$3/1; 🕑 9am-4:30pm Fri-Sun Dec 15-Mar 15, Sat & Sun only rest of year), 82km west of Ovalle, is an ecological island of Valdivian cloud forest in a semiarid region. Of its original 10,000 hectares, there remain only 400 hectares of this truly unique vegetation – enough, though, to make it a Unesco World Biosphere Reserve. **El Arrayancito** (campsites US$10), 3km from the visitors center, has sheltered sites with fire pits, picnic tables, potable water and toilets. Bring your own food and warm, rain-protective clothing.

Reach the park by taking a westward lateral off the Panamericana, about 20km north of the Ovalle junction. There's no public transport, but agencies in La Serena and Ovalle offer tours. A taxi from Ovalle will cost about US$40.

LA SERENA

Peaceful most of the year, pretty La Serena (population 120,000) is a trendy beach town come summer. Founded in 1544, the city sports a good deal of interesting architecture – some of it original colonial (this is Chile's second-oldest city), but most is neocolonial. There's also an impressive array of 29 churches. Nearby **Coquimbo** is quite a bit more rough-and-tumble, but is more alive at night. The **Feria Internacional del Libro** is held in late January/early February. Mornings in La Serena can be foggy and chilly.

She Transfer (☎ 051-295058) provides door-to-door transfers to/from the airport for US$1.50. Cabs to the airport cost only US$3–4. Many lodging options are within about six blocks of the bus terminal – an easy walk.

Information

Net Café (Cordovez 285), provides snack and log-on specials and good ambiance, but Internet prices are steep. There are loads of places with Internet access for about US$1 per hour around town. **Lavaseco** (Balmaceda 851) charges US$2 a kg for laundry. **Gira Tour** (Prat 689) exchanges money. **Edificio Caracol Colonial** (Balmaceda btwn Prat & Cordovez) has many exchange houses, most of them closed during lunch.

Hospital Juan de Dios (☎ 051-225569; Balmaceda 916) has an emergency entrance at Larraín Alcalde and Anfión Muñoz. The **post office** (Matta & Prat) is opposite the Plaza de Armas. You can phone from **Entel** (Prat 57). **Sernatur** (☎ 051-225199; Matta 461; ☉ 8:45am-8pm Jan & Feb; 8:45am-6pm Mon-Fri rest of year) is helpful and attentive. **Conaf** (☎ 051-225068; Cordovez 281) has brochures on Fray Jorge and Isla Choros.

Sights & Activities

On the east side of the Plaza de Armas is the 1844 **Iglesia Catedral**, while a block west and facing a smaller plaza is the mid-18th-century **Iglesia Santo Domingo**. The colonial **Iglesia San Francisco** (Balmaceda 640) was the first stone church built in town. It was constructed in the early 1600s.

Museo Histórico Casa Gabriel González Videla (Matta 495; admission US$1) is named after La Serena's native son and Chile's president from 1946 to 1952 who took over the Communist party, then outlawed it, driving Pablo Neruda out of the senate and into exile. The exhibits omit such episodes, but do include material about regional history. **Museo Arqueológico** (Cordovez & Cienfuegos) has some Atacameño mummies, a *moai* from Rapa Nui, Diaguita artifacts and a decent map showing the distribution of Chile's indigenous population. **Mercado La Recova** is a touristy, fun market full of dried fruits, papayas in all sorts of preparations, soapstone ashtrays, rain sticks and artisan jewelry.

Kokoro No Niwa (Jardín del Corazón; admission US$1) is a well-maintained Japanese garden at the south end of Parque Pedro de Valdivia. It's is a pleasant escape, with its trickling brooks and water lilies.

Wide sandy **beaches** stretch from La Serena's nonfunctional lighthouse to Coquimbo. Safe swimming beaches generally start south of Cuatro Esquinas and include most of the beaches around Coquimbo; those between the west end of Av Aguirre and Cuatro Esquinas are generally unsafe for swimming. A bike path runs about 4km by the beach.

Over in Coquimbo, **Cruz del Tercer Milenio** (Cross of the Third Millennium; admission US$1; ☉ 10am-7pm Mon-Fri, 11am-8pm Sat & Sun) is a 96m-high concrete cross, which is illuminated at night. The site includes a museum, praying rooms and an elevator ride to the top (US$2): you won't get to heaven on this ticket, but you will get a dizzying good view of the bay.

Loads of agencies sell tours to sites around town – you can easily visit most places on your own, except for Parque Nacional Fray Jorge (US$25) and Isla Damas in the Parque Nacional Pingüino de Humboldt (US$40). Agencies also provide tours to Mamalluca in Vicuña (US$20), but taking a tour direct from Vicuña is cheaper. The minimum number of passengers typically ranges from two to six; off-season it can be hard to gather up enough to make a tour possible.

Aquayaken (☎ 051-264671; Caleta de Guayacán) In Coquimbo, fishing in traditional boats, kayak tours.

Hector Moyano (☎ 051-253206) Provides transport to Punta de Choros (US$6 per person).

Ingservtur (☎ 051-220165, Matta 611) Very established, but can be arrogant. Will let you use Internet if you sign up with them.

Talinay Adventure Expeditions (☎ 051-218658; talinay@turismoaventura.com; Prat 470) Also rents mountain bikes.

Turismo Aventura Delfines (☎ 051-244058; call for office location) More adventurous, tailored trips.

Sleeping

The neighborhood just east of the bus terminal has a concentration of budget lodging. Many cab drivers receive commission from hotels. Insist on going to the one you choose, or walk – distances are short. Unless indicated otherwise, rates do not include breakfast.

Hostal Family Home (☎ 051-212099, 224059; El Santo 1056; r per person US$7, s/d with bath US$11/17) The annex house provides a large, equipped kitchen, comfy lounge area with TV and decent rooms. There's also bike rental and laundry.

Maria's Casa (☎ 051-229282; Las Rojas 18; r per person US$6) Maria fusses over weary travelers like a loving aunt. Simple rooms with flimsy locks, attractive outdoor seating areas, coffee upon arrival. A cobbler on the premises makes Chile's cutest shoes.

Hostal El Punto (☎ 051-228474; info@punto.de; Andrés Bello 979; r per person US$8.50, d with bath & TV US$20-25; P) Gorgeous – bright colors, flower gardens, patios. The beds make spines happy and the baths are kept clean. Run by a friendly German couple who speak English and provide traveling tips. Breakfast is included. Book exchange, laundry and a bistro serving sandwiches, cakes and fruit juices.

CHILE

LA SERENA

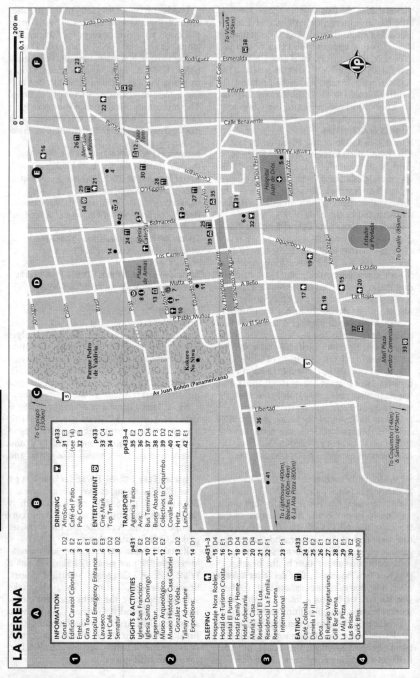

Hospedaje Nora Robles (☎ 051-216316; Amunategui 315; r per person US$8.50) Good for hermit couples – each double room has an equipped mini-kitchen, table and private bath, but little decor or character. Quiet inside, but on a busy street.

Residencial Lorena Internacional (☎ 051-223380; Cantournet 950; r per person without/with bath US$4.50/9) Large rambling place with a fun, youthful feel. Spacious rooms, large TV lounge and communal kitchen. During school, students live in the back rooms, so it can get noisy, or fun, depending on your outlook.

Residencial La Familia (☎ 051-215927; Infante 435; r per person US$8) Basic rooms, quiet with a delightful, thatch-roofed dining area.

Residencial El Loa (☎ 051-210304; O'Higgins 362; r per person US$7) In the heart of town, a basic place with high ceilings but some rooms are dark; check them first.

Hostal de Turismo Croata (☎ 051-224997; Cienfuegos 248; s/d US$13/20; P 🖳) Central, intimate and extra safe (smile at the security cameras). Laundry and bike rental available. Rooms have private baths; breakfast is US$2.

Hotel Soberanía (☎ 051 227672; Regimiento Coquimbo 1049; s/d US$15/25) Colonial-style family hotel on a quiet street; some rooms are a little cramped. Breakfast is US$2.50.

Eating

If you're coming from the north, La Serena's variety of restaurants is sure to please the palate.

AfroSon (Balmaceda 824; breakfast/lunch Mon-Fri US$1/2, dinner Thu-Sun US$4-7) Simple, healthful lunches (salad, main course, fruit salad). There's often live music with dinner.

Daniela I y II (Aguirre 456; lunch US$1.50, fish US$3.50) Local favorite for hearty portions of Chilean comfort food.

Quick Biss (Cienfuegos 545, 2nd fl; self-serve lunch US$2, dinner US$4) Cafeteria above a supermarket, with a variety of cheap, surprisingly good hot plate and salad options.

El Refugio Vegetariano (O'Higgins 685; lunch US$1.50) Strictly veg (dairy yes, eggs no), dishing up large plates of filling stews, soy burgers and fruit juices with spiritual serenity.

Café Colonial (Balmaceda 475; breakfast US$3-4, pizza US$6) Not cheap, but they've got pancakes for breakfast, great sandwiches made with fresh herb bread and strong espresso drinks.

La Mia Pizza (O'Higgins 360) Lots of different pizza toppings and pasta dishes. Try the branch at Av de Mar 2100 for better ambience.

Grill Bar Serena (Eduardo de la Barra 614; mains US$4-7) Popular place for grilled meats, cheap seafood and plentiful desserts.

For groceries, try **Deca** (next to Mercado La Recova) or **Las Brisas** (Cienfuegos 545).

Drinking

In summer, most of the fun is along the beach, but the 'in' venues change year to year, so ask around. Drink of choice in La Serena? A papaya sour or Serena libre. **Club de Jazz** (Aldunate 739, Coquimbo; cover US$5), in an old house with marble stairs, has live music on weekends starting at 11pm.

Other good year-round places include:
AfroSon (Balmaceda 824) Live music Thu-Sun evenings.
Café del Patio (Prat 470) Lively jazz and blues venue Fri and Sat night.
Pub Croata (Balmaceda 871) Serves up pitchers and rock music.

Entertainment

Top Ten (O'Higgins 327) Challenge the local pool sharks to a few rounds of billiards.

Cine Mark (Av Albert Solari 1490) In the Mall Plaza shows first-run movies. (Get discounts at Net Café.)

Getting There & Away

AIR

La Serena's **Aeropuerto La Florida** is a short distance east of downtown, on Hwy 41. **LanChile** (☎ 600-526-2000; Balmaceda 406) flies three to five times daily to Santiago (US$30 one way, 50 minutes) and once a day to Antofagasta (US$60). The office in the Mall Plaza is open longer hours and on Sunday.

BUS

The **bus terminal** (☎ 051-224573; cnr Amunátegui & Av El Santo) has a cash machine and luggage storage. To get to Vicuña (US$2.40, one hour) and towns in Valle Elqui, look for Buses Serenamar, Via Elqui, Expreso Norte or **Buses Abasto** (Peñí & Esmeralda). Buses Serenamar and Via Elqui leave almost continuously for Ovalle (US$1.50, 1¼ hours). Fares to other regional destinations range from US$3 to US$5.

Tur Bus and Pullman are the most reliable and comfortable, with *salón cama* service at night to Santiago and Calama. Typical destinations and fares (more expensive fares reflect *salón cama* service) are:

Destination	Duration in Hours	Cost
Antofagasta	13	US$16-40
Arica	23	US$24
Calama	16	US$22-35
Copiapó	5	US$6
Iquique	19	US$24-40
Santiago	7	US$11-17
Valparaíso	7	US$6-17

Covalle Bus (☎ 051-213127; Infante 538) goes to Mendoza (US$33, 12 hours) and San Juan (US$35, 14 hours) via the Libertadores pass Tuesday, Thursday, and Sunday at 11pm. **Tas Choapa** (bus terminal) also goes to Mendoza, but via Santiago, daily at 11:30pm.

COLECTIVOS
Agencia Tacso (Domeyko) and others run *colectivos* to Ovalle and Vicuña – faster than by bus (US$4–US$6). During the off-season, you may have to wait about 20 minutes for enough people to go.

Getting Around
For car rental, try **Hertz** (☎ 051-225471; Aguirre 0225) or **Avis** (☎ 051-227049; Aguirre 063). For quick beach access, take either bus Liserco or the *colectivo*, running between La Serena and Coquimbo, and get off at Peñuelas and Cuatro Esquinas, a block from the beach. *Colectivos* to Coquimbo (US$0.75) leave from Aguirre between Balmaceda and Los Carrera.

VICUÑA
Vicuña (population 24,000), 62km east of La Serena, is a quiet town at the base of the Elqui Valley. It's mainly a service town for the valley, but has an impressive assortment of museums, better access to Observatorio Mamalluca, and a relaxed pace. Around the **Plaza de Armas** (Gabriela Mistral, San Martín, Chacabuco & Prat) there are all the regular tourist services: **Oficina de Información Turística** (Torre Bauer), Banco de Estado which changes US cash or traveler's checks and has an ATM (better to change money in La Serena), post office, and the call centers Telefónica and Entel. **Mami Sabina** (cnr Mistral & Infante) has Internet (US$0.90/per hour) and bike rental.

Sights & Activities
Museo Gabriela Mistral (Av Gabriela Mistral; admission US$1), near the eastern edge of town, celebrates the life of one of Chile's most famous literary figures. A 20-minute walk outside of town is the snooty, over-marketed **Planta Pisco Capel**, where you can get a quick tour and a few skimpy samples, then get herded into the sales room. Head southeast of town and across the bridge, then turn left. It's closed from 12:30pm to 2:30pm.

Look at the stars through the 30cm telescope at **Observatorio Cerro Mamalluca**. Tours (US$5, two hours), which also include a quick video or talk about the cosmos in either Spanish or English, run every two hours from nightfall to 3am. Reservations are required (book one month ahead in summer, one week ahead in winter) and can be made by phone, email or visiting the **office** (☎ 051-411352; obser@mamalluca.org; Av Gabriela Mistral 260). Shuttles (US$2) leave from the office.

Sleeping & Eating
Hostal Rita Klamt (☎ 051-419611; Condell 443; r per person US$9) Cozy home with a bunch of guest rooms with private and shared bath, backyard pool and greenhouse. Rita is wonderfully helpful and speaks German. Includes a good breakfast.

Hostal Michel (☎ 051-411060; Gabriela Mistral 573; r per person US$8) Plain and spacious rooms with private bath, no breakfast.

Restaurant Mi Casa (☎ 051-411214; Chacabuco 199; r per person US$3.50) Cluttered, familiar and cheap! Rents to workers in the off-season; lunch US$2.50.

Residencial La Elquina (☎ 051-411317; O'Higgins 65; camping/r per person US$3.50/7, s/d with bath US$18/30; P) A backyard full of grapevines and fruit trees, small communal kitchen and plant-filled patio make this a favorite, although some rooms are cramped. Breakfast is included for lodgers.

Hostal Valle Hermoso (☎ 051-411206; Gabriela Mistral 706; s/d US$11/20) Century-old Spanish-style adobe. Rates include private bath and breakfast. Friendly and quiet.

Yo y Soledad (Mistral 448) and **Pizzería Virgos** (Prat 234) Have cheap eats.

Halley (Mistral 404) Well known for its roast goat (US$7) and plentiful salads.

Solar Villaseca (☎ 051-412189; lunch US$3.50) Six kilometers from Vicuña, Solar cooks tasty, organic food in spacey glass boxes. It's popular so reservations are a must. Take a *colectivo* from the bus station.

Getting There & Away
The **bus terminal** (Prat & O'Higgins) is a block south of the plaza. There are many buses to La Serena, Coquimbo and Pisco Elqui (US$2). Across Prat from the bus terminal is the Terminal de Taxis Colectivos; they charge US$3 to La Serena, US$1.50 to Monte Grande.

VALLE DEL ELQUI
East of La Serena, Valle del Elqui is a prominent agricultural region, especially for papaya and muscatel grapes, from which **pisco** is made. With the eclectic mix of *pisco* distilleries, some of the largest observatories in the world, seekers of geomagnetic energies and inviting villages, this valley is a fascinating place to kick back for a couple of days.

Pisco Elqui, a bucolic town nestled in the valley, is the most accessible place to experience this area. Sample locally made *pisco* at **Solar de Pisco Elqui**, which produces the Tres Erres brand, or 3km south of town at the original 'pisquería' **Los Nichos**. Next door to Hotel Elqui, Ramón offers **horse rides** for US$4.50 per hour.

About 100m past the Elqui Market on O'Higgins, **El Refugio del Angel** (☎ 051-1952248; campsites per person US$3.50) has campsites next to the river, under willow trees. Baths are clean, sites are flat and the place ordinarily serene. **Hostal Don Juan** (☎ 051-451087; Arturo Prat s/n; r per person US$7) looks like a mystery mansion. Most rooms have private bath. Breakfast is extra and you can use the kitchen for quick meals.

Hotel Elqui (☎ 051-451-083; O'Higgins s/n; r per person US$11) In a ranch-style house with grapevines and a pool, includes breakfast.

El Tesoro de Elqui (☎ 051-1982609; tesoro@pisco.de; Prat; s/n; s US$15-19, d US$37-50; P) By far the best and most romantic place, with lush gardens and flowering vines. Cabins are attractively furnished, have modern baths and skylights; breakfast is included. Menu items at the restaurant are US$4.50–6. Opposite the plaza, Los Jugos/Mandarino serves huge fresh juices (US$1.70) and crispy pizzas (US$3).

Buses Via Elqui run between Pisco Elqui and Vicuña (US$2.50) throughout the day; catch a bus across from Los Jugos at the plaza. Occasional buses continue on to the hamlets of Horcón and Alcohuaz.

COPIAPÓ
Copiapó (population 128,000) is the point of departure for treks to Argentine peaks, Parque Nacional Nevado Tres Cruces and Laguna Verde. The discovery of silver at nearby Chañarcillo in 1832 provided Copiapó with several firsts: South America's first railroad and Chile's first telegraph and telephone lines. Copiapó is 800km north of Santiago and 565km south of Antofagasta.

Information
Sernatur (☎ 052-212838; Los Carrera 691), at Plaza Prat, is helpful and well informed. Change money at **Cambios Fides** (Centro Comercial Coimbra, Atacama 541). **Conaf** (☎ 052-213404; Juan Martínez 55) has park info. **Añañucas** (Chañarcillo near Chacabuchas) has a drop-off laundry service.

Sights
The **Museo Mineralógico** (Colipí & Rodríguez; admission US$1; ⌚ 10am-1pm Mon-Sat & 3:30-7pm Mon-Fri) displays more than 2000 samples, organized according to chemical elements and structure, and a number of mineral curiosities. Notable buildings from Copiapó's mining boom include the **Iglesia Catedral** and the **Municipalidad**, on Plaza Prat. At the foot of Batallón Atacama, directly south of the station, the **Palacete Viña de Cristo** was the town's most elegant mansion.

Sleeping
Residencial Benbow (☎ 052-217634; Rodríguez 541; r per person without/with bath US$5/15) Friendly, but a bit noisy.

Residencial Chañarcillo (☎ 052-213281; Chañarcillo 741; r per person US$8, s/d with bath US$14/24) Small but clean rooms.

Residencial Rocio (☎ 052-215360; Yerba Buenas 581; s/d US$7/12) Cool with decent, but basic rooms.

Palace Hotel (☎ 052-212852; Atacama 741; s/d with bath US$21/31) More expensive with a delightful patio and helpful staff.

Eating
Empanadopolis (Colipí 320) Offers mouthwatering take-away empanadas.

El Pollo Loco (O'Higgins 461; ⌚ Mon-Sat) The spot for grilled chicken.

CHILE

Di Tito (Chacabuco 710) Serves pizzas and pastas.

El Corsario (Atacama 245) Offers varied Chilean food in a patio setting.

Chifa Hao Hwa (334 Yerba Buenas) One of northern Chile's better Chinese restaurants.

Getting There & Away

Aeropuerto Chamonate (☎ 052-214360) is 15km west of town. **LanChile** (☎ 600-526-2000; Colipí 484) flies daily to La Serena, Santiago and Antofagasta. **Transfer** (☎ 09-5540364) runs a service to the airport for US$3. *Colectivos* charge about US$8; a taxi costs US$5–8.

The **bus terminal** (☎ 052-212577; Chacabuco 112) is three blocks southwest of Plaza Prat; lodging options are nearby. **Tur Bus** (terminal, Chañarcillo 680) has a **ticket office** (Colipí 510). Fénix Pullman has a direct bus to Mendoza and Buenos Aires. Caldera-bound (US$2.50) *colectivos* leave from Buena Esperanza, half a block from the bus terminal. Across the street, Recabarren costs less, with fewer departures. Sample fares include Antofagasta (US$12, eight hours), Arica (US$21, 18 hours), Calama (US$18, 11 hours), Iquique (US$20, 14 hours), La Serena (US$5, five hours) and Santiago (US$10, 11 hours).

PARQUE NACIONAL NEVADO TRES CRUCES

International Hwy 31 curves some 140km east of Copiapó cutting through the northern sector of the 61,000-hectare **Parque Nacional Nevado Tres Cruces** (admission US$5). Sector Laguna Santa Rosa includes the Salar de Maricunga (3,700m) covering some 8000 hectares. A few kilometers past the border control another road goes 85km south to **Laguna del Negro Francisco**. Here, flamingos spend the summer and Conaf maintains a **refugio** (per person US$7.50) with a kitchen and hot water; bring bedding, potable water and food; camping is allowed. From the northern sector, Hwy 31 continues east, flanked by clusters of snow-capped volcanoes, to pass **Laguna Verde** (4325m), appearing like a surreal watercolor, before coming to the border crossing at Paso de San Francisco.

Outside the park boundaries to the south, 6893m **Ojos del Salado** is Chile's highest peak and just 69m shorter than Aconcagua. *Refugios* are at the 5100m and 5750m levels. Climbing it requires permission from Chile's **Dirección de Fronteras y Límites** (Difrol; ☎ 02-6983502; www.difrol.cl in Spanish; 5th fl, Bandera 52, Santiago), which can be requested prior to arriving in Chile.

Erik Galvez (☎ 052-319038; erikgalvez@latinmail .com) is a well-recommended, responsible mountain guide. **Puna Atacama Expediciones** (☎ 052-211273; Piloto Marcial Arredondo No 154, Copiapó) organizes tours of the area.

There is no public transportation; take a high-clearance vehicle, water and extra gas, and check with Conaf before departing.

CALDERA & BAHÍA INGLESA

The beach town of Caldera, 75km west of Copiapó, is quiet most of the year, but gets crowded in January and February. Between the plaza and the fishing pier are some distinctive 19th-century buildings. Bahía Inglesa has pretty, protected whitesand beaches.

Camping Bahía Inglesa (☎ 052-315424; Playa Las Machas; campsites US$30, cabins US$40) has good facilities but is expensive, unless you're a group of six. Cabins have kitchenettes. In low season, prices are discounted. Across from the plaza in Caldera, **Residencial Millaray** (☎ 052-315528; Cousiño 331; r per person US$7) is the best budget choice with clean, comfortable rooms and shared bath. **Hotel Montecarlo** (☎ 052-315388; Caravallo 627; s/d US$17/20) has quality rooms with private baths; breakfast is included.

In Caldera, popular **New Charles** (Ossa Cerda 350) has seafood options at palatable prices. Bahía Inglesa's upscale **El Coral** (El Morro 564) serves superb seafood, including local scallops.

Bus stations are in Caldera and served by **Pullman** (Gallo & Vallejo), **Recabarren** (Cousiño 260) and **Tur Bus** (Gallo 149). Buses and *colectivos* run between Caldera and Bahía Inglesa for US$1. Buses to Copiapó cost US$2.50 (one hour).

PARQUE NACIONAL PAN DE AZÚCAR

Just 30km north of the ugly, forgotten mining port of Chañaral, **Pan de Azúcar** (admission US$7) comprises 44,000 hectares of coastal desert and *cordillera*. From the Conaf office in the park (not the entrance), it's an 8km hike to El Mirador and a 12km hike to Quebrada Castillo. **PingüiTour** (☎ 09-7430011; per boat US$35) runs boat tours to see penguins and other bird life on an island. Off-season this area is sleepy and fog thick.

Camping (campsites without/with shade US$5/10) at Playa Piqueros, Playa Soldado and Caleta Pan de Azúcar have toilets, cold showers and tables. **Cabins** (☎ 052-213404; 6-8 persons US$60) in the park have kitchens; reserve with Conaf in Copiapó. In Chañaral, you can wild-camp on the beach across from the Esso gas station (which has showers, a restaurant and ATM). Places in town are very basic, try **Hotel La Marina** (Merino Jarpa 562; s/d US$5/9). San Pedro, below Aliccinto at La Caleta, serves humble but good fish dishes.

Turismo Chango runs shuttles to the park in the summer from opposite Pullman Bus. A taxi costs about US$20 – one-way. **Pullman Bus** (Los Baños) and **Tur Bus** (Merino Jarpa 854) go – mainly at night – to Antofagasta and Calama.

ANTOFAGASTA

Antofagasta (population 245,000) has the reputaton among many travelers of being too chaotic and more trouble than it's worth. Most travelers heading to San Pedro de Atacama continue straight on to Calama. Founded in 1870, the city earned its importance by offering the easiest route to the interior, and was soon handling the highest tonnage of any South American Pacific port. Today it exports most of the minerals found in Atacama, especially copper. Around Antofagasta, the desolate land has little to offer except small, forgotten seaside port towns and eerie deserted nitrate towns that line both sides of the Baquedano–Calama Rd and the Panamericana north of the Tocopilla–Chuquicamata Hwy, all easily appreciated from a bus window. A photogenic natural arch **La Portada** is an offshore sea stack 16km north of Antofagasta. Take bus No 15 from Sucre to the *cruce* (junction) at La Portada, then walk 3km to the arch.

Orientation

Antofagasta sits on a terrace at the foot of the coastal range, some 1350km north of Santiago and 700km south of Arica. Downtown has a basic grid. Av JM Carrera and Av Bernardo O'Higgins – with a pedestrian park in the middle – run north-south and merge to become Angamos, on which *colectivos* run to the southern beaches and campgrounds.

Information

Internet businesses south of Plaza Colón charge less than US$1 per hour. Change money at **Cambio San Marcos** (Baquedano 524) or **Cambio Ancla Inn** (Baquedano 508). **Laverap** (14 de Febrero 1802) charges about US$6 a load for a wash, dry and fold. Emergency? **Hospital Regional** (☎ 055-269009; Av Argentina 1962). The **post office** (Washington 2613) is opposite Plaza Colón. **Telefónica** (Condell 2529) has long-distance call facilities. **Sernatur** (☎ 055-451818; Maipú 240; ✆ 8:30am-5:30pm Mon-Fri) has good listings.

Sights & Activities

Evidence of the good ol' Nitrate-era days is seen in the architecture – wooden Victorian and Georgian buildings – in the **Barrio Histórico** between the plaza and old port. British influence is seen in the **Plaza Colón**, with its **Torre Reloj** replica of Big Ben. The **Museo Regional** (Balmaceda & Bolívar; admission US$1), in the former Custom House, is worth a peak. The **Puerto Antiguo** (old port) has a fish market that is especially lively on Saturday morning.

Desértica (Latorre 2732) organizes 4WD trips along the Tropic of Capricorn and through the *salares* – an exciting way to access off-track places and get to San Pedro de Atacama (US$60/100 one/two days all included).

Sleeping

Camping Las Garumas (☎ 055-247764; Anexo 42, km 6; campsites US$7) On the coast road south of Antofagasta, has four-person sites, picnic tables and shared baths. Family style.

Camping El Griego Viejo (☎ 09-8244027; km 9; campsites US$11) Up to six people per site in a more attractive, smaller area but needs better baths.

Hotel Brasil (☎ 055-267268; JS Ossa 1978; s/d US$9/13, d with bath US$20) Good value, with clean, spacious rooms.

Hotel Rawaye (☎ 055-225339; Sucre 762; s/d US$5.50/8.50) Parchment-board walls and large rooms on a busy street, but good for the price.

Hotel Frontera (☎ 055-281219; Bolívar 558; s/d US$10/14, d with bath US$20) Convenient to buses; clean, safe and collects empty perfume bottles. Breakfast costs US$1.50.

Hotel Isla Capri (☎ 055-263703; Copiapó 1208; s/d US$8/16) Has a fig tree, squeaky-clean rooms, kind staff, breakfast as early as 5am and a Brazilian restaurant.

CHILE

ANTOFAGASTA

0 — 500 m
0 — 0.3 mi

INFORMATION
Argentine Consulate................1 C5
Bolivian Consulate...................2 B2
Cambio Ancla Inn....................3 C2
Cambio San Marcos................4 C3
Hospital Regional....................5 C6
Laverap Laundry.....................6 B5
Sernatur..................................7 C2
Telefónica...............................8 C2

SIGHTS & ACTIVITIES   p437
Desértica................................9 C2
Museo Regional...................10 C1
Torre Reloj............................11 C2

SLEEPING   pp437–9
Hotel Brasil..........................12 B4
Hotel Costa Marfil................13 D3
Hotel Frontera......................14 C2
Hotel Isla Capri....................15 C5
Hotel Rawaye.......................16 D3

EATING   p439
Bavaria.................................17 C2
Bongo...................................18 C3
Don Pollo.............................19 C3
El Arriero..............................20 C2
Gelatomania........................21 C2
Pizzanté................................22 B4

TRANSPORT   p439
Avis......................................23 B2
Flota Barrios........................24 C2
Géminis................................25 D1
Hertz....................................26 B2
LanChile...............................27 C2
Pullman Bus........................28 C2
Terminal Pesquero...............29 C1
Tur Bus.................................30 C2

Hotel Costa Marfil (☎ 055-225569; Prat 950; s/d US$18/24; P) Looks a bit like a prison block of stairs and halls, with stuffy/musty tile-floored rooms, but you can order breakfast in bed. Professionally run.

Eating

Mercado Central (Ossa btwn Maipú & Uribe) Good for cheap weekday fish and seafood lunches.

Bavaria (Ossa 2424) Does fresh fruit juices (US$2–3) and decent sandwiches.

Don Pollo (Ossa 2594) Serves grilled chicken under a grass-hut patio.

Bongo (Baquedano 743) Popular for draft beer and sandwiches.

El Arriero (Condell 2644, mains US$6-10) Has large slabs of beef.

Pizzanté (Av JM Carrera 1857; U$4-7) Imaginative toppings on yummy pizzas.

Desértica (Latorre 2732; lunch US$2.50; ✆ Mon-Sat) Too exposed to the street; has veg-inspired fare, breakfast cereals and tasty sandwiches. Fun spot.

Gelatomania (Baquedano & Latorre) Satisfies ice-cream cravings.

Getting There & Away

AIR

Aeropuerto Cerro Moreno (airport) is 25km north of town. **LanChile** (☎ 600-526-2000; Washington 2552) has daily nonstop flights to Santiago and Iquique. **Sky Airline** (☎ 055-459090; General Velásquez 890) has discounted flights.

BUS

Nearly all northbound services now use coastal Ruta 1, via Tocopilla, en route to Iquique and Arica. Companies include **Flota Barrios** (Condell 2764), **Géminis** (Latorre 3055), **Pullman Bus** (Latorre 2805) and **Tur Bus** (Latorre 2751), with direct service to San Pedro de Atacama at 3pm daily.

Destination	Duration in Hours	Cost
Arica	11	US$12
Calama	3	US$4
Copiapó	7	US$12
Iquique	6	US$10
La Serena	12	US$18
San Pedro de Atacama	4	US$5
Santiago	19	US$23

Géminis goes to Salta and Jujuy, Argentina via Calama, and San Pedro on Wednesday and Sunday at 7:30am (US$36, 14 hours).

Getting Around

Aerobus (☎ 055-262727) and **Transfer** (☎ 055-244422) run shuttles to/from Aeropuerto Cerro Moreno (US$3 to US$4). From the Terminal Pesquero, local bus No 15 goes to the airport (US$0.50), but only every two hours or so. Buses arrive at their individual terminals along Latorre, in the city center.

Micro No 2 from Mercado Central goes south to the campgrounds. *Micro* No 14 goes all over downtown, accessing laundry and Hotel Brasil. Car rentals include **Avis** (☎ 055-221073; Balmaceda 2556) and **Hertz** (☎ 055-269043; Balmaceda 2492).

CALAMA

For travelers, Calama (population 137,000; altitude 2700m), 220km from Antofagasta, is a quick stopover to pick up supplies and money before heading to San Pedro de Atacama. For the copper miners, it's a service center to Chuquicamata, a distraction with *schops con piernas* (same ideas as the *cafés con piernas*, but with beer) and home in a couple of years: the entire population of nearby Chuqui is being relocated here. **Parque El Loa**, at the southern end of Av O'Higgins, has a scale model of Chiu Chiu, a typical Andean village northeast of Calama, a couple of museums and river-side swimming holes.

At the end of March, villagers from around the region come with crafts, food, music and farm animals for the colorful Feploa fair.

Information

Lavaexpress (Sotomayor 1887) offers a fast laundry service for US$2 per kilo. **Marbumor Money Exchange** (Sotomayor 1837) pays good rates and changes traveler's checks. **Hospital Carlos Cisterna** (☎ 055-342347; Av Granaderos & Cisterna) is five blocks north of the Plaza 23 de Marzo. There's a **post office** (Vicuña Mackenna 2167) and the call centers **Entel** (Sotomayor 2027) and **Telefónica** (Abaroa 1986). The municipal **tourist office** (☎ 055-345345; Latorre 1689) is very helpful and organizes tours to Chiu Chiu and the Tatio Geysers (via Atacameño towns) in summer.

Sleeping

For camping, there's **Casas del Valle** (☎ 055-340056; Francisco Bilbao 1207; US$3), or **Extracción** (☎ 055-342797; Av La Paz 1556; US$1.50), which is 500m from the train station.

CHILE

NORTHERN CHILE (NORTE GRANDE)

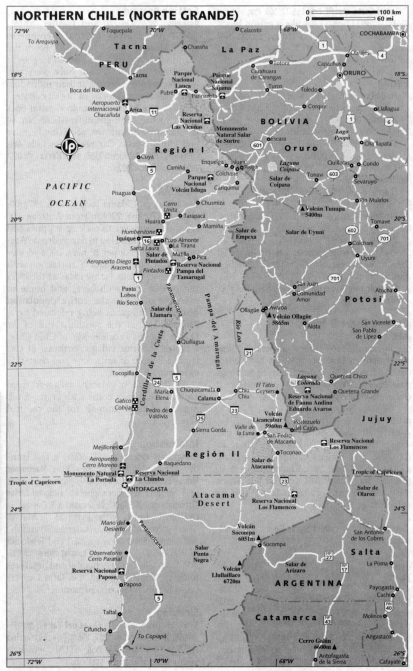

Most budget places in Calama don't provide breakfast.

Gran Chile (☎ 055-317455; Latorre 1474; s/d/tr US$11/17/25; P) Motel-like and nondescript, but quiet with private baths and hot water.

Residencial Casa de Huéspedes (☎ 055-346132; Sotomayor 2073; r per person US$5) Close to bus stops and the plaza. Basic but safe.

Residencial Toño (☎ 055-341185; Vivar 1970; s/d US$7/14, with bath US$12/21) Popular, fairly tranquil, provides lots of blankets.

Hotel El Loa (☎ 055-341963; Abaroa 1617; r US$10, d with bath US$18) Double rooms have cable TV; good water pressure. Friendly and helpful management.

Eating & Drinking

Along the north side of the large market **Feria Modelo** (Vivar & Antofagasta), *cocinerías* such as La Chilenita or Las Palmas prepare quality cheap meals (US$1.50–2) in a lively ambience. Also look for Zenteno, a juice bar with a great assortment (US$0.60–1.20), and stands selling rotisserie chicken, nuts, olives, and cheeses. Closer to the center, check out:

Bavaria (Sotomayor 2093) Open for breakfast when others aren't.

Cactus (Sotomayor & Vivar) Cocktail lounge with Tex-Mex inspired attempts at *fajitas* and stiff cocktails.

Café Viena (Abaroa 2023) Espresso and a decent selection of salads and sandwiches.

Club Croata (Plaza 23 de Marzo) For linen service and hearty good fixed-price lunches.

Pizzería D'Alfredo (Abaroa 1835) Smallish pizzas and espresso drinks.

Getting There & Away

AIR

LanChile (☎ 600-526-2000; Latorre 1499) flies four times daily to Santiago from Aeropuerto El Loa. **Sky Airline** (☎ 055-310190; Latorre 1497) has cheaper rates.

BUS

In the high season, buy tickets for long-distance trips a couple of days in advance. For frequent buses to Antofagasta or overnights to Iquique, Arica or Santiago, try **Tur Bus** (Ramírez 1852), **Pullman Santa Rosa** (Balmaceda 1902), **Pullman Bus** (Sotomayor 1808) and **Géminis** (Antofagasta 2239). Tur Bus and Pullman also have large terminals outside of town. Sample fares include the following: Antofagasta (US$5.50, three hours), Arica (US$22, nine

hours), Copiapó (US$25, 11 hours), La Serena (US$35, 16 hours) and Santiago (US$44, 20 hours).

For San Pedro de Atacama (US$2, 1½ hours) head to **Buses Frontera** (Antofagasta 2041), **Buses Atacama 2000** (Géminis terminal) or Tur Bus.

For international destinations, make reservations as far in advance as possible. Uyuni, Bolivia, is served by **Buses Manchego** (Alonso de Ercilla 2142), which depart at midnight Wednesday and Sunday (US$12, 15 hours). To get to Salta, Argentina, both **Pullman** and **Géminis** leave Wednesday and Sunday at 10am (US$32–39, 12 hours).

TRAIN

Get out your warm clothing and sleeping bag and get on board the only passenger train in the north, between Calama and Uyuni (US$10). The train leaves Wednesday at 11pm, spends time at the border (passport handy) then supposedly arrives at 5pm. Call **Estación de Ferrocarril** (train station; ☎ 055-348908; Balmaceda & Ramírez) to reserve seat. Purchase tickets on Tuesday from 3:30 to 6:30pm or the day of travel. Seats are basic and uncomfortable. The café serves sandwiches, but bring food and drink. Temperatures drop below freezing.

Getting Around

From the airport, 5km away, taxis charge US$2.50. Bus companies have large terminals just a bit outside town center. Ask to be dropped off at their office in 'el centro' to avoid the taxi ride back.

Rental car agencies include **Avis** (☎ 055-319797; León Gallo 1883) and **Hertz** (☎ 055-340018; Latorre 151). If heading to the geysers, you'll need a high clearance jeep or pickup.

CHUQUICAMATA

'Chuqui' – the copper mine just north of Calama – is enormous: 4.3km long, 3km wide and 850m deep. Some 600,000 tons of copper are extracted each year: 43% of the country's total copper output and around 17% of annual export income. Diesel trucks carry 170- to 330-ton loads on tires more than 3m high (and that cost US$12,000 each).

The US Anaconda Copper Mining Company began excavations in 1915. The mine is now operated by Corporación del Cobre de Chile (Codelco). The once orderly town that Anaconda built is soon to be a ghost town: over the next few years Chuqui's employees and families will be relocated to a new city being built for them in Calama.

Bus tours (US$1.50, 1½ hours) of the facilities run daily from December to March and weekdays from April to November. Report to the Oficina Ayuda a la Infancia, at the top of Av JM Carrera by 9am with your passport and wear long-sleeved shirts, pants and closed-toe shoes. Demand is high in January and February, so get there early; with enough demand, there are afternoon tours. *Colectivos* to Chuqui (US$1.25) leave Calama from Abaroa between Vicuña Mackenna and Sotomayor. Don't arrange the tour through agencies in Calama, which may charge more than Codelco's nominal fee.

SAN PEDRO DE ATACAMA

San Pedro de Atacama (population 2800; altitude 2440m) is *the* backpackers' gathering point of northern Chile. What was once a serene Atacameño village on the cattle drive from Argentina to the nitrate mines is now an adobelandia catering to the cattle drive of tourists in both good ways (familiar music, activities aplenty, variety of cuisine) and bad (rip-off tours, false promises of free drinks). Once you get over the steep prices and the cash cow feeling, it can be fun, and that laid-back, high-altitude feel makes it easy to relax. The town is near the north end of the Salar de Atacama, a vast saline lake, 120km southeast of Calama. Buses stop right near the plaza. Everything in town is within easy walking distance. San Pedro's water is not potable; most stores sell bottled water. The town now has electricity 24 hours a day.

Information

Log on to the Internet (US$1.40 per hour) at **Café Etnico** (Tocopilla 423) and **Apacheta Café** (Toconao & Plaza). **Laundry Alana** (Caracoles 162-B) charges about US$2.50 per kilo of washing. **Posta Médica** (☎ 055-851010; Toconao s/n), east of the plaza, is the local health clinic. There are no ATM facilities in San Pedro. Exchange houses include **Money Exchange** (Toconao 492) and Apacheta Café; rates in

town are poor. Tell your friends all about San Pedro through the **post office** (Toconao s/n) and **Telefónica** (Caracoles s/n). The **tourist office** (☎ 055-851084; Toconao & Gustavo Le Paige; ☺ 9:30am-1pm & 3-7pm Fri-Wed, till 8pm in summer) has a *libro de reclamos* (complaints book). **Conaf** (Solcor; ☺ 8:30am-7pm) is about 2km past customs and immigration on Toconao road. It has good free information about the area.

Sights

Museo Archeológico Padre Le Paige (Gustavo Le Paige; admission US$2; ☺ 9am-noon & 2-6pm Mon-Fri, from 10am Sat & Sun) has an impressive collection of artifacts, including mummies on display, that trace the Atacameño culture through the Inca invasion and Spanish conquest. There are also fragments of ancient weavings, pottery, tools, jewelry and paraphernalia for smoking hallucinogenic plants.

The modified 17th-century **Iglesia San Pedro** was built with local materials – adobe, wood from the cardón cactus and leather straps in lieu of nails. To the north of the plaza is the **Paseo Artesanal**, with alpaca sweaters, trinkets made of cardón cactus and jewelry.

Activities

Go swimming at **Oasis Alberto Terrazas** (Pozo Tres; admission US$1.50 all day) 3km east off the road to Paso Jama. Try sand-boarding on the dunes or mountain biking (US$5/9 a half/full-day): rent from **H20** (Caracoles 295A) and **Vulcano** (Caracoles 329).

Tours

Altiplano Lakes (US$26-36) Bolivian trip: go all the way to Laguna Colorado. Take passport.

Tatio Geysers (US$16-20) Wear layers, hat and warm socks. Below freezing in morning at geysers. Tours going to villages (US$33-42) can drop you in Calama.

Uyuni, Bolivia (US$70-100) Expect little, take extra food and a sense of humor.

Valle de la Luna (US$5-8) Make sure you'll be there for sunset, better yet, bike it.

Competition keeps prices low, and the quality of service suffers. The following are simply some of the more established tour agencies. When choosing an operator, ask lots of questions, talk to other travelers and trust your judgment. For more Uyuni details, see p445. Agencies come and go; try the following:

Atacama Inca Tour (☎ 055-851034; Toconao 421-A) Specializing in general tours to main destinations.

Cosmo Andino (☎ 055-851069; Caracoles s/n) Slightly more expensive, but good quality. A bit snobby.

Planeta Aventura/Vulcano (☎ 055-851373; www .vulcanochile.cl in Spanish; Caracoles 329) Plan your own adventure – they provide guides (some speak English). Volcano ascents and mountain descents. Bike, sand-board rental.

Southern Cross Adventure (☎ 055-851451; www .scadventure.com; Caracoles 119) Multilingual; good variety; mountaineering specialists.

Sleeping

Many budget places will request that solo travelers share the room, and few include

breakfast in the price. Cheapest lodging (sometimes private homes) is along Ckilapana and Lasana, about five blocks from the plaza.

Camping Oasis Alberto Terrazas (☎ 055-851042; camping per person US$3.50; ☒) This place has ample sites, lovely shaded areas, a barbecue and tables, as well as good baths and facilities. It's popular with family groups on weekends. There's even a dance hall with an onyx floor. Swimming pool use is included. A long, hot walk, it's 3km on the road to Paso Jama.

Camping Los Chañares (☎ 09-3548833; Ckilapana 624; camping per person US$2.50; ☒ Jan 1-Mar 15, Jul 15-Aug 15) Small sites with shade; showers and communal kitchen.

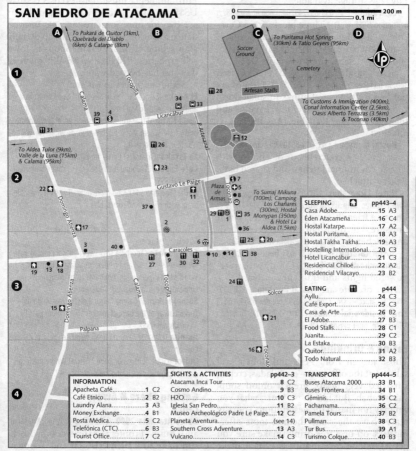

SAN PEDRO DE ATACAMA

INFORMATION	
Apacheta Café	1 C2
Café Etnico	2 B2
Laundry Alana	3 A3
Money Exchange	4 B1
Posta Médica	5 C2
Telefónica (CTC)	6 B3
Tourist Office	7 C2

SIGHTS & ACTIVITIES	pp442–3
Atacama Inca Tour	8 C2
Cosmo Andino	9 B3
H2O	10 C3
Iglesia San Pedro	11 B2
Museo Arqueológico Padre Le Paige	12 C2
Planeta Aventura	(see 14)
Southern Cross Adventure	13 A3
Vulcano	14 C3

SLEEPING	pp443–4
Casa Adobe	15 A3
Éden Atacameña	16 C4
Hostal Katarpe	17 A2
Hostal Puritama	18 A3
Hostal Takha Takha	19 A3
Hostelling International	20 C3
Hotel Licancábur	21 C3
Residencial Chiloé	22 A3
Residencial Vilacayo	23 B2

EATING	p444
Ayllu	24 C3
Café Export	25 C3
Casa de Arte	26 B2
El Adobe	27 B3
Food Stalls	28 C1
Juanita	29 C2
La Estaka	30 B3
Quitor	31 A2
Todo Natural	32 B3

TRANSPORT	pp444–5
Buses Atacama 2000	33 B1
Buses Frontera	34 B1
Géminis	35 C2
Pachamama	36 C2
Pamela Tours	37 B2
Pullman	38 C3
Tur Bus	39 A1
Turismo Colque	40 B3

CHILE

Hostal Takha Takha (☎ 055-851038; Caracoles 101-B; camping per person US$5, r US$11, d with bath US$31-47; P 💻) Attractive garden areas, superb hot showers, basic private rooms ones with original décor; mellow and secure. Breakfast included for lodgers, Internet access available and a good restaurant.

Éden Atacameña (☎ 055-851154; Toconao 592; camping per person US$3.50, r without/with bath US$7/10) Large campsites with shade and mediocre baths. Communal outdoor kitchen area and laundry basins and pleasant patios for chilling out.

Residencial Vilacayo (☎ 055-851006; Tocopilla 387; r per person US$7) Small, friendly and helpful with kitchen, gravel common area with hammocks. Rooms are a bit dark, but clean. Luggage storage available.

Casa Adobe (☎ 055-851249; Domingo Atienza 582; r per person US$5-8; P) Three blocks from Caracoles, with a long adobe corridor of rooms, shared kitchen and sufficient baths with hot showers; mellow. Breakfast costs US$2.

Hostelling International (☎ 055-851426; Caracoles 360; HI members/nonmembers US$7.50/9.50) Rates are per bed in three-level bunks in small dorm rooms. Lockers, laundry, towel rental and luggage storage available. A cute café is attached.

Hostal Monypan (☎ 055-851097; Lasana 687; r per person US$4.50) A concrete box of a house with a basic communal kitchen and shared bath. Bakery attached.

Hotel Licancábur (☎ 055-851007; Toconao s/n; r with shared bath US$7, s/d with bath US$14/31; P) Enjoys a friendly family atmosphere. Water pressure is inconsistent, but has decent beds and kitchen facilities. Breakfast is US$2.

Hostal Katarpe (☎ 055-851033; Diego Atienza s/n; d without/with bath US$20/42; P) Comfy with solar-powered lights and tranquil courtyard.

Also of note are **Hostal Puritama** (☎ 055-851049; Caracoles s/n; camping US$2.60, dm US$4, US$7) and **Residencial Chiloé** (☎ 055-851017; Domingo Atienza s/n; r per person US$8; P).

Eating & Drinking

Those just in from Peru and Bolivia will salivate at the offerings – enchiladas, crepes, stir-fried veg, pesto, French onion soup, shish kebab. But like those tours, what you get may not match the description. Touristy places have the same themes: touts offering 10% off or a free drink (make sure you get it), adobe cave motifs, fires that make

clothes smell like bonfire pits and repetitive Euro-ambience music. Dishes costs US$6 to US$8, set-price lunches US$5. Happy hours are two for one. Some restaurants turn on dance music on weekend nights; all of them stop selling alcohol at 1am. Shops in town sell groceries. **H2O** (Caracoles 295-A) is open all day and has bottled water.

Standout places to eat are:

El Adobe (Caracoles; 🕑 before 9am) Good breakfasts and consistently good meals.

Todo Natural (Caracoles) Refreshing juices, *empanadas* and whole-wheat stove-top bread made while you wait; it's slow, but worth it.

La Estaka (Caracoles) Better for drinks.

Café Export (Toconao & Caracoles) For coffee and small pizzas (US$5).

Ayllu (Toconao 544) A bit more relaxed and off the main drag, with crepes and cozy tables.

Cheaper eating in town includes the following places:

Casa de Arte (Tocopilla s/n) Sweet outdoor dining with whole-wheat bread and crepes; breakfast at 8am.

Food stalls (parking lot) *Humitas* (corn dumplings), *empanadas* etc for about US$0.60 each.

Sumaj Mikuna (Galería Cultural de Pueblos Andinos) Tucked away at the back of market about 100m past HI. *Menú del día* US$2.

Juanita (Plaza de Armas) Cheap *menú del día*; truly Chilean.

Quitor (Licancábur & Domingo Atienza) Where the locals eat. Simple and nourishing meals for about US$4.

Getting There & Away
CHILE
Buses Atacama 2000 (Licancábur & Paseo Artesanal) and Buses Frontera, a few doors down, run daily to Calama (US$2) and Toconao

(US$1). **Tur Bus** (Licancábur 11) has six daily buses to Calama.

ARGENTINE BORDER CROSSING

Géminis (Toconao s/n) and **Pullman** (Atacama Connection; Toconao & Caracoles) leave Wednesday and Sunday at 11:30am (US$33, 12 hours). Buses originate in Antofagasta, delays are possible; check latest schedule.

BOLIVIAN BORDER CROSSING

Operators herd backpackers on three-day trips to Uyuni in 4WD Jeeps. The cost of US$65–70 includes transport, lodging and meals. *Do not expect quality at these prices.* **Turismo Colque** (☎ 055-851109; Caracoles & Calama) has most departures. Staff are rude and arrogant and there are many reports of drivers falling asleep at the wheel. They have their own lodging, outside of towns. The success of the trip depends largely on travelers' attitudes and getting a good driver. Bring extra drinks, snacks and warm clothes. Other agencies to check out are **Pachamama** (☎ 055-851064; Toconao s/n) and **Pamela Tours** (☎ 09-6766841; Tocopilla 405). None get glowing reports.

AROUND SAN PEDRO DE ATACAMA

Near town, ruins of the 12th-century **Pukará de Quitor** (admission US$1.75; 3km northwest of town) fortress sit atop a hill, affording great views of the entire oasis. Another 3km on the right, **Quebrada del Diablo** (Devil's Gorge) is a mountain-biking delight, with serpentine single tracks going deep into a silent maze. About 2km further north are the Inca ruins of **Catarpe**. At **Valle de la Luna**, 15km west of town, the strikingly eroded landforms are awash with color at sunset. Wild camping in this area is strictly prohibited due to the existence of landmines. **Aldea Tulor** (admission US$2), 9km south of town, are the ruins of a pre-Columbian Atacameño village with intriguing circular dwellings. If you are biking or hiking to any of these places, make sure you take plenty of water, snacks and sunblock.

Pungent **Laguna Chaxa** (admission US$3), 67km south of town, within the **Salar de Atacama**, is home to three species of flamingo (James, Chilean and Andean), as well as plovers, coots and ducks. It is gorgeous at sunset. **Lagunas Miscanti & Miñiques** (155km south of town), at 4300m above sea level, are shimmery-blue

freshwater lakes. They are very peaceful; check with Conaf about *refugios*.

The volcanic hot springs of **Puritama** (admission US$10), 30km north of town, are in a box canyon en route to El Tatio. A restful place with good facilities, it's a 20-minute walk from the junction along an obvious gravel track. The temperature of the springs is about 33°C, and there are several falls and pools. Bring food and water. Transport is difficult and expensive – the options are a taxi or tour.

At an altitude of 4300m, **El Tatio Geysers** (95km north of town) is the world's highest geyser field, and tourists galore descend upon this dragon field every sunrise to watch the fumaroles bellow. Tours leave at the forbidding hour of 4am in order to get to geysers by 6am. Currently, no toilets or snack shops, but they're in the plans. Camping possible but nights are freezing; no-frills refugio is about 2km before the geysers; take sleeping bag.

TOCONAO

Tidy and tiny Toconao, 40km south of San Pedro, is a smart choice if you're looking for the authentic feel of the Atacama. It is known for its finely hewn volcanic stone called *laparita*. **Iglesia de San Lucas**, with a separate bell tower, dates from the mid-18th century. About 4km from town, **Quebrada de Jerez** (admission US$0.75) is an idyllic oasis bursting with fruit trees, herbs and flowering plants. Several inexpensive *residenciales* and restaurants are near the plaza, such as Valle de Toconao. Camping is possible near the Quebrada de Jerez. Ask locals for current options. See p444 for bus services; tours to the *altiplano* lakes stop here for about a half hour.

IQUIQUE

Surfers, paragliding pros, casino snobs and frenzied merchants mix together in Iquique (population 215,000). Lots of effort is being made to turn this into Chile's premier beach resort; they've already got the glitzy casino, large mall and a pleasant boardwalk along some beaches. Refurbished Georgian-style architecture from the 19th-century mining boom is well preserved, and the pedestrian street Baquedano sports charming wooden sidewalks. Iquique's main claim for now, however, is its duty-free status, with a chaotic *zona franca* (duty-free shopping center).

CHILE

IQUIQUE

0 — 500 m
0 — 0.3 mi

Puerto de Iquique

Muelle de Pasajeros

PACIFIC OCEAN

To Zona Franca (400m)

Train Station

To Hospital Regional Dr Torres (500m)

Plaza Prat

Plaza Condell

Mercado Centenario

Playa Bellavista

To Humberstone (45km), Santa Laura (44km), Pica (113km), Mamiña (125km) & Arica (315km)

To Escuela de Parapente Manutara & Residencial Manutara (100m)

La Gaviota

To Playa Cavancha (100m) Altazor Skysports (100m), Península Cavancha (120m), Mall de las Americas (2km), Playa Brava (3km), Airport (41km) & Antofagasta (490km)

CHILE

Orientation

Iquique, 1853km north of Santiago and 315km south of Arica, is squeezed between the ocean and desolation-brown coastal range rising abruptly some 600m. South of the center, Peninsula de Cavancha houses the casino, luxury hotels and an attractive rocky coastline.

Information

Internet services can be found in just about every block, and even right across from Playa Cavancha. For laundry service, try **Vaporito** (☎ 057-421652; Bolívar 505), which also has a another **branch** (Juan Martínez 832), or **Lavarápido** (Labbe 1446). **Hospital Regional Dr Torres** (☎ 057-422370; Tarapacá & Av Héroes de la Concepción) is 10 blocks east of Plaza Condell. **Afex Money Broker** (Serrano 396) changes cash and traveler's checks. Banks around Plaza Prat have ATMs; the *zona franca* has more *casas de cambio*. Send mail at the **post office** (Bolívar 458). Phones are at **Telefónica** (Ramírez 587) and **Entel** (Gorostiaga 251).

Sernatur tourist office (☎ 057-312238; Anibal Pinto 436; ☼ 9am-8pm Mon-Sat, 9am-1pm Sun Jan & Feb, 8:30am-1pm & 3-5pm Mon-Fri Mar-Dec) is mildly helpful.

Sights & Activities

At the Plaza Prat, take a look at the 1877 **Torre Reloj** (clock tower) and the 1890 neoclassical **Teatro Municipal**. At the northeastern corner, the Moorish 1904 **Casino Español** has elaborate interior tile work and *Don Quixote*-themed paintings. The 1871 **Edificio de la Aduana** (customs house; Av Centenario) now houses a small **Museo Naval** (admission free).

Baquedano, the main thoroughfare to the beach, has an impressive array of Georgian-style buildings. The **Museo Regional** (Baquedano 951; admission US$0.60; ☼ 8:30am-4pm Mon-Fri, 10:30am-1pm Sat), housed in the 1892 courthouse, features pre-Columbian artifacts, Aymara crafts and historical photos. Also on Baquedano is the grand Georgian-style **Palacio Astoreca** (O'Higgins 350; admission US$0.70; ☼ 10am-1pm & 4-7:30pm Tue-Fri, 10am-1:30pm Sat, 11am-2pm Sun) and the **Iquique English College** at the far end. **Harbor tours** (Muelle de Pasajeros; US$2.50) go to sea lion colonies and a buoy marking the place where Arturo Prat's ship *Esmeralda* sank after a confrontation with the Peruvian ironclad *Huáscar* during the War of the Pacific.

North of downtown, the **Zofri** (zona franca; ☼ 11am-9pm Mon-Sat) covers some 240 hectares of duty-free shops. Take any northbound *colectivo* from downtown.

Playa Cavancha (Av Arturo Prat & Amunátegui) is the best beach for swimming and bodysurfing. Along the rocky northern parts are good surf breaks. Further south, **Playa Brava** is too rough for swimming, but there's plenty of space to sunbathe; take a *colectivo* from downtown or walk. **Playa Huaiquique**, further south, has good surfing.

Tours

Public transportation to Humberstone, Mamiña and the geoglyphs (see p449) is limited, so tours are worth considering. Tours to Pica include the Cerro Pintados. Try **Coki Tour** (☎ 057-428984; Baquedano 982), which offers tours in Spanish or, by prior arrangement, in English, French or German, and **Mane Tour** (☎ 057-473032; Baquedano 1067). **Civet Adventure** (☎ 057-428483; civetcor@yahoo.es; Bolívar 684) organizes small, fully equipped 4WD adventure tours to *altiplano* destinations, as well as landsailing. German and English spoken.

Sleeping

Taxi drivers get commissions from some hostels and *residenciales*, so may try to convince you that your choice is unsafe or closed. Places they'll take you to are usually fine, but your money pays their commission. The cheapest beds (US$5) are around the *mercado* central, but they are no-frills, no smiles, no breakfast. Try **Hostal Sol del Norte** (☎ 057-421546; Juan Martínez 852), **Pleamar**

SPLURGE!

Go jump off a cliff...and fly! Iquique's unique geography makes it one of the best places for paragliding in South America. It'll cost you about US$40–60 for a tandem flight. For general information, log on to www.parapenteiquique.cl in Spanish. Check out French-run **Escuela de Parapente Manutara** (☎ 057-418280; manutarachile@hotmail.com; 18 de Septiembre 1512), the first to 'take the leap', and more recent **Altazor Skysports** (☎ 057-437437; altazor@entelchile.net; Av Diego Portales 920, 1502A) at Playa Cavancha. Bring along a windbreaker, sunblock...and guts.

CHILE

Hostal (☎ 057-411840; LaTorre 1036; r per person with bath US$7; **P**) or **Hostal San Francisco** (☎ 057-422186; Latorre 990; r per person with bath US$7).

Hostal Beach (☎ 057-429653; Vivar 1707; US$7; s/d with bath US$9/14) Surfer dudes' home away from home, with a communal kitchen. The kind owners will stash your board till next season.

Casa de Huespedes Profesores (☎ /fax 057-475175; Ramírez 839; r per person without/with bath US$6/8; 🖳) Full of character, from the eccentric owner to the high ceilings and peeling floral wallpaper. The beds are soft; breakfast is included. Tours are available.

Residencial Manutara (☎ 057-418280; 18 de Septiembre 1512; r per person US$8) Staging place for *parapentistas* (paragliders), with casual atmosphere; communal kitchen in a modern house.

Residencial Baquedano (☎ 057-422990; Baquedano 1315; r per person US$8) Has small and clean singles without breakfast; ask for hot water.

Hostal Cuneo (☎ 057-428654; Baquedano 1175; r with shared/private bath US$7/10) Family-run with rooms of varying quality. Rooms in back are poorly maintained; breakfast is included.

Hostal Catedral (☎ 057-426372; Obispo Labbé 253; r per person US$8.50, s/d with bath US$12/20) Well located for early or late Tur Bus connections. Stuffy, with fluorescent lights and fake and real plants; breakfast is included.

Hotel de La Plaza (☎ 057-419339; Baquedano 1025; s/d with bath US$11/17) Fancy stained-glass reception at front, a quaint café serving inexpensive lunches and spick-and-span rooms in the back. Maria, the owner, is very courteous, especially to the French. Single rooms are a bit small, but the baths are large.

TiKoo Hotel (☎ 057-475031; Ramirez 1051; s/d US$20/30) Clean but boxy rooms and attentive staff; rates include breakfast; request rates without IVA.

Eating
Mercado Centenario (Barros Arana btwn Sargento Aldea & Latorre) Lined with fruit juice and sandwich stalls along the north side. Upstairs *cocinerías* have pushy touts but cheap seafood meals.

Club Croata (Plaza Prat 310; US$3.50) Elegant and bedecked in Croatian coats of arms; has the best fixed-price lunch on the plaza.

Don Giuseppe (Rodriguez btwn Vivar & Barros Arana; lunch US$3) Close to the beach, popular for lunch.

Boulevard (Baquedano 790) Ah, *c'est bon*. A bit expensive, but they've got delicious fondues, crepes and enormous salads with zesty dressings.

Café Cappuccino (Baquedano & Gorostiaga) Elegant, with attentive service, canned music, huge cups of ice cream, scrumptious cakes and sandwiches.

La Picá Cavanchina (Filomena Valenzuela 205, Peninsula Cavancha; mains US$7) The place to go for platters of fresh fish and seafood, and *empanadas* (on weekends). Worth the walk.

Win Li (San Martín 439; combos US$2-3) and **Hong Fa** (Serrano 489) are reputable *chifas* (Chinese restaurants).

Supermercado Rossi (Tarapacá btwn Labbé & Ramírez) has decent variety and fresh produce.
Bavaria (Anibal Pinto & Wilson) has a take-out deli.

Entertainment
Taberna Barracuda (Gorostiaga 601) The two-for-one happy hour (8–10pm) makes outlandishly expensive drinks (US$5) more reasonable in this popular English pub meets US sports bar.

Mall de las Americas (Héroes de la Concepción) Has a multiplex cinema.

Getting There & Away
AIR
LanChile (☎ 600-526-2000; Tarapacá 465) flies about four times daily to Arica (US$36, 40 minutes), six times to Santiago (US$130, 2½ hours), twice to Antofagasta (US$45, 45 minutes) and to La Paz, Bolivia, daily except Tuesday and Saturday (US$130, two hours).
Sky Airline (☎ 057-415013; Ramírez 411) has cheaper flights with comparable service.

LAB (Lloyd Aéreo Bolivano; ☎ 057-426750; Serrano 442) flies four times a week to Santa Cruz, Bolivia (US$290). The first leg is operated by LanChile. **TAM** (☎ 057-390600; Serrano 430) can help with any flights from Santiago to Asunción, Paraguay, and within Paraguay.

BUS & COLECTIVO
Most buses leave from the **terminal** (☎ 057-416315; Patricio Lynch); some companies have ticket offices along west and north sides of the Mercado Centenario. **Tur Bus** (Esmeralda & Ramírez) has a cash machine. Sample fares include:

Destination	Duration in Hours	Cost
Antofagasta	8	US$10
Arica	5	US$5
Calama	7	US$9
Copiapó	14	US$19
La Serena	18	US$24
Santiago	26	US$25-40

Faster *colectivos* to Arica (US$12, 3½ hours) include **Taxis Tamarugal** (☎ 057-470035; Barros Arana 897-B) and **Taxitur** (☎ 057-414875; Sargento Aldea 791). To get to Pica, **Pullman Santa Angela** (☎ 057-423751; Barros Arana 971) leaves every couple of hours starting at 8am (US$2, two hours). Otherwise, Tamarugal (see above) runs tours leaving at 8am, returning at 6pm (US$9). For Mamiña, Taxitur leaves at 8am, and leaves Mamiña at 4pm (US$9 round trip).

To get to La Paz, Bolivia (US$36, 24 hours), try **Chile Bus** (☎ 057-474363; Esmeralda 978) or head to Arica for better prices. To Jujuy and Salta, Argentina, Pullman leaves from the bus terminal Tuesday at 11pm (US$65).

Getting Around

Aerotransfer (☎ 057-310800) has a door-to-door shuttle service from the airport, 41km south of town.

For car rental, try **Nippan Rent-a-Car** (☎ 057-470998; O'Higgins 410). An international driver's license may be required. By the time this book is out, a tram service is due to be running along Baquedano from the beach and up to the Zofri.

AROUND IQUIQUE

Agencies in Iquique offer tours to the following sites, but they don't combine Pica and Mamiña in the same tour.

The influence and wealth of the nitrate boom whisper through the eerie ghost town of **Humberstone** (admission US$1.50), 45km northeast of Iquique. Built in 1872, this town was hopping in the 1940s: Santiago-based performers came to the theater, workers relaxed at the enormous cast-iron pool after a few games of tennis, families had all amenities: schools, hospitals, stores. By 1960, the town closed, due to the collapse of the nitrate industry. Some buildings are restored, but others are unstable; take care when walking through places. At the western end are the power plant and old railway

to the older **Oficina Santa Laura**, just a half-hour walk southwest. Eastbound buses can drop you off, and it's usually easy to catch a return bus if you're willing to wait. Take food, water and a camera.

The pre-Columbian geoglyphic **El Gigante de Atacama** (Giant of the Atacama), 14km east of Huara on the slopes of Cerro Unita, is, at 86m, the largest archaeological representation of a human figure in the world, with a rectangular head with a dozen rays, enormous feet and odd protrusions from the knees and thighs. The best way to see it is to stand several hundred meters back from the base of the hill. Don't climb the hill; this damages the site. The best way to visit this impressive site is to hire a car or taxi, or go on a tour.

Lining the Panamericana south of Pozo Almonte are groves of tamarugo (*Prosopis tamarugo*), which once covered thousands of square kilometers until woodcutting for the mines nearly destroyed it. They are protected within the **Reserva Nacional Pampa del Tamarugal**, where you can also find over 300 restored geoglyphs of humans, llamas and geometric shapes blanketing the hillside at **Cerro Pintados** (admission US$1.50), nearly opposite the turnoff to Pica. Pass by the derelict railroad yard, a dry and dusty but easy walk from the highway, about 1½ hours each way. A Conaf-operated **campground** (camping/guesthouse bed US$7/10) has flat, shaded sites with tables and limited space in guesthouses. It's 24km south of Pozo Almonte.

Pica, an attractive oasis 113km southeast of Iquique is well known for its limes, a key ingredient in any decent *pisco sour*. It's a good day trip to cool down at the attractive freshwater pool, **Cocha Resbaladero** (General Ibáñez; admission US$2), and slurp on fresh fruit drinks. Exposed **Camping Miraflores** (☎ 057-741338; Miraflores s/n; camping per person US$2) gets crowded, especially on weekends. Simple but clean **Hotel Palermo** (☎ 057-741129; Arturo Prat & Balmaceda; r per person US$7) has large, airy three-bed rooms with private bath, and has a restaurant. Friendly **Hotel San Andrés** (☎ 057-741319; Balmaceda 197; r US$8) has spacious rooms, including bath and breakfast, as well as a good quality restaurant with cheap, filling lunches. The rickety, historic 1906 **El Tambo** (☎ 057-741041; General Ibáñez 68; r per person US$5, 4-person cabin US$27) has simple but airy rooms with loads of character.

Mamiña, 125km east of Iquique (not on the same road to Pica), is a quizzical terraced town with thermal baths, a 1632 church and a pre-Columbian fortress, **Pukará del Cerro Inca**. At **Barros Chino**, 1km from the entrance, sit in a flimsy lawn chair and get plastered with restorative mud for US$1.50. Or for soaks in individual concrete tubs head to **Baños Ipla** or **Baños Rosario**, below Refugio del Salitre. **Cerro Morado** (campsite US$9) serves up fixed-price lunches and offers camping in the backyard. **Residencial Inti Raimi** (Ipla s/n; r US$5) has spartan rooms. **Residencial Cholele** (r per person US$11) has a few comfortable rooms, the tariff includes breakfast. All places offer full board. See Iquique (p448) for transport details.

ARICA

Hailed as a beach 'resort,' Arica (population 191,000) has long stretches of beach and a few neat historic buildings scattered among an otherwise unattractive city center. Lording over the city is the dramatic headland, El Morro de Arica, a major battle site during the War of the Pacific. You'll find loads of craft stands where Aymara people sell their goods. Near the port, beware the *yeco* birds that nest in the palm trees and whose droppings turn trees into ghostly silhouettes and splatter on tourists' heads.

Orientation

Chacalluta airport is 18km north. **Radio Taxi Chacalluta** (☎ 058-254812; Patricio Lynch 371) has taxis (US$10) and *colectivos* (US$4 per person). *Colectivos* run daily to/from Tacna, Peru, 20km north.

Most traveler services are in the commercially chaotic center between the coast and Av Vicuña Mackenna. Part of 21 de Mayo is a pedestrian mall. The best beaches are south of the *morro* (headland) and north of Parque Brasil. The bus terminals are on Diego Portales, just after Av Santa María. Take *Colectivo* No 8 (US$0.40) along Diego Portales to get to the city center. It's about a 3km walk.

Information

INTERNET ACCESS

Interface (Thompson & Paseo Bolognesi) There's Internet access (US$0.60 per hour) in lots of places, but here it's quiet as well.

LAUNDRY

La Moderna (18 de Septiembre 457) Has drop-off laundry service for US$3/kilo.

MEDICAL SERVICES

Hospital Dr Juan Noé (☎ 058-229200; 18 de Septiembre 1000)

MONEY

There are plenty of ATMs along 21 de Mayo. **Cambio Yanulaque** (21 de Mayo 175) and **Turismo Sol y Mar** (Colón 610) change US, Peruvian, Bolivian and Argentine currency. Also try **freelance changers** (cnr 21 de Mayo & Colón).

POST & TELEPHONE

Entel (21 de Mayo 372)
Post office (Prat 305)
Telefónica (Colón 476)

TOURIST CARD EXTENSIONS

Departamento de Extranjería (☎ 058-250377; Angamos 990) Replaces lost tourist cards and extends visas.

TOURIST OFFICES

Automóvil Club de Chile (☎ 058-252678; Chacabuco 460) Sells maps and offers road information.
Conaf (☎ 058-250207; Vicuña Mackenna 820; ☺ 8:30am-5:30pm Mon-Fri) Take bus No 12 from downtown.
Sernatur (☎ 058-252054; San Marcos 101; ☺ 8:30am-7pm Mon-Sat & 10am-2pm Sun Dec-Feb; 8:30am-5:20pm Mon-Fri Mar-Nov) Useful city map, plus brochures.

Dangers & Annoyances

Arica has a reputation for petty thievery. Be especially cautious at bus terminals and beaches (take just the essentials).

Remember to change your watches: from October 15 to March 15, Chile is two hours ahead of Peru, and April to September one hour ahead.

Sights & Activities

For good views, take the footpath from the south end of Calle Colón to **El Morro de Arica**, with a museum commemorating the June 7, 1880, battle between Peru and Chile. At the base of El Morro, one of downtown's most imposing buildings is the blue-and-white **Casa Bolognesi** (cnr Colón & Yungay). Alexandre Gustave Eiffel (yes, the Eiffel Tower guy) designed the 1875 **Iglesia San Marcos** on Plaza Colón and the **Aduana de Arica**, the former customs house at Parque General Baquedano (before landfill, it

ARICA

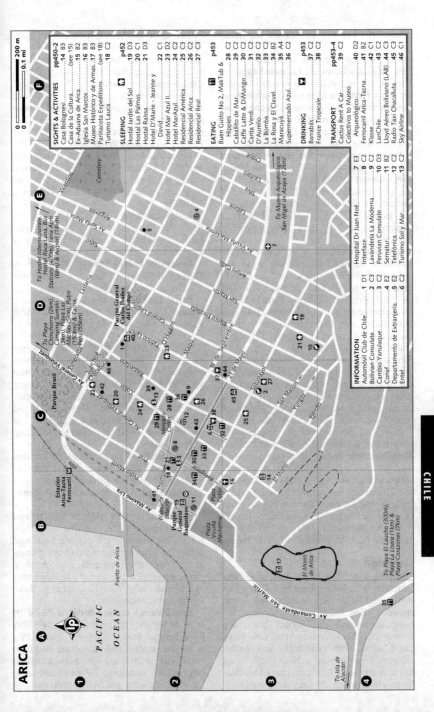

0   200 m
0   0.1 mi

SIGHTS & ACTIVITIES	pp450-2
Casa Bolognesi	14 B3
Casa de la Cultura	(see 15)
Ex-Aduana de Arica	15 B2
Iglesia San Marcos	16 B3
Museo Histórico y de Armas	17 B3
Parinacota Expeditions	(see 18)
Turismo Lauca	18 C2

SLEEPING	p452
Hostal Jardín del Sol	19 D3
Hostal Las Palmas	20 C1
Hostal Raissa	21 D3
Hotel D'Marie – Jeanne y	
David	22 C1
Hotel Mar Azul II	23 D2
Hotel MarAzul	24 C1
Residencial América	25 C3
Residencial Arica	26 C3
Residencial Real	27 C3

EATING	p453
Buen Gusto No 2, MakTub &	
Hippies	28 C2
Caballito de Mar	29 C2
Caffe Latte & DiMango	30 C2
Canta Verdi	31 C2
D'Aurelio	32 C2
La Bomba	33 C2
La Rosa y El Clavel	34 B2
Maracuyá	35 A4
Supermercado Azul	36 C2

DRINKING	p453
Barrabás	37 C2
France Tropicale	38 C2

TRANSPORT	pp453-4
Cactus Rent A Car	39 C2
Colectivos to Museo	
Arqueológico	40 D2
Ferrocarril Arica-Tacna	41 B2
Klasse	42 C1
LanChile	43 C3
Lloyd Aéreo Boliviano (LAB)	44 C3
Radio Taxi Chacalluta	45 C3
Sky Airline	46 C1

INFORMATION	
Automóvil Club de Chile	1 D1
Bolivian Consulate	2 C3
Cambio Yanulaque	3 C2
Conaf	4 E2
Departamento de Extranjería	5 E2
Entel	6 C2
Hospital Dr Juan Noé	7 E3
Interface	8 C2
Lavandería La Moderna	9 C2
Peruvian Consulate	10 D3
Sernatur	11 B2
Telefónica	12 C2
Turismo Sol y Mar	13 C2

CHILE

452 NORTHERN CHILE •• Arica

fronted the harbor). Except for the door, the church is made entirely of cast iron. Both buildings were prefabricated in Eiffel's Parisian studios. At **Plazoleta Estación** is a small, free museum with railroad-related antiques. **Feria Agro**, 6km from downtown at the junction with Panamericana Sur, is an attractive produce market with lots of variety and friendly vendors. Take any *micro* or *colectivo* with 'Agro' on destination board.

Museo Arqueológico San Miguel de Azapa (12km east of Arica; admission US$1.50; ☺ 9am-8pm Jan & Feb, 10am-6pm Mar-Dec) has superb displays of the archaeological and cultural heritage of the area. Well-written booklets in English are available. Taxi *colectivos* (US$1) at Chacabuco and Patricio Lynch provide transport.

South of town, along Av Comandante San Martín, beaches that are good for swimming and lounging around are **Playa El Laucho**, just past the Club de Yates, followed by much prettier, sheltered **Playa La Lisera**, with change rooms and showers. Take bus No 8 either from 18 de Septiembre or from the northeast corner of General Velásquez and Chacabuco. About 7km south, past a fishmeal processing plant, is **Playa Corazones**, with wild camping and a kiosk. Just past the beach, a neat trail accesses impressive caves, cormorant colonies, crashing waves, tunnels and a sea lion colony. No buses serve Corazones: hire a cab or bike it.

North of downtown, the beaches are longer and a bit more rough, but cleaner. **Playa Chinchorro**, 2km north, is playland, with loads of overpriced restaurants, ice cream shops and jet ski rental. **Playa Las Machas**, a few kilometers further north, is a popular surfing destination. Take bus No 12 from General Velásquez and Chacabuco. Expert surfers hit the breaks El Gringo and El Buey at Isla de Alacrán, south of Club de Yates.

Sleeping

Camping is possible at the dark-sand **Playa Corazones** (Av San Martín; camping free), 7km south at the end of Av San Martín, with dirty, crowded sites; bring water. You can also camp at the established **Sumaki** (Arica; camping per person US$3), 5km north of Arica, near Playa Las Machas, with volleyball court, baths, showers. Sernatur runs a cheap youth hostel from December to February; check the office for location, which changes every season.

Taxi drivers earn commission from some *residenciales* and hotels; be firm in your decision. Besides those listed, cheap places spring up along Prat and Velásquez. Better-quality ones come and go on Sotomayor.

For convenience to the bus terminal, consider the safe and clean **Hostal Internacional** (☎ 058-222119; Diego Portales 905; s US$4.50-7, tr US$13) or **Hostal Roca Luna** (☎ 058-264624; Diego Portales 861; r per person US$4.50).

Residencial Real (☎ 058-253359; Sotomayor 578; s/d US$5.50/10) Quiet, clean and friendly. Rooms on the top floor are the best bet. There's no breakfast available but use of the kitchen is US$0.75.

Residencial Arica (☎ 058-255399; 18 de Septiembre 466; r per person US$5.50) Central, with huge shared baths. There's no breakfast or kitchen use.

Residencial América (☎ 058-254148; Sotomayor 430; s/d US$7/10) Rooms are clean with cable TV and private bath, but soft beds.

Hostal Las Palmas (☎ 058-255753; Av General Velásquez 730; r per person without/with bath US$7/9) Plenty of rooms and an airy upstairs dining room.

Hotel MarAzul (☎ 058-256272; Colón 665; r per person US$10; 🖳) Professional hotel atmosphere with cable TV, banana trees, pet birds and an overly chlorinated pool. Single rooms are closet-tiny and baths suffer from mildew. **Hotel Mar Azul II** (☎ 058-233653; Patricio Lynch 681; r per person US$9) isn't as soundproof, but smells better. Good breakfasts are included at both places.

Hostal Jardín del Sol (☎ 058-232795; Sotomayor 848; r per person US$10) Peaceful and popular with lovely interior gardens, private bath and breakfast. Upstairs rooms are better quality.

Hostal Raissa (☎ 058-251700; San Martín 281; r per person with breakfast US$10) Raissa has a kitchen for guests, rooms with private bath and cable TV. Interior courtyards have mango and papaya trees, an aviary of chirping parakeets and a pet parrot. Independent apartments may also be available. Bike rental and laundry.

Hotel D'Marie – Jeanne y David (☎ 058-258231; Av General Velásquez 792; r per person US$12; 🅿) Run by a helpful French/Chilean couple, this is an immaculate and safe white-and-blue oasis with frangipani and hibiscus trees, large rooms with fans, TV and maid service, great showers and basic breakfasts.

Eating & Drinking

Tap water here has a high percentage of chemicals. Buy bottled and benefit from the many fresh fruit juice stands.

Supermercado Azul (18 de Septiembre & Baquedano) Large supermarket.

Have a juice and a condiment-heavy hot dog (US$0.75–1.25) at such stands as **Buen Gusto No 2** (Baquedano 559) and, next-door, Mak-Tub and Hippies.

For cheap fixed-price lunches (three courses for US$2–4), your best bets are **La Bomba** (Colón 357), which is part of the fire station, and **La Rosa y El Clavel** (Sangra 380), which is decked out in Coca-Cola propaganda. Both are popular with the locals and provide quick attentive service and hearty portions.

D'Aurelio (Baquedano 369; pasta US$3.50-6) A linen-service Italian restaurant with excellent four-course lunch deals for only US$4.50, including a beverage.

Mercado Colón (Colón & Maipú) Has stands with even cheaper lunches (US$1.50), usually *cazuela* (a soupy stew of broth, rice, a half ear of corn and some meat).

Caballito del Mar (Colón & Maipú; dishes US$3–5) Inside the Mercado Colón and specializing in fish dishes.

CaffeLatte (21 de Mayo 248; US$1.50-5) Has tacky bright decor, but good huge sandwiches, fruit juices and cakes.

DiMango (21 de Mayo) Next door to Caffe-Latte. Serves huge scoops of Arica's best ice cream. (There's another DiMango at the north end of Playa Chinchorro.)

SPLURGE!

You've been traveling hard, sweating it at border crossings, roughing it in the desert, and eating way too many white bread rolls and *pollo con arroz* (chicken and rice). Now's your chance to slink into elegance, watch the sun set over crashing waves and renew the gourmet in you. Let bow-tied waiters serve you a knockout *pisco sour* followed by exquisitely prepared seafood specialties at **Maracuyá** (☎ 057-227600; Av San Martín 0321; mains US$10-15), perched on the rocky shoreline of Playa El Laucho. Even the smoked salmon salad (US$5), with hearts of palm and avocado, is enough to restore a weary spirit.

Canta Verdi (Bolgnesi 453) One of the best meeting points for dinners of pizzas, sandwiches, pitchers of beer and cocktails. Great music and fun ambience on an attractive pedestrian alley.

Popular with travelers are **France Tropicale** (21 de Mayo 384) with good music, plenty of drinks and pizzas, and **Barrabás** (18 de Septiembre 520) for strong drinks and a slightly younger crowd.

In summer, discos along Playa Chinchorro charge about US$5 cover.

Getting There & Away

AIR

LanChile (☎ 600-526-2000; 21 de Mayo 345) has several daily flights to Santiago and one daily to La Paz, Bolivia. **Sky Airline** (☎ 058-231951; Chacabuco 314, local 82a) has domestic flights. **LAB** (☎ 058-251919; 21 de Mayo 423) flies to La Paz, Bolivia (US$100), Santa Cruz (US$155) and Cochabamba (US$130).

BUS & COLECTIVO

At **Terminal Rodoviario** (☎ 058-248709; Diego Portales & Santa María) many bus companies serve several destinations, including several daily departures to Iquique (US$6, four hours; faster *colectivos* charge US$12); Antofagasta (US$13, 12 hours) and Santiago (US$38, 26 hours). For Calama (US$12, 10 hours), Geminis has direct buses with connections to San Pedro de Atacama at 10pm. On all southbound buses you will go through a regional border inspection. Fruits and vegetables are not permitted. Keep your passport handy and take any unused film out of your backpack, as luggage goes through X-ray screening. (Your luggage may be screened at the bus terminal before departure.)

For La Paz, Bolivia (US$10–17, eight hours), Cuevas y González and Chilebus depart daily in the morning. There are more services to La Paz from the shabbier Terminal Internacional, just to the east, with Buses Humire, from Tuesday to Friday at 11:30am. Hop on these buses at Lago Chungara; enquire about arrival times there. Also from this terminal are Tacna *colectivos* (US$3). Call **Chile Lintur** (☎ 058-225028) for a hotel pickup (US$0.50). Peruvian *colectivos* leave from outside the terminal, Chilean ones from inside. Peruvian ones reportedly take longer at the border (more exhaustive car searches).

CHILE

Give the driver your passport – he'll deal with the border formalities. Don't take any fruits or veg.

For Putre, **La Paloma** (☎ 058-222710) has a direct bus at 6:30am (US$3, 1½ hours), leaving from Germán Riesco 2071. Or take the stop-and-go Tuesday and Friday 11am bus from the terminal, which drops you off at the Putre road junction, 5km above town (3½ hours). The bus continues to Parinacota (US$4). To get to the bus terminals, hop on *colectivo* No 8 from Maipú downtown.

CAR

If driving to Peru, check with the consulate about the latest required forms. You'll need multiple copies of the Relaciones de Pasajeros form, found in most stationery stores, allowing 60 days in Peru; no charge. The border at Chacalluta is open 8am to midnight (Chilean time) and 24 hours from Friday to Sunday. To Bolivia, take extra gas, water and antifreeze.

TRAIN

Trains to Tacna (US$1, 1½ hours) depart from the **Ferrocarril Arica-Tacna** (☎ 058-231115; Máximo Lira 889) Monday, Wednesday, Friday and Saturday around 3pm.

Getting Around

For car rental, **Cactus** (☎ 058-257430; Baquedano 635, Local 36) and **Klasse** (☎ 058-254498; General Velásquez 762, local 25) charge US$50 per day for 4WD with unlimited mileage. Cactus also rents mountain bikes for US$4/12 per hour/day.

RUTA 11 & PUTRE

On Ruta 11 heading to Putre, you'll pass hillside geoglyphs, **Poconchile**, with one of the country's oldest churches, candelabra cacti that grow a mere 5–7mm annually, and the ruins of a 12th-century fortress, **Pukará de Copaquilla**.

Putre, 150km northeast of Arica, is a small (population 2200; altitude 3500m) Aymara village surrounded by ancient stone-faced terraces on which local farmers grow alfalfa and oregano. Most visitors just stop here for a night to acclimatize before continuing to Parque Nacional Lauca; it's not overrun by tourists and has great hiking and tranquil village ambiance. Originally a 16th-century *reducción* (a Spanish settle-

ment established to try to control the Indians), many buildings retain colonial features, most notably the restored adobe **Iglesia de Putre** (1670). The town hosts a colorful Carnaval in February.

There's a post office and an Entel office in town. Baquedano is the main strip, on which the following places can be found, unless otherwise indicated.

Altiplanet Turismo (altiplanet@hotmail.com) leads typical tours and more adventurous hiking or biking; has laundry service and mellow owners. **Birding Alto Andino** (☎ 058-300013; www.birdingaltoandino.com) leads tailored nature tours; personalized nature tours and five-day theme excursions; make reservations early. Freddy Torrejón and Valentina Alave are recommended guides to the area.

Residencial La Paloma (dm with shared bath US$4.50, d with private bath US$19, lunch US$2.50; **P**) has hot showers and OK beds but thin walls – it can get noisy and chilly at night. The restaurant caters to tour groups, but is quite good. **Hostal Cali** (☎ 058-261066; r without/with bath US$10/19) is smaller, with thicker walls, limited kitchen use, a store attached and laundry service. **Pachamama** (☎ 058-251354; s/d US$12/20), a block south of Baquedano, is a sun-yellow adobe hostel appealing to foreigners; good amenities and local info.

Kuchu Marka dishes up quinoa soup, alpaca steaks, veg specials and great ambience; Wednesday is karaoke night; every night it's open late (3am to 4am) and Gloria, the owner, has information on lodging in private homes.

See opposite for transport options to Putre. Bus La Paloma leaves Putre for Arica at 2pm daily. Hop on buses to Parinacota, and Parque Nacional Lauca at Putre turnoff, 5km uphill from town.

PARQUE NACIONAL LAUCA

Lauca, 160km northeast of Arica, is northern Chile's treasure. Within the park (138,000 hectares; altitude 3000m–6300m) are herds of vicuña, vizcachas and over 100 bird species, including flamingos, giant coots and Andean gulls, plus cultural and archaeological landmarks.

At 22km from Putre, termas de Las Cuevas has a small rustic thermal bath, accessed along a cute path where vizcachas hide under rocks. Another 4km east, domestic llamas and alpacas graze on emerald green pastures among crystalline lagoons with *guallatas* (Andean geese) and ducks. Great photo op here.

Another 20km away and 5km off the highway is the beautiful **Parinacota**, a tiny Aymara village of whitewashed adobe and stone streets. The 18th-century church has an intriguing museum and interior murals and a table tethered down like a dog; it once escaped, walked through town and stopped in front of someone's house; the next day, that man died. So, to avoid anymore unnecessary announcements… But, you can go on hikes all you want; a few worthwhile ones explore the area. Ask the Conaf ranger in town for details.

The twin **Payachata volcanoes** – Parinacota (6350m) and Pomerape (6240m) – are dormant. At their feet is **Lago Chungará**, at 4500m, one of the world's highest lakes. Just to the south Volcán Guallatire smokes ominously.

Adapt to the altitude gradually; do not exert yourself at first, and eat and drink moderately. If you suffer altitude sickness try the herbal tea remedy *chachacoma*, or some *Mate de coca*, both are available from village vendors. Pack sunblock, shades and a hat.

Tours

Lots of places in Arica offer tours to sights along Ruta 11 (see p454) up to the Lago Chungara section of the park. Unless you can tolerate *soroche* (altitude sickness), do not take a one-day tour. This area has too much to offer to slam dunk it all in one day. However, multiday trips are expensive. It's easy enough to get to Putre on your own, but if you want the ease of a tour, shop wisely. A tour of 1½ days (US$55–60) includes a night in Putre; 2½-day tours (US$120–130) to Lauca also visit Salar de Surire. Most agencies don't have English-speaking guides, but this can be arranged in advance.

Latinorizons (☎ 058-250007; latinor@entelchile.net; Bolognesi 449) Belgian-run and friendly; 2–5-day trips; may also rent bikes. If the office is closed, check at Thompson 236 (Hostal Chez Charlie).

Parinacota Expeditions (Map p451; ☎ 058-256227; Arturo Prat 430, Local 5) Longer trips, volcano ascents and mountain bike descents from 4500m along llama trails.

Turismo Lauca (Map p451; ☎ 058-252322; Arturo Prat 430, Local 10) The most promoted agency with the biggest buses and the least amount of personality; mainly one-day *soroche* tours.

Sleeping

Conaf has **refugios** (per person US$6) at Las Cuevas, Parinacota and Lago Chungará, the latter having the best accessibility and most beds (six). Camping costs US$8 per tent. Bring enough food and a warm sleeping bag.

Francisca Morales (beds per person US$3.50) In Parinacota, a drafty five-bed *refugio* with lots of crocheted blankets, adjacent to her humble abode. You can use her sunken kitchen (the only place to escape the night chill) or she'll prepare meals (US$1/2 for breakfast/dinner). Camping is possible for a nominal charge. Look for her at the kiosk near the church.

Getting There & Away

The park straddles the paved Arica–La Paz Hwy. See Arica (p453) for bus details. If you are renting a car, or have your own, carry extra fuel and antifreeze.

MIDDLE CHILE

Rodeos, wineries and less frequented national parks in the Andes characterize this area of Chile, often skipped over by backpackin' just-the-highlights travelers. This is the country's main agricultural zone, with acre after acre of orchards and vineyards. The area south of Concepción was a bonanza for the Spaniards, who found small gold mines, good farmland and a large potential workforce, but the tenacious Mapuche continuously defended their land rights. Such disturbances, coupled with natural disasters, led the Spanish to abandon most of their settlements by the mid-17th century. Present-day Mapuche influence is evident south of the Río Biobío.

RANCAGUA

Rancagua (population 212,000) is known for two things: the national rodeo championship held in late March and the 1814 Desastre de Rancagua (Disaster of Rancagua) when the Spanish beat the Chilean patriots. It's 86km south of Santiago and has some late-colonial buildings.

Traveler services include **Sernatur** (☎ 072-230413; Germán Riesco 277), money-changer **Forex** (Campos 363) and **Conaf** (☎ 072-297505; Cuevas 480) for park information.

CHILE

Rancagua is best visited as a day trip from Santiago. Barebones **Hotel Rosedal de Chile** (☎ 072-230253; Calvo 435; r per person with breakfast US$9) is a couple of blocks from Tur Bus. **Casino Carabineros en Retiro** (Bueras 255; lunch US$3) serves huge portions at good prices. Fancy **Reina Victoria** (Independencia 667; lunch US$4) has excellent ice cream and a supermarket.

Long-distance buses use the **terminal** (Dr Salinas 1165) north of the Mercado Central. **Tur Bus** (Calvo & O'Carrol) and **Buses al Sur** (O'Carrol 1039) have their own terminals. Buses to Santiago (US$2, one hour) leave every 10 or 15 minutes. From the **train station** (Av Viña del Mar, btwn O'Carrol & Carrera Pinto) the commuter, Metrotren, goes to Santiago every hour (US$2) and EFE's long-distance trains to

Chillán, Concepción and Temuco stop at least once a day.

SANTA CRUZ

This unspoiled town is the locus of the area's winemaking activities. A lively **Fiesta de la Vendimia** (grape-harvest festival) takes place in the plaza at the beginning of March. Worth a detour is Chile's largest private museum, **Museo de Colchagua** (Errázuriz 145; admission US$4; ✆ Tue-Sat), with unusual fossils; amber-trapped insects; Mapuche textiles; masses of pre-Columbian anthropomorphic ceramics from all over Latin America; exquisite gold work; and conquistador equipment, documents and maps. The **bus terminal** (Rafael Casanova 478) is about

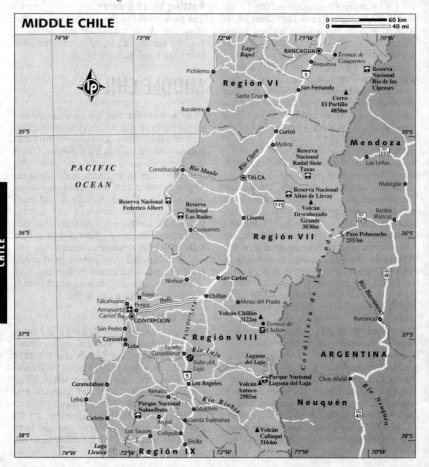

four blocks west of the town plaza. Catch buses to Pichilemu (US$2, two hours) and Santiago every half-hour or so.

PICHILEMU

Pichilemu is Chile's surfer paradise, with one of the best left-breaks along the long coast. The **tourist office** (☎ 072-842109; Municipalidad, Angel Gaete 365) also has a **kiosk** (cnr Angel Gaete & Aníbal Pinto; ☼ summer). Learn to surf with **Lobos del Pacífico** (☎ 09-7180255; lobosdelpacifico@hotmail.com).

Pequeño Bosque (☎ 072-842071; cnr Santa Teresa & Paseo del Sol; 4-person sites US$11) has all campground amenities and is accessible to the beach. Lots of *residenciales* pop up along Aníbal Pinto in season, such as **Las Salinas** (☎ 072-841071; Aníbal Pinto 51; per person US$6). **Gran Hotel Ross** (☎ 072-841038; Av Ross 130; r & cabañas per person US$10) is an old rambling place opposite Parque Ross. Rooms are musty; the cabins are a better option. **Hotel Asthur** (☎ 072-841495; Av Ortúzar 540; s/d with breakfast & bath US$12/25; ☒) is a huge place with a big common space that has a great view; there's also a laundry, bar and restaurant. The rooms are a little on the dark side, but pleasant.

From Rancagua, take Gal Bus or Andimar, connecting with San Fernando, or Sextur, which leaves at 7am (US$3). From Pichilemu's **bus terminal** (cnr Av Millaco & Los Alerces) buses run frequently to Santa Cruz (US$2, two hours) and San Fernando (US$3, three hours), where there are connections north and south.

CURICÓ

Off the backpacker radar, relaxed Curicó (population 120,300) is a service center for surrounding orchards and vineyards Their famous **Festival de la Vendimia** (grape-harvest festival) lasts three days in mid-March. It has one of the prettiest **Plaza de Armas**, with a wrought-iron bandstand on stilts. The **Miguel Torres** (☎ 075-564100) vineyard, 5km south of town, conducts tours by reservation only. Their elegant restaurant serves French-inspired cuisine (lunch US$20) Take *colectivos* going to Molina and ask to be dropped off. In summer, **Sernatur** (Plaza de Armas) has an information kiosk. **Forex** (Carmen 477) is the only *casa de cambio*; there are many ATMs.

With a shady grape arbor and old-world charm, **Hotel Prat** (☎ 075-311069; Peña 427; r per person without/with bath US$6/12) has some spacious rooms, while others are drab with sagging beds. **Residencial Rahue** (☎ 075-312194; Peña 410; r per person US$9), across the street, is a comfy, brightly painted alternative to Prat. **Casino Bomberos** (Membrillar 690; lunch US$2.50) has the best deal on lunches.

The **Terminal de Buses** (Maipú & Prat) and the **Estación de Ferrocarril** (Maipú & Prat) are four blocks west of the Plaza de Armas, at Maipú and Prat. Buses to Santiago (US$4, 2½ hours) leave about every half-hour. Or head to **Bus Pullman Sur** (Camilo Henríquez), three blocks north of the plaza. **Tur Bus** (Manso de Velasco 0106) has buses to Talca (US$2), Pucón (US$6) and Concepción (US$8). *Micros* to Molina (for wineries and Reserva Nacional Radal Siete Tazas) leave almost continuously from in front of the train station. Trains run north and south five times daily: Santiago (US$3–4), Chillán (US$3–5) and Temuco (US$7–10).

RESERVA NACIONAL RADAL SIETE TAZAS

In a ballet of waterfalls and robin's-egg blue water, the upper Río Claro descends through seven pools, each one leading to the next and ending at the 50m **Cascada Velo de la Novia** (Bridal Veil Falls). **Parque Inglés** is another beauty spot with a nice lodge serving meals. Conaf charges US$1.50 entrance fee here. Trails lead to Cerro El Fraile and into Valle del Indio, and across the Claro drainage to Altos del Lircay.

Radal Eco Adventure (☎ 09-3338719; 5-person sites US$21), 1km from the road to Radal Siete Tazas and 45km from Molina, has spacious sites with stunning views. Rates include firewood. Camping is also possible at the reserve's entrance (US$4) and at Parque Inglés (US$1.50). In summer the place is a zoo, so try to come in the off-season. Bring food from Molina.

Parque Inglés is 50km from Molina; take the *micro* bus from Av San Martín in Curicó to get to Molina. From November to March, there are five buses daily from Terminal de Molina on Maipú, starting at 8am, the last one returning at 8pm (US$2, two hours). The rest of the year, there's one bus a day, at 5:30pm, returning at 8:30am.

TALCA

Talca (population 172,000) is a smart base from which to explore wineries and national reserves, and offers better long-distance bus connections than nearby towns. It's 257km south of Santiago. Traveler services include **Sernatur** (1 Poniente 1281), **Conaf** (3 Sur & 2 Poniente) and **Forex Money Exchange** (2 Oriente 1133). The **Museo O'Higginiano y de Bellas Artes** (1 Norte 875; admission free; ⏰ Tue-Sun) occupies the house where Bernardo O'Higgins signed Chile's declaration of independence in 1818. It has paintings by Chilean artists and period furnishings.

Sleeping & Eating

Residencial Elsa Labrín (☎ 071-231482; 5 Oriente 1186, Dpto 8; r per person US$8) Above the Galería Talca. The chatty owner offers clean rooms and ample breakfast.

Hostal del Puente (☎ 071-220930; 1 Sur 411; s/d with bath US$16/26) Beside the river, it's the nicest accommodation in town, with friendly English-speaking management, a pretty garden and cozy rooms.

Casa Chueca (☎ 197-0096; 09-4190625; casachueca@ hotmail.com; bunks US$11, s/d/tr with bath & breakfast US$22/30/36) On Talca's outskirts, is a backpacker favorite, and with reason. Stay in rustic cabañas set amid beautiful gardens with river views. There's a cozy dining room and a pool and the owners have loads of information about the region and lead hiking trips in the mountains. Hop on a bicycle here and explore many nearby wineries.

The cheapest belch-inducing hotdogs are along 5 Oriente.

Mercado Central (1 Norte, 5 Oriente, 1 Sur & 4 Oriente) Cheap *cocinerías*.

Ibiza (1 Sur 1168) Dispatches rotisserie chicken (US$4) and other grills.

Kebabs House (6 Oriente) Sandwiches and snacks; open Sundays too.

Rubin Tapia (2 Oriente 379) Great regional dishes (including fried frogs!) and a large selection of wines.

Las Brisas supermarket (1 Norte & 5 Oriente) Open until 10pm.

Getting There & Away

Most of the north–south buses stop at the **Rodoviario Municipal** (2 Sur 1920) or there's **Tur Bus** (3 Sur 1960). Sample fares and times are: Chillán (US$6, four hours), Puerto Montt (US$18, 11 hours) and Temuco or Valparaíso (US$13, six hours). Buses Biotal is the agent for Transporte Pehuenche, which crosses the 2553m Paso Pehuenche to the Argentine cities of Malargüe and San Rafael in the summer.

The **train station** (11 Oriente 1000) is at the eastern end of 2 Sur. There are five trains a day to Chillán (US$3, two hours), Curicó (US$2, one hour), San Fernando (US$3, 1½ hours) and Rancagua (US$4, 2¼ hours), and one per day to Concepción (US$5, 5½ hours) and Temuco (US$8, 10 hours).

RESERVA NACIONAL ALTOS DE LIRCAY

In the Andean foothills, 65km east of Talca, this **national reserve** (admission US$1.50) offers a number of hiking options, including **El Enladrillado**, a strenuous 12-hour hike to a unique basaltic plateau, affording stunning views and **Laguna del Alto** a 10-hour hike. Trekkers can loop to Radal Siete Tazas, but a guide is needed as the trail is not marked. **El Caminante** (☎ 09-8371440, 071-1970097; www.trekking chile.com) has years of experience and can organize guided hikes.

The **Conaf campground** (camping for 5 people US$13) is a one-hour hike from the bus stop; you can also camp at backcountry sites. From Talca, Buses Vilches goes directly to the park entrance, usually in the morning, returning in afternoon; check for latest schedules (US$1.50, 2½ hours).

CHILLÁN

Of the towns on the Panamericana between Santiago (400km north) and Temuco (270km south), Chillán (population 163,000) most deserves a stopover. Today's Chillán consists of two cities. Chillán Viejo was crippled by Mapuche sieges and earthquakes. As a consequence, Chillán Nuevo was built in 1835. When another quake in 1939 destroyed the new city, the Mexican government donated the still-operating **Escuela México** (O'Higgins 250; ⏰ 10am-noon & 3-6pm Mon-Fri, 10am-6pm Sat & Sun). Mexican artist David Alfaro Siqueiros painted murals honoring indigenous and post-Columbian figures in each country's history – the northern wall devoted to Mexico and the southern wall to Chile in the school's library; donations are accepted (and encouraged).

One of Chile's most colorful markets, the **Feria de Chillán** has a great selection of Chilean-style crafts (leather, basketry and weaving). It's especially lively on Saturday, occupying the entire Plaza de la Merced and spilling into adjacent streets.

Take a short bus or cab ride from downtown to visit **Chillán Viejo**, the original town and Bernardo O'Higgins' birthplace. A 60m-long mosaic wall illustrates scenes from his life. The Centro Histórico, next to the wall, displays objects from the liberator's life.

Information

Places that are good to know in town include **Sernatur** (☎ 042-223272; 18 de Septiembre 455), located half a block north of the plaza; the **post office** (Libertad 505); **Telefónica** (Arauco 625); **Banco de Chile** (cnr El Roble & 5 de Abril); the travel agency **Centrotur** (☎ 042-221306; 18 de Septiembre 656), which sells train tickets; and **Hospital Herminda Martín** (☎ 042-212345;

Constitución & Av Argentina), seven blocks east of the plaza.

Sleeping

Residencial 18 (☎ 042-211102; 18 de Septiembre 317; r per person US$7) Central, with pool tables.

Hostal Canadá (☎ 042-234515; Libertad 269; r per person US$6) Pleasant and cozy rooms.

Residencial Su Casa (☎ 042-223931; Cocharcas 555; r per person US$9) Cramped but run by a friendly *señora* who may allow kitchen use.

Hotel Libertador (☎ 042-223255; Av Libertad 85; s/d US$11/20, with bath US$17/25) The Libertador is family-run and close to the bus station; make sure you ask for an upstairs room – they're much nicer.

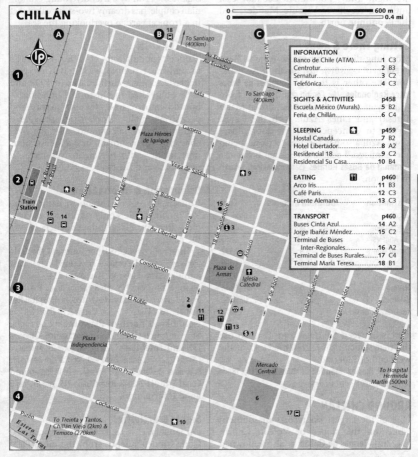

CHILLÁN

0	600 m
0	0.4 mi

INFORMATION
Banco de Chile (ATM).............................1 C3
Centrotur..2 B3
Sernatur...3 C2
Telefónica...4 C3

SIGHTS & ACTIVITIES   p458
Escuela México (Murals)..........................5 B2
Feria de Chillán....................................6 C4

SLEEPING   p459
Hostal Canadá.......................................7 B2
Hotel Libertador....................................8 A2
Residencial 18.......................................9 C2
Residencial Su Casa...............................10 B4

EATING   p460
Arco Iris...11 B3
Café Paris...12 C3
Fuente Alemana....................................13 C3

TRANSPORT   p460
Buses Cinta Azul..................................14 A2
Jorge Ibañéz Méndez.............................15 C2
Terminal de Buses
  Inter-Regionales.................................16 A2
Terminal de Buses Rurales.......................17 C4
Terminal María Teresa...........................18 B1

CHILE

Eating

Mercado Central (Maipón btwn 5 de Abril & Isabel Riquelme) Has the cheapest lunches, where *cocinerías* serve up excellent meals; try the *longaniza* (long pork sausage).

Arco Iris (El Roble 525) The only veg restaurant in town.

Fuente Alemana (Arauco 661) For sandwiches and *Kuchen* (cake).

Café Paris (Arauco; ☿ 24hr) Across from Alemana, it has the same type of fare. Trendy.

Trienta y Tantos (Chillán Viejo) Worth the trek for 30 varieties of *empanadas* and great *pisco sours*; ask a local for its location.

Restaurant Pub Santos Pescadores (Av Vicente Méndez 275) A big, late-night place with candles on the tables; order a *tabla* and drink the night away. Follow Av Ecuador east until you reach Av Vicente Méndez, and then continue north.

Getting There & Away

Most long-distance buses use **Terminal María Teresa** (Av O'Higgins 010), just north of Av Ecuador. The other is the old **Terminal de Buses Inter-Regionales** (Av Constitución & Brasil), from which you can catch Tur Bus (also at María Teresa) and Línea Azul, with the fastest service to Concepción. Next door, Buses Cinta Azul also has services to Concepción and Santiago. Local and regional buses use **Terminal de Buses Rurales** (Sargento Aldea), south of Maipón.

Destination	Duration in Hours	Cost
Angol	3	US$4.30
Concepción	1½	US$3
Los Ángeles	1½	US$3
Puerto Montt	9	US$12
Santiago	6	US$9
Talca	3	US$4
Temuco	5	US$6
Valdivia	6	US$8.50
Valparaíso/Viña del Mar	8	US$12

Trains between Santiago and Temuco use the **train station** (☎ 042-222424; Av Brasil), at the west end of Libertad.

Jorge Ibañez Méndez (☎ 042-211218; 18 de Septiembre 380) rents cars.

AROUND CHILLÁN

One of the largest ski resorts in southern Chile, on the slopes of Volcán Chillán (3122m), **Termas de Chillán** is also renowned for its high-end hot springs (adult/child US$20/16) – heated pools, really. Check travel agencies for day trips. **Cabañas Rucahue** (☎ 042-220-817; www.rucahueescalador.cl in Spanish; r per person US$10; 🏊), in Valle Las Trancas, 7km before Termas de Chillán, offers fully equipped cabins in the woods and there's a restaurant on site. The owners organize trekking, transport to Termas and rent ski equipment. Buses Línea Azul goes to Valle Las Trancas year-round at 8am (returning at 4pm) and continues to Termas in summer.

Coastal areas west of Chillán are worth exploring. **Buchupureo**, 13km north of Cobquecura (about 100km from Chillán), is a tranquil village popular with surfers. **La Joya del Mar Cabañas** (☎ 042-1971733; 4-person cabin with kitchen US$50), run by a friendly young Californian couple, has dreamy two-story cabins set in a tropical garden overlooking the sea.

CONCEPCIÓN

'Conce' (population 214,500) is Chile's second-most populous city. It's not particularly scenic – earthquakes in 1939 and 1960 obliterated the historical buildings – but downtown has pleasant plazas and pedestrian malls. Universities provide a youthful buzz. Talcahuano, another sizeable city 15km north, has an enormous port facility with petroleum refineries, a naval base and fisheries.

Orientation & Information

Concepción sits on the north bank of the Río Biobío, Chile's only significant navigable waterway. Plaza Independencia marks the center.

Internet costs US$1 per hour at **CyberC@fé** (Portales 530) and **Portal** (Caupolicán 314). For fast laundry, try **Laverap** (Caupolicán 334). To exchange money, try **Afex** (Barros Arana 565, Local 57). Many ATMs are downtown. **Hospital Regional** (☎ 041-237445; San Martín & Av Roosevelt) is eight blocks north of Plaza Independencia. Stay in touch through the **post office** (O'Higgins 799) and **Entel** (Barros Arana 541, Local 2). **Sernatur** (☎ 041-227976; Aníbal Pinto 460; ☿ 8:30am-8pm daily in summer, 8:30am-1pm & 3-6pm Mon-Fri in winter) and **Conaf** (☎ 041-248048; Barros Arana 215, 2nd fl) have good information.

Sights & Activities

On January 1, 1818, O'Higgins proclaimed Chile's independence from the city's **Plaza**

Independencia. On the grounds of the Barrio Universitario, the **Casa del Arte** (cnr Chacabuco & Larenas) has the massive mural by Mexican Jorge González Camarena, *La Presencia de América Latina* (1965). On the edge of Parque Ecuador, the **Galería de Historia** (Av Lamas & Lincoyán) features vivid dioramas of local and regional history. Subjects include Mapuche subsistence, battles with the Spaniards (note Mapuche tactics), literary figure Alonso de Ercilla, the 1939 earthquake and a finely detailed model of a local factory. Both museums are open weekends, closed Monday, and have admission free.

Once the center of Chile's coal industry, the town of **Lota**, south of Concepción, is home to the magnificently landscaped 14-hectare **Parque Isidora Cousiño** (admission US$2.50; 9am-8pm), complete with peacocks and a lighthouse. Nearby, **Chiflón del Diablo** (Devil's Whistle; ☎ 041-871565; 9am-6:30pm) was a working mine until 1976, but now laid-off coal miners take tourists through the mine (US$7–14 depending on length – and depth – of tour; arrive before 4pm if taking the long tour). Ask the *micro* bus driver to drop you off at Parada Calero. Go down Bajada Defensa Niño street and you'll see a long wall with the name.

Sleeping

Catering more to businesses than back-packs, lodging in Conce is not a bargain and kitchen use rarely an option. During

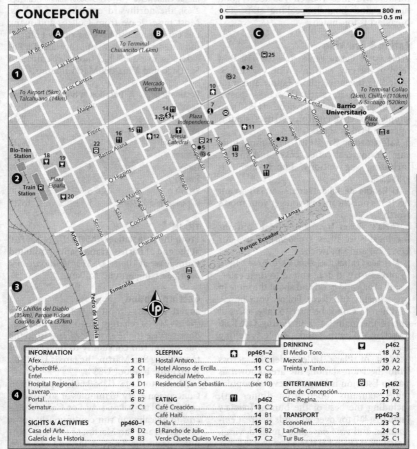

CONCEPCIÓN

0 — 800 m
0 — 0.5 mi

CHILE

the school year, university students fill up many *residenciales*; call before trekking around town.

Hostal Antuco (☎ 041-235485; Barros Arana 741 Depto 33; s/d with breakfast US$12/22) Decent rooms above an arcade; ring the buzzer at the gate to the stairs, right after entering the arcade.

Residencial San Sebastián (☎ 041-242710; Barros Arana 741, Depto 35; s/d US$12/22) Down the hall from Antuco; just about the same, with slightly nicer rooms.

Residencial Metro (☎ 041-225305; Barros Arana 464; s/d with breakfast US$10/16) One of the better deals, with spacious high-ceilinged rooms.

Hotel Alonso de Ercilla (☎ 041-227984; Colo Colo 334; s/d with breakfast US$33/55) Clean and comfortable with nice wooden '70s decor, good heating and English-speaking staff. The breakfast is top-notch.

Eating & Drinking

Verde Quete Quiero Verde (Colo Colo 174) Best food in the city with inspiring veg dishes, including inventive juices (apple and mint US$2), unusual salads (US$3–5), pastas (US$6) and hearty sandwiches (US$3), in simple, attractive environs. Artists' studios open on Friday nights.

Café Creación (San Martín 756) Sunny little café serving real coffee, cakes and snacks, including veg options. Lunch menu is US$2.25.

El Rancho de Julio (Barros Arana 337) Want beef? It's not cheap, but you get your moo's worth.

Chela's (Barros Arana 405) Great options for local specialties (*cazuela de ave* for US$1.75) and sandwiches.

Mercado Central (Caupolicán, Maipú, Rengo & Freire) Waitresses try to drag you in to their eateries; all cheap and good and about the same in price, quality and decor. Follow your nose.

When in Conce be sure to take *onces* at one of the many cafés including **Café Haití** (Caupolicán 511) with good people-watching seats.

West of Plaza Independencia, across from the train station, the area known as Barrio Estación is home to several popular pub/restaurants (open from dinner on), including the best of the bunch, **Treinta y Tanto** (Prat 404) for over 30 kinds of great *empanadas* and *vino navegado* (mulled wine), **Mezcal** (Prat 532) and **El Medio Toro** (Prat 592).

Entertainment

Cine de Concepción (O'Higgins 650) and **Cine Regina** (Barros Arana 340) show flicks.

Getting There & Away

AIR

Aeropuerto Carriel Sur is 5km northwest of downtown, on the road to Talcahuano. **LanChile** (☎ 600-526-2000; Barros Arana 600) has up to eight daily flights to Santiago and four to Punta Arenas. **Sky Airline** (☎ 041-218941; Freire 746, Local 54) has competitive rates.

BUS

There are two long-distance bus terminals: **Collao** (Puchacay; ☎ 041-316666; Tegualda 860), on the northern outskirts of town, and **Terminal Chillancito** (☎ 041-315036; Camilo Henríquez 2565), the northward extension of Bulnes. Most buses leave from Collao, and many bus companies also have downtown offices, indicated below where appropriate. **Tur Bus** (ticket office Tucapel 530) has most departures to Santiago and Viña del Mar/Valparaíso.

Destination	Duration in Hours	Cost
Angol	1½	US$4
Chillán	2	US$3
Los Ángeles	2	US$3
Puerto Montt	7	US$13
Santiago	7	US$7-15
Talca	4	US$8
Temuco	4	US$6
Valdivia	6	US$10
Valparaíso/Viña del Mar	9	US$13

TRAIN

From the **train station** (☎ 041-227777; Arturo Prat) at the end of Barros Arana, Santiago-bound trains leave at 10pm (US$13/34 *salón/cama baja*), arriving around 6:30am.

Getting Around

Airport Express (☎ 041-236444) and **Taxivan** (☎ 041-248748) charge US$3 for door-to-door service to the airport. *Micros* from the bus station run constantly to the center of town along San Martín; the fare is US$0.40. A taxi ride is about US$4.

Micros to Lota (US$0.60) depart from Concepción every 15 minutes or so from the corner of Tucapel and Av Los Carrera. *Micros* to Talcahuano run continuously down O'Higgins and San Martín, or take the commuter train Bio-Trén, at the end of Freire, leaving every half-hour. For car rental, try **EconoRent** (☎ 041-225377; Castellón 134).

LOS ÁNGELES

Stop here if you're planning jaunts into Parque Nacional Laguna de Laja and upper Biobío. The **Museo de la Alta Frontera** (Caupolicán & Colón) has an impressive collection of Mapuche silverwork. The best information can be found at **Automóvil Club de Chile** (Caupolicán 201). **InterBruna travel agency** (Caupolicán 350) changes money and rents cars.

The best place to stay around this region is **Hospedaje El Rincón** (☎ 09-4415019; elrincon@ cvmail.cl; Panamericana km 494; r without/with bath US$12/ 15), where hospitable German owners offer weary backpackers tranquility, excellent homemade food and comfortable rooms. They also arrange intensive Spanish courses, bike rentals and guided hikes to Laguna del Laja. A substantial breakfast is included. Call to arrange a pickup from Los Ángeles or from Cruce La Mona if you're coming from the north. In town, good places to sleep are **Residencial El Angelino** (☎ 043-325627; Colo Colo 335; r per person US$10) with cheerful rooms, shared bath and **Hotel Oceano** (☎ 043-342432; Colo Colo 327; s/d with bath & breakfast US$18/35) is clean and pleasant. Eats include **Café Prymos** (Colón 400) for breakfast and coffee, **Julio's Pizza** (Colón 452) for pizza and pasta, and **Las Brisas supermarket** (Villagrán).

The **bus terminal** (Av Sor Vicenta 2051) is on the northeastern outskirts of town. **Tur Bus** (Av Sor Vicenta 2061) is nearby. Antuco-bound buses leave from **Terminal Santa Rita** (Villagrán & Rengo).

PARQUE NACIONAL LAGUNA DEL LAJA

Lava from the 2985m-high Volcán Antuco dammed the Río Laja to form **Parque Nacional Laguna Del Laja's** (admission US$1) centerpiece lake, 95km east of Los Ángeles, with forests of mountain cypress and pehuén (monkey-puzzle tree). Nearly 50 bird species, including the condor, frequent the area. Most trails are for easy day hikes; the best is around Antuco. The higher **Sierra Velluda**, to the southwest, shows off a series of impressive glaciers. Bring supplies from Los Ángeles.

Near the park entrance, at km 90, is **Camping Lagunillas** (☎ 043-321086; 5-person sites US$7.50). **Hostería El Bosque** (☎ 043-372719; US$6), 12km from Lago Laja at the last bus stop, is locally recommended for a very basic (no showers) mountain shack.

Take buses from Los Ángeles to Antuco. Buses also leave for Abanico (two hours) every two hours. Conaf's administrative offices and visitor's center at Chacay is an 11km walk.

PARQUE NACIONAL NAHUELBUTA

Pehuéns, up to 50m tall and 2m in diameter, cover the slopes of **Parque Nacional Nahuelbuta** (admission US$3), one of the tree's last non-Andean refuges. Angol, 35km to the east, is the closest town. Conaf's **Centro de Informaciones Ecológicas** is at Pehuenco, 5km from the park entrance. From Pehuenco, a 4km trail winds through pehuén forests to the granite outcrop of **Piedra del Aguila**, a 1379m overlook with views from the Andes to the Pacific. **Cerro Anay**, 1450m above sea level, has similar views; the trail itself, reached via Coimallín, is relatively short and has countless wildflowers and huge stands of araucarias.

The park is open all year, but there's snow on the summits in winter. **Camping** (per site US$9) is available at Pehuenco, which has water and flush toilets, and at more rustic Coimallín (5km north of Pehuenco).

From Angol, **Buses Angol** (Terminal Rural; Ilabaca 422) goes to Vegas Blancas (US$1.70), 7km from the entrance, Monday, Wednesday and Friday at 6:45am and 4pm, returning at 9am and 6pm. **Buses Nahuelbuta** (cnr Ilabaca & Caupolicán) travels to Vegas Blancas Tuesday, Thursday and Saturday at 6:45am, returning at 4pm.

THE LAKE DISTRICT

Few landscapes surpass the beauty of the Lake District, where volcanic cones tower above deep blue lakes, ancient forests and verdant farmland. Dive into the green by getting off Ruta 5 and exploring bumpy dirt roads in the wild and undeveloped countryside. There's a little bit of everything, from rafting to climbing, from hiking to hot-springs hopping, from taking *onces* in colonial towns to sharing a maté (Paraguayan tea) with the local *huasos* cowboys. Along the way, the warmth and hospitality of the *sureños* (southerners) and the region's magic are sure to enrapture.

The area between the Río Biobío and the Río Toltén, just south of Temuco, was once Mapuche-controlled and not

CHILE

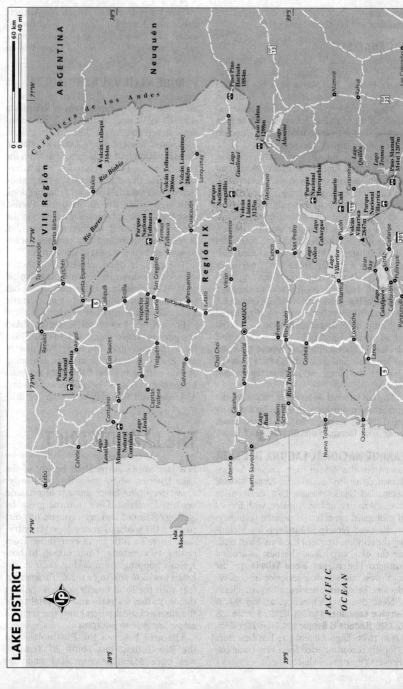

CHILE

LAKE DISTRICT

ARGENTINA

Neuquén

VIII Región

Cordillera de los Andes

Región IX

PACIFIC OCEAN

60 km
40 mi

Isla Mocha

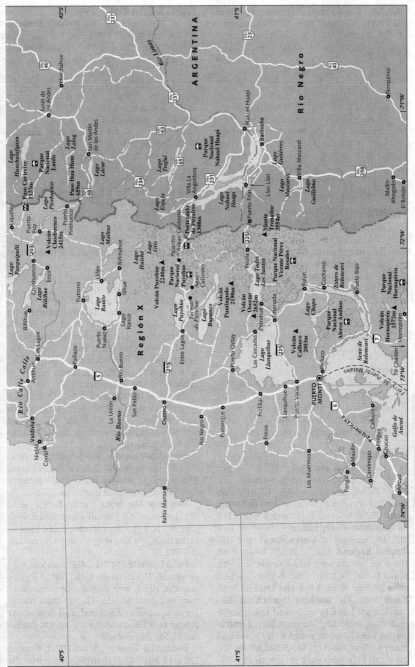

safe for European settlement up until the 1880s. Valdivia, now the cultural gem of the country, was the only settlement not abandoned and became a main stage of German immigration. Today, several hundred thousand Mapuche still live in La Frontera, the area between the two rivers, earning a precarious livelihood from farming and crafts. Valdivia and the towns to the south have considerable German influence, most evidenced in the architecture and appearance of cream-laden *Kuchen* on every menu. This section takes in the IX Region and part of the X, including Puerto Montt, gateway to the Chiloé archipelago and Chilean Patagonia.

TEMUCO
Chaotic and ill-planned, Temuco (population 244,000) was founded in 1881 after the Chilean government and the Mapuche signed a landmark treaty on Cerro Ñielol. Temuco is one of the fastest growing cities in the south and it's the main business center for the region's industries. This gives the city a sense of white-collar pomp that contrasts with its other traditional identity – as the main market town for the surrounding Mapuche community.

Orientation
On the north bank of the Río Cautín, Temuco is 675km south of Santiago via the Panamericana. Cerro Ñielol is north of the city center. Affluent west Temuco is a more relaxed area with better restaurants.

Information
Internet centers are cheap (US$0.70 per hour) and come and go too fast to list here. ATMs are abundant. Change US cash and traveler's checks at **Casa de Cambio Global** (Bulnes 655, Local 1), **Intercam** (Bulnes 743) or **Christopher Money Exchange** (Bulnes 667, Local 202). Do laundry at **Marva** (Manuel Montt 415). **Hospital Regional** (☎ 045-212525; Manuel Montt 115) is six blocks west and one block north of the plaza. To stay in touch there's a **post office** (cnr Diego Portales & Prat) and **Entel** (cnr Prat & Manuel Montt). The **municipal tourist kiosk** (Mercado Municipal) has city maps and informative materials, including lodgings lists. **Sernatur** (cnr Claro Solar & Bulnes) distributes city maps and many leaflets. **Conaf** (☎ 045-298100; Av Bilbao 931, 2nd fl) can help with park information.

Sights & Activities
In a 1929 building, the **Mercado Municipal** (⏰ 8am-8pm Mon-Sat, 8:30am-3pm Sun) occupies most of a block bounded by Bulnes, Portales, Aldunate and Rodríguez. It caters mainly to tourists looking to dine and shop away from hustle and bustle. The quality of the artisanship varies substantially. **Feria Libre** (⏰ 8am-5pm) is a much more dynamic and colorful Mapuche produce and crafts market along Barros Arana. **Museo Regional de la Araucanía** (Av Alemania 084; admission US$1, Sun free; ⏰ 9am-5pm Mon-Fri, 11am-2:30pm Sat, 11am-2pm Sun) has exhibits recounting the history of the Araucanian peoples before, during and since the Spanish invasion. Take *Micro* No 9 from downtown; it's also reasonable walking distance.

Chile's national flower, the copihue, flowering from March to July, grows in abundance at **Cerro Ñielol** (Calle Prat; admission US$1.25), with trails and an environmental information center.

Sleeping
Patience and tolerance are required to find decent accommodations. Around the train station and Feria Libre are the cheapest, least reputable places, while the neighborhood between the plaza and university has better options. Rates below are per person, with shared bath. Budget places rarely include breakfast in the price.

Hospedaje La Araucaría (☎ 045-322820; Antonio Varas 568; r per person US$8.50) Clean, large rooms and firm beds in an old home, plus a great self-serve kitchen and eating area overlooking back garden.

Hospedaje Araucanía (☎ 045-219089; General Mackenna 151; r per person US$7) Quiet upstairs rooms in a grand old wooden house in the heart of downtown. Lots of character and kids.

Hospedaje Flor Aroca (☎ 045-234205; Lautaro 591; r per person US$7) Just off Caupolicán, with cheerful and spacious rooms, could use another bath. No kitchen privileges; breakfast is US$1.50.

Hotel Espelette (☎ 045-234805; Claro Solar 492; r per person US$11, s/d with bath US$25/35; ⓟ) Central, safe and strict, with florist shop, art collection and great towels. The upstairs rooms are cute, small and ignored; and downstairs rooms face the common TV room. Breakfast (US$1.50) is drab.

Residencial Temuco (☎ 045-233721; Rodriguez 1341 2nd fl; dm US$8.50) HI affiliate with friendly

TEMUCO

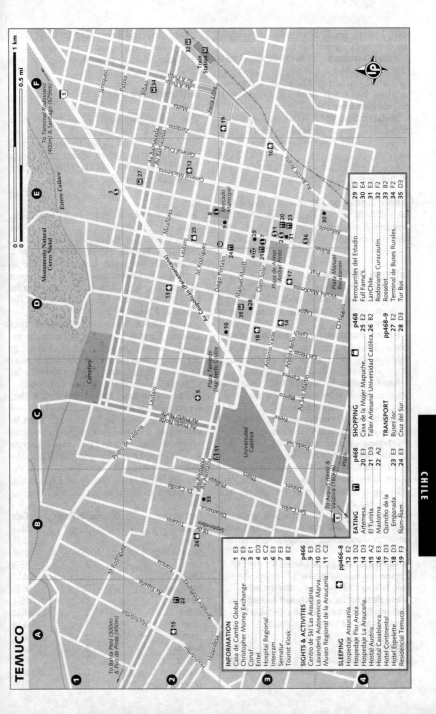

INFORMATION	
Casa de Cambio Global............	1 E3
Christopher Money Exchange.....	2 E3
Conaf...............................	3 E1
Entel...............................	4 D3
Hospital Regional..................	5 C2
Intercam...........................	6 E3
Sematur............................	7 E3
Tourist Kiosk......................	8 E2

SIGHTS & ACTIVITIES	p466
Centro de Ski Las Araucanas......	9 E3
Lavandería Autoservicio Marva...	10 D3
Museo Regional de la Araucanía..	11 C2

SLEEPING	pp466-8
Hospedaje Araucaria...............	12 E2
Hospedaje Flor Arora..............	13 D2
Hospedaje La Araucanía...........	14 D3
Hostal Austria....................	15 A2
Hostal Casablanca.................	16 E3
Hotel Continental.................	17 D3
Hotel Espelette...................	18 D3
Residencial Temuco................	19 F3

EATING	p468
Artemesa..........................	20 E3
El Turista........................	21 D3
Madonna...........................	22 A2
Quincho de la	
Empanada..........................	23 E3
Nam-Nam...........................	24 E3

SHOPPING	p468
Casa de la Mujer Mapuche.........	25 E2
Taller Artesanal Universidad Católica.	26 B2

TRANSPORT	pp468-9
Buses Jac.........................	27 E2
Cruz del Sur......................	28 D3
Ferrocarriles del Estadio.........	29 E3
Full Fama's.......................	30 E4
LanChile..........................	31 E3
Rodoviario Curacautín............	32 F2
Rosselot..........................	33 B2
Terminal de Buses Rurales.........	34 F2
Tur Bus...........................	35 D3

CHILE

staff, but it's small, near noisy streets and the thin beds squeak too much.

Hostal Casablanca (☎ 045-212740; Manuel Montt 1306; s without/with bath US$10/16) In a rambling old white building, Casablanca requires earplugs, but offers breakfast. Rooms with private bath have cable TV.

Hostal Austria (☎ 045-247169; hostalaustria@terra .cl; Hochstetter 599; r per person with breakfast US$20-35; ℗ ✕) Peaceful (except for the dog), non-smoking, frilly rooms with cable TV. The annex is not as impressive. There's loads of hot water and heat; the breakfast is good.

Hotel Continental (☎ 045-238973; Antonio Varas 709; s US$12-20, d US$21-26, s/d with bath US$23/33) Reserve Neruda's favorite room at this pre-eminent hotel. Historic, with renovated rooms.

Eating & Drinking

Feria Libre (⏲ 8am-5pm) Cheap eats can be found here, where vendors dice, boil and fry fresh produce, fish and meat into tasty stews at many stalls.

Mercado Municipal (⏲ 8am-8pm Mon-Sat, 8:30am-3pm Sun) Touristy restaurants with lots of seafood options, including *caldillo* (soup). Main course dishes cost about US$4–US$8.

Ñam Ñam (Diego Portales 802 & No 855) Student-oriented with heaping sandwiches, draft beer and nonsmoking sections.

Quincho de la Empanada (Aldunate 698) Excellent *empanadas*, many of them veg.

Artemesa (☎ Aldunate 620; Local 801) Veg restaurant, open lunch and dinner.

El Turista (Claro Solar 839) Serves coffees with butter-laden cookies, cakes and chocolates.

In west Temuco, many restaurants are also the place for drinks:

Madonna (Av Alemania 0660) Tops for pizza, with almost 30 different pies to choose from plus mix-and-match pasta and salsas. Fun and informal, individual/shared pizzas cost US$5/8-12.

Bahía Perú (cnr Av Alemania & Recreo) Not cheap, but dishes out enormous platters of spicy food. Come after dinner for fancy drinks and a lively, affluent crowd.

Pub de Pinte (cnr Recreo & Alessandri) Has candles on tables, woodsy decor and tranquil vibe. Best place for a decent draft beer and snacks.

Shopping

Casa de la Mujer Mapuche (Prat 283) Cooperative selling indigenous crafts, most notably textiles and ceramics.

Taller Artesanal Universidad Católica (Av Alemania 0422) Sells silver reproductions of Mapuche jewelry, created by artisans and local students.

Getting There & Away

AIR

Temuco's Aeropuerto Maquehue is 6km south of town. **LanChile** (☎ 600-526-2000; Bulnes 687) has plenty of flights to Santiago and daily flights to Puerto Montt and Punta Arenas. **Sky Airline** (☎ 045-747300; Bulnes 655, Local 4) has competitive rates.

BUS

Terminal Rodoviario (☎ 045-255005; Pérez Rosales 01609) is at the northern approach to town. Companies have ticket offices downtown, including **Tur Bus** (☎ 045-278161; cnr Lagos & Montt), with the most frequent service to Santiago; **Tas Choapa** (Varas 609), for northern destinations up to Antofagasta; and **Cruz del Sur** (☎ Claro Solar 599), which also serves the island of Chiloé.

Argentina is more easily accessed from Osorno. Cruz del Sur goes to Bariloche via Paso Cardenal Samoré, east of Osorno, at 2:45am; however, the Thursday and Sunday 8am departure is more time efficient. Tas Choapa has similar service.

Terminal de Buses Rurales (Balmaceda & Pinto) serves local destinations, such as Chol Chol (about every hour) and Melipeuco. **Buses Jac** (cnr Balmaceda & Aldunate) offers the most frequent service to Villarrica and Pucón, plus service to Santiago, Lican Ray and Coñaripe. The **Rodoviario Curacautín** (Barros Arana 191) is the departure point for buses to Curacautín, Lonquimay and the upper Biobío.

Destination	Duration in Hours	Cost
Ancud	7	US$11
Angol	2	US$3.50
Bariloche (Arg)	10½–12	US$18
Castro	8	US$14
Chillán	4	US$6.50
Concepción	4½	US$5
Curacautín	1½	US$3
Osorno	3	US$5
Pucón	1	US$3.50
Puerto Montt/Puerto Varas	5	US$7
Santiago	8	US$15–30
Valdivia	3	US$3
Valparaíso–Viña del Mar	10	US$18–20
Zapala & Neuquén (Arg)	10	US$30

TRAIN

Santiago-bound trains leave at 10:30pm nightly, stopping at various stations en route (US$11–35, 11½ hours). Buy tickets at **Estación de Ferrocarril** (☎ 045-233416; Av Barros Arana) or at the downtown office of **Ferrocarriles del Estado** (EFE; ☎ 045-233522; Bulnes 582).

Getting Around

From the airport, taxis cost about US$5 to the city center. Bus No 1 runs between downtown and the train station. From the bus terminal, hop on *colectivos* 11P and 25A. *Colectivo* 9 services west Temuco. Car rental is available at **Rosselot** (☎ 045-952525; Av Alemania 0180) and **Full Famas** (☎ 045-215420; Andrés Bello 1096).

PARQUE NACIONAL CONGUILLÍO

A popular national park, but rarely visited in the off-season, **Conguillío** (admission US$5) is about 80km east of Temuco and covers 60,835 hectares of alpine lakes, canyons and forests surrounding the smoldering 3125m Volcán Llaima, which last erupted in 1957.

The **Sierra Nevada trail** (10km, approx three hours one way) leaves from the parking lot at Playa Linda, at the east end of Laguna Conguillío and climbs northeast through coigue forests, passes a pair of lake overlooks; from the second and more scenic, you can see solid stands of araucarias begin to supplant coigues on the ridge top. **Sendero de Chile** (18km, approx six hours one way) links Laguna Captrén with Guardaría Truful-Truful. At **Laguna Captrén, Los Carpinteros** (8km, approx 2½ hours one way) accesses the 1800-year-old, 3m-wide Araucaría Madre, considered the largest tree in the park.

From April to November call to find out which parts of the park are open: in the winter 3m of snow can accumulate here. Conaf's **Centro de Información Ambiental** (Laguna Conguillío) sells some trail maps. **Centro de Ski Las Araucarias** (☎ 045-562313) also has an office in **Temuco** (Map p467; ☎ 045-274141; Bulnes 351, Oficina 49). The Curacautín **tourist office** (☎ 045-881726; cnr M Rodríguez & Yungay) has park information.

Sleeping & Eating

Campgrounds in the park cost US$21 per five-person site, but at Lago Conguillío,

El Estero (☎ 045-644388 in Temuco) reserves sites for backpackers (US$5 per person). Camping is also available at **Laguna Captren**, 6km from Lago Conguillío. Rates are heavily discounted off-season.

Centro de Ski Las Araucarias (☎ 045-562-313; dm without/with bedding US$10/12) Convenient location; bring a sleeping bag.

Suizandina (☎ 09-884-9541; www.suizandina.com; camping per person US$4, dm US$8-10, cabañas for 2 people US$22, r per person with bath US$22) North of the park, on the road to Lonquimay, this is a great base from which to explore the park and surrounding areas. The young Swiss family organize treks and horse rides. Evening meals may include Swiss specialties such as raclette or fondue, and a hearty breakfast is included. No kitchen use.

Santa Elvira de Tracura (☎ 171-2-1968-503; km 18; cabins per person US$8) Near Melipeuco, off-the-beaten-track. Fully equipped cabins with breakfast included. They will also prepare homemade lunches (US$5) and rent horses for day treks (or longer).

Getting There & Away

For Los Paraguas, take a Chequenco bus (US$2) from Temuco's Terminal de Buses Rurales, then walk or hitch the 17km to the ski lodge.

For the northern entrance, take a bus to Curacautín, from where a shuttle (US$1) runs to the park border at Guardería Captrén Monday to Friday. From December to March, if conditions allow, it continues to Laguna Captrén. For the southern entrance, take Nar-Bus in Temuco to Melipeuco (US$2), where Hostería Huentelén can arrange a cab to park headquarters. The lodgings listed can arrange transport.

VILLARRICA

On the southwest shore of Lago Villarrica, 86km southwest of Temuco, Villarrica (population 45,000) is a quieter and cheaper alternative to nearby Pucón, but not nearly as much fun. Founded in 1552, the town was repeatedly attacked by Mapuche until treaties were signed in 1882. The **museum**, next to the tourist office, displays Mapuche jewelry, musical instruments and rough-hewn wooden masks. Behind the tourist office, the **Feria Artesanal** has a selection of crafts. Many of the same tours organized in Pucón can be arranged here; try the agency **Politur**

CHILE

(☎ 045-414547; Henríquez 475) and the operators working out of **Touring** (V Letelier 712).

Information

Todo Lavado (☎ 045-414452; General Urrutia 699, Local 7) has efficient same-day laundry service. For medical care, go to **Hospital Villarrica** (☎ 411-169; San Martín 460). **Turcamb** (Pedro de Valdivia 1061) exchanges US cash. Banks with ATMs are plentiful, including Banco Santander and **Banco de Chile** (cnr Alderete & Pedro de Valdivia).

Stay in contact with the **post office** (Anfión Muñoz 315), **Telefónica** (Henríquez 544) and **Entel** (Henríquez 446). The municipal **Oficina de Turismo** (Pedro de Valdivia 1070; ☉ until 11pm in summer) has helpful staff and useful leaflets. The **Cámara de Turismo** (cnr General Urrutia & A Bello) lists *hospedajes*.

Sleeping

Prices rise considerably in summer and during the ski season.

Camping Dulac (☎ 045-412097; camping per site US$19) A convenient campground, 2km east of town.

Hostal Berta Romero (☎ 045-411276; Pedro de Valdivia 712; r US$9) A few rooms in a simple, elegant home. It's slightly noisy, but excellent value, including kitchen use. Breakfast is US$2.

Hospedaje Balboa (☎ 045-411098; San Martín 734; r per person without/with bath US$9/11) Cozy and clean rooms, breakfast is available and some kitchen use. There are loads of deer antlers on the living room walls. A good resource for fishing enthusiasts.

Hospedaje Maria Elena (☎ 045-411951; General Körner 380; r per person with breakfast US$8, cabins for 2-4 people US$15-33) There are just a few rooms in the main house, but the cabins are a great deal – quiet, clean and well lit.

El Arrayán (☎ 045-411235; General Körner 442; r per person with breakfast US$8-10, cabins for 4 people US$36-40) Rooms in the house are good value and includes possible kitchen use.

La Torre Suiza (☎ /fax 045-411213; info@torresuiza.com; Bilbao 969; camping US$5, dm US$8, dm without/with bath US$18/25) Well known among European travelers, has a fully equipped kitchen, laundry, bike rental, Internet access and lots of information.

Eating & Drinking

Café Bar 2001 (Henríquez 379) Has coffee, sandwiches and an impressive key ring collection.

Touring (V Letelier 712) Tiny, noisy and crowded with cheap lunches and sandwiches. Can arrange tours.

Hotel Fuentes (Vicente Reyes 665) Dishes up filling meals of *cazuela* and steak under a large-screen TV.

The Travellers (V Letelier 753) Ambitious menu of Chilean, Chinese, Thai and Mexican dishes (US$4–8), but can be disappointing. Best to enjoy the fun surroundings at night when the jazz club takes over.

Getting There & Away

Villarrica has a main **bus terminal** (Pedro de Valdivia 621), though a few companies have separate offices nearby. Long-distance fares are similar to those from Temuco (an hour away), which has more choices.

Buses Jac (Bilbao 610) goes to Pucón (US$0.60), Temuco (US$3), Lican Ray (US$0.60) and Coñaripe (US$1.25). **Buses Regional Villarrica** (Vicente Reyes 619) also has frequent buses to Pucón.

For Argentine destinations, Igi Llaima leaves at 6:45am Monday, Wednesday and Friday for San Martín de los Andes (US$23), Zapala and Neuquén (US$35, 16 hours) via Paso Mamuil Malal. Buses San Martín has a similar service, and both leave from the main bus terminal.

PUCÓN

Adventure travel and tourist navel of the Lake District, Pucón (population 21,000) has an outlandish casino and enough adrenaline activities to keep you pumped. It's the most convenient place in Chile to do it all: climb

---

SPLURGE!

Hostería de la Colina (☎ /fax 045-411503; Las Colinas 115; aldrich@entelchile.net; s/d US$70/84, ste US$84-98) is homegrown luxury at its finest, with a Japanese-style hot tub in the garden, classical music CDs, lots of books and games and charming expat owners. Even if spending the night is too costly, climb the hill to get here and *mmm* your way through lunch or dinner, where the changing menu may include gazpacho or Chinese carrot soup, lasagna or pot roast, just to name a few. The price is more than reasonable, and you'll want to save room for their famous handmade, hand-cranked ice cream.

that active volcano, raft or kayak a river, soak in hot springs (lots of 'em), discuss the plight of the environment, trek in native forest, eat well and party like you're in Santiago again. That said, it is touristy, and high season can be a downright drag with snooty staff and off-the-charts prices.

Orientation

Pucón is 25km from Villarrica at the east end of Lago Villarrica. It's a compact town, easy to get around. The lake beaches are west and north. O'Higgins, the main strip, runs southeast out of town and becomes the international highway. The Buses Jac terminal is downtown. Tur Bus is just on the outskirts, along O'Higgins – you can walk there from downtown.

Information

INTERNET ACCESS

Café Brinck (Ansorena 243) One of the better places (US$1 per hr). Most budget lodgings have service.

LAUNDRY

Laundry Express (O'Higgins 660, Local 2)
Lavandería Alemana (☎ 045-441106; Fresia 224)
Lavandería Esperanza (☎ 045-441379; Colo Colo 475)

MEDICAL SERVICES

Hospital San Francisco (☎ 045-441177; Uruguay 325)

MONEY

Exchange rates are better in Temuco. *Casas de cambio* include:
Supermercado Eltit (O'Higgins 336) Will change US cash and has an ATM.
TravelSur (Fresia 285)
Turismo Christopher (O'Higgins 335)

POST & TELEPHONE

Entel (Ansorena 299)
Post office (Fresia 183)

TOURIST OFFICES

Conaf (☎ 045-443781; Lincoyán 336) Information on the nearby national parks.
Oficina de Turismo (☎ 045-293002; O'Higgins & Palguín; ☺ 8:30am-10pm daily summer, to 7pm in winter) Stacks of brochures and usually an English speaker on staff.
Sernatur (cnr Brasil & Caupolicán) Similar info, not as helpful.

Activities

Prices are similar, but quality of service can vary among the agencies providing activi-

ties. Climbing Volcán Villarrica is a full-day excursion, leaving at 7:30am (US$45–60). All equipment can be rented. Bring extra snacks. Note that trips may be delayed for days, cancelled due to bad weather, or required to turn back halfway up. Check cancellation policies carefully.

Rafting-trip durations include transport time. On offer are 2½-hour trips down the lower Río Trancura (US$10–15), or three-hour trips on the Class IV upper Trancura (US$25–35).

For mountain biking, places that rent bikes should have a map of how to get to Ojos de Caburgua. Check shocks and brakes before renting bikes.

Courses

For those who would like to get a handle on the local lingo, **Pucón Language & Cultural Center** (☎ 045-443315, 09-935-9417; Uruguay 306) is a good option. Or try Hostería ¡école!, La Tetera and Hospedaje La Casita (see p473 for details).

Tours

Outfitters include:
Aguanieve Travel Adventure (☎ 045-443690; O'Higgins 448-B) Small, but sound.
Aquaventura (☎ 045-444246; Palguín 336) Rafting and kayaking, also rappeling and canyoning, snowshoeing in winter; arranges trips to El Cañi.
Campo Antilco (☎ 09-7139758; www.antilco.com) Fifteen kilometers east of Pucón on Río Liucura; recommended horse treks in Liucura Valley.
Centro Ecuestre Huepil-Malal (☎ 09-6433204; www.huepil-malal.cl; km 27 on Cam Pucón-Huife) Reputable equestrian center with half-day to multiday treks in the *cordillera*, run by a charming couple.
Politur (☎ 045-441373; O'Higgins 635) Well established and straightforward.
Rancho de Caballos (☎ 045-441575) Palguín Alto; three-hour to six-day horse treks near Parque Nacional Villarrica.
Trawen Outdoor Center (☎ 045-442024; O'Higgins 311, Local 5) Fun youthful guides lead the gamut of activities, but their passion is kayaking.

Festivals & Events

Mid-January's **Jornadas Musicales de Pucón** is an annual music festival. The first week of February the town fills with the überathletes competing in the **Triatlón Internacional de Pucón** (Pucón International Triathlon).

CHILE

Sleeping

The following prices are for the high season unless otherwise indicated; prices drop about 20% the rest of the year. Rates are higher here than elsewhere; reservations are advisable. You may find cheap, unregistered family homestays on and around Lincoyán, Perú and Ecuador.

Camping Parque La Poza (☎ 045-441435; Av Costanera Roberto Geis 769; camping per person US$4) Car camping facility with a place to cook, storage lockers and hot water. Sites are flat with shade. It's mainly quiet, but with hum of nearby road.

About 18km east, off road to Lago Caburgua, three campgrounds charge US$9 per six-person site. Look for signs after

crossing Río Pucón. There are more campsites between Pucón and Villarrica.

The following all charge around US$8–10 per person for rooms with shared bath and kitchen use. Many places offer discounts with tour operators. Check out the operators before you sign up.

Hostal Donde Germán (☎ 045-442444; dondegerman@latinmail.com; 640 Brasil) A new backpacker favorite. This place has a living room with TV and fireplace, backyard garden for barbecues and chilling; young, friendly owners; free Internet access, book exchange and laundry. It also has rooms with private bath (around US$12 per person) and cabins. Staff are very helpful, and there's loads of information.

PUCÓN

0 ___ 500 m
0 ___ 0.3 mi

Hospedaje M@yra (☎ 045-442745; Palguín 695) Next to Buses Jac, with comfortable common areas, some cozy double rooms and congenial owners.

Hospedaje La Casita (☎ 045-441712; Palguín 555) Quaint place with Spanish classes, near Buses Jac; few single rooms.

Hospedaje Juan Torres (☎ 045-441248; Lincoyán 445) Quiet and friendly, with gorgeous flower gardens.

Hospedaje Lucía (☎ 045-441271; Lincoyán 565) Friendly and organizes fishing trips.

Hospedaje Irma (☎ 045-442226; Lincoyán 545) Gregarious owner in cute house with nice, but small common areas.

Residencial Graciela (☎ 045-441494; Roland Matus 521) With distracted staff and tidy rooms (no singles), many of which look out onto the central corridor. There's a restaurant on the premises.

Hostería ¡école! (☎ 045-441675; ecole@entelchile .net; Urrutia 592; dm US$4.50, shared r US$12.50, s/d with bath US$25/31, 4-person r US$38) This HI affiliate attracts gringos like bears to honey. A good place to meet others, and one of the few places with dorm lodging. Whimsical signs and artwork, eco-focused with loads of excursions. Good for solo travelers, but thin walls mean it's not great for couples.

La Tetera (☎ 045-441462; Urrutia 580; info@tetera.cl; r US$17-35) Just like afternoon tea: warm, cozy, tidy and a bit uptight. Rooms with shared or private bath. One double room with an attractive balcony. Breakfasts (your choice!) included. **Multilingual. Good for quiet couples.**

Hostal Gerónimo (☎ 045-443762; Alderete 665; s/d US$25/40) Reputable and worth checking out.

Eating

For quick bites, try **Tío Pablo** (Urrutia 215; US$2.50) for filling fries and *cazuela*, or **Rap Hamburger** (O'Higgins & Arauco; US$1.50), for cheeseburgers (open very late).

Coppa Kavana (Urrutia 407) and **El Rinconcito** (O'Higgins 660) have sandwiches and OK fixed-price lunches (US$2.50).

Trawen (O'Higgins 311; mains US$3-7) Hip adventure outfitter doubles as veg haven, with huge bowls of soup, overstuffed *empanadas*, fresh juices, wheat bread, and fixed-price meals. Scrumptious.

El Rincón de la Pasta (Fresia 284; pasta US$6-8.50) Best pasta in town: fresh, homemade with loads of sauces (even the veg options are good) and served with swift efficiency.

Buonatesta (Fresia 243; pizzas US$5-8) Crispy thin crusts and a long list of toppings. Ordering a half portion is quite acceptable.

Hostería ¡école! (Urrutia 592; mains US$4-7) Very sociable and popular, with a wide variety of hearty veg cuisine (a few fish dishes too). Service is a bit slow, but worth the wait.

Marmonhi (☎ 441-972; Ecuador 175; mains US$4-6) Regional cuisine, including *empanadas* and *humitas*. Large (but not super cheap) fixed-price lunches.

La Tetera (Urrutia 580) Best breakfasts, plus spaghetti lunches, raclette (US$33 for four people) and afternoon tea.

Arabian Café (Fresia 354; mains US$5-8) Service is a bit distracted, the lights too bright, but where else can you find baba ganoush?

Drinking

Pucón's nightlife has a big-city buzz and attitude to match.

Vagabundo (Fresia 135) Small, vibrant bar/café packed with a fun-loving sporty crew, serving mixed drinks and quiche.

Bar Del Pelao (O'Higgins & Arauco) The place to drink till drunk and dance till dawn.

Mama's & Tapas (O'Higgins 587) If you can push open the door, you'll find cool, black clad hipsters around the round bar. Unimpressive tapas and weekday happy hour until 10pm.

Entertainment

Hotel del Lago (Ansorena 23) Movie theater and glitzy casino inside a lux hotel.

Getting There & Away

LanChile (☎ 600-526-2000; Urrutia 102) has occasional summer flights to Santiago, but normally flies from Temuco. Bus transportation to/from Santiago (US$13 to US$27) is with **Tur Bus** (O'Higgins), which is east of town, **Buses Jac** (cnr Uruguay & Palguín), **Cóndor Bus** (Colo Colo 430) and **Buses Power** (Palguín 550), the cheapest (and least comfortable) option.

Tur Bus also goes to Puerto Montt daily (US$9, five hours). For Temuco, Tur Bus leaves every hour and Buses Jac every half-hour (US$3.50). For Valdivia, Jac has five daily buses (US$3.50, three hours). Buses Jac and **Minibuses Vipu Ray** (Palguín 550) have a continuous service to Villarrica and Curarrehue. Buses Jac also has a service to Caburgua, Paillaco and Parque Nacional Huerquehue. For San Martín de los Andes, Argentina, **Buses San Martín** (Tur Bus terminal) has six weekly departures (US$16, five hours) stopping in Junín.

Getting Around

Travel agencies rent cars and prices can be competitive, especially off-season. Daily rates range from US$46 for passenger cars to US$70 for 4WD pickups. Try **Sierra** (☎ 045-444210; O'Higgins 524A), which also rents bikes (US$10 per day), or **Hertz** (☎ 045-441664; cnr Alderete & Fresia). A taxi is a viable option to get to parks and hot springs. **Radio Taxi Araucaria Tour** (☎ 045-442323; Palguín & Uruguay) charges, for a maximum of four passengers round trip, US$12 to Ojos del Caburgua, US$26 to Termas Los Pozones (both with a two-hour wait).

AROUND PUCÓN
Río Liucura Valley

East of Pucón, the Camino Pucón–Huife accesses hot-spring spas of varying luxury. At the end of the road is the best and cheapest: **Termas Los Pozones** (km 36; day/night use US$5/6.50, 3hr max stay) with the six natural stone pools open 24 hours. Light some candles and soak under the stars. *Hospedajes* and agencies arrange transport, but gather a group together, rent a car and do the hot-spring hop in your own time. Also along this road is access to **Santuario El Cañl** (km 21; entrance without/with guide US$5/10), protecting some 400 hectares of ancient araucaria forest. It's the first private park in Chile with an emphasis on education and scientific research. Not much different from Huerquehue in looks, but coming here fills you up with the good feeling of doing something good for mother earth. There's a gorgeous lookout at the top of the very steep **hiking trail** (9km, approx three hours).

Ruta 119

Accessing the Argentine border at Mamuil Malal, this route provides some off-the-road delights.

Curarrehue is a quiet little town with Mapuche cultural influences. Camping is available at **Municipal Camping** (Cruce a Panqui). **Hospedaje La Mamy** (O'Higgins 973) offers lodging and breakfast in an old frontier style house. Before town, **Kila Leufu** (☎ 09-711-

8064; s/d US$10/23) provides a fun farmland alternative; learn to milk cows and enjoy a comfy night's sleep. Buses leave frequently to Curarrehue from Pucón (US$1.20) and Villarrica (US$2). There is also service to San Martín de los Andes from Curarrehue: come here first to save pesos on the bus ticket.

Only 5km northeast of Curarrehue, quiet and rustic **Recuerdo de Ancamil**, on the banks of Río Maichín, has eight natural pools, including one in a grotto. There's camping and a few cabins. Another 10km, **Termas de Panqui** (day use US$10, meals US$5-7.50, tepee/hotel r per person US$15/20) has serene baths and an emphasis on 'spiritual healing' – but some find such sentiments contrived. It gets pricey and transport can be difficult.

PARQUE NACIONAL HUERQUEHUE

A gem of the area, **Parque Nacional Huerquehue** (admission US$3.50) protects 12,500 hectares of rivers and waterfalls, alpine lakes and araucaria forests.

The trail **Los Lagos** (9km, three to four hours one way) switchbacks from 700m to 1300m through dense lenga forests to solid stands of araucaria surrounding a cluster of pristine lakes. At Laguna Huerquehue, the trail **Los Huerquenes** (two days) continues north then east to cross the park and access **Termas de San Sebastián** (Río Blanco; ☎ 045-341961), just east of the park boundary. From there a gravel road connects to the north end of Lago Caburgua and Cunco.

Conaf's Lago Tinquilco and Renahue **campgrounds** charge US$14 per site. **Refugio Tinquilco** (☎ 02-7777673 in Santiago; www.tinquilco.cl; bunks without/with sheets US$9/10.50, d without/with bath US$31/39), at the base of the Lago Verde trailhead, is a two-story cozy wooden dream house. Come in for a French-press coffee and you'll want to stay a couple of days. Meals are extra or you can cook your own.

Buses Jac has a regular service to/from Pucón in the morning and afternoon (US$2.50, one hour); reserve your seat beforehand. Otherwise join a tour or share a taxi.

PARQUE NACIONAL VILLARRICA

Established in 1940, Parque Nacional Villarrica protects 60,000 hectares of remarkable volcanic scenery and the dragons that made it that way: 2847m-high Villarrica,

2360m-high Quetrupillán and, along the Argentine border, a section of 3746m-high Lanín. (The rest of Lanín is protected in an equally impressive park in Argentina, from where it may be climbed.) Its enormity is broken into three sectors and has an array of trails for day trippers and traversers.

Rucapillán is directly south of Pucón along a well-maintained road and takes in the most popular hikes up and around Villarrica. The climb to the sulfur-smoky summit is physically, but not technically demanding, requiring equipment and either experience or a guide; usually with a group tour. However, Conaf will let you go it alone if you show you know what you're doing and have the proper equipment. (For more climb details, see p471.) The trail **Challupen Chinay** (23km, 12 hours) rounds the volcano's southern side crossing through a variety of scenery to end at the entrance to the **Quetrupillán** sector.

Centro de Esquí Villarrica (☎ 045-441001; Gran Hotel Pucón, Holzapfel 190) has five lifts leading to slopes of varying difficulty, all on the volcano's north face. Full-day lift tickets are US$23–27. There is no scheduled transport to Sector Rucapillán; the cost of a shared taxi is reasonable. Buses Regional Villarrica go to Sector Puesco.

LAGO CALAFQUÉN

During summer, visitors crowd this island-studded lake, especially at fashionable **Lican Ray** (30km south of Villarrica) and more down-to-earth **Coñaripe** (22km east of Lican Ray), which has black-sand beaches. Out of season, it's very tranquil. Lican Ray's **tourist office** (☎ 045-431201; Urritia 310) is directly on the plaza. Coñaripe's **Chumay Turismo Aventura** (☎ 045-317287; Las Tepas 201) rents bikes and has area information and tours. Coñaripe has good access to rustic hot springs and other sides of the park that tourists rarely tread.

Sleeping & Eating

In Coñaripe, campgrounds by the lake are small, cramped lots charging a negotiable US$13–17 per site. Try **Millaray** (☎ 045-317210) or **Rucahue** (☎ 045-317210).

Hospedaje Plaza (☎ 045-317227; Beck Ramberga 458; r per person with breakfast US$9) A simple and quaint option.

Hostal Chumay (☎ 045-317287; Las Tepas 201; r per person US$10, d with bath US$25) Behind the plaza,

this is a great deal, and has a restaurant serving delicious lunches (US$4).

Lodgings that are open year-round in Lican Ray include:

Hostal Hofmann (☎ 045-431109; Cam Coñaripe 100; r per person US$20) Very comfortable, personable with filling breakfasts.

Residencial Temuco (☎ 045-431130; Gabriela Mistral 515; r per person US$8) Basic, but some beds are a bit bumpy.

Neither town has many stand-out restaurants. But do be on the lookout for fresh-caught trout – a local specialty.

Getting There & Away

Buses Jac goes through both towns en route to Villarrica; both run along main street in towns. At 7:30am, a local Lican Ray bus goes to Panguipulli (US$2, two hours) via back roads, while Coñaripe has more departures. Bus services are very limited on Sunday and in the off-season.

LAGO PANGUIPULLI

If taking the Puerto Fuy ferry to Argentina you'll end up along this lake. At the northwest end of Lago Panguipulli the town of **Panguipulli** is a main service center, with a surprising amount of restaurants and a view of Volcán Choshuenco (2415m). The municipal **tourist office** (☎ 063-312202; east side of Plaza Prat) is helpful and has area information. At the lake's east end is the cute hamlet **Choshuenco**, a study in serenity. Further south is **Enco**, the access point for hikes on Mocho Choshuenco, the most accessible of the volcano's two tops.

Sleeping & Eating

Camping El Bosque (☎ 063-311489; r per person US$4.50) In Panguipulli, 200m north of the plaza. Has 15 tent sites.

Hospedaje Berrocal (☎ 063-311812; Portales 72; r per person US$8-10) Simple, personable, with home-cooked meals.

Hotel Central (☎ 09-319-5640; Pedro de Valdivia 115; r per person US$11) Friendly, with airy rooms and clean baths (even bathtubs).

Camping Choshuenco (☎ 063-318220; per tent US$5; ☺ Dec-Mar) In Choshuenco, with beachfront sites.

Hotel Rucapillán (☎ 063-318220; San Martín 85; d without/with bath US$20/23) Heated rooms and a good restaurant.

CHILE

Girasol (Martínez de Rozas 664) and **Gardylafquen** (☎ 063-311887; Martínez de Rozas 722) are the best places for meals.

Getting There & Away

Panguipulli's main **bus terminal** (Gabriela Mistral 100), at the corner of Diego Portales, has regular departures, except Sunday, to Coñaripe and Lican Ray; Choshuenco, Neltume and Puerto Fuy; and to Valdivia and Temuco. Buses from Panguipulli to Puerto Fuy (two hours) pass through Choshuenco and return to Panguipulli early the following morning.

LAGO PIREHUEICO

A fabulously scenic way to get to San Martín de los Andes, Argentina, is from Lago Pirehueico. The **ferry Hua-Hum** (☎ 063-311-334 in Panguipulli) transports passengers and vehicles between Puerto Fuy and Puerto Pirehueico (1½ hours), from where land transportation departs, crossing the border at Paso Hua Hum and continuing onto San Martín. The ferry leaves twice a day in each direction from January to mid-March, and once daily the rest of the year. Automobiles cost US$16; jeeps and pickups US$25; pedestrians US$1; and bicycles US$3. Basic lodging is available at both ends of the lake.

VALDIVIA

A lively university scene, a strong emphasis on the arts, plenty of history and surrounded by rivers and natural beauty – Valdivia just may be Chile's most attractive and enjoyable city. Valdivia (population 137,000) is also known as the 'City of Rivers'.

Pedro de Valdivia founded the town in 1552, but the Mapuche ransacked it in the 1599 revolt. Dutch privateers then occupied it, but were also driven out by the Mapuche. In 1645 the Peruvian viceroy ordered a wall to be built around the town and forts built on strategic points of Corral, Niebla and Mancera. In 1820, Chilean patriots launched a surprise attack on Spanish loyalists from Corral. Large German immigration in the 1850s and '60s influenced the town's architecture and cuisine. The 1960 earthquake obliterated much of the town, but luckily many classic mansions and forts remain.

Orientation

Valdivia is 160km southwest of Temuco and 45km west of the Panamericana. From the bus terminal, any bus marked 'Plaza' will take you to Plaza de la República. Many lodgings are within walking distance.

Information

The best place for Internet access and long-distance phone rates is **Café Phonet** (Libertad 127). Laundry services are available at **Lavandería Manantial** (Henríquez 809) and **Supermatic Lavandería** (Henríquez 316). **Hospital Regional** (☎ 063-214066; Bueras 1003) is south of town, near Aníbal Pinto. To change money, try **Cambio Arauco** (Arauco 331, Local 24), open on Saturday, or **Cambio La Reconquista** (Carampangue 329). Downtown ATMs are abundant. There is a **post office** (O'Higgins 575) and call centers include **Telefónica** (Valdés & Picarte) and **Entel** (Pérez Rosales 601). **Sernatur** (☎ 063-213596; Prat 155; ☺ 8:30am-5:30pm Mon-Fri Mar-Dec, daily Jan & Feb) is on the riverfront. There is also a tourist kiosk at the bus terminal.

Sights & Activities

Head to the colorful **Feria Fluvial**, a riverside fish and vegetable market, where sea lions will come up close for handouts. In a riverfront mansion on Isla Teja, the **Museo Histórico y Arqueológico** (Los Laureles 47; admission US$1.25; ☺ 9am-1pm & 2:30-6pm Dec-Mar, 10am-1pm & 2-6pm Apr-Nov) has a large, well-labeled collection from pre-Columbian times to the present, with displays of Mapuche Indian artifacts and household items from early German settlements. It's across the Río Valdivia, turn left at the first intersection and walk about 200m; the entrance is on the left (east) side. Nearby is **Museo de Arte Contemporáneo** (☎ 063-221968; ☺ 10am-1pm & 3-7pm Tue-Sun), sitting atop the foundations of the former Cervecería Anwandter, the one-time brewery that tumbled during the 1960 earthquake. Also on Isla Teja, shady **Parque Saval** has a riverside beach and a pleasant trail that leads to a lily-covered lagoon.

At Corral, Niebla and Isla Mancera, at the mouth of the Río Valdivia, is a series of 17th-century Spanish forts. The largest and most intact of these is the 1645 **Fuerte de Corral**. Boat cruises (US$22-26; 6½ hr) leave from the **Puerto Fluvial**. Save money by taking **colectivos** (cnr Chacabuco & Yungay; US$0.75)

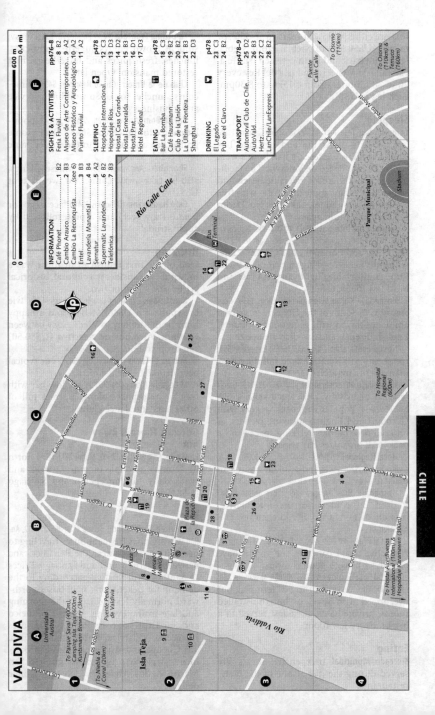

VALDIVIA

CHILE

that are either yellow or marked 'T-350', or *micros* (US$0.50), to Niebla. From Niebla, ferries jot back and forth between Isla Teja, Corral, Isla Mencera and Isla del Rey every 20 to 30 minutes, from 8:15am to 8:30pm; each leg is US$1.

Sleeping

Camping Isla Teja (☎ 063-225855; Los Cipreses 1125; campsites US$10-15) At the end of Calle Los Robles and Los Cipreses, a half hour's walk across Puente Pedro de Valdivia. The facilities are good, there's a riverside beach and sites in a pleasant apple orchard – with free apples in late summer. Take Bus No 9 from the Mercado Municipal.

AiresBuenos International (☎ 063-206304; General Lagos 1036; r per person US$8.50, s/d with bath US$18/22; **P**) Great addition to the backpacker scene, with Internet access; luggage storage; travel info; comfortable, light, airy rooms; and breakfast that satisfies.

Hospedaje Karamawen (General Lagos 1334; r per person US$10) South of the city center, artistic ambience mixed with generous hospitality. English, French and Swedish are spoken.

Hostal Esmeralda (☎ 063-215659; Esmeralda 651; r per person US$11) Rambling old building near many of the nightclubs.

Hospedaje Internacional (☎ 063-212015; García Reyes 660; s/d US$10/19, s with bath US$20-25, d with bath US$26-30) Popular with backpackers, with German- and English-speaking owners. A bit cramped, but has relaxing spaces and a backyard; organizes day trips.

Hotel Regional (☎ 063-216027; Picarte 1005; s US$6, d with bath US$20) A friendly, plain and clean place to stay.

Hospedaje Ríos (Arauco 869; r per person US$8) Praised by readers for its informative, friendly owners who offer kitchen use and breakfast.

Hostal Prat (☎ 063-222020; Prat 575; s/d US$20/27) Attractive wood paneling and rooms have private baths with good showers.

Hostal Casa Grande (☎ 063-202035; Anwandter 880; s/d US$17/26) Convenient to bus terminal, but overpriced with spacious but thin-walled rooms, private baths. Breakfast served in a bright, river-view room.

Eating

Mercado Municipal Inexpensive meals are served during the day at one of the many restaurants.

La Última Frontera (Pérez Rosales 787) An artsy, student crowd enjoys superb sandwiches, lunches, fresh juices and huge beers, in a restored mansion. Open late.

Club de la Unión (Camilo Henríquez 540) Three-course lunches for US$6 with linen service and a business crowd.

Bar La Bomba (Caupolicán 594) A good, popular choice for lunch (US$5–6). Order some grilled fish and tune in to the soccer game on the TV.

Shanghai (Andwandter 898) Chinese fixings, also for take-away. Dinner for two starts at US$10.

Café Hausmann (O'Higgins 394) Place to go for *crudos* (raw beef) and a pint, followed by apple strudel.

Drinking

One of the first industries in town was a brewpub, so consider it a cultural, historical act to sink a pint or two.

Kunstmann Brewery (Isla Teja) Large US-style brewpub with US$6 pitchers and a happy hour from Monday to Wednesday between 7–10pm. Any bus or *colectivo* (US$0.50) can drop you off.

Pub en el Clavo (Av Alemania 290) Your typical beer-drinkin' establishment.

El Legado (Esmeralda 657) A mellow bar with trendy atmosphere along a street full of other bars and dance clubs.

Getting There & Away

AIR

LanChile (☎ 600-526-2000; Maipú 271) flies north to Temuco a couple of times a week and twice daily to Concepción and Santiago (US$150).

BUS

Valdivia's **Terminal de Buses** (☎ 063-212212; Anfión Muñoz 360) has frequent buses traveling to destinations on or near the Panamericana between Puerto Montt and Santiago. Prices to Santiago will fluctuate according to the demand for tickets; long-haul buses northward normally leave early in the morning and late in the evening. Buses Pirehueico and Sur Express access Panguipulli; Buses Jac access Villarrica, Pucón and Temuco. Tas Choapa and Andesmar travel to Bariloche, Argentina. Igi Llaima goes to San Martín de los Andes and Neuquén once daily.

Destination	Duration in Hours	Cost
Ancud	5½	US$9
Bariloche (Arg)	5	US$16.50
Neuquén (Arg)	14	US$25
Osorno	1½	US$2
Panguipulli	2½	US$1.75
Pucón	3	US$3.50
Puerto Montt	3½	US$4.50
San Martín de los Andes (Arg)	8	US$17.50
Santiago	10	US$13-36
Temuco	3	US$3.50

Getting Around

Aeropuerto Pichoy is located north of the city via the Puente Calle Calle. **Transfer** (☎ 063-204111) provides a minibus service (US$3.50).

Both **Autovald** (☎ 063-212786; Henríquez 610) and **Hertz** (☎ 063-218317; Picarte 640) rent vehicles. **Automóvil Club de Chile** (☎ 063-212376; Garcia Reyes 440) is also helpful.

OSORNO

The town of Osorno (population 142,000), 910km south of Santiago, is an access point to Parque Nacional Puyehue and a convenient base for bus trips to Argentina. There's not much of note, but if spending the day here check out the **Museo Histórico Municipal** (Matta 809; admission free), a good summary of Mapuche culture and German colonization. Also worth a look is the **Historic District** between Plaza de Armas and the 1912 train station, which may lose ground to new construction.

Orientation & Information

The main bus station is in the eastern section of downtown, five blocks from Plaza de Armas. Many budget lodgings are one block north and one block west. Laundry facilities are available at **Lavandería Limpec** (Prat 678). Change money at **Turismo Frontera** (☎ 064-236394; Ramírez 959, Local 12) or **Cambiotur** (☎ 064-234846; Juan Mackenna 1004, Local B). There is a **post office** (O'Higgins 645) and an **Entel** (Ramírez 1107). **Hospital Base** (☎ 064-235572; Av Bühler) is on the southward extension of Arturo Prat. **Sernatur** (☎ 064-237575; O'Higgins 667) is on the west side of the Plaza de Armas. There's a **tourist booth** (☺ until 11pm) at the bus station, and **Conaf** (☎ 064-234393; Martínez de Rosas) has details on Parque Nacional Puyehue.

Sleeping

Camping Olegario Mohr (☎ 064-204860; camping per site US$8.50) On Río Damas' south bank, east of town, but the gate closes between midnight and 8am. *Colectivos* on Av Buschmann can drop you within a few minutes' walk.

Rates at the following places include breakfast.

Hospedaje Webar (☎ 064-319034; Los Carreras 872; r per person US$8.50) The most charming of the bunch is in an old house with fading wallpaper and lots of artistic expression.

Residencial Ortega (☎ 064-232592; Colón 602; r per person US$9; P) A backpackers' favorite and gets a bit crowded, but it has a large eating area, and even the smallest of rooms has cable TV. Limited kitchen use.

Residencial Alemana (☎ 064-250588; Colón 666; r per person US$11; P) Comfortable and quiet rooms with either shared or private bath, and a large breakfast.

Hotel Villa Eduviges (☎ /fax 064-235023; Eduviges 856; s/d US$23/36; P) In a residential area, has spacious rooms with large beds, thin walls and lots of plants.

Eating & Drinking

Mercado Municipal (cnr Prat & Errázuriz) Has an array of *cocinerías* serving good and inexpensive seafood.

Bell'Italia (Mackenna 1027; US$6-9) Part of an Italian culinary arts school housed in an attractive colonial mansion; has a tantalizing variety of pastas and sauces, plus daily lunch specials. Very good deal.

Club de Artesanos (Mackenna 634) In an old union house; serves locally brewed Märzen and Chilean specialties. The bar, perhaps the most interesting place in town, stays open until 11pm.

Salón de Té Rhenania (Ramírez 977; ☺ Mon-Sat) Enormous empanadas. The sandwiches are equally good.

Café Migas (Freire 584) Cozy café with US$3 lunches and an English-speaking owner who likes helping travelers.

Pizzería Donnatelo (Cochrane & Ram'rez; ☺ dinner only) Locals claim this is the best pizza in town.

Supermercado Las Brisas (Mackenna & Arturo Prat) Has a slightly highbrow café, Kaffeestube, inside, which is good for a quick coffee and something sweet. There's another **supermarket** (Colón & Errázuriz) a block from the bus terminal.

Shopping
Asociación Futa Huillimapu (Mackenna & Portales) Sells quality woven and wooden goods, supporting an association of indigenous women.

Climent (Angulo 603) Specializes in camping supplies.

Getting There & Away
Long-distance and Argentine-bound buses use the **main bus terminal** (Av Errázuriz 1400 near Angulo). Most services going north on the Panamericana start in Puerto Montt, departing about every hour, with mainly overnight services to Santiago. Services to Argentina daily and to Coyhaique, Punta Arenas and Puerto Natales once or twice a week, via Ruta 215 and Paso Cardenal Antonio Samoré.

Sample travel times and fares follow:

Destination	Duration in Hours	Cost
Chile		
Coyhaique	22	US$30
Puerto Montt	1½	US$2
Punta Arenas	28	US$30–41
Santiago	12	US$21–40
Temuco	3	US$5
Argentina		
Bariloche	5	US$13
Zapala-Neuquén	17	US$28

Local and regional services leave from **Terminal Mercado Municipal** (cnr Errázuriz & Prat), two blocks west of the main terminal, in the Mercado Municipal, destinations include: Entre Lagos (US$1, front of market), Termas Puyehue/Aguas Calientes (US$1.50, back of market), Anticura (US$3, 1½ hours), Pajaritos (customs; US$3). *Colectivos* go to Entre Lagos all year, and to Aguas Calientes in summer only. To get to coastal towns, cross the Río Rahue to the bus stops at Feria Libre Ráhue or catch a *colectivo* on the corner of República and Victoria.

Getting Around
Automóvil Club de Chile (☎ 064-255555; Bulnes 463) rents jeeps and cars. **ViaCar** (☎ 064-252000; Bilbao 1011) also has decent rates.

AROUND OSORNO
Along the coast, **Maicolpué** is a great escape from the regular gringo grid. **Campsites** (per tent US$1.50) are at the southern section of town. **Cabañas Rosenburg** (per person US$6.50) has gnome-like, wood-shingled A-frames with views of the crashing surf. Trails south access pristine, almost deserted beaches.

On the southwest shore of Lago Puyehue, **Entre Lagos**, 50km from Osorno, is a restful alternative to Osorno. **Camping No Me Olvides** (☎ 064-371633; camping per person US$5, cabins per person US$13-17), 6km east of town on Ruta 215, is a topnotch campground divided by pruned hedges. Lodgers can also buy hearty, economic lunches here.

Hospedaje Panorama (☎ 064-371398; Gral Lagos 687; r per person US$7.50) is brimming with fruit trees, with friendly German shepherds. Beds have wool duvets, and the breakfasts may include fresh pie, enjoyed on the back porch. **Hostal Millaray** (☎ 064-371251; r per person US$10) is a quieter choice run by retired teachers.

Another 16km east is **Termas de Puyehue**, a hoity-toity resort with hot-springs; day use of pools (rest those weary trekkin' muscles) costs US$7.50–12.50. From here, Ruta 215 forks; the north fork goes to Anticura and the Argentine border, while its south fork goes to Parque Nacional Puyehue.

PARQUE NACIONAL PUYEHUE
Volcán Puyehue, 2240m tall, blew its top the day after the earthquake in 1960, turning a large chunk of dense humid evergreen forest into a stark landscape of sand dunes and lava rivers. Today, **Parque Nacional Puyehue** (admission US$1.20) protects 107,000 hectares of this contrasting environment. **Aguas Calientes** (day use US$2-4.50) is an unpretentious hot-springs resort. Conaf has an information center and collects admission here. **Camping Chanleufú** (4-person sites US$20) doesn't have hot showers, but fees entitle you to use the outside hot-springs pool and facilities.

Antillanca (lift tickets US$24, rentals US$18-23), at the foot of 1990m Volcán Casablanca, is a small ski resort 18km beyond Aguas Calientes. A trail leads to a crater outlook with views of the mountain range.

Anticura is 17km northwest of the Aguas Calientes turn-off. There are good short walks from here to a lookout and waterfall. **Camping Catrué** (2-person sites US$6.50) has woodsy, level sites with tree-trunk picnic tables, limited electricity and decent baths.

Two kilometers west of Anticura, **El Caulle** (☎ 09-641-2000; admission US$11) is the entrance for the popular trek across the desolate plateau of Volcán Puyehue. While officially within park boundaries, the access land is privately owned. The admission fee is steep, but is used to maintain the free *refugio* and trails. Trekkers can stash extra gear at entrance. The **Puyehue Traverse** (three to four days) starts with a steep hike through lenga forest and loose volcanic soil to a campsite and *refugio* with a woodstove and water. From there, trudge to the top of the crater or continue four hours to Los Baños, a series of riverbank thermal baths (not obvious – test the waters to find them) with wild camping. The trail continues to an impressive geyser field. The trail does continue north to Riñinahue, at the south end of Lago Ranco, although these trails are not maintained and may be difficult to follow. (Hikers report being charged to cross private land leaving the park as well.) Another hike, **Ruta de los Americanos** (six to eight days), branches off the Los Baños trail and loops around the eastern side of the volcano. Wild camping is possible.

Buses and *colectivos* from Osorno's **Mercado Municipal** (cnr Errázuriz & Prat) go to Termas de Puyehue, Aguas Calientes, Anticura and Chilean customs and immigration at Pajaritos. Any bus heading to Anticura can drop off trekkers at El Caulle. In winter there may be a shuttle to the ski lodge at Antillanca; contact the **Club Andino Osorno** (☎ 064-232297; O'Higgins 1073, Osorno). Otherwise, you'll need to arrange your own transportation.

PUERTO OCTAY

Bucolic Puerto Octay linked Puerto Montt and Osorno via Lago Llanquihue in the early days of German settlement. Nowadays travelers find it a serene alternative to the lake's more touristed towns. It has an impressive assortment of original German buildings and the **Museo El Colono** (Independencia 591) includes displays on German colonization, relevant and well-labeled historical photographs and local architecture. The **tourist office** (Esperanza 555) is on the east side of the Plaza de Armas. Ask for the map of the town's historic houses. February is the month for the **Festival de Canción Salmon de Oro**.

Camping Centinela (Península Centinela; 7-person sites US$13) will discount for just two people.

Sites are right near the lakeshore with lots of shade. Amiable and fun **Zapato Amarillo** (☎ /fax 064-391575; dm/doubles US$9/21, lunch or dinner US$5), on a small farm about 2km north of town, is reason enough to come here. The hospitable Chilean-Swiss owners provide a separate kitchen for lodgers, farm-fresh veg, excursions and bike rental. **Hospedaje Barrientos** (☎ 064-391381; Independencia 488; r per person US$8), in a rickety old house on a hill, has mattresses that might be as old as the house, and the matrons seem equally tired. Good for ghost stories. **Hostería La Baja** (☎ 09-444-6884; Península Centinela; s without/with bath US$9/10), a few kilometers south of town, has views over town. Rates include breakfast. **Baviera** (Germán Wulf 582) has special lunches for US$2.50, with veg alternatives. **Tante Valy** (km 3, Frutillar Hwy) has cheaper *onces* than you get in Frutillar. One order is easily shared by two.

Puerto Octay's **bus terminal** (cnr Balmaceda & Esperanza) has regular services to Osorno, Frutillar, Puerto Varas, Puerto Montt and Cruce de Rupanco, from where Osorno–Las Cascadas buses can be picked up.

LAS CASCADAS

On the eastern shore of Lago Llanquihue, Las Cascadas is a tiny settlement fronting a black-sand beach. The supermarket has maps with hikes in the area. The road south to Ensenada is a popular bicycle route, but it's very exposed and cyclists are vulnerable to the irritating, biting insects *tábanos*.

Hostería Irma (☎ 064-396227; r per person US$10), 1km south of town on the road to Ensenada, is a slanting ranch-style home; rates include breakfast. Opposite the *hostería*, alongside the lake, is a free campsite with few facilities. At **Camping Las Cañitas** (☎ 09-643-4295; 6-person sites US$17.50), 5km down the Ensenada road, sites are clustered together – not private. **Donde 'Don Pancho'** (Vicente Pérez Rosales 210; per person US$7) has a couple of rooms with shared bath, and a diner with US$2.50 breakfasts and US$1.50 burgers.

Buses Cordillera runs direct to/from Osorno three times per day. From Puerto Octay, there is a 5pm bus each weekday, leaving Las Cascadas at 7:30am.

FRUTILLAR

When people speak of Frutillar they refer to lakeside Frutillar Bajo (the popinjay of Lago

CHILE

Llanquihue), on a beautiful crescent beach with well-restored German architecture, *Kuchen* cafés and where everything is just a bit too neat. Views of Volcán Osorno are fabulous here. An enormous concert hall is being built at the beach. From late January to early February, Frutillar hosts the **Semana Musical de Frutillar**, which draws jazz and classical musicians. The **tourist kiosk** (Av Philippi; 🕓 10am-9pm Dec-Mar) is just south of the municipality, between San Martín and O'Higgins. Around the municipality, you can find the regular banks, post office and call centers. Frutillar Alto is no-frills working town.

Museo Colonial Alemán (Pérez Rosales & Prat; admission US$1.50; 🕓 Tue-Sun) features nearly perfect reconstructions of a water-powered mill, a smithy and a mansion set among manicured gardens. **Centro Forestal Edmundo Winkler** (Calle Caupolicán), on the spit of land north of town, has an 800m loop trail along which species of trees are identified.

Hotel Posada Campesina (☎ 064-339123; 6-person sites US$17), on a peninsula at the south end of the beach, has 50 campsites with dividing bushes, hot showers, electricity and firepits. **Hospedaje Kaiserseehaus** (☎ 064-421387; Philippi 1333; per person without/with bath US$7.50/10) has loads of character, comfortable upstairs rooms and generous breakfasts too. **Hostería Winkler** (☎ 064-421388; Philippi 1155; dm US$10) opens an annex to HI card holders. Some roadside stands sell snacks, but restaurant meals are expensive. Best value is **Casino de Bomberos** (Philippi 1065). **Hotel Klein Salzburg** (Philippi 663) is a smart choice if you're after *onces*.

Buses to Puerto Varas, Puerto Montt and Osorno leave from Frutillar Alto. Inexpensive *colectivos* shuttle the short distance of Av Carlos Richter between Frutillar Alto and Frutillar Bajo.

PUERTO VARAS

Adventure seekers, fly-fishing fanatics and Bariloche-bound casino goers mix in Puerto Varas (population 33,000), on the southern tip of Lago Llanquihue. With well-preserved Middle European architecture, a friendly community, gorgeous views of Volcán Osorno and easy access to Parque Nacional Vicente Pérez Rosales, Puerto Varas is a top destination – and a quick 20km from Puerto Montt.

Orientation & Information

From the Puerto Montt airport, taxis cost US$18, while a door-to-door shuttle costs US$13. *Micros* shuttle back and forth from Puerto Montt's bus terminal (US$0.75). **Crell** (San Francisco 430; US$1 per hr) has Internet access with fast connections. Laundry service is available at **Lavandería Schnell** (San Pedro 26-A). **Clínica Alemana** (☎ 065-232336; Hospital 810, Cerro Calvario) is near Del Salvador's southwest exit from town. There's also the **Centro Médico Puerto Varas** (☎ 065-232792; Walker Martínez 576). **Afex Exchange** (Del Salvador 257, Local 8), in Galería Real, changes cash and traveler's checks. There are numerous ATMs downtown. There's a **post office** (cnr San Pedro & San José) and an **Entel** (San José 413). **Casa de Turista** (☎ 065-237956; Av Costanera), on the pier, is a private organization with good information about their members; it's the best place to pick up details of the area. **Informatur** (cnr San José & Santa Rosa) has lists of *hospedajes* around town. The municipality's **tourist office** (☎ 065-232437; San Francisco 431) has brochures and free maps.

Sights & Activities

The colorful 1915 **Iglesia del Sagrado Corazón** (cnr San Francisco & Verbo Divino) is based on the Marienkirche of Black Forest, Germany.

Nearby lakes, mountains and rivers provide enough for a week's worth of activities. Climbing Volcán Osorno (2652m) costs around US$150 per person in groups of three, or US$200 for solo climbers, including all equipment. The trip lasts 12 hours, leaving at 5am. If weather turns and the trip is aborted, agencies refund 50%. Río Petrohué churns up Class III and IV rapids. Rafting trips range from US$30 (5½ hours, two hours on the river) to US$70, including canyoning. All-day kayaking on Lago Todos Los Santos is about US$50. This is prime fly-fishing territory, but knowing where will cost you – up to US$150 a day, all inclusive.

Tours

Local activity outfitters in town include:
Adriazola Turismo Expediciones (☎ 065-233477; Santa Rosa 340) Fly-fishing.
Aqua Motion (☎ 065-232747; San Francisco 328) All activities on offer; more high-end but has rafting and climbing trips.
Campo Aventura (☎ 065-232910; info@campoaventura.com; San Bernardo 318) Quality horse-riding trips from Cochamó.

Ko'Kayak (☎ 065-346433; www.paddlechile.com; San José 320) Sea and river kayaking and rafting trips (1-3 days), with the option to connect with horse treks; French is spoken.

Sleeping

Several historic houses serve as cute B&Bs, including the 1941–42 **Casa Schwerter** (Del Carmen 873), the 1930 **Casa Hitschfeld** (Arturo Prat 107)

and the 1930 **Casa Wetzel** (O'Higgins 608). **Museo Antonio Felmer** (Fundo Bellavista, Nueva Braunau; ☾ Tue-Sun), 8km west of town, exhibits a collection of colonial knickknacks, including cuckoo clocks and gramophones.

Cabañas Camping Trauco (☎ 065-233325; Imperial 433; campsites US$7; [P]) Offers pleasant but cramped garden camping.

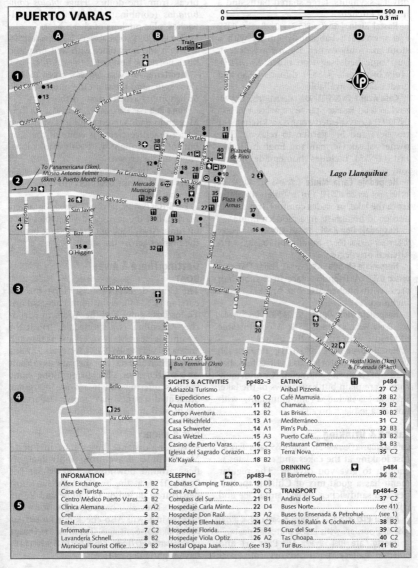

PUERTO VARAS

0 — 500 m
0 — 0.3 mi

Lago Llanquihue

To Panamericana (3km),
Museo Antonio Felmer
(8km) & Puerto Montt (20km)

To Cruz del Sur
Bus Terminal (2km)

To Hostal Klein (1km)
& Ensenada (45km)

SIGHTS & ACTIVITIES	pp482–3
Adriazola Turismo	
Expediciones	10 C2
Aqua Motion	11 B2
Campo Aventura	12 B2
Casa Hitschfeld	13 A1
Casa Schwerter	14 A1
Casa Wetzel	15 A3
Casino de Puerto Varas	16 C2
Iglesia del Sagrado Corazón	17 B3
Ko'Kayak	18 B2

SLEEPING	pp483–4
Cabañas Camping Trauco	19 D3
Casa Azul	20 C3
Compass del Sur	21 B1
Hospedaje Carla Minte	22 D4
Hospedaje Don Raúl	23 A2
Hospedaje Ellenhaus	24 C2
Hospedaje Florida	25 B4
Hospedaje Viola Optiz	26 A2
Hostal Opapa Juan	(see 13)

EATING	p484
Aníbal Pizzeria	27 C2
Café Mamusia	28 B2
Chamaca	29 B2
Las Brisas	30 B2
Mediterráneo	31 C2
Pim's Pub	32 B3
Puerto Café	33 B2
Restaurant Carmen	34 B3
Terra Nova	35 C2

DRINKING	p484
El Barómetro	36 B2

TRANSPORT	pp484–5
Andina del Sud	37 C2
Buses Norte	(see 41)
Buses to Ensenada & Petrohué	(see 1)
Buses to Ralún & Cochamó	38 B2
Cruz del Sur	39 C2
Tas Choapa	40 C2
Tur Bus	41 B2

INFORMATION	
Afex Exchange	1 B2
Casa de Turista	2 C2
Centro Médico Puerto Varas	3 B2
Clínica Alemana	4 A2
Crell	5 B2
Entel	6 B2
Informatur	7 C2
Lavandería Schnell	8 B2
Municipal Tourist Office	9 B2

CHILE

Compass del Sur (☎ 065-232044; Klenner 467; r per person US$14; 🖵) Gets warm praise from well-rested lodgers. It has Scandinavian touches, a garden, kitchen for lodgers and comfortable beds; breakfast is US$4 more.

Hospedaje Ellenhaus (☎ 065-233577; Walker Martínez 239; r per person with breakfast US$9) Small but very clean upstairs rooms with fluffy duvets, skylights, large shared baths and a limited kitchen.

Hostal Klein (☎ /fax 065-233109; Ramírez 1255; r per person US$11) Fabulously quirky with a stout matronly owner. Rooms are decent, but some beds sag (too much *Kuchen*?). Huge breakfasts (US$3), dinners US$6 and great cake are available.

Casa Azul (☎ 065-232904; casaazul@telsur.cl; Manzanal 66 & Del Rosario; r per person without/with bath US$10/13) Cozy heated rooms, a kitchen for travelers and big garden to relax in. The owners speak German and English. Breakfast (US$3) includes homemade muesli and yogurt.

Hospedaje Carla Minte (☎ 065-232880; Maipó 1010; r per person US$14) On a quiet street up from the lake, provides comfort, tranquility and good breakfasts in a modern home.

Hospedaje Don Raúl (☎ 065-310897; Del Salvador 928; r per person US$7) Small and basic, with kitchen privileges.

Hospedaje Florida (☎ 233-387; Florida 1361; r per person US$7) A friendly place in a suburban area, with kitchen use but breakfast isn't included.

Hospedaje Viola Optiz (☎ 232-890; Del Salvador 408, Depto 302; r per person US$10) A comfortable old house with an attentive owner.

Hostal Opapa Juan (☎ 232-234; Arturo Prat 107; s/d US$23/33) In historic Casa Hitschfeld, has loads of historic character. Comfortable rooms are plain but have views of the lake. Breakfast is included (and abundant), with homemade black bread.

Eating & Drinking

Café Mamusia (San José 316; lunch US$5, cakes US$1.50) Just looking at the cakes and chocolates is enough to give you cavities. The regular menu has a good mix of Chilean specialties and sandwiches, served amid lace and frills.

Aníbal Pizzeria (Del Salvador & Santa Rosa; pizzas US$3-6) Popular, with large plates of pasta.

Puerto Café (Del Salvador 328) Part art and cultural gallery, part Internet café, part sandwich shop – makes for an inviting place to relax.

Terra Nova (Santa Rosa 580; crepes US$2.50-4) Tiny and with a French touch, Terra Nova serves savory and sweet crepes and imaginative cocktails.

Restaurant Carmen (San Francisco 669; sandwiches US$2-3) Typical Chilean diner feel offers a break from the doilies. Huge *platos combinados* (combination plates) and sandwiches, plus pitchers of cheap beer.

Chamaca (Del Salvador, above the market; mains US$4-8) Bright and busy place with well-prepared huge portions; best bet is the *caldillo*.

Mediterráneo (Santa Rosa 068; dinners US$7-15) *Pisco sours* and tapas on the outdoor deck, or heaping, flavorful pasta dishes.

Pim's Pub (San Francisco 712; mains US$5-10) Tex-Mex and salads served amid lots of stylized bric-a-brac. Ice cream is some of the best. Lots of fun at night, with stiff drinks loosening up the crowd.

El Barómetro (San Pedro 418) Swap tales of ascents and descents over beers in this always popular bar.

Las Brisas (San Bernardo & Del Salvador) Big supermarket, but the fruits and vegetables are a bit limp. Also check out the produce behind the market across the street.

Getting There & Away
BOAT

The Cruce de Lagos touristy boat–bus excursion (US$140, eight hours) across Lago Todos Los Santos and the Andes to Bariloche, Argentina, is a spectacular trip if the weather is clear. Make reservations through **Andina del Sud** (☎ 065-232511; Del Salvador 72, Puerto Varas), which also has a branch at **Puerto Montt** ☎ 065-257797; A Varas 437). Bring along some food as offerings on board are marginal. Student discounts may apply. Departures are limited in the off-season.

BUS & MICRO

Most long-distance buses start in Puerto Montt. Buses leave from individual offices around downtown. **Cruz del Sur** (San Francisco 1317), at the bus terminal has most departures, including to Chiloé and Punta Arenas. They also have an **office** (Walker Martínez 230) in town. Also check out **Tur Bus** (San Pedro 210). For Santiago, Tur Bus, **Tas Choapa** (Walker Martínez 227) and **Buses Norte** (San Pedro 210) have nightly departures.

For Bariloche, Argentina, Tas Choapa leaves Monday and Saturday, while Cruz del Sur leaves every day. Minibus services include: to/from Ensenada (US$1.25) and Petrohué (US$2.50) from in front of **Afex Exchange** (Del Salvador & San Pedro), or along Del Salvador; to Puerto Montt, Frutillar and Puerto Octay from along San José between the plaza and San Francisco; to Ralún and Cochamó from the corner of Walker Martínez and San Bernardo.

ENSENADA

Views of Volcán Osorno are stunning from Ensenada, between Puerto Varas and Petrohué on Ruta 225. Lots of campgrounds are on or near the beach, such as fun artsy **Caleta Trauco Camping** (☎ 065-212033; km 43; camping per site US$4-7) with hot water and fire pits, or **Camping Montaña** (☎ 065-235285; camping per site US$8) in front of the police station. **Hospedaje Ensenada** (☎ 065-212050; km 43; r per person with bath US$13-17) is a spacious, lakeside house that's tranquil (except for the doorbell) with a yard large enough for volleyball and a patio just begging for loungers. Breakfast is included. It's open December to late April (or early May).

PARQUE NACIONAL VICENTE PERÉZ ROSALES

Chile's first **national park** (admission US$2) protects 251,000 hectares, taking in Lago Todos Los Santos and the rivers that feed it as well as volcanoes Osorno, Puntiagudo (2190m) and Mt Tronador (3554m). Sounds like heaps, but most of it is inaccessible to the average hiker. Ruta 225 accesses the park, 50km east of Puerto Varas.

If you've wondered why rafting trips don't start at the lake, you'll find out at **Saltos del Petrohué** where the waters boom and froth over basalt columns. Another 6km is **Petrohué** where a new hotel is being constructed to replace one that burned down in 2002. The lake is a glorious slate blue here. By taking the passenger-only cruise to Peulla, you'll get spectacular views of mountains and changing hues of the lake. From there, bus/boat combos continue to Bariloche. This is a hyper-touristy trip (more like a group organized tour), but it's the only way to cross the lake. From the cruise landing and old hotel site, a dirt track leads to **Playa Larga**, a long black-sand beach,

from where **Sendero Los Alerces** heads west to meet up with **Sendero La Picada**, which climbs past Paso Desolación on Volcán Osorno, and continues on to Refugio La Picada on the volcano's north side. What are the chances of rain? Very good: more than 200 rainy days a year keep this park dizzyingly green.

On **Volcán Osorno**, the ski slopes of **Centro de Esquí La Burbuja** (adults/children US$16/13) have seven different runs with spectacular views. Climbing groups depart from here. Views of Lago Llanquihue are spectacular.

Sleeping & Eating

Küschel (Petrohué; campsites/r per person US$5/10) Cross the river by rowboat (US$0.50) to reach this basic farmhouse. Rooms with breakfast included, or camp with the cows. It's an incredible setting.

Refugio Teski Ski Club (La Burbuja; dm US$10; year-round) Small but well-kept dorm rooms (bring sleeping bag). Breakfast (US$5), lunch and dinner (both US$9) are served, and kitchen use is possible.

Getting There & Away

In summer, shuttles from Puerto Montt and Puerto Varas to Petrohué are frequent, but limited to twice daily the rest of the year. For details on the boat trip across the lake and to Bariloche see p484.

To get to 'La Burbuja' and the *refugio*, take the Ensenada–Puerto Octay road to a signpost about 3km from Ensenada and continue 9km up the lateral. This road is supposed to be improved in the future, but at press time was still a very steep, muddy mess, accessible only with high-clearance, 4WD vehicles. Ask tour operators in town about the latest conditions and transport options.

COCHAMÓ

Cochamó, with its Chilote-style, *alerce*-shingled **church** standing proudly against a backdrop of milky blue water, is one of the most picturesque villages in this region. On the eastern shore of Estuario Reloncaví, it's unaltered by the growing tourism and committed to preserving its natural environment. From here, long-distance trekkers can access upper Río Cochamó Valley, where granite domes rise above verdant rain forest.

CHILE

The municipal office on the main road provides information on horse-trek outfitters, and **Avenco**, in the section of Cochamó referred to as 'Pueblo Hundido,' has loads of area information. At both places and in Puerto Varas, look for the very useful Cochamó hiking map and brochure. **Campo Aventura** (campsite/dm per person US$4/15, breakfast US$5-8, lunch US$10, dinner US$14; ✆ Oct 1-Apr 15) has three shared cabins, a kitchen and indoor and outdoor dining areas at its riverside camp. Facilities are primarily for horse-riding tour clients, but are open to the public if space is available. For horse trekking and contact information, see Puerto Varas, p482.

Charging US$9 per person for adequate rooms with breakfast and shared bath, are **Hospedaje Edicar** (✆ 065-216256; Av Prat & Sargento Aldea), with views and a little balcony, and **Hospedaje Maura** (✆ 09-913-0106; J Molina 12), with good beds and very low ceilings.

There are five daily departures to/from Puerto Montt, stopping in Puerto Varas and Ensenada. Most buses continue to Río Puelo.

PUERTO MONTT

One of Chile's fastest growing cities, Puerto Montt (population 175,000) hustles and bustles with everybody and everything heading further south, including Navimag to Puerto Natales, ferries to Chaitén, and buses to Chiloé. While away the hours at craft markets and *cocinerías* at **Angelmó**, 3km from downtown, or at one of the malls in the city center. **Casa del Arte Diego Rivera** (Quillota 116), a joint Mexican–Chilean project with contemporary art, the **church** across from the plaza, and **Museo Juan Pablo II** (Portales 991), with exhibits on regional history, are worth a look. Offshore **Isla Tenglo**, reached by inexpensive launches from the docks at Angelmó, is a favorite local beach with mountain range views if you're here on a clear day.

Orientation

Sitting 1020km south of Santiago, Puerto Montt's downtown stretches along the waterfront; Av Diego Portales is the main street, turning into Av Angelmó to the west, and accessing the beach resort Pelluco and the Carretera Austral to the east. Hills of suburban sprawl rise abruptly to the north.

The bus station is toward the west side of the city center. The ferry terminal is about 500m west. Eleven blocks to the west is the plaza. *Micros* roar along Diego Portales, linking east and west ends.

Information

INTERNET ACCESS

Lots of Internet places line Av Angelmó, including:

Latin Star (Av Angelmó 1672) Also has a call center and book exchange.

Travel & Adventure (✆ 065-348888; Av Angelmó 1760) Internet access, maps, money exchange and excursion planning.

LAUNDRY

Arco Iris (San Martín 232)

Full Fresh supermarket On Portales across from the bus terminal, this supermarket has laundry facilities inside that offer cheap rates.

MEDICAL SERVICES

Hospital Regional (✆ 065-261134; Seminario) Near the intersection with Décima Región.

MONEY

Lots of ATMs, try **Banco de Chile** (Pedro Montt & Diego Portales). For money exchange try:

Afex (Portales 516)

Eureka Tour (Antonio Varas 445)

Exchange (Talca 84)

POST & COMMUNICATIONS

Entel (cnr Rancagua & Urmeneta)

Post office (Rancagua 126)

TOURIST OFFICES

Municipal tourist office (Varas & O'Higgins) In a kiosk across from the plaza, is only slightly more helpful than Sernatur.

Sernatur (Plaza de Armas) On the plaza's western side.

Sleeping

A mob of *hospedaje* hawkers hovers at the bus terminal. Many of these represent 'pirate' operations. There's a kiosk just outside the bus terminal at which licensed *hospedajes* can post and linger.

Camping Los Paredes (✆ 065-258394; campsites US$14) En route to Chinquihue 6km west of town; pleasant sites with hot showers; ask about per person rates. Local buses from the bus terminal will drop you at the entrance.

Hostal Don Teo (☎ 065-251625; Andrés Bello 990, 2nd fl; r per person with bath & breakfast US$12) Highly regarded, this HI-affiliated hostal has clean rooms with satellite TV.

Near the bus terminal, Av Juan Mira has many cheap options to choose from: **Hospedaje Anita** (☎ 065-315479; Mira 1094; r per person US$8) is decent with kitchen access, but bring your own padlock, and **San Sebastián** (☎ 065-257719; Mira 1096; r per person US$5) is bleak but cheap.

Residencial Los Helechos (☎ 065-259525; Chorrillos 1500; r per person US$7) A comfortable place. Breakfast is US$2 extra.

Casa Gladys (☎ 065-260247; Ancud 112; r per person US$9) Conscientious owners and very cool kitchen.

Hostal Sur (☎ 065-292535; Andrés Bello 973; r per person US$10) Clean rooms with shared bath and cable TV.

Casa Almondacid (☎ 065-257565; Independencia 247; r per person with breakfast US$10) Small, just a family home. Or try next door **Hospedaje Eliana** (Independencia 251).

Hostal Marazul (☎ 065-256567; Ecuador 1558; r without/with bath US$7.50/10) Convenient to the ferry port at Angelmó and includes breakfast.

Eating & Drinking

The *cocinerías* at the far end of Angelmó have loads of ambience and good meals for about US$6 to US$8. Try *picorocos* (giant barnacles) in herb sauce.

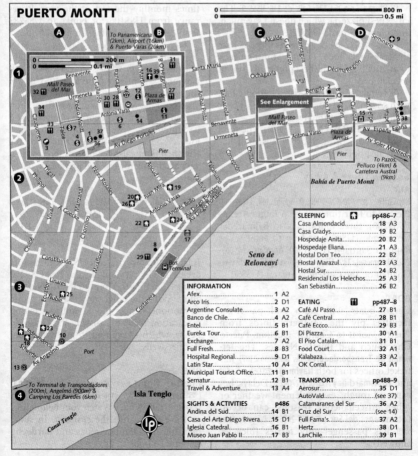

PUERTO MONTT

0 ———— 800 m
0 ———— 0.5 mi

To Panamericana (2km), Airport (16km) & Puerto Varas (20km)

0 ———— 200 m
0 ———— 0.1 mi

Mall Paseo del Mar

Plaza de Armas

See Enlargement

Bahía de Puerto Montt

To Pazos, Pelluco (4km) & Carretera Austral (9km)

Seno de Reloncaví

Bus Terminal

To Terminal de Transportadores (200m), Angelmó (900m) & Camping Los Paredes (6km)

Isla Tenglo

Canal Tenglo

SLEEPING		pp486–7
Casa Almondacid	18	A3
Casa Gladys	19	B2
Hospedaje Anita	20	B2
Hospedaje Eliana	21	A3
Hostal Don Teo	22	B2
Hostal Marazul	23	A3
Hostal Sur	24	B2
Residencial Los Helechos	25	A3
San Sebastián	26	B2

INFORMATION		
Afex	1	A2
Arco Iris	2	D1
Argentine Consulate	3	A2
Banco de Chile	4	A2
Entel	5	B1
Eureka Tour	6	B1
Exchange	7	A2
Full Fresh	8	B3
Hospital Regional	9	D1
Latin Star	10	A4
Municipal Tourist Office	11	B1
Sernatur	12	B1
Travel & Adventure	13	A4

SIGHTS & ACTIVITIES		p486
Andina del Sud	14	B1
Casa del Arte Diego Rivera	15	D1
Iglesia Catedral	16	B1
Museo Juan Pablo II	17	B3

EATING		pp487–8
Café Al Passo	27	B1
Café Central	28	B1
Café Eccco	29	B3
Di Piazza	30	A1
El Piso Catalán	31	B1
Food Court	32	A1
Kalabaza	33	A2
OK Corral	34	A1

TRANSPORT		pp488–9
Aerosur	35	D1
AutoVald	(see 37)	
Catamaranes del Sur	36	A2
Cruz del Sur	(see 14)	
Full Fama's	37	A2
Hertz	38	D1
LanChile	39	B1

CHILE

Café Eccco (Pueblito de Melipulli; snacks US$2-4) Best place to meet friends and wait out the hours for the boat to leave. Veg goodies, coffee and juice bar, plus lots of area info. Ask about the brewpub.

Café Al Passo (Varas 350; hot dogs US$1, lunches US$3) Large, cafeteria style; watch the masses go by while filling up with *completos*.

Café Central (☎ 254-721; Rancagua 117; US$1.50-4) Tasty drinks, snacks and cakes all in a smoky room.

El Piso Catalán (Quillota 185; meals US$2-5) Great-value fixed-price menus in a low key, artistic dining room. Drinks, tapas and music in evenings.

Kalabaza (Varas 629; US$3-4.50) Attractive and central, with sandwiches, Kuntsmann beer and fixed-price lunches.

Di Piazza (☎ 254-174; Gallardo 118; US$5-9) The city's best pizzeria, which doesn't say much, and plenty of pasta choices.

Pazos (☎ 252-552; Liborio Guerrero 1; US$5-9) Take the trek to Pelluco, Puerto Montt's beach town, to fill up on the best prepared Chilean specialties.

OK Corral (Cauquenes 128) Also a hopping bar, with soccer-sized burgers and loads of beer with an Old West theme.

Mall Paseo del Mar (Talca & Urmeneta) The food court on the third floor of this mall has many fast options.

Getting There & Away
AIR
LanChile (☎ 600-526-2000; O'Higgins 167, Local 1-B) flies up to four times daily to Punta Arenas (US$200), three times daily to Balmaceda/Coyhaique (US$90) and up to eight times daily to Santiago (US$180). **AeroSur** (☎ 065-252523; Urmeneta 149) flies daily except Sunday to Chaitén on the Carretera Austral (US$50).

BOAT
Cargo boats with auto and passenger facilities ply the southern fjords from Puerto Montt to Chaitén, Quellón, Puerto Chacabuco and Puerto Natales. The **Terminal de Transbordadores** (Av Angelmó 2187) has ticket offices for both **Navimag** (☎ 065-253318) and **Transmarchilay** (☎ 065-270420). Delays, because of rough seas, inclement weather or other miscellaneous reasons, can occur. **Catamaranes del Sur** (☎ 065-267533; Diego Portales 510) has passenger-only ferries (bicycles allowed).

To Chaitén, Catamaranes del Sur has a faster (four to five hours) ferry that leaves Monday, Wednesday and Thursday at 9–10am. Twice weekly they continue to Castro (US$35 one-way, US$66 round trip). Transmarchilay and Navimag sail to/from Chaitén and Quellón regularly in high season, but less often off-season. Prices are US$20–US$25 per person, US$11 for bicycles, US$20 motorcycles of US$100 for cars or pickups.

To Puerto Chacabuco you can hop on Navimag's M/N *Puerto Edén* (18 hours). Prices from US$40 for a *butaca* (reclining chair) to US$297 per person for a dorm bed with shared bath. M/N *Evangelistas* stops en route to Laguna San Rafael every four or five days in high season, and only three or four times monthly the rest of the year. Prices range from US$106 for bunks to US$283 for a cabin with private bath per person.

To Puerto Natales, Navimag's M/N *Magallanes* sails the popular three-night journey through Chile's fjords; check with Navimag's Santiago offices (p405) or on the website for departure dates and confirm your booking with the Santiago office. High season is December–February; mid-season is September–November and March; and low season is April–August. Prices for the trip include meals. Per person fares, which vary according to view and private or shared bath, are as follows:

Class	High season	Mid-season	Low season
AA	US$398	US$354	US$166
A	US$345	US$302	US$131
Berths	US$250	US$210	n/a

In addition, bicycles cost US$9 and motorcycles US$30; cars and pickups cost US$250 going from Puerto Montt to Puerto Natales, and US$200 the other way. Travelers prone to motion sickness should consider taking medication prior to crossing the Golfo de Penas, which is exposed to gut-wrenching Pacific swells.

BUS
Puerto Montt's waterfront **bus terminal** (☎ 065-253143; Av Portales & Lillo) is the main transportation hub. Watch your belongings or leave them with the *custodia*. In summer, buses to Punta Arenas and Bariloche sell out, so book in advance.

Minibuses to Puerto Varas (US$0.70), Frutillar (US$1.40) and Puerto Octay (US$1.70) leave from the eastern side of the terminal. Buses leave five times daily for Cochamó (US$3.50, four hours).

For Hornopirén, where summer-only ferries connect to Caleta Gonzalo, Buses Fierro has three daily departures (US$5, five hours). Off-season (mid-March to mid-December) bus transportation to Hornopirén and the upper Carretera Austral is very limited.

Cruz del Sur (Varas 437) has frequent buses to Chiloé. Santiago-bound buses usually leave around 10pm, stopping at various cities. **Tur Bus** (☎ 065-253329) has daily buses to Valparaíso/Viña del Mar. For Coyhaique and Punta Arenas via Argentina, try Cruz del Sur or Turibús. For Bariloche, Argentina, try **Tas Choapa** (☎ 065-254828), **Río de La Plata** (☎ 065-253841) and Cruz del Sur, which travel daily via the Cardenal Samoré pass east of Osorno.

Destination	Duration in Hours	Cost
Ancud	2½	US$4
Bariloche (Arg)	8	US$19
Castro	3½	US$6
Concepción	9	US$15
Osorno	1½	US$2
Pucón	6	US$7
Punta Arenas	30–36	US$50
Quellón	6	US$9
Santiago	13–16	US$11–23
Temuco	7	US$8
Valdivia	3½	US$5
Valparaíso/Viña del Mar	18	US$25

Getting Around

ETM buses (US$1.50) run between Aeropuerto El Tepual, 16km west of town, and the bus terminal. A door-to-door shuttle from the airport costs about US$4.

Car rental agencies include **Acchi** (Automóvil Club; ☎ 065-252968; Esmeralda 70), **Hertz** (☎ 065-259585; Varas 126), **AutoVald** (☎ 065-313158; Portales 504) and **Full Fama's** (☎ 065-258060; Portales 506). These last two can help get permission to take rental vehicles into Argentina. Rates range from US$45 for a normal car to US$100 for a pickup or jeep.

PARQUE NACIONAL ALERCE ANDINO

Despite being only 40km from Puerto Montt, the mountainous 40,000-hectare **Parque Nacional Alerce Andino** (admission US$2) is little visited, though it offers some great hiking through old growth alerce forest. It may be a rainy hike: up to 4.5m of rain falls annually. The easiest way to enjoy the park is on an organized day-tour. Public transport is limited. *Tábanos* are nasty on exposed trails in January and February. A trail linking the sectors Correntoso and Río Chaica lead deep into thick vegetation and to the alerce. Conaf maintains a five-site **campground** (campsites US6.50) at Correntoso on Río Chamiza and a six-site facility at Lago Chaiquenes, at the head of the Río Chaica valley. There's camping also near Lenca, a 7km walk from the entrance.

From Puerto Montt's bus terminal, Buses Fierro goes four times daily to Correntoso, 3km from the Río Chamiza entrance on the northern boundary of the park; there are five buses daily to the crossroads at Lenca (US$1.50), on the Carretera Austral.

CHILOÉ

Island insularity gives Chiloé a magic all its own. Rich in folkloric tradition and myth (ask locals about the Trauco or Pincoya), as well as having some of its own culinary specialties, this archipelago can be a fun jaunt. The main island is a lush patchwork of pastureland on undulating hills, 180km long but just 50km wide, and surrounded by smaller islands. Most of the towns and farming are on the eastern side, while the western shores are nearly roadless, and the interior still thick with forest. More than half of the 154,000 Chilotes (residents of Chiloé) make a living from subsistence agriculture, while others depend on fishing. Throughout the island are shingled houses and wooden churches, some up to 200 years old, many now preserved as an Unesco World Heritage Site.

Huilliche Indians first raised potatoes and other crops in the fertile volcanic soil. Jesuits were among the earliest European settlers. A Spanish royalist stronghold, Chiloé resisted *criollo* attacks on Ancud until 1826. In February, each town hosts a festival rich in folk music, dancing and loads of feasting.

ANCUD

Founded in 1767 to defend the coastline, Ancud, at the north end of Isla Grande, is

Chiloé's largest town (population 40,000) and a worthwhile stop.

Information

Clean Center (Pudeto 45) does your laundry. Change money in Puerto Montt for better rates. ATMs at banks around the plazas, include Banco de Estado. **Hospital de Ancud** (☎ 065-622356; Almirante Latorre 405) is at the corner of Pedro Montt. There's a **post office** (Pudeto & Blanco Encalada) and **Entel** (Pudeto 219), below Hotel Lacuy, which also has Internet access. **Sernatur** (☎ 065-622800; Libertad 665; ☒ 8:30am-8pm in summer, 8:30-6pm Mon-Fri in winter), across from the plaza, is the only formal tourist office on the island, with helpful staff, brochures and accommodations listings.

Sights & Activities

The **Museo Regional de Ancud** (Libertad; adult/child US$1/0.25; ☒ 10:30am-7:30pm Jan-Feb, 9:30am-5:30pm Mon-Fri, 10am-2pm Sat & Sun Mar-Dec) just south of the Plaza de Armas, has displays tracking island history, including outstanding photographs, a natural history display and a patio of Chilote folklore creatures. **Fuerte San Antonio** at the northwest corner of town was Spain's last Chilean outpost. The **Mercado Municipal**, on Prat, is brimming with woolens, carvings and pottery.

Austral Adventures (☎ 065-625977; www.austral-adventures.com; Lord Cochrane 432) organizes beach hiking, trips to penguin colonies, kayaking, and rural tourism home stays. Day rates for hiking and penguin colonies are US$60, kayaking US$40. Guides speak English. Excursions to farming communities and private homes that offer meals and lodging can be arranged through them or **Agroturismo** (☎ 065-628-333; Ramírez 207).

Sleeping

Camping Arena Gruesa (☎ 065-623428; Costanera Norte 290; camping/r per person US$3/11) Northeast of Fuerte San Antonio. Grassy sites with hot water, lights and use of a large kitchen in house. Rooms are clean and decent.

Casa del Apostulado (☎ 065-623256; Chacabuco 841; dm US$3; ☒ Dec-Mar) At the end of the street, offers dorm-style rooms with flimsy beds. No smoking or alcohol.

Hospedaje Vista al Mar (☎ 065-622617; Costanera 918; r per person US$10, full cabin US$35) Has an annex cabin where HI members can shack up. Great for a small group, with a decent kitchen and shared baths.

Hospedaje Patricia (☎ 065-623781; Monseñor Aguilera 756; r per person US$6) Cute rooms with good, firm beds in a lively family environment. The owner recommends bringing your own padlock.

Residencial María Carolina (☎ 065-622458; Almirante Latorre 558; r per person US$10) Receives accolades for its quiet residential area, attractive common spaces and spacious gardens.

Hospedaje Capri (☎ 065-622830; Mocopulli 323; r per person US$9) Above a restaurant, with basic rooms and a very caring matron.

Hostal Lluhay (☎ 065-622656; Cochrane 458; s/d US$16/25) Near the water, with comfortable rooms, welcoming owners, roaring fireplace, mini-grand piano and bread 'n' cake heavy breakfasts.

Eating & Drinking

El Sacho (Dieciocho btwn Libertad & Blanco Encalada; dishes US$3-6) In the Mercado Municipal; has enormous plates of steamed mussels and clams.

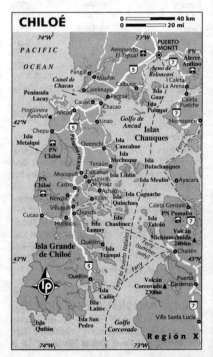

CHILE

La Hormiguita (Pudeto 44; snacks US$2-4) Offers pies and sandwiches (veg choices), fruit juices and real coffee.

Retro Pub (Maipú 615; mains US$3-6) Dark pub style with rock 'n' roll posters; varied menu, including overpriced but good Tex-Mex; best ambience at night.

Pedersen Salón de Té (Sargento Aldea 470) Bakes fresh *Kuchen* daily in this cute spot overlooking the pier.

Café Lidia (Pudeto 256) serves hearty lunches and dinners, as does **Capri** (Mocopulli 323).

Getting There & Away

The **bus terminal** (Aníbal Pinto & Marcos Vera) is a couple of kilometers east of downtown. Taxis from the terminal to downtown cost US$1.50. Cruz del Sur has a dozen buses daily to Puerto Montt and to Castro and Quellón.

CASTRO

If it weren't for the *palafitos* (wood-shingled houses on stilts hovering precariously over the waters), where parking means roping up the fishing boat, Castro would look like any other mainland Chilean town. Founded in 1567, 90km south of Ancud, Castro is the capital of Chiloé province and is the main transport center for the island.

Information

For the best exchange rates try **Julio Barrientos** (Chacabuco 286). There are ATMs at the main banks at the plaza. There's a **post office** (O'Higgins 388) and **Entel** (O'Higgins 480). **Turismo Isla Grande** (☎ 065-632384; Thompson 241) organizes tours and makes Navimag bookings. **Hospital de Castro** (☎ 065-632445; Freire 852) is at the foot of Cerro Millantuy. A **tourist kiosk** (Plaza de Armas) has town maps and limited material on lodging and nearby towns.

Sights & Activities

The neo-Gothic yellow-lavender 1906 **Iglesia San Francisco de Castro** (Plaza de Armas) has a soothing well-crafted wood interior. **Museo Regional de Castro** (cnr Esmeralda & Blanco Encalada) houses Huilliche Indian relics and photos of the 1960 earthquake. Waterfront **Feria Artesanal** (Costanera; ☼ daily) has a selection of woolens – caps, gloves, sweaters, ponchos – and basketry; it's at Costanera's southern end. **Palafitos** are along Costanera Pedro Montt, at the north end of town, the Feria Artesanal and both ends of the Río Gamboa bridge, at the western exit from the city.

Sleeping

Some lodging is seasonal – look for handwritten signs along San Martín and O'Higgins, near Sargento Aldea. Barros Arana is another *hospedaje* ghetto.

Albergue Juvenil (☎ 065-632766; Freire 610; beds US$2.50; ☼ summer only) In the Gimnasio Fiscal, throw down your sleeping bag on the floor.

Hospedaje Mirador (☎ 065-633795; Barros Arana 127; r per person US$9) Seaside views, large breakfasts and great showers.

Hospedaje Central (☎ 065-637026; Los Carrera 316; r per person US$7) Spotless but small rooms with firm beds.

Hospedaje Agüero (☎ 065-635735; Chacabuco 449; r per person US$10) Quiet, with views of the *palafitos*.

Hostal Chilote (☎ 065-635021; Aldunate 456; r per person US$9) Lively, family-run hostel with spotless, spacious rooms and breakfast at the kitchen table. Rates with private bath are US$13.

Hospedaje Corchito (☎ 065-632806; Ramírez 251 & 240; r per person US$8; **P**) Comfortable and secure with amicable management, but marginal breakfast. With private bath is US$12.

Hostal O'Higgins (☎ 065-632016; O'Higgins 831, Interior; d US$17) Set away from road, with quiet, clean rooms.

Eating

Behind the Feria Artesanal the waterfront restaurants have the best food for the fewest pesos – try **Brisas del Mar** or **Curanto** for US$3 set lunches as well as seafood specialties.

Años Luz (San Martín 309; mains US$4.50-8; ☼ Mon-Sat) Has a boat hull for a bar and creative, somewhat pricey cuisine – including exceptional salads, juices, veg entrees and delicious desserts.

La Tavolata (Balmaceda 245 US$3-5) Serves up zesty pizza and pastas, including veg ravioli and lasagna in cute dining room.

Sacho (Thompson 213; mains US$5-9) Fancy, but the fixed-price lunches are worthwhile.

Getting There & Away
BOAT

Catamaranes del Sur (☎ 065-267533; Diego Portales 510, Puerto Montt) runs passenger ferries to

Chaitén at 9am Tuesday and Thursday, January and February only. One way is US$20, round trip US$36. The ferry leaves from the port.

BUS & COLECTIVO

There are two main bus terminals. The municipal **Terminal de Buses Rurales** (San Martín near Sargento Aldea) has buses to Huillinco and Cucao (US$2), and the entrance to Parque Nacional Chiloé. Services are very limited off-season.

The **Cruz del Sur terminal** (San Martín 486) services the main Chilote cities (Quellón and Ancud) and long-distance destinations, but buses to Dalcahue and Isla Quinchao leave from here.

Destination	Duration in Hours	Cost
Ancud	1	US$2
Bariloche (Argentina)	12	US$21
Puerto Montt	3	US$5
Quellón	2	US$1.50
Santiago	19	US$29–48
Temuco	8	US$15

For nearby destinations, *colectivos* provide a faster alternative. Colectivos Chonchi leave from Chacabuco near Esmeralda (US$1) as well as from Ramírez near San Martín. Colectivos Quellón leave from Sotomayor and San Martín (US$3), as do Colectivos Achao (US$1).

DALCAHUE & ISLA QUINCHAO

Dalcahue, 20km northeast of Castro, has an intriguing 19th-century church, well-preserved vernacular architecture, and a Sunday market with picturesque *cocinerías* with stout cooks filling orders for *curanto* (Chiloé's specialty; a hearty pile of fish, shellfish, chicken, pork, lamb, beef and potato cooked together) and mussels. Isla Quinchao, southeast of Dalcahue, is one of the most accessible islands, and worth a day trip. Midway between Dalcahue and Achao, **Curaco de Vélez** dates from 1660 and has a treasure of Chilote architecture, plus an open-air oyster bar at the beach. Buses between Achao and Dalcahue stop in Curaco.

In **Achao**, Isla Quinchao's largest town, 18th-century **Iglesia Santa María de Achao** is the oldest church in Chiloé; note the elaborate woodwork on the ceiling and the

wooden pegs that were used instead of nails. In summer, informal camping– for free or negligible cost – is possible on Delicias between Sargento Aldea and Serrano. Good lodging options at **Hostal Plaza** (☎ 065-661283; Amunátegui 20; r per person US$6.50), across from the plaza, and **Hospedaje Sol y Lluvias** (☎ 065-253996; Gerónimo de Urmeneta 215; r without/with bath US$10/26). Overlooking the pier, **Mar y Velas** (Serrano 02) is the place for mussels or clams with a couple of cold beers.

Minibuses and *colectivos* go directly to/from Castro. From Dalcahue, **Dalcahue Expreso** (Freire btwn San Martín & Eugenio) has half-hourly buses to Castro (US$0.50) weekdays, fewer on weekends. **Cruz del Sur** (San Martín 102) runs buses to Puerto Montt twice daily (US$5). Ferries leave continuously from Dalcahue to Isla Quinchao (pedestrians free, cars US$6 round trip).

CHONCHI

Chonchi, 23km south of Castro and nestled on Canal Lemuy, was a pirates' delight and a port for the export of cypress. Founded in 1767, the town is known as the Ciudad de los Tres Pisos (City of Three Levels) but its more colorful indigenous name literally means 'slippery earth'. **Iglesia San Carlos**, with its three-story tower and multiple arches, is a 19th-century landmark. The townspeople take pride in their easy-going community and enjoy a cottage industry of *licor de oro* (golden liqueurs). Most tourist services are on Centenario, including a **tourist office** (cnr Sargento Candelaria & Centenario; ☽ Jan-Mar). A good day trip is to **Isla Lemuy**. The ferry (free) leaves every half-hour from Puerto Huichas, 5km to the south; on Sunday and in the off-season, the service is approximately hourly.

With great views, cozy **Hospedaje El Mirador** (☎ 065-671351; Ciriaco Álvarez 198; r per person US$7) includes breakfast. Beachfront **Hospedaje La Esmeralda** (☎ 065-671954; Irarrázabal s/n; bunks US$5.50, r per person US$7.50-10), run by the inexhaustible Carlos Gredy, offers rowboat use, fishing, salmon dinners, possible tours of his mussel farm, laundry and valuable advice on what to do in the area. *Hospedajes* serve meals; otherwise try **El Trébol**.

Catch Castro-bound buses opposite the plaza on the upper level or take a *colectivo* (US$1) opposite the church. Transport to Parque Nacional Chiloé (US$2, 1½ hours) tends to be sporadic, with not enough departures to meet demand in summer and hardly any departures the rest of the year. Ask around for the latest (eg at La Esmeralda).

PARQUE NACIONAL CHILOÉ
Wild coast meets native coniferous and evergreen forests in this 43,000-hectare national park (admission US$1.50) about 54km southwest of Castro. The park protects the chilote fox; trauco; pudú (miniature deer), which is rarely seen; and bird species including the Magellanic penguin. Huilliche communities live in the park; some manage campsites.

At Sector Chanquín – the most accessible, and the starting point for most hikes – Conaf has a visitors center with information on the trails. The 1km **Sendero Interpretivo El Tepual** winds along tree trunks through dense forest. The 2km **Sendero Dunas de Cucao** leads to a series of dunes behind a long, white-sand beach. The most popular route is the 20km **Sendero Chanquín-Cole Cole** along the coast, past Lago Huelde to Río Cole Cole; it is possible to do the hike there and back in one long day. The hike continues 8km north to Río Anay, with another rustic *refugio*. Cucao is the service town to the park. A suspension bridge connects the two.

Sleeping
Camping Chanquín (sites/cabin r per person US$5/9) Within the park, about 200m beyond the visitors center offers good amenities and a covered area for rainy nights. Cabins are perched on the hill; ask about availability at La Madrigüera, a small café.

Cole Cole (campsites/floor space per person US$1.50) There are no kitchen facilities here and sand fleas may be a problem.

El Arrayán (☎ 09-219-3565; r per person US$5) Across from the bus stop by the park entrance; has a kitchen (with woodstove) for the guest use. Rooms in the main house are warmer; meals are available.

El Paraíso (☎ 09-296-5465; camping per person US$1.50, r US$9) Best choice in Cucao, with an attentive owner and breakfast included.

Getting There & Away
Buses go to/from Castro four to five times daily (US$2.50). Service from Chonchi is sporadic.

QUELLÓN
The last outpost at the end of the Panamericana, 92km south of Castro, Quellón is, for travelers, most often a destination of necessity rather than desire. Change money before coming here; **Banco del Estado** (cnr Ladrilleros & Freire) has an ATM. Phone home at **Entel** (cnr Ladrilleros & La Paz).

Lodgings per person, no breakfast, include **Club Deportivo Torino** (La Paz 316; floor space US$1.50), with floor space for you and your sleeping bag; **Casa del Profesor** (☎ 065-681516; La Paz & Santos Vargas; beds US$9; ☼ summer only), with comfortable dorm beds and kitchen facilities; **Hotel Playa** (☎ 065-681278; Pedro Montt 427; r US$6), which has large rooms and clean shared baths; and **Hotel El Chico Leo** (☎ 065-681567; Pedro Montt 325; r without/with bath US$10/15), with attentive staff, comfortable beds, a good, popular restaurant (lunches US$2.50–6) and pool tables. **Café Nuevo Amanecer** (22 de Mayo 344) is a sandwich café by day and a crowded bar by night.

Buses Cruz del Sur and **Transchiloé** (cnr Aguirre Cerda & Miramar) travel to Castro frequently (US$4, two hours). **Navimag** (Pedro Montt 457) sails to Chaitén twice weekly. Ferry schedules change seasonally; verify all departures at the Navimag office in Puerto Montt. Contact the Transmarchilay office in Puerto Montt for the current status of their ferries.

CARRETERA AUSTRAL

Beyond the Lake District and Chiloé, Chile thins into a snake of fjords, glaciers, hidden lakes, raging rivers, impenetrable rain forest and Patagonian steppe. This beginning and middle of Chilean Patagonia looks like it shouldn't be at all accessible, but is, due to the Carretera Austral, which was begun in the 1980s and is now being paved over stretch by stretch. Starting in Puerto Montt, the road links widely separated towns and hamlets all the way to Villa O'Higgins, a total of just over 1200km. The population of the entire region is only 87,000, and nearly half of those people live in the city of Coyhaique.

During Chile's push to colonize the land with grazing and timber leases, a single company controlled nearly a million hectares near Coyhaique. Land laws rewarding

CHILE

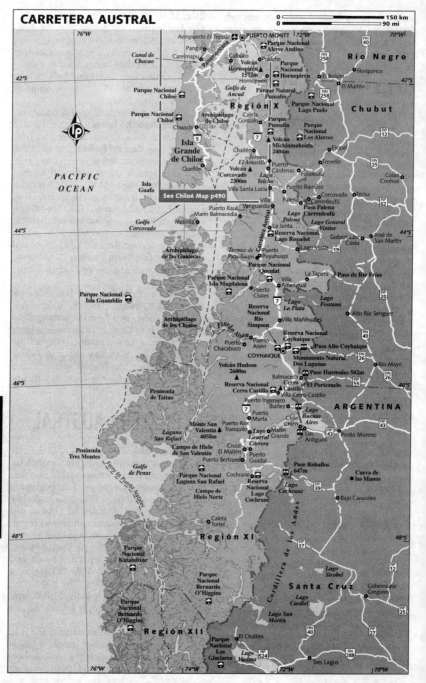

CARRETERA AUSTRAL

0 — 150 km
0 — 90 mi

CHILE

clearance led to the company and colonists burning nearly three million hectares of lenga forest in the 1940s, evidenced by the many whitened, felled trees you'll see along the way.

Going the whole length is possible only in high season (from mid-December through February) due to a limited ferry service between Puerto Montt and Caleta Gonzalo. Most travelers opt to take a ferry from Puerto Montt or Chiloé to Chaitén or Puerto Chacabuco, fly to Chaitén or Coyhaique, or go overland via Argentina, accessing the region through Futaleufú. This section covers Chaitén to Lago General Carrera. Buses from Chaitén or Coyhaique can drop passengers at points along the Carretera.

If you've got the time and moxie, keep going south to the hamlets of Cochrane, Puerto Bertrand and Villa O'Higgins, in some of the most beautiful, desolate regions of the country. Transportation in these extremes is limited and information changes fast; go to the Sernatur office in Coyhaique for details, and enjoy the incredible adventure.

CHAITÉN & PARQUE PUMALÍN

Hugged by rugged hills and a peaceful bay, outpost Chaitén is little more than a six by eight grid of wide streets. It's the only town near Parque Pumalín and is a transport stop for the Carretera Austral. Most travelers arrive by ferry; the port is a 10-minute walk northwest of town. **Bellavista al Sur** (☎ 065-731469; Riveros 479) has Internet access and organizes rock-climbing trips. **Banco del Estado** (cnr Libertad & O'Higgins), at the plaza, exchanges cash only at poor rates and has an ATM, but not for Visa cards. The post office and Entel are also at the plaza. The **tourist office** (Costanera & O'Higgins; ☺ 9am-9pm Jan-Feb) has lodgings lists. **Pumalín Information Center** (O'Higgins 62) has park information and reserves cabins.

Sights & Activities

Parque Pumalín (www.pumalinpark.org; admission free) is the controversial privately owned park, 68km north of Chaitén, protecting native rain forest and the immense alerce trees. Most of the land is impenetrable. Developed hikes are along a length of road through the park; you'll have to choose which one and ask the driver to drop you off, or hitch from one to the next (difficult off-season). **Sendero Cascadas** (Caleta Gonzalo) climbs to impressive waterfalls. **Sendero Laguna Tronador**, 12km south, leads to views of Michinmahuida and a secluded lake with two campsites. Another kilometer south, **Sendero Los Alerces** is an easy interpretive trail through majestic groves of alerce. More hikes, including three to four day routes, are in development; check at the park offices.

About 25km southeast of Chaitén, **Termas El Amarillo** (admission US$3; camping per tent US$5) is a riverside hot spring. **Chaitur** (☎ 065-731429), at the bus terminal, dispatches most of the buses and organizes trips to nearby sites.

Sleeping & Eating

In Pumalín, camping costs US$2 to US$3 per person, or US$9 for a covered site, some of which are on elevated platforms. Information centers and the park's website have details.

Camping Río Gonzalo (camping per tent US$5) This is the most accessible in the park. Termas El Amarillo also has camping.

Los Arrayanes (☎ 065-218202; campsites per person US$2.50) Boasts beachfront sites and hot showers in Chaitén, 4km north of town.

Casa de Rita (cnr Almirante Riveros & Prat; r per person US$6) A basic family-run place; it's nonsmoking and quiet and has kitchen access.

Don Carlos (☎ 065-731287; Almirante Riveros 53; r without/with bath & breakfast US$9/16) Has a newer upstairs area with firm beds in cramped rooms. There's a patio where you can do laundry.

Santa Anita (Pedro de Valdivia 129; r US$6.50) Bit small and stuffy, but clean.

The following are good places to eat:

Flamengo (Corcovado 218) Portions here large enough to share, and the *caldillo* is hearty.

La Unión (Riveros 242) Simple and basic; try it for lunch.

Getting There & Away

AIR

AeroSur (☎ 065-731228; cnr Pinto & Riveros) flies Monday through Saturday to Puerto Montt (US$36–US$43).

BOAT

Ferry schedules change, so confirm them at the relevant office before making plans. See p488 for price information.

CHILE

Catamaranes del Sur (☎ 065-731199; Juan Todesco 118) Passenger-only ferries to Puerto Montt Mon, Wed and Fri; and to Castro Mon and Thu at 6pm.

Navimag (☎ 065-731570; Ignacio Carrera Pinto 188) Auto-passenger ferry *Alejandrina* to Quellón 3 times a week, and to Puerto Montt Sat.

Transmarchilay (☎ 065-731272; Corcovado 266) Auto-passenger ferry *Pincoya* to Puerto Montt (10 hours) 3 times a week. In summer only to Quellón, Chiloé (6 hours) 3 times a week; and daily from Caleta Gonzalo in Parque Pumalín to Hornopirén, where buses depart for Puerto Montt.

BUS

Buses and minivans to Caleta Gonzalo and Parque Pumalín (US$5, two hours), Futaleufú (US$10, five to six hours) and Coyhaique (US$24, 12–15 hours) leave from **B y V Tour** (Libertad 432) and the **bus terminal** (O'Higgins 67). Departures depend on demand and conditions. In high season there are usually daily departures, in low season two to three times a week. Transport to the park may mean having to spend a night if you want to hike. The trip to Coyhaique stops in many towns along Carretera Austral. If you want to break up the trip and take a bus another day, buy the ticket in advance to secure a seat.

FUTALEUFÚ

The 'Fu' or 'Futa' river, crystalline blue and impressively wild, has international fame as one of the best white-water runs and kayaking play rivers around. Spain-based Endesa, a utility company, has its eye on developing plans to build a series of dams along this river. **FutaFriends** (www.futafriends.org) is a good resource to learn more about protecting the river. The town of Futaleufú, 155km from Chaitén, is a worthwhile side trip from the Carretera Austral if you want to take to the rapids or head into Argentina through some gorgeous green scenery. Otherwise, it's a long trip to a town with little on offer.

Information

The **tourist office** (O'Higgins 536) seems to be open only on occasion. Bring all the money you'll need; **Banco del Estado** (cnr O'Higgins & Manuel Rodríguez) is the only place to change cash.

Tours

Rafting trips on Río Espolón and segments of the more difficult Futaleufú are expen-sive (US$60–70). Outfitters pop up in season; some of the more steady are:

Bio Bio Expeditions (☎ 800-246-7238; www.bbx rafting.com) US-based company that may take walk-ons to their mainly package-oriented trips.

Centro Aventura Futaleufú (☎ 065-721320; O'Higgins 397) At the Hostería Río Grande.

Club de Rafting y Kayak (☎ 065-721298; Pedro Aguirre Cerda 545)

Sleeping & Eating

Cara del Indio (camping per person US$5) Camp here, 15km after Puerto Ramírez, and you'll wish you'd packed a kayak. Private riverfront with put-in sites, hot showers, sauna, homemade bread and loads of space.

Camping Puerto Espolón (camping per person US$3; ☼ Jan-Feb only) Before the entrance to town; has flat sites, some more remote and without lights for stargazers; along a peaceful stretch of river.

In town, lodgings include:

Hospedaje Adolfo (☎ 065-721256; O'Higgins 302; r per person US$8) With a good breakfast and pleasant family atmosphere.

Hotel Continental (☎ 065-721222; Balmaceda 595; r per person US$5.50) A simple, ramshackle place with firm beds, breakfast is US$2.50.

Residencial Ely (☎ 065-721205; Balmaceda 409; r per person US$14)

The town is known for its apples and pears. For meals you could try:

El Encuentro (cnr O'Higgins & Rodríguez) Has passable meals.

SurAndres (Cerda 308) Serves sandwiches and fruit juices.

Getting There & Away

A bus service to the Argentine border with **Buses Cordillera** (Prat 262; ☼ 8am-8pm; US$3; 1½ hr) is daily in high season, less often off-season. Buses to Chaitén (US$8, four to five hours) leave daily except Sunday; stopping in Villa Santa Lucía, which is the transfer point for Coyhaique-bound buses. Check with **Transportes Sebastián** (Piloto Carmona 381) and the tourist office for up-to-date schedules.

PUERTO PUYUHUAPI

Settled by German immigrants in the 1940s, Puerto Puyuhuapi was one of the earliest settlements in the area. Across the inlet, **Termas de Puyuhuapi** is a high-end hot-springs resort. The **Fábrica de Alfombras** (tours US$2) makes handmade carpets.

Camping Puyuhuapi (by donation) is alongside the gas station. **Hostería Marily** (☎ 067-325102; Uebel s/n; r without/with bath US$10/12) is your best choice with firm beds and breakfast included. **Hostería Elizabeth** (☎ 067-325106; Circunvalación s/n; r per person US$8.50) is comfortable and has good meals; breakfast is included. **Casa Ludwig** (☎ 067-325220; Uebel s/n; share/no-share r per person US$11/16) is a cozy B&B with some room for budget backpackers. Details, like hot water bottles and real coffee, make it a favorite. About 15km south, **Hospedaje Las Toninas** (km 205; campsites US$9, r per person US$7) has beachfront campsites with fire pits and rooms in a cute wood-shingled house. Meals (about US$4) are available. **Aonikenk Cabañas** (Hamburgo 16) has a delightful café. The owner is very helpful with area information.

Buses going south usually arrive around 3–5pm. Transportes Emanuel leaves from the store next to the police station.

PARQUE NACIONAL QUEULAT

Queulat (admission US$3) is a wild domain of steep-sided fjords, rushing rivers, evergreen forests, creeping glaciers and high volcanic peaks. Conaf's **Centro de Información Ambiental** is at the parking lot for the lookout toward the Ventisquero Colgante, the visible hanging glacier. A 3km hike accesses good views.

Just north of the southern entrance at Pudú, at km 170, a damp trail climbs the valley of the **Río de las Cascadas** through a dense forest to an impressive granite bowl where half a dozen waterfalls drop from hanging glaciers.

Basic camping is available at **Ventisquero** (per site US$6), convenient to the Ventisquero Colgante, and at **Angostura** on Lago Risopatrón, 12km north of Puyuhuapi.

COYHAIQUE

Coyhaique (population 45,000) spreads over the barren Patagonian steppe, lorded over by the impressive basalt massif of Cerro Macay. Housing strips, windmill energy farms and herds of semitrucks may shock travelers emerging from the forests of the northern Carretera Austral. It's the regional capital and base for settlements and elite fly-fishing resorts further south.

Orientation

Coyhaique's street plan around its plaza is based on a disorienting pentagonal plan.

Av General Baquedano skirts the northeastern side of town and connects with the highway to Puerto Chacabuco. Av Ogano heads south to Balmaceda and Lago General Carrera.

Information

Internet access is at **Visual.com** (12 de Octubre 485-B; US$0.80 per hr) and at main call centers. Laundry is available at **Lavamatic** (Simpson 417) and **Lavandería QL** (Bilbao 160). Change cash or traveler's checks at **Turismo Prado** (21 de Mayo 417) or **Cambios Emperador** (Bilbao 222). Banks with ATMs are along Condell near the plaza. **Hospital Base** (☎ 067-231286; Calle Hospital) is at the western end of JM Carrera. There's a **post office** (Cochrane 202) and **Entel** (Prat 340). Helpful staff at **Sernatur** (☎ 067-233949; Bulnes 35) post updated listings of lodgings and transportation. **Conaf** (☎ 067-212125; 12 de Octubre 382) has park details.

Sights & Activities

Museo Regional de la Patagonia (cnr Baquedano & Eusebio Lillo; admission US$0.75) is worth a quick visit, with pioneer artifacts and Jesuit regalia. **Feria Artesanal** (Plaza de Armas) has woolens, leather and wooden knick-knacks.

There are good hiking possibilities in the **Reserva Nacional Coyhaique** (admission US$1), 5km from town: take Baquedano north across the bridge, then go right at the gravel road; from the entrance it's another 3km to Laguna Verde. Recommended and English-speaking, **Patagonia Adventure Expeditions** (☎ 067-219894; www.adventurepatagonia.com; Dussen 357) runs kayaking trips (US$25 to US$60). **Cabot** (☎ 067-230101; General Parra 1777) also plans adventurous trips in the area.

Sleeping

Reserva Nacional Coyhaique (camping per site US$6) There's camping at Caja Bruja, 2.5km from the entrance, and at Laguna Verde, 4km from the entrance.

Camping Alborado (☎ 067-238868; camping per person US$3.50) Clean with good amenities and sheltered sites; 1km from the city.

Albergue Las Salamandras (☎ 067-211865; campsites US$5, beds per person US$10) In a woodsy area about 2km south of town. An attractive lodge with ample common spaces, two kitchens, large baths and cozy dorm rooms with loads of blankets.

CHILE

COYHAIQUE

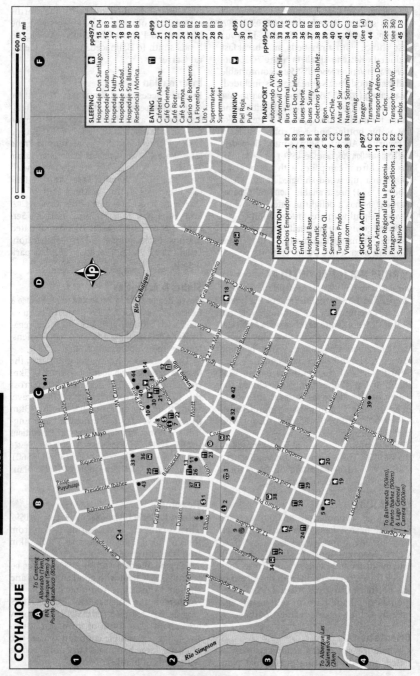

0   600 m
0   0.4 mi

To Camping
Alborada (1km),
RN Coyhaique (5km) &
Puerto Chacabuco (800km)

Río Coyhaique

Río Simpson

To Albergue Las
Salamandras
(2km)

To Balmaceda (50km),
Puerto Aisén (30km)
& Lago General
Carrera (200km)

Rates listed below are per person with shared bath, unless indicated. Many *hospedajes* line Almirante Simpson.

Hospedaje Nathy (☎ 067-231047; Simpson 417; r US$9) Amiable and helpful with cozy but slightly cramped rooms; breakfast included.

Hospedaje Sra Blanca (☎ 067-232158; Simpson 459; r US$11.50) Large rooms in an independent annex and an abundant breakfast make this good value. A couple of doubles with private bath are available.

Hospedaje Don Santiago (☎ 067-231116; Errázuriz 1040; r US$6) Family-run and friendly, with bright rooms and kitchen use.

Hospedaje Soledad (☎ 067-254764; 21 de Mayo 935; camping/r US$3.50/9) Has an annex house with independent lodging, kitchen use and garden camping.

Residencial Mónica (☎ 067-234302; Eusebio Lillo 664; r with bath & breakfast US$13) A well-regarded small place with cozy rooms; there's a restaurant downstairs.

Hospedaje Lautaro (☎ 067-238116; Lautaro 269; r US$9; ☼ summer only) Spacious, clean and handy for bus terminal; locks up around midnight.

Eating & Drinking

Casino de Bomberos (General Parra 365) Another top bet for set menus at lunch.

Café Oriente (Condell 201; US$3-5) A decent sandwich place.

Cafetería Alemana (Condell 119) Also has OK sandwiches, but is a bit too smoky; the best deal is roasted chicken.

La Fiorentina (Prat 230; large pizzas US$9) Serves hearty pizzas with lots of toppings, plus cold beers.

Café Ricer (Horn 48) Over-touristy and over-priced. Full menu with a variety of breakfasts, open when everywhere else is closed.

Two large supermarkets are near each other on Lautaro, one is at Prat, the other at Cochrane.

Piel Roja (Mordela 495) Colorfully designed with a swank bar serving mixed drinks and good mini-pizzas; the upstairs dance floor stays hopping till late.

Pub Z (Moraleda 420) A converted *galpón* (shed); hosts art exhibits and live music performances.

Getting There & Away

AIR

The region's main airport is in Balmaceda, 50km southeast of Coyhaique. **LanChile** (☎ 600-526-2000; General Parra 402) has daily flights to Puerto Montt and Santiago. **Sky Airline** (☎ 067-240825; Arturo Prat 203) is another choice. **Transporte Aéreo Don Carlos** (☎ 067-231981; Subteniente Cruz 63) flies to Chile Chico (US$32) weekdays except Thursday, and Cochrane (US$60) and Villa O'Higgins (US$93) Monday and Thursday.

BOAT

Ferries to Puerto Montt leave from Puerto Chacabuco, two hours from Coyhaique by bus. Schedules are subject to change.

Ask **Navimag** (☎ 067-223306; Presidente Ibáñez 347) about the ferry service to Puerto Montt; departing about twice weekly, once weekly in low season (US$47 to US$85, meals included) and to Quellón, Chiloé. **Naviera Sotramin** (☎ 067-233515; Bolívar 254) and **Mar del Sur** (☎ 067-231255; Baquedano 146-A) run ferries to/from Puerto Ibáñez and Chile Chico. If you're driving, make reservations at the offices.

BUS

Bus transportation in and out of Coyhaique changes continuously; check with Sernatur for the latest information. The small **bus terminal** (cnr Lautaro & Magallanes) has limited services; most companies operate from offices elsewhere in town.

For Puerto Aisén and Puerto Chacabuco, **Buses Don Carlos** (Cruz 63) and **Buses Suray** (Arturo Prat 265) leave approximately every 1½ hours (US$2, one hour).

Companies going to Chaitén include **Buses Norte** (Gral Parra 337) and **Transporte Muñoz** (Gral Parra 337). Otherwise, from the bus terminal, take a bus to La Junta (US$12, 7 to 10 hours), from where there are more buses to Chaitén.

Colectivos and shuttle buses head to Puerto Ingeniero Ibáñez (US$5, 1½ hours) to connect with the Chile Chico ferry. These include **Colectivos Puerto Ibáñez** (cnr Arturo Prat & Errázuriz) and **Transportes Ali** (☎ 067-219009; 250-346), with a door-to-port shuttle service.

Acuario 13 and Buses Ñadis, at the bus terminal, go to Cochrane four times weekly. Don Carlos goes to Puerto Río Tranquilo (US$10, five hours) at 4pm Thursday and Monday, from where connections can be made to Chile Chico. Transportes Ali leaves Wednesday and Sunday mornings for Chile Chico (US$16, six hours) via Puerto Río Tranquilo; returning Tuesday.

CHILE

Turíbus (Baquedano 1171) goes to Osorno and Puerto Montt via Argentina (US$30, 22 hours) on Saturday (and Tuesday in summer). For Punta Arenas, **Bus Sur** (bus terminal) leaves Tuesday (US$49, 17 hours), or take Turíbus to Comodoro Rivadavia on Monday and Friday (US$26, eight hours) and transfer there.

Getting Around

The door-to-door shuttle service (US$4) to the airport is with **Transfer Coyhaique** (☎ 067-210495, 09-838-5070) and **Transfer Aisén Tour** (☎ 067-217070, 09-489-4760). They leave two hours before flight departure. Buses drop off downtown.

Car rental is expensive at about US$70 a day for a double-cabin pickup, which you'll need on the rough roads. Try **Traeger** (☎ 067-231648; Baquedano 457), **Automundo AVR** (☎ 067-231621; Bilbao 510), and **Automóvil Club de Chile** (☎ 067-231847; Carrera 333). **Figon** (Simpson 888) rents and repairs bikes.

LAGO GENERAL CARRERA

Although public transport is limited around the lake, extending your Carretera Austral road trip around Lago General Carrera and further south presents a unique experience of complete isolation, barren Patagonian steppe, and a gut-churning road snaking along the brilliantly blue lake. About a third of its 224,000-hectare mass is in Argentina, as Lago Buenos Aires. This section follows the Carretera Austral south from Coyhaique, around the lake's western border.

Just before reaching Balmaceda from Coyhaique, a right-hand turn-off (the sign points to Cochrane) heads toward **Reserva Nacional Cerro Castillo**. This national reserve encompasses some 180,000 hectares of southern beech forest and the towering basalt castle spires of Cerro Castillo, flanked by three major glaciers on its southern slopes. At km 104, in Villa Cerro Castillo, there's lodging and food at **La Querencia** (O'Higgins 522; r US$8).

Along the western shore, **Puerto Río Tranquilo** has a petrol station. Pricey tours are arranged to **Capilla de Mármol** (marble chapel), but don't bother in rough water. North of town a road to Parque Nacional San Rafael is underway. **Residencial Darka** (Arrayanes 330; r per person US$9) includes breakfast. Wild camping is possible on the windy beach, or 10km west at Lago Tranquilo.

About 13km east of Cruce El Maitén, where the Carretera Austral continues to Puerto Bertrand, **Puerto Guadal** has petrol and provisions. Pitch a tent along the lake, or hunker down at **Hostería Huemules** (Las Magnolias 382; r per person US$9), with a good restaurant. If it is closed, go to the blue house next door.

Chile Chico

After a hair-raising roller coaster of a ride from Puerto Guadal, the road ends in this flat windswept lakeside town with a sunny microclimate that makes it a large producer of fruit. From here, buses connect to Los Antiguos and Ruta 40 leading to southern Argentine Patagonia. There is **tourist information** (cnr O'Higgins & Lautaro) and a **Banco del Estado** (González 112) for money exchange. Camping options are at tranquil, small and friendly **Camping Chile Chico** (Pedro Burgos 6; camping per person US$4) and sweet **Hospedaje No Me Olvides** (campsites per person US$2; r US$7.50), 200m from town on the highway to Argentina; also with large clean rooms, kitchen use and meals available.

Stuffy **Hospedaje Eben Ezer** (☎ 067-411535; Rodríguez; beds US$5.50) has kitchen use and large shared rooms. **Hospedaje Brisas del Lago** (☎ 067-411204; Manuel Rodríguez 443; beds US$8) offers the best value rooms but service can be apathetic. For meals and drinks, head to **Café Refer** (O'Higgins 424).

SPLURGE!

Watching icebergs calve off the giant San Rafael glacier into **Laguna San Rafael**, 225km southwest of Puerto Chacabuco, is impressive, but getting there is expensive. You've got two choices: by air or sea. Flights (US$140 to US$180) from Coyhaique permit about two hours at the glacier; contact **Patagonia Explorer Aviación** (☎ 09-8172172). Navimag's ferry *Evangelistas* goes once a week in summer from Puerto Chacabuco (US$208 to US$320 round trip, all inclusive; two days), but only two or three times a month the rest of the year. Transmarchilay has a similar service. See p496 for contact information. Ideally, find a boat trip that travels to the glacier by day.

Getting There & Away
BOAT
Auto-passenger ferries, Naviera Sotramin's *Pilchero* and Mar del Sur's *Chelenco*, chug across the lake to/from Puerto Ingeniero Ibañéz (2½ hours), with a combined schedule of at least once a day, with limited service Sunday. Departure days and times change often: check at the Entel office in Chile Chico for the latest posting. Rates are: passengers US$3, bicycles US$2.50, motorcycles US$6.50 and vehicles US$31 to US$37. Reservations for vehicles are highly recommended; for contact information, see p499.

BUS
For transportation from Coyhaique to Puerto Ibáñez, Puerto Río Tranquilo and Chile Chico, see p496. From Chile Chico, **Turismo Padilla** (O'Higgins 42) goes to Los Antiguos, Argentina, four to five times daily (US$2.50).

MAGALLANES

Rugged, mountainous and stormy, the Magallanes region is the heart of Chilean Patagonia. Its wild geography is a playground for trekkers, many of whom tackle Torres del Paine before or after continuing on to Argentine Patagonia. And for the more sedate, the pristine nature and proximity to Tierra del Fuego and Antarctica is enough reason to explore. You can wonder at how or why anyone got here in the first place while watching the sky change color and shape across an endless horizon.

The region's original inhabitants were the subject of zealous Salesian missions, and all but wiped out by disease and warfare in attempts to push them off lands claimed for sheep herding. When 300 purebred sheep were brought over from the Falkland Islands in the late 19th century, the wool boom took off; soon two million animals were grazing the territory's pastures. English, Scottish and Croatian immigrants flocked to the area to seek work in the wool boom and in gold rushes. Their influence, as well as the great wealth spun from wool and gold, is evident in the opulence of Punta Arenas' mansions as well as the many place names and faces of the region.

Chile did not assume definite control of the area until 1843. Today, petroleum and fishing are boom industries. For a map of the area, refer to the Tierra del Fuego section in the Argentina chapter (p146).

PUNTA ARENAS
On the western shore of the Strait of Magellan, Punta Arenas (population 121,000) has elaborate mansions dating from the wool boom of the late 19th and early 20th centuries and good traveler's services. Nearby penguin colonies and historic sites make it a worthwhile stopover. The city is dead quiet on Sunday.

Orientation
Punta Arenas' regular grid street plan, with wide streets and sidewalks, makes it easy to walk around. The Plaza de Armas, or Plaza Muñoz Gamero, is the center of town. Street names change on either side of the plaza. Most landmarks and accommodations are within a few blocks of here.

Information
Internet access is available at most hostels, including **Hostal Calafate II** (Magallanes 926), and at **GonFish** (Croacia 1028), with notebook hookups.

For laundry, try **Record** (☎ 061-243607; O'Higgins 969), which charges US$6 per basket, or **Backpackers Laundry** (☎ 061-241516; Sarmiento 726). For money exchange, try the travel agencies along Lautaro Navarro between Errázuriz and Pedro Montt and along Roca; they're open from Monday to Saturday. Finding a compatible ATM is no problem. The **Hospital Regional** (☎ 061-244040) is at Arauco and Angamos. The **post office** (Bories 911) is one block north of the plaza. For phone service, there's **Entel** (Navarro 957; ◷ until 10pm) and **Telefónica** (Nogueira 1116). **Sernatur** (☎ 061-241330; Waldo Seguel 689; ◷ 8:15am-6:45pm Mon-Fri, 8:15am-8pm in summer) has well-informed staff, and accommodations and transportation lists. There's also an **information kiosk** (Plaza de Armas; ◷ 8am-7pm Mon-Fri, 9am-8pm Sat). **Conaf** (☎ 061-223841; José Menéndez 1147) has details on the nearby parks.

Sights & Activities
The heart of the city, **Plaza Muñoz Gamero** is surrounded by opulent mansions, including the former **Sara Braun mansion** and the

CHILE

PUNTA ARENAS

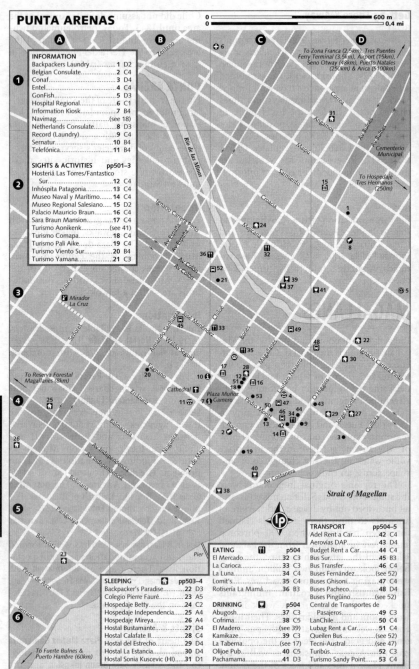

INFORMATION
Backpackers Laundry..............1 D2
Belgian Consulate..................2 C4
Conaf...................................3 D4
Entel....................................4 C4
GonFish................................5 D3
Hospital Regional..................6 C1
Information Kiosk...................7 B4
Navimag.........................(see 18)
Netherlands Consulate...........8 D3
Record (Laundry)...................9 C4
Sernatur...............................10 B4
Telefónica............................11 B4

SIGHTS & ACTIVITIES   pp501–3
Hostería Las Torres/Fantastico
   Sur....................................12 C4
Inhóspita Patagonia................13 C4
Museo Naval y Marítimo.........14 C4
Museo Regional Salesiano.......15 D2
Palacio Mauricio Braun...........16 C4
Sara Braun Mansion...............17 C4
Turismo Aonikenk...........(see 41)
Turismo Comapa....................18 C4
Turismo Pali Aike..................19 C4
Turismo Viento Sur................20 B4
Turismo Yamana....................21 C3

To Zona Franca (2.5km), Tres Puentes
Ferry Terminal (3.5km), Airport (15km),
Seno Otway (48km), Puerto Natales
(250km) & Arica (5100km)

To Hospedaje
Tres Hermanos
(250m)

Río de las Minas

Mirador
La Cruz

To Reserva Forestal
Magallanes (8km)

Cathedral

Plaza Muñoz
Gamero

Strait of Magellan

Pier

To Fuerte Bulnes &
Puerto Hambre (60km)

Cementerio
Municipal

SLEEPING   pp503–4
Backpacker's Paradise.........22 D3
Colegio Pierre Fauré............23 A5
Hospedaje Betty..................24 C2
Hospedaje Independencia......25 A4
Hospedaje Mireya................26 A4
Hostal Bustamante...............27 D4
Hostal Calafate II................28 C4
Hostal del Estrecho..............29 D4
Hostal La Estancia................30 D4
Hostal Sonia Kuscevic (HI)....31 D1

EATING   p504
El Mercado..........................32 C3
La Carioca...........................33 C3
La Luna...............................34 C4
Lomit's................................35 C4
Rotisería La Mamá................36 B3

DRINKING   p504
Abugosh...............................37 C3
Cofrima................................38 C5
El Madero.......................(see 39)
Kamikaze.............................39 C4
La Taberna......................(see 17)
Olijoe Pub............................40 C5
Pachamama...........................41 D3

TRANSPORT   pp504–5
Adel Rent a Car....................42 C4
Aerovías DAP.......................43 D4
Budget Rent a Car.................44 C4
Bus Sur...............................45 B3
Bus Transfer........................46 C4
Buses Fernández...............(see 52)
Buses Ghisoni.......................47 C4
Buses Pacheco......................48 D4
Buses Pingüino................(see 52)
Central de Transportes de
   Pasajeros..........................49 C3
LanChile..............................50 C4
Lubag Rent a Car..................51 C4
Queilen Bus.....................(see 52)
Tecni-Austral...................(see 47)
Turibús................................52 C3
Turismo Sandy Point.............53 C4

0   600 m
0   0.4 mi

former Sociedad Menéndez Behety, now housing the Turismo Comapa offices.

Palacio Mauricio Braun (Magallanes 949; admission US$1.50; 🕑 10:30am-5pm in summer, 10:30am-2pm in winter) was the luxurious dwelling of the powerful 19th-century Braun-Menéndez family of land holders and sheep farmers. Note the French-nouveau furnishings and intricate wooden inlay floors. **Cementerio Municipal** (Bulnes 949) tells the story of the town's founding, with extravagant tombs of the town's first families hovering over more humble graves of the immigrants whose labor made such fortunes possible. There is also a monument to the Selk'nam, an indigenous group that was wiped out during the wool boom.

Museo Regional Salesiano (Av Bulnes 374; admission US$2.50; 🕑 10am-12:30pm & 3-6pm Tue-Sun) portrays missionaries as peacemakers between Indians and settlers. The rotting natural history specimens are nothing to speak of; the best materials are on the mountaineer priest Alberto de Agostini and the various indigenous groups.

Museo Naval y Marítimo (🕾 Pedro Montt 981; admission US$0.75; 🕑 Tue-Sat) displays model ships, naval history and an account of the Chilean mission that rescued Sir Ernest Shackleton's crew from Antarctica.

Only 8km from downtown, **Reserva Forestal Magallanes** has good hiking and mountain-biking trails. A steady uphill hike goes to the top of Mt Fenton; views are spectacular and the wind impressively strong. In winter, ski while admiring the strait.

Tours

Worthwhile day trips include tours to the **Seno Otway pingüinera** (tours US$9, admission US$4; 🕑 Dec-Mar) and to the town's first settlements at **Fuerte Bulnes & Puerto Hambre** (tours US$12, admission US$2). Lodgings can help arrange tours, or try one of the following:

Turismo Aonikenk (🕾 061-228332; Magallanes 619) Well regarded with multilingual staff.

Turismo Pali Aike (🕾 061-223301; Lautaro Navarro 1129)

Turismo Viento Sur (🕾 061-225167; Fagnano 565)

Tours on the *Barcaza Melinka* to see penguin colonies on **Isla Magdalena** (Monumento Natural Los Pingüinos; adult/child US$30/15) leave Tuesday, Thursday and Saturday, December through February. Book tickets through **Turismo Comapa** (🕾 061-200200; Magallanes 990). For more adventure, check with **Inhóspita Patagonia** (🕾 061-224510; Lautaro Navarro 1013), which offers treks to Cape Froward; and **Turismo Yamana** (🕾 061-221130; Colón 568) for kayaking on the Magellan Strait.

Sleeping

Colegio Pierre Fauré (🕾 061-226256; Bellavista 697; camping/beds US$4/6; 🕑 Dec-Mar) A private school, six blocks south of the plaza. Has garden camping, shared baths but plenty of hot water.

Hostal Bustamante (🕾 061-222774; Jorge Montt 847; r per person US$10) Although you can't tell from the outside, it's elegant inside. Strong showers, good breakfast and homemade jam.

Hospedaje Tres Hermanos (🕾 061-225450; Angamos 1218; r per person US$7) Quiet, comfortable rooms in an old converted house; rates include breakfast.

Hospedaje Independencia (🕾 061-227572; Independencia 374; camping/dm US$3/5) Casual place run by a young couple, with decent dorm rooms, kitchen use and camping in the small front yard. Breakfast is US$3.

Hospedaje Betty (🕾 061-249777; Mejicana 576; r US$7) Family atmosphere with kitchen use; breakfast included.

Hospedaje Mireya (🕾 061-247066; Boliviana 375; r US$9) Has an independent annex with full kitchen, but tiny baths and lacks heat. Includes breakfast.

Backpacker's Paradise (🕾 061-240104; Ignacio Carrera Pinto 1022; dm US$6) Crowded rooms divided by flimsy curtains, well-stocked kitchen, Internet access, fun atmosphere and a friendly house dog.

Hostal Sonia Kuscevic (🕾 061-248543; Pasaje Darwin 175; shared r HI members US$14, s/d US$22/32) Cozy but cramped rooms with private bath and breakfast. A bit formal; good for solo travelers.

Hostal La Estancia (🕾 061-249130; O'Higgins 765; s/d US$13/23) Run by a friendly young couple; attractive upstairs rooms with shared bath, decent beds, rock hard pillows and thin walls. A large breakfast is included and has Sky TV.

Hostal Calafate II (🕾 061-241281; Magallanes 926; s/d with breakfast US$23/32, with bath US$37/45) In the heart of downtown, has a laid-back hotel feel with long hallways and large rooms with TV, but lots of street noise.

CHILE

Hostal del Estrecho (☎ 061-241011; José Menéndez 1048; s/d US$17/28, with bath US$33/40) Kind owners and huge rooms, each full of bunk beds. Breakfast is included and served in the cozy dining area.

Eating & Drinking

La Luna (O'Higgins 974; seafood pastas US$5) Has some of the tastiest food and best ambiance in town. Service is attentive, the music good and the world maps fun to stick pins into.

La Carioca (José Menéndez 600; pizzas US$3-7) Praised for pizzas, sandwiches and cold lager beer, plus a daily lunch special.

Rotisería La Mamá (Sanhueza 720; mains US$4-9) Homemade pastas, including a hearty bowl of lasagna (the veg option is bland).

Lomit's (José Menéndez 722; sandwiches US$3-5) Open late and on Sunday with generous, made-to-order sandwiches but has slow service.

El Mercado (Mejicana 617; mains US$5-10; ☾ 24 hr) Heaps on the seafood specials, from scallops to baked *centolla* (king crabs) to mussels *a la parmesana*. There's a 10% surcharge between 1am and 8am. A must-go.

For drinks and snacks, check out **Olijoe Pub** (Errázuriz 970), **La Taberna** in the basement of the former Sara Braun mansion, or **El Madero** (Bories 655), above the dance club Kamikaze.

Pachamama (Magallanes 698) Sells dried nuts and fruits.

Abugosh (Bories 647) and **Cofrima** (Navarro & Balmaceda) are supermarkets; they are large and well-stocked.

Shopping

Punta Arenas is a duty-free zone.

Zona Franca (Zofri; ☾ Mon-Sat) A chaotic maze of vendors; it may prove fruitful if you're looking for camera equipment and film. *Colectivos* shuttle back and forth from downtown throughout the day.

Getting There & Away

Check with Sernatur about recent transportation, especially for maritime schedules. *La Prensa Austral* newspaper lists transportation availability, contact details and schedules.

AIR

Aeropuerto Presidente Carlos Ibáñez del Campo is 20km north of town. **LanChile** (☎ 600-526-2000; Lautaro Navarro 999) flies at least four times daily to Santiago via Puerto Montt. **Aerovías DAP** (☎ 061-223340; www.aeroviasdap.cl; O'Higgins 891) flies to/from Porvenir (US$22) twice daily except Sunday; Puerto Williams on Isla Navarino (US$70) Tuesday to Saturday; Ushuaia (US$100) on Monday and Wednesday; El Calafate (US$50) twice daily on weekdays; and Río Grande (US$79) about once a week in summer. Luggage is limited to 10kg per person.

BOAT

Transbordadora Austral Broom (☎ 061-218100; www.tabsa.cl; Av Bulnes 05075) sails to Porvenir, Tierra del Fuego (US$7, 2½ to four hours), from the Tres Puentes ferry terminal (*colectivos* leave from Palacio Mauricio Braun). A faster way to get to Tierra del Fuego (US$2, 20 minutes) is via the Punta Delgada–Bahía Azul crossing northeast of Punta Arenas. Ferries leave every 1½ hours from 8:30am to 10:15pm. Call ahead for vehicle reservations (US$17).

Broom also runs the ferry *Patagonia*, which sails from Tres Puentes to Puerto Williams, Isla Navarino, two or three times a month, Wednesday only, returning Friday (US$120 to US$150 including meals, 38 hours). Paying extra for a bunk is advisable.

BUS

Minibuses (US$4), Bus Pacheco (US$2.50) and taxis (US$9) meet flights at the airport. There is also a bus direct to Puerto Natales, but it usually stops downtown first. Bus Transfer (US$3) has scheduled departures throughout the day to coincide with flight departures. **Turismo Sandy Point** (☎ 061-246954; Pedro Montt 840) runs shuttles (US$2.50 from it's office or US$3 for door-to-door service). Aerovías DAP (see Air above) provides a shuttle service for its clients.

Punta Arenas has no central bus terminal, but at the time of writing plans to build one near the port were underway. If traveling to Ushuaia, it may be cheaper and easier to go to Río Grande and hop on *micros* heading to Ushuaia.

Companies and destinations include:

Bus Sur (Menéndez 565) Puerto Natales, Coyhaique.
Bus Transfer (Pedro Montt 966) Puerto Natales.
Buses Fernández, Turíbus, Queilen Bus & Buses Pingüino (Armando Sanhueza 745) Puerto Natales, Puerto Montt, Río Gallegos.

Buses Ghisoni (Lautaro Navarro 975) Río Grande, Río Gallegos, Ushuaia.

Buses Pacheco (Colón 900) Puerto Natales, Puerto Montt, Río Grande, Río Gallegos, Ushuaia; recommended.

Central de Transportes de Pasajeros (cnr Magallanes & Colón) All destinations.

Destination	Duration in Hours	Cost
Coyhaique	20	US$44
Puerto Montt	30	US$44
Puerto Natales	3	US$4
Río Gallegos	4	US$12
Río Grande	8	US$19
Ushuaia	12	US$36

Getting Around

Colectivos (US$0.50, a bit more at night and Sunday) zip around town; catch northbound ones on Av Magallanes or Av España and southbound along Bories or Av España.

Adel Rent a Car (☎ 061-235471; Pedro Montt 962) provides attentive service, competitive rates and good travel tips for the area. Other choices include **Budget Rent a Car** (☎ 061-225983; O'Higgins 964) and **Lubag** (☎ 061-242023; Magallanes 970). All agencies can arrange papers for crossing into Argentina.

PUERTO NATALES

Usually a quiet, slightly depressed but welcoming fishing port town, Puerto Natales (population 19,000) turns into a hub of activity and fun come springtime. Navimag ferries dump trek-ready travelers here and buses to/from El Calafate and Torres del Paine keep them churning in and out. All of this on the shores of Seno Última Esperanza (Last Hope Sound), 250km northwest of Punta Arenas.

Information

Internet connections are very slow throughout town; try **CyberCafe** (Blanco Encalada 226). **Servilaundry** (Bulnes 513) is the main washhouse in town, but many hostels offer service. There's a **hospital** (☎ 061-411533; O'Higgins & Ignacio Carrera Pinto) and **Redfarma** (Arturo Prat 158) is a good pharmacy. **Stop Cambios** (Baquedano 386) changes cash, as do many agents along Blanco Encalada. Most banks in town have ATMs. **Banco del Estado** (Plaza de Armas) changes US cash. Stay in touch via the **post office** (Eberhard 429), **Telefónica** (Blanco Encalada 298) and **Entel** (Baquedano 270). The municipal **tourist**

office (☎ 061-411263; Bulnes 285) in the museum is useful and has good listings. **Sernatur** (☎ 061-412125; Costanera Pedro Montt) isn't as helpful. **Conaf** (☎ 061-411438; O'Higgins 584) has an administrative office. For adventure outfitters, see Torres del Paine p509.

Sleeping

Puerto Natales has loads of lodgings, but in the high season the most popular ones fill up fast, so call to reserve before you get there. Off-season, rates tumble.

Josmar 2 (☎ 061-414417 Esmeralda 517; camping US$3) You can camp behind a restaurant with crummy toilets.

Charging US$5 per person are:

Hospedaje Dumestre (☎ 061-411347; Ignacio Carrera Pinto 540) With a large living room with fireplace and TV, kitchen use, and country fresh eggs right from their farm.

Backpacker's Magallania (☎ 061-414950; Rogers 255) With dorm beds and kitchen privileges, but no breakfast.

The following places all charge US$7 to US$8 per room with breakfast. Rooms may be shared in high season.

Residencial Mwono (☎ 061-411018; Eberhard 214) Small and personable, with kitchen use, wood-burning stove and relaxing, warm living room.

Casa Teresa (☎ 061-410472; Esmeralda 483) Very kind and pleasant with dorm beds. No kitchen access, but a good breakfast.

Patagonia Aventure (☎ 061-411028; Tomás Rogers 179) Hip and mellow, with a great kitchen and homemade breads. Lots of help with organizing trips.

Residencial Danicar (☎ 061-412170; O'Higgins 707; ✗) Run by a conscientious family, good dorm beds.

Residencial Oasis (☎ 061-411675; Señoret 332) Rooms in the back have outstanding views. There are also rooms with private baths.

Niko's (☎ 061-412810; Ramírez 669) Separate kitchen for travelers, plus some organized dinners; bring your own towel and toilet paper, though. Rooms with private bath US$11 per person.

Also try checking out **Hospedaje Tequendama** (☎ 061-412951; Ladrilleros 141) and **Hospedaje Nancy** (☎ 061-411186; Bulnes 343).

Charging a bit more, around US$9 to US$11, are the following:

Residencial Bernardita (☎ 061-411162; O'Higgins 765) With quiet back annex rooms and kitchen use.

CHILE

Hostal Dos Lagunas (☎ 61-415733; Barros Arana 104) Small place with a few large rooms (heaters brought in), great showers, filling breakfasts and loads of travel tips.

Casa Cecilia (☎ 061-411797; Tomás Rogers 64; s/d US$15/21) Popular with the European crowd, lots of rooms close together, but usually stays quiet. Small kitchen, great showers, delicious morning toast. Owners provide equipment rentals.

Eating & Drinking

El Living (Prat 156; US$2.50-5) Understands gringo cravings, such as peanut butter and jelly, baked beans on toast and fresh, crunchy salads, just to name a few. Sink into the sofas with a cup of real coffee and a muffin in the morning or a choice of strong drinks in the evening.

Concepto Indigo (Ladrilleros 105) Another good gathering place. Has whole-wheat sandwiches, a fun bar and views across the sound.

El Rincón de Tata (Prat 236) For pizza; it's dark.

Masay (Bulnes 427; US$3.50-5) Has fast service and oversized sandwiches and burgers.

Andrés (Ladrilleros 381; US$5) Small, but come with a big appetite: the owner/chef knows how to treat his clients right.

El Marítimo (Costanera Pedro Montt 214) Has heaping platters of fish and seafood, but has become too touristy.

Don Chicho (Baquedano s/n; US$10) Carnivore heaven, with all-you-can-eat lamb *parrilla*; evenings only.

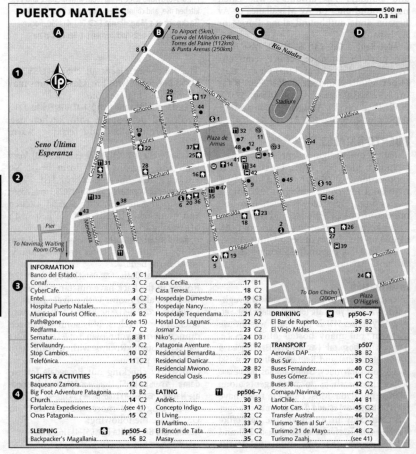

PUERTO NATALES

0 — 500 m
0 — 0.3 mi

To Airport (5km),
Cueva del Milodón (24km),
Torres del Paine (112km)
& Punta Arenas (250km)

Río Natales

Rodríguez

Bernardo Phillipi

Stadium

Señoret

Magallanes

Tomás Rogers

Plaza de Armas

Valdivia

Seno Última Esperanza

Barros Arana

Bories

Eberhard

Andúamos

Ramírez

Calvarino

Manuel Bulnes

Arturo Prat

Blanco Encalada

Baquedano

Pier

Esmeralda

Golfo Carrera Pinto

To Navimag Waiting Room (75m)

O'Higgins

Chorrillos

To Don Chicho (200m)

Plaza O'Higgins

Miraflores

INFORMATION			
Banco del Estado.............................	1 C1	Casa Cecilia.............................	17 B1
Conaf...	2 C2	Casa Teresa............................	18 C2
CyberCafe.....................................	3 C3	Hospedaje Dumestre.................	19 C3
Entel...	4 C2	Hospedaje Nancy....................	20 B2
Hospital Puerto Natales................	5 C3	Hospedaje Tequendama............	21 A2
Municipal Tourist Office...............	6 B2	Hostal Dos Lagunas.................	22 B2
Path@gone................................	(see 15)	Josmar 2...............................	23 C2
Redfarma....................................	7 C2	Niko's...................................	24 D3
Sernatur.....................................	8 B1	Patagonia Aventure................	25 B2
Servilaundry...............................	9 C2	Residencial Bernardita.............	26 D2
Stop Cambios.............................	10 D2	Residencial Danicar.................	27 D2
Telefónica..................................	11 C2	Residencial Mwono................	28 B2
		Residencial Oasis....................	29 B1
SIGHTS & ACTIVITIES	p505		
Baqueano Zamora.......................	12 C2	EATING 🍴	pp506–7
Big Foot Adventure Patagonia......	13 B2	Andrés..................................	30 B3
Church.......................................	14 C2	Concepto Indigo....................	31 A2
Fortaleza Expediciones...............	(see 41)	El Living...............................	32 B2
Onas Patagonia.........................	15 C2	El Marítimo...........................	33 A2
		El Rincón de Tata...................	34 C2
SLEEPING 🏠	pp505–6	Masay.................................	35 C2
Backpacker's Magallania..............	16 B2		

DRINKING 🍸	pp506–7
El Bar de Ruperto......................	36 B2
El Viejo Midas..........................	37 B2

TRANSPORT	p507
Aerovías DAP...........................	38 B2
Bus Sur...................................	39 D3
Buses Fernández.......................	40 C2
Buses Gómez...........................	41 C2
Buses JB.................................	42 C2
Comapa/Navimag.....................	43 A2
LanChile.................................	44 B1
Motor Cars.............................	45 C2
Transfer Austral........................	46 D2
Turismo 'Bien al Sur'.................	47 B2
Turismo 21 de Mayo.................	48 C2
Turismo Zaahj.........................	(see 41)

CHILE

El Viejo Midas (Tomás Rogers 169) and **El Bar de Ruperto** (cnr Bulnes & Magallanes) serve oversized drinks; both are fun haunts.

Getting There & Away

AIR

Aerovías DAP (☎ 061-415100; Bulnes 100) flies to El Calafate, Argentina (US$50, 30 minutes), at 9am and 6:30pm weekdays from the small airfield, a few kilometers north of town. **LanChile** (☎ 600-526-2000; Tomás Rogers 78) can help with flights from Punta Arenas.

BOAT

To find out when Navimag's *Magallanes* ferry to/from Puerto Montt is arriving, head to **Comapa/Navimag** (☎ 061-414300; www.navimag .com; Costanera Pedro Montt 262) a couple of days before and on the estimated date. Dates and times can vary according to weather conditions and tides. See Puerto Montt, p488 for rate information.

BUS

Puerto Natales has no central bus terminal. Carriers include **Buses Fernández** (Eberhard 555), **Bus Sur** (Baquedano 534), **Transfer Austral** (Baquedano 414), **Buses JB** (Arturo Prat 258), **Turismo Zaahj** (Arturo Prat 236) and **Buses Gómez** (Prat 234). Expect limited service in the off-season.

To Torres del Paine, buses leave two to three times daily. Morning buses start picking up at lodgings around 7am. The afternoon bus leaves around 2:30pm. If you're heading to Refugio Pehoé in the off-season, take the morning bus (US$10 round trip, two hours) to meet the catamaran at Pudeto.

To Punta Arenas (US$4, three hours), Buses Fernández is the best regarded, but also try Transfer Austral and Bus Sur. Book morning departures early the day before.

To Río Gallegos, Argentina (US$12, four hours), Bus Sur leaves Tuesday and Thursday; El Pingüino, at the Fernández terminal, goes at 11am Wednesday and Sunday.

To El Calafate, Argentina (US$21, 5½ hours), Zaahj and Bus Sur have the most service.

To Coyhaique (US$48, 22 hours), Bus Sur leaves Monday.

Getting Around

You'll get better car rental rates in Punta Arenas. **Motor Cars** (☎ 061-413593; Blanco Encalada 330) rents high-clearance vehicles for US$75 to US$90 daily with 400km free. **Turismo 'Bien al Sur'** (☎ 061-415064; Bulnes 433) charges around US$75; it also rents mountain bikes for US$16 per day.

PARQUE NACIONAL TORRES DEL PAINE

Torres del Paine is Chile's most popular backpacker destination, and rightly so. A well-developed trail network accesses granite pillars, turquoise lakes, roaring rivers, creeping glaciers and dense forests to create a hiker's paradise. Most people come to either circuit or 'do the W' around the main mountain peaks of Torres del Paine (2800m), Paine Grande (3050m) and Los Cuernos (2200m to 2600m), in this 181,000-hectare Unesco Biosphere Reserve, while other trails remain almost deserted. If planning to camp or sleep in *refugios* along the most popular trails, make reservations as soon as possible. Avoid the crunch by coming either in November or March/April when the weather is less temperamental and the autumn colors brilliant. And be prepared for unpredictable rain showers and wind strong enough to break tent poles. Bring waterproof gear, *synthetic* sleeping bag, and, if you're camping, a good tent (much of this can be rented in Puerto Natales).

Orientation & Information

Parque Nacional Torres del Paine is 112km north of Puerto Natales via a decent but sometimes bumpy gravel road that passes Villa Cerro Castillo, where there is a seasonal border crossing into Argentina at Cancha Carrera. The road continues 40km north and west to **Portería Sarmiento** (admission US$11), the park's main entrance where entrance fees are collected. It's another 37km to the *administración* (park headquarters) and the **Conaf Centro de Visitantes** (✆ 9am-8pm in summer), with good information on park ecology and trail status.

Parque Nacional Torres del Paine is open year-round, subject to your ability to get there. Conaf and the concessions in charge of many of the lodgings may have to start regulating the flow of people into the most popular parts of the park in the near future. JLM maps of the park are found in Puerto Natales.

Activities

HIKING

The most popular hiking routes are the 'W' and the circuit. Doing the circuit (basically the 'W' plus the backside of the peaks) takes from seven to nine days, while the 'W' takes four to five. Add another day or two for transportation connections.

Most trekkers start both routes from Laguna Amarga and head west. However, it is also possible to hike from the Administración or take the catamaran from Pudeto to Pehoé and start from there (see Getting Around later in this section); hiking from these starting points, roughly southwest to northeast along the 'W', presents more

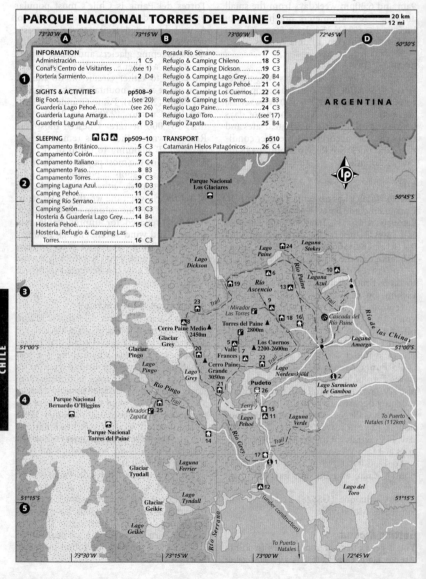

PARQUE NACIONAL TORRES DEL PAINE

INFORMATION	
Administración..................................	**1** C5
Conaf's Centro de Visitantes	(see 1)
Portería Sarmiento...........................	**2** D4

SIGHTS & ACTIVITIES	pp508–9
Big Foot..	(see 20)
Guardería Lago Pehoé......................	(see 26)
Guardería Laguna Amarga................	**3** D4
Guardería Laguna Azul......................	**4** D3

SLEEPING	pp509–10
Campamento Británico......................	**5** C3
Campamento Coirón..........................	**6** C3
Campamento Italiano........................	**7** C4
Campamento Paso.............................	**8** B3
Campamento Torres...........................	**9** C3
Camping Laguna Azul........................	**10** D3
Camping Pehoé.................................	**11** C4
Camping Río Serrano........................	**12** C5
Camping Serón..................................	**13** C3
Hostería & Guardería Lago Grey.......	**14** B4
Hostería Pehoé.................................	**15** C4
Hostería, Refugio & Camping Las Torres..	**16** C3

Posada Río Serrano...........................	**17** C5
Refugio & Camping Chileno..............	**18** C3
Refugio & Camping Dickson..............	**19** C3
Refugio & Camping Lago Grey...........	**20** B4
Refugio & Camping Lago Pehoé.........	**21** C4
Refugio & Camping Los Cuernos.......	**22** C4
Refugio & Camping Los Perros..........	**23** C3
Refugio Lago Paine...........................	**24** C3
Refugio Lago Toro............................	(see 17)
Refugio Zapata.................................	**25** B4

TRANSPORT	p510
Catamarán Hielos Patagónicos.........	**26** C4

Scale: 0 — 20 km / 0 — 12 mi

73°30'W A   73°15'W B   73°00'W C   72°45'W D

50°30'S

ARGENTINA

Parque Nacional Los Glaciares

50°45'S

Lago Dickson

Lago Paine **24** Laguna Stokes

6 Río Ascencio **19** **13** Laguna Azul **10** **4**

Río Paine

Trail

23 Trail Mirador Las Torres

9 Torres del Paine ▲ 2800m **18** **16** Cascada del Río Paine

Cerro Paine Medio ▲ 2450m Glaciar Grey **20** **5** Valle **7** Los Cuernos ▲ 2200-2600m **3** Laguna Amarga

51°00'S Glaciar Pingo Lago Pingo Río Pingo Cerro Paine Grande 3050m **22** Trail Lago Nordenskjöld **2** Lago Sarmiento de Gamboa 51°00'S

Lago Grey **21** Pudeto **26**

Parque Nacional Bernardo O'Higgins Mirador Zapata **25** Trail Ferry **15** **11** Laguna Verde To Puerto Natales (112km)

Parque Nacional Torres del Paine **14** Lago Pehoé Río Grey Trail

17 **1**

Glaciar Tyndall Laguna Ferrier Lago Tyndall **12** Lago del Toro

51°15'S Glaciar Geikie Lago Geikie Río Serrano (under construction) 51°15'S

To Puerto Natales

73°30'W 73°15'W 73°00'W 72°45'W

CHILE

views of Los Cuernos. Trekking alone, especially on the backside of the circuit is inadvisable (and restricted by Conaf).

The 'W'

The trail to **Mirador Las Torres** is relatively easy, except for the last hour's scramble up boulders. The trail to Refugio Los Cuernos is the most windy along the W. **Valle Frances** is not to be missed. Plan time to get all the way to the lookout Campamento Británico. From Valle Frances to Pehoé can get windy, but is relatively easy. The stretch to **Lago Grey** is moderate, with some steep parts. The glacier lookout is another half-hour past the *refugio*.

The Circuit

The landscape along the backside of the peaks is a lot more desolate, holding its own special kind of beauty. Around Paso John Garner (the most extreme part of the trek) you may encounter knee-deep mud and snow. There's one basic *refugio* at Los Perros, the rest is rustic camping. Factor from four to six hours between each camp.

Other Trails

Trails away from the main jams offer welcome solitude and a chance to experience other treasures of the park. From the Laguna Amarga Guardería, a four-hour hike leads through barren land to **Laguna Azul**, where there is camping on the northeastern shore. Another two hours north the trail reaches Lago Paine. From Administración, the three-hour hike to Refugio Pehoé is an easy, mainly flat trail with fantastic views. For true remoteness, plus a chance to view glaciers, a four-hour trail from Guadería Lago Grey follows Río Pingo to Conaf's Refugio Zapata, from where hikes (about another 1½ to two hours) continue to a lookout of **Glaciar Zapata** and to **Lago Pingo**.

GLACIER TREKKING & KAYAKING

Big Foot Adventure Patagonia (☎ 061-414611; www.bigfootpatagonia.com; Bories 206, Puerto Natales) leads ice hikes (US$75) on Glaciar Grey, including a lesson in ice climbing. To leave the park, let your arms do the hiking: both Big Foot and **Onas Patagonia** (☎ 061-412707; Eberhard 599, Puerto Natales) run two- to three-day kayaking trips down Río Serrano. It's

not quite budget travel, but a unique way to experience the park.

HORSE RIDING

Due to property divisions within the park, horses cannot cross between the western sections (Lagos Grey and Pehoé, Río Serrano) and the eastern part managed by Hostería Las Torres (Refugio Los Cuernos is the approximate cut-off). **Baqueano Zamora** (☎ 061-412911; baqueano@terra.cl; Eberhard 566, Puerto Natales) runs excursions to Lago Pingo, Laguna Amarga, Lago Paine and Lago Azul (half-day US$47, lunch included).

Sleeping

Make reservations. Arriving at the park without them, especially in the high season, means you may be without any place to stay. The reservation system is slow and can be very nerve racking. Make sure that you receive a voucher for each reservation made; give these to the staff at the *refugios* upon arrival. A number of travel agencies in Puerto Natales (Big Foot, Casa Cecilia, Fortaleza Expediciones) can call in reservations; they also rent camping equipment. Or go directly to the offices of **Andescape** (☎ 061-412592; andescape@terra.cl) in the Path@gone (Map p506) office in Puerto Natales and the **Hostería Las Torres/ Fantástico Sur** (Map p506; ☎ 061-226054; Magallanes 960, Punta Arenas). The latter manages Torres, Chileno and Los Cuernos *refugios* and campgrounds; the former manages Pehoé, Grey, Dickson and Los Perros.

CAMPING

Camping at the *refugios* costs between US$4 and US$5 per site. *Refugios* rent equipment – tent (US$8 per night), sleeping bag (US$4), mat (US$1) and stove (US$3) – and have small stores with pasta, soup packets and butane gas. Other sites are administered by Conaf, are free and very basic. Many campers have reported rats lurking around campsites; don't leave food in packs or in tents, instead hang it from a tree.

REFUGIOS

Refugios have rooms with four to eight bunk beds each, kitchen privileges (for lodgers and during specific hours only), hot water and meals. A bed costs US$17 to US$19, sleeping bag rental US$4, meals US$5 to US$11. Should the *refugio* be full, staff provide all necessary camping equipment. Refugios Los Torres, Chileno and Cuernos close at the end of March; Lago Grey in mid-April. Refugio Lago Pehoé is the only one that stays open after that. Conaf-controlled Refugio Lago Toro at Administración costs US$5 in one large dorm room with kitchen and hot water (showers US$1 more). All other Conaf-managed *refugios* in the park are basic rain shelters.

Getting There & Away

For details of transportation to the park, see p507 in Puerto Natales. A new road is being built from Puerto Natales to Administración, but it currently ends at Río Serrano, where the government has yet to finish a bridge.

Buses drop off and pick up passengers at Laguna Amarga, the Hielos Patagónicos catamaran launch at Pudeto and at park headquarters, coordinating with the catamaran schedule. Each transfer within the park costs US$3. The catamaran (US$14 per person with one backpack) leaves Pudeto for the Refugio Pehoé at 9:30am, noon and 6pm from December to mid-March, noon and 6pm in late March and November, and at noon only in October and April. Another tourist boat runs between Hostería Lago Grey and Refugio Lago Grey, but does not have a regular schedule.

PARQUE NACIONAL BERNARDO O'HIGGINS

Running every day in summer (if the weather permits), **Turismo 21 de Mayo** (Map p506; ☎ 061-411176; Eberhard 560, Puerto Natales) has boat excursions (US$55) to the otherwise inaccessible **Parque Nacional Bernardo O'Higgins** (admission US$3). Here you can admire Glaciar Serrano. Whether the trip justifies the cost is debatable; rather than expect tour excellence, consider this simply as a way to access a very privileged corner. If weather is bad the trips are aborted and a percentage of the cost refunded. Path@gone sells a similar tour for the same price on the galleon-style *Nueva Galicia*.

Zodiacs continue up Río Serrano arriving at the southern border of the park at 4:30pm, where a bus waits to take passengers further into the park. (US$33). Trips are available until mid-March. Outfitters 21 de Mayo and Onas Patagonia provide foul-weather gear and sack lunch.

TIERRA DEL FUEGO

Chile's half of Tierra del Fuego isn't as accessible as Argentina's, but for those determined to go the length of the country, the 'island of fire' is a must. This island used to be home to roaming herds of guanaco and to groups of Yahgan and Selk'nam. The landscape of the entire island drastically changed in the mid-1900s, once gold was discovered and sheep introduced. Indigenous groups were massacred, as were the guanaco, to make room for the sheep. Ambitious immigrants, many from Croatia and Chiloé, moved here in search of work. Missionaries arrived in hopes of taming the 'wild peoples' but found the extreme weather too wild to handle. Many ended in starvation and disaster. Shepherding still dominates the island, along with extraction of natural gas.

Porvenir

The largest settlement on Chilean Tierra del Fuego, Porvenir (population 5400) is most often visited as a day trip from Punta Arenas, but this usually means spending only a couple of hours in town and more time than a belly might wish crossing the choppy strait. The **tourist office** (Padre Mario Zavattaro 402) is upstairs from the intriguing **Museo de Tierra del Fuego** (Plaza de Armas), which has some unexpected materials, including Selk'nam mummies and skulls, musical instruments used by the mission Indians on Isla Dawson, and an exhibit on early Chilean cinematography.

Explore Patagonia (☎ 061-580206; www.explore patagonia.cl; Croacia 675) organizes excursions, including a visit to Peale's dolphins around Bahía Chilote (US$65, including meals).

Stay at **Residencial Colón** (☎ 061-581157; Damián Riobó 198; r per person US$7) or **Hotel España** (☎ 061-580160; Croacia 698; s/d US$9/11). For a meal, **El Chispa** (cnr Viel & Señoret; breakfast US$1.50-3, lunch US$5-7) is a good choice.

To get to Río Grande, Argentina (US$15, 5½ hours), **Tecni-Austral** (Map p502) buses leave from the corner of Philippi and Manuel Señoret Wednesday, Friday and Sunday. **Transbordadora Broom** (☎ 061-580089) operates the auto-passenger ferry *Melinka* to Punta Arenas (US$7 per person, US$45 per vehicle, 2½ to 4 hours) at 2pm Tuesday through Saturday, and at 5pm Sunday and holidays. Travel times depend on weather conditions.

Isla Navarino

Across the Beagle Channel from Argentine Tierra del Fuego, Isla Navarino (population 2200) has a truly end-of-the-world feel to it. Trekkers seeking isolation and challenge are increasingly drawn to the **Dientes de Navarino** chain, through which there's a five-day circuit. Throughout the island, beavers introduced to Tierra del Fuego from Canada in the 1940s have wreaked havoc on the landscape. The only town, **Puerto Williams**, is a naval settlement and an official port of entry for yachts en route to Cape Horn and Antarctica. It is one of Chile's most unique towns. Within minutes from town you can be deep in lenga and ñire forests dripping in old man's beard.

INFORMATION

In town, head to the Centro Comercial and **Turismo SIM** (☎ 061-621150; www.simltd.com) for information about the island. Money exchange (US cash only) or Visa advances are possible at Banco de Chile; there is no ATM.

SIGHTS

The **Museo Martín Gusinde** honors the German priest and ethnographer who worked among the Yahgans from 1918 to 1923. It has mediocre exhibits on natural history and ethnography. The most southerly ethno-botanical park in South America, **Omora** contains trails showing regional foliage. Take the road to the right of the **Virgen**, 4km toward Puerto Navarino. A lookout point, **Cerro Bandera**, can be reached via the beginning of the 'Dientes Circuit'. The trail ascends steeply through the mossy forest to a sparse alpine terrain with great vistas.

SLEEPING

Refugio Coirón (☎ 061-621150; Ricardo Maragano 168; dm US$13) Caters to backpackers with shared rooms, a welcoming atmosphere, kitchen privileges and a large communal table.

Residencial Onashaga (☎ 061-621081; Upachun 290; dm US$14) Has plenty of rickety bunks,

shared baths and a furnace made out of a ship's exhaust pipe.

Residencial Pusaki (☎ 061-621020; Piloto Pardo 242; r US$12) has clean, warm rooms with shared bath and pleasant family surroundings.

Hostería Camblor (meals US$3–8) Overlooking the town, serves the best bread in town. Thursday night is disco night.

Club de Yates Micalvi (at the harbor) No trip to the island is complete without a night out at this club down at the harbor, where you can sip a cocktail, munch on a crab sandwich (US$5) and listen to yacht hotties and Antarctic explorers from around the world hold forth amid souvenirs of former adventurers.

GETTING THERE & AWAY

Aerovías DAP (☎ 061-621051; Centro Comercial) flies to Punta Arenas from Tuesday to Saturday (US$64). Seats are limited and advance reservations are essential. The *Transbordadora Austral Broom* ferry departs once weekly for the 30-hour trip to Punta Arenas (US$120 including meals, US$150 for a bunk). Regular connections between Puerto Williams and Ushuaia, on Argentine Tierra del Fuego, should be up and running. Private yachts making the trip sometimes take on extra passengers, usually for about US$50 each. For the most up-to-date information ask at the Club de Yates or Turismo SIM.

ISLA ROBINSON CRUSOE

Strange but true: the island on which the real-life Robinson Crusoe lived in complete isolation from 1704–09 is 670km off the coast of Valparaíso. In 1574, Juan Fernández discovered the Archipiélago Juan Fernández. For over two centuries the islands sheltered sealers and pirates, including the British corsairs from whom Scotsman Alexander Selkirk sought exile and left to live on Isla Masatierra, renamed Robinson Crusoe in the 1960s. Spain founded the village of San Juan Bautista in 1750, but there was no permanent presence until 1877. During WWI the British navy sank a German cruiser in Cumberland Bay.

The island is only 93 sq km. Its unusual shape (22km long and 7km wide) means

CHILE

that the climate can be rather erratic. Dress for both warm and cool, wet and dry weather. The average temperature is about 22°C. April to September is the rainy season. Both Robinson Crusoe and the further off island of Masafuerra are a storehouse of rare plants and animals that evolved in isolation and adapted to specific ecological niches. The islands have been a national park since 1935 and are also a Unesco World Biosphere Reserve. Keep your eyes peeled for the bright-red male Juan Fernández hummingbird; the female is a more subdued green, with a white tail.

San Juan Bautista

Most visitors stay in very tranquil San Juan Bautista (population 500), overlooking Bahía Cumberland and surrounded by steep peaks. The Municipalidad, near the plaza, has tourist information. Bring cash money from the mainland, preferably in small bills. Hotels accept US dollars for accommodations. Conaf's Centro Información Turista is at the top of Vicente González, about 500m inland from the Costanera.

SIGHTS & ACTIVITIES

Around town, visit the **cementerio**, near the lighthouse, were survivors of the WWI battleship Dresden are buried. More than 40 participants in Chile's independence movement spent many years imprisoned in the **Cuevas de los Patriotas** after defeat at Rancagua in 1814. Directly above the caves is **Fuerte Santa Bárbara**, built by the Spaniards in 1749 to discourage pirate incursions. The **national park** (admission US$5 for 7 days) takes in most of the island. Many areas have restricted access; arrange with Conaf for a guided hike. Hikes you can do on your own are to **Mirador de Selkirk**, with a couple of plaques about the castaway, and down the other side to **Punta La Isla**, up to **Salsipuedes**, or, for a short jaunt, to **Plazoleta El Yunque**.

SLEEPING & EATING

Camping Los Cañones (Vincente González; camping per person US$2) The in-town campground, with baths and cold showers.

Rates listed here are for breakfast/half-board. Full board is also available.

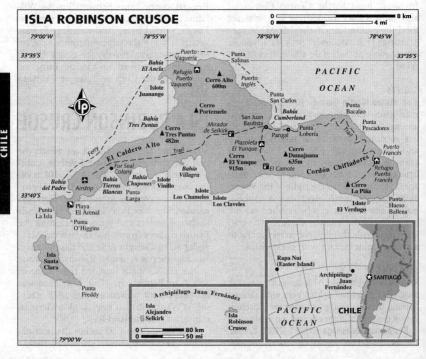

ISLA ROBINSON CRUSOE

Refugio Náutico (☎ 032-751077; Carrera Pinto; r per person US$20/30) Airy, spacious rooms with an independent entrance. Owners are charming and they have a great deck.

Residencial Mirador Selkirk (☎ 032-751028; Pasaje del Castillo; per person without/with breakfast US$16/25) A family home up the hill from town.

Cabaña Paulentz (☎ 032-751108; Costanera El Palillo; per person without/with breakfast US$18/33) Set in beautiful gardens with an independent entrance and kitchen.

The best meals will be where you are staying, but in town try **El Remo** (Plaza) for sandwiches and drinks into the wee hours, and **Hostería Aldea Daniel Defoe** (Costanera El Palillo) for the most character of all.

Getting There & Away

Two companies fly air taxis to the island from Santiago a few times a week, depending on demand, from October to April, and almost daily from December to February. Travelers should allow for an extra two or three days' stay when poor weather makes landings risky.

Lassa (☎ 02-2735209; Aeródromo Tobalaba, Av Larraín 7941) has the most flights, in a 19-seat Twin Otter. **Transportes Aéreos Robinson Crusoe** (☎ 02-5344650; Av Pajaritos 3030, Oficina 604) flies from Aeropuerto Los Cerrillos. Fares are about US$405 to US$490 round trip, including a 1½-hour shuttle from the airstrip by a combination of 4WD (to the jetty at Bahía del Padre) and motor launch to San Juan Bautista.

RAPA NUI (EASTER ISLAND)

Tiny Polynesian Rapa Nui (117 sq km), one of the most isolated places on earth, is entirely off the map for most South American trekkers, but those who do go the distance rarely regret it. Locals refer to their island as *Te Pito o Te Henua*, (The Navel of the World), but since becoming a Chilean territory in 1888, it is officially known by its Spanish name, Isla de Pascua (Dutch admiral Roddeveen was the first European to land on the island, on Easter Sunday, 1722, thus that name). It's 1900km east of even tinier Pitcairn, the nearest populated

landmass, and is 3700km west of the South American coast.

How such an isolated island became inhabited has stumped historians and archaeologists for years. While Thor Heyerdahl's *Kon Tiki* expedition theorized that Polynesians came from South America, the most accepted answer is that they came from South-East Asia, populating what is now the triangle of Polynesia, created by Hawaii, New Zealand and Rapa Nui.

On Rapa Nui, two civilizations formed, the Long Ears of the east and the Short Ears of the west, both of whom built large stone altars, *ahu*, and the enormous stone sculptures, *moai*, to honor their ancestors. Warfare led to destruction of the *ahu* and the toppling of the *moai* (in recent years many have been restored to their upright position). How were the *moai* moved from where they were carved at Rano Raraku volcano to their *ahu* around the coast? Legend says that priests moved the *moai* by the power of mana, with the statues themselves 'walking' a short distance each day. Other theories suggest that a sledge was fitted to the *moai*, which was then lifted with a bipod and dragged forward. The use of timber to help move the statues may partly explain the island's deforestation. Another religious cult, that of the birdman, equally intriguing, had its ceremonial center on **Orongo**.

Islanders speak Rapa Nui, an Eastern Polynesian dialect related to Cook Islands Maori, but also Spanish. Essential expressions include: *iorana* – hello; *Maururu* – thank you; *pehe koe* – how are you?; and *riva riva* – fine, good.

For a fortnight in February the island celebrates its culture in the elaborate and colorful Tapati Rapa Nui festival. Allow at least three days to see the major sites. Rapa Nui is two hours behind mainland Chile, six hours behind GMT, or five hours behind GMT in summer.

Surfers will enjoy big swells off the north and south coasts, but bring your own board.

HANGA ROA

Hanga Roa is a peaceful sprawl of irregular, uncrowded streets. The main road is north–south Av Atamu Tekena, on which are a number of shops, the main supermarket,

CHILE

an arts fair and several eateries. Some maps show this as Policarpo Toro, which now is just below, along the waterfront (names of the two main streets keep switching). Caleta Hanga Roa is the town's small bay from which fishing boats come and go, and body surfers catch small swells.

Information

Internet cafés come and go, but stay relatively expensive at around US$4 or more an hour. Ask at your lodging where the latest service is. *Residenciales* provide laundry service. **Hospital Hanga Roa** (☎ 032-100215) is one long block east of the church.

Most businesses, especially *residenciales* and rental agencies, prefer US cash dollars. **Banco del Estado** (Tu'u Maheke), next to Sernatur, changes US dollars but charges commission on traveler's checks. An ATM is expected on the island, but it is prudent to bring money with you. Exchange rates are better at the petrol station on Av Hotu Matua.

The **post office** (Av Te Pito o Te Henua) is a half block from Caleta Hanga Roa. **Entel** is in a cul-de-sac opposite Sernatur. **Sernatur** (☎ 032-100255; Tu'u Maheke) distributes basic maps of the island. The useful **Cámara de Turismo** (☎ 032-550055; Atamu Tekna s/n) near Av Pont has lists of registered lodgings and tour operators. **Conaf** (☎ 032-100236), on the road to Rano Kau, may give suggestions on hiking and camping.

Dangers & Annoyances

Petty thievery is on the rise on the island, and some travelers have reported break-ins at some *residenciales*. Ask lodging owners to store valuables in a strong box. The sun is strong here! Bring good sunblock, sunglasses, long sleeved shirts and a hat.

Sights & Activities

The interesting **Museo Antropológico Sebastián Englert** (admission US$2; ⊙ 9:30am-12:30pm & 2-5:30pm Tue-Fri; 9:30am-12:30pm Sat & Sun), north of town, uses text and photographs to explain the Rapa Nui people's history. It also displays *moai* kavakava (the strange 'statues of ribs') and replica rongo-rongo tablets. **Iglesia Hanga Roa**, the island's Catholic church, has intricate wood carvings, which

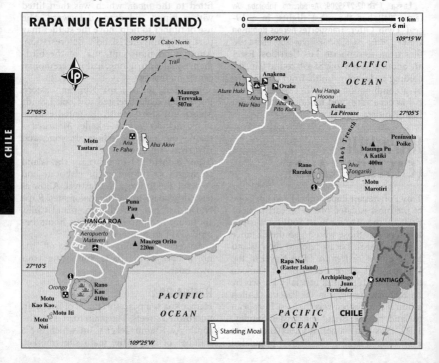

integrate Christian doctrine and Rapa Nui tradition.

Steep drop-offs, abundant marine life and clear water make for good diving, available at **Orca Diving Center** (☎ 032-100375; Caleta Hanga Roa). Dives cost from US$50 to US$80. Bring proof of certification. **Hare Orca**, next door, rents body boards (per half-/full-day US$16/27), surfboards (US$22/33), ocean kayaks (single kayak US$22/33, double US$33/55) and snorkeling gear (US$10 per day).

Plenty of operators do tours of the island's main sites, such as well-established **Kia Koe Tour** (☎ 032-100852; Atamu Tekena s/n), for US$20/35 per person for a half/full-day.

Sleeping

Upon arrival at the airport, locals and *residenciale* proprietors will attempt to woo you, sometimes with discounts. Make sure you are talking with a person from the *residenciale* and not an agent. Reservations are only necessary in the peak times of August, and January to February.

Conaf operates a barebones campsite across the street from Anakena on the north coast of the island; during the day barbecues are set up, but you might want to bring your own food and water.

Residencial Miru (☎ 032-100365; Atamu Takena s/n; r without/with bath US$10/15) Super sweet owners provide kitchen use and are very welcoming. Rooms are basic with shared bath; breakfast is US$5.

Cabañas Vaianny (☎ 32-100650; Tu Haka He Vari; r per person US$15) Friendly, well run with good breakfast, laundry and Internet.

Chez Oscar (☎ 032-100404; Av Pont; US$15) Spotless and relaxed; breakfast costs US$5 extra, but you can use the kitchen.

Residencial Kona Tau (☎ 032-100321; Avariepua s/n; HI members/nonmembers US$15/20) The island's HI affiliate, in a family house serving large breakfasts. Rooms outside the main house are better.

Residencial Mahina Taka Taka Georgia (☎ 032-100452; Atamu Tekena & Calle Tahai; r per person US$30) Gregarious family encourages guests to mingle, and provides lots of personality. Meals are plentiful, but rooms are a bit musty and basic.

Hotel Taura'a (☎ 32-100463; tauraa@entelchile.net; Av Atamu Tekena; s/d US$40/60) Across from the supermarket, with modern rooms, multilingual welcoming and helpful owners and pleasant gardens.

Residencial Chez Goretti (☎ 032-100459; Av Atamu Tekena s/n; r per person with breakfast US$40) A 30-minute walk north of town (or a short, US$2 taxi ride) with marvelous gardens spread out over the spacious grounds. The rooms are large and bright. Great value.

Eating

Besides the great fruit juices and fish, the island's cuisine is bland and expensive.

Supermercado Kai Nene (Atamu Tekena) Has the best selection of basic goods.

Aeropuerto (Plaza Policarpo Toro) Has the best fresh bread and cheeses, but get there early.

Ariki o Te Pana (Atamu Tekena; lunches US$5-8) Has *empanadas* that are a lunch in themselves, cold drinks and large lunches.

Avarei Pua (Av Policarpo Toro & Av Te Pito o Te Henua; mains US$9) Serves filling, well-priced meals including excellent *ceviche*.

Bar Restaurant Pub Café Tavake (Atamu Tekena) Can't quite decide what it is, but it is open late for snacks, sandwiches and drinks.

Gringo's Pizza (Residencial Miru) Pizza, *empanadas*, veg meals and great, big juices.

Drinking

Aloha Pub (cnr Atamu Tekena & S Englert) Good for a drink and pub food.

Banana Pub (Atamu Tekena) Shoot a game of pool here, with cold beers and loud music.

Dancing through the night is a way of life here. **Toroko** (Policarpo Toro) is best on Thursday and Friday, while **Piditi** (Av Hotu Matua) is slightly less frenetic and best on Saturday. Cover charge at both is about US$4, drinks are expensive, and nothing gets going until after 1am.

PARQUE NACIONAL RAPA NUI

Much of Rapa Nui's land and all the archaeological sites are part of the **national park** (admission US$10). The admission fee is paid once in Orongo (p516) and you can then visit the park as many times as you like. What is listed below skims the surface of things to see around the island. Respecting archaeological sites is essential – avoid walking on the *ahu* or removing/relocating rocks of archaeological structure. Handle the land gently and the *moai* will smile upon you.

Near Hanga Roa

A short hike north of town, **Ahu Tahai** has three restored *ahu*, which are especially photogenic at sunset. Ahu Tahai proper is in the middle, with a solitary *moai*. Ahu Ko Te Riku is to the north, with a top knotted and eyeballed *moai*. Ahu Vai Uri has five eroded *moai* of varying sizes. Along the hills are foundations of *hare paenga* (elliptical houses) and walls of 'chicken houses.'

Four kilometers north of Tahai, **Ahu Tepeu** has several fallen *moai* and an extensive village site. Nearby, at the coast, is **Ana Kakenga** (cave of the two windows). Going inland, **Ahu Akivi** has seven *moai*. They are the only ones that face the sea, but like all *moai* they overlook the site of a village.

Anakena

The legendary landing place of Hotu Matua, Anakena is the only accessible white-sand beach, with **Ahu Nau Nau** and a picture perfect row of *moai*. On a rise south of the beach stands **Ahu Ature Huki** and its lone *moai* (the one that Heyerdahl and a dozen islanders took nine days to lever up).

Ahu Te Pito Kura

Overlooking La Perouse Bay, a massive 10m-high *moai* lies facedown with its neck broken. It is the largest *moai* ever moved from Rano Raraku and erected on an *ahu*. Its resemblance to the uncompleted figures at Rano Raraku suggest that this *moai* is also one of the most recent. Its name derives from the nearby polished round stone, *te pito kura* (navel of light).

Ahu Tongariki

The most stunning in scale and location, 15 *moai* line up along the largest *ahu* built. A 1960 tsunami demolished several of the *moai* and scattered topknots far inland, but the Japanese company Tadano restored the site in the early 1990s.

Rano Raraku

Referred to as 'the nursery', the *moai* were cut out of the slopes of this extinct volcano. Along the hills, *moai* stand partially buried, while on the rocky surface is a jigsaw puzzle of partially carved *moai*, the largest of which is a 21m giant – but most range from 5.5m to 7m. More than 600 of these wonderful figures stand and lie around Rano Raraku.

Inside the crater is a silent reedy lake and an amphitheater full of handsome heads. At the top is a fabulous 360° view.

Rano Kau

With its witch's cauldron of a crater, Rano Kau dominates the island's southwest corner. On the edge of the crater wall overlooking the ocean is the **Orongo Ceremonial Village**, 9km south of Hanga Roa, where bird cult rituals were performed. One of the more elaborate, used to decide the next leader, involved a competition to retrieve an egg of the sooty tern which breeds on the small *motu* (islets) just offshore. Young men descended the cliffs, swam out to the islands (with the aid of rafts), and stayed on the island to search for an egg. The first one to find an egg, and communicate that back successfully, became birdman for the year. A cluster of boulders is covered in petroglyphs depicting Tangata Manu (the birdman) and Make Make (their god). Walking or biking is possible; it's a rather steep 9km trip from town.

GETTING THERE & AWAY

LanChile (☎ 600-526-2000; Atamu Tekena, Hanga Roa) is the only airline serving Rapa Nui. It has two flights per week to/from Santiago and to/from Papeete (Tahiti). Round-trip fares from Santiago range from US$650 to US$900. Flights are often overbooked, so it is essential to reconfirm your ticket two days before the flight at both ends.

For travelers coming from Asia or Australia, consider stopping here en route to/from South America, via Auckland (New Zealand) and joining a Qantas flight to Papeete, connecting with LanChile's Papeete–Rapa Nui–Santiago service. The airport departure tax is US$13, but is usually included in your ticket.

GETTING AROUND
Bicycle

Mountain bikes can be rented at many places in Hanga Roa for US$11 to US$16 per eight hours or US$20 per day. Take it for a test spin – the quality of bikes is questionable and the seats can be uncomfortable. There's an air pump at the gas station.

Car

In Hanga Roa, **Comercial Insular** (☎ 032-100480; Atamu Tekena) rents jeeps at US$50 to US$60 for eight hours. Also ask at established hotels and tour agencies, or look for signs in windows of businesses. Make sure the car has all the necessary equipment should a tire go flat (not uncommon).

Taxi
Taxis cost a flat US$2 for most trips around town. Longer trips can be negotiated, with the cost depending mainly on the time. The round trip from Hanga Roa to Anakena costs US$16.

CHILE DIRECTORY

ACCOMMODATIONS
In the most popular towns during high season, places book up fast, so make reservations before you arrive. Summer prices may be 10%–20% higher than the rest of the year. Most municipal tourist offices have lists of budget lodgings. Sernatur does as well, but only of places that are licensed, ie they pay their taxes. Hostelling International has a hostel in almost every main city; but aren't always the best value. Cards can be purchased at affiliated hostels and at their **office** (☎ 02-2333220; Hernando de Aguirre 201, Oficina 602, Providencia, Santiago) for US$14.

A couple of pamphlets highlight some of the more popular places; look for 'Backpacker's Best of Chile', 'Hostels for Backpackers' and SCS Scott's listings. From north to south, you'll find a definite network of German-, Swiss- or Austrian-run hostels. These have all the amenities a packer could dream up, plus an added level of comfort, maintenance and familiarity. Especially in the Lake District, families offer inexpensive rooms in their homes, most often with kitchen privileges, hot showers and breakfast. Fancier hotels often include the 18% IVA in the price, which should be subtracted from the tourist price for foreign travelers (smaller hotels may not be equipped to handle this step though). Make sure to agree on this before taking a room.

For camping, your best resource is Turistel's *Rutero Camping* guide. Most organized campgrounds are family oriented with large sites, full baths and laundry, fire pits, a restaurant or snack bar.

Many campgrounds charge a five-person minimum, so they may cost more than staying under a roof. Try asking for per person rates. Free camping – no facilities – is possible in some remote areas. Camping gas, referred to as butan gas, is carried in *ferreterias* (hardware stores) or larger supermarkets.

ACTIVITIES
Chile is all about enjoying the great outdoors. First on everyone's list is **trekking**, with the Torres del Paine (p508) 'W' or circuit topping the list. Areas around Parinacota and Lago Chungara (p455), Parque Pumalín (p495), Nahuelbuta (p463), Huerquehue (p474) and Puyehue (p480), Cochamó Valley (p485) and Isla Navarino (p511) are other favorites. Trails in many parks are not well-marked or maintained. Some trails are simply old cattle roads. Ask around for the latest developments of Sendero de Chile – sure to be a new trekking highlight. For those going **climbing**, get permission to scale peaks on the border (Ojos de Salado) from Chile's **Dirección de Fronteras y Límites** (Difrol; ☎ 02-6714110, fax 02-6971909; 4th fl, Bandera 52, Santiago).

Surfing breaks run up and down the coast of Middle and Northern Chile; Pichilemu (p457) is one well-known destination, as is Iquique (p447). Iquique also has South America's best conditions for **paragliding** and **landsailing**.

Rafting or **kayaking** is world-class here. Most popular is the Futaleufú River (p496), but don't overlook the Liucura (p474) and Trancura (p471) outside Pucón, or the Petrohué near Puerto Varas (p482). For sea kayaking, just head to Chiloé (p490) and the fjords around Parque Pumalín (p495).

Mountain biking favorites include around San Pedro de Atacama (p442), Lago Llanquihue (p481), to Ojos de Caburgua (p471), and along the challenging Carretera Austral (p493). Taking to two wheels is not without its drawbacks: on gravel roads cars kick up rocks, summer in the south brings *tábanos* that fly around and bite, winds along the southern stretch of Carretera Austral are fierce. Most towns have a repair shop.

Exploring the Andes on multi-day **horse-riding** trips accesses terrain you can't get to

CHILE

otherwise. Places to go are around Pucón (p471), Cochamó (p485), Puyehue (p480) in Valle Elqui (p428), and around Torres del Paine (p508).

The **skiing** season runs from June to September, but Chilean slopes are no bargain. Santiago has some rental shops; otherwise resorts rent full packages. Head out to Volcán Villarrica (p469), Chillán (p458) and any of the resorts near Santiago (p418).

Now for the more relaxing stuff. **Bathing** in hot springs is not only good for you, it's relaxing too. With a line of volcanic activity running down its spine, Chile has an abundance of hot springs, from the kind you dig for on your own, to fancy ones that'll bring fluffy towels to you. Try Puritama (p445) outside San Pedro de Atacama, Los Pozones (p474) by Pucón, riverside ones at Puyehue (p480). Also check out areas around Liquiñe and Coñaripe. Considering the growing reputation of Chile's wines, **wine tasting** is a fun detour. In Middle Chile (p455) and around Santiago (p418) are a plethora of wineries, however, visiting them requires advance reservations.

BOOKS

Lonely Planet's *Chile & Easter Island* provides detailed travel information and coverage. The annually updated, very informative Turistel series has separate volumes on northern, central and southern Chile, plus an additional one on camping. Sara Wheeler's *Travels in a Thin Country*, Charles Darwin's *Voyage of the Beagle* and Nick Reding's *The Last Cowboys at the End of the World: The Story of the Gauchos of Patagonia* are good travel companions.

BUSINESS HOURS

Shops in Chile open by 10am, but some close at about 1pm for two to three hours for lunch then reopen until about 8pm. Government offices and businesses have a more conventional 9am to 6pm schedule. Banks are open 9am to 2pm weekdays. Tourist offices stay open long hours daily in summer, but have abbreviated hours in the off-season. Museums are often closed Monday.

CLIMATE

Northern Chile is good to visit any time of year. Pack warm clothes – even in the summer – to deal with foggy mornings and high altitude destinations. January and February are the rainy months, making some traveling to off-the-trail destinations difficult.

Santiago and Middle Chile are best enjoyed from September to April, with the autumn harvest being a main reason to spend time in this wine-growing region. Santiago can be unbearably hot and smoggy from December through February. Ski resorts are open roughly from June through October.

Head to the Lake District and Patagonia from October through April – but be prepared for rainy weather throughout and windy weather the further south you go. Sun protection – hats, sunglasses, blocks etc – is essential. If camping in Patagonia, bring a synthetic sleeping bag.

Throughout Chile, including the islands, mid-December to mid-March is the high season, which means increased prices, crowded lodgings, tons of tourists (this is when most Chileans travel), and overbooked flights and buses. However, in the south, this is the only season with regularly scheduled ferry and bus service.

For more information and climate charts, see the South America Directory (p1028).

DANGERS & ANNOYANCES

Compared with other South American countries, Chile is remarkably safe. But still, in larger cities, most noticeably Santiago, and in bus terminals (most notably Arica), petty thievery is not uncommon. Keep an eye on all belongings, and take advantage of the secure left-luggage services at bus terminals and *hospedajes*. Beach resorts are prime territory for thievery in summer, and some of Valparaíso's neighborhoods are best avoided. Photographing military installations may lead to the film being confiscated and possibly a visit to jail.

Earthquakes happen. If you're hypersafety conscious, make contingency plans for safety or evacuation before going to sleep. Many of the most popular beach areas have dangerous offshore currents. Look for signs *'apta para bañar'* (swimming okay) and *'no apta para bañar'* (no swimming).

Summertime in the south brings about the pesty *tábano* (a large biting horsefly);

more an annoyance than a health risk. Chile's canine gangs involve a good deal of high-end dogs. They'll follow you everywhere, but are usually harmless.

DISABLED TRAVELERS

Chile still ignores the needs of people with disabilities. Employees of buses will help you on and off buses, but finding lodgings that don't have stairs, or have hallways large enough for wheelchairs, is close to impossible.

EMBASSIES & CONSULATES

For information on visas, see p524. Chile has embassies and consulates in Argentina and Peru, and also in the following countries:

Embassies & Consulates in Chile

Argentina Antofagasta (☎ 055-220440; Blanco Encalada 1933); Puerto Montt (☎ 253-996; Cauquenes 94, 2nd fl); Punta Arenas (☎ 061-261912; 21 de Mayo 1878); Santiago (☎ 02-6359863; Vicuña Mackenna 41); Valparaíso (☎ 32-217419; Blanco 890)

Australia Santiago (☎ 02-2285065; Gertrudis Echeñique 420, Las Condes)

Belgium Punta Arenas (☎ 061-241472; Roca 817)

Bolivia Antofagasta (☎ 055-221403; Jorge Washington 2675); Arica (☎ 058-231030; Patricio Lynch 292); Calama (☎ 055-344413; Vicuña Mackenna 1984); Iquique (☎ 057-421777; Gorostiaga 215, Dept E); Santiago (☎ 02-2328180; Av Santa María 2796, Las Condes)

Canada Santiago (☎ 02-3629660; 12th fl, Nuevo Tajamar 481, Las Condes)

France Santiago (☎ 02-2251030; Condell 65, Providencia)

Germany Santiago (☎ 02-4632500; 7th fl, Agustinas 785)

Israel Santiago (☎ 02-7500500; 5th fl, San Sebastián 2812, Providencia)

Netherlands Punta Arenas (☎ 061-248100; Magallanes 435)

New Zealand Santiago (☎ 02-2909809; Isidora Goyenechea 3516, Las Condes)

Peru Arica (☎ 058-231020; San Martín 235); Iquique (☎ 057-411584; 2nd fl, Zegers 570); Santiago (☎ 02-2354600; Calle Padre Mariano 10, Oficina 309, Providencia); Valparaíso (☎ 32-215621; Errazuríz 1178)

UK Punta Arenas (☎ 061-211535; Cataratas de Niaguara 01325); Santiago (☎ 02-3704100; 3rd fl, Av El Bosque Norte 0125, Las Condes); Valparaíso (☎ 32-213063; Blanco 1199)

USA Santiago (☎ 02-H3356550; Andrés Bello 2800, Las Condes)

Chilean Embassies & Consulates Abroad

Australia Canberra (☎ 06-6286 2430; 10 Culgoa Circuit, O'Malley, ACT 2606); Sydney (☎ 02-9299 2533; 18th fl, National Market Centre, 44 Market St, Sydney 2000); Melbourne (☎ 03-9654 4982; Level 43, Nauru House, 80 Collins St, Melbourne 3000)

Canada Ottawa (☎ 613-235-4402; 50 O'Connor St, Suite 1413, Ottawa, Ontario); Toronto (☎ 416-924-0106; Suite 1801, 2 Bloor St W, Toronto, Ontario); Vancouver (☎ 604-681-9162; 1185 W Georgia, Suite 1250, Vancouver, BC)

France Paris (☎ 01-4705 4661; 64 Blvd de la Tour Maubourg, Paris, 75007)

Germany Frankfurt (☎ 069-550194; Humboldtstrasse 94, Frankfurt); Berlin (☎ 030-2044990; Leipzigerstrasse 63, Berlin)

New Zealand Wellington (☎ 4-471 6270; 19 Bolton St, Wellington)

UK London (☎ 207-580 1023; 12 Devonshire Rd, London)

USA Washington (☎ 202-331-5057; 1140 Connecticut, Suite 703, Washington, DC 20036); New York (☎ 212-980-3366; 866 United Nations Plaza, Room 302, New York, NY 10017); Los Angeles (☎ 310-785-0047; 1900 Avenue of the Stars, Suite 1250, Los Angeles, CA 90067); San Francisco (☎ 415-982-7662; 870 Market St, Suite 1058, San Francisco, CA 94102); Miami (☎ 305-373-8623; 1110 Brickell Ave, Suite 616, Miami, FL 33131); Chicago (☎ 708-654-8780; 875 N Michigan Ave, Suite 3352, Chicago, IL 60611)

FESTIVALS & EVENTS

January and February are festive months in Chile. Every town and city puts on some sort of show, from exhibiting local artisans, to lots of live music, special meals and fireworks. Check with tourist offices for exact dates. Other festivities take place at religious holidays and during the mid-September Fiestas Patrias.

Semana Ancuditana (Ancud Week; second week in January) Includes Encuentro Folklórico de Chiloé, promoting the island's music, dance and cuisine.

Brotes de Chile (Second week of January) A folksong festival in Angol with music, dance, food and crafts.

Festival de Huaso Chilote (Late January) Celebrated in the town of Castro in Chiloe.

Festival Costumbrista For an authentic Patagonian rodeo go to Villa Cerro Castillo.

Carnaval Ginga (Mid-February) Arica; features regional *comparsas* (groups of musicians and dancers).

Festival Costumbrista (Mid-February) Castro; folk music and dance and traditional foods.

Noche de Valdivia (Third Saturday in February) Decorated riverboats and fireworks.

Carnaval (February/March) San Pedro de Atacama.

Semana Ariqueña (Arica Week; early June)

CHILE

Fiesta de San Pedro y San Pablo (June 29) San Pedro de Atacama; folk dancing groups, rodeo and processions.
Festival de la Virgen del Carmen (Mid-July) In Tirana some 40,000 pilgrims pay homage to Chile's virgin, with lots of street dancing and masks.
Carnaval de Invierno (End of July) Punta Arenas; fireworks and parades.
Año Nuevo (New Years Eve; December 31) Go to Valparaíso for lots of fireworks and partying.

FOOD & DRINK
Chilean Cuisine

What Chilean cuisine lacks in spice and variety it makes up for in abundance and superb seafood. Breakfast is usually coffee (instant Nescafé) or tea and a couple of white-flour bread rolls with jam. Occasionally places offer *paila de huevos* (scrambled eggs). *Menú del día* is the cheapest lunch at about US$2 to US$3. First course is usually *cazuela*, a soupy stew of broth, rice, a half ear of corn and some meat, followed by a main dish of fish or meat and some overcooked veg. Good places to find cheap meals are at the central markets and the *casinos de bomberos* (restaurants for firefighters and unionized workers). The most prolific snack is the *completo*, a hot dog smothered in mayo and other sauces. *Empanadas* are either fried, with cheese, or *al horno* with meat, called *pino*. They are larger than the Argentine variety.

A cold ham and cheese sandwich is an *aliado*, which, when melted, is a *Barros Jarpa*. Steak with melted cheese is a *Barros Luco*, while beefsteak with tomato and other vegetables is a *chacarero*. *Lomo a lo pobre* is an enormous slab of beef topped with two fried eggs and buried in fries. The *chorrillana*, a platter full of fried potatoes, grilled onions, eggs (usually fried) and strips of fried steak, can easily feed two. *Curanto*, a specialty of Chiloé, is a hearty pile of fish, shellfish, chicken, pork, lamb, beef and potato that has all been cooked together.

The best deal in the country is seafood. *Caldillo de...*is a hearty soup of a variety of fish (often congrio), with potato chunks, spiced up with lemon, cilantro and garlic. *Chupe de...*is a 'stew' of some sort of seafood, cooked in a thick sauce of butter, bread crumbs, cheese and spices. *Paila marina* is a fish and shellfish chowder.

German influence in the south provides a variety of strudel, *Kuchen* and cheesecake.

Drinks

Chileans guzzle a lot of soft drinks. Bottled water is available. In the south, tap water is safe to drink. *Mote con huesillo*, sold by street vendors in summer, is a refreshing peach nectar with barley kernels and rehydrated peaches. *Licuados* are blended fruit drinks, made with milk or water and often with too much sugar. *Vitamina* is the same thing, but with vegetables (carrots and beets) thrown in.

Coffee is mainly instant, but espresso bars are found in most towns. Tea is normally served black, with at least three packets of sugar. *Maté* (Paraguayan tea) is consumed to some degree in Patagonia, but not as much as in Argentina. Herbal teas are very common and often use the leaves or flowers rather than the bagged tea.

Don't miss the powerful *pisco* (grape brandy), often served in the form of a *pisco sour* (with lemon juice, egg white and powdered sugar). *Pisco* may also be served with coke, called a *piscola*, or ginger ale, called *chilcano*.

Kunstmann is Chile's best beer. Most others are refreshing but lack taste. A draft beer is called *schop*. Chilean wine receives international recognition. The microclimate of central Chile provides excellent conditions, especially for cabernets and merlots. Treat yourself to a decent bottle (US$3 to US$4) once in a while.

GAY & LESBIAN TRAVELERS

While Chile is a strongly Catholic country and many frown upon homosexuality, there are enclaves of tolerance, most notably in Santiago. Since Chilean males are often more physically demonstrative than their counterparts in Europe or North America, behaviors like a vigorous embrace will seem innocuous. Likewise, lesbians walking hand-in-hand will attract little attention, since Chilean women frequently do so. The website gaychile.com is a fine resource with lodging recommendations, listings of basic services – legal, medical and otherwise, plus information on the nightlife in Santiago. **Tempo Travel** (☎ 02-281-8547; novellus@tempotravel.cl; Almirante Pastene 7, Oficina 54, Providencia, Santiago) can provide all sorts of help to plan a gay-friendly trip through the country. While in Santiago look for *Opus Gay*, a magazine covering gay issues around Chile.

CHILE

HEALTH

Hospitals in Chile are decent and clean. The best places are the private *clínicas Alemanas* (German clinic) found in many towns, especially in the south. Except for in the Atacama desert and in Santiago, tap water is safe to drink. Altitude sickness and dehydration are the most common concerns in the north, while in the south - the area most affected by ozone depletion - it is essential to apply sunscreen and wear sunglasses. No vaccinations are required to travel in Chile, but if you are planning to travel to Rapa Nui, ask your travel agent about any current restrictions or documentation requirements. Women should purchase tampons before heading to smaller towns or to the islands.

For more information, see the Health chapter (p1053).

HOLIDAYS

Government offices and businesses close on the following national holidays:
Año Nuevo (New Year's Day; January 1)
Semana Santa (Easter Week; March/April, dates vary)
Día del Trabajador (Labor Day; May 1)
Glorias Navales (Naval Battle of Iquique; May 21)
Corpus Christi (May/June; dates vary)
San Pedro y San Pablo (St Peter's & St Paul's Day; June 29)
Asunción de la Virgen (Assumption; August 15)
Día de Unidad Nacional (Day of National Unity; first Monday of September)
Día de la Independencia Nacional (Independence Day; September 18)
Día del Ejército (Armed Forces Day; September 19)
Día de la Raza (Columbus Day; October 12)
Todos los Santos (All Saints' Day; November 1)
Inmaculada Concepción (Immaculate Conception Day; December 8)
Navidad (Christmas Day; December 25)

INTERNET ACCESS

Most large towns and all cities in Chile have Internet cafés charging US$1 to US$2 per hour, but it can be more expensive in more remote areas. The *main centro de llamadas* (call centers) often have one or two computers with fast lines for Internet use, but charge more. In the southern mountainous areas, particularly in Puerto Natales, connections can take an unbearably long time.

INTERNET RESOURCES

Many websites are geared more to those with bigger wallets, but provide background information.
Chile.com (www.chile.com) Kind of like Yahoo, but more specific; has good sections on nightlife and slang vocab, but in Spanish.
Chile Information Project (www.chip.cl) Well written, informative materials on everything from human rights to out of the way destinations; in English.
Chiloé (www.chiloeweb.com) Best source of information about the island of Chiloé.
Patagonia Chile (www.patagonia-chile.com) Comprehensive listings of all touristy things in Patagonia.
Rehue Foundation (www.xs4all.nl/~rehue) Links to Mapuche history, issues and events.
Sernatur (www.sernatur.cl) Information from the national tourism organization.
South America Travel Directory (www.planeta.com /chile) Worthwhile links to ecotourism, environmental organizations, towns and more.

MAPS

In Santiago, the **Instituto Geográfico Militar** (Map pp412-13; ☎ 02-4606800; Dieciocho 369, Centro; ⏰ 9am-5:30pm Mon-Fri) sells 1:50,000 topographic regional maps for about US$15 per sheet. These may be helpful for trekkers but their city maps are very out-of-date. The Conaf office in Santiago allows photocopying of national parks maps. The Turistel guidebooks, found in large bookstores such as Feria del Libro, have detailed maps of towns and regions, but lack scale. JLM Mapas has maps for all major regions and trekking areas at scales ranging from 1:50,000 to 1:500,000. Catering mainly to tourists, the maps are easy to use and provide decent information, but don't claim 100% accuracy.

MEDIA

Santiago's daily papers are all rather conservative. The oldest and the best is *El Mercurio* (www.elmercurio.cl). *La Segunda*, *La Tercera* and *Últimas Noticias* are daily rags most always with a butt shot on the cover. The *Estrategia* (www.estrategia.cl) is the voice of the financial sector and the best source for exchange rate information. The weekly *News Review* serves the English-speaking population. Most regions have their own papers with local news and event information. The *Clinic* provides the most open and cutting-edge editorials and satire about politics and Chilean society.

CHILE

Radio broadcasting is less regulated than in the past, with many stations on both AM and FM bands. TV stations include state-owned TVN (Televisión Nacional), the Universidad Católica's Channel 13, and several private stations. An alarming number of people have satellite Sky TV.

MONEY
ATMs
ATMs are called *redbanc*, and can be found in almost all banks, many large supermarkets, pharmacies and in well-trafficked areas. Just head to the town plaza and there's usually a bank or two at the corners. Even smaller towns usually have one. However, do not rely on ATMs in San Pedro de Atacama (doesn't have one), Rapa Nui or in small Patagonian towns. Most accept the Star, Plus system. Make sure you have a four-digit PIN. Select 'Foreign Client' to access system.

Bargaining
Buying items in a crafts market is the only acceptable time to bargain. Transport and accommodation rates are generally fixed and prominently displayed, but during a slow summer or in the off-season, try asking very politely for a discount, '*¿Me podría hacer precio?*'

Cash
The unit of currency is the peso (Ch$). There are banknotes for 500, 1000, 2000, 5000, 10,000 and 20,000 pesos, and coins for one, five, 10, 50 and 100 pesos. One-peso coins are disappearing, and even fives and tens are uncommon. Carry small bills with you; trying to make change can be a challenge, but liquor stores are sometimes able to, just make a deeply worried face and ask, '*¿Tiene suelto?*'

Credit Cards
Credit cards are useful, particularly when buying cash from a bank. Visa and MasterCard are the most widely accepted. Many adventure travel outfitters will accept credit cards, but will charge you up to 6% extra for the convenience.

Exchange Rates
Exchange rates at press time included the following:

Country	Unit		Ch$ (Peso)
Australia	A$1	=	457
Canada	C$1	=	487
euro zone	€1	=	742
Japan	¥100	=	590
New Zealand	NZ$1	=	397
United Kingdom	UK£1	=	1080
United States	US$1	=	644

Exchanging Money
US dollars are the preferred currency for exchange. To exchange cash and traveler's checks, *casas de cambios* are quicker and simpler than banks. Cash earns a better rate than traveler's checks and avoids commissions (though these are usually modest). Basically, the more desolate a destination, the higher the commission rates, so plan to exchange in larger cities. In very touristy areas, hotels, travel agencies and some shops also change cash. A few places have street changers, but they don't offer much difference in rate. The American Express representative is **Blanco Viajes** (☎ 02-6369100; Gral Holley 148, Providencia).

POST
Post offices (*Correos de Chile*) are open from 9am to 6pm weekdays and 9am to noon Saturday. Send essential overseas mail certificado to ensure its arrival. Parcel post is efficient, though customs may inspect your package before a clerk will accept it. Vendors near the post office wrap parcels for a small charge. Within Chile, an ordinary letter costs about US$0.45. An airmail letter or postcard costs about US$0.45 to North America and US$0.50 to Europe and Australia.

To send packages within Chile, the bus system is a much more reliable service, called *encomienda*. Simply take the package to a bus company that goes to the destination. Label the package clearly with the destination and the name of the person who will pick it up.

In Santiago, poste restante or *lista de correos* (general delivery mail), costs approximately US$0.25 per letter. Instruct correspondents to address letters clearly and to precede your name with either Señora or Señor, as post offices divide lists of correspondence by gender. Mail is held for one month.

RESPONSIBLE TRAVEL

Indigenous groups have a history of oppression, and homestays in indigenous communities help them make a living, but some consider it exploitation: you be the judge. Take out your litter in the parks. Avoid walking off the trail – it damages the ecosystem and you might get lost. Walking all over *ahus* in Rapa Nui is simply disrespectful to the gods. Avoid eating *locos* (abalone) or *centolla* when in *veda* (quarantine) for their breeding season. Lots of articles made of cardón cactus are for sale in the north, but this is a protected species. Same applies for the alerce in the south. If a place requests that you throw used toilet paper in the trash basket (most places), do it. The best and easiest way to earn karma points in Chile is to be pleasant and courteous to the locals.

SHOPPING

In Chiloé and Patagonia sheep-wool products are plentiful and great deals. In the Lake District, look for Mapuche design jewelry and basketry. Items with lapis lazuli can be found in many places. In the north, much of the artisanry is similar to Peru's and Bolivia. Edibles include *miel de ulmo*, a very aromatic honey special to Patagonia, *mermelada de murtilla*, a jam made of a red blueberry-like fruit, and canned papayas from Elqui Valley. Many cities have good antiques markets, most notably Valparaíso's Plaza O'Higgins.

STUDYING

Santiago and Pucón have the best variety of Spanish-language courses. That said, Spanish learners find Chile, with all its modismos and lazy pronunciation, not the best country in South America to pick up the language.

With Chilean headquarters at Coyhaique, the **National Outdoor Leadership School** (NOLS; ☎ 307-332-5300; www.nols.edu; 284 Lincoln St, Lander, WY 82520, USA) offers a 75-day 'Semester in Patagonia' program, emphasizing mountain wilderness skills, sea kayaking and natural-history courses, with university credit available. Santiago's **Vinoteca** (☎ 02-3352349; Isidora Goyenechea 2966, Las Condes) organizes wine courses. **Abtao** (☎ 02-2115021; www.abtao.cl; El Director 5660, Las Condes) organizes selective courses on Chilean ecosystems and wildlife.

TELEPHONE

Chile's country code is ☎ 56. All telephone numbers in Santiago and the metropolitan region have seven digits; all other telephone numbers have six digits. Finding a place to make a phone call is not a problem in Chile. The two largest telephone companies, Entel and Telefónica, have call centers from which you call directly from private, clean cabins. Other privately operated call centers will place the call for you then tell you in which *cabina* your call is transferred (this transition can be confusing for folks back home). Long distance calls are based on a carrier system: to place a call precede the number with the telephone company's code – **Entel** (☎ 123), **Telefónica** (☎ 188), for example. To make a collect call, dial ☎ 182 to get an operator.

Each telephone company installs its own public phones. Many take coins, but most use magnetic phone cards. A local call costs Ch$100 (about US$0.20) for five minutes, but outside peak hours (8am to 8pm weekdays, 8am to 2pm Saturday) costs only Ch$50. Phone cards are sold at kiosks and are compatible only with the phone booth of the same company. Rates for international calls are cheap, due to the competition among carriers.

Cell phone numbers have seven digits, prefixed by ☎ 09. When making a cell-to-cell phone call, drop the 09 prefix, but if making a cell-to-landline call, add the landline's area code. Numbers are often duplicated, so not adding the area code often means calling up a stranger. Cell phones sell for as little as US$50 and can be charged up by prepaid phone cards. Cell phones have a 'caller-pays' format. Calls between cell and landlines are expensive and quickly eat up prepaid card amounts.

TOILETS

Most public toilet facilities charge a small fee (US$0.10) in exchange for some toilet paper. Almost everywhere, they are clean and well maintained. In older buildings, where plumbing is an issue, soiled paper goes in the trash and not down the loo.

TOURIST INFORMATION

The national tourist service, Sernatur, has offices in Santiago and most cities. Their job is to inform, and they do so by burying

CHILE

you in brochures and leaflets, but not by advising or making suggestions. Many towns have municipal tourist offices, usually on the main plaza or at the bus terminal, which may be more helpful.

TOURS

There are lots of opportunities to go on tour here, but most things can be done on your own. In San Pedro de Atacama, competition keeps tour prices insanely low, so don't expect top-notch service. If going the distance to Rapa Nui, tours help explain the mystic archaeology. The only way to get to Laguna San Rafael, or climb an active volcano, or slam down a river, is on tour. Operators may say they have English-speaking guides, but sometimes you have to pay extra for this service – ask first.

VISAS

Nationals of US, Canada, Australia and the EU do not need a visa to visit Chile. Passports are obligatory and are essential for cashing traveler's checks, checking into hotels and other routine activities.

On arrival, you'll be handed a 90-day tourist card. Don't lose it! If you do, go to the **Policía Internacional** (☎ 02-7371292; General Borgoño 1052, Santiago; ⏰ 8:30am-5pm Mon-Fri), or to the nearest police station. You will be asked for it upon leaving the country.

It costs US$100 to renew a tourist card for 90 more days at the **Departamento de Extranjería** (☎ 02-5502400; Agustinas 1235, 2nd fl, Santiago; ⏰ 9am-2pm Mon-Fri).

See p519 for information regarding embassies and consulates.

VOLUNTEERING

If you are an experienced rafting guide, horse trekking guide etc, operators may enjoy your free labor during the busy high season, and may be able to work out some form of accommodation compensation for you. Be committed to riding out the entire season. **Experiment Chile** (www.experiment.cl) organizes 14-week language–learning/volunteer programs. Language schools often place students in volunteer work as well.

WOMEN TRAVELERS

The sight of women traveling, be it in a group or alone, is not met with much surprise or curiosity. Chilean men are usually courteous and respectful. They are quick with a *piropo* (comment or compliment), but this is usually a simple gesture and is not a come on. If attention is aggressive and unwanted, either ignore it or shame the bloke by responding aggressively '*¿Me estás hablando?*' ('You talking to me?') If problems persist, seek out a security guard or *carabinero* (police officer). While young Chilean women wear skin-tight revealing outfits without too much hassle, foreign women wearing similar styles will be more objectified. On long bus rides, if the person next to you looks like trouble don't be shy about asking the drivers to switch your seat. Many Chilean women look at their foreign counterparts as competition and can be initially catty, but this quickly subsides after some chatter. In smaller towns, tampons are hard to come by and pads are stashed away in the most discreet corner possible.

WORKING

Finding work as an English-language instructor in Santiago is feasible, but wages are fairly low and full-time employment is rare. Reputable employers insist on work or residence permits (increasingly difficult to obtain) from the **Departamento de Extranjería** (☎ 02-5502400; Agustinas 1235, 2nd fl, Santiago; ⏰ 9am-2pm Mon-Fri).

Colombia

HIGHLIGHTS

- **Cartagena** – the living museum of Spanish colonial architecture, legendary for its history and its beauty (p561)
- **Parque Nacional Tayrona** – the most beautiful part of the Colombian Caribbean coast, graced with deep bays and charming beaches (p560)
- **San Agustín** – a pre-Hispanic ceremonial funeral site noted for hundreds of enigmatic stone statues (p588)
- **Bogotá** – great cosmopolitan metropolis with splendid museums, cultural life and night scene (p536)
- **Off-the-beaten track** – hike to Ciudad Perdida, one of the greatest pre-Hispanic cities found in the Americas, hidden in a lush rain forest (p561)
- **Best journey** – most roads in Colombia wind up and down the Andean chains and provide for scenic, often dramatic, vistas. A great example of these is the legendary Carretera Panamericana, running across the country from Venezuela to Ecuador via Cúcuta–Bucaramanga–Bogotá–Cali–Pasto–Ipiales

FAST FACTS

- **Area:** 1,141,748 sq km
- **Budget:** US$15–25 a day
- **Capital:** Bogotá
- **Costs:** double room in a budget hotel US$5–12, set meal in a budget restaurant US$1.50–2.50, 100km intercity bus fare US$3–4
- **Country code:** ☎ 57
- **Electricity:** 110V, 60 Hz; US-type plugs
- **Famous for:** Gabriel García Márquez, coffee, emeralds, cocaine
- **Language:** Spanish
- **Money:** US$1 = 2945 pesos
- **Phrases:** *chévere, bacano* (cool), *asqueroso* (disgusting, horrible), *rumba* (party)
- **Population:** 45 million (2003 estimate)
- **Time:** GMT minus 5 hours (no daylight-saving time)
- **Tipping:** customary (not compulsory) 10% in upmarket restaurants
- **Traveler's checks:** cashed in some major banks
- **Visas:** not required from nationals of major Western countries

TRAVEL HINTS

Don't wear any khaki-colored clothing or army surplus uniforms, as the military may take you for a guerrilla, or the guerrilla for a military – it's not clear which is worse. Be sure to try as many exotic fruits as you can – Colombia is famous for them. For both safety and scenery, do your overland travel during daytime only.

COLOMBIA

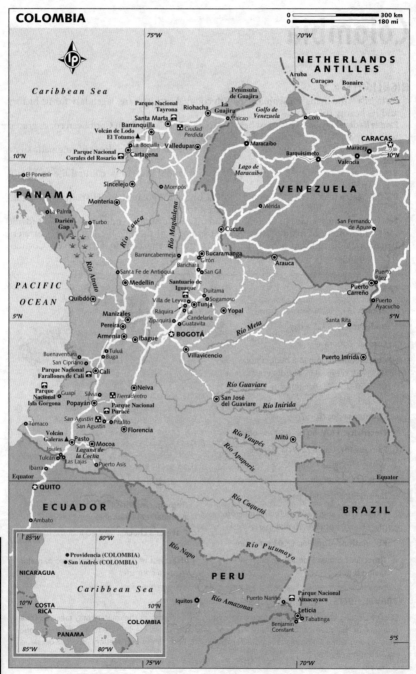

COLOMBIA

0 — 300 km
0 — 180 mi

Caribbean Sea

NETHERLANDS ANTILLES

Aruba
Curaçao
Bonaire

Península de Guajira

Golfo de Venezuela

Coro

CARACAS
Maracay
Valencia
Barquisimeto

Parque Nacional Tayrona
Riohacha
La Guajira
Santa Marta
Barranquilla
Maicao
Volcán de Lodo El Totumo
Ciudad Perdida
La Boquilla
Valledupar
Cartagena
Parque Nacional Corales del Rosario

Maracaibo

Lago de Maracaibo

VENEZUELA

Mérida

San Fernando de Apure

El Porvenir

Sincelejo
Mompós

PANAMA

Montería

La Palma
Turbo
Darién Gap

Río Cauca
Río Magdalena

Cúcuta

Barrancabermeja
Bucaramanga
Girón
Barichara
San Gil
Arauca

Puerto Páez
Puerto Carreño
Puerto Ayacucho

Santa Fe de Antioquia
Río Atrato

PACIFIC OCEAN

Quibdó
Medellín

Santuario de Iguaque
Villa de Leyva
Ráquira
La Candelaria
Duitama
Sogamoso
Tunja
Yopal

Manizales
Pereira
Armenia
Ibagué
Zipaquirá
Guatavita
BOGOTÁ

Río Meta
Santa Rita

Buenaventura
San Cipriano
Parque Nacional Farallones de Cali
Tuluá
Buga
Cali

Villavicencio
Puerto Inírida

Parque Nacional Isla Gorgona
Guapí
Silvia
Popayán
Neiva
Tierradentro
Parque Nacional Puracé
Río Guaviare

San José del Guaviare
Río Inírida

Tumaco
San Agustín
San Agustín
Pitalito
Florencia

Volcán Galeras
Pasto
Mocoa
Ipiales
Laguna de la Cocha
Tulcán
Las Lajas
Puerto Asís
Ibarra

Río Vaupés
Mitú
Río Apaporis

Equator
Equator

QUITO

ECUADOR

Ambato

BRAZIL

Río Caquetá

Río Putumayo

Río Napo

PERU

Iquitos
Río Amazonas
Puerto Nariño
Parque Nacional Amacayacu
Leticia
Tabatinga
Benjamín Constant

5°S

Inset map

85°W   80°W

Providencia (COLOMBIA)
San Andrés (COLOMBIA)

NICARAGUA

Caribbean Sea

COSTA RICA
10°N
10°N

COLOMBIA

PANAMA

85°W   80°W

75°W   70°W

75°W   70°W

5°N   5°N

10°N   10°N

For most travelers, Colombia is unknown territory – a land of myths, cocaine barons, guerrillas, emeralds and the mysterious El Dorado. It is the land of Gabriel García Márquez and his famous novel, *One Hundred Years of Solitude* – a tale as magical as the country itself. And it is the land that bears the name of Columbus, who never got as far as Colombia, but where people have rearranged the name to spell 'Locombia' (the mad country), and not without reason.

Colombia's geography is among the most varied in South America, as are its flora and fauna. The inhabitants form a palette of ethnic blends uncommon elsewhere on the continent and include 80 different Indian groups, some of which still maintain traditional lifestyles. It's a country of amazing natural and cultural diversity and contrast, where climate, topography, wildlife, crafts, music, cuisine and architecture change within hours of overland travel.

Through its turbulent history, Colombia has been soaked with blood in innumerable civil wars and has endured the continent's largest and fiercest guerrilla insurgency. The country is also the world's major producer of cocaine. With such a background, it's no wonder that violence occurs here more frequently than in neighboring countries, and that Colombia is not as safe.

However, if you take the necessary precautions, Colombia is worth the challenge. It's exotic, sensual, wild, complex and fascinating. And it's hard to find such hospitable, spirited and stimulating people as Colombians.

HISTORY
Pre-Columbian Times

Colombia is the only overland gateway to South America and undoubtedly part of the route pioneered by the continent's first inhabitants who migrated from North and Central America. Some tribes headed further south, while others established permanent settlements in what is now Colombia and, in time, reached a remarkably high level of development. They left behind three important archaeological sites – San Agustín, Tierradentro and Ciudad Perdida – and an impressive collection of gold work, considered the continent's best, both for the techniques used and for its artistic design.

In contrast to the Aztecs or Incas, who dominated vast regions, several independent Colombian groups occupied relatively small areas scattered throughout the Andean region and along the Pacific and Caribbean coasts. Despite trading and cultural contacts, these cultures developed largely independently. Among the most outstanding were the Calima, Muisca, Nariño, Quimbaya, San Agustín, Sinú, Tayrona, Tierradentro, Tolima and Tumaco.

San Agustín, one of the most extraordinary ceremonial centers in South America, is famous for hundreds of monolithic statues and tombs scattered over a wide area. Another culture flourished in nearby Tierradentro, and is noted for developed funeral rites with elaborate underground burial chambers (unique in the Americas), laboriously carved out of the soft rock and decorated with paintings.

The Tayrona, in the Sierra Nevada de Santa Marta, had long been considered one of the most advanced early Indian civilizations, yet it was only after the accidental discovery of Ciudad Perdida (Lost City), in 1975, that their greatness as architects was confirmed. Ciudad Perdida, thought to be their major center, is one of the largest ancient cities ever found in the Americas. Resplendent with several hundred stone terraces linked by a network of stairs, it's spectacularly set in the heart of a tropical rain forest.

The Muisca group was known far and wide for its wealth, and had a flourishing civilization that occupied what are now the Boyacá and Cundinamarca departments. It's particularly known for the myth of El Dorado, created by the Spaniards.

Spanish Conquest

In 1499, Alonso de Ojeda was the first conquistador to set foot on Colombian soil and to see indigenous people using gold objects. Attracted by the presumed riches of the Indians, the shores of present-day Colombia became the target of numerous coastal expeditions by the Spaniards.

Several short-lived settlements were founded, but it was not until 1525 that Rodrigo de Bastidas laid the first stones of Santa Marta, the earliest surviving town. In 1533, Pedro de Heredia founded Cartagena, which soon became the principal center of trade.

In 1536, a general advance toward the interior began independently from the north and south. Jiménez de Quesada set off from Santa Marta, pushed up the Magdalena valley, then climbed the Cordillera Oriental, arriving in Muisca territory early in 1537. After conquering the Muiscas, he founded Santa Fe de Bogotá in 1538. Quesada didn't actually find gold, despite the elaborate rituals of the Indians, who threw gold offerings into the waters of their sacred lake, Laguna de Guatavita, and thus gave birth to the mysterious legend of El Dorado.

Sebastián de Benalcázar (known in Colombia as Belalcázar) deserted from Francisco Pizarro's army, which was conquering the Inca empire, and mounted an expedition from Ecuador. He subdued the southern part of Colombia, founding Popayán and Cali along the way, and reached Bogotá in 1539.

The two groups fought tooth and nail for supremacy, and it was not until 1550 that King Charles V of Spain, in an effort to establish law and order, created the Real Audiencia del Nuevo Reino de Granada, a tribunal based in Bogotá. Administratively, the new colony was subject to the Viceroyalty of Peru.

With the growth of the Spanish empire in the New World, a new territorial division was created in 1717, and Bogotá became the capital of its own viceroyalty, the Virreinato de la Nueva Granada. It comprised the territories of what are today Colombia, Panama, Ecuador and Venezuela.

Independence Wars

Toward the end of the 18th century, the general disillusionment with Spanish domination gave rise to open protests and rebellions. This, together with events such as the North American and French revolutions and, more importantly, the invasion of Spain by Napoleon Bonaparte, paved the way to independence. When Napoleon placed his own brother on the Spanish throne in 1808, the colonies refused to recognize the new monarch. One by one, Colombian towns declared their independence.

In 1812, Simón Bolívar, who was to become the hero of the independence struggle, arrived in Cartagena to take the offensive against the Spanish armies. In a brilliant campaign to seize Venezuela, he won six battles but was unable to hold Caracas, and had to withdraw to Cartagena. By then, Napoleon had been defeated at Waterloo, and Spain set about reconquering its colonies. Colonial rule was re-established in 1817.

Bolívar took up arms again. After assembling an army of horsemen from the Venezuelan Llanos, strengthened by a British legion, he marched over the Andes into Colombia. The last and most decisive battle took place at Boyacá on August 7, 1819. Colombia's independence was won.

After Independence

A revolutionary congress was held in Angostura (present-day Ciudad Bolívar, Venezuela) in 1819. Still euphoric with victory, the delegates proclaimed the Gran Colombia, a new state uniting Colombia, Venezuela and Ecuador (although Venezuela and Ecuador were still under Spanish rule). The congress was followed by another, held in Villa del Rosario, near Cúcuta, in 1821. It was there that the two opposing tendencies, centralist and federalist, came to the fore. Bolívar, who supported a centralized republic, succeeded in imposing his will. The Gran Colombia came into being and Bolívar was elected president.

From its inception, the state started to disintegrate. It soon became apparent that a central regime was incapable of governing such a vast and diverse territory. The Gran Colombia had split into three separate countries in 1830.

The two political currents, centralist and federalist, were formalized in 1849 when two political parties were established: the Conservatives (with centralist tendencies) and the Liberals (with federalist leanings). Colombia became the scene of fierce rivalries between the two forces, resulting in complete chaos. During the 19th century, the country experienced no less than eight civil wars. Between 1863 and 1885, there were more than 50 antigovernment insurrections.

In 1899, a Liberal revolt turned into a full-blown civil war, the so-called War of a Thousand Days. That carnage resulted in a Conservative victory and left 100,000 dead. In 1903, the USA took advantage of the country's internal strife and fomented a secessionist movement in Panama (at that time a Colombian province). By creating a new republic, the USA was able to build a canal across the Central American isthmus.

La Violencia

After a period of relative peace, the struggle between Liberals and Conservatives broke out again in 1948 with La Violencia, the most destructive of Colombia's many civil wars, which left a death toll of some 300,000. Urban riots broke out on April 9, 1948 in Bogotá following the assassination of Jorge Eliécer Gaitán, a charismatic populist Liberal leader. Liberals soon took up arms throughout the country.

By 1953, some groups of Liberal guerrillas had begun to demonstrate a dangerous degree of independence. As it became evident that the partisan conflict was taking on revolutionary overtones, the leaders of both the Liberal and Conservative parties decided to support a military coup as the best means to retain power and pacify the countryside. The 1953 coup of General Gustavo Rojas Pinilla was the only military intervention the country experienced in the 20th century.

The dictatorship of General Rojas was not to last. In 1957, the leaders of the two parties signed a pact to share power for the next 16 years. The agreement, later approved by a plebiscite (in which women were, for the first time, allowed to vote), became known as the Frente Nacional (National Front). During the life of the accord, the two parties alternated in the presidency every four years. The party leaders repressed all political activity that remained outside the scope of their parties, thus sowing the seeds for the appearance of guerrilla groups.

Guerrillas & Paramilitaries

Guerrillas have been quite an important part of Colombian political life, and a headache for the government. With roots that extend back to La Violencia, they are the oldest insurgent forces in Latin America. They continue to engage in armed struggle and are more active than ever.

Colombia saw the birth of perhaps a dozen different guerrilla groups, each with its own ideology and its own political and military strategies. The movements that have had the biggest impact on local politics (and left the largest number of dead) include the FARC (Fuerzas Armadas Revolucionarias de Colombia), the ELN (Ejército de Liberación Nacional) and the M-19 (Movimiento 19 de Abril).

Until 1982, the guerrillas were treated as a problem of public order and persecuted by the military forces. President Belisario Betancur (1982–86) was the first to open direct negotiations with the guerrillas in a bid to reincorporate them into the nation's political life. Yet the talks ended in failure. The rupture was poignantly symbolized by the takeover of Bogotá's Palacio de Justicia by the M-19 guerrillas in November 1985.

The Liberal government of President Virgilio Barco (1986–90), after long and complex negotiations with the M-19, signed an agreement under which this group handed over its arms, ceased insurgent activity and transformed itself into a political party. However, the two other major groups – the 18,000-strong FARC and the 5000-strong ELN – remain under arms and currently control about 40% of the country. Having lost support from Moscow and Havana, they now rely on extortion and kidnapping to finance their struggle. They are also deeply involved in the production and trafficking of drugs, principally cocaine.

Since the state has been unable to control areas lost to the guerrillas, private armies – the so-called *paramilitares* or *autodefensas* – have mushroomed, with the army turning a blind eye or even supporting them. These right-wing armies operate against rebels in many regions, including Urabá, Cesar, Córdoba, Antioquia, Magdalena Medio, Santander, Cundinamarca and Caquetá, and have committed some horrendous massacres on civilians allegedly supporting the guerrillas. They form a loosely woven alliance known as the AUC (Autodefensas Unidas de Colombia), with an estimated 10,000 fighters nationwide.

COLOMBIA

Drug Cartels

Colombia is the biggest producer of co-caine, controlling some 80% of the world market. The mafia started in a small way in the early 1970s but, within a short time, developed the trade into a powerful industry, with its own plantations, laboratories, transport services and protection.

The boom years began in the early 1980s. The Medellín Cartel, led by Pablo Escobar, became the principal mafia and its bosses lived in freedom and luxury. They even founded their own political party and two newspapers, and in 1982 Escobar was elected to the Congress.

In 1983 the government launched a campaign against the drug trade, which gradually turned into an all-out war. The cartel responded violently and managed to liquidate many of its adversaries. The war became even bloodier in August 1989, when Luis Carlos Galán, the leading Liberal contender for the 1990 presidential election, was assassinated. The government responded with the confiscation of nearly 1000 mafia-owned properties, and announced new laws on extradition – a nightmare for the drug barons. The cartel resorted to the use of terrorist tactics, principally car bombs.

The election of the Liberal President César Gaviria (1990–94) brought a brief period of hope. Following lengthy negotiations, which included a constitutional amendment to ban extradition of Colombians, Escobar and the remaining cartel bosses surrendered and the narco-terrorism subsided. However, Escobar escaped from his palace-like prison following the government's bumbling attempts to move him to a more secure site. An elite 1500-man special unit sought Escobar for 499 days, until it tracked him down in Medellín and killed him in December 1993.

Despite this, the drug trade continued unaffected. While the military concentrated on hunting one man and persecuting one cartel, the other cartels were quick to take advantage of the opportune circumstances. The Cali Cartel, led by the Rodríguez Orejuela brothers, swiftly moved into the shattered Medellín Cartel's markets and became Colombia's largest trafficker. It also diversified into opium poppies and heroin. Although the cartel's top bosses were captured in 1995 and put behind bars, the drug trade continues to flourish, with other regional drug cartels, paramilitaries and, principally, the guerrillas filling the gap left by the two original mafias. And until the USA rethinks its drug strategy, including the legalization of drugs, there's little hope that the Colombian bad guys will simply walk away from a US$6-billion-a-year business.

Into the 21st Century

Following a troubled term of office of the Liberal President Ernesto Samper (1994–98), plagued by drug-money scandals, the voters in the 1998 election opted for the independent conservative President Andrés Pastrana (1998–2002). Just after the election Pastrana met secretly with the FARC's top commander Manuel Marulanda, known as Tirofijo (Sure Shot), in order to end 34 years of bloody guerrilla war.

Before entering into talks, the FARC insisted on the withdrawal of government troops from the guerrilla-controlled areas of Caquetá and Putumayo departments. In a politically risky move to start the peace process, Pastrana ceded to the FARC a 42,000-sq-km demilitarized zone the size of Switzerland, which effectively became the rebels' country.

Talks began in January 1999 and inched on and off practically without any results. The guerrillas refused a cease-fire as a precondition to the peace dialogue, so the war went on as it had been for decades. By February 2002, the government eventually lost its patience and reclaimed the demilitarized zone, but the FARC was already well established in the region. In April 2002, shortly before the presidential election, the FARC began a campaign of terror including car bombs aimed at the civil population.

New Hope

The May 2002 election was carried out in a climate of violence, with a fragile economic situation and crises for the two traditional parties. Six presidential candidates campaigned for the top post, but one of them, Ingrid Betancourt, was kidnapped by the FARC (and by the time we were going to press, she was still in the guerrillas' hands). Álvaro Uribe, who ran as an independent hard-liner, claimed a landslide first-round victory, capturing 53% of the vote.

Uribe ran on a strong anti-guerrilla ticket, promising more intensive military campaigns against the two enduring rebel groups as the best way to end Colombia's 38-year bloody civil war. Predictably, his program won him the votes of a large part of the electorate, fed up with the never-ending guerrilla war, their bombs, kidnappings and extortions.

Uribe's term is likely to be a difficult period for the nation and crucial for the future of the country. Both the government and the guerrillas are determined to win, but what will come out of their strong declarations is yet to be seen. The first year of the new government hasn't brought any radical changes, although the war has intensified, claiming more victims on both sides. Despite that (or perhaps thanks to it), Uribe has enjoyed remarkable popular support, more than any other president in recent history.

THE CULTURE
The National Psyche & Lifestyle
Decades of internal social and political conflict have molded, marked and scarred a complex national psyche. The national mood swings between hope and despair, courage and fear, resilience and inflexibility, enthusiasm and pessimism. Most Colombians feel victims of the never-ending war they didn't start or want, and from which they can't escape. They feel trapped in their own country, with increasingly limited means of escape for a while or for good.

Trying to adapt to the generations-long violence, many Colombians have developed a sort of siege mentality. In cities particularly, children and teenagers are often under strict supervision, residential buildings have 24-hour security guards and sniffer dogs are omnipresent. Many people will travel inter-city only under the umbrella of the *caravanas turísticas* organized during holiday peaks (which involve placing an enormous number of soldiers along major roads in order to discourage robberies and kidnappings).

In the countryside, plagued by armed conflict, rural dwellers sometimes have little choice other than fleeing the area. Since 1985, 2.9 million people have been internally displaced, mainly peasants and ethnic minori-ties. Under fire from all fronts, these refugees flee their homeland and go to the cities and towns where they live in extreme poverty.

Given all the internal problems, it's amazing to see how orderly and normal the everyday life of most families appears, and how easy-going, open and hospitable Colombians are.

People
About 75% of the population is of mixed ancestry, comprising 50% to 55% *mestizos* (of European–Indian blood) and 15 to 20% *mulatos* (of European–African blood). There are also 3% *zambos* (of African–Indian blood).

Whites constitute about 20% of the population and are mainly descendants of the Spaniards. Blacks represent about 4% of the population and are most numerous on the Caribbean and Pacific coasts.

Indians number between 400,000 and 600,000, representing just a bit more than 1% of the total population. This seemingly insignificant number comprises about 80 different Indian groups speaking about 65 languages and nearly 300 dialects belonging to several linguistic families. They live in communities scattered throughout the country, usually occupying quite small areas.

ARTS
Architecture
The most outstanding example of pre-Columbian urban planning is the Ciudad Perdida of the Tayronas in the Sierra Nevada de Santa Marta. Although the dwellings haven't survived, the stone structures, including a complex network of terraces, paths and stairways remain in remarkably good shape.

After the arrival of the Spaniards, bricks and tiles became the main construction materials. The colonial towns followed rigid standards laid down by the Spanish Crown. They were constructed on a grid plan, centered on the Plaza Mayor (main square). This pattern was applied during the colonial period and long after, and is the dominant feature of most Colombian cities, towns and villages.

Spain's strong Catholic tradition left behind loads of churches and convents in the colony – the central areas of Bogotá,

Cartagena, Popayán and Tunja are good examples.

In the 19th century, despite independence, the architecture continued to be predominantly Spanish in style. Modern architectural trends only began to appear in Colombia after WWII. This process accelerated during the 1960s when city skyscrapers appeared.

Literature

During the independence period and up to WWII, Colombia produced few internationally acclaimed writers other than José Asunción Silva (1865–96), perhaps the country's best poet, considered the precursor of modernism in Latin America.

A postwar literary boom thrust many great Latin American authors into the international sphere, including the Colombian Gabriel García Márquez (born 1928). His novel *One Hundred Years of Solitude*, published in 1967, immediately became a worldwide best seller. It mixed myths, dreams and reality, and amazed readers with a new form of expression which critics dubbed *realismo mágico* (magic realism). In 1982, García Márquez won the Nobel Prize for literature. His most recent book, the first volume of his memoirs titled *Vivir Para Contarla*, was released in 2002 and hit all sales records in Colombia and all over the Spanish-language world.

Music

In broad terms, Colombia can be divided into four musical zones: the two coasts, the Andean region and Los Llanos. The Caribbean coast vibrates with hot African-related rhythms such as the *cumbia*, *mapalé* and *porro*. The coast is also the cradle of the *vallenato*, based on the European accordion, which emanated a century ago from the regions of La Guajira and Cesar and has successfully conquered just about the whole of the country. This is the most popular Colombian musical genre today.

The music of the Pacific coast, such as the *currulao*, is based on a strong African drum pulse, but tinged with Spanish influences. Colombian Andean music has been strongly influenced by Spanish rhythms and instruments, and differs notably from the Indian music of the Peruvian and Bolivian highlands. Among the typical forms are

the *bambuco*, *pasillo* and *torbellino*, all of which are instrumental and predominantly feature string instruments. The music of Los Llanos, *música llanera*, is sung and usually accompanied by a harp, *cuatro* (a sort of four-string guitar) and maracas.

Colombia's most famous musical export is Shakira, whose album *Laundry Service* stormed pop charts in the USA and elsewhere in 2002, making her a global, not just Latin, superstar. Other Colombian artists known beyond the country's borders include Carlos Vives (a Latin pop vocalist), Totó La Momposina (a traditional Afro-Caribbean music singer), Juanes (Latin rock vocalist) and Los Aterciopelados (Colombia's most popular rock group).

Visual Arts

The colonial period was dominated by Spanish religious art, and although the paintings and sculptures of this era were generally executed by local artists, they reflected the Spanish trends of the day. With the arrival of independence, visual arts departed from strictly religious themes, but it was not until the turn of the 19th-century revolution in European painting that Colombian artists began to experiment and create original work.

Among the most distinguished modern painters and sculptors are Pedro Nel Gómez, known for his murals, watercolors, oils and sculptures; Luis Alberto Acuña, a painter and sculptor who used motifs from pre-Columbian art; Alejandro Obregón, a painter tending to abstract forms; Edgar Negret, an abstract sculptor; Rodrigo Arenas Betancur, Colombia's most famous monument creator; and Fernando Botero, the most internationally renowned Colombian artist, whose somewhat ironic style of painting and sculpture is easily recognizable by the characteristic fatness of the figures.

RELIGION

The great majority of Colombians are Roman Catholic. Other creeds are officially permitted but their numbers are small. However, over the past decade there has been a proliferation of various Protestant congregations, which have succeeded in converting some three million Catholics. Many Indian groups have adopted the

Catholic faith, sometimes incorporating some of their traditional beliefs.

SPORT

Soccer and cycling are the most popular spectator sports. Colombia regularly takes part in international events in these two fields, such as the World Cup and the Tour de France, and has recorded some successes. The national soccer league has matches most of the year.

Colombians are passionate about *corrida* (bullfighting), which was introduced by the Spaniards. Most cities and towns have *plaza de toros* (bullrings). The bullfighting season usually peaks in January, when the top-ranking matadors are invited from Spain.

ENVIRONMENT
Land

Colombia covers 1,141,748 sq km, roughly equivalent to the area of France, Spain and Portugal combined. It occupies the northwestern part of the continent and is the only South American country with coasts on both the Pacific (1448km long) and the Caribbean (1760km). Colombia is bordered by Panama, Venezuela, Brazil, Peru and Ecuador.

Colombia's physical geography is amazingly diverse. The western part, almost half of the total territory, is mountainous, with three Andean chains – the Cordillera Occidental, Cordillera Central and Cordillera Oriental – running roughly parallel north–south across most of the country. More than half of the territory east of the Andes is a vast lowland, which is divided into two regions: the savanna-like Los Llanos in the north and the mostly rain forest-covered Amazon in the south.

Colombia has several small islands. The major ones are the archipelago of San Andrés and Providencia (in the Caribbean Sea, 750km northwest of mainland Colombia), the Islas del Rosario (near the Caribbean coast) and Isla Gorgona (in the Pacific Ocean).

Wildlife

Colombia has more plant and animal species per unit area than any other country in the world. This abundance reflects Colombia's numerous climatic zones and microclimates, which have created many different habitats and biological islands in which wildlife has evolved independently.

Colombia is home to the jaguar, ocelot, peccary, tapir, deer, armadillo, spectacled bear and numerous species of monkey, to mention just a few of the 300-odd species of mammals. There are more than 1920 recorded species of birds (nearly a quarter of the world's total), ranging from the huge Andean condor to the tiny hummingbird. Colombia's flora is equally impressive and includes some 3000 species of orchid alone. The national herbariums have classified more than 130,000 plants, including many endemic species.

National Parks

Colombia has 35 national parks and 12 other state-run nature reserves. Their combined area constitutes 8.2% of the country's territory. Only a handful of parks provide accommodation and food for visitors. The remaining parks have no tourist amenities at all and some, especially those in remote regions, are virtually inaccessible. Many parks can be unsafe for tourists because of guerrilla presence.

National parks are operated by the Unidad Administrativa Especial del Sistema de Parques Nacionales, a department of the Ministry of the Environment. Their central office is in Bogotá, and there are regional offices in other cities. The Bogotá office handles all parks, whereas subsidiary offices only service the parks in their regions. The most popular parks include Tayrona, Corales del Rosario, Isla Gorgona, Amacayacu and the Santuario de Iguaque.

Environmental Issues

Colombia's environment is under various serious threats, one of which is deforestation. Every year vast areas of rain forest and other fragile habitats are indiscriminately cleared for industry, housing, farming and ranching. Even national parks are not safe because of lack of funds and personnel to properly guard them. In many areas, simply decreeing a national park has not eliminated settling, logging, ranching and poaching.

For over 20 years, guerrillas have targeted oil pipelines in order to stop multinationals depleting natural resources. Since 1986, there have been over 950 attacks that have spilled more than two million barrels of crude oil into the environment (11 times the amounts spilled by *Exxon Valdez*), polluting rivers and land.

On the other hand, the US has made its military aid to Colombia conditional on the aerial fumigation of coca and poppy crops. In 2002 alone, 130,000 hectares of coca and 3,400 hectares of poppy were fumigated with a herbicide containing Glyphosate, an ingredient that besides coca plants kills traditional crops, impoverishing and displacing thousands of peasants and indigenous people and compromising their health. Furthermore, many scientists claim that the herbicide is killing microbes and fungi necessary within the rain forest ecosystem and that therefore it is altering the whole nutrient cycling system.

TRANSPORT

GETTING THERE & AWAY
Air
Sitting on the northwestern edge of the continent, Colombia is a convenient and reasonably cheap gateway to South America from the USA and Central America, and even from Europe. Bogotá has Colombia's major international airport, but some other cities, including Cartagena, Medellín and Cali, also handle international flights. The country is serviced by a number of major intercontinental airlines, including British Airways, Air France, Iberia and American Airlines, and a dozen national carriers.

The airport tax on international flights out of Colombia is US$28 if you have stayed in the country up to 60 days, and US$43 if you have stayed longer. The tax is payable either in US dollars or pesos at the exchange rate of the day.

BRAZIL & PERU
Direct flights between these countries and Colombia are expensive. It will be cheaper to fly through Leticia in the Colombian Amazon. See the Leticia section (p601).

CENTRAL AMERICA
Colombia has regular flight connections with most Central American capitals. Sample fares include: Guatemala City–Bogotá US$356, San José (Costa Rica)–

Bogotá US$312 (60-day return US$377) and Panama City–Bogotá US$151 (60-day return US$274). It may work out cheaper to go via the Colombian island of San Andrés and then get a domestic flight to the Colombian mainland. See the San Andrés section (p573).

ECUADOR
There are daily flights between Quito and Bogotá with Alianza Summa and Continental Airlines (one way US$242, 30/60-day return US$192/258). Tame (an Ecuadorian carrier) has flights between Cali and Tulcán in Ecuador (one way US$84) and between Cali and Quito (US$118).

VENEZUELA
There are several daily flights between Caracas and Bogotá, with Alianza Summa and Aeropostal. One-way fares are US$160 to US$180; a discount 60-day round-trip ticket costs US$250 to US$270.

Boat
BRAZIL & PERU
The only viable border crossing between these two countries and Colombia is via Leticia in the Colombian Amazon. Leticia is reached from Iquitos (Peru) and Manaus (Brazil) by boat; see p602.

PANAMA
There are sailboats between Colón in Panama and Cartagena in Colombia. See the Cartagena section (p566).

Bus
ECUADOR
Almost all travelers use the Carretera Panamericana border crossing through Ipiales and Tulcán. See Ipiales (p597) and Tulcán (Ecuador).

VENEZUELA
There are several border crossings between Colombia and Venezuela. By far the most popular with travelers is the route via Cúcuta and San Antonio del Táchira, on the main Bogotá–Caracas road. See the Cúcuta section (p557) and the San Antonio del Táchira section (p982).

Another border crossing is at Paraguachón, on the Maicao–Maracaibo road. There are buses and shared taxis between Maicao and Maracaibo, and direct buses between Cartagena and Caracas. See Maracaibo (p975) and Cartagena (p566).

There's also a popular little border crossing between Colombia's Puerto Carreño and either Puerto Ayacucho (p1016) or Puerto Páez (both in Venezuela).

GETTING AROUND

Air

Colombia has a well-developed airline system and a good network of domestic flights. Main passenger airlines include Avianca, Sam, Aces, Aires, Intercontinental de Aviación, AeroRepública, Satena and West Caribbean Airways, most of which also have international flights. In 2002, Avianca, Sam and Aces entered into an alliance known as Alianza Summa to control about 75% of the domestic air traffic. However, it suffered a serious financial crisis in 2003 and had to cut down the number of its destinations and frequency of services.

Airfares differ significantly between the carriers, so if the route you're going to fly is serviced by several airlines, check their fares before buying your ticket. The Alianza Summa is normally more expensive than the remaining airlines, but may have some occasional good deals.

Additionally, every airline may offer different fares on the same route, depending on a number of factors such as what season it is, how long in advance you book, whether it's a weekday or a weekend etc, and there may be various promotional and discounted fares.

There's a US$4 airport tax on domestic flights, which you normally pay while buying your ticket (this tax is included in the airfares listed in this chapter). Always reconfirm your booking at least 72 hours before departure.

Boat

With more than 3000km of Pacific and Atlantic coastline, there is a considerable amount of shipping traffic, consisting mostly of irregular cargo boats, which may also take passengers. Rivers are important transport routes in the Chocó and the Amazon, where there is no other way of getting around. Few riverboats run on regular schedules, and as most are primarily cargo boats, they are far from fast and conditions are primitive.

Bus

Buses are the main means of getting around Colombia. The bus system is well developed and extensive, reaching even the smallest villages. There are three principal classes of buses: ordinary (called *corriente* or *ordinario*), 1st class (which goes by a variety of names, such as *pullman*, *metropolitano* or *directo*) and the air-con buses (known as *climatizado* or *ejecutivo*).

The *corriente*-type buses are usually old crates and mostly service side roads. The *pullmans* are more modern and comfortable. They ply both side and main routes. *Climatizados* are the most luxurious. They have plenty of leg room, reclining seats, large luggage compartments, and some have toilets. They are predominantly long-distance buses covering main routes. The *climatizado* is the dominant means of inter-city transport. Carry warm clothes – drivers usually set the air-con to full blast.

On the main roads buses run frequently, so there is little point in booking a seat in advance. In some places off the main routes, where there are only a few buses daily, it's better to buy a ticket some time before departure. The only time you really need to book is during the Christmas and Easter periods, when hordes of Colombians are on holiday.

There is one more kind of bus – the *chiva*. This trolley-type vehicle was the principal means of transport several decades ago. Its body is made almost entirely of wood, covered with colorful decorative patterns. Today, the *chivas* have disappeared from the main roads, but they still play an important role on back roads between small villages.

The *colectivo* is a cross between a bus and a taxi. They are usually large cars (sometimes jeeps or minibuses) that cover fixed routes, mainly over short and medium distances. They leave when full, not according to a schedule, and are a good option if there is a long wait for the next bus or if you are in a hurry.

Bus travel is reasonably cheap in Colombia. As a rule of thumb, the climatizado bus costs roughly US$4 every 100km. *Pullmans* cost about 20% less than *climatizados* and the *corrientes* 20% less than *pullmans*. If various companies service the same route, the fare is much the same with all of them (though some may offer temporary promotions, so shop around).

BOGOTÁ

The capital of the country, Bogotá is the quintessence of all things Colombian. It's a huge Latin American city, which offers just about every modern Western convenience and suffers from every third-world problem. It's a city of brilliant museums, splendid colonial churches, universities, futuristic architecture, intellectuals and artists, offering a vibrant and diverse cultural life. Yet it is also a city of vast shantytowns, street urchins, beggars, thieves, itinerant vendors, wild traffic and graffiti.

Bogotá is a bustling and noisy metropolis – amazing but awful, fascinating but dangerous. It's a bizarre mixture of everything from oppressive poverty to sparkling prosperity – you may love it or hate it, but it won't leave you indifferent.

The city was founded in 1538 and named Santa Fe de Bogotá, but after independence the name was shortened to Bogotá. Though it always played an important political role as the capital, its rapid progress only came in the 1940s, with industrialization and consequent migrations from the countryside. Over the past 50 years, Bogotá has grown 20-fold to its present population of about seven million.

Bogotá lies at an altitude of about 2600m, and at this height altitude sickness can occur. You may feel a bit dizzy when you arrive. Take it easy for a day or two – it should soon go away. The city's average temperature is 14°C year-round, with cool nights and warm days. The dry seasons are from December to February and June to September.

ORIENTATION

Bogotá has grown along its north–south axis and is bordered to the east by a mountain range topped by the two peaks of Mt Monserrate and Mt Guadalupe. Having expanded up the mountain slopes as far as possible, Bogotá is now developing to the west and north.

The city center divides the metropolis into two very different parts. The northern sector consists mainly of upmarket residential districts, while the southern part is a vast spread of undistinguished lower-income suburbs. The western part, away from the mountains, is the most hetero-

GETTING INTO TOWN

If arriving in Bogotá by air, you can get from El Dorado airport to the center (13km) by *busetas* (small buses) or *colectivos* marked 'Aeropuerto'; they park about 50m from the terminal. From the center to the airport, you catch them on Calle 19 or Carrera 10. Alternatively, take a taxi (US$6).

If arriving in Bogotá by bus at the main bus terminal, you can get to the center (9km) by a *buseta* or *colectivo*, or by taxi (US$4).

geneous and is more industrial. This is where the airport and the bus terminal are located.

Bogotá has enough sights to keep you busy for several days. It also has a far more vibrant and diversified cultural and artistic life than any other city in the country. Most major attractions are in the city center, within easy walking distance of each other.

INFORMATION
Emergency

Emergency numbers operate 24 hours daily unless otherwise indicated.

Ambulance (☎ 125)
Fire (☎ 119)
Police (☎ 112)
Tourist police (☎ 1-337-4413; Carrera 13 No 26-62; ☼ 7am-noon & 2-7pm) The bilingual staff can provide advice and assist travelers to make a police statement when documents and valuables are lost or stolen.

Internet Access

Central Bogotá has plenty of Internet facilities (most cost US$1 to US$1.50 per hour).
Café Internet Doble-Click (Calle 19 No 6-68)
K@binas (Av Jiménez No 5-61)
mes@net.com (Calle 19 No 4-42)
OfficeNET (Carrera 4 No 19-16, Oficina 112)

Medical Services

Bogotá has a number of public hospitals, private clinics and specialist medical centers.
Clínica de Marly (☎ 1-343-6600; Calle 50 No 9-67) Good outpatient clinic with doctors of just about all the specialties.
Fundación Santa Fe de Bogotá (☎ 1-629-0766; Calle 116 No 9-02) One of Colombia's best medical facilities, which provides excellent services at prices to match. It has both outpatient and in-patient clinics.
Hospital San Ignacio (☎ 1-288-8188; Carrera 7 No 40-62) University hospital with high medical level but long lines.

Money

Bogotá's banks keep different opening hours than the banks elsewhere in the country: they open 9am to 3pm Monday to Thursday, and 9am to 3:30pm Friday. Most banks have ATMs. Banks that change traveler's checks include:

Banco Unión Colombiano (Carrera 8 No 14-45)
Bancolombia (Carrera 8 No 12-55)
Lloyds TSB Bank (Carrera 8 No 15-46)

Changing cash may be better and quicker in *casas de cambio*, which include:

Casa de Cambio La Candelaria (☎ 1-342-1184; Av Jiménez No 5-81)
Casa de Cambio Unidas (☎ 1-341-0537; Carrera 6 No 14-72)
Titán Intercontinental (☎ 1-336-0549; Carrera 7 No 18-42)

American Express is represented by **Expreso Viajes & Turismo** (☎ 1-593-4949; Calle 85 No 20-32). It doesn't cash checks but gives a replacement if your checks are lost or stolen.

Post

Both Avianca and Adpostal have their main offices in the city center (where they have post restante service) and branch offices in other districts. Have letters sent to you c/o Avianca, Lista de Correo Aéreo Avianca, Edificio Avianca, Carrera 7 No 16-36, Bogotá. If you want your letters sent via Adpostal, they should be addressed to Lista de Correo Adpostal, Edificio Murillo Toro, Carrera 8 entre Calles 12 y 13, Bogotá.

Telephone

Apart from the Telecom public telephones, there is an increasing number of new ETB phones, which operate on phone cards and are more reliable.

Tourist Offices

There are tourist information desks at the bus terminal and El Dorado airport.
Instituto Distrital de Cultura y Turismo City (☎ 1-327-4900; Carrera 8 No 9-83; 🕑 8:30am-4:30pm Mon-Fri) On the corner of Plaza de Bolívar; Teatro Jorge Eliécer Gaitán (☎ 1-334-6800; Carrera 7 No 22-47; 🕑 10am-5pm Mon-Sat, 10am-3pm Sun)
Oficina de Ecoturismo (☎ 1-243-3095; 1-243-1634; Carrera 10 No 20-30, Piso 4; 🕑 8am-4:30pm Mon-Fri) Provides information about national parks, issues permits and books accommodation in the parks.

Travel Agencies

Useful student agencies include:
Educamos Viajando (☎ 1-620-5359; Calle 108A No 18-64)
Trotamundos (☎ 1-599-6413; Diagonal 35 No 5-73) Represents STA Travel and may have attractive discounted airfares for students and young people.
Trotamundos (☎ 1-341-2027; Carrera 6 No 14-13, Oficina 208) Central outlet of the above.

Visas

For details of embassies and consulates in Bogotá, see p606. Visa and tourist-card extensions are issued at the **DAS office** (☎ 1-610-7315; Calle 100 No 11B-27; 🕑 7:30am-3:30pm Mon-Fri). A 30-day extension costs US$20 and is issued on the spot. Your onward ticket may be required.

DANGERS & ANNOYANCES

Bogotá is not a perfectly safe place, but parts of the city center, including La Candelaria, appear to be safer now than they were a few years ago. The center has been largely restored over recent years and policing has improved. The northern districts are generally regarded as safer than the center, but it's best to observe some security precautions there as well.

Try to keep night-time strolls to a minimum and don't carry money or other valuables, but don't get paranoid about going out at night. Just use common sense and travel by taxi.

SIGHTS
Plaza de Bolívar & Around

Plaza de Bolívar is the heart of the historic town, but what you see around it is a mishmash of architectural styles. The massive stone building in classical Greek style on the southern side is the **Capitolio Nacional**, the seat of the Congress. Opposite is the equally monumental **Palacio de Justicia**. It replaces an earlier building that was taken by the M-19 guerrillas in November 1985 and gutted in a fierce 28-hour offensive by the army, which left more than 100 dead, including 11 Supreme Court justices.

The western side of the plaza is taken up by the French-style **Alcaldía** (mayor's office), dating from the early 20th century. The neoclassical **Catedral Primada**, on the eastern side of the square, was completed in 1823 and is Bogotá's largest church. Next door,

COLOMBIA

COLOMBIA

BOGOTÁ

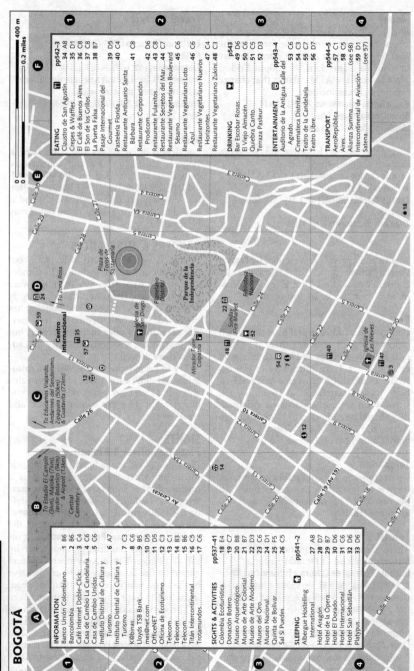

INFORMATION
Banco Unión Colombiano................1 B6
Bancolombia.................................2 B6
Café Internet Doble-Click..............3 C4
Casa de Cambio La Candelaria........4 C6
Casa de Cambio Unidas..................5 C6
Instituto Distrital de Cultura y
  Turismo...................................6 A7
Instituto Distrital de Cultura y
  Turismo...................................7 C3
K@binas......................................8 C6
Lloyds TSB Bank...........................9 B5
mesi@net.com............................10 D5
OfficeNET.................................11 D5
Oficina de Ecoturismo..................12 C3
Telecom....................................13 C1
Telecom....................................14 B3
Telecom....................................15 B6
Titán Intercontinental.................16 C5
Trotamundos.............................17 C6

SIGHTS & ACTIVITIES   pp537–41
Colombia Ecoturística...................18 E4
Donación Botero..........................19 C7
Museo Arqueológico......................20 B8
Museo de Arte Colonial..................21 B7
Museo de Arte Moderno.................22 D3
Museo del Oro............................23 C6
Museo Nacional...........................24 D1
Quinta de Bolívar........................25 F5
Sal Si Puedes..............................26 C5

SLEEPING   pp541–2
Albergue Hostelling
  International............................27 A8
Hotel Aragón..............................28 D7
Hotel de la Ópera........................29 B7
Hotel El Dorado..........................30 D6
Hotel Internacional......................31 C6
Hotel San Sebastián.....................32 D6
Platypus....................................33 D6

EATING   pp542–3
Claustro de San Agustín................34 A8
Crepes & Waffles.........................35 D1
El Café de Buenos Aires.................36 C8
El Son de los Grillos.....................37 C8
La Puerta Falsa...........................38 B7
Pasaje Internacional del
  Gourmet.................................39 D5
Pastelería Florida.........................40 C4
Restaurante Anticuario Santa
  Bárbara..................................41 C8
Restaurante Corporación
  Prodicom.................................42 D6
Restaurante Fulanitos...................43 C8
Restaurante Secretos del Mar.........44 C7
Restaurante Vegetariano Boulevard
  Sésamo..................................45 C6
Restaurante Vegetariano Loto
  Azul.....................................46 C6
Restaurante Vegetariano Nuevos
  Horizontes.............................47 C4
Restaurante Vegetariano Zukiní.....48 C3

DRINKING   p543
Bar Escobar Rosas........................49 D6
El Viejo Almacén..........................50 C6
Quiebra Canto.............................51 C5
Terraza Pasteur...........................52 D3

ENTERTAINMENT   pp543–4
Auditorio de la Antigua Calle del
  Agrado..................................53 C6
Cinemateca Distrital.....................54 C3
Teatro de la Candelaria..................55 C7
Teatro Libre...............................56 D7

TRANSPORT   pp544–5
AeroRepública.............................57 C1
Aires...58 C5
Alianza Summa........................(see 58)
Intercontinental de Aviación..........59 D1
Satena....................................(see 57)

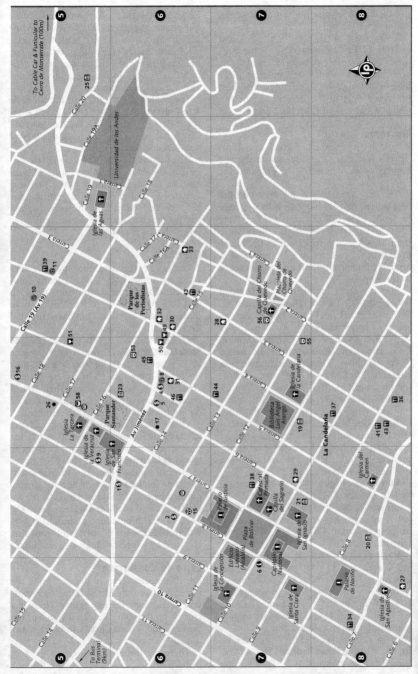

COLOMBIA

the **Capilla del Sagrario** is the only colonial building on the square.

To the east of the plaza is the colonial quarter of **La Candelaria**. The sector preserves an agreeable old-world appearance, even though a number of modern edifices have replaced historic buildings. The best preserved part of the district is between Calles 9 and 13 and Carreras 2 and 5.

Museums

Bogotá has a number of good museums. There's free entry to museums on the last Sunday of each month – be prepared for big crowds.

The star attraction is the **Museo del Oro** (Gold Museum; ☎ 1-343-0545; Calle 16 No 5-41; adults Tue-Sat US$1.50, Sun US$0.75, students US$0.10; ☺ 9am-4:30pm Tue-Sat, 10am-4:30pm Sun). It houses more than 34,000 gold pieces from all the major pre-Hispanic cultures in Colombia and is arguably the most important gold museum in the world.

Bogotá's other highlight is the **Donación Botero** (☎ 1-343-1331; Calle 11 No 4-41; admission free; ☺ 10am-8pm Mon & Wed-Fri, 10am-7pm Sat, 10am-4pm Sun). It's a permanent exhibition of paintings and sculptures donated by Fernando Botero, Colombia's most famous artist, to the Banco de la República. The 208-piece collection contains 123 of Botero's own works, including his paintings, drawings and sculptures, plus 85 works by international artists, sporting such names as Picasso, Chagall, Miró, Dalí, Renoir, Matisse, Léger and Monet. In effect, this is one of South America's richest art collections. Botero has made another impressive gift to Medellín, his natal city – see the Medellín section (p577).

Museo Arqueológico (☎ 1-243-1048; Carrera 6 No 7-43; admission US$1.50; ☺ 8:30am-5pm Tue-Fri, 9:30am-5pm Sat, 10am-4pm Sun), in a beautiful colonial mansion, has an extensive collection of pottery from Colombia's main pre-Hispanic cultures.

Museo de Arte Colonial (☎ 1-284-1373; Carrera 6 No 9-77; admission US$1; ☺ 9am-5pm Tue-Fri, 10am-4pm Sat & Sun) features a remarkable collection of colonial art, including 76 oil paintings and 106 drawings by Gregorio Vásquez de Arce y Ceballos (1638–1711), the most important painter of the colonial era.

In the northern part of the city center, be sure to visit the **Museo Nacional** (☎ 1-334-8366; Carrera 7 No 28-66; admission US$1.50; ☺ 10am-5:30pm Tue-Sat, 10am-3:30pm Sun). Accommodated in an old prison, it gives an insight into Colombian history, from the first settlers to modern times, through a wealth of exhibits that include historic objects, photos, maps, artifacts, paintings, documents and weapons. Don't miss the mummies.

For contemporary art, visit the **Museo de Arte Moderno** (☎ 1-286-0466; Calle 24 No 6-00; admission US$1.50; ☺ 10am-6pm Tue-Sat, 10am-3pm Sun), which has frequently changing displays of national and foreign artists.

The **Quinta de Bolívar** (☎ 1-336-6419; Calle 20 No 2-91 Este; admission US$1.50; ☺ 9am-5pm Tue-Sat, 10am-4pm Sun), is an old country house that was donated to Simón Bolívar in gratitude for his services. Today, it's a museum displaying documents, maps, weapons, uniforms and Bolívar's personal effects.

Churches

A center of evangelism since the early days of Spanish rule, Bogotá boasts many colonial churches, most dating from the 17th and 18th centuries. Bogotá's churches have quite austere exteriors, but their internal decoration is often quite elaborate.

One of the most impressive is the **Iglesia de Santa Clara** (☎ 1-337-6762; Carrera 8 No 8-91; admission US$2; ☺ 9am-5pm Tue-Fri, 10am-4pm Sat & Sun), now open as a museum. Its walls are entirely covered with paintings (more than 100 of them), statues of saints and altarpieces, all dating from the 17th and 18th centuries.

Other churches worth a look include: **Iglesia de San Francisco** (Av Jiménez at Carrera 7), for the extraordinary decoration of its chancel; **Iglesia de la Concepción** (Calle 10 No 9-50), home of Bogotá's most beautiful Mudejar vault; **Iglesia de San Ignacio** (Calle 10 No 6-35), distinguished by both its size and its valuable art collection; and **Iglesia de San Diego** (Carrera 7 No 26-37), a charming country church (it was well outside the town when built) now surrounded by a forest of high-rise buildings.

Cerro de Monserrate

For spectacular views of the city, go to the top of the Cerro de Monserrate, the mountain overlooking the city center. There is a church on the summit, with a statue of the Señor Caído (Fallen Christ), to which many miracles have been attributed.

There are three ways to get to the top: by *teleférico* (cable car), funicular railway or footpath. The cable car operates every 15 minutes from 9:30am to midnight Monday to Saturday, 6am to 5pm Sunday. The funicular normally only runs from 6am to 6pm on Sundays and public holidays. The return fare on either is US$4.

If you want to go on foot (one hour uphill), do it only on Sunday, when crowds of pilgrims go; on weekdays, take it for granted that you will be robbed along the way. The lower joint station of the cable car and the funicular is close to the city center, but the access road leads through a poor suburb, so don't walk; instead take the bus marked 'Funicular' from Calle 19, or a taxi.

Other Sights

For another impressive bird's-eye view go to the **Mirador Torre Colpatria** (☎ 1-283-6697; Carrera 7 No 24-89; admission US$1.25; ☽ 11am-5pm Sat, Sun & holidays) nearby Parque de la Indepencia. The 360° lookout atop this 48-storey 162m-high skyscraper (built in 1975–79) provides excellent views in all directions.

On Sunday, don't miss the colorful **Mercado de San Alejo**, a flea market held at the car park on Carrera 7 between Calles 24 and 26.

Jardín Botánico José Celestino Mutis (☎ 1-630-0949; Calle 57 No 61-13; admission US$1.50; ☽ 8am-4pm Tue-Fri, 9am-4pm Sat & Sun) has a variety of national flora from different climatic zones; some are in gardens, others in greenhouses. The airport *buseta* or *colectivo* will let you off nearby.

Maloka (☎ 1-427-2707; Carrera 68D No 40A-51; adult/student US$3.50/2; ☽ 9am-6pm Tues-Sun) is an interactive center of science and technology, possibly the continent's largest and best. It features a variety of thematic exhibitions, such as the universe, human being, technology, life, water and biodiversity, plus a hi-tech Cine-Domo cinema. The best way to get here is via the airport *buseta* or *colectivo*.

COURSES

Bogotá's best known school of Spanish language is the **Centro Latinoamericano de la Universidad Javeriana** (☎ 1-320-8320; Carrera 10 No 65-48), which offers regular one-year courses and three-week intensive courses. Other providers to check include:
Universidad Nacional (☎ 1-316-5335)
Universidad de los Andes (☎ 1-286-9211)
Universidad Externado de Colombia (☎ 1-282-6066)

TOURS

Eco-Guías (☎ 1-347-5736, 1-212-1423; www.ecoguias .com; Carrera 7 No 57-39, Oficina 501) is an adventure travel company that focuses on ecotourism and offers individualized tours to various regions of the country, including some national parks. It also organizes reasonably priced Sunday walks in Bogotá's environs.

Sal Si Puedes (☎ 1-283-3765; Carrera 7 No 17-01, Oficina 639) is an association of outdoor-minded people who organize weekend walks in the countryside. These are mostly one-day excursions to Cundinamarca, though longer trips to other regions are also arranged during holiday periods and long weekends. Other associations of this type include:
Andarines del Senderismo (☎ 1-617-8857; Transversal 48 No 96-48)
Colombia Ecoturística (☎ 1-241-0065, 1-366-3059; Carrera 3 No 21-46, Apto 802B)
Viajar y Vivir (☎ 1-211-1368, 1-211-1205; Carrera 13 No 61-47, Local 125)

FESTIVALS & EVENTS

Festival Iberoamericano de Teatro The theater festival, featuring groups from Latin America and beyond takes place in March/April of every even-numbered year.
Festival de Cine de Bogotá Bogotá's film festival in October usually attracts a strong selection of Latin American films.
Expoartesanías This crafts fair in December gathers together artisans along with their crafts from all around the country. It's an excellent place to buy crafts.

SLEEPING

Bogotá has loads of places to stay in every price bracket. A good share of budget accommodation is concentrated in the city center. Coincidently, this is the most convenient area to stay in, as most tourist attractions are here. The historic suburb of La Candelaria is the most popular area with foreign travelers, and it has a reasonable choice of budget hotels. The alternative area is the northern part of the city, which has a good selection of upmarket accommodation, but there are very few budget hotels there.

Platypus (☎ 1-341-2874, 1-341-3104; www.platypus bogota.com; Calle 16 No 2-43; dm/s/d US$5/8/11) By far the most popular budget place among backpackers, Platypus has three four-bed dorms and several singles and doubles. Although conditions are quite simple and only a couple of rooms have private baths, the place is safe, clean and pleasant and has hot water.

The hostel offers book exchange, Internet access, laundry and kitchen facilities and free coffee. The friendly owner, Germán (pronounced Hermann), a longtime traveler himself, speaks several languages and is an excellent source of practical information. The hostel has no sign on the door, just a picture of the platypus, so don't be confused.

If the Platypus is full, you can try one of the following places in the same area, though none of these provides such a wide range of facilities or extensive information.

Hotel Aragón (☎ 1-284-8325; Carrera 3 No 14-13; r per person US$5) One of the cheapest places around, with bright rooms and large windows, but no private baths.

Hotel El Dorado (☎ 1-334-3988; Carrera 4 No 15-00; d without/with bath US$10/12) A convenient option close to nightspots. It has fairly small rooms, but most of them have private baths.

Hotel Internacional (☎ 1-341-8731; Carrera 5 No 14-45; s/d/t US$5/10/13, with bath US$6/11/15) A favorite haunt among Israeli travelers, it provides Internet access and the use of the kitchen.

Hotel San Sebastián (☎ 1-480-0503; Av Jiménez No 3-97; s/d/t US$18/25/32) More comfortable than any of the above, San Sebastián has airy rooms with TV and private bath, and is well located just a couple of blocks from the Museo del Oro (Gold Museum).

Albergue Hostelling International (☎ 1-280-3202; Carrera 7 No 6-10; dm US$4-5) The only genuine youth hostel in Colombia, four blocks south of Plaza de Bolívar. It has six- and eight-bed dorms, most with shared bath (hot water in the morning only). Everybody can stay here, but an HI membership card will save you a dollar.

SPLURGE!

Hotel de la Ópera (☎ 1-336-2066; www.hotel opera.com.co; Calle 10 No 5-72; d/ste US$95/115) By far the best lodging option in La Candelaria, accommodated in two meticulously restored historic buildings right next door to the Teatro Colón. This five-star hotel has much charm and character, and a rooftop restaurant with views over red-tiled roofs of the nearby colonial houses. The atmosphere and service are great, and the place is small enough that you receive personal attention.

La Casona del Patio Amarillo (☎ 1-212-8805; Carrera 8 No 69-24; s/d/t US$12/20/24, with bath US$14/24/33) One of the cheapest options in northern Bogotá, located in a quiet residential neighborhood with good transport to the center. The rooms are spotlessly clean and airy, and the place offers various services, including breakfast (US$2), laundry and Internet.

EATING

Innumerable places have set lunches for US$1.50 to US$3 – the best way to choose is to drop into one, see what people are eating and stay or move on to the next one.

Restaurante Corporación Prodicom (Calle 15A No 2-21; set lunches US$1.50-2) One of the locals' favorites thanks to its great-value tasty lunches.

Pasaje Internacional del Gourmet (Carrera 4 No 19-44/56; lunches US$1.50-4) A dozen budget restaurants under one roof.

There's a choice of budget vegetarian restaurants in the center, which serve set lunches for around US$2. Most of them operate from Monday to Friday only, and close late afternoon. They include:
Restaurante Vegetariano Loto Azul (Carrera 5A No 14-00)
Restaurante Vegetariano Boulevard Sésamo (Av Jiménez No 4-64)
Restaurante Vegetariano Zukini (Calle 24 No 7-12)
Restaurante Vegetariano Nuevos Horizontes (Calle 20 No 6-37)

La Puerta Falsa (Calle 11 No 6-50; snacks US$0.50-1.50) Bogotá's, and for that matter Colombia's, oldest operating place to eat, serves typical local snacks (including *tamales* and chocolate *santafereño*) and sweets just as it has since 1816.

Pastelería Florida (Carrera 7 No 21-46) In its new locale, Florida is famous for its chocolate *santafereño*. It's also a good place for breakfast.

Crepes & Waffles (Centro Internacional, Carrera 10 No 27-91, Piso 2, Local 2-33; crepes US$2-5) Delicious crepes with a range of fillings and great salads. There are several outlets of this chain in the northern suburbs.

Restaurante Secretos del Mar (Carrera 5 No 13-20; mains US$2-5) Solid food typical of the Pacific coast at budget prices.

El Son de los Grillos (Calle 10 No 3-60; mains US$2.50-5) Charming, cozy place that serves good food at reasonable prices.

Claustro de San Agustín (in Museo de Artes y Tradiciones Populares, Carrera 8 No 7-21; mains US$3-5) Fine regional cuisine at lunch time (until about 3pm). It has a different menu every day of the week.

Restaurante Fulanitos (Carrera 3 No 8-61; mains US$4-7) Beautifully arranged, informal place that offers food typical of the Valle del Cauca in southern Colombia.

DRINKING
Bars & Clubbing

Bogotá is alive 24 hours a day and there's a lot of activity going on at night. There are plenty of nightspots, including nightclubs, bars and discos, offering a variety of moods and any musical rhythms you wish for, including rock, reggae, rap, tango, samba, techno, hip-hop and salsa. The latter is perhaps the most popular among the hot-blooded city dwellers, and a worthwhile experience for travelers. There are plenty of disco-type places called *salsotecas*, which play predominantly, or exclusively, salsa. Don't miss trying one, if only to listen to the music and watch people dancing.

The main area of night-time entertainment is the Zona Rosa, in the northern sector of the city, between Carreras 11 and 15, and Calles 81 and 84. There's a maze of music spots, bars, restaurants and cafés in the area, which become particularly vibrant on weekend nights. This is the best time to come, hang around and see Bogotá's more affluent revelers in action. On a less pleasant note, most of the nightspots are expensive, especially drinks and cover charges.

Galería Café Libro (Calle 81 No 11-92) One of the best *salsotecas*, with great music and atmosphere.

Salomé Pagana (Carrera 14A No 82-16) Another recommended *salsoteca*, with fine salsa and *son cubano* (traditional Cuban music).

Mister Babilla (Calle 82 No 12-15) Popular disco in a warm tropical style, playing a ragbag of musical rhythms, including rock, merengue and salsa.

Gótica (Calle 14 No 82-50) Large disco offering different musical ambiences on different levels, including salsa, techno and trance.

The Pub (Carrera 12A No 83-48) Irish addition to the Zona Rosa, which has become hugely popular with some more affluent locals and expats.

The city center has revived over recent years and many nightspots have mushroomed all over the place, particularly in La Candelaria. Most are reasonably cheap, with a bottle of beer below a dollar.

Quiebra Canto (Carrera 5 No 17-76) One of the most popular night-time hangouts in the center.

El Viejo Almacén (Calle 15 No 4-18) Nostalgic tango bar with 4000-plus old tango vinyls.

Bar Escobar Rosas (cnr Calle 15 & Carrera 4) Trendy bar with good music and atmosphere.

Terraza Pasteur (Carrera 7 No 23-56) Former shopping mall turned into a night-time entertainment complex packed with 30-something bars spread over three floors and playing everything from salsa to vallenato and rock to reggae.

Gay & Lesbian Venues

Gay and lesbian life is pretty active in Bogotá. Popular hangouts include:

Chase (Calle 67 No 4A-91) Three-level restaurant-cum-bar, with a quiet atmosphere and good food.

La Capilla (Carrera 7 No 48-93) Pub/disco with cheap beer and loud music. Check its fortnightly theme parties which might include carnival nights, esoteric nights, Brazilian dance etc.

Ponto De Encontro (Carrera 7 No 48A-70) Tiny bar with a few tables and good music.

Theatron (Calle 58 No 10-36) One of the most popular gay discos in town, but it's not that cheap.

Village Café (Carrera 8 No 64-29) Quiet, reasonably-priced bar-cum-restaurant. Very good coffee.

ENTERTAINMENT

Bogotá has far more cultural activities than any other city in Colombia. Have a look at the entertainment columns of the leading local paper, *El Tiempo*. The Friday edition carries a 'what's-on' section called

COLOMBIA

Eskpe. Also check **Terra** (www.terra.com.co/bogota in Spanish), which covers cinemas, theatres, nightclubs, cultural events and more.

Cinemas

Bogotá has about 60 cinemas offering the usual Hollywood fare. For something more thought provoking, check the programs of the *cinematecas* (arthouse cinemas). Regular cinemas of that type include:

Auditorio de la Antigua Calle del Agrado (☎ 1-281-4671; Calle 16 No 4-75)

Cinemateca Distrital (☎ 1-334-3451; Carrera 7 No 22-79)

Museo de Arte Moderno (☎ 1-286-0466; Calle 24 No 6-00)

Theater

Leading theaters include:

Teatro de la Candelaria (☎ 1-281-4814; Calle 12 No 2-59)

Teatro Libre (☎ 1-281-4834; Calle 13 No 2-44 & ☎ 1-217-1988; Calle 62 No 10-65)

Teatro Nacional (☎ 1-217-4577; Calle 71 No 10-25)

Sport

Soccer is Colombia's national sport. The principal venue is the **Estadio El Campín** (Carrera 30 at Calle 55). Matches are played on Wednesday nights and Sunday afternoons. Tickets (US$4 to US$40) can be bought at the stadium before the matches. For local games, tickets can also be bought at **Millonarios** (Carrera 24 No 63-68) and **Santa Fe** (Calle 64A No 38-08). For international matches (Selección Colombia), you can buy tickets in advance at **Federación Colombiana de Fútbol** (Av 32 No 16-22).

Bullfighting

Bullfighting is invariably popular, with fights held at the **Plaza de Toros de Santamaría** (Carrera 6 at Calle 27) on most Sundays in January and February. Tickets are available from the bullring's box office (US$10 to US$100).

GETTING THERE & AWAY

Air

Bogotá's airport, Aeropuerto El Dorado, has two terminals and handles all domestic and international flights. The main terminal, **El Dorado** (☎ 1-425-1000; Av El Dorado) is 13km northwest of the city center and offers plenty of facilities, including tourist information (in the luggage claim area), Internet access (in the Telecom office) and

money exchange. Three *casas de cambio* (Aerocambios, City Exchange and Cambios Country), next to each other on the ground floor, change cash and are open 24 hours a day. The Banco Popular, at the next window (also open 24 hours), changes both cash and traveler's checks. There are a dozen ATMs on the upper level.

The other terminal, **Puente Aéreo** (☎ 1-413-9511; Av El Dorado), is 1km from El Dorado towards the city center. It handles some of Alianza Summa's international and domestic flights. Make sure to check which terminal your flight departs from.

There are plenty of domestic flights to destinations all over the country, including Cali (US$50 to US$110), Cartagena (US$70 to US$120), Leticia (US$100 to US$120), Medellín (US$50 to US$110) and San Andrés (US$100 to US$140). You can buy tickets from travel agents or directly from the airlines, most of which have their main offices in the city center:

AeroRepública (☎ 1900-331-5656, 1-320-9090; www.aerorepublica.com.co; Carrera 10 No 27-51, Oficina 303)

Aires (☎ 1-294-0300, 1-413-8500; www.aires.com.co; Carrera 7 No 16-36)

Alianza Summa (☎ 01800-051-7862, 1-401-2237; www.summa.aero; Carrera 7 No 16-36)

Intercontinental de Aviación (☎ 1-217-6452, 1-413-8888; www.intercontinental.com.co; Carrera 10 No 28-31)

Satena (☎ 1-423-8500, 1-570-0893; www.satena.com; Carrera 10 No 26-21, Oficina 210)

West Caribbean Airways (☎ 01800-094-1333; www.wca.com.co) No offices in Bogotá.

Bus

The **bus terminal** (☎ 1-295-1100; Calle 33B No 69-13) is 9km northwest of the city center. It's large, functional and well organized, and has a tourist office, restaurants, cafeterias, showers and left-luggage rooms. It also has a number of well-dressed thieves who will wait for a moments inattention to grab your stuff and disappear – watch your bags closely.

The terminal handles buses to just about every corner of the country. On the main roads, buses run frequently round the clock to: Bucaramanga (US$19, 10 hours), Cali (US$20, 12 hours) and Medellín (US$17, nine hours). There are also direct buses to Cartagena (US$40, 20 hours), Cúcuta (US$29, 16 hours), Ipiales (US$35, 23 hours), Popayán (US$24, 15 hours), San Agustín (US$15, 12 hours) and Santa Marta (US$32, 16 hours).

All prices are for air-con buses, the dominant class on long-distance routes.

GETTING AROUND
Bus & Buseta

TransMilenio apart, Bogotá's public transport is operated by buses and *busetas*. They all run the length and breadth of the city, usually at full speed if the traffic allows.

Except on a few streets, there are no bus stops – you just wave down the bus or *buseta* wherever you happen to be. The fare (US$0.30 to US$0.50 depending on the class and generation of the vehicle) is posted by the door or on the windscreen. The fare is flat, so you will be charged the same to go one block as to go right across the city. There are also *colectivos*, which operate on the major routes and cost about US$0.50.

Taxi

Bogotá's taxis all have meters and you should insist that the driver uses it. A 10km ride should cost no more than US$4. There's a US$1.25 surcharge on rides to the airport.

A warning: When taxiing from the bus terminal or the airport to a budget hotel, your driver may insist that your chosen hotel no longer exists, is now a brothel, has security problems or some other story, and will offer a 'much better option.' Don't trust a word – many taxi drivers have agreements with hotel owners and get kickbacks for delivering tourists.

TransMilenio

TransMilenio is a revolution in Bogotá's public transport. After numerous plans and studies drawn up over the past 30 years to build a metro, the project was eventually buried and a decision to introduce a fast urban bus service called TransMilenio was taken instead.

Inaugurated in 2000 on Av Caracas, the system employs large buses which run on their own street lines, uninterrupted by other vehicles. The service is cheap (US$0.40), frequent and fast, and operates from 5am to 11pm. Buses get very crowded at rush hour. The system is being gradually extended by introducing the buses on other streets. In the center, there's already a side line along Av Jiménez up to Carrera 3. Portal del Norte, TransMilenio's northern terminus, is on Autopista del Norte at Calle 170.

AROUND BOGOTÁ

ZIPAQUIRÁ

Zipaquirá, 50km north of Bogotá, is noted for its salt mines. The mines date back to the Muisca period and have been intensively exploited, but they still contain vast reserves; they tap into a huge mountain of rock salt. In the heart of the mountain, an underground **salt cathedral** (☎ 1-852-4035; admission US$4, Wed US$2; ☼ 10am-4pm Tue-Sun) has been carved out of the solid salt and was opened to the public in 1995. It's 75m long and 18m high and can accommodate 8400 people. Visits are by guided tours that take one hour. You can also visit the adjacent **salt museum** (admission US$1; ☼ 10am-4pm Tue-Sun) which features the history of salt exploitation, the model of the local mine and other exhibits.

Buses from Bogotá to Zipaquirá (US$0.80, 1¼ hours) run every 10 minutes, departing from the northern terminus of TransMilenio, known as Portal del Norte, on Autopista del Norte at Calle 170. TransMilenio from Bogotá's center will take you to Portal del Norte in 40 minutes. The mines are a 15-minute walk uphill from Zipaquirá's center.

GUATAVITA

Also called **Guatavita Nueva**, this town was built from scratch in the late 1960s when the old colonial Guatavita was flooded by the waters of a hydroelectric reservoir. The town is an interesting architectural blend of old and new, and is a popular weekend destination for people from Bogotá.

About 15km from the town is the famous **Laguna de Guatavita**, the sacred lake and ritual center of the Muisca Indians, and a cradle of the myth of El Dorado. The lake was an object of worship, where gold pieces, emeralds and food were offered by the Muiscas to their gods. The myth of incalculable treasures at the bottom gave rise to numerous attempts to salvage the riches. Despite enormous efforts by the Spanish and later the Colombians, very little has actually been recovered. Legend claims that the lake retains its treasures.

Buses from Bogotá to Guatavita (US$2, two hours) depart every half an hour from the northern terminus of TransMilenio. For the lake, get off 11km before town (drivers will let you off at the right place) and walk

7km uphill along a dirt road. There are several farms around so ask for directions if in doubt. On weekends, it's possible to hitch a lift with tourists coming in their jeeps.

NORTH OF BOGOTÁ

Covered by three departments – Boyacá, Santander and Norte de Santander – the region north of Bogotá is scenic and picturesque due to the Cordillera Oriental, which takes up much of the area. While traveling around, you'll enjoy a variety of landscapes, from verdant valleys to arid highlands and the snowy peaks of the Sierra Nevada del Cocuy.

Once the territory of the Muiscas (Boyacá) and the Guane Indians (Santander), the region was explored and settled early on by the Spaniards. Consequently, the mountains and valleys are dotted with old colonial towns, of which Villa de Leyva, Barichara and Girón are among the finest examples.

Of the three departments, Boyacá is perhaps the safest and most pleasant in which to travel. It is also the most traditional province, widely known for its handicrafts, particularly pottery, basketwork and weaving.

TUNJA

Today a city of 150,000 people and the capital of Boyacá, Tunja was founded in 1539 on the site of Hunza, the pre-Hispanic Muisca seat. Although almost nothing is left of the Indian legacy, much colonial architecture remains. The central sector was restored for the town's 450-year anniversary and many historic public buildings have recovered their original splendor. Tunja is a city of churches: several imposing examples dating from the 16th century stand almost untouched by time.

Tunja sits at an altitude of 2820m and has a cool climate; you'll need warm clothing, especially at night.

Information

INTERNET ACCESS

There are several convenient facilities on or just off Plaza de Bolívar, including:

Café Internet (Calle 20 No 8-94)
Internet Cibertienda (Carrera 10 No 19-83)
Internet Orbitel (Calle 20 No 10-26)

MONEY

Useful money-changing facilities include the following:

Bancolombia (Carrera 10 No 22-43) One of the few banks in town that is likely to exchange traveler's checks and perhaps cash as well.
Banco de Bogotá (Calle 20 No 10-60) May also exchange traveler's checks but not cash.
Giros & Finanzas (Carrera 10 No 16-81) *Casa de cambio*, nestled at the back of the Supermercado Comfaboy. It exchanges traveler's checks and cash and is an agent of Western Union.

TOURIST OFFICES

Secretaría de Educación, Cultura y Turismo
(☎ 8-742-3272; Carrera 9 No 19-68; ☺ 8am-noon & 2-6pm Mon-Fri) The Municipal tourist office is in the Casa del Fundador on Plaza de Bolívar.

Sights

The **Casa del Fundador Suárez Rendón** (☎ 8-742-3272; Carrera 9 No 19-68; admission US$1; ☺ 8am-noon & 2-6pm) and **Casa de Don Juan de Vargas** (☎ 8-742-6611; Calle 20 No 8-52; admission US$1; ☺ 9am-noon & 2-5pm Tue-Fri, 10am-4pm Sat & Sun) have both been converted into colonial art museums. The ceilings in both houses are covered with intriguing paintings featuring human figures, animals and plants, coats of arms and mythological scenes – an impressive and unusual view.

Iglesia de Santa Clara La Real (☎ 8-742-5659; Carrera 7 No 19-58; admission US$1; ☺ 8am-noon & 2-6pm) is one of the most beautiful and richly decorated churches in Colombia. It has been converted into a museum. The **Iglesia de Santo Domingo** (Carrera 11 No 19-55) is another extraordinary example of the Spanish colonial art; be sure to see the exuberant Capilla del Rosario, just to the left as you enter the church.

Other churches worth a visit include the **Iglesia de Santa Bárbara** (Carrera 11 No 16-62), **Iglesia de San Francisco** (Carrera 10 No 22-23) and the **Catedral** (Plaza de Bolívar). Tunja's churches are noted for their Mudejar art, an Islamic-influenced style that developed in Christian Spain between the 12th and the 16th centuries. It is particularly visible in the ornamented, coffered vaults.

Sleeping

There are a number of hotels around Plaza de Bolívar, and this is the most pleasant area to stay.

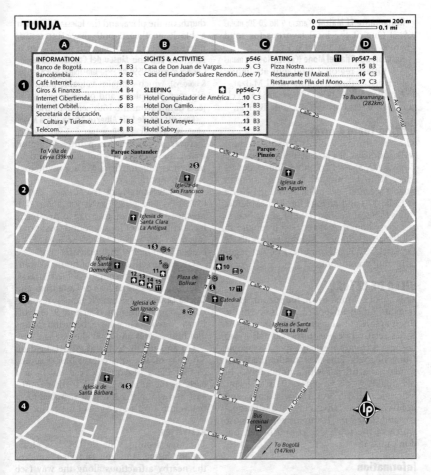

TUNJA

0 — 200 m
0 — 0.1 mi

INFORMATION			SIGHTS & ACTIVITIES	p546		EATING	pp547–8	
Banco de Bogotá	**1** B3		Casa de Don Juan de Vargas	**9** C3		Pizza Nostra	**15** B3	
Bancolombia	**2** B2		Casa del Fundador Suárez Rendón	(see 7)		Restaurante El Maizal	**16** C3	
Café Internet	**3** B3					Restaurante Pila del Mono	**17** C3	
Giros & Finanzas	**4** B4		SLEEPING	pp546–7				
Internet Cibertienda	**5** B3		Hotel Conquistador de América	**10** C3				
Internet Orbitel	**6** B3		Hotel Don Camilo	**11** B3				
Secretaría de Educación,			Hotel Dux	**12** B3				
Cultura y Turismo	**7** B3		Hotel Los Virreyes	**13** B3				
Telecom	**8** B3		Hotel Saboy	**14** B3				

Hotel Saboy (☎ 8-742-3492; Calle 19 No 10-40; r without/with bath per person US$4/5) One of the cheapest central options, accommodated in a historic building with a glass-roofed patio. Basic but clean and pleasant with hot water in the morning.

Hotel Los Virreyes (☎ 8-742-3556; Calle 19 No 10-64; r without/with bath per person US$5/6) Simple, central budget accommodation just a few paces from the main plaza.

Hotel Dux (☎ 8-742-5736; Calle 19 No 10-78; r without/with bath per person US$5/7) Another nearby option, offering acceptable if rudimentary lodging with a touch of old-world style and atmosphere.

Hotel Don Camilo (☎ 8-742-6574; Carrera 10 No 19-57; r per person without/with bath US$4/6) Conveni-ent budget shelter, but basic and slightly unkempt. Right on but not overlooking the Plaza Bolívar.

Hotel Conquistador de América (☎ 8-742-3534; Calle 20 No 8-92; s/d/t US$12/17/22) Good option for those who need somewhere less basic yet still at a low price. Housed in a colonial-style building at the corner of Plaza Bolívar, it has 20 ample rooms, all with private baths.

Eating

Plenty of restaurants in Tunja serve inexpensive set lunches for US$1.50 to US$2. There are also a number of outlets serving regional cuisine, snacks, fast food and chicken.

COLOMBIA

Restaurante El Maizal (Carrera 9 No 20-30; mains US$3-5) One of the local favorites for solid regional dishes at budget prices.

Restaurante Pila del Mono (Calle 20 No 8-19; mains US$5-7) Offers regional food, but at slightly higher prices than Restaurante El Maizal.

Pizza Nostra (Calle 19 No 10-36; pizza US$3-6) Welcoming pizzeria just off Plaza de Bolívar.

Getting There & Away

The bus terminal is on Av Oriental, a short walk southeast of Plaza de Bolívar. Buses to Bogotá (US$5, 2½ to three hours) depart every 10 to 15 minutes. If you're going to Bogotá's center, get off at Portal del Norte at Calle 170 and change for TransMilenio. Buses to Bucaramanga (US$14, seven hours) run every hour or less and pass through San Gil (US$9, 4½ hours). Minibuses to Villa de Leyva (US$1.50, 45 minutes) depart regularly until about 6pm.

VILLA DE LEYVA

This small colonial town, founded in 1572, remains largely unspoiled, and is one of the finest architectural gems in the country. As it lies relatively close to the capital, it has become a trendy weekend spot for people from Bogotá. This has made the town somewhat artificial, with a noticeably split personality – on weekdays it is a sleepy, lethargic village, but on weekends and holidays it comes alive, crammed with tourists and their cars. It's up to you to choose which of the town's faces you prefer, but don't miss it.

Information

The **Oficina de Turismo** (☎ 8-732-0232; cnr Carrera 9 & Calle 13; ☼ 8am-1pm & 3-6pm Mon-Sat, 9am-1pm & 3-6pm Sun) is on the corner of the main plaza.

Traveler's checks are useless in Villa de Leyva. You can change cash (at a poor rate) at the photocopier's business, five doors up from the parish church. The **Banco Popular** (Calle 12), on the main plaza, gives cash advances on Visa cards. Servientrega, nine doors from the church (four doors past the photocopier), provides access to the Internet.

Sights

The **Plaza Mayor**, an impressive central square, is paved with massive cobblestones and lined with whitewashed colonial houses. The **parish**

church, on the plaza, and the **Iglesia del Carmen**, a block northeast, both have interesting interiors. Next to the latter is a museum of religious art, the **Museo del Carmen** (Plazuela del Carmen; admission US$0.80; ☼ 10am-1pm & 2-5pm Sat, Sun & holidays), which contains valuable paintings, carvings, altarpieces and other religious objects dating from the 16th century onward.

Casa Museo de Luis Alberto Acuña (Plaza Mayor; admission US$0.80; ☼ 10am-1pm & 3-5pm Tue-Sun) features works by this painter, sculptor, writer and historian who was inspired by influences ranging from Muisca mythology to contemporary art.

Museo Paleontológico (Vía Arcabuco; admission US$0.80; ☼ 10am-1pm & 3-5pm Tue-Sun), about 1km northeast of town on the road to Arcabuco, has a collection of locally found fossils dating from the period when the area was a seabed (100 to 150 million years ago).

Give yourself a couple of hours to wander about the charming cobbled streets. Pop into the **Casa de Juan de Castellanos** and **Casona La Guaca**, two meticulously restored colonial mansions on Carrera 9 just off Plaza Mayor. They have beautiful patios and house cafés and craft shops.

Go and see the colorful **market**, held on Saturday on the square three blocks southeast of Plaza Mayor. It's best and busiest early in the morning. Walk further southeast and climb the hill to a **viewpoint** for a marvelous bird's-eye view of the town.

Activities

The area around Villa de Leyva is pleasant for **hiking**, and you can visit some of the nearby attractions along the way (see Around Villa de Leyva p550), or go trekking in the Santuario de Iguaque (p551). The region is also good for **cycling** and you can hire a bicycle in Villa de Leyva – see the following Tours section.

Horse riding is another popular activity. Many locals rent out horses (US$2.50 per hour) – ask at your hotel or go to the corner of Carrera 9 and Calle 16.

Tours

The **Guías & Travesías** (☎ 8-732-0742; Calle 12 No 8A-31) organizes tours around the region and rents out bicycles (US$1.50/9 per hour/day). **El Arca Verde** (☎ 8-732-0177; cnr Calle 13 & Carrera 8) is a French-run agency offering ecological walks.

Taxi drivers parking in front of the bus terminal offer return taxi trips around the surrounding sights. Standard routes include El Fósil, El Infiernito and Convento del Santo Ecce Homo (US$20) and Ráquira and La Candelaria (US$25). Prices are per taxi for up to four people and include stops allowing visits to the sights.

Sleeping

The town has a good choice of places to stay and most hotels, particularly the upmarket ones, are stylish and pleasant. Accommodation may become limited on weekends, and can fill up completely on *puentes* and during Easter week, despite the fact that the prices tend to rise, sometimes significantly,

at these times. Prices listed below are weekday rates.

Dino's (☎ 8-732-0803; Plaza Mayor; r per person US$5) Next to the parish church on the main plaza, Dino's is one of the cheapest places and offers good value. It has six neat rooms, all with private baths.

Hospedería La Villa (☎ 8-732-0848; Calle 12 No 10-11; r per person US$5) Basic budget option on the corner of the main plaza. Some rooms have private bath.

Hospedería Colonial (☎ 8-732-1364; Calle 12 No 10-81; r per person US$5-6) Another basic but acceptable option, just a block off the plaza, marginally better than La Villa.

Posada San Martín (☎ 8-732-0428; Calle 14 No 9-43; r per person US$7.50) This new, small place is

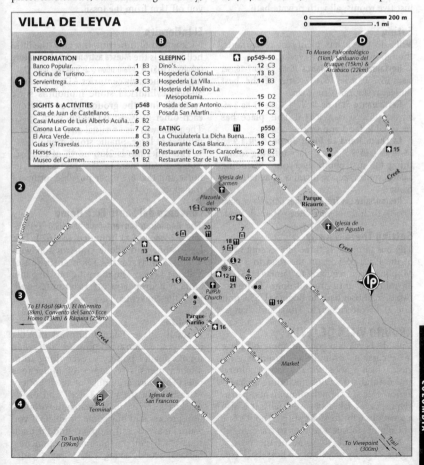

VILLA DE LEYVA

0 —————— 200 m
0 —————— .1 mi

INFORMATION		SLEEPING	☐ pp549–50
Banco Popular	1 B3	Dino's	12 C3
Oficina de Turismo	2 C3	Hospedería Colonial	13 B3
Servientrega	3 C3	Hospedería La Villa	14 B3
Telecom	4 C3	Hostería del Molino La	
		Mesopotamia	15 D2
SIGHTS & ACTIVITIES	p548	Posada de San Antonio	16 C3
Casa de Juan de Castellanos	5 C3	Posada San Martín	17 C2
Casa Museo de Luis Alberto Acuña	6 B2		
Casona La Guaca	7 C2	EATING	☐ p550
El Arca Verde	8 C3	La Chucalatería La Dicha Buena	18 C3
Guías y Travesías	9 B3	Restaurante Casa Blanca	19 C3
Horses	10 D2	Restaurante Los Tres Caracoles	20 B2
Museo del Carmen	11 B2	Restaurante Star de la Villa	21 C3

To Museo Paleontológico (1km), Santuario del Iguaque (15km) & Arcabuco (22km)

Iglesia del Carmen

Plazuela del Carmen

Parque Ricaurte

Iglesia de San Agustín

Creek

Plaza Mayor

Parish Church

Parque Nariño

To El Fósil (6km), El Infiernito (8km), Convento del Santo Ecce Homo (13km) & Ráquira (25km)

Market

Iglesia de San Francisco

Bus Terminal

To Tunja (39km)

To Viewpoint (300m)

Trail

Via Circunvalar

Carrera 12A
Carrera 11
Carrera 10
Carrera 9
Carrera 8
Carrera 7
Carrera 6
Carrera 5
Carrera 4

Calle 18
Calle 16
Calle 15
Calle 14
Calle 13
Calle 12
Calle 11
Calle 10

Creek

COLOMBIA

SPLURGE!

Villa de Leyva has a collection of charming hotels, most of which are set in restored colonial mansions.

Posada de San Antonio (☎ 8-732-0538; Carrera 8 No 11-90; d US$35-45, suites US$50-60) Small beautiful hotel with comfortable rooms and good service.

Hostería del Molino La Mesopotamia (☎ 8-732-0235; Carrera 8 No 15A-265; s/d/t US$38/ 44/55) Legendary 435-year-old place (the oldest building in town), originally a flour mill, today an atmospheric hotel.

---

set up in a beautiful historic house. It has just five rooms, all with private bath.

Eating

Villa de Leyva has plenty of restaurants, though not all open on weekdays.

Restaurante Casa Blanca (Calle 13 No 7-16; set meals US$2.50, mains US$4-5) One of the best budget restaurants in town.

Restaurante Star de la Villa (Calle 13 No 8-85; set meals US$2.50, mains US$4-5) This place has reasonable food and prices.

La Chuculatería La Dicha Buena (Carrera 9 No 13-41; dishes US$2-5) Cozy place offering something for just about everyone, including salads, soups, crepes, tortillas, spaghetti and trout.

Restaurante Los Tres Caracoles (Plaza Mayor; mains US$6-10) Rich if not very cheap Spanish food.

Getting There & Away

The bus terminal is three blocks southwest of the Plaza Mayor, on the road to Tunja. Minibuses run regularly to Tunja (US$1.50, 45 minutes) until around 6pm. There are two direct buses daily to Bogotá (US$6, four hours), or you can go to Tunja and change.

AROUND VILLA DE LEYVA

Villa de Leyva is a good jumping-off place for excursions around the surrounding region, which is noted for a variety of cultural and natural attractions, including archaeological relics, colonial monuments, petroglyphs, caves, lakes and waterfalls. It is also a great place for fossil hunting. And it's one of Colombia's safest regions to travel in.

You can walk to some of the nearest sights, or go by bicycle or on horseback (see

p548). You can also use local buses or go by taxi, or arrange a tour (see p548).

A return taxi trip (up to four people) from Villa de Leyva to El Fósil, El Infiernito and Ecce Homo will cost about US$20, including waits allowing for visiting the three sights.

El Fósil

This is a reasonably complete **fossil of a kronosaurus** (admission US$1; ☺ 9am-noon & 2-5pm Fri-Wed), a 120-million-year-old prehistoric marine reptile vaguely resembling a crocodile. It's off the road to Chiquinquirá, 6km east of Villa de Leyva. You can walk there by a path in just over an hour, or take the Chiquinquirá or Ráquira bus, which will drop you off 1km from the fossil.

El Infiernito

Nicknamed El Infiernito (literally 'the little hell'), this is the **Muisca astronomic observatory** (admission US$1; ☺ 9am-noon & 2-5pm Tue-Sun), dating from the early centuries AD. It contains 30-odd cylindrical stone monoliths sunk vertically into the ground about 1m from each other in two parallel lines 9m apart. The place was also a ritual site, noted for a number of large, phallic stone monoliths.

The Infiernito is 2km north of El Fósil. You can walk there in 25 minutes. Bicycle, horse and taxi are other possible means of transport.

Convento del Santo Ecce Homo

The **Dominican convent** (admission US$1; ☺ 9am-noon & 2-5pm Tue-Sun), founded in 1620, is a large stone and adobe construction with a lovely courtyard. It's 13km northwest of Villa de Leyva. The morning bus to Santa Sofía will drop you off 15-minutes walk from the convent.

Ráquira

A small village 25km southwest of Villa de Leyva, Ráquira is known countrywide for its quality pottery – everything from kitchen utensils to copies of indigenous pots. There are a number of small pottery workshops in the village itself and on its outskirts, where you can watch the production process and buy some products if you want. Plenty of craft shops around the main square sell pottery, hammocks, ponchos, baskets, woodcarving etc. Many facades have been painted in bright colors, which gives the village much life and charm.

There are three budget hotels near the main plaza and a handful of restaurants. Three or four minibuses run daily from Villa de Leyva to Ráquira (US$1.50, 35 minutes) and back, plus occasional *colectivos* if there's a demand.

La Candelaria

This tiny hamlet set amid arid hills, 7km beyond Ráquira, is noted for the **Monasterio de La Candelaria** (☉ 9am-5pm). The monastery was founded in 1597 by Augustine monks and completed about 1660. Part of it is open to the public. Monks will show you through the chapel, a small museum, the library, and the courtyard flanked by the cloister with a collection of 17th-century canvasses.

Only two buses a day call at La Candelaria, both of which come from Bogotá. Otherwise, walk by a path from Ráquira (one hour). You can also go by taxi: a return taxi trip from Villa de Leyva to Ráquira and La Candelaria can be arranged for US$25 (for up to four people), allowing some time in both villages.

Santuario de Iguaque

Iguaque is a 67.5-sq-km nature reserve northeast of Villa de Leyva. It covers the highest part of the mountain range that stretches up to Arcabuco. There are eight small mountain lakes in the northern part of the reserve, sitting at an altitude of between 3550m and 3700m. The Laguna de Iguaque, which gave its name to the whole reserve, is the most important one, mostly because it was a sacred lake for the Muiscas.

The **visitor center** (dm US$8, 3 meals US$8) is at an altitude of 2950m, 3km off the Villa de Leyva–Arcabuco road. It offers accommodation in dorms, meals and collects the reserve's entrance fee (US$7.50). If you plan on staying there overnight, check accommodation availability in advance at Bogotá's park office.

The usual starting point for the reserve is Villa de Leyva. Take a bus to Arcabuco (four departures a day), get off 12km from Villa at a place known as Los Naranjos and walk to the visitor center (3km). A walk from the visitor center uphill to the Laguna de Iguaque takes two to three hours. A leisurely return trip is likely to take four

to six hours, unless you plan on visiting some other lakes as well.

SAN GIL

This 300-year-old town on the Bogotá–Bucaramanga road has a pleasant main square with huge old ceibas and an 18th-century cathedral. However, San Gil's main attraction is **Parque El Gallineral** (☎ 7-724-4372; Malecón at Calle 6; admission US$1.50; ☉ 8am-6pm), a beautiful riverside park where the trees are covered with *barbas de viejo*, long silvery fronds of tillandsia that form spectacular transparent curtains of foliage.

If you stop in San Gil, be sure to make the short trip to Barichara, an amazing small colonial town (p552). San Gil is the place to go rafting with some of the local tour companies.

Information

The tourist office, the **CAI de Turismo** (☎ 7-724-3433; Malecón at Calle 7; ☉ 7am-noon & 1-6pm) is near the entrance to the Parque El Gallineral.

The town has a collection of banks, including **Bancolombia** (Calle 12 No 10-44) and **Bancafé** (Carrera 10 No 11-16).

Internet access is provided by **Compugu@nes** (Carrera 10 No 12-37, Piso 2) in the Centro Comercial El Edén on the main plaza.

Tours

The major product of all four tour companies in San Gil is white-water rafting on local rivers. A standard 10km run on Río Fonce costs US$12 per person and takes 1½ hours, but longer, more adventurous trips are available on request. Most operators also offer horse riding, caving, paragliding and ecological walks.

The first three tour operators listed operate together and their desks are at the entrance to the Parque El Gallineral:

Aventura Total (☎ 7-723-8888) The stand of this fourth tour agency is about 100m away, next to the tourist office.
Planeta Azul (☎ 7-724-0000)
Rafting Club Brújula (☎ 7-723-7000)
Ríos y Canoas (☎ 7-724-7220)

Sleeping

San Gil has plenty of hotels, predominantly budget ones, all across the center of town.

Hotel San Carlos (☎ 7-724-2542; Carrera 11 No 11-25; s/d/t US$2.50/4.50/6, with bath US$5/7/10) One of the cheapest acceptable places and it's friendly.

Hotel El Viajero (☎ 7-724-1965, Carrera 11 No 11-07; s/d US$3.50/6, with bath US$6/8) Next door to San Carlos, marginally better and a bit more expensive.

Hotel Victoria (☎ 7-724-2347; Carrera 11 No 10-40; s/d/t with bath US$5/9/11) Another reasonable option, providing 15 rooms, all with baths, arranged around a large central courtyard.

Getting There & Away

The bus terminal is 2km west of the town center on the road to Bogotá. Urban buses shuttle regularly between the terminal and the center, or take a taxi (US$1).

Frequent buses run south to Bogotá (US$15, 7½ hours) and north to Bucaramanga (US$5, 2½ hours). There are also half-hourly minibuses that run to Bucaramanga (US$5, 2¼ hours). Buses to Barichara (US$1, 40 minutes) leave every 45 minutes from **Cotrasangil** (Carrera 10 No 14-82), in the town center.

BARICHARA

Barichara was founded in 1705 on Guane Indian territory. Most of the streets in this tiny town are paved with massive stone slabs and lined with fine whitewashed single-story houses. The town's real charm lies in its beauty as a whole, and its sleepy, old-world atmosphere. Authentic, well preserved and clean, this is one of the most beautiful small colonial towns in the country.

Strolling about, have a look at the massive 18th-century sandstone **Catedral de la Inmaculada Concepción**, on the main plaza, the largest and most elaborate single piece of architecture in town. The **Casa de la Cultura** (☎ 7-726-7002; Calle 5 No 6-29; admission US$0.25; ☺ 8am-noon & 2-6pm Wed-Sat, 9am-1pm Sun) features a small collection of fossils and pottery of the Guane Indians.

From Barichara, you can visit the tiny old village of **Guane**, 10km to the northwest, where time seems to have frozen a century or two ago. It has a fine rural church and a museum with a collection of fossils and Guane Indian artifacts.

Sleeping & Eating

Barichara has half a dozen hotels, plus some locals who rent rooms in their homes.

Aposentos (☎ 7-726-7294; Calle 6 No 6-40; r per person US$5) This small, friendly hotel, right

---

> **SPLURGE!**
>
> **Hostal Misión Santa Bárbara** (☎ 7-726-7163; Calle 5 No 9-12; s/d/t US$22/36/48) Housed in a meticulously refurbished beautiful colonial mansion, this charming place has comfortable, old-fashioned rooms with bath, a restaurant and a swimming pool. Room prices include breakfast. Bookings (☎ 1-288-4949) can be made in Bogotá.

---

on the main plaza, offers five rooms with private baths. It's very good value and one of the cheapest places to stay.

Hospedaje Los Tiestecitos (☎ 7-726-7224; Carrera 6 No 4-57; r per person US$5) Another small budget place, just off the plaza.

Hotel Coratá (☎ 7-726-7110; Carrera 7 No 4-08; r per person US$7) Likeable historic mansion with neat, ample rooms with baths.

There are quite a number of simple, budget restaurants around the plaza and neighboring streets, including **Restaurante La Braza Misifú** (Carrera 6 No 6-31) and **Restaurante La Casona** (Calle 6 No 5-68). Both serve cheap set meals and typical local dishes.

Getting There & Away

Buses shuttle between Barichara and San Gil every 45 minutes (US$1, 40 minutes). Two buses a day (except Saturday) go to Guane, or you can walk there by an old Spanish trail in less than two hours.

BUCARAMANGA

Bucaramanga, the capital of Santander, is a fairly modern, busy commercial and industrial center of 600,000 people with an agreeable climate. It is noted for its numerous parks, cigars and the famous *hormiga culona*, a large ant that is fried and eaten.

Information

The tourist office, the **Corporación Mixta de Promoción de Santander** (☎ 7-630-7589; Carrera 19 No 35-02, Oficina 215; ☺ 8am-noon & 2-6pm Mon-Fri) is on the corner of Parque Santander.

Internet access in the city center is provided by **Click and Play** (Calle 34 No 19-46) in the Centro Comercial La Triada. In the eastern sector of the city, there are a number of facilities, including **Mundo Internet** (Carrera 33 No 34-45) and **SAI Telecom** (Carrera 33 No 45-86).

COLOMBIA

BUCARAMANGA

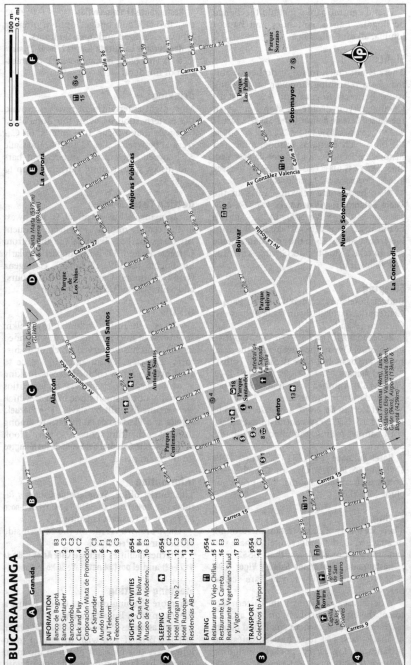

INFORMATION		
Banco de Bogotá...................	1	B3
Banco Santander..................	2	C3
Bancolombia........................	3	C3
Click and Play.....................	4	C2
Corporación Mixta de Promoción		
de Santander....................	5	C3
Mundo Internet....................	6	F1
SAI Telecom.........................	7	F3
Telecom..............................	8	C3

SIGHTS & ACTIVITIES	p554	
Museo Casa de Bolívar........	9	B4
Museo de Arte Moderno......	10	E3

SLEEPING	p554	
Hotel Amparo......................	11	C2
Hotel Morgan No 2..............	12	C3
Hotel Ruitoque....................	13	C3
Residencias ABC..................	14	C2

EATING	p554	
Restaurante El Viejo Chiflas...	15	F1
Restaurante La Carreta.........	16	E3
Restaurante Vegetariano Salud		
y Vigor..............................	17	B3

TRANSPORT	p554	
Colectivos to Airport............	18	C3

COLOMBIA

Useful central banks include the Banco de Bogotá, Banco Santander and Bancolombia, all on Calle 35.

Sights

There is not much to see or do here, but it may be a refreshing stopover on the long route between Bogotá and the coast or Cúcuta. If you decide to stop here, visit the **Museo Casa de Bolívar** (☎ 7-630-4258; Calle 37 No 12-15; admission US$0.50; ⏲ 8am-noon & 2-5:50pm Mon-Fri), which contains ethnographic and historic collections, and **Museo de Arte Moderno** (☎ 7-645-0483; Calle 37 No 26-16; admission US$0.50; ⏲ 9am-noon & 3-6pm Tue-Sat).

Also, have some relaxing walks in the **Jardín Botánico Eloy Valenzuela** (☎ 7-648-0729; admission US$0.25; ⏲ 8am-5pm), in the suburb of Bucarica. To get there, take the Bucarica bus from Carrera 15 in the city center. Make sure to take a side trip to Girón, 9km away (see following).

Sleeping

Budget hotels are centered on the Parque Centenario, particularly on Calle 31 between Carreras 19 and 22.

Residencias ABC (☎ 7-633-7352; Calle 31 No 21-44; s/d/t US$3/5/6) One of the cheapest in the area, rooms are basic but have their own baths.

Hotel Amparo (☎ 7-630-4098; Calle 31 No 20-29; s/d/t US$4/6/7) Another basic if acceptable accommodation in the area.

Hotel Morgan No 2 (☎ 7-630-4226; Calle 35 No 18-83; s/d US$12/17) Very central budget place with ample rooms equipped with baths and fans.

Hotel Ruitoque (☎ 7-633-4567; Carrera 19 No 37-26; s/d/t US$20/28/35) One of the cheapest hotels with air-con rooms. The prices include breakfast.

Eating

There are plenty of cheap restaurants around, or attached to, the budget hotels, where you can grab a set meal for less than US$2.

Restaurante Vegetariano Salud y Vigor (Calle 36 No 14-24) Inexpensive lunches are served here.

A better area for dining is the eastern sector of the city, particularly on and around Carreras 27 and 33, where you'll find plenty of snack bars, fast food outlets, cafés and restaurants for every pocket, including some of the city's best eateries.

Restaurante El Viejo Chiflas (Carrera 33 No 34-10; mains US$3-6) Good budget option, offering typical local food and open 24 hours.

Restaurante La Carreta (Carrera 27 No 42-27; mains US$6-12) This place has a 40-year long tradition of fine food.

Drinking

Most night entertainment revolves around the eastern suburbs, with the Zona Rosa being the major focus. It's centered on Carrera 31 between Calles 33 and 34, and Calle 33 between Carreras 31 and 33, but bars and discos spread along Carrera 33 up to Calle 45.

Getting There & Away

Bucaramanga's bus terminal is southwest of the center, midway to Girón; frequent city buses marked 'Terminal' go there from Carreras 15 and 33. Buses depart regularly for Bogotá (US$19, 10 hours), Cartagena (US$27, 12 hours), Cúcuta (US$10, six hours) and Santa Marta (US$20, nine hours).

GIRÓN

Girón is a beautiful colonial town 9km southwest of Bucaramanga. It was founded in 1631 and has preserved much of its historic character. It's an agreeable place to stroll about narrow cobbled streets, looking at white-washed old houses, shaded patios and half a dozen small stone bridges, which were reputedly built by slaves. The **Plazuela Peralta** and **Plazuela de las Nieves** are among its most enchanting spots. Also have a look at the eclectic **Catedral del Señor de los Milagros** on the main plaza.

Information

The tourist office, **Secretaría de Cultura y Turismo** (☎ 7-646-1337; Calle 30 No 26-64; ⏲ 8am-noon & 2-6pm) is in Casa de la Cultura.

There are two ATMs on the eastern side of the Parque Principal.

Internet facilities include **Café Arles** (Calle 31 No 23-48) and **el port@l.net** (Calle 30 No 25-03).

Sleeping & Eating

For more sleeping options, Girón is just a short trip from Bucaramanga.

Hotel Las Nieves (☎ 7-646-8968; Calle 30 No 25-71; s/d/t US$8/15/22) If you wish to stay in town longer, try this pleasant place on the main plaza. It has large, comfortable rooms with private bath. The hotel has a budget restaurant serving set meals and regional dishes.

You can also dine out in any of several finer restaurants that serve hearty, typical food in charming, colonial-style surroundings, including:

Mansión del Fraile (Calle 30 No 25-27; mains US$4-6)
Restaurante Villa del Rey (Calle 28 No 27-49; mains US$3-6)
Restaurante La Casona (Calle 28 No 28-09; mains US$5-8)

Getting There & Away

Frequent city buses from Carreras 15 and 33 in Bucaramanga will deposit you at Girón's main plaza in half an hour.

CÚCUTA

Cúcuta is a hot, uninspiring city of around half a million people. It's the capital of Norte de Santander and a busy commercial center, fueled by its proximity to Venezuela, just 12km away. The city doesn't have significant tourist attractions, so unless you're en route to or from Venezuela, there's little reason to visit.

Information
IMMIGRATION
The DAS immigration post (where you have to get an exit/entry stamp in your passport) is just before the border on the Río Táchira, on the left side of the road going towards Venezuela. There's also a DAS post at Cúcuta's airport – convenient if you're coming or leaving by air.

INTERNET ACCESS
Cúcuta has plenty of cybercafés, including:
Biblioteca Pública Julio Pérez Ferrero (Av 1 btwn Calles 12 & 13; US$0.80 per hr) The largest and cheapest Internet facility.
Café Cadena Internet (Edificio Domus Center, Local 105, Av 0 No 12-66)
OpinoNet (Centro Comercial Gran Bulevar, Piso 6, Oficina 606B, Av 0 at Calle 11)
SIS Café Internet (Calle 14 No 4-47)

MONEY
No banks in Cúcuta will change cash dollars, but there are plenty of *casas de cambio*, including two dozen at the bus terminal and a number in the center. They all change dollars, pesos and bolívares. There's also a rash of *casas de cambio* in San Antonio (on the

Venezuelan side of the border), paying much the same as those in Cúcuta. Only a few of Cúcuta's banks, including **Bancolombia** (Av 5 No 9-80 & Av 0 No 14-50), change traveler's checks.

TOURIST OFFICES
Corporación Mixta de Promoción de Norte de Santander (☎ 7-571-3395; Calle 10 No 0-30; ♻ 8am-noon & 2-6pm Mon-Fri) The tourist office is in the city center.

Sights

With a few hours to spare, you can visit the **Casa de la Cultura** (☎ 7-571-6689; Calle 13 No 3-67; ♻ 8am-noon & 2-6pm Mon-Fri), noted for its impressive clock tower, which has temporary art exhibitions. **Banco de la República** (☎ 7-575-0131; Av Diagonal Santander at Calle 11; ♻ 8am-noon & 2-6pm Mon-Fri) also stages temporary exhibitions in its Area Cultural.

You can also take a short trip to **Villa del Rosario**, 10km southeast of Cúcuta, on the road to the border, where the constitution of Gran Colombia was drawn up and passed in 1821. To commemorate the event, the Parque de la Gran Colombia was laid out. It features the ruins of the Templo del Congreso (the church where sessions of the congress were held, which was destroyed by an earthquake in 1875) and Casa de Santander (the house where Santander was born, now a small museum). To get to these sights from Cúcuta, take a San Antonio bus, not the Villa del Rosario bus.

Sleeping

There are a number of cheapies just south of the bus terminal, but they are mostly basic and the area is not attractive and may get unsafe at night. It's safer and more pleasant to stay further south, in the city center, though hotels there are not as cheap.

Hotel Internacional (☎ 7-571-2718; Calle 14 No 4-13; s/d/t US$6/11/15) One of the cheapest acceptable central options. The hotel has a spacious patio, a swimming pool and rooms with bath and fan.

Hotel La Bastilla (☎ 7-571-2576; Av 3 No 9-42; s/d/t US$7/11/15) Another central budget establishment, offering rooms with private facilities, though it's not as pleasant as the Internacional.

Hotel Real Cúcuta (☎ 7-571-6841; Av 4 No 6-51; s/d/t with fan US$7/11/14, with air-con US$11/14/17) One of the cheapest options providing air-con, but otherwise undistinguished.

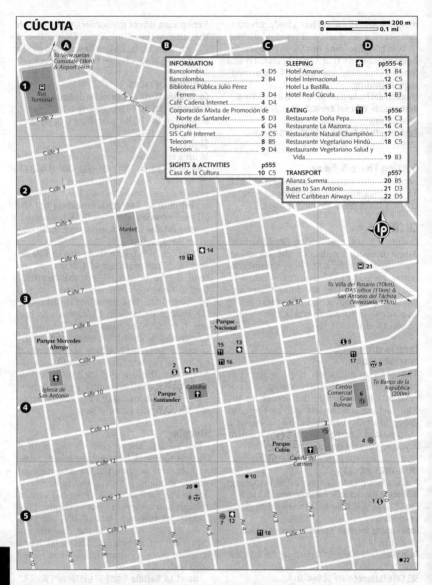

CÚCUTA

INFORMATION		**SLEEPING**	pp555-6
Bancolombia.............................1 D5		Hotel Amaruc..........................11 B4
Bancolombia.............................2 B4		Hotel Internacional..................12 C5
Biblioteca Pública Julio Pérez		Hotel La Bastilla......................13 C3
Ferrero..................................3 D4		Hotel Real Cúcuta...................14 B3
Café Cadena Internet..............4 D4		
Corporación Mixta de Promoción de		**EATING**	p556
Norte de Santander...............5 D3		Restaurante Doña Pepa...........15 C3
OpinoNet................................6 D4		Restaurante La Mazorca...........16 C4
SIS Café Internet.....................7 C5		Restaurante Natural Champiñón...17 D4
Telecom..................................8 B5		Restaurante Vegetariano Hindú...18 C5
Telecom..................................9 D4		Restaurante Vegetariano Salud y
		Vida.....................................19 B3
SIGHTS & ACTIVITIES	p555	
Casa de la Cultura..................10 C5		**TRANSPORT**	p557
		Alianza Summa........................20 B5
		Buses to San Antonio...............21 D3
		West Caribbean Airways...........22 D5

Hotel Amaruc (☎ 7-571-7625; Calle 10 at Av 5; s/d with fan US$16/24, with air-con US$22/30) Very central place overlooking the Parque Santander.

Eating

There are plenty of budget eateries across the center, including **Restaurante La Mazorca** (Av 4 No 9-67; set meals US$2; mains US$5-7) and **Res-**taurante Doña Pepa** (Av 4 No 9-57; set meals US$2, mains US$4-6). Both serve tasty *almuerzos* and typical Colombian dishes à la carte.

For budget vegetarian set lunches on weekdays, choose between the following: **Restaurante Vegetariano Salud y Vida** (Av 4 No 6-60) **Restaurante Natural Champiñón** (Calle 10 No 0-05) **Restaurante Vegetariano Hindú** (Calle 15 No 3-48)

COLOMBIA

Getting There & Away

AIR

The airport is 4km north of the city center. Minibuses marked 'El Trigal Molinos', which you catch on Av 1 or Av 3 in the center, will drop you 350m from the terminal, or take a taxi (US$3). The airport handles flights to most major Colombian cities (either direct or with connection), including Bogotá (US$70 to US$130), Medellín (US$80 to US$130) and Cartagena (US$90 to US$130).

There are no direct flights to Venezuela – go to San Antonio del Táchira (p982), the Venezuelan border town, 12km from Cúcuta.

BUS

The **bus terminal** (Av 7 at Calle 1) is very dirty and very busy – one of the poorest in Colombia. Watch your belongings closely. If you are arriving from Venezuela, you may be approached by well-dressed English-speaking characters who will kindly offer their help in buying bus tickets. They may also advise that you need to insure your cash and invite you to 'their office.' Ignore them – they are con men. Buy tickets directly from company offices.

There are frequent buses to Bucaramanga (US$10, six hours). At least two dozen buses daily run to Bogotá (US$29, 16 hours).

If you're heading to Venezuela, take one of the frequent buses or shared taxis that run from Cúcuta's bus terminal to San Antonio del Táchira (US$0.30 and US$0.50 respectively, paid in either pesos or bolívares). You can also catch *colectivos* and buses to San Antonio from the corner of Av Diagonal Santander and Calle 8, in the center. Don't forget to get off just before the bridge to have your passport stamped at DAS.

CARIBBEAN COAST

The Colombian Caribbean coast stretches 1760km from the dense jungles of the Darién Gap, on the border with Panama, to the desert of La Guajira, near Venezuela. To the south, the region extends to the foot of the Andes. Administratively, the area falls into the departments of La Guajira, Cesar, Magdalena, Atlántico, Bolívar, Sucre and Córdoba, plus the northern tips of Antioquia and Chocó.

The coast is steeped in sun, rum and tropical music. Its inhabitants, the *costeños*, are an easygoing, fun-loving people who give the coast a touch of carnival atmosphere.

Special attractions include Cartagena, one of the most beautiful colonial cities in Latin America, and the town of Mompós, a small architectural gem. You can take it easy on the beach – some of the best are in the Parque Nacional Tayrona – or go snorkeling or scuba diving amid the coral reefs of the Islas del Rosario. There's also Ciudad Perdida, the pre-Hispanic lost city of the Tayrona Indians, hidden deep in the lush tropical forest on the slopes of the Sierra Nevada de Santa Marta.

SANTA MARTA

Founded in 1525, Santa Marta is the oldest surviving town in Colombia, though its colonial character has largely disappeared. The climate is hot, but the sea breeze, especially in the evening, cools the city and makes it pleasant to wander about, or to sit over a beer in any of the numerous open-air waterfront cafés.

Santa Marta has become a popular tourist center mostly because of its surroundings rather than for the city itself. El Rodadero, just to the south (today within the city limits) is a fashionable beach resort. North of Santa Marta is the popular fishing village of Taganga, and further northeast, the beautiful Parque Nacional Tayrona. Santa Marta is also a jumping-off point for Ciudad Perdida.

Information

INTERNET ACCESS
Casa Familiar (Calle 10C No 2-14)
DialNet (Calle 13 No 3-13, Centro Comercial San Francisco Plaza) Cheap and open daily.
Hotel Miramar (Calle 10C No 1C-59)

MONEY
Bancolombia (Carrera 3 No 14-10) Of the local banks, probably only Bancolombia will change your traveler's checks and cash.

Before you change money, check the *casas de cambio*, which may give comparable rates and are faster. The two *casas* with a good reputation are:
Titán Intercontinental (Calle 14 No 3-08)
Todo Arte (Calle 14 No 4-45, Local 25) In the Centro Comercial Royal Plaza.

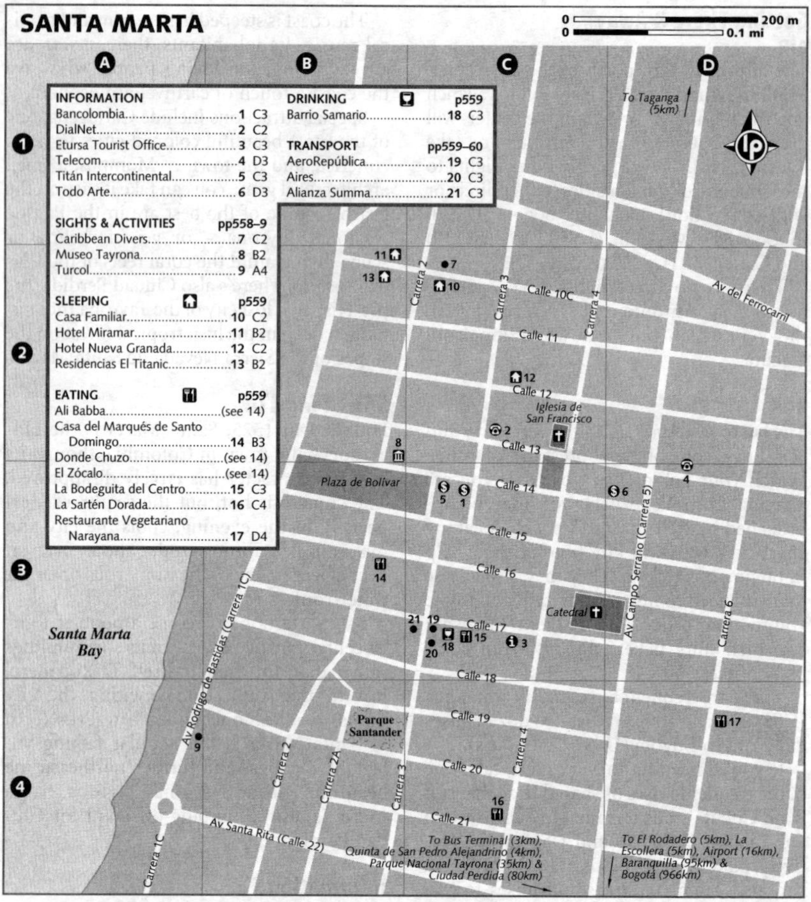
SANTA MARTA
0 200 m
0 0.1 mi
A
B
C
D
1
2
3
4
INFORMATION
Bancolombia....................1 C3
DialNet..........................2 C2
Etursa Tourist Office.............3 C3
Telecom..........................4 D3
Titán Intercontinental.............5 C3
Todo Arte........................6 D3
SIGHTS & ACTIVITIES pp558–9
Caribbean Divers...................7 C2
Museo Tayrona......................8 B2
Turcol.............................9 A4
SLEEPING p559
Casa Familiar.....................10 C2
Hotel Miramar.....................11 B2
Hotel Nueva Granada...............12 C2
Residencias El Titanic.............13 B2
EATING p559
Ali Babba.....................(see 14)
Casa del Marqués de Santo Domingo.....14 B3
Donde Chuzo...................(see 14)
El Zócalo.....................(see 14)
La Bodeguita del Centro...........15 C3
La Sartén Dorada..................16 C4
Restaurante Vegetariano Narayana..17 D4
DRINKING p559
Barrio Samario....................18 C3
TRANSPORT pp559–60
AeroRepública.....................19 C3
Aires.............................20 C3
Alianza Summa.....................21 C3
To Taganga (5km)
Av del Ferrocarril
Calle 10C
Calle 11
Calle 12
Calle 13
Calle 14
Calle 15
Calle 16
Calle 17
Calle 18
Calle 19
Calle 20
Calle 21
Carrera 2
Carrera 3
Carrera 4
Carrera 2A
Carrera 6
Carrera 1C
Av Campo Serrano (Carrera 5)
Av Rodrigo de Bastidas (Carrera 1C)
Av Santa Rita (Calle 22)
Iglesia de San Francisco
Plaza de Bolívar
Catedral
Parque Santander
Santa Marta Bay
To Bus Terminal (3km), Quinta de San Pedro Alejandrino (4km), Parque Nacional Tayrona (35km) & Ciudad Perdida (80km)
To El Rodadero (5km), La Escollera (5km), Airport (16km), Baranquilla (95km) & Bogotá (966km)

TOURIST OFFICES

Etursa (☎ 5-421-1833; Calle 17 No 3-120; 8am-noon & 2-6pm Mon-Fri) The city tourist office is diagonally opposite the cathedral.

Sights

The **Museo Tayrona** (☎ 5-421-0953; Calle 14 No 2-07; admission free; 8-11:45am & 2-5:45pm Mon-Fri) has an interesting collection of Tayrona objects, mainly pottery and gold. Don't miss the impressive model of Ciudad Perdida, especially if you plan on visiting the real thing.

The massive whitewashed **Catedral** (Carrera 4 at Calle 17) claims to be Colombia's oldest church, but work was not actually completed until the end of the 18th century. It holds the ashes of the town's founder, Rodrigo de Bastidas (just to the left as you enter the church).

The **Quinta de San Pedro Alejandrino** (☎ 5-433-0589; admission US$4; 9:30am-4:30pm) is the hacienda where Simón Bolívar spent his last days and died. You can visit the house, arranged in the style of Bolívar's day, and the Museo Bolivariano, which features works of art donated by Latin American artists. The Quinta is in the far eastern suburb of Mamatoco; take the Mamatoco bus from the waterfront to get there.

Activities

Santa Marta is an important **scuba-diving** center. Most dive schools have settled in

COLOMBIA

nearby Taganga (see p560), but there are also some operators in the city center, including the French-run **Caribbean Divers** (☎ 5-431-1568; www.caribbeandiverscol.com; Calle 10C No 2-11).

Tours

Santa Marta's tour market revolves principally around Ciudad Perdida. Tours are organized by **Turcol** (☎ 5-421-2256, 5-433-3737; Carrera 1C No 20-15). You can book and pay for the tour through some hotels (eg, the Hotel Miramar or Casa Familiar), which will then transfer your application and payment to Turcol. See Ciudad Perdida (p561) for more information.

Sleeping

There are plenty of hotels in the city center.

Hotel Miramar (☎ 5-423-3276, 5-421-4756; Calle 10C No 1C-59; hammock/dm US$1/2, d without/with bath US$4/5) Some of the cheapest accommodation in town. The place has long been the archetypal gringo hotel, with a noisy, hippie-type atmosphere, but it's very basic and unkempt. It has a café serving budget meals and drinks.

Residencias El Titanic (☎ 5-421-1947; Calle 10C No 1C-68; s/d US$4/6) A better and quieter alternative to Miramar, right across the street. It has 10 rooms, all of which have private baths and cable TV.

Casa Familiar (☎ 5-421-1697; Calle 10C No 2-14; dm US$3, s/d/t US$4/7/9) Another popular backpacker shelter just a few steps away from Hotel Miramar. Rooms have private baths but dorms have shared facilities.

Hotel Nueva Granada (☎ 5-421-1337; Calle 12 No 3-17; dm/s/d/t US$3/6/11/14) Quiet and well kept option. Rooms with bath overlook a spacious flowered patio.

Eating

There are a lot of cheap restaurants around the budget hotels, particularly on Calles 11 and 12 near the waterfront, where you can get an unsophisticated set meal for under US$2. The restaurant of the Hotel Miramar serves reasonable budget meals.

Restaurante Vegetariano Narayana (Carrera 6 No 18-15; set meals US$3) Tasty vegetarian lunches.

The waterfront is packed with cafés and restaurants offering almost anything from burgers and pizzas to local cuisine and seafood. It's a pleasant area for an evening stroll and dinner or just a snack.

Casa del Marqués de Santo Domingo (Calle 16 No 2-08) This beautiful colonial mansion shelters three restaurants: **Donde Chuzo** (mains US$5-8) serves seafood, **El Zócalo** (dishes US$3-6) serves Mexican food, and **Ali Babba** (dishes US$3-6) dishes up Middle-Eastern fare.

La Sartén Dorada (Carrera 4 at Calle 21; mains US$4-7) Reasonably priced restaurant that does good seafood.

La Bodeguita del Centro (Calle 17 No 3-38; mains US$5-9) One of the best restaurants in the center, serving beautiful seafood and beef dishes.

Drinking

Nightspots include:

Barrio Samario (Calle 17 No 3-36) A popular bar in Santa Marta's center. It has cheap beer, and plays a ragbag of music.

La Escollera (Calle 5 No 4-107) This trendy disco is in the northern end of El Rodadero.

Getting There & Away

AIR

The airport is 16km south of the city on the road to Barranquilla/Bogotá. City buses marked 'El Rodadero Aeropuerto' will take you there in 45 minutes from Carrera 1C. Alianza Summa, AeroRepública and Aires service Santa Marta. Flights include Bogotá (US$80 to US$130) and Medellín (US$80 to US$130).

BUS

The bus terminal is on the southeastern outskirts of the city. Frequent minibuses go there from Carrera 1C in the center.

Half a dozen buses run daily to Bogotá (US$32, 16 hours) and about the same number travel to Bucaramanga (US$20, nine hours). Buses to Barranquilla (US$4, 1¾ hours) depart every 15 to 30 minutes. Some of them go direct to Cartagena (US$8, four hours), but if not, there are immediate connections in Barranquilla.

Half-hourly buses depart for **Maicao** (US$9, four hours), where you change for a *colectivo* to Maracaibo (Venezuela). *Colectivos* depart regularly from about 5am to 3pm (US$10, 2½ hours) and go as far as Maracaibo's bus terminal. Note that Maicao is widely and justifiably known as a lawless town and can be unsafe – stay there as briefly as possible and don't move outside the bus terminal.

There are also three buses daily from Santa Marta direct to Maracaibo (US$25, seven hours), operated by Expreso Brasilia, Expresos Amerlujo and Unitransco/Bus Ven. They come through from Cartagena, go to Maracaibo and continue to Caracas.

All passport formalities are done in Paraguachón on the border. Change Colombian pesos to Venezuelan bolívares in Maicao or Paraguachón. They will be very difficult to change beyond Maracaibo. Wind your watch one hour forward when crossing from Colombia to Venezuela.

AROUND SANTA MARTA
Taganga
Taganga is a small fishing village set in a beautiful horseshoe-shaped bay, 5km northeast of Santa Marta, easily accessible by frequent minibuses from Carrera 1C. The village's beach is packed with boats and open-air restaurants and bars blasting out music at full volume. Locals offer boat excursions along the coast, or you can walk around the surrounding hills, which provide good views.

Playa Grande is a magnificent bay northwest of the village. You can either walk there (20 minutes) or take a boat from Taganga (US$1). The beach is lined with palm-thatched restaurants serving fried fish.

ACTIVITIES
Taganga is a popular scuba-diving center, with half a dozen dive schools offering dives and courses. Local services are among the cheapest you can find in Colombia (some say in the world). A four-day open-water PADI/NAUI course including six dives costs US$160 and a mini-course with two dives is US$40. The best local schools include **Centro de Buceo Tayrona** (☎ 5-421-9195; www.buceotayrona.net; Calle 18 No 1-45) and **Centro de Buceo Poseidon** (☎ 5-421-9224; www.poseidondive center.com; Calle 18 No 1-69).

SLEEPING & EATING
Taganga offers heaps of options for accommodation.

La Casa de Felipe (☎ 5-421-9101; www.lacasa defelipe.com; Carrera 5A No 19-13; r/ste per person US$4/6) A quiet and pleasant place that offers four rooms with bath and three suites with bath

and kitchenette. Run by a friendly Frenchman, Jean-Philippe, the hotel is a few blocks uphill from the beach, past the soccer pitch.

Casa Blanca (☎ 5-421-9232; Carrera 1 No 18-161; r per person US$5) New hotel right on the beach. Each of its 10 rooms has a private bath and a balcony with a hammock overlooking the bay. Guests can use the kitchen free of charge.

Chalet Suizo (☎ 5-421-9070; Calle 4 No 1B-12; r per person US$5) Swiss-run hostel, tucked behind the beach. It has five double rooms with baths.

There are a string of open-air restaurants along the waterfront, where a fresh fried fish with rice and salad shouldn't cost more than US$4.

Parque Nacional Tayrona
One of Colombia's most popular national parks, **Tayrona** (admission US$7.50) is on the jungle-covered coast just east of Santa Marta. The park's beaches, set in deep bays and shaded with coconut palms, are among the loveliest in Colombia. Some are bordered by coral reefs, and snorkeling is good, but be careful of the treacherous offshore currents. The region was once the territory of the Tayrona Indians and some remnants have been found in the park, the most important being the ruins of the pre-Hispanic town of Pueblito.

The park's main entrance is in **El Zaíno** (where you pay the entrance fee), 35km from Santa Marta on the coastal road to Riohacha. From El Zaíno, a 4km paved side road goes to **Cañaveral**, on the seaside. Here you'll find the park's administrative center, a campground, *cabañas*, a restaurant and a small Museo Arqueológico Chairama, which displays some archaeological finds excavated in Pueblito.

From Cañaveral, most visitors take a 45-minute walk west to Arrecifes, where there are budget lodging and eating facilities and the coast is spectacular, dotted with massive boulders.

From Arrecifes, a 20-minute walk northwest along the beach will bring you to La Piscina, a deep bay partly cut off from the open sea by an underground rocky chain. It's a good place for snorkeling. Another 20-minute walk will take you to the Cabo San Juan de la Guía, a beautiful cape with good beaches and views. From the Cabo, a scenic path goes inland uphill to Pueblito, a

1½-hour walk away, providing some splendid tropical forest scenery.

SLEEPING & EATING

Most travelers stay in Arrecifes, where there are three places to stay and eat.

Rancho Lindo (Arrecifes; campsites per person/hammock US$1.50/2, meals US$4-6) Offers a campsite, rents out hammocks under the roof and has a restaurant.

Finca El Paraíso (Arrecifes; campsites US$2, hammock US$2.50, 2/4/6-person cabañas US$15/25/35, meals US$5-7) Just behind the Rancho Lindo, this place has cabañas, under-cover hammocks, campsites and a restaurant.

Bucarú (Arrecifes) A 10-minute walk further west along the beach, is an offspring of El Paraíso, offering similar facilities as its parent.

GETTING THERE & AWAY

You can get to El Zaíno (US$1.25, one hour) by Palomino buses which depart regularly from Santa Marta's market (corner Carrera 11 and Calle 11). From El Zaíno, walk for 50 minutes to Cañaveral or catch the jeep which shuttles between the two places (US$0.60, 10 minutes).

CIUDAD PERDIDA

Ciudad Perdida (literally, the 'Lost City') is one of the largest pre-Columbian towns discovered in the Americas. It was built between the 11th and 14th centuries on the northern slopes of the Sierra Nevada de Santa Marta and was most probably the Tayrona's biggest urban center. During their conquest, the Spaniards wiped out the Tayronas, and their settlements disappeared without trace under the lush tropical vegetation. So did Ciudad Perdida for four centuries, until its accidental discovery in 1975 by *guaqueros* (robbers of pre-Columbian tombs).

Ciudad Perdida lies on the slopes of the Buritaca valley, at an altitude of between 950m and 1300m. The central part of the city is set on a ridge, from which various stone paths descend to other sectors on the slopes. There are about 150 stone terraces – some in remarkably good shape – which once served as foundations for the houses. Originally, the urban center was completely cleared of trees, before being reclaimed by the jungle. Today, the city is quite overgrown, which gives it a somewhat mysterious air.

Ciudad Perdida lies about 40km southeast of Santa Marta as the crow flies. It's hidden deep in the thick forest amid rugged mountains, far away from any human settlements and without access roads. The way to get there is by foot and the return trip takes six days. The trail begins in El Mamey and goes up along the Río Buritaca. The section between Santa Marta and El Mamey is done by vehicle.

Access to Ciudad Perdida is by tour only, organized by Turcol in Santa Marta. You cannot do the trip on your own, nor hire an independent guide. The all-inclusive six-day tour (about US$150 per person) includes transport, food, accommodation (in hammocks), porters, guides and all necessary permits. Tours are in groups of four to 12 people, and depart year-round as soon as a group is assembled. You carry your own personal belongings. Take a flashlight, water container and insect repellent.

The trip takes three days uphill to Ciudad Perdida, one day at the site and two days back down. The hike may be tiring due to the heat, and if it's wet (as it is most of the year) the paths are pretty muddy. The driest period is from late December to February or early March. There are several creeks to cross on the way; be prepared to get your shoes wet and carry a spare pair.

As in most parts of Colombia guerilla activity is rife – be extra careful when traveling around these parts.

CARTAGENA

Cartagena de Indias is legendary, for both its history and its beauty. It is Colombia's most amazing colonial city, and shouldn't be missed. Don't be in a hurry either, as the city's charm will keep you here for at least several days.

Founded in 1533, Cartagena swiftly blossomed into the main Spanish port on the Caribbean coast and the gateway to the north of the continent. Treasure plundered from the Indians was stored here until the galleons could ship it back to Spain. As such, it became a tempting target for pirates and, in the 16th century alone, it suffered five dreadful sieges, the best known of which was that led by Francis Drake in 1586.

In response to pirate attacks, the Spaniards decided to make Cartagena an impregnable port and constructed elaborate walls

CARTAGENA – OLD TOWN

0 ____ 200 m
0 ____ .1 mi

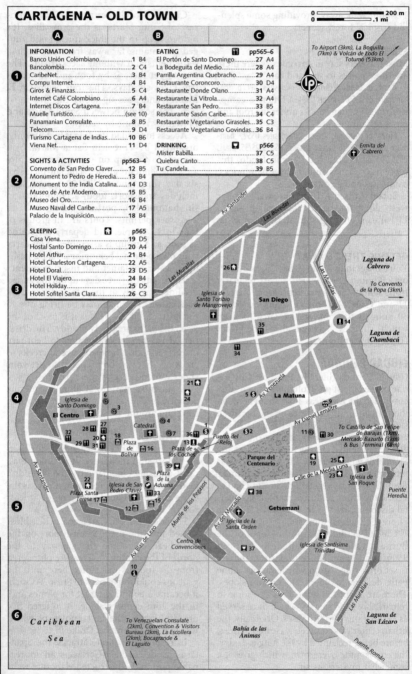

INFORMATION
Banco Unión Colombiano...............1 B4
Bancolombia..................................2 C4
CaribeNet......................................3 B4
Compu Internet.............................4 B4
Giros & Finanzas............................5 C4
Internet Café Colombiano..............6 A4
Internet Discos Cartagena..............7 B4
Muelle Turístico.......................(see 10)
Panamanian Consulate...................8 B5
Telecom...9 D4
Turismo Cartagena de Indias.......10 B6
Viena Net....................................11 D4

SIGHTS & ACTIVITIES   pp563–4
Convento de San Pedro Claver.....12 B5
Monument to Pedro de Heredia...13 B4
Monument to the India Catalina...14 D3
Museo de Arte Moderno..............15 B5
Museo del Oro.............................16 B4
Museo Naval del Caribe...............17 A5
Palacio de la Inquisición..............18 B4

SLEEPING   p565
Casa Viena...................................19 D5
Hostal Santo Domingo.................20 A4
Hotel Arthur................................21 B4
Hotel Charleston Cartagena..........22 A5
Hotel Doral..................................23 D5
Hotel El Viajero............................24 B4
Hotel Holiday...............................25 D5
Hotel Sofitel Santa Clara..............26 C3

EATING   pp565–6
El Portón de Santo Domingo.........27 A4
La Bodeguita del Medio................28 A4
Parrilla Argentina Quebracho........29 A4
Restaurante Coroncoro.................30 D4
Restaurante Donde Olano.............31 A4
Restaurante La Vitrola..................32 A4
Restaurante San Pedro.................33 B5
Restaurante Sasón Caribe.............34 C4
Restaurante Vegetariano Girasoles...35 C3
Restaurante Vegetariano Govindas...36 B4

DRINKING   p566
Mister Babilla..............................37 C5
Quiebra Canto.............................38 C5
Tu Candela..................................39 B5

To Airport (3km), La Boquilla
(7km) & Volcán de Lodo El
Totumó (53km)

Ermita del
Cabrero

Laguna del
Cabrero

To Convento
de la Popa (3km)

Av Santander

Las Bóvedas

Las Murallas

Laguna de
Chambacú

26

Iglesia de
Santo Toribio
de Mangrovejo

San Diego

35

34

Las Murallas

21
24

5   Av Venezuela   La Matuna

9

Av Daniel Lemaître

11   30

To Castillo de San Felipe
de Barajas (1km),
Mercado Bazurto (3km)
& Bus Terminal (6km)

Iglesia de
Santo Domingo

El Centro

6
3
4

Catedral

1
36   Puerto del
Reloj

2

19   25
23

Iglesia de
San Roque

32
28   27
29   31
18   16
Plaza de
Bolívar

7

Plaza de
los Coches

39

Plaza
de la
Aduana

8
33
15

Parque del
Centenario

Calle de la Media Luna

Puente
Heredia

22
Plaza Santa
Teresa 17

12

Iglesia de San
Pedro Claver

38

Muelle de los Pegasos

Getsemaní

Iglesia de
Santa Orden

Iglesia de Santísima
Trinidad

Av Blas de Lezo

10

Centro de
Convenciones

37

Av del Arsenal

Las Murallas

Laguna de
San Lázaro

Av Santander

Caribbean
Sea

To Venezuelan Consulate
(2km), Convention & Visitors
Bureau (2km), La Escollera
(2km), Bocagrande &
El Laguito

Bahía de las
Ánimas

Puente Román

COLOMBIA

encircling the town, and a chain of forts. These fortifications helped save Cartagena from subsequent sieges, particularly the fiercest attack of all, led by Edward Vernon in 1741. In spite of these attacks, Cartagena continued to flourish. During the colonial period, the city was the key outpost of the Spanish empire, and influenced much of Colombia's history.

Today, Cartagena has expanded dramatically and is surrounded by vast suburbs. It is now Colombia's largest port and an important industrial center of 850,000 inhabitants. Nevertheless, the old walled town has changed very little. It's a living museum of 16th- and 17th-century Spanish architecture, with narrow winding streets, palaces, churches, monasteries, plazas and large mansions with overhanging balconies.

Over the past decades, Cartagena has become a fashionable seaside resort. A modern tourist district has sprung up on Bocagrande and El Laguito, an L-shaped peninsula south of the old town. This sector, packed with top-class hotels and expensive restaurants, has become the main destination for moneyed Colombians and international charter tours. Most backpackers, however, stay in the historic part of town.

Cartagena's climate is hot, but a fresh breeze blows in the evening, making this a pleasant time to stroll around the city. Theoretically, the driest period is from December to April, while October and November are the wettest months.

Information

INTERNET ACCESS

There are a number of facilities in El Centro. Expect to pay US$1 to US$2 per hour.

CaribeNet (Calle Santo Domingo)
Compu Internet (Calle del Arzobispado)
Internet Café Colombiano (Plaza Santo Domingo)
Internet Discos Cartagena (Calle Román)
Viena Net (Calle Tripita y Media) The major facility in Getsemaní.

MONEY

Cartagena is the only Colombian city where you are likely to be propositioned (sometimes quite persistently) by street moneychangers. Give the street changers a big miss – they are all con men. Central banks that change traveler's checks and/or cash include:

Bancolombia (Av Venezuela)
Banco Unión Colombiano (Av Carlos Escallón)
Lloyds TSB Bank (Av San Martín No 10-21, Bocagrande)

There are plenty of *casas de cambio* in the center, many of which are around Plaza de los Coches. Try:

Titán Intercontinental (Av San Martín No 7-88) In Bocagrande.
Giros & Finanzas (Av Venezuela) In El Centro. Represents Western Union.

TOURIST OFFICES

Turismo Cartagena de Indias (☎ 5-665-1843; Av Blas de Lezo; ✆ 8am-noon & 2-6pm Mon-Fri) The main tourist office is in the Muelle Turístico.
Convention & Visitors Bureau (☎ 5-655-1484; Carrera 1 No 6-130; ✆ 8am-noon & 2-6pm Mon-Fri) An alternative in Bocagrande.

Sights

Cartagena's old town is its principal attraction, particularly the inner walled town, consisting of the historical districts of El Centro and San Diego. Almost every street is worth strolling down. Getsemaní, the outer walled town, is less impressive and not so well preserved, but it is also worth exploring. Be careful – this part of the city may not be safe, especially after dark.

The old town is surrounded by **Las Murallas**, the thick walls built to protect it. Construction was begun toward the end of the 16th century, after the attack by Francis Drake; until that time, Cartagena was almost completely unprotected. The project took two centuries to complete, due to repeated storm damage and pirate attacks.

The main gateway to the inner town was what is now the **Puerta del Reloj** (the clock tower was added in the 19th century). Just behind it is the **Plaza de los Coches**, a square once used as a slave market. Note the fine old houses with colonial arches and balconies, and the monument to Pedro de Heredia, the founder of the city.

A few steps southwest is the **Plaza de la Aduana**, the oldest and largest square in the old town. It was used as a parade ground, and all governmental buildings were gathered around it. At the southern outlet from the plaza is the **Museo de Arte Moderno** (☎ 5-664-5815; Plaza de San Pedro Claver; admission US$0.50; ✆ 9am-noon & 3-7pm Mon-Fri, 10am-1pm Sat), which presents temporary exhibitions.

COLOMBIA

Close by is the **Convento de San Pedro Claver**, built by the Jesuits, originally under the name of San Ignacio de Loyola. The name was changed in honor of the Spanish-born monk Pedro Claver, who lived and died in the convent. He spent his life ministering to the slaves brought from Africa. The convent is a monumental three-story building surrounding a tree-filled courtyard, and part of it, including Claver's cell, is open to visitors as a **museum** (☎ 5-664-4991; Plaza de San Pedro Claver; admission US$2; ☼ 8am-6pm Mon-Sat, 8am-5pm Sun).

The church alongside, **Iglesia de San Pedro Claver**, has an imposing stone facade. The remains of San Pedro Claver are kept in a glass coffin in the high altar. Behind the church, the **Museo Naval del Caribe** (☎ 5-664-9672; Calle San Juan de Dios; admission US$1.50; ☼ 10am-6pm Tue-Sun) traces the naval history of Cartagena and the Caribbean.

Nearby, the **Plaza de Bolívar** is in a particularly beautiful area of the old town. On one side of the square is the **Palacio de la Inquisición**, a fine example of late colonial architecture dating from the 1770s, with its overhanging balconies and magnificent Baroque stone gateway. It is now a **museum** (☎ 5-664-4113; Plaza de Bolívar) that displays Inquisitors' instruments of torture, pre-Columbian pottery and works of art from the colonial and independence periods. It was closed for refurbishing when this book was being researched.

Across the plaza, the **Museo del Oro** (☎ 5-660-0778; Plaza de Bolívar; admission free; ☼ 8am-noon & 2-6pm Tue-Fri, 9am-noon Sat) has a good collection of gold and pottery from the Sinú culture. The **Catedral** was begun in 1575 but was partially destroyed by Drake's cannons in 1586, and not completed until 1612. The dome on the tower was added early in the 20th century.

One block west of the plaza is **Calle Santo Domingo**, a street which has hardly changed since the 17th century. On it stands the **Iglesia de Santo Domingo**, the city's oldest church. It is a large, heavy construction, and buttresses had to be added to the walls to support the naves.

At the northern tip of the old town are **Las Bóvedas**, 23 dungeons built in the defensive walls at the end of the 18th century. This was the last construction done in colonial times, and was destined for military purposes. Today, the dungeons are tourist shops.

While you're wandering around, call in at the **Muelle de los Pegasos**, a lovely old port full of fishing, cargo and tourist boats, just outside the old town's southern walls.

Several forts were built at key points outside the walls to protect the city from pirates. By far the greatest is the **Castillo de San Felipe de Barajas** (☎ 5-656-0590, 5-666-4790; Av Arévalo; admission US$3; ☼ 8am-5pm), east of the old town and a huge stone fortress, begun in 1639 but not completed until some 150 years later. Don't miss the impressive walk through the complex system of tunnels, built to facilitate the supply and evacuation of the fort.

The **Convento de la Popa** (☎ 5-666-2331; admission US$2; ☼ 9am-5pm), perched on top of a 150m hill beyond the San Felipe fortress, was founded by the Augustinians in 1607. It has a nice chapel and a lovely flower-filled patio, and offers panoramic views of the city. There have been some cases of armed robbery on the zigzagging access road to the top – take a taxi (there's no public transport).

Activities

Taking advantage of extensive coral reefs along Cartagena's coast (particularly around the Islas del Rosario), Cartagena has grown into an important scuba-diving center. Virtually all the local dive schools are in Bocagrande and El Laguito and include:

Caribe Dive Shop (☎ 5-665-3517; caribediveshop@ yahoo.com; Hotel Caribe, Bocagrande)

Dolphin Dive School (☎ 5-665-2792; www.pavito .com; Edificio Costamar, Av San Martín No 6-105, Bocagrande)

Eco Buzos (☎ 5-655-1129; Edificio Alonso de Ojeda, Av Almirante Brion, El Laguito)

La Tortuga Dive School (☎ 5-665-6994; Edificio Marina del Rey, Av del Retorno, El Laguito)

Festivals & Events

Cartagena's major annual events include:

Festival Internacional de Cine International film festival, held in March/April, usually shortly before Easter.

Feria Artesanal y Cultural Regional craft fair taking place in June/July, accompanied by folk music concerts and other cultural events.

Reinado Nacional de Belleza National beauty pageant held on 11 November to celebrate Cartagena's independence day. The fiesta strikes up several days before and the city goes wild. The event, also known as the Carnaval de Cartagena or Fiestas del 11 de Noviembre, is the city's most important annual bash.

Sleeping

Cartagena has a reasonable choice of budget accommodations and despite its touristy status, the prices of its hotels are no higher than in other large cities. The tourist peak is from late December to late January but, even then, it's relatively easy to find a room.

A vast majority of travelers stay in the walled city. This is Cartagena's most pleasant and convenient area to stay and the one that offers plenty of lodging options, everything from rock bottom to top notch. Within the walled city, Getsemaní is the principal area of budget accommodation, whereas El Centro and San Diego shelter the city's top-end hotels. All hotels listed below have rooms with fans, unless specified.

Casa Viena (☎ 5-664-6242; hotel@casaviena.com; Calle San Andrés, Getsemaní; dm/s/d US$/4/7, d with bath US$9) One of the most popular and cheapest backpacker haunts has simple rooms, most with shared baths. The hotel offers a typical range of facilities that Western travelers seek, including laundry service, Internet access, book exchange, individual strongboxes, cooking facilities, tours and tourist information. Dorms have air-con.

Hotel Holiday (☎ 5-664-0948; Calle de la Media Luna, Getsemaní; r without/with bath per person US$3.50/4.50) Another popular and friendly travelers' hangout. Its 13 neat airy double rooms with bath are good value, and there are four smaller rooms without private facilities.

Hotel Doral (☎ 5-664-1706; Calle de la Media Luna, Getsemaní; r without/with bath per person US$4/5) Hotel Doral's attractive, spacious courtyard is filled with potted shrubs and flowers and umbrella-shaded tables. Rooms, distributed on two levels around the courtyard, are simple but spacious. The rooms on the 1st floor are more airy and pleasant but they don't have private baths.

Hotel El Viajero (☎ 5-664-3289; Calle del Porvenir, El Centro; s/d US$5/10) One of the best budget bets in El Centro, and good value. This new 14-room hotel provides good beds, spacious courtyard and free use of the kitchen. All rooms have private baths.

Hostal Santo Domingo (☎ 5-664-2268; Calle Santo Domingo, El Centro; s/d/t US$14/20/25) Small, quiet hotel ideally located on one of the loveliest streets in El Centro, but probably overrated.

Hotel Arthur (☎ 5-664-2633; Calle San Agustín, El Centro; d with fan/air-con US$12/15) Nothing particu-

larly stylish or special, but one of the cheapest central options with air-conditioning.

Eating

Cartagena is a good place to eat, particularly at the upmarket level, but cheap places are also plentiful. Dozens of simple restaurants in the old town serve set *almuerzos* for less than US$2, and many also offer set *comidas*. Among the cheapest are **Restaurante Coroncoro** (Calle Tripita y Media, Getsemaní) and **Restaurante Sasón Caribe** (Calle La Tablada, San Diego).

Tasty, budget vegetarian meals are served at **Restaurante Vegetariano Govinda's** (Plaza de los Coches, El Centro) and **Restaurante Vegetariano Girasoles** (Calle Quero, San Diego).

A dozen stalls on the Muelle de los Pegasos operate round the clock and offer an unbelievable selection of fruit juices – try *níspero* (round fruit with soft, fleshy meat), *maracuyá* (passion fruit), *lulo* (prickly fruit with very soft flesh), *zapote* (eggplant-shaped fruit with orange, fleshy-fibred meat) and *guanábana* (soursop) – and plenty of local snacks. Also, try typical local sweets at the confectionery stands at El Portal de los Dulces on the Plaza de los Coches.

Plaza Santo Domingo hosts six open-air cafés, serving a varied menu of dishes, snacks, sweets and drinks. The cafés are not that cheap but the place is trendy and invariably fills up in the evening.

Restaurante San Pedro (Plaza San Pedro Claver; mains US$4-8) A variety of cuisines, including Italian pastas, Mexican burritos and Indonesian nasi goreng. Facing the mighty San Pedro Church, the restaurant has an air-con interior and tables outdoors.

Restaurante Donde Olano (Calle Santo Domingo; mains US$5-8) A cozy place that cooks fine

---

SPLURGE!

Hotel Charleston Cartagena (☎ 5-664-9494; reserv-charlesctg@hoteles-charleston.com; Plaza Santa Teresa; d US$100-120, ste US$130-150) The former Convento de Santa Teresa is one of two convents in the walled city that has been turned into a luxurious hotel. It features 91 rooms and 22 suites distributed around two amazing historic courtyards straight out of a postcard. The rooftop swimming pool offers good views over the colonial quarter.

COLOMBIA

> **SPLURGE!**
>
> There are some classy restaurants in the old town, most of which are set in historic interiors. Some worth trying include:
>
> **El Portón de Santo Domingo** (☎ 664 8897; Calle Santo Domingo; mains US$8-15) Fine international food, including seafood, with live music on weekend nights.
>
> **Restaurante La Vitrola** (☎ 5-664-8243; Calle de Baloco; mains US$10-15) Top-quality international cuisine and live music, played nightly.
>
> **Parrilla Argentina Quebracho** (☎ 5-664-1300; Calle de Baloco; mains US$8-12) Argentine cuisine, including famous juicy steaks, in appropriately decorated surroundings, plus tango shows in the evening.

French and Creole specialties at reasonable prices.

Restaurante Pelíkanos (cnr Calle Santo Domingo & Calle Gastelbondo; menu US$10) This arty bohemian two-level restaurant is different from any other. It has just one set menu daily, consisting of six courses (four entrees, a main course and dessert), plus unlimited Chilean wine included in the price.

La Bodeguita del Medio (Calle Santo Domingo; mains US$5-9) Charming Cuban affair serving Cuban food surrounded by old Cuban photos.

Drinking

A number of bars, taverns, discos and other venues stay open late. Plenty of them are on Av del Arsenal in Getsemaní, Cartagena's Zona Rosa.

Mister Babilla (Av del Arsenal) This is one of the most popular discos in this area, yet also one of the most expensive ones. You will find cheaper venues nearby; just walk along the street, as everybody does, and take your pick.

Quiebra Canto is a good salsa spot overlooking the Parque del Centenario.

Tu Candela (Portal de los Dulces) An informal bar that serves beer and plays taped music till late.

La Escollera (Carrera 1 at Calle 5) This disco in a large, thatched open hut in Bocagrande goes wild nightly until 4am. It has three bars serving expensive spirits and soft drinks and the music is played at extra-high volume.

You can also go on a night trip aboard a *chiva*, a typical Colombian bus, with a band playing *vallenato*, a popular local rhythm. *Chivas* depart around 8pm from Av San Martín between Calles 4 and 5 in Bocagrande for a three- to four-hour trip, and leave you at the end of the tour in a discotheque – a good point from which to continue partying for the rest of the night.

Getting There & Away
AIR
All major Colombian carriers operate flights to and from Cartagena. There are flights to Bogotá (US$70 to US$120), Cali (US$80 to US$130), Cúcuta (US$90 to US$130), Medellín (US$70 to US$120), San Andrés (US$80 to US$130) and other major cities.

The airport is in the suburb of Crespo, 3km northeast of the old city, and is serviced by frequent local buses which depart from various points, including India Catalina and Av Santander. *Colectivos* to Crespo depart from India Catalina; the trip costs US$2.50 by taxi. The terminal has two ATMs and the Casa de Cambio América (in domestic arrivals) changes cash and traveler's checks.

BOAT
There's no ferry service between Cartagena and Colón in Panama, and there are very few cargo boats. A more pleasant way of getting to Panama is by sailboat. There are various boats, mostly foreign yachts, that take travelers from Cartagena to Colón via San Blas Archipelago (Panama), and vice versa, but this is not a regular service. The trip takes four to six days and normally includes a couple of days at San Blas for snorkeling and spear fishing. It costs around US$200. Keep an eye out for information on the boats at popular backpacker hotels, or inquire at the Club Náutico.

While strolling about Cartagena, you may be approached by men offering fabulous trips around the Caribbean in 'their boats' for a little help on board; if you seem interested, they will ask you to pay some money for a boarding permit or whatever. Don't pay a cent – you'll see neither the man, nor your money, again.

BUS
The bus terminal is on the eastern outskirts of the city, a long way from the center. Large

green-and-white air-con Metrocar buses shuttle between the two every 10 minutes (US$0.50, 40 minutes). In the center, you can catch them on Av Daniel Lemaitre. Catch the one with red letters on the board, which goes by a more direct route and is faster.

Half a dozen buses go daily to Bogotá (US$40, 20 hours) and another half a dozen to Medellín (US$27, 13 hours). Buses to Barranquilla run every 15 minutes or so (US$4, two hours), and some continue on to Santa Marta; if not, just change in Barranquilla. Unitransco has one bus to Mompós (US$10, eight hours); see Mompós (p570).

Three bus companies – **Expreso Brasilia** (☎ 5-665-0469), **Expresos Amerlujo** (☎ 5-653-2536) and **Unitransco/Bus Ven** (☎ 5-663-2065) – operate daily buses to Caracas (US$60, 20 hours) via Maracaibo (US$35, 10 hours). Unitransco is a bit cheaper than the other two, but you have to change buses on the border in Paraguachón. All buses go via Barranquilla, Santa Marta and Maicao. You'll save if you do the trip to Caracas in stages by local transport, with changes in Maicao and Maracaibo.

AROUND CARTAGENA
Islas del Rosario
This archipelago, about 35km southwest of Cartagena, consists of 27 small coral islands, including some tiny islets only big enough for a single house. The archipelago is surrounded by coral reefs, where the color of the sea ranges from turquoise to purple. The whole area has been decreed a national park, the Corales del Rosario.

Cruises through the islands are well-established. Tours depart year-round from the Muelle Turístico in Cartagena. Boats leave between 8am and 9am daily and return about 4pm to 6pm. The cruise office at the Muelle sells tours in big boats for about US$18, but independent operators hanging around may offer cheaper tours in smaller vessels, for US$15 or even less. It's probably best (and often cheapest) to arrange the tour through one of the budget gringo hotels. Tours normally include lunch, but not the entrance fee to the aquarium (US$4) on one of the islands, the port tax (US$1.50) and the national park entrance fee (US$1.50).

Playa Blanca
This is one of the most beautiful beaches around Cartagena. It's about 20km south-west of the city, on the Isla de Barú, and it's the usual stop for the boat tours to the Islas del Rosario. The place is also good for snorkeling as the coral reef begins just off the beach (take snorkeling gear).

The beach has some rustic places to stay and eat. The most popular with travelers is **Campamento Wittenberg**, run by a Frenchman named Gilbert. It offers accommodation in beds (US$4) or hammocks (US$2) and serves meals.

The easiest way of getting to the beach is with Gilbert, who comes to Casa Viena in Cartagena once a week (usually on Wednesday) and takes travelers in his boat (US$4, 45 minutes). If this doesn't coincide with your itinerary, go to Cartagena's main market, Mercado Bazurto, and go by boat or bus. Boats depart from about 9am to 10:30am daily except Sunday, when an early morning bus runs directly to the beach.

La Boquilla
This small fishing village is 7km north of Cartagena on a peninsula between the sea and the seaside lagoon. There's a pleasant place known as El Paraíso, a five-minute walk from the bus terminus, where you can enjoy a day on the beach. The locals fish with their famous *atarrayas* (a kind of net) at the lagoon, and you can arrange boat trips with them along the narrow water channels cutting through the mangrove woods. Negotiate the price and only pay after they bring you back.

Plenty of beachfront palm-thatched restaurants attract people from Cartagena on weekends; most are closed at other times. Frequent city buses run to La Boquilla from India Catalina in Cartagena (US$0.40, 30 minutes).

Volcán de Lodo El Totumo
About 50km northeast of Cartagena, on the bank of the shallow Ciénaga del Totumo, is an intriguing 15m mound, looking like a miniature volcano. It's indeed a volcano but instead of lava and ashes, it spews mud, a phenomenon caused by the pressure of gases emitted by decaying organic matter underground.

El Totumo is the highest mud volcano in Colombia. Lukewarm mud with the consistency of cream fills its crater. You can climb to the top by specially built stairs, then go down into the crater and have a refreshing mud bath (US$1). It's a unique experience – surely volcano-dipping is something you haven't yet tried! The mud contains minerals acclaimed for their therapeutic properties. Once you've finished your session, go down and wash the mud off in the *ciénaga* (lagoon). There are several restaurants around the volcano.

To get to the volcano from Cartagena, take a bus from Mercado Bazurto, from where hourly buses depart in the morning to Galerazamba. They travel along the old Barranquilla road up to Santa Catalina then, shortly after, turn north onto a side road to Galerazamba. Get off on the coastal highway by the petrol station at Lomita Arena (US$1.50, 1½ hours) and walk along the highway 2.5km towards Barranquilla (30 minutes), then to the right (southeast) 1km to the volcano (another 15 minutes). The last direct bus from Lomita Arena back to Cartagena departs at around 3pm.

Several tour operators in Cartagena organize minibus trips to the volcano (transport only US$10; with lunch in La Boquilla US$13), which can be booked through popular backpacker hotels.

Jardín Botánico Guillermo Piñeres

A pleasant half-day escape from the city rush, this **botanical garden** (☎ 5-663-7172; admission US$1.50; ☽ 9am-4pm Tue-Sun) is on the outskirts of the town of Turbaco, 15km southeast of Cartagena. Take the Turbaco bus departing regularly from next to the Castillo de San Felipe in Cartagena and ask the driver to drop you at the turnoff to the garden (US$0.50, 45 minutes). From there it's a 20-minute stroll down the largely unpaved side road. The 20-acre garden features plants typical of the coast, including two varieties of coca plant.

MOMPÓS

Mompós, about 230km southeast of Cartagena, was founded in 1537 on the eastern branch of the Río Magdalena, which in this region has two arms: Brazo Mompós and Brazo de Loba. The town soon became an important port through which all merchandise from Cartagena passed to the interior of the colony. Several imposing churches and many luxurious mansions were built.

Toward the end of the 19th century, shipping was diverted to the other branch of the Magdalena, ending the town's prosperity. Mompós has been left in isolation and little has changed since. Its colonial character is very much in evidence, as are the airs of a bygone era. It's fun to wander about this tranquil town, discovering its rich architectural legacy and absorbing the old-time atmosphere.

The region around Mompós is known for the presence of the guerrillas and there have been some cases of assaults on buses over recent years. Check for news before you set off for the trip.

Information

The **tourist office** (Plaza de la Libertad; ☽ 8am-noon & 2-6pm Mon-Fri) is in the Alcaldía building. There are a couple of ATMs around Plaza de Bolívar, but it's best to bring pesos with you, just in case. **Compartel** (Calle Real del Medio) provides Internet access.

Sights

Most of the central streets are lined with fine whitewashed colonial houses with characteristic metal-grill windows, imposing doorways and lovely hidden patios. Six colonial churches complete the scene; all are interesting, though rarely open. Don't miss the **Iglesia de Santa Bárbara** (Calle 14), with its Moorish-style tower, unique in Colombian religious architecture.

The **Casa de la Cultura** (Calle Real del Medio; admission US$0.50; ☽ 8am-noon & 2-5pm Mon-Fri) displays memorabilia relating to the town's history. **Museo Cultural** (Calle Real del Medio; admission US$1; ☽ 9:30am-noon & 3-5pm Tue-Fri, 9:30am-noon Sat & Sun) features a collection of religious art. There's a small **Jardín Botánico** (Calle 14), with lots of hummingbirds and butterflies. Knock on the gate to be let in.

Festivals & Events

Holy Week celebrations are very elaborate in Mompós. The solemn processions circle the streets for several hours on Maundy Thursday and Good Friday nights.

Sleeping

There are a dozen hotels in town, most of them pleasant and friendly. Among the cheapest options are these simple *residencias*:

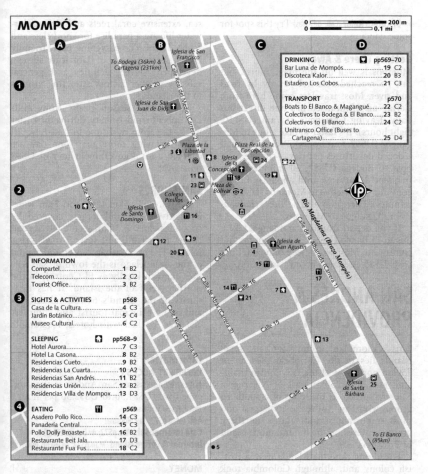

MOMPÓS

0 — 200 m
0 — 0.1 mi

To Bodega (36km) &
Cartagena (231km)

To El Banco
(85km)

Residencias La Cuarta (☎ 5-685-6040; Calle Nueva; r per person US$3)

Residencias Cueto (Calle de Atrás; r per person US$4)

Residencias Unión (☎ 5-685-5723; Calle 18; r per person US$4)

Better places to stay line Calle Real del Medio.

Hotel La Casona (☎ 5-685-5307; Calle Real del Medio; s/d with fan US$6/10, with air-con US$9/15) This friendly and comfortable hotel has good rooms with bath.

The following places charge US$4 to US$6 per person in rooms with fan and bath.

Residencias Villa de Mompox (☎ 5-685-5208; Calle Real del Medio)

Hotel Aurora (☎ 5-685-5930; Calle Real del Medio)

Residencias San Andrés (☎ 5-685-5886; Calle Real del Medio)

Eating

There are a number of budget restaurants in town, including **Restaurante Fua Fus** (Plaza de Bolívar) and **Restaurante Beit Jala** (Calle de la Albarrada). For chicken, try **Asadero Pollo Rico** (Calle 16) or **Pollo Dolly Broaster** (Calle 18). **Panadería Central** (Calle Real del Medio) is a good breakfast option.

Drinking

Bar Luna de Mompós (Calle de la Albarrada) A great place for a drink.

Estadero los Cobos (Calle 16) This open-air place has cheap beer and plays good music until late.

COLOMBIA

Discoteca Kalor (Calle de Atrás) Try this spot for some dancing.

Getting There & Away

Mompós is well off the main routes, but can be reached relatively easily by road and river. Most travelers come here from Cartagena. Unitransco has one direct bus daily, leaving Cartagena at 7am (US$10, eight hours). It's faster to take a bus to Magangué (US$7, four hours); Brasilia has half a dozen departures per day – change for a boat to Bodega (US$2, 20 minutes) with frequent departures until about 3pm, and continue by *colectivo* to Mompós (US$2, 40 minutes). There may also be direct *chalupas* from Magangué to Mompós.

If you depart from Bucaramanga, take a bus to El Banco (US$10, seven hours) and continue to Mompós by jeep or boat (either costs US$5 and takes about two hours).

SAN ANDRÉS & PROVIDENCIA

This Colombian archipelago of small islands lies in the Caribbean Sea about 750km northwest of the Colombian mainland and only 230km east of Nicaragua. The archipelago is made up of a southern group, with San Andrés as its largest and most important island, and a northern group, centered on the mountainous island of Providencia.

For a long time the islands were a British colony and, although Colombia took possession after independence, the English influence on language, religion and architecture remained virtually intact until modern times. It wasn't until the 1950s, when a regular domestic air service was established with the Colombian mainland and San Andrés was declared a duty-free zone, that the situation began to change. A significant migration of Colombians to the islands and a boom in tourism and commerce have meant that much of San Andrés' original character has been lost. Providencia has managed to preserve much more of its colonial character.

The islands, especially Providencia, provide a good opportunity to experience the unique Caribbean ambience. The turquoise sea, extensive coral reefs and rich underwater life are a paradise for snorkelers and scuba divers. The easygoing pace, friendly locals (descendants of Jamaican slaves), developed tourist facilities and general safety are other factors attracting visitors to the islands.

The tourist season peaks from mid-December to mid-January, during the Easter week, and from mid-June to mid-July. All visitors staying more than one day are charged a local government levy of US$8 on arrival.

SAN ANDRÉS

San Andrés, 12.5km long and 3km wide, is relatively flat and largely covered by coconut palms. A 30km scenic paved road circles the island, and several roads cross inland. The main urban center and capital of the archipelago is the town of San Andrés (known locally as El Centro), in the northern end of the island. It has two-thirds of the island's 60,000 inhabitants and is the principal tourist and commercial area, packed with hotels, restaurants and stores.

Information

INTERNET ACCESS

Internet access on San Andrés is slow and expensive (US$1.50 to US$2.50 per hour). Facilities include:

AMI (Map p572; Av Colombia)
Café Internet Sol (Map p572; Av Duarte Blum)
Internet & Coffee Island (Map p572; Av 20 de Julio)

MONEY

Some banks exchange traveler's checks and cash, including:

Bancolombia (Map p572; Av Costa Rica)
Banco Popular (Map p572; Av Las Américas)

Banks useful for credit-card holders include Bancafé, Banco de Bogotá and Banco Occidente.

Both traveler's checks and cash can be more easily and quickly exchanged in *casas de cambio*, which include:

Cambios y Capitales (Map p572; Centro Comercial New Point Plaza, Local 106, Av Providencia)
Giros & Finanzas (Map p572; Centro Comercial San Andrés, Local 12, Av Costa Rica)
Titán Intercontinental (Map p572; Edificio Leda, Local 5, Av Providencia)

Secretaría de Turismo Departamental (Map p572; ☎ 8-512-4284; Av Newball; ☑ 8am-noon & 2-6pm Mon-Fri) In the building of the Gobernación, Piso 3.

Tourist information desk (Map p572; ☎ 8-512-6110; ☑ 10am-6pm) The Secretaría operates a desk at the airport.

VISAS

Only Costa Rica and Honduras maintain consulates on the island (see p606 for details). Try to get visas on the mainland, as consuls do not always stay on the island and you may be stuck for a while waiting for one to return.

Sights

Most people stay in El Centro, but take some time to look around the island. El Centro's beach, along Av Colombia, is handy and fine but it may be crowded in tourist peak seasons. There are no beaches along the island's western shore, and those along the east coast are nothing special, except for the good beach in San Luis.

A 50m rocky hill known as **El Cliff** (Map p571), a 20-minute walk southeast of the airport, provides views over the town and the surrounding coral reefs. The small village of **La Loma**, in the central hilly part of the island, is noted for its Baptist church, the first established on San Andrés.

The **Cueva de Morgan** (Map p571) is an underwater cave where the Welsh pirate Henry Morgan is said to have buried some of his treasure. **Hoyo Soplador** (Map p571), at the southern tip of the island, is a sort of small geyser where the sea water spouts into the air through a natural hole in the coral rock. This phenomenon can be observed only when the winds and tide are right.

There are several small cays off San Andrés, of which the most popular are **Johnny Cay** (Map p571), opposite El Centro, and **Acuario** (Map p571), off the island's eastern coast.

Activities

Thanks to the beautiful coral reefs surrounding it, San Andrés has become an important scuba-diving center. The water is pleasantly warm and visibility is better than that on the mainland's coast. There are more than 35 different spots for div-

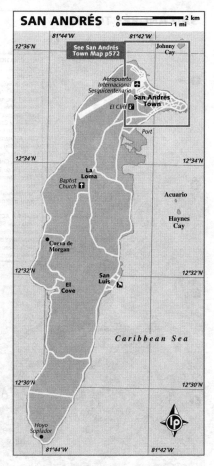

SAN ANDRÉS

ing around the island. San Andrés' diving schools include:

Banda Dive Shop (Map p572; ☎ 8-512-2507; banda@sol.net.co; in Hotel Lord Pierre, Av Colombia) A reliable, reasonably priced facility.

Buzos del Caribe (Map p572; ☎ 8-512-8930; www.buzosdelcaribe.com; Av Colombia) The oldest and largest facility. It has good equipment and a good reputation, but it's expensive (US$250 for the open water PADI or NAUI course).

Divers Dream (Map p572; ☎ 8-512-7701, 8-512-6923; www.diversdream.com; in Hotel Aquarium Decameron, Av Newball) Experienced, reasonably priced school.

Karibik Diver (Map p572; ☎ 8-512- 0101; wernersai@gmx.net; Av Newball) This small school is also expensive (US$300) but provides quality equipment, personalized service and long dives.

COLOMBIA

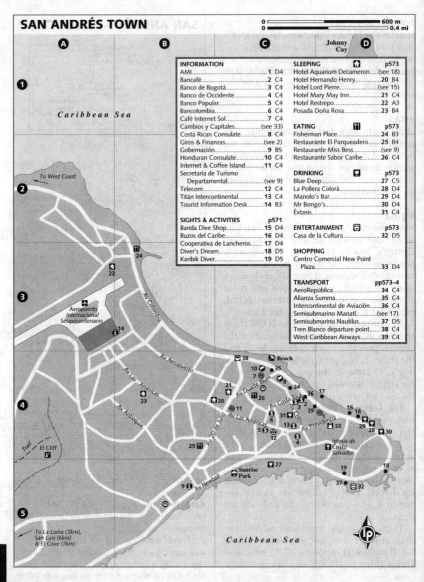

SAN ANDRÉS TOWN

0 — 600 m
0 — 0.4 mi

INFORMATION
AMI..1 D4
Bancafé....................................2 C4
Banco de Bogotá.......................3 C4
Banco de Occidente...................4 C4
Banco Popular...........................5 C4
Bancolombia.............................6 C4
Café Internet Sol........................7 C4
Cambios y Capitales..............(see 33)
Costa Rican Consulate................8 C4
Giros & Finanzas...................(see 2)
Gobernación.............................9 B5
Honduran Consulate.................10 C4
Internet & Coffee Island.............11 C4
Secretaría de Turismo
  Departamental.................(see 9)
Telecom..................................12 C4
Titán Intercontinental...............13 C4
Tourist Information Desk............14 B3

SIGHTS & ACTIVITIES   p571
Banda Dive Shop......................15 D4
Buzos del Caribe......................16 D4
Cooperativa de Lancheros.........17 D4
Diver's Dream..........................18 D5
Karibik Diver...........................19 D5

SLEEPING   p573
Hotel Aquarium Decameron.....(see 18)
Hotel Hernando Henry...............20 B4
Hotel Lord Pierre...................(see 15)
Hotel Mary May Inn..................21 C4
Hotel Restrepo.........................22 A3
Posada Doña Rosa.....................23 B4

EATING   p573
Fisherman Place.......................24 B3
Restaurante El Parqueadero.......25 B4
Restaurante Miss Bess............(see 9)
Restaurante Sabor Caribe..........26 C4

DRINKING   p573
Blue Deep................................27 C5
La Pollera Colorá......................28 D4
Manolo's Bar............................29 D4
Mr Bongo's..............................30 D4
Éxtasis....................................31 C4

ENTERTAINMENT   p573
Casa de la Cultura....................32 D5

SHOPPING
Centro Comercial New Point
  Plaza....................................33 D4

TRANSPORT   pp573–4
AeroRepública..........................34 C4
Alianza Summa.........................35 C4
Intercontinental de Aviación......36 C4
Semisubmarino Manatí...........(see 17)
Semisubmarino Nautilus............37 D5
Tren Blanco departure point......38 C4
West Caribbean Airways............39 C4

Caribbean Sea

Johnny Cay

To West Coast

Aeropuerto
Internacional
Sesquicentenario

Av Colombia

Av Aeropuerto

Av Las Américas

Av Antioquia

Av 20 de Julio

Av Las Américas

Av Duarte Blum

Av Costa Rica

Av Providencia

Beach

Iglesia de
Cristo
Salvador

El Cliff

Trail

Av Newball

Sunrise
Park

Caribbean Sea

To La Loma (3km),
San Luis (6km)
& El Cove (7km)

COLOMBIA

Tours

The Tren Blanco, a sort of road train pulled by a tractor dressed up like a locomotive, departs every morning from the corner of Av Colombia and Av 20 de Julio to circle the island, stopping at several sights along the way (US$3, three hours). The same route can be done by taxi (US$18 for up to four people). Other, shorter or longer arrangements with taxi drivers are available.

Cooperativa de Lancheros (Map p572; Av Colombia), on the town's beach, provides trips to Johnny Cay (US$3) and Acuario (US$4), plus a combined tour to both cays (US$5).

Semisubmarino Manatí is a specially designed boat with large windows below the waterline. It departs once or twice daily for a 1½-hour tour (US$12 per person) around the nearby reefs. If you are not planning on scuba diving or snorkeling, this trip is probably the next best option for having a look at San Andrés' rich marine life. Tickets can be bought from the Cooperativa de Lancheros. There's another boat, *Semisubmarino Nautilus*, which does similar trips from the wharf just west of the Casa de la Cultura (US$12, two hours).

Sleeping

On the whole, accommodation in San Andrés is plentiful but more expensive than on the mainland. All the places listed can be found on the San Andrés Town map (p572).

Hotel Restrepo (☎ 8-512-6744; r per person US$5) The cheapest place to stay, just north of the airport terminal. It's extra basic and unkempt but friendly. Some rooms have their own bath.

Posada Doña Rosa (☎ 8-512-3649; Av Las Américas; s/d/t US$8/15/20) Small guesthouse with eight rooms, all of which have a bath and fan. It's good value and much better than the Restrepo.

Hotel Mary May Inn (☎ 8-512-5669; Av 20 de Julio; s/d/t US$15/18/22) Small and friendly place that is one of the best inexpensive hotels in town. All of its eight rooms have bath, hot water and air-con.

Hotel Hernando Henry (☎ 8-512-3416; Av Las Américas; s/d with fan US$12/18, with air-con US$18/23) A good affordable option; all 30 rooms have private bath and balcony.

Eating

There are a number of simple restaurants in El Centro that serve the usual set meals for US$2 to US$3. All the places listed can be found on the San Andrés Town map (p572). Try **Restaurante El Parqueadero** (Av 20 de Julio) or **Restaurante Miss Bess** (Av Newball) in the building of Gobernación.

Fisherman Place (Av Colombia) Open-air beach restaurant offering typical local food, including crab soup (US$3), fried fish (US$3) and seafood stew (US$7).

Restaurante Sabor Caribe (Av Los Libertadores; mains US$4-5) One of the best inexpensive restaurants serving seafood and other local specialties, including *rondón* (soup prepared with coconut milk, vegetables, fish and sea snails).

Drinking & Entertainment

There are several nightspots on Av Colombia between Hotel Lord Pierre and Hotel Aquarium Decameron. Popular bars with dance floors in the area include **Mr Bongo's** (Av Colombia), **La Pollera Colorá** (Av Colombia) and **Manolo's Bar** (Av Colombia), all on the waterfront.

Some upmarket hotels have discotheques, the most trendy (and expensive) of which is **Blue Deep** (Av Newball) in Sunrise Beach Hotel, followed by **Éxtasis** (Av Colón) in Hotel Sol Caribe San Andrés.

Casa de la Cultura (Av Newball) organizes folkloric shows on Friday night, which feature live music, dance and typical local food.

Getting There & Away

AIR

International connections change frequently. At press time, West Caribbean Airways was the only carrier with direct flights between San Andrés and Central America. It had flights to and from San José (one way/30-day return US$145/236) and Panama City (US$120/206). Both destinations were serviced three times weekly on Monday, Wednesday and Friday.

The airport tax on international departures from San Andrés is the same as elsewhere in Colombia: US$28 if you have stayed in the country for less than 60 days, and US$43 if you've stayed longer.

Alianza Summa (Avianca, Sam and Aces), AeroRepública and Intercontinental have flights to and from the major Colombian cities, including Bogotá (US$100 to US$140), Cali (US$100 to US$150), Cartagena (US$80 to US$130) and Medellín (US$100 to US$140).

West Caribbean Airways operates flights between San Andrés and Providencia (one way US$42). There are three to seven flights daily (depending on the season) in each direction. In the high season, book in advance.

Flights between Central America and Colombia via San Andrés were once cheap and popular with travelers, but the routes and prices have changed and the flights are no longer that attractive. However, the San José–San Andrés–Cartagena route may still be worth its money.

If San Andrés is not your stopover on the Central–South American route, but a destination in its own right from the

Colombian mainland, it's best to check for package deals in weekend papers. Good deals can be found in the low season, with offers including return airfare and a decent hotel for far less than you'd pay buying your ticket and accommodation separately.

BOAT
There are no ferries to the Colombian mainland or elsewhere. Cargo boats to Cartagena and Providencia don't take passengers.

Getting Around
Local buses run along the circular coastal road, and along the inner road to La Loma and El Cove, and can drop you near any of the sights. Otherwise, hire a bicycle (from US$1.50/5 per hour/day). Motorbikes, scooters and cars can also be hired at various locations throughout the town. Shop around, as prices and conditions vary.

PROVIDENCIA
Providencia, 90km north of San Andrés, is the second-largest island in the archipelago at 7km long and 4km wide. It is a mountainous island of volcanic origin, much older than San Andrés. It's highest peak is El Pico (320m).

An 18km road skirts the island, and virtually the entire population of 5000 lives in houses scattered along it, or in one of the several hamlets. Santa Isabel, a village at the northern tip of the island, is the administrative seat. Santa Catalina, a smaller island just to the northwest, is separated from Providencia by the shallow Canal Aury, spanned by a pedestrian bridge.

Providencia is much less affected by tourism than San Andrés. English is widely spoken, and there's still much Caribbean English-style architecture to be seen. The locals are even friendlier than those on San Andrés, and the duty-free business fever is unknown. However, the island is becoming a fashionable spot for Colombian tourists. Aguadulce, on the west coast, has already been converted into a tourist village, with hotels and restaurants, boat and motorbike rental, and scuba diving facilities. So far, the rest of the island is largely unspoiled, though the situation is changing.

The coral reefs around Providencia are extensive and snorkeling and scuba diving are excellent. The interior of the island

provides pleasant walks, with El Pico being the major goal. The trail to the peak begins from Casabaja, on the south side of the island. It's a steady 1½ hours' walk to the top.

Getting around the island is pretty straightforward – just wave down any of the taxi-*colectivos* or pickups that run the circular road (US$1 for any distance).

Information
The tourist office at the airport has closed down. Try **Body Contact** (Aguadulce ☎ 8-514-8283; Santa Isabel ☎ 8-514-8107). Both outlets of this travel agency can provide some tourist information and both have Internet service, albeit painfully slow. The Aguadulce branch also offers tours, bicycle rental (US$7 a day) and may change your cash dollars at a poor rate.

Banco Agrario de Colombia (Santa Isabel) gives cash advances on Visa card, whereas the ATM next door to the bank services Master Card. However, it's best to bring enough pesos with you from San Andrés.

Activities
Scuba-diving at Providencia is as good as at San Andrés. There are three dive schools on the island, all offering roughly similar programs and prices, with an open water or advance course for about US$180 to US$200:

Centro de Buceo Scuba Town (☎ 8-514-8481; Pueblo Viejo) Also known as Buceo Beda.
Sirius Dive Center (☎ 8-514-8213; Bahía Suroeste)
Sonny Dive Shop (☎ 8-514-8231; Aguadulce)

Sleeping & Eating
Accommodation and food are expensive on Providencia, even more so than on San Andrés. The overwhelming majority of places to stay and eat are in Aguadulce.

Mr Mac (☎ 8-514-8366; s/d US$10/18) This is one of Aguadulce's cheapest hotels. It has just a few rooms, all of which are simple but have private baths, some overlooking the beach.

Posada del Mar (☎ 8-514-8168; d with fan/aircon US$25/32) A good affordable option next door to Mr Mac. All rooms have baths and balconies facing the beach.

Cabañas El Encanto (☎ 8-514-8131; r per person US$15) Tucked away a bit from the beach, this good-value place has comfortable, airy rooms, all of which have bath, fan, air-con and fridge. Add US$7 for breakfast and dinner in its in-house restaurant.

Residencias Sofía (☎ 8-514-8109; r per person US$5) This ultra-basic place in Pueblo Viejo, 2km south of Santa Isabel, is one of the cheapest places to stay on the island. Get off by the SENA center and take the rough track that branches off the main road and leads toward the seaside; the hotel is just 100m away. It has very rustic doubles and triples with shared baths, and simple meals are available on request.

Eating is generally not cheap in Aguadulce, though there are some basic eateries that offer budget breakfasts (US$3) and dinners (US$5). Most of the hotels have their own restaurants and will be more than happy to provide a bed-and-board package.

There are also lodging and eating facilities in other areas of the island, including Santa Isabel and Bahía Suroeste.

Getting There & Away

West Caribbean Airways flies between San Andrés and Providencia several times a day (one way US$42). Buy your ticket in advance, and be sure to reconfirm your return flight.

NORTHWEST COLOMBIA

A vast central part of northwestern Colombia is taken up by Antioquia, one of Colombia's largest, most populated and wealthiest departments. Its inhabitants, commonly known as *paisas*, have traditionally been reluctant to mix with either blacks or Indians, and consequently, this is the country's 'whitest' region, with a large Creole population.

Antioquia, or the *país paisa* (*paisa* country) as its inhabitants call it, is a picturesque mountainous land, spread over parts of the Cordillera Occidental and the Cordillera Central. It's crisscrossed by roads linking little *pueblos paisa* (paisa towns) noted for their distinctive architectural style.

Most of the region has an enjoyable mild climate, rich vegetation and is pleasant to travel. Sadly, some areas of rural Antioquia, particularly its eastern part, can be unsafe because of guerrilla and paramilitary presence. Check the safety conditions before you set off for the countryside.

MEDELLÍN

The capital of Antioquia, Medellín is a dynamic industrial and commercial center of 2.2 million people, Colombia's second largest city after Bogotá. It is spectacularly set in the deep Aburrá Valley in the Central Cordillera, with a modern center and vast slum barrios perched all over the surrounding slopes. The town was founded in 1675, but only at the beginning of the 20th century did it begin to expand rapidly, first as a result of the coffee boom in the region, and then as the center of the textile industry. Medellín became a large metropolitan city in a relatively short period of time.

Perhaps not a top travelers' destination, Medellín is a thriving city with an agreeable climate and friendly people. It does have some good museums and other attractions, as well as developed tourist facilities. With its three large universities and half a dozen smaller ones, the city has a sizeable student population, which gives it a vibrant and cultured air.

Information
INTERNET ACCESS
There are plenty of cybercafés in the center of town (most charge around US$1 per hour).

Café Internet Doble-Click (Calle 50 No 43-135) Medellín's largest cybercafé (80 computers). It's open longer than most other places and is one of very few that opens on Sunday.

EMP.Net (Carrera 45 No 52-49)

Internet Villanueva (Calle 57 No 49-44, Centro Comercial Villanueva, Local 9957)

MONEY
Banks likely to change traveler's checks at reasonable rates include:

Bancolombia (Av Colombia at Carrera 52)
Banco Santander (Av Oriental at Av La Playa)

The banks may also change cash, but you'll probably get similar or even better rates (and will save time) at *casas de cambio*.

There are half a dozen *casas de cambio* in **Centro Comercial Villanueva** (Calle 57 No 49-44), including **Giros & Finanzas** (Local 241), the Western Union agent. Another collection of *casas de cambio* is in the **Edificio La Ceiba** (Calle 52 Av La Playa No 47-28). Also check **Titán**

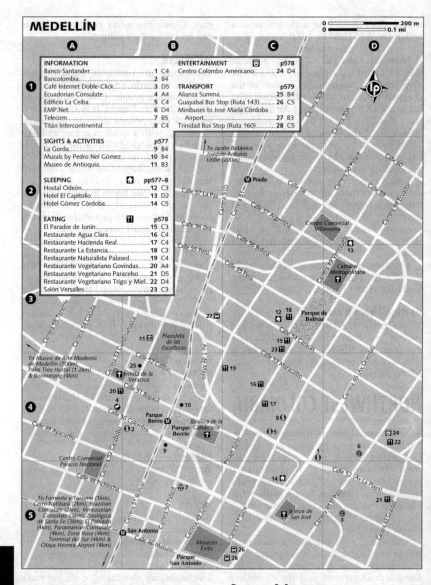

MEDELLÍN

0 — 200 m
0 — 0.1 mi

INFORMATION	
Banco Santander.....................................1 C4	
Bancolombia..2 B4	
Café Internet Doble-Click......................3 D5	
Ecuadorian Consulate.............................4 A4	
Edificio La Ceiba.....................................5 C4	
EMP.Net..6 D4	
Telecom..7 B5	
Titán Intercontinental...........................8 C4	

SIGHTS & ACTIVITIES	p577
La Gorda...9 B4	
Murals by Pedro Nel Gómez................10 B4	
Museo de Antioquia.............................11 B3	

SLEEPING	pp577–8
Hostal Odéon..12 C3	
Hotel El Capitolio................................13 D2	
Hotel Gómez Córdoba.........................14 C5	

EATING	p578
El Parador de Junín..............................15 C3	
Restaurante Agua Clara.......................16 C4	
Restaurante Hacienda Real..................17 C4	
Restaurante La Estancia.......................18 C3	
Restaurante Naturalista Palased...........19 C4	
Restaurante Vegetariano Govindas.....20 A4	
Restaurante Vegetariano Paracelso......21 D5	
Restaurante Vegetariano Trigo y Miel..22 D4	
Salón Versalles......................................23 C3	

ENTERTAINMENT	p578
Centro Colombo Americano...............24 D4	

TRANSPORT	p579
Alianza Summa.....................................25 B4	
Guayabal Bus Stop (Ruta 143)............26 C5	
Minibuses to José María Córdoba	
Airport...27 B3	
Trinidad Bus Stop (Ruta 160)............28 C5	

To Jardín Botánico
Joaquín Antonio
Uribe (200m)

To Museo de Arte Moderno
de Medellín (700m);
Palm Tree Hostal (1.2km)
& Boomerang (4km)

To Fomento y Turismo (1km),
Cerro Nutibara (2km), Brazilian
Consulate (2km), Venezuelan
Consulate (3km), Zoológica
de Santa Fe (3km), El Poblado
(4km), Panamanian Consulate
(4km), Zona Rosa (4km),
Terminal del Sur (4km) &
Olaya Herrera Airport (4km)

Intercontinental (Edificio Coltejer, Carrera 46 No 52-65, Local 103).

TOURIST OFFICES

Fomento y Turismo (☎ 4-232-4022; Av Alfonso López; ⏱ 7:30am-12:30pm & 1:30-5:30pm Mon-Fri) Medellín's main tourist office is in the Palacio de Exposiciones, 1km southwest of the center.

Dangers & Annoyances

Although no longer the world's cocaine trafficking capital, Medellín isn't the safest place on the globe; like any large Colombian city, it has security problems. It is notorious for crime, but most of it happens in the poor outer suburbs. The city center appears quite safe during the daytime, but keep your evening strolls to a minimum. If you're going to party at night, use taxis.

Sights

The **Museo de Antioquia** (☎ 4-251-3636; Carrera 52 Carabobo No 52-43; admission US$2.50; ☯ 9:30am-5pm Mon & Wed-Fri, 10am-4pm Sat & Sun) is Colombia's second oldest museum and one of the most significant ones. It features pre-Hispanic, colonial, independence and modern art collections, spanning Antioquia's 400-year-long history, plus Fernando Botero's donation of 92 of his own works and 22 works by other international artists. Additionally, his 23 large bronze sculptures have been placed in front of the museum, in what is known as Plazoleta de las Esculturas. Born in Medellín in 1932, Botero is the most internationally known Colombian contemporary artist and has some of his sculptures gracing city squares and parks, including a massive woman's torso, popularly known as **La Gorda**, in Parque Berrío, and three sculptures in Parque San Antonio.

Across the Parque Berrío are two large murals depicting Antioquia's history, the 1956 work by another of Medellín's illustrious sons, Pedro Nel Gómez (1899–1984). The **Casa Museo Pedro Nel Gómez** (☎ 4-233-2633; Carrera 51B No 85-24; admission US$2; ☯ 9am-noon & 2-5pm Mon-Fri, 9am-noon Sat), set in the house where the artist lived and worked, shelters nearly 2000 of his works, including watercolors, oil paintings, drawings, sculptures and murals. Pedro Nel Gómez is said to have been Colombia's most prolific artist.

Another important city museum, the **Museo de Arte Moderno de Medellín** (☎ 4-230-2622; Carrera 64B No 51-64; admission US$1.50; ☯ 10:30am-7pm Mon-Fri, 10am-5pm Sat) stages changing exhibitions of contemporary art.

Apart from a few old churches, the city's colonial architecture has virtually disappeared. The most interesting of the historic churches is the **Basílica de la Candelaria** (Parque Berrío), built in the 1770s and functioning as the city's cathedral until 1931. Also worth a visit is the gigantic neo-Romanesque **Catedral Metropolitana** (Parque de Bolívar), completed in 1931 and thought to be South America's largest brick church (1.2 million bricks were used).

Medellín has a fine botanical garden, the **Jardín Botánico Joaquín Antonio Uribe** (☎ 4-233-7025; Carrera 52 No 73-182; admission US$1; ☯ 9am-5pm Mon-Sat, 10am-5pm Sun). The local zoo, the **Zoológico de Santa Fe** (☎ 4-235-1326; Carrera 52 No 20-63; admission US$2; ☯ 9am-5pm), specializes in species typical of Colombia.

For views of the city, go to the **Cerro Nutibara**, an 80m-tall hill 2km southwest of the city center. The **Pueblito Paisa**, a replica of a typical Antioquian village, has been built on the summit and is home to several handicrafts shops.

Activities

Medellín is regarded as Colombia's main center of paragliding thanks to favorable conditions provided by the winds and rugged topography. Best gliding schools include:

Boomerang (☎ 4-412-3886; piloto_x@hotmail.com; Calle 38B No 79-16, Barrio Laureles) Offers courses (about US$300 for a week-long course), equipment rental and tandem flights over the city (US$25).

Luisito Escuela (☎ 4-388-0493; luisitoescuela@hotmail.com) Similar services and prices to Boomerang, but its flights are in the mountainous area 30km north of Medellín.

Festivals & Events

Feria Nacional de Artesanías Craft fair held in July at the Atanasio Girardot sports complex. Good for cheap buys.

Feria de las Flores Held for a week in early August, this is Medellín's biggest event. Its highlight is the Desfile de Silleteros, on 7 August, when hundreds of *campesinos* come down from the mountains and parade along the streets carrying *silletas* full of flowers on their backs.

Mercado de San Alejo Colorful craft market held in the Parque de Bolívar on the first Saturday of every month.

Sleeping

Palm Tree Hostal (☎ 4-260-2805; www.palmtreemedellin.com; Carrera 67 No 48D-63; dm US$5) Medellín's major traveler haunt. It offers a range of facilities typical of a Western backpacker hostel, including laundry service, Internet access, bicycle rental, book exchange and the use of the kitchen. It has half a dozen four-bed dorms without bath and one room with bath. The hostel is in the suburb of Suramericana, about 1.5km west of the center, easily accessible by metro (Suramericana Station) or by bus along Calle 50 Av Colombia. A taxi from either bus terminal is US$2.

The city center is the main area of budget accommodation. There are plenty of cheap hotels here, though nothing as traveler-friendly or popular as the Palm Tree Hostal.

COLOMBIA

Many cheapies double as love hotels and raise prices on the weekend.

Hotel Gómez Córdoba (☎ 4-513-1676; Carrera 46 No 50-29; s/d with bath US$6/9) This is a reasonably orthodox and clean option – one of the few popular with travelers.

Hostal Odeón (☎ 4-511-1360; Calle 54 No 49-38; s/d/t with bath US$9/15/22) Small, quiet and very central with fridges in rooms.

Hotel El Capitolio (☎ 4-512-0004; Carrera 49 Venezuela No 57-24; s/d/t with bath US$20/24/28) Fully renovated and affordable accommodation right behind the cathedral. Price includes breakfast.

Eating

Like every big city, Medellín has hundreds of places to eat for every budget. The center is literally flooded with restaurants, snack bars and cafés and provides some of the cheapest meals.

Restaurante La Estancia (Carrera 49 Venezuela No 54-15; set meals US$1) One of the cheapest places to eat. It's not particularly clean, good or pleasant but it has cheap set meals.

El Parador de Junín (Pasaje Junín No 53-53; set meals US$1.50, breakfast US$1) Another rock-bottom eatery, serving budget set meals and breakfasts.

Salón Versalles (Pasaje Junín No 53-39; set lunches US$3) Two-level restaurant-cum-café invariably popular with the locals. It has a varied menu including tasty set lunches, delicious Argentine and Chilean *empanadas* (fried pastry stuffed with rice, vegetables and meat; US$1 each) and a choice of high-calorie cakes and pastries.

Restaurante Hacienda Real (Pasaje Junín No 52-98; mains US$4-6) Pleasant second-story restaurant with a wide balcony, serving typical local food, including the omnipresent *bandeja paisa* (Antioquian dish of beef, sausage, red beans, rice, banana, egg, salt pork and avocado).

Restaurante Agua Clara (Pasaje Junín No 52-145; mains US$4-6) Regional food is served here and a band plays typical music on weekends.

Several budget vegetarian options offer set lunches for about US$2, including:
Restaurante Vegetariano Govinda's (Calle 51 No 52-17)
Restaurante Naturalista Palased (Carrera 50 Palacé No 52-50, Centro Comercial Unión Plaza)
Restaurante Vegetariano Trigo y Miel (Calle 53 Maracaibo No 43-54)

Restaurante Vegetariano Paracelso (Calle 52 Av La Playa No 43-17)

Drinking

The major scene of night-time dance and drink is the Zona Rosa in El Poblado, spreading approximately between Calles 9 and 10A, and Carreras 36 and 42. The area is packed with restaurants, cafés, clubs, bars, pubs and discos, which become vibrant after about 10pm, particularly on weekends. A taxi from the center will bring you to the Zona Rosa from the center of town for US$2.

La Cantera (Calle 10A No 38-20) One of the most popular haunts, with good, mostly Latin music and excellent sound quality.

Sam Pués (Calle 10A No 40-37) A trendy disco/bar with Caribbean music and often a great atmosphere.

República (Calle 10 No 40-15) A primarily Latin affair, blasting with salsa, merengue and the like.

Blue (Calle 10 No 40-20) Rock-music venue, with a sober modern interior.

Mango's (Carrera 42 No 67A-151) Arguably Medellín's best disco, with charming decor, five bars and a ragbag of good music. It's on Autopista Sur in Itagüí, away from El Poblado.

Entertainment

Check the local dailies, *El Colombiano* and *El Mundo*, for what's going on. Get a copy of the **Opción Hoy** (www.supernet.com.co/opcionhoy; price US$1), a local what's-on monthly that lists art exhibitions, theatre, concerts, arthouse cinema and sports and cultural events. You can read it online.

Museo de Arte Moderno (☎ 4-230-2622; Carrera 64B No 51-64) Medellín's best *cinemateca* (arthouse cinema) with a diverse and interesting program. Other arthouse cinemas are in the **Museo de Antioquia** (☎ 4-251-6888; Carrera 52 No 52-43) and the **Centro Colombo Americano** (☎ 4-513-4444; Carrera 45 No 53-24).

Teatro Matacandelas (☎ 4-239-1245; Carrera 47 No 43-47) One of the best experimental groups in town.

Teatro Pablo Tobón Uribe (☎ 4-239-2674; Carrera 40 No 51-24) Medellín's major mainstream theatre.

Pequeño Teatro de Medellín (☎ 4-269-9418; Carrera 42 No 50A-12) The varied repertoire here combines the traditional with more contemporary performances.

Getting There & Away

AIR
The main José María Córdoba airport, 35km southeast of the city, takes all international and most domestic flights, except for some regional flights on light planes, which use the old Olaya Herrera airport right inside the city. Frequent minibuses shuttle between the city center and the main airport from the corner of Carrera 50A and Calle 53 (US$2, one hour). A taxi costs US$15.

There are domestic flights throughout the country – to Bogotá (US$50 to US$110), Cali (US$80 to US$120), Cartagena (US$70 to US$120) and San Andrés (US$100 to US$140).

BUS
Medellín has two bus terminals. The Terminal del Norte, 3km north of the city center, handles buses to the north, east and southeast, including Santa Fe de Antioquia (US$3, three hours), Bogotá (US$17, nine hours), Cartagena (US$27, 13 hours) and Santa Marta (US$32, 16 hours). It's easily reached from the center by metro in seven minutes, or by taxi (US$2).

The Terminal del Sur, 4km southwest of the center, handles all traffic to the west and south, including Manizales (US$10, five hours), Cali (US$16, nine hours) and Popayán (US$20, 12 hours). It's accessible from the center by the Guayabal bus (Ruta No 143) and the Trinidad bus (Ruta No 160), both of which you catch on Av Oriental next to the Éxito San Antonio store. Alternatively, go by taxi (US$2).

Getting Around
Medellín is Colombia's first (and for the foreseeable future the only) city to have the metro, or fast metropolitan train. It is clean, cheap, safe and efficient, and has become a pride of the *paisas*. It took 10 years to build before it opened in 1995.

The metro consists of the 23km north–south line and a 6km western leg, and has 25 stations. The trains run on ground level except in the 5km stretch through central area where they go on viaducts above the streets, providing good views.

The metro operates 5am to 11pm Monday to Saturday, 7am to 10pm Sunday and holidays, with trains running every five

to 10 minutes. Single/double tickets cost US$0.35/0.60, or buy a 10-ride *multiviaje* for US$2.80.

Apart from the metro, urban transport is serviced by buses and *busetas*, and is quite well organized. All buses are numbered and display their destination point. The majority of routes originate on Av Oriental and Parque Berrío, from where you can get to almost anywhere within the metropolitan area.

AROUND MEDELLÍN
The picturesque, rugged region surrounding Medellín is sprinkled with haciendas and lovely little pueblos *paisas*, looking as if the 20th century got bogged somewhere down the road. With a few days to spare, take a trip around Medellín to see what Antioquia is really like. Before you set off however, check travel safety conditions.

Interesting places include the towns of **La Ceja**, **El Retiro** and **Marinilla**, which offer good examples of the regional architecture; **Carmen de Viboral**, known for its hand-painted ceramics; and the spectacular, 200m granite rock of **El Peñol**. Food and accommodation are available in all these places, and bus connections are frequent (all depart from Medellín's Terminal del Norte).

The last addition to the region's attractions is the **Parque de las Aguas**, an enjoyable amusement park full of waterslides, pools and other distractions. It's about 20km northeast of Medellín and has good transportation links with the city. Take the metro to the northern end of the line at Niquía and change to a bus.

SANTA FE DE ANTIOQUIA
Founded in 1541, this is the oldest town in the region. It was an important and prosperous center during Spanish days and the capital of Antioquia until 1826. The town's historic urban fabric has survived largely intact, with narrow cobbled streets, one-storey whitewashed houses and four churches. This is actually the only town in Antioquia which has preserved its colonial character. The town is 79km northwest of Medellín, on the road to Turbo.

Sights
Give yourself a couple of hours to wander about the streets to peruse the houses'

COLOMBIA

decorated doorways, windows with carved wooden guards and flower-bedecked patios. Of the town's churches, the 18th-century **Iglesia de Santa Bárbara** (Calle 11 at Carrera 8) is the most interesting, noted for its fine wide Baroque stone facade.

The **Museo de Arte Religioso** (☎ 4-853-2345; Calle 11 No 8-12; admission US$1; ❧ 10am-5pm Sat, Sun & holidays), next door to Santa Bárbara church, has a collection of religious objects, including paintings by Gregorio Vásquez de Arce y Ceballos.

The **Puente de Occidente**, an unusual 291m bridge over the Río Cauca, is 5km east of town. When completed in 1895, it was one of the first suspension bridges in the Americas. Walk there or negotiate a taxi in Santa Fe.

Sleeping & Eating

The town has a dozen hotels catering for different budgets and they are usually empty except for weekends when Medellín's city dwellers come to warm up.

Hospedaje Franco (☎ 4-853-1654; Carrera 10 No 8A-14; r without/with bath per person US$3/5) This basic but acceptable place is one of the cheapest in town and also serves some of the cheapest meals.

El Mesón de la Abuela (☎ 4-853-1053; Carrera 11 No 9-31; r per person US$4) Also known as Hospedaje Rafa, this place offers basic but acceptable rooms, some with bath. There's an attached restaurant.

Hostal del Viejo Conde (☎ 4-853-1091; Calle 9 No 10-56; r with bath per person US$4) A small budget place, much in the same class as the other two options here. It serves cheap meals.

Apart from the hotel restaurants, there are a dozen other places to eat. Don't miss the *pulpa de tamarindo*, a local tamarind sweet sold in the market on the main plaza.

Getting There & Away

There are half a dozen buses daily (US$3, three hours) and another half a dozen minibuses (US$4, 2½ hours) to and from Medellín's northern terminal.

SOUTHWEST COLOMBIA

The southwest covers the departments of Cauca, Valle del Cauca, Huila and Nariño. The region is widely diverse, both culturally and geographically. The biggest tourist attractions are the two outstanding archaeological sites of San Agustín and Tierradentro, and the colonial city of Popayán. Cali is the region's largest urban center.

CALI

Cali is a prosperous and lively city with a fairly hot climate. Although founded in 1536, its growth came only in the 20th century, primarily with the development of the sugar industry, followed by dynamic progress in other sectors. Today, Cali is Colombia's third-largest city, home to nearly two million people.

Apart from a few fine churches and museums, the city doesn't have many tourist attractions. Its appeal lies in its vibrant atmosphere and its amiable inhabitants, who are generally friendly and easygoing.

Cali is also noted for its salsa music. These hot rhythms originated in Cuba in the 1940s and spread throughout the Caribbean, reaching Colombia in the 1960s. The Cali region and the Caribbean coast remain Colombia's major centers of salsa music.

The women of Cali, *las caleñas*, are considered the most beautiful in the nation.

Orientation

The city center is split in two by the Río Cali. To the south is the historic heart, laid out on a grid plan and centered around the Plaza de Caycedo, which contains most tourist sights, including historic churches and museums.

To the north of the river is the new center, whose main axis is Av Sexta (Av 6N). This modern sector contains trendy shops and restaurants, and comes alive in the evening when a refreshing breeze tempers the daytime heat. This is the area to come to dine, drink and dance after a day of sightseeing on the opposite side of the river.

Information

INTERNET ACCESS

Internet access is fast and cheap (US$1 to US$1.50 per hour). Most cybercafés are in the new center, around Av Sexta. They include:

Cosmonet (Av 6N No 17N-65)
Cy@ncopias (Av 6N No 13N-23)
CyberMax (☎ 661 5945; Calle 12N No 4N-68)
Sc@nner (Av 6N No 15N-37)
SCI Sala de Internet (Av 6N No 13N-66) Largest and possibly the fastest central facility.

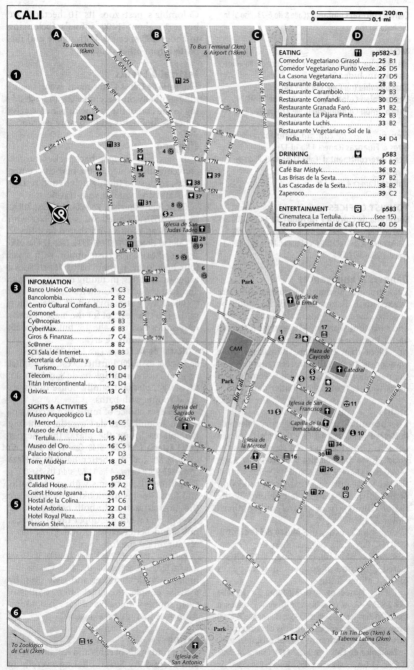

CALI

| 0 | 200 m |
| 0 | 0.1 mi |

EATING pp582–3
- Comedor Vegetariano Girasol....25 B1
- Comedor Vegetariano Punto Verde.26 D5
- La Casona Vegetariana.....27 D5
- Restaurante Balocco.....28 B3
- Restaurante Carambolo.....29 B3
- Restaurante Comfandi.....30 D5
- Restaurante Granada Faró.....31 B2
- Restaurante La Pájara Pinta.....32 B3
- Restaurante Luchis.....33 B2
- Restaurante Vegetariano Sol de la India.....34 D4

DRINKING p583
- Barahunda.....35 B2
- Café Bar Mistyk.....36 B2
- Las Brisas de la Sexta.....37 B2
- Las Cascadas de la Sexta.....38 B2
- Zaperoco.....39 C2

ENTERTAINMENT p583
- Cinemateca La Tertulia.....(see 15)
- Teatro Experimental de Cali (TEC)....40 D5

INFORMATION
- Banco Unión Colombiano.....1 C3
- Bancolombia.....2 B2
- Centro Cultural Comfandi.....3 D5
- Cosmonet.....4 B2
- Cy@ncopias.....5 B3
- CyberMax.....6 B3
- Giros & Finanzas.....7 C4
- Sc@nner.....8 B2
- SCI Sala de Internet.....9 B3
- Secretaría de Cultura y Turismo.....10 D4
- Telecom.....11 D4
- Titán Intercontinental.....12 D4
- Univisa.....13 C4

SIGHTS & ACTIVITIES p582
- Museo Arqueológico La Merced.....14 C5
- Museo de Arte Moderno La Tertulia.....15 A6
- Museo del Oro.....16 C5
- Palacio Nacional.....17 D3
- Torre Mudéjar.....18 D4

SLEEPING p582
- Calidad House.....19 A2
- Guest House Iguana.....20 A1
- Hostal de la Colina.....21 C6
- Hotel Astoria.....22 D4
- Hotel Royal Plaza.....23 C3
- Pensión Stein.....24 B5

To Juanchito (6km)
To Bus Terminal (2km) & Airport (18km)
To Zoológico de Cali (2km)
To Tin Tin Deo (1km) & Taberna Latina (2km)

COLOMBIA

Centro Cultural Comfandi (Calle 8 No 6-23, Piso 5) In the historic center.

MONEY

Banks changing foreign cash and traveler's checks include:

Bancolombia (cnr Calle 15N & Av 8N)
Banco Unión Colombiano (Carrera 3 No 11-03)
Banco Unión Colombiano (Calle 22N No 6N-22)

Central *casas de cambio* include:
Giros & Finanzas (Carrera 4 No 10-12)
Titán Intercontinental (Calle 11 No 4-48, Plaza de Caycedo)
Univisa (Carrera 4 No 8-67)

TOURIST OFFICES

Secretaría de Cultura y Turismo (☎ 2-620-0000 ext 2410; ⊗ 8am-12:30pm & 2:30-6pm Mon-Fri) The city tourist office is on the 1st floor of the building of Gobernación del Valle del Cauca.

Dangers & Annoyances

Even though Cali may look quieter and more relaxed than Bogotá or Medellín, don't be deceived by its easy-going air, summery heat and beautiful women. Muggers and thieves aren't inactive here, nor are they less clever or violent than elsewhere. Be careful while wandering around the streets at night. Avoid the park along Río Cali in the evening, and don't walk east of Calle 13 after dark.

Sights

The beautiful, mid-16th-century **Iglesia de la Merced** (cnr Carrera 4 & Calle 7) is Cali's oldest church. The adjacent monastery houses the good **Museo Arqueológico La Merced** (☎ 2-889-3434; Carrera 4 No 6-59; admission US$1; ⊗ 9am-1pm & 2-6pm Mon-Sat) featuring an extensive collection of pre-Hispanic pottery left behind by the major cultures from central and southern Colombia.

One block away, the **Museo del Oro** (☎ 2-684-7757; Calle 7 No 4-69; admission free; ⊗ 8am-11:30am & 2-6pm Mon-Fri) has a small but well-selected collection of gold and pottery pieces of the Calima culture.

The **Museo de Arte Moderno La Tertulia** (☎ 2-893-2942; Av Colombia No 5 Oeste-105; admission US$1; ⊗ 9am-1pm & 3-7pm Tue-Sat, 3-7pm Sun & Mon) presents temporary exhibitions of contemporary painting, sculpture and photography.

Zoológico de Cali (☎ 2-892-7474; Carrera 2A Oeste at Calle 14 Oeste; admission US$2.50; ⊗ 9am-5pm) is

Colombia's best zoo. Its 10 hectares are home to about 1200 animals (belonging to about 180 species), both native and imported from other continents.

Festival & Events

The **Feria de Cali** is Cali's main event, beginning annually on December 25 and extending to the end of the year with parades, salsa concerts, bullfights and a beauty pageant.

Sleeping

Cali has two budget backpacker hostels conveniently located in the new city center. They are close to the nightclubs and restaurants and are popular with travelers.

Guest House Iguana (☎ 2-661-3522; Calle 21N No 9N-22; s/d US$7/10) Quiet, Swiss-run place with ample clean rooms with shared facilities.

Calidad House (☎ 2-661-2338; Calle 17N No 9AN-39; r per person US$5) A basic option with small four-bed dorms without baths. It provides a range of facilities, including laundry service and free use of the kitchen.

There are not many budget hotels south of the Río Cali, except for the maze of seedy *hospedajes* east of Calle 15, but don't walk there – it's an unsafe area.

Hostal de la Colina (☎ 2-893-7991; Carrera 12 No 2-54; s/d US$15/20) Further west, in a quiet residential area near Iglesia de San Antonio, this large, pleasant family house offers six good rooms with baths.

There's a choice of mid-price accommodation around Plaza de Caycedo, including two places lining the plaza: the cheaper **Hotel Astoria** (☎ 2-883-0140; Calle 11 No 5-16; s/d/t US$14/18/22) and the better **Hotel Royal Plaza** (☎ 2-883-9243; Carrera 4 No 11-69; s/d/t US$25/30/35). Both hotels have rooms with private baths and fans. Rooms overlooking the plaza are the most attractive. In both hotels, ask for a room on one of the upper floors, for less noise and better views. Royal Plaza has a restaurant on the top floor.

Pensión Stein (☎ 2-661-4999; Av 4N No 3N-33; s/d with fan US$24/40, with air-con US$34/48) Castle-like mansion with character and style. Run by a Swiss couple, the hotel offers spotlessly clean rooms with bath and has a restaurant. All prices include breakfast.

Eating

You'll find loads of cafés and restaurants on and around Av Sexta, offering everything from simple snacks, burgers and pizzas to regional Colombian specialties and ethnic cuisines. The historic center also has plenty of budget eateries, but not many upmarket restaurants.

Restaurante Balocco (Av 6N No 14N-04; set meals US$1.75) This long-established budget restaurant in the mid-section of Av Sexta is popular with locals.

Restaurante Luchis (Calle 18N No 9N-111; set meals US$2, mains US$3) Small, family-run place in the new center, which offers both vegetarian and nonvegetarian dishes.

Restaurante Comfandi (Carrera 6 No 8-22; set lunches US$2) Simple self-service lunchtime restaurant in the old center, hugely popular among locals.

The old center provides a choice of budget vegetarian eateries, including:

La Casona Vegetariana (Carrera 6 No 6-56; set meals US$2)

Restaurante Vegetariano Sol de la India (Carrera 6 No 8-48; set meals US$2)

Comedor Vegetariano Punto Verde (Carrera 6 No 7-40; set meals US$2)

Comedor Vegetariano Girasol (Av 5BN No 20N-30; set meals US$1.75) Try this place in the new center.

For fine dining, try some of the well-appointed restaurants on or just off Av 9N in the new center.

Restaurante Carambolo (Calle 14N No 9N-18; mains US$6-10) This cozy and charmingly informal place is spread over two levels and is full of flowers. It cooks fine Mediterranean food.

Restaurante Granada Faró (Av 9N No 15AN-02; mains US$7-10) In a trendy locale with an artistic touch, and decorated with paintings, Granada Faró serves international, mostly Mediterranean cuisine, including great salads.

Restaurante La Pájara Pinta (Av 9N No 12N-76; mains US$7-10) This spacious rambling mansion provides different ambiences with each room and a great outdoor eating area. The service is first class, as is the food (international cuisine), even though the portions are rather small.

Drinking

There are lots of bars, discos and night-clubs in the new center. You'll find half a dozen discos around the corner of Av 6N and Calle 16N. Most places don't have a cover fee, so it's easy to move from one to the next.

Las Brisas de la Sexta (Av 6N No 15N-94) One of the largest and most popular haunts.

Las Cascadas de la Sexta (Av 6N No 16N-18) Boasting seven large screens and four dance floors, just across the street from Las Brisas de la Sexta.

Zaperoco (Av 5N No 16N-52) Tucked away a bit, this cozy and likeable *salsoteca* has magnetic salsa rhythms and a hot atmosphere.

Several attractive bars have mushroomed on Calle 17N between Av 8N and Av 9N.

The **Barahunda** (Calle 17N No 8N-60) This was the happening place at the time of research, but check the others, including Café Bar Mistyk, directly across the street.

Another center of night-time entertainment is on and around Calle 5 in southern Cali, where you'll find two trendy discos: **Taberna Latina** (Calle 5 No 38-75) and **Tin Tin Deo** (Carrera 22 No 4A-27). Both are frequented by university students and professors, adding an intellectual feel to the action.

Cali's best known salsa nightlife is in the legendary Juanchito, a popular, predominantly black outer suburb on the Río Cauca. Far away from the center, Juanchito was traditionally an archetypal salsa haunt dotted with dubious cafés and bars. Today, sterile and expensive *salsotecas* have replaced most of the old shady but charming watering holes.

Juanchito's most famous salsa place is Changó, which is also probably the priciest. Agapito, next door, is cheaper and not necessarily poorer. Parador is frequented by some of the most acrobatic dancers in town. Come on the weekend and take a taxi. Note that the action starts late: places open at around 10pm and get rowdy by midnight, peaking at about 2am.

Entertainment

Check the entertainment columns of the local newspaper *El País*.

Cinemateca La Tertulia (☎ 2-893-2942; Av Colombia No 5 Oeste-105) Cali's best arthouse cinema, in the Museo de Arte Moderno La Tertulia.

Teatro Experimental de Cali (TEC; ☎ 2-884-3820; Calle 7 No 8-61) Colombia's national theatre started with the foundation of this company. It continues to be one of the city's most innovative theatre companies.

COLOMBIA

Getting There & Away

AIR

The Palmaseca airport is 16km northeast of the city. Minibuses between the airport and the bus terminal run every 10 minutes until about 8pm (US$1, 30 minutes), or take a taxi (US$12).

There are plenty of flights to most major Colombian cities, including Bogotá (US$50 to US$110), Cartagena (US$80 to US$130), Medellín (US$80 to US$120), Pasto (US$50 to US$100) and San Andrés (US$100 to US$150). Aires and Satena fly to Ipiales (US$60 to US$100). Satena has daily flights to Guapí (US$50).

Avianca flies to Panama City (60-day return ticket US$268), while Tame has three flights a week to Tulcán in Ecuador (one way US$84) and to Quito (US$118).

BUS

The bus terminal is a 25-minute walk northeast of the city center, or 10 minutes by one of the frequent city buses. Buses run regularly to Bogotá (US$20, 12 hours), Medellín (US$16, nine hours) and Pasto (US$12, nine hours). Pasto buses will drop you off at Popayán (US$4, three hours) and there are also hourly minibuses to Popayán (US$5, 2½ hours).

AROUND CALI
Historic Haciendas

There are a number of old haciendas in the Cauca Valley around Cali. Most of them date from the 18th and 19th centuries and were engaged in the cultivation and processing of sugar cane, the region's major crop. The two best known are the **Hacienda El Paraíso** (☎ 2-256-2378; admission US$1.50; ☻ 9am-4pm Tue-Sun) and **Hacienda Piedechinche** (☎ 2-438-4950; admission US$1.50; ☻ 9am-4pm Tue-Sun), both about 40km northeast of Cali and open as museums. There are tours from Cali on weekends, or you can visit them on your own using public transport, though both places are off the main roads. Take any bus to Buga and get off on the outskirts of **Amaime** (the drivers know where to drop you). Then walk to Piedechinche (5.5km) or negotiate a taxi. El Paraíso is still further off the road.

San Cipriano

This village is lost deep in the tropical forest near the Pacific coast, off the Cali–Buenaventura road. There's no road leading to the village, just a railway with occasional trains, but the locals have set up their own rail network with small man-propelled trolleys. This ingenious means of transport is a great attraction and justifies a San Cipriano trip if only for the ride.

San Cipriano has a crystal-clear river, ideal for swimming, informal budget accommodation and some simple places to eat. The village is a popular weekend destination with *caleños* (residents of Cali), but it's quiet on weekdays.

To get there from Cali, take a bus or *colectivo* to Buenaventura, get off at the village of Córdoba (US$3, two hours) and walk down the hill into the village to the railway track. From here, locals will take you to San Cipriano in their rail cars (US$1) – a great journey through the rain forest.

Check for safety conditions before setting off from Cali. There have been occasional reports of guerrillas along the Cali–Buenaventura road.

ISLA GORGONA

Lying 56km off the mainland, the 9km-long and 2.5km-wide Gorgona is Colombia's largest Pacific island. It's a mountainous island of volcanic origin, with the highest peak reaching 330m. It's covered with lush tropical rain forest and shelters diverse wildlife, including various monkeys, lizards, turtles, snakes and bird species, a number of which are endemic. There are some beaches and coral reefs along the shores, and the surrounding waters seasonally host dolphins, humpback whales and sperm whales. The climate is hot and wet, with high humidity and no distinctive dry season.

The island was a cruel high-security prison during La Violencia until 1984, but is now a **national park** (admission US$7.50; dm US$12; 3 set meals US$12). It offers accommodations in a four-bed dorm with bath, food and trips around the island (all excursions are accompanied by guides). You can also swim, sunbathe and snorkel (bring your own gear).

To visit Gorgona, you need a permit from the national park office in Bogotá. Booking long in advance is advisable, especially for Colombian vacation periods. All visits are fixed four-day/three-night stays, which must be paid for in advance.

The usual departure point for Isla Gorgona is Buenaventura (a three-hour bus trip from Cali), where you catch a (usually overcrowded) cargo boat for a 10- to 12-hour night trip to the island (about US$30). It can be a hellish experience if the sea is rough. Since the access road to Buenaventura was targeted by the guerrillas on various occasions in the past and may be not 100% safe, some travelers and most tours began to use Guapí as a launching pad for Gorgona. Guapí is a seaside village in Cauca, just opposite Gorgona. Guapí is not connected by road with the rest of the country but can be reached by air on daily flights from Cali with Satena (US$50). From Guapí, boats take up to 10 tourists to Gorgona in less than two hours (about US$200 per boat). For information and reservations, call ☎ 2-825-7137 or ☎ 2-825-7136.

If you desire more comfort, several Cali tour companies organize trips to Gorgona for US$250 to US$300. Try **Ecolombia Tours** (☎ 2-557-1957; ecolombiatours@yahoo.com; Carrera 37A No 6-18), which is arguably Cali's best specialist for tours to Isla Gorgona.

POPAYÁN

Popayán is one of the most beautiful colonial cities in Colombia. Founded in 1537, the town quickly became an important political, cultural and religious center, and was an obligatory stopover on the route between Cartagena and Quito. Its mild climate attracted wealthy Spanish settlers from the sugar haciendas of the hot Cali region. Several imposing churches and monasteries were built in the 17th and 18th centuries, when the city was flourishing.

During the 20th century, while many Colombian cities were caught up in the race to modernize and industrialize, Popayán somehow managed to retain its colonial character. Ironically, many historic structures, including most of the churches, were seriously damaged by an earthquake in March 1983, just moments before the much-celebrated Maundy Thursday religious procession was due to depart. The difficult and costly restoration work continued for nearly two decades, and the results are admirable – little damage can be seen today and the city looks even better than it did before the disaster.

Apart from its beauty, Popayán is a friendly, tranquil and clean city. It has competent tourist offices, a range of places to stay and eat and is not expensive by Colombian standards. And it's also pretty safe, unlike some parts of the surrounding region.

Information

INTERNET ACCESS

Popayán's cybercafés are cheap (US$1 per hour or less) and include:

C@feto (Carrera 9 No 5-42)
El Universitario (Carrera 6 No 3-47)
Todo Punto Com (Calle 3 No 5-81)

MONEY

Few of Popayán's banks change cash and/or traveler's checks, but fortunately, there are several *casas de cambio*, including:

Cambios Country (Carrera 7 No 6-41)
Titán Intercontinental (Carrera 7 No 6-40, Centro Comercial Luis Martínez, Interior 106)
Unidas (Carrera 6 No 5-44)

TOURIST OFFICES

Popayán has two tourist offices:
Oficina de Turismo de Popayán (☎ 2-824-2251; Carrera 5 No 4-68; ✆ 8am-noon & 2-6pm Mon-Fri, 9am-1pm Sat & Sun)
Policía de Turismo (☎ 2-822-0916; Edificio de Gobernación, Parque Caldas; ✆ 8am-noon & 2-6pm Mon-Fri)

Sights

Popayán has some good museums, most of which are set in splendid historic buildings. **Casa Museo Mosquera** (☎ 2-824-0683; Calle 3 No 5-38; admission US$1; ✆ 8:30am-noon & 2-5:30pm Tue-Sun) is a great colonial mansion that was home to General Tomás Cipriano de Mosquera, Colombia's president between 1845 and 1867. The museum contains personal memorabilia and a collection of colonial art, including some religious objects.

Museo Arquidiocesano de Arte Religioso (☎ 2-824-2759; Calle 4 No 4-56; admission US$1; ✆ 8:30am-12:30pm & 2:30-5:30pm Mon-Fri, 10am-3pm Sat) has an extensive collection of religious art, including paintings, statues, altarpieces, silverware and liturgical vessels, most of which date from the 17th to 19th century. **Museo Guillermo Valencia** (☎ 2-824-2081; Carrera 6 No 2-65; admission US$1; ✆ 10am-noon & 2-5pm Tue-Sun), dedicated to the Popayán-born poet who once lived here, is full of period

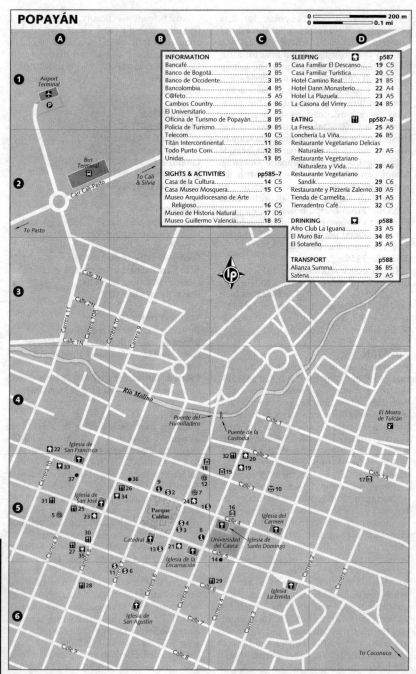

POPAYÁN

0 — 200 m
0 — 0.1 mi

INFORMATION
Bancafé................................**1** B5
Banco de Bogotá...................**2** B5
Banco de Occidente.............**3** B5
Bancolombia.........................**4** B5
C@feto..................................**5** A5
Cambios Country...................**6** B6
El Universitario......................**7** B5
Oficina de Turismo de Popayán.....**8** B5
Policía de Turismo................**9** B5
Telecom...............................**10** C5
Titán Intercontinental.........**11** B6
Todo Punto Com..................**12** B5
Unidas.................................**13** B5

SIGHTS & ACTIVITIES pp585–7
Casa de la Cultura................**14** C5
Casa Museo Mosquera.........**15** C5
Museo Arquidiocesano de Arte
  Religioso............................**16** C5
Museo de Historia Natural....**17** D5
Museo Guillermo Valencia....**18** B5

SLEEPING p587
Casa Familiar El Descanso.....**19** C5
Casa Familiar Turística..........**20** C5
Hotel Camino Real...............**21** B5
Hotel Dann Monasterio.........**22** A4
Hotel La Plazuela.................**23** A5
La Casona del Virrey.............**24** B5

EATING pp587–8
La Fresa...............................**25** A5
Lonchería La Viña................**26** B5
Restaurante Vegetariano Delicias
  Naturales...........................**27** A5
Restaurante Vegetariano
  Naturaleza y Vida...............**28** A6
Restaurante Vegetariano
  Sandik................................**29** C6
Restaurante y Pizzería Zalerno.....**30** A5
Tienda de Carmelita.............**31** A5
Tierradentro Café.................**32** C5

DRINKING p588
Afro Club La Iguana.............**33** A5
El Muro Bar.........................**34** B5
El Sotareño.........................**35** A5

TRANSPORT p588
Alianza Summa.....................**36** B5
Satena.................................**37** A5

Airport Terminal

Bus Terminal

Carr Cali-Pasto

To Cali & Silvia

To Pasto

Calle 3N
Calle 2N
Calle 1N
Carrera 11
Carrera 10A
Carrera 10
Carrera 9

Río Molino

Puente del Humilladero
Puente de la Custodia
Calle 1
Calle 2
Calle 3

El Morro de Tulcán

Iglesia de San Francisco
Carrera 10
Iglesia de San José
Carrera 9

Parque Caldas

Catedral
Iglesia de la Encarnación

Iglesia del Carmen

Universidad del Cauca
Iglesia de Santo Domingo

Calle 1A

Calle 4
Calle 5

Iglesia La Ermita

Iglesia de San Agustín
Calle 6
Carrera 6
Carrera 5
Carrera 4
Carrera 3
Carrera 2
Carrera 1

Calle 7
Calle 8
Calle 9

To Coconuco

COLOMBIA

furniture, paintings, old photos and documents related to him.

Museo de Historia Natural (☎ 2-820-1952; Carrera 2 No 1A-25; admission US$1.50; ☽ 8:30am-noon & 2-5pm Tue-Sun) is noted for its collections of insects, butterflies and, in particular, stuffed birds. Part of the top floor is taken up by an archaeological display of pre-Columbian pottery from southern Colombia.

All the colonial churches were meticulously restored after the 1983 earthquake. The **Iglesia de San Francisco** (Carrera 9 at Calle 4) is the city's largest colonial church and arguably the best, with its fine high altar and a collection of seven amazing side altarpieces. Other colonial churches noted for their rich original furnishings include the **Iglesia de Santo Domingo** (Carrera 5 at Calle 4), **Iglesia de San José** (Calle 5 at Carrera 8) and the **Iglesia de San Agustín** (Calle 7 at Carrera 6).

Iglesia La Ermita (Calle 5 at Carrera 2) is Popayán's oldest church (1546), worth seeing for its fine main retable and for the fragments of old frescoes, which were only discovered after the earthquake. The neoclassical **Catedral** (Parque Caldas) is the youngest church in the center, built between 1859 and 1906. It was almost completely destroyed by the earthquake and subsequently rebuilt from the ground up.

Walk to the river to see two unusual old bridges. The small one, the **Puente de la Custodia**, was constructed in 1713 to allow the priests to cross the river to bring the holy orders to the sick of the poor northern suburb. About 160 years later, the solid 178m-long 12-arch **Puente del Humilladero** was built alongside the old bridge, and it's still in use.

Museums, churches and bridges are only a part of what Popayán has to offer. The best approach is to take a leisurely walk along the streets lined with whitewashed colonial mansions, savor the architectural details and drop inside to see the marvelous patios (many are open to the public).

Festivals & Events

If you are in the area during Holy Week, you'll have the chance to see the famous night-time processions on Maundy Thursday and Good Friday. Popayán's Easter celebrations are the most elaborate in the country. The festival of religious music is held concurrently.

> **SPLURGE!**
>
> Popayán features some splendid historic mansions that have been refashioned as stylish hotels, including **Hotel La Plazuela** (☎ 824 1084; Calle 5 No 8-13; s/d/t US$30/40/50) and **Hotel Camino Real** (☎ 2-824-3595; Calle 5 No 5-59; s/d/t US$35/45/55). All rooms have private baths and the prices include breakfast.
>
> **Hotel Dann Monasterio** (☎ 2-824-2191; Calle 4 No 10-14; s/d US$50/60) In a great colonial building with a vast courtyard that was once a Franciscan monastery, this is Popayán's top-notch offering. It has 48 spacious refurbished rooms, a fine restaurant and a swimming pool (the only hotel with a pool in town).

Sleeping

Popayán has an array of accommodation to suit every pocket. Many hotels are set in old colonial houses and are stylish and atmospheric.

Casa Familiar Turística (☎ 2-824-4853; Carrera 5 No 2-07; r per person US$3) One of the cheapest hotels in town. Basic but acceptable. It has just four rooms, all with shared facilities.

Casa Familiar El Descanso (☎ 2-824-0019; Carrera 5 No 2-41; r per person US$5) A slightly better but pricier option with shared baths.

La Casona del Virrey (☎ 2-824-0836; Calle 4 No 5-78; r per person US$6, s/d/t with bath US$11/17/24) Colonial building with style and character. Choose one of the ample rooms facing the street. There are also some cheaper rooms without bath.

Eating

Popayán has plenty of places to eat and the food is relatively cheap.

Lonchería La Viña (Calle 4 No 7-79; set meals US$1.75, mains US$3-5) One of the best and most popular budget eateries. It has tasty food, generous portions and is open until midnight or even longer.

Restaurante y Pizzeria Zalermo (Carrera 8 No 5-100; set meals US$1.75, mains US$3-7) This new place has already become popular with locals. It's open until late and has a wide selection including pizzas and chicken.

La Fresa (Calle 5 No 8-89) From a small cubbyhole with no sign on the door, delicious, cheap *empanadas de pipián* (a type of fried pastry) are served.

Tienda de Carmelita (Calle 5 No 9-45) An unsigned place that serves good *tamales de pipián*.

Tierradentro Café (Carrera 5 No 2-12) The best choice of espressos and cappuccinos in town, with 90 different flavors. An important stop for coffee addicts.

Try the following places for tasty, budget vegetarian meals.

Restaurante Vegetariano Sandik (Calle 6 No 4-52)

Restaurante Vegetariano Delicias Naturales (Calle 6 No 8-21)

Restaurante Vegetariano Naturaleza y Vida (Carrera 8 No 7-19)

Drinking

El Sotareño (Calle 6 No 8-05) Legendary rustic bar with a 40-year history. It plays nostalgic old rhythms such as tango, bolero, ranchera and milonga from scratched vinyls probably as old as the place itself, and serves some of the cheapest beer in town.

Afro Club La Iguana (Calle 4 No 9-67) Bar with excellent salsa and Cuban son music at high volume, which is so hot and exciting that people rush to dance all over the place, especially on weekends.

El Muro Bar (Carrera 8 No 4-11) Quiet bar playing soft rock and Latin ballads. There are several other places in the same area, which came to be regarded as Popayán's Zona Rosa.

Getting There & Away

AIR

The airport is just behind the bus terminal, a 15-minute walk north of the city center. Satena have daily flights to Bogotá (US$70 to US$80).

BUS

The bus terminal is a short walk north of the city center. Note that traveling on some roads out of Popayán may be risky. Read the information listed here and check for recent news with the tourist offices.

Plenty of buses run to Cali (US$4, three hours), and there are also minibuses and *colectivos* every hour or so. Buses to Bogotá run every hour or two (US$24, 15 hours).

You shouldn't wait more than an hour for a bus to Pasto (US$8, six hours), but this spectacular road may be unsafe to travel. Buses have been ambushed (mostly at night) and passengers robbed over the past decade. More recently, guerrillas have been stopping the traffic and burning buses or trucks, thus blocking the road, but passengers were not harassed or robbed. If you plan to travel on this road, do it during daytime only.

For Tierradentro, take the Sotracauca bus at 8am or 10:30am, which will take you directly to San Andrés de Pisimbalá (US$6, five to six hours), passing the museum en route. Other buses (three daily) will drop you off in El Cruce de San Andrés, from where you have to walk 20 minutes to the museum plus another 25 minutes to San Andrés. The region between Popayán and Tierradentro is known for guerrilla presence.

Three buses daily (two with Cootranshuila and one with Sotracauca) run to San Agustín via Coconuco and Isnos (US$8, seven to eight hours). The road is rough, but the trip through the lush cordillera cloud forest is spectacular. Part of this road is controlled by guerrillas and they have even put up permanent checkpoints on the road. They stop passing traffic, check tourists' passports and let them go. So far, there haven't been any life-threatening incidents involving travelers, nor any hostages taken here.

SILVIA

A small town 60km northeast of Popayán, Silvia is the center of the Guambianos, one of the most traditional Indian communities in Colombia. Though the Indians don't live in the town, they come to Silvia for the Tuesday market to sell fruit, vegetables and handicrafts. This is possibly the most colorful Indian gathering in the country and the best day to visit Silvia, an attractive day trip from Popayán. You'll see plenty of Indians in traditional dress, the women in hand-woven garments and beaded necklaces, busily spinning wool. Bring a sweater – it can get cold when the weather is cloudy. If you decide to stay longer in Silvia, there are at least half a dozen budget hotels.

To get to Silvia from Popayán, take the Coomotoristas bus or Tax Belalcázar minibus (US$1.50, 1½ hours). On Tuesday, there are also *colectivos* between Popayán and Silvia.

SAN AGUSTÍN

This is one of the continent's most important archaeological sites. The area was inhabited by a mysterious pre-Columbian civilization

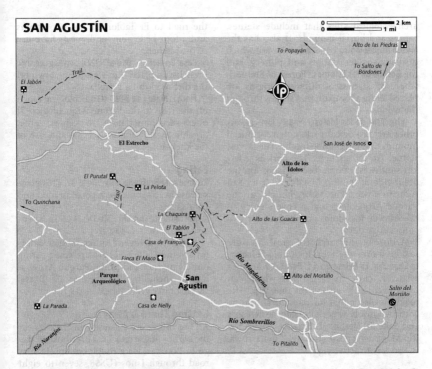

SAN AGUSTÍN

that left behind hundreds of freestanding monumental statues carved in stone. The site was a ceremonial center where locals buried their dead and placed the statues next to the tombs. Pottery and gold objects were left in the tombs of the tribal elders.

San Agustín culture flourished between the 6th and 14th centuries AD. The best statuary was made only in the last phase of the development, and the culture had presumably vanished before the Spaniards came. The statues were not discovered until the middle of the 18th century.

So far, some 500 statues have been found and excavated. A great number are anthropomorphic figures – some of them realistic, others very stylized, resembling masked monsters. Others are zoomorphic, depicting sacred animals such as the eagle, the jaguar and the frog. The statues vary both in size, from about 20cm to 7m, and in their degree of detail.

The area around San Agustín has witnessed some intensive guerrilla activity over recent years. Fewer travelers come these days to visit the statues and a number of

hotels and restaurants have closed. Check the current state of safety conditions before you come.

Orientation & Information

The statues and tombs are scattered in groups over a wide area on both sides of the gorge formed by the upper Río Magdalena. The main town of the region, San Agustín, shelters most of the accommodations and restaurants. From there, you can explore the region on foot, horseback or by jeep; give yourself three days for leisurely visits to the most interesting places.

It's hard to change traveler's checks in San Agustín. US currency can be exchanged at some travel businesses but at poor rates. It's best to come with a cache of pesos. The **Banco Agrario** (Carrera 13 at Calle 4) gives peso advances on Visa, but not on MasterCard.

Sights

The 78-hectare **Parque Arqueológico** (admission US$2; ☼ 8am-6pm), 2.5km west of the town of San Agustín, features some of the best of San Agustín statuary. The park covers several archaeological sites that include statues, tombs and burial mounds. It also has the **Museo Arqueológico** (8am-5pm Tue-Sun) which displays smaller statues and pottery, and the **Bosque de las Estatuas** (Forest of Statues), where 35 statues of different origins are placed along a footpath that snakes through the woods.

The **Alto de los Ídolos** (8am-4pm) is another archaeological park, noted for burial mounds and large stone tombs. The largest statue, 7m tall, is here. The park is a few km southwest of San José de Isnos, on the other side of the Río Magdalena from San Agustín town. The ticket bought at the Parque Arqueológico also covers entry to the Alto de los Ídolos and is valid for two consecutive days.

A dozen other archaeological sites are scattered over the area, including **El Tablón**, **La Chaquira**, **La Pelota** and **El Purutal**, four sites relatively close to each other which can be conveniently visited on one trip. The region is also noted for its natural beauty, with two lovely waterfalls, **Salto de Bordones** and **Salto del Mortiño**. **El Estrecho**, where the Río Magdalena passes through 2m narrows, is also an attractive sight.

Sleeping

There's a dozen budget hotels in and around San Agustín, most of which are clean and friendly and have hot water. Unless stated otherwise, the hotels listed below charge US$2 to US$3 per person in rooms without bath, US$3 to US$4 with private bath.

Hospedaje El Jardín (8-837-3455; Carrera 11 No 4-10) Basic but neat option near the bus offices, offering rooms with and without private baths.

Hotel Colonial (8-837-3159; Calle 3 No 11-54) Close to the bus offices, Hotel Colonial has rooms with and without baths, and a reasonable restaurant.

Hotel Ullumbe (8-837-3799; Carrera 13 No 3-36) Central location. Rooms have private baths and there's a laundry service.

Residencias Menezú (8-837-3693; Carrera 15 No 4-74) Clean rooms with shared baths and hot water.

There are more budget options outside the town, and these are possibly the most popular with travelers.

Casa de François (8-837-3847) Pleasant French-run hostel 1km north of town, off the road to El Tablón. It has two rooms and a four-bed cabin, and guests have use of the kitchen.

Casa de Nelly (8-837-3221) An agreeable French-run place 1km west of the town off the dirt road to La Estrella.

Finca El Maco (8-837-3437) Ecological ranch off the road to the Parque Arqueológico. It offers accommodation in cabins, great organic meals, laundry service and use of the kitchen.

Eating

Restaurante Brahama (Calle 5 No 15-11) This place serves cheap set meals, vegetarian food and fruit salads.

Restaurante Surabhi (Calle 5 No 14-09) Inexpensive meals are served here.

You'll find several other budget eateries around Calle 5. There are some eating outlets on the road to the Parque Arqueológico, including Restaurante La Brasa, serving tasty grilled meat.

Getting There & Away

All bus offices are clustered on Calle 3 near the corner of Carrera 11. Three buses a day go to Popayán via a rough but spectacular road through Isnos (US$8, seven to eight hours). Guerrillas stop the traffic on this route but so far have let tourists pass by without problems.

Coomotor has two buses daily to Bogotá (US$15, 12 hours). There's also a faster and more comfortable Taxis Verdes van service (US$18, 10 hours).

There are no direct buses to Tierradentro; go to La Plata (US$7, five hours) and change for a bus to El Cruce de San Andrés (US$3, 2½ hours), from where it's a 20-minute walk to the Tierradentro museum. La Plata has several cheap hotels.

Getting Around

The usual way of visiting San Agustín's sights (apart from the Parque Arqueológico) is by jeep tours and horse riding excursions. The standard jeep tour includes El Estrecho, Alto de los Ídolos, Alto de las Piedras, Salto de Bordones and Salto de Mortiño. It takes seven to eight hours and costs US$10 per person if there are six people to fill the jeep, or US$13 if there are four. Since few tourists come here these days, there are few jeep tours, or you pay for the empty seats.

Horse rental can be arranged through hotel managers or directly with horse owners who frequently approach tourists. Horses are hired out for a specific route, or by the hour (US$2), half day (US$6) or full day (US$10). One of the most popular horse riding trips (US$6 per horse, around five hours) includes El Tablón, La Chaquira, La Pelota and El Purutal. If you need a guide to accompany your party, add US$6 for the guide and another US$6 for his horse.

TIERRADENTRO

Tierradentro is an archaeological site noted for its underground burial chambers, the only such example in the Americas. They are elaborate circular tombs ranging from 2m to 7m in diameter, scooped out of the soft rock in the slopes and tops of hills. The dome-like ceilings of the larger vaults are supported by massive pillars. The chambers have been hewn out to house the cremated remains of tribal elders. They were painted in geometric patterns in red and black (representing life and death, respectively) on a white background, and the decoration

in some of them has been remarkably well preserved.

About a hundred tombs have been discovered to date, as well as several dozen stone statues similar to those of San Agustín, probably the product of a broad cultural influence. Not much is known about the people who built the tombs and statues. Most likely, they were from different cultures, and the people who scooped out the tombs preceded those who carved the statues. Today, the region is inhabited by the Páez Indians, who have lived here since before the Spanish conquest, but it is doubtful whether they are the descendants of the statue sculptors.

Much like San Agustín, the Tierradentro region has been notorious for guerrilla presence in recent years. Guerillas have been held responsible for various cases of killings and the kidnapping of locals. Very few foreigners visit Tierradentro these days. Check for the safety conditions before you go.

Orientation & Information

Tierradentro is far away from any significant urban centers and is only accessible by

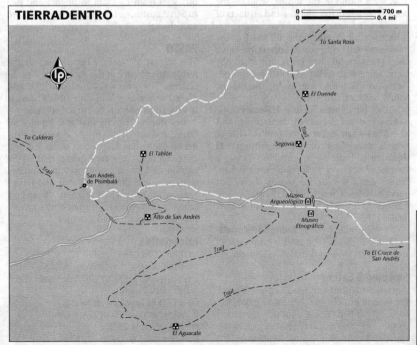

TIERRADENTRO

0 ——— 700 m
0 ——— 0.4 mi

To Santa Rosa

El Duende

To Calderas

Segovia

El Tablón

San Andrés de Pisimbalá

Museo Arqueológico

Alto de San Andrés

Museo Etnográfico

To El Cruce de San Andrés

Trail

El Aguacate

dirt roads. You can get there from Popayán and San Agustín, but in each case it's a rough half-day bus ride.

Once in Tierradentro, you have four sites with tombs and one with statues, as well as two museums and the village of San Andrés de Pisimbalá. Except for the burial site of El Aguacate, all the sights are within easy walking distance. You can also visit them on horseback; horses are rented out near the museums and in San Andrés (US$8 per day). A flashlight is necessary for almost all the tombs – make sure to bring one with you.

There are no tourist office or money changing facilities in Tierradentro. General information is available from the museum staff and hotel managers.

Sights

Begin your visit from the two museums, right across the road from one another. One combined ticket (US$2) is valid for two consecutive days to all archaeological sites and the **museums** (🕙 8am-5pm). The **Museo Arqueológico** contains pottery urns that were found in the tombs, whereas the **Museo Etnográfico** has utensils and artifacts of the Páez Indians.

A 20-minute walk up the hill north of the museums will bring you to **Segovia**, the most important burial site. There are 28 tombs here, some with well-preserved decoration. Seven of the tombs are lit; for the others, you'll need a flashlight.

Other burial sites include **El Duende** (four tombs without preserved decoration) and the **Alto de San Andrés** (five tombs, two of which have their original paintings). **El Aguacate** is high on a mountain ridge, a two-hour one-way walk from the museum. There are a few dozen tombs there, but most have been destroyed by the *guaqueros*. Statues have been gathered together at **El Tablón**.

The tiny village of **San Andrés de Pisimbalá**, a 25-minute walk west of the museums, is noted for its beautiful thatched church.

Sleeping & Eating

Accommodations and food in Tierradentro are simple but cheap – expect to pay US$2 to US$3 per bed. There's nothing upmarket in the area. You can stay either close to the museums or in San Andrés de Pisimbalá.

Residencias Lucerna This house just up the road from the museums, is clean, pleasant and friendly.

Hospedaje Pisimbalá (set meals US$1.50) About 150m beyond Residencias Lucerna, this is one of the cheapest places for accommodation and food. Another 150m further up the road is the budget Residencias Ricabet.

Hotel El Refugio (s/d US$10/15) Next to Residencias Ricabet is this more expensive hotel, but prices fall in the low season. The hotel has a swimming pool and a restaurant.

Los Lagos de Tierradentro In San Andrés de Pisimbalá, there are three budget *residencias*, of which this is the cheapest. The family who run it serve meals and rent horses.

Getting There & Away

Only two buses a day call at San Andrés de Pisimbalá. Most buses just pass El Cruce de San Andrés, from where you need to walk to the museums (20 minutes).

Three or four buses daily pass via El Cruce on their way to Popayán (US$6, five to six hours), and the same number to La Plata (US$2.50, 2½ hours). Two direct buses go from La Plata to Bogotá and two to San Agustín, or take a *colectivo* to Pitalito and change.

PASTO

The capital of Nariño, Pasto is set in the fertile Atriz Valley at the foot of the Volcán Galeras. The town was founded in 1537 and played an active role in Colombia's history. It was an important cultural and religious center during the colonial and republican times, and is today home to 350,000 inhabitants. Pasto has lost much of its historic character because of earthquakes that hit the city on various occasions, yet its churches were rebuilt in the original style and reflect some of the town's past splendor. It can be a relaxing stop on a long Panamericana route between Colombia and Ecuador.

Information

INTERNET ACCESS

Internet access is relatively slow in Pasto. Expect to pay US$1 to US$2 per hour. Central facilities include:

Ciber C@fe PC Rent (Calle 18A No 25-36)
Global System (Calle 18A No 25-51)
Infonet (Calle 18 No 29-15)
Net Conección (Carrera 30 No 16B-82)

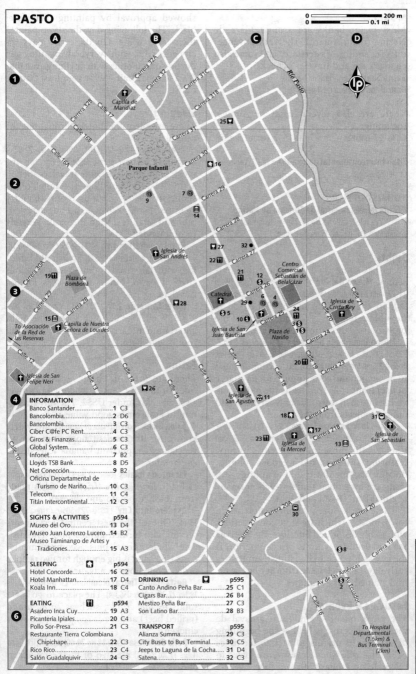

PASTO

0 — 200 m
0 — 0.1 mi

Capilla de Maridíaz

Parque Infantil

Plaza de Bombona

Iglesia de San Andrés

Catedral

Capilla de Nuestra Señora de Lourdes

To Asociación de la Red de las Reservas

Iglesia de San Felipe Neri

Centro Comercial Sebastián de Belalcázar

Iglesia de Cristo Rey

Iglesia de San Juan Bautista

Plaza de Nariño

Iglesia de San Agustín

Iglesia de la Merced

Iglesia de San Sebastián

Río Pasto

Av de las Américas

Av Ecuador

To Hospital Departamental (1.5km) & Bus Terminal (2km)

COLOMBIA

INFORMATION
Banco Santander	1 C3
Bancolombia	2 D6
Bancolombia	3 C3
Ciber C@fe PC Rent	4 C3
Giros & Finanzas	5 C3
Global System	6 C3
Infonet	7 B2
Lloyds TSB Bank	8 D5
Net Conección	9 B2
Oficina Departamental de Turismo de Nariño	10 C3
Telecom	11 C4
Titán Intercontinental	12 C3

SIGHTS & ACTIVITIES p594
Museo del Oro	13 D4
Museo Juan Lorenzo Lucero	14 B2
Museo Taminango de Artes y Tradiciones	15 A3

SLEEPING p594
Hotel Concorde	16 C2
Hotel Manhattan	17 D4
Koala Inn	18 C4

EATING p594
Asadero Inca Cuy	19 A3
Picantería Ipiales	20 C4
Pollo Sor-Presa	21 C3
Restaurante Tierra Colombiana Chipichape	22 C3
Rico Rico	23 C4
Salón Guadalquivir	24 C3

DRINKING p595
Canto Andino Peña Bar	25 C1
Cigars Bar	26 B4
Mestizo Peña Bar	27 C3
Son Latino Bar	28 B3

TRANSPORT p595
Alianza Summa	29 C3
City Buses to Bus Terminal	30 C5
Jeeps to Laguna de la Cocha	31 D4
Satena	32 C3

MONEY

Most major banks are around Plaza de Nariño (main square). They pay advances on Visa and/or MasterCard, and some also change cash and traveler's checks.

Banco Santander (Plaza de Nariño)
Bancolombia (Plaza de Nariño)

There are also several *casas de cambio*, including:

Giros & Finanzas (Carrera 26 No 17-12, Centro Comercial El Liceo)
Titán Intercontinental (Carrera 26 No 18-71, Centro Comercial Galerías)

TOURIST OFFICES

Oficina Departamental de Turismo de Nariño
(☎ 2-723-4962; Calle 18 No 25-25; ⏰ 8am-noon & 2-6pm Mon-Fri) Just off Plaza de Nariño.

Sights

Pasto has some small but interesting museums. **Museo del Oro** (☎ 2-721-9108; Calle 19 No 21-27; admission free; ⏰ 9am-6pm Mon-Fri, 9am-1pm Sat), in the building of the Banco de la República, features gold and pottery of the pre-Columbian cultures of Nariño.

Museo Taminango de Artes y Tradiciones (☎ 2-723-5539; Calle 13 No 27-67; admission US$0.50; ⏰ 8am-noon & 2-6pm Mon-Fri, 9am-1pm Sat), accommodated in a meticulously restored *casona* (large house) from 1623 (reputedly the oldest surviving house in town), displays artifacts and antique objects from the region.

Museo Juan Lorenzo Lucero (☎ 2-731-4414; Calle 18 No 28-87; admission US$1; ⏰ 8am-noon & 2-4pm Mon-Fri) is the museum of the city's history, featuring antiques, old weapons, photos, documents, furniture and paintings. All visits are by guided tours, which normally begin at 8am, 10am and 2pm.

There are a dozen colonial churches in town, most of which are large constructions with richly decorated interiors. **The Iglesia de San Juan Bautista**, with its ornate interior, is the city's oldest church, dating from Pasto's early days. The **Iglesia de Cristo Rey** has beautiful stained-glass windows.

Festivals & Events

The city's major event, the Carnaval de Blancos y Negros, is held at the beginning of January. Its origins go back to the times of Spanish rule when slaves were allowed to celebrate on January 5th and their masters showed approval by painting their faces black. The following day, the slaves painted their faces white. On these two days the city goes wild, with everybody painting and dusting one another with anything available. It's a serious affair – wear your least favorite outfit.

Sleeping

There are plenty of hotels throughout the central area.

Koala Inn (☎ 2-722-1101; Calle 18 No 22-37; r without/with bath per person US$4/5) By far the most popular place with travelers. Set in a fine historic building, the hotel offers spotlessly clean, spacious rooms, laundry facilities, book exchange, a budget restaurant and satellite TV on the patio. Warmly recommended.

Hotel Manhattan (☎ 2-721-5675; Calle 18 No 21B-14; s/d US$4/6, with bath US$5/7) Stylish old building with fair-sized rooms and a spacious covered patio, but it rarely sees foreign travelers.

Hotel Concorde (☎ 2-731-0658; Calle 19 No 29A-09; s/d US$10/15) Small hotel close to the night entertainment area. It has cozy tranquil rooms with bath.

Eating

There are loads of cheap restaurants and cafés in the city center, where you can get a set meal for under US$2. The tiny restaurant in **Koala Inn** is good value.

Salón Guadalquivir (Plaza de Nariño) Café widely known for its *tamales* (chopped meat with vegetables wrapped in banana leaves) and *empanadas*.

Picantería Ipiales (Calle 19 No 23-37) Local specialist in *lapingachos* (fried pancakes made from mashed potato and cheese).

Asadero Inca Cuy (☎ 2-723-8050; Carrera 29 No 13-65) One of the best central restaurants serving *cuy* (grilled guinea pig). The dish (the whole animal plus accompaniments) costs US$9 and is big enough for two people; order it one hour in advance.

Restaurante Tierra Colombiana Chipichape (Calle 18 No 27-19; mains US$3-4) The place to go for a solid *comida criolla*, such as *carne asada* (grilled beef) and *arroz con pollo* (rice with chicken).

Pollo Sor-Presa (Calle 18 No 26-60) and **Rico Rico** (Calle 17 No 22-03) are two of the best chicken outlets.

Drinking

Several pleasant bars are located in the center.

Cigars Bar (Carrera 25 No 14-06) A cozy bar.

Son Latino Bar (Calle 16 No 26-78) This place plays salsa, merengue and vallenato and has a dance floor.

For some Andean rhythms, try **Mestizo Peña Bar** (Calle 18 No 27-67) or **Canto Andino Peña Bar** (Calle 20 No 30-41); both have live music on weekends.

The local Zona Rosa, roughly between Calles 19 and 20 and Carreras 31C and 32, features some fast food joints, bars and discos, and comes alive on weekend nights. Another concentration of central bars and discos is on Calle 19 between Carreras 26 and 28, where you'll find about a dozen watering holes.

Getting There & Away

AIR

The airport is 33km north of the city on the road to Cali. *Colectivos* go there from Calle 18 at Carrera 25 (US$2.50, 45 minutes). Pay the day before your flight at the airline office or at a travel agency, and the *colectivo* will pick you up from your hotel.

Avianca, Intercontinental and Satena service Pasto, with daily flights to Bogotá (US$70 to US$125) and Cali (US$50 to US$100), and connections to other cities.

BUS

The bus terminal is 2km south of the city center. Urban buses go there from different points in the central area, including Carrera 20A at Calle 17, or take a taxi (US$1.25).

Frequent buses, minibuses and *colectivos* go to Ipiales (US$2 to US$3, 1½ to two hours); sit on the left for better views. Plenty of buses ply the spectacular road to Cali (US$12, nine hours). These buses will drop you off in Popayán in six hours. Avoid traveling this route at night – buses have been ambushed and passengers robbed. A dozen direct buses depart daily to Bogotá (US$32, 21 hours).

AROUND PASTO
Volcán Galeras

Galeras volcano (4267m) is 8km west of Pasto as the crow flies or 22km by rough road (no public transport). The volcano's

activity rose dangerously in 1989, putting the city and the surrounding region in a state of emergency. Since that time, the volcano has erupted several times but has since calmed down. Tourists are again allowed to hike or ride to the top. The hike from Pasto to the top takes four to five hours. Pasto's tourist office can organize guides (US$20) and vehicles (US$35).

Laguna de la Cocha

This is one of the biggest and most beautiful lakes in Colombia, about 25km east of Pasto. The small island of La Corota is a nature reserve, covered by dense forest and home to highly diverse flora. It is accessible by boat from the lakeshore.

Scattered around the lake are two dozen small private nature reserves, collectively known as the Reservas Naturales de la Cocha, established by locals on their farms. They will show you around, and some provide accommodation and food. However, some have been closed due to guerrilla presence in the region. For the current situation, inquire at the **Asociación de la Red de las Reservas** (☎ 2-723-1022; Calle 10 No 36-28) in Pasto.

Jeeps for the lake (US$1.50, 45 minutes) depart on weekdays from the Iglesia de San Sebastián in central Pasto, and on weekends from the back of the **Hospital Departamental** (Calle 22 at Carrera 7).

IPIALES

Ipiales, close to the Ecuadorian border at Rumichaca, is an uninspiring commercial town of 70,000 inhabitants, driven by trade across the frontier. There is little to see or do in town, except for the colorful Saturday market, where the *campesinos* from surrounding villages come to buy and sell goods. A short side trip to the Santuario de las Lajas is a must (see p597).

Information
IMMIGRATION

All passport formalities are processed in Rumichaca, not in Ipiales or Tulcán. The DAS office is on the Colombian side of the border and the Ecuadorian post is just across the Rumichaca River. Few nationals need a visa for Ecuador, but if you do need one, the consulate is in the center of Ipiales (see p606 for details).

COLOMBIA

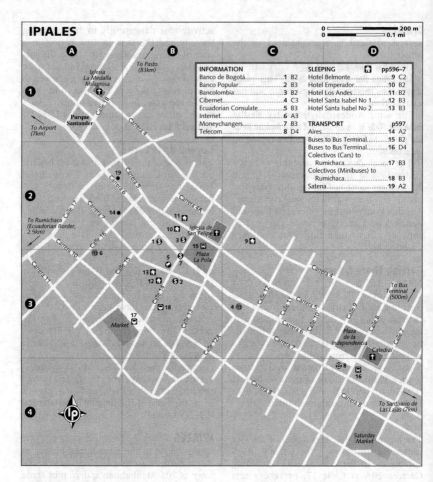

IPIALES

INFORMATION	
Banco de Bogotá................1	B2
Banco Popular..................2	B3
Bancolombia....................3	B2
Cibernet.........................4	C3
Ecuadorian Consulate........5	B3
Internet..........................6	A3
Moneychangers................7	B3
Telecom.........................8	D4

SLEEPING	pp596–7
Hotel Belmonte................9	C2
Hotel Emperador..............10	B2
Hotel Los Andes...............11	B2
Hotel Santa Isabel No 1.......12	B3
Hotel Santa Isabel No 2.......13	B3

TRANSPORT	p597
Aires.............................14	A2
Buses to Bus Terminal........15	B2
Buses to Bus Terminal........16	D4
Colectivos (Cars) to Rumichaca...................17	B3
Colectivos (Minibuses) to Rumichaca...................18	B3
Satena...........................19	A2

INTERNET ACCESS

Ipiales has several cybercafés but the access can be slow.

Internet (Calle 16 No 6-51)

Cibernet (Carrera 6 No 12-43, Centro Comercial Polo)

MONEY

No bank in Ipiales changes cash or traveler's checks, but they are likely to give advances on credit cards. Both the following have ATMs.

Bancolombia (Plaza La Pola)

Banco de Bogotá (Carrera 6 at Calle 15)

Plenty of moneychangers on Plaza La Pola will change your US, Colombian and Ecuadorian currency, as will a number of *casas de cambio* in the town's center. There are also moneychangers at the border in Rumichaca.

Sleeping & Eating

There are plenty of budget hotels and restaurants all across the town's center.

Hotel Belmonte (☎ 2-773-2771; Carrera 4 No 12-111; r without/with bath per person US$3/4) One of the cheapest acceptable hotels. It's small, friendly, family-run and popular with backpackers. There's hot water and some rooms have private baths.

Hotel Emperador (☎ 2-773-2311; Carrera 5 No 14-43; s/d US$6/10) This hotel is not particularly memorable, but its rooms, with private baths, are OK.

Hotel Santa Isabel No 1 (☎ 2-773-3851; Calle 14 No 7-30; s/d/t US$7/12/15) A budget option with private baths.

Hotel Santa Isabel No 2 (☎ 2-773-4172; Carrera 7 No 14-27; s/d/t US$12/17/20) Just round the corner from its older brother, No 2 provides more comfort and space.

Hotel Los Andes (☎ 2-773-4338; Carrera 5 No 14-44; s/d/t US$20/27/37) One of Ipiales' best hotels, offering neat, quiet rooms, a gym, sauna and a restaurant, which is also among the best in town.

You'll find numerous budget restaurants all over town, but don't expect too much as they are all pretty basic.

Getting There & Away
AIR
The airport is 7km northwest of Ipiales, on the road to Cumbal, accessible by taxi (US$3). Satena and Aires have flights to Cali (US$60 to US$100) and Bogotá (US$80 to US$130).

BUS
Ipiales has a large bus terminal, about 1km northeast of the center. It's linked to the center by urban buses (US$0.20) and taxis (US$1).

Expreso Bolivariano has a dozen buses daily to Bogotá (US$33, 23 hours) and several companies run regular buses to Cali (US$13, 11 hours). All these buses will drop you in Popayán in eight hours. Don't travel at night on this route – buses have been ambushed and passengers robbed.

There are plenty of buses, minibuses and *colectivos* to Pasto (US$2 to US$3, 1½ to two hours). They all depart from the bus terminal. Sit on the right for better views.

Frequent *colectivos* (cars and minibuses) travel the 2.5km to the border at Rumichaca (US$0.50), leaving from the bus terminal and the market area near the corner of Calle 14 and Carrera 10. After crossing the border on foot, take another *colectivo* to Tulcán (6.5km).

SANTUARIO DE LAS LAJAS
The Santuario de las Lajas, 7km southeast of Ipiales, is a neo-Gothic church built between 1926 and 1944 on a bridge spanning a spectacular river gorge. The church was constructed to commemorate the appearance of the Virgin, whose image, according to a legend, appeared on an enormous vertical rock 45m above the river. The church is set up against the gorge cliff in such a way that the rock with the image forms its main altar.

Pilgrims from all over Colombia and from abroad come here year-round. Many leave thanksgiving plaques along the alley leading to the church. Note the number of miracles that are said to have occurred.

Colectivos run regularly from Ipiales to Las Lajas (US$0.50, 15 minutes), leaving from Carrera 6 at Calle 4. A taxi from Ipiales to Las Lajas costs US$2.50. A return taxi trip (for up to four people), including one hour of waiting in Las Lajas, shouldn't cost more than US$6.

AMAZON BASIN

Colombia's Amazon covers the entire southeast portion of the country, comprising more than a third of the national territory. Almost all the region is thick tropical rain forest crisscrossed by rivers and sparsely inhabited by Indian communities. There are no roads; transport is either by air or by river. Parts of the region are controlled by guerrillas and may be unsafe to travel.

LETICIA
Set in the southeast tip of the country, Leticia is a small hot town on the Amazon River where the borders of Colombia, Peru and Brazil converge. The town is the only significant tourist center in Colombian Amazonia, serving as a base for jungle trips around the region. For foreign travelers, Leticia is also a gateway to further Amazonian adventures, as it is linked via the Amazon with Iquitos (Peru) upriver and Manaus (Brazil) downriver.

The town has reasonable tourist facilities and flight connections with Bogotá. Importantly, Leticia is a secure and easygoing place – guerrillas are not active in the region. Tourists arriving at Leticia's airport are charged a compulsory US$5 tax.

July and August are the only relatively dry months. The wettest period is from February to April. The Amazon River's highest level is in May to June, while the lowest is from August to October. The difference

COLOMBIA

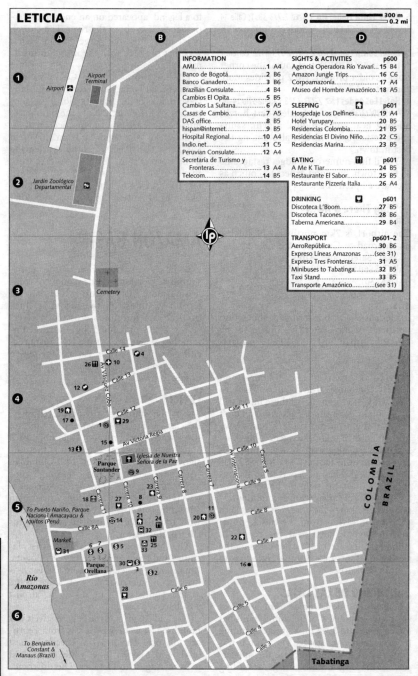

LETICIA

| 0 | 300 m |
| 0 | 0.2 mi |

INFORMATION
AMI	1	A4
Banco de Bogotá	2	B6
Banco Ganadero	3	B6
Brazilian Consulate	4	B4
Cambios El Opita	5	B5
Cambios La Sultana	6	A5
Casas de Cambio	7	A5
DAS office	8	B5
hispan@internet	9	B5
Hospital Regional	10	A4
Indio.net	11	C5
Peruvian Consulate	12	A4
Secretaría de Turismo y Fronteras	13	A4
Telecom	14	B5

SIGHTS & ACTIVITIES　p600
Agencia Operadora Río Yavarí	15	B4
Amazon Jungle Trips	16	C6
Corpoamazonía	17	A4
Museo del Hombre Amazónico	18	A5

SLEEPING　p601
Hospedaje Los Delfines	19	A4
Hotel Yurupary	20	B5
Residencias Colombia	21	B5
Residencias El Divino Niño	22	C5
Residencias Marina	23	B5

EATING　p601
A Me K Tiar	24	B5
Restaurante El Sabor	25	B5
Restaurante Pizzería Italia	26	A4

DRINKING　p601
Discoteca L'Boom	27	B5
Discoteca Tacones	28	B6
Taberna Americana	29	B4

TRANSPORT　pp601–2
AeroRepública	30	B6
Expreso Líneas Amazonas	(see 31)	
Expreso Tres Fronteras	31	A5
Minibuses to Tabatinga	32	B5
Taxi Stand	33	B5
Transporte Amazónico	(see 31)	

Airport Terminal

Airport

Jardín Zoológico Departamental

Cemetery

Calle 14

Calle 13

Calle 12

Calle 11

Av Vásquez Cobo

Av Victoria Regia

Iglesia de Nuestra Señora de la Paz

Parque Santander

Calle 10

Calle 9

Calle 8

Carrera 11

Carrera 10

Carrera 9

Carrera 8

Carrera 7

Av Internacional

To Puerto Nariño, Parque Nacional Amacayacu & Iquitos (Peru)

Calle 8A

Market

Parque Orellana

Calle 7

Río Amazonas

Calle 6

Calle 5

Calle 4

Calle 3

To Benjamin Constant & Manaus (Brazil)

COLOMBIA

BRAZIL

Tabatinga

COLOMBIA

between low and high water can be as great as 15m.

Orientation

Leticia lies right on the Colombia–Brazil border. Just south across the frontier sits Tabatinga, a Brazilian town much the same size as Leticia, with its own port and airport. Leticia and Tabatinga are virtually merging together, and there are no border checkpoints between the two. Frequent *colectivos* link the two towns, or you can just walk. Both locals and foreigners are allowed to come and go between the two towns without visas, but if you plan on heading further into either country, you must get your passport stamped at DAS in Leticia and at Polícia Federal in Tabatinga (not on the actual border).

On the island in the Amazon opposite Leticia/Tabatinga is Santa Rosa, a Peruvian village. Boats go there from both Tabatinga and Leticia.

On the opposite side of the Amazon from Leticia, about 25km downstream, is the Brazilian town of Benjamin Constant, the main port for boats downstream to Manaus. Tabatinga and Benjamin Constant are connected by regular boats.

Of the four border towns, Leticia has the best-developed tourist facilities and is the most pleasant – the best place to hang your hat no matter which way you are headed. Nonetheless, we've included in the following sections information on various Tabatinga services (money exchange, Internet access, hotels, restaurants) to allow you to easily move around the place and flexibly plan your itinerary.

Information

IMMIGRATION

The DAS office in Leticia, on Calle 9, no longer stamps passports. You now need to get an entry or exit stamp in your passport from DAS officials at Leticia's airport (open daily).

Entry and exit stamps for Brazil must be obtained at the Polícia Federal in Tabatinga, Av da Amizade 650, near the hospital. A yellow fever vaccination certificate is likely to be required by officials when you enter Brazil.

If heading for or coming from Iquitos, you get your entry or exit stamp in Santa Rosa.

For details of consulates in Leticia and Tabatinga, see p606.

INTERNET ACCESS

The cybercafés listed here will charge US$1 to US$1.50 an hour. Connections are rather slow.

Leticia has several cybercafés, including:
AMI (Carrera 10 No 11-119)
hispan@internet (Calle 10 No 9-82)
Indio.net (Centro Comercial Acuarios, Carrera 7 at Calle 8)

There are also Internet facilities in Tabatinga, including:
Digital Net Internet Café (Rua Pedro Texeira)
D'Joy Internet Café (Rua da Pátria 568)

MONEY

Leticia has two banks. MasterCard is so far useless in Leticia.
Banco Ganadero (cnr Carrera 10 & Calle 7) Changes Amex traveler's checks (but not cash) and gives peso advances on Visa.
Banco de Bogotá (cnr Carrera 10 & Calle 7) Won't touch your traveler's checks or cash dollars, but has an ATM that accepts Visa cards.
Cambios El Opita (Carrera 11 No 7-96) Changes traveler's checks.

Don't carry pesos further into Brazil or Peru as it will be difficult to change them. By the same token, don't bring reais to Bogotá. Change all the money of the country you're leaving in Leticia/Tabatinga.

There are plenty of *casas de cambio* on Calle 8 between Carrera 11 and the market in Leticia. They change US dollars, Colombian pesos, Brazilian reais and Peruvian soles. They open weekdays from 8am or 9am until 5pm or 6pm and Saturday until around 2pm. Shop around, as rates vary.

There are also money-changing facilities in Tabatinga.
Banco do Brasil (Av da Amizade) Offers cash advances in reais on Visa.
CNM Câmbio e Turismo (Av da Amizade 2017) About 500m from the border, exchanges cash and traveler's checks, and pays in reais or pesos, as you wish, but the rate may be a bit lower than in Leticia.

TOURIST OFFICES
Secretaría de Turismo y Fronteras (☎ 8-592-7505; Carrera 11 No 11-35; ☺ 7am-noon & 2-5:30pm Mon-Fri) Just off Parque Santander.

COLOMBIA

Sights

The **Jardín Zoológico Departamental** (Av Vásquez Cobo; admission US$1; 🕑 8am-noon & 2-5pm Mon-Fri, 8am-5:30pm Sat & Sun), near the airport, houses animals typical of the region, including anacondas, tapirs, monkeys, caimans, ocelots, eagles, macaws and a friendly manatee named Polo.

The small **Museo del Hombre Amazónico** (☎ 8-592-7729; Carrera 11 No 9-43; admission free; 🕑 9am-noon & 2:30-5pm Mon-Fri, 9am-1pm Sat) features artifacts and household implements of Indian groups living in the region.

Have a look around the market and stroll along the waterfront. Visit the Parque Santander before sunset for an impressive spectacle, when thousands of small screeching parrots (locally called *pericos*) arrive for their nightly rest in the park's trees.

Tours

JUNGLE TRIPS

There are a dozen tour operators in Leticia focusing on jungle trips. Most agencies offer standard one-day tours, which go up the Amazon to Puerto Nariño and include lunch, a short walk in the forest and a visit to an indigenous village. These excursions are usually well organized, comfortable and trouble-free, but will hardly give you a real picture of the rain forest or its inhabitants.

The real wilderness begins well off the Amazon proper, along its small tributaries. The further you go, the more chance you have to observe wildlife in relatively undamaged habitat and visit indigenous settlements. This involves more time and money, but the experience can be much more rewarding.

Multiday tours are run from Leticia by several companies, three of which have established small nature reserves and built jungle lodges. All three reserves are along the lower reaches of the Río Yavarí, on the Brazil–Peru border.

Reserva Natural Zacambú is the nearest to Leticia, about 70km by boat. Its lodge is on Lake Zacambú, just off Río Yavarí, on the Peruvian side of the river. The lodge is simple, with small rooms without baths, and the total capacity for about 30 guests. The lodge and tours are run from Leticia by **Amazon Jungle Trips** (☎ 8-592-7377; amazonjungle trips@yahoo.com; Av Internacional No 6-25).

Reserva Natural Río Yavarí is about 20km upriver from Zacambú, on the opposite (Brazilian) side of the Río Yavarí. The lodge is lovely, as is its location overlooking a small lake off the Río Itaquai. Rooms have private baths and there's a *maloca* (large, usually round constructions thatched with palm leaves) with hammocks. The lodge is run from Leticia by the **Agencia Operadora Río Yavarí** (☎ 8-592-7457; Carrera 10 No 11-27). If you find the office closed, inquire at Hospedaje Los Delfines (p601).

Reserva Natural Palmarí is another 20km further upstream of Río Yavarí, about 110km by river from Leticia. Its rambling lodge sits on the high south (Brazilian) bank of the river, overlooking a wide bend where pink and gray dolphins are often seen. The lodge features several cabañas with baths and a round *maloca* with hammocks. The reserve is managed from Bogotá by its owner, **Axel Antoine-Feill** (☎ 1-236-3813, 1-623-4265; www.palmari.org; Carrera 10 No 93-72, Bogotá), who speaks several languages, including English. His representative in Leticia is **Marcela Torres** (☎ 8-592-7344).

All three operators offer three- to six-day all-inclusive packages, based at the lodges. The packages include accommodation (in beds), meals, excursions with guides and return transport from Leticia. The cost largely depends on the number of people in the party, length of the stay, season etc; count on US$40 to US$80 per person per day. Tours don't usually have a fixed timetable; the agents normally wait until they have enough people, unless you don't want to wait and are prepared to pay more. Contact the operators in advance. Legally, you should have a Brazilian or Peruvian visa to stay in the reserves, so check this issue with the agencies (unless nationals of your home country don't need a visa).

Palmarí is the only operator that, apart from tours, has a budget offer for independent travelers who want to stay in the reserve but don't want to pay for an all-inclusive tour. The **lodge** (hammock/r per person US$7/10, breakfast/lunch/dinner US$3/4/5) simply charges for accommodation and food, and you can plan your stay and excursions as you wish, using the reserve's canoes and guides if they are not too busy with tours or other tasks.

Apart from the Palmarí's backpacker offer, other budget ways of getting a taste of the jungle include guided excursions in the Parque Nacional Amacayacu (p602) and trips with the locals from Puerto Nariño (p602). Bring enough mosquito repellent from Bogotá because you can't get good quality repellant in Leticia. Take high-speed film – the jungle is always dark.

Sleeping

There are a dozen places to stay in Leticia, which is generally sufficient to cope with the tourist traffic.

Residencias Colombia (Carrera 10 No 8-52; s/d US$4/7) One of the cheapest but most basic places. Rooms have hard double beds and fans, but baths are shared.

Residencias Marina (☎ 8-592-6014; Carrera 9 No 9-29; s/d/t US$7/10/15) Acceptable central hotel providing rooms with bath, fan and fridge.

Residencias El Divino Niño (☎ 8-592-5598; Av Internacional No 7-23; s/d US$6/10) A cheap but undistinguished option with private baths, but it's tucked a bit away from the center.

Hospedaje Los Delfines (☎ 8-592-7388; Carrera 11 No 12-81; s/d US$10/15) Small family-run place offering nine neat rooms with bath, fan and fridge, arranged around a leafy patio.

Hotel Yurupary (☎ 8-592-7983; Calle 8 No 7-26; s/d/t US$18/28/36) One of the best affordable bets in town. It has ample air-con rooms with fridge and cable TV, and the price includes breakfast.

Tabatinga also has a good range of accommodation, and it's a bit cheaper than Leticia.

Traveler Jungle Home (☎ 92-412-5060; mowgly discovery@hotmail.com; Rua Marechal Rondon 86; r per person US$5) In the house of jungle guide Tony 'Mowgly' Vargas, there are two basic rooms for tourists, with use of the kitchen. He also organizes tours.

Hotel Pajé (☎ 92-412-2774; Rua Pedro Texeira 367; r with fan/air-con US$4/6) One of the cheapest places in town. All rooms have one double bed and private bath.

Hotel Cristina (☎ 92-412-2558; Rua Marechal Mallet 248; s/d with fan US$6/8, with air-con US$8/12) Convenient basic shelter if you plan on taking the early-morning boat to Iquitos (see Getting There & Away).

Hotel Rio Mar (☎ 92-412-3061; Rua Marechal Rondon 1714; d with fan & bath US$10) Small, friendly place just next to the market and Porto da Feira.

Posada do Sol (☎ 92-412-3987; Rua General Sampaio; s/d/t US$20/24/36) One of the most pleasant places around. This large family-run mansion has seven air-con rooms with bath and fridge; prices include breakfast.

Eating

Food in Leticia is generally good and not too expensive. The local specialty is fish, including the delicious *gamitana* and pirarucu.

Restaurante El Sabor (Calle 8 No 9-25; set meals US$2; ⏰ 24hr Tue-Sun) Leticia's best budget eatery, with excellent-value set meals, vegetarian burgers, banana pancakes, fruit salad, plus unlimited free juices with your meal.

A Me K Tiar (Carrera 9 No 8-15; mains US$3-5) Some of the best *parrillas* and barbecued meat in town, at very reasonable prices.

Restaurante Pizzería Italia (Av Vásquez Cobo No 13-77; mains US$3-6) Delicious spaghetti, lasagna and pizza, cooked by a friendly Italian.

Tabatinga's culinary picture has improved over recent years.

Restaurante Tres Fronteiras do Amazonas (Rua Rui Barbosa; mains US$4-7) Attractive palm-thatched open-air restaurant with a wide choice of fish and meat dishes.

Restaurante Fazenda (Av da Amizade 1961; mains US$3-7) Good-value Brazilian food served in a pleasant interior.

Drinking

Discoteca Tacones (Carrera 11 No 6-14) is probably the trendiest disco in Leticia, closely followed by **Discoteca L'Boom** (Calle 9 No 10-40). Both play a mixed bag of music.

Taberna Americana (Carrera 10 No 11-108) A cheap, rustic bar playing salsa music till late.

Getting There & Away

AIR

The only passenger airline that services Leticia is **AeroRepública** (☎ 8-592-7666; Calle 7 No 10-36). It flies between Leticia and Bogotá several days a week (US$100 to US$120). It may be difficult to get on flights out of Leticia in the holiday season – book as early as you can.

There are no flights into Brazil from Leticia, but from Tabatinga, Varig has flights to Manaus on Monday, Wednesday and Friday (one way US$170), while Rico flies on Tuesday, Thursday, Saturday and Sunday (US$165). Tickets can be bought from Tabatinga's travel agency, **Turamazon** (☎ 92-412-2244; Av da Amizade 2271), or **CNM Câmbio e Turismo** (☎ 92-412-3281; Av da Amizade 2017), both near the border. The airport is 2km south of Tabatinga; *colectivos* marked 'Comara' from Leticia will drop you off nearby.

A small Peruvian airline, TANS, flies its 15-seat hydroplane from Santa Rosa to Iquitos, on Wednesday and Saturday (US$65). Information and tickets are available from **Cambios La Sultana** (☎ 8-592-7071; Calle 8 No 11-57) in Leticia. You need to go by boat to Santa Rosa to catch the plane, from Leticia or Tabatinga.

BOAT

Leticia is a jumping-off point for travelers looking for backwater Amazonian adventures, downstream to Manaus (Brazil) or upriver to Iquitos (Peru).

Boats down the Amazon to Manaus leave from Porto Fluvial de Tabatinga, beyond the hospital, and call at Benjamin Constant. There are two boats per week, departing from Tabatinga on Wednesday and Saturday around 2pm, and from Benjamin Constant on the same evenings. More boats may go on other days so check.

The trip to Manaus takes three days and four nights and costs US$40 in your own hammock, or US$180 for a double cabin. (Upstream from Manaus to Tabatinga, the trip usually takes six days, and costs about US$70 in your hammock or US$220 for a double cabin.) Food is included but is poor and monotonous. Bring snacks and bottled water. Boats come to Tabatinga one or two days before their scheduled departure back down the river. You can string up your hammock or occupy the cabin as soon as you've paid the fare, saving on hotels. Food, however, is only served after departure. Beware of theft on board.

Three small boat companies, **Transtur** (☎ 92-412-3186; Rua Marechal Mallet 306), **Mayco** and **Mi Reyna** (☎ 92-412-2945; Rua Marechal Mallet 248), in Tabatinga, run high-powered passenger boats *(rápidos)* between Tabatinga and Iquitos. Each company has a few departures a week, so there is at least one boat almost every day. The boats depart Tabatinga's Porto da Feira at 5am and arrive in Iquitos about 10 hours later. The boats call at Santa Rosa's immigration post. The journey costs US$50 in either direction, including breakfast and lunch. Don't forget to get an exit stamp in your passport from DAS at Leticia's airport the day before.

There are also irregular cargo boats from Santa Rosa to Iquitos, once or twice a week. The journey takes about three days and costs US$25 to US$30, including food. Downstream from Iquitos to Santa Rosa, it generally doesn't take any longer than two days.

Note that there are no roads out of Iquitos into Peru. You have to fly or continue by river to Pucallpa (five to seven days), from where you can go overland to Lima and elsewhere.

PARQUE NACIONAL AMACAYACU

Amacayacu national park takes in 2935 sq km of jungle on the northern side of the Amazon, about 75km upstream from Leticia. A spacious **visitor center** (hammock/dm US$7/9, 3 meals about US$8), with food and accommodation facilities, has been built on the bank of the Amazon. The park entry fee is US$7.50. You can book and pay at the national park office in Bogotá, or in Leticia at **Corpoamazonía** (☎ 8-592-7124; Carrera 11 No 12-45).

From the visitor center, you can explore the park either by marked paths or by water. Local guides accompany visitors on all excursions and charge roughly US$10 to US$20 per group, depending on the route. In the high-water period (May to June), much of the land turns into swamps and lagoons, significantly reducing walking options; trips in canoes are organized at this time. Bring plenty of mosquito repellent, a flashlight, long-sleeve shirt and waterproof gear.

Boats from Leticia to Puerto Nariño (see following) will drop you off at the park's visitor center (US$10, 1½ hours).

PUERTO NARIÑO

About 90km up the Amazon from Leticia (15km upstream from the Amacayacu park), Puerto Nariño is a tiny town on the bank of the great river in the middle of nowhere. It can be a good base for budget jungle trips into the surrounding area. About 10km west of Puerto Nariño is the Lago Tarapoto, a beautiful lake accessible only by river, where you can see the pink dolphins. A half-day trip to the lake in a small motorized boat can be organized from Puerto Nariño (around US$20 per boat for up to four people). Locals can take you on boat or walking excursions to many other places, including the Parque Nacional Amacayacu, or you can just rent a canoe (US$7 per day) and do your own tour.

Sleeping & Eating

Puerto Nariño has quite a few choices.

Cabañas Manguaré (r per person US$4) A basic but acceptable option.

Brisas del Amazonas (s/d/t US$7/11/14) Simple rooms in a stylish, if dilapidated, mansion.

Casa Selva (hammock US$4, r per person US$9-12, meals US$2-3.50) Casa Selva has impeccably clean rooms with private baths and a six-hammock dorm. Breakfast, lunch and dinner are available.

El Alto del Águila (dm US$5, d US$10) This charming place is a 20-minute walk from town, with sightings of monkeys, macaws and great river views. Budget jungle trips can be organized.

For cheap meals, try one of the two basic town restaurants near the waterfront: Doña María or Las Margaritas.

Getting There & Away

Three small boat companies, Expreso Tres Fronteras, Transporte Amazónico and Expreso Líneas Amazonas (all with offices near the waterfront in Leticia), operate scheduled fast passenger boats to Puerto Nariño at 2pm from Monday to Friday and at 1pm on weekends (US$11, two hours). Buy your ticket in the morning or a day before departure.

COLOMBIA DIRECTORY

ACCOMMODATIONS

There is a constellation of places to stay in Colombia, in the largest cities and smallest villages. A vast majority are straight Colombian hotels where you are unlikely to meet foreigners, but some budget traveler haunts have appeared over the past decade. You'll find them in most large cities (Bogotá, Medellín, Cali, Cartagena) and popular tourist destinations.

Accommodation appears under a variety of names including *hotel*, *residencias*, *hospedaje*, *hostería* and *posada*. *Residencias* and *hospedaje* are the most common names for budget places. A hotel generally suggests a place of a higher standard, or at least a higher price, though the distinction is often academic.

On the whole, *residencias* and *hospedajes* are unremarkable places without much style or atmosphere, but there are some pleasant exceptions. Many cheapies have a private bathroom (referred to as 'bath' in this book), which includes a toilet and shower. Note that cheap hotel plumbing can't cope with toilet paper, so throw it in the box or basket that is usually provided.

In hot places (ie, the lowland areas), a ceiling fan or table fan is often provided. Always check the fan before you take the room. On the other hand, above 2500m, where the nights can be chilly, count how many blankets you have, and check the hot water if they claim to have it.

By and large, *residencias* (even the cheapest) provide a sheet and some sort of cover (another sheet or blankets, depending on the temperature). Most will also give you a towel, a small piece of soap and a roll of toilet paper. The cheapies cost US$3 to US$7 for a single room, US$5 to US$12 a double.

Many *hospedajes* have *matrimonios*, rooms with a double bed intended for couples. A *matrimonio* is usually cheaper than a double and slightly more expensive than a single (or even the same price). Traveling as a couple considerably reduces the cost of accommodation.

Many cheap *residencias* double as love hotels, renting rooms by the hour. Intentionally or not, you are likely to find yourself in such a place from time to time. This is actually not a major problem, as love hotels are normally as clean and safe as other hotels, and the sex section is usually separated from the genuine hotel.

Colombia has just one youth hostel, in Bogotá. Camping is not popular and there are only a handful of campsites in the country. Camping wild is possible outside the urban centers but you should be extremely careful. Don't leave your tent or gear unattended.

ACTIVITIES

With its amazing geographical diversity, Colombia offers many opportunities for hiking, though some regions are infiltrated by guerrillas and should be avoided.

Colombia's coral reefs provide good conditions for snorkeling and scuba diving. The main centers are San Andrés (p571), Providencia (p574), Santa Marta (p558),

Taganga (p560) and Cartagena (p564), each of which has several diving schools offering courses and other diving services. Colombia is considered one of the world's cheapest countries for diving.

Colombia has also developed greatly as a center of paragliding. The main hub is Medellín (p577), but there are also gliding schools in Bogotá, Cali and elsewhere. Paragliding in Colombia is cheap.

White-water rafting is pretty new in Colombia but is developing fast, with its major base in San Gil (p551). Like most other outdoor activities, rafting is also cheap in Colombia.

Cycling is one of Colombia's favorite spectator sports, yet bicycle-rental agencies have only begun to appear in recent years.

Other possible activities include horse riding, mountaineering, rock climbing, windsurfing, fishing, caving and even bathing in a mud volcano (see Around Cartagena p567).

BOOKS

For more detailed travel information, pick up a copy of Lonely Planet's *Colombia*.

In Focus: Colombia – A Guide to the People, Politics and Culture, by Colin Harding, is a good brief introduction to the country's history, economy and society. *Colombia: Portrait of Unity and Diversity,* by Harvey F Kline, is a balanced overview of Colombian history.

Titles covering Colombia's modern history include: *The Politics of Colombia,* by Robert H Dix; *Colombia: Inside the Labyrinth,* by Jenny Pearce; *The Politics of Coalition Rule in Colombia,* by Jonathan Hartlyn; and *The Making of Modern Colombia: A Nation in Spite of Itself,* by David Bushnell.

Killing Peace: Colombia's Conflict and the Failure of US Intervention, by Garry M Leech, is an excellent overview of the history of the bloody internal conflict, which is often so difficult for outsiders to understand.

BUSINESS HOURS

The office working day is, theoretically at least, eight hours long, usually from 8am to noon and 2pm to 6pm Monday to Friday. Many offices in Bogotá have adopted the so-called *jornada continua*, a working day without a lunch break, which finishes

two hours earlier. Banks (except for those in Bogotá – see p537) are open 8am to 11:30am and 2pm to 4pm Monday to Thursday, and 8am to 11:30am and 2pm to 4:30pm on Friday.

As a rough guide only, the usual shopping hours are from 9am to 6pm or 7pm Monday to Saturday. Some shops close for lunch while others stay open. Large stores and supermarkets usually stay open until 8pm or 9pm or even longer. Most of the better restaurants in the larger cities, particularly in Bogotá, tend to stay open until 10pm or longer, whereas restaurants in smaller towns often close by 9pm or earlier.

The opening hours of museums and other tourist sights vary greatly. Most museums are closed on Monday but are open on Sunday.

CLIMATE

Colombia's proximity to the equator means its temperature varies little throughout the year, and lacks the four seasons of Europe or the USA. Instead, Colombia has dry and wet seasons, the pattern of which varies in different parts of the country. As a rough guideline only, in the Andean region and the Caribbean coast (where you are likely to spend most of the time) there are two dry and two rainy seasons per year.

The main dry season falls between January and March, with a shorter, less-dry period between June and August. The most pleasant time to visit Colombia is in the dry season. This is particularly true if you plan on hiking or some other outdoor activities. The dry season also gives visitors a better chance to savor local cultural events, as many festivals and fiestas take place during these periods.

For more information and climate charts, see the South America Directory (p1028).

CUSTOMS

Customs procedures are usually a formality, both on entering and on leaving the country. However, thorough luggage checks occasionally occur, more often at the airports than at the overland borders, and they can be very exhaustive, with a body search included. They aren't looking for your extra Walkman, but for drugs. Trying to smuggle dope through the border is the best way to see what the inside of a Colombian jail looks like, for quite a few years.

DANGERS & ANNOYANCES

Colombia definitely isn't the safest of countries, and you should be careful at all times. Keep your passport and money next to your skin and your camera inside your bag, and don't wear jewelry or expensive watches. Always carry your passport with you, as document checks on the streets are not uncommon. Some police officers may accept a photocopy of the passport, but legally, only the genuine document is valid.

Theft & Robbery

If you can, leave your money and valuables somewhere safe before walking the streets. In practice, it's good to carry a decoy bundle of small notes, the equivalent of US$5 to US$10, ready to hand over in case of an assault; if you really don't have a peso, robbers can become frustrated and, as a consequence, unpredictable.

Armed hold-ups in the cities can occur even in some more upmarket suburbs. If you are accosted by robbers, it is best to give them what they are after, but try to play it cool and don't rush to hand them all your valuables at once – they may well be satisfied with just your decoy wad. Don't try to escape or struggle – your chances are slim. Don't count on any help from passers-by.

Be careful when drawing the cash from an ATM – some cases of robbery have been reported. The criminals just watch who is drawing money, and then assault people either at the ATM or at a convenient place a few blocks down the street.

Drugs

Cocaine is essentially an export product but it is also available locally. More widespread is marijuana, which is more easily available. However, be careful with drugs – never carry them. The police and army can be very thorough in searching travelers, often looking for a nice fat bribe.

Sometimes you may be offered to buy dope on the street, in a bar or a disco, but never accept these offers. The vendors may well be setting you up for the police, or their accomplices will follow and stop you later, show you false police documents and threaten you with jail unless you pay them off. There have been reports of drugs being planted on travelers, so keep your eyes open.

The *burundanga* is more bad news. It is a drug obtained from a species of tree that is widespread in Colombia and is used by thieves to render a victim unconscious. It can be put into sweets, cigarettes, chewing gum, spirits, beer – virtually any kind of food or drink – and it doesn't have any particular taste or odor. The main effects are loss of will and memory, and sleepiness lasting from a few hours to several days. An overdose can be fatal. Think twice before accepting a cigarette from a stranger or a drink from a new 'friend.'

Guerrillas

There's intense guerrilla and paramilitary activity in many regions, and consequently areas reasonably safe for traveling have become limited. As a general rule, avoid any off-the-beaten-track travel. It's best to stick to the main routes and travel during daytime only. Yet even main routes may sometimes be risky – there have been assaults on buses and cars on the Popayán–Pasto, Bogotá–Medellín, Bogotá–Santa Marta and Medellín–Cartagena roads, to name just a few.

Many regions may be unsafe for travel. The entire area east of the Andes (except Leticia and its environs) should be avoided, as it's guerrilla heartland. Parts of Cundinamarca, eastern Antioquia, Chocó, Córdoba, Bolívar, Magdalena, Cesar, La Guajira, southern Tolima, Valle de Cauca, Huila, Cauca and Nariño are considered security risk areas.

Kidnapping for ransom has been part of guerrilla activity for quite a while and is on the increase. The main targets are well-off locals and foreign executives and the ransoms go up to US$1 million or more. In 2002 about 3000 people were kidnapped in Colombia (a world record), including some foreigners. Guerrillas don't specifically target tourists, but cases have been reported. One of the most recent ones is the case of eight travelers kidnapped (one escaped) by the ELN guerrillas in Ciudad Perdida in September 2003.

Ambushing of car and bus travelers for their valuables is also frequent. These surprise attacks mostly happen at night at roadblocks set up by common criminals and also by guerrillas.

There's no need to be paranoid, but you should be aware of the potential risk, and

COLOMBIA

avoid the regions that are notorious for guerrilla activity. Air travel may be worth considering to skip over some unsafe regions, even though it may eat a bit into your pocket.

Monitor current guerrilla movements. It's not that easy because things change rapidly and unexpectedly, but take the most of various resources. Regional press and TV news can be useful. Possibly better and more specific is advice from the locals who best know what's going on in their region. Inquire at regional tourist offices, travel agents and bus terminals. Ask other travelers along the way and check online resources.

DISABLED TRAVELERS

Colombia offers very little to people with disabilities. Wheelchair ramps are available only at a few upmarket hotels and restaurants, and public transport will be a challenge for any person with mobility problems. Hardly any office, museum or bank provides special facilities for disabled travelers, and wheelchair-accessible toilets are virtually nonexistent.

EMBASSIES & CONSULATES
Embassies & Consulates in Colombia

Foreign diplomatic representatives in Bogotá include (embassy and consulate are at the same address unless specified otherwise) the following. For locations of these and other consulates, see individual city maps.

Australia Bogotá honorary consulate (☎ 1-636-5247; Carrera 18 No 90-38)

Brazil Bogotá (☎ 1-218-0800; Calle 93 No 14-20, Piso 8); Leticia (☎ 8-592-7530; Carrera 9 No 13-84); Medellín (☎ 4-265-7565; Calle 29D No 55-91)

Canada Bogotá (☎ 1-657-9800; Carrera 7 No 115-33, Piso 14)

Costa Rica San Andrés (☎ 8-512-4938; Av Colombia, in Novedades Regina shop)

Ecuador Bogotá (☎ 1-635-0322; Calle 89 No 13-07); Ipiales consulate (☎ 2-773-2292; Carrera 7 No 14-10); Medellín (☎ 4-512-1303; Calle 50 No 52-22, Oficina 603)

France Bogotá (☎ 1-638-1400; Carrera 11 No 93-12)

Germany Bogotá (☎ 1-423-2600; Carrera 69 No 43B-44, Piso 7)

Honduras San Andrés (☎ 8-512-3235; Av Colombia, in Hotel Tiuna)

Israel Bogotá (☎ 1-288-4637; Calle 35 No 7-25, Piso 14)

Panama Bogotá (☎ 1-257-4452; Calle 92 No 7-70); Cartagena (☎ 5-655-1055; Plaza de San Pedro Claver, El Centro); Medellín (☎ 4-268-1358; Carrera 43A No 7-50, Oficina 1607)

Peru Bogotá embassy (☎ 1-257-0505; Calle 80A No 6-50), Bogotá consulate (☎ 1-257-3147; Calle 90 No 14-26); Leticia (☎ 8-592 7204; Calle 13 No 10-70)

UK Bogotá (☎ 1-317-6690; Carrera 9 No 76-49, Piso 9)

USA Bogotá (☎ 1-315-0811; Calle 22D Bis No 47-51)

Venezuela Bogotá embassy (☎ 1-640-1213; Carrera 11 No 87-51, Piso 5), Bogotá consulate (☎ 1-636-4011; Av 13 No 103-16); Cartagena (☎ 5-665-0382; Carrera 3 No 8-129, Bocagrande); Cúcuta (☎ 7-579-1956; Av Camilo Daza); Medellín (☎ 4-351-1614; Calle 32B No 69-59)

Colombian Embassies & Consulates Abroad

Colombia has embassies and consulates in all neighboring countries, and also in:

Australia (☎ 02-9955 0311; 100 Walker St, North Sydney, NSW 2060)

Brazil (☎ 92-412-2104; Rua General Sanpaio 623, Tabatinga)

Canada (☎ 514-849 4852; 1010 Sherbrooke St West, Suite 420, Montreal, Quebec H3A 2R7; ☎ 416-977 0475; 1 Dundas St West, Suite 2108, Toronto, Ontario M5G 1Z3)

France (☎ 01-53 93 91 91; 12 rue de Berri, Paris 75008)

Germany (☎ 030-263 96 10; Kurfürsternstrasse 84, 10787 Berlin)

UK (☎ 020-7495 4233; Suite 14, 140 Park Lane, London W1Y 3AA)

USA (☎ 202-387 8338; 2118 Leroy Place NW, Washington, DC 20008; ☎ 305-441 1235; 280 Aragon Ave, Coral Gables, Miami, FL 33134; ☎ 212-949 9898; 10 East 46th St, New York, NY 10017)

FESTIVALS & EVENTS

Colombians love fiestas. There are more than 200 festivals and events ranging from small, local affairs to international festivals lasting several days. Most of the celebrations are regional, and the most interesting ones are listed in individual destination sections.

FOOD & DRINK
Colombian Cuisine

Colombian cuisine is varied and regional. Among the most typical regional dishes are:

Ajiaco Soup with chicken and three varieties of potato, served with corn and capers; a Bogotán specialty.

Bandeja paisa Typical Antioquian dish made up of ground beef, a sausage, red beans, rice, fried green banana, a fried egg, a piece of fried salt pork and avocado.

Chocolate santafereño Cup of hot chocolate accompanied by a piece of cheese and bread (traditionally, you put the cheese into the chocolate); another Bogotán specialty.

Cuy Grilled guinea pig, typical of Nariño.

Hormiga culona Large fried ants; probably the most exotic Colombian specialty, unique to Santander.

Lechona Pig carcass stuffed with its own meat, rice and dried peas and then baked in an oven; a specialty of Tolima.

Tamal Chopped pork with rice and vegetables folded in a maize dough, wrapped in banana leaves and steamed; there are many regional varieties.

Variety does not, unfortunately, apply to the basic set meal *(comida corriente)*, which is the principal diet of the majority of Colombians eating out. It is a two-course meal consisting of *sopa* (soup) and *bandeja* or *seco* (main course). At lunchtime (from noon to 2pm), it is called *almuerzo*; at dinnertime (after 6pm), it becomes *comida*, but it is in fact identical to lunch. The *almuerzos* and *comidas* are the staple, sometimes the only, offering in countless budget restaurants. They are the cheapest way to fill yourself up, costing between US$1.50 and US$2.50 – roughly half the price of an à la carte dish.

Colombia has an amazing variety of fruits, some of which are endemic to the country. You should try *guanábana, lulo, curuba, zapote, mamoncillo, uchuva, feijoa, granadilla, maracuyá, tomate de árbol, borojó, mamey* and *tamarindo,* to name just a few.

Drinks

Coffee is the number one drink – *tinto* (a small cup of black coffee) is served everywhere. Other coffee drinks are *perico* or *pintado,* a small milk coffee, and *café con leche,* which is larger and uses more milk.

Tea is of poor quality and not very popular. On the other hand, the *aromáticas* – herb teas made with various plants like *cidrón* (citrus leaves), *yerbabuena* (mint) and *manzanilla* (chamomile) – are cheap and good. *Agua de panela* (unrefined sugar melted in hot water) is tasty with lemon.

Beer is popular, cheap and generally not bad. This can't be said about Colombian wine, which is best avoided.

Aguardiente is the local alcoholic spirit, flavored with anise and produced by several companies throughout the country; Cristal from Caldas and Nectar from Cundinamarca are the most popular. *Ron* (rum) is another popular distilled spirit, particularly on the Caribbean coast.

In some regions, mostly in rural areas, you will find *chicha* and *guarapo* (fermented maize or fruit drinks), which are homemade and low (or not so low) in alcohol.

GAY & LESBIAN TRAVELERS

In a deeply Catholic country such as Colombia, the gay and lesbian movement is still very much underground, yet there has been an increasing number of gay hangouts appearing over recent years, principally in the major cities. Bogotá has the largest gay and lesbian community and the most open gay life, and therefore is the best place to make contacts and get to know what's going on. Visit www.geocities.com /WestHollywood/Heights/1424/, which lists bars, discos, events, activities, publications and other related matters.

HEALTH

Colombia has an extensive network of pharmacies, and those in the large cities are usually well stocked. The country also has a developed array of clinics and hospitals, including some world-class private facilities in Bogotá. Tap water in the large cities is said safe to drink, but it's best avoided anyway. See the general Health chapter (p1053) for more information.

HOLIDAYS

The following holidays and special events are observed as public holidays in Colombia. When the dates marked with an asterisk do not fall on a Monday, the holiday is moved to the following Monday to make a three-day long weekend, referred to as a *puente*.

Año Nuevo (New Year's Day; January 1)
Los Reyes Magos (Epiphany; January 6*)
San José (St Joseph; March 19)
Jueves Santo (Maundy Thursday; March/April – dates vary)
Viernes Santo (Good Friday; March/April – dates vary)
Día del Trabajo (Labor Day; May 1)
La Ascensión del Señor (Ascension; May – dates vary)
Corpus Cristi (Corpus Christi; May/June* – dates vary)
Sagrado Corazón de Jesús (Sacred Heart; June*)
San Pedro y San Pablo (St Peter and St Paul; June 29*)
Día de la Independencia (Independence Day; July 20)
Batalla de Boyacá (Battle of Boyacá; August 7)
La Asunción de Nuestra Señora (Assumption; August 15*)
Día de la Raza (Discovery of America; October 12*)
Todos los Santos (All Saints' Day; November 1*)
Independencia de Cartagena (Independence of Cartagena; November 11*)
Inmaculada Concepción (Immaculate Conception; December 8)
Navidad (Christmas Day; December 25)

COLOMBIA

Apart from the weather, you may also consider Colombian holiday periods. There are basically three high seasons when Colombians rush to travel: late December to mid-January, during the Semana Santa, and mid-June to mid-July. During these three periods transport gets more crowded, airfares rise and hotels tend to fill up faster. If you travel at this time, you will have to plan your trip a little ahead, but you'll also enjoy more contact with traveling Colombians, who will be in a relaxed, holiday spirit.

INTERNET ACCESS

Virtually all large cities and many smaller urban centers have cyber cafés. Bogotá alone has probably more than 100 of them. Most cafés provide a range of related services such as printing, scanning and faxing, and some offer cheap international calls. Internet connections are fastest in the major urban centers, while they can be pretty slow in some remote places such as San Andrés or Leticia. Access normally costs US$0.80 to US$2 per hour.

INTERNET RESOURCES

Useful online resources of general and tourist information about Colombia include:

www.colombiaupdate.com Comprehensive site on news, politics, environment, travel etc, with plenty of links to history and culture.

www.colombiareport.org Excellent site providing information on current politics, the economy, human rights issues etc.

www.lanic.utexas.edu/la/colombia Plenty of links to just about everything related to Colombia, provided by the Latin American Network Information Center of the University of Texas.

www.onlinenewspapers.com/colombia.htm Links to 19 Colombian online newspapers.

www.poorbuthappy.com/colombia Lots of tourist and practical information.

www.quehubo.com Web site comprising 93 categories and over 4500 links to Colombian pages (mostly in Spanish), including hotels, tourist attractions and sporting events.

www.zmag.com/CrisesCurEvts/Colombia/colombiatop.htm Analytical articles on current issues including war on drugs, guerrillas, paramilitaries, human rights and refugees.

MAPS

The widest selection of maps of Colombia is produced and sold by the **Instituto Geográfico Agustín Codazzi** (IGAC; Carrera 30 No 48-51; Bogotá), the government mapping body. Folded national road maps are produced by several publishers and distributed through bookstores.

MEDIA
Newspapers & Magazines

All major cities have daily newspapers. Bogotá's leading newspaper, *El Tiempo*, has reasonable coverage of national and international news, culture, sports and economics. It has the widest distribution nationwide. The leading newspapers in other large cities include *El Mundo* and *El Colombiano* in Medellín, and *El País* and *El Occidente* in Cali.

Semana is the biggest national weekly magazine. It features local and international affairs and has an extensive cultural section. *Cambio*, is another popular weekly magazine.

Radio & TV

Hundreds of AM and FM radio stations operate in Colombia and mainly broadcast music programs. There are three nationwide and four regional TV channels. Satellite and cable TV has boomed in Bogotá and in other major cities.

MONEY

Given the country's hazards, it's better to carry traveler's checks (American Express traveler's checks are by far the most easy to change) rather than cash, though some US dollar bills may be useful (euros are far less popular). With the proliferation of ATMs, however, the best way to carry money in Colombia is on a credit card.

Note that large amounts of counterfeit US dollars 'made in Cali' circulate on the market. According to rough estimates, about a quarter of all fake US dollars circulating worldwide are printed in Colombia. They are virtually indistinguishable from the genuine article.

ATMs

There are plenty of *cajeros automáticos* (ATMs) in the cities and major towns. Most major banks have their own ATMs, usually in the bank's wall, but also at other key locations (at the main plaza, in a shopping center, airport etc). Many ATMs are linked to Cirrus and Plus and accept MasterCard and Visa. Advances are in Colombian pesos.

Bargaining

Bargaining is limited to informal trade and services, such as markets, street stalls, taxis, and sometimes long-distance buses.

Credit Cards

Credit cards are increasingly popular as a method of payment for goods and services. They are also useful for getting peso advances at the bank, either from the cashier or from the ATM. These transactions are calculated on the basis of the official exchange rate, so you effectively get more money than when changing traveler's checks or cash.

Visa is by far the best card for Colombia, as most banks will give advance payments on it. MasterCard is the next best, it's accepted in fewer banks (including Bancolombia and Banco de Occidente). Make sure you know the number to call if you lose your credit card, and be quick to cancel it if it's lost or stolen.

Currency

Colombia's official currency is the peso. There are 50-, 100-, 200-, 500- and 1000-peso coins, and paper notes of 1000, 2000, 5000, 10,000, 20,000 and 50,000 pesos. Forged peso notes do exist, so watch exactly what you get. In contrast to perfect dollar fakes, peso forgeries are usually of poor quality and easy to recognize.

Exchange Rates

Exchange rates at press time included the following:

Country	Unit		Col$ (peso)
Australia	A$1	=	2085
Canada	C$1	=	2233
euro zone	€1	=	3415
Japan	¥100	=	2681
New Zealand	NZ$1	=	1805
United Kingdom	UK£1	=	4996
United States	US$1	=	2945

Exchanging Money

Some major banks change cash (mostly US dollars, less often euros) and traveler's checks (principally Amex). The most useful banks include Lloyds TSB Bank, Banco Unión Colombiano, Bancolombia, Bancafé and Banco Santander.

Banks change traveler's checks at rates 2% to 5% lower than the official rate, and usually pay about a further 1% to 3% less for cash. Exchange rates vary from bank to bank, so shop around. Some banks charge a commission for changing checks. Banks usually offer currency exchange services within limited hours, which may mean only a few hours daily, usually in the morning. Banks are often crowded and there's much paperwork involved in changing money, so the process may be time-consuming – set aside up to an hour. Your passport is required for any banking transaction.

You can also change cash (and often traveler's checks) at *casas de cambio* (authorized money-exchange offices), found in virtually all major cities and border towns. They are open until 5pm or 6pm on weekdays, and usually until noon on Saturday. They deal mainly with US dollars, less often with euros, offering rates comparable to, or slightly lower than, banks. The whole operation takes seconds.

You can change cash dollars on the street, but it's not recommended. The only street money markets worth considering are those at the borders, where there may be simply no alternative. There are money-changers at every land border crossing.

Never change money that is not yours, particularly on behalf of Colombians you meet in the street. Travelers have been arrested and jailed for this favor after the bank discovered that the dollars were fake.

POST

The Colombian postal service is operated by two companies, Avianca and Adpostal, and is expensive. Both companies cover domestic and international post, but Avianca only deals with airmail, so if you want to ship a parcel overseas, you'll need Adpostal. Both companies seem to be efficient and reliable but Avianca is far more expensive than Adpostal: a 20-gram letter sent with Avianca to Europe costs US$4 (US$2 with Adpostal). The poste restante system is operated by both Avianca and Adpostal. The most reliable offices are in Bogotá (see p537).

RESPONSIBLE TRAVEL

A responsible tourist is, perhaps, one who treats the visited place as if it were home. Would you wander into your hometown church during a service and start taking flash photos? Would you point your camera at your friends while they go about their daily business? Would you leave rubbish scattered in your favorite park?

Respect rituals and ceremonies, traditions and beliefs. Be aware that some customs can challenge your own belief system and avoid trying to impose your own view of the world on the locals. Encourage ecotourism projects that aim to preserve or restore local environments. Support native communities by buying their crafts but avoid those made from corals, turtles or fossils.

STUDYING

Colombia can be a good place to study Spanish. The Spanish spoken in Colombia is clear and easy to understand and there are language school in the big cities. You can also find a teacher and arrange individual classes. Inquire in popular travelers' hostels (in Bogotá, Cartagena, Medellín, Cali), which usually have contacts with Spanish tutors. They are often students and their rates are reasonable.

TELEPHONE

The telephone system is largely automated for both domestic and international calls. Until not long ago, Telecom was the only national telecommunication company, but in 1998 two new companies, Orbitel and ETB, entered the market.

Public telephones exist in cities and large towns but, except for the centers of the largest cities, they are few and far between, and many are out of order. As a rule, Telecom offices have some operable phones. Public telephones use coins, although newly installed telephones accept phone cards *(tarjeta telefónica)*. Phone cards can be used for international, inter-city and local calls. Local calls are charged by timed rate (not flat rate), costing around US$0.10 for a three-minute call.

You can call direct to just about anywhere in Colombia. All phone numbers are seven digits long countrywide. Area codes are single digits (they are included before all the local numbers listed in this chapter), but before them you need to dial the index of the provider you want to use: ☎ 05 for Orbitel, ☎ 07 for ETB and ☎ 09 for Telecom. As yet, Orbitel and ETB only provide connections between some major cities, so in most cases you'll be using Telecom.

All three companies provide international service and may temporarily offer significant discounts – watch out for their ads in the press and TV. To call abroad from Colombia, dial ☎ 005, ☎ 007 or ☎ 009, respectively, then dial the country code, followed by the area code and number.

Colombia's country code is ☎ 57. If you are dialing a Colombian number from abroad, drop the prefix (05, 07 or 09) and dial only the area code and the local number.

TOILETS

There are virtually no self-contained public toilets in Colombia. If you are unexpectedly caught in need, use a toilet in a restaurant. Museums and large shopping centers are other rescue options, as are bus and airport terminals. Carry some toilet paper with you at all times.

Except for toilets in some upmarket establishments, the plumbing might not be of a standard you are accustomed to. The pipes are narrow and water pressure is weak, so toilets can't cope with toilet paper, which you should throw into a wastebasket (normally provided).

TOURIST INFORMATION

Tourist information is administered by municipal tourist information offices in departmental capitals and other tourist destinations. Some are better than others, but on the whole they lack city maps and brochures. Staff members may be friendly but often don't speak English. The practical information they provide can be lacking, and the quality of information largely depends on the person who attends you.

In some cities, tourist offices are supported by the Policía de Turismo, the police officers specially trained to attend tourists. They are mainly to be found on the street and at the major tourist attractions.

VISAS

Nationals of some countries, including most of Western Europe, the Americas, Japan, Australia and New Zealand, don't need a visa to enter Colombia. It's a good idea for you to check this before your planned trip, because visa regulations change frequently. Over recent years, Colombia has reintroduced visas for nationals of various countries, partly as a response to the decision of these countries to re-introduce visas for Colombians.

All visitors get an entry stamp or print in their passport from DAS (the security police who are also responsible for immigration) upon arrival at any international airport or land border crossing. Make sure they've stamped your passport, otherwise you are illegally in Colombia. The stamp indicates how many days you can stay in the country. The maximum allowed is 90 days, but DAS officials often stamp 60 or just 30 days. An onward ticket is legally required and you may be asked to show one.

Upon departure, immigration officials put an exit stamp in your passport. Again, be sure to check if they've done it; without the stamp you may have problems entering Colombia next time around.

You are entitled to a 30-day visa extension (US$20), which can be obtained from DAS in any departmental capital. Apply shortly before the expiration of your allowed stay because the extension runs from the day it is stamped in your passport. Most travelers apply for an extension in Bogotá – see that section (p537).

VOLUNTEERING

There are few options for volunteers in Colombia, mostly because local organizations are afraid to take responsibility for visitors, given the precarious safety condition of life, work and travel in the country. That said, your best chance is to work as a ranger in one of Colombia's national parks. A minimum commitment of one month and at least basic Spanish-speaking skills are required. For information (in Spanish) check www.parquesnacionales.gov.co/parques /gpvhtml.htm. For other possible voluntary

work (in social areas), contact federations of nongovernmental organizations:
Confederación Colombiana de ONGs (☎ 1-215-6519; www.ccong.org.co; Carrera 13A No 107-02, Bogotá)
Federación de ONGs de Bogotá y Cundinamarca (☎ 1-677-1088; Calle 175 No 40-56, Bogotá)

WOMEN TRAVELERS

Like most of Latin America, Colombia is very much a man's country. Machismo and sexism are palpable throughout society. Women travelers will attract more curiosity, attention and advances from local men than they would from men in the West. Many Colombian men will stare at women, use endearing terms, make comments on their physical appearance and, in some cases, try to make physical contact. It is just the Latin-American way of life, and local males would not understand if someone told them their behavior was sexual harassment. On the contrary, they would argue that they are just paying the woman a flattering compliment.

The best way to deal with unwanted attention is simply to ignore it. Maintain your self-confidence and assertiveness and don't let macho behavior disrupt your holiday. Dressing modestly may lessen the chances of you being the object of macho interest, or at least make you less conspicuous to the local peacocks. Wearing a wedding band and carrying a photo of a make-believe spouse may minimize harassment.

There isn't much in the way of women's support services in Colombia, let alone resources specifically for women travelers.

WORKING

Legally, you need a work visa to get a job in Colombia. Without one, you can try to teach English, but it may be difficult to get a job without bona fide teaching credentials.

Ecuador

HIGHLIGHTS

- **Galápagos Islands** – snorkel with harmless sharks, have staring contests with meter-long iguanas, scuba dive with manta rays and stand face-to-face with spectacular seabirds (p696)
- **Cuenca** – wander the splendid colonial streets of Ecuador's third-largest city, shop for panama hats, dance the night away and spend tomorrow in the misty moors of Parque Nacional Cajas (p659)
- **The Oriente** – hike, visit indigenous communities, white-water raft, fish for piranhas and spot caimans, freshwater dolphins, monkeys and more in one of the world's greatest rain forests (p668)
- **The Quilotoa loop** – get around this spectacular high-Andean road and stop to hike, buy indigenous crafts and gaze into Ecuador's most stunning crater lake, Laguna Quilotoa (p649)
- **Off the beaten track** – from Coca in the Oriente to Iquitos Peru, the two-week (at least!) journey down the Río Napo to the Amazon River by canoe and cargo boat is way off the beaten track (p671)
- **Best journey** – Riobamba–Guaranda and Guaranda–Ambato: short but sweet, this bus ride skirts the highest mountain in Ecuador (Volcán Chimborazo), affording mind-boggling views (p655)

FAST FACTS

- **Area:** 283,560 sq km (roughly the size of New Zealand or the US state of Nevada)
- **Budget:** US$15–20 a day
- **Capital:** Quito
- **Costs:** budget hotel in Quito US$6, bottle o' beer US$1, national park entrance fee US$10–20
- **Country code:** ☎ 593
- **Electricity:** 110V, 60Hz; US-type plugs
- **Famous for:** the Galápagos Islands and the panama hat
- **Languages:** Spanish, Quechua
- **Money:** US dollar
- **Phrases:** bacán (cool), ¡guácala! (disgusting), farra (party)
- **Population:** 12 million
- **Time:** GMT minus 5 hours
- **Tipping:** 10% in better restaurants; tip all guides
- **Traveler's checks:** cashed at major banks; ATMs are easier
- **Visas:** North American and most European citizens need only a valid passport

TRAVEL HINTS

Pack reasonably lightly and you can almost always carry your backpack inside the bus. If you're setting up a last-minute tour, get a few people together to increase your bargaining power.

If you can't decide whether to climb snowcapped volcanoes, lounge on sunny beaches or slosh through rain forests spying on monkeys, have no fear – in Ecuador you can change your world as fast as you can change your mind. One day your cold fingers are picking through hand-woven woolen sweaters at a chilly indigenous market in the Andean highlands, and the next day you're slapping mosquitoes off your ass on a tropical beach. That is, if you decide to head to the ocean. Because you could easily head east to the jungle, leaving those towering Andean peaks for a romp through the rain forests of the upper Amazon Basin, which is also only a day's journey away. The beauty of Ecuador is that it's three different worlds in one little country: the spectacular Andes, the sun-drenched Pacific Coast and the lush Oriente (the tropical lowlands east of the Andes). Add to this the Galápagos Islands, only 1000km off the coast, and it's surprising every adventurous soul among us isn't roaming around Ecuador. And did we mention the cloud forests? The bird-watching? The trekking? The mountain biking? The white-water rafting...?

HISTORY
Early Cultures
The oldest tools found in Ecuador date back to 9000 BC, meaning people were mucking about the region in the Stone Age. Signs of a more developed culture – mainly ceramics from the coastal Valdivia period – date back to 3400 BC.

Pre-Inca Ecuador is less well known than pre-Inca Peru, but the existence of numerous *camellones* (raised-field earthworks) for cultivation suggests a large population inhabited the Guayas lowlands in very early times. In the 11th century AD, Ecuador had two dominant cultures: the expansionist Cara along the coast and the peaceful Quitu in the highlands. These cultures merged to form the Shyri nation. Around 1300, the Puruhá of the southern highlands became powerful, and a Shyri princess married a Puruhá prince named Duchicela, which forged a successful alliance. Duchicela's descendants ruled more or less peacefully for about 150 years.

Inca Empire
By the mid-1400s, Duchicela's descendants dominated the north. The south was ruled by the Cañari people, who defended themselves fiercely against the Inca invaders. It was some years before Inca Tupac-Yupanqui was able to subdue the Cañari and turn his attention north. During this time, a Cañari princess bore him a son, Huayna Capac.

The subjugation of the north took many years, and Huayna Capac grew up in Ecuador. He succeeded his father to the Inca throne and spent years traveling all over his empire, from Bolivia to Ecuador, constantly suppressing uprisings. Wherever possible, he strengthened his position by marriage. His union with a secondary wife, Paccha, the daughter of the defeated Cacha Duchicela, produced a son, Atahualpa, while from his principal marriage came Huáscar, his son born entirely of Inca tradition.

Huayna Capac died in 1526 and left his empire not to one son, as was traditional, but to the two half brothers, thus dividing the Inca empire for the first time. In the same year, the first Spaniards, led by Bartolomé Ruiz de Andrade, landed near Esmeraldas in northern Ecuador.

Meanwhile, the rivalry between the Inca, led by Huáscar of Cuzco and Atahualpa of Quito, flared into civil war. After years of fighting, Atahualpa defeated Huáscar in a battle near Ambato in central Ecuador. Atahualpa thus ruled a weakened and still divided Inca empire when Francisco Pizarro landed in Peru in 1532.

Colonial Era
Pizarro appointed his brother Gonzalo governor of Quito in 1540. Gonzalo, hoping to find more gold, sent his lieutenant Francisco de Orellana to explore the Amazon. Orellana and his force ended up floating clear to the Atlantic – the first men to descend the Amazon and cross the continent.

Lima was the seat of Ecuador's political administration during the first centuries of colonial rule. Ecuador was at first a *gobernación* (province), but in 1563 it became the Audiencia de Quito, a more important political division. In 1739, the *audiencia* was transferred from the viceroyalty of Peru to the viceroyalty of Colombia (then known as Nueva Grenada).

ECUADOR

ECUADOR

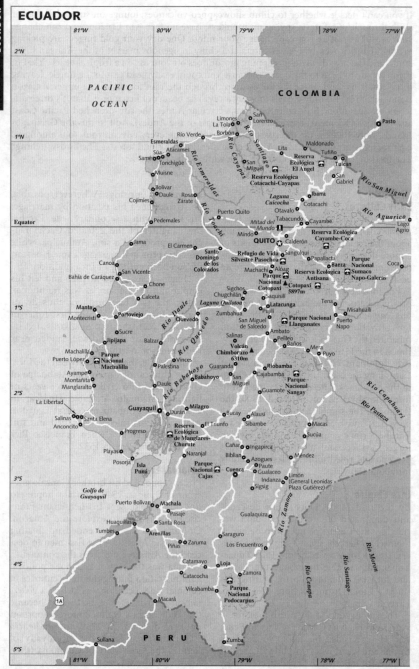

PACIFIC
OCEAN

COLOMBIA

2°N

1°N

Equator

1°S

2°S

3°S

4°S

5°S

81°W 80°W 79°W 78°W 77°W

Pasto

Limones
La Tola
Borbón
San
Lorenzo
Río Verde
Esmeraldas
Atacames
Súa
Same
Tonchigüe
Muisne
Bolívar
Daule
Rosa
Zárate
Cojimíes
Pedernales
Jama
El Carmen
Canoa
San Vicente
Bahía de Caráquez
Chone
Calceta
Manta
Montecristi
Portoviejo
Sucre
Jipijapa
Machalilla
Puerto López
Ayampe
Montañita
Manglaralto
La Libertad
Salinas
Anconcito
Santa Elena
Progreso
Playas
Posorja
Isla Puná

Río Santiago
Río Cayapas
San
Miguel
Reserva Ecológica
Cotacachi-Cayapas
Lita
Maldonado
Tufiño
Reserva
Ecológica
El Ángel
Tulcán
San
Gabriel
Ibarra
Cotacachi
Laguna
Cuicocha
Otavalo
Tabacundo
Cayambe
Río San Miguel
Río Aguarico
Lago
Agrio
Puerto Quito
Mindo
Mitad del
Mundo
QUITO
Calderón
Reserva Ecológica
Cayambe-Coca
Papallacta
Baeza
Parque
Nacional
Sumaco
Napo-Galeras
Coca
Santo
Domingo
de los
Colorados
Refugio de Vida
Silvestre Pasochoa
Sangolquí
Machachi
Alóag
Parque
Nacional
Cotopaxi
Reserva Ecológica
Antisana
Cotopaxi
5897m
Sigchos
Chugchilán
Saquisilí
Laguna Quilotoa
Zumbahua
Pujilí
Latacunga
Tena
Misahuallí
Puerto
Napo
Quevedo
San Miguel
de Salcedo
Parque Nacional
Llanganates
Salinas
Ambato
Pelileo
Baños
Mera
Puyo
Guaranda
Volcán
Chimborazo
6310m
San
Miguel
Riobamba
Cajabamba
Parque
Nacional
Sangay
Balzar
Vinces
Palestina
Daule
Babahoyo
Guamote
Guayaquil
Durán
Milagro
Bucay
Alausí
Macas
Reserva
Ecológica
de Manglares-
Churute
El Triunfo
Sibambe
Sucúa
Naranjal
Cañar
Ingapirca
Biblián
Azogues
Paute
Méndez
Parque
Nacional
Cajas
Cuenca
Gualaceo
Limón
(General Leonidas
Plaza Gutiérez)
Indanza
Sígsig
Golfo de
Guayaquil
Puerto Bolívar
Machala
Pasaje
Huaquillas
Santa Rosa
Tumbes
Arenillas
Zaruma
Piñas
Saraguro
Gualaquiza
Río Zamora
Río Capahuari
Río Pastaza
Río Morona
Catamayo
Loja
Zamora
Catacocha
Parque
Nacional
Podocarpus
Río Cenepa
Río Santiago
Río Nangaritza
Vilcabamba
Macará
Los Encuentros
Sullana
Zumba

PERU

Río Esmeraldas
Río Toachi
Río Daule
Río Quevedo
Río Babahoyo

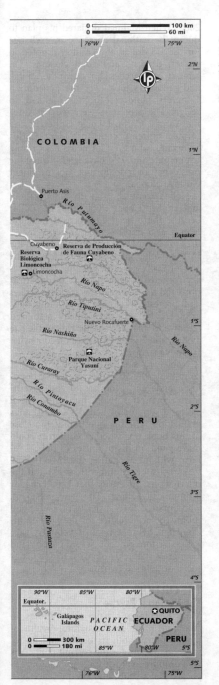

Ecuador remained peaceful during these centuries, and agriculture and the arts flourished. Europeans introduced cattle, bananas and other agricultural products. They also built an abundance of churches and monasteries, which they decorated with unique carvings and paintings blending Spanish and indigenous artistic influences.

Life was comfortable for the ruling Spaniards, but the indigenous people and *mestizos* (people of mixed Spanish and indigenous descent) were treated abysmally. Systems of forced labor and tribute were not only tolerated but encouraged, and this led to several 18th-century uprisings against the Spanish rulers.

One of the best remembered heroes of the early revolutionary period was Eugenio Espejo, born in Quito in 1747 of an indigenous father and a *mulata* (of mixed African and European ancestry) mother. A brilliant man who obtained his doctorate by the age of 20, Espejo became a major literary voice for independence. He wrote political satire, founded a liberal newspaper and spoke out strongly against colonialism. He was imprisoned several times and died in jail in 1795.

Independence

The first serious attempt at independence was made on August 10, 1809, by a partisan group led by Juan Pío Montúfar. The group took Quito and installed a government, but royalist troops regained control in only 24 days.

A decade later, Simón Bolívar, the Venezuelan liberator, freed Colombia in his march southward from Caracas. Bolívar then supported the people of Guayaquil when they claimed independence on October 9, 1820. It took another two years for Ecuador to be entirely liberated from Spanish rule. The decisive battle was fought on May 24, 1822, when Mariscal (Field Marshall) Sucre, one of Bolívar's best generals, defeated the royalists at Pichincha and took Quito.

Bolívar's idealistic dream was to form a united South America. He began by amalgamating Venezuela, Colombia and Ecuador into the independent state of Gran Colombia. This lasted only eight years with Ecuador becoming fully independent in 1830. That same year, a treaty was signed with Peru, establishing a boundary between the two nations. Unfortunately, the treaty didn't hold up.

War with Peru

In 1941, after Peru tried to take nearly half of Ecuador's territory, war broke out between the two nations. The boundary was finally redrawn by a conference of foreign government ministers in the 1942 Protocol of Rio de Janeiro. Ecuador never recognized this border, and minor skirmishes with Peru have occurred because of it – the most serious was the short war in early 1995, when several dozen soldiers on both sides were killed. Finally, after more fighting in 1998, Peru and Ecuador negotiated a settlement, in which Peru retained a majority of the land in question.

Liberals & Conservatives

Independent Ecuador's internal history has been a typically Latin American turmoil of open political warfare between liberals and conservatives. Quito emerged as the main center for the Church-backed conservatives, while Guayaquil has traditionally been considered liberal and socialist. The rivalry between these groups has frequently escalated to extreme violence: conservative president García Moreno was shot and killed in 1875, and liberal President Eloy Alfaro was killed and burned by a mob in Quito in 1912. The military began assuming control, and the 20th century saw more periods of military rather than civilian rule. The rivalry between the two factions continues on a social level today (see The National Psyche, following).

Recent Political Developments

In 1996, left-wing populist Abdalá Bucaram was elected president, but after just six months, the Ecuadorian Congress deemed Bucaram (known as 'El Loco' – The Madman) mentally unfit and removed him from office. Congress named Fabián Alarcón interim president until the 1998 elections, in which Jamil Mahuad, former mayor of Quito, emerged victorious.

Mahuad had his political savvy put to the test. The effects of El Niño and the sagging oil market of 1997–98 sent the economy into a tailspin in 1999. The sucre depreciated from about 7000 per US dollar at the start of 1999 to about 25,000 by January 2000. When Mahuad declared his plan to dump the national currency in exchange for the US dollar, the country erupted in strikes, protests and road closures. On January 21, marches shut down the capital, and protesters took over the Ecuadorian Congress building, forcing Mahuad to resign. The protesters were led by Antonio Vargas, Coronel Lucio Gutiérrez and former supreme court president Carlos Solorzano, who then formed a brief ruling triumvirate and, two days later, turned the presidency over to former vice president Gustavo Noboa.

Noboa went ahead with dollarization, and in September 2000, the US dollar became the official currency of Ecuador. Noboa also implemented austerity measures to obtain US$2 billion in aid from the IMF and other international lenders. At the end of 2000, gas and cooking fuel prices sky-rocketed (largely because of dollarization) and the new year saw frequent strikes and protests by unions and indigenous groups. The economy finally stabilized (relative to its roller coaster ride in the late 1990s), and Noboa left office on somewhat favorable terms.

Noboa was succeeded in 2002 by former coup-leader Lucio Gutiérrez, whose populist agenda and promises to end government corruption won him the crucial electoral support of Ecuador's indigenous population. The big question at the close of this book was whether Gutiérrez could make good on his promises of radical reform without alienating the IMF (whose loans Ecuador continued to seek) and the international investors that kept Ecuador economically afloat. The new president, who opposed IMF austerity measures and promised social justice for the poor in his campaign, held the reins of a country with a massive foreign debt, severe poverty and a congress staunchly opposed to any major social or political reform.

THE CULTURE
The National Psyche

Most Ecuadorians have three things in common: pride in the natural wealth of their country (both its beauty and its resources); disdain for the corrupt politicians who promise to redistribute yet continue to pocket that wealth; and the presence of a relative in another country (over 10% of the population – some 1.3 million people – have left Ecuador in search of work elsewhere).

From there, the psyche blurs, and attitude becomes a matter of altitude. *Serranos* (people from the mountains) and *costeños* (people from the coast) can spend hours telling you what makes themselves different (ie better) to the other. Largely based on the competition between Quito in the mountains and Guayaquil on the coast, *serranos* call *costeños* '*monos*' (monkeys) and say they're lazy and would rather party than keep their cities clean. *Costeños* say *serranos* are uptight and elitist and that they pepper their interactions with shallow formalities. Of course, *serranos* still pour down to the coast in droves for holidays and *costeños* speak longingly of the cool evenings of the highlands.

Lifestyle
How an Ecuadorian lives is a matter of geography, ethnicity and class. A poor *campesino* (peasant) family that cultivates the thin volcanic soil of a steep highland plot lives very differently to a coastal fishing family living in the mangroves of Esmeraldas Province, or a family living in the slums of Guayaquil. An indigenous Saraguro family that tends communally owned cattle in the southern highlands lives a dramatically different life to that of an upper-class *quiteño* family (family from Quito), who might have three maids, a big-screen TV and a Mercedes in the garage.

An estimated 70% of the population live below the poverty line, and paying for cooking fuel and putting food in the belly is a constant concern for most Ecuadorians. But, as most first-time visitors are always astounded to experience, even the poorest Ecuadorians exude an openness, generosity and happiness all too rare in developed countries. Fiestas are celebrated with fervor by everyone, and you'll sometimes roll around in bed, kept awake until dawn by the noise of a nearby birthday bash.

People
Ecuador has the highest population density of any South American country – about 45 people per sq km. The birth rate is 25.47 per 1000 inhabitants, which means the population will double by around 2028.

About 65% of the Ecuadorian people are *mestizos*, 25% are indigenous, 7% are Spanish and 3% are black. Other ethnicities account for less than 1%. Most of the indigenous people speak Quechua and live in the highlands. A few other small groups live in the lowlands.

Nearly half of the country's people live on the coast (including the Galápagos), while about 46% live in the highlands. The remainder live in the Oriente, where colonization is slowly increasing. The urban population is 65%.

RELIGION
The predominant religion is Roman Catholicism, although a small minority of other churches are found. Indigenous peoples tend to blend Catholicism with their own traditional beliefs.

ARTS
Architecture
Many of Quito's churches were built during the colonial period, and the architects were influenced by the Quito school (see Visual Arts, p618). In addition, churches often have Moorish influences. The overall appearance of the architecture of colonial churches is overpoweringly ornamental and almost cloyingly rich – in short, baroque.

Many colonial houses have two stories, with the upper floors bearing ornate balconies. The walls are whitewashed and the roofs are red tile. Quito's Old Town and Cuenca are Unesco World Cultural Heritage Sites and both are full of beautifully preserved colonial architecture.

Literature
Ecuadorian literature is not very well known outside Latin America, but indigenous novelist Jorge Icaza's *Huasipungo*, a naturalistic tale of the miserable conditions on Andean haciendas in the early 20th century, is available in English translation as *The Villagers*. Also worth checking out is *Fire from the Andes: Short Fiction by Women from Bolivia, Ecuador & Peru*, edited by Susan E Benner and Kathy S Leonard.

Music
Cumbia has the rhythm of a galloping three-legged horse, and you'd better get used to it. Originally from Colombia, Ecuadorian

cumbia has a sharper, faster sound than that of its northern counterpart, and it's played *everywhere,* especially on buses (which makes those high-speed rides seem even more psychotic).

Salsa is favored on the coast, especially in Esmeraldas Province. Esmeraldas is also famous for marimba music, played mostly by Afro-Ecuadorians.

Traditional Andean music – *música folklórica* – has a distinctive, haunting sound that has been popularized in Western culture by songs such as Paul Simon's version of 'El Cóndor Pasa' ('If I Could'). Its otherworldly quality results from use of a pentatonic, or five-note, scale (rather than the eight-note octaves common in most Western music) and the use of pre-Columbian wind and percussion instruments that conjure the windswept quality of *páramo* (highland) life. It is best heard at a *peña* (a folk-music club or performance).

Visual Arts

The colonial religious art found in many churches and museums – especially in Quito – was produced by indigenous artists trained by the Spanish conquistadors. The artists portrayed Spanish religious concepts, yet infused their own indigenous beliefs, giving birth to a unique religious art known as the *escuela quiteña* (Quito school). The Quito school died out with independence.

The 19th century is referred to as the Republican period, and its art is characterized by formalism. Favorite subjects included heroes of the revolution, important members of the new republic's high society, and florid landscapes.

The 20th century saw the rise of the indigenist school, whose unifying theme is the oppression of Ecuador's indigenous inhabitants. Important *indigenista* (indigenist school) artists include Camilo Egas (1889–1962), Oswaldo Guayasamín (1919–99), Eduardo Kingman (1913–97) and Gonzalo Endara Crow (1936–). You can (and should!) see the works of these artists in Quito's galleries and museums. The former homes of Egas and Guayasamín, also in Quito, are now museums featuring their respective works.

SPORT

The national sport – go on, guess – is *futból* (soccer). Major-league games are played every Saturday and Sunday in Quito and Guayaquil, and impromptu games are played everywhere. The country's best team is Barcelona (from Guayaquil), although you should avoid shouting that around Quito. Volleyball is also huge. Bullfighting is popular in the highlands; the biggest season is the first week of December in Quito. Finally, the *pelea de gallos* (cockfight) is a national favorite – a town ain't a town without a cockfighting ring.

ENVIRONMENT
Land

Despite its pipsqueak size, Ecuador has some of the world's most varied geography. The country can be divided into three regions. The Andes form the backbone of Ecuador. West of the mountains lie the coastal lowlands, while to the east is the Oriente, comprising the jungles of the upper Amazon Basin. In only 200km, as the condor flies, you can climb from the coast to snowcaps over 6km above sea level, then descend to the jungle on the country's eastern side. The Galápagos Islands (Islas Galápagos) lie on the equator, 1000km west of Ecuador's coast, and constitute one of the country's 21 provinces.

Wildlife

Ecuador is one of the most species-rich countries on the globe, deemed by ecologists as a 'megadiversity hot spot.' The country has more than 20,000 plant species, with new ones discovered every year. In comparison, there are only 17,000 plant species on the entire North American continent. The tropics, in general, harbor many more species than do more temperate regions, but another reason for Ecuador's biodiversity is simply that the country holds a great number of habitat types. Obviously, the Andes will support very different species from the tropical rain forests, and when intermediate biomes and the coastal areas are included, the result is a wealth of different ecosystems, a riot of life that draws nature lovers from the world over.

Bird-watchers flock to Ecuador for the great number of bird species recorded here – some 1500, or about twice the number found in any one of the continents of North America, Europe or Australia. But Ecuador isn't just for the birds: some 300 mammal species have been recorded, from monkeys in the Amazonian lowlands to the rare Andean spectacled bear in the highlands.

National Parks

Ecuador's first national park was Islas Galápagos (p696, established in 1959. It's the most famous of the country's parks, thanks to Charles Darwin and the islands' unique flora and fauna.

Scattered across mainland Ecuador are eight other national parks, including (from north to south):

Cotopaxi A park high in the Andes between Quito and Latacunga, surrounding 5897m Volcán Cotopaxi (p650).

Yasuní A Unesco International Biosphere Reserve and Ecuador's largest mainland national park, encompassing a vast tract of nearly uninhabited rain forest southeast of Coca (p669).

Machalilla The country's only coastal national park, with scuba diving, whale watching, beaches, pre-Columbian ruins and islands (p685).

Sangay Near Riobamba, this park encompasses three of Ecuador's highest peaks (p653).

Cajas West of Cuenca, this park holds hundreds of high mountain lakes (p663).

Podocarpus Near Loja and Zamora, this park is named for Ecuador's only native conifer and holds a variety of habitat, from jungle to cloud forest (p666).

In addition to these national parks are various national reserves and protected areas, as well as private nature reserves. Most parks and reserves lack the tourist infrastructure found in other parts of the world. Entrance fees are between US$10 and US$20 on the mainland and US$100 in the Galápagos.

Environmental Issues

Ecuador is fraught with environmental problems. Texaco discovered oil in the Oriente in 1968, and the subsequent large-scale oil drilling (which continues today by several multinational companies) has had a devastating impact on the rain forest and its indigenous populations. Toxic waste water and raw crude were spilled or dumped into lakes and streams; oil roads opened once-pristine rain forest to colonists who cleared the forests for farming and ranching; and indigenous communities have been devastated (and, in the case of the Cofán, practically wiped out). One oil pipeline already pumps crude from the Oriente to the coast, and, in June, 2001 the Ecuadorian government granted a consortium of international oil companies the license to build a second. This is one of the most high-profile, recent environmental issues in Ecuador, as the pipeline runs through seven ecologically sensitive areas on its way over the Andes to Esmeraldas city. One of those areas was virgin cloud forest near the town of Mindo (p677), which has made international news for its local protests against the pipeline.

On the coast, the opening of shrimp farms in the 1980s and 1990s resulted in the complete destruction of 80% to 90% of Ecuador's mangrove forests. In 1999, the industry was hard hit when shrimp diseases decimated farms. Esmeraldas Province has some of the last large stands of mangroves in the country. Opening new shrimp farms is now prohibited.

Ecuador has one of the highest deforestation rates in Latin America. In the Andes, poor *campesinos* have (as a means of survival) burnt large tracts of forest for farming and ranching. Over 90% of the tropical forests in the western lowlands (between the Andes and the coast) have been cleared to develop banana plantations and other forms of agriculture.

Ecuador lacks the financial resources to commit itself to strong government-funded conservation. Various local and international conservation agencies, indigenous groups, which survive on their natural resources (such as the rain forest), combined with nature-oriented tourism have brought international attention to Ecuador's environmental crises and contribute to an ever-increasing demand to protect the environment. But, as any environmentalist in Ecuador will tell you, this is no time to rest. New mining, oil, logging and other projects are continuously implemented, and pressure is needed from all sides to minimize or eliminate their impacts on the environment.

TRANSPORT

GETTING THERE & AWAY
Air

The main international airports are in Guayaquil (p694) and Quito (p635). Unless they are merely in transit, passengers on outbound international flights must pay a

US$25 departure tax from Quito and US$10 from Guayaquil (both cash-only).

Direct flights go to Bogotá (Colombia), Buenos Aires (Argentina), Caracas (Venezuela), Curaçao, Guatemala City, Havana (Cuba), Lima (Peru), Panama City, Rio de Janeiro (Brazil), San José (Costa Rica), Santiago (Chile) and São Paulo (Brazil). Connecting flights (via Lima) are available to Asunción (Paraguay) and La Paz (Bolivia). There are also three flights per week between Tulcán (in the northern highlands of Ecuador) and Cali (Colombia).

Boat

For information on boat travel between Nuevo Rocafuerte (Ecuador) and Iquitos (Peru), see p671.

Bus

International bus tickets sold in Quito often require a change of bus at the border. It's usually cheaper and just as convenient to buy a ticket to the border and another ticket in the next country. The exceptions are the international bus companies listed under Guayaquil (p694) which run to Peru via Huaquillas; on these, you do not have to change buses, and the immigration officials usually board the bus to take care of your paperwork.

The main bus route between Colombia and Ecuador is via Tulcán (p646). The main bus routes between Peru and Ecuador are via Huaquillas (p696) or Macará (p668). Zumba, south of Vilcabamba (p668), is gaining popularity as an alternative route to/from Peru due to its scenic location and lack of use.

GETTING AROUND

You can usually get anywhere quickly and easily. Bus is the most common mode of transport, followed by airplanes. Buses can take you from the Colombian border to Peru's border in 18 hours. Boats are used in the northern coastal mangroves and in the Oriente.

Whatever form of transport you use, remember to have your passport with you, as you will need to show it when you board planes, and document checks are frequent on buses. People without documents may be arrested. If your passport is in order, these procedures are cursory. If you're traveling anywhere near the borders or in the Oriente, expect more frequent passport checks.

Air

With the exception of flying to the Galápagos, most internal flights are fairly cheap. One-way flights are all US$58 or less, except to the Galápagos (see p702 for details). Almost all flights originate or terminate in Quito or Guayaquil.

Ecuador's major domestic airline is **TAME** (www.tame.com.ec). **Icaro** (www.icaro.com.ec) is the second biggest, with fewer flights but newer planes.

Between these two airlines, you can fly from Quito to Guayaquil, Coca, Cuenca, Esmeraldas, Lago Agrio, Loja, Macas, Machala, Manta, Portoviejo, Tulcán and the Galápagos. From Guayaquil you can fly to Quito, Coca, Cuenca, Loja, Machala and the Galápagos. There are no Sunday flights to the Oriente.

Seats on domestic flights are unreserved, so there's always a race to get the choice seats. Some flights have marvelous views of the snowcapped Andes. When flying from Quito to Guayaquil, sit on the left.

If you can't get a ticket for a particular flight (especially out of small towns), go to the airport early and get on the waiting list in the hope of a cancellation. If you have a reservation, confirm it and then reconfirm it or you may be bumped.

Boat

Motorized dugout canoes are the only transportation available in some roadless areas. Regularly scheduled boats are affordable, although not as cheap as a bus for a similar distance. Hiring your own boat and skipper is possible but extremely expensive. The northern coast (near San Lorenzo and Borbón) and the lower Río Napo from Coca to Peru are the places you'll most likely travel to by boat (if you get out that far). Pelting rain and glaring sun can induce serious suffering, and an umbrella is excellent defense against both. Use good sunscreen or wear long sleeves, pants and a hat. A light jacket is worth having in case of chilling rain, and insect repellent is useful during stops along the river. Bring a water bottle and a stash of food, and you're set. Keep your spare clothes in plastic bags or they'll get soaked if it storms.

Bus

Buses are the lifeblood of Ecuador and the easiest way to get around. Most towns have a *terminal terrestre* (central bus terminal) for long-distance buses, although in some towns, buses leave from various places. *Busetas* are fast, small buses offering direct, and sometimes frighteningly speedy, service. Larger coaches usually allow standing passengers and can get crowded, but are often more interesting.

To get your choice of seat, buy tickets in advance from the terminal. Some companies have frequent departures and don't sell advance tickets. During holiday weekends, buses can be booked up for several days in advance. For immediate travel, go to the terminal and listen for your destination to be yelled out. Make sure your bus goes direct to your destination if you don't want to change.

If you're traveling light, keep your luggage with you inside the bus. Otherwise, heave it onto the roof or stuff it into the luggage compartment and keep an eagle eye on it.

Long-distance buses rarely have toilets, but usually stop for 20-minute meal and bladder-relief breaks at fairly appropriate times. If not, drivers will stop to let you fertilize the roadside.

Local buses are usually slow and crowded, but cheap. You can get around most towns for about US$0.12 to US$0.15. Local buses often go out to nearby villages (a great way to explore an area).

Hitching

Private cars are uncommon and trucks are used as public transport in remote areas, so trying to hitch a free ride isn't easy. If the driver is stopping to drop off and pick up other passengers, assume that payment will be expected. If you're the only passenger, the driver may have picked you up just to talk to a foreigner.

Taxi

Taxis are cheap. Bargain the fare beforehand, or you're likely to be overcharged. A long ride in a large city (Quito or Guayaquil) shouldn't go over US$5, and short hops in small towns usually cost about US$1. Meters are obligatory in Quito but rarely seen elsewhere. On weekends and at night,

fares are always about 25% to 50% higher. A full-day taxi hire should cost from US$50 to US$60.

Train

Little remains of Ecuador's railways after the damage to lines during the 1982–83 El Niño rains. Only the sections with tourist appeal have received enough funding to reopen. A train runs three times a week between Riobamba and Sibambe, which includes the hair-raising Nariz del Diablo (Devil's Nose) – the country's railway pride and joy. The Ibarra–San Lorenzo line, which used to link the highlands with the coast, is on its deathbed; *autoferros* (buses mounted on railway chassis) only make it a fraction of the way to San Lorenzo. One easy way to ride the rails is on the weekend Quito–Cotopaxi route, which stops at El Boliche train station (no food or lodging) in the national park and waits about two hours before returning.

Truck

In remote areas, *camiones* (trucks) and *camionetas* (pickup trucks) often double as buses. If the weather is OK, you get fabulous views; if not, you have to crouch underneath a dark tarpaulin and suck dust. Pickups can be hired to remote places such as climbers' refuges.

QUITO

Ecuador's capital city, cradled in a high Andean valley 2850m above sea level, is two cities in one. Its colonial Old Town – a Unesco World Cultural Heritage Site – is majestically preserved, yet big and busy enough that it absorbs tourism like a sponge, allowing you to escape into a world that is magically South American. The modern New Town, only a 20-minute walk away, is a whipped-up mixture of multistory hotels, city parks, mirrored high-rises and drab government complexes. For travelers, its heart is the Mariscal Sucre neighborhood, which is block after block of trendy cafés, international restaurants, travel agencies, raucous bars and imaginative, small hotels. Quito is one of the best places in South America to study Spanish and a great place to set up climbing, jungle, rafting, mountain biking and Galápagos tours.

ECUADOR

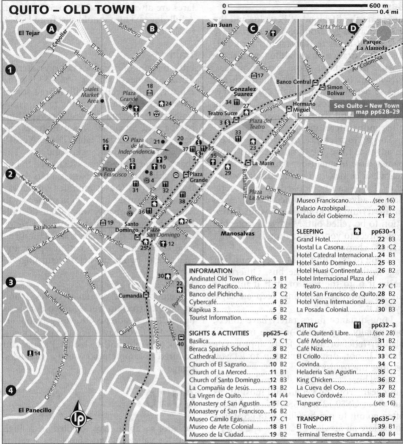

QUITO – OLD TOWN

0 ———— 600 m
0 ———— 0.4 mi

See Quito – New Town
map pp628–29

INFORMATION	
Andinatel Old Town Office.....1	B1
Banco del Pacifico.................2	B2
Banco del Pichincha.............3	C2
Cybercafé............................4	B2
Kapikua 3............................5	B2
Tourist Information...............6	B2

SIGHTS & ACTIVITIES	pp625–6
Basilica................................7	C1
Beraca Spanish School.........8	B2
Cathedral............................9	B2
Church of El Sagrario.........10	B2
Church of La Merced..........11	B1
Church of Santo Domingo...12	B3
La Compañía de Jesús.........13	B2
La Virgen de Quito.............14	A4
Monastery of San Agustín...15	C2
Monastery of San Francisco..16	B2
Museo Camilo Egas............17	C1
Museo de Arte Colonial......18	B1
Museo de la Ciudad............19	B2

Museo Franciscano..............(see 16)	
Palacio Arzobispal.............20	B2
Palacio del Gobierno..........21	B2

SLEEPING	pp630–1
Grand Hotel.......................22	B3
Hostal La Casona...............23	C2
Hotel Catedral Internacional.24	B1
Hotel Santo Domingo.........25	B3
Hotel Huasi Continental.....26	B2
Hotel Internacional Plaza del	
Teatro.............................27	C1
Hotel San Francisco de Quito.28	B2
Hotel Viena Internacional...29	C2
La Posada Colonial.............30	B3

EATING	pp632–3
Cafe Quiteñö Libre...............(see 28)	
Café Modelo......................31	B2
Café Niza...........................32	B2
El Criollo...........................33	C2
Govinda............................34	C1
Heladería San Agustin........35	C2
King Chicken......................36	B2
La Cueva del Oso...............37	B2
Nuevo Cordovéz.................38	B2
Tianguez............................(see 16)	

TRANSPORT	pp635–7
El Trole.............................39	B1
Terminal Terrestre Cumandá..40	B4

Quito was a major Inca city that was destroyed by Atahualpa's general, Rumiñahui, shortly before the arrival of the Spanish conquistadors. The present capital was founded atop the Inca ruins by Sebastián de Benalcázar on December 6, 1534. Unfortunately, no Inca structures remain.

ORIENTATION

Quito is Ecuador's second-largest city. It can be divided into three segments. In the center is the colonial Old Town. The north is modern Quito – known as the New Town – with major businesses, airline offices, embassies and shopping centers. The New Town also contains the airport, middle- and upper-class homes and the Mariscal Sucre

neighborhood (the travelers' ghetto known simply as El Mariscal). Av Amazonas, with its banks, crafts stores, cafés and corporate business offices, is the New Town's best-known street, although Avs 10 de Agosto and 6 de Diciembre are the most important thoroughfares. The south comprises mostly working-class housing areas.

The **Instituto Geográfico Militar** (IGM; Map pp628-9; ☎ 02-254-5090, 02-222-9075/76; map sales r ☺ 8am-1pm & 1:30-4:30pm Mon-Thu, 7am-3pm Fri), on top of steep Calle Paz y Miño, publishes and sells Ecuador's best topographical maps. Lines are shorter (and the views from the hilltop are better) in the morning. You'll need to leave your passport at the gate.

GETTING INTO TOWN

The airport is on Av Amazonas, about 10km north of the Mariscal Sucre neighborhood (where most of the budget hotels are). As you walk out of the airport, south is to your left. Cross Av Amazonas and flag a south-bound bus. It costs about US$0.25 to get from here to the Mariscal. From there, you can catch a bus or El Trole (trolley) to the Old Town, about 2km further south. A taxi from the airport to the Mariscal costs about US$4; to the Old Town about US$5 or US$6. Cabs are cheaper if you walk outside the airport drive-through and hail one on either side of Amazonas. Make sure the driver turns on the *taxímetro* (taximeter).

The bus terminal is a few blocks south of Plaza Santo Domingo in the Old Town. Take a cab into town if you arrive at night. The nearest *trole* stops (for transport to the Mariscal) are Santo Domingo (at Plaza Santo Domingo) and Cumandá, just south of the terminal.

INFORMATION
Bookshops
Confederate Books (Map pp628-9; J Calamá 410) Used-books heaven – hundreds of titles in French, English and German line the shelves.
Libri Mundi (Map pp628-9; JL Mera 851) Quito's best bookshop has an excellent selection of books in Spanish, English, German and French.
Libro Express (Map pp628-9; Av Amazonas 816 & General Veintimilla) Good for guidebooks, coffee-table books and magazines.

Cultural Centers
Alliance Française (Map pp628-9; ☎ 02-224-9345/50; Av Eloy Alfaro N32-468 near Av 6 de Diciembre) Films, language classes and information on Ecuador and France.
Asociación Humboldt (Map pp628-9; ☎ 02-254-8480; www.asociacion-humboldt.org in Spanish & German; Vancouver & Polonia) German center and Goethe Institute with local arts information, language courses, films and events.
Centro Cultural Afro-Ecuatoriano (Map pp628-9; ☎ 02-252-2318; JL Tamayo 985) Information on black Ecuadorian culture and events in Quito.

Emergency
Fire Department (☎ 102)
General Emergency (☎ 911)
Police (☎ 101)
Red Cross Ambulance (☎ 131, 02-258-0598)

Internet Access
The Mariscal area (especially along J Calamá) is bursting with cybercafés. They're trickier to find in the Old Town. In the New Town, you'll pay about US$0.60 per hour; in the Old Town US$0.90 to US$1.20.
Cybercafé (Map p622; Sucre 350, Galería Sucre, Old Town) Sharpest café in the Old Town.
Kapikua 3 (Map p622; Venezuela near Bolívar, Old Town)
La Sala (Map pp628-9; Reina Victoria 1137 & J Calamá, New Town) Bright café with espresso drinks and fast computers.
Papaya Net (Map pp628-9; J Calamá 469 & JL Mera, New Town) Internet, beer, espresso, snacks, groovin' tunes and bad postures.
Sambo.net (Map pp628-9; JL Mera at J Pinto, New Town) Comfy place, fast connection, drinks and snacks.

Internet Resources
Gay Guide to Quito (http://gayquitoec.tripod.com)
Municipal website (www.quito.gov.ec in Spanish)

Laundry
The following laundries will wash, dry and fold your whiffy clothes within 24 hours. All charge between US$0.75 and US$1 per kg.
Opera de Jabón (Map pp628-9; J Pinto 325 near Reina Victoria)
Rainbow Laundry (Map pp628-9; JL Mera 1337 at Cordero)
Sun City Laundry (Map pp628-9; Foch at JL Mera)
Wash & Go (Map pp628-9; J Pinto 340 at JL Mera)

Medical Services
Clínica de la Mujer (☎ 02-245-8000; Av Amazonas 4826 at Gaspar de Villarroel) Private clinic specializing in women's health.
Hospital Voz Andes (☎ 02-226-2142; Juan Villalengua 267 near América & 10 de Agosto) American-run hospital with outpatient and emergency rooms. Fees are low.
Metropolitano (☎ 02-226-1520; Av Mariana de Jesús at Occidental) Better, but pricier than Voz Andes.

Recommended doctors and dentists include:
Dr Alfredo Jijon (☎ 02-245-6259, 02-246-6314; Centro Meditropoli, office 215, Mariana de Jesús & Occidental) Gynecologist.
Dr John Rosenberg (Map pp628-9; ☎ 02-252-1104, ext 310, 09-973-9734, pager 02-222-7777; Foch 476 & D de Almagro) Internist specializing in tropical medicine; speaks English and German. He makes house calls.
Dr Roberto Mena (☎ 02-256-9149; Coruña E24-865 at Isabel La Católica) Dentist; English and German spoken.
Sixto & Silvia Altamirano (☎ 02-224-4119; Av Amazonas 2689 & Av de la República) Orthodontists.

Money

Banks are plentiful on Av Amazonas between Patria and Orellana. The following change traveler's checks and have ATMs:

Banco de Guayaquil Av Amazonas N22-147 (Map pp628-9; at General Veintimilla, New Town; ⊘ 9am-4pm Mon-Fri); Av Cristobal Colón (Map pp628-9; cnr Reina Victoria, New Town)

Banco del Pacífico New Town (Map pp628-9; Av 12 de Octubre & Cordero; ⊘ 8:30am-4pm Mon-Fri); Old Town (Map p622; cnr Guayaquil & Chile; ⊘ 8:30am-4pm Mon-Fri)

Banco del Pichincha (Map p622; Guayaquil at Manabí, Old Town; ⊘ 8am-3:30pm Mon-Fri)

You can also cash traveler's checks or cash at *casas de cambio* (currency-exchange houses); hours are usually 9am to 6pm weekdays and on Saturday mornings. The *casas de cambio* at the airport, at hotel **Hilton Colón** (Map pp628-9; Av Amazonas & Av Patria) and at **Centro Comercial El Jardín** (Av Amazonas & Av de la República) are open daily. You could also try **Producambio** (Map pp628-9; Av Amazonas 350; ⊘ 8:30am-6pm Mon-Fri, 9am-2pm Sat). **Western Union** (Map pp628-9; ☎ 02-256-5059; Av de la República 433 near D de Almagro; ⊘ 8am-7pm) charges US$85 for a US$1000 transfer from the USA. There's also a branch at **Av Cristobal Colón 1333** (Map pp628-9; ☎ 02-290-1505).

You can receive cash advances with your credit card at the following offices:

American Express (Map pp628-9; ☎ 02-256-0488; Av Amazonas 339; ⊘ 8:30am-6pm Mon-Fri, 9am-1pm Sat)

Diners Club (☎ 02-298-1300; Av Amazonas 4560 at Pereira; ⊘ 8:30am-6:30pm Mon-Fri, 9am-1:30pm Sat)

MasterCard (☎ 02-226-2770; Naciones Unidas 8771 at Shyris; ⊘ 8:30am-5pm Mon-Fri, 9am-1pm Sat)

Visa (☎ 02-256-6800; at Banco de Guayaquil, Av Cristobal Colón at Reina Victoria)

Post

The following are open from 8am to 6pm Monday through Friday and 8am to noon on Saturday. Arrive before 5:40pm.

Central post office (Correo Central; Map p622; Espejo 935 at Guayaquil, Old Town) Pick up *lista de correos* (general delivery) mail here (see Post, p712).

Mariscal Sucre post office (Map pp628-9; Av Cristobal Colón at Reina Victoria)

New Town parcels office (Map pp628-9; Ulloa 273 near Ramírez Dávalos) Send packages weighing over 2kg from here.

New Town post office (Map pp628-9; Av Eloy Alfaro 354 at 9 de Octubre, New Town) To receive *lista de correos* mail here, the sender should drop the 'Correo Central' line in the address and insert 'Av Eloy Alfaro'.

South American Explorers

The **South American Explorers** (SAE; Map pp628-9; ☎ 02-222-5228; quitoclub@saexplorers.org; www.samexplo.org; Jorge Washington 311 & Leonidas Plaza Gutiérrez; ⊘ 9:30am-5pm Mon-Fri, 9:30am-8pm Thu, 9am-noon Sat) has a clubhouse in the New Town. On Wednesdays, members meet to arrange day hikes in different areas around Quito. On Thursdays at 6pm, the club hosts presentations by guest speakers. The SAE's mailing address is Apartado 17-21-431, Av Eloy Alfaro, Quito, Ecuador.

Telephone

For information on Pichincha Province's new seven-digit telephone numbers, see the boxed text (p713).

Local, national and international calls can be made at **Andinatel** (main office Map pp628-9; Av Eloy Alfaro 333 near 9 de Octubre; ⊘ closed Sun; Mariscal branch JL Mera 741 Map pp628-9; at General Baquedano; Mariscal branch Reina Victoria Map pp628-9; near J Calamá; Old Town office Map p622; Benalcázar at Mejía). There are also branches at the airport and the main bus terminal.

Tourist-Card Extensions

For tourist-card extensions, go to the **immigration office** (Migraciones; Map pp628-9; ☎ 02-245-4122/6249; Av Amazonas 2639 at Av de la República; ⊘ 8am-noon & 3-6pm Mon-Fri). Onward tickets out of Ecuador and 'sufficient funds' are rarely asked for, but bring airline tickets and traveler's checks if you have them, just in case.

Tourist Offices

The **Cámara Provincial de Turismo de Pichincha** (Captur; www.captur.com in Spanish) operates the following tourist-information offices:

Mariscal Tourist Information (Map pp628-9; ☎ 02-255-1566; Reina Victoria & Cordero; ⊘ 9am-5pm Mon-Fri) Some English spoken.

Old Town Tourist Information (Map p622; ☎ 02-295-4044; Venezuela & Chile; ⊘ 9am-5pm Mon-Sat) Usually only Spanish is spoken.

DANGERS & ANNOYANCES

If you are arriving from sea level, Quito's 2850m elevation might make you somewhat breathless and give you headaches or cottonmouth. This symptom of *soroche* (altitude sickness) usually disappears after a day or two. To minimize symptoms, take it easy upon arrival, drink plenty of water and lay off the smokes and alcohol.

The Mariscal area and the Old Town are dangerous after dark and you should always take a taxi, even for short distances. As usual, pickpockets work crowded buses, the bus terminal and markets. Definitely avoid the climb up El Panecillo hill; take a tour or hire a taxi for the trip to the top and back. If you are robbed, obtain a police report within 48 hours from the **Old Town police station** (Map p622 ; Mideros & Cuenca) between 9am and noon.

Quito's streets are pretty safe during the day.

SIGHTS

Sundays are pleasant days to explore the city on foot. Traffic is light, crowds in the Old Town are thinner and the parks are full of people.

Old Town   Map p622

If you're not already staying there, beeline it to the Old Town, where it's block after block of marvelous colonial architecture, bustling plazas, yelling street vendors, ambling pedestrians, belching buses and whistle-blowing traffic cops trying to keep the narrow, congested one-way streets orderly (yeah, right). It's well worth spending several hours – if not several days – wandering this historic area. The best place to start is probably Plaza de la Independencia. To get there from the Mariscal, jump a southbound *trole* (trolley) on Av 10 de Agosto and get off at the Plaza Grande stop (Map p622).

PLAZA DE LA INDEPENDENCIA

Quito's small, exquisitely restored central plaza (also known as Plaza Grande) is a great spot for bench-sitting in the sun to the sound of shoeshine boys and photographers peddling their services around the park. The plaza is flanked by several important buildings. The low white building on the northwestern side is the **Palacio del Gobierno** (Presidential Palace). The prez does indeed carry out business inside, so sightseeing is limited to the entrance area. On the southwestern side of the plaza stands Quito's recently painted **cathedral** (admission US$1, free during Sun services; ☯ 10am-4pm Mon-Sat, Sun services hourly 6am-noon & 5-7pm). Although not as ornate as some of the other churches, it's worth a peek. Paintings by several notable

artists of the Quito school adorn the inside walls. Mariscal Sucre, the leading figure of Quito's independence, is buried inside. The **Palacio Arzobispal** (Archbishop's Palace), now a colonnaded row of small shops, stands on the northeastern side of the plaza.

NORTH OF PLAZA DE LA INDEPENDENCIA

Two blocks northwest of Plaza Grande stands one of colonial Quito's most recently built churches, **La Merced** (cnr Cuenca & Chile; admission free; ☯ 6am-noon & 3-6pm), finished in 1742. Among the wealth of fascinating art inside, paintings depict such calming scenes as glowing volcanoes erupting over the church roofs of colonial Quito and the capital covered with ashes.

Three blocks north of the plaza, the impressive **Museo de Arte Colonial** (☎ 02-221-2297; Mejía 915 at Cuenca; admission US$0.50) houses Ecuador's best collection of colonial art. The museum was closed for restoration in 2002, with plans to reopen in late 2003 or early 2004; call or ask at one of the tourist offices for the latest.

The **Museo Camilo Egas** (Venezuela 1302; admission US$1; ☯ 10am-1pm & 3-5:30pm Tue-Fri, 10am-2pm Sat & Sun) contains works by the late Egas – one of the country's foremost indigenous painters – and others.

High on a hill on Venezuela stands the unfinished **basilica** (admission US$1; ☯ 9:30am-5:30pm). Construction commenced in 1926, so the tradition of taking decades to build a church is obviously still alive. Climb the church's clock tower for **superb views** of the city.

PLAZA & MONASTERY OF SAN FRANCISCO

With its sweeping cobblestone plaza, its mountainous backdrop of Volcán Pichincha, and the bustling street market flanking its northeastern side, the **Monastery of San Francisco** (admission free; ☯ 7-11am daily, 3-6pm Mon-Thu) is a marvelous sight – both inside and out. It's the city's largest colonial structure and its oldest church (built 1534–1604). And it's free.

Although much of the church has been rebuilt because of earthquake damage, some of it is original. The **Chapel of Señor Jesús del Gran Poder**, to the right of the main altar, has original tilework, and the **main altar** itself is a spectacular example of baroque carving. To the right of the church's main entrance is the **Museo Franciscano** (☎ 02-228-2545; admission US$2.50; ☺ 9am-6pm Mon-Sat, 9am-noon Sun), which contains some of the church's finest artwork.

To the right of the monastery begins the sprawling, chaotic **Ipiales street market** (☺ daily), whose streets were packed daily. The market has grown with Quito over the years, as more streets succumb to the blue overhead tarps and vendors who sell everything from pirate CDs and pocket watches to braziers and barbwire. It's a fascinating area to wander around, but watch for pickpockets and think twice before whipping that camera out.

CALLES GARCÍA MORENO & SUCRE
Beside the cathedral on García Moreno stands the 17th-century **Church of El Sagrario** (García Moreno; admission free; ☺ 6am-noon & 3-6pm). Around the corner on Sucre is Ecuador's most ornate church, **La Compañía de Jesús** (admission US$2.50; ☺ 9:30-11am & 4-6pm). Seven tons of gold were supposedly used to gild the walls, ceilings and altars inside, and quiteños (people from Quito) proudly call it the most beautiful church in the country. Construction of this Jesuit church began in 1605 and it took 163 years to build.

Occupying a beautifully restored building dating from 1563, the **Museo de la Ciudad** (☺ 02-228 3882; García Moreno & Rocafuerte; admission US$3; ☺ 9:30am-5:30pm Tue-Sun) is near the southwestern end of García Moreno. The historic building (originally a hospital) houses a fascinating museum with well-conceived exhibits depicting daily life in Quito through the centuries. There are also temporary exhibits of contemporary artists.

PLAZA & CHURCH OF SANTO DOMINGO
Plaza Santo Domingo is a regular haunt for street performers, and crowds fill the plaza to watch pouting clowns and half-cocked magicians do their stuff. The interior of the **church** (Flores & Rocafuerte; admission free; ☺ 7am-1pm & 4:30-7:30pm), even during the day, is almost spooky. Giant hardwood boards creak beneath your feet as you approach the dramatic Gothic-like altar ahead. Construction of the church began in 1581 and continued until 1650.

EL PANECILLO
The small, ever-present hill to the south of the old town is called **El Panecillo** (The

Little Bread Loaf) and it's a major Quito landmark. It's topped by a huge statue of **La Virgen de Quito** and offers marvelous **views** of the whole city and of the surrounding volcanoes. Go early in the morning, before the clouds roll in. Definitely don't climb the stairs at the end of García Moreno on the way to the statue – there have been numerous reports of travelers being robbed on the way up. A taxi from the Old Town costs US$10 to US$20, including waiting time and the return trip.

New Town   Map pp628–9
PARQUE LA ALAMEDA & PARQUE EL EJIDO
From the northeastern edge of the Old Town, the long, triangular **Parque La Alameda** begins its grassy crawl toward the New Town.

In the center of the park is the **Quito Observatory** (☎ 02-257-0765; admission US$0.20, night viewings US$0.40; ☺ 8am-noon & 3-5pm Mon-Fri, 8am-noon Sat), the oldest (European) observatory on the continent. On very clear nights the observatory opens for star and planet gazing; call ahead of time if the weather looks promising. The north end of La Alameda is popular with weekend picnickers.

Northeast of La Alameda, the pleasant, tree-filled **Parque El Ejido** is the biggest park in downtown Quito. It's a popular spot for impromptu soccer games and volleyball. The northern end of the park teems with activity on weekends when open-air **art shows** are held along Av Patria. Just inside the northern end of the park, artisans and crafts vendors set up stalls on the weekend and turn the sidewalks into Quito's largest **handicrafts market**.

CASA DE LA CULTURA ECUATORIANA
A landmark, circular, glass building, **Casa de la Cultura Ecuatoriana** (www.cce.org.ec in Spanish), across from Parque El Ejido, houses two important museums. The **Museo de Arte Ecuatoriano** (☎ 02-222-3392; cnr Patria & Av 12 de Octubre; admission US$1; ☺ 9am-5pm Tue-Fri, 10am-3pm Sat & Sun) boasts a large collection of contemporary, modern and 19th-century Ecuadorian art, including canvases by Ecuador's most famous artists – Oswaldo Guayasamín, Eduardo Kingman and Camilo Egas.

The **Museo del Banco Central** (☎ 02-222-3259; admission US$1; ☺ 9am-5pm Tue-Sun, 10am-3pm Sat & Sun) is Quito's best archaeology museum.

Allow at least a couple of hours to eyeball all the goods, which include pottery, gold ornaments, skulls showing deformities, early surgical methods and much more. For information on events, see the website.

AMAZONAS & THE MARISCAL

A solitary stone archway at the northern end of Parque El Ejido marks the beginning of modern Quito's showpiece street, **Amazonas**. It's the main artery of the **Mariscal Sucre**, where the avenue is lined with modern hotels, airline offices, travel agencies, banks and restaurants.

On Av 12 de Octubre, just south of the Mariscal, the **Museo Amazónico** (☎ 02-256-2663; Av 12 de Octubre 1436; admission US$1; 8am-4pm Mon-Fri, 9am-1pm Sat & Sun) houses a small but interesting display of indigenous artifacts from the Amazon Basin.

Just northeast of the Mariscal, is a small museum run by **Fundación Sinchi Sacha** (☎ 02-223-0609; www.sinchisacha.org in Spanish; Reina Victoria N26-166 & La Niña), a nonprofit organization supporting Amazonian cultures. The **museum** (8am-6:30pm Mon-Fri, 10am-6pm Sat) exhibits the artwork and utensils of the peoples of the Oriente and sells a variety of related literature.

MUSEO GUAYASAMÍN

In the former home of the world-famous indigenous painter Oswaldo Guayasamín (1919–99), **Museo Guayasamín** (☎ 02-246-5265; Calle Bosmediano 543; admission US$2; 9am-1:30pm & 3-6:30pm Mon-Fri) houses the most complete collection of his work. It also houses Guayasamín's collection of pre-Columbian and colonial pieces, as well as a jewelry workshop with plenty of original pieces for sale. The museum is in the residential district of Bellavista, northeast of downtown. You can walk uphill or take a bus along Av 6 de Diciembre to Av Eloy Alfaro, then a Bellavista bus up the hill.

Guápulo   Map pp628–9

If you follow Av 12 de Octubre up the hill from the Mariscal, you'll reach **Hotel Quito** (González Suárez N27-142) at the top. Behind the hotel (which has a top-floor bar with magnificent views), stairs lead steeply down to the neighborhood of El Guápulo, set in a precipitous valley. At the center of this small neighborhood stands the lovely **Santu-**ario de Guápulo** (Sanctuary of Guápulo; 9am-noon), built between 1644 and 1693.

The best views of the church are from the **Mirador de Guápulo**, behind the Hotel Quito, at the **Statue of Francisco de Orellana** (Calle Larrea near González Suárez). In the statue, Francisco de Orellana is looking down into the valley that was the beginning of his epic journey from Quito to the Atlantic – the first descent of the Amazon by a European.

COURSES
Dancing

Tired of shoe-gazing when you hit the *salsotecas* (salsa clubs)? Try salsa dance classes – they're a blast! Merengue, *cumbia* and other Latin dances are also taught. The following two schools both offer excellent one-on-one instruction:

Ritmo Tropical (Map pp628-9; ☎ 02-222-7051; ritmotropical5@hotmail.com; Av 10 de Agosto 1792, Office 108) One-on-one per hour US$5, group lessons per hour US$4.

Tropical Dancing School (Map pp628-9; ☎ 02-222-4713; tropicaldancing@hotmail.com; Foch E4-256 at Av Amazonas) One-on-one per hour US$4, group lessons per hour US$3.

Language

Quito is one of the better places in South America to learn Spanish. Most schools offer all levels of instruction, in private or group lessons, and can arrange home-stays with families. Some programs also include dance classes, cooking courses or cultural events. Most schools charge between US$4 and US$10 per hour. The following schools have consistently received favorable reports from students:

Amazonas (Map pp628-9; ☎ 02-252-7509; www.eduamazonas.com; Jorge Washington 718 at Av Amazonas)

Atahualpa (Map pp628-9; ☎ 02-254-5914, 02-225-1229; www.atahualpa.com; J Pinto 375 at JL Mera)

Beraca (beraca@interactive.net.ec); Old Town (Map p622; ☎ 02-228-8092; García Moreno 858); New Town (Map pp628-9; ☎ 02-290-6642; Av Amazonas 1114)

Bipo & Toni's (Map pp628-9; ☎ 02-255-6614, 02-256-3309; homepage.iprolink.ch/~bipo//index.htm; J Carrion E8-183 at Leonidas Plaza Gutiérrez)

Instituto Superior de Español (☎ 02-222-3242; www.instituto-superior.net; Darquea Terán 1650 near 10 de Agosto)

TOURS

Organized tours are sometimes cheaper if they are booked in the town closest to where you want to go, although this demands a

ECUADOR

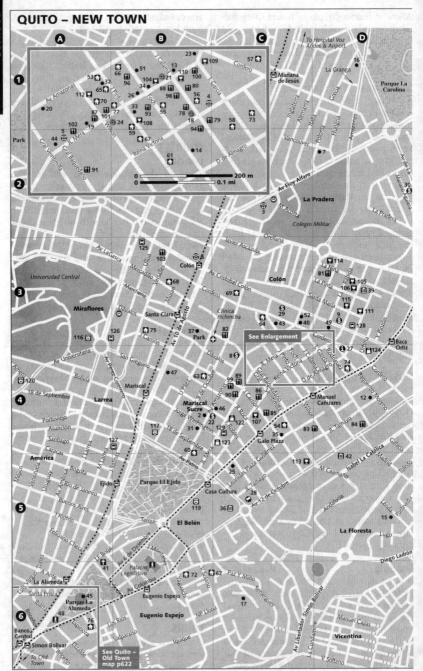

Map scale: 0 – 1 km / 0 – 0.5 mi

more flexible schedule. If you prefer to start in Quito, the following agencies and operators are well received and reliable:

Biking Dutchman (Map pp628-9; ☎ 02-254-2806; www.bikingdutchman.com; Foch 714 at JL Mera) Quito's original mountain-biking outfitter; experienced guides, great reports.

Fundación Golondrinas (Map pp628-9; ☎ 02-222-6602; www.ecuadorexplorer.com/golondrinas; Isabel La Católica 1559, La Casa de Eliza hotel) Conservation project with volunteer community; also arranges walking tours in the *páramo* west of Tulcán (see p645).

Galasam (Map pp628-9; ☎ 02-250-7080; www.galasam.com; Av Amazonas 1354 at Cordero) All types of Galápagos tours, but especially popular for economy cruises. Some complaints, some raves – know what you're getting into.

Native Life (Map pp628-9; ☎ 02-255-0836; natlife1@natlife.com.ec; Foch E4-167 at Av Amazonas) Specializes in tours of Río Aguarico and Cuyabeno Reserve.

Pamir Adventure (Map pp628-9; ☎ 02-222-0892; info@pamirtravels.com.ec; JL Mera 721 at General Veintimilla) Does it all, but it's best for climbing; experienced guides.

Rainforestur (Map pp628-9; ☎ 02-223-9822; www.rainforestur.com; Av Amazonas 420 at F Robles) Excellent for Cuyabeno Reserve jungle trips. Also rafting trips near Baños.

Safari Tours (Map pp628-9; ☎ 02-255-2505; admin@safari.com.ec; J Calamá 380 at JL Mera) Arranges everything from jungle treks and Galápagos cruises to volcano climbing; 10% discounts to SAE members.

Tropic Ecological Adventures (Map pp628-9; ☎ 02-222-5907; www.tropiceco.com; Av de la República E7-320 at D de Almagro) Winner of international ecotourism awards for work with indigenous jungle communities and sustainable use of the rain forest.

Yacu Amu Rafting/Ríos Ecuador (Map pp628-9; ☎ 02-223-6844; www.yacuamu.com; Foch 746 near JL Mera) White-water rafting, and kayaking trips and courses. Australian owned, highly experienced.

FESTIVALS & EVENTS

The city's biggest party is the founding of Quito, celebrated the first week of December when bullfights are held daily at the Plaza de Toros. On New Year's Eve, life-size puppets (often of politicians) are burned in the streets at midnight. Carnaval is celebrated with intense water fights – no one is spared. Colorful religious processions are held during Easter week.

SLEEPING

Most people shack up in the New Town – particularly in the Mariscal neighborhood – so they can be near the cybercafés, bars and restaurants in the area (it definitely makes

the cab ride home from the bar cheaper). If you prefer a more traditional slice of Quito, however, stay in the Old Town – you may not find banana pancakes around the corner, but you will find a world that feels more traditionally South American. Hotels in the Old Town tend to be slightly cheaper. Both areas are dangerous after dark. Always take a cab at night.

Old Town   Map p622

Plenty of cheapies can be found south of Plaza Santo Domingo. Travelers regularly stay in this area, but some (particularly single women) do not feel comfortable lodging here.

La Posada Colonial (☎ 02-228-2859; Paredes N9-188; s/d with bath US$5/10; P) Arguably the best hotel south of Plaza Santo Domingo. It's in a handsome, old building with simple but clean rooms, some balconies, a roof terrace and a very friendly staff. The beds are saggy but the showers are hot. Creaky wood floors add nostalgia.

Grand Hotel (☎ 02-228-0192; www.geocities.com/grandhotelquito; Rocafuerte 1001; s/d with shared bath US$3.50/5.50, with private bath US$6/10). The Grand is big and busy and popular with locals and travelers alike. Showers are hot, and there's laundry service and a restaurant. Rooms with shared bath are miniscule.

Hotel Santo Domingo (☎ 02-251-2810, 02-221-1598; Rocafuerte 1345; s US$3-6, d US$5-8) Worn-out, old-fashioned clunker right on Plaza Santo Domingo. The older rooms lack baths but a few have balconies over the plaza (great for views, lousy for street noise). The 'newer' rooms are tired, musty and dark but have private baths.

Hotel Catedral Internacional (☎ 02-295-5438; Mejía 638; s/d with private bath & TV US$7/12) Good deal if you don't mind the bustling vendors that crowd the streets out front. Rooms are spacious but musty, and there's a restaurant and laundry service.

Hotel Huasi Continental (☎ 02-295-7327; Flores 332; s/d with shared bath US$4/7, with private bath US$6/11; P) Large, professionally run hotel with lonely rooms. Plusses: the mattresses are firm, the staff is friendly and the restaurant is good. Rooms vary wildly, so choose carefully.

Hostal La Casona (☎ 02-258-8809; Manabí 255; s/d with bath US$6/9) Occupying an interesting colonial-style building, La Casona has three floors of dark, clean rooms with hot water opening onto a dimly lit, covered courtyard. Decent.

Hotel Internacional Plaza del Teatro (☎ 02-295-9462, 02-295-4293; Guayaquil N8-75; s/d with private bath & TV US$8/14; **P**) Historic old-timer with a marble staircase entry, wide hallways and balconied rooms with hot water. The off-street rooms lack balconies but are quieter.

Hotel Viena Internacional (☎ 02-295-9611, 02-295-4860; Flores 600; s/d with bath & TV US$12/24) Modernish, no-frills rooms offer a touch of comfort in the Old Town. They're large and carpeted, with hot-water baths, and some have balconies.

Hotel San Francisco de Quito (☎ 02-228-7758; hsfquito@andinanet.net; Sucre 217 at Guayaquil; s/d with private bath & TV US$14/24, mini apt with kitchenettes US$18/25) If you want to sleep in style (old style, that is) in colonial Quito, try this centuries-old beauty. There's a pool table, and for US$1.50 extra you can use the Jacuzzi, sauna and steam room (soak it up!). Breakfast is included in the price.

Between the Old & New Towns

L'Auberge Inn (Map pp628-9; ☎ 02-255-2912; www .ioda.net/auberge-inn; Av Colombia N12-200 at Yaguachi; s/d with shared bath US$6/12, with private bath US$9/15) With a pool table, sauna, safe-deposit facilities, fireplace in the common room, courtyard, kitchen, luggage storage, laundry service, in-house travel agency and a great pizzeria (say no more), this is an excellent deal. Airport pickup is available.

Hostal Bambú (Map pp628-9; ☎ 02-222-6738; V Solano 1758 near Av Colombia; r per person US$5-10) Traveler oriented and popular, Bambú boasts a kitchen, library, laundry facilities and spectacular views from the hammocks on the roof. Great deal.

Residencial Marsella (Map pp628-9; ☎ 02-295-5884; Los Ríos 2035; r per person US$4-6) About a block south of Parque La Alameda, Marsella has an empty rooftop terrace and 35 clean rooms (which vary widely in quality) with shared baths and thin mattresses. Popular for the price.

New Town   Map pp628–9

The following small hostels are great places to meet other travelers, and they almost always have a relaxed common area. It is best to phone ahead for availability and prices.

La Casa de Eliza (☎ 02-222-6602; manteca@uio .satnet.net; Isabel La Católica N24-679; dm US$5, d US$10)

This is a homey place (it's a converted house, after all), with a big guest kitchen, a sociable common area and modest, comfortable rooms. Breakfast is available for US$1 extra.

El Centro del Mundo (☎ 02-222-9050; centrode lmundo@hotmail.com; L García E7-22; dm with breakfast US$5, s/d with bath US$9/16) Run by travelers (an Ecuadorian/French-Canadian couple) for travelers, this old favorite is often a nonstop party. Amenities include hot water, laundry and kitchen facilities and a TV room.

Amazonas Inn (☎ 02-222-5723, 02-222-2666; J Pinto E4-324 & Av Amazonas; s/d/tr US$9/18/27) Excellent value. The rooms are straightforward and spotless, with private baths, constant hot water and cable TV; those on the 1st floor have windows. Friendly staff, central location.

El Cafecito (☎ 02-223-4862; cafecito@ecuadorexplorer .com; Cordero 1124; dm US$6, s/d US$9/14) Popular budget choice with clean rooms, a mellow vibe and an excellent café. Baths are shared.

Crossroads (☎ 02-223-4735; www.crossroadshostal .com; Foch E5-23; dm US$5.50-6.60, d with shared bath US$24.50, s/d with private bath US$15.50/27; **P**) Big, converted house with bright rooms and a welcoming communal atmosphere. Facilities include a good café, cable TV, kitchen privileges, luggage-store and a patio with a fireplace.

Hostal Mundo Net (☎ 02-223-0411; mundonet@ netscape.net; J Pinto E6-37; dm US$3.50, s/d US$5/10) It's cheap and the water's hot, but cleanliness isn't always up to snuff. Handy Internet café below.

Hostal Vamara (☎ 02-222-6425; hostalvamara@yahoo .com; Foch 753 & Av Amazonas; dm US$3, s/d with shared bath US$6/12, with private bath & TV US$8/16) Cheap? Now we're talkin'. Vamara is friendly and clean to boot. It's simple and reliable and there's a laundry next door.

Daugi's (☎ 02-222-8151; J Calamá E6-05; shared r per person US$5) Cheap, busy and basic. The attached patio café is good for soaking up the Mariscal scene over a plate of eggs. The shared rooms have two to three beds in each.

Magic Bean (☎ 02-256-6181; www.ecuadorexplorer .com/magic/home; Foch 681; dm US$7, s/d/tr with private bath US$25/29/36) Located smack in the middle of the Mariscal above the extremely popular café of the same name. There's only one dorm room, so call ahead. Rates include breakfast. Clean.

Hostal El Taxo (☎ 02-222-5593; acordova@ramt.com; Foch E4-116; dm US$5, s/d with shared bath US$10/14) Converted house with hammocks and a bar out front. Rooms are a bit shabby (which goes with the relaxed atmosphere), and the dimly lit common area has a fireplace.

Loro Verde (☎ 02-222-6173; Rodríguez 241; s/d US$8/14) Spacious rooms with a bath and a great location on a leafy Mariscal street.

Casa Helbling (☎ 02-222-6013; www.casahelbling .de; General Veintimilla E18-166; s/d with shared bath US$10/16, with private bath US$14/24) This homey, converted, colonial-style house in the Mariscal is clean, relaxed, friendly and has a guest kitchen, laundry facilities and plenty of common areas for chilling out.

Hostal Déjà Vu (☎ 02-222-4483; dejavu_hostal@ hotmail.com; 9 de Octubre 599; dm US$5, s/d with shared bath US$8/12, with private bath US$10/15) Two private rooms, two dorm rooms, one friendly family running the place. Rates include breakfast in the café downstairs.

Tortuga Verde (☎ 02-255-6829; cnr JL Mera & J Pinto; dm US$5) Busy backpackers hotel that some love and others prefer to leave. Clean dorm rooms sleep six and have lockers. It's worth a peek for the price.

HI Youth Hostel (☎ 02-254-3995; J Pinto E16-12; dm US$6-7, s/d with bath US$11/18) The only HI-affiliated youth hostel in Quito is impersonal but spotless, with four floors of rooms. There's a guest kitchen and breakfast is included.

SPLURGE!

If city life is driving you nuts but you want to be near Quito, try the 25-room **Hostería San Jorge** (☎ 02-256-5964, 02-223-9287; www .hostsanjorge.com.ec; s/d US$50/60, ste US$85). This converted hacienda is situated at an altitude of 3200m on the flanks of Rucu Pichincha, overlooking Quito. Its 30 hectares make for great hiking, horse riding, bird-watching and mountain biking – all of which can be arranged for a fee. There's an indoor heated pool, sauna, whirlpool and steam room. A restaurant serves local and international food, and the bar boasts a pool table, darts and other games. All rooms have rustic fireplaces and hot showers. Airport pickup costs US$10, and all meals are available at moderate rates. The *hostería* (inn) is 4km west of Av Occidental, on the road to Nono.

Other reliable cheapies include **Hostal Alpa Aligu** (☎ 02-256-4012; alpaaligu@yahoo.com; J Pinto 240; dm US$4) and **Hostal Nassau** (☎ 02-256-5724; J Pinto E4-340; r with private bath per person about US$7).

If you prefer a place that doesn't exude 'international backpacker', try one of the following hotels. All deal in private rooms with TV, telephone and private hot bath.

Hotel Majestic (☎ 02-254-3182; Mercadillo Oe2-58 at Versalles; s/d US$12/17; (P)) Orderly and well guarded with over 10 floors of carpeted rooms.

Hotel Nueve de Octubre (☎ 02-255 2424; 9 de Octubre 1047 at Av Cristobal Colón; s/d/tr US$9/11/15; (P)) Secure, no-frills rooms. Good value.

Hotel Pickett (☎ 02-255-1205; Wilson at JL Mera; s/d US$12/16) Comfortable, straightforward rooms. Mariscal location.

Residencial Carrión (☎ 02-223-4620; Carrión 1250; s/d/tr US$11/15/19; (P)) Flowery rooms that are popular with Ecuadorian families and business folk.

EATING

In Quito, you can eat however you want, from down-home to downright extravagant. Restaurants in the New Town cater to everyone from working locals to foreigners and upper-class quiteños, but you'll have to search to find the cheaper deals. The city's best restaurants are in the New Town.

Most restaurants in the Old Town cater to lunching locals and are therefore fairly cheap and close early. The majority serve unembellished Ecuadorian standards – the food might not blow your mind, but it fills the stomach. Many places close on Sunday.

If you're pinching pennies, stick to the standard *almuerzos* or *meriendas* (set lunches and dinners). If you're tempted to indulge, Quito's the place to do it.

Old Town   Map p622

Café Quiteño Libre (Sucre 217; almuerzos US$1.30, mains US$2-3) In the brick-wall cellar of the Hotel San Francisco de Quito (p631), this local favorite does a booming lunchtime business. Cheap.

Nuevo Cordovéz (Guayaquil 774; almuerzos US$1.40-1.75, mains US$2-3) Down-home family eatery with colorful booths and a bullfighting theme.

King Chicken (Bolívar 236; mains US$2-4) Good fried chicken and Ecuadorian standards, big vinyl booths, ice-cream sundaes and a blind organ player. What more do you need?

El Criollo (Flores 825) Good, cheap, home-style Ecuadorian fare. *Yaguarlocro* (potato and blood-sausage soup) served on Saturdays and *caldo de patas* (cow-foot soup) served Sundays – two classic dishes.

Tianguez (Plaza San Francisco; mains US$3-5) Snacks, juices, well-prepared Ecuadorian specialties and an unbeatable location outside the Monastery of San Francisco. Great for afternoon beers.

Govinda (Esmeraldas 853; mains US$1-3) Vegetarian restaurant run by the Hare Krishnas. Cheap and wholesome.

La Cueva del Oso (Chile 1046 at Venezuela; mains US$5-10) Snazziest restaurant in the Old Town with dim lighting, vaulted, pressed-tin ceilings and exquisite Ecuadorian specialties. Pricey, but worth it.

Heladería San Agustín (Guayaquil 1053) This place is an absolute must for *helados de paila* (handmade ice cream). It's been around for over a century. Try *leche y mora* (cream and blackberry).

Café Modelo (Sucre 391 at García Moreno) Strong coffee and good breakfasts, milk shakes and pastries.

Cafe Niza (Venezuela near Sucre; ⊘ from 7:30am) Whips out good, cheap breakfasts – share a table.

New Town
Map pp628–9

CAFÉS
Sidewalk cafés (Av Amazonas near R Roca) Popular meeting places and good spots to watch the world go by. They're affordable, they serve decent coffee and the waiters don't hassle you if you sit there for hours. For inexpensive fast food, walk down J Carrión east of Av Amazonas; several places there whip out burgers and other artery-blockers such as *papi pollo* (fried chicken and French fries) and *salchipapas* (sausage and fries).

Sugar Mammas (JL Mera 921 & Wilson; mains US$2-4, juices US$1-2.50) Cozy little juice-bar/café with excellent fresh juices, smoothies and lots of vegetarian dishes. The three-course *almuerzos* (served with juice of course) are great value. Get breakfast here too.

Magic Bean (Foch 681) Longtime favorite café for monstrous breakfasts, good coffee (that's the magic bean!) and fresh juices. Open all day for appetizing snacks and meals. Pricey.

El Cafecito (Cordero 1124) Warm fireplace and a variety of light eats. Veggie options.

Mango Tree Café (Foch 721) Friendly, comfortable café with good prices and tasty food (which includes pastas, vegetarian dishes, bagels and soup).

El Español (cnr JL Mera & Wilson; ⊘ daily) European delicatessen – good place to stock up for picnic lunches.

Super Papa (JL Mera N23-41; ⊘ daily) Baked potatoes served with your choice of about a dozen different fillings. Great notice board for apartments, events and the like too.

Café Sutra (J Calamá 380; food US$2-6; ⊘ noon-2am Mon-Sat, 3pm-2am Sun) Dim lighting, mellow music and a cool crowd make Sutra a great place for a snack and a beer before a night out. The free bowls of popcorn are never-ending, and goodies such as falafel, hummus and fried cheese balls hit the spot.

Grain de Café (General Baquedano 332; mains US$3-5) Laid-back café/restaurant where you can kick back over coffee or order a full meal. Lots of vegetarian options.

Mirador de Guápulo (Rafael León Larrea y Pasaje Stübel) Cozy café on the cliff side overlooking the Sanctuary of Guápulo. Great views, tasty Ecuadorian snacks.

RESTAURANTS
Mama Clorindas (Reina Victoria 1144) Great place for well-prepared, traditional Ecuadorian dishes at good prices. Best for lunch.

Cevichería y Marisquería 7 Mares (La Niña 525; mains US$1-3; ⊘ 7:45am-5:30pm) This is the place for cheap *encebollado* (a delicious seafood, onion and yucca soup). Bowls – served cafeteria-style to loads of locals – are only US$1 and make an excellent breakfast or lunch (it's rarely eaten for dinner).

Cevichería Viejo José (General Veintimilla 1254) Friendly service and good, cheap seafood.

Su Cebiche (JL Mera 1232 at J Calamá) Knockout *ceviches* (uncooked, well-marinated seafood), great seafood soup and a handful of other coastal specialties. Pricier, but still reasonable.

La Bodeguita de Cuba (Reina Victoria 1721; mains US$3-5) Great Cuban food, graffiti-covered walls, fun atmosphere. Thursday nights are best, when Cuban musicians perform to a standing-room-only crowd, and the bar stays open till 2am.

Varadero (Reina Victoria 1721; ⊘ noon-2am Mon-Sat) Cuban sandwiches and light meals; live music Wednesday, Friday and Saturday nights. Owned by La Bodeguita, next door.

634 QUITO •• Drinking

Red Hot Chili Peppers (Foch 713 at JL Mera) Popular Mexican restaurant with a big-screen TV. Go straight for the fajitas and daiquiris.

If you're hankering for Chinese, try **Chifa Mayflower** (J Carrión 442 at Av 6 de Diciembre) or the more expensive **Chifa Hong Kong** (Lizardo García 235 at 12 de Octubre).

El Maple (cnr JL Calamá & JL Mera; mains US$2-4) Small menu of organic vegetarian dishes. Some are a bit bland, but the soy burgers are big and delicious.

Sakti (Carrión 641; almuerzos US$1.50, mains US$2-3; ☯ 8am-6pm Mon-Fri) Mostly vegetarian cafeteria serving cheap, wholesome soups, veggies, fruit salad, pastas and lasagna. It's popular with the local lunch crowd and a good deal.

Windmill Vegetarian Restaurant (Av Cristobal Colón 2245) Good, reasonably priced vegetarian food.

El Arabe (Reina Victoria 627) Great for quick, inexpensive falafel, hummus or schwarma.

Siam (J Calamá E5-10; mains US$5-8) Delicious Thai food.

Fried Bananas (JL Mera 539; mains US$3.50-4.50) Varied menu of steak, seafood, trout, chicken, soups and salads, all creatively prepared.

Boca del Lobo (J Calamá 284; mains US$6-10; ☯ 4pm-1am Mon-Sat) Ultra-hip restaurant with ambient grooves and a mind-boggling menu of delicacies such as rosemary sea bass, salmon *ishpungo* (a spice similar to cinnamon), stuffed plantain tortillas, raclette, focaccias, pizzas and excellent desserts. Fun place to splurge.

Adams Ribs (J Calamá 329) Get messy over a plate of barbequed ribs (the best around). Lots of grilled meats and hungry North American expats.

Le Arcate (General Baquedano 358; ☯ closed Mon) Delicious brick-oven pizzas, as well as pasta and seafood at reasonable prices.

La Briciola (☎ 02-254-7138; Toledo 1255; mains US$6-10) Outstanding Italian food, large portions and friendly waiters with thick Italian accents. Pricey. Make a reservation if you hope to eat before 9:30pm.

Sake (☎ 02-252-4818; Rivet N30-166) Kick-ass sushi. Expensive, yes, but it's sushi. Expect to drop US$20 on a *full* meal.

DRINKING

The Mariscal is loaded with bars, and the big nights out are Thursday through Saturday. There are several bar-cum-discos near the intersection of Reina Victoria and Santa María – although this area is busy with midnight hotdog vendors, taxis and bar hoppers, it's very sketchy at night. Don't stray far from club entrances and *always* take a cab home. Inside it's fine (aside from the danger of sweating to death). Most bars with dancing charge a small cover, which usually includes a drink.

La Reina Victoria (Map pp628-9; Reina Victoria 530) For British pub atmosphere, this one's tough to beat. Great chili and fish and chips too.

Other comfortable British or American bars with pool tables, pub-grub and plenty of drinking include:
Patatu's Bar (Map pp628-9; Wilson E4-229)
Turtle's Head (Map pp628-9; La Niña 626)
King's Cross (Map pp628-9; ☎ 02-252 3597; Reina Victoria 1781)
Bloom's Bar (Map pp628-9; JL Mera 1117)
Ghoz Bar (Map pp628-9; La Niña 425)

No Bar (Map pp628-9; J Calamá 380 & JL Mera; admission US$3; ☯ 6pm-3am) Four small, dark dance floors surround a chaotic bar (always with dancing on top), and beer-bongs and the spraying of Pilsener are a common sight. Expect high-energy dance pop and lots of pickup lines.

Tijuana (Map pp628-9; cnr Reina Victoria & Santa María; admission US$3) Locals pack this small dance floor so tight, it's amazing they can still bump and grind. Edgy.

Papillon (Map pp628-9; cnr Santa María & Diego de Almagro; admission US$3) Fun place once you succumb to the Latin and international dance pop.

Matrioshka (Map pp628-9; J Pinto 376; admission US$5; ☯ Tue-Sat) Possibly the best disco in town, and one of Quito's more openly gay nightclubs.

Seseribó (Map pp628-9; General Veintimilla & Av 12 de Octubre, Edificio Girón; minimum consumption US$6) Quito's premier *salsoteca* shouldn't be missed. It's small and friendly and the music is tops. Finding dance partners is rarely a problem (women: expect to be asked – guys: better start asking). The action is usually polite.

Mayo 68 (Map pp628-9; L García 662) This fun *salsoteca* is smaller (and some say, for that reason, better) than Seseribó.

ENTERTAINMENT
Cinemas
Check *El Comercio*, section D, for complete cinema listings. The first two are state-of-the-art multiplexes which usually screen Hollywood hits with Spanish subtitles.

Cinemark 7 (☎ 02-226-0301; www.cinemark.com.ec in Spanish; Naciones Unidas & Av América; admission US$4)

Multicines (☎ 02-225-9677; www.multicines.com.ec in Spanish; CCI – Centro Comercial Iñaquito; admission US$4)

Ocho y Medio (Map pp628-9; ☎ 02-290-4720/21/22; www.ochoymedio.net in Spanish; Vallodolid N24-353 & Vizcaya) Shows art films (often in English) and has occasional dance, theater and live music. Small café attached.

Cine Universitario (Map pp628-9; Indoamerican Plaza, Av América & Av Pérez Guerrero; admission US$2) University cinema.

Live Music

Peñas are usually bars that feature live *música folklórica* (traditional folk music).

Ñucanchi Peña (Map pp628-9; ☎ 02-254-0967; Av Universitaria 496; admission US$5; ☉ 8pm-2am Thu-Sat) In the New Town, it's Quito's best known *peña*. The music kicks in around 9:30pm.

La Taberna del Duende (Map pp628-9; U Páez 141) A comfy local bar with traditional music Thursday to Saturday nights.

La Bodeguita de Cuba (Map pp628-9; Reina Victoria 1721) Features excellent live Cuban music on Thursday nights from about 9pm to 2am (see Eating, p633). Get there early.

Varadero (Map pp628-9; Reina Victoria) Next door to La Bodeguita has live music Wednesday, Friday and Saturday nights (see Eating, p633).

Theater & Dance

Dances, concerts and plays in Spanish are presented at various venues; check the entertainment listings in *El Comercio* newspaper.

Teatro Prometeo (Map pp628-9; ☎ 02-222-6116; Av 6 de Diciembre 794) Across from (and affiliated with) the Casa de la Cultura (p626), often hosts a variety of performances. Check out the **Casa de la Cultura website** (www.cce.org.ec in Spanish) for events.

Humanizarte (☎ 02-222-6116; Leonidas Plaza Gutiérrez N24-226; admission US$3-4) Presents both contemporary and Andean dance.

SHOPPING

Numerous stores in the Mariscal (especially along and near Av Amazonas and JL Mera) sell traditional indigenous crafts. Quality is often high, but so are the prices. The best prices can be found at the two crafts markets listed here, where indigenous (mostly *otavaleño* – people from Otavalo) vendors

sell their goods. The quality is sometimes lower, but your money stays within the communities producing the crafts.

Crafts Stores

Folklore Olga Fisch (Map pp628-9; Av Cristobal Colón 260) The store of legendary designer Olga Fisch. Highest quality (and prices) around. Pretend it's a museum.

Fundación Sinchi Sacha (Map pp628-9; Reina Victoria N26-166 & La Niña) Excellent Amazonian crafts. Profits go to indigenous groups who make the crafts.

MCCH (Map pp628-9; JL Mera & F Robles) Women's artisans cooperative.

Productos Andinos (Map pp628-9; Urbina 111) Artisans' cooperative with reasonably priced crafts.

Markets

On Saturday and Sunday, the northern end of Parque El Ejido turns into Quito's biggest crafts market and sidewalk art show. Two blocks north, on JL Mera between Jorge Washington and 18 de Septiembre, the **Mercado Artesanal La Mariscal** (Map pp628-9; ☉ daily) is an entire block filled with craft stalls.

The chaotic **Ipiales street market** (Map p622; ☉ daily) is good for cheap everything: knock-off designer jeans, hardware items, pirate CDs, bad batteries, shoes, underwear, sunglasses, odd medicinal products, switchblades, rubber boots and much more. As usual, watch for pickpockets.

GETTING THERE & AWAY
Air

The **airport** (☎ 02-243-0555, 02-244-0080) is 10km north of the center. Many of the northbound buses on Av Amazonas and 10 de Agosto go there – some have 'Aeropuerto' placards and others say 'Quito Norte.' Also see Getting Into Town (p623).

In order of importance, Ecuador's principal domestic airlines are:

TAME (Map pp628-9; ☎ 02-250-9375/76/77/78, 02-290-9900; Av Amazonas 1354 at Av Cristobal Colón)

Icaro (☎ 02-245-0928, 02-245-1499; Palora 124 at Av Amazonas) Across from the airport.

AeroGal (☎ 02-225-7301/8087/8086; Av Amazonas 7797) Near the airport.

Prices for internal flights vary little between the airlines. Most travel agents also sell domestic airline tickets for the same price as the airline offices. The following price information and schedule is subject to change. Prices quoted are one-way. All flights last under an hour, except to the Galápagos (3¼ hours from Quito, 1½ from Guayaquil).

Coca US$57, 3 per day Mon-Sat with Icaro and TAME.

Cuenca US$58, 2 per day Mon-Fri & 1 per day Sat & Sun with Icaro, 3 per day Mon-Fri, 2 per day Sat & Sun with TAME.

Esmeraldas US$37, 1 per day Mon, Wed, Thu, Fri & Sun with TAME.

Galápagos US$389 (round trip), 2 every day with TAME.

Guayaquil US$58, 1 per day with AeroGal, 3 per day Mon-Fri & 1 per day Sat & Sun with Icaro, 10-12 per day with TAME. Flights on TAME are rarely full and last-minute tickets can usually be purchased at the airport on the day of the flight.

Lago Agrio US$56, 1 per day Mon-Sat with Icaro, 2 per day Mon, Thu & Fri & 1 per day Tue, Wed & Sat with TAME.

Loja US$55, 2 per day Mon-Fri, 1 per day Sat & Sun with Icaro, 2 per day Mon-Sat with TAME.

Macas US$57, 1 per day Mon-Thu with TAME.

Machala US$66, via Guayaquil only, 1 per day Mon-Fri with TAME.

Manta US$50, 1 per day with TAME.

Portoviejo US$50, 1 per day Mon, Wed & Fri with TAME.

Tulcán US$33, 1 per day Mon, Wed & Fri with TAME.

Anyone flying out of the country must pay a US$25 international departure tax (cash only) before boarding.

Bus

The **Terminal Terrestre Cumandá** (main bus terminal; Map p622; Morales) is in the Old Town, a few hundred meters south of Plaza Santo Domingo. Take Maldonado if you're walking. By El Trole, get off at the Cumandá stop. If arriving by taxi at night, ask to be taken inside the station to the passenger drop-off; you'll probably have to pay the US$0.10 vehicle entrance fee, but you'll be safer.

From the terminal several buses a day go to most major destinations around the country, and several per hour run to some places, including Ambato and Otavalo. Book in advance to travel during holiday periods and on Friday evening.

Approximate one-way fares and journey times are shown in the following table. More expensive luxury services are available for long trips.

Destination	Duration in Hours	Cost
Ambato	2½	US$2
Atacames	6-8	US$8
Bahía de Caráquez	8	US$7
Baños	3½	US$3
Coca	10	US$8
Cuenca	9	US$10
Esmeraldas	6	US$7
Guayaquil	8	US$7
Ibarra	2½	US$2
Lago Agrio	8	US$8
Latacunga	1½	US$1.50
Loja	14	US$12
Machala	10	US$9
Manta	8-10	US$6-8
Otavalo	2¼	US$1.80
Portoviejo	8-9	US$6
Puerto López	11	US$8
Puyo	5½	US$4
Riobamba	4	US$3
San Lorenzo	6	US$6
Santo Domingo	3	US$2
Tena	6	US$5
Tulcán	5½	US$4

For comfortable (and slightly pricier) buses to Guayaquil from the New Town, avoiding the trip to the terminal, ride with **Transportes Ecuador** (Map pp628-9; ☎ 02-222-5315; JL Mera N21-44 at Jorge Washington) or **Panamericana** (Map pp628-9; ☎ 02-255-3690/1839; Av Cristobal Colón & Reina Victoria). Panamericana also has long-distance buses to Machala, Loja, Cuenca, Manta and Esmeraldas.

Train

The **train station** (☎ 02-265-6142; Sincholagua near Maldonado) is 2km south of the Old Town. The only train service from Quito is the weekend tourist train to El Boliche recreation area at Parque Nacional Cotopaxi. The train leaves at 8am on Saturday and Sunday and arrives at El Boliche about 11:30am. Passengers have about 2½ hours to hike or picnic before the train leaves El Boliche at 2pm for the return to Quito. The fare is US$4.60 each way. Train schedules change frequently so call the station or ask at SAE (p624).

GETTING AROUND
Bus

The crowded local buses, usually blue and marked *populares*, charge a flat fare of about US$0.15, which you pay as you board. The *especiales*, which are usually red, charge

US$0.20 and don't allow standing. Generally, buses run north–south and have a fixed route. The *especiales* are found primarily on 10 de Agosto and Av 6 de Diciembre. Buses have destination placards in their windows and drivers will usually tell you which bus to take if they're not going your way. Traffic in the Old Town is very heavy, and it's sometimes faster to walk than to take a bus, particularly during rush hour.

Taxi

Cabs are yellow and have taxi-number stickers in the window. Quito cabs have meters (US$0.80 minimum charge), and drivers should use them (although at night and on Sundays they usually refuse). If the driver won't turn on the meter, arrange the fare before you get in the cab. Taxis cost US$1 to US$2 for short journeys, and up to US$5 for a long trip. You can hire them by the hour or longer; figure about US$60 for a day.

Trolley

Quito's efficient trolley service, El Trole, runs between the Estación Trolebús Sur, on Maldonado south of Villaflora, and the Estación Trolebús Norte, on 10 de Agosto just north of Av de La Prensa. With its own lane, it is often the fastest mode of transport through the Old Town. Trolleys run along Maldonado and 10 de Agosto and along Guayaquil in the Old Town about every 10 minutes from 6am to 12:30am. They stop every few blocks and are usually crowded. The fare is US$0.20.

A new trolley, called the Ecovía, runs along Av 6 de Diciembre between Río Coca in the north and La Marin in the Old Town.

The tourist offices usually provide free pocket maps for both lines.

AROUND QUITO

MITAD DEL MUNDO & AROUND

The most famous nearby excursion from Quito is to the equator at **Mitad del Mundo** (Middle of the World; admission US$0.50; 9am-6pm Mon-Fri, 9am-7pm Sat & Sun), 22km north of Quito. It's touristy, sure, but hopping back and forth between hemispheres is quite a sensation (freak yourself out!). On Sunday afternoons live bands rock the equatorial line in the central plaza area, and *quiteños*

pour in for the fun. A planetarium, a wonderful scale model of Quito's Old Town and other attractions cost extra. Check out the **Museo Solar Inti Ñan** (02-239-5122; admission US$1) just outside the complex. Besides housing fascinating exhibits of astronomical geography, it has some fun demonstrations of tasks that can only be performed at the equator.

Rumicucho is a small pre-Inca site under excavation about 3.5km north of Mitad del Mundo. On the way to the village of Calacalí, about 5km north of Mitad del Mundo, is the ancient, massive volcanic crater of **Pululahua** – the views are great from the rim or you can hike down to the crater floor.

From Quito, pink buses marked 'Mitad del Mundo' (US$0.35, 45 minutes) leave frequently from Av América. Buses continue past the complex and will drop you at the entrance road to Pululahua – ask for the Mirador de Ventanillas (the lookout point where the trail into the crater begins). Pululahua is easy to reach from Mitad del Mundo.

REFUGIO DE VIDA SILVESTRE PASOCHOA

This unique **reserve** (day admission US$7), 30km southeast of Quito, has one of the last stands of undisturbed humid **Andean forest** left in central Ecuador. It's a recommended day trip for naturalists and bird-watchers, as more than 100 bird species and many rare plants have been recorded here. Trails range from easy to strenuous, and overnight **camping** (per person US$0.75) is allowed in designated areas; campsites may be full on weekends. Facilities include latrines, picnic areas and water. Basic **accommodations** (cots per person US$3) are available. The reserve is operated by **Fundación Natura** (02-250-3385/86/87 through 3394, ext 202, 203; Av República 481 & D de Almagro) in Quito; it offers directions, maps and information.

To reach the reserve, take the bus from La Marín in Quito's Old Town to the village of **Amaguaña** (US$0.35, one hour), then hire a pickup (about US$7 per group/truck) to take you the last 7km to the park entrance.

VOLCÁN PICHINCHA

Quito's closest volcano is **Pichincha**, which looms over the city's western side. The volcano has two summits: the closer Rucu

Pichincha (about 4700m) and the higher Guagua Pichincha (4794m). Both can be climbed from Quito in a very long day. Rucu Pichincha, however, has been plagued with rape and armed robbery (local authorities have done nothing to stop this) and is rarely climbed. You're seriously advised to skip it, regardless of your group size, unless local information indicates otherwise. SAE in Quito stays abreast of safety in the area. Guagua Pichincha is most easily reached by joining a hiking tour (see Tours in Quito, p627), although reaching the summit is currently not permitted.

NORTHERN HIGHLANDS

The Andean highlands north of Quito are among the most popular destinations in Ecuador. Few travelers spend any good amount of time in the country without visiting the famous indigenous market in the small town of Otavalo, where you can buy a wide variety of weavings, clothing and handicrafts. The dramatic mountain scenery of the region is dotted with shining white churches set in tiny villages, and includes views of Cayambe, the third-highest peak in the country, as well as a beautiful lake district. Several small towns are noted for specialty handicrafts such as wood carving and leatherwork, and the people are wonderfully friendly.

OTAVALO

The small town of Otavalo (population 26,000) is justly famous for its friendly people and their giant Saturday market. The market dates back to pre-Inca times, when jungle products were brought up from the eastern lowlands and traded for highland goods. Today's market serves two different groups: locals who buy and barter animals, food and other essentials; and tourists looking for crafts. The latter flood the place on weekends, but that shouldn't deter you from visiting one of the most important markets in South America – the setting is beautiful and the shopping is fun.

The most evident feature of the *otavaleños'* culture is their traditional dress. The men wear long single pigtails, calf-length white pants, rope sandals, reversible gray or blue ponchos and dark felt hats. The women are very striking, with beautifully embroidered blouses, long black skirts and shawls, and interesting folded head cloths.

Information

Banco del Pacífico (Modesto Jaramillo near Calderón) and **Banco del Pichincha** (Bolívar at García Moreno) change traveler's checks and have ATMs. **Vaz Cambios** (cnr Modesto Jaramillo & Saona) also changes traveler's checks.

The **post office** (Sucre at Salinas, 2nd fl) is just off Plaza de Ponchos. Make telephone calls at **Andinatel** (Calderón near Modesto Jaramillo); there's also another **branch** (Salinas 509) in town.

For Internet access, try **Native C@ffee Net** (Sucre at Colón), **Caffé Net** (Sucre 10-14) or **Samarina Net** (Bolívar at Quiroga). All charge about US$1.20 per hour.

Sights

In the wee hours of every Saturday morning, while the tourists are still sawing logs in their hotel rooms, vendors pour into town lugging massive bundles of crafts to sell at the **Saturday market**. By 8am, things are in full swing and by 10am – after the tourist buses pull in and spill their contents – **Plaza de Ponchos** (the center of the crafts market) and nearly every street around it is jammed with people. Both traditional crafts (such as weavings, shawls and ponchos) and crafts tailored toward tourists (such as woolen sweaters with Rasta motifs) vie for buyers' dollars. Bargaining is tough but possible, and the *otavaleño* sellers are always friendly.

The **animal market**, on the western edge of town, offers an interesting break from the hustle of the crafts market. Beneath the volcanic backdrop of Cotacachi and Imbabura, indigenous men and women mill around with pigs, cows, goats and chickens and inspect, haggle and chat in the crisp morning air. It generally winds down by 8am. The **food market** is near the southern end of Modesto Jaramillo

The **Instituto Otavaleño de Antropología** (admission free; ☽ 8:30am-noon & 2:30-6pm Tue-Fri, 8:30am-noon Sat), just off the Panamericana north of town, houses a small archaeological and ethnographical museum of the area, a library and a bookstore selling books (in Spanish) about the anthropology and culture of Otavalo.

You can close the afternoon at the weekly **cockfight** (Montalvo; admission US$0.50), which begins

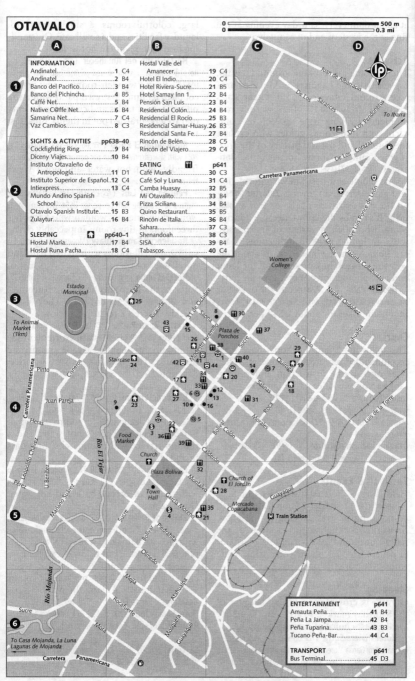

OTAVALO

0 ─── 500 m
0 ─── 0.3 mi

INFORMATION
Andinatel.................................1 C4
Andinatel.................................2 B4
Banco del Pacifico....................3 B4
Banco del Pichincha..................4 B5
Caffé Net................................5 B4
Native C@ffe Net.....................6 B4
Samarina Net...........................7 C4
Vaz Cambios............................8 C3

SIGHTS & ACTIVITIES   pp638–40
Cockfighting Ring.....................9 B4
Diceny Viajes..........................10 B4
Instituto Otavaleño de
   Antropología........................11 D1
Instituto Superior de Español..12 C4
Intiexpress.............................13 C4
Mundo Andino Spanish
   School...............................14 C4
Otavalo Spanish Institute......15 B3
Zulaytur................................16 B4

SLEEPING   pp640–1
Hostal María.........................17 B4
Hostal Runa Pacha................18 C4

Hostal Valle del
   Amanecer..........................19 C4
Hotel El Indio........................20 C4
Hotel Riviera-Sucre...............21 B5
Hotel Samay Inn 1.................22 B4
Pensión San Luis....................23 B4
Residencial Colón..................24 B4
Residencial El Rocío..............25 B3
Residencial Samar-Huasy.....26 B3
Residencial Santa Fe.............27 B4
Rincón de Belén....................28 C5
Rincón del Viajero................29 C4

EATING   p641
Café Mundi.............................30 C3
Café Sol y Luna.......................31 C4
Camba Huasay........................32 B5
Mi Otavalito...........................33 B4
Pizza Siciliana.........................34 B4
Quino Restaurant....................35 B5
Rincón de Italia.......................36 B4
Sahara....................................37 C3
Shenandoah...........................38 C3
SISA..39 B4
Tabascos.................................40 C4

ENTERTAINMENT   p641
Amauta Peña...........................41 B4
Peña La Jampa.........................42 B4
Peña Tuparina.........................43 B3
Tucano Peña-Bar......................44 C4

TRANSPORT   p641
Bus Terminal...........................45 D3

ECUADOR

at about 6pm every Saturday evening at the ring at the western end of Montalvo.

Activities

There's some great hiking around Otavalo, especially in the Lagunas de Mojanda area (see Around Otavalo, p641). **Diceny Viajes** (☎ 06-921-217; Sucre 10-11) offers warmly recommended hiking trips up Volcán Cotacachi with indigenous guides who explain the cultural and natural history of the area. If you'd rather roam by horse, contact **Intiexpress** (☎ 06-921-436; Sucre 11-06).

The oldest and best-known information and guide service in town is **Zulaytur** (☎ 06-921-176; www.geocities.com/zulaytur; cnr Sucre & Colón, 2nd fl). It's run by the knowledgeable Rodrigo Mora, who offers a variety of inexpensive tours, including visits to indigenous weavers' homes, where you can learn about the weaving process, buy products off the loom and take photographs. People love the guy.

Hostal Valle del Amanecer (☎ 06-920-990; amanacer@uio.satnet.net; cnr Roca & Quiroga) rents mountain bikes for about US$8 per day.

Courses

The following Spanish schools have been recommended repeatedly by travelers. They offer one-on-one instruction and can arrange accommodations with families.

Instituto Superior de Español (☎ 06-922-414; www.instituto-superior.net; Sucre 11-10)

Mundo Andino (☎ 06-921-864; espanol@interactive .net.ec; Salinas 4-04)

Otavalo Spanish Institute (☎ 06-925-475; www .otavalospanish.com; 31 de Octubre 4-76)

Festivals & Events

Held during the first two weeks of September, the Fiesta del Yamor features processions, music and dancing in the plaza, fireworks, cockfights, the election of the fiesta queen and, of course, lots of *yamor* (a delicious nonalcoholic corn drink made with seven varieties of corn).

Sleeping

Otavalo is crowded on Friday because of the Saturday market, so arrive on Thursday for the best choice of accommodations.

Hotel Riviera-Sucre (☎ 06-920-241; rivierasucre@ hotmail.com; García Moreno 3-80; r with shared/private bath per person US$5/8) This Belgian-owned hotel, in a handsomely converted old house, boasts large colorful rooms, a small courtyard, laundry facilities and a small café. Outstanding deal with plenty of hot water.

Hostal Valle del Amanecer (☎ 06-920-990; cnr Roca & Quiroga; r with shared/private bath per person US$7/9) Rustic wooden rooms open onto a cobbled, hammock-strewn patio with a fire pit and lots of tables and chairs (and plenty of travelers sprawled out in them). Breakfast is included.

Residencial El Rocío (☎ 06-920-584; Morales 11-70; r with shared/private bath per person US$4/5) Clean, friendly, with hot water and good views from the roof.

Pensión San Luis (☎ 06-920-614; Calderón 6-02; r with shared/private bath per person US$4/5) Run by a wonderfully friendly woman who keeps her three floors of tiny rooms impeccably clean.

Residencial Samar-Huasy (Modesto Jaramillo 6-11; s/d US$2/4) Small rooms with shared bath and unreliable hot water.

Hotel El Indio (☎ 06-920-060; Sucre 12-14; d US$7) Some of the 10 rooms here have balconies, and all have private hot bath. They fill up quickly. There's a restaurant below.

Hotel Runa Pacha (☎ 06-921-730; Roca 10-02; r per person US$7-9) Great staff, convenient location, brightly painted facade and private hot baths. The plain rooms vary in price, depending on the season and whether or not you want a TV.

Rincón del Viajero (☎ 06-921-741; rincondelviajero@ hotmail.com; Roca 11-07; r shared/private bath per person US$6/8; P) Clean, well-lit rooms are small but comfortable. There's hot water and a rooftop terrace with hammocks. Breakfast included.

Hostal María (☎ 06-920-672; Modesto Jaramillo near Colón; s/d US$4/8; P) Large, clean rooms with shared or private bath and hot water. Good value.

Rincón de Belén (☎ 06-921-860; Roca near Montalvo; d US$7-10; P) Good price for clean doubles with private bath, hot water, TV and telephone. The restaurant below is excellent.

Several decent places with hot water charge about US$4 per person for rooms with shared bath. Among them are:

Residencial Santa Fe (☎ 06-920-161; Colón 507)

Hotel Samay Inn 1 (☎ 06-922-871; Calderón 10-05)

Residencial Colón (Colón near Ricuarte)

La Luna (☎ 09-973-7415; campsites US$2, dm with/ without breakfast US$4.50/3, s without bath US$6, d without/ with bath US$12/16) For a marvelous setting outside of town, try the tranquil La Luna, 4km along the road to Lagunas de Mojanda. The breakfasts are filling and perks include kitchen facilities, fireplace, dining room, views and free pickup from Otavalo if you call ahead. A cab ride out costs about US$4. The owners will arrange mountain biking and hiking tours in the area. Great place!

Eating
With all those kitchenless travelers sauntering around town, it's hardly surprising Otavalo has plenty of restaurants.

Shenandoah (Salinas 5-15; pie slices US$1) Perennially popular for whopping slices of homemade fruit pie.

Café Mundi (Quiroga 6-08; mains US$2-4; Plaza de Ponchos) Café Mundi has been turning out good, cheap, wholesome food for years. Check it out: 16 types of pancakes, seven vegetarian plates, nachos, hummus and several traditional Ecuadorian dishes grace the menu.

Café Sol y Luna (Bolívar 11-10; mains US$2-3) Friendly, American-owned café serving healthy portions of well-prepared organic food, including hearty soups, veggie burgers and tofu (tofu!?) sandwiches.

Camba Huasay (Bolívar near Calderón; mains US$1.50-3) Tiny, family-run place with a filling US$2 *almuerzo*. US$1 buys you a big plate of lentils and rice, and there's good fried chicken too.

Mi Otavalito (Sucre 11-19; mains US$2-4) Great for Ecuadorian dishes and family atmosphere.

Pizza Siciliana (Morales 510) Decent pizzas, steep prices (figure about US$5 per person). Best on Friday and Saturday nights when *música folklórica* (folk music) groups play for a packed house.

Rincón de Italia (Sucre 9-19; till 11pm) Small place, delicious thin-crust pizzas (about US$3.50 per person). Spaghetti, cannelloni and lasagna too.

Sahara (Quiroga at Sucre; mains US$2-4) Good Middle Eastern food such as falafel, hummus and shawermas. For dessert, smoke a fat bowl of fruit-flavored tobacco from a giant hookah.

Quino Restaurant (Roca near García Moreno) Great, pricey seafood and more. Popular.

Tabascos (cnr Salinas & Sucre; mains US$3-5) Pricey Mexican food, decent breakfasts. The 2nd-floor patio overlooks Plaza de Ponchos.

SISA (Calderón 409; mains US$2-5) Café and restaurant-cum-arts complex with good coffee, OK breakfasts and a wide variety of lunch and dinner meals.

Entertainment
Otavalo is dead midweek but lively on the weekend. *Peñas* are the main hangouts.

Peña La Jampa (cnr Modesto Jaramillo & Morales; admission US$2-3; 10pm-3am Fri & Sat) Showcases live salsa, merengue, *rock en español* (Spanish rock) and *folklórica*.

Peña Tuparina (Morales near 31 de Octubre) A mainstay of the local music scene.

Amauta Peña (Modesto Jaramillo 614) and **Tucano Peña-Bar** (Morales 5-10) are also good.

Getting There & Around
Otavalo is 95km from Quito. The **bus terminal** (Atahualpa & Jacinto Collahuazo) is two blocks north of Av Quito. Transportes Otavalo and Transportes Los Lagos are the only buses from Quito (under US$2, 2½ hours) that enter the terminal. Other companies drop passengers on the Panamericana (a 10-minute walk from town) on their way north (or south). Transportes Otavalo offers frequent buses to Ibarra (US$0.35, 35 minutes).

AROUND OTAVALO
The spectacular countryside surrounding Otavalo is scattered with lakes, indigenous villages and hiking trails, all easily accessible to anyone with the slightest inkling to beat the Otavalo market scene and take to the hills. Tour agencies in Otavalo (p640) can provide information or organize hikes, or you can explore on your own.

The beautiful **Lagunas de Mojanda**, in the high *páramo* some 17km south of Otavalo, make for unforgettable hiking. The area acquired protected status (primarily through the hard work of Casa Mojanda – see the boxed text, p642) in 2002. Taxis from Otavalo charge about US$8 each way. You could also walk up and camp. For information about the lakes, stop at the Mojanda Foundation/Pachamama Association directly across from Casa Mojanda (which also has information) on the road to the park. You could also ask at one of the tour agencies in Otavalo (see p640).

Strung along the eastern side of the Panamericana, a few kilometers north of Otavalo, are the mostly indigenous villages of **Peguche**, **Ilumán** and **Agato**. You can walk or take local buses to all three. Sunday,

SPLURGE!

The country inn and organic farm of **Casa Mojanda** (☎ 09-973-1737; www.casamojanda .com; s low season/high season US$75/90, d year-round US$120) is the perfect place to replenish your body and mellow your mind. The setting – about 4km south of Otavalo on the road to Lagunas de Mojanda – is spectacular. The friendly owners speak perfect English and have implemented several widely praised eco- and community-tourism projects. The inn itself consists of eight individual cottages, each built using rammed-earth construction and natural building materials. Some have fireplaces, and all have sweeping views of the magnificent Andean countryside. Rates include use of the Jacuzzi and two meals made entirely of ingredients from the organic farm.

however, is not a good day to visit: many people would rather get blind drunk than deal with gringos. In Peguche, **Hostal Aya Huma** (☎ 06-922-663; www.ayahuma.com in Spanish; s/d with shared bath US$8/12, with private bath US$14/20) is a mellow, Dutch/Ecuadorian-owned *hostal* that serves good, cheap homemade meals (veggie options too) and hosts live Andean music on Saturday night. You can also hike to a pretty **waterfall** 2km south of Peguche.

Laguna San Pablo can be reached on foot from Otavalo by heading roughly southeast on any of the paths heading over the hill behind the railway station. You can then walk the paved road that goes all the way around the lake.

The village of **Cotacachi**, some 15km north of Otavalo, is famous for its leatherwork, which is sold in stores all along the main street. **Hostal Plaza Bolívar** (☎ 06-915-755; cotacachi@ turismoaventura.net; Bolívar 12-26 at 10 de Agosto, 3rd fl; r with shared/private bath per person US$4/6) is the best budget hotel in town. There are hourly buses from Otavalo.

About 18km west of Cotacachi, the spectacular crater-lake **Laguna Cuicocha** lies within an extinct, eroded volcano. The lake is part of the **Reserva Ecológica Cotacachi-Cayapas**, established to protect the large area of western Andean forest that extends from Volcán Cotacachi (4939m) to the Río Cayapas in the coastal lowlands. A walk around the

lake takes about six hours (ask about safety at the ranger station at the park entrance). Trucks, taxis (both US$4, one way) and occasional buses go from Cotacachi.

IBARRA

The busy capital of Imbabura Province is a fascinating little town. Its colonial architecture, leafy plazas and cobbled streets make it a relaxing sort of place, while its unique blend of students, *mestizos*, highland Indians and Afro-Ecuadorians give it an exciting multicultural edge. And the ice cream? Can't beat it.

Information

Banco del Pacífico (cnr Olmedo & Moncayo) changes traveler's checks and has an ATM. Post your letters at the **post office** (Salinas 6-64) and make calls at **Andinatel** (Sucre 4-48). You can get online at **Zonanet** (Moncayo 5-74; US$1 per hr) or at the cybercafé below **Hotel El Ejecutivo** (Oviedo 9-33; US$1 per hr).

The **tourist office** (☎ 06-955-711; García Moreno 7-44; ☯ 8:30am-1pm & 2-5pm Mon-Fri) is slim on handouts, but the staff is helpful.

Sleeping

Ibarra is bursting with cheap hotels. The cheapest (and skuzziest) are near the bus terminals.

Residencial Majestic (☎ 06-950-052; Olmedo 7-63; r with shared/private bath per person US$2/2.50) Bare-bones but will do for a night.

Hotel Imbabura (☎ 06-950-155; Oviedo 9-33; r per person US$4-5) Old building with thick walls, creaky wood floors and clean communal baths. It has a relaxing, flower-filled courtyard and a small café. Dark rooms, popular place.

Hostal El Ejecutivo (☎ 06-956-575; Bolívar 9-69; s/d US$5/10) Some rooms have balconies, and all have private hot baths, telephone and TV. Plain, but a great deal.

Hostal Ecuador (☎ 06-956-425; Mosquera 5-54; r per person US$5) Family-run hotel with several floors of clean, spacious rooms with rock-hard beds and private hot showers.

Hostería Casona de Los Lagos (☎ 06-957-844; Sucre 3-50; s/d US$6/12) HI-affiliate in an expansive old building with a relaxing courtyard. Rooms vary, but most are a good deal and have TV and private hot bath.

Hotel Madrid (☎ 06-956-177; Moncayo 7-41; s/d US$10/20; Ⓟ) For something a bit plusher,

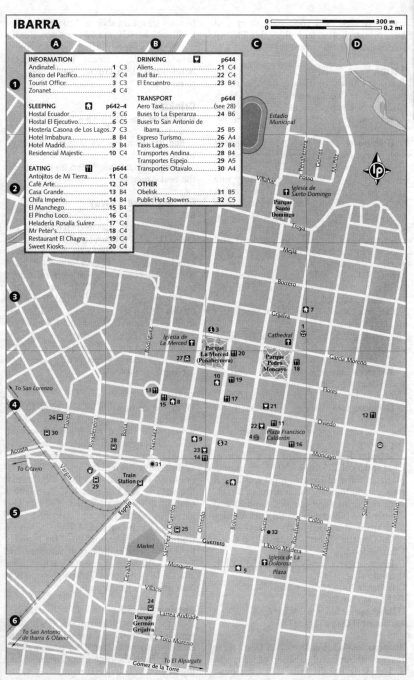

IBARRA

0		300 m
0		0.2 mi

INFORMATION
Andinatel.................................**1** C3
Banco del Pacífico..................**2** C4
Tourist Office.........................**3** C3
Zonanet..................................**4** C4

SLEEPING 🏠 p642–4
Hostal Ecuador......................**5** C6
Hostal El Ejecutivo................**6** C5
Hostería Casona de Los Lagos.**7** C3
Hotel Imbabura......................**8** B4
Hotel Madrid..........................**9** B4
Residencial Majestic.............**10** C4

EATING 🍴 p644
Antojitos de Mi Tierra...........**11** C4
Café Arte...............................**12** D4
Casa Grande.........................**13** B4
Chifa Imperio.........................**14** B4
El Manchego..........................**15** B4
El Pincho Loco......................**16** C4
Heladería Rosalía Suárez.......**17** C4
Mr Peter's..............................**18** C4
Restaurant El Chagra............**19** C4
Sweet Kiosks........................**20** C4

DRINKING 🍸 p644
Aliens....................................**21** C4
Bud Bar.................................**22** C4
El Encuentro..........................**23** B4

TRANSPORT p644
Aero Taxi.........................(see 28)
Buses to La Esperanza..........**24** B6
Buses to San Antonio de
Ibarra..................................**25** B5
Expreso Turismo....................**26** A4
Taxis Lagos...........................**27** B4
Transportes Andina...............**28** B4
Transportes Espejo................**29** A5
Transportes Otavalo..............**30** A4

OTHER
Obelisk..................................**31** B5
Public Hot Showers...............**32** C5

Estadio
Municipal

To San Lorenzo

To Otavalo

Acosta

To San Antonio
de Ibarra & Otavalo

Train
Station

Market

Parque
Santo
Domingo

Iglesia de
Santo Domingo

Iglesia de
La Merced

Parque
La Merced
(Peñaherrera)

Cathedral

Parque
Pedro
Moncayo

Plaza Francisco
Calderón

Iglesia de La
Dolorosa

Plaza

Parque
Germán
Grijalva

To El Alpargate

To San Lorenzo

try the Madrid. The rooms are sharp and have private, hot-water baths, cable TV and telephone. The restaurant is good too.

Eating

Ibarra is known for its tasty *nogadas* (nougats) and its sweet *arrope de mora* (a thick blackberry syrup). You can purchase (and taste) these treats at the sweets kiosks across from Parque La Merced.

El Alpargate (☎ 06-644-062; Barrio El Alpargate 1-59; ☽ noon-6pm) El Alpargate is famous in Ibarra for serving the best *plato típico* (traditional meal) in town. There's only one plate on the menu: marinated beef cubes with sausage, fresh cheese, avocado, *mote* (similar to hominy), potatoes and *empanadas* (turnovers filled with vegetable, egg, olive, meat or cheese). It's excellent and well worth the US$4. The restaurant is in Barrio El Alpargate and reached easiest by taxi (US$1). To walk (about 20 minutes), head east on Gomez de la Torre to the end, turn right and look for the sign.

Café Arte (Salinas 5-43; mains US$2-3) Specializes in art, music and Mexican snacks. There's live music every Friday and Saturday night, and the atmosphere (warmed up by photography and painting exhibits) is welcoming.

Mr Peter's (Sucre 5-36; mains US$2-4) Good set meals and big, cheap plates of *menestra* (lentils or beans) and rice. Big breakfasts.

El Pincho Loco (Moncayo 4-61; mains US$2-3) Whips out cheap *asados* (grilled meats) to the sonic onslaught of sports TV, hence its popularity.

Antojitos de Mi Tierra (Plaza Francisco Calderón) Chef and local TV-show host Marta Jduregi prepares some of Ibarra's most traditional treats, including *chicha de arroz* (a sweetened rice drink) and *tamales, humitas* and *quimbolitos* (all variations on corn dumplings steamed in corn husks or leaves).

Chifa Imperio (Olmedo 9-79; mains US$2-4) Good Chinese food.

Cheap, hearty meals can also be had at the following:

Casa Grande (Narváez 6-97; almuerzos US$1.70; ☽ lunch only Mon-Sat)

El Manchego (cnr Narváez & Oviedo)

Restaurant El Chagra (Olmedo 7-48)

Heladería Rosalía Suárez (Oviedo 7-82) Don't leave Ibarra without having a scoop of ice cream at Heladería Rosalía Suárez. It's the most famous ice cream shop in Ecuador, opened by Rosalía herself over 90 years ago. Rosalía is credited with perfecting the tradition of *helados de paila* (ice cream – usually sorbets – hand-turned in a copper bowl); she lived to be 104.

Drinking

El Encuentro (Olmedo 9-35) An eclectic little hideaway bar.

Bud Bar (Plaza Francisco Calderón) Slick and trendy.

Aliens (Oviedo at Bolívar; ☽ 9pm-late Mon-Sat) Has the best dance floor.

Getting There & Away

BUS

Each bus company has its own terminal. For Quito (US$2, 2½ hours) and Tulcán (US$2, 2½ hours), use **Transportes Andina** (Velasco), **Aero Taxi** (Velasco) or **Expreso Turismo** (cnr Flores & Moncayo). These companies also offer five daily buses to Esmeraldas (US$8, eight hours) and Guayaquil (US$8, 10 hours). **Transportes Otavalo** (Velasco) serves Otavalo (US$0.35, 35 minutes) between 5:30am and 9:30pm.

Transportes Espejo (off Vargas) heads regularly to the coastal town of San Lorenzo (US$4, 3½ to four hours), a spectacular ride; sit on the right for views.

TRAIN

With the completion of the road to San Lorenzo, the Ibarra–San Lorenzo railway, which once linked the highlands to the coast, no longer runs. However, *autoferros* (buses mounted on a train chassis) go as far as the point known as Primer Paso (US$3.80 one way, 1¾ hours), less than a quarter of the way to San Lorenzo. It's essentially a round-trip tourist attraction. You can also get off at Primer Paso and wait for a passing bus to San Lorenzo. A daily departure from Ibarra is scheduled for 7am Monday through Friday and 8am on Saturday and Sunday, although it doesn't leave without at least 16 passengers. Tickets go on sale at 6am on the day of departure.

Getting Around

Ibarra's various bus terminals (each company has its own) are scattered about southeast of the town center. They're all walking distance from the hotels, but consider taking a cab if you arrive at night.

AROUND IBARRA

Almost a suburb of Ibarra, **San Antonio de Ibarra** is famous for its wood carving, and numerous shops on and just off the main plaza sell carvings. Buses leave frequently for San Antonio from the intersection of Guerrero and Sánchez y Cifuentes in Ibarra, or you can walk 5km south along the Panamericana (the western extension of Velasco).

The pretty little village of **La Esperanza**, 7km south of Ibarra, is the place to stay if you're looking for peace and quiet. There's nothing to do here except talk to the locals and stroll through the surrounding countryside. The basic but friendly **Casa Aida** (☎ 06-642-020; Calle Gallo Plaza; r per person US$3-4) has simple rooms and serves good, cheap meals, including vegetarian dishes. Buses from Ibarra leave from the terminal near Parque Germán Grijalva, or you can walk.

TULCÁN

At 3000m above sea level, the drab, wind-whipped city of Tulcán is the principal gateway to Colombia. Colombians come here to shop (Thursday and Sunday are market days, when shopping takes on a feverish pitch), but travelers come to cross the border. Its only real tourist attraction is its topiary gardens.

Information

Tulcán's **tourist information office** (☎ 06-984-184; 🕙 8:30am-5pm Mon-Fri) is at the border.

Banco del Pichincha (cnr 10 de Agosto & Sucre) changes currency and traveler's checks on weekdays only. The **casa de cambio** (Ayacucho 3-74; 🕙 7am-6pm) changes cash. Exchange rates in Tulcán and at the border are usually lower than in Quito, so it's best to change only what you need.

Make calls at **Andinatel** (Olmedo near Junín; 🕙 8am-10pm).

Sights

The big tourist attraction is the **topiary garden** in the cemetery. Behind the cemetery, the locals play *pelota de guante* (glove ball) on weekends. It's a strange game, played with a small, soft ball and large, spiked paddles. Thursday and Sunday **market** days are crowded with Colombian bargain hunters.

West of Tulcán, the **Reserva Ecológica El Ángel** covers nearly 16,000 hectares of *páramo* which drops down to the Cerro Golondrinas cloud forests. The Cerro Golondrinas Cloud-

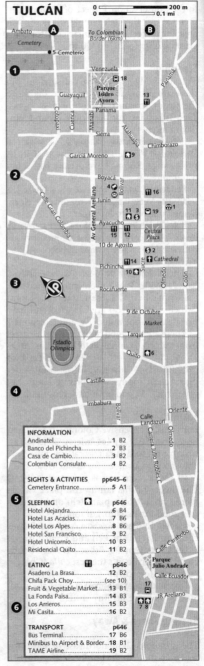

TULCÁN

INFORMATION	
Andinatel............................1	B2
Banco del Pichincha..............2	B3
Casa de Cambio....................3	B2
Colombian Consulate............4	B2

SIGHTS & ACTIVITIES	pp645-6
Cemetery Entrance................5	A1

SLEEPING	p646
Hotel Alejandra.....................6	B4
Hotel Las Acacias..................7	B6
Hotel Los Alpes....................8	B6
Hotel San Francisco...............9	B2
Hotel Unicornio...................10	B3
Residencial Quito................11	B2

EATING	p646
Asadero La Brasa.................12	B2
Chifa Pack Choy...............(see 10)	
Fruit & Vegetable Market.....13	B1
La Fonda Paisa....................14	B3
Los Arrieros.......................15	B3
Mi Casita............................16	B2

TRANSPORT	p646
Bus Terminal.......................17	B6
Minibus to Airport & Border..18	B1
TAME Airline........................19	B2

forest Conservation Project offers a recommended trek through remote villages in this area; the project can be contacted through La Casa de Eliza (p631) in Quito.

Sleeping

Tulcán's budget hotels are a dismal lot, but there are plenty to choose from, thanks to the steady stream of Colombian shoppers. They fill up fast for the Thursday and Sunday markets.

Hotel San Francisco (☎ 06-980-760; Bolívar near Atahualpa; s/d US$3.50/7) One of the best in its price range. Rooms have private baths, hot water and TV.

Residencial Quito (☎ 06-980-541; Ayacucho 450; s/d US$2/4) Very basic but reasonably clean. Bring your own toilet paper.

Hotel Alejandra (☎ 06-981-784; Sucre at Quito; s/d US$4/8; ℗) Score! Carpeted rooms, private baths and hot water – hard to beat for US$4 a head.

Hotel Unicornio (☎ 06-980-638; cnr Pichincha & Sucre; s/d US$6/12; ℗) Conveniently located over the town's best Chinese restaurant. Rooms (which vary widely) are carpeted and have private bath, hot water, TV and telephone.

There are two good hotels across the street from the bus terminal: **Hotel Las Acacias** (☎ 06-982-501; JR Arellano; s/d US$4/8) and **Hotel Los Alpes** (☎ 06-982-235; JR Arellano; s/d US$4/8). Both offer plain, clean rooms with private baths, hot water and TV, and both have restaurants.

Eating

For good, inexpensive Colombian food and huge breakfasts try **Los Arrieros** (Bolívar near Ayacucho) or **La Fonda Paisa** (Bolívar at Pichincha), where you can stuff yourself for about US$2.

Mi Casita (Sucre near Boyacá; mains US$1-2.50) The owner of this family-run place swears there's not a Colombian item on his menu (it's good for Ecuadorian food).

Asadero La Brasa (Ayacucho near Sucre) Serves cheap rotisserie chicken and French fries.

Chifa Pack Choy (cnr Pichincha & Sucre) Below Hotel Unicornio, it's the best *chifa* (Chinese restaurant) in town.

Fruit and vegetable market (Sucre at Panamá) Stock up on the healthy stuff.

Getting There & Away
AIR

The airport is 2km northeast of the town center en route to the border. **TAME** (☎ 06-980-

675; Sucre near Ayacucho) has offices in town and at the **airport** (☎ 06-982-850). It offers daily flights to/from Quito (US$32). TAME also flies Monday, Wednesday and Friday to Cali, Colombia (US$78, plus US$25 international departure tax).

BUS
Ecuador

Buses run to/from Ibarra (US$2.20, 2½ hours) and Quito (US$4, five hours). Long-haulers go to Cuenca (US$16, 17 hours, once a day), Guayaquil (US$13, 13 hours) and other cities. Buses to Otavalo usually drop you along the Panamericana on the outskirts.

Colombian Border Crossing

The Rumichaca border crossing, 6.5km north of Tulcán, is the principal gateway to/from Colombia. All formalities – which are very straightforward – are taken care of at the border, which is open 24 hours every day. Minibuses (US$0.60) and taxis (US$4) run regularly between the border and Parque Isidro Ayora. The buses accept Colombian pesos or US dollars. Be absolutely certain that you have your papers in order and be ready for drugs and weapons searches on both sides. Stay abreast of the conflict in Colombia and inquire locally about the safety of travel in Colombia before you pounce across the country line.

Entering Ecuador, you get a stamp in your passport and on a separate tourist card. Leaving Ecuador, you get an exit stamp in your passport and you hand in your tourist card. If you lose your tourist card, they *should* give you another one free (see Visas & Documents, p714).

Getting Around

The bus terminal (Bolívar at JR Arellano) is 2.5km southwest of the town center. City buses (US$0.10) run along Bolívar to the center. Taxi fare to/from the center is around US$1.

CENTRAL HIGHLANDS

The Panamericana heads south from Quito through the wildly scenic central Andean valley, snaking past nine of the country's 10 highest peaks (several of which are active volcanoes) and scores of tiny indigenous villages. The central highlands boast Ecuador's most important mountain climbing, including Volcanes Chimborazo (6310m) and Cotopaxi (5897m), the country's two highest mountains. Riobamba and Baños are the best towns to hire guides and equipment. If climbing doesn't pull your rope, rest assured – there's plenty more to do. You can hike between remote Andean villages near the Quilotoa loop, gorge yourself on homemade cheeses and chocolate in Guaranda and Salinas, bomb downhill to the Oriente on a rented mountain bike from Baños, hike or trek in spectacular national parks or ride the roof of a boxcar down the famous Nariz del Diablo.

LATACUNGA

The two-hour drive from Quito to Latacunga (population 54,000) is magnificent. Volcán Cotopaxi is the cone-shaped, snow-capped mountain looming to the east of the Panamericana, while the two Ilinizas (Sur and Norte) stand to the west. From the city itself, several volcanoes are visible in the distance, provided you can drag yourself out of bed early on a clear morning (it's worth it!). Latacunga is a good base for climbing or day-tripping to Parque Nacional Cotopaxi (p650), and is the starting point for bussing around the spectacular Quilotoa loop (p649). It's also the best place to stay for a visit to the indigenous market in Saquisilí (p649).

Information

Banco de Guayaquil (Maldonado 7-20) changes traveler's checks and has an ATM. There's also an **Andinatel** (Quevedo near Maldonado) and **post office** (Quevedo near Maldonado) in town. Internet access is available at **Gato Azul** (Guayaquil 6-14; US$1 per hr) and **AJ Cyber Café** (Quito 16-19; US$1 per hr).

Activities

Several tour operators have sprung up in recent years offering day trips and two- to three-day climbing trips to Cotopaxi (p650). Day trips cost US$25 to US$35 per person, depending on the size of your group. Two-day summit trips to Cotopaxi cost about US$120 per person – but make sure your guide is qualified and licensed if you're attempting the summit. Many hotels in town also offer day trips to Cotopaxi. The following offer all sorts of excursions.

Expediciones Volcán Route (☎ 03-812-452; volcanroute@hotmail.com; Salcedo 4-55)

Tierra Zero (☎ 03-801-170, 03-804-327; guiller moneiges@latinmail.com; Guayaquil 5-13)

Tovar Expeditions (☎ 03-811-333; Guayaquil 5-38)

Festivals & Events

Latacunga's major annual fiesta (September 23–24) honors La Virgen de las Mercedes. More popularly known as the Fiesta de la Mama Negra, the event features processions, costumes, fireworks, street dancing and Andean music. This is one of those festivals that, although superficially Christian, has much indigenous influence and is truly worth seeing.

Sleeping

Hotels fill fast on Wednesday afternoon for the Thursday-morning indigenous market at Saquisilí.

Hotel Estambul (☎ 03-800-354; Quevedo 73-40; r with shared/private bath per person US$6/8) Friendly, popular budget hotel with large rooms, hot water and spotless communal showers. Good choice.

Hotel Cotopaxi (☎ 03-801-310; Salcedo 5-61; s/d US$7/14) Popular with climbers, this friendly hotel offers spacious, comfortable rooms with TV, private bath and hot water. Some have giant windows and views of the central plaza.

Hotel Central (☎ 03-800-912; Sanchez de Orellana at Salcedo; s/d US$7/14) Same building as Hotel Cotopaxi and similar services.

Residencial Amazonas (☎ 03-812-673; El Valencia 47-36; r with shared/private bath per person US$3/5) Small, basic, dark rooms, but clean enough and good for the price.

Hotel Tilipulo (☎ 03-810-611; hoteltilipulo@hotmail .com; Guayaquil & Quevedo; s/d US$9/16) This homey favorite offers comfy rooms with hot water, TV and telephone, and the downstairs restaurant is great for breakfast.

Residencial Santiago (☎ 03-800-899; 2 de Mayo & Guayaquil; r per person US$8) Large, no-frills rooms have private hot bath and TV. Downstairs rooms were being remodeled during our visit, promising spiffy rooms (that may be pricier).

Eating

Latacunga's traditional dish is the *chugchucara*, a tasty, heart-attack-inducing plate of *fritada* (pieces of fried pork meat); *mote*

ECUADOR

LATACUNGA

0 _____ 200 m
0 _____ 0.1 mi

INFORMATION	
AJ Cyber Café	1 C2
Andinatel	2 C3
Banco de Guayaquil	3 D3
Gato Azul	4 D2

SIGHTS & ACTIVITIES	p647
Expediciones Volcán Route	5 C2
Tierra Zero	6 C2
Tovar Expeditions	7 C2

SLEEPING	p647
Hotel Central	8 D2
Hotel Cotopaxi	9 D2
Hotel Estambul	10 C2
Hotel Tilipulo	11 C2
Residencial Amazonas	12 B1
Residencial Santiago	13 C2

EATING	pp647-8
Casa Grande	14 C2
Chifa China	15 B2
Pingüino	16 C2
Pizzería Bon Giorno	17 D3
Restaurant Rodelu	18 C2
Restaurante El Mashca	19 D1
Restaurante La Borgoña	(see 19)

TRANSPORT	pp648-9
Main Bus Terminal	20 A2

with *chicharrón* (bits of fried pork skin); potatoes; fried banana; *tostada* (toasted corn); popcorn; and cheese *empanadas*. There are several *chugchucara* restaurants on Quijano y Ordoñez, a few blocks south of the center. They're busiest on weekends, when families fill the tables and musicians stroll door to door. One of the best is **Chugchucaras La Mamá Negra** (☎ 03-805-401; Quijano y Ordoñez 1-67; chugchucara US$4; ♥ closed Mon).

Restaurante La Borgoña and **Restaurant El Mashca** (both on F Valencia near Sanchez de Orellana) – for chicken – are both cheap and quite good. Other good restaurants include the following:

Casa Grande (cnr Quito & Guayaquil; almuerzos US$1) Family run, *almuerzos* only.

Chifa China (Antonio Vela near 5 de Junio; mains US$2.50-4) Decent Chinese food.

Pizzería Bon Giorno (cnr Sanchez de Orellana & Maldonado; mains US$4-7; ♥ noon-10pm) Best pizzas and Italian food in town.

Pingüino (Quito near Guayaquil) Good ice cream, great coffee (for Latacunga).

Restaurant Rodelu (Quito) Good breakfasts, espresso drinks and pizza.

Getting There & Away

Buses from Quito (US$1.50, two hours) will drop you at the **bus terminal** (Panamericana) if Latacunga is their final destination. If you're taking a bus that's continuing to Ambato or Riobamba it will either drop you on the Panamericana at Av 5 de Junio, or at the corner of 5 de Junio and Cotopaxi, about five blocks west of the Panamericana. Buses to Ambato (US$0.80, one hour) and Quito (US$1.50, 1½ to two hours) leave the bus terminal. If you're heading south to Riobamba, it's easiest to catch a passing bus from the corner of 5 de Junio and Cotopaxi, although these are often full during holidays. Otherwise, bus it to Ambato and change there.

From the terminal, Transportes Cotopaxi departs hourly for the rough but spectacular descent to Quevedo (US$3, five hours) via Zumbahua (US$1.80, two hours). For transport information to other destinations on the Quilotoa loop, see below.

THE QUILOTOA LOOP

The beat-up and bumpy unpaved road known as the Quilotoa loop begins and ends in Latacunga and winds through some of the most spectacular high Andean scenery in Ecuador. Allow yourself *at least* two days to bounce around this circuit, and more if you wish to hike some of the fabulous trails along the route. Bring warm clothes (it gets painfully cold up here) and bring water and snacks.

Ten kilometers west of Latacunga, **Pujilí** has a Sunday market and interesting Corpus Christi and All Souls' Day celebrations. The tiny village of **Zumbahua**, 67km west of Latacunga, sits at an altitude of 3500m and has a small but fascinating Saturday market. The town's three lodgings fill up fast on Friday, so get there early; the best of them is **Condor Matzi** (r per person US$4), on the square. Accommodations and food are basic.

From Zumbahua, buses and hired trucks trundle up the 14km of unpaved road leading north to the beautiful volcanic **Laguna Quilotoa**, where there are several extremely basic accommodations owned by friendly indigenous folks. Camping is possible near the lake.

About 14km north of the lake is the little village of **Chugchilán**, which is an excellent base for hiking in the area and has three traveler-friendly hotels. The best of them is the much-loved, North American–owned **Black Sheep Inn** (☎ 03-814-587; www.blacksheepinn .com; bunk beds US$20-22.50, s US$40-42.50, d US$49-53.50, tr US$70.50-77), where rates include two delicious vegetarian meals. **Hostal Mama Hilda** (☎ 03-814-814, in Quito ☎ 02-258-2957; mama_hilda@

hotmail.com; dm US$8, s/d US$9/18) is friendly and popular with backpackers; rates include breakfast and dinner.

Another 23km north is the village of **Sigchos**, which has a couple of basic lodgings. From here, it's about 52km east to **Saquisilí**.

Saquisilí's Thursday-morning market is for the inhabitants of remote indigenous villages, most of whom are recognized by their felt porkpie hats and red ponchos. Ecuadorian economists consider this to be the most important indigenous village market in the country, and many travelers rate it as the most interesting in Ecuador. Accommodations are available in a couple of cold-water cheapies in town.

Getting There & Around

No buses go all the way around the loop. From Latacunga, they only go as far as Chugchilán, and they either go clockwise (via Zumbahua and Quilotoa) or counterclockwise (via Sigchos). The bus via Zumbahua departs Latacunga's bus terminal daily at noon, passing Zumbahua at around 1:30pm, Laguna Quilotoa at around 2pm, arriving in Chugchilán at about 4pm. The bus via Sigchos departs daily at 11:30am, passing Saquisilí just before noon and Sigchos at around 2pm, arriving in Chugchilán at around 3:30pm; the Saturday bus via Sigchos leaves at 10:30am on Saturdays.

From Chugchilán, buses returning to Latacunga via Zumbahua leave Chugchilán Monday through Friday at 4am (good morning!), passing Quilotoa at around 6am, Zumbahua at around 6:30am, arriving in Latacunga at around 8am. On Saturday this bus leaves at 3am, and on Sunday at 6am and 10am. Buses via Sigchos leave Monday through Friday at 3am, passing Sigchos at around 4am, Saquisilí at around 7am, arriving in Latacunga at around 8am. On Saturday this bus departs at 7am. On Sunday you must switch buses in Sigchos.

A morning milk truck between Chugchilán and Sigchos will take passengers, allowing you to skip the predawn wakeup of the bus (ask around). In Zumbahua, trucks can be hired to Laguna Quilotoa (or anywhere on the loop for the right amount of cash).

Buses to Pujilí (US$0.25) and Saquisilí (US$0.25, 30 minutes) leave regularly from Latacunga's bus terminal.

PARQUE NACIONAL COTOPAXI

Mainland Ecuador's most frequently visited national park, **Cotopaxi** (admission US$10) has excellent hiking and mountaineering possibilities. Its centerpiece is the active **Volcán Cotopaxi** (5897m), the country's second-highest peak. Outfitters in Riobamba offer downhill mountain-biking tours of Cotopaxi that will really spin your wheels (p656). The park is almost deserted midweek, when nature freaks can have the breathtaking (literally) scenery nearly to themselves. The park has a small **museum**, an information center, a climbers' refuge (*refugio*) and camping and picnicking areas. The gate is open 8am to 6pm (longer on weekends), but hikers can slip through just about anytime. Camping costs about US$2 per person. A bunk in the climbers' refuge costs US$10; cooking facilities are available. Be sure to bring a warm sleeping bag. Near the Clirsen entrance to the park, about 2km west (and across the Panamericana), the **Albergue Cuello de Luna** (☎ 09-970-0330, in Quito ☎ 02-224-2744; www.cuellodeluna.com; dm from US$11, s/d/tr without bath US$20/26/36, with bath US$23/34/45) is the cheapest place in the area. It's friendly and popular, and good food (US$4 to US$6) is available.

Two park entrances are on the Panamericana, north of Latacunga. One is about 20km north, and the other, Clirsen, about 26km north. Buses will drop you at both of these entrances – you can then follow the signposted dirt roads to the administration building and museum, about 15km from either entrance. You can walk or hitchhike into the park, but traffic is minimal except on weekends. Pickups from Latacunga cost about US$20 to US$30. Many hotels in Latacunga provide truck service to the park.

The **Laguna de Limpiopungo** area, with camping (it gets very cold) and picnicking, is about 4km beyond the museum, and the climbers' refuge is about 12km further on. You can drive up a very rough road to a parking area about 1km before the refuge. The lake itself is at 3800m and the refuge is 1000m higher; it is very hard walking at this altitude if you are not used to it. Altitude sickness is a very real danger, so acclimatize for several days in Quito or elsewhere before attempting to walk in; see p1059.

Continuing beyond the climbers' refuge requires snow- and ice-climbing gear and expertise. Guides and gear are available in Quito, Baños, Riobamba and Latacunga. Ask at the SAE (p624) in Quito for advice.

AMBATO

About 47km south of Latacunga, the capital of Tungurahua Province has two claims to fame: its flower festival, held in the second half of February, and its huge, chaotic Monday market, the largest in Ecuador. With little else to offer, travelers usually zip through Ambato (population 174,261) on their way to Baños or Riobamba. It's a busy yet manageable city.

From the bus terminal, city buses marked 'Centro' go to Parque Cevallos (US$0.10), on the central plaza. To return, take one marked 'Terminal' from the plaza.

Information

The **tourist office** (☎ 03-821-800; cnr Guayaquil & Rocafuerte; ☼ 9am-3pm Mon-Fri) is by Hotel Ambato. **Banco del Pacífico** (cnr Lalama & Cevallos, Parque Cevallos), **Banco de Guayaquil** (cnr Sucre & Mera) and **Banco del Pichincha** (Lalama near Sucre, Parque Cevallos) all change foreign currency and have ATMs.

Sleeping & Eating

The area around Parque 12 de Noviembre and the nearby Mercado Central has numerous cheap and basic hotels. Of these, the best are **Residencial América** (JB Vela 737; s/d US$3/6), which has tepid shared showers, and **Hostal La Union** (☎ 03-822-375; cnr Espejo & 12 de Noviembre; s/d US$3/6), where the baths are shared, the water's hot and the beds are saggy.

Hostal Señorial (☎ 03-825-124; cnr Cevallos & Quito; s/d US$12/24) In a more attractive area, this hostel has spacious, carpeted rooms with bath, telephone, TV and big windows.

Chifa Nueva Hong Kong (Bolívar 768; mains US$2-3) Whips out good but standard Chinese food.

Parrilladas Farid (Bolívar 16-74; mains US$5-7) A great Argentine grill.

Pizzería Fornace (Cevallos 17-28; mains US$4-7). The best pizza and pasta in town.

Cuba Son (cnr Cevallos & Montalvo; ☼ 1pm-2am) A cool little 2nd-floor bar serving Cuban snacks and light meals.

Getting There & Away

The bus terminal, 2km from the center of town, has many buses to Baños (US$1, one hour), Riobamba (US$1, one hour), Quito (US$2, 2½ hours) and Guayaquil (US$4, six hours). Less frequent are buses to Guaranda (US$1.60, 2½ hours), Cuenca (US$7, seven hours) and Tena (US$4, six hours).

BAÑOS

The idyllic town of Baños is surrounded by lush, green mountains offering great hiking and mountain biking. It's a popular gateway to the jungle (Puyo, in the Oriente, is only two hours east by bus), and its hot springs are cherished by Ecuadorian and foreign visitors alike. But behind Baños (and its tranquil feel) sits Volcán Tungurahua, which began erupting in October 1999. After volcanologists gave Tungurahua red-alert status, ex-President Mahuad ordered Baños and the surrounding areas evacuated. With no major eruption by January 2000, thousands forced their way through the military blockades and returned to their homes.

In September 2002 Baños was demoted to yellow alert (down from orange, earlier in the year), and at the close of this edition, life and tourism in Baños were back to normal. To keep the public apprised of the situation, **El Comercio** (www.elcomercio.com in Spanish) posts daily updates on its website and in its newspaper. Also visit the Spanish-language website of **Instituto Geofísico** (www.igepn.edu.ec).

Baños' annual fiesta is held on December 16 and preceding days.

Information

The **post office** (Halflants) and **Andinatel** (cnr Rocafuerte & Halflants) are both on Parque Central. Internet access is available at **Linknet** (16 de Diciembre; US$2 per hr) and **Direct Connect** (Martínez near Alfaro; US$2 per hr). You can change traveler's checks at **Banco del Pacífico** (cnr Halflants & Rocafuerte) and at **Banco del Pichincha** (cnr Ambato & Halflants); both have ATMs. The semi-useful **tourist office** (E Espejo & Reyes) is at the bus terminal.

Sights

Pop into the **Basílica de Nuestra Señora de Agua Santa** for a look at the bizarre paintings of people being saved from auto accidents and natural disasters by the Virgin of the Holy Water – Baños' patron saint. The Virgin is honored for the entire month of October, when indigenous musicians flock to the streets. Above the church, a small **museum**

(admission US$0.30) houses an odd taxidermic display and traditional crafts exhibits.

Activities

HOT BATHS

Soaking in the hot baths with vacationing families and screaming children is what Baños is traditionally all about. Go early in the morning (before 7am) if you want peace. All the baths have changing rooms and bathing suit rental. The only complex in town with hot baths is **Piscina de La Virgen** (admission US$2; ☽ 4:30am-5pm & 6-10pm), by the waterfall. **Piscina El Salado** (admission US$2; ☽ 8am-5pm Fri-Sun), 2km west of town, is similar but has more pools of different temperatures. Catch the bus on Rocafuerte, near the market.

HIKING

There are some great hikes around Baños and most offer superb views. From the bus terminal, a short trail leads to Puente San Francisco (San Francisco Bridge), across Río Pastaza. Continue up the other side as far as you want. Trails are well pounded.

At the southern end of Maldonado is a footpath to Bellavista (the white cross high over Baños) and then to the settlement of **Runtún**, two hours away. South on Mera, a footpath leads to the **Mirador de La Virgen del Agua Santa** and on to Runtún.

CLIMBING & TREKKING

Clarify with all tour operators whether you will be entering a park and, if so, who will pay the entrance fees. Although contracting a tour with unlicensed guides may be financially tempting, think twice – you usually get what you pay for, including security.

At the time of writing, hikers were officially not allowed to ascend beyond the defunct climbers' refuge on **Tungurahua**

ECUADOR

BAÑOS

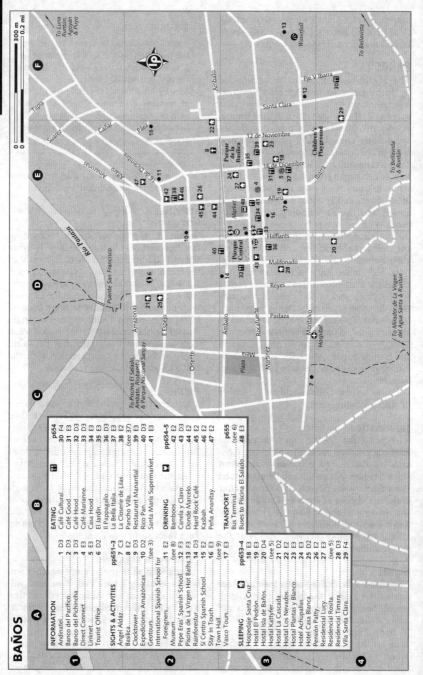

0   300 m
0   0.2 mi

INFORMATION
Andinatel......................................1 D3
Banco del Pacífico...........................2 D3
Banco del Pichincha.........................3 D3
Direct Connect................................4 E3
Linknet...5 E3
Tourist Office.................................6 D2

SIGHTS & ACTIVITIES pp651-3
Angel Aldaz...................................7 C3
Basílica..8 E2
Clocktower....................................9 D3
Expediciones Amazónicas.................10 D2
Geotours...................................(see 3)
International Spanish School for
 Foreigners..................................11 E2
Museum.....................................(see 8)
Pepe Eras' Spanish School................12 F3
Piscina De La Virgen Hot Baths........13 F3
Rainforestur.................................14 D3
Si Centro Spanish School................15 E2
Stay In Touch...............................16 E3
Town Hall..................................(see 9)
Vasco Tours................................17 E3

SLEEPING pp653-4
Hospedaje Santa Cruz.....................18 E3
Hostal El Pedrón............................19 E3
Hostal Isla de Baños.......................20 D4
Hostal Kattyfer...........................(see 5)
Hostal La Cascada.........................21 D2
Hostal Los Nevados.......................22 E2
Hostal Plantas y Blanco...................23 E3
Hotel Achupallas...........................24 E3
Hotel Casa Blanca..........................25 D2
Pensión Patty...............................26 E2
Residencial Lucy............................27 E3
Residencial Rosita........................(see 5)
Residencial Timara.........................28 D3
Villa Santa Clara............................29 F4

EATING p654
Café Cultural.................................30 F4
Café Good....................................31 E3
Café Hood....................................32 D3
Café Marianne...............................33 D3
Casa Hood....................................34 E3
El Jardín......................................35 E3
Il Pappagallo.................................36 D3
La Bella Italia................................37 E3
La Closerie de Lilas.........................38 E2
Pancho Villa..................................39 E3
Restaurant Manantial.......................40 D3
Rico Pan...................................(see 37)
Santa María Supermarket..................41 E3

DRINKING pp654-5
Bamboos......................................42 E2
Canela y Clavo..............................43 D3
Donde Marcelo..............................44 E2
Hard Rock Café..............................45 E2
Kasbah..46 E2
Peña Ananitay...............................47 E2

TRANSPORT p655
Bus Terminal...............................(see 6)
Buses to Piscina El Salado................48 E3

(5016m). With crampons it can normally be climbed in two days. The volcano is part of **Parque Nacional Sangay**, which charges a US$20 entrance fee. Check with any of the operators recommended in this section for current conditions.

Guided two- and three-day climbs up **Cotopaxi** and two-day climbs on **Chimborazo** are offered by **Geotours** (☎ 03-741-344; www.ecuadorexplorer.com/geotours; Ambato at Halflants) and **Expediciones Amazónicas** (☎ 03-740-506; amazonicas2002@yahoo.com; Oriente 11-68). The going rate is about US$60 to US$80 per person per day (minimum two people), plus park fees. Refuge accommodations, equipment, transportation and experienced guides are included in the price. **Rainforestur** (☎ 03-740-743; rainfor@interactive.net.ec; Ambato 800) offers similar climbs using experienced guides at similar prices.

MOUNTAIN BIKING
Numerous companies rent bikes for about US$5 per day. Check the equipment carefully. A popular ride is the dramatic descent to Puyo, about 60km away by paved road. Be sure to stop at the spectacular **Pailón del Diablo**, a waterfall about 20km from Baños. There is a passport control at the town of Shell so carry your documents. From Puyo (or anywhere along the way) take a bus back to Baños with the bike on the roof.

HORSE RIDING
You can rent horses for about US$10 per half day (more with a guide) through **Ángel Aldáz** (☎ 03-740-175; Montalvo & Mera). Christián, at **Hostal Isla de Baños** (☎ 03-740-609; islabanos@andinanet.net; Halflants 1-31), offers guided half-day and multiday horse-riding trips.

RIVER-RAFTING
Geotours (☎ 03-741-344; www.ecuadorexplorer.com/geotours; Ambato at Halflants) offers half-day river-rafting trips on the Río Patate (class III; per person US$30); full-day trips on Río Pastaza (class III; per person US$100) and Río Misahuallí (IV+); and two-day trips on Río Anzu (III). Prices include food, transportation, guides and equipment. **Rainforestur** (☎ 03-740-743; rainfor@interactive.net.ec; Ambato 800) also offers excellent rafting trips.

JUNGLE TRIPS
Visiting the Amazon is generally cheaper (although more time-consuming) from the Oriente. If you're looking for a *Heart of Darkness* type of jungle experience, make sure your trip begins in Coca or Lago Agrio. For those with time constraints, however, jungle tours are available closer to Baños. Three- to seven-day jungle tours cost about US$35 to US$45 per person per day (three- or four-person minimum), depending on destination. Some focus more on indigenous culture and plants, others more on wildlife. Don't expect to see many animals in the rain forest; you need patience and luck.

Rainforestur (☎ 03-740-743; rainfor@interactive.net.ec; Ambato 800) has been repeatedly recommended for tours in Cuyabeno Reserve and other areas. **Vasco Tours** (☎ 03-547-832; Alfaro near Martínez) has also been recommended.

Courses
For one-on-one instruction at about US$6 per hour try any of the following, well-received Spanish schools:
International Spanish School for Foreigners (☎ 03-740-612; 16 de Diciembre at E Espejo)
Pepe Eras' Spanish School (☎ 03-740-232; Montalvo 5-26)
Sí Centro Spanish School (☎ 03-740-360; Páez)

Sleeping
There are scores of hotels in Baños, and competition is stiff, so prices are low. Rates are highest Friday evenings, and holiday weekends when every hotel in town can fill up.

Pensión Patty (☎ 03-740-202; Alfaro 556; r per person US$2) Rooms at this climbers' favorite range from downtrodden to decent. Baths are communal, one shower has hot water and a communal kitchen is available. Popular with broke gringos.

Hostal Plantas y Blanco (☎ 03-740-044; option3@hotmail.com; Martínez at 12 de Noviembre; r with shared/private bath per person US$6/7) This extremely popular hotel has small rooms, laundry facilities, a steam bath and a rooftop restaurant serving great breakfasts in the sun. Lots of socializing on the roof at night. Single rooms are miniscule.

Hospedaje Santa Cruz (☎ 03-740-648; santa_cruz@bacan.com; 16 de Diciembre; s/d US$4/8) Excellent value for clean, spacious rooms with bath and hot water.

Hostal El Pedrón (☎ 03-740-701, 03-824-390; Alfaro; r with shared/private bath per person US$3/5, with TV US$8) This rustic old-timer boasts the biggest garden in town, complete with a few hammocks and chairs strewn around. Rooms are well worn but clean.

Villa Santa Clara (☎ 03-740-349; 12 de Noviembre; s/d US$6/12) Comfy, motel-style rooms open onto a sparse patio area. You get a private hot shower and kitchen privileges, and there's a restaurant to boot.

Hostal Isla de Baños (☎ 03-740-609; islabanos@ andinanet.net; Halflants 1-31; r per person US$7-10) This German-owned hostal is set in attractive gardens with cheerful, clean rooms with private bath and hot water.

Hotel Casa Blanca (☎ 03-740-092; hcasablanca@ latinmail.com; Maldonado & Oriente; s/d US$5/10) Clean and modern with private hot showers and cable TV. Some rooms are a bit cramped.

Residencial Rosita (☎ 03-740-396; 16 de Diciembre near Martínez; s/d US$3/6, apt per person US$4) Plain, clean rooms with hard beds and shared baths. A large apartment sleeps six to eight and has a kitchen (reserve it if you want it).

Hotel Achupallas (☎ 03-740-389; 16 de Diciembre; s/d with bath US$4/8) On Parque de la Basílica, Achupallas is a good deal if you get a window over the plaza (and don't mind a bit of street noise).

Residencial Timara (☎ 03-740-599; s/d US$3/6) Ten simple rooms share two hot-water baths and a well-equipped communal kitchen.

Numerous run-of-the-mill hotels offer simple accommodations at cheap prices, including:

Hostal Los Nevados (☎ 03-740-673; s/d US$4/8; Ambato) Good value.

Residencial Lucy (☎ 03-740-466; Rocafuerte 2-40; r with shared/private bath per person US$3/4) Friendly; hot water.

Hostal Kattyfer (☎ 03-740-856; 16 de Diciembre; r with shared/private bath per person US$3/4) Large, simple rooms; guest kitchen.

Hostal La Cascada (☎ 03-740-946; s/d US$3/6) Clean; next to the bus terminal.

Eating

Restaurants line the pedestrian section of Ambato between the basilica and Parque Central; they're great for people-watching, but the food is generally mediocre. Hit the side streets for the best restaurants. Most restaurants cater to travelers and stay open late. Baños is famous for its *melcocha*, a delicious chewy toffee; makers pull it from wooden pegs in doorways around town.

Café Hood (Maldonado; mains US$3-6) Some of the dishes here are simply excellent, such

as the chickpeas and spinach in curry sauce. Several Mexican and Thai dishes as well.

Café Good (16 de Diciembre; mains US$2-4, almuerzos US$1.20) Offers vegetarian food, curries, pastas, chicken, a small book exchange and a nightly 8pm movie.

Casa Hood (Martínez; mains US$2-4.50) Best book exchange in town, with equally first-rate comfort food (much of it vegetarian). Nightly 8pm movies.

El Jardín (Parque de la Basílica; mains US$3-6) Popular hangout with a leafy outdoor patio and a variety of dishes and sandwiches.

Restaurante Manantial (Martínez; mains US$2-6) An absurdly diverse menu features plates from over a dozen different countries.

La Closerie de Lilas (Alfaro 6-20; mains US$3-5) Great little family-run place (kids included) serving steaks, trout and pastas.

Pancho Villa (12 de Diciembre; mains US$2-3) Festive atmosphere and good, cheap Mexican standbys such as tacos, burritos, nachos and fajitas.

Café Cultural (Pje V Ibarra; mains US$2-4) Homemade breads, veggie burgers, Swedish meatballs, fruit pies, fresh fish, pastries, fruit juices and other delectable items make choosing difficult.

Santa María Supermarket (cnr Alfaro & Rocafuerte) Stock up on picnic supplies here.

Rico Pan (Ambato) Best bread in town, including whole-grain loaves. Healthy breakfasts too.

Café Mariane (Halflants & Rocafuerte; mains US$3-6) Excellent French-Mediterranean cuisine at reasonable prices.

For Italian food, hit **Il Pappagallo** (Martínez; mains US$4-5) or **La Bella Italia** (16 de Diciembre; mains US$3-6).

Rotisserie chicken restaurants (Ambato near Alfaro) Great for cheap, fill-the-belly lunches.

Drinking

You can bar-hop your brains out on Alfaro, north of Ambato, where several hip bars draw the crowds. The most popular are the knock-off Hard Rock Café (Alfaro), Donde Marcelo (Alfaro), which has a dance floor, and the cool, new Kasbah (Alfaro), just up the street.

Bamboos (cnr Alfaro & E Espejo) The local salsa club.

Canela y Clavo (cnr Rocafuerte & Maldonado) A fun new *peña*; the *música folklórica* kicks in nightly around 9pm.

ECUADOR

Peña Ananitay (16 de Diciembre) Has live *folk-lórica* on weekends.

Getting There & Away
From many towns, it may be quicker to change buses in Ambato, where there are frequent buses to Baños (US$0.90, 45 minutes).

From the Baños **bus terminal** (E Espejo & Reyes), many buses leave for Quito (US$3, 3½ hours), Puyo (US$1.50, two hours) and Tena (US$3.50, five hours). The road to Riobamba is currently closed; buses go via Ambato.

GUARANDA
Getting to Guaranda is half the fun. The wild, unpaved road from Riobamba and the paved road from Ambato offer mind-blowing views of Chimborazo. Once you're in town, there's nothing to do but suck in the mountain air, stroll the colonial streets and eat the delicious cheeses that Bolívar Province is famous for. Saturday is market day. Guaranda celebrates Carnaval vigorously.

Information
Banco del Pichincha (Azuay) has an ATM but does not change traveler's checks. **Andinatel** (Rocafuerte near Pichincha) and the **post office** (Azuay near Pichincha) are both downtown.

Sleeping
Hostal de las Flores (☎ 03-980-644; Pichincha 4-02; r with shared/private bath per person US$7/8) The cheerful rooms in this beautifully renovated building open onto a small interior courtyard and have private baths, hot water and cable TV.

Hotel Bolívar (☎ 03-980-547; Sucre 7-04; r with shared/private bath per person US$5/7) The next-best hotel in town. It is pleasant and has a small patio and a good, cheap restaurant.

The cheapest hotels are pretty ratty and include:

Pensión San José (Sucre near Rocafuerte; s/d US$2/4)
Pensión Tequendama (Rocafuerte near José García; s/d US$2/4)
Residencial Acapulco (☎ 03-981-953; 10 de Agosto 8-06; r with shared/private bath per person US$3/5)
Residencial Santa Fé (☎ 03-981-526; 10 de Agosto; r with shared/private bath per person US$4/6) Both residencials have hot water and decent restaurants.

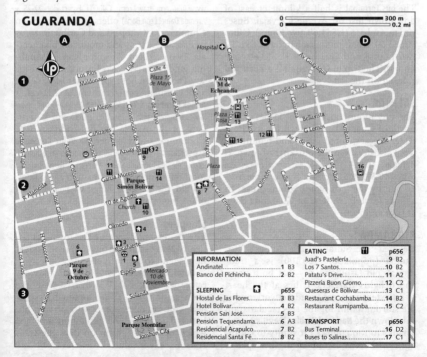

GUARANDA

0 —————— 300 m
0 —————— 0.2 mi

Eating & Drinking

Restaurant Rumipamba (cnr Av Gral Enriquez & Av E de Carvajal) Of the several eateries around Plaza Roja, this is the best (although still simple).

Queseras de Bolívar (Av Gral Enriquez) Also on Plaza Roja, Queseras de Bolívar is a co-operative of Andean cheese makers and one of the best reasons to visit Guaranda.

Pizzería Buon Giorno (García Moreno; pizzas US$3.50-7) Serves fluffy-crust pizzas, pasta and lasagna.

Juad's Pastelería (cnr Convención de 1884 & Azuay) For cakes, pastries and coffee, this is the place.

Restaurant Cochabamba (García Moreno) Good but pricey.

Los 7 Santos (Convención de 1884 near 10 de Agosto; mains US$1-3) You can bump softly into midnight at Los 7 Santos, a groovy little café/bar with a fireplace in back. It serves breakfast, snacks and coffee.

Patatu's Drive (García Moreno near Sucre; ☾ Thu-Sat) For dancing.

Getting There & Away

The **bus terminal** is half a kilometer east of downtown just off Ave de Carvajal. Buses run to Ambato (US$1.60, two hours), Quito (US$3.60, five hours), Riobamba (US$1.75, two hours) and Guayaquil (US$3.60, five hours). The trip to Guayaquil is a beautiful ride; sit on the left.

SALINAS

The tiny mountain village of **Salinas**, 35km north of Guaranda, is known for its chocolate, cheeses, cured meats and handmade wool sweaters. On the outskirts of town, **El Refugio** (☎ 03-981-253/574/266; fugjs@ecnet.ec; dm US$6, s/d US$10/20) is a clean, comfortable hostal run by the local youth group. Buses to Salinas leave Plaza Roja in Guaranda daily at 6am and 7am.

RIOBAMBA

Deemed 'the Sultan of the Andes', Riobamba (population 126,100) is a traditional, old-fashioned city that both bores and delights travelers. It lies at the heart of an extensive scenic road network and is the starting point for the spectacular train ride down the **Nariz del Diablo** (Devil's Nose). Thanks to Riobamba's proximity to Chimborazo, the city is one of the best places

to arrange mountain-climbing guides and tours.

Information

Internet access is available at **Bambario Net** (Rocafuerte near 10 de Agosto; US$0.60 per hr). Cash traveler's checks at **Banco del Pichincha** (cnr Moreno y Primera Constituyente) or next door at **Banco de Guayaquil** (Primera Constituyente). The **post office** (Espejo & 10 de Agosto) and **Andinatel** (Tarqui at Veloz) are both downtown.

Sights

On **market day** (Saturday), the streets become a hive of activity, especially around the intersection of 5 de Junio and Argentinos.

The renowned **Museo de Arte Religioso** (☎ 03-965-212; Argentinos; admission US$2; ☾ 9am-noon & 3-6pm Tue-Sat), in the restored Iglesia de La Concepción, houses many paintings, sculptures and religious artifacts. On clear mornings great views can be had from **Parque 21 de Abril** (Orozco & Ángel León).

Activities

Expediciones Julio Verne (☎ 03-963-436, 960-398; www.julioverne-travel.com; Calle El Espectador 22-25 y Avenida Daniel Leon Borja) offers guided climbs on Chimborazo, Cotopaxi and Carihuairazo, as well as jungle trips and mountain-bike rentals. Two excellent, Aseguim-licensed climbing guides are Marcelo Puruncajas and his son Pablo, who both speak Spanish, English and German; contact them at Marcelo's **Andes Climbing & Trekking** (☎ 03-940-963/64; www.andes-trek.com; Colón 22-25). Enrique Veloz is president of the Asociación de Andinismo de Chimborazo and owner of **Veloz Coronado Expeditions** (☎ 03-960-916; velozexpediciones@hotmail.com; Chile 33-21 at Francia); he's an excellent source for mountaineering information and guides. **Pro Bici** (☎ 03-942-468; Primera Constituyente 23-51) offers mountain-bike rentals and tours.

Sleeping

The better hotels are in the town center, nearly 2km east of the bus terminal. Budget hotels tend to be pretty dingy.

Hotel Tren Dorado (☎ 03-964-890; htrendorado@hotmail.com; Carabobo 22-35; s/d US$7/14) Near the train station, the Tren Dorado has spotless, comfortable rooms with private hot baths. There's a good restaurant attached which opens at 5:30am on days the train runs. Excellent value.

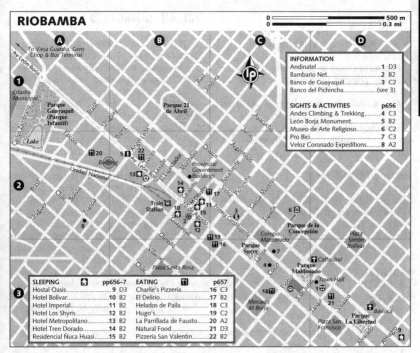

RIOBAMBA

0 — 500 m
0 — 0.3 mi

INFORMATION
Andinatel.....................................1 D3
Bambario Net..............................2 B2
Banco de Guayaquil....................3 C2
Banco del Pichincha..............(see 3)

SIGHTS & ACTIVITIES   p656
Andes Climbing & Trekking........4 C3
León Borja Monument................5 B2
Museo de Arte Religioso............6 C2
Pro Bici.......................................7 C3
Veloz Coronado Expeditions......8 A2

SLEEPING	pp656–7	EATING	p657
Hostal Oasis.....................9 D3		Charlie's Pizzería.............16 C3	
Hotel Bolívar..................10 B2		El Delirio........................17 B2	
Hotel Imperial................11 B2		Helados de Paila.............18 C3	
Hotel Los Shyris.............12 B2		Hugo's...........................19 C2	
Hotel Metropolitano.......13 B2		La Parrillada de Fausto....20 A2	
Hotel Tren Dorado..........14 B2		Natural Food..................21 D3	
Residencial Ñuca Huasi...15 B2		Pizzería San Valentín.......22 B2	

Hotel Los Shyris (☎ 03-960-323; Rocafuerte & 10 de Agosto; s/d US$8/14) Large, friendly and recommended for its central location and clean rooms with TV and hot showers.

Hostal Oasis (☎ 03-961-210; Veloz 1532 at Almagro; r per person US$5, with kitchen US$7; P) The Oasis has three excellent rooms with private hot baths; two of them have kitchens. The friendly owner will provide transport to and from the bus terminal.

Hotel Imperial (☎ 03-960-429; Rocafuerte 22-15; r with shared/private bath per person US$5/6) Clean and friendly (but noisy) place with hot water. The manager will arrange trips to Chimborazo.

Other reliable cheapies include:
Residencial Ñuca Huasi (☎ 03-966-669; 10 de Agosto 10-24; r with shared/private bath per person US$2/3) Grimy rooms, clean sheets; popular.
Hotel Bolívar (☎ 03-968-294; cnr Carabobo & Guayaquil; s/d US$3/6) Dark, no-frills rooms and hot water.
Hotel Metropolitano (☎ 03-961-714; Av León Borja & Lavalle; s/d US$5/10) Adequate rooms with TV and bath.

Eating
Pizzería San Valentín (Av León Borja & Torres; mains US$3-5) Order your pizza at the counter and

hang with the young locals while you eat (and the pizza's good). This place doubles as a bar (p658).

Hugo's (Pichincha near Guayaquil; sandwiches US$1-3) Great, old-school sandwich shop with a fridge full of cold beer and lots of submarine-style sandwiches prepared by a tie-clad barman.

Natural Food (Tarqui near Primera Constituyente; set lunch US$1.50; ☼ 8:30am-3pm) The two choices for lunch at Natural Food are vegetarian or seafood *almuerzos*. It's so popular the owner may be open for dinner by the time this book is out.

El Delirio (☎ 03-966-441; Primera Constituyente 28-16; mains US$5-9) In a restored historic home, this atmospheric eatery serves pricey but delicious traditional Ecuadorian food.

Charlie's Pizzería (García Moreno 24-42) Good pizza, lasagna and calzones.

La Parrillada de Fausto (Uruguay 20-38; mains US$4-5) Dark-wood tables and a *rancho*-esque atmosphere complement outstanding grilled steaks, trout and chicken.

Helados de Paila (Espejo 21-43) Best handmade ice cream in town.

Drinking

For nightlife, head northwest along Av León Borja (and watch for the flocks of night owls).

Pizzería San Valentin (Av León Borja & Torres) An eternally popular hangout in the area; see p657.

Vieja Guardia (Flor 40-43) Further up from San Valentin, this is a decent *discoteca*.

Gens Chop (Av León Borja) North of the *estadio municipal* (stadium), Gens Chop also has dancing.

Getting There & Away

BUS

The main bus terminal is 2km northwest of the city center. Buses run frequently to Quito (US$3, four hours), Guayaquil (US$3.60, 4½ hours) and Alausí (US$1.20, two hours), and less frequently to Cuenca (US$5, five hours). Two night buses travel to Machala (10 hours) and Huaquillas (12 hours). Local buses run along Av León Borja, connecting the terminal with downtown.

Buses to Baños (US$0.80, one hour) and the Oriente leave from the Oriente bus terminal, on Espejo some 2km northeast of town. The direct road to Baños may be closed due to mudslides from erupting Tungurahua; if so go via Ambato (US$1, 1½ hours). No local buses link the two terminals. A taxi is about US$1.

TRAIN

The spectacular train ride to Sibambe (US$11, five hours) begins in Riobamba. The train stops in Alausí just before trudging down the hair-raising switchbacks called the Nariz del Diablo. From Sibambe, the train immediately makes a return trip to Riobamba (US$14.40 round trip), stopping again in Alausí (if you get off at Alausí on the way back, the cost is only US$11 total). Most people get off at Alausí and either spend the night or head back to Riobamba by bus. The train departs Riobamba on Wednesday, Friday and Sunday at 7am. Buy tickets between 7pm and 8pm the night before, or from 6am on the day of departure. Roof riding, of course, is permitted.

The train schedule changes regularly so inquire at the **train station** (☎ 03-961-909; 10 de Agosto) for the latest information.

VOLCÁN CHIMBORAZO

Ecuador's highest peak, Volcán Chimborazo (6310m), is part of **La Reserva de Producción de Fauna Chimborazo** (admission US$10), which also encompasses **Volcán Carihuairazo** (5020m). The Chimborazo **climbers' refuge** (beds US$10) at 5000m can almost be reached by taxi or hired truck from Riobamba (you have to walk the last 200m). Nearly all of Riobamba's hotels can arrange transport out here, although it's slightly cheaper if you hire your own taxi or truck from the train station; figure on US$25 per vehicle with hard bargaining. Climbers who plan on staying more than a day can arrange a return trip for a later day, most likely paying another US$12 per person. The refuge has mattresses, water and cooking facilities; bring warm sleeping bags.

Climbing beyond the refuge requires snow- and ice-climbing gear and mountaineering experience, as does the ascent of Carihuairazo. Contact one of the recommended guide outfits listed under Riobamba (p656), Baños (p651) or Quito (p627). Be wary of cheaper guides who may be inexperienced; a climb at this altitude is not to be taken lightly.

There are also excellent trekking opportunities between the two mountains. Topographical maps of the region are available at the IGM in Quito (p622). June through September is the dry season in this region, and the nights are very cold year-round.

ALAUSÍ

Alausí is the last town the Riobamba–Sibambe train passes through before beginning its switchback descent down the famous Nariz del Diablo, just below Alausí. This spectacular ride is the main reason to visit this small town.

Many hotels are found along the one main street (Av 5 de Junio), and most fill up on Saturday night. The clean, family-run **Hotel Tequendama** (☎ 03-930-123; s/d US$4/8) has hot water and breakfast is available. Other possibilities are the friendly **Hotel Panamericano** (☎ 03-930-156; s/d US$5/10), which has hot showers and a basic restaurant below. The best is **Hotel Americano** (☎ 03-930-159; García Moreno 159; s/d with shared bath only US$4/8), near the railway station.

Apart from the hotel restaurants, you'll find a couple of basic eateries along the main street.

Buses run hourly to/from Riobamba (US$1.20, 1½ hours) and several buses a day also go to Cuenca (US$3, five hours). Riobamba–Cuenca buses leave passengers on the Panamericana, 1km from town. *Camionetas* act as buses to various local destinations.

The train from Riobamba to Sibambe stops in Alausí to pick up passengers before heading down the Nariz del Diablo (US$11 round trip). Tickets go on sale at 7am. It takes about two hours to reach Sibambe, where the train immediately changes course to return to Riobamba. During the high season, it's best to start in Riobamba for a guaranteed seat. Riding on the roof is allowed (and encouraged!), although it's often full with passengers from Riobamba.

CUENCA & THE SOUTHERN HIGHLANDS

As you roll down the Panamericana into the southern highlands, the giant snow-capped peaks of the central highlands fade from the rearview mirror, the climate gets a bit warmer, distances between towns become greater, and the decades seem to clunk down by the wayside. The region's isolation until relatively recently (paved roads didn't reach Cuenca until the 1960s) has given the southern highlands a rich and tangible history.

The beautiful cities of Cuenca and Loja are the region's only sizable towns. The misty, lake-studded Parque Nacional Cajas has great hiking and superb trout fishing, and Parque Nacional Podocarpus, which tumbles from the highlands down the tropical forests of the Oriente, is easily accessible from either Loja or the delightful Oriente town of Zamora. From the laid-back gringo hangout of Vilcabamba you can spend days walking or horse riding through the mysterious mountainside. Ingapirca, Ecuador's most important Inca ruins, is a two-hour bus ride (an easy day trip) from Cuenca.

CUENCA

When it comes to colonial splendor, Cuenca arguably reigns supreme in Ecuador. Its narrow cobblestone streets and whitewashed red-tiled buildings, its hand-

some plazas and domed churches and its setting above the grassy banks of the Río Tomebamba, where women still wash and dry clothes in the sun, all add up to a city that's definitely one of Ecuador's highlights. With its large student population and its popularity with foreigners, Ecuador's third-largest city also has a modern edge, with international restaurants, art galleries, cool cafés and welcoming bars all tucked into its colonial architecture.

Information

INTERNET ACCESS

The numerous cybercafés in town all charge about US$1 per hour and include:

Café Oficina (Luís Cordero & Jaramillo)
Cuenca Net (cnr Calle Larga & Hermano Miguel)
Golden Net (Presidente Córdova 9-21)

LAUNDRY

For same-day laundry service, take your clothes to **Lavahora** (Honorato Vásquez 6-76; up to 5kg US$3) or **Fast Klín** (Hermano Miguel 4-21; per kg US$1).

MEDICAL SERVICES

Of several hospitals and clinics, **Clínica Santa Inés** (☎ 07-817-888; Daniel Córdova) has been recommended.

MONEY

Numerous banks have ATMs. **Banco de Guayaquil** (Sucre at Borrero) changes traveler's checks (go to the 3rd floor), as does **Banco del Pichincha** (cnr Solando & 12 de Abril).

POST & TELEPHONE

The post office is on the corner of Gran Colombia and Borrero. Make telephone calls at **Etapa** (Benigno Malo 7-26).

TOURIST OFFICES

The friendly **tourist information office** (Mariscal Sucre at Luís Cordero), facing Parque Calderón, provides free city maps and sells good trail maps (US$0.50) of Parque Nacional Cajas. There's also an **information office** (☎ 07-843-888) in the bus terminal.

Sights

Be sure to take a walk along 3 de Noviembre, which follows the northern bank of the **Río Tomebamba**. The river is lined with colonial buildings and folks still dry their laundry on the river's grassy banks. A

ECUADOR

CUENCA

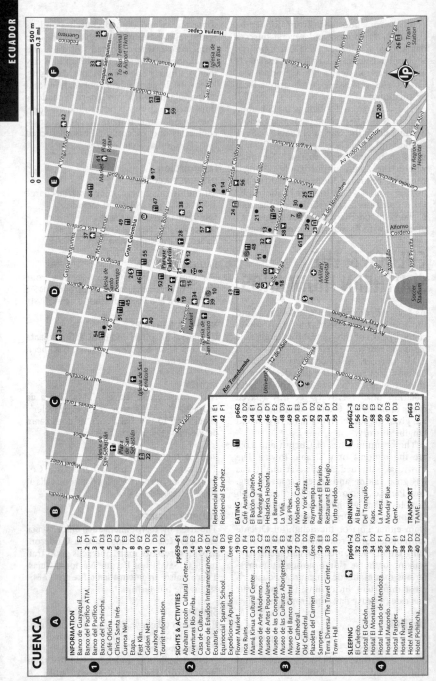

500 m
0.3 mi

INFORMATION
Banco de Guayaquil...................1 E2
Banco del Pacifico ATM...............2 D1
Banco del Pacifico....................3 F1
Banco del Pichincha...................4 D3
Café Oficina.........................5 D3
Clinica Santa Inés....................6 C3
Cuenca Net...........................7 E3
Etapa................................8 D2
Fast Klin............................9 E2
Golden Net..........................10 D2
Lavahora............................11 D3
Tourist Information..................12 D2

SIGHTS & ACTIVITIES   pp659-61
Abraham Lincoln Cultural Center......13 E3
Aventuras Río Arriba.................14 E2
Casa de Cultura......................15 D2
Centro de Estudios Interamericanos...16 D1
Ecuaturis............................17 E2
Equinoccial Spanish School.........(see 16)
Expediciones Apullacta...............18 D3
Flower Market........................19 D2
Inca Ruins...........................20 F4
Mamá Kinua Cultural Center...........21 E3
Museo de Arte Moderno................22 C2
Museo de Artes Populares.............23 E3
Museo de Conceptas...................24 E3
Museo de las Culturas Aborígenes.....25 E3
Museo del Banco Central..............26 F4
New Cathedral........................27 D2
Old Cathedral........................28 D2
Plazoleta del Carmen...............(see 19)
Sampere..............................29 E3
Terra Diversa/The Travel Center......30 E3
Town Hall............................31 D2

Residencial Norte....................41 E1
Residencial Sánchez..................42 F1

EATING   p662
Café Austria.........................43 D2
El Balcón Quiteño....................44 E1
El Pedregal Azteca...................45 D1
Heladería Holanda....................46 D1
La Barranca..........................47 E2
La Viña..............................48 D3
Los Pibes............................49 E1
Moliendo Café........................50 E1
New York Pizza.......................51 D1
Raymipampa...........................52 D2
Restaurant El Paraíso................53 F2
Restaurant El Refugio................54 D1
Tutto Freddo.........................55 D2

SLEEPING   pp661-2
El Cafecito..........................32 D3
Hostal El Galeón.....................33 E1
Hostal El Monasterio.................34 D2
Hostal Hurtado de Mendoza............35 F1
Hostal Macondo.......................36 D1
Hostal Paredes.......................37 E1
Hostal Nusta.........................38 E2
Hotel Milan..........................39 D2
Hotel Pichincha......................40 D2

DRINKING   pp662-3
Al Bar...............................56 E2
Del Tranquilo........................57 E2
Kaos.................................58 E3
La Mesa..............................59 F2
Monday Blue..........................60 D3
QenK.................................61 D3

TRANSPORT   p663
TAME.................................62 D3

patch of **Inca ruins** lie near the river, between the east end of Calle Larga and Av Todos Los Santos. Most of the stonework was destroyed to build colonial buildings, but there are some fine niches and walls. A small museum is at the site.

Parque Calderón, the main plaza, is dominated by the handsome **'new' cathedral** (c. 1885), with its huge blue domes. Opposite is the squat **old cathedral**, known as El Sagrario. At the southwestern corner is the **Casa de Cultura** (cnr Benigno Malo & Mariscal Sucre; ☺ 9am-1pm & 3-6:30pm Mon-Fri, 9am-1pm Sat), which features changing exhibits of local art.

Go smell the flowers (or at least snap a photo of them) at the **flower market** in front of the wee colonial church on **Plazoleta del Carmen**, at the corner of Sucre and Padre Aguirre. Afterwards, hoof it over to the quiet **Plaza de San Sebastián**, which has a mural and a couple of art galleries. On the southern side of the plaza, the **Museo de Arte Moderno** (Mariscal Sucre; ☺ 9am-6pm Mon-Fri, 9am-3pm Sat & Sun) has a small exhibit of contemporary local art.

Cuenca's vibrant **markets** are aimed more at locals than tourists. Market day is Thursday, and there's a smaller market on Saturday. The main market areas are around Iglesia de San Francisco and at the plaza by the corner of Mariscal Lamar and Hermano Miguel.

The interesting **Museo del Banco Central** (Calle Larga at Huayna Capac; admission US$0.50; ☺ 9am-5pm Mon-Fri, 9am-1pm Sat) has old B&W photographs of Cuenca, ancient musical instruments and some great temporary exhibitions.

Museo de las Culturas Aborígenes (Calle Larga 5-24; admission US$2; ☺ 9am-6pm Mon-Sat) houses an excellent collection of over 5000 archaeological pieces representative of about 20 Ecuadorian pre-Columbian cultures.

Museo de Artes Populares (CIDAP; Hermano Miguel 3-23; admission free; ☺ 9:30am-1pm & 2:30-6pm Mon-Fri, 10am-1pm Sat) has a small but good exhibit of traditional instruments, clothing and crafts.

Museo de las Conceptas (Hermano Miguel 6-33; admission US$1; ☺ 9am-5pm Tue-Fri, 10am-1pm Sat) is Cuenca's best religious museum.

Activities

Cuenca is an excellent base for exploring – by foot, horse or bike – nearby attractions such as Parque Nacional Cajas, the Inca ruins of Ingapirca and indigenous villages.

Head out on your own or set yourself up at one of the following tour operators:

Aventuras Río Arriba (☎ 07-830-116; Hermano Miguel 7-14) Naturalist guide Edgar Aguirre speaks English.

Ecuaturis (☎ 07-823-018; equito@az.pro.ec; Hermano Miguel 9-56) Local guide Eduardo Quito is highly recommended and speaks English and Italian.

Expediciones Apullacta (☎ 07-837-681; Gran Colombia 11-02) Day tours to Ingapirca and Cajas.

Humberto Chico (contact Cabañas Yanuncay – see Sleeping, p662) Overnight tours to Cajas (three days, US$100), the southern Oriente (five days, US$250) and other areas.

Mamá Kinua Cultural Center (Juan Jaramillo 6-35) Excellent Quechua-run cultural tours. Great organization; stop by for brochures.

Terra Diversa/The Travel Center (☎ 07-823-782; www.terradiversa.com; Hermano Miguel 4-46) Horse-riding and mountain-biking trips and rentals.

Courses

Centro de Estudios Interamericanos (☎ 07-839-003; info@cedei.org; Gran Colombia 11-02) offers courses in Spanish, Quechua, Portuguese, Latin American literature and indigenous culture. Other recommended schools include:

Abraham Lincoln Cultural Center (☎ 07-823-898; rboroto@cena.or.ec; Borrero 5-18)

Equinoccial Spanish School (☎ 07-884-353; ece@cue.satnet.net; Calle Larga near Benigno Malo)

Sampere (☎ 07-841-986; www.sampere.com/cuenca; Hermano Miguel 3-43)

Festivals & Events

Cuenca's independence is celebrated on November 3 with a major fiesta. Christmas Eve parades are very colorful. The founding of Cuenca (April 10–13) and Corpus Christi are also busy holidays. Carnaval is celebrated with boisterous water fights.

Sleeping

Hotels fill up fast (and charge more) for the celebrations mentioned under Festivals & Events above.

Hostal El Monasterio (☎ 07-824-457; Padre Aguirre 7-24; r with shared/private bath per person US$5/6) This six-floor gem boasts stunning views from its communal kitchen and eating areas, and the rooms are comfy and clean. Very backpacker-friendly, excellent value.

Hostal Macondo (☎ 07-840-697, 07-830-836; macondo@cedei.org; Tarqui 11-64; s/d with shared bath US$11/17, with private bath US$16/22) In a beautifully converted old house, this friendly HI affiliate

ECUADOR

offers kitchen privileges and has a sunny, plant-filled courtyard and several indoor sitting areas. Breakfast included.

Hostal Paredes (☎ 07-835-674; Luís Cordero 11-29; r with shared/private bath per person US$4/6) In an early-20th-century building, Hostal Paredes offers spacious rooms furnished with period furniture. Beds are saggy, and the hot water is a bit erratic, but it's a great deal.

Hotel Milan (☎ 07-831-104, 07-835-351; Presidente Córdova 9-89; s/d US$8/16) Comfortable, modernish hotel with a pool table and a 4th-floor café serving breakfast (included in the price). Nab a balcony and you're set. Private showers, telephone and cable TV too.

El Cafecito (☎ 07-832-337; elcafec@cue.satnet.net; Honorato Vásquez 7-36; dm US$4, s/d with bath US$7/14) Party paaad! That, and it has a great café full of cigarette-smoking, coffee-jacked travelers munchin' tasty snacks. It can be noisy, but some love the scene.

Residencial Norte (☎ 07-827-881; Cueva 11-63; r with shared/private bath per person US$3/5) Of the several cheap hotels in the busy market area near Mariscal Lamar and Cueva, this is the best. The rooms are unimpressive but large and have plenty of hot water.

Hotel Pichincha (☎ 07-823-868; karolina7a@hotmail .com; Torres 8-82; s/d US$4.50/9) The Pichincha is a big, impersonal 60-room hotel, but it's good value, clean and popular with backpackers. Baths are shared and have hot water.

Residencial Sánchez (☎ 07-831-519; Muñoz 4-32; r with shared/private bath per person US$4/7) Odd fauxbrick interior and dark rooms with private bath. It's friendly, but don't expect much.

Hostal Ñusta (☎ 07-830-862; Borrero 8-44; s/d US$9/18) About eight large rooms sleep one to six people. Rates include breakfast, private baths and a TV lounge.

Between downtown and the bus terminal, **Hostal El Galeón** (☎ 07-831-827; Gaspar Sangurima 2-42; s/d US$8/16) and **Hostal Hurtado de Mendoza** (☎ 07-831-909; Huayna Capac & Gaspar Sangurima; s/d US$15/25) are clean and have private hot baths and TV.

Cabañas Yanuncay (☎ 07-810-265; Calle Canton Gualaceo 21-49; s/d US$12/24). About 3km southwest of the center Cabañas Yanuncay is warmly recommended. Rooms are in a private house or in two cabins in the garden. The rates include breakfast, and, for US$6 more, you can get a delicious organic dinner. English is spoken. Take a taxi or bus

out on Av Loja, then take the first right after 'Arco de la Luz', 200m along the river.

Eating

Many restaurants close on Sunday.

Restaurant El Paraíso (Tomás Ordóñez 10-19) Filling vegetarian *almuerzos* cost US$1.

El Balcón Quiteño (Gaspar Sangurima 6-49; mains US$2-4) Tasty Ecuadorian food served in a bright, plastic environment.

Moliendo Café (Honorato Vásquez 6-24; light meals US$1-2) Excellent café serving Colombian *antojitos* (appetizers), some of which are meals in themselves. Cheap.

Mamá Kinua Cultural Center (Juan Jaramillo 6-35; set lunch US$1.80) This Quechua cultural center serves one of the best *almuerzos* around. They're mostly vegetarian, always wholesome and always filling.

Los Pibes (Gran Colombia 7-66; pizza US$1.50-6) Dark pizza joint serving slices, whole pies and pastas.

New York Pizza (Gran Colombia 10-43; mains US$1.50-3.50) Cheap slices, *empanadas*, calzones and Ecuadorian standards such as *chaulafán* (fried rice).

Raymipampa (Benigno Malo 8-59; mains US$3-5; ☮ daily) Locals and travelers flock to this diner-like café for the large portions, varied menu and good prices.

La Viña (Juan Jaramillo 7-79; mains US$3-6) Cozy Italian-owned restaurant serving delicious homemade spaghetti, tortellini, lasagna, gnocchi, risotto, fresh salads and more. Skip the pesto unless you *love* salt.

El Pedregal Azteca (Gran Colombia 10-33; mains US$5-9) Excellent Mexican food, but the portions can be small (fill up on the free corn chips).

La Barranca (Borrero 9-68; mains US$3-8) Hip, casual atmosphere; good, reasonably priced local dishes and premier international plates.

Café Austria (Benigno Malo 5-45) Austrian-style cakes, coffee and sandwiches.

Restaurant El Refugio (Gran Colombia 11-24) Good value for Ecuadorian lunches.

Heladería Holanda (Benigno Malo 9-55) and **Tutto Freddo** (Benigno Malo 9-60), across the street, vie for best ice cream in town. Better try both!

Drinking

Discos are open Thursday through Saturday nights. Midweek Cuenca's as dead as Pizarro. There's a slew of bars on Honorato Vásquez near El Cafecito (above); they're all small, friendly and popular with travelers.

Along Presidente Córdova, east of Hermano Miguel, are several popular bars with dance floors. They're all tucked into old buildings in a dark area so they're pretty cool.

La Mesa (Gran Colombia 3-55) Cuenca's premier *salsoteca*. Great.

Del Tranquilo (Borrero near Mariscal Sucre) Fun but tame bar in an old converted house. Live music Thursday through Saturday nights.

WunderBar (Hermano Miguel at Calle Larga) Hip, hoppin' hangout over the river.

QenK (Calle Larga at Borrero) Good for a mellow night of beer and pool.

Monday Blue (cnr Calle Larga & Luís Cordero) Friendly low-key bar with a young crowd. Pizza and tacos are served.

Al Bar (Presidente Córdova; drink minimum US$2) A favorite that's loud and trendy.

Popular discos include the following. None of these places get moving till after midnight. Taxi drivers know them all.

Cuenca Tropicana (10 de Agosto s/n)

Ego (12 de Abril & Unidad Nacional) Mixes salsa, merengue and Latin rock.

Kaos (Honorato Vásquez 6-11) Laid-back with couches, pool tables and snacks.

Getting There & Away

AIR

Local buses (US$0.15) to the airport pass the flower market on Aguirre. **TAME** (☎ 07-843-222; Benigno Malo 5-08) flies daily to Quito (US$58) and from Monday through Saturday to Guayaquil (US$58). There's also a branch of TAME at the **airport** (☎ 07-862-400).

BUS

Buses to Guayaquil (US$7) go either via Parque Nacional Cajas (3½ hours) or Cañar (4½ to five hours). There are regular departures to Quito (US$6 to US$10, eight to 11 hours). Several go to Machala (US$3.60, four hours); a few continue on to Huaquillas. Hourly buses go to Azogues (US$0.50, 45 minutes), many continuing to Cañar (US$1, 1½ hours) and Alausí (US$3, four hours). Several buses a day leave for Loja (US$6, five hours), Macas (US$5, 11 hours) and several Oriente towns. Buses for Gualaceo ($1.20, 1½ hours) leave from the corner of the terminal.

Getting Around

Cuenca is easy to negotiate. The **bus terminal** (España) is 1.5km northeast of the center and

the airport is a further 500m past that. A taxi to the center costs about US$2. Buses to the center leave just outside both terminals.

AROUND CUENCA
Ingapirca

The Inca site of **Ingapirca** (admission US$5), 50km north of Cuenca, was built with the same mortarless, polished-stone technique used by the Inca in Peru. Although less impressive than sites in Peru, it's definitely worth a visit. A **museum** (admission US$6; ⊙ 8am-6pm) explains the site, and guides (both the human and the written varieties) are available. **Ingapirca village**, 1km away, has a craft shop, simple restaurants and a basic *pensión*.

For an economical visit, catch a direct Transportes Cañar bus (US$2, two hours) from Cuenca's bus terminal at 9am or 1pm Monday through Friday, or at 9am on Saturday and Sunday. Buses return to Cuenca at 1pm and 4pm Monday through Friday and at 9am and 1pm on Saturday and Sunday.

Gualaceo, Chordeleg & Sígsig

These villages are famous for their Sunday markets. If you start early from Cuenca, you can visit all three and be back in the afternoon. **Gualaceo** has the biggest market, with fruit and vegetables, animals and various household goods. **Chordeleg's market**, 5km away, is smaller and more touristy. **Sígsig's market** is 25km from Gualaceo and less visited by tourists; it's a good place to see the art of panama-hat making.

Buses from Cuenca to Gualaceo leave about every hour (more often on Sunday). From there, walk or take a local bus or pickup to Chordeleg. Another 40-minute bus ride will take you to Sígsig, from where there are buses to Cuenca.

Parque Nacional Cajas

Only 30km west of Cuenca, the stunning, chilly, moor-like *páramo* of **Parque Nacional Cajas** (admission US$10) is famous for its many lakes, great trout fishing and rugged camping and hiking. It's a good day trip from Cuenca, or you can stay a few days. **Camping** (free with admission) is allowed, and a small refugio has eight cots and a kitchen; it fills up fast. Hiking solo in Cajas can be dangerous – the abundance of lakes and fog is disorienting. It's best to be finished by 4pm when the fog gets thick. Shorter trails are

ECUADOR

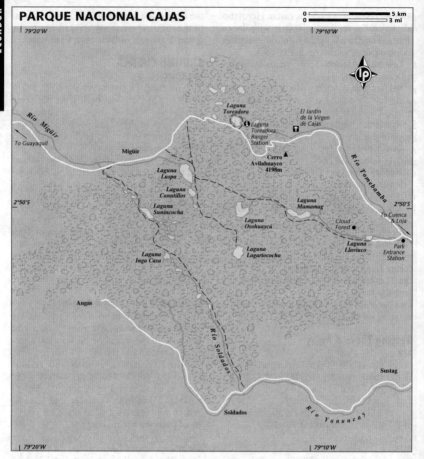

PARQUE NACIONAL CAJAS

well marked. Good trail maps (US$0.50) are available in Cuenca at the tourist information office on Parque Calderón (see p659).

From Cuenca's bus terminal, Ejecutivo San Luis buses leave every hour starting at 4am (US$2, two hours). Ask to be let off at **Laguna Toreadora** (the main visitors' and hiking area). To return to Cuenca, flag a Cuenca-bound bus on the highway.

LOJA

An attractive provincial city surrounded by beautiful countryside, Loja makes a convenient stopover on the route to Peru via Macará. One of the country's best universities is here, and the streets are vibrant, with plenty of cozy little hideaways. For

views of the town, take a short walk east across Río Zamora and up a hill to the **statue of the Virgen de Loja**. Delightful attractions near Loja include the village of Vilcabamba and Parque Nacional Podocarpus.

The main market day is Sunday. The annual fiesta of the Virgen del Cisne is on September 8; it's celebrated with huge parades and a produce fair.

Information

Internet access is available at **Jungle Net** (Riofrío 13-64; US$1 per hr) and **World Net** (Colón 14-69; US$1.20 per hr). **Banco de Guayaquil** (Eguiguren) changes traveler's checks and has an ATM. The good **Clínica San Agustín** (☎ 07-570-314; cnr 18 de Noviembre & Azuay) handles medical emergencies. **Pacifictel** (Eguiguren) and the **post office** (cnr Sucre & Colón) are downtown.

The **tourist office** (☎ 07-570-407; Eguiguren) is across from Parque Central. Call into the **Ministerio del Medio Ambiente** (☎ 07-585-421, 07-571-534; podocam@impsat.net.ec; Sucre 4-35) for information about Parque Nacional Podocarpus.

Sleeping

Hotel Londres (☎ 07-561-936; Sucre 07-51; s/d US$4/8) Arguably the best cheapie in town. Clean, simple rooms share three baths, two of which have hot water.

Hotel Internacional (☎ 07-578-486; 10 de Agosto 15-28; r with shared/private bath per person US$5/6) Rooms have private bath, TV and plenty

of hot water. This place is friendly and has a restaurant.

Hotel Metropolitano (☎ 07-570-007/244; 18 de Noviembre 6-41; s/d US$8/16) Friendly management and comfortable, wood-floored rooms with private hot shower and cable TV. Great choice.

Hotel México (☎ 07-570-581; Eguiguren 15-89; s/d US$3/6) Reliable cheapie with hard beds, dark rooms (get a window) and shared baths.

Hostal Las Orquideas (☎ 07-587-008; Bolívar 08-59; s/d US$8/16) The clean, windowless rooms aren't as cheerful as the flowery lobby suggests, but the place is friendly.

Hotel Caribe (☎ 07-572-902; Rocafuerte 15-52; s/d US$4/8) Noisy and impersonal, but fine. Shared hot baths, hard beds.

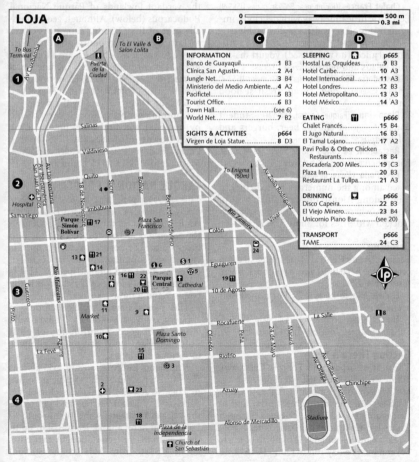

LOJA

INFORMATION	
Banco de Guayaquil	1 B3
Clínica San Agustín	2 A4
Jungle Net	3 B4
Ministerio del Medio Ambiente	4 A2
Pacifictel	5 B3
Tourist Office	6 B3
Town Hall	(see 6)
World Net	7 B2

SIGHTS & ACTIVITIES	p664
Virgen de Loja Statue	8 D3

SLEEPING		p665
Hostal Las Orquídeas	9	B3
Hotel Caribe	10	A3
Hotel Internacional	11	A3
Hotel Londres	12	B3
Hotel Metropolitano	13	A3
Hotel México	14	A3

EATING		p666
Chalet Francés	15	B4
El Jugo Natural	16	B4
El Tamal Lojano	17	A2
Pavi Pollo & Other Chicken Restaurants	18	B4
Pescadería 200 Miles	19	C3
Plaza Inn	20	B3
Restaurant La Tullpa	21	A3

DRINKING		p666
Disco Capeira	22	B3
El Viejo Minero	23	B4
Unicornio Piano Bar	(see 20)	

TRANSPORT		p666
TAME	24	C3

Eating

El Tamal Lojano (18 de Noviembre 05-12; mains US$0.60-2) People flock here for the excellent *quimbolitos*, *humitas* and *tamales lojanos* (all delicious variations on corn dumplings); and *empanadas de verde* (a savory plantain pastry stuffed with seasoned chicken). Try them all!

Salon Lolita (Salvador Bustamante Celi at Guayaquil, El Valle; mains US$3-8) This is *the* place for traditional *lojano* food. Try the roast *cuy* (guinea pig); they come whole in US$8-, US$10- or US$12-sizes. The bigger ones serve two. It's in the neighborhood of El Valle, just below the church. Buses signed 'El Valle' leave Parque Bolívar heading north up Av Universitaria.

Chalet Francés (Riofrío near Bolívar; mains US$5-9) Eccentric little hideaway with delicious, imaginative food served at candlelit tables.

El Jugo Natural (Eguiguren 14-20; US$1-2) All-natural juices (no water used), yogurt shakes, fruit salads and personalized pizzas.

Pescadería 200 Miles (Peña 07-41; mains US$3-4; ✪ 9am-3:30pm) Good, cheap, fresh seafood lunches.

Plaza Inn (Parque Central, Bolívar) Student hangout – join 'em for beer, burgers and *salchipapas*.

Restaurant La Tullpa (18 de Noviembre) Good, cheap Ecuadorian standards.

Pavi Pollo (Alonso de Mercadillo 14-99) A good place among the numerous grilled-chicken joints along Alonso de Mercadillo, west of Bolívar, where you can pick up a quarter-chicken with fries for about US$2.

Drinking

Facing Parque Central is the loungelike **Unicornio Piano Bar** (Bolívar) and, two doors down, **Disco Capeira** (Bolívar).

El Viejo Minero (Sucre 10-76) For a mellower scene Minero is cozy.

Enigma (Zoilo Rodríguez near 24 de Mayo; ✪ Wed-Sat) The biggest, loudest disco in town.

Getting There & Away

The nearest airport is La Toma in Catamayo, 30km west of Loja. **TAME** (☎ 07-570-248; Ortega near 24 de Mayo) offers morning flights to Quito (US$49) Monday through Saturday and to Guayaquil (US$36) on Tuesday through Thursday. Catamayo has basic hotels.

Loja's bus terminal is 1km north of town. Several buses a day run to Quito (US$12, 12 to 14 hours), Macará (US$4.50, six hours), Guayaquil (US$6, nine hours), Machala (US$3.50, four hours; seven hours via Piñas), Huaquillas (US$4, six hours), Zamora (US$2, three hours) and Cuenca (US$4, six hours), as well as other destinations.

Buses for Vilcabamba (US$1, 1½ hours) leave every hour, as do buses for Catamayo. Shared taxis to Vilcabamba (US$1, 40 minutes) leave from the lot at Aguirre, 10 blocks south of Alonso de Mercadillo.

Transportes Loja goes three times daily to Piura, Peru (US$8, eight hours), via Macará.

ZAMORA

The tranquil, humid, easy-going town of Zamora is the best base for exploring the verdant lowlands of Parque Nacional Podocarpus (below). Although geographically part of the Oriente, Zamora is closer to Loja by bus (two hours) than to other jungle towns, most of which are a long way north. Decent budget hotels include **Hostal Seyma** (☎ 07-605-583; s/d US$3/6), northeast of the plaza, and **Hotel Maguna** (☎ 07-605-219; s/d US$6/12), on Diego de Vaca by the river.

Continuing north through the Oriente by bus, you will find basic hotels in the small towns of **Gualaquiza** (five hours), **Limón** (about nine hours), **Méndez** and **Sucúa**. Macas (p676) is 13 to 15 hours away.

PARQUE NACIONAL PODOCARPUS

This **national park** (admission US$10) protects many habitats in the southern Ecuadorian Andes at altitudes ranging from 3600m in the *páramo* near Loja to 1000m in the rain forests near Zamora. The topography is rugged and complex, and the park is full of different plant and animal species. This is one of the most biologically rich areas in the country and a fun park to explore.

The park's namesake, Podocarpus, is Ecuador's only native conifer. Trails provide visitors with good opportunities for bird-watching, plant study and maybe glimpses of various mammals.

Maps and information are available at the Ministerio del Medio Ambiente office in Loja. Reach the highland sector of the park on a Vilcabamba bus and get off at the **Cajanuma entrance**, some 10km south of Loja. From here, a track leads 8.5km up to the Cajanuma ranger station. A taxi costs about US$10 from Loja to the station.

Camping is allowed, but carry everything you need. Access from Vilcabamba is possible by horseback. To visit the tropical, lowland sector, head to Zamora and get a taxi (US$6) or walk the 8km dirt road to the **Bombuscaro entrance**, where there is a ranger station, trails, swimming, waterfalls, a **camping area** (per person US$3) and a small **refugio** (cots per person US$3).

VILCABAMBA

People come here to take a break – an easy task once you're here, considering the tranquility of the village and its stunning mountainous surroundings. The gentle, somewhat surreal peaks which practically engulf Vilcabamba make for excellent day hikes from town. The town offers access to some of the most biodiverse sections of Podocarpus (p666) and is a good stopping point en route to or from Peru via **Zumba**. Vilcabamba has for many years been famous as 'the valley of longevity.' Inhabitants supposedly live to be 100 or more.

Most of the town surrounds the main square. **Pacifictel** (Bolívar), **Aventur Net** (Sucre; Internet US$3 per hr) and the **post office** (Agua de Hierro) are all within a block of the square.

Activities

Orlando Falco, a trained, English-speaking naturalist guide, leads recommended tours to Parque Nacional Podocarpus and other areas for about US$20 to US$35 per person, plus the US$10 park fee. Find him at Primavera, his craft shop on the plaza. New Zealander Gavilan Moore, of **Caballos Gavilan** (☎ 07-571-025; gavilanhorse@yahoo.com; Sucre), leads affordable, highly recommended horse treks, which can last from four hours to three days. Several readers and numerous locals have recommended local guide Jorge Mendieta of **Caminatas Andes Sureños** (☎ 07-673-147; jorgeluis222@latinmail.com; Parque Central) for his guided hikes.

Sleeping

Hotel Valle Sagrado (☎ 07-580-686; r with shared/private bath per person US$3/4) This simple place facing the plaza is popular with roaming budgeteers and has laundry facilities, kitchen privileges, a garden with hammocks and a vegetarian restaurant.

Hidden Garden (☎ 07-580-281; hiddengarden@latinmail.com; r with shared/private bath per person US$6/7)

The best place in the center really does have a hidden garden – and clean, airy rooms, a pool and kitchen facilities.

Rumi Wilco Ecolodge/Pole House (ofalcoecolodge@yahoo.com; r per person US$4-4.50, d/tr US$16/18) About a 30-minute walk from town, Rumi Wilco consists of the four-person Pole House, a serene hideaway with hammocks, kitchen and a private drinking well; and several other exquisitely set cabins. Wonderfully relaxing.

Hostal Madre Tierra (☎ 07-580-269; hmtierra@ecua.net.ec; r per person US$12-25, cabin d US$36) About 2km north of town, Madre Tierra is a rustic, laid-back hostel run by an Ecuadorian-Canadian couple. Rooms are in cabins spread over a steep hillside and some have fabulous views. Rates include excellent organic vegetarian meals. A plethora of spa treatments are available.

Hostería y Restaurante Izhcayluma (izhcayluma@yahoo.de; www.izhcayluma.com; dm US$7, r per person with shared/private bath US$8/10; 🔊) Great-value, German-owned place with an excellent restaurant and 11 comfortable *cabañas*. Rates include an American breakfast. It's 2km south of town on the Zumba road.

Cabañas Río Yambala (charlie@loja.telconet.net; cabins with dinner & breakfast per person US$10-14, without meals US$5-9) About 4km southeast of town along the Yamburara road, this friendly, British-run favorite boasts six homey, rustic cabins of varying sizes, all with private hot showers and views. A vegetarian restaurant and kitchen privileges are available, and the owners can arrange camping, hiking and horse riding. You can walk up or hire a taxi (US$4) from the plaza.

Hostería Las Ruinas de Quinara (☎ 07-580-314; dm US$7-9, private r per person US$10-11) Also on the Yamburara road is this expansive, resort-like *hostería*.

Cabañas La Tasca (cabins per person US$7) Further up, the warmly recommended, somewhat rugged La Tasca rents spacious cabins on a steep hillside. Owner Rene bakes excellent bread, and his French wife Elena prepares delicious French cuisine and sandwiches in her restaurant (open to the public) below.

Eating & Drinking

Several good cafés and restaurants are on or near the plaza including:

La Terraza (mains US$2.50-4) Italian, Mexican and Thai food with plenty of vegetarian options.

El Jardín (mains US$3-5; ⏰ Wed-Mon) Delicious Mexican food; garden setting.

El Che (mains US$3-4; ⏰ Tue-Sun) Steaks, pizzas and pastas.

Shanta's Bar, on the road to Río Yambala, serves great trout, pizza and frogs' legs; it's also the town's best bar. On the way out, you'll pass Manolo's, a thatched-roof place serving pizzas and sandwiches.

Getting There & Away

Transportes Loja runs buses every 90 minutes to Loja (US$1, 1½ hours). Shared taxis leave from the bus terminal and take five passengers to Loja (US$1, 40 minutes). Transportes Nambija goes about twice daily to Zumba, on the Peruvian border.

MACARÁ

The small border town of Macará lies along a more scenic and less traveled route to Peru than the conventional border crossing at Huaquillas.

Sleeping & Eating

Cheap, basic, cold-water hotels in the town center charge about US$3 to US$6 per person. Among the better ones are **Hotel Paraíso** (Veintimilla 553), **Hotel Amazonas** (M Rengel 418) and Hotel Espiga de Oro, which also has a restaurant. A few basic restaurants are near the corner of Bolívar and M Rengel.

Getting There & Away

ECUADOR

Transportes Loja offers six buses a day (the last one is at 3pm) to Loja (US$5, six hours), a morning bus to Guayaquil and a morning bus to Quito. Transportes Cariamanga has two morning buses to Loja.

PERUVIAN BORDER CROSSING

Before heading into Peru get an exit stamp at the Ecuadorian immigration office near the market plaza. (Arrivals from Peru need to stop here for entry stamps.) Pickup trucks and taxis leave the market plaza for the border (US$1 to US$2), less than 3km away. Walking is cheaper. Border hours are 8am to 6pm daily. Formalities are straightforward if your papers are in order. Peru doesn't have many accommodations until Sullana, 150km away. Cross in the morning for bus connections.

Moneychangers are found in the market and at the border. Banks don't change money. If you're coming into Ecuador, arrive with minimal Peruvian money and change it into US dollars before crossing the border.

THE ORIENTE

El Oriente – that is, all of the Amazon Basin lowlands east of the Andes – is one of Ecuador's most thrilling travel destinations, offering the visitor the chance to experience one of the most biodiverse regions on the planet. It's a land of exotic animals, forested hills, wetland marshes, big rivers and blackwater lagoons. It's also home to isolated indigenous groups struggling for self-determination, two gigantic oil pipelines, rugged jungle towns, oil workers, roving environmentalists, clearcut pasture land, encroaching colonists, jungle lodges, crude-hungry oil companies and curious tourists. All these combine to offer the open-eyed visitor a sometimes mindboggling, but always fascinating look at the state of one of the earth's greatest rain forests. There are many superb opportunities for wildlife viewing, river trips and cross-cultural exchanges out here, and it's possible – although arduous – to travel down the Río Napo to Peru and the Amazon River.

The northern Oriente, including the towns of Puyo, Tena, Misahuallí, Coca and Lago Agrio, sees more travelers. Buses from Quito frequently go to Puyo, Tena, Coca and Lago Agrio. There are many passport checks en route. The region south of Río Pastaza has a real sense of remoteness and it's a good place to get off the beaten track. Buses from Cuenca go through Limón (officially known as General Plaza Gutiérrez) to Macas. Buses from Loja go via Zamora to Limón and on to Macas. From Macas, a road leads to Puyo and the northern Oriente.

This section describes the Oriente from north to south (see Cuenca & the Southern Highlands, p659, for the region's southernmost towns.)

LAGO AGRIO & AROUND

Built in virgin jungle after oil was discovered in the 1970s, Lago Agrio (Nueva Loja on some maps) is Ecuador's largest new oil town. It has an edgy, frontier, border-town feel and is the jumping-off point for visits to the nearby **Reserva de Producción de Fauna Cuyabeno** (admission US$20). This reserve protects the rain-forest home of the Siona and Secoya people and conserves the Río Cuyabeno watershed, but there have been numerous oil spills. Nevertheless, huge parts of the reserve are still pristine and well worth a visit. Most visitors make arrangements in Quito or Coca.

A Sunday morning **market** is visited by the local Cofan people. They may take you to their village of **Dureno**, from which further explorations are possible with Cofan guides.

Dangers & Annoyances

With an increased pitch in the conflict in neighboring Colombia, border towns such as Lago Agrio have become safe havens for Colombian guerrillas, anti-rebel paramilitaries and drug smugglers. Bars can be sketchy and side streets unsafe, so stick to the main drag, especially at night. Tourists rarely have problems but be careful.

Tours

Booking a tour from Lago can be difficult. Most people arrive with a tour already booked, the guides show up, and everyone's gone the next morning. You may be able to squeeze in at the last minute. A good place to hang out and await arriving groups and other travelers is the Hotel D'Mario (see Sleeping & Eating, below).

Sleeping & Eating

Most of the hotels are on Av Quito, and they're all run-of-the-mill at best. Mosquitoes can be a problem, especially from June to August, so look for fans or mosquito nets. Most lack hot water.

Hotel La Cabaña (☎ 06-830-608; Av Quito; r with shared/private bath per person US$4/6) Clean and friendly with on-site laundry facilities. Rooms have fans.

Residencial Ecuador (☎ 06-830-124; s/d US$6/12) Decent value for rooms with bath, fan and TV.

Hotel Willigram (☎ 06-830-163; s/d without bath US$4/5, with bath US$5/6) Basic but tolerable.

Hotel D'Mario (☎ 06-830-172; Av Quito 1171; s US$14-27, d US$17-32; 🕮) In the middle of the hotel strip, D'Mario is the hub of Lago's

tourist scene. All rooms have private bath and fan or air-conditioning.

There are many hole-in-the-wall restaurants, chicken rotisserie stalls and fast-food vendors along Av Quito.

The two dining mainstays are **Restaurant D'Mario** (Av Quito), at the hotel of the same name, and **Restaurant Machala** (Av Quito), next door. Both have good food and cold beer.

Panadería Jackeline (Amazonas at Av Quito) Serves tasty, cheap breakfasts and fresh juices.

Getting There & Away

The airport is 5km east of town; taxi fare is US$2. **TAME** (☎ 06-830-113; Orellana near 9 de Octubre) and **Icaro** (☎ 06-832-370/71), at the airport, fly Monday through Saturday to Quito (US$51); it's best to book in advance.

The bus terminal is about 2km northwest of the center. Buses head regularly to Quito (US$6 to US$8, eight hours). There are one or two daily departures, mainly overnight, to Tena (US$7, nine hours), Cuenca, Guayaquil and Machala. Buses to Coca aren't usually found in the bus terminal; flag one on Av Quito in the center – ask locally for where to wait.

COCA

At the junction of the Ríos Coca and Napo, this dusty, sweltering oil town is unattractive but manageable and – if you're one of those people who digs sitting around in the heat guzzling beer and watching small-town street life – oddly appealing. Officially named Puerto Francisco de Orellana, it's a good place to hire a guide for visits to Pañacocha, Cuyabeno and **Parque Nacional Yasuní**.

Information

The **tourist office** (García Moreno; diturorellana@andina net.net) is helpful. There is an **Andinatel** (cnr Eloy Alfaro & 6 de Diciembre) and a **post office** (9 de Octubre). Internet service is available at **Imperial Net** (García Moreno; US$1.80 per hr). **Casa de Cambio 3R** (cnr Napo & García Moreno) charges 4% commission on traveler's checks.

Tours

Coca is closer than Misahuallí to large tracts of virgin jungle, but to hire a guide you should have a group of four or more to make it affordable. Trips down the Río Tiputini and into Parque Nacional Yasuní are possible, but require at least a week. Yasuní

ECUADOR

COCA

0 _____ 300 m
0 _____ 0.2 mi

A   B   C   D

To Bus Terminal (500m) & Municipal market   Rodríguez

Guayaquil

Cemetery

INFORMATION
Andinatel.............................1 B3
Casa de Cambio 3R................2 C2
Imperial Net.........................3 C3
Tourist Office.......................4 C3

SIGHTS & ACTIVITIES   p670
Emerald Forest Expeditions.....5 C3
River Dolphin Expeditions.......6 C2

SLEEPING   pp670-1
Hostería La Misión.................7 D3
Hotel El Auca.......................8 C2
Hotel Florida........................9 D2
Hotel Lojanita.....................10 C2
Hotel Oasis........................11 D3

EATING   p671
Asadero El Gran Chaparral.....12 C3
Medianoche........................13 C2
Pollo El Campero.................14 C3

DRINKING   p671
Café Rock.......................(see 6)
Emerald Forest Blues............15 C3
La Jungla Disco................(see 8)
Papa Dan's........................16 C3

TRANSPORT   p671
Boats to Nuevo Rocafuerte......17 D3
Coop de Transportes Fluviales
   de Orellana.....................18 C3
Icaro.............................(see 7)
TAME.................................19 C2

Montalvo   Bolívar   Cuenca
Quito   Rocafuerte
9 de Octubre
6 de Diciembre
17 de Febrero
Alejandro Labaka
Inez Arango
Padre de Vidana
García Moreno   Napo   Amazonas   Inez Arango
Eloy Alfaro
Espejo
Chimborazo
Capitanía (Port Captain)

To Hospital, Airport (1km), Lago Agrio, Tena
To Nuevo Rocafuerte
La Misión
To Río Tiguino
Río Napo
To Misahuallí

---

is the country's largest national park and contains a variety of rain-forest habitats, wildlife and a few Huaorani communities. Unfortunately, poaching and, increasingly, oil exploration are damaging the park.

Visiting a Huaorani village requires written permission from the community. An excellent source of information about this is **Randy Smith** (☎ 09-830-2650; bufeo2me@yahoo.ca). He doesn't have an office, but you can contact him anytime on his cellular phone or by email; he sets up some great tours. Also try Ramiro Viteri at **River Dolphin Expeditions** (☎ 06-880-600/127, 09-917-7529; www.aamazon-green-magician .com; García Moreno). Among other interesting tours, the company offers a 10-day canoe trip (you paddle!) down the Río Napo to Iquitos, Peru.

Hotel El Auca (see following) doesn't arrange tours but is probably one of the best places in town to meet guides looking for work, as well as to meet other travelers who can tell you of their experiences or help form a group. Luís García, who runs **Emerald Forest Expeditions** (☎ 06-882-285; www.emeraldexpeditions .com; Napo), is also highly recommended for

a variety of trips. **Whimper Torres** (☎ 06-880-336/017, 06-881-196, in Quito ☎ 02-265-9311; ronoboa@ latinmail.com) is a well-known local guide with over 18 years experience.

Sleeping

Coca's cheaper hotels are dingy, overpriced and fill up quickly with oil workers. Water shortages are frequent.

Hotel Oasis (☎ 06-880-206; yuturilodge@yahoo.com; r with cold/hot private bath per person US$5/7) Oasis is the best of Coca's cheapies and one of the few hotels that gets more travelers than oil workers.

Hotel El Auca (☎ 06-880-127/600; helauca@ecuanex .net.ec; Napo; s US$12-35, d US$20-50; 🐾) Popular with tour groups and upper-rank oil folks, El Auca has the nicest garden in Coca and perhaps the best restaurant.

Hostería La Misión (☎ 06-880-260/544; s/d with fan US$17/25, with air-con US$20/29; 🐾) Popular with oil execs; great river-side location; comfortable.

Hotel Lojanita (☎ 06-880-032; Napo at Cuenca; r with/without bath per person US$5/4) is just bearable if you're in a pinch, and **Hotel Florida** (☎ 06-

880-177; s/d with shared bath US$6/12, with private bath US$10/18) is overpriced but secure enough.

Eating & Drinking

The restaurants at Hostería La Misión and Hotel El Auca are considered to be the best in town.

Medianoche (mains US$2-2.50; ☾ 6pm-1am) Has four plates of chicken on the menu and is extremely popular.

Pollo El Campero (García Moreno) Good for rotisserie chicken.

Asadero El Gran Chaparral (Espejo) Good for grilled meats.

La Jungla Disco (admission US$10, hotel guests free; ☾ Wed-Sat) Over the restaurant of Hotel El Auca, this is the place to dance on weekends.

Emerald Forest Blues (Quito) and **Café Rock** (García Moreno) are both fun, friendly hangouts.

Papa Dan's (Napo) A Coca institution.

Getting There & Away

AIR

The airport is 2km north of town. **TAME** (☎ 06-881-078, 06-880-768; Napo) and **Icaro** (☎ 06-880-997/546; in Hostería La Misión) fly to Quito (US$56) Monday through Saturday. Book ahead or chance on getting lucky on departure day.

BOAT

On Monday and Thursday at 7am, **Coop de Transportes Fluviales Orellana** (Napo near Chimborazo) offers passenger service to Nuevo Rocafuerte (US$15, nine to 15 hours) on the Peruvian border. It returns to Coca, departing Nuevo Rocafuerte at 7am on Sunday and Thursday. Although there's usually a stop for lunch, be sure to bring food and water for the long trip. With the completion of the Coca–Tena road, boats no longer go to Misahuallí unless you cough up about US$250 total. It's 14 hours upstream (six coming down).

BUS

There are bus offices in town and at the bus terminal, north of town. Several buses a day go to Quito (US$8, nine hours via Loreto; US$10, 13 hours via Lago Agrio), Tena (US$6, six hours) and Lago Agrio (US$2, three hours), as well as other jungle towns. Night buses go to Ambato. *Chivas* (open-sided trucks) leave from the terminal to

most jungle destinations. They're fun but uncomfortable for long hauls.

RÍO NAPO

Several villages and lodges east of Coca can be reached down the Río Napo; lodges provide transportation as part of their packages or you can join a tour (see Tours under Coca, p669). Traveling independently by canoe is expensive. About an hour downstream from Coca, Yarina Lodge is a good choice for budget travelers seeking a comfortable introduction to the jungle. Rates include English- or Spanish-speaking guides and meals. Make arrangements through Hotel Oasis in Coca (p670) or in Quito at **Yuturi Jungle Adventure** (Map pp628-9; ☎ 02-250-4037/3225; www.yuturilodge.com; Amazonas N24-236 & Colón).

Two hours east of Coca is the mission of **Pompeya**, where you can get basic food and lodging. From here an 8km road goes north to **Limoncocha** village, which also has a basic **hotel** (r per person US$2.50) and restaurant. Nearby is the locally run **Reserva Biológica Limoncocha** (admission US$16), which has a rustic **lodge** (per person per night with food about US$20) and a beautiful lake with outstanding birdwatching. Rooms in the lodge have private cold showers and four beds. Limoncocha can also be reached by one of the several buses a day leaving from the oil base of **Shushufindi** (which is a two- or three-hour bus trip from either Coca or Lago Agrio).

Pañacocha village, near the stunning **Laguna Pañacocha**, is five hours downstream from Coca and has a couple of simple places to stay. Food and local guides are available.

NUEVO ROCAFUERTE

About five more hours downstream from Pañacocha brings you to the border at Nuevo Rocafuerte, where a basic **pensión** (per person US$3-5) and local guides are available. Tours up the Río Yasuní into Parque Nacional Yasuní (p669) can be arranged. For details on boat travel between Nuevo Rocafuerte and Coca, see above.

For travelers continuing on to Peru, exit and entry formalities on the Ecuador side are taken care of here; in Peru they're settled in **Iquitos**. The official border crossing is at **Pantoja**, a short ride downstream from Nuevo Rocafuerte. Timing is the key:

ECUADOR

A cargo boat called the *Torres Causana* leaves Iquitos, Peru around the 18th of every month, arriving in Pantoja around the 24th. Catch this boat in Pantoja for its six-day return trip (about US$70) to Iquitos. To get to Pantoja, ask for a ride (about US$5) with the Peruvian *militares* (soldiers) who visit Nuevo Rocafuerte daily by boat. Conditions on the *Torres Causana* are extremely basic (you sleep in hammocks). Food is available, but you're better off bringing your own. Definitely bring water-purifying tablets.

TENA

Tena is the de facto white-water rafting and kayaking capital of Ecuador. It's an attractive little town where kayaks lay around hotel-room entrances and boaters hang out in pizza joints rapping about their day on the rapids. Rafting trips are easily arranged, and several tour operators also offer jungle trips. The town sits at the confluence of the lovely Ríos Tena and Pano and has a comfortable climate.

Information

Internet access is available at **Piraña.net** (Orellana; US$3.50 per hr). **Banco del Austro** (15 de Noviembre) changes traveler's checks and **Banco del Pichincha** (Mera) has an ATM. **Andinatel** (Olmedo) and the **post office** (cnr Olmedo & García Moreno) are east of the river. **Tourist Information** (☎ 06-887-305; García Moreno) is near the footbridge.

Tours

The popular **Amarongachi Tours** (☎ 06-886-372; www.amarongachi-tours.com; 15 de Noviembre 438) offers various good-time jungle tours for US$45 per person per day, including food, transport and lodging. Also offering tours at this price is the well-recommended **Sacharicsina** (☎ 06-886-839; sacharicsinatour@yahoo.com; Montsedeoca 110), operated by the Quechua-speaking Cerda brothers. For emphasis on Quechua culture, visit **Ricancie** (☎ 06-887-953; http://ricancie.nativeweb.org; 15 de Noviembre 774), an organization of 10 Quechua communities on the upper Río Napo. **Sachamazónica** (☎ 06-887-979), in the bus terminal, is run by local indigenous guides who know their stuff.

For river-running trips, stop by the excellent **Ríos Ecuador/Yacu Amu Rafting** (☎ 06-886-727; www.riosecuador.com; 15 de Noviembre). Day trips cost between US$50 and US$65, and a four-day kayaking class costs US$260.

Sleeping

Welcome Break (☎ 06-886-301; cofanes@hotmail.com; Agusto Rueda 331; s/d US$4/8) Family-run favorite with simple rooms, shared showers, guest kitchen and laundry facilities. Basic but loved.

Residencial Austria (☎ 06-887-205; Tarqui; s/d US$7/11) Great deal. Rooms are airy and have fan, bath and hot water.

Hostal Limoncocha (☎ 06-887-583; limoncocha@andinanet.net; Sangay 533; r with shared/private bath per person US$3.50/5) German-owned with a guest kitchen and cheerful, clean rooms and firm beds. Hammocks grace the outside deck with lovely views.

Hostal Travellers Lodging (☎ 06-886-372; 15 de Noviembre 438; r per person US$6 & US$12) The US$12-rooms have great views; cheaper rooms are small, thin-walled and dark (but still comfortable). All have private baths and hot water. Popular.

Residencial Hilton (☎ 06-886-329; 15 de Noviembre; r with shared/private bath per person US$4/6) Tidy little place with small rooms; cheerful if you score a window.

If you just need a place to crash, sans the hot water and other mod-cons, try:

Hotel Amazonas (☎ 06-886-439; cnr Juan Montalvo & Mera; s/d US$3/6)
Residencial Enmita (☎ 06-886-253; Bolívar; s/d US$4/8)
Hostal Camba Huasi (☎ 06-887-429; s/d US$3/6)
Residencial Nápoli (☎ 06-886-194; s/d US$3/6)

Eating

Cositas Ricas (15 de Noviembre; mains US$3-4.50) Popular place whipping up tasty vegetarian and Ecuadorian dishes.

Los Chuquitos (mains US$3-5) Just off the plaza, has a balcony with river views, a large menu of local food and the best lemonade in town.

Pizzaría La Massilia (Orellana at Pano; pizzas US$4.25-6; 5-11pm) Bakes great pizza.

Restaurant Safari (15 de Noviembre & Monteros) Serves good, cheap Ecuadorian fare.

Pollo Sin Rival (15 de Noviembre) Two blocks south of the bus terminal, makes good rotisserie chicken.

Drinking

Discos open from 8pm to 2am or 3am Thursday through Saturday.

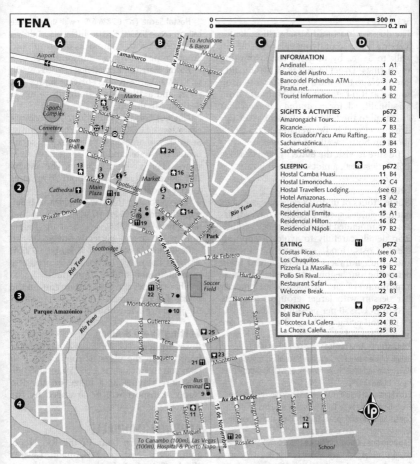

TENA

0 — 300 m
0 — 0.2 mi

INFORMATION
Andinatel..1 A1
Banco del Austro.......................................2 B2
Banco del Pichincha ATM.......................3 A2
Piraña.net..4 B2
Tourist Information...................................5 B2

SIGHTS & ACTIVITIES   p672
Amarongachi Tours....................................6 B2
Ricancie..7 B3
Rios Ecuador/Yacu Amu Rafting..............8 B2
Sachamazónica...9 B4
Sacharicsina...10 B3

SLEEPING   p672
Hostal Camba Huasi...............................11 B4
Hostal Limoncocha................................12 C4
Hostal Travellers Lodging...............(see 6)
Hotel Amazonas.....................................13 A2
Residencial Austria.................................14 B2
Residencial Enmita.................................15 A1
Residencial Hilton...................................16 B2
Residencial Nápoli..................................17 B2

EATING   p672
Cositas Ricas.....................................(see 6)
Los Chuquitos...18 A2
Pizzería La Massilia................................19 B2
Pollo Sin Rival..20 C4
Restaurant Safari....................................21 B4
Welcome Break.......................................22 B3

DRINKING   pp672–3
Boli Bar Pub..23 C4
Discoteca La Galera................................24 B2
La Choza Caleña......................................25 B3

La Choza Caleña (15 de Noviembre; admission US$2)
The thatched Caleña gets packed.

At **Canambo** (admission US$1) and **Las Vegas**
(admission US$1) local kids do the communal
soft-shake to pop tunes.

Discoteca La Galera (admission US$2) A poppy
little disco with a roller-rink attached (now
we're talking!).

Boli Bar Pub (15 de Noviembre) Good for pool,
beer and rock and roll.

Getting There & Away

The bus terminal is less than 1km south
of the town center. Several buses a day
head for Quito (US$5, six hours), Baeza
(US$4, six hours), Lago Agrio (US$7, nine
hours), Coca (US$6, six to seven hours),

Baños (US$3.50, five hours) and other
places. Buses for Misahuallí (US$0.75, one
hour) depart hourly from in front of the
terminal.

MISAHUALLÍ

The tranquil village of Misahuallí, on Río
Napo, is popular for jungle tours, but
don't expect virgin jungle: the area has
been colonized and most of the animals
are gone, although you still can see many
birds, tropical flowers, army ants and dazzling butterflies. Excursions deeper into the
jungle are also possible but require patience
and money.

Change money and make phone calls in
Tena (p672).

Activities

The dirt roads around Misahuallí make for relaxing walks to outlying villages. You can walk to a nearby **waterfall** for swimming and picnics. To get there, take a Misahuallí–Puerto Napo bus and ask the driver to drop you off at Río Latas, about 20 minutes from Misahuallí; ask for *el camino a las cascadas* ('the trail to the falls'). Follow the river upstream to the falls. Be prepared to wade; it's about an hour's walk up the river.

Be sure to visit the **Butterfly Farm** (admission US$2; ☉ 9am-4pm), a block off the plaza.

Tours

Guided tours of up to 18 days are available, but few guides speak English. Longer tours are recommended if you hope to see wildlife. Plan details carefully to avoid disappointment. Costs, food, equipment, itinerary and group numbers must be agreed upon before the tour begins. Tours usually require a minimum of four people and are cheaper per person with larger groups. Costs are US$25 to US$50 per person per day.

The following guides and operators are all recommended.

Adventuras Amazónicas (☎ 06-890-031/113) Below Residencial La Posada, this place offers tours in the Pañacocha and upper Napo regions, as well as shorter trips closer to Misahuallí.

Ecoselva (☎ 06-890-019; ecoselva@yahoo.es) Run by English-speaking Pepe Tapia González, who has a biology background and speaks English. He is also extremely knowledgeable about plants and insects.

Expediciones Douglas Clarke (☎ 06-887-584; douglasclarkeexpediciones@yahoo.com) In Hostal Marena Internacional, this place offers one- to 10-day trips, some of which use the company's well-equipped lodge, Cabañas Shinchi. Longer trips should be booked in advance.

Jaime Recalde (☎ 06-890 077/087; jaimerecalde@yahoo.com) Private guide with many recommendations. Inquire at Restaurant Doña Gloria on the plaza.

Sleeping & Eating

Water and electricity failures are frequent here, and most of the hotels are very basic (forget about hot water), but friendly and safe.

El Paisano (☎ 06-890-027; s/d US$5/10) A pleasant garden with hammocks and an open-air restaurant serving vegetarian dishes (with advance notice) make this place one of the best. It's just off the plaza. Rates include private baths, fans and mosquito nets.

Hostal Sacha (☎ 06-886-679; r with shared/private bath per person US$3/4) Rustic little place down by the river with hammocks out front and an open-air bar. Bring a mosquito net.

Hostal Marena Internacional (☎ 06-890-002; s/d US$6/12) Large rooms, private baths, hot water and a 4th-floor restaurant – quite a deal for Misahuallí.

Albergue Español (☎ 06-890-127; www.albergue espanol.com; s/d US$8/16) Rooms at this comfy, Spanish-run hotel have private baths, solar-heated hot water and fans; some have river views. There's a restaurant too. The owners run Jaguar Lodge (p675), about 90 minutes away by boat.

Two places on the plaza, **Residencial El Balcón del Napo** (☎ 06-890-117/045; s/d US$2/4) and **Hotel Shaw** (s/d US$3/6), are beat-up jungle junkers but they're perfectly fine.

Residencial La Posada (☎ 06-890-113; s/d US$5/10) Near the plaza, La Posada was recently renovated, so it's more comfortable.

There are several little restaurants on the plaza. Try Restaurant Doña Gloria, where the juice is made with boiled water.

Getting There & Away

Buses to Tena (US$0.75, one hour) leave hourly from the plaza. Hiring a canoe to take you to Coca costs US$250 to US$300. If you're staying at a lodge on the Río Napo, transport will be arranged by the lodge.

AROUND MISAHUALLÍ

On the southern bank of the Río Napo, about 7km east of Misahuallí, **Cabañas Aliñahui/Butterfly Lodge** (www.ecuadorexplorer.com /alinahui; r & board per person per day US$25-35) is a comfortable eight-cabin lodge adjacent to the 2000-hectare **Jatun Sacha Biological Reserve** (admission US$6). The cabins are set in a 1.6-hectare tropical garden and have solar electricity and showers, shady patios with hammocks and upstairs verandas with stunning river views. Guided naturalist hikes through the reserve and on Aliñahui's property cost US$15 per person. The Jatun Sacha reserve, administered by the Ecuadorian nonprofit **Fundación Jatun Sacha** (in Quito ☎ 02-243-2240/173; www.jatunsacha.org; Pasaje Eugenio de Santillán N34-248 & Maurián, Urbanización Rumipamba), has a staggering rate of biodiversity, with a greater concentration of reptile, plant and bird species than nearly anywhere on the planet. Cabañas Aliñahui has recorded 537 bird species in the area!

Make lodge reservations at Cabañas Aliñahui's **Quito office** (☎ 02-222-7094; alinahui@i nteractive.net.ec; Mosquera Narváez 668 & Av América) or by email. You could also just show up and chance a vacancy.

Both the lodge and the reserve are reached by bus from Tena. Take an Ahuano or Santa Rosa bus and ask the driver to drop you at either entrance (all drivers know them). Aliñahui is about 3km east of (past) Jatun Sacha research station, or 27km east of Tena on the road to Santa Rosa.

Albergue Español in Misahuallí operates **Jaguar Lodge** (☎ 06-890-127, 06-890-004; www.albergueespanol.com; packages per person 2-nights/ 3-days US$105, 3-nights/4-days US$135, 4-nights/5-days US$155), about 1½ hours downstream from Misahuallí. The lodge's 10 cabins have private baths with solar-heated water. It's a good deal, considering the price includes meals, kayaks, and various activities. Inquire at Albergue Español about river transport.

PUYO

Puyo is a busy, rickety, friendly old jungle town and an important stopover for travelers. It's only two hours by bus from the highland town of Baños (p651) and three hours south of Tena. There are often impressive views of the volcanoes to the west – quite a sight from a little lowland town on the edge of the jungle.

Orientation & Information

Marín and Atahualpa are the main downtown streets with the most services. North of downtown, a bridge crossing the Río Puyo leads to the **Paseo Turístico**, a short trail through the woods.

Cyber Té (Marín 5-69; US$2 per hr) has the fastest Internet connection, but **Guanábanet** (Atahualpa; US$1.80 per hr) is livelier. **Amazonía Touring** (Atahualpa) charges 3% on traveler's checks. **Banco del Austro** (Atahualpa) has an ATM. The **post office** (27 de Febrero) and **Andinatel** (cnr Orellana & Villamil) are southwest of the main plaza. For basic tourist information visit the **Cámara de Turismo** (☎ 03-886-737; Marín, Centro Comercial Zuñiga, 2nd fl).

Tours

The highly recommended **Papangu-Atacapi Tours** (☎ 03-883-875; papangu@andinanet.net; 27 de Febrero near Sucre) is a unique Quechua-run tour operator specializing in cultural tourism, offering travelers the opportunity to visit Quechua villages, stay with local families and learn about Quechua lifestyles. The money you spend here goes directly to the communities you visit. One- to 10-day tours (two-person minimum) cost US$35 to US$40 per person per day.

Sleeping

Hotel Araucano (☎ 03-883-834; Marín 5-75; per person US$6.50-11.50) With a dusty hat collection and odd artifacts dangling from the lobby walls, Araucano is an appealing place, despite the

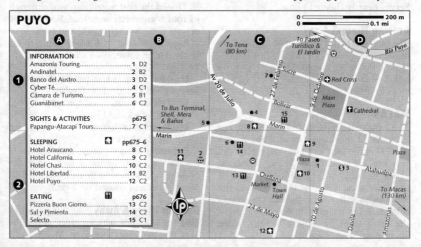

fact that the rooms are a bit disheveled. Rooms have private bath and hot water.

Hotel Libertad (☎ 03-883-282; Orellana; s/d US$5/10) A new, sparkling-clean hotel and one of the best value in town. The rooms have good beds and TVs, but all have shared baths.

Hotel Puyo (☎ 03-884-497, 03-886-525; 9 de Octubre; s/d US$8/16) Boasts spotless rooms with firm beds, TV, telephone and private hot-water baths.

Hotel Chasi (☎ 03-883-059; 9 de Octubre; s/d US$5/10) and **Hotel California** (☎ 03-885-189; 9 de Octubre; s/d US$5/10) are both worn down but clean.

Eating

Selecto (Marín; mains US$1.50-2.50) A simple but good place and one of several cheap eateries on Calles Marín and Atahualpa. You could also join the folks lingering around the sidewalk vendors snacking on *chuzos* (grilled sausage and steak shish kebabs) and hotdogs.

El Jardín (Paseo Turístico; mains US$4-5; ☘ Tue-Sun) A casual, intimate restaurant on the bank of the Río Puyo. Sofia, the chef/owner, has won province-wide awards for her regional cooking, and you'll see why if you eat here. It's just across the footbridge leading to the Paseo Turístico, a short walk north of downtown.

Sal y Pimienta (Atahualpa near 27 de Febrero; set meals US$2) Good for cheap, fast meals.

Pizzería Buon Giorno (Orellana near 27 de Febrero) Serves heavily cheesed pizzas.

Getting There & Away

The bus terminal is 3km out of town. Many buses run to Baños (US$1.50, two hours), Quito (US$3, six hours), Macas (US$4, six hours) and Tena (US$2, three hours). Services to other towns are also available.

MACAS

The handsome capital of Morona Santiago Province is the biggest town (population 30,177) in the southern Oriente, yet it's still very much a small town. Macas is situated above the banks of the wild Río Upano, and there are great views of the river and the Río Upano valley from behind the town's cathedral. On a clear day you can glimpse the often smoking Volcán Sangay, some 40km northwest.

Information

Internet service is available at **Cyber Vision** (Soasti at Sucre; US$1.50 per hr). **Banco del Austro** (cnr 10 de Agosto & 24 de Mayo) changes traveler's checks. The **post office** (9 de Octubre) is south of the main plaza. **Pacifictel** (24 de Mayo) is two blocks north of the main plaza.

Tours

Ikiaam Shuar Travel (☎ 07-701-690, 07-700-120; ikiaamjungle_tour@yahoo.com; Barrio Las Palmeras, Sevilla) offers several recommended jungle trips emphasizing Shuar culture. Owner Andres Vizuma speaks the Shuar language and has a good relationship with interior communities. Tours have a five-day minimum and cost US$50 to US$70 per person per day, depending on the number in your group. It also offers less expensive tours to Parque Nacional Sangay. Make arrangements in advance by email or phone.

Sleeping & Eating

Residencial Macas (☎ 07-700-254; r with shared/private bath per person US$3/4) If you don't mind miniscule rooms it's a great deal.

Hotel Orquidea (☎ 07-700-970; r with cold/hot water per person US$7/8) Clean, spacious rooms, although all doubles have twin beds only (no snuggling).

Hotel Los Gemelos (☎ 07-701-770; Amazonas; per person US$8) A sparkling, modest, new hotel with five immaculate rooms with firm beds and cable TV. Downside? Baths are shared.

Hotel Peñon del Oriente (☎ 07-700-124; s/d US$8/16) One of the best hotels in town, although its rooms are pretty worn-out. Rooms have private bath, hot water, TV and fans.

Pagoda (cnr Amazonas & Comín) The finest restaurant in town, it's a *chifa* across from Peñon del Oriente.

El Jardín (Amazonas btwn Comín & 10 de Agosto) Serves good Ecuadorian stand-bys.

Eros Café (Amazonas) Good for hamburgers, ice cream, snacks and beer.

Rincón Manabita (Amazonas) Serves filling set meals for US$1.50.

Comedores (cheap restaurants; Comín near Soasti) Several sell *ayampacos*, a local specialty of either chicken, beef or fish, wrapped in *bijao* leaves and cooked on a grill.

Getting There & Away

TAME (☎ 07-700-162), with an office at the airport, flies to Quito (US$56) on Monday and

Thursday. The bus terminal has several daily departures for Cuenca (US$7, nine hours), Gualaquiza (US$4, eight to 10 hours), Riobamba and Ambato. Several buses a day leave for Puyo (US$4, five hours); you have to cross Ríos Pastaza and Pano by footbridges. Buses wait on the other side to continue to Puyo. It's well synchronized.

PACIFIC COAST & LOWLANDS

A spell on Ecuador's coast makes an excellent complement to the chill of the highlands. Although less than one-third of its shoreline is beaches, there are still plenty of stunning stretches of sand where you can char yourself in the hot tropical sun and swim in the warm water that bathes the Ecuadorian coast year-round.

Esmeraldas is the northernmost coastal province, and north of the provincial capital (also called Esmeraldas) are some of the wildest mangrove and lowland coastal rain forests imaginable. The region is very poor, and travel (often by boat through the mangroves) is challenging. South of the provincial capital, Atacames, Same, Súa, Muisne and especially Canoa all have popular beaches with good swimming.

The next province south is Manabí, home of Parque Nacional Machalilla, Ecuador's only coastal national park. South of Puerto López – the park's main access point – the coastal highway winds through low-key beach villages and finally reaches Guayaquil, Ecuador's biggest city. The next city south is Machala, an important (and rather ugly) port city and the common gateway to Peru.

Costeño (anyone from the coast is a *costeño*) culture is markedly different to that of the rest of the country. Esmeraldas has Ecuador's highest population of Afro-Ecuadorians. And if you like seafood, you're in for a real treat – Ecuador's best food comes from the coast.

The north coast is wet from December to June, and the south coast (the provinces of Guayas and El Oro) is drier and more barren, with a rainy season from January to April. All these months are hot and humid, and Ecuadorians flock to the beaches for relief on weekends. Mosquitoes are plentiful in the wet months, so bring repellent and consider using antimalarial medication in the north.

Getting There & Away

Most places along the northern coast can be reached from Quito in a day's travel. San Lorenzo (in Esmeraldas Province) can be reached by paved road from Ibarra (in the northern highlands) in only four hours. From Cuenca, Guayaquil is less than four hours away via the new road through Parque Nacional Cajas. Nearly the entire coastal highway is now paved south from Esmeraldas city. A spectacular road links Latacunga in the highlands to the lowland city of Quevedo, an important junction en route to the south coast.

FROM QUITO TO THE COAST
The New Road

The main, fastest route to the coast passes through the lowland city of **Santo Domingo de los Colorados**, an important transport hub, but little more than a convenient place to break the journey west should the need arise. **Hostal Patricia** (☎ 02-276-1906; s/d US$4/8) is a reliable budget hotel by the bus terminal, or you could taxi or bus the 2km into town and stay at the friendly **Hostal Jennefer** (☎ 02-275-0577; 29 de Mayo near Ibarra; s/d US$6/10). Most buses from Quito just pull into Santo Domingo for a break before continuing to the coast. The new road to Santo Domingo is as steep as it is spectacular and should be done in the morning (before the fog sets in).

The Old Road

The old road to Santo Domingo is a bit slower, but has some fabulous opportunities to stop and smell the cloud forest on the way to the coast. The best place to do this is the village of **Mindo**, which is famous for its bird-watching and local environmentalism (it was the only town to protest the new OCP or Oleoducto de Crudos Pesados oil pipeline running from the Oriente to the coast). There are several cheap accommodations in the village, the best being **Hostal Bijao** (in Quito ☎ 02-276-5740; r with shared/ private bath per person US$4/7.50) near the village entrance. Once in Mindo you can hike in the cloud forest, hire bird-watching guides, swim in the Río Mindo and *relax*.

ECUADOR

Direct buses from Quito to Mindo (US$2, 2½ hours) leave from the **Cooperativa Flor de Valle bus terminal** (Map pp628-9; M Larrea, west of Ascunción, near Parque El Ejido, Quito) at 3:20pm daily and at 8am on Friday, Saturday and Sunday.

After passing the turnoff to Mindo, the old road meanders down through the lowland villages of **Puerto Maldonado** and **Puerto Quito** before meeting the north–south road between Santo Domingo and Esmeraldas. From the Mindo turnoff you can flag a bus to Santo Domingo.

SAN LORENZO & AROUND

Spread haphazardly about the banks of the estuary created by Ríos Mataje and Cayapas, lively San Lorenzo is hardly attractive, but it's friendly. The town is easily reached by bus from Ibarra in the highlands, and the main reason to visit is to explore the infrequently visited mangroves of the area. Boat tours can be arranged down at the port.

If you're heading south, the road from San Lorenzo to Esmeraldas passes a recommended hostel in Río Verde (p679). You could also travel by boat through the mangroves via **Limones**, and stop at the muddy fishing village of **Olmedo** (a short walk from La Tola; see Getting There & Away, following), where there's a tiny hostel run by local Afro-Ecuadorian women. There are few beaches in this area – it's all mangroves.

Orientation & Information

Calle Imbabura is the main drag. Buses roll into town, pass the train station (on the left) and stop at the end of Imbabura at the plaza. The port is a couple of blocks further down. Money-changing opportunities are poor.

Sleeping & Eating

Hotels are *all* basic. Mosquito nets and fans are recommended and water shortages are frequent.

Hotel Pampa de Oro (☎ 06-780-214; s/d US$5) Off Calle Imbabura, this hotel has cheerful, clean rooms with fan, mosquito net and private bath.

Hotel Continental (☎ 06-780-125/304; Calle Imbabura; r with fan/air-con per person US$6/10; 🞩) Another block toward the plaza, it's about as swanky as San Lorenzo gets.

Hotel Carondolet (☎ 06-780-202; r with shared/private bath per person US$3.50/4) On the inland side of the plaza, has small, clean rooms, private baths and a communal balcony overlooking the park.

Ballet Azul (Imbabura) At the street's western end, serves excellent seafood and knockout *batidos* (fruit shakes).

El Condorito (off Imbabura) Popular for its basic US$2 *almuerzos*.

La Red (Isidro Ayora near Imbabura) Serves good seafood.

Getting There & Away

Buses leave from the central plaza. There are several buses daily to Ibarra (US$4, four hours) and eight to Esmeraldas (US$4, five hours), Borbón (US$2, two hours) and intermediate points. The last Esmeraldas bus leaves at 2:30pm.

Train service to/from Ibarra has been suspended indefinitely.

Although boat traffic has dwindled with the completion of the road to Borbón and Esmeraldas, there are still hourly departures from 7am to 3pm for La Tola (US$2, 2½ hours), via Limones (US$3.50, 1½ hours). The ride through the coastal mangroves to these tiny, predominantly Afro-Ecuadorian fishing villages, with pelicans and frigate birds soaring overhead, is quite an experience. Prepare for sun, wind and spray. In La Tola, boats connect with buses to Esmeraldas (four to five hours). Boats to Borbón leave La Tola at 7am and 4pm daily.

BORBÓN & AROUND

This small port with a predominantly Afro-Ecuadorian population of 5000 is on the Río Cayapas. Boats travel from here up Ríos Cayapas and San Miguel to Reserva Ecológica Cotacachi-Cayapas – an interesting trip to a remote area. Ángel Cerón runs **Hotel Pampa de Oro** (per person US$3) and is a good source of information. There are several simple restaurants in town.

An hour beyond Borbón is the friendly seaside village of **Río Verde**, where the recommended **Hostería Pura Vida** (☎ 06-744-203/4; pura_vida_verde@yahoo.com; r per person US$10-15) offers clean rooms or *cabañas* near the beach. It also has a restaurant. Swiss co-owner Thomas Meier speaks five languages and arranges mountain-biking and fishing excursions.

Buses to Esmeraldas (US$3, three hours) and San Lorenzo (US$2, two hours) leave frequently from Borbón. Esmeraldas-bound buses will drop you at Pura Vida, 2km past the Río Verde bridge.

Boats to San Lorenzo leave at 7am and 11am.

RESERVA ECOLÓGICA COTACACHI-CAYAPAS

Five hours by boat up the Río Cayapas, the primarily Afro-Ecuadorian community of **San Miguel** is the jumping-off point for trips into this rarely visited **reserve** (admission US$20). The park boasts waterfalls, rain-forest trails, great bird-watching and opportunities to see monkeys and other wildlife. A shop in San Miguel sells a few supplies and basic meals are available for about US$5. Indigenous Cayapas people live across the river and can be visited.

The **ranger station** (beds per person US$5) here has four beds, but there's no running water or mosquito nets, or you may camp outside. Beware of ferocious chiggers. Rangers will guide you into the reserve by dugout and on foot for about US$15 per guide per day (two guides are needed on some trips), plus food. Camping is possible. The best time to visit is from September to December.

A passenger boat leaves at 11am daily for San Miguel (US$8, five hours), passing the Catholic mission of **Santa María** and then the Protestant mission of **Zapallo Grande** (both of which have basic accommodations). The boat back to Borbón leaves San Miguel be-

fore dawn. Arrange in advance which day you want to return.

ESMERALDAS

Esmeraldas has been an important port for centuries and the oil refinery here is a major source of income and employment. It's a lively, noisy city with a reputation for being dangerous, and most travelers pass through it quickly. Avoid the southern end of Malecón Maldonado.

Sleeping & Eating

The cheapest hotels are in poor condition.

Hotel Diana (☎ 06-726-962; Cañizares 224; r per person US$3-5) Probably the best of the cheapies.

Sandry Hotel (☎ 06-726-861; Bolívar near Montalvo; s/d US$5/10; 🞕) Across from the market, this is also good.

Las Redes Restaurant (Bolívar near 10 de Agosto) On the plaza, it is good for seafood.

Fuente de Soda Estrecho de Bering (Bolívar) Good for ice cream and people-watching.

Chifa Asiática (Cañizares near Sucre) Two blocks south of the plaza, offers dependable Chinese food.

Getting There & Away

AIR

The airport is 25km up the road to San Lorenzo; taxi fare is US$5. **TAME** (☎ 06-726-862/3; Bolívar at 9 de Octubre), near the plaza, offers late-morning flights to Quito (US$37) on weekdays, plus an evening flight on Friday and Sunday.

BUS

Buses leave from different stops within walking distance of each other and the main plaza. **Aero Taxi** (Sucre near Rocafuerte), **Transportes Occidentales** (9 de Octubre near Sucre), **Transportes Esmeraldas** (10 de Agosto, Plaza Central) and **Panamérica International** (Piedrahita near Olmedo) all go to Quito (US$6, six hours). Occidentales and Esmeraldas both have many buses to Guayaquil (US$5.50 to US$7, eight hours), Ambato, Machala and other cities. **CITA** (Sucre near Rocafuerte) has buses to Ambato. **Reina del Camino** (Piedrahita near Bolívar) has buses to Manta and Bahía de Caráquez.

Transportes La Costeñita (Malecón Maldonado) and **Transportes del Pacífico** (Malecón Maldonado) head frequently to Atacames and Súa (US$0.70, about one hour) and Muisne (US$1.50, 2½ hours). The company also goes to La

Tola, Borbón (US$3, three hours) and San Lorenzo (US$4.50, five hours). These buses pass the airport.

ATACAMES

Atacames is at its rip-roaring riotous best (or worst, depending on your mindset) when *serranos* (people from the highlands) pour into town to party down. They arrive in droves during the high season (July to mid-September, Christmas through New Year's, Carnaval and Easter), and the beach and *malecón* (beachfront road) turn into a chaotic family fiesta. The rest of the season, it's dead.

Foreigners tend to visit from April to October, when things are quieter, although they definitely miss the *farra* (party).

Orientation

Buses drop passengers off in the center of town, on the main road from Esmeraldas. The center is on the inland side of the highway, and the beach is reached by a small footbridge over the Río Atacames. The *malecón*, where most of the hotels and bars are located, is the main drag along the beach.

Dangers & Annoyances

A powerful undertow here causes drownings every year, so keep within your limits. There have been many reports of assaults on late-night beach walkers, so skip the moonlight necking. Camping is unsafe. Don't leave anything unattended on the beach.

Sleeping

Hotels are full on weekends and holidays, so arrive early. During high season, prices rise and hotels usually charge a four-person minimum (the number of beds in most hotel rooms).

At the west end of the *malecón*, Calle Las Acacias runs away from the beach toward the highway. Atacames' cheapest hotels are along this street. Most of them are simple but just fine.

El Reina Isabel (☎ 06-731-665; Las Acacias; low/high season per person US$4/7) A good choice and doubles are always available.

Cabañas Sol y Mar (☎ 06-731-524, 06-726-649; r low/high season per person US$7/10; ℗) Just off the *malecón*, one of the few places that actually has (and charges for) double rooms. It's a great deal.

Hostal Jennifer (☎ 06-710-482; r low/high season per person US$5/8) Next door to Sol y Mar, Jennifer is also good.

Casa del Manglar (☎ 06-731-464; r with shared/private bath per person US$6/7) The bamboo-walled Manglar, near the footbridge, rents clean but miniscule rooms with bath.

Hotel El Tiburon (☎ 06-731-145/622; antonia_tiburon@hotmail.com; Malecón; low/high season per person US$5/10; ℗) A large, clean hotel smack in the center of the *malecón*. Rooms have TV, bath and fan. It has a popular restaurant.

Hotel Villa Hermosa (☎ 06-731-547; r per person US$4-6) Behind El Tiburon, this place is better.

Eating

Restaurants near the beach all serve the same thing – the morning catch.

La Cena (Malecón; mains US$2-4) Serving good, cheap *almuerzos* (US$1.50) and inexpensive seafood dishes.

Walfredo's (Calle Principal) For a seafood selection as giant as its open-air dining area, try this place (the street is parallel to and behind the *malecón*).

Pizzería No Name (Malecón; pizzas US$4-12) The place for pizza.

Getting There & Away

There are regular buses to Esmeraldas (US$0.70, one hour), as well as south to Súa (US$0.50, 10 minutes), Same and Muisne (US$1, 1½ hours). Transportes Occidentales and Aerotaxi, whose offices are near the highway, both go daily to Quito (US$8, six to seven hours).

SÚA

This friendly fishing village, 6km west of Atacames, is far more tranquil than its party-town neighbor. It's a good place to kick the feet up in the sun and swim in the mellow bay.

Lodgings here are fewer than in Atacames, but they're also quieter and often better value if you aren't looking for nightlife. **Hotel Chagra Ramos** (☎ 06-731-006; r per person US$6-8) has a good, inexpensive restaurant, a little beach and nice views. **Hotel El Peñón de Súa** (☎ 06-731-013; r per person US$5) isn't on the beach but has nice rooms with bath. At the ramshackle but friendly **Las Acacias** (☎ 06-731-021; tent-pitch US$2, cabin per person US$6), you can pitch a tent in its sandy yard or sleep in a cabin. On the beach, **Hotel Bouganvilla** (☎ 06-731-008; r per person US$7) has cheery rooms with private bath.

SAME & TONCHIGÜE

The small village of Same (*sah*-may) is a small beach resort about 6km southwest of Súa, but its hotels are pricier. **Azuca** (☎ 06-733-343; Entrada Las Canoas, Carretera), on the highway, is the cheapest place in town. It's an eclectic, artsy, Colombian-owned place with just a few rooms over a good restaurant.

About 3km past Same, Tonchigüe is a tiny fishing village whose beach is a continuation of the Same beach. **Playa Escondida** (☎ 09-973-3368; campsites per person US$5, r per person US$8-12) is 3km west of Tonchigüe and 10km down the road to Punta Galeras. It's an isolated, quiet, beautiful spot, run by a Canadian named Judy. It has a restaurant and lots of empty, hidden beach.

MUISNE

An hour from Atacames by bus, Muisne has a long, wide, usually empty beach backed by a few sandy little hotels and simple restaurants. Most of the town is on an island, separated from the mainland by the Río Muisne. Buses stop at the dock at the end of the road from Esmeraldas, where boats (US$0.15) cross the river to the town. On the island, the main road heads from the dock through the 'center' of town and crumbles slowly away to the beach, 1.5km away. Hire an 'ecotaxi' (tricycle) for a ride to the beach if you're feeling lazy.

Hotels Playa Paraíso and Calade (see Sleeping & Eating, below) both offer boat trips into the area's remaining mangroves and to the nearby isolated beach of **Mompiche**, where there is world-class surf (during big swells only).

Sleeping & Eating

The beach is the reason to be here, so head straight for the sand. When you hit it, hang a left for the two best hotels.

Playa Paraíso (☎ 06-480-192; r per person US$4) Rustic, wooden and extremely friendly this place rents small rooms with shared baths and mosquito nets. It has a good restaurant and a bar, and you can pitch a tent on the grass for US$2.

Hotel Calade (☎ 06-480-279) Just up the beach, Italian-owned Calade is also good.

Many of the restaurants scattered along the beach serve *encocado* (seafood cooked in a savory coconut sauce); it's usually excellent.

Getting There & Away

La Costeñita runs hourly buses to Esmeraldas (US$1.50, 2½ hours) via Atacames. Transportes Occidentales has night buses to Quito (US$8, eight hours). There are regular departures for the junction known as El Salto, where buses stop en route to Pedernales (with connections inland and south). Five buses head daily to Santo Domingo de los Colorados, with connections to Quito and Guayaquil. Buses leave regularly for Daule.

SOUTH OF MUISNE

The northernmost point of Manabí Province is the quiet, isolated town of **Cojimíes**, which is reached either by boat from **Daule** or by bus from the south. The easiest way to work south from Muisne, however, is by bussing to **El Salto** (a road junction) and then grabbing a passing bus to **Pedernales**. Between El Salto and Pedernales, you sometimes have to change buses in **San José de Chamanga** (you'll recognize Chamanga by the floating piles of garbage and stilted houses). Pedernales has connections further south and into the highlands. It also has an unsightly but locally popular beach and several cheap hotels. On the way to Canoa, you'll pass **Jama**, which has a basic *pensión*.

CANOA

Friendly little Canoa sits on the edge of one of the coast's widest beaches, perhaps the best along this stretch. **Caves** at the northern end of the beach can be reached at low tide.

Hotel Bambu (☎ 05-616-370; www.ecuadorexplorer .com/bambu; tent-pitch US$2, s/d with shared bath US$7/10, with private bath US$12/14, with private bath & balcony US$15/18) The Dutch-owned Bambu rents spotless, cottagelike rooms on the beach. The grounds are scattered with hammocks, the restaurant is excellent and surfboards are available for about US$6 per hour.

Posada de Daniel (☎ 05-616-373; posadadedaniel@ hotmail.com; cabañas per person low/high season US$6/9) Three blocks inland, has spacious cabins around a clean swimming pool.

Hostal Shelmar (☎ 05-674-476; r with shared/private bath per person US$2/4) Two blocks off the beach, rents comfortable, basic rooms with fan and mosquito net.

Restaurante Torbellino, three blocks up from the beach, serves excellent seafood and delicious US$1 *almuerzos*.

Arenabar (Malecón; pizzas US$2-3) Serves good pizza and has dancing on Saturday nights.

SAN VICENTE

This busy town is a short ferry ride across the Río Chone from the more popular resort of Bahía de Caráquez. Most travelers stop only for bus connections or to catch the ferry to Bahía.

Hostal San Vicente (☎ 05-674-182; r per person US$4-5) Basic but expansive rooms with private bath. Several fancier hotels with decent restaurants are nearby.

Buses leave from the market area near the pier. Costa del Norte offers hourly service to Pedernales (three hours), as well as one or two buses a day to Cojimíes. Coactur runs buses to Manta, Portoviejo and Guayaquil daily. Launches to Bahía de Caráquez (US$0.20, 10 minutes) leave often from the pier between 6am and 10pm. A car ferry takes passengers for free.

BAHÍA DE CARÁQUEZ

Thanks to the white, high-rise vacation condos climbing out of the town center, this resort town (popular with wealthy Ecuadorians) looks bigger than it actually is. The town was devastated by a massive earthquake in 1998, and in 1999 it declared itself an 'eco-city.' The town market may be the only one in Ecuador that recycles its waste. There are several interesting eco and cultural tours worth checking out, but if you're after beaches you'll have to head elsewhere. There's a decent one about 500m north of the center on Av Montúfar.

Orientation & Information

The town is on a small peninsula only four blocks wide at its narrowest, northern point. Ferries from San Vicente cross the Río Chone and dock at the piers along Malecón Alberto Santos, on the peninsula's eastern side. Most services are on and around the *malecón* and the parallel street of Bolívar, one block west.

Genesis Net (Malecón Alberto Santos 1302; US$2 per hr) offers Internet access. **Banco de Guayaquil**

(Bolívar & Riofrío) cashes traveler's checks and has an ATM.

Tours

Tours in Bahía are unique. The two operators listed here devote themselves to ecotourism and will show you local environmental projects and take you to handmade-paper cooperatives. Both companies offer day trips to Islas Fragatas in the Chone estuary. **Guacamayo Bahíatours** (☎ 05-691-107/412; www.riomuchacho.com; cnr Bolívar & Arenas) also arranges stays at nearby Río Muchacho Organic Farm. **Bahía Dolphin Tours** (☎ 05-692-097/86/88; www.bahiadolphin.com; Bolívar 1004) offers visits to its nearby archaeological site.

Sleeping

The cheapest places have water-supply problems.

Bahía B&B (☎ 05-690-146; Ascázubi 322; r with shared/private bath per person US$4/7) A decent choice for the price, with a friendly staff and an English- and French-speaking owner. Breakfast is included.

Bahía Hotel (☎ 05-690-509; Malecón Alberto Santos at Vinueza; r without/with TV per person US$7/9) Forty clean, straightforward rooms with firm beds, private bath, fan and, if you want, TV.

Other cheapies include:

Residencia Vera (☎ 05-691-581; Ante 212 near Bolívar; r per person US$3) Fair value, shared baths.

Hotel Palma (☎ 05-690-467; Bolívar 910; r per person US$2) Basic, but fine for a night.

Hostal Los Andes (☎ 05-690-587; Ascázubi; d US$3) Thin-walled dump, but cheap.

Eating

Several restaurants line the waterfront near the pier. The best are **La Chozita** (Malecón Alberto Santos; mains US$3-6) and **Muelle Uno** (Malecón Alberto Santos; mains US$4-6). Both do grilled meat and fish.

Colombiu's (Bolívar near Ante) Serves good, filling *almuerzos* for US$1.30 and tasty plates of seafood for under US$4.

Picantería la Patineta (Ascázubi near Malecón Alberto Santos; soup US$0.80; ☻ 8:30am-12:30pm) Serves delicious *encebollado*, a seafood, yucca and onion soup garnished with *chifles* (crispy banana slices). It's a breakfast tradition (and it's cheap!).

Rincón Manabita (cnr Malecón Alberto Santos & Aguilera) The place to go for grilled chicken (evening only).

Getting There & Away

For boat information, see San Vicente (p682). Coactur buses serve Portoviejo (US$1.50, two hours) and Manta (US$2.20, 2½ hours) every hour. Reina del Camino runs buses to Portoviejo, Quito (US$6 to US$8, eight hours), Esmeraldas (US$6, eight hours), Santo Domingo (US$4, four hours) and Guayaquil (US$4.50 to US$6, six hours). Buses stop at the southern end of Malecón Alberto Santos, near the Bahía Hotel.

MONTECRISTI

Montecristi is known throughout the world for producing the finest straw hat on the planet, the 'Montecristi,' better known as – and mistakenly labeled – the **panama hat**. In Ecuador they're called *sombreros de paja toquilla* (hats made of *toquilla* straw, a fine fibrous straw endemic to the region). Countless places in town sell hats, but for a proper *super-fino* (the finest, most tightly woven hat of all) visit the shop and home of **José Chávez Franco** (☎ 05-606-343; Rocafuerte 386), behind the church. You can pick up a beauty for less than US$100, cheaper than just about anywhere else in the world.

Montecristi is 15 minutes by bus from Manta (US$0.25). It has no hotels and only a couple of basic restaurants.

MANTA

Despite its popularity among Ecuadorian tourists, foreign travelers tend to zip through Manta on their search for quieter and cleaner beaches. Sure Manta's not the place for empty, paradisiacal beaches, but it's an interesting place to soak up the atmosphere of a relatively safe and always busy Ecuadorian port city. Manta has a strong seafaring tradition, and giant wooden fishing boats are still built by hand on Tarqui beach. Nearby, fishing crews drag their daily catches onto the sand each morning, turning the beach into a bustling, impromptu fish market with lots of chatter, barter and standing around in the sun.

Manta (population 183,000) is named after the Manta culture (AD 500 to 1550), known for its pottery and navigational skills. The Mantas sailed to Central America, Peru and possibly the Galápagos. Traditional balsa sailing rafts are still seen along the coast.

Orientation

A stinky inlet divides the town into Manta (west side) and Tarqui (east side); the two sides are joined by a vehicle bridge. Manta has the main offices, shopping areas and bus terminal, while Tarqui has the cheaper hotels.

The airport is 3km east of Tarqui, and the bus terminal, conveniently, is in Manta, one block off the *malecón*.

Information

Get online at **Publicomp** (Av 3 245; US$0.70 per hr) or **Manta Cyber Café** (Av 1 near Calle 14). The **post office** (Calle 8) is at the town hall, and **Pacifictel** (Malecón de Manta) is on the Manta waterfront.

Change traveler's checks at **Banco del Pacífico** (cnr Av 2 & Calle 13) or **Banco del Pichincha** (Av 2 at Calle 11); both have ATMs. There's also a **Banco del Pacífico ATM** (cnr Av 107 & Calle 103) in Tarqui.

The friendly **municipal tourist office** (☎ 05-611-471/79; Calle 9, Municipio) is below the town hall.

Sights

The clean, wide **Playa Murciélago**, 2km west of Manta's center, is popular with residents and Ecuadorian tourists. **Tarqui beach** is less picturesque, but it's interesting in the early morning when fisherfolk haul their catches ashore in front of the boat-building area.

The **Museo del Banco Central** (admission US$1, free Sun; 🕙 9am-5pm Mon-Sat, 11am-3pm Sun), near the bus terminal, houses a small but interesting exhibit on the Manta culture.

Sleeping

Prices rise during holiday weekends and the December-to-March and June-to-August high seasons, when single rooms are hard to find.

Hotel Panorama Inn (☎ 05-611-552; Calle 103; r per person US$6-12; 🖳 🖳) Bare-bones but spacious rooms have private baths, TV and large windows. Drab, yes, but it's a good deal. Pricier rooms have air-conditioning.

Boulevard Hotel (☎ 05-625-333/627; Calle 103; s/d US$6/12) Rooms run the gamut from decent to dismal. All have baths. Choose carefully.

Hotel Miami (☎ 05-611-743; cnr Malecón de Tarqui & Calle 108; s/d US$4/8) Quirky old wooden place near the beach with tolerable rooms with

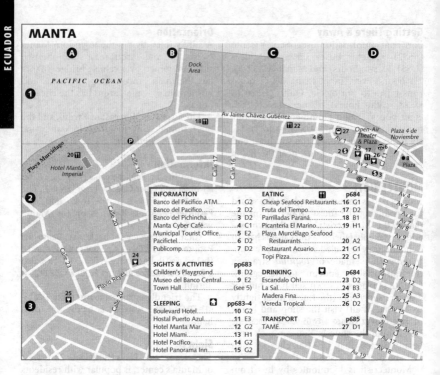

MANTA

INFORMATION
Banco del Pacífico ATM	1 G2
Banco del Pacífico	2 D2
Banco del Pichincha	3 D2
Manta Cyber Café	4 C1
Municipal Tourist Office	5 E2
Pacifictel	6 D2
Publicomp	7 D2

SIGHTS & ACTIVITIES pp683
Children's Playground	8 D2
Museo del Banco Central	9 E2
Town Hall	(see 5)

SLEEPING pp683–4
Boulevard Hotel	10 G2
Hostal Puerto Azul	11 E3
Hotel Manta Mar	12 G2
Hotel Miami	13 H1
Hotel Pacífico	14 G2
Hotel Panorama Inn	15 G2

EATING p684
Cheap Seafood Restaurants	16 G1
Fruta del Tiempo	17 D2
Parrilladas Paraná	18 B1
Picantería El Marino	19 H1
Playa Murciélago Seafood Restaurants	20 A2
Restaurant Acuario	21 G1
Topi Pizza	22 C1

DRINKING p684
Escandalo Oh!	23 D2
La Sal	24 B3
Madera Fina	25 A3
Vereda Tropical	26 D2

TRANSPORT p685
TAME	27 D1

TV and bath. It's pretty basic, but has an alluring nostalgia.

Hotel Pacífico (☎ 05-623-584, 05-622-475; Av 106; s with fan US$10, d with fan/air-con US$15/20; ❄) White monstrosity near the river with appealing rooms (avoid the noisy ones facing the river) and only a shell's throw from Tarqui beach (not the best beach, but still the beach).

Hotel Puerto Azul (☎ 05-623-167; 24 de Mayo; s with shared bath US$6, d with bath & fan/air-con US$20/30; ❄) Clean, carpeted, no-frills rooms. Next to the bus terminal.

Hotel Manta Mar (☎ 05-624-670; Malecón de Tarqui; s/d US$5/7) Good deal if you get a window.

Eating

Cheap outdoor seafood restaurants line the eastern end of Tarqui beach. The Playa Murciélago seafood restaurants are newer but still cheap.

Restaurant Acuario (mains US$5-9) At the far end of Playa Murciélago it's one of the best (and priciest). Its sand floor, thatch umbrellas and maritime bric-a-brac make for excellent atmosphere, and the portions are massive.

Picantería El Marino (Malecón Tarqui & Calle 110; ⏰ 8am-5pm) Serves good seafood and has a salty-dog, seafaring feel.

Fruta del Tiempo (cnr Av 1 & Calle 12; mains US$1-3) Pop in for filling, cheap *almuerzos*, fruit juices, shakes and ice cream.

Topi Pizza (Malecón de Manta; mains US$3-6) Bakes good pizza and other Italian dishes.

Parrilladas Paraná (Malecón de Manta at Calle 17; mains US$3-6) Grills delicious meats.

Drinking

The epicenter of Manta's nightlife is the intersection of Flavio Reyes and Calle 20, uphill from Playa Murciélago.

La Sal (Flavio Reyes & Calle 20; admission US$3-8) Folks swear by this for disco.

Madera Fina (Flavio Reyes near Calle 23) A more tropical feel (both inside and out), favoring salsa, reggae and tropical rhythms.

If you're not too musically selective and want something that's closer to Tarqui, then try **Escandalo Oh!** (Calle 12) or **Vereda Tropical** (Av 1).

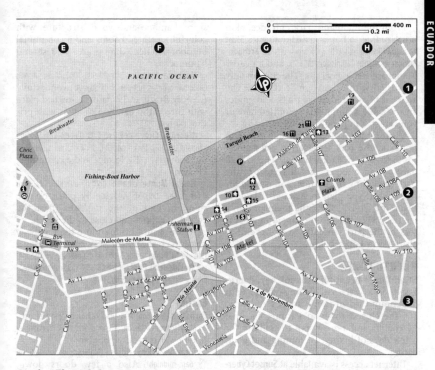

Getting There & Away

TAME (☎ 05-622-006, 05-613-210; Malecón de Manta) flies daily to Quito (US$50).

Buses depart frequently to Portoviejo (US$0.70, 40 minutes), Guayaquil (US$4.50, four hours), Quito (US$8, nine hours) and Bahía de Caráquez. Three companies depart frequently to Puerto López (US$2.40, 2½ hours) and Montañita (US$4.70, 3½ hours). Coactur goes regularly to Pedernales (US$4.60, seven hours) and Canoa. Most other major destinations are served regularly.

PARQUE NACIONAL MACHALILLA

Ecuador's only coastal **national park** (admission US$20) preserves isolated beaches, coral formations, two offshore islands, unusual tropical dry forest, coastal cloud forest, several archaeological sites and 20,000 hectares of ocean. In other words, it's time for some fun.

The tropical dry forest seen here used to stretch along much of the Pacific coast of Central and South America, but it has been whacked nearly into extinction. Plants in the park include cacti, various figs and the giant kapok tree. Parrots, parrotlets and parakeets inhabit the forest interior, while the coastal edges are home to frigate birds, pelicans and boobies, some of which nest in colonies on the offshore islands.

The beautiful beach of **Playa Los Frailes** is about 10km north of Puerto López, just before the town of Machalilla. Buses stop in front of the ranger station, from where a 3km road and a 4km trail lead to the beach. The swimming is good, seabirds are plentiful and camping is allowed.

The barren, sun-charred **Isla de la Plata**, an island 40km northwest of Puerto López, is a highlight of the park, especially from mid-June to mid-October when humpback whales mate offshore and sightings from tour boats (arranged in Puerto López, p686) are practically guaranteed. The island itself hosts nesting seabird colonies, and a short hike is usually included in the whale-watching tours. Outside whale season, you may see dolphins. It takes two to three hours to reach the island. Camping is not permitted.

From the mainland park entrance, 6km north of Puerto López, a dirt road goes 5km to **Agua Blanca**, a little village with an **archaeological museum** (admission US$1.25) and a nearby Manta archaeological site. The site can only be visited with a local guide (US$3). The area has hiking and horse trails, and guides are available. Camping is permitted here or you can stay in people's homes.

Visitor information is available in Puerto López at the **park headquarters and museum** (☎ 05-604-170; ☉ 8am-5pm Mon-Fri). The US$20 park entrance fee covers all sectors of the park (including the islands) and is valid for five days. If you plan to visit *only* Isla de la Plata, the fee is US$15; the mainland-only fee is US$12. The fee is charged in all sectors of the park, so carry your ticket. See also Puerto López below.

PUERTO LÓPEZ

Straddling a beautiful fishhook bay, Puerto López is a dirt-road fishing village with a booming down-home tourist industry. It's the closest town to Parque Nacional Machalilla and a great spot to chill out for a few days of hiking, swimming and good eating.

Internet access is available at **Sunset Cybercafé** (General Córdova; US$2 per hr). There's no ATM in town, but **Banco del Pichincha** (cnr Machalilla & Córdova) changes traveler's checks and gives cash advances on Visa.

Tours

Numerous outfits offer trips to Isla de la Plata and/or tours of the mainland area of the park. Most agencies charge US$30 per person (not including the park entrance fee) for a trip to the island and seasonal whale watching. Licensed companies have better boats and more equipment (such as life jackets, radio and backup) than the unlicensed guides, who offer the trip for nearly half the price. Companies with good reputations include **Exploratur** (☎ 05-604-123; Malecón) and **Mantaraya Travel** (☎ 05-604-233; Malecón), which also rent diving equipment and offer diving trips to certified divers.

Sleeping

Sol Inn (Juan Montalvo near Eloy Alfaro; r with shared/private bath per person US$3/4) Definitely has a *buena onda* (good vibe) thanks to its young and friendly owners. It's an attractive two-

story bamboo-and-wood structure with colorfully painted rooms and a communal outdoor kitchen, dining area and several hammocks.

Hostería Itapoá (☎ 09-984-3042; Calle Abdón Calderón; cabañas per person US$5) A wonderfully friendly Brazilian/Ecuadorian-owned place with three little bamboo *cabañas* with private baths.

Albergue Cueva del Oso (☎ 05-604-124; Lascano 116; s/d US$4/8) Part of the IYH chain, it has hot showers, a TV lounge and a communal kitchen.

Hostal Monte Libano (☎ 05-601-850; Malecón; r per person US$3-5) A friendly place on the southern end of the *malecón* (past the creek). It's quiet and close to the beach.

If you want nothing more than a cheap place to crash, try the very basic **Residencial Isla de la Plata** (☎ 05-604-114; Córdova; s/d US$2/4) or **Residencial Paola** (☎ 05-604-162; r with shared/private bath per person US$2/3).

Eating

Carmita's (Malecón) A good, cheap restaurant.

Mayflower (Malecón) Next door to Carmita's, Mayflower is locally popular.

Picantería Rey Hojas (Malecón; mains US$2-4; ☉ 6am-midnight) Also a few doors down, has outdoor tables, longer hours (good for breakfast before you head out whale watching) and lots of seafood.

Café Bellena/The Whale Café (Malecón) Serves great breakfasts (the apple-cinnamon pancakes are divine), sublime desserts and pizzas and vegetarian meals.

Bellitalia (☉ from 6pm) In a private house a few blocks north of the center, serves delicious Italian dinners in an enchanting candlelit garden environment.

Getting There & Away

Transportes Carlos A Aray has direct buses (one in the morning, one in the evening) to Quito (US$5, 11 hours). It also has the only direct bus from Quito, a night bus. Buses to Jipijapa can drop you at the national park entrance and at other coastal points. Hourly buses head south to Santa Elena and can drop you at points along the way.

SOUTH OF PUERTO LÓPEZ

About 14km south of Puerto López (right after the village of Puerto Rico), **Hostería Alándaluz** (☎ 04-278-0690, in Quito ☎ 02-254-3042;

info@alandaluz.com; campsites with/without tent US$3/4, s/d with shared bath US$16/26, with private bath US$26/36, beach cabins US$30/46) is one of Ecuador's very first self-sustaining, low-impact resorts. It's Ecuadorian-run and built from fast-growing (and easily replaceable) local bamboo and palm leaves. You can bask on the undisturbed nearby beach, ride horses, play volleyball or just hang out – the atmosphere is very relaxed. Meals are provided at reasonable prices.

The next village south (blink and you'll miss it) is **Las Tunas**. The beach here is long, wide and empty. You'll know you're in Las Tunas when you spot the grounded bow of a giant wooden boat, which is actually the restaurant-half of a hotel built by an inspired Swiss expat. It's appropriately called **La Barquita** (☎ 04-278-0051; barquita2000@yahoo.com; dm US$6, d/tr US$24/30) and has clean, comfortable doubles with hammocks out front and a few nice *cabañas* and dorm beds for budget travelers.

Sandwiched between verdant tropical hills and another long, wide beach, the sandy little village of **Ayampe** is about 17km south of Puerto López, right on the Guayas–Manabí provincial line. Of the three excellent hotels here, the tiny, delightful **Cabañas de la Iguana** (☎ 04-278-0605; www.designalltag.com /ayampe; r with shared/private bath per person US$6/8) is the cheapest.

The next coastal village is **Olón**, which has a nice beach, a cheap *pensión* and a pricey hotel.

MONTAÑITA

Blessed with the country's best surf – and more budget hotels than you can shake your board at – Montañita means bare feet, banana pancakes, surf and scene. Some dig it, others despise it. It's growing but still friendly, and prices rise with the surf. Several shops in town rent boards.

Hotels in the village are cheaper than those along the beach toward 'La Punta' (The Point). Definitely book a room in advance if you're coming in December or January. Hotel-hopping is easy here, so check out a few before deciding.

La Casa Blanca (☎ 04-290-1340; lacasablanca@ hotmail.com; r low/high season per person US$5/10) In town, Blanca has three floors of rustic, cane-wall doubles with balconies, hammocks and baths.

Cabañas Tsunami (☎ 09-714-7344; r with shared/ private bath per person US$8/10, low-season US$3/4) Next door to La Casa Blanca, Tsunami is slightly cramped but similar.

Cabañas Pakaloro (☎ 04-290-1366; low/high season per person US$5/6) Behind La Casa Blanca, Pakaloro is a masterfully crafted, two-story, wooden place with immaculate rooms, blazing-hot showers, firm beds, mosquito nets and individual terraces.

El Centro del Mundo (dm US$5, r with shared/private bath per person US$6/8) Also in town, the main attractions of this place are its small communal balconies facing the ocean and the pool table; prices are halved in the low season. The 20-mattress dorm area is dismal.

Hostal D' Lucho (Calle Principal; r per person US$5, low season US$2-3) A tin-roof dump, but it's the cheapest in town.

Hotel Brisas Marina (r low/high season US$7/15) Just south of Calle Principal, it has paper-thin walls but a great little balcony right over the seawall.

Hostal de Ricky (☎ 04-290-1363; s/d US$7/14, low season US$4/8) Owned by a pair of surfers, Ricky is a friendly place near the main road.

Restaurants are plentiful; stroll around and take your pick.

MANGLARALTO

Walk 4km down the beach from Montañita (or take the bus) and you hit Manglaralto, a small town on a wide-open beach. There are a few basic hotels and restaurants in town. Just north of town on the beach, **Kamala Hostería** (☎ 09-942-3754; kamalahosteria@hotmail.com; dm US$10, private cabaña per person US$20) is an easygoing beachside *hostería* owned by four backpackers looking to let their guests relax. PADI dive courses, horse riding and day tours are offered, and dinner is included in the rate. Monthly full-moon parties too!

Fundación Pro Pueblo (☎ 04-290-1208/1195/1114/ 1343; propueble1@propueblo.org.ec) arranges stays with families in local villages at about US$8 per day, including all meals. Pro Pueblo is a nonprofit organization promoting sustainable development, local artisans and handicrafts and responsible tourism.

South of Manglaralto, **Valdivia** is home to Ecuador's oldest archaeological site.

SANTA ELENA & LA LIBERTAD

If you're heading south to Guayaquil, you'll have to change buses in one of these two cities.

Go for Santa Elena – the driver will drop you where the road forks; cross the street and flag a bus on the other fork. Otherwise deal with the ugly, dusty, busy port of La Libertad. There, buses for Guayaquil (US$2, 2½ hours) leave from several places along 9 de Octubre. Buses going north along the coast leave from the market on Guayaquil.

PLAYAS

The nearest beach resort to Guayaquil, Playas is slammed from January to April, when prices rise, tents and litter adorn the beach, discos thump into the night and the open-air seafood restaurants (half the fun of Playas) are packed all day. It's almost deserted at other times.

There's some good **surf** around Playas; get information at the local surf club **Playas Club Surf** (☎ 09-725-9056; cnr Paquisha & Av 7) at Restaurant Jalisco. Friendly club president, Juan Gutierrez, can turn you on to the local breaks (or take you water skiing).

The cheapest hotels have brackish running water. **Residencial El Galeón** (☎ 04-276-0270; cnr Guayaquil & A Garay; r with shared/private bath per person US$4/5), one block east of the central plaza, is clean and friendly, and has a good, cheap restaurant.

For something closer to the beach, **Hotel Brisas del Pacífico** (☎ 04-276-1730/31; s/d US$10/20), on the east side of town, is one of the best deals.

Transportes Villamil runs buses to Guayaquil (US$1.90, 1¾ hours) every half-hour.

GUAYAQUIL

Ecuador's largest city (population 2,117,553) is wrestling its reputation as a sweltering, dangerous port town and standing it on its hot head. The city has transformed the once dangerous waterfront along the wide Río Guayas into a 2.5km outdoor architectural showpiece. The historical neighborhood of Las Peñas, as well as Guayaquil's principal downtown thoroughfare, Calle 9 de Octubre, have also been restored. These areas, as well as the city's downtown parks, plazas and museums, are safe and fun to explore.

Sure, Guayaquil is still an oppressively hot, noisy and chaotic city, but *guayacos* (people from Guayaquil) are damn proud of the place (and of themselves), and it's well worth hanging out for a while to fig-

GETTING INTO TOWN

The main airport is on Av de las Américas, 5km north of the center, and the bus terminal is 2km north of the airport. A taxi to the center should cost about US$4 from either, provided you cross Av de las Américas (rather than hailing one from inside) and bargain. From the bus terminal, buses run down Av de las Américas past the airport to the center; No 71 is a good one to take.

ure out why. If you're not enamored of big cities, however, you won't like this one.

All flights to the Galápagos either stop or originate in Guayaquil. Subsequently, it's the next best place (after Quito) to set up a trip to the islands.

Orientation

The city center is an easily navigable grid, with Malecón Simón Bolívar and the Río Guayas on its eastern side. The relatively subdued northern suburbs of Los Sauces, La Garzota, Alborada and Kennedy are closer (and more convenient) to the airport and bus terminal. The northern burbs have few hotels, although many travelers hunker down in the ones that do exist to avoid the chaos of downtown. The northwestern suburb of Urdesa is home to Calle VE Estrada, Guayaquil's Champs-Élysées, where you'll find countless restaurants, bars and stores.

For regional topographical maps, go to the **Instituto Geográfico Militar** (Map pp690-1; IGM; ☎ 04-239-3351; Quito & Padre Solano).

Information
BOOKSHOPS

A small selection of English-language travel guides are available at **Librería Científica** (Map pp690-1; Luque 225).

INTERNET ACCESS

The following cybercafés charge about US$1 per hour.

American Cyber (Map p692; Oxandaberro near Isidro Ayora, Alborada)

Cyber@City (Map pp690-1; Unicentro Shopping Center, Ballén near Chile)

Cyberin@Net (Map p692; off Av Guillermo Pareja Rolando) A few blocks south of Garzocentro Shopping Center, La Garzota.

CyberTek (Map pp690-1; cnr 9 de Octubre & Chimborazo)

SCI Cyber Center (Map pp690-1; cnr Chile & Ballén)

ECUADOR

MEDICAL SERVICES

The best hospital is **Clínica Kennedy** (☎ 04-228-6963/9666; Av del Periodista) in the northwest suburb of Nueva Kennedy.

MONEY

The following banks change traveler's checks and have ATMs.

Banco de Guayaquil (Map pp690-1; cnr Rendón & Panamá)

Banco del Pacífico Paula de Icaza 200 (Map pp690-1); 9 de Octubre (Map pp690-1; cnr Ejército); Plaza Mayor Shopping Center (Map p692; RB Nazur near JM Egas, Los Sauces)

POST & TELEPHONE

There's a main **post office** (Carbo near Aguirre) and **Pacifictel** (Map pp690-1; Chile) is around the block. There's also a **Pacifictel branch** (Map p692; Av José María Egas) in Alborada/Los Sauces.

For information on Guayas Province's new seven-digit telephone numbers, see Telephone in the Directory chapter (p713).

TOURIST-CARD EXTENSIONS

T-3 tourist-card extensions are available from the **immigration office** (☎ 04-229 7002/4; Av de las Américas), across from the bus terminal.

TOURIST OFFICES

The friendly **Dirección Municipal de Turismo** (Map pp690-1; ☎ 04-252-4100; dturgye@telconet.net; www.guayaquil.gov.ec in Spanish; Malecón Simón Bolívar & 10 de Agosto) is in the Palacio Municipal. The **Subsecretario de Turismo Litoral** (Map pp690-1; ☎ 04-256-8764; infotour@telconet.net; Paula de Icaza 203, 6th fl) provides information about coastal attractions of Guayas and Manabí Provinces.

TRAVEL AGENCIES

The agencies listed here arrange affordable Galápagos trips.

Dreamkapture Travel (Map p692; ☎ 04-224-2909; www.dreamkapture.com; Alborada 12a etapa, Benjamín Carrión at Francisco Orellana) French-Canadian owned.

Galápagos Sub-Aqua (Map pp690-1; ☎ 04-230-5514; Orellana 211 & Panamá, Office 402) Highly recommended Galápagos scuba-diving operator.

Galasam Tours (Map pp690-1; ☎ 04- 230-4488; www.galapagos-islands.com; 9 de Octubre 424, Office 9A) Great deals; bargain hard. Some complaints.

Dangers & Annoyances

The downtown area is fine during the day, but sketchy after dark. The Malecón and the main stairway up Cerro Santa Ana are

perfectly safe, even at night. Watch your belongings in the bus terminal and in the Bahía street market.

Sights

MALECÓN 2000   Map pp690–1

If you've just arrived and you're frazzled and sweaty, get down to the newly reconstructed **waterfront promenade** (⏱ 7am-midnight) and take in the breeze blowing (if you're lucky) off the wide Río Guayas. Known as Malecón 2000, the waterfront is Guayaquil's flagship redevelopment project, stretching 2.5km along the river, from the **Mercado Sur** at the southern end to Cerro Santa Ana and Las Peñas (see below) to the north. The area is heavily policed and completely safe, even at night (which is when it's most pleasant).

Just north of the Mercado Sur, in the area bound by Olmedo, Chile, Colón and the waterfront, is the crowded and colorful street market **La Bahía**, a fascinating area to explore (but watch for pickpockets).

Calle 9 de Octubre is Guayaquil's principal downtown street and oh what a feeling to bounce among the hordes of business people, junk sellers and newspaper vendors beneath some of the city's more austere buildings. The street meets the Malecón at the impressive **La Rotonda** monument. Further north is the new **Museo Antropológico y de Arte Contemporáneo** (MAAC; Malecón at Loja), a museum of anthropology, archaeology and contemporary art (planned to open in stages beginning in late 2003). MAAC also has a 400-seat noncommercial art cinema, an open-air stage and an indoor fast-food patio.

LAS PEÑAS & CERRO SANTA ANA   Map pp690–1

At the northern end of the Malecón, to the right of the stairs leading up Cerro Santa Ana, the historic cobbled street of Calle Numa Pompillo Llon winds past elegantly decaying wooden colonial houses propped half-heartedly on bamboo supports. Many of the houses over the river are art galleries – peek in, if only to check out the architecture.

The stairway winding up Cerro Santa Ana past the brightly painted buildings is quite touristy, but views from the hilltop fort (called **Fortín del Cerro**) and the **lighthouse** are wonderful.

ECUADOR

GUAYAQUIL – CITY CENTER

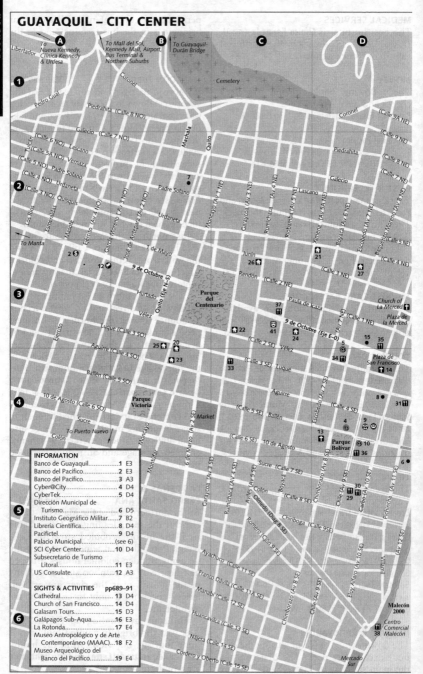

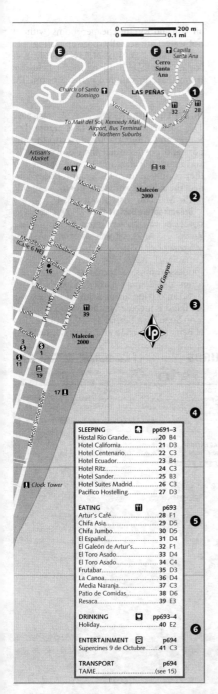

DOWNTOWN AREA   **Map pp690–1**

Dinosaurian iguanas roam around the handsome, tree-filled Parque Bolívar (also called Parque Seminario) and stare down small children for their snacks. They're an odd sight. The modern cathedral is on the plaza's western side.

Guayaquil's biggest plaza, **Parque del Centenario**, covers four blocks, is full of monuments and marks the center of the city. The city's most impressive church is the **Church of San Francisco**, which has been reconstructed and beautifully restored since the devastating 1896 fire.

The **Museo Arqueológico del Banco del Pacífico** (Paula de Icaza 113; admission free; ⊙ 9am-6pm Tue-Fri, 11am-1pm Sat & Sun) houses ceramics and other artifacts documenting the development of Ecuadorian cultures from 3000 BC to AD 1500.

CITY CEMETERY   **Map pp690–1**

This dazzling-white hillside **cemetery** (Moncayo & Coronel), with hundreds of tombs, monuments and huge mausoleums, is a Goth's wet dream. A walk through the palm trees leads to the impressive grave of President Vicente Rocafuerte. The cemetery is best reached with a short cab ride.

Festivals & Events

The whole city parties during the last week of July, celebrating Simón Bolívar's birthday (July 24) and Guayaquil Foundation Day (July 25). Hotels may be full then and banks and other services are also disrupted. Another important local holiday period comes in October, with Guayaquil's Independence Day (October 9) and Día de la Raza (October 12). New Year's Eve is celebrated with bonfires.

Sleeping

Few single rooms are available during festivals, and budget hotels are generally poor and fairly pricey.

CITY CENTER   **Map pp690–1**

Hotel Sander (☎ 04-232-0030/944; Luque 1101; r with fan/air-con per person US$9/11; ✳) One of the best budget options downtown it's a big place with plain but pleasant rooms, tiled floors, private baths and TV.

Hotel Ecuador (☎ 04-232-1460; Moncayo 1117; s/d US$8.50/10; ✳) Decent place for basic rooms with cramped baths, fan and TV. Dark interior rooms are slightly quieter and cheaper than the brighter outside rooms. A few have air-con.

Pacífico Hostelling (☎ 04-256-8093, 04-230-2077; Escobedo 811; s/d US$9; 🛇) This hotel doesn't belong to a hostel chain but does provide good clean rooms with firm beds, bath, TV and fan. Some have air-con for the same price.

Hostal Río Grande (☎ 04-251-8972; Luque 1035; interior s/d US$12/14, d with window US$15) Gloomy, but the rooms are clean and have air-con, cable TV and bath.

Hotel Suites Madrid (☎ 04-230-7804, 04-231-4992; Quisquis 305; s with fan/air-con US$10/12, d US$12/15; 🛇) Some rooms are dark and cramped, but overall it's fair value. Rooms have hot showers and TV.

Hotel Centenario (☎ 04-252-4467; Garaycoa 931; r US$12) Rooms vary – some have fans and others have air-con; most have TVs and telephones.

Hotel California (☎ 04-230-2538; Urdaneta 529; d with cold water/hot water US$18/24) Big friendly place with adequate rooms, private baths,

air-con and TV; the cheaper rooms (without hot water) are actually more appealing.

Hotel Ritz (☎ 04-253-0120, 04-251-6610; 9 de Octubre 709; s/d US$19/22) Bland soccer-field-size rooms have private hot baths, air-con, TV and telephone.

NORTHERN SUBURBS   Map p692
The northern suburbs of La Garzota, Los Sauces and Alborada are closer to the airport and bus terminal than downtown is, and many travelers opt to stay out here if they're only in town for a night. Buses connect the suburbs with downtown; a cab ride to the Malecón costs about US$4.

Dreamkapture Hostal (☎ 04-224-2909; info@dreamkapture.com; www.dreamkapture.com; Alborada 12a etapa, Manzana 2, Villa 21; s/d with shared bath US$12/20, with private bath US$15/23) This small, friendly Canadian/Ecuadorian-owned hostal boasts spotless rooms, a breakfast room, a TV room and a small garden. There's lots of travel info lying around, and a wholesome breakfast is included in the price. The hostal is on Sixto Juan Bernal near the intersection of Benjamín Carrión and Francisco de Orel-

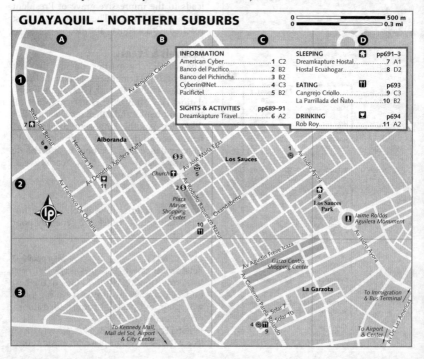

GUAYAQUIL – NORTHERN SUBURBS

0   500 m
0   0.3 mi

INFORMATION	
American Cyber	1 C2
Banco del Pacífico	2 B2
Banco del Pichincha	3 B2
Cyberin@Net	4 C3
Pacifictel	5 B2

SIGHTS & ACTIVITIES	pp689–91
Dreamkapture Travel	6 A2

SLEEPING	pp691–3
Dreamkapture Hostal	7 A1
Hostal Ecuahogar	8 D2

EATING	p693
Cangrejo Criollo	9 C3
La Parrillada del Ñato	10 B2

DRINKING	p694
Rob Roy	11 A2

lana. There's no sign; look for the dreamy paintings. Airport pickup costs US$5.

Hostal Ecuahogar (☎ 04-224-8357; youthhost@telconet.net; Av Isidro Ayora, Los Sauces 1, Manzana F-31, Villa 20; dm 1/2 people US$15/22, s/d US$20/25) In Los Sauces neighborhood, Ecuahogar seems a bit overpriced, but it's friendly and clean. Perks include hot baths, kitchen privileges, an on-site travel agency and pickup service from the airport or bus station. Prices include continental breakfast. Discounts for HI members. Take bus No 22 from the bus terminal.

Eating

CITY CENTER   Map pp690–1

There's a slough of bright, clean fast-food restaurants in the **Patio de Comidas** (Malecón Simón Bolívar near Olmedo); several in front of MAAC (see p689); and dozens more in the Mall del Sol, north of downtown. Calle 9 de Octubre has lots of modern cafeterias, restaurants and fast-food joints, although none are very cheap. There are several cafés on the steps of Cerro Santa Ana which cater to tourists.

El Toro Asado (cnr Chimborazo & Vélez; mains US$2-4, almuerzos US$1.50) Casual joint with good, reasonably priced grilled meats. *Asado y menestra* (grilled beef with lentils or beans) is the specialty. There's also a branch on **Garaycoa** (cnr Luque).

Media Naranja (9 de Octubre & Aviléz) The beer's on tap, the *asado* is cheap and the tables are outdoors.

Pique y Pase (Lascano 1617 near Carchi; mains US$2.50-5) Excellent *menestra* with chicken or beef costs only US$2.50. Vegetarians should go straight for *menestra* with rice.

Resaca (☎ 09-942-3390; Malecón Simón Bolívar at Roca; mains US$4-6; 🕙 11am-midnight Sun-Thu, 11-3am Fri & Sat) This hip new restaurant/bar on the Malecón serves tasty, fairly priced food (mostly seafood and salads). Make a reservation if you hope to dine after 8pm. Because it's also a popular bar (see Drinking following), it's packed (and fun) on weekend nights.

Artur's Café (Numa Pompilio Llona 127; mains US$3-7) Longtime local favorite for its unbeatable hideaway atmosphere and superb location over the Río Guayas in Las Peñas. Ecuadorian cuisine is the specialty.

El Galeón de Artur's (Cerro Santa Ana) Good traditional Ecuadorian food. The atmosphere is cozy, but avoid the upstairs tables unless

you like eating *seco de chivo* (goat stew) to the cacophony of karaoke singers. Same management as Artur's Café (previous).

Frutabar (9 de Octubre 410, 1st fl) Choose from over 20 types of *batidos* and dozens of juice creations.

Chifa Asia (Sucre 321 at Chile; mains US$2-5) The best of several cheap *chifas* around this area. **Chifa Jumbo** (Sucre 309), a few doors down, is also good.

La Canoa (Chile 510; mains US$3-5; 🕙 24hr) In the Hotel Continental. Superb traditional Ecuadorian fare; reasonable prices.

El Español (Pichincha at Luque) Good sandwiches, deli food.

NORTHERN SUBURBS   Map p692

Guayaquil's best restaurants are out in the burbs, especially along VE Estrada in Urdesa, and well worth the trek.

La Parrillada del Ñato (VE Estrada 1219 at Laureles, Urdesa; mains US$6-10) Guayaquil's most famous grill is *well* worth the splurge. Seriously! It's an institution. There's also a **branch** (cnr Demetrio Aguilera Malta & RB Nazur) in Alborada.

Cangrejo Criollo (Guillermo Pareja Rolando, Villa 9, La Garzota; mains US$7-12) Like crab? Eat here. Look for the giant crab over the door. Guillermo Pareja Rolando is commonly called Av Principal in La Garzota.

Tsuji (VE Estrada 813, Urdesa) Delicious Japanese food. Expensive.

Drinking

The *farra* (party or nightlife) in Guayaquil is out in the northern suburbs.

Kennedy Mall (Kennedy Norte) Basically a bar mall. Each bar charges about US$10 cover, but you can drink all you want for free. Most have dancing. Have a cab drop you off and you can walk between them.

La Creme (CC Albán Borja, Av Carlos Julio Arosemena, Km 2.7; admission US$10-15) One of the largest *discotecas* in town, with international DJs and house, techno and similar beats. **Suruba** (Francisco de Orellana 796) and **La Sal** (Puntilla Mall Shopping Center) are similar. Cabbies know them.

Holiday (Map pp690-1; Rocafuerte 410; admission US$7; 🕙 Thu-Sat) For something downtown, try Holiday where international DJs, fire-breathers and go-go dancers tickle three floors of happy clubbers.

Resaca (Malecón Simón Bolívar at Roca) A slick new bar/restaurant on the Malecón (see Eating, previous).

Rob Roy (Map p692; Av Demetrio Aguilera Malta 739) In the suburb of Alborada, near Burger King, draws a hospitable blend of expats, travelers and locals.

El Jardín de Salsa (Av de las Américas) On the road between the airport and the bus terminal (every cab driver knows it), is the place for salsa (often live).

Entertainment

El Telégrafo and *El Universo* publish entertainment listings.

Supercines 9 de Octubre (Map pp690-1; 9 de Octubre 823 at Avilés) With six screens, it's the best cinema downtown.

Cinemark (www.cinemark.com.ec in Spanish) In the Mall del Sol, Cinemark is state-of-the-art.

Getting There & Away

AIR

The airport is on Av de las Américas, 5km north of the center. International flights are subject to a US$10 departure tax.

TAME (Map pp690-1; ☎ 04-256-077/920; Paula de Icaza 424, Gran Pasaje) offers several flights daily to Quito (US$58), one or two daily to Cuenca (US$58), three a week to Loja (US$37) and one every weekday to Machala. The airline also flies twice daily to Baltra Airport in the Galápagos (US$344 round trip, US$299 mid-January to mid-June and September through November). There's also a branch at the **airport** (☎ 04-228-2062/7155).

BOAT

Cargo boats steam every few weeks for the Galápagos (p703); one accepts passengers.

BUS

The bus terminal is 2km beyond the airport. There is service to most major towns in the country. Many buses go daily to Quito (US$7, eight hours), Manta (US$3, 3½ hours), Esmeraldas (US$5 to US$7, eight hours) and Cuenca (US$4, 3½ to 4½ hours).

Several companies at the terminal go to Machala and Huaquillas on the Peruvian border. The easiest way to Peru, however, is with one of the international lines. **Rutas de America** (☎ 04-245-2844, 04-245-0342; Los Rios 3012 at Letamendi), whose office and terminal is southeast of downtown, has direct buses to Lima (US$50, 24 hours) every day at 6am. **Expresso Internacional Ormeno** (☎ 04-229-

7362; Centro de Negocios El Terminal, Bahía Norte, Office 34, Bloque C) goes daily to Lima (US$55) at 2pm, stopping in Tumbes (US$20, five hours). Its office and terminal is on Av de las Américas just north of the main bus terminal. These services are very convenient because you do not have to get off the bus (let alone change buses) at the border – formalities are taken care of on the bus. Both companies also go to several other South American countries.

Getting Around

Buses to the airport from the center run along the Malecón (US$0.25, 30 minutes to one hour); allow plenty of time if catching a flight. Buses to the bus terminal from the center leave from Parque Victoria, near 10 de Agosto and Moncayo.

MACHALA

Machala, capital of El Oro Province, is the self-proclaimed 'banana capital of the world.' With 216,900 inhabitants, it's Ecuador's fourth-largest city. Most travelers to and from Peru pass through here, but few stay more than a night – with reason. It's a chaotic city whose highlight is probably the presence of free bananas on restaurant tables. Páez is a pedestrian-only zone between Rocafuerte and 9 de Octubre.

Information

For Internet access try **Copy@Comp** (Sucre near Montalvo) or **Ciber Yogur** (9 de Mayo near Pichincha). They each charge US$0.80 per hour. The **hospital** (☎ 07-930-420, 07-937-581; Boyacá) is located across from the park. **Banco de Guayaquil** (cnr Rocafuerte & Guayas) and **Banco del Pichincha** (cnr Rocafuerte & Guayas) change traveler's checks and have ATMs. **Pacifictel** (Montalvo near 9 de Octubre) is a block southeast of the plaza. The **tourist office** (☎ 07-932-106; 9 de Octubre 1017, Edificio Galarza) offers basic information about El Oro Province.

Sleeping

Most hotels have only cold water, and mosquito nets come in handy.

Hostal Mercy (☎ 07-920-116; Junín 609; r with fan/air-con per person US$4/5; ❒ P) One of the best cheap hotels, often full by lunchtime; it's clean.

Hotel Suites Guayaquil (☎ 07-922-570; Montalvo near 9 de Octubre; s/d US$5/10) Large, empty wooden-floor rooms with private bath. Choose carefully – they vary greatly.

Gran Hotel Machala (☎ 07-930-530; Montalvo near Rocafuerte; r with shared/private bath per person US$4/5) If you don't mind seatless toilets, you'll be fine at the bare-bones but clean Machala.

Hotel Estefania (☎ 07-960-087; r per person US$3-5) In a busy spot near the market, the cheaper rooms are small and stuffy, while the large, 4th-floor rooms have a haggard swanky feel.

Hotel International San Francisco (☎ 07-930-445/457; Tarqui near Sucre; s/d with fan US$12/18, with air-con US$17/23; ❊) This comfortable hotel has five floors of large, clean rooms with fan or air-conditioning. The restaurant is also comfortable and popular.

Eating

Bar Restaurant El Bosque (9 de Mayo near Bolívar) Simple but decent meals at outdoor tables.

Restaurant Chifa Central (Tarqui near 9 de Octubre) Whips out massive portions of Chinese food.

Parrillada restaurants (Sucre) Around the corner from Chifa Central, several cheap *parrilladas* serve inexpensive grilled chicken and steaks. They're best for dinner.

Don Angelo's (9 de Mayo; ☽ 7-4am) A completely unembroidered little restaurant with a reputation for serving some of the town's better food, namely chicken and seafood.

Restaurant América (Olmedo near Guayas; mains US$2-3) Gets packed for its good US$1.50 set lunches and dinners.

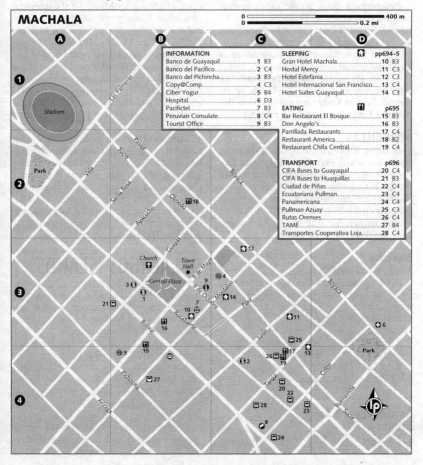

| MACHALA | 0 —— 400 m |
| | 0 —— 0.2 mi |

INFORMATION	
Banco de Guayaquil	1 B3
Banco del Pacifico	2 C4
Banco del Pichincha	3 B3
Copy@Comp	4 C3
Ciber Yogur	5 B4
Hospital	6 D3
Pacifictel	7 B3
Peruvian Consulate	8 C4
Tourist Office	9 B3

SLEEPING	pp694–5
Gran Hotel Machala	10 B3
Hostal Mercy	11 C3
Hotel Estefania	12 C3
Hotel Internacional San Francisco	13 C4
Hotel Suites Guayaquil	14 C3

EATING	p695
Bar Restaurant El Bosque	15 B3
Don Angelo's	16 B3
Parrillada Restaurants	17 C4
Restaurant America	18 B2
Restaurant Chifa Central	19 C4

TRANSPORT	p696
CIFA Buses to Guayaquil	20 C4
CIFA Buses to Huaquillas	21 B3
Ciudad de Piñas	22 C4
Ecuatoriana Pullman	23 C4
Panamericana	24 C4
Pullman Azuay	25 C3
Rutas Orenses	26 C4
TAME	27 B4
Transportes Cooperativa Loja	28 C4

Getting There & Away

AIR

The airport is 1km southwest of town along Montalvo; a taxi from town costs US$1. **TAME** (☎ 07-930-139; Montalvo near Pichincha) flies weekdays to Guayaquil (US$31); it continues on to Quito (US$65).

BUS

There is no central terminal. Buses with **CIFA** (cnr Bolívar & Guayas) run regularly to Huaquillas (US$1.20, 1½ hours) at the Peruvian border. CIFA buses also go to Guayaquil (US$3, 3½ hours) from 9 de Octubre near Tarqui. **Rutas Orenses** (9 de Octubre near Tarqui) and **Ecuatoriana Pullman** (9 de Octubre near Colón) also serve Guayaquil, the latter has air-conditioned buses.

Panamericana (Bolívar at Colón) offers several buses a day to Quito (US$7.50, 10 to 12 hours). **Ciudad de Piñas** (Colón at Rocafuerte) runs several buses daily to the pretty mountain village of Piñas (the 6am bus continues to Loja) and one or two buses daily to Cuenca (US$3.50, 4½ hours). **Transportes Cooperativa Loja** (Tarqui) goes to Loja (US$3.50, seven hours). **Pullman Azuay** (Sucre near Tarqui) has departures for Cuenca every 30 minutes.

HUAQUILLAS

Huaquillas, 80km from Machala, is the main border town with Peru. It's called Aguas Verdes on the Peruvian side. A busy street market on the Ecuadorian side is full of Peruvians shopping on day passes. Almost everything happens on the long main street. Banks don't change money, but briefcase-toting money-changers do, albeit at poor rates.

Sleeping

Machala has better hotels.

Hotel Hidalgo (Teniente Cordovez near 10 de Agosto; s/d US$4/8) Rents basic rooms with bath and mosquito nets.

Hotel Gaboeli (☎ 07-907-149; Teniente Cordovez 311; s/d US$3/5) Tolerable for a night.

Hotel Mini (☎ 07-907-031; Callejón Rocafuerte; r per person US$3-6) Better than Hotel Gaboeli.

Hotel Lima (☎ 07-907-899; cnr Machala & Portobelo; r with fan/air-con per person US$4/5; ☒) Tops the barrel.

Getting There & Away

ECUADOR

CIFA buses run frequently to Machala (US$1.20, 1½ hours) from the main street,

two blocks from the border. Panamericana goes daily to Quito (US$8, 13 hours). Ecuatoriana Pullman has buses to Guayaquil (US$4, 5½ hours). For Loja (US$4, six hours), use Transportes Loja.

PERUVIAN BORDER CROSSING

The Ecuadorian **immigration office** (☒ 24hr) is 5km outside of Huaquillas. Entrance and exit formalities are carried out here. The bus doesn't wait, but taxis are about US$2, or you can jump on another passing bus for US$0.20 (free if you've saved your ticket).

Those entering Ecuador need an exit stamp in their passport from the Peruvian authorities. Entrance formalities are usually straightforward. Travelers need a T-3 tourist card, which is available free at the immigration office. Usually only 30 days are given, but it is easy to obtain a renewal in Quito (p624) or Guayaquil (p689). Show of funds or onward tickets are very rarely asked for.

Those leaving Ecuador need an exit stamp from the Ecuadorian immigration office before entering Peru. If you have lost your T-3 card, you should be able to get a free replacement, as long as the stamp in your passport has not expired.

After showing your passport to the international bridge guard, take a shared moto-taxi (US$0.70) to the Peruvian immigration building, about 2km beyond the border. Officially, an onward ticket is required to enter Peru, but this is not often asked for and, if it is, you can (usually) talk your way out of it. From here, *colectivos* (buses) go to Tumbes (US$1.50).

GALÁPAGOS ISLANDS

A visit to the Galápagos Islands is, very literally, the wildlife experience of a lifetime. It's a mind-blowing lesson in natural history set in a barren, volcanic land with a haunting beauty all of its own. Here, you can swim with sea lions, float eye-to-eye with a penguin, scuba dive with hammerhead sharks, stand next to a blue-footed booby feeding its young, watch a giant 200kg tortoise lumbering through a cactus forest and try to avoid stepping on iguanas scurrying over the lava. Most of the animal species on the islands are found nowhere else in the world – and surely nowhere else

THE GALÁPAGOS ISLANDS

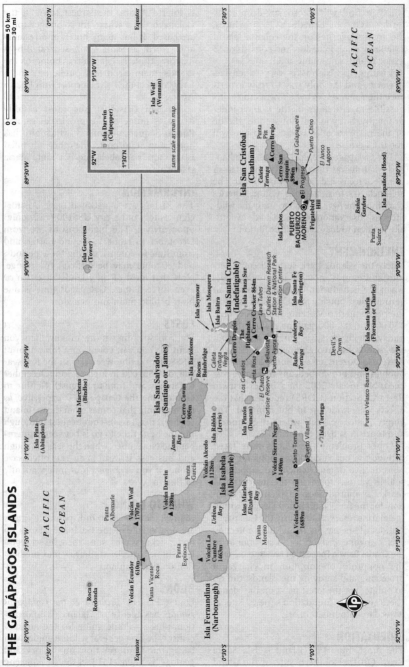

same scale as main map

0 — 50 km
0 — 30 mi

PACIFIC OCEAN

PACIFIC OCEAN

Isla Darwin (Culpepper)

Isla Wolf (Wenman)

Roca Redonda

Volcán Ecuador 610m

Punta Vicente Roca

Punta Albemarle

Volcán Wolf 1707m

Isla Pinta (Abingdon)

Isla Marchena (Bindloe)

Isla Genovesa (Tower)

Punta Espinosa

Volcán La Cumbre 1463m

Isla Fernandina (Narborough)

Volcán Darwin 1280m

Punta García

Volcán Alcedo 1128m

Isla San Salvador (Santiago or James)

Cerro Cowan 905m

James Bay

Rocas Bainbridge

Isla Bartolomé

Caleta Tortuga Negra

Isla Seymour
Isla Mosquera
Isla Baltra

Isla Santa Cruz (Indefatigable)

Isla Plaza Sur

Urbina Bay

Isla Rábida (Jervis)

Isla Pinzón (Duncan)

Los Gemelos

Cerro Dragón
The Highlands
Santa Rosa
El Chato Tortoise Reserve
Bellavista
Puerto Ayora

Cerro Crocker 864m
Lava Tubes
Charles Darwin Research Station & National Park Information Center

Isla Marisla Elizabeth Bay

Isla Isabela (Albemarle)

Bahía Tortuga
Academy Bay

Isla Santa Fe (Barrington)

Punta Moreno

Volcán Sierra Negra 1490m

Santo Tomás
Puerto Villamil

Isla Tortuga

Puerto Velasco Ibarra

Isla Santa María (Floreana or Charles)

Devil's Crown

Isla San Cristóbal (Chatham)

Punta Pitt
Cerro Brujo
Caleta Tortuga
Cerro San Joaquín 896m
La Galápaguera
Puerto Chino
El Junco Lagoon
El Progreso
PUERTO BAQUERIZO MORENO
Frigatebird Hill

Isla Lobos

Punta Suárez

Bahía Gardner

Isla Española (Hood)

Volcán Cerro Azul 1689m

Equator

0°30'N
0°30'S
1°00'S

92°00'N
92°00'W
91°30'W
91°00'W
90°30'W
90°00'W
89°30'W
89°00'W

will you find wildlife so jaw-droppingly fearless. One of Ecuador's 21 provinces, the archipelago lies on the equator, about 1000km west of Ecuador, and consists of 13 major islands and many small ones.

Visiting the islands is very expensive, however, and the only way to truly experience their marvels is by taking a cruise. It's possible to visit four of the islands independently, but you will not see the wildlife or the many smaller islands that you will aboard a cruise.

The Galápagos archipelago was uninhabited when it was discovered by the Spanish in 1535. Five islands are now inhabited. The archipelago's most famous visitor, Charles Darwin, came here in 1835 to study the wildlife. His observations on the islands eventually led him to his theory of evolution.

ENVIRONMENT

Lately the islands have suffered some serious abuse, most notably in January 2001, when the Ecuadorian oil tanker *Jessica* ran aground just outside San Cristóbal Island's Puerto Baquerizo Moreno, spilling between 150,000 to 180,000 gallons of fuel. Fortunately, much of it was carried away from the islands by favorable winds and ocean currents. Dozens of sea lions, blue-footed boobies and brown pelicans had to be rescued, but in late 2002 the Charles Darwin Research Station (CDRS) reported that the effects were widespread but minimal. The empty *Jessica* was left where it grounded, and tourism is back to normal.

Other problems the islands have faced include the poaching of sea lions for their reproductive organs, which are supposedly sold in various forms on the international market as aphrodisiacs. Shark, usually taken only for the fins, is still fished illegally within the marine reserve. Obviously the Galápagos National Park has its hands full protecting itself. Anyone wishing to donate money to the **Charles Darwin Foundation** (www.galapagos.org), the nonprofit organization in charge of protecting and studying the islands, can do so online. For the latest news on the islands check out the foundation's news site at www.darwinfoundation.org.

ORIENTATION

The most important island is Isla Santa Cruz. On the southern side of the island is Puerto Ayora, the largest town in the Galápagos and where most budget tours are based. It has many hotels and restaurants. North of Santa Cruz, separated by a narrow strait, is Isla Baltra, home of the islands' main airport. A public bus and a ferry connect the Baltra airport with Puerto Ayora.

Isla San Cristóbal, the most easterly island, is home to the provincial capital, Puerto Baquerizo Moreno, which also has hotels and an airport. The other inhabited islands are Isla Isabela and Isla Santa María (Floreana).

INFORMATION

The islands are a national park. All foreign visitors must pay US$100 (cash only) upon arrival. The high seasons are from December to January, around Easter, and from June to August; during these periods, budget tours may be difficult to arrange. Note that most of the islands have two or even three names. Galápagos time is one hour behind mainland Ecuador.

COSTS

Plan on spending more money than you want to. You can count on a minimum of US$800 for a one-week trip in the low season, or US$1000 in high season (December to January and June to August). Getting to and touring the Galápagos is expensive, as is everything that comes from the mainland (eg beer, rice, taxis). The cheapest (although not the best) time to go is between September and November, when the seas are rough and business is dead. You can often save money if you arrange a tour independently in Puerto Ayora.

WHAT TO BRING

Many handy (or even indispensable) items are unavailable in the Galápagos. Stock up on seasickness pills, sunscreen, insect repellent, film, batteries, toiletries and medication on the mainland.

BOOKS

Lonely Planet's *Ecuador & the Galápagos Islands* has plenty of Galápagos information, plus a wildlife guide for the nonspecialist. The best general wildlife guide, with background information on history and geology, is Michael H Jackson's *Galápagos:*

A *Natural History Guide*. Bird-watchers consult *A Field Guide to the Birds of the Galápagos* by Michael Harris. There is also *A Field Guide to the Fishes of Galápagos* by Godfrey Merlen. Most of these are available at major bookstores in Quito (p623) and Guayaquil (p688) or from the SAE (p624).

VOLUNTEERING

Once a month between July and February, the national park sends a fishing boat out to collect trash among the islands. Four volunteers do the work. There's no cost, and food (usually fish caught en route) and water are provided. Quarters are very cramped and primitive. If you're interested, inquire at the **Recursos Marinos office** (☎ 05-526-511/189, ext 126) behind the Charles Darwin Research Station in Puerto Ayora. This is not recommended for weak swimmers or anyone prone to seasickness.

On Isla San Cristóbal, the community organization **Nueva Era** (☎ 05-520-489; www .neweragalapagos.org) needs volunteers to work with local kids on environmental issues, art, dance, crafts, beach cleanup etc. Volunteers pay only room and board. It's an admirable local organization. Check out the website.

VISITOR SITES

To protect the islands, the national park authorities allow access to about 50 visitor sites, in addition to the towns and public areas. Other areas are off-limits. The visitor sites are where the most interesting wildlife and geology are seen. Apart from the ones mentioned later (near Puerto Ayora and Baquerizo Moreno), most sites are reached by boat.

Normally, landings are made in a *panga* (skiff). Landings are either 'wet' (where you hop overboard and wade ashore in knee-deep water) or 'dry' (where you get off onto a pier or rocky outcrop). People occasionally fall in the surf (ha ha ha! not funny) of a wet landing or slip on the algae-covered rocks of a dry one. Take it slow and put your camera in a watertight bag. Boat captains will not land groups in places other than designated visitor sites.

In addition to the sites on land, many marine sites have been designated for snorkeling or diving.

ITINERARIES
Less than One Week

On a cruise of less than a week, try to visit the following places:

Isla Plaza Sur (South Plaza Island) The island has land iguanas, sea lions and swallow-tailed gulls, an Opuntia cactus forest and good snorkeling.

Isla Seymour Nesting colonies of both blue-footed boobies and magnificent frigate birds.

Caleta Tortuga Negra (Black Turtle Cove) On the north shore of Isla Santa Cruz, has marine turtles and white-tipped sharks.

Isla Bartolomé A volcanic cone that's easy to climb and gives great views of the islands. The island also has resident penguins and sea lions, along with good snorkeling.

Isla San Salvador A lava flow you can walk on (by Bahía Sullivan), as well as marine iguanas, sea lions, fur seals, Galápagos hawks and many kinds of seabirds near Puerto Egas.

Isla Rábida A flamingo colony and a colony of irascible bachelor sea lions.

You'll see common species almost everywhere, such as masked and blue-footed boobies, pelicans, mockingbirds, finches, Galápagos doves, frigate birds, lava lizards and red Sally Lightfoot crabs.

More than One Week

If you have a full week or more, visit some outlying islands.

Isla Genovesa is the best place to see red-footed boobies. Colonies of masked boobies, great frigate birds and red-billed tropicbirds also make Genovesa home. **Isla Isabela** and **Isla Fernandina**, in the west, are home to the flightless Galápagos cormorant. **Isla Española**, about 90km southeast of Isla Santa Cruz, has the archipelago's only colony of waved albatross. These spectacular birds can be seen between late March and early December at **Punta Suárez**, on the island's western side. **Bahía Gardner**, on the eastern side, has a beautiful white-sand beach with good swimming and a sea lion colony.

TOURS

Two kinds of trips are within reach of budget travelers: day trips and boat tours (cruises), with nights spent aboard. Arranging trips in Puerto Ayora is the cheapest way to go, although deals can be found in Guayaquil or Quito. Note that tips are not included. On a cheap one-week tour, the crew and guide are tipped at least US$20 per passenger (about half to the guide).

Day Tours

Most day trips are based in Puerto Ayora, but a few are offered in Puerto Baquerizo Moreno. Several hours are spent sailing to the visitor site(s), the island is visited in the middle of the day and you'll probably be part of a large group. Only a few islands are close enough to either Santa Cruz or San Cristóbal to be visited on day trips.

Because time is spent going back and forth and because you don't visit the islands early or late in the day, we don't recommend day tours. The island visits may be too brief, the guides poorly informed and the crew lacking an adequate conservationist attitude.

Day-trip operators in Puerto Ayora charge about US$25 to US$60 per person per day. Talk to other travelers about how good the guide and boat are. Make sure there will not be a fuel stop at Seymour South – these can take hours.

Boat Tours

Most visitors go on longer boat tours and sleep aboard overnight. Tours from four to eight days are the most common. You can't really do the Galápagos justice on a tour shorter than a week, although five days gives a reasonable look. To visit the outlying islands of Isabela and Fernandina, two weeks are recommended. On the first day of a prearranged tour, you arrive from the mainland by air at about noon, so this leaves only half a day in the Galápagos; on the last day, you have to be in the airport in the morning. Thus a 'five-day' tour gives only three full days in the islands. Arranging a tour in Puerto Ayora avoids this.

Tour boats range from small yachts to large cruise ships. The most common type of boat is a motor sailer carrying six to 16 passengers.

Tours are usually categorized as economy, tourist or luxury level. Seven-night/eight-day economy tours are generally aboard small boats with six to 12 bunks in double, triple and quadruple cabins. Bedding is provided and the accommodations are clean but damp and cramped, with little privacy. Plenty of simple but fresh food and juice is served at all meals and a Naturalista

II guide accompanies the boat (few guides on economy tours speak English).

There are toilets and fresh water is available for drinking. Bathing facilities may be saltwater deck hoses or freshwater showers on some boats. The pre-set itineraries allow you to visit most of the central islands and give enough time to see the wildlife.

Occasionally, things go wrong, and when they do, a refund is extremely difficult to obtain. Problems have included last-minute changes of boat (which the contractual small print allows), poor crew, lack of bottled drinks, not sticking to the agreed itinerary, mechanical breakdowns and overbooking. Passengers have to share cabins and are not guaranteed that their cabin mates will be of the same gender; if you are uncomfortable sharing a cabin with a stranger of the opposite sex, make sure you are guaranteed in writing that you won't have to do this. Generally speaking, the cheaper the tour the less comfortable the boat and the less knowledgeable the guide.

Arranging Tours On-site

It's slightly cheaper to arrange a tour independently in Puerto Ayora than to pay for a prearranged tour from the mainland, although the better boats may be full. Arranging a tour can take days or more in the high season, so although you might get lucky and find a boat leaving the next day, this is not a reliable option for people with a limited amount of time. July and August are especially busy months, when cheap tours are difficult to organize. In the low season, tour operators will chase you down as you alight from the bus.

If you are alone or with a friend, find some more people, as even the smallest boats take four passengers and most take eight or more. Your hotel manager can often introduce you to a boat owner. After all, Puerto Ayora is a tight little town.

The cheapest and most basic boats are available for about US$50 per day per person, and this should include everything (except park fees, tips and bottled drinks). The cheaper the boat, the simpler the food and more crowded the accommodations. Bargaining over the price is acceptable and sometimes necessary.

The most important thing is to find a boat whose crew you like and which has a good, enthusiastic guide who can point out and explain the wildlife and other items of interest. It is worth paying a little more for a good guide. The cheapest boats employ Spanish-speaking Naturalista II guides, whose function is to fulfill the legal obligation that every boat have a certified guide. Most Naturalista II guides know a bit about the wildlife, but they primarily act as rangers, making sure groups stay together on the trails and don't molest the wildlife. (You cannot land on any of the islands without a guide, and you must always walk around more or less in a group.) Naturalista III guides, on the other hand, are trained, multilingual guides with degrees in biology. They work only on the more expensive boats.

Dealing with tour agencies in Puerto Ayora can be tricky because most are booking the same boats and fighting for the same tourist dollar, but it's worth checking several of them. Ask travelers coming off tours for their impressions.

Get the itinerary in writing – before you hand over your money – to avoid disagreements between you and other passengers and the crew during the cruise. It is particularly important to discuss seasickness and what happens if you have to turn back with a sick passenger. This is more common than anyone will admit and hospitalization is not unheard of. Get it in writing. Even with a written agreement, the itinerary may sometimes be changed, but at least it gives you some bargaining power. The SAE in Quito (p624) has a current Galápagos information packet, which includes a detailed contract in Spanish and English.

Conditions can be cramped and primitive. Washing facilities vary from a bucket of sea water on the cheapest boats to freshwater deck hoses or showers on the better boats. However, it is possible to find a cheap boat with adequate freshwater showers. If you don't want to stay salty, ask about washing facilities. Also inquire about drinking water. We recommend treating the water on most of the cheaper boats or bringing your own fresh water. Agree on the price of bottled drinks before you leave and make sure that enough of your favorite refreshments are aboard. There have been reports of thefts on boats, so watch your stuff.

Owners, captains, guides and crews change frequently, and many boats make changes and improvements from year to year. Because of this, it is difficult to make foolproof recommendations. The Cámara de Turismo in Puerto Ayora keeps a record of all complaints about boats. Check this file and make any complaints you have here.

Although arranging your own boat tour on-site is the cheapest option, even in the low season total costs (with flight) will be US$750 minimum for a week-long tour. Mainland operators often discourage travelers from attempting to make arrangements on the islands (it's not in their interest), but as long as you avoid the high season and are flexible with your schedule, you shouldn't have major problems.

Arranging Tours in Advance

If you don't have the time or patience to arrange a tour on-site, you can arrange one in Quito or Guayaquil. Still, you may have to wait several days or weeks during the high season.

You might get a substantial discount by checking various agencies and seeing if they have any spaces to fill on boats leaving in the next day or two. This applies to the cheaper tours and some of the more expensive ones. Particularly when business is slow, agencies may let you travel cheaply at the last minute rather than leave berths empty. This depends on luck and your bargaining skills.

Safari Tours (Map pp628-9; ☎ 02-255-2505; admin@safari.com.ec; J Calamá 380 at JL Mera, Quito), in Quito, runs a booking service for a number of Galápagos boats and agencies. Safari has a wide variety of contacts and can help you make the best choice, saving you a lot of legwork and uncertainty.

Some of the cheapest prearranged tours are through **Galasam**, which has offices in **Quito** (Map pp628-9; ☎ 02-250-7079/080; www.galasam.com; Amazonas 1354 at Cordero) and in **Guayaquil** (Map pp690-1; ☎ 04-230-4488; www.galapagos-islands.com; 9 de Octubre 424, Office 9A). Reports have been very mixed, so deal with this company with your eyes wide open.

Eight-day economy tours start at about US$500 to US$600 per person. The US$100 park fee, airfare and bottled drinks are not included. There are weekly departures. Typically, you'll leave Quito on a specific morning, say Monday, and begin the boat tour on Monday evening. The tour may finish on Sunday night or, possibly, Monday morning at the airport for your flight back. Shorter and cheaper tours are available. Often, a one-week tour is two shorter tours combined, for example a Monday to Thursday tour combined with a Thursday to Monday tour. Try to avoid one-week trips such as this, as you'll spend most of Thursday dropping off and picking up passengers.

If you add up the cost of the cheapest one-week tour plus airfare and park fees, you get almost no change out of US$1000. If you're going to spend that much, the Galápagos are an important destination for you and you want to get as much out of it as possible. The economy-class boats are usually OK, but if something is going to go wrong, it's more likely to happen on the cheaper boats. If this is all you can afford and you really want to see the Galápagos, go! It'll probably be the adventure of a lifetime. But you might consider spending an extra few hundred dollars to go on a more comfortable, reliable boat and get a decent guide. All that said, most people have the time of their lives. Good luck!

INDEPENDENT TRAVEL

Visiting the Galápagos on your own is – for better or worse – a wholly different experience than touring the islands on a cruise. Only four of the islands – Santa Cruz, San Cristóbal, Isabela and Santa María – can be visited independently. When you add up hotel costs, day tours (which you'll surely want to take) and interisland travel, it probably won't be much cheaper than a cruise. Most importantly, you will not see the many islands, nor the wildlife (the main attraction) that require a guide (ie a cruise) to see. But you *can* have an amazing time – and more time – hanging out and getting to know these four islands in ways you cannot on a short cruise.

You can fly independently to either Santa Cruz or San Cristóbal, and a passenger ferry (see Getting Around, p703) runs regularly between the two islands. Puerto Ayora on Santa Cruz is a bit pricey, although there are some great visitor sites (namely Bahía Tortuga) that you can visit on your own. Setting up diving trips and day cruises is easy from here. Baquerizo Moreno on San Cristóbal is cheaper and more laid-back

and has world-class surf, good snorkeling, places to camp and several interesting visitor sites that you can visit without a guide. Puerto Villamil, on Isabela, is even cheaper. It's rarely visited, and you may be the only one around for days on end (and with only two ferry boats calling at Isabela each month, you'll have plenty of days on end!). Finally, Floreana can be reached (and left) only once a month by boat, and there's only one place to stay and eat (not cheap, although you may be able to camp), but it's truly an escape.

Going it alone in the Galápagos is worth it only if you have *at least* two weeks, preferably three or more. The best time for this type of travel is in the off season, when hotels are cheaper and unlikely to be booked solid (as they often are in high season).

GETTING THERE & AWAY
Air
Most visitors fly to Isla Baltra, from where public buses and a ferry go to Puerto Ayora on Isla Santa Cruz. Flights are available to Puerto Baquerizo Moreno on Isla San Cristóbal, but Puerto Ayora has more facilities, so travelers wanting to arrange tours on-site should go there.

TAME flies twice daily from Quito (US$389 round trip, 3¼ hours) via Guayaquil (US$344 round trip, 1½ hours) to Baltra. It flies Monday, Wednesday and Saturday mornings to San Cristóbal (same fare). Flights are cheaper – US$333 from Quito and US$300 from Guayaquil – in low season (May 1 to June 14 and September 15 to October 31).

You can buy one-way tickets to one island and leave from the other, or fly with an open return. To change an already ticketed return date (US$7 fee) you must do so in person at **TAME** (☎ 05-526-165/527; cnr Av Charles Darwin & 12 de Febrero; ☯ 7am-noon Mon-Sat & 1-4pm Mon-Fri) in Puerto Ayora, or at the airport office in Baquerizo Moreno; changes are more difficult in high season. Get there early to avoid an excruciating wait. Always reconfirm flights.

If you are signed up with a tour, make sure you are flying to the right island! People occasionally end up in the wrong place and miss their tour.

If flights are full, try going to the airport. Agencies book blocks of seats for their tours and release unsold seats on the day of the flight (these are full-price tickets). Tuesday is the quietest day to fly.

Boat

Cargo ships leave Guayaquil's Muelle Sur Naval every few weeks and charge about US$150, one way. Conditions are extremely basic. The journey takes about 3½ days. If you stay aboard while the boat spends about a week making deliveries around the islands, you are charged about US$50 a day. In 2003, the old, rusty **Marina 91** (in Guayaquil ☎ 04-239-7370) was the only boat authorized to carry passengers. Be sure you see the boats before you drop any cash.

GETTING AROUND

Arriving air passengers in Baltra are met by a crew member (if on a prearranged tour) or take a bus-ferry-bus combination to Puerto Ayora (US$2.50, two hours). From Puerto Ayora, buses start leaving at 7am from the park for the return trip to Baltra.

Air passengers arriving in Puerto Baquerizo Moreno can walk into town in a few minutes.

Ingala (in Puerto Ayora ☎ 05-526-151/199) operates *Ingala II*, an interisland passenger ferry. It goes from Santa Cruz to San Cristóbal about three times per week, from Santa Cruz to Isabela about twice monthly (usually on a Friday) and once a month from Isabela to Floreana. The office in Puerto Ayora can give you up-to-date details, as can the Cámara de Turismo in Puerto Ayora. Departure times change often. Fares are US$50 for foreigners (sometimes cheaper in low season if you bargain) on any passage and are purchased on the day of departure.

The cheapest rides are usually on the smaller (but often faster) private boats that zip between the islands with supplies and occasional passengers. Ask around the harbors. These are easiest to find in the busier ports of Puerto Ayora on Santa Cruz and Puerto Baquerizo Moreno on San Cristóbal.

ISLA SANTA CRUZ
Puerto Ayora

This clean little town is the Galápagos' main population center and the heart of the tourist industry. It's a friendly place to chill out and the best place in the islands to set up a cruise.

INFORMATION

Have your clothes washed at **Lavandería Central** (Charles Binford). Internet service is available at **Compu-matic** (Bolívar Naveda; US$2 per hr). **Banco del Pacífico** (Av Charles Darwin) changes money and traveler's checks and has a MasterCard/Cirrus ATM. The post office is near the harbor.

Tourist information is available at the **Cámara de Turismo** (Capturgal; ☎ 05-526-206; infocptg@ capturgal.org.ec; Av Charles Darwin). Report here any complaints about boats, tours, guides or crew.

ACTIVITIES

The **Red Mangrove Hotel** (Av Charles Darwin), near the cemetery, rents sea kayaks, sailboards and bikes. **Galápagos Tour Center** (cnr Pelícano & Padre Julio Herrera) rents surfboards (half-day/full-day US$8/18) and mountain bikes (US$8/15) and offers fun snorkeling trips (US$25).

The best dive centers in town are **Scuba Iguana** (☎ 05-526-296, ☎ /fax 05-526-497; mathiase@ pa.ga.pro.ec), in the Hotel Galápagos, near the cemetery, and **Galápagos Sub-Aqua** (☎ 05-526-350; sub_aqua@ga.pro.ec; Av Charles Darwin). Both are excellent and offer a variety of tours that include gear, boat and guide. Full PADI-certification courses are available.

TOURS

If you're setting up a cruise from Puerto Ayora visit all the following agencies to compare prices and tours. They all offer last-minute deals (when they exist).

Galápatour (☎ 05-526-088; Av Rodríguez Lara & Genovesa) Behind the municipal market.

Galasam (☎ 05-526-126; www.galasam.com; Av Padre Julio Herrera) Very popular for economy packages. Some complaints, some raves.

Moonrise Travel (☎ 05-526-403/348; sdivine@ga.pro .ec; Av Charles Darwin) Reputable agency long in the business; great for cheap, last-minute tours.

SLEEPING

Try bargaining in the off season.

Residencial Los Amigos (☎ 05-526-265; Av Charles Darwin; s/d with shared bath US$6/10, with private bath US$7/ 12) Popular but unimpressive budget hotel with eight plain rooms and cot-like beds.

La Peregrina B&B (☎ 05-526-323; Av Charles Darwin; r with/without breakfast per person US$7/10) Friendly place with a garden and four rooms with private baths.

Hotel Santa Cruz (☎ 05-526-573; Av Padre Julio Herrera; s/d US$5/10) Six-room, family-run hotel with shared baths. Cheapest in town.

Hotel Lirio del Mar (☎ 05-526-212; Bolívar Naveda; s/d US$8/16) Three-story hotel with orange walls and a bare, 2nd-story terrace. The rooms are fine and have private, hot-water baths. Good deal.

Hotel Sir Francis Drake (☎ 05-526-221; Av Padre Julio Herrera; s/d US$8/15) Thirteen plain rooms above a shoe store have cold showers and fans, but the ones lacking windows are stuffy.

Hotel Salinas (☎ 05-526-107; Bolívar Naveda; s/d US$10/16) Two-story hotel with spacious but plain rooms, private cold showers and fans.

Estrella del Mar (☎ 05-526-427; s/d without view US$15/20, with ocean view US$18/30) Near the police station, this is the only place at this price with ocean views; only about four rooms have the views, however. All the rooms are clean and have private hot showers.

EATING
Proinsular supermarket (Av Charles Darwin) Near the harbor, the place to stock up on food supplies. There's also a **municipal market** (Av Padre Julio Herrera).

Restaurant Salvavidas (mains US$6-11; ☯ 9am-8pm Mon-Sat) A dockside favorite for beers, snacks and seafood.

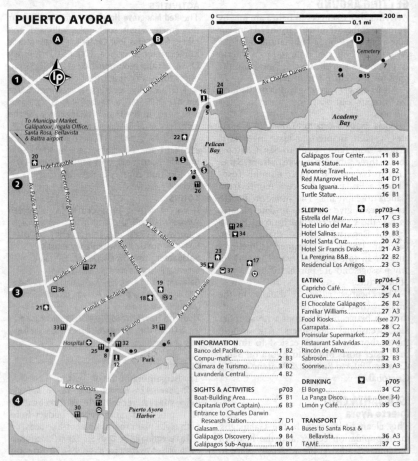

Familiar Williams (☾ 6-10pm Tue-Sun) Famous for its *encocado,* Familiar Williams is one of the best of the great food kiosks that line Charles Binford.

The cheapest places to eat are found out along Av Padre Julio Herrera.

Cucuve (Av Padre Julio Herrera) At the *avenida*'s southeastern end, sells a variety of hot snacks.

Sabrosón (Av Padre Julio Herrera) Across the street from Cucuve, does open-air *parrilladas* (grilled meats).

Soonrise (Av Padre Julio Herrera) Good for breakfasts and cheap set lunches.

El Chocolate Galápagos (Av Charles Darwin) Has great breakfasts and burgers.

Capricho Café (Av Charles Darwin) Good for coffee and juices.

Garrapata (Av Charles Darwin) The place for pasta and it's open late.

Rincón de Alma, near the harbor, serves good *ceviche* and seafood at reasonable prices.

DRINKING
La Panga (Av Charles Darwin) Next to Garrapata, it's the most popular disco in town.

Most people start out with drinks at the equally popular bar El Bongo, downstairs. Always busy on weekends, Limón y Café is a laid-back little hangout with a pool.

Around Puerto Ayora
Much of the island is off-limits to visitors without a guide. Unless otherwise noted, you can visit the following sites by yourself. The **Charles Darwin Research Station** (Map p697; www.darwinfoundation.org; admission free) is about a 20-minute walk by road northeast of Puerto Ayora. The station features an information center, a museum, a baby tortoise nursery and a walk-in adult tortoise enclosure where you can meet these Galápagos giants face to face. Paths wind through weird arid-zone vegetation such as prickly pear and other cacti, salt bush and mangroves.

Southwest of Puerto Ayora, a 3km trail takes you to the paradisiacal **Bahía Tortuga** (Turtle Bay; Map p697), which has a beautiful, white, coral-sand beach and protected swimming behind a spit. The beach is backed by mangroves, and you may spot harmless sharks (worry not), pelicans and even flamingos. Marine iguanas abound.

Beware of strong currents on the exposed side of the spit. Follow the sign from Av Padre Julio Herrera.

Buses from Puerto Ayora go to the villages of **Bellavista** (Map p697) and **Santa Rosa** (Map p697), from where you can explore some of the interior. Neither of these villages has hotels. Buses to Santa Rosa (12km west of Bellavista) leave from the corner of Av Padre Julio Herrera and Charles Binford. If there's room, you can hop on the airport bus at 8am from the park. To ensure you don't get stuck, put together a group and hire a truck for the day. You could also rent a bike (it's uphill to the villages) or go with a tour.

From the village of Bellavista, 7km north of Puerto Ayora, you can turn either west on the main road toward Santa Rosa, or east and go about 2km to some **lava tubes** (Map p697; admission US$2). These are underground tunnels more than 1km in length; bring a flashlight.

A footpath north from Bellavista leads toward the highlands, including **Cerro Crocker** (Map p697) and other hills and extinct volcanoes. This is a good chance to see local vegetation and birds. It is about 6km from Bellavista to the crescent-shaped hill of Media Luna and another 3km to the base of Cerro Crocker. This is national park land, and a guide is required.

The twin craters called **Los Gemelos** (Map p697) are 5km beyond Santa Rosa. They are sinkholes rather than volcanic craters and are surrounded by Scalesia forest. Vermilion flycatchers are often seen and short-eared owls are spotted on occasion. Although less than 100m from the road, the craters are hidden by vegetation, so go with a guide.

Near Santa Rosa, **El Chato Tortoise Reserve** protects giant tortoises roaming in the wild. A trail from the village (ask for directions) leads through private property to the reserve, about 3km away. The trail is downhill and often muddy. It forks at the reserve boundary, with the right fork going up to the small hill of Cerro Chato (3km further) and the left fork going to La Caseta (2km). A guide is required. All manner of locals will offer to guide you and competition is tough. If you want an informed, bilingual guide, stop in at any of the boat-tour offices and ask for a recommendation. Otherwise, find your own and bring plenty of water. Horses can be hired in Santa Rosa.

Near the reserve is a ranch owned by the Devine family. This place always has dozens of giant tortoises. You can wander around at will and take photos for a US$3 fee, which includes a cup of coffee or herbal tea that's welcome if the highland *garúa* (mist) has soaked you. Remember to close the gates as you go through.

ISLA SAN CRISTÓBAL
Puerto Baquerizo Moreno
Often simply called Cristóbal, its capital Puerto Baquerizo Moreno is a laid-back little town, busy with tourists during the high season and dead the rest of the year. Arranging tours is difficult, but hanging out is a cinch. Three world-class surf breaks are nearby.

Hotel San Francisco (☎ 05-520-304; s/d US$6/12) The cheapest hotel in town; it's basic but fine.

Mar Azul (☎ 05-520-139; s/d US$12/20) Has pleasant patios and rooms with hot showers and fan.

Hotel Chatham (☎ /fax 05-520-137; d US$15) Plain, clean rooms with corrugated tin roofs, hot showers and fans; they open onto a hammock-filled patio.

Restaurants abound and *almuerzos* are cheap. Be sure to have a *batido* at El Grande; surfers swear the '4x4' – made with *borojó* (a gooey, bitter Colombian fruit), alfalfa, malt, raw egg and your choice of one other fruit – keeps them energized all day.

Around Puerto Baquerizo Moreno
You can visit the following sites without a guide. About 1.5km southeast of Puerto Baquerizo Moreno, **Frigatebird Hill** (Cerro de las Tijeretas; Map p697) provides good views and can be reached on a trail without a guide. You'll pass a national park information office en route, and there's excellent snorkeling on the ocean side.

A few buses a day go from Baquerizo Moreno to the farming center of **El Progreso** (Map p697), about 8km east at the base of the Cerro San Joaquín (896m), the highest point on San Cristóbal. From El Progreso, you can catch one of the occasional buses (or hire a jeep, hitch or walk the 10km) to **El Junco Lagoon** (Map p697), a freshwater lake about 700m above sea level with superb

views. The road continues beyond the lagoon and branches to the isolated beach of **Puerto Chino** (Map p697), where you can camp with permission from the information office on Cerro de las Tijeretas. The other branch goes to **La Galapaguera** (Map p697), where giant tortoises can be seen.

About an hour north of Puerto Baquerizo Moreno by boat is tiny, rocky **Isla Lobos** (Map p697), the main sea lion and blue-footed booby colony open to visitors (a guide is required) to San Cristóbal. The island has a 300m trail and you can see lava lizards here.

ISLA ISABELA
Puerto Villamil (Map p697) is the main town on seldom-visited Isla Isabela. An 18km road leads from the town up to the tiny village of Santo Tomás.

The island has a handful of places to stay, all of which are fairly affordable. In Puerto Villamil, **Posada San Vicente** (☎ 05-529-140; s/d US$3/5) is clean, recommended and fills up fast. **Hotel Ballena Azul** (☎ 05-529-125; isabela@ga.pro.ec; s/d US$8/16) is likely to be the best budget hotel. Singles have shared bath, and doubles and triples have private solar-heated showers. Other places to stay include the **Tero Real** (☎ 05-529-195; s/d US$5/8), with clean rooms and private cold showers, and **Hotel Loja** (☎ 05-529-174), on the road to the highlands.

Hotel Loja has a good restaurant. Most hotels can arrange meals. There are some cheap restaurants in the port, but you need to ask them in advance to cook a meal for you – giving you an idea of how few visitors there are to this island.

ISLA SANTA MARÍA
Also known as Floreana, this island has fewer than 100 inhabitants, most centered around **Puerto Velasco Ibarra** (Map p697), the island's only settlement. There you will find a **hotel and restaurant** (☎ 05-520-250; s/d/tr US$30/50/70), run by the family of the late Margaret Wittmer, who is famous for being one of the islands' first settlers and the author of the book *Floreana,* in which she tells of her early years on the island. Beachfront rooms have hot water and fan, and the place is rarely full. Puerto Velasco Ibarra also has a small gift shop and post office.

ECUADOR DIRECTORY

ACCOMMODATIONS

There is no shortage of places to stay in Ecuador, but during major fiestas or the night before market day, accommodations can be tight, so plan ahead. If you are going to a town specifically for a market or fiesta, try to arrive a day early, or at least by early afternoon the day before the event. Most hotels have single-room rates, although busy tourist towns often charge for the number of beds in the room, regardless of the number of people checking in.

Ecuador has several youth hostels, although they're rarely the best value. *Pensiones* (small hotels) are the cheapest accommodations, although the rooms are sometimes rented by the hour and cleanliness may be suspect. Staying with families is another option. The SAE (p624) can provide information about homestays. Ask about discounts at hotels for SAE members.

Most beds in Ecuador will challenge tall people: expect to hang off the end if you're at all lanky.

ACTIVITIES

What do you wanna do? Climb? The volcanic, snowcapped peaks of Ecuador's central highlands – including Chimborazo (a doozy at 6310m, p658), Cotopaxi (5897m, p650) and the Ilinizas (p647) – attract mountaineers from around the world. Quito (p627), Riobamba (p656), Baños (p651) and Latacunga (p647) are the best towns to hire guides and gear.

How 'bout hiking? The moor-like landscape of Parque Nacional Cajas (p663); the cloud forests of Parque Nacional Podocarpus (p666) or Mindo (p677); the windswept *páramo* of Lagunas de Mojanda, near Otavalo (p641); the spectacular high-Andean Quilotoa loop area (p649); and the coastal dry forests of Parque Nacional Machalilla (p685) are just a few of Ecuador's hiking possibilities.

If bird-watching ruffles your feathers, you're in for a real treat. Mindo is famous for its fowl, the Oriente is awesome – Cabañas Aliñahui (p674) has a bird list numbering 537 species in the lodge's immediate vicinity –

and, of course, the Galápagos, where the seabirds are fearless, is truly mind-altering.

Tena (p672) in the Oriente is Ecuador's kayaking and river-rafting capital, where it's easy to set up day-runs down the nearby upper Río Napo (class III; p671) or Río Misahuallí (class IV+).

The surfing is world class at Montañita (p687) and on Isla San Cristóbal (p706) in the Galápagos. Playas (p688) has some decent nearby breaks, but you'll have to get in with the locals (try the Playas Club Surf) to find them. The Galápagos are also famous for scuba diving and snorkeling (think hammerhead sharks and giant manta rays, baby), while Parque Nacional Machalilla (p685) qualifies as 'pretty damn cool.'

And mountain biking? You can rent bikes for about US$5 per hour in places such as Baños (p653) and Riobamba (p656) or go for the extreme downhill day trips offered by outfitters in those towns, as well as in Quito (p627) and Cuenca (p661).

Beer swilling is also practiced just about everywhere at the end of the day.

BOOKS

Lonely Planet's *Ecuador & the Galápagos Islands* offers more detailed travel information on the country. *Climbing & Hiking in Ecuador* by Rob Rachowiecki and Mark Thurber is a guide to climbing and hiking Ecuador's mountains. Tom Miller's *The Panama Hat Trail* is a wonderful travel book bent around Ecuador's panama hat industry. For a look into the oil industry's effects on the Oriente and the indigenous Huaorani, read Joe Kane's *Savages*.

For a more literary (and surreal) impression of Ecuador, read Henri Michaux's *Ecuador: A Travel Journal*, or Kurt Vonnegut's *Galápagos*, which takes place in futuristic Guayaquil as well as the islands.

BUSINESS HOURS

Banks are generally open Monday through Friday, from 8am or 9am to between 3pm and 5pm. Often they will change money only until around 2pm. In bigger cities, most business and government offices are open Monday through Friday between 9am and 5:30pm, and closed for an hour at lunch, which is sometime between noon and 2pm. On the coast and in smaller towns, the lunch break can be dragged on for two or more hours. Many businesses operate midday hours on Saturday, but nearly everything – including restaurants – closes on Sunday.

CLIMATE

Ecuador's climate consists of wet and dry seasons, with significant variation among the different geographical regions (depending on whether you're in the Andes, on the coast or in the Oriente).

The Galápagos and the coast are influenced by ocean currents. These areas have a hot and rainy season from January to April; you can expect short torrential downpours with skin-cooking sunshine in between. You'll be a walking pool of sweat if you travel on the coast during this time. From May to December it rains infrequently, but the skies are often overcast and the beaches cool. Travel is definitely more pleasant, but you may find the beach a little too nippy for sunbathing at times. Ecuadorians hit the beaches during the wet season.

In the Oriente, it rains during most months, especially during the afternoon and evening. August and December through March are usually the driest months, and April through June are the wettest, with regional variations. Malaria is more common during the wet season, but river travel is usually easier due to higher water levels.

Travel is pleasant in the highlands year-round, although you'll definitely be dodging raindrops in the wet season (October through May). It doesn't rain daily, however, and even April, the wettest month, averages one rainy day in two. The highland dry season is from June through September, with another short, dry season around Christmas.

Daytime temperatures in Quito average a high of 21°C (70°F) and a low of 8°C (48°F) year-round.

For more information and climate charts see the South America Directory (p1028).

DANGERS & ANNOYANCES

Ecuador is a fairly safe country, but you should still be careful. Pickpocketing is definitely on the increase and is common in crowded places, such as markets. Armed robbery is still unusual in most of Ecuador, although parts of Guayaquil, the stairs up El Panecillo in Quito and Rucu Pichincha, near Quito, have a reputation for being very dangerous. Holdups in Quito's New Town are not unheard of.

Every year or so, a couple of long-distance night buses are robbed on the way to the coast. Avoid taking night buses through the provinces of Guayas or Manabí unless you have to.

Take the normal precautions as outlined under Dangers & Annoyances in the South America Directory (see p1030). If you are robbed, get a *denuncia* (police report) from the local police station within 48 hours – they won't process a report after that.

DISABLED TRAVELERS

Unfortunately, Ecuador's infrastructure for disabled travelers is virtually nonexistent. Disabled travelers are, however, eligible for 50% discounts on domestic airfares.

EMBASSIES & CONSULATES
Embassies & Consulates in Ecuador

Embassies and consulates are best visited in the morning.

Australia Guayaquil (☎ 04-268-0823/700; Nahín Isaías & Luís Orrarte, Edificio Tecniseguros, Kennedy Norte)

Canada Guayaquil (☎ 04-256-3580/6747; Córdova 810, 21st fl); Quito (Map pp628-9; ☎ 02-223-2114, 02-250-6162/63; Av 6 de Diciembre 2816 & P Rivet, 4th fl)

Colombia Guayaquil (☎ 04-263-0674/75; Francisco de Orellana, World Trade Center, Tower B, 11th fl); Quito (☎ 02-245-8012; Atahualpa 955 & República, 3rd fl); Tulcán (☎ 06-980-559; Bolívar 3-68 & Junín; ☺ 8am-1pm Mon-Fri)

France Guayaquil (☎ 04-232-8442; J Mascote 909 & Hurtado, Ground fl); Quito (Map pp628-9; ☎ 02-254-3101/10, 02-256-9883; Diego de Almagro 1550 & Pradera)

Germany Quito (☎ 02-297-0820; Naciones Unidas & República de El Salvador, Edificio Citiplaza, 14th fl)

Holland Quito (Map pp628-9; ☎ 02-222-9229/30, 02-256-7606; Av 12 de Octubre 1942 & Cordero, World Trade Center, Tower 1, 1st fl)

Ireland Quito (☎ 02-245-1577; Antonio de Ulloa 2651 & Rumipamba)

Peru Guayaquil (☎ 04-228-0114/35/42; Francisco de Orellana, Edificio Porta, 14th fl); Machala (☎ 07-930-680; cnr Bolívar & Colón; ☺ mornings Mon-Fri); Quito (☎ 02-246-8410/389; El Salvador 495 & Irlanda)

UK Guayaquil (☎ 04-256-0400/3850; Córdova 623 at Padre Solano); Quito (☎ 02-297-0800/01; Naciones Unidas & República de El Salvador, Edificio Citiplaza, 14th fl)

USA Guayaquil (Map pp690-1; ☎ 04-232-3570; 9 de Octubre and García Moreno); Quito (Map pp628-9; ☎ 02-256-2890; Av Patria & Av 12 de Octubre)

Venezuela Quito (☎ 02-226-8636; Av Los Cabildos 115)

Ecuadorian Embassies & Consulates Abroad

Ecuador has embassies in Colombia and Peru, and also in the following countries.

Australia Canberra (☎ 02-6262 5282; embecu@hotkey .net.au; 1st fl, Law Society Bldg, 11 London Circuit, Canberra, ACT 2601)

Canada Ottawa (☎ 613-563-8206; mecuacan@sprint.ca; 50 O'Connor St, Suite 316, Ottawa K1P 6L2)

France Paris (☎ 01-45 61 10 21; ambecuad@wanadoo.fr; 34 Avenue de Messine, 75008 Paris)

Germany Berlin (☎ 030 238 6217; Kaiser-Friedrich Strasse 90,10585 Berlin)

UK London (☎ 020-7584 1367; embajada@ecuador.fr eeserve.co.uk; 3 Hans Crescent, Knightsbridge, London SW1X 0LS)

USA Washington (☎ 202-234-7200; mecuawaa@pop .erols.com; 2535 15th St NW, Washington, DC 20009)

FESTIVALS & EVENTS

Many of Ecuador's major festivals are oriented around the Roman Catholic liturgical calendar. These are often celebrated with great pageantry, especially in highland indigenous villages, where a Catholic feast day is often the excuse for a traditional indigenous fiesta with drinking, dancing, rituals and processions. The most important are:

Carnaval (February – dates vary) Celebrated throughout Ecuador.

Fiesta de Frutas y Flores (Fruit and flower festival) Held in Ambato on the last two weeks of February.

Corpus Christi (June – dates vary) Religious feast day (the Thursday after the eighth Sunday after Easter) combined with the traditional harvest fiesta in many highland towns; includes processions and street dancing.

Día de San Juan (St John the Baptist; June 24) Fiestas in Otavalo area.

Día de San Pedro y San Pablo (St Peter & St Paul; June 29) Fiestas in Otavalo area and other northern highland towns.

Fiesta del Yamor (September 1–15) Held in Otavalo.

Fiesta de la Mamá Negra (September 23–24) Held in Latacunga.

Fundación de Quito (Founding of Quito; December 6) Celebrated the first week of December with bullfights, parades and dancing.

FOOD & DRINKS
Ecuadorian Cuisine

For breakfast, eggs and bread rolls or toast are available. A good alternative is a *humita*, a sweet-corn tamale often served with coffee.

Lunch is the main meal of the day for many Ecuadorians. A cheap restaurant will serve a decent *almuerzo* (lunch of the day) for as little as US$1.25. An *almuerzo* consists of a *sopa* (soup) and a *segundo* (second dish), which is usually a stew with plenty of rice. Sometimes the segundo is *pescado* (fish), *lentejas* (lentils) or *menestras* (generally, whatever legume stew – usually it's beans or peas – happens to be in the pot). Some places serve salad (often cooked), juice and *postre* (dessert), as well as the two main courses.

The *merienda* (evening meal) is a set meal usually similar to lunch. If you don't want the *almuerzo* or *merienda*, you can choose from the menu, but this is always more expensive.

A *churrasco* is a hearty dish of fried beef, fried eggs, a few veggies, fried potatoes, slices of avocado and tomato, and the inevitable rice.

Arroz con pollo is a mountain of rice with little bits of chicken mixed in. *Pollo a la brasa* is roast chicken, often served with fries. *Gallina* is usually boiled chicken, as in soups, and *pollo* is more often chicken that's been spit-roasted or fried.

Parrilladas are grill houses. Steaks, pork chops, chicken breasts, blood sausage, liver and tripe are all served (together or individually, depending on the establishment). Some *parrilladas* do the Argentine thing and serve everything together on a tabletop grill.

Seafood is good, even in the highlands, as it is brought in fresh from the coast. The most common types of fish are *corvina* (white sea bass) and *trucha* (trout). Popular throughout Ecuador, *ceviche* is uncooked seafood marinated in lemon and served with popcorn and sliced onions. It's delicious. *Ceviche* can be *de pescado* (fish), *de camarones* (shrimp), *de concha* (shellfish) or *mixto* (mixed). Unfortunately, improperly prepared *ceviche* is a source of cholera, so avoid it if in any doubt.

Chifas (Chinese restaurants) are generally inexpensive. They serve *chaulafan* (rice dishes) and *tallarines* (noodles mixed with your choice of meat or vegetables). Portions tend to be filling, with a good dose of MSG. Vegetarians will find that *chifas* are the best choice for meatless dishes. Vegetarian restaurants are rare in Ecuador.

Restaurants usually offer a wide range of dishes, including the following:

Caldo Soup or stew. Often served in markets for breakfast. *Caldo de gallina* (chicken soup) is the most popular. *Caldo de patas* is soup made by boiling cattle hooves.

Cuy Whole-roasted guinea pig. A traditional food dating back to Inca times, cuy tastes rather like a cross between rabbit and chicken. They're easily identified on grills with their little paws and teeth sticking out and tightly closed eyes. It's a local delicacy.

Lechón Suckling pig, often roasted whole. This is a common sight at Ecuadorian food markets. Pork is also called *chancho*.

Llapingachos Fried mashed-potato-and-cheese pancakes, often served with *fritada* (scraps of fried or roast pork).

Seco Literally 'dry' (as opposed to a 'wet' soup), this is stew, usually meat served with rice. It may be *seco de gallina* (chicken stew), *de res* (beef), *de chivo* (goat) or *de cordero* (lamb).

Tortillas de maíz Tasty fried corn pancakes.

Yaguarlocro Another classic. Potato soup with chunks of fried blood sausage floating in it. Many people prefer straight *locro*, which usually has potatoes, corn and an avocado or cheese topping – without the blood sausage.

Drinks

Purify all tap water or buy bottled water. *Agua mineral* is carbonated; Güitig (pronounced weetig) is the most famous brand. *Agua sin gas* is not carbonated.

Bottled drinks are cheap and all the usual soft drinks are available. The local ones have endearing names such as Bimbo or Lulu. Ask for your drink *helada* if you want it out of the refrigerator, *al clima* if you don't. Remember to say *sin hielo* (without ice) unless you really trust the water supply.

Jugos (juices) are available everywhere. Make sure you get *jugo puro* (pure) and not *con agua* (with water). The most common kinds are *mora* (blackberry), *tomate de árbol* (a strangely appetizing fruit with a greenish taste), *naranja* (orange), *toronja* (grapefruit), *maracuyá* (passion fruit), *piña* (pineapple), *sandía* (watermelon), *naranjilla* (a local fruit that tastes like bitter orange) and papaya.

Coffee is widely available but is often disappointing. Instant – served either *en leche* (with milk) or *en agua* (with water) – is the most common. Espresso is available in the better restaurants.

Té (tea) is served black with lemon and sugar. *Té de hierbas* (herb tea) and hot chocolate are also popular.

For alcoholic drinks, local *cervezas* (beers – memorize it) are good and inexpensive.

Pilsener is available in 650mL bottles, while Club comes in 330mL bottles. Imports are tough to find. Local wines are terrible and imported wines are expensive.

Ron (rum) is cheap and good. The local firewater, *aguardiente,* is sugarcane alcohol, and is an acquired taste but can be good. It's very cheap. Imported spirits are expensive.

GAY & LESBIAN TRAVELERS

Ecuador is probably not the best place to be outwardly affectionate with a partner of the same sex. Homosexuality was illegal until 1997, giving an idea of how far off tolerance lies. Quito and Guayaquil have underground social scenes, but outside the dance club, they're hard to find. Pick up a copy of *Conexión G&L* at **Hostal El Ciprés** (Map pp628-9; Lérida 381 & Pontevedra, La Floresta) in Quito – it will plug you into whatever scenes do exist in the major cities. Also check out **Syberian's Gay Guide to Quito** (http://gayquitoec.tripod.com) or **Gayecuador** (www.gayecuador.com in Spanish).

HEALTH

Decent, affordable health care is available at hospitals and clinics in most towns. Treat tap water with caution. A yellow fever vaccination and malaria precautions are advisable for the Oriente or the northern coastal lowlands (the highlands are unaffected by those diseases). Dengue fever is occasionally a problem on the coast. Condoms are widely sold.

For more information, see the Health chapter (p1053).

HOLIDAYS

On major holidays, banks, offices and other services are closed and public transport is often very crowded; book ahead if possible. The following are Ecuador's major national holidays; they may be celebrated for several days around the actual date:

Año Nuevo (New Year's Day; January 1)

Epifanía (Epiphany; January 6)

Semana Santa (Holy Week; dates vary)

Día del Trabajador (Labor Day; May 1)

Batalla de Pichincha (Battle of Pichincha; May 24) National holiday commemorating the decisive battle for independence from Spain in 1822.

Cumpleaños de Simón Bolívar (Simón Bolívar's Birthday; July 24)

Fundación de Guayaquil (Founding of Guayaquil; July 25)

Independencia de Quito (Quito's Independence Day; August 10)
Independencia de Guayaquil (Guayaquil's Independence Day; October 9)
Día de la Raza (Columbus Day; October 12)
Todos los Santos (All Saints' Day/All Souls' Day; November 1–2) Celebrated by flower-laying ceremonies in the cemeteries; especially colorful in rural areas.
Independencia de Cuenca (Cuenca's Independence Day; November 3)
Fundación de Quito (Founding of Quito; December 6) Celebrated throughout the first week of December with bullfights, parades and dancing.
Nochebuena/Navidad (Christmas Eve/Christmas Day; December 24–25)
Año Nuevo (End-of-year celebrations; December 28–31) Parades and dances culminate in the burning of life-size effigies in the streets on New Year's Eve.

INTERNET ACCESS

All but the smallest of towns have cybercafés. The smaller the town, however, the higher the rates (up to about US$3 per hour) and the slower the service.

INTERNET RESOURCES

Best of Ecuador (www.bestofecuador.com) Comprehensive tourist information.
Ecuador Explorer (www.ecuadorexplorer.com) Covers just about everything visitors might want to know.
Ecuadorian Embassy in the US (www.ecuador.org) Current events, visa requirements, news and more.
Lanic (http://lanic.utexas.edu/la/ecuador/) Outstanding collection of links from the University of Texas.

MAPS

Ecuadorian bookstores carry a limited selection of Ecuadorian maps. The best selection is available from the **Instituto Geográfico Militar** (IGM; Map pp628-9; ☎ 02-254-5090, 02-222-9075/76; map sales r ⌚ 8am-1pm & 1:30-4:30pm Mon-Thu, 7am-3pm Fri) in Quito (see p622). *The Pocket Guide to Ecuador*, published in Quito, includes maps of the country and the major cities.

MEDIA

The country's best newspapers are *El Comercio* (www.elcomercio.com in Spanish) and *Hoy* (www.hoy.com.ec in Spanish), published in Quito, and *El Telégrafo* and *El Universo* (www.eluniverso.com), published in Guayaquil. An abbreviated version of the *Miami Herald* is available in Quito for about US$0.50. The *Explorer* is a free monthly booklet printed in English and Spanish listing what's on in Quito.

MONEY

ATMs

ATMs are the easiest way of getting cash – period. They're found in most cities and even in smaller towns, although they are sometimes out of order. Make sure you have a four-digit PIN. Bancos del Pacífico and Bancos del Pichincha have MasterCard/Cirrus ATMs. Bancos de Guayaquil and Bancos La Provisora have Visa/Plus ATMs.

Change

Change is difficult to come by. Trying to purchase inexpensive items with a US$20 bill (or even a US$10 bill) generally results in either you or the proprietor running shop to shop until someone has change. If no one does, you're out of luck. Change bills whenever you can. To ask for change, make a deeply worried face and ask, '*¿Tiene suelto?*' (Do you have change?).

Credit Cards

Credit cards are useful, particularly when buying cash from a bank. Visa and MasterCard are the most widely accepted.

Currency

Ecuador's currency was the sucre until it switched to the US dollar in 2000 – a process called dollarization (see Recent Political Developments under History, p616 for more information). Bills are identical to those used in the US and come in denominations of 1, 5, 10, 20, 50 and up. Coins are identical in shape, size and material to their US counterparts and have the same denominations of 1, 5, 10, 25 and 50 cents. Instead of the heads of US presidents, however, they feature the faces and symbols of Ecuador.

Exchange Rates

Exchange rates at press time included the following:

Country	Unit		US$
Australia	A$1	=	0.70
Canada	C$1	=	0.75
euro zone	€1	=	1.15
Japan	¥100	=	0.91
New Zealand	NZ$1	=	0.61
United Kingdom	UK£1	=	1.68

ECUADOR

Exchanging Money

Foreign currencies can be exchanged into US dollars easily in Quito, Guayaquil and Cuenca, where rates are the best. You can also change money at major border crossings. In some places, notably the Oriente, it is difficult to exchange money. Exchange houses, or *casas de cambio*, are normally the best places; banks will also exchange money but are slower. Usually, exchange rates are within 2% of one another in any given city. There is little difference between exchange rates for cash and traveler's checks. Most banks and nearly all exchange houses will cash traveler's checks, but only top-end hotels and restaurants will consider them.

Major towns have a black market for currency, usually near the big *casas de cambio*. Rates are about the same, but street changing is illegal, and forged currency and cheating have been reported.

International Transfers

The fastest way to have money transferred from abroad is with Western Union. It has offices in all major cities and charges US$85 for a US$1000 transfer. Your bank can also wire money to a cooperating Ecuadorian bank. This is cheaper than Western Union, but takes about three business days.

POST

It costs US$0.85 to send a letter to North America and US$1.05 to Europe. For a few cents extra, you can send them *certificado* (certified). Sending parcels of 2kg to 20kg is best done in Quito, at the post office on Calle Ulloa near Calle Dávalos.

To receive mail in Ecuador, have the sender mail your item to the nearest post office, eg Joan SMITH, Lista de Correos, Correo Central, Quito (or town and province of your choice), Ecuador. Mail is filed alphabetically, so make sure that your last name is clear.

Clients of **American Express** (Map pp628-9; ☎ 02-256-0488; Amazonas 339, 5th fl) can receive mail sent to them c/o American Express, Apartado 17-01-02-605, Quito, Ecuador. The **SAE** (p624) will hold mail sent to the clubhouse. If your incoming mail weighs over 2kg, you have to recover it from customs (and pay high duty).

RESPONSIBLE TRAVEL

Responsible travel in Ecuador is a tricky issue. 'Ecotourism' is a major buzzword used by nearly every tour operator in the country, and it really comes down to your own impression of the company you're dealing with as to whether it practices the responsibility it espouses. The SAE in Quito (p624) is an excellent resource for finding tour operators and hotels or lodges that truly practice ecotourism.

On the level of personal behavior, there are several things you can do to leave a minimal impact (or maximize your positive impact) on the country. If you're taking a tour in the Oriente, make sure your guide does not hunt game for the cooking pot or cut trees for firewood. If you plan to visit an indigenous community, make sure the guide is from the community or has a good working relationship with the community (or written permission to visit, in the case of the Huaorani). In the Galápagos, do not approach the animals (no matter how tempting) or wander off the trails. With the sheer number of tourists visiting the islands, this is incredibly important. On the islands, as well as on the coast, think twice before eating lobster or shrimp – lobster is overfished and shrimp farming is one of the most ecologically damaging practices in the country. Do not buy anything made from coral, particularly black coral. Don't litter, even though many Ecuadorians do.

With all the stories travelers love to tell about slashed or stolen packs, it's easy to get paranoid. Remember that Ecuadorians travel their country too, but you'll never see an Ecuadorian with a fandangled, wire-mesh locking bag around their luggage. Items like this simply shout that you don't trust the people you're supposedly here to get to know.

See Responsible Travel at the front of this book for more information.

SHOPPING

Souvenirs are good, varied and cheap. If you have time for only one big shopping expedition, the Saturday market at Otavalo (p638) is both convenient and varied. In markets and smaller stores, bargaining is expected, although don't expect to reduce the price by more than about 20%. In Quito's 'tourist stores,' prices are usually fixed.

ECUADOR

Woolen goods are popular and are often made of a pleasantly coarse homespun wool. The price of a thick sweater will begin at less than US$10, depending on size and quality. Wool is also spun into a much tighter textile used for making ponchos. *Otavaleño* indigenous ponchos are among the best in Latin America.

Panama hats are worth buying. A really good panama is so finely made that it can be rolled up and passed through a man's ring. Montecristi and Cuenca are the best places to buy them.

Weavings are found all over the country. Cotacachi and Ambato are centers for leather goods.

San Antonio de Ibarra, between Otavalo and Ibarra, is Ecuador's major woodworking center. Balsa-wood models, especially of brightly colored birds, are popular; these are made in the Oriente.

STUDYING

Ecuador is one of the best places to study Spanish on the continent. Quito (p627) and Cuenca (p661), and to a lesser extent Otavalo (p640) and Baños (p653), are the best places to shack up with the books and go one-on-one with your teacher. Prices range from US$5 to US$10 per hour.

TELEPHONE

Andinatel (mainly in the highlands and Oriente) and Pacifictel (mainly on the coast) provide long-distance national and international telephone services. Offices are generally open 8am to 10pm daily (except in small towns or airports, where they keep shorter hours). The city of Cuenca uses Etapa, a private telephone service. Calls cost about US$0.38 per minute to the USA, about US$0.50 to the UK and about US$1.05 to Australia.

Reverse-charge (collect) phone calls are possible to North America and most European countries. Direct dialing to a North American or European operator is also possible; the numbers are available from your long-distance service provider. From a private phone within Ecuador, dial ☎ 116 for an international operator. You can also make Internet phone calls in larger towns for about US$0.25 a minute to the USA and Europe. The connection isn't great and the delay is annoying, but it's cheap.

NEW '2' FOR TELEPHONE NUMBERS

Days before this book went to print, Ecuador added a '2' to the beginning of all telephone numbers (except cellular numbers). Telephone numbers now have seven digits, the first always being a '2.' (Telephone numbers within Guayas and Pichincha Provinces already had seven digits, so the numbers listed in this book for those provinces are complete). Throughout Ecuador, people still regularly quote only six numbers. If you come across a six-digit number for a noncellular telephone number, simply add a '2' to the beginning to make it complete. For example, if a Riobamba telephone number was 683-456, it is now 268-3456. You must still dial the area code (in this example, ☎ 03 for Chimborazo province) when calling from outside the province.

Two-digit area codes change by province. Dial ☎ 09 for mobile phones. Throughout this book, the area code is given with each telephone number. Drop the area code if you're calling within a province. If calling from abroad, drop the 0 from the code. Ecuador's country code is ☎ 593.

To call locally, you can use either a Pacifictel or Andinatel office or a phone box on the street or in a bar or restaurant. Phone boxes are usually Porta or Bell South cellular pay-phone boxes and operate with a prepaid phone card. The cards come in various denominations and are available wherever the phones are found. You can also call internationally with these cards.

TOILETS

Ecuadorian plumbing has very low pressure. Putting toilet paper into the bowl may clog the system, so a waste receptacle is provided for paper. A basket of used toilet paper may seem unsanitary, but is much better than clogged bowls and water overflowing onto the floor. A well-run hotel will ensure that the receptacle is emptied and the toilet cleaned daily. The same applies to restaurants and other public toilets. The more expensive hotels have adequate flushing capabilities.

Public toilets are limited mainly to bus terminals, airports and restaurants. Lavatories are called *servicios higiénicos* and are usually marked 'SS.HH.' People needing to use the lavatory often ask to use the *baño* in a restaurant; toilet paper is rarely available, so the experienced traveler carries a personal supply.

TOURIST INFORMATION

The government-run **Ministerio de Turismo** (www.vivecuador.com) maintains tourist offices in most towns. They're generally underfunded, but staffed by friendly folks who usually do what they can to answer your questions (in Spanish). The private Cámara de Turismo (Chamber of Tourism) operates offices in most major towns and can be a useful source of information.

TOURS

Most of the Galápagos archipelago is accessible to visitors only by guided tour (ie a cruise). Many travelers also opt to visit the Amazon on organized tours, as these are efficient, educational and often the only way to get deep into the rain forest.

VIDEOS

Lonely Planet's *Ecuador & the Galápagos Islands* video (which is available at www.lonelyplanet.com under Propaganda) is an excellent predeparture warm-up to the country's attractions.

VISAS & DOCUMENTS

Most tourists entering Ecuador need a passport (valid for six months or more from the date of entry) and a T-3 tourist card, which is obtainable on arrival. The T-3 is free, but don't lose it – you'll need it for stay extensions, passport checks and leaving the country. Lost cards can be replaced at the immigration office in Quito or Guayaquil or at exit points in Ecuador.

On arrival, you get identical stamps on both your passport and T-3, indicating how long you can stay. The maximum is 90 days, but less is often given. You can get an extension at the immigration offices in Quito (p624) or Guayaquil (p689).

Tourists can stay for a total of 90 days in any 12-month period. UK citizens may stay longer. Trying to extend your stay by leaving the country and returning doesn't usually work because the border officials check entry and exit dates (although they aren't always thorough).

Officially, to enter the country you must have a ticket out of Ecuador and sufficient funds for your stay, but border authorities rarely ask for proof of this.

Always carry your passport and T-3 card for document checks on public transport. You can be arrested if you have no ID and deported if you don't have a visa or T-3.

International vaccination certificates are not required by law, but some vaccinations, particularly against yellow fever, are advisable.

VOLUNTEERING

Nearly all organizations accepting volunteers in Ecuador require a minimum commitment of one month, and many require at least basic Spanish-speaking skills. Most also *charge* volunteers between US$100 and US$300 per month, so don't expect free room and board in exchange for your work – it's rarely given. By far, the best place to get information in Ecuador is the Quito clubhouse of **SAE** (p624). **Ecuador Explorer** (www.ecuadorexplorer.com) has a great classified page listing numerous organizations that need volunteers. Go to its homepage and click Classifieds under Ecuador, Tours & Things to Do.

WOMEN TRAVELERS

Ecuador is among the least (outwardly) macho of the Latin American countries, but machismo can still manifest itself subtly. For instance, if you speak Spanish and have a male traveling companion who doesn't, Ecuadorian men may still ignore you and try to converse with your language-challenged friend. Brazen come-ons and whistles are rare, but become less so with some alcohol-induced courage.

Tampons are expensive and available in regular sizes only in major cities; sanitary pads are cheaper and more common. Condoms are widely sold, but spermicidal jelly for diaphragms is hard to find. The choice of oral contraceptives is limited, so bring your preferred brand from home.

WORKING

Officially you need a work visa to get a job in Ecuador. You might, however, teach English in language schools without one, usually in Quito or Cuenca. The pay is low but enough to live on.

The Guianas

Occupying the northeast shoulder of South America, the republics of Guyana and Suriname and the department of French Guiana are the continent's undiscovered jewels of ecotourism. The region exhibits a curious political and social geography left by British, Dutch and French colonization. Collectively referred to as the Guianas, these regions are culturally more Caribbean than South American, and they offer a fascinating contrast to the rest of the continent. Each capital city is its own unique microcosm, wonderfully diverse in everything from language to religion to cuisine. The interior regions promise some of the best off-the-beaten-track traveling around; never dominated by Europeans, they retain some of the world's purest remaining tropical forests. Traveling in any of the Guianas can be challenging and relatively expensive yet, despite the hardships and costs, incredibly rewarding.

Of the three Guianas (which all offer unique yet comparable ecotourism opportunities), French Guiana is tops for comfort, ease of transport and variety of sights – it is also primarily (and in some places, exclusively) French-speaking. Guyana is English-speaking and less expensive (except for tours into the interior) than French Guiana, but its reputation as an unsafe and desperate country strengthens daily. Suriname has a vibrant capital and is cheaper than Guyana, but its minimalist infrastructure makes exploration costly and primarily guide-dependent.

THE GUIANAS

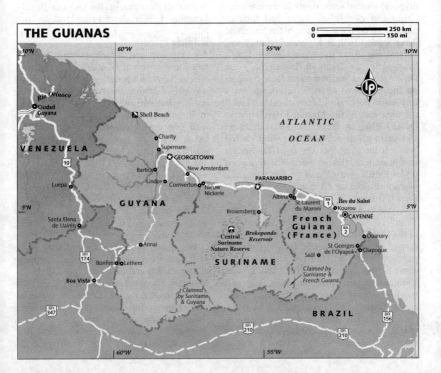

THE GUIANAS

0 ————— 250 km
0 ————— 150 mi

HISTORY

The muddy Guiana coastline, covered by mangroves and sparsely populated with warlike Carib Indians, did not attract early European settlement. Spaniards first saw the coast in 1499, but they found no prospect of gold or cheap labor, though they made occasional slave raids. Several 16th-century explorers, including Sir Walter Raleigh, placed the mythical city of El Dorado in the region, but Spain's European rivals displayed no sustained interest in the region until the mid-17th century.

The Netherlands began to settle the land in 1615. After forming the Dutch West India Company in 1621, the colonists traded with Amerindian peoples of the interior and established plantations of sugar, cocoa and other tropical commodities. Indigenous peoples were almost wiped out by introduced diseases, so the Dutch imported West African slaves to construct dikes and work the plantation economies. Beginning in the mid-18th century, escaped slaves (descendants of whom are now called Maroons, or Bushnegroes) formed settlements in the interior.

England established sugar and tobacco plantations on the west bank of the Suriname River around 1650 and founded what is now Paramaribo. After the second Anglo-Dutch War, under the Treaty of Breda (1667), the Dutch retained Suriname and their colonies on the Guyanese coast (in exchange for a tiny island now called Manhattan) but ceded the area east of the Maroni (Marowijne in Dutch) River to the French. For the next 150 years sovereignty of the region shifted between the three powers; by 1800 Britain was dominant, though Suriname remained under Dutch control, and France retained a precarious hold on Cayenne in what is now French Guiana.

At the end of the Napoleonic Wars, the Treaty of Paris reaffirmed the sovereignty of the Dutch in Suriname and of the French east of the Maroni, while Britain formally purchased the Dutch colonies in what became British Guyana. By 1834 slavery was abolished in all British colonies, and and the Royal Navy suppressed the slave trade in the Caribbean. This created a need for more plantation labor, and the subsequent immigration of indentured labor from other colonies (especially India) created a unique ethnic mix in each of the Guianas.

ENVIRONMENT
Land

Although Caribbean in culture, the Guianas actually front the Atlantic Ocean. The most prominent geological feature is the Guiana Shield, an extensive, crystalline upland that extends throughout northeast Brazil, French Guiana, Suriname, Guyana and Venezuela. Once part of the larger Brazilian Shield to the south, it became separated in Tertiary times, when the rising Andes reversed the course of west-flowing rivers and created the Amazon Basin. The shield falls away in steps from 2810m Mt Roraima, on the Guyana–Brazil–Venezuela border, down to sea level.

Wildlife

An extensive and largely pristine tropical rain forest covers the Guianas' interior and offers a habitat for countless plant and animal species (although these ecosystems are threatened by both uncontrolled gold mining and multinational timber companies operating with few environmental safeguards). The jaguar is the most magnificent wild mammal, but the region teems with relatively undisturbed populations of splendid creatures, such as the scarlet macaw, the giant anteater and the sun parakeet. The Guianas are also home to flourishing numbers of creatures – like the tapir, black caiman and giant river otter – endangered in other parts of lowland South America.

The many waterways abound with side-neck turtles, electric eels, spectacled caimans, black piranhas and *tucunares* (peacock bass). Along the coasts are seasonal nesting sites for the awe-inspiring giant leatherback turtle, as well as green and olive ridley turtles. The Guianas are probably the best place in South America to see two of the most memorable species of Amazonian birds: the harpy eagle and the cock-of-the-rock.

Environmental Issues

The Guianas are at a collective conservation crossroads, trying to balance the pressing need to boost their economies (which can be accomplished most quickly through logging, mining and oil exploration) and the longer-term prospects for ecotourism. All three have been actively putting aside lands as protected nature reserves. Starting with a US$1 million donation, Suriname established the 16,187 sq km Central Suriname Nature Reserve in 1998, followed by a conservation foundation to protect nearly 15% of the nation's total area. That conservation effort is supported by a US$15 million endowment from the UN Development Program.

In Suriname, Conservation International is trying to promote biodiversity as a way to conserve the forest, and in Guyana the organization is aiming to develop more national preservation areas. Guyana is also hoping that the discovery of a giant sloth fossil in the Mazaruni area of the interior will draw tourists.

All three Guianas have leatherback turtle sites, under threat by hunters.

RESPONSIBLE TRAVEL

Whether spoken in French, Sranan Tongo or Amerindian, 'ecotourism' means the same thing throughout the Guianas. However, some operators have their own take on what it means as far as practice goes. Poke around and get a feel for a company's 'ecostrategy' before going with it. Rest assured that Suriname's Stinasu (see p742) is environmentally sensitive; a percentage of every tour booking goes directly to nature conservation.

On an individual level, make your ecotourist impact by making no impact. As well as always keeping the basics in mind, tread lightly in the interior in particular. Bring fishhooks and knives as trade goods (Maroons also like welcoming gifts of rum, but don't take rum into Amerindian villages), and ask locals' permission before photographing them. In some communities, like Amerindian villages in Guyana, you must obtain permission to visit. If you go with a guide, ensure that he or she shows environmental respect – no hunting, gathering, littering etc – and, ideally, is from the culture of the village that you're visiting. In cities, keep an eye out for and steer clear of rare animals (like turtle) on menus, buy local products and, no matter where you are, conserve energy and water (many establishments filter their own water or collect precious rainwater).

TRANSPORT

For more information about traveling in the Guianas see the individual transport sections for French Guiana (p721), Suriname (p739) and Guyana (p752–3).

Air

Most visitors to the Guianas visit one region and thus arrive and depart from the same city – international flights arrive in Georgetown (Guyana), Paramaribo (Suriname) and Cayenne (French Guiana). From North America, flights go to all three cities, but won't avoid Miami and probably one or multiple Caribbean islands. For example, Air France offers regular flights from Miami to Cayenne via Guadeloupe, Martinique and Haiti, but believe it or not it can sometimes be more cost- and time-efficient to fly via Paris. Thanks to lingering colonial ties, you can fly direct to Cayenne from Paris, and from Amsterdam you can arrive in Paramaribo blissfully unburdened by plane changes.

Car & Motorcycle

It is possible to travel overland across all three Guianas but only in the coastal area. Be forewarned that road travel here is difficult – it helps to be well trained in the art of auto repair and to carry spare tires and fuel. Rainy seasons drastically affect road conditions, especially in Guyana and Suriname, where roads are iffy even when dry. Cars (especially rentals) aren't always allowed over borders and are particularly unwelcome into Suriname from French Guiana.

From the west, you can get into Guyana from Boa Vista in northern Brazil, but the road connection to Georgetown is not always open, and you may have to take a flight. From Georgetown, roads follow the coast eastward, with a river crossing into Suriname and another into French Guiana, plus several others along the way. A road from Régina, in French Guiana, to the Brazil border is expected to open in early 2004.

There is a lot of illegal immigration (called 'backtracking') across all of these borders, and papers are scrutinized carefully. Note that entry into French Guiana and Suriname requires onward tickets.

THE GUIANAS

THE GUIANAS

FRENCH GUIANA

HIGHLIGHTS

- **Awala-Yalimopo during turtle egg-laying season** – observe by moonlight the amazing ritual of giant leatherback turtles storming the beach to lay eggs, and of their newborn offspring waddling to the sea (p732)
- **Îles du Salut** – visit two of these fascinating former penal-settlement islands by private catamaran or sailboat (avoiding the crowded, fumigating ferry that visits only one island; p729)
- **Centre Spatial Guyanais (Guianese Space Center)** – learn everything you always wanted to know about rockets but were afraid to ask, and enjoy one of French Guiana's few English-language displays, in the Musée de L'Espace (Space Museum; p728)
- **Best journey** – St Laurent du Maroni to Awala-Yalimopo via Javouhey and Mana: spot wildlife in the engulfing greenery of the thick, lush rain forest that lines this entire route to the sea (p732)
- **Off the beaten track** – be humbled in the Trésor Nature Reserve (or just about anywhere in the interior) amid age-old stands of virgin rain forest (p727)

FAST FACTS

- **Area:** 91,000 sq km (slightly smaller than Portugal or the US state of Indiana)
- **Budget:** US$50–60 a day
- **Capital:** Cayenne
- **Costs:** hammock space on Île Royale free, savory crepe US$3, guava nectar US$1
- **Country code:** ☎ 594
- **Electricity:** 220/127V, 50Hz
- **Famous for:** penal settlements (particularly Devil's Island), Centre Spatial Guyanais
- **Languages:** French, French Guianese, Creole, Amerindian languages, Sranan Tongo (Surinaams)
- **Money:** US$1 = €0.87
- **Phrases:** *chébran* (cool), *infect* (disgusting), *une teuf* (party)
- **Population:** 182,400 (2002 estimate)
- **Time:** GMT minus 3 hours
- **Tipping:** 10% in restaurants and hotels if not included; none in taxis
- **Traveler's checks:** cashed at nationwide banks and *casa de cambios* (currency-exchange houses); commission varies
- **Visas:** US$25 for three months; not issued at borders

TRAVEL HINTS

Learn to *parler français*. Reserve ahead (it's hard to wing it here). When leaving Cayenne, don't lug your stuff to the Gare Routière – go there in advance and arrange for a *taxi collectif* (shared taxi) to pick you up at your hotel for no extra charge.

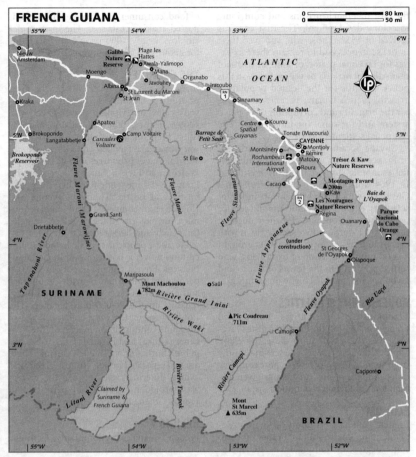

FRENCH GUIANA

THE GUIANAS

The smallest of the Guianas, French Guiana (Guyane – pronounced gwee-*ahn* – locally) is an overseas department of France, and therefore part of the EU. The urban areas of Cayenne and Kourou have excellent facilities and an infrastructure comparable to rural France, but the hinterland is sparsely populated and little developed. Once renowned for the penal colony where Captain Alfred Dreyfus (a French army officer wrongfully convicted of treason in 1894) and Papillon (see Books p733) were imprisoned, today Guyane attracts visitors to not only the ruins of these prisons, but to its unspoiled interior regions and the Centre Spatial Guyanais – launch site for the European Space Agency's Ariane rockets.

HISTORY

The earliest French settlement was in Cayenne in 1643, but tropical diseases and hostile local Amerindians limited plantation development. After various conflicts with the Dutch and British and an eight-year occupation by Brazil and Portugal, the French resumed control only to see slavery abolished (1848), and the few plantations almost collapsed. The 1850s' gold rush saw more laborers desert the plantations and led to border disputes with Suriname and Brazil.

About the same time, France decided that penal settlements in Guyane would reduce the cost of French prisons and contribute to colony development. The first convicts arrived in 1852. Those who survived their initial sentences had to remain there as exiles for an equal period of time, but 90% of them died of malaria or yellow fever, so this policy did little for the desired population growth. French Guiana became notorious for the brutality and corruption of its penal system and for some infamous cases. The last penal settlement closed in 1953.

Guyane became an overseas department of France in 1946, and it receives substantial economic support from the *metropole*. In 1964 work began on the Centre Spatial Guyanais, which has brought an influx of scientists, engineers, technicians and service people from Europe and elsewhere, turning the city of Kourou into a sizable town with every modern amenity. The 1970s brought a good number of Hmong from Laos, who settled primarily in the towns of Cacao and Javouhey and survive chiefly on farming.

GOVERNMENT & POLITICS

Traditionally, conservatives have ruled French Guiana, but the Parti Socialiste Guyanaise has done well since the early 1980s. Some Guianese favor greater autonomy from France, but very few support complete independence – not surprising, given the high level of French economic assistance.

ECONOMY

French Guiana's economy is mainly dependent on metropolitan France and, to some degree, benefits from its EU membership. Successive French governments have provided state employment and billions of francs in subsidies, resulting in a near-European standard of living in urban areas. Rural villages are much poorer, and in the hinterland many Amerindians and Maroons still lead a subsistence lifestyle. Ironically, locals have criticized the French government's relatively generous welfare benefits, arguing that the assistance provides a disincentive to work.

Historically the main export product has been rain forest timber. Now the main industries are fishing (particularly shrimp), forestry and mining (particularly gold). The tourist industry is embryonic but growing. Agriculture consists of a few plantations and Hmong market gardens – the vast majority

of food, consumer goods and energy are imported, making costs soar. The space center employs nearly 1000 people and accounts for about 15% of economic activity.

THE CULTURE

Imagine a part of France without the tourist-riddled landmarks, pretentious sidewalk cafés and yipping poodles, yet with visible history, fabulous cuisine and the sultry French language; then toss a dash of warmth and congeniality into its people and a sprinkling of palm trees into its landscape. Welcome to French Guiana, dependent on France yet independent of her European hustle and bustle. Though Cayenne and Kourou enjoy somewhat continental economies, the majority of the populace struggles financially and lives a modest lifestyle.

Guianese people take pride in their multicultural universe borne of multiregional influences. French Guiana has about 150,000 permanent inhabitants, with temporary and migrant workers from Haiti and Brazil making up the 30,000-plus balance. The Boni represent the only endemic tribe of Maroons, although members of the Aucaner (Djuka) and Paramaccaner tribes live in both Suriname and French Guiana. There are two separate Hmong groups: 'green' and 'white.' Intermarriage between the groups was forbidden in Laos but permitted in French Guiana to prevent inbreeding.

RELIGION

French Guiana is predominantly Catholic, but Maroons and Amerindians follow their own religious traditions. The Hmong also tend to be Roman Catholics due to the influence of Sister Anne-Marie Javouhey, the nun who brought them to French Guiana.

ARTS

Music and dance are the liveliest art forms in French Guiana – think Caribbean rhythms with a French accent. Maroon woodcarvings and Hmong tapestries are sold in markets and along the roadside. Maroon art is also available in Suriname, but Hmong products are not found elsewhere in the Guianas.

ENVIRONMENT
Land

French Guiana borders Brazil to the east and south, while to the west the Maroni and Litani Rivers form the border with Suriname (the southern part is disputed).

The majority of Guianese people live in the Atlantic coastal zone, which has most of French Guiana's limited road network. The coast is mostly mangrove swamp, but there are a few sandy beaches. The densely forested interior, whose terrain rises gradually toward the Tumac-Humac Mountains on the Brazilian frontier, is largely unpopulated.

Wildlife

Blissfully devoid of a considerable plantation history, French Guiana's rain forest is 90% intact. It's also more botanically diverse than Surinamese and Guyanese forests – one hectare of Trésor Nature Reserve's forest contains 164 tree species! French Guiana is also home to myriad animal and insect species, such as tapirs, jaguars, poison arrow frogs and caiman.

TRANSPORT
Getting There & Away
AIR

All international passengers experience Cayenne's Rochambeau International Airport (see p723). If you're headed to Suriname, Brazil and other international destinations (besides France), the departure tax is US$20 and often included in the ticket price. Flights to Paris are regarded as domestic, thus there's no departure tax.

BOAT & BUS

River transport into French Guiana, with *taxi collectif* connections to major municipalities, passes through the border towns of St Laurent du Maroni, on the Suriname border (locally called just St Laurent; see Getting There & Around p732) and St Georges de l'Oyapok, on the Brazilian border (see p728).

Getting Around
AIR

From Cayenne, small flights go to interior destinations such as St Georges and Saül (see Air p725). Air Guyane operates most internal flights.

BOAT

River transport into the interior is possible but requires patience and good timing, unless you are taking a tour. The best places to try to catch a boat are Kaw and Régina.

CAR

Roads in French Guiana are considerably better than in neighboring Suriname or in Guyana, and as a result it's easier and cheaper to see more of the area, especially by car. Secondary and tertiary roads can be bad, especially in the rainy season – have a spare tire, spare gas and spare time. Because public transport is minimal, car rental is worth considering; see Cayenne (p726) and Kourou (p729) for details. An International Driving Permit is recommended but not legally required.

HITCHING

Because private cars are numerous and roads are good in French Guiana, some budget travelers choose to hitchhike, but competition is considerable in certain areas, such as on the outskirts of Cayenne on the highway to Kourou. Major interchanges are the best venues for lifts. Note that hitching is *not* recommended and can be dangerous, especially at night.

TAXI COLLECTIF

Taxis collectifs (actually minibuses) are the second-best wheeled option. They run frequently from Cayenne (see p726) and not as frequently from St Laurent (see p732).

CAYENNE

Cayenne (population 50,750) is one of the loveliest capital cities in South America. In lieu of soaring grandeur and modern urban vibrancy are bustling, colorful markets amid charming French colonial buildings ribbed with flowered balconies. The excellent Creole and Guianese food and the unique ethnic mix – locals, French expatriates, Brazilian fisherfolk, Surinamese Maroons and Hmong farmers – make this a fun place to spend a few days and eat, eat, eat while planning trips to the lush interior or along the populated coast.

Orientation

Cayenne is at the western end of a small, somewhat hilly peninsula between the Cayenne and Mahury Rivers. The center of action is the Place des Palmistes, in the northwest corner, where cafés and outdoor food stalls skirt stands of palm trees. To its west, Place Léopold Héder (aka Place Grenoble) is one of the oldest parts of Cayenne.

THE GUIANAS

CAYENNE

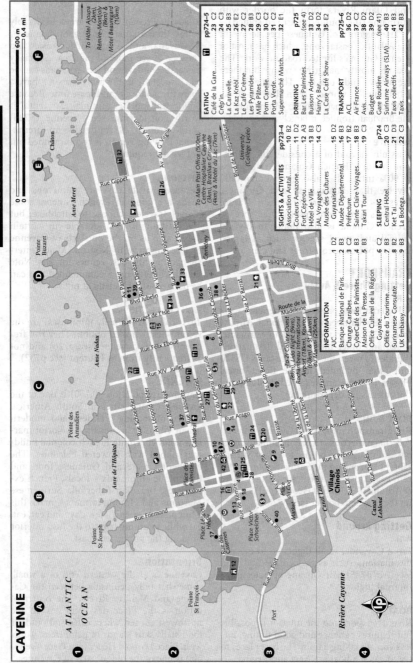

ATLANTIC OCEAN

Pointe St-Joseph

Pointe des Amandiers

Pointe Buzaret

Anse de l'Hôpital

Anse Nadau

Anse des Amandiers

Anse Merct

Château

Pointe St François

Port

Rivière Cayenne

Canal Laussat

Canal Leblond

Village Chinois

0   600 m
0   0.4 mi

To Hôtel Ajoupa (2km);
Rémire-Montjoly (8km) &
Motel Beauregard (10km)

To Main Post Office (500m);
Centre Hospitalier Cayenne
(3km); Brazilian Consulate
(4km) & Motel du Lac (7km)

To 727 Gallery Ouest
(8m); Ludo Night (5km);
Rochambeau International
Airport (18km); Kourou
(60km) & St-Laurent
du Maroni (250km)

INFORMATION
AJC.............................1 D2
Banque National de Paris......2 B3
Change Caraïbes................3 C2
CyberCafé des Palmistes.......4 B3
Maison de la Presse............5 B3
Office Culturel de la Région Guyane......6 C2
Office du Tourisme..............7 B3
Surinamese Consulate..........8 B2
UK Embassy.....................9 B3

SIGHTS & ACTIVITIES   pp723-4
Association Aratai..............10 D2
Couleurs Amazone..............11 D2
Fort Cépérou...................12 A3
Hôtel de Ville..................13 B3
Musée des Cultures Guyanaises...14 C3
Musée Départemental..........15 D2
Préfecture......................16 B3
Sainte Claire Voyages..........17 B2
Takari Tour.....................18 B3
JAL Voyages.....................19 C3

SLEEPING   p724
Central Hôtel...................20 C2
Ket Tai.........................21 B2
La Bodega......................22 B3

EATING   pp724-5
Café de la Gare................23 C2
Crêp'in.........................24 C2
La Caravelle....................25 B3
La Kaz Kréol....................26 E2
Le Café Crème..................27 C2
Les Pyramides..................28 C3
Mille Pâtes.....................29 C3
Pom Canelle....................30 C2
Porta Verde....................31 C2
Supermarché Match............32 E1

DRINKING   p725
Bar Les Palmistes..............(see 4)
Buisson Ardent.................33 D2
Harry's Bar.....................34 D2
La Case Café Show.............35 E2

TRANSPORT   pp725-6
ACL.............................36 D2
Air France......................37 C2
Avis............................38 D2
Budget.........................39 D2
Gare Routière..................(see 41)
Suriname Airways (SLM)........40 B3
Taxis collectifs.................41 B3
Taxis...........................42 B3

Place Léopold Héder
Place des Palmistes
Place Victor Schœlcher
Place du Coq

Cemetery
University (Collège Lycée)

Blvd Jubelin
Blvd de la République

Av du G Virgile
Av A Aron
Rue Gippet
Rue Lubin
Rue Pichevin
Rue Vermont Polycarpe
Av G Decaesse
Av Voltaire
Av d'Estrées
Rue Rouget de l'Isle
Av Pasteur
Blvd Jubelin
Rue Félix Éboué
Rue Christophe-Colomb
Rue L Becker
Rue Dr Barrat
Rue XIV Juillet
Rue Schœlcher
Av Léopold Héder
Rue Mme Payé
Rue du Cap Bernard
Rue Lalouette
Rue de l'Église
Av du Général de Gaulle
Rue J Catayée
Rue Arago
Rue de la Liberté
Av de la Liberté
Rue L Brasse
Rue René Jadfard
Rue R Barthélémy
Rue Ronjon
Rue Amusant
Rue Gobert
Rue E Prévot
Rue Mole
Av Monnerville
Rue Lallouette
Rue Guisan
Rue de Remire
Rue Victor Hugo
Rue Louis Blanc
Rue Malouet
Rue Friemond
Rue des Casernes
Rue du Port
Rue Dr Henri
Rue Defous
Route de la Madeleine

Cathédrale

Market

GETTING INTO TOWN

Rochambeau International Airport is located 18km southwest of Cayenne. From the airport, consider sharing a taxi (day/night US$25/30); the trip takes about 20 minutes. To the airport, it's far cheaper to take a *taxi collectif* to Matoury, then a bus or taxi the remaining 5km. Don't let taxi drivers tack on bogus surcharges for each piece of luggage.

Grab a free map of Cayenne from the airport's tourist information desk before you head out, or get one from a hotel or the tourist office in town (see Tourist Offices, opposite).

Information

BOOKSHOPS

AJC (33 Blvd Jubelin) Offers the biggest selection of books and maps, including Institut Géographique National topographic maps.

Maison de la Presse (14 Av du Général de Gaulle) Carries French, Brazilian and a few English-language newspapers and magazines; they're often out of maps.

CULTURAL CENTERS

Office Culturel de la Région Guyane (☎ 28-94-00; 82 Av du Général de Gaulle) Hosts art exhibitions, plays and other events in celebration of Guianese culture.

EMERGENCY

Fire (☎ 18)
Police (☎ 17)

INTERNET ACCESS

CyberCafé des Palmistes (12 Av du Général de Gaulle, in Bar Les Palmistes; ☒ 7am-midnight Mon-Sat) At this Internet bar/café, you buy a US$15/21 access card that's good for one/two hours, then refill it for US$7/13 per additional one/two hours.

Post office (US$6 per hr) The Internet terminal here is usually on the fritz.

MEDICAL SERVICES

Centre Hospitalier Cayenne (☎ 39-50-50; 3 Av Flamboyants)

MONEY

Banks and ATMs are easily found throughout the city.

Banque National de Paris (BNP; 2 Place Victor Schoelcher) Be prepared to wait in line.

Change Caraïbes (64 Av du Général de Gaulle; ☒ 7:30am-12:30pm & 3:30-5:30pm Mon-Fri, 8am-noon Sat) Offers competitive rates.

POST

Post office (La Poste; ☒ 7:30am-1:30pm Mon-Fri, 7:30-11:45am Sat) This is the most convenient post office, on the south side of Place Léopold Héder.

Main post office (☎ 39-40-00; Rte Baduel; ☒ 7:15am-6:15pm Mon-Fri, 7am-12:15pm Sat) Poste restante goes to this location, 2km outside the center.

TELEPHONE

There is no central telephone office, but there are plenty of pay phones, especially on and near Place des Palmistes.

TOURIST OFFICES

Office du Tourisme (☎ 31-29-19; 19 Rue Arago; ☒ 8am-1pm & 3-6pm Mon-Fri, 8am-noon Sat) The only tourist office in town has good maps of Cayenne and French Guiana, a few English-speaking staff, brochures, and a list of *gîtes* (long-stay studios or apartments) in French Guiana.

Comité du Tourisme de la Guyane (☎ 29-65-00) This desk at the airport is open late for arriving flights.

TRAVEL AGENCIES

Sainte Claire Voyages (☎ 30-00-38, 8 Rue de Rémire) Helpful staff can book flights within the Guianas and beyond.

Dangers & Annoyances

The Village Chinois (aka Chicago) area, south of the market, is not entirely safe unless you're with a local, especially at night; take taxis to and from its bars and clubs.

Sights

Between superb meals, don't forget to check out Cayenne's (mostly free!) attractions – mainly its lively squares, colonial architecture, local museums, and main market (read: food opportunity). Stroll over to the remains of 17th-century **Fort Cépérou**, up a narrow alleyway off the gardened **Place Léopold Héder** (on which looms the **Préfecture** and near which sits the hulking **Hôtel de Ville**), for good views of the town and river. In the heat of the day, people-watch from the shady refuge of palm trees in the manicured **Place des Palmistes**. After siesta, cruise Av du Général de Gaulle, the main commercial street – if you're on a budget, don't expect to do more than window-shop.

Cut through **Place Victor Schoelcher,** which commemorates the man most responsible for ending slavery in French Guiana, to find Cayenne's main **market** (🕑 6:30am-1pm Wed, Fri & Sat), where folks peddle everything from tropical fruits to caged finches and mysterious-looking syrups and tonics in unlabeled bottles. This produce bazaar is sensory ecstasy – go and gawk, sniff and, best of all, *mangez* (eat). The indoor soup stalls serve up the best Vietnamese *pho* (US$4) in the Guianas.

The centrally located **Musée Départemental** (1 Rue de Rémire; adult/child or student US$2.50/1.50; 🕑 8am-1:15pm & 3-5:45pm Mon & Thu, 8am-1:15pm Wed & Fri, 8:30am-12:45pm Sat) features a frighteningly large stuffed black caiman that once washed up on the beach near Cayenne, as well as other preserved local critters, an ethno-botanical display, and an air-conditioned 'butterfly room,' easily missed because it is poorly marked. The upstairs area recaptures life in the old penal colony and displays some Amerindian handicrafts. The smaller **Musée des Cultures Guyanaises** (🕿 31-41-72; 78 Rue Madame Payé; admission free; 🕑 8am-12:45pm & 3-5:45pm Mon, Tue, Thu & Fri, 8am-12:45pm Wed, 8am-11:45am Sat) conserves traces of traditional culture, catalogs French Guiana's vicious penal history, features exhibitions and houses a thorough library (upstairs) of English-language and other publications.

Tours

For most travelers, organized tours are the easiest and best way to experience French Guiana's unrivaled ecotourism opportunities. **Takari Tour** (🕿 31-19-60; www.takaritour.gf; 8 Rue du Cap Bernard) is the oldest and perhaps the best-regarded tour operator. It runs road and river adventures just about anywhere in French Guiana and can customize trips for groups. Other reputable local outfits are **JAL Voyages** (🕿 31-68-20; www.jal-voyages.com in French; 26 Av du Général de Gaulle), whose popular jaunts include Îles du Salut (from US$32) and one-day or longer trips to Kaw (from US$50) and along the Approuague and Mana Rivers (from US$140), and **Couleurs Amazone** (🕿 28-70-00; www.couleursamazone.fr in French; 2 Av Pasteur), which features numerous excursions and *Survivor*-esque extreme wilderness adventures (from US$289).

Festivals & Events

Carnaval is *the* annual fête, and it gets bigger and wilder every year, with near-perpetual live bands and parades. Schools are often closed during the last week of Carnaval, so don't be surprised if businesses are closed and hotels are more crowded.

Sleeping

Staying in central Cayenne is best for sightseeing, but some places beyond the center are good value (and have ice machines!).

Central Hôtel (🕿 25-65-65; www.centralhotel-cayenne .fr; cnr Rues Molé & du Lieutenant Becker; s/d US$46/54; 🍴 🅿) This is the best value in the city center, and is complemented by the helpful, knowledgeable staff and prime location.

La Bodega (🕿 30-25-13; 42 Av du Général de Gaulle; s/d from US$30/35; 🅿 🍴) Rooms in this hotel/bar/restaurant are pretty basic but pretty popular, so book ahead. The downstairs bar can make for noisy nights. You'll pay more for rooms with a view during Carnaval.

Ket Tai (🕿 28-97-77; 72 Blvd Jubelin; s/d from US$39/43; 🍴) The multilingual staff here help you feel at home in otherwise un-homey but (relatively) affordable rooms.

Hôtel Ajoupa (🕿 30-33-08; Rte du Cabassou; s/d US$35/37; 🅿 🍴 🛏) Comfortable rooms surround the inviting pool, which is just beyond the often-hectic front desk. From central Cayenne, take bus No 5 to the *gendarmerie* and hoof the extra few hundred meters.

Motel du Lac (🕿 38-08-00; Chemin Poupon – Rte de Montjoly; d US$62; 🅿 🍴 🛏) Relax in quiet comfort at this peaceful site between Cayenne and Montjoly.

Eating

For the best bang for your buck, slurp noodles at Cayenne's daytime market (see above) and browse the nighttime **food stalls** (Place des Palmistes) for delicious crepes, Indonesian fried rice or colossal hamburgers and sandwiches (all from US$2.50). For a few more cents, follow families to the popular Chinese and Vietnamese fast-food restaurants, such as **Pom Canelle** (44 Rue XIV Juillet). Or whip up your own feast with goodies (and even a sandwich maker and 'J'aime Guyane' apron) from **Supermarché Match** (73 Av Voltaire; 🕑 8am-8pm Mon-Sat, 8am-12:45pm Sun). Myriad other mouthwatering sit-down options include:

Le Café Crème (44 Rue J Catayée; 🕑 6:15am-4:30pm Mon-Fri, 6:15am-3:30pm Sat) This Parisian-style café serves great coffee, sizable sandwiches (from US$3) and yummy pastries.

Crêp'in (5 Rue du Lieutenant Becker; dishes US$2-6; 8am-8pm Mon-Sat) Start your day with a delectable *crêpe forestière* (a savory crepe of mushrooms and cheese; US$5), and then come back for fresh salads, giant sandwiches, sweet crepes and fresh juices (US$2).

Mille Pâtes (52 Rue J Catayée; pizzas US$5-9, pastas US$7-11; noon-11pm) This pizzeria makes a thin-crust pie (New Yorkers, don't get excited) and doesn't close for siesta!

Café de la Gare (42 Av Léopold Héder; mains US$8-12) This hip bar/restaurant has excellent French and Creole cuisine (menu changes daily), great atmosphere and occasional live music.

Les Pyramides (28-16-28; cnr Rues Christophe Colomb & Malouet; mains US$9-20; noon-3pm & 7-11pm Tue-Sun) Bring a mate and share the *baba ganoush* (US$6) and a heaping order of couscous (US$9 to US$16) in this superb eat-in-or-take-out Middle Eastern restaurant.

Porta Verde (29-19-03; 58 Rue du Lieutenant Goinet; mains US$6-10; 11:45am-2:45pm Mon-Sat) This Brazilian eatery features lunch priced by weight (US$12 per kg), as well as meaty mains. Dinner is by reservation only.

La Kaz Kréòl (39-06-97; 35 Av d'Estrées; mains US$13-16; 12:30-2:30pm & 7:30-11:30pm) Traditional and modern Creole fare are elaborately presented at this restaurant, near the university.

Drinking

Lots of drinking establishments feature live music, and some restaurants moonlight as bars as the late hours approach. Bottles of red wine and beer from local grocery shops make good, cheap liquid fodder to start with at the hotel as some places can be expensive.

Bar Les Palmistes (12 Av du Général de Gaulle; 7am-midnight Mon-Sat) This is quite the indoor-outdoor, see-and-be-seen scene, as is the cheaper and much hipper bar at **La Bodega** (p724).

Harry's Bar (20 Rue Rouget de l'Isle; 7am-2pm & 5pm-1am Mon-Thu, until 2am Fri & Sat) For great ambience, cozy couches and darts, this lounge boasts 50 brands of whiskey, nearly as many beers,' and Havana cigars. Even the bathrooms – replete with beach-scene toilet seats – are fun.

La Case Café Show (55 Av Voltaire; 5:30pm-1am Wed-Mon) Ease into the evening (or morning) at this piano bar with a pool table and toasted ham-and-cheese sandwiches.

Buisson Ardent (3 Av d'Estrées) Madame Serotte's reggae bar is popular with university students.

More reggae music rocks small clubs in Village Chinois, where a few Brazilian and Dominican bars also dot Av de la Liberté.

Away from the center, nightclubs like **Lido Night** (35-79-69; Sentier Cotonnière Ouest, Matoury) pump out Zouk and international music.

Shopping

This is a hit-or-miss event in Cayenne; the best way is to just wander around the center. You'll find several souvenir shops and general stores (clothing, electronics etc) along Av du Général de Gaulle. Warning: Prices can rival those in Paris.

Getting There & Away

Rochambeau International Airport (29-97-00) offers flights to local, regional and international destinations.

Airline offices in town or at Rochambeau include:

Air France (29-87-00; 17-19 Rue Lalouette & airport)

Air Guyane (29-36-30; airport)

AOM (29-36-30; airport)

Nouvelles Frontières/Corsair (29-30-30; airport)

Penta (30-39-10; Centre commercial Katoury)

Surinam Airways (SLM; 29-30-00; 15 Rue L Blanc & airport)

Airfares within the region vary; buying tickets in the Guianas may be cheaper than at home. Destinations and one-way flight details include:

Belém (Brazil) SLM, US$215, 1¼ hours, two weekly; Penta, US$258, 1¼ hours, six weekly

Georgetown (Guyana) SLM, US$172, 2½ hours (via Paramaribo), two weekly

Macapá (Brazil) Penta, US$195, 1 hour, six weekly

Maripasoula Air Guyane, US$67, 45 minutes, daily

Paramaribo (Suriname) SLM, US$116, 35 minutes, two weekly

Saül Air Guyane, US$53, 40 minutes, five weekly

St Georges Air Guyane, US$53, 30 minutes, daily

Getting Around

BUS

Local **SMTC buses** (25-49-29 for schedule) service the region around Cayenne, including Hôtel Ajoupa (line No 5) and Montjoly's beaches (US$2.50). There are limited routes and buses don't run on Sundays, so you'll probably need taxis.

CAR

Rental cars are the best way to see lots of French Guiana. Both companies and roads can be dodgy; check the cars thoroughly, and know how to put on your spare tire. Most companies give deals for rentals of one week or longer; most also have desks at the airport. Reputedly, ACL and Service Auto Location are the cheapest (from US$22 per day) and best, respectively.

ACL (☎ 30-47-56; 44 Blvd Jubelin)
Avis (☎ 30-25-22; 58 Blvd Jubelin)
Budget (☎ 31-31-32; 13 Blvd Jubelin)
Europcar (☎ 35-18-27; ZI Collery Ouest)
Hertz (☎ 29-69-30; ZI Collery Ouest)
Service Auto Location (☎ 35-67-87; airport)

TAXI

Taxis have meters and charge a hiring fee of US$1.50 plus US$0.75 per kilometer (US$1.10 from 7pm to 6am, Sunday and holidays). There's a taxi stand on the southeast corner of Place des Palmistes.

TAXI COLLECTIF

Taxis collectifs leave when full from Gare Routière on Av de la Liberté until 6pm daily. From the corner of Rue Molé, they head to Matoury (US$1.25, 15 minutes, 10km) and St Laurent (US$30, three to four hours, 250km). From the corner of Rue Malouet, they depart for Rochambeau airport (US$25, 20 minutes, 18km), Kourou (US$10, one hour, 60km) and Régina (US$23, two hours, 100km). Settle rates in advance.

AROUND CAYENNE

There's heaps to explore around the capital city, and the best way to do it is by renting a car for a day or two.

Rémire-Montjoly

The beach area around Cayenne is referred to collectively as Rémire-Montjoly, though Rémire and Montjoly are actually two separate towns. **Plage Montjoly** (which giant leatherback turtles visit to spawn in the summer) is Cayenne's best beach, reachable by bus or taxi. Montjoly also features historical ruins at **Fort Diamant** and hiking trails along the lakes at Le Rorota and to the top of **Montagne du Mahury**, offering stunning views. The 5km hike into the **Grand Matoury Nature Reserve** at La Mirande is good for bird-watching.

The comfy complex at **Motel Beauregard** (☎ 35-41-00; PK9, 2 Rte de Rémire; s/d US$51/55; P ☒ ☒), 10km from Cayenne, also features private bungalows (from US$63); prices include use of the health club and tennis court. For a refreshing ice cream or cocktail, grab a beachfront table at **La Baie des Îles** (PK11, Rte des Plages; ☾ noon-3pm & 7:30-11pm).

Montsinéry

Along the Montsinéry River, 45km west of Cayenne and 8.5km off RN1, is the **Réserve Animalière Macourienne** (adult/child US$12/7; tours US$5; ☾ 9am-6pm). The biggest attraction is the feeding of the spectacled caimans at 6pm Sunday; otherwise, it's your best chance to see jaguars, tapirs, ocelots, capuchins, anteaters, toucans, anacondas and other regional inhabitants up close. Artisanal huts dot the side of the road (D5), while the tiny, riverfront town of Montsinéry is a good launching point for **canoe trips.**

At the intersection of D5 and RN2, 25km south of Cayenne, is one of the best ecotourism opportunities in the vicinity: **Emerald Jungle Village** (☎ 28-00-89; emeraldjungle village@wanadoo.fr; Carrefour du Gallion; s/d US$29/32). Dutch expats Joep Moonen, a biologist and conservationist of the Trésor Nature Reserve, and his wife, Marijke, run this tropical nature center. The solar-powered lodge holds only eight people (reserve in advance!) and has a botanical trail on the premises. Joep organizes ecoexcursions throughout eastern French Guiana – call ahead to customize an unforgettable adventure – and rents canoes (US$25 per day) and mountain bikes (US$10 per day).

Cacao

Cacao, about 75km southwest of Cayenne, is a beautiful little town of Hmong refugees who left Laos in the 1970s. Sunday, market day, is the best time for a visit (go by 10am, before the tour buses arrive). Hmong embroidery and weaving are sold alongside tables of local produce and fresh, authentic Asian food – the specialty is noodle soup (US$3). After lunch, visit **Le Planeur Bleu** (ecoledecacao.free.fr/planeur.html; adult/child US$2.50/ free; ☾ 10am-1pm Thu-Tue, 10am-1pm & 2-4:30pm Sat, 9am-1pm & 2-4pm Sun) for incredible butterfly and arachnid displays – dead and alive.

For lodging, try the lovely **L'Auberge des Orpailleurs** (☎ 27 06 22; PK62, Rte de Régina; s/d

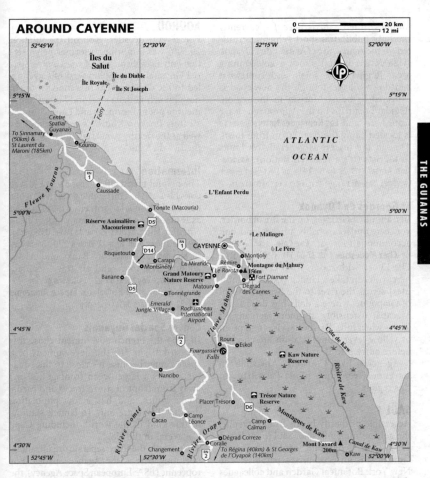

AROUND CAYENNE

US$23/28), which also rents canoes; reserve beds ahead. For tasty homemade Laotian specialties, eat at **Chez By et Daniel** (☎ 27-09-98; 111 Bourg de Cacao).

Trésor & Kaw Nature Reserves
The Trésor Nature Reserve is one of French Guiana's most accessible primary rain forest areas. Drive (17km from Roura) to Trésor's 1.75km **botanical trail** to experience its rich diversity and protected wildlife. Trésor borders the mysterious forests and swamps of the Kaw Nature Reserve, an excellent place to observe caiman (best at night) and spectacular waterfowl like the scarlet ibis (best in summer). **Mont Favard** features hiking trails and petroglyphs.

Independent exploration of Kaw is difficult but not impossible. The road into the area is good and ends right at the Kaw River. Basic **lodging** is available in the village of Kaw (accessible by boat only), but most visitors take all-inclusive trips with Cayenne-based tour operators (see Tours p724) or bird-watching boat tours with Emerald Jungle Village (see Montsinéry p726).

Régina
On the Approuague River, 116km south of Cayenne, Régina sits at the end of RN2, which is being connected to a road that will bridge the river and travel onward to St Georges and then Brazil by mid-2004. Until then, catch a river launch (US$4, 10

minutes), then a *taxi collectif* – currently the only public-transport vehicles permitted on the road – to St Georges de l'Oyapok (US$35, 2½ hours). Once a gold-mining area, Régina is a small and somewhat run-down village, though the new road is expected to boost tourism in the region. Regular boat trips up the Approuague leave from here, and **Les Nouragues Nature Reserve** is located along the river 40km from town. Though the reserve is generally off-limits to tourists (it's a research station), **Association Arataï** (☎ 28-40-20; 2 Rue du Lieutenant Goinet, Cayenne) can arrange trips to certain areas.

St Georges de l'Oyapok

In tranquil St Georges, on the Brazil border, you can find reasonably priced food and accommodations at **Caz-Calé** (☎ 37-00-54) or **Chez Modestine** (☎ 37-00-13), both on Rue Elie-Elfort, with rooms from US$28. From here, you can take a launch (US$5, 15 minutes) across the river to the Brazilian town of Oiapoque, where a daily bus departs for Macapá, ostensibly at noon (actually, it leaves when full). Passports, visas and proof of yellow-fever immunization are checked before entry into Brazil.

Agencies like Couleurs Amazone in Cayenne (see Tours p724) runs trips to this region.

SAÜL

Accessible primarily by air from Cayenne, the gold-mining village of Saül (population 175) – the geographic center of French Guiana – is an ecotourist's paradise. The New York Botanical Garden and colleagues from ORSTOM, the French Overseas Research Institute, have established study sites in the surrounding undisturbed **rain forest**. Trails crisscross the area, and the Approuague, Mana and Inini Rivers flow nearby.

Extremely basic accommodations include **Les Eaux Claires** (6km north of town; hammock/bed US$7/25) and **Gîte Municipal** (near town hall; s/d US$11/17); call ☎ 37-45-00 to reserve for either and ask what utilities are available; power is iffy. Book trips through the trails with Takari Tour in Cayenne (see Tours p724). You can also organize an eight-day river-jungle-villages adventure to Saül; inquire at tour agencies in Cayenne or Kourou.

KOUROU

For several decades, Kourou (population 20,500) was a moribund former penal settlement. Establishment of the Centre Spatial Guyanais here, 60km west of Cayenne, led to the development of a modern town, now French Guiana's second largest and a melting pot of European and Latin cultures. Visitors flock to Kourou's space center, as well as the nearby penal settlement ruins on the Îles du Salut.

Information

The helpful **tourist office** (Centre d'Accueil; 30 Av du Général de Gaulle) has miserable **dorms** (US$12) but can book rooms for you elsewhere, as well as tours. It has good city maps, too. Check email at **Micromarket** (5 Rue du Lycée; US$9 per hr; ◷ 2:30-7:30pm Mon, 8am-12:30pm & 2:30-7:30pm Tue-Fri, 8am-noon & 4-7:30pm Sat). Banks and ATMs abound. For tours and air travel, contact **GuyanEspace Voyages** (☎ 22-31-01; www.guyanespace .com in French; 39 Av Berlioz) or **Espace Amazonie** (☎ 32-34-30; Place de la Condamnie).

Centre Spatial Guyanais

In 1964 the French government chose this 900-sq-km site for the development of a space center because it's close to the equator, enjoys a large ocean frontage (50km) away from tropical storm tracks and earthquake zones, and has a low population density. There are only 16 launch stations of this kind in the world, including Cape Canaveral in the US.

Currently the three separate organizations operating here – the Agence Spatiale Européenne (ESA; European Space Agency), the Centre National d'Études Spatiales (CNES; French Space Agency) and Arianespace (a private commercial enterprise developing the Ariane rocket) – employ about 1600 people and run eight or nine launches per year.

Cool (and free!) three-hour **tours** (☎ 32-61-23; www.csg-spatial.tm.fr; ◷ 7:45am & 12:45pm Mon-Thu & 7:45am Fri) include a launch-pad visit; phone ahead for reservations, and bring your passport. Tour guides sometimes speak English or German; ask when you book. Don't miss the excellent **Musée de l'Espace** (Space Museum; adult/child US$6/4, with tour US$4/2.50; ◷ 8am-6pm Mon-Fri, 2-6pm Sat); the informative displays are in English and French.

Ideally, coordinate your visit with a launch. To see one, email well ahead, to

CSG-accueil@cnes.fr, providing your full name, address, phone number and age.

Sleeping

Accommodations are expensive; most budget travelers stay in Cayenne. The best beds are at **Hotel Ballahou** (☎ 22-00-22; 1-3 Rue Amet Martial; r from US$33; P)), which can be tricky to find but they'll pick you up from the Centre d'Accueil, and **Le Gros Bec** (☎ 32-91-91; 56 Rue du De Floch; s/d US$50/58; P)), whose spacious split-level studios with kitchenette are the best deal in town, especially for couples and groups. Sleeping on Île Royale is another cheap option (see the Îles du Salut, opposite). Locals have reported that you can sling a hammock – and mozzie net! – on Roches beach for free.

Eating & Drinking

Affordable eateries are abundant, including many appetizing Asian places such as **Le Swan** (79 Av Monnerville; mains US$5-9) and **Les Rayons du Soleil** (56 Cité Angélique; mains US$5-7; ☺ Mon-Sat).

Délifrance (56-58 Av Monnerville; sandwiches from US$4) Stop by this central bakery for hearty sandwiches and pastries.

La Case à Crêpes (48 Av du Général de Gaulle; dishes US$3-10) Even if you're not hungry, stop here and make room for an amazing savory or sweet crepe, or be good and have a wholesome salad.

La Pizzeria (38 Rue ML King; pizzas from US$5; ☺ noon-11pm) This large eatery does Italian dishes and pizzas.

Le Glacier des 2 Lacs (68 Av des Deux Lacs; ☺ 8am-11:30pm Wed-Sun) For sinful ice cream and other sweets made on the premises, this is the best creamery in French Guiana.

Self-catering is easy thanks to the produce **market** (Place de la Condamine; ☺ Tue & Fri) and **Supermarché Match** (Rond-point Monnerville).

Watering holes include the Brazilian **Bar des Sports** (4 Av des Frères Kennedy), airy **Le 13** (Place Monnerville) and clubby **Le Vieux Montmartre** (67 Av du Général de Gaulle; admission US$8; ☺ from 10pm Wed-Mon).

Getting There & Away

Taxis collectifs run to Cayenne (US$10, one hour, 60km) and St Laurent (US$15, two to three hours, 190km); inquire at hotels about times and departure locations. Some rental companies in Cayenne are in Kourou too, enabling one-way jaunts:

Avis (☎ 32-52-99; 4 Av de France)
Europcar (☎ 35-25-55; Hotel Mercure Atlantis, Lac Bois Diable)
Service Auto Location (☎ 32-01-01; Centre Commercial Simarouba)

AROUND KOUROU
Îles du Salut

Best known for the notorious prison at Île du Diable (Devil's Island), the must-see Îles du Salut (Salvation Islands) is 15km north of Kourou over choppy, shark-infested waters. For 18th-century colonists the islands were an escape from mainland fever and malaria because the sea breezes kept mosquitoes away. The prisons came later, along with more than 2000 convicts. The prison closed in 1947.

Île Royale, the largest of the three islands, was the administrative headquarters of the penal settlement, while the smaller Île St Joseph was reserved for solitary confinement. Île du Diable, a tiny islet now covered with coconut palms, was home to political prisoners, including Alfred Dreyfus. Nearly inaccessible (and now closed to the public) because of hazardous currents, the island was linked to Île Royale by a 225m supply cable.

The Centre Spatial Guyanais has a huge infrared camera on Île Royale, but the atmospheric ruins are the main attractions; only those on Île Royale are being preserved. See St Joseph's eerie remaining isolation cells before the jungle fully reclaims them. The old **director's house** (☺ 10am-4:30pm Tue-Sun) contains an interesting English-language history display and temporary exhibits; two-hour guided tours of Royale (usually in French, US$6) begin here. Surprisingly abundant wildlife includes macaws, agoutis, capuchins and sea turtles. Carry a swimsuit and towel to take advantage of refreshing swimming holes on St Joseph. Note that the islands are evacuated when there is an eastward launch from the space center.

SLEEPING & EATING
Auberge des Îles du Salut (☎ 32-11-00; Île Royale; hammock space US$9, dm US$12.50, bungalows US$54, s/d US$115/168; meals US$20) Offers hammock space in former prison cells, dormitory accommodations, and pricier bungalows (one to three people) and single/double rooms. Some adventurous backpackers just sling their hammocks (bring tarps and mosquito nets, too)

THE GUIANAS

in abandoned cell blocks or on St Joseph's beach. The Auberge restaurant's fixed-price meal is good but expensive as are drinks and coffee at the bar. Solution: unless you can subsist on fallen mangoes, bring your own food and water; the water is not potable.

GETTING THERE & AWAY

Boats to the islands depart around 8am from Kourou's *ponton des pêcheurs* (fishermen's dock, at the end of Av de Gaulle) and return between 4pm and 6pm (but inquire about two-day trips). Call to reserve, or book in Cayenne. Getting to Kourou from Cayenne in time can be a problem – even the first *taxis collectifs* may not make it. Seafaring options include:

Albatros (☎ 32-16-12; US$45, two hours) and **Brava** (☎ 0694 42-48-46; US$44, three hours) Relaxing sailboats (nine passengers maximum) visit Îles Royale and St Joseph; book ahead.

La Navette (☎ 32-09-95; US$35, 1 hr one way) This crowded and fumy ferry visits Île Royale only; book ahead or pay at dock (cash only).

Royal Ti'Punch (☎ 32-09-95; US$46, 1½ hr) and **La Hulotte** (☎ 32-33-81; US$46, 1½ hours) Festive catamarans (20 to 28 passengers) visit Îles Royale and St Joseph; book ahead.

Alternatively, hook up with a tour from Cayenne (see p724).

Sinnamary & Around

Sixty km northwest of Kourou, Sinnamary, a friendly village of 3500 people, includes an Indonesian community that produces excellent woodwork, jewelry, pottery and other folk arts. Warning: local artwork made from bird feathers is based on the wholesale slaughter of the scarlet ibis! **Corossal Artisanat** (Rue Verderosa) is a nice crafts shop.

Don't leave the area without hiking at least part of the 20km **Pripri Yiyi trail** (trailhead at La Maison de la Nature, a few kilometers out of town) for great bird-watching. Also stop in **Iracoubo** on your way west – a prisoner painted the ornate interior of its 1893 parish church.

Roadside **Restaurant-Hôtel Floria** (RN1 at southeastern entrance to Iracoubo; r US$23) has clean, simple rooms for up to three people, while **Hôtel du Fleuve** (☎ 34-54-00; www.hoteldufleuve.com in French; 11 Rue Mine at southeastern entrance to Sinnamary; s/d US$65/76.50; P 🍴 🖥 🖳) has all the mod cons.

ST LAURENT DU MARONI

Once a reception camp for arriving convicts, St Laurent (population 21,500) retains some picturesque colonial buildings and a certain backwater charm. It sits 250km from Cayenne on the east bank of the Fleuve Maroni (Marowijne River), which borders Suriname. Linger here for a bit and explore the town's historical and cultural offerings, perhaps by arranging a boat trip up the river, which has many Maroon and Amerindian settlements along its banks.

Information

St Laurent's **Office du Tourisme** (☎ 34-23-98; www.97320.com in French; Esplanade Baudin; 🕑 7:30am-6pm Mon-Fri, 7:45am-12:45pm & 2:45-5:45pm Sat, 9am-1pm Sun) stocks maps and brochures, and books mountain-biking and rum-factory tours. It maintains a list of the area's accommodations, which it can book for you (list posted on door when closed). Another good place for getting one's bearings is the **Rainforest Information Center** (Le Pou d'Agouti; ☎ 34-20-97; 9 Rue Victor Hugo), which sells maps and books.

For euros, try **Banque Française Commerciale** (BFM; 11 Av Félix Eboué; 🕑 7:45am-12:45pm & 3:15-4:45pm Mon & Wed, 7:45am-12:45pm Thu, 7:45am-12:30pm Fri, 7:45am-noon Sat) or **Cambio COP** (23 Rue Montravel; 🕑 8am-noon). There's also an ATM at the **post office** (3 Av du Général de Gaulle). Internet access is at **www.ouest-elites** (30 Rue Thiers; 1-/2-/5-hr card US$10/15/25; 🕑 9am-12:30pm & 3:30-7:30pm Mon-Fri, 9am-12:30pm Sat).

Plan big trips or book flights with **Ouest Voyages** (☎ 34-44-44; 10 Av Félix Eboué), the ticket agent for Air France, AOM and others.

For emergencies, go to **Hôpital Franck Joly** (☎ 34-10-37; 16 Av du Général de Gaulle).

Sights & Activities

At the creepy **Camp de la Transportation** (1857), prisoners arrived for processing and transfer to various prison camps throughout the territory. Each boat on which they traveled carried 500 to 600 men and took 20 days to cross the Atlantic. You are free to walk through the same gates as Dreyfus and Papillon and see some of the deteriorating buildings, but the must-see cell blocks with open toilets and shackles and the solitary confinement cells with their tiny windows are only open to 1½-hour **tours** (adult/student/child US$4/2/1; 🕑 8am, 9:30am, 11am, 3pm & 4:30pm Mon-Sat, 9:30am & 11am Sun); pay at the tourist office.

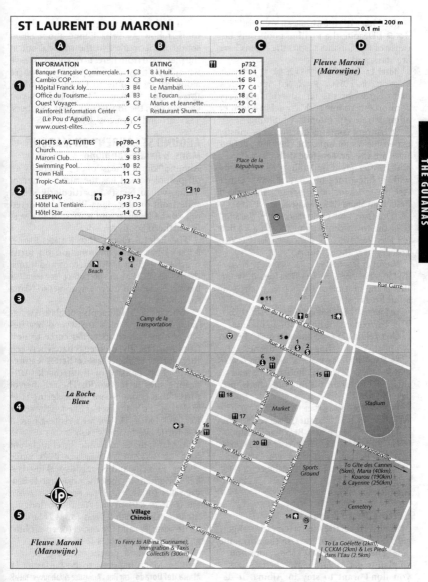

ST LAURENT DU MARONI

0 — 200 m
0 — 0.1 mi

INFORMATION
Banque Française Commerciale....**1**	C3
Cambio COP....................................**2**	C3
Hôpital Franck Joly.........................**3**	B4
Office du Tourisme.........................**4**	B3
Ouest Voyages...............................**5**	C3
Rainforest Information Center	
(Le Pou d'Agouti)........................**6**	C4
www.ouest-elites...........................**7**	C5

SIGHTS & ACTIVITIES   pp780–1
Church..**8**	C3
Maroni Club....................................**9**	B3
Swimming Pool.............................**10**	B2
Town Hall.......................................**11**	C3
Tropic-Cata....................................**12**	A3

SLEEPING   pp731–2
Hôtel La Tentiaire..........................**13**	D3
Hôtel Star......................................**14**	C5

EATING   p732
8 à Huit..**15**	D4
Chez Félicia...................................**16**	B4
Le Mambari....................................**17**	C4
Le Toucan......................................**18**	C4
Marius et Jeannette.......................**19**	C4
Restaurant Shum...........................**20**	C4

Fleuve Maroni (Marowijne)

Place de la République

Av Malouet

Rue Nonon

Av Franklin Roosevelt

Av Dannas

Esplanade Baudin

Beach

Rue Barrat

Rue Talon

Rue Garre

Camp de la Transportation

Rue du Lt Colonel Chandon

Rue Montravel

La Roche Bleue

Rue Schoelcher

Rue Victor Hugo

Stadium

Market

Rue Rousseau

Rue Félix Éboué

Av Monnerville

Av du Général de Gaulle

Rue Marceau

Rue du Lieutenant Colonel Tourtet

Sports Ground

To Gîte des Cannes (5km), Maria (40km), Kourou (190km) & Cayenne (250km)

Cemetery

Rue Thiers

Rue Simon

Village Chinois

Rue Guynemer

Fleuve Maroni (Marowijne)

To Ferry to Albina (Suriname), Immigration & Taxis Collectifs (300m)

To La Goélette (2km), CCKM (2km) & Les Pieds dans l'Eau (2.5km)

THE GUIANAS

The Maroni is perfect for **canoeing**; rent canoes from the **Maroni Club** (☎ 23-52-51; Esplanade Baudin; 2 hrs US$12) or **CCKM** (☎ 34-49-03; 15 Rue des Amazones; US$14 per day; ☼ Tue-Sat), next to La Goélette (see Sleeping & Eating, following). **Tropic-Cata** (☎ 34-25-18; www.tropic-cata.com in French; Esplanade Baudin) offers two-hour (US$13) to two-day (US$160) **boat tours** of the Maroni.

The Rainforest Information Center (see Information p730) arranges **ecotours** and employs English-speaking guides.

Sleeping & Eating

Gîte des Cannes (35 Chemin de la Crique Tafia; d from US$22; **P**) About 5km before town, this secluded, family-run place is great for backpackers.

Hôtel Star (☎ 34-10-84; 26 Rue Thiers; d from US$35; ❄ ⊠) Despite the inviting pool (only because of the Guianese heat) the rooms here are stark and ramshackle.

Hôtel La Tentiaire (☎ 34-26-00; 12 Av Franklin Roosevelt; d from US$42; P ❄ ⊠) Sport a few extra euros for the far superior and very comfortable rooms at this hotel in a former administrative penitentiary building.

St Laurent contains delicious but mostly expensive restaurants; the cheapest alternatives are the **Javanese food stalls** (Av Félix Eboué), which offer good and filling bami goreng with a side order of satay (US$3). Other Asian eateries include the reasonably priced **Restaurant Shum** (14 Rue Rousseau; mains US$3-5).

The fruit-and-vegie **market** (☾ Wed & Sat) is in the town center, and there's a **8 à Huit** (cnr Rues Montravel & du Lieutenant Colonel Tourtet) grocery near the stadium.

Marius et Jeannette (11 Rue Victor Hugo; breakfast US$4.50, pizzas US$6-8; ☾ 6am-10pm Tue-Sat) By far, this is the best place for pizzas, pastries or a full breakfast.

Le Toucan (17 Av du Général de Gaulle; breakfast US$5-7) This bar/restaurant does a filling brekkie.

Chez Félicia (23 Av du Général de Gaulle) Félicia whips up mighty fine Creole cuisine.

Le Mambari (7 Rue Rousseau; salads US$6-7, pizzas US$4.50-10, grills US$8.50-15) Fun will be had at this bar/restaurant dishing out salads, pizzas and grills.

La Goélette (Balate Plage; mains US$12-18) The well-known boat-restaurant serves a combination of French and Brazilian cuisine.

Les Pieds dans L'Eau (29 Pointe St Louis; meals US$12-23) Forget everything you just read and eat here, 2.5km south of the center, for phenomenal French cuisine and a charming beach setting.

Getting There & Around

Minibuses meet the Albina ferry (passenger/car US$4/23, 30 minutes) on the Suriname side. The entire trip takes about four hours, so plan to get to Paramaribo before dark – you don't want to stay in Albina. It departs at 7am, 9am, 2pm and 5pm Monday, Tuesday, Thursday and Friday, 7am and 5pm Wednesday, 8am and 9am Saturday, 3:30pm and 5pm Sunday. Schedules can vary; call ☎ 39-80-00 to confirm. At other times, you can hire a *pirogue* (motorized dugout canoe; US$5 but haggle for US$3, 10 to 15 minutes).

To find the ferry, immigration and customs, follow Av Félix Eboué about 800m south of the market to the roundabout at the pier. Also from here, *taxis collectifs* leave when full; they can drop you anywhere along RN1 en route to Cayenne (US$30, three hours, 250km). At other times you can call one; the tourist office has numbers. Taxis around town cost US$3 to US$4.

AROUND ST LAURENT DU MARONI
Mana & Awala-Yalimopo

About 50km northeast of St Laurent by an oft-potholed road lies the rustic village of Mana, which boasts a particularly scenic waterfront on the Mana River, considered one of the loveliest and least-spoiled rivers in northern South America.

The helpful **tourist office** (cnr Rues Jahouvey & Bastille) has maps, information on turtle beaches, and lists of accommodations; there's an ATM at the **post office** (east end of Rue Bastille). There's no other way to get to Mana than by car.

Amerindian settlements populate Awala-Yalimopo, near which are several beaches where **giant leatherback turtles** come to nest from April to July; their eggs hatch between July and September. **Plage Les Hattes** features the highest density of leatherback-turtle nesting sites in the world. The number of turtles that come ashore in the spring is so high that one biologist has likened the scene to a tank battle. Do *not* miss visiting here if it is turtle egg-laying season.

In Mana, the nuns beside the church rent **beds** (☎ 34-82-70; 1 Rue Bourguignon; US$8), while cheery French- and Spanish-speaking Isabelle brightens up the otherwise drab **Le Bougainvillier** (☎ 34-80-62; 33 Rue Frères; d with/without bath US$35/25; ❄). Awala-Yalimopo lodging includes **Chez Judith & Denis** (☎ 34-24-38; US$23 with breakfast; P) and the *carbet* (open-air hut) at **Pointe les Hattes** (☎ 34-38-06; d US$23).

The best (and practically only) restaurant in Mana happens to be fantastic: **Le Mana del Dorado** (cnr Rues Armistice & Jahouvey; meals US$15; ☾ 11:30am-3pm & 7-10:30pm Tue-Sat, 7-10:30pm Sun) specializes in local game and fish – be adventurous! – prepared by the exuberant, English-speaking proprietor.

Javouhey

Thirteen kilometers off the sketchy St Laurent–Mana road, this Hmong refugee village is where many local farmers reside. If you're not here for the popular Sunday market, at least stop at the wonderfully remote and clean **Auberge du Bois Diable** (☎ 34-19-35; PK8 Rte de l'Acarouany; d US$39) for the night or for a multiday canoe trip on the Mana or St Laurent River. In the nearby dot-of-a-town of Acarouany, rustic **Relais Acarouany** (☎ 34-17-20; d US$23) offers simple rooms, a home-cooking restaurant, and canoe rental.

FRENCH GUIANA DIRECTORY
Accommodations
Places to stay in French Guiana are generally good but expensive – cheap hotels start at around US$25 for a single, and around US$35 for a double. Most hotels have some English-speaking staff. Generally, skip the overpriced breakfasts (generally US$5 to US$8) and hit a local café.

There are modern *gîtes* (long-stay studios or apartments; inquire at Cayenne's tourist office) in Cayenne, Kourou and St Laurent, which can save long-term visitors some cash, and rustic *carbets* (open-air huts) for hammocks. In rural areas, it's possible to hang a hammock in some camping areas from US$5 and elsewhere for free, and many accommodations offer hammock space (from US$4) or have hammocks and mosquito nets to rent (generally US$8 to US$16).

Activities
Bird-watching, hiking and canoeing are popular in French Guiana. Canoes can be launched from most rivers without the need for a tour operator; those seeking more-strenuous activities might want a guide, however. Surfing, windsurfing and sailing are possible on nice beaches at Montjoly (p726), near Cayenne (beware of sharks) and Kourou (p729), but there are few public facilities.

Books
The best-known book on French Guiana's penal colony is Henri Charrière's autobiographical novel, *Papillon*, which was made into a legendary Hollywood film starring Steve McQueen and Dustin Hoffman. Alexander Miles' *Devil's Island: Colony of the Damned* is a factual but very readable account. For a good overview of the region, pick up *France's Overseas Frontier* by R Aldrich and J Connell. Ann Fadiman's brilliant *The Spirit Catches You and You Fall Down,* though set mostly in California, is the best work explaining the Hmong diaspora.

Business Hours
If you want to accomplish something, get up early. Many businesses close up shop in the heat of the day; generally hours are 8am to noon and 2pm to 5pm, while restaurants tend to serve from noon to 2pm and again from 7pm to 10pm or later. The country stops on Sunday and sometimes Monday, especially in St Laurent. Nightclubs open at around 10pm.

Climate
Carnaval (February and March) is an experience to be had, but note that the rainy season runs from January to June, with the heaviest rains occurring in May. The dry season, from July to December, may be the most comfortable time to visit. French Guiana maintains a toasty (average 83°F/28°C) and humid climate year round. Travel with light clothing and a poncho.

Dangers & Annoyances
Generally, French Guiana is very safe, but parts of Cayenne are not, especially at night. There has been an increase in crime and drug trafficking around Cayenne in recent years, and you'll often find a customs roadblock staffed by gendarmes at Iracoubo. Both locals and foreigners may be thoroughly searched for drugs. For the most part, only eastward traffic is stopped.

Embassies & Consulates
For information on Visas see p735.

EMBASSIES & CONSULATES IN FRENCH GUIANA
Brazil (☎ 29-60-10; 444 Chemin St Antoine)
Netherlands (☎ 34-05-04; ZI Dégrad des Cannes, Rémire-Montjoly)
Suriname (Map p722; ☎ 30-04-61; 3 Av Léopold Héder)
UK (Map p722; ☎ 31-10-34; 16 Av Monnerville) Consular representative is Georges NouhChaia.
US The nearest US representative is in Suriname (see p746).

FRENCH GUIANESE EMBASSIES & CONSULATES ABROAD
France's many representatives outside South America include:

Australia (☎ 02-6216-0100; 6 Perth Ave, Yarralumla, ACT 2600)
Canada (☎ 613-789-1795; 42 Sussex Dr, Ottawa, Ontario K1M 2C9)
Germany (☎ 0211-49-77-3-0; Cecilienallee 10, 40474 Dusseldorf)
Ireland (☎ 01-260 1666; 36 Ailesbury Rd, Dublin 4)
New Zealand (☎ 04-384-2555; 34–42 Manners St, PO Box 11-343, Wellington)
UK (☎ 020-7201-1000; 58 Knightsbridge, London SW1X 7JT)
USA (☎ 202-944-6000; 4101 Reservoir Rd, NW, Washington, DC 20007)

Festivals & Events

Carnaval is a gigantic, colorful occasion, with festivities rocking towns from Epiphany to several solid days of partying before Ash Wednesday. Other fabulous celebrations include the Hmong New Year (usually in December) in Cacao, and Chinese New Year (January or February) in Cayenne.

Food & Drink

One of French Guianas main attractions is the excellent food available just about everywhere. Don't be shy to try local (but not endangered!) meats and fishes. Prevalent Asian restaurants and food stalls serve truly delicious and truly cheap Chinese, Vietnamese and Indonesian dishes, including numerous vegetarian delights. Cafés and delis offer tasty meals for a few euros more, but better restaurants are expensive (rarely less than US$8 for a meal).

Note that in this chapter's French Guiana section, 'mains' often refers to *menus* (two or three courses) or a full meal.

Self-catering is a cinch thanks to frequent local produce *marchés* (markets) as well as megamarkets in Cayenne and Kourou and smaller shops (locally called *chinois,* pronounced sheen-*wah*) in every town. Imported alcoholic and soft drinks are pricey in bars and restaurants but are reasonable at groceries.

Health

Chloroquine-resistant malaria is present in the interior, and French Guiana is considered a yellow-fever–infected area. If you need a vaccination while there, contact the **Centre de prévention et de vaccination** (☎ 30-25-85; rue des Pommes Rosas, Cayenne; ⊗ 8:30am-noon Mon & Thu). Typhoid prophylaxis is recommended. Excellent medical care is available, but few doctors speak English. Water is fine in bigger towns; drink bottled or boiled elsewhere.

See the Health chapter (p1053) for more information.

Holidays

New Year's Day (January 1)
Epiphany (January 6) Carnaval begins.
Ash Wednesday (February/March – dates vary) Carnaval ends.
Good Friday/Easter Monday (March/April – dates vary)
Labor Day (May 1)
Pentecost (May/June – dates vary)
Bastille Day (July 14)
Assumption (August 15)
All Saints Day (November 1)
All Souls Day (November 2)
Armistice (Veterans Day; November 11)
Christmas Day (December 25)

Internet Access

Internet surf spots are scarce (one each in Cayenne, Kourou and St Laurent) and costly, especially in the capital.

Internet Resources

Guiana Shield Media Project (www.gsmp.org) Good information on environmental issues (in five languages).
Welcome to Guyane (www.destination.fr) General tourist information in English and French.

Maps

France's Institut Géographique National publishes a 1:500,000 map of French Guiana, with fine city maps of Cayenne and Kourou as well as more detailed maps of the populated coastal areas. There are also 1:25,000 topographic maps and heaps of tourist maps available throughout the country.

Media

The *International Herald Tribune* arrives regularly at local newsstands. *France-Guyane* is Cayenne's daily French-language newspaper, with good local and international coverage. French newspapers and magazines are everywhere. *Loisirs Hebdo,* a free mini-magazine with entertainment listings and upcoming events throughout French Guiana, comes out on Thursday.

Money

French Guiana is one of the most expensive regions in South America, with prices comparable to metropolitan France (from where nearly everything is imported). Being a department of France, French Guiana's local currency is the euro. It's easy to change cash or traveler's checks in US dollars or euros in Cayenne, yet the rates are about 5% lower than official rates – bring some euros with you. Credit cards are widely accepted, and you can get Visa or MasterCard cash advances at ATMs (*guichets automatiques*), which are on the Plus and Cirrus networks. Eurocard and Carte Bleu are also widely accepted. Credit cards and ATMs give the best exchange rates.

EXCHANGE RATES

Exchange rates at press time included the following:

Country	Unit		€ (euro)
Australia	A$1	=	0.62
Canada	C$1	=	0.65
Japan	¥100	=	0.79
New Zealand	NZ$1	=	0.54
United Kingdom	UK£1	=	1.46
United States	US$1	=	0.87

Post

The postal service is very reliable, although all mail is routed through France. To receive mail in French Guiana, it's best to have the letters addressed to France but using the French Guianese postal code.

Shopping

Elaborate tapestries, produced by the Hmong peoples who emigrated here from Laos in the 1970s, cannot be found elsewhere in South America and can be good value, though they are not cheap. The best place to look for tapestries outside of Cayenne is Cacao. Excellent Maroon carvings are sold along the roadside, but they tend to be much more expensive here than in Suriname. Other souvenirs include gold items (jewelry, flakes in fancy glass bottles etc), pinned gigantic bugs and stunning butterflies (though it's not recommended to support this industry by buying such products!), and Amerindian handicrafts (similar to but more expensive than those in Suriname).

Telephone

There are no central telephone offices, but you can make an international call from any pay phone: dial ☎ 00, then the country code, then the area code, then the local number. For an operator, dial ☎ 00, then 594. You need a telephone card to use public telephones; cards are available at post offices, newsstands and tobacconists.

Tourist Information

Amazingly, nearly every city and town in French Guiana has a tourist office of some sort, even if it's just a desk in the local *marché*. Abroad, French tourist offices can supply basic information about French Guiana.

Australia (☎ 02-9231-5244) 25 Bligh St, Level 22, Sydney 2000, NSW

Canada (☎ 514-288-2026) 1981 Av McGill College, Suite 490, Montreal, QC H3A 2W9

South Africa (☎ 2711-880-8062) PO Box 41022, Craighall 2024

UK (☎ 090-6824-4123) 178 Piccadilly, London W1V OAL

USA (☎ 410-286-8310) 676 N Michigan Ave, Suite 3360, Chicago, IL 60611

Tours

Because public transport is so limited, especially in the interior, tours are the best way to see French Guiana. Operators and their offerings are provided in individual town sections.

Visas

Passports are obligatory for all visitors, except those from France. Visitors should also have a yellow-fever vaccination certificate. Australian, New Zealand, Japanese, EU and US nationals, among others, do not need a visa. Those who need visas should apply with two passport photos at a French embassy and be prepared to show an onward or return ticket, to pay about US$25 and to wait for two or three days (it might take a lot longer at a consulate if officials have to refer to an embassy). Within the Guianas, it's reputedly easier to obtain a visa from the French representative in Suriname than in Guyana. Officially, all visitors, even French citizens, should have onward or return tickets, though they may not be checked at land borders.

If you are traveling from Suriname but plan to return to the republic after your travels, be sure to obtain a multiple-entry Surinamese visa (p748).

THE GUIANAS

THE GUIANAS

SURINAME

HIGHLIGHTS

- **Central Suriname Nature Reserve** – climb to the summit of the Voltzberg at sunrise for a breathtaking panorama (p744)
- **Galibi Nature Reserve** – visit one of the world's few nesting sites for giant leatherback turtles (p745)
- **Best journey** – into or out of the interior in a small plane: survey the mind-boggling expanse of the unspoiled rain forest from a six-seater Cessna. Can you say broccoli?
- **Off the beaten track** – conquer Mt Kasikasima after days of canoeing, trekking and becoming one with nature (p742)

FAST FACTS

- **Area:** 163,270 sq km (roughly the size of four Netherlands, or the US state of Georgia)
- **Budget:** US$25–30 a day
- **Capital:** Paramaribo
- **Costs:** guesthouse in Paramaribo US$14, chicken-and-vegetable roti US$2.50, *djogo* of Parbo beer US$1.50
- **Country code:** ☎ 597
- **Electricity:** 110/220V, 60Hz
- **Famous for:** having the second-worst national football team in South America
- **Languages:** Dutch, English, Sranan Tongo (Surinaams), Hindustani, Javanese, Maroon and Amerindian languages, Chinese
- **Money:** US$1 = 2502 Suriname guilders
- **Phrases:** *tof* (cool) in Dutch; *walgelijk* in Dutch, *viestie* in Sranan Tongo (disgusting); *feest* in Dutch, *vissa* in Sranan Tongo (party)
- **Population:** 436,500 (2002 estimate)
- **Time:** GMT minus 3 hours

- **Tipping:** 10–15% in restaurants and hotels if not included; none in taxis
- **Traveler's checks:** cashed at large banks for considerable fee; useless elsewhere
- **Visas:** Americans/others US$50/30 for two months (single entry); not issued at borders

TRAVEL HINTS

Pack light – it's *hot* here. If you can sneak in without a visa, don't – you'll have a heck of a time getting out.

Suriname is a unique cultural enclave whose extraordinary ethnic variety derives from indigenous cultures, British and Dutch colonization, the early importation of African slaves and, later, workers from China and indentured laborers from India and Indonesia. Paramaribo, the capital, retains some fine Dutch colonial architecture, but the country's greatest attractions are the extraordinary nature parks and reserves, notably the enormous Central Suriname Nature Reserve.

HISTORY

Suriname was the last outpost of what was once a substantial Dutch presence in South America. The Netherlands controlled large parts of Brazil and most of the Guianas until territorial conflicts with Britain and France left them control of only Dutch Guiana and a few Caribbean islands.

Suriname's 19th-century influx of Hindustanis and Indonesians (locally referred to as 'Javanese') resulted in less overt racial tension than in Guyana. Despite limited autonomy, Suriname remained a colony until 1954, when the area became a self-governing state; it became independent in 1975. Since then, political developments have been uneven. A widely popular coup in 1980, led by Sergeant Major (later Lieutenant Colonel) Desi Bouterse, brought a military regime to power that brutally executed 15 prominent opponents in 1982. The government then carried out a vicious campaign to suppress a 1986 rebellion of Maroons, many of whom fled to French Guiana as their villages were destroyed or severely disrupted.

In 1987 a civilian government was elected, but it was deposed by a bloodless coup in 1990. Another civilian government was elected in 1991, and a treaty was signed with the Jungle Commando (the Maroon military) and other armed bands in 1992. A series of strikes and street demonstrations in 1999 protested economic instability and called for the government to hold elections a year ahead of schedule. Elections were subsequently held in May 2000, producing little change, though the Netherlands stepped up its level of aid into Suriname, helping to stabilize the economy. That same year, Guyana granted the right to a foreign company to drill for oil in an area claimed by Suriname. The two nations clashed in a dispute over territorial waters; the issue is contentious and ongoing.

GOVERNMENT & POLITICS

Most political parties run along ethnic lines, but a broad coalition of Hindu, Creole and Indonesian parties, known as the Front for Democracy and Development (later the New Front), came to power in 1991 and won a provisional total of 24 national assembly seats (out of 51) in the 1996 election. The New Front's Ronald Venetiaan became president but, unable to assemble a working majority, was replaced by Jules Wijdenbosch, a candidate from Bouterse's party (the National Democratic Party, or NDP).

ECONOMY

Suriname relies on bauxite for 70% of its foreign exchange, though its ore deposits are less accessible than those of its neighbor, Guyana. Agriculture, particularly irrigated rice cultivation and bananas, is a major industry for the republic, and the fishing industry (including aquaculture) is growing. The country is also making a conscious effort to develop ecotourism in the interior.

After independence Suriname benefited from a massive aid program from the Netherlands, but the former colonial power suspended assistance in 1983. The economic situation has become increasingly difficult; despite restoration of limited aid, a fall in the world price of aluminum brought Suriname to economic crisis. Inflation is an incredibly high 170%.

THE CULTURE

Suriname is a cultural free-for-all of incredibly friendly and generous people. Paramaribo's level of acceptance and unity is primarily undisturbed by religious and racial tension, which is remarkable given the intimacy of so many groups living in such a small corner of the world. Yet many individuals, especially in the interior, are scarred by the nation's civil war in the 1980s. Some who had fled are still returning slowly, looking forward and rebuilding their damaged homeland and their lives in Suriname.

Many Surinamese live or have lived in the Netherlands, partly because of its greater economic opportunities and partly to escape military repression. The majority of the population lives in Paramaribo and along the coast. Dutch is the official national language, but most people understand standard English.

RELIGION

About 40% of the country's well-integrated population is nominally Christian, but some also adhere to traditional African beliefs. Hindus compose 26% of the population (most of the East Indian community), while 19% are Muslim (ethnic Indonesians plus a minority of East Indians). There are also small numbers of Buddhists, Jews and followers of Amerindian religions.

ARTS

Some cultural forms – such as Indonesian gamelan music, which can be heard at some special events – derive from the immigrant populations. Other art forms that visitors enjoy include intricate basketry woven by Amerindians, paintings done by a number of excellent artists and the carvings produced by the Maroons, who are widely regarded as the best woodcarvers in tropical America.

SPORT

Sports are important to the Surinamese, and it was a source of great pride when swimmer Anthony Nesty won a gold medal in the 100m butterfly at the 1988 Olympics. Though not typically South American in some ways, Suriname has soccer fields in even the tiniest villages. Dutch footballer Clarence Seedorf, who was born in Suriname and plays for Inter Milan, developed a national team, and provided the land and funds to build a major-league stadium and training facility 30 minutes outside of Paramaribo.

ENVIRONMENT

Suriname is divided into quite diverse topographical regions, primarily dense tropical forest and savannas. To its west, the Corantijn (Corentyne in Guyana) River forms the border, disputed in its most southerly reaches, with Guyana; the Marowijne (Maroni in French Guiana) and Litani Rivers form the border (also disputed in the south) with French Guiana.

The majority of Surinamese inhabit the Atlantic coastal plain, where most of the country's few roads are located. The major links to the interior are by air or north–south rivers, though there is a road to the Brownsberg Nature Reserve. The nearby Afobaka Dam created one of the world's largest reservoirs (1550 sq km), Brokopondo, on the upper Suriname River. Rapids limit the navigability of most rivers. Interior mountain ranges are not as high as those in Guyana; 1230m Julianatop is the highest point in the country.

TRANSPORT

Getting There & Away

International flights land at Suriname's simple and numbingly air-conditioned Zanderij airport (see p743). Suriname's departure tax is about US$20 (usually lumped with the ticket price).

From Albina (in the east) and Nieuw Nickerie (in the west), boats traverse the rivers to the borders of French Guiana and Guyana, respectively. See those towns' sections for details.

Getting Around

Air and river transport are the only ways to penetrate the interior, due to lack of roads.

AIR

Small planes, operated by Surinam Airways (SLM) and Gum Air (mostly a charter airline), shuttle people between Paramaribo and remote destinations, including some nature reserves (see p743).

BOAT

Rivers offer scenic routes to parts of the interior that are often inaccessible. There are few scheduled services, and prices are negotiable. Your best bet is to arrange something ahead of time in Paramaribo. Ferries and launches cross some major rivers, such as the Suriname and the Coppename, and are very cheap.

BUS

Medium-sized, often lavishly painted buses (referred to locally as 'jumbos') on the coastal highway are frequent and cheap. Arrange your fee with the driver before you get on. Government buses cost less than private buses but may be more crowded. There are very few buses off the main routes.

CAR

Suriname's roads are limited and navigating them can be dicey; some are still damaged from bombs dropped during the 1980s civil war. Passenger cars can handle the roads along the coast and to Brownsberg, but tracks into the interior are for 4WDs only. Rental cars are available but expensive and you can't take them over borders. Driving is on the left (a legacy of the British). An International Driving Permit is required.

TAXI

Shared taxis cover routes along the coast; though several times more expensive than buses, they are markedly faster. Cab fares are negotiable and generally reasonable; set a price before getting in.

PARAMARIBO

With a population of 217,300, Paramaribo (a corruption of the Amerindian term meaning 'place where the maramara tree grows'), locally called simply 'Parbo,' is a fascinatingly curious hybrid of northern Europe, tropical Asia, tropical Africa and tropical America. Imposing buildings

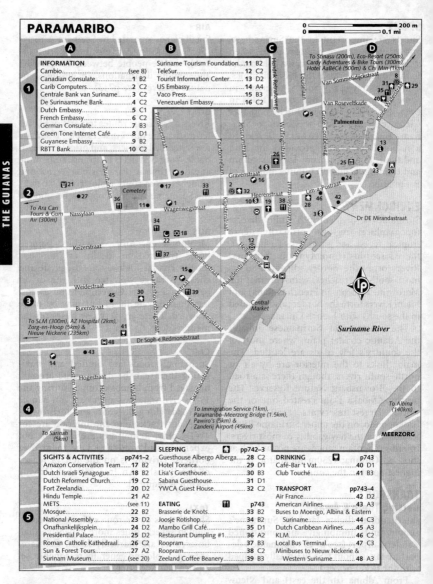

PARAMARIBO

0 ————————— 200 m
0 ————————— 0.1 mi

INFORMATION	
Cambio	(see 8)
Canadian Consulate	1 B2
Carib Computers	2 C2
Centrale Bank van Suriname	3 C2
De Surinaamsche Bank	4 C2
Dutch Embassy	5 C1
French Embassy	6 C2
German Consulate	7 B3
Green Tone Internet Café	8 D1
Guyanese Embassy	9 B2
RBTT Bank	10 C2
Suriname Tourism Foundation	11 B2
TeleSur	12 C2
Tourist Information Center	13 D2
US Embassy	14 A4
Vaco Press	15 B3
Venezuelan Embassy	16 C2

To Stinasu (200m), Eco-Resort (250m), Cardy Adventures & Bike Tours (300m), Hotel AaBéCé (500m) & Chi Min (1km)

Van Sommelsdijckstraat

Van Roseveltkade

Palmentuin

Suriname River

To Albina (140km)

MEERZORG

To Immigration Service (1km), Paramaribo-Meerzorg Bridge (1.5km), Pawiro's (5km) & Zanderij Airport (45km)

To Sarinah (5km)

To SLM (300m), AZ Hospital (2km), Zorg-en-Hoop (5km) & Nieuw Nickerie (235km)

To Ara Cari Tours & Gum Air (300m)

Central Market

SIGHTS & ACTIVITIES	pp741–2
Amazon Conservation Team	17 B2
Dutch Israeli Synagogue	18 B2
Dutch Reformed Church	19 C2
Fort Zeelandia	20 D2
Hindu Temple	21 A2
METS	(see 11)
Mosque	22 B2
National Assembly	23 D2
Onafhankelijksplein	24 D2
Presidential Palace	25 D2
Roman Catholic Kathedraal	26 C2
Sun & Forest Tours	27 A2
Surinam Museum	(see 20)

SLEEPING	pp742–3
Guesthouse Albergo Alberga	28 C2
Hotel Torarica	29 D1
Lisa's Guesthouse	30 B3
Sabana Guesthouse	31 D1
YWCA Guest House	32 C2

EATING	p743
Brasserie de Knots	33 B2
Joosje Rotishop	34 B2
Mambo Grill Café	35 D1
Restaurant Dumpling #1	36 A2
Roopram	37 B3
Roopram	38 B2
Zeeland Coffee Beanery	39 B3

DRINKING	p743
Café-Bar 't Vat	40 D1
Club Touché	41 B3

TRANSPORT	pp743–4
Air France	42 D2
American Airlines	43 A3
Buses to Moengo, Albina & Eastern	
Suriname	44 C3
Dutch Caribbean Airlines	45 A3
KLM	46 C2
Local Bus Terminal	47 C3
Minibuses to Nieuw Nickerie &	
Western Suriname	48 A3

overlook grassy squares, wooden balconied houses crowd narrow streets, mosques and synagogues play neighbors and enticing aromas waft from streetside food stalls. Parbo is also the hub for Suriname's myriad tour operators, so shop around for your ideal ecoadventure – you're sure to find it here.

Orientation

Sprawling Parbo sits on the west bank of the meandering Suriname River. Its core is a compact triangular area whose boundaries are Gravenstraat on the north, Zwartenhovenbrugstraat on the west, and the river to the southeast. The recent Paramaribo–Meerzorg bridge spans the river to its east

GETTING INTO TOWN

From Johan Pengel International Airport, usually referred to as Zanderij, 45km south of Parbo, you can grab a taxi into town (US$25, one hour). Better yet, have your hotel arrange for a cab to meet you. To the airport, **De Paarl** (☎ 403610) and **Le Grand Baldew** (☎ 474713) airport services are cheaper (US$8) and will pick you up at your hotel. Still cheaper minibuses go to Zanderij (US$1.20) and the Zorg-en-Hoop airfield (US$0.50) from Heiligenweg in daytime hours only. A taxi to Zorg-en-Hoop is about US$8.

bank. The letters 'bv' in an address stand for *'boven'* ('above' or 'upstairs').

Information

BOOKSHOPS
Vaco Press (Domineestraat 26; ☽ 8am-4:30pm Mon-Fri, 8am-1pm Sat) Parbo's best bookshop sells publications in various languages and is the only reliable source for maps.

EMERGENCY
Academisch Ziekenhuis (AZ; ☎ 442222; Flustraat) Paramaribo's only hospital for emergency services.
Police, fire & rescue (☎ 115)

INTERNET ACCESS
The post office (see opposite) has access for US$2 per hour.
Green Tone Internet Café (Kleine Waterstraat 11; US$2 per hr; ☽ 9am-10pm) Across from Hotel Torarica.
Carib Computers (Heerenstraat 22; US$1.50 per hr; ☽ 9am-10pm Mon-Sat, 2-9pm Sun) Several locations throughout Parbo.

INTERNET RESOURCES
An excellent introduction to Paramaribo and Suriname is the **'Welcome to Parbo' website** (www.parbo.com), maintained by the Suriname Tourism Foundation.

MEDICAL SERVICES
AZ (see Emergency above) has **GPs** (☽ 6-10pm Mon-Fri, 9am-10pm Sat & Sun) who provide excellent care and speak perfect English.

MONEY
Across from the Hotel Torarica is a safe **cambio** (Kleine Waterstraat 11; ☽ 9am-10:30pm). Major banks include:

Centrale Bank van Suriname (Waterkant 20)
De Surinaamsche Bank (DSB; Gravenstraat 26-30)
RBTT Bank (Kerkplein 1)

POST
The **post office** (Korte Kerkstraat 1), opposite the Dutch Reformed Church, can be a madhouse. To send urgent or important packages, call **DHL** (☎ 474007) or **FedEx** (☎ 494290).

TELEPHONE
You can make long-distance calls and buy cards for payphones at **TeleSur** (Heiligenweg 1).

TOURIST OFFICES
You can pick up some valuable information about Suriname's natural attractions at Stinasu (see Tours p742).

Your first stop in town should be the **Tourist Information Center** (☎ 479200; www.sr.net/users /stsur; Waterkant 1; ☽ 9am-3:30pm Mon-Fri). Claudia and her staff know all, and the office includes a Conservation International (CI) exhibit of different ecotourism projects in the country. The center is run by the **Suriname Tourism Foundation** (STF; Stichting Toerisme Suriname; ☎ 410357; stsur@sr.net; Dr JF Nassylaan 2; ☽ 7am-3pm Mon-Thu), whose staff at this administrative office speak English, Dutch and German but refer you to Claudia for all tourist info.

VISA EXTENSIONS
For stays over eight days, regardless of the length of your visa, you must get an exit stamp from the **Vreemdelingenpolitie** (Immigration Service; ☎ 403609; Havenkomplex, Van't Hogerhuystraat, Nieuwe Haven; ☽ 7am-2pm Mon-Fri).

Dangers & Annoyances
Paramaribo has been one of the safest cities in tropical America, but that is changing. Be careful after dark, as crime is on the rise – stick to busier streets. Do not enter the Palmentuin at night.

Sights
This 17th-century capital offers a day or two of lovely colonial architecture, lively main streets, a two-story **central market**, at the foot of Jodenbreestraat, and impressive religious buildings. Surrounding the central **Onafhankelijksplein** (Independence Square), which features a statue of legendary former prime minister Pengel, are the

contrasting stately 18th-century **Presidential Palace** (open to the public November 25 only), aging colonial government buildings and an ultramodern finance building. Behind the palace is the **Palmentuin**, a shady haven of tall royal palms, home to some tropical birds and a troop of capuchin monkeys.

Inside well-restored **Fort Zeelandia**, a pentagonal 17th-century fort built on the site where the first colonists alighted, is the **Surinam Museum** (☎ 425871; ⌚ 9am-2pm Tue-Sat, 10am-2pm Sun; tours 11am & 12:30pm Sun or by appointment), which features colonial-era relics, period rooms, and temporary exhibitions. Southwest along Waterkant are some of the city's most impressive colonial buildings, mostly merchants' houses built after the fires of 1821 and 1832. The streets inland from here, particularly **Lim-a-Postraat**, have many old wooden buildings, some restored, others in picturesque decay.

On Gravenstraat is the **Roman Catholic Kathedraal** (1885), one of the largest wooden buildings in South America, which is closed indefinitely (since 1979) until its sagging superstructure can be repaired. A few blocks away are some of the continent's finest examples of other religious buildings – the biggest **mosque** in the Caribbean and the expansive **Dutch Israeli synagogue** – sitting harmoniously side by side on Keizerstraat.

Tours

Most of Suriname's exemplary system of national parks and reserves is accessible via Parbo-based tour operators. **Stinasu** (Foundation for Nature Conservation in Suriname, Stichting Natuurbehoud Suriname; ☎ 476597; www.stinasu.sr; Cornelis Jongbawstraat 14), the Foundation for Nature Conser-

---

TWEETY FEST

On Sunday people engage in peaceful yet underlyingly cutthroat bird-song competitions on the Onafhankelijksplein. Everyone brings his or her favorite *twatwa*, usually a seed finch purchased from Amerindians in the interior. The *twatwa* that can best belt it out wins it. Something of a national obsession, this competition is well worth observing, though its popularity is petering out. It tends to be a male-oriented gathering.

---

vation in Suriname, donates a percentage of all trip proceeds to nature conservation. It coordinates research and ecotourism expeditions, runs excellent guided trips to Brownsberg (from US$45), Galibi (from US$150), Raleighvallen/Voltzberg/Foengoe Island (US$375, four days) and Coppename (US$80, one day), and helps unguided visitors explore the Central Suriname Nature Reserve more-or-less independently.

METS (Movement for Eco-Tourism in Suriname; ☎ 477088; www.metsresorts.com; JF Nassylaan 2) conducts a wide range of trips, from a sightseeing tour of Paramaribo (US$22, half-day) to a jungle expedition to Mt Kasikasima (US$675, eight days). A popular offering is a river tour of the Awarradam, in the heart of Maroon country (US$350, five days). It also books other operators' tours.

Ara Cari Tours (☎ 499705; www1.sr.net/~t100908; Kwattaweg 254) runs excellent trips to Tafelberg, the easternmost of the 'Lost World Mountains,' and Frederik Willem Falls in southwest Suriname.

Sun & Forest Tours (☎ 478383; www.surinamesun forest.nl; Gravenstraat 155) and **Suriname Safari Tours** (☎ 400925; safaritours@sr.net; Dr S Kaffulidistraat 27) run multiday trips into the interior. **Amar's Ecotours** (☎ 400372; Estabrielstraat 16) offers shorter trips (Jodensavanne is the specialty). **Cardy Adventures** (see Getting Around p744) specializes in bike (US$40) and boat (US$50) tours to the nearby Commewijne plantations.

Sleeping

Guesthouse Albergo Alberga (☎ 520050; www.guest housealbergoalberga.com; Lim-A-Postraat 13; s/d US$12/20; ⌧) This guesthouse is Paramaribo's best budget accommodation. In a beautiful colonial building, rooms without air-con can be toasty, but the flowered balcony, which overlooks one of Parbo's loveliest streets, is perfect for staying cool and enjoying a *djogo*. Notify the staff the night before if you want breakfast (US$2.50).

YWCA Guest House (☎ 472009; ywca@sr.net; Heerenstraat 14-16; s/d US$15/20; Ⓟ) The highly regarded 'why-kuh' offers clean, simple rooms to men and women. It often fills up, so reserve ahead. The adjacent **café** is affordable and reliable for decent eats.

Sabana Guesthouse (☎ 424158; Kleine Waterstraat 7; s/d US$25/28; Ⓟ ⌧) Sabana is central and popular with travelers, but the rooms are simpler than even some cheaper places.

Lisa's Guesthouse (☎ 476927; Burenstraat 6; s/d US$16/20; 🖳) In central Parbo, Lisa's has a slew of mediocre rooms that are invariably popular with Peace Corps volunteers. There are basic cooking facilities.

Hotel AaBéCé (☎ 422950; Mahonylaan 55; s/d US$35/40; 🖳) Within walking distance from the center of town, this long-standing establishment offers comfortable rooms and good value.

Eco-Resort (☎ 425522; Cornelis Jongbawstraat 16; s/d US$67/77; P 🖳) This first-rate, comfortable hotel is surprisingly popular with backpackers. Though not cheap, the price includes a buffet breakfast and use of the swanky facilities at the exclusive **Hotel Torarica** (☎ 471500; www.torarica.com; Mr Rietbergplein 1; s/d US$100/110; P 🖳 🖳). The Torarica is the best and most expensive hotel (and casino) in the country and is something of a national crossroads. The high prices at both hotels include free transport to and from the airport, which can be quite a saving. Even if you don't stay at the Torarica, be sure to visit on a Friday or Saturday night to people-watch at the bar or behind the hotel at the pavilion built above the Suriname River.

Eating
It's highly recommended to eat as often as possible – there's *great* food here. Locals and tourists alike frequent 'the strip' across from the Torarica, and other central restaurants, as well as spots on the outskirts of town, are worth the journey. The cheapest options in the center are the frenetic central market (see Sights p741) and Javanese stalls along Waterkant (try the salt fish or *petjil*, a type of green bean). For a few thousand guilders more, try the following places.

Brasserie de Knots (Heerenstraat 42; US$3-5) Everything at this little breakfast and lunch spot is delicious: eggs, cheese, bread, coffee, salad, sandwiches, burgers…

Zeeland Coffee Beanery (cnr Domineestraat & Steenbakkerijstraat; ⏱ 7am-9pm Sun-Wed, 7am-11pm Thu-Sat) This is a popular hang-out for caffeine and sweets addicts. It makes good coffee, pastries and cakes (from US$1.25) and sandwiches (US$2.25).

Roopram (Watermolenstraat; rotis US$2-5) When the locals want *roti*, a tasty Hindustani concoction made by filling a flatbread with meat or vegetables and a fiery curry sauce, they come to a Roopram (there are several

in the city, including at Zwarthovenbrugstraat 23).

There's equally yummy (if not yummier and, allegedly, less salty) competition for Roopram at **Joosje Rotishop** (Zwartenhovenbrugstraat 9; rotis US$2-5; ⏱ 8:30am-10pm Mon-Sat), which has been serving since 1942!

Mambo Grill Café (Kleine Waterstraat 5; fish US$11-12, meats US$10-25) This popular open-air 'strip' venue serves tremendous portions of grilled fish and meats, with more budget options such as fantastic burgers (US$5 to US$6) and generous appetizers (US$3 to US$9).

Restaurant Dumpling #1 (Nassylaan 12; ⏱ 7am-2pm & 5-11pm Tue-Sun) The name says it all: the best wontons in South America, with lightweight prices and heavyweight portions.

Chi Min (☎ 412155; Cornelis Jongbawstraat 83; ⏱ 11am-3:30pm & 6:30-11pm) Known for excellent Chinese food, Chi Min is a short taxi ride north of the center; a group is fine to walk.

Pawiro's (Samson Greenstraat 114) Paramaribo's Javanese neighborhood, Blauwgrond, features people cooking in their kitchens and serving dinner to customers on their patios. This is the best of the lot, though there are many to choose from.

Sarinah (☎ 430661; Verlengde Gemenelandsweg 187; 10/15 dishes per person US$8/10.50) The best upscale Indonesian restaurants are a bit further out of town, but are worth the trip. Sarinah outshines them all. Get ravenous before trying a multicourse *rijstaffel* (literally 'rice table').

Drinking
Café-Bar 't Vat (Kleine Waterstraat 1) On evenings and weekends (until 3am), people gather at this spot with outdoor tables and live music.

Club Touché (cnr Waldijkstraat & Dr Sophie Redmondstraat) For dancing, try this place.

The Hotel Torarica offers live music at the Saramacca Bar on Friday and Saturday night, as well as moonlit cocktails at the Country House Bar on the pier behind the hotel.

Getting There & Away
AIR
Paramaribo has two airports: nearby Zorgen-Hoop (for domestic flights and some flights to Georgetown, Guyana) and the larger Johan Pengel International Airport

(for all other international flights), in, and usually referred to as, Zanderij, 45km south of Parbo.

Airlines with offices in Paramaribo include **Air France** (☎ 473838; Waterkant 12), **American Airlines** (☎ 420083; Dr Sophie Redmondstraat 93), **Dutch Caribbean Airlines** (DCA; ☎ 476066; Burenstraat 34), **Gum Air** (☎ 498760; Kwattaweg 254), **KLM** (☎ 472421; Dr DE Mirandastraat 9) and **SLM** (☎ 432700; Dr Sophie Redmondstraat 219).

Regional destinations and sample one-way airfares include:

Belém (Brazil) SLM, US$263, 2½ hours, two per week.
Cayenne (French Guiana) SLM, US$116, 45 minutes, two per week.
Georgetown (Guyana) SLM, US$91, 45 minutes, two per week.

There are also direct flights to Curaçao, Barbados, Martinique and Trinidad.

BUS
Minibuses to Nieuw Nickerie (US$4, four hours, 235km) and other western destinations leave when full from the corner of Dr Sophie Redmondstraat and Hofstraat. Eastbound minibuses to Moengo (US$2, two hours, 95km) and Albina (US$4, four hours, 140km) leave at hourly intervals (or when full) from Waterkant at the foot of Heiligenweg. For connecting boat information, see the Albina (p745) and Nieuw Nickerie (p745) sections.

CAR
The most reliable rental agency in town is **Avis** (☎ 421567), which has offices in the Hotel Torarica and at Zanderij. Other car rental agencies include **Spac** (☎ 490877; Verl Gemenelandsweg 1391) and 24-hour **Wheelz** (☎ 442929; HD Benjaminstraat 20). Rental cars are expensive (from $35 per day) and may not be in perfect condition; be somewhat car savvy.

TAXI
Taxis leave from the same areas as the minibuses, or have your hotel call one. Choose a reputable company like **Ashruf** (☎ 450102). Going east, it might be better to catch a taxi on the Meerzorg side of the river.

Getting Around
The new Paramaribo–Meerzorg bridge has displaced ferry service, but long dugout canoes are cheap (about US$0.50), fast and frequent.

Bicycles are a great way to see Parbo and its environs, including the old plantations across the Suriname River. **Cardy Adventures & Bike Rental** (☎ 422518; Cornelis Jongbawstraat 31; US$4 per day; ☉ 8am-4pm Mon-Fri, 8:30am-1pm Sat, by appointment Sun) has 'reliable Dutch' road and mountain bikes, and provides maps of good biking routes. It also rents one **studio** (s/d US$20/35) with kitchenette – a great deal in a great area.

The tourist office carries photocopied route maps of Paramaribo's extensive and inexpensive bus system. Most buses leave from Heiligenweg.

Taxis are usually reasonably priced but unmetered, so agree on the fare in advance (a short trip will cost around US$2); most drivers speak passable English.

NATURE PARKS & RESERVES
Suriname's extensive system of protected nature reserves and parks is Eden for nature lovers. For tour operators' contact information, see Tours p742.

Central Suriname Nature Reserve
This 1.6-million-hectare World Heritage Site, established in 1998 thanks to a US$1 million donation from CI and efforts by local and international environmental groups to set aside areas of Suriname's vast rain forest, covers a massive 12% of Suriname's total land surface. It is known for its abundant wildlife (about 40% of which is found only in the Guianas), diverse and pristine ecosystems, and dramatic geological formations and waterfalls. Limited areas of the reserve are accessible.

RALEIGHVALLEN & VOLTZBERG
Raleighvallen (Raleigh Falls) is situated on the upper Coppename River and is known for its rich bird life, many monkey species and, of course, spectacular waterfalls. Stinasu has tourist lodges on Foengoe Island, accessible by a five-hour drive and two-hour boat ride. Voltzberg is a 240m granite dome accessible by a 2½-hour jungle trail and then a steep ascent of its face; the summit offers an unbelievable view of the forest canopy.

TAFELBERG
This remote region of mountains, forest and savanna has no surrounding human

populations. Ara Cari Tours operates fabulous journeys involving a flight and two solid days of hiking before ascending the 1026m mountain.

Brownsberg Nature Reserve & Tonka Island

Brownsberg is a beautiful area of trail-covered montane tropical rain forest overlooking Brokopondo Reservoir, about 100km south of Paramaribo by paved highway and bumpy bauxite road. Park headquarters is on the plateau, as are some very nice Stinasu-run tourist lodges. Birds and primates are particularly plentiful, though the area is so heavily visited (relatively speaking) that you may have to hike quite a way to see them.

Worth a special trip from Brownsberg is the lake's Tonka Island, a rustic ecotourism project run by the Saramaccan Maroons and US-based **Amazon Conservation Team** (ACT; ☎ 421770; actsur@sr.net; 123 Gravenstraat, Paramaribo). For ecotour details, contact ACT (ask for Angela) or Stinasu.

Galibi & Coppename Nature Reserves

Galibi's turtle-nesting area hosts hordes of sea turtles, including the giant leatherback, during egg-laying season (April through August). You can get there from Albina with permission from Carib Indians and a hired canoe, or more easily from Paramaribo with Stinasu.

The Coppename wetland reserve, at the mouth of the Coppename River, is home to the endangered manatee and is a haven for bird-watchers. Stinasu organizes trips by request.

NIEUW NICKERIE

Near the mouth of the Nickerie River, Nieuw Nickerie (population 13,300) is Suriname's second port city, exporting rice and bananas. A daily ferry runs to Springlands (Corriverton).

The four-bed dorms at **YWCA Nickerie** (☎ 232322; Waterloostraat; dm US$4) are as simple as can be, and **Hotel de Vesting** (☎ 231365; Balatastraat 6; d US$25; ⊠) is a motel-style place. **Hotel Ameerali** (☎ 231212; Maynardstraat 32; r with cold/hot water US$25/50; ⊠), with clean but smallish rooms, is second in comfort only to the **Residence Inn** (☎ 210950; RP Bharosstraat 84; s/d US$51/56.50; P ⊠).

Places to eat include the Chinese restaurants **Pak Hap** (Gouverneurstraat 97) and New Kowloon.

The Suriname–Guyana ferry (US$8, 25 minutes, 10am Monday to Saturday) traverses the Corantijn (Corentyne in Guyana) River to Springlands (Corriverton). Expect a thorough customs check and tedious formalities on each side. See p758 for details.

Government buses traveling to Paramaribo (US$4, four hours, 235km, 6am and 1pm daily) leave from the market on Maynardstraat. A private bus (US$7) leaves when full, but only after the government bus leaves. Parbo-bound taxis (US$60, three to four hours) also leave from the market.

ALBINA

A small village on the west bank of the Marowijne River, which forms the border with French Guiana, Albina (population 4100) was destroyed in the Maroon rebellion of the 1980s and early '90s and is still recovering. There is little to see and even less to do here; most pass through town en route to Galibi (see opposite) or French Guiana.

If you must stay overnight, try the **Creek Guesthouse** (☎ 458075; US$15), a clean and friendly place whose proprietors speak some English and may be able to help find a guide to the turtle beaches.

The French ferry (passenger/car US$4/23, 30 minutes, 8am, 10am, 3pm and 5:30pm Monday, Tuesday, Thursday and Friday, 7:30am and 5:30pm Wednesday, 8:30am and 9:30am Saturday, 4pm and 5:30pm Sunday) cross the Marowijne River to St Laurent du Maroni in French Guiana; from there, a good road leads to Cayenne (see p732). At other times, you can hire a dugout canoe (about US$5; haggle for less) for the short crossing. When arriving by bus or taxi, you'll be swarmed by dugout operators eager to take you across the river; not all are reliable. Go to the Surinamese immigration office first and get your passport stamped, then ask the official to recommend someone.

Minibuses (US$4, four hours, 235km) and taxis to Paramaribo leave from just outside the customs and immigration office. The road is not great.

THE GUIANAS

SURINAME DIRECTORY
Accommodations
Fairly affordable hotels and guesthouses are readily found in Paramaribo, while sleeping in the interior can involve more rustic accommodations or hammocks. Nights can be hot and buggy; your mozzie net will be your friend. Most places charge extra (US$2.50 to US$4) for breakfast.

Activities
As in the other Guianas, the best activity in Suriname is experiencing the interior. Bird-watching is fabulous, as are other animal-spotting opportunities, most of which involve boating and/or trekking.

Books
The most popular book on Suriname is Mark Plotkin's *Tales of a Shaman's Apprentice*, which also includes information on Brazil, Venezuela and the other Guianas. *The Guide to Suriname* by Els Schellekens and famous local photographer Roy Tjin is published in English; grab it at Vaco Press (see p741) or order it from **Brasa Publishers** (sranansani@aol.com). Other good introductions to the region are *Surinam: Politics, Economics & Society* by Henk E Chin and Hans Buddingh.

Business Hours
Days begin and end early in Suriname. General business hours are 7:30am or 8am to 3pm weekdays, perhaps with a few hours on Saturday. Restaurant kitchens tend to close at around 10pm or 11pm.

Climate
Temperatures and humidity are high year-round. The major rainy season is from late April to July, with a shorter one in December and January. Suriname's dry seasons – February to late April and August to early December – are the best times for a visit, though most travelers visit July through August, and prices inflate slightly. Consider coming between April and July, when several species of sea turtles come ashore to nest at Wia Wia and Galibi Reserves.

Dangers & Annoyances
Certain urban neighborhoods are subject to petty crime (mainly muggings); ask locally for places to avoid, if any. Visitors to the interior are seeing incidents of theft as well, and it's not recommended to travel inland alone.

Embassies & Consulates
For information on visas see p748.

EMBASSIES & CONSULATES IN SURINAME
Most foreign representatives are in central Paramaribo.
Brazil (☎ 400200; Maratakkastraat 2, Zorg-en-Hoop)
Canada (Map p740; ☎ 471222; Wagenwegstraat 50 bv)
France (Map p740; ☎ 476455; Gravenstraat 5-7, 2nd fl)
Germany (Map p740; ☎ 471150; Domineestraat 34-36)
Guyana (Map p740; ☎ 477895; Gravenstraat 82)
Netherlands (Map p740; ☎ 477211; Van Rosevelt-kade 5)
UK (☎ 402870; VSH United Bldg, Van't Hogerhuys-straat 9-11)
USA (Map p740; ☎ 472900; Dr Sophie Redmondstraat 129) Also responsible for US citizens in French Guiana.
Venezuela (Map p740; ☎ 475401; Gravenstraat 23-25)

SURINAMESE EMBASSIES & CONSULATES ABROAD
Suriname's representatives outside South America include:
Germany Munich (☎ 089-55-33-63; Adolf-Kolping-Strasse 16, Munich)
Netherlands The Hague (☎ 3170-36-50-844; Alexander Gogelweg 2, The Hague); Amsterdam (☎ 3120-64-26-137; De Cuserstraat 11, Amsterdam)
USA Washington (☎ 202-244-7488; 4301 Connecticut Ave NW, Suite 108, Washington, DC 20008); Miami (☎ 305-593-2163; 7235 NW 19th St, Suite A, Miami, FL 33126)

Food & Drink
Surinamese cooking reflects the nation's ethnic diversity and is often superb. Many varieties of Asian cuisine make Suriname a relative paradise for vegetarians; Chinese and Hindustani food is cheap and flavorsome. The cheapest eateries are *warungs* (Javanese food stalls), serving *bami goreng* (fried noodles) and *nasi goreng* (fried rice), but some of the best upmarket restaurants are also Javanese. Creole cooking mixes African and Amerindian elements into unique combinations. Nearly all restaurants have English-speaking staff, and menus are often in English.

Parbo, the local beer, is quite good; it's customary to share a *djogo* (1L bottle) among friends. Borgoe and Black Cat are the best local rums.

Health

A yellow-fever vaccination certificate is required for travelers arriving from infected areas. Typhoid and chloroquine-resistant malaria are present in the interior. Tap water is safe to drink in Paramaribo but not elsewhere.

See the Health chapter (p1053) for more information.

Holidays

New Year's Day (January)
Day of the Revolution (February 25)
Holi Phagwah (Hindu New Year; March/April – dates vary)
Good Friday/Easter Monday (March/April – dates vary)
Labor Day (May 1)
National Union Day/Abolition of Slavery Day (July 1)
Independence Day (November 25)
Christmas Day (December 25)
Boxing Day (December 26)
Eid-ul-Fitr (*Lebaran* or *Bodo* in Indonesian; dates vary) End of Ramadan.

Internet Access

Parbo and Nieuw Nickerie have affordable (around US$2 per hour) Internet cafés. Major hotels offer Internet access to guests with laptops (for a fee).

Internet Resources

Amazon Conservation Team (www.ethobotany.org) Articles on local conservation projects.
Stinasu (www.stinasu.sr) Ecotours and calls for conservation volunteers.
Suriname Online Tourist Guide (www.suriname tourism.com) Comprehensive tourism site.
Suriname Tourism Foundation (www.sr.net/users /stsur) Wealth of valuable information.

Maps

The one map of Suriname that is available in the country – the excellent and current Hebri BV *toeristenkaart* (US$11) – as well as a book of Parbo maps (US$10) – are stocked at Vaco Press and the Hotel Torarica gift shop, both situated in Paramaribo. The good **International Travel Maps** (www.itmb.com) country map is not sold in Suriname.

Media

There are two daily newspapers, *De Ware Tijd* and *De West.* The *Suriname Weekly,* in both English and Dutch, is a bit skeletal.

Five TV stations and 10 commercial radio stations operate in Suriname. TV broadcasts are in Dutch, but radio transmissions are also in Hindustani, Javanese and Sranan Tongo.

Money

Though the main unit of currency is the Surinamese guilder (Sf) some businesses quote prices in and accept US dollars. Most **banks** (7am-2pm Mon-Fri) accept Dutch guilders and other major foreign currencies, but you may run into difficulty trying to change Guyanese dollars and sometimes even Brazilian *reais.*

CREDIT CARDS

The ATMs around town don't accept foreign cards, and credit cards are accepted (often for a fee) at major hotels and travel agencies but hardly anywhere else. The country is trying to increase credit-card acceptance but has a way to go.

EXCHANGE RATES

Exchange rates at press time included the following:

Country	Unit		Sf (Surinamese guilder)
Australia	A$1	=	1774
Canada	C$1	=	1878
euro zone	€1	=	2862
Japan	¥100	=	2276
New Zealand	NZ$1	=	1541
United Kingdom	UK£1	=	4189
United States	US$1	=	2502

EXCHANGING MONEY

Except at *cambios*, getting cash can involve time-consuming paperwork. Slowly but surely, banks (and only banks) cash traveler's checks, give advances on credit cards and stamp foreign-exchange transaction forms. Black-market rates are much higher than bank rates – generally more than 50%. This type of currency exchange is technically illegal and not without risk; short-changing is the most frequent problem. This leaves the only other – and perhaps the best – option: changing money at hotels (and some shops). Haggle for good exchange rates.

THE GUIANAS

Post
Postal services in Paramaribo are reliable but may be less so in other parts of Suriname.

Shopping
Maroon handicrafts, especially tribal wood-carvings, are stunning and are cheaper in Suriname than in Guyana or French Guiana. Amerindian and Javanese crafts are also attractive. Paramaribo is the best place to shop; the commercial center is along Domineestraat and nearby streets.

Telephone
TeleSur (Telecommunicatiebedrijf Suriname) is the national telephone company. Calls abroad can be made from yellow public telephone booths. You can pay with *fiches* (coin-like tokens) purchased from a TeleSur office, make reverse-charge (collect) calls or use a home-country direct service (☎ 156 to the US, ☎ 157 to the Netherlands).

Tourist Information
Abroad, Suriname information and maps are most readily found in the Netherlands. In Suriname, the STF, which also has a representative in the Netherlands, runs a fabulous tourist office (see p741).

Tours
Suriname's must-see interior is best experienced with a professional tour company. See p742 for details on a few of the 30-something operators that specialize in numerous regions and activities, often combining the environmental and the sociocultural (visiting Amerindian or Maroon villages). Tour prices tend to vary based on duration and the number of people, and many trips are on demand or customized for groups.

Tours include all meals, accommodations, transport and guides. There is usually a minimum of four and maximum of eight people for each trip, so it's wise to make arrangements in advance.

Visas
Passports are obligatory, and those who don't need a visa are given a tourist card. Suriname is becoming somewhat liberal with its entry requirements; for example, Guyanese, Israeli and Japanese citizens don't require visas, but Australian, Canadian, Dutch, French, German, New Zealand, UK and US nationals still do.

Suriname's overseas representation is very limited. You can contact the nearest embassy for an application form, but allow four weeks for a postal application. Consulates in Georgetown (Guyana) and Cayenne (French Guiana) charge US$30 (US$50 for US citizens) for two-month single-entry visitor visas and issue them within a couple of hours or days; prices rise for multiple-entry and longer-stay visas. Some say that the process of obtaining a visa is easier in Cayenne than in Georgetown. Bring a passport-sized photo and your ticket out of South America.

Even with a multiple-month visa, you get a one-week entry stamp upon arrival. Visitors spending more than eight days in Suriname require an exit visa (stamp) from immigration in Paramaribo (see p741).

Women Travelers
Female travelers, especially those traveling alone, will find local males verbally aggressive (sometimes extremely), but rarely physically threatening. Constant brazen attention can be annoying, if not truly disconcerting.

GUYANA

HIGHLIGHTS

- **Kaieteur Falls** – revel in the spray of one of South America's most majestic waterfalls (p758)
- **Iwokrama** – support Guyana's biodiversity effort in the heart of her vast rain forest (p759)
- **Best journey** – Georgetown–Kurupukari–Linden–Lethem: climb into the back of a truck during the dry season for an unforgettable overland crossing (p757)
- **Off the beaten track** – take a wildlife-viewing excursion to a local ranch in the Rupununi Savanna (p759)

THE GUIANAS

FAST FACTS

- **Area:** 214,970 sq km (about the size of the UK)
- **Budget:** US$20–30 a day
- **Capital:** Georgetown
- **Costs:** guesthouse bed US$19, delicious pepperpot US$3, refreshing Banks beer US$0.75
- **Country code:** ☎ 592
- **Electricity:** 127V, 60Hz
- **Famous for:** Jim Jones tragedy, having the worst national football team in South America
- **Languages:** English, Creole, Hindi, Urdu, Amerindian
- **Money:** US$1 = 179 Guyanese dollars
- **Population:** 698,200 (2002 estimate)
- **Time:** GMT minus 4 hours
- **Tipping:** 10% in restaurants and hotels if not included; none in taxis
- **Traveler's checks:** cashed at nationwide banks and *cambios*; commission varies
- **Visas:** US$16 for three months; if not required, 30-day visas granted at borders

TRAVEL HINTS

Bring warm clothes for excursions into the interior – it gets damp and cold overnight. Avoid traveling solo; explore towns in groups, and visit the interior with experienced guides.

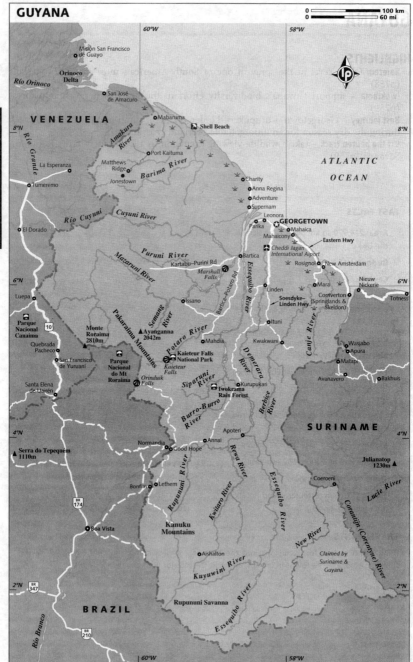

GUYANA

0 ——————— 100 km
0 ——————— 60 mi

VENEZUELA

Misión San Francisco de Guayo

Orinoco Delta

Río Orinoco

San José de Amacuro

La Esperanza

Tumeremo

Río Cuyuni

El Dorado

Luepa

Parque Nacional Canaima

Quebrada Pacheco

San Francisco de Yuruaní

Santa Elena de Uairén

Serra do Tepequem 1110m

Boa Vista

BRAZIL

Río Branco

Mabaruma

Shell Beach

Port Kaituma

Matthews Ridge

Jonestown

Amakura River

Barima River

Río Cuyuni   *Cuyuni River*

Charity

Anna Regina

Adventure

Supernam

Leonora

Parika

Puruni River

Mazaruni River

Kartabu–Purini Rd

Bartica

Marshall Falls

Issano

Semang River

Monte Roraima 2810m

Parque Nacional do Mt Roraima

Ayanganna 2042m

Potaro River

Kaieteur Falls National Park

Kaieteur Falls

Orinduik Falls

Pakaraima Mountains

Siparuni River

Iwokrama Rain Forest

Burro-Burro River

Normandia

Good Hope

Bonfim

Lethem

Rupununi River

Kanuku Mountains

Aishalton

Kuyuwini River

Rupununi Savanna

Annai

Apoteri

Rewa River

Kwitaro River

Essequibo River

Mahdia

Kurupukari

Kwakwani

Ituni

Linden

Soesdyke–Linden Hwy

Demerara River

Berbice River

Cane River

GEORGETOWN

Mahaica

Mahaicony

Cheddi Jagan International Aiport

Eastern Hwy

Rosignol   New Amsterdam

Mara   Canje River   Corriverton (Springlands & Skeldon)

Nieuw Nickerie

Totness

Wasjabo

Apura

Matapi

Avanavero

Bakhuis

SURINAME

Julianatop 1230m

Coeroeni

New River

Lucie River

Corantijn (Corenyne) River

Claimed by Suriname & Guyana

ATLANTIC OCEAN

8°N

6°N

4°N

2°N

60°W   58°W

BR 174

BR 347

BR 210

10

Many find Guyana's ecotourism opportunities worth the challenge of the country's little infrastructure, high prices and growing safety concerns. While most visitors come on business, trolling for gold or timber, the country has been trying to boost tourism into its less-touched rain forest areas and beautiful waterfall areas. (Expensive) adventure guides and resorts are on the increase, though even with a healthy budget, it'll take advance planning – and patience – to book a tour operator. Unfortunately, going it alone isn't always possible, affordable or safe.

HISTORY

Both Carib and Arawak tribes inhabited the land that is now Guyana before the Dutch arrived in the late 16th century. The British took over in 1796. Halfway between rulers, in 1763, the locals staged the Berbice Slave Revolt; Kofi, the revolt's leader, remains the country's national hero.

In 1831 the three colonial settlements of Essequibo, Demerara and Berbice merged to become British Guiana. After the abolition of slavery (1834), Africans refused to work on the plantations for wages, and many established their own villages in the bush. Plantations closed or consolidated because of the labor shortage. A British company, Booker Bros, resurrected the sugar industry by importing indentured labor from India, drastically transforming the nation's demographic and laying the groundwork for fractious racial politics that continue to be a problem today. The late 19th century forced Guyana to start diversifying its economy by penetrating its interior: revenue from mining and logging allowed the country to ride out collapses in the sugar market.

British Guiana was run very much as a colony until 1953, when a new constitution provided for home rule and an elected government. Ten years later, riots left almost 200 dead after black laborers were hired to replace striking Indian plantation workers. In 1966 the country became an independent member of the British Commonwealth with the name Guyana, and in 1970 it became a republic with an elected president.

Guyana attracted the world's attention in 1978 with the mass suicide-murder of over 900 cultists in American Jim Jones' expatriate religious community of Jonestown.

Today the country struggles to conserve land and develop ecotourism while it continues to develop logging and mining concessions; Guyana's government has allowed Malaysian, American and other multinationals to move in on some lands. To top it off, racial tensions soured into street violence after the People's Progressive Party, largely backed by the East Indian population, won a third consecutive term in 2001.

GOVERNMENT & POLITICS

Guyana's 1980 constitution established an executive branch with an elected president and a prime minister appointed by the president. The main political parties are the People's National Congress (PNC) and the Marxist-oriented People's Progressive Party (PPP/Civic). The PPP/Civic is supported principally by the East Indian community, while the PNC is supported by Afro-Guyanese. In October 1992, in an election marred by violence, PPP/Civic candidate Cheddi Jagan easily defeated the incumbent PNC president, Desmond Hoyte.

Since independence, most of the important posts in the Guyanese Defense Force, the police and the civil service have been occupied by Afro-Guyanese, but with the change of government more East Indians have been appointed to influential positions. Jagan died in office (1997) and was replaced by his US-born wife, Janet. Negotiations ended the resulting PNC-led violence, but the political situation remained somewhat tense. In 1999 Janet Jagan retired from the presidency and named Bharrat Jagdeo her successor.

Elections scheduled for January 2001 were delayed until March 2001, a move that many feared would antagonize already sensitive race relations; even former US president Jimmy Carter traveled to Guyana to monitor the elections. Nonetheless, entire blocks of Georgetown were set ablaze by opposition supporters as the ruling PPP/Civic was declared victor of a third consecutive term, and the police and protesters clashed in the capital for weeks.

ECONOMY

Guyana's economy relies on exports of primary commodities, especially bauxite but also gold, sugar, rice, timber and shrimp. East Indians control most of the small business, while the Afro-Guyanese have, until the late '90s, dominated the government sector. Guyana is a member of the Caribbean economic group, Caricom.

Guyana Sugar Company (Guysuco), the state-controlled sugar enterprise, employs more Guyanese than any other industry and produces 28% of Guyana's export earnings. Multinational corporations, including US-based Reynolds Metals and Canada's Alcan, are major investors in the mineral sector. Substantial gold-mining ventures pose a risk to the environment; one gold-extraction plant spilled a huge quantity of cyanide into the Essequibo River in 1995. The Barama Company, owned by Koreans and Malaysians, has an enormous logging concession in the northwest (8% of the country), and most of the local and many international environmentalists are skeptical of this company's capacity (or intention) to carry out a truly sustainable operation.

But the infrastructure, once very run-down, is slowly improving, with more reliable phones and fewer electricity blackouts. However, one in three Guyanese is said to live in poverty, and the country has had recent bouts of negative growth.

THE CULTURE
There are about 697,000 people in Guyana, but some 500,000 Guyanese live abroad, mostly in Canada, the UK, the USA, Trinidad and other English-speaking Caribbean countries. The main groups of Amerindians, who reside in scattered interior settlements, are Arawak, Carib, Macushi and Wapishana. The vast majority of the population lives in Georgetown or along the coast.

Dress is informal, though Guyanese people seldom wear shorts; women, in fact, are usually in skirts.

RELIGION
Most Afro-Guyanese are Christian, usually Anglican, but a handful are black Muslim. The East Indian population is mostly Hindu, with a sizable Muslim minority, but Hindu-Muslim friction is uncommon. Since independence, efforts have been made to recognize all relevant religions in national holidays.

SPORT
In racially polarized Guyana, sport is one of the few unifying factors, and sport mainly means cricket. Internationally, Guyanese play with the West Indies; Clive Lloyd and Carl Hooper are the best-known local cricketers. Soccer is also played, but not as fervently as cricket. Guyana has only had one Olympian: boxer Michael Parris, who won a bronze medal in 1980.

ENVIRONMENT
Like Suriname, Guyana is swarming with rivers; its three principal waterways – the Demerara, Essequibo and Berbice (listed east to west) – are all north-flowing. The narrow strip of coastal lowland, 16km to 60km wide and 460km long, comprises 4% of the total land area but is home to 90% of the population. The Dutch, using a system of drainage canals, seawalls and groins, reclaimed much of the marshy coastal land from the Atlantic. These polders support most of Guyana's agriculture. There are very few sandy beaches.

Tropical rain forest covers most of the interior, though southwestern Guyana features an extensive savanna between the Rupununi River and the Brazil border.

TRANSPORT
Getting There & Away
Travelers flying to Guyana arrive at Cheddi Jagan International Airport, south of the capital (see p757 and p761). Outbound passengers pay a departure tax of around US$14 (payable in Guyanese dollars only).

BOAT & BUS
From Bonfim (Brazil), you can cross the river to Lethem, in Guyana's southwestern Rupununi Savanna. Bonfim has a good road connection to the Brazilian city of Boa Vista, but the road from Lethem to Georgetown is rough and may be impassable in wet weather.

In the northeast, a ferry connects Corriverton (Springlands) to the Surinamese border town of Nieuw Nickerie, from which you can four-wheel it to Paramaribo and on to French Guiana (see p758).

There are no road connections west to Venezuela and no legal border crossing points. The only overland route is through Brazil via Boa Vista and Bonfim.

Getting Around
Charter air services to the interior are available from the Ogle Aerodome in Georgetown (see p757).

Ferries cross most major rivers. There is regular service on the Essequibo between Charity and Bartica, with a stop at Parika (reached by paved highway from Georgetown). A ferry also crosses from Rosignol to New Amsterdam, along the Eastern Hwy on the way to the Suriname border. More frequent, but relatively expensive, speedboats (river taxis) carry passengers from Parika to Bartica. Ferry docks are known as *stellings,* a term adopted from Dutch.

Unscheduled minibuses link Georgetown with secondary towns. Rental cars are available in Georgetown, though not from the airport at the time of writing.

For more details about traveling around Guyana, see Getting Around (p757).

An International Driving Permit is recommended and is required for car rental.

Hitchhiking is not recommended – the threat of robbery is *very* real.

GEORGETOWN
Originally designed by the Dutch on a regular grid pattern with canal-lined (read: often smelly) streets, Georgetown (population 250,000) is Guyana's capital and only large city. It retains some 19th-century colonial architecture, though many buildings are in poor condition. There is little to see and less to do in Georgetown, but it's the best place to get information before setting off into the interior. Be aware that the rumors are true: Georgetown is a dangerous city (see Dangers & Annoyances p755).

Orientation
Low-lying Georgetown sits on the east bank of the Demerara River, where it empties into the Atlantic. A long seawall prevents flooding, while the Dutch canal system drains the town, and its position seven feet below sea level helps keep the city relatively cool. Pedestrian paths pass between the traffic lanes of the town's broad avenues.

Georgetown is divided into several districts: Kingston (in the northwest); Cummingsburg, Alberttown, Queenstown and Newtown (in the center); Robbstown, Lacytown, Stabroek and Bourda (south of Church St; Bourda lines the western border

---

GETTING INTO TOWN
Minibuses (US$1, one hour) at Stabroek Market connect Georgetown with Cheddi Jagan International Airport; they are safe enough in the daytime, but at night a taxi (US$20; may be shared) is a much wiser choice. For early-morning flights from Jagan, make taxi arrangements the day before.

---

of the botanical gardens); Werk-en-Rust, Wortmanville, Charlestown and Le Repentir (further south); Thomas Lands (east; where many of the city's sports clubs and fields are); and Kitty (further east).

Note that street numbering is discontinuous in Georgetown's various boroughs – the same number may appear twice on the same street or may not go in the order that you expect, say, in Cummingsburg and Lacytown. Thus, districts are often cited in addresses. Some streets change names west of Main St and Ave of the Republic.

A decent map (US$2) of Georgetown is available at **Kojac Marketing Agency** (☎ 225-2387; 140B Quamina St, Cummingsburg).

Information
BOOKSHOPS
The Bookseller (☎ 227-1244; 78 Church St; ☉ 8am-4pm Mon-Fri, 8am-1pm Sat) Offers a reasonable selection of paperback novels, mostly by Caribbean writers.

CULTURAL CENTERS
National Cultural Centre (☎ 226-2161; Mandela Ave in D'Urban Park) Frequently puts on plays, concerts and other cultural events.

INTERNET ACCESS
Web access in Georgetown goes for about US$2 per hour.
Internet cafe (☎ 223-7614; 125 Carmichael St; ☉ 8am-8pm Mon-Fri, 10am-4pm Sat)
Le Bureau Business Centre (cnr Church & Thomas Sts; US$5 per hr) Internet access and other services, including computer rental; also in Le Meridien Pegasus Hotel (see Sleeping p756).
Net Zone (☎ 227-3235; 42 Water St; ☉ 8am-5:30pm Mon-Sat)

MEDICAL SERVICES
Travelers may prefer private clinics and hospitals, such as **St Joseph's Mercy Hospital** (☎ 227-2072; 130-132 Parade St), to **Georgetown**

THE GUIANAS

THE GUIANAS

GEORGETOWN

INFORMATION
Brazilian Embassy.....1 E3
Canadian High Commission.....2 E3
Colombian Embassy.....3 E3
Georgetown Public Hospital.....4 C2
Globe Trust & Investment.....5 B2
Guyana Telephone &
  Telegraph.....6 B3
Immigration Office.....7 C1
Internet Café.....8 B3
Kayman Sankar.....9 B2
Kojac Marketing Agency.....10 B3
Le Bureau Business Centre.....11 C3
Ministry of Amerindian Affairs in the
  Office of the President.....12 D4
Ministry of Tourism, Industry
  & Commerce.....13 B4
NetZone.....14 B1
St Joseph's Mercy Hospital.....15 B1
Surinamese Embassy.....16 E2
The Bookseller.....17 B3
Tourism & Hospitality Association
  of Guyana.....18 B2
UK High Commission.....19 C3
US Embassy.....20 C3
Venezuelan Embassy.....21 C3

SIGHTS & ACTIVITIES pp755-6
Basket Shop.....22 B3
Horizons Travel Service.....23 B3
Museum of Guyana.....24 B3
National Library.....25 B3
Parliament Building.....26 B4
Rainforest Tours.....(see 39)
Shell Beach Adventures.....(see 40)
Square of the Revolution.....27 E4
St George's Cathedral.....28 B3
Stabroek Market.....29 A4
State House.....30 B2
Timberhead Rainforest Resort.....(see 40)
Town Hall.....31 B4
Victoria Law Courts.....32 B4
Wilderness Explorers.....(see 35)
Zoo.....33 E3

SLEEPING p756
Campala International.....34 C4
Cara Suites.....35 B2
Florentene's Hotel.....36 B3
Friends Apartment Hotel.....37 C3
Hotel Ariantze.....38 B2
Hotel Tower.....39 B3
Le Meridien Pegasus Hotel.....40 B1
Rima Guest House.....41 B2
The New Tropicana Hotel,
  Restaurant & Bar.....42 B3
Woodbine International Hotel.....43 B2

EATING pp756-7
Browne's 24 Hour Café.....(see 40)
Caribbean Rose.....44 B2
Cazabon.....(see 39)
Club del Casa.....45 C2
Coal Pot.....46 B3
Country Pride.....47 B3
Forest Hills.....48 C4
Hack's Halaal.....49 B4
IDIHO Health Bar.....50 B4
Main Street Café.....(see 39)
New Orient Chinese
  Restaurant.....51 C2
Palm Court.....52 B2
Rice Bowl.....53 B3
Salt & Pepper Restaurant and
  Bakery.....54 B3

DRINKING p757
Club Blue Note.....55 C3

SHOPPING p757
Creations Craft.....56 A3
Hibiscus Craft Plaza.....57 B3
Houseproud.....58 B3

TRANSPORT p757
Budget.....59 C3
BWIA.....60 B3
LIAT.....(see 6)
Minibuses to Airport.....61 B4
Minibuses to Parika, Rosignol
  & Linden.....62 B4
SLM.....63 B2

Demerara River

Kingston
National Park
Cummingsburg
Promenade Garden
Independence Square
Tiger Bay
Robbstown
Lacytown
Stabroek
Werk-en-Rust
Bourda
Queenstown
Newtown
Wortmanville
Lodge

Roman Catholic Cathedral
Botanical Gardens
D'Urban Park

To Kitty & Thomas Lands
To Alberttown
To Back to Eden, Old Roadstand, Subryanville & Eastern Hwy
To Le Repentir
To Charlestown
To National Cultural Centre & Lands & Survey Dept, Ministry of Agriculture
To Parika

0 ------ 0.5 mile
0 ------ 1 km

Public Hospital (☎ 225-6900; New Market St), which has inadequate and run-down facilities.

MONEY
Reliable *cambios* include:
Kayman Sankar (☎ 227-1560; 217 Lamaha St, North Cummingsburg)
Globe Trust & Investment (92 Middle St)

POST
Main post office (☎ 225-7071; Robb St) This central postal hub can be hectic; go early.

TELEPHONE
Guyana Telephone & Telegraph (GT&T; Church St at Ave of the Republic; ☺ 7am-10pm) Phone home.

TOURIST OFFICES
The **Ministry of Tourism, Industry & Commerce** (☎ 226-2505; www.sdnp.org.gy/mtti; 229 South St, Lacytown; ☺ 8am-4:30 pm Mon-Fri) is not nearly as helpful as the privately run **Tourism & Hospitality Association of Guyana** (THAG; ☎ 225-0807; www.exploreguyana.com; 157 Waterloo St, North Cummingsburg; ☺ 8am-5pm Mon-Fri), which publishes the useful *Guyana Tourist Guide.*

VISA EXTENSIONS
To stay longer than 30 days, appeal to the **immigration office** (☎ 225-1744; Camp Rd; ☺ 8-11:30am & 1-3pm Mon-Fri).

Dangers & Annoyances
Georgetown is dangerous. Period. Street crime, often violent, is common even in broad daylight. Don't walk *any*where alone, carry next to nothing (ie, small change) and wear nothing of value – not even flash trainers. Don't walk anywhere at night; even locals take cabs to restaurants two blocks from their homes. Electricity blackouts are quite frequent, and street lighting is poor at the best of times. *Never* enter the Tiger Bay area (north of Church St and west of Main St), avoid Middle St between Main and Waterloo Sts, and stay out of the Promenade Garden.

Sights
Georgetown can be seen in a day. The best 19th-century buildings are along Main St and especially along Ave of the Republic, just east of the Demerara River.

Gothic-style **St George's Cathedral** (North Rd), said to be the world's tallest wooden building, was built mostly with local materials, most notably a hardwood called greenheart. Further south is the distinctive neo-Gothic **Town Hall** (1889), beyond which are the **Victoria Law Courts** (1887). At the south end of Ave of the Republic is the well-kept **Parliament Building** (1833) and, nearby, the landmark **Stabroek Market** (Water St), a striking cast-iron building with a corrugated-iron clock tower. This main shopping venue, once described as quite a 'bizarre bazaar,' dates back to 1792.

Andrew Carnegie built the **National Library** (cnr Ave of the Republic & Church St), three blocks north of which stands the 1852 **State House** (cnr Main & New Market Sts), now the president's residence.

The **Museum of Guyana** (cnr North Rd & Hincks St; admission free) is a curious institution with some very old-fashioned exhibits documenting the nation's cultural, social, and political history. Also interesting is the **Walter Roth Museum of Anthropology** (61 Main St), the first such museum in the English-speaking Caribbean.

Georgetown's **botanical gardens** (Regent Rd) are worth visiting, but stick to the main paths and avoid the southeastern corner. The garden's **zoo** (www.guyanazoo.org.gy; Regent & Vlissnegen Rds; adult/child US$0.50/0.25, with video camera US$11; ☺ 7:30am-5:30pm) focuses on local fauna. There's a stunning jaguar (in a miserably small cage), and manatees swim in the zoo canal, offering remarkably close glimpses of these shy creatures. The open court on the block south of the botanical gardens is the **Square of the Revolution**, which houses the monument to Cuffy, famous leader and hero of the 1763 rebellion on the Berbice sugar estate.

Tours
The safest (for you and the environment) way to see inland Guyana is with an experienced, ecofriendly tour guide. For operators headquartered in hotels, see the boxed text Splurge! on p756.

Horizons Travel Service (☎ 223-9794; 133A Church St, South Cummingsburg) puts together superb customized trips to the interior, as does **Evergreen Adventures** (☎ 226-0605; www.evergreen-adventures.com; 159 Charlotte St, Lacytown), which visits the Rupununi Savannas, as well as other destinations. **Shell Beach Adventures** (☎ 225-4483; www.sbadventures.com; Le Meridien Pegasus Hotel) specializes in three-day trips to the coast (US$450) to observe the egg-laying of the sea turtle, including the giant leatherback, during egg-laying season (March/April to August). **Timberhead Rainforest Resort** (☎ 225-3760; www.lemeridien -pegasus.com/timberhead.htm; Le Meridien Pegasus Hotel) offers trips to the Timberhead Lodge (day/ overnight US$55/105) and other parts of the interior.

Frank Singh's **Rainforest Tours** (☎ 227-5632; www.hoteltowerguyana.com/rainforesttours.htm; Hotel Tower) can arrange tours up the Essequibo and Mazaruni Rivers (US$80), as well as an adventurous five-day overland journey (US$550) to Kaieteur Falls. The reader-recommended **Wilderness Explorers** (☎ 227-7698; www.wilderness-explorers.com; Cara Suites) runs day trips to the Santa Mission of Carib Indians (US$50) and around Georgetown (US$30), and numerous interior treks including a five-day overland (US$750) or one-day with flight (US$210) to Kaieteur Falls.

Sleeping

Prices here are for 'singles' (usually for two, with double beds) with fans unless otherwise indicated.

The New Tropicana Hotel, Restaurant & Bar (☎ 227-2864; 177 Waterloo St; r with/without bath US$9/6) One of Georgetown's cheapest lodgings, this place is very basic but has character, a lively bar and disco, and a good location.

Florentene's Hotel (☎ 226-2283; 3 North Rd; r with/without bath US$18/12) This highly recommended hotel offers very clean rooms.

Rima Guest House (☎ 225-7401; 92 Middle St; r US$19) For a friendly family place, try this central and secure spot. It's open for registration only 8am to 4pm weekdays and 8am to noon Saturday.

Pricier options include nice and clean **Friends Apartment Hotel** (☎ 227-2383; 82 Robb St; r from US$24); **Campala International** (☎ 225-2950; 10 Camp St, Werk-en-Rust; s/d US$33/43); further south, modern **Woodbine International Hotel** (☎ 225-9430; 41 New Market St; s/d US$50/60); and pleasant **Hotel Ariantze** (☎ 226-5363; 176 Middle St; s/d US$55/65 with breakfast).

Eating

The cuisine in Georgetown is not as phenomenal as in the other Guianas, but there are some noteworthy eateries. In the Hotel Tower (see the boxed text), Main Street Café makes a good stop for breakfast and

---

SPLURGE!

Georgetown's city life can be taxing, so treat yourself to a swankier-than-thou night – or three. The capital's upscale options (which are cheaper than French Guiana and Suriname's cushiest hotels) include:

Cara Suites (☎ 226-1612; www.carahotels .com/cara_suites.htm; carasuites@carahotels.com; 176 Middle St; s/d US$85/95; 🔀 💻) Business-folks and backpackers alike enjoy Cara's fine suites with kitchenettes, *free* Internet access and computer services, and use of Cara Inn's pool, tennis courts and full-service BBQ pits. Email or call ahead to arrange for a taxi from the airport.

Hotel Tower (☎ 227-2011; www.hoteltower guyana.com; 74-75 Main St; d with breakfast from US$85; 🔀 💻 🖳) With a gym, pool, beauty salon, 24-hour café and room service, three restaurants, two bars and two shops, where do you begin? Start with trying to negotiate a slightly better rate, especially in the off-season.

Le Meridien Pegasus Hotel (☎ 225-2856, toll-free from USA or Canada 800-543-4300; www.lemeridien-pegasus.com; Seawall Rd, Kingston; d from US$150; 🔀 🔀 💻 🖳) It's worth totally splurging at this 132-rooms-and-suites-with-river-and-ocean-views, cream-of-the-Georgetown-hotel-crop landmark. Enjoy a 24-hour café, a popular Latin-style bar/club, a poolside BBQ, gym, tennis court...and forget it all on the massage table.

---

sandwiches, while the Cazabon specializes in spicier meat dishes. Le Meridien Pegasus Hotel (see the boxed text) features good but relatively expensive restaurants, including Browne's 24 Hour Café, which, as its name indicates, stays open all day and has great coffee. Robb St offers cheap, authentic local food at places like **Salt & Pepper Restaurant and Bakery, Rice Bowl** (34 Robb St) and **Country Pride** (64 Robb St).

It's worth roaming the streets for other venues, including:

Coal Pot (17 Hincks St; meals US$2-3) Often crowded thanks to its diverse lunch menu, Coal Pot's seafood is much cheaper than elsewhere in town.

Hack's Halaal (Commerce St near Hincks St) This place is quite popular for fast East Indian food.

IDIHO Health Bar (Brickdam St near Stabroek Market) Mmm…snacks. And healthy ones!

Forest Hills (Campsite, cnr Camp & South Sts) This restaurant offers Chinese food, pastries and snacks.

Back to Eden (85 David St, Subryanville) Ask for the daily special at this good vegetarian restaurant.

Palm Court (35 Main St) This is a lively and popular spot, with good seafood and daily lunch specials.

Caribbean Rose (175 Middle St) Enjoy tasty Indian- and Caribbean-influenced fare at this rooftop restaurant.

Club del Casa (232 Middle St) Fairly expensive and formal, with a dress code and surprisingly indifferent service, the good meat and seafood is worth the stuffiness.

New Orient Chinese Restaurant (218 Lamaha St) There's good service at this fine Chinese place.

Drinking

You'll find some nightlife in Georgetown, where quite a few places feature live reggae and rock until the early hours. Most discos in central Georgetown are safe and welcome foreigners, but discos on the outskirts may harbor thieves.

The best nightlife is along Sheriff St, east of the town center, where Sheriff, Buddy's Night Club & Pool Hall, C&S and Tennessee are all popular spots that feature local dance music. Night Flight is Georgetown's most happening disco, jammed with locals and visitors on the weekend. Other hot spots include **Club Blue Note** (202 Camp St). Most places have a cover charge of a few dollars.

Shopping

For pottery, paintings and woodcarvings, try **Houseproud** (6 Ave of the Republic) or **Creations Craft** (7A Water St). The multiple shops at **Hibiscus Craft Plaza**, in front of the post office, specialize in local handicrafts.

Getting There & Away

AIR

Cheddi Jagan International Airport is 41km south of Georgetown. These airlines, with offices in Georgetown, link the capital to Caribbean islands, Suriname (where you can connect to French Guiana and Brazil) and beyond: **BWIA** (☎ 225-8900; www.bwee.com; 4 Robb St), **LIAT** (☎ 226-1260; Bank of Guyana Bdg, Church St near Ave of the Republic) and **Surinam Airways** (SLM; ☎ 225-3473; www.slm.firm.sr; 91 Middle St). **Roraima Airways** (☎ 225-9648; www.roraimaairways.com; 101 Cummings St, Bourda) and **Trans Guyana Airways** (TGA; ☎ 222-2525; www.transguyana.com; Ogle Aerodome) send small planes into the interior from the Ogle Aerodome, East Coast Demerara, Georgetown. Availability varies, so inquire well ahead of when you plan to travel.

One-way airfares within Guyana and the Guianas include:

Kaieteur TGA, US$123, 1 hour, weekly

Lethem Roraima, US$100, 2 hours, three per week; TGA, US$117, 1½ hours, daily

Paramaribo (Suriname) SLM, US$91, 45 minutes, two weekly

Cayenne (French Guiana) SLM, US$172, 2½ hours (via Paramaribo), two weekly

BUS

Minibuses to Parika (No 32), Rosignol (No 44) and Linden leave from Stabroek Market. (At Parika, you can make ferry connections to Bartica and Charity; at Rosignol, catch the ferry to New Amsterdam, with connecting service to Corriverton.) These have no fixed schedules and leave whenever they fill up.

If you're interested in overland travel to Lethem, ask around at Stabroek Market about trucks going that way or, better yet, arrange it through Horizons Travel Service (US$50 one way). Either way this is a remarkable trip, but it is rustic and not for the rushed or fainthearted (12 to 18 hours in a 4x4 with eight other people). Bring your own food, tent or hammock with mosquito net and warm clothes; nights can be chilly.

Getting Around

Budget (☎ 225-5595; 75 Church St, Alberttown; ☼ Mon-Sat) rents quite expensive cars (US$35 per day, three-day minimum, includes 100km per day). With bad road conditions and fellow drivers, you're better off in a taxi or bus.

For simplicity and safety, taxis are *the* way to get around central Georgetown (around center/to outskirts US$1/2 or US$5 per hour). Try **Tower Taxi Service** (☎ 225-7202), in front of Hotel Tower, or have your hotel call one for you. Legit cabs have license plates that begin with an H.

COASTAL PLAIN

The coastal plain, an area heading east from Georgetown to the Suriname border, can be (painstakingly) traversed via the Eastern Hwy. The road travels through town after unremarkable town, passing potholes, suicidal dogs (oblivious to cars), unfenced livestock and the resultant roadkill. **Rosignol**, about a two-hour drive from Georgetown, is where the road ends; a ferry then travels over the Berbice River to **New Amsterdam** and the continuing road to the border.

Corriverton

Together known as Corriverton (population 12,500), the towns of Springlands and Skeldon, on the west bank of the Corentyne River about 195km from Georgetown, are at the south eastern end of the coastal road from Georgetown. The town's Main St is a long strip with mosques, churches, a Hindu temple, cheap hotels, eateries and bars. Brahman (zebu) cattle roam round the market like the sacred cows of India. At the north end of town, the Skeldon Estate of Guysuco is the biggest local employer.

SLEEPING & EATING

Everything of note is on Main St.

Hotel Par Park (r with bath US$10-12) is a clean, cheap and secure spot. Check the room before you part with your cash.

Mahogany Hotel (☎ 339-2289; r US$13-33) Further south, this nice old place has some rooms offering good river views. Its **restaurant** serves some tasty food, which you can enjoy at a table on the veranda overlooking Main St.

Station View is a good place for lunch. There are a couple of 'snackettes' and Chinese restaurants, but avoid the one next to Hotel Par Park.

GETTING THERE & AWAY

From Springlands, a ferry (US$8, Surinamese guilders and US dollars only, 30 minutes), crosses the Corentyne River to the Surinamese border town of Nieuw Nickerie at noon Monday to Sat except holidays. The ferry can carry cars, and the roads are decent enough to drive the rest of the way to Paramaribo. The crossing takes about 30 minutes, but everything before and after that can be a hassle. The booking office near the *stelling* opens at around 8am, but people begin queuing as early as 7am. There's a US$2 booking fee (payable in Guyanese dollars only, which changes according

to the exchange rate) and the paperwork is a headache. Around 10am you queue for Guyanese emigration formalities; after giving you an exit stamp, staff members hold your passport until you board the boat.

Smuggling and backtracking are rampant here; frequent small boats cross the river in about 15 minutes. Travelers may be tempted to take one to save the hassle of the ferry, but this is highly inadvisable. These boats are prone to robbery and, at best, you'll wind up in Suriname without the proper stamps in your passport.

Moneychangers on the *stelling* sell Surinamese guilders and buy excess Guyanese currency at fair rates. Although it is reasonably safe to change money with them, you should still be careful. You'll need enough guilders to pay for the ferry and for your first night in Suriname.

NORTHWEST COAST

The west bank of the Essequibo River can be reached by boat from **Parika** to **Supernam**. A coastal road takes you as far as the charming town of **Charity**, about 50km away. From there, you need a boat to get any further. There are several jungle lodges in the western part of the country, mainly reachable by air. Boats also travel from Parika southward to the mining town of **Bartica**. Near Bartica, the Essequibo meets the Mazaruni River and **Marshall Falls**, a series of rapids and a jungle waterfall that can be hiked from shore. Tour operators offer day trips from Georgetown (see Tours p755). **Shanklands** and **Timberhead** are among the beachside resorts (about US$60 per night) stationed along the Mazaruni.

Shell Beach extends for about 140km along the coast near the Venezuela border and is a nesting site for four of the eight sea turtle species, including olive ridleys, hawksbills and the magnificent giant leatherbacks. These turtles used to be slaughtered for their meat and eggs but are now part of a nongovernment conservation program. The area is in pretty much the same shape as when the early explorers first arrived. See p755 for tour information.

THE INTERIOR
Kaieteur National Park & Orinduik Falls

Guyana's best-known attraction, majestic **Kaieteur Falls**, is the most impressive of a series of three falls on the upper Potaro River. In its own way, Kaieteur – which is home to stunning creatures like the silver fox and the Kaieteur swift – is nearly as impressive than the better-known Iguazú Falls of Argentina and Brazil. In fact, Kaieteur's waters drop precipitously 250m from a sandstone tableland, making the falls much higher than Iguazú and allegedly the world's highest single-drop falls. Depending on the season, the falls are from 76m to 122m wide. Swifts nest under the falls' overhang and dart in and out of the waters.

Camping is possible, but there are no formal facilities. The hike to the foot of the falls is spectacular, with some climbing involved. Many people just go for the day, by air, from Georgetown, and can often arrange to see both falls in the same day. Orinduik is a 15-minute flight south of Kaieteur and drops 80 feet.

Several operators offer day trips in small planes (about US$210); make early inquiries and be flexible, since the flights go only when a full load of five to eight passengers can be arranged (usually on weekends).

It's possible to reach the falls overland, but expect a challenging trip that takes five to seven days. Call Rainforest Tours or Horizons Travel Service.

For more details, see Tours p755.

Iwokrama Rain Forest

Iwokrama, established in 1996, is a rainforest conservation and development center. Created with a mandate to promote sustainable use of tropical rain forests everywhere, it comprises 360,000 hectares of virgin rain forest in the heart of Guyana, along the road that travels south from Georgetown to Lethem. The Smithsonian Institution is just one of the international organizations that's involved in surveying and cataloging the forest's flora and fauna, an estimated 30% of which is still unidentified.

The cheapest and most ecofriendly way to visit Iwokrama is through the center itself. Its Georgetown office (☎ 225-1504; www.iwokrama.org; 67 Bel Air) arranges flights and accommodations for longer tours, or you can show up at its field station for a shorter visit. A two-day tour (about US$225 per person, depending on group size) includes stops in Amerindian villages and a hike through the forest.

Lethem

In the Rupununi Savanna along the Brazil border, Lethem (population 7600) itself has little of interest, but it serves as the stepping-off point to the incredible Kanuku Mountains nearby. 'Kanuku' means 'rich forest' in the Macushi language, a reflection of the fact that these mountains harbor an extraordinary diversity of wildlife – 70% of all bird species found in Guyana reside in the Kanukus.

The ranches near Lethem are home to Guyana's *vaqueros* (cowboys), and there's an annual Easter rodeo.

The Guyanese are suspicious about drug smuggling in this area, so definitely go through proper bureaucratic channels when crossing the border. Keep in mind that you need permission to visit Amerindian communities; inquiries can be made at the **Ministry of Amerindian Affairs in the Office of the President** (☎ 226-5167; New Garden & Vlissengen Rd, Georgetown). If traveling with an organized tour, this should be taken care of for you.

Don & Shirley's shop at the airstrip is the best place to get information about the local attractions, guides and other points of interest in the area.

SLEEPING & EATING

Takatu Guest House (☎ 772-2084; r US$20; meals US$5-8) has just-OK rooms and serves three meals a day.

The **Savanna Inn** (☎ 772-2035; s US$40, meals US$3.50-5) About 100m north of Takatu, Savanna Inn offers more comfortable accommodations and also has meals and airport transport.

Karanambu Ranch (houses tourists/researchers/students with meals & some activities US$120/75/50) It feels more like East Africa than tropical America at Karanambu, 95km from Lethem (about US$200 round-trip flight). Owned and run by the extraordinary Diane McTurk, Karanambu is a nature lover's paradise and is one of the best places to see two spectacular endangered species: the giant river otter and the black caiman. The ranch also offers great fishing (US$15 to US$60) and bird-watching. The houses are modeled after traditional Amerindian dwellings.

If Karanambu is full, try less-expensive **Dadanawa Ranch** (per person with meals US$107), south of town; the country's largest working cattle ranch, the **Pirara Ranch** (US$50), north of town; or **The Rock View Lodge** (☎ 226-5412; r & meals per person US$95, camp without meals per person US$10), near the Macushi village of Annai at the foothills of the scenic Pakaraima mountains. It's possible to negotiate better long-stay rates. For more information on any of the ranches, contact Shell Beach Adventures (see Tours p755).

GETTING THERE & AWAY

Two local airlines, Roraima and TGA (see p757), make trips from Georgetown to Lethem or Annai (both from US$100 one way). Flights tend to leave early in the morning, and it can be hard to get on one at a moment's notice, so plan ahead. Conveniently, the airlines schedule flights to connect with service to and from Boa Vista, Brazil, a two-hour drive from Lethem. If you're coming overland, try booking a ticket by phone from Brazil, through **Weiting & Richter Travel Agency** (in Brazil ☎ 226-5121) in Georgetown and paying with a credit card.

In the dry season, overland truck transport is feasible between Lethem and Georgetown (via Kurupukari and Linden); see Bus p757 for details.

To reach and enter Guyana from Brazil, take an early bus from Boa Vista (see p380) to Bonfim, get off at the last stop (after the bus station) and walk about 2½ km to the Brazilian customs police post. After obtaining an exit stamp in your passport, hire a small boat (about US$3) to cross the Takatu River to Guyana. Officially the border crossing closes at 6pm. Go immediately to the police station in Lethem (about 1½ km from the crossing point) to have your passport stamped. There's also an immigration office at the airport, which is usually open only in the morning.

Going to Brazil is the same in reverse; do it early to ensure you are in time for a bus to Boa Vista. Make sure your papers are in order, as illegal immigration and smuggling are rife here, and checks can be thorough. Note also that US nationals need a visa – and all need yellow-fever vaccinations – to enter Brazil.

GUYANA DIRECTORY
Accommodations

In Georgetown, modest hotels that are clean, secure and comfortable charge US$15 to US$25. Better accommodations, with air-con,

start at US$40, while the growing number of rain-forest lodges and savanna ranches are more expensive (US$100 and up).

Activities

Guyana has few facilities for recreational activities, but the interior offers possibilities for river rafting and trekking, best arranged through local tour operators.

Books

The classic account of travel in Guyana is Charles Waterton's 1825 *Wanderings in South America*. Though out of print, it is widely available in used bookstores and libraries in the USA and the UK. Guyana-born Jan Shinebourne's *The Last English Plantation* is about the political chaos in Guyana in the 1950s. Evelyn Waugh described a rugged trip from Georgetown across the Rupununi Savanna in *Ninety-Two Days*. Shiva Naipaul wrote a moving account of the Jonestown tragedy in *Journey to Nowhere: A New World Tragedy*, published in the UK as *Black and White*. *Georgetown Journal* by Andrew Salkey is a first-person account of life in Georgetown in 1970 during independence.

Business Hours

Commerce awakens around 8:30am and tends to last until 4pm or so. Saturdays are half-days if shops open at all, and Sundays are quietest; Georgetown becomes an utter ghost town.

Climate

The equatorial climate features high temperatures with little seasonal variation, though coastal breezes moderate the heat. Guyana has two distinct rainy seasons: May to mid-August and mid-November to mid-January. August through October are the hottest months.

The best time to visit Guyana may be at the end of either rainy season, when the discharge of water over Kaieteur Falls is greatest. Some locals recommend mid-October to mid-May, which may be wet but not as hot. If you want to travel overland to the interior, visit during the dry seasons. Note that downpours can occur even in the 'dry' seasons.

Dangers & Annoyances

Guyana (Georgetown in particular) is notorious for street crime and physical violence, especially around elections. Avoid potentially hazardous situations and be aware of others on the street. For details, see Dangers & Annoyances p755.

At Cheddi Jagan International Airport, try to arrive during daylight and use only registered airport taxis. Drivers are easily recognizable, as they all have official IDs attached to their shirt pockets. All baggage should be locked. Backpacks are particularly prone to pilfering hands.

See Dangers & Annoyances in the South America Directory (p1030) for more information.

Embassies & Consulates

EMBASSIES & CONSULATES IN GUYANA

Foreign representatives in Guyana, all of which are in Georgetown, include:

Brazil (Map p754; ☎ 225-7970; 308-309 Church St)
Canada (Map p754; ☎ 227-2081; cnr High & Young Sts)
Colombia (Map p754; ☎ 227-1410; 306 Church St)
France (☎ 227-5435; 46 First Ave)
Suriname (Map p754; ☎ 226-7844; 171 Crown St)
UK (Map p754; ☎ 226-5881; 44 Main St)
USA (Map p754; ☎ 225-4902; 100 Young St)
Venezuela (Map p754; ☎ 226-6749; 296 Thomas St)

GUYANESE EMBASSIES & CONSULATES ABROAD

Guyana's representatives abroad include:
Belgium (☎ 323-675 62 16; 13-17 Rue de Praetere, 1050 Brussels)
Canada (☎ 613-235-7249; 151 Slater St, Suite 309, Ottawa, K1P 5H3); (☎ 416-494-6040; 505 Consumers Rd, Suite 206, Willowdale, M2J 4V8)
UK (☎ 4471-229-7684; 3 Palace Court, Baywater Court, London W2 4LP)
USA (☎ 202-265-6900; 2490 Tracy Place NW, Washington, DC, 20008); (☎ 212-527-3215; 866 United Nations Plaza, 3rd fl, New York, NY, 10017)

Festivals & Events

Republic Day celebrations in February are the most important national cultural events of the year, though Hindu and Muslim religious festivals are also significant. The recently established **Amerindian Heritage Month** (September) features a series of cultural events, such as handicraft exhibits and traditional dances. **Regatta**, an aquatic event attracting innumerable speedboats of different design, takes place every Easter at both Bartica and Canaan. An annual Easter rodeo is held in the Rupununi Savanna at Lethem.

Food & Drink

Guyanese food ranges from the tasty pepperpot (an Amerindian game stew made with cassava) to the challenging souse (jellied cow's head). Chinese food is widespread but not noteworthy; Indian food is as widespread and quite noteworthy. Two ubiquitous dishes in local restaurants are 'cook-up' (rice and beans – boring) and 'roti' (chicken curry in Indian flatbread – delicious). Overall, Guyanese like spice, so if you don't, say so.

Local rum is available everywhere; D'Aguiar's 5-Year-Old and El Dorado 5 Star are two of the best local brands. Banks beer, brewed at Thirst Park in South Georgetown, comes in both regular and premium versions. Also try fruit punch (or, effectively, rum punch) at any of Georgetown's better restaurants.

Health

Adequate medical care is available in Georgetown, at least at private hospitals, but facilities are few elsewhere. Chloroquine-resistant malaria is endemic, and dengue fever is also a danger, particularly in the interior and even in Georgetown – protect yourself against mosquitoes and take a malaria prophylaxis. Typhoid, hepatitis A, diphtheria/tetanus and polio inoculations are recommended. Guyana is regarded as a yellow-fever infected area, and your next destination may require a vaccination certificate, as does Guyana if you arrive from another infected area. Tap water is suspect, especially in Georgetown. Cholera outbreaks have occurred in areas with unsanitary conditions, but precautions are recommended everywhere.

See the Health chapter (p1053) for more information.

Holidays

New Year's Day (January 1)
Youman Nabi (early January)
Republic Day (February 23) Slave rebellion of 1763.
Phagwah (Hindu New Year; March/April – dates vary)
Good Friday/Easter Monday (March/April – dates vary)
Labor Day (May 1)
CARICOM Day (July – 1st Monday)
Emancipation Day (August 1)
Diwali (November – dates vary)
Christmas Day (December 25)
Boxing Day (December 26)

Internet Access

Georgetown is your best bet for Internet cafés (about US$2 per hour); some nicer hotels also offer web access.

Internet Resources

Land of Six Peoples (www.landofsixpeoples.com) Smorgasbord of information, from news to weather to history.
Guyana Online Tourist Guide (www.turq.com /guyana) Comprehensive tourism site.
Guyana Outpost (guyana.gwebworks.com/websites .shtml) Collection of links to other sites about Guyana.
Guyana News and Information (www.guyana.org) Wealth of data with heavy emphasis on current affairs.
Sustainable Development Networking Programme (SDNP; www.sdnp.org.gy/guylink.html) Guyana links, links and more links.

Maps

Country and Georgetown maps can sometimes be found in the gift shops of the higher-end hotels or Kojac Marketing Agency (see Orientation p753). Otherwise, for detailed maps of the country, visit Georgetown's **Lands & Surveys Dept, Ministry of Agriculture** (☎ 226-4051; 22 Upper Hadfield St, Durban Backlands). Have a taxi take you, because it's difficult to find.

Media

Georgetown has two daily newspapers, *Stabroek News* (www.stabroeknews.com) and the **Guyana Chronicle** (guyanachronicle.com), plus the weekly *Kaieteur News* and influential *Catholic Standard*. The *Guyana Review* is a monthly news magazine published in Georgetown. The 'Voice of Guyana' radio program can be found on 102 FM or 560 AM.

Money

The Guyanese dollar (G$) is more or less stable, but it's declining in line with domestic inflation. Guyanese dollars add up to large amounts – a Coke is G$100, for example – so don't faint when you see meals costing thousands of dollars on local menus.

CREDIT CARDS

Credit cards are accepted at many of Georgetown's better hotels and restaurants, though not at gas stations or many stores.

EXCHANGE RATES

Exchange rates at press time included the following:

Country	Unit		G$ (Guyanese dollar)
Australia	A$1	=	126
Canada	C$1	=	134
euro zone	€1	=	204
Japan	¥100	=	162
New Zealand	NZ$1	=	110
United Kingdom	UK£1	=	299
United States	US$1	=	179

EXCHANGING MONEY

Cash and traveler's checks can be exchanged in **banks** (☒ 8am-noon Mon-Fri & 3-5pm Fri) and **cambios** (exchange houses; ☒ 9am-3:30pm Mon-Thu, 9am-2:30pm Fri), which offer better rates and less red tape than banks. Sometimes you can change cash unofficially at hotels for 10% or 15% less; there is no real black market. Rates are almost the same for traveler's checks and cash. ATMs are hard to come by.

Post

Postal services are generally unreliable; use registered mail for essential correspondence. For important shipments, try these international shippers, all in Georgetown: **UPS** (☎ 227-1853; 210 Camp St), **DHL** (☎ 225-7772; 50 E 5th St, Alberttown) and **FedEx** (☎ 227-6976; 125 D Barrack St, Kingston).

Shopping

Nibbee fiber, extracted from forest vines, is the most distinctive and appealing local product and is used to make everything from hats to furniture. The Macushi of the southwest have developed a unique art form based on carving forest scenes and creatures from the hardened latex of the *balata* tree. Pieces created by master craftsman George Tancredo are particularly prized. Georgetown is the best place to shop.

Telephone

US-based Atlantic Tele-Network Inc operates GT&T, a joint venture with the government which has made major improvements in the telephone service. At blue public telephones scattered around towns, you can make direct and reverse-charge (collect) calls abroad. Credit-card calls have been suspended because of frequent fraud, but you can purchase prepaid phone cards in Georgetown. For a USA direct line, dial ☎ 165 (AT&T) or 151 (Sprint); for Canada, dial ☎ 161; and for the UK, dial ☎ 169. For the international operator, dial ☎ 002, and for directory assistance in Georgetown, dial ☎ 92 (092 for numbers outside Georgetown). Yellow public telephones are for local calls, which are free. Hotels and restaurants generally allow free use of their phones for local calls.

Tourist Information

The government has no official tourism representative abroad. THAG (see Tourist Offices p755) is more active in promoting the country. Guyanese embassies and consulates abroad provide relatively up-to-date information.

Tours

As in the other Guianas, limited infrastructure plus tour operators equals unforgettable trips into the amazing interior. Many Guyanese companies promote 'adventure tourism' in rain-forest and riverside lodges. These tours can be costly, as can domestic airfares, which are often not included, but food and lodging are always covered. Most operators require a minimum number of people (usually five) to be booked for a tour before they'll commit to the date. Friday and Saturday are your best bet for a trip into the interior or to a resort. For details on tour operators, see p755.

Visas

All visitors must carry a passport, but travelers from the USA, Canada, EU countries, Australia, New Zealand, Japan and the UK do not need a visa; confirm with the nearest embassy or consulate. A 30-day stay is granted on arrival in Guyana with an onward ticket. If you do need a visa, file your application at least six weeks before you leave your home country.

As well as a passport, carry an international yellow-fever vaccination certificate with you, and keep other immunizations up to date.

Women Travelers

Guyana's not-so-safe reputation should put women travelers on particular alert. Don't go out alone. On the street, verbal attention from men isn't as bad as in neighboring Suriname, but it can be irksome.

Paraguay

HIGHLIGHTS

- **Trans-Chaco Road to Bolivia** – lookin' to watch the road eat a bus? Test your luck on the continent's most bumpy dust-ways (see p768)
- **Trinidad** – explore the picturesque remnants of the Jesuits at one of the world's least-visited Unesco sites (see p780)
- **Parque Nacional Ybycuí** – wend your way through blue-butterfly-filled subtropical rain forest to dreamlike waterfalls (see p781)
- **Parque Nacional Defensores del Chaco** – watch a jaguar race through the scrub, sleep under billions of stars, experience the absence of humanity (see p787)
- **Off the beaten track** – well-organized, gorgeous, historically significant and not hard to reach, Parque Nacional Cerro Corá is still way off the travel radar (see p785)
- **Best journey** – up the Río Paraguay – this ain't your mama's river cruise. Sleep next to dinner, watch wildlife from your hammock and become one with lazy river (see 'Up the lazy Río Paraguay' p784)

FAST FACTS

- **Area:** 406,752 sq km (bigger than Germany, about the size of California)
- **Budget:** US$15–25 a day
- **Capital:** Asunción
- **Costs:** *residencial* in Asunción US$5–8, bus rides per hour US$1, *chipa* (p788) US$0.15
- **Country code:** ☎ 595
- **Electricity:** 220V, 50Hz; two rounded prongs
- **Famous for:** contraband, corruption, the Chaco
- **Languages:** Spanish (official), Guaraní, Plattdeutsch, Hochdeutsch, Lengua, Nivaclé, Aché
- **Money:** US$1 = 6373 guaraní
- **Phrases:** *porã* (cool), *vai* (disgusting), *arete* (party)
- **Population:** 5.8 million
- **Time:** GMT minus 4 hours
- **Tipping:** 10% in restaurants only
- **Traveler's checks:** cashed at *casas de cambio* (3–5% commission)
- **Visas:** most non-EU citizens, including Americans, Australians, Canadians and New Zealanders need a visa (US$50)

TRAVEL HINTS

The cheapest lodgings with the best Guaraní lessons are in homes with *'se aquila pieza'* (room for rent) signs. Hitching is the cheapest and often fastest way to get around.

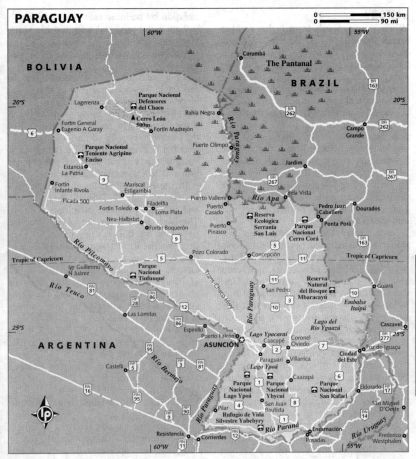

PARAGUAY

| 0 | | 150 km |
| 0 | | 90 mi |

BOLIVIA

Corumbá

The Pantanal

BRAZIL

Lagerenza

Parque Nacional
Defensores
del Chaco

Bahía Negra

Fortín General
Eugenio A Garay

Cerro León
500m   Fortín Madrejón

Parque Nacional
Teniente Agripino
Enciso

Fuerte Olimpo

Campo
Grande

Estancia
La Patria

Jardim

Fortín
Infante Rivola

Mariscal
Estigarribia

Picada 500

Filadelfia
Fortín Toledo   Loma Plata

Puerto Vallemí

Río Apa   Bela Vista

Pedro Juan
Caballero   Dourados

Neu-Halbstat

Puerto
Casado

Reserva
Ecológica
Serranía
San Luis

Ponta Porã

Fortín Boquerón

Puerto
Pinasco

Parque
Nacional
Cerro Corá

Pozo Colorado

Concepción

Tropic of Capricorn

Tropic of Capricorn

Igr Guillermo
N Juárez

Parque
Nacional
Tinfunqué

Río Teuco

Río Pilcomayo

San Pedro

Reserva
Natural
del Bosque
Mbaracayú

Guairá

Embalse
Itaipú

Las Lomitas

Espinillo

Lago del
Río Yguazú

Cascavel

ARGENTINA

Río Bermejo

Puerto Falcón

ASUNCIÓN

Lago Ypacaraí
Caacupé
Coronel
Oviedo

Ciudad
del Este

Foz do Iguaçu

Castelli

Paraguarí   Villarrica

Río Paraguay

Lago Ypoá

Caazapá

Parque
Nacional
Lago Ypoá

Parque
Nacional
Ybycuí

Parque
Nacional
San Rafael

Eldorado

Pilar

San Juan
Bautista

São Miguel
D'Oeste

Rufugio de Vida
Silvestre Yabebyry

Río Paraná

Encarnación

Río Uruguay

Resistencia

Corrientes

Posadas

Frederico
Westphalen

Travelers are scarce in Paraguay and backpackers are less common than jaguars. Paraguay is a seldom-visited subtropical rain forest decorated with metallic butterflies, exotic bird-filled wetlands and the Gran Chaco, a wild frontier. It's where you can experience river life aboard rickety boats lugging the edible, inedible, breathing and not, up the jungle-lined Río Paraguay and beyond into the pristine Pantanal. Crumbling colonial towns and striking Jesuit ruins tell volumes of history, much of it unchanged by time. The residual effects of dictators, corruption and contraband contribute to an overall sense that much of Paraguayan life happens behind closed doors. That said, Paraguay's real highlights are its people, who are unaccustomed to travelers but are always curious, helpful and kind.

HISTORY

When 350 Spaniards from Pedro de Mendoza's expedition fled Buenos Aires and founded Asunción in 1537, Guaraní cultivators dominated what is now southeastern Paraguay. Eager to strengthen themselves against the Chaco's hostile hunter-gatherers, the Guaraní absorbed the conquistadors by providing them with food and an abundance of Guaraní women. This mixing resulted in a *mestizo* culture of Guaraní food, customs and language and Spanish politics.

Asunción was the most significant Spanish settlement east of the Andes for nearly 50 years before Buenos Aires was fully established. During the colonial period Paraguay covered much of northern Argentina and western Brazil.

In the early 17th century, Jesuit missionaries created *reducciones* (settlements) where Guaraní were introduced to European high culture, new crafts, new crops and new methods of cultivation. Until their expulsion in 1767 (because of local jealousies and Madrid's concern that their power had become too great), the Jesuits were remarkably successful. They deterred Portuguese intervention in the region and are credited with protecting the Guaraní from bands of ruthless slavers from the Portuguese colony of São Paulo. The Jesuits were less successful among the Guaycurú, the indigenous groups of the Chaco.

Within a few years of Paraguay's uncontested independence from Spain in 1811, José Gaspar Rodríguez de Francia emerged as the strongest member of a governing junta. Until his death in 1840, the xenophobic and sinister 'El Supremo' sealed the country's borders to promote national self-sufficiency, expropriated the properties of landholders, merchants and even the Church, thus establishing the state as the dominant political and economic power.

Like most of his successors, Francia ruled by fear. His secret police force jailed and tortured his opponents, many of which met their end in Francia's most notorious dungeon, the 'Chamber of Truth.' After escaping an assassination attempt in 1820, El Supremo had his food and drink checked for poison, allowed no one to get closer than six paces and slept in a different bed every night.

By the early 1860s, Francia's successor, Carlos Antonio López, ended Paraguay's isolation by building railroads, a telegraph system, a shipyard and a formidable army. His megalomaniac son, Francisco Solano López, succeeded him and declared war simultaneously on Argentina, Brazil and Uruguay in 1865. This disastrous War of the Triple Alliance proved to be one of the bloodiest and most savage in Latin American history. Allied forces outnumbered Paraguayans 10 to one, and by the end of the campaign boys as young as 12 years old were fighting on the front lines. In five years, Paraguay had lost half of its pre-war population and 26% of its national territory.

In the early 1900s, tensions arose with Bolivia over the ill-defined Chaco border and in 1932 full-scale hostilities erupted. The exact reasons for the Chaco War are uncertain, but Bolivia's new desire for a sea port (via the Río Paraguay) and rumors of petroleum deposits in the area were likely factors. The tenacity and guerrilla tactics of Paraguayan troops overcame Bolivia's numerically stronger forces and the Paraguayans made it as far as the lower slopes of the Andes. A 1935 cease-fire left no clear victor but more than 80,000 dead. A treaty awarded Paraguay three-quarters of the disputed territory.

After the Chaco War, Paraguay endured a decade of disorder before a brief civil war brought the Colorado party to power in 1949. A 1954 coup installed General Alfredo Stroessner, whose brutal 35-year, military-dominated rule was characterized by repression and terror. Political opponents, real or imagined, were persecuted, tortured and 'disappeared,' elections were fraudulent, corruption became institutionalized and the country became a safe haven for Nazis and other international criminals. By the time Stroessner was overthrown, 75% of Paraguayans had known no other leader.

Even today the Colorado (Red) party maintains political control despite having provided nothing but scummy leaders who've benefited from economic corruption, been thrown in jail and sought asylum in Brazil. In 2001, ex-Central Bank official Luis Ángel González Macchi, who was caught embezzling millions of dollars, was appointed caretaker president.

In April 2003, Nicanor Duarte, another Red party member, won the presidential election with 37%, lower than any other past party member. The ex-journalist claims he'll 'break the stronghold of the elite' while dogmatically claiming that he is 'the one who directs.' With the country's economy beyond the toilet (the government barely makes payroll, is able to collect less than 25% of due taxes and has been denied International Monetary Fund support), no one is exactly jealous of the challenges he faces.

THE CULTURE
The National Psyche

Paraguayans proudly speak at least two languages, boast about their beef and *fútbol* (soccer) teams, and accept that they live in the most bribe-hungry country outside of Africa. Paraguay is saturated with corruption; its people (and politicians) know it, live with it and, often, die by it. The politicians lead by example by rollin' in stolen BMWs while their cronies are busy pumping US$1 billion worth of bootlegged cigarettes into Brazil's economy. It's no wonder Paraguayans prefer to focus on the strength of their soccer teams and the quality of their beef when it comes to comparing themselves to their neighbors, especially Argentina.

Don't let the headlines fool you. Paraguayans are famously laid-back. Sipping *tereré* (super-sweet iced *maté*) in the 40°C shade while shooting the breeze, interrupted only by a passing horse-drawn cart, takes the better part of a day. Paraguayans are rightly renowned for their warmth and hospitality, as you will discover when you accept their inevitable invitation to join them. The slightest suggested interest in learning Guaraní will induce spontaneous blurtings of all sorts of indecipherable (to English speakers) sounds.

Lifestyle

Paraguay is the third-poorest South American country (after Bolivia) with 37% living below the poverty line and some 800,000 unemployed. However, it's not uncommon to see souped-up Mercedes Benz' whizzing around town. Aside from the shacks inhabited by subsistence farmers, and the ultra-well-to-do, most Paraguayan homes are somewhere between semi-modern two-story affairs and crumbling colonial mansions.

The disparity between the lifestyle of Guaraní cotton-pickers and prosperous Mennonite landowners is enormous. Living side by side, many Mennonites enjoy German-made appliances and new trucks, while their counterparts live from hand to mouth, sleeping in semi-permanent shacks.

The Paraguayan siesta is the most infectious slice of Paraguayan life. Even the disciplined Mennonites have adopted the afternoon break, albeit limited by loud horns reminding workers to get back on the job. In some communities, the siesta may extend from noon to sunset, making the early morning and dusk the busiest times of day.

People

Some 95% of Paraguayans are considered *mestizos* – most speak Guaraní as their first preference and Spanish as their second choice. The remaining 5% are descendants of European immigrants, including Mennonite farmers and indigenous tribes mostly living in the Chaco. Small but notable Asian, Arab and Brazilian communities are found in the southern and eastern regions, respectively.

More than 95% of the population lives in eastern Paraguay, only half in urban areas. The government reports a literacy rate of 92.1%, an infant mortality rate of 2.8% and an average life expectancy of 74 years. Some 38.7% of the population is under 14 years old.

RELIGION

Ninety percent of the population claims to be Roman Catholic, but folk variants are common. Most indigenous peoples have retained their religious beliefs, or modified them only slightly, despite nominal allegiance to Catholicism or evangelical Protestantism.

ARTS

Paraguay's major literary figures are poet-novelist Augusto Roa Bastos –winner of the 1990 Cervantes Prize, and poet-critic Josefina Plá. Despite many years in exile, Bastos has focused on Paraguayan themes and history drawing from personal experience. For example, *Son of Man*, is a novel tying together several episodes in Paraguayan history, including the Francia dictatorship and the Chaco War.

Roland Joffe's 1986 epic film the *Mission* is a must-see even if you're not a Jesuit buff.

PARAGUAY

Theater is popular in Asunción, with occasional offerings in Guaraní as well as Spanish. Numerous art galleries emphasize modern, sometimes very unconventional artworks.

Paraguayan music is entirely European in origin. The most popular instruments are the guitar and the harp, while traditional dances include the lively *polkas galopadas* and the *danza de la botella*, with dancers balancing bottles on their heads.

SPORT

Paraguayans are soccer-mad. It's not uncommon to see large groups of men crowded around the *pancho* (hot dog) stand watching the Copa Libertadores on a communal TV. The most popular teams, Olimpia and Cerro Porteño, often beat the best Argentine sides. Tennis, basketball, volleyball, hunting and fishing are also popular.

ENVIRONMENT

Land

The country is divided into two distinct regions; east and west of the Río Paraguay. The east is a well-watered plateau of savanna grasslands, with patches of subtropical forest that extends to the Río Paraná (borders with Brazil and Argentina). The west is the Gran Chaco; a marshy bird habitat near Río Paraguay and a dusty, thorny forest further northwest toward Bolivia.

Wildlife

Wildlife is diverse, but the dense rural population is pressuring southeastern Paraguay's fauna. Mammals in danger of extinction include the giant anteater, giant armadillo, maned wolf, river otter, Brazilian tapir, jaguar, pampas deer and marsh deer. One modest but notable wildlife success has been the rediscovery in the mid-1970s of the Chacoan peccary, which was thought to be extinct for at least half a century, and its nurture by conservationists.

Bird life is abundant, especially in the Chaco. Paraguay has 365 bird species, including 21 species of parrots and parakeets, jabiru and wood storks, plumed ibis and waterfowl, among many others. Many reptiles, including caiman and anaconda, inhabit the riverine lowlands.

National Parks

Paraguay has 12 official national parks and several other reserves protecting a variety of habitats. The three covered in this edition are Cerro Corá (p785), Defensores del Chaco (p787) and Ybycuí (p781). Because of corruption, economic pressure and traditionally weak political will, park development is constantly disrupted. With every new politician a totally new team and name for the national park management arrives. Thus, the parks depend heavily on outside funding and guidance from nonprofit organizations like the Nature Conservancy.

Secretariat of the Environment (SEAM), the Dirección General de Protección & Conservación de la Biodiversidad and Senatur (Secretaria Nacional de Turismo) are now working together to promote ecotourism in Paraguay.

TRANSPORT

GETTING THERE & AWAY

Air

Paraguay's only international airport is in Asunción (see p776). Travelers spending more than 24 hours in the country must pay a US$18 departure tax (cash only).

Direct international flights from Asunción are limited to neighboring countries: Buenos Aires, Argentina; La Paz, Bolivia; Santa Cruz, Bolivia; São Paulo, Brazil; Rio de Janeiro, Brazil; Iquique and Santiago, Chile.

Boat

Boats cross into Asunción and Encarnación from Argentina, but immigration procedures are more complicated if entering by boat. With patience and stamina, unofficial river travel from Concepción to Isla Margarita on the Brazilian border is possible. See Getting There & Away in Concepción for details (p784).

Bus

Negotiating Paraguayan borders can be schizophrenic; on the bus, off the bus, on the bus... Ask the driver to stop at immigration since locals don't always need to and be sure your papers are in order. Buses enter Argentina via Puerto Falcón for

THE TRANS-CHACO: EATING DUST

Gotta get to Bolivia? The journey up the paved **Ruta Trans-Chaco** and the dirt **Picada 500** to Santa Cruz, Bolivia, takes 30 hours (US$32) in optimal weather, much more in the wet. Get your exit stamp in Asunción or wake up the immigration officer at the Shell station in **Pozo Colorado** before crossing into Bolivia at **Fortín Infante Rivola**. You can get off in **Boyuibe**, Bolivia, if your ass is tired of bouncin'. *Común* buses (very basic buses that make plenty of stops) leave daily. Bring food and water, your dust rag in dry weather and your shovel in the wet.

Clorinda from Asunción, via Puerto Iguazu from Ciudad del Este and via Posadas from Encarnación. Brazilian border crossings are at Foz de Iguaçu and Ponta Porã. Note: many bus companies claim to travel further into Brazil than border towns, but actually change buses after crossing the border.

GETTING AROUND

Buses dominate transportation with cheap fares and reasonably efficient service. Journeys from the Brazilian or Argentine border to Bolivia (and everywhere in between) take 30 hours or less, depending on the start and end destinations. Boats are used between Asunción and central cities along the Río Paraguay.

Always carry your passport but use your discretion (especially at night) when asked to show it. You will need it to board planes and aboard buses when crossing contraband checkpoints.

Air

Flights save time but cost much more than buses. The private carrier Arpa (Aerolíneas Paraguayas), in the same offices as TAM (Transportes Aéreos Mercosur), flies to Asunción and Ciudad del Este (US$65–91, 50 minutes) three to four times daily (once Sunday). Bolivian carrier LAB shuttles between La Paz, Santa Cruz and Asunción.

Boat

Several cargo boats take passengers up the Río Paraguay. Two have regular departures from Asunción to Concepción (US$8, 30 hours): *Cacique II* (Wednesday at 6am) and the larger *Guaraní* (every other Friday at 10am). More boats head on from Concepción to Puerto Vallemí (US$12, 2½ days): *Guaraní* (every other Monday), *Aquidabán* (late Tuesday morning), *Carmenleticia* (Friday morning), and the *Cacique II* (Saturday morning). You can pay a bit more for a double-occupancy *camarote* (cabin) or hang in your hammock below deck with the other passengers and their unbelievable assortment of cargo – ranging from chickens to motorbikes. Two very basic cheap meals are served on board, but it's best to bring your own drinking water and toilet paper (unless you prefer river water and your hand). You get more bang for your buck beyond Concepción.

Bus

Bus quality varies. No buses go from start to end without picking up someone (or something). *Servicio removido* makes flag stops; *servicio directo* collects passengers only at fixed locations; *común* is a basic bus that stops at fewer locations; *ejecutivo* is a faster, deluxe bus with toilets, tea and coffee service and other facilities. Sometimes paying more means better service, sometimes not. It's best to travel during the day and always ask for a ticket or receipt. Larger towns have central terminals. Elsewhere companies are within easy walking distance of each other. If you want a choice of seats buy your ticket early. If you want the best price, wait until the driver starts his engine and start bargaining.

Asunción has an extensive public transportation system, but late-night buses are infrequent; also see p777.

Hitching

Hitching is relatively safe but solo women should exercise caution. You usually won't have to wait very long for a *lleva* (lift), but beware of the afternoon heat and carry water. Most drivers will not ask for any money.

Taxi

Most taxi fares are metered. Drivers legally levy a 30% *recargo* (surcharge) after 10pm and on Sunday and holidays. They may try to tack on the surcharge at other times; agree on a ballpark fare before getting in.

ASUNCIÓN

As the heart of a sleepy country, Asunción crawls along at an un-citylike pace. Although home to some 1.2 million people, its central streets are stunningly empty during siesta and at weekends. Asunción's treasures are its sprinkling of original colonial and beaux arts buildings, its selection of international cuisine, shady plazas, incredibly helpful and friendly people, and its nearly hidden Río Paraguay backdrop. Asunción's blemishes are its diesel-spewing buses, stark utilitarian architecture, dengue fever–carrying mosquitoes, oppressive heat and streets that become rivers in the frequent tropical rain.

ORIENTATION

Asunción's riverside location and the haphazard growth in the 19th and 20th centuries has created irregularities in Asunción's conventional grid, centered on Plaza de los Héroes. Names of east–west streets change at Independencia Nacional. Nearby Plaza Uruguaya offers shade from the midday heat, but can be unsavory at night. North, along the riverfront, Plaza Constitución contains the Palacio Legislativo. Below the bluff and subject to flooding sprawl *viviendas temporarias*, Asunción's shantytowns.

INFORMATION

Bookshops

Plaza Uruguaya holds two semi-open-air bookstalls with a good selection of postcards and Paraguayana.

Books SRL (Villa Mora shopping center, Av Mariscal López 3971) New and used English-language books and magazines.

Guarani Raity (Las Perlas 3562; www.quanta.net.py /guarani) Books in and about Guaraní.

GETTING INTO TOWN

Asunción's **bus terminal** (☎ 021-551740; Av Fernando de la Mora & República Argentina) is several kilometers southeast of downtown. Bus No 8 (US$0.30) takes the most direct route to the center, but Nos 10, 25, 31 and 38 also end up on Oliva. From the airport, hop on a bus headed for the center via Av Aviadores del Chaco, or grab a cab (US$15).

Cultural Centers

Asunción's international cultural centers offer reading material, film and art exhibitions at little or no cost.

Alianza Francesa (☎ 021-210382; Mariscal Estigarribia 1039)

Centro Cultural de España Juan de Salazar (☎ 021- 449221; Tacuary 745)

Centro Cultural Paraguayo-Americano (☎ 021- 224831; Av España 352)

Instituto Cultural Paraguayo Alemán (☎ 021- 226242; Juan de Salazar 310)

Emergency

Fire Department (☎ 131)

Medical Emergency (☎ 021- 204800)

Police (☎ 130; Mariscal López at Iturbe)

Internet Access

Numerous locutorios offer decent Internet access for around US$1 per hour.

Cyber SPC (Chile 862) Cool, clean, fast and friendly.

Easy.com.py (25 de Mayo) Across from Plaza Uruguaya. Convenient, but a little slow.

Laundry

The following laundries charge around US$1.25 per kg; other laundries often charge per piece.

Burbujas Lavandería (Independencia Nacional 738)

Lavabien (Hernandarias 636) Drop-off and self-service.

Maps

Most maps in Paraguay don't have a scale and are out of date, but Senatur sells a decent *Plano Turistico de Asunción* (US$1).

Medical Services

Hospital Privado Frances (☎ 021-295250; Av Brasilia 1194) Offers better services than the Hospital Central.

Hospital Central (☎ 021-206896; Av Sacramento s/n) In the *barrio* of Santo Domingo.

Money

Northeast of Plaza de los Heroes *casas de cambio* crowd Av Palma and side streets (see the Asunción map). Moneychangers on the 2nd floor of the bus terminal give acceptable rates.

Banco Sudameris (Cerro Corá & Independencia) 24hr ATM.

Citibank (Estrella & Chile) 24hr ATM.

Lloyds Bank (Palma & Juan O'Leary) 24hr ATM.

Inter-Express (☎ 021-490111; Yegros 690) The American Express representative.

Post & Telephone

Main post office (Alberdi at Paraguayo Independiente; 7am-7pm Mon-Fri)

Antelco (14 de Mayo & Oliva; 8am-10pm) Has card phones outside for making collect or credit-card calls that require dialing toll-free numbers. Otherwise, private competitors with better prices for non-card calls are everywhere.

Tourist Offices

Secretaria Nacional de Turismo (Senatur; ☎ 021-441530; www.senatur.gov.py; Palma 468; 7am-7pm Mon-Fri & 8am-noon Sat) Friendly but you may need to give some encouragement to actually get the information you want.

Dirección General de Protección & Conservación de la Biodiversidad (☎ 021-615 812, 021-615 805; Av Madame Lynch 3500; 7am-1pm Mon-Fri) Has the only reliable national park information. The office is reachable via bus 44A from Olivia and takes at least 20 minutes. Rides with rangers to hard-to-reach parks are occasionally available.

DANGERS & ANNOYANCES

Consider insect repellent a new cologne because dengue fever is a problem in Asunción. Muggings have been known to happen even in broad daylight so keep your pockets light. Police call the area between Palma and Río Paraguay the 'Zona Roja,' meaning don't schedule a pre-dawn stroll there.

SIGHTS

Everyone's favorite, **Museo del Barro** (☎ 021-607996; Grabadores del Cabichui s/n; admission US$0.50; 3:30-8pm Wed-Sun), is east of the center in a slick modern neighborhood. It displays everything from modern paintings to pre-Columbian and indigenous crafts to political caricatures of prominent Paraguayans. Take any No 30 bus from Olivia and ask the driver to drop you at Av Molas López; the museum is to the south off of Callejón Cañada in a contemporary building.

The free anthropological and archaeological **Museo Etnográfico Andrés Barbero** (☎ 021-441696; Av España 217; admission free; 7:30-11:30am & 3-5:30pm Mon-Fri) displays indigenous tools, ceramics and weavings, plus superb photographs and maps showing where each item comes from.

The well-organized **Museo Boggiani** (☎ 021-584717; Coronel Bogado 888; admission free; 3-6pm Tue-Fri, 9am-noon & 3-6pm Sat) houses much of the feather art collection of Italian ethnographer Guido Boggiani, who conducted fieldwork with the Chamacoco Indians of the upper Río Paraguay. It's well worth the 45-minute bus ride from downtown at Av Mariscal López at Yegros on Línea 27.

The **Museo de Historia Natural** (inside the Jardín Botánico; admission US$0.40; 8am-4pm Mon-Fri, 8am-1pm Sat) is notable only for its spectacular display of insects – including a butterfly with a 274mm wingspan. From downtown, the most direct bus is No 44-B ('Artigas') from Oliva and 15 de Agosto, which goes right to the gates.

WALKING TOUR

When Francia was in charge, 'every person observed gazing at the front of his palace should be shot in the act,' but today the **Palacio de Gobierno (1)**, on Paraguayo Independiente near Juan O'Leary, is guarded only by semi-alert youths in military attire.

Across the street, the free **Centro Cultural Manzana de la Rivera (2**; ☎ 021-442448; Ayolas & Paraguayo Independiente; 8am-10:30pm) is a complex of eight beautifully restored houses. The oldest is Casa Viola (1750), where the Museo Memoria de la Ciudad houses a history of Asunción's urban development.

Two blocks east, at 14 de Mayo, the **Cámara de Diputados (3)** is where Paraguay's Congress meets. Across the Plaza de Armas is the **Cámara de Senadores (4)**, built in 1857, which was once Carlos Antonio López's residence and now houses the Senate.

At the east end of Plaza Constitución is the 19th-century **Catedral Metropolitana**

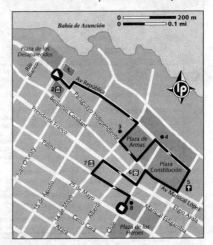

DOWNTOWN ASUNCIÓN

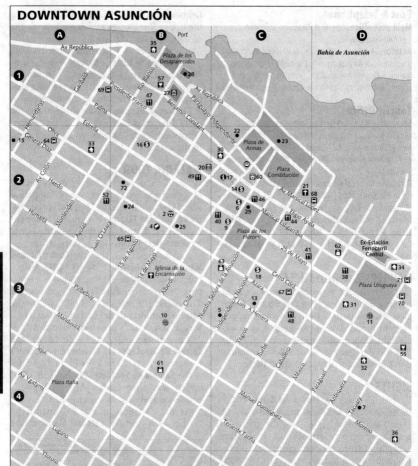

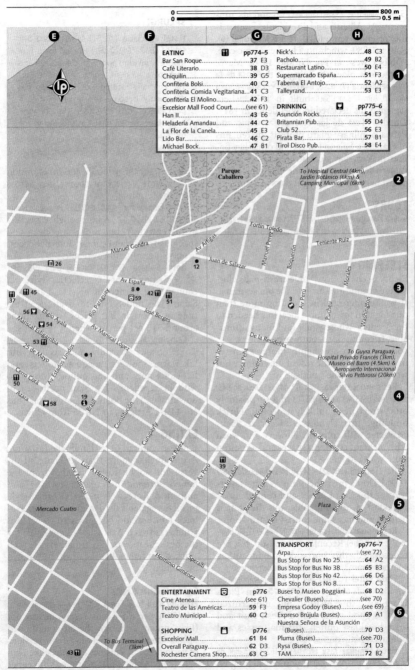

EATING 🍴 pp774–5
Bar San Roque	37 E3
Café Literario	38 D3
Chiquilin	39 G5
Confitería Bolsi	40 C2
Confitería Comida Vegitariana	41 C3
Confitería El Molino	42 F3
Excelsior Mall Food Court	(see 61)
Han II	43 E6
Heladería Amandau	44 C2
La Flor de la Canela	45 E3
Lido Bar	46 C2
Michael Bock	47 B1
Nick's	48 C3
Pacholo	49 B2
Restaurant Latino	50 E4
Supermacado España	51 F3
Taberna El Antojo	52 A2
Talleyrand	53 E3

DRINKING 🍸 pp775–6
Asunción Rocks	54 E3
Britannian Pub	55 D4
Club 52	56 E3
Pirata Bar	57 B1
Tirol Disco Pub	58 E4

Parque Caballero

To Hospital Central (4km),
Jardín Botánico (6km) &
Camping Municipal (6km)

Fortín Toledo

Av Artigas
Manuel Gondra
Manuel Pérez
Boquerón
Teniente Ruiz
Juan de Salazar
12
Morales
Av España
8
42 59
51
Río Paraguay
José Berges
Av Mariscal López
Av Perú
Pucheu
Washington
3
De la Residenta
26
37 45
56
Eligio Ayala
Mariscal Estigarribia
53
25 de Mayo
San José
Rosa Peña
Boquerón
To Guyra Paraguay,
Hospital Privado Francés (3km),
Museo del Barro (4.5km) &
Aeropuerto Internacional
Silvio Pettirossi (20km)
1
Cerro Corá
50
Azara
58
19
Brasil
Av Estados Unidos
Constitución
Curupayty
Pa'i Pérez
Escobar
Ríos
José Berges
Río de Janeiro
Découd
Melgarejo
Av Luis A Herrera
Av Pettirossi
Luis Irrazábal
Av Perú
República Francesa
Fulgencio R Moreno
Fulgencio R Moreno
Aquino
Bulnes
Bróquez
22 de Septiembre
Plaza
5
Mercado Cuatro
39
Herminio Giménez
Speratti

ENTERTAINMENT 🎭 p776
Cine Atenea	(see 61)
Teatro de las Américas	59 F3
Teatro Municipal	60 C2

SHOPPING 🛍 p776
Excelsior Mall	61 B4
Overall Paraguay	62 D3
Rochester Camera Shop	63 C3

TRANSPORT pp776–7
Arpa	(see 72)
Bus Stop for Bus No 25	64 A2
Bus Stop for Bus No 38	65 B3
Bus Stop for Bus No 42	66 D6
Bus Stop for Bus No 8	67 C3
Buses to Museo Boggiani	68 D2
Chevalier (Buses)	(see 70)
Empresa Godoy (Buses)	(see 69)
Expreso Brújula (Buses)	69 A1
Nuestra Señora de la Asunción (Buses)	70 D3
Pluma (Buses)	(see 70)
Rysa (Buses)	71 D3
TAM	72 B2

To Bus Terminal (3km)
43

PARAGUAY

0 ———— 800 m
0 ———— 0.5 mi

(**5**; admission free; 8-11am Mon-Sat) and its museum. At Alberdi and Presidente Franco is the recently remodeled **Teatro Municipal (6)**, built in 1889, which now houses a chic café. A block west, at Franco and 14 de Mayo, Asunción's oldest building is the **Casa de la Independencia (7**; 021-493918; 7.30am-6:30pm Mon-Fri, 8am-12:30pm Sat), built in 1772, where Paraguayans declared independence in 1811. On the Plaza de los Héroes, at Chile and Palma, a military guard protects the remains of Francisco Solano López, and other key figures of Paraguay's catastrophic wars in the **Panteón de los Héroes (8)** – the changing of the guard happens every eight days at 10am.

TOURS

Guyra Paraguay (021-227777; Comandante Franco 281) Organizes monthly bird-watching trips with English-speaking guides.

SLEEPING

Plenty of cheap, acceptable crash-pads clutter the chaotic area around the bus terminal. If you're interested in spending more than one night in town, hop a local bus headed to the 'Centro' where you'll find many affordable, friendly, clean, but worn, options. Accommodations are slightly more expensive in Asunción than the rest of the country but won't bust anyone's budget.

Residencial Itapúa (021-445121; Moreno 943; per person US$5, with bath US$7) On a surprisingly quiet street, in an unlikely neocolonial brick building, this signless *residencial* packs character with comfort. Flowery and worn with pleasant common spaces and a rooftop suite with city views.

Hotel Miami (021-444950; México 449; s/d US$7/12;) Don't miss the John Wayne tapestries at this clean, quiet and central hotel. Breakfast is unremarkable, but the staff is helpful and has some tourist information.

Residencial Ambassador (021-445901; Río Blanco 110; s/d US$4/6) Recently cleaned-up, but not redecorated, this port-side lodging offers spartan rooms, some with Palace views.

Plaza Hotel (021-444772; www.plazahotel.com.py; Eligio Ayala 609; s/d US$12/19;) On Plaza Uruguaya, this historic but modernized hotel is good value with a fresh fruit and juice breakfast buffet, stiff mattresses and full-sized bathrooms.

Hotel Familiar Yasy (021-551623; Fernando de la Mora 2390; s/d US$5.50/8) If you're catching an

early bus, try this friendly and quiet option with a wide variety of rooms just across from the terminal.

Hotel Embajador (021-493393; Presidente Franco 514; s/d US$7/10;) A little rough, especially in the entryway, but rooms are clean and spacious with high ceilings. Internet access is only intermittently available.

Hotel Sahara (021-494935; Oliva 920;) Known for its eclectic style, pet caiman and garden of objects d'arte, the Sahara was undergoing renovations at the time of research, but prices will likely be around $10 per person when it re-opens.

Camping Municipal (Jardín Botánico; campsites US$1.50) Shady, friendly and secure with lukewarm showers, adequate toilets and ferocious ants and mosquitoes (don't go without repellent). It's 5km northwest of downtown in the Botanical Garden; take bus No 44-B ('Artigas') or No 35 from Olivia.

EATING

For the capital of a landlocked nation, Asunción has more than its share of diverse and sophisticated cuisine: from the famed *surubíal ajo* (garlic catfish) and authentic Korean *kim chi* (Korean-style pickled vegetables) to nighttime under-a-buck *panchos* and burgers. Cruise Estados Unidos between Azara and Eligio Ayala for the best cheap eats. Supermarkets are well stocked but remember the town shuts down on Sunday.

Cafés & Quick Eats

Excelsior Mall Food Court (Chile near Manduvirá; mains US$1.50-3) Open when most restaurants are not (like Sunday evening), the air-conditioned upstairs food court offers fast-food versions of various ethnic cuisines at outlets like Don Vito (*empanadas* – patties stuffed with either chicken, cheese and ham, or beef), Sabor Brasil and Apolo (Chinese); there's also an Austria Pub with good homebrews.

Café Literario (Mariscal Estigarribia & México; ⊗ 4-10pm) Artsy, comfy café-con-bookstore makes a good afternoon spot to read or write.

Confitería El Molino (Av España 382; snacks US$1-2) Serves minutas (short orders), salads, soups, sandwiches, pizza and excellent banana licuados (blended fruit drinks).

Michael Bock (Presidente Franco 820; snacks US$0.50-2) This excellent German bakery features goods from surrounding Mennonite communities.

Confitería Comida Vegitariana (25 de Mayo 241; almuerzo US$2.25) Get here before 2pm for the Chinese-style veg lunches and sandwiches.

Pacholo (Palma 547; pizza US$1-3) Beer, hot dogs, burgers and delicious pizza. There's also another branch at Brasilia 1493.

Heladería Amandau (Eligio Ayala & Independencia Nacional) C'mon it's hot, have some ice cream.

Supermercado España (Brasil 469) Stocked with everything from colored flip-flops to bulk peanuts to chocolate bars, this is the best place to load up on the way out of town.

Restaurants

Nick's (Azara 348; almuerzo US$2) Set lunches and dinners aren't the only good deals here. Rotisserie chicken and pay-by-the-kilo vegie salads also come cheap.

Taberna El Antojo (☎ 021-441743; Ayolas 631; lunch US$3.50, dinner US$6) The energetic ambience of proverb-covered walls, dangling shells, bottles and bells are only the backdrop for good-value Spanish set-price meals.

Lido Bar (Chile & Palma; mains US$2-5) A diner-style, local favorite, with sidewalk seating opposite the Pantheon that serves a variety of Paraguayan specialties (excellent sopa paraguaya – cornbread with cheese and onion) in generous portions for breakfast and lunch.

Han II (Av Perú 1090; mains US$2.50-5) The sign and the menu bear only Korean characters, but behind the smoked glass Paulina will help you order kim chi and bulgogi (delicious marinated meat grilled at your table; ask for garlic).

Bar San Roque (☎ 021-446015; Tacuary & Eligio Ayala; mains US$3-5) Traditional Paraguayan dishes made with fresh ingredients from the owner's farm, all served in a turn-of-the-20th-century atmosphere.

> **SPLURGE!**
>
> **Talleyrand** (☎ 021-441163; Mariscal Estigarribia 932) Hankerin' for gourmet comida (food)? Treat yourself to a French-influenced meal served by polite white-collared waiters in a cozy colonial atmosphere. A three-course meal of Greek salad, carrot soup and salmon with wine will only set you back about US$20 a head.

Confitería Bolsi (Estrella 399; mains US$1-3) More than a confitería, this place serves everything from sandwiches and short orders to escargots, curried rabbit and garlic pizza. Readers recommend the surubí casa nostra, the pasta and the soothing air-con.

La Flor de Canela (☎ 021-498928; Tacuary 167; mains US$3-9) Excellent Peruvian seafood, with faux Inca sculptures to compliment. If offered, don't refuse the homemade after-dinner liqueurs.

Restaurante Latino (Cerro Corá 948; mains US$3-7) A humble hole-in-the-wall with inexpensive Peruvian fare, including tasty pisco sours (grape brandy with lemon juice, egg white and powdered sugar).

Chiquilín (Av Perú & Mariscal Estigarribia; mains US$3-5) Artesanal pizza and pasta, plus hamburgers and empanadas.

DRINKING

Bars hosting theme nights, whenever they can charge a cover, can be crowded at weekends. Several late-night hotspots line the 900 blocks of Estigarribia, but most of the flashy, all-decked-out clubs are a short cab ride east of downtown on Av Brasilia.

Britannia Pub (Cerro Corá 851; ⊗ Wed-Sun) Casually hip with an air-conditioned international ambience and outdoor patio. You can sip cans of Guinness while throwing darts or challenge a stranger to a game of chess. The 'Brit Pub' is a favorite among foreigners and locals alike.

Asunción Rocks (Mariscal Estigarribia 991; admission $3; ⊗ 10pm-6am) The spot for late-night after-parties (especially with Peace Corp volunteers), but not totally uncool before 1am.

Club 52 (Eligio Ayala 848) This trendy, downtempo, modern sculpture-filled, art nouveau club is the spot for dimly lit drinks. Happy hour is from 5pm to 8pm.

PARAGUAY

Pirata Bar (Benjamín Constant & Ayolas) Popular, pirate-themed club playing American and English beats.

Tirol Disco Pub (Estados Unidos & Cerro Corá) Spicy Latin music in an '80s atmosphere.

Mouse Cantina (Patria & Brasilia) Ultra-popular, fashionable MTV-esque dancehall.

ENTERTAINMENT
Cinemas

Downtown cinemas are notorious for showing cheap porn and low-budget action-adventure flicks on reels that rarely make it through a screening. More reliable, though less endearing, are the cinemas of Asunción's shopping malls, such as the four-screen **Cine Atenea at Excelsior Mall** (Manduvirá & Chile; tickets US$2). Check *Tiempo Libre* for showtimes.

Music & Theater

Asunción has several venues for live music theater; the major season is March to October. Check *Tiempo Libre* (a free weekly) for showtimes.

Centro Cultural Manzana de la Rivera (☎ 021-442448; Ayolas & Paraguayo Independiente)

Teatro de las Américas (☎ 021-224831; José Berges 297)

Teatro Municipal (Alberdi & Presidente Franco) Check the listing outside for showtimes.

SHOPPING

Asunción offers Paraguay's best souvenir shopping – the ground floor of the **Senatur** tourist office has the best of the best from around the country.

Plaza de los Héroes The open-air market at the plaza is stocked with *ao po'i* or *lienzo* (loose-weave cotton) garments and other indigenous crafts.

Overall Paraguaya (☎ 021-448 657; Mariscal Estigarribia 397) The place for *ñandutí* lace and leather goods.

Mercado Cuatro A lively trading lot occupying the wedge formed by the intersection of Dr Francia and Pettirossi, stretching several blocks west toward Brasil. Shops along Palma near Av Colón offer everything from digital cameras to leather bags for your *tereré* thermos at reasonable prices.

Rochester Camera Shop (632 Nuestra Señora de la Asunción) Has an impressive selection of cameras and accessories and offers a one-hour film-processing service.

GETTING THERE & AWAY
Air

Aeropuerto Internacional Silvio Pettirossi (☎ 021-672855) is in the suburb of Luque, 20km east of Asunción. It's easily reached by buses displaying 'Aeropuerto' signs and headed out Av Aviadores del Chaco.

Paraguay's only national airlines, **Arpa** (☎ 021-495265; Oliva 761) and **Transportes Aéreos Mercosur** (TAM; ☎ 021-495265; www.tam.com.py; Oliva 761), share an office.

The only scheduled domestic flights within Paraguay are between Asunción and Ciudad del Este (US$65–91 one way, 50 minutes). TAM Mercosur flies between the two cities four times daily from Monday through Friday, three times on Saturday and once on Sunday. Tickets should be reserved and purchased at least one day before. Occasional flights are available to Concepción (US$40) and Vallemi (US$50).

Direct international flights to and from Asunción and the following cities in neighboring countries are regularly available. Prices are one-way and are subject to change. All flights are with TAM Mercosur.

Buenos Aires, Argentina US$279, 2 daily.
Santa Cruz, Bolivia US$324 1 daily Mon-Sat.
Santiago, Chile US$359, 1 per day Mon, Wed, Fri, Sat & Sun.
São Paolo, Brasil US$325, 1 daily.

Anyone who has spent more than 24 hours in the country must pay a US$18 international departure tax (cash only) before boarding.

Boat

Two cargo boats carry passengers up the Río Paraguay from the port (east of Aduana at the end of Calle Montevideo) to Concepción; *Cacique II* (US$6, 30 hours; departs 6am Wed) and the larger *Guaraní* (US$8, 30 hours; departs 10am every other Friday). It's possible for adventurous travelers to float as far as Brazil (see p784).

Crossing into Argentina via launch from Puerto Itá Enramada, southwest of downtown, to Puerto Pilcomayo (Argentina) is possible. Launches leave every half-hour from 7am to 5pm weekdays, and irregularly from 7am to 10am on Saturday. You must visit immigration before you leave Asunción.

Bus

Some companies such as Rysa and Empresa Godoy maintain convenient offices on Plaza Uruguaya and around town (see the Asunción map for other locations). Otherwise the bus terminal is the place for tickets. Bus No 8 runs downtown along Cerro Corá to the terminal, as do No 25 from Colón and Oliva, No 38 from Haedo, and No 42 from Rodríguez de Francia. See the Asunción map for suggested intersections.

Destination	Duration in Hours	Cost
Paraguay		
Ciudad del Este	5	US$6–8
Concepción	6	US$6–8
Encarnación	5	US$6–8
Filadelfia	7	US$7
Pedro Juan Caballero	7½	US$7–9
Argentina		
Buenos Aires	16–20	US$24–57
Clorinda	1	US$1
Cordoba	18	US$46
Posadas	6	US$11
Bolivia		
Santa Cruz	30+	US$30
Brazil		
Curitiba	14	US$30
Foz do Iguaçu	5	US$7
Rio De Janeiro	24	US$45
São Paulo	20	US$30
Chile		
Santiago	28	US$70
Uruguay		
Montevideo	20	US$40

GETTING AROUND

City buses (US$0.20) go almost everywhere, but few run after 10pm. Nearly all city buses start their route at the western end of Olivia.

Taxis are metered and reasonable, but tack on a surcharge late at night and on Sunday. A taxi to the bus terminal costs about US$3.

AROUND ASUNCIÓN

Hop on a local bus, hope you get a seat and prepare yourself for a taste of rural and historical Paraguay. Humble communities dominated by colonial buildings observe long siestas, disturbed only by occasional ox- or horse-drawn carts clacking up cobbled streets that surround the capital city. The tourist industry plugs the area as the 'Circuito Central,' which includes the weaving center of **Itauguá**, the lakeside resorts of **Areguá** and **San Bernardino**, the shrine of **Caacupé** and colonial villages like **Piribebuy** and **Yaguarón**. You can hire a cab to drive you through the whole circuit (US$40 for up to four people), but you'll get more flavor on the bus (less than US$1). The circuit's highlights are described below in order of the author's preference.

SAN BERNARDINO

Pizza pubs, discos and upmarket hotels and restaurants line the shady cobbled streets of Lago Ypacaraí's eastern shore. Known as 'San Ber' by locals, this pleasant resort town is the perfect spot to soak your heated bones in the lake, dance the night away with vacationing Asunciónites, or just chill in the shade by the pool. Some of the elite spend weekends here but there's plenty for budget travelers as well. In summer, a pleasure boat takes passengers for short cruises on the lake (US$1.40).

Visitor information, including an area map, is available at **Casa Hassler** (☎ 0512-2974; Vache at Hassler).

Hotel Balneario (☎ 0512-2252; Hassler at Asunción; per person US$9) is nothin' special, but it is clean and it's cheap. On the lakeside of the plaza is the worn, but still romantically Victorian **Hotel del Lago** (☎ 0512-2201; Caballero & Teniente Weiler; US$11 per person with breakfast; ⊠ ⚑), full of antique furniture. **Camping** (☎ 0512-2459/2291; campsites per person US$2) is available near town, but call ahead for details.

The **Aleman Panadería & Confitería** (Colonos Alemanes below Estigarribia) has basic sandwiches, buttery baked treats, ice cream and a full restaurant upstairs.

From Asunción, Transporte Villa del Lago (bus No 210) and Transporte Cordillera de los Andes (bus No 103) run frequent buses to San Ber (US$0.70, 1½ hours, 48km); ask the driver to drop you near the plaza.

YAGUARÓN

Yaguarón's 18th-century **Franciscan church** is a landmark of colonial architecture. The nearby **Museo del Doctor Francia** (admission free;

⊙ 7-11am & 2-5pm Tue-Sat) has some good period portraiture.

Across from the church is a nameless restaurant with mediocre food, excellent homemade ice cream and basic **accommodations** (per person US$5). Ciudad Paraguarí bus No 193 (US$0.60, 1½ hours, 48km, every 15 minutes) departs Asunción from 5am to 8:15pm.

ITAUGUÁ

For the women of Itauguá weaving multicolored spiderweb *ñandutí* (lace) is a cottage industry from childhood to old age. Pieces range in size from doilies to bedspreads; smaller ones cost only a few dollars but larger ones range upward of US$50. In July the town celebrates its annual **Festival de Ñandutí**.

Two blocks south of Ruta 2, the dilapidated **Museo Parroquial San Rafael** (US$0.30; ⊙ 8-11:30am & 3-6pm Mon-Fri) displays Franciscan and secular relics, plus early *ñandutí* samples. From the Asunción bus terminal, buses leave for Itauguá (US$0.50, one hour, 30km, every 15 minutes) all day and night.

SOUTHERN PARAGUAY

East of the Río Paraguay is the center of historical Paraguay. About 90% of Paraguayans live within 100km of Asunción, but the border towns of Encarnación and Ciudad del Este have grown because of contraband smuggling and the hydroelectric projects.

ENCARNACIÓN

Encarnación is a cut-rate shopping center, the heart of the Paraguayan Carnaval and the gateway to the nearby Jesuit ruins at Trinidad and Jesús. Sadly its pleasant riverfront is drowning because of the reservoir created by the nearby Yacyretá Dam. Most established businesses have fled to higher ground, leaving the old town a tawdry bazaar of imported trinkets – Discmans, DVD players etc – among decaying public buildings.

Information

INTERNET ACCESS

More places advertise than actually deliver Internet services.

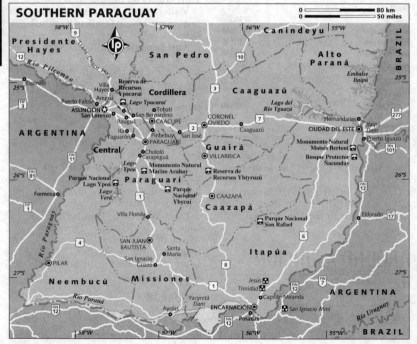

Century.com (Av Mariscal JF Estigarribia btwn Constitución & 25 de Mayo; US$0.60 per hr; ⏰ 8am-midnight)
Ciber KFE (Av Mariscal JF Estigarribia btwn Constitución & 25 de Mayo; US$0.60 per hr; ⏰ 8am-midnight; 🐾)

LAUNDRY

Lavacenter (☎ 071-206210; Monseñor Weissen) Will get the mud from your seams in less than 24 hours.

MONEY

Several banks, including Citibank and Banco Continental, face the Plaza Artigas and have 24-hour ATMs that dispense US dollars.

The following moneychangers are recommended for swapping currencies.
Cambio Parapiti (Av Mariscal JF Estigarribia 1405)
Cambio CIFESA (Cerro Corá & Av Mariscal JF Estigarribia)

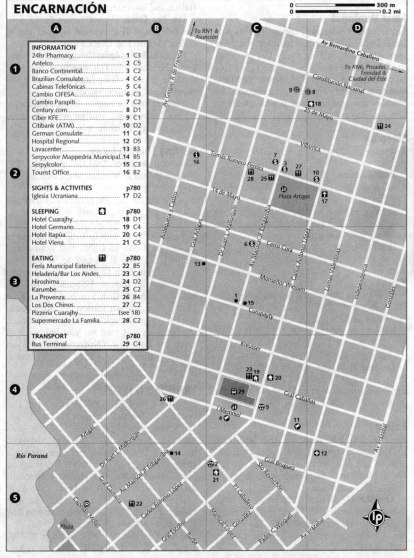

TELEPHONE
Cabinas Telefónicas (Carlos Antonio López 810; ✆ 7am-10pm) Across from the bus terminal.
Antelco (PJ Caballero & Carlos Antonio López; ✆ 7am-10pm) Has phones that accept phone cards.

TOURIST OFFICES
Tourist office (☎ 071-203508; Tomas Romero Pereira 126; ✆ 7am-noon Mon-Fri) English-speaking staff.

Fería Municipal
On General Gamarra, between Carlos Antonio López and Mariscal Estigarribia, petty merchants are milking every last peso out of visiting Argentines before the rising tide completely devours the old town. The **Fería Municipal market**'s liveliness transcends its baubles and gadgets, and it's an inexpensive place to eat.

Sleeping
There are plenty of clean, reasonably priced places to choose from in Encarnación.
Hotel Germano (☎ 071-203346; General Cabañas & Carlos Antonio López; s/d US$4/6; ☒) Across from the bus terminal, Hotel Germano is the best value in town with spotless rooms and helpful staff. Rooms cost less without bath, more with air conditioning.
Hotel Cuarajhy (☎ 071-202155; 25 de Mayo 415; per person US$6; ☒) Modern and homey with in-room TVs and a popular pizzeria downstairs.
Hotel Itapúa (☎ 071-205045; Carlos Antonio López 814; s/d US$3/4; P ☒) For cheaper digs try the large and impersonal Hotel Itapúa.
Hotel Viena (☎ 071-203486; PJ Caballero 568; s/d US$5/6.50; P) A tranquil hotel that is closed on Sunday – supposedly for cleaning.
Camping El Paraiso (campsites US$3.50) Five kilometers east of town on Ruta 6; take any bus from downtown. Buses may be caught at the bus terminal or from Plaza Artigas.

Eating
Encarnación has some of the best eats in Paraguay. Budget meals are available around the bus terminal anytime, in the Fería Municipal for lunch and at night around Plaza Artigas.
Karumbe (Av Mariscal JF Estigarribia & Tomas Romero Pereira; meals US$2) Popular with visiting Argentines and locals alike, has a killer *tenedor libre* (a buffet lunch of meat, pizza and pasta).

Hiroshima (☎ 071-203505; 25 de Mayo & Lomas Valentinas; set lunch US$3, mains US$2-5) No one should deny themselves the opportunity to eat at Hiroshima. With great service, superb sushi, pickles and udon this signless Japanese community center is deservedly a local favorite.
La Provenza (☎ 071-204618; Dr Juan L Mallorquín 609; mains US$3.50-5.25) A comfy place that serves Italian and international dishes.
Los Dos Chinos (Tomás Romero Pereira across from Plaza Artigas) If ice cream is what you're cravin', hit up Los Dos Chinos.
Heladería/Bar Los Andes (General Cabañas; ✆ closed Sunday) Next to Hotel Germano, this place has the killer trio of *helados* (ice cream), beer and super cheap Japanese noodles.
Supermercado La Familia (Dr Juan L Mallorquín & Tomas Romero Pereira) Stuffed with prepared meals and fresh produce.

Getting There & Away
Although **launches** (US$1.15) cross the Río Paraná to/from Posadas, there are no immigration procedures on this route; you don't want to face Paraguayan authorities without proper paperwork – the fines are ridiculous.

Frequent buses run from Encarnación to Asunción (US$6 to US$8, five hours) and Ciudad del Este (US$4.50 to US$6, four hours). From 6am to 11pm, local Servicio International buses (US$0.50) cross to Posadas in Argentina. You must get off the bus at immigration stations in both countries. Take your pack and keep your ticket, the bus may not wait for you but you can catch the next one. (Note the Paraguayan Tourist Information Office next to immigration is rarely open.)

TRINIDAD & JESÚS
Set atop a lush green hill northeast of Encarnación, **Trinidad** (admission US$0.50; ✆ 7am-7pm summer, 7am-5:30pm winter) is Paraguay's best-preserved Jesuit *reducción*. Although it's been a Unesco world heritage site since 1993, don't expect the usual information and conveniences. The closest bathrooms are in the nearby **Hotel León** (s/d US$5/7), where meals, refreshments and spacious rooms with bath are available. **Camping** (free) is possible outside the ruins.

Easily accessible **Jesús** (admission US$0.50), 12km north, is the nearly complete reconstruction of the Jesuit mission that was interrupted by the Jesuit's expulsion in 1767.

From Encarnación, frequent buses go to Trinidad ($0.80, 28km) between 6am and 7pm, but any bus headed east along Ruta 6 to Ciudad del Este or Hohenau will drop you off there. There are two morning buses to Jesús (6:30am and 10am) or it is possible to catch a bus from Trinidad.

PARQUE NACIONAL YBYCUÍ
This popular national park preserves one of eastern Paraguay's last stands of Brazilian subtropical rain forest. Its steep hills, dissected by creeks with attractive waterfalls and pools, reach 400m. The dense forest makes it difficult to see animals, which hide, rather than run, with the exception of the stunningly colorful butterflies, including the metallic blue morpho.

Rangers at the **visitors center**, at the park entrance, distribute a self-guided nature-trail brochure and claim that no one has ever been bitten by any of the poisonous snakes. The **Salto Guaraní** waterfall is near the **campground** (campsites per person US$1.50), which has cold showers and bothersome insects; bring your own food. Below it, a bridge leads to a pleasant creekside trail with a wealth of butterflies, but watch for snakes. The trail continues to **La Rosada**, an iron foundry destroyed by Brazilian forces in the War of the Triple Alliance. There is also a **museum** (admission free) with irregular hours.

In Ybycuí village, 4km from the park, **Hotel Pytu'u Renda** (☎ 0534-364; Av Quyquyho s/n; r per person US$7) has decent rooms and a restaurant.

Empresa Salto Cristal has hourly buses from Asunción to Ybycuí village (US$2, three hours) from 4am to 6pm. From there buses to the park entrance leave at 10am Monday, Wednesday and Saturday. At least two buses, at 11am and noon Monday to Saturday, enter the park and stop at the *administración*. Six buses make the return trip to the village between 7am and 3:30pm (ask rangers for the schedule). Salto Cristal runs one Sunday bus direct from Asunción; it leaves the park at 3:30pm.

CIUDAD DEL ESTE
Grubby, crumbling Ciudad del Este (population 167,000) has a justifiable reputation as one of South America's most corrupt cities, frequented by smugglers and money launderers. It's a busy border crossing where you can watch human pack-horses hump suspicious black boxes back and forth across the international bridge. During the day the streets are alive with Brazilian and Argentine shoppers searching for cheap electronic goods, cigarettes and liquor, but by 5pm all business has cleared away and the city takes on a deserted and sinister feel. New Brazilian customs laws and an economic depression in Argentina have hit Ciudad del Este hard.

Orientation & Information
On the west bank of the Paraná, across the Puente de Amistad from Foz do Iguaçu, Ciudad del Este has an irregular plan. The downtown area is compact and easily managed on foot but watch your step – the sidewalk is extremely irregular.

INTERNET ACCESS
Cíber Café (Pampliega; US$1 per hr) South of Av Adrián Jara. Offers fast connections in a modern atmosphere.
Cibertronic (Av de los Pioneros & Adrián Jara; US$1 per hr) Crowded with digital addicts.

LAUNDRY
Laverap (☎ 061-561511; Pampliega btwn Av Adrián Jara & Paí Pérez) It will clean 'em how you need 'em.

MONEY
Street moneychangers lounge around the Pioneros de Este rotunda.
Citibank (Av Adrián Jara s/n) ATM.
ABN AMRO (Av Adrián Jara s/n) ATM.
Banco Sudameris (Av Monseñor Rodríguez & Curupayty) Also changes currency.

POST
Post office (Av de los Pioneros & Oscar Rivas Ortellado) Across from the bus terminal.

TELEPHONE
Antelco (Av de los Pioneros & Paí Pérez)
PRV (Capitan Miranda s/n)

TOURIST OFFICES
Tourist office (☎ 061-511113) Next to immigration on Puente de Amistad. It looks intimidating with its blacked-out windows, but inside the staff are friendly and armed with an extensive supply of brochures. Immigration formalities must be completed at both ends of the bridge.

CIUDAD DEL ESTE

0 — 500 m
0 — 0.3 mi

Río Paraná

To Ruta 6, Ruta 2, Airport (30km);
Encarnación (130km) & Asunción

To Puente de Amistad (300m),
Foz do Iguaçu (Brazil) (1km) &
Puerto Iguazú (Argentina) (5km)

To Bus Terminal,
Post Office &
Hotel Tía
Nancy (all 2km)

To TAM
(100m)

SLEEPING		p782
Hotel Austria	11	A1
Hotel Caribe	12	A1
Hotel Mi Abuela	13	A2
Hotel Munich	14	A1

EATING		p782
Arco Iris & New Tokio		
Restaurant	15	A2
Bovolo	16	B2
Doli Bar	17	B2
Kokorelia	18	B2
Lebanon	19	B2
Restaurant Oriental	20	B2

INFORMATION		
ABN AMRO (ATM)	1	A2
Antelco	2	A2
Banco Sudameris	3	A2
Brazilian Consulate	4	A2
Cibertronic	5	A2
Citibank (ATM)	6	A2
Ciber Café	7	A2
Immigration & Customs Tourist		
Office	8	D1
Laverap	9	A2
PRV	10	A1

TRANSPORT		p783
Buses for Foz do Iguaçu &		
Puerto Iguazú	21	D2

Sleeping

Ciudad's mid-range places are definitely worth the extra couple of bucks, especially once you sample the mega-value breakfast buffets, which are included in the price.

Hotel Munich (☎ 061-500347; Emiliano R Fernández 71; s/d US$8/11; ✷) Enthusiastically recommended for its spacious rooms with frigobar and cable TV.

Hotel Austria (☎ 061-500883; Emiliano R Fernández 165; s/d US$9/12; ✷) Slightly bigger rooms than the Munich, with bigger baths and bigger prices.

Hotel Caribe (☎ 061-512460; Emiliano R Fernández s/n; s/d US$5/7; ✷) In the downright rugged category Caribe might have a new paint job by the time you arrive.

Hotel Mi Abuela (☎ 061-500348; Alejo García & Av Adrián Jara; s/d US$4/5) Wears a semipermanent 'En Venta' sign and provides dark rooms with ceiling fans around a wannabe garden courtyard.

Hotel Tía Nancy (☎ 061-502974; Garcete & Cruz del Chaco; s/d US$5/7) Near the bus terminal is this friendly place.

Eating

The cheapest options are the stalls along Captain Miranda and Av Monseñor Rodriguez. Otherwise, Asian cuisine fans dig in.

Kokorelia (Av Boquerón 169; mains US$3-12) A hole-in-the-wall that serves authentic Korean fare like crisp *kim chi*, grilled meats and noodles.

Restaurant Oriental (Av Adrián Jara; mains US$1.50-5.50) For a divine bowl of *agropicante* (hot-and-sour) soup and other eastern delights. It's near Av Boqueró.

Doli Bar (Av Adrián Jara & Abay; almuerzos US$1-3) The popular diner-style Doli Bar is the best choice for Paraguayan food.

Bovolo (Av Boquerón 148) For real coffee and baked goods.

Lebanon (Av Adrián Jara & Abay, Edifico Salah I) For something more exotic and upscale but not expensive, Lebanon serves scrumptious Middle Eastern fare.

Arco Iris (Av de los Pioneros & Av Adrián Jara) A supermarket with everything from ramen noodles to granola bars.

New Tokio (Av de los Pioneros & Av Adrián Jara) Has a Japanese-style lunch buffet for under US$2.

Getting There & Away

AIR

The airport is 30km west of town on Ruta 2. **TAM Mercosur** (☎ 061-506030; Curupayty & Ayala) flies between Ciudad del Este and Asunción four times daily Monday to Friday, three times a day on Saturday and once on Sunday.

BUS

The bus terminal is 2km south from the center on Av Bernardino Caballero. City buses (US$0.15) with 'Terminal' signs run to and from all day.

Taxi fares are about US$2 from the bus terminal to downtown. There are daily buses to Asunción (US$5–8, five hours) and Encarnación (US$4.50–6, four hours); less frequently to Pedro Juan Caballero (US$9, seven hours) in the north. Daily buses run to São Paulo, Brazil (US$30, 17 hours); and Buenos Aires, Argentina (US$35, 20 hours).

Buses to Foz do Iguaçu (US$1) and nonstop buses to Puerto Iguazu, Argentina (no Brazilian visa necessary; US$1), both pass by immigration (until 8pm) after departing from outside the terminal. Note that if you require a Brazilian visa, you cannot visit for the day without one, officially. Unless you're already at the terminal, it's most convenient (if a bit sketchier) to walk or taxi to immigration and catch the bus from there.

ITAIPÚ DAM

Paraguay is the world's largest exporter of hydropower and Itaipú, the world's largest hydroelectric project, is why – hence its image on the 100,000 guaraní bill. Itaipú's generators supply nearly 80% of Paraguay's electricity and 25% of Brazil's entire demand. In 1997 it churned out a staggering 88.2 billion kilowatts per hour. Dam fans should not miss touring this massive yet disconcerting human accomplishment.

Project propaganda omits the US$25 billion price tag (mostly from over-invoicing) and ignores environmental concerns. The 1350-sq-km reservoir, 220m deep, drowned Sete Quedas, a set of waterfalls that was more impressive than Iguazú, and stagnant water has provided a new habitat for anopheles mosquitoes, a malaria vector.

Tours (adults free; ☼ 8am, 9am, 10am, 1:30pm, 2:30pm & 3:30pm Mon-Fri; 8 & 9:30am Sat) leave from the **visitor's center** (☎ 061-5998592), north of Ciudad del Este near the town of Hernandarias; passports are required. **Light shows** (☎ 061-5998700; admission free; ☼ 7:30pm Fri) take place in the summer and require reservations.

From Ciudad del Este, Transtur and Tacurú Pucú buses traveling to Hernandarias (US$0.25, every 15 minutes) depart from west of the traffic circles at San Blás and Av de los Pioneros and will drop you at the entrance.

NORTHERN PARAGUAY & THE CHACO

The Gran Chaco is a vast plain of thorny scrub and swampy wetlands that encompasses the entire western half of Paraguay and stretches into Argentina and Bolivia. During the rainy season, large tracts of the plain are flooded. In dry weather, it's an arid dustbowl.

Although the Chaco accounts for over 60% of Paraguayan territory, less than 3% of the population actually live here. Historically, it was a refuge for indigenous hunter-gatherers, and most of Paraguay's remaining indigenous groups still live here. Close to the Río Paraguay, *campesinos* have built picturesque houses of palm logs, and Mennonite farmers have successfully settled in the middle Chaco. Only army bases and cattle *estancias* inhabit the denser thorn forests of the high Chaco beyond Mariscal Estigarribia, where the pavement ends and the fun begins.

Brazilian settlers are moving into northeastern Paraguay, deforesting the countryside to plant coffee and cotton and squeezing out the existing population, including the few remaining Aché. The northeast is also contraband country with numerous marijuana plantations.

Controversy hit the area in 2000 when the Reverend Sun Myung Moon's Unification Church (the Moonies) purchased 360,000 hectares of the Chaco, including the entire town of Puerto Casado, for an estimated US$15 million. The Moonies claim they have plans for the economic reactivation of the area, including the export of timber.

PARAGUAY

CONCEPCIÓN

On the Río Paraguay, Concepción (population 50,000) is an attractive, easygoing city of poetically crumbling early-20th-century buildings. It's connected to the rest of the country by road (via Pozo Colorado in the Chaco), but still depends largely on the river, the original means of communication. Horse-drawn carts haul watermelons and other goods through town from the port to market. Upriver, locals gather on sandy beaches in late afternoon to swim and play guitars. Increasingly popular on weekends, some independent boat owners have started taking people across the river to explore the nearby islands and delta; ask around the old port.

Information

Some banks have ATMs but they're not linked internationally.

Cyberc@t (Franco near Garay; around US$1 per hr) Has a quick connection in a quiet, air-conditioned space.
Tourist information station (Agustín Pinedo) This is a brand-new place, below the colorful monument in the center divider.

Museo del Cuartel de la Villa Real

The **Museo del Cuartel de la Villa Real** (CA López & Cerro Cordillera; admission free; ☯ 7am-noon Mon-Fri) is a beautifully restored Hispaño-Paraguayo building that exhibits historical and war paraphernalia and a curious collection of prehistoric bones.

Sleeping & Eating

Hospedaje Puerta del Sol (across from old port; s/d US$2/3) The walls may be thin enough to hear your neighbors but it's clean(ish) and the owners are sweet.

Hotel Frances (☎ 031-42383; Franco & CA López; per person US$7; ☒ ☒) Away from the port, Hotel Frances has a groomed pool area, small rooms with TVs and includes a breakfast buffet.

Hotel Center (Franco near Yegros; s/d US$3/4) A few beer cans line the hallway but there are decent rooms and a restaurant.

El Quincho del Victoria (Presidente Franco & Caballero; mains US$1-4) A lively *parrillada* (restaurant serving grilled meats) with courtyard seating.

Heladería Amistad (Presidente Franco & Concepción) Stopping at Heladería Amistad for ice cream, soda and snacks is a local pastime.

UP THE LAZY RÍO PARAGUAY

Forget creature comforts – this is the Pantanal. South of Concepción river commerce is lively, but further north the pace slackens and cargo exchanges are replaced by wildlife sightings. From your hammock you'll see caimans, capybaras, monkeys and birds galore: jabiru, herons, egrets, spoonbills, even macaws. Upriver from Vallemí is Isla Margarita (aka Puerto Esperanza), where you can disembark and catch a skiff to Porto Murtinho, Brazil, which has bus connections to Corumbá. Note: Fuerte Olimpo is the only place between Concepción and Bahía Negra where you can get a Paraguayan exit stamp.

Rivals **Pollería El Bigote** (Presidente Franco) and **Pollería Bulldog** (Presidente Franco & Garay; US$1 portions) duke it out for the best cheap wood-roasted chicken.

Getting There & Away

BOAT

The most traditional (but not the most comfortable) way to get to or from Concepción is by riverboat. **Cacique II** (☎ 031-42621) boats to Asunción leave Thursday at 1pm (US$6, 30 hours). Boats heading upriver to Puerto Vallemí (US$8, 24 hours) or as far as Bahía Negra (US$15, 2½ days) include the *Aquidabán* (late Tuesday morning), *Cacique II* (Saturday morning), *Carmenleticia* (Friday morning) and *Guaraní* (every other Monday). Ask around the old port about heading as far north as Isla Margarita on the Brazilian border. (See Getting There & Away in Asunción for details on getting to Concepción, p776.)

BUS

The bus terminal is eight blocks north of the lone stoplight, which is as close to the center as Colectivo Línea 1 (US$0.20) will take you. Car or motorcycle taxis cost about US$2; *karumbes* (horse-carts) are twice as much fun and cost less.

Several buses pass Pozo Colorado (US$3, 1½ hours) en route to Filadelfia (US$5, five to six hours, 7:30am only) and Asunción (US$6 to US$8, six hours). There's a daily service to Pedro Juan Caballero (US$4, four hours) with some services continuing to Campo Grande, Brazil.

PEDRO JUAN CABALLERO

Literally across the street from Ponta Porã in Brazil, Pedro Juan Caballero is a dusty, former shopping destination. The only real reasons to shack up here are to visit the picturesque Parque Nacional Cerro Corá (see below) or en route to/from Brazil.

Information

Money-exchange houses are numerous. Other tourist facilities include:

Immigration (Naciones Unidas 144; ☼ 8am-noon Mon-Sat) Locals cross the border freely, but to continue any distance you must visit the immigration office.

Vitalinfo (Mariscal López; US$1 per hr) Has reasonable Internet access.

Sleeping & Eating

Hotel La Siesta (☎ 0367-3022; Alberdi & Francia; s/d US$6/11) A dusty lounge atmosphere with carpeted rooms, some with vibrating beds, others with Jacuzzis.

Hotel Guavirá (☎ 0367-2743; Mariscal López 1325; per person US$2.25) Scruffy but damn cheap rooms, with breakfast.

Banana Azul (Mariscal López; US$1-2) Near Julia Estigarribia, this place serves good sandwiches, chicken salad, burgers and fruit drinks with and without alcohol.

Getting There & Away

The bus terminal is a few blocks east of the border, with frequent services to Concepción (US$4, four hours) and Asunción (US$7-9, 7½ hours), but only two daily buses to Ciudad del Este (US$8, 8½ hours). Nasa goes daily to Campo Grande, Brazil (US$4.50, five hours) and São Paulo (US$28, 16 hours). Connections to many more Brazilian destinations available in Ponta Porã.

PARQUE NACIONAL CERRO CORÁ

Visitors to northeastern Paraguay should not overlook **Parque Nacional Cerro Corá** (☎ 036-72069), 40km west of Pedro Juan Caballero. It protects an area of dry tropical forest and savanna in a landscape of steep, isolated hills. Cultural and historical features include pre-Columbian caves, petroglyphs and the site of Francisco Solano López's death at the end of the War of the Triple Alliance.

The park has **nature trails** and a **camping area** (bring insect repellent and watch out for the bats in the bathrooms). There is also a small **visitor's center/museum** (admission free) with a very curious monkey, where guests who phone ahead can bunk for free.

Buses running between Concepción and Pedro Juan Caballero (US$0.80, one hour) will stop at the park entrance; walk a few kilometers uphill to the visitor's center. The helpful staff can tell you the bus schedule for your return trip. One-way taxis from Pedro Juan Caballero cost US$12.

FILADELFIA

Filadelfia, the administrative and service center of Fernheim, has a surprising collection of modern teenagers in big trucks

---

LOS MENNOS (MENNONITE COLONIES)

Some 14,000 Mennonites inhabit the Chaco in near harmony with 30,000 indigenous people. According to their history, Canadian Mennonites en route to Argentina were invited, and offered free land, by the Paraguayan president, who was on the same boat. In 1927, the Canadians formed **Menno Colony** around **Loma Plata**. A few years later, refugees from the Soviet Union established **Fernheim** (Distant Home), with its capital at **Filadelfia**. In 1947 Ukrainian Germans, many of whom served unwillingly in WWII, founded **Neuland** (New Land) with the capital of **Neu-Halbstadt**.

Mennonites believe in adult baptism, separation of church and state, and pacifist opposition to military service. They speak Plattdeutsch (Low German) and also Hochdeutsch (High German). Most adults, and all children, speak Spanish. Canadian descendants speak English and some have attended Canadian universities. Mennonite farmers speak some Guaraní as well.

As more *mestizo* Paraguayans settle in the Chaco, Mennonite leaders worry that the government may eliminate their privileges; some have begun to participate in national politics. Others are disgruntled with developments in Filadelfia, where material prosperity has spawned a generation more interested in motorcycles and Jackie Chan than traditional values. Alcohol and tobacco, once absolutely *verboten*, are now sold openly, except at the Cooperativa Mennonita in Filadelfia.

PARAGUAY

tight jeans, and who even sport facial piercings. Mennonite dairy products are the cream of the Paraguayan crop. Indigenous day laborers from nearby *pueblos* line the streets where Fernheim's cotton and dairy farmers pick them up in the morning and drop them off again in the afternoon. The town is exceptionally quiet at midday – it stays that way until 2pm, when a conspicuous siren blast shatters the stillness of the adopted siesta.

Orientation & Information

Filadelfia's dusty streets form an orderly grid whose Hauptstrasse (main street) is Hindenburg. Perpendicular Av Trébol leads east to Loma Plata and west to the Trans-Chaco and Fortín Toledo.

Filadelfia has no tourist office, but Hotel Florida (see Sleeping & Eating below) shows a video on the Mennonite colonies, will help organize transportation and runs the local museum.

The well-stocked **Cooperativa Mennonita** (Unruh & Hindenburg) supermarket has excellent dairy products and might change cash, but the Mennonites deal in barter more than hard currencies. Antelco and the post office are at the same corner.

Unger Museum

Opposite Hotel Florida, the **Unger Museum** (Hindenburg s/n; admission free; ☿ 7-11:30am Mon-Fri) displays colony-specific items downstairs (take a peak in the refrigerator) and everything from 15th century coins and stuffed jaguars to colorful Nivaclé headdresses upstairs. Tours are possible in Spanish, German and English; or just get the keys from Hotel Florida.

Sleeping & Eating

Hotel Florida (☎ 0491-32151; Postfach 214; dm beds US$3, d US$24; P ✖ ✚) Filadelfia's nicest accommodation has hostel beds with fan or upscale private rooms with modern, quiet air conditioners.

Camping (campsites free) In shady Parque Trébol, 5km east of Filadelfia, but there is no water and only a pit toilet.

Churrascuría Girasol (Unruh) Apart from Hotel Florida's restaurant, try Girasol, which serves delicious all-you-can-eat Brazilian *asados* (barbeque), or the drunken *parrillada* at **La Estrella**.

Getting There & Away

There's no bus terminal, but companies have offices along and near Hindenburg. There's a limited daily service to Mariscal Estigarribia (US$3, 1½ hours) and Asunción (US$7, seven hours, 480km). Packed buses to Santa Cruz, Bolivia, pass through Filadelfia, but remember you must get an exit stamp in Pozo Colorado or you may face a stiff fine (up to US$100) at Bolivian immigration.

Getting between colonies by bus is tricky, but not impossible. A local bus connects Filadelfia with Loma Plata (25km) at 7:30am and 10pm daily (timed to meet arriving buses from Asunción). Some buses stop in Loma Plata after Filadelfia en route to Asunción and fewer continue to Neu-Halbstadt. During the school year there are early morning and noon buses connecting the colonies; ask locals for specifics. Hitching is worth a try.

AROUND FILADELFIA
Loma Plata

The Menno Colony's administrative center is the oldest and most traditional of the Mennonite settlements. It's also the best place to organize Chaco adventures. Its excellent **museum**, in a typical pioneer house, has a remarkable display of original photographs chronicling the colony's history. The museum is usually shut but you can ask for the keys at the informal **tourist office** (☎ 0492-2301) next door in the *municipalidad* (town hall), where you may be able to arrange free tours of the Mennonite cooperative.

Visit **Ecoturismo Boquerón** (☎ 04925-2060; www .desdelchaco.org.py; Quebracho 865) to organize a 4x4 tour of the surrounding Chaco or Parque Nacional Defensors del Chaco (p787).

Hotel Mora (☎ 04925-2255; Calle Sandstrasse 803; s/d US$7/11; P ✖) has spotless rooms and friendly hosts who can organize tours to the nearby wilderness, including the recommended Laguna Capitán. **Chaco's Grill** serves quality meats Brazilian style, or try **Pizzeria Primavera**, across from the *municipalidad*.

Neu-Halbstadt

Neu-Halbstadt is the center of Neuland Colony. Nearby **Fortín Boquerón** preserves a sample of trenches dating from the Chaco War. South of Neuland are several indigenous reserves, where many Lengua and Nivaclé have become settled farmers. Neu-Halbstadt is a good place to buy native handicrafts such as bags, hammocks and woven goods.

Hotel Boquerón (☎ 0493-311; cfiss@telesurf.com.py; s/d US$8.50/12; 🈺), across from Supermercado Neuland, fires up the grill on Wednesdays and Saturdays. Owners Osmar and Rosana lead and organize tours to the surrounding highlights.

Some buses from Asunción to Filadelfia continue to Neu-Halbstadt, while some come direct from Asunción.

PARQUE NACIONAL DEFENSORES DEL CHACO

Once the province of nomadic Ayoreo foragers, **Defensores del Chaco** is a wooded alluvial plain; isolated **Cerro León** (500m) is its greatest landmark. The dense thorn forest harbors large cats such as jaguar, puma, ocelot and Geoffroy's cat, which survive despite threats posed by poaching.

Defensores del Chaco is a long 830km from Asunción, over roads impassable to ordinary vehicles. There is no regular public transportation, but the Dirección General de Protección & Conservación de la Biodiversidad (see p771) may be able to put you in contact with rangers who have space in their vehicle. Still interested? Good. Heinrich Gossen Delegado of **TACPy** (☎ 021-210550; www.elgranchaco.com; 25 de Mayo & Brasil, 1st fl) in Asunción organizes camping tours starting at US$90 per person for groups of five.

PARAGUAY DIRECTORY

ACCOMMODATIONS

Though worn and of a distant era, hotels and *residenciales* (guesthouses) are usually *muy limpio* (very clean). Camping facilities, while less common, are cheaper and in remote areas you can usually pitch your tent anywhere – but beware of tent-eating ants! In the Chaco, formal accommodations are sparse outside the few towns, but *campesinos* may offer a bed with mosquito net. For information on visiting working *estancias* (ranches), contact TACPy (p790) in Asunción.

ACTIVITIES

Paraguay's biodiversity makes it a notable destination for nature-watching, particularly bird-watching. River activities such as fishing and swimming are also popular.

BOOKS

Lonely Planet's *Argentina, Uruguay & Paraguay* guidebook has more detailed coverage of Paraguay. For more about Paraguay's notorious wars, pick up Harris Gaylord Warren's *Rebirth of the Paraguayan Republic*, or Augusto Roa Bastos' novel *Son of Man*. For a look into Paraguay's heinous dictators, check out Bastos' book *I the Supreme* about Francia, or Carlos Miranda's *The Stroessner Era*. For a more anthropological slant check out Pierre Clastres' *Chronicle of the Guayaki Indians* or Matthew J Pallamary's novel *Land Without Evil*. Mark Jacobs' *The Liberation of Little Heaven and Other Stories* is a collection of fictional Paraguayan shorts.

BUSINESS HOURS

Because of the much disputed law ordering government offices to remain open continuously, most are now open 7am to 2pm or 3pm, without siesta time. Most shops are open weekdays and Saturday from 7am to noon and from 2pm or 3pm until 7pm or 8pm. Banking hours are 7:30am to noon weekdays, but *casas de cambio* keep longer hours.

CLIMATE

Because of Paraguay's intense summer heat, winter months (May to September) are preferable. The weather is variable and nightly frosts are not unusual.

Southern Paraguay's climate is humid, with rainfall distributed fairly evenly throughout the year. In the east, near the Brazilian border, it averages an abundant 2000mm a year, declining to about 1500mm near Asunción. Since elevations do not exceed 600m, temperatures are almost uniformly hot in summer – the average high in December, January and February is 35°C (95°F), with daily temperatures ranging between 25°C and 43°C (77°F to 109°F). Winter temperatures are more variable and can reach freezing or hover at 6°C (42°F), though the average high in July, the coldest month, is 22°C (71°F).

DANGERS & ANNOYANCES

Paraguay's economy continues to deteriorate. Crime is supposedly on the rise, but it's still a relatively safe country. It's best not to wander around on your own late at night in Asunción and border towns. There have been reports of armed robbery on buses traveling at night. Many Paraguayans carry handguns, even in the cities. Police and military officers operate with less impunity than they used to, but try not to aggravate them and always carry a copy of your passport. Poisonous snakes are common in the Chaco, but mosquitoes are a likelier nuisance. Beware of strong currents when swimming in rivers. Request a receipt or ticket whenever you give someone money – especially if they are wearing a questionable uniform.

DISABLED TRAVELERS

Infrastructure for disabled travelers is negligible and unfortunately there are really no services for disabled travelers or for people with special needs.

EMBASSIES & CONSULATES
Embassies & Consulates in Paraguay
For information about Visas see p790. For locations of these embassies see individual city maps.

Argentina Asunción (Map pp772-3; ☎ 021-212320; Av España btwn Boquerón & Av Perú)

Bolivia Asunción (Map pp772-3; ☎ 021-227213, 203654; America 200)

Brazil Asunción (Map pp772-3; ☎ 021-448084; General Díaz 521; 3rd fl); Ciudad (Map p782; ☎ 061-500984; Pampliega 205; ☒ 7am-noon Mon-Fri); Encarnación (Map p779; ☎ 071-203950; Memmel 452), Best visited in the morning; Pedro Juan Caballero (Mariscal Estigarribia west of CA López; ☒ 7am-5pm Mon-Fri, 7-11am Sat) Near the border in Ponta Porã.

Canada Asunción (☎ 021-226196; Profesor Ramírez at Juan de Salazar)

Chile Asunción (☎ 021- 662756; Capitán Nudelman 351)

France Asunción (Map pp772-3; ☎ 021-212439; Av España 893)

Germany Asunción (Map pp772-3; ☎ 021-214009; Av Venezuela 241)

Paraguay Pedro Juan Caballero (☎ 067-724-4934; Av Presidentes Vargas 120; ☒ 7am-2pm Mon-Fri) Near the border in Ponta Porã.

UK Asunción (Map pp772-3; ☎ 021-612611; Av Boggiani 5848)

USA Asunción (☎ 021-213715; Mariscal López 1776)

Paraguayan Embassies & Consulates Abroad
Paraguay has representatives in neighboring countries (see those chapters for details) and in the following countries:

Canada Ottawa (☎ 613-567-1283; 151 Slater St, Suite 401, Ottawa, Ontario K1P 5H3)

France Paris (☎ 01 42 22 85 05; 113 Rue de Courcelles, 76017 Paris)

Germany Bonn (☎ 0228-356 727; Uhlandstrasse 32, 53173 Bonn 2)

UK London (☎ 020-7937 1253; Braemar Lodge, Cornwall Gardens, London SW7 4AQ)

USA Washington (☎ 202-483-6960; 2400 Massachusetts Ave NW, Washington, DC 20008)

FESTIVALS & EVENTS
Paraguay's celebration of **Carnaval** (February; dates vary) is liveliest in Asunción, Encarnación, Ciudad del Este and Villarrica. Caacupé is the most important site for the Roman Catholic **Día de la Virgen** (December 8).

Other curious events include:

Día de San Blás (Day of San Blás; February 3) Paraguay's patron saint.

Election of Miss Paraguay (March – dates vary) Asunción.

Rally Transchaco (First week in September) Transchaco car race.

FOOD & DRINK
Parrillada (grilled meat) is popular, but nourishing tropical and subtropical foodstuffs play a greater role in the typical Paraguayan diet. Grains, particularly maize, and tubers like manioc (cassava) are part of almost every meal. *Chipas*, made with manioc flour, eggs and cheese, are sold every-where, as are cheap and filling *empanadas* (patties stuffed with either chicken, cheese and ham, or beef). During Easter's Holy Week, the addition of eggs, cheese and spices transforms ordinary food into a holiday treat.

Paraguayans consume massive quantities of *maté*, most commonly as ice-cold *tereré* (super-sweet iced *maté*) and generously spiked with *yuyos* (medicinal herbs). Roadside stands offer *mosto* (sugarcane juice), while *caña* (cane alcohol) is the fiery alcoholic alternative. Local beers, especially *Baviera*, are excellent.

The following are some other common foods you'll likely encounter:

Bori-bori Chicken soup with cornmeal balls.
Locro Maize stew.
Mazamorra Corn mush.
Mbaipy he-é A dessert of corn, milk and molasses.
Mbaipy so-ó Hot maize pudding with meat chunks.

Mbeyú or **torta de almidón** A grilled manioc pancake resembling the Mexican tortilla.
Sooyo sopy Thick soup of ground meat, accompanied by rice or noodles.
Sopa paraguaya Cornbread with cheese and onion.

GAY & LESBIAN TRAVELERS
Paraguay is a rather old-fashioned country, with conservative views. Public displays of affection are uncommon between heterosexual couples, and invisible between same-sex couples.

HEALTH
Paraguay presents relatively few health problems for travelers. The private hospitals are definitely better than public and those in Asunción are the best. Beware of Dengue fever in Asunción's suburbs and other wetland areas in the southeast. It's not advisable to drink the tap water, even though it is said to come from wells. In the Chaco it can be undrinkably salty. Be sure to carry sunscreen, a hat and plenty of bottled water at all times to avoid becoming dehydrated. Condoms are available in most pharmacies. For more information, see the Health chapter (p1053).

HOLIDAYS
Government offices and businesses in Paraguay are closed for the following official holidays.
Año Nuevo (New Year's Day; January 1)
Cerro Corá (Death of Mariscal Francisco Solano López; March 1)
Viernes Santo/Pascua (Good Friday/Easter; March/April – dates vary)
Día del Trabajad (Labor Day; May 1)
Independencia Patria (Independence Day; May 15)
Paz del Chaco (End of Chaco War; June 12)
Día de San Juan (Day of St John; June 24)
Fundación de Asunción (Founding of Asunción; August 15)
Victoria de Boquerón (Battle of Boquerón; September 29)
Día de la Virgen (Immaculate Conception Day; December 8)
Navidad (Christmas Day; December 25)

INTERNET ACCESS
Internet is *muy popular* in cities, but limited in smaller towns. An hour of use costs less than US$1 and some places offer cheap Net2Phone calls.

INTERNET RESOURCES
Guarani Dictionary (www.uni-mainz.de/~lustig/guarani/diccion.html) Basic Guaraní language tools.
Lanic (http://lanic.utexas.edu/la/sa/paraguay/) Excellent collection of links from the University of Texas.
Paraguayan Current Events (www.paraguay.com) Links to news stories about Paraguay in English.
Paraguayan Search Engine (www.quanta.com.py) Spanish-language search engine.
Senatur (www.senatur.gov.py) Official tourist information homepage.

MAPS
The *Guía Shell* ($7.50) road atlas is sold at most Shell gas stations and at **Touring y Automóvil Club Paraguayo** (TACPy; Map pp772-3) offices. It includes a general 1:2,000,000-scale country map, and a map of Asunción with street index at 1:25,000. The **Instituto Geográfico Militar** (IGM; ☎ 021-206344; Artigas 920, Asunción) sells 1:50,000 topographic maps.

MEDIA
The following is a list of Paraguay's more important newspapers:
ABC Color (www.abc.com.py) Asunción's daily paper made its reputation opposing the Stroessner dictatorship.
Ultima Hora (www.ultimahora.com) An editorially bold independent daily with an excellent cultural section.
Neues für Alle Asunción's German community publishes this newspaper twice-monthly.
Rundschau Weekly.

MONEY
The unit of currency is the *guaraní* (plural *guaraníes*), indicated by ₲. Banknote values are 500, 1000, 5000, 10,000, 50,000 and 100,000 guaraníes; there are rare 50, 100 and 500 coins. Breaking big bills, like the 100,000 guaraníes from ATMs, can be tough, but most *casas de cambios* will do it for free.

ATMs & Credit Cards
ATMs in Asunción, Encarnación and Ciudad del Este are connected to Visa, MasterCard and Cirrus networks. Some even dispense US dollars. You may stumble upon an ATM in other towns but they are not linked internationally. As a traveler with an international ATM card you can only get cash from the ones in the three major cities listed.

Plastic is rarely accepted outside Asunción, and even there, only in mid- to top-end hotels, restaurants and shops.

Exchange Rates

Exchange rates at press time included the following:

Country	Unit		Par G (guaraní)
Australia	A$1	=	4516
Canada	C$1	=	4784
euro zone	€1	=	7291
Japan	¥100	=	5799
New Zealand	NZ$1	=	3926
United Kingdom	UK£1	=	10671
United States	US$	=	6373

Exchanging Money

Casas de cambio are abundant in Asunción and border towns and change both cash and traveler's checks (3% to 5% commission); try banks in the interior. Some *cambios* will not cash traveler's checks without the original proof of purchase receipt. Street changers give slightly lower rates for cash only and can be helpful on evenings and weekends.

PHOTOGRAPHY

Most Paraguayans will gladly smile for the camera, if you ask before shooting. Professional-quality color print and slide film is available in Asunción, Encarnación and Ciudad del Este. Two good places in Encarnación to stock up on print and slide film are:

Serpylcolor (Av Mariscal JF Estigarribia & Curupayty)

Serpylcolor mappedria municipal (Av Mariscal JF Estigarribia & Mariscal López)

POST

To send a letter to the USA costs about US$0.25 and it's US$0.35 to Europe. Essential mail should be registered for a small fee.

RESPONSIBLE TRAVEL

Avoid buying crafts made from endangered species like armadillos, jaguars, pumas and other exotic animals. Visitors interested in natural history and conservation should contact the **Fundación Moisés Bertoni** (☎ 021-608740; www.mbertoni.org.py; Prócer Carlos Argüello 208, Asunción), a nonprofit conservation organization that also arranges tours to reserves it helps manage.

TELEPHONE

Antelco, the state telephone company, has central long-distance offices throughout the country. Private *locutorios* (phone offices) have sprung up everywhere, often with Internet service as well. Despite deregulation, international calls still run over US$1 per minute, even with lower nighttime rates.

Public phone boxes are rare, but they are the best places to make credit card or calling-card calls.

For phone codes use the following: country code (☎ 595) – when calling Paraguay from another country drop the '0' in the area code; international operator (☎ 0010); and International Direct Dial (☎ 002).

TOILETS

Public toilets are so rare you are likely to see locals going on the street more often than you'd like. Bus terminals usually have one you can use for a small fee, but it is best to go when you can in restaurants, hotels or museums. Most restaurants will charge you a nominal fee if you don't buy anything. Carry your own toilet paper and don't throw it down the pipes. Few buses have one that won't spill over onto your shoes but drivers will stop and let you go if you ask nicely.

TOURIST INFORMATION

The government-run **Senatur** (www.senatur.com .py) has tourist offices in large towns only. They may lack colorful brochures but the staff do what they can to answer your questions (in Spanish). **Asociación de Colonias Mennonitas del Paraguay** (☎ 021-226059; acomepa@rieder.net.py; Republica de Columbia 1050, Asunción) has information about Mennonite communities. **Touring y Automóvil Club Paraguayo** (TACPy; Map pp772-3; ☎ 021-215010; www.turis morural.org.py; Av Brasil & Cerro Corá, Asunción; ⏱ 8am-5pm Mon-Fri, 8am-2pm Sat) can help make reservations for overnight visits (US$20 to US$100 per person, per day including meals) to 20 working *estancias*.

VISAS

Visitors from Australia, Canada, Japan, New Zealand and the USA need visas. Others only need a valid passport. Get your visa in advance, either in a neighboring country or at home. Visas may be requested and obtained in the same day at most consulates. You will need three passport photos, proof of onward travel, proof of sufficient funds, several copies of your passport and US$50 in cash for single entry or US$65 for multiple entry (30 to 90 days). Be sure to get your passport stamped on entering the country or you may be subject to fines upon leaving. The only place where daily visits without a visa were possible at the time of writing was Ciudad del Este – be sure to check in with Senatur before subjecting yourself to a shake-down by immigration officials.

For information about immigration points (such as Pozo Colorado en route to Bolivia), entrance or exit stamps or visa paperwork, visit the **Immigration Office** (☎ 021-446673, 021-492 908; Juan O'Leary & General Díaz, 1st fl; ☉ 7am-1pm Mon-Fri) in Asunción.

WOMEN TRAVELERS
Paraguay is comparatively safe for women but modest dress is important.

Peru

HIGHLIGHTS

■ **Machu Picchu & the Inca Trail** – the awesome and ethereal 'Lost City of the Inca,' reached by train from Cuzco or an exhilarating four-day trek from one ancient ruin to the next (p854)

■ **Lake Titicaca** – breathtakingly beautiful lake straddling the Peru–Bolivia border, dotted with storybook isles and whole villages that float on a bed of reeds (p832)

■ **Nazca Lines** – one of the world's greatest archaeological mysteries: vast and elaborate lines and designs etched starkly across the *pampa* (plains) (p820)

■ **Arequipa** – framed by smoldering volcanoes, the 'White City' is packed with colonial architecture and is home to Inca ice-mummies; nearby Cañón del Colca is your best bet to see wild condors (p824 & p830)

■ **Cordillera Blanca** – over 50 snowcapped peaks of 5700m or higher crown this as one of South America's most spectacular mountain ranges, with excellent trekking (p882)

■ **Off the beaten track** – head for the jungle: Manu (p862), Puerto Maldonado (p900) and Iquitos (p896) areas are all home to countless tropical mammal and bird species

■ **Best journey** – get off the gringo trail: make for Pucallpa, buy a hammock, pick up a slow boat along the Amazon and swing lazily all the way to Brazil (p800)

FAST FACTS

■ **Area:** 1,285,215 sq km (five times larger than Great Britain)

■ **Budget:** US$20–30 a day

■ **Capital:** Lima

■ **Costs:** bedding down in Lima dorm/single US$6/10, 650ml beer US$2, three-hour bus ride US$3

■ **Country code:** ☎ 51

■ **Electricity:** 220V, 60 cycles AC; two rounded prongs

■ **Famous for:** Machu Picchu

■ **Languages:** Spanish, Quechua, Aymara

■ **Money:** US$1 = 3.60 soles

■ **Phrases:** *chevere*, *bacán* (cool), *asqueroso* – or *asco* for short (disgusting), *fiesta*, *juerga* (party)

■ **Population:** 28 million

■ **Time:** GMT minus 5 hours

■ **Tipping:** 10% in better restaurants; tip all guides

■ **Traveler's checks:** cashed at larger banks

■ **Visas:** North American, Australian and most European citizens need only a valid passport

---

TRAVEL HINTS

Book tours with travel agents in the city or largest town closest to the area or attraction you want to visit. Bring high-speed film to photograph in the low light of the rainforest.

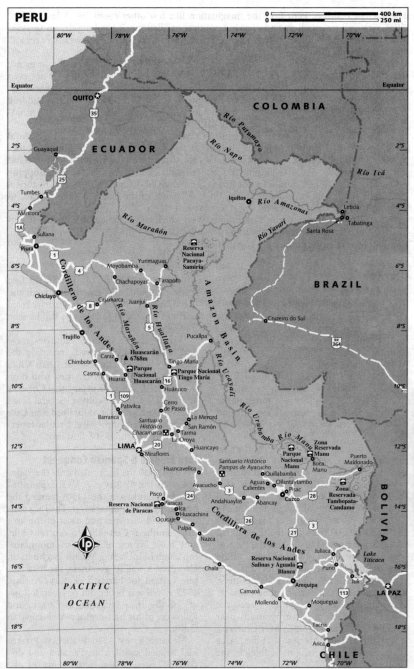

The ancient realm of Peru fires the imagination like few other countries. A land of lost cities, rich cultural medleys and dizzying political oscillations, it has long drawn treasure hunters and travelers alike, united in the search to uncover the secrets and wealth of remote and exotic civilizations.

So you've seen pictures of cloud-topping Inca city Machu Picchu? And the immense desert designs stretching for miles around Nazca? Well, these incredible sites are not even half of what Peru has to offer, as this is a region jam-packed with dazzling archaeology, and new and ever-more-exciting sites are continually being discovered. If you're a budding Indiana Jones, all you need to do is whack a pack on your back, take your pick of a mind-boggling array of ancient ruins and you're off.

And while you're at it, you'll find yourself exploring a country of astounding natural diversity – from drifting through parched expanses of desert sands to dipping your toes in the cool sapphire-blue waters of Lake Titicaca, from tramping through lush lowland jungle replete with wildlife to gasping in wonder (and lack of oxygen) at the jaw-dropping pinnacles of the Andes. And let's not forget the wealth of diverse cultures and historical cityscapes you'll pass en route, from the floating islands of the Uros on Lake Titicaca to the centuries-old colonial treasures of Arequipa and Cuzco.

But wherever your wanderings take you in Peru, you'll be welcomed by a singularly big-hearted folk that tackle their lot with gusto and a deep lust for life. Small wonder, then, that Peru is one of the continent's top destinations.

HISTORY
Early Cultures

The infamous Inca civilization is merely the tip of Peru's archaeological iceberg. The country's first inhabitants were nomadic hunters and gatherers, living in caves, and hunting fearsome (and now extinct) animals like giant sloths, saber-toothed tigers and mastodons. Domestication of the llama, alpaca and guinea pig began between 7000 BC and 4000 BC, and various forms of the faithful potato were domesticated around 3000 BC (Peru now boasts almost 4000 varieties!).

From 1000 to 300 BC, the Early Horizon or Chavín Period seen at Chavín de Huántar (which is the archaeological site near Huarez) saw widespread settled communities, plus the interchange of ideas, enhanced skills and cultural complexity, although the Chavín culture inexplicably disappeared around 300 BC. The next 500 years saw the rise and fall of the Salinar near Trujillo and the Paracas south of Lima, who produced some of the most exquisite textiles in the Americas.

Between AD 100 and AD 700, pottery, metalwork and textiles reached new heights of technological development, and the Moche built their massive pyramids near Trujillo (p872) and at Sipán near Chiclayo. It was also around this time that the Nazca sculpted their giant enigmatic lines in the southern desert (p820).

From about AD 600 to AD 1000 the first Andean expansionist empire emerged, and the influence of the Wari (Huari), from north of Ayacucho (p864), can still be seen throughout most of Peru.

During the next four centuries, several regional states thrived, including the Chimú, who built the city of Chan Chan near Trujillo, the Chachapoyas, who built the forested site of Kuélap, the Chancay and the Ica-Chincha culture. Several small and warlike highland groups lived near Lake Titicaca and left impressive, circular funerary towers like those at Sillustani.

Inca Empire & Spanish Conquest

Prior to 1430 the Inca ruled only the valley of Cuzco, but victory over local expansionists the Chankas in the 1430s marked the beginning of a rapid takeover. The Inca conquered and incorporated most of the area from southern Colombia to central Chile, and built scores of fabulous mountain-top citadels, including Machu Picchu itself. However, for all its greatness, the Inca empire existed for barely a century. Around 1525 a civil war broke out between followers of the Inca Huáscar, in Cuzco, and followers of his half-brother Atahualpa, in Quito.

Meanwhile, by 1526 Francisco Pizarro had headed south from Panama and discovered rich coastal settlements of the

MUST-SEE ANCIENT SITES

If you're ripe for ruins you've come to the right country.

■ **Machu Picchu** (p854) The world-famous mountaintop 'Lost City of the Inca'

■ **Nazca Lines** (p820) Ancient designs covering vast areas of the southern desert

■ **Chavín de Huántar** (p888) Go underground at this 3000-year-old site near Huaraz

■ **Chan Chan** (p875) Vast Chimú mud-brick capital stretching for kilometers around Trujillo

■ **Pisac** (p852) Imposing Inca citadel presiding over the Sacred Valley

■ **Sillustani** (p837) Dramatic hilltop funerary towers of the Colla culture near Puno

■ **Sacsayhuamán** (p850) Awesome Inca fortress in Cuzco and site of the festival of Inti Raymi

■ **Kuélap** (p892) Massive Chachapoyan site in the cloud forest; no crowds

■ **Sipán** (p878) Visit the Lord of Sipán's grave, and don't miss his new museum too

■ **Choquequirau** (p863) Newly rediscovered Inca city reached by several days hiking

Inca empire. After returning to Spain to court money and men for the conquest he returned, landing on the Ecuadorian coast, and marching overland toward Peru and the heart of the Inca empire, reaching Cajamarca in November 1532. Here he captured the northern Inca leader, Atahualpa, ransomed him for rooms filled with gold, but then murdered him anyway once he had cash in hand. Taking advantage of the chaos following the civil war, Pizarro was able to enter Cuzco as conqueror by 1533. Despite sporadic rebellions, the Inca empire was forced to retreat into the mountains and jungle, and never recovered its once glorious prestige and extent.

For more details on this period of history, see p839 and p854.

Colonial Peru

In 1535 Pizarro founded the capital city of Lima. A 30-year period of turmoil ensued, with the Inca resisting their conquerors, who were fighting among themselves for control of the rich colony. Pizarro was assassinated in 1541 by the son of conquistador Diego de Almagro, whom Pizarro had put to death in 1538. Manco Inca nearly regained control of the highlands in 1536, but by 1539 had retreated to his rainforest hideout at Vilcabamba, where he was killed in 1544. Inca Tupac Amaru also attempted to overthrow the Spaniards in 1572, but was defeated and executed.

The next 200 years were relatively peaceful. Lima became the major political, social and commercial center of the Andean nations, while Cuzco became a backwater. However, this peaceful period came to an abrupt end as the indigenous people were exploited as expendable laborers under the *encomienda* system (whereby settlers were granted a parcel of land and native inhabitants). This led to the 1780 uprising under the self-proclaimed ruler Inca Tupac Amaru II. This uprising was likewise quelled and its leaders cruelly executed.

Independence

By the early 1800s rebellion was stirring among the colonists due to high taxes imposed by Spain plus a desire to take control of the country's rich mineral deposits – beginning with the seemingly inauspicious guano (seabird droppings) used for fertilizer (see p816). Change came from two directions. José de San Martín liberated Argentina and Chile from Spain, and in 1821 he entered Lima and formally proclaimed independence. Meanwhile, Simón Bolívar had freed Venezuela, Colombia and Ecuador. San Martín and Bolívar met in Ecuador, and as a result of this mysterious one-to-one – the details of which are unknown – San Martín left Latin America altogether to live in France, and Bolívar continued into Peru. Two decisive battles were fought at Junín and Ayacucho in 1824, and the Spanish finally surrendered on January 22, 1826.

Peru also won a brief war with Spain in 1866 and lost a longer war with Chile (1879–83) over the nitrate-rich northern Atacama Desert. Chile annexed much of coastal southern Peru, but returned some areas in 1929. Only a decade later, Peru went to war with Ecuador over a border dispute. A 1942 treaty gave Peru the area north of the Río Marañón, but Ecuador disputed this and skirmishes occurred every few years. Only in 1998 did a peace treaty finally put an end to hostilities.

Modern Times

Politics in Peru are never boring. Coups and military dictatorships have characterized Peru's 20th-century government, despite periods of civilian rule. In the late 1980s, the country experienced severe economic and guerrilla problems, and demonstrations protesting the disastrous handling of the economy by then-president Alán García Pérez were an everyday occurrence. At one point, inflation even reached 10,000%! His 10 years of rule were also mirrored by the disruptive activities of Maoist organization Sendero Luminoso (Shining Path), which waged a guerrilla war resulting in the death or 'disappearance' of between 40,000 and 60,000 people, especially in the Central Andes. However, Sendero leaders were captured and imprisoned in 1992, ameliorating guerrilla problems.

In June 1990 Alberto Fujimori, the 52-year-old son of Japanese immigrants, was elected president. Strong, semi-dictatorial actions led to unprecedented improvements in the economy. The ensuing popular support propelled Fujimori to a second term in 1995 (only after he amended the constitution to allow himself to run again), but by late 1998 support was dwindling due to economic crisis.

In 2000 Fujimori again ran for office but came up 0.1% short of the 50% votes needed to win outright. His main challenger, the leftist Alejandro Toledo, claimed the elections had been rigged and refused to enter the scheduled runoff, which Fujimori promptly won.

However, in October 2000 a video was released showing Vladimiro Montesinos, Fujimori's hawkish head of intelligence, bribing a congressman, and Fujimori's 10-year presidency spiraled out of control. Fujimori ordered Montesinos' arrest, but the spymaster fled. Within days, 2600 so-called 'Vladivideos' were discovered, implicating key figures in money laundering and

government corruption. Fujimori claimed innocence, but then resigned during a state trip to Asia and stayed in Japan despite continuing extradition efforts. Montesinos was later captured and faced televised trials that gripped the nation in 2003.

Elections were held in 2001, and Toledo's highland-Indian heritage won through in a country where the majority of the population is of Indian or mixed-Indian lineage. He took over a country struggling to come to terms with its upheavals. By 2003 Peruvians were again facing increased unemployment, stagnant wages and a higher cost of living, and for the first time in almost a decade, the country was again plagued by strikes and demonstrations.

THE CULTURE
The National Psyche

Peruvians have been caught up in a political roller-coaster ride for decades, with public opinion leaping to and fro' in time with the rise and usually thunderous fall of each new president. Entirely unshakable, however, is the Peruvians' fierce pride in their heritage. But because Peru is such a prime destination for tourists, it has seen decades of well-off gringos splashing their cash around, and many shoestringers may feel themselves caught up in an 'us and them' mentality where foreigners equal profit potential. Don't let this superficial shell blind you to what are a supremely warm and generous people. Peruvians work on the principle that it only takes a second to make a friend and that you can never have too many, and hospitality is more than commonplace – it's a way of life.

Lifestyle

Just as Peru's geography varies hugely between desert, sierra and jungle, so does the lifestyle and attitude of its inhabitants. For example, a poor *campesino* (peasant practicing subsistence agriculture) family that scratches out a living cultivating scraps of infertile ground in a remote highland hamlet lives very differently from a city slicker in Lima with a holiday home on the coast, or a hunter-gatherer Amazonian tribe isolated from the outside world.

That said, even within a single city the gaps between rich and poor can be astounding. The introduction of TV to the impoverished highlands in the 1950s fueled a first wave of migration to the coast in pursuit of the privileged lives they saw on their screens. The vast influx of migrants that followed spawned *pueblos jovenes* (young towns) that surround Lima, many of which still lack electricity, water and adequate sanitation.

Indeed 50% of the Peruvian population lives below the poverty line; jobs are scarce and often pay a pittance. However, entrepreneurial energy is exceptionally strong. Many of the jobless work as *ambulantes* (street vendors), selling anything from chocolates to clothespins in the frenetic streets, while teachers and policemen top up their public-sector pay by driving taxis in their free time.

People

Peru is essentially a society split between the mainly white and *mestizo* middle and upper classes, and the mostly poor Indian *campesinos*. Over half of Peru's 27 million inhabitants are concentrated in the narrow coastal desert, while the other half are mostly to be found in the highlands. These highlanders are mostly *campesinos,* many of whom live at or below poverty levels. In contrast, more than 60% of Peru lies east of the Andes in the Amazon Basin, but only 6% of the population lives there.

About 45% of Peru's population is indigenous and 37% *mestizo*. Most *indígenas* are Quechua-speaking highlanders, though a few speak Aymara in the Lake Titicaca region. About 15% of the population is white and 3% are black or of Asian descent. There is a sizeable community of Japanese and Chinese Peruvians that immigrated at the turn of the century to set up trading enterprises. Alberto Fujimori (president 1990–2000) is of Japanese descent and the many *chifas* (Chinese restaurants) are testimony to the widespread Chinese presence.

ARTS

For details of Andean crafts, see p908.

Architecture

While the Inca stonework of Machu Picchu is Peru's star attraction, many other pre-Columbian cultures have left us with magnificent examples of their architecture. Colonial architecture is well represented by the many imposing cathedrals, churches, monasteries and convents built during the 16th, 17th and 18th centuries, with both interiors and exteriors equally ornate.

Literature

Peru's most famous novelist is the internationally recognized Mario Vargas Llosa (1936–), who ran for president in 1990. His complex novels, including *The Time of the Hero,* delve deeply into Peruvian society, politics and culture. César Vallejo (1892–1938), considered Peru's greatest poet, wrote *Trilce,* a book of 77 avant-garde poems, which some critics say is one of the best books of poetry ever written in Spanish.

Two writers noted for their portrayals of indigenous communities are José María Arguedas (1911–69) and Ciro Alegría (1909–67), while women writers can be read in *Fire From the Andes: Short Fiction by Women from Bolivia, Ecuador and Peru.*

A recent arrival on the literary scene is Sergio Bambarén (1960–), who lived in the USA and Australia before returning to Lima. His self-published *The Dolphin – Story of a Dreamer* became a bestseller.

Music & Dance

ANDEAN

Haunting pre-Columbian music is inescapable in the highlands. It features wind and percussion instruments, some of which date back as far as 5000 BC. Called *música folklórica,* traditional Andean music is heard all over Peru, but bars that specifically cater to it are called *peñas.*

The most representative wind instruments are the *quena* and the *zampoña.* The *quena* (or *kena*) is a flute, usually made of bamboo and of varying lengths depending on the pitch desired. The *zampoña,* or *siku* in Quechua, is a set of panpipes with two rows of bamboo canes. They come in sizes ranging from the tiny, high-pitched *chuli* to the meter-long, bass *toyo.*

Percussion instruments include the inevitable drum *(bombo),* usually made from a hollowed-out segment of a cedar, walnut or other tree and using stretched goatskin for the head. *Shajshas* (rattles) are made of polished goat hooves.

Today's *música folklórica* groups also use stringed instruments adapted from Spanish instruments; the most typical is the *charango,* a tiny, five-stringed guitar with a resonance box traditionally made of an armadillo shell.

PERU

COASTAL

In contrast with its Andean counterpart, sassy *música criolla* (coastal music) has its roots in Spain and Africa. Its main instruments are guitars and *cajón*, a wooden box on which the player sits and pounds out a rhythm. The *cajón* is attributed to African slaves brought to Peru by the Spanish. The most popular coastal dance is the *marinera*, a romantic routine employing much waving of handkerchiefs. *Marinera* competitions are frequent in coastal Peru, especially in Trujillo. Afro-Peruvian music has also enjoyed a comeback, particularly around Chincha (see p814). A great introductory compilation is *Afro-Peruvian Classics: The Soul of Black Peru* (LuakaBop), which is headlined by the incomparable Susan Baca – one of the only Afro-Peruvian singers to have toured Europe and North America.

MODERN

Also popular in Peru is the omnipresent Caribbean salsa, as well as *cumbia* and *chicha*, both originally from Colombia. All three can be enjoyed in the *salsotecas* (salsa clubs), which cram in hundreds of Peruvians for all-night dance-fests. Deriving from *cumbia* is the Peruvian *tecno cumbia* of which prime exponents were Euforia and Rosy War, while newer bands include Agua Marina and Armonía 10. In the Andes, *chicha* is a cheerful modern fusion music combining traditional panpipes with electronic percussion and guitars. Peruvian rock is represented by groups such as '80s band Arena Hash and its bassist Christian Meier, who also pursued a solo career, and more recently, Aliados, Dolores Delirio and the singer Pedro Suárez Vertiz.

Painting & Sculpture

Much of Peru's religious art was created by indigenous artists under strong colonial influence. This unique cross-pollination gave rise to the *escuela cuzqueña* (Cuzco school) of art – a syncretic blend of Spanish and indigenous sensibilities. *Cuzqueña* canvases are on display in many of Lima's museums and highland churches.

SPORT

Fútbol (soccer) inspires passionate fanaticism in Peru, though its squad hasn't qualified for the World Cup since 1982. The big-boy teams are mostly from Lima, and the traditional *clásico* (classic) pitches Alianza Lima against rivals Universitario (La U). The soccer season is late March to November.

Bloodthirsty bullfighting is also part of the national culture. The Lima season is October to early December and attracts top international talent (see p812). In remote Andean hamlets, condors are tied to the back of the bull – an expression of indigenous solidarity against the Spanish conquerors.

RELIGION

More than 90% of Peruvians are declared Roman Catholics, and Catholicism is the official religion. However, while indigenous Peruvians are outwardly Catholic, they often combine elements of their traditional beliefs.

ENVIRONMENT
The Land

The third-largest country in South America, Peru has three distinctive regions – a narrow coastal belt, the wide Andean mountains and the Amazon rainforest. The coastal strip is mainly desert, punctuated by cities and rivers from the Andes forming about 40 agricultural oases. The country's best highway, the Carretera Panamericana, also slices through coastal Peru from border to border.

The Andes rise rapidly from the coast to spectacular heights of up to 6000m just 100km inland. Most of Peru's Andes lie between 3000m and 4000m, with jagged ranges separated by deep, vertiginous canyons. Huascarán (6768m) is Peru's highest mountain.

The eastern Andes get more rainfall than the dry western slopes and so are covered in cloud forest, which slips and slides it way down to merge with the rainforest of the Amazon Basin.

Wildlife

With long coastal deserts, glaciated mountain ranges, vast tropical rainforests and almost every imaginable habitat in between, Peru hosts one of the world's most varied menageries of wildlife.

Starting with birds: Peru has 1700 species – more than any country except Brazil, and twice as many as any one of the continents of North America, Europe or Australia.

Travel down to the Islas Ballestas (Ballestas Islands) (p816) and you'll spot thousands of cormorants and boobies, gulls galore, and a few flamingoes and penguins thrown in to boot.

Then head into the highlands to see the Andean gull (just don't call it a sea-gull), torrent ducks with a taste for whitewater, a gaggle of Andean geese and, of course, the majestic Andean condor, weighing as much as 10kg. Swoop down towards the Amazon and with luck you'll spot all the iconic tropical birds – parrots, macaws, toucans and an assortment of thousands more.

But for many, it is the diminutive hummingbird that steals the show, with about 120 species recorded native to Peru, each with a fittingly extravagant name, such as 'spangled coquette,' or 'amethyst-throated sunangel.'

Turning to mammals: Peru's highlands are home to all four South American camelids: llama, alpaca, guanaco and vicuña. The Amazon is also home to prolific plant life and mammals, including over 20 species of monkeys, while cloud forests rimming the Amazon are also the haunts of jaguars, tapirs and the endangered spectacled bear. Other Amazonian creatures include frogs, reptiles, fish and insects galore. Snakes? Don't panic. Many species live here, but they're mostly human-shy.

National Parks

In 2003 an impressive 12.74% of the country contained 56 protected areas. Following are the principle parks and other top wildlife-spotting destinations:

Parque Nacional Manu (p862) Remote jungle; your best chance to see jaguars, tapirs and myriad monkeys
Reserva Nacional Paracas (p816) Coastal reserve with abundant boobies, flamingoes and sea lions
Reserva Nacional Pacaya-Samiria (p896) Little-known rainforest reserve
Parque Nacional Huascarán (p883) Condors, giant Puya raimondii plants, vicuña and vizcachas
Puerto Maldonado (p900) Capybara sightings highly likely while cruising to a lowland macaw lick
Cruz del Condor (p832) The surest place to see Andean condors
Iquitos Area (p896) Canopy Walkways, jungle lodges and river cruises

Environmental Issues

Farming, grazing and logging all cause serious environmental problems in Peru.

While rainforest deforestation has caught international attention, deforestation and overgrazing in the highlands is also acute, causing highland soil to deteriorate and get blown or washed away. This also leads to decreased water quality, particularly in the Amazon Basin, where silt-laden water is unable to support microorganisms at the base of the food chain.

Other water-related problems are pollution from mine tailings in the highlands and from industrial waste and sewage along the coast. Because of sewage contamination, some coastal beaches have been declared unfit for swimming and Peru's rich marine resources are threatened.

Protected areas also lack infrastructure and are still subject to illegal hunting, fishing, logging or mining. The government simply doesn't have the money to patrol the parks, though various international agencies contribute money and resources to assist conservation and local projects.

TRANSPORT

GETTING THERE & AWAY
Air

Lima's Aeropuerto Internacional Jorge Chávez is the main hub for flights to Andean countries, Europe and North America. There is one additional international connection from Cuzco to La Paz in Bolivia. June to September is the high season; discount fares may be available in other months.

Lima's international departure tax is US$28, payable in dollars or nuevos soles when you check in. Other airports charge US$10 international airport tax. Tickets bought in Peru are subject to 18% tax.

Students with international student ID cards and anyone under 26 can get discounts with most airlines. Following are some sample one-way fares from Peru to other South American countries:

Bolivia Lloyd Aéreo Boliviano (LAB) Airlines has daily flights between La Paz and Lima (US$160), and several weekly flights from Santa Cruz to Lima (US$220 round trip).
Brazil There are several weekly flights between Rio de Janeiro, São Paulo and Lima (US$800) on Varig.
Chile LanChile has daily flights between Santiago and Lima (from US$260 round trip).

PERU

Colombia There are daily flights from Bogotá to Lima (US$220) with Alianza Summa (Aces) and other airlines.
Ecuador TACA flies to Lima from Quito and Guayaquil (US$250 round trip).

Boat

Boats ply the Amazon from Iquitos (p899) to Leticia, Colombia (US$50, 12 hours) or Tabatinga, Brazil (US$15 to US$20, two to three days). It's also possible, but difficult, to reach Bolivia by river from Puerto Maldonado (p902).

Bus & Car

Border crossing is straightforward as long as your passport is valid for at least six months. The major border crossings are Tacna to Chile (p824) and Tumbes (p882) or La Tina (p880) to Ecuador. Bolivia is normally reached via Yunguyo (p837) or Desaguadero (p837). Brazil is reached (not easily) via Iñapari (p902).

GETTING AROUND

When traveling, keep your passport with you, not packed in your luggage. Buses may go through police checkpoints. A US$3.50 domestic departure tax is charged on local flights from most airports. Lima charges US$5.

Air

Domestic flights are competitively priced. **Aero Continente/Aviandina** (www.aerocontinente.com in Spanish) and **LanPeru** (www.lanperu.com) serve most of the major and some minor domestic routes. **TANS** (www.tans.com.pe) is good for Cuzco and the jungle cities. Connecting flights between smaller cities are becoming less common. Small airlines like **AeroCóndor** (www.aerocondor.com.pe) provide important links to smaller Andean highland towns, such as Ayacucho, Andahuaylas, Cajamarca and Trujillo. Offices are listed under the appropriate cities.

Flights are often late. Morning flights are more likely to be on time, but by afternoon schedules fall an hour or more behind. Show up at least an hour early for all domestic flights

One-way flights are half the cost of round-trip flights, but prices can vary as much as 35% for seats on the same flight. Early bookers get cheaper seats. Lima–Cuzco fares cost US$59 to US$109 one way. Flights are often fully booked during holiday periods. *Confirm and reconfirm* 72 and 24 hours in advance; airlines are notorious for bumping passengers off flights. An 18% tax is charged on domestic fares. On internal flights, 20kg of checked luggage is allowed.

A useful air schedule website is www.traficoperu.com.

Boat

Small motorboats that take about 20 passengers go from Puno to Lake Titicaca's islands. There are departures every day and the costs are low; see p838.

In Peru's eastern lowlands, dugout canoes, usually powered by an outboard engine, act as water buses on the smaller rivers. Where the rivers widen, larger cargo boats are normally available. This is the classic way to travel down the Amazon – swinging in your hammock aboard a banana boat piloted by a grizzled old captain who knows the waters better than the back of his hand. You can travel from Pucallpa or Yurimaguas to Iquitos, where you change boats to the Brazilian border, and on to the mouth of the Amazon. The boats are small but have two or more decks. The lower deck is for cargo, the upper for passengers and crew. Bring a hammock. Food provided is basic and you may want to bring some of your own.

To get a passage, go down to the docks and ask for a boat going to your destination. Arrange this with the captain (nobody else). Departure time depends, more often than not, on filling up the hold. Sometimes you can sleep on the boat while waiting for departure, thus saving on hotel bills.

Bus

Peru's buses are cheap and go just about everywhere, except the deep jungle and Machu Picchu. Less-traveled routes are served by ramshackle old chicken buses, which see long-legged travelers tucking knees under chins, but popular destinations also have fast, luxury services (called *Imperial* or similar), charging 30% to 100% more than *económico* (economy) buses. Some companies offer *bus-camas* (bed buses), which have seats that almost fully recline. Students with ISIC cards may be able to get a 10% discount.

Many cities now have central bus terminals, while others have bus companies clustered around a few city blocks or scattered all over town. It's best to buy your ticket in advance. Schedules and fares change frequently and vary from company to company. Occasionally buses don't leave from the ticket office – just ask.

Long-distance buses generally stop for meals, though toilet stops are highly unpredictable. Many companies have their own restaurants in the middle of nowhere, so you have to eat there or bring your own food.

At low travel periods, some companies offer discounted fares; conversely, fares can double around holidays such as Christmas, Easter or Independence Day (July 28), when tickets may be sold out several days ahead of time. Buses can be much delayed during the rainy season due to landslides and bad road conditions. It can get freezing cold on night buses in the highlands, so dress warmly.

Car & Motorcycle

With the exception of the Panamericana Hwy and one or two new roads leading inland from the coast, road conditions are generally poor, distances are great and rental cars are not always in the best condition. That said, there is nothing to stop you from driving in Peru other than the expense (US$60 to US$80 per day) of rental cars. Importing your car or motorcycle temporarily is no big hassle and an expensive *carnet de passage* is not required. Customs officers at the border issue a temporary import license, which you simply display on your windscreen. Keep in mind that road signage is sometimes deficient and most major roads are also toll roads: US$1 to US$2 for every 100km or so. Renting a taxi for long-distance trips costs little more than renting a car.

Local motorcycle rental is an option mainly in jungle towns, and there are a few lone outfitters in Cuzco.

Local Transport

Taxis have no meters, so ask the going rate in advance and haggle; drivers often double or triple the standard rate for unsuspecting foreigners. For a short run in Lima, the fare is about US$1.50; in other cities, US$1 or under. Unregulated taxis are recognizable by fluorescent 'TAXI' stickers on the windshield, while safer, but more expensive,

authorized taxis are called for by telephone in all major cities.

Colectivos – a cross between a bus and a taxi – and trucks (in the Amazon) run between various local and not-so-local destinations.

Train

Frequent trains link Cuzco with Machu Picchu (see p849), and there is an unpredictable, expensive thrice-weekly service to Juliaca and Puno on Lake Titicaca. The Puno/Juliaca–Arequipa route has been discontinued. Another train line runs between the Central Andean towns of Huancayo and Huancavelica (see p866 and p869).

Perurail (reservas@perurail.com) operates much of the train network. You can view its current timetables and passenger fares on the Web at www.perurail.com.

LIMA

For fans of *Paddington Bear*, Lima in 'darkest Peru' may conjure up images of an exotic city in the heart of a tropical jungle, but that couldn't be further from the bustling reality of this modern metropolis. Sprawled untidily on the coastal desert, Lima was founded and dubbed the City of Kings by Francisco Pizarro in 1535, on the Catholic feast of Epiphany, or the Day of the Kings. The capital, home to 7,7000,000 people, now houses almost a third of Peru's inhabitants and the influx of rural poor continues to spawn extensive *pueblos jovenes* (young towns) that surround the capital.

It's inevitable that the ensuing overpopulation problems have earned Lima a hardened reputation as a polluted, frenetic and dangerous city. But to submit to such one-sided caricatures undermines its position as an ever-evolving city filled with fascinating contrasts and nuances that in no time can transport you from the waning splendor of its colonial architecture to pre-Inca pyramids and ultramodern shopping malls.

Lima's climate also echoes its contrasting faces: from April to December, a melancholy coastal fog *(garúa)* blankets the city's skyline, but during the coastal summer the sun breaks through and the high-spirited *limeños* (people from Lima) make a break for the nearby beaches. Indeed, coastal

PERU

CENTRAL LIMA

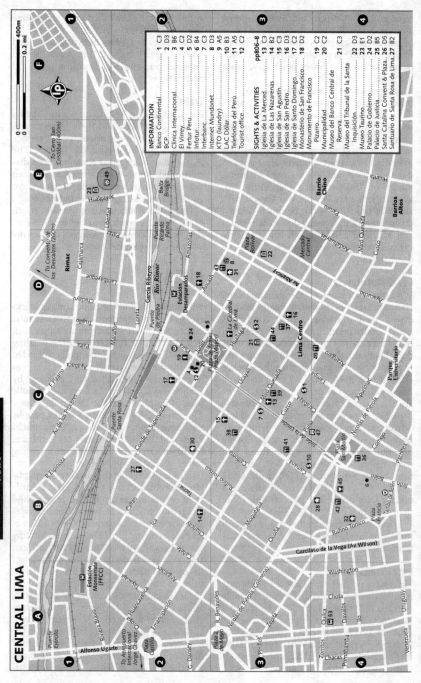

INFORMATION			
Banco Continental	1	C3	
BCP	2	D3	
Clínica Internacional	3	B6	
El Virrey	4	C2	
Fertur Perú	5	D2	
Infotur	6	B4	
Interbanc	7	C3	
Internet Mundonet	8	D3	
KTO (laundry)	9	A5	
LAC Dólar	10	B3	
Telefónica del Perú	11	A5	
Tourist office	12	C2	

SIGHTS & ACTIVITIES			pp806–8
Iglesia de La Merced	13	C3	
Iglesia de Las Nazarenas	14	B2	
Iglesia de San Agustín	15	C3	
Iglesia de San Pedro	16	D3	
Iglesia de Santo Domingo	17	C2	
Monasterio de San Francisco	18	D2	
Monumento de Francisco			
Pizarro	19	C2	
Municipalidad	20	C2	
Museo del Banco Central de			
Reserva	21	C3	
Museo del Tribunal de la Santa			
Inquisición	22	D3	
Museo Taurino	23	E1	
Palacio de Gobierno	24	D2	
Palacio de Justicia	25	B5	
Santa Catalina Convent & Plaza	26	D5	
Santuario de Santa Rosa de Lima	27	B2	

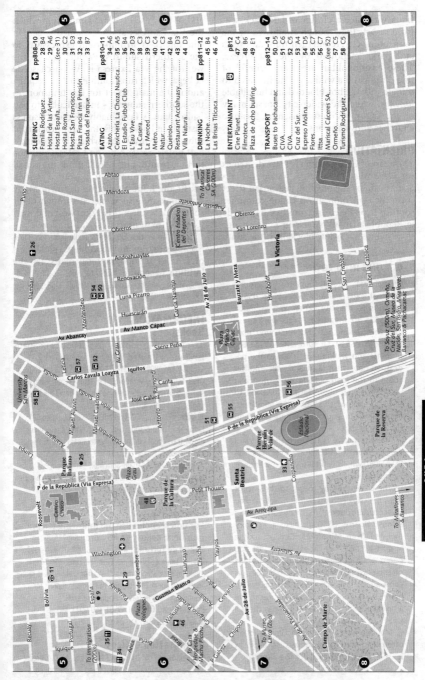

SLEEPING	pp808-10
Familia Rodríguez	28 B4
Hostal de las Artes	29 A6
Hostal España	(see 31)
Hostal Roma	30 C2
Hostal San Francisco	31 D3
Plaza Francia Inn Pensión	32 B4
Posada del Parque	33 B7

EATING	pp810-11
Azato	34 A6
Cevichería La Choza Náutica	35 A5
El Estadio Fútbol Club	36 B4
L'Eau Vive	37 D3
La Casera	38 C3
La Merced	39 C3
Metro	40 C4
Natur	41 C3
Queirolo	42 B4
Restaurant Acchahuasy	43 D3
Villa Natura	44 D3

DRINKING	pp811-12
La Noche	45 B4
Las Brisas Titicaca	46 A6

ENTERTAINMENT	p812
Cine Planet	47 C4
Filmoteca	48 B6
Plaza de Acho bullring	49 E1

TRANSPORT	pp812-14
Buses to Pachacamac	50 D5
CIVA	51 C6
CIVA	52 C5
Cruz del Sur	53 A4
Expreso Molina	54 D5
Flores	55 C7
Ittsa	56 C7
Mariscal Cáceres SA	(see 52)
Ormeño	57 C5
Turismo Rodríguez	58 C5

PERU

Lima was once a cluster of laid-back sea-front resorts that, though swallowed by the burgeoning city, retain their tranquil streets and parks mellowed by the sea breeze. These cosmopolitan areas are brimful of fine dining and a wild nightlife in which to mingle with the hot-blooded and hospitable *limeños*, while the wider city boasts many of the country's best museums, historic churches and mansions.

ORIENTATION

The heart of Central Lima is Plaza de Armas (or Plaza Mayor), which is linked to Plaza San Martín by the bustling pedestrian street Jirón (de la) Unión. Jirón Unión continues south as Jirón Belén and runs to the Paseo de la República (many streets in Lima change their names every few blocks). At the south end of the Paseo is Plaza Grau, from which the Vía Expresa, also nicknamed *el zanjón* (the ditch), is an important expressway to the southern suburbs. Parallel and to the west of the Vía Expresa is Av Garcilaso de la Vega, which runs south into Av Arequipa and is the main street for bus transport to the southern suburbs – in particular, to San Isidro, Lima's fashionably elegant business district, and below this, the ritzy beachfront suburb of Miraflores, which hosts Lima's best hotels, restaurants and cafés. Continue further south and you'll find the small cliff-top community of Barranco, which boasts the hottest nightlife in town. Many museums are also scattered through other suburbs. The airport is 12km west of downtown or 16km northwest of Miraflores.

South American Explorers (Calle Puira 135, Miraflores) has hiking and road maps, plus maps of Lima. For topographical maps, try the **Instituto Geográfico Nacional** (IGN; ☎ 01-475-9960; ventaign@ignperu.gob.pe; Aramburu 1198, Surquillo; 🕙 9am-4pm Mon-Fri).

INFORMATION
Bookshops

The following bookshops sell books in Spanish (and a limited number in English).

Crisol (Map p809; ☎ 01-221-1010; Av Santa Cruz 816, Óvalo Gutuiérrez, Miraflores; 🕙 10am-11pm) A big and showy bookshop, with some novels and travel guides in English and French.

El Virrey (Map pp802-3; ☎ 01-440-0607; Dasso 141, Lima; 🕙 10am-6:30pm Mon-Sat) A limited selection of glossy travel books in the city center near Plaza de Armas.

Zeta Books Miraflores (Map p809; ☎ 01-446-5139; Av Espinar 219; 🕙 10am-8pm Mon-Sat); Miraflores (Larcomar shopping mall) A small but helpful shop, with a varied foreign-language selection.

Emergency

For emergencies use the following telephone numbers: **police** (☎ 105); **fire** (☎ 116).

Policía de Turismo (Map pp802-3; ☎ 01-424-2053; Pasaje Tambo de Belén 106, Pachitea, Lima; 🕙 24 hr) Advice and assistance on anything from robberies to rabies. Some staff speak English, and will provide reports for insurance claims or traveler's check refunds.

Policía Head Office (☎ 01-460-0921; Moore 268, Magdalena del Mar; 🕙 24 hr)

Immigration Offices

Migraciónes (☎ 01-330-4144; Av España 734, Breña; 🕙 8am-1pm Mon-Fri) Go first thing in the morning if

---

you want to get your tourist card extension (US$27) on the same day. You need your passport and immigration slip. You may be asked to show a ticket out of the country, or prove that you have the sufficient funds.

Internet Access

Many hotels have Internet access, and fast public access for about US$0.60 an hour is available. Following are some Internet cafés:

Dragon Fans Internet (Map p809; Pasaje Tarata 230, Miraflores; ☷ 24 hr)

Full Screen Internet (Map p809; Angamos Oeste 401, Miraflores)

Internet Mundonet (Map pp802-3; Ancash 105, Lima)

Telefónica del Peru (Map p809; Alfredo Benavides 4th block, Miraflores; ☷ 24hr)

Laundry

KTO (Map pp802-3; España 481, Lima; less than 5kg US$1.40 per kg, over 5kg US$1 per kg; ☷ 7am-8pm Mon-Sat)

Lavandaría 40 minutos (Map p809; Av Espinar 154, Miraflores; 4kg US$4.20; ☷ 8am-8pm Mon-Sat, 9am-1pm Sun)

Servirap (Map p809; cnr Schell & Grimaldo del Solar, Miraflores; US$2.25 per kg; ☷ 8am-10pm Mon-Sat, 9am-6pm Sun) Also has self-service.

Medical Services

Clínica Anglo-American (☎ 01-221-3656; 3rd block Salazar, San Isidro; consultation up to US$60) Stocks yellow-fever vaccines (US$17) .

Clínica Internacional (Map pp802-3; ☎ 01-433-4306; Washington 1471 & 9 de Diciembre, Lima; consultation US$17-35)

Clínica San Borja (☎ 01-475-4000; Av Guardia Civil 337, San Borja)

Other medical options:

Jorge Bazan (☎ 01-9735-2668; jrbazanj@yahoo .com) An English-speaking backpacker medic recommended by readers. He doesn't have rooms, but makes housecalls.

Dr Victor Aste (☎ /fax 01-421-9169; Antero Aspillaga 415, office 101, San Isidro) Well-recommended, English-speaking dentist.

The following pharmacies are modern and well stocked. They often deliver free of charge.

Botica Fasa (Map p809; ☎ 01-619-0000; cnr Av José Larco & Av Ricardo Palma, Miraflores; ☷ 24hr)

Superfarma (Map p809; ☎ 01-440-9000; Av Armendariz 215, Miraflores; ☷ 24 hr)

Money

If you've got plastic in your pocket, you'll find accommodating ATMs throughout Lima. Opening hours in town are generally 9am to 6pm Monday to Friday and 9am to 1pm Saturday. Banks at the airport are open late; one bank in the international arrivals area is open 24 hours.

American Express Miraflores (☎ 01-221-8204; amexcard@travex.com.pe; Santa Cruz 621, Miraflores) Replaces lost AmEx traveler's checks.

Banco Continental Lima (Map pp802-3; Cuzco 286, Lima); Miraflores (Map p809; cnr Av José Larco & Tarata, Miraflores) ATMs take Visa/MasterCard.

Banco Wiese Miraflores (Map p809; Av José Larco 1123, Miraflores) MasterCard representative, and changes AmEx and Citicorp traveler's checks.

BCP (Banco de Crédito) Miraflores (Map p809; Av José Pardo 491, Miraflores); Miraflores (Map p809; cnr Av José Larco & José Gonzales, Miraflores); Miraflores (Map p809; cnr Av José Larco & Schell, Miraflores); Lima (Map pp802-3; Lampa 499, Lima) 24-hr Visa/Plus ATMs and cash advances on Visa. Also changes AmEx, Citicorp and Visa traveler's checks.

Interbanc Miraflores (Map p809; Av José Pardo 413, Miraflores); Miraflores (Map p809; Av José Larco 690, Miraflores); Lima (Map pp802-3; Jirón de la Unión 600, Lima) ATMs with Cirrus/MasterCard/Plus/Visa.

LAC Dólar Lima (Map pp802-3; ☎ 01-428-8127; Camina 779, Lima); Miraflores (Map p809; ☎ 01-242-4069; Av de la Paz 211, Miraflores) A reliable *casa de cambio* that will deliver if you phone ahead with traveler's check numbers.

Other *casas de cambio* (authorized money-exchange office) can be found downtown on Ocean and Camina, as well as along Av José Larco in Miraflores.

Post

Main post office (Map pp802-3; ☎ 01-427-9370; Pasaje Piura, Lima; ☷ 8:15am-8:15pm Mon-Fri, 9am-1:30pm Sat, 8am-4pm Sun) Mail sent to Poste Restante, Correos Central, Lima, can be collected here, though it is not 100% reliable. Bring identification.

Miraflores post office (Map p809; ☎ 01-445-0697; Av Petit Thouars 5201)

DHL (☎ 01-422-5232; Los Castaños 225, San Isidro)

South American Explorers

South American Explorers (Map p809; ☎ 01-445-3306; www.saexplorers.org; Calle Piura 135, Miraflores; ☷ 9:30am-5pm Mon-Fri, 9:30am-8pm Wed, 9:30am-1pm Sat) The clubhouse is just off the 49th block of Arequipa. The club is a member-supported, nonprofit organization that functions primarily as an information center for travelers.

PERU

Annual membership costs US$50 per person (US$80 for a couple), which includes full use of clubhouse facilities and four issues of its quarterly magazine. It also has a members-only book exchange. Members can have their mail held at the clubhouse.

Telephone & Fax
Telefónica del Peru has pay phones on almost every street corner in Lima (many accept only telephone cards, see p908 for more details). There are telephone offices that also have fax services in **Miraflores** (Benavides 4th block; ☪ 24 hr) and **Lima** (Bolivia 347; ☎ 7am-11pm).

Tourist Offices
The *Peru Guide* is a free tourist booklet published monthly that can be found at hotels and tourist spots in Lima. The South American Explorers Club also has tourist information.

iPeru Aeropuerto (☎ 01-574-8000; iperulimaapto@prom peru.gob.pe; Aeropuerto Internacional Jorge Chávez); Miraflores (Map p809; ☎ 01-445-9400; Larcomar; ☪ noon-8pm) Only a tiny office in the shopping mall, but useful on weekends; San Isidro (☎ 01-421-1627; iperulima@ promperu.gob.pe; Jorge Basadre 610; ☪ 8:30am-6:30pm Mon-Fri) This office combines services of the tourist protection agency (INDECOPI) and the information office PromPeru. It dispenses maps and useful advice, as well as dealing with tourist complaints.

Tourist office (Map pp802-3; ☎ 01-427-6080 ex 222-83; Pasaje de los Escribanos 145, Lima; ☪ 9am-6pm Mon-Fri, 11am-3pm Sat & Sun) Offers limited information.

SIGHTS
Museums
Museum hours are often shortened drastically from January to March, when it is best to go in the morning. Photography is usually not allowed.

The dominating concrete block of **Museo de la Nación** (☎ 01-476-9878; Javier Prado Este 2466, San Borja; adult/student US$2/1, special shows US$3.30; ☪ 9am-5pm Tue-Sun) is a state-run museum and the best place in the country to get your head around Peru's myriad pre-historic civilizations. It's great value. A taxi there from Miraflores will cost about US$1.40.

Museo Larco (☎ 01-461-1312; webmaster@museo larco.org; Bolívar 1515, Pueblo Libre; adult/student US$6/3; ☪ 9am-6pm) contains one of world's most impressive collections of ceramics, stacked high to the ceilings. There are approximately 55,000 pots here, as well as exhibits of gold and silver work, textiles made from feathers and a Paracas weaving that contains 398 threads to a linear inch – a world record. But many tourists are lured here simply by the infamous collection of pre-Columbian erotic pots, illustrating, with remarkable explicitness, the sexual practices of ancient Peruvian men, women, animals and skeletons in all combinations of the above. Catch a bus marked 'Todo Bolivar' from Arequipa in Miraflores to its 15th block.

The **Museo del Tribunal de la Santa Inquisición** (Map pp802-3; ☎ 01-311-7801; Junín 548, Lima; admission free; ☪ 9am-1pm & 2:30-5pm Mon-Fri) is in the building used by the Spanish Inquisition from 1570 to 1820. Visitors can explore the basement where prisoners were tortured, and there's a ghoulish waxwork exhibit of life-size unfortunates on the rack or having

---

PACHACAMAC

This sprawling, desert complex of palaces and temple-pyramids is the closest major archaeological site to Lima, 31km south of the city. **Pachacamac** (☎ 01-430-0168; http://wpro.com/pachacamac; adult/child/student US$1.40/0.30/0.60; ☪ 9am-5pm Mon-Fri) predates the Incas by 1000 years, and each sand-blasted palace and temple has its own story to tell from a different culture and historical period. The name Pachacamac comes from the powerful Wari god, whose wooden two-faced image can be seen in the on-site museum. Most of the buildings are now little more than walls of piled rubble, except for the huge temple-pyramids and one of the Inca complexes, the Mamacuña (House of the Chosen Women), which have been excavated and reconstructed.

A thorough visit of this extensive site takes several hours, following a dirt road leading from site to site. Guided tours from Lima start at US$20 per person. Going solo? Catch a minibus signed 'Pachacamac' from the corner of Ayacucho and Grau in central Lima (US$0.60, 45 minutes, leaves every 15 minutes). From Miraflores, catch a taxi to Angamos at the Panamericana, also known as the Primavera Bridge (US$1.20), then take the bus signed 'Pachacamac/Lurin' (US$0.30, 25 minutes). In both cases, tell the driver to let you off near the *ruinas* or you'll end up at Pachacamac village, 1km beyond the entrance.

their feet roasted. Student guides give tours in Spanish and English: tips are expected.

The now-notorious **Museo de Oro del Perú** (☎ 01-345-1292; Alonso de Molina 1100, Monterrico; adult/child US$8.50/4.20; ☾ 11:30am-7pm) was at the top of Lima's must-see list until 2001, when it was rocked by a scandal that claimed large numbers of the museum's gold collection were fakes. The thousands of remaining gold pieces range from gold-encrusted ponchos to huge earrings that make your ears ache just looking at them. Upstairs, the Arms Museum has a mammoth collection of ancient and bizarre firearms. A taxi from Miraflores costs US$2 to US$2.50.

Religious Buildings

Lima's many churches, monasteries and convents are a welcome break from the city's incessant hustle and bustle, though they are often closed for restoration or because the caretaker fancies an extended lunch.

The original **Catedral de Lima** (Map pp802-3; ☎ 01-427-9647; Plaza de Armas; adult/child US$1.40/1; ☾ 9am-4:30pm Mon-Fri, 10am-4:30pm Sat) was built on the southeastern side of the Plaza de Armas in 1555, but has been destroyed by earthquakes and rebuilt several times, most recently in 1746. Look for the coffin of Francisco Pizarro in the mosaic-covered chapel to the right of the main door. A debate over the authenticity of the remains raged for years after a mysterious body with multiple stab wounds and a disembodied head were unearthed in the crypt in the late 1970s. After a battery of tests and speculation, the authorities concluded that the remains previously on display was an unknown church official and the body from the crypt was indeed Pizarro's, and was transferred to the chapel (where the head is kept in a separate casket). Also of interest are the beautifully carved choir and the small religious museum at the back of the cathedral.

The **Monasterio de San Francisco** (Map pp802-3; cnr Lampa & Ancash, Lima; adult/student US$1.40/0.75; ☾ 9:30am-5:30pm) is famous for its catacombs and remarkable library, which has thousands of antique texts, some dating back to the Spanish conquest. The church is one of the best-preserved of Lima's early colonial churches, and much of it has been restored to its original baroque style with Moorish influence. Admission includes a 45-minute guided tour in English or Spanish. The underground catacombs are the site of an estimated 70,000 burials; the faint-hearted may find the bone-filled crypts unnerving – if only for the conservationists' decision to rearrange skulls and femurs into pretty patterns.

The **Iglesia de Santo Domingo** (Map pp802-3; ☎ 01-427-6793; cnr Camaná & Conde de Superunda, Lima; admission US$1; ☾ 9am-12:30pm & 3-6pm Mon-Sat, 9am-1pm Sun) was begun in 1540 and finished in 1599, and contains the tombs of Santa Rosa and San Martín de Porres (the Americas' first black saint).

Plazas

The oldest part of **Plaza de Armas** (Plaza Mayor) is the central bronze fountain, erected in 1650. The exquisitely balconied Palacio Arzobispal, to the left of the cathedral, dates from around 1924, as does the **Palacio de Gobierno**, on the northeastern flank. The changing of the guard takes place at 11:45am. On the corner of the plaza, opposite the cathedral, there is a statue of Francisco Pizarro on horseback. This statue once stood in the center of the plaza, but the clergy took a dim view of the horse's rear end facing the cathedral, so the statue was moved to its present position with its backside safely averted.

Five blocks of the pedestrian mall **Jirón Unión** connect Plaza San Martín with the Plaza de Armas, packed with a multitude of fashion stores, cinemas and fast-food joints, as well as the church of **La Merced**.

Plaza San Martín dates from the early 1900s. The bronze statue of the liberator General José de San Martín was erected in 1921, but get closer and you'll discover the largely overlooked statue of Madre Patria. Commissioned in Spain under instruction to give the good lady a crown of flames, nobody thought to iron out the double meaning of the word flame in Spanish (*llama*), and the hapless craftsmen duly placed a delightful little llama on her head.

ACTIVITIES
Swimming & Surfing

Limeños hit the beaches in their droves during the summer months of January to March despite publicized warnings of pollution. If you join them, don't leave anything unattended for a second.

Nearby surfing hotspots **Punta Hermosa** and **San Bartolo** have hostels near the beach. **Punta Rocas** is for experienced surfers, and has one basic hostel for crashing. You'll have to buy or rent boards in Lima.

To get to the beaches, take a 'San Bartolo' bus from the Panamericana Sur at the intersection with Angamos, also known as the Primavera Bridge (taxi from Miraflores US$1.20). Get off where you want and hike down to the beaches, which are mostly 1km or 2km from the highway.

Other Activities

For **paragliding** trips around Peru and the cliff-tops of Lima itself, contact **Peru Fly** (Map p809; ☎ 01-444-5004; www.perufly.com; Jorge Chavez 658, Miraflores; US$25). Tandem flights take off near Parque del Amor in Miraflores. Be sure to wave at the bemused coffee-drinkers in the cliff-side Larcomar shopping mall as you glide past.

Explore Bicycle Rentals (Map p809; ☎ 01-241-7494; iexplore@terra.com; Bolognesi 381, Miraflores; US$3/8/45 per hour/day/week; ☺ 9am-7pm Mon-Fri, 9am-2pm Sat) rents mountain bikes with helmet and lock. **Cabalgatas** (☎ 01-221-4591; informes@cabalgatas.com.pe) has Peruvian Paso horses and runs horse-riding trips around Pachacamac for US$35.

You can go tenpin bowling at **Cosmic Bowling** (Map p809; Larcomar, Miraflores; US$12 per hr; ☺ 10am-midnight) in Larcomar shopping mall. At night, the lanes are illuminated by 'cosmic' lighting. There's also bowling and pool at the more run-down **Brunswick Bowl** (Map p809; Malecón Balta 135, Miraflores; bowling US$7 per hr plus drink, pool US$1.40 per hr; ☺ 9am-3pm Mon-Sat).

TOURS

City tours with English-speaking guides start at US$25. Two recommended agencies are **Fertur Peru** (Map pp802–3; ☎ 01-427-1958; fertur@terra.com.pe; Junín 211, Lima; ☺ 9am-7pm Mon-Sat), which is also good for countrywide information and student flight deals; and **Infotur** (Map pp802–3; ☎ 01-431-0117; Jirón Belén 1066, Lima; ☺ 9:30am-6pm Mon-Fri & 10am-2pm Sat).

The Río Cañete, three or four hours drive south of Lima, has river rafting opportunities (see p814).

SLEEPING

Apart from the tourist mecca of Cuzco, hotels are more expensive here than in any other Peruvian city. The cheapest are generally in central Lima, though it's not as safe here as in the more upmarket neighborhoods of Miraflores and Barranco.

Central Lima   Map pp802–3

Hostal España (☎ 01-428-5546; hotel_espana@hotmail .com; Azangaro 105; dm per person US$3, s/d US$6/9) España is in a rambling old mansion full of classical busts, stuffed birds and paintings. It's an established gringos-only scene with basic accommodations. There are shared bathrooms with hot showers in the early morning or late evening, a laundry and a rooftop café surrounded by a veritable jungle of trailing plants.

Hostal San Francisco (☎ 01-426-2735; hostal_san _francisco@terramail.com.pe; Azangaro 127; dm US$5-6; ☐) This is a clean and modern escape from the travelers' scene next door and, though it has less character, is friendly and has good beds.

Familia Rodríguez (☎ 01-423-6465; jjr-art@mail .cosapidata.com.pe; Nicolás de Piérola 730, 2nd fl, No 3; dm with breakfast US$6) This is an informal and very friendly family home in a central position.

Plaza Francia Inn Pensión (☎ 01-330-6080; francia squareinn@yahoo.com; Rufino Torrico 1117; dm US$7, s/d US$11/14) This good, simple choice has clean dorm rooms with shared hot showers, small personal safes in each room and a lounge with cable TV.

Hostal Roma (☎ 01-427-7576; resroma@terra.com.pe; Ica 326; s/d US$13/20, with bath US$25/36; ☐) This friendly old hostel is clean, central and a little camp with quirky, varied rooms – some are windowless so look at a few first. Low-season discounts are available.

Hostal de las Artes (☎ 01-433-0031; artes@terra.com .pe; Chota 1469; s/d US$8/14-17) This gay-friendly Dutch/Peruvian-owned hostel has well-maintained rooms with private hot showers. It is located on a quiet street in an atmospheric high-ceilinged *casa antigua* (old house) with colorful tiling.

Posada del Parque (☎ 01-433-2412; 01-9945-4260; posada@incacountry.com; Parque Hernán Velarde 60; s/d/tr US$27/33/48) This well-recommended mid-range spot is on a quiet cul-de-sac just south of central Lima. It's run by a helpful English-speaking couple, and boasts spotless rooms with private hot showers and cable TV.

Miraflores   Map p809

Albergue Juvenil Internacional (☎ 01-446-5488; hostel@terra.com.pe; Av Casimiro Juan Ulloa 328; dm US$11, d with bath US$26) This newly renovated hostel

LIMA – MIRAFLORES

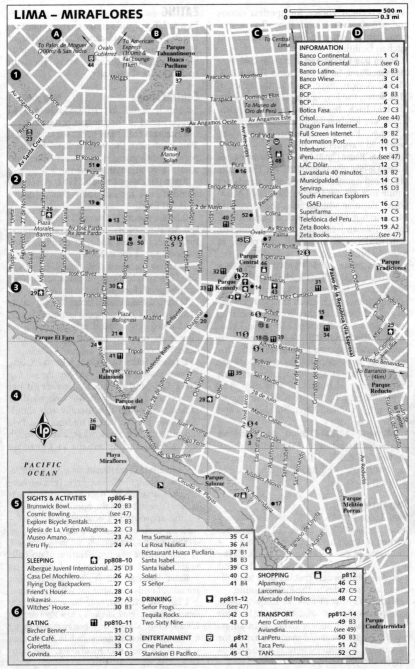

INFORMATION

Banco Continental	1 C4
Banco Continental	(see 6)
Banco Latino	2 B3
Banco Wiese	3 C4
BCP	4 C4
BCP	5 B3
BCP	6 C3
Botica Fasa	7 C3
Crisol	(see 44)
Dragon Fans Internet	8 C3
Full Screen Internet	9 B2
Information Post	10 C3
Interbanc	11 C3
iPeru	(see 47)
LAC Dólar	12 C3
Lavandaria 40 minutos	13 B2
Municipalidad	14 C3
Servirap	15 D3
South American Explorers (SAE)	16 C2
Superfarma	17 C5
Telefónica del Peru	18 C3
Zeta Books	19 A2
Zeta Books	(see 47)

SIGHTS & ACTIVITIES   pp806–8

Brunswick Bowl	20 B3
Cosmic Bowling	(see 47)
Explore Bicycle Rentals	21 B3
Iglesia de La Virgen Milagrosa	22 C3
Museo Amano	23 A2
Peru Fly	24 A4

SLEEPING   pp808–10

Albergue Juvenil Internacional	25 D3
Casa Del Mochilero	26 A2
Flying Dog Backpackers	27 C3
Friend's House	28 C4
Inkawasi	29 A3
Witches' House	30 B3

EATING   pp810–11

Bircher Benner	31 D3
Café Café	32 C3
Glorietta	33 C3
Govinda	34 D3
Ima Sumac	35 C4
La Rosa Nautica	36 A4
Restaurant Huaca Pucllana	37 B1
Santa Isabel	38 B3
Santa Isabel	39 B3
Solari	40 C3
Sí Señor	41 B4

DRINKING   pp811–12

Señor Frogs	(see 47)
Tequila Rocks	42 C3
Two Sixty Nine	43 C3

ENTERTAINMENT   p812

Cine Planet	44 A1
Starvision El Pacífico	45 C3

SHOPPING   p812

Alpamayo	46 C3
Larcomar	47 C5
Mercado del Indios	48 C2

TRANSPORT   pp812–14

Aero Continente	49 B3
Aviandina	(see 49)
LanPeru	50 B3
Taca Peru	51 A2
TANS	52 C2

PERU

is an excellent choice for spotless dorms and private rooms, and also offers a spacious garden, sociable lounge and excellent kitchen facilities.

Flying Dog Backpackers (☎ 01-445-0940; flying dog@mixmail.com; Ernesto Diez Canseco 117; dm US$9, d US$25) A neat place right in the heart of Miraflores, the Flying Dog is run by youthful laid-back hosts who speak English. There are kitchen facilities, cable TV and a lounge. Prices include breakfast at the nearby El Parquetito café.

Witches' House (☎ 01-446-7722; gizik@hotmail.com; Bolognesi 364; dm US$5, s/d US$10/20; P) This oddly misplaced nouveau-Tudor house stands out a mile in a quieter residential area of Miraflores. Popular with Israelis, the hostel has 24-hour hot water, a kitchen, DVDs and cable TV, and the surrounding concrete courtyard boasts basketball and plenty of room to breathe.

Friend's House (☎ 01-446-6248; Jr Manco Capac 368; dm US$6, d US$14) This backpacker-friendly hostel has a highly sociable atmosphere – perhaps inescapable given the cramped nature of the dorms. Kitchen access is available, and there's a small lounge with cable TV.

Casa Del Mochilero (☎ 01-444-9089; pilaryv@hotmail .com; Chacaltana 130A, 2nd fl; per person US$4) This homestay is so popular the neighbors are having a stab at stealing customers with copy-cat named outfits of their own. The original is best, but all are welcoming spots with simple rooms, shared hot showers and kitchen access.

Inkawasi (☎ 01-241-8218; backpackerinkawasi@hot mail.com; Martin Narpánga; dm US$10, d with bath/Jacuzzi with breakfast US$25/30) This small budget newbie is modern, well furnished and close to cliff-top parks.

Barranco

Point Lodge (☎ 01-247-7997; the_point_barranco@ hotmail.com; Junín 300; dm US$7-8; 🖳) This whitewashed seafront hostel is run by a couple of laid-back, ex-pat backpackers. It has all the toys – DVDs, games, ping-pong, kitchen and a garden, plus owners that are only too willing to act as guides to the local nightlife.

Mochilero's (☎ 01-477-4506; backpackers@back packersperu.com; Pedro de Osma 135; dm US$10) This long-established budget haunt is in an atmospheric 100-year-old mansion handy for Barranco's nightlife. There is a boisterous bar on the premises.

EATING

Beware! Taxes and service charges (*impuestos*; IGV) on meals can be an exorbitant 30% in fancier restaurants. Lima boasts high-quality restaurants of every type, with seafood a local specialty.

Central Lima   Map pp802–3

Set-lunch menus that cost US$1.50 to US$2 can be found in the cheaper restaurants.

Restaurant Accllahuasy (Ancash 400; mains US$2-5) This spot near the backpackers' hotels is popular with gringos and locals alike, with a have-a-go-at-anything menu.

Azato (Arica 298; set menu US$1.20-2) A recommended spot for fast spicy *criollo* (native of Peru) food.

Queirolo (Camaná 900; mains US$3-5; ☺ lunch only Sun) An atmospheric old restaurant popular for its set lunches and as a drinking-and-gathering spot for *limeños*.

La Casera (Huancavelica 244; menu US$2; ☺ closed Sun) This simple, brusque place serves typical Peruvian food for loose change.

La Merced (Miró Quesada 158; mains US$2-6) Usually bustling with businesspeople doing lunch, La Merced has a bland exterior giving no clue to its spacious interior and intricately carved wooden ceiling.

El Estadio Futbol Club (Nicolás de Piérola 926, Lima; ☺ noon-midnight Mon-Wed, noon-2am Thu-Sat) On Plaza San Martín, this soccer-themed bar serves good food on indoor and outdoor tables, where you can literally rub shoulders with the likes of Maradona and Pele (admittedly just waxworks), and as much soccer-related paraphernalia as will fit on the walls.

Cevichería La Choza Nautica (Breña 204; mains US$6-10) This popular little *cevichería* (place where *ceviche* – marinated, uncooked seafood – is served) doesn't miss the opportunity to play on the aphrodisiacal qualities of seafood – look for their excellent 'ceviche erotica.'

Villa Natura (Ucayali 326; set menu US$1.50-2; ☺ Mon-Sat) One of a proliferation of no-frills vegetarian pit-stops in central Lima.

Natur (Moquegua 132; ☺ closed Sun) Another friendly, family-run spot for vegetarian fare.

L'Eau Vive (☎ 01-427-5612; Ucayali 370; set lunch/ dinner US$10/25; ☺ 12:30-3pm & 7:30-9:30pm Mon-Sat) L'Eau Vive is a unique restaurant run by a French order of nuns and is a welcome relief from the Lima madhouse. The nuns sing 'Ave María' at 9pm.

Miraflores   Map p809
Restaurants are pricier in Miraflores, but if you keep your eyes peeled there's still a few hole-in-the-wall cafés selling cheap set menus. Fast-food joints cluster around Óvalo Gutiérrez, but the trendiest spot to dine is in Larcomar shopping mall, with its spectacular location teetering on the brink of the coastal cliffs.

Ima Sumac (Colón 241; set menu US$2; ☻ lunch only) A warm and friendly little place with great value set meals.

Santa Isabel (Alfredo Benavides 487; mains US$2.50-6; ☻ 24 hr) Open for midnight munchies, this supermarket café-restaurant has a varied buffet.

Solari (Av José Pardo 216; mains US$4-9) Serving a mix of international dishes in a flashy modern glass building complete with plants and an artificial waterfall, the atmosphere only slightly resembling that of an indoor swimming pool.

Sí Señor (Bolognesi 706; mains US$6-10; ☻ evenings only) This lively central American place serves kick-ass Tex-Mex food with Mexican beer and, as you'd expect, plenty of tequila.

Glorietta (Diagonal 181; mains US$5-10) On what is locally dubbed 'Pizza Street' for all its open-fronted Italian joints.

Café Café (Martír Olaya 250 & Larcomar; Larcomar; snacks/sandwiches US$2-3.50, drinks US$1.50-6; ☻ till 3am Fri-Sat) Advertises 120 different gourmet coffees, snacks and desserts. The Larcomar branch has a great cliff-top location looking down to the surfers below: not for sufferers of vertigo.

Govinda (Schell 634; set menu US$2-3; ☻ lunch only Sun) Cheap and cheerful vegetarian café run by Hare Krishnas; you'll see Govindas popping up all across Peru.

Bircher Benner (Diez Canseco 487; mains US$3-7; ☻ Mon-Sat) This long-established restaurant makes an excellent place for vegetarians to treat themselves.

Restaurant Huaca Pucllana (☎ 01-445-4042; General Borgoño block 8; mains US$7.50-20) Sophisticated establishment overlooking pre-Inca pyramidal temple.

La Rosa Nautica (☎ 01-445-0149; Circuito de Playas; set menu US$17, mains US$11-25) Famous restaurant in a fabulous building at the end of Playa Costa Verde's historic pier. Worth grabbing a coffee or dessert if you can't afford the meals.

Barranco
La Canta Rana (Génova 101; mains US$7-10; ☻ lunch only) Literally translated as 'The Singing Frog,' this unpretentious place is a topnotch *cevichería*, with all manner of seafood. Great ambiance.

Tío Dan (cnr Grau & Piérola; mains US$2.50-5) Reasonably priced pizza and pasta served around a circular bar.

Self-Catering
Santa Isabel (Map p809; Benavides 487, Miraflores; ☻ 24 hr) rivals any North American mall hang-out. There is also a branch on **Pardo** (☻ 8am-10:30pm), and on Camino Real in **San Isidro** (☻ 8am-10:30pm). In central Lima, try **Metro** (Map pp802-3; Cuzco; ☻ 8am-10pm).

DRINKING
Bars & Nightclubs
Lima is overflowing with bars – from San Isidro's pricey havens for the modern elite to Barranco's cheap-and-cheerful stomping grounds. The tight-knit clubs around Barranco's Parque Municipal are the best place to go club-hopping; walking just a few steps here will transport you to entirely different vibes. Lima's center has little action, however. Weekends from January to March also see the fresh-from-the-beach summer crowds heading down to km 97 on the Panamericana, where DJs happily crank up the volume with a clear conscience.

Tai Lounge (Conquistadores 325; ☻ Mon-Sat) In San Isidro, this place draws the cream of young *limeños*, appreciative of the plush lounging areas, cool outside patios and suave clientele.

Juanito's (Grau 274; ☻ Mon-Sat) Was a leftist *peña* of the 1960s and is still popular for the quirky antics of its bar staff.

La Noche (Bolognesi 307; admission US$3; ☻ Mon-Sun) A well-known, three-level bar in the thick of things.

La Posada del Mirador (Ermita 104; ☻ Mon-Sun) A cliff-top bar great for catching the sunset while knocking back a chilled pint or three.

Wahio's (Boulevard de los Bomberos; ☻ Thu-Sat) A lively little bar with its fair share of dreadlocks, and a classic soundtrack of reggae, ska and dub.

Sargento Pimienta (Bolognesi 755; ☻ Wed-Sat) Alcohol is cheap at this barn-like place, which plays a knock-out mix of international retro.

PERU

El Estadio Futbol Club (Nicolás de Piérola 926, Lima; noon-midnight Mon-Wed, noon-2am Thu-Sat) This bar gives a great taste of Peruvian-style soccer-fanaticism.

La Noche (Map pp802-3; cnr Camaná & Quilca; Mon-Sat) Live music after 11pm.

Palos de Moguer (Cavenecia 129; Mon-Sat) Just north of Óvalo Gutiérrez in Miraflores, this tavern-like, international beerhouse boasts by far the best real-ale pints in town.

Tequila Rocks (Map p809; Diez Canseco 146; admission US$3; Mon-Sat) For clubbing, this long-established place plays all the crowd-pleasers and has a deserved reputation as a travelers pick-up joint.

Señor Frogs (Larcomar; admission US$8-10; Mon-Sat) A flashy, electric club that attracts a young local crowd, who later spill out into the mall's late-night cafés to cool their aching feet.

Live Music

Peruvian music and dance is performed at *peñas* from Wednesday to Saturday. **Las Brisas de Titicaca** (Map pp802-3; ☎ 01-332-1901; Walkuski 168, Lima; admission US$7; 9:30pm-late Wed-Sat) and **La Candelaria** (☎ 01-247-2941; Bolognesi 292, Barranco; admission US$7; 9:30-late Fri-Sat) are both popular with *limeños*.

Gay & Lesbian Venues

Lima hosts Peru's most open gay scene. For the most up-to-date ideas, see http://gaylimape.tripod.com. A couple of gay-friendly bars include **Two Sixty Nine** (Map p809; Pasaje Tello 269, Miraflores; 8pm-5am Mon-Sat) and **Kitch** (Bolognesi 743, Barranco; Thu-Sat).

ENTERTAINMENT

Cinemas

Some cinemas offer half-price entry midweek. Listings are in the newspapers' cultural-events section.

Cine Planet Lima (Map pp802-3; ☎ 01-452-7000; Jirón de la Unión 819, Lima; US$2); Miraflores (Map p809; ☎ 01-452-7000; Av Santa Cruz 814, Miraflores; US$4)

Filmoteca (Map pp802-3; ☎ 01-423-4732; Museo de Arte, Paseo Colón 125, Lima; US$1.60-4.20) In Parque de la Cultura.

Starvision El Pacífico (Map p809; ☎ 01-445-6990; Av Ricardo Pardo 121; Miraflores; US$3.50)

Sport

The Estadio Nacional on the 7th, 8th and 9th blocks of the Paseo de la República is the venue for most important soccer matches.

Bullfighting also has a good fan-base in Lima. The season is late October to late November, plus a shorter season in March. Matadors fight in the **Plaza de Acho bullring** (Map pp802-3; ☎ 01-481-1467; Hualgayoc 332, Rímac; US$20-100; 3pm Sun). Tickets can be bought at the stadium from 9am to 1pm or at **Farmacia Deza** (☎ 01-222-3195; Conquistadores 1140, San Isidro).

SHOPPING

Haggle your heart out at the enormous **Mercado del Indios** (Map p809; Petit Thouars 5245) in Miraflores, which is crammed with handicrafts from all over Peru. Lima's American-style malls include the fancy **Larcomar** (Map p809) hiding below the Parque Salazar in Miraflores, with a spectacular location built into the cliffs. For camping gear, try **Alpamayo** (Map p809; ☎ 01-445-1671; Av José Larco 345, Miraflores).

GETTING THERE & AWAY

Air

Lima's **Aeropuerto Internacional Jorge Chávez** (☎ 01-595-0606; www.lap.com.pe) is in Callao, 12km west of the city center (16km from Miraflores). There is a post office (open during the day), ATMs, a 24-hour restaurant upstairs and a 24-hour luggage storage room (US$6 per item per day).

About 30 international airlines have offices in Lima – check 'Aviación' in the *Yellow Pages*. Airlines offering domestic flights:

AeroCóndor (☎ 01-441-1354; reservas@aerocondor.com.pe; Juan de Arona 781, San Isidro)

Aero Continente/Aviandina (Map p809; ☎ 01-242-4260/113, airport 01-447-8080; www.aerocontinente.com.pe in Spanish; Av José Pardo 651)

LanPeru (Map p809; ☎ 01-213-8200; www.lanperu.com; Av José Pardo 513, Miraflores)

Taca Peru (Map p809; ☎ 01-213-7000; ventasgt@grupotaca.com.pe; Av Espinar 331, Miraflores)

TANS (Map p809; ☎ 01-213-6000; ventaslima@tans.com.pe; Av Arequipa 5200, Miraflores)

See regional sections for details of which airlines fly where.

Flight schedules and ticket prices change frequently; one-way fares from Lima to interior destinations cost US$40 to US$90. There is a US$28 international-departure tax, and tax on domestic flights is US$5.

Getting flight information, buying tickets and reconfirming flights is best done at airline offices (or a reputable travel agent) rather than at the airport counters. You can buy tickets at the airport on a space-available basis, however, if you want to leave for somewhere in a hurry.

Overbooking is the norm on domestic flights, so be at the airport early. For all flights, domestic and international, reconfirm several times, especially during July and August.

The official ISIC card site in Lima is **Intej** (☎ 01-247-3230; intej@intej.org; San Martín 240, Barranco), which organizes student airfares and can change dates for flights booked through student or youth travel agencies, such as STA Travel.

Bus
PERU

Lima has no central bus terminal; each bus company runs its own office and station, many of which are clustered around the main bus station at Av Javier Prado Este, in La Victoria. Other bus stations are found in Central Lima, just north of Av Grau, and just south of 28 de Julio on both sides of Paseo de la Republica. Make sure you verify which station your bus departs from. Lima's bus stations are notorious for theft, so find the station and buy your tickets in advance, unencumbered by luggage.

Use reputable bus services whenever possible. There are countless choices in Lima, but look at the quality of the bus before traveling. The most reputable bus companies utilize modern buses, some of which are also sleeping buses, with seats that convert into beds for overnight trips.

Following are two particularly reliable companies:

Cruz del Sur www.cruzdelsur.com.pe (in Spanish); Lima (Map pp802-3; ☎ 01-424-1005/6158; Quilca 531); La Victoria (☎ 01-225-6163/5748; Javier Prado Este 1109)

Ormeño Lima (Map pp802-3; ☎ 01-427-5679; Carlos Zavala Loayza 177); La Victoria (☎ 01-472-1710; Javier Prado Este 1059)

Also good:

CIVA www.civa.com.pe (in Spanish); Lima (Map pp802-3; ☎ 01-332-5236/5264/0656; cnr Av 28 de Julio & Paseo de la Republica 575); Lima (Carlos Zavala 211)

Expreso Molina (Map pp802-3; ☎ 01-428-4852; Ayacucho 1141-1145, Lima)

Flores (Map pp802-3; ☎ 01-424-3278; cnr Paseo de la República & 28 de Julio)

Ittsa (Map pp802-3; ☎ 01-423-5232; Paseo de la República, block 6)

Mariscal Cáceres SA Lima (Map pp802-3; ☎ 01-427-2844; Carlos Zavala 211); Lima (☎ 474-7850; 28 de Julio 2195)

Soyuz (☎ 01-226-1515; cnr Mexico 333 & Paseo de la República)

Turismo Rodríguez (Map pp802-3; ☎ 01-428-0506; Roosevelt 354)

Approximate one-way fares and journey times from Lima are shown in the following table.

Destination	Duration in Hours	Cost
Arequipa	16	US$10–28
Ayacucho	8½	US$11.50–14
Cajamarca	13	US$11.50–28
Chachapoyas	25	US$20
Chiclayo	12	US$10–26
Cuzco	30	US$18.50–28.50
Huancayo	7	US$7–11.50
Huaraz	8	US$5.70–10
Ica	4½	US$4.50–13
Nazca	8	US$5.70–17
Pisco	3	US$3–8.50
Piura	14	US$10–28
Puno	21	US$17–37
Tacna	18	US$12–31
Trujillo	9	US$7–15
Tumbes	20	US$8.50–28

INTERNATIONAL

Ormeño (Av Javier Prado Este) runs buses to Bogotá, Buenos Aires, Caracas, Quito, La Paz and Santiago.

GETTING AROUND
Bus

Local buses around Lima are startlingly cheap (fares are US$0.30 to US$0.40). Bus lines are identifiable by windscreen destination cards and you can flag them down or get off anywhere. The most useful routes link central Lima with Miraflores along Av Arequipa. Buses are labeled 'Todo Arequipa' and 'Larco/Schell/Miraflores' when heading to Miraflores, and likewise 'Todo Arequipa' and 'Wilson/Tacna' when leaving Miraflores for Lima. From Plaza Grau in central Lima, buses travel along the Vía Expresa, stopping at Ricardo Palma and Benavides for Miraflores.

A regular bus running from the city center through Miraflores and on to Barranco is the green bus marked 73A, which passes through Tacna and Garcilaso de la Vega, down Arequipa and Av José Larco in Miraflores.

PERU

Taxi

Taxis don't have meters so negotiate a price before getting in. The majority of taxis in Lima are unofficial. Hawkers sell florescent taxi stickers at busy intersections throughout the city, and anybody who fancies a bit of spare cash can stick one in their windscreen. Officially registered taxis are generally safer. Taxi companies can be phoned or you can catch official yellow taxis from taxi stands, such as the one outside Larcomar shopping mall in Miraflores. Official taxis cost 30% to 50% more than regular street taxis. **Moli Taxi** (☎ 01-479-0030), **Taxi Miraflores** (☎ 01-446-3953) and **Taxi Móvil** (☎ 01-422-6890) all work 24 hours and accept advance reservations.

SOUTH COAST

The arid southern lowlands, interspersed with oases and spanned by the Carretera Panamericana, is the preferred route to Lake Titicaca and Cuzco but boasts far more diversity than seen in the kilometer upon numbing kilometer of barren desert viewed from a bus window. Pisco is particularly famous for its rich marine wildlife and rugged coastline, while neighboring Ica is surrounded by vineyards and monstrous sand dunes, irresistible to sand-boarders. The region also played host to the extraordinary Nazca civilization, remembered for its striking lines and figures etched across 500 sq km.

CAÑETE & LUNAHUANÁ

Cañete, 144km south of Lima, is the turn-off for Lunahuaná, 40km away. River rafters ride the Río Cañete from Lunahuaná from December to April. February is the best month, with Class III rapids. Contact **Río Cañete Expediciones** (☎ 01-9815-7858; expriocanete@terra.com.pe). Short trips generally cost US$10 to US$15. Lunahuaná also has wineries serving generous samples year-round; there's a harvest festival in March. Nearby archaeological sites include the large, rough-walled **Incawasi**.

Camping San Jerónimo (☎ 056-9633-7093; per person US$1.50), bordering the river, has a campsite, climbing wall and river-running equipment. **Hostal Lunahuana** (☎ 056-284-1089; Malecón; s/d US$6/9, with bath US$12/14) is a decent budget hostel.

From Lima, buses for Pisco or Ica can drop you at Cañete (US$2, 2½ hours). In Cañete, catch a combi to the annex of Imperial (US$0.15, 10 minutes); micros run from there to Lunahuaná (US$0.70, 30 minutes).

CHINCHA

This small town is famous for its wild Afro-Peruvian music heard in the *peñas* of the El Carmen district, a 30-minute minibus ride from the main plaza. The best times to visit are during Verano Negro (February 22 to March 1), Fiestas Patrias (in late July), a local fiesta in late October, and Christmas. During these times, minibuses run from Chincha to El Carmen all night long, and the *peñas* are full of frenzied *limeños* and the local African population shaking that ass. One dance not to try at home is El Alcatraz, when a gyrating male dancer attempts to set his partner's skirt on fire with a candle.

During the festivals, hotels double or triple their prices. Try **La Rueda** (☎ 056-9850-7121; Santo Domingo 228; s/d/tr US$7/8.50/10), a friendly cacti-lined place, or the rudimentary **Hotel Sotelo** (☎ 056-26-1681; Benavides 260; s/d US$4.50/7, with bath US$6/10). **Palacio de los Mariscos** (☎ 056-26-2556; km 195), in the Hostal El Valle, is the best seafood restaurant in town.

PISCO

Sharing its name with the white-grape brandy produced in this region, Pisco is an important port 235km south of Lima. Generally used as a base from which to see the abundant wildlife of the nearby Islas Ballestas and Península de Paracas, the area is also of historical and archaeological interest, having hosted one of the most highly developed pre-Inca civilizations – the Paracas culture – from 1300 BC until AD 200. In addition, it later acted as a base for the revolutionary fever of the 1800s.

Information

Embassy Internet (Comercio; US$0.60 per hr; ☺ 9am-2am) is very fast and good; for snail-mail, there's a **post office** (Callao 176; ☺ 8am-9pm Mon-Sat). **BCP** (Perez de Figueroa 162) has a Visa ATM, and changes cash and traveler's checks in US dollars. For laundry, try **El Pacifico** (Callao 274).

Dangers & Annoyances

Take great care on the road to the beach area and the beach annex itself (2km west of town) – never walk alone here.

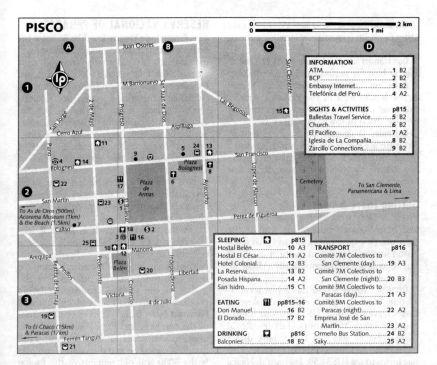

PISCO

INFORMATION
ATM...1 B2
BCP...2 B2
Embassy Internet..........................3 B2
Telefónica del Perú........................4 A2

SIGHTS & ACTIVITIES   p815
Ballestas Travel Service................5 B2
Church...6 B2
El Pacífico......................................7 A2
Iglesia de La Compañía................8 B2
Zarcillo Connections.....................9 B2

SLEEPING   p815
Hostal Belén..............................10 A3
Hostal El César...........................11 A2
Hotel Colonial............................12 B3
La Reserva..................................13 B2
Posada Hispana..........................14 A2
San Isidro...................................15 C1

EATING   pp815–16
Don Manuel................................16 B2
El Dorado...................................17 B2

DRINKING   p816
Balconies....................................18 B2

TRANSPORT   p816
Comité 7M Colectivos to
  San Clemente (day)........19 A3
Comité 7M Colectivos to
  San Clemente (night)....20 B3
Comité 9M Colectivos to
  Paracas (day)...............21 A3
Comité 9M Colectivos to
  Paracas (night)...............22 A2
Empresa José de San
  Martín.........................23 A2
Ormeño Bus Station.........24 B2
Saky.............................25 A2

Sights
Acorema Museum (☎ 056-53-2046; Av San Martín 1471; admission US$1; ☽ 10am-1pm & 2-6pm) has exhibits on conservation in Paracas. The **cemetery** also has a few hidden secrets: local taxi drivers like to tell the story of a 19th-century English witch, Sarah Ellen, who claimed that she would arise again after 100 years. Much to everyone's disappointment, she didn't.

Tours
Recommended agencies pitching their sales at local tours to the Islas Ballestas and the Península de Paracas include **Zarcillo Connections** (☎ 056-53-6543; zarcillo@terra.com.pe; San Francisco 111) and **Ballestas Travel Service** (☎ 056-53-3095; jpachecot@terra.com.pe; San Francisco 249). Both run similarly organized tours to the Islas Ballestas (US$10) and the Reserva Nacional de Paracas (US$8).

Sleeping
San Isidro (☎ 056-53-6471; San Clemente 103; hostals anisidro@hotmail.com; dm US$6, s/d with bath $10/16) A highly recommended spot near the cemetery, with a kitchen and free games room

with all the toys, plus secure, good-value rooms and plentiful hot water.

Posada Hispana (☎ 056-53-6363; posahispana@ terra.com.pe; Bolognesi 236; s/d per person US$10) Another justifiably popular choice, with bamboo fittings, a café and a great terrace for kicking back with a *pisco* sour. All rooms have private hot showers.

Hostal Belén (☎ 056-53-3046; Arequipa 128; per person US$4, s/d with bath US$7/10) A faded but very decent, clean option with electric showers.

Hostal El César (☎ 056-53-2512; 2 de Mayo; s/d US$6/ 8.50) Friendly and in reasonably good nick, though with mostly shared bathrooms.

Hotel Colonial (☎ 056-53-2035; Comercio 194; dm US$3) For penny pinchers, this is a rickety old place with outdoor showers.

La Reserva (☎ 056-53-5643; lareserva_hostal@hotmail .com; San Francisco 327; s/d/tr US$10/20/30) For something a bit sharper, the whitewashed, oval-shaped La Reserva has sparkling rooms, private hot showers and cable TV.

Eating & Drinking
A few cafés are open early enough for breakfasts before Ballestas tours.

PERU

El Dorado (Progreso 171; set menu US$1.70; ☺ early) Offers a cheap have-a go-at-anything menu on Plaza de Armas.

Don Manuel (Comercio 179; mains US$3-12) One of Pisco's best for seafood and *criollo* dishes.

As de Oros (San Martín 472; mains US$3-12; ☺ noon) A few blocks west of the Plaza de Armas, this good modern restaurant hosts the only notable disco in town on weekends.

Balconies (Jr Comercio 108; 2nd fl; ☺ 6pm-2am) An intimate bar from which to peer down on passing folk below, but take great care negotiating its wonky staircase after a few *piscos*.

Getting There & Away

Pisco is 5km west of the Panamericana, and many coastal buses drop you at the turn-off. Ask for a direct bus to Pisco from both Lima and Ica. From the turn-off, local buses go into Pisco sporadically (US$0.30, 10 minutes).

Ormeño (☎ 056-53-2764) has a bus terminal one block from the Plaza de Armas. Buses leave for Lima (US$3.50, four hours) roughly every two hours. Luxury Royal Class services also run twice daily direct from Pisco to Lima (US$10). Ormeño also has buses to Ica (US$1.50, 1½ hours), Nazca (US$4.20 to US$11.20, four hours) and two to Arequipa (US$11.20 to US$15.40, 12 to 15 hours). To Ayacucho (US$7 to US$11.20, seven hours) there are three daily buses.

Other bus companies covering long journeys include **Empresa José de San Martín** (☎ 056-53-2052), with 10 direct buses daily to Lima (US$3, three hours). **SAKY** (☎ 056-53-4309) has direct services to Ica every half-hour from 5:30am until 7:30pm (US$0.70, one hour).

Getting Around

Combis to Paracas leave from near the market about every half-hour during the day (US$0.50, 20 minutes). Buses for the San Clemente turn-off (where you catch long-distance northbound and southbound buses on the Panamericana) leave frequently from the market. At night, they leave from Libertad near Comercio to avoid the dangerous market area.

A taxi around town charges about US$0.50, to San Clemente about US$1.60 and to Paracas about US$3.

RESERVA NACIONAL DE PARACAS

The **Península de Paracas** and **Islas Ballestas** together form the most important bird and marine sanctuary on the Peruvian coast. Though all-too-often referred to as 'the poor man's Galapagos,' a trip to the offshore Ballestas is a particularly memorable experience. Guano-producing **birds** include the booby, pelican, Humboldt penguins and Chilean flamingos. See the boxed text. Large colonies of **sea lions** are also found on the islands. Flotillas of jellyfish, some reaching about two-thirds of 1m in diameter and with stinging tentacles trailing a meter or more behind them, often get washed up onto the shore (swimmers beware!). Beachcombers also find sea hares, ghost crabs and seashells.

On the peninsula itself is **Museo JC Tello** (adult/child/student US$2/0.30/0.60; ☺ 9am-5pm), with a collection of weavings, trophy heads and trepanned skulls (this was a medical technique used by several ancient cultures whereby a slice of the skull is removed, relieving pressure on the brain caused by injuries). **Flamingos** often hang out in the bay in front of the complex, and there's now a walkway down to a *mirador* (watchtower). Also, a few hundred meters behind the visitor's complex is the 5000-year-old remains of the **Paracas Necropolis**.

The coastline between Pisco and Paracas is home to a large and smelly fish-meal fac-

---

DROPPINGS TO DIE FOR

Layers of sun-baked, nitrogen-rich seabird droppings (guano) have been deposited over millennia on the Islas Ballestas and Península de Paracas by their large resident bird colonies – in places the droppings are as much as 50m deep. Guano's reputation as a first-class fertilizer dates back to pre-Inca times, but few could have predicted that these filthy riches were to become Peru's principal export during the mid-19th century. In fact, the trade was so lucrative that Spain precipitated the so-called Guano War of 1865–66 over possession of the nearby guano-rich Chincha Islands. Nowadays, however, over-exploitation and synthetic fertilizers have taken their toll and the birds are largely left to their steady production process in peace, if it weren't for boatloads of day-trippers from Pisco.

RESERVA NACIONAL DE PARACAS

SIGHTS & ACTIVITIES	pp816–17
Archaeological Site	(see 4)
Candelabra	1 B2
Cliff-Top Trail	(see 8)
Fish-Meal Factories	2 B2
Flamingos Often Seen Here	3 B3
Museo JC Tello	4 B3
Obelisk	5 C3
Paracas Necropolis	6 B3
Playa El Chaco	7 B2
Seabirds & Sea Lions	8 B3
Ship Graveyard	9 B3

SLEEPING	p817
El Amigo	10 B2
El Mirador	11 B3
Hotel Paracas	12 B3

TRANSPORT	p817
Boats to Islas Ballestas	(see 12)

OTHER	
Watch Tower	13 B3

tory and an **obelisk** marking the landing of the liberator General José de San Martín. A **ship graveyard** is to be found at the western end of the bay.

Most people stay in Pisco but places to stay in the area include **El Amigo** (☎ 056-54-5042; s/d US$10/17) which has cute rooms with TV. It's up to 50% cheaper in the low season.

Tours

Resident bird and sea-lion colonies are visited on fun, inexpensive and worthwhile organized boat tours. See p815 for agencies.

Tours leave daily at 7am (US$7 to US$10, depending on your bargaining skills and the season). Minibuses go to Paracas, where slow motorboats are boarded; there's no cabin, so dress for wind and spray. The outward boat journey takes about 1½ hours, and en route you see the famous three-pronged **Candelabra**, a giant figure etched into the coastal hills, over 150m high and 50m wide.

An hour is spent cruising around the island's arches and caves, watching the large colonies of sea lions sprawl on the rocks and swim around your boat. Be sure

to wear a hat, as it's not unusual to receive a direct guano hit from the thousands-strong bird colonies.

Back on shore, minibuses wait to take you back to Pisco in time for lunch. Alternatively, continue on an afternoon tour of the Península de Paracas (US$6 to US$10), which visits coastal sea-lion and flamingo colonies and geological formations. The Paracas tour requires an extra US$1.20 reserve fee and the museum entrance fee.

ICA

The capital of its department, the oasis town of Ica boasts a thriving wine and *pisco* industry, an excellent museum and colorful annual fiestas. Its slightly elevated position sits above the coastal mist, and the climate is dry and sunny. Many travelers choose to visit Ica from the chilled Huacachina oasis (see p819).

Information

Velox Net (Lima 2nd block; US$0.40 per hr) has about 50 fast machines for Internet access, while the **main post office** (San Martín 556; ⏲ 8am-7pm

PERU

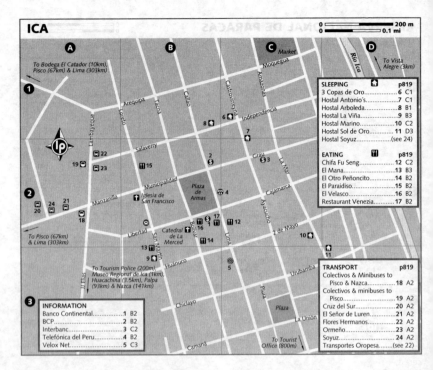

ICA

0   200 m
0   0.1 mi

To Bodega El Catador (10km),
Pisco (67km) & Lima (303km)

Market

Río Ica

To Vista
Alegre (3km)

Moquegua

Arequipa

Tacna

Callao

Catiouovequa

Amazonas

Independencia

Salaverry

Lambayeque

Loreto

☐ 22
19 ☐
☐ 23

🏨 15

Municipalidad

Iglesia de
San Francisco

Grau
ⓢ

ⓢ 2

La Mar

Grau
ⓢ 3

8 🏨

6 🏨

7

Plaza
de
Armas

🏠 4

Cajamarca

Ayacucho

Manzanilla

24 21
☐ 20
☐ 18

Libertad

San Martín

Catedral
de La
Merced

🏨 🏨 17
🏨 16

🏨 12

Lima

Bolívar

🏨 14

2 de Mayo

10 🏨

13 🏨
9 🏨

Huánuco

ⓢ 5

Urubamba

🏨
11

To Pisco (67km)
& Lima (303km)

JJ Elias

To Tourism Police (200m),
Museo Regional de Ica,
Huacachina (3.5km), Palpa
(93km) & Nazca (141km)

Chiclayo

Piura

Plaza

La Unión

Camaná

To Tourist
Office (800m)

SLEEPING	🏨	p819
3 Copas de Oro	**6**	C1
Hostal Antonio's	**7**	C1
Hostal Arboleda	**8**	B1
Hostal La Viña	**9**	B3
Hostal Marino	**10**	C2
Hostal Sol de Oro	**11**	D3
Hostal Soyuz	(see 24)	

EATING	🍴	p819
Chifa Fu Seng	**12**	C2
El Mana	**13**	B3
El Otro Peñoncito	**14**	B2
El Paraidiso	**15**	B2
El Velasco	**16**	B2
Restaurant Venezia	**17**	B2

INFORMATION		
Banco Continental	**1**	B2
BCP	**2**	B2
Interbanc	**3**	C2
Telefónica del Peru	**4**	B2
Velox Net	**5**	C3

TRANSPORT		p819
Colectivos & Minibuses to		
Pisco & Nazca	**18**	A2
Colectivos & minibuses to		
Pisco	**19**	A2
Cruz del Sur	**20**	A2
El Señor de Luren	**21**	A2
Flores Hermanos	**22**	A2
Ormeño	**23**	A2
Soyuz	**24**	A2
Transportes Oropesa	(see 22)	

Mon-Sat) is also close at hand. **BCP** (Plaza de Armas) changes traveler's checks and cash, and has a Visa ATM, and **Interbanc** (2nd block Grau) has a Visa/MasterCard ATM. The **tourism police** (☎ 056-22-7673; JJ Elias 4th block; ☻ 8am-1pm & 5-8pm) are located in the southwest end of town, and the **tourist office** (☎ 056-22-7287; Av Gerónimo de Cabrera 426, Urbanisacion Luren; ☻ 8am-noon & 2-4pm Mon-Fri) is a US$1 taxi ride from the city center.

Sights
MUSEO REGIONAL DE ICA
Don't miss this gem of a **museum** (☎ 056-23-4383; adult/child/student US$2.80/0.30/0.60, cameras/video recorders US$1.15/1.40; ☻ 8am-7pm Mon-Fri, 9am-6pm Sat & Sun) in the southwestern suburbs; it's about 1.5km from the city center and can be reached by *colectivo* from the Plaza de Armas (US$0.50, 10 minutes). It has an excellent collection of artifacts from the Paracas, Nazca and Inca cultures, and some superb examples of Paracas weavings. There are some scarily well-preserved mummies of everything from children to a small macaw, trepanned skulls and

shrunken trophy heads, enormous wigs and tresses of hair, plus a fascinating scientific display on the skeletal remains.

WINERIES
Fancy some free samples? Wines and *piscos* can be tracked down at year-round *bodegas* near Ica; the best time to visit is late February until early April. Producing the right stuff close to Ica is **Bodega El Catador** (☎ 056-40-3295; off km 296 Panamericana), 10km north of Ica, which runs tours and wine-tastings all year. Catch a combi from the 2nd block of Moquegua before noon, or from Loreto afterwards (US$0.40, 20 minutes). The **Vista Alegre winery** (☎ 056-23-2919; ☻ 9am-noon & 1-4pm Mon-Fri, 9am-noon & 2-5pm Sat & Sun), 3km northeast of Ica, is the easiest large commercial winery to visit (US$1 taxi *tico* – small three-wheeled vehicle).

Festivals & Events
Ica has more than its share of fiestas. Early March sees the famous wine-harvest Fiesta de la Vendimia, with all manner of processions, beauty contests, cockfights, music

and dancing, and of course, free-flowing pisco and wine. Most events are held evenings and weekends at the festival site of Campo Feriado, on the outskirts.

In October, Ica holds the religious pilgrimage of El Señor de Luren, which culminates in an all-night procession. In February, the Carnaval de Yunza inspires water-throwing plus colorful dances. The founding of Ica on June 17 in 1563 is also celebrated, and late September sees the Ica Tourist Festival.

Sleeping

Hotels double their prices during festivals, especially during the wine harvest in March. Prices below are low-season rates. Consider heading for the oasis of Huacachina (p819) for more hospitable options.

Hostal Arboleda (☎ 056-21-3207; Independencia 165; s/d US$3/4.50, with bath US$4.50/9)A cheerful, bare-bones place offering straightforward value and cold showers.

Hostal Marino (☎ 056-21-7201; Av La Mar 330; s/d US$4/8.50) New, clean and good value, with private cold showers and local TV.

Hostal Antonio's (☎ 056-21-5565; Castrovirreyna 136; s/d US$4.50/7) Also good, with neat, well-cared-for rooms with private bathrooms.

3 Copas de Oro (☎ 056-80-2920; cnr Independencia & Castrovirreyna 209; s/d US$7/10) A new and thoroughly disinfected place with small rooms and local TV.

Hostal Soyuz (☎ 056-22-4743; Manzanilla 164; s/d US$11/16) Sitting directly over Soyuz bus terminal, this place has exceptionally good-value carpeted rooms with cable TV, but is only for heavy sleepers on account of the rumpus below.

Also try the simple **Hostal Sol de Oro** (☎ 056-23-3735; La Mar 371; dm US$3, s/d with bath US$6/8.50) or **Hostal La Viña** (☎ 056-21-8188; San Martín 256; s/d/tr US$6/9/10) with hot private showers.

Eating

El Otro Peñoncito (Bolívar 255; mains US$4-10) The oldest restaurant in the city center; serves a mean *pisco* sour.

Restaurant Venezia (Lima 230; mains US$4-9) This popular little Italian place is near the plaza.

Chifa Fu Seng (Lima 243; mains US$2.50-5.50) Opposite Restaurant Venezia, this typical *chifa* place serves various set meals.

El Velasco (Libertad 133; set menu US$4, mains US$3-7) On the plaza itself, this place serves

lip-smackingly good cakes, desserts and coffee, and is a popular drinking den in the evening.

Two no-frills vegetarian places are **El Mana** (San Martín; set menu US$1; ☏ Sun-Fri) and **El Paraidiso** (Loreto; set menu US$1.50; ☏ Sun-Fri), which both serve filling menus for loose change.

Getting There & Away

Most bus companies are clustered around the west end of Salaverry. For Lima (US$3 to US$5, 4½ hours), **Soyuz** (☎ 056-23-3312) has departures every 15 minutes. Services are also available with **Cruz del Sur** (☎ 056-22-3333), **Ormeño** (☎ 056-21-5600) and **El Señor de Luren** (☎ 056-22-3658), and every 20 minutes with **Flores Hermanos** (☎ 056-21-2266). For Pisco, simply listen for conductors yelling 'Pisco' at the end of Salaverry. Most companies have daytime buses to Nazca (US$1.70, two hours), but services to Arequipa (US$10 to US$27, 12 hours) are mostly at night. *Colectivos* and minibuses for Pisco and Nazca leave from Lambayeque at Municipalidad, but charge a bit more than buses.

Transportes Oropesa (☎ 056-22-3650), by the Flores terminal, has overnight buses to Ayacucho at 7:30pm (US$5) and Huancavelica at 5pm (US$8, 14 hours).

HUACACHINA

Four kilometers west of Ica, this tiny resort is dominated by giant sand dunes and nestles next to a picturesque lagoon. As a softer, warmer and safer alternative to snowboarding, rent sand boards for US$1.50 an hour to slide, surf and ski your way down the irresistible dunes, getting sand lodged into every bodily nook and cranny imaginable.

Casa de Arena (☎ 056-21-5439; casadearena@hotmail .com; dm US$3, s/d US$3/4.50, with bath US$4.50/6; ☒ 🖳) is a funky sociable place with clean new rooms, an outdoor bar and disco: women should expect attention.

Hostal Rocha (☎ 056-22-2256; kikerocha@hotmail .com; shared r per person US$3; ☒) This place has the same carefree atmosphere, though its rooms are older and all share bathrooms. The owner runs desert dune-buggy trips.

A taxi here from Ica costs US$1.

NAZCA

As the Panamericana rises through coastal mountains and stretches across the arid flats to Nazca (population 53,000), you'd be

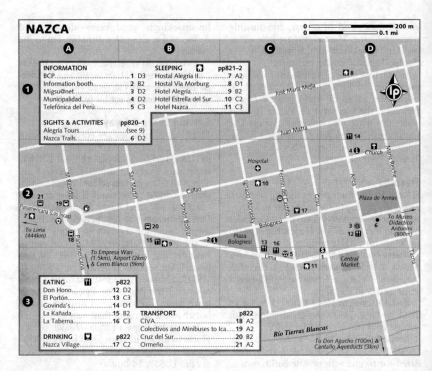

NAZCA

0 —————— 200 m
0 —————— 0.1 mi

INFORMATION	
BCP	1 D3
Information booth	2 B2
Migsu@net	3 D2
Municipalidad	4 D2
Telefónica del Perú	5 C3

SIGHTS & ACTIVITIES	pp820-1
Alegría Tours	(see 9)
Nazca Trails	6 D2

SLEEPING	pp821-2
Hostal Alegría II	7 A2
Hostal Vía Morburg	8 D1
Hotel Alegría	9 B2
Hotel Estrella del Sur	10 C2
Hotel Nazca	11 C3

EATING	p822
Don Hono	12 D2
El Portón	13 C3
Govindu's	14 D1
La Kañada	15 B2
La Taberna	16 C3

DRINKING	p822
Nazca Village	17 C2

TRANSPORT	p822
CIVA	18 A2
Colectivos and Minibuses to Ica	19 A2
Cruz del Sur	20 B2
Ormeño	21 A2

forgiven for thinking that this desolate pampa could hold little of interest. And indeed this sun-bleached expanse was largely ignored by the outside world until 1939, when plane pilots stumbled across one of ancient Peru's most impressive and enigmatic achievements: the Nazca Lines. Today the small town of Nazca is continually inundated by travelers who come to scratch their heads over the mysterious designs.

Information

Hotels and agencies provide information promoting their own tours, but for independent advice, try the **Municipalidad** (☎ 056-52-2418; Plaza de Armas; ⏲ 7am-2pm Mon-Fri) or the student-run **information booth** (cnr Bolognesi & Lima). **BCP** (cnr Lima & Grau) has a Visa ATM and changes traveler's checks. **La Kañada** (Lima 160; US$1.40 per hr) has fast but few Internet machines, while the larger **Migsu@net** (Plaza de Armas; US$0.60 per hr) has clunkier machines.

Dangers & Annoyances

Arriving by bus in Nazca means being harassed by numerous hotel and tour touts

that meet every major bus arrival. Never conduct any business or choose a hotel at the bus stop.

Sights & Activities

NAZCA LINES

Spread across an incredible 500 sq km of arid, rock-strewn plain, the mysterious Nazca Lines form a striking network consisting of over 800 lines, 300 figures, and some 70 animal and plant drawings. The most elaborate designs include a curvaceous 90m-long monkey, a condor with a 130m wingspan, a hummingbird, spider and an intriguing figure popularly referred to as an astronaut because of its goldfish-bowl head. The ancient lines were mostly made by removing sun-darkened stones from the desert surface to expose the lighter stones below.

But who constructed the gigantic lines and for what reason? And why bother when they can only be properly appreciated from the air? Maria Reiche, a German mathematician and longtime researcher of the lines, theorized that they were made by the Paracas and Nazca cultures from 900 BC to 600 AD, with additions by the Wari in the 7th century. She claimed the lines were an astronomical calendar mapped out by sophisticated mathematics (and a long rope), while other theories claim the lines were ritual walkways connected to a water/fertility cult, giant running tracks, extraterrestrial landing sites and representations of shamans' dreams brought on by hallucinogenic drugs. Take your pick.

You can visit the *mirador* (observation tower), on the Panamericana 20km north of Nazca, which has an oblique view of three figures: the lizard, tree and hands (or frog, depending on your angle). Signs warning of landmines are a humorous reminder that walking on the lines is strictly forbidden. To get to the tower, catch a northbound bus (US$0.60) and hitchhike back.

Flights above the lines can be arranged through tour operators or hotels (see below).

Lectures on the lines are held at **Maria Reiche Planetarium** (☎ 056-52-2293; Nazca Lines Hotel; adult/student US$6/3) at 7pm and 9:15pm, and at **Viktoria Nikitzki** (☎ 056-969-9419; Los Espinales 300; admission US$3) at 7pm.

OTHER SIGHTS & ACTIVITIES

The excellent little **Museo Didactico Antonini** (☎ 056-52-3444; Av de la Cultura 600; admission US$3, cameras US$1.50; ☒ 9am-7pm) is highly informative on local sites, and boasts an aqueduct running through the back garden, plus a scale model of the lines.

Local tours take you to the **Cantallo aqueducts** (admission US$1), 2km outside town, where you can see and walk down to working water channels accessed by spiraling wells.

The popular **Cemetery of Chauchilla** (admission US$1.20), 30km away, will satisfy any urges you have to see Nazca bones, skulls and mummies. A dirt road also travels 25km west from Nazca to **Cahuachi**, an important Nazca center.

One off-the-beaten-track expedition is a sand-boarding trip down the nearby **Cerro Blanco**, the highest known sand dune in the world at 2078m, and a real challenge for budding sand-boarders fresh from Huacachina.

Tours

Tour operators are aggressive in Nazca and meet arriving buses to sell you tours before you've even picked up your pack. Don't rush: most tour operators are clustered around the southwest end of Lima where you can pick and choose at will.

Two of the more reliable operators are the well-recommended **Nasca Trails** (☎ 056-52-2858; nascatrails@terra.com.pe; Bolognesi 550) and **Alegría Tours** (☎ /fax 056-52-2444; info@alegriatours peru.com; Hotel Alegría), though flights can also be booked at many of the hotels.

Flights over the lines are made in light aircraft in the mornings and last 30 minutes. The standard flight costs US$35 per person, but low-season deals are available and prices climb to US$50 from June to August. There is a US$5 airport tax. There are also combination flights that include nearby Palpa geoglyphs (US$75). The airport is 2km south of town.

The small aircraft bank left and right, so sufferers of motion sickness may want to skip breakfast.

Sleeping

Prices increase by 25% to 50% between May and August.

Hotel Estrella del Sur (☎ 056-52-2106; estrelladel surhotel@yahoo.com.mx; Callao 568A; s/d/tr/q with breakfast US$7/10/13/18) Offers small but very well-cared for rooms with private electric shower and TV. Service is cheerful and there's a sociable outdoor café.

Hotel Alegría (☎ 056-52-2702; alegriatours@hot mail.com; Lima 168; per person US$4) A mid-range hotel that keeps 13 basic but clean rooms for budget travelers sharing two bathrooms with hot showers.

Hostal Alegría II (☎ 056-52-2497; alegriatours@ hotmail.com; Los Incas 117; per person US$3, s/d with bath US$6/8.50) The sister hotel to Hotel Alegriá is run by second-generation Alegrías and, though it's plain, the staff is helpful and there's hot water.

Hotel Nazca (☎ 056-52-2085; Lima 438; per person US$3) Offers very basic rooms with communal tepid showers. Ticket touts hang around here offering cheap tours – don't pay for anything until you have it in writing.

Hostal Vía Morburg (☎ 056-52-2141; hotelvia morburg@yahoo.es; José María Mejía at Maria Reiche; s/d US$8.50/14; ☒) A cozy place outside the town center, this is cozy, with private showers and lots of hot water. The miniature swimming pool is the size of a bathtub, but there is a decent rooftop restaurant.

Don Agucho (☎ 056-52-2048; donagucho@hotmail .com; Av San Carlos 100; s/d/tr/q US$25/30/40/50; 🖭) Good for a splurge; has chatty service, nice rooms, and a great terrace for lounging, filled with cacti, wickerwork and wagon wheels.

The mid-range **Nido del Condor** (☎ 056-52-3520; km 447; s/d US$25/35; 🖭) and **Hostal Maison Suisse** (☎ 056-52-2434; km 447; s/d/tr US$49/58/79; 🖸 🖭) by the airport also allow campers to stay on their grassy lawns for about US$3 per person.

Eating & Drinking

La Kañada (Lima 160; set menu US$3; ☻ early) Offers good Peruvian food and often gives a free *pisco* sour. A decent list of cocktails includes Algarrobina, made with syrup from the huarango tree.

La Taberna (Lima 321; mains US$2.50-5) An intimate hole-in-the-wall place, the scribbles covering every inch of wall testament to its popularity.

El Portón (cnr Ignacio Morsesky & Lima; mains US$5-10) More upmarket, with a stone courtyard and a varied menu strong on *criollo* and Italian fare.

Don Hono (Arica 254; mains US$2-6; ☻ closed Sat) Just off the Plaza; serves fresh farm produce and is justifiably proud of its *pisco* sour.

Govinda's (Arica 450; set menu US$1.20) The ubiquitous Govinda's has also made it to Nazca. This tiny Hare Krishna–run place serves healthy vegetarian fare.

Nazca Village (Bolognesi; ☻ 10am-11pm) An open-air bar, swish by local standards, in a town with scant nightlife.

Getting There & Away

Ormeño (☎ 056-52-2058) has four buses daily to Lima (US$5 to US$20, eight hours), as well as to intermediate points such as Ica and Pisco. **Cruz del Sur** (☎ 056-52-3500) and **CIVA** (☎ 056-52-3019) also have several buses daily.

Most Arequipa buses (nine to 11 hours) leave late afternoon or at night. Ormeño has three daily services between 4pm and 4am (US$7 to US$2.50). CIVA (US$10 to US$20, three daily) and Cruz del Sur (US$8.50 to US$22.50, seven daily) also have buses.

To go direct to Cuzco, several companies take the newly paved road east via Abancay (US$15.50 to US$22.50, 20 hours). **Empresa Wari** (☎ 056-52-3746), located 2km south of town, leaves at 5pm, 9pm and 11pm. Cruz

del Sur also goes to Cuzco (US$20 to US$28, two daily). The route gets cold; wear warm clothes.

For those heading to Chile, CIVA and Cruz del Sur have twice-daily buses to Tacna (US$12 to US$24, 14 hours).

Frequent combis leave central Nazca for the airport, 2km away (US$0.30, 10 minutes). Fast *colectivos* (US$4, 1½ hours) and minibuses (US$3, 2½ hours) to Ica leave from the Panamericana at Lima when they are full.

NAZCA TO TACNA

Apart from Arequipa, places to stay on the Carretera Panamericana include the small ramshackle seaside town of **Chala**, **Camaná** and the inland colonial town of **Moquegua**, all of which have a few inexpensive hotels from US$3 to US$25.

Mollendo, a small beach resort of about 15,000 people, is another option for accommodations. This normally sleepy little town gets busy during the January to March summer season when *arequipeños* (people from Arequipa) descend in their masses. Buses connect Mollendo with Lima directly (US$15, 17 hours) and Arequipa (US$2.50, three hours).

TACNA

Located 1293km southeast of Lima, Tacna is Peru's southernmost city. It is only 36km from the Chilean border, and was occupied by Chile in 1880 after the War of the Pacific, until its people voted to return to Peru in 1929. Tacna has some of the best schools and hospitals in Peru; whether this is due to its Chilean ties is a matter of opinion.

Information

There's a Chilean consulate near the train station, though most travelers head straight for the border. Chilean pesos, Nuevo Soles and US dollars can all be easily exchanged in Tacna. **BCP** (San Martín 574) has a Visa/MasterCard ATM, changes traveler's checks and gives cash advances on Visa cards. For a decent Internet connection, try **Tacna Net** (Hipolito Unanue; US$0.45 per hr; ☻ 10am-9pm) or **UPT** (Plaza de Armas; US$0.60 per hr; ☻ 8am-11pm Mon-Sat). **Lavandería Latina** (Vizcarra 264b; US$1.40 per kg; ☻ 8am-9:30pm Mon-Sat) will wash your gear. In medical emergencies, there is the **general hospital** (☎ 052-72-3361; Blondell).

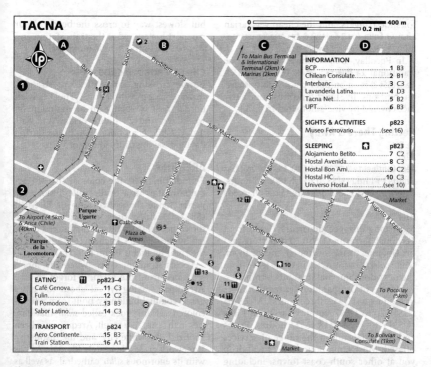

TACNA

INFORMATION	
BCP	1 B3
Chilean Consulate	2 B1
Interbanc	3 C3
Lavandería Latina	4 D3
Tacna Net	5 B2
UPT	6 B3

SIGHTS & ACTIVITIES	p823
Museo Ferroviario	(see 16)

SLEEPING	p823
Alojamiento Betito	7 C2
Hostal Avenida	8 C2
Hostal Bon Ami	9 C2
Hostal HC	10 C3
Universo Hostal	(see 10)

EATING	pp823–4
Café Genova	11 C3
Fulin	12 C2
Il Pomodoro	13 B3
Sabor Latino	14 C3

TRANSPORT	p824
Aero Continente	15 B3
Train Station	16 A1

Sights

The plaza, which is studded with palm trees and pergolas topped by bizarre mushroom-like bushes, features a fountain and cathedral created by French engineer Eiffel (of tower fame).

The **Museo Ferroviario** (☎ 052-72-4981; admission US$0.30; ⏰ 8am-5:30pm), in the train station, lets you wander amid beautiful though poorly maintained 20th-century engines and rolling stock, plus atmospheric salons filled with historic paraphernalia.

A British locomotive, built in 1859 and used as a troop train in the War of the Pacific, is the centerpiece of **Parque de la Locomotora**.

Sleeping

Marinas (☎ 052-74-6014; Circunvalación Sur; s/d US$4/7, with bath US$7/10) Positioned by the bus terminals; secure and very handy for dropping your stuff when arriving late at night. There's cable TV in en-suite rooms.

Hostal Bon Ami (☎ 052-71-1873; miriiam@hotmail .com; 2 de Mayo 445; s/d US$4/6.50, with bath US$6/8) In the city center; shabby but secure with limited hot water.

Alojamiento Betito (☎ 052-70-7429; 2 de Mayo 493; s/d US$3.50/7) Near Hostal Bon Ami in a quirky, old high-ceilinged building with a likeably shambolic feel and cold-water communal baths.

Hostal HC (☎ 052-74-2042; Zela 734; s/d US$7/10) A clean place with a familiar atmosphere, cable TV and private hot showers.

Universo Hostal (☎ 052-71-5441; Zela 724; s/d US$7/10) Next door to Hostal HC; has neat, compact rooms with hot shower, cable TV and telephone.

Hostal Avenida (☎ 052-72-4582; Bolognesi 699; s/d/tr US$10/13/16) Offers clean, businesslike rooms with bath and hot water if requested in advance.

Eating & Drinking

Café Genova (San Martín 649; mains US$4-10; ⏰ till late) Brush shoulders with local socialites at this open-fronted streetside café.

Il Pomodoro (San Martín 521; mains US$4-10) For something more substantial, try this long-established Italian restaurant.

Other options include **Sabor Latino** (Vigil 68; mains US$1.50-5), a recommended small café for shoestringers, and the cheap vegetarian *chaufa* **Fulin** (cnr 2 de Mayo & Aria Araguez; set menu US$1; ❧ closed evenings & weekends).

In Pocollay, 5km southeast of Tacna, the traditional **La Huerta** (☎ 052-71-3080; Zela 1327; mains US$4-8) is an outdoor place with uproarious birdsong, live lunchtime music and a terrace covered by vine-smothered trellising.

Getting There & Away
PERU
Air
Aero Continente (☎ 052-74-7300; Apurímac 265) has flights to Lima (US$70 to US$80, 1½ hours, daily). A US$3.50 departure tax is charged.

Bus
Most long-distance departures leave from Terminal Terrestre (US$0.30 departure tax) on Unanue, at the northeast end of town, while *colectivos* for Arica in Chile leave from the next-door international bus terminal.

Dozens of companies offer regular buses to Moquegua (US$2, three hours), Arequipa (US$4.20 to US$7, seven hours) and Lima (US$11 to US$35, 18 to 22 hours). Prices and times depend on the range of services offered. Most Lima-bound buses will drop you at other south-coast towns, including Nazca (14 hours). Cruz del Sur also has a direct bus to Cuzco at 4:30pm (US$20, 14 hours) via Puno and Desaguadero on the Bolivian border.

Most bus companies to Puno (US$5 to US$17, 12 hours) via Desaguadero (eight hours) leave from Av Circumvalación, north of the city.

Numerous *colectivos* (US$3, one hour) and infrequent buses (US$2) to Arica in Chile leave between 7am and 11pm from the neighboring international bus terminal. On Friday and Saturday you may also find taxis willing to go outside these times, but expect to pay over the odds. Taxi drivers help you through the border formalities.

Note that northbound buses are frequently stopped and searched by immigration and/ or customs officials: have your passport handy.

Train
Tacna's **train station** (☎ 052-72-4981) is on the western side of town, just north of 2 de Mayo. Trains to Arica (US$1.50, 1½ to 2 hours, two to three per day) are the cheapest but slowest way to cross the border. Your passport is stamped at the train station and you receive entry stamps on arrival.

CHILEAN BORDER CROSSING
Border-crossing formalities are straightforward in both directions. The Peruvian border post is open 8am to midnight on weekdays, and 24 hours Friday and Saturday. Chile is an hour (two hours during daylight-saving time) ahead of Peru.

AREQUIPA
Founded in 1540, the colonial city of Arequipa nestles in a fertile valley under the perfect cone-shaped volcano of El Misti (5822m), which rises majestically behind the cathedral from the plaza, flanked to the left by the ragged Chachani (6075m) and to the right by Pichu Pichu (5571m).

Locals sometimes say 'when the moon separated from the earth, it forgot to take Arequipa,' waxing lyrical about the city's grand colonial buildings, built from a light-colored volcanic rock called *sillar* that dazzles in the sun. As a result, Arequipa has been baptized 'the white city' and the distinctive stonework graces the stately Plaza de Armas with its enormous *sillar* cathedral, as well as numerous beautiful colonial churches and mansions dotted throughout the city.

Information
BOOKSHOPS
Librería el Lector (☎ 054-28-8677; San Francisco 221; ❧ 9am-9pm) Book exchange, plus good selection of new titles and guidebooks.
Colca Trek (☎ 054-20-6217, 054-960-0170; Jerusalén 401B) Best place for maps of the region.

EMERGENCY
Clínica Arequipa (☎ 054-25-3424; cnr Bolognesi & Av Puente Grau; consultation US$17; ❧ 7am-8:30pm Mon-Sat)
Inka Farma (☎ 054-20-3275; Santa Domingo 103; ❧ 24 hr) Well-stocked pharmacy.
Paz Holandesa Policlinic (☎ 054-20-6720; info@paz holandesa.com; Av Jorge Chavez 527; ❧ Mon-Sat)
Policía de Turismo (☎ 054-20-1258; Jerusalén 317; ❧ 24 hr)

IMMIGRATION OFFICES
Migraciónes (☎ 054-42-1759; at Parque 2, cnr Bustamante & Rivero, Urb Quinta Tristán; ❧ 8am-11am & 2-3pm Mon-Fri) For tourist-card extensions.

INTERNET ACCESS
Cibermarket (☎ 054-22-7055; Santa Catalina 115B; US$0.60 per hr)
Chips Internet (☎ 054-20-3651; San Francisco 202A; US$0.60 per hr)

LAUNDRY
Jerusalén has plenty of spots for washing your kit.
Magic Laundry (Jerusalén 404; US$1.20 per kg; 🕑 8am-7pm Mon-Sat)

MONEY
Moneychangers and ATMs are found on nearby streets.
Interbanc (Mercaderes 217) ATM with Visa/Plus/Cirrus/MasterCard, and the bank accepts a broad range of traveler's checks.
BCP (San Juan de Dios 125 at Jerusalén) Has a Visa ATM and changes traveler's checks; there's also an ATM on the northeast corner of Plaza de Armas.

POST
Main post office (Moral 118; 🕑 7:30am-8:30pm Mon-Sat, 7:30am-1pm Sun)

TELEPHONE
Telefónica del Perú (Alvarez Thomas 201)

TOURIST OFFICES
iPeru (☎ 054-22-1228; iperuarequipa@promperu.gob.pe; Portal Municipal 112, Plaza de Armas; 🕑 8:30am-7:30pm) The iPeru office combines Prom Peru and INDECOPI, the tourist protection agency, and deals with complaints against tour agencies. It also has a branch at the airport.

Sights
CHURCHES
Even if you've already overdosed on colonial edifices of yesteryear, the **Monasterio de Santa Catalina** (☎ 054-22-9798; Santa Catalina 300; admission US$7; 🕑 9am-4pm) shouldn't be missed. Occupying a whole city block between Bolívar and Santa Catalina, and surrounded by imposing high walls, this huge convent is practically a city within a city. A wealthy widow that chose her nuns from the richest Spanish families founded it in 1580, but her new nuns generally lived it up in the style they had always been accustomed to. After about three centuries of these hedonistic goings-on, a strict Dominican nun arrived to straighten things out. From this point, the vast majority of the 450 people who once lived here never ventured outside the convent's imposing high walls and the convent was shrouded in mystery until it finally opened to the public in 1970.

The imposing **cathedral** (Plaza de Armas; admission free; 🕑 7am-10am & 5-7pm) was originally built in 1656, but was gutted by fire in 1844, rebuilt, then promptly flattened by the earthquake of 1868. The earthquake of June 2001 also toppled one enormous tower while the other slumped precariously, yet by late 2002 the cathedral was as good as new once again.

One of the oldest churches in Arequipa is the Jesuit **Iglesia de La Compañía** (☎ 054-21-2141; admission free; 🕑 10am-noon & 5-7pm) on the southeast corner of the Plaza de Armas. It's noted for its ornate main façade and the **San Ignacio chapel** (admission US$0.60; 🕑 9am-noon & 3-6pm Sun-Fri, 11am-noon & 3-6pm Sat), with its polychrome cupola smothered with lush murals of tropical flowers, fruits and birds, among which mingle warriors and angels.

The Franciscan **Monasterio de la Recoleta** (☎ 054-27-0966; convrecoleta@terra.com.pe; La Recoleta 117; adult/student US$1.40/1; 🕑 9am-7pm Mon-Sat) was built in 1648, but has been completely rebuilt since. The fascinating library on the grounds contains more than 20,000 historic books.

COLONIAL BUILDINGS
A few of the stately *sillar* mansions can also be visited. Built in 1730, **Casa de Moral** (☎ 054-22-1084; Moral 318; adult/student US$1.40/1; 🕑 9am-5pm Mon-Sat) is now one of the most accessible for snooping, and bilingual guides are available. **Casa Ricketts** (San Francisco; admission free; 🕑 9:15am-1pm & 4:30-6:30pm Mon-Fri, 9:30am-noon Sun), built in 1738, is also worth a look.

MUSEUMS
Museo Santuarios Andinos (☎ 054-20-0345; www.ucsm.edu.pe/santury; Santa Catalina 210; adult/child US$4.20/1.40; 🕑 9am-6pm Mon-Sat, 9am-3pm Sun) exhibits 'Juanita, the Ice Princess' – the frozen Inca maiden sacrificed on the summit of Mt Ampato (6288m) over 500 years ago. For the Incas, mountains were gods who could kill by volcanic eruption, avalanche or climatic catastrophes. These violent deities could only be appeased by sacrifices, and over 20 similar child sacrifices have now been discovered atop various Andean mountains since 1954. Multilingual tours consist of a video followed by a reverent look at burial

PERU

AREQUIPA

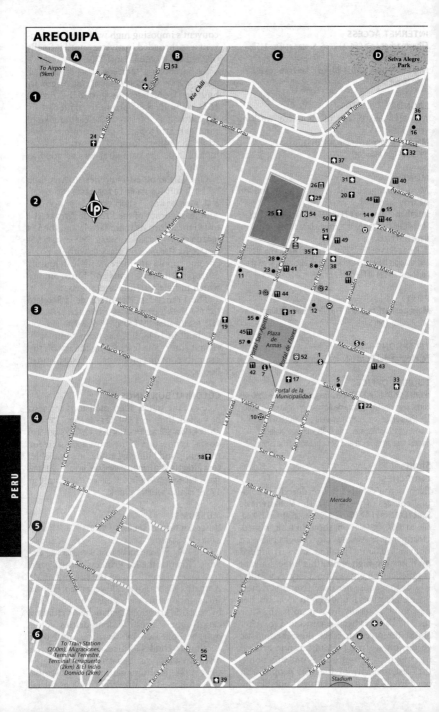

artifacts culminating with a viewing of the star herself plus another frozen mummy preserved in glass-walled freezers under carefully monitored conditions. Note that Juanita herself is not on display from January to April each year, but is replaced by another child sacrifice.

The **Museo Histórico Municipal** (San Francisco 407; adult/student US$0.60/0.30; ☉ 7am-3pm Mon-Fri) houses paintings, satirical caricatures, photographs, maps and other paraphernalia.

Courses

To book in for a language course, contact the following organizations:

Centro de Intercambio Cultural (☎ 054-22-1165; ceica@terra.com.pe; Urb Universitaria G-9) US$120 for 20 hours of private lessons per week.

Rocio Oporto (☎ 054-28-6929; claro@unas.edu.pe; La Perlita 103) US$6.50 per individual class of 90 minutes. Group lessons cost less.

CEPESMA (☎ 054-40-5927; La Marina 141; cepesma .idiomas@peru.com) US$6 per hour for private classes.

Tours

Santa Catalina and Jerusalén host dozens of travel agencies offering city tours, excursions to the Cañón del Colca, and trekking, mountaineering and rafting trips; there are plenty of carpet-baggers muscling in on the action here, so shop carefully. Never accept tours from street touts.

Colca Trek (☎ 054-20-6217, 054-960-0170; colcatrek@ hotmail.com; Jerusalén 401B) Excellent adventure tour agency run by the English-speaking Vlado Soto.

Cusipata (☎ 054-20-3966, 054-931-1576; gvellutino@ terra.com.pe; Jerusalén 408; ☉ closed Dec-Feb) Currently the best river-running company.

Giardino (☎ 054-22-1345; giardino@terra.com.pe; Jerusalén 604)

Illary Tours (☎ 054-22-0844; Santa Catalina 205)

Naturaleza Activa (☎ 054-69-5793; naturaleza@ yahoo.com; Santa Catalina 211) New company making its name in adventure tours, especially mountain biking. It's also possible to hire bikes here.

Pa'Enrique (☎ 054-44-3789; tourecuestre@mixmail.com; Chilina) Short horse-riding tours. Based outside of the city so prefers to be contacted by phone or email.

Zárate Adventura (☎ 054-26-3107; www.zarateadventures.com; Santa Catalina 204) The great grandfather of Arequipeño climbing agencies.

Festivals & Events

The *arequipeños* are a proud people, and their passionate celebration of the city's founding on August 15, renews a stubborn sense of aloofness from their coastal capital.

Sleeping

Unless otherwise indicated, all hostels listed have hot water. Many are unmarked, or recognizable by a sign proclaiming 'Room For Tourist.'

Hospedaje El Caminante Class (☎ 054-20-3444; Santa Catalina 207A, 2nd fl; s/d US$5.60/9.80, with bath US$9.80/14) Central, clean and repeatedly recommended by readers, this place offers spotless rooms, kitchen privileges, friendly English-speaking service and all the *maté de coca* (coca-leaf tea) you can possibly drink. There's a terrace and fine views from the rooftop.

El Indio Dormido (☎ 054-42-7401; the_sleeping_indian@yahoo.com; Av Andrés Avelino Cáceres B9; per person US$4, s/d with bath US$5.60/8.40) By Terminal Terrestre, this new hostel is cheap, popular and has a cute (but noisy) terrace garden with hammocks on top.

Colonial House Inn II (☎ 054-28-4249; colonialhouseinn@star.com.pe; Rivero 504; s/d US$7/13, with bath US$9/14) This is a top-notch new hostel housed in a colonial building. Rooms combine a rustic style with cleanliness and convenience. It doesn't have a sign.

Le Foyer (☎ 054-28-6473; hostallefoyer@yahoo.com; Ugarte 114; s/d US$5/9, with bath US$10/13) Though pervaded with hunger-inducing smells from the Mexican restaurant below, this clean place is a stone's throw from Arequipa's nocturnal action.

Casa La Reyna (☎ 054-28-6578; Zela Melgar 209; dm per person US$4, s/d US$5/10) An old favorite, La Reyna has rooftop balconies with mountain and monastery views. It's cheek-to-jowl with Arequipa's nightlife – a plus or minus point depending on your sleep requirements.

Tambo Viejo (☎ 054-28-8195; room@tamboviejo.com; Malecón Socabaya 107; dm US$5, s/d US$9/12, with bath US$12/18) This longtime travelers' hang-out has a garden with tiny outdoor bar, and a terrace with volcano views and raucous pet parrots.

Hostal Tumi de Oro (☎ 054-28-1319; San Agustín 311A; s/d US$8.40/11.20) Run by a chirpy old lady, this informal hostel has a prettily tiled terrace, book exchange and table football. Rooms have private bath and there are kitchen facilities.

Other recommendations:

Hostal Residencial Núñez (☎ 054-21-8648; hostal_nunez@terra.com.pe; Jerusalén 528; s/d with bath & TV US$10/17) A frilly, friendly hostel popular with gringos.

La Posada del Cacique (☎ 054-20-2170; posadadelcacique@yahoo.es; Calle Puente Grau 219; s/d US$4/7, bath US$7/9.80) Friendly, family-run option with a central patio for lazing.

Colonial House Inn (☎ 054-22-3533; colonialhouseinn@hotmail.com; Av Puente Grau 114; s/d US$7/11.20) Peaceful colonial house.

Hotel Regis (☎ 054-22-6111; Ugarte 202; s/d US$5/10, d with bath US$14) Clean, safe and close to the action.

Hostal Tito (☎ 054-23-4424; Peru 107; s/d US$2.50/3.40, with cold-water bath US$4.70/7.20) Friendly rock-bottom option.

Eating
RESTAURANTS

El Turko (San Francisco 216; mains US$2.50-6; 🕐 24 hr Fri & Sat) This funky little joint serves a hungry crowd its late-night kebabs, but also makes a good coffee-stop during the day. Its big brother, in the thick of things at San Francisco 315, is also highly recommended for Turkish/Italian fare.

La Serenata (Portal San Agustín 115, 2nd fl; mains US$4.50-12) One of several restaurants overlooking the Plaza de Armas from surrounding balconies. The food is so-so value, but the views are more than worth the price of an espresso.

Ary Quepay (Jerusalén 502; mains US$4-7) This place offers traditional plates (including alpaca and guinea pig) in a colonial building that extends into a dimly lit rustic area dripping with plants. There's enthusiastic *música folklórica* nightly (7:30pm to 8:30pm).

Pizzería Los Leños (Jerusalén 407; mains US$1.60-17; 🕐 evening only, closed Sun) One of the best wood-burning pizzerias in southern Peru. If you're impressed, add your personalized scribble to the already-covered walls.

La Viñeda (San Francisco 319; mains US$6-10) An intimate spot, this is one of the best places to knock back 'as-thick-as-you-like' Argentine steaks plus typical food.

Tradición Arequipeña (☎ 054-42-6467; Av Dolores 111; US$4-10; 🕐 closes 7pm Sun-Thu, 10pm Fri-Sat) This excellent Arequipeño restaurant has maze-like gardens, and locals come from miles around to discuss the hot topics of Peruvian politics over a similarly spicy Arequipeñan meal. Located 2km southeast of the city center, taxis here cost US$1.20.

El Gaucho Parrilladas (☎ 054-22-0301; Portal de Flores 112; mains US$6-16; ✆ evenings only, closed Sun) Experts in steak and steak alone; no skimping on portions here.

Bistrot (Santa Catalina 208) Cultural café in the Alianza Francesa to get your caffeine fix.

Trattoria Gianni (San Francisco 304; mains US$4.50-9; ✆ Mon-Sat) Old favorite for pizza.

SELF-CATERING

Stock up at the two branches of **El Super** (Pierola & Portal de la Municipalidad, Plaza de Armas; ✆ 9am-2pm & 4-8:30pm Mon-Sat, 9am-2pm Sun).

VEGETARIAN

Mandala (Jerusalén 207; set menu US$1.20-2; ✆ closed Sun) A great vegetarian option with quick, cheap and quality offerings. Recommended.

Lakshimivan (Jerusalén 402; mains US$2-3.50) Set in a colorful old building with a tiny outdoor courtyard, this vegetarian place has set menus and an extensive à la carte selection. Service can be slow.

Govinda (Santa Catalina 120; set menu US$4.20) Run by the Hare Krishnas, this large vegetarian restaurant has a line-up of menus that change daily, including Italian, Hindu and traditional Arequipeño.

Entertainment

Beyond the tourist haunts, the hottest local action is to be had along Av Dolores, 2km southeast of the city center.

Déjà Vu (San Francisco 319B; ✆ 6pm-2am) A popular watering hole. Has a rooftop terrace overlooking San Francisco, and makes it easy by combining movies, meals and booze. It also has a long list of cocktails – try Cucaracha (US$3).

Forum Rock Café (San Francisco 317; admission Fri-Sat US$4; ✆ 10pm-4am Tue-Sat) A gutsy Latin rock bar with a thing for bamboo and waterfalls; it's currently the most happening club in town.

La Casa de Klaus (Melgar Zela 207; ✆ 11am-2am Mon-Sat, 11am-5pm Sun) Attracts a rowdy crowd. Serves Holsten, Guinness and Heineken for those hankering after home.

Las Quenas (Santa Catalina 302; admission US$1.40; ✆ Mon-Sat) This place features nightly performances of *folklórica*.

A handful of local cinemas include **Cinessur el Portal** (☎ 054-20-2202; Portal de Flores 112).

For sports, **Club Internacional** (☎ 054-25-3384; admission Mon-Fri US$3, Sat & Sun US$4.50; ✆ 6am-8pm Mon-Sat & 7am-5pm Sun) has swimming, soccer and bowling near Puente Grau.

Getting There & Away
AIR

The **airport** (☎ 054-44-3464) is 9km northwest of the city center (there's a US$3.50 departure tax). There are several daily flights to Lima (US$72 to US$80) and Cuzco (US$43 to US$70), and connections to Puerto Maldonado and Iquitos.

Aero Continente/Aviandina (☎ 054-20-3294; Portal San Augustín 113) and **LanPeru** (☎ 054-20-1100; Portal de San Agustín 118) serve Lima and Cuzco daily, while **TANS** (☎ 054-20-5231; Portal de San Agustín 143A) has flights to Iquitos and Puerto Maldonado via Cuzco and Lima.

BUS

Terminal Terrestre and Terrapuerto bus station are located 3km south of the city center (US$0.30 departure tax). All busy companies are located at either of these two terminals. Check which terminal your bus leaves from in advance. Travel agents will book tickets for a commission of around US$1.50 – less than a round-trip taxi fare and less hassle.

For Lima (US$9 to US$32, 16 hours), **Ormeño** (☎ 054-42-4187), **Cruz del Sur** (☎ 054-42-7375) and **CIVA** (☎ 054-42-6563) have several buses a day, mostly in the afternoon. Most buses stop in Nazca (US$6 to US$25, 10 to 12 hours) and Ica (13 to 14 hours) en route. These and other companies also have buses to Cuzco (US$12 to US$15, 12 to 16 hours) on a partially paved direct road or the asphalted route via Puno.

Ormeño (US$10), Cruz del Sur (US$6) and CIVA (US$4.50) also have several buses a day to Juliaca (five hours) and Puno (5½ hours). **Señor de los Milagros** (☎ 054-42-3260) continues all the way to Desaguadero (US$7, nine hours) on the Bolivian border. Flores and Cruz del Sur have many buses to Tacna (US$4 to US$7, seven hours).

For Chivay (US$3, three hours), continuing to Cabanaconde (US$4, seven hours) on the upper Cañón del Colca, try **La Reyna** (☎ 054-43-0612), **Transportes Colca** (☎ 054-42-6357) or **Turismo Pluma** (☎ 054-28-4721). Buses leave around 1am, 11am and 2pm daily.

Transportes del Carpio (☎ 054-42-7049) goes to Valle de Majes (US$2.50, four hours, hourly)

PERU

for river running. For Cotahuasi (US$7 to US$9, 12 hours), La Reyna has a 5pm departure and **Transportes Alex** (☎ 054-42-4605) has a 3:45pm departure.

TRAIN
Services to Juliaca/Puno were suspended in 2002.

Getting Around
Combis go south along Bolívar and Sucre bound for Terminal Terrestre (US$0.30, 10 minutes). A taxi will cost about US$1. Buses marked 'Río Seco,' 'Cono-Norte' or 'Zamacola' go along Puente Grau and Ejército and pass within 700m of the airport. A taxi from downtown costs US$3. Two local taxi numbers to call are **Ideal Taxi** (☎ 054-28-8888) and **Gino Taxi** (☎ 054-27-2828).

AROUND AREQUIPA

Arequipa is surrounded by some of the wildest terrain in Peru. This is a land of active volcanoes, thermal springs, high-altitude deserts and the world's deepest canyons – not least, the famous Cañón del Colca, shadowed by snow-topped volcanoes, replete with opportunities for hiking, and moreover the best place in Peru to spot the wild Andean condor.

CAÑÓN DEL COLCA
For years there was raging controversy over whether or not this was the world's deepest canyon at 3191m, but it has recently drawn in a close second to the neighboring Cañón del Cotahuasi, which is all of 163m deeper. The sections seen on a standard guided tour are impressive in themselves, but to witness the deepest sections you have to make an overnight trip and put in some legwork hiking. As you pass through the canyon's traditional villages, look out for the local women's painstakingly embroidered traditional clothing and hats.

Activities
MOUNTAINEERING
Superb mountains for climbing surround Arequipa. Problems are extreme weather conditions, altitude and lack of water (carry 4L per person per day). Though many climbs in the area are not technically difficult, they

should never be undertaken lightly. Be aware of the main symptoms of altitude sickness (see p1059).

Always check the ID of guides carefully, and ask to see the little black book that identifies trained and registered guides. **Colca Trek** (☎ 054-20-6217, 054-960-0170; colcatrek@hotmail.com) and **Zárate Adventura** (☎ 054-26-3107; www.zarateadventures.com) are recommended agencies, and rent tents, ice axes and crampons. Colca Trek also sells maps of the area.

Looming above Arequipa is the city's guardian volcano **El Misti** (5822m), the most popular local climb. It can be tackled solo, but going with a guide protects against robberies, which have been reported on the Apurímac route. Ask in Arequipa for advice. One popular route is from Chiguata, an eight-hour hard uphill slog on rough trails to base camp. From there to the summit and back takes eight more hours and there's no water. The summit is marked by a 10m-high cross. The return from the base camp to Chiguata takes three hours or less.

Chachani (6075m) is one of the easiest 6000m peaks in the world. You will need crampons, an ice axe and good equipment. Other nearby peaks of interest include **Sabancaya** (5976m), **Hualca Hualca** (6025m), **Ampato** (6288m), **Ubinas** (5675m), **Mismi** (5556m) and **Coropuna** (6425m).

RIVER RAFTING
The **Río Chile**, 7km from Arequipa, is the most frequently run local river, with a half-day trip suitable for beginners leaving daily from April to December (US$25 to US$30). Further afield, the **Río Majes** passes grade II and III rapids. The **Casa de Mauro** (camping per person US$2, dm US$3), in the village of Ongoro, 190km by road west of Arequipa, is a convenient base for rafting the Majes (US$20 to US$35). The lodge can be contacted through **Colca Trek** (☎ 054-20-6217, 054-960-0170; colcatrek@hotmail.com) or **Cusipata** (☎ 054-20-3966, 054-931-1576; gvellutino@terra.com.pe; ☉ closed Dec-Feb). It is cheapest to take a bus from Arequipa with Trebul to Aplao (US$2, three hours) and then take a minibus to Ongoro (or taxi for US$3.50).

Tours
Guided day trips cost US$18 to US$20, but are rushed and not recommended. The

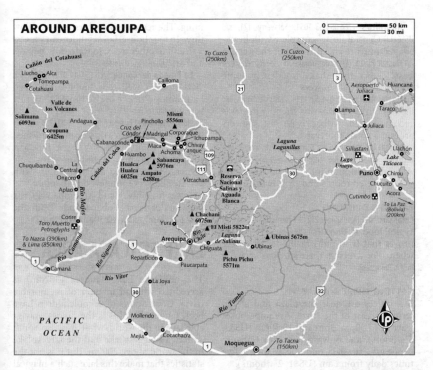

AROUND AREQUIPA

two-day guided trip is far more relaxed, and costs US$18 to US$70 per person depending on your hotel. Two-day tours leave between 7am and 9am and arrive in Chivay for lunch. Some agencies take their groups on a hike, and the hot springs of Chivay are almost always visited, followed by a visit to a *peña* in the evening. Next morning, groups leave at 6am to reach Cruz del Cóndor around 8am to 8:30am, for an hour of condor spotting before returning.

Agencies also offer a mish-mash of other tours, including an array of off-the-beaten-track trekking routes. The best time to hike is from May to November, and the canyon has a scattering of **camping zones** (camping per person US$1.40), but it's forbidden to camp by Cruz del Condor.

Arequipa to Chivay

The road from Arequipa climbs northwest to **Reserva Nacional Salinas y Aguada Blanca**, where vicuñas – the delicate wild cousins of llamas and alpaca – are often sighted. The road continues through bleak *altiplano* (high Andean plateau) over the highest point of 4800m, before dropping spectacularly to Chivay.

Chivay

There are no money-changing facilities in the canyon, so bring plenty of cash. Internet access is available at **Albicsa Hotel** (Jose Galvez 109; US$2.25 per hr; ☾ 8am-10pm). Don't miss the **hot springs** (adult US$1.40, locker deposit US$1.40; ☾ 4am-7pm), 4km northeast of Chivay by road. The steaming-hot, mineral-laden water does a good job of boiling eggs and it's particularly handy when the hot-water supply in Chivay packs up. There are occasional *colectivos* (US$0.30) or you can easily walk.

SLEEPING

Though a tiny town, Chivay has plenty of hostels to choose from.

Hospedaje Rumi Wasi (☎ 054-53-1101; Sucre 714; s/d/tr US$6/9/12) A recommended family-run hostel, with a central garden and decent rooms with private bath. Also hires bikes.

Hostal Municipal (☎ 054-53-1093; Plaza de Armas; s/d US$7/12) Central hostel with private hot showers.

Ricardito's (☎ 054-53-1051; Salaverry 121; s/d US$6/12) Central hostel complete with heart-shaped mirrors and private hot showers.

Hostal Plaza (Plaza de Armas; s/d US$3/6) A very basic choice in a shaky wooden building with shared cold showers.

Hostal Anita (☎ 054-52-1114; Plaza de Armas; s/d US$6/12) On the plaza, this friendly hostel is recommended, with private hot showers around a small courtyard.

Hostal La Pascana (☎ 054-53-1019; gromup@latin mail.com; cnr Siglo xx & Puente Inca; s/d/tr US$10/20/35) A good new option for a few dollars more, with carpeted rooms and firm mattresses.

EATING & DRINKING

Calamarcito's (José Gálvez 232; set menu US$4) serves typical food. **M´elroys** (Plaza de Armas; ☺ 4pm-1am) proves that Irish pubs really do get everywhere. For dancing, there's **Latigo's** (cnr Puente Inca & Bolognesi).

GETTING THERE & AWAY

Bus offices are near the plaza and at the terminal, east of the plaza. Arequipa buses leave at 12:30pm, 3pm and 10:30pm (US$3, 3½ hours), and onward buses for Cabanaconde via Cruz del Condor leave four to five times daily from 6am (US$1, 2¾ hours).

Chivay to Cabanaconde

The road following the south bank of the upper Cañón del Colca leads past several villages and some of the most extensive pre-Inca terracing in Peru until it comes to **Cruz del Cóndor** (admission US$2). For many, this viewpoint is the highlight of their trip to the Colca. A large family of Andean condors nests by the rocky outcrop and can be seen gliding effortlessly on thermal air currents rising from the canyon, often swooping low over watchers' heads. It's a mesmerizing scene, heightened by the spectacular 1200m drop to the river below and the sight of 5556m-high Mismi reaching 3200m above sea level on the other side of the ravine. Early morning or late afternoon are the best times to see the birds.

Cabanaconde

Cabanaconde is a good base for some spectacular hikes into the canyon, including the popular two-hour trek down to Sangalle (the Oasis) at the bottom of the canyon, where there are two natural pools for swim-

ming. The return trek is thirsty work; allow three to four hours. Local guides can suggest a wealth of other treks, to waterfalls, geysers and archaeological sites.

La Posada del Conde (☎ 054-44-0197; per person US$7) Modern, well-kept doubles with clean bathrooms. Prices can rise to US$15 in July through August.

Hostal Valle del Fuego (☎ 054-28-0367; per person US$3) Although basic, this is an established travelers' scene, with DVDs, a full bar, solar-powered showers and knowledgeable owners. There's also a newer annex with private showers for a few dollars more.

Buses for Chivay and Arequipa via Cruz del Condor leave Cabanaconde from the plaza at 5am, 8am, 10:30am and 8pm.

LAKE TITICACA AREA

The immense Lake Titicaca (3820m) is accredited with all manner of memorable trivia. Generations of schoolchildren have been taught that this is the highest navigable lake in the world, while it is also South America's biggest lake and the largest lake in the world above 2000m. But it is not the statistics that make this lake such a magical place to visit.

At this altitude, the air is unusually clear, and the luminescent quality of the sunlight suffuses the highland *altiplano* and sparkles on the deep waters of the lake. Horizons here seem limitless, and the environs boast a liberal scattering of ancient funerary towers and crumbling colonial churches. The port of Puno is a convenient base from which to visit far-flung islands dotted across Titicaca – from the artificial reed islands constructed by the Uros culture to isolated communities where islanders live their lives much as they have for centuries.

See Bolivia p191 for a map.

JULIACA

The large, brash town (elevation 3822m) has the department's only commercial airport, though it sees far less tourists than smaller lakeside neighbor Puno.

Information

Clínica Americana Adventista (☎ 051-32-1001, emergency 051-32-1071; Loreto 315; ☺ emergencies only Sat) is the best hospital in the department.

Interbanc (Nuñez, 2nd block) and **BCP** (Nuñez 138) have ATMs, and the latter changes traveler's checks.

Sleeping & Eating

Hostal Luquini (☎ 051-32-1510; Bracesco 409; s/d US$4.50/7.50, with bath US$7.50/12.50) This recommended hostel has simple, clean rooms around a courtyard and is run by a charmingly absent-minded family. There is hot water from 5pm till morning.

Hostal San Antonio (☎ 051-32-1803; San Martín 347; s/d US$3/5, with bath US$8/11.50) Offers a large array of basic but clean rooms; the better options are in the new wing with private hot showers and national TV. For those without bath, hot showers are an extra US$0.75 for 20 minutes. There is also an attached sauna for US$3.

La Fonda del Royal (☎ 051-32-1561; San Román 158; mains US$3-5) Housed in the Hotel Royal Inn, this is the best restaurant in town.

Getting There & Away

AIR

Juliaca **airport** (☎ 051-32-1391) serves both Juliaca and Puno. Between **LanPeru** (☎ 051-32-2228; San Roman 125) and **Aero Continente** (☎ 051-33-3004; San Roman 754) there are three flights a day to Lima (from US$74, 1½ hours) via Arequipa (from US$43, 40 minutes). The airport tax is US$3.50. Minibuses to Puno (US$1.50, one hour) await arriving flights and can be found outside the arrival hall.

BUS

Cruz del Sur (☎ 051-32-2011), **CIVA** (☎ 051-32-6229) and **Ormeño** (☎ 051-54-5057), located on the 12th block of San Martín, 1km to the east of town, travel to the same destinations as from Puno (see p836). **San Martín** (☎ 051-32-7501) has night buses to Moquegua and Tacna (US$6, 11 hours). Minibuses to Puno (US$0.60, 50 minutes) leave when they are full from the southeast corner of Plaza Bolognesi.

TRAIN

For details about trains, times and fares to Cuzco, see p836. Trains leave Juliaca one to two hours after the Puno departure time. Juliaca train station has had a reputation for luggage snatching, so keep a sharp eye on your stuff.

AROUND JULIACA

Almost 56km northwest of Juliaca, the sleepy village of **Pucara** (pop 2500) is famous for its earthy **ceramic bulls** seen perched on the roofs of Andean houses for luck. There is also a **museum** (adult/student US$1.40/1; ⏱ 8am-5pm) displaying a good little selection of anthropomorphic monoliths from the town's pre-Inca site.

From here, the route climbs 170km through bleak *altiplano* to the **Abra La Raya**, a pass at 4319m and the highest point on the trip to Cuzco.

PUNO

The small port of Puno is the best departure point for forays to Lake Titicaca's various islands or surrounding archaeological sites. The town was founded in 1668, though few colonial buildings remain in the claustrophobic streets, which bustle with *trici-taxis* (rickshaws) and markets. Nights here get especially cold, particularly during the winter months of June to August, when temperatures can drop well below freezing.

Information

IMMIGRATION OFFICES

Migraciónes (☎ 051-35-7103; Ayacucho 240; ⏱ 8am-2pm Mon-Fri) Extends visas and tourist cards, though it's cheaper to go to Bolivia and return.

INTERNET ACCESS

Choza@net (Lima 339, 2nd fl; US$0.60 per hr; ⏱ 8am-11pm)

Puno Line (Lima 288; US$0.45 per hr; ⏱ 8am-11pm)

LAUNDRY

Lavaclin (Valcárcel; US$1.40 per kg; ⏱ 8am-noon & 2-7pm Mon-Sat)

Lavandería Don Manuel (Lima 4th block; US$1.40 per kg; ⏱ 7am-6pm Mon-Sat)

MEDICAL SERVICES

Botica Fasa (☎ 051-36-5543; Arequipa 314) Good 24-hour pharmacy.

Regional Hospital (☎ 051-35-2931; El Sol 1022)

MONEY

Bolivian pesos can be exchanged in Puno or at the border near Yunguyo; rates vary so ask travelers coming from Bolivia which is currently the best choice.

BCP (cnr Lima & Grau) Visa ATM and gives cash advances from Visa cards.

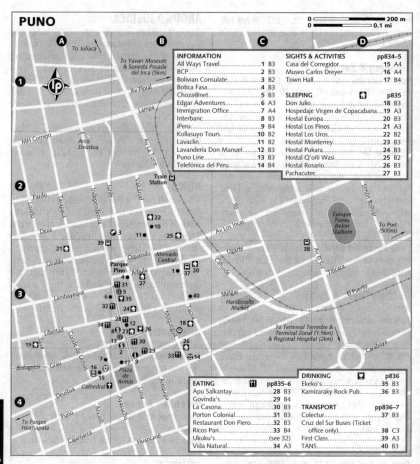

PUNO

INFORMATION		SIGHTS & ACTIVITIES	pp834–5
All Ways Travel................1 B3		Casa del Corregidor...........15 A4	
BCP................................2 B3		Museo Carlos Dreyer..........16 A4	
Bolivian Consulate............3 B2		Town Hall........................17 B4	
Botica Fasa.....................4 B3			
Choza@net....................5 B3		SLEEPING	p835
Edgar Adventures.............6 A3		Don Julio........................18 B3	
Immigration Office............7 A4		Hospedaje Virgen de Copacabana...19 A3	
Interbanc.......................8 B3		Hostal Europa..................20 B3	
iPeru............................9 B3		Hostal Los Pinos...............21 A3	
Kollasuyo Tours...............10 B3		Hostal Los Uros................22 B3	
Lavaclin........................11 B2		Hostal Monterrey..............23 B3	
Lavandería Don Manuel......12 B3		Hostal Pukara..................24 B3	
Puno Line......................13 B4		Hostal Q'oñi Wasi..............25 B2	
Telefónica del Peru...........14 B4		Hostal Rosario..................26 B3	
		Pachacutec......................27 B3	

EATING	pp835–6
Apu Salkantay...............28 B3	
Govinda's....................29 B4	
La Casona....................30 B3	
Porton Colonial.............31 B3	
Restaurant Don Piero.......32 B3	
Ricos Pan.....................33 B4	
Ukuku's.......................(see 32)	
Vida Natural.................34 A3	

DRINKING	p836
Ekeko's........................35 B3	
Kamizaraky Rock Pub.......36 B3	

TRANSPORT	pp836–7
Colectur......................37 B3	
Cruz del Sur Buses (Ticket office only)...38 C3	
First Class....................39 A3	
TANS..........................40 B3	

Interbanc (Lima 4th block) ATM for Visa/Plus/ MasterCard/Cirrus networks, and changes traveler's checks.

POST
Post office (☎ 051-35-1141; Moquegua 267; ⏰ 8am-6pm Mon-Sat, 8am-1pm Sun)

TELEPHONE
Telefónica del Peru (cnr Moquegua & El Puerto)

TOURIST OFFICE
iPeru (☎ 051-36-5088; iperupuno@promperu.gob.pe; cnr Lima & Deustua; ⏰ 8:30am-7:30pm) Puno's very helpful and friendly main tourist office.
Policía de Turismo (Deustua 588; ⏰ 24 hr) Provides help in cases of emergency.

TRAVEL AGENCIES
Never part with your money until you are in a hotel or travel agency.
All Ways Travel (☎ 051-35-5552; awtperu@terra.com.pe; Tacna 234) An excellent agency run by multilingual staff. Also good for more off-the-beaten track options.
Edgar Adventures (☎ 051-35-3444; edgaradventures@ terra.com.pe; Lima 328) Gets mostly good recommendations.
Kollasuyo Tours (☎ 051-36-8642; kollasuyos@terra.com; Valcárcel 155) Newer agency recommended for its flexibility.

Sights & Activities
The **Yavari Museum** (☎ 051-36-9329; www.yavari.org; admission free; ⏰ 8am-10pm) is an iron-hulled boat built in England in 1862 in no less

than 1383 pieces that were shipped to Arica, transported to Tacna by train, then hauled by mule over the Andes to Puno (taking a mere six years), where it was reassembled and finally launched on Lake Titicaca in 1870. Due to a shortage of coal, the engines were often powered by dried llama dung. After over a century of service, the Yavari was beached, but in 1987 it was acquired by the Yavari Project, and is once again afloat and open to the public as an example of one of the oldest seaworthy iron-hulled boats. The ship is moored by the Sonesta Posada Hotel.

Just off the plaza is the 17th-century **Casa del Corregidor** (☎ 051-35-1921; www.casadelcorregidor .com.pe in Spanish; Deustua 576; admission free; ☺ 10am-10pm Tue-Fri, 10am-2:30 & 5-10pm Sat), housing a café/bar great for hobnobbing with the local well-to-do over a cappuccino.

A 10-minute walk southwest of town brings you to **Huajsapata Park**, atop a little hill crowned by a larger-than-life white statue of the first Inca Manco Capac looking out over the legendary site of his birth. The view is excellent, but do not walk here alone; robberies have been reported.

Festivals & Events

Puno is often said to be the folklore capital of Peru, boasting as many as 300 wild and colorful traditional dances, and celebrating numerous fiestas throughout the year. The dazzlingly ornate and imaginative costumes worn on these occasions are often worth more than an entire household's everyday clothes. Following are a selection of fiestas that are particularly important in the region:

Epiphany January 6
Candlemas (or Virgen de la Candelaria) February 2
Saint John March 7–8
Alacitas (miniature handicrafts fair), Holy Cross (Taquile) May 2–4
Saint James (Taquile) July 25
Our Lady of Mercy September 24
Puno Week November 1–7

Sleeping

The prices given are for the June to August high season and during fiestas. Bargaining reaps dramatic rewards in other months. Some barest-bones hostels have only cold showers: if you want to economize yet avoid freezing off appendages, use the public hot showers dotted around town.

Hostal Los Uros (☎ 051-35-2141; Valcárcel 135; s/d/ tr US$5/8/12, with bath US$6/10/14) This clean, quiet and decent choice, which is often full, has hot water in the morning and evening, plus a cafeteria open for early simple breakfasts.

Hospedaje Virgen de Copacabana (☎ 051-36-3766; llave 228; per person US$4) This friendly YHA-affiliated hostel has clean homey rooms with shared bathrooms, tucked off the road on a narrow passageway.

Hostal Q'oñi Wasi (☎ 051-36-5784; qoniwasi@mundo mail.net; Av La Torre 119; s/d US$4/7, with bath US$7/10) The small and quirky Q'oni Wasi has snug, older rooms, electric showers and smiley service.

Hostal Europa (☎ 051-35-3026; heuropa@puno almundo.com; Ugarte 112; s/d US$4/6, with bath US$7/12) Surrounded by local flower sellers, Europa has standard good-value rooms and hot water all day. Rooms with private bath also have thick duvets and TV.

Hostal Los Pinos (☎ 051-36-7398; hostalpinos@hot mail.com; Tarapacá 182; s/d US$10/15) A highly recommended budget hostel, Los Pinos has large, spotless rooms and an exceptionally warm welcome.

Don Julio (☎ 051-36-3358; hostaldonjulio@hotmail .com; Tacna 336; s/d/tr with breakfast US$10/15/20) Run by a very friendly family, Don Julio has a relaxed atmosphere, set back from the road in a quiet courtyard. Rooms have cable TV and heating on request.

Pachacutec (☎ 051-36-4827; Arbulu 235; s/d with breakfast US$11/15.50) A popular, neat little place, Pachacutec has well cared for rooms with private hot showers, and accommodating hosts.

Hostal Pukara (☎ 051-36-8448; pukara@terra.com .pe; Libertad 328; s/d with breakfast US$25/40) Pukara is a quirky mid-range hostel that strives to leave no corner undecorated. It has an eye-catching four-story-high relief, plus murals, tiling and other unusual touches. Rooms are heated, and have cable TV and telephone

Hostal Rosario (☎ 051-35-2272; Moquegua 325; per person US$3) Cold shared showers, but consistently cheap.

Eating

Tourist haunts huddle together on the glitzy pedestrian street of Calle Lima. Many don't advertise their set meals (el menú), which are cheaper than à la carte. All serve the requisite banana pancakes and many welcome visitors with a flaming cauldron to warm your hands by.

Vida Natural (Libertad 449; set menu US$1.40-3; ☺ Sun-Fri) Friendly little vegetarian place run by a certified nutritionist and offering an excellent, wide-ranging menu.

Govinda's (Deustua 312; set menu US$1-2; ☺ closes 8pm) True to form, Govinda's serves its usual hearty vegetarian menus without burning a hole in your pocket.

Restaurant Don Piero (Lima 364; mains US$3-5) Don Piero doesn't match the other restaurants on Calle Lima for glitz, but has excellent local food and an elegant simplicity.

Ukuku's (Lima 332; mains US$2.50-6; ☺ closed Sat) Crowds of travelers and locals thaw out in this balmy restaurant based in the heart of gringo central, which serves good typical food and pizza.

Porton Colonial (Lima 345; mains US$3-6) This tiny, backpacker-friendly place has a low, curvaceous ceiling woven with bamboo and seating insulated with llama skins. The food can be so-so, but it has a good atmosphere.

La Casona (☎ 051-35-1108; Lima 517; mains US$2-6) La Casona, which calls itself a 'restaurant-museum,' retains an old-fashioned 1920s air with its collection of antique irons lining walls. It serves typical local food and lovingly prepared fish.

Apu Salkantay (☎ 051-36-3955; Lima 425; mains US$3-6) This rustic, popular place serves local dishes as well as good pizza, and has live *música folklórica* nightly.

Ricos Pan (Moquegua 330; ☺ early, closed Sun) The best bakery in town with great coffees and melt-in-the-mouth cakes.

Drinking

Musicians do the rounds of all the restaurants, playing a half-hour set of *música folklórica*, passing the hat and moving on.

Ekeko's (Lima 355; ☺ 7pm-late) Travelers often gravitate to the tiny, ultraviolet dance floor splashed with psychedelic murals.

Kamizaraky Rock Pub (Pasaje Grau 148; ☺ 5pm-late) This laid-back pub also hands out free *cuba libres* to lure its punters in and plays a classic travelers' soundtrack to keep them there.

Getting There & Away

PERU

Air

The nearest airport is in Juliaca. **TANS** (☎ 051-36-7227; Tacna 299) is the only airline with an office in Puno.

Bus

Terminal Terrestre (departure tax US$0.30), 2km southeast of the town center, now houses all of Puno's long-distance bus companies. The roads to Arequipa and Cuzco are now paved, and regular fast services run to Lima (US$17 to US$35, 21 to 25 hours), Arequipa (US$4.20 to US$9, five hours) and Cuzco (US$3.70 to US$7, six hours), as well as to the Bolivian border. **Ormeño** (☎ 051-962-2155) has the most luxurious buses with its Royal Class service.

For Tacna (US$6 to US$7, 10 hours), try **San Martín** (☎ 051-36-3631), which has four daily departures.

Buses for Arequipa and Cuzco go via Juliaca (US$0.60, 50 minutes), and minibuses also run there from Terminal Zonal, the new local bus terminal located just a few blocks before Terminal Terrestre.

First Class (☎ 051-36-5192; firstclass@terra.com.pe; Lima 177) has comfortable tour buses to Cuzco every morning. The US$25 fare includes beverages and an English-speaking tour guide, who explains sites that are briefly visited en route, including Pucara, La Raya, Sicuani, Raqchi, Andahuayillas and Piquillaqta (see p852).

For information on buses to south-shore towns and the Bolivian border, see p837 and below, respectively.

Train

Puno's **train station** (☎ 051-36-9179; puno@perurail.com; ☺ 7am-noon & 2-5pm Mon-Fri, 7am-11am Sat & Sun) is on Av La Torre. First-class/Turismo fares to Cuzco are now US$83/14. This line has a 50% reduction on Inca class tickets if you purchase them 24 hours in advance.

The train leaves at 8am on Monday, Wednesday and Thursday from June to August, supposedly arriving at 6pm, though it's often hours late. During other months, the service officially runs on Monday, Wednesday and Saturday, though it suffers routine cancellations.

Check the website of **Perurail** (www.perurail.com) for the latest schedules as well as ticket prices. Most travelers now take the faster, smoother bus service to Cuzco.

BOLIVIAN BORDER CROSSING

There are two overland routes from Puno to La Paz, Bolivia: via Yunguyo or via Desaguadero. The Yunguyo route is more attractive and some travelers like to break the trip in the mellow lakeshore resort of Copacabana, but the Desaguadero route is faster, less complicated and slightly cheaper. It can also be combined with a visit to the ruins at Tiahuanaco. Usually, there's little hassle entering Bolivia at either border crossing, and you can get 30- to 90-day permits without difficulty. Beware of immigration officials trying to charge an illegal 'entry tax' or searching luggage for 'fake dollars' to confiscate. There's a Bolivian Consulate in Puno (Map p834).

Via Yunguyo

The most convenient way to get from Puno to La Paz is with a company such as **Colectur** (☎ 051-35-2302; colectur@latinmail.com; Tacna 221), which has daily departures at 1:30pm, stopping at a money exchange, the border, then Copacabana (US$3 to US$4, three hours), where you are met by a Bolivian bus for La Paz (US$6 to US$7, five hours). **Tour Peru** (☎ 051-36-5517) at Puno's Terminal Terrestre leaves at 8am daily.

Alternatively, buses leave from Terminal Zonal, 1.5km from central Puno on Simón Bolívar for the border town of Yunguyo (US$1.20, 2½ hours), which has a couple of basic hotels. You'll find moneychangers in Yunguyo's plaza and by the border, 2km away in Casani (combis US$0.30); count your money carefully. The border is open from 8am to 6pm.

From the border, it's 10km more to Copacabana (combis US$0.45).

Via Desaguadero

Buses and minibuses leave Puno's Terminal Zonal and Terminal Terrestre regularly until 4pm for Desaguadero (US$2, 2½ hours), where there are basic hotels, moneychangers and a *casa de cambio*. Border hours are 7:30am to 8pm, though remember that Bolivia is an hour ahead of Peru, so plan to cross before 7pm Peru time. Many buses go to La Paz (US$1.75, 3½ hours) until 8pm, passing the turn-off to the ruins of Tiahuanaco. The best bus from Puno to La Paz via this route is with Ormeño's Royal Class service (US$14, six hours).

Getting Around

Tricycle taxis are the most popular way of getting around Puno and are cheaper than ordinary taxis (US$0.75 per ride).

AROUND PUNO

Sillustani

The ancient Colla people were a warlike tribe that later became the southeastern arm of the Incas. They buried their nobility in impressive funerary towers called *chullpas*, made from massive coursed blocks and reaching heights of up to 12m. Some of the best examples can be found at this large windswept **site** (admission US$1.40), set against a bleak backdrop on the Lake Umayo peninsula.

Agencies run 3½-hour tours that usually leave at 2:30pm and cost upwards of US$6, including entrance. To go solo, catch any bus to Juliaca and ask to be let off where the road splits to Sillustani. From here, occasional combis run to the village of Atuncolla (US$0.60, 10 minutes), 4km from the ruins. In high season they will occasionally continue to the ruins, but expect to have to walk it.

South Shore Towns

Terminal Zonal, 1.5km from central Puno on Simón Bolívar, has cheap, slow minibuses and faster combis for all destinations to the Bolivian border (US$1.20, 2½ hours). For a map of this region, see Bolivia (p191).

The road east of Puno follows the edge of the lake. After 8km, you reach the village of **Chimú**, famous for its totora-reed industry. Bundles of reeds are seen piled up to dry, and there are often reed boats in various stages of construction.

The next village is **Chucuito**, 10km southeast of Chimu. Chucuito has two colonial churches, but the principal attraction is the outlandish **Templo de la fertilidad** (Inca Uyu; admission free; ☷ 6am-8pm), which consists of dozens of large stone phalluses, some up to 4 foot in length. Local guides tell various entertaining stories about the structures: good for giggles.

Juli, 80km southeast of Puno, is called Peru's Pequeña Roma (Little Rome) on account of its four colonial churches dating from the 16th and 17th century. **Pomata**, 106km from Puno, is also dominated by a Dominican church atop a small hill.

ISLAND HOPPING

By far the best way to see Lake Titicaca is by spending a few days visiting the culturally fascinating islands of the lake itself. With two regular islands and a whole colony of

PERU

floating islands, travelers can easily hop between them and spend a few days chilling out.

Islas Flotantes

The unique **Islas Flotantes** (Floating Islands; admission US$0.60) of the Uros people are Lake Titicaca's top tourist attraction, and though their popularity has led to shocking overcommercialization, there is still nothing quite like them anywhere else.

Intermarriage with Aymara-speaking Indians has seen the demise of the pureblooded Uros. Always a small tribe, they began their floating existence centuries ago in an effort to isolate themselves from the aggressive Collas and the Incas. Today, several hundred people still live on the islands.

The islands are built using many layers of the buoyant totora reeds that grow abundantly in the shallows of Lake Titicaca. Indeed, the lives of the Uros are totally interwoven with these reeds, which are used to make their homes, boats and the crafts they churn out for tourists. The islands' reeds are constantly replenished from the top as they rot away, so the ground is always soft and springy: mind your step.

The Uros usually have an elaborate and tightly bundled reed boat on hand to offer **rides** (US$0.60 to US$1).

GETTING THERE & AWAY

Boats (US$3) leave from 7am until early afternoon according to demand; it's best to leave before 8am to avoid tour groups. Pay on the boat rather than the pier as you may be overcharged there. The standard trip to the main island and one or two others, takes around two hours. Agencies arrange tours with a guide from US$6 per person.

Isla Taquile

Isla Taquile (admission US$1) is an island inhabited for many thousands of years. The Quechua-speaking islanders maintain lives largely untrammeled by the modernities of the mainland and have a deeply ingrained tradition of weaving. Their creations can be bought in the island's cooperative store on the main plaza. Look for the menfolk's tightly woven woolen hats, resembling floppy nightcaps, which they take great pride in knitting themselves.

Taquile, which is only 1km wide but about 6km or 7km long, often feels like its own little world. Several hills have pre-Inca terracing and small ruins, and visitors are free to wander, but you can't do this on a day trip without skipping lunch or missing the returning boat, so stay overnight if you can.

SLEEPING & EATING

A steep stairway leads up from the dock. Travelers will be met by islanders next to the arch at the top; these villagers can arrange **homestays** (per person US$3). Beds are basic but clean, and facilities are minimal. You will be given blankets, but bring a sleeping bag too. A flashlight is essential.

The San Santiago restaurant on the main plaza is the only communally owned restaurant, the profits of which benefit the entire community. You can buy bottled drinks, though it's worth bringing purifying tablets or a filter as backup. Bring small bills (change is limited) and extra money for the exquisite crafts on sale.

GETTING THERE & AWAY

A passenger boat for the 24km trip to Taquile leaves the Puno dock every day by 7:30am (US$6/8.50 one way/round trip, four to five hours), and tour boats leave around 8am. Get to the dock early and pay the captain directly. The return trip leaves at 2pm, arriving in Puno around nightfall. Remember to bring sunscreen for the journey.

Tour agencies offer this trip for about US$10 with a guide, or US$14 with an overnight stay, including accommodation and meals, though the islanders benefit much more directly from travelers who go independently.

Isla Amantaní

This less frequently visited **island** (admission US$1.50) is a few kilometers north of Taquile. Trips here usually involve an overnight stay with islanders and a rousing traditional dance, where travelers dress in the islanders' traditional partying gear.

Several hills are topped by **ruins**, which date to the Tiahuanaco culture.

Boats to Amantaní (round trip US$5.50) leave Puno between 7:30am and 8:30am most mornings: pay the captain directly. Boat connections make it easiest to travel from Puno to the Islas Uros then to Amantaní and on to Taquile, rather than in reverse. A daily boat runs to Taquile for US$1.50 one way.

A bed and full board costs around US$3 per night. Puno travel agencies charge US$12 and up for a two-day tour to Amantaní, with a quick visit to Taquile and the floating islands.

CUZCO & THE SACRED VALLEY

As the heart of the once-mighty Inca empire, the magnetic city of Cuzco heads the list of many a traveler's itinerary. Each year it draws hundreds of thousands of tourists to its cobble-stoned streets, lured by the city's unique combination of colonial splendor built on hefty stone foundations of the Incas. And lying within easy hopping distance of the city is the country's biggest draw card of all, the lost city of the Incas, Machu Picchu, perched high on its isolated mountaintop.

But the department of Cuzco also encompasses much more of the most fascinating and accessible archaeology on the continent, not least in the Sacred Valley of the Río Urubamba. The department also offers unmissable opportunities for rafting and trekking, as well as hosting a long list of flamboyant fiestas and carnivals.

CUZCO

The beautiful city of Cuzco, or Qosq'o in Quechua (population 350,000, elevation 3326m), was once the foremost city of the Inca empire, and is now the undisputed archaeological capital of the Americas as well as the continent's oldest continuously inhabited city. Massive Inca-built walls line the city's central streets and form the foundations of both colonial and modern buildings, and the cobbled streets are often stepped, narrow and thronged with Quechua-speaking descendants of the Incas. But while Cuzco was long ruled by Inca or Conquistador, there's no question of who rules the roost now: the city's economy is almost totally at the whim of the international tourist, and every second building in the city center is now a touristy restaurant, shop or hotel.

History

Cuzco is a city so steeped in history, tradition and legend that it can be difficult to know where fact ends and myth begins. Legend tells that in the 12th century, the first Inca, Manco Capac, was charged to find *qosq'o* (navel of the earth). When at last Manco discovered such a point, he founded the city. Traditionally, the Incas dominated all but a modest area close to Cuzco, though frequently skirmishing with other highland tribes. However, the bloodthirsty Chanka tribe's expansion provoked the ninth Inca, Pachacutec, to rally the Inca army and rout their enemies around 1438, and during the next 25 years he went on to conquer most of the central Andes.

But Pachacutec wasn't only a warmonger: he also proved himself a sophisticated urban developer, devising Cuzco's famous puma shape and diverting rivers to cross the city. He also built the famous Coricancha temple and his palace on what is now the western corner of the Plaza de Armas.

By 1532 Atahualpa had defeated his half-brother Huáscar in the Inca civil war. The conquistador Francisco Pizarro exploited this situation, marching into Cuzco in 1533 after taking Atahualpa hostage, and later having him killed. Pizarro was permitted into the heart of the empire by a people whose sympathy lay more with the defeated Huáscar than with Atahualpa, and Pizarro was able to appoint Manco Inca as a puppet ruler of the Inca. For more on the empire, see p854.

But once Cuzco had been safely captured, looted and settled, the seafaring Spaniards turned their attentions to Lima on the coast, and Cuzco's importance waned, becoming just another quiet colonial town. Few events of historical significance have rocked Cuzco since Spanish conquest. Indeed it was the rediscovery of Machu Picchu in 1911 that has affected Cuzco far more than any event since 1533, changing the city from provincial backwater to Peru's foremost tourist center.

Orientation

Cuzco's heart is the Plaza de Armas (each side of the plaza's arches have different names), and Av Sol is the main business street. Streets to the north or east of the plaza have changed little in centuries; many are for pedestrians only. The central street leading from the northwest side of the plaza is

PERU

officially named Procuradores, but has long been called Gringo Alley thanks to its huddle of budget haunts, cafés and predatory street-sellers. Recently, the city's had a resurgence of Quechua pride and the official names of many streets have changed from Spanish to Quechua spellings (Cuzco has become Qosco, Cuichipunco is now K'uychipunko etc). Maps usually retain the old spellings, however, and most people still use them.

Information
BOOKSHOPS
Jerusalen (☎ 084-23-5428; Heladeros 143; ⏱ 9am-9pm Mon-Sat) Book exchange in several languages, as well as new titles and music.

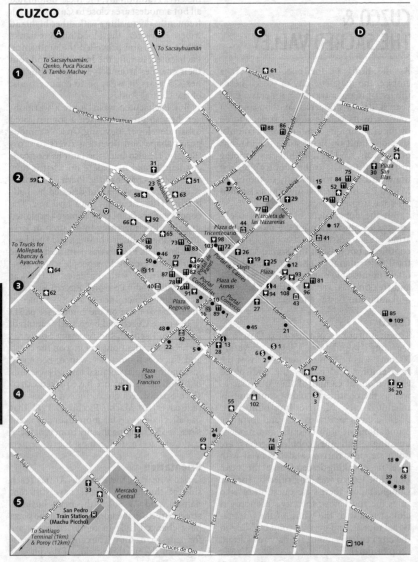

CUZCO

Los Andes (☎ 084-23-4231; Portal Comercio 125, Plateros; ☺ 10am-2pm & 5-9pm Mon-Sat)
SBS Bookshop (☎ 084-24-8106; Av Sol 781; ☺ 8am-1pm & 3:30-7pm Mon-Fri, 8am-1pm Sat) Specializes in foreign-language books.

Book exchanges abound throughout Cuzco. Try the following places:

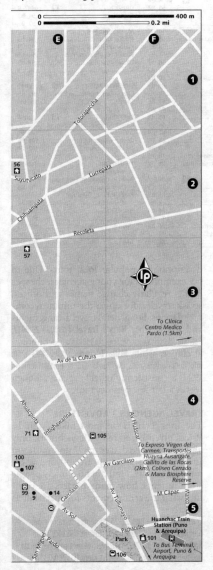

Granja Heidi (Cuesta San Blas 525, 2nd fl; ☺ closed Sun)
Norton Rats Tavern (Calle Loreto 115; ☺ 9am-late)
South American Explorers (☎ 084-24-5484; Choquechaca 188; cuscoclub@saexplorers.org; ☺ 9:30am-5pm Mon-Fri, 9:30am-1pm Sat Oct-Apr, 9:30am-5pm Mon-Fri, 9:30am-5pm Sat, 9:30am-1pm Sun May-Sep) Members only.

EMERGENCY
Policía de Turismo (☎ 084-24-9654; Saphi 510; ☺ 24 hours) Staff are trained to deal with problems pertaining to tourists, and can give details of foreign consulate representatives.

IMMIGRATION OFFICES
Migraciónes (☎ 084-22-2741; Av Sol 612; ☺ 8am-noon Mon-Fri) You can renew your tourist card for US$27 per 30 days here, but consider going to Bolivia for a day — most nationalities get 90 days on their return and save the renewal cost.

INTERNET ACCESS
MundoNet (Santa Teresa 344; US$0.60 per hr; ☺ 8am-10pm Mon-Sat, 5-10pm Sun)
Telser (Calle del Medio 117; US$0.60 per hr; ☺ 7am-midnight)
Trotamundos (Portal Comercio 177, Plateros)

LAUNDRY
There's a high concentration of *lavandarías* on Suecia, Procuradores, Plateros and Espaderos that will wash, dry and fold your clothes for US$1 to US$2 per kilogram. However, during the busiest months, it's best not to stake your last pair of socks on their promise of 'in by 10am, ready by 6pm.'

MEDICAL SERVICES
Clínica Centro Medico Pardo (☎ 084-24-0387; Av de la Cultura 710; consultation US$14)
Inka Farma (☎ 084-24-2601; Av Sol 174; ☺ 24 hr) Well-stocked pharmacy.

MONEY
Several banks on Av Sol have foreign-card friendly ATMs (see the map), and you'll find several more strategically positioned in shops around the Plaza de Armas and in Huanchac train station.
Casas de cambio All give similar exchange rates and are scattered around the Plaza de Armas and along Av Sol.
LAC Dolar (☎ 084-25-7969; Av Sol 150; ☺ 9am-7pm Mon-Sat) Will deliver to your hotel if you phone with your traveler's check numbers.

INFORMATION		
BCP	1	C4
Inka Farma	2	C3
Interbanc	3	D4
iPeru	4	C3
Jerusalen	5	B4
LAC Dolar	6	C4
Los Andes	7	C3
Mayuc	8	B3
Migraciones	9	E5
Milla Turismo	10	C3
MundoNet	11	B3
Naty's Travel	12	C3
Regional Tourist Office	13	C3
SBS Bookshop	14	E5
South American Explorers	15	D2
Telser	16	B3
SIGHTS & ACTIVITIES	**pp843–5**	
12-sided stone	17	D2
Academia Latinoamericana	18	D5
Cathedral	19	C3
Coricancha	20	D4
Craft Market	21	C3
Cusco Spanish School	22	B4
Don Quijote	23	B2
Eric Adventures	(see 97)	
Excel Language Center	24	C3
Iglesia de El Triunfo	25	C3
Iglesia de Jesús María	26	B3
Iglesia de La Compañía	27	C3
Iglesia de La Merced	28	C3
Iglesia de San Antonio	29	C2
Iglesia de San Blas	30	D2
Iglesia de San Cristóbal	31	B2
Iglesia de San Francisco	32	B4
Iglesia de San Pedro	33	A5
Iglesia de Santa Clara	34	B4
Iglesia de Santa Teresa	35	B3
Iglesia de Santo Domingo	36	D4
La Casona de la Esquina	37	C2
Loreto Tours	(see 16)	
Manu Expeditions	38	D5
Milla Turismo	39	D5
Municipalidad	40	B3
Museo de Arte Religioso	41	D3
Museo de Historia Regional	42	B3
Museo de Santa Catalina	43	C3
Museo Inka	44	C2
OFEC Office	45	C3
Panticolla Tours	46	B3
Pre-Columbian Art Museum	47	C2
Q'ente	48	B3
SAS	49	B3
United Mice	50	B3
SLEEPING 🏠	**pp845–6**	
Albergue Municipal	51	B2
Amaru Hostal	52	D2
El Dorado Inn	53	D4
El Mirador de la Ñusta	54	D2
Gran Hostal Machu Picchu	55	C4
Hospedaje Inka	56	E2
Hospedaje Iquique	57	E3
Hostal Corihuasi	58	B2
Hostal Familiar	59	A2
Hostal Incawasi	60	B3
Hostal Kuntur Wasi	61	C1
Hostal Los Niños	62	A3
Hostal Resbalosa	63	B2
Hostal Rikch'arty	64	A3
Hostal Royal Qosco	65	B3
Hostal Suecia II	66	B2
Hotel Cristina	67	C4
Hotel Don Carlos	68	D5
Hotel Wiracocha	69	B4
Residencia de la Solidaridad	70	A5
Residencial Madres Dominicanas	71	E4
EATING 🍴	**pp846–7**	
Café Bagdad	72	C3
Chez Maggy	73	B3
Coco Loco	(see 76)	
Dimart	74	C4
El Buen Pastor Bakery	75	D2
El Mesón de los Espaderos	76	B3
Fallen Angel	77	C2
Govinda	78	B3
Granja Heidi	79	D2
Greens	80	D2
I Due Mondi	81	D3
Inka Grill	82	B3
La Tertulia	83	B3
Macondo	84	D2
Moni	85	D3
Pi Shop	86	C2
Pucará	87	B3
Quinta Eulalia	88	C2
Trotamundos	89	C3
Victor Victoria	90	B3
DRINKING 🍷	**pp847–8**	
Cross Keys	91	B3
Los Perros	92	B2
Mama Africa Pub	93	C3
Norton Rat's	94	C3
Paddy O'Flaherty's	95	C3
Rosie O'Grady's Irish Pub	96	C3
Ukuku's Bar	97	B3
X'ss	98	C3
ENTERTAINMENT 🎭	**p848**	
Qosqo Center of Native Dance	99	E5
Sunset	(see 65)	
SHOPPING 🛍	**p848**	
Center for Traditional Textiles of Cusco	100	E5
Centro Artesanal Cuzco	101	F5
Inca Craft Market	102	C4
TRANSPORT	**pp848–50**	
Aero Continente	103	C3
Buses to Chinchero, Urubamba & Ollantaytambo	104	D5
Buses to Pisac, Calca and Urubamba	105	E4
First Class	106	F5
LanPeru	107	C3
Lloyd Aereo Boliviano	108	C3
Taca	(see 99)	
TANS	109	D3

POST

Post office (☎ 084-22-4212; Av Sol 800; ⏰ 7:30am-8pm Mon-Sat, 8am-2pm Sun)

SOUTH AMERICAN EXPLORERS

South American Explorers (☎ 084-24-5484; cusco club@saexplorers.org; Choquechaca 188; ⏰ 9:30am-5pm Mon-Fri, 9:30am-1pm Sat Oct-Apr, 9:30am-5pm Mon-Fri, 9:30am-5pm Sat, 9:30am-1pm Sun May-Sep) Traveler's information, maps and a long list of local discounts to members. For more information about the club, see p805.

TOURIST OFFICES

iPeru Aeropuerto (☎ 084-23-7364; iperucuscoapto@ prompperu.gob.pe; Aeropuerto Alejandro Velasco Astete; ⏰ 6am-2pm); Plaza de Armas (☎ 084-25-2974/23-4498; iperucusco@promperu.gob.pe; Portal Carrizos 250, Plaza de Armas; ⏰ 8:30am-7:30pm) Also runs INDECOPI, the tourist protection society.
Regional Tourist Office (☎ 084-26-3176; cusco@mincetur .gob.pe; Mantas 117-A; ⏰ 8am-7pm Mon-Fri, 8am-2pm Sat)

TRAVEL AGENCIES

There are over 200 registered travel and tour agencies in Cuzco. See Tours (p845) for a description of popular local tours. Due to tax exemptions for young agencies, cheaper outfits regularly change names and offices, so ask travelers for up-to-the-minute recommendations. For general travel arrangements and local trips, **Naty's Travel** (☎ 084-23-9437; natystravel@terra.com.pe; Triunfo 338) is an economical choice, while **Milla Turismo** (☎ 084-23-1710; info@millaturismo.com; Av Pardo 675 & Portal Comercio 195) is a consistently reliable agency, though worth a fair few pennies more.

TRAVEL AGENCIES – ADVENTURE

The Inca Trail is on most hikers' minds. Prices given here are as a benchmark only and are *not* fixed (see p857 for more on Inca Trail tours). Shop around and ask a lot of questions. Find out how many people sleep in tents, how many porters are coming, what the arrangements for special diets are etc.

Q'ente (☎ /fax 084-22-2535; qente@terra.com.pe; Garcilaso 210; Inca Trail adult/student US$300/275)
SAS (☎ 084-23-7292; sastravel@planet.com.pe; Portal de Panes 143; Inca Trail adult/student US$260/235)

United Mice (☎ 084-22-1139; unitedmi@terra.com.pe; Plateros 351; Inca Trail adult/student US$250/215) Consistently recommended.

Cuzco is also a destination for river rafters and mountain bikers. Following are some companies offering trips for beginners and experts alike:

Eric Adventures (☎/fax 084-22-8475; cusco@ericadventures.com; Plateros 324) Good rafting agency.

Loreto Tours (☎ 084-22-8264; loretotours@planet.com .pe; Calle del Medio 111) Offers short rafting trips and is recommended for mountain-biking.

Mayuc (☎ 084-23-2666; chando@mayuc.com; Portal Confiturias 211) Resident rafting experts.

The city is also a great place to organize trips to the jungle, especially to Manu and Puerto Maldonado. None are cheap. Some recommended operators:

Manu Ecological Adventures (☎ 084-26-1640; www .manuadventures.com; Plateros 356)

Manu Expeditions (☎ 084-22-6671/23-9974; www .manuexpeditions.com; Pardo 895)

Pantiacolla Tours (☎ 084-23-8323; www.pantiacolla .com; Plateros 360)

Dangers & Annoyances

Many tourists attract many thieves. Watch your back around the train stations and central market as these are prime areas for pickpockets and bag-slashers. Use only official taxi firms – look for the company's number on top of the taxi, lock your doors and never allow the driver to admit a second passenger. Late-night revelers returning from bars or lone travelers setting off for the Inca trail before sunrise can be vulnerable to muggings, so take extra care at these times.

Also, beware of altitude sickness if you're flying in from sea level (see p1059).

Sights

For admission to many major sites in and around Cuzco, you have to buy a Boleto Turístico (Tourism Ticket), which costs US$10 or US$5 for students under 26 and is valid for 10 days. The ticket can be purchased from **Oficina Ejecutiva del Comité** (OFEC; ☎ 084-22-6919; Av Sol 103; ☺ 8am-6pm Mon-Fri, 8: 30am-1pm Sat). Boletos Turísticos are valid for 10 days.

Within Cuzco, this ticket is valid for the cathedral, San Blas church, Santa Catalina,

---

OVER THE RAINBOW

A common sight in Cuzco's Plaza de Armas is the city's much-loved flag – a brightly striped banner developed in the 1970s to represent the *arco iris* (rainbow) that was sacred to the beliefs of the Cuzqueñans forebears, the Incas. Whatever you do, don't mistake this flag for the international gay pride banner to which it bears a remarkable resemblance – a similarity so striking, in fact, the powers that be are reportedly considering redesigning their city's flag to prevent confusion!

Museo Histórico Regional, Museo de Arte Religioso and more. The ticket also covers Sacsayhuamán, Qenko, Puca Pucara, Tambo Machay, Pisac, Chinchero, Ollantaytambo, Pikillacta and Tipón – all outside Cuzco. It's also possible to buy partial *boletos* costing US$6 that are valid for one day only.

PLAZA DE ARMAS

Colonial arcades surround the plaza. On the northeastern side is the cathedral, while on the southeastern side is the very ornate church of La Compañía. Some Inca walls remain, notably from Pachacutec's palace on the western corner. The pedestrian alleyway of Loreto is enclosed by solid Inca walls.

CHURCHES

Begun in 1559, the **cathedral** (admission with Boleto Turístico; ☺ 10am-11:30am & 2-5:30pm Mon-Wed & Fri-Sat, 2-5:30pm Thu, 2-5pm Sun) is positioned on the site of Inca Viracocha's Palace and was built using blocks from Sacsayhuamán (see p850). It is one of the city's greatest repositories of colonial art, especially the Cuzco school, which mingled colonial styles with those of the Andean Indian artists. Look for *The Last Supper* by Marcos Zapata in the northeastern corner, with a plump, juicy-looking roast *cuy* (guinea pig) stealing the show with its feet held plaintively in the air. Opposite the silver altar is the magnificently carved choir, dating from the 17th century.

The cathedral is joined with the **Iglesia de Jesús María** (1733) to the left, and the **Iglesia de El Triunfo** (1536) to the right, which is the oldest church in Cuzco. It contains the vault of the famous Inca historian Garcilaso de la Vega, born in Cuzco in 1539.

PERU

The painstaking baroque façade of **Iglesia de La Compañía** (admission free), also on the plaza, makes it one of Cuzco's most ornate churches (so intricate, in fact, it provoked an almighty squabble between the Jesuits and the bishop of Cuzco, who complained that the church's splendor shouldn't rival the cathedral). Its foundations contain stones from the palace of the Inca Huayna Capac.

Iglesia de La Merced (☎ 084-23-1821; Mantas; adult/student US$1/0.60; ☺ 9am-noon & 2-5pm Mon-Sat) dates from 1654; an earlier church was destroyed in the 1650 earthquake. Left of the church is the monastery and museum, which contains conquistador/friar Vicente de Valverde's vestments, religious art and a priceless gold monstrance, covered with 1500 diamonds and 1600 pearls – just don't try to count them.

The adobe **Iglesia de San Blas** (Plaza San Blas; admission with Boleto Turístico; ☺ 10am-11:30am & 2-5: 30pm Mon-Wed & Fri-Sat, 2-5:30pm Thu, 2-5pm Sun) has a pulpit some call the finest example of colonial woodcarving in the Americas. Legend claims the skull of its creator is nestled in the topmost part of the carving.

Museo de Santa Catalina (☎ 084-22-8613; Arequipa; admission with Boleto Turístico; ☺ 9am-5:30pm Sat-Thu, 8am-4pm Fri) has a colonial- and religious-art museum and a dramatically friezed baroque side chapel, with the convent's main altar behind steel bars.

On the site of Coricancha is the **Iglesia de Santo Domingo**, which was destroyed by the 1650 earthquake and badly damaged by the 1950 earthquake. Compare the colonial building with the Inca walls within and outside, most of which survived both of these earthquakes with hardly a hairline crack.

INCA RUINS

The Inca site of **Coricancha** (☎ 084-24-9176; Plazoleta Santo Domingo; adult/student US$1.60/1; ☺ 8:30am-5:30pm Mon-Sat, 2-5pm Sun) forms the base of the colonial church of Iglesia de Santo Domingo, creating a combination of Inca and colonial architecture, topped with a modern roof. Coricancha is Quechua for 'Golden Courtyard' and in Inca times the walls of the temple were lined with a mind-boggling 700 solid-gold sheets each weighing 2kg. No wonder then that the Spaniards' greed kicked in and that, today, only the excellent stonework remains after the conquistadors looted the rest. The fitting

of the remaining stone blocks is so precise that, in some places, you can't tell where one block ends and the next begins.

Coricancha was used for religious rites – mummified bodies of Incas were kept here and brought out into the sunlight every day. Food and drink were offered to them and then ritually burnt. The site was also an observatory, where priests kept track of major celestial events.

A perfectly fitted, curved, 6m wall can be seen from outside the site. It has withstood all of Cuzco's earthquakes. The courtyard inside has an octagonal font, once covered with 55kg of solid gold. There are Inca temples to either side of the courtyard. The largest, to the right, are said to be temples to the moon and stars, and perhaps were covered with solid silver.

Back in the town center, leave the Plaza de Armas along Loreto alley, and you'll have **Inca walls** on both sides. On the right is Amarucancha (Courtyard of the Serpents), the site of the palace of Inca Huayna Capac. After the conquest, the Iglesia de La Compañía was built here. On the left side of Loreto is the oldest Inca wall in Cuzco, part of the Acllahuasi (House of the Chosen Women). After the conquest, it became part of Santa Catalina, so went from housing Virgins of the Sun to pious Catholic nuns.

Exiting the plaza along Calle Triunfo you reach the street of Hatunrumiyoc, named after the great **12-sided stone** on the right of the second city block – recognizable by the small knot of souvenir-sellers next to it. This excellently fitted stone is part of the palace of the sixth Inca, Roca. There are dozens of other Inca walls dotted around town.

MUSEUMS

Museo Inka (☎ 084-23-7380; cnr Ataúd & Tucumán; adult/under-15 US$1.40/free; ☺ 9am-5pm Mon-Fri, 9am-4pm Sat) is housed in one of the city's finest colonial buildings, and packed with metal and gold work, jewelry, pottery, textiles, mummies, *queros* (Inca vases) and more. Look out for the massive stairway guarded by sculptures of mythical creatures. A corner window column looks like a statue of a bearded man, until you go outside, from where it appears to be a naked woman. The ceilings are ornate and the views are good, but the collection is labeled in Spanish.

A new **Pre-Columbian Art Museum** (☎ 084-23-3210; Plaza de las Nazarenas; adult/child/student US$4.20/1.40/2.50; ☼ 9am-10pm) was founded in June 2003 to showcase a varied collection of 450 archaeological pieces that were previously buried in the vast storerooms of Lima's Larco Museum.

Also known as the Archbishop's Palace, the **Museo de Arte Religioso** (Hatunrumiyoc; admission with Boleto Turístico; ☼ 8am-11:30am & 3-5:30pm Mon-Sat) has a fascinating religious art collection noted for its period detail and insight into the interaction of conquistadors with Indians. There are some impressive ceilings and colonial-style tile work (not original).

Museo de Historia Regional (☎ 084-22-3245; cnr Garcilasco at Heladeros; admission with Boleto Turístico; ☼ 8am-5pm Mon-Sat) is in the home of the famous Cuzco chronicler Garcilaso de la Vega. There is a small, chronologically arranged archaeological collection.

Courses

Cuzco is one of the best places in Peru to study Spanish, and can learn Quechua and Aymara too. Following are some language schools:

Academia Latinoamericana (☎ 084-24-3364; info@latinoschools.com; Av Sol 580)

Cusco Spanish School (☎ 084-22-6928; info@cuscospanishschool.com; Garcilaso 265, 2nd fl)

Don Quijote (Amauta; ☎ 084-24-1422; www.donquijote.org; Calle Suecia 480)

Excel Language Center (☎ 084-23-5298; contact@excelinspanish.com; Cruz Verde 336)

La Casona de la Esquina (☎ 084-23-5903; spanish lessonscusco@yahoo.es; Calle Purgatorio 395)

Tours

Standard tours include a half-day city tour for US$5 to US$10, a half-day tour of the nearby ruins for US$5.50 to US$13 (Sacsayhuamán, Qenko, Puca Pucara and Tambo Machay; see p850), a half-day trip to the Sunday markets at Pisac or Chinchero, or a full-day tour to the Sacred Valley (Pisac, Ollantaytambo and Chinchero).

Many visitors also buy a Machu Picchu combined tour from agencies in Cuzco for US$95 to US$130. This includes train fares, the bus to/from the ruins, admission to the ruins, an English-speaking guide and lunch. You get to spend two or three hours in the ruins before it's time to return to the train station. To prolong the experience, a two-day trip costs US$135 to US$160, including accommodation.

Many agencies run adventure trips. Rafting the Urubamba for one or two days is popular (around US$25 to US$30 a day) and can be combined with seeing the Sacred Valley. Other, longer rafting trips include the exhilarating Río Apurímac from May to November.

Hikers should note that it is now compulsory to hire a guide or take a guided tour along the Inca Trail to Machu Picchu (see p857). A wealth of other treks surround Cuzco, and agencies also run hiking trips to Ausangate (p863) and to Inca ruins, such as Choquequirau (p863), Vilcabamba (p862) and Corihuayrachina, a recent rediscovery. Ask trekking agencies or the **South American Explorers** (☎ 084-24-5484; cuscoclub@saexplorers.org; Choquechaca 188) for advice and maps of this place, as it's still very much off-the-beaten track. Mountaineering, horse riding, paragliding, mountain-biking and jungle-trekking trips are also available.

Festivals & Events

Inti Raymi (Festival Of The Sun), on June 24, is Cuzco's most important festival attracting tourists from all over the world. The entire city seems to celebrate in the streets. The festival culminates in a re-enactment of the Inca winter solstice festival at Sacsayhuamán. Reserved tourist tickets are available or you can sit on the stone ruins for free.

Held on the Monday before Easter, the procession of El Señor de los Temblores (Lord of the Earthquakes) dates from the 1650 earthquake. The feast of Corpus Christi takes place in early June (usually the ninth Thursday following Easter), with fantastic religious processions and celebrations in the cathedral.

Sleeping

Albergue Municipal (☎ /fax 084-25-2506; albergue@municusco.gob.pe; Kiskapata 240; dm US$6-7) The Albergue is up a steep hill that affords great city views from the balcony. The rooms are spotless and have bunk beds for four to eight people, and there is hot water, a common room, café, laundry facilities and luggage storage.

Hostal Resbalosa (☎ 084-22-4839; Resbalosa 494; s/d/tr US$4.20/7/10) Resbalosa's main attraction is a fabulous terrace overlooking the plaza. It has shared warm showers, decent rooms, luggage storage and a helpful owner. It's on a steep pedestrian-only street; taxis can only reach within 100m of the hostel.

Hospedaje Inka (☎ 084-23-1995; americopache co@hotmail.com; Suytuccato 848; per person US$3.50-6) This is a scruffy but charming converted hillside farmhouse above San Blas, popular with backpackers and affording some great views. There's erratic hot water, private bathrooms and a large farm kitchen. Taxis can't climb the final stepped stretch, so be prepared to put in some puff.

Hostal Kuntur Wasi (☎ 084-22-7570; Tandapata 352A; per person US$5, s/d with bath US$10/15) Kuntur Wasi has a friendly environment, with warm showers and kitchen access.

Hostal Rikch'arty (☎ 084-23-6606; Tambo de Montero 219; per person with breakfast US$5) Rikch'arty is a relaxed, family-run hostel, with kids usually scampering around the small garden. Rooms are very basic and share small bathrooms with hot showers.

Hostal Royal Qosco (☎ /fax 084-22-6221; royalqos@ hotmail.com; Tecsecocha 2; s/d/tr US$5/9/12, s/d with bath US$10/20) Royal Qosco is popular largely for its position just a stone's throw from Gringo Alley. Rooms are basic, dark and have hot water in the morning.

Gran Hostal Machu Picchu (☎ 084-23-1111; Quera 282; s/d/tr US$10/20/30) This friendly spot set around two pretty courtyards with intricate old wooden balconies has hot water most of the time.

Hostal Familiar (☎ 084-23-9353; hostalfamiliar@ hotmail.com; Saphi 661; s/d US$8.50/13, with bath & breakfast US$11.50/18.50) Hostal Familiar has a well-kept colonial courtyard and clean, spartan rooms.

Hostal Suecia II (☎ 084-23-9757; Tecsecocha 465; s/d US$5.60/8.40, with bath US$8.40/14) This safe, popular colonial-style place has friendly staff and a central position (no huffing and puffing to get *here*). There is reliable hot water and a glassed-in courtyard.

Residencia de la Solidaridad (☎ 084-23-1118; hspedro@hotmail.com; Ccascaparo 116; s/d/tr US$15/20/ 30) You'll be greeted with dozens of smiling faces at this new option situated in a home for girls near the Machu Picchu train station. The hostel is run by missionaries, and has several courtyard gardens, surprisingly comfortable rooms and a convenient wake-up call from church bells.

Amaru Hostal (☎ /fax 084-22-5933; amaru@telser.com .pe; Cuesta San Blas 541; s/d US$14/16, with bath US$17/25) Taller travelers should note to duck through the colonial doorframes of this exceptionally friendly choice in a character-filled old building. Rates include national TV and breakfast.

Other recommendations:

Residencial Madres Dominicanas (☎ 084-22-5484; Ahuacpinta 600; per person US$7) Run by nuns in Colegio Martín de Porres.

El Mirador de la Ñusta (☎ 084-24-8039; elmirador delanusta@hotmail.com; Calle Tandapata 682; s/d/tr with bath US$10/20/30) Takes 30 seconds to be seated on Plaza San Blas for your morning maté.

Hospedaje Iquique (☎ 084-22-5880; hicuzco@terra .com.pe; Recoleta; s/d US$4.20/8.40, with bath US$8.40/ 16.80) Homey hostel hidden down backstreets.

Hotel Wiracocha (☎ 084-22-1014; Cruz Verde 364; s/d with bath & breakfast US$15/25) Freshly renovated colonial house and courtyard.

Hostal Incawasi (☎ 084-22-3992; Portal de Panes 147; s/d/tr US$10/16/21, with bath US$15/23/30) It's the position, smack on the plaza, that you're paying for here.

Hostal Los Niños (☎ 084-23-1424; ninoshotel@ terra.com.pe; Meloc 442; s/d US$12/24, with bath US$30; 🖳) Dutch-run hostel dedicated to helping street kids.

Eating
CAFÉS

El Buen Pastor Bakery (Cuesta San Blas 575; ⊙ closed Sun) The warm glow isn't just from supping hot chocolate with your morning pastries here, but also the knowledge that all profits go towards a charity-run home for girls.

La Tertulia (Procuradores 44; breakfasts US$2.50-4.50, mains US$2.50-6; ⊙ Oct-Mar mornings only) La Tertulia makes homemade bread, strong coffee and you won't leave hungry after its 'eat-as-mucho-as-you-want' breakfast.

Granja Heidi (Cuesta San Blas 525, 2nd fl; ⊙ closed Sun) Follow the pictures of cows to this light, Alpine-feel café, with terrific fresh produce, yogurts, cakes and other light snacks on offer.

Coco Loco (Calle Espaderos 135; snacks US$1.50-2.50; ⊙ till 5am Mon-Sat) For post-clubbing burger cravings.

Trotamundos (Portal Comercio 177; snacks US$1.50-4; 🖳) Popular bar/café with a great view of the cathedral.

I Due Mondi (Santa Catalina Ancha 366) Chic café with 15 seductive ice-cream flavors (including *chicha* – corn-beer!).

RESTAURANTS

A multitude of tourist restaurants litter Cuzco's center, each with its own pastiche of Peruvian and international dishes.

Quinta Eulalia (Choquechaca 384; mains US$2-6; ☻ noon-6pm) This is a no-nonsense open-air spot serving authentic Andean specialties – no opt-out hamburgers for the suddenly faint of heart. It sells *cuy* cheaper than most city-center places (US$6).

Fallen Angel (Plazoleta Nazarenas 221; mains US$4.50-7, cocktails US$2.50-5) Fallen Angel is an ultra-funky restaurant almost falling over itself in the rush to cram in as much kitsch as possible: glitterballs, fake fur and even bathtub-cum-aquarium tables complete with goldfish. The cocktails, though distinctly unangelic, are recommended.

Macondo (Cuesta San Blas 571; mains US$2.80-5.60; ☻ evening only Sun) A trendy spot serving nuevo-Andean and jungle dishes, Macondo gets busy with backpackers in the evening – evidenced by the hundreds of grinning faces on the photo-bedecked tables.

Pucará (Plateros 309; ☻ closed Sun) This Japanese-run place has good food and menus with handy photographs, so even the linguistically challenged can order chicken and not get eggdrop soup.

Inka Grill (☎ 084-26-2992; Portal de Panes 115; mains US$7-14) This grill, on the corner of the Plaza de Armes, is deservedly popular for both food and service: order *cuy* dishes in advance.

El Mesón de los Espaderos (☎ 084-23-5307; Calle Espaderos 105, 2nd fl; mains US$9-12) The huge photo of a juicy steak on entry to this place is a large clue for what is to come.

Pi Shop (Atoqsaykuchi 599; ☻ Tue-Sun) Travelers looking for a few home comforts can find everything from apple pies to Vegemite in this welcoming, informal spot.

Chez Maggy (Procuradores 344, 365, 374; set menu US$4) Chez Maggy has virtually taken over Gringo Alley with three deja-vu-inducing branches and another on Plateros 348, all serving reasonable pizza and pasta.

Other recommendations:

Greens (☎ 084-24-3820; Tandapata 700; mains US$4.50-7.50) Cheery den hidden away in San Blas; serves Sunday roasts by reservation.

Café Bagdad (Portal de Carnes 216; mains US$6-9) Open-fronted balcony restaurant overlooking the plaza.

Victor Victoria (Tigre 130; mains US$2.50-6) No-frills restaurant that slips in a few French and Israeli dishes.

SELF-CATERING

The best supermarket in the city center is **Dimart** (Ayacucho 248; ☻ 7am-10pm).

VEGETARIAN

Moni (San Agustin 311; mains US$3-4.50; ☻ closed Sun) Moni has a laid-back, coffee-bar ambiance and great à la carte vegetarian fare, including a mean veg curry and adapted Peruvian dishes.

Café Cultural Ritual (Choquechaca 140; set menu US$1.40, mains US$1.40-4.20) This is a bright, cute little option with gaudy decorations and a mild stuffed-toy fixation.

Govinda (Espaderos 128; set menu US$2.50-4.50) Veg stalwart with an incense-infused atmosphere.

Drinking

Savvy travelers soon twig to the fact that competition is intense between Cuzco's nocturnal establishments, and that they can count on enough free drinks and happy hours to forget any aching feet fresh from the Inca trail and can set out on lengthy bar crawls. The drinks in question are almost exclusively *cuba libre* and *pisco* sour, however, so beer-lovers may prefer more sedentary tactics.

Los Perros (Tecsecocha 436; ☻ 11am-1am) One of Cuzco's best drinking dens with a funky, laid-back couch bar and a top-notch music collection.

Cross Keys (Portal Confiturías 233; ☻ 11am-late) The most established watering hole in town is this British-style pub in a rickety old building on the plaza. You can talk without having to scream, or, if you're pressed for conversation, there's cable TV, darts and a pool table with an unparalleled banana-like trajectory.

Paddy O'Flaherty's (Triunfo 124; ☻ 11am-late) This cramped little Irish bar is full of high stools, games and a sizeable foam Leprechaun.

Rosie O'Grady's Irish Pub (Santa Catalina Ancha 360; ☻ 11am-late) Paddy O'Flaherty's newer, shinier compatriot has more room to breathe.

Norton Rat's (Loreto 115; ☻ 9am-late) Down-to-earth US-run biker bar with reputedly the best burgers in town, plus cable TV, darts and a pool table to keep your thirst whetted.

Also try **Fallen Angel** (Plazoleta Nazarenas 221) and **Macondo** (Cuesta San Blas 571).

PERU

Clubbing

Ukuku's Bar (Plateros 316; admission US$1.50) The most popular spot in town, playing crowd-pleasers and Latin pop, and hosting live local bands nightly. Usually full to bursting after midnight, it's good, sweaty dance fun with as many locals as tourists.

X'ss (Portal de Carnes 298) Has the most up-to-the-minute music collection, with techno, trance and hip-hop mixed with the mainstream. There are chill-out sofas upstairs but this isn't the place for chat. Free drinks offered on entry.

Mama Africa Pub (Portal de Belén 115) The city's classic backpackers' hang-out, usually packed with people sprawled across cushions or swaying to rock and reggae rhythms. It has a happy hour from 3pm to 9pm and a 'very happy hour' between 11pm and midnight.

Entertainment

FOLK MUSIC

For folklore music and dance, visit **Qosqo Center of Native Dance** (☎ 084-22-7901; Av Sol 604; admission US$4.20), with daily shows at 7pm.

CINEMAS

Sunset (☎ 084-80-7434; Calle Tecsecocha 2; admission US$0.85) A small video bar showing movies daily at 4pm, 7pm and 9:30pm. Several nightclubs also show movies during the day.

Shopping

Cuzco offers a tremendous variety of woolens, textiles, ceramics, jewelry and art. A great starting point is the sizeable **Centro Artesenal Cuzco** (cnr Av Sol & Tullumayo; 🕓 8am-10pm), where you can literally shop till you drop. Also, the area surrounding Plaza San Blas is Cuzco's artisan quarter, packed with the workshops and showrooms of local craftsmen.

The **Center for Traditional Textiles of Cusco** (☎ 084-22-8117; Av Sol 603A) is a non-profit organization promoting the survival of traditional weaving, and has shop-floor demonstrations of techniques in all their finger-twisting complexity.

There are also craft markets on the corner of Quera and San Bernardo and on the Loreto, just off Plaza de Armas. The **Mercado Central** isn't the place for crafts, but can be a good spot to pick up fruit or that vital spare pair of clean socks. Go in a group and don't take valuables, as thieves are professional and persistent.

Getting There & Away

AIR

Almost all flights from Cuzco's **airport** (☎ 084-22-2611), 2km southeast of the city center, are in the morning. Frequent *colectivos* run from Av Sol (US$0.30) to just outside the airport precinct. Airport departure tax is US$3.50/10 for domestic/international flights. There are regular daily flights to Lima (from US$59, one hour). A few airlines also have flights to Puerto Maldonado (from US$43, 30 minutes), Juliaca (from US$89, 30 minutes), Arequipa (from US$43, 30 minutes) and La Paz, Bolivia (US$106, one hour).

Following are some airlines flying these routes:

Aero Continente/Aviandina (☎ 084-24-3031, toll-free 0800-42420; www.aerocontinente.com in Spanish; Portal de Carnes 254)

LanPeru (☎ 084-25-5552, Airport 084-25-5550; Av Sol 627-B)

Lloyd Aéreo Boliviano (LAB; ☎ 084-22-2990; Santa Catalina Angosta 160)

Taca (☎ 084-24-9921, Airport 084-24-6858; www.taca.com; Av Sol 602-B)

TANS (☎ 084-24-2727; San Agustín 315)

Flights tend to be overbooked, so confirm and reconfirm flights. Many also get cancelled or lumped together during low periods. Earlier flights are less likely to be cancelled.

BUS

Peru

Cuzco has a long-distance bus terminal (departure tax US$0.30), 2km southeast of the city center, where you'll find the following bus companies. Note that there are no buses to Machu Picchu. You must take the train from Cuzco or Ollantaytambo (p854).

Bus services to Puno (US$6 to US$7, six hours) via Juliaca include **Ormeño Royal Class** (☎ 084-22-7501), **Cromotex** (☎ 084-24-9573) and **Imexso** (☎ 084-22-9126). **First Class** (☎ 084-22-3102; firstclass@terra.com.pe; Av Sol 930) has tour buses that stop at significant sites en route. This road route now beats the train for convenience.

Frequent buses also run to Arequipa (US$6 to US$14, 11 hours) with Ormeño Royal Class, **Cruz del Sur** (☎ 084-22-1909) and **CIVA** (☎ 084-24-9961).

PERU

There are two options to get to Lima. The first is via Abancay, Puquio and Nazca (US$17 to US$25, 22 to 26 hours), which is quicker but can be a rough ride and prone to crippling delays from December to April. Companies include the most luxurious Cruz del Sur, the cheapest **Palomino** (☎ 084-22-2694) and the most frequent **Expreso Molino** (☎ 084-24-9512). The alternative is to go via Arequipa, a longer but more reliable route (US$17 to US$40, 30 to 34 hours). Ormeño Royal Class has a daily departure at 9am and a cheaper option at 7pm.

Transportes San Jeronimo (☎ 084-20-1142) goes to Abancay (US$4, six hours) and Andahuaylas (US$7, 10 hours) at 11am and 6pm; there are several other companies. To continue on to Ayacucho, you have to change at Andahuaylas. The road to these towns is rough and cold at night.

Buses to Quillabamba (US$4.20 to US$5, nine hours) leave from the Santiago bus terminal in eastern Cuzco (taxi US$0.85), including **Ampay** (☎ 084-22-7541; Santiago terminal), which has three departures daily. For other jungle destinations, you have to fly, go by truck or on an expedition. There are daily trucks to Puerto Maldonado during the dry season along a wild and difficult road, taking anything from two to eight days in the wet season. Trucks leave from near Plaza Túpac Amaru, two blocks east of Tacna along Av Garcilaso.

Traveling to the Manu reserve is problematic. **Expreso Virgen del Carmen** (☎ 084-22-6895) has buses to Paucartambo (US$2, five hours) leaving from Diagonal Angamos 1952 behind the Coliseo Cerrado daily at 3am, 11am and 3pm. Continuing from Paucartambo to Manu, there are only passing trucks or expedition buses, though **Gallito de las Rocas** (Av Angamos) has buses from Cuzco to Pillcopata at 10am on Monday, Wednesday and Friday (US$5.60, 12 hours). Trucks from the Coliseo Cerrado also go to Pillcopata (12 hours), Atalaya (16 hours) and Shintuya (20 hours).

Buses to Oropesa (US$0.45), Urcos and Sicuani (US$2) leave from near the Coliseo Cerrado on Manco Capac, about five blocks east of Tacna. Buses for Urcos (US$1) also leave from Av de la Cultura opposite the regional hospital. Take these buses to visit the ruins of Tipón, Pikillacta, Rumicolca and Raqchi. For Ausangate, **Transportes**

Huayna Ausangate (☎ 084-965-0922; Av Tomasa Tito Condemayta) has buses to Ocongate and Tinqui (US$3.40, seven hours) at 10am from Monday to Saturday.

Note that long delays are possible from January to April.

Sacred Valley
Buses to Pisac (US$0.85, one hour), Calca and Urubamba (US$0.80, two hours) leave frequently from Tullumayo 800 between Aropunco and Garcilaso from 5:30am until 8pm. There are also micros and *colectivos* to Pisac from Calle Puputi off Av de la Cultura. Buses for Urubamba via Chinchero (US$0.45, 50 minutes) leave from the 300 block of Grau near Puente Grau every 15 minutes from 5am to 8pm.

To get to Ollantaytambo, change at Urubamba or catch the 7:45am or 7:45pm buses from Puente Grau. Buses to Quillabamba stop in Ollantaytambo, but charge the full fare (US$4.20).

International
Several companies offer buses to Copacabana (US$10, 13 hours) and La Paz (US$12 to US$15, 18 hours) in Bolivia. Many will swear blind that their service is direct, though evening buses usually stop in Puno for several hours until the border opens. These services include **Transportes Zela** (☎ 084-24-9977) and **Litoral** (☎ 084-24-8989), both in the main bus terminal, as well as Imexso, and all depart between 9pm and 10pm. Ormeño Royal Class has the only direct service to La Paz (US$25, 15 hours), but goes via Desaguadero.

To get to Tacna, by the Chilean border, Cruz del Sur has a daily service at 4:30pm (US$17, 16 hours).

TRAIN
Cuzco has two unlinked stations. **Estación Huanchac** (Wanchaq; ☎ 084-23-8722; reservas@perurail.com; ⏰ 7am-5pm Mon-Fri, 7am-noon Sat & Sun) serves Juliaca and Puno, with trains leaving at 8am Monday, Wednesday and Saturday (for more details, see p836). Tickets for the Machu Picchu train to Ollantaytambo and Aguas Calientes are also sold from Estación Huanchac (bring ID to buy tickets), but leave from **Estación San Pedro** (☎ 084-22-1992) near the central market. Get tickets as far ahead as possible – seats sell out fast.

It's no longer possible for foreigners to use the cheaper local train. There are three *trenes de turismo* (tourist trains) a day, with more during the high season. Trains leave Cuzco between 6am and 6:35am and stop at Poroy (6:40am to 7:25am), Ollantaytambo (8:05am to 9am) and Aguas Calientes for Machu Picchu (9:40am to 10:40am). Services return between 3:30pm and 4:20pm, arriving back between 7:20pm and 8:45pm. You can cut 45 minutes off the return journey by getting off at Poroy and catching a waiting bus (US$1.40) back to Cuzco center.

Round-trip/one-way tickets cost US$53.10/41.30 on 'Backpacker' trains, or US$88.50/59 in the 1st-class 'Vistadome', which is first and fastest off the marks.

If you'll be visiting the Sacred Valley, you can travel for less from Ollantaytambo to Machu Picchu (see p854).

The journey begins with four back-and-forth switchbacks that take about 30 minutes to negotiate, so late-risers who miss the train can often make a dash for the station at Poroy to catch up. The tracks then drop gently to Ollantaytambo station and down a narrow gorge alongside the lower Urubamba. The last station on the line is at Aguas Calientes, the end-of-the-line station for Machu Picchu.

For the most up-to-date schedules, check the website www.perurail.com.

Getting Around

A taxi from the airport to the center of Cuzco costs about US$2.50. A taxi around town should cost no more than US$1. Official taxis, identified by a roof light and company telephone number, are far safer than 'pirate' taxis with a sticker in the window. A company to call is **Aló Taxi** (☎ 084-22-2222), whose drivers are all licensed and carry photo ID. The **Tranvia** (US$2) is a free-rolling tram service that conducts a two-hour tour of Cuzco, leaving from the Plaza de Armas at 10am and 1pm daily.

NORTH OF CUZCO

The four ruins closest to Cuzco are **Sacsayhuamán**, **Qenko**, **Puca Pucara** and **Tambo Machay** (admission to all with Boleto Turístico; ☉ 7am-6pm). Take a Cuzco–Pisac bus and get off at Tambo Machay, the ruin furthest from Cuzco (and, at 3700m, the highest). From here, walk 8km back to Cuzco, visiting all four

ruins along the way. Locals in all their finery plus their most photogenic llamas wait near each site, hoping to be photographed for a tip (US$0.30 to US$60). Go in a group and return before nightfall.

Sacsayhuamán

This immense ruin is the most impressive in the immediate Cuzco area. The name means 'Satisfied Falcon,' though most tourists remember it by the mnemonic 'sexy woman.'

To reach the site from Cuzco, you can climb the steep street of Resbalosa, turn right past the Church of San Cristóbal and continue to a hairpin bend in the road. Here, you'll join the old Inca road between Cuzco and Sacsayhuamán to the top and left. The climb is steep and takes 20 to 40 minutes. Arriving at dawn will give you the site almost to yourself, though a few opportunistic robberies have been reported, so go in a group.

Although Sacsayhuamán seems huge, what today's visitor sees is only about 20% of the original structure. Soon after the conquest, the Spaniards tore down walls and used the blocks to build their own houses in Cuzco.

The most striking area left is the magnificent three-tiered zigzag fortifications – one stone incredibly weighs over 300 tons. The Incas envisioned Cuzco in the shape of a puma, with Sacsayhuamán as the head, and these 22 zigzagged walls form the teeth of the puma.

Opposite is the hill called Rodadero, with retaining walls, curiously polished rocks and a series of stone benches known as the throne of the Inca. Between the zigzag ramparts and Rodadero Hill lies a large, flat parade ground used for Inti Raymi, held June 24.

The fort saw one of the most bitter battles of the conquest between the Spanish and the rebellious Manco Inca, who used Sacsayhuamán to lay siege to the conquistadors in Cuzco. Only a desperate last-ditch attack by 50 Spanish cavalry succeeded in retaking Sacsayhuamán and putting an end to the rebellion. Manco Inca retreated to the fortress of Ollantaytambo. Thousands of dead littered the site and attracted swarms of carrion-eating Andean condors, leading to the inclusion of eight condors in Cuzco's coat of arms.

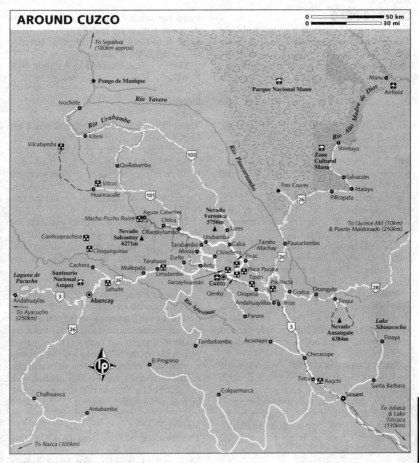

AROUND CUZCO

0 — 50 km
0 — 30 mi

To Sepahua
(180km approx)

Pongo de Manique

Ivochote

Río Yavero

Parque Nacional Manu

Manu
Airfield

Río Urubamba

Kiteni

Río Alto Madre de Dios

Vilcabamba

103

Quillabamba

Río Paucartambo

Shintuya

Zone
Cultural
Manu

Vitcos

101

Salvación

Huancacalle

Tres Cruces

Atalaya

26

Pillcopata

Machu Picchu Ruins

Aguas Calientes

Chilca

Nevado
Veronica
5750m

Lares

To Quince Mil (10km)
& Puerto Maldonado (250km)

Corihuayrachina

Nevado
Salcantay
6271m

Ollantaytambo

Urubamba

Choquequirao

Tarabamba

Calca

Tambo
Machay

Paucartambo

26

Moray

Chinchero

Pisac

Cachora

Tarahuasi

Zurite

Anta

Puca Pucara

Mollepata

Limatambo

Tipón

Pikillacta

Laguna de
Pacucha

Santuario
Nacional
Ampay

Sacsayhuamán

Cuzco

Ocongate

28

Sahuite

Qenko

Oropesa

Andahuaylillas

Urcos

Ccatca

Tinqui

Andahuaylas

26

Abancay

Río Apurímac

Paruro

3

Nevado
Ausangate
6384m

Lake
Sibinacocha

Finaya

To Ayacucho
(250km)

Tambobamba

Acomayo

Checacupe

26

El Progreso

Tinta

Raqchi

Santa Barbara

Chalhuanca

Colquemarca

Sicuani

Antabamba

To Juliaca
& Lake
Titicaca
(130km)

To Nazca (300km)

Other Ruins

On the left side of the road descending from Tambo Machay, 4km before Cuzco, **Qenko** is a small yet fascinating ruin whose name means 'zigzag.' It's a large limestone rock riddled with niches, steps and extraordinary symbolic carvings, including zigzagging channels that may have been used for the ritual sacrifice of *chicha* or, perhaps, blood. Scrambling up to the top of the boulder you'll find a flat surface used for ceremonies, and if you look carefully, laboriously etched representations of animals. Back below, explore the tunnels and mysterious subterranean cave with altars hewn into the rock.

The commanding ruin of **Puca Pucara** appears red in certain light, and the name means 'red fort,' though its function is unknown. **Tambo Machay**, a small ruin about 300m from the main road, is a beautifully wrought ceremonial bath, still channeling clear spring water that earns it the title as El Baño del Inca (The Bath of the Inca); theories connect the site to an Inca water cult.

Action Valley

The perfect antidote to ruin-fatigue, this **adventure park** (☎ 084-24-0835; www.actionvalley.com; ☷ 10am-4pm Sun-Fri Apr-Nov) has a climbing pole (US$19), climbing wall (US$9), 120m bungee jump (US$59) and a bungee sling shot (US$59) ready to sweep you off your feet. The park is 11km outside Cuzco on the road to Poroy (taxi US$2).

CUZCO TO PUNO

The railway and the road to Puno and Lake Titicaca head southeast from Cuzco. En route are several sites that make great daytrips. **Tipón** (admission with Boleto Turístico; ☼ 7am-6pm) is a little-known Inca site noted for its ingenious irrigation system – a demonstration of the Inca's mastery over their environment. Take an Urcos bus from Cuzco to the Tipón turn-off, 23km away. A steep dirt road from the turn-off climbs 4km to the ruins.

Pikillacta (admission with Boleto Turístico; ☼ 7am-6pm), 32km from Cuzco, is the only major pre-Inca ruin near Cuzco and was built around AD 1100 by the Wari culture. Literally translated as 'The Place Of The Flea,' Pikillacta is a large city of crumbling, two-story buildings, all with entrances strategically located on the upper floor.

About 1km away on the highway is the huge Inca gate of **Rumicolca**, built on Wari foundations. To get to either site, take the Urcos or Puno-bound bus from Cuzco.

Andahuaylillas, 40km from Cuzco and 7km before Urcos, is famous for its lavishly decorated 17th-century **church** (admission US$1), almost oppressive in its heavy, baroque embellishments. Take a bus from Cuzco bound for Puno.

Raqchi (adult/student US$1.40/1; ☼ 7am-6pm) are the ruins of the Temple of Viracocha, which once supported the largest known Inca roof. They are visible from the road and the railway at San Pedro, a few kilometers before Sicuani, and look like a huge aqueduct. Buses from Cuzco to Puno pass the site (US$1.75, 2½ hours).

THE SACRED VALLEY

The Valle Sagrado, or Sacred Valley of the Río Urubamba, is 15km north of Cuzco as the condor flies. The valley's star attractions are the lofty Inca citadels of Pisac and Ollantaytambo. A multitude of tour companies in Cuzco offer whirlwind tours to these spots, but it's more fun to explore at your leisure.

Pisac

Pisac lies 32km northeast of Cuzco and is the most convenient starting point for visits to the Sacred Valley. It consists of a somnolent rural colonial village alongside the river, and an Inca site dramatically located on a mountain spur 600m above. Colonial Pisac comes alive on Sunday mornings, when the famous weekly market swamps its center with every craft imaginable, from llama finger-puppets to panpipes practically as tall as their makers.

There's a small **cyber café** (US$0.85 per hr; ☼ 3-11pm Mon-Sat, noon-11pm Sun) on Bolognesi.

SIGHTS
Ruins

The hilltop **Inca citadel** (admission with Boleto Turístico) lies high above the village on a triangular plateau with a plunging gorge on either side. A taxi up the 10km road costs US$5 return or take the steep 5km footpath starting on the left-hand side of the church. On market days, combis also make the trip (US$0.60).

The stiff but spectacular path climbs through terraces, sweeping around the flanks of the mountain, and along cliff-hugging footpaths, defended by massive stone doorways, steep stairs and a short tunnel carved out of the rock.

Topping the terraces is the site's ceremonial center, with an Intihuatana (or hitching post of the sun), several working water channels and some painstakingly neat masonry in the well-preserved temples. From here a path leads up the hillside to a series of ceremonial baths and round to the military area. A cliff behind the site is honeycombed with hundreds of Inca tombs that were plundered by *huaqueros* (grave robbers).

Markets

The bustling Sunday market kicks into life in the early morning, and between 10am and 11am the tourist buses deposit their hoards into an already chaotic scene, thronging with buyers and overrun with colorful stalls packed with crafts of every description. Despite drawing tourists from the world over, the market also retains a traditional side, and good-natured haggling over everyday produce goes on alongside the craft circus. Watch for when the Quechua mass finishes, as the congregation leaves the church in a colorful procession led by the mayor. There are also smaller markets on Tuesday and Thursday, and some mercantile activity daily.

SLEEPING & EATING

Hostal Pisaq (☎ /fax084-20-3062; hotelpisaq@terra.com.pe; Plaza Constitución; per person US$10, d with bath

US$26) Recognizable by its funky geometric designs, this place has good rooms and an underground sauna.

Kisay Cchocha (☎ 084-20-3101; Plaza Constitución & Arequipa; per person US$5) and **Parador de Pisaq** (☎ 084-20-3061; Plaza Constitución; s/d US$7) also provide cheap, no-frills lodging with shared bathrooms, or you can camp at **Royal Inka Pisac** (☎ 084-20-3064/5; per person US$3, tent hire 1-person/2-person/4-person US$10/12/15), 1.5km along the road to the ruins.

Ulrike's Café (Plaza Constitución; set menu US$3) Serves the best (vegetarian) menu, home-made pasta and melt-in-the-mouth muffins (US$0.60) of the several eateries in town.

Also visit the clay-oven bakery on Mariscal Castilla for hot-out-of-the-oven flat-bread rolls typical of the area.

GETTING THERE & AWAY

To return to Cuzco or continue to Urubamba, wait for a bus by the bridge between 5:30am and 8pm. Note that buses to Cuzco start in Urubamba and often have standing room only.

Urubamba

Urubamba is located at the junction of the valley road with the Chinchero road. Surrounded by beautiful countryside, it makes a serene base from which to explore the amphitheater-like Inca terracing of **Moray** (10km east of Urubamba) and the extraordinary Salinas. It's also a great place to enjoy some of the valley's best outdoor activities.

The village of **Tarabamba** is about 6km further down the valley. Here, cross the river by footbridge and continue on a footpath, climbing roughly southward up a valley for 3km further to the **Salinas** (admission US$0.60), thousands of saltpans that have been exploited since Inca times.

There's a Visa ATM on the main road by Quinta Los Geranios, and Internet access is available at **Academia de Internet Urubamba** (cnr Grau & Belén; US$0.70 per hr; ☺ 8am-10pm).

SIGHTS & ACTIVITIES

Perol Chico (☎ 084-20-1694; info@perolchico.com) has an excellent ranch outside Urubamba with Peruvian Paso horses. Horse-riding tours cost roughly US$60 per day. **Viento Sur** (☎ 084-20-1620; www.aventurasvientosur.com; Hotel Sol y Luna) also organizes horse-riding tours, plus paragliding (high-season only, US$100) and mountain biking.

SLEEPING & EATING

Hotel Urubamba (☎ 084-20-1062; Bolognesi 605; s/d US$3/6, with bath US$6/9) A basic but friendly choice in the town center. Some shared showers have hot water on request.

Señor de Torrechero (☎ 084-20-1033; Mariscal Castilla 114; s/d/tr US$6/9/12) Offers fair value rooms with private bath.

Quinta Los Geranios (☎ 084-20-1093; Cabo Conchatupa; per person US$10) Has spotless new rooms with private baths, and a garden running down to the river. It also has a **restaurant** (mains US$3-7; ☺ noon-6pm).

Los Cedros (☎ 084-20-1416; camping US$4-6 per person) Los Cedros has a campsite located 4km above the town on winding country roads.

Che Mary (☎ 084-20-1003; cnr Comercio & Grau; set menu US$2.50) A cozy little restaurant on the plaza.

GETTING THERE & AWAY

Buses going to Cuzco (US$0.85, two hours), Pisac (US$0.60, one hour) or via Chinchero (US$0.50, 30 minutes) and combis to Ollantaytambo (US$0.30, 25 minutes) all leave every 20 minutes from the bus terminal.

Ollantaytambo

Ollantaytambo, dominated by the massive Inca fortress above, is the best surviving example of Inca city planning, with narrow cobble-stoned streets that have been constantly inhabited since the 13th century. The spectacular, steep terraces guarding the **Inca complex** (admission with Boleto Turístico; ☺ 7am-6pm) also mark one of the few places where the conquistadors lost a major battle, when Manco Inca showered a force of 70 cavalrymen with missiles and flooded the plain below.

But Ollantaytambo was as much a temple as a fort to the Incas. The finely worked ceremonial area sits on top of the terracing. The stone was quarried from the mountainside 6km away, high above the opposite bank of the Río Urubamba. Transporting the huge blocks was a stupendous feat involving the sweat and blood of thousands of workers.

Museo CATCCO (☎ 084-20-4024; admission US$1.50; ☺ 10am-1pm & 2-4pm Tue-Sun) has information and Internet access for a whopping US$3 per hour.

SLEEPING & EATING

Chaska Wasi (☎ 084-20-3061; chaskawasihostal@hot mail.com; Chaupicalle; US$5-6 per person) Cheap and cheerful spot with shared electric showers.

Hostal Tambo (☎ 084-20-4003; Costado; per person US$3) This hostel is run-down, with shared cold-water showers.

Hostal La Ñusta (☎ 084-20-4035; per person US$4.50, with breakfast US$8) Slightly chaotic, with a miniature terrace with ruin views.

Hospedaje Los Andenes (☎ 084-20-4095; Ventiderio; per person US$4.50, s/d with bath US$7/14) Recommended, with hot water and a cute café outside.

El Albergue Ollantaytambo (☎ /fax 084-20-4014; albergue@rumbosperu.com; s/d US$15/30) Try Albergue Ollantaytambo for more luxury. It's on the train platform 800m from the town center – no fear of missing your train here.

Restaurants are found in the plaza and by the ruins, and Bar Amazonica serves colorful jungle cocktails.

GETTING THERE & AWAY

Frequent combis run here from Urubamba's bus terminal (US$0.30, 25 minutes); services peter out in late afternoon. To get to Cuzco it's often quickest to change in Urubamba, or several buses daily go direct to Cuzco (US$1, 2½ hours).

Ollantaytambo's **train station** (ticket office ✆ 6:30am-noon & 5-8pm) is the half-way point for trains running between Cuzco and Machu Picchu (see p849 and p857 for details). These trains charge the same fare as from Cuzco. However, Ollantaytambo itself also runs two daily Vistadome services (one way/round trip US$35/69), a high-season Backpacker train (one way/round trip US$29.50/41.30), plus a local train with two Backpacker coaches that leaves at 7:45pm daily (one way/round trip US$11.80/23.60); this limited service is currently the cheapest option to get to Machu Picchu. Vistadome one-way tickets are reduced by 50% when purchased within 48 hours.

Chinchero

Known as the 'birthplace of the rainbow,' Chinchero combines Inca ruins with a typical Andean village and an elaborate colonial church on Inca foundations, as well as mountain views and a colorful Sunday market. Access requires a Boleto Turístico.

Buses running between Cuzco and Urubamba (US$0.45, 50 minutes) stop here.

MACHU PICCHU

For many visitors to Peru and even South America itself, a visit to the lost Inca city of Machu Picchu is the whole purpose of their trip. This spectacular and awe-inspiring location is the best-known and most spectacular archaeological site on the continent, and from June to September as many as a thousand people arrive daily. Despite this great tourist influx, the site manages to retain its air of grandeur and mystery, and is a must for all visitors to Peru. Many tourists choose to approach Machu Picchu on foot, taking up to four days to walk the Inca Trail (p857) across spectacular mountains and valleys.

History

For all its glory, Inca pre-eminence only lasted around 100 years. The reign of the first eight Incas spanned the period from the 12th century to the early 15th century, but it was the ninth Inca, Pachacutec, that gave the empire its first bloody taste of conquest. A growing thirst for expansion led neighboring highland tribe, the Chanka, to Cuzco's doorstep in around 1438, and Viracocha Inca fled in the belief that his small empire was lost. However, his third son Pachacutec rallied the Inca army and, in a desperate battle, he famously routed the Chanka. Buoyed by his victory, he then embarked upon the first wave of Incan expansion, promptly bagging much of the central Andes.

Over the next 25 years, the Inca empire grew and grew until it stretched from the present day border of Ecuador and Colombia to the deserts of northern Chile. Pachacutec's successor, Tupac Yupanqui, was every bit his father's son and it was upon his death in 1493 that the Inca empire had reached its territorial apogee as a colonial force.

Huayna Capac, the 12th Inca, ruled over an empire that was united for the last time. By this time the Europeans had arrived in the New World and were making inroads into the continent via Central America and the Caribbean. Shortly before his death from a European disease, Huayna Capac divided his empire between his two sons,

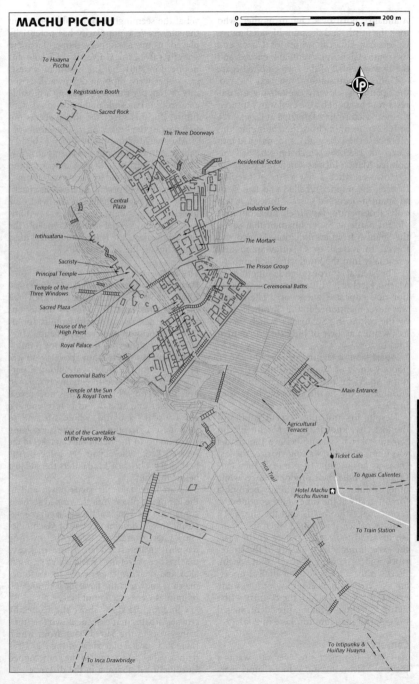

MACHU PICCHU

0 — 200 m
0 — 0.1 mi

To Huayna Picchu

Registration Booth

Sacred Rock

The Three Doorways

Residential Sector

Central Plaza

Industrial Sector

Intihuatana

The Mortars

Sacristy

Principal Temple

The Prison Group

Temple of the Three Windows

Ceremonial Baths

Sacred Plaza

House of the High Priest

Royal Palace

Ceremonial Baths

Temple of the Sun & Royal Tomb

Main Entrance

Hut of the Caretaker of the Funerary Rock

Agricultural Terraces

Ticket Gate

Inca Trail

To Aguas Calientes

Hotel Machu Picchu Ruinas

To Train Station

To Inca Drawbridge

To Intipunku & Huiñay Huayna

PERU

Atahualpa, born of a Quitan mother, who took the north, and the pure-blooded native Cuzqueñan Huáscar, who took Cuzco and the south. Civil war eventually ensued and the slow downfall of the Inca empire began.

Under conquistador Francisco Pizarro, the Spaniards, cleverly capitalizing on unrest brought about by the civil war, captured the near-victorious Atahualpa at Cajamarca in 1532 (ransoming him, then bumping him off once he had the gold), and marched into Cuzco in 1533, by which time he had appointed Manco Inca as a new puppet Inca.

However, after a few years of keeping to heel, the puppet rebelled and laid siege to Spanish-occupied Cuzco. Indeed, it was only a desperate, last-ditch breakout and violent battle at Sacsayhuamán that saved the Spanish from annihilation. Manco was forced to retreat to Ollantaytambo and eventually into the jungle at Vilcabamba.

The actual purpose and function of Machu Picchu is still a matter of speculation and educated guesswork. The citadel was never mentioned in the chronicles kept by the colonizing Spaniards, which served as a written archive of hitherto unrecorded Inca history.

Apart from a few indigenous Quechuas, nobody knew of Machu Picchu's existence until American historian Hiram Bingham stumbled upon the thickly overgrown ruins in 1911.

Despite his and more recent studies of the lost city, knowledge of Machu Picchu remains sketchy. Some believe the citadel was founded in the waning years of the last Incas as an attempt to preserve Inca culture or rekindle their predominance, while others think it may have already become a forgotten city at the time of the conquest. A recent suggestion holds that the site was a country palace abandoned when the Spanish invasion took grip. Whatever the case, the exceptionally high quality of the stonework and ornamentation tell that Machu Picchu must once have been vitally important as a ceremonial center. Indeed, to some extent, it still is; Toledo, the country's first native Quechua-speaking president, staged his colorful inauguration here in 2001.

Conservation

As Peru's showpiece site, everyone wants a piece of Machu Picchu. While visitors mar-vel at the seemingly untouchable beauty of the site, its very popularity has potentially placed it on a slippery slope. Japanese scientists from the University of Kyoto announced in 2001 that the mountain's western slopes were slipping downwards at the rate of 1cm per month, prefacing a possible catastrophic landslide in the not-too-distant future. But this suggested threat seems not to have put the brakes on visitor numbers.

Also, while a long-mooted plan to build a cable car to the summit has been put firmly on the backburner following condemnation from the national and international community, the threat of private interests encroaching on the site continually rears its head. One unbelievable accident even saw a crew filming a beer commercial smash a crane into the site's showpiece, the Intihuatana, breaking a large chip off the principle block!

The Site

Machu Picchu (adult/student under 26 US$20/10; ⊙ 6am-9:30pm) is both the best and the least known of the Inca sites, tantalizing for its mysterious past and deservedly world-famous for its stunning location and craftsmanship.

Unless you arrive on the Inca Trail – which enters the site from above – you will proceed from the ticket gate along a narrow path to the maze-like main entrance to Machu Picchu, where the ruins now reveal themselves and stretch out before you. To get a visual fix of the whole site and to take the classic photo, take the zigzagging staircase up to the **Hut of the Caretaker of the Funerary Rock**, where you get some of the best views. The Inca Trail enters the site just below this hut.

From here, take the steps down and to the left of the plazas into the ruined sections containing the **Temple of the Sun**, a curved, tapering tower containing some of Machu Picchu's finest stonework. Below the towering temple is an almost hidden, natural rock cave that has been carefully carved with a step-like altar and sacred niches by the Inca's stonemasons, known as the **Royal Tomb**, though no mummies were ever found here.

Climbing the stairs above the 16 nearby **ceremonial baths** that cascade down the ruins brings you to the **Sacred Plaza**, from which there is a spectacular view of the Río Urubamba valley and across to the snowcapped Cordillera Vilcabamba in the distance.

Further on, the **Intihuatana** (Hitching Post of the Sun) is the major shrine of Machu Picchu, and lies atop a small hill. The carved rock at the summit is often called a sundial, though it was connected to the passing of the seasons rather than the time of day. This post is unique; the Spaniards smashed most of such shrines in an attempt to wipe out the pagan blasphemy of sun worship.

Immediately below and to the northeast of the Intihuatana is the **Central Plaza**, which divides the ceremonial sector of Machu Picchu from the more mundane **residential** and **industrial** sectors. At the lower end of this area is the **Prison Group**, a labyrinthine complex of cells, niches and passageways. The centerpiece of the group is a carving of the head of a condor.

A further US$10 gets you into the ruins at night, but tickets are only sold during the day and may not be offered during the wet season. You aren't allowed to bring large backpacks, food or water bottles into the ruins; there's a locker-room at the main entrance. Guards check the ruins at closing time, so you can't spend the night. The ruins are most heavily visited between about 10am and 2pm.

Hiking

Behind the ruins is the steep-sided mountain of **Huayna Picchu** (Young Peak); it takes an hour to scramble up the steep path, but for all the puffing it takes to get there, you'll be rewarded with spectacular views. Take care in wet weather as the steps get dangerously slippery. The entrance to the trail is at the back of the ruins to the right and closes at 2pm (be back by 4pm).

Part of the way up Huayna Picchu, another path plunges down to your left, hugging the rear of Huayna Picchu to the small **Temple of the Moon**, from where you can climb steeply to Huayna Picchu – a circuitous route taking two hours.

Another option is to walk to the **Inca Drawbridge**, a scenic and flatter walk from the Hut of the Caretaker of the Funerary Rock, taking you out along a narrow cliff-clinging trail (20 minutes each way) with vertical drops to the valley below.

Getting There & Away

Unless hiking the Inca Trail, visitors must come by train to Aguas Calientes (p861).

There is no other way. Buses depart from Aguas Calientes every hour or so for Machu Picchu (p861). Alternatively, you can walk from Aguas Calientes to Puente Ruinas – where the road crosses the Río Urubamba; it's about a 20-minute walk. From Puente Ruinas there is a marked, steep walking trail to Machu Picchu, taking a good hour (less coming down!).

INCA TRAIL

The most famous hike in South America, the four-day Inca Trail to Machu Picchu is walked by many thousands of people every year. Although the total distance is only 33km, the ancient trail laid by the Incas winds its way up and down and around the mountains, taking three high passes en route, which have collectively led to the route being fondly dubbed 'The Inca Trial.' The views of snowcapped mountains and high cloud forest can be stupendous, and walking from one cliff-hugging ruin to the next is a mystical and unforgettable experience.

When to Go

Groups leave year-round, except for February when the annual clean up of the trail takes place (generally collecting over 400kg of unburnable garbage!). However, in the wettest months from December to April, trails can be slippery and campsites muddy, and views are often obscured behind a thick bank of rolling clouds. In contrast, the dry season from May to September is the most popular time, as well as the most crowded.

Regulations & Tours

The Peruvian government has introduced a string of reforms to the Inca Trail since 2001 in an attempt to reduce the number of hikers and prevent further damage to the trail. As a result, all Inca trail hikers must now go with a licensed guide, and groups should not exceed 16, with one guide per 10 hikers. Registered tour agencies also have to pay huge fees and trail prices have shot up in response.

This all adds up to the four-day Inca Trail costing the barest minimum of US$170 for adults, or US$145 for students on presentation of a valid ISIC card, but to be sure of a reliable company, even shoestringers should look to pay over US$220. This price includes a tent, food, porters, a cook, admission to Machu Picchu and the train fare back to

Cuzco. For details of outfitters, see p842. Tickets must be bought at least 72 hours before the trek, but tour agents will handle this (note that the INC ticket office is closed Saturday afternoon and Sunday, so plan to wait four to five days if booking at the weekend). Booking ahead and reconfirming four to five days in advance will avoid delays caused by bottlenecks in the high season. Also, campsites are allotted in advance, so late-comers are more likely to spend the last night several hours short of the final stretch. This necessitates getting up at 3am and hiking down a perilously steep trail in order to catch the sunrise at the Sun Gate (you also miss the fantastic views on the way down and the ruins at Huiñay Huayna).

Another recent change has been to order all tourists to carry their passport (a copy will not do) and student cards where appropriate to present at checkpoints throughout the trail.

Preparation & Conservation

Sleeping bags and other gear can be found at travel agencies in Cuzco. The trail gets extremely cold at night, so make sure sleeping bags are warm enough and bring plenty of snug clothing. Also remember sturdy shoes, rain gear, insect repellent, sunscreen, a flashlight (with fresh batteries), water-purification tablets, high-calorie snacks and a basic first-aid kit. Take a small stash of cash for tipping the guide, cook and the slave-driven porters. Detailed maps are available from South American Explorers in Cuzco (see p842). Keep all gear inside your tents at night.

Don't litter or defecate in the ruins, or pick plants in the national park. Also remember that it is illegal to graffiti any trees or stones en route. When choosing your tour group, be aware that the cheaper guided tours have less idea about ecologically sensitive camping, while more expensive trips make some effort to camp cleanly and provide adequate facilities for porters.

The Hike

Most agencies run minibuses to the start of the trail near the village of Chilca at Piscacucho (km 82 on the railway to Aguas

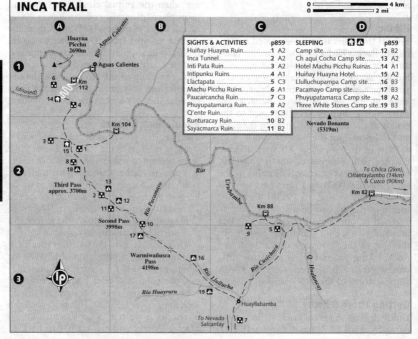

INCA TRAIL

0 —————— 4 km
0 —————— 2 mi

SIGHTS & ACTIVITIES	p859
Huiñay Huayna Ruin	1 A2
Inca Tunnel	2 A2
Inti Pata Ruin	3 A2
Intipunku Ruins	4 A1
Llactapata	5 C3
Machu Picchu Ruins	6 A1
Paucarcancha Ruin	7 C3
Phuyupatamarca Ruin	8 A2
Q'ente Ruin	9 C3
Runturacay Ruin	10 B2
Sayacmarca Ruin	11 B2

SLEEPING	p859
Camp site	12 B2
Ch aqui Cocha Camp site	13 A2
Hotel Machu Picchu Ruinas	14 A1
Huiñay Huayna Hotel	15 A2
Llulluchupampa Camp site	16 B3
Pacamayo Camp site	17 B3
Phuyupatamarca Camp site	18 A2
Three White Stones Camp site	19 B3

Calientes). After crossing the Río Urubamba (2200m) and taking care of trail fees and registration formalities, the trail climbs gently alongside the river to the first archaeological site of **Llactapata** (Town on Hillside), before heading south down a side valley of the Río Cusichaca. The trail south leads 6km to the hamlet of **Huayllabamba** (Grassy Plain; 2750m), where many tour groups camp nearby. You can buy bottled drinks and high-calorie snacks in houses here, and take a breather to appreciate views of the snow-capped Veronica (5750m).

Huayllabamba is situated near the fork of the Llullucha and Cusichaca Rivers. You will cross Río Llullucha on a log bridge then climb steeply up along the river. This area is known as **Llulluchayoc** (Three White Stones), and from here it is a long, very steep climb, through humid Polylepis woodlands for about 1½ hours. At some points, the trail and stream bed become one, but stone stairs keep hikers above the water. The trail eventually emerges on the high, bare mountainside of **Llulluchupampa**, where the flats are dotted with campsites (these sites get very cold at night). This is as far as you can reasonably expect to get on your first day, though many groups will spend their second night here.

From Llulluchupampa, a good path up the left-hand side of the valley climbs for the two- to three-hour ascent to the pass of **Warmiwañusca**, also colorfully known as 'Dead Woman's Pass.' At 4198m above sea level, this is the highest point of the trek, and leaves many a seasoned hiker gasping. From Warmiwañusca, you can see the Río Pacamayo (Sunrise River) far below, as well as the ruin of Runturacay halfway up the hill.

The trail continues down a long and knee-jarringly steep descent to the river, where there are large campsites. At an altitude of about 3600m, the trail crosses the river over a small footbridge and climbs to the right toward **Runturacay** (Basket-Shaped Building), a round ruin with superb views about an hour's walk above the river.

Above Runturacay, the trail climbs to a false summit before continuing past two small lakes to the top of the second pass at 3998m, which has views of the snow-capped Cordillera Vilcabamba. The clear trail descends past a lurid green lake to the ruin of **Sayacmarca** (Dominant Town),

a tightly constructed complex perched on a small mountain spur with incredible views. The trail continues downward crossing a tributary of the Río Aobamba, and passing a campsite and shower block.

The trail leads on across an Inca causeway and up again through cloud forest and an Inca tunnel carved into the rock to the third pass at 3700m. Soon afterwards, you'll reach the beautiful and well-restored ruin of **Phuyupatamarca** (Town Above The Clouds), about 3650m above sea level and two or three hours beyond Sayacmarca. The site contains a beautiful series of ceremonial baths with water running through them. A ridge here offers campsites where some groups spend their final night, with the advantage of watching the sun set over a truly spectacular view, but the disadvantage of having to leave at 3am in the race to reach the Sun Gate in time for the sunrise.

From Phuyupatamarca, the trail takes a dizzying dive into the cloudforest below, following an incredibly well-engineered flight of many hundreds of Inca steps (a nerve-racking experience in the early hours). After two to three hours, the trail eventually zigzags its way down to a red-roofed, white building that provides youth-hostel facilities, with hot showers and meals, for those who want to pay a bit extra.

A 500m trail behind the hostel leads to the exquisite little Inca site of **Huiñay Huayna** (Growing Young).

From the Huiñay Huayna guard post, the trail contours around through cliff-hanging cloudforest for about two hours to reach **Intipunku** (Sun Gate) – where you can catch your first glimpse of majestic Machu Picchu and wait for the sun to rise over the encompassing mountaintops.

The final triumphant descent takes almost an hour. Backpacks are not allowed into the ruins, and park guards will pounce on you to check your pack and to stamp your trail permit. Trekkers generally arrive long before the morning trainloads of tourists, so you can enjoy the exhausted exhilaration of reaching your goal without having to push past sweet-smelling tour parties fresh from Cuzco.

Other Inca Trails
A shorter version of the Inca Trail leaves from km 104. You will be let off the train

shortly before Aguas Calientes where a trail crosses the river before climbing steeply to Huiñay Huayna, which takes about three hours. Trekkers can stay overnight at the hostel near Huiñay Huayna or carry on to Machu Picchu and down to Aguas Calientes. The average price for the all-inclusive two-day trek is around US$60 to US$150 (regulations for the four-day trek still apply).

The village of **Mollepata**, a few kilometers off the main Cuzco–Abancay road, is the starting point for a longer, more spectacular approach to the Inca Trail, climbing over 4800m-high passes near the magnificent glacier-clad peak of **Salcantay** (6271m) and joining the Inca Trail after three to four days.

AGUAS CALIENTES
Also known as Machu Picchu Pueblo, this village is nestled in the deep valley below Machu Picchu (8km away) enclosed by towering walls of stone and cloud forest. All travelers to and from Machu Picchu will pass through the town, and many choose to stick around and indulge in a spot of serious R&R after the Inca Trail.

Orientation & Information
The path from the tourist train station to the Machu Picchu bus stop passes through a scrum of handicraft sellers and over the railway footbridge. There is no bank, but small amounts of money and traveler's checks can be changed in tourist shops. There are card phones scattered around the village, and you can email your mates from **Ink@net** (Imperio de los Incas; US$1.50 per hr). A small tourist information office is in the municipality (town hall), and a medical center, post office and **police station** (☎ 084-21-1178) are shown on the Aguas Calientes map.

Sights & Activities
Just staggered in from the Inca Trail? Soak your aches and pains away in the **hot springs** (admission US$1.50; ☯ 5am-8:30pm), 10-minutes' walk up Pachacutec. Footsore trekkers may also be interested in to-your-door **massage services** (☎ 084-974-5617; US$10-20), which can also be arranged through your hotel.

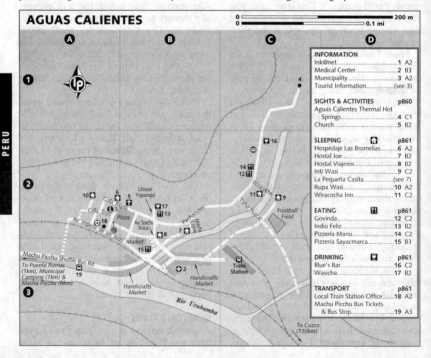

AGUAS CALIENTES

0	200 m
0	0.1 mi

INFORMATION
Ink@net.................................1 A2
Medical Center......................2 B3
Municipality..........................3 A2
Tourist Information...........(see 3)

SIGHTS & ACTIVITIES p860
Aguas Calientes Thermal Hot
  Springs...............................4 C1
Church...................................5 B2

SLEEPING 🏠 p861
Hospedaje Las Bromelias........6 A2
Hostal Joe.............................7 B2
Hostal Viajeros......................8 B2
Inti Wasi...............................9 C2
La Pequeña Casita............(see 7)
Rupa Wasi............................10 A2
Wiracocha Inn......................11 C2

EATING 🍴 p861
Govinda................................12 C2
Indio Feliz.............................13 B2
Pizzeria Manu.......................14 C2
Pizzeria Sayacmarca.............15 B3

DRINKING 🍷 p861
Blue's Bar.............................16 C2
Wasicha................................17 B2

TRANSPORT p861
Local Train Station Office.....18 A2
Machu Picchu Bus Tickets
  & Bus Stop.........................19 A3

To Cuzco
(110km)

Sleeping

Prices listed in this section are for the high season: Expect to pay 20% to 40% less for the rest of the year. Check-out times before 10am are the norm.

Rupa Wasi (☎ 084-21-1101; rupawasi@hotmail.com; dm US$10-15) Sociable hostel with dorm-like rooms and private hot showers in wood-cabins built haphazardly into the hillside off a dirt track.

Hostal Joe (☎ 084-21-1190; trasoc@latinmail.com; Mayta Cápac 103; per person US$5, s/d with bath US$10/15) Toward the hot springs; has clean rooms and hot water, though some communal showers are a mite exposed.

Hospedaje Las Bromelias (☎ 084-21-1145; Colla Raymi; s/d US$4/6) On the plaza, has plain rooms but good value with private hot showers.

Other options for a shade more comfort include **Hostal Viajeros** (☎ 084-21-1237; info@sas travelperu.com; Av Sinchi Roca 4; per person US$15), **Wiracocha Inn** (☎ 084-21-1088; wiracocha-inn@peru.com; Wiracocha; s/d US$15/20) and **La Pequeña Casita** (☎ 084-21-1153; Hermanos Ayar 13; s/d US$20/30), where you can be lulled to sleep by the rushing river below.

Inti Wasi (☎ 084-21-1151; hanan65@latinmail.com; dm US$6) Offers bunk beds in four- to six-bed dorms, with shared bathrooms. It also has camping space.

Municipal Campsite (per person US$1.40) On the road to Machu Picchu, about 20-minutes' walk west of the town center, this campsite offers basic facilities.

Eating

A cluster of restaurants exists along the railway tracks and Pachacutec on the way to the hot springs.

Indio Feliz (Lloque Yupanqui Lote; set menu US$10-14) Cozy restaurant with a French cook who whips up some fantastic meals.

Pizzería Manu (Pachacutec; mains US$4-8, set menu US$5.50) For a cheaper option try this open-fronted pizzeria, which also has an international flavor to its food and atmosphere.

Govinda (Pachacutec; set menu US$2.50-7) Has a stone floor and good-value vegetarian fare.

Pizzería Sayacmarca (Hermanos Ayar; mains US$3.50-7; ☯ lunch only) A meeting point for weary trekkers near the train station.

Drinking

Blue's Bar (Pachacutec; ☯ 9am-11:30pm) A funky gringo bar near the springs.

Wasicha (Lloque Yupanqui Lote) Four dance floors open till the wee hours.

Getting There & Away

Aguas Calientes is the final train stop for Machu Picchu. The Vistadome leaves for Cuzco at 3:30pm daily, arriving in Cuzco at 7:20pm. Backpacker services leave at 3:55pm and 4:20pm, arriving in Cuzco at 8:20pm and 8:45pm. Catch a bus from Poroy to speed things along. For more information, see Cuzco's Getting There & Away section (p849).

For Ollantaytambo (see p854), three Vistadome services return at 8:35am, 1:20pm and 4:45pm. There's also a high-season backpacker train at 5pm and a local service with two cheap backpacker carriages at 5:45am.

Buses to Machu Picchu (US$4.50 one way, 20 minutes) leave hourly between 6:30am and 12:30pm, plus 1pm, and there are enough extra buses to handle fresh-off-the-train crowds. Buses return when full; the last departure is 5:30pm.

CUZCO TO THE JUNGLE

There are three routes into the jungle from Cuzco. One starts in the Sacred Valley and continues down to the town of Quillabamba, while two poor roads head eastwards – one to Paucartambo, Tres Cruces and Shintuya for Parque Nacional Manu, and the other through Ocongate and Quincemil to Puerto Maldonado. You should travel on these in the dry months (June to September), as they are muddy and slow in the wet months, especially from January to April.

Quillabamba

This hot and humid town of the high jungle lies on the Río Urubamba at the end of a spectacular route high over the breathtaking pass of Abra de Malaga. It can be used as a base for trips further into the jungle.

BCP (Libertad) has a Visa ATM and changes dollars. There's Internet access at **Cybermaster** (Espinar 229; US$0.60 per hr; ☯ 7am-11pm).

SLEEPING & EATING

Hostal Urusayhua (☎ 084-28-1426; Lima 114; s/d/tr US$3/4.50/6) A friendly bare-bones place with a cold-water communal bathroom.

Hostal Pineda (☎ 084-28-1447; Libertad 530; s/d US$4/7; ☯ closed Dec-May) Although welcoming, it has pokey rooms with cold private bath above the owner's grocery store.

Hostal Alto Urubamba (☎ 084-28-2616; 2 de Mayo 333; s/d/tr US$5/7/10, with bath US$10/13/18) Recommended, with comfortable rooms, some with fans, circling a sunny courtyard.

Hostal Quillabamba (☎ 084-28-1369; chisaluna@ hotmail.com; Grau 590; s/d/tr/q US$13/18/24/29; ☒) A large, professional affair recommended for clean rooms with hot showers and TV, a good rooftop restaurant and garden.

Heladería La Esquina (cnr Espinar & Libertad; ⓥ evening only Sun) A modern café, with good-value juices and snacks.

GETTING THERE & AWAY

Buses for Cuzco leave daily at 8am, 2pm and 7pm (US$4.20, nine hours) traveling through Ollantaytambo and Urubamba. They leave from the bus terminal, six blocks from Plaza Grau.

Pickup trucks and buses leave every morning from the market area to the village of Ivochote, further into the jungle (US$4.20, 12 to 16 hours). Combis make the long, bumpy trip to Huancacalle from Plaza Grau in Quillabamba in the morning at 9am and 11am (US$3, eight hours), from where you can proceed to Vilcabamba.

Vilcabamba

The beleaguered Manco Inca fled to his jungle retreat in Vilcabamba after finally being defeated by the Spaniards in 1536. This hideout, Espíritu Pampa, was later forgotten until expeditions in the mid-1960s. The hike takes several days from the village of **Huancacalle**, reached from Quillabamba (see p861). There's one basic hostel, called Manco Sixpac, where you can hire mules and guides.

Paucartambo

This village, 115km northeast of Cuzco, is reached by a cliff-hanging dirt road with exhilarating views of the Andes dropping away to the Amazon Basin. Paucartambo is famous for its riotously colorful celebration of the **Fiesta de la Virgen del Carmen**, held around July 15 to 17, with hypnotic street dancing, processions, and all manner of weird and wonderful costumes. For accommodations, camp, rent a room in one of the two extremely basic hotels or ask locals for floor space. Agencies in Cuzco run buses for the fiesta.

Expreso Virgen del Carmen (☎ 084-27-7755; Diagonal Angamos 1952) has three daily bus services from Cuzco (US$2, five hours).

Tres Cruces

Tres Cruces is 45km beyond Paucartambo. The view of the mountains dropping away into the Amazon Basin here is gorgeous in itself, but from May to July it is made all the more magical by the sunrise phenomenon that optically distorts the dawn into a multi-colored light show with double images, halos and unusual tints. During these months, agencies run sunrise-watching trips from Cuzco.

Parque Nacional Manu

Parque Nacional Manu covers almost 20,000 sq km (about the size of Wales) and is one of the best places in South America to see tropical wildlife. The park starts in the eastern slopes of the Andes and plunges down into the lowlands, covering a wide range of remote cloudforest and virgin rainforest habitats that contain hundreds of bird species, not to mention monkeys, tapirs, giant anteaters, capybaras, giant river otters, and countless insects, reptiles and amphibians.

It's illegal to enter Parque Nacional Manu without a licensed guide and permit, which can only be arranged at travel agencies in Cuzco. Transportation, accommodations, food and guides are also part of tour packages. Not all companies enter the park itself, but some offer cheaper 'Manu Tours' outside the park, that still boast exceptional wildlife viewing.

Costs depend on whether you camp or stay in a lodge, and whether you arrive/depart overland or by air (see p842 for suggested agencies), but generally start at US$750 for five days/four nights, flying in and out, or US$800 for nine days/eight nights, all overland. Camping trips using tents on the beaches of the national park can bring costs down to roughly US$75 per day.

Independent travelers can reach the reserve's environs without taking a tour. However, you'll need to hire a guide to get the most out of your trip, who generally charge US$60 per day plus food so little is saved. If you're determined to go solo, you can get to Pillcopata with the Gallito de las Rocas bus (US$6, 12 hours in good weather) from Cuzco's Av Angamos or trucks from the Coliseo Cerrado.

Boats can travel from Pilcopata and the subsequent villages of Atalaya, Salvación or Shintuya toward Manu. People on tours often start river travel from Atalaya after a night in a lodge. The boat journey down the Alto Madre de Dios to the Río Manu takes almost a day. A few minutes from the village of Boca Manu is an airstrip, often the starting or exit point for commercial trips into the park. There is a park entrance fee of US$20, and continuing is only possible with a guide and permit.

The best time to go is from June to November; Manu may be closed from January to April or open only to people staying in the expensive Manu Lodge or the Casa Machiguenga at Cocha Salvador.

Further information can be obtained from South American Explorers or travel agencies in Cuzco (p842).

To Ocongate & Puerto Maldonado

The journey to Puerto Maldonado (see p900) is a spectacular but difficult journey on nightmarish roads that takes two to three days in the dry season (a week or more in the wet) and costs US$15. The journey can be broken at Ocongate or Quincemil (both with basic hotels). Trucks leave Cuzco from the little plaza just east of Tacna and Pachacutec a few times a week. It may be better to wait in Urcos: all trucks to Puerto Maldonado go via Urcos. This trip involves a degree of hardiness, self-sufficiency and good luck.

From Ocongate, trucks take an hour to reach the village of **Tinqui**, which is the start of the five- to seven-day trek encircling 6384m **Ausangate**, southern Peru's highest peak, and taking three spectacular passes higher than 5000m. Tinqui has a very basic hotel, and mules can be rented for the trek.

CUZCO TO THE CENTRAL HIGHLANDS
Choquequirau

The recently rediscovered ridge-top Inca site of **Choquequirau** (admission US$3) is a remote ruin fast becoming a popular and cheaper alternative to the Inca Trail. It has an incredible location at the junction of three valleys, and can currently only be reached on foot: get to it quick before it's accessible to the masses. The most common route

begins from Cachora, a village off the road to Abancay – the turn-off is shortly after Sahuite, about four hours from Cuzco.

Abancay

This sleepy, rural town is one welcome resting place between Cuzco and Ayacucho. The **BCP** (Arequipa) has a Visa ATM. Several Internet cafés cluster near the bus companies. Abancay also has a particularly colorful **Carnaval**, uncluttered by the trappings of tourism.

Places to stay include **Hostal Gran Hotel** (☎ 083-32-1144; Arenas 196; s/d US$3/5, with bath US$4/6), a noisy, old hostel with cold water. **Hostal Victoria** (☎ 083-32-1301; Arequipa 305; s/d US$4.50/7, with bath US$6/8.50) is an excellent, clean little hostel opposite the BCP, while **Hostal El Dorado** (☎ 083-32-2005; Arenas 131; s/d US$7/10) has decent whitewashed rooms with private hot showers and TV.

Restaurant La Delicia (Elias 217; set menu US$2; closed Sat) is a health-food joint with vegetarian food and there are plenty of cheap cafés near the bus companies.

GETTING THERE & AWAY

Buses leave from Arenas near Núñez for Cuzco (US$3, five hours) and Andahuaylas (US$4, five hours) at 6am, 1pm and 8pm in both directions. Journeys may take longer in the wet season. For Ayacucho, change in Andahuaylas.

Andahuaylas

Andahuaylas (2980m) is another convenient stop on the cold and rough but scenic route between Cuzco and Ayacucho. The BCP has a Visa ATM and changes dollars. The best Internet connection is in the back of the **Telefónica del Peru** (JF Ramos 317) office.

SLEEPING & EATING

Hostal Los Libertadores Wari (☎ 083-72-1434; JF Ramos 424; s/d US$3.50/5, with bath US$4.50/7) This bare-bones hostel is clean, safe and has hot water.

Hostal Delicias (☎ 083-72-1104; JF Ramos 525; s/d US$6/10) A better-kept place run by welcoming folks and with private hot baths.

Encanto de Apurimac Hotel (☎ 083-72-3527; JF Ramos 401; s/d/tr US$6/8.50/13) Offers shiny new rooms with private hot baths.

Sol de Oro (☎ 083-72-1152; JA Trelles 164; s/d/tr US$13/17/20) The best in town, boasting modern rooms with cable TV and attentive service.

PERU

Places to eat include **Chifa El Dragón** (cnr JF Ramos & JA Trelles; set menu US$1.70) and dinky vegetarian **Nuevo Horizonte** (Constitución 572; set menu US$1.50; ☒ closed Sat), just off the plaza.

GETTING THERE & AWAY

AeroCóndor (☎ 083-72-2877; Cáceres 326) has Lima flights daily except Saturday (US$59, one hour). It runs minibuses (US$1.70) to the airport. **Señor de Huanca** (☎ 083-72-1218; Martinelly 170) has buses to Abancay (US$4, five hours) at 6:30am, 1pm and 8pm, and **Empresa Transportes San Jeronimo** (☎ 083-72-1400; Andahuaylas 116) has a 6:30pm bus on to Cuzco (US$7, 10 hours).

Expreso Los Chankas (☎ 083-72-2441; Grau 232) has a twice-daily service to Ayacucho at 6:30am and 6:30pm, and **Empresa Wari** (☎ 083-72-1936; Los Sauces) has three daily buses to Lima (US$14, 22 to 24 hours).

CENTRAL HIGHLANDS

The central Peruvian Andes is one of the most neglected areas of Peru. A combination of harsh mountain terrain and terrorist unrest in the 1980s (the Sendero Luminoso, or Shining Path, was born in Ayacucho) made travel difficult for many decades. However, the power of the guerrilla organizations was broken in the 1990s, and roads have improved in recent years to make the region ripe for exploration. Indeed traveling between the unspoilt highland towns is an exciting experience in itself, with memorable mountain views and ear-popping passes.

AYACUCHO

Since the capture of the Sendero's founder in 1992 and the paving of the road to Lima in 1999, the fascinating colonial city of Ayacucho has embraced the 21st century and welcomed flocks of adventurous travelers. The city is particularly famous for its wild Semana Santa celebrations.

Information

iPeru (☎ 066-81-8305; iperuayacucho@promperu.gob.pe; Portal Municipal 48; ☒ 8:30am-7:30pm) is good for information. Travel agencies are also helpful; **Warpa Picchu Eco-Aventura** (☎ 066-81-5191; Portal Independencia 66) and **Wari Tours** (☎ 066-81-3115; Portal Independencia 70), on the main square, are among the better. **BCP** (Portal Unión 28) has a

Visa ATM and cashes traveler's checks, and there's also an **Interbanc** (9 de Diciembre 183). You can access email at **JB Internet** (Portal Constitución 3) and many other places. In emergencies, contact the **Policía de Turismo** (☎ 066-81-2179; 2 de Mayo 100; ☒ 7:30am-8pm).

Sights

The town center has three small museums, a 17th-century cathedral, dozens of ornate churches from the 16th, 17th and 18th centuries, and several old mansions around the plaza.

The extensive ruins of **Wari** (Huari; admission US$0.60; ☒ 8am-5:30pm), capital of the Wari empire, which predated the Inca by 500 years, are well worth seeing. The site sprawls for several kilometers along the roadside. Beyond is the village of **Quinua**, where a huge monument and small museum mark the site of the Battle of Ayacucho (1824). Wari is 20km and Quinua about 40km northeast of Ayacucho. Agencies run tours, or you can use public transport.

Festivals & Events

Ayacucho's **Semana Santa** celebration, held the week before Easter, is Peru's finest religious festival and attracts folks from all around the country. The celebrations begin on the Friday before Palm Sunday and rage for 10 days until Easter Sunday. The Friday before Easter Sunday is marked by a procession in honor of La Virgen de los Dolores (Our Lady of Sorrows), during which it is customary to inflict 'sorrows' on bystanders by firing pebbles out of slingshots. Gringos are popular targets, so watch out! Every day sees a procession, culminating in an all-night party on Easter Saturday and a dawn fireworks display on Easter Sunday.

Sleeping

Prices rise by 25% to 75% over Semana Santa.

Hotel Yañez (☎ /fax 066-81-4918; M Cáceres 1210; s/d with breakfast US$8/12) Comfy mattresses, kitsch wall art, cable TV and hot private showers are the hallmarks of this well-run hotel.

Hotel La Crillonesa (☎ 066-81-2350; hotelcrillonesa@latinmail.com; Nazareno 165; s/d US$5/8, with bath US$8/11.50) Small hotel offering a roof-top terrace with photogenic church-tower views, and there's a café, cable TV room and 24-hour hot water.

Hostal Huamanga (☎ 066-81-3527; Bellido 535; s/d US$3/6, with bath US$6/12) This basic place manages to crank out hot water all day.

La Colmena Hotel (☎ 066-81-2146; Cuzco 140; s US$4.50, s/d with bath US$7/9) Just steps from the plaza; it's often full.

Hostal El Marqués de Valdelirios (☎ 066-81-8944; Bolognesi 720; s/d US$13/18; P) In a lovely colonial building 10-minutes' walk from the town center, with beautiful furniture, cable TV and hot showers, this place is good for a splurge.

Other recommendations:

Hotel Samary (☎ 066-81-2442; Callao 329; s/d US$5.75/7.25, with bath US$8/10; P) Simple.

Hotel Florida (☎ 066-81-2565; Cuzco 310; s/d US$10/16) Has a garden, private baths and TV.

Gran Hotel Los Alamos (☎ /fax 066-81-2782; Cuzco 215; s/d US$6/11.50)

Eating

El Niño (9 de Diciembre 205; mains US$2.75-6) In a colonial mansion overlooking a garden; specializes in grills.

Urpicha (Londres 272; mains US$4) A homey place with a flower-filled patio, familial attention and traditional dishes, including *cuy*. Take a taxi here after dark.

Wallpa Suwa (G de la Vega 240; mains US$2-5; ⌚ Mon-Sat) A chicken restaurant translated as 'Chicken Thief.'

Los Alamos (Cuzco 215; mains US$3) This place offers a long menu, including a few vegetarian dishes.

Also recommended are **La Casona** (Bellido 463; mains US$2-6) for big portions and **Pizzería Italiana** (Bellido 490; pizzas US$4-8) for being cozy on cold nights.

Centro Turístico Cultural San Cristobal (28 de Julio 178) is a remodeled colonial building transformed into a hip little mall with bars and coffee shops.

Drinking

Los Balcones (Asamblea 187, 2nd fl) This popular student bar has occasional Andean bands and a variety of music.

La Nueva Ley (Cáceres 1147) does disco and salsa.

Shopping

Ayacucho is famous as a crafts center. The area around the Plazuela Santa Ana has various workshops, and there is also a **crafts market** (Independencia & Quinua).

Getting There & Away

AIR

The airport is 4km from the town center (taxis cost under US$2). **Aero Continente** (☎ 066-81-3177; 9 de Diciembre 160) and **AeroCóndor** (☎ 066-81-2418; 9 de Diciembre 123) have flights four times a week from Lima (US$59 to US$94), sometimes continuing to Andahuaylas. **LC Busre** (Lima 178) has daily flights to Lima.

BUS & TRUCK

A new Terminal Terrestre is planned to open in late 2004. For Lima (US$6 to US$18, nine hours), **Cruz del Sur** (☎ 066-81-2813; M Cáceres 1264) has the priciest buses. Cheaper services with **Ormeño** (☎ 066-81-2495; Libertad 257) leave at 7:30am and 9:30pm; Ormeño also goes to Ica at 9pm. **Empresa Molina** (☎ 066-81-2984; 9 de Diciembre 459) has five daily buses to Lima and two to Huancayo (US$7.25, 10 hours). **Expreso Wari** (☎ 066-89-1686; Pasaje Cáceres 171) also goes to Lima, as well as Cuzco (US$14, 24 hours) daily. Another company going to Cuzco is **Expreso Turismo Los Chancas** (☎ 066-81-2391; Pasaje Cáceres 150). It's a rough trip, and the journey can be broken at Andahuaylas (US$6, 10 hours).

For Huancavelica, try **Turismo Nacional** (☎ 066-81-5405; M Cáceres 884).

Pickup trucks and buses go to Quinua (US$0.75, one hour) and the Wari ruins, departing from the Paradero Magdalena at the traffic circle at the east end of M Cáceres.

HUANCAVELICA

The beautiful but forgotten Huancavelica is in a high area 147km south of Huancayo; so remote the listings for the entire department take up just over half a page in the telephone directory's yellow pages. It was once a strategic Inca center, a Spanish mercury and silver mining area, and still has seven 16th- and 17th-century churches with silver-plated altars.

Information

Dirección de Turismo (☎ 067-75-2938; V Garma 444, 2nd fl; ⌚ 8am-1pm & 2-5pm Mon-Fri) gives good orientation information. **BCP** (V Toledo 384) has a Visa ATM and changes money. Internet access is at **@Internet** (Segura 166) on the Plaza de Armas. The **INC** (☎ 067-75-2544; Raimondi 205; admission free; ⌚ 10am-1pm & 3-6pm Tue-Sun) has information about the area.

Sleeping & Eating

Most hotels have only cold water, but with the **San Cristóbal mineral springs** (pool US$0.30, shower US$0.45; ⏱ 5:30am-4pm Sat-Thu, 5:30am-noon Fri) in town, this is no great hardship.

Hostal Camacho (☎/fax 067-75-3298; Carabaya 481; s/d US$2.50/4, s/d with bath US$4/6.50) A well-run choice with small rooms, but piles of blankets. Hot water is available in the morning only.

Hotel Ascensión (☎ 067-75-3103; Manco Capac 481; s/d US$3/4.50; s/d with bath US$4.50/6.50) On the main plaza, with larger rooms and hot water.

Hotel Tahuantinsuyo (☎ 067-75-2968; Carabaya 399; s/d US$4/5.75) Offers basic rooms with private baths and hot water in the morning.

The best restaurant is **Restaurant Joy** (V Toledo 216; set menu US$2, mains US$2.50-6). **Mochica Sachun** (V Toledo 303) is another good choice.

Getting There & Away

BUS

Most buses depart from near Parque Santa Ana. Companies serving **Huancayo** (US$3, five hours, six buses daily) include **Transportes Ticlas** (☎ 067-75-1562; O'Donavan 505). *Colectivos* (US$6, four hours) leave when full from Plaza Santa Ana.

For Lima (US$10, 12 to 15 hours) companies go via Huancayo or Pisco. **Transportes Oropesa** (☎ 067-75-3181; O'Donovan 599) goes via Pisco at 6pm and also has an overnight bus to Ica. **Expreso Lobato** (☎ 067-75-2964; M Muñoz 489) has comfortable overnight buses that go via Huancayo. Also try **Expreso Huancavelica** (☎ 067-75-2964; M Muñoz 516).

For Ayacucho, Transportes Ticllas leaves at dawn, or take the local buses to Santa Inés, 78km south on the Pisco–Ayacucho Hwy and look for a Lima–Ayacucho bus (115 km).

TRAIN

The train from Huancayo is faster than buses, but the road goes higher and has better views. **Trains** (☎ 067-75-2898) leave Huancavelica for Huancayo at 6:30am daily and 12:30pm Monday to Saturday. A faster *autovagón* (electric train) leaves at 5:30pm Friday. See Huancayo for more information (p869).

HUANCAYO

This modern commercial hub, at 3260m, lies in the flat and fertile Río Mantaro valley, and is famous for its Sunday market.

The bus trip is spectacular as you rise from the coast to a *soroche*-inducing 4700m before dropping quickly into the Mantaro valley. Huancayo is a great base for extended forays into the Central Highlands, and has some excellent Spanish classes, crafts and fun nightlife.

Information

The **tourist office** (☎ 064-23-8480; Real 481; ⏱ 8am-1:30pm & 4-6pm Mon-Fri) is in the Casa del Artesano and has information on local sightseeing. There is a clutch of Internet stops along Giráldez, and **Lavandería Chic** (Breña 154; ⏱ 8am-10pm Mon-Sat, 10am-6pm Sun) has both self-service and a drop-off laundry service. For emergencies, there is **Clínica Ortega** (☎ 064-23-2921; Carrión 1124; ⏱ 24 hr) and the **Policía de Turismo** (☎ 064-23-4714; Ferrocarril 580), and for money, BCP, Interbanc and other banks are on Real.

Sights

The **Mercado Mayorista** (daily produce market) overflows onto the railway tracks from the covered market off Ica, east of the tracks. The meat section sells every imaginable Andean delicacy, from fresh and dried frogs to guinea pigs. But unless you fancy a crusty amphibian to remember Huancayo by, you might also want to check out the Sunday souvenirs **crafts market** along Calle Huancavelica, with weavings, sweaters, embroidered items, ceramics, woodcarvings and *mates burilados* (carved gourds) that are a local specialty. Watch your wallet.

The **Parque de la Identidad Huanka**, 2km northwest of the Plaza de la Constitución, is a fanciful park full of stone statues and miniature buildings representing the area's culture. There are colorful Indian food stalls and it's a great spot to soak up the atmosphere at night. Take a taxi to get here at night.

Walk (or take a taxi) 2km northeast on Giráldez to the **Cerro de la Libertad**, which has good city views and more nightly food stalls. Continue 2km to see the eroded **sandstone towers** at Torre Torre.

Courses

Incas del Peru (☎ 064-22-3303; www.incasdelperu.org; Giráldez 652) also arranges Spanish lessons, which include meals and accommodations with a local family (if you wish) for about

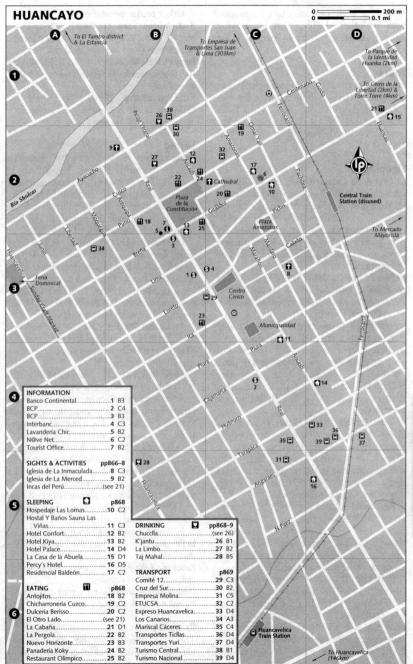

HUANCAYO

0 — 200 m
0 — 0.1 mi

To El Tambo district & La Estancia
To Empresa de Transportes San Juan & Lima (303km)
To Parque de la Identidad Huanka (2km)
To Cerro de la Libertad (2km) & Torre Torre (4km)
To Mercado Mayorista
To Huancavelica (146km)

Río Shulcas
Feria Dominical
Nunahy Craft Market
Plaza de la Constitución
Cathedral
Plaza Amazonas
Central Train Station (disused)
Centro Cívico
Municipalidad
Huancavelica Train Station

INFORMATION
Banco Continental................1 B3
BCP...2 C4
BCP...3 B3
Interbanc...............................4 C3
Lavandería Chic...................5 B2
N@ve Net.............................6 C2
Tourist Office.......................7 B2

SIGHTS & ACTIVITIES pp866–8
Iglesia de La Inmaculada.........8 C3
Iglesia de La Merced.............9 B2
Incas del Perú......................(see 21)

SLEEPING p868
Hospedaje Las Lomas...........10 C2
Hostal Y Baños Sauna Las Viñas................................11 C3
Hotel Confort.......................12 B2
Hotel Kiya............................13 B2
Hotel Palace.........................14 D4
La Casa de la Abuela............15 D1
Percy's Hotel........................16 D5
Residencial Baldeón.............17 C2

EATING p868
Antojitos...............................18 B2
Chicharronería Cuzco...........19 C2
Dulcería Berisso....................20 C2
El Otro Lado.........................(see 21)
La Cabaña............................21 D1
La Pergola............................22 B2
Nuevo Horizonte..................23 B3
Panadería Koky....................24 B2
Restaurant Olímpico............25 B2

DRINKING pp868–9
Chuccla................................(see 26)
K'jantu.................................26 B1
La Limbo..............................27 B2
Taj Mahal.............................28 B5

TRANSPORT p869
Comité 12............................29 C3
Cruz del Sur.........................30 B2
Empresa Molina....................31 C5
ETUCSA................................32 C2
Expreso Huancavelica...........33 A3
Los Canarios.........................34 A3
Mariscal Cáceres..................35 C4
Transportes Ticllas...............36 D4
Transportes Yuri...................37 D4
Turismo Central....................38 B1
Turismo Nacional.................39 D4

PERU

US$200 a week. Lessons can be combined with its other classes, such as weaving, dancing, cooking, *zampoña* (panpipes) and Quechua.

Tours

Incas del Peru (☎ 064-22-3303; www.incasdelperu.org; Giráldez 652) offers a whole range of services, including day hikes (US$25), local tours, mountain-bike rental (US$15 per day) and guided cycling/horse-riding tours (both US$35).

Sleeping

La Casa de la Abuela (Giráldez 691; dm US$5.50; d with/without bath US$14/17; ✗) Backpackers get mothered by *la Abuela* (the owner's mom) at this clean and friendly hostel in an older house, with a garden, hot water and laundry, games and cable TV. Rates include home-made bread and jam and killer coffee for breakfast.

Peru Andino (☎ 064-22-3956; www.geocities.com/peruandino_1; Pasaje San Antonio 113; dm US$3, s/d US$5/10; with bath US$6/12 incl breakfast) Another shoestringer favorite, a few blocks northwest of the town center, Andino offers hot showers, a kitchen and laundry, book exchange, bike rental, tour information and Spanish lessons. **Hospedaje Las Lomas** (☎ 064-23-7587; Giráldez 327; s/d US$7/10) Spotless private hot-water bathrooms and excellent mattresses make this a fine choice. Rooms vary in size.

Hotel Confort (☎ 064-23-3601; Ancash 237; s/d US$6/9; P) This huge barn of a hotel echoes with institutional corridors leading to scores of stark, faded rooms. But clean, large rooms with private hot showers, good mattresses, desks and cable TV (US$1.50) make up for any characterless convenience.

Residencial Baldeón (☎ 064-23-1634; Amazonas 543; s/d US$3/6) In a friendly family house, teeny rooms line a small courtyard. Shared hot showers (advance notice is needed to ensure hot water), a kitchen, laundry and a secure entrance make this basic place fair value.

Hotel Kiya (☎ 064-21-4955; hotelkiya@terra.com.pe; Giráldez 107; s/d US$17/20) Kiya is a six-story hotel with rooms painted in pink stencil to look like wallpaper. It has a restaurant, good beds and hot private showers (some with tubs), telephone and optional cable TV. Some rooms have plaza views (but also plaza noise).

Other recommendations:

Hostal y Baños Sauna Las Viñas (☎ 064-23-1294; Piura 415; s/d US$10/13) Small rooms squeeze in private hot bath, cable TV and telephone. Sauna costs US$2.

Percy's Hotel (☎ 064-21-2749; Real 1339; s/d US$4.50/7.25) Good-sized rooms with private showers (hot with 30 minutes' notice).

Hotel Palace (☎ 064-23-8501; Ancash 1127; s/d US$3/6, with bath US$6/9) Spacious rooms with decent mattresses. Hot water mornings only.

Eating

Antojitos (Puno 599; mains US$1.50-8; ☺ Mon-Sat) This restaurant-cum-bar, housed in an antique-filled, wood-beamed building with the obligatory Lennon and Santana posters, brings in friendly crowds of upscale locals to trade banter over the sounds of anything from cumbia to Pink Floyd.

La Cabaña (Giráldez 652; mains US$2-6) The house drink here is sangria, which fuels a party crowd of locals and travelers alike, along with pizza, hamburgers and pasta. *Folklórico* bands perform at 9pm Thursday to Saturday. It's connected to the café El Otro Lado, which does *cuy* and has an art gallery.

Restaurant Olímpico (Giráldez 199; set lunch US$2, mains US$4-8) Huancayo's oldest restaurant has a large open kitchen where you can see traditional dishes prepared.

Nuevo Horizonte (Ica 578; mains US$1-1.50; ☺ Sun-Fri) Inside an atmospheric older house with great ceilings, this place has an excellent vegetarian menu using soy and tofu to recreate Peruvian plates like *lomo saltado* (chopped steak, fried onions, potatoes and tomatoes).

La Estancia (☎ 064-22-3279; M Castilla 2815; mains US$7) Northwest of town, Real becomes Av Mariscal Castilla in the El Tambo district. La Estancia does a great lunchtime *pachamanca*, containing a meaty mix of *cuy*, pork and lamb, wrapped in leaves and cooked in an underground earth oven.

Following are more recommendations:

La Pergola (Puno 444; set lunch US$2) Upstairs with a plaza view.

Panadería Koky (Puno 298) Bakery/coffeeshop serving good empanadas and espressos.

Chicharronería Cuzco (Cusco 173; snacks US$2) Hole-in-the-wall with excellent *chicharrones*.

Drinking

The local *calientes* are hot, spicy toddies ideal to warm the cockles of your heart on cold Andean nights.

La Cabaña (Giráldez 652) Has the liveliest action at night and live *folklórico* and rock from Thursday to Saturday.

K'jantu (Ayacucho 308) A nightclub with live *folklórica* music and dancing; Chucclla and a couple of other places on the same block are worth checking out.

La Limbo (Cuzco 374) Offers live local rock bands.

Taj Mahal (Huancavelica 1052) A club with video karaoke and dancing.

Getting There & Away

BUS
Services change depending on season and demand. Lima (US$5 to US$10, six to seven hours) is served by **Mariscal Cáceres** (☎ 064-21-6633; Real 1241), **ETUCSA** (☎ 064-23-6524; Puno 220), which has the most departures, and **Cruz del Sur** (☎ 064-23-5650; Ayacucho 251), which has the most expensive and comfortable service.

For Ayacucho (US$7.25, 10 to 12 hours) the best service is **Empresa Molina** (☎ 064-22-4501; Angaraes 334), with morning and night departures on a rough road.

Huancavelica (US$3, five hours) is served most frequently by **Transportes Ticllas** (cnr Ancash & Angaraes) with 10 daily buses. Others include the nearby Turismo Nacional, Expreso Huancavelica and Transportes Yuri, with night buses only.

Empresa de Transportes San Juan (☎ 064-21-4558; Ferrocarril 131) has minibuses almost every hour to Tarma (US$2.50, 3½ hours), and can drop you off at Concepción or Jauja. **Los Canarios** (Puno 739) also serves Tarma.

Turismo Central (☎ 064-22-3128; Ayacucho 274) has buses north to Cerro de Pasco, Huánuco (US$5, eight hours), Tingo María and Pucallpa (US$11.50, 20 hours).

Local buses to most of the nearby villages leave from the street intersections indicated by arrows on the Huancayo map (p867).

CAR
Comité 12 (☎ 064-23-3281; Loreto 421) has *colectivos* to Lima (US$14, five hours).

TRAIN
Passenger trains run up from Lima a few times a year, usually on holiday weekends for US$30 round trip. They pass through La Galera (4781m), the world's highest station on a single-gauge track.

Huancayo has two unlinked train stations in different parts of town. The **Huancavelica station** (☎ 064-23-2581) is at the south end of town. The *Expreso* (five hours, 6:30am Monday to Sunday) and *Ordinario* (6¼ hours, 12:30pm Monday to Saturday) services cost US$2/3/4 in 2nd/1st/buffet class. On Sunday and Monday, there's a faster *autovagón* that leaves at 6pm (US$6, 4¾ hours).

Trains depart from Huancavelica at the same times as from Huancayo (see p866).

TARMA

This pleasant town (altitude 3050m) is nicknamed 'the pearl of the Andes.' There are many little-known and overgrown ruins to discover in the surrounding hills.

Information
The **tourist office** (☎ 064-32-1010 ext 20; turist arma@hotmail.com; 2 de Mayo 775; ☉ 8am-1pm & 3-6pm Mon-Fri), on Plaza de Armas, stocks brochures and information about local tours (in Spanish). The **BCP** (☎ 064-32-2149; cnr Lima & Paucartambo) will change money and has a Visa ATM. Internet access is at Paucartambo 567.

Sights & Activities
Trips are made to the village of Acobamba, 9km away, to see the famous religious sanctuary of **El Señor de Muruhuay**. From the village of Palcamayo, 28km northwest of Tarma, it's 4km to the **Gruta de Guagapo**, a huge limestone cave protected as a national speleological area. Expeditions have reached 2745m into the cave, but no one knows how much further its seemingly bottomless depths go. A guide lives opposite the entrance and can provide ropes and lanterns to enter the first sections; caving and scuba gear is required for a thorough exploration.

Festivals & Events
The Semana Santa processions, including several candlelit after dark, are the big attraction. The Easter Sunday procession to the cathedral follows a route carpeted with flower petals, as does the procession on the annual fiesta of El Señor de Los Milagros, in late October. Other fiestas include Semana de Tarma in late July and San Sebastián on January 20.

PERU

> **SPLURGE!**
>
> Hankering after the Hacienda life? Try the 18th-century **Hacienda La Florida** (☎ 064-34-1041; laflorida@terra.com.pe; s/d US$25/50; **P**), 6km from Tarma on the road to Acobamba. It's now a B&B owned by a Peruvian/German couple only too happy to let guests help out. Visitors can gather firewood, collect eggs, feed lambs, milk cattle and ride horses – but the hands-on approach doesn't sacrifice those all-important comforts like private hot showers. Camping is also possible for US$5 per person. From here, it's a one-hour hike to El Señor de Muruhuay sanctuary.

Sleeping

Hostal Vargas (☎ 064-32-1460; 2 de Mayo 627; s US$5.75, s/d with bath US$7.25/11.50) This clean hostel has spacious rooms and hard beds for those fed up with sagging mattresses. Note that hot water is available from 5am to 10am only.

Hostal Aruba (☎ 064-32-2057; Moquegua 452; s/d US$10/14.50) Very secure, with private hot showers and cable TV.

Hotel El Dorado (☎ 064-32-1598; Huánuco 488; s/d US$3/5.75, with bath US$5.75/8.75) Can be noisy, but is reasonably clean.

Hostal Central (☎ 064-32-3134; Huánuco 614; s/d US$4.50/5.75, with bath US$6.75/8.75) An old but adequate hotel, with an observatory open for stargazers on Friday night.

Eating & Drinking

Restaurant Señorial (Huánuco 138; mains US$1-5) and **El Braserito** (Huánuco 140; mains US$1-5) are the locals' favorites, judging by the non-stop crowds.

Restaurant Grima (Lima 270; set menu US$1-2) Good for breakfasts and set lunches.

Inti Killa (Huánuco 190; mains US$1-4) Boasts coastal, highland and jungle dishes.

Getting There & Away

Terminal Terrestre has frequent buses for Lima (US$3 to US$7, six hours), as does **Transportes Junín** (☎ 064-32-1234; Amazonas 667). **Los Canarios** (☎ 064-32-3357; Amazonas 694) and **Transportes San Juan** (☎ 064-32-3139) go regularly to Huancayo (US$2.50, three hours). *Colectivos* to Huancayo (US$5) also leave from Jauja at Amazonas. A bus stop next to

Transportes San Juan has minibuses going to Acobamba and Palcamayo.

TARMA TO PUCALLPA

The main road from Lima to Pucallpa (in the jungle) goes through the central Andes north of La Oroya, via Cerro de Pasco, Huánuco and Tingo María. This route is reasonably safe, but there are several police controls around Tingo María. This route is used by travelers heading for the first navigable Amazon Basin port, from where it is possible to head inland into the Amazon Basin and Iquitos along the Río Ucayali. It is a long, tiring route to Pucallpa from Lima and is probably best broken with an overnight stop in Tingo María (see p871).

Huánuco

This town (elevation 1894m) is another possible stopover between Lima and Pucallpa. It is also the site of one of Peru's oldest Andean archaeological sites: the **Temple of Kotosh** (adult/student US$0.90/0.45 includes guide; ☼ 9am-3pm), aka Temple of the Crossed Hands.

SLEEPING & EATING

Hostal Huánuco (☎ 062-51-2050; Huánuco 777; s US$5.75, s/d with bath US$7.25/8.75) A traditional mansion that exudes character with old-fashioned tiled floors, a lush garden, and walls covered with art and newspaper clippings. Ask for hot water in advance.

Gran Hotel Cuzco (☎ 062-51-3578; Huánuco 616; s/d US$5.75/11.50; **P**) An old hotel with clean, bare but good-sized rooms with private hot showers and cable TV on lower floors.

Hotel Caribe (☎ 062-51-3645; Huánuco 546; s/d US$2/3, with bath US$3/4.50) This hotel has cold showers and a karaoke café downstairs.

Hostal Las Vegas (☎ /fax 062-51-2315; 28 de Julio 934; s/d US$7.25/10.25) On the plaza; basic but popular. Hot water in private showers is available morning and evening.

Others include the bland, but spotless **Hotel Confort** (☎ 062-51-7880; Huánuco 736; s/d US$5.75/11.50) and **Hotel Continental** (☎ 062-51-9898; Huánuco 602; s/d US$7.25/11.50).

Hotel Real (2 de Mayo 1125; ☼ 24 hr) The 24-hour restaurant at the Hotel Real is the place for midnight munchies or pre-dawn breakfasts.

Cheers (2 de Mayo 1201; mains US$2-3) Also good, the neon-bright, cheaply chic Cheers is on the plaza.

Shorton Grill (D Beraún 685; mains US$2-3) Chicken, chips and beer is where this place is at.

There are also excellent vegetarian meals at **Govinda** (2 de Mayo 1044; mains US$1-2; ☺ lunch only Sun) and **Nature's Vida** (Abtao 951; mains US$1-2).

GETTING THERE & AWAY

The airport is 8km north of town. **LC Busre** flies from Lima on Tuesday, Thursday and Saturday mornings (US$94).

Buses go to Lima (US$6 to US$10, eight hours), Pucallpa (US$6, nine hours) and Huancayo (US$5, six hours), with companies all over town. Among the best are **León de Huánuco** (☎ 062-51-1489; Robles 821), with three daily buses to Lima and one to Pucallpa, **Bahía Continental** (☎ 062-51-9999; Valdizán 718), with luxury buses to Lima (US$10), **Transportes Rey** (☎ 062-51-3623; 28 de Julio 1215), with buses to Lima and Huancayo, and **Transmar** (28 de Julio 1067), with a bus to Pucallpa daily at 6am.

For Tingo María (US$2, 3½ hours), take a Pucallpa-bound bus or a *colectivo* (US$3.50) with **Comite 15** (☎ 062-51-8346) at General Prado near the river.

Tingo María

Tingo María, which lies in the *ceja de la selva* (eyebrow of the jungle), as the lush, tropical slopes of the eastern Andes are called, is surrounded by mountains, waterfalls and caves, and is hot most of the year. North is the dangerous drug-growing Río Huallaga valley. After the high and bleak hinterland of the Andes, Tingo María is a breath of fresh air. It is a good place to break your trip to Pucallpa.

The 18,000-hectare **Parque Nacional Tingo María** (admission US$1.50) lies on the south side of town.

SLEEPING & EATING

Showers are cold unless stated otherwise.

Hotel Royal (☎ 062-56-2166; Tito Jaime 214; s/d from US$4.50/7.25; P) Well kept; offers private showers, and US$3 more buys hot water and cable TV.

Hotel Palacio (☎ 062-56-2319; hospedajepalacio@ terra.com.pe; A Raimondi 158; s/d 4.50/7.25, with bath US$7.25/12) Also good, with rooms surrounding a plant- and parrot-filled courtyard.

Other possibilities are quiet **Hotel Nueva York** (☎/fax 062-56-2406; Alameda Peru 553; s/d from US$7/10), popular **Hostal Cuzco** (☎ 062-56-2095; A

Raimondi 671; s/d US$2/3.50) and family-run **Hospedaje La Cabaña** (☎ 062-56-2178; A Raimondi 634; s/d US$2/3.50). **Villa Jennifer** (☎ 062-969-5059; villajen nifer53@hotmail.com; km 3.4 Castillo Grande; s/d US$14/22; ♨ P), north of the airport, is a farm and lodge run by a Danish/Peruvian couple, with hammocks, a barbecue and games.

Hotel Nueva York has an OK restaurant.

GETTING THERE & AWAY

Star Up (☎ 062-56-2250; Raimondi 210) flies to Lima on Saturday. Schedules change frequently – ask around. As a general rule, avoid night travel and be careful in the Río Huallaga region north of Tingo María. **León de Huánuco** (☎ 062-56-2030), **Transmar** (☎ 062-56-3076), **Transportes Rey** (☎ 062-56-2565) and **TransInter** have buses to Lima (US$7 to US$12, 12 hours), mostly leaving at 7am or 7pm. Some of these go to Pucallpa (US$5, eight hours). Faster service to Pucallpa is with **Turismo Ucayali**, which has *colectivos* (US$12).

NORTH COAST

The coast road north of Lima passes huge, rolling sand dunes, dizzying cliffs, mind-boggling pre-Inca cities and temples, and beaches with some of the best surf in South America. If you're heading north to Ecuador, take your time to visit this laid-back part of Peru, which is largely ignored by the traveler hoards that follow the well-beaten path of the gringo trail in the south. And the further north you go, the better the weather gets – more sunshine, more beach time.

CASMA

The small town of Casma is 370km north of Lima, and the archaeological site of **Sechín** (admission US$1.50; ☺ 8am-5pm) is 5km away. This surprisingly well-preserved site dates from 1600 BC, and the outside walls of the main temple are covered with gruesomely realistic bas-relief carvings of warriors and captives being eviscerated. To get there, go 3km south of Casma on the Panamericana, then left on the paved road to Huaraz for 2km more.

Sleeping & Eating

Hostal Gregori (☎ 043-71-1073; L Ormeño 579; s/d US$4.50/5.75, d with bath US$7.25) This friendly place is a popular choice, with hot water and TV on request.

Hostal Selene (☎ 043-71-1065; L Ormeño 595; s/d US$4.50/8.50, s/d with bath US$5.75/10; P) Offers large rooms with hot water and cable TV.

Hostal Indoamericano (☎ 043-71-1395; Huarmey 132; s/d US$4.50/5.75, d with bath US$7.25) Clean, but the showers are tepid unless you request hot water.

Chifa Tío Sam (Huarmey 138; mains US$3.50) One of the better restaurants.

Getting There & Away

For Trujillo (US$2.50, three hours) or Lima (US$4.50, five hours), ask where you can flag down a passing bus, and hope for a seat. Buses often stop by the gas station on the Panamericana at the Lima end of town. Small offices along the Panamericana sell a few tickets.

Near the plaza are frequent *colectivos* north to Chimbote (US$1.10, one hour), where there are better connections.

TRUJILLO

Trujillo (population 620,000), 560km north of Lima, is northern Peru's main city. Founded in 1535 by Francisco Pizarro, it's an attractive town that retains much of its colonial flavor. Nearby are the 1500-year-old Las Huacas del Sol y de la Luna (Moche Pyramids of the Sun and Moon) and the ancient Chimú capital of Chan Chan, which preceded the Incas. And if so much ancient culture wears you out, relax at nearby beach village Huanchaco.

Information

The tourist office is **iPeru** (☎ 044-29-4561; Pizarro 412; ◷ 9am-1pm & 2-5pm Mon-Fri), and there is also a branch of the **Policía de Turismo** (☎ 044-29-1705; Independencia 630). For Internet access, try **DeltaNet** (Orbegoso 641), and for laundry, **Lavanderías Unidas** (Pizarro 683; US$1.75 per kg). The best clinic is **Clínica Americano-Peruano** (☎ 044-23-1261; Mansiche 702). Banks include **Banco Continental** (Pizarro 620) and **Interbanc** (Gamarra at Pizarro), which have good rates for travelers' checks and a Visa/MasterCard ATM. **Guía Tours** (☎ 044-24-5170; Independencia 580) has daily tours of local archaeological sites for US$13 to US$18.

Sights

The spacious and attractive **Plaza de Armas**, with its impressive statue representing work, the arts and liberty, is fronted by the **cathedral**, which was begun in 1647, destroyed in 1759 and rebuilt soon afterward. It has a famous basilica, and is often open in the evenings around 6pm.

There are several elegant **colonial mansions** in the city center. Their wrought-iron grillwork and pastel shades are typical of Trujillo. The recommended **Casa de la Emancipación** (Pizarro 610) was restored in 1970 by the Banco Continental. Don't miss the 16th-century fountain made of Carabamba marble in the last patio. The **colonial churches** are worth a look, though hours are erratic. La Merced, El Carmen and San Agustín are three of the best.

The **Museo Cassinelli** (N de Piérola 601; admission US$2; ◷ 9:30am-1pm & 3-6pm Mon-Sat, 9am-1pm Sun) has an excellent private archaeological collection – in the basement of a gas station! The university-run **Museo de Arqueología** (☎ 044-24-9322; Junín 682; adult/student US$1.50/0.30; ◷ 9:30am-2pm Mon, 9:15am-1pm & 3-7pm Tue-Fri, 9:30am-4pm Sat & Sun), in the restored Casa Risco, has an interesting collection of art and pottery, and a reproduction of the murals in the Huaca de la Luna.

The cathedral and **Iglesia El Carmen** (admission US$0.90; ◷ 9am-1pm Mon-Sat) have **art museums** featuring religious and colonial art. **Casona Orbegoso** (Orbegoso 553) is a beautiful 18th-century mansion with a period art exhibit. Several colonial buildings contain **art galleries** with changing shows. The **Casa Ganoza Chopitea** (Independencia 630), recognized by the two lions on the front, deserves a look. Opening hours vary.

Festivals & Events

The marinera dance is the highlight of many of Trujillo's festivals. Caballos de paso (dressage displays) are another highlight. The Fiesta de la Marinera, at the end of January, is the biggest in Peru. The Fiesta de la Primavera, held in late September, has Peru's most famous parade, and much dancing and entertainment. Hotels are often booked during festivals.

Sleeping

Consider staying in nearby beachside Huanchaco, as it's much more chilled than the city (p876).

Hostal Colonial (☎ 044-25-8261; hostcolonialtruji@ hotmail.com; Independencia 618; s/d US$11.50/17.25) A great location just a block from the Plaza

TRUJILLO

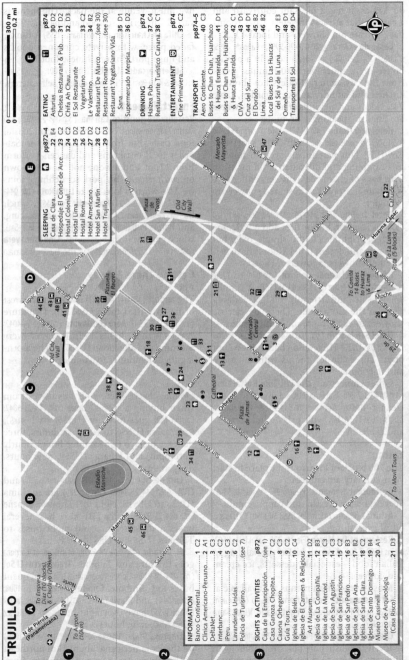

0   300 m
0   0.2 mi

INFORMATION
Banco Continental....................1 C2
Clinica Americano-Peruano..........2 A1
DeltaNet..................................3 C3
Interbanc................................4 C2
iPeru.....................................5 C3
Lavanderías Unidas....................6 C2
Policia de Turismo......................(see 7)

SIGHTS & ACTIVITIES   p872
Casa de la Emancipación............(see 1)
Casa Ganoza Choplea..................7 C2
Casona Orbegoso......................8 C3
Guía Tours..............................9 C4
Iglesia de Belén........................10 C4
Iglesia de El Carmen & Religious
    Art Museum.........................11 D2
Iglesia de La Compañía...............12 B3
Iglesia de La Merced..................13 C3
Iglesia de San Agustín................14 C3
Iglesia de San Francisco..............15 C3
Iglesia de San Pedro..................16 B3
Iglesia de Santa Ana..................17 B2
Iglesia de Santa Clara................18 C2
Iglesia de Santo Domingo...........19 B4
Museo Cassinelli.......................20 A1
Museo de Arqueología
    (Casa Risco).........................21 D3

SLEEPING   pp872-4
Casa de Clara............................22 E4
Hospedaje El Conde de Arce........23 C2
Hostal Colonial..........................24 C2
Hostal Lima..............................25 D4
Hostal Roma.............................26 D4
Hotel Americano........................27 D2
Hotel San Martín........................28 C2
Hotel Trujillo............................29 D3

EATING   p874
Asturias..................................30 D2
Chelsea Restaurant & Pub...........31 D2
Chifa Ah Chau..........................32 D3
El Sol Restaurante
    Vegetariano..........................33 C2
Le Valentino.............................34 B2
Restaurant De Marco..................(see 30)
Restaurant Romano...................(see 30)
Restaurant Vegetariano Vida
    Sana...................................35 D1
Supermercado Merpisa................36 D2

DRINKING   p874
Haizea Pub...............................37 C4
Restaurante Turístico Canana........38 C1

ENTERTAINMENT   p874
Cine Primavera..........................39 C2

TRANSPORT   pp874-5
Aero Continente........................40 C3
Buses to Chan Chan, Huanchaco
    & Huaca Esmeralda.................41 D1
Buses to Chan Chan, Huanchaco
    & Huaca Esmeralda.................42 C1
CIVA......................................43 D1
Cruz del Sur.............................44 D1
El Dorado................................45 B2
Linea.....................................46 B2
Local Buses to Las Huacas
    del Sol y de la Luna................47 E3
Ormeño..................................48 D1
Transportes El Sol.....................49 D4

PERU

de Armas, it has a pleasant courtyard and a garden that attracts travelers. Cozy rooms have private hot showers and local TV.

Casa de Clara (☎ 044-29-9997; Cahuide 495; s/d US$6/10; P 💻) A small hotel in a private house on a quiet park 10-minutes' walk from the city center, it offers hot showers, kitchen and laundry access, a garden, cable TV, videos and all kinds of help. The owners are English-speaking tour guides.

Hotel Americano (☎ 044-24-1361; Pizarro 792; s/d US$4.50/7.50, with cold shower US$6/9, with hot shower US$9/11.50) This perennially popular hotel is in a rambling and dilapidated old mansion with bags of character. Travelers either love it or hate it. Rooms with shared shower are grungier.

Hotel Trujillo (☎ 044-24-3921; Av Grau 581; s/d US$6/10) The floral floor tiles add a welcome touch of brightness to this simple, older but well-run and decent hotel. Rooms have private hot showers, a towel and soap.

Hospedaje El Conde de Arce (☎ 044-994-3236; Independencia 577; dm US$4.50, d US$11.50) A simple, small, safe and friendly budget lodging right in the city center. There are electric showers in each room and a quiet patio.

Hotel San Martín (☎ /fax 044-25-2311; San Martín 745; s/d US$12/20) Huge and characterless, but offers fair value for rooms with cable TV and telephone.

Other choices are the jail-like **Hostal Lima** (☎ 044-23-2499; Ayacucho 718; s/d US$3/4) and the cleaner **Hostal Roma** (☎ 044-25-9064; Nicaragua 238; s/d US$11.50/16), with private hot showers and cable TV.

Eating
The 700 block of Pizarro is the place to start your culinary adventures.

Restaurant Romano (Pizarro 747; mains US$3-6) Serves good espressos and cappuccinos.

Asturias (Pizarro 741; mains US$3.50-6.50) Offers a bit of everything.

Restaurant De Marco (Pizarro 725; breakfasts US$2, mains US$3-7.50) A small bistro specializing in Italian food – especially desserts, ice cream and coffees.

Mostly vegetarian menus are available at **El Sol Restaurante Vegetariano** (Pizarro 660; mains US$1-2) and **Restaurant Vegetariano Vida Sana** (Pizarro 917; mains US$1-2).

Chelsea Restaurant & Pub (Estete 675; mains US$5.50) A lovely English pub plus restaurant with different rooms to meet your tastes, plus a live music venue at the back. The menu is varied with grills, seafood and pasta.

Chifa Ah Chau (Gamarra 769; mains US$5) A funky, faded place, with private curtained booths and huge portions of Chinese food.

Supermercado Merpisa (Pizarro 700; ⏰ 9:15am-1:15pm & 4:30-9pm) Will take care of self-caterers.

Entertainment
Restaurante Turístico Canana (☎ 044-23-2503; San Martín 791; admission US$3) is open for good coastal food daily, but from late Thursday to Saturday local musicians and dancers perform from 11pm, and anyone not chowing down on *chicharrones* (big pork scratchings) joins in. Also worth a look are **La Luna Rota** (☎ 044-22-8877; América Sur 2119; admission free-US$3), which has a restaurant, live music and dancing, and **Haizea Pub** (Bolognesi 420; ⏰ 7pm-late Mon-Sat), which gets lively on weekends. **Cine Primavera** (☎ 044-24-1277; Orbegoso 239) is the best cinema.

Getting There & Away
AIR
The **airport** (☎ 044-46-4013) is 10km northwest of the city (taxi there US$3.50). Departure tax is US$3.50. **Aero Continente** (☎ 044-24-4042; Pizarro 470) has flights to/from Lima every morning and afternoon (US$71). The morning flight continues to Tumbes.

BUS
Double-check where your bus leaves from when buying a ticket. **Linea** (☎ 044-23-5847; Carrión 142) goes to Piura (US$6, six hours), Cajamarca (US$6 to US$9, six hours, three daily), Chiclayo (US$3, three hours, hourly until 6pm) and Huaraz (US$9, nine hours, daily at 9pm).

Cruz del Sur (☎ 044-26-1801; Amazonas 237) and **CIVA** (☎ 044-25-1402; Ejército 285) go to Lima (US$8 to US$18, eight to 10 hours). **Ormeño** (☎ 044-25-9782; Ejército 233) also has several buses a day to Lima and night buses to Tumbes (US$9 to US$14, 10 hours).

El Dorado (☎ 044-29-1778; Mansiche at Carrión) goes to Piura and Tumbes. **Transportes El Sol** (☎ 044-29-0328; Lloque Yupanqui 282) has frequent buses to Chimbote. **Comité 14** (☎ 044-26-1008; Moche 544) and **Movil Tours** (☎ 044-28-6538; América Sur 3955) have overnight buses to Huaraz (US$7.50, nine hours).

Empresa Díaz (☎ 044-20-1237; N de Piérola 1079) on the Panamericana, about 1km northeast of the city center, goes to Cajamarca. Connections from Chiclayo to Cajamarca are better than those from Trujillo.

For buses to Moyobamba, Tarapoto and Chachapoyas, go from Chiclayo.

Getting Around

White-yellow-and-orange B *colectivos* to La Huaca Esmeralda, Chan Chan and Huanchaco pass the corners of España and Ejército, España and Industrial every few minutes. Minibuses (red, blue and white) or buses (green and white) for Esperanza go northeast along Mansiche and can drop you off at La Huaca Arco Iris. Minibuses leave every half-hour from Suarez for the Huacas del Sol y de la Luna. Fares are US$0.25 on these routes.

AROUND TRUJILLO

The Moche and the Chimú are the two cultures that have left the greatest mark on the Trujillo area. The Moche (AD 0–700) were famous for their massive ceremonial pyramids, while the Chimú (AD 1000–1470) are remembered for their capital, Chan Chan, which is the largest pre-Columbian city in the Americas, covering 28 sq km and originally housing about 60,000 people.

Chan Chan museum and site, plus Huaca Esmeralda and Huaca Arco Iris are all entered with a **Chimu Combined Ticket** (adult/student US$2.75/1.40) that must be used within two days. All sites are open from 9am to 4:30pm daily. The ticket is sold at each site, except Huaca Esmeralda.

Chan Chan

The city of Chan Chan, 5km west of Trujillo, must once have been a dazzling site. As you approach along the Panamericana, it's still impossible not to be impressed by the vast area of crumbling mud walls stretching away into the distance. This site once formed the largest pre-Columbian city in the Americas and the largest mud-brick city in the world. It was built around AD 1300 and contained about 10,000 structures, from huge walk-in wells, canals and temple pyramids, to royal palaces lined with precious metals.

Although the Incas conquered the Chimú around 1460, the city was not looted – that is, not until the gold-hungry Spanish arrived, and the graverobbers finished their work.

The Chimú capital consisted of nine subcities, called the Royal Compounds. The **Tschudi compound**, which is restored and open to visitors, is to the left of the main road about 1km beyond the site museum and to the left.

The highest of Tschudi's walls once stood over 10m high, and impressive friezes of

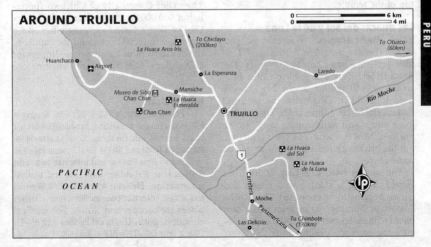

fish, waves and sea life can be seen interspersed with square- and diamond-shaped fishing-net designs. Also look for the mausoleum, where a king was once buried, along with plenty of (specially sacrificed) people and a treasure trove of grave goods to keep him company.

La Huaca Esmeralda

This temple was built by the Chimú at about the time of Chan Chan. Huaca Esmeralda is at Mansiche, halfway between Trujillo and Chan Chan, and it is possible to walk there (but don't go alone). Returning from Chan Chan to Trujillo, the *huaca* (temple) is to the right of the main road, about four blocks behind the Mansiche church. The temple consists of two stepped platforms, and an onsite guard will take you around (for a tip) to see the characteristic designs of fish, seabirds, waves and fishing nets.

La Huaca Arco Iris

This Chimú site meaning Rainbow Temple (also called La Huaca del Dragón) is left of the Panamericana, in La Esperanza, 4km northwest of Trujillo.

It's one of the best-preserved Chimú temples, because it was covered by sand until 1963. The site has a defensive wall enclosing 3000 sq km. Inside is the temple itself, which is about 800 sq meters and has two levels with a combined height of about 7.5m. The walls are covered with repeated rainbow designs and ramps lead to the very top of the temple.

Las Huacas del Sol y de la Luna

These **Moche temples** (admission incl guide US$2.75; 9am-4pm), 10km southeast of Trujillo, predate Chan Chan by 700 years. The **Huaca del Sol** is Peru's largest pre-Columbian structure; 140 million adobe bricks were used to build it. Originally, the pyramid had several levels, connected by steep stairs, huge ramps and walls sloping at 77° to the horizon. Now it resembles a giant sand pile, but the brickwork remains impressive from some angles.

The smaller **Huaca de la Luna**, 500m from Huaca del Sol, is riddled with rooms and friezes begging to be excavated. The Moche custom of 'burying' old temples under new ones facilitated preservation, and archaeologists are currently peeling away the layers

and uncovering more and more intriguingly stylized friezes. Also look for the Peruvian hairless dog that hangs out here. The body temperature of these dogs is higher than that of normal dogs, and they've traditionally been used as body-warmers for people with arthritis!

HUANCHACO

The fishing village of Huanchaco, 12km northwest of Trujillo, is famous for the high-ended, cigar-shaped, totora (reed) boats called *caballitos* on which fishermen paddle beyond the breakers then surf back to the beach with their catch. Totora-like boats were even depicted on 2500-year-old ceramics from this area – the world's first surfer dudes? Paying fishermen about US$1.50 will get you paddled out and surfed back in a wet rush.

La Casa Suiza (044-46-1825; www.casasuiza.com; Los Pinos 451/310; per person US$4, d with bath US$9.25; P) Friendly German- and English-speaking owners, this place has a rooftop barbecue area, hot showers, free boogie-board use, and surfboard and wet suits for rent.

Naylamp (044-46-1022; naylamp@terra.com.pe; Victor Larco 3; camping US$2, dm US$3, d with bath US$9) The beachside Naylamp is also recommended.

Combis will take you from Industrial at España in Trujillo to Huanchaco's beachfront for US$0.30.

CHICLAYO

The major coastal city of Chiclayo (population 400,000) is 200km north of Trujillo. One of Peru's fastest growing cities, it's a major commercial center and the capital of the department of Lambayeque. Important archaeology sites Sipán and Túcume are nearby.

Information

The **Policía de Turismo** (074-23-6700; Saenz Peña 830) is useful for reporting problems and for basic tourist information. Both **Centro de Informacion Turístico** (074-23-3132; Saenz Peña 838; 7:30am-4:30pm Mon-Fri) and **information booths** (Plaza de Armas & elsewhere) have limited tourist information. **EfeNet** (E Aguirre 181; US$0.90 per hr) has a fast Internet connection; many other places are cheaper and slower. For medical attention, go to **Clínica del Pacífico** (074-23-6378; JL Ortiz 420). The **BCP** (J Balta 630) has a 24-

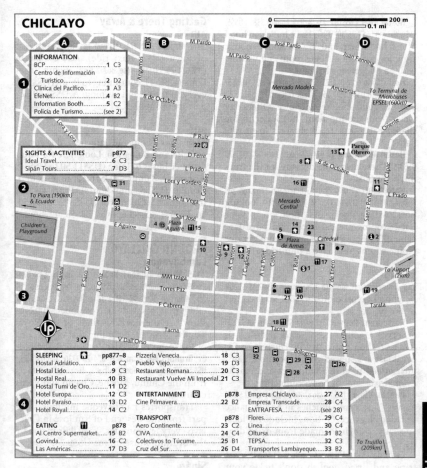

CHICLAYO

INFORMATION	
BCP	1 C3
Centro de Información Turístico	2 D2
Clínica del Pacífico	3 A3
EfeNet	4 B2
Information Booth	5 C2
Policia de Turismo	(see 2)

SIGHTS & ACTIVITIES	p877
Ideal Travel	6 C3
Sipán Tours	7 D3

SLEEPING	pp877–8
Hostal Adriático	8 C2
Hostal Lido	9 C3
Hostal Real	10 B3
Hostal Tumi de Oro	11 D2
Hotel Europa	12 C3
Hotel Paraíso	13 C2
Hotel Royal	14 C2

EATING	p878
Al Centro Supermarket	15 B2
Govinda	16 C2
Las Américas	17 D3
Pizzería Venecia	18 C3
Pueblo Viejo	19 D3
Restaurant Romana	20 C3
Restaurant Vuelve Mi Imperial	21 C3

ENTERTAINMENT	p878
Cine Primavera	22 B2

TRANSPORT	p878
Aero Continente	23 C2
CIVA	24 C4
Colectivos to Túcume	25 B1
Cruz del Sur	26 D4
Empresa Chiclayo	27 A2
Empresa Transcade	28 C4
EMTRAFESA	(see 28)
Flores	29 C4
Linea	30 C4
Oltursa	31 B2
TEPSA	32 C3
Transportes Lambayeque	33 B2

hour Visa ATM and is one of several banks on the 600 block of J Balta.

Sights

Need a love potion or a cure for warts? Don't miss the southwest corner of the enormous, sprawling **Mercado Modelo**, where the herbalist and *brujo* (witchdoctor) stalls sit side by side with their dried herbs, bones, claws, hooves, and other weird and wonderful healing charms. Also look for *alforjas*, heavy woven saddlebags typical of the area.

Sipán Tours (☎ 074-22-9053; sipantours@terra.com .pe; 7 de Enero 772) and **Ideal Travel** (☎ 074-22-2991; indianatours@terra.com.pe; Colón 556) have tours in English or Spanish.

Sleeping

Hotel Paraíso (☎ 074-22-8161; hotelparaiso@terra.com .pe; P Ruiz 1064; s/d US$10/13) Good value at this price, with modern rooms boasting decent furniture, hot shower and cable TV.

Hotel Royal (☎ 074-23-3421; San José 787; s/d US$6.50/9.25) For aficionados of older, run-down characterful hotels, Hotel Royal is right on the Plaza de Armas. Large rooms have private baths with hot water.

Hotel Europa (☎ 074-23-7919; hoteleuropachiclayo@ terra.com.pe; E Aguirre 466; s US$4.50, s/d with bath US$10/13) Clean but aging; has a spacious feel to it and rooms with electric showers have cable TV.

Hostal Tumi de Oro (☎ 074-22-7108; L Prado 1145; s/d US$6/9.50) Simple but decent; has private hot showers.

PERU

Hostal Real (☎ 074-23-7829; E Aguirre 338; s US$5, s/d with bath US$7.25/10) This basic but clean hotel offers hot water and TV in some rooms. Couples can rent a single room and use one bed – a budgeteer's bargain.

Hostal Lido (☎ 074-23-6752; E Aguirre 412; s/d US$3/4.50, with bath US$4.50/7.25) This friendly place is another good shoestring choice. Offers city views from the top floor, hot water in the shared baths, but tepid showers in private baths.

Hostal Adriático (☎ 074-24-0065; J Balta 1009; s/d US$3/5) These desperate digs are for the truly impecunious.

Hotel Kalu (☎ 074-23-9195; hotelkalu@terra.com.pe; P Ruiz 1038; s/d US$14/17; **P**) A spiffy-looking hotel with a doorman – hold on to your hats! Rooms are carpeted, and have fan, cable TV, hot showers and room service (some rooms also have a minifridge).

Eating

Las Américas (E Aguirre 824; mains US$2.25-5) A perennial favorite off the southeast corner of the plaza.

Restaurant Romana (J Balta 512; mains US$2.50-6) Serves a wide variety of local dishes. If you're feeling brave, try its *chirimpico* for breakfast; it's stewed goat tripe and organs, guaranteed to cure a hangover and maybe even swear you off booze altogether.

Pueblo Viejo (MM Izaga 900; mains US$2.50-5) Serves Chiclayano lunches in an ambiance of faded elegance. Options include the local specialty, *chingirito*, made from dried dogfish (chewy!).

Govinda (Balta 1029; set lunch US$1.50) If goat tripe and dried dogfish don't tickle your tastebuds, the lovingly prepared vegetarian fare at Govinda will.

Pizzería Venecia (J Balta 413; large pizzas US$8) A rip-roaring pizzeria that attracts young locals listening to Latin favorites while chugging beer with their pie.

Restaurant Vuelve Mi Imperial (J Balta 535; mains US$1.50-6.60) A cheap but unlovely hole-in-the-wall that specializes in grills.

Al Centro Supermarket (cnr E Aguirre & L Gonzalez) Stock up on do-it-yourself meal supplies at this modern supermarket.

Entertainment

Cine Primavera (☎ 074-20-7471; L Gonzales 1235) has five screens, often with some Hollywood flicks.

Getting There & Away
AIR

The **airport** (☎ 074-23-3192) is 2km southeast of town (US$1 taxi ride). **Aero Continente** (☎ 074-20-9916; S José 867) has flights from Lima (US$71), continuing to Piura (US$39), every morning and evening. A US$3.50 departure tax applies.

BUS

Many bus companies are near the corner of Balta and Bolognesi. Look here for long-distance buses to Lima (US$11.50 to US$30, 12 hours), Tumbes (US$6.50, nine hours), Trujillo (US$6, four hours), Piura (US$3, three hours), Cajamarca (US$6 to US$7.50, six hours), Chachapoyas (US$8, 12 hours) and elsewhere.

AROUND CHICLAYO
Lambayeque

The **Museo Tumbas Reales De Sipán** (☎ 074-28-3977/8; adult/student US$2/0.75; 🕒 9am-noon & 2:30-4pm Tue-Sun; 🕱 **P**) is a world-class facility that opened in November 2002 to showcase the dazzling finds of the Royal Tombs of Sipán, including that of the Lord of Sipán himself. Also in town is the older **Bruning Museum** (☎ 074-28-2110; adult/student US$2/0.75; 🕒 9am-5pm), which houses artifacts from the Chimu, Moche, Chavín and Vicus cultures.

Transportes Lambayeque minibuses depart from the west end of San José in Chiclayo every few minutes. They'll drop you by the Bruning Museum for US$0.25.

Sipán

The story of this **site** (☎ 074-80-0048; adult/student US$2/0.75; 🕒 8am-5pm) is an exciting one of buried treasure, *huaqueros* (grave robbers), the black market, police, archaeologists and at least one killing. Hundreds of exquisite and priceless artifacts have now been recovered, and a gold-smothered royal Moche burial site – the Lord of Sipán – was discovered in 1987. One tomb has a replica of this burial, but the most spectacular finds are in Lambayeque's museums.

Sipán is 30km southeast of Chiclayo. Buses leave from Chiclayo's Terminal de Microbuses, on Nicolás de Pierola at Oriente, northeast of downtown; departures are frequent in the morning, less so in the afternoon.

Túcume

This vast and little-known **site** (☎ 074-80-0052; adult/student US$2/0.75; ☺ 8am-4:30pm) can be seen from a spectacular cliff-top viewpoint about 30km north of Lambayeque on the Panamericana. It's worth the climb to see over 200 hectares of crumbling walls, plazas and no less than 28 pyramids. **Guides** (US$3) are available, or you can hire one in Chiclayo or Lambayeque's museums. Buses go from Chiclayo (Angamos near M Pardo) or from the Bruning museum; the site is about a 1km walk from the bus stop.

PIURA

Founded by Pizarro in 1532, Piura is Peru's oldest colonial city. The cathedral dates from 1588. The city center has some colonial buildings, though many were destroyed in a 1912 earthquake. The city's focal point is the large, shady and pleasant Plaza de Armas.

Information

The Consejo Provincial on the Plaza de Armas has **tourist information** (☎ 073-30-3208; ☺ 8am-1pm Mon-Sat & 4-8pm Mon-Fri). BCP (Visa ATM), Banco Wiese (MasterCard ATM) and Banco Continental are all on the main plaza. *Casas de cambio* are at the intersection of Ica and Arequioa.

Internet access is available at **Piura@online** (Arequipa 728), **KFE Net** (S Cerro 273) and others on Sanchez Cerro.

The best medical attention is at **Clínica San Miguel** (☎ 073-30-9300; Los Cocos 111; ☺ 24 hr). **Piura Tours** (☎ 073-32-8873; piuratours@mail.udep.edu .pe; Ayacucho 585) is recommended for tours.

Sights

Museo de Oro Vicus (☎ 073-30-9267; Huánuco 893; admission US$0.90; ☺ 9am-5pm Tue-Sun) has an underground gold museum, which features a belt with a life-sized gold cat's head for a buckle. **Casa Grau** (☎ 073-32-6541; Tacna 662; admission by donation; ☺ 8am-noon & 3-6pm Mon-Fri), where Almirante Miguel Grau was born, on July 27, 1834, is now a naval museum, strong on the War of the Pacific (1879-80).

Sleeping

Hostal California (☎ 073-32-8789; Junín 835; s/d US$4/7.25) Friendly, clean and popular with

PIURA

0 — 500 m
0 — 0.3 mi

INFORMATION	
Banco Continental	1 C2
Banco Wiese	2 D2
BCP	3 C2
Clínica San Miguel	4 B2
Consejo Provincial Tourist Office	5 D2
KFE Net	6 D1
Piura@online	7 C1

SIGHTS & ACTIVITIES	p879
Bolognesi Monument	8 C2
Casa Grau	9 C2
Grau Monument	10 B2
Iglesia de San Francisco	11 D1
Iglesia de San Sebastián	12 D2
Iglesia del Carmen	13 D1
Museo de Oro Vicus	14 B1

SLEEPING	pp879-80
Hostal California	15 C2
Hostal Continental	16 C2
Hostal El Almirante	17 B1
Hostal El Sol	18 C1

Hostal Moon Night	19 C2
Hostal Oriental	20 C1
Hostal San Jorge	21 B2
Hotel Peru	22 C1

EATING 🍴	p880
Capuccino	23 D2
Carburmer	(see 23)
Ganimedes	24 D1
Heladería El Chalan	25 C2
Heladería El Chalan	26 C1
Heladería El Chalan	27 C2
Picantería Los Santitos	(see 23)

TRANSPORT	p880
Aero Continente	28 D2
Chinchaysuyo	29 B1
Cruz del Sur	30 D2
EPPO	31 B1
ITTSA	(see 29)
Linea	32 A1
TANS	33 D1
TEPSA	34 C2
Transportes El Dorado	(see 31)

PERU

shoestring travelers. Has small bright rooms with fans, shared cold showers and enough security to bring to mind its namesake song.

Hostal Oriental (☎ 073-30-4011; Callao 446; s/d US$3.50/7, with bath US$5/8.75) Helpful and with an English-speaking owner; offers basic but clean rooms with fans and cold showers.

Hostal San Jorge (☎ 073-32-7514; Loreto 960; s/d US$7.25/10) Small and homey, offers rooms with table fans and reliable hot showers, so it's often full.

Hostal El Almirante (☎ 073-32-9137; Ica 860; s/d US$10/13) Offers rooms with table fans, reliable hot showers and cable TV, and is clean but otherwise spartan.

Hotel Peru (☎ 073-33-3421; Arequipa 476; s/d US$11.25/17, with air-conditioning US$23; ✕) An elegant lobby and restaurant make a welcome first impression. The rooms are good, and have hot showers, cable TV and fans.

Other recommendations:

Hostal Continental (☎ 073-33-4531; Junín 924; s/d US$4/5.75, with bath US$5.75/7.25)

Hostal Moon Night (☎ 073-33-6174; Junín 899; s/d US$4/5.75, with bath US$7/10) Modern, with hot water and cable TV.

Hostal El Sol (☎ 073-32-4461; elsol@mail.udep.edu.pe; S Cerro 455; s/d 14/20; 🖭 🅿) Good value, with private hot showers, fan and cable TV.

Eating

Picantería Los Santitos (Libertad 1014; mains US$2.50-6; 🕑 lunch only; ✕) Inside a small mall is this old-fashioned restaurant with mud-plastered walls, cane ceilings and coastal music.

Carburmer (Libertad 1014; mains US$5-8; ✕) A cozy, romantic place, the best Italian joint in town.

Capuccino (Libertad 1048) An excellent spot for coffees and desserts.

Heladería El Chalan (Tacna 520; Grau 173 & 453; US$1.50-3) Popular; has several outlets of freshly prepared fast-food. It does a good ice-cream trade too.

Ganimedes (Jirón Lima 440; mains US$1.50-3) The purest vegetarian restaurant in Piura. No goat-head soups here.

Getting There & Away
PERU
Air
The **airport** (☎ 073-34-4505) is 2km southeast of the city center (departure tax costs US$3.50). **Aero Continente** (☎ 073-32-5635; Libertad 951) has

daily morning and evening flights to Lima via Chiclayo (US$69).

Bus & Truck
Services to Lima (US$11 to US$30, 12 to 16 hours) include **Cruz del Sur** (☎ 073-33-7094; cnr Bolognesi & Lima) and **TEPSA** (☎ 073-32-3721; Loreto 1198).

EPPO (☎ 073-30-4543; S Cerro 1141) has slow buses to Máncora (US$3.20, 3½ hours) six times a day. **Transportes El Dorado** (☎ 073-32-5875; S Cerro 1119) has buses for Tumbes (US$4.50, five hours). **ITTSA** (☎ 073-33-3982; S Cerro 1142) has buses to Trujillo (US$4.50 to US$7.50), Chimbote, and bus-camas (bed buses) to Lima. **Linea** (☎ 073-32-7821; S Cerro 1215) has 17 buses daily to Chiclayo and a 6pm bus to Cajamarca (10 hours). For Cajamarca and the northern Andes, it's best to connect in Chiclayo. **Chinchaysuyo** (S Cerro 1156) has overnight buses to Huaraz via Trujillo.

The standard route to Ecuador is via Tumbes to Machala, Ecuador. The route via La Tina/Macará to Loja, Ecuador, is more scenic but less used because it goes to minor towns. **Transportes Loja** (☎ 073-30-9407; S Cerro 228) has direct buses to Machala (US$7.50, seven hours) at 10:30pm, and to Macará (US$3.50, four hours) and Loja (US$7.25, eight hours) at 9:30am and 9pm. These buses stop for border formalities, then continue.

ECUADORIAN BORDER CROSSING
Formalities are fairly relaxed at the **border** (🕑 24 hr), which is the international bridge over the Río Calvas. There are no banks, but moneychangers in Macará, Ecuador, will change cash. Taxis will take travelers entering Ecuador to Macará (3km), where the Ecuadorian Immigration building is found on the 2nd floor of the Municipalidad, on the plaza (stop here for entry stamps).

After crossing the international bridge, travelers entering Peru will find immigration on the right and the police on the left.

MÁNCORA
For sun-worshippers of the non-Inca variety, Máncora is the most-visited coastal resort on the north coast. It's sunny year-round and becomes a real scene during the surfing months of November to February. Several budget hotels rent surfboards (US$4 per day). From January to mid-March rates jump 50% higher.

PERU

Cheap sleeps are found in the center of town, all close to the beach. **HI La Posada** (☎ 073-85-8328; Panamericana km 1164; camping per person US$1.50, dm US$4.50-6; **P**) has a garden, hammocks and kitchen, while **Hostal Sol y Mar** (☎ 073-85-8106; Piura 220; per person from US$4.50, d with bath US$13; **P** **R**) is a sprawling place close to good waves that has pumping music and dancing till late, plus games and a bar/restaurant. As for food – if you love seafood, you'll be happy. If not, there ain't much else.

Most southbound bus trips to Lima and intermediates originate in Tumbes. Combis leave for Tumbes (US$1.50, two hours) every hour along the main drag.

TUMBES

Tumbes is a languid town half an hour from the Ecuadorian border, and is where transportation and accommodations for border-crossers are found. It's hot, dusty or mosquito-bugged, and most travelers pass through quickly, though it's not a bad spot to catch your breath and plan onward travels.

Information

There's an Ecuadorian consul on the Plaza de Armas. For Internet access, there's **Micro Tecni** (Bolognesi 116), **EFE Net** (Bolívar 227) and many others. **BCP** (Bolívar 261) changes traveler's checks and has an ATM. The only currencies you will be dealing with are US dollars for Ecuador and Peruvian soles. Avoid the dollar doldrums: change nuevos soles to dollars while still in Peru for the best rates. Beware of 'fixed' calculators, short-changing and other rip-offs at the border. The **Ministerio de Turismo** (☎ 072-52-3699; Bolognesi 194, 2nd fl; ⏲ 7:30am-1pm & 2-4:30pm Mon-Fri) has patchy information.

Sleeping

Many hotels have only cold water, but most have fans, handy for repelling mozzies during the twice-yearly harvests of local rice paddies. During holidays, hotels are often full by noon and single rooms difficult to find.

Hospedaje Chicho (☎ 072-52-2282; Tumbes 327; s/d US$8.50/13.50) Small but neat rooms with private hot shower, cable TV, fan, minifridge, telephone and helpful staff. Mosquito nets are provided on request.

TUMBES

| 0 | 200 m |
| 0 | 0.1 mi |

To Flores, CIVA, Cial; CIFA (1 block); Hotel Chilimasa & Airport (8km)

Abad Puell

Paell

Plaza Bolognesi

Hilscol

Tiapaca

Arica

Navarrete

6

19

20

Piura

8 17

Bolívar

San-Martin

Market

Tacna

16

1 3

A Ugarte

Tumbes Teniente Vásquez

9

Mayor Bocero

11

Catedral

Bolognesi

Los Andes

7

Ramon Castilla

21

15 12

Grau

13 14

2

Plaza de Armas

5

10

18

José Gálvez

Malecon Lizner

Río Tumbes

7 de Enero

Filipuidi

To Lima (1264km)

Panamericana

4

Gral Vidal

PERU

Hostal Roma (☎ 072-52-4137; hotelromatumbes@ hotmail.com; Bolognesi 425; s/d US$11.50/17.25) A more modern hotel with a great Plaza de Armas location. Offering clean, comfortable rooms with private hot shower, fans, telephone and cable TV.

Hostal Lourdes (☎ 072-52-2126; Mayor Bodero 118; s/d US$11.50/17.25) Clean, safe and friendly, and has a top floor restaurant. The simple rooms have fans, telephones, TV and hot showers.

No-frills, cold-shower options include **Hospedaje Amazonas** (☎ 072-52-5266; Tumbes 317; s/d US$6/9), the especially spartan **Hospedaje Sudamericano** (San Martín 130; s/d US$3/4, with bath US$4/5), which has no telephone, and the more spacious **Hospedaje Tumbes** (☎ 072-52-2203; Grau 614; s/d US$4.50/7.50).

Also worthy of a peek are **Hospedaje El Estoril** (☎ 072-52-4906; Huáscar 361; s/d US$5/7.50) and **Hospedaje Florian** (☎ 072-52-2464; Piura 414; s/d US$6/9).

Eating

The Plaza de Armas sports many bars and restaurants with shaded tables outside that are ideal for watching the world go by.

Classic Restaurant (Tumbes 185; set lunch US$1.75, mains US$3-5; 🕖 7:30am-5pm; ✿ ✗) This small, dignified restaurant is a great escape from torrid Tumbes to relax with a long lunch amid the town's better-connected locals. Food is mainly coastal.

Studio 307 (Grau 307; mains US$2.50-5; 🕗 8am-midnight) On the north side of the plaza, this is a hip place attracting a younger crowd who enjoy burgers, pizza and beers late into the night. It does decent breakfasts as well.

Restaurant Latino (Bolívar 165; mains US$3-6) Lots of choices (especially seafood) and you can eat outside on the shaded pavement.

Getting There & Away
PERU
Air

Aero Continente (☎ 072-52-2350; Tumbes 217) has daily flights to/from Lima (US$69) stopping in Trujillo (US$39). Flights are often full, so reconfirm; schedules, carriers and routes change frequently. Departure tax is US$3.50. The **airport** (☎ 072-52-5102) is 8km north of town. A taxi there costs US$2 to US$4.

Bus

Most bus companies are on Av Tumbes, near the intersection with Av Piura. Fares to Lima are US$12 to US$39 (18 to 20 hours). The **Cruz del Sur** (☎ 072-52-4001; Tumbes 319) Cruzero service to Lima costs US$39, but takes less time than less-luxurious services and has air-con, toilets and video. There are several buses a day; most stop at Piura (US$4.50, five hours), Chiclayo (US$7, eight hours), Trujillo (US$10, 12 hours) and other intermediates. For Máncora, see the map (p881) for combi stops.

If going to Ecuador, the best service is with **CIFA** (☎ 072-52-7120; Tumbes 572), an Ecuadorian company that stops at the border for passport formalities. Alternatively, *colectivos* leave from the 300 block of Tumbes (US$1). A taxi charges US$5 to US$7.

ECUADORIAN BORDER CROSSING

The Peruvian border town of Aguas Verdes is linked by an international bridge across the Río Zarumilla with the Ecuadorian border town of Huaquillas. For more border crossing information, see p696).

Exit formalities as you cross from Peru to Ecuador are fairly quick. Immigration is open 24 hours. The Peruvian border post is 2km from the border; mototaxis take you to the border for US$0.50. In Aguas Verdes, there are a few simple restaurants and a bank, but no hotels. The bridge between Aguas Verdes and Huaquillas marks the actual border. The Ecuadorian immigration office is 5km outside Huaquillas (taxi US$2).

There are no entry fees into either country, so be polite but insistent with any border guards trying their luck. Change your Peruvian soles into dollars before you enter Ecuador, as you will get better exchange rates in Peru than Ecuador.

Getting Around

A taxi to the airport is around US$4, to the border about US$7. *Colectivos* for Aguas Verdes leave from the corner of Bolívar and Piura (US$1, 26km).

HUARAZ & THE CORDILLERA BLANCA

The Cordillera Blanca is Peru's climbing, trekking and mountain-biking heartland. Though only 20km wide and 180km long, it packs in more than 50 peaks of 5700m or higher (North America has only three such mountains, and Europe has none!). Huascarán, at 6768m, is Peru's highest mountain and the highest peak in the tropics anywhere in the world. But once you're here, forget the figures: it's the shining glaciers, sparkling streams, awesome vertical walls, impressive pre-Inca sites and glistening lakes that will stay in your memory.

And if the Cordillera Blanca isn't enough to wear a hole in your hiking boots, just look south to the majestic Cordillera Huayhuash, a tightly bound mountain range looking up to Yerupajá (6634m), Peru's second highest mountain.

HUARAZ

Huaraz (elevation 3091m), capital of its department, has a population of 80,000 and lies in the valley called El Callejón de Huaylas. Although now rebuilt, most of the town was destroyed by the 1970 earthquake, which killed 70,000 people in central Peru.

All the equipment and help you need can be rented, hired or bought here, including trail maps, guidebooks, muleteers and guides. The best time for hiking is the dry season, from late May to September.

Information
EMERGENCY
Casa de Guías (☎ 043-72-1811; Plaza Ginebra 28-G) Can arrange mountain rescue. All trekkers and climbers should carry rescue insurance, best purchased before leaving home. Register before heading out on a climb.
Local Police (☎ 043-72-1221) On Sucre at San Martín.
Policía de Turismo (☎ 043-72-1341; ☺ 9am-1pm Mon-Sat & 4-6pm Mon-Fri) Located on an alley on west side of Plaza de Armas. Staff speak limited English.

INTERNET ACCESS
There are about 10 places clustered on Plaza Ginebra and the corresponding block of Luzuriaga.

LAUNDRY
B&B/Pressmatic (José de la Mar 674; US$1.25 per kg)

MEDICAL SERVICES
Clínica San Pablo (☎ 043-72-8811; Huaylas 172; ☺ 24 hr) A few blocks north of the map (see p884); some doctors speak English.
Farmacia Recuay (☎ 043-72-1391; Luzuriaga 497) Will restock expedition medical kits.

MONEY
BCP (Luzuriaga 691) Visa ATM
Banco Wiese (José Sucre 760) MasterCard ATM
Interbanc (José Sucre 687) Visa ATM

POST
Serpost (Luzuriaga 702; ☺ 8am-8pm Mon-Sat)

TOURIST OFFICES
Café Andino (Lucar y Torre 530, 3rd fl) Owner specializes in Cordillera Huayhuash travel information, maps etc.
Parque Nacional Huascarán (☎ 043-72-2086; Sal y Rosas 555; ☺ 8:30am-1pm & 2:30-6pm Mon-Fri) Staff have limited information on the park.

Sights & Activities
PARQUE NACIONAL HUASCARÁN
Register with your passport at the park office (see above) and pay the US$2/20 day/multiday visit park fee. The US$20 fee is valid for 30 days. You can also pay at control stations (sometimes unstaffed in the low season) at the Lagunas Llanganuco, Pastoruri glacier or Musho village, west of Huascarán. Don't begrudge the fee: Parque Nacional Huascarán and the Cordillera Blanca are some of the most magical places on the planet and need to be preserved.

The most popular backpacking circuit, the Llanganuco–Santa Cruz loop, takes four days and rises to 4700m at the Punta Unión pass, which arguably has the best mountain views in Peru. Many other trails are available ranging from day hikes to ambitious two-week treks.

OTHER SIGHTS & ACTIVITIES
The **Museo Regional de Ancash** (☎ 043-72-1551; adult/student US$1.50/0.60; ☺ 9am-5pm Mon-Sat, 9am-2pm Sun), on the Plaza de Armas, has a small archaeology exhibit.

Monumento Nacional Wilcahuaín (adult/student US$1.20/0.60; ☺ 7am-5pm) is a small Wari site with a three-story temple. To get there, head north on Av Centenario to a dirt road on your right a few hundred meters past the Real Hotel Huascarán. The dirt road climbs 6km (passing through the communities of Jinua and Paria) to the ruins and can be reached by taxi (US$3).

Tours
Plentiful outfitters rent climbing and hiking gear, sell maps and guidebooks, and provide information and guides. **Casa de Guías**

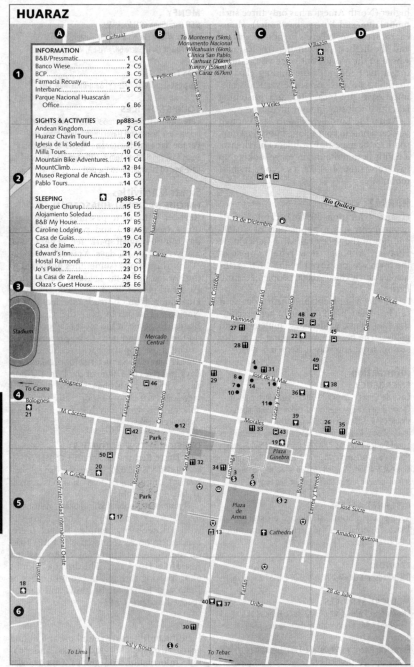

HUARAZ

INFORMATION
B&B/Pressmatic	1	C4
Banco Wiese	2	C5
BCP	3	C5
Farmacia Recuay	4	C4
Interbanc	5	C5
Parque Nacional Huascarán Office	6	B6

SIGHTS & ACTIVITIES pp883–5
Andean Kingdom	7	C4
Huaraz Chavín Tours	8	C4
Iglesia de la Soledad	9	E6
Milla Tours	10	C4
Mountain Bike Adventures	11	C4
MountClimb	12	B4
Museo Regional de Ancash	13	C5
Pablo Tours	14	C4

SLEEPING 🏠 pp885–6
Albergue Churup	15	E5
Alojamiento Soledad	16	E5
B&B My House	17	B5
Caroline Lodging	18	A6
Casa de Guías	19	C4
Casa de Jaime	20	A5
Edward's Inn	21	A4
Hostal Raimondi	22	C3
Jo's Place	23	D1
La Casa de Zarela	24	E6
Olaza's Guest House	25	E6

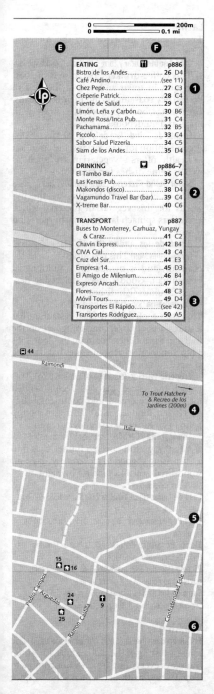

EATING   p886
Bistro de los Andes.....................26 D4
Café Andino............................(see 11)
Chez Pepe...................................27 C3
Crêperie Patrick..........................28 C4
Fuente de Salud...........................29 C4
Limón, Leña y Carbón..................30 B6
Monte Rosa/Inca Pub...................31 C4
Pachamama.................................32 B5
Piccolo.......................................33 C4
Sabor Salud Pizzería....................34 C5
Siam de los Andes.......................35 D4

DRINKING   pp886-7
El Tambo Bar................................36 C4
Las Kenas Pub..............................37 C6
Makondos (disco)........................38 D4
Vagamundo Travel Bar (bar)........39 C4
X-treme Bar.................................40 C6

TRANSPORT   p887
Buses to Monterrey, Carhuaz, Yungay
   & Caraz...................................41 C2
Chavin Express.............................42 B4
CIVA Cial.....................................43 C4
Cruz del Sur.................................44 E3
Empresa 14..................................45 D3
El Amigo de Milenium...................46 B4
Expreso Ancash............................47 D3
Flores...48 C3
Móvil Tours..................................49 D4
Transportes El Rápido...............(see 42)
Transportes Rodríguez..................50 A5

(☎ 043-72-1811; casa_de_guias@hotmail.com; Plaza Ginebra 28G) has a list of registered guides that are a great source of information. Other good rental agencies are **MountClimb** (☎ 043-72-6060; M Caceres 421) and **Andean Kingdom** (Luzuriaga 522), which also has a bouldering cave. **Mountain Bike Adventures** (☎ 043-72-4259; julio .olaza@terra.com.pe; Lúcar y Torre 530, 2nd fl) rents bikes and has English-speaking guides. Rental starts at US$20 per day.

Bus tours are another option. One visits the ruins at Chavín de Huantar, another goes through Yungay to the beautiful Lagunas Llanganuco, where there are spectacular views of Huascarán and other mountains, and a third goes to see the extraordinary giant *Puya raimondii* plant (boasting the tallest flower spike on the planet, which takes about 100 years to grow to its full height – often 10m!) and ice caves at Nevado Pastoruri. For more information, see p887. Prices cost US$8 to US$10 per person, including a guide. There are daily departures in the high season. Following are some recommended agencies:

Huaraz Chavín Tours (☎ 043-72-1578; hct@chavintours .com.pe; Luzuriaga 502)
Milla Tours (☎ 043-72-1742; Luzuriaga 528)
Pablo Tours (☎ 043-72-1145; pablotours@terra.com.pe; Luzuriaga 501)

Sleeping

Prices given are dry-/high-season rates, but bargains can be had throughout the October-to-April low season. Locals meet buses to offer rooms in their houses, and hostels do the same: don't pay until you've seen the room.

La Casa de Zarela (☎ 043-72-1694; zarelaz@hotmail .com; Arguedas 1263; d/tr with breakfast US$15/18) Zarela's helpfulness is legendary, and assistance with expedition planning is available. Rooms have private hot showers and kitchen access. Check out the rooftop terrace, and try Zarela's famous 'megaburrito' in her café.

Albergue Churup (☎ 043-72-2584; www.churup.com; A Figueroa 1257; dm US$4, d/tr/q with bath US$15/22/25) A super-popular hotel with a pretty garden, mountain views, a lounge with open fireplace, book exchange, laundry and trekking-gear rental.

Olaza's Guest House (☎ 043-72-2529; info@andean explorer.com; J Arguedas 1242; s/d US$10/15) A small, spotless hotel, this place has excellent private hot showers, book exchange, laundry and wonderful views from the rooftop terrace – a great place to wolf down breakfast (US$2.50 to US$5). Bus station pick-up is free with reservation.

Casa de Guías (☎ 043-72-1811; casa_de_guias@ hotmail.com; Plaza Ginebra 28G; dm US$5) Fourteen-bed dorm sharing several hot showers, kitchen and laundry facilities, and a popular pizza restaurant are on the premises. This is a youth hostel and climbers' meeting place, and there are bulletin boards of information. The Mountain Guide Association has an office here.

Alojamiento Soledad (☎ 043-72-1196; ghsoledad@ hotmail.com; Amadeo Figueroa 1267; d without/with bath US$11.50/14.50; 💻) This cozy family house has a rooftop terrace with one of the best views in town, plus a barbecue for sunset cook-outs. The owners speak English and German, and have a book exchange, cable TV, kitchen and laundry plus rental gear.

Jo's Place (☎ 043-72-5505; josplacehuaraz@hotmail .com; D Villayzan 278; dm US$3, s/d US$5/10) A chamingly chaotic place with a huge grassy yard (camping allowed), this hostel attracts hardcore trekkers. Some rooms have private baths. English ex-pat Jo provides the Sunday papers and makes bacon and eggs for breakfast. There's a common room with cable TV and a welcome fireplace.

Caroline Lodging (☎ 043-72-2588; trojas@viabcp .com; Urb Avitentel Mz-D, Lt 1; dm US$3) Shoestringers rave about this friendly place, southwest of the city center. Call – staff will pick you up and throw a free breakfast into the bargain. Kitchen and laundry facilities, hot showers – a steal for the price.

B&B My House (☎ 043-72-3375; bmark@ddm.com .pe; 27 de Noviembre 773; s/d with breakfast US$12/20) This hospitable B&B has a bright little patio and rooms decorated as if you were a family member being welcomed home. Rates include private hot showers. English and French spoken.

Other recommendations:

Hostal Raimondi (☎ 043-72-1082; Raimondi 820; s/d US$6/9) Old property with private showers; morning/ evening hot water.

Casa de Jaime (☎ 043-72-2281; A Gridilla 267; dm US$2, s/d with bath US$3/6; 💻) Basic, friendly, noisy; tepid shower.

Edward's Inn (☎ 043-72-2692; edwardsinn@viabcp .com; Bolognesi 121; dm US$3-5, s/d with bath US$10/20) Solar showers; perennially popular.

Eating

The cheapest meals are in the Mercado Central.

Café Andino (Lucar y Torre 530, 3rd fl; breakfast US$2-4) This coffee-drinkers' paradise is the best java-joint in town and one of the best in Peru. They roast and grind their own beans. Great vistas, board games and a library, with maps and guidebooks.

Fuente de Salud (José de la Mar 562; mains US$1-4) A good option for vegetarians, the 'fountain of health' offers a vegetarian set lunch, as well as some dishes for carnivores.

Sabor Salud Pizzería (Luzuriaga 672, 2nd fl; mains US$1.50-4) 'Flavor and Health' are the by-words for this vegetarian pizzería, which also offers spinach lasagna, soy burgers and more.

Bistro de los Andes (Morales 823; mains US$5; ☾ evening only Mon) This restaurant has a European air, and is owned by a multilingual Frenchman. Good coffees, delectable desserts, fabulous fish dishes.

Pachamama (San Martín 687; snacks & mains US$1.50-6) This glass-roofed, plant-filled restaurant/bar features a pool table, Ping-Pong, art on the wall and a giant chessboard on the floor – it's a hip, fun locale that sometimes has dancing at weekends (*not folklórico*!).

Crêperie Patrick (Luzuriaga 422; mains US$5) This French-influenced place is recommended for crepes, ice cream and continental dinners (trout, fondue, pasta). There is a rooftop patio open for breakfast under the sun.

Limón, Leña y Carbón (Luzuriaga 1014; mains US$4.50-6) A funky, graffiti-covered tunnel leads into a surprisingly good *cevichería* by day and wood-fired grill and *pizzería* by night.

Also consider:

Casa de Guías (Plaza Ginebra 28G; mains US$3-9) Good breakfasts and open all day.

Chez Pepe (Raimondi 624; mains US$4) An institution for pizza.

Monte Rosa/Inca Pub (José de la Mar 661; mains US$5-8) Excellent Alpine vibe.

Piccolo (Morales 632; mains US$3-6) Pavement café, pizzería and Peruvian restaurant in one.

Siam de los Andes (Gamarra 560; mains US$7-11) Superb Thai food worth the pricetag.

Drinking

El Tambo Bar (José de la Mar 776; admission US$3) The longest-lasting of the dance clubs, El Tambo Bar plays everything from technocumbia to Top Twenty, with occasional salsa to spice things up. Downside: it's the smokiest bar in town.

X-treme Bar (cnr Uribe & Luzuriaga) Accomplishes a wild and woolly atmosphere, with bizarre art, drunken graffiti, strong cocktails and good rock and blues.

Las Kenas Pub (Uribe 620) Usually overflowing with young Peruvians, bent on the techno-cumbia craze and lack of a cover most nights.

You could also try **Vagamundo Travel Bar** (Morales 753) or **Makondos** (José de la Mar 812), which has plenty of dark corners to hide in.

Getting There & Away

AIR

Anta (23km north of Huaraz) is the nearest airport, but lacks regular commercial flights; only charters are possible.

BUS

A plethora of companies go to Lima (US$6 to US$12, eight hours) in mid-morning or late evening. **Cruz del Sur** (☎ 043-72-8726; Raimondi 242) has nightly Imperial non-stop service (the most expensive). Others include **CIVA Cial** (☎ 043-72-1947; Morales 650), **Móvil Tours** (☎ 043-72-2555; Bolívar 542), **Transportes Rodríguez** (☎ 043-72-1353; Tarapaca 622) and **Flores** (☎ 043-72-6598; Raimondi 813).

Buses to Chimbote (US$5 to US$7, eight hours) go north through the spectacular Cañón del Pato, or west over the 4225m Punta Callán. Both are worth seeing, though most buses travel at night. Transportes Rodríguez and Cruz del Sur go to Chimbote, some continuing to Trujillo (US$6 to US$9, 10 hours).

Buses north to Monterrey (10 minutes), Carhuaz (45 minutes), Yungay (one hour) and Caraz (US$1.25, 1½ hours) leave every few minutes during daylight from Centenario on the north side of the river. **Chavín Express** (☎ 043-72-4652; M Cáceres 338) goes to Chavín de Huantar (US$3.50, four hours) at 7:30am, 11am and 2pm, with some buses continuing on to Huari (US$6, seven hours) and other towns east of the Cordillera Blanca. For Chiquián (and the Cordillera Huayhuash), El Amigo de Milenium, on the south side of the market, and **Transportes El Rápido** (☎ 043-72-2887; cnr M Cáceres & Tarapaca) have several daily buses.

Brave, beat-up buses also go to many other villages in the region: ask around.

NORTH OF HUARAZ

The road through the Callejón de Huaylas follows the Río Santa and is paved to Caraz. Five kilometers north of Huaraz is **Monterrey**, with **hot springs** (admission US$1; ☯ 8am-6pm Tue-Sun). **Carhuaz**, 26km further north, has plenty of basic hotels and is the best entrance/exit to the Cordillera Blanca via the beautiful Quebrada Ulta.

Yungay

The rubble-strewn area of old Yungay is the site of the single worst natural disaster in the Andes. The earthquake of 1970 loosened 15 million cubic meters of granite and ice, and almost all of the town's 18,000 inhabitants were buried. New Yungay has been rebuilt just beyond the avalanche path, about 59km north of Huaraz.

Lagunas Llanganuco

The trip to Lagunas Llanganuco begins from new Yungay and is one of the loveliest excursions in the Cordillera Blanca, with killer views of the giant surrounding mountains. Take a tour from Huaraz (see Bus earlier), or buses or taxis from Yungay. From June to August, minibuses (US$5 round trip) leave from the plaza in Yungay, stopping for two hours near the lakes. (Trips in other months depend on passenger demand.) National park entry is US$2. Llanganuco is the start of the popular and spectacular five-day backpacking loop to Santa Cruz (US$20).

There are several basic hostels near the plaza.

Caraz

This pretty little town (elevation 2270m), 67km north of Huaraz, has survived many an earthquake and landslide, and is the end of the Llanganuco to Santa Cruz trek. The Plaza de Armas is attractive, hotels are inexpensive and you can take pleasant walks in the surrounding hills. **Pony Expeditions** (☎ 043-79-1642; www.ponyexpeditions.com; José Sucre 1266; ☯ 8am-10pm) offers gear and bike rental, maps, trekking services and Internet access.

SLEEPING & EATING

Alojamiento Caballero (☎ 043-79-1637; Daniel Villar 485; s/d US$3/6) This simple, family-run place has shared hot showers and good views.

Albergue Los Pinos (☎ 043-79-1130; lospinos@terra .com.pe; Parque San Martín 103; camping US$2.50, s/d US$8/16, with bath US$10/20; (P)(🖳)) A YHA-affiliated hostel, with hot water, kitchen and laundry. Rates halve in the low season.

Hostal La Casona (☎ 043-79-1334; Raimondi 319; s/d US$4/6, with bath US$6/8) An attractive patio also makes this a favored budget choice.

Hostal Chavín (☎ 043-79-1171; hostalchavin@latin mail.com; San Martín 1135; s/d US$8/11) This place has a knowledgeable owner and simple rooms with hot showers.

Café de Rat (above Pony Expeditions; mains US$1-3, large pizzas US$6-8; 🕙 closed Sun) An atmospheric, wood-beamed restaurant open all day.

GETTING THERE & AWAY
Minibuses to Yungay and Huaraz leave from the station on the Carretera Central. *Colectivos* for Cashapampa (US$1.50, two hours), for the north end of the Llanganuco-to-Santa Cruz trek, leave from Ramón Castilla at Santa Cruz.

SOUTHEAST OF HUARAZ
Chavín de Huantár
Located near this small village are the ruins of **Chavín** (admission US$1; 🕙 8am-4pm), Peru's oldest major culture (1300 to 400 BC), predating the Incas by an incredible two millennia. The site contains highly stylized cultist carvings of the feline (a jaguar or puma), Chavín's principal deity, and of condors, snakes and human deities. The site's snaking underground tunnels (which are electrically lit) are a stupendous feat of 3000-year-old engineering and are exceptionally well ventilated. In the heart of the underground complex at the intersection of four passageways lies an exquisitely carved, 4m dagger-like rock, the Lanzón de Chavín.

SLEEPING & EATING
La Casona de JB (☎ 043-75-4020; Plaza de Armas 130; s/d US$3/6, with bath US$4.50/8.50; (P)) An old house with erratic hot water, but friendly and recommended.

Hotel Chavín Arqueológico (☎ 043-75-4055; Inca Roca 141; s/d US$8/14) Modern, has hot water and TVs. Around the corner is its more basic partner, Hostal Chavín.

Camping is possible by the ruins with permission of the guard.

Restaurants close around sunset, so you'll need to eat early. The best is **Chavín Turístico** (17 de Enero 439).

GETTING THERE & AWAY
See p887 for details of tours and buses that make the trip (US$2.75).

Chiquián
At 3400m, this village is the gateway to the spectacular Cordillera Huayhuash. Few supplies are available, but mules can be hired here.

The clean and attractive **Hotel Los Nogales** (☎ 043-74-7121; hotel_nogales_chiquian@yahoo.com; Comercio 1301; s/d US$3/6, with bath US$6/12) is three blocks from the central plaza. Rooms surround a pretty colonial-style courtyard and there is hot water. The more modern **Gran Hotel Huayhuash** (☎ 043-74-7049; 28 de Julio 400; s/d US$3/6, with bath from US$6/12) has some rooms with cable TV, views and hot water, plus the town's best **restaurant** (mains US$1.20-4.50). Cheaper and adequate, the **Hostal Chavín** (San Martín 1st block; d US$5) attracts shoestringers.

El Rápido buses return from Chiquián to Huaraz at 5am and 2pm, leaving from Gran Hotel Huayhuash. **Transfysa** (☎ 043-74-7063; 2 de Mayo 1109) and **Turismo Cavassa** (☎ 043-74-7036; Bolognesi 421) have buses to Lima (US$5, nine hours).

THE NORTHERN HIGHLANDS

Travelers heading upcountry to the northern highlands will be rewarded by a region relatively off the beaten track but offering unique destinations. How about soaking up the steam in hot springs where Inca Atahualpa himself bathed before his last stand against the Spanish? Or being one of the few to visit the isolated pre-Inca city of Kuélap? This is also the best route to forge a slow trail across the highlands to one of the Amazon Basin's less-visited ports at Yurimaguas.

CAJAMARCA
Cajamarca (2750m), five hours east of the coast, is a tranquil, traditional city of 111,000 people. Once a major Inca stronghold, it was here that Francisco Pizarro tricked and captured the Inca Atahualpa, before demanding ransom and subsequently having him killed off. The surrounding countryside is lush and attractive, particularly during the rainy season.

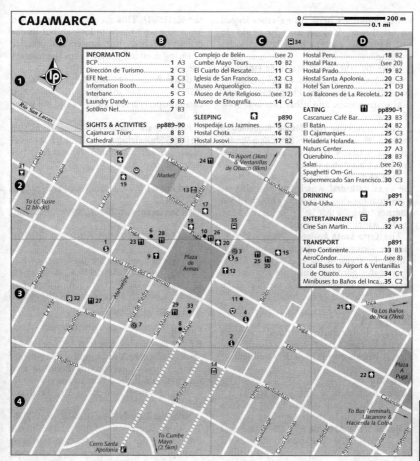

CAJAMARCA

0 — 200 m
0 — 0.1 mi

INFORMATION
BCP.................................1 A3
Dirección de Turismo..............2 C3
EFE Net............................3 C3
Information Booth..................4 C3
Interbanc..........................5 C3
Laundry Dandy.....................6 B2
Sot@no Net........................7 B3

SIGHTS & ACTIVITIES pp889–90
Cajamarca Tours...................8 B3
Cathedral.........................9 B3

Complejo de Belén................(see 2)
Cumbe Mayo Tours................10 B2
El Cuarto del Rescate.............11 C3
Iglesia de San Francisco..........12 C3
Museo Arqueológico...............13 B2
Museo de Arte Religioso......(see 12)
Museo de Etnografía..............14 C4

SLEEPING p890
Hospedaje Los Jazmines..........15 C3
Hostal Chota.....................16 B2
Hostal Jusovi....................17 B2

Hostal Peru......................18 B2
Hostal Plaza....................(see 20)
Hostal Prado....................19 B2
Hostal Santa Apolonia...........20 C3
Hotel San Lorenzo...............21 D3
Los Balcones de La Recoleta....22 D4

EATING pp890–1
Cascanuez Café Bar...............23 B3
El Batán.........................24 B2
El Cajamarques...................25 C3
Heladería Holanda................26 B2
Naturs Center....................27 A3
Querubino........................28 B3
Salas...........................(see 26)
Spaghetti Om-Gri.................29 B3
Supermercado San Francisco.......30 C3

DRINKING p891
Usha-Usha........................31 A2

ENTERTAINMENT p891
Cine San Martín..................32 A3

TRANSPORT p891
Aero Continente..................33 B3
AeroCóndor......................(see 8)
Local Buses to Airport & Ventanillas
de Otuzco.....................34 C1
Minibuses to Baños del Inca....35 C2

Information

For tourist information try **Dirección de Turismo** (☎ 076-82-2903; El Complejo de Belén; ⏲ 7:30am-1:30pm & 3:30-5:30pm Mon-Fri) or the **information booth** (Lima at Belén). Internet access is available at **EFE Net** (2 de Mayo 568) and **Sot@no.Net** (Junín at Cruz de Piedra). **Laundry Dandy** (☎ 076-92-3454; Puga 545) charges US$1.40 per kg. **Clínica Limatambo** (☎ 076-82-4241; Puno 265), west of town, is the medical service. Banks include **BCP** (cnr Lima & Apurímac) and **Interbanc** (2 de Mayo 546), which changes traveler's checks and has an ATM. Tour agencies running inexpensive tours of the surroundings include **Cumbe Mayo Tours** (☎ 076-82-2938; Puga 635) and **Cajamarca Tours** (☎ 076-82-2813; 2 de Mayo 323).

Sights

The only remaining Inca building in Cajamarca is **El Cuarto del Rescate** (The Ransom Chamber; admission US$1; ⏲ 9am-noon & 3-5pm). Despite the name, this is actually where Pizarro kept Atahualpa prisoner, not where his ransom was stored. The admission price includes El Complejo de Belén and El Museo de Etnografía if visited on the same day.

Construction of **Complejo de Belén** (⏲ 9am-noon & 3-5pm) began in the 17th century. Inside what once was the women's hospital is a small archaeology museum and a few minuscule patient cells. In the kitchen and dispensary there is an **art museum**.

Next door is the **church**, with a fine cupola and a carved pulpit. Woodcarvings include

PERU

a tired-looking Christ sitting cross-legged on his throne, looking as if he could do with a *pisco* sour after a hard day's miracle-working.

Close by, the small **Museo de Etnografía** (🕙 9am-noon & 3-5pm) exhibits local costumes, domestic and agricultural implements, musical instruments, and other bits and bobs of Cajamarcan culture.

The university-run **Museo Arqueológico** (Del Batán 289; admission free; 🕙 8am-2:30pm Mon-Fri) displays artifacts from the under-studied pre-Inca Cajamarca culture.

Two churches face the Plaza de Armas: the squat **cathedral**, which has no belfry as a colonial tax dodge, and the church of **San Francisco** (admission US$0.50; 🕙 9am-noon & 3-5pm Mon-Fri), which has catacombs.

The **Cerro Santa Apolonia** (admission US$0.50) hill overlooks the city from the southwest. Climb the stairs at the end of 2 de Mayo. There are gardens and pre-Columbian carvings, including one throne-like niche known as the Seat of the Inca.

Festivals & Events

Water throwing during Carnaval is without respite. Corpus Christi is very colorful, and Fiestas Patrias events include a bullfight.

Sleeping

Some cheapies have only cold water, but you can always hop over to Baños del Inca (p891) for a dip in the hot springs.

Hostal Santa Apolonia (🕿 076-82-7207; Puga 649; s/d US$14.50/23) The best budget hotel on the plaza, featuring a small plant-filled courtyard and smart rooms with solid mattresses, 24-hour hot showers, cable TV and minifridges.

Hostal Plaza (🕿 076-82-2058; Puga 669; s/d US$4.50/8.50, s/d with bath US$7.25/13) In a colorful old building on the plaza, rooms are creaky and basic, but those with bath are fun, with plaza views and some balconies. Hot water is available 7am to 10am and 7pm to 10pm.

Los Balcones de La Recoleta (🕿 /fax 076-82-3302; Puga 1050; s/d US$14.50/17.50) This 19th-century place has well-presented rooms around a grassy, plant-filled courtyard. Private hot showers all day, cable TV and comfortable beds with a candy on the pillow at night.

Hospedaje Los Jazmines (🕿 /fax 076-82-1812; assado@hotmail.com; Amazonas 775; s/d US$8.50/13, with bath US$11.50/17) This six-room German-run *hospedaje* isn't much to look at, but its excellent café, beds, hot showers and practice of hiring disabled people keeps the punters coming.

Hostal Prado (🕿 076-82-6093; La Mar 582; s/d US$7.25/10, with bath US$12/20) This well-kept, clean property has a café, TVs and hot water all day.

Hostal Chota (🕿 076-82-8704; La Mar 637; s/d US$3/4.50) Shoestringers find this basic hostel nicely priced; communal showers have hot water on request.

Other recommendations:

Hostal Jusovi (🕿 076-82-2920; Amazonas 637; s/d US$8.50/14.50)

Hotel San Lorenzo (🕿 076-82-2909; Amazonas 1060; s/d US$10/16)

Hostal Peru (🕿 076-82-4030; Puga 605; s/d US$8/13)

Also worth a splurge are the bungalows at **Complejo Turístico Baños del Inca** (🕿 /fax 076-83-8249; bungalow US$35; 🅿), right behind the Baños del Inca, which have views of the water steaming Danté-esquely.

Eating

El Batán (Del Batán 369; set menu US$3.50, mains US$4-8; 🕙 closed some Mon) A restaurant-gallery-*peña*-cum-cultural-center serving Peruvian and international dishes. Live music on weekends ranges from Andean to Afro-Peruvian rhythms.

Heladería Holanda (Puga 657; double scoop US$0.60) The tiny entrance opens into a large, bright café selling the best ice cream in northern Peru, plus excellent espressos, creamy cappuccinos and pukka pies.

Spaghetti Om-Gri (San Martín 360; mains US$2.25-5) This five-table restaurant serves the best lasagna in town and the chef chats with guests as he cooks.

Salas (Puga 637; mains US$2.25-6) This barn-like place has been a local favorite since 1947, but the faint-hearted might want to avoid the *sesos* (cow brains), a local specialty.

El Cajamarques (Amazonas 770; mains US$4-7) An upscale restaurant adjoining a colonial courtyard containing tropical birds.

Cascanuez Café Bar (Puga 554; desserts US$1-2) Serves meals, but it's the delectable desserts that bring people flocking.

Querubino (Puga 589; mains US$4-7.50) Stylish and colorful, and has among Cajamarca's best steaks and seafood.

Other recommendations:

Naturs Center (Apurímac 614; mains US$2) For mostly vegetarian dishes.

Supermercado San Francisco (Amazonas 780) For self-catering.

Entertainment

Cine San Martín (☎ 076-82-3260; Junín 829; US$1.50) screens movies. **Usha-Usha** (Puga 142; admission US$1.50) is a local, hole-in-the-wall bar, run by a local musician who likes to tell stories, and can be a blast or a bust.

Getting There & Away

AIR

The **airport** (☎ 076-82-2523) is 3km north of town. **AeroCóndor** (☎ 076-82-2813; in Cajamarca Tours) has a daily flight from Lima (US$59 to US$94), returning via Trujillo on demand. **Aero Continente** (☎ 076-82-3304; 2 de Mayo 381) and **LC Busre** (Lima 1020) also have Lima flights.

Local buses for Otuzco pass the airport (US$0.30) from the north end of Del Batán. Taxis cost US$1.50.

BUS

Most bus terminals are on the third block of Atahualpa (not in the town center, but another street of the same name), 1.5km southeast of town on the road to the Baños del Inca.

Many companies have buses to Trujillo (US$5 to US$9, six hours), Chiclayo (US$4.50 to US$7, six hours) and Lima (US$9 to US$30, 13 hours). Lima buses go overnight. **CIVA** (☎ 076-82-1460; Atahualpa 753), **Cruz del Sur** (☎ 076-82-4421; Via de Evitamiento 750) and **Ormeño** (☎ 076-82-9889; Via de Evitamiento 740) all have comfortable buses. **Atahualpa** (☎ 076-82-3060; Atahualpa 322), **Tepsa** (☎ 076-82-3306; Atahualpa 300) and **Cial** (☎ 076-82-8701; Atahualpa 300) have cheap buses.

For Trujillo, buses leave in the afternoon and arrive late at night. **Linea** (☎ 076-82-3956; Atahualpa 318) is one recommended company for Trujillo. For Chiclayo (US$7, seven hours), **El Cumbe** (☎ 076-82-3088; Independencia 236) has three or four daily buses during the day. **Diaz** (☎ 076-82-8289; Sucre 422) goes to Chota (US$6, nine hours of wild scenery), an alternative route for Chiclayo if you're not in a hurry. Atahualpa also goes to Celendín (US$3, five hours). Beyond Celendín to Chachapoyas transport is unreliable. It is easier to travel to Chachapoyas from Chiclayo.

AROUND CAJAMARCA

Baños del Inca

These natural **hot springs** (per hr US$0.50-1.50) are 7km east of Cajamarca. The water is channeled into private cubicles, some large enough to hold six people. *Colectivos* for Baños del Inca leave frequently from 2 de Mayo near Amazonas (US$0.50). Buses also pass through the Plaza de Armas to the Baños. Atahualpa was camped by these natural hot springs before his fateful run-in with Pizarro (see p888).

Cumbe Mayo

Pre-Inca channels run for several kilometers across the bleak mountaintops, 23km southwest of Cajamarca. Nearby are caves with petroglyphs, and the countryside is high, windswept and slightly eerie. The site can be reached on foot from Cerro Santa Apolonia via a signposted road. The walk takes about four hours, if you take shortcuts and ask for directions. Daily tours (US$6) are sold in Cajamarca (p889).

Ventanillas de Otuzco

This pre-Inca graveyard has hundreds of funerary niches built into the hillside. The site is in superb countryside, and you can walk here from Cajamarca or Baños del Inca. Local buses from Cajamarca (US$0.50) leave from the north end of Del Batán, or tours cost US$5. To walk, take the airport road for about 8km.

CHACHAPOYAS

This quiet, friendly little town sits at about 2400m on the eastern slopes of the Andes. Nearby are many remote, little-known archaeological sites. One of the most accessible is the magnificent ruin of Kuélap, one of the largest stone structures in the Americas.

Cyber Club (Triunfo 769; ☽ 8am-midnight) has Internet access. **BCP** changes US cash and traveler's checks, and has a Visa/AmEx ATM. The regional **tourist office** (Junín 801; ☽ 8am-1pm & 2-5pm Mon-Fri) dispenses some information.

Gran Vilaya Tours (☎ 041-77-7506; www@vilaya tours.com; Grau 624) arranges excursions, including archaeology, trekking, climbing and horse riding.

Chachapoyas has a small **museum** (Ayacucho 904; admission free; ☽ 9am-noon & 3-5pm Mon-Sat).

PERU

Sleeping

Hostal Kuélap (☎ 041-77-7136; kuelaphotel@hotmail .com; Amazonas 1057; s US$3, s/d with bath US$6/8; **P**) Clean enough and has hot water.

Hostal Johumaji (☎ 041-77-7279; olvacha@terra .com.pe; Ayacucho 711; s/d US$4.50/6) The best of the cheap hotels, with small, tidy rooms and electric showers.

Hotel Continental (☎ 041-77-8352; Arrieta 431; s US$4.50, s/d with bath US$6/8) This place is modern and adequate.

Hostal El Tejado (☎ 041-77-7654; eltejado@viabcp .com; Grau 534; s/d with bath & breakfast US$9/13) For a few bucks more, this recommended hostel has quiet, well-kept rooms with hot water.

Hostal Revash (☎ 041-77-7391; Grau 517; s/d with bath US$10/14) The older, classic hostel has endless hot water, a thickly forested courtyard and wooden floors.

Casa Vieja Hostal (☎ /fax 041-77-7353; casavieja@ viabcp.com; Chincha Alta 569; s/d US$9/15; 🖳) Rooms are located in this converted mansion.

Eating & Drinking

Restaurant Matalacha (Ayacucho 616; mains US$1.50-4.50) Popular locally.

El Tejado (Grau 534; set lunch US$2) This atmospheric place is also popular with locals

Las Rocas (Ayacucho 932; mains US$1.50-3.50; evening only Sun) Excellent value.

Chacha (Grau 545; set lunch US$1, mains US$2-4) Situated on the plaza. This old stand-by is excellent value.

El Eden (Grau 505; set lunch US$0.90; 🕑 8:30am-5pm) A tiny, friendly vegetarian restaurant.

Panificadora San José (Ayacucho 816; breakfasts US$1-2) An early opening bakery.

La Noche (Triunfo 1061) Dancing can be had here.

Getting There & Away

LC Busre (☎ 041-77-7610; Puno 368) has flights to Lima on Tuesday and Saturday mornings (US$79). Departure text costs US$3.50.

Buses go along the mostly paved route to Chiclayo (US$7 to US$10, 10 to 12 hours) and on to Lima (US$17 to US$22, 20 to 25 hours). These services leave with **Transervis Kuélap** (☎ 041-77-8128; Arrieta 412), **CIVA** (☎ 041-77-8048; La Libertad 812) and **Movil Tours** (☎ 041-77-8545; La Libertad 1084).

Virgen del Carmen (Salamanca 650) goes to Celendín on Tuesday and Friday. **Transportes Roller** (Grau 302) has buses to Kuélap (US$3.50, 3½ hours) at 4:30am. This block also has

colectivos for Tingo (US$1.75, 1½ hours). *Colectivos* go to Pedro Ruíz (US$3, 1½ hours), from where you continue east to Moyobamba and the Amazon Basin.

KUÉLAP

An immense, oval-shaped pre-Inca city, **Kuélap** (admission US$3; 🕑 8am-5pm) is perched at 3100m on a ridge above the Río Utcubamba, southeast of Chachapoyas. It's a major site with very little tourism. *El Tintero* (The Inkpot) is a mysterious underground chamber where, locals claim, pumas were kept and human sacrifices were thrown in.

A bare-bones **hostel** (per person US$2.25) has a few beds and floor space, or you can camp here. Bring water-purification equipment. Basic meals are available. The friendly guardian will give tours for a small tip.

To get to Kuélap, take the Transportes Roller bus from Chachapoyas to within 1km of the site or a *colectivo* to Tingo, which has a few basic hotels. A steep trail leads from the southern end of Tingo to the ruins, 1200m above. Allow five hours for the climb and take water.

EAST OF CHACHAPOYAS

First go north to Pedro Ruíz (see Getting There & Away, earlier), where there are a couple of basic hotels. From here a rough road goes east to Yurimaguas (definitely off the gringo trail).

Tarapoto

About 3½ hours southeast of Moyobamba, Tarapoto is the largest and most important town in the area. It has plenty of hotels, but is pricier than most of Peru. Travel from Moyobamba and on to Yurimaguas is safe, but the route south along the Río Huallaga valley to Tingo María goes through Peru's major coca-growing region and therefore is not recommended. Tarapoto's geography is rugged, and waterfalls and lakes are abundant. Money can be changed at the BCP.

SLEEPING & EATING

Hospedaje Misti (☎ 042-52-2439; L Prado 341; s/d US$4.50/7) Rooms have tiny bathrooms (the cold shower splashes the toilet), but you get a TV and ceiling fan.

Hospedaje Las Palmeras (☎ 042-52-5475; M Grau 229; s US$2, d with bath US$4.50) Less recommended and very basic; cold-water showers.

Hostal Miami (☎ /fax 042-52-2038; Urzua 257; s/d US$5/8) Also less-recommendable and very basic; cold-water showers.

El Mirador (☎ 042-52-2177; La Cruz 517; s/d US$13/16) Super-friendly, with a rooftop terrace complete with hammocks.

Alojamiento Arevalo (☎ 042-52-5265; Moyobamba 223; US$9/13; **P**) Spacious.

La Patarashca (☎ 042-52-3899; lapatarashca@hotmail.com; Lamas 261; s/d US$10/13) A tropical vibe encompasses this cute place, which has a plant-filled courtyard with hammocks, private cold showers and cable TV.

Hostal San Antonio (☎ 042-52-5563; Pimentel 126; s/d US$7.50/11) Good value, with private hot showers and cable TV just steps from the main plaza.

La Patarashca (Lamas 261; mains US$4-8) Offers regional Amazonian cuisine.

Las Terrazas (Hurtado 183; mains US$1.50-5) An economical choice on the plaza.

Natur Micuna (Maynas 257; set lunch US$2) Great for vegetarians.

La Alternativa (Grau 401) Hole-in-the-wall bar with shelves of dusty bottles containing various homemade concoctions based on soaking roots, lianas etc in cane liquor. Amazonian aphrodisiac, anyone?

GETTING THERE & AWAY

The **airport** (☎ 042-52-2278) is 2.5km from town (US$1.50 by mototaxi). **Aero Continente** (☎ 042-52-4332; Moyobamba 101), **LC Busre** (www.lcbusre.com.pe in Spanish; Airport) and **TANS** (☎ 042-52-5339; Plaza Mayor 491) have flights to Lima (US$71) and Iquitos (US$56). **SAOSA** (☎ 042-52-4185; Airport) has daily flights to Pucallpa.

Several companies head west on the paved road via Moyobamba, Chiclayo (US$15, 15 to 17 hours) and Trujillo to Lima (US$25, 25 to 30 hours). Most companies are along Salaverry in the Morales district. The best companies are **Movil** (☎ 042-52-9193; Salaverry 858) and **El Sol Peruano** (☎ 042-52-8322). Cheaper companies include **Paredes Estrella** (☎ 042-52-8552; Salaverry 7th block) and **Expreso Huamanga** (☎ 042-52-7272; Salaverry 7th block).

Minibuses, pickup trucks and *colectivos* traveling to Yurimaguas (US$4 to US$7, six hours) leave from the market in the eastern suburb of Banda de Shilcayo. Paredes Estrella and Expreso Huamanga have buses.

AMAZON BASIN

You'll feel a dramatic sense of remoteness and a frontier spirit when exploring this region. About half of Peru is in the Amazon Basin, but this wilderness is penetrated by few roads and has few towns of any size. Furthermore, this vast area contains only about 5% of the nation's population. Pucallpa and Yurimaguas can be reached by long road trips. Both have slow boats on to Iquitos, which can only be reached by boat or air. Puerto Maldonado can be reached by air or a very wearing trip by truck from Cuzco.

PUCALLPA

Bustling boomtown Pucallpa, capital of Ucayali department, is an unlovely, fast-growing jungle town linked to Lima by road. The main reasons to visit are jungle trips from the nearby Yarinacocha and the river trip to Iquitos.

Information

There's a **tourist office** (☎ 061-57-1303; 2 de Mayo 111), and several banks change money and traveler's checks and have ATMs. Exchange houses are found along the 4th, 5th and 6th blocks of Raimondi. Western Union is at **Viajes Laser** (☎ 061-57-1120; Raimondi 470), which is one of the better travel agencies in Pucallpa, but for jungle guides, go to Yarinacocha. **Trial Internet** (Portillo 398) has fast machines.

The **Clínica Santa Rosa** (☎ 061-57-1689; Inmaculada 529; ☆ 24 hr) has good medical services. **Lavandería Gasparin** (Portillo 526) offers self-service and drop-off laundry.

Sights

Usko Ayar (☎ 061-57-3088; www.egallery.com/pablo.html; Sánchez Cerro 465), near Iglesia Fray Marcos, is the gallery of Pablo Amaringo, a visionary local artist who has used the hallucinogenic ayahuasca vine for inspiration. Some of the work of famed local woodcarver Agustín Rivas can be seen at his house, now the **Gallery of Agustín Rivas** (☎ 061-57-1834; Tarapaca 861, 2nd fl).

Sleeping

Hostería del Rey (☎ 061-57-5815; Portillo 747; s/d US$5/6) High ceilings, cold showers and fans to help you keep your cool.

Hospedaje Sisley (☎ 061-57-5137; Portillo 658, upstairs; s/d US$8.50/12) Decent place run by

PUCALLPA

```
0        300 m
0        0.2 mi
```

To Yarinacocha (10km) / To Docks
Arahuaiba
To Dock (3km) & Capitania
To TANS

INFORMATION
Banco Continental	1 C3
BCP	2 D2
Clinica Santa Rosa	3 C1
Interbanc	4 C3
Lavandería Gasparin	5 D3
Tourist Office	6 D1
Trial Internet	7 D2
Viajes Laser	8 C2

SIGHTS & ACTIVITIES p893
Clock Tower	9 D3
Gallery of Agustín Rivas	10 D2

To Parque Natural (4km), Airport & Lima

Plaza de Armas

Market

Market

Parque San Martín

Swamp (Docks in high water)

SLEEPING p893–4
Hospedaje Amazonas	11 C3
Hospedaje Barbtur	12 C3
Hospedaje El Gran Dorado	13 C1
Hospedaje Komby	14 B2
Hospedaje Sisley	15 C3
Hostal Perú	16 C3
Hostal Tariri	17 C3
Hostería del Rey	18 C3

EATING p894
C'est Si Bon	19 C2
Cebichería El Escorpión	20 C2
Chez Maggy	21 D1
Chifa Mey Lin	22 D1
Don José's	23 C3
El Paraíso	24 C2
El Portal Chicken	25 C2
Fuente Soda Tropitop	26 C2
Supermercado Los Andes	27 D3

TRANSPORT pp894–5
Aero Continente	28 C3
León de Huánuco (to Lima)	29 C2
Motorbike Rental	30 B2
Servicios Generales	31 B2
Transmar (to Lima)	32 C3
Transportes Amazonas (to Lima)	33 C2
Transportes El Rey (to Lima)	34 C3
Transportes Palcazu (to Amazon Towns)	35 C3

friendly older ladies, with tidy rooms, private cold showers, fans and TV.

Hospedaje Barbtur (☎ 061-57-2532; Raimondi 670; s/d US$4/5.50, s/d with bath US$7.25/10) Well-maintained and family-run option, with cold showers and cable TV in en-suite rooms.

Hostal Perú (☎ 061-57-5128; Raimondi 639; s/d US$4.25/5.50, with bath US$5.50-9/7.25-11.50) A Shipibo pot collection brightens the faded entry stairs. Rooms are tiny but clean with small fans. Showers are cold.

Other recommendations:

Hospedaje Amazonas (☎ 061-57-1080; Portillo 729; s/d US$4.50/6) Dingy but cheap.

Hostal Tariri (☎ 061-57-5147; Raimondi 733; s/d US$4.50-6/6-9)

Hospedaje Komby (☎ 061-57-1562; Ucayali 360; s/d US$10/13; ⊠) Offers private baths, fans and cable TV.

Hospedaje El Gran Dorado (☎ /fax 061-57-4592; Independencia 204; s/d US$11.50/17.25) Check out the electric-blue tiles.

Eating

Many restaurants are closed Sunday.

Don José's (Ucayali 661; mains US$1.50-5) The old stand-by for freshly squeezed juices.

C'est Si Bon (Independencia 560) On the plaza, great for ice cream and breakfast.

Fuente Soda Tropitop (Sucre 401) Opposite corner of the plaza to C'est Si Bon. Another bright spot for ice cream and breakfast.

Cebichería El Escorpión (Independencia 430; mains US$3-6) Boasting a prime plaza location is this seafood-oriented place.

El Portal Chicken (Independencia 510; mains US$3) Another plaza place, with open-air plaza views, is this choice chicken joint.

Chez Maggy (Inmaculada 643; mains US$3-7) Good for pizza.

Chifa Mey Lin (Sucre 698; mains US$3) Serves Chinese food.

El Paraíso (Tarapacá 653; set lunch US$1; ⊙ Sun-Fri) This plaza-side vegetarian place uses soy and vegetables to make typical Peruvian dishes.

For long trips, stock up at **Supermercado Los Andes** (Portillo 545). The local beer, San Juan, is Peru's only beer brewed in the Amazon.

Getting There & Away
AIR

Pucallpa's airport is 5km northwest of town (departure tax costs US$3.50). **Aero**

PERU

Continente (☎ 061-57-5643; 7 de Junio 861) has daily direct flights to Lima (US$79), while Iquitos (US$69) is served by **TANS** (☎ 061-59-1852; Arica 500). **SAOSA** (☎ 061-57-2637) flies most days to Tarapoto; also try **Servicios Generales** (☎ 061-57-8003; Progreso 564).

BOAT
La Hoyada, Pucallpa's port, is 2.5km northeast of town. During low water (June to October) boats leave from the El Mangual docks, 3km further. In high water (February to April) boats reach the Parque San Martín. Crowded boats to Iquitos (US$15 to US$25) take three to five days; many other destinations are also served. Passengers can sleep aboard on hammocks, which are sold in the market by Parque San Martín.

BUS
Several companies go to Lima (US$13, 21 hours) via Tingo María and Huánuco. These include **León de Huánuco** (☎ 061-57-2411; Tacna 655), **Transportes El Rey** (☎ 061-57-5545; cnr Raimondi & 7 de Junio), **Transmar** (☎ 061-57-4900; Raimondi 793) and **Transportes Amazonas** (☎ 061-57-1292; Tacna 628).

Getting Around
Motocarros (three-wheeled motorcycle rickshaws) cost US$2 to the airport or Yarinacocha; car taxis charge 50% more. Buses (US$0.20) and *colectivos* (US$0.25) leave from 9 de Diciembre near the market and San Martín at Ucayali. Alternatively, you can rent a motorbike for US$2 per hour or US$15 to US$20 for 12 hours. See the Pucallpa map for rental locations (p894).

YARINACOCHA
This lovely oxbow lake is 10km northeast of Pucallpa. You can take canoe rides, observe wildlife, visit Shipibo communities and purchase handicrafts. Internet access is available at the Restaurant Latino, and Maroti Shobo sells handmade Shipibo ceramics.

Tours
Peki-peki boats with drivers cost about US$5 per hour (four passengers). Overnight trips are US$30 per person per day. Recommended guides include **Gilber Reategui Sangama** (leave message at ☎ 061-57-9018; junglesecrets@yahoo.com), with his boat *La Normita*; **Miguel TANS** (☎ 061-59-7494) and his boat *Pituco*; and

Gustavo Paredes with *Poseidon*. It's easy to find their boats, which are all pulled up along the waterfront. Ask around, but don't fall for the old 'Oh, that boat sank. Why don't you take a tour with me?' tactic.

Popular trips include to the **botanical gardens** (US$0.60; ☺ 8am-4pm), and the **Shipibo villages** of San Francisco and Santa Clara.

Sleeping & Eating
On the waterfront is the basic **Hotel El Pescador** (s/d US$4/6). **Los Delfínes** (☎ 061-59-6423; r US$4-12) has some private showers. Gilber Reategui Sangama provides beds at his **house** (leave message at ☎ 061-57-9018; junglesecrets@yahoo.com; per person with meals & transport US$15) across the lake. Three pricier **lodges** (per person US$25-35) are across the lake.

The Shipibo village of San Francisco offers lodging at US$3 per person.

YURIMAGUAS
This quiet, sleepy little port on the Río Huallaga has boats to Iquitos. Reaching Yurimaguas involves a tiring road trip from the coast or northern highlands.

Manguare Expediciones (Lores 126) arranges tours, sells handicrafts and gives information. BCP or Banco Continental (Visa ATMs) will change US cash or traveler's checks. **JC's Internet** (US$1.20 per hr; ☺ 8am-midnight) is on Plaza de Armas. **Paraíso Azul** (Huallaga at M Castilla) has a swimming pool.

Sleeping & Eating
Few hotels have hot water, though most have private bathrooms.

Hostal César Gustavo (☎ 065-35-1585; Atahualpa 102; s/d with bath US$4.50/6) Clean and quiet, and it's recommended by readers. Rooms have decent beds and fans.

Quinta Lucy (☎ 065-35-1575; Jáuregui 305; s US$3, s/d with bath US$3.50/4.50) Decently run, although rooms look like they're in a jail block.

Hostal de Paz (☎ /fax 065-35-2123; Jáuregui 431, s/d with bath US$6/8) Good value, with fans and TVs. Note that there is no sign out the front.

Leo's Palace (☎ 065-35-1499; Lores 108; s/d with bath US$6/9) An older place, with a few basic but spacious rooms with fan. Some rooms have a balcony overlooking the plaza.

Hostal El Naranjo (☎ 065-35-2650; elnaranjo_yms@hotmail.com; Arica 318; s/d with bath US$10/15) Quiet and recommended. Rooms have fans and

PERU

cable TV. A pool and hot water are planned, and there's a good restaurant.

Hostal Luis Antonio (☎ 065-35-2065; Jáuregui 407; s/d US$10-20/20-30; 🔂 🕸) All rooms have fan; cable TV and/or air-con cost more. It has a decent restaurant and a small pool.

Hotel restaurants are among the best places to eat. Also OK is **La Prosperidad** (☎ 065-35-2057; Progreso 107) for tropical juices, burgers and chicken.

Getting There & Around

TANS, Star Up and AviaSelva share an **office** (☎ 065-35-2387; Libertad 221), which is located in front of the airport. AviaSelva flies Iquitos–Yurimaguas–Tarapoto–Yurimaguas–Iquitos on Saturday (subject to change). Connections from Tarapoto can be made for Lima and other cities.

Companies with buses from Tarapoto (US$3 to US$6, four to six hours) include Estrella and Huamanga.

Mototaxis charge US$0.60 to the port, 13 blocks north of the town center. Cargo boats, stopping in Lagunas, leave a few times a week to Iquitos (US$12 to US$24, two days).

LAGUNAS & RESERVA NACIONAL PACAYA-SAMIRIA

Lagunas is a remote village with no money-changing facilities and limited food. Spanish-speaking guides for visiting Reserva Nacional Pacaya-Samiria charge less than those in Iquitos. Going rates are US$15 per person per day, including accommodation but not food. To avoid price-cutting, there is now an official guides association, **ESTPEL** (☎ 065-40-1007).

The best hotel is **Hostal Miraflores** (☎ 065-40-1001; Miraflores 249; s/d US$3/5), with clean rooms and a shared shower. **Hostal La Sombra** (☎ 065-40-1063; per person US$2) has hot, stuffy little rooms with a shared shower. Both hotels provide cheap meals.

Boats from Yurimaguas take 10 to 12 hours and leave most days.

IQUITOS

With almost 500,000 inhabitants, Iquitos is a friendly, sassy and slightly manic jungle metropolis that holds the title of the largest city in the world without road links. Originally founded as a remote Jesuit mission in the 1750s, the town spent many of its early years fending off attacks from Indian tribes who didn't particularly want to be converted, thank you very much. However, the city's principle growth spurt came with a rubber boom in the late 19th century, and traces of boom-town opulence can still be seen in central mansions and attractive tiled walls.

Then, in the 1960s, oil propelled Iquitos to become a prosperous modern town once again. Be warned that everything must be 'imported' by boat or air, so costs are high. There are also few cars; most people get around on *motocarros*, and the streets buzz incessantly with revving motorbikes zipping past.

Information

EMERGENCY

Clínica Ana Stahl (☎ 065-25-2535; Av La Marina 285; 🕒 24 hr)

Tourism Police (☎ 065-24-2081; Lores 834)

IMMIGRATION OFFICES

Brazil has a consul in Leticia, Colombia.

Migraciónes (☎ 065-23-5371; M Cáceres cuadra 18) Extends tourist cards, but get entry/exit stamps at the border.

INTERNET ACCESS

Manugare Internet (Próspero 273)

Sured Internet (☎ 065-23-6119; Morona 213; 🕸)

LAUNDRY

Lavandería Imperial (Putumayo 150; 🕒 8am-8pm Mon-Sat) Coin-operated.

MONEY

Banks (see map, p897) change traveler's checks, give credit-card advances and have ATMs. Changing Brazilian or Colombian currency is best done at the border.

Western Union (☎ 065-23-5182; Napo 359)

POST

Serpost (Arica 402; 🕒 8am-6pm Mon-Fri, 8am-4:30pm Sat)

TOURIST OFFICES

Iquitos Monthly is a free newspaper in English aimed at tourists.

Gerald Mayeaux (cajafesa@hotmail.com) A former tourist office director who now dispenses information from Yellow Rose of Texas at Putumayo 180.

INRENA's Reserva Nacional Pacaya-Samiria office (☎ 065-23-2980; Ricardo Palma 113, 4th fl; 🕒 8am-4pm Mon-Fri)

IQUITOS

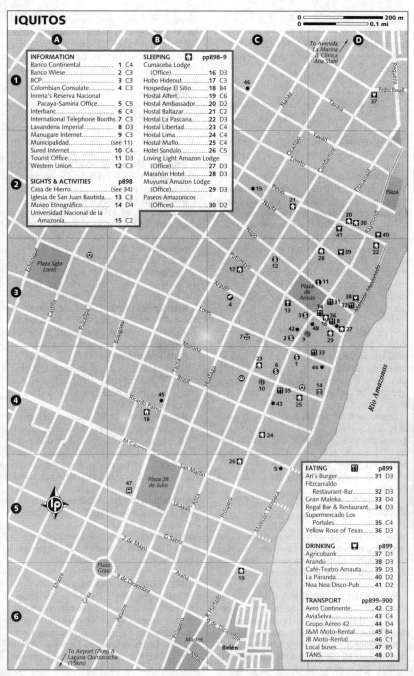

INFORMATION			
Banco Continental	1	C4	
Banco Wiese	2	C3	
BCP	3	C3	
Colombian Consulate	4	C3	
Inrena's Reserva Nacional			
Pacaya-Samiria Office	5	C5	
Interbanc	6	C4	
International Telephone Booths	7	C3	
Lavandería Imperial	8	D3	
Manugare Internet	9	C3	
Municipalidad	(see 11)		
Sured Internet	10	C4	
Tourist Office	11	D3	
Western Union	12	C3	

SIGHTS & ACTIVITIES		**p898**	
Casa de Hierro	(see 34)		
Iglesia de San Juan Bautista	13	C3	
Museo Etnográfico	14	D4	
Universidad Nacional de la			
Amazonía	15	C2	

SLEEPING		**pp898–9**	
Cumaceba Lodge			
(Office)	16	D3	
Hobo Hideout	17	C3	
Hospedaje El Sitio	18	B4	
Hostal Alfert	19	C6	
Hostal Ambassador	20	D2	
Hostal Baltazar	21	C2	
Hostal La Pascana	22	D3	
Hostal Libertad	23	C4	
Hostal Lima	24	C4	
Hostal Maflo	25	C4	
Hotel Sandalo	26	C5	
Loving Light Amazon Lodge			
(Office)	27	D3	
Marañón Hotel	28	D3	
Muyuma Amazon Lodge			
(Office)	29	D3	
Paseos Amazonicos			
(Offices)	30	D2	

EATING		**p899**	
Ari's Burger	31	D3	
Fitzcarraldo			
Restaurant-Bar	32	D3	
Gran Maloka	33	D4	
Regal Bar & Restaurant	34	D3	
Supermercado Los			
Portales	35	C4	
Yellow Rose of Texas	36	D3	

DRINKING		**p899**	
Agricobank	37	D1	
Arandú	38	D3	
Café-Teatro Amauta	39	D3	
La Paranda	40	D2	
Noa Noa Disco-Pub	41	D2	

TRANSPORT		**pp899–900**	
Aero Continente	42	C3	
AviaSelva	43	C4	
Grupo Aéreo 42	44	D4	
J&M Moto-Rental	45	B4	
JB Moto-Rental	46	C1	
Local buses	47	B5	
TANS	48	D3	

PERU

iPerú (☎ 065-26-0251; Airport; ☺ 8:30am-1:30pm & 4:30-8:30pm)
Tourist Office (☎ 065-23-5621; Napo 232; ☺ 8am-8pm Mon-Fri, 9am-1pm Sat) Poorly signed on the Plaza de Armas.

Sights

The **Casa de Hierro** (Iron House; cnr Putumayo & Raymondi), designed by Eiffel, was made in Paris and imported piece by piece into Iquitos around 1890, though it looks like what it is – a bunch of metal sheets bolted together.

The **Museo Etnográfico** (Malecón at Morona; ☺ Mon-Fri), inside one of Iquitos' oldest houses, features 76 startlingly lifelike statues of different Amazonian Indians made by covering Indians with mud to obtain a mold!

The floating shantytown of **Belén** houses thousands of people living on huts that rise and fall with the river, and canoes float from hut to hut selling and trading jungle produce. Boatmen will paddle you around during the November to May high-water season; it's difficult to navigate in other months. This is a poor area, but relatively safe in daylight. The **market**, on the west side of Belén, has piles of dried frogs and fish, armadillo shells, piranha teeth and almost everything else, including the kitchen sink. Look for the bark of the Chuchuhuasi tree that is soaked in rum and used as a tonic in local bars.

Laguna Quistacocha (admission US$1), 15km south of Iquitos, features a small zoo of local fauna, a museum, swimming areas and a fish hatchery with paiche (2m-long Amazonian river fish; good eating but becoming overfished). Minibuses leave frequently from Plaza 28 de Julio.

Sleeping

IN TOWN

Mosquitoes are rarely a serious problem, so mosquito netting is not provided. The May to September high season sees a slight rate increase. All hotels listed have private baths and fans unless otherwise indicated.

Hostal Alfert (☎ 065-23-4105; G Saenz 001; s/d US$4.50/7.25) With a view of the river and warm showers, this place attracts shoestringers, though the neighborhood is dodgy.

Hobo Hideout (☎ 065-23-4099; hobohideout@yahoo.com; Putumayo 437; dm US$5, s/d US$7.50/9, with bath US$10/11.50) A cool travelers' vibe reaches out

through the iron-grill gate, and kitchen, laundry, 2 sq meter plunge pool with waterfall, bar and cable TV room draw international hobos. One (pricier) room towers above the rest on jungle-style stilts; others are small and dark.

Hostal Lima (☎ 065-23-5152; Próspero 549; s/d US$7.50/10) A small courtyard opens onto tight but tidy rooms (the fans are window-mounted for lack of space), with baths so small the hot shower sprays the toilet. Upstairs rooms are better and breezier.

Hospedaje El Sitio (☎ 065-23-4932; R Palma 545; s/d US$7.50/10) Clean, extra-large rooms with TVs are the draw.

Hostal Maflo (☎ 065-24-1257; hostalmaflo@mixmail.com; Morona 177; s/d US$7.50/11) Simple, plain rooms are set back from the street and feature hot water and cable TV, and include continental breakfast – a good deal.

Hostal La Pascana (☎ 065-23-1418; pascana@tsi.com.pe; Pevas 133; s/d/tr US$9/12/15) With a small plant-filled garden, this safe and friendly place is deservedly popular with travelers.

Hotel Sandalo (☎ 065-23-4761; sandalo@iquitos.net; Próspero 616; s/d with breakfast US$20/25; ☒) Modern, motel-style carpeted rooms with cable TV, minifridge, hot private baths and phone.

Hostal Ambassador (☎ 065-23-3110; Pevas 260; s/d with breakfast US$20/30; ☒) Comfortable rooms, cable TV, hot private baths and free airport transfers are provided, and a restaurant offers room service.

Marañón Hotel (☎ 065-24-2673; hotel.maranon@terra.com.pe; Nauta 285; s/d with breakfast US$30/35; ☒ ☒) Sparklingly new, with light tiles everywhere and a restaurant with room service. The rooms have notably good-sized bathrooms by Iquitos standards, with hot water.

Other recommendations:
Hostal Baltazar (☎ 065-23-2240; Condamine 265; s/d US$7.50/10, with bath US$12/17; ☒) Quiet, clean and decent.
Hostal Libertad (☎ 065-23-5763; Arica 361; s/d US$7.50/11.50, d with air-con US$15; ☒) Simple rooms with electric showers; some with cable TV.

JUNGLE LODGES & CAMPS

Over a dozen jungle lodges in the Iquitos area have prices from US$25 to over US$100 per day depending on services, number of days, number of guests and your bargaining abilities. Lodge offices are found in central Iquitos (see the Iquitos map for locations, p897), or ask at the tourist office. Lodges further off into the Amazon itself offer better chances of seeing wildlife. Budget travelers have recommended Sinchicuy, Cumaceba, Muyuma, Yarapa River and Loving Light Amazon lodges.

Check carefully if arranging jungle camping trips; some guides are crooks! Try to avoid street touts and self-styled guides selling jungle tours as they tend to bump up prices.

Eating

Lidia's (Bolognesi 1181; mains US$2-4; ☼ Mon-Sat) So homey it's practically inside Lidia's living room, with plenty of sizzling grills straight from the barbecue. Note that there is no sign out the front.

Ari's Burger (Próspero 127; mains US$2-6; ☼ 7am-3am) Squeaky clean and on the main plaza. Locally dubbed 'gringolandia' and great for American-style food.

Yellow Rose of Texas (Putumayo 180; breakfasts US$1.50, mains US$5-7.50; ☼ 24 hr) Specializes in Texas barbecue, and has games, sports TV and heavenly ice-cold beers.

Regal Bar & Restaurant (Putumayo 182; mains US$4-9) Inside the Iron House, with a balcony overlooking the plaza; a great spot for a pint.

Fitzcarraldo Restaurant-Bar (Napo 100; mains US$3-7) Anchors a block of upscale riverside restaurants.

Gran Maloka (Lores 170; mains US$3.50-9; ☼) Inside an atmospheric mansion from rubber-boom days. The menu is adventurous (curried caiman anyone?) but has plenty of less-startling options. Good for a splurge.

For DIY, stop by **Supermercado Los Portales** (cnr Próspero & Morona).

Drinking

Ready for an all-nighter? A good beer bar is **Arandú** (Napo), next to the Fitzcarraldo. **Café-Teatro Amauta** (Nauta 250) has live Peruvian music and a well-stocked bar of local drinks. **Jungle Jim's** is a bar that's great for darts, beer and chat, and totally surrounded by **Yellow Rose of Texas** (Putumayo 180; ☼ 24 hr).

For dancing, **Agricobank** (cnr Condamine & Pablo Rosell; admission US$1.75) is a huge, outdoor place where hundreds of locals gather to let loose. The trendier **Noa Noa Disco-Pub** (Pevas 292) charges a US$6 cover. Also popular for dancing, **La Paranda** (Pevas 174) sees locals strutting their stuff on weekends.

Getting There & Away
PERU
Air
Iquitos' airport is 7km south of town. **Aero Continente** (☎ 065-24-3489; Próspero 232) and **TANS** (☎ 065-23-1071; Próspero 215) are the main airlines serving Lima (US$71), with two or more flights a day. TANS flies daily to Pucallpa. Some Lima flights stop at Tarapoto, Chiclayo or Trujillo. **AviaSelva** (Próspero 439) is a new airline with twice-weekly flights to Leticia, Colombia, and to Yurimaguas and Tarapoto on Saturday. **Grupo Aéreo 42** (☎ 065-23-4632; Lores 127) is a military airline with flights to small jungle towns, though schedules are highly unreliable. Airport departure tax on domestic/international flights is US$3.50/10.

Boat
Boat departures are much more reliable than flights. Large boats leave Puerto Masusa, on Av La Marina, 3km north of the town center. Boats have blackboards with departure information (though boats often leave hours or days late). Passengers can sleep aboard (usually in hammocks) while waiting for departure. Watch luggage carefully.

Boats to Pucallpa (four to seven days) or Yurimaguas (three to six days) cost US$20 to US$30 per person. Boats leave about three times a week to Pucallpa, more often to Yurimaguas, but less if the river is low.

COLOMBIAN, BRAZILIAN & ECUADORIAN BORDER CROSSINGS
Colombia, Brazil and Peru share a three-way border. The biggest town is Leticia (Colombia), linked with Tabatinga (Brazil) by road (a short walk). Leticia has the best choice of hotels, restaurants, money-changing facilities and a hospital. On the south bank, opposite Leticia/Tabatinga, is Santa Rosa (Peru), which lacks hotels.

Boats to Santa Rosa at the border with Brazil and Colombia leave Peru every few days, take two to three days and cost US$15 to US$20 (bargain hard). The tourist office can call the riverboat captain for departure dates.

Fast launches to Leticia (Colombia) and Tabatinga (Brazil) charge US$50 and take 12 hours. Several companies on Raymondi at Loreto offer 6am departures every two days.

PERU

Amazon Tours & Cruises (☎ 065-23-3931; www .amazontours.net; Requena 336) has expensive weekly cruises on comfortable ships that go to Leticia (Colombia).

Ask the riverboat captain to stop at the Peruvian guard post in Santa Rosa for entry/ exit formalities.

To enter or leave Colombia, get your passport stamped in Leticia. For Brazil, formalities are normally carried out in Tabatinga, although the town of Benjamin Constant, an hour downriver, also has an immigration office. You don't need stamps for all three countries – just the one you are leaving and the one you are entering. Regulations change, but the riverboat captains know where to go. Don't try to enter a country without first getting the required exit stamp.

You can travel between the three countries without formalities, as long as you stay in the tri-border area. As soon as you leave the border ports, however, your documents must be in order.

Boats to Iquitos leave from Tabatinga every few days (about US$20, 2½ days). Alternatively, the express boat (US$50, 10 hours) leaves most days with various companies.

Boats to Manaus (Brazil) leave from Tabatinga. The fare is about US$100 in a stuffy shared cabin (less for your hammock) for the four- to six-day trip, including very basic meals. Bottled soft drinks and beer are available.

Leticia and Tabatinga have airports, with flights into Colombia and Brazil, respectively. Santa Rosa has three flights a week to Iquitos.

It is also possible, though arduous, to travel by cargo boat between Iquitos and Coca, Ecuador, via the Amazon and Napo Rivers. For more information see Coca (p671) and Nuevo Rocafuerte (p671) in the Ecuador chapter.

Getting Around

Buses and trucks for nearby destinations, including the airport, leave from Plaza 28 de Julio. Taxis to the airport cost US$3 or *moto-carros* US$2. **JB Moto-Rental** (Yavari 702) and **J&M Moto-Rental** (Tacna at R Palma) rent motorcycles, both for US$2.50 an hour. Boats to take you around the floating shantytown of Belén can be hired on the Belén waterfront.

PUERTO MALDONADO

Founded a century ago, Puerto Maldonado has been a rubber boom town, a logging center and, recently, a gold and oil center. It's a fast-growing town with a frontier feel and is the most important port of the department of Madre de Dios. The jungle around Puerto Maldonado is second growth rather than virgin forest. The most inexpensive activity is to take the five-minute ferry ride across the Río Madre de Dios; from here you can pick up the road that eventually leads to Iñapari. Most people come here to participate in a jungle lodge experience.

Information
EMERGENCY
Social Seguro Hospital (☎ 082-57-1711; km 3 on the road to Cuzco)

IMMIGRATION OFFICES
To leave Peru via Puerto Heath for Bolivia, check first with officials in Puerto Maldonado. Iñapari now has a border post.
Migraciónes (☎ 082-57-1069; 26 de Diciembre 356)

INTERNET ACCESS
UnAMad (2 de Mayo 287; US$1.50 per hr)
ZonaVirtual.com (Velarde near Plaza de Armas)

LAUNDRY
Lavandería (Velarde 898)

MONEY
BCP (Plaza de Armas) Changes US cash or traveler's checks and has a Visa ATM.
Casa de Cambio (cnr Puno & G Prada) Good rates for US dollars. Brazilian cruzeiros and Bolivian pesos are hard to negotiate.

TOURIST OFFICES
INRENA (☎ 082-57-1604; Cuzco 135) National park office, which also collects entrance fees; US$8.50 on the north side of the Río Tambopata, US$20 if you enter from the south.
Ministerio de Industria y Turismo (☎ 082-57-1413; Fitzcarrald 252)

Courses
Tambopata Language Center (☎ 082-57-6014; www.tambopata-language.com; Cajamarca 895) Spanish classes, homestays and jungle tours.

Tours
If you haven't organized a prearranged river and jungle tour (see p845), local ar-

PUERTO MALDONADO

INFORMATION	
Banco de la Nación	1 C2
BCP	2 C2
Bolivian Consulate	3 C1
Casa de Cambio	4 B2
Inrena	5 C2
Lavandería	6 B3
Migraciones (Immigration) office	7 C2
Ministerio de Industria y Turismo	8 A3
UnAMad	9 B2
ZonaVirtual.com	10 C2

SIGHTS & ACTIVITIES	p900
Tambopata Language Center	11 B2

SLEEPING	pp901–2
Corto Maltes office	12 C1
Hospedaje Rey Port	13 C2
Hospedaje Royal Inn	14 B2
Hostal Cahuata	15 A3
Hostal El Solar	16 B2
Hostal Moderno	17 B2
Hotel Wilson	18 B2

EATING	p902
Chifa Wa-Seng	19 C2
El Califa	20 A1
El Tigre	21 A2
La Casa Nostra	22 B2
La Estrella	23 B2
Pizzería El Hornito/Chez Maggy	24 C1
Pollería Astoria	25 B3

DRINKING	p902
Discoteca Anaconda	26 C1
Discoteca Witite	27 C1

TRANSPORT	p902
Aero Continente	28 B2
Empresa Transportes Imperial (colectivo taxi to Iñapari)	29 A2
Ferry Crossing Dock	(see 30)
River-Boat Hire	30 D1
TANS	31 C1
Trucks to Cuzco	32 A3

rangements are possible. There are several local guides, some very reputable and experienced, others just interested in making quick money. Shop around, never pay for a tour beforehand and, when you agree on a price, make sure that it includes the return trip!

Guides charge US$25 to US$60 per person per day depending on destination and number of people. **Victor Yohamona** (☎ 082-968-6279; victorguideperu@hotmail.com) is a well-known guide. Also recommended is **Hernán Llavé** (☎ 082-57-2243), who speaks some English. Another honest freelancer with infectious enthusiasm is **Willy Wither** (☎ 082-57-2014; compured@compured.limaperu.net), who speaks some English and German. Readers have recommended **Nadir Gnan** (☎ 082-57-1900), who speaks English and Italian.

Sleeping

Watch for overcharging and expect cold showers at these places to stay.

Hostal Moderno (☎ 082-57-1063; Billinghurst 359; s/d/tr US$4.50/6/7.50) Despite the name, this is a simple, family-run place that has been around for decades, though receiving a regular lick of paint.

Hostal Cahuata (☎ 082-57-1526; Fitzcarrald 517; s/d US$3/6, with bath US$6/9) Market-side; quietens down at night and has small, neat rooms with fans.

Also worth a peek are basic **Hostal El Solar** (☎ 082-57-1634; G Prada 445; s/d 4.50/7.50, with bath US$6/10), **Hotel Wilson** (☎ 082-57-2838; G Prada 355; s/d US$4.50/7.50, with bath US$7.50/10.50), the clean **Hospedaje Royal Inn** (☎ 082-57-1048; 2 de Mayo 333; s/d with bath US$7.50/10.50) and **Hospedaje Rey Port** (☎ 082-57-1177; Velarde 457; s/d US$6/9, with bath US$10/14), which has good views from upper floors.

Iñapari Lodge (☎ 082-57-2575; per person US$6) Five kilometers from the town center near the airport, this is a rustic hostel with communal showers, restaurant and bar. Inexpensive horse-riding, bicycle and other tours can be arranged.

Hotel Don Carlos (☎ 082-57-1323; hdoncarlosmaldonado@viabcp.com; León Velarde 1271; s with breakfast US$20-29, d US$25-36 with breakfast; 🛏 🖵) Wood-paneled rooms have hot showers, minifridge and TV. The tranquil location 1km southwest of the

PERU

town center overlooks the Río Tambopata. Airport transfer is included.

Outside Puerto Maldonado are a dozen jungle lodges.

Eating

There are no fancy restaurants in Puerto Maldonado, though prices are high.

Pizzería El Hornito/Chez Maggy (Carrión 271; pizzas US$3.50-8.50; ☺ evening only) Popular hangout serving the best Italian in town.

Chifa Wa-Seng (Cuzco 244; mains US$4-6; ☺ evening only Mon) Offers the Amazon version of Chinese food.

El Califa (Piura 266; mains US$2-5; ☺ 10am-4:30pm Mon-Sat) A rustic, sultry place with good regional specialties, including palm-heart salad, *juanes*, fried plantains and game dishes.

El Tigre (Tacna 456; mains US$4) Recommended for its *ceviche* and local fish dishes.

La Casa Nostra (Velarde 515; snacks US$1-3) The best café/meeting spot in town. Serves breakfasts, great juices, snacks and coffee.

La Estrella (Velarde 474; mains US$2) This neonlit chicken restaurant resembles an American fast-food joint.

Pollería Astoria (Velarde 701; mains US$2) A dimly lit wooden *pollería*, with more of an Amazonian feel.

In the Mercado Modelo, look for freshly squeezed fruit juices and other jungle staples, such as *fariña*, a muesli-like yucca concoction and *pan de arroz* (rice bread) in the early morning.

Drinking

A handful of nightclubs sputter into life late on weekend nights. The best known is **Discoteca Witite** (Velarde 153). Also try **Discoteca Anaconda** (Loreto 2nd block) on the Plaza de Armas.

Getting There & Away
PERU
Air

The airport is 7km west of town. *Colectivos* from the airport are US$1.50, mototaxis are US$2. Flights go every morning to Lima (US$68) via Cuzco (US$43) with **Aero Continente** (☎ 082-57-2004; Velarde 584) and **TANS** (☎ 082-57-1429; Velarde 147). LanPeru has three flights a week.

Boat

Boats at the Madre de Dios ferry dock make local excursions and travel down to the Bolivian border (US$80 per boat). Upriver boats to Manu are hard to find and expensive.

Truck

Trucks to Cuzco during the highland dry season leave from the Mercado Modelo. The rough 500km trip (US$15) takes three days, depending on road and weather conditions. Fly if you can afford it.

BRAZILIAN BORDER CROSSING

A track to Iñapari, on the Brazilian border, is open. Wet-season travel is reportedly not possible but, during the drier months, *colectivos* to Iñapari (US$8, four hours) leave from **Empresa Transportes Imperial** (☎ 082-57-4274), on the fifth block of Ica, when they have four passengers. Other companies on the same block also advertise this trip.

Iberia, 170km north of Puerto Maldonado, has a couple of basic hotels. Iñapari, 70km beyond Iberia, has a basic hotel and an airport. Both towns have occasional flights from Cuzco, but most people come by road. From Iñapari, wade across the Río Acre to Assis, Brazil, which has a better hotel and a dry-season road to Brasiléia and Río Branco. Peruvian exit and entry formalities are conducted in Puerto Maldonado.

BOLIVIAN BORDER CROSSING

Boats can be hired to the Bolivian border at the village of Puerto Pardo (about US$100, half a day). Cheaper passages are available on cargo boats, but these run infrequently. From Puerto Heath, on the Bolivian side, it takes several days (even weeks) to arrange a boat (expensive) to Riberalta, where road and air connections are available. Travel in a group to share costs and try to avoid months when the water is too low. Make sure to get exit stamps at the immigration office in Puerto Maldonado before leaving Peru. The Peruvian and Bolivian border guards can stamp you out of and into their respective countries if your passport is in order. Few foreigners travel this route. Trips are more frequent during the dry season.

Getting Around

There are several motorcycle-rental outlets, mainly on G Prada between Velarde and Puno, charging US$1.15 per hour for small, 100cc bikes.

AROUND PUERTO MALDONADO

There are about a dozen jungle lodges along the Ríos Tambopata and Madre de Dios, running either upstream (east) or downstream (southwest) of Puerto Maldonado. Lodges and jungle tours are expensive, but to get the most out of your visit to this jungle town, it's well worth forking out the extra cash.

An inexpensive lodge in Puerto Maldonado itself is the family-run **Willy Mejía Cepa Lodge** (Velarde 487; per person US$20), which has been offering basic accommodations and expeditions (in Spanish) for 16 years. Further down the Madre de Dios, the comfortable **Reserva Amazonica Lodge** (in Cuzco ☎ 084-24-5314; www.inkaterra.com; 3 days & 2 nights standard s/d US$183/314, ste US$292/480) is run by Inkaterra.

Inotawa (☎/fax 82-57-2511; Fonavi J9, Puerto Maldonando; 3 days & 2 nights per person US$120; each extra night US$35) is a good budget option, with German-, French- and English-speaking guides available on advance request.

But perhaps the pick of the bunch for budget travelers is the **Picaflor Research Center** (Picaflor_rc@yahoo.com – allow up to two weeks for response; www.picaflor.org), 74km from Puerto Maldonado. Visitors can volunteer, research or take guided tours. Volunteers work three hours daily and pay US$140 for 10 nights of food and accommodations (plus park fees and US$3 transportation from Puerto Maldonado). Researchers pay about US$20 a night and tourists pay US$190 for an all-inclusive three-day, two-night tour.

There are plenty of other – pricier – options.

PERU DIRECTORY

ACCOMMODATIONS

Hotels and hostels are the norm, and camp sites are rare. Cuzco and Lima are by far the most expensive places to stay. During the high season (June to August) and major festivals (p905), accommodations are more likely to be full and top prices can be charged. Out of prime time, however, you can find incredibly good deals, so rates mentioned (generally US$3 to US$14 per person) are highly variable. Budget hotels usually have hot (or more likely, tepid) showers at least some of the time. They may not accept or honor phone reservations. In other months (except for major holidays) expect lower prices and try bargaining.

ACTIVITIES

Trekkers pack your boots – the variety of trails in Peru is staggering. The Cordillera Blanca (p882) can't be beat for peaks, while the nearby Cordillera Huayhuash (p882) is similarly stunning. But if you've heard of *any* trek in Peru, you will have heard of the world-famous Inca Trail to Machu Picchu (p857). The spectacular six-day Ausangate Circuit (p863) or the trek to the newly rediscovered Inca site Choquequirau (p863) are just a few other possibilities. Alternatively, get down in one of the world's deepest canyons – the Cañón del Colca (p830).

But why stop with hiking? Peru has plenty more high-adrenaline activities to get your pulse racing. River running around Cuzco (p842) and Arequipa (p830) offers a multitude of day runs and longer hauls (grade III to IV+ rapids).

Gearing up for some downhill adventures? Easy or demanding single-track trails also await mountain bikers in Huaraz (p883), Cuzco (p842) and Arequipa (p827), or for something completely different, slide down humungous dunes in the desert on sand boards in Huacachina (p819).

Fancy something more uplifting? Paragliding is an up-and-coming sport in Peru, with promising companies in Lima (p808) and Urubamba (p853). Also on the up is mountaineering (p830). Huascarán (6768m) is for experts, but easier peaks abound near Huaraz and Arequipa.

Horse riding can be arranged widely, but for a real splurge, take a ride on a graceful Peruvian Paso horse near Lima (p808) or Urubamba (p853). Surfing (p807) also has a big fan base in Peru and there are some radical waves up north, especially around Huanchaco (p876) and Máncora (p880).

Alternatively, if bird watching gets you in a flap, head for the Amazon, Paracas and the Cañón del Colca just for starters. See p798 for more information).

BOOKS

If you read only one book about the Incas, make it the lucid and lively *Conquest of the Incas* by John Hemming. Or to get a grip of *all* of Peru's scores of bygone cultures, *The*

PERU

Ancient Kingdoms of Peru by Nigel Davies is excellent.

Travel writing on Peru also abounds. *The White Rock* by Hugh Thomson is an account of an explorer's search for Inca archaeological sites throughout the Peruvian Andes, ending at Machu Picchu.

Tahir Shah's book *Trail of Feathers* describes the author's quest to uncover what lies behind the 'birdmen' legends in the Peruvian desert, eventually leading him into the remote Amazon.

Inca-Kola by Matthew Parris is a tongue-in-cheek account of the backpacking author's travels in Peru.

Joe Kane's *Running the Amazon* describes an exciting expedition from the source of the Amazon (high in the Peruvian Andes) to the Atlantic.

Touching the Void by Joe Simpson is a harrowing account of surviving a mountaineering accident in Peru's Cordillera Huayhuash.

BUSINESS HOURS

Shops open at 9am or 10am and close between 6pm and 8pm. A two- or three-hour lunch break is common. There are 24-hour supermarkets in Lima, and shops may stay open through lunch in big cities. Most shops close on Sunday. Banks and offices keep highly variable hours.

CLIMATE

June to August, the highland dry season, is the most popular time to travel in Peru. During the coastal summer (late December to early April), the sky clears and sun breaks through. January to March are the summer months on the coast, and many Peruvians vacation at this time. During the rest of the year, the *garúa* (coastal fog) moves in on the central and south coasts. Inland, above the coastal *garúa*, however, it is sunny for most of the year.

In the Andes proper, the dry season runs from May to September. The mountains can reach freezing temperatures at night, but enjoy glorious sunshine during the day. The wet season in the mountains extends from October to May, at its worst in late January and February. The Amazon lowlands have a similar weather pattern.

For more information and climate charts see the South America Directory (p1028).

DANGERS & ANNOYANCES

Peru has its fair share of traveler hassles, but they can mostly be avoided by exercising common sense. The most common problem is theft, either stealth or snatch – theft by violent mugging is rare, though not to be ruled out. Keep your wits about you and you will have few problems. Avoid unlicensed taxis and take good quality buses to lower the risk of being delayed or having an accident. Do not get involved in drugs. Lima's prisons have more than their fair share of gringos and gringas who did, and are being repaid with long-term incarceration.

Terrorism is largely a thing of the past in Peru, but narco-trafficking is a risk. Areas to avoid are the Río Huallaga valley between Tingo María and Tarapoto (these towns are safe but the area between is prime drug country).

Soroche (altitude sickness) can be quite discomforting and can even be fatal. For more information, see p1059.

EMBASSIES & CONSULATES
Embassies & Consulates in Peru

Australia Lima (Map pp802-3; ☎ 01-222-8281; fax 221-4996; losani@ibm.net.pe; Victor Belaúnde 398, San Isidro) Limited services only at Honorary Consul.

Bolivia Lima (Map pp802-3; ☎ 01-422-8231; Los Castaños 235, San Isidro; ☎ 9:30-12:30pm); Puerto Maldonado (Map p901; Loreto 268, upstairs)

Brazil Lima (Map p809; ☎ 01-421-5650; fax 445-2421; José Pardo 850, Miraflores; ☼ 9:30am-1pm & 2-5pm); Puno (Map p834; ☎ 051-35-1251; Arequipa 120; ☼ 8:30am-2pm Mon-Fri)

Canada Lima (Map p809; ☎ 01-444-4015; lima@dfait-maeci.gc.ca; Federico Gerdes 130, Miraflores; ☼ 8am-5pm)

Chile www.minrel.cl in Spanish; Lima (Map pp802-3; ☎ 01-221-2817, 221-2818; Javier Prado Oeste 790, San Isidro; ☼ 9am-1pm); Tacna (Map p823; ☎ 052-72-3063; ☼ 8am-1pm Mon-Fri)

Colombia Iquitos (Map p897; ☎ 065-23-1461; Araujo 431); Lima (Map pp802-3; ☎ 01-441-0954; fax 441-9806; Jorge Basadre 1580, San Isidro; ☼ 9am-1pm)

Ecuador Lima (Map pp802-3; ☎ 01-440-9991; fax 442-4182; Las Palmeras 356, San Isidro; ☼ 9am-1pm & 3-6pm); Tumbes (Map p881; Bolívar 123; ☼ 9am-1pm & 4-6pm Mon-Fri)

France Lima (Map pp802-3; ☎ 01-215-8400; embajada@ambafrance-pe.org; Arequipa 3415, San Isidro; ☼ 9-11am)

Germany Lima (Map p809; ☎ 01-212-5016; kanzlei@embajada-alemana.org.pe; Arequipa 4202, Miraflores; ☼ 9am-noon)

Israel Lima (Map pp802-3; ☎ /fax 01-433-4431; Natalio Sánchez 125, 6th floor, Santa Beatriz; ☾ 10am-1pm)
The Netherlands Lima (Map pp802-3; ☎ 01-476-1069; fax 475-6536; Principal 190, Santa Catalina; ☾ 9am-noon)
New Zealand Lima (Map pp802-3; ☎ 01-222-5022; Alfonso.Rey@newzealandmilk.com; S.A. Av Victor Andres Belaunde 147, Edificio Real Tres-Oficina 1102, San Isidro)
UK Iquitos (Map p897; ☎ 065-22-2732; at Regal Bar &Restaurant, Putumayo 182); Lima (Map p809;
☎ 01-617-3000; britemb@terra.com.pe; José Larco 1301, piso 22, Miraflores; ☾ 8am-noon)
USA Lima (Map pp802-3; ☎ 01-434-3000; http://us embassy.state.gov/lima; Av Encalada, Cuadra 17, Surco; ☾ 8am-5pm)

Peruvian Embassies & Consulates

Peruvian embassies are found in all neighboring countries. There are also representatives in the following locations:
Australia Canberra (☎ 02-6273-8752; embassy@emba peru.org.au; Suite 8, 40 Brisbane Ave, Barton, ACT 2600)
Canada Ottawa (☎ 613-238-1777; emperuca@bellnet.ca; Suite 1901, 130 Albert St, Ottawa, Ontario K1P 5G4)
France Paris (☎ 331-5370-4200; amb.perou@noos.fr; Av Kleber, 75116 París 50)
Germany Berlin (☎ 030-206-4103; eprfa@aol.com; Mohrenstrasse 42, 10117 Berlín)
Japan Tokyo (☎ 3-346-4243; fax 3-3409-7589; embperu tokyo@embperujapan.org; 4-4-27, Higashi 1-Chome, Shibuya-ku, Tokyo)
The Netherlands The Hague (☎ 70-365-3500; info@ embassyofperu.nl; Nassauplein 4, 2585 EA, The Hague)
New Zealand Wellington (☎ 04-499-8087; embassy .peru@xtra.co.nz; Level 8, Cigna House, 40 Mercer St, Wellington, PO BOX 2566)
UK London (☎ 0207-235-1917; postmaster@peruembassy -uk.com; 52 Sloane St, London SW1X 9SP)
USA Washington (☎ 202-833-9860/9; lepruwash@aol.com; 1700 Massachusetts Ave NW, Washington DC 20036)

FESTIVALS & EVENTS

La Virgen de la Candelaria (Candlemas; February 2) A colorful highland fiesta, particularly in the Puno area.
Carnaval (February/March) Water fights galore.
Semana Santa (Holy Week; March/April) Religious processions throughout the week.
Corpus Christi (June) Dramatic processions in Cuzco.
Inti Raymi (Winter solstice; June 24) The greatest Inca festival, which brings thousands of visitors to Cuzco.
La Virgen del Carmen (July 16) Street dancing in Paucartambo and Pisac near Cuzco, and Pucara near Lake Titicaca.
El Señor de los Milagros (Lord of the Miracles; October 18) Huge (and purple) religious processions in Lima.

Puno Day (November 5) Spectacular costumes and dancing in Puno commemorate the legendary emergence of the first Inca, Manco Capac, from Lake Titicaca.

FILMS & VIDEOS

Lonely Planet's *Peru* video is worth investing in for a peek at the country before you go. *Manu* in PBS' Living Eden series is phenomenal, as is *Keep the River on Your Right*, the story of Tobias Schneebaum, who lived in the Peruvian jungle for several months, and participated in village raids and cannibalism. The 2002 movie *The Dancer Upstairs* is a cool, tense political thriller based on the search for the leader of the Shining Path. Shot partly in Ecuador, and featuring dialogue in Quechua, the film is a fascinating if grim portrait of the Peruvian psychological landscape.

FOOD & DRINK

Travelers with a tight budget and a strong stomach can indulge in food from street and market stalls if it's freshly cooked. *Chifas* (Chinese restaurants) are often good value, and many restaurants offer a *menú del día* (set lunch), consisting of a soup and second course for only US$1 to US$3. Better restaurants add 18% to 31% in tips and tax – ask before you eat.

Food tends towards the spicy, but *aji* (chili condiments) are generally served separately. Vegetarianism is a small but fast-growing industry in Peru, and hole-in-the-wall joints are popping up in all major cities and tourist destinations. Or if you're sick of seafood, crying off *cuy* or feeling ill at the very idea of Cajamarca's specialty, cow brains, every town has its resident *pollería*, grills churning out chickens for the masses, plus other international favorites like pizza and pasta.

Peruvian Cuisine

The following list includes some of the most typical Peruvian snacks and dishes.
  We dare you to try:
Ceviche erótico Mixed seafood marinated in lemon, chili and onions, served cold with a boiled potato or yam; considered an aphrodisiac!
Chirimoya Reptilian-looking custard apple with sweet interior that looks like frogspawn; tastes better than it looks.
Cuy chactado Grilled guinea pig.
Lomo de Alpaca Alpaca meat tastes like beef, but has only about half the fat.

PERU

WARNING

Avoid food prepared from endangered animals. Sometimes *chanco marino* (dolphin) may be served up or, in the jungle areas, *huveos de charapa* (tortoise eggs), *motelo* (turtle) or even *mono* (monkey).

Lomo saltado Chopped steak fried with onions, tomatoes and potatoes, served with rice.
Palta a la jardinera Avocado stuffed with cold vegetables and mayonnaise; *a la reina* is stuffed with chicken salad.
Roccoto relleno Spicy bell pepper stuffed with ground meat; very hot!
Sopa a la criolla Lightly spiced noodle soup with beef, egg, milk and vegetables; *a la criolla* describes spicy foods.

Drinks
ALCOHOLIC DRINKS
There are about a dozen kinds of palatable and inexpensive beer, both light, lager-type beers and sweet, dark beers. Dark beer is *malta* or *cerveza negra*. Cuzco and Arequipa are known for their beers, Cuzqueña and Arequipeña.

The traditional highland *chicha* (corn beer), dating back to pre-Columbian times, is stored in earthenware pots and served in huge glasses in small Andean villages and markets, but is not usually commercially available. It is homemade and an requires acquired taste, plus the fermentation process begins with chewing the corn, which inevitably puts some folks off.

Peruvian wines are good but not up to the standard of Chilean or Argentine tipple. The best labels are Tacama and Ocucaje.

Ron (rum) is cheap and good quality. A white grape brandy called *pisco* is the national drink, most frequently served in a *pisco* sour, a tasty cocktail made from *pisco*, egg white, lemon juice, syrup, crushed ice and bitters. Local *aguardiente*, sugarcane alcohol, is an acquired taste but very cheap. *Salud!*

NONALCOHOLIC DRINKS
Agua mineral (mineral water) is sold *con gas* (with carbonation) or *sin gas* (without carbonation).

The usual soft drinks are available, plus a plethora of local varieties. Don't leave without trying Peru's top-selling, fizzy-bubble-gum-flavored Inca Kola at least once. Ask for *helada* if you want a refrigerated drink, *al tiempo* if you don't. Remember *sin hielo* (without ice) unless you really trust the water supply.

Jugos (fruit juices) are available everywhere. Make sure you get *jugo puro* and not *con agua*. The most common kinds of juices are *mora* (blackberry), *naranja* (orange), *toronja* (grapefruit), *maracuyá* (passion fruit), *naranjilla* (a local fruit tasting like bitter orange) and papaya. *Chicha morada* is a sweet, bland non-carbonated drink made from purple corn.

Maté and *té de hierbas* are herbal teas. The iconic highland drink is *maté de coca*, a coca leaf tea that is supposed to help with acclimatization.

GAY & LESBIAN TRAVELERS
Gays and lesbians tend to keep a low profile in Peru where 'rights' and 'status' don't exist as such. There are a few discreet gay bars in Lima, but that's about it. Peru's only open gay movement is **Movimiento Homosexual-Lesbiana** (MHOL; ☎ 01-433-6375; mhol@terra.com.pe; Mariscal Miller 828, Jesús María, Lima). It has English-speaking staff in the evenings. The best resource for travelers in Lima is the excellent website http://gaylimape.tripod.com.

HEALTH
Yellow-fever vaccinations and malaria tablets are recommended for the Amazon but generally not needed in the highlands or coast. For more information, see the Health chapter, p1053).

HOLIDAYS
The following dates are all bank holidays. If traveling on or around these dates, plan to book buses and hotels ahead of time and expect prices to rise significantly. This is particularly true for Fiestas Patrias – the biggest national holiday – when buses and hotels are booked long in advance and hotel prices can triple.
Año Nuevo (New Year's Day; January 1)
Semana Santa (Holy Week; Thu & Fri, March/April)
Día del Trabajador (Labor Day; May 1)
Inti Raymi (Winter solstice; June 24)
San Pedro y San Pablo (St Peter & St Paul; June 29)
Fiestas Patrias (Peru's Independence; July 28-29)
Santa Rosa de Lima (August 30)
Battle of Angamos (October 8)
Todos Santos (All Saint's Day, November 1)

Fiesta de la Purísima Concepción (Feast of the Immaculate Conception, December 8)
Navidad (Christmas Day, December 25)

INTERNET ACCESS

'Internet Cabinas' are found on every second or third block in most major Peruvian towns and cities. Even small towns will have at least one *cabina* tucked away. Access in cities is generally fast and cheap – around US$0.60 in major towns to US$1.25 in more remote areas. Many are also equipped for Net-to-phone calls.

INTERNET RESOURCES

Andean Travel Web (www.andeantravelweb.com/peru) Travel site with dozens of links to hotels, tour companies etc.
Latin America Network Information Center (www.lanic.utexas.edu/la/peru/) The University of Texas provides hundreds of links from Academics to Sport.
Peru Links (www.perulinks.com) Over 2500 links, many in Spanish, some in English.
PromPerú (www.promperu.gob.pe) Official government tourist office, in Spanish, English and German.

MAPS

Topographical maps are sold at the Instituto Geográfico Nacional in Lima (p804). South American Explorers (p805) has hiking maps. The best (and most recent) road map of the entire country is the 1:2,200,000 *Mapa Vial* published by Lima 2000 and available in better bookshops.

MEDIA

The best newspapers are the dry, conservative *El Comercio*, good for what's going on in Lima; the conservative *Expreso*, and the moderately left-wing *La República* – all published in Lima. A shorter *El Comercio* (lacking the Lima cultural section) is sold in other cities.

MONEY
ATMs

Most cities and many small towns have 24-hour ATMs on the Plus (Visa) or Cirrus (MasterCard) system, and will accept your debit card. Visa is more the more widespread option. This is a convenient way of obtaining cash at rates usually about 2% lower than exchange houses. Both US dollars and nuevo soles are available. Check the ATM locators on www.visa.com or www.mastercard.com. Your bank will

charge a fee (usually US$2) for each foreign ATM transaction.

Cash

The currency is the *nuevo sol* (S/.), divided into 100 *céntimos*. The following bills are in circulation: S/.10, S/.20, S/.50, S/.100. Counterfeit bills abound, so try to exchange money at banks or *casas de cambio*. Coins of S/.0.10, S/.0.20, S/.0.50, S/.1, S/.2 and S/.5 are also in use.

When changing money ask for plenty of small bills. Trying to buy toilet roll with anything above a S/.20 (US$5.50) note will often result in the owner dashing from store to store until change is found.

Credit Cards

Many upscale restaurants and shops accept Visa and MasterCard credit cards, but usually charge you a 7% or greater fee for using them.

Exchange Rates

Exchange rates at press time included the following:

Country	Unit		S/. (nuevo sol)
Australia	A$1	=	2.55
Canada	C$1	=	2.72
euro zone	€1	=	4.14
Japan	¥100	=	3.29
New Zealand	NZ$1	=	2.22
United Kingdom	UK£1	=	6.03
United States	US$	=	3.60

Exchanging Money

Currencies other than US dollars can be exchanged only in major cities and at a high commission, so it pays to obtain US dollars before your trip. Worn, torn or damaged bills are not accepted. In the summer (January to March), banks in Lima may open only from 8:30am to 11:30am. *Casas de cambio* open longer and are much faster. Moneychangers are useful for exchange outside banking hours or at borders where there are no banks, but beware of 'fixed' calculators, counterfeit notes or short-changing.

With the abundance of counterfeit bills, street vendors now sell devices to detect false currency.

Recommended banks include BCP, Interbanc and Banco Continental.

PERU

Taxes & Refunds

Departure taxes are charged in airports. Better hotels and restaurants may tack on a tax and service charge, which can be as high as 31%. *Incluye impuesto* (IGV) or means service charge is included in the price. Ask before ordering to avoid nasty surprises. There is no system of tax refunds.

Traveler's Checks

Commissions on traveler's checks mean that you can lose from 3% to 7% when exchanging checks, and they may be hard to exchange in small towns. AmEx is the most widely accepted brand, followed by Visa and Thomas Cook.

POST

The privatized postal system is now run by Serpost. It's relatively efficient, but more expensive than in more developed nations. Airmail postcards and letters are about US$1 to most foreign destinations and arrive in about seven to 10 days from Lima, longer from provincial cities.

Poste restante is called 'Lista de Correos' and can be sent to any major post office. Make sure your surname is clearly printed to avoid confusion. South American Explorers (see p805) will also hold, return or forward mail for members as indicated.

RESPONSIBLE TRAVEL

Archaeologists are fighting a losing battle with *huaqueros* (grave robbers), particularly along the coast. Refrain from buying original pre-Columbian artifacts, and do not contribute to wildlife destruction by purchasing souvenirs made from skins, feathers, horns or turtle shells.

Some indigenous communities, like Taquile on the Titicaca, make their living from tourism. Visiting these communities supports their initiatives.

SHOPPING

Souvenirs from Peru are good, varied and cheap. You can buy everything in Lima, be it an Amazonian blowpipe or a highland poncho. Although Lima is more expensive, the choice is varied and the quality high. Cuzco also has a great selection of craft shops. Old and new weavings, ceramics, paintings, woolen clothing and jewelry are all available.

The Puno-Juliaca area is good for knitted alpaca sweaters and knickknacks made from the totora reed, which grows on Lake Titicaca. The Huancayo area is the place for carved gourds, and excellent weavings and clothing are available in the cooperative market. The Ayacucho area is famous for modern weavings and stylized ceramic churches. The Shipibo pottery sold in Yarinacocha (near Pucallpa) is the best jungle craft available. Superb reproductions of Moche and Mochica pottery are available in Trujillo; make sure that they are labeled as copies.

TELEPHONE

Peru's country code is ☎ 51. Public phones are available in even the smallest towns. Most work with phonecards, and many with coins.

Each department has its own area code, which begins with 0 (01 in Lima, 0 plus two digits elsewhere; these are given with phone numbers throughout this chapter). To call long distance within Peru, include the 0 in the area code. If calling from abroad, dial your access code, the country code (51), then the area code without the 0, then the local number.

Dial 129 to make a collect call anywhere in Peru. Dial 109 for a Peruvian operator, 108 for an international operator and 103 for information. There's a telephone directory online at www.amarillastelefonica.com (in Spanish). Fax services are also available at most Telefónica del Perú offices.

To call a foreign country, dial 00, the country code, area code and number.

Phonecards

Called *tarjetas telefonicas*, phonecards are widely available in many price ranges from street vendors or kiosks. Some have an electronic chip, but most use a code system whereby you dial your own personal code to obtain access; these can be used from almost any phone. The most common are the 147 cards: dial 147, enter the code on the back of the card, listen to a message in Spanish telling you your balance, dial the number, listen to how much time you have, then your call connects. For long-distance calls, the Hola Peru card is cheaper: begin by dialing 141. A card for S/.30 (US$8.40) lasts about nine minutes to the USA, less to Europe. Rates are cheaper on Sunday and after 9pm.

TOILETS

The most important rule for budget travelers looking to avoid blocked toilets and irritated hotel owners is to realize that the bowlside basket is there for a reason – to get filled with your used paper! Apart from those in restaurants, hotels and bus stations, public toilets are rare in Peru.

TOURIST INFORMATION

The official tourism website www.promperu.gob.pe has tourist information. PromPeru also runs information offices called **iPerú** (24-hour hotline ☎ 01-574-8000; iperu@promperu.gob.pe) in Lima, Cuzco, Puno, Trujillo, Arequipa, Ayacucho and Iquitos. Municipal tourist offices are also found in many other cities, as listed in this chapter.

South American Explorers (SAE), based in Lima and Cuzco, are an excellent source of traveler information, but you'll get more help as a paid member (see p805).

TOURS

Some protected areas, such as the Inca Trail and Manu National Park, can only be entered as part of a guided tour. Trips into the Amazon can also be more rewarding with an expert guide.

VISAS & DOCUMENTS

With very few exceptions (a handful of Asian, African and communist countries), visas are not required for tourism. Passports should be valid for at least six months. Travelers are permitted a 30- to 90-day stay, stamped into their passports and onto a tourist card that you keep and return upon leaving the country. Extensions can be obtained in the immigration offices of the major cities, with Lima (p804) being the easiest place to do so. This costs about US$27 and you can stay up to 180 days total. When your time is up, you can leave the country overland and return a day later to begin the process again.

To enter Peru, you officially need an onward ticket, though travelers are rarely asked to show such proof and evidence of sufficient funds is usually enough to convince border police that you will eventually leave the country.

Carry your passport and tourist card at all times, since you can be arrested if you don't have identification. When walking around town, carry a photocopy and leave the original in a safe place.

Showing your international student card (ISIC) will save you money at several sites and museums.

VOLUNTEERING

Language schools usually know of several volunteer programs suitable for their students. South American Explorers (see p805) also have reports by many foreign volunteers, especially in Lima and Cuzco. If you contact them in advance, **ProPeru Student Service Corporations** (☎ 084-20-1340; www.properu.org; Grau 654, Urubamba) can organize two- to 26- week cultural, service and academic placements in the Sacred Valley and the Peruvian Amazon. Most organizations charge volunteers for room and board.

WOMEN TRAVELERS

Most women – both solo and in groups – encounter no serious problems in Peru, though they should come mentally prepared for being the center of attention. Machismo is alive and well in Peruvian towns and cities, where curious staring, whistling, hissing and *piropos* (flirtatious remarks) are an everyday occurrence. Ignoring provocation is generally the best response, but in the case of persistent harassment, keep in store a number of ardor-smothering phrases, such as *soy casada* (I'm married) or *déjame en paz* (leave me alone). Appealing to locals is also recommended, as you'll find most Peruvians to be extremely warm and protective towards women traveling alone. Exercise common sense: avoid suspect areas, take only authorized taxis and perhaps wear a ring on your wedding finger.

WORKING

Officially you need a work visa to work in Peru, though language centers in Lima or Cuzco sometimes hire native speakers to teach English. Casual bar work is often available in destinations like Cuzco where there is a high turnover of staff.

PERU

Uruguay

HIGHLIGHTS

- **Colonia del Sacramento** – explore the maze of cobbled streets and take in a tango show in this old smugglers' port (p921)
- **Punta del Este** – lounge on the beach all day and party all night with South America's bright young things (p930)
- **Mercado del Puerto (Montevideo)** – some come to feast from the huge *parrilla* racks, others to see, be seen and (possibly) meet that special someone. Whatever your motivation, a Saturday afternoon in the Mercado is an unforgettable experience (p920)
- **Grappa con miel** – it's grappa, it's honey...goes down smooth and knocks your socks off
- **Off the beaten track** – the rugged fishing village of Punta del Diablo, where surfers, artists and nature lovers converge to escape the crowds at Punta del Este (p932)

FAST FACTS

- **Area:** 187,000 sq km (roughly the size of the US state of North Dakota)
- **Budget:** US$15–25 a day
- **Capital:** Montevideo
- **Costs:** budget hotel in Montevideo US$6, three-hour bus ride US$3, set lunch US$2
- **Country code:** ☎ 598
- **Electricity:** 220V, 50Hz; various types of plugs in use
- **Famous for:** winning the first World Cup (1930), beach resorts
- **Languages:** Spanish; Portuguese near the Brazilian border
- **Money:** US$1 = 28.82 pesos
- **Phrases:** *bárbaro* (cool), *¡garca!* (disgusting), *jodita* (party – very colloquial and slightly rude; for use with young people only)
- **Population:** 3.5 million
- **Time:** GMT minus 3 hours
- **Tipping:** 10% appreciated but not mandatory in restaurants; round up taxi fares
- **Traveler's checks:** cashed at major banks and *casas de cambio*; ATMs are easier
- **Visas:** North American and most European citizens need only a valid passport

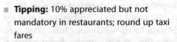

TRAVEL HINTS

Pack reasonably lightly. Taxis are cheap enough to rival local buses. Eat plenty of desserts. Tap water's safe if you don't mind the taste of chlorine. A little bit of Spanish will make you a lot of friends. Bargaining isn't really part of the culture, nor is ripping off the tourists (yet).

URUGUAY

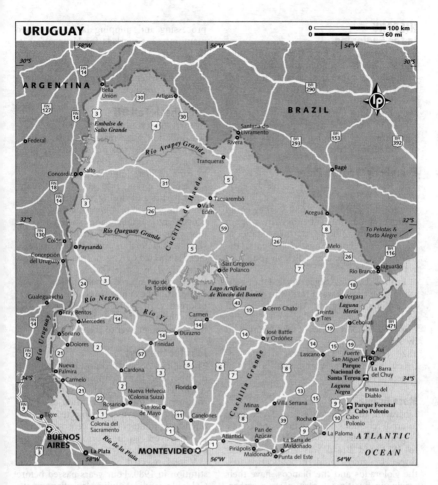

URUGUAY

0 ———— 100 km
0 ———— 60 mi

Some people think 'real' backpacking is all about varying degrees of discomfort – maybe they should avoid Uruguay. It's hard to feel hardcore when your hotel's spotless, the buses are roomy, the streets immaculate, you're eating home-made pasta and sipping espresso coffee, and nobody's hassling you to buy a half-plucked chicken.

There's really no choice here...for years Uruguay was considered the Switzerland of South America. Not much has changed, except it's like if Switzerland had an economic meltdown – the price to quality ratio is so good it's ridiculous; you'll find yourself chuckling as you come out of restaurants, rubbing your belly and gleefully planning your next meal.

Which is great for visitors, but not so much for the locals. Uruguayans are doing it tough, but their famous easy-going nature makes for an air of optimism that might surprise you.

With stunning beaches, atmospheric colonial streetscapes and super-friendly locals, it's strange how few people visit Uruguay... At some places you're the only gringo in town, but there's definitely the feeling that this, at least, is all about to change.

HISTORY
In the Beginning...
The Charrúa were here first, huntin' and fishin'. They had no gold and a nasty habit of killing European explorers, so the Spanish left them alone. Eventually they mellowed out, got some horses and cattle, and started trading. Once the big cattle farmers moved in, the Charrúa got pushed out and they now exist in isolated pockets around the Brazilian border.

Everybody Wants a Piece
The Jesuits were on the scene as early as 1624, and the Portuguese established present-day Colonia in 1680 so they could smuggle goods into Buenos Aires. Spain responded by building its own citadel at Montevideo. For almost 200 years, the Portuguese, Spanish and British fought to get a foothold.

From 1811 José Artigas repelled the Spanish invaders, but it was Brazil who ended up controlling the region. Artigas was exiled to Paraguay where he died in 1850, after inspiring the 33 Orientales who, reinforced by Argentine troops, liberated the area in 1828, establishing Uruguay as a buffer between the emerging continental powers of Argentina and Brazil.

More Drama
Liberation didn't bring peace. There were internal rebellions, insurrections and coups. Argentina besieged Montevideo from 1838 to 1851 and Brazil was an ever-present threat. Uruguay's modern political parties, the Colorados and the Blancos, have their origins in this time – early party membership comprised large numbers of armed *gauchos* (cowboys). By the mid-19th century, the economy was largely dependent on beef and wool production. The rise of the *latifundios* (large landholdings) and commercialization of livestock led to the demise of the independent gaucho.

José Batllé, We Love You
In the early 20th century, visionary president José Batllé y Ordóñez introduced such innovations as pensions, farm credits, unemployment compensation and the eight-hour workday. State intervention led to the nationalization of many industries and general prosperity. The invention of refrigerated processing and shipping facilities opened many overseas markets for Uruguay's cattle industry. However, Batllé's reforms were largely financed through taxing the livestock sector and, when this sector faltered, the welfare state crumbled.

The Wheels Fall Off
By the 1960s economic stagnation and massive inflation were reaching crisis points, and social unrest was increasing. President Oscar Gestido died in 1967 and was replaced by running mate Jorge Pacheco Areco.

Pacheco sprang into action, outlawing leftist parties and closing leftist newspapers, which he accused of supporting the guerrilla Movimiento de Liberación Nacional (commonly known as Tupamaros). The country slid into dictatorship. After Tupamaros executed suspected CIA agent Dan Mitrione (as dramatized in Costa-Gavras' film *State of Siege*) and engineered a major prison escape, Pacheco put the military in charge of counter-insurgency. In 1971 Pacheco's chosen successor, Juan Bordaberry, handed control of the government over to the military.

Jobs for the Boys
The military occupied almost every position of importance in the 'national security state'. Arbitrary detention and torture became routine. The forces determined eligibility for public employment, subjected political offenses to military courts, censored libraries and even required prior approval for large family gatherings.

Voters rejected a military-drawn constitution in 1980. Four years passed before Colorado candidate Julio María Sanguinetti became president under the existing constitution. His presidency implied a return to democratic traditions, but he also supported a controversial amnesty, ratified by voters in 1989, for military human rights abuses.

Later in 1989, the Blancos' Luis Lacalle succeeded Sanguinetti in a peaceful transition. Sanguinetti returned to office in the November 1994 elections and was succeeded by Jorge Battle Ibañez, another Colorado candidate, in March 2000.

Oh No, Not this Again
The military were still lurking around, though – one of Ibañez's first official duties was to dismiss the head of the army for

suggesting that another coup might be in order. The Frente Amplio (Broad Front) – a coalition of leftist parties – became a serious political contender, winning popularity for its anti-privatization, pro-welfare stance. In December 2000, Ibañez called for the legalization of cocaine in the US (¡olé!) as a means of stamping out the black market. His calls were met with a resounding silence from Washington.

Bad Omens

When the spread of foot and mouth disease led to the banning of Uruguayan beef exports, it was bad news for the economy. When Argentine banks froze deposits and thousands of Argentineans withdrew their cash from Uruguayan banks, it was *really* bad news. Argentinean deposits made up 80% of foreign reserves in Uruguay's banks. Uruguayans watched in horror as their economy – previously one of the strongest in South America – crumbled, and inflation (3.6% in 2001) rocketed to 40% by the end of 2002. The tourist industry (heavily reliant on prosperous Argentines) suffered. The peso plummeted in value, the economy minister resigned and the government declared a bank holiday to prevent a run on the banks.

Independence?

What followed was a massive bailout – Ibañez's emergency measures (cutting public spending, increasing sales tax) were rewarded by a series of loans from the US, IMF and World Bank totalling US$1.5 billion. Despite that, Uruguay is still showing some pluck politically – condemning the sanctions against Cuba, the coup in Venezuela and, most recently, the war in Iraq.

THE CULTURE
The National Psyche

The one thing that Uruguayans will tell that they're *not* is anything like their *porteño* (people from Buenos Aires) cousins across the water. In many ways they're right. Where the Argentines are brassy and sometimes arrogant, the Uruguayans are relaxed and self-assured. Where the former have always been a regional superpower, the latter have always lived in the shadow of one. Those jokes about Punta del Este being a suburb of Buenos Aires don't go down so well on this side of the border. There are

plenty of similarities, though – the near universal appreciation for the arts and the Italian influence, with its one-ingredient pizzas and love of wine and cheese. The gaucho thang plays a part, too, and the rugged individualism and disdain that many Uruguayans hold for *el neoliberalismo* (neoliberalism) can be traced directly back to those romantic cowboy figures.

Lifestyle

Uruguayans like to take it easy, and pride themselves on being the opposite of the hot-headed Latino type. They're big drinkers, but bar-room brawls are rare. Sunday's the day for family and friends, to throw half a cow on the *asado* (spit roast), sit back, sip some maté, maybe go for a walk along the river. The population is well educated, although public school standards are slipping. The chasm between rich and poor may widen as private universities become the main providers of quality education.

Uruguay's small population produces a surprising amount of talented artists and literary figures. While Juan Carlos Ornetti is probably the most famous Uruguayan writer, most young Uruguayans have a big soft spot for Eduardo Galeano who has written many books and poems.

People

The Uruguayan population is predominately white (88%) with 8% *mestizo* (people with mixed Spanish and indigenous blood) and 4% black. Amerindian are practically nonexistent. The population growth rate is 0.8%, with a doubling time of about 90 years. Population density is 19.7 people per sq km.

ARTS

Uruguay has an impressive literary and artistic tradition; Uruguay's major contemporary writers are Juan Carlos Onetti and poet, essayist and novelist Mario Benedetti.

There aren't that many films made in or about Uruguay. Probably the most famous exception is Costa-Gavras' famous and engrossing *State of Siege* (1973), filmed in Allende's Chile, deals with the Tupamaro guerrillas' kidnapping and execution of suspected American CIA officer Dan Mitrione.

Theater is popular and playwrights such as Mauricio Rosencof are prominent. The most renowned painters in Uruguay are the late Juan Manuel Blanes and Joaquín Torres García. Sculptors include José Belloni, whose awesome life-size bronzes can be seen in Montevideo's parks.

Tango is big in Montevideo – Uruguayans claim tango legend Carlos Gardel as a native son (although the Argentines have other ideas). During Carnaval, Montevideo's streets reverberate to the energetic African drum beats of *candombe*, which is an African-derived rhythm brought to Uruguay by slaves from 1750 onwards, thought to have been influential in the birth of tango.

SPORT
Sexo, droga y Peñarol
Montevideo graffito

In Uruguay, sport means football and football means soccer. Uruguay has won the World Cup twice, including the very first match, which was played in Uruguay in 1930. The most notable teams are Montevideo-based Nacional and Peñarol. If you go to a match between these two, sit on the sidelines, not behind the goal, unless you're up for some serious passion-induced rowdiness.

The **Asociación Uruguayo de Fútbol** (☎ 02-400-7101; Guayabo 1531) in Montevideo can provide information on matches and venues.

RELIGION
Seventy eight percent of Uruguayans are Roman Catholic, but church and state are officially separate. There's a small Jewish minority, numbering around 25,000, almost all of whom live in Montevideo. Evangelical Protestantism has made some inroads, and Sun Myung Moon's Unification Church owns the afternoon daily, *Últimas Noticias*.

ENVIRONMENT
The Land
Uruguay's rolling northern hills extend from southern Brazil with two main ranges of interior hills, the Cuchilla de Haedo, west of Tacuarembó, and the Cuchilla Grande, south of Melo, neither of which exceeds 500m in height. West of Montevideo, the terrain is more level, while the Atlantic coast has impressive beaches, dunes and headlands.

Wildlife
Uruguay's grasslands and forests resemble those of Argentina's Pampas or southern Brazil. Patches of palm savanna persist in the southeast, along the Brazilian border.

Nearly all large land animals have disappeared, but the occasional rhea still races across northwestern Uruguay's grasslands. Some offshore islands harbor southern fur seal and sea lion colonies.

National Parks
Uruguay isn't big on national parks. Santa Teresa is the country's only park, but it doesn't have a whole lot going on naturewise.

TRANSPORT

GETTING THERE & AWAY
Air
Most international flights to/from Montevideo's Aeropuerto Carrasco pass through Buenos Aires. Many others stop at Rio de Janeiro or São Paulo. International passengers leaving from Carrasco pay US$6 departure tax if headed to Argentina, US$12 to other destinations.

Direct flights go to Porto Alegre, Florianópolis, Rio and São Paulo (Brazil), Asunción (Paraguay) and Santiago (Chile). There are also flights to Santa Cruz de la Sierra and La Paz (Bolivia), and Havana (Cuba) via Buenos Aires.

Boat
Most travelers cross from Montevideo to Argentina by ferry, sometimes with bus combinations to Colonia or Carmelo.

Bus
There are direct buses from Montevideo to Buenos Aires via Gualeguaychú, but these are slower and less convenient than the land/river combinations across the Río de la Plata. Further north, there are bridge crossings over the Río Uruguay from Fray Bentos to Gualeguaychú, Paysandú to Colón and Salto to Concordia. There are plenty of land crossings to Brazil, including Chuy to Chuí and Pelotas, Río Branco to Jaguarão, Rivera to Santana do Livramento, Artigas to Quaraí and Bella Unión to Barra do Quaraí. Buses generally

continue through the border and passport formalities are conducted on the bus.

GETTING AROUND

Uruguayan buses and roads are generally well maintained. Montevideo is *the* transport hub. If you stay on the coast or river roads, you'll never be waiting long for a bus. Try something tricky (Chuy to Tacuarembó, for example) and you might experience otherwise. Due to its small size, Uruguay is perfect for bus travel – the longest ride you're likely to have is a measly six hours.

Air

If you really need to get somewhere in a hurry, internal flights are available. **Aeromas** (www.aeromas.com) flies from Montevideo to Salto, Tacuarembó, Paysandú, Rivera and Artigas.

Bus

Bus travel in Uruguay is a lot less painful than in many parts of the world. Most towns have a *terminal de omnibus* (central bus terminal) for long-distance buses. To get your choice of seat, buy tickets in advance from the terminal. The clerk will have a map of the bus and you can point out where you want to sit.

If you're traveling light, take your luggage inside the bus. Otherwise, put it underneath. Tipping the luggage handler is not essential, but most Uruguayans hand over a few pesos.

Local buses are usually slow and crowded, but cheap. You can get around most towns for about US$0.10 to US$0.15.

Hitching

Hitch-hikers are rare in Uruguay, so you might get picked up for novelty value. It's not a particularly dangerous country, but hitching is a gamble anywhere in the world. Take the usual precautions.

Taxi

Taxis are so cheap they're hard to resist. Meters are always out of whack, so drivers consult a photocopied chart to calculate the fare. A long ride in Montevideo shouldn't go over US$5; short hops in small towns usually cost less than US$1. On weekends and at night, fares are 25% to 50% higher.

MONTEVIDEO

Montevideo is probably South America's most laid-back capital. The population is only 1.3 million, but a lot of those folks are students and young workers, and the city has a lively buzz. It also has a decidedly European feel, thanks to a large influx of Spanish and Italian immigrants who arrived during the late-19th and early-20th centuries.

Most of the grand 19th-century neoclassical buildings, legacies of the beef boom, have all but crumbled, although vestiges of Montevideo's colonial past still exist in the Ciudad Vieja (Old Town), the picturesque historic center.

ORIENTATION

Montevideo lies on the east bank of the Río de la Plata. Its functional center is Plaza Independencia, east of the Ciudad Vieja. Av 18 de Julio is its key commercial and entertainment area. At the northeast end of 18 de Julio, Parque José Batlle y Ordóñez contains a 75,000-seat stadium, the Estadio Centenario.

Across the harbor, the 132m Cerro de Montevideo was a landmark for early navigators of this region. East of downtown, the riverfront Rambla leads past residential suburbs and sandy beaches frequented by *montevideanos* (people from Montevideo) in summer and on weekends – catch bus No 64, which goes from 18 de Julio along the coast road – the beaches get better the further out of town you go.

INFORMATION
Bookshops

Linardi y Risso (Juan Carlos Gómez 1435) Carries a sizable selection of out-of-print books, especially in history and literature.

Plaza Libros (18 de Julio 892) Stocks a selection of books in English.

GETTING INTO TOWN

Bus Nos 21, 61, 180, 187 and 188 go from Tres Cruces bus terminal to 18 de Julio. A taxi from the airport will cost approximately US$7; the airport bus costs US$0.70.

URUGUAY

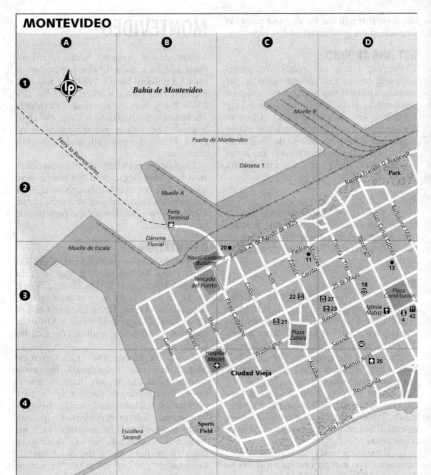

MONTEVIDEO

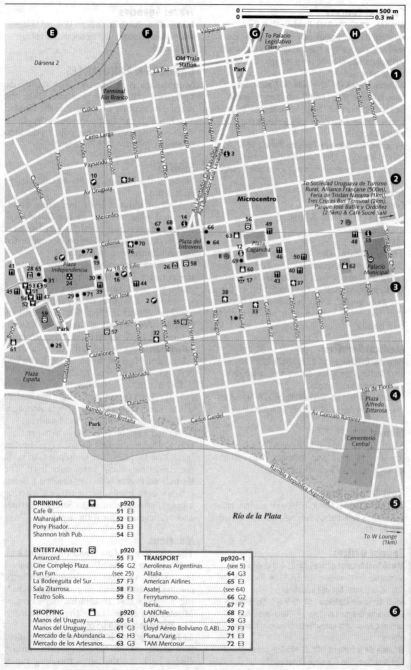

URUGUAY

Cultural Centers

Alianza (☎ 02-901-7423; Paraguay 1217; ☻ 7am-8pm Mon-Thu) The American-Uruguayan cultural center contains a bookstore, a theater and a substantial library with publications in English. The center also sponsors special programs and lectures.

Alliance Française (☎ 02-408-6012; www.alianza francesa.edu.uy; 18 de Julio 1772; ☻ 8am-7:30pm) A well-stocked library with books, magazines and CDs. Short-term visitors can avoid membership fees by paying a US$50 refundable deposit.

Sociedad Uruguaya de Turismo Rural (☎ 02-322-7477; Maximo Tajes 7249) An information center that can put you in touch with *estancias* that accept paying guests.

Internet Access

Cybercafé (18 de Julio 966).

Cybermix (cnr 18 de Julio & Paraguay)

Media

The invaluable *Guía del Ocio*, which lists cultural events, cinemas, theaters and restaurants, comes with the Friday edition of *La Republica*. Ask at the tourist office for a copy of *Pimba!*, a free pocket-sized booklet that has more information on bars, clubs and bands.

Medical Services

Hospital Británico (☎ 02-280-0020; Av Italia 2420) You'll find English-speaking doctors at this private, but highly recommended hospital.

Hospital Maciel (☎ 02-915-3000; cnr 25 de Mayo & Maciel) Located in the Ciudad Vieja, this is the public hospital.

Money

Most downtown banks have ATMs. **Exprinter** (cnr Sarandí & Juncal) and **Indumex** (Plaza Cagancha) change traveler's checks and cash.

Post & Telephone

Post office (Buenos Aires 451) This is the main post office. Antel has **Telecentros** (San José 1108; ☻ 24hr) and (Rincón 501).

Tourist Offices

Municipal tourist office (☎ 02-903-0649; Palacio Municipal; ☻ 10am-6pm Mon-Fri, 11am-6pm Sat & Sun) This office is small but well informed.

Ministerio de Turismo (☎ 02-908-9141; Colonia & Liberatador General Lavalleja; ☻ 10am-noon Mon-Fri summer, noon-5pm winter) Better equipped than offices.

Oficina de Informes (☎ 02-409-7399; bus terminal; ☻ 9am-9pm) This office is well equipped.

Travel Agencies

Asatej (☎ 02-908-0509; Río Negro 1354, 2nd fl) Argentina's nonprofit student travel agency, this is an affiliate of STA Travel.

DANGERS & ANNOYANCES

Montevideo is sedate by most standards, but street crime is on the rise. Take the usual precautions, especially in the Ciudad Vieja, which can be dangerous at night. If you want to report a crime, contact the **tourist police** (☎ 02-924-7277; Paysandú 1234).

SIGHTS

None of the listings in this section charge admission.

Most of Montevideo's interesting buildings and museums are in the **Ciudad Vieja**. Many refugees from rural poverty live here in *conventillos*, large, older houses converted into multifamily slum dwellings.

On **Plaza Independencia**, a huge statue of the country's greatest hero tops the eerie underground **Mausoleo Artigas** (☻ 9am-5pm), where fans of famous dead people can tick another one off the list. The 18th-century **Palacio Estévez** served as the Casa de Gobierno until 1985, while the striking 26-story **Palacio Salvo** was once South America's tallest building. Just off the plaza, the **Teatro Solís** (1856) is Montevideo's leading theater.

Beyond the colonial **Puerto de la Ciudadela** (1742) is **Plaza Constitución**, where the austere white marble **Iglesia Matriz** (1799; Sarandí & Ituzaingó) is the city's oldest public building.

Further west, on 25 de Mayo between Solís and Colón, is the **Casa Garibaldi** (☻ 11am-5pm Tue-Fri, 11am-4pm Sat), where Guiseppe Garibaldi, the Italian nationalist hero, once lived. The **Mercado del Puerto** (1868; Pérez Castellano & Piedras) is a wrought-iron superstructure sheltering a gaggle of restaurants. On Saturday, artists and musicians frequent the area.

Museums

The neoclassical **Casa Rivera** (1802; Rincón & Misiones; ☻ 11am-5pm Tue-Fri, 11am-6pm Sat) houses a fascinating collection of indigenous artifacts, colonial treasures and oil paintings, including a spectacular panoramic depiction of Montevideo at the end of the 18th century. The **Museo Romántico** (25 de Mayo 428; ☻ 11am-5pm Tue-Fri, 11am-4pm Sat) is filled with the opulent furnishings of Montevideo's 19th-century elite. Check out the ladies traveling vanity case, replete with brushes, combs, scissors, perfume bottles and fold-out candleholders – you can bet there were some arguments about whose backpack *that* monster was going in. The **Casa Lavalleja** (1783; Zabala & 25 de Mayo; noon-5pm Mon-Fri, 11am-4pm Sat) is a well-preserved example of colonial architecture.

The **Museo del Gaucho y de la Moneda** (18 de Julio 998; 10am-5pm Mon-Fri) in the Banco de la República is having a bit of an identity crisis – one half displays exquisite specimens of antique horsefittings and other gaucho paraphernalia, while the other is devoted to the troubled history of the Uruguayan economy.

The **Museo Torres García** (Sarandí 683; 10am-7pm, 10am-6pm Sat) displays the works of Joaquín Torres García (1874–1949), the Uruguayan artist who spent much of his career in France producing abstract and Cubist work, and unusual portraits of figures like Columbus, Mozart and Beethoven.

COURSES

The following courses don't cater for the casual learner – you'd want to be staying at least a month to get your money's worth.

Afro Mundo (02-915-0247; Mercado Central, 1st fl) Classes in African drumming, *capoeira* and *candombe* dance.

Berlitz (02-901-5535; www.berlitz.com; Plaza Independencia 1380) One-on-one Spanish tuition.

Joventango (02-901-5561; Mercado de la Abundancia) Tango classes for all levels, from gringo to expert.

FESTIVALS & EVENTS

Montevideo's Carnaval takes place the first Monday and Tuesday before Ash Wednesday. Highlights include *candombe* dance troops beating out African-influenced rhythms on large drums. The Semana Criolla (during Semana Santa) is part rodeo, part arts fair, part outdoor concert – it's *gaucho*-rama out there. Festivities take place at Prado, easily reached by bus No 149 or 152.

SLEEPING

Albergue Juvenil (02-908-1324; Canelones 935; dm member/nonmember US$6/8) The official HI facility is well set up, with kitchen and Internet facilities, and a spacious central area.

Hotel Windsor (02-901-5080; Zelmar Michelini 1260; s/d without bath US$4/6, with bath US$5.50/7) Spacious and clean enough.

Pensión Nuevo Ideal (02-908-2913; Soriano 1073; d without/with bath US$3.50/7) This central hotel is bright, friendly and clean.

Hotel City (02-915-6427; Buenos Aires 462; d US$5) A clean family place with kitchen facilities. The amiable Brazilian *dueña* can lodge guests in two other properties as well.

Hospedaje del Centro (02-900-1419; Soriano 1126; d with bath US$6) Once a luxurious single-family residence, it's clean but crumbling. Some rooms are very dark.

Hotel Ideal (02-901-6389; Colonia 914; s/d with bath US$7/9) Spotless rooms with wooden floors, TV and balconies.

Hotel Arapey (02-900-7032; Uruguay 925; s/d US$8/12) Gorgeous (if slightly over-the-top) furniture, tiled floors, curvy balconies, TV, piped music – a good place to rest up if you've been doing it hard.

EATING

Lobizón (Zelmar Michelini 1325) Popular with young *montevideanos*, with inexpensive lunch specials including *gramajo*, a calorie-packed house special of eggs, ham and French fries. It has live music some nights.

La Vegetariana (cnr Mitre & Sarandi) Offers a good range of meat-free mains and some excellent desserts.

Buffet Grand Dragon (San José 1216) All you can eat Chinese food for US$2. Undeniable value for those with big stomachs and small budgets.

Café Pedamonte (Mitre 1375) A lunchtime favorite for its wide range of sandwiches on a variety of breads. Live music Saturday and Sunday nights.

Bolero (Plaza Independencia 848) An upscale restaurant (check the waterwall behind the bar!) serving good-value breakfasts and set lunches.

Café Sucré Salé (18 de Julio 1772) Run by a real live French chef, this place in the Alliance Française has excellent breakfasts (brióche!) and a shady courtyard area with tinkling fountain.

Mangrullo (Bacacay 1327) A cute little restaurant serving excellent meat, pasta and seafood. The salmon in shrimp sauce (US$6) pushes the outer limits of indulgence.

Mesón del Club Espanol (18 de Julio 1332; meals US$1-4) Spanish food in classy surrounds. A cover charge of US$1.50 applies Thursday to Saturday nights when there's live music and dancing.

Euskal Erria (San José 1168) Excellent Basque food in a relaxed dining room. It has the best paella in town.

Pizza Bros (Plaza Cagancha 1364) A lively, informal place, with good pizza, calzones and draft beer.

Viejo Sancho (San José 1229) Good-value set meals and all your *parrillada* (mixed grill) faves.

La Torre (Convención 1324; meals US$3) Serves as much pasta and meat as you can eat.

Confitería La Pasiva (Plaza Constitución) Reasonably priced *minutas* (snacks) and a superb *flan casero* (crème caramel) in a traditional atmosphere.

The steaks served at *parrillas* (steakhouses) inside the Mercado del Puerto are so large they're almost obscene. Saturday lunchtime, when the market is crammed with locals (who also use the market as a pick-up joint), is the best time to visit. La Posada del Puerto has two stalls serving seafood, while **El Corralín**, just outside, is a sidewalk café with entrées starting at about US$3.

The Mercado de la Abundancia is a popular and atmospheric spot for lunch or dinner. **El Rincon de las Poetas** (set meals US$2-3) and **Las Refranes** (set meals US$2-3) both have good set meals. **El Esquinazo** has a wider menu and **La Pizzeria** is open for dinner only.

DRINKING

The most convenient and happening bar precinct in town is in Bartholomew Mitre in the old city. **The Pony Pisador** (Mitre 1326), **Café @** (Mitre 1322), **Shannon Irish Pub** (Mitre 1318) and **Maharajah** (Mitre 1316) all have reasonably priced drinks, DJs, occasional live music and young crowds who party 'til late. And they're all next door to each other – perfect stumbling distance!

W Lounge (☎ 02-712-1177; Rambla Wilson s/n; admission US$3; ☯ 11pm-4am Mon-Sat) In the Parque Rodó, this club is *the* place to shake your thang. A taxi from the center should cost around US$3.

ENTERTAINMENT

Amarcord (Julio Herrera y Obes 1231; admission US$1) One of the last places in Montevideo still giving young bands a go. Styles vary greatly – hip hop, blues, metal and jazz, but the smoky ambience of this underground student hangout is a constant.

La Bodeguita del Sur (☎ 02-902-8649; Soriano 840) The place for live folkloric music, Cuban salsa and the like.

Sala Zitarrosa (☎ 02-901-7303; cnr 18 de Julio & Herrera y Obes) Hosts rock bands and occasional live theater.

Fun Fun (☎ 02-915-8005; Ciudadela 1229) Located in the Mercado Central, Fun Fun attracts an older crowd of tango enthusiasts, with live bands on weekends and a pleasant deck area out the front.

Cine Complex Plaza (Plaza Cagancha) Shows Hollywood blockbusters.

Cinemateca Uruguaya (☎ 02-408-2460; Lorenzo Carnelli 1311; membership per month US$3) For more arty flicks, this cinema is also a film club with a modest membership fee allowing unlimited viewing at its five cinemas.

Teatro Solís (Buenos Aires 678) Montevideo has an active theater community and this is the most prestigious playhouse in town, but there are many others. Admission starts around US$3. Check the *Guía del Ocio* for listings.

SHOPPING

Feria de Tristán Narvaja (Calle Tristán Narvaja, btwn Av 18 de Julio & Calle La Paz, El Cordón; ☯ 9am-3pm Sun) This is a bustling outdoor market selling everything from antique knick-knacks and jewelry to artisan crafts and fried fish. The market stalls sprawl for seven blocks.

Mercado de los Artesanos (Plaza Cagancha) This has some excellent handicrafts at ridiculously low prices.

You'll find most of the same stuff at the **Mercado de la Abundancia** (San José & Yaguarón). Plaza Constitución hosts an enjoyable flea market on Saturday.

Manos del Uruguay (San José 1111 & Reconquista 602) This is famous for its range of slightly pricey, high-quality goods.

GETTING THERE & AWAY
Air

Montevideo international airport (☎ 02-604-0329) is 20km east of the city at Carrasco. Besides the usual international carriers, commuter airlines also provide services to Argentina. Aéromas has three flights weekly for Salto, Tacuarembó, Paysandú, Rivera and Artigas, all for around US$50. The following is a list of airline offices in Montevideo:

Aerolíneas Argentinas (☎ 02-902-3694; Convención 1343, 4th fl)

URUGUAY

Aéromas (☎ 02-604-0011; Montevideo international airport)

American (☎ 02-916-3929; Sarandí 699)

Iberia (☎ 02-908-1032; Colonia 975)

LanChile(☎ 02-902-3881; Colonia 993, 4th fl)

LAPA (☎ 02-900-8765; Plaza Cagancha 1339)

Lloyd Aéreo Boliviano (LAB; ☎ 02-902-2656; Colonia 920, 2nd fl)

Pluna/Varig (☎ 02-902-1414; Colonia 1001)

TAM Mercosur (☎ 02-901-8451; Colonia 820)

Boat

Ferryturismo (☎ 02-900-0045; Río Branco 1368) does bus-ferry combinations to Buenos Aires, via Colonia (US$9, six hours), and with their faster Sea Cat (US$21, four hours). They also have a branch at **Terminal Tres Cruces** (☎ 02-409-8198) *Buqueaviones* (high-speed ferries) cross directly to Buenos Aires from Montevideo (2½ hours). Fares start at US$41.

Cacciola (☎ 02-401-9350), at Terminal Tres Cruces, runs a bus-launch service to Buenos Aires (US$12/21 one way/return, eight hours) via Carmelo and the Argentine Delta suburb of Tigre.

Bus

Montevideo's **Terminal Tres Cruces** (☎ 02-401-8998; Bulevar Artigas & Av Italia) has decent restaurants, clean toilets, a left-luggage facility, a *casa de cambio* and ATMs.

COT, Rutas del Sol and Rutas del Plata go to various destinations daily, with departures for Punta del Este and Fray Bentos. Many companies, including Agencia Central, Núñez Chadre and Sabelín, go west and north.

Destination	Duration in Hours	Cost
Bella Unión	8	US$14
Chuy	5	US$9
Colonia	2½	US$4
Fray Bentos	4½	US$7
Maldonado	2	US$3.50
Mercedes	4	US$6.50
Minas	2	US$3
Nueva Helvecia	2	US$3
La Paloma	3½	US$6
Paysandú	5	US$9
Punta del Diablo	4½	US$8
Punta del Este	2½	US$3.50
Rivera	6	US$12
Rocha	3	US$5
Salto	6	US$12
Tacuarembó	5	US$9
Treinta y Tres	4	US$6.50

Bus de la Carrera has three buses daily to Buenos Aires (US$18, eight hours) via Fray Bentos.

There are several departures for other destinations in Argentina, including Rosario (US$23, 10 hours), Córdoba (US$29, 15 hours), Santa Fe (US$21, eight hours), Paraná (US$20, 10 hours) and Mendoza (US$40, 20 hours).

EGA goes to Santiago de Chile (US$61, 30 hours), Porto Alegre (US$33, 11 hours), Florianópolis (US$51, 18 hours) and Curitiba, Brazil (US$61, 24 hours). TTL also goes to Porto Alegre and other Brazilian destinations.

Brújula and Coit go to Asunción, Paraguay (US$41, 20 hours).

GETTING AROUND

Buses to the airport leave from Terminal Suburbana, at Rambla Franklin D Roosevelt and Río Branco (US$0.70, 40 minutes). A taxi from the airport will cost approximately US$7. Local buses go everywhere for about US$0.40. Bus Nos 21, 61, 180, 187 and 188 go from Tres Cruces bus terminal to 18 de Julio.

WESTERN URUGUAY

West of Montevideo are the wheat fields and gardens that feed the capital. Its main attraction is the 17th-century Portuguese contraband port and fortress of Colonia, but overland travelers from Argentina may find towns along the Río Uruguay pleasant stopovers.

COLONIA DEL SACRAMENTO

Colonia's a superstar, and rightly so. No town can be this cute, with winding cobblestone streets, funky little restaurants and gorgeous river views without becoming a major tourist attraction.

The Portuguese founded Colonia in 1680 to smuggle goods across the Río de la Plata into Buenos Aires. The Spanish captured it in 1762 and held it until 1777, when tax reforms finally permitted foreign goods to proceed directly to Buenos Aires.

Orientation & Information

The Barrio Histórico is on a small peninsula – the commercial downtown, near

URUGUAY

URUGUAY

COLONIA DEL SACRAMENTO

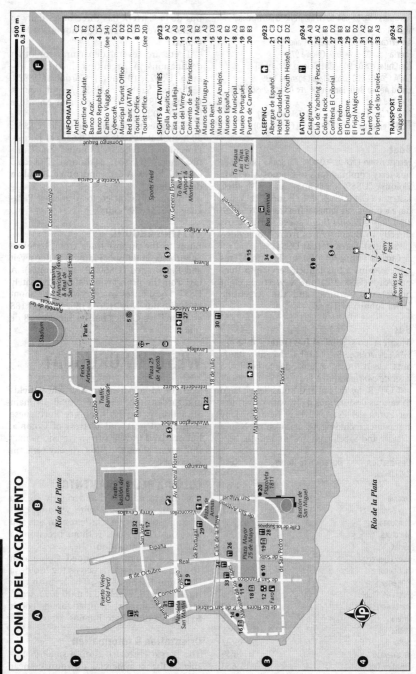

0   500 m
0   0.3 mi

INFORMATION	
Antel..	1 C2
Argentine Consulate................	2 B2
Banco Acac..............................	3 C2
Banco Republica.......................	4 D4
Cambio Viaggio........................	(see 34)
Cybercafé................................	5 D2
Municipal Tourist Office...........	6 D2
Red Banc (ATM).......................	7 D2
Tourist Office..........................	8 D3
Tourist Office..........................	(see 20)

SIGHTS & ACTIVITIES	p923
Capilla Jesuítica.......................	9 A2
Casa de Lavalleja......................	10 A3
Casa del Virrey.........................	11 A3
Convento de San Francisco.......	12 A3
Iglesia Matriz...........................	13 B2
Manos del Uruguay..................	14 A3
Moto Rent...............................	15 D3
Museo de los Azulejos..............	16 A3
Museo Español.........................	17 B2
Museo Municipal......................	18 A3
Museo Portugués......................	19 B3
Puerta de Campo......................	20 B3

SLEEPING	p923
Albergue de Español.................	21 C3
Hotel Ciudadela.......................	22 C2
Hotel Colonial (Youth Hostel)...	23 D2

EATING	p924
Casagrande..............................	24 A3
Club de Yachting y Pesca..........	25 A2
Colonia Rock............................	26 B3
Confitería El Colonial................	27 D2
Don Pedro...............................	28 B3
El Drugstore.............................	29 B2
El Frijol Mágico........................	30 D2
La Luna...................................	31 A2
Puerto Viejo.............................	32 B2
Pulpería de los Faroles.............	33 A3

TRANSPORT	p924
Viaggio Renta Car....................	34 D3

Río de la Plata

Puerto Viejo
(Old Port)

Stadium

Feria
Artesanal

Park

Colombo
Traffic
Barricade

Rambla de las
Américas

Coronel Arroyo

Vicente P. García

Sports Field

Av General Flores

To Camping
Municipal (4km)
& Real de
San Carlos (5km)

Daniel Fosalba

To Ruta 1,
Airport &
Montevideo

Av Artigas

Av FD Roosevelt

Bus Terminal

To Posada
Las Tejas
(1.5km)

Rivera

Alberto Méndez

Lavalleja

Plaza 25
de Agosto

Intendente Suárez

Rivadavia

Washington Barbot

Ituzaingó

Av General Flores

Manuel de Lobos

Florida

18 de Julio

Teatro
Bastión del
Carmen

Virrey Cevallos

San José

España

Vizconcillos

de San Antonio

Plaza de
Portugal

Calle de la Playa

Real

Plaza de
Armas

San Miguel

Plazoleta
1811

Bastión de
San Miguel

Ferry
Port

Ferries to
Buenos Aires

Río de la Plata

Colegio

Comercio

8 de Octubre

Plazoleta
San Martín

Mendoza

de San Francisco

Plaza Mayor
25 de Mayo

Calle de los Suspiros

de San Pedro

de las Flores

P de San Gabriel

de Solís

Faro

Plaza 25 de Agosto, and the river port are a few blocks east. Information services are as follows:

Antel (Rivadavia 420)

Banco Acac (Flores & Washington Barbot) This has an ATM.

Banco República Operates exchange facilities at the port.

Cambio Viaggio (General Flores 350; ⊙ closed Sun)

Cybercafé (Méndez, btwn Fosalba & Rivadavia)

Main tourist office (☎ 052-26141; General Flores 499; ⊙ 8am-7pm)

Post office (Lavalleja 226)

Tourist office (☎ 052-28506; Plaza 1811; ⊙ 9am-7pm)

Walking Tour

Colonia's museums are open 11am to 5pm daily. The US$0.30 entrance ticket covers all of the following.

The Barrio Histórico begins at the restored **Puerta de Campo (1**; 1745), on Manuel de Lobos, where a thick fortified wall runs to the river. A short distance west, off Plaza Mayor 25 de Mayo, tile-and-stucco colonial houses line narrow, cobbled **Calle de los Suspiros**; just beyond is the **Museo Portugués (2)**, where you'll find some great old seafaring maps and a very fanciful depiction of the Lobo family tree.

At the southwest corner of the plaza are the **Casa de Lavalleja (3)**, formerly General Lavalleja's residence, ruins of the 17th-century **Convento de San Francisco (4)** and the restored 19th-century **faro (5**; lighthouse). At the west end, on Comercio, the **Museo Municipal (6)** has antique homewares, dinosaur remains and

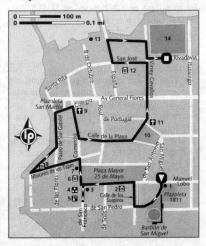

huge petrified mushrooms...magic! The **Casa del Virrey (7)** – which was never home to a viceroy – is just to the north.

At the west end of Misiones de los Tapes, the tiny **Museo de los Azulejos (8)** is a 17th-century house with colonial tilework. The riverfront **Paseo de San Gabriel** leads to Colegio, where a right turn onto Comercio heads to the ruined **Capilla Jesuítica (9**; Jesuit chapel). Turning east along Calle de la Playa will take you to Vasconcellos and the **Plaza de Armas (10)**, where you'll find the landmark 1680 **Iglesia Matriz (11)**, Uruguay's oldest church. Nearly destroyed by fire in 1799, it was rebuilt by Spanish architect Tomás Toribio. During the Brazilian occupation of 1823, lightning ignited a powder magazine, causing serious damage. Changes since have been mainly cosmetic. The interior retains its simple aesthetic appeal.

Across Av General Flores, the **Museo Español (12**; España & San José) exhibits replicas of colonial pottery, clothing and maps. At the north end of the street is the **Puerto Viejo (13**; Old Port). Although it has long ceased to function as a port, it's a picturesque place to soak up some of the atmosphere of the old smuggling days. One block east, the **Teatro Bastión del Carmen (14**; Virrey Cevallos & Rivadavia) incorporates part of the ancient fortifications.

Sleeping

Albergue de Español (☎ 099-624129; Manuel del Lobos 377; s/d US$4/7, with bath US$5/8) Large multi-bed rooms in an atmospheric old building. Some are a bit dark.

Hotel Colonial (☎ 052-28151; barlocel@adinet.com.uy; Av General Flores 440; dm US$5) Four-bed dorms with free bikes, Internet access, kitchen and laundry facilities.

Posada Las Tejas (☎ 052-24096; Rosenthal & Fray Bentos; r per person US$4) Eight blocks southeast of the port, this place is hardly central, but it's comfortable and quiet. Call first to arrange transport.

Hotel Ciudadela (☎ 052-21183; 18 de Julio 315; s/d with bath & breakfast US$7/13; ❄) Bright, modern and fairly forgettable rooms.

Camping Municipal de Colonia (☎ 052-24662; sites per person US$1.50, 2-person cabañas US$5) Near the beach at Real de San Carlos, 5km northwest of the Barrio Histórico. There are hot showers on site and a handful of restaurants nearby.

Eating

Confitería El Colonial (Flores 432) Good breakfasts and set meals, an extensive menu and free Internet access.

Casagrande (Misiones de los Tapes 143) An atmospheric café doubling as a handicrafts market. Fondue for four is US$8.

Colonia Rock (Real & Misiones de las Tapes) A hip restaurant/bar serving excellent *chivitos al plato* (small steaks). Live music on Saturday and a healthy cocktail list.

El Frijol Mágico (18 de Julio & Méndez) OK, so you can order a steak, but Colonia's only vegetarian restaurant still delivers the goods – soy and lentil burgers, brown bread, spinach cannelloni and an excellent-value *tenedor libre* (all-you-can-eat buffet; US$3).

Club de Yachting y Pesca (Santa Rita s/n) Excellent seafood, standard Uruguayan fare and stunning views of the river.

Pulpería los Faroles (del Comercio & Misiones de los Tapes) Rustic decor, tasty seafood and a good wine list. The *pescado mar del plata* (fish in a creamy, seafood sauce; US$4) comes recommended.

Drugstore (Vasconcellos 179) Reasonable set meals for two, eclectic decor (try dining in the vintage car on the street) and live music on weekends.

Don Pedro (Manuel de Lobo 144) Serves sandwiches, pasta, meats and ice cream. The shady outdoor seating on Plaza Mayor makes this a great lunch spot.

Puerto Viejo (San Jose 170; meals US$7) Nightly tango shows in a beautiful old building by the old port. Meals are a bit pricey, but you're really paying for the atmosphere. Performances start around 9:30pm.

La Luna (General Flores 43) This laidback pub/restaurant with a great rooftop terrace is perfect if you enjoy drinking a beer at sunset.

Getting There & Away

BOAT

From the port at the foot of Av Roosevelt, **Buquebus** (☎ 052-22975) has two daily ferries to Buenos Aires (US$13, 2½ hours) and three high-speed *buqueaviones* (US$22, one hour) – literally 'flying boat.' **Ferryturismo's** (☎ 052-22919) catamaran goes twice daily and charges US$22. Immigration is at the port.

BUS

Colonia's new **terminal** (Artigas & Roosevelt) is near the port. Departures include Monte-
video (US$4.50, 2½ hours), Colonia Suiza (US$1.50, 50 minutes), Mercedes (US$4, three hours), Carmelo (US$2, one hour), Paysandú (US$8, six hours), Salto (US$10, eight hours) and Bella Unión (US$13.50, 10 hours).

Getting Around

Local buses leave from Flores to the Camping Municipal. Bicycles and mopeds can be rented in the port area; try **Viaggo Renta Car** (☎ 052-22266; Manuel del Lobos 503; bikes US$2/day, mopeds US$6/day, scooters US$10/day). Otherwise, walking is enjoyable in compact Colonia.

COLONIA SUIZA

Sixty kilometers east of Colonia del Sacramento, Colonia Suiza was settled by Swiss immigrants in 1862, and soon provided wheat for Montevideo. It's a quiet destination with a demonstrably European ambience. Its dairy goods are known throughout the country.

Hotel del Prado (☎ 0554-4169; r per person US$8) On the outskirts of town, this 80-room hotel dates from 1884. It once functioned as a brewery. Rooms have huge balconies The hostel wing offers beds in dorms with shared bathroom for the same price, somehow.

Don Juan (18 de Julio 1214) Pizza, pasta, coffee, cocktails and an excellent bakery. **Pizza y Pico** (Herrera & 25 de Agosto; ☽ evenings) is also recommended.

COT (☎ 0554-4093) and **Turil** (☎ 0554-4998) run numerous buses to Colonia (US$1.50, 50 minutes) and Montevideo (US$3, two hours), and fewer services westbound to Fray Bentos and Paysandú.

CARMELO

Carmelo's the sort of place you just fall for. Why? Who knows...it's small, nothing happens, there's no famous landmarks, but still, you go there for a day and find yourself a week later, planning to move on...tomorrow...maybe...

The town provides an interesting crossing to Argentina via the islands and channels of the Paraná delta. From Plaza Independencia in the center of town, Av 19 de Abril leads to Arroyo de las Vacas. A large park on the other side of the *arroyo* (river) offers camping, swimming and a monstrous casino.

The **main tourist office** (☎ 0542-2001; 19 de Abril 246; ☽ 8am-6pm Mon-Fri) is in the Casa de

Cultura. It has lots of information (some in English) and a decent city map. There's also a small tourist office in the park at Playa Seré. There are *casas de cambio* (authorized foreign currency-exchange houses) near Plaza Independencia.

Sleeping & Eating

Hotel Bertoletti (☎ 0542-2030; Uruguay 171; s/d US$5/8) Friendly and clean with a gee-it's-just-like-grandma's-house decor.

Hotel Centro (☎ 0542-2028; Uruguay 368; s/d with bath & breakfast US$10/13) Clean and spacious, some rooms have good light.

Camping Náutico Carmelo (☎ 0542-2058; sites US$3) This is on the south side of Arroyo de las Vacas.

Perrini (19 de Abril 440) Serves good *chivitos* (steak sandwiches with cheese, lettuce, tomato, bacon and condiments), pasta and sandwiches.

Piccolino (19 de Abril & Roosevelt) A good breakfast spot on the plaza. It also serves ice cream and is open for late-night snacking.

Getting There & Away

All bus companies are on or near Plaza Independencia. **Chadre** (☎ 0542-2987) goes to Montevideo (US$6, four hours), and north to Fray Bentos, Paysandú and Salto. **Turil** goes to Colonia (US$2, one hour), as do **Klüver** (☎ 0542-3411), Intertur and Berruti. Klüver also goes to Mercedes (US$2.50, two hours).

Cacciola (☎ 0542-3042; Constituyentes 219) has launches to the Buenos Aires suburb of Tigre (US$7, 3½ hours).

FRAY BENTOS

Three hundred kilometers west of Montevideo, across the Río Uruguay from Gualeguaychú, Argentina, Fray Bentos (population 23,3000) will always be best remembered for its famous meat factory, now a museum (see below).

Barren Plaza Constitución has only a few palms and a Victorian band shell, but the helpful **tourist office** (☎ 0562-2233; ⏰ 9am-8pm) occupies a room in the Museo Solari, on the west side of Plaza Constitución. There's another **tourist office** (☎ 0562-22737; ⏰ 24hr) in the bus terminal

Sights

The landmark 400-seat **Teatro Young** (25 de Mayo & Zorrilla), bearing the name of the Anglo-

Uruguayan *estanciero* who sponsored its construction from 1909 to 1912, hosts cultural events throughout the year.

In 1865 the Liebig Extract of Meat Company located its pioneer South American plant in the **Barrio Histórico del Anglo**, southwest of downtown. British-run El Anglo took over operations in the 1920s and by 1940 the factory employed a workforce of 4000, slaughtering up to 2000 cattle a day. Most of the defunct Frigorífico Anglo del Uruguay has become the **Museo de la Revolución Industrial** (☎ 0562-2918; ⏰ 10am-3pm Tue-Sun), a fascinating maze of corrals, walkways and slaughterhouses. You can only visit the museum on a guided tour (US$1).

Sleeping, Eating & Drinking

Nuevo Hotel Colonial (☎ 0562-2260; 25 de Mayo 3293; s/d with bath US$5/9) Clean but stuffy, the rooms have a TV.

Hotel 25 de Mayo (☎ 0562-2586; 25 de Mayo & Lavalleja; s/d US$6/8) Small but quiet and clean, with a lovely courtyard.

Balneario Las Cañas (☎ 0562-22224; sites for 2 people US$5) This sprawling municipal campground is 8km south of town.

La Enramada (España 1242) For dining, this is cheap but basic.

Juventud Unida (18 de Julio 1124) Try this popular, good-value local choice serving *parrillada*, sandwiches and pasta.

Ninos Bar (25 de Mayo 3373) This is a great place for a few drinks – there's a young crowd, pool tables and the occasional movie on the big screen.

Getting There & Away

The **bus terminal** (☎ 0562-2737; 18 de Julio & Varela) is 10 blocks east of Plaza Constitución. ETA goes to Gualeguaychú (US$3.50, one hour). Buses stop at immigration on the international bridge. **CUT** (☎ 0562-2286) has buses to Mercedes (US$1, 30 minutes) and Montevideo (US$7, 4½ hours). Chadre goes to Bella Unión via Salto and Paysandú, and south to Montevideo via Mercedes, Dolores, Carmelo and Colonia.

MERCEDES

The livestock center of Mercedes (population 40,900) is also a pretty resort on the Río Negro, popular for boating, fishing and swimming.

Plaza Independencia, the center of downtown, is dominated by the imposing neoclassical **cathedral** (1860).

The center is 10 blocks from the bus terminal. Either walk straight up Calle Colón with Plaza Artigas on your right, catch any local bus or fork out US$1 for a taxi.

The **tourist office** (☎ 053-22733; Artigas 215; 9:30am-12:30pm Mon-Fri, 6:30-9:30pm Sat & Sun) has friendly, enthusiastic staff and a good city map. Two nearby *casas de cambio* change cash but not traveler's checks. There is a **post office** (Rodó 650) and telephone office, **Centro Telefónico** (Artigas 290).

Sleeping & Eating

Club Remeros Mercedes (☎ 053-22534; De la Rivera 949; dm US$4-5) A classy old club with a big fireplace, pool and pingpong tables. The small dorms have a bathroom, fridge and microwave.

Hotel Mercedes (☎ 053-23204; Giménez 659; r without/with bath per person US$4/5) Central with a shady courtyard, the rooms have cable TV.

Camping del Hum (sites per person US$1, plus per tent US$1) On an island in the Río Negro, linked by a bridge to the mainland. It has excellent swimming, fishing and sanitary facilities. The campground closes when the river floods.

Parador La Rambla (Rambla de la Ribera s/n) Cheap *parrillada*, a good range of pasta and some seafood at this riverside joint with no-frills decor but some pleasant outdoor seating.

Pizza Uno (Colón & Castro y Careaga) Vaguely atmospheric, serving the standard range of pizza, sandwiches and ice cream.

Getting There & Away

The **bus terminal** (☎ 053-30515) is on Plaza Artigas, 10 blocks south of downtown. There are departures to Colonia (US$4, three hours) and Montevideo (US$6.50, four hours). ETA has services to Gualeguaychú, Argentina (US$14) and interior destinations.

PAYSANDÚ

Uruguay's third-largest city, Paysandú (population 78,200) is quiet during the week, crazy on weekends and absolute mayhem during the annual **beer festival** (in Semana Santa). Processing beer, sugar, textiles and leather, the city has a slightly gritty edge.

Av 18 de Julio, the main commercial street, runs along the south side of Plaza Constitución. The flood-prone riverfront mostly consists of parkland. The **tourist office** (☎ 072-26221; 18 de Julio 1226; 7am-7pm Mon-Fri, 8am-6pm Sat & Sun) is opposite Plaza Constitución. Cambio Fagalde is at 18 de Julio 1002. **Banco Acac** (18 de Julio 1020) has an ATM.

To get to the center from the bus terminal, walk seven blocks north on Av Zorilla. A taxi should cost around US$1.

The **Museo Histórico** (Zorrilla 874; admission free; 9am-5pm Mon-Fri) is housed in a fine 19th-century building with indigenous and colonial artifacts.

Sleeping & Eating

Hotel Concordia (☎ 072-22417; 18 de Julio 984; s/d with bath US$4/6) A grand old hotel offering good, quiet rooms with wooden floors, TV and some lovely tilework.

Hotel Rafaela (☎ 072-24216; 18 de Julio 1181; s/d with bath & breakfast US$5/8) Downstairs rooms have their own bathrooms, but are a bit airless. Upstairs, the cheaper rooms with shared bath are a much better deal, and you get a bit of a balcony, too.

Pan Z (18 de Julio & Pereda) 'Panceta' is the most popular eating place in town – it serves pizza, pasta, *chivitos* and half decent jugs of *sangria* (US$1.50).

Los Tres Pinos (Av España 1474) A busy, upmarket restaurant with reasonable prices. Steak, chicken and pasta go for around US$3. The local specialty is *chajá*, a creamy dessert.

Drinking

Sahara (Ave de los deportistas s/n; admission US$2) Paysandú's biggest club sleeps all week and goes crazy on Friday and Saturday, playing Latin pop, dance and techno later in the night. The crowd really starts to thicken around 2am.

Edelle (Paz & Brasil) This is *the* place to go for pre-clubbing drinks. Or else fill a bottle with something 'n' cola and hang out with everybody else in Plaza Artigas.

Getting There & Away

Paysandú's **bus terminal** (☎ 072-23225; Zorrilla & Artigas) is south of Plaza Constitución. Regular buses leave for Montevideo (US$8.50, five hours), Salto (US$3, two hours) and Tacuarembó (US$9, six hours). Copay goes to Colón, Argentina (US$2, 45 minutes).

SALTO

Directly across the river from Concordia, Argentina, Salto's main attractions are the nearby **hot springs** at Daymán and Arapey, but the city itself is also a pleasant destination.

The **Museo del Hombre y la Tecnología** (Brasil & Zorrilla; ☺ 2-7pm) in the former market features displays on local history. **Plaza Artigas** has an enchanting simplicity and is a great place to people watch.

The **tourist office** (☎ 073-25194; Uruguay 1052; ☺ 8am-8pm) is vaguely useful and can supply information about visiting the local hot springs. There are *casas de cambio* downtown.

Eight kilometers south of Salto, the **Termas de Daymán** is the largest and most developed of several thermal bath complexes in northwestern Uruguay. Surrounded by a cluster of motels and restaurants, it's a popular destination for Uruguayan and Argentine tourists, offering facilities for a variety of budgets.

Bus No 1 goes from the bus terminal to the center of town.

Sleeping & Eating
Hotel Concordia (☎ 073-32735; Uruguay 749; s/d US$6/11) Reputedly Uruguay's oldest hotel, rooms overlook an attractive interior patio and are filled with wonderful antique furniture. Ask to see room 32, where Carlos Gardel, the famous tango singer, stayed in 1933.

Hotel Plaza Artigas (☎ 073-34824; Artigas 1146; s/d US$4/8) Aging but atmospheric, this place could do with a few more windows.

Club Remeros (☎ 073-33418; Gutiérrez s/n; dm members/nonmembers US$2.50/3, bedding extra US$1) The local HI affiliate has basic hostel accommodations in a great old brick building at the river's edge. Rooms have two to 18 beds; some face the water.

Gran Hotel Salto (25 de Agosto 5) This has an excellent-value breakfast buffet (US$2.50).

Azabache (Uruguay 702) This has better atmosphere than most snack joints, serving good cheap pasta, sandwiches and fresh juices.

La Terraza (Costanera norte & Apolon) Two kilometers north of Club Remeros, this is a great place to while away an afternoon on the riverside munching on pasta and *parrillada*.

Drinking
Down near the port, the little strip of bars on Chinazzaro between Artigas and 19 de Abril gets lively on weekends. Also look out for Sensaciónes disco in the same area.

Getting There & Around
From Plaza Artigas, catch the bus marked 'Termas' for the Daymán hot springs. The US$1 fare includes entrance to the hot springs.

Chadre/Agencia Central and **Flecha Bus** (☎ 099-732052) go to Concordia, Argentina (US$1.50, one hour; immigration procedures are carried out on the bus).

Domestic buses go to Montevideo (US$12, six hours), Bella Unión (US$3, three hours) and Paysandú (US$3, two hours).

From the port at the foot of Brazil, launches cross the river to Concordia (US$1.50).

TACUAREMBÓ
In the rolling hills of the Cuchilla de Haedo, 390km north of Montevideo, Tacuarembó's sycamore-lined streets are home to monuments honoring not just the usual military heroes, but also writers, clergy and educators. The late-March **Fiesta de la Patria Gaucho** (Gaucho Festival) merits a visit from travelers in the area.

Tacuarembó's center is Plaza 19 de Abril. The **tourist office** (☎ 063-27144; ☺ 1-7pm Mon-Fri, 8am-1pm Sat & Sun) is in the bus terminal. The post office is at Ituzaingó 262. Antel is at Sarandí 240. The bus terminal is 2km from the center. Turn left on exiting, walk through the small plaza, veer right onto Herrera and walk four blocks to 18 de Julio. A taxi costs US$0.80

The **Museo del Indio y del Gaucho** (Flores & Artigas; admission free; ☺ 1-7pm Mon-Fri, 2-6pm Sat & Sun) pays romantic tribute to Uruguay's Indians and *gauchos*.

Sleeping & Eating
Hospedaje Bertiz (☎ 063-23324; Ituzaingó 211; s/d with bath US$6/8) Friendly with clean, basic rooms. Ask to see a few.

Hotel Plaza (☎ 063-27988; 25 de Agosto 247; s/d US$6/10) Clean but cramped rooms with TV.

Balneario Municipal Iporá (☎ 063-25344; sites free-US$2) Seven kilometers north of town, the free sites have clean toilets but lack showers. Buses leave from near Plaza 19 de Abril.

La Rueda (Beltrán & Flores) An inexpensive, atmospheric *parilla* decorated with gaucho paraphernalia.

La Sombrilla (25 de Mayo & Suárez) Located on Plaza 19 de Abril, this place is good for breakfast and late-night snacking.

Getting There & Away

The **Terminal Municipal** (Ruta 5 & Av Victorino Perera) is on the northeastern outskirts of town. Sample fares include Montevideo (US$9, five hours), Salto (US$6, five hours) and Paysandú (US$7, six hours).

EASTERN URUGUAY

East of Montevideo, countless resorts dot a scenic coastline, whose sandy beaches, vast dunes and dramatic headlands extend to the Brazilian border.

Conflicts between Spain and Portugal, then between Argentina and Brazil, left eastern Uruguay with historical monuments such as the fortresses of Santa Teresa and San Miguel. The interior's varied landscape of palm savannas and marshes is rich in bird life.

In summer the area attracts hordes of tourists, but by early March prices drop, the weather's still ideal and the pace more leisurely.

PIRIÁPOLIS

In the 1930s entrepreneur Francisco Piria built the landmark Hotel Argentino and an eccentric residence known as 'Piria's castle,' and ferried tourists directly from Argentina. Almost everything in Piriápolis is within walking distance of the waterfront Rambla de los Argentinos and defined by proximity to Hotel Argentino. The nearby countryside offers features like Cerro Pan de Azúcar and the hill resort of Minas.

The **tourist office** (☎ 043-22560; Rambla de los Argentinos 1348; ☺ 10am-8pm) has maps, brochures and current hotel prices. There's another tourist office in the bus terminal that is open odd hours during summer.

There's an ATM at Piria and Buenos Aires. You can change cash, but not traveler's checks, at Hotel Argentino.

Sleeping & Eating

Many hotels are open from December to April only; nearly all raise prices from mid-December to March.

Albergue Antón Grassi (☎ 043-20394; Simón del Pino 1106/36; dm member/nonmember US$3/4.50; ☺ year-round) Reservations are essential in January and February. It has fairly ordinary five-bed rooms with kitchen facilities.

Hotel Centro (☎ 043-22516; Sanabria 931; r per person with bath US$5) Hotel Centro has bright, airy and spacious rooms with a TV.

Hotel Lujan (☎ 043-22216; Sanabria 939; d US$9) This has friendly owners and rooms with a TV and fridge.

Camping Piriápolis FC (☎ 043-23275; Misiones & Niza; sites per person US$1.50, dm US$2.50; ☺ mid-Dec–late Apr) Opposite the bus terminal, this has plenty of sporting facilities.

La Langosta (Rambla de los Argentinos 1214; meals from US$2) Serving fine seafood and *parrillada*.

El Epignon (Rambla de los Argentinos & Sanabria; meals US$4) *Parrillada*, pasta and a great range of seafood, including paella.

Getting There & Away

The **bus terminal** (Misiones & Niza) is three blocks from the beach. There are numerous departures for Montevideo (US$3), Punta del Este (US$1.50) and Pan de Azúcar (US$1), where there are connections to Minas.

AROUND PIRIÁPOLIS
Pan de Azúcar

Ten kilometers north of town, there's a trail to the top of **Cerro Pan de Azúcar** (493m), Uruguay's third-highest point, crowned by a 35m-high cross and a conspicuous TV aerial. At the nearby Parque Municipal is the small but well-kept **Reserva de Fauna Autóctona**, with native species such as capybara and gray fox. Across the highway is the **Castillo de Piria**.

Minas & Around

Sixty kilometers north of Piriápolis, this amiable hill town draws its name from nearby quarries. There's a **tourist office** (☎ 044-29796; Batlle & Ordóñez) and **post office** (Rodó 571), and Antel at Beltrán and Rodó.

For lodging, try friendly **Posada Verdún** (☎ 044-24563; Washington Beltrán 715; s/d US$7/12). Inexpensive camping is possible at leafy **Parque Arequita** (☎ 0440-2503; sites per person US$1, 2-bed cabañas US$15), 9km north on the road to Polanco (public transport is available). For food, **Confitería Irisarri** (Plaza Libertad) is a local institution, famous for its *alfajores* (cookie sandwiches).

Every April 19, up to 70,000 people visit the pilgrimage site of **Cerro y Virgen del Verdún**, 6km west of Minas. Among the eucalyptus groves in **Parque Salus**, 10km west of town, is the source of Uruguay's best-known mineral water.

MALDONADO

In 1755 Spanish authorities founded Maldonado at the mouth of the Río de la Plata as an outpost to provision ships. Downtown retains colonial airs, but the town has sprawled because of tourist development in the area. It remains an economical alternative to Punta del Este (5km to the southeast, but strictly speaking also part of Maldonado) for food and accommodations.

Orientation & Information

The town's original grid centers on Plaza San Fernando, but streets are irregular between Maldonado and Punta del Este. West, along the river, Rambla Claudio Williman is the main thoroughfare, while to the east, Rambla Lorenzo Batlle Pacheco follows the Atlantic coast. Locations along these routes are usually identified by numbered *paradas* (bus stops). Both routes have fine beaches; the ocean beaches have rougher surf.

The **tourist office** (25 de Mayo s/n; 9am-8pm) is on Plaza San Fernando. A **desk** (042-250490) at the bus terminal keeps longer hours.

Casas de cambio are clustered around Plaza San Fernando. The post office is at Ituzaingó and San Carlos. Antel is at Florida and Joaquin de Viana. The **Bookshop** (Sarandi & Alegre) has a decent selection of books in English.

Sights

On Plaza San Fernando is the neoclassical **Catedral de Maldonado** (1895) with its striking gold-leaf altar. At Pérez del Puerto, between Solís and Michelini, the colonial watchtower at the **Plaza de la Torre del Vigía** was built with peepholes for viewing the approach of hostile forces.

Built between 1771 and 1797, the **Cuartel de Dragones y de Blandengues** is a block of military fortifications along 18 de Julio and Pérez del Puerto. Its **Museo Didáctico Artiguista** (admission free; 10am-11pm, guided visits 5-11pm) honors Uruguay's independence hero. Artigas was a very busy guy – check out the maps of his battle campaigns, and don't miss the room with the bronze busts of the Liberators of the Americas (and, yes... Washington gets a guernsey).

The **Museo San Fernando** (Sarandí & Pérez del Puerto; admission free; 1-6pm) is a fine-arts facility. Maldonado's oddest museum is the **Museo Mazzoni** (Ituzaingó 789; 9am-1pm), built in 1782, displaying a bathtub that reputedly belonged to Darwin and a copper pot used by Napoleon, among other things.

Sleeping

Hotel Le Petit (042-223044; Florida & Sarandí; s/d US$5/8) With chintzy, small rooms, this is almost over-friendly. It has a bit of street noise.

Hotel Sancar (223563; Juan Edye 597; s/d US$7/10) Well-kept and quieter than most hotels in town. Some rooms have TV.

Hotel 25 (042-223717; 18 de Julio 1092; s/d US$5/6) Basic, but cheap.

Camping San Rafael (042-486715; sites for 2 people US$7; summer only) On the eastern outskirts of town, with fine facilities on leafy grounds. Take bus No 5 from downtown.

Eating

Pizza y Pasta (Trienta y Tres 729) Friendly service and home-style cooking in a great old building. The house red is a ripper.

Lo de Ruben (Santa Teresa 846; set meals US$5) Good *parrillada*, and draft beer for US$1.50.

Taberna Patxi (Dodera 944) Basque specialties, including fish and shellfish, for around US$5. An extensive wine list and cozy seating.

Mundo Natural (Román Guerra 918) Most items US$2. This small, cheerful vegetarian place serves tasty *tartas*, soy- and seitan burgers, and brown rice.

Pizzapata (Ituzaingó & Román Guerra) Serves pizza by the meter, *chivitos* and seafood.

Getting There & Away

Terminal Maldonado (042-250490; Av Roosevelt & Sarandí) is eight blocks south of Plaza San Fernando. There are plenty of buses to Montevideo (US$3.50, two hours), Rocha (US$2, 1½ hours), La Paloma (US$3, two hours), Chuy (US$5, three hours), Minas (US$2, two hours) and Treinta y Tres (US$5, 3½ hours).

Codesa, Olivera and Maldonado Turismo buses link Maldonado with Punta del Este and other local destinations, including the beach circuit.

AROUND MALDONADO

Casa Pueblo (admission US$3) is an unconventional Mediterranean villa and art gallery at scenic Punta Ballena, 10km west of Maldonado. It was built by Carlos Páez Vilaró and is without right angles. It now includes the expensive **Hotel Casa Pueblo** (042-578485),

URUGUAY

but nearby **Camping Internacional Punta Ballena** (☎ 042-78902; sites US$5, 4-person cabins US$18) is a more economical option.

PUNTA DEL ESTE

The 'Punta' checklist: skimpy bikini (men and women), designer sunglasses (imitations will be sniggered at), dancing shoes.

Bring plenty of: cash, attitude, all-night party stamina.

Orientation & Information

Rambla General Artigas circles the peninsula, passing the protected beach of Playa Mansa and the yacht harbor on the west side and rugged Playa Brava on the east.

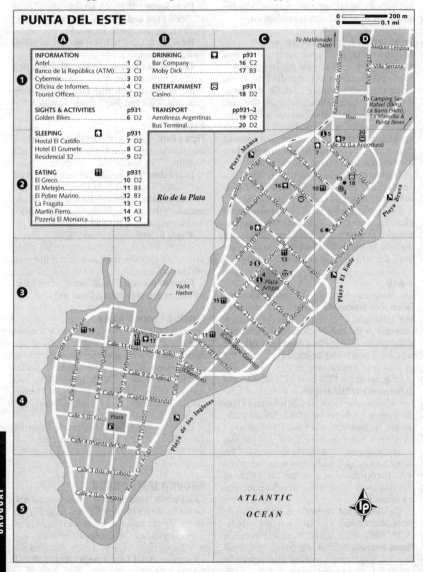

PUNTA DEL ESTE

INFORMATION		DRINKING	🍸	p931
Antel	1 C3	Bar Company		16 C2
Banco de la República (ATM)	2 C3	Moby Dick		17 B3
Cybermix	3 D2			
Oficina de Informes	4 C3	ENTERTAINMENT	🎭	p931
Tourist Offices	5 D2	Casino		18 D2
SIGHTS & ACTIVITIES	p931	TRANSPORT		pp931–2
Golden Bikes	6 D2	Aerolineas Argentinas		19 D2
		Bus Terminal		20 D2
SLEEPING	🛏 p931			
Hostal El Castillo	7 D2			
Hotel El Grumete	8 C2			
Residencial 32	9 D2			
EATING	🍴 p931			
El Greco	10 D2			
El Metejón	11 B3			
El Pobre Marino	12 B3			
La Fragata	13 C3			
Martin Fierro	14 A3			
Pizzería El Monarca	15 C3			

To Maldonado (5km)

Joaquin Lenzina

Villa Serrana

To Camping San Rafael (8km), La Barra (9km), La Marocha & Punta News

Rambla Claudio Williman

Bvar Artigas

Riso

Playa Mansa

Rambla Gral Artigas

Calle 30 (Las Focas)

Calle 31 (El Itajurú)

Calle 32 (La Angostura)

Calle 29 (Los Gaviotas)

Calle 28 (Los Meros)

Calle 18 (Baupres)

Los Muergos)

Río de la Plata

Calle 24 (El Mesana)

Playa Brava

Calle 20 (El Remanso)

Calle (Los Muergos)

Calle 19 (Los Gorteri)

Calle 22 (Av Juan Gorteri)

Calle 21 (Arrecifes)

Plaza Artigas

Rambla Gral Artigas

Playa El Emir

Yacht Harbor

Calle 23 (El Coral)

Calle 21 (La Galerna)

Calle 26 (Recalero)

Calle 19 (Comedero Gorteri)

Calle 13 (Marentes)

Calle 17 (El Estrecho)

Calle 11 (Juan Díaz de Solís)

Calle 9 (La Salina)

Calle 15 (Obenque)

Calle 14 (El Foque)

Rambla Gral Artigas

Calle 6 (El Pampero)

Calle 8 (El Tinquete)

Calle 10 (2 de Febrero)

Calle 7 (Capitán Miranda)

Calle 5 (El Faro)

Plaza

Calle 12 (Virazon)

Calle 4 (Puesta del Sol)

Playa de los Ingleses

Calle 3 (Isla de Lobos)

Rambla Gral Artigas

Calle 2 (Los Sargos)

ATLANTIC OCEAN

0 — 200 m
0 — 0.1 mi

Punta has two separate grids. North of a constricted neck east of the harbor is the high-rise hotel zone; the southern area is largely residential. Streets bear both names and numbers. Av Juan Gorlero is the main commercial street.

The **tourist office** (☎ 042-446510; cnr Baupres & Inzaurraga; ⏰ 8am-midnight summer) has shorter hours in winter. It also maintains an **Oficina de Informes** (☎ 042-446519) on Plaza Artigas.

Nearly all banks and *casas de cambio* are along Gorlero. The post office is at Los Meros between Gorlero and El Remanso. Antel is at Arrecifes and El Mesana. There is Internet access at **Cybermix** (Gorlero & Las Focas).

Activities

Twelve kilometers off Punta's east coast, **Isla de los Lobos** is home to large colonies of southern fur seals and sea lions. **Don Quico** (☎ 042-443963) runs tours to the island (US\$20, three hours) that leave from the port daily in the high season, on weekends in the low season. Make reservations in advance.

During summer, **parasailing, windsurfing** and **jet skiing** are possible on the Río de la Plata. Operators set up on the beach along Rambla Claudio Williman between paradas 7 and 20.

Blessed with the rough Atlantic ocean to the east and the calm waters of the Río de la Plata on the west, Punta's main attraction is its beaches. Beach-hopping is common, depending on local conditions and the general level of action. The most popular (and fashionable) beaches, such as Bikini, are north along Playa Brava.

Bikes can be rented for US\$1/3 per hour/day at **Golden Bikes** (☎ 042-447394; El Mesana), near Las Gaviotas.

Sleeping

Prices listed here are for the off season. For summer, add at least 30%.

Hostal El Castillo (☎ 09-409799; hostalelcastillo@hotmail.com; Inzaúrraga, btwn El Remanso & Baupres; dm/d US\$5/14) Minutes from the bus terminal with dorm-style accommodations and kitchen facilities.

Residencial 32 (☎ 042-491464; Angostura 640; s/d with bath US\$10/15) Clean but simple rooms.

Hotel El Grumete (☎ 042-447080; El Remanso & Los Muergos; s/d with bath US\$12/14) Basic but good-value rooms.

Eating

El Greco (Gorlero & Las Focas) A good spot for breakfast. It also does great sandwiches and homemade cakes.

El Pobre Marino (Solís 665) An absolute gem with fishnets, buoys and...dreamcatchers hanging from the roof. It's run by local fishermen and serves food for half the price (mains US\$4) of other seafood restaurants.

El Metejón (Gorlero 578) Popular for *parrillada* – be prepared to wait for a table.

Pizzería El Monarca (Gorlero 631) Reasonably priced pizza, pasta and *minutas*.

La Fragata (Gorlero 800; dishes US\$3, set meals US\$8) A good choice for seafood.

Martín Fierro (Rambla Artigas & Solís) A classy but pricey alternative with stunning ocean views.

Drinking

Punta's dynamic social scene kicks off with drinks at **Moby Dick** (Rambla Artigas, btwn Virazón & 2 de Febrero), or **Bar Company** (Las Gaviotas, btwn Baupres & Remanso). Clubbers then head north along Rambla Batlle to fashionable venues such as **La Morocha** and **Punta News**. Early in the night you'll have the dancefloor to yourself – nobody turns up at clubs until at least 2am.

Entertainment

There are many **cinemas** along Gorlero, as well as a **casino** (Gorlero & Inzaurraga).

Getting There & Away

AIR

Pluna (☎ 042-490101; Parada 8-1/2 on Rambla Batlle Pacheco) has daily flights to Buenos Aires (US\$120), plus summer schedules to São Paulo and other Brazilian destinations. **Aerolíneas Argentinas** (☎ 042-442949; Las Focas, btwn Gorlero & El Mesana), in the Edificio Santos Dumont, flies to Buenos Aires frequently, as does **LAPA** (☎ 042-490840; Av Roosevelt Parada 14-1/2) on Friday and Sunday.

BUS

Terminal Punta del Este (☎ 042-489467; Riso & Bulevar Artigas) has services that are an extension of those to Maldonado. International carriers include **TTL** (☎ 042-86755) to Brazil (US\$72).

Nationally, **COT** (☎ 042-483558) covers the Uruguayan coast from Montevideo to the Brazilian border. **Copsa** (☎ 042-489205) goes to Montevideo (US\$3.50, 2½ hours).

URUGUAY

Getting Around

Aeropuerto Laguna del Sauce (☎ 042-559777), west of Maldonaldo, can be reached by COT bus (US$3).

Frequent buses leaving from Rambla Artigas connect Punta del Este with Maldonado (US$0.50).

ROCHA

Late colonial and early independence era houses line the alleyways of Rocha, 220km east of Montevideo. It merits an afternoon's visit for those traveling to La Paloma.

The **tourist office** (☎ 0472-8202) is on the highway at the turn-off to La Paloma. The post office is at 18 de Julio 131. Antel is at General Artigas and Rodó.

Hotel Arrarte (☎ 0472-26756; Ramirez 118; s, d & t with bath US$7) Right on the plaza, this large hotel has a variety of rooms with TV and balcony. Ask to see a few.

City Café (Jose Ribot & Ramirez) A refreshingly inspired menu – downstairs is ordinary, but upstairs is cozy and comfy, with a good wine list.

Bus offices are on the main plaza. Sample fares include Montevideo (US$5, three hours), Chuy (US$3, 2½ hours) and La Paloma (US$1, one hour).

LA PALOMA

La Paloma (population 5000) is definitely up there for inclusion on the surfie/beachbum pilgrimage map. The surf breaks on both sides of the headland, and if one side's flat, the other should have a swell. The town's got a good vibe, too – you can slouch around in your flip flops and boardshorts to your heart's content.

The **tourist office** (☎ 0479-6008; Av Nicolás Solari s/n; ☜ 10am-noon & 2-4pm) is in the Liga de Fomento building. The post office is on Av Nicolás Solari, as is Antel.

Bikes can be rented from **Bicicletas El Topo** (Canopus, btwn de la Virgen & Antares) for US$2 per day. **Peteco** (Av Solari) rents surfboards for US$4 per day.

Sleeping & Eating

Albergue Altena 5000 (☎ 0479-6396; dm members/nonmembers US$3/4; ☜ year-round) In Parque Andresito, it has comfortable dorm rooms and a good party atmosphere in summer.

Hotel Embeleco (☎ 0479-6108; Av El Sol & de la Virgen; d US$8) All of the good-sized rooms at

this well-run establishment have balconies, minibars and TV.

Camping La Aguada (☎ 0479-6239; sites for 2 people US$3, 6-person cabins US$18) At the northern approach to town, this campground has excellent beach access, hot showers, a supermarket, restaurant and electricity.

All of the restaurants in La Paloma generally fall into two categories – very ornery or very snazzy. Of the former, **La Farola** (Av Solari) is good for *minutes*, pizza and coffee. Swankier restaurants include **La Marea** (Av Antares, btwn Av Solari & Canopus), which has reasonably priced seafood.

Getting There & Away

Cynsa (☎ 0479-6304) goes to Rocha (US$1) and Montevideo (US$6, 3½ hours). **Rutas del Sol** (☎ 0479-6019) goes to Montevideo and Punta del Diablo via Rocha.

PUNTA DEL DIABLO

Now *this* is a wild place – stuck out here, waves pounding against the shore, miles of wide sandy beach to wander along. It's getting developed, but in a totally low-key way; little huts and cabins, no high-rises. Let's hope it stays this way. **Parque Nacional Santa Teresa** is within easy hiking distance. **Horse riding** can be arranged for about US$3 an hour; ask in town for Sr José Vega.

Hotel La Posada (☎ 0477-2041; r at back/front US$10/17) A quaint little hotel perched on top of the bluff – the front rooms have awesome sea views. It has plenty of driftwood-styled furniture and seashells around the place.

There are a few private **cabañas** (US$14) for rent in the village; ask around for availability and bring your own bedding.

Camping Punta del Diablo (☎ 0477-2060; sites for 2 people US$7, 5-person cabins US$28) Two kilometres northwest of town, it has excellent facilities, including a supermarket and restaurant.

Locally caught seafood is a specialty. Try the excellent *corvina a la Provencal* (Croaker Provencal) at La Gaviotas Coiner, one of the best restaurants in town. **Los Varales** (opposite La Posada) has the usual range of seafood offerings, but the setting is the star here, with great ocean views. Little bars open up along the seafront during the summer, but the best parties happen on the beach where locals and visitors gather around beachfires to play guitars, sing songs and share aromatic, hand-rolled cigarettes.

Rutas del Sol has buses to La Paloma, Chuy and Montevideo (US$7, 4½ hours).

PARQUE NACIONAL SANTA TERESA

More an historical than a natural attraction, this coastal park 35km south of Chuy contains the hilltop **Fortaleza de Santa Teresa**, begun by the Portuguese but captured and finished by the Spaniards. Santa Teresa's a humble place, but Uruguayan and Brazilian visitors enjoy its uncrowded beaches and decentralized forest **camping** (sites US$5), with basic facilities.

The park gets crowded during Carnaval, but otherwise absorbs visitors without much difficulty. Services at park headquarters include telephones, a post office, supermarket, bakery, butcher and restaurant. Rutas del Sol travels from Punta del Diablo at 9am directly to the park headquarters and returns at 4:35pm. Buses traveling east to Chuy can also drop you off at the park entrance on Ruta 9.

CHUY & AROUND

Border towns often have a distinct atmosphere, and Chuy's no exception – it feels like the Wild West, and you half expect to see cowboys clanking down the main street in spurs. Mostly, though, it's old ladies flogging duty-free cigarettes and pirated CDs from Brazil.

If you're proceeding to Brazil, complete Uruguayan immigration formalities on Ruta 9, 2.5km south of town.

Seven kilometers west of Chuy, don't miss restored **Fuerte San Miguel** (Tue-Sun), a pink-granite fortress built in 1734 during hostilities between Spain and Portugal and protected by a moat.

Ten kilometers south of Chuy, a coastal lateral heads to **Camping Chuy** (0474-9425; sites US$6); catch a local bus from Chuy.

Hotel Internacional (0474-2055; Río San Luis 121; s/d with bath US$5/10) Well-kept rooms with a TV and vertigo-inducing murals.

For dining, try **Parrillada Jesús** (Av Brasil 603) or the nearby Los Leños for pasta, *parilla* and an excellent range of pizzas.

Several bus companies on Av Brasil connect Chuy with Montevideo (US$9, five hours).

URUGUAY DIRECTORY

ACCOMMODATIONS

Uruguay has a substantial network of youth hostels and several campgrounds, especially along the coast. An HI or International Student Identity Card (ISIC) will often help with discounts in hostels and (very) occasionally with bus fares. In towns, *hospedajes, residenciales* and *pensiones* offer budget accommodations from about US$4 per person (*hospedajes* have shared bathrooms and *pensiones* are usually a family home).

ACTIVITIES

Charlie may not surf, but plenty of visitors to Uruguay do. Punta del Diablo (p932) and La Paloma (p932) both get excellent waves and have shops that hire equipment. Punta del Este (p931) is the place to head for the upmarket beach scene, bars and snazzier beach activities, like parasailing, windsurfing and jet skiing.

Horse riding is popular in the interior. Many *estancias* now take paying guests – an excellent way of seeing the real heart of Uruguay (the Sociedad Uruguaya de Turismo Rural in Montevideo can hook you up). Bike riders can easily while away a day or two cycling around the atmospheric streets of Colonia del Sacramento (p921).

BOOKS

Lonely Planet's *Argentina, Uruguay & Paraguay* has greater coverage of the country. Worth tracking down is William Henry Hudson's 19th-century classic *The Purple Land*. For an account of Uruguay's own Dirty War, see Lawrence Weschler's *A Miracle, A Universe: Settling Accounts with Torturers*. Onetti's novels *No Man's Land*, *The Shipyard*, *Body Snatcher* and *A Brief Life* are mostly available in Spanish and English translation. *The Tree of Red Stars*, Tessa Bridal's acclaimed novel set in Montevideo during the 1970s, provides one of the best descriptions of life in Uruguay available to English readers.

BUSINESS HOURS

Most shops are open weekdays and Saturday from 8:30am to 12:30 or 1pm, then close until mid-afternoon and reopen until

URUGUAY

7pm or 8pm. Food shops are also open Sunday mornings.

From mid-November to mid-March, government offices are open weekdays from 7:30am to 1:30pm; the rest of the year, they are open noon to 7pm. Banks are open weekday afternoons in Montevideo; elsewhere, mornings are the rule.

CLIMATE

Since Uruguay's major attraction is its beaches, most visitors come in summer. Between late April and November strong winds sometimes combine with rain and cool temperatures (July's average temperature is a chilly 11°C). Along the Río Uruguay in summer, temperatures can be smotheringly hot, but the interior hill country is slightly cooler (January's average maximum is between 21°C and 26°C).

DANGERS & ANNOYANCES

Uruguay is one of the safest countries in South America, but street crime is on the rise. Take the normal precautions outlined in Dangers & Annoyances in the South America Directory (p1030).

DISABLED TRAVELERS

A modern country in many other ways, Uruguay hasn't kept up with developments for travelers with special needs. Footpaths are level(ish), but ramps and easy access buses are non-existent. Many budget hotels have at least one set of stairs and no elevator. On the bright side, taxis are cheap and plentiful, and the locals more than happy to help out when they can.

EMBASSIES & CONSULATES
Embassies & Consulates in Uruguay

Argentina Montevideo (☎ 02-902-8623; WF Aldunate 1281); Carmelo (☎ 054-22266; Roosevelt 442); Colonia del Sacramento (☎ 052-22093; General Flores 350); Paysandú (☎ 072-22253; Leandro Gómez 1034); Salto (☎ 073-32931; Artigas 1162)

Brazil Montevideo (☎ 02-901-2024; Convención 1343, 6th fl); Chuy (Fernández 147)

Canada Montevideo (☎ 02-902-2030; Plaza Independencia 749, Oficina 102)

France Montevideo (☎ 02-902-0077; Av Uruguay 853)

Germany Montevideo (☎ 02-902-5222; La Cumparsita 1435)

Paraguay Montevideo (☎ 02-408-5810; Bulevar Artigas 1191)

Switzerland Montevideo (☎ 02-710-4315; Federico Abadie 2936, 11th fl)

UK Montevideo (☎ 02-622-3630; Marco Bruto 1073)

USA Montevideo (☎ 02-203-6061; Lauro Muller 1776)

Uruguayan Embassies & Consulates Abroad

Uruguay has diplomatic representation in the following countries and also in most South American countries.

Canada Ottawa (☎ 613-234-2937; Ste 1905, 130 Albert St, Ottawa, Ontario K1P 5G4)

France Paris (☎ 01-45008137; 15 Le Sueur – 1er, 75116, Paris)

Germany Berlin (☎ 4930-2291424; Dorotheenstrasse 97, 10117 Berlin)

UK London (☎ 020-7589-8735; 140 Brompton Rd, 2nd fl, London SW3 1HY)

USA Washington (☎ 202-331-1313; 2715 M St NW, 3rd fl, Washington, DC 20007)

FESTIVALS & EVENTS

Uruguay's Carnaval, which takes place the Monday and Tuesday before Ash Wednesday, is livelier than Argentina's but more sedate than Brazil's. Montevideo's Afro-Uruguayan population celebrates with traditional *candombe* ceremonies. Semana Santa (the holy week of Easter) has become known as Semana Tourismo, with everybody from all over the country apparently going somewhere else. Accommodation is tricky during this time, but well worth the hassle are Montevideo's Creole Week (a gaucho extravaganza) and Paysandú's beer festival (no explanation needed).

FOOD & DRINK
Uruguayan Cuisine

Breakfast to a Uruguayan generally means *café con leche* and a croissant or two, followed by serious amounts of maté. Most restaurants will be able to offer at least some *tostados* (toasted sandwiches) to those accustomed to actually eating something in the morning. Any later than, say 10am, huge slabs of beef are the norm, usually cooked over hot coals on a *parrilla*. The most popular cut is the *asado de tira* (ribs) but *pulpo* (fillet steak) is also good, and *morcilla* (blood sausage) comes in both sweet and savory forms. Seafood is good on the coast.

The standard snack is *chivito*, a steak sandwich with cheese, lettuce, tomato, bacon and condiments. Other typical items are *puchero*, a beef stew, and *olímpicos* (club sandwiches).

Vegetarians can usually find something on the menu, often along the lines of pizza and pasta. Most vegans end up very familiar with the Uruguayan supermarket scene.

Regional desserts include *chajá*, a meringue and ice-cream concoction so good you'll be wondering how to smuggle some home, *flan casero* (crème caramel) and *masini*, a custard cream pastry topped with burnt sugar.

Drinks
NONALCOHOLIC DRINKS
The tap water's OK to drink in most places, but bottled water is cheap if you still have your doubts

Bottled drinks are inexpensive, and all the usual soft drinks are available. Try the *pomelo* (grapefruit) flavor – it's very refreshing and not too sickly sweet.

Jugos (juices) are available everywhere. The most common options are *naranja* (orange), *piña* (pineapple) and papaya. *Licuados* are juices mixed with either *leche* (milk) or water.

Coffee is available everywhere and always good, coming mostly *de la máquina* (from the machine). Uruguayans consume even more maté than Argentines and Paraguayans. If you get the chance, you should try to acquire the taste – there's nothing like whiling away an afternoon passing the maté with a bunch of newfound friends. *Té* (tea) drinking is not that common, but most cafés and bars will have some lying around somewhere. *Té de hierbas* (herb tea) are more popular, particularly *manzanilla* (chamomile) and *menta* (mint).

ALCOHOLIC DRINKS
Local beers, including Pilsen, Norteño and the sweeter Patricia, are good. The 330ml bottles are rare outside tourist areas – generally *cerveza* (beer) means a liter bottle and some glasses, which is a great way of meeting people – pour your neighbor a beer and no doubt they'll return the favor soon.

Cleric is a mixture of white wine and fruit juice, while *Medio y Medio* is a mixture of sparkling wine and white wine. A shot of *Grappa con miel* (grappa with honey) is worth a try – you might just like it.

GAY & LESBIAN TRAVELERS
Uruguay's not what you'd call G & L paradise. The progressive spirit hasn't transposed to matters of sexuality, and many gay and lesbian Uruguayans take the path of least resistance and simply migrate to Buenos Aires where the scene's a lot healthier. The **Grupo Diversidad website** (www .geocities.com/diversidad2000 in Spanish) has detailed information about gay and lesbian organizations in Argentina and Uruguay.

HEALTH
Uruguay does not require a yellow fever vaccination certificate and malaria isn't a problem. For more information, see the Health chapter (p1053).

HOLIDAYS
Año Nuevo (New Year's Day; January 1)
Epifanía (Epiphany; January 6)
Viernes Santo/Pascua (Good Friday/Easter; March/April – dates vary)
Desembarco de los 33 (Return of the 33 Exiles; April 1)
Día del Trabajador (Labor Day; May 1)
Batalla de Las Piedras (Battle of Las Piedras; May 18)
Natalicio de Artigas (Artigas' Birthday; June 19)
Jura de la Constitución (Constitution Day; July 18)
Día de la Independencia (Independence Day; August 25)
Día de la Raza (Columbus Day; October 12)
Día de los Muertos (All Souls' Day; November 2)
Navidad (Christmas Day; December 25)

INTERNET ACCESS
There are Internet cafés in cities and most resort towns; access costs around US$1 an hour. Some are set up for making Web calls, although varying connection speeds can make this a frustrating process.

INTERNET RESOURCES
Red Uruguaya (www.reduruguaya.com) A guide to Uruguayan Internet resources.
Ministerio de Turismo del Uruguay (www.turismo .gub.uy in Spanish) Government tourist information.
Mercopress News Agency (www.mercopress.com in English and Spanish) Montevideo-based Internet news agency.
Uruguayan Embassy in Washington, DC (www .embassy.org/uruguay) Historical, cultural and economic information on Uruguay.

MAPS
Uruguayan road maps are only a partial guide to the highways, but see the Automóvil Club del Uruguay, and Shell and Ancap stations

URUGUAY

for the best ones. For more detailed maps, try the **Instituto Geográfico Militar** (☎ 02-481-6868; 12 de Octubre & Abreu) in Montevideo.

MEDIA

Montevideo dailies include the morning *El Día*, *La República*, *La Mañana* and *El País*. *Gaceta Comercial* is the voice of the business community. Afternoon papers are *El Diario*, *Mundocolor* and *Últimas Noticias*. Most are identified with political parties, but the weekly *Búsqueda* takes a more independent stance.

MONEY

ATMs

For speed and convenience, nothing beats ATMs. They're found in most cities and smaller towns. Red Banc and Banco de la República Oriental del Uruguay seem to have the least temperamental machines.

Change

Change isn't the drama that it is in many South American countries. That said, you're not going to be making any friends by handing over a 1000 peso note for that pack of gum. Try to pay hotel and higher restaurant bills with large notes, even if you have exact change. Otherwise, any bank or *casa de cambio* will break unwieldy bills.

Credit Cards

Credit cards are useful, particularly when buying cash from a bank. Most better hotels, restaurants and shops accept credit cards.

Currency

The unit of currency is the peso *uruguayo* (Ur$). Banknote values are five, 10, 20, 50, 100, 200, 500 and 1000. There are coins of 50 *centésimos*, and one and two pesos.

Exchange Rates

Exchange rates at press time included the following:

Country	Unit		Ur$ (peso)
Australia	A$1	=	20.44
Canada	C$1	=	21.80
euro zone	€1	=	33.19
Japan	¥100	=	26.37
New Zealand	NZ$1	=	17.78
United Kingdom	UK£1	=	48.28
United States	US$1	=	28.82

Exchanging Money

There's plenty of *casas de cambio* in Montevideo, Colonia, and the Atlantic beach resorts, but banks are the rule in the interior. *Casas de cambio* offer slightly lower rates and sometimes charge commissions. There's no black market for dollars or other foreign currencies.

POST

Postal rates are reasonable, though service can be slow. If something is truly important, send it by registered mail or private courier.

For poste restante, address mail to the main post office in Montevideo. It will hold mail for up to a month, or two months with authorization.

RESPONSIBLE TRAVEL

Responsible tourism in Uruguay is mostly a matter of common sense, and the hard and fast rules here are ones that apply all over the globe.

Travelers should also be aware that Uruguayans are having a pretty tough time economically. Prices, profits and tourist arrivals are all down. Bargaining isn't part of the culture and serious red-in-the-face, veins-out-on-forehead haggling is completely out of phase with the whole Uruguayan psyche. Chances are you're paying exactly what the locals are, so ask yourself how important that 25 cents is before things get really nasty.

SHOPPING

Bargains include leather clothing and accessories, woolen clothing and fabrics, agates and gems, ceramics, woodcrafts and decorated maté gourds.

STUDYING

Cafés in tourist areas often have notice boards advertising private Spanish tuition and there are options for more organized classes in Montevideo. Dance and music tuition is also available in Montevideo.

TELEPHONE

Antel is the state telephone company, but there are private *locutorios* (telephone offices) as well. Magnetic cards are sold in values of 50, 100, 200 and 300 pesos. Discount rates (40% off) for international calls are available from 9pm to 9am weekdays, and all day Saturday, Sunday and holidays.

Making credit-card or collect calls to the US and other overseas destinations is often cheaper than paying locally.

TOILETS

Toilets in Uruguay are generally clean and of a similar design to what you're probably used to. If there's a wastepaper basket next to the toilet, put used toilet paper in there. Unless you want to block up the system and make a flood that is.

TOURIST INFORMATION

Almost every municipality has a tourist office, usually on the plaza or at the bus terminal. Maps can be mediocre, but many brochures have excellent historical information. The Ministerio de Turismo in Montevideo answers general inquiries on the country and has a fact-filled Web site (in Spanish) at www.turismo.gub.uy. Uruguayan embassies and consulates overseas can sometimes help with tourist inquiries.

TOURS

Organized tours haven't taken off in Uruguay – you're just going to have to get out there and do it yourself, tiger.

VISAS & DOCUMENTS

Uruguay requires passports of all foreigners, except those from neighboring countries (who need only national identification cards). Nationals of Western Europe, Australia, the USA, Canada and New Zealand automatically receive a 90-day tourist card, renewable for another 90 days. Other nationals may require visas. For extensions, visit the immigration office in Montevideo or local offices in border towns.

Passports are necessary for many everyday transactions, such as cashing traveler's checks and checking into hotels.

VOLUNTEERING

All Uruguayan organizations accepting volunteers require a minimum commitment of one month, and many require at least basic Spanish proficiency. Following are some of the many Montevideo-based NGOs.

Comisión de la Juventud (☎ 1950-2046; Santiago de Chile & Soriano) Social workers concentrating on youth issues.

Cruz Roja (Red Cross; ☎ 02-480-0714; 8 de Octubre 2990) The Red Cross helps people avoid, prepare for and cope with emergencies.

Liga Uruguaya de Voluntarios (☎ 02-481-F3763; Juancio 3216) Cancer prevention and education.

UNICEF (☎ 02-707-4972; España 2565) The local branch of the United Nations Children's Fund.

WOMEN TRAVELERS

Uruguayans are no slouches when it comes to *machismo,* but their easygoing nature means that in all but the most out of the way places, this will probably only manifest as the odd wolf-whistle or sleazy remark (or compliment, depending on your point of view).

Venezuela

HIGHLIGHTS

- **Mérida** – adventure-sports capital of the continent, offering paragliding, canyoning, rafting and mountaineering, to name just a few (see p976)
- **Salto Ángel (Angel Falls)** – the world's highest waterfall, sheltered in a spectacular natural setting (see p1007)
- **Los Roques** – beautiful archipelago of small coral islands and reefs – a paradise for fishing, snorkeling and scuba diving (see p962)
- **Los Llanos** – Venezuela's largest repository of wildlife, providing amazing safari-like opportunities (see p981)
- **Gran Sabana road** – a spectacular drive across the rolling savannah dotted with massive table mountains (see p1009)
- **Off the beaten track** – hike to the top of Roraima, a giant flat-topped mountain with moonscape scenery and unique plant life (see p1011)
- **Best journeys** – Maracay to Puerto Colombia: a short but dramatic ride through fabulous scenery ranging from beaches to cloud forest (see p967)

FAST FACTS

- **Area:** 916,445 sq km
- **Budget:** US$20–30 a day
- **Capital:** Caracas
- **Costs:** double room in a budget hotel US$7–15, set meal in a budget restaurant US$2–4, 100km intercity bus fare US$1.50–2
- **Country code:** ☎ 58
- **Electricity:** 110V, 60 Hz; US-type plugs
- **Famous for:** oil, beauty queens, *tepuis* and Simón Bolívar
- **Language:** Spanish
- **Money:** US$1 = 1600 bolívares
- **Phrases:** *de pinga*, *chévere* (cool), *asqueroso*, *guácala* (disgusting), *rumba*, *bonche* (party)
- **Population:** 25 million (2003 estimate)
- **Time:** GMT minus 4 hours
- **Tipping:** voluntary tips up to 10% in upmarket restaurants
- **Traveler's checks:** cashed in some major banks
- **Visas:** not required from nationals of major Western countries

TRAVEL HINTS

Have warm clothes at hand while traveling in air-con buses; they are often like freezers. Show respect for Bolívar – he is a saint to many Venezuelans.

Venezuela has a developed tourism infrastructure, spectacular new architecture and an extensive road network – a result of rapid growth achieved due to oil money. Yet deep in the countryside, people still live traditional lives, as if the modern era got lost somewhere down the road.

Venezuela's varying landscapes are unlikely to disappoint visitors. In the west, the northern tip of the Andes crowns the horizon with snowcapped peaks; in the east, the vast Orinoco Delta spreads a maze of crisscrossed natural channels out to the Atlantic. The south is a wild region of dense rainforest and includes a swath of the legendary Amazon Basin, while the north is bordered by 2800km of Caribbean coast lined with countless beautiful beaches.

Venezuela's most unusual natural formations are the *tepui,* flat-topped mountains looming more than 1000m above rolling savannas, with moonlike landscapes and peculiar endemic flora. From one *tepuis* spills Salto Ángel (Angel Falls), the world's highest waterfall (979m) and Venezuela's most famous tourist sight.

Visitors can travel as easily and safely, and even more cheaply, than a year or two ago. It has South America's cheapest air links to both Europe and the USA, and is thus a convenient gateway to the continent. Don't treat Venezuela as just a bridge, though; give yourself some time to discover this land – it's well worth it.

HISTORY
Pre-Columbian Times

By the time of the Spanish Conquest, some 300,000 to 400,000 indigenous people inhabited the region that is now Venezuela. They were isolated communities of various backgrounds, belonging to three main linguistic families: Carib, Arawak and Chibcha.

The warlike Carib tribes inhabited the central and eastern coast, living off fishing and shifting agriculture. Various Arawak groups were scattered over the western plains and north up to the coast. They lived off hunting and food-gathering, and occasionally practiced farming.

The Timote-Cuica, of the Chibcha linguistic family, were the most advanced of Venezuela's pre-Columbian societies. They inhabited the Andes and developed advanced agricultural techniques, including irrigation and terracing.

Spanish Conquest

Christopher Columbus was the first European to set foot on Venezuelan soil – indeed, Venezuela was the only country in the South American continent that Columbus landed on. On his third trip to the New World, in 1498, he anchored at the eastern tip of the Península de Paria, opposite Trinidad. At first he thought he had discovered yet another island, but continuing along the coast, he found the voluminous mouth of the Río Orinoco – sufficient proof that the place was much more than an island.

A year later another explorer Alonso de Ojeda, accompanied by the Italian Amerigo Vespucci, sailed up to the Península de la Guajira, on the western end of present-day Venezuela. On entering Lago de Maracaibo, the Spaniards saw the local indigenous people living in *palafitos,* thatched huts on stilts above the water. Perhaps as a sarcastic sailor joke, they called the land 'Venezuela' (literally, 'Little Venice'), as these rustic reed dwellings didn't exactly match the opulent palaces of the Italian city they knew. The first Spanish settlement on Venezuelan soil, Nueva Cádiz, was established in around 1500 on the small island of Cubagua, just south of Isla de Margarita. Pearl harvesting provided livelihood for the settlers, and the town developed into a busy port, which was subsequently destroyed by an earthquake and tidal wave in 1541. The earliest Venezuelan town still in existence, Cumaná (on the mainland directly south of Isla Cubagua), dates from 1521.

Officially, most of Venezuela was ruled by Spain from Santo Domingo (present-day capital of the Dominican Republic) until 1717, when it fell under the administration of the newly created Viceroyalty of Nueva Granada (with its capital in Bogotá), where it remained until independence. In practice, however, the region was allowed a large degree of autonomy. It was, after all, such an unimportant and sparsely populated backwater with an uninviting, steamy climate that the Spaniards gave it low priority,

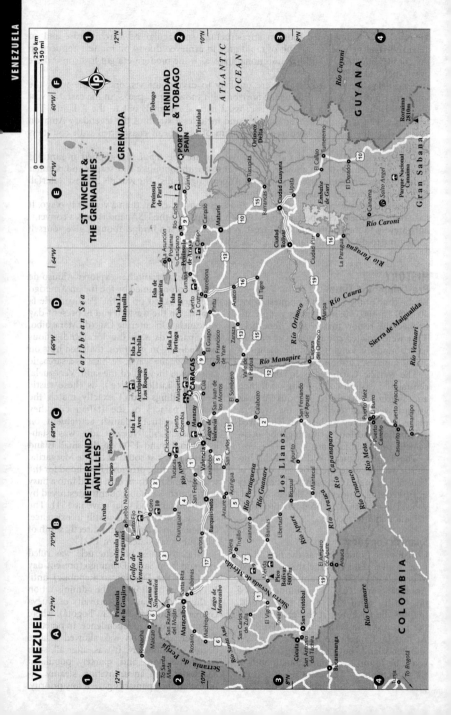

VENEZUELA

250 km
150 mi

Caribbean Sea

ATLANTIC OCEAN

NETHERLANDS ANTILLES

Aruba Curaçao Bonaire

ST VINCENT & THE GRENADINES

GRENADA

Tobago

TRINIDAD & TOBAGO

PORT OF SPAIN

Trinidad

GUYANA

COLOMBIA

Península de la Guajira

Laguna de Sinamaica

Golfo de Venezuela

Península de Paraguaná

Pueblo Nuevo

Punto Fijo

Coro

Peninsula de Paraguaná

Riohacha Maicao

To Santa Marta

San Rafael del Moján

Maracaibo

Santa Rita Cabimas

Rosario

Río Santa Ana

Machiques

San Carlos de Zulia

Lago de Maracaibo

El Vigía

Tovar

San Cristóbal

San Antonio del Táchira

Cúcuta

Bucaramanga

Tunja

To Bogotá

Río Casanare

Arauca

El Amparo de Apure

Apure

Río Apure

Río Arauca

Barinas

Libertad

Guanare

Trujillo

Valera

Carora

Acarigua

Sierra Nevada de Mérida

Pico Bolívar 5007m

Mérida

Barquisimeto

San Felipe

Churuguara

Tucacas

Río Aroa

Valencia

Carabobo

San Carlos

Río Portuguesa

Río Guanare

Buzual

Manteca

Río Cinaruco

Río Meta

Puerto Carreño

Casuarito Puerto Ayacucho

Samariapo

Puerto Páez

Río Capanaparo

San Fernando de Apure

Calabozo

El Sombrero

Valle de la Pascua

Río Manapire

San Juan de los Morros

Güa

CARACAS

Maiquetía

Puerto Colombia

Chichiriviche

Archipiélago Los Roques

Isla Las Aves

Isla La Orchila

Isla La Tortuga

Isla La Blanquilla

Isla La Orchila

El Guapo

San Francisco de Yare

Zaraza

Caicara del Orinoco

Maripa

Río Caura

Río Orinoco

El Tigre

Anaco

Pirtu

Puerto La Cruz

Barcelona

Cumaná

Isla de Margarita

Isla Cubagua

La Asunción

Porlamar

Península de Araya

Península de Paria

Río Caribe

Carúpano

Carúpano

Güiria

Maturín

Caripito

Barrancas

Tucupita

Orinoco Delta

Ciudad Guayana

Upata

El Callao

Tumeremo

El Dorado

Canaima

Salto Ángel

Parque Nacional Canaima

Roraima 2810m

Gran Sabana

Río Cuyuni

Ciudad Bolívar

Ciudad Piar

La Paragua

Río Paragua

Embalse de Guri

Río Caroní

Los Llanos

Río Ventuari

Sierra de Maigualida

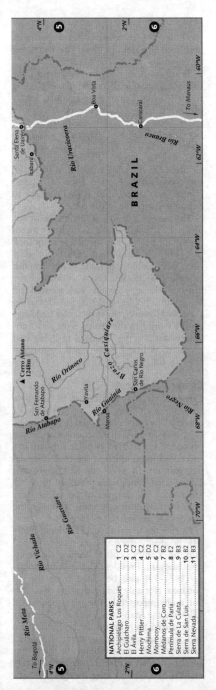

focusing instead on gold- and silver-rich Colombia, Peru and Bolivia. In many ways, Venezuela remained a backwater until the oil boom of the 1920s.

Independence Wars

Colonial Venezuela had a relatively uneventful history. All this changed at the beginning of the 19th century, when Venezuela gave Latin America its greatest hero, Simón Bolívar, who came to be largely responsible for ending colonial rule all the way to the borders of Argentina.

The revolutionary flame was lit by Francisco de Miranda in 1806, but his efforts to set up an independent administration in Caracas ended when fellow conspirators handed him over to the Spanish. He was shipped to Spain and died in jail. Bolívar then assumed leadership of the revolution. After unsuccessful initial attempts to defeat the Spaniards at home, he withdrew to Colombia, then to Jamaica, until the opportune moment came in 1817.

The Napoleonic Wars had ended, and Bolívar's agent in London was able to raise money and arms to recruit 5000 British veterans of the Peninsular War. With this force and an army of horsemen from Los Llanos, Bolívar marched over the Andes and defeated the Spanish at the Battle of Boyacá, bringing independence to Colombia in August 1819. Four months later in Angostura (present-day Ciudad Bolívar), the Angostura Congress proclaimed Gran Colombia a new state, unifying Colombia, Venezuela and Ecuador (though the last two were still under Spanish rule).

The liberation of Venezuela was completed with Bolívar's victory over Spanish forces at Carabobo in June 1821, though the royalists put up a desultory rearguard fight from Puerto Cabello for another two years. Gran Colombia existed for only a decade before splitting into three separate countries. Bolívar's dream of a unified republic fell apart before he died in 1830.

After Independence

Venezuela's post-independence period was marked by serious governmental problems that continued for more than a century. These were times of despotism and anarchy, with the country being ruled by a series of military dictators known as *caudillos*. It wasn't until 1947 that the first democratic government was elected.

The first of the *caudillos,* General José Antonio Páez, controlled the country for 18 years (1830–48). Despite his tough rule, he established a certain political stability and put the weak economy on its feet. The period that followed was an almost uninterrupted chain of civil wars that was only stopped by another long-lived dictator General Antonio Guzmán Blanco (1870–88). He launched a broad program of reform, including a new constitution, and assured some temporary stability, yet his despotic rule triggered wide popular opposition, and when he stepped down the country plunged again into civil war.

Things were not going much better on the international front. In the 1840s, Venezuela raised the question of its eastern border with British Guiana (present-day Guyana), claiming as much as two-thirds of Guiana, up to the Río Essequibo. The issue was finally settled in 1899 by an arbitration tribunal, which gave rights over the questioned territory to Great Britain. Despite the ruling, Venezuela maintains its claim to this day. All maps produced in Venezuela have this chunk of Guyana within Venezuela's boundaries, labeled *'Zona en Reclamación.'*

20th-Century Dictatorships

The first half of the 20th century was dominated by five successive military rulers from the Andean state of Táchira. The longest-lasting and most despotic was General Juan Vicente Gómez, who seized power in 1908 and didn't relinquish it until his death in 1935. Gómez phased out the parliament, squelched the opposition and monopolized power.

Thanks to the discovery of oil in the 1910s, the Gómez regime was able to stabilize the country. By the late 1920s, Venezuela became the world's largest exporter of oil, which not only contributed to economic recovery but also enabled the government to pay off the country's entire foreign debt.

Little of the oil-related wealth filtered down to people on the street. The vast majority continued to live in poverty with little or no educational or health facilities, let alone reasonable housing. Oil money also resulted in the neglect of agriculture. Food had to be imported and prices rose rapidly. When Gómez died in 1935, the people of Caracas went on a rampage, burning down the houses of his relatives and supporters, and even threatening to set fire to the oil installations on Lago de Maracaibo.

Tensions rose dangerously during the following *caudillo* dictatorships, exploding in 1945 when Rómulo Betancourt, leader of the left-wing Acción Democrática party (AD), took control of the government. A new constitution was adopted in 1947, and noted novelist Rómulo Gallegos became president in Venezuela's first democratic election. On the wave of political freedom, the conservative Partido Social Cristiano (Copei) was founded by Rafael Caldera to counterbalance the leftist AD.

The pace of reform was too fast, however, given the strength of the old military forces greedy for power. The inevitable coup took place only eight months after Gallegos' election, with Colonel Marcos Pérez Jiménez emerging as leader. Once in control, he crushed the opposition and plowed oil money into public works and modernizing Caracas. However, the spectacular buildings mushrooming in the capital were poor substitutes for a better standard of living and access to political power, and opposition grew rapidly.

Democracy at Last

Pérez Jiménez was overthrown in 1958 by a coalition of civilians and navy and air force officers. The country returned to democratic rule, and Rómulo Betancourt was elected president. He enjoyed popular support and succeeded in completing the constitutional five-year term in office – the first democratically elected Venezuelan president to do so. Since then, all changes of president have been by constitutional means, although the last decade has seen a few hiccups.

During the term of Rafael Caldera (1969–74) the steady stream of oil money flowed into the country's coffers keeping the economy buoyant. President Carlos Andrés Pérez (1974–79) also benefited from the oil bonanza. Not only did production of oil rise but, more importantly, the price quadrupled following the Arab–Israeli war in 1973. Pérez nationalized the iron-ore and oil industries and went on a spending spree. Imported luxury goods crammed shops, and the nation got the impression that El Dorado had finally materialized. Not for long, though.

Back to Instability

In the late 1970s, the growing international recession and oil glut began to shake Venezuela's economic stability. Oil revenues declined, pushing up unemployment, inflation and once more forcing the country to incur foreign debt. The 1988 drop in world oil prices cut the country's revenue in half, casting doubt on Venezuela's ability to pay off its foreign debt. Austerity measures introduced in 1989 by President Carlos Andrés Pérez (elected for the second time) triggered a wave of protests, culminating in three days of bloody riots, known as El Caracazo, and the loss of more than 300 lives. All further measures (basically price increases) spurred protests that often escalated into riots. Strikes and street demonstrations became part of everyday life.

To make matters worse, there were two attempted coups d'état in 1992. The first, in February, was led by paratrooper Colonel Hugo Chávez. Shooting throughout Caracas claimed more than 20 lives, but the government retained control. Chávez was sentenced to a long term in prison. The second attempt, in November, was led by junior air force officers. The air battle over Caracas, with warplanes flying between skyscrapers, gave the coup a cinematic, if not apocalyptic, dimension. The Palacio de Miraflores (Presidential Palace) was bombed and partially destroyed. The army was called to defend the president, and more than 100 people died.

Things became even more complicated in 1993 when Pérez was charged with embezzlement and misuse of public funds. He was automatically suspended from office, then judged, sentenced and placed under house arrest.

Amid the Pérez corruption scandals, Rafael Caldera was elected president for a second, nonconsecutive term, but his term was plagued by financial problems. The domino-like failure of a dozen banks in 1994 cost the government US$10 billion in payments to depositors, and several more banks failed in 1995. In all, the disaster cost the state coffers 20% of the GDP, making it one of the largest financial collapses experienced by a country in recent history.

In 1995 Caldera was forced to devalue the currency by more than 70%, and a year later the government introduced drastic rescue measures, including the increase of gas prices by 500%. By the end of 1998, two-thirds of Venezuela's 23 million inhabitants were living below the poverty line; drug-trafficking and crime had increased; and Colombian guerrillas had dramatically expanded their operations into Venezuela's frontiers.

Turn to the Left

The 1998 election put Hugo Chávez, the leader of the 1992 failed coup, into the presidency. After being pardoned by Caldera in 1994, Chávez embarked on an aggressive populist campaign, with nationalist Bolivarian rhetoric targeting the poor majority. He showed little enthusiasm for privatization and a free-market economy, vowing instead to produce a great if unspecified 'peaceful and democratic social revolution.'

Shortly after taking office, Chávez held a referendum in which a constituent assembly was approved to rewrite the existing constitution. The new document was approved in another referendum and came into force in December 1999. The new constitution gave the chief executive sweeping powers. It also introduced extensive changes – so extensive, in fact, that general elections had to be held again. In July 2000, still enjoying widespread popular support, Chávez easily won the new elections.

Since then, however, Chávez's 'social revolution' has been anything but peaceful. The introduction of a package of new decree laws in 2001 was met with angry protests, and was followed by a massive strike in April 2002. The strike turned violent, claimed 24 lives, and culminated in a coup d'état run by military leaders sponsored by a business lobby, in which Chávez was forced to resign. Miraculously, thanks to the help of his supporters, he regained power two days later, but this only intensified the conflict and left people poised for violence. Meanwhile, the economy continued to slump.

While the popular tensions rose, in December 2002 the opposition called a general strike in an attempt to oust the president. The nationwide strike paralyzed the country, including its vital oil industry and a good part of the private sector. After 63 days, the opposition finally called off the strike, which had cost the country 7.6% of its GDP and further devastated the oil-based economy.

Chávez again survived and claimed the victory, yet he has been increasingly isolated. According to the polls in mid-2003, his support had dropped to a record low of about 30%. The opposition has been divided and dispirited after the failure of the strike, and lacks a clear strategy and leader. The bitter political conflict is likely to continue, while Venezuela's future seems uncertain.

THE CULTURE
The National Psyche & Lifestyle
If there's one person who stands out in the nation's history it's Simón Bolívar, *the* national hero. His presence is ubiquitous (try to find a town without a Plaza Bolívar), and no matter which side of politics you are on, you can claim him as yours. Never show any disrespect for Bolívar – he's venerated by Venezuelans. Even innocent actions such as sitting on a bench in Plaza Bolívar with your feet on the bench, crossing the plaza wearing shorts or carrying a bulky backpack may be considered an insult, and police may hassle you.

Another source of national pride is the beauty of Venezuelan women, who have won all the major international beauty contests, including four Miss Universe pageants and five Miss Worlds. Supported by an enormous industry that includes cosmetics, plastic surgery and fashion, girls are trained from a very young age to become queens.

Venezuelans are also great sport aficionados but, intriguingly, soccer is not the top sport here, as it is just about anywhere else in Latin America. In Venezuela, baseball is the rage. Provided you're not a serious player, baseball goes very well with rum, the national drink. Beer is also a popular drink, particularly Polar beer, the dominant brand, sold in small 0.22L bottles and drunk at close to freezing temperature. If you ever wonder why Venezuelans don't like larger bottles, the answer is simple: the beer could get warm before you finish it.

For decades Venezuelans lived within a petrol bubble, in which wealth, comfort and stability seemed assured. Education in US universities, weekend shopping sprees in Margarita or even Miami and overseas holidays were a way of life. But when the oil crisis hit, the economy turned terribly sour. Venezuelans were some of the most apolitical folks on the continent. With petrol revenue flooding the country, there was no need to waste time thinking about politics. Then came President Hugo Chávez in his trademark scarlet beret, and all changed overnight. His unconventional style and populist rhetoric divided the nation. Today the spirit of revolution is everywhere. There are daily demonstrations in favor of or against his government, and everybody has taken a political stand. The society has become so polarized that it's effectively paralyzed.

It's probably not a coincidence that in such a volatile environment Venezuelans have been seeking spiritual and religious support. The country's most important holy figure, José Gregorio Hernández, is gaining more and more followers. You'll see his portraits and statuettes in homes, shops, offices and churches. It's the guy with a black felt hat and Chaplin's moustache that seems to have been taken from a silent movie – don't be confused.

People
Venezuela is a young nation of mixed races – more than half the population is under 18 years old. About 70% of the population has a blend of European, African and indigenous ancestry, or any two of the three. Of the remainder, 21% are white, 8% are black and 1% are full-blooded members of one of the country's many indigenous groups. Venezuela's indigenous people form 27 culturally distinct communities living in various regions of the country. Major groups include the Guajiro (north of Maracaibo), the Piaroa, Guajibo, Yekuana and Yanomami (in Amazonas), the Warao (in the Orinoco Delta) and the Pemón (in southeastern Guayana).

ARTS
Architecture
Since colonial Venezuela was a backwater of Spain, local architecture never reached the grandeur that marked the colony's wealthier neighbors, Colombia, Ecuador and Peru. Churches were mostly small and unpretentious, and houses followed the modest Andalusian style. More splendid residences were only built in the last 50 years of the colonial era, and only a handful of those have survived, including some in Coro. Local architectural style largely followed Spanish fashion for long after independence.

A real rush toward modernity came with oil money and culminated in the 1970s. This period was characterized by the indiscriminate demolition of the historic urban fabric and its replacement with modern architecture. Many dilapidated colonial buildings fell prey to greedy urban planners. Accordingly, Venezuela's colonial legacy can be disappointing when compared to that of other Andean countries. On the other hand, Venezuela has some remarkable modern architecture. Carlos Raúl Villanueva, who began work in the 1930s, is considered the most outstanding Venezuelan architect. The campus of Universidad Central de Venezuela in Caracas is regarded as one of his best and most coherent designs, and has been included on Unesco's Cultural Heritage list.

Literature
Simón Bolívar left an extensive written heritage, including letters, proclamations, discourses and dissertations. Bolívar was influenced by his close friend Andrés Bello, the first Venezuelan poet of note.

Andrés Eloy Blanco is often considered the best poet Venezuela has produced, while Rómulo Gallegos is perhaps the most internationally renown Venezuelan writer. *Doña Bárbara*, his most famous novel, was first published in Spain in 1929 and has been translated into a dozen languages.

Arturo Uslar Pietri stands out as an authority in the field of literature. A novelist, essayist, historian, literary critic and journalist, he has also been a prominent figure in politics.

Music
Venezuela's most popular folk rhythm is the *joropo*, which developed in Los Llanos. The *joropo* is usually sung and accompanied by harp, *cuatro* (a small, four-stringed guitar) and maracas. There's also a dance form of *joropo*.

Regional beats are plentiful. In the east, depending on where you are, you might hear the *estribillo, polo margariteño, malagueña, fulía* or *jota*. In the west, the *gaita* is typical of the Maracaibo region, while the *bambuco* is a popular Andean rhythm. The central coast echoes with African drumbeats. Caracas has absorbed all the influences, both local and international, and blasts as much with *joropo* and *merengue* as with salsa and Western rock.

Oscar D'León is Venezuela's most internationally renown musician and one of the world's top salsa stars. With his 40-year-long musical career, he has already entered the books of Latin American music history, yet hasn't slowed down on concerts and hectic tour schedules. He has recorded 60 albums and performed with most of salsa's luminaries, including Celia Cruz and Tito Puente.

Visual Arts
Visual art of the pre-Hispanic period is best reflected in petroglyphs, which have been found at about 200 locations across the country, mostly in the central coastal region and along the Orinoco and Caroní Rivers. A number of cave paintings have also been discovered, almost all of them in Guayana.

The art of the colonial period had an almost exclusively religious character and followed the Spanish style. Works from this era, consisting mainly of paintings of saints, carved wooden statues and retables, can be seen in old churches and museums.

After independence, painting turned to historical themes; noted representatives of the genre include Martín Tovar y Tovar, remembered for his monumental works in Caracas' Capitolio Nacional, and Tito Salas, who commemorated Bolívar's life and achievements.

Modern painting in Venezuela began with Armando Reverón, while Francisco Narváez is acclaimed as the country's first modern sculptor. Remarkable contemporary artists include Héctor Poleo (painting), Marisol Escobar (sculpture) and Jacobo Borges (painting). The most internationally renowned Venezuelan artist of recent decades is Jesús Soto, noted for his kinetic art.

SPORT
Baseball is the country's most popular sport, followed by basketball. Venezuelans don't seem to be as crazy about soccer as most other South Americans. Venezuela has several horseracing tracks, including La Rinconada in Caracas. Most cities have bullrings that attract crowds of *corrida* (bullfighting) fans, with the season peaking during Carnaval.

RELIGION

Most Venezuelans are Roman Catholics. Many indigenous people adopted Catholicism, and only a few, primarily those living in isolation, still practice ancient beliefs. Various Protestant churches in Venezuela have lately gained importance, taking adherents away from Catholicism. There are small Jewish and Muslim populations.

ENVIRONMENT
Land

Venezuela occupies the northernmost part of the continent, including the 2800km-long Caribbean coastline, and borders Colombia, Brazil and Guyana. Just south of the coast looms the Cordillera de la Costa, a chain of mountain ranges with a number of peaks exceeding 2000m. The mountains recede southward into a vast region of plains known as Los Llanos, which occupy one-third of the country's territory.

The 2150km Río Orinoco is Venezuela's main river, its entire course lying within national boundaries. The land south of the Orinoco (half of the country's area), known as Guayana, includes a chunk of the Amazon Basin, the Orinoco Delta, and a plateau of open savannas known as the Gran Sabana. The latter harbors several dozen *tepuis* (table mountains). These gigantic mesas, with vertical walls and flat tops, are all that's left of the upper layer of a plateau that has gradually eroded over millions of years.

Northwest Venezuela is another area of geographic contrast. The Sierra Nevada de Mérida, northern terminus of the Andes and Venezuela's highest mountain range, reaches its zenith here atop snowcapped Pico Bolívar (5007m). Just north of the lofty peaks lies the marshy lowland basin containing Lago de Maracaibo, South America's largest lake (about 200km long and 120km wide) and the center of Venezuela's oil-producing area.

Venezuela possesses 72 islands scattered along the Caribbean coast, the largest of which is Isla de Margarita.

Wildlife

As a tropical country with a diverse geography, Venezuela enjoys varied and exuberant flora and fauna. Distinctive habitats, each with its own peculiar wildlife, have evolved in different regions.

The country is home to about 1360 bird species, including the macaw, parrot, toucan, heron, pelican, flamingo, hummingbird, condor and oilbird. Mammals are also well represented (about 340 species) and include the jaguar, capybara, armadillo, anteater, tapir, puma, ocelot and peccary. Among the country's numerous reptiles are iguanas, snakes and five species of caiman (American crocodile).

The *tepuis* support some of Venezuela's most unusual flora. Isolated from the savanna below and from other *tepuis* for millions of years, the plant life on each of these plateaus developed independently. Half the plant life is considered endemic and typical of only one or a group of *tepuis*.

National Parks

Venezuela has 43 national parks and 21 *monumentos naturales* (small nature reserves intended to protect a particular natural feature, such as a lake, a mountain peak or a cave). The whole system of parks and reserves covers about 15% of the country's area.

The Instituto Nacional de Parques, commonly referred to as Inparques, is the governmental body created to administer the national parks and nature reserves. Only a handful of parks have Inparques-built visitor facilities. Many other parks are either wilderness or have been taken over by private operators, who offer their own tourist facilities and provide transport.

No permits are needed to enter national parks, but some parks charge admission, among them Los Roques (US$10), the western part of Canaima (US$6) and a half-dozen others with fees around US$1.

Environmental Issues

Tropical forest still covers a quarter of the country but is threatened by indiscriminate deforestation. Every year large areas of forest are logged and the land is cleared for agricultural use, pastureland, construction and industrial projects, and for its timber. A catastrophic drought in 2003 largely contributed to the loss of large chunks of forest, which have been burned, both deliberately and by bushfires. The shrinking forest area reduces the habitat for the wildlife and promotes erosion.

Lago de Maracaibo has been so heavily contaminated by decades of oil drilling and untreated sewage from the city of Maracaibo that cleaning it would cost billions of dollars. The discovery and exploitation of oil deposits in the Delta del Orinoco have put at risk the ecological balance of one of the best-preserved regions, including the pristine Parque Nacional Mariusa. Mercury is widely used in gold and diamond mining in Guayana, polluting rivers and causing health hazards for local inhabitants and wildlife.

Ironically, Venezuela was at the forefront of Latin America's green movement. An environmental protection law was enacted in 1975, and three years later the Ministerio del Ambiente (Ministry of the Environment) was created, becoming the first ministry of its kind on the continent. In 1992 Venezuela passed an environmental law specifying dozens of punishable crimes, including the pollution of soil, water and air; damaging the ozone layer; and setting forest fires.

All this looks highly impressive on paper, yet compliance has been minimal. The lack of personnel to enforce the law, a weak judicial system, widespread bureaucracy and notorious corruption are all obstacles to the successful prosecution of violators. If decisive measures aren't implemented promptly, the country's forests and wildlife resources face bleak prospects.

TRANSPORT

GETTING THERE & AWAY
Air

Set at the northern edge of South America, Venezuela is the cheapest gateway to the continent from both Europe and North America. Caracas is Venezuela's major international air hub, and most visitors arrive at Caracas' airport in Maiquetía. Other cities served by international flights include Valencia and Maracaibo.

International flights to/from Venezuela are offered by British Airways, Air France, KLM, American Airlines, and several Venezuelan carriers, including Aeropostal (Miami Lima, Havana, Port of Spain, Miami), Santa Bárbara (Aruba, Barranquilla) and Aserca (Aruba, Santo Domingo).

DEPARTURE TAX

The *tasa aeroportuaria* (airport tax) is US$25. An additional *impuesto de salida*

(departure tax) of US$13 must be paid by all visitors. The taxes are payable in either US dollars or bolívares, but not by credit card.

BRAZIL
Flying between Brazil and Venezuela is expensive. The one-way flight from São Paulo or Rio de Janeiro to Caracas will cost around US$840, or US$905 for a 60-day round trip. There are no direct flights between Manaus and Caracas, nor between Boa Vista and Santa Elena de Uairén.

COLOMBIA
Avianca and Aeropostal fly between Bogotá and Caracas (one way US$229, 30-/60-day round trip US$251/281). Santa Bárbara flies daily between Barranquilla and Maracaibo (one way US$135, 30-day round trip US$190).

GUYANA
There are no direct flights between Venezuela and Guyana. You have to fly via Port of Spain, Trinidad, with BWIA (one way/ 30-day round trip US$257/347).

NETHERLAND ANTILLES
KLM has flights from Caracas to Aruba, Curaçao and Bonaire. Aeropostal serves Aruba and Curaçao from Caracas. Aserca flies between Caracas and Aruba, and between Maracaibo and Aruba. Expect to pay about US$120 (one way) for any of these routes. Discount fares are available on seven- and 14-day round-trip flights with all three carriers.

Charter flights on light planes are available from Aruba and Curaçao to Coro. See the Coro section (p975).

TRINIDAD
Aeropostal and BWIA fly daily between Port of Spain and Caracas (one way/21-day round trip US$150/205). Aeropostal and Rutaca fly between Porlamar and Port of Spain.

Boat
Weekly passenger boats operate between Venezuela and Trinidad, but there are no longer ferries between Venezuela and the Netherland Antilles. For more information, see the Güiria section (p994).

Bus

BRAZIL

Only one road connects Brazil and Venezuela; it leads from Manaus through Boa Vista to Santa Elena de Uairén and continues to Ciudad Guayana. For details see Santa Elena de Uairén (p1013).

COLOMBIA

You can enter Venezuela from Colombia at several border crossings. In the northwest is a coastal route between Maicao and Maracaibo (see the Maracaibo section, p975). Further south is the most popular border crossing, between Cúcuta and San Antonio del Táchira (see the San Antonio del Táchira section, p982). There's also an uncommon outback route from Puerto Carreño in Colombia to either Puerto Páez or Puerto Ayacucho in Venezuela. See the Puerto Ayacucho section for details (p1016).

GUYANA

No roads link Guyana and Venezuela; you must go via Brazil.

GETTING AROUND

Air

Venezuela has a number of airlines and a reasonable network of air routes. Caracas (Caracas' airport is actually located in Maiquetía) is the country's major aviation hub and handles flights to most cities around the country.

Venezuela's major passenger airlines include Aeropostal, Aserca, Avior, Laser and Santa Bárbara. There are also perhaps a dozen minor passenger carriers that cover mostly regional routes.

Flying in Venezuela is reasonably cheap. Fares vary between carriers (sometimes substantially), so if the route you're flying is served by several airlines, check alternative fares before buying a ticket. Information on routes and fares is included in the relevant sections.

Reconfirm your flight at least 72 hours before departure and arm yourself with patience, as not all flights depart on time.

Boat

Venezuela has a number of islands, but only Isla de Margarita is serviced by regular scheduled boats and ferries; see Puerto La Cruz (p985), Cumaná (p990) and Isla de Margarita (p996).

The Río Orinoco is the country's major inland waterway. It's navigable from its mouth up to Puerto Ayacucho, but there's no regular passenger service on any part of it.

Bus

As there is no passenger train service in Venezuela, most traveling is done by bus. Buses are generally fast, and they run regularly day and night between major population centers.

Venezuela's dozens of bus companies run buses ranging from archaic pieces of junk to the most recent models. Many major companies offer *servicio ejecutivo,* comfortable air-con buses, which now cover most of the major long-distance routes. Note that the air-con can be very efficient, so have plenty of warm clothing at hand to avoid being frozen solid. The standard of service may differ from one company to another, as may fares. Figures given in particular sections later in this chapter are approximate average fares for air-con service.

All intercity buses depart from and arrive at the *terminal de pasajeros.* Every city has such a terminal, usually outside the city center but always linked to it by local transport. Caracas is the most important transport hub, handling buses to just about every corner of the country. In general, there's no need to buy tickets in advance for major routes, except around Christmas, Carnaval and Easter.

Many short-distance regional routes are served by the *por puesto* (literally, 'by the seat'). It's a cross between a bus and a taxi – the same kind of service as a *colectivo* in Colombia or Peru. *Por puestos* are usually large cars (or minibuses) that ply fixed routes and depart when all seats are filled. They cost about 40% to 80% more than buses, but are faster and usually more comfortable. On some routes, they're the dominant or even the exclusive means of transport.

Car & Motorcycle

Traveling by car is a comfortable and attractive way of getting around Venezuela. The country is sufficiently safe, and the network of roads is extensive and usually in acceptable shape. Gas stations are numerous and fuel is just about the cheapest in the world: US$0.05 to US$0.10 per liter, depending on the octane level.

A number of international and local car-rental companies, including Hertz, Avis, Budget and National, have offices at major airports throughout the country and in the centers of the main cities. Check with tourist offices, travel agencies or top-class hotels for information.

As a rough guide, a small car will cost US$40 to US$60 per day, with discount rates applying for a full week or longer. A 4WD vehicle is considerably more expensive and difficult to obtain.

Local Transport
BUS & METRO
All cities and many major towns have their own urban transportation systems, which in most places are small buses or minibuses. They are called, depending on the region, *busetas, carros, carritos, micros* or *camionetas*, and fares are usually not more than US$0.25. In many larger cities, you will also find urban *por puestos*, swinging faster than buses in the often chaotic traffic. Caracas is the only city in Venezuela with a subway system.

TAXI
Taxis are fairly inexpensive and are worth considering, particularly for transport between the bus terminal and city center when you are carrying all your bags. Taxis don't have meters, so always fix the fare with the driver before boarding. It's a good idea to find out the correct fare beforehand from an independent source, such as terminal officials or a hotel reception desk.

CARACAS

A spectacular setting in a valley amid rolling hills, striking modern architecture and a spider's web of motorways make Caracas unique among South American capitals. Fast-paced, progressive and cosmopolitan, it's a cocktail of all things Latin American, with a dash of the Caribbean and an aftertaste of Miami. In a race towards modernity, this love-it-or-hate-it city has almost buried 440 years of history beneath the gleaming monuments to oil-fueled affluence.

Home to five million people, Caracas is an important travel destination in itself, and a popular gateway to the country and

the continent. At an altitude of about 900m, the city enjoys an agreeable, sunny climate often described as eternal summer.

The unquestioned center of Venezuela's political and economic life, the size and status of the city make it the cultural capital as well. It has a vibrant theater scene, arthouse cinemas and cutting-edge art galleries. Its acclaimed Museum of Contemporary Art is perhaps the best on the continent, where the collection of Picasso, Matisse and Chagall is matched by stunning works by Venezuelan and Latin American artists.

Caracas' frenetic, eclectic nightlife provides myriad options for night clubbers, bar hoppers and live salsa aficionados, and an opportunity to rub shoulders with local hipsters. Upmarket restaurants abound in gastronomic hubs like Las Mercedes, where every international gourmet can be indulged. For less affluent visitors and hungry locals there are inexpensive eateries on every other corner.

Caracas' northern edge abuts directly onto the steep, wooded slopes of El Avila national park. Just minutes from the city bustle there are miles of walking trails where you can stroll through scented forests. A longer trek or a ride on the cable car will take you to the top of Pico El Avila providing bird's-eye views of the sprawling metropolis that is modern Caracas.

ORIENTATION
Nestled in a long and narrow valley, the city spreads for 25km west to east. To the north looms the steep green wall of Parque Nacional El Ávila, refreshingly free of human dwellings. To the south, by contrast, modern *urbanizaciones* (suburbs) and ramshackle *barrios* (shantytowns) expand up the hillsides, occupying every acceptably flat piece of land. The valley itself is cloaked edge to edge in a dense urban fabric; through a solid mass of low-rise architecture, skyscrapers poke up like needles through a quilt.

The city's historic quarter, at the west end of the greater downtown area, is clearly recognizable on the map by the chessboard layout of its streets. About 1.5km to the east is Parque Central, noted for museums, theaters and cinemas. Another 2km east is Sabana Grande, centered on a pedestrian mall. Continuing east is the commercial district of Chacao and, further on, the trendy Altamira,

VENEZUELA

CENTRAL CARACAS

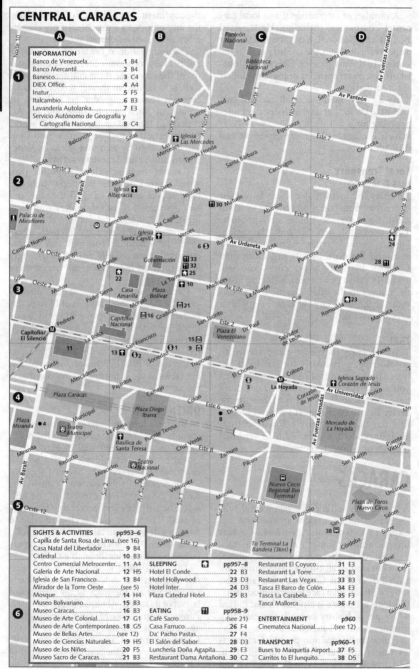

INFORMATION
Banco de Venezuela	**1** B4
Banco Mercantil	**2** B4
Banesco	**3** C4
DIEX Office	**4** A4
Inatur	**5** F5
Italcambio	**6** B3
Lavandería Autolanka	**7** E3
Servicio Autónomo de Geografía y Cartografía Nacional	**8** C4

SIGHTS & ACTIVITIES   pp953–6
Capilla de Santa Rosa de Lima	(see 16)
Casa Natal del Libertador	**9** B4
Catedral	**10** B3
Centro Comercial Metrocenter	**11** A4
Galería de Arte Nacional	**12** H5
Iglesia de San Francisco	**13** B4
Mirador de la Torre Oeste	(see 5)
Mosque	**14** H4
Museo Bolivariano	**15** B3
Museo Caracas	**16** B3
Museo de Arte Colonial	**17** G1
Museo de Arte Contemporáneo	**18** G5
Museo de Bellas Artes	(see 12)
Museo de Ciencias Naturales	**19** H5
Museo de los Niños	**20** F5
Museo Sacro de Caracas	**21** B3

SLEEPING   pp957–8
Hotel El Conde	**22** B3
Hotel Hollywood	**23** D3
Hotel Inter	**24** D3
Plaza Catedral Hotel	**25** B3

EATING   pp958–9
Café Sacro	(see 21)
Casa Farruco	**26** F4
Da' Pacho Pastas	**27** F4
El Salón del Sabor	**28** D3
Lunchería Doña Agapita	**29** E3
Restaurant Dama Antañona	**30** C2
Restaurant El Coyuco	**31** E3
Restaurant La Torre	**32** B3
Restaurant Las Vegas	**33** B3
Tasca El Barco de Colón	**34** E3
Tasca La Carabela	**35** F3
Tasca Mallorca	**36** F4

ENTERTAINMENT   p960
Cinemateca Nacional	(see 12)

TRANSPORT   pp960–1
Buses to Maiquetía Airport	**37** F5
Carritos to El Junquito	**38** D5

VENEZUELA

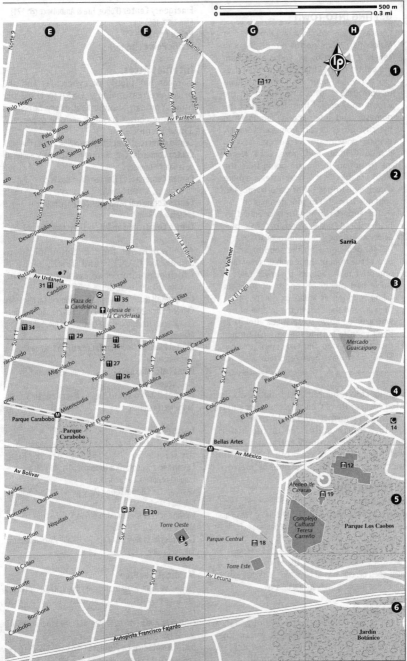

GETTING INTO TOWN

Caracas' main commercial airport is at Maiquetía, 26km northwest of the city center. If arriving by air, you can get from the airport to the city by bus or taxi. Buses run every half-hour from about 5:30am to 8pm (US$3, 30 to 50 minutes). At the airport, they depart from the front of the domestic and international terminals. In the city, buses depart from Calle Sur 17, directly underneath Av Bolívar, next to Parque Central, and from Gato Negro metro station. If you are going from the airport to the city, it may be faster and more convenient to get off at Gato Negro and continue by metro to your destination.

The airport taxi service is operated by black-colored Ford Explorers of the Corporación Anfitriones de Venezuela (US$12 to US$16, depending on the suburb), which park at the front of the terminal. Never take unofficial taxis, allured by lower fares – we've had plenty of reports of travelers being mugged at knife- or gun-point on the way and then left in the middle of nowhere. If you arrive at Maiquetía after dark, don't venture outside the terminal further than the bus stop and taxi stand. Holdups at gun-point have been reported.

with its chic restaurants and nightspots. Las Mercedes, south of Chacao, is another suburb catering to gourmets and night-trippers.

Most tourist sights are in the historic center and the Parque Central area, within walking distance of each other. Sights further away are easily accessible by metro.

INFORMATION
Bookshops

American Book Shop (☎ 0212-263-5455; Av San Juan Bosco, Altamira) Leading bookshop specializing in English-language publications.

Tecni-Ciencia Libros (☎ 0212-264-1765; Centro Comercial Sambil, Nivel Acuario, Chacao) One of Venezuela's best general-interest bookshops. It has half a dozen branches in shopping malls around the city.

Emergency

Services listed here operate 24 hours a day. Don't expect the attendants to speak English. If your Spanish is not up to scratch, try to get a local to call on your behalf.

Emergency Center (Police, Fire & Ambulance ☎ 171)
Fire (☎ 166)
Police (☎ 169)
Traffic Police (☎ 167)

Internet Access

Caracas has plenty of cybercafés and the prices are reasonable – US$1 to US$2 per hour. You can assume that every fair-sized shopping center has at least one cybercafé. These include:

Centro Comercial Chacaíto (Map pp954-5; Plaza Chacaíto)
Centro Comercial City Market (Map pp954-5; Boulevard de la Sabana Grande)
Centro Comercial El Recreo (Map pp954-5; Av Casanova, Sabana Grande)
Centro Comercial Metrocenter (Map pp950-1; Pedrera a La Bolsa)
Centro Comercial Sambil (Av Libertador, Chacao)

Also watch out for the communications centers of CANTV and Telcel, many of which offer Internet access. Other convenient facilities include:

CompuMall (Edificio CompuMall, Av Orinoco, Las Mercedes)
Cyber Office 2020 (Map pp954-5; Edificio San Germán, Calle Pascual Navarro con Av Francisco Solano, Sabana Grande)
Digital Planet (Yamin Family Center, Piso 1, Av San Juan Bosco, Altamira)
Point Café (Map pp954-5; Torre Capriles, Planta Baja, Plaza Venezuela)
Postnet (Estación Metro Chacaíto, Mezzanina, Local C-3) At the metro station.

Laundry

All the listed laundries provide wash and dry service for US$2 to US$3 per 5kg load:
Lavandería Autolanka (Map pp950-1; Av Urdaneta, Esquina Candilito, La Candelaria)
Lavandería Chapultepex (Map pp954-5; Calle Bolivia, Sabana Grande)
Lavandería El Metro (Map pp954-5; Calle Los Manguitos, Sabana Grande)
Lavandería El Rey (Map pp954-5; Calle Pascual Navarro, Sabana Grande)

Medical Services

Caracas has a number of hospitals, clinics and specialist medical centers. The best facilities include:
Clínica El Ávila (☎ 0212-276-1111; Av San Juan Bosco con 6a Transversal, Altamira)
Instituto Médico La Floresta (☎ 0212-285-2111; Av Principal de la Floresta con Calle Santa Ana)

OLD CARACAS CURIOUS STREET-ADDRESS SYSTEM

A curiosity of Caracas is the street-address system in the historic quarter. It's actually not the streets that bear names, but the *esquinas* (street corners). A place is identified by the street corners on either side, and its address is given 'corner to corner.' For example, the address 'El Conde a Carmelitas' means that the place is between these two street corners. Street numbers are seldom used. If the place is right on the corner, its address would be 'Esquina El Conde.' In modern times, authorities have given numbers and cardinal-point designations to the streets (*este, oeste, norte, sur* – east, west, north, south), but locals continue to stick to the *esquinas*.

Policlínica Metropolitana (☎ 0212-908-0100; Av Principal de Caurimare con Calle A)

Money

Italcambio, Caracas' major *casa de cambio* (authorized money-exchange office), has several outlets throughout the city, plus a couple at Maiquetía airport. All change foreign currency and most major brands of traveler's checks. American Express traveler's checks can also be cashed (at a better rate than at Italcambio) at any branch of Corp Banca.

Cash advances on Visa and/or MasterCard credit cards can be obtained at Banco de Venezuela, Banco Mercantil, Banesco, Banco Provincial and some other banks. Virtually all of these have ATMs.

Post

Ipostel (Map pp950-1; Av Urdaneta, Carmelitas a Llaguno) The main post office handles poste restante service. Letters sent to you here should be addressed with your name, Lista de Correos, Ipostel, Carmelitas, Caracas 1010. Ipostel has branch offices in most suburbs.

Telephone

You can easily call long-distance domestic and international telephone numbers from public phones. Should you need operator assistance, make your call from one of the numerous offices called Centro de Comunicaciones CANTV or Centro de Conexiones Telcel.

Tourist Offices

Inatur (Map pp950-1; ☎ 0800-462-8871, 0212-574-8712, 0212-574-9556; Torre Oeste (West Tower), 35 fl, Parque Central; ☟ 8:30am-12:30pm & 2-5pm Mon-Fri) Inatur also has outlets in the international and domestic terminals at Maiquetía airport.

Travel Agencies

IVI Idiomas Vivos (☎ 0212-993-6082, 0212-993-7174; www.ividiomas.com; Residencia La Hacienda, Piso Bajo, Final Av Principal de Las Mercedes) Issues ISIC and ITIC cards, and offers discounted airfares to Europe and elsewhere for foreign students, teachers and people under 26 years of age.

DANGERS & ANNOYANCES

Caracas is the least secure of all Venezuelan cities. Petty crime, robbery and armed assaults are increasing, especially at night. Central districts are OK during the day, though armed robberies occasionally occur. The eastern suburbs (Altamira, Las Mercedes) are safer than the historic center and Sabana Grande. Travelers should be cautious and aware of their surroundings.

SIGHTS
Historic Center & Around

Caracas' historic center lost much of its original identity following the rush toward modernization, when many colonial houses were replaced with modern buildings. The best preserved sector is around **Plaza Bolívar**, sporting the inevitable monument to the hero at its center. The equestrian statue was cast in Europe, shipped in pieces, assembled and unveiled in 1874.

The **Catedral** (Map pp950-1; Plaza Bolívar) was built between 1665 and 1713 after an earthquake destroyed the previous church. A wide, five-nave interior supported on 32 columns was largely remodeled in the late 19th century. In the middle of the right-hand aisle is the Bolívar family chapel, recognizable by the modern sculpture of Bolívar mourning his parents and wife.

Next to the cathedral is the **Museo Sacro de Caracas** (Map pp950-1; ☎ 0212-861-6562; Plaza Bolívar; admission US$0.40; ☟ 10am-4:30pm Tue-Sun), which has a fine collection of religious art.

The **Museo Caracas** (Map pp950-1; ☎ 0212-409-8236; Plaza Bolívar; admission free; ☟ 10:30am-noon & 2-4:30pm Tue-Fri, 10:30am-4:30pm Sat & Sun), in the colonial Palacio Municipal, features exhibits related to the town's history. The

VENEZUELA

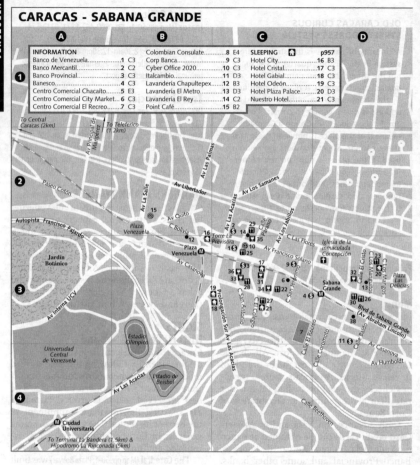

CARACAS - SABANA GRANDE

INFORMATION		Colombian Consulate............8 E4		SLEEPING 🏠 p957
Banco de Venezuela..............1 C3		Corp Banca...........................9 C3		Hotel City.............................16 B3
Banco Mercantil...................2 C2		Cyber Office 2020..............10 C3		Hotel Cristal.........................17 C3
Banco Provincial..................3 C3		Italcambio..........................11 D3		Hotel Gabial.........................18 C3
Banesco...............................4 C3		Lavandería Chapultepex.....12 B3		Hotel Odeón.........................19 C3
Centro Comercial Chacaíto....5 E3		Lavandería El Metro............13 D3		Hotel Plaza Palace................20 D3
Centro Comercial City Market..6 C3		Lavandería El Rey...............14 C2		Nuestro Hotel.......................21 C3
Centro Comercial El Recreo....7 C3		Point Café...........................15 B2		

west side of the building accommodates the **Capilla de Santa Rosa de Lima**, where, on July 5, 1811, congress declared Venezuela's independence (though it was another 10 years before this became fact).

The entire block southwest of Plaza Bolívar is taken up by the neoclassical **Capitolio Nacional**, a complex of two buildings erected in the 1870s. In the northern building is the **Salón Elíptico** (admission free; ☺ 9am-noon & 1-4:30pm Tue-Fri, 10am-1pm & 2-4:30pm Sat & Sun), an oval hall boasting a large mural on its domed ceiling. The mural, depicting the battle of Carabobo, was painted in 1888 by Martín Tovar y Tovar.

Just south of the Capitolio is the **Iglesia de San Francisco** (Map pp950-1; Av Universidad), which

shelters a number of richly gilded baroque altarpieces. It was here that Bolívar was first proclaimed El Libertador (in 1813) and where his much-celebrated funeral was held (in 1842, 12 years after his death, when his remains were finally brought back from Colombia).

Two blocks east is the **Casa Natal del Libertador** (Map pp950-1; ☎ 0212-541-2563; San Jacinto a Traposos; admission free; ☺ 9am-4:30pm Tue-Fri, 10am-4:30pm Sat & Sun), the house where Bolívar was born in 1783. Its reconstructed interior is decorated with paintings by Tito Salas depicting Bolívar's battles and other scenes from his life. Just to the north, in another colonial house, the **Museo Bolivariano** (Map pp950-1; ☎ 0212-545-9828; San Jacinto a Traposos;

| 0 | 800 m |
| 0 | 0.5 mi |

Av Libertador

Av Francisco Solano

Chacao (1km),
La Castellana (2km),
Los Palos Grandes (2km),
Parque del Este
& Altamira (2km)

Chacaíto
Plaza
Chacaíto

Centro
Comercial
Arta

Av Tamanaco

El Rosal

Calle Monroe

To Las Mercedes (500m),
Real Past (500m),
La Castanuela (750m),
La Punta Grill (250m),
CompuMall (1km),
Los Riviera (1km),
La Casa del Llano (1km),
(VI Idiomas Vivos (1.5km)
& El Hatillo (12km)

Autopista Francisco Fajardo

admission free; 🕙 9am-4:30pm Tue-Fri, 10am-4:30pm Sat & Sun) displays independence memorabilia, period weapons, and banners and portraits of Bolívar.

The **Panteón Nacional**, (☎ 0212-862-1518; Av Norte; admission free; 🕙 9am-4pm Tue-Fri, 10am-4pm Sat & Sun), five blocks north of Plaza Bolívar, was originally built as a church, but after being wrecked by the 1812 earthquake, it was rebuilt to serve as the last resting place for eminent Venezuelans. The central nave is dedicated to Bolívar – his bronze sarcophagus occupies the chancel in place of the high altar, while the tombs of 140 other distinguished figures (including only three women) have been pushed out to the aisles. The vault of the pantheon is covered by

paintings depicting scenes from Bolívar's life, all done by Tito Salas in the 1930s.

About 1.5km east of the pantheon is the **Museo de Arte Colonial** (Map pp950-1; ☎ 0212-551-8517; Av Panteón, San Bernardino; admission US$1.50; 🕙 9am-11:30am & 2-4:30pm Tue-Fri, 10am-5pm Sat & Sun), housed in a colonial country mansion known as the Quinta de Anauco, surrounded by a lush garden. You'll be guided around meticulously restored interiors filled with works of art, furniture and household implements.

Parque Central & Around

Parque Central, 1.5km southeast of Plaza Bolívar, is not, as you might expect, a park, but a concrete complex consisting of five high-rise residential slabs of rather apocalyptic appearance, crowned by two 53-story octagonal towers, the tallest in the country. The complex and its environs boast some important museums and other sights.

To start with, go to the **Mirador de la Torre Oeste** (Map pp950-1; ☎ 0212-573-5386; admission free; 🕙 9am-11am & 2-4pm Tue-Fri), an open-air viewpoint on the top of the West Tower, which provides an impressive 360° bird's-eye view of the city. Inquire at the CSB División y Departamento de Seguridad, on the tower's basement level (called Nivel Sótano Uno), and somebody will accompany you to the top.

The **Museo de Arte Contemporáneo** (Map pp950-1; ☎ 0212-573-0075; admission free; 🕙 10am-6pm Tue-Sun), at the east end of Parque Central, is by far the best contemporary art museum in the country and also one of the best in South America. It features works by major national artists, including Jesús Soto, and works by some great international painters such as Miró, Chagall, Léger and Picasso. The museum's pride is its collection of about 100 engravings by Picasso, created between 1931 and 1934. Part of the exhibition space is given to changing displays.

In the opposite, west end of Parque Central is the good, hands-on **Museo de los Niños** (Map pp950-1; Children's Museum; ☎ 0212-573-3022; admission US$3; 🕙 9am-noon & 2-5pm Wed-Sun), where adults have as much fun as kids. Avoid weekends, when the museum is besieged by families.

Just east of Parque Central is the **Complejo Cultural Teresa Carreño** (☎ 0212-574-9122), a modern performing-arts center that hosts concerts, ballet and theater in its

2400-seat auditorium. Hour-long guided tours (US$0.50) around the complex are run several times a day from Tuesday to Saturday. At the back of the building is a small museum dedicated to Teresa Carreño (1853–1917), widely considered the best pianist Venezuela has ever produced.

North of the complex is the **Museo de Ciencias Naturales** (Map pp950-1; ☎ 0212-577-5786; Plaza de los Museos; admission US$1.50; ☼ 9am-5pm Mon-Fri, 10:30am-6pm Sat & Sun).

Opposite, the **Galería de Arte Nacional** (Map pp950-1; ☎ 0212-578-1818; Plaza de los Museos; admission free; ☼ 9am-5pm Tue-Fri, 10am-5pm Sat & Sun) has a collection of some 4000 works of art embracing four centuries of Venezuelan artistic expression, plus some pre-Hispanic art. Adjoining the gallery is the **Museo de Bellas Artes** (☎ 0212-578-1816; Plaza de los Museos; admission free; ☼ 10am-4pm Tue-Sun), which features mainly temporary exhibitions. Go to the rooftop terrace for views over the city, including a modern mosque to the north. Both art museums are closed on Monday.

Other Areas

Visit the **Jardín Botánico** (Map pp950-1 & pp954-5; Botanical Garden; ☎ 0212-662-9254; Av Interna UCV; admission US$0.80; ☼ 8:30am-4:30pm Tue-Sun), southwest of Plaza Venezuela. South of the garden is the **Universidad Central de Venezuela** (Map pp954-5; ☎ 0212-605-4050), Caracas' largest university, which occupies a vast campus dotted with sculptures and murals. The campus was designed in the 1950s by Venezuela's most prominent architect, Carlos Raúl Villanueva, and was included on Unesco's Cultural Heritage list. There's a good concert hall, Aula Magna, on the grounds – it's worth checking what's going on.

In the eastern part of the city is the **Parque del Este** (☎ 0212-273-2818; Av Francisco de Miranda; admission US$0.20; ☼ 5-9am Mon, 5am-5pm Tue-Sun), the city's largest park. It's good for walks, and you can visit the snake house, aviary and cactus garden. You can also enjoy a show in the Planetario Humboldt on weekend afternoons. Next to the park is the **Museo del Transporte** (☎ 0212-234-2234; admission US$0.80; ☼ 8am-1pm Wed, 9am-4pm Sun), which features collections of old horse-drawn carts, carriages and vintage cars.

At the southwestern outskirts of the city is Caracas' main zoo, the **Parque Zoológico de Curicuao** (☎ 0212-431-2045; admission US$1; ☼ 9am-4pm Tue-Sun), which features a selection of native birds, reptiles and mammals. It's easily accessed by metro.

El Hatillo, 15km southeast of the city center, was once a small, colonial town, but today is a city suburb. Centered on Plaza Bolívar, it retains some of its colonial architecture, including the parish church. Restored houses have been painted in bright colors, giving the place an attractive and lively look. Every second house is either an eating establishment or a handicrafts shop. El Hatillo has become a trendy getaway for *caraqueños* (residents of Caracas), and is packed with cars and people on weekends. Frequent *carritos* (US$0.30) run to El Hatillo from Av Humboldt, just off Boulevard de Sabana Grande.

Don't miss the **Teleférico** (☎ 0212-905-8811; round-trip fare US$10; ☼ noon-7pm), a cable-car trip up to El Ávila in the Parque Nacional El Ávila, north of the city. Originally built by a German company in 1956–57, the 3.4km cable-car line runs from Caracas up to Pico El Ávila (2105m). It was closed down in 1988, before a wholly new Austrian construction with 76 Swiss cars was built on the same site and opened in 2002. The *teleférico* departs from the Maripérez station (accessible by taxi, not by bus) and the trip to the top takes 15 minutes. Take a jacket or a sweater if you plan to stay until late afternoon. A collection of food stalls will keep you going. The area around Pico El Ávila provides splendid views of Caracas and the Caribbean coast. The park also offers great hikes – see Parque Nacional El Ávila (p961).

TOURS

Plenty of travel agencies in Caracas offer tours to virtually every corner of the country, but it will be cheaper to arrive in a region on your own and contract a local operator.

Akanan Travel & Adventure (☎ 0212-234-2323; www.akanan.com; Edificio Claret, Av Sanz con Calle La Laguna, El Marqués) is one of Caracas' best adventure tour companies, offering ecological trips to off-the-beaten-track natural attractions.

The Centro Excursionista Caracas (CEC) is an association of outdoor-minded people who organize weekend trips around Caracas and the central states (longer journeys to other regions are scheduled for holiday periods). The excursionists use public transport and take their own food and camping gear.

Foreign travelers are welcome. For details contact **Andrea Würz** (☎ 0212-235-3053), who speaks English and German, and German-speaking **Fritz Werner** (☎ 0212-945-0946).

Another club of this kind is the Centro Excursionista Universitario (CEU), which bands together mostly university students. Contact persons include **Roberto González** (☎ 0212-762-0424), English-speaker **José Daniel Santana** (☎ 0212-371-1871, 0414-253-2384) and **Mirna Carolina Ríos** (☎ 0212-661-5644, 0412-738-7473).

FESTIVALS & EVENTS

Caracas' main event is the Festival Internacional de Teatro, held in March/April of every even-numbered year. Other cultural events include the Festival de Música El Hatillo (September/November) and the Temporada de Danza (July/August).

SLEEPING

Accommodation in Caracas is more expensive than elsewhere in the country. On the whole, Caracas' budget hotels are styleless and usually in unprepossessing, sometimes unsafe areas. Many of the budget hotels double as love hotels; business is particularly brisk on Friday and Saturday. Consequently, some hotels may turn you down on weekends.

Sabana Grande   Map pp954–5

By far the city's most popular lodging area among travelers, Sabana Grande has plenty of places to stay. It feels pretty safe during the daytime, but may be dangerous at night.

Nuestro Hotel (☎ 0212-761-5431; bhostelccs@yahoo .com; Calle El Colegio; s/d with bath US$10/14) The most popular haunt among backpackers. Friendly and safe, yet it also rents rooms by the hour. Almost all the rooms are *matrimoniales* (with a double bed intended for couples) and have fans.

Hotel Odeón (☎ 0212-793-1345; Av Las Acacias con Av Casanova; s/d/t with bath US$13/15/18; ☒) One of the cheapest acceptable options providing air-con rooms, yet not the quietest one. The airy rooms can be a bit noisy due to the hotel's location on a busy intersection.

Hotel Gabial (☎ 0212-793-1156; Prolongación Sur Av Las Acacias; d with bath US$25-28; ☒) A better and more comfortable choice than the Odeón, just a few paces away. It has *matrimoniales* and doubles with silent air-con and good beds.

Hotel Cristal (☎ 0212-761-9131; Boulevard de Sabana Grande con Pasaje Asunción; d/tr US$18/20; ☒) Fair-sized rooms with bath and air-con, and perfectly located on the lively boulevard. Choose the one with a balcony overlooking the busy mall.

Hotel City (☎ 0212-793-5785; Calle Bolivia; s/d US$24/26) This hotel has reasonable standards and rates, and a good location just off Plaza Venezuela metro station, next to the landmark Torre La Previsora. Ask for a room on one of the upper floors.

Hotel Plaza Palace (☎ 0212-762-4821; Calle Los Mangos; d/tr with bath & air-con US$30/33, d/tr suites US$35/38; ☒) Respectable mid-range hotel close to Boulevard de Sabana Grande. Air-con rooms are airy and comfortable, but it's worth to add a mere US$5 and stay in an excellent spacious suite.

Central Caracas   Map pp950-1

Central Caracas is not famous for its safety at night, but it shelters some of the cheapest hotels in town. The cheapest accommodations in the center are south of Av Lecuna, between Av Balart and Av Fuerzas Armadas, but the area is unattractive and can be positively unsafe. It's more convenient for sightseeing and possibly safer to stay north of Av Universidad.

Hotel Hollywood (☎ 0212-561-4989; Av Fuerzas Armadas, Esquina Romualda; d with bath US$15; ☒) One of the cheapest options around. Fully refurbished over recent years, it has 30 spacious rooms with silent air-con. Good value.

Hotel Inter (☎ 0212-564-6448; Esquina Calero; s/d/tr with bath US$14/17/20; ☒) Quiet, well-kept small hotel with air-con rooms, and popular with businesspeople.

Plaza Catedral Hotel (☎ 0212-564-2111; Esquina La Torre; d/tr with bath US$20/24; ☒) Very central option, overlooking Plaza Bolívar and the cathedral. Choose one of the front corner rooms for best views. It's not a proposition for light sleepers, as the cathedral bells ring every quarter hour. The hotel's rooftop restaurant provides reasonably priced food and great views.

Hotel El Conde (☎ 0212-860-1171; hotelconde@cantv .net; Esquina El Conde; s/d/tr with bath US$25/30/32; ☒) The oldest hotel in the historic center, and possibly the best one. Comfortable lodging with air-con at affordable prices just a block from Plaza Bolívar.

VENEZUELA

SPLURGE!

Caracas has a number of upmarket hotels, but **La Posada Ejecutiva** (☎ 0212-283-4817; gerdschad@cantv.net; 8a Transversal No 2, Los Palos Grandes; d/ste US$70/90 with breakfast; 🖫) is something different and special. It's a complex of cabins and small houses loosely scattered within a large garden. The *posada* has just two double rooms and three double suites (all with bath and air-con), plus a swimming pool, gym, seven bars, a library and a business room with Internet access. Advance booking is recommended, preferably for several days rather than just one night.

Altamira

Altamira is one of the eastern residential suburbs renowned for its upmarket restaurants and nightspots. There are few budget hotels here, but some travelers might be interested in paying a little bit more for the location, since the area is reasonably safe.

Hotel Residencia Montserrat (☎ 0212-263-3533; Av Ávila, Plaza Altamira Sur; d/tr with bath US$25/30; 🖫) Convenient accommodation within spitting distance of the Altamira metro station. Choose one of the spacious air-con studio apartments with kitchenette and fridge. The hotel has long passed its best days, but it's still worth its price.

Hotel Altamira (☎ 0212-267-4255; Av José Félix Sosa; d/tr with bath US$26/35; 🖫) Undistinguished if perfectly acceptable lodging with air-con, and just one block south of the metro station.

EATING

Caracas has loads of places to eat; you could easily stay in town a full year and eat out three times a day without visiting the same restaurant twice. The food is generally OK, even in the budget eateries, so you can safely explore the culinary market by yourself. Some restaurants offer the so-called *menú ejecutivo*, a set two-course lunch (US$3 to US$5), which is usually reasonable value. The annually updated, bilingual Spanish/English *Caracas Gastronomic Guide*, published by Miro Popic and available from local bookshops, covers more than 600 restaurants and is a great help in discovering the local food scene.

Sabana Grande   Map pp954-5

Sabana Grande boasts heaps of restaurants, cafés and snack bars to suit any budget and taste. Cheap restaurants usually nest in the back streets, but you'll also find some on the Boulevard de Sabana Grande, Av Francisco Solano and Av Casanova.

Budget vegetarian meals are served at **Restaurant Vegetariano Sabas Nieves** (Calle Pascual Navarro; set lunch US$3) and **El Chalet Vegetariano** (Calle Los Manguitos; set lunch US$3).

Delicatesses Indú (Calle Villaflor; set lunch US$3, mains US$4-5) You can also enjoy appetizing Indian vegie dishes here.

El Gran Café (Boulevard de Sabana Grande) A fully remodeled and refurbished café with a 50-year-long tradition. Breakfasts, snacks and light meals are served indoors and al fresco on the boulevard.

Mi Tasca (Av Francisco Solano) One of the cheapest *tascas* (Spanish-style bar/restaurants) in the area, serving tasty fare including a variety of *tapas* (traditional Spanish snacks).

Tasca Rías Gallegas (Av Francisco Solano) A popular local Spanish-style restaurant.

El Fogón del Pollo (Av Tamanaco) One of the best chicken outlets in the area. Half a chicken with potatoes or yucca makes for a filling meal for US$4.

Restaurant Shich Kabab (Calle El Colegio; mains US$3-5) Ask for its copious *plato especial* at this small Middle-Eastern eatery – it has a bit of everything.

Restaurant El Arabito (Av Casanova; meals US$3-4) A budget Middle-Eastern fast-food outlet with attached shop selling a variety of typical snacks.

Centro Comercial El Recreo (Av Casanova) This is the largest shopping mall in the area, featuring a food court on its top floor, with a collection of fast-food outlets serving anything from pizza and chicken to falafel and Chinese fried rice.

Central Caracas   Map pp950-1

The center is packed with mostly low- to mid-priced eateries, many of which serve local fare known as *comida criolla*.

Restaurant La Torre (La Torre a Veroes; mains US$3-5) This basic central option just off Plaza Bolívar gets packed with office employees at lunchtime.

Restaurant Las Vegas (La Torre a Veroes; mains US$3-5) It's more basic than La Torre but has good *cachapas* (corn cakes with ham and/or cheese). You'll find more places like these around the central streets.

El Salón del Sabor (Edificio Iberia, Av Urdaneta, Esquina Ánimas; set lunches US$4) Tasty vegetarian and non-vegetarian meals are served until 4pm.

Restaurant Dama Antañona (Jesuitas a Maturín; mains US$5-7) Traditional regional cooking at affordable prices in pleasant old-fashioned surroundings.

Café Sacro (in Museo Sacro de Caracas, Plaza Bolívar) Delicious fresh salads and sandwiches, plus great espresso.

Restaurant El Coyuco (Av Urdaneta, Platanal a Candilito; mains US$3-5) Popular budget eatery serving chicken and barbecued beef.

Lunchería Doña Agapita (Miguelacho a La Cruz; cachapas US$1-50-2.50) Some of the best and cheapest *cachapas* in town.

Da' Pacho Pastas (Peligro a Alcabala; pasta US$2) New simple restaurant serving tasty pasta and pizza at bottom-end prices.

La Candelaria, the area east of Av Fuerzas Armadas is brimming with *tascas*, where you can either try some traditional Spanish cooking, including a variety of tapas and paellas, or dedicate yourself to drinks, as many locals do. The best places include the following, all near Plaza de la Candelaria:

Tasca La Carabela (Esquina Urapal; mains US$5-9)
Tasca El Barco de Colón (Esquina Ferrenquín; mains US$6-9)
Tasca Mallorca (Esquina Alcabala; mains US$5-8)
Casa Farruco (Peligro a Puente República; US$6-10).

Las Mercedes

Las Mercedes has a long-standing reputation as a fashionable dining district that becomes particularly lively in the evening. Most restaurants here cater to an affluent clientele, but there are also some budget options.

Real Past (Av Río de Janeiro; pasta US$2-3) The cheapest pasta house in the area.

Los Riviera (Calle París; mains US$4-6) A budget spot for spit-roasted chicken and barbecued meats.

La Casa del Llano (Av Río de Janeiro, mains US$4-7; 24hr) Hearty *comida típica*, such as *arepas, cachapas*, chicken and *parrilla* (mixed grill of different kinds of meat).

DRINKING

Las Mercedes and La Castellana hold most of the city's nightlife, but bars and discos

SPLURGE!

Caracas has plenty of classy restaurants (prices are about US$8 to US$16), including:

La Castañuela (☎ 0212-993-2205; Calle París; Las Mercedes) Fine Spanish cuisine in atmospheric surroundings.

La Punta Grill (☎ 0212-993-2855; Calle París; Las Mercedes; mains US$8-12) Some of the best grilled meat in town.

La Estancia (☎ 0212-261-4223; Av Principal de La Castellana, La Castellana) Tradition and quality at their best in grilled meats.

dot other suburbs as well, including Sabana Grande, El Rosal and Altamira.

Bars & Clubbing

El León (Plaza La Castellana) One of the most popular watering holes in La Castellana, basically due to the cheap beer. It's a vast open-air bar that gets packed with young folks in the evening.

Birras Pub & Café (Av Principal de Las Mercedes) Possibly the cheapest bar in Las Mercedes, frequented by student-like clientele. A few dozen plastic tables and chairs on the sidewalk plus beer at US$0.40 a bottle is all that's needed to have it full every night. You may have to queue to sit down.

Auyama Café (Calle Londres, Las Mercedes) Alfresco bar-restaurant with live music on some evenings and a good atmosphere.

Boo Caffe (Calle Londres, Las Mercedes) Likeable budget bar open till late, which also has reasonable food.

Wassup Bar & Fun Place (Calle New York, Las Mercedes) New bar-cum-restaurant with live rock music, which has swiftly come to be one of the trendiest places in town.

Dady's Latino (Calle Madrid, Las Mercedes) A new disco playing hot Latin music. It's popular with salsa aficionados.

Kazoo (Av Principal de Las Mercedes) Large, multilevel disco playing a rag bag of music, with a well-stocked bar, pool tables, and all the bells and whistles.

U Bar (Av La Trinidad, Las Mercedes) One of the cheapest discos in the area. There's no cover fee, so just enter to see what's happening and stay or move on.

El Maní es Así (Map pp945-5; Calle El Cristo, Sabana Grande) One of Caracas' best-known salsa spots, with a 15-year-long tradition. Salsa bands play nightly except Monday.

Juan Sebastián Bar (Av Venezuela, El Rosal) A long-established bar-restaurant that's one of the leading jazz venues in town. Live jazz, performed by various groups, plays from the afternoon until 2am.

Little Rock Café (Av 6 entre 3a y 5a Transversales, Altamira) A bastion of rock music at full volume, played by local groups on most nights.

Gay & Lesbian Venues

Gay and lesbian establishments in Caracas have mushroomed. Check www.republica gay.com for details. Popular hangouts in Sabana Grande include:

Bar Don Sol (Map pp954-5; Pasaje Asunción; ☿ nightly) A two-level place with a bar downstairs and disco upstairs frequented by gays and lesbians.

Tasca La Fragata (Map pp954-5; Calle Villaflor) A two-level bar-disco which is popular with gays and lesbians of all ages.

Tasca Pullman (Map pp954-5; Av Francisco Solano) One of the most popular gay bars in the area.

El Rincón del Gabán and **Vía Libre** (Map pp954-5; Calle San Antonio) Two small neighboring bars.

ENTERTAINMENT

The Thursday edition of *El Universal* carries a what's-on section called *Guía de la Ciudad*, which gives brief descriptions of selected coming events, including music, theater, cinema and exhibitions.

Cinemas, Theater & Music

Cinemateca Nacional, (Map pp950-1; ☎ 0212-576-7118; in Galería de Arte Nacional) For thought-provoking films, check the program of Caracas' leading arthouse cinema.

Celarg (☎ 0212-285-2990; Casa de Rómulo Gallegos, Av Luis Roche, Altamira) Cinemateca also presents its films at Celarg.

Ateneo de Caracas (☎ 0212-573-4622, 0212-573-4479) It's worth checking whether something interesting is playing in this theater, home to Rajatabla, Venezuela's best-known theater company.

Complejo Cultural Teresa Carreño (☎ 0212-574-9122) The main venue for concerts, ballet and other performances.

Aula Magna (Map pp954-5; ☎ 0212-605-4516; in Universidad Central de Venezuela) Hosts concerts by the local symphony orchestra, usually on Sunday morning.

Sport

Professional baseball league games are played from October to February in the stadium at Universidad Central de Venezuela. The neighboring soccer stadium hosts major soccer matches, most of which are held between December and March, with major events usually scheduled on Saturday evening.

Caracas' horse-racing track, the Hipódromo La Rinconada, has racing on Saturday and Sunday afternoon from 1pm. The track is 6km southwest of the city center, off the Caracas–Valencia freeway.

GETTING THERE & AWAY
Air

The Simón Bolívar International Airport is in Maiquetía on the Caribbean coast, 26km from central Caracas. It's linked to the city by a freeway with three tunnels cutting through the coastal mountain range. The airport has separate domestic and international terminals, 400m apart. Both terminals have tourist offices, ATMs, bars and restaurants, travel agencies and car-rental companies. The international terminal also has Ipostel and CANTV, plus several *casas de cambio*, which change both cash and traveler's checks.

Maiquetía airport services direct flights to most cities in the country, including Barcelona (one way US$40 to US$60), Ciudad Bolívar (US$45 to US$70), Ciudad Guayana (US$50 to US$75), Coro (US$50 to US$70), Maracaibo (US$50 to US$75), Mérida (US$40 to US$65), Porlamar (US$35 to US$65), Puerto Ayacucho (US$80 to US$100) and San Antonio del Táchira (US$45 to US$80).

All major national airlines have offices at the airport and in Caracas. Reservation phone numbers and websites include:

Aeropostal (☎ 0800-237-6252, 0800-284-6637; www .aeropostal.com)

Aserca (☎ 0212-905-5214, 0212-953-3004; www.aserca airlines.com)

Avior (☎ 0212-202-5811; www.avior.com.ve)

LAI (☎ 0212-355-2333, 0212-355-2322)

Laser (☎ 0800-237-3200, 0212-232-6533; www.laser.com)

Santa Bárbara (☎ 0212-204-4000; www.santabarbara airlines.com)

Bus

The central Nuevo Circo long-distance bus terminal has closed (although the terminal for shorter routes remains open); its services are now handled by the following two new bus terminals.

The Terminal La Bandera, 3km south of the center near La Bandera metro station (and easily accessible by metro), handles all intercity runs to the west and southwest of the country, including Coro (US$8, seven hours), Maracaibo (US$12, 10½ hours), Maracay (US$2, 1½ hours), Mérida (US$15, 12 hours), San Antonio del Táchira (US$15, 14 hours) and San Cristóbal (US$14, 13 hours).

The Terminal de Oriente, is in the eastern outskirts of Caracas on the highway to Barcelona, 5km beyond the suburb of Petare, and is accessible by local *carritos* from both the city center and Petare. It handles all traffic to the east and southeast, including Ciudad Bolívar (US$11, nine hours), Ciudad Guayana (US$12, 10½ hours), Cumaná (US$9, 6½ hours), Güiria (US$13, 12 hours) and Puerto La Cruz (US$7, five hours). All the fares given here are for air-con buses.

GETTING AROUND
Bus
The bus network is extensive, covering all suburbs within the metropolitan area and some beyond. Small buses called *carritos* run frequently, but may often be trapped in traffic jams. Use *carritos* only if going to destinations that are inaccessible by metro.

Metro
The French-made metro is fast, cheap, easy to use and clean, and provides access to most major city attractions and tourist facilities. The metro system has three lines and 39 stations. The longest line, No 1, goes east–west along the city axis. Line No 2 leads from the center southwest to the distant suburb of Caricuao and the zoo. The newest and shortest line, No 3, runs from Plaza Venezuela southwest to El Valle suburb, passing by the bus terminal at La Bandera. The system also includes *metrobús*, a network of bus routes linking some of the suburbs to metro stations.

The metro operates from 5:30am to 11pm daily. Yellow tickets cost US$0.20 for a ride up to three stations away from your starting point; US$0.25 for four to seven stations; and US$0.30 for any longer route. Yellow double tickets (*ida y vuelta*; US$0.40) are valid for two rides of any distance, or consider buying the *multiabono* (US$1.75), an orange ticket valid for 10 metro rides of any distance. Not only do you save money, but you also avoid lines at the ticket counters.

Bulky packages are not allowed in the metro. Use common sense and avoid carrying large bags, at least during rush hours. The metro is generally safe, though be careful of pickpockets operating in groups on the escalators of some busy stations.

AROUND CARACAS

This section covers attractions that are usually visited on day trips out of Caracas. Also included here is Los Roques, an archipelago of coral islands about 180km north of Caracas, for which the city is a main jumping off point.

PARQUE NACIONAL EL ÁVILA
This national park encompasses about 90km of the coastal mountain range north of Caracas, that runs east–west along the coast and separates the city from the sea. The highest peak in the range is Pico Naiguatá (2765m), while the most visited is Pico El Ávila (2105m), accessible by the *teleférico*. For more information about the *teleférico*, see the Caracas section (p956).

The southern slope of the range, overlooking Caracas, is uninhabited but is crisscrossed with about 200km of walking trails. El Ávila provides better facilities for walkers than any other national park in Venezuela. Most of the trails are well signposted, and there are a number of campgrounds.

A dozen entrances lead into the park from Caracas; all originate from Av Boyacá, commonly known as Cota Mil (which runs at an altitude of 1000m). All routes have a short ascent before reaching a guard post, where you pay a nominal entrance fee. Get a copy of the useful *Mapa para el Excursionista – Parque Nacional El Ávila* (scale 1:40,000) before you arrive; it shows trails and camping facilities.

Options abound for half- and full-day hikes. A popular destination is Pico El Ávila – at least four routes lead there. Start early as it gets pretty hot by mid-morning. If you are prepared to camp, you can enjoy one of the most scenic routes: the two-day hike to Pico Naiguatá. Take rain gear, warm clothes, water (scarce in the park) and plastic bags (for bringing your rubbish back down). The dry season is December to April, but even then some rain may fall in the upper reaches.

COLONIA TOVAR

This unusual mountain town, about 60km west of Caracas, sits at an altitude of 1800m amid the rolling forests of the Cordillera de la Costa. It was founded in 1843 by a group of 376 German settlers from the Black Forest, who came when Venezuela was soliciting immigrants to cultivate land devastated by independence wars.

Effectively isolated by a lack of roads and internal rules prohibiting marriage outside the colony, the village followed its mother culture, language and architecture for a century. Only in the 1940s was Spanish introduced as the official language and the ban on marrying outside the community abandoned. It was not until 1963 that a paved road reached Colonia Tovar from Caracas, marking a turning point in the history of the town, which by then had a mere 1300 souls.

Today, Colonia Tovar has five times as many inhabitants and is a classic example of a tourist town, drawing hordes of *caraqueños* curious to see a bit of old Germany lost in the Venezuelan mountains. They come on weekends to glimpse the German-style architecture, enjoy a German meal, and buy bread, jam or sausage made according to traditional recipes.

You can visit the **Museo Histórico**, the **Museo Arqueológico** (both ☽ 9am-5pm Sat & Sun) and the local **church**, a curious L-shaped building with two perpendicular naves (originally, one for women, the other for men).

On weekends the town is swamped with visitors and their cars; on weekdays it's almost dead, and many restaurants are closed. Whenever you come, bring warm clothing.

Sleeping & Eating

By and large, accommodations are good and stylish, but not cheap by Venezuelan standards. Rates start at US$20 per double. Private bath and hot water are the norm, and some places also have heated rooms. Many hotels offer full board, and most hotels listed here have their own restaurants.

Among the cheapest options are **Cabañas Breidenbach** (☎ 0244-355-1211; d US$20-30) and **Residencias Baden** (☎ 0244-355-1151; d US$20-30).

For more comfort try **Hotel Edelweiss** (☎ 0244-355-1260; d US$25-35), **Hotel Drei-Tannen** (☎ 0244-355-1246; d US$30-40) or, possibly the best, **Hotel Bergland** (☎ 0244-355-1229; d US$25-40).

Hotel Selva Negra (☎ 0244-355-1415; d US$35-50) The oldest and best-known lodge in town.

Getting There & Away

The trip from Caracas to Colonia Tovar by public transport requires a change at El Junquito. *Carritos* to El Junquito (US$0.80) depart from Esquina San Roque, the corner of Av Lecuna and Calle Sur 9, just south of the Nuevo Circo bullring. Large buses also run to El Junquito (US$0.50); catch them on Av Lecuna or Av Universidad. From El Junquito, *por puestos* take you the remainder of the journey (US$1). The whole trip takes about two hours.

If you don't want to go back to Caracas the same way (or want to continue to Maracay or further west), you can take an exciting ride south down to La Victoria. Over a distance of 30km, the road descends about 1300m. *Por puestos* depart from Colonia Tovar (US$1.50, 1½ hours); grab a seat on the left side for better views. There's regular bus transport from La Victoria to both Caracas and Maracay.

SAN FRANCISCO DE YARE

This small town, about 70km southeast of Caracas, is famous for its impressive celebrations of **Diablos Danzantes**, annually on Corpus Christi, when up to 1000 devil dancers wearing giant monstrous masks take to the streets and perform their ceremonial dance to the beat of drums for most of the day. It's well worth coming to San Francisco de Yare at this time to take part in the unusual spectacle. See the boxed text (p963).

San Francisco has no regular hotels, but it's easy to come just for the day. From Caracas, take one of the frequent buses to Ocumare del Tuy (US$0.80, 1½ hours) from the Nuevo Circo regional bus terminal, and change for the bus to Santa Teresa del Tuy, which will drop you off in San Francisco (US$0.40, 20 minutes). Come early.

ARCHIPIÉLAGO LOS ROQUES

Los Roques is a beautiful archipelago of small coral islands lying about 160km north of the central coast. Stretching 36km east to west and 25km north to south, it consists

DANCING WITH THE DEVILS

Diablos Danzantes (Dancing Devils) invade the streets of Venezuela's coastal towns on the morning of Corpus Christi. Clad in their red costumes and monstrous masks, hundreds of devils dance through the streets and plazas for the whole day to the clamor of drums. The dance can be anything from ceremonial marching movements to spasmodic squirms and frenetic leaps.

Corpus Christi is one of the major feast days in the Roman Catholic tradition, falling on the 60th day after Easter Sunday and held in honor of the Eucharist. So, why do the devils come out on this holiest of days?

The ceremony manifests the struggle between Good and Evil, and the eventual triumph of the former. No matter how profane the devil dances may look, the devils come at some stage to the steps of the church to submit themselves to the Eucharist. They get the priest's blessing and can then return to their whirling dances. The event has a magical-religious appearance and meaning; locals believe it will ensure abundant crops, welfare, prosperity, and protection against misfortune and natural disasters.

Diablos Danzantes is a blend of Spanish and African traditions. The event's roots go back to medieval Andalusia, where the devils' images and masks featured in Corpus Christi festivities. When the feast was brought to the New World by the Spanish missionaries, black slaves reinterpreted the Catholic devotion in their own way. They happily put on their old masks from their homeland and danced to the rhythm of familiar drumbeats.

Even though the dances today are not performed exclusively by blacks, the ceremony has been preserved only in areas that have traditionally had a significant black population. The event is still very much alive in a dozen towns and villages on Venezuela's central coast. The celebrations in San Francisco de Yare and Chuao are best known throughout the country, as are their masks.

Today's masks are commonly made of papier-mâché, but they show direct similarities to the traditional wooden masks from some West African countries, mostly Congo, Benin and Nigeria. The devils masks from San Francisco de Yare are the most elaborate and colorful, depicting horned demons, monsters and fantastic animals. They make popular and attractive souvenirs, and are sold by every second craft shop across Venezuela.

of some 40 islands big enough to deserve names, and perhaps 250 other unnamed islets, sandbars and cays. The archipelago, complete with the surrounding waters, makes up the Archipiélago Los Roques National Park.

Gran Roque, on the northern edge of the archipelago, is the main island and transport hub. It has a fishing village of about 1200 people, an airstrip and a wharf. From here tourists visit other islands. The soft, white-sand beaches are clean and lovely, although shadeless, and the coral reefs offer a snorkeling and scuba-diving paradise.

Orientation & Information

On arrival at the Gran Roque airstrip, you are charged a US$10 national park entry fee. Just off the airstrip is **Oscar Shop** (☎ 0237-414-5515, 0414-291-9160; oscarshop@hotmail.com), where you can get information about the archipelago. It's a combination of shop, tour agency, boat operator and tourist office, all run by Oscar. He provides boat transporta-

tion to the islands, organizes boat tours and rents snorkeling equipment. Next door to Oscar is Pluto Shop, which offers much the same.

About 200m west is Plaza Bolívar, where Pizzería La Chuchera provides Internet access. Opposite, you'll find Banesco, along with its ATM giving advances on Visa and MasterCard.

About 500m further west is the office of **Inparques** (☎ 0237-221-1073, 0414-323-2821), which can be another source of information. You can also camp here for free.

Activities

Los Roques provide some of Venezuela's best **snorkeling** and **scuba diving**. There are several diving schools based at Gran Roque, including:

Aquatics Diving Center (☎ 0237-414-5555; www.scubavenezuela.com)

Ecobuzos (☎ 0237-221-1235; www.ecobuzos.com)

Sesto Continente Dive Resort (☎ 0414-924-1853; www.scdr.com)

VENEZUELA

Other activities available on the archipelago include **game fishing**, **windsurfing** and **sailing**.

Tours

The easiest and most popular way of visiting the archipelago is by tour. Tours are offered by most of the airlines that fly to Los Roques. For details see Getting There & Away in this section (p964).

The one-day tour (about US$130 to US$150) includes the round-trip flight, a boat excursion from Gran Roque to nearby islands, lunch, soft drinks, and one hour of snorkeling (equipment provided) and free time on the beach. The two-day tour (US$200 to US$300) also includes accommodations in Gran Roque and all meals.

If you plan on staying two or more days, consider going on your own, which is easy to organize and much cheaper than a tour. Just buy a round-trip ticket from one of the airlines and arrange all the rest in Gran Roque. Avoid tourist peaks, when flights and accommodations are in short supply.

Sleeping & Eating

Gran Roque has more than 50 *posadas* (family-run guest houses), providing a total of about 500 beds. Most of the *posadas* are small and simple, usually offering both lodging and dining. The minimum you'll pay in the low season is about US$15 per person for bed, breakfast and dinner.

The following recommended places have neat rooms with private baths and fans, and are among the cheapest; prices include breakfast and dinner.

Posada Doña Magalys (☎ 0414-373-1090; Plaza Bolívar; r per person US$16)

Posada Doña Carmen (☎ 0414-318-4926; Plaza Bolívar; r per person US$20)

Posada Roquelusa (☎ 0414-369-6401; r per person US$16) Nearby Inparques office.

Posada Karlin (☎ 0414-288-1654; Calle La Laguna; r per person US$18)

Camping is allowed on Gran Roque and the nearby islands; get a free camping permit from the Inparques office. Boats can take you to the island of your choice and pick you up either later that day or on another day. If you plan on camping on any island other than Gran Roque, take food and water. Bring along snorkeling gear and sun protection – there's almost no shade on the islands.

Getting There & Away

Los Roques is served from Maiquetía airport by a number of small airlines, all of which have desks at the domestic or auxiliary terminal. These include:

AeroEjecutivos (☎ 0212-355-1259; www.aeroejecutivos .com.ve)

LTA (Línea Turística Aereotuy; ☎ 0212-355-1297; www .tuy.com) The largest operator, with its main office in Caracas (☎ 0212-762-3009; Edificio Gran Sabana; Boulevard de Sabana Grande)

Sol de América (☎ 0212-355-1797)

Transavén (☎ 0212-355-1179; www.transaven.com)

Round-trip flights are US$80 to US$120 – shop around as they may differ between the carriers. LTA may offer budget one-way fares on late afternoon flights to Los Roques and on early morning flights to Maiquetía.

THE NORTHWEST

Venezuela's northwest shelters such diverse natural features as coral islands, beaches, rainforests, the country's only desert (near Coro) and South America's largest lake, Lago de Maracaibo. The region combines the traditional with the contemporary, from living indigenous cultures (such as that of the Guajiros) and colonial heritage (in Coro) to the modern city of Maracaibo. Favorite travel destinations in the region are Henri Pittier, Morrocoy and Sierra San Luis national parks. Administratively, the northwest encompasses the states of Aragua, Carabobo, Yaracuy, Lara, Falcón and Zulia.

MARACAY

The capital of Aragua state, Maracay is a thriving city of about 600,000 people. It was founded in 1701, but its growth only really came with the rule of Juan Vicente Gómez (1908–35), an enduring and ruthless *caudillo*. He made Maracay his home and commissioned a number of projects, including the government house, a bullring, an aviation school, an opera house, a zoo and his own mausoleum.

Maracay may not make the 'not-to-be-missed' list, but it has some attractions and a number of parks, including Venezuela's largest Plaza Bolívar, and is a gateway to Parque Nacional Henri Pittier.

Information

Internet facilities include **Net Café** (Centro Comercial La Capilla, Av Santos Michelena), **Telefonía Internet** (Av Bolívar) and **CANTV** (in Torre Sindoni). There are

also a few small cybercafés in the Centro Comercial Paseo Las Delicias.

Most central banks, including Banco de Venezuela, Banesco and Corp Banca have ATMs. Foreign cash and traveler's checks can be exchanged at **Italcambio** (Centro Comercial Maracay Plaza, Av Aragua at Av Bermúdez), 1.5km south of Plaza Bolívar.

The **tourist office** (☎ 0243-242-2284; in Hotel Maracay, Av Las Delicias; ☼ 8am-4pm Mon-Fri) is 2km north of the city center.

Sights

Plaza Girardot, the historic heart of Maracay, features the fair-sized **cathedral**, completed in 1743. The arcaded building on the plaza's south side was erected by Gómez as the seat

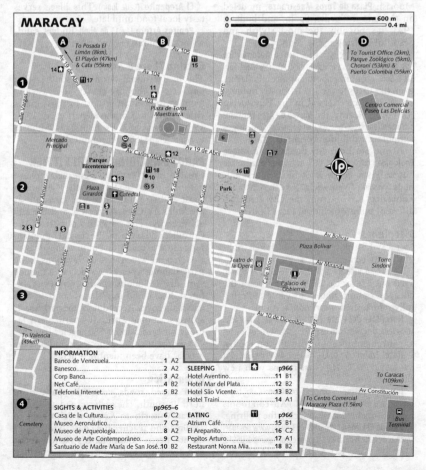

MARACAY

0 — 600 m
0 — 0.4 mi

To Posada El Limón (8km), El Playón (47km) & Cata (55km)

To Tourist Office (2km), Parque Zoológico (5km), Choroní (53km) & Puerto Colombia (55km)

Av 105
Av 104
Av 103
Plaza de Toros Maestranza
Av Carlos Michelena
Av 19 de Abril
Centro Comercial Paseo Las Delicias

Calle Vargas
Mercado Principal
Parque Bicentenario
Plaza Girardot
Catedral
Park
Calle Pérez Almarza
Calle 5 de Julio
Calle Sucre
Calle Junín
Calle López Aveledo

Av Sucre

Av Bolívar
Plaza Bolívar
Teatro de la Opera
Calle Soublette
Calle Mariño
Calle Brión
Palacio de Gobierno
Torre Sindoni
Av Miranda

To Valencia (49km)

Av 10 de Diciembre

Cemetery

Av Bermúdez

To Caracas (109km)
Av Constitución

To Centro Comercial Maracay Plaza (1.5km)

Bus Terminal

INFORMATION	
Banco de Venezuela	1 A2
Banesco	2 A2
Corp Banca	3 A2
Net Café	4 B2
Telefonía Internet	5 B2

SIGHTS & ACTIVITIES	pp965–6
Casa de la Cultura	6 C2
Museo Aeronáutico	7 C2
Museo de Arqueología	8 A2
Museo de Arte Contemporáneo	9 C2
Santuario de Madre María de San José	10 B2

SLEEPING	p966
Hotel Aventino	11 B1
Hotel Mar del Plata	12 B2
Hotel São Vicente	13 B2
Hotel Traini	14 A1

EATING	p966
Atrium Café	15 B1
El Arepanito	16 C2
Pepitos Arturo	17 A1
Restaurant Nonna Mia	18 B2

of government. Today, it houses the **Museo de Arqueología** (☎ 0243-247-2521; admission free; ☉ 8am-3:30pm Tue-Fri, 9am-12:30pm Sat & Sun), featuring pre-Hispanic pottery from the region and crafts of various Indian groups.

One block east of the plaza is the **Santuario de Madre María de San José** (Calle López Aveledo; admission free; ☉ 8:30am-noon & 2:30-5pm Tue-Fri, 8:30am-5pm Sat & Sun). Madre María (1875–1967), a Choroní-born nun who dedicated her life to the service of the poor, was beatified in 1995 by a papal bull. Her remains were exhumed and, to everybody's surprise, the corpse was allegedly intact. You can see it in a crystal sarcophagus in the Santuario (though the face is covered with a mask).

Just to the north is the large Spanish-Moorish **Plaza de Toros Maestranza**, modeled on the one in Seville, Spain, and built in 1933; it's possibly the most stylish and beautiful bullring in the country.

Two blocks east, the **Museo Aeronáutico** (☎ 0243-233-3812; admission US$0.80; ☉ 10am-5pm Sat & Sun) contains about 50 aircraft dating from the 1910s to the 1950s, mostly military planes that once served in the Venezuelan Air Force. Nearby, the **Museo de Arte Contemporáneo** (admission free; ☉ 9am-5pm Tue-Sun) stages temporary exhibitions of modern art.

At the northern city limits is the **Parque Zoológico** (☎ 0243-241-3933; Av Las Delicias; admission US$0.50; ☉ 9am-4pm Tue-Sun), which features animals typical of Venezuela. Take the Castaño-Zoológico *carrito* from the city center at different points, including Plaza Bolivar.

Sleeping

Maracay has quite a choice of hotels right in the city center.

Hotel São Vicente (☎ 0243-247-0321; Av Bolívar; d with bath & fan/air-con US$7/10; ✷) One of the cheapest options in the city center, offering fully refurbished *matrimonial* rooms.

Hotel Mar del Plata (☎ 0243-246-4313; Av Carlos Michelena; d/tr with bath US$12/15; ✷) Quiet hotel at convenient location with air-con rooms.

Hotel Traini (☎ 0243-245-5502; Av 19 de Abril; d/tr with bath US$16/20; ✷) Neat rooms with new silent air-con.

Hotel Aventino (☎ 0243-245-0656; Calle López Aveledo; d/tr with bath US$18/20; ✷) Air-con rooms in a reasonable location facing the bullring.

Posada El Limón (☎ 0243-283-4925; www.posadael limon.com; Calle El Piñal No 64; mattress or hammock US$10, d with bath US$30; ✷) A charming Dutch-run

place that offers beds and hammocks, meals, Internet access, a laundry, swimming pool, tours and transfers. If you are not up to the rooms, go for a mattress or hammock on the spacious balcony. The *posada* is in the leafy residential suburb of El Limón, about 8km northwest of the city center (US$4 by taxi).

Eating

The center is packed with budget eateries.

Restaurant Nonna Mia (Calle López Aveledo; mains US$2-3) Simple Italian place serving set meals and pastas.

Atrium Café (Calle Coromoto; set meals US$2, mains US$3-5) Pleasant café arranged around a patio.

Mercado Principal (Av Santos Michelena) Offers some of the cheapest meals in town.

El Arepanito (Calle Junín) This place serves tasty local food until late.

Pepitos Arturo (Av 19 de Abril) Budget sandwiches, hamburgers and *parrillas*.

Getting There & Away

The bus terminal is on the southeastern outskirts of the city center. It's vast and handles frequent transport to most major cities. Buses to Caracas depart every 10 or 15 minutes (US$2, 1½ hours), as do buses to Valencia (US$1, 45 minutes).

PARQUE NACIONAL HENRI PITTIER

Created in 1937, this is Venezuela's oldest national park. It starts at the Caribbean coast and stretches almost as far south as the Valencia–Caracas freeway and the city of Maracay. The park covers part of the Cordillera de la Costa, the coastal mountain range that exceeds 2000m in some areas.

Given the wide range of elevations in the park, habitat types vary widely and include semi-dry deciduous woods, evergreen rainforest, lush cloud forest, arid coastal scrub and mangroves. Accordingly, the park boasts a diverse animal world. It's particularly famous for birds; about 580 species (roughly 43% of the total bird species found in Venezuela) have been identified here.

Orientation

Two paved roads cross the park from north to south. The eastern road goes from Maracay north to Choroní (climbing to 1830m) and reaches the coast 2km further on at Puerto Colombia. It's narrow, poor and twisting, but amazingly spectacular.

The western road leads from Maracay to Ocumare de la Costa and El Playón, then continues to Cata; it ascends to 1128m at Paso Portachuelo. Both roads are about 55km long. There's no road connection between the coastal ends of these roads.

The coast features rocky cliffs in some parts, interspersed with bays ringed by beaches and coconut groves. The town of Puerto Colombia is the major destination, with boat-rental facilities, and a choice of hotels and restaurants.

The park has something for nearly everyone, including beachgoers, bird-watchers, hikers, architecture buffs and fiesta lovers. Unless you are particularly interested in bird-watching, it's better to take the eastern road, which provides access to more attractions and leads along a more spectacular route.

The Eastern Road

If traveling along the eastern road, stop in **Choroní**, a tiny colonial town whose narrow streets are lined with old, pastel houses. The leafy Plaza Bolívar boasts a lovely parish church, **Iglesia de Santa Clara**, with a finely decorated interior. The **feast of Santa Clara**, the town's patron saint, is celebrated in August.

A 20-minute walk north will bring you to **Puerto Colombia**, the main travelers' haunt. Its major magnet is **Playa Grande**, a fine coconut palm-shaded beach just a five-minute walk east of town.

Boats from town take tourists further down the coast to isolated beaches, such as **Playa Aroa** (round trip per boat for up to 10 people US$25), **Playa Chuao** (US$30) or **Playa Cepe** (US$40). From Playa Chuao, walk up a rough 4km track to the old village of **Chuao**, which is surrounded by cocoa plantations. The village lives in almost complete isolation, with no road links to the outside world, and is known for its **Diablos Danzantes** celebrations.

Drumbeats are an integral part of life in Chuao and Puerto Colombia, and can be heard year-round on weekend nights and particularly during the **Fiesta de San Juan** on June 23 and 24. The pulsating beat immediately sparks dancing, and the atmosphere is invigorating.

The Western Road

The western road also leads to fine beaches, of which **Playa Cata** is the most popular and developed. Boats from Cata take tourists to the smaller but quieter **Playa Catita**, on the east side of the same bay. Further east is **Playa Cuyagua**, accessible by a 2.5km sand track from the town of Cuyagua or by boat from Cata (round trip US$25).

The highlight of the western road is **Paso Portachuelo**, the lowest pass in the mountain ridge. It's a natural corridor for migratory birds and insects flying inland from the sea (and vice versa), en route to such distant places as Argentina and Canada.

Close to the pass is **Estación Biológica Rancho Grande**, a biological station run by the Universidad Central de Venezuela. An ecology path, traced through the forest behind the station, provides an opportunity to watch local wildlife, particularly birds. You may also see monkeys, agoutis, peccaries, butterflies and snakes.

Sleeping & Eating

Accommodations and food are available in various areas. You can camp free on the beaches, but should never leave your tent unattended.

PUERTO COLOMBIA

Some two dozen places to stay are available here – everything from rock bottom to luxury. Locals often rent rooms if demand is high. Prices usually rise on weekends and during major holidays (rates listed here are for low-season times). Restaurants, too, are in good supply; fried fish is the local staple.

Hostal Colonial (☎ 0243-991-1087; Calle Morillo; d US$9) German-operated *posada* opposite the bus terminus. One of the cheapest options and the most popular with travelers.

Posada Los Guanches (☎ 0243-991-1209; Calle Trino Rangel; d/tr US$10/13) Small simple place. Neat rooms have fan and bath.

Posada Alemania (☎ 0243-991-1036; Calle Morillo; d US$12) Reasonable rooms with bath and guest use of the kitchen.

Posada La Montañita (☎ 0243-991-1132; Calle Morillo; d US$20) Colonial-style mansion just off the waterfront.

Posada La Parchita (☎ 0243-991-1233; Calle Trino Rangel; d US$28) Well-maintained, quiet place with rooms arranged around a leafy patio.

EL PLAYÓN

Like Puerto Colombia on the eastern road, El Playón is the major lodging center on the western road, gathering together more than a dozen places to stay. Many of them are within two blocks of the waterfront, where tourist life concentrates.

De La Costa Eco-Lodge (☎ 0243-993-1986; Calle California; d/tr with bath US$24/30; 🐕) One of the best facilities around. It has reasonable rooms, a pool, restaurant, Internet access, boat trips, bike rental, snorkeling and scuba diving.

RANCHO GRANDE

The **Rancho Grande biological station** (☎ 0243-550-7085, 0414-589-6163; ranchogrande@saib.agr.ve; dm US$4) has four simple dormitories with shared facilities. Students with an ISIC card get a 25% discount on accommodation. No camping is allowed and no food is provided, but you can use the kitchen facilities. Bring a sleeping bag, flashlight and food.

Getting There & Away

Buses to El Playón (marked 'Ocumare de la Costa') depart every hour (US$1.50, two hours). They can let you off at Rancho Grande (28km from Maracay), but the fare is the same as to El Playón. From El Playón, you can take a *carrito* to Playa Cata (US$0.60, 10 minutes).

The last buses from El Playón and Puerto Colombia back to Maracay depart at 5pm (later on weekends) but are not reliable.

PARQUE NACIONAL MORROCOY

This is one of the most popular parks among those looking for beaches and snorkeling opportunities. Set at the eastern edge of Falcón state, the park comprises a strip of the coast and the offshore area dotted with islands, islets and cays. Many islands are skirted with white-sand beaches and surrounded by coral reefs, though some of the coral has died as the result of a chemical leak from an oil refinery.

The most popular of the islands is Cayo Sombrero, which has fine coral reefs and some of the best beaches. Other places good for snorkeling include Cayo Borracho, Playuela and Playuelita.

Orientation & Information

The park lies between the towns of Tucacas and Chichiriviche, which are its main gateways. Tucacas is an ordinary hot town on the Valencia–Coro highway, with nothing to keep you for long. With the park just a

stone's throw away, though, the town has developed into a holiday center dotted with hotels and restaurants. The park's nearest island, Cayo Punta Brava, is accessible by a bridge from the town's waterfront and has some good palm-shaded beaches. To visit other islands, go to the wharf close to the bridge, where boats await tourists.

Chichiriviche is smaller than Tucacas, but equally drab and unattractive. Here, too, accommodations, food and boats are in good supply. Boats depart from the wharf at the end of Av Zamora, the main street.

Both towns have Internet facilities. In Tucacas, use CANTV in the Centro Comercial Morrocoy; in Chichiriviche, go to Bit Manía near the Hotel Caribana.

Cash advances on Visa and MasterCard are available from ATMs at Banco Mercantil and Banco Provincial, and from the cashier in Banesco (all three banks are in Tucacas). In Chichiriviche, Banco Industrial de Venezuela gives advances on Visa cards only.

Neither Tucacas nor Chichiriviche have reliable tourist offices; try the staff at travelers' hotels. The office of **Inparques** (☎ 0259-812-2905) is close to the bridge in Tucacas.

Activities

The park offers sunbathing, diving and snorkeling. Tucacas has two diving schools: the cheaper **Amigos del Mar Divers** (☎ 0259-812-1754; amigos-del-mar@cantv.net; Calle Democracia) and the pricier **Submatur** (☎ 0259-812-4640; Calle Ayacucho). Both offer diving courses and guided dives, and sell diving and snorkeling equipment, some of which can be rented. There are no diving operators in Chichiriviche.

Snorkeling gear can also be rented from some boat operators and hotel managers for about US$4 per day. Some hotels have their own boats or have arrangements with the boat owners, and offer beach, snorkeling and bird-watching excursions.

Sleeping & Eating

ISLANDS

With a tent, or hammock and mosquito net, you can stay on the islands; otherwise, you'll be limited to day trips out of Tucacas or Chichiriviche. Camping is officially permitted on four islands: Sal, Sombrero, Muerto and Paiclás. All four have beach restaurants or food kiosks, but some may be closed on weekdays in the low season, so come prepared. Take sufficient fresh water, snorkeling gear, good sun protection and a reliable insect repellent.

Before you go camping, you have to contact the Inparques office in Tucacas and shell out a camping fee of US$1 per person per night, payable at Banesco in Tucacas.

TUCACAS
Many of Tucacas' hotels and restaurants are on or nearby the 1km-long Av Libertador, the town's lifeline.

Posada Amigos del Mar (☎ 0259-812-3962; Calle Nueva; d/tr US$9/12) Pleasant 10-room facility run by a Belgian named André (manager of the diving school of the same name), with spacious rooms with bath and fan. Guests have use of the kitchen. The *posada* is beyond the Hospital Viejo, a three-minute walk from the bus stop.

Posada de Carlos (☎ 0259-812-1493; Av Libertador; s/d US$8/12) Named after the owner, this small hotel has *matrimoniales* and doubles with bath and fan, and you can use the kitchen.

Hotel La Suerte (☎ 0259-812-1332; Av Libertador; s/d with fan US$8/13, with air-con US$13/19; 🅿) Next door to Carlos, the 70-room hotel is undistinguished but possibly the cheapest air-con option in town.

Arepera La Esperanza (Av Libertador; arepas under US$1; 🕐 24 hours) Serving a variety of *arepas* across the road from Carlos.

Restaurant El Timón (Av Libertador; mains US$4-6) Solid satisfying food at good prices.

CHICHIRIVICHE
The town has quite a choice of hotels and restaurants, many of which are budget options.

Morena's Place (☎ 0259-815-0936; posadamorenas@ hotmail.com; r with fan per person US$5) This inviting *posada*, in a fine old house near the waterfront, has five rooms with fans and is one of the cheapest in town. It's run by friendly English-speaking Carlos. Meals and tours available.

Villa Gregoria (☎ 0259-818-6359; Calle Mariño; d with fan/air-con US$13/18) Spanish-run *posada* near the bus terminus. Good rooms with bath. Choose a room on the upper floor – they are brighter and more attractive.

Posada Milagro (☎ 0259-8150864; Av Zamora; d US$13) Just 60m from the seaside. There are seven *matrimoniales* with bath, fan and sea

views. Ask for rooms in the Licorería Falcón downstairs.

Hotel Capri (☎ 0259-818-6026; Av Zamora; d US$20; 🅿) Reasonable air-con option close to the waterfront.

Hotel Caribana (☎ 0259-818-6837; d US$22; 🅿) Comfortable air-con accommodation just off Av Zamora. Tours available.

There are plenty of budget eateries along Av Zamora. Among the best places in town are **Restaurant Casamare** (Av Zamora) and **Restaurant Txalupa** (Av Zamora), both on the waterfront.

Getting There & Away
Tucacas lies on the Valencia–Coro highway, and buses run frequently to/from both Valencia (US$2, two hours) and Coro (US$3.50, 3½ hours). Chichiriviche is 22km off the highway and is served by half-hourly *busetas* (small buses) from Valencia (US$2.50, 2½ hours).

There are no direct buses to Chichiriviche from Caracas or Coro. To get there from Caracas, take any of the frequent buses to Valencia (US$2.50, 2½ hours) and change there. From Coro, take any bus to Valencia, get off in Sanare at the turn-off for Chichiriviche (US$3.50, 3¼ hours), and catch the Valencia–Chichiriviche *buseta*.

Getting Around
Boats to the islands from both Tucacas and Chichiriviche take up to eight people and charge the same for one as for eight. Popular destinations from Tucacas include Playa Paiclás (round trip US$22), Playuela (US$26) and Cayo Sombrero (US$38). From Chichiriviche, popular trips include the close cays of Cayo Muerto (US$10), Cayo Sal (US$14) and Cayo Pelón (US$14), and Cayo Sombrero (US$38). Boats will pick you up from the island in the afternoon or on a later date. On weekdays during the low season, you can usually beat the price down.

Before you decide to go to one particular island or beach, check for excursions with stops on various islands, organized by some boat operators and hotel managers. They may be an interesting proposition and not so expensive. For example, a full-day boat trip organized by Posada Amigos del Mar costs about US$10 per person. For details see p969.

CORO

Set at the base of the Península de Paraguaná, Coro is a pleasant, peaceful city of 160,000 people. It has some of the best colonial architecture in the country and a few good museums. In 1993 Coro was included on Unesco's World Heritage list.

Founded in 1527, the city became the first capital of Venezuela. Four years later, the Episcopal See, the first in the New World, was established in Coro. Despite its early and promising start, the town was almost deserted a century later and was only revived thanks to contraband trade with Curaçao and Bonaire during the 18th century. Most of its historical legacy dates from that time.

Once in Coro, it's worth visiting the arid Península de Paraguaná and the lush, mountainous Sierra de San Luis, two interesting if completely different regions. You can choose to explore them on your own or take a tour (the best tours are run from Posada Turística El Gallo, for details see p971).

Information

INTERNET ACCESS

Internet access in Coro is cheap: US$0.50 to US$0.80 an hour. There are several facilities in the city center, but they close early (the following close at 8pm or earlier):

ATC Micro Suply (in Centro Comercial Punta del Sol, cnr Av Manaure & Calle Falcón)

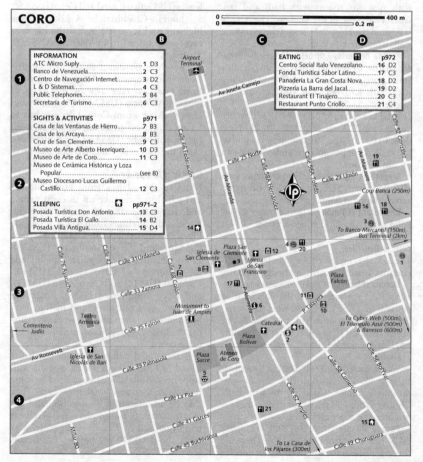

CORO

0 — 400 m
0 — 0.2 mi

INFORMATION	
ATC Micro Suply	1 D3
Banco de Venezuela	2 C3
Centro de Navegación Internet	3 D2
L & D Sistemas	4 C3
Public Telephones	5 B4
Secretaría de Turismo	6 C3

SIGHTS & ACTIVITIES	p971
Casa de las Ventanas de Hierro	7 B3
Casa de los Arcaya	8 B3
Cruz de San Clemente	9 C3
Museo de Arte Alberto Henríquez	10 D3
Museo de Arte de Coro	11 C3
Museo de Cerámica Histórica y Loza Popular	(see 8)
Museo Diocesano Lucas Guillermo Castillo	12 C3

SLEEPING	pp971–2
Posada Turística Don Antonio	13 C3
Posada Turística El Gallo	14 B2
Posada Villa Antigua	15 D4

EATING	p972
Centro Social Italo Venezolano	16 D2
Fonda Turística Sabor Latino	17 C3
Panadería La Gran Costa Nova	18 D2
Pizzería La Barra del Jacal	19 D2
Restaurant El Tinajero	20 C3
Restaurant Punto Criollo	21 C4

Map labels: Airport Terminal; Av Josefa Camejo; Calle 52 González; Calle 66 Federación; Calle 25 Norte; Calle 58A Hernández; Calle 56A Toledo; Av Manaure; Av Miranda; Calle 29 Unión; Corp Banca (250m); To Banco Mercantil (150m), Bus Terminal (2km); Plaza San Clemente; Iglesia de San Clemente; Iglesia de San Francisco; Calle 31 Urdaneta; Calle 76 Ayacucho; Calle 42; Calle 66 Colón; Calle 33 Zamora; Plaza Falcón; Monument to Juan de Ampíes; Calle 35 Falcón; Teatro Armonía; Cementerio Judío; To Cyber Web (500m), El Triángulo Azul (500m) & Banesco (600m); P T Alvarez; Catedral; Plaza Bolívar; Av Roosevelt; Iglesia de San Nicolás de Bari; Calle 39 Palmasola; Plaza Sucre; Ateneo de Coro; Calle 58 Comercio; Calle 56 Bolívar; Calle La Paz; Calle 62 Ampíes; Calle 41 Garcés; Millar 80; Calle 45 Buchivacoa; To La Casa de los Pájaros (300m); Calle 49 Churuguara

Centro de Navegación Internet (cnr Av Manaure & Calle Zamora)
L & D Sistemas (Calle Zamora)

If you need Internet access later at night, there are some cybercafés away from the city center that are open until midnight, including **Cyber Web** (Av Manaure near Banesco) and **El Triángulo Azul** (Av Manaure near Banesco), which are both in Castillo Don Leoncio.

MONEY

Most of the major banks have branches in the city center:
Banco de Venezuela (Paseo Talavera)
Banco Mercantil (Calle Falcón) Two blocks east of Av Manaure.
Banesco (Av Manaure) Eight blocks south of Calle Falcón.
Corp Banca (Calle Zamora) Three blocks east of Av Manaure.
Italcambio (airport terminal) Changes cash & traveler's checks.

TOURIST OFFICES

Secretaría de Turismo (☎ 0268-251-8033; Paseo La Alameda; 🕒 8am-noon & 2-6pm Mon-Fri) On the central pedestrian mall.

Sights

The massive fortresslike **cathedral** (Plaza Bolívar) is the oldest surviving church in Venezuela. Its construction began in the 1580s and was completed half a century later.

One block east, the **Museo de Arte de Coro** (☎ 0268-251-5658; Paseo Talavera; admission free; 🕒 9am-12:30pm & 3-7:30pm Tue-Sat, 9am-4pm Sun) presents temporary exhibitions of modern art. Diagonally opposite, the **Museo de Arte Alberto Henríquez** (☎ 0268-252-8661; Paseo Talavera; admission free; 🕒 9am-noon & 3-6pm Tue-Sat, 9am-noon Sun) also features modern art and shelters Venezuela's oldest synagogue.

The **Museo Diocesano Lucas Guillermo Castillo** (☎ 0268-251-5645; Calle Zamora; admission US$0.40; 🕒 9am-noon & 3-6pm Tue-Sat, 9am-2pm Sun), in an old convent building, has an extensive collection of religious and secular art from the region and beyond. All admissions are by a 45-minute tour (in Spanish only). Adjacent to the museum is the 18th-century **Iglesia de San Francisco**.

Continuing west along Calle Zamora, you'll pass a string of sites. The **Cruz de San Clemente** (Plaza San Clemente) is said to be the cross used in the first mass celebrated after the founding of the town. The 18th-century **Iglesia de San Clemente** (Plaza San Clemente) was laid out on the Latin-cross plan. It's one of the few examples of this design in the country.

The **Casa de los Arcaya** (☎ 0268-251-5645; Calle Zamora) is noted for its long, tile-roofed balconies. Inside is the **Museo de Cerámica Histórica y Loza Popular** (admission free; 🕒 9am-noon & 3-6pm Tue-Sat, 9am-1pm Sun), which features antique pottery and ceramics. One block further west, the **Casa de las Ventanas de Hierro** (Calle Zamora; admission US$0.40; 🕒 9am-noon & 3-6pm Tue-Sat, 9am-2pm Sun), noted for its splendid 8m plaster doorway, shelters a private collection of historic objects.

The **Cementerio Judío** (Calle Zamora at Calle 23 de Enero) was established in the 1830s and is the oldest Jewish cemetery still in use in South America. It's normally locked – to visit, inquire at the Museo de Arte Alberto Henríquez.

Northeast of town spreads the **Médanos de Coro National Park** (admission free; 🕒 7am-7:30pm), a unique mini-Sahara with sandy dunes rising up to 30m. To get there from the city center, take the city bus marked 'Carabobo' and get off 300m past the huge Monumento a la Federación. Then walk 10 minutes north along a wide avenue to another public sculpture, Monumento a la Madre. A few paces north, there is nothing but sand.

Sleeping

There are several budget places conveniently located in the historic center.

Posada Turística El Gallo (☎ 0268-252-9481; posadaelgallo2001@hotmail.com; Calle Federación No 26; d/tr US$10/12) The cheapest place in town, run by a friendly Frenchman named Eric. It's simple and lacks private baths, but otherwise is clean, pleasant and perfectly acceptable. The owner provides good tourist information and organizes full-day jeep tours to the Península de Paraguaná and Sierra de San Luis (each US$30).

Posada Turística Don Antonio (☎ 0268-253-9578; Paseo Talavera No 11; d US$16; ❄) Brand new *posada* in the city's heart. It has nine *matrimoniales* and three larger rooms, all with bath, air-con and cable TV.

Posada Villa Antigua (☎ 0414-682-2924; Calle Comercio No 46; d US$16; ❄) A small six-room place, providing comfortable rooms with bath and noiseless air-con.

La Casa de los Pájaros (☎ 0268-252-8215; Calle Monzón No 74; d with bath US$15, tr without bath US$16)

A private home with three small rooms rented out to guests. Pleasant but a bit outside the historic center.

Eating

Coro is a cheap place to eat and there are plenty of budget restaurants.

Fonda Turística Sabor Latino (Paseo La Alameda; breakfasts US$1-2, lunches US$2-3) Some of the cheapest meals in town.

Restaurant El Tinajero (Calle Zamora; mains US$2-4) An enjoyable eatery providing popular Venezuelan fare on the patio of an historic house.

Restaurant Punto Criollo (Calle Federación; meals US$2-4) A small simple place that gets packed with patrons at lunchtime.

Centro Social Italo Venezolano (Calle Urdaneta; mains US$2-4) Budget food, including good pizza.

Pizzería La Barra del Jacal (Calle Unión; mains US$3-6; 🕑 until late) An open-air restaurant popular with locals. It offers more than just pizza.

Panadería La Gran Costa Nova (Av Manaure) Fully refurbished, with tables inside and out. It serves good breakfasts, lunches and snacks.

Getting There & Away

AIR

The airport, just a five-minute walk north of the city center, handles daily flights to Caracas (US$50 to US$70), where you need to change for other destinations. Aerocaribe Coro and Dutch Caribbean Airlines fly light planes to Aruba and Curaçao (round trip around US$100, valid for only 14 days).

BUS

The **bus terminal** (Av Los Médanos), about 2km east of the city center, is accessible by frequent city transport. Ordinary buses to Maracaibo (US$5, four hours) and Valencia (US$5.50, 5½ hours) run every half-hour until about 6pm. Most of the direct buses to Caracas (US$8, seven hours) depart in the evening, but you can easily take one of the buses to Valencia and change. Several direct buses go nightly to Mérida (US$13, 13 hours) and to San Cristóbal (US$12, 12 hours).

MARACAIBO

Hot as hell and rich with oil, Maracaibo is Venezuela's second largest urban center, with a population of 1.5 million people. It's a mostly modern city with tall but soulless tower blocks, wide streets and a few shady parks. Visibly prosperous, Maracaibo becomes a ghost town in the middle of the day when the scorching heat drives everyone indoors for three hours or more of air-conditioned siesta. In sharp contrast to the urban modernity are the many Guajiro women in their long colorful dresses, sometimes even with their faces painted in a dark pigment. The Guajiros, who inhabit the region, are among the most traditional indigenous groups in the country.

Founded as a trading post in 1574, Maracaibo was a backwater on the shores of Lago de Maracaibo, South America's largest lake, until 1914, when drillers struck oil. By the late 1920s Venezuela had become the world's largest exporter of oil, the Saudi Arabia of South America, while Maracaibo developed into the country's oil capital, with two-thirds of the nation's output coming from beneath the lake. Even with the oil industry in its current slump, the Maracuchos, as local inhabitants are called, still feel they are producing the money that the rest of the country is spending.

Today, Maracaibo is a sweltering stop for travelers on the way to or from Colombia's Caribbean coast. Stay a day or so to visit the old holy basilica and the brightly painted houses on restored Calle Carabobo, and be sure to make a 60km detour to see the old *palafitos* on the shores of Laguna de Sinamaica. Five hundred years ago, Spanish sailors saw these over-water houses on stilts and named the place 'Little Venice' – Venezuela.

Information

INTERNET ACCESS

Central facilities include:

CANTV (in Centro Comercial Plaza Lago, Local 43, Av Libertador)

Telcel (in Centro Comercial La Redoma, Local 52-53, Av Libertador)

MONEY

Central banks include:

Banco de Venezuela (Calle 97)

Banco Provincial (Av El Milagro)

Corp Banca (Av Libertador)

Cash and traveler's checks can be exchanged at *casas de cambio*:

Casa de Cambio Maracaibo Av 9B (btwn Calles 77 & 78); Centro Comercial Plaza Lago (Av El Milagro)

VENEZUELA

MARACAIBO

0 ———————— 400 m
0 ———————— 0.2 mi

To Cazutur (2km)
& Museo de Arte
Contemporáneo
del Zulia (4km)

Cementerio El
Cuadrado

To Airport
(12km)

To Hotel Nuevo Montevideo (1.3km);
Corpozulia (1.5km); Nuevo Hotel
Unión (1.5km); Hotel Oasis Garden
(1.7km); Hotel San Martin
(2km); Hotel Astor (2.2km) &
Laguna de Sinamaica (60km)

Av Bella Vista

To Italcambio (4km) &
Casa de Cambio /
Maracaibo (4km)

Iglesia de
Santa Lucía

Basílica de
Chiquinquirá

Parque
Urdaneta

Iglesia de
Santa Bárbara

Iglesia de
San Francisco

Plaza
Baralt

Plaza
Bolívar

Catedral

Iglesia de
San Felipe
Neri

Teatro
Baralt

Lago de Maracaibo

Bus Terminal

Centro Comercial
Plaza Lago

Centro Comercial
La Redoma

Paseo de las Ciencias

INFORMATION	
Banco de Venezuela........................	1 D3
Banco Provincial............................	2 E3
CANTV...	3 B3
Corp Banca....................................	4 B3
Telcel..	5 B3

SIGHTS & ACTIVITIES	pp974
Casa de la Capitulación.................	6 E2
Centro de Arte de Maracaibo..........	7 D3
Mercado Artesanal San Sebastián...	8 E3
Museo Urdaneta............................	9 D1

SLEEPING	pp974-5
Hotel Caribe..................................	10 D2
Hotel El Milagro............................	11 F2
Hotel Victoria................................	12 D3

EATING	p975
Restaurant El Enlosao.....................	13 D2
Restaurant El Zaguán.....................	14 D2

Italcambio Centro Comercial Montielco (Av 20 at Calle 72); Centro Comercial Plaza Lago (**Av El Milagro**); La Chinita airport (inside terminal)

TOURIST OFFICES
Maracaibo has two tourist offices, none of which is in the historic center:
Corpozulia (☎ 0261-791-5555; Av Bella Vista btwn Calles 83 & 84; ⏱ 8:30-11:30am & 1:30-3:30pm Mon-Fri) Two-kilometers north of the city center, accessible by the Bella Vista *por puestos* from Plaza Bolívar.
Corzutur (☎ 0261-783-4928; Edificio Lieja, cnr Av 18 & Calle 78; ⏱ 8am-4pm Mon-Fri) Two-kilometers northwest of the city center.

Sights

If you are in Maracaibo in transit, you probably won't go far beyond downtown, the oldest part of the city. The axis here is the **Paseo de las Ciencias**, a wide greenbelt seven blocks long that was created after the demolition of old buildings.

At the western end of the *paseo* is the **Basílica de Chiquinquirá**, which features opulent interior decor. In the high altar is the venerated image of the Virgen de Chiquinquirá, to whom numerous miracles are attributed. Pilgrims flock here year-round, but the major celebrations are held for a full week in November, culminating in a procession on the 18th.

The eastern end of the paseo is bordered by **Plaza Bolívar**, which has a 19th-century **cathedral** on one side. To the north is the mid-18th-century **Casa de la Capitulación** (☎ 0261-725-1194; admission free; ⏱ 8am-6pm Mon-Fri), where the Spaniards – defeated in the naval battle of Lago de Maracaibo – signed the act of capitulation, sealing the independence of Gran Colombia. This is the only residential colonial building left in the city.

A short walk north from the city center is **Museo Urdaneta** (Calle 91A No 7-70; admission free; ⏱ 8am-3pm Mon-Fri), dedicated to Maracaibo-born General Rafael Urdaneta, the city's greatest independence hero.

Calle 94, also known as **Calle Carabobo**, has been partly restored to its former appearance, and is notable for its brightly colored facades and grilled windows. The most spectacular part of the street is between Av 6 and Av 8. Also worth visiting is the **Mercado Artesanal San Sebastián** (Av El Milagro at Calle 96 Ciencias), a colorful Guajiro craft market full of beautiful hammocks and other articrafts.

The sector south of the *paseo* is a wonder of heat, dirt and chaos. Many streets are crammed with stalls, making the area feel like a market. The imposing old market-building, restored and opened as the **Centro de Arte de Maracaibo** (☎ 0261-723-0166; Av Libertador; admission free; ⏱ 9:30am-6pm Tue-Fri, 10am-5pm Sat & Sun) stages temporary exhibitions.

Away from the historic center, you can visit the **Museo de Arte Contemporáneo del Zulia** (☎ 0261-759-4866; Av Universidad; admission free; ⏱ 9am-5pm Tue-Sun), on the grounds of the Universidad del Zulia, north of town.

The most popular tourist sight around Maracaibo is **Laguna de Sinamaica**, 60km north of the city. It's noted for the *palafitos* (houses built on piles) along the lakeshore. Perhaps it was here that in 1499 the Spaniards first saw indigenous people living in similar houses and gave Venezuela its name. Pleasure boats take tourists for a trip around the lagoon (US$20 per boat for up to six people). To get there from Maracaibo, take a bus heading for Guana or Los Filuos, get off in the town of Sinamaica (US$1.50, two hours) and take a *por puesto* to Puerto Cuervito (US$0.30, 10 minutes).

Sleeping

If you're trapped for the night in the city, you can try any of half a dozen ultrabasic hotels on the west side of the bus terminal; none deserves to be named here. The historic center doesn't offer anything special in the way of accommodations either. Moreover, it gets deserted after 8pm or so and can be unsafe.

Hotel Victoria (☎ 0261-722-9697; Plaza Baralt; s/d/tr with bath US$9/11/13; ❄) This character-filled and stylish place is attractively located overlooking the old market-building. Sadly, it's unkempt and run down, though some refurbishing was planned at the time of research. Choose a room with a balcony and a view over the plaza.

Hotel Caribe (☎ 0261-722-5986; Av 7; s/d/tr with bath US$9/11/13; ❄) Not much style or comfort, yet one of very few central shelters to choose from.

Hotel El Milagro (☎ 0261-722-8934; Av El Milagro; s/d with bath US$9/12; ❄) An undistinguished proposition in the old center, with small dim rooms.

If you plan on hanging around for a while, it's probably better and safer to stay further north of the historic center. The following budget hotels in the area have air-con rooms with private bath, and are accessible by *por puestos* running along Av Bella Vista.

Hotel Nuevo Montevideo (☎ 0261-722-2762; Calle 86A No 4-96; d US$10; 🏠) Old style.

Nuevo Hotel Unión (☎ 0261-793-3278; Calle 84 No 4-60; d US$10; 🏠) A small place.

Hotel Oasis Garden (☎ 0261-797-9582; Calle 82B No 8-25; d US$13; 🏠) Family run.

Hotel San Martín (☎ 0261-791-5095; Av 3Y No 80-11; d US$12; 🏠)

Hotel Astor (☎ 0261-791-4510; Plaza República; d US$10; 🏠) A simple spot.

Eating

A lot of ordinary cheap eateries in the city center serve set lunches for about US$2, but they close early and the quality of the food often mirrors the price.

Restaurant El Enlosao (in Casa de los Artesanos, Calle 94; mains US$3-5) A pleasant place serving tasty Venezuelan dishes at low prices.

Restaurant El Zaguán (Calle 94 at Av 6; mains US$4-6) A few steps away from El Enlosao, this also serves reasonable food.

Most upmarket restaurants are in the northern sector of the city. Many of them are concentrated around Av 5 de Julio and Av Bella Vista, Maracaibo's new center.

Getting There & Away

VENEZUELA

La Chinita airport is about 12km southwest of the city center. It's not linked by public transport; a taxi will cost about US$6. Flights are available to major cities, including Caracas (US$50 to US$75) and Mérida (US$35 to US$45).

The bus terminal is about 1km southwest of the city center. Buses run regularly to Coro (US$5, four hours) and Caracas (US$12, 10½ hours). Several night buses run to Mérida (US$11, nine hours) and San Cristóbal (US$10, eight hours).

COLOMBIAN BORDER CROSSING

Three bus companies – Bus Ven, Expreso Brasilia and Expresos Amerlujo – run air-conditioned buses to Cartagena via Maicao, Santa Marta and Barranquilla (all in Colombia). **Bus Ven** (☎ 0261-723-9084) has two morning departures daily from Maracaibo's bus terminal and is cheaper than its competitors: Cartagena (US$30, 10 hours), Santa Marta (US$22, 6½ hours). The two other companies depart from elsewhere.

You can also go by *por puesto* to Maicao and change there. *Por puestos* depart regularly from about 5am to 3pm (US$8, 2½ hours) and go as far as Maicao's bus terminal. There are also infrequent buses to Maicao (US$5, four hours). From Maicao, several Colombian bus companies operate buses to Santa Marta (US$9, four hours) and further on; buses depart regularly until about 5 pm.

All passport formalities are done in Paraguachón on the border. Venezuelan immigration charges a US$13 *impuesto de salida* (exit tax), paid in cash bolívares by all tourists leaving Venezuela.

You can change bolívares into Colombian pesos at the Maracaibo terminal or in Paraguachón or Maicao, but don't take them further into Colombia. They are very difficult to change beyond Maicao. Wind your watch back one hour when crossing from Venezuela to Colombia.

THE ANDES

The Venezuelan Andes extend from the Táchira depression on the Colombian border northeast to the state of Trujillo. This part of the range, about 400km long and 70km to 100km wide, is Venezuela's highest outcrop. Administratively, the mountains are covered by the states of Táchira, Mérida and Trujillo.

Mérida state is the center of the Venezuelan Andes. The mountains here form two roughly parallel chains separated by a verdant mountain valley. The southern chain culminates at the Sierra Nevada de Mérida, crowned with snowcapped peaks. The country's highest summits are here, including Pico Bolívar (5007m), Pico Humboldt (4942m) and Pico Bonpland (4883m). All this area is in the Parque Nacional Sierra Nevada. The northern chain, the Sierra de La Culata, reaches 4660m and is also the focus of a national park. In the deep valley between the two ranges sits the city of Mérida, the region's major urban center and the country's mountain capital.

MÉRIDA

Mérida is arguably Venezuela's most popular destination among foreign backpackers. It has an unhurried and friendly atmosphere, plenty of tourist facilities, the famous *teleférico* and is surrounded by beautiful mountains, including the country's rooftop, Pico Bolívar, just 12km away. It's Venezuela's major center for outdoor activities.

Home to the large Universidad de los Andes (Venezuela's second-oldest university), Mérida has a sizable academic community that gives it a cultured and bohemian air. The city enjoys a pleasant, mild climate, with an average temperature of 19°C (66°F). Furthermore, it's inexpensive and reasonably safe by Venezuelan standards.

Mérida was founded in 1558, but its transition from a town into a city really took place only over the last few decades. It sits on a flat *meseta*, a terrace stretching for a dozen kilometers between parallel rivers, its edges dropping abruptly to the riverbanks. Having filled the *meseta* as densely as possible, Mérida is now expanding beyond it and is approaching 300,000 inhabitants.

Information
INTERNET ACCESS
Mérida has plenty of Internet facilities and they are about the cheapest in Venezuela: US$0.40 to US$0.80 an hour. Central locations include:

CANTV (Calle 26 at Av 3)
Ciber Café El Russo (Av 4 No 17-74)
Interplanet (Av 4 No 19-28)
La Abadía (in restaurant; Av 3 No 17-45)
Telcel (Calle 20 No 4-64)

LAUNDRY
Many *posadas* offer laundry service; if not, there are several central facilities, including:
Lavandería Andina (Av 7 No 22-45)
Lavandería Marbet (Calle 25 No 8-35)
Lavandería Yibe (Av 6 No 19-25)

MONEY
Banks generally do not exchange cash; you can do it at **Italcambio** (airport terminal), which also changes traveler's checks. **Corp Banca** (Av Las Américas), located outside the city center, changes American Express traveler's checks. Central banks, including Banco de Venezuela, Banco Mercantil and Banesco, all have ATMs.

TOURIST OFFICES
Cormetur (☎ 0274-263-0814; Av Urdaneta at Calle 45) The local tourist office is near the airport. Cormetur operates several tourist information outlets, including one at the airport, one at the bus terminal and another in Parque Las Heroínas.

Most major tour companies (see p978) provide information about trekking, mountaineering and other activities.

Sights
CITY CENTER
The city center is pleasant for leisurely strolls, even though it has little in the way of colonial architecture or outstanding sights. Plaza Bolívar is the city's heart, but is not a colonial square. Work on the **cathedral** was begun in 1800 but not completed until 1958. Next to it is the **Museo Arquidiocesano** (☎ 0274-252-5786; Plaza Bolívar, Av 4; admission US$0.75; ☼ 9am-noon Tue-Sat) featuring a collection of religious art. Note the bell cast in 909, thought to be the world's second-oldest surviving bell.

The **Museo Arqueológico** (☎ 0274-240-1111; cnr Av 3 & Calle 23; admission US$0.50; ☼ 8-11am & 2-5pm Tue-Sun) has a collection related to the pre-Hispanic times of the region.

The large, modern Complejo Cultural shelters the **Museo de Arte Moderno** (☎ 0274-252-4380; cnr Calle 21 & Av 2; admission free; ☼ 9am-noon & 2-5pm Tue-Sun). The **Museo de Arte Colonial** (☎ 0274-252-7860; cnr Av 4 & Calle 20; admission US$0.50; ☼ 8am-noon & 2-6pm Tue-Sun) has a collection of mostly sacred art.

TELEFÉRICO
The highlight of any visit to Mérida is the *teleférico*, the world's highest and longest cable-car system, now running again after a period of being out of order. It was constructed in 1958 by a French company and runs 12.6km from the bottom station of Barinitas (1577m) in Mérida to the top of Pico Espejo (4765m), covering the ascent in four stages. The three intermediate stations are La Montaña (2436m), La Aguada (3452m) and Loma Redonda (4045m).

The cable car normally operates from Wednesday to Sunday, though in tourist season it runs daily. The first trip up is at 7:30am and the last at noon (7am and 2pm, respectively, in peak season). The last trip down is at about 1:30pm (4pm or even later

VENEZUELA

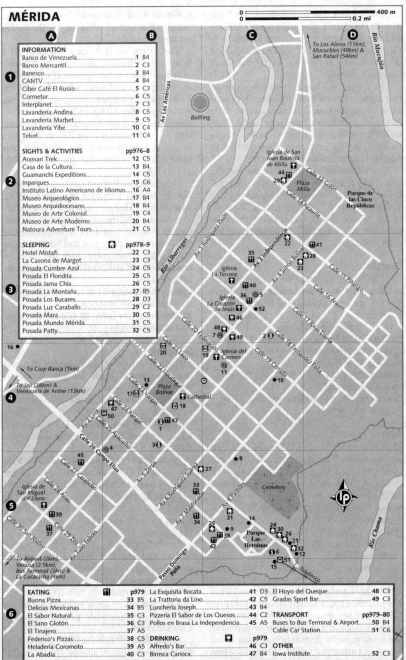

MÉRIDA

0 |————————| 400 m
0 |————————| 0.2 mi

INFORMATION
Banco de Venezuela..........................1 B4
Banco Mercantil................................2 C3
Banesco..3 B4
CANTV..4 B4
Ciber Café El Russo...........................5 C3
Cormetur..6 C5
Interplanet..7 C3
Lavandería Andina.............................8 C5
Lavandería Marbet.............................9 C5
Lavandería Yibe...............................10 C4
Telcel...11 C4

SIGHTS & ACTIVITIES   pp976–8
Arassari Trek....................................12 C5
Casa de la Cultura............................13 B4
Guamanchi Expeditions....................14 C5
Inparques..15 C6
Instituto Latino Americano de Idiomas....16 A4
Museo Arqueológico........................17 B4
Museo Arquidiocesano.....................18 B4
Museo de Arte Colonial....................19 C4
Museo de Arte Moderno...................20 B4
Natoura Adventure Tours..................21 C5

SLEEPING   pp978–9
Hotel Mistafí....................................22 C3
La Casona de Margot........................23 C3
Posada Cumbre Azul.........................24 C5
Posada El Floridita...........................25 C5
Posada Jama Chía............................26 C5
Posada La Montaña..........................27 B5
Posada Los Bucares..........................28 D3
Posada Luz Caraballo........................29 C2
Posada Mara....................................30 C5
Posada Mundo Mérida......................31 C5
Posada Patty....................................32 C5

To Los Aleros (11km),
Mucuchíes (48km) &
San Rafael (54km)

Río Mucujún

Av Las Américas

Bullring

Iglesia de San
Juan Bautista
de Milla

Calle 13 Colón

Plaza
Milla

Parque de
las Cinco
Repúblicas

Calle 14 Picaurte

Av 1 Rodríguez Picón

Av 3 Independencia

Calle 15 Piñango

Río Albarregas

Iglesia
La Tercera

Av 4 Simón Bolívar

Calle 16 Arauíe

Calle 17 Rivas Dávila

Iglesia
La Corazón
de Jesús

Calle 18 Fernández Peña

Calle 20 Federición

Calle 21 Lazo

Iglesia del
Carmen

Calle 19 Cerrada

To Corp Banca (1km)

To Jají (38km) &
Venezuela de Antier (12km)

Calle 22 Lizcategui

Plaza
Bolívar

Calle 23 Vargas

Calle 24 Rangel

Cathedral

Calle 25 Ayacucho

Av 2 Lora

Calle 26 Campo Elías

Calle 27 Carabobo

Av 5 Zerpa

Calle 28 Arias

Iglesia de
San Miguel
del Llano

Calle 29 Zea Tulio Fabres

Calle 30 San Mateo

Av 6 Paredes

Cemetery

Av 6 Rodríguez Suárez

Av 7 Maldonado

Parque
Las
Heroínas

Río Chama

To Airport (2km),
Venusa (2.5km),
Bus Terminal (3km) &
La Cucaracha (4km)

Paseo Domingo
Peña

Teleférico

EATING   p979
Buona Pizza.....................................33 B5
Delicias Mexicanas...........................34 B5
El Sabor Natural...............................35 C3
El Sano Glotón................................36 C3
El Tinajero.......................................37 A5
Federico's Pizzas.............................38 C5
Heladería Coromoto.........................39 A5
La Abadía..40 C3

La Exquisita Bocata..........................41 D3
La Trattoria da Lino..........................42 C5
Lunchería Joseph.............................43 B4
Pizzería El Sabor de Los Quesos.......44 C2
Pollos en Brasa La Independencia.....45 A5

DRINKING   p979
Alfredo's Bar...................................46 C3
Birosca Carioca................................47 B4

El Hoyo del Queque.........................48 C3
Gradas Sport Bar.............................49 C3

TRANSPORT   pp979–80
Buses to Bus Terminal & Airport.......50 B4
Cable Car Station............................51 C6

OTHER
Iowa Institute..................................52 C3

in peak season). The round-trip ticket from Mérida to Loma Redonda costs US$10, and the last stage from Loma Redonda to Pico Espejo is another US$3; no student discounts are available. To take a large backpack costs US$2 extra.

The ascent to Pico Espejo takes one to two hours. It's best to go up as early as possible, as clouds usually obscure views later in the day. You can then take some short walks around Pico Espejo and/or Loma Redonda before returning. Don't forget to take warm clothes and sunscreen.

Apart from splendid views during the trip itself, the cable car provides easy access for high-mountain hiking, saving you a day or two of puffing uphill. Bear in mind, however, that acclimatization problems can easily occur by quickly reaching high altitudes.

Courses

Mérida is a great place to study Spanish. It has plenty of students and tutors offering private lessons (inquire at the popular travelers' hotels and tour companies) and several language schools, including:

Instituto Latino Americano de Idiomas (☎ 0274-244-5463; ildi@bolivar.funmrd.gov.ve; Centro Comercial Mamayera, Av Las Américas)

Iowa Institute (☎ 0274-244-6404; www.iowainstitute.com; Av 4 at Calle 18)

Venusa (☎ 0274-263-8855; www.venusa.net; Edificio Tibisay, Av Urdaneta No 49-49)

Tours

Mérida is easily Venezuela's main center of active tourism. The region provides excellent conditions for hiking, mountaineering, rock climbing, bird-watching, paragliding and rafting, and local operators have been quick to make these activities accessible to visitors. Tour companies abound, and prices are reasonable. See the Around Mérida section (p980) for more about trips and activities mentioned here.

Understandably, mountain trips figure prominently on tour-company agendas and include treks to Pico Bolívar and Pico Humboldt; expect to pay about US$30 to US$50 per person per day, all-inclusive.

The village of Los Nevados is probably the most popular destination among those who don't attempt to climb the peaks. Most companies offer trips there, but you can easily do it on your own. Tour companies listed in this section will give you the details on how to do it.

The Sierra de la Culata National Park is another attractive destination, available as a tour from most agents. It's a two- to three-day trip and costs around US$30 to US$50 per person per day, all-inclusive. See Activities in the Around Mérida section for more details (p980). A recommended excursion out of Mérida is a wildlife safari in Los Llano, and many companies offer this trip, most often as a four-day tour for US$100 to US$160.

Other special-interest tours readily available in Mérida focus on mountain biking, paragliding, rafting, canyoning, rock climbing, fishing and horse riding. Some companies handle rental of mountaineering equipment, camping gear and bikes. Among the best local tour companies are:

Arassari Trek (☎ 0274-252-5879; www.arassari.com; Calle 24 No 8-301)

Guamanchi Expeditions (☎ 0274-252-2080; www.guamanchi.com; Calle 24 No 8-86)

Natoura Adventure Tours (☎ 0274-252-4216; www.natoura.com; Calle 24 No 8-237)

Sleeping

Mérida has heaps of places to stay all across the city center. Most budget places are *posadas.*. Many have hot water and provide laundry facilities, and some offer guest use of the kitchen.

Posada Jama Chía (☎ 0274-252-5767; Calle 24 No 8-223; r per person US$4) Nine pleasant rooms with shared facilities.

Posada Patty (☎ 0274-251-1052; Calle 24 No 8-265; r per person US$3) One of the cheapest places, with six basic rooms and shared facilities.

Posada Mundo Mérida (☎ 0274-252-2644; Calle 24 No 8-14; r per person US$4) A simple place offering rooms without bath. Guests can use the kitchen.

Posada Cumbre Azul (☎ 0274-416-3231; Calle 24 No 8-153; r per person US$3.50) This is essentially an equipment rental company, but it offers three rooms with shared facilities.

Posada El Floridita (☎ 0274-251-0452; Calle 25 No 8-44; r with bath per person US$3.50) One of the cheapest options with private facilities. Clean and OK.

Posada Mara (☎ 0274-252-5507; Calle 24 No 8-215; d/tr with bath US$8/12) A simple choice but all rooms have private baths.

Posada La Montaña (☎ 0274-252-5977; Calle 24 No 6-47; s/d with bath US$10/13) This charming colonial-style place has its own restaurant. All rooms have cable TV.

Posada Luz Caraballo (☎ 0274-252-5441; Av 2 No 13-80; s/d/tr with bath US$9/12/18) A three-story stylish lodging facing Plaza Milla. It has a good budget restaurant.

Posada Los Bucares (☎ 0274-252-2841; Av 4 No 15-05; s/d/tr with bath US$11/13/18) Fine historic mansion with a patio turned into an enjoyable *posada*.

La Casona de Margot (☎ 0274-252-3312; Av 4 No 15-17; d/tr with bath US$13/16) Next door to Los Bucares, another old-fashioned building with style and atmosphere.

Hotel Mistafi (☎ 0274-251-0729; cnr Av 3 & Calle 15; s/d/tr US$20/23/26; ✴) New comfortable hotel, with ample rooms, good beds and its own restaurant. Some rooms have air-con.

Eating

Mérida is one of the cheapest places to eat in Venezuela and the food is generally good. Plenty of restaurants serve set lunches for around US$2 or even less. One of these is the consistently popular **Lunchería Joseph** (Calle 23 off Plaza Bolívar).

Cheap lunchtime vegetarian meals are served at **El Sano Glotón** (Av 4 No 17-84), **El Sabor Natural** (Av 3 No 16-80) and **El Tinajero** (Calle 29 No 3-54).

Pollos en Brasa La Independencia (Av 3 No 26-52; ✴ until late) One of the best budget outlets for chicken.

Pizzería El Sabor de Los Quesos (Plaza Milla, Av 2; pizza US$2-4) Some of the town's cheapest pizza, and they aren't bad.

Buona Pizza (Av 7 No 24-46; pizza US$3-4) A recommended budget pizza outlet.

Delicias Mexicanas (Calle 25 No 7-48; mains US$3-4) A colorful place bringing Mexican flavor to town.

Federico's Pizzas (Pasaje Ayacucho; pasta US$3-4) Nicely decorated two-level pasta and pizza house.

La Trattoria da Lino (Pasaje Ayacucho; mains US$4-7) Well-appointed Italian restaurant with fine home-cooked food.

La Exquisita Bocata (Av 4 No 14-99) Delicious *bocata* (a sort of sandwich with a variety of fillings).

La Abadía (Av 3 No 17-45; mains US$4-6) A beautifully reconstructed colonial mansion with different dining spaces, plus a cybercafé.

One of the loveliest places to eat in town, serving salads, meats and pasta.

Heladería Coromoto (Av 3 No 28-75) Perhaps the most famous ice-cream parlor on the continent, appearing in the *Guinness Book of Records* for having the greatest number of ice-cream flavors. The place offers more than 800 flavors, though not all are available on an average day. Among the more unusual varieties, you can try polar beer, shrimp, trout or chicken with spaghetti. You can even have the Lonely Planet flavor (which appears under its Spanish name, Planeta Solitario).

Drinking

There are three bars on the corner of Calle 19 at Av 4.

Alfredo's Bar (cnr Calle 19 & Av 4) This noisy spot has long been one of the most popular watering holes in town, largely due to its incredibly cheap beer.

El Hoyo del Queque (cnr Calle 19 & Av 4) Marginally more expensive, El Hoyo is an attractive alternative and has live music on weekends.

Gradas Sport Bar (cnr Calle 19 & Av 4) Also worth checking out.

Other poles of nighttime entertainment include the following options.

Birosca Carioca (Calle 24 No 2-04) Invariably popular central bar-disco for fast drinking and dancing in a 'student' atmosphere.

La Cucaracha (in Centro Comercial Las Tapias, Av Urdaneta) The city's oldest, largest and loudest disco. The main hall blasts with disco/techno music, while the Latin Caribbean rhythms are played downstairs.

Getting There & Away

AIR

The airport is right inside the city, 2km southwest of Plaza Bolívar, accessible by buses from Calle 25 at Av 2. Avior and Santa Bárbara fly daily to/from Caracas (US$40 to US$65). There are also direct flights to Maracaibo (US$35 to US$45) and San Antonio del Táchira (US$35 to US$45).

BUS

The bus terminal is on Av Las Américas, 3km southwest of the city center; it's linked by frequent public buses, which depart from Calle 25 at Av 2, or you can take a taxi (US$2). Half a dozen buses a day run to Caracas (US$15, 12 hours) and to Maracaibo (US$11, eight hours). Busetas to San Cristóbal depart every 1½ hours from 5:30am to 7pm (US$6, five hours). *Por puestos* operate on many regional routes, including Apartaderos and Jají.

AROUND MÉRIDA

The region surrounding Mérida offers plenty of natural and cultural attractions, and you could easily spend a week or two here, walking in the mountains or exploring old villages. Virtually every sizable village on the Trans-Andean Hwy has some budget places to stay and eat.

The region is sprinkled with old mountain villages, the best known of which is **Jají**, 38km west of Mérida and accessible by *por puesto*. It was extensively reconstructed in the late 1960s to become a manicured typical Andean town. There are two budget *posadas* in the village.

For something more authentic, try **Mucuchíes**, a 400-year-old town 48km east of Mérida. Several kilometers up the road is the village of **San Rafael**, noted for an amazing small stone chapel built by a local artist Juan Félix Sánchez.

Two theme parks in the vicinity of Mérida are loved by Venezuelans, though they may look a bit tacky to some foreign travelers. **Los Aleros**, near Tabay, on the road to Mucuchíes, is a re-creation of an Andean village from the 1930s, with period events, crafts, food and a few surprises. *Por puestos* from the corner of Calle 19 and Av 4 in Mérida will take you there. **Venezuela de Antier**, on the Jají road, 12km from Mérida, is a sort of Venezuela in a capsule, encompassing landmarks, costumes and traditions. Take a *por puesto* from Calle 26 between Av 3 and Av 4. Admission to either park is US$12. Don't go if it's raining as most of the action takes place outdoors.

Activities
HIKING & MOUNTAINEERING

Climbing Venezuela's highest peaks, **Pico Bolívar** and **Pico Humboldt**, shouldn't be attempted without a guide unless you have climbing experience. Trips to both are offered by a number of tour operators in Mérida.

On your own, you can hike along the trails leading up to both peaks. The trail to Pico Bolívar roughly follows the cable-

car line, but don't go alone from Loma Redonda to Pico Espejo – the trail is not clear and it's easy to get lost. The starting point for the trek up to Pico Humboldt is La Mucuy, accessible by road from Mérida.

An easier and more popular destination is **Los Nevados**, a charming mountain village sitting at an altitude of about 2700m (budget accommodations and food are available). One way of getting there is by jeep along a breathtaking, cliffside-hugging track (US$50 per jeep for up to five people, four to five hours; you can find a jeep for hire in Mérida, at the Parque Las Heroínas). You can stay the night in Los Nevados, then walk or ride on muleback to Loma Redonda (five to six hours) the next day. Return by cable car to Mérida or walk downhill for about 2½ hours to the beautiful Valle Los Calderones for another night, returning to Mérida on the third day.

Possibly a more attractive way to do the trip is to go by cable car up to Pico Espejo, have a look around and go down (also by cable car) to Loma Redonda. Then walk to Los Nevados (four to five hours), spend the night and return the next day by jeep to Mérida.

Sierra de La Culata National Park also offers some amazing hiking territory and is particularly noted for its desert-like highland landscapes. Take a *por puesto* to La Culata (departing from Calle 19 in Mérida), from where it's a three- to four-hour hike uphill to a primitive shelter known as El Refugio at about 3700m. Continue the next day for about three hours to the top of Pico Pan de Azúcar (4660m). Return before 4pm, in time for the last *por puesto* to Mérida.

Another interesting area for hiking is further east, near **Pico El Águila** (4118m). Take a morning bus to Valera and get off at Venezuela's highest road pass (4007m), at the foot of the peak, about 60km from Mérida. Locals with mules wait on the pass to take tourists to **Laguna Mucubají** (3540m), 5km due south, but it's better to walk there to get a closer look at the splendid *páramo* (an open highland moor). From Laguna Mucubají, it's an hour's walk through the reforested pine woods to **Laguna Negra**, a small but beautiful mountain lake with amazingly dark water.

Some of Mérida's tour operators can provide information about these and other do-it-yourself tours. Don't ignore their comments about safety measures. Bear in mind that weather can change frequently and rapidly even in the dry season.

If you are going to stay overnight in the Parque Nacional Sierra Nevada you need a permit from Inparques (so far, La Culata doesn't require permits). Permits are issued by Inparques outlets at the park entry points, including the one next to the cable-car station. The permit is issued on the spot (you have to show your passport) and costs US$1 per person per night.

MOUNTAIN BIKING
Several tour companies in Mérida organize bike trips and rent bikes. One of the most popular bike tours is the loop around the remote mountain villages south of Mérida known as Pueblos del Sur. Ask for recommended bike trips to do on your own. Bike rental is around US$8 to US$10 a day.

PARAGLIDING
Most tour operators offer tandem flights with a skilled pilot, so no previous experience is necessary. The usual starting point for flights is Las González, an hour-long jeep ride from Mérida, from where you glide for 20 to 30 minutes down 850 vertical meters. The cost of the flight (US$40 to US$50) includes jeep transport.

HORSE RIDING
From short leisurely rides to horse treks of several days, horse riding is organized by most tour operators. Contact the companies for details, as offerings and prices vary considerably.

RIVER-RAFTING & CANYONING
Rafters run some rivers at the southern slopes of the Andes. Rafting can be included in the tour to Los Llanos or done on a two-day exclusive rafting tour (US$80 to US$100 per person). It's a wet-season activity, normally possible from May to November, but climate anomalies over recent years make it difficult to pinpoint the season.

The newest craze, described by travelers as 'awesome, terrifying, beautiful, insane but amazing' or 'possibly the maddest thing you can do without getting killed,' is canyoning – climbing, rappelling and hiking down a river canyon. Full-day all-inclusive canyoning tours go for around US$50.

Arassari Trek offers the most adventurous rafting and canyoning tours.

WILDLIFE WATCHING
Some of the agencies organize bird-watching tours in the mountains, but by far the most popular wildlife-watching destination is Los Llanos, an immense plain savannah south of the Andes. Los Llanos is Venezuela's greatest repository of wildlife, particularly birds, but it's also excellent ground to get a close touch with caimans, capybaras, piranhas and anacondas, to name just a few. Several ecotourism camps in Los Llanos offer wildlife-watching tours on their ranches, but they are expensive (US$100 to US$150 per person per day). Mérida's companies provide similarly fascinating excursions for US$25 to US$40 per day. They are offered as three- to four-day all-inclusive packages.

SAN CRISTÓBAL
Set 40km from the Colombian border, San Cristóbal is the capital of Táchira state and a thriving commercial center of 350,000 people. Spread over a mountain slope at an altitude of about 800m, the city has an attractive location and an agreeable climate, with an average temperature of 21°C (70°F). However, San Cristóbal has little to offer tourists and is really just a transit point on the Pan-American route between Venezuela and Colombia. You are likely to pass through if you come from or go to Bogotá in Colombia. With a couple of hours to spare, you can visit the **Museo del Táchira** (☎ 0276-353-0543; Av Universidad Paramillo; admission free; 🕑 9am-5pm Tue-Fri, 10am-6pm Sat & Sun), which features exhibitions on the archaeology, history and ethnography of the region.

Information
Central Internet facilities include **Telcel** (Av 7 No 9-97), **CANTV** (Av 5 at Calle 5) and **Atelcom** (Av 7 at Calle 12). More cybercafés are in Barrio Obrero north of the city center. Some major banks are close to Plaza Bolívar. The local tourist office, **Cotatur** (☎ 0276-357-9655; Av España at Av Carabobo; 🕑 8am-noon & 2-5:30pm Mon-Fri) is 2km northeast of the city center.

Sleeping
If you're coming by bus and just need a budget shelter for the night, check one of several basic hotels on Calle 4, a short block

south of the bus terminal. Alternatively, try one of the budget hotels in the city center (a 10-minute ride by local bus). All the hotels listed have rooms with private baths and fans.

Hotel Rossio (☎ 0276-343-2330; Carrera 9 No 10-98; s/d/tr US$8/10/12)

Hotel Parador del Hidalgo (☎ 0276-343-2839; Calle 7 No 9-35; s/d/tr US$6/8/10)

Hotel Bella Vista (☎ 0276-343-7866; Carrera 9 at Calle 9; s/d/tr US$10/12/13)

Hotel Horizonte (☎ 0276-343-0011; Calle 7 at Carrera 4; s/d/tr US$12/14/15)

Eating

The city center has lots of restaurants, including numerous greasy spoons serving set lunches for US$1 to US$2. More decent central eateries include **Restaurant Bologna** (Calle 5 No 8-54; mains US$2-5), **Restaurant El Maizal** (Carrera 9 No 10-82; US$3-6) and **El Bistrot del Gordo Barón** (Carrera 4 No 5-34; mains US$3-5).

Tienda Vegetariana Tropical (Carrera 6 No 6-11) Budget vegetarian lunches are served here.

Getting There & Away

San Cristóbal's airport is in Santo Domingo, about 35km southeast of the city, but not much air traffic goes through there. The airport in San Antonio del Táchira is far busier and just about the same distance from San Cristóbal.

The bus terminal is 2km south of the city center and linked by frequent city bus services. About 10 buses daily go to Caracas (US$14, 13 hours). Most depart in the late afternoon or early evening for an overnight trip via El Llano highway. Busetas to Mérida depart every 1½ hours until 7pm (US$6, five hours). *Por puestos* to San Antonio del Táchira, on the Colombian border, run every 15 minutes or so (US$1, 1¼ hours).

SAN ANTONIO DEL TÁCHIRA

San Antonio is a Venezuelan border town of 60,000 people, sitting on a busy San Cristóbal–Cúcuta road and living off trade with neighboring Colombia. You'll pass through it if taking this route between the two countries; otherwise, there's no point in coming here as the town has no significant attractions. Wind your watch back one hour when crossing from Venezuela to Colombia.

Information

Internet facilities include **Infoplanet Cybercafé** (Calle 4 No 3-45), **Cyber World** (Carrera 6 No 6-11) and **Compunet Cybercafé** (Calle 6 No 8-28).

The city center has plenty of *casas de cambio*, particularly on Av Venezuela and around the DIEX office. They don't cash traveler's checks but they do change US dollars, bolívares and Colombian pesos. **Banco de Venezuela** (Calle 3 at Carrera 9) and **Banco Mercantil** (Calle 3 at Carrera 10) have ATMs.

A tourist information desk at the airport is open during flight times only. The following travel agencies in the town center will answer your transportation queries and sell air tickets.

Turismo Internacional (☎ 0276-771-5555; Av Venezuela No 4-04)

Turismo Uribante (☎ 0276-771-1779; Av Venezuela No 5-59)

Turismo Turvinter (☎ 0276-771-0311; Av Venezuela at Calle 7)

The office of **DIEX** (Carrera 9 btwn Calles 6 & 7; ⌚ 6am-9pm) puts exit or entry stamps in passports. A US$13 departure tax, paid in bolívares, is required from all tourists leaving Venezuela.

Nationals of most Western countries don't need a visa for Colombia, but all travelers must get an entry stamp from DAS. For details see Cúcuta in the Colombia chapter (p555).

Sleeping & Eating

Hotel Colonial (☎ 0276-771-2679; Carrera 11 No 2-51; s/d with bath US$6/8) and **Hotel Terepaima** (☎ 0276-771-1763; Carrera 8 No 1-37; d/tr with bath US$8/10) are both quite simple but have rooms with fans, as well as budget restaurants.

The best accommodations in town are at **Hotel Don Jorge** (☎ 0276-771-1932; Calle 5 No 9-20; s/d/tr US$10/16/18; 🖥) and **Hotel Adriático** (☎ 0276-771-5757; Calle 6 No 5-51; s/d/tr US$10/15/20; 🖥). Both have air-con rooms and reasonable restaurants.

Getting There & Away
AIR

The airport, 2km northeast of town, is reachable by buses heading to Ureña (catch them on Calle 6). It handles direct flights to Caracas (US$45 to US$80), Maracaibo (US$45 to US$65) and Mérida (US$35 to US$45). There are no direct flights to Colombia from

SAN ANTONIO DEL TÁCHIRA

INFORMATION	
Banco de Venezuela	1 B2
Banco Mercantil	2 B3
Compunet Cybercafé	3 C2
Cyber World	4 C1
DAS Office (Colombian Immigration)	5 A1
DIEX Office	6 C2
Infoplanet Cybercafé	7 C1
Turismo Internacional	8 B1
Turismo Turvinter	9 C1
Turismo Uribante	10 C1

SLEEPING	p982
Hotel Adriático	11 C1
Hotel Colonial	12 B3
Hotel Don Jorge	13 C2
Hotel Terepaima	14 B2

TRANSPORT	pp982-3
Buses to Ureña	15 C1
Expresos Los Llanos	16 C1
Expresos Mérida	17 C1
Expresos San Cristóbal	18 B1
Por Puestos to Cúcuta	19 C2
Por Puestos to San Cristóbal	20 D2

San Antonio; instead, go to Cúcuta across the border, from where you can fly to Bogotá, Medellín and other major cities.

BUS

The bus terminal is halfway to the airport. Five bus companies – Expresos Mérida, Expresos Los Llanos, Expresos Alianza, Expresos Occidente and Expresos San Cristóbal – operate buses to Caracas, with a total of six buses daily. All depart between 4pm and 7pm and use the El Llano route (US$15, 14 hours). Most bus companies also have offices in the town center, where they sell tickets.

No direct buses run to Mérida; go to San Cristóbal and change there. *Por puestos* to San Cristóbal leave frequently from Av Venezuela at Carrera 10 (US$1, 1¼ hours).

Buses and *por puestos* run frequently to Cúcuta in Colombia, 12km from San Antonio. You can catch buses (US$0.40) at stops on Av Venezuela, but remember to get off at DAS just behind the bridge for your Colombia entry stamp (or walk from San Antonio across the bridge to DAS), then take another bus. Buses go as far as the Cúcuta bus terminal, passing through the town center. You can pay in bolívares or pesos.

THE NORTHEAST

Venezuela's northeast region is a mosaic of diverse natural features, including whitesand beaches, coral reefs, fresh mountains and verdant valleys. The coast has some amazing stretches here, especially within Parque Nacional Mochima and around Río Caribe. The region also boasts Venezuela's best cave, the Cueva del Guácharo.

Most of the cultural and historic attractions are close to the sea, for it was essentially the coast that the Spanish conquered and settled. However, little remains of the colonial legacy except for the partly preserved old quarters of Barcelona and Cumaná, and some old churches and forts scattered over the region. Administratively, the northeast covers the states of Anzoátegui, Sucre and Monagas.

BARCELONA

The capital of Anzoátegui state, Barcelona was founded in 1671 by a group of Catalan colonists, who named the initial settlement after their hometown in Spain. Today it's a city of about 300,000 people and is gradually merging into a single urban sprawl with its dynamic young neighbor, Puerto La Cruz.

Central Barcelona has several leafy plazas and also some colonial architecture. The historic quarter has been partly restored and whitewashed throughout, giving it a pleasant general appearance. The urban fabric, however, is an architectural mishmash dating from many different periods.

Information

Internet facilities include **CANTV** (Centro Comercial La Llovizna, Av 5 de Julio) and **Centro de Navegación** (Centro Comercial Marinelli, Av 5 de Julio).

Banesco (Av 5 de Julio), **Banco de Venezuela** (Plaza Boyacá) and **Banco Mercantil** (Plaza Bolívar) advance cash on Visa and MasterCard, while **Corp Banca** (Plaza Bolívar) changes American Express traveler's checks.

The local tourist office, **Coranztur** (☎ 0281-275-0474; Av 5 de Julio; ✆ 9am-noon & 2-5pm Mon-Fri), is in the government building.

Sights

The city's historic center, **Plaza Boyacá**, features a statue of General José Antonio Anzoátegui, the Barcelona-born hero of

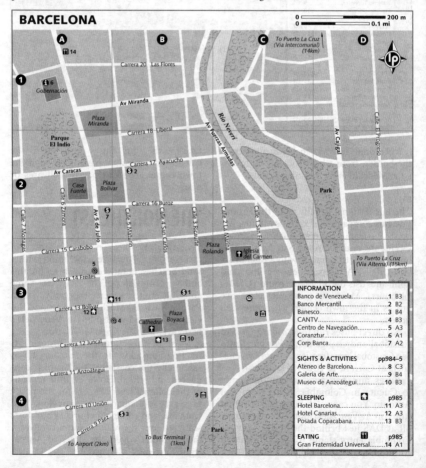

BARCELONA	
0	200 m
0	0.1 mi

INFORMATION
Banco de Venezuela.................1 B3
Banco Mercantil........................2 B2
Banesco.....................................3 B4
CANTV.......................................4 B3
Centro de Navegación..............5 A3
Coranztur..................................6 A1
Corp Banca...............................7 A2

SIGHTS & ACTIVITIES   pp984–5
Ateneo de Barcelona.................8 C3
Galería de Arte..........................9 B4
Museo de Anzoátegui.............10 B3

SLEEPING   p985
Hotel Barcelona......................11 A3
Hotel Canarias........................ 12 A3
Posada Copacabana................13 B3

EATING   p985
Gran Fraternidad Universal......14 A1

the War of Independence. Overlooking the plaza is the **cathedral**, built a century after the town's founding.

The **Museo de Anzoátegui** (☎ 0281-277-3481; Plaza Boyacá; admission free; 🕑 9am-noon & 2-5pm Tue-Fri, 9am-3pm Sat, 9am-1pm Sun), in the town's oldest surviving building, features a variety of interesting objects related to Barcelona's history. The **Ateneo de Barcelona** (Calle San Félix; admission free; 🕑 9am-noon & 2-5pm Mon-Fri) houses a collection of 44 paintings by modern Venezuelan artists.

The **Casa Fuerte** (Plaza Bolívar; admission free; 🕑 9am-noon & 2-5pm Tue-Sun) was once a Franciscan hospice. It was destroyed by royalists in an attack in 1817, and more than 1500 people died in a massacre following the takeover. Surviving parts of the walls have been left in ruins as a memorial.

The Palacio Legislativo, two blocks south of Plaza Boyacá, houses the **Galería de Arte** (☎ 0281-276-0622; Av Fuerzas Armadas; admission free; 🕑 8am-3pm Mon-Fri), which hosts temporary exhibitions.

Sleeping & Eating

Barcelona has a few hotels right in the historic center.

Hotel Canarias (☎ 0281-277-1034; Carrera Bolívar; d/tr with bath US$8/12) One of the cheapest options, and not a bad one. Rooms have fans and there are some slightly cheaper *matrimoniales*.

Posada Copacabana (☎ 0281-277-3473; Carrera Juncal; d/tr with bath US$16/24; 🗷) A new inviting place next to the cathedral with 11 air-con rooms. Great value.

Hotel Barcelona (☎ 0281-277-1076; Av 5 de Julio; d/tr with bath US$20/24; 🗷) The largest hotel in the city center, refurbished over recent years. Ask for a room on one of the top floors.

Av 5 de Julio is the main culinary artery, clogged with budget restaurants, *luncherías*, *fuentes de soda* and street-food vendors.

Gran Fraternidad Universal (Av 5 de Julio) Serves cheap vegetarian lunches.

Getting There & Away

The airport is 2km south of the city center and is accessible by urban transport. There are direct flights to Caracas (US$40 to US$60) and Porlamar (US$25 to US$40).

The bus terminal is 1km southeast of the city center, but it handles only regional routes; for long-distance service, you need to go to Puerto La Cruz and take a bus from there.

To reach Puerto La Cruz, catch a city bus going north along Av 5 de Julio (US$0.30). These buses use two routes: 'Vía Intercomunal' and 'Vía Alterna.' Either will set you down in the center of Puerto La Cruz. There are also *por puestos*; they depart from Av 5 de Julio, two blocks south of the Banesco, and are faster than the buses. A taxi to Puerto La Cruz will cost about US$5.

PUERTO LA CRUZ

Puerto La Cruz is a young, dynamic and expanding city of 200,000 people. Until the 1930s it was no more than an obscure village, but it boomed after rich oil deposits were discovered in the region to the south. The oil is piped to an export terminal just east of the city, where port facilities have been built.

Puerto La Cruz is the major gateway to Isla de Margarita. It's also a jumping-off point to the beautiful Parque Nacional Mochima. Taking advantage of its strategic position, the city has grown into a watersports center, with marinas and yacht clubs, sailing and diving schools, yacht-rental facilities, and diving and fishing tours.

The city has become a popular destination among Venezuelan holiday-makers. Its 10-block waterfront boulevard, Paseo Colón, is lined with hotels, tour agencies, bars and restaurants, and it comes to life in the late afternoon and evening, when craft stalls open (it was being remodeled when this book was researched). Apart from the Paseo, the city has little to offer tourists; a block or two back from the beach it's just an ordinary place. International travelers may be disappointed.

Information

Puerto La Cruz has plenty of cybercafés. There are half a dozen of them in the Centro Comercial Cristoforo Colombo alone and many more along the Paseo. Most charge around US$1 an hour.

Most banks are just south of Plaza Colón. They include:

Banco de Venezuela (Calle Miranda)
Banco Mercantil (Calle Arismendi)
Banco Provincial (Calle Carabobo)
Corp Banca (Av 5 de Julio)

VENEZUELA

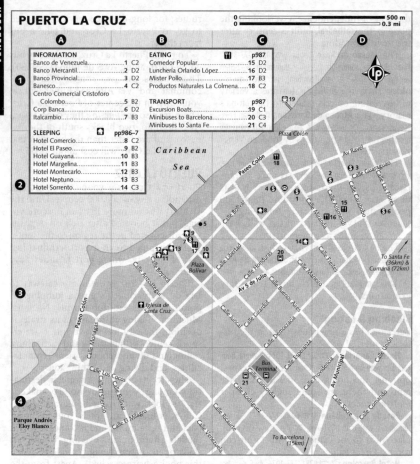

PUERTO LA CRUZ

0 ————————— 500 m
0 ————————— 0.3 mi

Ⓐ	Ⓑ	Ⓒ

INFORMATION
Banco de Venezuela...................1 C2
Banco Mercantil.........................2 D2
Banco Provincial.........................3 D2
Banesco....................................4 C2
Centro Comercial Cristoforo
  Colombo.................................5 B2
Corp Banca...............................6 D2
Italcambio.................................7 B3

SLEEPING 🛏 pp986–7
Hotel Comercio..........................8 C2
Hotel El Paseo...........................9 B2
Hotel Guayana........................10 B3
Hotel Margelina......................11 B3
Hotel Montecarlo.....................12 B3
Hotel Neptuno.........................13 B3
Hotel Sorrento........................14 C3

EATING 🍴 p987
Comedor Popular......................15 D2
Lunchería Orlando López...........16 D2
Mister Pollo.............................17 B3
Productos Naturales La Colmena...18 C2

TRANSPORT p987
Excursion Boats........................19 C1
Minibuses to Barcelona.............20 C3
Minibuses to Santa Fe...............21 C4

Caribbean
Sea

Plaza Colón

Paseo Colón

Av Ravel

Calle Guaraguao

Calle Las Flores

Calle Carabobo

Calle Arismendi

Calle Miranda

Calle Bolívar

Iglesia de
Santa Cruz

Plaza
Bolívar

Calle Libertad

Calle Honduras

Av 5 de Julio

Calle Buenos Aires

Calle Maneiro

Calle Freites

To Santa Fe
(36km) &
Cumaná (72km)

Calle Anzoátegui

Calle Boyacá

Calle Juncal

Calle Girardot

Calle Democracia

Paseo Colón

Calle Montagas

Calle Los Cocos

Calle El Silencio

Calle Bolívar

Calle El Milagro

Calle Esperanza

Calle Providencia

Av Municipal

Calle Sucre

Calle Comando

Calle Unión

Bus
Terminal

Calle Concordia

Calle Rodríguez

Calle Ricaurte

Calle Venezuela

Parque Andrés
Eloy Blanco

To Barcelona
(15km)

Italcambio (Calle Sucre at Paseo Colón) changes cash and traveler's checks. You'll find more *casas de cambio* in upmarket hotels on the Paseo.

The Coranztur tourist office, midway along Paseo Colón, was closed due to the boulevard's reconstruction at the time of research.

Tours

Tours to the Parque Nacional Mochima are offered by a number of agencies nestled along Paseo Colón. You can also use the cheaper services of the excursion boats that dock at the wharf near Plaza Colón, which organize tours around the park's islands and beaches, as well as provide transport service to the three of the most

popular island beaches: Playa Puinare, Playa El Saco and Playa El Faro (US$5 round trip to any of the three). Boats go to the beaches throughout the morning and return in the afternoon. All three beaches have restaurants and you can camp if you have a tent (US$1 per person a night).

Sleeping

Accommodations in Puerto La Cruz are expensive by Venezuelan standards, and hotels fill up fast in the tourist season. Many hotels are on Paseo Colón and the adjoining streets, which is the liveliest and most enjoyable area to stay. All the hotels listed have rooms with private bath and air-con. None is anything special.

Hotel El Paseo (☎ 0414-482-8293; Paseo Colón; d/tr US$12/16; 🏠) One of the cheapest, if pretty basic, options on the waterfront.

Hotel Montecarlo (☎ 0281-268-5677; Paseo Colón; d US$12; 🏠) Cheap and basic on the waterfront.

Hotel Margelina (☎ 0281-268-7545; Paseo Colón; d/tr US$14/16; 🏠) A bare-bone establishment facing the beach.

Hotel Guayana (☎ 0281-265-2175; Plaza Bolívar; d/tr US$12/16; 🏠) Basic choice one block back from the beach.

Hotel Neptuno (☎ 0281-265-3261; Paseo Colón; d/tr US$18/22; 🏠) Marginally better option.

Hotel Sorrento (☎ 0281-268-6745; Av 5 de Julio; s/d/tr US$14/19/23; 🏠) A bit noisy but an acceptable choice on a busy avenue away from the waterfront.

Hotel Comercio (☎ 0281-265-1429; Calle Maneiro; d/tr US$16/18; 🏠) A quiet place two blocks back from the beach.

Eating

Paseo Colón boasts plenty of restaurants, including half a dozen reasonably priced Middle-Eastern eateries serving the usual falafel and schwarma; most also offer set lunches for about US$3.

Productos Naturales La Colmena (Paseo Colón; lunches US$3) Serves budget vegetarian lunches (weekdays only) near Plaza Colón.

Hotel Neptuno (Paseo Colón; mains US$3-5) The restaurant on the top floor of this hotel is acceptable and relatively cheap.

Mister Pollo (Calle Sucre) Just off Paseo Colón, this place doesn't look very elegant, but serves tasty chicken at low prices.

For more budget eating, comb the streets back from the beach.

Comedor Popular (Calle Arismendi; meals US$1.50-2.50) One of the cheapest eateries in town, but it closes early in the afternoon.

Lunchería Orlando López (Calle Miranda; meals US$2-4) One of the better options, it offers hearty breakfasts and lunches.

Getting There & Away

AIR

The nearest airport is in Barcelona (see p985).

BOAT

Conferry provides ferry service for passengers, cars and trucks between Puerto La Cruz and Isla de Margarita. The standard ferries make four departures a day (1st/2nd class US$10/8, 4½ hours). The faster *Margarita Express* ferry makes two trips a day (US$15,

2¼ hours), as does the *Gran Cacique* fast passenger boat (US$14, 2¾ hours). There may be fewer departures in the low season. Do this trip in the daytime – it's a spectacular journey among the islands of Parque Nacional Mochima. The Conferry terminal, 1km southwest of the city center, is accessible by *por puestos*.

BUS

The busy bus terminal is just three blocks from Plaza Bolívar. Frequent buses travel to Caracas (US$7, five hours) and Cumaná (US$2, 1½ hours); some of the latter continue as far as Güiria (US$8, 6½ hours). If you go eastward (to Cumaná or further on), grab a seat on the left side of the bus for some spectacular views of the islands of Parque Nacional Mochima. Minibuses run from the bus terminal to Santa Fe (US$1, 50 minutes). Buses to Ciudad Guayana (US$8, six hours) depart roughly every two hours, and all go via Ciudad Bolívar (US$6, 4½ hours).

To Barcelona, take a city bus or the faster *por puesto* minibus from Av 5 de Julio; both will deposit you in Barcelona's center in 40 to 60 minutes, depending on traffic.

PARQUE NACIONAL MOCHIMA

Mochima National Park covers the offshore belt of the Caribbean coast between Puerto La Cruz and Cumaná, encompassing 36 islands and a strip of the mountainous hinterland complete with bays and beaches. Most islands are barren and partly rocky, but some have beaches and are surrounded by coral reefs good for snorkeling. There are also some fine beaches along the mainland coast.

Some of the islands are serviced by excursion boats from Puerto La Cruz (see earlier). Trips to the islands are also organized from the popular tourist destinations of Santa Fe and Mochima. On weekends, beaches swarm with boisterous holiday-makers. Deserted beaches can be unsafe, particularly at night – use common sense.

Playa Colorada

Parts of the Puerto La Cruz–Cumaná road skirt the seafront, providing some spectacular glimpses of the islands. The road passes a dozen beaches, the most popular of which is Playa Colorada, 27km east of Puerto La Cruz. It's not long or wide, but it does have fine orange sand and is pleasantly shaded with coconut groves. A line of rustic restaurants sits at the back of the beach and, further inland, there are several budget places to stay, including the following:

Jakera Lodge (☎ 0281-276-3112; www.jakera.com; beds/hammock US$6/4) Scottish-managed camp offering accommodation, meals, Internet access, kayak and bicycle rental, tours, Spanish courses and more.

Quinta Jaly (☎ 0416-681-8113; d/tr with bath US$10/13) Canadian-owned *posada* with five rooms. Guests can use the kitchen.

Posada Nirvana (☎ 0414-803-0101; d without/with bath US$10/12) Swiss-run six-room place. Great breakfasts on request.

Santa Fe

The fishing town of Santa Fe, about 8km east of Playa Colorada, has become popular with foreign backpackers thanks to its beach and tourist infrastructure. A dozen budget lodgings have sprung up along the beach, and various facilities and activities are available, such as boat excursions, scuba diving, snorkeling, horse riding and Spanish lessons. Santa Fe has regular bus and *por puesto* service to/from Puerto La Cruz and Cumaná. Accommodations include the following places, all with baths and fans.

Posada Café del Mar (☎ 0293-231-0009; d US$8) Run by a German, this is one of the cheapest places, and has a good budget restaurant. Offers full-day boat tours at US$6 per person.

Posada Los Siete Delfines (☎ 0293-431-4166; d/tr US$8/10) A simple option with its own restaurant.

Posada La Sierra Inn (☎ 0293-231-0042; d US$10) A small quiet lodge in a garden. Kayak rental and tours are available.

Posada Bahía del Mar (☎ 0293-231-0073; d US$10) Seven-room *posada* run by a French Canadian. Grab the room upstairs – it's the best.

Hotel Las Palmeras (☎ 0293-231-0008; d with fan/air-con US$14/20) A French-managed comfortable 10-room lodging 100m back from the beach.

Mochima

The village of Mochima, about 20km northeast of Santa Fe, sits on the shore of the deep Bahía de Mochima and is a jumping-off point for nearby beaches that are inaccessible by road. Boat operators wait for tourists at the village's wharf to take them to the beach of their choice (US$12 to US$16 round trip per boat for up to seven people) or on a tour with stops on several different beaches. The most visited of the beaches are Playa Blanca and Playa Las Maritas, both of which have places to eat.

The village of Mochima has a dozen budget accommodation options, several restaurants and two diving schools. Jeeps run regularly to/from Cumaná (US$0.80, 40 minutes), but there's no direct transport to/from Puerto La Cruz; you have to change.

The following recommended places have rooms with baths.

Posada Villa Vicenta (☎ 0293-416-0916; d with fan/air-con US$11/14; 🖭) Four-story building with 11 rooms on various levels. Cheap tours available.

Posada El Mochimero (☎ 0414-773-8782; d with fan/air-con US$11/14; 🖭) A good budget option; the restaurant cooks fine Spanish food.

CUMANÁ

The capital of Sucre state, Cumaná is a city of 300,000 inhabitants, and an important port for sardine fishing and canning. Founded by the Spaniards in 1521, it takes pride in being the oldest existing town on South America's mainland. Most of its colonial architecture, however, has been destroyed by earthquakes, which have rocked the town several times.

Cumaná has some attractions but is noted more for its environs than for the city itself. To the west is the beautiful Parque Nacional Mochima with its islands and beaches, to the north is the intriguing Península de Araya, while to the southeast is the Cueva del Guácharo. Cumaná is also one of the gateways to Isla de Margarita.

Information

Internet access in the city center is available at **Pacho's Café** (Calle Sucre), **Capme Computers** (Calle Montes) and **Inversiones OneWorld** (Calle Catedral).

Most major banks are on Calle Mariño and Av Bermúdez. Banesco is on Calle Mariño at Calle Carabobo. **Corp Banca** (Av Bermúdez at Av Aristides Rojas) is 1km west of Plaza Miranda. The *casa de cambio* **Oficambio** (Calle Mariño) is 600m west of Plaza Miranda.

The **Dirección de Turismo** (☎ 0293-431-6051; Calle Sucre; 🕑 8am-noon & 2:30-5:30pm Mon-Fri) is in the city center.

Sights

The streets around **Iglesia de Santa Inés** retain some of their former appearance. The church itself is a 1929 construction and has few objects of an earlier date inside. The **cathedral** (Plaza Blanco) is also relatively young and has a hodgepodge of altarpieces in its largely timbered interior.

Castillo de San Antonio de la Eminencia (admission free; 9am-noon & 3-5pm Mon-Fri), on a hill southeast of the city center, was constructed in 1659 on a four-pointed star plan. It suffered pirate attacks and earthquakes, but the coral-rock walls have survived in remarkably good shape. The fort commands good views over the city and the bay. Next to the fort, the small **Museo de Arte Contemporáneo de Cumaná** (admission free; 9am-noon & 3-5pm Tue-Sat) stages changing exhibitions of modern art.

The city has more museums, though they are pretty modest. **Casa Natal de Andrés Eloy Blanco** (Plaza Bolívar; admission free; 9am-noon & 3-5pm Mon-Fri) is the house in which this poet, considered one of Venezuela's most extraordinary literary talents, was born in 1896. **Casa Ramos Sucre** (Calle Sucre; admission free; 9am-noon & 3-5pm Mon-Fri) is dedicated to another local poet José Antonio Ramos Sucre, who was born here in 1890. **Museo Gran Mariscal de Ayacucho** (Av Humboldt; admission free; 9am-noon & 3-5pm Tue-Sat) is dedicated to the Cumaná-born hero of the War of Independence, General Antonio José de Sucre.

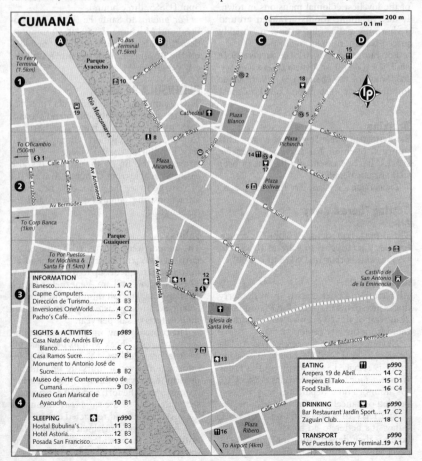

CUMANÁ

0 — 200 m
0 — 0.1 mi

INFORMATION	
Banesco	1 A2
Capme Computers	2 C1
Dirección de Turismo	3 B3
Inversiones OneWorld	4 C2
Pacho's Café	5 C1

SIGHTS & ACTIVITIES	p989
Casa Natal de Andrés Eloy Blanco	6 C2
Casa Ramos Sucre	7 B4
Monument to Antonio José de Sucre	8 B2
Museo de Arte Contemporáneo de Cumaná	9 D3
Museo Gran Mariscal de Ayacucho	10 B1

SLEEPING	p990
Hostal Bubulina's	11 B3
Hotel Astoria	12 B3
Posada San Francisco	13 C4

EATING	p990
Arepera 19 de Abril	14 C2
Arepera El Tako	15 D1
Food Stalls	16 C4

DRINKING	p990
Bar Restaurant Jardín Sport	17 C2
Zaguán Club	18 C1

TRANSPORT	p990
Por Puestos to Ferry Terminal	19 A1

Sleeping & Eating

Many of the central cheap hotels are on or just off Calle Sucre in the city center. Most are unremarkable places, but there are some pleasant exceptions. The following places have rooms with baths and air-con.

Hotel Astoria (☎ 0293-433-2708; Calle Sucre; s/d/tr US$7/9/10; ⊠) Arguably the best bet among the cheapies. It has a budget restaurant.

Hostal Bubulina's (☎ 0293-431-4025; Callejón Santa Inés; d US$16; ⊠) Remodeled historic building offering six modern *matrimoniales* and six doubles, all with TV, bath and hot water. The hotel restaurant, next door, provides tasty budget meals.

Posada San Francisco (☎ 0293-431-3926; posadas anfrancisco@hotmail.com; Calle Sucre; d US$20; ⊠) One of the loveliest colonial mansions in town. It has 10 ample rooms arranged around a charming patio, plus a fine, reasonably priced restaurant open to all.

For budget *arepas*, try the **Arepera 19 de Abril**, (Calle Catedral) or **Arepera El Tako** (Calle Boyacá). Some of the cheapest *parrillas* can be found at the food stalls on Calle Urica just off Plaza Ribero.

Drinking

Bar Restaurant Jardín Sport (Plaza Bolívar) This informal open-air bar serves inexpensive snacks, but it's essentially the cheap beer that attracts people.

Zaguán Club (Calle Sucre) Try this arty place.

Getting There & Away

AIR

The airport, 4km southeast of the city center, handles direct flights to Caracas (US$35 to US$55) and Porlamar (US$25 to US$40).

BOAT

All ferries and boats depart from the ferry docks next to the mouth of Río Manzanares, 2km west of the city center; *por puestos* go there from the city center.

Naviarca operates two ferries a day to Isla de Margarita (US$9, 3½ hours). The same route is serviced twice daily by the faster *Gran Cacique* boat (1st/2nd class US$13/10, 2½ hours). Some departures may be suspended or canceled in the low season.

The ferry to Araya runs once or twice a day. It's better to go by small passenger boats – they depart from the same docks every 20 to 30 minutes until about 4pm or

5pm (US$0.80, 20 minutes) and go to Manicuare, not Araya. From Manicuare, *por puestos* travel the rest of the way to Araya on a paved road (US$0.30, 10 minutes).

BUS

The bus terminal, 1.5km northwest of the city center, is linked to town by frequent city buses. From the terminal, buses run regularly to Caracas (US$9, 6½ hours) via Puerto La Cruz (US$2, 1½ hours). Half a dozen buses go daily to Ciudad Bolívar (US$8, six hours) and Güiria (US$6, five hours).

For Cueva del Guácharo, take the Caripe bus (US$4, 3½ hours), which theoretically departs at 7am. More reliable is the private minibus, which is supposed to depart at 3pm (US$5, three hours).

Por puestos to Santa Fe (US$1, 50 minutes) and Mochima (US$0.80, 40 minutes) depart from near the Mercadito, one block off the Redoma El Indio, southwest of the city center.

PENINSULA DE ARAYA

This 70km-long arid peninsula stretches east to west along the mainland's coast, with its western end lying due north of Cumaná. The population is thinly scattered in a handful of coastal villages, of which Araya, on the tip, is the largest. It's also easily accessible from Cumaná. Araya is the place to go to see the peninsula's two major attractions: the *salinas* (salt pans) and the *castillo* (fort).

Salinas

The *salinas* were discovered by the Spaniards in 1499 and have been exploited almost uninterruptedly up to the present day. They were, and still are, Venezuela's largest salt deposits. The salt mining is done by the Salaraya company, which produces half a million tons of salt per year.

The company may organize tours around the saltworks – check with its **Departamento de Relaciones Públicas** (☎ 0293-437-1222) for information. Even if tours are unavailable, the trip to Araya is still worth considering, if only to visit the fort, and you can actually see quite a bit of the *salinas* from outside the installations and restricted areas.

A *mirador* (lookout), built on the hill 2km north of Araya, provides a good view over the rectangular pools filled in with saltwater and left to evaporate. The color of the water in pools ranges from creamy pink to deep purple.

Start early and be prepared for baking heat: a hat or other head protection is recommended, as are sunglasses and sunscreen. It's wise to carry a large bottle of water or other drink.

Castillo
This fort was built in the first half of the 17th century to protect the *salinas* from plunder. It was the most costly Spanish project in the New World up to that time. In 1726 a hurricane produced a tide that broke over the salt lagoon, flooding it and turning it into a gulf. Salt could no longer be exploited, and the Spanish decided to abandon the fortress. Before leaving, they tried to blow it up with huge charges of gunpowder, but the fort largely resisted destruction. The mighty bulwarks still proudly crown the waterfront cliff. The fort is a 10-minute walk along the beach from the wharf. You can wander freely around the place, as there's no gate.

Sleeping & Eating
Araya is normally visited on a day trip from Cumaná, but should you like to stay longer, there are half a dozen budget *posadas* to choose from. Good options include the pleasant **Posada Araya Wind** (☎ 0414-774-5485) and the larger **Posada Helen** (☎ 0414-7754043), both near the fort. There are a few basic restaurants in the same area.

CARIPE
Set in a verdant mountain valley 55km back from the coast, Caripe is a pleasant, small town renowned for its agreeable climate, attractive environs, coffee and orange plantations, and proximity to the spectacular Cueva del Guácharo. Home to 12,000 inhabitants, the town is little more than two parallel streets, around which most activities and services are centered. It's quite touristy, and on weekends it's full of people escaping the steamy lowlands that dominate most of the region.

Information
Internet facilities include **Telsenet** (off Plaza Bolívar) and **Cibernet** (Av Guzmán Blanco). **Banco de Venezuela** (Av Enrique Chaumer) and **Banesco** (Av Guzmán Blanco) give advances on Visa and

MasterCard. The town has no tourist office – chat to the manager of Hotel Samán, who may also organize tours.

Sights
The town itself has no special tourist baits, but the rugged surroundings are beautiful. The top attraction in the region is no doubt the Cueva del Guácharo (see p992).

El Mirador (1100m), north of town, commands sweeping views over the Valle de Caripe. It's an hour's walk from town, or you can go there by car. Other sights include two beautiful waterfalls: the 30m-high **Salto La Payla**, near the Cueva del Guácharo, and the 80m-high **Salto El Chorrerón**, an hour's walk from the village of Sabana de Piedra. Highlights further away include the **Puertas de Miraflores**, a spectacular river canyon, and the **Mata de Mango**, a group of 22 caves including the impressive Cueva Grande and Cueva Clara.

Sleeping & Eating
Caripe has a number of hotels and restaurants in town, and still more in its environs.

Parrilla Restaurant La Posada (Plaza Bolívar; d US$5; meals US$2-3) Budget restaurant offering three simple rooms with shared bath. One of the cheapest places to stay and eat.

Hotel San Francisco (☎ 0292-545-1018; Av Enrique Chaumer; d/tr US$7/9) It's pretty basic, but all the rooms have their own baths.

Hotel Venezia (☎ 0292-545-1035; Av Enrique Chaumer; d/tr US$8/10) Acceptable budget shelter, slightly better than San Francisco.

Hotel Samán (☎ 0292-545-1183; Av Enrique Chaumer; d/tr US$13/16) Comfortable and pleasant lodging; the manager offers special rates for backpackers (single/double US$8/10) – be sure to ask for one.

Trattoria da Stefano (Calle Cabello; pastas US$2-3) Mouthwatering pasta at low prices – ask for the home-made ones.

Getting There & Away
The bus terminal is at the northeastern end of town, behind the market. There's an evening bus to Caracas (US$12, 11 hours) via Maturín. To Cumaná, a bus departs daily at 6am (US$4, 3½ hours), or there's a private minibus at the same time (US$5, three hours). To Cueva del Guácharo, take a taxi (US$2, or US$5 round trip, including a wait).

CUEVA DEL GUÁCHARO

Twelve kilometers northwest of Caripe on the road toward the coast, **Cueva del Guácharo** (Guácharo Cave; adult/student US$5/2; ✆ 8am-4pm) is Venezuela's longest, largest and reputedly most magnificent cave. Known to the local Chaima people long before Columbus crossed the Atlantic, it was later explored by Europeans. Alexander von Humboldt penetrated 472m into the cave in 1799, and it was he who first classified its unusual inhabitant, the *guácharo* (oilbird), after which the cave has been named.

Depending on when you come, you'll find somewhere between 8000 to 18,000 birds living in the cave. The birds inhabit only the first chamber of the cave, the 750m-long Humboldt Hall. The cave also hosts a variety of other wildlife and amazing natural formations, including stalactites and stalagmites.

All visits are guided, and the tour – which covers a 1200m portion of the cave's total 10.2km length – takes about 1½ hours. A small museum holds cave-related exhibits. Cameras with flashes are permitted beyond the area where the *guácharos* live.

You can camp (US$2.50 per tent) near the entrance to the cave, but only after closing time. If you camp here, you can watch the hundreds of birds pouring out of the cave mouth at around 6:30pm and returning at about 4:30am.

RÍO CARIBE

Río Caribe, 25km east of Carúpano, is an old port that grew fat on cacao export, and

---

GUÁCHARO – AN UNUSUAL CAVE RESIDENT

The *guácharo* (oilbird) is a nocturnal, fruit-eating bird, the only one of its kind in the world. It inhabits caves in various parts of tropical America, living in total darkness and leaving the cave only at night for food, principally the fruit of some species of palm. The *guácharo* has a radarlike location system similar to that used by bats, which enables it to get around. The adult bird is about 60cm long, with a wingspan of a meter. In Venezuela, the *guácharo* has been seen in more than 40 caves; the biggest colony, estimated at about 15,000 birds, is in Cueva del Guácharo.

---

the air of its former splendor is still palpable along tree-shaded Av Bermúdez and some other central streets. Today a pleasant, peaceful town of 30,000 people, Río Caribe is fairly popular with holiday-makers and a good springboard for nearby attractions, including some of Venezuela's finest beaches. See Around Río Caribe for more information (p993).

Information

Infocentro (Calle Sucre) provides free Internet access, or use the facilities at **Parian@Café** (Av Bermúdez).

The town has a few banks, including **Banco de Venezuela** (Calle Rivero), which gives cash advances on credit cards.

The **Dirección de Turismo** (☎ 0294-646-1510; Calle Rivero; ✆ 8am-noon & 1-5pm Mon-Fri) is in the Alcaldía. You may also inquire for information at **Mareaje Tours** (☎ 0294-646-1543; Av Bermúdez).

Sleeping & Eating

The town has more than a dozen places to stay and most are cheap.

Posada Doña Eva (☎ 0294-646-1465; Calle Girardot; r per person US$4; meals US$3-4) One of the cheapest places around and good value. It has four neat rooms with fan and bath, and a restaurant downstairs. You can use the kitchen.

Posada Don Chilo (☎ 0294-646-1212; Calle Mariño; d/tr US$7/10) This place is ultra budget with only basic accommodation and shared facilities.

Pensión Papagayos (☎ 0294-646-1868; Calle 14 de Febrero; r per person US$5) A friendly four-room *posada* with shared baths. You can use the kitchen and fridge.

Hotel Mar Caribe (☎ 0294-416-6147; d US$18) Good hotel on the waterfront, with a swimming pool and restaurant.

Posada Caribana (☎ 0294-61242; Av Bermúdez; d/tr with breakfast US$36/44; ✖) This typical Caribbean mansion looks like something straight out of a picture postcard. It has good-sized rooms with fan (three with aircon) and a spacious patio.

Tasca Mi Cocina (Calle Juncal) This restaurant is frequented by both locals and visitors for good food at good prices.

Parian@Café (Av Bermúdez) Informal place serving local cuisine and plenty of drinks. Popular with travelers.

Getting There & Away

Frequent *por puestos* link Río Caribe with Carúpano (US$0.60, 30 minutes), where you can get regular buses to Güiria, Puerto La Cruz, Caracas and elsewhere.

Pickup trucks depart in the morning to the villages of Medina (US$1), Puy Puy (US$1.50) and San Juan de las Galdonas (US$2.50). They don't get as far as the beaches of Medina and Puy Puy; you need to walk the rest of the way (a pleasant half-hour stroll in either case).

AROUND RÍO CARIBE

The region around Río Caribe features a beautiful stretch of coast backed by picturesque mountains and dotted with some of the country's loveliest beaches, including the postcard-perfect sands of Playa Medina and the almost as nice Playa Puy Puy. The charming fishing village of San Juan de las Galdonas, 47km east of Río Caribe, also has fine beaches. Attractions further inland include Hacienda Aguasana (hot springs), Hacienda Bukare (a cacao plantation) and Hato Río de Agua (a buffalo ranch). Information and tours to these places are available from most tour agencies and hotel managers.

Sleeping

PLAYA MEDINA

There are eight lovely **cabañas** (per person incl 3 meals US$34) right on the beach that are booked through **Corpomedina** (☎ 0294-331-5241; in Carúpano). Budget options nearby include the following *posadas*.

Posada El Milagro (☎ 0416-794-5291; r with bath per person US$10, with breakfast & dinner US$16) A fine country house 2km back from the beach.

Posada del Ángel (☎ 0416-794-7477; r with bath per person US$10, with breakfast & dinner US$18) In the village of Medina, 3km back from the beach.

PLAYA PUY PUY

This beach too, has a colony of fine beachfront **cabañas** (per person incl 3 meals US$22). You can book at **Corpomedina** (☎ 0294-331-5241) in Carúpano or directly at the beach. You can also **camp** (per tent US$2) on the beach.

Posada El Rincón de Puy Puy (r with bath per person US$10) The last house at the eastern end of the beach. Four *matrimoniales* with bath, plus a restaurant. Budget option at convenient location.

Posada El Hijo de Paula (d US$10) Basic but very cheap *posada* in the village of Puy Puy, 2km back from the beach. Two rooms share one bath.

SAN JUAN DE LAS GALDONAS

The village has several places to stay, most of which have their own eating facilities and organize tours.

Posada Las Tres Carabelas (☎ 0416-894-0914; r with bath per person US$9, with breakfast & dinner US$15) Charming place spectacularly set atop a cliff high above the beach. Rooms have fans, and there's a restaurant serving palatable Spanish and vegetarian food.

Casa Marcos (☎ 0416-813-2054; d with bath US$12) New budget place facing the beach.

Habitat Paria (☎ 0414-779-7955; d/tr US$16/24, r per person with breakfast & dinner US$20) Beautiful *posada* on the beach with a rooftop terrace and an enjoyable restaurant offering some first-class Italian fare.

Hotel La Pionera (☎ 0294-808-1509; d/tr US$24/28, r per person with breakfast & dinner US$22) Beach location, good facilities, satisfactory standards, swimming pool and restaurant, plus tour offer.

OTHER AREAS

There are some facilities on other beaches and further inland.

Hacienda Bukare (☎ 0294-808-1505; bukare@cantv.net; hammock US$4, d/tr US$25/30) About 14km east of Río Caribe, this is an old cacao hacienda with comfortable rooms and an atmospheric restaurant. It's one of the best places to stay inland. Rates include healthy breakfast. All guests can enjoy a free tour of the cacao plantation. The owner, Billy, provides good information and organizes tours around the region.

Getting There & Around

You can explore the region on your own, or arrange a tour through almost any hotel manager or through **Mareaje Tours** (☎ 0294-646-1543; Av Bermúdez) in Río Caribe.

GÜIRIA

Güiria, 275km east of Cumaná, is the easternmost point on Venezuela's coast that you can reach by road. Home to 30,000 people, it's the largest town on Península de Paria and an important fishing port. The town itself is rather undistinguishable, with no significant tourist attractions, but it's a springboard for Trinidad. Near the eastern tip of the peninsula, about 40km east of Güiria, is the small fishing village of Macuro (accessible by boat), the place where Columbus supposedly came ashore in August 1498.

Information

Ceicca (Calle Juncal at Calle Bolívar) provides Internet access. You can get cash advances at **Banco Mercantil** (Calle Juncal), **Banco de Venezuela** (Calle Concepción) and **Banesco** (Calle Bolívar). There's no tourist office here.

Sleeping & Eating

There are quite a number of facilities, including the following two options:

Hotel Plaza (☎ 0294-982-0022; Calle Bolívar; d with fan/air-con US$8/13; ✂) Popular budget place providing rooms of different standards, but all have baths. Its restaurant serves good, inexpensive food.

La Posada de Chuchú (☎ 0294-982-1266; Calle Bideau; d/tr US$12/15; ✂) Good central option, with air-con rooms and its own restaurant, El Timón de Máximo.

Getting There & Away

BOAT

Windward Lines no longer operates its ferry to Trinidad. Now the comfortable, air-con passenger boat *Sea Prowler* makes the trip, arriving from Chaguaramas, near Port of Spain, every Wednesday at 1pm and departing for the return trip at 3pm the same day (one way US$48, four hours; round trip US$96). Add US$23 tax to the listed fares going from Güiria to Trinidad (in Trinidad, the tax is US$12). For information and tickets, contact **Acosta Asociados** (☎ 0294-982-0058; grupoacosta@cantv.net; Calle Bolívar).

Peñeros (open fishing boats) go to Macuro every morning, except Sunday, normally around 11am (US$2.50, 1½ to two hours). There are a few simple *posadas* in Macuro that can also provide meals.

BUS

Several bus companies have offices around the triangular Plaza Sucre, two blocks west of Plaza Bolívar. A half-dozen buses head to Caracas (US$13, 12 hours) daily. They all go via Cumaná (US$6, five hours) and Puerto La Cruz (US$8, 6½ hours). *Por puestos* run frequently to Carúpano (US$5, two hours).

ISLA DE MARGARITA

Venezuela's largest island (1071 sq km), Isla de Margarita stretches 69km east to west and 35km north to south. It lies about 40km off the mainland, due north of Cumaná. Once two neighboring islands, the two sides of Isla de Margarita are now linked by a narrow, crescent-shaped natural sandbank called La Restinga.

The eastern side of Margarita is larger and more fertile, and contains 95% of the island's total population of 360,000. The thriving city of Porlamar and all the major towns are here, connected by a well-developed array of roads. The western side, known as the Península de Macanao, is arid and sparsely populated, with people living in a dozen villages mostly along the coast. Both sections of the island are mountainous, with their highest peaks approaching 1000m.

The island is popular both with Venezuelans and with international visitors, a majority of whom arrive on package tours. Most are drawn to the island for the beaches that skirt its coast. Actually, Margarita has become a prime destination for vacationers seeking white sand and sunbathing opportunities with decent facilities at hand. The island's tourism infrastructure is well developed, and Margarita has a collection of posh hotels comparable only to those in Caracas.

The island's other magnet has been shopping. Margarita is a duty-free zone, so the prices of imported goods are supposed to be lower than on the mainland, although in many cases there's no significant difference. Moreover, the country is in deep economical crisis these days, and few Venezuelans have the money to go on a shopping spree to Margarita.

The island's varied geography includes mangrove swamps, cloud forests and semi-desert areas. Five nature reserves, among them two national parks, have been established on Margarita. The island also has some interesting historic monuments, including two fine Spanish forts and one of the oldest churches in the country.

Administratively, Isla de Margarita and the two small islands of Cubagua and Coche make up the state of Nueva Esparta. Although Porlamar is by far the largest urban

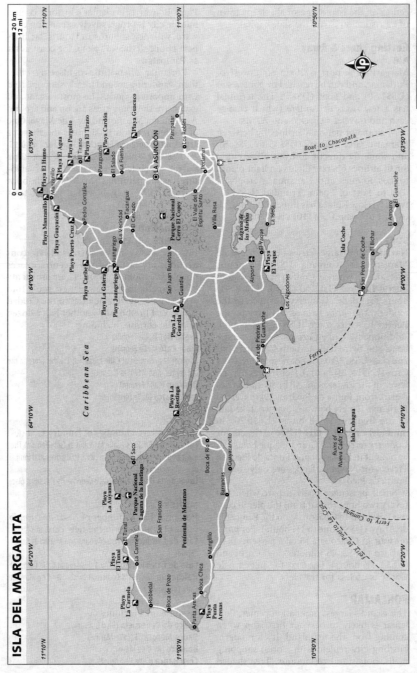

ISLA DEL MARGARITA

20 km
12 mi

Caribbean Sea

Playa La Carmela
Playa El Tunal
El Tunal
Robledal
Boca de Pozo
Punta Arenas
Playa Punta Arenas
Boca Chica
Manglillo
Barrancas
San Francisco
La Carmela
Playa La Auyama
Parque Nacional Laguna de la Restinga
El Saco
Boca de Río
Guayacancito
Peninsula de Macanao

Playa La Restinga

Playa La Guardia
La Guardia
San Juan Bautista
La Vecindad
Juangriego
Playa Juangriego
Playa La Galera
Playa Caribe
Playa Puerto Cruz
Playa Guayacán
Playa Manzanillo
Manzanillo
Pedro González
El Maco
La Asunción
El Cercado
Tacarigua
El Valle del Espíritu Santo
Villa Rosa
Parque Nacional Cerro El Copey
Paraguachí
El Salado
La Fuente
Playa El Agua
Playa Parguito
Playa El Tirano
El Tirano
Playa Cardón
Playa Guacuco
LA ASUNCIÓN
Pampatar
Los Robles
Portamar
Laguna de las Marites
La Isleta
El Yaque
Playa El Yaque
Airport
Los Algodones
Punta de Piedras
El Guamache
El Guamache

Boat to Chacopata

Isla Coche
San Pedro de Coche
El Bichar
El Amparo
El Guamache

Ferry

Ferry to Puerto La Cruz
Ferry to Cumaná

Ruins of Nueva Cádiz
Isla Cubagua

11°10'N
11°00'N
10°50'N
64°20'W
64°10'W
64°00'W
63°50'W

center on the island, the small, sleepy town of La Asunción is still the state capital.

Getting There & Away

AIR

Margarita's airport is 20km southwest of Porlamar, and can be reached by *por puestos* (US$1.50) and taxis (US$5). The terminal has a few *casas de cambio* (which change cash and traveler's checks) and ATMs.

Most major national airlines fly between Margarita and Caracas (US$35 to US$65), and some fly directly to/from other cities. Small airlines operate flights on light planes to Los Roques and Canaima. Aeropostal flies to Port of Spain, Trinidad (US$120) twice weekly. Rutaca has three flights a week to Port of Spain (US$110) via Maturín.

BOAT

Naviarca runs large ferries between Isla de Margarita and Cumaná (US$9, 3½ hours, twice daily), whereas Conferry run ferries to Puerto La Cruz (1st/2nd class US$10/8, 4½ hours, four daily). Conferry also operates the modern *Margarita Express* fast ferry on the Puerto La Cruz route (US$15, 2¼ hours). Additionally, *Gran Cacique* fast passenger boats run twice daily to both Cumaná (1st/2nd class US$13/10, 2½ hours) and Puerto La Cruz (US$14, 2¾ hours). Departures may be fewer in the low season. All boats and ferries depart from Punta de Piedras, 29km west of Porlamar. To get between the two, take one of the frequent small buses (US$0.70, 40 minutes) or go by taxi (US$6). Tickets for Conferry ferries and Gran Cacique boats can be bought in Porlamar and Punta de Piedras. Tickets for Naviarca ferries are only sold in Punta de Piedras.

Small passenger boats depart when full (every two hours or so) from the pier in central Porlamar to Chacopata on the Península de Araya (US$4, one to 1½ hours). *Por puestos* wait in Chacopata to take passengers to Cariaco (US$2, 45 minutes) and Carúpano (US$4, 1½ hours). The ferry to San Pedro de Coche is useless for travelers.

PORLAMAR

The island's largest population center, Porlamar is likely to be your first stop when coming from the mainland. It's a modern, bustling city replete with stores, shopping malls, hotels and restaurants. Tree-shaded

Plaza Bolívar is Porlamar's historic center, but the city is progressively expanding eastward, with new suburbs and tourist facilities being built all the way along the coast as far as Pampatar.

Porlamar offers little sightseeing other than wandering around trendy shops packed with imported goods. The most elegant and expensive shopping areas are on and around Av Santiago Mariño and Av 4 de Mayo. One of the few real tourist sights is the **Museo de Arte Contemporáneo Francisco Narváez** (☎ 0295-261-8668; Calle Igualdad; admission free; ☒ 9am-3:30pm Mon-Fri), which features a collection of sculptures and paintings by Margarita-born Narváez (1905–82), as well as various temporary exhibitions.

Information

INTERNET ACCESS

Internet access in Porlamar is cheap, connections are fast, and most central places open until 10pm or 11pm. There are plenty of cybercafés in the new center; you'll find at least half a dozen facilities in the Ciudad Comercial Jumbo, and another half a dozen on Calle Fermín, including:

Arena Net (Calle Fermín)
Ciber Café (Calle Fermín)
Digicel (Av Miranda at Calle Igualdad) Try this place in the old center, just off Plaza Bolívar.
Digicom (Calle Fermín)
La Comarca (Calle Fermín)

LAUNDRY

Porlamar has a number of laundry facilities.
Lavandería Edikö's (Calle Marcano at Calle Fermín) The most popular place for good service, low prices and long opening hours.
Lavandería Divino Niño (Calle Cedeño) Try this small place.

MONEY

Porlamar has a number of *casas de cambio*, most of which are in the new center.
Casa de Cambio For You (Av Santiago Mariño at Calle Patiño)
Casa de Cambio Triple (Av 4 de Mayo at Calle Campos)
Italcambio (in Ciudad Comercial Jumbo, Av 4 de Mayo at Calle Campos).

Useful banks include:
Banco de Venezuela (Blvd Guevara)
Banco Mercantil (Calle Mariño)
Banesco (Av 4 de Mayo)
Corp Banca (Calle Velázquez)

VENEZUELA

PORLAMAR

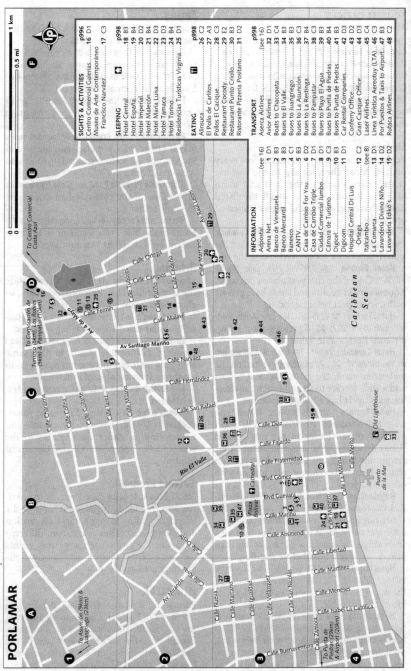

0   0.5 mi
0   1 km

SIGHTS & ACTIVITIES   **p996**
Centro Comercial Galerías...............16 D1
Museo de Arte Contemporáneo
   Francisco Narváez.......................17 C3

SLEEPING   **p998**
Hotel Central...................................18 B3
Hotel España...................................19 B4
Hotel Imperial.................................20 D2
Hotel Malecón.................................21 B4
Hotel María Luisa............................22 D3
Hotel Tamaca..................................23 D3
Hotel Torino...................................24 B4
Residencias Turísticas Virginia......25 D1

EATING   **p998**
Alinsuca...26 C2
El Pollo de Carlitos.........................27 A3
Pollos El Cacique............................28 C3
Restaurant Cocody...........................29 E2
Restaurant Punto Criollo................30 B3
Ristorante Pizzería Positano............31 D2

TRANSPORT   (see 16)
Aserca Airlines...............................32 D1
Avior Airlines..................................33 C4
Boats to Chacopata.........................34 B3
Buses to El Valle.............................35 B3
Buses to Juangriego........................36 C3
Buses to La Asunción.....................37 B4
Buses to La Restinga.......................38 C3
Buses to Pampatar.........................39 B3
Buses to Playa El Agua...................40 B4
Buses to Punta de Piedras..............41 B3
Car Rental Companies.....................42 D2
Conferry Office................................43 D2
Gran Cacique Office........................44 D3
Laser Airlines..................................45 C4
Línea Turística Aereotuy (LTA)......46 C3
Por Puestos & Taxis to Airport......47 B3
Rutaca Airlines................................48 C2

INFORMATION
Adpostal...(see 16)
Arena Net...1 D1
Banco de Venezuela...........................2 B3
Banco Mercantil..................................3 B3
Banesco..4 C1
CANTV..5 B3
Casa de Cambio For You......................6 D2
Casa de Cambio Triple.........................7 B4
Ciudad Comercial Jumbo......................8 D1
Cámara de Turismo..............................9 B3
Digicel...10 B3
Digicom..11 D1
Hospital Central Dr Luis
   Ortega...12 C2
Italcambio..(see 8)
La Comarca.......................................13 D1
Lavandería Divino Niño.....................14 D2
Lavandería Edikó's............................15 D2

Caribbean
Sea

Old Lighthouse

Puerto
de la Mar

TOURIST OFFICES

Margarita has two bodies providing tourist information:

Cámara de Turismo (☎ 0295-263-9024; Av Santiago Mariño at Calle Hernández; ☽ 8am-12:30pm & 2-5pm Mon-Fri) Private corporation bureau, in Porlamar.

Corporación de Turismo (☎ 0295-262-2322; Centro Artesanal Gilberto Menchini, Los Robles; ☽ 9am-noon & 2-5pm Mon-Fri) Government-run office, midway between Porlamar and Pampatar.

Sleeping

Porlamar has plenty of hotels for every pocket. Most cheapies are in the historic center, particularly to the west and south of Plaza Bolívar. Rooms at all the listed hotels have private bath, unless indicated otherwise.

Hotel Malecón (☎ 0295-514-7332; Calle La Marina; d with bath US$6-8) Small friendly lodge on the waterfront. Get a room overlooking the sea.

Hotel España (☎ 0295-261-2479; Calle Mariño; d US$6-8) One of the cheapest places, but basic. Rooms vary in quality and some have private baths, so inspect before deciding.

Hotel Torino (☎ 0295-261-7186; Calle Mariño; s/d/tr with bath US$7/10/12; ✼) Spacious rooms with air-con. Reasonable value.

Hotel Central (☎ 0414-791-0042; Blvd Gómez; d/tr with bath US$8/10; ✼) Attractively seated on the pedestrian mall, the hotel has neat rooms and a wide terrace to sit and watch the street life pass by. It has a budget restaurant.

Hotel Tamaca (☎ 0295-261-1602; Av Raúl Leoni; d with bath & fan/air-con US$12/14; ✼) The most popular gringo haunt in the new center. It has a variety of rooms and an open-air restaurant in its front garden where you can share a beer and exchange information with other travelers.

Residencias Turísticas Virginia (☎ 0295-261-2373; Calle Fermín; d with bath & fan/air-con US$9/12; ✼) Undistinguished but acceptable accommodation at convenient location. Rooms range from singles to quads. Some are better than others, so have a look before deciding.

Hotel Imperial (☎ 0295-261-6420; Av Raúl Leoni; d/tr with bath US$18/22; ✼) Ask for a room on one of the upper floors with a view of the sea. Quiet location with cable TV.

Hotel María Luisa (☎ 0295-261-0564; www.hotel marialuisa.com; Av Raúl Leoni; s/d US$20/24, ste US$30) Seven-story three-star hotel with swimming pool, bar and fine restaurant. Be sure to ask for a room with sea views. Good value.

Eating

Budget eateries are plentiful across the city, particularly in the old town.

Alinsuca (Calle Cedeño at Calle Díaz; ☽ lunch) Some of Porlamar's cheapest pastas and pizza.

El Pollo de Carlitos (Calle Marcano; ☽ until late) Excellent chicken at bargain prices.

Pollos El Cacique (Calle Igualdad) Another good chicken affair, better located, but a bit more expensive.

Restaurant Punto Criollo (Calle Igualdad; mains US$4-6) Deservedly popular with locals and visitors for its solid Venezuelan food and reasonable prices.

Ristorante Pizzeria Positano (Calle Fermín; mains US$4-8) One of the better Italian eateries in the new center.

Restaurant Cocody (Av Raúl Leoni; mains US$6-12) Some of the best French cuisine in town, in charming waterfront surroundings.

Drinking

Most of the trendy night haunts are outside the city center. The scene often changes, so check what's 'in' when you arrive.

Señor Frog's (in Centro Comercial Costa Azul, Av Bolívar) Popular disco with a ragbag of music.

Latino's (in Centro Comercial Costa Azul, Av Bolívar) Another fashionable disco in the same shopping mall, but this one has mostly Latin rhythms, such as salsa and merengue.

The British Bulldog (in Centro Comercial Costa Azul, Av Bolívar) A lively bar.

Woody's Pub (Av 4 de Mayo) Enjoyable wood-decked pub with a bar in the middle and a surrounding dance floor. Close to the center (200m beyond the Ciudad Comercial Jumbo).

Getting Around

Small buses, locally called *micros* or *carritos*, run frequently throughout most of the island, including to Pampatar, La Asunción and Juangriego. They leave from different points in the city center; departure points for some of the main tourist destinations are indicated on the map.

PAMPATAR

Pampatar, a town of 15,000 people just northeast of Porlamar, is gradually merging into a single conurbation with Porlamar. Founded in the 1530s, it was one of the earliest settlements on Margarita and still has some colonial buildings.

The 17th-century **Castillo de San Carlos Borromeo** (admission free; ☼ 9am-noon & 2-5pm Tue-Sun), on the waterfront, is the best preserved and restored of seven forts built on the island to protect it from pirate attacks. Across the road, the mid-18th-century **parish church** shelters Cristo del Buen Viaje, an old crucifix much venerated by local fisherfolk. Nearby, the neoclassical **Casa de la Aduana** stages temporary exhibitions. The beach, which extends for 1km east of the fort, has old-world charm; rustic fishing boats lie anchored in the bay while their crews repair nets along the shore.

Few travelers stay in Pampatar, but if you want to, there are several budget lodgings on Calle Almirante Brion, one block back from the beach. You'll also find many open-air eateries along the beach. Buses between Porlamar and Pampatar run every five to 10 minutes (US$0.25, 20 minutes).

LA ASUNCIÓN

Set in a fertile valley in the inland portion of the island, La Asunción is the capital of Nueva Esparta state, even though it's far smaller than Porlamar. It's distinguished by its tranquility and its verdant environs. Duty-free commerce is virtually nonexistent here, and hotels and restaurants are scarce. Frequent buses link La Asunción with Porlamar (US$0.30, 20 minutes).

The late-16th-century **cathedral**, facing Plaza Bolívar, is one of the oldest surviving colonial churches in the country. Diagonally opposite is **Museo Nueva Cádiz** (admission free; ☼ 9am-4pm Tue-Sun), named after the first Spanish town in South America (established around 1500 on nearby Isla Cubagua). The museum displays a small collection of exhibits related to the region's history.

A 10-minute walk south up the hill is **Castillo de Santa Rosa** (admission free; ☼ 9am-4pm Tue-Sun), which provides a good view over the town and the valley, and has some old armor on display.

JUANGRIEGO

Set on the edge of a fine bay in the northern part of Margarita, Juangriego is a relaxing backwater sort of town. It has become popular with tourists, most of whom hang around the beach, by the picturesque fishing boats and visiting yachts. Far away on the horizon, the peaks of Macanao are visible –

they're particularly spectacular when the sun sets behind them. **Fortín de la Galera**, the fort crowning the hill just north of town, draws tourists for the sunset view, though you can get just as good a vista right from the beach. Juangriego is easily accessible from Porlamar by frequent buses (US$0.60, 45 minutes).

Juangriego has some attractive lodging options.

Hotel Nuevo Juangriego (☎ 0295-253-2409; Calle La Marina; d with bath & fan/air-con US$14/20; ⌘) Dutch-operated small hotel right in the middle of the beach. Five rooms facing the bay have balconies from where you can enjoy a postcard snap of the sunset.

Posada Los Tucanes (☎ 0295-253-1716; Calle El Fuerte; d with bath US$18; ⌘) A quiet, four-room place. It doesn't provide sea views.

Hotel Patrick's (☎ 0295-253-6218; Calle El Fuerte; d with bath & fan/air-con US$12/15; ⌘) French-run hotel with good rooms and its own restaurant offering – you guessed it – some French cuisine.

There are a number of places to eat around town. Particularly pleasant are several beach restaurants, including **El Búho**, **El Fortín** and **El Viejo Muelle**. All provide reasonable food and perfect settings for the sunset view.

BEACHES

Isla de Margarita has some 50 beaches big enough to deserve a name, not to mention the smaller bits of sandy coast. Many beaches have been developed with restaurants, bars and other facilities. Though the island is no longer a virgin paradise, you can still find a relatively deserted strip of sand. On the whole, Margarita's beaches have little shade, and some are virtually barren. You can camp on the beaches, but use common sense and be cautious. Don't leave your tent unattended. Swimmers should be aware of dangerous undertows on some beaches, including Playa El Agua and Playa Puerto Cruz.

Playa El Agua

Picture-postcard Playa El Agua is Margarita's trendiest and most developed beach. It's shaded with coconut groves and densely dotted with palm-thatched restaurants and bars offering a good selection of food, cocktails and frequent live music. Behind the beach is a collection of hotels and holiday homes. Most of these are upmarket establishments but there are some budget options in the back streets.

Chalets de Belén (☎ 0295-249-1707; Calle Miragua; d with bath & fan/air-con US$13/20) A recommended six-room family-run place just 150m back from the beach.

Residencia Vacacional Playa El Agua (☎ 0295-249-1975; Calle Miragua; d with bath US$10, 4-/6-person cabins US$18/20) Basic but about the cheapest accommodation in the area, 100m beyond the Chalets. Rooms have fans and cabins have a kitchenette.

Costa Linda Beach Hotel (☎ 0295-249-1303; Calle Miragua; d/tr US$28/35; 🗷) A charming colonial-style place with 25 comfortable air-con rooms, swimming pool and its own restaurant. Prices include rich buffet breakfast.

Other Beaches

Other popular beaches include **Playa Guacuco** and **Playa Manzanillo**. Perhaps Margarita's finest beach is **Playa Puerto Cruz**, which arguably has the island's widest, whitest stretch of sand and still isn't overdeveloped. **Playa Parguito**, next to Playa El Agua, has strong waves good for surfing, whereas **Playa El Yaque**, south of the airport, has tranquil waters and steady winds perfect for windsurfing. If you want to escape from people, head for **Península de Macanao**, the wildest part of the island.

GUAYANA

Occupying all of southeast Venezuela, half of the country's area, the amazing and wildly diverse region of Guayana features mysterious *tepuis*, spectacular waterfalls, wild jungles and sweeping savannas. Highlights include Salto Ángel, the world's highest waterfall, and the unique Gran Sabana (p1009), a rolling savanna dotted with *tepuis*; both are part of the huge, 30,000-sq-km Parque Nacional Canaima. For more information on *tepuis*, see the boxed text (p1010).

The only two important cities in the region are Ciudad Bolívar and Ciudad Guayana, both on the lower Orinoco River; apart from these, Guayana is sparsely populated, with no other significant cities.

CIUDAD BOLÍVAR

Ciudad Bolívar is a hot city on the southern bank of the Orinoco, 420km upstream from the Atlantic Ocean. Founded in 1764 on a rocky elevation at the narrowest point of the river, the town was originally named Angostura (literally, 'narrows'). As a sleepy river port hundreds of miles from any important population centers, Angostura grew slowly at first. Then, suddenly and unexpectedly, it became the place where much of the country's (and the continent's) history was forged.

It was here that Bolívar came in 1817, soon after the town had been liberated from Spanish control, to set up a base for military operations against the Spaniards. It was here that the British Legionnaires joined Bolívar before all set off on a long and strenuous march across Los Llanos and up the Andes to gain independence for Colombia. And it was here that the Angostura Congress convened in 1819 to give birth to Gran Colombia, a unified republic comprising Venezuela, Colombia and Ecuador. In honor of 'El Libertador,' the town was renamed Ciudad Bolívar in 1846.

Today, Ciudad Bolívar is the capital of Venezuela's largest state, Bolívar, and a city of 300,000 inhabitants. It has retained the flavor of an old river-town and still conserves some of the architecture dating from its colonial era. It's a popular stop on travelers' routes, partly for the city itself and partly as a jumping-off point for Angel Falls.

Information

Central Internet facilities include **Galaxia.com** (in Abboud Center, Paseo Orinoco), **CANTV** (Paseo Orinoco) and **Estrella de Oriente** (Calle Bolívar).

Banesco (Calle Dalla Costa) and **Banco de Venezuela** (Paseo Orinoco), in the city center, give advances on credit cards. The **Corp Banca** (Paseo Meneses), 2km south of the city center, changes American Express traveler's checks. **Casa de Cambio Febres Parra** (in Hotel Laja Real, Av Andrés Bello), near the airport, exchanges cash and traveler's checks.

The **Corporación de Turismo** (☎ 0285-632-2362; Quinta Yeita, Av Bolívar; 🕒 8am-noon & 2-5:30pm Mon-Fri) is four blocks north of the airport.

Sights

Paseo Orinoco, the lively waterfront, is lined with old arcaded houses, some of which remember Bolívar days. Midway along the Paseo is **Mirador Angostura**, a rocky headland that juts into the river at its narrowest

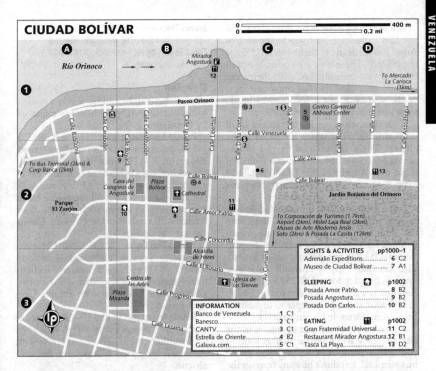

CIUDAD BOLÍVAR

0 .... 400 m
0 .... 0.2 mi

Río Orinoco →

Mirador Angostura 12

To Mercado La Carioca (1km)

Paseo Orinoco

3   1   5   Centro Comercial Abboud Center

Calle Babliona
Calle Carabobo
Calle Constitución
Calle Boyacá
Calle Igualdad
Calle Libertad
Calle Dalla Costa
Calle Venezuela
Calle Piar
Calle Roscio
Calle Urica
Calle Anzoátegui

7
9

Calle Zea

To Bus Terminal (2km) & Corp Banca (2km)

Casa del Congreso de Angostura
Plaza Bolívar
Cathedral
4
6

Calle Bolívar
Calle Bolívar

13

Parque El Zanjón

10
8
11

Jardín Botánico del Orinoco

Calle Amor Patrio

To Corporación de Turismo (1.7km), Airport (2km), Hotel Laja Real (2km), Museo de Arte Moderno Jesús Soto (2km) & Posada La Casita (12km)

Calle Concordia

Alcaldía de Heres

Av Cumaná

SIGHTS & ACTIVITIES   pp1000–1
Adrenalin Expeditions.............. 6 C2
Museo de Ciudad Bolívar......... 7 A1

Calle El Rosario

Centro de las Artes

Iglesia de las Siervas

SLEEPING   p1002
Posada Amor Patrio................. 8 B2
Posada Angostura.................... 9 B2
Posada Don Carlos................. 10 B2

Plaza Miranda

Calle Progreso

INFORMATION
Banco de Venezuela.............1 C1
Banesco................................2 C1
CANTV.................................3 C1
Estrella de Oriente................4 B2
Galaxia.com..........................5 C1

EATING   p1002
Gran Fraternidad Universal.... 11 C2
Restaurant Mirador Angostura.12 B1
Tasca La Playa...................... 13 D2

Calle Lezama

point. The lookout commands good views up and down the Orinoco, taking in, among other things, the **Puente de Angostura**, a suspension bridge 5km upriver from the city. This is the only bridge across the Orinoco along the river's entire course.

Three blocks west of the lookout is the **Museo de Ciudad Bolívar** (☎ 0285-632-4121; Paseo Orinoco; admission US$0.20; 9am-noon & 2-5pm Mon-Fri). The republic's first newspaper was printed in this building (1818–21), and you can see the original press on which it was done, plus a collection of modern paintings.

South up the hill is **Plaza Bolívar**, the historic heart of the city. Five allegorical statues on the square personify the five countries Bolívar liberated. The massive **cathedral** was begun right after the town's founding and completed 80 years later. Also on the plaza, the **Casa del Congreso de Angostura** (admission free; 9am-5pm Tue-Sun) was the site of the lengthy debates of the 1819 Angostura Congress. You can have a look around the interior.

Three blocks south of Plaza Bolívar is **Plaza Miranda**, bordered by the sizable **Centro de las Artes** (☎ 0285-630-1306; admission free;

9am-5pm Tue-Sun), which features temporary modern art exhibitions.

Casa San Isidro (Av Táchira; admission free; 9am-5pm Tue-Sun) occupies a fine colonial mansion where Bolívar stayed during the Angostura Congress. The interior of the house is maintained in the style of the Bolívar era.

Museo de Arte Moderno Jesús Soto (☎ 0285-632-0518; Av Germania; admission free; 9:30am-5:30pm Tue-Fri, 10am-5pm Sat & Sun) has a good collection of works by this kinetic artist (born in Ciudad Bolívar in 1923) and works by other modern artists.

In front of the airport terminal stands the legendary **airplane of Jimmie Angel** – see the Salto Ángel section (p1007).

Tours

Ciudad Bolívar is the main gateway to Angel Falls, and tours to the falls are the staple of most tour operators in the city. One of the most popular tours is a one-day package that includes a round-trip flight to Canaima, a flight over Angel Falls, lunch in Canaima and a short boat excursion (US$160 to US$200 per person).

Another popular offer is a three-day package that includes a boat trip to the foot of Angel Falls instead of a flight over it (US$200 to US$260). These trips are normally run in the rainy season only, but with the recent climatic anomalies they are organized most of the year with just a few months break, somewhere between January and April.

Tour companies use the services of small local airlines, all of which are based at the airport. These airlines can fly you to Canaima (one way US$50), and can include a flight over Angel Falls for US$40 to US$50 extra. You can buy tickets directly from the airlines or from tour operators.

Other tours available from Ciudad Bolívar include trips to the Gran Sabana, Río Caura and Roraima. Gran Sabana tours are offered by most agents, often as a four-day jeep trip (about US$200 per person, all-inclusive). The Río Caura trip is normally done as a four- to five-day tour (US$200 to US$300). Roraima is a six- to eight-day tour (US$250 to US$300); it will be cheaper to organize it from Santa Elena de Uairén (p1012).

There are plenty of tour operators in the city and they will hunt for you as soon as you arrive. Some may wait for you at the bus terminal, but don't buy any tour on the street. Check the offer of several companies, as prices and programs may vary widely. It's probably best to start by inquiring at hotels – most of the hotels listed in the Sleeping section, following, have tour agencies:

Gekko Tours (☎ 0285-632-3223, 0414-854-5146; www.gekkotours-venezuela.de) Run by Posada La Casita; office in the airport terminal.

Sakaika Travel (☎ 0414-854-4925; plazabolivar@ hotmail.com) In Posada Amor Patrio.

Soana Travel (☎ 0285-632-6017, 0414-854-6616; soanatravel@gmx.de) In Posada Don Carlos.

Other tour companies you may want to check include:

Adrenalin Expeditions (☎ 0285-617-0633, 0414-854-2940; adrenalinexptours@hotmail.com; Centro Comercial Roque Center, Calle Bolívar)

Turi Express Dorado (☎ 0285-632-9764, 0414-893-9576; turiexpress@cantv.net) In the airport terminal.

If you are interested in Salto Ángel tours, you can also buy the package directly from either of the two major Canaima boat-tour operators, both of which have offices at Ciudad Bolívar's airport terminal:

Bernal Tours (represented by Sapito Tours; ☎ 0285-632-7989; 0414-854-8234; www.sapitotours.com)

Tiuna Tours (☎ 0285-632-8697, 0414-893-3003; www.tiunatours.com)

Sleeping

Ciudad Bolívar has some lovely *posadas;* coincidentally, all listed here are managed by Germans.

Posada Amor Patrio (☎ 0285-632-8819, 0414-854-4925; plazabolivar@hotmail.com; Calle Amor Patrio; hammock US$4, d/tr US$10/14) The most popular backpackers' shelter, right behind the cathedral. Set in a historic house, it has just five rooms with fan and shared bath. If all rooms are taken you can sleep in a hammock on a top-floor terrace with views over the Orinoco. Guests can use the kitchen.

Posada Don Carlos (☎ 0285-632-6017, 0414-854-6616; soanatravel@gmx.de; Calle Boyacá; d with fan/air-con US$10/25; 🐾) Brand new *posada* in a meticulously restored historic mansion with two ample patios. Great bar with antique German furniture.

Posada Angostura (☎ 0285-632-4639; www.posada angostura.com; Calle Boyacá; s/d/tr with bath US$20/24/28; 🐾) Another charming colonial house with character. Its seven rooms have fan and air-con.

Posada La Casita (☎ 0285-617-0832, 0414-854-5146; www.gekkotours-venezuela.de; Urbanización 24 de Julio; tent site US$2, hammock US$3, s/d/tr US$8/12/15) Something different – a country estate on the city outskirts, 12km east of the city center. You can stay in bungalows and cabins with bath, or you can sleep in a hammock. Camping is also permitted. It has good meals available on request, a swimming pool and free pickup service.

Eating

The city center is full of cheap eateries.

Restaurant Mirador Angostura (Paseo Orinoco; mains US$1-2) Ultra-cheap food at the great river's bank.

Mercado La Carioca (Paseo Orinoco; mains US$2-4) A market at the eastern end of the Paseo Orinoco, with a row of restaurants lining the riverfront. Good, inexpensive local fare includes some delicious fish.

Tasca La Playa (Calle Urica; mains US$3-5) Solid food at reasonable prices.

Gran Fraternidad Universal (Calle Amor Patrio; set meals US$2.50; ☀ lunch Mon-Fri) Tasty vegetarian meals.

Getting There & Away

The airport is 2km southeast of the riverfront and is linked to the city center by local transport. Avior flies daily to Caracas (US$45 to US$70). The city is the major jumping-off point for Canaima. For information see Tours under Ciudad Bolívar (p1001).

The bus terminal is on Av República at Av Sucre, 2km south of the city center. To get there, take the westbound *buseta* marked 'Terminal' from Paseo Orinoco.

Buses to Caracas depart mostly in the evening (US$11, nine hours). A dozen buses a day go to Puerto Ayacucho (US$10, 10 hours). Several bus companies run to Santa Elena de Uairén (US$8 to US$10, nine to 11 hours), with a total of eight departures daily. To Ciudad Guayana, buses depart every 15 to 30 minutes (US$1.50, 1½ hours).

CIUDAD GUAYANA

Set on the southern bank of the Orinoco at its confluence with the Río Caroní, Ciudad Guayana is an unusual city. Officially 'founded' in 1961 as a regional industrial center, it embraced within its metropolitan boundaries two urban components: the old town of San Félix, on the eastern side of the Caroní, and the newborn Puerto Ordaz on the opposite bank. At the time of its founding, the total population of the area was about 40,000. Forty years later, Ciudad Guayana is Venezuela's fastest growing city, and its two components have merged into an urban sprawl populated by more than 600,000. Despite the official unified name, people continue to refer to San Félix and Puerto Ordaz.

San Félix was founded in the 16th century, but has few historical remnants of importance. Puerto Ordaz is modern and well planned, with a good infrastructure of roads, shopping malls and services, yet it lacks the soul of cities that have evolved in a natural way. However, it's worth stopping here to visit the city's three scenic parks.

Information

Internet access is available at the **Cyber Café Continental** (Av Principal de Castillito) and **Web Celular** (in Torre Loreto, Planta Baja, Av Las Américas).

Italcambio (airport terminal) changes traveler's checks and cash. Useful central banks include: **Banco de Venezuela** (Av Las Americas), **Banco Mercantil** (Av Ciudad Bolivar), **Banco Provin-** cial (Av Ciudad Bolivar), **Banesco** (Via Caracas) and **Corp Banca** (Calle Urbana). The tourist office, **Almacaroní** (☎ 0286-924-4077; Calle 1 at Carrera 1; ☺ 8am-4pm Mon-Fri), is in central San Félix.

Sights

The riverside **Parque Cachamay** (Av Guayana; admission US$0.30; ☺ 7am-5pm Tue-Sun) is 2km southeast of Puerto Ordaz' center. Here the Río Caroní turns into a series of rapids and eventually into a spectacular 200m-wide line of waterfalls. Adjoining the park is **Parque Loefling** (Av Guayana; admission free; ☺ 7am-5pm Tue-Sun), which has a small zoo with some animals in cages and others wandering freely.

Another park noted for its falls, **Parque La Llovizna** (Av Leopoldo Sucre Figarella; admission free; ☺ 5am-5pm Tue-Sun) is on the 26 islands in the Río Caroní. Its highlight is the 20m Salto La Llovizna, which produces the *llovizna* (drizzle) for which both the waterfall and park are named. Several vantage points provide views over the falls from various angles.

Tours

Local tour operators focus on Guayana's highlights, such as the Salto Ángel, Gran Sabana and Delta del Orinoco. Most of these tours can be arranged cheaper elsewhere, but if you plan on a Delta de Orinoco trip it may be worth checking with **Sacoroco River Tours** (☎ 0286-961-5526; sacoroco@yahoo.com; Calle Gahna No 19, Villa Africana, Manzana 32, Puerto Ordaz). The English- and German-speaking French manager, Roger, personally runs boat trips to the southern part of the delta, in the Río Grande area (US$45 to US$50 per person per day).

Sleeping

Both San Félix and Puerto Ordaz have a range of hotels, but it's advisable to stay in the latter for convenience, surroundings and security.

La Casa del Lobo (☎ 0286-961-6286; Calle Zambia No 2, Villa Africana, Manzana 39; s/d US$7/10) Budget accommodation in the private house of a German guy, Wolf, who rents out four rooms with fan and bath in his home. It's a friendly, cheap and safe place, with excellent value and meals on request. Free pickup from Puerto Ordaz bus terminal, or take a taxi (US$2.50).

Residencias Tore (☎ 0286-923-0679; Calle San Cristóbal at Carrera Los Andes; d with bath US$25; ☯)

VENEZUELA

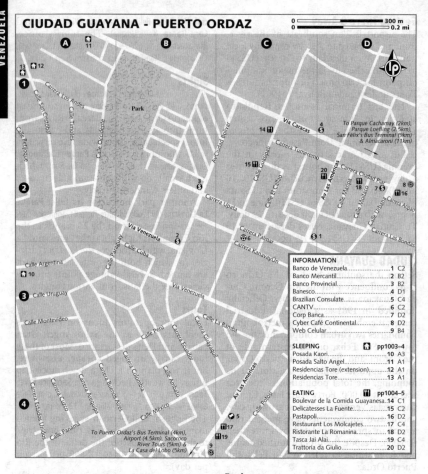

CIUDAD GUAYANA - PUERTO ORDAZ

INFORMATION	
Banco de Venezuela..................1	C2
Banco Mercantil.......................2	B2
Banco Provincial......................3	B2
Banesco...................................4	D1
Brazilian Consulate...................5	C4
CANTV....................................6	C2
Corp Banca.............................7	D2
Cyber Café Continental............8	D2
Web Celular.............................9	B4

SLEEPING	🏠 pp1003–4
Posada Kaori...........................10	A3
Posada Salto Angel..................11	A1
Residencias Tore (extension).......12	A1
Residencias Tore.....................13	A1

EATING	🍴 pp1004–5
Boulevar de la Comida Guayanesa.14	C1
Delicatesses La Fuente..............15	C2
Pastapoli.................................16	D2
Restaurant Los Molcajetes.........17	C4
Ristorante La Romanina............18	D2
Tasca Jai Alai...........................19	C4
Trattoria da Giulio....................20	D2

One of Puerto Ordaz's first *posadas*, in a quiet residential suburb. It now has an extension diagonally across the street. It has simple but comfortable air-con rooms with bath and breakfast – though they are possibly a bit overpriced. Its restaurant has good food, including a budget *menú ejecutivo*.

Posada Kaori (☎ 0286-923-4038; Calle Argentina; d/tr with bath US$20/24; ❄) New 12-room *posada* with air-con and private baths. Reasonable standards and value.

Posada Salto Ángel (☎ 0286-922-6516; Vía Caracas; d with breakfast US$24) A new kid on the block. It's on a main road but the rooms are at the back of the building. It has its own restaurant and bar.

Eating

All the places listed are in Puerto Ordaz's center.

Boulevar de la Comida Guayanesa (Calle Guasipati; meals US$2-4) A dozen budget food stalls serving typical local fare until 3pm to 4 pm.

Delicatesses La Fuente (Calle Guasipati; set meals US$3) A good place for an appetizing set lunch.

Pastapoli (Calle Urbana; pastas US$2-3) Tasty pasta at bargain prices till about 3pm.

Trattoria da Giulio (Av Las Américas; mains US$3-6) Simple Italian restaurant adjoining the Hotel La Guayana, offering more than just pasta.

Tasca Jai Alai (Av Las Américas; mains US$5-8) A touch of Spain, with well-prepared meat, fish and seafood.

Restaurant Los Molcajetes (Av Las Américas; mains US$5-7) Fairly authentic Mexican cuisine at reasonable prices.

Ristorante La Romanina (Carrera Ciudad Piar; mains US$5-9) Respectable Italian restaurant.

Getting There & Away

AIR

The airport is at the west end of Puerto Ordaz on the road to Ciudad Bolívar (note that the airport appears in all schedules as Puerto Ordaz, not Ciudad Guayana). It handles direct flights to Caracas (US$50 to US$75) and Porlamar (US$40 to US$65), and has connections to other cities.

BUS

Ciudad Guayana has two bus terminals. The main one is in San Félix, on Av Gumilla, about 1.5km south of San Félix's center. The environs of the terminal can be unsafe, particularly after dark, so don't walk there; take a bus or taxi. The other terminal is in Puerto Ordaz, on Av Guayana, 1km east of the airport. It's smaller, cleaner, quieter and safer, and handles far fewer buses than the San Félix station.

From the San Félix terminal, buses depart regularly to Caracas (US$12, 10½ hours), most stopping en route at the Puerto Ordaz terminal. Buses to Ciudad Bolívar (US$1.50, 1½ hours) depart from both terminals every half-hour or so.

Nine buses daily come through from Ciudad Bolívar on their way to Santa Elena de Uairén (US$7 to US$9, nine to 10 hours); all call at San Félix, but only a few stop in Puerto Ordaz.

Expresos La Guayanesa has two buses a day from San Félix to Tucupita (US$3, 3½ hours), or go by *por puesto* (US$5, 2¼ hours), which depart regularly. The trip involves a ferry ride across the Orinoco from San Félix to Los Barrancos.

TUCUPITA

The largest town of the Orinoco Delta, Tucupita is a hot river port of 70,000 people. The town was founded in the 1920s as one of the Capuchin missions that were established in the delta to convert the Indigenous communities. For travelers, Tucupita is essentially a jumping-off point for exploring the delta rather than an attraction in itself.

Covering about 25,000 sq km, the Orinoco Delta is the second-largest delta on the continent after the Amazon. The river splits into 40-odd major *caños* (channels), which carry the waters down to the Atlantic. Their mouths are distributed along 360km of coast. The southernmost channel, Río Grande, is the main one and is used by ocean-going vessels sailing upriver to Ciudad Guayana.

The climate of the delta is hot and humid, with an average annual temperature around 27°C (81°F). The driest period is from January to March. The water reaches its highest level from August to September, when parts of the delta become marshy or flooded.

The delta is inhabited by the Warao people, the second-largest indigenous group in Venezuela after the Guajiro. Numbering about 24,000, they live along the *caños*, constructing *palafitos* (rudimentary huts built on stilts over the water) on riverbanks and living off fishing.

Information

Internet facilities have mushroomed over recent years and include **Compucenter.com** (Plaza Bolívar), **Copicom** (Calle Petión), **Cyber Computer** (Calle Bolívar) and **Go's Computer** (Calle Petión).

Banco de Venezuela (Calle Manamo) and **Banesco** (Calle Petión) give cash advances on credit cards. There's also the convenient **Mi Casa ATM** (Plaza Bolívar).

The tourist office, **Dirección de Turismo** (Edificio San Juan, Piso 3, Oficina 18, Calle Bolívar; ☾ 8am-noon & 2-5pm Mon-Fri) is just off Plaza Bolívar.

Tours

All local tour operators focus on trips into the delta. Tours are usually all-inclusive two- to four-day excursions and the going rate is US$40 to US$80 per person a day, depending on the company, the routes and conditions, and particularly on the number of people in the group. All the agents listed here offer tours to the northern part of the delta, toward Pedernales. If you want a trip to the southern delta, check Sacoroco River Tours in the Ciudad Guayana section (p1003). All tour companies have *campamentos* that serve as a base for boat trips around the area.

Aventura Turística Delta (☎ 0287-721-0835; a_t_d_1973@hotmail.com; Calle Centurión) The most popular company with travelers, and probably the cheapest. Accommodation in hammocks only.

VENEZUELA

Campamento Mis Palafitos (☎ 0287-721-1733; www.deltaorinocomispalafitos.com; Centro Comercial Delta Center, Plaza Bolívar) Comfortable *campamento* providing rooms with bath, two hours by boat from Tucupita.

Tucupita Expeditions (☎ 0287-721-0801; www.orinocodelta.com; Calle Las Acacias) Possibly the most expensive agency. It works principally with organized groups and generally doesn't focus on individual travelers.

Sleeping

There are four or five hotels in the town center, and a few more outside the central area. All the hotels listed have rooms with private baths, but otherwise are pretty poor quality.

Pequeño Hotel (☎ 0287-721-0523; Calle La Paz; d/tr with bath & fan US$6/8) Perhaps the most primitive option with dim rooms and bumpy beds, but the cheapest. The door is locked at 10pm, so don't be late.

Hotel Sans Souci (☎ 0287-721-0132; Calle Centurión; d/tr with bath & fan US$8/10, with air-con US$12/14; 🕸) On the basic side and a bit run-down, but has some rooms with air-con.

Hotel Delta (☎ 0287-414-5877; Calle Pativilca; d/tr with bath US$12/14; 🕸) An unmemorable but clean establishment with air-con rooms.

Hotel Amacuro (☎ 0287-721-0404; Calle Bolívar; d/tr with bath & fan US$12/14, with air-con US$16/20; 🕸) Possibly the best hotel in the town center; and its air-con is marginally quieter than that of the others, yet it's really nothing special.

Eating

Don't worry, you won't starve here; restaurants are in good supply, and food stalls open on Paseo Manamo in the evening.

Mi Tasca (Calle Dalla Costa; mains US$3-5) Now enlarged and revamped, this place remains one of the town's best budget eateries, with generous portions and quick service.

El Rincón de Pedro (Calle Petión; mains US$1.50-2.50) Acceptable meals at basic prices.

Restaurant Cen China Tonw (Calle Petión; mains US$2-3) Perhaps not the most authentic Chinese cuisine in your life, but not expensive either.

For breakfast, choose from a few central *panaderías*, including **Panadería Pan Center** (Calle Dalla Costa) and **Panadería Tucupita** (Calle Tucupita).

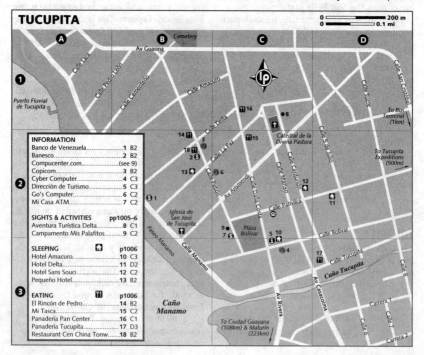

TUCUPITA

0 — 200 m
0 — 0.1 mi

INFORMATION
Banco de Venezuela	1 B2
Banesco	2 B2
Compucenter.com	(see 9)
Copicom	3 B2
Cyber Computer	4 C3
Dirección de Turismo	5 C3
Go's Computer	6 C2
Mi Casa ATM	7 C2

SIGHTS & ACTIVITIES pp1005-6
Aventura Turística Delta	8 C1
Campamento Mis Palafitos	9 C1

SLEEPING 🏠 p1006
Hotel Amacuro	10 C3
Hotel Delta	11 D2
Hotel Sans Souci	12 C2
Pequeño Hotel	13 B2

EATING 🍴 p1006
El Rincón de Pedro	14 B2
Mi Tasca	15 C2
Panadería Pan Center	16 C1
Panadería Tucupita	17 D3
Restaurant Cen China Tonw	18 B2

Puerto Fluvial de Tucupita

Cemetery

Av Guasina

Calle Lara
Calle Pedro León
Calle Cementerio
Calle Amacuro
Calle Delta
Calle Sucre
Calle San Cristóbal
Calle La Paz
Calle Petión
Av Arismendi
Calle Dalla Costa
Calle 5 de Julio
Calle Centurión
Calle Mamo
Calle Patricia
Calle Bolívar
Calle Tucupita
Caño Tucupita
Av Cascolma
Av Rivera
Carrera 1
Carrera 2
Calle B
Calle 7

Catedral de la Divina Pastora

Iglesia de San José de Tucupita

Plaza Bolívar

Caño Manamo

To Bus Terminal (1km)
To Tucupita Expeditions (500m)
To Ciudad Guayana (108km) & Maturín (223km)

Getting There & Away

The bus terminal is 1km southeast of the town center; walk or take a taxi (US$1). There are five departures nightly to Caracas (US$10, 10 hours). Expresos La Guayanesa runs two buses daily to Ciudad Guayana (US$3, 3½ hours), but *por puestos* (US$5, 2½ hours) serve this route regularly. For Caripe and Cueva del Guácharo, take a bus (US$4, four hours) or one of the more frequent, faster *por puestos* (US$7, three hours) to Maturín and change there.

SALTO ÁNGEL

Commonly know to the English-speaking world as Angel Falls, this is the world's highest waterfall and Venezuela's number-one promotional landmark. Its total height is 979m, of which the uninterrupted drop is 807m, about 16 times the height of Niagara Falls. The cascade spills off the heart-shaped Auyantepui, one of the largest of the *tepuis,* into Cañón del Diablo (Devil's Canyon).

The waterfall's volume much depends on the season, and the contrast can be quite dramatic. In the dry months (normally January to May), it can be pretty faint – just a thin ribbon of water fading into mist halfway down its drop. In the rainy season, and particularly in the wettest months (August and September), it's often voluminous and spectacular, but frequently covered by clouds.

The waterfall is in a distant wilderness with no road access. The village of Canaima, about 50km northwest, is the major gateway to the falls. Canaima doesn't have an overland link to the rest of the country either, but it does have an airport.

A visit to Angel Falls is normally undertaken in two stages, with Canaima as the stepping stone. Most tourists fly into Canaima, where they take a light plane or boat to the falls. No walking trails go all the way from Canaima to the falls.

Two other popular waterfalls are in the Canaima area. **Salto El Sapo** is a 10-minute boat trip from Canaima plus a short walk. It's beautiful and unusual in that you can walk behind the curtain of water (take a swimsuit with you). A short walk from El Sapo is **Salto El Sapito**, another attractive waterfall, normally included in the same excursion.

ANGEL FALLS' DIVINE NAME

The Angel Falls is not named, as one might expect, after a divine creature, but after an American bush pilot Jimmie Angel, who landed on the boggy top of the Auyantepui in 1937 in his four-seater airplane in search of gold. The plane stuck in the marshy surface and Angel couldn't take off again. He, along with his wife and two companions, trekked through rough, virgin terrain to the edge of the plateau, then descended 1km of almost vertical cliff, finally returning to civilization after an 11-day odyssey. The plane was later removed from the top of the *tepui,* restored and placed in front of the airport terminal in Ciudad Bolívar, where it now resides.

Salto Ángel, Auyantepui, Canaima and the surrounding area lie within the boundaries of 30,000-sq-km Parque Nacional Canaima, Venezuela's second-largest national park, and the country's only park appearing on the Unesco World Natural Heritage list. All visitors coming to Canaima pay a US$6 national park entrance fee.

CANAIMA

Canaima is an indigenous-tourist village that serves as a springboard for Angel Falls. It lies along a peaceful stretch of the Río Carrao known as Laguna de Canaima, just below the point where the river turns into a line of magnificent falls (Saltos Hacha).

The center of the village is Campamento Canaima, a tourist camp spectacularly set right on the bank of the lake. The airport is just a few minutes walk to the west. Bring a swimsuit, plenty of film and efficient insect repellent.

Information

Canaima has no specific tourist office (try tour operators for information) and no banks. The Tienda Quincallería Canaima (souvenir-cum-grocery shop), near the airport, changes US dollars and traveler's checks. The rate is lower than in the cities, so it's best to come with bolívares. Most of Canaima's tour operators will accept payment in US dollars, but not credit cards, or will charge 10% more if you pay with plastic money.

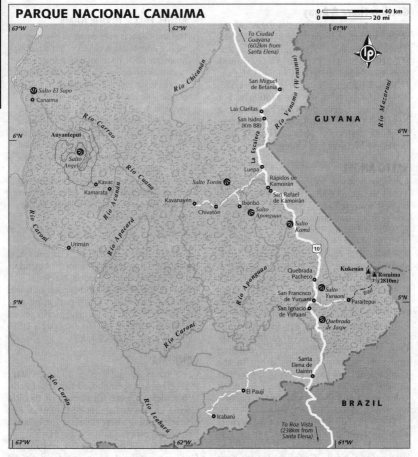

PARQUE NACIONAL CANAIMA

0 — 40 km
0 — 20 mi

To Ciudad
Guayana
(602km from
Santa Elena)

San Miguel
de Betania

Las Claritas

San Isidro
(Km 88)

GUYANA

Río Chicanán
Río Venamo (Wenamu)
Río Mazaruni

Salto El Sapo
Canaima

Río Carrao

Auyantepui

Salto
Angel

Kavac

Kamarata

Río Aicanán

Río Cuana

La Escalera

Luepa

Rápidos de
Kamoirán

San Rafael
de Kamoirán

Salto Torón

Kavanayén

Chivatón

Iboribó

Salto
Aponguao

Salto
Kamá

Río Caroní

Urimán

Río Apacará

Río Aponguao

Quebrada
Pacheco

Kukenán

Roraima
(2810m)

10

San Francisco
de Yuruaní

San Ignacio
de Yuruaní

Salto
Yuruaní

Trail

Paraitepui

Quebrada
de Jaspe

Santa
Elena de
Uairén

Río Caroní

Río Caribí

Río Icabarú

El Paují

Icabarú

BRAZIL

To Boa Vista
(238km from
Santa Elena)

63°W
62°W
61°W
6°N
5°N

VENEZUELA

Tours

You can get to Angel Falls by boat or plane. The flights are in light (usually five-seat) planes of various small airlines mostly coming from Ciudad Bolívar. The pilots fly two or three times back and forth over the face of the falls, circle the top of the *tepui* and then return. The round-trip flight from Canaima (about 40 minutes) costs US$40 to US$50.

Motorized canoes to the foot of Angel Falls operate when the water level is sufficiently high, usually nine to 10 months a year, with some breaks between January and April. One-day tours are available (US$90 to US$120 per person, all-inclusive), but more popular and relaxing are three-day/two-night tours (US$100 to US$150).

All Canaima-based tour companies run boat trips and can arrange flights. The main operators include:

Bernal Tours (☎ 0414-852-3293; www.bernaltours .com) Small family-run company based on an island on Laguna de Canaima, with a rustic *campamento*.

Canaima Tours (☎ 0286-625560) Based at its upmarket Wakü Lodge, this is by far the most expensive operator, rarely used by backpackers.

Excursiones Kavac (☎ 0414-884-0511) Agency managed by the local Pemón Indigenous community.

Tiuna Tours (☎ 0286-962-4255; www.tiunatours.com) The biggest local player, with a large *campamento* in Canaima and another one up the Río Carrao.

Save for Canaima Tours, all other companies wait for incoming flights at the airport; the prices of their tours can be negotiated. Tiuna and Bernal have outlets at Ciudad Bolívar's airport, where you can buy their tours. See Tours in the Ciudad Bolívar section (p1001) for tours organized from that city, which may work out to be cheaper and more convenient than coming to Canaima and buying a tour.

Sleeping & Eating

There are a dozen *campamentos* and *posadas* in Canaima, some of which also serve meals. Most accommodations are relatively inexpensive; expect to pay US$4 to US$7 for a hammock and US$8 to US$15 for a bed. The prices are volatile and largely depend on demand.

Campamento Canaima (☎ 0286-961-3071; per person with 3 meals US$70) Canaima's oldest and best-known lodging and dining facility, consisting of 35 palm-thatched *cabañas* (featuring 109 rooms with baths), a restaurant and bar. Accommodations are available as part of an expensive tour package or can be bought in Canaima. The buffet-style restaurant is open to all, but it's expensive.

Posada Kaikusé (r with bath per person US$10) Small budget place in the northern end of Canaima. Rooms have fans, but are pretty basic.

Posada Kusarí (hammock US$5, r per person US$16) Near Kaikusé, this one is a bit better – inquire at the Tienda Quincallería Canaima near the airport for vacancies and current rates.

Posada Wey Tepuy (☎ 0414-850-2059; r with bath per person US$8) One of the cheapest options, opposite the school in the south part of the village. Basic doubles and triples.

Campamento Churún Vená (☎ 0414-884-0511; hammock US$6, r per person US$13) Opposite the soccer pitch, this is the camp for the clients of Excursiones Kavac, but it often has vacancies available to all. Ask its agent at the airport upon arrival.

Campamento Tiuna (☎ 0286-962-4255; hammock US$6, r per person US$12) Camp of Tiuna Tours. It also offers student beds and hammocks to tourists, and can provide meals. Ask its agent at the airport when you arrive.

If you have your own tent, you can **camp** (free) in Canaima, but get a permit from the Inparques officer at the airport. The usual place to camp is on the beach next to the Guardia Nacional post, just behind Campamento Canaima. You may be able to arrange with guards to leave your stuff at the post while you are away.

A few shops in Canaima sell basic supplies, such as bread, pasta, canned fish and biscuits, but prices are high. Consider bringing some food with you.

Getting There & Away

Avior flies between Caracas and Canaima (one way US$100 to US$125). Several regional carriers fly between Ciudad Bolívar and Canaima on a semi-regular or charter basis (US$50) – see Tours in the Ciudad Bolívar section (p1001). Rutaca has daily flights between Canaima and Santa Elena de Uairén (US$70).

GRAN SABANA

A rolling grassy highland in Venezuela's far southeastern corner, the Gran Sabana is vast, wild, beautiful, empty and silent. The only real town in the region is Santa Elena de Uairén, near the Brazilian border. The remainder of the sparsely populated region is inhabited mostly by the indigenous Pemón, who live in scattered villages and hamlets.

Not long ago, the Gran Sabana was virtually inaccessible by land. It wasn't until 1973 that a road between El Dorado and Santa Elena was completed, and the last stretch of this road was finally paved in 1991. Today, it's one of the best highways in the country and one of the most spectacular. The road is signposted with kilometer marks from the El Dorado fork (km 0) southward to Santa Elena (km 316) – a great help for orientation.

The most striking natural features of Gran Sabana's skyline are gigantic table mountains called *tepuis*. More than 100 such plateaus dot the vast region from the Colombian border in the west up into Guyana and Brazil in the east. The largest concentration is in the Gran Sabana. Roraima, one of the *tepuis*, can be climbed and this trip is an extraordinary adventure (see p1011).

The Sabana holds many other sights as well, including some amazing waterfalls. One of the best examples easily accessible from the road is the lovely, 50m-high **Salto Kamá** (km 202). Go down to the foot of the waterfall for the best view.

THE MYSTERIOUS WORLD OF THE TEPUIS

Tepuis are flat-topped, cliff-edged mountains typical of southern Venezuela. 'Tepui' (also spelled 'tepuy') is a Pemón Indian word for 'mountain', and it has been adopted internationally as the term to identify this specific type of table mountain.

Geologically, these sandstone tablelands are the remnants of a thick layer of Precambrian sediments (some two billion years old) that gradually eroded, leaving behind only the most resistant rock 'islands.' Effectively isolated over millions of years from each other and from the eroded lower level, the tops of tepuis saw the independent evolution of flora and fauna. Developing in such a specific environment, many species have preserved features of their remote ancestors, and outside of their tepuis they can be seen only in fossilized remains.

Every tepui has a characteristic plant life, different from any of its neighbors. Scientific explorations show that roughly half of some 2000 plant species found on top of the tepuis are endemic – that is, they grow only there. This is about the highest percentage of endemic flora found anywhere in the world.

Salto Yuruaní (km 247) is a wonderful mini-Niagara, about 6m high and 60m wide, with an unusual water coloration reminiscent of beer. **Quebrada de Jaspe** (km 273) is a small cascade made particularly beautiful by the red jasper rock of the creek bed.

The star attraction is probably the 105m **Salto Aponguao**, also known by its Pemón name, Chinak Merú. This one is harder to get to, as it's about 40km off the highway, near the small Pemón hamlet of Iboribó, accessible by a rough road.

Make sure you bring plenty of good insect repellent. The Sabana is infested by small gnats known as jejenes. They are particularly voracious in the morning and late afternoon, and the bites itch for days.

Sleeping & Eating

Simple accommodations and meals are available in a number of places throughout the Gran Sabana, including Kavanayén, Chivatón, Iboribó, Rápidos de Kamoirán (km 172), Salto Kamá (km 202), Quebrada Pacheco (km 237) and San Francisco de Yuruaní (km 250). You can camp virtually anywhere you wish.

Getting Around

The Ciudad Guayana–Santa Elena de Uairén Hwy provides access to this fascinating land, but public transport on this road is infrequent, making individual sightseeing inconvenient and time consuming. A comfortable solution is a tour from Ciudad Bolívar (p1001) or Santa Elena de Uairén (p1012).

RORAIMA

With its plateau at about 2700m, Roraima, on the tripartite border of Venezuela, Guyana and Brazil, is one of the highest tepuis. It was the first of the tepuis on which a climb was recorded (in 1884) and has been much explored by botanists. It's also the easiest table mountain to ascend and is popular among travelers. The climb can be done by anyone reasonably fit and healthy, yet it's a long and strenuous hike. Five days is a minimum for the Roraima trip, and you'll need camping equipment and food.

Dry season is from January to April, but the top of the tepui receives year-round rain off the Atlantic. Weather can change in a matter of minutes, with bright sunshine or heavy rain possible at any time.

A good tent, preferably with a zip, is a must. It gets bitterly cold at night on the top, so bring a good sleeping bag and warm clothes. You also need reliable rain gear, sturdy shoes, a cooking stove and the usual hiking equipment. Bring enough food to last you one or two days more than planned, just in case.

The top of Roraima is mercifully free of jejenes, but you'll have to deal with plenty of nasty biting gnats on the way, so take an effective insect repellent. Don't forget to bring a good supply of film. Make sure to bring along plastic bags to take all your garbage back down to civilization. Don't remove anything that belongs to the mountain – no plants, rocks or crystals. Searches are sometimes conducted on returning travelers, and those caught with crystals are subject to heavy fines.

Most travelers take a tour from Santa Elena de Uairén (see p1012), instead of organizing everything by themselves and only hiring a (compulsory) guide. Given fairly reasonable tour prices, the difference in cost between going solo and taking a tour may not be so drastic, and the advantages of a tour quite significant.

San Francisco de Yuruaní

This small village, 67km north of Santa Elena de Uairén by highway, is the starting point for the Roraima trip. There's nothing much to do here, except possibly arrange guides (US$25 a day per group) and porters (US$20 a day). Both guides and porters are easier to be hired (for much the same) in the village of Paraitepui, your next stop on the way to Roraima.

San Francisco has a few accommodation options along the main road near the bus stop (US$5 to US$10 per person). Food stalls at the Indian market and a few basic eateries will keep you going.

Paraitepui

Paraitepui is a nondescript Pemón village of about 250 people whose identity has been largely shattered by tourism. It's 26km east of San Francisco; to get there, hire a jeep in San Francisco (US$50 for up to eight passengers) or walk. The road to Paraitepui branches off the highway 1km south of San Francisco. It's a hot, steady, seven-hour walk, mostly uphill, to Paraitepui (back to San Francisco, it's six hours). You may be lucky enough to hitch a jeep ride on this road, but traffic is sporadic and drivers are likely to charge you for the lift.

Upon arrival at Paraitepui, you will be greeted by Inparques rangers, who will arrange a guide for you. Although you don't really need a guide to follow the track up to the *tepui*, you won't be allowed to continue without one. The village has no hotels or restaurants, but you can camp near the Inparques post.

Climbing Roraima

Once a guide has been arranged, you can set off for Roraima. The trip to the top normally takes two days; the total walking time is about 12 hours up and 10 hours down. There are several good places to camp (with water) on the way. The most popular campsites are on the Río Tek (four hours from Paraitepui), on the Río Kukenán

(30 minutes further on) and the so-called *campamento base* (base camp) at the foot of Roraima (three hours uphill from the Río Kukenán). The steep and tough four-hour ascent from the base camp to the top is the most spectacular (yet demanding) part of the hike.

Once you reach the top, you walk for 15 minutes to a place called El Hotel, one of the few sites good for camping. It's actually a patch of sand large enough for a few tents and partly protected by an overhanging rock. Half a dozen other 'hotels' are in the area.

The scenery all around is a dreamscape, evocative of a science-fiction movie: impressive blackened rocks of every imaginable shape, gorges, creeks, pink beaches and gardens filled with unique flowering plants. Frequent and constantly changing mist and fog add to the mysterious air.

It's here that the guide finally becomes handy, as it's very easy to get lost on the vast plateau. Your guide will take you to some of the attractions, including El Foso, an intriguing round pool in a deep rocky hole. It's a three-hour walk north from El Hotel. On the way, you'll pass by the amazingly lush Valle Arabopo. Beyond the pool are the Valle de los Cristales and the Laberinto. Another fascinating area is the southwestern part of Roraima, where attractions include La Ventana (Window), El Abismo (Abyss) and La Piscina (Swimming Pool). Plan on staying at least two days on the top.

Getting There & Away

San Francisco de Yuruaní is on the Ciudad Guayana–Santa Elena Hwy, eight buses a day run in either direction.

SANTA ELENA DE UAIRÉN

Santa Elena is a pleasant, easygoing border town of 20,000 people, with an agreeable, if damp, climate. Its Brazilian flavor is thanks to the significant number of residents from across the border.

Founded in 1924, Santa Elena began to grow when diamonds were discovered in the 1930s in the Icabarú region, 115km to the west. However, since the village was isolated from the center of the country by a lack of roads, it remained small. The second development push came with the opening of the highway from El Dorado.

Information

Internet facilities in Santa Elena include **Globalstar** (Calle Urdaneta), **Ramiprint** (Calle Bolívar) and **detodo.com** (Calle Lucas Fernández Peña).

Banco Industrial de Venezuela (Calle Bolívar) gives cash advances on Visa, but not on Master-Card. US dollars can easily be exchanged with the moneychangers who hang around the corner of Calle Bolívar and Calle Urda-neta, popularly known as Cuatro Esquinas. There are a couple of *casas de cambio* on the same corner, which may cash traveler's checks, albeit at a poor rate. If you're heading south for Brazil, get rid of all your bolívares in Santa Elena and buy Brazilian currency (from the moneychangers).

There's no tourist office, but try one of the tour operators.

Both Venezuelan and Brazilian passport formalities are now processed at the border itself, locally known as La Línea, 15km south of Santa Elena. Be sure to have your passport stamped upon leaving or entering Venezuela. The Brazilian consulate (p1018) is opposite the petrol station. If you want to play it safe, get your visa beforehand – the

nearest Brazilian consulate before Santa Elena is in Ciudad Guayana. A yellow-fever vaccination certificate is likely to be required before you're issued with a visa.

Tours

Santa Elena has about a dozen tour agencies. Their staples are one-, two- or three-day jeep tours around the Gran Sabana, with visits to the most interesting sights. Count on roughly US$25 per person per day in a group of four or more. This price includes transportation and a guide, but no accommodations or food. However, tours normally stop in budget places to stay and eat.

Another local specialty is the Roraima tour, which is normally offered as an all-inclusive six-day package for US$120 to US$300. The operators who organize this tour usually also rent out camping equipment and can provide transportation to Paraitepui, the starting point for the Roraima trek, for US$60 to US$80 per jeep each way (up to six people).

Some operators may offer tours to the El Pauji area, noted for some natural attractions

SANTA ELENA DE UAIRÉN

0 — 200 m
0 — 0.1 mi

To New Bus Terminal (2km), Ciudad Guayana (603km) & Ciudad Bolívar (718km) →

Av Mariscal Sucre

Calle Bolívar

Calle Roscio

Av Perimetral

Calle Urdaneta

Calle Lucas Fernández Peña

Calle Zea

Calle Icabarú

Av Perimetral

Plaza Bolívar

Capilla de San Francisco

To Airport (7km) & Boa Vista (Brazil) (238km)

INFORMATION	
Banco Industrial de Venezuela	1 A2
Brazilian Consulate	2 C1
detodo.com	3 B3
Globalstar	4 B2
Moneychangers	5 A2
Ramiprint	6 A2

SIGHTS & ACTIVITIES	pp1012–13
Kamadac	7 C2
Mystic Tours	8 B2
New Frontiers Adventure Tours	9 C2
Ruta Salvaje Tours	10 C1

SLEEPING		
		p1013
Hotel Augusta	11 A2
Hotel Lucrecia	12 C2
Hotel Michelle	13 C2
Hotel Panzarelli	14 A2
La Casa de Gladys	15 B2
Posada Michelle	(see 13)

EATING		
		p1013
Pollo Asado La Dorada	16 B3
Restaurant Mi Casa	17 B3
Restaurant Michelle	(see 13)
Restaurant Nova Opção Sucursal I	18 A2
Restaurant Nova Opção	19 A3
Restaurant Oriental	20 A3

TRANSPORT	
	p1013
Old Bus Terminal	21 C1

and gold and diamond mines. These are usually two-day trips, with prices and conditions similar to those of the Gran Sabana tours.

Popular local tour companies include:

Kamadac (☎ 0289-995-1408; www.abenteuer-venezuela .de; Calle Urdaneta) German-run agency offering popular tours to Gran Sabana and Roraima, as well as some more adventurous projects.

Mystic Tours (☎ 0414-886-1055; www.mystictours .com.ve; Calle Urdaneta) Good tours to Roraima at some of the lowest prices. Also, one of the few operators that offers El Pauji tours.

New Frontiers Adventure Tours (☎ 0289-995-1584; www.newfrontiersadventures.com; Calle Urdaneta) Specialist in trekking tours, including trips to the top of Roraima, with experienced guides and good equipment.

Ruta Salvaje Tours (☎ 0289-995-1134; www.geocities .com/rutagransabana; Av Mariscal Sucre) Reliable all-round company. Tours include Gran Sabana and Roraima. Also rafting day trips, and kayak and bicycle rental.

Sleeping

Santa Elena has no shortage of accommodations. It's easy to find a room, except perhaps in mid-August, when the town celebrates the feast of its patron saint. Hotel rooms come with fan and private bath.

La Casa de Gladys (☎ 0289-995-1171; Calle Urdaneta; d/tr with bath US$9/11) Popular travelers' lodge. Gladys provides laundry facilities and offers tours, and guests can use the kitchen and fridge.

Posada Michelle (☎ 0289-995-1415; Calle Urdaneta: s/d/tr with bath US$4/7/10) Brand-new place offering eight neat rooms.

Hotel Michelle (☎ 0289-995-1415; Calle Urdaneta: s/d/tr with bath US$6/11/15) Next door to the *posada*, this marginally better hotel is administered by the same manager.

Hotel Panzarelli (☎ 0289-995-1196; Calle Bolívar; d with bath US$8) Clean spacious rooms at good prices.

Hotel Augusta (☎ 0289-995-1654; Calle Bolívar; d with bath US$7) Pleasant 17-room hotel with fair-sized rooms. Good value.

Hotel Lucrecia (☎ 0289-995-1130; Av Perimetral; d/tr with bath US$18/22; 🏊) Charming old-style house with a lovely patio and air-con rooms.

Eating

The central streets are full of inexpensive eateries.

Restaurant Mi Casa (Calle Lucas Fernández Peña; meals US$1.50-2.50) Home-cooked meals at bargain prices.

Pollo Asado La Dorada (Calle Zea) The place for savory, cheap chicken.

Restaurant Nova Opção (Plaza Bolívar; meals US$2-3) Brazilian self-service budget eatery selling food (chicken, beef, potatoes, rice etc) by weight, so you can choose what you want and how much you want.

Restaurant Nova Opção Sucursal I (Calle Urdaneta; meals US$2-3) New outlet of the above, but with a traditional restaurant menu.

Restaurant Michelle (Calle Urdaneta; mains US$2-4) Pretty authentic and tasty Chinese food.

Restaurant Oriental (Calle Roscio; mains US$2-4) A Chinese affair particularly good for vegetarian dishes.

Getting There & Away

AIR

The airport is 7km southwest of town, off the road to the border. There's no public transport; a taxi will cost around US$4. Rutaca has daily flights on five-seater Cessnas to Ciudad Bolívar (US$80), via Canaima (US$70).

BUS

Santa Elena has a new bus terminal, on the Ciudad Guayana highway about 2km east of the town center, though some bus companies still maintain their ticket offices at the old bus terminal near the corner of Av Mariscal Sucre and Av Perimetral.

Eight buses depart daily to Ciudad Bolívar (US$8 to US$10, nine to 11 hours), and they all pass through Ciudad Guayana. Two buses a day run to Boa Vista, Brazil (US$8, three to four hours). The road is now paved all the way. The bus calls at the Venezuelan and Brazilian immigration posts on the border for passport formalities.

AMAZONAS

Venezuela's southernmost state, Amazonas, covers an area of 175,000 sq km (one-fifth of the national territory), yet it holds, at most, only 1% of the country's population. Despite its name, most of the region lies in the Orinoco Basin, while the Amazon Basin takes up only the southwestern portion of the state. The two basins are linked by the unusual Brazo Casiquiare, a natural channel that sends a portion of the water from the Orinoco to Río Negro and down to the Amazon. The state boasts four large national parks that protect a good chunk of the region.

Amazonas is predominantly a thick rainforest crisscrossed by rivers and sparsely populated by a mosaic of indigenous communities. The current indigenous population, estimated at 40,000 (half of what it was in 1925), comprises three main groups – the Piaroa, Yanomami and Guajibo – and a number of smaller communities, among them the Yekuana (Maquiritare), Curripaco, Guarekena and Piapoco.

Puerto Ayacucho, at the northwestern tip of Amazonas, is the region's only town of significance, and is the main gateway and supply center for the entire state. It's also the chief transport hub, from where a couple of small regional airlines fly in light planes to the region's major settlements. Roads are scarce – most transport is by river or air. And since there's virtually no regular passenger-boat service on any stretch of any river, travel on your own here is difficult, if not impossible. Tour operators in Puerto Ayacucho have swiftly filled the gap and can take you just about everywhere – at a price, of course.

PUERTO AYACUCHO

Set on the middle reaches of the Orinoco, Puerto Ayacucho is the capital of Amazonas. It was founded in 1924, together with another port, Samariapo, 63km upriver. The two ports have been linked by road to bypass an unnavigable stretch of the Orinoco cut by a series of rapids.

For a long time, particularly during the oil boom, Amazonas was a forgotten territory, and the two ports were just obscure villages. The link between them was the only paved road in the whole region; connection to the rest of the country was by a rough track. Only in the late 1980s, when this track was improved and surfaced, did Puerto Ayacucho start to grow toward its present population of 75,000. The town is the main gateway to Venezuelan Amazonia and is a regional tourist center. It has a range of hotels and restaurants, and numerous tour operators. Puerto Ayacucho is also a transit point for travelers heading to/from Colombia.

Information

Internet facilities include **CANTV** (Av Río Negro), **Cibercafé Compuserv** (Calle Evelio Roa), **Cibercafé**

Maniack (Av Aguerrevere at Av Río Negro), **Windows PC** (in Centro Comercial Rapagna, Av Orinoco) and **El Navegante** (in Centro Comercial Maniglia, Av Orinoco).

Banesco (Av Orinoco) changes American Express traveler's checks and gives cash advances on Visa and MasterCard. **Banco de Venezuela** (Av Orinoco) and **Banco Provincial** (Calle La Guardia) only serve credit-card holders. Some tour agencies may change your dollars; all will happily accept them as payment for tours.

The tourist office, **Dirección de Turismo** (☎ 0248-521-0033; Plaza Bolívar; ⊙ 8am-noon & 2-5:30pm Mon-Fri), is in the building of the Gobernación (government offices).

You'll need to get your passport stamped at the office of **DIEX** (Av Aguerrevere; ⊙ 8am-noon & 1-5pm Mon-Fri) when leaving or entering Venezuela. It doesn't seem to keep to its opening hours very strictly.

Sights

Puerto Ayacucho is hot, but pleasantly shaded by luxuriant mango trees. The **Museo Etnológico de Amazonas** (Av Río Negro; admission free; ⊙ 8:30-11:30am & 2:30-6pm Tue-Fri, 9am-noon & 3:30-7pm Sat, 9am-1pm Sun) gives insight into the culture of regional indigenous groups, including the Piaroa, Guajibo, Yekuana and Yanomami.

The **Mercado Indígena**, held every morning (it's busiest from Thursday to Saturday) on the square opposite the museum, has indigenous crafts for sale. A few paces away is the **cathedral**, noted for its colorful interior.

Cerro Perico, southwest of the town center, provides views over the Río Orinoco and the town. Another hill, Cerro El Zamuro, commonly known as **El Mirador**, 1.5km south of the town center, overlooks the Raudales Atures, the spectacular rapids that block river navigation. The rapids are most impressive in the wet season, when the water is high.

There are some attractions near Puerto Ayacucho. The **Parque Tobogán de la Selva** is a popular weekend picnic area developed around a large, steeply inclined smooth rock with water running over it – a sort of natural slide. It's 30km south of town along the Samariapo road, then 6km off to the east. There's no direct transport to the park. Take a *por puesto* to Samariapo, get off at the turn-off and walk the remaining distance, or negotiate a taxi ride from Puerto Ayacucho.

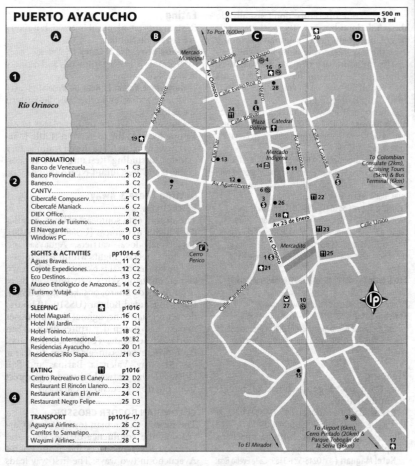

PUERTO AYACUCHO

0 — 500 m
0 — 0.3 mi

To Port (600m)

Río Orinoco

INFORMATION
Banco de Venezuela.....................1 C3
Banco Provincial..........................2 D2
Banesco.......................................3 C2
CANTV...4 C1
Cibercafé Compuserv...................5 C1
Cibercafé Maniack.......................6 C2
DIEX Office..................................7 B2
Dirección de Turismo....................8 C1
El Navegante...............................9 D4
Windows PC..............................10 C3

SIGHTS & ACTIVITIES   pp1014–6
Aguas Bravas.............................11 C2
Coyote Expediciones..................12 C2
Eco Destinos..............................13 C2
Museo Etnológico de Amazonas..14 C2
Turismo Yutajé...........................15 C4

SLEEPING   p1016
Hotel Maguarí............................16 C1
Hotel Mi Jardín..........................17 D4
Hotel Tonino..............................18 C2
Residencia Internacional.............19 B2
Residencias Ayacucho.................20 D1
Residencias Río Siapa.................21 C3

EATING   p1016
Centro Recreativo El Caney........22 D2
Restaurant El Rincón Llanero.......23 D2
Restaurant Karam El Amir...........24 C1
Restaurant Negro Felipe.............25 D3

TRANSPORT   pp1016–17
Aguaysa Airlines.........................26 C3
Carritos to Samariapo.................27 C3
Wayumi Airlines.........................28 C1

Mercado Municipal

Calle Atabapo
Av Orinoco
Calle Evelio Roa
Av Río Negro
Calle Bolívar
Plaza Bolívar
Catedral
Mercado Indígena
Av Aguerrevere
Av Amazonas
Calle La Guardia
Cerro Perico
Av 23 de Enero
Calle Unión
Mercadito
Av Orinoco
Calle Píar
Calle Luisa Cáceres
Calle Carabobo

To Colombian
Consulate (2km),
Cruising Tours
(5km) & Bus
Terminal (6km)

To El Mirador

To Airport (6km),
Cerro Pintado (20km) &
Parque Tobogán de
la Selva (36km)

A lesser-known natural water slide lies further upriver.

Cerro Pintado is a large rock with pre-Columbian petroglyphs carved high above the ground in a virtually inaccessible place. It's 17km south of town and a few kilometers off the main road to the left. The best time to see the carvings is in the afternoon.

Tours

Operators have some standard tours, but most can arrange a tour according to your interests and time. Be sure to carry your passport and tourist card on all trips. If there's a serious discrepancy between what an agency promises and what it actually provides, complain to the tourist office and insist on having part of your money reimbursed.

Among the popular shorter tours are a three-day trip up the Río Cuao and a three-day trip up the Sipapo and Autana Rivers to the foot of Cerro Autana. Expect to pay US$30 to US$60 per person a day, all-inclusive.

The Ruta Humboldt, following the route of the great explorer, is a longer and more adventurous trip. It goes along the Orinoco, Casiquiare and Guainía Rivers up to Maroa. From there, the boat is transported overland to Yavita, and you then return down the Atabapo and Orinoco to Puerto Ayacucho. This trip takes 10 to 14 days and will cost you around US$60 to US$90 per person per day. Tour operators don't usually do the whole loop but only its most attractive fragments, including Casiquiare, skipping over the less interesting parts by plane.

The far southeastern part of Amazonas, where the Yanomami live, is a restricted area requiring special permits that are virtually impossible to get.

Tour operators worth checking include:

Aguas Bravas (☎ 0248-521-0541; aguasbravas@cantv .net; Av Río Negro) Three-hour-long rafting trips over the Atures rapids (US$35).

Coyote Expediciones (☎ 0248-521-4583; coyotexpe dition@cantv.net; Av Aguerrevere) A company popular with travelers. Its main offerings are three-day Autana and Cuao tours, but it also runs longer trips.

Cruising Tours (☎ 0416-785-5033; cruisingtours@ hotmail.com; Valle Verde Triángulo) One-man agency run by a friendly German Axel, who has lived in the region for over 20 years, offers diverse tours and expeditions in the region and beyond at reasonable prices (from US$30 a day).

Eco Destinos (☎ 0248-521-3964; ecodestinosvzla@ hotmail.com; Calle Piar) Roughly similar tour offer as Coyote Expediciones, which often work jointly.

Turismo Yutajé (☎ 0248-521-0664; turismoama zonas@cantv.net; Barrio Monte Bello) One of the longest-running companies, with good experience and low tour prices.

Sleeping

The town has a good choice of budget accommodations.

Residencia Internacional (☎ 0248-521-0242; Av Aguerrevere; d with bath & fan/air-con US$10/14; ⚡) The most popular choice with backpackers. Simple, pleasant, friendly.

Hotel Maguarí (☎ 0248-521-3189; Calle Evelio Roa; d with bath & fan/air-con US$8/12; ⚡) Central and cheap but nothing special.

Residencias Ayacucho (Calle Atabapo; d/tr with bath US$5/6) Something for those who always hunt for the cheapest place in town regardless of the quality. Super basic.

Hotel Tonino (☎ 0248-521-1464; Av 23 de Enero; d/tr with bath & air-con US$12/14; ⚡) Clean ample rooms at very central location.

Residencias Río Siapa (☎ 0248-521-0138; Calle Carabobo; d/tr with bath & air-con US$12/14; ⚡) A reasonable central place, even more pleasant and tranquil than the Tonino.

Hotel Mi Jardín (☎ 0248-521-4647; Av Orinoco; d/tr with bath & air-con US$15/18; ⚡) South of the town center, with rooms arranged around a central patio-garden.

Eating

Restaurants are plentiful in town, but many are closed on Sunday.

Centro Recreativo El Caney (Av Amazonas; meals US$2) Simple breakfasts, lunches and dinners at rock-bottom prices.

Restaurant Karam El Amir (Av Orinoco) Hearty falafel, schwarma and other Middle-Eastern specialties.

One of the favorite budget places to eat among locals is the Mercadito (Little Market), which boasts half a dozen rudimentary eateries, including Restaurant El Rincón Llanero and Restaurant Negro Felipe.

Getting There & Away
VENEZUELA

The airport, 6km southeast of town, handles daily flights to Caracas (US$80 to US$100). Two small local carriers, Aguaysa and Wayumi, operate flights within Amazonas.

The bus terminal is 6km east of the town center, on its outskirts. City buses go there from Av 23 de Enero, or take a taxi (US$2). Buses to Ciudad Bolívar (US$10, 10 hours) depart regularly throughout the day. Buses make a half-dozen departures daily to San Fernando de Apure (US$8, seven hours), from where you can get buses to Caracas, Maracay, Valencia, Barinas and San Cristóbal. One or two buses a day go direct from Puerto Ayacucho to Caracas.

COLOMBIAN BORDER CROSSING

The nearest Colombian town, Puerto Carreño, at the confluence of the Meta and Orinoco Rivers, is accessible from Puerto Ayacucho in two ways. The first way leads via Casuarito, a Colombian hamlet right across the Orinoco from Puerto Ayacucho. A boat between Puerto Ayacucho's port (at the northwestern end of town) and Casuarito shuttles regularly throughout the day (US$1). From Casuarito, the *voladora* (high-speed boat) goes once daily to Puerto Carreño (US$7, one hour). In the dry season (December to April), there may also be some jeeps between Casuarito and Puerto Carreño.

The other way goes via Puerto Páez, a Venezuelan village 95km north of Puerto Ayacucho. Get there by San Fernando bus (US$2, two hours); the trip includes a ferry crossing of the Orinoco from El Burro to Puerto Páez. Take a boat from the village's wharf across the Río Meta to Puerto Carreño (US$1); it runs regularly during the day. Whichever way you go, remember to get an exit stamp in your passport at DIEX in Puerto Ayacucho before setting off.

Puerto Carreño is a long, one-street town with an airport, a half-dozen budget hotels and a number of places to eat. Go to the DAS office, one block west of the main square, for an entry stamp in your passport. A number of shops will change bolívares to pesos.

There are two flights per week to Bogotá (US$105) from Puerto Careño. Buses go only in the dry season, roughly from mid-December to mid-March. They depart once a week for the two-day journey by rough road to Villavicencio (US$60), which is four hours by bus from Bogotá. Bus travel is not recommended because the bus route goes through the areas where guerrillas are present.

VENEZUELA DIRECTORY

ACCOMMODATIONS

Venezuela has heaps of hotels for every budget and it's usually easy to find a room, except perhaps on major feast days. With some exceptions, low-budget hotels are uninspiring and styleless, but most do have rooms with private toilet and shower (simply called baths in this chapter). As most of the country lies in the lowland tropics, rooms have either fan or air-con, but there's no hot water. Always have a look at the room and check the fan or air-con before you book in and pay.

An interesting kind of budget accommodation is the *posada*, a small, family-run guest house. They have mushroomed in the cities and countryside over past decades. They often, but not always, have more character and offer more personalized attention than other budget lodgings.

Few budget hotels or *posadas* have single rooms but many have *matrimoniales*, rooms with a double bed intended for couples. These rooms usually cost much the same for one as for two, so traveling as a couple significantly reduces the cost of accommodation. Single travelers are at a disadvantage. By and large, expect to pay roughly US$5 to US$10 per single or couple, and US$7 to US$15 per double. A double has two single beds.

Many cheap hotels double as love hotels (places that rent rooms by the hour), and it's often impossible to avoid staying in one from time to time.

Venezuela has no youth hostels. Camp sites, as the term is understood in the West, are virtually nonexistent, but you can camp rough in the countryside. Camping on the beach is popular, but be cautious and don't leave your tent unattended.

Over the past decades, places to stay called *campamentos* (literally, 'camps') have multiplied throughout the countryside. Not to be confused with camp sites, *campamentos* can be anything from rustic shelters with a few hammocks to posh country lodges with swimming pools. They usually provide accommodation, food and often also tours, sometimes selling these services as all-inclusive packages.

ACTIVITIES

Venezuela's national parks provide good opportunities for walking, ranging from easy, well-signposted trails to wild jungle paths. Sierra Nevada de Mérida (p980) is the country's best region for high-mountain trekking; if you're up to it, you can also try mountaineering there. The Mérida region is also Venezuela's main center for mountain biking, paragliding, rafting and canyoning. Coincidentally, Mérida is also the best place to arrange safari-like trips to Los Llanos (p981), noted for its rich and diverse wildlife.

Some national parks, such as Henri Pittier (p966) are good for bird-watching. Others, including Mochima (p987) and Archipiélago Los Roques (p962), have coral reefs, providing good conditions for snorkeling and scuba diving. Other possible activities in Venezuela include sailing, fishing and caving, to name just a few.

BOOKS

For more detailed travel information, get a copy of Lonely Planet's *Venezuela*. Of the useful local publications, *Ecotourism Guide to Venezuela* by Miro Popic is a bilingual Spanish/English guidebook focusing on ecological tourism, while *Guide to Camps, Posadas and Cabins in Venezuela* by Elizabeth Kline is a bilingual edition detailing 1200 mostly rural accommodation options. Both are updated yearly.

A captivating overview of the Spanish colonization period is provided by John Hemming's *The Search for El Dorado*. *In Focus: Venezuela – A Guide to the People, Politics and Culture* by James Ferguson is a good, concise introduction to the country. *Venezuela: the Search for Order, the Dream of Progress* by John V Lombardi provides general reading on history, politics, geography and people.

For 20th-century history, try *Venezuela: a Century of Change* by Judith Ewell or *Venezuela, Politics in a Petroleum Republic* by David Eugene Blank.

Travelers with a serious interest in bird-watching may want to check *A Guide to the Birds of Venezuela* by Rodolphe Meyer de Schauensee and William H Phelps. *Birding in Venezuela* by Mary Lou Goodwin is also a good reference.

BUSINESS HOURS

The working day is theoretically eight hours, from 8am to noon and 2pm to 6pm, Monday to Friday. Most offices, including tourist offices, are closed on Saturday and Sunday. Banks are normally open from 8:30am to 11:30am and 2pm to 4:30pm Monday to Friday, but in some major cities they're open 8:30am to 3:30pm without a lunch break.

Usual shopping hours are 9am to 6pm or 7pm weekdays, and a half-day in the morning on Saturday. Many shops close for lunch but some work the *horario corrido*, ie, without a lunch break. Many restaurants are closed on Sunday. Most museums are open on Sunday but closed Monday.

CLIMATE

Venezuela's climate features dry and wet seasons, though the tourist season runs year-round. The dry season runs roughly from December to April, while the wet season lasts the rest of the year. The dry season is more pleasant for traveling, but some sights – such as waterfalls – are more impressive in the wet season. There are many regional variations in the amount of rainfall and the length of the seasons.

For more information and climate charts, see the South America Directory (p1025).

CUSTOMS

Customs regulations are not that much different from those in other South Ameri-can countries. You are allowed to bring in personal belongings and presents that you intend to give to Venezuelan residents. You can bring cameras (still, video and movie), camping equipment, sports accessories, a personal computer and the like without problems.

According to Venezuelan law, possession, trafficking and the consumption of drugs are all serious offenses subject to heavy penalties. You would be crazy to try smuggling drugs across the border.

DANGERS & ANNOYANCES

Venezuela is a relatively safe country, though robbery is becoming a problem. Common crime is increasing in the large cities; Caracas is by far the most dangerous place in the country, and you should take care while strolling the streets, particularly at night. Venturing into poor shantytowns is asking for trouble.

When traveling around the country, there are plenty of *alcabalas* (checkpoints), though not all are actually operating. They check the identity documents of passengers, and occasionally the luggage as well. In cities, police checks are uncommon, but they do occur, so always have your passport with you. If you don't, you may end up at the police station.

Some travelers have commented on the risks of using ATMs. In some cases cards were swallowed by the machine. In others, the card came out but not the requested money. Back at home, they discovered that their home bank statement featured records of the withdrawals. We've also had some reports about muggers targeting ATM users in Caracas; they simply watch the machine discreetly and then approach the victims, robbing them of their freshly withdrawn cash and the card in one go.

DISABLED TRAVELERS

Sadly, Venezuela offers almost no facilities to disabled travelers. Wheelchair-accessible toilets and ramps are virtually nonexistent, and public transport is not adapted for people with mobility limitations.

EMBASSIES & CONSULATES
Embassies & Consulates in Venezuela
Australia Caracas (☎ 0212-263-4033; Av Francisco de Miranda con Av Sur Altamira, Altamira)

Brazil Caracas (☎ 0212-261-5505; Centro Gerencial Mohedano, Av Mohedano con Calle Los Chaguaramos, La Castellana); Puerto Ordaz (☎ 0286-923-5243; Edificio Amazonas, Av Las Américas); Santa Elena de Uairén (Av Mariscal Sucre; ⏰ 8am-noon Mon-Fri)

Canada Caracas (☎ 0212-264-0833; Av Francisco de Miranda con Av Sur Altamira, Altamira)

Colombia Caracas (☎ 0212-951-3631; Edificio Consulado de Colombia, Calle Guaicaipuro, Chacaíto); Puerto Ayacucho (☎ 0248-521-0789; Calle Yapacana near Av Rómulo Gallegos)

France Caracas (☎ 0212-909-6500; Edificio Embajada de Francia, Calle Madrid con Av Trinidad, Las Mercedes)

Germany Caracas (☎ 0212-261 01 81; Edificio Pan-american, Piso 2, Av San Juan Bosco con 3a Transversal, Altamira)

Guyana Caracas (☎ 0212-977-1158; Quinta Roraima, Av El Paseo, Prados del Este)

Trinidad & Tobago Caracas (☎ 0212-261-5796; Quinta Serrana, 4a Av entre 7a y 8a Transversales, Altamira)

UK Caracas (☎ 0212-263-8411; Torre La Castellana, Piso 11, Av Principal La Castellana, La Castellana)

USA Caracas (☎ 0212-975-6411; Calle F con Calle Suapure, Colinas del Valle Arriba)

Venezuelan Embassies & Consulates Abroad

Venezuela has embassies and consulates in neighboring countries and also in the following:

Australia (☎ 02-6290 2967; 5 Culgoa Circuit, O'Malley, Isaacs, ACT 2606)

Canada (☎ 613-235-5151; 32 Range Rd, Ottawa, Ontario K1N 8J4)

France (☎ 01-45 53 29 98; 11 Rue Copernic, 75116 Paris)

UK (☎ 020-7581 2776; 1 Cromwell Rd, London SW7 2HW)

USA (☎ 202-342-2214; 1099 30th St NW, Washington, DC 20007)

FESTIVALS & EVENTS

Given the strong Catholic character of Venezuela, a good number of feasts and celebrations follow the Church calendar. Possibly the biggest event celebrated throughout the country is **Carnaval**, which takes place on the Monday and Tuesday prior to Ash Wednesday, although feasting breaks out by the end of the preceding week.

One of Venezuela's most colorful events is the **Diablos Danzantes** (Dancing Devils). It's held on Corpus Christi in San Francisco de Yare, about 70km southeast of Caracas. The ceremony consists of a spectacular parade and the dance of devils, performed by dancers in elaborate masks and costumes.

FOOD & DRINK

On the whole, food is good and relatively inexpensive. Various local dishes, international cuisine and an array of Western fast foods are available. Spanish and Italian restaurants are well represented, thanks to a sizable immigrant population from those two countries. The major cities also hold some good Chinese and Middle-Eastern restaurants. Gourmands will enjoy their stay in Caracas, which offers the country's widest range of eating establishments and international cuisines.

Budget travelers should look for restaurants that offer a *menú del día* or *menu ejecutivo*, a set meal consisting of soup and a main course. It will cost roughly US$3 to US$5 (a little more in Caracas), which is cheaper than any à-la-carte dish. A budget alternative might be spit-roasted chicken, usually called *pollo en brasas*. Or just grab an *arepa*, a wonderful local snack. For more information see Venezuelan Cuisine below.

As in most of South America, markets are a good cheap option, offering usually tasty and fresh local food. For breakfast, visit any of the ubiquitous *panaderías* (bakeries), which serve sandwiches, croissants, pastries and a variety of snacks, plus delicious espresso.

In almost every dining or drinking establishment, a 10% service charge will automatically be added to the bill. In budget eateries, tipping is uncommon, but it's customary to leave a small tip at upmarket places.

Venezuelan Cuisine

The following list includes some of the most typical Venezuelan snacks and dishes:

Arepa Small grilled maize pancake stuffed with cheese, beef, ham, sausage, octopus, shrimp, eggs, salad or just about anything you might think of. *Arepas* cost about US$1 to US$2 and are served in snack bars called *arepera*s.

Cachapa Round juicy pancake made of fresh corn, usually served with cheese and/or ham.

Cachito Croissant filled with chopped ham and served hot.

Hallaca Maize dough with chopped pork, beef or chicken with vegetables and olives, wrapped in banana leaves and steamed; particularly popular during Christmas.

Mondongo Seasoned tripe cooked in bouillon with maize, potatoes, carrots and other vegetables.

Muchacho Roasted beef served in sauce.

Pabellón Main course consisting of shredded beef, rice, beans and fried plantain; it's Venezuela's national dish.

Sancocho Vegetable stew with fish, meat or chicken.

Drinks

Espresso coffee is strong and good in Venezuela. Ask for *café negro* if you want it black; *café marrón* if you prefer half coffee, half milk; or *café con leche* if you like milkier coffee.

Fruit juices are readily available in restaurants, *fuentes de soda* (soda fountains), *fruterías*, *refresquerías* and other eating outlets. Given the variety of fruit in the country, you have quite a choice. Juices come as *batidos* (pure or watered down) or as *merengadas* (milk shakes).

The number-one alcoholic drink is *cerveza* (beer), particularly Polar beer, the dominant brand. It's sold everywhere in cans or small bottles at close to freezing temperature. Among spirits, *ron* (rum) heads the list and comes in numerous varieties and qualities.

GAY & LESBIAN TRAVELERS

Check local gay website www.republicagay.com. Caracas has the largest gay and lesbian community and the most open gay life. See the Caracas section (p960). The city's contact links include **Movimiento Ambiente de Venezuela** (☎ 0212-321-9470) and the gay 'what's on' guide **En Ambiente** (☎ 0414-219-1837; enambiente@latinmail.com).

HEALTH

Venezuela has a wide array of pharmacies, private clinics and hospitals, but health services have deteriorated over the past decade due to the disastrous economic situation. Be sure to have a good health-insurance policy to cover an emergency flight home or to the USA if something goes terribly wrong. If you need hospital treatment in Venezuela, by far the best facilities are in Caracas.

Avoid drinking tap water – a fairly easy task as bottled water and soft drinks are sold everywhere.

See the Health chapter (p1053) for more information.

HOLIDAYS

Keep in mind that Venezuelans usually take holidays over Christmas, Carnaval (several days prior to Ash Wednesday) and Holy Week (the week before Easter Sunday). In these periods, you'll have to plan ahead and do more legwork to find a place to stay, but it may be worth it – these times are colorful and alive with a host of festivities. Official public holidays include:

Año Nuevo (New Year's Day; January 1)
Carnaval (February/March– dates vary)
Jueves Santo/Viernes Santo (Maundy Thursday/Good Friday; March/April – dates vary)
Declaración de la Independencia (Declaration of Independence; April 19)
Día del Trabajo (Labor Day; May 1)
Batalla de Carabobo (Battle of Carabobo; June 24)
Día de la Independencia (Independence Day; July 5)
Nacimiento de Bolívar (Bolívar's birthday; July 24)
Día de la Raza (Discovery of America; October 12)
Navidad (Christmas Day; December 25)

INTERNET ACCESS

Virtually all cities and most towns have cyber-cafés. An hour of Internet access will cost between US$0.50 and US$2, depending on the region, city and particular place. Mérida has some of the cheapest facilities.

INTERNET RESOURCES

Some useful websites for information on Venezuela include:

www.think-venezuela.net General information on Venezuela, including politics, geography, economy, culture, education and national parks.

www.venezuelavirtual.com Spanish-language site with lots of background information for travelers (history, tourist destinations, news etc).

www.latinworld.com/sur/venezuela Useful directory with links to English- and Spanish-language sites. Categories include arts, traditions, travel, sports and books.

www.lanic.utexas.edu/la/venezuela Impressive directory of Venezuelan websites provided by the Latin American Network Information Center of the University of Texas.

www.auyantepuy.com Another good directory for Venezuelan websites.

www.internet.ve/wildlife Site focusing on eco-tourism and adventure trips.

www.venezuelavoyage.com Travel-focused website created by a journalist and photographer. Worth visiting.

www.onlinenewspapers.com/venezuel.htm Links to at least 30 Venezuelan online newspapers.

www.zmag.org/venezuela_watch.htm Website containing articles analyzing the current political and economic issues from a pro-government perspective.

fossil.energy.gov/international/venzover.html All you wanted to know about petrol in Venezuela...only for petrol heads.

MAPS

The best general map of Venezuela (scale 1:1,750,000) is published by International

Travel Maps (Canada). Within Venezuela, folded road maps of the country are produced by several local publishers.

For large-scale regional maps, contact the Caracas-based state map publisher, **Servicio Autónomo de Geografía y Cartografía Nacional** (☎ 0212-408-1115; Calle Este 6, Colón a Dr Díaz).

MEDIA
Newspapers & Magazines
All major cities have daily newspapers. The two leading Caracas papers, *El Universal* and *El Nacional*, have countrywide distribution. Both have reasonable coverage of national and international affairs, sports, economics and culture. The *Daily Journal* is the main English-language newspaper published in Venezuela. It's available at major newsstands and select bookshops in Caracas. Elsewhere in Venezuela, it can be difficult to find.

Radio & TV
Most of Venezuela's numerous radio stations are dominated by musical programs, principally Latin music, imported pop, rock, disco and the like. Jazz and classical music are less popular but some stations do grant them airtime.

Two government and three private TV stations operate out of Caracas and reach most of the country. They all offer the usual TV fare, including newscasts, music, feature films, sports and culture. Prime-time hours are dominated by *telenovelas* (soap operas), some of which can literally paralyze the country when the drama reaches its peak. Venezuela is one of Latin America's major producers and exporters of this genre. All programming is in Spanish, including foreign films, which are dubbed.

Several pay-TV providers, including Cablevisión, Supercable, Intercable and DirecTV, offer mixed Spanish/English packages of feature films, sports, music, soap operas and news.

MONEY
ATMs
ATMs *(cajeros automáticos)* are the easiest way of getting cash. They can be found at most major banks, including Banesco, Banco de Venezuela, Banco Provincial and Banco Mercantil (we've marked these banks on the maps in this chapter). Many ATMs are linked to Cirrus and Plus and

---

PRICE WARNING
Venezuela is in the most profound economic crisis in living memory. State-imposed restrictions on exporting and importing foreign currency and the introduction of currency exchange control (which doesn't represent the actual value of the local currency) have contributed greatly to the financial chaos. This makes prices of goods and services volatile, and the changes unpredictable. As such, the prices listed in this chapter are particularly vulnerable to change, probably more so than elsewhere on the continent. They should be regarded as guidelines and pointers only.

---

accept international Visa and MasterCard. Advances are in bolívares.

Bargaining
As in most Latin American countries, bargaining in Venezuela is part of everyday life. Since part of the economy is informal, quasi-legal or uncontrolled, prices for some goods and services, including products purchased at the market, taxi fares, rates in some budget hotels or even bus and *por puesto* fares, are to some extent negotiable.

Black Market
Early in 2003, the Chávez' government introduced restrictions on importing and exporting currency, and fixed the exchange rate of the local currency against the US dollar (US$1 = Bs 1595). Predictably, the move sparked the appearance of the black market, where the US dollar buys up to 70% more bolívares than it does at the official rate. Visitors coming with cash dollars and changing them on the black market can take advantage of this, but should be very careful as high fines are likely to be introduced. Check if the exchange controls still apply before arriving. They have been introduced several times in the past in Venezuela, but never worked. The government was always forced to abolish the controls, and then faced the inevitable hyper-inflation.

Credit Cards
Visa and MasterCard are the most useful credit cards in Venezuela. Both are widely accepted as a means of payment for goods and

VENEZUELA

services (though many tour operators may refuse payment by credit card or charge 10% more for the service). They are also useful for taking cash advances from the banks, either from the bank's ATM or from the cashier.

Currency

The unit of currency is the bolívar, abbreviated to Bs. There are 50-, 100- and 500-bolívar coins, and paper notes of 1000, 2000, 5000, 10,000, 20,000 and 50,000 bolívares. Two different kinds of notes in 1000, 2000, 5000 and 10,000 bolívares denominations are in circulation, and both are legal. Watch the notes carefully before you pay (and also those you receive) because some notes have similar colors and are easy to confuse.

Exchange Rates

Exchange rates at press time included the following:

Country	Unit		Bs (bolívar)
Australia	A$1	=	1144
Canada	C$1	=	1219
euro zone	€1	=	1841
Japan	¥1	=	1471
New Zealand	NZ$1	=	1000
United Kingdom	UK£1	=	2664
United States	US$1	=	1600

Exchanging Money

US dollars and American Express traveler's checks are the most popular and accepted in Venezuela, so try to stick to them. Theoretically, they can be exchanged in some banks, but very few banks handle foreign-exchange transactions these days. Corp Banca is likely to exchange American Express traveler's checks, while Unibanca and sometimes Banco de Venezuela may exchange your cash dollars. The picture changes from city to city and from bank to bank.

The *casas de cambio* (authorized money-exchange offices) are more likely to exchange your money, but may pay less and charge higher commission. The best-known *casa de cambio* is Italcambio, which has offices in most major cities and exchange both cash and traveler's checks.

POST

The postal service is run by Ipostel, which has post offices throughout the country. Airmailing a letter up to 20g costs US$0.50

to anywhere in the Americas, US$0.60 to Europe or Africa and US$0.80 to the rest of the world. Sending a package of up to 500g will cost US$6/8/12, respectively. Ipostel also handles poste restante.

RESPONSIBLE TRAVEL

Visiting a different culture can pose a great deal of challenges and you'll need to remind yourself how important it is to minimize the negative impact of your visit. Be sensitive to the needs and beliefs of the local people, and resist imposing your standards and way of life.

Also resist the temptation of stuffing your pockets and backpack with crystals, jasper or jade from the waterfalls and creeks of the Gran Sabana. Refrain from purchasing articles made from tropical shells, tortoises or corals, no matter how beautiful they'd look back at home. Don't even dream of the shoes you could make from the caiman leather you saw in the market. Avoid buying pre-Columbian pieces of art as they promote looting and destroy the cultural patrimony of the country.

Encourage and use truly ecological tourist companies and projects. Many tourist operators use the 'eco' label as a simple sales strategy – often as genuine as, say, an alcohol-free vodka would be. Find out what they do for the protection of the environment and the preservation of the traditional culture.

Use the memories of your trip to write a book, draw a picture, name a dish or simply tell a story to a friend who's never had the chance to experience another culture.

STUDYING

Venezuela has a number of language schools in most big cities. You can also find an independent teacher and arrange individual classes. Possibly the best place to learn Spanish is Mérida, which is an attractive city offering many activities and has plenty of language-teaching facilities (see p978). It's one of the cheapest places to learn Spanish in Venezuela.

TELEPHONE

The telephone system is operated by CANTV and is largely automated for both domestic and international connections. All phone numbers are seven-digits long countrywide, whereas area codes are three-digits long.

Public telephones exist in the cities and larger towns, though some are out of order. All public phones operate only on phone cards, not coins. It's worth buying a phone card *(tarjeta CANTV)* as soon as you arrive, unless you don't plan on using public phones at all. Cards come in denominations of 3000 and 5000 bolívares (US$1.90 and US$3.20, respectively). A three-minute local call costs about US$0.10. You can also phone from the public phones of Telcel, another telecommunications operator that has its own array of phones operating on its own phone cards *(tarjeta Telcel),* but it has far fewer phones than CANTV. Telcel is the major operator of cellular telephones (its numbers begin with ☎ 0414), followed by Mobilnet (☎ 0416) and Digitel (☎ 0412).

Long-distance and international calls can be made from public phones or from the offices of CANTV and Telcel. They are called Centro de Comunicaciones CANTV and Centro de Conexiones Telcel, respectively, and are easily found in cities. Most of them also offer Internet facilities.

Sample per-minute phone rates of CANTV/Telcel are US$0.35/0.20 to the USA, US$0.50/0.40 to the UK and US$0.80/0.80 to Australia. You can save using the Multiphone or Entel pre-paid phone cards, available from newsagents and some other businesses, but they can only be used from private phones. Also, some cybercafés provide cheap Internet phone calls. Finally, you can call reverse-charge (collect) to most countries.

The country code for Venezuela is ☎ 58. To call a number in Venezuela from abroad, dial the international access code of the country you're calling from, then Venezuela's code (☎ 58), the area code (drop the initial '0') and the local phone number.

TOILETS

Since there are no self-contained public toilets in Venezuela, use the toilets of the establishments that normally have them, such as restaurants, museums, shopping malls and bus terminals. Carry toilet paper with you at all times and throw it into the waste basket provided.

The most common word for toilet is *baño.* Men's toilets will usually bear a label reading *señores* or *caballeros,* whereas women's toilets will be marked *señoras* or *damas.*

TOURIST INFORMATION

Inatur (www.inatur.gov.ve) is the Caracas-based government agency that promotes tourism and provides tourist information. Outside the capital, tourist information is handled by regional tourist bodies that have offices in their respective state capitals and in some other cities. Some are better than others, but on the whole they lack city maps and brochures, and the staff members rarely speak English.

TOURS

Taking tours is the usual way to visit some of Venezuela's attractions, largely because vast areas of the country are virtually inaccessible by public transport (eg, the Orinoco Delta or Amazon Basin), or because a solitary visit to scattered sights in a large territory (eg, the Gran Sabana) may be more time-consuming and eventually more expensive than a tour.

Tours booked from abroad are expensive; you are likely to save a lot of money by arranging a tour in Venezuela. It's cheapest to arrange a tour from the regional center closest to the area you are going to visit. For hikes in the Andes, the place to look for a guide is Mérida; for excursions around the Gran Sabana, the cheapest organized trips are from Santa Elena de Uairén; for the Amazon Basin, book a tour in Puerto Ayacucho; and for tours to Salto Ángel, Ciudad Bolívar is the place to shop around. Information about local tour operators is included in relevant sections.

VISAS

Nationals of the USA, Canada, Australia, New Zealand, Japan, the UK, and most of Western and Scandinavian Europe don't need a visa to enter Venezuela; a free *tarjeta de ingreso* (tourist card) is all that's required. The card is normally valid for 90 days (unless immigration officers note a shorter period on the card) and can be extended. Airlines flying into Venezuela provide the cards to their passengers onboard the plane. Overland visitors bearing passports of the countries listed above can obtain the card from the immigration official at the border crossing (it's best to check this beforehand at the nearest consulate).

On entering Venezuela, your passport and tourist card will be stamped (make sure this happens) by Dirección de Identificación y Extranjería (DIEX or DEX) border officials. You may be asked to show an onward ticket, though that rarely happens these days.

Visa and tourist-card extensions are handled by the DIEX office in Caracas.

VOLUNTEERING

The options of voluntary work in Venezuela are currently virtually nonexistent.

WOMEN TRAVELERS

Like most of Latin America, Venezuela is very much a man's country. Women travelers will attract more curiosity, attention and advances from local men than they would from men in the West. Local males will quickly pick you out in a crowd and use a combination of body language and flirtatiousness to capture your attention. These advances may often be lighthearted but can sometimes be more direct and rude.

The best way to deal with unwanted attention is simply to ignore it. Dressing modestly may lessen the chances of you being the object of macho interest, or at least make you less conspicuous to the local peacocks. If you don't want added attention, don't follow the local style of dressing. Most Venezuelan women are dressed up and beautifully turned out – whether it's on the beach or on the bus. You can take it for granted they will wear lots of makeup, high heels and trendy, usually skintight clothes.

WORKING

Travelers looking for a paid job in Venezuela may be disappointed. The economic situation is a mess, unemployment is around 20% and over three-quarters of the population live in poverty. Qualified English teachers have perhaps the best chance of getting a job, yet it's not that easy. Try English-teaching institutions such as the British Council, private-language schools or linguistic departments at universities. Note that you need a work visa to work legally in Venezuela.

South America Directory

This directory provides general information on South America, from activities and books to toilets and telephones. Specific information for each country is listed in the Directory sections at the end of each country chapter.

ACCOMMODATIONS

Obviously there are many more places to stay in South America than we're able to include in this book, but we've visited most of them and included those we think are the best. Throughout the book's Sleeping sections, we list accommodations in order of our preference – the best value in the best location comes first. For those nights when the thought of another cold, shared shower and a hard, over-used bed is enough to make you toss in your pack, we've also included our favorite splurges – places where an extra $20 or so will get you a nurturing night in a comfy hotel.

Accommodation costs vary greatly from country to country, with Andean countries (especially Bolivia) being the cheapest (from as little as US$2 per night) and Chile, Brazil and the Guianas the costliest (more than US$30).

Camping

Camping is an obvious choice in parks and reserves and a useful budget option in the pricier countries of southern South America. In Andean countries, there are few organized campgrounds. In Argentina, Chile, Uruguay and parts of Brazil, however, camping holidays have long been popular. It's better to bring your own equipment than to buy locally. Camping gear can be rented in areas with substantial camping and trekking action (eg the Lake District, Mendoza and Huaraz). Another option is staying in *refugios* (simple structures within parks and reserves), where a basic bed and kitchen access are usually provided.

Hotels

Good *hostales* (small hotels) and hotels proper are generally costlier, but distinctions can be unclear. In some countries, especially southern Chile and Argentina, the cheapest places may be *casas familiares*, family houses whose hospitality makes them excellent value.

The cheapest places are *hospedajes, casas de huéspedes, residenciales, alojamientos, pensiones* or *dormitorios*. An *albergue* is a hostel, and may or may not be an official *albergue juvenil* (youth hostel). The terminology varies in each country. Basic accommodations in these places include a bed with (hopefully) clean sheets and a blanket, table and chair, sometimes a fan, but rarely any heating in colder climes. Showers and toilets are shared, and there may not be hot water. Cleanliness varies widely, but some places are remarkably good.

Some cheap hotels specialize in renting rooms by the hour. These 'love hotels' can be acceptable budget accommodations, although they may be reluctant to take travelers who want a room for the whole night. This applies especially on weekends, when the hotel can make more money from a larger number of quickies.

In Brazil and some other places, room prices usually include breakfast, which can be very good. It's worth paying a little extra for a place with a quality breakfast.

Hot-water supplies are often erratic, or may be available only at certain hours of the day. It's something to ask about (and consider paying extra for), especially in the highlands where it gets *cold*.

Beware the electric shower – a cold-water shower head hooked up to an electric heating element. Don't touch the heating unit, or anything metal, while in the shower or you may get a shock – never strong enough to throw you across the room, but hardly pleasant. Wearing rubber sandals will protect you from shock. Regulate the temperature by adjusting the water flow – more water means less heat.

ACTIVITIES
Diving
Major destinations for divers are the Caribbean coast of Colombia and Venezuela, islands such as Providencia (a Colombian island that is actually nearer to Nicaragua; p574) and the Galápagos, and Brazil's Arraial do Cabo (p287).

Mountaineering
On a continent with one of the world's greatest mountain ranges, climbing opportunities are almost unlimited. Ecuador's volcanoes, the high peaks of Peru's Cordillera Blanca (p882), Bolivia's Cordillera Real (p189) and Argentina's Aconcagua (p114) (the continent's highest verified peak) are all suitable for mountaineering, but perhaps the most challenging technical climbs are in Argentina's Fitz Roy range (p140).

River Rafting
Chile churns with good white water: the Maipó (p418), Trancura (p471) and Futaleufú (p496) Rivers are all world class. River running is also possible on the Urubamba (p845), other rivers near Cuzco and in the very difficult Río Colca canyon near Arequipa (p830), in Peru; on several rivers around Bariloche (p124) and Mendoza (p110) in Argentina; and near Tena (p672) and Baños (p653) in Ecuador.

Skiing & Snowboarding
South America's most important downhill ski areas are in Chile and Argentina – see those chapters for more details. The season is from about June to September. There's also plenty of snow in the Andes of Bolivia, Peru, Ecuador, Colombia and Venezuela, where ski touring is a challenging possibility. Chris Lizza's *South America Ski Guide* is the best source of information.

Surfing
South America's best surfing is in Peru, especially the northern coast, but the water's chilly (so what?). Brazil has thousands of kilometers of coast, mostly characterized by beach breaks, with the best breaks in the southeast. Chile's central and northern coasts get good waves. Uruguay, Ecuador and Venezuela all have decent surf with a handful of top-notch waves. For more far-flung possibilities there's the Galápagos Islands (p706) and Rapa Nui (Easter Island) (p513).

For detailed information, get a copy of the *Surf Report* from **Surfer Publications** (☎ 949-661-5147; www.surfermag.com; PO Box 1028, Dana Point, CA 92629, USA). It has individual reports on most parts of the South American coast. On the Web, check out www.wannasurf.com.

Trekking
South America is a brilliant trekking destination. In the Andean countries, many of the old Inca roads are ready-made for scenic excursions, but lesser-known mountain ranges, such as Colombia's Sierra Nevada de Santa Marta, also have great potential. The national parks of southern South America, such as Chile's Torres del Paine (p507) and Argentina's Nahuel Huapi (p127), are superb, with good trail infrastructure and accessibility. Books on trekking are listed under Books (p1028).

BOOKS
The list of South America-related books varies as wildly as the continent itself.

Art & Literature

Get a handle on the region's art history with *A Cultural History of Latin America: Literature, Music and the Visual Arts in the 19th and 20th Centuries*, edited by Leslie Bethell. Andean art is supremely discussed, illustrated and photographed in Rebecca Stone-Miller's lush volume *Art of the Andes*. Celluloid enthusiasts will want to see John King's seminal *Magical Reels: A History of Cinema in Latin America*.

For notable literature by South American authors, see the Arts section within individual country chapters.

Flora & Fauna

Neotropical Rainforest Mammals: A Field Guide, by Louise Emmons and François Feer, provides color illustrations for identification. Bird-watchers in the Amazon region might try *South American Birds: A Photographic Aid to Identification* by John S Dunning. Covering more territory is Rodolphe Meyer de Schauensee's *A Guide to the Birds of South America*. Martin de la Peña's *Birds of Southern South America and Antarctica* is an excellent resource for southern Bolivia and Brazil, as well as points south.

The superb *Ecotravellers' Wildlife Guides* will tell you everything you need to know about wildlife, ecotourism, and threats and conservation efforts in specific habitats. Currently available in the series are *Ecuador and the Galápagos Islands* and *Peru*, both by David Pearson and Les Beletsky.

Henry Walter Bates' *The Naturalist on the River Amazons* is a classic 19th-century account. More or less contemporaneous is Alfred R Wallace's *A Narrative of Travels on the Amazon and Rio Negro*. Anthony Smith's *Explorers of the Amazon* is a series of essays on explorers of various kinds, from conquerors and scientists to plant collectors and rubber barons.

Despite some shortcomings, Betty J Meggers' *Amazonia: Man and Culture in a Counterfeit Paradise* is essential reading for its description of traditional rain-forest cultures and the environment. Perhaps the best overall account of the plight of the world's rain forests is journalist Catherine Caufield's *In the Rainforest*, which contains substantial material on Amazonia, but also covers other imperiled areas. More recent is *The Fate of the Forest: Developers, Destroyers and Defenders of the Amazon*, by Susanna Hecht and Alexander Cockburn.

Julie Sloan Denslow and Christine Padoch's *People of the Tropical Rainforest* is an edited and well-illustrated collection of articles on tropical ecology and development that deals with rain-forest immigrants and indigenous peoples. For everything you ever wanted to know about flora in the Amazon region, see *A Field Guide to Medicinal and Useful Plants of the Upper Amazon* by James L Castner et al.

Guidebooks

William Leitch's beautifully written *South America's National Parks* is essential background for trekkers, superb on environment and natural history, but weaker on practical matters.

To glimpse day-to-day realities you'll likely face in your travels, check out the *Culture Shock!* series. Recommended country overviews are provided by the *In Focus* series. Both of these cover most South American countries.

History & Contemporary Issues

Eduardo Galeano's *Open Veins of Latin America: Five Centuries of the Pillage of a Continent* is an eloquent polemic from a leftist perspective on the continent's cultural, social and political struggles by the famous Uruguayan writer. Galeano's *Memories of Fire* trilogy is readable and highly recommended. John A Crow's *The Epic of Latin America* is a daunting but accessible volume that covers Mexico to Tierra del Fuego, from prehistory to the present. George Pendle's *A History of Latin America* is a readable but very general account of the region since the European invasions.

Conquest of the Incas, by John Hemming, is a fine interpretation of the clash between the Spaniards and the lords of Cuzco. Hemming's *Search for El Dorado* is a very readable, illustrated account of the European quest for South American gold.

Carl O Sauer's *The Early Spanish Main* casts Columbus as an audacious bumbler whose greed colored his every perception of the New World.

For a general analysis of both the cocaine and anti-cocaine industries, read *Snowfields: The War on Cocaine in the Andes* by Clare Hargreaves. *Green Guerrillas: Environmental*

Conflicts and Initiatives in Latin America and the Caribbean, edited by Helen Collinson, focuses on the struggle between environmental conservation and the survival of local communities, with many voices and alternative views presented throughout. For an overview of social problems in Latin America, see Eric Wolf and Edward Hansen's *The Human Condition in Latin America.*

Lonely Planet

It's impossible to cover every element of South American travel in this book, so if you want greater detail on specific places, consider supplementing it with other guides.

Lonely Planet produces regularly updated travel guides for individual South American countries, with heaps of information, numerous maps, illustrations and color photos. Titles to look for are *Argentina, Uruguay & Paraguay; Bolivia; Brazil; Chile & Easter Island; Colombia; Ecuador & the Galápagos Islands; Peru;* and *Venezuela.*

For even more detailed information, see the Lonely Planet city guides to *Buenos Aires* and *Rio de Janeiro.*

Also useful are the *Brazilian phrasebook,* the *Latin American Spanish phrasebook* and the *Quechua phrasebook.*

For detailed trekking information, look at Lonely Planet's *Trekking in the Patagonian Andes* and *Trekking in the Central Andes.* If you're planning to visit Central America as well as South America, get a copy of Lonely Planet's *Central America on a shoestring,* which covers the region from Panama to Belize.

First-time travelers to the region can learn lots from Lonely Planet's *Read This First: Central & South America.*

Chilean writer Luis Sepúlveda's gripping personal odyssey takes him to different parts of the continent and beyond in *Full Circle: A South American Journey,* translated into English for Lonely Planet's travel literature series. An engaging combination of travelogue and botanical guide, *Tales of a Shaman's Apprentice* is the wonderful story of Mark Plotkin's travels in Amazonia and the Guianas in search of medicinal plants.

Travel Literature

Driving from Tierra del Fuego to the North Slope of Alaska in 23½ days takes a little extra something and Tim Cahill's got it in spades – hilarious run-ins with customs officials and other bureaucrats make his *Road Fever* worth reading. Another funny road yarn is *Inca-Kola: A Traveller's Tale of Peru,* by Matthew Parris. *Eight Feet in the Andes,* by Dervla Murphy, is an insightful description of the author's trip through Peru with her 10-year-old daughter and Juana the mule. Motorheads and *comandante* buffs shouldn't miss *Chasing Che: A Motorcycle Journey in Search of the Guevara Legend,* by Patrick Symmes.

Peter Matthiessen describes a journey from the rivers of Peru to the mountains of Tierra del Fuego in *The Cloud Forest.* Alex Shoumatoff's *In Southern Light* explores firsthand some of the fantastic legends of the Amazon.

BUSINESS HOURS

Generally, businesses are open from 8am or 9am to 8pm or 9pm Monday through Friday, with a nice, fat two- to three-hour lunch break around noon. Businesses are often open on Saturday, usually with shorter hours. Banks usually only change money Monday through Friday. Forget about getting anything done on Sunday, when nearly everything is closed. In the Andean countries, business tend to close a little earlier. See Business Hours in each country's Directory for more precise hours.

CLIMATE

Climate in South America is a matter of latitude and altitude, although warm and cold ocean currents, trade winds and topography play their part. More than two-thirds of South America is tropical, including the Amazon Basin, northern Brazil, the Guianas and the west coasts of Colombia and Ecuador. These areas of tropical rain forest have average daily maximum temperatures of about 30°C (86°F) year-round and more than 2500mm of rain annually. Less humid tropical areas, such as the Brazilian highlands and the Orinoco Basin, are still hot but enjoy cool nights and a distinct dry season.

South of the Tropic of Capricorn, Paraguay and southern Brazil are humid subtropical zones, while most of Argentina, Chile and Uruguay have temperate mid-latitude climates with mild winters and warm summers ranging from 12°C (54°F) in July to 25°C (77°F) in January, depending

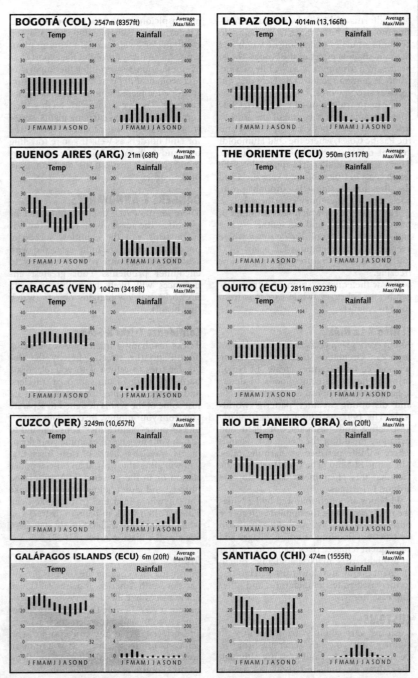

on landforms and latitude. Rainfall, occurring mostly in winter, varies from 200mm to 2000mm annually, depending on winds and the rain-shadow effect of the Andes. (Most of the rain dumps on the Chilean side, while Argentina remains relatively dry, but receives strong winds.)

The main arid regions are northern Chile (the Atacama Desert is one of the world's driest) and Peru, between the Andes and the Pacific Coast, where the cold Humboldt current creates a cloudy but dry climate. There are two smaller arid zones, along the north coast of Colombia and Venezuela and the Brazilian *sertão* (the drought-prone backlands of the country's northeast).

The high Andes, which have altitudes of more than 3500m, and far southern Chile and Argentina are cool climate zones, where average daily temperatures fall below 10°C (50°F) and temperatures can dip below freezing.

Below the equator, summer is from December to February, while winter is from June to August.

El Niño & La Niña

About every seven years, large-scale changes in ocean circulation patterns and rising sea-surface temperatures create 'El Niño,' bringing heavy rain and floods to desert areas, plunging tropical areas into drought and disrupting weather patterns worldwide. The 1997–98 winter was particularly destructive and traumatic for Peru and Ecuador, including the Galápagos Islands where wildlife perished at alarming rates. The name El Niño (The Child) refers to the fact that this phenomena usually appears around Christmas.

El Niños are often followed by La Niñas the next year, where the opposite effects are observed and can include bridge and road destruction, flooding of entire villages and subsequent refugee crises, raging forest fires in drought areas, malaria epidemics due to stagnant floodwater, lower fish catches due to increased water temperatures and other unpleasantness.

CUSTOMS

Customs vary slightly from country to country, but you can generally bring in personal belongings and presents, although their quantity and kind shouldn't arouse any suspicions that you'll be reselling them. You can bring camera equipment, a laptop computer or a video camera without problems. All countries prohibit the export (just as home countries prohibit the import) of archaeological items and goods made from rare or endangered animals (no snake skins, cat pelts, jewelry made with teeth – that sort of thing). Avoid carrying plants, seeds, fruits and fresh meat products. This is true for land borders as well. If you're traveling overland to/from Colombia, expect thorough customs inspections on both sides of the border.

DANGERS & ANNOYANCES

There are potential dangers, but don't be put off – the media only reports the few tragic trips, not the countless successful ones. Most areas are quite safe, and with sensible precautions, you are unlikely to encounter problems. Your greatest annoyances will likely be pollution, fiesta fireworks and low-hanging objects (watch that head!).

Confidence Tricks & Scams

Tricks involving a quantity of cash being 'found' on the street, whereby the do-gooder tries to return it to you, elaborate hard-luck stories from supposed travelers, and 'on-the-spot fines' by bogus police are just some of the scams designed to separate you from your money. Be especially wary if one or more 'plainclothes' cops demand to search your luggage or examine your documents, traveler's checks or cash. Insist that you will allow this only at an official police station or in the presence of a uniformed officer, and don't allow anyone to take you anywhere in a taxi or unmarked car. Thieves often work in pairs to distract you while lifting your wallet. Simply stay alert. See also the Black Market (p1035).

Drugs

Marijuana and cocaine are big business in parts of South America, and are available in many places but illegal everywhere. Penalties are severe. Beware that drugs are sometimes used to set up travelers for blackmail and bribery. Avoid any conversation with someone proffering drugs. If you're in an area where drug trafficking is prevalent, ignore it entirely, with conviction.

Don't accept food, drinks, sweets or cigarettes from strangers. They may be laced with powerful sedatives, and you could be robbed (or worse) while you're unconscious.

Roll-your-own cigarettes or cigarette papers may arouse suspicion.

In Bolivia and Peru, coca leaves are sold legally in *tiendas* (stores) or markets for about US$4/kilo. *Maté de coca* is a tea made by infusing coca leaves in boiling water. It's served in many cafés and restaurants in the Andean region, and coca-leaf 'tea bags' are also available. Although *maté de coca* is widely believed to combat the effects of altitude, there is no evidence that conclusively supports this, and a cup of *maté de coca* has no immediate stimulant effect.

The practice of chewing coca leaves goes back centuries and is still common among *campesinos* (peasant farmers) of the Andean *altiplano*. The icky tasting leaves are chewed with a little ash or bicarbonate of soda, as the alkalinity releases the mild stimulant contained in the leaf cells. Prolonged chewing dulls the pangs of hunger, thirst, cold and fatigue, but the initial effect just makes your mouth go numb. Without the alkaline catalyst, chewing coca leaves doesn't do much at all.

Be aware that someone who has chewed coca leaves or taken *maté de coca* may test positive for cocaine in the following weeks.

More refined forms of coca are illegal everywhere and transporting coca leaves over international borders is also illegal.

Natural Hazards

The Pacific Rim 'ring of fire' loops through eastern Asia, Alaska and all the way down through the Americas to Tierra del Fuego in a vast circle of earthquake and volcanic activity that includes the whole Pacific side of South America. In 1991, for example, Volcán Hudson in Chile's Aisén region erupted, burying parts of southern Patagonia knee-deep in ash. In 2002 Volcán Reventador (literally the 'exploder') erupted and blanketed Quito and other areas in northern Ecuador in ash. Volcanoes usually give some notice before blowing and are therefore unlikely to pose any immediate threat to travelers. Earthquakes are common, occur without warning and can be very serious. Andean construction rarely meets seismic safety standards; adobe buildings are particularly vulnerable. If you're in an earthquake, get in a doorway or dive under a table immediately; don't go outside.

Police & Military

Corruption is a very serious problem among Latin American police, who are generally poorly paid, trained and supervised. In many places, they are not beyond planting drugs on travelers or enforcing minor regulations in hopes of extracting *coimas* (bribes).

If you are stopped by 'plainclothes policemen', never get into a vehicle with them. Don't give them any documents or show them any money, and don't take them to your hotel. If the police appear to be the real thing, insist on going to a police station on foot.

The military often maintains considerable influence, even under civilian governments. Avoid approaching military installations, which may display warnings such as 'No stopping or photographs – the sentry will shoot.' In the event of a coup or other emergency, state-of-siege regulations suspend civil rights. Always carry identification and be sure someone knows your whereabouts. Contact your embassy or consulate for advice.

Theft

Theft can be a big problem, especially in Colombia, Peru and parts of Brazil, but remember that fellow travelers can also be accomplished crooks, so where there's a backpacker scene, there may also be thievery. Here are some common sense suggestions to limit your liability:

- A small padlock is useful for securing your pack zippers and hostel door, if necessary. When used to secure your pack zippers, twist ties, paper clips or safety pins can be another really effective deterrent.
- Always conceal your money belt and its contents, preferably beneath your clothing.
- Don't flash the expensive stuff.
- Keep your spending money separate from the big stuff (credit cards, traveler's checks, tickets etc).

- Pack lightly and you can stash your pack under your seat on the bus. Otherwise you'll enjoy the anxiety of wondering if your pack is staying on the roof every time you stop. It usually does, but… Some swear by grain sacks – buy one at a market, stick your pack in it and it looks just like the local haul, as well as keeping your pack from getting dirty.
- To deter pack slashers, keep moving when you're wearing a backpack and wear your daypack on your chest in crowded markets or terminals.

Trouble Spots

Some countries and areas are more dangerous than others. The more dangerous places (see individual country chapters for details) warrant extra care, but don't feel you should avoid them altogether. Due to the armed conflict in Colombia, parts of the country are simply off limits. For more detailed information about trouble spots in specific countries see the Dangers & Annoyances sections in the individual country Directory.

DISABLED TRAVELERS

In general, South America is not well set up for disabled travelers, but the more modernized, Southern Cone countries are slightly more accommodating – notably Chile, Argentina and perhaps the main cities of Brazil. Unfortunately, cheap local lodgings probably won't be well-equipped to deal with physically challenged travelers; air travel will be more feasible than local buses (although this isn't impossible); and well-developed tourist attractions will be more accessible than off-the-beaten-track destinations.

In the US, **Mobility International** (☎ 541-343-1284; www.miusa.org; PO Box 10767, Eugene, OR 97440) advises disabled travelers on mobility issues. It runs educational-exchange programs, which could be a good way to visit South America. In Australia and New Zealand, try the **National Information Communication Awareness Network** (Nican; ☎ 02-6285 3713; www.nican.com.au; PO Box 407, Curtin, ACT 2605). In the UK, there's the **Royal Association for Disability and Rehabilitation** (Radar; ☎ 020-7250 3222; www.radar.org.uk; 12 City Forum, 250 City Rd, London EC1V 8AF).

Resources on the Internet include **Accessable Travel Source** (www.access-able.com), which has little information specifically on South America, but provides some good general travel advice, and **Emerging Horizons** (www.emerginghorizons.com), which has well-written articles and regular columns full of handy advice. For a list of services available to disabled passengers by airline, check out **All Go Here Airline Directory** (www.everybody.co.uk/airindex.htm).

DISCOUNT CARDS

A Hostelling International-American Youth Hostel (HI-AYH) membership card can be useful in Brazil, Chile, Argentina and Uruguay, where there are many hostels, and accommodations tend to be (or traditionally have been) costlier. Elsewhere on the continent, cheap hotels and *pensións* typically cost less than affiliated hostels.

An International Student Identity Card (ISIC) can provide discounted admission to archaeological sites and museums. It may also entitle you to reductions on bus, train and air tickets. In less developed countries, student discounts are rare, although high-ticket items such as the entrance to Machu Picchu (discounted 50% for ISIC holders under 26) may be reduced. In some countries, such as Argentina, almost any form of university identification will suffice where discounts are offered.

DISCRIMINATION

Discrimination in South America – and it's a different beast in every country – is complex and full of contradictions. The most serious reports of racism we've received recently have been from black travelers who were denied access to nightclubs, in some cases until the doorperson realized they were foreigners. Some black travelers describe experiencing genuine curiosity from people who simply aren't used to seeing folks of black African descent. A recent posting on the **Lonely Planet Thorntree** (www.lonelyplanet.com) generated several responses from travelers of color who felt perfectly safe traveling in South America. Mixed-race couples may also receive curious looks from time to time. South Americans love to nickname people based on their appearance – *flaca* (skinny), *gordo* (chubby) – and a favorite for dark-skinned people is *negro/a* (literally 'black'). If you have darker skin, regardless of your heritage, you can expect to be called this – it's nearly always used affectionately.

See also Women Travelers (p1040) and Gay & Lesbian Travelers (p1033).

DRIVING LICENCE

If you're planning to drive anywhere, obtain an International Driving Permit or Inter-American Driving Permit (Uruguay theoretically recognizes only the latter). For about US$10, any motoring organization will issue one on presentation of a current state or national driver's license. See also Car & Motorcycle in the Transport chapter (p1049).

EMBASSIES & CONSULATES

For embassy and consulate addresses and phone numbers, see the Directory in individual country chapters.

As a visitor in a South American country, it's important to realize what your own embassy – the embassy of the country of which you are a citizen – can and can't do. Generally speaking, it won't be much help in emergencies where you're even remotely at fault. Remember that you are bound by the laws of the country you are in. Your embassy will not be sympathetic if you end up in jail after committing a crime locally, even if such actions are legal in your own country.

In genuine emergencies you may get some assistance, but only if other channels have been exhausted. For example, if you have all your money and documents stolen, it might assist in getting a new passport, but a loan for onward travel is out of the question.

FESTIVALS & EVENTS

South America has some fabulous fiestas, from indigenous harvest festivals to wild New Year parties. Some festivals, such as **Carnaval** in Salvador (p328) and Rio (p277) (celebrated around Lent in February/March), are worth planning your trip around, however, it's worth taking into account that some places are crowded, expensive and it might be difficult to find accommodations. Remember, Carnaval is celebrated throughout the continent if you can't make it to Brazil.

For more information, see Festivals & Events in the individual country directories. Also see Best Festivals & Events in the Destination South America chapter (p12).

GAY & LESBIAN TRAVELERS

Brazil is the most gay-friendly country on the continent, especially in Rio de Janeiro, São Paulo and Salvador. Buenos Aires also has a lively, 'out' gay scene (although same-sex couples may be harassed in other parts of Argentina), as does Santiago. Elsewhere on the continent, where public displays of affection by same-sex couples may provoke negative reactions, do as the locals do – be discreet and you shouldn't encounter problems.

Despite a growing number of publications and websites devoted to gay travel, few have specific advice on South America. The gay travel newsletter *Out and About* occasionally covers South America – its website, **Out & About** (www.outandabout.com), has general information and lets you order back issues on Argentina, Rio and São Paulo.

Global Gayz.com (www.travelandtranscendence.com) has a South America section full of news, tips and links about gay travel in the region.

Viajar Travel (www.viajartravel.com) is geared toward adventure travel and has some decent coverage. There are heaps of helpful links at **Pridelinks.com** (www.pridelinks.com).

INSURANCE

A travel insurance policy covering theft, loss, accidents and illness is highly recommended. Many policies include a card with toll-free numbers for 24-hour assistance, and it's good practice to carry that with you. Note that some policies compensate travelers for misrouted or lost luggage. Baggage insurance is worth its price in peace of mind. Also check that the coverage includes worst-case scenarios: ambulances, evacuations or an emergency flight home. Some policies specifically exclude 'dangerous activities,' which can include scuba diving, motorcycling, even trekking. If such activities are on your agenda, you don't want this sort of policy.

There is a wide variety of policies available and your travel agent will be able to make recommendations. The policies handled by STA Travel and other student-travel organizations usually offer good value. If a policy offers lower and higher medical-expense options, the low-expenses policy should be OK for South America – medical costs are not nearly as high here as elsewhere.

If you have baggage insurance and need to make a claim, the insurance company may demand a receipt as proof that you bought the stuff in the first place. You must usually inform the insurance company by airmail and report the loss or theft to local police within 24 hours. Make a list of stolen items and their value. At the police station, you complete a *denuncia* (statement), a copy of which is given to you for your insurance claim. The denuncia usually has to be made on *papel sellado* (stamped paper), which you can buy for pennies at any stationer.

INTERNET ACCESS

Internet access is available nearly everywhere, except the smallest towns, for anywhere from US$0.25 to US$5 per hour. This book lists Internet access points in most towns and cities. Either 'Alt + 64' or 'Alt-Gr 2' is the command to get the @ symbol on almost any Spanish-language keyboard.

INTERNET RESOURCES

There's no better place to start your Web explorations than the **Lonely Planet website** (www.lonelyplanet.com). Here you'll find succinct summaries on traveling to most places on earth, postcards from other travelers and the Thorn Tree bulletin board, where you can ask questions before you go or dispense advice upon your return. You'll also find travel news and updates to many of our most popular guidebooks, and the sub-WWWay section links you to the most useful travel resources elsewhere on the Web. The site has destination profiles on all South American countries, feedback from travelers on the road and links to other sites.

Most of the other interesting Internet sites about South America are devoted to specific countries within the continent – see the individual country chapters for suggestions. The following are all useful sites related to the continent as a whole:

Latin American Network Information Center (Lanic; http://lanic.utexas.edu/subject/countries.html) University of Texas' outstanding list of links to all things Latin American.

Latin American Travel Advisor (www.amerispan.com /lata/) Offers all the up-to-date, on-the-spot information that made its newsletter indispensable in the past.

Latin World (www.latinworld.com) Latin American search engine with loads of links.

South American Explorers (www.saexplorers.org) Excellent starting point for Internet research.

UK Foreign & Commonwealth Office (FCO; www.fco .gov.uk) British government site with travel advisories and the like.

US State Department (www.state.gov) Travel advisories and tips; rather alarmist.

LANGUAGE

Spanish is the first language of the vast majority of South Americans; Brazilians speak Portuguese, but may understand Spanish as well. Without a basic knowledge of Spanish, travel in South America can be difficult, and your interaction with local people will be limited. French is spoken in French Guiana, Dutch and English are spoken in Suriname, and English is spoken in Guyana.

Lonely Planet publishes the handy, pocket-size *Latin American Spanish phrasebook*, and *Brazilian phrasebook*. For a very brief introduction to Spanish and some useful phrases, see the Language chapter (p1064).

There are hundreds of distinct indigenous languages in South America, although some of them are spoken by only a few people. In the Andean countries and parts of Chile and Argentina, millions of people speak Quechua (called Quichua in Ecuador) or Aymara as a first language, and many do not use Spanish at all. Quechua was the official language of the Inca empire, and is most widely spoken in the Inca heartland of Peru and Ecuador. Aymara was the language of the pre-Inca Tiahuanaco culture, and their language survives around Lake Titicaca and in much of Bolivia. For a few useful words and phrases, see the Language chapter (p1064). If you're serious about learning more, or will be spending a lot of time in remote areas, look around La Paz or Cuzco for a good language course. Lonely Planet's *Quechua phrasebook* is primarily for travelers to Peru and contains grammar and vocabulary in the Cuzco dialect, but will also be useful for visitors to the Bolivian and Ecuadorian highlands.

LEGAL MATTERS

In city police stations, you might find an English-speaking interpreter, but don't bank on it: in most cases you'll either have to speak the local language or provide an interpreter. Some cities have a tourist police service, which can be more helpful.

Replacing a lost or stolen passport will likely be expensive and time-consuming. Apart from the cost of backtracking to the nearest embassy or consulate, there will be telex charges to your home country to check the details of your previous passport plus the cost of a new passport.

If you are robbed, photocopies (even better, certified copies) of original passports, visas and air tickets and careful records of credit card numbers and traveler's checks will prove invaluable. Replacement passport applications are usually referred to the home country, so it helps to leave a copy of your passport details with someone back home.

For more information, see Dangers & Annoyances (p1030) and Embassies & Consulates (p1033).

MAPS

International Travel Maps & Books (ITMB; ☎ 604-879-3621; www.itmb.com; 530 W Broadway, Vancouver, BC, V5Z 1E9, Canada) produces a range of excellent maps of Central and South America. For the whole continent, they have a reliable three-sheet map at a 1:4,000,000 scale and a memorial edition of their classic 1:500,000 map. The maps are huge for road use, but they're helpful for pre-trip planning. More detailed ITMB maps are available for the Amazon Basin, Ecuador, Bolivia and Venezuela. All are available on the ITMB website.

World Map has a good, but expensive, three-sheet set at 1:4,000,000. Collins and Halliwag both have OK maps of the continent at 1:7,000,000, but detail is sacrificed to fit the entire continent on one sheet. These maps are widely available; check any well-stocked map or travel bookstore.

South American Explorers (SAE; ☎ 607-277-0488; www.saexplorers.org; 126 Indian Creek Rd, Ithaca, NY 14850, USA) has scores of reliable maps, including topographical, regional and city maps. See the individual country chapters for more suggestions.

MONEY

Prices throughout this book are quoted in US dollars. We've found that in a multicountry book such as this, it's easier for the traveler to budget and compare costs if prices are all given in a common currency. Some national South American currencies are unstable and we've found that using a stable currency reference can be helpful for the traveler over the life of the book.

ATMs

Bring an ATM card. ATMs are available in most cities and large towns, and are almost always the most convenient, reliable and economical way of getting cash. The rate of exchange is usually as good as, or better than, any bank or legal money-changer. Many ATMs are connected to the Cirrus or Plus network, but many countries prefer one over the other. To search for ATMs in specific countries honoring either network, see www.mastercard.com and www.visa.com and click on ATM Locator. If you are relying on ATMs, take two or more cards in case one gets swallowed by a machine or disappears.

Many ATMs will accept a personal identification number (PIN) of only four digits; find out whether this applies to the countries you're traveling to before heading off.

Bargaining

Bargaining is accepted and expected when contracting long-term accommodations and shopping for craft goods, the prices of which are normally very negotiable. Haggling is a near sport in the Andean countries, with patience, humor and respect serving as the ground rules of the game. Bargaining is much less common in the Southern Cone. When you head into the bargaining trenches, remember that the point is to have fun while reaching a mutually satisfying end: the merchant should not try to fleece you, but you shouldn't try to get something for (nearly) nothing either.

Black Market

The unofficial exchange rate for the US dollar can be higher than the official bank rate because official rates do not always reflect the market value of local currency. The unofficial rate is often known as the *mercado negro* (black market) or *mercado paralelo* (parallel market). Nowadays, official exchange rates are quite realistic in most South American countries, so the role of the black market is declining.

You might still want to use street money-changers if only because they are so much faster and more convenient than banks (and also at border crossings where there may not be a bank). Use the following common sense: be discreet, as it's often illegal, although it may be tolerated. Have the exact amount handy to avoid flashing large wads of cash. Beware of sleight-of-hand tricks – insist on personally counting out the notes you are handed one by one, and don't hand over your dollars until you're satisfied you have the exact amount agreed upon. One common trick is to hand you the agreed amount, less a few pesos, so that, on counting it, you complain that it's short. They take it back, recount it, discover the 'mistake,' top it up and hand it back, in the process spiriting away some of the larger bills. For certainty, recount it yourself and don't be distracted by supposed alarms such as 'police' or 'danger.' Decline to accept torn, smudged or tattered bills. Other scams to watch out for include the old fixed calculator trick and passing counterfeit bills.

Cash

It's convenient – but not crucial – to have a small wad of US cash tucked away because it's exchangeable for local currency just about anywhere. Of course, unlike traveler's checks, nobody will give you a refund for lost or stolen cash (if you find someone, let us know). When you're about to cross from one country to another, it's handy to change some small dollar bills rather than a traveler's check. Dollars are also useful when there's a black/parallel market or unofficial exchange rate. In some places you can exchange US-dollar traveler's checks for US cash at banks and *casas de cambio* (currency-exchange houses), in order to replenish your stash (or you can stock up in Ecuador, where the US dollar is the official currency). Trying to exchange ragged notes can be a hassle, so procure crisp bills before setting out.

Credit Cards

The big-name credit cards are accepted at most large stores, travel agencies and better hotels and restaurants. Credit card purchases sometimes attract an extra *recargo* (surcharge) on the price (2% to 5% or more), but they are usually billed to your account at quite favorable exchange rates. Some banks issue cash advances on major credit cards. The most widely accepted card is Visa, followed by MasterCard (those with UK Access should insist on its affiliation with Master-Card). American Express and Diners Club are also accepted in many places. Beware of credit card fraud (especially in Brazil) – never let the card out of your sight.

Exchanging Money

Traveler's checks and foreign cash can be changed at *casas de cambio* or banks. Rates are usually similar, but *casas de cambio* are quicker, less bureaucratic and open longer

hours. Street moneychangers, who may or may not be legal, will only handle cash. Sometimes you can also change money unofficially at hotels or in shops that sell imported goods (electronics dealers are an obvious choice).

It is preferable to bring money in US dollars, although banks and *casas de cambio* in capital cities will change euros, pounds sterling, Japanese yen and other major currencies. Changing these currencies in smaller towns and on the street is next to impossible.

Traveler's Checks

The safest way to carry money is in traveler's checks, although they're not nearly as convenient as ATM cards. American Express are the most widely accepted checks, while Visa, Thomas Cook and Citibank are equally the next best. Forget checks from smaller banks with limited international affiliations – they'll be difficult, if not impossible, to cash. To facilitate replacement in case of theft, keep a record of check numbers and the original bill of sale in a safe place. Even with proper records, replacement can take time.

Have some traveler's checks in small denominations, say US$50. If you carry only large denominations, you might find yourself stuck with copious amounts of local currency when leaving a country.

In some countries, notably Argentina and to a lesser extent Peru, traveler's checks are more difficult to cash, and banks and *casas de cambio* charge commissions as high as 10%.

PASSPORT

A passport is essential – make sure it's valid for at least six months beyond the projected end of your trip and has plenty of blank pages for stamp-happy officials. Carrying a photocopy of your passport (so you can leave the original in your hotel) is sometimes enough if you're walking around a town, but *always* have the original if you travel anywhere. To reduce the risk of hassles in the event you are asked for your papers, keep the original with you at all times.

PHOTOGRAPHY & VIDEO
Film & Equipment

Consumer electronics are readily available throughout South America, but taxes can kick prices through the roof. A good range of reasonably priced film, including B&W and slide, is obtainable in the biggest cities. For low-light conditions in the rain forests, carry a few rolls of high-speed (ASA 400 or faster) film and a flash.

Photo processing is relatively expensive, but widely available. Have one roll processed and check the results before you hand over your whole stash.

Photographing People

Ask for permission before photographing individuals, particularly indigenous people. If someone is giving a public performance (such as a street musician or a dancer at Carnaval), or is incidental to a photograph (in a broad cityscape, for example), permission is not usually necessary – but if in doubt, ask or refrain. If you're after local-market pictures, purchasing items from a vendor may result in permission to photograph them or their wares. Paying folks for their portrait is a personal decision; in most cases, the subject will tell you right off the going rate for a photo.

Restrictions

Some tourist sites charge an additional fee for tourists with cameras. It's unwise and possibly illegal to take photos of military installations and personnel or security-sensitive places such as police stations. In most churches, flash photography (and sometimes photography period) is not allowed.

Video

Go digital. If you can't, 8mm cassettes for video cameras are available. Tourist sites that charge for still cameras probably charge more for a video camera. If you want to buy a prerecorded videocassette or record a local TV program for your VCR at home, remember that different countries use different TV and video systems. For example, Colombia and Venezuela use the NTSC system (as in the USA), while Brazil uses PAL, and French Guiana uses the French SECAM system.

POST

International postal rates can be quite expensive. Generally, important mail and parcels should be sent by registered or certified service. Sending parcels can be awkward: often an *aduana* (customs) officer must inspect the contents before a postal clerk can accept them, so wait to seal your package until after it has been checked. Most post offices have a parcels window, usually signed *'encomiendas'* (parcels). The place for posting overseas parcels is sometimes different from the main post office.

UPS, FedEx, DHL and other private postal services are available in most countries.

Local Addresses

Many South American addresses in this book contain a post-office box number as well as a street address. A post-office box is known as an *apartado* (abbreviated 'Ap' or 'Apto') or a *casilla de correos* (abbreviated 'Casilla' or 'CC').

Receiving Mail

The simplest way to receive mail is to have letters sent to you c/o Lista de Correos ('Posta Restante' in Brazil), followed by the name of the city and country where you expect to be. Mail addressed like this will always be sent to that city's main post office. In most places, the service is free or almost so. Most post offices hold mail for a month or two. American Express operates a mail service for clients.

Bring ID, preferably a passport, when collecting mail. If awaited correspondence seems to have gone missing, ask the clerk to check under every possible combination of your initials. To simplify matters, have your letters addressed with only your first and surnames, with the latter underlined and in capital letters.

STUDYING

Spanish-language courses are available in most South American cities, with Quito (Ecuador; p627), Cuzco (Peru; p845) and Buenos Aires (Argentina; p50; especially now that it's cheap) being the most popular. For Portuguese, Rio de Janeiro (Brazil; p393) is a great place to spend some time studying. For Quechua and Aymara, try Cochabamba (Bolivia) or Cuzco. For details, see individual country chapters.

TELEPHONE

Traditionally, governments have operated the national and international telecommunications systems and, traditionally, services have been horrid. Many countries have privatized their phone systems, choosing high charges over poor service, but sometimes getting both. International calls are particularly expensive from Bolivia and Colombia; they are perhaps cheapest from Chile.

Direct lines, accessed via special numbers and billed to an account at home, have made international calls much simpler. There are different access numbers for each telephone company in each country – get a list from your phone company before you leave.

It is sometimes cheaper to make a reverse-charge (collect) or credit-card call overseas than to pay for the call at the source. Often the best way is to make a quick international call and have the other party call you back (some telephone offices allow this, others don't). Keep your eyes peeled for 'net-to-phone' (Internet) capabilities, where calls can be as cheap as US$0.25 per minute to the USA and US$0.50 to Europe.

Nearly every town and city has a telephone office with a row of phone booths for local and international calls.

TOILETS

There are two toilet rules for South America: always carry your own toilet paper and don't throw anything into the toilet bowl. Except in the most developed places, South American sewer systems can't handle toilet paper, so all paper products must be discarded in the wastebasket. Another general rule is to use public bathrooms whenever you can, as you never know when your next opportunity will be. Folks posted outside bathrooms proffering swaths of paper require payment. For a list of clean bathrooms worldwide – and proof you can find anything online – check out **The Bathroom Diaries** (www.thebathroomdiaries.com).

USEFUL ORGANIZATIONS

South American Explorers (SAE; www.saexplorers.org) is by far one of the most helpful organizations for travelers to South America. Founded in 1977, SAE functions as an information center for travelers, adventurers and researchers. It supports scientific fieldwork, mountaineering and other expeditions, wilderness conservation and social development in Latin America. It has traveler clubhouses in Lima, Cuzco and Quito (for contact information, see the Peru and Ecuador chapters), as well as the **US office** (☎ 607-277-0488; 126 Indian Creek Rd, Ithaca, NY 14850), which

publishes the quarterly magazine, *South American Explorer*. The clubhouses have extensive libraries of books, maps and traveler's reports, plus a terrific atmosphere. The club sells maps, books and other items at its offices and by mail order.

Membership to the organization costs US$50 per person per year (US$80 for a couple) and includes four issues of *South American Explorer* magazine. Members receive access to the club's information service, libraries, storage facilities, mail service and book exchange, and discounts at some hotels and travel services. Joining online is easy.

VISAS & DOCUMENTS

A visa is an endorsement in your passport (p1036), usually a big stamp, permitting you to enter a country and remain for a specified period of time. It's obtained from a foreign embassy or consulate of that country. You can often get them in your home country, but it's also usually possible to get them en route, which may be better if you have a flexible itinerary: most visas are only good for a limited period after they're issued. Ask other travelers about the best places to get visas, since two consulates of the same country may enforce different requirements.

If you really need a visa fast, kiss ass and explain your needs. Consulates can often be very helpful if the officials sympathize and your papers are in order. Sometimes they will charge a fee for fast processing, but don't mistake this for a bribe.

Nationals of most European countries and Japan require few visas, but travelers from the USA need some, and those from Australia, New Zealand or South Africa might need several. Carry a handful of passport-size photographs for visa applications (although most border towns have a photographer who can do the honors).

Visa requirements are given in the Fast Facts section at the beginning of each country chapter, but a summary follows. Some countries issue tourist cards to visitors on arrival; while traveling within those countries, carry your tourist card with you at all times. Residents of most countries will not need visas for Argentina, Bolivia, Chile, Colombia, Ecuador, French Guiana or Peru; consult the following list for other destinations. If you plan on entering Panama or elsewhere in Central America, check up on those visa requirements as well.

Brazil Residents of Canada, the USA, Australia, New Zealand and Japan require visas (p394).

Falkland Islands For non-Britons, visa requirements are generally the same as those for foreigners visiting the UK, although Argentines must obtain an advance visa. Any queries regarding entry requirements for the Falkland Islands should be directed to the British embassy in your home country (p36).

Paraguay Residents of Canada, the USA, Australia and New Zealand require visas (p790).

Suriname Residents of Canada, the USA, Australia, New Zealand, France, Germany, the UK and the Netherlands require visas (p748).

Uruguay Residents of Canada, Australia and New Zealand require visas (p937).

Venezuela Officially, no one needs a visa if arriving by air, but everyone must obtain a tourist card or visa before arriving at a land border (p1023).

If you need a visa for a certain country and arrive at a land border without one, be prepared to backtrack to the nearest town with a consulate to get one. Airlines won't normally let you board a plane for a country to which you don't have the necessary visa. Also, a visa in itself does not guarantee entry: you may still be turned back at the border if you don't have 'sufficient funds' or an onward or return ticket.

Onward or Return Tickets

Several countries require you to have a ticket out of their country before they will admit you at the border, grant you a visa or let you board their national airline. The onward or return ticket requirement can be a major nuisance for travelers who want to fly into one country and travel overland through others. Officially, Peru, Colombia, Ecuador, Venezuela, Bolivia, Brazil, Suriname and French Guiana demand onward tickets, but only Brazil, Suriname and French Guiana are strict about it. Still, if you arrive in one of the countries technically requiring an onward ticket or sufficient funds and aggravate or in any way piss off a border guard, they *can* enforce these rules (yet another reason to be pleasant and neatly dressed at border crossings). Panama can also be prickly about onward tickets: a pain for folks flying there over the Darién Gap.

Sometimes you can satisfy the return ticket requirement by purchasing an MCO (miscellaneous charge order), a document that looks like an airline ticket but can be re-funded in cash or credited toward a specific flight with any International Air Transport Association (IATA) carrier. Check whether consular or immigration officials will ac-cept an MCO as an onward ticket. If not, try to buy a refundable onward or return ticket – ask specifically where you can get a refund, as some airlines will only refund tickets at the office of purchase or at their head office.

Any ticket out of South America plus sufficient funds might be an adequate sub-stitute for an onward ticket. Having a major credit card or two may help.

Airlines flying to Colombia or Venezuela may be reluctant to sell a one-way ticket – if you're not admitted they will have to fly you back.

Sufficient Funds

Immigration officials may ask (verbally or on the application form) about your finan-cial resources. If you lack 'sufficient funds' for your proposed visit, officials may limit the length of your stay, but once you are in the country, you can usually extend your visa by showing a wad of traveler's checks or producing a credit card.

VOLUNTEERING

Adequate Spanish (or Portuguese in Brazil) is usually essential for any volunteer work in South America. With many organizations, expect to provide your own food and lodg-ing, or pay up to $300 per month. If you're setting up from home, you usually have to pay an application fee to boot. Some people prefer to check out volunteer opportunities on the spot to get a closer look at exactly what they'll be doing before they start and to avoid extraneous fees. One good place to do this is the South American Explor-ers (SAE; see Useful Organizations), which maintains a database of volunteer work. If you want to peek at what's available before you go, check the following websites:

Amerispan (www.amerispan.com/volunteer_intern) Volunteer and internship programs in Argentina, Bolivia, Brazil, Chile, Ecuador and Peru.

Australian Volunteers International (www.ozvol .org.au) Sends qualified Australian volunteers to several spots in South America for one- to two-year volunteer stints.

Tx Serve (www.txserve.org/general/volopp2.html) Lots of links to organizations currently needing volunteers in South America.

WOMEN TRAVELERS

At one time or another, solo women travelers will find themselves the object of curiosity – sometimes well-intentioned, sometimes not. Avoidance is an easy, effective self-defense strategy. In the Andean region, particularly in smaller towns and rural areas, modest dress and conduct are the norm, while in Brazil and the more liberal Southern Cone, standards are more relaxed, especially in beach areas; note, however, that virtually nowhere in South America is topless or nude bathing customary. When in doubt, follow the lead of local women.

Machista attitudes, stressing masculine pride and virility, are fairly widespread among South American men (although less so in indigenous communities). They are often expressed by boasting and in exaggerated attention toward women. Snappy put-down lines or other caustic comebacks to unwanted advances may make the man feel threatened, and he may respond aggressively. Most women find it easier to invent a husband and leave the guy with his pride intact, especially in front of others.

Consider a Spanish (or Portuguese) class (see Language in this chapter; p1034) – a command of the language can sometimes be the best way to ward off unwanted attention.

There have been cases of South American men raping women travelers. Women trekking or taking tours in remote or isolated areas should be especially aware. Some cases have involved guides assaulting tour group members, so it's worth double-checking the identity and reputation of any guide or tour operator. Also be aware that women (and men) have been drugged, in bars and elsewhere, using drinks, cigarettes or pills. Police may not be very helpful in rape cases – if a local woman is raped, her family usually seeks revenge rather than calling the police. Tourist police may be more sympathetic, but it's possibly better to see a doctor and contact your embassy before reporting a rape to police.

Tampons are generally difficult to find in smaller towns, so stock up in cities or bring a supply from home. Birth control pills may be tricky to find outside metropolitan areas, so you're best off bringing your own supply from home. Morning after pills are readily available in some countries, notably Brazil. The **International Planned Parenthood Federation website** (www.ippf.org) offers a wealth of information on member clinics (Family Planning Associations) throughout South America that provide contraception (and abortions where legal).

WORKING

Except for teaching or tutoring English, opportunities for employment are few, low-paying and usually illegal. Even tutoring, despite good hourly rates, is rarely remunerative because it takes time to build up a clientele. The best opportunities for teaching English are in the larger cities, and, although you won't save much, it will allow you to stick around longer. Santiago, Rio and the larger cities of Brazil are the best bets for decent pay. Other work opportunities may exist for skilled guides or in restaurants and bars catering to travelers.

The **Association of American Schools in South America** (AASSA; www.aassa.com) places accredited teachers in many academic subjects in preparatory schools throughout South America.

Transport

GETTING THERE & AWAY

AIR

Every South American country has an international airport in its capital or its major cities. Main gateways include Buenos Aires (Argentina); Caracas (Venezuela); La Paz (Bolivia); Lima (Peru); Quito (Ecuador); Rio de Janeiro (Brazil); and Santiago (Chile). Less frequently used international gateways include Asunción (Paraguay); Bogotá (Colombia); Guayaquil (Ecuador); Manaus, Recife, Salvador and São Paulo (Brazil); Montevideo (Uruguay); Río Gallegos (Argentina); and Santa Cruz (Bolivia).

The most frequent and direct flights to a South American country are likely to be with its national 'flag carrier' airline. Many of these airlines have websites, including the following:

Aero Continente (www.aerocontinente.com.pe in Spanish; Peru)
Aerolíneas Argentinas/Austral (www.aerolineas .com.ar; Argentina)
Alianza Summa (www.summa.aero; Colombia) Umbrella for Avianca, Sam and Aces airlines.
Avensa/Servivensa (www.avensa.com.ve in Spanish; Venezuela)
LanChile (www.lanchile.cl; Chile)
Lloyd Aéreo Boliviano (www.labairlines.com in Spanish; Bolivia)
Varig (www.varig.com.br; Brazil)

North American and European airlines offering regular South American connections include the following:

Air France (www.airfrance.com)
American Airlines (www.aa.com)
British Airways (www.britishairways.com)
Continental Airlines (www.continental.com)
Iberia (www.iberia.com)
KLM (www.klm.com)
Swiss (www.swiss.com)

Tickets

Airfares to South America depend on your point and date of departure, your destination, your access to discount travel agencies and whether you can take advantage of advance-purchase fares and special offers. Airlines are the best source for finding information on routes, timetables and standard fares, but they rarely sell the cheapest tickets. Start shopping around as soon as you can, because the cheapest tickets must be bought months in advance, and popular, affordable flights sell out early.

Flights from North America, Europe, Australia and New Zealand may permit a stopover in South America en route to your destination city. This gives you a free air connection within the region, so it's worth considering when comparing flights. For example, a Varig flight from London to La Paz may offer a free stopover in Rio de Janeiro. International flights may also include an onward connection at a much lower cost than a separate fare.

THINGS CHANGE...

The information in this chapter is particularly vulnerable to change. Check directly with the airline or a travel agent to make sure you understand how a fare (and ticket you may buy) works and be aware of the security requirements for international travel. Shop carefully. The details given in this chapter should be regarded as pointers and are not a substitute for your own careful, up-to-date research.

TRANSPORT

COURIER FLIGHTS

These offer outstanding value, if you can tolerate the restrictions. For one thing, folks angling for a courier flight from remote outposts will likely be out of luck: only the major cities are serviced, with London, Los Angeles and New York being the most common departure points. Still, a New York to Rio de Janeiro round-trip fare can cost as little as US$250 on a courier flight, so if you can get to one of these gateway cities and connect with a courier flight, you might save a big amount. Some of the larger courier operators (all US-based) include the following:

Air Courier Association (☎ 800-822-0888; www .aircourier.org)
International Association of Air Travel Couriers (☎ 308-632-3273; www.courier.org)
Now Voyager (☎ 212-431-1616; www.nowvoyager travel.com)

RTW TICKETS

Nearly all airlines that fly to South America offer round-the-world (RTW) tickets in conjunction with their alliances. Rules and regulations vary depending on the airline you fly with, but nearly all require an advance purchase of at least 14 days. Generally, you must arrange in advance your departure and arrival cities. Most airlines allow you to change your mid-trip flight dates for free, but charge a minimum fee (US$25 to US$50) for changing destination/ departure cities.

British Airways' 'Oneworld Explorer' fare is a good RTW for South America, allowing you to fly with Qantas, Aer Lingus, Cathay Pacific, American Airlines, Iberia, Finnair, LanChile and their affiliates. Visit the website of **British Airways** (www.britishairways.com) for more information.

US-based **Airtreks** (in North America ☎ 800-350-0612, outside North America ☎ 415-365-1698; www .airtreks.com) offers customized RTW tickets that don't require you to stick within airline affiliates. The staff is also excellent at helping clients work out itineraries.

The following websites advertise RTW tickets:

■ www.airfare.com.au
■ www.bridgetheworld.co.uk
■ www.e-ticket-travel.com.au
■ www.flightcentre.com.au
■ www.lastminute.com
■ www.statravel.com.au
■ www.trailfinders.co.uk
■ www.travel.com.au
■ www.travelshop.com.au

Although you can sometimes purchase a RTW ticket online, it's usually best (and often required) that you purchase this type of ticket through a travel or airline agent due to the complexity of the ticket. And for your own sanity, nothing is better than a good agent when planning this type of ticket.

FREE STOPOVERS

If your flight to South America connects through Miami, Los Angeles, Houston or other cities in the US, or through cities in Mexico or Central America, you may be able to arrange a free stopover. This would allow you to spend some time in these countries before continuing south. Ask your travel agent about this possibility.

From Australia

Excursion fares from Australia to South America aren't cheap. The most direct routes on Qantas and its partners are from Sydney to Santiago or Buenos Aires. Fares are usually the same from Melbourne, Sydney or Brisbane, but from other Australian cities you may have to add the cost of getting to Sydney. Check for low-season 'Discover South America' excursion fares from Sydney or Melbourne.

The other South American route is with Qantas or Air New Zealand and travels from Sydney to Papeete, Tahiti, connecting with a LanChile flight via Easter Island to Santiago, with a free onward flight to either Rio or Buenos Aires. Connections can be awkward on this route, making for a long trip.

In terms of airfare only, it may be marginally cheaper to go to South America via the US, but even a day in Los Angeles would cost more than the savings in airfares, so it's not a good value unless you want to visit the US anyway. It may be worth it for travel to Colombia or Venezuela, but not for cities further south.

The best RTW options are probably those with Aerolíneas Argentinas combined with other airlines, including Air New Zealand, British Airways, Iberia, Singapore Airlines, Thai Airways or KLM. The Qantas version of a RTW ticket is its 'Oneworld Explorer' fare, which allows you to visit up to six continents with three stopovers in each one.

Many agents offer cheap air tickets out of Australia. **STA Travel** (☎ 1300-733 035; www.statravel.com.au) has offices in all capital cities and on many university campuses. **Flight Centre** (☎ 1300-133 133; www.flightcentre.com.au) also specializes in cheap airfares and has offices countrywide. **Inca Tours** (☎ 02-4351 2133, 800-024 955) is staffed by very knowledgeable people who arrange tours to South America in addition to giving advice and selling tickets to independent travelers. **Destination Holidays** (☎ 03-9725 4655, 800-337 050; www.south-america.com.au) also specializes in Latin American travel. Also, check the advertisements in Saturday editions of newspapers, such as Melbourne's *Age* or the *Sydney Morning Herald*. You can buy airline tickets online at www.travel.com.au.

The following South American airlines have offices in Australia:

Aerolíneas Argentinas Melbourne (☎ 03-9650 7111; Level 6, Nauru House, 80 Collins St, Melbourne 3000); Sydney (☎ 02-9283 3660; Level 2, 580 George St, Sydney 2000)

LanChile Sydney (☎ 02-9321 9333; 64 York St, Sydney 2000)

Varig Melbourne (☎ 03-9920 3856; 310 King St, Melbourne 3000); Sydney (☎ 02-9244 2179; 403 George St, Sydney 2000)

From Central America

Flights from Central America are usually subject to high tax, and bucket-shop deals are almost unobtainable. Nevertheless, it's cheaper, easier and safer to fly between Central and South America than to go overland.

You must have an onward ticket to enter Colombia, and airlines in Panama and Costa Rica are unlikely to sell you a one-way ticket to Colombia unless you already have an onward ticket or are willing to buy a round-trip flight. Venezuela and Brazil also demand an onward ticket. If you have to purchase a round-trip ticket, check whether the airline will give you a refund for unused portions of the ticket. One way to avoid the onward or return ticket requirement is to fly from Central America to Ecuador or Peru.

For other countries that require onward tickets, see p1039.

VIA ISLA DE SAN ANDRÉS

From San José, Costa Rica and Panama City, **West Caribbean Airways** (www.wca.com.co) flies to the Colombian island of Isla de San Andrés, off the coast of Nicaragua. One-way fares at press time were about US$145 from either city. From San Andrés, you can continue on a domestic Colombian flight to Bogotá (US$100 to US$140), Cali (US$100 to US$150), Cartagena (US$80 to US$130) or Medellín (US$100 to US$140). For more information, see p573.

FROM COSTA RICA

Flights to Quito from Costa Rica (one way about US$325) are about US$100 more than from Panama. The Costa Rican student organization **OTEC** (www.turismojoven.com) offers some cheap tickets.

FROM PANAMA

Like Colombia, Panama requires an onward or return ticket before you enter the country (a bus ticket is acceptable, but the return half is not refundable). The cost of living is higher in Panama than nearby countries, so time spent looking for a ticket can punish your budget. There are direct services from Panama City to Bogotá (US$174), Cartagena (US$173) and Medellín (US$182). The Colombian airline, **Alianza Summa** (www.avianca.com), composed of Avianca, Sam and Aces airlines, and the Panamanian carrier **Copa** (www.copaair.com), a Continental partner, generally offer the cheapest deals to these places. Copa offices in Cartagena, Barranquilla and Medellín should refund unused return halves of tickets, but check in advance. If possible, apply for a refund in Barranquilla, since applications in Cartagena are referred to Barranquilla anyway. Refunds, in Colombian currency only, take up to four days. A Panama City to Quito flight will cost around US$250.

From Continental Europe

The best places in Europe for cheap airfares are 'student' travel agencies (you don't have to be a student to use them) in Amsterdam, Berlin, Brussels, Frankfurt and Paris, and sometimes in Athens. If airfares are expensive where you live, try contacting a London agent, who may be able to issue a ticket by mail. The cheapest destinations in South America are generally Caracas, Buenos Aires and possibly Rio de Janeiro, or Recife, Brazil. High-season months are from early June to early September, and mid-December to mid-January. The cheapest flights from Europe are typically charters, usually with fixed dates for both outward and return flights.

In Paris, student/discount travel agencies include **Nouvelles Frontières** (www.nouvelles-frontieres .com), with offices throughout the country, and **Havas Voyages** (www.havasvoyages.fr).

STA Travel (www.statravel.com) has offices in Austria, Denmark, Finland, Sweden, Switzerland and throughout Germany. In the Netherlands, the official student agency, **NBBS Reizen** (☎ 0900-10 20 300; www.nbbs.nl), is good.

Or you can search for cheap airfares from Europe at **DiscountAirfares.com** (www.etn.nl).

From New Zealand

The two chief options are to fly **Aerolíneas Argentinas** (☎ 09-379 3675; aerolineas@repworld.co.nz; Level 15, 135 Albert St, Auckland) from Auckland to Buenos Aires (with connections to neighboring countries) or to fly with **Air New Zealand** (☎ 0800-737 000; www.airnz.co.nz) from Auckland to Papeete, Tahiti, connecting with a **LanChile** (in Auckland ☎ 09-912 7435, 309 8673; www.lanchile.com) flight via Easter Island to Santiago. Onward tickets, eg, to Lima, Rio de Janeiro, Guayaquil, Bogotá or Caracas, are much cheaper if purchased in conjunction with a long-haul flight from the same carrier. A 'Visit South America' fare, valid for three months, allows you two stops in South America plus one in the US, then returns to Auckland. Various open-jaw options are possible, and you can make the trip in either direction.

For discount fares, try **STA Travel** (☎ 09-309 9723, 0508 782 872; www.statravel.co.nz) or **Flight Centre** (☎ 0800-24 35 44, in Auckland ☎ 09-368 5370; www.flightcentre.co.nz). Both companies have offices in Auckland and other cities.

Check the *New Zealand Herald* for discounted fares advertised by travel agencies.

From the UK

Fares from London used to be the cheapest in Europe, but some other cities now have similar fares. The cheapest destinations in South America are generally Caracas and Bogotá. Some of the best sources of information about cheap fares are weekend editions of national newspapers. In London, try the *Evening Standard,* the listings magazine *Time Out* and *TNT,* a free weekly magazine. *TNT* comes out every Monday and is found in dispensers outside underground stations.

Some London agencies specialize in South American travel. One very good agency is **Journey Latin America** (JLA; www.journeylatinamerica .co.uk; London ☎ 020-8747 8315; 12 & 13 Heathfield Terrace, Chiswick, London W4 4JE; Manchester ☎ 0161-832 1441; sales@jlamanchester.co.uk). Ask for *Papagaio*, JLA's useful free magazine. JLA is very well informed about South American destinations, has a good range of air passes and can issue tickets from South America to London and deliver them to any of the main South American cities (this can be much cheaper than buying the same ticket in South America).

Other places to try are **South American Experience** (☎ 020-7976 5511; www.southamericanexperience .co.uk; 47 Causton St, Pimlico, London SW1P 4AT) and **Austral Tours** (☎ 020-7233 5384; www.latinamerica.co.uk; 20 Upper Tachbrook St, London SW1).

London has countless bucket shops with well-advertised services and prices. Travel agents that are bonded (eg by ATOL, ABTA or AITO) give you some protection if the company goes broke. A good general agency is **Trailfinders** (☎ 020-7938 3939; www.trailfinders.com; 194 Kensington High St, London W8 7RG), which has cheap flights to many destinations. Its useful travel newspaper, *Trailfinder,* is free. Check its website for office addresses in Birmingham, Bristol, Dublin, Glasgow, Manchester and other cities. Another well-established budget travel agency is **STA Travel** (☎ 020-7465 0484; www.statravel.co.uk), which has offices in nearly every city in the UK.

From the USA & Canada

Major gateways are Los Angeles, Miami and New York; Miami is usually cheapest. Newark, New Jersey; Washington, DC; and Dallas and Houston, Texas, also have direct connections to South America. As a general rule, Caracas and Lima are probably the cheapest South American cities to fly to, while Buenos Aires, Santiago and La Paz are the most expensive.

Inexpensive tickets from North America usually have restrictions; often there's a two-week advance-purchase requirement, and usually you must stay at least one week and no more than three months (prices often double for longer periods). High season for most fares is from early June to early September, and mid-December to mid-January. Look in major newspapers and alternative weeklies for sample fares and deals.

Travel agencies known as 'consolidators' typically have the best deals. They buy tickets in bulk, then discount them to their customers, or sell 'fill-up fares', which can be even cheaper (with additional restrictions). Look for agencies that specialize in South American travel, such as **eXito** (☎ 800-655-4053, 925-952-9322; www.exitotravel.com; 108 Rutgers St, Fort Collins, CO, 80525). eXito has a very knowledgeable staff (most of them have lived in Latin America), offers great deals and is excellent for travelers with special interests.

The largest student travel company in the USA is **STA Travel** (☎ 1-800-777-0112; www.statravel.com). Its US offices are listed on its website, or you can book tickets online.

Most flights from Canada involve connecting via one of the US gateways. Canada's national student travel agency is **Travel Cuts** (in Canada ☎ 800-667-2887, in USA ☎ 800-593-2887; www.travelcuts.com), which has over 50 locations throughout the country. It offers great deals for students and under-26s and can get good fares for the general public as well. It has offices in several US cities. The **Adventure Travel Company** (in USA ☎ 1-800-467-4595; www.atcadventure.com) deals with the general public as much as it does with students and offers some excellent prices. The agency has offices in the US and Canada.

The Internet is a great way to begin digging through prices to South American destinations. The following are all reputable, US-based online sellers:
Cheap Tickets (www.cheaptickets.com)
Expedia.com (www.expedia.com)
Orbitz (www.orbitz.com)
Travelocity (www.travelocity.com)

For occasional steals, try an air-ticket auction site such as **Priceline.com** (www.priceline.com) or **SkyAuction.com** (www.skyauction.com), where you bid on your own fare. These tickets are with major airlines flying to most international destinations, and the concept actually works! The restrictions are not crippling, either; see the websites for more information.

LAND

From North America, you can journey overland only as far south as Panama. There is no road connection onward to Colombia: the Carretera Panamericana (Pan-American Hwy) ends in the vast wilderness of the Darién Province, in southeast Panama. This roadless area between Central and South America is called the Darién Gap. In the past it has been difficult, but possible, to trek across the gap with the help of local guides, but since around 1998 it has been prohibitively dangerous, especially on the Colombian side. The region is effectively controlled by guerrillas and is positively unsafe.

SEA

A few cruise ships from Europe and the US call on South American ports, but they are much more expensive than any air ticket. Some cargo ships from Houston, New Orleans, Hamburg and Amsterdam will take a limited number of passengers to South American ports, but they are also expensive.

The ferry that used to run between Colón, Panama, and Cartagena, Colombia, no longer runs due to lack of traffic. Some small cargo ships sail between Colón and the Colombian port of Barranquilla, but many of them are involved in carrying contraband and may be too shady for comfort. Nevertheless, some of these ships will take paying passengers, and some will also take motorcycles and even cars. Prices are very negotiable – maybe US$50 for a passenger, US$150 to US$200 for a motorcycle. For more information on shipping a vehicle, see p1049.

It is also possible – and increasingly popular – to secure passage on a sailboat between Cartagena and the San Blás islands, with some boats continuing to Colón. The typical passage takes four to six days and costs about US$200. The best place for up-to-date information regarding schedules and available berths is at Hotel Holiday and Casa Viena in Cartagena (see p565).

Officially, both Panama and Colombia require an onward or return ticket as a condition of entry. This may not be enforced in Colombia, but it's wise to get a ticket anyway, or have plenty of money and a plausible itinerary. Panama requires a visa or tourist card, an onward ticket and sufficient funds, and has been known to turn back arrivals who don't meet these requirements. The Panamanian consulate in Cartagena is reportedly helpful.

TRANSPORT

GETTING AROUND

AIR

There is an extensive network of domestic flights, with refreshingly low price tags, especially in the Andean countries. After 18-hour bus rides across 350km of mountainous terrain on atrocious roads, you may decide, as many travelers do, to take the occasional flight. Flying allows you to cover a lot of ground in a flash – definitely an advantage for those short on time but long on finances.

There are drawbacks to flying, however. Airports are often far from city centers, and public buses don't run all the time, so you may end up spending a lot on taxis (it's usually easier to find a cheap taxi *to* an airport than *from* one). Airport taxes also add to the cost of air travel; they are usually higher for international departures. If safety concerns you, check out the 'Fatal Events by Airline' feature at **AirSafe.com** (www.airsafe.com).

In some areas, planes rarely depart on time. Avoid scheduling a domestic flight with a close connection for an international flight or vice versa. Many a traveler has been stranded after setting too tight an itinerary that hinges on their international flight arriving on time and connecting with a domestic leg to a far-flung outpost. Reconfirm all flights 48 hours before departure and turn up at the airport at least an hour before flight time.

Flights from North America and Europe may permit stopovers on the way to the destination city. It's worth considering this when shopping for an international flight, as it can effectively give you a free air connection within South America. On-ward connections in conjunction with an international flight can also be a cheap way to get to another South American city (for more, see p1041).

Air Passes

Air passes offer a number of flights within a country or region, for a specified period, at a fixed total price. Passes offer an economical way to cover long distances if your time is limited, but they have shortcomings. Some passes are irritatingly inflexible – once you start using the pass, you're locked into a schedule and can't change it without paying a penalty. The validity period can be restrictive and certain passes require that you enter the country on an international flight – you can't travel overland to the country and then start flying around with an air pass. Citizens of some countries are not eligible for certain air passes and on and on. For a concise overview of the various passes and their minutiae, see the air passes pages on the **Last Frontiers** (www.lastfrontiers.co.uk/airpass.htm) or **eXito** (www.exitotravel.com) websites.

MULTICOUNTRY AIR PASSES

The number of multicountry air passes for South America are few, but a handful do exist that will save you money if you can deal with a fixed itinerary. One such pass is the Mercosur Pass. This mileage-based pass offered by LanChile allows travelers to fly to cities in Argentina, Brazil, Chile (excluding Easter Island), Paraguay and Uruguay on the major airlines of those countries. The flights must be completed over a minimum of seven days and a maximum of 30 days, and there's a maximum of four flights in any country, eight flights in all. If it's well organized, this can be cheaper than some domestic air passes. The cost is based on the number of standard air miles (not kilometers) you want to cover; prices range from US$225 to US$780, for 1200 to 7200 miles.

Another one to ask your travel agent about is Grupo Taca's Latin Airflex Pass, but it's available only if you start and end your trip in the US. It allows you to stop in Mexico, Central America and eight South American countries within a total of 180 days. If Central America figures into your travel, and you're flying originally from the USA, ask your travel agent about the Copa Pass, offered by Copa Airlines in partner-

---

FLYING HIGH

You know you're in South America when...your one-hour 'direct' flight is delayed for half a day (there's no radar and when the fog finally clears the pilots are busy eating lunch), then you get a free, three-stop, two-plane-change aerial tour of the country, only to arrive 16 hours later, just beating the 18-hour bus ride you were initially trying to avoid.

Andrew Dean Nystrom

ship with Continental. With this pass you can fly from certain US cities to, say, Guatemala City and/or San José, Costa Rica, and on to one or more South American cities and return from South America.

SINGLE-COUNTRY AIR PASSES
Most air passes are only good within one country and are usually purchased in combination with a return ticket to that country. In addition, most air passes must be purchased outside the destination country; check with a travel agent. Argentina, Chile, Colombia, Bolivia and Brazil all offer domestic air passes; for more details, see Getting Around in the Transport section of each country chapter.

Sample Airfares
The following chart includes sample low-season, one-way airfares (unless otherwise specified) for getting around the continent; of course, with some savvy you may get substantially better fares.

Origin	Destination	Cost
Asuncíon	Buenos Aires	US$188
Asuncíon	La Paz	US$224
Bogotá	Quito	US$158
Buenos Aires	La Paz	US$300
Buenos Aires	Río Gallegos	US$141
Buenos Aires	Santiago	US$110
Guayaquil	Galápagos Islands	US$300 (round trip)
Guayaquil	Lima	US$179-250
La Paz	Arica	US$119
Lima	La Paz	US$189
Manaus	Tabatinga	US$161
Punta Arenas	Falkland Islands	US$280
Punta Arenas	Santiago	US$332
Quito	Galápagos Islands	US$333 (round trip)
Río Gallegos	Ushuaia	US$33
Rio	Asuncíon	US$395
Rio	Manaus	US$232
Rio	Montevideo	US$358
Rio	Santa Cruz	US$325
Salvador	Rio	US$139
Santa Cruz	Manaus	US$215
Santiago	Easter Island	US$499 (round trip)
Santiago	Juan Fernández Islands	US$405-490 (round trip)
Santiago	La Paz	US$362
Santiago	Lima	US$219-428

BICYCLE
Cycling is an interesting and inexpensive alternative, especially in Southern Cone countries, where roads are better and transport costs higher. Touring bikes are suitable for paved roads and long trips, but on the mostly dirt roads of the Andes, a *todo terreno* (mountain bike) is a better choice. Bring your own bicycle, since locally manufactured ones are less dependable, and secure a good map that shows side roads, as you'll have the enviable ability to get off the beaten track at will.

Advise your airline far in advance of traveling that you will be checking in your bike; on some airlines it's free, while others charge a fee (as much as US$100 each way). It's best to get to the airport early if you're taking a bike so you're not handed the old 'limited space availability' line. You'll need to loosen the handle bar nut and turn the handles 90 degrees and remove any attachments like panniers or lights. Consider purchasing a bike box or wrapping the bike in bubble wrap to avoid dings, dents or worse.

There are many good cycling routes, especially in the lake districts of Chile and Argentina. Mountain bikers have even cycled the length of Brazil's Trans-Amazon Hwy and more than one adventurous cyclist has made the transcontinental journey from North to South America.

Bicycle mechanics are common even in small towns, but will almost invariably lack the parts you'll need. Before setting out, make an effort to become a competent bicycle mechanic and purchase spares for the pieces most likely to fail. A basic road kit will include extra spokes and a tightener, a tire patch kit, extra inner tubes, spare cables, a wrench and a pair of pliers.

Drawbacks to cycling include the weather (rain in Brazil or wind in Patagonia can slow your progress to a crawl) and high altitude and poor roads in the Andean countries. In addition, motorists may have a total disregard for anyone but themselves and can be a serious hazard to cyclists. Safety equipment such as reflectors, mirrors and a helmet are highly recommended. Security is another issue: always take your panniers with you, pay someone to watch your bike while you sightsee and bring your bike into your hotel room overnight.

TRANSPORT

For further tips on bike travel, get the well-recommended *Latin America by Bike: A Complete Touring Guide (By Bike)* by Walter Sienko.

BOAT
Lake Crossings

There are outstanding lake excursions in southern Chile and Argentina and on Lake Titicaca in Bolivia and Peru. For details, see the individual country chapters. Here are some of the most popular:

- Puerto Montt and Puerto Varas (Chile) to Bariloche (Argentina).
- Lago General Carrera (Chile) to Chile Chico and Puerto Ingeniero Ibáñez (Chile).
- Puno (Peru) to the Lake Titicaca islands.
- Copacabana (Bolivia) to Lake Titicaca islands of Isla del Sol and Isla de la Luna.

Riverboat

Cruising down mighty rivers like the Orinoco or Amazon is a nice fantasy, but you'll have a more idyllic time on one of the smaller rivers such as the Mamoré or Beni, where boats hug the shore and you can see and hear the wildlife. Another alternative is the Río Paraguay, upstream from Asunción (Paraguay) to Brazil.

The Amazon is quite densely settled in its lower reaches, and its upper reaches have fewer passenger boats than in the past. Also, the Amazon is so broad that your boat may be miles from anything interesting on the riverbanks.

Boats vary greatly in size and standards, so check the vessel before buying a ticket and shop around. Hammock space on the slow boat between Manaus and Belém, Brazil, for example, costs around US$70, including food; from Trinidad to Guayaramerín, Bolivia (three to four days), it costs US$28. When you pay the fare, get a ticket with all the details on it. Downriver travel is faster than upriver, but boats going upriver travel closer to the shore and offer more interesting scenery. The time taken between ports is unpredictable: from Manaus to Belém should be about four days, but it commonly takes six or more. River travel is not for those on a tight schedule.

Food is usually included in ticket prices and means lots of rice and beans and perhaps some meat, but bring bottled water, fruit and snacks as a supplement. The evening meal on the first night of a trip is not usually included. Drinks and extra food are generally sold on board, but at high prices. Bring some spare cash and insect repellent.

Unless you have cabin space, you'll need a hammock and rope to string it up. It can get windy and cool at night, so a sleeping bag is also recommended. There are usually two classes of hammock space, with space on the upper deck costing slightly more; it's cooler there and worth the extra money. Be on the boat at least eight hours prior to departure to get a good hammock space away from engine noise and toilet odors.

Overcrowding and theft on boats are common complaints. Don't allow your baggage to be stored in an insecure locker – bring your own padlock. Don't entrust your bag to any boat officials unless you are quite certain about their status – bogus officials have been reported.

Sea Trips

The best sea trip is down the Chilean coast from Puerto Montt to Puerto Natales. Short boat rides in some countries take you to islands not far from the mainland, including Ilha Grande and Ilha de Santa Catarina in Brazil, Isla Grande de Chiloé in Chile and Isla Grande de Tierra del Fuego in Argentina. More distant islands are usually reached by air, but ocean trips to the Galápagos and Juan Fernández Islands are a possibility for those with the stomach and patience for the journey.

BUS

Bus transport is well developed throughout the continent, but road conditions, bus quality and driver professionalism vary widely. One seasoned traveler observed that South American bus drivers never seem to wear spectacles – scary, but largely true.

Highland Peru, Bolivia and Ecuador have some of the worst roads, and bad stretches can be found in parts of Colombia and the Brazilian Amazon. Much depends on the season – vast deserts of red dust in the dry season become oceans of mud in the rainy season. In Argentina, Uruguay, coastal and southern Brazil, and most of Venezuela, roads are generally better. Chile has some of the best-maintained roads and most comfortable and reliable bus services in South America.

Especially in the Andean countries (Peru, Bolivia and Ecuador), buses may be stripped nearly bare, tires are often treadless and rock-hard suspensions ensure every bump is transmitted directly to your ass before shooting up your spine, resulting in killer neck aches and headaches. After all seats are taken, the aisle is packed beyond capacity, and the roof is loaded with cargo to at least half the height of the bus, topped by the occasional goat or pig. You may have serious doubts about ever arriving at your destination, but the buses usually make it.

At the other extreme, you'll find luxurious coaches in Argentina, Brazil, Chile, Colombia, Uruguay, Venezuela and even Bolivia along main routes. The most expensive buses usually feature reclining seats, and snack, beverage and movie services. You can get a deluxe sleeper bus, called a *bus cama*, on some long routes, but it may cost double the fare of a regular bus. Still, overnighters negate the need for a hotel room, thereby saving you money.

Most major cities and towns have a *terminal de autobuses* (long-distance bus terminal); in Brazil, it's called a *rodoviária* and in Ecuador it's a *terminal terrestre*. Often this is on the outskirts of town, and you'll need a local bus or taxi to reach it. The biggest and best terminals also have restaurants, shops, showers and other services, and the surrounding area is often a good (but frequently ugly) place to look for cheap sleeps and eats. At best, bus companies will have ticket offices at central terminals and information boards showing routes, departure times and fares. Seats will be numbered and booked in advance. At worst, you'll find yourself in the middle of a dirt lot flanked by dilapidated metal hulks called 'buses' and men hawking various destinations to passersby; listen for your town of choice. Whatever the depot situation, all the seats may be filled on major routes at holiday times, but generally you will get a seat if you turn up an hour or so before the scheduled departure.

Some cities have several terminals, each serving a different route. Sometimes each bus company has its own terminal, which is particularly inconvenient. This is most common in Colombia, Ecuador and Peru, particularly in smaller towns, but notably in Lima.

The width of the highway provided drivers the opportunity to pull out into the middle lane, evaluate their chances of success or death, then swerve back into their own lane, cutting off other drivers who leaned bitterly on their horns… 'The Pan-American,' Alejandro had said, 'is war.'

Road Fever, Tim Cahill

CAR & MOTORCYCLE

In parts of South America where distances are great and buses infrequent (think Patagonia), a rental car may be worth the hassle and expense. If you've driven your own vehicle from up north somewhere, so much the better.

Driving around South America is not all fun and glory. First off, if you're driving, you need an International or Inter-American Driving Permit to supplement your license from home (see p1033). Vehicle security can be a problem, most notably in the Andean countries and Brazil. Avoid leaving valuables in your car, and always lock it up. Parking is not always secure or even available; be mindful of where you leave your car, lest it be missing when you return. Contracting a local kid to keep an eye on things works wonders; agree on terms beforehand. Familiarizing yourself with phrases for 'nearest gas,' 'busted fan belt' and the like can mitigate road-trip stress. In the same vein, the more you know about vehicle maintenance and repair, the smoother your travels will be.

South American Explorers (SAE; www.samexplo.org /docum.htm) sells the very useful *Central/South American Driving Packet,* as well as Chris Yelland's *Driving through Latin America: USA to Argentina.* SAE gives a quick rundown on driving in South America on its website.

Bring Your Own Vehicle

Taking your own car or motorcycle to South America can involve a lot of money up front, mostly for paperwork. Also, remember there is no road connecting Panama and Colombia, so any vehicle making it that far will have to be shipped around the Darién Gap (see Land, p1045).

Quite a few people ship their own motorcycle and ride it around South America. Before getting outfitted, bikers should keep

TRANSPORT

in mind the changeable weather and real threat of wet conditions.

It is generally cheaper to ship from US Atlantic ports than Pacific ports. You must usually book transport for your vehicle at least two weeks ahead, and often you can't travel on the same ship as your vehicle.

One alternative is to drive through Central America and ship your vehicle from Panama to South America. There's no regular boat service from Panama to Colombia, and the cargo ships between Colón and the Colombian port of Barranquilla are not very safe or reliable. Prices are highly negotiable; they might start at US$1500 and eventually come down to half that; bank on about US$1000. More established shippers are more expensive, but they may help you with the paperwork, which must be handled at both the Colombian and Panamanian ends.

DOCUMENTS

You must submit three notarized copies of the vehicle's title to the shipper, plus a letter of permission from the lien holder if it is not completely paid for. In practice, most countries seem to have dispensed with the requirement for a *carnet de passage* or a *libreta de pasos por aduana,* but officially one of these documents is still required; check with the appropriate consulates, especially for any country where your vehicle will arrive by air or sea. Some travelers have had horrendous experiences taking vehicles, especially motorcycles, from Panama to South America without proper documentation.

On arrival, make it clear to customs officials that the vehicle is only in transit; in the case of Chile, for example, the maximum stay is 90 days. Once you have entered South America, border crossings should be routine in a vehicle from your home country.

SECURITY

Anticipate that something will be stolen from your vehicle – stealing from vehicles being shipped is big business. Remove everything removable (hubcaps, wipers, mirrors), and take everything visible from the interior. Shipping your vehicle in a container is more secure, but more expensive.

Purchase

If you're spending several months in South America, purchasing a car is worth consid-

ering. It will be cheaper than renting if you can resell it at the end of your stay. On the other hand, any used car can be a financial risk, especially on rugged roads.

The best countries in which to purchase cars are Argentina, Brazil and Chile, but expect exasperating bureaucracies. By reputation, Santiago de Chile is the best place to buy a car, and Asunción, Paraguay, is the best place to sell one. Be certain of the title; as a foreigner, getting a notarized document authorizing your use of the car is a good idea, since the bureaucracy may take its time transferring the title. Taking a vehicle purchased in South America across international borders may present obstacles.

Officially, you need a *carnet de passage* or a *libreta de pasos por aduana* to cross most land borders in your own vehicle, but you'll probably never have to show these documents. The best source of advice is the national automobile club in the country where you buy the car. In North America, the Canadian Automobile Association may be more helpful in getting a carnet than the American Automobile Association.

Rental

Major international rental agencies such as Hertz, Avis and Budget have offices in South American capitals and other major cities, but there are also local agencies. To rent a car, you must be at least 25 and have a valid driver's license from home. It may also be necessary to present a credit card or pay a large cash deposit. If your itinerary calls for crossing borders, know that some rental agencies restrict or forbid this; ask before renting.

Even at smaller agencies, rental charges are very high (eg between US$50 and US$100 per day): get a group together to defray costs. If the vehicle enables you to camp out, the saving in accommodations may offset much of the rental cost, especially in Southern Cone countries.

Road Rules

In South America you drive on the right-hand side of the road, except in Guyana and Suriname. Road rules are frequently ignored and seldom enforced, conditions can be hazardous and many drivers, especially in Argentina and Brazil, are very reckless and even willfully dangerous. Driving at night is riskier than the day, due to lower visibility and the preponderance of tired and/or intoxicated nighttime drivers sharing the road.

Road signs can be confusing, misleading or nonexistent – good humor and patience are key attributes. Honking your horn on blind curves is a simple, effective safety measure; the vehicle coming uphill on a one-way road usually has the right of way. If you're cruising along and see a tree branch or rock in the middle of the road, slow down: this means there's a breakdown, rock slide or some other trouble up ahead. Speed bumps can pop up anywhere, most often smack in the center of town, but sometimes inexplicably in the middle of a highway.

HITCHING

Hitching is never entirely safe in any country. Travelers who decide to hitch should understand they are taking a potentially serious risk. Hitching is less dangerous if you travel in pairs and let someone know where you are planning to go.

Though it is possible to hitch all over South America, free lifts are the rule only in Argentina, Chile, Uruguay and parts of Brazil. Elsewhere, hitching is virtually a form of public transport (especially where buses are infrequent) and drivers expect payment. There are generally fixed fares over certain routes – ask the other passengers what they're paying. It's usually about equal to the bus fare, marginally less in some places. You get better views from the top of a truck, but if you're hitching on the Andean altiplano, take warm clothing. Once the sun goes down or is obscured by clouds, it gets very cold.

There's no need to wait at the roadside for a lift, unless it happens to be convenient. Almost every town has a central truck park, often around the market. Ask around for a truck going your way and how much it will cost; be there about 30 minutes before the departure time given by the driver. It is often worth soliciting a ride at *servicentros* on the outskirts of large cities, where drivers refuel their vehicles.

LOCAL TRANSPORT

Local and city bus systems tend to be thorough and reliable throughout South America. Although in many countries you can flag a bus anywhere on its route, you're best off finding the official bus stop. Still, if you can't find the stop, don't hesitate to throw your arm up to stop a bus you know is going your direction. Never hesitate to ask a bus driver which is the right bus to take; most of them are very generous in directing you to the right bus.

Taxis in most big cities (but definitely not all) have meters. When a taxi has a meter, make sure the driver uses it. When it doesn't, always agree on a fare *before* you get in the cab. In most cities, fares are higher on Sundays and after around 9pm.

TRAIN

South American trains, covering some of the most spectacular routes on earth, are often cheaper than buses (even in 1st class) but they're slower. Many services are obsolete, but railway enthusiasts should note the following routes:

Curitiba–Paranaguá (Brazil) Descending steeply to the coastal lowlands, this trip offers some unforgettable views.

Oruro–Uyuni–Calama (Bolivia–Chile) The Oruro–Uyuni run offers great altiplano scenery all the way to Uyuni, where a branch line goes southwest to the Chilean border. After a tedious border crossing, there's a dramatic descent to Calama, through wild moonlike landscapes and extinct volcanoes. This is a long, tiresome trip and can get very cold at night. Bundle up and bring along extra food and water.

Oruro–Uyuni–Tupiza–Villazón (Bolivia) The main line from Oruro continues south from Uyuni to Tupiza (another scenic rail trip through gorge country) and on to Villazón at the Argentine border. This is a great trip if you can do it in daylight.

Puno–Juliaca–Cuzco (Peru) From the shores of Lake Titicaca and across a 4600m pass, this train runs for group bookings during high season. Departures are unpredictable, but when it does run, it's open to nongroup passengers.

Riobamba–Sibambe (Ecuador) This ride navigates the hairy Nariz del Diablo (Devil's Nose) and is known for its exhilarating steep descent via switchbacks.

Salta–San Antonio de los Cobres (Argentina) The Tren a las Nubes (Train to the Clouds) runs through the arid foothills on the eastern slope of the Andes, offering hair-raising bridge and tunnel crossings en route. It's usually done as an expensive excursion from Salta.

There are several types of passenger trains in the Andean countries. The *ferrobus* is a relatively fast, diesel-powered single or double car that caters to passengers going from A to B but not to intermediate stations. Meals are often available on board. These are the most expensive trains and can be an excellent value.

The *tren rápido* is more like an ordinary train, pulled by a diesel or steam engine. It is relatively fast, makes few stops and is generally cheaper than a *ferrobus*. Ordinary passenger trains, sometimes called *expresos*, are slower, cheaper and stop at most intermediate stations. There are generally two classes, with 2nd class being very crowded. Lastly, there are *mixtos,* mixed passenger

and freight trains; these take everything and everyone, stop at every station and a lot of other places in between, take forever and are dirt cheap.

The few remaining passenger trains in Chile and Argentina are generally more modern, and the salon and Pullman classes are very comfortable and quite inexpensive. The *economía* or *turista* classes are slightly cheaper, while the *cama* (sleeper class) is even more comfortable. Brazil still has a few interesting train trips, but they're quite short.

Health

CONTENTS

Medically speaking, there are two South Americas: tropical South America, which includes most of the continent except for the southernmost portion, and temperate South America, which includes Chile, Uruguay, southern Argentina and the Falkland Islands. The diseases found in tropical South America are comparable to those found in tropical areas in Africa and Asia. Particularly important are mosquito-borne infections, including malaria, yellow fever and dengue fever, which are not a significant concern in temperate regions.

Prevention is the key to staying healthy while in South America. Travelers who receive the recommended vaccines and follow common-sense precautions usually come away with nothing more than a little diarrhea.

BEFORE YOU GO

Bring medications in their original, clearly labeled, containers. A signed and dated letter from your physician describing your medical conditions and medications, including generic names, is also a good idea.

If carrying syringes or needles, be sure to have a physician's letter documenting their medical necessity.

INSURANCE

If your health insurance doesn't cover you for medical expenses abroad, consider getting extra insurance – check Subwwway on www.lonelyplanet.com for more information. Find out in advance if your insurance plan will make payments directly to providers or reimburse you later for overseas health expenditures. (In many countries doctors expect payment in cash.)

RECOMMENDED VACCINATIONS

Since most vaccines don't produce immunity until at least two weeks after they're given, visit a physician four to eight weeks before departure. Ask your doctor for an International Certificate of Vaccination (otherwise known as the yellow booklet), which will list all the vaccinations you've received. This is mandatory for countries that require proof of yellow-fever vaccination upon entry, but it's a good idea to carry it wherever you travel.

The only required vaccine is yellow fever, and that's only if you're arriving from a yellow fever–infected country in Africa or the Americas. (The exception is French Guiana, which requires yellow-fever vaccine for all travelers.) However, a number of vaccines are recommended.

MEDICAL CHECKLIST

- acetaminophen (Tylenol) or aspirin
- acetazolamide (Diamox; for altitude sickness)
- adhesive or paper tape
- antibacterial ointment (eg Bactroban; for cuts and abrasions)
- antibiotics
- antidiarrheal drugs (eg loperamide)
- antihistamines (for hay fever and allergic reactions)
- anti-inflammatory drugs (eg ibuprofen)
- bandages, gauze, gauze rolls
- insect repellent containing DEET for the skin

HEALTH

Vaccine	Recommended for	Dosage	Side effects
chickenpox	travelers who've never had chickenpox	two doses one month apart	fever; mild case of chickenpox
hepatitis A	all travelers	one dose before trip; booster 6–12 months later	soreness at injection site; headaches; body aches
hepatitis B	long-term travelers in close contact with the local population	3 doses over 6-month period	soreness at injection site; low-grade fever
measles	travelers born after 1956 who've had only one measles vaccination	one dose	fever; rash; joint pains; allergic reactions
rabies	travelers who may have contact with animals and may not have access to medical care	Three doses over 3–4 week period	soreness at injection site; headaches; body aches
tetanus-diphtheria	all travelers who haven't had booster within 10 years	one dose lasts 10 years	soreness at injection site
typhoid	all travelers	four capsules by mouth, one taken every other day	abdominal pain; nausea; rash
yellow fever	travelers to jungle areas at altitudes above 2300m	one dose lasts 10 years	headaches; body aches; severe reactions are rare

- iodine tablets (for water purification)
- oral rehydration salts
- permethrin-containing insect spray for clothing, tents and bed nets
- pocket knife
- scissors, safety pins, tweezers
- steroid cream or cortisone (for poison ivy and other allergic rashes)
- sun block
- syringes and sterile needles
- thermometer

ONLINE RESOURCES

There is a wealth of travel health advice on the Internet. For further information, the **Lonely Planet website** (www.lonelyplanet.com) is a good place to start. The **World Health Organization** (www.who.int/ith) also publishes a superb book called *International Travel and Health*, which is revised annually and is available online at no cost. Another website of general interest is the **MD Travel Health website** (www.mdtravelhealth.com), which provides complete travel health recommendations for every country; information is updated daily.

It's usually a good idea to consult your government's travel health website before departure, if one is available:

Australia (www.dfat.gov.au/travel)
Canada (www.travelhealth.gc.ca)
UK (www.doh.gov.uk/traveladvice)
US (www.cdc.gov/travel)

FURTHER READING

For further information, see *Healthy Travel Central & South America*, also from Lonely Planet. If you're traveling with children, Lonely Planet's *Travel with Children* may be useful. The *ABC of Healthy Travel*, by E. Walker et al, is another valuable resource.

IN TRANSIT

DEEP VEIN THROMBOSIS

Blood clots may form in the legs (deep vein thrombosis or DVT) during plane flights, chiefly because of prolonged immobility. The longer the flight, the greater the risk. Although most blood clots are reabsorbed uneventfully, some may break off and travel through the blood vessels to the lungs, where they could cause life-threatening complications.

The chief symptom of DVT is swelling or pain of the foot, ankle or calf, usually – but not always – on just one side. When a blood clot travels to the lungs, it may cause chest pain and difficulty with breathing. Travelers with these symptoms should immediately seek medical attention.

To prevent the development of DVT on long flights, you should walk about the cabin, perform isometric compressions of the leg muscles (ie flex the leg muscles while sitting), drink plenty of fluids and avoid alcohol and tobacco.

JET LAG & MOTION SICKNESS

Jet lag is common when crossing more than five time zones, resulting in insomnia, fatigue, malaise or nausea. To avoid jet lag try drinking plenty of (nonalcoholic) fluids and eating light meals. Upon arrival, get exposure to natural sunlight and readjust your schedule (for meals, sleep etc) as soon as possible.

Antihistamines such as dimenhydrinate (Dramamine) and meclizine (Antivert, Bonine) are usually the first choice for treating motion sickness. Their main side effect is drowsiness. An herbal alternative is ginger, which works like a charm for some people.

IN SOUTH AMERICA

AVAILABILITY & COST OF HEALTH CARE

Good medical care may be more difficult to find in smaller cities and impossible to locate in rural areas. Many doctors and hospitals expect payment in cash, regardless of whether you have travel health insurance. If you develop a life-threatening medical problem, you'll probably want to be evacuated to a country with state-of-the-art medical care. Since this may cost tens of thousands of dollars, be sure you have insurance to cover this before you depart. You can find a list of medical evacuation and travel insurance companies on the **US State Department website** (travel.state.gov/medical.html).

INFECTIOUS DISEASES
Cholera

Cholera is an intestinal infection acquired through ingestion of contaminated food or water. The main symptom is profuse, watery diarrhea, which may be so severe that it causes life-threatening dehydration. The key treatment is drinking oral rehydration

solution. Antibiotics are also given, usually tetracycline or doxycycline, though quinolone antibiotics such as ciprofloxacin and levofloxacin are also effective.

Cholera is rare among travelers. Cholera vaccine is no longer required, and is in fact no longer available in some countries, including the US, because the old vaccine was relatively ineffective and caused side effects. There are new vaccines that are safer and more effective, but they're not available in many countries and are only recommended for those at particularly high risk.

Dengue

Dengue fever is a viral infection found throughout South America. Dengue is transmitted by Aedes mosquitoes, which bite preferentially during the daytime and are usually found close to human habitations, often indoors. They breed primarily in artificial water containers, such as jars, barrels, cans, cisterns, metal drums, plastic containers and discarded tires. As a result, dengue is especially common in densely populated, urban environments.

Dengue usually causes flu-like symptoms, including fever, muscle aches, joint pains, headaches, nausea and vomiting, often followed by a rash. The body aches may be quite uncomfortable, but most cases resolve uneventfully in a few days. Severe cases usually occur in children under age 15 who are experiencing their second dengue infection.

There is no treatment for dengue fever except to take analgesics such as acetaminophen/paracetamol (Tylenol) and drink plenty of fluids. Severe cases may require hospitalization for intravenous fluids and supportive care. There is no vaccine. The cornerstone of prevention is insect protection measures (see p1060).

Hepatitis A

Hepatitis A is the second most common travel-related infection (after travelers' diarrhea). It's a viral infection of the liver that is usually acquired by ingestion of contaminated water, food or ice, though it may also be acquired by direct contact with infected persons. The illness occurs throughout the world, but the incidence is higher in developing nations. Symptoms may include fever, malaise, jaundice, nausea, vomiting and abdominal pain. Most cases resolve without complications, though hepatitis A occasionally causes severe liver damage. There is no treatment.

The vaccine for hepatitis A is extremely safe and highly effective. If you get a booster six to 12 months later, it lasts for at least 10 years. You really should get it before you go to any developing nation. The safety of hepatitis A vaccine has not been established for pregnant women or children under two years – instead, they should be given a gammaglobulin injection.

Hepatitis B

Like hepatitis A, hepatitis B is a liver infection that occurs worldwide but is more common in developing nations. Unlike hepatitis A, the disease is usually acquired by sexual contact or by exposure to infected blood, generally through blood transfusions or contaminated needles. The vaccine is recommended only for long-term travelers (on the road more than six months) who expect to live in rural areas or have close physical contact with the local population. Additionally, the vaccine is recommended for anyone who anticipates sexual contact with the local inhabitants or a possible need for medical, dental or other treatments while abroad, especially if a need for transfusions or injections is expected.

Hepatitis B vaccine is safe and highly effective. However, a total of three injections are necessary to establish full immunity. Several countries added hepatitis B vaccine to the list of routine childhood immunizations in the 1980s, so many young adults are already protected.

Malaria

Malaria occurs in every South American country except Chile, Uruguay and the Falkland Islands. It's transmitted by mosquito bites, usually between dusk and dawn. The main symptom is high spiking fevers, which may be accompanied by chills, sweats, headache, body aches, weakness, vomiting or diarrhea. Severe cases may involve the central nervous system and lead to seizures, confusion, coma and death.

There is a choice of three malaria pills, all of which work about equally well. Mefloquine (Lariam) is taken once weekly in a dosage of 250mg, starting one to two weeks before arrival and continuing through the trip and for four weeks after your return. The problem is that a certain percentage of people (the number is disputed) develop neuropsychiatric side effects, which may range from mild to severe. Atovaquone/proguanil (Malarone) is a newly approved combination pill taken once daily with food starting two days before arrival and continuing through the trip and for seven days after departure. Side effects are typically mild. Doxycycline is a third alternative, but may cause an exaggerated sunburn reaction.

In general, Malarone seems to cause fewer side effects than mefloquine and is becoming more popular. The chief disadvantage is that it has to be taken daily. For longer trips, it's probably worth trying mefloquine; for shorter trips, Malarone will be the drug of choice for most people.

Protecting yourself against mosquito bites is just as important as taking malaria pills (for recommendations see p1060), since none of the pills are 100% effective.

If you do not have access to medical care while traveling, you should bring along additional pills for emergency self-treatment,

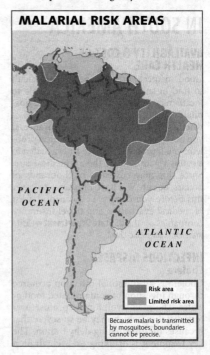

MALARIAL RISK AREAS

PACIFIC OCEAN

ATLANTIC OCEAN

Risk area

Limited risk area

Because malaria is transmitted by mosquitoes, boundaries cannot be precise.

which you should take if you can't reach a doctor and you develop symptoms that suggest malaria, such as high spiking fevers. One option is to take four tablets of Malarone once daily for three days. However, Malarone should not be used for treatment if you're already taking it for prevention. An alternative is to take 650mg quinine three times daily and 100mg doxycycline twice daily for one week. If you start self-medication, see a doctor at the earliest possible opportunity.

If you develop a fever after returning home, see a physician, as malaria symptoms may not occur for months.

Plague

The plague is usually transmitted to humans by the bite of rodent fleas, typically when rodents die off. Symptoms include fever, chills, muscle aches and malaise, associated with the development of an acutely swollen, exquisitely painful lymph node, known as a bubo, most often in the groin. Cases of the plague are reported from Peru, Bolivia and Brazil nearly every year. Most travelers are at extremely low risk for this disease. However, if you might have contact with rodents or their fleas, you should bring along a bottle of doxycycline, to be taken prophylactically during periods of exposure. Those less than eight years old or allergic to doxycycline should take trimethoprim-sulfamethoxazole instead. In addition, you should avoid areas containing rodent burrows or nests, never handle sick or dead animals, and follow the guidelines in this chapter for protecting yourself against insect bites (see p1060).

Rabies

Rabies is a viral infection of the brain and spinal cord that is almost always fatal. The rabies virus is carried in the saliva of infected animals and is typically transmitted through an animal bite, though contamination of any break in the skin with infected saliva may result in rabies. Rabies occurs in all South American countries.

Rabies vaccine is safe, but a full series requires three injections and is quite expensive. Those at high risk for rabies, such as animal handlers and spelunkers (cave explorers), should certainly get the vaccine. In addition, those at lower risk for animal bites should consider asking for the vaccine if they might be traveling to remote areas and might not have access to appropriate medical care if needed. The treatment for a possibly rabid bite consists of rabies vaccine with rabies immune globulin. It's effective, but must be given promptly. Most travelers don't need rabies vaccine.

All animal bites and scratches must be promptly and thoroughly cleansed with large amounts of soap and water and local health authorities contacted to determine whether or not further treatment is necessary (p1059).

Typhoid

Typhoid fever is caused by ingestion of food or water contaminated by a species of Salmonella known as *Salmonella typhi*. Fever occurs in virtually all cases. Other symptoms may include headache, malaise, muscle aches, dizziness, loss of appetite, nausea and abdominal pain. Either diarrhea or constipation may occur. Possible complications include intestinal perforation, intestinal bleeding, confusion, delirium or (rarely) coma.

Unless you expect to take all your meals in major hotels and restaurants, typhoid vaccine is a good idea. It's usually given orally, but is also available as an injection. Neither vaccine is approved for use in children under two years.

The drug of choice for typhoid fever is usually a quinolone antibiotic such as ciprofloxacin (Cipro) or levofloxacin (Levaquin), which many travelers carry for treatment of travelers' diarrhea. However, if you self-treat for typhoid fever, you may also need to self-treat for malaria, since the symptoms of the two diseases may be indistinguishable.

Yellow Fever

Yellow fever is a life-threatening viral infection transmitted by mosquitoes in forested areas. The illness begins with flu-like symptoms, which may include fever, chills, headache, muscle aches, backache, loss of appetite, nausea and vomiting. These symptoms usually subside in a few days, but one person in six enters a second, toxic phase characterized by recurrent fever, vomiting, listlessness, jaundice, kidney failure and hemorrhage, leading to death in up to half of the cases. There is no treatment except for supportive care.

YELLOW FEVER RISK AREAS

PACIFIC OCEAN

ATLANTIC OCEAN

Risk area

Because yellow fever is transmitted by mosquitoes, boundaries cannot be precise.

Yellow-fever vaccine is given only in approved yellow-fever vaccination centers, which provide validated International Certificates of Vaccination (yellow booklets). The vaccine should be given at least 10 days before any potential exposure to yellow fever and remains effective for approximately 10 years. Reactions to the vaccine are generally mild and may include headaches, muscle aches, low-grade fevers, or discomfort at the injection site. Severe, life-threatening reactions have been described but are extremely rare. In general, the risk of becoming ill from the vaccine is far less than the risk of becoming ill from yellow fever, and you're strongly encouraged to get the vaccine.

Taking measures to protect yourself from mosquito bites (p1060) is an essential part of preventing yellow fever.

Other Infections

BARTONELLOSIS (OROYA FEVER)
Bartonellosis (Oroya fever) is carried by sandflies in the arid river valleys on the western slopes of the Andes in Peru, Colombia and Ecuador between altitudes of 800m and 3000m. (Curiously, it's not found anywhere else in the world.) The chief symptoms are fever and severe body pains. Complications may include marked anemia, enlargement of the liver and spleen, and sometimes death. The drug of choice is chloramphenicol, though doxycycline is also effective.

CHAGAS' DISEASE
Chagas' disease is a parasitic infection that is transmitted by triatomine insects (reduviid bugs), which inhabit crevices in the walls and roofs of substandard housing in South and Central America. In Peru, most cases occur in the southern part of the country. The triatomine insect lays its feces on human skin as it bites, usually at night. A person becomes infected when he or she unknowingly rubs the feces into the bite wound or any other open sore. Chagas' disease is extremely rare in travelers. However, if you sleep in a poorly constructed house, especially one made of mud, adobe or thatch, you should be sure to protect yourself with a bed net and a good insecticide.

GNATHOSTOMIASIS
Gnathostomiasis is an intestinal parasite acquired by eating raw or undercooked freshwater fish, including *ceviche* (marinated, uncooked seafood).

HISTOPLASMOSIS
Histoplasmosis is caused by a soil-based fungus that is acquired by inhalation, often when the soil has been disrupted. Initial symptoms may include fever, chills, dry cough, chest pain and headache, sometimes leading to pneumonia. Histoplasmosis has been reported in spelunkers who have visited caves inhabited by bats.

HIV/AIDS
HIV/AIDS has been reported in all South American countries. Be sure to use condoms for all sexual encounters.

LEISHMANIASIS
Leishmaniasis occurs in the mountains and jungles of all South American countries except for Chile, Uruguay and the Falkland Islands. The infection is transmitted by sandflies, which are about one-third the size of mosquitoes. Leishmaniasis may be limited to the skin, causing slow-growing

ulcers over exposed parts of the body, or (less commonly) disseminate to the bone marrow, liver and spleen. The disease may be particularly severe in those with HIV. There is no vaccine. To protect yourself from sandflies, follow the same precautions as for mosquitoes (see p1060), except that netting must be finer-mesh (at least 18 holes to the linear inch).

LEPTOSPIROSIS

Leptospirosis is acquired by exposure to water contaminated by the urine of infected animals. Outbreaks often occur at times of flooding, when sewage overflow may contaminate water sources. The initial symptoms, which resemble a mild flu, usually subside uneventfully in a few days, with or without treatment, but a minority of cases are complicated by jaundice or meningitis. There is no vaccine. You can minimize your risk by staying out of bodies of fresh water that may be contaminated by animal urine. If you're visiting an area where an outbreak is in progress, you can take 200mg of doxycycline once weekly as a preventative measure. If you actually develop leptospirosis, the treatment is 100mg of doxycycline twice daily.

ENVIRONMENTAL HAZARDS
Altitude Sickness

Altitude sickness may develop in those who ascend rapidly to altitudes greater than 2500m. Being physically fit offers no protection. Those who have experienced altitude sickness in the past are prone to future episodes. The risk increases with faster ascents, higher altitudes and greater exertion. Symptoms may include headaches, nausea, vomiting, dizziness, malaise, insomnia and loss of appetite. Severe cases may be complicated by fluid in the lungs (high-altitude pulmonary edema) or swelling of the brain (high-altitude cerebral edema).

To protect yourself against altitude sickness, take 125mg or 250mg acetazolamide (Diamox) twice or three times daily starting 24 hours before ascent and continuing for 48 hours after arrival at altitude. Possible side effects include increased urinary volume, numbness, tingling, nausea, drowsiness, myopia and temporary impotence. Acetazolamide should not be given to pregnant women or anyone with a history of sulfa allergy. For those who cannot tolerate acetazolamide, the next best option is 4mg dexamethasone taken four times daily. Unlike acetazolamide, dexamethasone must be tapered gradually upon arrival at altitude, since there is a risk that altitude sickness will occur as the dosage is reduced. Dexamethasone is a steroid, so it should not be given to diabetics or anyone for whom steroids are contraindicated. A natural alternative is gingko, which some people find quite helpful.

When traveling to high altitudes, it's also important to avoid overexertion, eat light meals and abstain from alcohol.

If your symptoms are more than mild or don't resolve promptly, see a doctor. Altitude sickness should be taken seriously; it can be life threatening when severe.

Animal Bites

Do not attempt to pet, handle or feed any animal, with the exception of domestic animals known to be free of any infectious disease. Most animal injuries are directly related to a person's attempt to touch or feed the animal.

Any bite or scratch by a mammal, including bats, should be promptly and thoroughly cleansed with large amounts of soap and water, followed by application of an antiseptic such as iodine or alcohol. The local health authorities should be contacted immediately for possible post-exposure rabies treatment, whether or not you've been immunized against rabies. It may also be advisable to start an antibiotic, since wounds caused by animal bites and scratches frequently become infected. One of the newer quinolones, such as levofloxacin (Levaquin), which many travelers carry in case of diarrhea, would be an appropriate choice.

Snakes and leeches are a hazard in some areas of South America. In the event of a bite from a venomous snake, place the victim at rest, keep the bitten area immobilized, and move the victim immediately to the nearest medical facility. Avoid tourniquets, which are no longer recommended.

Cold Exposure

Cold exposure may be a significant problem in the Andes, particularly at night. Be sure to dress warmly, stay dry, keep active, consume plenty of food and water, get enough rest, and avoid alcohol, caffeine and tobacco. Watch out for the 'umbles' – stumbles,

HEALTH

mumbles, fumbles and grumbles – which are important signs of impending hypothermia.

Heatstroke

To protect yourself from excessive sun exposure, you should stay out of the midday sun, wear sunglasses and a wide-brimmed sun hat, and apply sunscreen with SPF 15 or higher, with both UVA and UVB protection. Sunscreen should be generously applied to all exposed parts of the body approximately 30 minutes before sun exposure and should be reapplied after swimming or vigorous activity. Travelers should also drink plenty of fluids and avoid strenuous exercise when the temperature is high.

Hypothermia

Hypothermia occurs when the body loses heat faster than it can produce it and the core temperature of the body falls. If you're trekking at high altitudes or simply taking a long bus trip over mountains, particularly at night, be prepared. In the Andes, you should always be prepared for cold, wet or windy conditions even if it's just for a few hours. It is best to dress in layers and a hat is important, as a lot of heat is lost through the head.

The symptoms of hypothermia include exhaustion, numbness, shivering, slurred speech, irrational or violent behavior, lethargy, stumbling, dizzy spells, muscle cramps and violent bursts of energy. To treat mild hypothermia, first get people out of the wind or rain, remove their clothing if it's wet and give them something warm and dry to wear. Make them drink hot liquids – not alcohol – and some high-calorie, easily digestible food. Do not rub victims, instead allow them to slowly warm themselves. This should be enough to treat hypothermia's early stages. Early detection and treatment of mild hypothermia is the only way to prevent severe hypothermia, which is a critical condition.

Insect Bites & Stings

To prevent mosquito bites, wear long sleeves, long pants, hats and shoes (rather than sandals). Bring along a good insect repellent, preferably one containing DEET, which should be applied to exposed skin and clothing, but not to eyes, mouth, cuts, wounds or irritated skin. Products containing lower concentrations of DEET are as effective, but for shorter periods of time. In general, adults and children over 12 years should use preparations containing 25% to 35% DEET, which usually lasts about six hours. Children between two and 12 years of age should use preparations containing no more than 10% DEET, applied sparingly, which will usually last about three hours. Neurologic toxicity has been reported from DEET, especially in children, but appears to be extremely uncommon and generally related to overuse. DEET-containing compounds should not be used on children under age two.

Insect repellents containing certain botanical products, including oil of eucalyptus and soybean oil, are effective but last only 1½ to two hours. DEET-containing repellents are preferable for areas where there is a high risk of malaria or yellow fever. Products based on citronella are not effective.

For additional protection, you can apply permethrin to clothing, shoes, tents and bed nets. Permethrin treatments are safe and remain effective for at least two weeks, even when items are laundered. Permethrin should not be applied directly to skin.

Don't sleep with the window open unless there is a screen. If sleeping outdoors or in an accommodations that allows entry of mosquitoes, use a bed net, preferably treated with permethrin, with edges tucked in under the mattress. The mesh size should be less than 1.5mm. If the sleeping area is not otherwise protected, use a mosquito coil, which will fill the room with insecticide through the night. Wristbands impregnated with repellent are not effective.

Parasites

Intestinal parasites occur throughout South America. Common pathogens include Cyclospora, amoebae and Isospora. A tapeworm called Taenia solium may lead to a chronic brain infection called cysticercosis. If you exercise discretion in your choice of food and beverages, you'll sharply reduce your chances of becoming infected.

A parasitic infection called schistosomiasis, which primarily affects the blood vessels in the liver, occurs in Brazil, Suriname, and parts of north-central Venezuela. The disease is acquired by swimming, wading, bathing or washing in fresh water that contains infected snails. It's therefore best to stay out of bodies of fresh water, such as lakes, ponds, streams and rivers, in places where schistosomiasis might occur. Toweling yourself dry after exposure to contaminated water may reduce your risk of becoming infected, but doesn't eliminate it. Chlorinated pools are safe.

A liver parasite called echinococcus (hydatid disease) is found in many countries, especially Peru and Uruguay. It typically affects those in close contact with sheep. A lung parasite called paragonimus, which is ingested by eating raw infected crustaceans, has been reported from Ecuador, Peru and Venezuela.

Travelers' Diarrhea
To prevent diarrhea, avoid tap water unless it has been boiled, filtered or chemically disinfected (with iodine tablets); only eat fresh fruits or vegetables if cooked or peeled; be wary of dairy products that might contain unpasteurized milk; and be highly selective when eating food from street vendors.

If you develop diarrhea, be sure to drink plenty of fluids, preferably an oral rehydration solution containing lots of salt and sugar. A few loose stools don't require treatment but if you start having more than four or five stools a day, you should start taking an antibiotic (usually a quinolone drug) and an antidiarrheal agent (such as loperamide). If diarrhea is bloody, persists for more than 72 hours or is accompanied by fever, shaking chills or severe abdominal pain you should seek medical attention.

Water
Tap water is generally not safe to drink. Vigorous boiling for one minute is the most effective means of water purification. At altitudes greater than 2000m, boil for three minutes.

Another option is to disinfect water with iodine. You can add 2% tincture of iodine to 1L of water (five drops to clear water, 10 drops to cloudy water) and let stand for 30 minutes. If the water is cold, longer times may be required. Or you can buy iodine pills such as Globaline, Potable-Aqua and Coghlan's, available at most pharmacies. Instructions are enclosed and should be carefully followed. The taste of iodinated water may be improved by adding vitamin C (ascorbic acid). Iodinated water should not be consumed for more than a few weeks. Pregnant women, those with a history of thyroid disease, and those allergic to iodine should not drink iodinated water.

A number of water filters are on the market. Those with smaller pores (reverse osmosis filters) provide the broadest protection, but they are relatively large and are readily plugged by debris. Those with somewhat larger pores (microstrainer filters) are ineffective against viruses, although they remove other organisms. Manufacturers' instructions must be carefully followed.

TRAVELING WITH CHILDREN
When traveling with young children, be particularly careful about what you allow them to eat and drink, because diarrhea can be especially dangerous in this age group and because the vaccines for hepatitis A and typhoid fever are not approved for use in children under two years.

Since there's little information concerning the medical consequences of taking children to high altitudes, it's probably safer not to do so. Also, children under nine months should not be brought to jungle areas at lower altitudes because yellow-fever vaccine is not safe in this age group.

The two main malaria medications, Lariam and Malarone, may be given to children, but insect repellents must be applied in lower concentrations.

WOMEN'S HEALTH
It may be difficult to find quality obstetric care, if needed, outside major cities. In addition, it isn't advisable for pregnant women to spend time at altitudes where the air is thin. Lastly, yellow fever vaccine is strongly recommended for travel to all jungle areas at altitudes less than 2300m, but should not be given during pregnancy because the vaccine contains a live virus that may infect the fetus.

TRADITIONAL MEDICINE
Some common traditional remedies include the following:

Problem	Treatment
altitude sickness	gingko
jet lag	melatonin
mosquito-bite prevention	eucalyptus oil, soybean oil
motion sickness	ginger

HEALTH

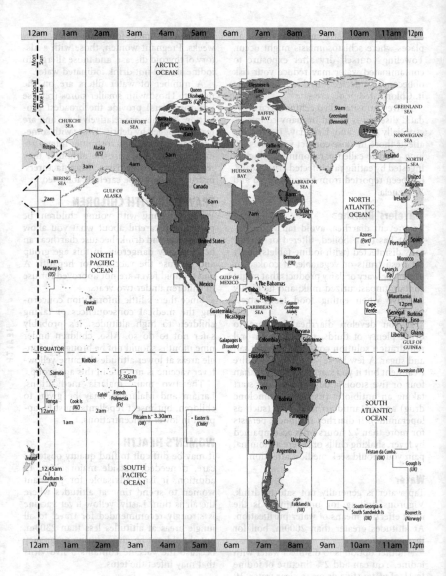

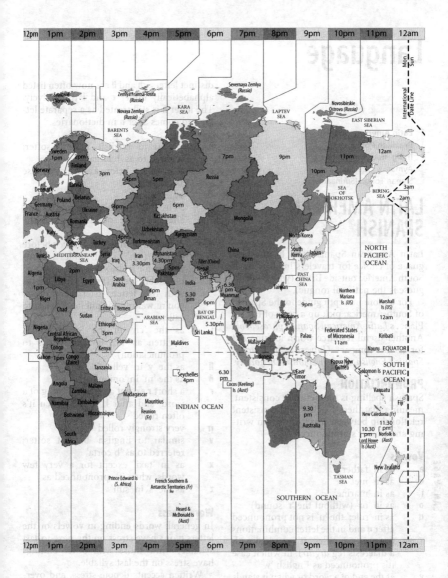

Language

CONTENTS

LATIN AMERICAN SPANISH

Latin American Spanish will be the language of choice for travelers in all parts of South America outside Brazil (where Portuguese is the national tongue).

For a more in-depth guide to the Spanish of South America, pick up a copy of Lonely Planet's *Latin American Spanish phrasebook*. Another useful resource worth looking out for is the compact *University of Chicago Spanish-English, English-Spanish Dictionary*.

PRONUNCIATION

Spanish spelling is phonetically consistent, meaning that there's a clear and consistent relationship between what you see in writing and how it's pronounced.

Vowels

a	as in 'father'
e	as in 'met'
i	as in 'marine'
o	as in 'or' (without the 'r' sound)
u	as in 'rule;' the 'u' is not pronounced after **q** and in the letter combinations **gue** and **gui**, unless it's marked with a diaeresis (eg *argüir*), in which case it's pronounced as English 'w'
y	at the end of a word or when it stands alone, it's pronounced as the Spanish **i** (eg *ley*); between vowels within a word it's as the 'y' in 'yonder'

Consonants

As a rule, Spanish consonants resemble their English counterparts. The exceptions are listed below. Note that while the consonants **ch**, **ll** and **ñ** are generally considered distinct letters, **ch** and **ll** are now often listed alphabetically under **c** and **l** respectively. The letter **ñ** is still treated as a separate letter and comes after **n** in dictionaries.

b	similar to English 'b,' but softer; referred to as 'b larga'
c	as in 'celery' before **e** and **i**; otherwise as English 'k'
ch	as in 'church'
d	as in 'dog,' but between vowels and after **l** or **n**, the sound is closer to the 'th' in 'this'
g	as the 'ch' in the Scottish *loch* before **e** and **i** ('kh' in our guides to pronunciation); elsewhere, as in 'go'
h	invariably silent. If your name begins with this letter, listen carefully if you're waiting for public officials to call you.
j	as the 'ch' in the Scottish *loch* (written as 'kh' in our guides to pronunciation)
ll	as the 'y' in 'yellow'
ñ	as the 'ni' in 'onion'
r	a short **r** except at the beginning of a word, and after **l**, **n** or **s**, when it's often rolled
rr	very strongly rolled
v	similar to English 'b,' but softer; referred to as 'b corta'
x	as in 'taxi' except for a very few words, when it's pronounced as **j**
z	as the 's' in 'sun'

Word Stress

In general, words ending in vowels or the letters **n** or **s** have stress on the next-to-last syllable, while those with other endings have stress on the last syllable.

Written accents denote stress, and override the rules above, eg *sótano* (basement), *América* and *porción* (portion).

GENDER & PLURALS

In Spanish, nouns are either masculine or feminine, and there are rules to help determine gender – with exceptions, of course! Feminine nouns generally end with -**a** or with the groups -**ción**, -**sión** or -**dad**. Other endings typically signify a masculine noun. Endings for adjectives also change to agree with the gender of the noun they modify (masculine/feminine **-o**/**-a**). Where both masculine and feminine forms are included in this language guide, they are separated by a slash, with the masculine form first, eg *perdido/a*.

If a noun or adjective ends in a vowel, the plural is formed by adding **s** to the end. If it ends in a consonant, the plural is formed by adding **es** to the end.

ACCOMMODATIONS

I'm looking for ...	Estoy buscando ...	e·stoy boos·kan·do ...
Where is ...?	¿Dónde hay ...?	don·de ai ...
a hotel	un hotel	oon o·tel
a guesthouse	una pensión/ casa de huéspedes/	oo·na pen·syon/ ka·sa de we·spe·des/
(Arg, Chi)	hostería	os·te·ree·a
a camping ground	un terreno de cámping	oon te·re·no de kam·peen
a youth hostel	un albergue juvenil	oon al·ber·ge khoo·ve·neel
I'd like a ... room.	Quisiera una habitación ...	kee·sye·ra oo·na a·bee·ta·syon ...
double	doble	do·ble
single	individual	een·dee·vee·dwal
twin	con dos camas	kon dos ka·mas
How much is it per ...?	¿Cuánto cuesta por ...?	kwan·to kwes·ta por ...
night	noche	no·che
person	persona	per·so·na
week	semana	se·ma·na

Does it include breakfast?
  ¿Incluye el desayuno? een·kloo·ye el de·sa·yoo·no
May I see the room?
  ¿Puedo ver la habitación? pwe·do ver la a·bee·ta·syon
I don't like it.
  No me gusta. no me goos·ta
It's fine. I'll take it.
  OK. La alquilo. o·kay la al·kee·lo
I'm leaving now.
  Me voy ahora. me voy a·o·ra

private/shared bathroom	baño privado/ compartido	ba·nyo pree·va·do/ kom·par·tee·do
too expensive	demasiado caro	de·ma·sya·do ka·ro
cheaper	más económico	mas e·ko·no·mee·ko
discount	descuento	des·kwen·to

MAKING A RESERVATION
(for phone or written requests)

To ...	A ...
From ...	De ...
Date	Fecha
I'd like to book ...	Quisiera reservar ... (see the list under 'Accommodations' for bed/ room options)
in the name of ...	en nombre de ...
for the nights of ...	para las noches del ...
credit card ...	tarjeta de crédito ...
number	número
expiry date	fecha de vencimiento
Please confirm ...	Puede confirmar ...
availability	la disponibilidad
price	el precio

CONVERSATION & ESSENTIALS

In their public behavior, South Americans are very conscious of civilities, sometimes to the point of ceremoniousness. Never approach a stranger for information without extending a greeting and use only the polite form of address, especially with the police and public officials. Young people may be less likely to expect this, but it's best to stick to the polite form unless you're quite sure you won't offend by using the informal mode. The polite form is used in all cases in this guide; where options are given, the form is indicated by the abbreviations 'pol' and 'inf.'

Hello.	Hola.	o·la
Good morning.	Buenos días.	bwe·nos dee·as
Good afternoon.	Buenas tardes.	bwe·nas tar·des
Good evening/ night.	Buenas noches.	bwe·nas no·ches
Goodbye.	Adiós.	a·dyos
Bye/See you soon.	Hasta luego.	as·ta lwe·go
Yes.	Sí.	see
No.	No.	no
Please.	Por favor.	por fa·vor
Thank you.	Gracias.	gra·syas
Many thanks.	Muchas gracias.	moo·chas gra·syas
You're welcome.	De nada.	de na·da
Pardon me.	Perdón.	per·don
Excuse me.	Permiso.	per·mee·so
(used when asking permission)		
Forgive me.	Disculpe.	dees·kool·pe
(used when apologizing)		

LANGUAGE

How are things?
| ¿Qué tal? | ke tal |

What's your name?
| ¿Cómo se llama? | ko·mo se ya·ma (pol) |
| ¿Cómo te llamas? | ko·mo te ya·mas (inf) |

My name is ...
| Me llamo ... | me ya·mo ... |

It's a pleasure to meet you.
| Mucho gusto. | moo·cho goos·to |

The pleasure is mine.
| El gusto es mío. | el goos·to es mee·o |

Where are you from?
| ¿De dónde es/eres? | de don·de es/e·res (pol/inf) |

I'm from ...
| Soy de ... | soy de ... |

Where are you staying?
| ¿Dónde está alojado? | don·de es·ta a·lo·kha·do (pol) |
| ¿Dónde estás alojado? | don·de es·tas a·lo·kha·do (inf) |

May I take a photo?
| ¿Puedo sacar una foto? | pwe·do sa·kar oo·na fo·to |

DIRECTIONS

How do I get to ...?
| ¿Cómo puedo llegar a ...? | ko·mo pwe·do lye·gar a ... |

Is it far?
| ¿Está lejos? | es·ta le·khos |

Go straight ahead.
| Siga/Vaya derecho. | see·ga/va·ya de·re·cho |

Turn left.
| Voltée a la izquierda. | vol·te·e a la ees·kyer·da |

Turn right.
| Voltée a la derecha. | vol·te·e a la de·re·cha |

I'm lost.
| Estoy perdido/a. | es·toy per·dee·do/a |

Can you show me (on the map)?
| ¿Me lo podría indicar (en el mapa)? | me lo po·dree·a een·dee·kar (en el ma·pa) |

SIGNS – SPANISH

Entrada	Entrance
Salida	Exit
Información	Information
Abierto	Open
Cerrado	Closed
Prohibido	Prohibited
Comisaria	Police Station
Servicios/Baños	Toilets
Hombres/Varones	Men
Mujeres/Damas	Women

north	norte	nor·te
south	sur	soor
east	este/oriente	es·te/o·ryen·te
west	oeste/occidente	o·es·te/ok·see·den·te

here	aquí	a·kee
there	allí	a·yee
avenue	avenida	a·ve·nee·da
block	cuadra	kwa·dra
street	calle/paseo	ka·lye/pa·se·o

EMERGENCIES – SPANISH

Help!
| ¡Socorro! | so·ko·ro |

Fire!
| ¡Incendio! | een·sen·dyo |

I've been robbed.
| Me robaron. | me ro·ba·ron |

Go away!
| ¡Déjeme! | de·khe·me |

Get lost!
| ¡Váyase! | va·ya·se |

Call ...!
¡Llame a ...!	ya·me a
an ambulance	una ambulancia	oo·na am·boo·lan·sya
a doctor	un médico	oon me·dee·ko
the police	la policía	la po·lee·see·a

It's an emergency.
| Es una emergencia. | es oo·na e·mer·khen·sya |

Could you help me, please?
| ¿Me puede ayudar, por favor? | me pwe·de a·yoo·dar por fa·vor |

I'm lost.
| Estoy perdido/a. | es·toy per·dee·do/a |

Where are the toilets?
| ¿Dónde están los baños? | don·de es·tan los ba·nyos |

HEALTH

I'm sick.
| Estoy enfermo/a. | es·toy en·fer·mo/a |

I need a doctor.
| Necesito un médico. | ne·se·see·to oon me·dee·ko |

Where's the hospital?
| ¿Dónde está el hospital? | don·de es·ta el os·pee·tal |

I'm pregnant.
| Estoy embarazada. | es·toy em·ba·ra·sa·da |

I've been vaccinated.
| Estoy vacunado/a. | es·toy va·koo·na·do/a |

I'm allergic to ...	Soy alérgico/a a ...	soy a·ler·khee·ko/a a ...
antibiotics	los antibióticos	los an·tee·byo·tee·kos
penicillin	la penicilina	la pe·nee·see·lee·na
nuts	las fruta secas	las froo·tas se·kas

I'm ...	Soy ...	soy ...
asthmatic	asmático/a	as·ma·tee·ko/a
diabetic	diabético/a	dya·be·tee·ko/a
epileptic	epiléptico/a	e·pee·lep·tee·ko/a

ROAD SIGNS – SPANISH

Acceso	Entrance
Aparcamiento	Parking
Ceda el Paso	Give way
Despacio	Slow
Dirección Única	One-way
Mantenga Su Derecha	Keep to the Right
No Adelantar/	No Passing
No Rebase	
Peaje	Toll
Peligro	Danger
Prohibido Aparcar/	No Parking
No Estacionar	
Prohibido el Paso	No Entry
Pare/Stop	Stop
Salida de Autopista	Freeway Exit

Is this the road to (...)?
¿Se va a (...) por   se va a (...) por
esta carretera?   es·ta ka·re·te·ra

Where's a petrol station?
¿Dónde hay una   don·de ai oo·na
gasolinera/un grifo?   ga·so·lee·ne·ra/oon gree·fo

Please fill it up.
Lleno, por favor.   ye·no por fa·vor

I'd like (20) liters.
Quiero (veinte) litros.   kye·ro (vayn·te) lee·tros

diesel	diesel	dee·sel
leaded (regular)	gasolina con	ga·so·lee·na kon
	plomo	plo·mo
petrol (gas)	gasolina	ga·so·lee·na
unleaded	gasolina sin	ga·so·lee·na seen
	plomo	plo·mo

(How long) Can I park here?
¿(Por cuánto tiempo)   (por kwan·to tyem·po)
Puedo aparcar aquí?   pwe·do a·par·kar a·kee

Where do I pay?
¿Dónde se paga?   don·de se pa·ga

I need a mechanic.
Necesito un   ne·se·see·to oon
mecánico.   me·ka·nee·ko

The car has broken down (in ...).
El carro se ha averiado   el ka·ro se a a·ve·rya·do
(en ...).   (en ...)

The motorbike won't start.
No arranca la moto.   no a·ran·ka la mo·to

I have a flat tyre.
Tengo un pinchazo.   ten·go oon peen·cha·so

I've run out of petrol.
Me quedé sin gasolina.   me ke·de seen ga·so·lee·na

I've had an accident.
Tuve un accidente.   too·ve oon ak·see·den·te

TRAVEL WITH CHILDREN

I need ...
Necesito ...
ne·se·see·to ...

Do you have ...?
¿Hay ...?
ai ...

a car baby seat
un asiento de seguridad   oon a·syen·to de se·goo·ree·da
para bebés   pa·ra be·bes

a child-minding service
un servicio de cuidado   oon ser·vee·syo de kwee·da·do
de niños   de nee·nyos

a children's menu
una carta infantil   oona kar·ta een·fan·teel

a creche
una guardería   oo·na gwar·de·ree·a

(disposable) diapers/nappies
pañoles (de usar y tirar) pa·nyo·les (de oo·sar ee tee·rar)

an (English-speaking) babysitter
una niñera   oo·na nee·nye·ra
(de habla inglesa)   (de a·bla een·gle·sa)

formula (milk)
leche en polvo   le·che en pol·vo

a highchair
una trona   oo·na tro·na

a potty
una pelela   oo·na pe·le·la

a pusher/stroller
un cochecito   oon ko·che·see·to

Do you mind if I breast-feed here?
¿Le molesta que dé   le mo·les·ta ke de
de pecho aquí?   de pe·cho a·kee

Are children allowed?
¿Se admiten niños?   se ad·mee·ten nee·nyos

BRAZILIAN PORTUGUESE

Given that 89% of the world's Portuguese speakers live in Brazil, South America's largest country, it's clear that a few words in the language will be very handy indeed. Regional variation within Brazil is minor, making the task of communicating in Portuguese even easier.

PRONUNCIATION
Vowels

a	as the 'u' in run
aa	as the 'a' in father
ai	as in 'aisle'

aw	as in 'saw'
ay	as in 'day'
e	as in 'bet'
ee	as in 'bee'
o	as in 'go'
oo	as in 'moon'
ow	as in 'how'
oy	as in 'boy'

Nasal Vowels

A characteristic feature of Brazilian Portuguese is the use of nasal vowels. Nasal vowels are pronounced as if you're trying to force the sound out of your nose rather than your mouth. English also has nasal vowels to some extent – when you say 'sing' in English, the 'i' is nasalized by the 'ng.' In Brazilian Portuguese, written vowels that have a nasal consonant after them (**m** or **n**), or a tilde over them (eg **ã**), will be nasal. In our pronunciation guide, we've used 'ng' after nasal vowels to indicate a nasal sound.

Consonants

The following lists a few of the letters used in our pronunciation guide that represent the trickier Portuguese consonant sounds.

ly	as the 'lli' in 'million'
ny	as in 'canyon'
r	as in 'run'
rr	as the 'r' in run but stronger and rolled
zh	as the 's' in 'pleasure'

Word Stress

Word stress generally occurs on the second-to-last syllable of a word, though there are exceptions. When a word ends in **-r** or is pronounced with a nasalized vowel, the stress falls on the last syllable. Another exception is that if a written vowel has an accent marked over it, the stress falls on the syllable containing that vowel.

In our transliteration system, we have indicated the stressed syllable with italics.

ACCOMMODATIONS

I'm looking for ...
Estou procurando por ...   es·to pro·koo·rang·do porr ...

Where is a ...?
Onde tem ...?   on·de teng ...
  a room
  um quarto   oom kwarr·to

bed and breakfast
  uma pensão   oo·maa pen·sowng
camping ground
  um local para   oom lo·kow paa·raa
  acampamento   aa·kam·paa·meng·to
guesthouse
  uma hospedaria   oo·maa os·pe·daa·ree·a
hotel
  um hotel   oom o·tel
youth hostel
  um albergue   oom ow·berr·ge
  da juventude   daa zhoo·veng·too·de

I'd like a ... room.
Eu gostaria um   e·oo gos·taa·ree·aa oom
quarto de ...   kwaarr·to de ...
  double
  casal   kaa·zow
  single
  solteiro   sol·tay·ro
  twin
  duplo   doo·plo

How much is it per ...?
Quanto custa por ...?   kwan·to koos·taa porr ...
  night
  noite   noy·te
  person
  pessoa   pe·so·aa
  week
  semana   se·ma·naa

What's the address?
Qual é o endereço?   kwow e o en·de·re·so
Do you have a ... room?
Tem um quarto de ...?   teng oom kwaarr·to de ...
For (three) nights.
Para (três) noites.   paa·raa (tres) noy·tes
Does it include breakfast?
Inclui café da manhã?   eeng·kloo·ee ka·fe da ma·nyang
May I see it?
Posso ver?   po·so verr
I'll take it.
Eu fico com ele.   e·oo fee·ko kom e·lee
I don't like it.
Não gosto.   nowng gos·to
I'm leaving now.
Estou indo embora   es·to een·do em·bo·raa
agora.   aa·go·raa

Can I pay ...?
Posso pagar com ...?   po·so paa·gaarr kom ...
  by credit card
  cartão de crédito   kaarr·towng de kre·dee·to
  by traveler's cheque
  traveler cheque   tra·ve·ler she·kee

MAKING A RESERVATION

(for phone or written requests)

To ...	Para ...
From ...	De ...
Date	Data
I'd like to book ...	Eu gostaria de fazer uma reserva ... (see the list under 'Accommodations' for bed/room options)
in the name of ...	no nome de ...
for the nights of ...	para os dias ...
from (...) to (...)	de (...) até (...)
credit card ...	cartão de credito ...
number	número
expiry date	data de vencimento
Please confirm ...	Por favor confirme ...
availability	a disponibilidade
price	o preço

CONVERSATION & ESSENTIALS

Hello.
Olá. o·*laa*
Hi.
Oi. oy
Good day.
Bom dia. bong *dee*·aa
Good evening.
Boa noite. bo·aa *noy*·te
See you later.
Até mais tarde. aa·te mais *taarr*·de
Goodbye.
Tchau. chau
How are you?
Como vai? *ko*·mo vai
Fine, and you?
Bem, e você? beng e vo·*se*
I'm pleased to meet you.
Prazer em conhecê-lo. praa *zerr* eng ko nye *se* lo (m)
Prazer em conhecê-la. praa *zerr* eng ko nye *se* laa (f)
Yes.
Sim. seem
No.
Não. nowng
Please.
Por favor. por faa·*vorr*
Thank you (very much).
(Muito) obrigado/ (mween·to) o·bree·*gaa*·do/
obrigada. (m/f) o·bree·*gaa*·daa
You're welcome.
De nada. de *naa*·daa

Excuse me.
Com licença kom lee·*seng*·saa
Sorry.
Desculpa. des·*kool*·paa
What's your name?
Qual é o seu nome? kwow e o se·oo *no*·me
My name is ...
Meu nome é ... me·oo *no*·me e ...
Where are you from?
De onde você é? de *ong*·de vo·se e
I'm from ...
Eu sou (da/do/de) ... e·oo so (daa/do/de)
May I take a photo (of you)?
Posso tirar uma foto po so te *raarr* oo ma *fo* to
(de você)? (de vo se)

DIRECTIONS

Where is ...?
Onde fica ...? *on*·de fee·kaa ...
Can you show me (on the map)?
Você poderia me o·se po·de·ree·aa me
mostrar (no mapa)? mos·*traarr* (no *maa*·paa)
What's the address?
Qual é o endereço? kwow e o en·de·*re*·so
How far is it?
Qual a distância kwow aa dees·*tan*·see·aa
daqui? daa·kee
How do I get there?
Como é que eu chego lá? ko·mo e ke e·oo she·go laa

Turn ...	Vire ...	vee·re ...
at the corner	à esquina	aa es·kee·naa
at the traffic lights	no sinal de trânsito	no see·now de tran·zee·to
left	à esquerda	aa es·kerr·daa
right	à direita	aa dee·ray·taa

here	aqui	a·kee
there	lá	laa
near ...	perto ...	perr·to ...
straight ahead	em frente	eng freng·te

SIGNS – PORTUGUESE

Delegacia de Polícia	Police Station
Hospital	Hospital
Polícia	Police
Pronto Socorro	Emergency Department
Banheiro	Bathroom/Toilet
Não Tem Vaga	No Vacancy
Tem Vaga	Vacancy

north	nort	norr·te
south	sul	sool
east	leste	les·te
west	oeste	o·es·te

EMERGENCIES – PORTUGUESE

Help!
Socorro! so·ko·ho

It's an emergency.
É uma emergência. e oo·maa e·merr·zheng·
see·aa

Call ...!
a doctor
um médico! oom me·dee·ko
an ambulance
uma ambulância oo·maa am·boo·lan·see·aa
the police
a polícia a po·lee·see·a

I'm lost.
Estou perdido. es·to perr·dee·do

Where are the toilets?
Onde tem um banheiro? on·de teng oom ba·nyay·ro

Go away!
Vai embora! vai eng·bo·raa

HEALTH

I'm ill.
Estou doente. es·to do·eng·te

I need a doctor (who speaks English).
Eu preciso de um médico e·oo pre·see·zo de oom me·dee·ko
(que fale inglês). (ke faa·le een·gles)

It hurts here.
Aqui dói. aa·kee doy

I've been vomiting.
Fui vomitando. foo·ee vo·mee·tan·do

(I think) I'm pregnant.
(Acho que) estou grávida. (aa·sho ke) es·to graa·vee·daa

Where's the nearest ...?
Onde fica ...is perto? on·de fee·kaa ... mais perr·to
(night) chemist
a farmácia (noturna) aa farr·maa·see·a (no·toor·naa)
dentist
o dentista o deng·tees·taa
doctor
o médico o me·dee·ko
hospital
o hospital o os·pee·tow
medical centre
a clínica médica aa klee·nee·kaa me·dee·kaa

I feel ...
Estou me sentindo ... es·to me seng·teeng·do ...
dizzy
tonto/tonta tong·to/tong·taa
nauseous
enjoado/enjoada (m/f) eng·zho·aa·do/en·zho·aa·daa

asthma	asma	aas·maa
diarrhea	diarréia	dee·aa·he·ee·aa
fever	febre	fe·bre
nausea	náusea	now·ze·aa
pain	dor	dorr

I'm allergic to ...
Tenho alergia à ... te·nyo aa·lerr·zhee·aa aa ...
antibiotics
antibióticos an·tee·bee·o·tee·kos
aspirin
aspirina aas·pee·ree·naa
bees
abelhas aa·be·lyaas
peanuts
amendoims aa·meng·do·eengs
penicillin
penicilina pe·nee·see·lee·naa

antiseptic
anti-séptico an·tee·sep·tee·ko
contraceptives
anticoncepcionais an·tee·kon·sep·see·o·now
painkillers
analgésicos aa·now·zhe·zee·ko

LANGUAGE DIFFICULTIES

Do you speak English?
Você fala inglês? vo·se faa·laa een·gles
Does anyone here speak English?
Alguém aqui fala inglês? ow·geng faa·laa een·gles
Do you understand?
Você entende? vo·se en·teng·de
I (don't) understand.
Eu (não) entendo. e·oo (nowng) en·teng·do
What does ... mean?
O que quer dizer ...? o ke kerr dee·zerr ...

Could you please ...?
Você poderia por favor ...? vo·se po·de·ree·a porr fa·vorr ...
repeat that
repetir isto he·pe·teerr ees·to
speak more slowly
falar mais devagar faa·laarr mais de·vaa·gaarr
write it down
escrever num papel es·kre·verr noom paa·pel

NUMBERS

0	zero	ze·ro
1	um	oom
2	dois	doys
3	três	tres
4	quatro	kwaa·tro
5	cinco	seen·ko
6	seis	says

7	sete	se·te
8	oito	oy·to
9	nove	naw·ve
10	dez	dez
11	onze	ong·ze
12	doze	do·ze
13	treze	tre·ze
14	quatorze	kaa·torr·ze
15	quinze	keen·ze
16	dezesseis	de·ze·says
17	dezesete	de·ze·se·te
18	dezoito	de·zoy·to
19	dezenove	de·ze·naw·ve
20	vinte	veen·te
21	vinte e um	veen·te e oom
22	vinte e dois	veen·te e doys
30	trinta	treen·taa
40	quarenta	kwaa·ren·taa
50	cinquenta	seen·kwen·taa
60	sessenta	se·seng·taa
70	setenta	se·teng·taa
80	oitenta	oy·teng·taa
90	noventa	no·veng·taa
100	cem	seng
200	duzentos	doo·zeng·tos
1,000	mil	mee·oo
1,000,000	um milhão	oom mee·lyowng

QUESTION WORDS

Who?
Quem? — keng
What?
(o) que? — (o) ke
When?
Quando? — kwang·do
Where?
Onde? — ong·de
Why?
Por que? — porr ke
Which/What?
Qual/Quais? (sg/pl) — kwow/kais

SHOPPING & SERVICES

I'd like to buy ...
Gostaria de comprar ... — gos·taa·ree·aa de kom·praarr ...
I'm just looking.
Estou só olhando. — es·to so o·lyan·do
May I look at it?
Posso ver? — po·so verr
How much?
Quanto? — kwan·to
That's too expensive.
Está muito caro. — es·taa mweeng·to kaa·ro
Can you lower the price?
Pode baixar o preço? — po·de baa·shaarr o pre·so

Do you have something cheaper?
Tem uma coisa mais barata? — teng oo·maa koy·zaa mais baa·raa·taa
I'll give you (five reals).
Dou (cinco reais). — do (seen·ko he·ais)
I don't like it.
Não gosto. — nowng gos·to
I'll take it.
Vou levar isso. — vo le·vaar ee·so

Where is ...?
Onde fica ...? — on·de fee·kaa ...
an ATM
um caixa automático — oom kai·sha ow·to·maa·tee·ko
a bank
o banco — o ban·ko
a bookstore
uma livraria — oo ma lee vraa ree aa
the ... embassy
a embaixada de ... — a eng bai shaa daa de
a foreign-exchange office
uma loja de câmbio — oo·maa lo·zhaa de kam·bee·o
a market
o mercado — o merr·kaa·do
the police station
a delegacia de polícia — aa de·le·gaa·see·aa de po·lee·see·aa
a pharmacy/chemist
uma farmácia — oo·ma faar·maa·syaa
the post office
o correio — o co·hay·o
a supermarket
o supermercado — o soo·perr·merr·kaa·do
the tourist office
a secretaria de turismo — aa se·kre·taa·ree·aa de too·rees·mo
a laundrette
uma lavanderia — oo·ma la·vang·de·ree·aa

less	*menos*	me·nos
more	*mais*	mais
large	*grande*	grang·de
small	*pequeno/a*	pe·ke·no/a

What time does ... open?
A que horas abre ...? — aa ke aw·raas aa·bre ...
Do you have any others?
Você tem outros? — vo·se teng o·tros
How many?
Quantos/Quantas? (m/f) — kwan·tos/kwan·taas

Do you accept ...?
Vocês aceitam ...? — vo·ses aa·say·tam ...
credit cards
cartão de crédito — kaarr·towng de kre·dee·to

traveler's cheques
traveler cheques — tra·ve·ler she·kes

letter
uma carta — oo·maa kaarr·taa
parcel
uma encomenda — oo·maa eng·ko·meng·daa

I want to buy ...
Quero comprar ... — ke·ro kom·praarr ...
  an aerogram
  um aerograma — oom aa·e·ro·gra·maa
  an envelope
  um envelope — oom eng·ve·lo·pe
  a phone card
  um cartão telefônico — oom kaar·towng te·le·fo·nee·ko
  a postcard
  um cartão-postal — oom kaarr·towng pos·tow
  stamps
  selos — se·los

Where can I ...?
Onde posso ...? — on·de po·so ...
  change a traveler's cheque
  trocar traveler cheques — tro·kaarr traa·ve·ler she·kes
  change money
  trocar dinheiro — tro·kaar dee·nyay·ro
  check my email
  checar meu e-mail — she·kaarr me·oo e·mail
  get Internet access
  ter acesso à internet — terr aa·se·so aa een·terr·ne·tee

TIME & DATES
What time is it?
Que horas são? — ke aw·raas sowng
It's (ten) o'clock.
São (dez) horas. — sowng (des) aw·raas

now	*agora*	aa·go·raa
this morning	*esta manhã*	es·taa ma·nyang
in the morning	*da manhã*	daa ma·nyang
this afternoon	*esta tarde*	es·taa taarr·de
in the afternoon	*da tarde*	daa taarr·de
today	*hoje*	o·zhe
tonight	*hoje à noite*	o·zhe aa noy·te
tomorrow	*amanhã*	aa·ma·nyang
yesterday	*ontem*	on·teng

Monday	*segunda-feira*	se·goon·daa·fay·raa
Tuesday	*terça-feira*	terr·saa·fay·raa
Wednesday	*quarta-feira*	kwaarr·taa·fay·raa
Thursday	*quinta-feira*	keen·taa·fay·raa
Friday	*sexta-feira*	ses·taa·fay·raa
Saturday	*sábado*	saa·baa·doo
Sunday	*domingo*	do·meen·go

January	*janeiro*	zha·nay·ro
February	*fevereiro*	fe·ve·ray·ro
March	*março*	marr·so
April	*abril*	aa·bree·oo
May	*maio*	maa·yo
June	*junho*	zhoo·nyo
July	*julho*	zhoo·lyo
August	*agosto*	aa·gos·to
September	*setembro*	se·teng·bro
October	*outubro*	o·too·bro
November	*novembro*	no·veng·bro
December	*dezembro*	de·zeng·bro

TRANSPORTATION
Public Transportation

Which ... goes	*Qual o ... que*	kwow o ... ke
to ...?	*vai para ...?*	vai paa·raa
boat	*barco*	baarr·ko
city/local bus	*ônibus local*	o·nee·boos lo·kow
inter-city bus	*ônibus inter-urbano*	o·nee·boos een·terr oorr·ba·no
ferry	*barca*	baarr·kaa
bus	*ônibus*	o·nee·boos
plane	*avião*	aa·vee·owng
train	*trem*	treng

When's the ...	*Quando sai o ...*	kwang·do sai o ...
(bus)?	*(ônibus)?*	(o·nee·boos)
first	*primeiro*	pree·may·ro
last	*último*	ool·tee·mo
next	*próximo*	pro·see·mo

What time does it leave?
Que horas sai? — ke aw·raas sai
What time does it get to (Parati)?
Que horas chega em (Parati)? — ke aw·raas she·gaa eng (paa·raa·tee)

A ... ticket	*Uma passagem*	oo·maa paa·sa·zhem
to (...)	*de ... para (...)*	de ... paa·raa (...)
1st-class	*primeira classe*	pree·may·raa klaa·se
2nd-class	*segunda classe*	se·goon·daa klaa·se
one-way	*ida*	ee·daa
round trip	*ida e volta*	ee·daa e vol·taa

How much is it?
Quanto é? — kwan·to e
Is this the bus to ...?
Este ônibus vai para ...? — es·te o·nee·boos vai paa·raa ...?
Do I need to change?
Preciso trocar de trem? — pre·see·so tro·kaarr de treng
the luggage check room
o balcão de guarda volumes — o baal·kowng de gwaarr·daa vo·loo·me

a luggage locker
um guarda volume oom *gwaarr*-daa vo-*loo*-me
Is this taxi free?
Este táxi está livre? es-te taak-see es-*taa* lee-vre
Please put the meter on.
Por favor ligue o porr fa-*vorr* lee-ge o
taxímetro. taak-*see*-me-tro
How much is it to ...?
Quanto custa até ...? kwan-to koos-taa aa-*te* ...
Please take me to (this address).
Me leve para este me *le*-ve paa-raa es-te en-de-*re*-so
endereço por favor. porr faa-*vorr*

Private Transportation

I'd like to hire	*Gostaria de*	gos-taa-*ree*-aa de
a/an ...	*alugar ...*	aa-loo-*gaarr* ...
4WD	*um quatro*	oom *kwaa*-tro
	por quatro	por *kwaa*-tro
bicycle	*uma bicicleta*	oo-maa bee-see-*kle*-taa
car	*um carro*	oom *kaa*-ho
motorbike	*uma motocicleta*	oo-maa mo-to-see-*kle*-taa

Is this the road to ...?
Esta é a estrada para ...? es-*taa* e aa es-*traa*-daa paa-raa
(How long) Can I park here?
(Quanto tempo) Posso (kwan-to teng-po) po-so
estacionar aqui? es-taa-see-o-*naarr* aa-*kee*
Where's a gas/petrol station?
Onde tem um posto on-de teng oom pos-to
de gasolina? de gaa-zo-*lee*-naa
Please fill it up.
Enche o tanque, por en-she o *tan*-ke porr
favor. faa-*vorr*
I'd like ... liters.
Coloque ... litros. ko-*lo*-ke ... *lee*-tros

diesel	*diesel*	*dee*-sel
LPG	*gás*	gas
ethanol	*álcool*	*ow*-kol
unleaded	*gasolina comum*	gaa-zo-*lee*-naa *ko-moon*

ROAD SIGNS – PORTUGUESE

Entrada	Entrance
Estrada dê Preferência	Give Way
Mão Única	One-way
Pare	Stop
Pedágio	Toll
Proibido Entrar	No Entry
Rua Sem Saída	Dead End
Saída	Freeway Exit

The (car/motorbike) has broken down ...
(O carro/A motocicleta) quebrou em ...
(a mo-to-se-*kle*-taa) ke-*bro* eng
The car won't start.
O carro não está pegando.
o *kaa*-ho nowng es-ta pe-*gang*-do
I need a mechanic.
Preciso de um mecânico.
pre-*see*-so de oom me-*ka*-nee-ko
I've run out of gas/petrol.
Estou sem gasolina.
es-*to* seng gaa-zo-*lee*-naa
I've had an accident.
Sofri um acidente.
so-*free* oom aa-see-*den*-te

TRAVEL WITH CHILDREN

I need a/an ...
Preciso de ...
pre-*see*-zo de ...
Do you have (a/an) ...?
Aqui tem ...?
aa-*kee* teng

baby change room	
uma sala para trocar	oo-maa saa-laa paa-raa tro-*kaarr*
bebê	be-*be*
baby seat	
um assento de criança	oom aa-*seng*-to de kree-*an*-saa
booster seat	
um assento de elevaçã	oom aa-*seng*-to de e-le-vaa-*sowng*
child-minding service	
um serviço de babá	oom serr-*vee*-so de baa-*baa*
children's menu	
um cardápio para	oom kaar-*daa*-pee-o paa-raa
criança	kree-*an*-saa
(English-speaking) babysitter	
uma babá	oo-maa baa-*baa*
(que fale ingles)	(ke *faa*-le een-*gles*)
formula (milk)	
leite em pó (para bebê)	*lay*-te (paa-raa be-*be*)
highchair	
uma cadeira de criança	oo-maa kaa-*day*-ra de kree-*an*-saa
potty	
um troninho	oom tro-*nee*-nyo
pusher/stroller	
um carrinho de bebê	oom kaa-*hee*-nyo de be-*be*
(disposable) nappies/diapers	
fraldas (descartáveis)	*frow*-daas (des-kaarr-*taa*-vays)

Do you mind if I breast-feed here?
Você se importa se eu amamentar aqui?
vo-*se* se eeng-*porr*-taa se *e*-oo aa-maa-meng-*taarr* aa-*kee*
Are children allowed?
É permitida a entrada de crianças?
e perr-mee-*tee*-daa aa eng-*traa*-daa de kree-*an*-saas

INDIGENOUS LANGUAGES

AYMARA & QUECHUA

The following list of words and phrases is obviously minimal, but it should be useful in areas where these languages are spoken. Pronounce them as you would a Spanish word. An apostrophe represents a glottal stop, which is the 'non-sound' that occurs in the middle of 'uh-oh.' For a comprehensive guide to Quechua, pick up a copy of Lonely Planet's *Quechua phrasebook*.

In the following list of phrases, Aymara is the first entry after the English, Quechua the second.

Hello.
Kamisaraki.   Napaykullayki.
Please.
Mirá.   Allichu.
Thank you.
Yuspagara.   Yusulipayki.
Yes/No.
Jisa/Janiwa.   Ari/Mana.
How do you say ...?
Cun sañasauca'ha ...?   Imainata nincha chaita ...?
It is called ...
Ucan sutipa'h ...   Chaipa'g sutin'ha ...
Please repeat.
Uastata sita.   Ua'manta niway.
How much?
K'gauka?   Maik'ata'g?

father	auqui	tayta
food	manka	mikiuy
mother	taica	mama
river	jawira	mayu
snowy peak	kollu	riti-orko
water	uma	yacu

1	maya	u'
2	paya	iskai
3	quimsa	quinsa
4	pusi	tahua
5	pesca	phiska
6	zo'hta	so'gta
7	pakalko	khanchis
8	quimsakalko	pusa'g
9	yatunca	iskon
10	tunca	chunca

SRANAN TONGO (SURINAAMS)

While Dutch is the official language of Suriname and English is understood by most people, in everyday situations the lingua franca is Sranan Tongo, a creole that combines elements of Dutch, English, Portuguese and African languages. Locals often speak Sranan Tongo among themselves as a form of casual, friendly conversation. While far from comprehensive, the following words and phrases will be useful.

Hello. Fi-go.
What's your name? Sah yu neng?
My name is ... Me neng ...
Thank you. Dan-key.
Yes. Ay.
No. No.
Do you speak Yu tah-key eng-els?
  English?
I mi
you yu
he, she, it a
we wi
you (plural) unu
they de
How much is it? Ow meh-nee?
What time does it Ow lah-tee ah gwa?
  leave?
Where is ...? Pa-ah da ...?
boat bo-to
near cros-by
far fah-rah
today tee-day
tomorrow tah-mah-rah
yesterday ess-day

1	wan
2	tu
3	dri
4	fo
5	feyfi
6	siksi
7	seybi
8	ayti
9	neygi
10	tin

Glossary

Unless otherwise indicated, the terms listed in this glossary refer to Spanish-speaking South America in general, but regional variations in meaning are common.

A

abra – in the Andes, a mountain pass

aerosilla – (Arg) chairlift

aguardente – (Bra) any strong drink, but usually *cachaça*

aguardiente – sugarcane alcohol or similar drink

alameda – street lined with trees, usually poplars

albergue – lodging house; youth hostel

alcabala – (Ven) roadside police checkpoint

alcaldía – town hall; virtually synonymous with *municipalidad*

alerce – large coniferous tree, once common in parts of the southern Argentine and Chilean Andes; it has declined greatly due to overexploitation for timber

almuerzo – lunch; often an inexpensive fixed-price meal

alojamiento – usually a rock-bottom (or close to it) accommodation choice with shared toilet and bathing facilities

altiplano – Andean high plain of Peru, Bolivia, Chile and Argentina

apartado – post-office box

apartamento – apartment or flat; (Bra) hotel room with private bath

api – in Andean countries, a syrupy *chicha* made of maize, lemon, cinnamon and sugar

arepera – (Ven) snack bar

arrayán – reddish-barked tree of the myrtle family; common in forests of southern Argentina and Chile

arriero – mule driver

artesanía – handicrafts; crafts shop

asado/a – roasted; (Arg) barbecue, often a family outing in summer

audiencia – colonial administrative subdivision under a president who held civil power in an area where no viceroy was resident

autopista – freeway or motorway

Aymara – indigenous people of highland Bolivia, Peru, Chile and Argentina (also called *Kolla*); also their language

azulejo – ceramic tile, mostly blue, of Portuguese origin

B

balneario – bathing resort or beach

bandeirante – (Bra) colonial slaver and gold prospector from São Paulo who explored the interior

barraca – (Bra) any stall or hut, including food and drink stands at the beach or the park

barrio – neighborhood, district or borough; (Ven) shantytown

bicho de pé – (Bra) literally, foot bug; burrowing parasite found near beaches and in some rain-forest areas

bloco – (Bra) group of musicians and dancers who perform in street parades during Brazil's Carnavals

bodega – winery or storage area for wine; (Bol) boxcar, sometimes used for train travel by 2nd-class passengers

boleadoras – heavily weighted thongs, once used for hunting guanaco and rhea; also called *bolas*

boletería – ticket office

bomba – among many meanings, a petrol (gasoline) station

burundanga – (Col) drug obtained from a plant commonly known as *borrachero* or *cacao sabanero*; used to intoxicate unsuspecting tourists in order to rob them

bus cama – very comfortable bus with fully reclining seats; usually travels at night and costs around double the regular fare

C

cabaña – cabin

cabildo – colonial town council

cachaça – (Bra) sugarcane rum, also called pinga or *aguardiente*, produced by hundreds of small distilleries throughout the country; Brazil's national drink

cachoeira – (Bra) waterfall

cacique – Indian chieftain; among Araucanian (Mapuche) Indians

cajero automático – automatic teller machine (ATM)

calle – street

cama matrimonial – double bed

camanchaca – (Chi) dense convective fog on the coastal hills of the Atacama Desert; equivalent to Peru's *garúa*

cambista – street moneychanger

camellones – (Ecu) pre-Columbian raised-field earthworks in the Guayas Basin; evidence of large early populations

camino – road, path, way

camión – open-bed truck; popular form of local transport in the Andean countries

camioneta – pickup or other small truck; form of local transport in the Andean countries

campesino/a – rural dweller who practices subsistence agriculture; peasant

campo – the countryside; field or paddock

Candomblé – (Bra) Afro-Brazilian religion of Bahia

capoeira – (Bra) martial art/dance performed to rhythms of an instrument called the *berimbau*; developed by Bahian slaves

carabinero – (Arg, Chi) police officer

caraqueño/a – native or resident of Caracas
carioca – native or resident of Rio de Janeiro
Carnaval – all over Latin America, pre-Lenten celebration
casa de cambio – authorized foreign-currency exchange house
casa de familia – modest family accommodations, usually in tourist centers in Southern Cone countries
casa de huésped – literally, guest house; form of economical lodging where guests may have access to the kitchen, garden and laundry facilities
casilla de correos – post-office box
casona – large house, usually a mansion; term often applied to colonial architecture in particular
catarata – waterfall
caudillo – in 19th-century South American politics, a provincial strongman whose power rested more on personal loyalty than political ideals or party organization
ceiba – common tropical tree; can reach a huge size
cena – dinner; often an inexpensive set menu
cerro – hill; term used to refer to even very high Andean peaks
ceviche – marinated raw seafood (be cautious about eating *ceviche* as it can be a source of cholera)
chachacoma – *Senecio graveolens;* this native Andean plant yields a tea that helps combat mild symptoms of altitude sickness
chacra – garden; small, independent farm
charango – Andean stringed instrument, traditionally made with an armadillo shell as a soundbox
chicha – in Andean countries, a popular beverage (often alcoholic) made from ingredients like *yucca*, sweet potato or maize
chifa – Chinese restaurant (term most commonly used in Peru and northern Chile)
Chilote – (Chi) person from the island of Chiloé
chiva – (Col) basic rural bus with wooden bench seats; until the 1960s, the main means of transport throughout the country
churrascaria – (Bra) restaurant featuring barbecued meat
cinemateca – art-house cinema
coima – in the Andean countries and the Southern Cone, a bribe
colectivo – depending on the country, either a bus, a minibus or a shared taxi
comedor – basic cafeteria or dining room in a hotel
confitería – café that serves coffee, tea, desserts and simple food orders
congregación – in colonial Latin America, the concentration of native populations in central settlements, usually to aid political control or religious instruction; also known as a *reducción*
Cono Sur – Southern Cone; collective term for Argentina, Chile, Uruguay and parts of Brazil and Paraguay
cordillera – mountain range

corregidor – in colonial Spanish America, governor of a provincial city and its surrounding area; the corregidor was usually associated with the *cabildo*
corrida – bullfight
cospel – token used for subway, public telephones etc, in lieu of coins
costanera – in the Southern Cone, a seaside, riverside or lakeside road
costeño – inhabitant of Colombia's Caribbean coast
criollo/a – Spaniard born in colonial South America; in modern times, a South American of European descent
cumbia – big on horns and percussion, a cousin to salsa, merengue and lambada
curanto – Chilean seafood stew
cuy – guinea pig, a traditional Andean food

D

DEA – US Drug Enforcement Agency
dendê – (Bra) palm-tree oil, a main ingredient in Bahian cuisine
denuncia – affidavit or statement, usually in connection with theft or robbery
desayuno – breakfast
dique – sea wall, jetty or dock; also a reservoir used for recreational purposes
dormitorio – extremely cheap accommodations where guests share rooms and sleep in bunks

E

edificio – building
empanada – baked or fried turnover filled with vegetables, egg, olive, meat or cheese
encomienda – colonial labor system under which Indian communities had to provide labor and tribute to a Spanish *encomendero* (landholder) in exchange for religious and language instruction; usually the system benefited the Spaniards far more than the Indians
esquina – corner (abbreviated to 'esq')
estancia – extensive grazing establishment, either for cattle or sheep, with a dominant owner or manager and dependent resident labor force
estanciero – owner of an *estancia*

F

farinha – (Bra) manioc flour; the staple food of Indians before colonization, and of many Brazilians today, especially in the Nordeste and the Amazon
farmacia – pharmacy
favela – (Bra) slum or shantytown
fazenda – (Bra) large ranch or farm, roughly equivalent to Spanish American *hacienda;* also cloth or fabric
ferrobus – bus on railway wheels
ferrocarril – railway, railroad
ferroviária – (Bra) railway station

flota – fleet; often a long-distance bus line
frigorífico – meat-freezing factory
fundo – *hacienda* or farm

G
garúa – (Per) convective coastal fog
gaucho – (Arg, Urg) cowboy, herdsman; in Brazil, *gaúcho* (*gaoo*-shoo)
golpe de estado – coup d'état
gringo/a – throughout Latin America, a foreigner or person with light hair and complexion; not necessarily a derogatory term; (Arg) a person of Italian descent
guanaco – undomesticated relative of the llama; (Chi) a water cannon
guaquero – robber of pre-Columbian tombs
guaraná – Amazonian shrub whose berry is believed to have magical and medicinal powers; (Bra) a popular soft drink
guardaparque – park ranger

H
hacienda – large rural landholding with a dependent resident labor force under a dominant owner; (Chi) the term *fundo* is more common; (Arg) a much less common form of *latifundio* than the *estancia*
hospedaje – budget accommodations with shared bathroom; usually a large family home with an extra room or two for guests
huaquero – grave robber

I
ichu – bunch grass of the Andean *altiplano*
iglesia – in Brazil, *igreja;* church
Inca – dominant indigenous civilization of the central Andes at the time of the Spanish conquest; refers both to the people and, individually, to their leader
indígena – native American (Indian)
indigenismo – movement in Latin American art and literature which extols aboriginal traditions, often in a romantic or patronizing manner
invierno – literally, winter; the rainy season in the South American tropics
invierno boliviano – (Chi) 'Bolivian winter'; summer rainy season in the *altiplano*
IVA – *impuesto de valor agregado,* a value-added tax (VAT)

K
Kolla – another name for the *Aymara*
Kollasuyo – 'Land of the Kolla'; early indigenous name for the area now known as Bolivia

L
lago – lake
laguna – lagoon; shallow lake
lanchonete – (Bra) stand-up snack bar

latifundio – large landholding, such as a *hacienda* or cattle *estancia*
leito – (Bra) luxury overnight express bus
licuado – fruit shake blended with milk or water
limeño/a – of Lima; native or resident of Lima
llanos – plains
llareta – *Laretia compacta,* a dense, compact *altiplano* shrub, used for fuel
locutorio – (Arg) small telephone office
loma – mound or hill; a coastal hill in the Atacama Desert
lunfardo – street slang of Buenos Aires

M
machismo – exaggerated masculine pride of the Latin American male
malecón – shoreline promenade
manta – shawl or bedspread
marcha espanol – (Arg) aggressive drum beats, bleepy noises and chanted lyrics
maté – see *yerba maté*
menú del día – inexpensive set meal
mercado – market
mercado negro – black market
mercado paralelo – euphemism for black market
meseta – interior steppe of eastern Patagonia
mestizo/a – a person of mixed Indian and Spanish descent
micro – small bus or minibus
mineiro – (Bra) miner; person from Minas Gerais state region and other parts of South America
minuta – (Arg) short-order snack
mirador – viewpoint or lookout, usually on a hill but often in a building
monte – scrub forest; any densely vegetated area
morro – hill or headland; (Bra) person or culture of the *favelas*
motocarro – (Per) three-wheeled motorcycle rickshaw
mulato/a – person of mixed African and European ancestry
municipalidad – city or town hall
museo – in Brazil, *museu;* museum
música folklórica – traditional Andean music

N
nevado – snow-covered peak
novela – novel; a TV soap opera
NS – (Bra) Nosso Senhor (Our Father) or Nossa Senhora (Our Lady); often used in the name of a church

O
oca – edible Andean tuber resembling a potato
oferta – promotional fare, often seasonal, for plane or bus travel
onces – literally, elevenses; morning or afternoon tea
orixá – (Bra) god of Afro-Brazilian religion

P

paceño/a – of La Paz; native or resident of La Paz

parada or **paradero** – bus stop

páramo – humid, high-altitude grassland of the northern Andean countries

parque nacional – national park

parrilla – steakhouse restaurant or the grill used to cook meat; see *parrillada*

parrillada – barbecued or grilled meat served at a *parrilla*

pasarela – catwalk

paseo – an outing, such as a walk in the park or downtown

paulistano – (Bra) native or resident of São Paulo city

peatonal – pedestrian mall

pehuén – *Araucaria araucana*, the monkey-puzzle tree of southern South America

peña – club/bar that hosts informal folk music gatherings; performance at such a club

pensión – short-term budget accommodations in a family home, which may also have permanent lodgers

pingüinera – penguin colony

piropo – sexist remark, ranging from relatively innocuous to very offensive

Planalto – enormous plateau that covers much of southern Brazil

por puesto – (Ven) shared taxi

porteño/a – (Arg) native or resident of Buenos Aires; (Chi) native or resident of Valparaíso

pousada – (Bra) hotel

prato feito, prato do día – (Bra) literally, made plate or plate of the day; typically an enormous and very cheap meal

precordillera – foothills of the Andes

propina – tip (eg in a restaurant or cinema)

pucará – an indigenous Andean fortification

pueblo jóven – literally, young town; (Per) shantytown surrounding Lima

puna – Andean highlands, usually above 3000m

Q

quarto – (Bra) hotel room with shared bath

quebracho – 'axe-breaker' tree *(Quebrachua lorentzii)* of the Chaco, a natural source of tannin

quebrada – ravine, normally dry

Quechua – indigenous language of the Andean highlands, spread by Inca rule and widely spoken today

quena – simple reed flute

quilombo – (Bra) community of runaway slaves; (Arg) slang term for a brothel or a mess

quinoa – native Andean grain, the dietary equivalent of rice in the pre-Columbian era

quiteño/a – of Quito; native or resident of Quito

R

rancho – rural house; (Ven) shantytown

recargo – surcharge; added by many businesses to credit-card transactions

reducción – see *congregación*

refugio – usually rustic shelter in a national park or remote area

residencial – budget accommodations, sometimes only seasonal; in general, *residenciales* are in buildings designed expressly for short-stay lodging

río – in Brazil, *rio;* river

rodeo – annual roundup of cattle on an *estancia* or *hacienda*

rodoferroviária – (Bra) combined bus and train station

rodoviária – (Bra) bus station

ruta – route or highway

S

salar – salt lake or salt pan, usually in the high Andes or Argentine Patagonia

salteña – meat and vegetable pastie, generally a spicier version of an *empanada*

santiaguino/a – native or resident of Santiago

selva – natural tropical rain forest

Semana Santa – all over South America, Holy Week, the week before Easter

sertão – dry interior region of northeast Brazil

siesta – lengthy afternoon break for lunch and, occasionally, a nap

s/n – *sin número;* indicating a street address without a number

soroche – altitude sickness

Southern Cone – see *Cono Sur*

stelling – (Gui) ferry dock or pier

suco – (Bra) fruit juice; fruit-juice bar

T

Tahuantinsuyo – Spanish name of the Inca Empire; in Quechua, Tawantinsuyu

tambo – in Andean countries, a wayside market and meeting place; an inn

tapir – large hoofed mammal; a distant relative of the horse

teleférico – cable car

telenovela – TV soap opera

tenedor libre – 'all-you-can-eat' restaurant

tepui – (Ven) elevated, sandstone-capped mesa; home to unique flora

termas – hot springs

tinto – red wine; (Col) small cup of black coffee

todo terreno – mountain bike

totora – type of reed, used as a building material

tranca – (Bol) police post

turismo aventura – 'adventure tourism' activities such as trekking and river rafting

V

vaquero – in Brazil, *vaqueiro;* cowboy

verano – literally, summer; the dry season in the South American tropics

vicuña – wild relative of the domestic llama and alpaca, found only at high altitudes in the south-central Andes

vivienda temporaria – literally, temporary dwelling; (Par) *viviendas temporarias* refers to any riverfront shantytown of Asunción

vizcacha – also written as *viscacha;* wild relative of the domestic chinchilla

voladora – (Col, Ven) river speedboat

Y

yacaré – South American alligator, found in tropical and subtropical river systems

yapa – variant spelling of ñapa

yareta – variant spelling of *llareta*

yerba maté – 'Paraguayan tea' *(Ilex paraguariensis); mate* is consumed regularly in Argentina, Paraguay, Uruguay and Brazil

yucca – manioc tuber; in Brazil, mandioca is the most common term

Z

zambo/a – a person of mixed African and Amerindian ancestry

zampoña – pan flute featured in traditional Andean music

zona franca – duty-free zone

zonda – (Arg) in the central Andes, a powerful, dry north wind

Behind the Scenes

THIS BOOK

This 9th edition of *South America on a Shoestring* was written by an able team of authors led by the tireless Danny Palmerlee. Danny wrote most of the front and back sections and the South America Directory, as well as the Ecuador chapter. Contributing authors Sandra Bao (Argentina), Charlotte Beech (Peru), Krzysztof Dydyński (Colombia and Venezuela), Molly Green (Brazil), Carolyn Hubbard (Chile), Morgan Konn (Paraguay), Andrew Dean Nystrom (Bolivia), Ginger Otis (Brazil), Regis St. Louis (Brazil), Lucas Vidgen (Uruguay and Argentina) and Emily K Wolman (The Guianas) wrangled the book into form. Dr David Goldberg wrote the Health chapter, and Regis St. Louis conducted the interview with Catherine Clark. The Peru chapter was adapted in part from writing and research by Rob Rachowiecki. The author team is indebted to the work of all authors from the eight previous editions, and particular thanks must be extended to Connor Gorry, the indefatigable coordinator of the 8th edition, and James Lyon, who coordinated the 7th edition.

THANKS FROM THE AUTHORS

Danny Palmerlee My research for this book was combined with research for LP's *Ecuador & the Galápagos Islands*, so to everyone who helped me on that project I extend the warmest of thanks again here. In Argentina (or London?), a big *abrazo* to Isabel Calvo. In the Bay Area, thanks to Ken Johnson at eXito Travel and Sherri Nakamura at The Adventure Travel Co. To the *South America on a Shoestring* crew: let's throw Felix on the fire and take the car downtown – thanks for keeping me up on the rest of the continent. A special thanks to Carolyn Hubbard whose support, help and sense of humor throughout this entire project kept me sane. Hey, Wendy Smith, see you at Squat & Gobble – it was a pleasure. Rebecca and Pete, thanks for all your help. For their friendship, support, critiques and shoulder massages, the hugest of hugs to Ken and Amy Shelf. Of course, I never would have been awake half those mornings if it weren't for Hucky 'Alarm Clock' Shelf. Love ya all!

Sandra Bao Countless Argentines and travelers on the road helped me research this book, but special thanks go to Lucas Markowiecki, Fernando Bischof

and Carolina Simón in Buenos Aires, Karina Scott in Bariloche and Danny Feldman in El Calafate. Co-authors Danny Palmerlee and Lucas Vidgen are pretty cool dudes to work alongside. Husband Ben Greensfelder was invaluable as an assistant and soul mate. And much appreciation, as always, to Mom, Dad and brother Daniel.

Charlotte Beech In Lima, particular thanks go to Leo Rovayo and Monica Moreno of the Posada del Parque, Simon Atkinson of the South American Explorers, the guys at The Point in Barranco for an insiders' guide to the local nightlife; and to Erwin of Pension Yolanda. Thanks also to William Hernandez and Luis Herrera in Pisco and Paracas, Vlado Soto in the White City, Tomas Tisnado Chura and Victor Pauca in Puno, Orfa Corrales for so generously giving up a bed for a stranded traveler on a stormy night, Ulrike Simic in Pisac, Carlos Milla and Russ Knutson in Cuzco.

Heartfelt thanks also to Emma Banks, Michael Button, Monica Acosta and especially John Beech and Alex Amelines for all their help back in London. I'd also like to thank Rob Rachowiecki for all his research in Peru's northern and central territories, and Wendy Smith for first involving me in the project.

Krzysztof Dydyński Many friends, colleagues and travelers have kindly contributed to the Colombia and Venezuela chapters and deserve the highest praise. I would like to thank all those people for their advice, information, hospitality and much else. Warmest thanks to Germán Escobar, Hans Kolland, Gert Altmann, Nico de Greiff, Billy Esser, Raquel and Tom Evenou, Jesús García, Axel Kelemen, Slawek Kociecki, Eric Migliore, Tulio Reyes, Peter Rothfuss, Roger Ruffenach, Claude Saint-Pierre and the Inatur tourist office in Caracas. My special appreciation goes to Angela Melendro.

Molly Green I'd like to warmly thank authors Susan Derby, Sandra Bao, Ben Greensfelder and Danny Palmerlee for their advice, Santa Cruzans Lynda Porter, Vanessa Millet, Sharon May, Jessica Damon, Flor Hunt *(cavalão)* and Dov Bock for sharing their Brazil expertise, adventurers Wayt Thomas, Greg Altman, Yariv Rotem, Abdel Oumarzoug, Joe Caccamo and unsuspecting travelers for divulging insider tips, Zoe Appleton and Alastair Jones for their company and help, locals Hestiveyrrevy Marino Guaster (Porto Seguro), João Lambadeiro (Arraial d'Ajuda), Ailton (Morro de São Paulo), Mônica Santos (Emtursa/Salvador), James Giangola (Salvador), Janie (Lençois), Isa (Olinda), Fernando (Olinda), Patricia Carvalheira (Empetur/Recife), Rosie (Praia da Pipa) and O Alemão (Ubajara) for their invaluable insights, 'fam' Frieda Krieger, Tom Green, Greg Green, Rebecca Nowlin and Jennifer Fosket for directly supporting this endeavor, Adrian Green and Eliza Fosket-Hydes for being born, and everyone who insisted I was capable of this.

Carolyn Hubbard *Un millón de gracias* to Scott Jones and Anne Keller, for a home in Santiago and scotch whisky lessons; to Clark Stede of Hacienda Los Andes, for end-of-trip escapes; to travelers in San Pedro de Atacama who inspired (Debbie), kept me healthy (Winfred) and kept me on track (Nicole and Lee, aka 'If I Ever Meet the Fuck'n' Author!...'). Thank you to the readers whose suggestions and criticisms shape the chapter. Thank you to Marcelo Diaz of America's Travel for travel help and encouragement. A toast to Danny Palmerlee, for a fabulous coordinating effort, and to LP staff for putting all of this together.

Morgan Konn *Muchas gracias* to Wendy Smith who gave me the opportunity to work on this edition and to Danny Palmerlee who kept the job organized and lighthearted. In Paraguay, my research would have been incomplete without Sofia Montiel de Afara at Senatur, Antonio with the National Parks, Helmut's personal tour of the Mennonite communities and the Peace Corps Volunteers' Guaraní lessons. Much thanks to Ben Greensfelder for his unedited advice and previous research, and Wayne Bernhardson for the original research. And finally, my infinite gratitude to Andrew and my family for their unfettered support and encouragement.

Andrew Dean Nystrom *Mil gracias a* Fabiola y Beatriz, Chris Sarge, Jazmin Caballero, Karen and Alistair, Sigrid Frönius, Stephan and Petra, Don Ricardo, Marcelo and Lizette de Mapajo, Martha Cáceres, Peter McFarren, Coco Cardenas, Oscar and Miriam de Abajo, Capítan Pibe, Saira Duque, Francisco Ishu, Pieter and Margarita, Amado Pacheco, Rusty Young, the San Joseanos, all the PCVs, Drs Patino and Orellana and the entire Hotel Rosario family for helping me feel at home during my whirlwind four month *de cabo a rabo recorrido* (head-to-toe tour). Much love to Morgan, Joe, Dolores and Mom and Dad for help keeping it all together back home.

Ginger Adams Otis A huge nod to all the authors who came before me – their excellent research and writing skills are the backbone of my chapters. Also, kudos to the Lonely Planet editorial team. In Brazil, a special thank you must go to Frances and Neri in Foz, Joel in Cuiabá, and all the many, many Brazilians who opened their hearts to me during my visit. *Un beijo grande para* (a big kiss to) Luis Nogueira, who graciously ferried me around São Paulo and generously shared his copious knowledge of the city. To my family, Joy, David, Trevor, Michael and Nana, a warm hug for the ongoing support and encouragement. And last, but not least, an *abraço bem apertado* (a warm hug) to Didem, Sinem, Shelley, Michael and all my fabulous friends!

Regis St. Louis Warmest thanks to Damian, Manoel and their families for their hospitality in the Amazon. *Abraços* to Edvan, Oliva and Flemish friends who made my stay in Belem so rewarding; Cynthia, the house of journalists and the Jedi warriors in Brasília for showing me a good time; Simon in Manaus for sharing great meals and conversation; and Jose in Rio. *Beijos* (kisses) to everyone on the Ilha de Marajó for being the most wonderful people on the planet and to Veronique for showing me the untainted beauty of Algodoal. In NYC, thanks to all my *amigos* who've nourished me with friendship and sometimes cocktails over the years, especially Jayson, Florence, Jim and Shannon. Thanks to Marina for the excellent crash course in Portuguese. I also want to thank Justine and France for being such great sisters and Mom for her tireless support. Deep thanks to Cassandra, who's always filling my head with wondrous ideas.

Lucas Vidgen Thanks to all the people of Argentina and Uruguay, for hating the government and loving the travelers – that's the way it should be. Thanks also to the hundreds of anonymous travelers who kept popping up with little tips and hints, many of which weren't even in The Book in the first place. Also to Paula and Teresa Armendariz for all their help, my introduction to one-ingredient pizzas, and their company on the fruitless search for organic champagne. To Sandra Bao for a lovely afternoon in the plaza, Ben Greensfelder for his speedy forwarding skills, Danny Palmerlee for good answers to dumb questions, and Wendy Smith for even better answers to even dumber questions.

In Montevideo, no set of thanks (or blame for alcohol poisoning) would be complete without the following names: Aida Martinez, Rosario Romero, Pablo Rebollo, Alejandra Cisneros, Jenisse Balcar (the *maté maestro*), Luar Roji, Dr Abuelo (surely the rockinest Dr in the whole wide world) and Tomas Laurenzo.

Thanks also to my family for some things, and to Alina, for everything.

Emily Wolman Solo traveling aside, many people – some of whose names I didn't even catch – aided me in my effort. Thanks to those nameless collaborators as well as the following kind, hospitable, wise, resilient, adventurous folks and innocent-by-stander-cum-tour-guides for guiding me along the oft indiscernible path of researching this chapter:

In French Guiana, Joep, Marijke and Bernie Moonen; Pascal 'Caiman Hunter' Studer and Guy-anEspace Voyages; Vic 'Camera in the Yiyi' Young and Ed 'Erm' McCloskey; and Patrice Bru.

In Suriname, Ed and Claire Suttie, Ayvin Rogers, Karen Tjon Pian Gi and Stinasu, and Maureen Libanon.

At home, Dr Mark Plotkin, Henk Reichart, Katherine Jamieson.

Finally, I would like to thank as well as dedicate my chapter to David Kohn, world traveler and grandfather extraordinaire, who will always be my spiritual travel companion.

CREDITS

South America on a Shoestring 9 was commissioned and developed in Lonely Planet's Oakland office by Wendy Smith. Cartography for this guide was developed by Graham Neale. Coordinating the production of this title were Nancy Ianni (editorial), Anneka Imkamp (cartography) and John Shippick and Vicki Beale (layout). Overseeing production were Glenn van der Knijff (project manager) and Alison Lyall (managing cartographer).

Editorial assistance was provided by Adrienne Costanzo, Melanie Dankel, Tony Davidson, Barbara Delissen, Susannah Farfor, Kim Hutchins, Emma Koch, Martine Lleonart, Lara Morcombe, Anne Mulvaney, Alan Murphy, Tegan Murray, Kristin Odijk, Nina Rousseau, Katrina Webb and Gabrielle Wilson.

Cartographic assistance was provided by Tony Fankhauser, Daniel Fennessy, Karen Fry, Pablo Gastar, Kim McDonald, Anthony Phelan, Lachlan Ross, Andrew Smith, Herman So, Natasha Velleley and Jody Whiteoak.

The language chapter was prepared by Quentin Frayne, the index was prepared by Nancy Ianni and the cover was designed by Pepi Bluck.

Series Publishing Manager Robert Reid oversaw the redevelopment of the shoestring guides series, and Regional Publishing Manager Maria Donohoe steered the development of this title. The series was designed by Maria Vallianos, with mapping development by Paul Piaia. The series development team included Shahara Ahmed, Anna Bolger, Jenny Blake, Erin Corrigan, Nadine Fogale, Virginia Maxwell, Dave McClymont, Leonie Mugavin, Rachel Peart, Lynne Preston, Howard Ralley, Kalya Ryan, Paul Smitz and Vivek Waglé.

THANKS from Lonely Planet
Many thanks to the hundreds of travelers who used the last edition and wrote to us with helpful hints, useful advice and interesting anecdotes:

A Gep Aadriaanse, Ebba Aakerman, Frederica Aalto, Beatriz Abad, Theodore Abbond, Tim Abbott, Kate A'Bear, Olivier Abon, Adriana Abreu, Anderson Abud, Allister Adams, Bob Adams, Esther Adams, Mitch Adams, Doug Adamson, David Addison, Sandi Addison, Stephen O Addison, Tolani Adeboye, Haydee Adel, Tamar Adelaar, Betty Adell, Carlijn Adema, Daniel Adorno, Peggy Aerts, Sebastian Agudelo, Jose Carlos Aguilar Malaga, Imran Ahmed, Hazel Ahrens, Chin-Joe Ajiet, Gilian Ajodha, Sarah Akber, Volkan Akkurt, Jason Alarcon, Fatima Albino, Ariel Albrecht, Erik Albrecht, Cristina Alcala, Andy Alcock, Lorraine Alcock, Marcelo Alexandre, Ximena Alfaro, Paul Alfers, Sytze Algera, Anwar Ali, Lucy W de Ali, Martin Allan, Jason Allard, Marjorie Allard, Ian Allen, Wayne Allen, Wendy Allen, Thomas Allerstorfer, Caroline Allerton, Alvaro Alliende, Kim Allin, Tim Allman, Bodil Almberg, Klaus Altman, Milagros Alvarez-Calderon, Marcos Amatucci, Brian Ambrosio, Xavier Amigo, Dov Amir, Karin Ammeraal, Regina M Anavy, Jennifer Anders, Ingvild W Andersen, Thomas Rude Andersen, C Anderson, Cath Anderson, Cherie Anderson, Clare Anderson, Geoff Anderson, Matt Anderson, Pat Anderson, Ryan Anderson, Diu Andhlam-Gardiner, Emma Andrews, B Androphy, Phillip Andrus, Guillermo Angel Peisina Lemos, Niels Anger, Rosemary Anton, Sayo Aoki, Joeri Apontoweil, Rob Appelboom, Katherine Appleton, Lilian Aquines, Betty Arbulu, Irene Arce, Carolynn Archibald, Judy Arday, Wilfredo Ardito, Molly Arevalo, Wayne Arizmendi, Diana Armstrong, David Armsworth-Maw, Tone Arneberg, Christina Arnet, John W Arnold, Vincent Arnold, Fran Arp, Francine Arpin, Paola Artola, Mieke Arts, Hilmir Asgeirsson, Liz Ashton, David Ashworth, Rubu Askvik, Edouard Asselin, John Atkins, Melissa Attebery, Ashu Atwal, Nicolas Atwood, Anne Auchatraire, Julie Aucoin, Alain Aucordier, Monica Auger, Nicole Avallone, Joe Avarne, Aria Avdal, Vivienne Avery, Ada Avrahami, Daniel Axelsson, Gloria Ayres, James Ayres, Jerry Azevedo **B** Roman Baba, Joy Babb, Megan Baccitich, Dirk Bachmann, Dorian BAchmann, Karl Backhaus, Ceri BAcon, Henry Bacon, Christine Badre, Erich Baechler, Myriam Baechler, Janina Baeder, Roman Baedorf, Serena Baehler, Werner Baer, Brooke Bailey, Courtney Bailey, Graham Bailey, Susie Bailey, Borut Bajzelj, Angie Baker, Richard Balcazar, Joeri Baldinger, Jorge Baldivieso, Davis Bales, Mandy Ball, Melinda Ballengee, Andrew Balmain, Mandy Baltar, Christian Balzer, Heike Balzer, Andrew Bambach, Martin Bamford, Johannes Bang, Carol Bank, Bill Baragano, Ann Barakat, Michael Baran, Julian Barbar, Alison Barber, Philip Barclay, Tamar Bar-El, Ben Barker, Fleur Barker, Arnold Barkhordarian, Angie

Barlow, Edward Barlow, Stephen Barnes, Sebastien Baron, Silke Baron, Norris Barr, Richard Barragan, Sue Barreau, Daniel Barrera, Florence Barrere, David Barriere, Kay, Jan & Andre Barth, Stéphane Barthe, Courtney Bartlett, Geoff Barton, Alistair Basendale, Christian Bass, Andrew Bassford, Floor Basten, Santiago Basualdo, Elise Batchelor, Gemma Bath, Patrizia Bathge, Angela Bauer, Florian Bauer, Nick Baughan, Daniel Baum, Jenna Baum, Christoph Baumgarten, K Baxter, Danilo Bayas, Jane Beamish, Marc Beaudin, Mirjam Beck, Peter Beckmann, Ralf Behrens, Jan-Willem Beijen, Aart Beijst, Adam Beird, Mike Beishuizen, Ben Beiske, Daphne Bell, Mary Bell, Sam Bell, Samantha Bellamy, Norma Viassone Beltrametti, Katie L Bendall, Diana Benedetto, Mira Benes, Maria & Tony Benfield, Lisbet Bengtsson, Arne Beniest, Cindy Benner, Dr Kae Bennetts, Erin Bennion, Overli Bente, Frederic Bequet, Anna Beran, Daniela Bercovitch, Annelies Van Den Berg, James Van Den Berg, Petter Berg, Timothy Bergen, Alex Berger, Brian Bergeron, Caryl Bergeron, Goran Berggren, Ingregerd Berghall, Soren Berghall, Aran Bergman, Stephen B Bergren, Mauricio Bergstein, Karin Berli, Alison Bermant, Denyse Bernard, Fergal Bernard, Edwin Bernbaum, Irene Bernhard, Tomas Berrin, Richard Berroa, Hermann Bersch, Joel Bertrand, John Bessant, John Beswetherick, Rene & Melissa Beukeboom, Katrin Beurger, Antoine Beurskens, Paul Beveridge, Simone Bianchi, Filippo Bianco, Karlheinz Biesinger, Christopher Billich, Sally Birchenough, Eliza Bird, Iain Bird, Vidar Birkeland, Tony Birkett, Simon Bishop, Corneliek Bisschop, Alastair Bisson, Ruth Bitterlin, Erwin Bittner, Jacob Bjoern, Camila Bjorkbom, Caroline Black, Martin Blain, Roberto Blanc, Greg Blanchard, Yaroslav Blanter, Maria-Jos Blass, Patrick Blattman, Pascal Bleuel, An Blevi, Charlotte Blixt, Esther Bloem, Oswald Bloemen, Neil Blood, Phillip Bloom, Nancy Bloomer, Sam Blowes, Daniel Boag, Ian Boag, Mykel Board, Annette Bodier, Juergen Boehler, Lenette & Joergen Boejgaard, Soren Boel, Chantal Boisvert, Andy Bolas, Tor Even Bole, Alberto Bollea, Inge Bollen, Michael Boller, Robin Bollweg, Camilla Bolum, Paul Bonavia, Jenefer Bonczyk, Stephane Bone, Gabriela Bonifaz, Jeohan Bonillo, Erick Bonnard, Luci Bonner, Claire Bonnet, Colin Bonnet, Yolanda Bons, Miguel Boo, Justin Boocock, Edgar Booth, Jon Booth, Craig Booker, William Bookhammer, Alistair Bool, Jasper Boon, Wilm-Jan Boon, Nila Boquin, Luis Borgeaud, Dirk Borowski, Arnaud Bos, Marleen Bos, Eric Boschmann, Peter Bossew, Marcel & Claudia Bot, Andres Botero, Stephen Bottomley, James G Botts, Robert Bough, RJ Boule, Anthony Boult, Martin Bourgon, Paul Bouwman, Joost Bouwmeester, Bernice Bovenkerk, L Bowers, Peter Bowie, Michelle Bowlen, Bill Bowles, Claire Boydell, Benjamin Boye, Jean-Yves Boyer, Gracijela Bozovic, Petra Braam, Ben Brabazon, Ben Brabazon, William Bradley, Mikael W Braestrup, Owen & Anna Brailsford, Michael Brandenburgsky, Ben Brazil, Kattis Brdnnlund, Justin Breen, Katja Breitenbncher, Benno Breitenmoser, Francis Brekke, T Brenan, Casey Brennan, John Breski, Nynke Brett, Karel Brevet, Ross Brevitt, Fran Brew, Gert Brienne, Mark Briggs, She Rise Bright, Marla Brin, Chuck Briscoe, Ian & Sally Britton, Montserrat Briz, Evelien Broeder, Caroline Bronkars, Richard Brooks, Tom Brooks, Liora Brosbe, Linda Broschofsky, Caroline Brouwer, Eric Brouwer, Peggy Browett, Christopher Brown, Dawson Brown, Hannah R Brown, Heather Brown, Jan Brown, Paul Brown, Suzanne Brown, Terry Brown, Tim Browne, Alison Bruce, Robert Bruce, Thomas Bruck, Jean-Yves Bruckert, Ulrike Bruckmann, Angela Bruderer, Andrea Brugnoli, Thomas Bruhin, Bouke Bruinsma, Emma Brunette, Paul Brunner, Uri Brutzkus, AM Bryant, Stephane Bryant, Dean Bubley, Ziemowit Buchalski, Martin Bucheli, Kristin buchenhorner, Julia Buckell, Quentin Buckingham, Quentin & Nicky Buckingham, Sarah & GB Bucknell, Peter Budd, Michael Buesing, Nicole Buettner, Peter Bugarski, Yasmin & Ricardo Buitinga, Kelly Buja, Werner Bull, Karen Bullen, Andrew Bunbury, Nicky Bunting, Claudia Burbaum, Peter Burkett, Agi & Shanf Burra, Mike Burrell, Tony Burson, Joel Burstyner, Lois Burton, Bruce Busch, Oscar Buse, Mike Buser, Debbie Busler, Martina Bussmann, Ben Buston, Ashley Butler, Helen Butler, Mimi Butler, Marie Butson, Stuart Buxton, Andrea A Byck, Nic Bye **C** Eduardo Caballero, Lorena Cabrera, Neko Cabrera Vasquez, Marcello Cafiero, Edward Cahill, John Cain, Matteo Calabresi, Miss Calderon, Lorena Caleffi, Josie Cali, Maximo Calla, Sanfous Calsaz, Daniel Calvete, David Cameron, Eileen Cameron, Jon Camfield, Alejandro Camino, Giulia Campanaro, Frank Campbell, Havelock Jimmy Campbell, Hyla Campbell, John Campbell, Louise Campbell, Richard Campero, Tamara Campero, Laurence Campo, Claudio Canazei, Jose Candeias, Robert Candey, Saul Candib, Stuart Candy, Laura Cangas, Edmur Caniato Arantes, Adam Canter, Robert Canter, Emma Cantrell, Janko Capel, Mike and Amy Capelle, Luca & Ann-Christin Cardholm, Francine Cardinal, Paul Cardoen, Agustfn Cardona M, Jason Cardwell, Gavin Carey, Anna Carin Gustafson, Germßn Bender-Pulido, Olivier Twiesselmann, Stephen Carlman, Jane Carlstrom, Nick Carney, Arnaud Caron, Johanna Carpenholm, Rulan Carr, Juan Carrera, Michael Carrigan, Mauricio Carvalho, Christian Carrigg, Rosmary Carrubba, Henry Carson, Roz Carter, James Carty, Miguel Carvalho, Ricardo Carvalho, Salvatore Casari, D Case, Anne Casement, Raheem Cash, Mick Cashman, Lucy Cass, Alan Casserly, Carmel Castellan, Fabian Castro, Marcus Castro, Jerome Catz, Nicola Cauchy, Michel Cavelier, Mike Cavendish, Sharon Cawood, Moira Cayetano, Adriana Caznoch Kurten, Sirman Celayir, Jeff Cenaiko, Sarah Cenaiko, Andzea Cesillo, Tanguy Ceulemans, Dennis Chambers, Dr Neil Chambers, Jane Chambers, Robert Chamerda, Bernard Champion, Parth Chanda, Simon Channon, Brandy Chapman, Brandyn Chapman, Carolynn Chaput, Matthias Chardon, Denton Chase, Dominique Chauvet, Nilson Chaves, Alexandra M Chciuk-Celt PhD, Jonathan Cheek, Matthew Chell, Philip P Chen, Andrew Chenoweth, Julie Ann Cheshire, Chris Childs, Ken Childs, Kim Childs, Marlene Chisholm, Andrea Chittleborough, Martin Chlodnicki, Claudia Cho, Na Choo, Rosemary Chopra, Frank Chou, Andreas Christen, Hansjuerg Christen, William Christian, Becky Christiansen, Willi Christiansen, R Christie, Robyn Christie, Maria Nordstedt, Ann Christofferson, Marie Chry, Yen Chuang, Felix-Leif Chue, Mark Churchill, Natalie Churnin, John Ciampi, Carolyn Cismoski, Liezy Claes, Kirsten Claiden-Yardley, Nicolas Claire, Liam Clancy, David Clapham, Helene Clappaz, Andy Clapperton, Lucy Claridge, Catherine Clark, Curtis Alan Clark, Peter Clark, Bjorn HB Clasen, Paul Class, Paolicelli Claudia, Pia Claudius, Aaron Clauson, Austin Clayton, Dan Clayton, Barry Clements, Julia Clements, Molly Clerk, Eleanor Clevenger, Bob Coats, Steve Coats, Jack Cobb, Nick Cocks, Magdalena Coelho, Karel Coenen, Kevin Coghlan, Shahar Cohen, Helen Cole, Neil Cole, Marcus Coleman, Pat Coleman, Colette Colfer, Phillip Colin, Philippa Collier, Ruth

Collinge, Greg Collings, Christian Collins, Tracey Collins, Simona Colombo, Reid Colvin, Andrea Com, Elena Como, Emma Connell, Paul Conroy, Norbert Conti, Chris Cook, Sophia Cook, Ron Coolen, Jack P Cooley, Mairead Cooley, Alisha Cooper, Crispin Cooper, Edward Cooper, Rob Cooper, Milton Copeland, Toyan Copeland, Brandi Copher, Dan Coplan, Aaron Corcoran, Kevin Corcoran, Xavier Cordero Lopez, Arnaud Corin, Paula Cormack, Josselin Cormier, Marieke Cornelissen, Robert Coronado, Nicole Correia, Len Corsbie, Briana Corso, Glenn Costello, Sandra Cottam, Vanessa Cottle, Brian Council, Rosa Couras, Chris Courtheyn, James Cowie, Nicko Coxon, John P Coy, Bob Coyne, Brooke Crabb, Chris Crabtree, Nina Craig, Carol Craven, Helen M Crawford, Susan Crawford, Timothy P Crawfurd, Steve Creamer, Zita Crener, Andrea Crenna, Tara Crete, Alessandro Crisanti, Tim Crockett, Daniel E Cronk, Jim Crooks, Juliette Croome, Hugh Cropp, Paula Crotty, Emma Crowe, Louis Crowe, Damien Croxton, Edmund Crozier, Brian Cruickshank, Dolores Cuadros, Marjolein Cuijpers, Amy Cummings, Heloisa Cunha, Benoit Cunningham, Tamara Cuppens, Mary Jean Currier, Fabio Cury, Ralf Czepluch **D** Sandra da Conceicao Fontinha, Sergio Da Gatta, Wojciech Dabrowski, Inge Daemen, Jan Daems, Natasha Dahanayake, Erin Daldry, Mara Dale, Megan Dale, Ivar Dalén, Ninna Dalgaard, Andrew Dalton, Maximillan Damberger, Leonne Damson, Beverly Dandurand, Vincent D'Angelo, Rachel Daniels, Elisabethe Dank, John Dank, Carolyn Dark, Cristine D'Arthuys Lohman, Aaron Daub, Robert D'Avanzo, Jonathan Davies, Phil & Ginny Davies, Steve Davies, Don Davis, Jennie-Lee Davis, Keith Davis, Nicki Davis, Anna Davison, Elizabeth Davison, Julie Davison, Joanie Dawson, Leanne Dawson, Marcelle Dawson, Melanie Day, Phill Day, Dan De Backer, Katia De Block, Koen De Boeck, Walter de Boef, Laura de Carvalho, Barbara De Fruytier, Ingrid de Graaf, Robert de graaf, Michel de Groot, Geby de Jong, Jan-Willem de Jong, Edu de la Combe, Maria de los Angeles Berg, Guy De Mondt, Lisa De Paoli, Koen De Rijcke, Martin de Ruiter, Laura de Vries, Sjoerd de Wit, Nelie de Wolff, John Deacon, Walter Deal, Catherine Dean, Johnathan Dean, Alan Dean Foster, Erwin Deckers, Liz Deeks, Edo Dekel, Peter Dekkers, Aaron Del La Garza, Hector Del Olmo, Maria del Pilar Costa, Maria del Soto, Silvia Del Zoppo, Ian Delahunt, Iris Delaney, Joseph Deleonardo, Fernando Delgado, Pascale Delhaye, M Dellar, Mark Dellar, Chris Demathieu, John Denison, Iglesias Denisse, Amy Denman, Kurt Dennis, Wendy Denton, Richard Derichs, Sanne Derks, Claire Derrick, Merel Dessens, Nathalie Desseaux, Danielle Deutscher, Christine Devane, Thea Devers, Vina Devi, Remmert DeVroome, Jeffrey Dhont, Andrea Di Napoli, Anna M Di Ponio, Damien Diament, Anne Dias, Rocio Diaz, Tomas Diaz Mathe, Angel Diaz Mendez, Nataly Mariela Mujica Diaz Valdes, Andrew Dick, Donald Dickson, Vanessa Dickson, Eric Diepstraten, Christa Dieterich, Eileen Dietrich, Bianca Dijkstra, Mike Dilley, Martin Dillig, Juan Carlos Dima, William Dinwoodie, Therese Dion-Renauld, Dave Diperna, Mr CJ Dippel, Kathleen Dirkens, Davien Dirkzwager, Tara Dittrick, Sasch Djumena, Mollie Dobson, Barbara Doersch, David Dolan, Jamie Donald, Annick Donkers, Gemma Dorritt, Sandra Dos Santos, Sergio dos Santos, Luis Eduardo Dosso, Tomas Dostal, Sarah Dotson, Keri Douglas, Jacqueline Dowling, Jo Dowling, A Downing, Ashley Downs, Christine Dowzer, Joey Doyle, Paisley Drab, Dan Dragonetti, Marja Dral, Deborah Dray, Inga Drechsel, Laura Cecilia Driau, Semeli Drymoniti,

Christina du Rietz, Ray Dubois, Lee Dubs, Zbynek Dubsky, Mettine Due, Andrea Duerr, Matt Dufort, Linda Duits, Ross Duke, Murray Dulac, Stephanie Dumack, Natasja Dumay, Jean-Marc Dumont, Tim Dun, Jennifer Duncan, James Dunlop, Mary Dunn, Julio Duran, Augusto Durand, Suzanne DuRard, Mike Durgerian, Alex Duss, Jacob Dutilh, Shaun Dwyer **E** Andy Eagleton, Catherine Early, Michael J Eatroff, Yasmin Ebrahim, Oliver Eck, Christian Eckstein, Justin Edgar, Todd Edgar, Bruce Edmunds, Carolann Edwards, Ian Edwards, Joel Edwards, Josse Eelman, Oivind Egeland, Alex Egger, Roland Ehrat, Noelle Ehrenkaufer, Michael Eiche, Katrin Eichenberger, Patrick Ekerot, John Eklund, Johan Ekstrom, Reneko Elema, Mette Elf, Jimena Elias, Paula Elias, David Eliason, Katrin Eliasson, Sarina Rita Eliyakim, Katherine Elizabeth ODonnell, Johan Ellborg, Ryan Elliott, Guy Ellis, Don Ellis III, Rolf J Ellmers, Patricia Elmore, Sarah-Jane Elvin, Jeroen en Esther, Elena Enache, Alex Encel, JOhn Endres, Honora Englander, Victor Englebert, Richard English, Ann-Charlotte Enstrom, Judy Ridgway Epp, Maren Erchinger, Chris Erhardt, Geoff Erickson, Kit Erickson, Magnus Eriksson, Susan Erk, Dimos Ermoupolis, Julie Escott, Scott Espie, Steven Espindola, Emmanuel Espino, Miguel Espinoza, Lucy Esplin-Jones, Otto & Uta Esser, Niebla Estival, Pily Estrada, Ingrid Estrella, Ruth Ettl, Heike Eujen, Cecilia Evans, Chris P Evans, Don Evans, Dr Karl Evans, Ian EVANS, Mark Evans, R G Evans, William Evelyn, Dr Yair Even-Zohar, Jane Ewbank **F** Camiel Faber, Joao Fabio Cese, Igor Fabjan, Elisabetta Fabris, Bruce Faecher, Brian Fagan, Caryll Fagan, Alexandre Fage-Moreel, Carlos Fagi, Sze Fairman, Kristen Faith, Roberto Falconi, Annabel Falk, Heinz Falter, Krista Farey, Jeff Faris, Jim & Carol Farmer, Paddy Farrell, Esther Farrerons, Thomas Fassbender, Enrica Fazio, Ed Fec, Michel Fecteau, Sven Feddern, Michael Feder, Csaba Feher, Mary Feher, Carole Feldman, Marek Feldman, Marvin Feldman, Angelo Fenili, Gabrielle Fennessy, Judy Fennessy, Eckhard Ferber, Andrew Ferguson, Michael Ferguson, Patrik Ferkl, Juvenal Fernandes, Salustiano Fernandes, Sara Fernandez, Berta Fernandez Rodriguez, Marcelo Ferrante, Tonino Ferrara, Tracy Ferrell, Andreas Fertin, Marjo Ferwerda, Christian Feustle, Eelco Fichtinger, Knut Andre Fiddan, Bjorn Fiedler, Lucia Cardenas Figueroa, Carsten Filthuth, Tara Findlay, John Finnerty, Renate Finsker, Ingrid Firmhofer, Alan Firth, Alistair Firth, Andrew Firth, Jonas Fischer, Martina Eva Fischer, Nadine Fischer, Gloria Fisher, Kimberly Fisher, Peter Fiske, Dairne Fitzpatrick, Julia Fizer, Andrea Flachsmann, Hubert Flahaux, Henrik Flamink, Marilyn Flax, Barbara Fleck, Heather Fleming, Jamie Fleming, Julia Fleminger, Amy Flickinger, Gabriel Flores, Orlando Flores, HC Florian Sorensen, Christopher Flynn, Robert Fogelnest, John Fogg, Pernille & Kennet Foh, Montse Fontellas, Robert Ford, Josh Forde, Matt Fordham, Judy Forney, Daniel Fortier, Robert Fortin, Dave Foster, Kent Foster, Neil Foster, Nicholas Foster, Peter Foster, Tim Foster, John Foster-Hill, Scott Fowler, Claudia Fraefel, Damian Francabandiera, Gustaaf Franck, Bernard Francou, Nicole Franken, Bryan & Sonja Fraser, Sharon Frazzini, Kay Freebern, Andrew Freeman, Anna Freeman, Reto & Sandra Frei, Bettina Freihofer, Marion Freijsen, Marcia Freire Cavalcante, Felix Freist, Patrick Frello, Bente K Fremmerlid, Audra French, Cash French, Erith French, Sarah Fretz, Achim Freund, Erika Fricke, Beth Fridinger, Tamar Friedlander, Carmen Frischenschalger, Burghard Fritzsch, Anita Frohli, Kate Frost, Caroline Frostick, Allan L Fruman, Tanya

Frymersum, Alejandro Fuentes, Johannes Fulcher, Rachel Fulcher, Dave Fuller, Dave & Lina Fuller, George Fullerlove, Patrick Po Kin Fung, Lesly Furness, B Sue Futrell, Erik Futtrup, Thomas Fux **G** Linus Gabrielsson, Michael Gacquin, Tim Gage, Carlos Gagliardi, Roman Gaiser, Markus Gajer, Tomasz Galka, Jim Gallagher, Katharina Gallauer, Margaret Gallery, Kathleen Gallichan, Maria Gallinger, Daryl Galloway, Carlos Galvalizi, Robert Galvan, Juan Galvan D, Cristian Gamarra, Jason Gamble, Cesar Gamio Brou, Ralf Gamper, Sanjay Gandhi, Robert Gantner, Rebecca Garbett, Fabian Garbolino, Ferdinando Garbuglio, Ignacio Garcia, Miss Garcia, Joanna Gardner, Marcel Gareau, Robert Garibay, Patrick Garland, Donovan Garnett, David Garrett, Maureen Garrigan, Samy Gasmi, Loredana Gatt, Ryan Gawn, Malachy Geelan, Bettina Gehri, Fabrice Gendre, Rag Gent, Rog Gent, Georgie George, Axarlis Georgios, Joe Geraci, Matija Gergolet, Kathy Gerst, Stecv Gerv, Matt Gervase, Stacy Gery, Christine Gesseney, Eva Geuder, Homer Geymer, Pawel Ghilardi, Michael Giacometti, Lara Giavi, Thomas Gibbins, Sheryl Gibbs, Brooke Gibson, James Gibson, Julie Gibson, Will Gibson, Annemarie Gielen, Marieke & Esther Gieteling, Julie Giguere, Kate Gilbert, Alice Gilbey, Shaun Giles, Shaun A B Giles, Nathalie Gilgenkrantz, Marlene Gilland, Beth Gilliam, Robert H Gillis, Charlie Gilmore, Nick Gilroy, Merel Gilsing, Michael Gimard, Paul W Gioffi, Giuseppe Giordano, Olivier Girard, Alex Girdwood, Sue Girling, Mirko Giulietti, Meghan Giulino, Todd Glaesmer, Tina Glahr, Roswit Glaubitz, Michael Gleeson, Katherine Glen, Roland Glockler, Jean-Francois Gloux, Barry Glover, Martin Gluckman, Florian Gmeiner, Marko Gnann, Jutta Gnilsen, David Gochman, Marc-Oliver Goebel, Matt Goff, V Gohl, Dan Goldberg, Nick Golding, Tone Golnar, Ricardo Gomes, Maria Gomez, Emilio Gómez Membrillera, Marc Goncher, Julian Gonzalez, Kim Gonzalez, Williams Gonzalez, Oscar Gonzalez van Eijk, Marne Good, Rebecca Goodall, Erik Goodbody, James Gooden, Diane B Goodpasture, Tress Goodwin, Charles Gordon, Gus Gordon, Lorenzo Gordon, Mathew Gore, Anthony J Gorski, Thorsten & Karina Gorski, Wolf Gotthilf, Leonardo Filipe Goulart, Claudia Grabner, Melissa Graboyes, Natalie Gracia, Greco Graciela, Cornel Grad, Andy Graham, Jerry Graham, Amanda Grant, Robert Grant, Asger Grarup, Rolf Grau, John P Graven, Kristoffer Gravgaard, Cathy Gray, Pat Gray, Frank Graziano, Giorgio Grazzini, Bob Greely, Nicholas Green, Julie Green, Megan Green, Steven Greenall, Alvaro Greene, Steven A Greenwald, Lance Greenwood, Vanessa Gregory, Alexander Grellmann, Harald Gries, Owen Griffith, DN Griffiths, Paul Griffiths, David Grill, Liz Grime, Peter Grip, Helma Groenen, Annabelle Groenendijk, Irena Grogan, Irene Grogan, Lianne Groothoff, Mario Grosso, Lynn Grout, Liz Groves, Aler Grubbs, Victor Gruber, Wendy Gruber, Chris Gudgin, Robson Guedes dos Santos, Monica Guerra, Stephen Guest, Philippe Guichard, Johan Guillaume, Jean Guillaumot, Dean Guirguis, Alf Amund Gulsvik, Anthony Gunn, Tim Gunn, Shira Gur Arie, Paul Gurn, Eddie Gustin, Diego Gutierrez, Kristina Gutschow, Joel Guzman, Rodrigo Guzman **H** Stephan Haag, Dr Joachim Haas, Moshe Haber, Emily Hadaway, Jennifer Haefeli, Katje Haeussler, Patrick Hagans, Jon Hagen, Andrea Hagenauer, Gary W Hahn, Jochen Hahn, Michael Hahne, Franz Haiboeck, Sarah Louisa Hails, Bethan Haines, Johannes Hajek, Frans Hakkemars, Ellen Hakstege, Louise Hall, Melody Hall, Richard Hall, Robert Hall, Lee Hallam, Gabriela Hallas, Chris Halliday, Daniel Halse, Jenni

Hamara, Sabrina Hambel, Mary Anne Hamer, JT Hamilton, Ross Hamilton, Wendy Hamilton, Andy Hammann, Vendela Hammarskjold, Robert Hammer, Anne Hammersbad, Karen Hammink, Rolf Hampel, Mike Hampshire, Leon Hamui, Helen Hanafin, Robert Hance, Michael Hancock, Roly Hancock, Gemma Handy, Ferdinand Hang, Bas Hangmatten, Roman Hanis, Jeff Hankens, Sarah Hankinson, Olivia Hanley, Maggie Hanlon, Paula Hanna, Fred Hanson, Tim Harcourt, Jenny Harding, Matt Harding, Rachel Hardisky, James Hardy, Kerry Hardy, Yso Hardy, Anne Pernille Harlem Dyrbekk, Michelle Harmon, Remco Harms, Aaron B Harnett, Cristina Harnischmacher, Eugenie Harper, Lynda Harpley, Warren Harrington, Deanna Harris, Fred Harris, Jude Harris, Kate Harris, Paul Harris, Rocky Harris, Scott Harris, Steve Harris, William Harris, Victoria Harrison, Jacquie Hart, Jaquie Hart, sherry hart, Martin Hartig, Imke und Markus Hartig-Jansen, Trudi Hartley, Claudio Hartmann, Michael Hartmann, Nils Hartmann, Rachel Hartsough, Philip Harvey, Sue Harvey, Zoe Harvey, Michael Haschka, Eric Haskell, Leslie Haskell, Ineke van Hassel, Or Hasson, Rob Haub, Haavard Haugen, Markus Hauk, Sabine Hauptmann, Gerlind Hauser, Dave Hawkin, Tom Hayes, Cindy Hayford, Julienne Heath, John Hebert, Kai Hecheltjen, Gerrit Hecking, Sven Hedinger, Michel Heemskerk, Birte Hegerlund, Sigrid Hegmann, Hendrik Heider, Rodrigo Heidorn, Christian Heindel, Raphaela Heinen, Heidi Heinzerling, Imogen Heldt, Robert Heller, Ivar Hellesnes, Burkhard Helmedag, Susan Henderson, Clive Henman, Gunnar Hennefrund, Tolima Henninghausen, Caroline Hennin, Adolfo Henriquez, Pearce Henry, Sandra van Henste, Padraig Heochaidh, Neil & Christine Hepburn, Byron Heppner, Lothar Herb, Anders Hermansen, Peter Hermens, Anne Hernaes, Sven Herr, Alexa Herrmann, Henrik Herrmann, Mark Herrmann, Kathleen Hershner, F Hertzberger, Eitan Hess, Tom Hetley, Larry W Heuple, Klaus-Peter Heussler, Joseph ven den Heuvel, Dawn Hewitt, Sandra van Heyste, Nicky Heyward, Carla Heyworth, Matt Hickey, Jesus Hidalgo, Rodrigo Hidalgo, Kathryn Hiestand, Dominic Higgins, David Higgs, Ernie Higgs, Jeroen Hilak, Francesca Hilbron, Rebecca Hill, Richard Hill, Steve Hill, Eva Himmelberg, Kay Hinchsliffe, Julie Hinckley, Julia Hinde, Amir Hindie, Raul Hinojosa, Jillian Hirasawa, Maximilian Hirn, Meral Hirsch, Erich Hirtler, Rado Hnath, Alison Hoad, Charmain Ho-A-Lim, Mike Hoave, Len Hobbs, Tamara Hocherl, Valerie Hodges, Cary Hodgkinson, Pettina Hodgson, Liesbeth Hoek, Merete Hoel, Andrea Hofer, Britta Hoffman, Rebecca Hoffman, Simon Hoffmann, Martine Hofstede, Debby & Jim Hogan, Ron Hohauser, Hillary Hohmann, Climmy Hoksbergen, Janette Hol, Jenny Holden, Daniela Holguin, Julie Hollar, Roos Hollenberg, Anne Hollier, Pierre Hollinger, Iris B Hollis, Karen S Hollweg, Sarah Holman, Andrew Holmes, Neil Holmes, NH Home, Johan van Hoof, Hester Hoogenboom, Rick Hoogenboom, Phil Hoopmann, Georgina Hopkins, Kevin Hopkins, Ned Hopkins, Joseph Horan, Rochus Horat, Philip Horchler, Tamir Horesh, Brian Horkan, Sheila Horkan, Miriam Horne, Danielle Horneman, Lina Hornton, Chris Horsfall, Petr Horsky, Koosje van der Horst, David Horton, Pat and Chris Horton, Sarah Horton, Amy Horwitz, Tom Hoskin, Bryan Houck, Patricia Houton, Armin Howald, Alan Howard, Jay Howarth, Laura Howell, Malcolm Howell, Richard Howitt, Danial Hoydal, Scott Hoyer, Elaine Hruschka, Victor Hskansson, Viktor Hskansson, Gloria Huang, Hilde Hublou, Damien Huffer, Katrina Hughes, Laura

Hughes, David M Hunt, Hernione Hunter, Lee Huntington, Mike Hurd, Andy Hurst, Hugo Hus, Cristian Huse, Jon Huss, Cameron Hutchison, Eva Huthoefer, Shelley Hutson, Alison Hutton, Nick Hutton, Paul Hyman I Tage Ibsen, Ernestein Idenburg, Paolo Ienne, Trebor Iksrazal, Jill Illidge, Ricardo Imai, Claudia Imhof, Lani Imhof, Hana Inai, Patricia Inarrea, Silvia Infanzon, Peter Ingerfeld, Adrienne Inglis, Kris Inglis, Henry Ionescu, Jeremy Ireland, Dan Irion, Annette Irvine, Vicki Irvine, David Irwin, Jim Isaacs, Laurent Iseli, Sabriya B. Ishoof, Olivier Issaverdens, David Issokson, Marijan Ivanua, Legarth Iversen, Pico Iyer J Bastiaan Jaarsma, Remco Jaasma, Joe Jabaily, Paul & Carole Jackman, Daniel Jacks, Michelle Jackson, Toni Jackson, Yves Jackson, Ellen Jacobs, Nico Jacobs, D Jagesar, Hellemans Jakke, Deborah James, Sam Jamison, Maria-Paz Jana, Ingo Janas, Santos Mamani Jancko, Lenka Janecek, Ariane Janér, Kazia Jankowski, Jack Janosik, Tjasa Janovljak, Gordon Janow, Juliette Jansen, M Jansen, Johana Janson, Susanne Janssen, Lauren Jarvis, Jan Jasiewicz, D Jax, Melanie Jay, Mikki Jee, Andy Jefferson, Myles Jelf, Bruno Jelk, Alden Jencks, Larry Jensen, Solveig Jeppesen, Tanja Jernss, Astrid Jirka, David Jiron, Kristine Jnrs, Fabio Joffe, Ronni Johansen, Lars Johansson, Eva Dagrun Johaug, Gerd Johnsen, Amanda Johnson, Carina Johnson, Denise Johnson, Lia Johnson, Paul and Liz Johnson, Peter Johnson, Ripton Johnson, Julie Johnston, Niels Johs, Schona Jolly, Christopher Jones, Kath Jones, Matt Jones, Megan Jones, Milly Jones, Nicky Jones, Richard Jones, Marika De Jong, Christian Jongeneel, Ard Jonker, Rebecca Jonson, Karel Jonsson, Arnold Joost, Paul Jorn, Catherine Joslyn, Isabelle & YC Jost, Amy Jozwiak, Jacqueline Judah, Andrew Juffermans, marc jumbert, Nina Junghans, Marc Jurgens, Cleve Justis K Hartmut Kahler, Katrin Kaempgen, Leonard Kahansky, Jean Kahe, Rebecca Kahn, David Kaiser, Mari Rose Kalile Passos, Claudia Kalin, Martin Kalista, Pamela Kalman, Andre Kalvin, Inge Kampfen, Sabrina Kandes, Jay Kane, Sabrina Kanji, Tony Kaperick, Ira Kaplan, Tuula Kareketo, Oda Karen Kvaal, Judith Karena, Pius Karena, Revital Kariv, Linda Karlbom, David Karlsson, Jan Karlsvik, Garben Karstens, Kenneth Kartchner, Tony Karton, Joanna Karwacka, Deborah Kashdan, Arne Kasper, Frank Kaspereit, Andreas Katechakis, Tessa Katesmark, Dave Katz, Dr Tobias Kaufmann, Yorgos Kechagioglou, Ute Keck, Sonja Keckeis, Ron Keesing, Kirby Keeton, Susan Keevil, Horst Kehler, Shane Kehoe, Christian Keil, Tom Keith-Roach, Michael Keller, Allan Kelly, Ben Kelly, Elisa Kelly, Helene Kelly, Jamie Kelly, Jane Kelly, Kristin Kelly, Shraga Kelson, Bill Kemball, Keith Kemp, Lucille Kemp, Dr Vera Kempe, Laura Kendal, Brad Kenedy, Abby Kennedy, Anne-Marie Kennedy, Letitia Kennedy, Mark Kennet, Pernillen og Kennet, Judy Kenning, Kieran Kenny, Mary Kenny, Patricia Kent, Julia Kentnor, Faiz Kermani, Christoph Kessel, Petra Kessler, Nathan Kesteven, Esther Keusch, Boris Keweloh, Khalid Khan, Zia Asad Khan, Kevin Kichinka, Sarah Kidd, Steve Kidd, Daniel Kiernan, Alfredo Kihien, Paul K Kim, Andrea Kinauer, Bob King, Dave King, Jay King, Susan King Lachance, Lucie Kinkorova, Justine Kirby, Hugh Kirkman, Scott Kistler, Arlo Kitchingman, Claus Kjaerby, Lucas Klamert, Konrad Klatt, AMJ Klaver, April Klavins, Kelly Klein, Ken Klein, Markus Klein, Kurt Kleiner, Lyn Kleiner, Karin Klitgaard, Alexandra Klitsch, Reiner Kloecker, Roman Klotsvog, Beate Klugmann, Hans Klugmann, Bill Klynnk, Barbara Knapton, Tina Knipping, Holger Knoedler, Brigitte Knoetig,

H Knoflach, Martin Knolle, Susie Knott, James Knox, Chris Knutson, D Koch, Carsten Koebisch, Stefan Koetter, Rok Kofol, Jeffrey Kok, Rob Kok, Cathrin Kolb, Gerd Kollakowski, Hans Kolland, Kirstin Koller, Edo Kolmer, Efrat Konforty, Heinke Konnerth, Matthew Konsa, Joyce Kool, Freek Koopmans, Fuat Koro, Kees-Jan Korving, Ilkka Koskinen, Johanna Koskinen, Adam Kosminski, Angela Kotsopoulos, Vera Kotz, Gary Kowalski, Thomas R Kraemer, Uwe Kraft, Dave Kramer, Andreas Krampe, Jeff and Diane Krans, Barbara Krantz, Oliver Krause, Frank Krautter, Joanna Kreckler, Adrienne De Kretser, Peter Kreuzaler, Uwe Krieger, Emma Kristensen, Kirstine Kristensen, Sten Kristensen, Horvath Krisztian, Nikki Kroan, Olga Kroes, Mike Krosin, Susie Krott, Gitta Krukenberg, Johan Kruseman, Frauke Kubischta, Stephanie Kubsch, Anne Kuiper, Annelies Kuipers, Eppo Kuipers, Lars Kuipers, Agnieszka Kula, Bob Kull, Oskar Kullingsjo, Peter Kunkel, Timo Kuntzsch, Matthias Kunz, John Kupiec, Lydia Kuster, Steven Kusters, Jan Kvet, Jan-Paul Kwasik, Kristin Bolenc & Nina Kyelby L Marcelo Labre, Rene Labrecque, Inga Labuhn, CR Lacy, David Lacy, Sandra Lafforgue, Ann Lager, Johannes Lahti, Gregor Laing, Nicolas Laisney, C Lamb, Colin & Clare Lamb, Jason Lamb, Costandi Lambaki, Paul Lambert, Fernanda Lamego, Selena Lamlough, Christel Lammertink, Stan Lampard, Selena Lamplough, Jeff Lamppert, Gert van Lancker, Mark Lander, Melanie Lander, CJ Lane, Evangeline Lane, John Lane, Kevin Lane, Xavier Lane-Mullins, Jerry Lang, David Langbroek, Frank-Michael Lange, Mauricio Lanos, Nick Lansdowne, Christy Lanzi, Christy Lanzl, Diana Laponder, Jasmin Lappalainen, Lisa Laria, Carl Lariviere, Pierre Larose, Erik Larsen, Jessica Larsen, Tony Larsen, Dr David Lasry, Monty Lasserre, Julie Lassonde, Chris Latterell, Michael Laudahn, Lewis Laura, Silvia Lavalle, Ebbe Lavendt, Angiolo Laviziano, Ian Lavoie, Christine Law, Chung Law, Emma Lawlor, Jenny Lawrence, Justin Lawson, Karen Lawson, Linda Layfield, Rachael Lazenby, Gregg Le Blanc, Sophie & Thomas Le Joille, Philip le Pelley, Danilo Leal, Chris Leary, Colleen LeBlanc Flanagan, Alexander Ledig, Andrea Lee, Avelyn & Hung Dhong Lee, Bill Lee, Brandon Lee, Emma Lee, Peter Lee, Sung Yun Lee, Richard Lee-Hart, Bernard Lefrançois, Anneliese Lehmann, Isabel Lehmann, Mirja Leibnitz, Diane Leighton, Zoe Leighton, Nanci Leitch, Brian Lema, Marie-Claire Lemay, Inga Lena, John Lengacher, Christoph Lenherr, Laura Lenyk, Sabrina Leombruni, Guy Leonard, Vanessa & Lucas Leonardi, Ronald Leong, Frank Lepannetier, Bernard & Marlene Leroudier, Philippe Lesne, Markus Lessky, Ludovico Lesti, Kristin Letcher, Chris Leuhery, Milton Lever, Sam Levitt, Idan Levy, Jon Levy, Stuart Levy, Colin Lewis, Laura Lewis, Lorna Lewis, matthew lewis, Pamela Lewis, Peter Lewis, Ralph Lewis, Rebecca Lewis, Robert Lewis, Larry Lewis, Alison Ley, Dawn Lezak, Gil Liberman, Jeff Libman, Steven Libralon, Kerstin Lichtenberg, Steve Lidgey, Jonathan Lieberman, Sigrid Liede, Arthur Liegeois, Ben Ligtvoet, Morten Lillesand, David Limacher, Louise Limoge, Andreas Lindberg, Corina and Alfred Lindenmann, Christian Linder, Claudia Linders, Anne Lindley, David Linford, John P Linstroth, Diane Lister, Alfred Little, Jen Little, Kylie Little, Dr RA Litton, Dmitriy Litvak, Daniel Lloyd, Elaine Lloyd, Shad Lloyd, Helen Lo, Katie Lo, Harriet Lock, James W Lockett, Martin Loebell, Paula Loeber, Joachim Loeblein, Anneli Lofgren, Sara Logie, Adrian Lohmueller, Mark Loney, Stacy Long, Ida Longeri, David Longman, Frederic Lopez,

Juan Jose Lopez, Aimee Lord, Antoine Lorgnier, Carola Lotz, Peter Loucks, Alexander Louis, Anna Lovejoy, Kate Low, Jessica Lowe, Richard J Lowe, Catherine Lowell, Lene Lubbert Hansen, Nancy Luberoff, Dieter Lubitz, Michael Luck, Andrew Ludasi, Dirk Luebbers, Jacqui Luff, Hannie Luijpen, A Lukosky, Francesco Lulli, Sophia Lund, Torbjoern Lundqvist, Mariam Lunrein, Ian Lunt, Joana Luplin, Joanna Luplin, Jacqui Lupp, Robert Lupp, Rebecca Lush, Veronica Lushington, Michael Lustenberg, Tanja Lutolf, Dikrßn P Lutufyan, Katie Luxton, PD Lynam, Toby Lynns **M** Casper Maasdam, Marco Macchi, Campbell Macdonald, Ian Mace, Steve Macfeely, Jim Macgillis, Gordon Machin, Mary Machin, JT Mack, Lachlan Mackenzie, Ian Mackley, Elizabeth Maclaine-Cross, Robert MacLellan, Karla Mader, Thomas Mader, Frederik Madsen, Fernanda Magalhaes Lamego, Antonia Maguire, Darcie Mahoney, Tristan Mainnevret, Denise Mainville, Volker Maiworm, Cedric Maizieres, Zukiso Makalima, Romain Mallard, George Malliaros, Philip Manchester, Giovani Mancilla, Francisco Mandiola, Katrin Mangold, Megan Mann, Axel Manthey, Lynette Manuel, Pablo Manzano Baena, Darryl Mar, Nick Marbach, Jean Marc Dugauquier, Jacques Marcais, Alessandro Marco Lindenmann, Rodrigo Marcus, Arnaud Marez, Mauro Janine Margiotta, Anne Margrethe, Felipe Mariani, Torsten Markert, George Markopoulos, Claire Marks, Sebastian Marks, Margit & Folke Markwardt, Milena Marmora, Sonalle Maroo, Sunny Maroo, Sandra Marquardt, Armenio Marques, Roy Marques, Sandra Marquez, David Marsden, June Marshall, Ann Martin, Jane Martin, John Martin, Roger Martin, Russel Martin, Trajan Martin, Andrea Martinez, Chip Martinson, Rebecca Martinsson, Okumura Masato, Al Mason, Ringo Massa, Dan Massey, Bob Masters, Beth Masterson, Fatimah Mateen, Marisa Maters, Michael Mathes, David Mathews, Mario Mathieu, Kyle and Terri Mathis, Anna Matova, Brent Matsuda, Carly Mattes, Dave Matthews, Bartholdi Matthias, Nara Mattoso, Gerd Maxl, Nicholas May, Thomas Mayes, Chris Mazur, Fraser McArthur, Geri McBride, Richard McCaig, AnneMarie McCarthy, Kelly McCarthy, Michael McCarthy, Thomas McCarthy, Wendy McCarty, Brendan McCauley, Lorraine McCreadie, David McCredie, Ralph B McCuen, Edward McDonagh, Tasha McDonald, Malcolm McDonaugh, Dan McDougall, Cathleen McGuire, Elizabeth McInerney, Philip McInerney, Alan McIntosh, Kenneth McIntosh, Alexander McIntyre, Norm McIver Jr, Melissa McKay, Anne McKendry, Mike McKenna, Sarah McKeown, Steve McKinney, Adam McKissack, Alexandra Scotti McLaren, Colin McLaren, John McLaverty, Barry McLean, Margaret McLean, Margaret McLenn, Brian McNicholas, Suzanne Mcparland, Phillip McRoberts, Lee Mead, Peter Meaker, Kerstin Mechlem, Alberto L Mederos, Bill Medhurst, Mitja Medved, Guus Meeuwsen, Moummad Mehdi, Olivia & Alain Meier, Sharon Meieran, Brett Meier-Tomkins, Liesbeth Meijnckens, Julia Meinke, Hans Meister, Osbaldo Mejia, Peter Mellas, Laura Mello, Harald Mellwig, Flavio Melo, Miranda Men, Erika Menamkat, Jaime Mendez, Manuel Menezes de Oliveira Neto, Anja Menkhaus, Gerard Menkhorst, Kerstin Menze, Silvia Merli, Yael Meroz, Gordon Merrick, Francois Mes, David Mesa Restrepo, Tessa Messenger, Juerg Messerli, Thomas Messerli, Frédéric Metey, Claire Metherell, Ellen Mette Finsveen, Astrid Metzger, Justin Meunier, Claudia Meyer, Matthew Meyer, Mariano Mezzatesta, Matthias Michael, Lloyd Michaels, Joshua Michaud, Lee Micholson, Sylvie Micolon, Monica

Middleton, Ross Middleton, Trikaliotis Mihalis, Birte Mikkelsen, Jakob Elm Mikkelsen, Lucas Mile, Aubree Miller, Deborah Miller, Jonathan and Jayme Miller, Leila Miller, Lynda Miller, Marisa Miller, Mark Miller, Fernando Milmo, Lennat Milsson, Rob Minnee, Robert Mirtsopoulos, Kavita Misra, Henrik Mitsch, Oded Mizrahi, Zachary Moavani, Jostein Moen, Hank Moffat, Jesper E Mogensen, Dennis Mogerman, Tanya Mohammadi, Alexis Molho, Angel Daniel Molina, Jamie Monk, Michael J Monsour, Darren Moody, Ian Moody, Martin Moorcroft, Ann Moore, Nicole Moore, Paul Moore, Ross Moorhouse, Arturo Mora, Jaime Mora, Gregorio Morales, Marina Morales, Amalia Moran, Lorn Moran, David Morawetz, Aksel Morch, Gina Morchio, Ricardo Moreno, David Morenoff, Chris Morey, Steffi Morgner, Paola Morich, Leonard Thomas Morin, Pierre Morin, Michael Moritz, Cyndi Morley, Dan Morris, David Morris, Jim Morris, Lisa Morris, Paul Morris, Samantha Mort, Itzik Morthehay, M Morton, Rohan Morton, Lars Mosbach, Thierry Moschetti, Fernando Moser, Ir Moshe, Lisa Moss, Ken Moxham, Carmen Moya, Daniel Moylan, Arun Mucherjee, Andreas Mueller, Annabelle Mueller, Christoph Mueller, Petra Mueller, Ellennita Muetze Hellmer, Debbie Muijsers, Arun Mukherjee, Patricia Mulkeen, Kerry Mullen, Gabriele Muller, Georg Muller, Jerry Muller, Jutta Muller, Kitty Muller, Patrick Mundy-O'Toman, Monica Munoc, Cristina Munoz, Karen Munro, Adam Munton, David Muntslag, Franklin Murillo, John Murphy, Kevin Murphy, Kieran Murphy, Lori Murphy, Angus Murray, Harriet Murray, Marcus Murray, R Murray, Charlotte Muspratt, Gus Musto, Gustavo Musto, Christopher Mutlow, Tan Mutlu, Asger Muurholm, Marco Mwaniki, Emile Myburgh, Sara Myers, Nicole Myerson, Mark Myles, Nicky Mylins **N** Ingrid Naden, David Naderi, Ishay Nadler, Goyo Nagai, Sean Nagle, Vandana Nair, Martin Najar, Kiran Nandra, Miguel Naranjo, Libe Narbarte, BJ Narkoben, Patricia Nascimento, Alex Nash, Gavin Nathan, John Naughton, Andreas Naujoks, Auke Nauta, Barbara Navarro, Neal Neal, Nathan Nebbe, Rike Nehlsen, Ric Neighbour, Danie Nel, Anne & John Nelson, Diana Nelson, Yannick Neron, Bruce Nesbitt, Marcia Nesbitt, Naomi Nestel, Manoel Netto, Steve Netto, David Neumann, Richard Neurink, Kirk Nevin, Lynea Newcomer, Paige Newman, Pete & Cath Newman, Lisanne Newport, Deborah Newton, Michael Newton, Tom Newton Chance, Lil Ng, Liv Ng, Tommy Nguyen, Ryan Nice, Katie Nicholls, Marcus Nicholson, Defossez Nicolas, Stefan Niederberger, Gitte Nielsen, Jan Nielsen, Marita Nieminen, Klarissa Nienhuys, Laurens Nieuwenhuizen, Helen Nigg, Anders Nilsson, Manuel Ninapaitan, Marco Nintzel, Max Nish, Jesper Nissen, Emanuel Nitsch, Linde Nobre, Thomas Nordenholz, Eva Nordenskjold, Linda Norman, Daniel Norton, Katharina Nothelfer, Renate Notter, Pedro Novak, Tom Novak, Mary Nowakowski, Paul Nugent, Matthias Nussbaum, Barbara Nusser, Steve Nutting, Michael Ny, Heather Nyberg **O** Colm O' Canainn, Mark O' Flaherty, Bearnard and Verne O'Riain, Steve Oades, Lisa Oakes, Penny Oakley, Evan Obercian, Rainer Oberguggenberger, Markus Oberli, Christopher Obetz, Izaskun Obieta, Michal Obrebski, Clare O'Brien, Jane O'Brien, Joan & Peter O'Brien, Kerry O'Brien, Matt O'Brien, Roo O'Brien, Olivia O'Callaghan, Etain O'Carroll, Neil O'Connell, Chris O'Connor, Diane O'Connor, Mark O'Day, Karen O'Donahoo, Deirdre O'Donnell, Katherine O'Donnell, J O'Donoghue, Theodor Oest, Patricia Oey, Anthony O'Hehir, Deirdre O'Kelly, Ole Olesen, Franco Olgiati, Jose Olimpio, Dahlia Olinsky,

Andres Olivares Pizarro, Morten Olsen, Gary Olson, Sissel Helen Ommedal, Katie O'Neill, Justin Ooi, Martijn Ophoff, Andre Oppe, Rebecca Oppenheimer, Caroline Oppl, Anne Lise Opsahl, Kara O'Reilly, Connie Orias, Cathal O'Riordain, Waltraud Orisich, Tommy Orme, Jeffrey L Orr, Melanie Ortlieb, Otto Ortner, Shannon Orton, Yoshitomo Osawa, Caroline Osborne, Sebastian Osenstetter, Aidan O'Shaughnessy, Thomas Ostergaard, Ibon Ostolaza, Olav Ostrem, Bernadette O'Sullivan, Christian Osvald, Adriana Otero, Miriam Otten, Jeroen Overmars, Ken Ow-Wing, Aleksandra Oziemska **P** Michael Pal, Edson Roberto Pacheco, Jeff Packman, Paddy Padmanaban, Conny Padt, Keir Paesel, Steve & Chris Page, Amarnath Pai, Graciela Pajuelo de Dahl Olsen, Jenny Paley, Norman Paley, Arvind Pallan, Juliane Palm, Andrew Palmer, Gary Palmer, Keasha Palmer, Josep Panella, Antje Pannenbecker, Irene Pappas, Sophia Pappas, Spiro Pappas, Vijay Parbat, Efrain Pardo, Lars Pardo, Melanie Pardo, Aristea Parissi, Jeremy Parker, Nick Parker, Joseph Parkhurst, Julia Parkin, Francesca Parnell, Sophie Parron, Adela Parzanese, Nirav V Patel, Fernando Patino, Vikki Patino, Michael Patrikeev, Ebony Pattenaude, Lynn H & Michele G Patterson, Stuart Pattullo, Thies-Peter Paukner, Johan Pauvert, Alexander Pavelka, Connie M Payne, Daniel Payne, Sam Payne, Rachel Peake, Henry Pearce, Theon Pearce, David Pearl, Lucy Pearson, Morten Pedersen, Lasse Pederson, Cristina Pedrazzini, Oscar Pedros, CJ Peereboom, Huub Peeters, Lucy Peile, Marzena Pejlak, Vicente Martin Peluffo, Richard Pendry, Jonathan Penny, Sabina Pensek, Rui Pereira, Fernanda Perez, Gualberto Perez, Vito Perillo, Janelle Perrin, Nathalie Perrot, Alan Perry, Andrew Perry, Earl Perry, Sian Perry, Claudia Peruccio, Darcy Peters, Brad Petersen, Don Peterson, Marshall Peterson, Pat Petronio, Flavio Germano Petry, Lin Petry, Debra Pett, Richard & Alison Pett, Lars E Pettersson, Severine Peudupin, Laura Pezzano, Dieter Pfeifer, Walter Pfeiffer, Barbara Pfister, Lili PGquet, Eric Phan-Kim, Jerson Philips, Jason Phillips, Rod Phillips, Roger Phillips, Saul Philpott, Tim Phipps, Phill Piddell, Dennis Piedra, Matthew Piercy, Julie Pike, Katherine Pike, Brydon Pilkington, Inger Pinkowsky, Stephanie Pinte, Cesar Piotto, Elisabeth & Gerd Pircher, Graham Pither, Jaroslav Plainer, Eduardo Planas, Mandy Planert, Marc Andre Plante, Mark Plattner, Thomas Pletzenauer, Cameron Plewes, Janice Plewes, Anne Podt, Anne-Marijke Podt, Andreas Poethen, Claudia Poffet, Oliver Pogatsnik, Daniela Pogliani, Bart Pogoda, Chris Pogson, Chantal Poiesz, Hans Polane, Thomas Polfeldt, Chris Pollard, John Polo, Ken Polspoel, Dominique Poncin, Claudia Ponikowski, Desmond Poon, Adrian Pope, Scott Pope, Boris Popov, Lutz Poppelbaum, Matt Popplewell, Simon Porges, Carine Porret, Lonnie Porro, Lucy C Porter, Steve Porter, Stephen Portnoy, Robert Pospiech, Filip Pospisil, Tal Potishman, Katja Potzsch, Brigitte Poulsen, Jeremy Pounder, Julianne Power, William Powers, Danielle Powley, Daniel Pozzi, MH Pratley, Chris Preager, Juergen Preimesberger, Barbara Preiswerk, Daniela Prenger, Carl Pressley, Trish Preston, Cath Priaulx, Adam Price, Ashley Price, David Price, Judy Price, Matt Price, Malte Priesmeyer, Dina Priess dos Santo Penha, Bart-Jan Prins, Mark Probst, Mirjam Pronk, Joop Proveniers, Lori Prucha, Leacy Pryor, Martina Puchir, Barbara Pukwana, Cam Pulham, Carolina Pulido, Celia Purdey **Q** Natascha Quadt, Joanna Querelle, Sebastian Querner, Mike Quick, Trish Quilaran, Rik Quint, Peter Quiros **R** Mark Rabine, Will Race, Maggie Racklyeft, Paddy Radford, Rob Rado, Barbara Radweiske, Bruce Rae, Andreas Raeder, Eynay Rafalin, Alan Rafferty, Scott Rains, Soni Rajeev, Sriram Ramakrishnan, Hanna Ramberg, Torsten Ramforth, Giselle Ramirez, Nicole Rankin, Verena Raschke, Nikolah Rasmussen, Erin & Chris Ratay, Kumi Rattenbury, Duilio Vargas Ratto, Thomas Rau, Sherry Rauh, Diederik Ravesloot, David Rawet, Johann Rawlinson, Sophie Raworth, Eric Rawson, Christopher Rea, Dr Luke Rea, Sally Reader, Robert Reagan, Albert Recknagel, Andrew Redfern, Bob Redlinger, Steven Reeves, Nora Regalado, David E Reibscheid, Chris Reicher, Frances Reid, Leonora Reid, Amanda Reidy, Ine Reijnen, Harald Reil, Ernst Reiner, Franziska Reinhard, Wim Reitsma, Natalie Rempel, Richard Remsberg, Cami Renfrow, Theo Rengelink, Doris Renggli, Charles Renn, Carlo Rettore, Helena Rex, Marco Antonio Reyes, Cory Reynolds, Harmony Reynolds, Heidi Rhodes, Judith Rhodes, Anabella & Maurizio Ribanelli, Carolina Ribeiro, Thomas Ribisel, Eliana Ricalde, Kathy Rice, Roberta Rice, Elise Richards, Jonathan Richards, Suzanne Richards, Valerie Richards, Fabian Richter, Mareike Richter-Oldekop, Michel Riemersma, Robert Riesinger, Marion Rimmer, Henrik Risvang, Fernando Rivas, Caroline Rix, Fabbio Robbi, Alex Robert, Camillo Roberti, Adam Roberts, Dr Alison Roberts, John Roberts, Julian Roberts, Kate Roberts, Martin Roberts, Scott Roberts, Ann Robertson, Jodi Robertson, Eric Robette, Becki Robinson, Edward Robinson, Helen Robinson, Nicola Robinson, Jacques Rocheteau, Noel Rochford, Simon Rochowski, Renaud Rodier, Cristiana Rodrigues, Walace Rodrigues, Alfredo Rodriguez, Ramiro Rodriguez, Stacey Roe, Machiel M Roelofsen, Margaret Roemer, Stephan Roess, Hubertine Roessingh, Michele Roessler, Wally Rogelstad, Becey Rogers, Elaine Rogers, Andrea Rogge, Britta Rohde, Yael Roitman, Ingrid Rol, Clive Rolfe, David Romain, Megan Romano, Robert Rome, Edu Romero, Suzy Romero Treuiller, Kathy & Jeff Rooney, Miranda Rooney, Ans Roovers, Professor Carlos Roquette, Bill Rose, Joachim Rose, Marilynn Rose, Simon Rose, Tim Rose, Derek Rosen, Assami Rosner, Bet Ross, Katherine Ross, Miga Rossetti, Andrea Rostek, Deborah Roth, Hans R Roth, Thomas Roth, Jeff Rothman, Delvenia Rounds, Erik Roupe, Catherine Rourke, Sonja & Marco Rouwenhorst, Martina & Brian Rowe, Karen Rowland, Harald Roy, Simone Royer Yamashita, Ori Rub, Giovanni Rubbiani, Andrew Ruben, Debra Ruben, Elad Rubin, Sean Rubin, Dario Rucco, Hansruedi Ruchti, Mattias Rudh, Aaron Rudner, Max Ruggier, Jan Ruis, Ben Rule, Thomas Runker, Anton Rupar, Erika Rupp, Michael Ruppert, Andrew Rurak, David Rusek, David Rusitschka, Alexandra Russell-Bitting, Erica Russo, Patrice Rutten, Hugh F Ryan, Stig Rygaard, Skarrn Rynine, Mark Ryser, Skarrn Ryvnine **S** Kathy Saad, Marcelo Saavedra, Claude Sabatier, Filippo Saccardo, Ofer Sadan, Andrea Sadlo, Patrick Sagmeister, Raul Saguillo, Amartya Saha, Silvana Saibene, Freddy Esteban Saieg, Marc Sajecki, Rania Salameh, Gabriela Salazar, Patricia Salazar, Monica & Noel Salazar Espinosa, Noel Salazar Medina, Terry Salguero, Rodrigo Salinas, Matt Salmon, Tom Salmon, Gil Salomon, Darren Salter, Andy Salzer, Hamadi Samia, Paola Samoggia, Ian Samways, Sofia San Martino, Victor Sanavia, Juan Cristobal Sanchez Gonzalez, Peter Sanders, Al Sandine, Gary Sands, Jen Sands, Julie Sands, Karen Sangster, Peter Sapper, Sarah Sarzynski, Alexandra Satori, Volker Sauer, Jeanette Sautner, Louise Savenborg, Todd Savitz, Ross Savoy, Barry Sayer, Elena Scanferla, Michael Scarlett,

Dr. Hanno Schaefer, Giada Schaeli, Elisabeth & Frank Schaettgen, Bettina Schaetzl, Hanno Schafer, Walter Schaffer, Natalie Schai, Nathaniel Scharer, Isabel Scharnbeck, Bettina Schatzl, Michaela Schau, Dr Peter Scheer, Emile Schenk, Iris Schick, Mark Schiffner, Frank Schilbach, Sandra Schilling, Vicki Schilling, Hannelore Schimmer, Henrik Schinzel, Susan Schirber, Luregn Schlapbach, Oliver Schleich, Marc Schlichtner, Beate Schmahl, Klaus-Dieter Schmatz, Peter Schmeitz, Marc A Schmenner, Gaetan Schmid, Judith Schmid, Hauke Schmidke, Ernst Schmidt, Gregg Schmidt, Stephen Schmidt, Susanne Schmidt, Caroline Andrews & Schmutz, Matthias Schmutz, Amy Schneider, Erin Schneider, Joerg Schneider, Katrina Schneider, Pia Schneider, Thomas Schneider, Nancy Schneider-Deacon, Matt Schoenfelder, Natasja Scholz, Jerad Schomer, Dieter Schoop, Herdis Helga Schopka, Mark Schottlander, Ramses Schouman, Mr & Mrs Gilbert Schouteet-Raes, Jaap & Maria Schouten, Peer Schouten, Eneas Schramm, Harald Schraut, Anne Schreiber, Toralf Schrinner, Silvia Schroder, Manfred Schroer, Andreas SchSfer, Ute Schuessler, Melisa Schuette, Ilja Schurink, Ralph Schurink, Matthias Schuster, Massimo Schutte, Deborah Schwagerman, Michael Schwartz, Vitor Schwartz Coelho, Robert Schweiger, Miguel Schweitzer, Dirk Schwensen, Torben Schwermann, Jens Schwyn, Falk Scleicher, Belinda Scotman, Martin Scott, Stephen Scott, Diego J Seckbach, John Sedlander, Meike Seele, Erich Seelye, Elana Sefton, Stephan Segers, Bill Seidel, Christina Seidler, Lawrence Seifert, Ulrike Seiler, Antonia Seilern, Jacob Seligmann, Davide Selva, Gour Sen, Claudia Senecal, Franck Senghor, Carlo Senna, Dawn Sentance, Emmanuel Serruys, Bobbi Setter, Benjamin Settle, Fabian Seul, Ana Severo, Eric Sevrin, Gavin Sexton, Jerome Sgard, Owen Shaffer, Saeed Shah, Sharlene Shah, Norman & Ruth Shanks, Myra Shapiro, Danielle Sharkan, Alexander Sharman, Warren Shauer, Aileen Shaw, Lydia Shaw, Nicola Shaw, Fred Sheckells, Mercedes Shelby, Rossie Shelty, Lisa Sherry, Tersina Shieh, Yusuke Shimada, Jennifer Shin, Peter Shinglewood, Yinon Shiryan, Mykel Shlub, Michael Shohat, Ross Shotton, Brooke Shuster, Kalpana Shyamapant, P Sibbles, Jonathan Sibtain, Itay Sidar, Afsheen Siddiqi, Veronika Siebenkotten, Shefa Siegel, Pete Siegfried, Paul Siegler, Jacob Silberberg, Ricardo Sillicani, Monica Silva, Amanda Silver, Charles Lustosa Silvestre, Oscar Silvius, Lydia Simbolon, Ondrej Simetka, Belinda Simmonds, Anthony Simmons, Carolina Simon, Horst Simon, Jane Simon, Dean Simonsen, John Simpkins, Anthony Simpson, Charlie Simpson, Dan & Kirsten Simpson, Gregg Simpson, Martin Sims, Diego Singer, Manpal Singh Sandhu, Anneke Sips, Tony Sirotkin, Wai Fung Sit, Jonathan Siverling, Milo Sjardin, Bo Sjoholm, Luke Skinner, Nathan Skon, Mette Skovbo, Diana Skroch, Siri Skroppa, Veronika Skvarova, Jeffrey Slater, Malcolm Slater, Rowan Slattery, Jenny Slepian, Kristoffer Sletten, Jacilda Slevin, Marc Sluisveld, John Smale, Monica Small, Stuart Smeeton, Anna Smet, Karen Smetana, Andrea Smith, Deborah Smith, Duncan Smith, Jason Smith, John Smith, Jonathan Smith, Pete Smith, Sally Smith, Stuart Smith, Tanya Smith, Terry Smith, Judeth Marie Smith Nussbaum, Peter Smolka, Carol J Snaith, Saskia Snik, Sandy Snively, Charlotte Snowden, Douglas Snyder, Vania Soares De souza Gomes, Paul Sodemann, Christoph Soekler, Jon Even Soerlie, Ioannis Sofilos, Vic Sofras, Ernie Soh, Tex Soh, Martin Sohngen, Alejandro Sola, Jennifer Sontag, Frank Sorauf, Heidi Sorensen, Matias Soriano, Fabio Sorrentino,

Susan Sotelo, Judy Soukup, Cristiane Spaccasassi, Eduardo Spaccasassi, Eduardo Spaccassi, Tracy Sparkes, Maike Sparrius, Clare Spauls, Erika Spencer, James Spencer, Ross Spencer Cohen, Fred Spengler, Amanda Spice, David L Spiegelberg, J S Spijker, Frans Spijkers, Ezra Spilke, Joshua Spillane, Bronwyn Spiteri, Ann & Frank Spowart Taylor, Elena Springer, Mary Ann Springer, Toby Sprunk, Anja Stacheder, Kimberlee Stack, Dorothee Staeheli Egger, John Staelens, Martine Staepelaere, John Stahle, Rob Stainsby, Andrea Stallkamp, Espen Stangeland, Pierre Stangherlin, Nicole Stania, Martin Staniforth, Jean Stanton, Peter Stapleton, Erik Stark, William K Stark, Andre Starobin, Lisa Starr, Jeremy Statham, Wolf Staub, Nancy Staus, Max Steden, Georg Steed, Mike Steele, Roland Steffen, Carl Stegman, Ernst Steigenga, Gabriela Steiglechner, Andrew Stein, Corri Stein, Yariv Steinberg, Juerg Steiner, Peter Steiner, Sibylle Steiner, J E Stellingwerf, Anja Stemmer, Signe Steninge, Rob Stephani, Craig Stephen Daly, Hal Stephens, Andrew Stephensen, Joachim Sterner, Colin Steward, Catherine Stewart, Don Stewart, Richard Stewart, Joe Stickler, Johannes Stigler, Patrick Stobbs, Lucy Stockbridge, Jo Stockhill, J M Stockill, Nicolas Stockmann, HP & G Stoffel, Carmine Stoffo, Emma Stone, Louis H Stone, Ralph E Stone, Cathy Storfer, Bill & Ann Stoughton, Edwina Strachen, Hannes Stradmann, Julia Straetmans, Lena Strandberg, John Strang, Tim Strang, Louie Strano, John Straube, Luis Streckman, Andreas Strein, Miki Strong, Clare Stubbins, Sarah Stubblefield, Marjorie Stuehrenberg, Adrian Stuerm, Stephanie Stump, Joseph R Sturgis, Tony Sturm, Wim Sturm, Matthias Suenkler, Michael Suesskind, Stuart Sugarbread, Daniel Suman, Jiri Surman, Melanie Surry, Gillian Suss, Nicole Suwito, Judy & Ariana Svenson, Stefan Svensson, Ed Swab, Kathryn Swan, Jeff Swartz, Deborah Sweeney, Peter Sweeny, Andrea Swintek, Catriona Syme, Joanne Symington, Peter Symons, Eileen Synnott, Ilona Szemzo, Micole Sztanski T Danko Taborosi, Eli Ragna Taerum, Gary C Tagalog, Diane Takeuchi, Vinay Talwar, L Tam, Nora Tam, Ron Tamari, Patricio Tamariz, Ariola Tamay, Ruth Tammaro, Jeroen Tamsma, Shona Taner, Gavin Tanguay, Claire & David Tarrant, Lee Tatham, Jocelyn Taub, Cristina Taubenschlag, Will Taygan, Alexandra Tayler, Alexandra Taylor, Graham Taylor, Jayne Taylor, Sarah R Taylor, Tania Taylor, Tom Taylor, Gill Teicher, Jesper Tejlgaard Pedersen, Ben Tellegen, Cami Tellez, Natascha Telling, Thomas Teltser, Joanne Tennyson, Carol Tepper, Renske Terpstra, Ruben A Terrazas, Annabel Terrill, Chris Terry, Paul Tetrault, Sonia Tevelow, Tim Tewsley, Dr Andra Thakur, Siddhartha Thanawala, Morgan Theorin, Rosemary Theroux, Marie-Josee Therrien, Robert Thi, Frank Thianer, Belinda Thiele, Sabine Thielicke, Andreas Thiess, Fiona Thiessen, Sara Thofte, David Thom, Janie Thomas, John Thomas, Oliver Thomas, Paul Thomas, Jorens Thomassen, Niels Thommesen, Ewan Thompson, Gordon Thompson, Isobel Thompson, J Thompson, Mark Thompson, Tim Thompson, Alex Thomson, John Thomson, Mark Thornburg, AG Thrift, Katrin Thuernau, Denise Tibbey, David Tickell, Aranea Tigelaar, Julie Tilghman, Frederik Tilmann, Bryan Tilson, Elizabeth Tilton, Edward Timpson, Julia Timpson, Marc Tissier, Robert Tissing, Sara Tizard, Theo Tjes, Nicole Tobin, Isabel Toebelmann, Juan Tohalino Vera, Dianne Tolentino, Heike Tölle, Jim Tomlinson, Mike Tompson, Diego Tonelli, Donald Toney, James Toplis, Oskar Olav Topnes, Pablo Torlaschi, Natalie Tornatore, Rodrigo Torres, Michele Tosi, Ryan Tott, Fred Tottenham,

Gilles Tournois, Carl Townsend, Nghia Tran, Chiara Trapani, Javier Travin, Lani Trenouth, Doyle Trent, Melanie Trevino, Robert Trevor, Jan Trien, Tu Trieu, Lina Troendle, Giovanni Troianiello, Allegra Troiano, Arnoud Troost, Jon Trost, Vangelio Trova, Bob Truett, Maria Trygger, Jacek Ture Nadzin, Melissa Turley, Mark Turner, Monika Tüscher, John Tustin, Susan Twombly, Markus Tyl **U** Jens Udsen, Silvia Ugarte, Marcela Ugaz, Michael Uhl, Laura Uittenbogaard, Andreas Ulrich, Christian D Ulrich, Craig Ungaro, Monique Unger, Heike Uphoff, Jacky Upson, Daniel Urbina **V** Nathan Valentine, Cheyenne Valenzuela, Xavier Valino, Marcelo Vallejos, Irma van Aalst, Wineke van Aken, Barbara van Amelsfort, Gerrie van Battum, Andre van Brussel, Henk van Caan, Serge Van Cauwenbergh, Catherine van Daele, Marius Van Dam, Balder Van de Velde, Carina van den Barg, Aukje van den Bent, Guido van den Berg, Kaspar van den Berg, Louis van den Berg, Rubin Van Den Berg, Sandra van den Berg, Floor van den Broek, Jaap van den Burg, Iris van den Ham, Fer van den Hurk, Ron Van Den Hurk, Theo van der Avoird, Richard van der Baan, Annette van der Donk, Esther van der Knaap, Jelmer van der Schaaf, Kris van der Starren, Hans van der Veen, Daphne van der Velden, Joke van der Wal, Bert van der woude, Gabriel van Diepen, Stefan Alexander van Dijk, Natalie van Eckendonk, Arjan van Egmond, Friso van Endt, Alex van Erp, Jann van Gaal, Fred van Geloof, Patti Van Ham, Dorine van Haselen, Luc van Hensberg, Pieter & Iris van Hoeken-Rusz, Paul van Homelen, Carna Van Hove, Dirk Van Hoydonck, Andre van Leeuwen, Elles van Loo, Ton van Maarsseveen, Jan-Eidse van Melle, Jack van Messel, Teun van Metelen, Silke & Ute van Os, Patrick van Riswick, Ron van Rooijen, Alma van Steenbergen, Gijs van Tilburg, Berry van Waes, Piet van Wesemael, Ronny van Zijl, Katrien Vanden Eynde, Oswaldo Vanegas, Pieter Vanhoeken, Koen Vanlerberghe, Robert Varga, Zoe Veater, Claudio Vecchi, Martin Veenendaal, Paola Vega, Andres Velasques, Fernando Velazquez, Leigh Anne Vellacott, Astrid Veninga, Edinildo Venturin, Eddy Veraghtert, Frits Verbeek, Georges Verbinnen, Karla Verhagen, Margot Verhagen, Tjen Verheye, Mariska Verplanke, Malin M Vestheim, Natalie Vial, Christian Vidal, Aurelie Vieillefosse, BJAM Viel, Jason Vigneron, Fredy Villamarin, Vickie Villavicencio, Marcella Vinciguerra, Marcel Vink, Niels Vink, Helen Vint, Linda Visser, Nalini Viswanathan, Michal Vit, Fernanda Vitalino, Eduardo Viteri Manticha, Bernard Vixseboxse, Eric Vlaanderen, Arlinde Vletter, Cees Vletter, Martijn Vlutters, Connie Voeten, Conny Vogel, Rick Vogel, Yanna Vogiazou, Ludwig Vogler, Axel Vogt, Thomas Vogt, Paul Volk, Marc-Andre Voll, Jan Vollebregt, JJH Vollenberg, Ruud Vollenberg, Scott Vomvolakis, Dinah von Badewitz, Rachel von Simson, Kristina von Stosch, Judith Vonwil, Michal Vossberg, Kfar Vradim, Jaron Vreman, Giuliette Vuerich **W** James Wade, Ute Waditschatka, Benj Wadsworth, Pam Wadsworth, Joo-Hee Waelzlein, Eric Wagensonner, Heike Wagner, Thomas Wagner, Jef Waibel, Carsten Waider, Robert Waite, Wolfgang Walch, Sandra Waldmann, Chenoa Walker, Clive Walker, Colin Walker, Julius Walker, Michael J Walker, Richard C Walker, Richard C Walker, Charmian Walker-Smith, Michael Wall, Mike Wallace, Karin Wallestad, Ross Wallis, Jen Walraven, Melanie Walsh, Jimmy Walter, Andy Walters, Nathaniel Walters, Julie Wang, Lillian Wang, Heather Wankling, Therese Wanzenried, Darren Wapplington,

Garth Ward, Michael Ward, Nathan Ward, Peter Ward, Richard Ward, Rowena Ward, Peter Wardle, Phil Waring, Trevor Warman, Yumi Watanabe, Etienne Waternal, Thomas Waters, Rachel Watkins, Herb Watson, Neil Watson, Paul Watson, Deborah Watt, Dal Watts, Steve Watts, Doug Waugh, Carol Weaver, Mark Weaver, Lenden Webb, Dora Webder, Joerg Weber, Karsten Weber, Susan Weber, Susanne Weber, Jonathan Weerts, Barbara Wegman, Lauretta Weimer, Elisabeth Weingraber-Pircher, Peter Weis, Jutta Weisenburger, Heidi W Weiskel, Jeffrey Weiss, Robin Weiss, Yishay Weiss, Douglas H Weller, Eugene Welling, Kelly Wells, Andreas Wenck, Anne Wendel, Lisa Wenzel, Sandi Wermes, Claude Werner, Goeran Werner, James West, Reto Westermann, Stefan Westmeier, Ling Weston, Annemieke Wevers, Sharon Whalley, Dalma Whang, Michael Whedahan, Michael Wheelahon, MC Whirter, Duanne White, Heather White, Linda White, Matt White, Sonia I White, Stephen White, Warwick White, Andy Whittaker, Eric Whittington, Dean Wickens, Glen Widmer, Ulrike Wiedenfels, Julie Wiedman, Chris Wigginton, John Wight, James Wigley, Ian Wikarski, Dianne Wild, Stephanie Wildes, Anita Wildi, Nills Alex Wilken, Cyprian Wilkowski, Harold Willaby, Eric Willemssens, Anna Williams, Byron Williams, Jennifer Williams, Jo Williams, John V. Williams, Lee Williams, Piers Williams, Sally Williams, Steve Williams, Matt Williamson, Janet Willoughby, Lawrence Wilmshurst, Anne Wilshin, Eldon R Wilson, Kyle Wilson, Mike Wilson, Steve Wilson, Tristan Wilson, Patricia Wim, Mikael Winblad, Lizzie Winborn, Michael Wingenroth, Robert Wingfield, Christina Winter, Karen Winter, Bert Winthorst, Leora Wise, Andrew Witlox, Robert Wittek, Christophe Wittwer, Alan H Witz, Caroline Witzier, Paul Witzier, Vincent WJ Eijt, Martin Woerner, Andreas Wolf, Kim Wolfenden, Tanja Wolk, Peter Wonacott, David Wong, Ting Hway Wong, Marjorie Wonham, Helen Wood, Martyn Wood, Nick Wood, Sophie Wood, Walter Wood, C Woodland, Kenneth J Woodside, Georgia Worrall, Robert Worthington, Rachel Worzencraft, Darren Wosol, Barrie Wraith, John Wray, Neil Wray, Rachel Wrench, Eoin Wrenn, Alister Wright, Bernie Wright, Sarah Wright, Slaney Wright, Steve Wright, Dieter Wrobel, Miriam Wu, Alexander Wuerfel, Katharina Wulf, Martin Wunderlich, Prescott Wurlitzer, Colin Wylie, Jules Wyman, Tom Wynne-Powell, Melanie Wynter **X** Christian & Stella X **Y** Masafumi Yamazaki, Irit Yanay, Mong Yang Loh, Yoav Yanir, Delia Yarrow, Brian Yates, Josh Yolish, Kim Yongsoo, Eric York, Andrew Young, Bill Young, Vincent Young, Bob Youngson **Z** Cathy Zacarovitz, Zdenek Zadrapa, Katarina Zak, Sher Zaman, Elles Zandhuis, Rosene Zaros, Suana Zavaleta Escobedo, John Zeeb, Manuel Zeh, Andrea Zeichner, S Zekkar, Lital Zelinger, Robert Zenyik, Tymoteusz Zera, GA Zevenboom, Johanna Zevenboom, Filippo Zimbile, Paula Zimbrean, Susanne Zimmer, Roland Zimmerman, Ralph Zimmermann, Judith Zingg, Oliver Zoellner, John Zubatiuk, Nicole Zuber, Georg Schulze Zumkley, Magda Zupancic, Margot Zylicz, Robert Zylstra.

ACKNOWLEDGMENTS

Many thanks to the following for the use of their content.

Mountain High Maps® Copyright © 1993 Digital Wisdom, Inc.